BARTLETT'S
FAMILIAR
QUOTATIONS

❖

BARTLETT'S FAMILIAR QUOTATIONS

A collection of passages, phrases, and proverbs traced to their sources in ancient and modern literature

SEVENTEENTH EDITION

John Bartlett

JUSTIN KAPLAN, GENERAL EDITOR

Little, Brown and Company

BOSTON · NEW YORK · LONDON

First Edition Published 1855
First Little, Brown Edition Published 1863
Seventeenth Edition Published 2002
First Printing

LIBRARY OF CONGRESS CATALOGING-IN-PUBLICATION DATA
Bartlett, John, 1820–1905.
Bartlett's familiar quotations: a collection of passages, phrases, and proverbs
traced to their sources in ancient and modern literature / John Bartlett;
edited by Justin Kaplan.—17th ed., rev. and enl.
p.   cm.
Includes indexes.
ISBN 0-316-08460-3
1. Quotations, English.   I. Kaplan, Justin.   II. Little, Brown and Company.   III. Title.
PN6081.B27 1992
808.88'2—dc20   91-21170

HML

Designed by Interrobang Design Studio

PRINTED IN THE UNITED STATES OF AMERICA

CONTENTS

PREFACE TO THE SEVENTEENTH EDITION

❖

A CENTURY AND A HALF AGO, JOHN BARTLETT, A CAMBRIDGE, MASSA-CHUSETTS, BOOKSELLER, EDITED AND SELF-PUBLISHED A 258-PAGE volume of prose and verse passages titled *A Collection of Familiar Quotations.* The quotations he chose came chiefly from the King James Bible, Shakespeare, and British writers, but he also drew on the work of a few Americans, among them Washington Irving and William Cullen Bryant, as well as his friends and neighbors Henry Wadsworth Longfellow and James Russell Lowell. A tireless reader and note-taker, Bartlett had made himself over the years an information bank for the local academic and literary community, a resource for someone wanting to know who said what, when, and where. *Familiar Quotations,* first issued in 1855 in a printing of one thousand copies, grew out of the commonplace books in which Bartlett kept the answers to frequently asked questions.

Bartlett sold his bookstore in 1863 and eventually became a partner in the Boston publishing house of Little, Brown. The company added *Familiar Quotations* to its list and, in subsequent revised and expanded editions, has been publishing it continuously ever since. By the time of his death in 1905 at the age of eighty-five, Bartlett had made his name as generic for quotations as Noah Webster's for definitions. Fame to the contrary, his gravestone in Cambridge's Mount Auburn Cemetery is unadorned with quotations of any sort and bears only his name and dates.

"The object of this work," Bartlett wrote in his original preface, "is to show, to some extent, the obligations our language owes to various authors for numerous phrases and familiar quotations which have become 'household words.'" Bartlett's modest collection, arranged chronologically by source date, evolved over the years and under subsequent editors into a book with an unusual double nature. It is an anthology of choice passages (the Greek root word for "anthology" means a gathering of flowers): a *reading book,* enjoyable in its own right and offering an informal intellectual and cultural history that ranges in time from ancient Egypt to the modern era. *Bartlett's Familiar Quotations* is also a *reference book* of first resort, like a dictionary or atlas. But even as this book has gone from edition to edition, it could never claim to be definitive, only up to date. To live up to its double nature it has had to remain open to change and responsive to the taste, temper, and events of its time. This requires shucking off tired or irrelevant quotations and replacing them with fresh material that answers the needs of new generations of readers. Many newly added quotations may turn out to have a life span of only years instead of centuries, but they belong nonetheless. (However uncomfortably, former president Bill Clinton's "I feel your pain" shares houseroom in this book with Hamlet's "To be, or not to be.")

John Bartlett's book remains literary in nature and loyal to prose and poetry sources of a traditional kind. The Bible and Shakespeare are still major components, just as they were in 1855. But recent editions have also broadened the cultural and geographical scope of the book, by drawing on the movies, television, politics, current events, and similar noncanonical or vernacular sources outside the bounds of Bartlett's original mandate of "ancient and modern literature." The sixteenth edition (1992) took large steps in this direction, at the price of disappointing a few readers who expected to find high and polite culture represented exclusively and felt the barbarians had breached the gates. The seventeenth edition continues to cast a wide net and at the same time reaffirms the traditional literary culture that is so gravely at risk. It's worth remembering that in the time of national shock and mourning that followed the devastating events of September 11, 2001, it was poetry (for example, W. H. Auden's "September 1, 1939") that many of us turned to for reassurance. As U.S. Poet Laureate Billy Collins said at the time, we needed "a human voice speaking directly in our ear."

The seventeenth edition of *Bartlett's Familiar Quotations* incorporates a number of significant changes in treatment and content. For the reader's convenience, and in order to unclutter the printed page, we've eliminated several hundred purely mechanical, nonsubstantive cross-references and footnotes. Similarly, we supply full citations of title and source in place of the traditional, often opaque and exasperating *"Ibid."* Around one hundred authors are represented here for the first time, among them Eric Ambler and Mother Teresa, Paul Celan and Richard Feynman, Alfred Hitchcock and Hillary Clinton, Jerry Seinfeld and J. K. Rowling, Isaiah Berlin and Potter Stewart, Maya Angelou and Princess Diana, Margaret Atwood and Katharine Graham, John Guare and Kingsley Amis. We give additional or enhanced space to about two dozen authors included in previous editions. Some of them are Jane Austen and Charles Darwin, Vladimir Nabokov and Edith Wharton, Virginia Woolf and Flannery O'Connor, Bob Dylan and Stephen Sondheim.

All of these author sources, however noncanonical by John Bartlett's standards, contribute to our common language of quotations and allusions. Directly or obliquely, all of us speak this language without necessarily being aware of it. We say "In my mind's eye" and "All hell broke loose" without recognizing that we're quoting *Hamlet* and *Paradise Lost.* Quotations are a form of capsule history, a way of summing up in a few words an entire era of event and spirit: for example, "With malice toward none, with charity for all," "The only thing we have to fear is fear itself," "Blood, toil, tears and sweat," "I have a dream," "I'm not a crook," "Mr. Gorbachev, tear down this wall," "Greed is good," "Show me the money." Quotations, to borrow from the preface to the sixteenth edition, are "telegraphic, a form of shorthand. We use them to lend point and luster to what we say. . . . We cherish and like to repeat, simply for the reassurance they give, proverbs, nursery rhymes, song lyrics, and the like that have so much talismanic force they function on a nearly pre-intellectual level. We use quotations, like the Biblical Shibboleth, as passwords and secret handshakes, socially strategic signals that say, 'I understand you. We speak the same language.'"

Bartlett's Familiar Quotations continues to welcome comments and nominations from readers. For their generous help in preparing this new edition I thank the following: Alex Beam, Anne Bernays, Ralph C. Bledsoe, Andrew Boyd, Paul Brooks, George Cronemiller, Peter Davison, John Dorenkamp, Carl Faith, Donald Fanger, Malcolm M. Ferguson, Joseph Finder, the late Sally Fitzgerald, James Gleick, Ralph Graves, Bill Grealish, John Guare, Scott Heller, Hester Kaplan, J. D. McClatchy, Victor McIlheny, Herbert Mitgang, Cynthia Ozick, Jaroslav Pelikan, Robert Pinsky, Nigel Rees, Philip Rule, S.J., Stacy Schiff, Mary Schmich, Heidi Jon Schmidt, Ralph Sipper, Eugene R. Sullivan, John M. Taylor, John Updike, and Helen Whall.

At Little, Brown, it's been a privilege to work with Pamela Marshall and to have the benefit of her vigilance, scholarship, and professional skill. We salute the memory of Betsy Pitha, longtime chief copyeditor, whose high standards for this book we've tried to uphold.

JUSTIN KAPLAN
Cambridge, Massachusetts

GUIDE TO THE USE OF *BARTLETT'S FAMILIAR QUOTATIONS*

·BASIC INFORMATION·

AUTHORS APPEAR CHRONOLOGICALLY IN THE ORDER OF THEIR BIRTH DATES; AUTHORS BORN IN THE SAME YEAR ARE ARRANGED ALPHABETICALLY. The quotations for each author are generally in chronological order according to the date of publication (in some instances according to the date of composition). Poetry generally precedes prose for authors who wrote both.

Anonymous quotations are located as follows: early miscellaneous and Latin quotations are placed at about A.D. 670. General anonymous quotations begin immediately after the last dated author and are arranged in roughly chronological order (no precise dates of origin being known). Specific groupings of anonymous quotations—African, Ballads, Cowboy Songs, and so on—follow the general Anonymous section in alphabetical order according to the heading.

A document without a specific author appears near the people with whom it is associated; for example, the Constitution of the United States (1787) appears among its creators, such as George Washington (born in 1732), John Adams (1735), James Madison (1751), and Alexander Hamilton (1755).

To find a particular author, consult the Index of Authors, page xv; to find a particular quotation, consult the Index, page 865. For information on the arrangement and use of the index, see below.

·QUOTATION SOURCES·

Each quotation has a source line supplying title, date if known (most often that of publication), and any other information the reader might find helpful. In the quotations from the Bible and from Shakespeare, the page headings provide blanket sources for the quotations on the particular page, while the source lines provide only chapter and verse or act, scene, and line references.

·FOOTNOTES·

The footnotes supply information about a quotation, such as the original text of a translated quotation, the name of a translator, background comments for the quotation, and other quotations related in phrase or content to the footnoted quotation.

·INDEX OF AUTHORS·

The Index of Authors provides birth and death dates and the page number for the quotations by each author, as well as the page numbers for any additional quotations by that author in the footnotes. When an author is better known by a name other than his or her given name, the author is listed under the more familiar name, with the given name provided in square brackets—for example, Bill [William Jefferson] Clinton. Bracketed parts of a name as listed in this index are those not used in the author's typical "signature"—for example, T[homas] S[tearns] Eliot. The Index of Authors also lists many pseudonyms, with cross-references from the less familiar name to the more familiar—for example, Karen Blixen is cross-referred to Isak Dinesen, the pseudonym under which she wrote. Authors who are quoted only in footnotes have their full names and birth and death dates given in the footnotes.

To find a particular book of the Bible, see the Bible entry, where the books are listed alphabetically. The same is true for Shakespeare; to find any work by Shakespeare, consult the Shakespeare entry. Anonymous quotations are listed under the heading "Anonymous," as well as by specific groupings, such as Ballads (Anonymous), Cowboy Songs (Anonymous), and so on.

·INDEX·

The *Bartlett's* index is arranged by keywords, not topics. The keywords are spelled according to *Webster's Tenth New Collegiate Dictionary* and *Webster's Third New International Dictionary*. The spelling and capitalization in the index entry are those of the quotation. Some older or variant spellings are indexed, as are "made" words, such as "hitherandthithering," "slithy," acronyms, and dialectal words. Compound expressions not found in *Webster's* are sometimes indexed: the hyphenated form "good-night," for example, is so indexed to allow grouping under this key expression rather than under "good" and "night." ("Human" and "being," however, are separately indexed.) Compound names, such as "Long Island," "South Vietnam," "United States," are indexed as one word. Elided letters found in many quotations (such as '*d* for *ed*) are supplied in the index entries. Quotations from other languages generally are indexed, usually at a keyword specific to the other language, but sometimes at a keyword that is also in English; see, for example, the entries at "Bourgeois."

Alphabetization of keywords is word-for-word, not letter-by-letter. Thus "New Zealand" precedes "Newborn." The order of plural and possessive keywords is from singular possessive to plural to plural possessive: for example, *Lover's, Lovers, Lovers'*.

The number at the end of each index entry shows the page on which the quotation starts and the number of the quotation on the page — 224:4, for example, is the fourth quotation on page 224. Entries for footnote quotations are cited by page and note number, such as 224:*n2* for the second footnote on page 224.

The index entry line is usually a short form of the indexed phrase, and the words in general appear in the same order, with the keyword abbreviated unless it starts the entry, in which case it is supplied by the keyword itself. Index entry lines are alphabetized, with articles, prepositions, and conjunctions included.

> Hope, all we h. in Heaven, 477:10
>   Americans h. of world, 340:7
>   animated by faith and h., 325:6
>   is waking dream, 79:10
>   the thing with feathers, 544:11
>   to see Pilot, 487:4

Occasionally words not in the actual quotations are supplied in the index entries to make the entries clear.

Readers who cannot find a particular quotation under one keyword are advised to scan any keyword entry in its entirety, since there are many ways of indexing one phrase, or to try other keywords.

PAMELA MARSHALL
Editor, Little, Brown and Company

INDEX OF AUTHORS

❖

BARTLETT'S FAMILIAR QUOTATIONS

❖

FAMILIAR QUOTATIONS

❖

The Song of the Harper[1,2]

c. 2650–2600 B.C.

1 There is no one who can return from there,
To describe their nature, to describe their
    dissolution,
That he may still our desires,
Until we reach the place where they have gone.
St. 5

2 Remember: it is not given to man to take his goods
    with him.
No one goes away and then comes back.
St. 10

Ptahhotpe

Twenty-fourth century B.C.

3   Teach him what has been said in the past; then he
will set a good example to the children of the magistrates, and judgment and all exactitude shall enter
into him. Speak to him, for there is none born wise.
The Maxims of Ptahhotpe [c. 2350 B.C.],[3]
introduction

4   Do not be arrogant because of your knowledge,
but confer with the ignorant man as with the
learned. . . . Good speech is more hidden than
malachite, yet it is found in the possession of
women slaves at the millstones.
The Maxims of Ptahhotpe, 1

5   Truth is great and its effectiveness endures.
The Maxims of Ptahhotpe, 5

6   Follow your desire as long as you live and do not
perform more than is ordered; do not lessen the
time of following desire, for the wasting of time is
an abomination to the spirit. . . . When riches are
gained, follow desire, for riches will not profit if one
is sluggish.   *The Maxims of Ptahhotpe, 11*

7   One who is serious all day will never have a good
time, while one who is frivolous all day will never
establish a household.
The Maxims of Ptahhotpe, 25

8   Be cheerful while you are alive.
The Maxims of Ptahhotpe, 34

The Teaching for Merikare[4]

c. 2135–2040 B.C.

9   Be skillful in speech, that you may be strong;
[. . .] it is the strength of [. . .] the tongue, and
words are braver than all fighting . . . a wise man is
a school for the magnates, and those who are aware
of his knowledge do not attack him.
Parable 4

10   Do justice, that you may live long upon earth.
Calm the weeper, do not oppress the widow, do not
oust a man from his father's property, do not degrade
magnates from their seats. Beware of punishing
wrongfully; do not kill, for it will not profit you.
Parable 8

11   Instill the love of you into all the world, for a
good character is what is remembered.   *Parable 24*

The Book of the Dead[5]

c. 1700–1000 B.C.

12 Hail to you gods . . .
On that day of the great reckoning.
Behold me, I have come to you,
Without sin, without guilt, without evil,
Without a witness against me,
Without one whom I have wronged. . . .
Rescue me, protect me,
Do not accuse me before the great god!

I am one pure of mouth, pure of hands.
The Address to the Gods

---

[1]Ancient Egyptian quotations from *The Song of the Harper*, Ptah-
hotpe, *The Teaching for Merikare*, and *Love Songs of the New King-
dom* are from WILLIAM KELLY SIMPSON, ed., *The Literature of
Ancient Egypt* [1973]. Those from *The Book of the Dead*, Suti and
Hor, *The Great Hymn to the Aten*, and Amenemope are from
MIRIAM LICHTHEIM, *Ancient Egyptian Literature, vol. II, The New
Kingdom* [1976].

[2]From the tomb of King Inyotef.
Translated by WILLIAM KELLY SIMPSON.

[3]Translated from the earliest manuscript of the *Maxims* (the
Prisse Papyrus in Paris) by R. O. FAULKNER.

---

[4]A treatise on kingship addressed by a king of Heracleopolis,
whose name is lost, to his son and successor Merikare.
Translated by R. O. FAULKNER.

[5]Translated by MIRIAM LICHTHEIM.
"The coming forth by day" . . . the Egyptians called it.—MIRIAM
LICHTHEIM, *Ancient Egyptian Literature, vol. II, The New King-
dom* [1976], *pt. III, introduction*

Love Songs of the New Kingdom[1]
c. 1550–1080 B.C.

1 My love for you is mixed throughout
   my body . . .

So hurry to see your lady,
like a stallion on the track,
or like a falcon swooping down to its
   papyrus marsh.

Heaven sends down the love of her
as a flame falls in the hay.

Song no. 2

2 The voice of the wild goose,
caught by the bait, cries out.
Love of you holds me back,
and I can't loosen it at all. . . .

I did not set my traps today;
love of you has thus entrapped me.

Song no. 10

3 Sweet pomegranate wine in my mouth
is bitter as the gall of birds.

But your embraces
alone give life to my heart;
may Amun give me what I have found
for all eternity.

Song no. 12

4 The voice of the turtledove speaks out. It says:
Day breaks, which way are you going?
Lay off, little bird,
must you so scold me?

I found my lover on his bed,
and my heart was sweet to excess.

Song no. 14

Suti and Hor[2]
Fifteenth–fourteenth centuries B.C.

5 Creator uncreated.
Sole one, unique one, who traverses eternity,
Remote one, with millions under his care;
Your splendor is like heaven's splendor.

First Hymn to the Sun God

6 Beneficent mother of gods and men . . .
Valiant shepherd who drives his flock,

Their refuge, made to sustain them. . . .
He makes the seasons with the months,
Heat as he wishes, cold as he wishes. . . .
Every land rejoices at his rising,
Every day gives praise to him.

Second Hymn to the Sun God

The Great Hymn to the Aten[3]
c. 1350 B.C.

7 Splendid you rise in heaven's lightland,
   O living Aten, creator of life!

St. 1

8 When you set in western lightland,
   Earth is in darkness as if in death.

St. 2

9 Every lion comes from its den,
   All the serpents bite;
   Darkness hovers, earth is silent,
   As their maker rests in lightland.

Earth brightens when you dawn in lightland,
When you shine as Aten of daytime;
As you dispel the dark,
As you cast your rays,
The Two Lands are in festivity.
Awake they stand on their feet,
You have roused them.

St. 2, 3

10 The entire land sets out to work,
   All beasts browse on their herbs;
   Trees, herbs are sprouting,
   Birds fly from their nests . . .
   Ships fare north, fare south as well,
   Roads lie open when you rise;
   The fish in the river dart before you,
   Your rays are in the midst of the sea.

St. 3

11 How many are your deeds,
   Though hidden from sight,
   O Sole God beside whom there is none!
   You made the earth as you wished, you alone.

St. 5

---

[1]Translated by WILLIAM KELLY SIMPSON.

[2]Architects to Amenhotep III (reigned c. 1411–1375 B.C.).
Translated by MIRIAM LICHTHEIM.

[3]From the reign [1365–1349 B.C.] of Amenhotep IV Akhenaten.
   Translated by MIRIAM LICHTHEIM.
   Amenhotep IV . . . converted the supreme god [Aten, the sun disk] into the sole god by denying the reality of all the other gods.
—MIRIAM LICHTHEIM, *Ancient Egyptian Literature, vol. II, The New Kingdom* [1976], *pt. II*

I Ching[1]
[The Book of Changes]
c. Twelfth century B.C.

1 The mountain rests on the earth: the image of splitting apart. Thus those above can insure their position only by giving generously to those below.
Bk. I, ch. 25, Po / Splitting Apart

2 Fire in the lake: the image of revolution.
I, 49, Ko / Revolution (Molting)

3 Wind over lake: the image of inner truth.
I, 61, Chung Fu / Inner Truth

Amenemope
c. Eleventh century B.C.

4 Beginning of the teaching for life,
The instructions for well-being . . .
Knowing how to answer one who speaks,
To reply to one who sends a message.
The Instruction of Amenemope,[2] prologue

5 The truly silent, who keep apart,
He is like a tree grown in a meadow.
It greens, it doubles its yield,
It stands in front of its lord.
Its fruit is sweet, its shade delightful,
Its end comes in the garden.
The Instruction of Amenemope, ch. 4

6 Do not move the markers on the border of the
fields.
The Instruction of Amenemope, 6

7 Better is poverty in the hand of the god,
Than wealth in the storehouse;
Better is bread with a happy heart
Than wealth with vexation.
The Instruction of Amenemope, 6

8 Do not set your heart on wealth . . .
Do not strain to seek increases,
What you have, let it suffice you.
If riches come to you by theft,
They will not stay the night with you. . . .
They made themselves wings like geese,
And flew away to the sky.
The Instruction of Amenemope, 7

The Holy Bible[3]
The Old Testament[4]

9 In the beginning God created the heaven and the earth.
And the earth was without form, and void; and darkness was upon the face of the deep. And the Spirit of God moved upon the face of the waters.
And God said, Let there be light:[5] and there was light.
The First Book of Moses, Called Genesis, chapter 1, verses 1–3

10 And the evening and the morning were the first day.
1:5

11 And God saw that it was good.
1:10

12 And God said, Let us make man in our image, after our likeness.
1:26

13 Male and female created he them.
1:27

14 Be fruitful, and multiply, and replenish the earth, and subdue it: and have dominion over the fish of the sea, and over the fowl of the air, and over every living thing that moveth upon the earth.
1:28

15 And on the seventh day God ended his work which he had made.
2:2

16 And the Lord God formed man of the dust of the ground, and breathed into his nostrils the breath of life; and man became a living soul.
2:7

17 And the Lord God planted a garden eastward in Eden.
2:8

18 The tree of life also in the midst of the garden.
2:9

19 But of the tree of the knowledge of good and evil, thou shalt not eat of it: for in the day that thou eatest thereof thou shalt surely die.
2:17

20 It is not good that the man should be alone; I will make him an help meet for him.
2:18

21 And the Lord God caused a deep sleep to fall upon Adam, and he slept: and he took one of his ribs, and closed up the flesh instead thereof.

---

[1]Translated from Chinese into German by RICHARD WILHELM, and into English by CARY F. BAYNES.

[2]Translated by MIRIAM LICHTHEIM.

---

[3]Bible quotations are from the Authorized (King James) Version [1611]. Numbers in Bible citations represent chapter and verse. The oldest part of the Bible, Song of the Sea (*Exodus 15:1–18;* see 8:25–8:28), dates from the tenth century B.C., the era of Solomon, but the material used by the author (called J, or the Yahwist) was much older. Next oldest is the Song of Deborah (*Judges 5:1–12, 10:29–10:30*).

[4]The Hebrew Scriptures. The first five books (the Pentateuch, or the five books of Moses) are the Jewish Torah, embodying the Law revealed to Moses on Mount Sinai.

[5]Fiat lux. — *The Vulgate*

And the rib, which the Lord God had taken from man, made he a woman.   *Genesis 2:21–22*

1   Bone of my bones, and flesh of my flesh.

2:23

2   Therefore shall a man leave his father and his mother, and shall cleave unto his wife: and they shall be one flesh.

And they were both naked, the man and his wife, and were not ashamed.   *2:24–25*

3   Now the serpent was more subtile than any beast of the field.   *3:1*

4   Your eyes shall be opened, and ye shall be as gods, knowing good and evil.   *3:5*

5   And they sewed fig leaves together, and made themselves aprons.[1]

And they heard the voice of the Lord God walking in the garden in the cool of the day.   *3:7–8*

6   The woman whom thou gavest to be with me, she gave me of the tree, and I did eat.   *3:12*

7   What is this that thou hast done? And the woman said, The serpent beguiled me, and I did eat.

And the Lord God said unto the serpent, Because thou hast done this, thou art cursed above all cattle, and above every beast of the field; upon thy belly shalt thou go, and dust shalt thou eat all the days of thy life.   *3:13–14*

8   And I will put enmity between thee and the woman, and between thy seed and her seed; it shall bruise thy head, and thou shalt bruise his heel.

3:15

9   In sorrow thou shalt bring forth children.

3:16

10   In the sweat of thy face shalt thou eat bread, till thou return unto the ground; for out of it wast thou taken: for dust thou art, and unto dust shalt thou return.

And Adam called his wife's name Eve; because she was the mother of all living.   *3:19–20*

11   So he drove out the man: and he placed at the east of the garden of Eden cherubims, and a flaming sword which turned every way, to keep the way of the tree of life.   *3:24*

12   And Abel was a keeper of sheep, but Cain was a tiller of the ground.   *4:2*

13   Am I my brother's keeper?   *4:9*

14   The voice of thy brother's blood crieth unto me from the ground.   *4:10*

15   A fugitive and a vagabond shalt thou be in the earth.   *4:12*

16   My punishment is greater than I can bear.

4:13

17   And the Lord set a mark upon Cain.   *4:15*

18   And Cain went out from the presence of the Lord, and dwelt in the land of Nod.   *4:16*

19   Jabal: he was the father of such as dwell in tents.

4:20

20   Jubal: he was the father of all such as handle the harp and organ.   *4:21*

21   Tubal-cain, an instructor of every artificer in brass and iron.   *4:22*

22   And Enoch walked with God.   *5:24*

23   And all the days of Methuselah were nine hundred sixty and nine years.   *5:27*

24   And Noah begat Shem, Ham, and Japheth.

5:32

25   There were giants in the earth in those days . . . mighty men which were of old, men of renown.

6:4

26   Make thee an ark of gopher wood.   *6:14*

27   And of every living thing of all flesh, two of every sort shalt thou bring into the ark.   *6:19*

28   And the rain was upon the earth forty days and forty nights.   *7:12*

29   But the dove found no rest for the sole of her foot.

8:9

30   And, lo, in her mouth was an olive leaf pluckt off.

8:11

31   For the imagination of man's heart is evil from his youth.   *8:21*

32   While the earth remaineth, seedtime and harvest, and cold and heat, and summer and winter, and day and night shall not cease.   *8:22*

33   Whoso sheddeth man's blood, by man shall his blood be shed: for in the image of God made he man.

9:6

34   I do set my bow in the cloud, and it shall be for a token of a covenant between me and the earth.

9:13

35   Even as Nimrod the mighty hunter before the Lord.   *10:9*

36   Therefore is the name of it called Babel; because the Lord did there confound the language of all the earth.   *11:9*

---

[1]The Geneva Bible [1560] was known sometimes as the Breeches Bible because in this passage "aprons" is rendered as "breeches."

1   Let there be no strife, I pray thee, between me and thee . . . for we be brethren. *13:8*

2   Abram dwelled in the land of Canaan, and Lot dwelled in the cities of the plain, and pitched his tent toward Sodom. *13:12*

3   In a good old age. *15:15*

4   His [Ishmael's] hand will be against every man, and every man's hand against him. *16:12*

5   Thy name shall be Abraham; for a father of many nations have I made thee. *17:5*

6   My Lord, if now I have found favor in thy sight, pass not away, I pray thee, from thy servant. *18:3*

7   But his [Lot's] wife looked back from behind him, and she became a pillar of salt. *19:26*

8   My son, God will provide himself a lamb for a burnt offering. *22:8*

9   Behold behind him a ram caught in a thicket by his horns. *22:13*

10   Esau was a cunning hunter, a man of the field; and Jacob was a plain man, dwelling in tents. *25:27*

11   And he [Esau] sold his birthright unto Jacob.
Then Jacob gave Esau bread and pottage of lentils. *25:33–34*

12   The voice is Jacob's voice, but the hands are the hands of Esau. *27:22*

13   Thy brother came with subtilty, and hath taken away thy blessing. *27:35*

14   He [Jacob] dreamed, and behold a ladder set up on the earth, and the top of it reached to heaven: and behold the angels of God ascending and descending on it. *28:12*

15   Surely the Lord is in this place; and I knew it not. *28:16*

16   This is none other but the house of God, and this is the gate of heaven. *28:17*

17   Jacob served seven years for Rachel; and they seemed unto him but a few days, for the love he had to her. *29:20*

18   And Laban said, This heap [of stones] is a witness between me and thee this day. Therefore was the name of it called Galeed;
And Mizpah; for he said, The Lord watch between me and thee, when we are absent one from another. *31:48–49*

19   And Jacob was left alone; and there wrestled a man with him until the breaking of the day. *32:24*

20   I will not let thee go, except thou bless me. *32:26*

21   And Jacob called the name of the place Peniel: for I have seen God face to face, and my life is preserved. *32:30*

22   Behold, this dreamer cometh. *37:19*

23   They stript Joseph out of his coat, his coat of many colors. *37:23*

24   The Lord made all that he did to prosper in his hand. *39:3*

25   And she [Potiphar's wife] caught him by his garment, saying, Lie with me: and he left his garment in her hand, and fled, and got him out. *39:12*

26   The seven good kine are seven years; and the seven good ears are seven years: the dream is one.
And the seven thin and ill-favored kine that came up after them are seven years; and the seven empty ears blasted with the east wind shall be seven years of famine. *41:26–27*

27   Then shall ye bring down my gray hairs with sorrow to the grave. *42:38*

28   But Benjamin's mess was five times so much as any of theirs. *43:34*

29   Wherefore have ye rewarded evil for good? *44:4*

30   God forbid. *44:7*

31   The man in whose hand the cup is found, he shall be my servant. *44:17*

32   And he fell upon his brother Benjamin's neck, and wept; and Benjamin wept upon his neck. *45:14*

33   And ye shall eat the fat of the land. *45:18*

34   And they came into the land of Goshen. *46:28*

35   But I will lie with my fathers, and thou shalt carry me out of Egypt, and bury me in their buryingplace. And he said, I will do as thou hast said. *47:30*

36   Unstable as water, thou shalt not excel. *49:4*

37   I have waited for thy salvation, O Lord. *49:18*

38   Unto the utmost bound of the everlasting hills. *49:26*

39   Now there arose up a new king over Egypt, which knew not Joseph.
The Second Book of Moses, Called Exodus 1:8

1   She took for him an ark of bulrushes, and daubed it with slime and with pitch.   *Exodus 2:3*

2   I have been a stranger in a strange land.   *2:22*

3   Behold, the bush burned with fire, and the bush was not consumed.   *3:2*

4   Put off thy shoes from off thy feet, for the place whereon thou standest is holy ground.   *3:5*

5   And Moses hid his face; for he was afraid to look upon God.   *3:6*

6   A land flowing with milk and honey.   *3:8*

7   And God said unto Moses, I AM THAT I AM.   *3:14*

8   I am slow of speech, and of a slow tongue.   *4:10*

9   Let my people go.   *5:1*

10   Ye shall no more give the people straw to make brick.   *5:7*

11   Thou shalt say unto Aaron, Take thy rod, and cast it before Pharaoh, and it shall become a serpent.   *7:9*

12   They [Pharaoh's wise men] cast down every man his rod, and they became serpents: but Aaron's rod swallowed up their rods.
And he hardened Pharaoh's heart.   *7:12–13*

13   This is the finger of God.   *8:19*

14   Darkness which may be felt.   *10:21*

15   Yet will I bring one plague more upon Pharaoh, and upon Egypt.   *11:1*

16   Your lamb shall be without blemish.   *12:5*

17   And they shall eat the flesh in that night, roast with fire, and unleavened bread; and with bitter herbs they shall eat it.   *12:8*

18   And thus shall ye eat it; with your loins girded, your shoes on your feet, and your staff in your hand; and ye shall eat it in haste: it is the Lord's passover.
For I will pass through the land of Egypt this night, and will smite all the firstborn in the land of Egypt, both man and beast; and against all the gods of Egypt I will execute judgment: I am the Lord.   *12:11–12*

19   This day [Passover] shall be unto you for a memorial; and ye shall keep it a feast to the Lord throughout your generations.   *12:14*

20   Seven days shall ye eat unleavened bread.   *12:15*

21   There was a great cry in Egypt; for there was not a house where there was not one dead.   *12:30*

22   Remember this day, in which ye came out from Egypt, out of the house of bondage.   *13:3*

23   And the Lord went before them by day in a pillar of a cloud, to lead them the way; and by night in a pillar of fire, to give them light.   *13:21*

24   And the children of Israel went into the midst of the sea upon the dry ground: and the waters were a wall unto them on their right hand, and on their left.   *14:22*

25   I will sing unto the Lord, for he hath triumphed gloriously: the horse and his rider hath he thrown into the sea.
The Lord is my strength and song, and he is become my salvation.   *15:1–2*

26   The Lord is a man of war.   *15:3*

27   Thy right hand, O Lord, is become glorious in power: thy right hand, O Lord, hath dashed in pieces the enemy.   *15:6*

28   Thou sentest forth thy wrath, which consumed them as stubble.
And with the blast of thy nostrils the waters were gathered together, the floods stood upright as an heap, and the depths were congealed in the heart of the sea.   *15:7–8*

29   Would to God we had died by the hand of the Lord in the land of Egypt, when we sat by the fleshpots, and when we did eat bread to the full.   *16:3*

30   It is manna.   *16:15*

31   I am the Lord thy God.   *20:2*[1]

32   Thou shalt have no other gods before me.
Thou shalt not make unto thee any graven image.   *20:3–4*

33   For I the Lord thy God am a jealous God, visiting the iniquity of the fathers upon the children unto the third and fourth generation of them that hate me;
And showing mercy unto thousands of them that love me, and keep my commandments.
Thou shalt not take the name of the Lord thy God in vain.   *20:5–7*

34   Remember the sabbath day, to keep it holy.
Six days shalt thou labor, and do all thy work:
But the seventh day . . . thou shalt not do any work.   *20:8–10*

---

[1] *Exodus 20:2–17* contains the Ten Commandments (the Decalogue), as handed down by God to Moses on Mount Sinai.

1 Honor thy father and thy mother: that thy days may be long upon the land which the Lord thy God giveth thee.

Thou shalt not kill.

Thou shalt not commit adultery.

Thou shalt not steal.

Thou shalt not bear false witness against thy neighbor.

Thou shalt not covet thy neighbor's house, thou shalt not covet thy neighbor's wife, nor his manservant, nor his maidservant, nor his ox, nor his ass, nor any thing that is thy neighbor's. *20:12–17*

2 But let not God speak with us, lest we die. *20:19*

3 He that smiteth a man, so that he die, shall be surely put to death. *21:12*

4 Eye for eye, tooth for tooth, hand for hand, foot for foot. *21:24*

5 Behold, I send an Angel before thee, to keep thee in the way. *23:20*

6 A stiffnecked people. *32:9*

7 Who is on the Lord's side? let him come unto me. *32:26*

8 Thou canst not see my face: for there shall no man see me, and live. *33:20*

9 And he [Moses] was there with the Lord forty days and forty nights; he did neither eat bread, nor drink water. And he wrote upon the tables the words of the covenant, the ten commandments. *34:28*

10 Whatsoever parteth the hoof, and is cloven-footed, and cheweth the cud, among the beasts, that shall ye eat.

The Third Book of Moses, Called Leviticus 11:3

11 And the swine . . . is unclean to you.

Of their flesh shall ye not eat. *11:7–8*

12 Let him go for a scapegoat into the wilderness. *16:10*

13 And when ye reap the harvest of your land, thou shalt not wholly reap the corners of thy field, neither shalt thou gather the gleanings of thy harvest.

And thou shalt not glean thy vineyard, neither shalt thou gather every grape of thy vineyard; thou shalt leave them for the poor and stranger. *19:9–10*

14 Thou shalt not go up and down as a talebearer among thy people. *19:16*

15 Thou shalt love thy neighbor as thyself.[1] *19:18*

16 Ye shall hallow the fiftieth year, and proclaim liberty throughout all the land unto all the inhabitants thereof:[2] it shall be a jubilee unto you. *25:10*

17 The Lord bless thee, and keep thee:

The Lord make his face shine upon thee, and be gracious unto thee:

The Lord lift up his countenance upon thee, and give thee peace.

The Fourth Book of Moses, Called Numbers 6:24–26

18 Sent to spy out the land. *13:16*

19 And your children shall wander in the wilderness forty years. *14:33*

20 Moses lifted up his hand, and with his rod he smote the rock twice: and the water came out abundantly. *20:11*

21 He whom thou blessest is blessed. *22:6*

22 The Lord opened the mouth of the ass, and she said unto Balaam, What have I done unto thee? *22:28*

23 Let me die the death of the righteous, and let my last end be like his! *23:10*

24 God is not a man, that he should lie. *23:19*

25 What hath God wrought![3] *23:23*

26 How goodly are thy tents, O Jacob, and thy tabernacles, O Israel! *24:5*

27 Be sure your sin will find you out. *32:23*

28 I call heaven and earth to witness.

The Fifth Book of Moses, Called Deuteronomy 4:26

29 Hear, O Israel: The Lord our God is one Lord. *6:4*

30 Thou shalt love the Lord thy God with all thine heart, and with all thy soul, and with all thy might.

And these words, which I command thee this day, shall be in thine heart:

And thou shalt teach them diligently unto thy children. *6:5–7*

31 Ye shall not tempt the Lord your God. *6:16*

32 The Lord thy God hath chosen thee to be a special people unto himself. *7:6*

---

[1]Also in *Matthew 19:19* and *22:39* (36:43), *Mark 12:31* and *33*, *Romans 13:9*, *Galatians 5:14*, *James 2:8*.

[2]From "proclaim" through "thereof": inscription on the Liberty Bell, Philadelphia [1751].

[3]Quoted by Samuel F. B. Morse in the first telegraph message he sent to his partner, Alfred Vail, from Washington to Baltimore [May 24, 1844].

1 Man doth not live by bread only,[1] but by every word that proceedeth out of the mouth of the Lord doth man live.   *Deuteronomy 8:3*

2 For the Lord thy God bringeth thee into a good land.   *8:7*

3 A land of wheat, and barley, and vines, and fig trees, and pomegranates; a land of oil olive, and honey;

A land wherein thou shalt eat bread without scarceness, thou shalt not lack any thing in it; a land whose stones are iron, and out of whose hills thou mayest dig brass.   *8:8–9*

4 A dreamer of dreams.   *13:1*

5 The wife of thy bosom.   *13:6*

6 The poor shall never cease out of the land.   *15:11*

7 Thou shalt not move a sickle unto thy neighbor's standing corn.   *23:25*

8 Thou shalt not muzzle the ox when he treadeth out the corn.   *25:4*

9 And thou shalt become an astonishment, a proverb, and a byword, among all nations.   *28:37*

10 In the morning thou shalt say, Would God it were even! and at even thou shalt say, Would God it were morning!   *28:67*

11 The secret things belong unto the Lord our God.   *29:29*

12 I have set before you life and death, blessing and cursing: therefore choose life, that both thou and thy seed may live.   *30:19*

13 He is the Rock, his work is perfect: for all his ways are judgment: a God of truth.   *32:4*

14 Jeshurun waxed fat, and kicked.   *32:15*

15 As thy days, so shall thy strength be.   *33:25*

16 The eternal God is thy refuge, and underneath are the everlasting arms.   *33:27*

17 No man knoweth of his [Moses'] sepulcher unto this day.   *34:6*

18 Be strong and of a good courage; be not afraid, neither be thou dismayed: for the Lord thy God is with thee whithersoever thou goest.   *The Book of Joshua 1:9*

19 And the priests that bare the ark of the covenant of the Lord stood firm on dry ground in the midst of Jordan, and all the Israelites passed over on dry ground, until all the people were passed clean over Jordan.   *3:17*

20 Mighty men of valor.   *6:2*

21 And it came to pass, when the people heard the sound of the trumpet, and the people shouted with a great shout, that the wall fell down flat, so that the people went up into the city [Jericho].   *6:20*

22 His fame was noised throughout all the country.   *6:27*

23 Hewers of wood and drawers of water.   *9:21*

24 Sun, stand thou still upon Gibeon; and thou, Moon, in the valley of Ajalon.   *10:12*

25 Old and stricken in years.   *13:1*

26 I am going the way of all the earth.   *23:14*

27 They shall be as thorns in your sides.   *The Book of Judges 2:3*

28 Then Jael, Heber's wife, took a nail of the tent, and took an hammer in her hand, and went softly unto him [Sisera], and smote the nail into his temples, and fastened it into the ground; for he was fast asleep, and weary: so he died.   *4:21*

29 I Deborah arose . . . I arose a mother in Israel.   *5:7*

30 Awake, awake, Deborah: awake, awake, utter a song: arise, Barak, and lead thy captivity captive.   *5:12*

31 The stars in their courses fought against Sisera.   *5:20*

32 She [Jael] brought forth butter in a lordly dish.   *5:25*

33 At her feet he bowed, he fell, he lay down: at her feet he bowed, he fell: where he bowed, there he fell down dead.   *5:27*

34 The mother of Sisera looked out at a window, and cried through the lattice, Why is his chariot so long in coming? why tarry the wheels of his chariots?   *5:28*

35 Have they not divided the prey; to every man a damsel or two?   *5:30*

36 The sword of the Lord, and of Gideon.   *7:18*

37 Is not the gleaning of the grapes of Ephraim better than the vintage of Abiezer?   *8:2*

38 Say now Shibboleth: and he said Sibboleth: for he could not frame to pronounce it right.   *12:6*

39 There was a swarm of bees and honey in the carcass of the lion.   *14:8*

---

[1] Man shall not live by bread alone. — *Matthew 4:4*

1   Out of the eater came forth meat, and out of the strong came forth sweetness.   *14:14*

2   If ye had not plowed with my heifer, ye had not found out my riddle.   *14:18*

3   He smote them hip and thigh.   *15:8*

4   With the jawbone of an ass . . . have I slain a thousand men.   *15:16*

5   The Philistines be upon thee, Samson.   *16:9*

6   The Philistines took him [Samson], and put out his eyes, and brought him down to Gaza, and bound him with fetters of brass; and he did grind in the prison house.   *16:21*

7   Strengthen me, I pray thee, only this once, O God, that I may be . . . avenged of the Philistines for my two eyes.   *16:28*

8   So the dead which he slew at his death were more than they which he slew in his life.   *16:30*

9   From Dan even to Beersheba.   *20:1*

10   All the people arose as one man.   *20:8*

11   In those days there was no king in Israel: every man did that which was right in his own eyes.   *21:25*

12   Whither thou goest, I will go; and where thou lodgest, I will lodge: thy people shall be my people, and thy God my God.   *The Book of Ruth 1:16*

13   Let me glean and gather after the reapers among the sheaves.   *2:7*

14   Go not empty unto thy mother in law.   *3:17*

15   In the flower of their age.   *The First Book of Samuel 2:33*

16   The Lord called Samuel: and he answered, Here am I.   *3:4*

17   Speak, Lord; for thy servant heareth.   *3:9*

18   Be strong, and quit yourselves like men.   *4:9*

19   And she named the child Ichabod, saying, The glory is departed from Israel: because the ark of God was taken.   *4:21*

20   Is Saul also among the prophets?   *10:11*

21   God save the king.   *10:24*

22   A man after his own heart.   *13:14*

23   Every man's sword was against his fellow.   *14:20*

24   But Jonathan heard not when his father charged the people with the oath: wherefore he put forth the end of the rod that was in his hand, and dipped it in an honeycomb, and put his hand to his mouth; and his eyes were enlightened.   *14:27*

25   For the Lord seeth not as man seeth; for man looketh on the outward appearance, but the Lord looketh on the heart.   *16:7*

26   I know thy pride, and the naughtiness of thine heart.   *17:28*

27   Let no man's heart fail because of him [Goliath].   *17:32*

28   Go, and the Lord be with thee.   *17:37*

29   And he [David] . . . chose him five smooth stones out of the brook.   *17:40*

30   So David prevailed over the Philistine with a sling and with a stone.   *17:50*

31   Saul hath slain his thousands, and David his ten thousands.   *18:7*

32   And Jonathan . . . loved him [David] as he loved his own soul.   *20:17*

33   Wickedness proceedeth from the wicked.   *24:13*

34   I have played the fool.   *26:21*

35   Tell it not in Gath, publish it not in the streets of Askelon.   *The Second Book of Samuel 1:20*

36   Saul and Jonathan were lovely and pleasant in their lives, and in their death they were not divided: they were swifter than eagles, they were stronger than lions.   *1:23*

37   How are the mighty fallen in the midst of the battle!   *1:25*

38   Thy love to me was wonderful, passing the love of women.
How are the mighty fallen, and the weapons of war perished!   *1:26–27*

39   Abner . . . smote him under the fifth rib.   *2:23*

40   Know ye not that there is a prince and a great man [Abner] fallen this day in Israel?   *3:38*

41   And David and all the house of Israel played before the Lord on all manner of instruments made of fir wood, even on harps, and on psalteries, and on timbrels, and on cornets, and on cymbals.   *6:5*

42   Uzzah put forth his hand to the ark of God, and took hold of it . . . and the anger of the Lord was kindled against Uzzah.   *6:6*

43   David danced before the Lord.   *6:14*

1   Tarry at Jericho until your beards be grown.
II Samuel 10:5

2   Set ye Uriah in the forefront of the hottest battle.
11:15

3   The poor man had nothing, save one little ewe lamb.   *12:3*

4   Thou art the man.   *12:7*

5   Now he is dead, wherefore should I fast? Can I bring him back again? I shall go to him, but he shall not return to me.   *12:23*

6   For we must needs die, and are as water spilt on the ground, which cannot be gathered up again.
14:14

7   Would God I had died for thee, O Absalom, my son, my son!   *18:33*

8   The Lord is my rock, and my fortress, and my deliverer.   *22:2*

9   David the son of Jesse . . . the sweet psalmist of Israel.   *23:1*

10   Went in jeopardy of their lives.   *23:17*

11   A wise and an understanding heart.
The First Book of the Kings 3:12

12   Many, as the sand which is by the sea in multitude.   *4:20*

13   Judah and Israel dwelt safely, every man under his vine and under his fig tree.   *4:25*

14   He [Solomon] spake three thousand proverbs: and his songs were a thousand and five.   *4:32*

15   The wisdom of Solomon.   *4:34*

16   So that there was neither hammer nor axe nor any tool of iron heard in the house,[1] while it was in building.   *6:7*

17   A proverb and a byword among all people.
9:7

18   When the queen of Sheba heard of the fame of Solomon . . . she came to prove him with hard questions.   *10:1*

19   The half was not told me: thy wisdom and prosperity exceedeth the fame which I heard.   *10:7*

20   Once in three years came the navy of Tharshish, bringing gold, and silver, ivory, and apes, and peacocks.   *10:22*

21   King Solomon loved many strange women.
11:1

22   My father hath chastised you with whips, but I will chastise you with scorpions.   *12:11*

23   To your tents, O Israel.   *12:16*

24   He [Elijah] went and dwelt by the brook Cherith, that is before Jordan.   *17:5*

25   And the ravens brought him bread and flesh in the morning, and bread and flesh in the evening; and he drank of the brook.   *17:6*

26   An handful of meal in a barrel, and a little oil in a cruse.   *17:12*

27   And the barrel of meal wasted not, neither did the cruse of oil fail.   *17:16*

28   How long halt ye between two opinions?
18:21

29   Either he [Baal] is talking, or he is pursuing, or he is in a journey, or peradventure he sleepeth, and must be awaked.   *18:27*

30   There ariseth a little cloud out of the sea, like a man's hand.   *18:44*

31   And he girded up his loins, and ran before Ahab.
18:46

32   But the Lord was not in the wind: and after the wind an earthquake; but the Lord was not in the earthquake:
And after the earthquake a fire; but the Lord was not in the fire: and after the fire a still small voice.
19:11–12

33   Let not him that girdeth on his harness boast himself as he that putteth it off.   *20:11*

34   Hast thou found me, O mine enemy?   *21:20*

35   The dogs shall eat Jezebel by the wall of Jezreel.
21:23

36   But there was none like unto Ahab, which did sell himself to work wickedness in the sight of the Lord, whom Jezebel his wife stirred up.   *21:25*

37   I saw all Israel scattered upon the hills, as sheep that have not a shepherd.   *22:17*

38   Feed him [Micajah] with bread of affliction, and with water of affliction, until I come in peace.
22:27

39   There appeared a chariot of fire, and horses of fire, and parted them both asunder; and Elijah went up by a whirlwind into heaven.
The Second Book of the Kings 2:11

40   The chariot of Israel, and the horsemen thereof. And he saw him no more.   *2:12*

41   He [Elisha] took up also the mantle of Elijah.
2:13

---

[1]Solomon's temple (the house of the Lord).

1   There is death in the pot.   *4:40*

2   Is thy servant a dog, that he should do this great thing?   *8:13*

3   What hast thou to do with peace? turn thee behind me.   *9:18*

4   The driving is like the driving of Jehu the son of Nimshi; for he driveth furiously.   *9:20*

5   Jezebel heard of it; and she painted her face, and tired her head, and looked out at a window.   *9:30*

6   The angel of the Lord went out, and smote in the camp of the Assyrians an hundred fourscore and five thousand: and when they arose early in the morning, behold, they were all dead corpses.
So Sennacherib king of Assyria departed.   *19:35–36*

7   Set thine house in order.   *20:1*

8   I will wipe Jerusalem as a man wipeth a dish, wiping it, and turning it upside down.   *21:13*

9   His mercy endureth for ever.
The First Book of the Chronicles 16:41

10   The Lord searcheth all hearts, and understandeth all the imaginations of the thoughts.   *28:9*

11   Thine, O Lord, is the greatness, and the power, and the glory, and the victory, and the majesty: for all that is in the heaven and in the earth is thine; thine is the kingdom, O Lord, and thou art exalted as head above all.   *29:11*

12   For all things come of thee, and of thine own have we given thee.   *29:14*

13   Our days on the earth are as a shadow.   *29:15*

14   He [David] died in a good old age, full of days, riches, and honor.   *29:28*

15   They which builded on the wall, and they that bare burdens, with those that laded, every one with one of his hands wrought in the work, and with the other hand held a weapon.   *The Book of Nehemiah 4:17*

16   And he [Ezra] read therein before the street that was before the water gate from the morning until midday, before the men and the women, and those that could understand; and the ears of all the people were attentive unto the book of the law.   *8:3*

17   Thou art a God ready to pardon, gracious and merciful, slow to anger, and of great kindness.   *9:17*

18   Mordecai rent his clothes, and put on sackcloth with ashes.   *The Book of Esther 4:1*

19   The man whom the king delighteth to honor.   *6:6*

20   They hanged Haman on the gallows.   *7:10*

21   One that feared God, and eschewed evil.
The Book of Job 1:1

22   Satan came also.   *1:6*

23   And the Lord said unto Satan, Whence comest thou? Then Satan answered the Lord, and said, From going to and fro in the earth, and from walking up and down in it.   *1:7*

24   Doth Job fear God for nought?   *1:9*

25   And I only am escaped alone to tell thee.   *1:15*

26   Naked came I out of my mother's womb, and naked shall I return thither: the Lord gave, and the Lord hath taken away; blessed be the name of the Lord.   *1:21*

27   Skin for skin, yea, all that a man hath will he give for his life.   *2:4*

28   Curse God, and die.   *2:9*

29   Let the day perish wherein I was born, and the night in which it was said, There is a man child conceived.   *3:3*

30   For now should I have lain still and been quiet, I should have slept: then had I been at rest,
With kings and counsellors of the earth, which built desolate places for themselves.   *3:13–14*

31   There the wicked cease from troubling; and there the weary be at rest.   *3:17*

32   Who ever perished, being innocent? or where were the righteous cut off?   *4:7*

33   Fear came upon me, and trembling.   *4:14*

34   Then a spirit passed before my face; the hair of my flesh stood up.   *4:15*

35   Shall mortal man be more just than God? shall a man be more pure than his maker?   *4:17*

36   Wrath killeth the foolish man, and envy slayeth the silly one.   *5:2*

37   Man is born unto trouble, as the sparks fly upward.   *5:7*

38   He taketh the wise in their own craftiness.   *5:13*

39   For thou shalt be in league with the stones of the field: and the beasts of the field shall be at peace with thee.   *5:23*

40   Thou shalt come to thy grave in a full age, like as a shock of corn cometh in in his season.   *5:26*

1   How forcible are right words!   *Job 6:25*

2   My days are swifter than a weaver's shuttle, and are spent without hope.   *7:6*

3   He shall return no more to his house, neither shall his place know him any more.   *7:10*

4   I would not live alway: let me alone: for my days are vanity.   *7:16*

5   But how should man be just with God?   *9:2*

6   The land of darkness and the shadow of death.   *10:21*

7   Canst thou by searching find out God?   *11:7*

8   And thine age shall be clearer than the noonday.   *11:17*

9   No doubt but ye are the people, and wisdom shall die with you.   *12:2*

10   The just upright man is laughed to scorn.   *12:4*

11   But ask now the beasts, and they shall teach thee; and the fowls of the air, and they shall tell thee:
Or speak to the earth, and it shall teach thee; and the fishes of the sea shall declare unto thee.   *12:7–8*

12   With the ancient is wisdom; and in length of days understanding.   *12:12*

13   He discovereth deep things out of darkness, and bringeth out to light the shadow of death.   *12:22*

14   Though he slay me, yet will I trust in him.   *13:15*

15   Man that is born of a woman is of few days, and full of trouble.
He cometh forth like a flower, and is cut down: he fleeth also as a shadow, and continueth not.   *14:1–2*

16   But man dieth, and wasteth away: yea, man giveth up the ghost, and where is he?   *14:10*

17   If a man die, shall he live again?   *14:14*

18   Should a wise man utter vain knowledge, and fill his belly with the east wind?   *15:2*

19   Miserable comforters are ye all.   *16:2*

20   My days are past.   *17:11*

21   I have said to corruption, Thou art my father: to the worm, Thou art my mother, and my sister.   *17:14*

22   The king of terrors.   *18:14*

23   I am escaped with the skin of my teeth.   *19:20*

24   Oh that my words were now written! oh that they were printed in a book!   *19:23*

25   I know that my redeemer liveth, and that he shall stand at the latter day upon the earth:[1]
And though, after my skin, worms destroy this body, yet in my flesh shall I see God.   *19:25–26*

26   Seeing the root of the matter is found in me.   *19:28*

27   Though wickedness be sweet in his mouth, though he hide it under his tongue.   *20:12*

28   Suffer me that I may speak; and after that I have spoken, mock on.   *21:3*

29   Shall any teach God knowledge?   *21:22*

30   They are of those that rebel against the light.   *24:13*

31   The womb shall forget him; the worm shall feed sweetly on him; he shall be no more remembered.   *24:20*

32   Yea, the stars are not pure in his sight.
How much less man, that is a worm? and the son of man, which is a worm?   *25:5–6*

33   But where shall wisdom be found? and where is the place of understanding?   *28:12*

34   The land of the living.   *28:13*

35   The price of wisdom is above rubies.   *28:18*

36   Behold, the fear of the Lord, that is wisdom; and to depart from evil is understanding.   *28:28*

37   I caused the widow's heart to sing for joy.   *29:13*

38   I was eyes to the blind, and feet was I to the lame.   *29:15*

39   I know that thou wilt bring me to death, and to the house appointed for all living.   *30:23*

40   I am a brother to dragons, and a companion to owls.   *30:29*

41   My desire is, that the Almighty would answer me, and that mine adversary had written a book.   *31:35*

42   Great men are not always wise.   *32:9*

43   For I am full of matter, the spirit within me constraineth me.   *32:18*

44   One among a thousand.   *33:23*

---

[1]Also in *Book of Common Prayer, Burial of the Dead.*

1   Far be it from God, that he should do wickedness.   *34:10*

2   He multiplieth words without knowledge.   *35:16*

3   Fair weather cometh out of the north.   *37:22*

4   Then the Lord answered Job out of the whirlwind, and said,
Who is this that darkeneth counsel by words without knowledge?
Gird up now thy loins like a man.   *38:1–3*

5   Where wast thou when I laid the foundations of the earth? declare, if thou hast understanding.   *38:4*

6   The morning stars sang together, and all the sons of God shouted for joy.   *38:7*

7   Hitherto shalt thou come, but no further: and here shall thy proud waves be stayed.   *38:11*

8   Hast thou entered into the springs of the sea? or hast thou walked in the search of the depth?   *38:16*

9   Hath the rain a father? or who hath begotten the drops of dew?   *38:28*

10   Canst thou bind the sweet influences of Pleiades, or loose the bands of Orion?   *38:31*

11   Canst thou guide Arcturus with his sons?   *38:32*

12   Who can number the clouds in wisdom? or who can stay the bottles of heaven.   *38:37*

13   Hast thou given the horse strength? hast thou clothed his neck with thunder?   *39:19*

14   He paweth in the valley, and rejoiceth in his strength: he goeth on to meet the armed men.   *39:21*

15   He swalloweth the ground with fierceness and rage; neither believeth he that it is the sound of the trumpet.
He saith among the trumpets, Ha, ha; and he smelleth the battle afar off, the thunder of the captains, and the shouting.   *39:24–25*

16   Doth the eagle mount up at thy command, and make her nest on high?
She dwelleth and abideth on the rock, upon the crag of the rock, and the strong place.
From thence she seeketh the prey, and her eyes behold afar off.
Her young ones also suck up blood: and where the slain are, there is she.   *39:27–30*

17   Behold, I am vile; what shall I answer thee?   *40:4*

18   Behold now behemoth, which I made with thee; he eateth grass as an ox.   *40:15*

19   Canst thou draw out leviathan with a hook?   *41:1*

20   Who can open the doors of his face? his teeth are terrible round about.
His scales are his pride, shut up together as with a close seal.   *41:14–15*

21   His heart is as firm as a stone; yea as hard as a piece of the nether millstone.   *41:24*

22   He maketh the deep to boil like a pot.   *41:31*

23   Upon earth there is not his like, who is made without fear.   *41:33*

24   He is a king over all the children of pride.   *41:34*

25   I have heard of thee by the hearing of the ear: but now mine eye seeth thee.   *42:5*

26   So the Lord blessed the latter end of Job more than his beginning.   *42:12*

27   Blessed is the man that walketh not in the counsel of the ungodly, nor standeth in the way of sinners, nor sitteth in the seat of the scornful.
But his delight is in the law of the Lord; and in his law doth he meditate day and night.
And he shall be like a tree planted by the rivers of water, that bringeth forth his fruit in his season; his leaf also shall not wither; and whatsoever he doeth shall prosper.
The ungodly are not so: but are like the chaff which the wind driveth away.
The Book of Psalms 1:1–4

28   Why do the heathen rage, and the people imagine a vain thing?   *2:1*

29   Blessed are all they that put their trust in him.   *2:12*

30   Lord, lift thou up the light of thy countenance upon us.   *4:6*

31   I will both lay me down in peace, and sleep.   *4:8*

32   Out of the mouth of babes and sucklings hast thou ordained strength, because of thine enemies; that thou mightest still the enemy and the avenger.
When I consider thy heavens, the work of thy fingers, the moon and the stars, which thou hast ordained;
What is man, that thou art mindful of him? and the son of man, that thou visitest him?
For thou hast made him a little lower than the angels.   *8:2–5*

1   How excellent is thy name in all the earth.
Psalms 8:9

2   Flee as a bird to your mountain.
11:1

3   How long wilt thou forget me, O Lord?
13:1

4   The fool hath said in his heart, There is no God.
14:1 and 53:1

5   Lord, who shall abide in thy tabernacle? who shall dwell in thy holy hill?
15:1

6   He that sweareth to his own hurt, and changeth not.
15:4

7   The lines are fallen unto me in pleasant places; yea, I have a goodly heritage.
16:6

8   Keep me as the apple of the eye, hide me under the shadow of thy wings.
17:8

9   He rode upon a cherub, and did fly: yea, he did fly upon the wings of the wind.
18:10

10   The heavens declare the glory of God; and the firmament showeth his handiwork.

Day unto day uttereth speech, and night unto night showeth knowledge.
19:1–2

11   Their line is gone out through all the earth, and their words to the end of the world. In them hath he set a tabernacle for the sun,

Which is as a bridegroom coming out of his chamber, and rejoiceth as a strong man to run a race.

His going forth is from the end of the heaven, and his circuit unto the ends of it: and there is nothing hid from the heat thereof.
19:4–6

12   The judgments of the Lord are true and righteous altogether.

More to be desired are they than gold, yea, than much fine gold: sweeter also than honey and the honeycomb.
19:9–10

13   Cleanse thou me from secret faults.   *19:12*

14   Let the words of my mouth, and the meditation of my heart, be acceptable in thy sight, O Lord, my strength, and my redeemer.
19:14

15   Thou hast given him his heart's desire.
21:2

16   My God, my God, why hast thou forsaken me?[1] why art thou so far from helping me, and from the words of my roaring?
22:1

17   They part my garments among them, and cast lots upon my vesture.
22:18

18   The Lord is my shepherd; I shall not want.

He maketh me to lie down in green pastures: he leadeth me beside the still waters.

He restoreth my soul: he leadeth me in the paths of righteousness for his name's sake.

Yea, though I walk through the valley of the shadow of death, I will fear no evil: for thou art with me; thy rod and thy staff they comfort me.

Thou preparest a table before me in the presence of mine enemies: thou anointest my head with oil; my cup runneth over.

Surely goodness and mercy shall follow me all the days of my life: and I will dwell in the house of the Lord for ever.
23

19   The earth is the Lord's, and the fullness thereof; the world, and they that dwell therein.

For he hath founded it upon the seas, and established it upon the floods.

Who shall ascend into the hill of the Lord? or who shall stand in his holy place?

He that hath clean hands, and a pure heart; who hath not lifted up his soul unto vanity, nor sworn deceitfully.
24:1–4

20   Lift up your heads, O ye gates; and be ye lift up, ye everlasting doors; and the King of glory shall come in.
24:7

21   Who is this King of glory? The Lord of hosts, he is the King of glory.
24:10

22   The Lord is my light[2] and my salvation; whom shall I fear? the Lord is the strength of my life; of whom shall I be afraid?
27:1

23   Though an host should encamp against me, my heart shall not fear: though war should rise against me, in this will I be confident.
27:3

24   The Lord is my strength and my shield.
28:7

25   Worship the Lord in the beauty of holiness.
29:2

26   Weeping may endure for a night, but joy cometh in the morning.
30:5

27   I am forgotten as a dead man out of mind: I am like a broken vessel.
31:12

28   My times are in thy hand.   *31:15*

29   From the strife of tongues.   *31:20*

30   Sing unto him a new song; play skillfully with a loud noise.
33:3

---

[1]This was the psalm Christ recited on the cross. See *Matthew 27:46, 38:9.*

[2]*Dominus illuminatio mea.* — *The Vulgate.* Motto of Oxford University.

1   O taste and see that the Lord is good.   *34:8*

2   Keep thy tongue from evil, and thy lips from speaking guile.
Depart from evil, and do good; seek peace, and pursue it.   *34:13–14*

3   Rescue my soul from their destructions, my darling from the lions.   *35:17*

4   How excellent is thy lovingkindness, O God!   *36:7*

5   The meek shall inherit the earth.   *37:11*

6   I have been young, and now am old; yet have I not seen the righteous forsaken, nor his seed begging bread.   *37:25*

7   I have seen the wicked in great power, and spreading himself[1] like a green bay tree.   *37:35*

8   Mark the perfect man, and behold the upright: for the end of that man is peace.   *37:37*

9   For thine arrows stick fast in me, and thy hand presseth me sore.   *38:2*

10   I said, I will take heed to my ways, that I sin not with my tongue.   *39:1*

11   My heart was hot within me, while I was musing the fire burned.   *39:3*

12   Lord, make me to know mine end, and the measure of my days, what it is; that I may know how frail I am.   *39:4*

13   Every man at his best state is altogether vanity.   *39:5*

14   Surely every man walketh in a vain show: surely they are disquieted in vain: he heapeth up riches, and knoweth not who shall gather them.   *39:6*

15   For I am a stranger with thee, and a sojourner, as all my fathers were.
O spare me, that I may recover strength, before I go hence, and be no more.   *39:12–13*

16   As the hart panteth after the water brooks, so panteth my soul after thee, O God.
My soul thirsteth for God, for the living God.   *42:1–2*

17   Why art thou cast down, O my soul? and why art thou disquieted in me?   *42:5*

18   Deep calleth unto deep.   *42:7*

19   My tongue is the pen of a ready writer.   *45:1*

20   The king's daughter is all glorious within.   *45:13*

21   God is our refuge and strength, a very present help in trouble.
Therefore will we not fear, though the earth be removed, and though the mountains be carried into the midst of the sea.   *46:1–2*

22   There is a river, the streams whereof shall make glad the city of God, the holy place of the tabernacles of the most High.
God is in the midst of her; she shall not be moved: God shall help her, and that right early.   *46:4–5*

23   Be still, and know that I am God.   *46:10*

24   Every beast of the forest is mine, and the cattle upon a thousand hills.   *50:10*

25   I was shapen in iniquity; and in sin did my mother conceive me.   *51[2]:5*

26   Purge me with hyssop, and I shall be clean: wash me, and I shall be whiter than snow.   *51:7*

27   Create in me a clean heart, O God; and renew a right spirit within me.   *51:10*

28   And take not thy holy spirit from me.   *51:11*

29   Open thou my lips; and my mouth shall show forth thy praise.   *51:15*

30   A broken and a contrite heart, O God, thou wilt not despise.   *51:17*

31   Oh that I had wings like a dove! for then would I fly away, and be at rest.   *55:6*

32   We took sweet counsel together.   *55:14*

33   The words of his mouth were smoother than butter, but war was in his heart: his words were softer than oil, yet were they drawn swords.   *55:21*

34   They are like the deaf adder that stoppeth her ear;
Which will not hearken to the voice of charmers, charming never so wisely.   *58:4–5*

35   Thou hast showed thy people hard things: thou hast made us to drink the wine of astonishment.   *60:3*

36   Moab is my washpot; over Edom will I cast out my shoe: Philistia, triumph thou because of me.   *60:8*

37   Lead me to the rock that is higher than I.   *61:2*

---

[1]Flourishing. — *Book of Common Prayer, Psalm 37:36*

[2]This psalm is known as the Miserere from its opening word in the *Vulgate.* The first line is: Have mercy upon me, O God.

1   He only is my rock and my salvation: he is my defense; I shall not be moved.   *Psalms 62:6*

2   Thou renderest to every man according to his work.   *62:12*

3   My soul thirsteth for thee, my flesh longeth for thee in a dry and thirsty land, where no water is.   *63:1*

4   Thou crownest the year with thy goodness.   *65:11*

5   Make a joyful noise unto God, all ye lands.   *66:1*

6   We went through fire and through water.   *66:12*

7   God setteth the solitary in families.   *68:6*

8   Cast me not off in the time of old age; forsake me not when my strength faileth.   *71:9*

9   He shall come down like rain upon the mown grass: as showers that water the earth.   *72:6*

10   His enemies shall lick the dust.   *72:9*

11   His name shall endure for ever.   *72:17*

12   A stubborn and rebellious generation.   *78:8*

13   Man did eat angels' food.   *78:25*

14   But ye shall die like men, and fall like one of the princes.   *82:7*

15   How amiable are thy tabernacles, O Lord of hosts!   *84:1*

16   They go from strength to strength.   *84:7*

17   A day in thy courts is better than a thousand. I had rather be a doorkeeper in the house of my God, than to dwell in the tents of wickedness.   *84:10*

18   Mercy and truth are met together; righteousness and peace have kissed each other.   *85:10*

19   Lord, why castest thou off my soul? why hidest thou thy face from me?   *88:14*

20   Lord, thou hast been our dwelling place in all generations.
    Before the mountains were brought forth, or ever thou hadst formed the earth and the world, even from everlasting to everlasting, thou art God.
    Thou turnest man to destruction; and sayest, Return, ye children of men.
    For a thousand years in thy sight are but as yesterday when it is past, and as a watch in the night.
    Thou carriest them away as with a flood; they are as a sleep: in the morning they are like grass which groweth up.

In the morning it flourisheth, and groweth up; in the evening it is cut down, and withereth.   *90:1–6*

21   We spend our years as a tale that is told.   *90:9*

22   The days of our years are threescore years and ten; and if by reason of strength they be fourscore years, yet is their strength labor and sorrow; for it is soon cut off, and we fly away.   *90:10*

23   So teach us to number our days, that we may apply our hearts unto wisdom.   *90:12*

24   Establish thou the work of our hands upon us; yea, the work of our hands establish thou it.   *90:17*

25   He that dwelleth in the secret place of the most High shall abide under the shadow of the Almighty.
    I will say of the Lord, He is my refuge and my fortress: my God; in him will I trust.
    Surely he shall deliver thee from the snare of the fowler, and from the noisome pestilence.
    He shall cover thee with his feathers, and under his wings shalt thou trust: his truth shall be thy shield and buckler.
    Thou shalt not be afraid for the terror by night; nor for the arrow that flieth by day.
    Nor for the pestilence that walketh in darkness; nor for the destruction that wasteth at noonday.
    A thousand shall fall at thy side, and ten thousand at thy right hand; but it shall not come nigh thee.   *91:1–7*

26   He shall give his angels charge over thee, to keep thee in all thy ways.
    They shall bear thee up in their hands, lest thou dash thy foot against a stone.
    Thou shalt tread upon the lion and adder: the young lion and the dragon shalt thou trample under feet.   *91:11–13*

27   The righteous shall flourish like the palm tree: he shall grow like a cedar in Lebanon.   *92:12*

28   Mightier than the noise of many waters.   *93:4*

29   O come, let us sing unto the Lord: let us make a joyful noise to the rock of our salvation.
    Let us come before his presence with thanksgiving, and make a joyful noise unto him with psalms.
    For the Lord is a great God, and a great King above all gods.
    In his hand are the deep places of the earth: the strength of the hills is his also.
    The sea is his, and he made it: and his hands formed the dry land.

O come, let us worship and bow down: let us kneel before the Lord our maker.

For he is our God; and we are the people of his pasture, and the sheep of his hand. *95:1–7*

1 O sing unto the Lord a new song. *96:1*

2 The Lord reigneth; let the earth rejoice. *97:1*

3 Make a joyful noise unto the Lord, all ye lands.
Serve the Lord with gladness: come before his presence with singing.
Know ye that the Lord he is God: it is he that hath made us, and not we ourselves; we are his people, and the sheep of his pasture.
Enter into his gates with thanksgiving, and into his courts with praise: be thankful unto him, and bless his name.
For the Lord is good; his mercy is everlasting; and his truth endureth to all generations. *100*

4 My days are consumed like smoke. *102:3*

5 I watch, and am as a sparrow alone upon the house top. *102:7*

6 As the heaven is high above the earth, so great is his mercy toward them that fear him. *103:11*

7 As for man, his days are as grass: as a flower of the field, so he flourisheth.
For the wind passeth over it, and it is gone; and the place thereof shall know it no more. *103:15–16*

8 Who layeth the beams of his chambers in the waters: who maketh the clouds his chariot: who walketh upon the wings of the wind. *104:3*

9 Wine that maketh glad the heart of man. *104:15*

10 The cedars of Lebanon. *104:16*

11 He appointed the moon for seasons: the sun knoweth his going down.
Thou makest darkness, and it is night: wherein all the beasts of the forest do creep forth.
The young lions roar after their prey, and seek their meat from God.
The sun ariseth, they gather themselves together, and lay them down in their dens.
Man goeth forth unto his work and to his labor until the evening.
O Lord, how manifold are thy works! in wisdom hast thou made them all: the earth is full of thy riches.
So is this great and wide sea, wherein are things creeping innumerable, both small and great beasts.
There go the ships: there is that leviathan, whom thou hast made to play therein.

These wait all upon thee; that thou mayest give them their meat in due season. *104:19–27*

12 The people asked, and he brought quails, and satisfied them with the bread of heaven. *105:40*

13 Such as sit in darkness and in the shadow of death. *107:10*

14 They that go down to the sea in ships, that do business in great waters. *107:23*

15 They mount up to the heaven, they go down again to the depths. *107:26*

16 They reel to and fro, and stagger like a drunken man, and are at their wit's end. *107:27*

17 For I am poor and needy, and my heart is wounded within me.
I am gone like the shadow when it declineth: I am tossed up and down as the locust. *109:22–23*

18 Thou hast the dew of thy youth. *110:3*

19 The fear of the Lord is the beginning of wisdom. *111:10*

20 From the rising of the sun unto the going down of the same the Lord's name is to be praised. *113:3*

21 The mountains skipped like rams, and the little hills like lambs. *114:4*

22 They have mouths, but they speak not: eyes have they, but they see not.
They have ears, but they hear not. *115:5–6*

23 I said in my haste, All men are liars. *116:11*

24 Precious in the sight of the Lord is the death of his saints. *116:15*

25 The stone which the builders refused is become the head stone of the corner. *118:22*

26 This is the day which the Lord hath made. *118:24*

27 Blessed be he that cometh in the name of the Lord. *118:26*

28 Thy word is a lamp unto my feet, and a light unto my path. *119:105*

29 I am for peace: but when I speak, they are for war. *120:7*

30 I will lift up mine eyes unto the hills, from whence cometh my help.
My help cometh from the Lord, which made heaven and earth.

He will not suffer thy foot to be moved: he that keepeth thee will not slumber.

Behold, he that keepeth Israel shall neither slumber nor sleep.

The Lord is thy keeper: the Lord is thy shade upon thy right hand.

The sun shall not smite thee by day, nor the moon by night.

The Lord shall preserve thee from all evil: he shall preserve thy soul.

The Lord shall preserve thy going out and thy coming in from this time forth, and even for evermore.   *Psalms 121*

1   I was glad when they said unto me, Let us go into the house of the Lord.   *122:1*

2   Peace be within thy walls, and prosperity within thy palaces.   *122:7*

3   They that sow in tears shall reap in joy.

He that goeth forth and weepeth, bearing precious seed, shall doubtless come again with rejoicing, bringing his sheaves with him.   *126:5–6*

4   Except the Lord build the house, they labor in vain that build it: except the Lord keep the city, the watchman waketh but in vain.   *127:1*

5   He giveth his beloved sleep.   *127:2*

6   As arrows are in the hand of a mighty man; so are children of the youth.

Happy is the man that hath his quiver full of them.   *127:4–5*

7   Out of the depths have I cried unto thee, O Lord.   *130:1*

8   My soul waiteth for the Lord more than they that watch for the morning.   *130:6*

9   I will not give sleep to mine eyes, or slumber to mine eyelids.   *132:4*

10   Behold, how good and how pleasant it is for brethren to dwell together in unity!   *133:1*

11   By the rivers of Babylon, there we sat down, yea, we wept, when we remembered Zion.

We hanged our harps upon the willows in the midst thereof.

For there they that carried us away captive required of us a song; and they that wasted us required of us mirth, saying, Sing us one of the songs of Zion.

How shall we sing the Lord's song in a strange land?

If I forget thee, O Jerusalem, let my right hand forget her cunning.

If I do not remember thee, let my tongue cleave to the roof of my mouth.   *137:1–6*

12   O Lord, thou hast searched me, and known me.

Thou knowest my downsitting and mine uprising; thou understandest my thought afar off.   *139:1–2*

13   Whither shall I go from thy Spirit? or whither shall I flee from thy presence?

If I ascend up into heaven, thou art there: if I make my bed in hell, behold, thou art there.

If I take the wings of the morning, and dwell in the uttermost parts of the sea;

Even there shall thy hand lead me, and thy right hand shall hold me.   *139:7–10*

14   The darkness and the light are both alike to thee.   *139:12*

15   I am fearfully and wonderfully made.   *139:14*

16   They have sharpened their tongues like a serpent.   *140:3*

17   Thou openest thine hand, and satisfiest the desire of every living thing.   *145:16*

18   The Lord is nigh unto all them that call upon him, to all that call upon him in truth.   *145:18*

19   Put not your trust in princes.   *146:3*

20   He telleth the number of the stars; he calleth them all by their names.   *147:4*

21   Praise him with the sound of the trumpet: praise him with the psaltery and harp.

Praise him with the timbrel and dance: praise him with stringed instruments and organs.

Praise him upon the loud cymbals: praise him upon the high sounding cymbals.

Let every thing that hath breath praise the Lord.   *150:3–6*

22   To give subtilty to the simple, to the young man knowledge and discretion.   *The Proverbs 1:4*

23   My son, if sinners entice thee, consent thou not.   *1:10*

24   Wisdom crieth without; she uttereth her voice in the streets.   *1:20*

25   Length of days is in her right hand; and in her left hand riches and honor.   *3:16*

26   Her ways are ways of pleasantness, and all her paths are peace.   *3:17*

27   Be not afraid of sudden fear.   *3:25*

28   Wisdom is the principal thing; therefore get wisdom: and with all thy getting get understanding.   *4:7*

1 The path of the just is as the shining light, that shineth more and more unto the perfect day.   *4:18*

2 Keep thy heart with all diligence; for out of it are the issues of life.   *4:23*

3 The lips of a strange woman drop as a honeycomb, and her mouth is smoother than oil:
But her end is bitter as wormwood, sharp as a two-edged sword.   *5:3–4*

4 Go to the ant, thou sluggard; consider her ways, and be wise:
Which having no guide, overseer, or ruler,
Provideth her meat in the summer, and gathereth her food in the harvest.   *6:6–8*

5 Yet a little sleep, a little slumber, a little folding of the hands to sleep:
So shall thy poverty come as one that traveleth, and thy want as an armed man.   *6:10–11*

6 Lust not after her beauty in thine heart; neither let her take thee with her eyelids.   *6:25*

7 Can a man take fire in his bosom, and his clothes not be burned?
Can one go upon hot coals, and his feet not be burned?   *6:27–28*

8 Jealousy is the rage of a man: therefore he will not spare in the day of vengeance.   *6:34*

9 He goeth after her straightway, as an ox goeth to the slaughter.   *7:22*

10 I love them that love me; and those that seek me early shall find me.   *8:17*

11 Wisdom hath builded her house, she hath hewn out her seven pillars.   *9:1*

12 Reprove not a scorner, lest he hate thee: rebuke a wise man, and he will love thee.   *9:8*

13 Stolen waters are sweet, and bread eaten in secret is pleasant.   *9:17*

14 A wise son maketh a glad father: but a foolish son is the heaviness of his mother.   *10:1*

15 Blessings are upon the head of the just: but violence covereth the mouth of the wicked.
The memory of the just is blessed: but the name of the wicked shall rot.   *10:6–7*

16 Hatred stirreth up strifes: but love covereth all sins.   *10:12*

17 In the multitude of counsellors there is safety.
He that is surety for a stranger shall smart for it.   *11:14–15*

18 As a jewel of gold in a swine's snout, so is a fair woman which is without discretion.   *11:22*

19 He that trusteth in his riches shall fall.   *11:28*

20 He that troubleth his own house shall inherit the wind.   *11:29*

21 A virtuous woman is a crown to her husband.   *12:4*

22 A righteous man regardeth the life of his beast: but the tender mercies of the wicked are cruel.   *12:10*

23 The way of a fool is right in his own eyes.   *12:15*

24 Hope deferred maketh the heart sick.   *13:12*

25 The way of transgressors is hard.   *13:15*

26 The desire accomplished is sweet to the soul.   *13:19*

27 He that spareth his rod hateth his son: but he that loveth him chasteneth him betimes.   *13:24*

28 Fools make a mock at sin.   *14:9*

29 The heart knoweth his own bitterness; and a stranger doth not intermeddle with his joy.   *14:10*

30 Even in laughter the heart is sorrowful.   *14:13*

31 The prudent man looketh well to his going.   *14:15*

32 In all labor there is profit: but the talk of the lips tendeth only to penury.   *14:23*

33 Righteousness exalteth a nation.   *14:34*

34 A soft answer turneth away wrath.   *15:1*

35 A merry heart maketh a cheerful countenance: but by sorrow of the heart the spirit is broken.   *15:13*

36 He that is of a merry heart hath a continual feast.
Better is little with the fear of the Lord, than great treasure, and trouble therewith.
Better is a dinner of herbs where love is, than a stalled ox and hatred therewith.   *15:15–17*

37 A wrathful man stirreth up strife: but he that is slow to anger appeaseth strife.   *15:18*

38 A word spoken in due season, how good is it!   *15:23*

39 Before honor is humility.   *15:33 and 18:12*

heart deviseth his way: but the Lord di-
teps. *Proverbs 16:9*

th before destruction, and an haughty
before a fall. *16:18*

3 The hoary head is a crown of glory, if it be found in the way of righteousness.

He that is slow to anger is better than the mighty; and he that ruleth his spirit than he that taketh a city.
16:31–32

4 Whoso mocketh the poor reproacheth his Maker.
17:5

5 He that repeateth a matter separateth very friends. *17:9*

6 Whoso rewardeth evil for good, evil shall not depart from his house. *17:13*

7 A merry heart doeth good like a medicine.
17:22

8 He that hath knowledge spareth his words: and a man of understanding is of an excellent spirit.

Even a fool, when he holdeth his peace, is counted wise. *17:27–28*

9 A fool's mouth is his destruction. *18:7*

10 A wounded spirit who can bear? *18:14*

11 A brother offended is harder to be won than a strong city: and their contentions are like the bars of a castle. *18:19*

12 Whoso findeth a wife findeth a good thing.
18:22

13 A man that hath friends must show himself friendly: and there is a friend that sticketh closer than a brother. *18:24*

14 Wealth maketh many friends. *19:4*

15 A foolish son is the calamity of his father: and the contentions of a wife are a continual dropping.
19:13

16 He that hath pity upon the poor lendeth unto the Lord. *19:17*

17 Wine is a mocker, strong drink is raging.
20:1

18 It is an honor for a man to cease from strife: but every fool will be meddling. *20:3*

19 Even a child is known by his doings, whether his work be pure, and whether it be right.

The hearing ear, and the seeing eye, the Lord hath made even both of them. *20:11–12*

20 It is naught, it is naught, saith the buyer: but when he is gone his way, then he boasteth.
20:14

21 Bread of deceit is sweet to a man; but afterwards his mouth shall be filled with gravel. *20:17*

22 Meddle not with him that flattereth with his lips.
20:19

23 It is better to dwell in a corner of the housetop, than with a brawling woman in a wide house.
21:9 and 25:24

24 A good name is rather to be chosen than great riches. *22:1*

25 Train up a child in the way he should go; and when he is old, he will not depart from it.
22:6

26 The borrower is servant to the lender. *22:7*

27 Bow down thine ear, and hear the words of the wise, and apply thine heart unto my knowledge.

For it is a pleasant thing if thou keep them within thee; they shall withal be fitted in thy lips.
22:17–18

28 Have I not written to thee excellent things in counsels and knowledge,

That I might make thee know the certainty of the words of truth; that thou mightest answer the words of truth to them that send unto thee?
22:20–21

29 Rob not the poor, because he is poor: neither oppress the afflicted in the gate. *22:22*

30 Remove not the ancient landmark. *22:28*

31 Seest thou a man diligent in his business? He shall stand before kings. *22:29*

32 Put a knife to thy throat, if thou be a man given to appetite. *23:2*

33 Labor not to be rich: cease from thine own wisdom. *23:4*

34 Riches certainly make themselves wings; they fly away as an eagle toward heaven. *23:5*

35 As he thinketh in his heart, so is he. *23:7*

36 The drunkard and the glutton shall come to poverty: and drowsiness shall clothe a man with rags.
23:21

37 Despise not thy mother when she is old.
23:22

38 Look not thou upon the wine when it is red, when it giveth his color in the cup, when it moveth itself aright.

At the last it biteth like a serpent, and stingeth like an adder. *23:31–32*

39 A wise man is strong; yea, a man of knowledge increaseth strength. *24:5*

1 If thou faint in the day of adversity, thy strength is small. *24:10*

2 A word fitly spoken is like apples of gold in pictures of silver. *25:11*

3 If thine enemy be hungry, give him bread to eat; and if he be thirsty, give him water to drink:
For thou shalt heap coals of fire upon his head. *25:21–22*

4 As cold waters to a thirsty soul, so is good news from a far country. *25:25*

5 For men to search their own glory is not glory. *25:27*

6 Answer a fool according to his folly. *26:5*

7 As a dog returneth to his vomit, so a fool returneth to his folly.
Seest thou a man wise in his own conceit? There is more hope of a fool than of him.
The slothful man saith, There is a lion in the way; a lion is in the streets. *26:11–13*

8 Whoso diggeth a pit shall fall therein: and he that rolleth a stone, it will return upon him. *26:27*

9 Boast not thyself of tomorrow; for thou knowest not what a day may bring forth. *27:1*

10 Let another man praise thee, and not thine own mouth. *27:2*

11 Open rebuke is better than secret love.
Faithful are the wounds of a friend; but the kisses of an enemy are deceitful. *27:5–6*

12 To the hungry soul every bitter thing is sweet. *27:7*

13 Better is a neighbor that is near than a brother far off. *27:10*

14 Iron sharpeneth iron; so a man sharpeneth the countenance of his friend. *27:17*

15 The wicked flee when no man pursueth: but the righteous are bold as a lion. *28:1*

16 He that maketh haste to be rich shall not be innocent. *28:20*

17 He that trusteth in his own heart is a fool. *28:26*

18 He that giveth unto the poor shall not lack. *28:27*

19 A fool uttereth all his mind. *29:11*

20 Where there is no vision, the people perish. *29:18*

21 A man's pride shall bring him low: but honor shall uphold the humble in spirit. *29:23*

22 Give me neither poverty nor riches. *30:8*

23 Accuse not a servant unto his master. *30:10*

24 The horseleach hath two daughters, crying, Give, give. *30:15*

25 There be three things which are too wonderful for me, yea, four which I know not:
The way of an eagle in the air; the way of a serpent upon a rock; the way of a ship in the midst of the sea; and the way of a man with a maid. *30:18–19*

26 Give strong drink unto him that is ready to perish, and wine unto those that be of heavy hearts.
Let him drink, and forget his poverty, and remember his misery no more. *31:6–7*

27 Who can find a virtuous woman? for her price is far above rubies.
The heart of her husband doth safely trust in her. *31:10–11*

28 Her husband is known in the gates, when he sitteth among the elders of the land. *31:23*

29 Strength and honor are her clothing. *31:25*

30 In her tongue is the law of kindness.
She looketh well to the ways of her household, and eateth not the bread of idleness.
Her children arise up, and call her blessed. *31:26–28*

31 Many daughters have done virtuously, but thou excellest them all.
Favor is deceitful, and beauty is vain: but a woman that feareth the Lord, she shall be praised.
Give her of the fruit of her hands; and let her own works praise her in the gates. *31:29–31*

32 Vanity of vanities, saith the Preacher, vanity of vanities; all is vanity.
What profit hath a man of all his labor which he taketh under the sun?
One generation passeth away, and another generation cometh: but the earth abideth for ever.
The sun also ariseth.
Ecclesiastes; or, The Preacher 1:2–5

33 All the rivers run into the sea; yet the sea is not full. *1:7*

34 The eye is not satisfied with seeing, nor the ear filled with hearing. *1:8*

35 The thing that hath been, it is that which shall be; and that which is done is that which shall be done: and there is no new thing under the sun. *1:9*

36 There is no remembrance of former things; neither shall there be any remembrance of things that are to come with those that shall come after. *1:11*

1   I have seen all the works that are done under the sun; and, behold, all is vanity and vexation of spirit. That which is crooked cannot be made straight: and that which is wanting cannot be numbered.

Ecclesiastes 1:14–15

2   In much wisdom is much grief: and he that increaseth knowledge increaseth sorrow.   *1:18*

3   Wisdom excelleth folly, as far as light excelleth darkness.   *2:13*

4   One event happeneth to them all.   *2:14*

5   How dieth the wise man? as the fool.   *2:16*

6   To every thing there is a season, and a time to every purpose under the heaven.

A time to be born, and a time to die; a time to plant, and a time to pluck up that which is planted;

A time to kill, and a time to heal; a time to break down, and a time to build up;

A time to weep, and a time to laugh; a time to mourn, and a time to dance;

A time to cast away stones, and a time to gather stones together; a time to embrace, and a time to refrain from embracing;

A time to get, and a time to lose; a time to keep, and a time to cast away;

A time to rend, and a time to sew; a time to keep silence, and a time to speak;

A time to love, and a time to hate; a time of war, and a time of peace.   *3:1–8*

7   Wherefore I praised the dead which are already dead more than the living which are yet alive.

4:2

8   Better is a handful with quietness, than both the hands full with travail and vexation of spirit.   *4:6*

9   A threefold cord is not quickly broken.

4:12

10   Better is a poor and a wise child than an old and foolish king.   *4:13*

11   God is in heaven, and thou upon earth: therefore let thy words be few.   *5:2*

12   Better is it that thou shouldest not vow, than that thou shouldest vow and not pay.   *5:5*

13   The sleep of a laboring man is sweet . . . but the abundance of the rich will not suffer him to sleep.   *5:12*

14   As he came forth of his mother's womb, naked shall he return to go as he came, and shall take nothing of his labor, which he may carry away in his hand.   *5:15*

15   A good name is better than precious ointment; and the day of death than the day of one's birth.

7:1

16   It is better to go to the house of mourning, than to go to the house of feasting.   *7:2*

17   The heart of the wise is in the house of mourning; but the heart of fools is in the house of mirth.

7:4

18   As the crackling of thorns under a pot, so is the laughter of the fool.   *7:6*

19   Better is the end of a thing than the beginning thereof.   *7:8*

20   In the day of prosperity be joyful, but in the day of adversity consider.   *7:14*

21   Be not righteous over much.   *7:16*

22   There is not a just man upon earth, that doeth good, and sinneth not.   *7:20*

23   And I find more bitter than death the woman, whose heart is snares and nets, and her hands as bands.   *7:26*

24   One man among a thousand have I found; but a woman among all those have I not found.

7:28

25   God hath made man upright; but they have sought out many inventions.   *7:29*

26   There is no discharge in that war.   *8:8*

27   A man hath no better thing under the sun, than to eat, and to drink, and to be merry.   *8:15*

28   A living dog is better than a dead lion.

For the living know that they shall die: but the dead know not any thing, neither have they any more a reward; for the memory of them is forgotten.

9:4–5

29   Whatsoever thy hand findeth to do, do it with thy might; for there is no work, nor device, nor knowledge, nor wisdom, in the grave, whither thou goest.

9:10

30   I returned, and saw under the sun, that the race is not to the swift, nor the battle to the strong, neither yet bread to the wise, nor yet riches to men of understanding, nor yet favor to men of skill; but time and chance happeneth to them all.

For man also knoweth not his time: as the fishes that are taken in an evil net, and as the birds that are caught in the snare; so are the sons of men snared in an evil time, when it falleth suddenly upon them.

9:11–12

1 A feast is made for laughter, and wine maketh merry: but money answereth all things.   *10:19*

2 A bird of the air shall carry the voice, and that which hath wings shall tell the matter.   *10:20*

3 Cast thy bread upon the waters: for thou shalt find it after many days.   *11:1*

4 He that observeth the wind shall not sow; and he that regardeth the clouds shall not reap.   *11:4*

5 In the morning sow thy seed, and in the evening withhold not thine hand.   *11:6*

6 Rejoice, O young man, in thy youth.   *11:9*

7 Remember now thy Creator in the days of thy youth, while the evil days come not, nor the years draw nigh, when thou shalt say, I have no pleasure in them;
    While the sun, or the light, or the moon, or the stars, be not darkened, nor the clouds return after the rain:
    In the day when the keepers of the house shall tremble, and the strong men shall bow themselves, and the grinders cease because they are few, and those that look out of the windows be darkened,
    And the doors shall be shut in the streets, when the sound of the grinding is low, and he shall rise up at the voice of the bird, and all the daughters of music shall be brought low.   *12:1–4*

8 The almond tree shall flourish, and the grasshopper shall be a burden, and desire shall fail; because man goeth to his long home, and the mourners go about the streets:
    Or ever the silver cord be loosed, or the golden bowl be broken, or the pitcher be broken at the fountain, or the wheel broken at the cistern.
    Then shall the dust return to the earth as it was: and the spirit shall return unto God who gave it.   *12:5–7*

9 The words of the wise are as goads, and as nails fastened by the masters of assemblies.   *12:11*

10 Of making many books there is no end; and much study is a weariness of the flesh.
    Let us hear the conclusion of the whole matter: Fear God, and keep his commandments: for this is the whole duty of man.
    For God shall bring every work into judgment, with every secret thing, whether it be good, or whether it be evil.   *12:12–14*

11 The song of songs, which is Solomon's.
    The Song of Solomon 1:1

12 I am black, but comely, O ye daughters of Jerusalem, as the tents of Kedar, as the curtains of Solomon.   *1:5*

13 O thou fairest among women.   *1:8*

14 I am the rose of Sharon, and the lily of the valleys.   *2:1*

15 As the apple tree among the trees of the wood, so is my beloved among the sons.   *2:3*

16 His banner over me was love.
    Stay me with flagons, comfort me with apples: for I am sick of love.   *2:4–5*

17 Rise up, my love, my fair one, and come away.
    For, lo, the winter is past, the rain is over and gone;
    The flowers appear on the earth; the time of the singing of birds is come, and the voice of the turtle is heard in our land.   *2:10–12*

18 Take us the foxes, the little foxes, that spoil the vines: for our vines have tender grapes.   *2:15*

19 Until the day break, and the shadows flee away.   *2:17 and 4:6*

20 By night on my bed I sought him whom my soul loveth: I sought him, but I found him not.   *3:1*

21 Thy two breasts are like two young roes that are twins, which feed among the lilies.   *4:5*

22 Thou art all fair, my love; there is no spot in thee.   *4:7*

23 How much better is thy love than wine!   *4:10*

24 Awake, O north wind; and come, thou south; blow upon my garden, that the spices thereof may flow out. Let my beloved come into his garden, and eat his pleasant fruits.   *4:16*

25 My beloved put in his hand by the hole of the door, and my bowels were moved for him.   *5:4*

26 His mouth is most sweet: yea, he is altogether lovely. This is my beloved, and this is my friend, O daughters of Jerusalem.   *5:16*

27 Who is she that looketh forth as the morning, fair as the moon, clear as the sun, and terrible as an army with banners?   *6:10*

28 Return, return, O Shulamite.   *6:13*

29 Thy belly is like a heap of wheat set about with lilies.   *7:2*

30 Thy neck is as a tower of ivory.   *7:4*

1   Like the best wine . . . that goeth down sweetly, causing the lips of those that are asleep to speak.
The Song of Solomon 7:9

2   I am my beloved's, and his desire is toward me.
7:10

3   Set me as a seal upon thine heart, as a seal upon thine arm: for love is strong as death; jealousy is cruel as the grave.
8:6

4   Many waters cannot quench love, neither can the floods drown it.
8:7

5   Make haste, my beloved, and be thou like to a roe or to a young hart upon the mountains of spices.
8:14

6   The ox knoweth his owner, and the ass his master's crib.   *The Book of the Prophet Isaiah 1:3*

7   The whole head is sick, and the whole heart faint.
1:5

8   As a lodge in a garden of cucumbers.   *1:8*

9   Bring no more vain oblations.   *1:13*

10   Learn to do well; seek judgment, relieve the oppressed, judge the fatherless, plead for the widow.
Come now, and let us reason together . . . though your sins be as scarlet, they shall be as white as snow.
1:17–18

11   They shall beat their swords into plowshares, and their spears into pruninghooks: nation shall not lift up sword against nation, neither shall they learn war any more.[1]
2:4

12   In that day a man shall cast his idols . . . to the moles and to the bats.
2:20

13   Cease ye from man, whose breath is in his nostrils.
2:22

14   The stay and the staff, the whole stay of bread, and the whole stay of water.
3:1

15   What mean ye that ye beat my people to pieces and grind the faces of the poor?
3:15

16   Walk with stretched forth necks and wanton eyes, walking and mincing as they go, and making a tinkling with their feet.
3:16

17   In that day seven women shall take hold of one man.
4:1

18   My wellbeloved hath a vineyard in a very fruitful hill.
5:1

19   And he looked for judgment, but behold oppression; for righteousness, but behold a cry.
Woe unto them that join house to house, that lay field to field, till there be no place, that they may be placed alone in the midst of the earth!
5:7–8

20   Woe unto them that rise up early in the morning, that they may follow strong drink.
5:11

21   Woe unto them that draw iniquity with cords of vanity, and sin as it were with a cart rope.
5:18

22   Woe unto them that call evil good, and good evil.
5:20

23   I saw also the Lord sitting upon a throne, high and lifted up, and his train filled the temple.
Above it stood the seraphims: each one had six wings; with twain he covered his face, and with twain he covered his feet, and with twain he did fly.
6:1–2

24   Holy, holy, holy, is the Lord of hosts: the whole earth is full of his glory.   *6:3*

25   Woe is me! for I am undone; because I am a man of unclean lips, and I dwell in the midst of a people of unclean lips: for mine eyes have seen the King, the Lord of hosts.
6:5

26   I heard the voice of the Lord, saying, Whom shall I send, and who will go for us? Then said I, Here am I; send me.
6:8

27   Then said I, Lord, how long?   *6:11*

28   Behold, a virgin shall conceive, and bear a son, and shall call his name Immanuel.
7:14

29   For a stone of stumbling and for a rock of offense.
8:14

30   The people that walked in darkness have seen a great light: they that dwell in the land of the shadow of death, upon them hath the light shined.   *9:2*

31   For unto us a child is born, unto us a son is given: and the government shall be upon his shoulder: and his name shall be called Wonderful, Counsellor, The mighty God, The everlasting Father, The Prince of Peace.
Of the increase of his government and peace there shall be no end.
9:6–7

32   The ancient and honorable, he is the head.
9:15

33   And there shall come forth a rod out of the stem of Jesse, and a Branch shall grow out of his roots:
And the Spirit of the Lord shall rest upon him, the spirit of wisdom and understanding, the spirit of counsel and might, the spirit of knowledge and of the fear of the Lord.
11:1–2

34   The wolf also shall dwell with the lamb, and the leopard shall lie down with the kid; and the calf and the young lion and the fatling together; and a little child shall lead them.

---

[1]Also in *Joel 3:10* and *Micah 4:3*.

And the cow and the bear shall feed; their young ones shall lie down together: and the lion shall eat straw like the ox.

And the suckling child shall play on the hole of the asp, and the weaned child shall put his hand on the cockatrice' den.

They shall not hurt nor destroy in all my holy mountain: for the earth shall be full of the knowledge of the Lord, as the waters cover the sea.

11:6–9

1   For the Lord JEHOVAH is my strength and my song; he also is become my salvation.   *12:2*

2   And I will punish the world for their evil, and the wicked for their iniquity; and I will cause the arrogancy of the proud to cease, and will lay low the haughtiness of the terrible.   *13:11*

3   How art thou fallen from heaven, O Lucifer, son of the morning!   *14:12*

4   Is this the man that made the earth to tremble, that did shake kingdoms.   *14:16*

5   The nations shall rush like the rushing of many waters.   *17:13*

6   And they shall fight every one against his brother.   *19:2*

7   The burden of the desert of the sea. As whirlwinds in the south pass through; so it cometh from the desert, from a terrible land.   *21:1*

8   Babylon is fallen, is fallen; and all the graven images of her gods he hath broken unto the ground.   *21:9*

9   Watchman, what of the night?   *21:11*

10   Let us eat and drink; for tomorrow we shall die.   *22:13*

11   I will fasten him as a nail in a sure place.   *22:23*

12   Whose merchants are princes.   *23:8*

13   As with the maid, so with her mistress.   *24:2*

14   For thou hast been a strength to the poor, a strength to the needy in his distress.   *25:4*

15   A feast of fat things, a feast of wines on the lees.   *25:6*

16   He will swallow up death in victory; and the Lord God will wipe away tears from off all faces.   *25:8*

17   Open ye the gates, that the righteous nation which keepeth the truth may enter in.

Thou wilt keep him in perfect peace, whose mind is stayed on thee.   *26:2–3*

18   Awake and sing, ye that dwell in dust.   *26:19*

19   Hide thyself as it were for a little moment, until the indignation be overpast.   *26:20*

20   Leviathan that crooked serpent . . . the dragon that is in the sea.   *27:1*

21   For precept must be upon precept, precept upon precept; line upon line, line upon line; here a little, and there a little.   *28:10*

22   We have made a covenant with death, and with hell are we at agreement.   *28:15*

23   It shall be a vexation only to understand the report.   *28:19*

24   They are drunken, but not with wine; they stagger, but not with strong drink.   *29:9*

25   Their strength is to sit still.

Now go, write it before them in a table, and note it in a book, that it may be for the time to come for ever and ever.   *30:7–8*

26   The bread of adversity, and the water of affliction.   *30:20*

27   This is the way, walk ye in it.   *30:21*

28   Behold, a king shall reign in righteousness.   *32:1*

29   And a man shall be as an hiding place from the wind, and a covert from the tempest; as rivers of water in a dry place, as the shadows of a great rock in a weary land.   *32:2*

30   An habitation of dragons, and a court for owls.   *34:13*

31   The desert shall rejoice, and blossom as the rose.   *35:1*

32   Then the eyes of the blind shall be opened, and the ears of the deaf shall be unstopped.

Then shall the lame man leap as an hart, and the tongue of the dumb sing.   *35:5–6*

33   Sorrow and sighing shall flee away.   *35:10*

34   Thou trustest in the staff of this broken reed.   *36:6*

35   Incline thine ear, O Lord, and hear.   *37:17*

36   I shall go softly all my years in the bitterness of my soul.   *38:15*

37   Comfort ye, comfort ye my people.   *40:1*

38   Speak ye comfortably to Jerusalem, and cry unto her, that her warfare is accomplished, that her iniquity is pardoned: for she hath received of the Lord's hand double for all her sins.

The voice of him that crieth in the wilderness, Prepare ye the way of the Lord, make straight in the desert a highway for our God.   *Isaiah 40:2–3*

1   Every valley shall be exalted, and every mountain and hill shall be made low: and the crooked shall be made straight, and the rough places plain.
40:4

2   The voice said, Cry. And he said, what shall I cry? All flesh is grass, and all the goodliness thereof is as the flower of the field.   *40:6*

3   The grass withereth, the flower fadeth; but the word of our God shall stand for ever.   *40:8*

4   Get thee up into the high mountain . . . say unto the cities of Judah, Behold your God!
40:9

5   He shall feed his flock like a shepherd: he shall gather the lambs with his arm, and carry them in his bosom, and shall gently lead those that are with young.   *40:11*

6   The nations are as a drop of a bucket, and are counted as the small dust of the balance.   *40:15*

7   Have ye not known? have ye not heard? hath it not been told you from the beginning?   *40:21*

8   They that wait upon the Lord shall renew their strength; they shall mount up with wings as eagles; they shall run, and not be weary, and they shall walk, and not faint.   *40:31*

9   They helped every one his neighbor; and every one said to his brother, Be of good courage.
41:6

10   A bruised reed shall he not break, and the smoking flax shall he not quench.   *42:3*

11   Shall the clay say to him that fashioneth it, What makest thou?   *45:9*

12   Behold, I have refined thee, but not with silver; I have chosen thee in the furnace of affliction.
48:10

13   O that thou hadst hearkened to my commandments! then had thy peace been as a river, and thy righteousness as the waves of the sea.   *48:18*

14   There is no peace, saith the Lord, unto the wicked.   *48:22*

15   Therefore the redeemed of the Lord shall return, and come with singing unto Zion.   *51:11*

16   Thou hast drunken the dregs of the cup of trembling.   *51:17*

17   Therefore hear now this.   *51:21*

18   How beautiful upon the mountains are the feet of him that bringeth good tidings, that publisheth peace.   *52:7*

19   They shall see eye to eye.   *52:8*

20   He is despised and rejected of men; a man of sorrows, and acquainted with grief.   *53:3*

21   Surely he hath borne our griefs, and carried our sorrows.   *53:4*

22   All we like sheep have gone astray.   *53:6*

23   He is brought as a lamb to the slaughter.   *53:7*

24   Ho, everyone that thirsteth, come ye to the waters.   *55:1*

25   Behold, I have given him for a witness to the people, a leader and commander to the people.
55:4

26   Let the wicked forsake his way, and the unrighteous man his thoughts.   *55:7*

27   For my thoughts are not your thoughts, neither are your ways my ways, saith the Lord.   *55:8*

28   Peace to him that is far off, and to him that is near.   *57:19*

29   Arise, shine; for thy light is come, and the glory of the Lord is risen upon thee.   *60:1*

30   A little one shall become a thousand, and a small one a strong nation.   *60:22*

31   Give unto them beauty for ashes, the oil of joy for mourning, the garment of praise for the spirit of heaviness.   *61:3*

32   I have trodden the winepress alone; and of the people there was none with me: for I will tread them in mine anger, and trample them in my fury; and their blood shall be sprinkled upon my garments, and I will stain all my raiment.   *63:3*

33   All our righteousnesses are as filthy rags; and we all do fade as a leaf.   *64:6*

34   We all are the work of thy hand.   *64:8*

35   I am holier than thou.   *65:5*

36   For, behold, I create new heavens and a new earth.   *65:17*

37   And they shall build houses, and inhabit them; and they shall plant vineyards, and eat the fruit of them.
They shall not build, and another inhabit; they shall not plant, and another eat.   *65:21–22*

1   As one whom his mother comforteth, so will I comfort you.   *66:13*

2   They were as fed horses in the morning: every one neighed after his neighbor's wife.
The Book of the Prophet Jeremiah 5:8

3   Hear now this, O foolish people, and without understanding; which have eyes, and see not; which have ears, and hear not.   *5:21*

4   But this people hath a revolting and a rebellious heart.   *5:23*

5   Saying, Peace, peace; when there is no peace.
6:14 and 8:11

6   Stand ye in the ways, and see, and ask for the old paths, where is the good way, and walk therein.
6:16

7   Amend your ways and your doings.
7:3 and 26:13

8   The harvest is past, the summer is ended, and we are not saved.   *8:20*

9   Is there no balm in Gilead?   *8:22*

10   Oh that I had in the wilderness a lodging place of wayfaring men!   *9:2*

11   Thus saith the Lord, Let not the wise man glory in his wisdom, neither let the mighty man glory in his might, let not the rich man glory in his riches:
But let him that glorieth glory in this, that he understandeth and knoweth me.   *9:23–24*

12   Can the Ethiopian change his skin, or the leopard his spots?   *13:23*

13   Our backslidings are many; we have sinned against thee.   *14:7*

14   Her sun is gone down while it was yet day.
15:9

15   A man of strife and a man of contention.
15:10

16   The sin of Judah is written with a pen of iron, and with the point of a diamond.   *17:1*

17   Cursed be the man that trusteth in man, and maketh flesh his arm, and whose heart departeth from the Lord.
For he shall be like the heath in the desert, and shall not see when good cometh; but shall inhabit the parched places in the wilderness, in a salt land and not inhabited.
Blessed is the man that trusteth in the Lord, and whose hope the Lord is.

For he shall be as a tree planted by the waters, and that spreadeth out her roots by the river, and shall not see when heat cometh, but her leaf shall be green; and shall not be careful in the year of drought, neither shall cease from yielding fruit.   *17:5–8*

18   The heart is deceitful above all things, and desperately wicked: who can know it?   *17:9*

19   As the partridge sitteth on eggs, and hatcheth them not; so he that getteth riches, and not by right, shall leave them in the midst of his days, and at his end shall be a fool.   *17:11*

20   Thou art my hope in the day of evil.   *17:17*

21   O earth, earth, earth, hear the word of the Lord.
22:29

22   A curse, and an astonishment, and a hissing, and a reproach.   *29:18*

23   The fathers have eaten a sour grape, and the children's teeth are set on edge.   *31:29*

24   With my whole heart and with my whole soul.
32:41

25   And seekest thou great things for thyself? seek them not.   *45:5*

26   How doth the city sit solitary, that was full of people! how is she become as a widow!
The Lamentations of Jeremiah 1:1

27   She weepeth sore in the night, and her tears are on her cheeks: among all her lovers she hath none to comfort her.   *1:2*

28   Is it nothing to you, all ye that pass by? behold, and see if there be any sorrow like unto my sorrow.
1:12

29   Remembering mine affliction and my misery, the wormwood and the gall.   *3:19*

30   It is good for a man that he bear the yoke in his youth.   *3:27*

31   As it were a wheel in the middle of a wheel.
The Book of the Prophet Ezekiel 1:16

32   As is the mother, so is her daughter.   *16:44*

33   The king of Babylon stood at the parting of the way.   *21:21*

34   The valley . . . was full of bones . . . and lo, they were very dry.   *37:1–2*

35   Can these bones live?   *37:3*

36   O ye dry bones, hear the word of the Lord.
37:4

1   Every man's sword shall be against his brother.
Ezekiel 38:21

2   His legs of iron, his feet part of iron and part of clay.   *The Book of Daniel 2:33*

3   Shadrach, Meshach, and Abednego, fell down bound into the midst of the burning fiery furnace.
3:23

4   Nebuchadnezzar . . . was driven from men, and did eat grass as oxen.   *4:33*

5   Belshazzar the king made a great feast to a thousand of his lords.   *5:1*

6   And this is the writing that was written, MENE, MENE, TEKEL, UPHARSIN.
This is the interpretation of the thing: MENE; God hath numbered thy kingdom, and finished it.
TEKEL; Thou art weighed in the balances, and art found wanting.
PERES; Thy kingdom is divided, and given to the Medes and Persians.   *5:25–28*

7   According to the law of the Medes and Persians, which altereth not.   *6:12*

8   They brought Daniel, and cast him into the den of lions.   *6:16*

9   So Daniel was taken up out of the den, and no manner of hurt was found upon him, because he believed in his God.   *6:23*

10   The Ancient of days.   *7:9 and 7:13*

11   Many shall run to and fro, and knowledge shall be increased.   *12:4*

12   Ye are the sons of the living God.
Hosea 1:10

13   Like people, like priest.   *4:9*

14   After two days will he revive us: in the third day he will raise us up, and we shall live in his sight.
6:2

15   He shall come unto us as the rain, as the latter and former rain unto the earth.   *6:3*

16   For I desired mercy, and not sacrifice; and the knowledge of God more than burnt offerings.
6:6

17   They have sown the wind, and they shall reap the whirlwind.   *8:7*

18   Ye have plowed wickedness, ye have reaped iniquity.   *10:13*

19   I drew them with . . . bands of love.   *11:4*

20   I have multiplied visions, and used similitudes, by the ministry of the prophets.   *12:10*

21   I will ransom them from the power of the grave; I will redeem them from death: O death, I will be thy plagues; O grave, I will be thy destruction.[1]
13:14

22   Your old men shall dream dreams, your young men shall see visions.   *Joel 2:28*

23   Multitudes in the valley of decision.   *3:14*

24   They sold the righteous for silver, and the poor for a pair of shoes.   *Amos 2:6*

25   Can two walk together, except they be agreed?
3:3

26   Woe to them that are at ease in Zion.   *6:1*

27   And Jonah was in the belly of the fish three days and three nights.   *Jonah 1:17*

28   What doth the Lord require of thee, but to do justly, and to love mercy, and to walk humbly with thy God?   *Micah 6:8*

29   The faces of them all gather blackness.[2]
Nahum 2:10

30   Write the vision, and make it plain upon tables, that he may run that readeth it.   *Habakkuk 2:2*

31   The stone shall cry out of the wall, and the beam out of the timber shall answer it.   *2:11*

32   The Lord is in his holy temple: let all the earth keep silence before him.   *2:20*

33   Your fathers, where are they? And the prophets, do they live forever?   *Zechariah 1:5*

34   I have spread you abroad as the four winds of the heaven.   *2:6*

35   Not by might, nor by power, but by my spirit, saith the Lord of hosts.   *4:6*

36   For who hath despised the day of small things?
4:10

37   Behold, thy King cometh unto thee . . . lowly, and riding upon an ass.   *9:9*

38   Prisoners of hope.   *9:12*

39   So they weighed for my price thirty pieces of silver.   *11:12*

40   What are these wounds in thine hands? . . . Those with which I was wounded in the house of my friends.   *13:6*

41   Have we not all one father? hath not one God created us?   *Malachi 2:10*

---

[1]See *Isaiah 25:8, 27:16*, and *I Corinthians 15:54, 44:33*.

[2]The faces of them all are as the blackness of a kettle. — *Douay Bible* [1609]

1   Behold, I will send my messenger, and he shall prepare the way before me.   *3:1*

2   Behold, the day cometh, that shall burn as an oven.   *4:1*

3   Unto you that fear my name shall the Sun of righteousness arise with healing in his wings.   *4:2*

4   Behold, I will send you Elijah the prophet before the coming of the great and dreadful day of the Lord.   *4:5*

The Apocrypha[1]

5   And when they are in their cups, they forget their love both to friends and brethren, and a little after draw out swords.   *I Esdras 3:22*

6   Great is Truth, and mighty above all things.[2]   *4:41*

7   What is past I know, but what is for to come I know not.   *II Esdras 4:46*

8   Now therefore keep thy sorrow to thyself, and bear with a good courage that which hath befallen thee.   *10:15*

9   I shall light a candle of understanding in thine heart, which shall not be put out.   *14:25*

10   If thou hast abundance, give alms accordingly: if thou have but a little, be not afraid to give according to that little.   *Tobit 4:8*

11   Put on her garments of gladness.
                                        Judith 10:3

12   The ear of jealousy heareth all things.
                        The Wisdom of Solomon 1:10

13   Our time is a very shadow that passeth away.
                                              2:5

14   Let us crown ourselves with rosebuds, before they be withered.   *2:8*

15   For God created man to be immortal, and made him to be an image of his own eternity.
    Nevertheless through envy of the devil came death into the world.   *2:23–24*

16   The souls of the righteous are in the hand of God, and there shall no torment touch them.

---

[1]The Apocrypha (The Hidden Books) is a term used to describe the books found in the Alexandrine Greek Scripture (the Septuagint) but absent from the Orthodox Hebrew Scripture (the Masoretic Text). These books are regarded as canonical only by Roman Catholics.

[2]Magna est veritas et praevalet. — *The Vulgate, Book III* (uncanonical)

In the sight of the unwise they seemed to die: and their departure is taken for misery,
    And their going from us to be utter destruction: but they are in peace.
    For though they be punished in the sight of men, yet is their hope full of immortality.
    And having been a little chastised, they shall be greatly rewarded: for God proved them, and found them worthy for himself.   *3:1–5*

17   They that put their trust in him shall understand the truth.   *3:9*

18   Even so we in like manner, as soon as we were born, began to draw to our end.   *5:13*

19   For the hope of the ungodly is like dust that is blown away with the wind . . . and passeth away as the remembrance of a guest that tarrieth but a day.   *5:14*

20   For the very true beginning of her [wisdom] is the desire of discipline; and the care of discipline is love.   *6:17*

21   And when I was born, I drew in the common air, and fell upon the earth, which is of like nature; and the first voice which I uttered was crying, as all others do.   *7:3*

22   All men have one entrance into life, and the like going out.   *7:6*

23   The light that cometh from her [wisdom] never goeth out.   *7:10*

24   Who can number the sand of the sea, and the drops of rain, and the days of eternity?
    The Wisdom of Jesus the Son of Sirach, or Ecclesiasticus, 1:2

25   To whom hath the root of wisdom been revealed?   *1:6*

26   For the Lord is full of compassion and mercy, long-suffering, and very pitiful, and forgiveth sins, and saveth in time of affliction.   *2:11*

27   The greater thou art, the more humble thyself.   *3:18*

28   Many are in high place, and of renown: but mysteries are revealed unto the meek.   *3:19*

29   Seek not out the things that are too hard for thee, neither search the things that are above thy strength.   *3:21*

30   Be not curious in unnecessary matters: for more things are showed unto thee than men understand.   *3:23*

31   Profess not the knowledge . . . that thou hast not.

A stubborn heart shall fare evil at the last.

Ecclesiasticus 3:25–26

1   Defraud not the poor of his living, and make not the needy eyes to wait long. *4:1*

2   Wisdom exalteth her children, and layeth hold of them that seek her.
He that loveth her loveth life. *4:11–12*

3   Observe the opportunity. *4:20*

4   Be not as a lion in thy house, nor frantic among thy servants.
Let not thine hand be stretched out to receive, and shut when thou shouldest repay. *4:30–31*

5   Set not thy heart upon thy goods; and say not, I have enough for my life. *5:1*

6   Winnow not with every wind, and go not into every way. *5:9*

7   Let thy life be sincere. *5:11*

8   Be not ignorant of any thing in a great matter or a small. *5:15*

9   If thou wouldest get a friend, prove him first. *6:7*

10   A faithful friend is a strong defense: and he that hath found such an one hath found a treasure. *6:14*

11   A faithful friend is the medicine of life. *6:16*

12   If thou seest a man of understanding, get thee betimes unto him, and let thy foot wear the steps of his door. *6:36*

13   Whatsoever thou takest in hand, remember the end, and thou shalt never do amiss. *7:36*

14   Rejoice not over thy greatest enemy being dead, but remember that we die all. *8:7*

15   Miss not the discourse of the elders. *8:9*

16   Forsake not an old friend; for the new is not comparable to him: a new friend is as new wine; when it is old, thou shalt drink it with pleasure. *9:10*

17   Pride is hateful before God and man. *10:7*

18   He that is today a king tomorrow shall die. *10:10*

19   Pride was not made for men, nor furious anger for them that are born of a woman. *10:18*

20   Be not overwise in doing thy business. *10:26*

21   Many kings have sat down upon the ground; and one that was never thought of hath worn the crown. *11:5*

22   In the day of prosperity there is a forgetfulness of affliction: and in the day of affliction there is no more remembrance of prosperity. *11:25*

23   Judge none blessed before his death. *11:28*

24   A friend cannot be known in prosperity: and an enemy cannot be hidden in adversity. *12:8*

25   He that toucheth pitch shall be defiled therewith. *13:1*

26   How agree the kettle and the earthen pot together? *13:2*

27   All flesh consorteth according to kind, and a man will cleave to his like. *13:16*

28   A rich man beginning to fall is held up of his friends: but a poor man being down is thrust also away by his friends. *13:21*

29   The heart of a man changeth his countenance, whether it be for good or evil. *13:25*

30   So is a word better than a gift. *18:16*

31   Be not made a beggar by banqueting upon borrowing. *18:33*

32   He that contemneth small things shall fall by little and little. *19:1*

33   Whether it be to friend or foe, talk not of other men's lives. *19:8*

34   A man's attire, and excessive laughter, and gait, show what he is. *19:30*

35   A tale out of season [is as] music in mourning. *22:6*

36   I will not be ashamed to defend a friend. *22:25*

37   All wickedness is but little to the wickedness of a woman. *25:19*

38   The discourse of fools is irksome. *27:13*

39   Many have fallen by the edge of the sword: but not so many as have fallen by the tongue. *28:18*

40   Better is the life of a poor man in a mean cottage, than delicate fare in another man's house. *29:22*

41   There is no riches above a sound body. *30:16*

42   Gladness of the heart is the life of a man, and the joyfulness of a man prolongeth his days. *30:22*

43   Envy and wrath shorten the life, and carefulness bringeth age before the time. *30:24*

44   Watching for riches consumeth the flesh, and the care thereof driveth away sleep. *31:1*

1 Let thy speech be short, comprehending much in few words. *32:8*

2 Consider that I labored not for myself only, but for all them that seek learning. *33:17*

3 Leave not a stain in thine honor. *33:22*

4 Let the counsel of thine own heart stand. *37:13*

5 Honor a physician with the honor due unto him for the uses which ye may have of him: for the Lord hath created him. *38:1*

6 When the dead is at rest, let his remembrance rest; and be comforted for him, when his spirit is departed from him. *38:23*

7 How can he get wisdom . . . whose talk is of bullocks? *38:25*

8 Let us now praise famous men, and our fathers that begat us. *44:1*

9 All these were honored in their generations, and were the glory of their times.
There be of them, that have left a name behind them, that their praises might be reported.
And some there be, which have no memorial; who are perished, as though they had never been; and are become as though they had never been born; and their children after them. *44:7–9*

10 Their bodies are buried in peace; but their name liveth for evermore. *44:14*

11 His word burned like a lamp. *48:1*

12 O all ye works of the Lord, bless ye the Lord: praise him and exalt him above all for ever.
The Song of the Three Holy Children 35

13 Daniel had convicted them of false witness by their own mouth. *The History of Susanna 61*

14 It is a foolish thing to make a long prologue, and to be short in the story itself.
The Second Book of the Maccabees 2:32

15 When he was at the last gasp. *7:9*

16 Speech finely framed delighteth the ears. *15:39*

The New Testament[1]

17 Behold, a virgin shall be with child, and shall bring forth a son, and they shall call his name Emmanuel, which being interpreted is, God with us.
The Gospel According to Saint Matthew 1:23

18 Now when Jesus was born in Bethlehem of Judaea in the days of Herod the king, behold, there came wise men from the east to Jerusalem,
Saying, Where is he that is born King of the Jews? for we have seen his star in the east, and are come to worship him. *2:1–2*

19 They saw the young child with Mary his mother, and fell down, and worshipped him: and . . . they presented unto him gifts; gold, and frankincense, and myrrh.
And being warned of God in a dream that they should not return to Herod, they departed into their own country another way. *2:11–12*

20 Out of Egypt have I called my son. *2:15*

21 Rachel weeping for her children, and would not be comforted, because they are not. *2:18*

22 He shall be called a Nazarene. *2:23*

23 Repent ye: for the kingdom of heaven is at hand. *3:2*

24 The voice of one crying in the wilderness, Prepare ye the way of the Lord, make his paths straight. *3:3*

25 And his meat was locusts and wild honey. *3:4*

26 O generation of vipers, who hath warned you to flee from the wrath to come? *3:7*

27 Now also the axe is laid unto the root of the trees: therefore every tree which bringeth not forth good fruit is hewn down, and cast into the fire. *3:10*

28 The Spirit of God descending like a dove. *3:16*

29 This is my beloved Son, in whom I am well pleased. *3:17*

30 And when he had fasted forty days and forty nights, he was afterward an hungred. *4:2*

31 The people which sat in darkness saw great light. *4:16*

32 Follow me, and I will make you fishers of men. *4:19*

33 Blessed are the poor in spirit: for theirs is the kingdom of heaven.
Blessed are they that mourn: for they shall be comforted.
Blessed are the meek: for they shall inherit the earth.
Blessed are they which do hunger and thirst after righteousness: for they shall be filled.
Blessed are the merciful: for they shall obtain mercy.

[1]The earliest Christian writings [A.D. c. 50–c. 64] are the Letters (Epistles) of Paul the Apostle. The Gospels are later, between the years 70 and 100.

Blessed are the pure in heart: for they shall see God.

Blessed are the peacemakers: for they shall be called the children of God.

Blessed are they which are persecuted for righteousness' sake: for theirs is the kingdom of heaven.

Blessed are ye, when men shall revile you, and persecute you, and shall say all manner of evil against you falsely, for my sake.   *Matthew 5:3–11*

1   Ye are the salt of the earth: but if the salt have lost his savor, wherewith shall it be salted?   *5:13*

2   Ye are the light of the world. A city that is set on an hill cannot be hid.

Neither do men light a candle, and put it under a bushel, but on a candlestick; and it giveth light unto all that are in the house.

Let your light so shine before men, that they may see your good works, and glorify your Father which is in heaven.

Think not that I am come to destroy the law, or the prophets: I am not come to destroy, but to fulfill.   *5:14–17*

3   Till heaven and earth pass, one jot or one tittle shall in no wise pass from the law, till all be fulfilled.   *5:18*

4   Whosoever looketh on a woman to lust after her hath committed adultery with her already in his heart.

And if thy right eye offend thee, pluck it out, and cast it from thee: for it is profitable for thee that one of thy members should perish, and not that thy whole body should be cast into hell.

And if thy right hand offend thee, cut it off.   *5:28–30*

5   Swear not at all; neither by heaven; for it is God's throne:

Nor by the earth; for it is his footstool.   *5:34–35*

6   Resist not evil: but whosoever shall smite thee on thy right cheek, turn to him the other also.   *5:39*

7   Love your enemies, bless them that curse you, do good to them that hate you, and pray for them which despitefully use you, and persecute you.   *5:44*

8   He maketh his sun to rise on the evil and on the good, and sendeth rain on the just and on the unjust.   *5:45*

9   Be ye therefore perfect, even as your Father which is in heaven is perfect.   *5:48*

10   When thou doest alms, let not thy left hand know what thy right hand doeth.   *6:3*

11   After this manner therefore pray ye: Our Father which art in heaven, Hallowed be thy name.

Thy kingdom come. Thy will be done in earth, as it is in heaven.

Give us this day our daily bread.

And forgive us our debts, as we forgive our debtors.[1]

And lead us not into temptation, but deliver us from evil: For thine is the kingdom, and the power, and the glory, for ever. Amen.   *6:9–13*

12   Lay not up for yourselves treasures upon earth, where moth and rust doth corrupt, and where thieves break through and steal:

But lay up for yourselves treasures in heaven.   *6:19–20*

13   For where your treasure is, there will your heart be also.   *6:21*

14   The light of the body is the eye.   *6:22*

15   If therefore the light that is in thee be darkness, how great is that darkness!   *6:23*

16   No man can serve two masters: for either he will hate the one, and love the other; or else he will hold to the one, and despise the other. Ye cannot serve God and mammon.   *6:24*

17   Is not the life more than meat, and the body than raiment?

Behold the fowls of the air: for they sow not, neither do they reap, nor gather into barns.   *6:25–26*

18   Which of you by taking thought can add one cubit unto his stature?   *6:27*

19   Consider the lilies of the field, how they grow; they toil not, neither do they spin.   *6:28*

20   Even Solomon in all his glory was not arrayed like one of these.   *6:29*

21   Seek ye first the kingdom of God, and his righteousness; and all these things shall be added unto you.   *6:33*

22   Take therefore no thought for the morrow: for the morrow shall take thought for the things of itself. Sufficient unto the day is the evil thereof.   *6:34*

23   Judge not, that ye be not judged.   *7:1*

24   With what measure ye mete, it shall be measured to you again.

And why beholdest thou the mote that is in thy brother's eye, but considerest not the beam that is in thine own eye?   *7:2–3*

---

[1]And forgive us our trespasses, As we forgive those who trespass against us. — *Book of Common Prayer, Morning Prayer*

1 Thou hypocrite, first cast out the beam out of thine own eye. *7:5*

2 Neither cast ye your pearls before swine. *7:6*

3 Ask, and it shall be given you; seek, and ye shall find; knock, and it shall be opened unto you. *7:7*

4 Or what man is there of you, whom if his son ask bread, will he give him a stone? *7:9*

5 Therefore all things whatsoever ye would that men should do to you, do ye even so to them: for this is the law and the prophets.[1] *7:12*

6 Wide is the gate, and broad is the way, that leadeth to destruction, and many there be which go in thereat:
  Because strait is the gate, and narrow is the way, which leadeth unto life, and few there be that find it. *7:13–14*

7 Beware of false prophets, which come to you in sheep's clothing, but inwardly they are ravening wolves. *7:15*

8 Ye shall know them by their fruits. Do men gather grapes of thorns, or figs of thistles? *7:16*

9 By their fruits ye shall know them. *7:20*

10 Not every one that saith unto me, Lord, Lord, shall enter into the kingdom of heaven; but he that doeth the will of my Father which is in heaven. *7:21*

11 [The house] fell not: for it was founded upon a rock. *7:25*

12 A foolish man, which built his house upon the sand. *7:26*

13 But the children of the kingdom shall be cast out into outer darkness: there shall be weeping and gnashing of teeth. *8:12*

14 The foxes have holes, and the birds of the air have nests; but the Son of man hath not where to lay his head. *8:20*

15 Follow me; and let the dead bury their dead. *8:22*

16 Why are ye fearful, O ye of little faith? *8:26*

17 He saw a man, named Matthew, sitting at the receipt of custom. *9:9*

18 They that be whole need not a physician, but they that are sick. *9:12*

19 I am not come to call the righteous, but sinners to repentance. *9:13*

20 Can the children of the bridechamber mourn, as long as the bridegroom is with them? *9:15*

21 Neither do men put new wine into old bottles. *9:17*

22 The maid is not dead, but sleepeth. *9:24*

23 The harvest truly is plenteous, but the laborers are few. *9:37*

24 Go rather to the lost sheep of the house of Israel. *10:6*

25 Freely ye have received, freely give. *10:8*

26 Whosoever shall not receive you, nor hear your words, when ye depart out of that house or city, shake off the dust of your feet. *10:14*

27 Be ye therefore wise as serpents, and harmless as doves. *10:16*

28 Ye shall be hated of all men for my name's sake. *10:22*

29 The disciple is not above his master, nor the servant above his lord. *10:24*

30 Are not two sparrows sold for a farthing? and one of them shall not fall on the ground without your Father.
  But the very hairs of your head are all numbered. *10:29–30*

31 I came not to send peace, but a sword. *10:34*

32 He that taketh not his cross, and followeth after me, is not worthy of me.
  He that findeth his life shall lose it: and he that loseth his life for my sake shall find it. *10:38–39*

33 He that hath ears to hear, let him hear. *11:15*

34 The Son of man came eating and drinking, and they say, Behold a man gluttonous, and a winebibber, a friend of publicans and sinners. But wisdom is justified of her children. *11:19*

35 Come unto me, all ye that labor and are heavy laden, and I will give you rest.
  Take my yoke upon you, and learn of me; for I am meek and lowly in heart: and ye shall find rest unto your souls.
  For my yoke is easy, and my burden is light. *11:28–30*

36 He that is not with me is against me. *12:30*

37 The tree is known by his fruit. *12:33*

38 Out of the abundance of the heart the mouth speaketh. *12:34*

---

[1]The Golden Rule. Common form: Do unto others as you would have others do unto you.
  See Confucius, 63:21; Aristotle, 79:16; Hillel, 106:1; and Chesterfield, 314:19.

1   Behold, a greater than Solomon is here.
Matthew 12:42

2   Some seeds fell by the way side.   *13:4*

3   Because they had no root, they withered away.
13:6

4   But other fell into good ground, and brought forth fruit, some an hundredfold, some sixtyfold, some thirtyfold.   *13:8*

5   The care of this world, and the deceitfulness of riches.   *13:22*

6   The kingdom of heaven is like to a grain of mustard seed.   *13:31*

7   Pearl of great price.   *13:46*

8   The kingdom of heaven is like unto a net, that was cast into the sea, and gathered of every kind.
13:47

9   Is not this the carpenter's son?   *13:55*

10   A prophet is not without honor, save in his own country.   *13:57*

11   [Salome] the daughter of Herodias danced before them, and pleased Herod.   *14:6*

12   Give me here John Baptist's head in a charger.
14:8

13   We have here but five loaves, and two fishes.
14:17

14   And they did all eat, and were filled: and they took up of the fragments that remained twelve baskets full.   *14:20*

15   And in the fourth watch of the night Jesus went unto them, walking on the sea.   *14:25*

16   Be of good cheer; it is I; be not afraid.   *14:27*

17   O thou of little faith, wherefore didst thou doubt?
14:31

18   Of a truth thou art the Son of God.   *14:33*

19   Not that which goeth into the mouth defileth a man; but that which cometh out of the mouth, this defileth a man.   *15:11*

20   They be blind leaders of the blind. And if the blind lead the blind, both shall fall into the ditch.
15:14

21   The dogs eat of the crumbs which fall from their masters' table.   *15:27*

22   When it is evening, ye say, It will be fair weather: for the sky is red.   *16:2*

23   The signs of the times.   *16:3*

24   Thou art the Christ, the Son of the living God.
16:16

25   Thou art Peter, and upon this rock I will build my church; and the gates of hell shall not prevail against it.
And I will give unto thee the keys of the kingdom of heaven.   *16:18–19*

26   Get thee behind me, Satan.   *16:23*

27   Whosoever will save his life shall lose it: and whosoever will lose his life for my sake shall find it.
For what is a man profited, if he shall gain the whole world, and lose his own soul?   *16:25–26*

28   Except ye be converted, and become as little children, ye shall not enter into the kingdom of heaven.   *18:3*

29   He rejoiceth more of that sheep, than of the ninety and nine which went not astray.   *18:13*

30   Where two or three are gathered together in my name, there am I in the midst of them.   *18:20*

31   Until seventy times seven.   *18:22*

32   What therefore God hath joined together, let not man put asunder.   *19:6*

33   If thou wilt be perfect, go and sell that thou hast, and give to the poor, and thou shalt have treasure in heaven.   *19:21*

34   It is easier for a camel to go through the eye of a needle, than for a rich man to enter into the kingdom of God.   *19:24*

35   Many that are first shall be last; and the last shall be first.   *19:30*

36   Borne the burden and heat of the day.   *20:12*

37   Is it not lawful for me to do what I will with mine own?   *20:15*

38   Overthrew the tables of the moneychangers.
21:12

39   My house shall be called the house of prayer; but ye have made it a den of thieves.   *21:13*

40   They made light of it.   *22:5*

41   Many are called, but few are chosen.   *22:14*

42   Render therefore unto Caesar the things which are Caesar's; and unto God the things that are God's.   *22:21*

43   Thou shalt love the Lord thy God with all thy heart, and with all thy soul, and with all thy mind.
This is the first and great commandment.
And the second is like unto it, Thou shalt love thy neighbor as thyself.[1]
On these two commandments hang all the law and the prophets.   *22:37–40*

---

[1]See *Leviticus 19:18*, 9:15.

1 Whosoever shall exalt himself shall be abased; and he that shall humble himself shall be exalted. *23:12*

2 Woe unto you, scribes and Pharisees, hypocrites! for ye pay tithe of mint and anise and cumin. *23:23*

3 Blind guides, which strain at a gnat, and swallow a camel. *23:24*

4 Whited sepulchers, which indeed appear beautiful outward, but are within full of dead men's bones. *23:27*

5 O Jerusalem, Jerusalem, thou that killest the prophets, and stonest them which are sent unto thee, how often would I have gathered thy children together, even as a hen gathereth her chickens under her wings, and ye would not! *23:37*

6 Ye shall hear of wars and rumors of wars: see that ye be not troubled: for all these things must come to pass, but the end is not yet.
For nation shall rise against nation. *24:6–7*

7 Abomination of desolation. *24:15*

8 Wheresoever the carcase is, there will the eagles be gathered together. *24:28*

9 And he shall send his angels with a great sound of a trumpet. *24:31*

10 Heaven and earth shall pass away, but my words shall not pass away. *24:35*

11 The one shall be taken, and the other left. *24:40*

12 Then shall the kingdom of heaven be likened unto ten virgins, which took their lamps, and went forth to meet the bridegroom.
And five of them were wise, and five were foolish. *25:1–2*

13 Well done, thou good and faithful servant . . . enter thou into the joy of thy lord. *25:21*

14 Unto every one that hath shall be given, and he shall have abundance: but from him that hath not shall be taken away even that which he hath. *25:29*

15 Cast ye the unprofitable servant into outer darkness. *25:30*

16 And before him shall be gathered all nations: and he shall separate them one from another, as a shepherd divideth his sheep from the goats. *25:32*

17 For I was an hungred, and ye gave me meat: I was thirsty, and ye gave me drink: I was a stranger, and ye took me in:
Naked, and ye clothed me: I was sick, and ye visited me: I was in prison, and ye came unto me. *25:35–36*

18 Inasmuch as ye have done it unto one of the least of these my brethren, ye have done it unto me. *25:40*

19 There came unto him [Jesus] a woman having an alabaster box of very precious ointment, and poured it on his head, as he sat at meat. *26:7*

20 To what purpose is this waste? *26:8*

21 For ye have the poor always with you; but me ye have not always. *26:11*

22 What will ye give me, and I will deliver him unto you? And they covenanted with him for thirty pieces of silver. *26:15*

23 My time is at hand. *26:18*

24 Verily I say unto you, that one of you shall betray me. *26:21*

25 And they were exceeding sorrowful, and began every one of them to say unto him, Lord, is it I? *26:22*

26 It had been good for that man [Judas] if he had not been born. *26:24*

27 Jesus took bread, and blessed it, and brake it, and gave it to the disciples, and said, Take, eat; this is my body.
And he took the cup, and gave thanks, and gave it to them, saying, Drink ye all of it;
For this is my blood of the new testament, which is shed for many for the remission of sins.
But I say unto you, I will not drink henceforth of this fruit of the vine, until that day when I drink it new with you in my Father's kingdom. *26:26–29*

28 My soul is exceeding sorrowful, even unto death. *26:38*

29 O my Father, if it be possible, let this cup pass from me: nevertheless, not as I will, but as thou wilt.
26:39

30 Could ye not watch with me one hour?
Watch and pray, that ye enter not into temptation: the spirit indeed is willing, but the flesh is weak. *26:40–41*

31 Behold, the hour is at hand, and the Son of man is betrayed into the hands of sinners. *26:45*

32 He came to Jesus, and said, Hail, Master; and kissed him. *26:49*

33 All they that take the sword shall perish with the sword. *26:52*

34 Thy speech bewrayeth thee. *26:73*

35 Then began he to curse and to swear, saying, I know not the man. And immediately the cock crew.

And Peter remembered the word of Jesus . . . Before the cock crow, thou shalt deny me thrice.[1] And he went out, and wept bitterly.   *Matthew 26:74–75*

1   The potter's field, to bury strangers in.   *27:7*

2   Have thou nothing to do with that just man.   *27:19*

3   Let him be crucified.   *27:22*

4   [Pilate] took water, and washed his hands before the multitude, saying, I am innocent of the blood of this just person: see ye to it.   *27:24*

5   His blood be on us, and on our children.   *27:25*

6   A place called Golgotha, that is to say, a place of a skull.   *27:33*

7   This is Jesus the King of the Jews.   *27:37*

8   He saved others; himself he cannot save.   *27:42*

9   Eli, Eli, lama sabachthani? that is to say, My God, my God, why hast thou forsaken me?[2]   *27:46*

10   And, behold, the veil of the temple was rent in twain from the top to the bottom; and the earth did quake, and the rocks rent.   *27:51*

11   His countenance was like lightning, and his raiment white as snow.   *28:3*

12   Go ye therefore, and teach all nations, baptizing them in the name of the Father, and of the Son, and of the Holy Ghost.   *28:19*

13   Lo, I am with you alway, even unto the end of the world.   *28:20*

14   There cometh one mightier than I[3] after me, the latchet of whose shoes I am not worthy to stoop down and unloose.

The Gospel According to Saint Mark 1:7

15   Arise, and take up thy bed, and walk.   *2:9*

16   The sabbath was made for man, and not man for the sabbath.   *2:27*

17   If a house be divided against itself, that house cannot stand.   *3:25*

18   The earth bringeth forth fruit of herself; first the blade, then the ear, after that the full corn in the ear.   *4:28*

19   What manner of man is this?   *4:41*

20   They came . . . into the country of the Gadarenes.   *5:1*

21   My name is Legion: for we are many.   *5:9*

22   And the unclean spirits went out, and entered the swine: and the herd ran violently down a steep place into the sea . . . and were choked in the sea.   *5:13*

23   Clothed, and in his right mind.   *5:15*

24   My little daughter lieth at the point of death.   *5:23*

25   Knowing in himself that virtue had gone out of him.   *5:30*

26   I see men as trees, walking.   *8:24*

27   Lord, I believe; help thou mine unbelief.   *9:24*

28   Suffer the little children to come unto me, and forbid them not; for of such is the kingdom of God.   *10:14*

29   Which devour widows' houses, and for a pretense make long prayers.   *12:40*

30   And there came a certain poor widow, and she threw in two mites.   *12:42*

31   Watch ye therefore: for ye know not when the master of the house cometh, at even, or at midnight, or at the cockcrowing, or in the morning:
Lest coming suddenly he find you sleeping.   *13:35–36*

32   He is risen.   *16:6*

33   Go ye into all the world, and preach the gospel to every creature.   *16:15*

34   Hail, thou that art highly favored, the Lord is with thee: blessed art thou among women.
The Gospel According to Saint Luke 1:28

35   For with God nothing shall be impossible.   *1:37*

36   Blessed is the fruit of thy womb.   *1:42*

37   My soul doth magnify the Lord.   *1:46*

38   For he hath regarded the low estate of his handmaiden: for, behold, from henceforth all generations shall call me blessed.   *1:48*

39   He hath scattered the proud in the imagination of their hearts.
He hath put down the mighty from their seats, and exalted them of low degree.   *1:51–52*

40   He hath filled the hungry with good things; and the rich he hath sent empty away.   *1:53*

41   Blessed be the Lord God of Israel; for he hath visited and redeemed his people.   *1:68*

42   As he spake by the mouth of his holy prophets, which have been since the world began:
That we should be saved from our enemies, and from the hand of all that hate us.   *1:70–71*

---

[1]This night, before the cock crow, thou shalt deny me thrice.— *Matthew 26:34*

[2]See *Psalm 22:1, 16:16.*

[3]John the Baptist.

1   Through the tender mercy of our God; whereby the dayspring from on high hath visited us,

To give light to them that sit in darkness and in the shadow of death.   *1:78–79*

2   And she brought forth her firstborn son, and wrapped him in swaddling clothes, and laid him in a manger; because there was no room for them in the inn.   *2:7*

3   There were in the same country shepherds abiding in the field, keeping watch over their flock by night.

And, lo, the angel of the Lord came upon them, and the glory of the Lord shone round about them: and they were sore afraid.

And the angel said unto them, Fear not: for, behold, I bring you good tidings of great joy, which shall be to all people.

For unto you is born this day in the city of David a Savior, which is Christ the Lord.   *2:8–11*

4   Glory to God in the highest, and on earth peace, good will toward men.   *2:14*

5   Lord, now lettest thou thy servant depart in peace.   *2:29*

6   A light to lighten the Gentiles, and the glory of thy people Israel.   *2:32*

7   Wist ye not that I must be about my Father's business?   *2:49*

8   Jesus increased in wisdom and stature, and in favor with God and man.   *2:52*

9   [The devil] showed unto him all the kingdoms of the world in a moment of time.   *4:5*

10   For it is written, He shall give his angels charge over thee, to keep thee:

And in their hands they shall bear thee up, lest at any time thou dash thy foot against a stone.   *4:10–11*

11   Physician, heal thyself.   *4:23*

12   Woe unto you, when all men shall speak well of you!   *6:26*

13   Her sins, which are many, are forgiven; for she loved much.   *7:47*

14   And he said to the woman, Thy faith hath saved thee; go in peace.   *7:50*

15   Nothing is secret, that shall not be made manifest.   *8:17*

16   No man, having put his hand to the plow, and looking back, is fit for the kingdom of God.   *9:62*

17   Nor scrip, nor shoes.   *10:4*

18   Peace be to this house.   *10:5*

19   The laborer is worthy of his hire.   *10:7*

20   I beheld Satan as lightning fall from heaven.   *10:18*

21   Many prophets and kings have desired to see those things which ye see, and have not seen them; and to hear those things which ye hear, and have not heard them.   *10:24*

22   A certain man went down from Jerusalem to Jericho, and fell among thieves.   *10:30*

23   A certain Samaritan . . . had compassion on him.   *10:33*

24   Go, and do thou likewise.   *10:37*

25   But Martha was cumbered about much serving.   *10:40*

26   But one thing is needful: and Mary hath chosen that good part, which shall not be taken away from her.   *10:42*

27   This is an evil generation: they seek a sign.   *11:29*

28   Soul, thou hast much goods laid up for many years; take thine ease, eat, drink, and be merry.   *12:19*

29   Thou fool, this night thy soul shall be required of thee.   *12:20*

30   Let your loins be girded about, and your lights burning.   *12:35*

31   For unto whomsoever much is given, of him shall be much required: and to whom men have committed much, of him they will ask the more.   *12:48*

32   The poor, and the maimed, and the halt, and the blind.   *14:21*

33   Which of you, intending to build a tower, sitteth not down first, and counteth the cost, whether he have sufficient to finish it?   *14:28*

34   Rejoice with me; for I have found my sheep which was lost.   *15:6*

35   [The prodigal son] wasted his substance with riotous living.   *15:13*

36   Bring hither the fatted calf, and kill it.   *15:23*

37   For this my son was dead, and is alive again; he was lost, and is found.   *15:24*

38   Son, thou art ever with me, and all that I have is thine.   *15:31*

39   What shall I do? . . . I cannot dig; to beg I am ashamed.   *16:3*

40   The children of this world are in their generation wiser than the children of light.   *16:8*

1   He that is faithful in that which is least is faithful also in much: and he that is unjust in the least is unjust also in much.   *Luke 16:10*

2   The beggar died, and was carried by the angels into Abraham's bosom.   *16:22*

3   Between us and you there is a great gulf fixed.   *16:26*

4   It were better for him that a millstone were hanged about his neck, and he cast into the sea.   *17:2*

5   The kingdom of God is within you.   *17:21*

6   Remember Lot's wife.   *17:32*

7   Two men went up into the temple to pray; the one a Pharisee, and the other a publican.   *18:10*

8   God, I thank thee, that I am not as other men are.   *18:11*

9   God be merciful to me a sinner.   *18:13*

10   Out of thine own mouth will I judge thee.   *19:22*

11   If these should hold their peace, the stones would immediately cry out.   *19:40*

12   He is not a God of the dead, but of the living.   *20:38*

13   In your patience possess ye your souls.   *21:19*

14   The Son of man coming in a cloud with power and great glory.   *21:27*

15   This do in remembrance of me.   *22:19*

16   Not my will, but thine, be done.   *22:42*

17   For if they do these things in a green tree, what shall be done in the dry?   *23:31*

18   The place, which is called Calvary.   *23:33*

19   Father, forgive them; for they know not what they do.   *23:34*

20   Lord, remember me when thou comest into thy kingdom.   *23:42*

21   To day shalt thou be with me in paradise.   *23:43*

22   Father, into thy hands I commend my spirit.   *23:46*

23   He gave up the ghost.   *23:46*

24   He was a good man, and a just.   *23:50*

25   Why seek ye the living among the dead?   *24:5*

26   Their words seemed to them as idle tales.   *24:11*

27   Did not our heart burn within us, while he talked with us?   *24:32*

28   The Lord is risen indeed.   *24:34*

29   In the beginning was the Word, and the Word was with God, and the Word was God.
The Gospel According to Saint John 1:1

30   And the light shineth in darkness; and the darkness comprehended it not.   *1:5*

31   There was a man sent from God, whose name was John.   *1:6*

32   The true Light, which lighteth every man that cometh into the world.   *1:9*

33   The Word was made flesh, and dwelt among us . . . full of grace and truth.   *1:14*

34   No man hath seen God at any time.   *1:18*

35   Behold the Lamb of God, which taketh away the sin of the world.   *1:29*

36   Can there any good thing come out of Nazareth?   *1:46*

37   Hereafter ye shall see heaven open, and the angels of God ascending and descending upon the Son of man.   *1:51*

38   Woman, what have I to do with thee? mine hour is not yet come.   *2:4*

39   The water that was made wine.   *2:9*

40   This beginning of miracles did Jesus in Cana of Galilee, and manifested forth his glory; and his disciples believed on him.   *2:11*

41   When he had made a scourge of small cords, he drove them all out of the temple.   *2:15*

42   Make not my Father's house an house of merchandise.   *2:16*

43   Except a man be born again, he cannot see the kingdom of God.   *3:3*

44   The wind bloweth where it listeth, and thou hearest the sound thereof, but canst not tell whence it cometh, and whither it goeth: so is every one that is born of the Spirit.   *3:8*

45   How can these things be?   *3:9*

46   God so loved the world, that he gave his only begotten Son, that whosoever believeth in him should not perish, but have everlasting life.   *3:16*

47   There cometh a woman of Samaria to draw water: Jesus saith unto her, Give me to drink.   *4:7*

48   The hour cometh, and now is, when the true worshippers shall worship the Father in spirit and in truth.   *4:23*

49   He was a burning and a shining light.   *5:35*

1   Search the scriptures.   *5:39*

2   What are they among so many?   *6:9*

3   Gather up the fragments that remain, that nothing be lost.   *6:12*

4   I am the bread of life: he that cometh to me shall never hunger; and he that believeth on me shall never thirst.   *6:35*

5   It is the spirit that quickeneth; the flesh profiteth nothing.   *6:63*

6   Judge not according to the appearance.   *7:24*

7   Never man spake like this man.   *7:46*

8   He that is without sin among you, let him first cast a stone at her.   *8:7*

9   Neither do I condemn thee: go, and sin no more.   *8:11*

10   I am the light of the world: he that followeth me shall not walk in darkness, but shall have the light of life.   *8:12*

11   The truth shall make you free.   *8:32*

12   Ye are of your father the devil . . . there is no truth in him. . . . he is a liar, and the father of it.   *8:44*

13   I must work the works of him that sent me, while it is day: the night cometh, when no man can work.   *9:4*

14   Whether he be a sinner or no, I know not: one thing I know, that, whereas I was blind, now I see.   *9:25*

15   I am the door.   *10:9*

16   I am come that they might have life, and that they might have it more abundantly.   *10:10*

17   I am the good shepherd: the good shepherd giveth his life for the sheep.   *10:11*

18   Other sheep I have, which are not of this fold.   *10:16*

19   I am the resurrection, and the life: he that believeth in me, though he were dead, yet shall he live:
And whosoever liveth and believeth in me shall never die.   *11:25–26*

20   Jesus wept.   *11:35*

21   It is expedient for us, that one man should die for the people.   *11:50*

22   Then saith one of his disciples, Judas Iscariot, Simon's son, which should betray him,
Why was not this ointment sold for three hundred pence, and given to the poor?   *12:4–5*

23   Yet a little while is the light with you. Walk while ye have the light, lest darkness come upon you.   *12:35*

24   That thou doest, do quickly.   *13:27*

25   A new commandment I give unto you, That ye love one another.   *13:34*

26   Let not your heart be troubled: ye believe in God, believe also in me.
In my Father's house are many mansions: if it were not so, I would have told you. I go to prepare a place for you.   *14:1–2*

27   I will come again, and receive you unto myself; that where I am, there ye may be also.   *14:3*

28   I am the way, the truth, and the life.   *14:6*

29   I will not leave you comfortless.   *14:18*

30   Peace I leave with you, my peace I give unto you: not as the world giveth, give I unto you. Let not your heart be troubled, neither let it be afraid.   *14:27*

31   Greater love hath no man than this, that a man lay down his life for his friends.   *15:13*

32   Ye have not chosen me, but I have chosen you.   *15:16*

33   Whither goest thou?[1]   *16:5*

34   Ask, and ye shall receive, that your joy may be full.   *16:24*

35   Be of good cheer; I have overcome the world.   *16:33*

36   Pilate saith unto him, What is truth?   *18:38*

37   Now Barabbas was a robber.   *18:40*

38   Behold the man![2]   *19:5*

39   Woman, behold thy son!   *19:26*

40   It is finished.   *19:30*

41   Touch me not.[3]   *20:17*

42   Then saith he to Thomas . . . be not faithless, but believing.   *20:27*

43   Blessed are they that have not seen, and yet have believed.   *20:29*

44   Suddenly there came a sound from heaven as of a rushing mighty wind.
The Acts of the Apostles 2:2

45   There appeared unto them cloven tongues like as of fire, and it sat upon each of them.

---

[1]Quo vadis? — *The Vulgate*

[2]Ecce homo. — *The Vulgate*

[3]Noli me tangere. — *The Vulgate*

And they were all filled with the Holy Ghost, and began to speak with other tongues.   *Acts 2:3–4*

1   Silver and gold have I none; but such as I have give I thee.   *3:6*

2   And distribution was made unto every man according as he had need.   *4:35*

3   If this counsel or this work be of men, it will come to nought:
But if it be of God, ye cannot overthrow it.   *5:38–39*

4   Thy money perish with thee.   *8:20*

5   In the gall of bitterness, and in the bond of iniquity.   *8:23*

6   Saul, yet breathing out threatenings and slaughter against the disciples of the Lord.   *9:1*

7   Saul, Saul, why persecutest thou me?   *9:4*

8   It is hard for thee to kick against the pricks.   *9:5*

9   He is a chosen vessel unto me.   *9:15*

10   Immediately there fell from his eyes as it had been scales.   *9:18*

11   What God hath cleansed, that call not thou common.   *10:15*

12   God is no respecter of persons.   *10:34*

13   The gods are come down to us in the likeness of men.   *14:11*

14   We also are men of like passions with you.   *14:15*

15   Come over into Macedonia, and help us.   *16:9*

16   Certain lewd fellows of the baser sort.   *17:5*

17   Ye men of Athens, I perceive that in all things ye are too superstitious.
For as I passed by, and beheld your devotions, I found an altar with this inscription, TO THE UNKNOWN GOD.   *17:22–23*

18   God that made the world, and all things therein, seeing that he is Lord of heaven and earth, dwelleth not in temples made with hands;
Neither is worshipped with men's hands, as though he needed any thing, seeing he giveth to all life, and breath, and all things;
And hath made of one blood all nations of men for to dwell on all the face of the earth.   *17:24–26*

19   For in him we live, and move, and have our being; as certain also of your own poets have said, For we are also his offspring.   *17:28*

20   Your blood be upon your own heads.   *18:6*

21   And Gallio, cared for none of those things.   *18:17*

22   Mighty in the Scriptures.   *18:24*

23   We have not so much as heard whether there be any Holy Ghost.   *19:2*

24   All with one voice about the space of two hours cried out, Great is Diana of the Ephesians.   *19:34*

25   It is more blessed to give than to receive.   *20:35*

26   I [Paul] am . . . a Jew of Tarsus, a city in Cilicia, a citizen of no mean city.   *21:39*

27   Brought up in this city at the feet of Gamaliel.   *22:3*

28   And the chief captain answered, With a great sum obtained I this freedom. And Paul said, But I was free born.   *22:28*

29   God shall smite thee, thou whited wall.   *23:3*

30   Revilest thou God's high priest?   *23:4*

31   I [Paul] am a Pharisee, the son of a Pharisee.   *23:6*

32   A conscience void of offense toward God, and toward men.   *24:16*

33   When I have a convenient season, I will call for thee.   *24:25*

34   I appeal unto Caesar.   *25:11*

35   Paul, thou art beside thyself; much learning doth make thee mad.   *26:24*

36   I am not mad . . . but speak forth the words of truth and soberness.   *26:25*

37   For this thing was not done in a corner.   *26:26*

38   Almost thou persuadest me to be a Christian.   *26:28*

39   Wherein thou judgest another, thou condemnest thyself.

The Epistle of Paul the Apostle to the Romans 2:1

40   These, having not the law, are a law unto themselves.   *2:14*

41   The things that are more excellent.   *2:18*

42   Where no law is, there is no transgression.   *4:15*

43   Who against hope believed in hope.   *4:18*

44   Where sin abounded, grace did much more abound.   *5:20*

45   Death hath no more dominion over him.   *6:9*

1   I speak after the manner of men.   *6:19*

2   The wages of sin is death; but the gift of God is eternal life.   *6:23*

3   The good that I would I do not: but the evil which I would not, that I do.   *7:19*

4   Who shall deliver me from the body of this death?   *7:24*

5   Heirs of God, and joint-heirs with Christ.   *8:17*

6   For we know that the whole creation groaneth and travaileth in pain together until now.   *8:22*

7   All things work together for good to them that love God.   *8:28*

8   For whom he did foreknow, he also did predestinate to be conformed to the image of his Son, that he might be the firstborn among many brethren.

Moreover whom he did predestinate, them he also called: and whom he called, them he also justified: and whom he justified, them he also glorified.   *8:29–30*

9   If God be for us, who can be against us?   *8:31*

10   Who shall lay any thing to the charge of God's elect? It is God that justifieth.   *8:33*

11   Who shall separate us from the love of Christ?   *8:35*

12   Neither death, nor life, nor angels, nor principalities, nor powers, nor things present, nor things to come,

Nor height, nor depth, nor any other creature, shall be able to separate us from the love of God, which is in Christ Jesus our Lord.   *8:38–39*

13   Hath not the potter power over the clay, of the same lump to make one vessel unto honor, and another unto dishonor?   *9:21*

14   For who hath known the mind of the Lord?   *11:34*

15   I beseech you therefore, brethren . . . that ye present your bodies a living sacrifice, holy, acceptable unto God, which is your reasonable service.   *12:1*

16   Let love be without dissimulation.   *12:9*

17   Be kindly affectioned one to another with brotherly love.   *12:10*

18   Given to hospitality.   *12:13*

19   Be not wise in your own conceits.
Recompense to no man evil for evil.   *12:16–17*

20   If it be possible, as much as lieth in you, live peaceably with all men.   *12:18*

21   Vengeance is mine; I will repay, saith the Lord.   *12:19*

22   Be not overcome of evil, but overcome evil with good.   *12:21*

23   The powers that be are ordained of God.   *13:1*

24   Render therefore to all their dues: tribute to whom tribute is due; custom to whom custom; fear to whom fear; honor to whom honor.
Owe no man anything, but to love one another.   *13:7–8*

25   Love is the fulfilling of the law.   *13:10*

26   The night is far spent, the day is at hand: let us therefore cast off the works of darkness, and let us put on the armor of light.

Let us walk honestly, as in the day; not in rioting and drunkenness, not in chambering and wantonness, not in strife and envying.

But put ye on the Lord Jesus Christ, and make not provision for the flesh, to fulfil the lusts thereof.[1]   *13:12–14*

27   Doubtful disputations.   *14:1*

28   Let every man be fully persuaded in his own mind.   *14:5*

29   For none of us liveth to himself, and no man dieth to himself.

For whether we live, we live unto the Lord; and whether we die, we die unto the Lord: whether we live therefore, or die, we are the Lord's.   *14:7–8*

30   Let us therefore follow after the things which make for peace.   *14:19*

31   We then that are strong ought to bear the infirmities of the weak, and not to please ourselves.   *15:1*

32   God hath chosen the foolish things of the world to confound the wise; and God hath chosen the weak things of the world to confound the things which are mighty.
The First Epistle of Paul the Apostle to the Corinthians 1:27

33   As it is written,[2] Eye hath not seen, nor ear heard.   *2:9*

34   I have planted, Apollos watered; but God gave the increase.   *3:6*

35   We are laborers together with God: ye are God's husbandry.   *3:9*

36   Every man's work shall be made manifest: for the day shall declare it, because it shall be revealed

---

[1]See Saint Augustine, 119:10, and note.

[2]Men have not heard, nor perceived by the ear, neither hath the eye seen. — *Isaiah 64:4*

by fire; and the fire shall try every man's work of what sort it is.   *I Corinthians 3:13*

1   For the temple of God is holy, which temple ye are.   *3:17*

2   We are made a spectacle unto the world, and to angels, and to men.   *4:9*

3   Absent in body, but present in spirit.   *5:3*

4   A little leaven leaveneth the whole lump.   *5:6*

5   For even Christ our Passover is sacrificed for us.   *5:7*

6   It is better to marry than to burn.   *7:9*

7   The fashion of this world passeth away.   *7:31*

8   Knowledge puffeth up, but charity edifieth.   *8:1*

9   I am made all things to all men.   *9:22*

10   Know ye not that they which run in a race run all, but one receiveth the prize?   *9:24*

11   Let him that thinketh he standeth take heed lest he fall.   *10:12*

12   All things are lawful for me, but all things are not expedient.   *10:23*

13   The earth is the Lord's, and the fullness thereof.   *10:26*

14   If a woman have long hair, it is a glory to her.   *11:15*

15   Take, eat: this is my body, which is broken for you: this do in remembrance of me.   *11:24*

16   This cup is the new testament in my blood: this do ye, as oft as ye drink it, in remembrance of me.   *11:25*

17   Though I speak with the tongues of men and of angels, and have not charity,[1] I am become as sounding brass, or a tinkling cymbal.   *13:1*

18   Though I have all faith, so that I could remove mountains, and have not charity, I am nothing.

And though I bestow all my goods to feed the poor, and though I give my body to be burned, and have not charity, it profiteth me nothing.

Charity suffereth long, and is kind; charity envieth not; charity vaunteth not itself, is not puffed up.   *13:2–4*

19   Beareth all things, believeth all things, hopeth all things, endureth all things.

Charity never faileth.   *13:7–8*

---

[1]In the Revised Standard Version *charity* throughout this chapter is translated as *love*—the love of mankind in the sense of the Greek *agapē* and the Latin *caritas*.

20   We know in part, and we prophesy in part.

But when that which is perfect is come, then that which is in part shall be done away.

When I was a child, I spake as a child, I understood as a child, I thought as a child: but when I became a man, I put away childish things.

For now we see through a glass, darkly; but then face to face: now I know in part; but then shall I know even as also I am known.

And now abideth faith, hope, charity, these three; but the greatest of these is charity.   *13:9–13*

21   If the trumpet give an uncertain sound, who shall prepare himself to the battle?   *14:8*

22   Let all things be done decently and in order.   *14:40*

23   And last of all he was seen of me also, as of one born out of due time.

For I am the least of the apostles, that am not meet to be called an apostle, because I persecuted the church of God.

But by the grace of God I am what I am.   *15:8–10*

24   But now is Christ risen from the dead, and become the firstfruits of them that slept.

For since by man came death, by man came also the resurrection of the dead.

For as in Adam all die, even so in Christ shall all be made alive.   *15:20–22*

25   The last enemy that shall be destroyed is death.   *15:26*

26   Evil communications corrupt good manners.   *15:33*

27   Thou fool, that which thou sowest is not quickened, except it die.   *15:36*

28   One star differeth from another star in glory.   *15:41*

29   It is sown in corruption; it is raised in incorruption.   *15:42*

30   The first man is of the earth, earthy.   *15:47*

31   Behold, I show you a mystery; We shall not all sleep, but we shall all be changed,

In a moment, in the twinkling of an eye, at the last trump: for the trumpet shall sound, and the dead shall be raised incorruptible, and we shall be changed.

For this corruptible must put on incorruption, and this mortal must put on immortality.   *15:51–53*

32   Death is swallowed up in victory.

O death, where is thy sting? O grave, where is thy victory?   *15:54–55*

1   Watch ye, stand fast in the faith, quit you like men, be strong.   *16:13*

2   If any man love not the Lord Jesus Christ, let him be Anathema Maranatha.   *16:22*

3   Not of the letter, but of the spirit: for the letter killeth, but the spirit giveth life.
The Second Epistle of Paul the Apostle to the Corinthians 3:6

4   Seeing then that we have such hope, we use great plainness of speech.   *3:12*

5   The things which are seen are temporal; but the things which are not seen are eternal.   *4:18*

6   We walk by faith, not by sight.   *5:7*

7   Now is the accepted time.   *6:2*

8   By honor and dishonor, by evil report and good report.   *6:8*

9   As having nothing, and yet possessing all things.   *6:10*

10   God loveth a cheerful giver.   *9:7*

11   Though I be rude in speech.   *11:6*

12   For ye suffer fools gladly, seeing ye yourselves are wise.   *11:19*

13   Forty stripes save one.   *11:24*

14   A thorn in the flesh.   *12:7*

15   My strength is made perfect in weakness.   *12:9*

16   The grace of the Lord Jesus Christ, and the love of God, and the communion of the Holy Ghost, be with you all.   *13:14*

17   The right hands of fellowship.
The Epistle of Paul the Apostle to the Galatians 2:9

18   Weak and beggarly elements.   *4:9*

19   It is good to be zealously affected always in a good thing.   *4:18*

20   Ye are fallen from grace.   *5:4*

21   For the flesh lusteth against the Spirit, and the Spirit against the flesh: and these are contrary the one to the other: so that ye cannot do the things that ye would.   *5:17*

22   The fruit of the Spirit is love, joy, peace, long-suffering, gentleness, goodness, faith,
Meekness, temperance.   *5:22–23*

23   Every man shall bear his own burden.   *6:5*

24   Be not deceived; God is not mocked: for whatsoever a man soweth, that shall he also reap.   *6:7*

25   Let us not be weary in well doing.   *6:9*

26   To be strengthened with might by his Spirit in the inner man.
The Epistle of Paul the Apostle to the Ephesians 3:16

27   Carried about with every wind of doctrine.   *4:14*

28   We are members one of another.
Be ye angry, and sin not: let not the sun go down upon your wrath.   *4:25–26*

29   Speaking to yourselves in psalms and hymns and spiritual songs, singing and making melody in your heart to the Lord.   *5:19*

30   Put on the whole armor of God.   *6:11*

31   For we wrestle not against flesh and blood, but against principalities, against powers, against the rulers of the darkness of this world, against spiritual wickedness in high places.
Wherefore take unto you the whole armor of God, that ye may be able to withstand in the evil day, and having done all, to stand.   *6:12–13*

32   To live is Christ, and to die is gain.
The Epistle of Paul the Apostle to the Philippians 1:21

33   Work out your own salvation with fear and trembling.   *2:12*

34   For it is God which worketh in you both to will and to do of his good pleasure.   *2:13*

35   This one thing I do, forgetting those things which are behind, and reaching forth unto those things which are before,
I press toward the mark.   *3:13–14*

36   Whose end is destruction, whose God is their belly, and whose glory is in their shame, who mind earthly things.   *3:19*

37   The peace of God, which passeth all understanding, shall keep your hearts and minds through Christ Jesus.   *4:7*

38   Whatsoever things are true, whatsoever things are honest, whatsoever things are just, whatsoever things are pure, whatsoever things are lovely, whatsoever things are of good report; if there be any virtue, and if there be any praise, think on these things.   *4:8*

39   I have learned, in whatsoever state I am, therewith to be content.   *4:11*

40   By him were all things created, that are in heaven, and that are in earth, visible and invisible . . . all things were created by him, and for him:

And he is before all things, and by him all things consist.
*The Epistle of Paul the Apostle
to the Colossians 1:16–17*

1   Touch not; taste not; handle not.   *2:21*

2   Set your affection on things above, not on things on the earth.   *3:2*

3   Where there is neither Greek nor Jew, circumcision nor uncircumcision, Barbarian, Scythian, bond nor free: but Christ is all, and in all.   *3:11*

4   Fathers, provoke not your children to anger, lest they be discouraged.   *3:21*

5   Let your speech be alway with grace, seasoned with salt.   *4:6*

6   Luke, the beloved physician.   *4:14*

7   Labor of love.
*The First Epistle of Paul the Apostle
to the Thessalonians 1:3*

8   Study to be quiet, and to do your own business.   *4:11*

9   The day of the Lord so cometh as a thief in the night.   *5:2*

10   Ye are all the children of light, and the children of the day: we are not of the night, nor of darkness.   *5:5*

11   Putting on the breastplate of faith and love; and for an helmet, the hope of salvation.   *5:8*

12   Pray without ceasing.   *5:17*

13   Prove all things; hold fast that which is good.   *5:21*

14   The law is good, if a man use it lawfully.
*The First Epistle of Paul the Apostle
to Timothy 1:8*

15   Christ Jesus came into the world to save sinners; of whom I am chief.   *1:15*

16   For if a man know not how to rule his own house, how shall he take care of the church of God?   *3:5*

17   Not greedy of filthy lucre.   *3:8*

18   Speaking lies in hypocrisy; having their conscience seared with a hot iron.   *4:2*

19   Every creature of God is good, and nothing to be refused, if it be received with thanksgiving.   *4:4*

20   Refuse profane and old wives' fables.   *4:7*

21   Let them learn first to show piety at home.   *5:4*

22   But if any provide not for his own, and specially for those of his own house, he hath denied the faith, and is worse than an infidel.   *5:8*

23   They learn to be idle, wandering about from house to house; and not only idle, but tattlers also and busybodies, speaking things which they ought not.   *5:13*

24   Drink no longer water, but use a little wine for thy stomach's sake.   *5:23*

25   We brought nothing into this world, and it is certain we can carry nothing out.   *6:7*

26   The love of money is the root of all evil.[1]   *6:10*

27   Fight the good fight of faith, lay hold on eternal life.   *6:12*

28   Rich in good works.   *6:18*

29   O Timothy, keep that which is committed to thy trust, avoiding profane and vain babblings, and oppositions of science falsely so called.   *6:20*

30   For God hath not given us the spirit of fear; but of power, and of love, and of a sound mind.
*The Second Epistle of Paul the Apostle to
Timothy 1:7*

31   A workman that needeth not to be ashamed.   *2:15*

32   Be instant in season, out of season.   *4:2*

33   I have fought a good fight, I have finished my course, I have kept the faith.   *4:7*

34   The Lord reward him according to his works.   *4:14*

35   Unto the pure all things are pure.
The Epistle of Paul to Titus 1:15

36   Making mention of thee always in my prayers.
The Epistle of Paul to Philemon 1:4

37   Who maketh his angels spirits, and his ministers a flame of fire.
The Epistle of Paul the Apostle to the Hebrews 1:7

38   The word of God is quick, and powerful, and sharper than any two-edged sword, piercing even to the dividing asunder of soul and spirit, and of the joints and marrow, and is a discerner of the thoughts and intents of the heart.   *4:12*

39   Strong meat belongeth to them that are of full age.   *5:14*

40   They crucify to themselves the Son of God afresh, and put him to an open shame.   *6:6*

41   Without shedding of blood is no remission.   *9:22*

42   Faith is the substance of things hoped for, the evidence of things not seen.   *11:1*

---

[1]Radix malorum est cupiditas. — CHAUCER, *The Canterbury Tales* [c. 1387], *The Pardoner's Prologue, l. 6*

1   Wherefore seeing we also are compassed about with so great a cloud of witnesses . . . let us run with patience the race that is set before us,

Looking unto Jesus the author and finisher of our faith.   *12:1–2*

2   Whom the Lord loveth he chasteneth.   *12:6*

3   The spirits of just men made perfect.   *12:23*

4   Let brotherly love continue.

Be not forgetful to entertain strangers: for thereby some have entertained angels unawares.   *13:1–2*

5   The Lord is my helper, and I will not fear what man shall do unto me.   *13:6*

6   Jesus Christ the same yesterday, and to day, and for ever.   *13:8*

7   For here have we no continuing city, but we seek one to come.   *13:14*

8   To do good and to communicate forget not: for with such sacrifices God is well pleased.   *13:16*

9   Let patience have her perfect work, that ye may be perfect and entire, wanting nothing.

If any of you lack wisdom, let him ask of God.
The General Epistle of James 1:4–5

10   Blessed is the man that endureth temptation: for when he is tried, he shall receive the crown of life.   *1:12*

11   Every good gift and every perfect gift is from above, and cometh down from the Father of lights, with whom is no variableness, neither shadow of turning.   *1:17*

12   Be swift to hear, slow to speak, slow to wrath:

For the wrath of man worketh not the righteousness of God.   *1:19–20*

13   Be ye doers of the word, and not hearers only.   *1:22*

14   Unspotted from the world.   *1:27*

15   As the body without the spirit is dead, so faith without works is dead also.   *2:26*

16   How great a matter a little fire kindleth!   *3:5*

17   The tongue can no man tame; it is an unruly evil.   *3:8*

18   This wisdom descendeth not from above, but is earthly, sensual, devilish.   *3:15*

19   Resist the devil, and he will flee from you.   *4:7*

20   What is your life? It is even a vapor, that appeareth for a little time, and then vanisheth away.   *4:14*

21   Be patient therefore, brethren, unto the coming of the Lord. Behold, the husbandman waiteth for the precious fruit of the earth, and hath long patience for it, until he receive the early and latter rain.   *5:7*

22   Ye have heard of the patience of Job.   *5:11*

23   The effectual fervent prayer of a righteous man availeth much.   *5:16*

24   Hope to the end.
The First Epistle General of Peter 1:13

25   The Father, who without respect of persons judgeth according to every man's work.   *1:17*

26   All flesh is as grass, and all the glory of man as the flower of grass. The grass withereth, and the flower thereof falleth away:

But the word of the Lord endureth for ever.   *1:24–25*

27   Abstain from fleshly lusts, which war against the soul.   *2:11*

28   Honor all men. Love the brotherhood. Fear God. Honor the king.   *2:17*

29   Ornament of a meek and quiet spirit.   *3:4*

30   Giving honor unto the wife, as unto the weaker vessel.   *3:7*

31   Charity shall cover the multitude of sins.   *4:8*

32   A crown of glory that fadeth not away.   *5:4*

33   Be sober, be vigilant; because your adversary the devil, as a roaring lion, walketh about, seeking whom he may devour.   *5:8*

34   And the day star arise in your hearts.
The Second Epistle General of Peter 1:19

35   The dog is turned to his own vomit again.   *2:22*

36   God is light, and in him is no darkness at all.
The First Epistle General of John 1:5

37   If we say that we have no sin, we deceive ourselves, and the truth is not in us.   *1:8*

38   If any man sin, we have an advocate with the Father, Jesus Christ the righteous:

And he is the propitiation for our sins: and not for ours only, but also for the sins of the whole world.   *2:1–2*

39   He is antichrist, that denieth the Father and the Son.   *2:22*

40   Whoso hath this world's good, and seeth his brother have need, and shutteth up his bowels of compassion from him, how dwelleth the love of God in him?   *3:17*

41   He that loveth not, knoweth not God; for God is love.   *4:8*

42   There is no fear in love; but perfect love casteth out fear.   *4:18*

1   Raging waves of the sea, foaming out their own shame; wandering stars, to whom is reserved the blackness of darkness for ever.

The General Epistle of Jude 13

2   I John, who also am your brother, and companion in tribulation, and in the kingdom and patience of Jesus Christ, was in the isle that is called Patmos, for the word of God, and for the testimony of Jesus Christ.   *The Revelation of Saint John the Divine 1:9*

3   What thou seest, write in a book, and send it unto the seven churches which are in Asia.   *1:11*

4   And being turned, I saw seven golden candlesticks.   *1:12*

5   His feet like unto fine brass, as if they burned in a furnace; and his voice as the sound of many waters.   *1:15*

6   When I saw him, I fell at his feet as dead.   *1:17*

7   I am he that liveth, and was dead; and, behold, I am alive for evermore, Amen; and have the keys of hell and of death.   *1:18*

8   I have somewhat against thee, because thou hast left thy first love.   *2:4*

9   To him that overcometh will I give to eat of the tree of life.   *2:7*

10   Be thou faithful unto death, and I will give thee a crown of life.   *2:10*

11   He shall rule them with a rod of iron.   *2:27*

12   I will give him the morning star.   *2:28*

13   I will not blot out his name out of the book of life.   *3:5*

14   I know thy works, that thou art neither cold nor hot: I would thou wert cold or hot.
So then because thou art lukewarm, and neither cold nor hot, I will spew thee out of my mouth.   *3:15–16*

15   Behold, I stand at the door, and knock.   *3:20*

16   The first beast was like a lion, and the second beast like a calf, and the third beast had a face as a man, and the fourth beast was like a flying eagle.
And the four beasts had each of them six wings about him; and they were full of eyes within: and they rest not day and night, saying, Holy, holy, holy, Lord God Almighty, which was, and is, and is to come.   *4:7–8*

17   Thou hast created all things, and for thy pleasure they are and were created.   *4:11*

18   A book . . . sealed with seven seals.   *5:1*

19   He went forth conquering, and to conquer.   *6:2*

20   Behold a pale horse: and his name that sat on him was Death, and Hell followed with him.   *6:8*

21   Four angels standing on the four corners of the earth, holding the four winds of the earth.   *7:1*

22   Hurt not the earth, neither the sea, nor the trees.   *7:3*

23   All nations, and kindreds, and people, and tongues.   *7:9*

24   These are they which came out of great tribulation, and have washed their robes, and made them white in the blood of the lamb.   *7:14*

25   They shall hunger no more, neither thirst any more; neither shall the sun light on them, nor any heat.   *7:16*

26   The name of the star is called Wormwood.   *8:11*

27   The kingdoms of this world are become the kingdoms of our Lord and of his Christ.   *11:15*

28   There was war in heaven: Michael and his angels fought against the dragon; and the dragon fought and his angels,
And prevailed not.   *12:7–8*

29   The great dragon was cast out, that old serpent, called the Devil, and Satan, which deceiveth the whole world.   *12:9*

30   No man might buy or sell, save he that had the mark, or the name of the beast.   *13:17*

31   The voice of many waters.   *14:2*

32   Babylon is fallen, is fallen, that great city.   *14:8*

33   Blessed are the dead which die in the Lord . . . that they may rest from their labours.   *14:13*

34   And he gathered them together into a place called in the Hebrew tongue Armageddon.   *16:16*

35   He is Lord of lords, and King of kings.   *17:14*

36   He treadeth the winepress of the fierceness and wrath of Almighty God.   *19:15*

37   Another book was opened, which is the book of life.   *20:12*

38   I saw a new heaven and a new earth: for the first heaven and the first earth were passed away; and there was no more sea.
And I John saw the holy city, new Jerusalem, coming down from God out of heaven, prepared as a bride adorned for her husband.   *21:1–2*

1   God shall wipe away all tears from their eyes; and there shall be no more death, neither sorrow, nor crying, neither shall there be any more pain: for the former things are passed away.   *21:4*

2   There shall be no night there.   *22:5*

3   He that is unjust, let him be unjust still: and he which is filthy, let him be filthy still: and he that is righteous, let him be righteous still: and he that is holy, let him be holy still.

And, behold, I come quickly.   *22:11–12*

4   I am Alpha and Omega, the beginning and the end, the first and the last.   *22:13*

The Roman Missal

5   Introibo ad altare Dei [I will go in to the altar of God].   *Antiphon*

6   Mea culpa, mea culpa, mea maxima culpa [Through my fault, through my fault, through my most grievous fault].   *Confession of Sins*

7   Dominus vobiscum [The Lord be with you].
Et cum spiritu tuo [And with your spirit].
Antiphon

8   Requiem aeternam dona eis, Domine: et lux perpetua luceat eis [Eternal rest give them, O Lord: and let perpetual light shine upon them].
Mass for the Dead

9   Dies irae, dies illa / Solvet saeclum in favilla / Teste David cum Sibylla [Day of wrath, that day, the earth will dissolve in ashes, as David and the Sibyl say].[1]   *Mass for the Dead*

10   Kyrie eleison [Lord, have mercy on us].   *Kyrie*

11   Gloria in excelsis Deo. Et in terra pax hominibus bonae voluntatis [Glory to God in the highest. And on earth peace to men of good will].   *Gloria*

12   Agnus Dei, qui tollis peccata mundi, miserere nobis; Agnus Dei, qui tollis peccata mundi, miserere nobis; Agnus Dei, qui tollis peccata mundi, dona nobis pacem [Lamb of God, who takes away the sins of the world, have mercy on us; Lamb of God, who takes away the sins of the world, give us peace].
Communion

13   Hoc est enim Corpus meum [For this is My Body].   *Consecration*

14   Hic est enim calix Sanguinis mei, novi et aeterni testamenti: mysterium fidei: qui pro vobis et pro multis effundetur in remissionem peccatorum [For this is the chalice of My Blood, of the new and eter-

nal covenant; the mystery of faith; which shall be shed for you and for many unto the forgiveness of sins].   *Consecration*

15   O felix culpa, quae talem ac tantum meruit habere Redemptorem [O happy fault, which has deserved to have such and so mighty a Redeemer].[2]
Exsultet on Holy Saturday

The Book of Common Prayer [1928][3]

16   Movable feasts.   *Tables and Rules, p. xxxi*

17   He is risen. The Lord is risen indeed.
Morning Prayer, Easter, p. 5

18   The Scripture moveth us, in sundry places, to acknowledge and confess our manifold sins and wickedness.
Morning Prayer, Minister's Opening Words, p. 5

19   We have erred, and strayed from thy ways like lost sheep.
Morning Prayer, A General Confession, p. 6

20   We have left undone those things which we ought to have done; And we have done those things which we ought not to have done.
Morning Prayer, A General Confession, p. 6

21   Have mercy upon us, miserable offenders.
Morning Prayer, A General Confession, p. 6

22   Who desireth not the death of a sinner, but rather that he may turn from his wickedness and live.
Morning Prayer, The Declaration of Absolution, p. 7

23   Let us come before his presence with thanksgiving; and show ourselves glad in him with psalms.
Morning Prayer, Venite, p. 9

24   In his hand are all the corners of the earth; and the strength of the hills is his also.
The sea is his, and he made it; and his hands prepared the dry land.   *Morning Prayer, Venite, p. 9*

25   Glory be to the Father, and to the Son, and to the Holy Ghost;

---

[2]Attributed to Saint Augustine and Saint Ambrose.

[3]Thomas Cranmer [1489–1556] gathered the western Latin rites as used in England, notably the Sarum rite of Salisbury Cathedral, when he compiled [1549] the English Prayer Book, known as the first Prayer Book of Edward VI. A revised second Prayer Book of Edward VI [1552] was revised again [1559]; finally, the present English Book of Common Prayer was published [1662]. The American Book of Common Prayer [1789], which derives from the English Prayer Book, was revised in 1892 and again in 1928. It is this revision from which the quotations in *Bartlett's* are taken.
See Newman, 450:1.

---

[1]Attributed to Thomas of Celano (c. 1185–c. 1255).

As it was in the beginning, is now, and ever shall be, world without end. Amen.
Morning Prayer, Gloria Patri, p. 9

1   We praise thee, O God [Te deum laudamus].
Morning Prayer, Te Deum, p. 10

2   The noble army of Martyrs.
Morning Prayer, Te Deum, p. 10

3   I believe in God the Father Almighty, Maker of heaven and earth:

And in Jesus Christ his only Son our Lord: Who was conceived by the Holy Ghost, Born of the Virgin Mary: Suffered under Pontius Pilate, Was crucified, dead, and buried: He descended into hell; The third day he rose again from the dead: He ascended into heaven, And sitteth on the right hand of God the Father Almighty: From thence he shall come to judge the quick and the dead.

I believe in the Holy Ghost: The holy Catholic Church; The Communion of Saints: The Forgiveness of sins: The Resurrection of the body: And the Life everlasting.
Morning Prayer, Apostles' Creed, p. 15

4   Begotten of his Father before all worlds, God of God, Light of Light, Very God of very God; Begotten, not made; Being of one substance with the Father; By whom all things were made: Who for us men and for our salvation came down from heaven, And was incarnate by the Holy Ghost of the Virgin Mary, And was made man.
Morning Prayer, Nicene Creed, p. 16

5   O God, who art the author of peace and lover of concord, in knowledge of whom standeth our eternal life, whose service is perfect freedom; Defend us thy humble servants in all assaults of our enemies.
Morning Prayer, A Collect for Peace, p. 17

6   O God, the Creator and Preserver of all mankind, we humbly beseech thee for all sorts and conditions of men; that thou wouldest be pleased to make thy ways known unto them, thy saving health unto all nations.
Morning Prayer, A Prayer for All Conditions of Men, p. 18

7   We commend to thy fatherly goodness all those who are any ways afflicted, or distressed, in mind, body, or estate.
Morning Prayer, A Prayer for All Conditions of Men, p. 19

8   We, thine unworthy servants, do give thee most humble and hearty thanks for all thy goodness and loving-kindness to us, and to all men; We bless thee for our creation, preservation, and all the blessings of this life; but above all, for thine inestimable love in the redemption of the world by our Lord Jesus Christ; for the means of grace, and for the hope of glory.
Morning Prayer, A General Thanksgiving, p. 19

9   Almighty God, who . . . dost promise that when two or three are gathered together in thy Name thou wilt grant their requests; Fulfill now, O Lord, the desires and petitions of thy servants, as may be most expedient for them.
Morning Prayer, A Prayer of Saint Chrysostom, p. 20

10   Lighten our darkness, we beseech thee, O Lord; and by thy great mercy defend us from all perils and dangers of this night.
Evening Prayer, A Collect for Aid against Perils, p. 31

11   From all blindness of heart, from pride, vainglory, and hypocrisy; from envy, hatred, and malice, and all uncharitableness,
Good Lord, deliver us.   *The Litany, p. 54*

12   From all the deceits of the world, the flesh, and the devil.   *The Litany, p. 54*

13   From battle and murder, and from sudden death.   *The Litany, p. 54*

14   Give to all nations unity, peace, and concord.
The Litany, p. 56

15   The kindly fruits of the earth.   *The Litany, p. 57*

16   Almighty God, unto whom all hearts are open, all desires known, and from whom no secrets are hid; Cleanse the thoughts of our hearts by the inspiration of thy Holy Spirit, that we may perfectly love thee, and worthily magnify thy holy Name.
Holy Communion, The Collect, p. 67

17   Ye who do truly and earnestly repent you of your sins, and are in love and charity with your neighbors, and intend to lead a new life.
Holy Communion, To those who come to receive the Holy Communion, p. 75

18   We acknowledge and bewail our manifold sins and wickedness, Which we, from time to time, most grievously have committed, By thought, word, and deed, Against thy Divine Majesty, Provoking most justly thy wrath and indignation against us. We do earnestly repent, And are heartily sorry for these our misdoings; The remembrance of them is grievous unto us; The burden of them is intolerable.
Holy Communion, General Confession, p. 75

19   Therefore with Angels and Archangels, and with all the company of heaven, we laud and magnify thy glorious Name; evermore praising thee.
Holy Communion, Proper Preface, p. 77

1 And here we offer and present unto thee, O Lord, our selves, our souls and bodies, to be a reasonable, holy, and living sacrifice unto thee.
Holy Communion, The Invocation, p. 81

2 The Peace of God, which passeth all understanding, keep your hearts and minds in the knowledge and love of God, and of his Son Jesus Christ our Lord.   *Holy Communion, Blessing, p. 84*

3 Miserable sinners.
Holy Communion, The Exhortations, p. 86

4 Read, mark, learn, and inwardly digest [the Scriptures].
The Second Sunday in Advent, The Collect, p. 92

5 Dost thou, therefore, in the name of this Child, renounce the devil and all his works, the vain pomp and glory of the world, with all covetous desires of the same, and the sinful desires of the flesh, so that thou wilt not follow, nor be led by them?
Holy Baptism, To the Godfathers and Godmothers, p. 276

6 An outward and visible sign of an inward and spiritual grace.
Offices of Instruction, Questions on the Sacraments, p. 292

7 Is not by any to be entered into unadvisedly or lightly; but reverently, discreetly, advisedly, soberly, and in the fear of God.
Solemnization of Matrimony, p. 300

8 If any man can show just cause, why they may not lawfully be joined together, let him now speak, or else hereafter for ever hold his peace.
Solemnization of Matrimony, p. 300

9 Wilt thou . . . forsaking all others, keep thee only unto [him; her], so long as ye both shall live?
Solemnization of Matrimony, p. 301

10 To have and to hold from this day forward, for better for worse, for richer for poorer, in sickness and in health, to love and to cherish, till death us do part.   *Solemnization of Matrimony, p. 301*

11 With this Ring I thee wed.
Solemnization of Matrimony, p. 302

12 Those whom God hath joined together let no man put asunder.
Solemnization of Matrimony, p. 303

13 In the midst of life we are in death.
Burial of the Dead, p. 332

14 Earth to earth, ashes to ashes, dust to dust; in sure and certain hope of the Resurrection unto eternal life.   *Burial of the Dead, p. 333*

15 The iron entered into his soul.
The Psalter, Psalm 105:18, p. 471

The Book of Common Prayer [English]

16 Give peace in our time, O Lord.
Morning Prayer, Versicles

17 Grant that the old Adam in this Child may be so buried, that the new man may be raised up in him.
Public Baptism of Infants, Blessing on the Child

18 To love, cherish, and to obey.
Solemnization of Matrimony

19 With all my worldly goods I thee endow.
Solemnization of Matrimony

The Upanishads
c. 800–500 B.C.

20 Lead me from the unreal to the real!
Lead me from darkness to light!
Lead me from death to immortality![1]
Brihadaranyaka Upanishad, 1.3.28

21 This Self is the honey of all beings, and all beings are the honey of this Self.
Brihadaranyaka, 2.5.14

22 The gods love the obscure and hate the obvious.[2]
Brihadaranyaka, 4.2.2

23 Da da da[3] (that is) Be subdued, Give, Be merciful.[1]
Brihadaranyaka, 5.2.3

24 If the slayer thinks he slays,
If the slain thinks he is slain,
Both these do not understand:
He slays not, is not slain.[4]
Katha Upanishad, 2.19

25 Om.[5]   *Passim*

26 Shanti.[6]   *Passim*

[1] Translated by F. MAX MÜLLER.

[2] Translated by R. C. ZAEHNER.

[3] The voice of the thunder. The full Sanskrit is: Da da da iti. Damyata datta dayadhvamiti.
"Datta, dayadhvam, damyata" (Give, sympathize, control).
—T. S. ELIOT, *The Waste Land* [1922], *note to line 401*
See T. S. Eliot, 719:2.

[4] See Emerson, 453:22.

[5] Om is a sacred syllable used especially to begin and end a scriptural recitation.

[6] Shanti means "peace." T. S. Eliot, in his note to line 434 of *The Waste Land*, says, " 'The Peace which passeth understanding' is our equivalent to this word."

Homer

c. 700 B.C.

1   Sing, goddess, the wrath of Peleus' son Achilles, a destroying wrath which brought upon the Achaeans myriad woes, and sent forth to Hades many valiant souls of heroes.   *The Iliad, bk. I, l. 1*

2   And the plan of Zeus was being accomplished.
    Iliad, I, l. 5

3   A dream, too, is from Zeus.   *Iliad, I, l. 63*

4   He knew the things that were and the things that would be and the things that had been before.
    Iliad, I, l. 70

5   If you are very valiant, it is a god, I think, who gave you this gift.   *Iliad, I, l. 178*

6   Speaking, he addressed her winged words.
    Iliad, I, l. 201

7   Whoever obeys the gods, to him they particularly listen.   *Iliad, I, l. 218*

8   From his tongue flowed speech sweeter than honey.   *Iliad, I, l. 249*

9   Rosy-fingered dawn appeared, the early-born.
    Iliad, I, l. 477 and elsewhere

10   The son of Kronos [Zeus] spoke, and nodded with his darkish brows, and immortal locks fell forward from the lord's deathless head, and he made great Olympus tremble.   *Iliad, I, l. 528*

11   The Olympian is a difficult foe to oppose.
    Iliad, I, l. 589

12   Uncontrollable laughter arose among the blessed gods.[1]   *Iliad, I, l. 599*

13   A councilor ought not to sleep the whole night through, a man to whom the populace is entrusted, and who has many responsibilities.   *Iliad, II, l. 24*

14   Proud is the spirit of Zeus-fostered kings — their honor comes from Zeus, and Zeus, god of council, loves them.   *Iliad, II, l. 196*

15   A multitude of rulers is not a good thing. Let there be one ruler, one king.   *Iliad, II, l. 204*

16   He [Thersites] was the ugliest man who came to Ilium.   *Iliad, II, l. 216*

17   I could not tell nor name the multitude, not even if I had ten tongues, ten mouths, not if I had a voice unwearying and a heart of bronze were in me.
    Iliad, II, l. 488

18   Yet with his powers of augury he [Chromis] did not save himself from dark death.
    Iliad, II, l. 859

19   The glorious gifts of the gods are not to be cast aside.   *Iliad, III, l. 65*

20   Young men's minds are always changeable, but when an old man is concerned in a matter, he looks both before and after.   *Iliad, III, l. 108*

21   Like cicadas, which sit upon a tree in the forest and pour out their piping voices, so the leaders of the Trojans were sitting on the tower.
    Iliad, III, l. 151

22   There is no reason to blame the Trojans and the well-greaved Achaeans that for such a woman they long suffer woes.   *Iliad, III, l. 156*

23   Words like winter snowflakes.
    Iliad, III, l. 222

24   The sun, which sees all things and hears all things.
    Iliad, III, l. 277

25   Son of Atreus, what manner of speech has escaped the barrier of your teeth?
    Iliad, IV, l. 350

26   Far away in the mountains a shepherd hears their thundering.   *Iliad, IV, l. 455*

27   He lives not long who battles with the immortals, nor do his children prattle about his knees when he has come back from battle and the dread fray.   *Iliad, V, l. 407*

28   Not at all similar are the race of the immortal gods and the race of men who walk upon the earth.
    Iliad, V, l. 441

29   Great-hearted Stentor with brazen voice, who could shout as loud as fifty other men.
    Iliad, V, l. 785

30   He was a wealthy man, and kindly to his fellow men; for dwelling in a house by the side of the road, he used to entertain all comers.[2]   *Iliad, VI, l. 14*

31   A generation of men is like a generation of leaves: the wind scatters some leaves upon the ground, while others the burgeoning wood brings forth — and the season of spring comes on. So of men one generation springs forth and another ceases.
    Iliad, VI, l. 146

32   Always to be bravest and to be preeminent above others.   *Iliad, VI, l. 208*

33   Victory shifts from man to man.
    Iliad, VI, l. 339

34   May men say, "He is far greater than his father," when he returns from battle.   *Iliad, VI, l. 479*

---

[1]Also in *The Odyssey, bk. VIII, l. 326.*

[2]He held his seat; a friend to human race. / Fast by the road, his ever-open door / Obliged the wealthy and relieved the poor. — ALEXANDER POPE, *translation of The Iliad* [1715]

1   Smiling through tears.   *Iliad, VI, l. 484*

2   Attach a golden chain from heaven, and all of you take hold of it, you gods and goddesses, yet would you not be able to drag Zeus the most high from heaven to earth.   *Iliad, VIII, l. 19*

3   Hades is relentless and unyielding.   *Iliad, IX, 1. 158*

4   Hateful to me as the gates of Hades is that man who hides one thing in his heart and speaks another.   *Iliad, IX, l. 312*

5   Even when someone battles hard, there is an equal portion for one who lingers behind, and in the same honor are held both the coward and the brave man; the idle man and he who has done much meet death alike.   *Iliad, IX, l. 318*

6   To be both a speaker of words and a doer of deeds.   *Iliad, IX, l. 443*

7   Prayers are the daughters of mighty Zeus, lame and wrinkled and slanting-eyed.   *Iliad, IX, l. 502*

8   A companion's words of persuasion are effective.   *Iliad, XI, l. 793*

9   It was built against the will of the immortal gods, and so it did not last for long.   *Iliad, XII, l. 8*

10   The single best augury is to fight for one's country.   *Iliad, XII, l. 243*

11   There is a strength in the union even of very sorry men.   *Iliad, XIII, l. 237*

12   There is a fullness of all things, even of sleep and of love.   *Iliad, XIII, l. 636*

13   You will certainly not be able to take the lead in all things yourself, for to one man a god has given deeds of war, and to another the dance, to another the lyre and song, and in another wide-sounding Zeus puts a good mind.   *Iliad, XIII, l. 729*

14   It is not possible to fight beyond your strength, even if you strive.   *Iliad, XIII, l. 787*

15   She [Aphrodite] spoke and loosened from her bosom the embroidered girdle of many colors into which all her allurements were fashioned. In it was love and in it desire and in it blandishing persuasion which steals the mind even of the wise.   *Iliad, XIV, l. 214*

16   There she met sleep, the brother of death.[1]   *Iliad, XIV, l. 231 and XVI, l. 672*

17   Ocean, who is the source of all.   *Iliad, XIV, l. 246*

18   The hearts of the noble may be turned [by entreaty].   *Iliad, XV, l. 203*

19   It is not unseemly for a man to die fighting in defense of his country.   *Iliad, XV, l. 496*

20   Of men who have a sense of honor, more come through alive than are slain, but from those who flee comes neither glory nor any help.   *Iliad, XV, l. 563*

21   The outcome of the war is in our hands; the outcome of words is in the council.   *Iliad, XVI, l. 630*

22   But he, mighty man, lay mightily in the whirl of dust, forgetful of his horsemanship.   *Iliad, XVI, l. 775*

23   Once harm has been done, even a fool understands it.   *Iliad, XVII, l. 32*

24   The most preferable of evils.[2]   *Iliad, XVII, l. 105*

25   Surely there is nothing more wretched than a man, of all the things which breathe and move upon the earth.   *Iliad, XVII, l. 446*

26   Sweeter it [wrath] is by far than the honeycomb dripping with sweetness, and spreads through the hearts of men.   *Iliad, XVIII, l. 109*

27   I too shall lie in the dust when I am dead, but now let me win noble renown.   *Iliad, XVIII, l. 120*

28   Zeus does not bring all men's plans to fulfillment.   *Iliad, XVIII, l. 328*

29   The Erinyes, who exact punishment of men underground if one swears a false oath.   *Iliad, XIX, l. 259*

30   Not even Achilles will bring all his words to fulfillment.   *Iliad, XX, l. 369*

31   Miserable mortals who, like leaves, at one moment flame with life, eating the produce of the land, and at another moment weakly perish.   *Iliad, XXI, l. 463*

32   It is entirely seemly for a young man killed in battle to lie mangled by the bronze spear. In his death all things appear fair. But when dogs shame the gray

---

[1]Sleep, the brother of Death. — HESIOD, *The Theogony, l. 756*
Sleep, Death's twin brother. — ALFRED, LORD TENNYSON, *In Memoriam* [1850], *pt. LXVIII*

[2]Of two evils, the least should be chosen. — CICERO, *De Officiis, III, 1*
Of harmes two, the lesse is for to chese. — CHAUCER, *Troilus and Criseyde* [c. 1385], *bk. II, l. 470*
Of two evils the less is always to be chosen. — THOMAS À KEMPIS, *Imitation of Christ, bk. III, ch. 12*
See West, 736:9.

head and gray chin and nakedness of an old man killed, it is the most piteous thing that happens among wretched mortals. *Iliad, XXII, l. 71*

1　Then the father held out the golden scales, and in them he placed two fates of dread death.
Iliad, XXII, l. 209

2　There are no compacts between lions and men, and wolves and lambs have no concord.
Iliad, XXII, l. 262

3　By the ships there lies a dead man, unwept, unburied: Patroclus. *Iliad, XXII, l. 386*

4　Remembering this, he wept bitterly, lying now on his side, now on his back, now on his face.
Iliad, XXIV, l. 9

5　The fates have given mankind a patient soul.
Iliad, XXIV, l. 49

6　Thus have the gods spun the thread for wretched mortals: that they live in grief while they themselves are without cares; for two jars stand on the floor of Zeus of the gifts which he gives, one of evils and another of blessings. *Iliad, XXIV, l. 525*

7　Tell me, muse, of the man of many resources who wandered far and wide after he sacked the holy citadel of Troy, and he saw the cities and learned the thoughts of many men, and on the sea he suffered in his heart many woes. *The Odyssey, bk. I, l. 1*

8　By their own follies they perished, the fools.
Odyssey, I, l. 7

9　Look now how mortals are blaming the gods, for they say that evils come from us, but in fact they themselves have woes beyond their share because of their own follies. *Odyssey, I, l. 32*

10　Surely these things lie on the knees of the gods.[1]
Odyssey, I, l. 267

11　You ought not to practice childish ways, since you are no longer that age. *Odyssey, I, l. 296*

12　For rarely are sons similar to their fathers: most are worse, and a few are better than their fathers.
Odyssey, II, l. 276

13　Gray-eyed Athena sent them a favorable breeze, a fresh west wind, singing over the wine-dark sea.
Odyssey, II, 420

14　A young man is embarrassed to question an older one. *Odyssey, III, l. 24*

15　All men have need of the gods.
Odyssey, III, l. 48

16　The minds of the everlasting gods are not changed suddenly. *Odyssey, III, l. 147*

17　A small rock holds back a great wave.
Odyssey, III, l. 296

18　No mortal could vie with Zeus, for his mansions and his possessions are deathless.
Odyssey, IV, l. 78

19　She [Helen] threw into the wine which they were drinking a drug which takes away grief and passion and brings forgetfulness of all ills.
Odyssey, IV, l. 220

20　The immortals will send you to the Elysian plain at the ends of the earth, where fair-haired Rhadamanthys is. There life is supremely easy for men. No snow is there, nor ever heavy winter storm, nor rain, and Ocean is ever sending gusts of the clear-blowing west wind to bring coolness to men.
Odyssey, IV, l. 563

21　Olympus, where they say there is an abode of the gods, ever unchanging: it is neither shaken by winds nor ever wet with rain, nor does snow come near it, but clear weather spreads cloudless about it, and a white radiance stretches above it.[2]
Odyssey, VI, l. 42

22　May the gods grant you all things which your heart desires, and may they give you a husband and a home and gracious concord, for there is nothing greater and better than this—when a husband and wife keep a household in oneness of mind, a great woe to their enemies and joy to their friends, and win high renown. *Odyssey, VI, l. 180*

23　All strangers and beggars are from Zeus, and a gift, though small, is precious. *Odyssey, VI, l. 207*

24　Their ships are swift as a bird or a thought.
Odyssey, VII, l. 36

25　We are quick to flare up, we races of men on the earth. *Odyssey, VII, l. 307*

26　So it is that the gods do not give all men gifts of grace—neither good looks nor intelligence nor eloquence. *Odyssey, VIII, l. 167*

27　Evil deeds do not prosper; the slow man catches up with the swift. *Odyssey, VIII, l. 329*

28　Even if you gods, and all the goddesses too, should be looking on, yet would I be glad to sleep with golden Aphrodite. *Odyssey, VIII, l. 341*

---

[1]Also familiar as: In the lap of the gods.

[2]The majesty of the gods is revealed, and their peaceful abodes, which neither the winds shake nor clouds soak with showers, nor does the snow congealed with biting frost besmirch them with its white fall, but an ever cloudless sky vaults them over, and smiles with light bounteously spread abroad.—LUCRETIUS, *De Rerum Natura, bk. III, l. 18*

1   Among all men on the earth bards have a share of honor and reverence, because the muse has taught them songs and loves the race of bards.

Odyssey, VIII, l. 479

2   Thus she spoke; and I longed to embrace my dead mother's ghost. Thrice I tried to clasp her image, and thrice it slipped through my hands, like a shadow, like a dream.

Odyssey, XI, l. 204

3   They strove to pile Ossa on Olympus, and on Ossa Pelion with its leafy forests, that they might scale the heavens.[1]

Odyssey, XI, l. 315

4   There is a time for many words, and there is also a time for sleep.

Odyssey, XI, l. 379

5   There is nothing more dread and more shameless than a woman who plans such deeds in her heart as the foul deed which she plotted when she contrived her husband's murder.

Odyssey, XI, l. 427

6   In the extravagance of her evil she has brought shame both on herself and on all women who will come after her, even on one who is virtuous.

Odyssey, XI, l. 432

7   Therefore don't you be gentle to your wife either. Don't tell her everything you know, but tell her one thing and keep another thing hidden.

Odyssey, XI, l. 441

8   There is no more trusting in women.

Odyssey, XI, l. 456

9   I should rather labor as another's serf, in the home of a man without fortune, one whose livelihood was meager, than rule over all the departed dead.   *Odyssey, XI, l. 489*

10   Friends, we have not till now been unacquainted with misfortunes.   *Odyssey, XII, l. 208*

11   It is tedious to tell again tales already plainly told.   *Odyssey, XII, l. 452*

12   The wine urges me on, the bewitching wine, which sets even a wise man to singing and to laughing gently and rouses him up to dance and brings forth words which were better unspoken.

Odyssey, XIV, l. 463

13   It is equally wrong to speed a guest who does not want to go, and to keep one back who is eager.

You ought to make welcome the present guest, and send forth the one who wishes to go.

Odyssey, XV, l. 72

14   Even his griefs are a joy long after to one that remembers all that he wrought and endured.

Odyssey, XV, l. 400

15   God always pairs off like with like.

Odyssey, XVII, l. 218

16   Bad herdsmen ruin their flocks.

Odyssey, XVII, l. 246

17   Wide-sounding Zeus takes away half a man's worth on the day when slavery comes upon him.

Odyssey, XVII, l. 322

18   Then dark death seized Argus, as soon as he had seen Odysseus in the twentieth year.

Odyssey, XVII, l. 326

19   The gods, likening themselves to all kinds of strangers, go in various disguises from city to city, observing the wrongdoing and the righteousness of men.   *Odyssey, XVII, l. 485*

20   Nothing feebler than a man does the earth raise up, of all the things which breathe and move on the earth, for he believes that he will never suffer evil in the future, as long as the gods give him success and he flourishes in his strength; but when the blessed gods bring sorrows too to pass, even these he bears, against his will, with steadfast spirit, for the thoughts of earthly men are like the day which the father of gods and men brings upon them.

Odyssey, XVIII, l. 130

21   Men flourish only for a moment.

Odyssey, XIX, l. 328

22   Dreams surely are difficult, confusing, and not everything in them is brought to pass for mankind. For fleeting dreams have two gates: one is fashioned of horn and one of ivory. Those which pass through the one of sawn ivory are deceptive, bringing tidings which come to nought, but those which issue from the one of polished horn bring true results when a mortal sees them.   *Odyssey, XIX, l. 560*

23   Endure, my heart: you once endured something even more dreadful.   *Odyssey, XX, l. 18*

24   Your heart is always harder than a stone.

Odyssey, XXIII, l. 103

25   Therefore the fame of her excellence will never perish, and the immortals will fashion among earthly men a gracious song in honor of faithful Penelope.   *Odyssey, XXIV, l. 196*

---

[1] Then the omnipotent Father with his thunder made Olympus tremble, and from Ossa hurled Pelion. —OVID, *Metamorphoses, I, l. 154*

I would have you call to mind the strength of the ancient giants, that undertook to lay the high mountain Pelion on the top of Ossa, and set among those the shady Olympus. —FRANÇOIS RABELAIS, *Works, bk. IV* [1548], *ch. 38*

Hesiod
c. 700 B.C.

1   With the muses of Helicon let us begin our singing.   *The Theogony, l. 1*

2   They once taught Hesiod beauteous song, when he was shepherding his sheep below holy Helicon.   *Theogony, l. 22*

3   We know how to speak many falsehoods which resemble real things, but we know, when we will, how to speak true things.   *Theogony, l. 27*

4   On his tongue they pour sweet dew, and from his mouth flow gentle words.   *Theogony, l. 83*

5   Love, who is most beautiful among the immortal gods, the melter of limbs, overwhelms in their hearts the intelligence and wise counsel of all gods and all men.   *Theogony, l. 120*

6   From their eyelids as they glanced dripped love.   *Theogony, l. 910*

7   There was not after all a single kind of strife, but on the earth there are two kinds: one of them a man might praise when he recognized her, but the other is blameworthy.   *Works and Days, l. 11*

8   Potter bears a grudge against potter, and craftsman against craftsman, and beggar is envious of beggar, and bard of bard.   *Works and Days, l. 25*

9   Fools, they do not even know how much more is the half than the whole.   *Works and Days, l. 40*

10   Often an entire city has suffered because of an evil man.   *Works and Days, l. 240*

11   He harms himself who does harm to another, and the evil plan is most harmful to the planner.   *Works and Days, l. 265*

12   Badness you can get easily, in quantity: the road is smooth, and it lies close by. But in front of excellence the immortal gods have put sweat, and long and steep is the way to it, and rough at first. But when you come to the top, then it is easy, even though it is hard.   *Works and Days, l. 287*

13   A bad neighbor is a misfortune, as much as a good one is a great blessing.   *Works and Days, l. 346*

14   Do not seek evil gains; evil gains are the equivalent of disaster.   *Works and Days, l. 352*

15   If you should put even a little on a little, and should do this often, soon this too would become big.   *Works and Days, l. 361*

16   At the beginning of a cask and at the end take your fill; in the middle be sparing.   *Works and Days, l. 368*

17   The dawn speeds a man on his journey, and speeds him too in his work.   *Works and Days, l. 579*

18   Observe due measure, for right timing is in all things the most important factor.   *Works and Days, l. 694*

19   Gossip is mischievous, light and easy to raise, but grievous to bear and hard to get rid of. No gossip ever dies away entirely, if many people voice it: it too is a kind of divinity.   *Works and Days, l. 761*

Archilochus
Early seventh century B.C.

20   I have saved myself—what care I for that shield? Away with it! I'll get another one no worse.   *Fragment 6*

21   Old women should not seek to be perfumed.   *Fragment 27*

22   The fox knows many things, but the hedgehog knows one great thing.[1]   *Fragment 103*

Mimnermus
c. 650–c. 590 B.C.

23   What life is there, what delight, without golden Aphrodite?   *Fragment 1*

The Seven Sages[2]
c. 650–c. 550 B.C.

24   Know thyself.
Inscription at the Delphic Oracle. From PLUTARCH, *Morals*

25   Hesiod might as well have kept his breath to cool his pottage.[3]
PERIANDER. *From* PLUTARCH, *The Banquet of the Seven Wise Men, sec. 14*

26   Every one of you hath his particular plague, and my wife is mine; and he is very happy who hath this only.
PITTACUS. *From* PLUTARCH, *Morals, On the Tranquillity of the Mind*

---

[1]The fox has many tricks, and the hedgehog has only one, but that is the best of all.—ERASMUS, *Adagia* [1500]. See Sir Isaiah Berlin, 782:3.

[2]Sayings throughout antiquity were variously attributed to the figures known as the Seven Sages. The list is commonly given as Thales, Solon, Periander, Cleobulus, Chilon, Bias, Pittacus. See Solon, 57.

[3]Spare your breath to cool your porridge.—FRANÇOIS RABELAIS, *Works, bk. V* [1552], *ch. 28*

1   Nothing too much.
From DIOGENES LAERTIUS, *Lives of Eminent Philosophers, bk. I, sec. 63*

2   Do not speak ill of the dead.[1]
From DIOGENES LAERTIUS, *Lives of Eminent Philosophers, I, 70*

3   Not even the gods fight against necessity.
From DIOGENES LAERTIUS, *Lives of Eminent Philosophers, I, 77*

4   Know the right moment.[2]
From DIOGENES LAERTIUS, *Lives of Eminent Philosophers, I, 79*

5   Rule will show the man.
BIAS. *From* ARISTOTLE, *Nicomachean Ethics, bk. V, ch. 1*

Solon
c. 638–c. 559 B.C.

6   Many evil men are rich, and good men poor, but we shall not exchange with them our excellence for riches.   *Fragment 4*

7   Poets tell many lies.   *Fragment 21*

8   I grow old ever learning many things.   *Fragment 22*

9   Speech is the image of actions.
From DIOGENES LAERTIUS, *Lives of Eminent Philosophers, bk. I, sec. 58*

10   Let us sacrifice to the Muses.
From PLUTARCH, *The Banquet of the Seven Wise Men*

11   Until he is dead, do not yet call a man happy, but only lucky.
From HERODOTUS,[3] *bk. I, ch. 32*

Stesichorus
c. 630–c. 555 B.C.

12   This tale is not true: you [Helen] did not even board the well-benched ships, and you did not go to the citadel of Troy.[4]   *Fragment 11*

Alcaeus
c. 625–c. 575 B.C.

13   Wine, dear boy, and truth.[5]   *Fragment 66*

14   Wine is a peep-hole on a man.[5]   *Fragment 104*

15   Let us run into a safe harbor.   *Fragment 120*

Anacharsis
fl. c. 600 B.C.

16   [On learning that the sides of a ship were four fingers thick:] The passengers are just that distance from death.[6]
From DIOGENES LAERTIUS, *Lives of Eminent Philosophers, Anacharsis, 5*

17   [Anacharsis] laughed at him [Solon] for imagining the dishonesty and covetousness of his countrymen could be restrained by written laws, which were like spiders' webs, and would catch, it is true, the weak and poor, but easily be broken by the mighty and rich.   *From* PLUTARCH, *Lives, Solon*

18   In Greece wise men speak and fools decide.[7]
From PLUTARCH, *Lives, Solon*

Sappho[8]
c. 612 B.C.

19   Deathless Aphrodite on your rich-wrought throne.[9]   *Fragment 1*

20   Equal to the gods seems to me that man who sits facing you and hears you nearby sweetly speaking and softly laughing. This sets my heart to fluttering in my breast, for when I look on you a moment, then can I speak no more, but my tongue falls silent, and at once a delicate flame courses beneath my skin, and with my eyes I see nothing, and my ears hum, and a cold sweat bathes me, and a trembling seizes me all over, and I am paler than grass, and I feel that I am near to death.   *Fragment 2*

---

[1]The Latin form: De mortuis nil nisi bonum [Of the dead, nothing but good].

[2]Occasionem cognosce.

[3]Herodotus attributed these words to Solon.

[4]Stesichorus allegedly went blind after writing an account of Helen's perfidy to Menelaus in his *Helen,* but he was cured after he composed a palinode denying that Helen ever went to Troy and blaming Homer for the story.

[5]Earliest references to what became the proverb "in vino veritas" (in wine is truth), which was known to Plato *(Symposium, 217)* and to Pliny the Elder, *Natural History, XIV, 141.*
See Anonymous: Latin, 124:3.

[6]"How thick do you judge the planks of our ship to be?" "Some two good inches and upward," returned the pilot. "It seems, then, we are within two fingers' breadth of damnation."—FRANÇOIS RABELAIS, *Works, bk. IV* [1548], *ch. 23*

[7]Literally: Anacharsis said [to Solon] that in Greece wise men spoke and fools decided.

[8]Some say there are nine Muses: but they're wrong. / Look at Sappho of Lesbos; she makes ten.—PLATO, *no. 36;* translated by PETER JAY in his edition of *The Greek Anthology* [1973]

[9]Or "with your intricate charms."

1   The stars about the lovely moon hide their shining forms when it lights up the earth at its fullest.

Fragment 4

2   I loved you once long ago, Athis . . . you seemed to me a small, ungainly child.

Fragments 40–41

3   The moon has set, and the Pleiades; it is midnight, and time passes, and I sleep alone.[1]

Fragment 94

4   Sweet mother, I cannot ply the loom, vanquished by desire for a youth through the work of soft Aphrodite.   *Fragment 114*

5   As an apple reddens on the high bough; high atop the highest bough the apple pickers passed it by — no, not passed it by, but they could not reach it.

Fragment 116

6   Hesperus, you herd homeward whatever Dawn's light dispersed: you herd sheep — herd goats — herd children home to their mothers.[2]

Fragment 120

Lao-tzu[3]

c. 604–c. 531 B.C.

7 The Tao [Way] that can be told of is not the eternal Tao;
The name that can be named is not the eternal name.
The Nameless is the origin of Heaven and Earth;
The Named is the mother of all things.
Therefore let there always be non-being, so we may see their subtlety,
And let there always be being, so we may see their outcome.
The two are the same,
But after they are produced, they have different names.
They both may be called deep and profound.
Deeper and more profound,
The door of all subtleties!   *The Way of Lao-tzu, 1*

8 When the people of the world all know beauty as beauty,
There arises the recognition of ugliness.
When they all know the good as good,
There arises the recognition of evil.

The Way of Lao-tzu, 2

9 In the government of the sage,
He keeps their hearts vacuous,
Fills their bellies,

Weakens their ambitions,
And strengthens their bones,
He always causes his people to be without knowledge [cunning] or desire,
And the crafty to be afraid to act.

The Way of Lao-tzu, 3

10 Heaven and Earth are not humane.
They regard all things as straw dogs.[4]

The Way of Lao-tzu, 5

11 The spirit of the valley never dies.
It is called the subtle and profound female.
The gate of the subtle and profound female
Is the root of Heaven and Earth.
It is continuous, and seems to be always existing.
Use it and you will never wear it out.

The Way of Lao-tzu, 6

12 The best [man] is like water.
Water is good; it benefits all things and does not compete with them.
It dwells in [lowly] places that all disdain.
This is why it is so near to Tao.

The Way of Lao-tzu, 8

13 To produce things and to rear them,
To produce, but not to take possession of them,
To act, but not to rely on one's own ability,
To lead them, but not to master them —
This is called profound and secret virtue.

The Way of Lao-tzu, 10

14 He who loves the world as his body may be entrusted with the empire.

The Way of Lao-tzu, 13

15 We look at it [Tao] and do not see it;
Its name is The Invisible.
We listen to it and do not hear it;
Its name is The Inaudible.
We touch it and do not find it;
Its name is The Subtle [formless].

The Way of Lao-tzu, 14

16 It is The Vague and Elusive.
Meet it and you will not see its head.
Follow it and you will not see its back.

The Way of Lao-tzu, 14

17 Manifest plainness,
Embrace simplicity,
Reduce selfishness,
Have few desires.   *The Way of Lao-tzu, 19*

18 Abandon learning and there will be no sorrow.

The Way of Lao-tzu, 20

19 To yield is to be preserved whole.
To be bent is to become straight.

---

[1]See Housman, 619:21.

[2]Translated by MARY BARNARD [1962].

[3]Translated by WING-TSIT CHAN.

[4]Straw dogs were used in sacrifices and then discarded.

To be empty is to be full.
To be worn out is to be renewed.
To have little is to possess.
To have plenty is to be perplexed.
The Way of Lao-tzu, 22

1 He who knows others is wise;
He who knows himself is enlightened.
The Way of Lao-tzu, 33

2 [The sage] never strives himself for the great, and
thereby the great is achieved.
The Way of Lao-tzu, 34

3 Tao invariably takes no action, and yet there is
nothing left undone.
Reversion is the action of Tao.
Weakness is the function of Tao.
All things in the world come from being.
And being comes from non-being.
The Way of Lao-tzu, 40

4 When the highest type of men hear Tao,
They diligently practice it.
When the average type of men hear Tao,
They half believe in it.
When the lowest type of men hear Tao,
They laugh heartily at it.
The Way of Lao-tzu, 41

5 The softest things in the world overcome the
hardest things in the world.
Non-being penetrates that in which there is no
space.
Through this I know the advantage of taking no
action. *The Way of Lao-tzu, 43*

6 There is no calamity greater than lavish desires.
There is no greater guilt than discontentment.
And there is no greater disaster than greed.
The Way of Lao-tzu, 46

7 One may know the world without going out of
doors.
One may see the Way of Heaven without looking
through the windows.
The further one goes, the less one knows.[1]
Therefore the sage knows without going about,
Understands without seeing,
And accomplishes without any action.
The Way of Lao-tzu, 47

8 He who possesses virtue in abundance
May be compared to an infant.
The Way of Lao-tzu, 55

9 He who knows does not speak.
He who speaks does not know.
The Way of Lao-tzu, 56

10 The more laws and order are made prominent,
The more thieves and robbers there will be.
The Way of Lao-tzu, 57

11 Tao is the storehouse of all things.
It is the good man's treasure and the bad man's
refuge. *The Way of Lao-tzu, 62*

12 A journey of a thousand miles must begin with a
single step.[2] *The Way of Lao-tzu, 64*

13 People are difficult to govern because they have
too much knowledge.
The Way of Lao-tzu, 65

14 I have three treasures. Guard and keep them:
The first is deep love,
The second is frugality,
And the third is not to dare to be ahead of the
world.
Because of deep love, one is courageous.
Because of frugality, one is generous.
Because of not daring to be ahead of the world,
one becomes the leader of the world.
The Way of Lao-tzu, 67

15 When armies are mobilized and issues joined,
The man who is sorry over the fact will win.
The Way of Lao-tzu, 69

16 To know that you do not know is the best.
To pretend to know when you do not know is a
disease. *The Way of Lao-tzu, 71*

17 Heaven's net is indeed vast.
Though its meshes are wide, it misses nothing.
The Way of Lao-tzu, 73

18 To undertake executions for the master executioner
[Heaven] is like hewing wood for the master
carpenter.
Whoever undertakes to hew wood for the master
carpenter rarely escapes injuring his own
hands. *The Way of Lao-tzu, 74*

19 The Way of Heaven has no favorites.
It is always with the good man.
The Way of Lao-tzu, 79

20 Let there be a small country with few people. . . .
Though neighboring communities overlook one
another and the crowing of cocks and barking
of dogs can be heard,
Yet the people there may grow old and die without
ever visiting one another.
The Way of Lao-tzu, 80

21 True words are not beautiful;[3]
Beautiful words are not true.
A good man does not argue;

---

[1] I.e., the more one studies, the further one is from the Tao.

[2] Traditional translation.

[3] I.e., they are not "fine-sounding."

He who argues is not a good man.
A wise man has no extensive knowledge;
He who has extensive knowledge is not a wise man.
The sage does not accumulate for himself.
The more he uses for others, the more he has himself.
The more he gives to others, the more he possesses of his own.
The Way of Heaven is to benefit others and not to injure.
The Way of the sage is to act but not to compete.

The Way of Lao-tzu, 81

Epimenides
Sixth century B.C.

1   All Cretans are liars.   *Attributed*

Pythagoras
c. 582–500 B.C.

2   Friends share all things.
From DIOGENES LAERTIUS, *Lives of Eminent Philosophers,*[1] *bk. VIII, sec. 10*

3   Don't eat your heart.
From DIOGENES LAERTIUS, *Lives of Eminent Philosophers, VIII, 17*

4   Reason is immortal, all else mortal.
From DIOGENES LAERTIUS, *Lives of Eminent Philosophers, VIII, 30*

Ibycus[2]
c. 580 B.C.

5   There is no medicine to be found for a life which has fled.   *Fragment 23*

6   An argument needs no reason, nor a friendship.
Fragment 40

Aesop[3]
fl. c. 550 B.C.

7   The lamb . . . began to follow the wolf in sheep's clothing.   *The Wolf in Sheep's Clothing*

8   Appearances often are deceiving.
The Wolf in Sheep's Clothing

9   Do not count your chickens before they are hatched.[4]   *The Milkmaid and Her Pail*

10   I am sure the grapes are sour.[5]
The Fox and the Grapes

11   No act of kindness, no matter how small, is ever wasted.   *The Lion and the Mouse*

12   Slow and steady wins the race.
The Hare and the Tortoise

13   Familiarity breeds contempt.[6]
The Fox and the Lion

14   The boy cried "Wolf, wolf!" and the villagers came out to help him.
The Shepherd Boy and the Wolf

15   A crust eaten in peace is better than a banquet partaken in anxiety.
The Town Mouse and the Country Mouse

16   Borrowed plumes.   *The Jay and the Peacock*

17   It is not only fine feathers that make fine birds.
The Jay and the Peacock

18   Self-conceit may lead to self-destruction.
The Frog and the Ox

19   People often grudge others what they cannot enjoy themselves.   *The Dog in the Manger*

20   It is thrifty to prepare today for the wants of tomorrow.   *The Ant and the Grasshopper*

21   Be content with your lot; one cannot be first in everything.   *Juno and the Peacock*

22   A huge gap appeared in the side of the mountain. At last a tiny mouse came forth.[7]
The Mountain in Labor

23   Any excuse will serve a tyrant.
The Wolf and the Lamb

24   Beware lest you lose the substance by grasping at the shadow.   *The Dog and the Shadow*

---

[1]Translated by R. D. Hicks (Loeb Classical Library).

[2]Associated with Ibycus is the phrase: the cranes of Ibycus. It derives from the legend that Ibycus was murdered at sea and his murderers were discovered through cranes that followed the ship. Hence, "the cranes of Ibycus" became a term for the agency of the gods in revealing crime.

[3]Animal fables from before Aesop's time and after were attributed to him. The first collection was made two hundred years after his death. See also La Fontaine, 276.

[4]To swallow gudgeons ere they're catched / And count their chickens ere they're hatched.—SAMUEL BUTLER, *Hudibras, pt. II* [1664], *canto III, l. 923*

[5]The fox, when he cannot reach the grapes, says they are not ripe.—GEORGE HERBERT, *Jacula Prudentum* [1651]

"They are too green," he said, "and only good for fools."—JEAN DE LA FONTAINE, *Fables, bk. III* [1668], *fable 11, The Fox and the Grapes*

[6]Familiarity breeds contempt—and children.—MARK TWAIN, *Notebooks* [1935]

[7]A mountain was in labor, sending forth dreadful groans, and there was in the region the highest expectation. After all, it brought forth a mouse.—PHAEDRUS, *Fables, IV, 22:1*

1   Who shall bell the cat?   *The Rats and the Cat*

2   I will have nought to do with a man who can blow hot and cold with the same breath.
The Man and the Satyr

3   Thinking to get at once all the gold the goose could give, he killed it and opened it only to find — nothing.   *The Goose with the Golden Eggs*

4   Put your shoulder to the wheel.
Hercules and the Wagoner

5   The gods help them that help themselves.[1]
Hercules and the Wagoner

6   We would often be sorry if our wishes were gratified.[2]   *The Old Man and Death*

7   Union gives strength.   *The Bundle of Sticks*

8   While I see many hoof marks going in, I see none coming out. It is easier to get into the enemy's toils than out again.   *The Lion, the Fox, and the Beasts*

9   The haft of the arrow had been feathered with one of the eagle's own plumes. We often give our enemies the means of our own destruction.[3]
The Eagle and the Arrow

Theognis

fl. c. 545 B.C.

10   One finds many companions for food and drink, but in a serious business a man's companions are very few.   *Elegies, l. 115*

---

[1]God loves to help him who strives to help himself. — AESCHYLUS, *Fragment 223*

Heaven helps not the men who will not act. — SOPHOCLES, *Fragment 288*

Try first thyself, and after call in God; / For to the worker God himself lends aid. — EURIPIDES, *Hippolytus, Fragment 435*

Help thyself, and God will help thee. — GEORGE HERBERT, *Jacula Prudentum* [1651]

God helps those who help themselves. — ALGERNON SIDNEY, *Discourses on Government* [1698], *sec. 23*, and BENJAMIN FRANKLIN, *Poor Richard's Almanac* [1733–1758]

[2]Granting our wish one of Fate's saddest jokes is! — JAMES RUSSELL LOWELL, *Two Scenes from the Life of Blondel, sc. II, st. 2*

Beware, my lord! Beware lest stern Heaven hate you enough to hear your prayers! — ANATOLE FRANCE, *The Crime of Sylvestre Bonnard* [1881], *pt. II, ch. 4*

When the gods wish to punish us they answer our prayers. — WILDE, *An Ideal Husband* [1895], *act II*

[3]So in the Libyan fable it is told / That once an eagle, stricken with a dart, / Said, when he saw the fashion of the shaft, / "With our own feathers, not by others' hands, / Are we now smitten." — AESCHYLUS, *Fragment 135;* translated [1868] by EDWARD HAYES PLUMPTRE

That eagle's fate and mine are one, / Which on the shaft that made him die / Espied a feather of his own, / Wherewith he wont to soar so high. — EDMUND WALLER, *To a Lady Singing a Song of His Composing*

11   Even to a wicked man a divinity gives wealth, Cyrnus, but to few men comes the gift of excellence.   *Elegies, l. 149*

12   Surfeit begets insolence, when prosperity comes to a bad man.   *Elegies, l. 153*

13   Adopt the character of the twisting octopus, which takes on the appearance of the nearby rock. Now follow in this direction, now turn a different hue.   *Elegies, l. 215*

14   The best of all things for earthly men is not to be born and not to see the beams of the bright sun; but if born, then as quickly as possible to pass the gates of Hades, and to lie deep buried.
Elegies, l. 425

15   No man takes with him to Hades all his exceeding wealth.   *Elegies, l. 725*

16   Bright youth passes swiftly as a thought.
Elegies, l. 985

Anacreon

c. 570–c. 480 B.C.

17   Bring water, bring wine, boy! Bring flowering garlands to me! Yes, bring them, so that I may try a bout with love.   *Fragment 27*

18   I both love and do not love, and am mad and am not mad.   *Fragment 79*

19   War spares not the brave, but the cowardly.
Fragment 101. From The Palatine Anthology, VII, 160

Xenophanes

c. 570–c. 475 B.C.

20   Homer and Hesiod attributed to the gods everything that is a shame and a reproach among men.
Fragment 11

21   If cattle and horses, or lions, had hands, or were able to draw with their feet and produce the works which men do, horses would draw the forms of gods like horses, and cattle like cattle, and they would make the gods' bodies the same shape as their own.   *Fragment 15*

22   One god, greatest among gods and men, similar to mortals neither in shape nor even in thought.
Fragment 23

23   It takes a wise man to recognize a wise man.
From DIOGENES LAERTIUS, Lives of Eminent Philosophers, bk. IX

Simonides

c. 556–468 B.C.

1   It is hard to be truly excellent, four-square in hand and foot and mind, formed without blemish.

Fragment 4

2   The city is the teacher of the man.

Fragment 53

3   Fighting in the forefront of the Greeks, the Athenians crushed at Marathon the might of the gold-bearing Medes.

Fragment 88

4 Go tell the Spartans, thou who passest by, That here, obedient to their laws, we lie.[1]

Fragment 92

5 If to die honorably is the greatest Part of virtue, for us fate's done her best. Because we fought to crown Greece with freedom We lie here enjoying timeless fame.

For the Athenian Dead at Plataia[2]

6 We did not flinch but gave our lives to save Greece when her fate hung on a razor's edge.

Cenotaph at the Isthmos[2]

7   Painting is silent poetry, and poetry painting that speaks.

From PLUTARCH, *De Gloria Atheniensium,* III, 346

Confucius

551–479 B.C.

8   Fine words and an insinuating appearance are seldom associated with true virtue.

The Confucian Analects,[3] *bk. 1:3*

9   A youth, when at home, should be filial, and, abroad, respectful to his elders.   *Analects, 1:6*

10   If a man withdraws his mind from the love of beauty, and applies it as sincerely to the love of the virtuous; if, in serving his parents, he can exert his utmost strength; if, in serving his prince, he can devote his life; if, in his intercourse with his friends, his words are sincere—although men say that he has not learned, I will certainly say that he has.

Analects, 1:7

---

[1]Translated by W. L. BOWLES.
   Epitaph for the Lacedaemonian [Spartan] king Leonidas and his small force at Thermopylae, who all died fighting to hold the pass against the invading Persian army [480 B.C.].

[2]Translated by PETER JAY in his edition of *The Greek Anthology* [1973].

[3]Sayings attributed to Confucius and his followers; from *The Chinese Classics* [1861–1886], *vol.* I, *The Confucian Analects,* translated by JAMES LEGGE.

11   Hold faithfulness and sincerity as first principles.

Analects, 1:8, ii

12   Have no friends not equal to yourself.

Analects, 1:8, iii

13   When you have faults, do not fear to abandon them.   *Analects, 1:8, iv*

14   He who exercises government by means of his virtue may be compared to the north polar star, which keeps its place and all the stars turn towards it.

Analects, 2:1

15   [The superior man] acts before he speaks, and afterwards speaks according to his actions.

Analects, 2:13

16   Learning without thought is labor lost; thought without learning is perilous.   *Analects, 2:15*

17   When you know a thing, to hold that you know it; and when you do not know a thing, to allow that you do not know it—this is knowledge.

Analects, 2:17

18   Things that are done, it is needless to speak about . . . things that are past, it is needless to blame.   *Analects, 3:21, ii*

19   I have not seen a person who loved virtue, or one who hated what was not virtuous. He who loved virtue would esteem nothing above it.

Analects, 4:6, i

20   If a man in the morning hear the right way, he may die in the evening without regret.

Analects, 4:8

21   The superior man . . . does not set his mind either for anything, or against anything; what is right he will follow.   *Analects, 4:10*

22   When we see men of worth, we should think of equaling them; when we see men of a contrary character, we should turn inwards and examine ourselves.   *Analects, 4:17*

23   The cautious seldom err.   *Analects, 4:23*

24   Virtue is not left to stand alone. He who practices it will have neighbors.   *Analects, 4:25*

25   Man is born for uprightness. If a man lose his uprightness, and yet live, his escape from death is the effect of mere good fortune.   *Analects, 6:16*

26   The man of virtue makes the difficulty to be overcome his first business, and success only a subsequent consideration.   *Analects, 6:20*

27   With coarse rice to eat, with water to drink, and my bended arm for a pillow—I have still joy in the

midst of these things. Riches and honors acquired by unrighteousness are to me as a floating cloud.

Analects, 7:15

1   I am not one who was born in the possession of knowledge; I am one who is fond of antiquity, and earnest in seeking it there.   *Analects, 7:19*

2   Is virtue a thing remote? I wish to be virtuous, and lo! virtue is at hand.   *Analects, 7:29*

3   The superior man is satisfied and composed; the mean man is always full of distress.

Analects, 7:36

4   The people may be made to follow a path of action, but they may not be made to understand it.

Analects, 8:9

5   While you are not able to serve men, how can you serve spirits [of the dead]? . . . While you do not know life, how can you know about death?

Analects, 11:11

6   To go beyond is as wrong as to fall short.

Analects, 11:15, iii

7   He with whom neither slander that gradually soaks into the mind, nor statements that startle like a wound in the flesh, are successful may be called intelligent indeed.   *Analects, 12:6*

8   In carrying on your government, why should you use killing [the unprincipled for the good of the unprincipled] at all? Let your evinced desires be for what is good, and the people will be good. The relation between superiors and inferiors is like that between the wind and the grass. The grass must bend when the wind blows across it.

Analects, 12:19

9   Good government obtains when those who are near are made happy, and those who are far off are attracted.   *Analects, 13:16, ii*

10   The firm, the enduring, the simple, and the modest are near to virtue.   *Analects, 13:27*

11   The scholar who cherishes the love of comfort is not fit to be deemed a scholar.   *Analects, 14:3*

12   The man who in the view of gain thinks of righteousness; who in the view of danger is prepared to give up his life; and who does not forget an old agreement however far back it extends—such a man may be reckoned a complete man.

Analects, 14:13, ii

13   He who speaks without modesty will find it difficult to make his words good.   *Analects, 14:21*

14   The superior man is modest in his speech, but exceeds in his actions.   *Analects, 14:29*

15   Recompense injury with justice, and recompense kindness with kindness.   *Analects, 14:36, iii*

16   The determined scholar and the man of virtue will not seek to live at the expense of injuring their virtue. They will even sacrifice their lives to preserve their virtue complete.   *Analects, 15:8*

17   If a man take no thought about what is distant, he will find sorrow near at hand.

Analects, 15:11

18   The superior man is distressed by his want of ability.   *Analects, 15:18*

19   What the superior man seeks is in himself. What the mean man seeks is in others.

Analects, 15:20

20   What you do not want done to yourself, do not do to others.[1]   *Analects, 15:23*

21   When a man's knowledge is sufficient to attain, and his virtue is not sufficient to enable him to hold, whatever he may have gained, he will lose again.   *Analects, 15:32, i*

22   The superior man cannot be known in little matters, but he may be entrusted with great concerns. The small man may not be entrusted with great concerns, but he may be known in little matters.

Analects, 15:33

23   Virtue is more to man than either water or fire. I have seen men die from treading on water and fire, but I have never seen a man die from treading the course of virtue.   *Analects, 15:34*

24   By nature, men are nearly alike; by practice, they get to be wide apart.   *Analects, 17:2*

25   To be able to practice five things everywhere under heaven constitutes perfect virtue. . . . [They are] gravity, generosity of soul, sincerity, earnestness, and kindness.   *Analects, 17:6*

26   There are three things which the superior man guards against. In youth . . . lust. When he is strong . . . quarrelsomeness. When he is old . . . covetousness.   *Analects, 17:8*

27   Without recognizing the ordinances of Heaven, it is impossible to be a superior man.

Analects, 20:3, i

28   Without an acquaintance with the rules of propriety, it is impossible for the character to be established.   *Analects, 20:3, ii*

29   Without knowing the force of words, it is impossible to know men.   *Analects, 20:3, iii*

---

[1]See *Matthew 7:12*, 35:5; Aristotle, 79:16; Hillel, 106:1; and Chesterfield, 314:19.

Heraclitus

c. 540–c. 480 B.C.

1   All is flux, nothing stays still.
From DIOGENES LAERTIUS, *Lives of Eminent Philosophers, bk. IX, sec. 8, and* PLATO, *Cratylus, 402A*

2   Nothing endures but change.
From DIOGENES LAERTIUS, *Lives of Eminent Philosophers, IX, 8, and* PLATO, *Cratylus, 402A*

3   It is wise to listen, not to me but to the Word, and to confess that all things are one.
On the Universe,[1] *fragment 1*

4   Nature is wont to hide herself.
On the Universe, 10

5   Much learning does not teach understanding.
On the Universe, 16

6   This world . . . ever was, and is, and shall be, ever-living Fire, in measures being kindled and in measures going out.   *On the Universe, 20*

7   God is day and night, winter and summer, war and peace, surfeit and hunger.   *On the Universe, 36*

8   You could not step twice into the same rivers;[2] for other waters are ever flowing on to you.
On the Universe, 41

9   The opposite is beneficial; from things that differ comes the fairest attunement; all things are born through strife.   *On the Universe, 46*

10   Couples are wholes and not wholes, what agrees disagrees, the concordant is discordant. From all things one and from one all things.
On the Universe, 59

11   The road up and the road down is one and the same.   *On the Universe, 69*

12   Man, like a light in the night, is kindled and put out.   *On the Universe, 77*

13   For when is death not within ourselves? . . . Living and dead are the same, and so are awake and asleep, young and old.   *On the Universe, 78*

14   The people should fight for their law as for a wall.   *On the Universe, 100*

15   It is better to hide ignorance, but it is hard to do this when we relax over wine.
On the Universe, 108

16   A man's character is his fate.
On the Universe, 121

---

[1]Translated by W. H. S. JONES (Loeb Classical Library).
[2]Usually quoted as: river.

Themistocles

c. 528–c. 462 B.C.

17   Tuning the lyre and handling the harp are no accomplishments of mine, but rather taking in hand a city that was small and inglorious and making it glorious and great.
From PLUTARCH, *Lives, Themistocles, sec. 2*

18   The wooden wall is your ships.[3]
From PLUTARCH, *Lives, Themistocles, 10*

19   Strike, but hear me.[4]
From PLUTARCH, *Lives, Themistocles, 11*

20   [Of his son:] The boy is the most powerful of all the Hellenes; for the Hellenes are commanded by the Athenians, the Athenians by myself, myself by the boy's mother, and the mother by her boy.
From PLUTARCH, *Lives, Themistocles, 18*

21   [Of two suitors for his daughter's hand:] I choose the likely man in preference to the rich man; I want a man without money rather than money without a man.
From PLUTARCH, *Lives, Themistocles, 18*

22   I have with me two gods, Persuasion and Compulsion.[5]
From PLUTARCH, *Lives, Themistocles, 21*

23   The speech of man is like embroidered tapestries, since like them this too has to be extended in order to display its patterns, but when it is rolled up it conceals and distorts them.
From PLUTARCH, *Lives, Themistocles, 29*

24   He who commands the sea has command of everything.
From CICERO, *Ad Atticum, X, 8*

25   [Upon being asked whether he would rather be Achilles or Homer:] Which would you rather be — a victor in the Olympic games, or the announcer of the victor?
From PLUTARCH, *Apothegms, Themistocles*

Aeschylus

525–456 B.C.

26   I would far rather be ignorant than knowledgeable of evils.   *The Suppliants, l. 453*

---

[3]This was Themistocles' interpretation to the Athenians in 480 B.C. of the second oracle at Delphi: "Safe shall the wooden wall continue for thee and thy children." The account appears in full in HERODOTUS, *Histories, bk. VII, sec. 141–143.*

[4]Said in reply to Eurybiades, commander of the Spartan fleet, when he raised his staff as though to strike.

[5]Said to the Andrians, when demanding money from them, to which they replied that they already had two great gods, Penury and Powerlessness, who hindered them from giving him money.

1   "Reverence for parents" stands written among the three laws of most revered righteousness.
The Suppliants, l. 707

2   His resolve is not to seem, but to be, the best.
The Seven Against Thebes [467 B.C.], l. 592

3   I pray the gods some respite from the weary task of this long year's watch that lying on the Atreidae's roof on bended arm, doglike, I have kept, marking the conclave of all the night's stars, those potentates blazing in the heavens that bring winter and summer to mortal men, the constellations, when they wane, when they rise.
Agamemnon [458 B.C.], l. 1

4   A great ox stands on my tongue.[1]
Agamemnon, l. 36

5   He who learns must suffer. And even in our sleep pain that cannot forget falls drop by drop upon the heart, and in our own despair, against our will, comes wisdom to us by the awful grace of God.
Agamemnon, l. 177

6   She [Helen] brought to Ilium her dowry, destruction.
Agamemnon, l. 406

7   It is in the character of very few men to honor without envy a friend who has prospered.
Agamemnon, l. 832

8   Only when man's life comes to its end in prosperity can one call that man happy.
Agamemnon, l. 928

9   Alas, I am struck a deep mortal blow!
Agamemnon, l. 1343

10   Death is better, a milder fate than tyranny.
Agamemnon, l. 1364

11   Zeus, first cause, prime mover; for what thing without Zeus is done among mortals?
Agamemnon, l. 1485

12   Do not kick against the pricks.
Agamemnon, l. 1624

13   I know how men in exile feed on dreams of hope.
Agamemnon, l. 1668

14   Good fortune is a god among men, and more than a god.
The Libation Bearers [458 B.C.], l. 59

15   Destiny waits alike for the free man as well as for him enslaved by another's might.
The Libation Bearers, l. 103

16   For a deadly blow let him pay with a deadly blow: it is for him who has done a deed to suffer.
The Libation Bearers, l. 312

17   What is pleasanter than the tie of host and guest?
The Libation Bearers, l. 702

18   Myriad laughter of the ocean waves.
Prometheus Bound, l. 89

19   For somehow this is tyranny's disease, to trust no friends.
Prometheus Bound, l. 224

20   Words are the physicians of a mind diseased.
Prometheus Bound, l. 378

21   Time as he grows old teaches all things.
Prometheus Bound, l. 981

22   God's mouth knows not how to speak falsehood, but he brings to pass every word.
Prometheus Bound, l. 1030

23   On me the tempest falls. It does not make me tremble. O holy Mother Earth, O air and sun, behold me. I am wronged.[2]
Prometheus Bound, l. 1089

Pindar

c. 518–c. 438 B.C.

24   Water is best. But gold shines like fire blazing in the night, supreme of lordly wealth.
Olympian Odes, I, l. 1

25   The days that are still to come are the wisest witnesses.
Olympian Odes, I, l. 51

26   If any man hopes to do a deed without God's knowledge, he errs.
Olympian Odes, I, l. 104

27   Do not peer too far.
Olympian Odes, I, l. 184

28   I have many swift arrows in my quiver which speak to the wise, but for the crowd they need interpreters. The skilled poet is one who knows much through natural gift, but those who have learned their art chatter turbulently, vainly, against the divine bird of Zeus.
Olympian Odes, II, l. 150

29   I will not steep my speech in lies; the test of any man lies in action.[3]
Olympian Odes, IV, l. 27

30   The issue is in God's hands.
Olympian Odes, XIII, l. 147

31   Zeus, accomplisher, to all grant grave restraint and attainment of sweet delight.
Olympian Odes, XIII, last line

---

[1]A proverbial expression of uncertain origin for enforced silence.

[2]Translated by EDITH HAMILTON.

[3]Translated by RICHMOND LATTIMORE.

1   Seek not, my soul, the life of the immortals; but enjoy to the full the resources that are within thy reach.   *Pythian Odes, III, l. 109*

2   They say that this lot is bitterest: to recognize the good but by necessity to be barred from it.   *Pythian Odes, IV, l. 510*

3   Creatures of a day, what is a man? What is he not? Mankind is a dream of a shadow. But when a god-given brightness comes, a radiant light rests on men, and a gentle life.   *Pythian Odes, VIII, l. 135*

4   When toilsome contests have been decided, good cheer is the best physician, and songs, the sage daughters of the Muses, soothe with their touch.   *Nemean Odes, IV, l. 1*

5   Words have a longer life than deeds.   *Nemean Odes, IV, l. 10*

6   Not every truth is the better for showing its face undisguised; and often silence is the wisest thing for a man to heed.   *Nemean Odes, V, l. 30*

7   One race there is of men, one of gods, but from one mother we both draw our breath.   *Nemean Odes, VI, l. 1*

8   If one but tell a thing well, it moves on with undying voice, and over the fruitful earth and across the sea goes the bright gleam of noble deeds ever unquenchable.   *Isthmian Odes, IV, l. 67*

9   It is not possible with mortal mind to search out the purposes of the gods.   *Fragment 61*

10   O bright and violet-crowned and famed in song, bulwark of Greece, famous Athens, divine city!   *Fragment 76*

11   Unsung, the noblest deed will die.   *Fragment 120*

12   What is God? Everything.   *Fragment 140d*

13   Convention is the ruler of all.   *Fragment 169*

14   Hope, which most of all guides the changeful mind of mortals.   *Fragment 214*

Anaxagoras
c. 500–428 B.C.

15   The descent to Hades is the same from every place.

From DIOGENES LAERTIUS, *Lives of Eminent Philosophers, Anaxagoras, 2*

The Pali Canon[1]
c. 500–c. 250 B.C.[2]

16   All that is comes from the mind; it is based on the mind, it is fashioned by the mind.[3]   *Suttapitaka. Dhammapada, ch. 1, verse 1*

17   For hatred does not cease by hatred at any time: hatred ceases by love—this is the eternal law.[3]   *Suttapitaka. Dhammapada, 1:5*

18   Avoid what is evil; do what is good; purify the mind—this is the teaching of the Awakened One [Buddha].[3]   *Suttapitaka. Dhammapada, 14:183*

19   Better to live alone; with a fool there is no companionship. With few desires live alone and do no evil, like an elephant in the forest roaming at will.   *Suttapitaka. Dhammapada, 23:330*

20   Be lamps [or islands] unto yourselves. Be a refuge unto yourselves. Do not turn to any external refuge. Hold fast to the teaching [dhamma] as a lamp.[3]   *Suttapitaka. Mahaparinibbana-sutta, 2:33*

21   Few and far between are the Tathagatas,[4] the Arahat Buddhas, who appear in the world.[3]   *Suttapitaka. Mahaparinibbana-sutta, 5:10*

22   Decay is inherent in all component things! Work out your salvation with diligence.   *Suttapitaka. Mahaparinibbana-sutta, 6:10*

23   The law that I have preached . . . and the discipline that I have established, will be your master after my disappearance.[3]   *Suttapitaka. Digha Nikaya, II*

24   This noble eightfold path . . . right views, right aspirations, right speech, right conduct, right livelihood, right effort, right mindfulness, and right contemplation.[5]   *Suttapitaka. Dhammacakkappavattanasutta, verse 4*

25   The wise and moral man
Shines like a fire on a hilltop,
Making money like the bee,
Who does not hurt the flower.[6]   *Suttapitaka. Singalavada-sutta, Digha-nikaya, 3:180*

---

[1]The sacred scriptures of Theravada Buddhists.

[2]Ancient Indian literary chronology is conjectural.

[3]Translated by JAN NATTIER-BARBARO.

[4]Tathagata: Thus-come-one, an Indian term designating an enlightened being.

[5]Translated by T. W. RHYS DAVIDS and H. OLDENBERG.

[6]Translated by WILLIAM THEODORE DE BARY.

A text addressed—exceptionally in the early Buddhist literature—to laity rather than monks.

1 I go for refuge to the Buddha.
I go for refuge to the Doctrine.
I go for refuge to the Order [of monks].
Traditional (liturgical), passim

Pericles[1]

c. 495–429 B.C.

2 Wait for that wisest of all counselors, Time.
From PLUTARCH, *Lives, Pericles, sec. 18*

3 Trees, though they are cut and lopped, grow up again quickly, but if men are destroyed, it is not easy to get them again.
From PLUTARCH, *Lives, Pericles, 33*

Sophocles[2]

c. 495–406 B.C.

4 Silence gives the proper grace to women.
Ajax, l. 293

5 Nobly to live, or else nobly to die,
Befits proud birth.
Ajax, l. 480

6 Of all human ills, greatest is fortune's wayward tyranny.
Ajax, l. 486

7 For kindness begets kindness evermore,
But he from whose mind fades the memory
Of benefits, noble is he no more.
Ajax, l. 522

8 Sleep that masters all.
Ajax, l. 675

9 I, whom proof hath taught of late
How so far only should we hate our foes
As though we soon might love them, and so far
Do a friend service as to one most like
Someday to prove our foe, since oftenest men
In friendship but a faithless haven find.[3]
Ajax, l. 678

10 Men of ill judgment oft ignore the good
That lies within their hands, till they have lost it.
Ajax, l. 964

11 It is not righteousness to outrage
A brave man dead, not even though you hate him.
Ajax, l. 1344

12 For God hates utterly
The bray of bragging tongues.
Antigone[4] [c. 442 B.C.], l. 123

13 Our ship of state, which recent storms have threatened to destroy, has come safely to harbor at last.
Antigone, l. 163

14 I have nothing but contempt for the kind of governor who is afraid, for whatever reason, to follow the course that he knows is best for the State; and as for the man who sets private friendship above the public welfare — I have no use for him, either.
Antigone, l. 181

15 Nobody likes the man who brings bad news.[5]
Antigone, l. 277

16 Money: There's nothing in the world so demoralizing as money.
Antigone, l. 295

17 How dreadful it is when the right judge judges wrong!
Antigone, l. 323

18 Numberless are the world's wonders, but none
More wonderful than man.
Antigone, l. 333 (Ode I)

19 It is a good thing
To escape from death, but it is not great pleasure
To bring death to a friend.
Antigone, l. 437

20 But all your[6] strength is weakness itself against
The immortal unrecorded laws of God.
They are not merely now: they were and shall be
Forever, beyond man utterly.
Antigone, l. 452

21 Grief teaches the steadiest minds to waver.
Antigone, l. 563

22 All that is and shall be,
And all the past, is his [Zeus's].
Antigone, l. 611 (Ode II)

23 Show me the man who keeps his house in hand,
He's fit for public authority.
Antigone, l. 660

24 Anarchy, anarchy! Show me a greater evil!
This is why cities tumble and the great houses rain down,
This is what scatters armies!
Antigone, l. 672

25 Reason is God's crowning gift to man.
Antigone, l. 684

26 The ideal condition
Would be, I admit, that men should be right by instinct;
But since we are all likely to go astray,

---

[1]See Thucydides, *Funeral Oration of Pericles,* 73:18–74:6.

[2]Sophocles said he drew men as they ought to be, and Euripides as they were. — ARISTOTLE, *Poetics, ch. 25*

[3]They love as though they will someday hate and hate as though they will someday love. — ARISTOTLE quoting BIAS [sixth century B.C.], *Rhetoric, II, 13*

---

[4]Translated by DUDLEY FITTS and ROBERT FITZGERALD.

[5]Don't shoot the messenger. — *Saying*

[6]Creon.

The reasonable thing is to learn from those who
    can teach.   *Antigone, l. 720*

1 Love, unconquerable,
Waster of rich men, keeper
Of warm lights and all-night vigil
In the soft face of a girl:
Sea-wanderer, forest-visitor!
Even the pure immortals cannot escape you,
And mortal man, in his one day's dusk,
Trembles before your glory.
      Antigone, l. 781 (Ode III)

2 Wisdom outweighs any wealth.
      Antigone, l. 1050

3 There is no happiness where there is no wisdom;
No wisdom but in submission to the gods.
Big words are always punished,
And proud men in old age learn to be wise.
      Antigone, l. 1347, closing lines

4 Ships are only hulls, high walls are nothing,
When no life moves in the empty passageways.
      Oedipus Rex [c. 430 B.C.],[1] *l. 56*

5 How dreadful knowledge of the truth can be
When there's no help in truth!
      Oedipus Rex, l. 316

6 The tyrant is a child of Pride
Who drinks from his great sickening cup
Recklessness and vanity,
Until from his high crest headlong
He plummets to the dust of hope.[2]
      Oedipus Rex, l. 872

7 The greatest griefs are those we cause ourselves.
      Oedipus Rex, l. 1230

8 Time eases all things.   *Oedipus Rex, l. 1515*

9   Look upon Oedipus
This is the king who solved the famous riddle [of
    the Sphinx].[3]   *Oedipus Rex, l. 1524*

---

[1]Translated by DUDLEY FITTS and ROBERT FITZGERALD.

[2]Pride will have a fall. — *English proverb* [c. 1509]
A variant is: Pride goeth before a fall.
Pride goeth before, and shame cometh behind. — *Treatise of a Gallant* [c. 1510]
Pride will have a fall; / For pride goeth before and shame cometh after. — JOHN HEYWOOD, *Proverbs* [1546], *pt. I, ch. 10*

[3]The riddle of the Sphinx: What creature walks in the morning on four feet, at noon upon two, and at evening upon three? Oedipus solved it: Man as a baby crawls on hands and knees, then strides erect on his feet, and in old age walks with a staff. The Sphinx, a monster with a woman's head and bust and a lion's body with wings, waylaid passers on the road to Thebes to propound the riddle, destroying anyone who failed to guess the answer. Oedipus solved the riddle, the Sphinx destroyed herself, and the grateful Thebans made him king.
See Seferis, 759:18.

10 Let every man in mankind's frailty
Consider his last day; and let none
Presume on his good fortune until he find
Life, at his death, a memory without pain.
      Oedipus Rex, l. 1529

11   A prudent mind can see room for misgiving, lest
he who prospers should one day suffer reverse.
      Trachiniae [c. 430 B.C.], l. 296

12   They are not wise, then, who stand forth to buffet against Love; for Love rules the gods as he will,
and me.   *Trachiniae, l. 441*

13   Knowledge must come through action; you can
have no test which is not fanciful, save by trial.
      Trachiniae, l. 592

14   Rash indeed is he who reckons on the morrow,
or haply on days beyond it; for tomorrow is not,
until today is past.   *Trachiniae, l. 943*

15 Death is not the worst; rather, in vain
To wish for death, and not to compass it.
      Electra [c. 418 B.C.], l. 1008

16 War never slays a bad man in its course,
But the good always![4]
      Philoctetes [409 B.C.], l. 436

17 Stranger in a strange country.
      Oedipus at Colonus[5] *[c. 406 B.C.], l. 184*

18 The good befriend themselves.
      Oedipus at Colonus, l. 309

19   The immortal
Gods alone have neither age nor death!
All other things almighty Time disquiets.
      Oedipus at Colonus, l. 607

20 Athens, nurse of men.
      Oedipus at Colonus, l. 701

21 Not to be born surpasses thought and speech.
The second best is to have seen the light
And then to go back quickly whence we came.
      Oedipus at Colonus, l. 1224

22   One word
Frees us of all the weight and pain of life:
That word is love.   *Oedipus at Colonus, l. 1616*

23 It made our hair stand up in panic fear.
      Oedipus at Colonus, l. 1625

24 A remedy too strong for the disease.
      Tereus, fragment 514[6]

---

[4]Translated by SIR GEORGE YOUNG.

[5]Translated by ROBERT FITZGERALD.

[6]The fragments are from the Everyman edition of *The Dramas of Sophocles.*

1 Truly, to tell lies is not honorable;
But when the truth entails tremendous ruin,
To speak dishonorably is pardonable.
Creusa, fragment 323

2 Sons are the anchors of a mother's life.
Phaedra, fragment 612

3 To him who is in fear everything rustles.
Acrisius, fragment 58

4 No falsehood lingers on into old age.
Acrisius, fragment 59

5 No man loves life like him that's growing old.
Acrisius, fragment 64

6 A woman's vows I write upon the wave.
Unknown Drama, fragment 694

Empedocles
c. 490–c. 430 B.C.

7   At one time through love all things come together
into one, at another time through strife's hatred they
are borne each of them apart.   *Fragment 17*

8   The blood around men's heart is their thinking.
Fragment 105

Euripides[1]
c. 485–406 B.C.

9 Never say that marriage has more of joy than pain.
Alcestis[2] *[438 B.C.], l. 238*

10   A second wife
is hateful to the children of the first;
a viper is not more hateful.   *Alcestis, l. 309*

11 A sweet thing, for whatever time,
to revisit in dreams the dear dead we have lost.
Alcestis, l. 355

12 Oh, if I had Orpheus' voice and poetry
with which to move the Dark Maid and her Lord,
I'd call you back, dear love, from the world below.
I'd go down there for you. Charon or the grim
King's dog could not prevent me then
from carrying you up into the fields of light.
Alcestis, l. 358

13 Light be the earth upon you, lightly rest.
Alcestis, l. 462

14   God, these old men!
How they pray for death! How heavy
they find this life in the slow drag of days!
And yet, when Death comes near them,
You will not find one who will rise and walk with him,
not one whose years are still a burden to him.
Alcestis, l. 669

15 You love the daylight: do you think your
father does not?   *Alcestis, l. 691*

16 Dishonor will not trouble me, once I am dead.
Alcestis, l. 726

17 Today's today. Tomorrow, we may be
ourselves gone down the drain of Eternity.
Alcestis, l. 788

18 O mortal man, think mortal thoughts!
Alcestis, l. 799

19 My mother was accursed the night she bore me,
and I am faint with envy of all the dead.
Alcestis, l. 865

20 You were a stranger to sorrow: therefore Fate
has cursed you.   *Alcestis, l. 927*

21 I have found power in the mysteries of thought,
exaltation in the chanting of the Muses;
I have been versed in the reasonings of men;
but Fate is stronger than anything I have known.
Alcestis, l. 962

22 Time cancels young pain.   *Alcestis, l. 1085*

23 Slight not what's near through aiming at
what's far.   *Rhesus [c. 435 B.C.], l. 482*

24 There is no benefit in the gifts of a bad man.
Medea [431 B.C.], l. 618

25 When love is in excess it brings a man nor honor
nor any worthiness.   *Medea, l. 627*

26 What greater grief than the loss of one's
native land.   *Medea, l. 650*

27 I know indeed what evil I intend to do,
but stronger than all my afterthoughts is my fury,
fury that brings upon mortals the greatest evils.
Medea, l. 1078

28 We know the good, we apprehend it clearly,
but we can't bring it to achievement.
Hippolytus [428 B.C.],[3] *l. 380*

29 There is one thing alone
that stands the brunt of life throughout its course:
a quiet conscience.   *Hippolytus, l. 426*

---

[1]All Greece is his monument, though his grave / Lies in Macedon, refuge of his last days. / Hellas of Hellas, Athens his land, who gave / so much joy by his art, whom so many praise.— THUCYDIDES, *Euripides;* translated by PETER JAY in his edition of *The Greek Anthology* [1973]

Sophocles said he drew men as they ought to be, and Euripides as they were.—ARISTOTLE, *Poetics, ch. 25*

[2]Translated by DUDLEY FITTS and ROBERT FITZGERALD.

[3]Translated by DAVID GRENE.

1 In this world second thoughts, it seems, are best.[1]
Hippolytus, l. 435

2 Love distills desire upon the eyes,
love brings bewitching grace into the heart
of those he would destroy.
I pray that love may never come to me
with murderous intent,
in rhythms measureless and wild.
Not fire nor stars have stronger bolts
than those of Aphrodite sent
by the hand of Eros, Zeus's child.
Hippolytus, l. 525

3 My tongue swore, but my mind was still unpledged.   *Hippolytus, l. 612*

4 Would that I were under the cliffs, in the secret
hiding-places of the rocks,
that Zeus might change me to a winged bird.
Hippolytus, l. 732

5 I would win my way to the coast,
apple-bearing Hesperian coast
of which the minstrels sing,
where the Lord of the Ocean
denies the voyager further sailing,
and fixes the solemn limit of Heaven
which giant Atlas upholds.
There the streams flow with ambrosia
by Zeus's bed of love,
and holy Earth, the giver of life,
yields to the gods rich blessedness.[2]
Hippolytus, l. 742

6   In a case of dissension, never dare to judge till
you've heard the other side.
Heraclidae[3] [c. 428 B.C.] (quoted by
ARISTOPHANES, *The Wasps)*

7   Leave no stone unturned.   *Heraclidae*

8   I care for riches, to make gifts
To friends, or lead a sick man back to health
With ease and plenty. Else small aid is wealth
For daily gladness; once a man be done
With hunger, rich and poor are all as one.
Electra [413 B.C.],[2] l. 427

9   A coward turns away, but a brave man's choice is
danger.
Iphigenia in Tauris [c. 412 B.C.], l. 114

10   The day is for honest men, the night for thieves.
Iphigenia in Tauris, l. 1026

11   Mankind . . . possesses two supreme blessings.
First of these is the goddess Demeter, or Earth—
whichever name you choose to call her by. It was she
who gave to man his nourishment of grain. But after
her there came the son of Semele, who matched her
present by inventing liquid wine as his gift to man.
For filled with that good gift, suffering mankind forgets its grief; from it comes sleep; with it oblivion of
the troubles of the day. There is no other medicine
for misery.[4]   *The Bacchae [c. 407 B.C.], l. 274*

12   Talk sense to a fool and he calls you foolish.
The Bacchae, l. 480

13   Slow but sure moves the might of the gods.
The Bacchae, l. 882

14 What is wisdom? What gift of the gods
is held in glory like this:
to hold your hand victorious
over the heads of those you hate?
Glory is precious forever.   *The Bacchae, l. 877*

15 Humility, a sense of reverence before the sons of
heaven—
of all the prizes that a mortal man might win,
these, I say, are wisest; these are best.
The Bacchae, l. 1150

16   Yet do I hold that mortal foolish who strives
against the stress of necessity.
Mad Heracles, l. 281

17   The company of just and righteous men is better
than wealth and a rich estate.   *Aegeus,[3] fragment 7*

18   A bad beginning makes a bad ending.
Aeolus,[3] fragment 32

19   Time will explain it all. He is a talker, and needs
no questioning before he speaks.
Aeolus, fragment 38

20   Waste not fresh tears over old griefs.
Alexander,[3] fragment 44

21   The nobly born must nobly meet his fate.[5]
Alcymene,[3] fragment 100

22   Man's best possession is a sympathetic wife.
Antigone,[3] fragment 164

23 When good men die their goodness does not perish,
But lives though they are gone. As for the bad,
All that was theirs dies and is buried with them.
Temenidae,[3] fragment 734

---

[1]Second thoughts, they say, are best. —JOHN DRYDEN, *The Spanish Friar* [1681], *act II, sc. ii*

Is it so true that second thoughts are best? —ALFRED, LORD
TENNYSON, *Sea Dreams* [1864]

[2]Translated by GILBERT MURRAY.

[3]Translated by MORRIS HICKEY MORGAN.

---

[4]Translated by WILLIAM ARROWSMITH.

[5]If there be any good in nobility, I trow it to be only this, that it
imposeth a necessity upon those which are noble, that they should
not suffer their nobility to degenerate from the virtues of their ancestors. —BOETHIUS, *De Consolatione Philosophiae*, III, 6, 25

1 An old man weds a tyrant, not a wife.
*Phoenix (quoted by ARISTOPHANES,
Thesmophoriazusae), fragment 413*

2 Every man is like the company he is wont to keep.[1]
*Phoenix (quoted by ARISTOPHANES,
Thesmophoriazusae), fragment 809*

3 Who knows but life be that which men call death,
And death what men call life?
Phrixus,[2] fragment 830

4 Whoso neglects learning in his youth,
Loses the past and is dead for the future.
Phrixus, fragment 927

5 The gods
Visit the sins of the fathers upon the children.[3]
Phrixus, fragment 970

6 Those whom God wishes to destroy, he first makes mad.[4]
Fragment

7 These men won eight victories over the Syracusans when the favor of the gods was equal for both sides. *Epitaph for the Athenians Slain in Sicily*

Herodotus
c. 485–c. 425 B.C.

8 Men trust their ears less than their eyes.
The Histories, bk. I, ch. 8

9 A woman takes off her claim to respect along with her garments. *Histories, I, 8*

10 In peace, children inter their parents; war violates the order of nature and causes parents to inter their children. *Histories, I, 87*

11 [The Persians] are accustomed to deliberate about the most important matters when they are drunk.
Histories, I, 133

12 It was a kind of Cadmean victory.[5]
Histories, I, 166

13 For great wrongdoing there are great punishments from the gods. *Histories, II, 120*

14 If a man insisted always on being serious, and never allowed himself a bit of fun and relaxation, he would go mad or become unstable without knowing it. *Histories, II, 173*

15 It is better to be envied than pitied.
Histories, III, 52

16 Envy is born in a man from the start.
Histories, III, 80

17 Force has no place where there is need of skill.
Histories, III, 127

18 From the foot, Hercules.[6]
Histories, IV, 82

19 It is the gods' custom to bring low all things of surpassing greatness.[7] *Histories, VII, 10*

20 Haste in every business brings failures.
Histories, VII, 10

21 When life is so burdensome, death has become for man a sought-after refuge.
Histories, VII, 46

22 Circumstances rule men; men do not rule circumstances. *Histories, VII, 49*

23 Great deeds are usually wrought at great risks.
Histories, VII, 50

24 Not snow, no, nor rain, nor heat, nor night keeps them from accomplishing their appointed courses with all speed.[8] *Histories, VIII, 98*

25 The king's might is greater than human, and his arm is very long. *Histories, VIII, 140*

26 This is the bitterest pain among men, to have much knowledge but no power. *Histories, IX, 16*

27 In soft regions are born soft men.
Histories, IX, 122

---

[1]Translated by MORRIS HICKEY MORGAN.
Familiar form: A man is known by the company he keeps.

[2]Translated by MORRIS HICKEY MORGAN.

[3]For the sins of your fathers you, though guiltless, must suffer. — HORACE, *Odes, III, 6, l. 1*
The sins of the father are to be laid upon the children. — SHAKESPEARE, *The Merchant of Venice, act III, sc. v, l. 1*

[4]In Boswell's *Life of Johnson* [1791], *vol. II, pp. 442–443* (Everyman edition), this is quoted as a saying which everybody repeats but nobody knows where to find.
Whom Fortune wishes to destroy she first makes mad. — PUBLILIUS SYRUS, *Maxim 911*
When falls on man the anger of the gods, / First from his mind they banish understanding. — LYCURGUS [fl. 820 B.C.]
For those whom God to ruin has designed, / He fits for fate, and first destroys their mind. — JOHN DRYDEN, *The Hind and the Panther* [1687], *pt. III, l. 1093*
Whom the Gods would destroy they first make mad. — HENRY WADSWORTH LONGFELLOW, *The Masque of Pandora* [1875], VI

[5]Polyneices and Eteocles, sons of Oedipus and descendants of Cadmus, fought for the possession of Thebes and killed each other. Hence, a Cadmean victory means one where victor and vanquished suffer alike.
See also Pyrrhus, 85:5 ("Pyrrhic victory").

[6]Ex pede, Herculem. From AULUS GELLIUS [c. 123–165] *(Noctes Atticae, I, 1)*, who tells how Pythagoras deduced the stature of Hercules from the length of his foot.

[7]It is the lofty pine that by the storm / Is oftener tossed; towers fall with heavier crash / Which higher soar. — HORACE, *Odes, II, 10, l. 9*
The bigger they come, the harder they fall. — *Boxing expression attributed to* ROBERT FITZSIMMONS [1862–1917] *and to* JOHN L. SULLIVAN [1858–1918]; *probably much earlier than either*

[8]Neither snow, nor rain, nor heat, nor gloom of night stays these couriers from the swift completion of their appointed rounds. — *Inscription, New York City General Post Office, adapted from* HERODOTUS *by architect* WILLIAM KENDALL [1913]

Protagoras

c. 485–c. 410 B.C.

1   Man is the measure of all things.

Fragment 1

2   There are two sides to every question.

From DIOGENES LAERTIUS, *Lives of Eminent Philosophers, bk. IX, sec. 51*

Agis

Fifth century B.C.

3   The Lacedemonians are not wont to ask how many the enemy are, but where they are.

From PLUTARCH, *Apothegms, Agis*

Socrates[1]

469–399 B.C.

4   Often when looking at a mass of things for sale, he would say to himself, "How many things I have no need of!"

From DIOGENES LAERTIUS, *Lives of Eminent Philosophers, bk. II, sec. 25*

5   Having the fewest wants, I am nearest to the gods.

From DIOGENES LAERTIUS, *Lives of Eminent Philosophers, II, 27*

6   There is only one good, knowledge, and one evil, ignorance.

From DIOGENES LAERTIUS, *Lives of Eminent Philosophers, II, 31*

7   My divine sign indicates the future to me.

From DIOGENES LAERTIUS, *Lives of Eminent Philosophers, II, 32*

8   I know nothing except the fact of my ignorance.[2]

From DIOGENES LAERTIUS, *Lives of Eminent Philosophers, II, 32*

9   Bad men live that they may eat and drink, whereas good men eat and drink that they may live.[3]

From PLUTARCH, *How a Young Man Ought to Hear Poems, 4*

10   I am not an Athenian or a Greek, but a citizen of the world.   From PLUTARCH, *On Banishment*

11   Crito, I owe a cock to Asclepius; will you remember to pay the debt?

From PLATO, *Phaedo (Socrates' last words)*

Democritus

c. 460–c. 370 B.C.

12   Whatever a poet writes with enthusiasm and a divine inspiration is very fine.   *Fragment 18*

13   In truth we know nothing, for truth lies in the depth.   *Fragment 117*

14   By convention there is color, by convention sweetness, by convention bitterness, but in reality there are atoms and space.   *Fragment 125*

15   Word is a shadow of deed.   *Fragment 145*

Hippocrates

c. 460–377 B.C.

16   I swear by Apollo Physician, by Asclepius, by Health, by Panacea, and by all the gods and goddesses, making them my witnesses, that I will carry out, according to my ability and judgment, this oath and this indenture. . . . I will use treatment to help the sick according to my ability and judgment, but never with a view to injury and wrongdoing. Neither will I administer a poison to anybody when asked to do so, nor will I suggest such a course. Similarly, I will not give to a woman a pessary to cause abortion. I will keep pure and holy both my life and my art. . . . In whatsoever houses I enter, I will enter to help the sick, and I will abstain from all intentional wrongdoing and harm, especially from abusing the bodies of man or woman, bond or free. And whatsoever I shall see or hear in the course of my profession in my intercourse with men, if it be what should not be published abroad, I will never divulge, holding such things to be holy secrets. Now if I carry out this oath, and break it not, may I gain forever reputation among all men for my life and for my art.   *The Physician's Oath*[4]

17   As to diseases make a habit of two things—to help, or at least, to do no harm.[5]

Epidemics, bk. I, ch. 11

18   Healing is a matter of time, but it is sometimes also a matter of opportunity.   *Precepts,[4] ch. 1*

---

[1]Much of Plato, especially in the *Apology* and *Phaedo,* is thought to be direct quotation from Socrates. See Plato, 76:15.

[2]See Milton, 268:28.

[3]He used to say that other men lived to eat, but that he ate to live. — DIOGENES LAERTIUS, *Lives of Eminent Philosophers, Socrates, sec. 14*

We must eat to live and live to eat. — HENRY FIELDING, *The Miser, act III, sc. iii*

[4]Translated by W. H. S. JONES (Loeb Classical Library).

[5]Often cited in Latin: *primum non nocere.*
See Nightingale, 522:5.

1   Time is that wherein there is opportunity, and opportunity is that wherein there is no great time.

Precepts, 1

2   Sometimes give your services for nothing, calling to mind a previous benefaction or present satisfaction. And if there be an opportunity of serving one who is a stranger in financial straits, give full assistance to all such. For where there is love of man, there is also love of the art. For some patients, though conscious that their condition is perilous, recover their health simply through their contentment with the goodness of the physician. And it is well to superintend the sick to make them well, to care for the healthy to keep them well, also to care for one's own self, so as to observe what is seemly.

Precepts, 6

3   If for the sake of a crowded audience you do wish to hold a lecture, your ambition is no laudable one, and at least avoid all citations from the poets, for to quote them argues feeble industry.

Precepts, 12

4   Opposites are cures for opposites.

Breaths, bk. I

5   Medicine is the most distinguished of all the arts, but through the ignorance of those who practice it, and of those who casually judge such practitioners, it is now of all the arts by far the least esteemed.   *Law, bk. I*

6   There are in fact two things, science and opinion; the former begets knowledge, the latter ignorance.   *Law, IV*

7   Things that are holy are revealed only to men who are holy.   *Law, V*

8   Idleness and lack of occupation tend—nay are dragged—towards evil.   *Decorum, bk. I*

9   A wise man should consider that health is the greatest of human blessings, and learn how by his own thought to derive benefit from his illnesses.

Regimen in Health,[1] bk. IX

10   Life is short, the art long,[2] opportunity fleeting, experiment treacherous, judgment difficult.

Aphorisms,[1] sec. I, 1

11   For extreme diseases extreme strictness of treatment is most efficacious.   *Aphorisms, I, 6*

12   Many admire, few know.

Regimen,[1] bk. I, sec. 24

13   Male and female have the power to fuse into one solid, both because both are nourished in both and because soul is the same thing in all living creatures, although the body of each is different.

Regimen, I, 28

14   Prayer indeed is good, but while calling on the gods a man should himself lend a hand.

Regimen, IV, 87

Thucydides[3]
c. 460–400 B.C.

15   Thucydides, an Athenian, wrote the history of the war between the Peloponnesians and the Athenians; he began at the moment that it broke out, believing that it would be a great war, and more memorable than any that had preceded it.

The History of the Peloponnesian War
[431–413 B.C.], bk. I, sec. 1

16   With reference to the narrative of events, far from permitting myself to derive it from the first source that came to hand, I did not even trust my own impressions, but it rests partly on what I saw myself, partly on what others saw for me, the accuracy of the report being always tried by the most severe and detailed tests possible. My conclusions have cost me some labor from the want of coincidence between accounts of the same occurrences by different eyewitnesses, arising sometimes from imperfect memory, sometimes from undue partiality for one side or the other. The absence of romance in my history will, I fear, detract somewhat from its interest; but I shall be content if it is judged useful by those inquirers who desire an exact knowledge of the past as an aid to the interpretation of the future, which in the course of human things must resemble if it does not reflect it. My history has been composed to be an everlasting possession, not the showpiece of an hour.

Peloponnesian War, I, 22

17   The great wish of some is to avenge themselves on some particular enemy, the great wish of others to save their own pocket. Slow in assembling, they devote a very small fraction of the time to the consideration of any public object, most of it to the prosecution of their own objects. Meanwhile each fancies that no harm will come of his neglect, that it is the business of somebody else to look after this or that for him; and so, by the same notion being entertained by all separately, the common cause imperceptibly decays.

Peloponnesian War, I, 141

18   Our constitution is named a democracy, because it is in the hands not of the few but of the many.

---

[1]Translated by W. H. S. JONES (Loeb Classical Library).

[2]*Vita brevis est, ars longa.* — SENECA, *De Brevitate Vitae, I, 1*

[3]Translated by RICHARD LIVINGSTONE unless otherwise noted.

But our laws secure equal justice for all in their private disputes, and our public opinion welcomes and honors talent in every branch of achievement, not for any sectional reason but on grounds of excellence alone. And as we give free play to all in our public life, so we carry the same spirit into our daily relations with one another. . . . Open and friendly in our private intercourse, in our public acts we keep strictly within the control of law. We acknowledge the restraint of reverence; we are obedient to whomsoever is set in authority, and to the laws, more especially to those which offer protection to the oppressed and those unwritten ordinances whose transgression brings admitted shame.

Peloponnesian War, II (Funeral Oration of Pericles), 37

1   We are lovers of beauty without extravagance, and lovers of wisdom without unmanliness. Wealth to us is not mere material for vainglory but an opportunity for achievement; and poverty we think it no disgrace to acknowledge but a real degradation to make no effort to overcome.

Peloponnesian War, II, 40

2   But the bravest are surely those who have the clearest vision of what is before them, glory and danger alike, and yet notwithstanding go out to meet it.   *Peloponnesian War, II, 40*

3   We secure our friends not by accepting favors but by doing them.[1]   *Peloponnesian War, II, 40*

4   In a word I claim that our city as a whole is an education to Greece.

Peloponnesian War, II, 41

5   Fix your eyes on the greatness of Athens as you have it before you day by day, fall in love with her, and when you feel her great, remember that this greatness was won by men with courage, with knowledge of their duty, and with a sense of honor in action . . . So they gave their bodies to the commonwealth and received, each for his own memory, praise that will never die, and with it the grandest of all sepulchers, not that in which their mortal bones are laid, but a home in the minds of men, where their glory remains fresh to stir to speech or action as the occasion comes by. For the whole earth is the sepulcher of famous men; and their story is not graven only on stone over their native earth, but lives on far away, without visible symbol, woven into the stuff of other men's lives. For you now it remains to rival what they have done and, knowing the secret of happiness to be freedom and the secret

of freedom a brave heart, not idly to stand aside from the enemy's onset.

Peloponnesian War, II, 43

6   Great is the glory of the woman who occasions the least talk among men, whether of praise or of blame.   *Peloponnesian War, II, 45*

7   You know as well as we do that right, as the world goes, is only in question between equals in power, while the strong do what they can and the weak suffer what they must.[2]

Peloponnesian War, V, 17

8   Men make the city, and not walls or ships without men in them.

Peloponnesian War, VII, 77 (Address of Nicias to the Athenians at Syracuse)

9   This was the greatest event in the war, or, in my opinion, in Greek history; at once most glorious to the victors and most calamitous to the conquered. They were beaten at all points and altogether; their sufferings in every way were great. They were totally destroyed — their fleet, their army, everything — and few out of many returned home. So ended the Sicilian expedition.

Peloponnesian War, VIII, 87

Aristophanes
c. 450–385 B.C.

10 For then, in wrath, the Olympian Pericles
   Thundered and lightened, and confounded Hellas
   Enacting laws which ran like drinking songs.[3]
   Acharnians [425 B.C.], l. 530

11 When men drink, then they are rich and successful
       and win lawsuits and are happy and help their
       friends.
   Quickly, bring me a beaker of wine, so that I may
       wet my mind and say something clever.
   Knights [424 B.C.], l. 92

12 You have all the characteristics of a popular politician: a horrible voice, bad breeding, and a vulgar manner.   *Knights, l. 217*

13 To make the worse appear the better reason.
   Clouds [423 B.C.], l. 114 and elsewhere

14 Haven't you sometimes seen a cloud that looked
       like a centaur?
   Or a leopard perhaps? Or a wolf? Or a bull?[4]
   Clouds, l. 346

---

[1] Rather by conferring than by accepting favors, they [the Romans] established friendly relations. — SALLUST, *The War with Catiline* [c. 42 B.C.], *sec. 6*

[2] Translated by RICHARD CRAWLEY.
[3] Translated by B. B. ROGERS (Loeb Classical Library).
[4] Translated by DUDLEY FITTS.

1 Old men are children for a second time.
Clouds, l. 1417

2 This is what extremely grieves us, that a man who
 never fought
 Should contrive our fees to pilfer, one who for his
 native land
 Never to this day had oar, or lance, or blister in his
 hand. *Wasps*[1] *[422 B.C.], l. 1117*

3 Let each man exercise the art he knows.
Wasps, l. 1431

4 You cannot teach a crab to walk straight.
Peace [421 B.C.], l. 1083

5 [On the nightingale:] Lord Zeus, listen to the little
 bird's voice; he has filled the whole thicket with
 honeyed song. *Birds [414 B.C.], l. 223*

6 Bringing owls to Athens. *Birds, l. 301*

7 The wise learn many things from their enemies.
Birds, l. 375

8 Full of wiles, full of guile, at all times, in all ways,
 Are the children of Men.[2] *Birds, l. 451*

9 Mankind, fleet of life, like tree leaves, weak creatures of clay, unsubstantial as shadows, wing-
 less, ephemeral, wretched, mortal and
 dreamlike. *Birds, l. 685*

10 Somewhere, what with all these clouds, and all this air,
 There must be a rare name, somewhere . . . How
 do you like "Cloud-Cuckoo-Land"?[2]
Birds, l. 817

11 Halcyon days.[3] *Birds, l. 1594*

12 A woman's time of opportunity is short, and if she
 doesn't seize it, no one wants to marry her,
 and she sits watching for omens.
Lysistrata [411 B.C.], l. 596

13 There is no animal more invincible than a woman,
 nor fire either, nor any wildcat so ruthless.
Lysistrata, l. 1014

14 These impossible women! How they do get around
 us!
 The poet was right: can't live with them, or without them![2] *Lysistrata, l. 1038*

15 Under every stone lurks a politician.[4]
Thesmophoriazusae [410 B.C.], l. 530

16 There's nothing worse in the world than shameless
 woman — save some other woman.
Thesmophoriazusae, l. 531

17 Shall I crack any of those old jokes, master,
 At which the audience never fail to laugh?
Frogs[2] *[405 B.C.], l. 1*

18 Brekekekex, ko-ax, ko-ax.
Frogs, l. 209 and elsewhere

19 A savage-creating stubborn-pulling fellow,
 Uncurbed, unfettered, uncontrolled of speech,
 Unperiphrastic, bombastiloquent.[5]
Frogs, l. 837

20 High thoughts must have high language.[2]
Frogs, l. 1058

21 Who knows whether living is dying, and breathing
 Is eating, and sleeping is a wool blanket?
Frogs, l. 1477

22 Blest the man who possesses a
 Keen intelligent mind. *Frogs, l. 1482*

23 I am amazed that anyone who has made a fortune
 should send for his friends.
Plutus [c. 388 B.C.], l. 340

24 We say that poverty is the sister of beggary.
Plutus, l. 549

25 Even if you persuade me, you won't persuade me.
Plutus, l. 600

26 A man's homeland is wherever he prospers.
Plutus, l. 1151

Agathon

c. 448–400 B.C.

27 This only is denied to God: the power to undo
the past.
*From ARISTOTLE, Nicomachean Ethics,
bk. VI, ch. 2*

Agesilaus

444–400 B.C.

28 If all men were just, there would be no need of
valor. *From PLUTARCH, Lives, Agesilaus, sec. 23*

29 It is circumstance and proper timing that give an
action its character and make it either good or bad.
From PLUTARCH, Lives, Agesilaus, 36

---

[1]Translated by B. B. ROGERS (Loeb Classical Library).

[2]Translated by DUDLEY FITTS.

[3]The appellation of Halcyon days, which was applied to a rare
and bloodless week of repose. — EDWARD GIBBON, *Decline and Fall
of the Roman Empire* [1776–1788], *ch. 48*

[4]A play on the proverb: Under every stone lurks a scorpion.

[5]Refers to Aeschylus.

Xenophon

c. 430–c. 355 B.C.

1   Apollo said that everyone's true worship was that which he found in use in the place where he chanced to be.

Recollections of Socrates, bk. I, ch. 3, sec. 1

2   The sea! The sea![1]   *Anabasis, IV, 7, 24*

3   I knew my son was mortal.[2]

From DIOGENES LAERTIUS, Lives of Eminent Philosophers, bk. II, sec. 55

Zeuxis

fl. 400 B.C.

4   Criticism comes easier than craftsmanship.

From PLINY THE ELDER, Natural History

Plato[3]

c. 428–348 B.C.

5   We who of old left the booming surge of the Aegean lie here in the mid-plain of Ecbatana: farewell, renowned Eretria once our country; farewell, Athens nigh to Euboea; farewell, dear sea.[4]

The Greek Anthology [1906],[5] III, 10

6   Beloved Pan, and all ye other gods who haunt this place, give me beauty in the inward soul; and may the outward and inward man be at one. May I reckon the wise to be the wealthy, and may I have such a quantity of gold as none but the temperate can carry.   *Phaedrus, sec. 279*

7   Friends have all things in common.

Phaedrus, sec. 279

8   And the true order of going, or being led by another, to the things of love, is to begin from the beauties of earth and mount upwards for the sake of that other beauty, using these steps only, and from one going on to two, and from two to all fair forms to fair practices, and from fair practices to fair notions, until from fair notions he arrives at the notion of absolute beauty, and at last knows what the essence of beauty is.   *Symposium, 211*

9   Beholding beauty with the eye of the mind, he will be enabled to bring forth, not images of beauty, but realities (for he has hold not of an image but of a reality), and bringing forth and nourishing true virtue to become the friend of God and be immortal, if mortal man may.   *Symposium, 212*

10   Socrates is a doer of evil, who corrupts the youth; and who does not believe in the gods of the state, but has other new divinities of his own. Such is the charge.   *Apology, 24*

11   The life which is unexamined is not worth living.

Apology, 38

12   Either death is a state of nothingness and utter unconsciousness, or, as men say, there is a change and migration of the soul from this world to another. . . . Now if death be of such a nature, I say that to die is to gain; for eternity is then only a single night.   *Apology, 40*

13   No evil can happen to a good man, either in life or after death.   *Apology, 41*

14   The hour of departure has arrived, and we go our ways—I to die, and you to live. Which is better God only knows.   *Apology, 42*

15   Man is a prisoner who has no right to open the door of his prison and run away. . . . A man should wait, and not take his own life until God summons him.   *Phaedo, 62*

16   Must not all things at the last be swallowed up in death?   *Phaedo, 72*

17   Will you not allow that I have as much of the spirit of prophecy in me as the swans? For they, when they perceive that they must die, having sung all their life long, do then sing more lustily than ever, rejoicing in the thought that they are going to the god they serve.[6]   *Phaedo, 85*

18   The partisan, when he is engaged in a dispute, cares nothing about the rights of the question, but is anxious only to convince his hearers of his own assertions.   *Phaedo, 91*

19   False words are not only evil in themselves, but they infect the soul with evil.   *Phaedo, 91*

20   The soul takes nothing with her to the other world but her education and culture; and these, it is said, are of the greatest service or of the greatest injury to the dead man, at the very beginning of his journey thither.   *Phaedo, 107*

---

[1]Thalatta! Thalatta! / Hail to thee, O Sea, ageless and eternal!—HEINE, *Thalatta! Thalatta!*, st. 1

[2]When his son was killed in battle.

[3]Translated by BENJAMIN JOWETT unless otherwise noted.

Asclepius cured the body: to make men whole / Phoebus sent Plato, healer of the soul.—*On Plato's Grave*, anonymous inscription translated by WILLIAM J. PHILBIN in *The Greek Anthology* [1973], edited by PETER JAY

[4]On the Eretrian exiles settled in Persia by Darius.

[5]Edited by J. W. MACKAIL.

[6]The jalous swan, ayens his deth that singeth.—CHAUCER, *The Parliament of Fowls* [1380–1386], *l. 342*

I will play the swan and die in music.—SHAKESPEARE, *Othello*, act V, sc. ii, *l. 245*

1 He who is of a calm and happy nature will hardly feel the pressure of age, but to him who is of an opposite disposition youth and age are equally a burden.
The Republic, bk. I, 329–D

2 No physician, insofar as he is a physician, considers his own good in what he prescribes, but the good of his patient; for the true physician is also a ruler having the human body as a subject, and is not a mere moneymaker. *Republic, I, 342–D*

3 When there is an income tax, the just man will pay more and the unjust less on the same amount of income. *Republic, I, 343–D*

4 Mankind censure injustice fearing that they may be the victims of it, and not because they shrink from committing it. *Republic, I, 344–C*

5 The beginning is the most important part of the work.[1] *Republic, I, 377–B*

6 The judge should not be young; he should have learned to know evil, not from his own soul, but from late and long observation of the nature of evil in others: knowledge should be his guide, not personal experience. *Republic, III, 409–B*

7 Everything that deceives may be said to enchant. *Republic, III, 413–C*

8 How, then, might we contrive . . . one noble lie to persuade if possible the rulers themselves, but failing that the rest of the city?[2]
Republic, III, 414–C

9 Wealth is the parent of luxury and indolence, and poverty of meanness and viciousness, and both of discontent. *Republic, IV, 422–A*

10 The direction in which education starts a man will determine his future life.
Republic, IV, 425–B

11 What is the prime of life? May it not be defined as a period of about twenty years in a woman's life, and thirty in a man's? *Republic, V, 460–E*

12 Until philosophers are kings, or the kings and princes of this world have the spirit and power of philosophy, and political greatness and wisdom meet in one, and those commoner natures who pursue either to the exclusion of the other are compelled to stand aside, cities will never have rest from their evils—no, nor the human race, as I believe—and then only will this our State have a possibility of life and behold the light of day.
Republic, V, 473–C

13 Let there be one man who has a city obedient to his will, and he might bring into existence the ideal polity about which the world is so incredulous.
Republic, V, 502–B

14 Behold! human beings living in an underground den . . . Like ourselves . . . they see only their own shadows, or the shadows of one another, which the fire throws on the opposite wall of the cave.
Republic, VII, 515–B

15 Astronomy compels the soul to look upwards and leads us from this world to another.
Republic, VII, 529

16 I have hardly ever known a mathematician who was capable of reasoning. *Republic, VII, 531–E*

17 Solon was under a delusion when he said that a man when he grows old may learn many things—for he can no more learn much than he can run much; youth is the time for any extraordinary toil.
Republic, VII, 536–D

18 Bodily exercise, when compulsory, does no harm to the body; but knowledge which is acquired under compulsion obtains no hold on the mind.
Republic, VII, 536–E

19 Let early education be a sort of amusement; you will then be better able to find out the natural bent.
Republic, VII, 537

20 Oligarchy: A government resting on a valuation of property, in which the rich have power and the poor man is deprived of it. *Republic, VIII, 550–C*

21 Democracy, which is a charming form of government, full of variety and disorder, and dispensing a sort of equality to equals and unequals alike.
Republic, VIII, 558–C

22 Democracy passes into despotism.[3]
Republic, VIII, 562–A

23 The people have always some champion whom they set over them and nurse into greatness. . . . This and no other is the root from which a tyrant springs; when he first appears he is a protector.
Republic, VIII, 565–C

24 In the early days of his power, he is full of smiles, and he salutes everyone whom he meets.
Republic, VIII, 566–D

25 When the tyrant has disposed of foreign enemies by conquest or treaty, and there is nothing to fear from them, then he is always stirring up some war or other, in order that the people may require a leader. *Republic, VIII, 566–E*

---

[1]Proverbial. Also in *Laws, VI, 2.*
[2]Translated by Paul Shorey (Loeb Classical Library).

[3]Translated by F. M. Cornford.

1   There are three arts which are concerned with all things: one which uses, another which makes, a third which imitates them.   *Republic, X, 601–D*

2   No human thing is of serious importance.   *Republic, X, 604–C*

3   The soul of man is immortal and imperishable.   *Republic, X, 608–D*

4   If a person shows that such things as wood, stones, and the like, being many are also one, we admit that he shows the coexistence of the one and many, but he does not show that the many are one or the one many; he is uttering not a paradox but a truism.   *Parmenides, 129*

5   The absolute natures or kinds are known severally by the absolute idea of knowledge.   *Parmenides, 134*

6   If a man, fixing his attention on these and the like difficulties, does away with ideas of things and will not admit that every individual thing has its own determinate idea which is always one and the same, he will have nothing on which his mind can rest; and so he will utterly destroy the power of reasoning.   *Parmenides, 135*

7   You cannot conceive the many without the one.   *Parmenides, 166*

8   Let us affirm what seems to be the truth, that, whether one is or is not, one and the others in relation to themselves and one another, all of them, in every way, are and are not, and appear to be and appear not to be.   *Parmenides, 166*

9   Well, my art of midwifery is in most respects like theirs; but differs, in that I attend men and not women, and I look after their souls when they are in labor, and not after their bodies: and the triumph of my art is in thoroughly examining whether the thought which the mind of the young man brings forth is a false idol or a noble and true birth.   *Theaetetus, 150*

10   He [the philosopher] does not hold aloof in order that he may gain a reputation; but the truth is, that the outer form of him only is in the city: his mind, disdaining the littlenesses and nothingnesses of human beings, is "flying all abroad" as Pindar says, measuring earth and heaven and the things which are under and on the earth and above the heaven, interrogating the whole nature of each and all in their entirety, but not condescending to anything which is within reach.   *Theaetetus, 173*

11   I would have you imagine, then, that there exists in the mind of man a block of wax, which is of different sizes in different men; harder, moister, and having more or less of purity in one than another, and in some of an intermediate quality. . . . Let us say that this tablet is a gift of Memory, the mother of the Muses; and that when we wish to remember anything which we have seen, or heard, or thought in our own minds, we hold the wax to the perceptions and thoughts, and in that material receive the impression of them as from the seal of a ring; and that we remember and know what is imprinted as long as the image lasts; but when the image is effaced, or cannot be taken, then we forget and do not know.   *Theaetetus, 191*

12   Let us now suppose that in the mind of each man there is an aviary of all sorts of birds — some flocking together apart from the rest, others in small groups, others solitary, flying anywhere and everywhere. . . . We may suppose that the birds are kinds of knowledge, and that when we were children, this receptacle was empty; whenever a man has gotten and detained in the enclosure a kind of knowledge, he may be said to have learned or discovered the thing which is the subject of the knowledge: and this is to know.   *Theaetetus, 197*

13   The greatest penalty of evildoing — namely, to grow into the likeness of bad men.   *Laws, 728*

14   Of all the animals, the boy is the most unmanageable.   *Laws, 808*

15   You are young, my son, and, as the years go by, time will change and even reverse many of your present opinions. Refrain therefore awhile from setting yourself up as a judge of the highest matters.   *Laws, 888*

16   And this which you deem of no moment is the very highest of all: that is whether you have a right idea of the gods, whereby you may live your life well or ill.   *Laws, 888*

17   Not one of them who took up in his youth with this opinion that there are no gods ever continued until old age faithful to his conviction.   *Laws, 888*

Iphicrates
c. 419–348 B.C.

18   My family history begins with me, but yours ends with you.[1]

From PLUTARCH, Apothegms, Iphicrates

---

[1]Iphicrates, a shoemaker's son who became a famous general, said this to Harmodius of distinguished ancestry when he reviled him for his mean birth.

Curtius Rufus seems to be descended from himself. — TIBERIUS [42 B.C.–A.D. 37]. From TACITUS, *Annals, XI, 21*

Phocion
c. 402–317 B.C.

1   Have I inadvertently said some evil thing?[1]
From PLUTARCH, *Apothegms, Phocion, sec. 10*

2   The good have no need of an advocate.
From PLUTARCH, *Apothegms, Phocion, 10*

Diogenes the Cynic
c. 400–c. 325 B.C.

3   [When asked by Alexander if he wanted anything:] Stand a little out of my sun.
From PLUTARCH, *Lives, Alexander, sec. 14*

4   Plato having defined man to be a two-legged animal without feathers, Diogenes plucked a cock and brought it into the Academy, and said, "This is Plato's man."[2] On which account this addition was made to the definition: "With broad flat nails."
From DIOGENES LAERTIUS, *Lives of Eminent Philosophers, Diogenes, sec. 6*

5   [When asked what was the proper time for supper:] If you are a rich man, whenever you please; and if you are a poor man, whenever you can.[3]
From DIOGENES LAERTIUS, *Lives of Eminent Philosophers, Diogenes, 6*

6   I am looking for an honest man.[4]
From DIOGENES LAERTIUS, *Lives of Eminent Philosophers, Diogenes, 6*

7   The sun too penetrates into privies, but is not polluted by them.[5]
From DIOGENES LAERTIUS, *Lives of Eminent Philosophers, Diogenes, 6*

Antiphanes
c. 388–c. 311 B.C.

8   We must have richness of soul.
Greek Comic Fragments, no. 570

Aristotle[6]
384–322 B.C.

9   Liars when they speak the truth are not believed.
From DIOGENES LAERTIUS, *Lives of Eminent Philosophers, bk. V, sec. 17*

10   Hope is a waking dream.
From DIOGENES LAERTIUS, *Lives of Eminent Philosophers, V, 18*

11   What soon grows old? Gratitude.
From DIOGENES LAERTIUS, *Lives of Eminent Philosophers, V, 18*

12   Beauty is the gift of God.
From DIOGENES LAERTIUS, *Lives of Eminent Philosophers, V, 19*

13   Educated men are as much superior to uneducated men as the living are to the dead.
From DIOGENES LAERTIUS, *Lives of Eminent Philosophers, V, 19*

14   What is a friend? A single soul dwelling in two bodies.[7]
From DIOGENES LAERTIUS, *Lives of Eminent Philosophers, V, 20*

15   I have gained this by philosophy: that I do without being commanded what others do only from fear of the law.[8]
From DIOGENES LAERTIUS, *Lives of Eminent Philosophers, V, 21*

16   We should behave to our friends as we would wish our friends to behave to us.
From DIOGENES LAERTIUS, *Lives of Eminent Philosophers, V, 21*

17   Education is the best provision for old age.
From DIOGENES LAERTIUS, *Lives of Eminent Philosophers, V, 21*

18   If purpose, then, is inherent in art, so is it in Nature also. The best illustration is the case of a

---

[1]Said when an opinion he delivered pleased the people.

[2]Seeing that the human race falls into the same classification as the feathered creatures, we must divide the biped class into featherless and feathered. — PLATO, *The Statesman, 266–E*

[3]The rich when he is hungry, the poor when he has anything to eat. — FRANÇOIS RABELAIS, *Works, bk. IV* [1548], *ch. 64*

[4]Attributed also to AESOP.

[5]The spiritual virtue of a sacrament is like light: although it passes among the impure, it is not polluted. — SAINT AUGUSTINE, *Tract on Saint John, ch. 5:15*
The sun shineth upon the dunghill, and is not corrupted. — LYLY, *Euphues* [1579]
The sun, which passeth through pollutions and itself remains as pure as before. — FRANCIS BACON, *Advancement of Learning* [1605], *bk. II*
Truth is as impossible to be soiled by any outward touch as the sunbeam. — JOHN MILTON, *The Doctrine and Discipline of Divorce* [1643]

---

[6]Chiefly from *The Basic Works of Aristotle,* edited by RICHARD MCKEON.

[7]Andrágathos, my soul's half. — MELEAGER. From *The Greek Anthology* [1906], edited by J. W. MACKAIL, *XII, 52*

[8]Also attributed to Xenocrates [396–314 B.C.] by Cicero.

man being his own physician, for Nature is like that—agent and patient at once.

Physics,[1] *bk. II, ch. 8*

1   Time crumbles things; everything grows old under the power of Time and is forgotten through the lapse of Time.   *Physics, IV, 12*

2   The least initial deviation from the truth is multiplied later a thousandfold.

On the Heavens, bk. I, ch. 5

3   In all things of nature there is something of the marvelous.

On the Parts of Animals, bk. I, ch. 5

4   All men by nature desire knowledge.

Metaphysics, bk. I, ch. 1

5   The final cause, then, produces motion through being loved.   *Metaphysics, I, 7*

6   The actuality of thought is life.

Metaphysics, XII, 7

7   It is of itself that the divine thought thinks (since it is the most excellent of things), and its thinking is a thinking on thinking.   *Metaphysics, XII, 9*

8   Every science and every inquiry, and similarly every activity and pursuit, is thought to aim at some good.   *Nicomachean Ethics, bk. I, ch. 1*

9   While both [Plato and truth] are dear, piety requires us to honor truth above our friends.[2]

Nicomachean Ethics, I, 6

10   One swallow does not make a summer.[3]

Nicomachean Ethics, I, 7

11   For the things we have to learn before we can do them, we learn by doing them.

Nicomachean Ethics, II, 1

12   It is possible to fail in many ways . . . while to succeed is possible only in one way (for which reason also one is easy and the other difficult—to miss the mark easy, to hit it difficult).

Nicomachean Ethics, II, 6

13   We must as second best . . . take the least of the evils.   *Nicomachean Ethics, II, 9*

14   A man is the origin of his action.

Nicomachean Ethics, III, 3

15   Without friends no one would choose to live, though he had all other goods.

Nicomachean Ethics, VIII, 1

16   To be conscious that we are perceiving or thinking is to be conscious of our own existence.

Nicomachean Ethics, IX, 9

17   To enjoy the things we ought and to hate the things we ought has the greatest bearing on excellence of character.   *Nicomachean Ethics, X, 1*

18   If happiness is activity in accordance with excellence, it is reasonable that it should be in accordance with the highest excellence.

Nicomachean Ethics, X, 7

19   We make war that we may live in peace.

Nicomachean Ethics, X, 7

20   With regard to excellence, it is not enough to know, but we must try to have and use it.

Nicomachean Ethics, X, 9

21   Man is by nature a political animal.

Politics, bk. I, ch. 1

22   Nature does nothing uselessly.[4]

Politics, I, 2

23   He who is unable to live in society, or who has no need because he is sufficient for himself, must be either a beast or a god.   *Politics, I, 2*

24   The two qualities which chiefly inspire regard and affection [are] that a thing is your own and that it is your only one.   *Politics, II, 4*

25   It is the nature of desire not to be satisfied, and most men live only for the gratification of it. The beginning of reform is not so much to equalize property as to train the noble sort of natures not to desire more, and to prevent the lower from getting more.   *Politics, II, 7*

26   Even when laws have been written down, they ought not always to remain unaltered.

Politics, II, 8

27   Again, men in general desire the good, and not merely what their fathers had.   *Politics, II, 8*

28   They should rule who are able to rule best.

Politics, II, 11

29   A state is not a mere society, having a common place, established for the prevention of mutual crime and for the sake of exchange. . . . Political society exists for the sake of noble actions, and not of mere companionship.   *Politics, III, 9*

30   If liberty and equality, as is thought by some, are chiefly to be found in democracy, they will be best attained when all persons alike share in the government to the utmost.   *Politics, IV, 4*

---

[1]Translated by PHILIP H. WICKSTEED and FRANCIS CORNFORD (Loeb Classical Library).

[2]Amicus Plato, sed magis amica veritas [Plato is dear to me, but dearer still is truth]. Adapted from a medieval life of Aristotle.

[3]One swallow maketh not summer.—JOHN HEYWOOD, *Proverbs* [1546], *pt. II, ch. 5*
One swallow makes a summer.—ROBERT LOWELL, *Fall, 1961*

---

[4]God and nature do nothing uselessly.—*On the Heavens, bk. I, ch. 4*

1   The best political community is formed by citizens of the middle class.   *Politics, IV, 11*

2   Democracy arises out of the notion that those who are equal in any respect are equal in all respects; because men are equally free, they claim to be absolutely equal.   *Politics, V, 1*

3   Inferiors revolt in order that they may be equal, and equals that they may be superior. Such is the state of mind which creates revolutions.
Politics, V, 2

4   In revolutions the occasions may be trifling but great interests are at stake.   *Politics, V, 3*

5   Well begun is half done.[1]   *Politics, V, 4*

6   The basis of a democratic state is liberty.
Politics, VI, 2

7   Law is order, and good law is good order.
Politics, VII, 4

8   Evils draw men together.
Rhetoric, bk. I, ch. 6

9   It is this simplicity that makes the uneducated more effective than the educated when addressing popular audiences.   *Rhetoric, II, 22*

10   A tragedy is the imitation of an action that is serious and also, as having magnitude, complete in itself . . . with incidents arousing pity and fear, wherewith to accomplish its catharsis of such emotions.   *Poetics, ch. 6*

11   A whole is that which has beginning, middle, and end.   *Poetics, 7*

12   Poetry is something more philosophic and of graver import than history, since its statements are of the nature of universals, whereas those of history are singulars.   *Poetics, 9*

13   A likely impossibility is always preferable to an unconvincing possibility.   *Poetics, 24*

14   Misfortune shows those who are not really friends.[2]   *Eudemian Ethics, bk. VII, ch. 2*

Demosthenes
c. 384–322 B.C.

15   Every advantage in the past is judged in the light of the final issue.   *First Olynthiac, sec. 11*

16   Nothing is easier than self-deceit. For what each man wishes, that he also believes to be true.
Third Olynthiac, sec. 19

17   You cannot have a proud and chivalrous spirit if your conduct is mean and paltry; for whatever a man's actions are, such must be his spirit.
Third Olynthiac, 33

18   I decline to buy repentance at the cost of ten thousand drachmas.[3]
From *AULUS GELLIUS, Noctes Atticae, bk. I, ch. 8*

Antigonus
c. 382–301 B.C.

19   But how many ships do you reckon my presence to be worth?[4]
From *PLUTARCH, Apothegms, Antigonus*

20   [When described by Hermodotus as "Son of the Sun":] My valet is not aware of this.
From *PLUTARCH, Apothegms, Antigonus*

Mencius[5]
372–289 B.C.

21   When one by force subdues men, they do not submit to him in heart. They submit, because their strength is not adequate to resist.
Works, bk. II, 1:3.2

22   There is no attribute of the superior man greater than his helping men to practice virtue.
Works, II, 1:8.5

23   The superior man will not manifest either narrowmindedness or the want of self-respect.
Works, II, 1:9.3

24   To give the throne to another man would be easy; to find a man who shall benefit the kingdom is difficult.   *Works, III, 1:4.10*

25   Never has a man who has bent himself been able to make others straight.   *Works, III, 2:1.5*

26   If you know that [a] thing is unrighteous, then use all dispatch in putting an end to it — why wait till next year?   *Works, III, 2:8.3*

27   The compass and square produce perfect circles and squares. By the sages, the human relations are perfectly exhibited.   *Works, IV, 1:2.1*

28   The root of the kingdom is in the state. The root of the state is in the family. The root of the family is in the person of its head.   *Works, IV, 1:5*

---

[3]In reply to the courtesan Laïs.

[4]His pilot had told him that the enemy outnumbered him in ships.

[5]From *The Chinese Classics* [1861–1886], *vol. II, The Works of Mencius*, translated by JAMES LEGGE.

---

[1]Aristotle is quoting a proverb.

[2]In prosperity it is very easy to find a friend, but in adversity it is the most difficult of all things. — EPICTETUS, *Fragment 127*

1   The people turn to a benevolent rule as water flows downwards, and as wild beasts fly to the wilderness.   *Works, IV, 1:9.2*

2   Benevolence is the tranquil habitation of man, and righteousness is his straight path.
Works, IV, 1:10.2

3   The path of duty lies in what is near, and man seeks for it in what is remote.
Works, IV, 1:11

4   Sincerity is the way of Heaven.
Works, IV, 1:12.2

5   There are three things which are unfilial, and to have no posterity is the greatest of them.
Works, IV, 1:26.1

6   Men must be decided on what they will not do, and then they are able to act with vigor in what they ought to do.   *Works, IV, 2:8*

7   The great man does not think beforehand of his words that they may be sincere, nor of his actions that they may be resolute—he simply speaks and does what is right.   *Works, IV, 2:11*

8   The great man is he who does not lose his child's-heart.   *Works, IV, 2:12*

9   Friendship with a man is friendship with his virtue, and does not admit of assumptions of superiority.   *Works, IV, 2:13.1*

10   The tendency of man's nature to good is like the tendency of water to flow downwards.
Works, VI, 1:2.2

11   From the feelings proper to it, [man's nature] is constituted for the practice of what is good.
Works, VI, 1:6.5–6

12   Benevolence, righteousness, propriety, and knowledge are not infused into us from without.
Works, VI, 1:6.7

13   Benevolence is man's mind, and righteousness is man's path.   *Works, VI, 1:11.1*

14   The great end of learning is nothing else but to seek for the lost mind.   *Works, VI, 1:11.4*

15   All men have in themselves that which is truly honorable. Only they do not think of it.
Works, VI, 1:17.1

16   If a scholar have not faith [in his principles], how shall he take a firm hold of things?
Works, VI, 2:12

17   When Heaven is about to confer a great office on any man, it first exercises his mind with suffering, and his sinews and bones with toil.
Works, VI, 2:15.2

18   Kindly words do not enter so deeply into men as a reputation for kindness.   *Works, VII, 1:14.1*

19   Is it only the mouth and belly which are injured by hunger and thirst? Men's minds are also injured by them.   *Works, VII, 1:27.1*

20   The people are the most important element in a nation; the spirits of the land and grain are next; the sovereign is the lightest.   *Works, VII, 2:14.1*

Chuang-tzu[1]
369–286 B.C.

21   Great wisdom is generous; petty wisdom is contentious. Great speech is impassioned, small speech cantankerous.   *On Leveling All Things*

22   Take, for instance, a twig and a pillar, or the ugly person and the great beauty, and all the strange and monstrous transformations. These are all leveled together by Tao. Division is the same as creation; creation is the same as destruction.
On Leveling All Things

23   I do not know whether I was then a man dreaming I was a butterfly, or whether I am now a butterfly dreaming I am a man.   *On Leveling All Things*

24   All men know the utility of useful things; but they do not know the utility of futility.
This Human World

25   He who pursues fame at the risk of losing his self is not a scholar.   *The Great Supreme*

26   Those who seek to satisfy the mind of man by hampering it with ceremonies and music and affecting charity and devotion have lost their original nature.   *Joined Toes*

27   In the days of perfect nature, man lived together with birds and beasts, and there was no distinction of their kind . . . they were in a state of natural integrity. . . . When Sages appeared, crawling for charity and limping with duty, doubt and confusion entered men's minds. . . . Destruction of Tao and virtue in order to introduce charity and duty—this is the error of the Sages.   *Horses' Hoofs*

28   Banish wisdom, discard knowledge, and gangsters will stop!
Opening Trunks; or, A Protest Against Civilization

29   For all men strive to grasp what they do not know, while none strive to grasp what they already know; and all strive to discredit what they do not

[1]From *The Wisdom of China and India* [1942], edited by LIN YUTANG.

excel in, while none strive to discredit what they do excel in. This is why there is chaos.
Opening Trunks; or, A Protest Against Civilization

1   Cherish that which is within you, and shut off that which is without; for much knowledge is a curse.   *On Tolerance*

2   "The prince keeps [a] tortoise carefully enclosed in a chest in his ancestral temple. Now would this tortoise rather be dead and have its remains venerated, or would it rather be alive and wagging its tail in the mud?"

"It would rather be alive . . . and wagging its tail in the mud."

"Begone!" cried Chuang-tzu. "I too will wag my tail in the mud."   *Autumn Floods*

Sun-tzu[1]
c. Fourth century B.C.

3   A military operation involves deception. Even though you are competent, appear to be incompetent. Though effective, appear to be ineffective.
The Art of War. Strategic Assessments

4   Victorious warriors win first and then go to war, while defeated warriors go to war first and then seek to win.   *Art of War. Strategic Assessments*

5   The best victory is when the opponent surrenders of its own accord before there are any actual hostilities. . . . It is best to win without fighting.
Art of War. Planning a Siege

6   Be extremely subtle, even to the point of formlessness. Be extremely mysterious, even to the point of soundlessness. Thereby you can be the director of the opponent's fate.
Art of War. Emptiness and Fullness

Pytheas
fl. 330 B.C.

7   They smell of the lamp.[2]
From PLUTARCH, Lives, Demosthenes

Alexander the Great
356–323 B.C.

8   [At Achilles' tomb:] O fortunate youth, to have found Homer as the herald of your glory!
From CICERO, Pro Archia, 24

9   If I were not Alexander, I would be Diogenes.
From PLUTARCH, Lives, Alexander, 14

Apelles
fl. 325 B.C.

10   Not a day without a line.[3]
Proverbial from PLINY THE ELDER, Natural History, XXXV, 36

11   A cobbler should not judge above his last.[4]
Proverbial from PLINY THE ELDER, Natural History, XXXV, 85

Menander[5]
c. 342–292 B.C.

12   We live, not as we wish to, but as we can.
Lady of Andros, fragment 50

13   Riches cover a multitude of woes.
The Boeotian Girl, fragment 90

14   Whom the gods love dies young.[6]
The Double Deceiver, fragment 125

15   At times discretion should be thrown aside, and with the foolish we should play the fool.
Those Offered for Sale, fragment 421

16   The man who has never been flogged has never been taught.[7]
The Girl Who Gets Flogged, fragment 422

17   The truth sometimes not sought for comes forth to the light.
The Girl Who Gets Flogged, fragment 433

18   This is living, not to live unto oneself alone.
The Brothers in Love, fragment 508

19   Deus ex machina [A god from the machine].
The Woman Possessed with a Divinity, fragment 227

---

[3]Nulla dies sine linea.

[4]Ne supra crepidam sutor iudicaret.
The more common rendering is: Cobbler, stick to your last.

[5]Translated by F. C. ALLINSON (Loeb Classical Library).

[6]Also in PLAUTUS, Bacchides, act IV, sc. vii, l. 816.
Those that God loves do not live long. —GEORGE HERBERT, Jacula Prudentum [2nd edition, 1651]
Heaven gives its favorites—early death. —LORD BYRON, Childe Harold, canto IV [1818], st. 102

[7]They spare the rod and spoil the child. —RALPH VENNING [c. 1621–1674], Mysteries and Revelations [1649]
Also in LUCIAN, Hermotimus, sec. 86.

---

[1]Translated by THOMAS CLEARY.

[2]Pytheas refers to the orations of Demosthenes, who worked in an underground cave lighted only by a lamp.

1   I call a fig a fig, a spade a spade.[1]
Unidentified fragment 545

2   Even God lends a hand to honest boldness.
Unidentified fragment 572

3   It is not white hair that engenders wisdom.
Unidentified fragment 639

4   Marriage, if one will face the truth, is an evil, but a necessary evil.[2]
Unidentified fragment 651

5   Health and intellect are the two blessings of life.
Monostikoi (Single Lines)

6   The man who runs may fight again.[3]
Monostikoi (Single Lines)

7   Conscience is a God to all mortals.
Monostikoi (Single Lines)

Epicurus
341–270 B.C.

8   Death is nothing to us, since when we are, death has not come, and when death has come, we are not.
From DIOGENES LAERTIUS, Lives of Eminent Philosophers, bk. X, sec. 125

9   Pleasure is the beginning and the end of living happily.
From DIOGENES LAERTIUS, Lives of Eminent Philosophers, X, 128

10   It is impossible to live pleasurably without living wisely, well, and justly, and impossible to live wisely, well, and justly without living pleasurably.
From DIOGENES LAERTIUS, Lives of Eminent Philosophers, X, 140

---

[1]Also attributed to Aristophanes by LUCIAN, *De Conscribend. Hist.*, 41.

The Macedonians are a rude and clownish people that call a spade a spade. — PLUTARCH, *Apothegms, Philip of Macedon*

I think it good plain English, without fraud, To call a spade a spade, a bawd a bawd. — JOHN TAYLOR [1580–1653], *A Kicksey Winsey*

[2]Marriage is an evil that most men welcome. — *Monostikoi (Single Lines)*

Motto of *The Spectator* [December 29, 1711].

[3]He who flees will fight again. — TERTULLIAN, *De Fuga in Persecutione, 10*

That same man that runneth away / May again fight another day. — ERASMUS, *Apothegms* [1542], *translated by* NICHOLAS UDALL [1505–1556]

Celuy qui fuit de bonne heure / Peut combattre derechef / [Who flies in good time / Can fight anew]. — ANONYMOUS [1594]; *translated from* VARRO, *Saturae Menippeae*

For he who fights and runs away / May live to fight another day; / But he who is in battle slain / Can never rise and fight again. — OLIVER GOLDSMITH, *The Art of Poetry on a New Plan* [1761]

A version similar to Goldsmith's appears in JAMES RAY, *History of the Rebellion* [1752].

Theophrastus
d. 278 B.C.

11   Time is the most valuable thing a man can spend.[4]
From DIOGENES LAERTIUS, Lives of Eminent Philosophers, bk. V, sec. 40

Zeno
335–263 B.C.

12   [When asked, "What is a friend?"] Another I.[5]
From DIOGENES LAERTIUS, Lives of Eminent Philosophers, bk. VII, sec. 23

13   The goal of life is living in agreement with nature.
From DIOGENES LAERTIUS, Lives of Eminent Philosophers, VII, 87

Cleanthes
c. 330–232 B.C.

14   For we are your offspring.
Hymn to Zeus, l. 4

15   Lead me, Zeus, and you, Fate, wherever you have assigned me. I shall follow without hesitation; but even if I am disobedient and do not wish to, I shall follow no less surely.
From EPICTETUS, Enchiridion, sec. 53

Euclid
fl. 300 B.C.

16   Q.E.D. [Quod erat demonstrandum: Which was to be proved.]   *Elements, bk. I, proposition 5[6]*

17   [To Ptolemy I:] There is no royal road to geometry.[7]
From PROCLUS, Commentary on Euclid, Prologue

Bion
c. 325–c. 255 B.C.

18   Old age is the harbor of all ills.
From DIOGENES LAERTIUS, Lives of Eminent Philosophers, bk. IV, sec. 47

---

[4]Nothing is so dear and precious as time. — FRANÇOIS RABELAIS, *Works*, bk. V [1564], ch. 5

[5]Alter ego.

[6]Proposition 5, too difficult for many students to pass beyond, became known as the asses' bridge [pons asinorum].

[7]Often quoted as: There is no royal road to learning.

1   Wealth is the sinews of affairs.
From DIOGENES LAERTIUS, *Lives of Eminent Philosophers, IV, 48*

2   The road to Hades is easy to travel.[1]
From DIOGENES LAERTIUS, *Lives of Eminent Philosophers, IV, 49*

3   He has not acquired a fortune; the fortune has acquired him.
From DIOGENES LAERTIUS, *Lives of Eminent Philosophers, IV, 50*

4   Though boys throw stones at frogs in sport, the frogs do not die in sport, but in earnest.
From PLUTARCH, *On Water and Land Animals, 7*

Pyrrhus
c. 318–272 B.C.

5   Another such victory over the Romans, and we are undone.[2]
From PLUTARCH, *Lives, Pyrrhus, sec. 21*

Aratus
c. 315–240 B.C.

6   From Zeus let us begin, whom we mortals never leave unnamed: full of Zeus are all streets and all gathering places of men, and full are the sea and harbors. Everywhere we all have need of Zeus. For we are also his offspring.
Phaenomena, sec. 1

Theocritus[3]
c. 310–250 B.C.

7   Sweet is the whispering music of yonder pine that sings.   *Idylls, I*

8   Our concern be peace of mind: some old crone let us seek,
To spit on us for luck and keep unlovely things afar.
Idylls, VII

9   Cicala to cicala is dear, and ant to ant,
And kestrels dear to kestrels, but to me the Muse and song.   *Idylls, IX*

10 The frog's life is most jolly, my lads; he has no care
Who shall fill up his cup; for he has drink enough to spare.   *Idylls, X*

11   Verily great grace may go
With a little gift; and precious are all things that come from friends.   *Idylls, XXVIII*

Callimachus
c. 300–240 B.C.

12   Big book, big bore.[4]
From The Greek Anthology [1973], PETER JAY, *ed., introduction to Callimachus*

13 You're walking by the tomb of Battiades,[5]
Who knew well how to write poetry, and enjoy
Laughter at the right moment, over the wine.
From The Greek Anthology, PETER JAY, *ed., no. 150, On Himself[6]*

14 Someone spoke of your death, Heraclitus.[7] It brought me
Tears, and I remembered how often together
We ran the sun down with talk . . . somewhere
You've long been dust, my Halicarnassian friend.
But your *Nightingales* live on. Though the Death-world
Claws at everything, it will not touch them.[6]
From The Greek Anthology, PETER JAY, *ed., no. 152*

Leonidas of Tarentum
c. 290–c. 220 B.C.

15 Far from Italy, far from my native Tarentum
I lie; and this is the worst of it—worse than death.
An exile's life is no life. But the Muses loved me.
For my suffering they gave me a honeyed gift:
My name survives me. Thanks to the sweet Muses
Leonidas will echo throughout all time.[8]
From The Greek Anthology [1973], PETER JAY, *ed., no. 189*

16 The season of ships is here,
The west wind and the swallows;
Flowers in the fields appear,
And the ocean of hills and hollows
Has calmed its waves and is clear.

---

[1]A passage broad, / Smooth, easy, inoffensive, down to Hell.—
JOHN MILTON, *Paradise Lost* [1667], *bk. II, l. 432*

[2]Pyrrhus, king of Epirus, refers to the dearly bought victory at Asculum, 280 B.C. Hence the phrase: Pyrrhic victory. See also Herodotus, 71:12 ("Cadmean victory").

[3]Translated by R. C. TREVELYAN.

[4]In reference to the traditional epics.

[5]Callimachus.

[6]Translated by PETER JAY.

[7]Elegiac poet from Halicarnassus, author of a collection of poems, *Nightingales,* and a friend of Callimachus.

[8]Translated by FLEUR ADCOCK.

Free that anchor and chain!
Set your full canvas flying,
O men in the harbor lane:
It is I, Priapus, crying.
Sail out on your trades again![1]

From The Greek Anthology, PETER JAY, *ed.,
no. 197*

Archimedes
c. 287–212 B.C.

1   Eureka! [I have found it!][2]

From VITRUVIUS POLLIO *[first century B.C.],
De Architectura, bk. IX, 215*

2   Give me where to stand, and I will move the earth.[3]

From PAPPUS OF ALEXANDRIA, *Collectio, bk.
VIII, prop. 10, sec. 11*

Quintus Fabius Maximus
c. 275–203 B.C.

3   To be turned from one's course by men's opinions, by blame, and by misrepresentation shows a man unfit to hold an office.

From PLUTARCH, *Lives, Fabius Maximus, sec. 5*

Lacydes
fl. c. 241 B.C.

4   [When asked late in life why he was studying geometry:] If I should not be learning now, when should I be?

From DIOGENES LAERTIUS, *Lives of Eminent
Philosophers, Lacydes, sec. 5*

Titus Maccius Plautus
254–184 B.C.

5   What is yours is mine, and all mine is yours.

Trinummus, act II, sc. ii, l. 48

6   Not by age but by capacity is wisdom acquired.

Trinummus, II, ii, l. 88

7   You are seeking a knot in a bulrush.[4]

Menaechmi, act II, sc. i, l. 22

8   In the one hand he is carrying a stone, while he shows the bread in the other.

Aulularia, act II, sc. ii, l. 18

9   There are occasions when it is undoubtedly better to incur loss than to make gain.

Captivi, act II, sc. ii, l. 77

10   Patience is the best remedy for every trouble.

Rudens, act II, sc. v, l. 71

11   Consider the little mouse, how sagacious an animal it is which never entrusts its life to one hole only.[5]

Truculentus, act IV, sc. iv, l. 15

12   No guest is so welcome in a friend's house that he will not become a nuisance after three days.[6]

Miles Gloriosus, act III, sc. i, l. 144

13   No man is wise enough by himself.

Miles Gloriosus, III, iii, l. 885

14   Nothing is there more friendly to a man than a friend in need.[7]

Epidicus, act III, sc. iii, l. 44

15   Things which you do not hope happen more frequently than things which you do hope.[8]

Mostellaria, act I, sc. iii, l. 40

16   To blow and swallow at the same moment is not easy.

Mostellaria, III, ii, l. 104

17   Practice yourself what you preach.[9]

Asinaria, act III, sc. iii, l. 644

Maharbal [Barca the Carthaginian]
fl. 210 B.C.

18   You know how to win a victory, Hannibal, but not how to use it.[10]

From LIVY, *History, XXII, 51*

---

[1]Translated by CLIVE SANSOM.

[2]On discovery of a method to test the purity of gold.

[3]Said with reference to the lever.

[4]A proverbial expression implying a desire to create doubts and difficulties where there really are none. It occurs in TERENCE, *Andria, l. 941;* also in ENNIUS, *Saturae, 46.*

[5]I holde a mouses herte nat worth a leek / That hath but oon hole for to sterte to, / And if that faille, thanne is al ydo. — CHAUCER, *The Canterbury Tales* [c. 1387], *The Wife of Bath's Prologue, l. 572*

The mouse that hath but one hole is quickly taken. — GEORGE HERBERT, *Jacula Prudentum* [1651]

The mouse that always trusts to one poor hole / Can never be a mouse of any soul. — ALEXANDER POPE, *Paraphrase of the Prologue* [1714], *l. 298*

[6]Fish and guests in three days are stale. — JOHN LYLY, *Euphues* [1579]

Fish and visitors stink in three days. — BENJAMIN FRANKLIN, *Poor Richard's Almanac* [1736], *January*

[7]A friend in need is a friend indeed. — WILLIAM HAZLITT, *English Proverbs*

[8]The unexpected always happens. — *Common saying*

[9]Facias ipse quod faciamus suades.

[10]Vincere scis, Hannibal, victoria uti nescis.

Maharbal was commander of cavalry under Hannibal, who had insisted on a day's rest for the army after the victory at Cannae [216 B.C.], thereby enabling the enemy to recoup.

Bhagavad Gita[1]

250 B.C.–A.D. 250[2]

1 For certain is death for the born
And certain is birth for the dead;
Therefore over the inevitable
Thou shouldst not grieve.[3]

Chapter 2, verse 27

2 This embodied [soul] is eternally unslayable
In the body of everyone, son of Bharata;
Therefore all beings
Thou shouldst not mourn.

Likewise having regard for thine own
[caste] duty
Thou shouldst not tremble;
For another, better thing than a fight required of
duty
Exists not for a warrior.   *2:30*

3 On action alone be thy interest,
Never on its fruits.
Let not the fruits of action be thy motive,
Nor be thy attachment to inaction.[4]
                                        2:47

4 Better one's own duty, [though] imperfect,
Than another's duty well performed.[5]
                           3:35 and 18:47

5 In whatsoever way any come to Me,
In that same way I grant them favor.[5]
                                        4:11

6 Who sees Me in all,
And sees all in Me,
For him I am not lost,
And he is not lost for Me.[5]

                                        6:30

7 Whatsoever state [of being] meditating upon
He leaves the body at death,
To just that he goes, son of Kunti,
Always being made to be in the condition
of that.[5]   *8:6*

8 If the radiance of a thousand suns were to burst forth at once in the sky, that would be like the splendor of the Mighty One [Krishna].[6]   *11:12*

9 I am mighty, world-destroying Time.   *11:32*

Quintus Ennius

239–169 B.C.

10 No sooner said than done—so acts your man of worth.   *Annals, bk. 9 (quoted by* PRISCIANUS*)*

11 I never indulge in poetics
Unless I am down with rheumatics.
Fragment of a satire (quoted by PRISCIANUS*)*

12 By delaying he preserved the state.[7]
From CICERO, *De Senectute, ch. IV, sec. 10*

13 Let no one pay me honor with tears, nor celebrate my funeral rites with weeping.
From CICERO, *De Senectute, XX, 73*

14 The ape, vilest of beasts, how like to us.[8]
From CICERO, *De Natura Deorum, bk. I, ch. 35*

15 No one regards what is before his feet; we all gaze at the stars.
Iphigenia. From CICERO, *De Divinatione, bk. II, ch. 13*

16 The idle mind knows not what it is it wants.
Iphigenia. From CICERO, *De Divinatione, II, 13*

17 Whom they fear they hate.
Thyestes. From CICERO, *De Officiis, bk. II, ch. 7*

Marcus Porcius Cato
[Cato the Elder][9]

234–149 B.C.

18 A farm is like a man—however great the income, if there is extravagance but little is left.
On Agriculture,[10] bk. I, sec. 6

19 Even though work stops, expenses run on.
On Agriculture, XXXIX, 2

---

[1]Sanskrit: The Lord's Song.

[2]Ancient Indian literary chronology is conjectural. The dates given are approximate.

[3]Translated by ANNIE BESANT.

[4]Translated by F. EDGERTON.
At the moment which is not of action or inaction / You can receive this: "on whatever sphere of being / The mind of a man may be intent / At the time of death"—that is the one action / (And the time of death is every moment) / Which shall fructify in the lives of others: / And do not think of the fruit of action, / Fare forward.—T. S. ELIOT, *Four Quartets* [1943], *The Dry Salvages, pt. III*

[5]Translated by F. EDGERTON.

---

[6]Translated by SWAMI NIKHILANANDA. See Oppenheimer, 769:n1.

[7]This refers to Quintus Fabius Maximus, "Cunctator." Hence the "Fabian policy" of waiting.

[8]Simia quam similis, turpissima bestia, nobis!

[9]Also known as Cato the Censor.

[10]Translated by WILLIAM D. HOOPER, revised by HARRISON BOYD ASH (Loeb Classical Library).

1   It is a hard matter, my fellow citizens, to argue with the belly, since it has no ears.[1]
From PLUTARCH, *Lives, Cato, sec. 8*

2   Wise men profit more from fools than fools from wise men; for the wise men shun the mistakes of fools, but fools do not imitate the successes of the wise.   *From* PLUTARCH, *Lives, Cato, 9*

3   I would much rather have men ask why I have no statue, than why I have one.
From PLUTARCH, *Lives, Cato, 19*

4   Carthage must be destroyed.[2]
From PLUTARCH, *Lives, Cato, 27*

5   Grasp the subject, the words will follow.[3]
From CAIUS JULIUS VICTOR, *Ars Rhetorica, I [4th century* A.D.*]*

6   An orator is a good man who is skilled in speaking.
From SENECA THE ELDER *[c. 45* B.C.*–*A.D. *40],
Controversiae, I, Preface, and elsewhere*

Caecilius Statius
220–168 B.C.

7   He plants trees to benefit another generation.[4]
Synephebi. Quoted by CICERO *in De Senectute, VII*

Polybius
c. 200–c. 118 B.C.

8   Those who know how to win are much more numerous than those who know how to make proper use of their victories.
History, bk. X, 36

9   There is no witness so dreadful, no accuser so terrible as the conscience that dwells in the heart of every man.   *History, XVIII, 43*

Terence[5] [Publius Terentius Afer]
c. 190–159 B.C.

10   Moderation in all things.
Andria (The Lady of Andros), l. 61

11   Hence these tears.[6]   *Andria, l. 126*

12   Lovers' quarrels are the renewal of love.[7]
Andria, l. 555

13   Charity begins at home.[8]   *Andria, l. 635*

14   I am a man: nothing human is alien to me.[9]
Heauton Timoroumenos (The Self-Tormentor), l. 77

15   Draw from others the lesson that may profit yourself.[10]   *Heauton Timoroumenos, l. 221*

16   Time removes distress.
Heauton Timoroumenos, l. 421

17   Nothing is so difficult but that it may be found out by seeking.[11]   *Heauton Timoroumenos, l. 675*

18   Some people ask, "What if the sky were to fall?"[12]
Heauton Timoroumenos, l. 719

19   Extreme law is often extreme injustice.[13]
Heauton Timoroumenos, l. 796

---

[1]The belly has no ears nor is it to be filled with fair words. — FRANÇOIS RABELAIS, *Works, IV* [1548], *67*

[2]Delenda est Carthago.
These words were added to every speech Cato made in the senate, preceded by *ceterum censeo* [in my opinion].

[3]Rem tene; verba sequentur.

[4]Serit arbores quae alteri seculo prosint.
He that plants trees loves others beside himself. — THOMAS FULLER [1654–1734], *Gnomologia* [1732]
A man does not plant a tree for himself; he plants it for posterity. — ALEXANDER SMITH, *Dreamthorp* [1863], *ch. 11*

[5]Translated by JOHN SARGEAUNT (Loeb Classical Library), with occasional adaptations.

[6]Hinc illae lacrimae.
The phrase is proverbial for "That's the cause of it," and was often quoted, by Horace in *Epistles, I, xix, 41,* and by others.
Hence rage and tears [Inde irae et lacrimae]. — JUVENAL, *Satires, bk. I, l. 168*

[7]Amantium irae amoris integratio est.
The anger of lovers renews the strength of love. — PUBLILIUS SYRUS, *Maxim 24*
The falling out of faithful friends renewing is of love. — RICHARD EDWARDS [c. 1523–1566], *The Paradise of Dainty Devices* [1576]
Let the falling out of friends be a renewing of affection. — JOHN LYLY, *Euphues* [1579]
The falling out of lovers is the renewing of love. — ROBERT BURTON, *Anatomy of Melancholy* [1621–1651], *pt. III, sec. 2*

[8]Proxumus sum egomet mihi.

[9]Homo sum: humani nil a me alienum puto. Quoted by CICERO in *De Officiis, I, 30.*

[10]Periclum ex aliis facito tibi quod ex usu siet. (A saying.)

[11]Nil tam difficile est quin quaerendo investigari possiet.

[12]Quid si nunc caelum ruat?
Some ambassadors from the Celtae, being asked by Alexander what in the world they dreaded most, answered, that they feared lest the sky should fall upon them. — FLAVIUS ARRIANUS [c. 100–170], *bk. I, 4*

[13]Ius summum saepe summa est malitia.
Extreme law, extreme injustice, is now become a stale proverb in discourse. — CICERO, *De Officiis, I, 33*
Extreme justice is often injustice. — JEAN RACINE, *La Thébaide* [1664], *act IV, sc. iii*
Mais l'extrême justice est une extrême injure. — VOLTAIRE, *Oedipe* [1718], *act III, sc. iii*

1   There is nothing so easy but that it becomes difficult when you do it reluctantly.
Heauton Timoroumenos, l. 805

2   While there's life, there's hope.
Heauton Timoroumenos, l. 981

3   In fact, nothing is said that has not been said before.
Eunuchus (The Eunuch), l. 41 (Prologue)

4   I have everything, yet have nothing; and although I possess nothing, still of nothing am I in want.
Eunuchus, l. 243

5   There are vicissitudes in all things.
Eunuchus, l. 276

6   I don't care one straw.[1]   *Eunuchus, l. 411*

7   Take care and say this with presence of mind.[2]
Eunuchus, l. 769

8   He is wise who tries everything before arms.
Eunuchus, l. 789

9   I know the disposition of women: when you will, they won't; when you won't, they set their hearts upon you of their own inclination.
Eunuchus, l. 812

10   I took to my heels as fast as I could.
Eunuchus, l. 844

11   Fortune helps the brave.[3]   *Phormio, l. 203*

12   So many men, so many opinions; every one his own way.[4]   *Phormio, l. 454*

13   I bid him look into the lives of men as though into a mirror, and from others to take an example for himself.   *Adelphoe (The Brothers), l. 415*

Huai-nan Tzu[5] [Liu An][6]
Second century B.C.

14   Before heaven and earth had taken form all was vague and amorphous. Therefore it was called the Great Beginning. The Great Beginning produced emptiness and emptiness produced the universe. . . . The combined essences of heaven and earth became the yin and yang, the concentrated essences of the yin and yang became the four seasons, and the scattered essences of the four seasons became the myriad creatures of the world.
Huai-nan Tzu, 3:1a

Tung Chung-shu[5]
c. 179–c. 104 B.C.

15   He who is the ruler of men takes non-action as his way and considers impartiality as his treasure. He sits upon the throne of non-action and rides upon the perfection of his officials.
Ch'un-ch'iu fan-lu

Lucius Accius
170–86 B.C.

16   Let them hate, so long as they fear.[7]
Fragment

Han Wu-ti[8]
157–87 B.C.

17   The sound of her silk skirt has stopped.
On the marble pavement dust grows.
Her empty room is cold and still.
Fallen leaves are piled against the doors.
   Longing for that lovely lady
How can I bring my aching heart to rest?
On the death of his mistress[9]

---

[1]Ego non flocci pendere.
Nor do they care a straw. —CERVANTES, *Don Quixote, pt. I* [1605], *bk. III, ch. 9*

[2]Fac animo haec praesenti dicas. Literally, "with a present mind"—equivalent to Caesar's "praesentia animi" (*De Bello Gallico, V, 43, 4*).

[3]Pliny the Younger says (*bk. VI, letter 16*) that Pliny the Elder said this during the eruption of Vesuvius: "Fortune favors the brave."

[4]Quot homines tot sententiae: suo quoque mos.
So many heads so many wits. —JOHN HEYWOOD, *Proverbs* [1546], *pt. I, ch. 2*
So many men so many minds. —GEORGE GASCOIGNE [c. 1525–1577], *The Glass of Government* [1575]

[5]From *Sources of Chinese Tradition* [1960], edited by WILLIAM THEODORE DE BARY.

[6]*Huai-nan Tzu* is from the scholarly court of Liu An (d. 122 B.C.), prince of Huai-nan, known also as Huai-nan Tzu.

[7]Oderint dum metuant.
From a lost tragedy. Frequently cited by Cicero and others. Suetonius (*Gaius Caligula, 30*) says that the Emperor Caligula was fond of quoting it.

[8]Sixth emperor of the Han dynasty.

[9]From *Chinese Poems*, ARTHUR WALEY, translator.

Marcus Terentius Varro

116–27 B.C.

1   The longest part of the journey is said to be the passing of the gate.

On Agriculture [De Re Rustica],[1] *bk. I, ii, 2*

2   When people come to inspect . . . farmsteads, it is not to see collections of pictures . . . but collections of fruit.

On Agriculture, I, ii, 10

3   Not all who own a harp are harpers.

On Agriculture, II, i, 3

4   It was divine nature which gave us the country, and man's skill that built the cities.[2]

On Agriculture, III, i, 4

Marcus Licinius Crassus

fl. 70 B.C.

5   Those who aim at great deeds must also suffer greatly.   *From* PLUTARCH, *Lives, Crassus, ch. 26*

Meleager

First century B.C.

6   Farewell, Morning Star, herald of dawn, and quickly come as the Evening Star, bringing again in secret her whom thou takest away.

The Greek Anthology [1906], J. W. MACKAIL, *ed., sec. 1, no. 21*

Marcus Tullius Cicero

106–43 B.C.

7   How long, Catiline, will you abuse our patience?[3]

In Catilinam, I, 1

8   O tempora! O mores! [Oh the times! The customs!]   *In Catilinam, I, 1*

9   He has departed, withdrawn, gone away, broken out.[4]   *In Catilinam, II, 1*

10   I am a Roman citizen.[5]   *In Verrem, V, 57*

11   Law stands mute in the midst of arms.[6]

Pro Milone, IV, 11

12   Cui bono? [To whose advantage?][7]

Pro Milone, XII, 32

13   These studies are a spur to the young, a delight to the old; an ornament in prosperity, a consoling refuge in adversity; they are pleasure for us at home, and no burden abroad; they stay up with us at night, they accompany us when we travel, they are with us in our country visits.

Pro Archia Poeta, VII, 16

14   Leisure with dignity.[8]

Pro Publio Sestio, XLV, 98

15   History is the witness that testifies to the passing of time; it illumines reality, vitalizes memory, provides guidance in daily life, and brings us tidings of antiquity.   *De Oratore, bk. II, ch. IX, sec. 36*

16   The first law for the historian is that he shall never dare utter an untruth. The second is that he shall suppress nothing that is true. Moreover, there shall be no suspicion of partiality in his writing, or of malice.   *De Oratore, II, XV, 62*

17   The freedom of poetic license.[9]

De Oratore, III, XXXVIII, 153

18   If a man aspires to the highest place, it is no dishonor to him to halt at the second, or even at the third.   *Orator, 4*

19   For just as some women are said to be handsome though without adornment, so this subtle manner of speech, though lacking in artificial graces, delights us.   *Orator, 78*

20   Nothing quite new is perfect.   *Brutus, 71*

21   There were poets before Homer.   *Brutus, 71*

22   The aim of forensic oratory is to teach, to delight, to move.

De Optimo Genere Oratorum, 16

23   The dregs of Romulus.[10]

Ad Atticum, II, 1

24   While there's life, there's hope.[11]

Ad Atticum, IX, 10

25   What is more agreeable than one's home?[12]

Ad Familiares, IV, 8

---

[1]Translated by WILLIAM D. HOOPER, revised by HARRISON BOYD ASH (Loeb Classical Library).

[2]Divina natura dedit agros, ars humana aedificavit urbes.

[3]Quo usque, Catilina, abutere patientia nostra?

[4]Abiit, excessit, evasit, erupit.

Depart — be off — excede — evade — erump! — OLIVER WENDELL HOLMES, *The Autocrat of the Breakfast-Table* [1858], *Aestivation, ch. II*

[5]Civis Romanus sum.

[6]Silent enim leges inter arma.

[7]In full: Cui bono fuerit? [To whose advantage was it?]

[8]Cum dignitate otium.

[9]Poetarum licentiae liberiora.

[10]In Romuli faece. That is, the lowest order of society.

[11]Dum anima est, spes est.

[12]Quae est domestica sede iucundior?

1   I like myself, but I won't say I'm as handsome as the bull that kidnapped Europa.

De Natura Deorum, I, 78

2   It was ordained at the beginning of the world that certain signs should prefigure certain events.

De Divinatione, I, 118

3   There is nothing so ridiculous but some philosopher has said it.   *De Divinatione, II, 119*

4   I would rather be wrong with Plato than right with such men as these [the Pythagoreans].

Tusculanae Disputationes, I, 17

5   O philosophy, you leader of life.[1]

Tusculanae Disputationes, V, 2

6   Socrates was the first to call philosophy down from the heavens and to place it in cities, and even to introduce it into homes and compel it to inquire about life and standards and goods and evils.

Tusculanae Disputationes, V, 4

7   The highest good.[2]   *De Officiis, I, 2*

8   Let arms yield to the toga, the laurel crown to praise.[3]   *De Officiis, I, 22*

9   Never less idle than when wholly idle, nor less alone than when wholly alone.

De Officiis, III, 1

10 Rome, fortunately natal 'neath my consulship![4]

De Consultatu Suo

11 The people's good is the highest law.[5]

De Legibus, III, 3

12 He used to raise a storm in a teapot.[6]

De Legibus, III, 16

13 Let the punishment match the offense.[7]

De Legibus, III, 20

14 The shifts of Fortune test the reliability of friends.

De Amicitia, XVII

15 A friend is, as it were, a second self.

De Amicitia, XXI

16 Give me a young man in whom there is something of the old, and an old man with something of the young: guided so, a man may grow old in body, but never in mind.   *De Senectute, XI*

17 Old men are garrulous by nature.

De Senectute, XVI

18 Old age: the crown of life, our play's last act.

De Senectute, XXIII

19 Endless money forms the sinews of war.[8]

Philippics, V, 2:5

Pompey [Gnaeus Pompeius]
106–48 B.C.

20 More worship the rising than the setting sun.[9]

From PLUTARCH, *Lives, Pompey, 14*

21 A dead man cannot bite.

From PLUTARCH, *Lives, Pompey, 77*

[Gaius] Julius Caesar
100–44 B.C.

22 All Gaul is divided into three parts.[10]

De Bello Gallico, I, 1

23 Men willingly believe what they wish.[11]

De Bello Gallico, III, 18

24 I love treason but hate a traitor.[12]

From PLUTARCH, *Lives, Romulus, sec. 17*

25 I wished my wife to be not so much as suspected.[13]

From PLUTARCH, *Lives, Caesar, sec. 10*

26 I had rather be the first man among these fellows than the second man in Rome.

From PLUTARCH, *Lives, Caesar, 11*

---

[1]O vitae philosophia dux.

[2]Summum bonum.
The nature of the good and the highest good. — HORACE, *Satires, II, 6, 76*

[3]Cedant arma togae, concedat laurea laudi.
He is quoting from his own poem *De suis temporibus, bk. III.*

[4]O fortunatam natam me consule Romam!
The verse is quoted disparagingly by Juvenal *(X, 122)*, Quintilian *(XI, 1, 24)*, and others.

[5]Salus populi suprema est lex.

[6]Excitabat enim fluctus in simpulo.
A tempest in a teapot. — *Proverb*

[7]Noxiae poena par esto.
See W. S. Gilbert, 565:14.

---

[8]He who first called money the sinews of affairs seems to have spoken with special reference to the affairs of war. — PLUTARCH, *Lives, Cleomenes 27*
Neither is money the sinews of war (as it is trivially said). — FRANCIS BACON, *Essays* [1625], *Of the True Greatness of Kingdoms*
Money is the sinew of love as well as of war. — THOMAS FULLER [1654–1734], *Gnomonologia* [1732], *no. 3442*

[9]Addressed to Sulla.

[10]Gallia est omnis divisa in partes tres.

[11]Fere libenter homines id quod volunt credunt.
See Demosthenes, 81:16, and Dryden, 283:3.

[12]Princes in this case do hate the traitor, though they love the treason. — SAMUEL DANIEL, *Tragedy of Cleopatra* [1594], *act IV, sc. i*
This principle is old, but true as fate, / Kings may love treason, but the traitor hate. — THOMAS DEKKER, *The Honest Whore* [1604], *pt. I, act IV, sc. iv*
Though I love the treason, I hate the traitor. — SAMUEL PEPYS, *Diary, March 7, 1667*

[13]Caesar's wife must be above suspicion. — *Traditional saying*

1   The die is cast.[1]

>   From PLUTARCH, *Lives, Caesar, 32*

2   Go on, my friend, and fear nothing; you carry Caesar and his fortune in your boat.

>   From PLUTARCH, *Lives, Caesar, 38*

3   The Ides of March have come.

>   From PLUTARCH, *Lives, Caesar, 63*

4   [In answer to a question as to what sort of death was the best:] A sudden death.

>   From PLUTARCH, *Lives, Caesar, 63*

5   I came, I saw, I conquered.[2]

>   From SUETONIUS, *Lives of the Caesars, Julius, sec. 37*

6   You also, Brutus my son.[3]

>   From SUETONIUS, *Lives of the Caesars, Julius, 82*

7   It is not these well-fed long-haired men that I fear, but the pale and the hungry-looking.[4]

>   From PLUTARCH, *Lives, Antony, sec. 11*

Lucretius[5] [Titus Lucretius Carus]
99–55 B.C.

8   Mother of Aeneas and his race, darling of men and gods, nurturing Venus.

>   *De Rerum Natura (On the Nature of Things), bk. I, l. 1 (Invocation)*

9   For thee the wonder-working earth puts forth sweet flowers.   *De Rerum Natura, I, l. 7*

10   The lively power of his mind prevailed, and forth he marched far beyond the flaming walls of the heavens,[6] as he traversed the immeasurable universe in thought and imagination.

>   *De Rerum Natura, I, l. 72*

11   Such evil deeds could religion prompt.[7]

>   *De Rerum Natura, I, l. 101*

12   Nothing can be created from nothing.[8]

>   *De Rerum Natura, I, l. 155*

13   The first beginnings of things cannot be distinguished by the eye.

>   *De Rerum Natura, I, l. 268*

14   The ring on the finger becomes thin beneath by wearing, the fall of dripping water hollows the stone.[9]   *De Rerum Natura, I, l. 312*

15   Nature works by means of bodies unseen.

>   *De Rerum Natura, I, l. 328*

16   Material objects are of two kinds, atoms and compounds of atoms. The atoms themselves cannot be swamped by any force, for they are preserved indefinitely by their absolute solidity.[10]

>   *De Rerum Natura, I, l. 518*

17   On a dark theme I trace verses full of light, touching all the muses' charm.[11]

>   *De Rerum Natura, I, l. 933*

18   Truths kindle light for truths.

>   *De Rerum Natura, I, l. 1117*

19   Pleasant it is, when over a great sea the winds trouble the waters, to gaze from shore upon another's great tribulation: not because any man's troubles are a delectable joy, but because to perceive what ills you are free from yourself is pleasant.[12]

>   *De Rerum Natura, II, l. 1*

20   O miserable minds of men! O blind hearts! In what darkness of life, in what great dangers ye spend this little span of years![13]

>   *De Rerum Natura, II, l. 14*

---

[1]Iacta alea est. Proverb quoted by Caesar as he crossed the Rubicon.
Also in SUETONIUS, *Lives of the Caesars, Julius.*

[2]Veni, vidi, vici. Inscription displayed in Caesar's Pontic triumph.
Also in PLUTARCH, *Apothegms, Caesar.*

[3]Et tu, Brute. Suetonius reports that Caesar said this in Greek.

[4]The reference is to Brutus and Cassius.

[5]Translated by W. H. D. ROUSE (Loeb Classical Library), with adaptations.

[6]Flammantia moenia mundi.

[7]Tantum religio potuit suadere malorum.
The reference is to Agamemnon's sacrifice of his daughter Iphigenia.
Translated by CYRIL BAILEY.

[8]Nil posse creari de nilo.

[9]Anulus in digito subter tenuatur habendo, / Stilicidi casus lapidem cavat.
See also the concluding lines of *Book IV:*
Nonne vides etiam guttas in saxa cadentis / Umoris longo in spatio pertundere saxa? [Do you not see that even drops of water falling upon a stone in the long run beat a way through the stone?]
Drops of water hollow out a stone, a ring is worn thin by use. — OVID, *Ex Ponto, IV, 10, l. 5*
Also in PLUTARCH, *Of the Training of Children.*
The drop of rain maketh a hole in the stone, not by violence, but by oft falling. — HUGH LATIMER, *Seventh Sermon Before Edward VI* [1549]
The soft droppes of rain perce the hard marble. — JOHN LYLY, *Euphues* [1579]
And drizling drops that often doe redound, / The firmest flint doth in continuance wear. — EDMUND SPENSER, *Amoretti* [1595], sonnet 18

[10]Translated by R. E. LATHAM.

[11]Translated by CYRIL BAILEY.

[12]It is a pleasure to stand upon the shore, and to see ships tost upon the sea: a pleasure to stand in the window of a castle, and to see a battle and the adventures thereof below: but no pleasure is comparable to the standing upon the vantage ground of truth . . . and to see the errors, and wanderings, and mists, and tempests, in the vale below. — FRANCIS BACON, *Essays* [1625], *Of Truth*

[13]Translated by CYRIL BAILEY.
Insensate care of mortals! Oh how false the argument which makes thee downward beat thy wings. — DANTE, *Divine Comedy* [c. 1310–1321], *Paradiso, canto XI, 1*

1 Life is one long struggle in the dark.
De Rerum Natura, II, l. 54

2 Thus the sum of things is ever being renewed, and mortals live dependent one upon another. Some nations increase, others diminish, and in a short space the generations of living creatures are changed and like runners pass on the torch of life.[1]
De Rerum Natura, II, l. 75

3 So far as it goes, a small thing may give analogy of great things, and show the tracks of knowledge.
De Rerum Natura, II, l. 123

4 All things must needs be borne on through the calm void, moving at equal rate with unequal weights.[2]   *De Rerum Natura, II, l. 238*

5 Never trust her at any time when the calm sea shows her false alluring smile.
De Rerum Natura, II, l. 558

6 What once sprung from the earth sinks back into the earth.[2]   *De Rerum Natura, II, l. 999*

7 That fear of Acheron be sent packing which troubles the life of man from its deepest depths, suffuses all with the blackness of death, and leaves no delight clean and pure.
De Rerum Natura, III, l. 37

8 So it is more useful to watch a man in times of peril, and in adversity to discern what kind of man he is; for then at last words of truth are drawn from the depths of his heart, and the mask is torn off, reality remains.   *De Rerum Natura, III, l. 55*

9 For as children tremble and fear everything in the blind darkness, so we in the light sometimes fear what is no more to be feared than the things children in the dark hold in terror and imagine will come true.   *De Rerum Natura, III, l. 87*

10 A tree cannot grow in the sky, nor clouds be in the deep sea, nor fish live in the fields, nor can blood be in sticks nor sap in rocks.
De Rerum Natura, III, l. 784

11 Therefore death is nothing to us, it matters not one jot, since the nature of the mind is understood to be mortal.[3]
De Rerum Natura, III, l. 830

12 When immortal Death has taken mortal life.[4]
De Rerum Natura, III, l. 869

13 Why dost thou not retire like a guest sated with the banquet of life, and with calm mind embrace, thou fool, a rest that knows no care?[2]
De Rerum Natura, III, l. 938

14 By protracting life, we do not deduct one jot from the duration of death.
De Rerum Natura, III, l. 1087

15 What is food to one, is to others bitter poison.[5]
De Rerum Natura, IV, l. 637

16 From the heart of this fountain of delights wells up some bitter taste to choke them even amid the flowers.[2]   *De Rerum Natura, IV, l. 1133*

17 But if one should guide his life by true principles, man's greatest riches is to live on a little with contented mind; for a little is never lacking.
De Rerum Natura, V, l. 1117

18 Men are eager to tread underfoot what they have once too much feared.
De Rerum Natura, V, l. 1140

19 Violence and injury enclose in their net all that do such things, and generally return upon him who began.   *De Rerum Natura, V, l. 1152*

20 [Epicurus] set forth what is the highest good, towards which we all strive, and pointed out the past, whereby along a narrow track we may strain on towards it in a straight course.[6]
De Rerum Natura, VI, l. 26

21 [The people] were given over in troops to disease[7] and death.
De Rerum Natura, VI, l. 1144

Gaius Valerius Catullus[8]

87–c. 54 B.C.

22 To whom am I to present my pretty new book, freshly smoothed off with dry pumice stone? To you, Cornelius: for you used to think that my trifles were worth something, long ago.
Carmina, poem I, l. 1

23 May it live and last for more than one century.
Carmina, I, l. 10

---

[1]Et quasi cursores vitae lampada tradunt.

[2]Translated by CYRIL BAILEY.

[3]Nil igitur mors est ad nos neque pertinet hilum, / Quandoquidem natura animi mortalis habetur.

[4]Mortalem vitam mors cum immortalis ademit.
Translated by CYRIL BAILEY.

[5]Ut quod ali cibus est aliis fuat acre venenum.
What's one man's poison, signor, / Is another's meat or drink. — BEAUMONT AND FLETCHER, *Love's Cure* [1647], act III, sc. ii
One man's meat is another's poison. — OSWALD DYKES [fl. c. 1709], *English Proverbs* [1709]

[6]Translated by CYRIL BAILEY.
The highest good [summum bonum]. See Cicero, 91:7.

[7]The devastating Athenian plague [430 B.C.] described by Thucydides.

[8]Translated by F. W. CORNFORD (Loeb Classical Library).

1   Mourn, ye Graces and Loves, and all you whom the Graces love. My lady's sparrow is dead, the sparrow, my lady's pet.[1]   *Carmina, III, l. 1*

2   Now he goes along the dark road, thither whence they say no one returns.   *Carmina, III, l. 11*

3   But these things are past and gone.[2]   *Carmina, IV, l. 25*

4   Let us live and love, my Lesbia, and value at a penny all the talk of crabbed old men. Suns may set and rise again: for us, when our brief light has set, there's the sleep of perpetual night. Give me a thousand kisses.[3]   *Carmina, V, l. 1*

5   Poor Catullus, you should cease your folly.   *Carmina, VIII, l. 1*

6   But you, Catullus, be resolved and firm.   *Carmina, VIII, l. 19*

7   And let her not look to find my love, as before; my love, which by her fault has dropped like a flower on the meadow's edge, when it has been touched by the plow passing by.   *Carmina, XI, l. 21*

8   Over head and heels.[4]   *Carmina, XX, l. 9*

9   Ah, what is more blessed than to put cares away!   *Carmina, XXXI, l. 7*

10   Whatever it is, wherever he is, whatever he is doing, he smiles: it is a malady he has, neither an elegant one as I think, nor in good taste.   *Carmina, XXXIX, l. 6*

11   There is nothing more silly than a silly laugh.   *Carmina, XXXIX, l. 16*

12   Oh this age! How tasteless and ill-bred it is!   *Carmina, XLIII, l. 8*

13   Now spring brings back balmy warmth.[5]   *Carmina, XLVI, l. 1*

14   Catullus, the worst of all poets, gives you [Marcus Tullius] his warmest thanks; he being as much the worst of all poets as you are the best of all patrons.   *Carmina, XLIX, l. 4*

15   He seems to me to be equal to a god, he, if it may be, seems to surpass the very gods, who sitting opposite you again gazes at you and hears you sweetly laughing.   *Carmina, LI, l. 1*

16   What an eloquent manikin![6]   *Carmina, LIII, l. 5*

17   I would see a little Torquatus, stretching his baby hands from his mother's lap, smile a sweet smile at his father with lips half parted.   *Carmina, LXI, l. 216*

18   The evening is come; rise up, ye youths. Vesper from Olympus now at last is just raising his long-looked-for light.   *Carmina, LXII, l. 1*

19   What is given by the gods more desirable than the fortunate hour?[7]   *Carmina, LXII, l. 30*

20   Not unknown am I to the goddess [Venus] who mingles with her cares a sweet bitterness.   *Carmina, LXVIII, l. 17*

21   It is not fit that men should be compared with gods.   *Carmina, LXVIII, l. 141*

22   What a woman says to her ardent lover should be written in wind and running water.   *Carmina, LXX, l. 3*

23   Leave off wishing to deserve any thanks from anyone, or thinking that anyone can ever become grateful.   *Carmina, LXXIII, l. 1*

24   If a man can take any pleasure in recalling the thought of kindnesses done.   *Carmina, LXXVI, l. 1*

25   It is difficult suddenly to lay aside a long-cherished love.   *Carmina, LXXVI, l. 13*

26   O ye gods, grant me this in return for my piety.   *Carmina, LXXVI, l. 26*

27   I hate and I love. Why I do so, perhaps you ask. I know not, but I feel it and I am in torment.[8]   *Carmina, LXXXV, l. 1*

28   Wandering through many countries and over many seas, I come, my brother, to these sorrowful obsequies, to present you with the last guerdon of death, and speak, though in vain, to your silent ashes.   *Carmina, CI, l. 1*

29   And forever, O my brother, hail and farewell![9]   *Carmina, CI, l. 10*

30   But you shall not escape my iambics.[10]   *Fragment*

---

[1]Passer, deliciae meae puellae.
This is also the opening line of *Carmina, II.*

[2]Sed haec prius fuere.

[3]Vivamus, mea Lesbia, atque amemus.../Soles occidere et redire possunt:/Nobis cum semel occidit brevis lux/Nox est perpetua una dormienda./Da mi basia mille.

[4]Per caputque pedesque.

[5]Iam ver egelidos refert tepores.

---

[6]Salaputium disertum!

[7]Quid datur a divis felici optatius hora?

[8]Odi et amo. Quare id faciam, fortasse requiris./Nescio, sed fieri sentio et excrucior.

[9]Atque in perpetuum, frater, ave atque vale.

[10]At non effugies meos iambos.

Sallust[1] [Gaius Sallustius Crispus]
86–34 B.C.

1   All our power lies in both mind and body; we employ the mind to rule, the body rather to serve; the one we have in common with the Gods, the other with the brutes.

The War with Catiline [c. 42 B.C.], sec. 1

2   The renown which riches or beauty confer is fleeting and frail; mental excellence is a splendid and lasting possession.   *The War with Catiline, 1*

3   Covetous of others' possessions, he [Catiline] was prodigal of his own.[2]   *The War with Catiline, 5*

4   Ambition drove many men to become false; to have one thought locked in the breast, another ready on the tongue.   *The War with Catiline, 10*

5   In truth, prosperity tries the souls even of the wise.[3]   *The War with Catiline, 11*

6   To like and dislike the same things, that is indeed true friendship.[4]   *The War with Catiline, 20*

7   Thus in the highest position there is the least freedom of action.[5]   *The War with Catiline, 51*

8   On behalf of their country, their children, their altars, and their hearths.[6]

The War with Catiline, 59

9   The soul is the captain and ruler of the life of mortals.[7] *The War with Jugurtha [c. 40 B.C.], sec. 1*

10   The splendid achievements of the intellect, like the soul, are everlasting.   *The War with Jugurtha, 2*

11   A city for sale and soon to perish if it finds a buyer![8]   *The War with Jugurtha, 35*

12   Punic faith.[9]   *The War with Jugurtha, 108*

13   Experience has shown that to be true which Appius[10] says in his verses, that every man is the architect of his own fortune.[11]

Speech to Caesar on the State, sec. 1

---

[1]Translated by J. C. ROLFE (Loeb Classical Library).

[2]Alieni appetens, sui profusus.

[3]Quippe secundae res sapientium animos fatigant.

[4]Idem velle atque idem nolle, ea demum firma amicitia est.

[5]Ita in maxima fortuna minima licentia est.

[6]Pro patria, pro liberis, pro aris atque focis suis.

[7]Dux atque imperator vitae mortalium animus est.

[8]Jugurtha's remark as he looked back at Rome upon being ordered by the senate to leave Italy.

[9]Punica fide (treachery).

[10]Appius Claudius Caecus, consul in 307 B.C., the earliest Roman writer known to us.

[11]His own character is the arbiter of everyone's fortune. — PUBLILIUS SYRUS, *Maxim 283*
The brave man carves out his fortune, and every man is the son of his own works. — CERVANTES, *Don Quixote, pt. I* [1605], *bk. I, ch. 4*

Virgil [Publius Vergilius Maro]
70–19 B.C.

14   A god has brought us this peace.

Eclogues, I, l. 6

15   To compare great things with small.

Eclogues, I, l. 23

16   Happy old man![12]   *Eclogues, I, l. 46*

17   Ah Corydon, Corydon, what madness has caught you?   *Eclogues, II, l. 69*

18   With Jove I begin.[13]   *Eclogues, III, l. 60*

19   A sad thing is a wolf in the fold, rain on ripe corn, wind in the trees, the anger of Amaryllis.

Eclogues, III, l. 80

20   A snake lurks in the grass.[14]

Eclogues, III, l. 93

21   Let us raise a somewhat loftier strain![15]

Eclogues, IV, l. 1

22   The great cycle of the ages is renewed. Now Justice returns, returns the Golden Age; a new generation now descends from on high.[16]

Eclogues, IV, l. 5

23   We have made you [Priapus] of marble for the time being.   *Eclogues, VII, l. 35*

24   We are not all capable of everything.[17]

Eclogues, VIII, l. 63

25   Draw Daphnis from the town, my songs, draw Daphnis home.   *Eclogues, VIII, l. 68*

26   Hylax barks in the doorway.

Eclogues, VIII, l. 107

27   Your descendants shall gather your fruits.[18]

Eclogues, IX, l. 50

28   Time bears away all things, even our minds.

Eclogues, IX, l. 51

29   Let us go singing as far as we go: the road will be less tedious.   *Eclogues, IX, l. 64*

---

[12]Fortunate senex!

[13]Ab Iove principium.

[14]Latet anguis in herba.

[15]Paulo maiora canamus!

[16]Magnus ab integro saeclorum nascitur ordo. / Iam redit et Virgo, redeunt Saturnia regna; / Iam nova progenies caelo demittitur alto.
Interpreted by the Middle Ages as a prophecy of the birth of Christ. Dante cites the lines in *Purgatorio, canto XXII, l. 70.*
A phrase altered from the first line (Novus ordo seclorum) appears on the reverse of the Great Seal of the United States of America. Virgil supplied the Latin for other phrases of the Great Seal.
See Virgil, 96:5 and 98:15.

[17]Non omnia possumus omnes.

[18]Carpent tua poma nepotes.

1   This last labor grant me, O Arethusa.
Eclogues, X, l. 1

2   What if Amyntas is dark? Violets are dark, too, and hyacinths.   *Eclogues, X, l. 38*

3   Love conquers all things; let us too surrender to Love.[1]   *Eclogues, X, l. 69*

4   Utmost [farthest] Thule.[2]
Georgics, I, l. 30

5   Look with favor upon a bold beginning.[3]
Georgics, I, l. 40

6   O farmers, pray that your summers be wet and your winters clear.   *Georgics, I, l. 100*

7   Practice and thought might gradually forge many an art.   *Georgics, I, l. 133*

8   Thrice they tried to pile Ossa on Pelion, yes, and roll up leafy Olympus upon Ossa; thrice the Father of Heaven split the mountains apart with his thunderbolt.   *Georgics, I, l. 281*

9   Frogs in the marsh mud drone their old lament.
Georgics, I, l. 378

10   Not every soil can bear all things.
Georgics, II, l. 109

11   Ah too fortunate farmers, if they knew their own good fortune!   *Georgics, II, l. 458*

12   May the countryside and the gliding valley streams content me. Lost to fame, let me love river and woodland.   *Georgics, II, l. 485*

13   Happy the man who could search out the causes of things.[4]   *Georgics, II, l. 490*

14   And no less happy he who knows the rural gods.[5]   *Georgics, II, l. 493*

15   This life the old Sabines knew long ago; Remus knew it, and his brother.   *Georgics, II, l. 532*

16   The best day . . . is the first to flee.[6]
Georgics, III, l. 66

17   Years grow cold to love.
Georgics, III, l. 97

18   Time is flying never to return.[7]
Georgics, III, l. 284

19   All aglow is the work.[8]
Georgics, IV, l. 169

20   A sudden madness came down upon the unwary lover [Orpheus]—forgivable, surely, if Death knew how to forgive.   *Georgics, IV, l. 488*

21   Sweet Parthenope nourished me, flourishing in studies of ignoble ease.[9]   *Georgics, IV, l. 563*

22   I who once played shepherds' songs and in my brash youth sang of you, O Tityrus, beneath the spreading beech.[10]   *Georgics, IV, l. 565*

23   Of arms and the man I sing.[11]
Aeneid, bk. I, l. 1

24   Can heavenly minds yield to such rage?
Aeneid, I, l. 11

25   So vast was the struggle to found the Roman state.   *Aeneid, I, l. 33*

26   Night, pitch-black, lies upon the deep.
Aeneid, I, l. 89

27   O thrice and four times blessed![12]
Aeneid, I, l. 94

28   Fury provides arms.   *Aeneid, I, l. 150*

29   You have suffered worse things; God will put an end to these also.   *Aeneid, I, l. 199*

30   Perhaps someday it will be pleasant to remember even this.[13]   *Aeneid, I, l. 203*

31   The organizer a woman.[14]   *Aeneid, I, l. 364*

32   Her walk revealed her as a true goddess.
Aeneid, I, l. 405

33   How happy those whose walls already rise!
Aeneid, I, l. 437

34   Here are the tears of things; mortality touches the heart.[15]   *Aeneid, I, l. 462*

---

[1]Omnia vincit amor: et nos cedamus amori.

[2]Ultima Thule.

The phrase, designating a far-off land, has been in use since the Greek mariner Pytheas discovered in the fourth century B.C. an island he named Thule six days north of England, thought to be Iceland.

[3]Audacibus annue coeptis.

This phrase also (see 95:*n*16) was adapted for use on the reverse of the Great Seal of the United States of America: Annuit coeptis. See Virgil, 98:*n*5, for the Latin on the face of the Great Seal.

[4]Felix qui potuit rerum cognoscere causas.

The reference is apparently to the scientist-philosopher-poet Lucretius (see 92:8–93:21).

[5]Fortunatus et ille deos qui novit agrestis.

[6]Optima . . . dies . . . prima fugit.

---

[7]Fugit inreparabile tempus.

[8]Fervet opus.

[9]Me . . . dulcis alebat / Parthenope, studiis florentem ignobilis otii.

Parthenope: ancient name of Naples.

[10]Tityrus is also referred to in *Eclogues I, 1.*

[11]Arma virumque cano. See Dryden, 285:6.

[12]O terque quaterque beati!

[13]Forsan et haec olim meminisse iuvabit.

[14]Dux femina facti.

[15]Sunt lacrimae rerum et mentem mortalia tangunt.

1   I make no distinction between Trojan and Tyrian.   *Aeneid, I, l. 574*

2   A mind aware of its own rectitude.[1]
                                        Aeneid, I, l. 604

3   As long as rivers shall run down to the sea, or shadows touch the mountain slopes, or stars graze in the vault of heaven, so long shall your honor, your name, your praises endure.
                                        Aeneid, I, l. 607

4   I have known sorrow and learned to aid the wretched.   *Aeneid, I, l. 630*

5   Unspeakable, O Queen, is the sorrow you bid me renew.   *Aeneid, II, l. 3*

6   Whatever it is, I fear Greeks even when they bring gifts.[2]   *Aeneid, II, l. 49*

7   From a single crime know the nation.
                                        Aeneid, II, l. 65

8   I shudder to say it.[3]   *Aeneid, II, l. 204*

9   O fatherland, O Ilium home of the gods, O Troy walls famed in battle!   *Aeneid, II, l. 241*

10   We have been Trojans; Troy has been.
                                        Aeneid, II, l. 325

11   There is but one safety to the vanquished — to hope not safety.   *Aeneid, II, l. 354*

12   Our foes will provide us with arms.
                                        Aeneid, II, l. 391

13   The gods thought otherwise.[4]
                                        Aeneid, II, l. 428

14   Thrice would I have thrown my arms about her neck, and thrice the ghost embraced fled from my grasp: like a fluttering breeze, like a fleeting dream.[5]
                                        Aeneid, II, l. 793

15   O accurst craving for gold!
                                        Aeneid, III, l. 57

16   Rumor flies.[6]   *Aeneid, III, l. 121*

17   I feel again a spark of that ancient flame.[7]
                                        Aeneid, IV, l. 23

18   Deep in her breast lives the silent wound.
                                        Aeneid, IV, l. 67

19   A woman is always a fickle, unstable thing.[8]
                                        Aeneid, IV, l. 569

20   Thus, thus, it is joy to pass to the world below.[9]
                                        Aeneid, IV, l. 660

21   Naked in death upon an unknown shore.
                                        Aeneid, V, l. 871

22   Yield not to evils, but attack all the more boldly.
                                        Aeneid, VI, l. 95

23   It is easy to go down into Hell; night and day, the gates of dark Death stand wide; but to climb back again, to retrace one's steps to the upper air — there's the rub, the task.[10]
                                        Aeneid, VI, l. 126

24   Faithful Achates.[11]
                                Aeneid, VI, l. 158 and elsewhere

25   Death's brother, Sleep.
                                        Aeneid, VI, l. 278

26   Unwillingly I left your land, O Queen.[12]
                                        Aeneid, VI, l. 460

27   Had I a hundred tongues, a hundred mouths, a voice of iron and a chest of brass, I could not tell all the forms of crime, could not name all the types of punishment.
                                        Aeneid, VI, l. 625

28   That happy place, the green groves of the dwelling of the blest.
                                        Aeneid, VI, l. 638

29   The spirit within nourishes, and the mind, diffused through all the members, sways the mass and mingles with the whole frame.
                                        Aeneid, VI, l. 726

30   Each of us bears his own Hell.
                                        Aeneid, VI, l. 743

31   Others, I take it, will work better with breathing bronze and draw living faces from marble; others will plead at law with greater eloquence, or measure the pathways of the sky, or forecast the rising stars.

---

[1]The mind, conscious of rectitude, laughed to scorn the falsehood of report. — OVID, *Fasti, bk. IV, l. 311*

[2]Quidquid id est, timeo Danaos et dona ferentis.

[3]Horresco referens.

[4]Dis aliter visum.

[5]Virgil here translates HOMER, *Odyssey, bk. XI, l. 204.* See 55:2.

[6]Fama volat.

[7]Agnosco veteris vestigia flammae.

[8]Varium et mutabile semper femina.
  Woman often changes; foolish the man who trusts her. — FRANCIS I OF FRANCE, written by him with his ring on a window of the château of Chambord (PIERRE DE BRANTÔME, *Oeuvres, VII, 395*)
  La donna è mobile. — FRANCESCO MARIA PIAVE [1810–1879], *libretto of Verdi's Rigoletto, Duke's song*

[9]Sic, sic, iuvat ire sub umbras.

[10]Facilis descensus Averni. / Noctes atque dies patet atri ianua Ditis; / Sed revocare gradum superasque evadere ad auras, / Hoc opus, hic labor est.

[11]Fidus Achates. Proverbial for a trusty friend; Achates was the faithful comrade of Aeneas.

[12]Aeneas to the ghost of Dido, who had killed herself when he left her.

Be it your concern, Roman, to rule the nations under law (this is your proper skill) and establish the way of peace; to spare the conquered and put down the mighty from their seat.

Aeneid, VI, l. 847

1 Give me handfuls of lilies to scatter.[1]

Aeneid, VI, l. 883

2 There are two gates of Sleep. One is of horn, easy of passage for the shades of truth; the other, of gleaming white ivory, permits false dreams to ascend to the upper air.   *Aeneid, VI, l. 893*

3 Prayed to the Genius of the place.

Aeneid, VII, l. 136

4 We descend from Jove; in ancestral Jove Troy's sons rejoice.   *Aeneid, VII, l. 219*

5 If I cannot bend Heaven, I shall move Hell.

Aeneid, VII, l. 312

6 An old story, but the glory of it is forever.

Aeneid, IX, l. 79

7 To have died once is enough.

Aeneid, IX, l. 140

8 I cannot bear a mother's tears.

Aeneid, IX, l. 289

9 Good speed to your youthful valor, boy! So shall you scale the stars![2]

Aeneid, IX, l. 641

10 Fortune favors the brave.[3]

Aeneid, X, l. 284

11 Believe one who has proved it. Believe an expert.[4]

Aeneid, XI, l. 283

12 His limbs were cold in death; his spirit fled with a groan, indignant, to the shades below.

Aeneid, XII, l. 951

13 One composed of many.[5]

Minor Poems. Moretum, l. 104

14 Death twitches my ear. "Live," he says; "I am coming."   *Minor Poems. Copa, l. 38*

Horace [Quintus Horatius Flaccus]
65–8 B.C.

15 How comes it, Maecenas, that no man living is content with the lot that either his choice has given him, or chance has thrown in his way, but each has praise for those who follow other paths?

Satires, bk. I [35 B.C.], satire i, l. 1

16 The story's about you.[6]   *Satires, I, i, l. 69*

17 There is measure in all things.[7]

Satires, I, i, l. 106

18 We rarely find anyone who can say he has lived a happy life, and who, content with his life, can retire from the world like a satisfied guest.

Satires, I, i, l. 117

19 And all that tribe.[8]   *Satires, I, ii, l. 2*

20 The limbs of a dismembered poet.[9]

Satires, I, iv, l. 62

21 A man without a flaw.[10]   *Satires, I, v, l. 32*

22 As crazy as hauling timber into the woods.

Satires, I, x, l. 34

23 Simplicity and charm.[11]   *Satires, I, x, l. 44*

24 This used to be among my prayers[12] — a piece of land not so very large, which would contain a garden, and near the house a spring of ever-flowing water, and beyond these a bit of wood.

Satires, II [30 B.C.], vi, l. 1

25 O nights and feasts of the gods![13]

Satires, II, vi, l. 65

26 In Rome you long for the country; in the country — oh inconstant! — you praise the distant city to the stars.   *Satires, II, vii, l. 28*

27 Happy the man who far from schemes of business, like the early generations of mankind, works

---

[1]Quoted by Dante in *The Divine Comedy, Purgatorio, canto XXX, l. 21.*

[2]Macte nova virtute, puer, sic itur ad astra.

[3]Audentes fortuna iuvat.

[4]Experto credite.
Believe an expert; believe one who has had experience. — Saint Bernard, *Epistle 106*
Believe the experienced Robert. Believe Robert, who has tried it. — Robert Burton, *Anatomy of Melancholy* [1621–1651], *Introduction*

[5]E pluribus unus.
Adapted (E pluribus unum) for the motto on the face of the Great Seal of the United States, adopted June 20, 1782. For the Latin on the reverse of the Great Seal, see Virgil, 95:*n*16 and 96:*n*3.

---

[6]De te fabula.

[7]Est modus in rebus.
See The Seven Sages, 57:1; Terence, 88:10; Horace, 99:23; Lucan, 110:3; and Anonymous: Latin, 124:9.

[8]Hoc genus omne.

[9]Disiecti membra poetae.
The reference is to Orpheus torn apart by the Maenads.

[10]Ad unguem factus homo.

[11]Molle atque facetum. This refers to Virgil's poetry.

[12]Hoc erat in votis.

[13]O noctes cenaeque deum!

his ancestral acres with oxen of his own breeding, from all usury free.

Epodes [c. 29 B.C.], II, st. 1

1   You ask me why a soft numbness diffuses all my inmost senses with deep oblivion, as though with thirsty throat I'd drained the cup that brings the sleep of Lethe.   *Epodes, XIV, st. 1*

2   But if you name me among the lyric bards, I shall strike the stars with my exalted head.

Odes, bk. I [23 B.C.], ode i, last lines

3   The half of my own soul.[1]   *Odes, I, iii, l. 8*

4   No ascent is too steep for mortals. Heaven itself we seek in our folly.   *Odes, I, iii, l. 37*

5   Pale Death with impartial tread beats at the poor man's cottage door and at the palaces of kings.

Odes, I, iv, l. 13

6   Life's brief span forbids us to enter on far-reaching hopes.[2]   *Odes, I, iv, l. 15*

7 What slender youth, bedewed with liquid odors,
Courts thee on roses in some pleasant cave,
Pyrrha? For whom bind'st thou
In wreaths thy golden hair,
Plain in thy neatness?[3]   *Odes, I, v, l. 1*

8   Never despair.[4]   *Odes, I, vii, l. 27*

9   Tomorrow once again we sail the Ocean Sea.[5]

Odes, I, vii, last line

10   Leave all else to the gods.[6]   *Odes, I, ix, l. 9*

11   Cease to ask what the morrow will bring forth, and set down as gain each day that Fortune grants.

Odes, I, ix, l. 13

12   Seize the day, put no trust in the morrow![7]

Odes, I, xi, last line

13   Happy, thrice happy and more, are they whom an unbroken bond unites and whose love shall know no sundering quarrels so long as they shall live.

Odes, I, xiii, l. 17

14   O fairer daughter of a fair mother![8]

Odes, I, xvi, l. 1

15   The pure in life and free from sin.[9]

Odes, I, xxii, l. 1

16   Grant me, sound of body and of mind, to pass an old age lacking neither honor nor the lyre.

Odes, I, xxxi, last lines

17   A grudging and infrequent worshipper of the gods.[10]   *Odes, I, xxxiv, l. 1*

18   Now is the time for drinking, now the time to beat the earth with unfettered foot.[11]

Odes, I, xxxvii, l. 1

19   Persian luxury, boy, I hate.[12]

Odes, I, xxxviii, l. 1

20   Cease your efforts to find where the last rose lingers.[13]   *Odes, I, xxxviii, l. 3*

21   In adversity remember to keep an even mind.[14]

Odes, II [23 B.C.], iii, l. 1

22   We are all driven into the same fold.[15]

Odes, II, iii, l. 25

23   Whoever cultivates the golden mean[16] avoids both the poverty of a hovel and the envy of a palace.

Odes, II, x, l. 5

24   It is the mountaintop that the lightning strikes.

Odes, II, x, l. 11

25   Nor does Apollo always stretch the bow.[17]

Odes, II, x, l. 19

26   I hate the common herd of men and keep them afar. Let there be sacred silence: I, the Muses' priest, sing for girls and boys songs not heard before.   *Odes, III [23 B.C.], i, l. 1*

27   It is sweet and honorable to die for one's country.[18]   *Odes, III, ii, l. 13*

28   The man who is tenacious of purpose in a rightful cause is not shaken from his firm resolve by the

---

[1]Animae dimidium meae.
The reference is to Virgil.

[2]Vitae summa brevis spem nos vetat incohare longam.

[3]Simplex munditiis.
Translated by JOHN MILTON.

[4]Nil desperandum.

[5]Cras ingens iterabimus aequor.
Translated by S. E. MORISON.

[6]Permitte divis cetera.

[7]Carpe diem, quam minimum credula postero.
See *The Wisdom of Solomon 2:8*, 31:14; Ronsard, 151:1; Spenser, 161:5; and Herrick, 248:8.

[8]O matre pulchra filia pulchrior.

[9]Integer vitae scelerisque purus.

[10]Parcus deorum cultor et infrequens.

[11]Nunc est bibendum, nunc pede libero / Pulsanda tellus.
Ode on the death of Cleopatra.

[12]Persicos odi, puer, apparatus.

[13]Mitte sectari, rosa quo locorum / Sera moretur.

[14]Aequam memento rebus in arduis / Servare mentem.

[15]Omnes eodem cogimur.

[16]Auream quisquis mediocritatem / Diliget.
Keep the golden mean. —PUBLILIUS SYRUS, *Maxim 1072*

[17]Neque semper arcum / Tendit Apollo.

[18]Dulce et decorum est pro patria mori.

frenzy of his fellow citizens clamoring for what is wrong, or by the tyrant's threatening countenance.

Odes, III, iii, l. 1

1   Force without wisdom falls of its own weight.

Odes, III, iv, l. 65

2   Our sires' age was worse than our grandsires'. We their sons are more worthless than they: so in our turn we shall give the world a progeny yet more corrupt.   *Odes, III, vi, l. 46*

3   Skilled in the works of both languages.

Odes, III, viii, l. 5

4   With you I should love to live, with you be ready to die.[1]   *Odes, III, ix, last line*

5   Gloriously perjured,[2] a maiden famous to all time.[3]   *Odes, III, xi, l. 35*

6   O fount Bandusian, more sparkling than glass.[4]

Odes, III, xiii, l. 1

7   I would not have borne this in my hot youth when Plancus was consul.[5]

Odes, III, xiv, l. 27

8   A pauper in the midst of wealth.[6]

Odes, III, xvi, l. 28

9   He will through life be master of himself and a happy man who from day to day can have said, "I have lived: tomorrow the Father may fill the sky with black clouds or with cloudless sunshine."[7]

Odes, III, xxix, l. 41

10   I have built a monument more lasting than bronze.[8]   *Odes, III, xxx, l. 1*

11   I shall not wholly die.[9]   *Odes, III, xxx, l. 6*

12   I am not what I was in the reign of the good Cinara. Forbear, cruel mother of sweet loves.[10]

Odes, IV [13 B.C.], i, l. 3

13   The centuries roll back to the ancient age of gold.   *Odes, IV, ii, l. 39*

14   We are but dust and shadow.

Odes, IV, vii, l. 16

15   Many brave men lived before Agamemnon; but all are overwhelmed in eternal night, unwept, unknown, because they lack a sacred poet.[11]

Odes, IV, ix, l. 25

16   It is not the rich man you should properly call happy, but him who knows how to use with wisdom the blessings of the gods, to endure hard poverty, and who fears dishonor worse than death, and is not afraid to die for cherished friends or fatherland.

Odes, IV, ix, l. 45

17   It is sweet to let the mind unbend on occasion.

Odes, IV, xii, l. 27

18   I am not bound over to swear allegiance to any master; where the storm drives me I turn in for shelter.   *Epistles, bk. I [c. 20 B.C.], epistle i, l. 14*

19   To flee vice is the beginning of virtue, and to have got rid of folly is the beginning of wisdom.

Epistles, I, i, l. 41

20   Make money, money by fair means if you can, if not, by any means money.[12]   *Epistles, I, i, l. 66*

21   The people are a many-headed beast.[13]

Epistles, I, i, l. 76

22   He who has begun has half done. Dare to be wise; begin!   *Epistles, I, ii, l. 40*

23   The covetous man is ever in want.

Epistles, I, ii, l. 56

24   Anger is a short madness.

Epistles, I, ii, l. 62

---

[1]Tecum vivere amem, tecum obeam libens.

[2]Splendide mendax.
Chosen by Swift as Gulliver's motto.

[3]Hypermestra.

[4]O fons Bandusiae splendidior vitro.

[5]In my hot youth, when George the Third was king. — LORD BYRON, *Don Juan* [1819–1824], *canto 1, st. 212*

[6]Magnus inter opes inops.

[7]Ille potens sui / Laetusque deget, cui licet in diem / Dixisse "Vixi: cras vel atra / Nube polum pater occupato / Vel sole puro."

[8]Exegi monumentum aere perennius.

[9]Non omnis moriar.

[10]Non sum qualis eram bonae / Sub regno Cinarae. Desine, dulcium / Mater saeva Cupidinum.
Mater saeva Cupidinum. — *Odes, bk. I, xix, l. 1*

[11]How many, famous while they lived, are utterly forgotten for want of writers! — BOETHIUS, *De Consolatione Philosophiae, II, 7*
Brave men were living before Agamemnon / And since, exceeding valorous and sage, / A good deal like him too, but quite the same none; / But then they shone not on the poet's page. — LORD BYRON, *Don Juan* [1819–1824], *canto I, st. 5*
See Pindar, 66:11, and Pope, 313:6.

[12]Get money; still get money, boy, no matter by what means. — BEN JONSON, *Every Man in His Humour* [1598], *act II, sc. iii*

[13]Belua multorum es capitum.
Plato describes the multitude as a "great strong beast." — *The Republic, bk. VI, 493–B*
The multitude of the gross people, being a beast of many heads. — ERASMUS, *Adagia, no. 122*
O weak trust of the many-headed multitude. — PHILIP SIDNEY, *The Arcadia* [1580], *bk. II*
The beast of many heads, the staggering multitude. — MARSTON AND WEBSTER, *The Malcontent* [1604], *act III, sc. iii*
If there be any among those common objects of hatred I do contemn and laugh at, it is that great enemy of reason, virtue, and religion, the multitude . . . one great beast and a monstrosity more prodigious than Hydra. — THOMAS BROWNE, *Religio Medici* [1643], *pt. II, sec. 1*
Sir, your people is a great beast. — *Attributed to* ALEXANDER HAMILTON

1 Think to yourself that every day is your last; the hour to which you do not look forward will come as a welcome surprise. As for me, when you want a good laugh, you will find me, in a fine state, fat and sleek, a true hog of Epicurus' herd.
Epistles, I, iv, l. 13

2 You may drive out Nature with a pitchfork, yet she still will hurry back. *Epistles, I, iv, l. 24*

3 They change their clime, not their disposition, who run across the sea. *Epistles, I, xi, l. 27*

4 He is not poor who has enough of things to use. If it is well with your belly, chest and feet, the wealth of kings can give you nothing more.
Epistles, I, xii, l. 4

5 Harmony in discord.[1] *Epistles, I, xii, l. 19*

6 For joys fall not to the rich alone, nor has he lived ill, who from birth to death has passed unknown.
Epistles, I, xvii, l. 9

7 It is not everyone that can get to Corinth.[2]
Epistles, I, xvii, l. 36

8 Once a word has been allowed to escape, it cannot be recalled.[3] *Epistles, I, xviii, l. 71*

9 It is your concern when your neighbor's wall is on fire. *Epistles, I, xviii, l. 84*

10 No poems can please for long or live that are written by water-drinkers. *Epistles, I, xix, l. 2*

11 O imitators, you slavish herd!
Epistles, I, xix, l. 19

12 And seek for truth in the groves of Academe.[4]
Epistles, II [14 B.C.], ii, l. 45

13 Barefaced poverty drove me to writing verses.
Epistles, II, ii, l. 51

14 The years as they pass plunder us of one thing after another. *Epistles, II, ii, l. 55*

15 I have to submit to much in order to pacify the touchy tribe of poets.[5] *Epistles, II, ii, l. 102*

16 "Painters and poets," you say, "have always had an equal license in bold invention." We know; we claim the liberty for ourselves and in turn we give it to others.
Epistles, III (Ars Poetica) [c. 15 B.C.], l. 9

17 It was a wine jar when the molding began: as the wheel runs round why does it turn out a water pitcher? *Epistles, III, l. 21*

18 It is when I struggle to be brief that I become obscure. *Epistles, III, l. 25*

19 Scholars dispute and the case is still before the courts.[6] *Epistles, III, l. 78*

20 Foot-and-a-half-long words.[7]
Epistles, III, l. 97

21 If you wish me to weep, you yourself Must first feel grief.[8] *Epistles, III, l. 102*

22 Taught or untaught, we all scribble poetry.
Epistles, III, l. 117

23 The mountains will be in labor, and a ridiculous mouse will be brought forth.[9]
Epistles, III, l. 139

24 From the egg.[10] *Epistles, III, l. 147*

25 In the midst of things.[11] *Epistles, III, l. 148*

26 A praiser of past time.[12] *Epistles, III, l. 173*

27 Let a play have five acts, neither more nor less.
Epistles, III, l. 189

28 Turn the pages of your Greek models night and day. *Epistles, III, l. 268*

29 He wins every hand who mingles profit with pleasure, by delighting and instructing the reader at the same time. *Epistles, III, l. 343*

---

[1]Concordia discors.

[2]A rendering of a Greek proverb, "It's not everyone that can make the voyage to Corinth," which referred to the expense of the life there.

There is but one road that leads to Corinth. —WALTER PATER, *Marius the Epicurean* [1885], *ch. 24*

[3]Semel emissum volat irrevocabile verbum.

The written word, unpublished, can be destroyed, but the spoken word can never be recalled. — *Ars Poetica* [c. 8 B.C.], *l. 389*

It is as easy to recall a stone thrown violently from the hand as a word which has left your tongue. —MENANDER, *Fragment 1092K*

Four things come not back: the spoken word; the sped arrow; time past; the neglected opportunity. —OMAR IBN AL-HALIF, *Aphorism*

A word once spoken revoked cannot be. —ALEXANDER BARCLAY [c. 1475–1552], *The Ship of Fools* [1509]

Thoughts unexpressed may sometimes fall back dead; / But God Himself can't kill them when they're said. —WILL CARLETON, *The First Settler's Story, st. 21*

[4]Atque inter silvas Academi quaerere verum.

[5]Genus irritabile vatum.

[6]Grammatici certant et adhuc sub iudice lis est.

[7]Sesquipedalia verba.

[8]Si vis me flere, dolendum est / Primum ipsi tibi.

[9]Parturient montes, nascetur ridiculus mus.

[10]Ab ovo.

Helen, the cause of the Trojan War, sprang from an egg engendered by Leda and the Swan (Zeus).

[11]In medias res.

[12]Laudator temporis acti.

1   Sometimes even good old Homer nods.[1]
Epistles, III, l. 359

2   As in painting, so in poetry.[2]
Epistles, III, l. 361

3   He has defiled his father's grave.
Epistles, III, l. 471

Augustus Caesar
63 B.C.–A.D. 14

4   Quintilius Varus, give me back my legions![3]
From SUETONIUS, Augustus, sec. 23

5   More haste, less speed.[4]
From SUETONIUS, Augustus, 25

6   Well done is quickly done.[5]
From SUETONIUS, Augustus, 25

7   I found Rome a city of bricks and left it a city of marble.   *From SUETONIUS, Augustus, 28*

8   After this time I surpassed all others in authority, but I had no more power than the others who were also my colleagues in office.
Res Gestae, bk. I, sec. 34

9   Young men, hear an old man to whom old men hearkened when he was young.
From PLUTARCH, Apothegms, Caesar Augustus

Livy [Titus Livius]
59 B.C.–A.D. 17

10   We can endure neither our evils nor their cures.[6]
History, Prologue

11   Better late than never.[7]   *History, bk. IV, sec. 23*

12   Beyond the Alps lies Italy.[8]   *History, XXI, 30*

---

[1]Quandoque bonus dormitat Homerus.
Homer himself, in a long work, may sleep. — ROBERT HERRICK, *Hesperides* [1648], *no. 95*

[2]Ut pictura poesis.

[3]Quintili Vare, legiones redde!

[4]A Greek proverb, a familiar rendering of which is the Latin Festina lente.

[5]A Latin proverb: Sat celeriter fieri quidquid fiat satis bene. See Publilius Syrus, 102:14, and Anonymous: Latin, 123:11.

[6]The two reasons for writing a history.

[7]Potius sero quam numquam.
It is better to learn late than never. — PUBLILIUS SYRUS, *Maxim 864*

[8]In conspectu Alpes habeant, quarum alterum latus Italiae sit.
Au-delà des Alpes est l'Italie. — NAPOLEON [1797]

Publilius Syrus[9]
First century B.C.

13   As men, we are all equal in the presence of death.
Maxim 1

14   He doubly benefits the needy who gives quickly.
Maxim 6

15   To do two things at once is to do neither.
Maxim 7

16   A god could hardly love and be wise.[10]
Maxim 25

17   The loss which is unknown is no loss at all.
Maxim 38

18   A good reputation is more valuable than money.
Maxim 108

19   It is well to moor your bark with two anchors.
Maxim 119

20   Many receive advice, few profit by it.
Maxim 149

21   While we stop to think, we often miss our opportunity.
Maxim 185

22   Whatever you can lose, you should reckon of no account.
Maxim 191

23   For a good cause, wrongdoing is virtuous.[11]
Maxim 244

24   You should hammer your iron when it is glowing hot.[12]
Maxim 262

25   What is left when honor is lost?
Maxim 265

26   A fair exterior is a silent recommendation.
Maxim 267

27   Fortune is not satisfied with inflicting one calamity.
Maxim 274

28   When Fortune is on our side, popular favor bears her company.   *Maxim 275*

---

[9]Commonly called Publius, but spelled Publilius by Pliny in his *Natural History, 35, sec. 199*. Translated mainly by DARIUS LYMAN. The numbers are those of the translator.

[10]It is impossible to love and be wise. — FRANCIS BACON, *Essays* [1597–1625], *Of Love*

[11]Honesta turpitudo est pro causa bona.

[12]Strike while the iron is hot. — FRANÇOIS RABELAIS, *Gargantua and Pantagruel, bk. II* [1534], *ch. 31*
When the iron is hot, strike. — JOHN HEYWOOD, *Proverbs* [1546], *pt. I, ch. 2*
Nothing like striking while the iron is hot. — CERVANTES, *Don Quixote, pt. II* [1615], *bk. IV, ch. 71*

1 When Fortune flatters, she does it to betray.
Maxim 277

2 Fortune is like glass—the brighter the glitter, the more easily broken. *Maxim 280*

3 It is more easy to get a favor from Fortune than to keep it. *Maxim 282*

4 There are some remedies worse than the disease.[1]
Maxim 301

5 A cock has great influence on his own dunghill.[2]
Maxim 357

6 Anyone can hold the helm when the sea is calm.
Maxim 358

7 The bow too tensely strung is easily broken.
Maxim 388

8 Treat your friend as if he might become an enemy.[3] *Maxim 402*

9 No pleasure endures unseasoned by variety.
Maxim 406

10 The judge is condemned when the criminal is absolved.[4] *Maxim 407*

11 Practice is the best of all instructors.[5]
Maxim 439

12 He who is bent on doing evil can never want occasion. *Maxim 459*

13 Never find your delight in another's misfortune.
Maxim 467

14 It is a bad plan that admits of no modification.
Maxim 469

15 It is an unhappy lot which finds no enemies.
Maxim 499

16 The fear of death is more to be dreaded than death itself. *Maxim 511*

17 A rolling stone gathers no moss.[6] *Maxim 524*

18 Never promise more than you can perform.
Maxim 528

19 No one should be judge in his own case.[7]
Maxim 545

20 Necessity knows no law except to prevail.[8]
Maxim 553

21 Nothing can be done at once hastily and prudently. *Maxim 557*

22 We desire nothing so much as what we ought not to have. *Maxim 559*

23 It is only the ignorant who despise education.
Maxim 571

24 Do not turn back when you are just at the goal.[9]
Maxim 580

25 It is not every question that deserves an answer.
Maxim 581

26 No man is happy who does not think himself so.[10]

Maxim 584

27 Never thrust your own sickle into another's corn.[11] *Maxim 593*

28 You cannot put the same shoe on every foot.
Maxim 596

29 Every day should be passed as if it were to be our last. *Maxim 633*

30 Money alone sets all the world in motion.
Maxim 656

31 You should go to a pear tree for pears, not to an elm.[12] *Maxim 674*

---

[1]Marius said, "I see the cure is not worth the pain." — PLUTARCH, *Lives, Caius Marius*

The remedy is worse than the disease. — FRANCIS BACON, *Essays* [1597–1625], *Of Seditions*

I find the medicine worse than the malady. — BEAUMONT AND FLETCHER, *Love's Cure* [1647], *act III, sc. ii*

[2]Every cock is proud on his own dunghill. — JOHN HEYWOOD, *Proverbs* [1546], *pt. I, ch. 2*

[3]Treat your friend as if he will one day be your enemy, and your enemy as if he will one day be your friend. — LABERIUS [105–43 B.C.], *Fragment*

See Sophocles, 67:9.

[4]Iudex damnatur ubi nocens absolvitur. — *Motto adopted for the Edinburgh Review*

[5]Practice makes perfect. — *Proverb*

The saying "Practice is everything" is Periander's. — DIOGENES LAERTIUS, *Lives of Eminent Philosophers, Periander, 6*

[6]The rolling stone never gathereth mosse. — JOHN HEYWOOD, *Proverbs* [1546], *pt. I, ch. 2*

The stone that is rolling can gather no moss. — THOMAS TUSSER, *A Hundred Good Points of Husbandry* [1557]

[7]It is not permitted to the most equitable of men to be a judge in his own cause. — BLAISE PASCAL, *Pensées* [1670], *sec. 2, ch. 82*

[8]Proverbial; attributed to Syrus.

Necessity gives the law and does not itself receive it. — *Maxim 399*

[9]When men are arrived at the goal, they should not turn back. — PLUTARCH, *Of the Training of Children*

[10]No man can enjoy happiness without thinking that he enjoys it. — SAMUEL JOHNSON, *The Rambler* [1750–1752]

[11]Did thrust as now in others' corn his sickle. — DU BARTAS, *Divine Weeks and Works* [1578], *Second Week, pt. 2*

Not presuming to put my sickle in another man's corn. — NICHOLAS YONGE [d. 1619], *Musica Transalpina, Epistle Dedicatory* [1588]

[12]You may as well expect pears from an elm. — CERVANTES, *Don Quixote, pt. II* [1615], *bk. IV, ch. 40*

1   It is a very hard undertaking to seek to please everybody.   *Maxim 675*

2   Look for a tough wedge for a tough log.   *Maxim 723*

3   Pardon one offense, and you encourage the commission of many.   *Maxim 750*

4   It takes a long time to bring excellence to maturity.   *Maxim 780*

5   No one knows what he can do till he tries.   *Maxim 786*

6   It is vain to look for a defense against lightning.   *Maxim 835*

7   Everything is worth what its purchaser will pay for it.   *Maxim 847*

8   Better be ignorant of a matter than half know it.   *Maxim 865*

9   Prosperity makes friends, adversity tries them.   *Maxim 872*

10   Let a fool hold his tongue and he will pass for a sage.   *Maxim 914*

11   You need not hang up the ivy branch over the wine that will sell.[1]   *Maxim 968*

12   It is a consolation to the wretched to have companions in misery.   *Maxim 995*

13   Unless degree is preserved, the first place is safe for no one.   *Maxim 1042*

14   Confession of our faults is the next thing to innocence.   *Maxim 1060*

15   I have often regretted my speech, never my silence.[2]   *Maxim 1070*

16   Speech is a mirror of the soul: as a man speaks, so is he.   *Maxim 1073*

Dionysius of Halicarnassus
c. 54–c. 7 B.C.

17   The contact with manners then is education; and this Thucydides appears to assert when he says history is philosophy learned from examples.
    Ars Rhetorica, XI, 2

Sextus Propertius
c. 54 B.C.–A.D. 2

18   Never change when love has found its home.
    Elegies, bk. I, elegy i, l. 36

19   The seaman's story is of tempest, the plowman's of his team of bulls; the soldier tells his wounds, the shepherd his tale of sheep.   *Elegies, II, i, l. 43*

20   Let each man pass his days in that wherein his skill is greatest.   *Elegies, II, i, l. 46*

21   What though strength fails? Boldness is certain to win praise. In mighty enterprises, it is enough to have had the determination.[3]
    Elegies, II, x, l. 5

22   Let no one be willing to speak ill of the absent.[4]
    Elegies, II, xix, l. 32

23   Let each man have the wit to go his own way.
    Elegies, II, xxv, l. 38

24   Absence makes the heart grow fonder.[5]
    Elegies, II, xxxiii, l. 43

25   There is something beyond the grave; death does not end all, and the pale ghost escapes from the vanquished pyre.[6]   *Elegies, IV, vii, l. 1*

Albius Tibullus
c. 54–c. 19 B.C.

26   May I look on you when my last hour comes; may I hold you, as I sink, with my failing hand.[7]
    Elegies, bk. I, elegy i, l. 59

27   Jupiter laughs at the perjuries of lovers.[8]
    Elegies, III, vi, l. 49

Ovid [Publius Ovidius Naso]
43 B.C.–A.D. c. 18

28   I have faith that yields to none, and ways without reproach, and unadorned simplicity, and blushing modesty.   *Amores, bk. I, poem iii, l. 13*

---

[1]Good wine needs no bush.—SHAKESPEARE, *As You Like It, Epilogue, l. 4*
    Good wine needs neither bush nor preface / To make it welcome.—WALTER SCOTT, *Peveril of the Peak* [1822], *ch. 4*
    Bush . . . *archaic:* a bunch of ivy formerly hung outside a tavern to indicate wine for sale.—*Merriam-Webster's Collegiate Dictionary* (10th ed.) [1998]
    I.e., good wine needs no advertising.

[2]Simonides said that "he never repented that he held his tongue, but often that he had spoken."—PLUTARCH, *Rules for the Preservation of Health*

[3]Quod si deficiant vires, audacia certe / Laus erit: in magnis et voluisse sat est.

[4]Absenti nemo non nocuisse velit.

[5]Semper in absentes felicior aestus amantes.

[6]Our souls survive this death.—OVID, *Metamorphoses, XV, l. 158*

[7]Te spectem, suprema mihi cum venerit hora. / Te teneam moriens deficiente manu.

[8]Periuria ridet amantum Iupiter.
    Also in OVID, *Ars Amatoria, I, 633*
    And Jove but laughs at lovers' perjury.—JOHN DRYDEN, *Palamon and Arcite* [1680], *bk. II, l. 758,* and *Amphitryon* [1690], *act I, sc. ii*

1   The rest who does not know?[1]
Amores, I, v, l. 25

2   Every lover is a warrior, and Cupid has his camps.[2]
Amores, I, ix, l. 1

3   Run slowly, horses of the night.[3]
Amores, I, xiii, l. 39

4   Stay far hence, far hence, you prudes![4]
Amores, II, i, l. 3

5   So I can't live either without you or with you.[5]
Amores, III, xi, l. 39

6   They come to see; they come that they themselves may be seen.[6]
Ars Amatoria, bk. I, l. 99

7   It is convenient that there be gods, and, as it is convenient, let us believe there are.[7]
Ars Amatoria, I, l. 637

8   To be loved, be lovable.
Ars Amatoria, II, l. 107

9   Nothing is stronger than habit.
Ars Amatoria, II, l. 345

10   Perhaps too my name will be joined to theirs[8] [the names of famous poets].
Ars Amatoria, III, l. 339

11   Now there are fields of corn where Troy once was.
Heroides, letter I, l. 53

12   [Chaos] A rough, unordered mass of things.[9]
Metamorphoses, bk. I, l. 7

13   Your lot is mortal: not mortal is what you desire.
Metamorphoses, II, l. 56

14   You will be safest in the middle.[10]
Metamorphoses, II, l. 137

15   I am Actaeon: recognize your master![11]
Metamorphoses, III, l. 230

16   The cause is hidden, but the result is well known.[12]
Metamorphoses, IV, l. 287

17   We can learn even from our enemies.[13]
Metamorphoses, IV, l. 428

18   I see and approve better things, but follow worse.[14]
Metamorphoses, VII, l. 20

19   The gods have their own rules.[15]
Metamorphoses, IX, l. 500

20   Time the devourer of all things.[16]
Metamorphoses, XV, l. 234

21   And now I have finished a work that neither the wrath of love, nor fire, nor the sword, nor devouring age shall be able to destroy.
Metamorphoses, XV, l. 871

22   Resist beginnings; the prescription comes too late when the disease has gained strength by long delays.
Remedia Amoris, l. 91

23   Love yields to business. If you seek a way out of love, be busy; you'll be safe then.[17]
Remedia Amoris, l. 143

24   Poetry comes fine-spun from a mind at peace.
Tristia, bk. I, poem i, l. 39

25   So long as you are secure you will count many friends; if your life becomes clouded you will be alone.
Tristia, I, ix, l. 5

26   Whatever I tried to write was verse.
Tristia, IV, x, l. 26

27   It is annoying to be honest to no purpose.
Epistulae Ex Ponto, bk. II, letter iii, l. 14

28   Note too that a faithful study of the liberal arts humanizes character and permits it not to be cruel.
Epistulae Ex Ponto, II, ix, l. 47

---

[1]Cetera quis nescit?

[2]Love is a kind of warfare. — OVID, *Ars Amatoria, II, 233*
A batallas de amor campo de pluma [A field of feathers for the strife of love]. — LUIS DE GÓNGORA Y ARGOTE [1561–1627], *Soledad, I*

[3]At si, quem malis, Cephalum complexa teneres, / Clamares "lente currite noctis equi."
See Marlowe, 171:4.

[4]Procul hinc, procul este, severi!

[5]Sic ego nec sine te nec tecum vivere possum.

[6]Spectatum veniunt, veniunt spectentur ut ipsae.
And for to se, and eek for to be seye. — CHAUCER, *The Canterbury Tales* [c. 1387], *The Wife of Bath's Prologue, l. 552*
To see and to be seen. — BEN JONSON, *Epithalamion, III, 4*

[7]See Voltaire, 316:22.

[8]Forsitan et nostrum nomen miscebitur istis.

[9]Rudis indigestaque moles.

[10]Medio tutissimus ibis.

---

[11]Actaeon ego sum, dominum cognoscite vestrum!

[12]Causa latet, vis est notissima.

[13]Fas est et ab hoste doceri. Imitated from ARISTOPHANES, *The Birds, l. 370*: People before this have learned from their enemies.

[14]Video meliora, proboque, deteriora sequor.
I know and love the good, yet, ah! the worst pursue. — PETRARCH, *Sonnet 225, Canzone 21, To Laura in Life* [c. 1327]

[15]Sunt superis sua iura.

[16]Tempus edax rerum.

[17]Qui finem quaeris amoris / Cedit amor rebus; res age, tutus eris.

Hillel
fl. 30 B.C.–A.D. 10

1   What is hateful to you do not do to your neighbor. That is the whole Torah. The rest is commentary.[1]
From Talmud [compiled sixth century]. Shabbath

2   God says: If you come to My House, I will come to yours.   *From Talmud. Sukkah*[2]

3   If I am not for myself, who is for me? And when I am for myself, what am I? And if not now, when?
From Talmud. The Wisdom of the Fathers[3]

4   The more flesh, the more worms. The more possessions, the more worry.
From Talmud. The Wisdom of the Fathers

Phaedrus[4]
fl. A.D. c. 8

5   Submit to the present evil, lest a greater one befall you.   *Fables, bk. I, fable 2, l. 31*

6   He was the author, our hand finished it.
Fables, I, 6, l. 20

7   It has been related that dogs drink at the river Nile running along, that they may not be seized by the crocodiles.[5]   *Fables, I, 25, l. 3*

8   Come of it what may, as Sinon said.
Fables, III, prologue, l. 27

9   Things are not always what they seem.[6]
Fables, IV, 2, l. 5

10   To add insult to injury.   *Fables, V, l. 3*

11   Once lost, Jupiter himself cannot bring back opportunity.[7]   *Fables, VII, l. 4*

Lucius Annaeus Seneca[8]
c. 4 B.C.–A.D. 65

12   What fools these mortals be.[9]
Epistles, letter 1, l. 3

13   It is not the man who has too little, but the man who craves more, that is poor.
Epistles, 2, l. 2

14   Live among men as if God beheld you; speak to God as if men were listening.
Epistles, 10, l. 5

15   The best ideas are common property.
Epistles, 12, l. 11

16   Men do not care how nobly they live, but only how long, although it is within the reach of every man to live nobly, but within no man's power to live long.   *Epistles, 22, l. 17*

17   A great pilot can sail even when his canvas is rent.   *Epistles, 30, l. 3*

18   Man is a reasoning animal.
Epistles, 41, l. 8

19   It is quality rather than quantity that matters.
Epistles, 45, l. 1

20   You can tell the character of every man when you see how he receives praise.
Epistles, 52, l. 12

21   Not lost, but gone before.[10]
Epistles, 63, l. 16

22   All art is but imitation of nature.
Epistles, 65, l. 3

23   It is a rough road that leads to the heights of greatness.   *Epistles, 84, l. 13*

24   The pilot . . . who has been able to say, "Neptune, you shall never sink this ship except on an even keel," has fulfilled the requirements of his art.[11]
Epistles, 85, l. 33

25   I was shipwrecked before I got aboard.
Epistles, 87, l. 1

26   It is better, of course, to know useless things than to know nothing.   *Epistles, 88, l. 45*

27   Do not ask for what you will wish you had not got.   *Epistles, 95, l. 1*

28   We are mad, not only individually, but nationally. We check manslaughter and isolated murders; but what of war and the much vaunted crime of slaughtering whole peoples?
Epistles, 95, l. 30

---

[1]See *Matthew 7:12*, 35:5; Confucius, 63:20; Aristotle, 79:16; and Chesterfield, 314:19.

[2]Translated by ISRAEL W. SLOTKIN.

[3]Translated by JACOB NEUSNER.

[4]Translated by HENRY THOMAS RILEY [1816–1878].

[5]"To treat a thing as the dogs do the Nile" was a common proverb, signifying superficial treatment.

[6]Non semper ea sunt quae videntur.

[7]Opportunity knocks only once. — *Proverb*

[8]Translated by R. M. GUMMERE, J. W. BASORE, W. H. D. ROUSE, and F. J. MILLER (Loeb Classical Library).

[9]Tanta stultitia mortalium est.

[10]Non amittuntur, sed praemittuntur.
Not dead, but gone before. — SAMUEL ROGERS, *Human Life* [1819]

[11]The mariner of old said thus to Neptune in a great tempest, "O God! thou mayest save me if thou wilt, and if thou wilt, thou mayest destroy me; but whether or no, I will steer my rudder true." — MONTAIGNE, *Essays* [1580–1595], *bk. II, ch. 16*

1   A great step towards independence is a good-humored stomach, one that is willing to endure rough treatment.

Epistles, 123, l. 3

2   Fire is the test of gold; adversity, of strong men.
Moral Essays. On Providence, chap. 5, sec. 9

3   Time discovers truth.[1]
Moral Essays. On Anger, 2, 22

4   Whom they have injured they also hate.[2]
Moral Essays. On Anger, 2, 33

5   There is no great genius without some touch of madness.[3]
Moral Essays. On the Tranquillity of the Mind, 17, 10

6   A great fortune is a great slavery.
Moral Essays. To Polybius on Consolation, 6, 5

7   Wherever the Roman conquers, there he dwells.
Moral Essays. To Helvia on Consolation, 7, 7

8   You roll my log, and I will roll yours.
Apocolocyntosis, sec. 9

9   Do you seek Alcides' equal? None is, except himself.[4]   *Hercules Furens, act 1, sc. 1, l. 84*

10   Successful and fortunate crime is called virtue.
Hercules Furens, 1, 1, l. 255

11   An age will come after many years when the Ocean will loose the chains of things, and a huge land lie revealed; when Tiphys[5] will disclose new worlds and Thule no more be the ultimate.[6]

Medea, 2, 2, l. 374

12   A good mind possesses a kingdom.
Thyestes, l. 380

Marcus Manilius
First century A.D.

13   [Human reason] freed men's minds from wondering at portents by wresting from Jupiter his bolts and power of thunder, and ascribing to the winds the noise and to the clouds the flame.[7]

Astronomica,[8] bk. I, l. 102

14   Who could know heaven save by heaven's gift and discover God save one who shares himself in the divine?   *Astronomica, II, l. 115*

Caligula [Gaius Caesar]
A.D. 12–41

15   Strike so that he may feel he is dying.[9]
From SUETONIUS, *The Lives of the Caesars, Caligula, sec. 30*

16   Would that the Roman people had a single neck [to cut off their head].[10]
From SUETONIUS, *The Lives of the Caesars, Caligula, 30*

---

[1] Veritatem dies aperit. Omnia tempus revelat [Time reveals all]. — TERTULLIAN, *Apologeticus, 7*
Time reveals all things. — ERASMUS, *Adagia*

[2] It is human nature to hate those whom you have injured. — TACITUS, *Agricola, 42, 15*
Chi fa ingiuria non perdona mai [He never pardons those he injures]. — *Italian proverb*
The offender never pardons. — GEORGE HERBERT, *Jacula Prudentum* [1651]
Forgiveness to the injured does belong; / But they ne'er pardon who have done the wrong. — JOHN DRYDEN, *The Conquest Of Granada* [1670], *pt. II, act I, sc. ii*

[3] An ancient commonplace, which Seneca says he quotes from ARISTOTLE, *Problemata, 30, 1:* "No excellent soul is exempt from a mixture of madness." It is also in PLATO, *Phaedrus, 245-A.*
Good sense travels on the well-worn paths; genius, never. And that is why the crowd, not altogether without reason, is so ready to treat great men as lunatics. — CESARE LOMBROSO, *The Man of Genius,* preface

[4] And but herself admits no parallel. — PHILIP MASSINGER, *Duke of Milan* [1623], *act IV, sc. iii*
None but himself can be his parallel. — LEWIS THEOBALD [1688–1744], *The Double Falsehood*

[5] Jason's pilot.

[6] Venient annis / Saecula seris, quibus Oceanus / Vincula rerum laxet, et ingens / Pateat tellus, Tiphysque novos / Detegat orbes nec sit terris / Ultima Thule.
Translated by S. E. MORISON.
As one much addicted to prophecies, and who had already voyaged beyond Thule (Iceland), Columbus was much impressed by the passage in Seneca's *Medea.* — S. E. MORISON, *Admiral of the Ocean Sea* [1942], *vol. I, ch. 6*
Next to these lines from *Medea* in an early edition of Seneca's tragedies that belonged to Columbus's son Ferdinand, there is this annotation in the son's hand: Haec profetia impleta est per patrem meum . . . almirantem anno 1492 [The prophecy was fulfilled by my father the Admiral in the year 1492]. — S. E. MORISON, *Admiral of the Ocean Sea* [1942], *vol. I, ch. 6*

[7] Cur imbres ruerent, ventosque causa moveret pervidit, solvitque animis miracula rerum eripuitque Jovi fulmen viresque tonandi et sonitum ventis concessit, nubibus ignem.
See Shakespeare, 224:28, and Benjamin Franklin, 319:*n*1.

[8] Translated by G. P. GOULD (Loeb Classical Library).

[9] Ita feri ut se mori sentiat.
Translated by J. C. ROLFE (Loeb Classical Library).

[10] Utinam populus Romanus unam cervicem haberet.

Pliny the Elder
[Gaius Plinius Secundus]
A.D. 23–79

1   In comparing various authors with one another, I have discovered that some of the gravest and latest writers have transcribed, word for word, from former works, without making acknowledgment.

Natural History, bk. I, dedication, sec. 22

2   Everything is soothed by oil, and this is the reason why divers send out small quantities of it from their mouths, because it smooths every part which is rough.[1]   *Natural History, II, 234*

3   It is far from easy to determine whether she [Nature] has proved to man a kind parent or a merciless stepmother.[2]   *Natural History, VII, 1*

4   Man alone at the very moment of his birth, cast naked upon the naked earth, does she abandon to cries and lamentations.[3]

Natural History, VII, 2

5   To laugh, if but for an instant only, has never been granted to man before the fortieth day from his birth, and then it is looked upon as a miracle of precocity.   *Natural History, VII, 2*

6   Man is the only one that knows nothing, that can learn nothing without being taught. He can neither speak nor walk nor eat, and in short he can do nothing at the prompting of nature only, but weep.   *Natural History, VII, 4*

7   With man, most of his misfortunes are occasioned by man.   *Natural History, VII, 5*

8   Indeed, what is there that does not appear marvelous when it comes to our knowledge for the first time? How many things, too, are looked upon as quite impossible until they have been actually effected?   *Natural History, VII, 6*

9   The human features and countenance, although composed of but some ten parts or little more, are so fashioned that among so many thousands of men there are no two in existence who cannot be distinguished from one another.[4]

Natural History, VII, 8

10   There is always something new out of Africa.[5]

Natural History, VIII, 17

11   When a building is about to fall down, all the mice desert it.[6]   *Natural History, VIII, 103*

12   Bears when first born are shapeless masses of white flesh a little larger than mice, their claws alone being prominent. The mother then licks them gradually into proper shape.[7]

Natural History, VIII, 126

13   The best plan is to profit by the folly of others.   *Natural History, XVIII, 31*

14   With a grain of salt.[8]

Natural History, XXIII, 8

15   Why is it that we entertain the belief that for every purpose odd numbers are the most effectual?[9]   *Natural History, XXVIII, 23*

Persius [Aulus Persius Flaccus]
A.D. 34–62

16   The stomach is the teacher of the arts and the dispenser of invention.[10]   *Satires, prologue, l. 10*

---

[1]Why does pouring oil on the sea make it clear and calm? Is it for that the winds, slipping the smooth oil, have no force, nor cause any waves? — PLUTARCH, *Natural Questions, IX*

Bishop Adain [651] gave to a company about to take a journey by sea some holy oil, saying, 'I know that when you go abroad you will meet with a storm and contrary wind; but do you remember to cast this oil I give you into the sea, and the wind shall cease immediately.' — BEDE, *Ecclesiastical History, bk. III, ch. 14*

[2]To man the earth seems altogether / No more a mother, but a stepdame rather. — DU BARTAS, *Divine Weeks and Works* [1578], *First Week, Third Day*

[3]He is born naked, and falls a-whining at the first. — ROBERT BURTON, *Anatomy of Melancholy* [1621–1651], *pt. I, sec. 2, member 3, subsec. 10*

[4]It is the common wonder of all men, how among so many millions of faces there should be none alike. — THOMAS BROWNE, *Religio Medici* [1643], *pt. II, sec. 2*

Of a thousand shavers, two do not shave so much alike as not to be distinguished. — SAMUEL JOHNSON [1777]; from BOSWELL, *Life of Johnson* [1791], *vol. II, p. 120* (Everyman edition)

[5]Ex Africa semper aliquid novi.
Quoted as a Greek proverb.

[6]Compare the modern proverb: Rats desert a sinking ship.

[7]Not unlike the bear which bringeth forth / In the end of thirty days a shapeless birth; / But after licking, it in shape she draws, / And by degrees she fashions out the paws, / The head, and neck, and finally doth bring / To a perfect beast that first deformed thing. — DU BARTAS, *Divine Weeks and Works* [1578], *First Week, First Day*

I had not time to lick it into form, as a bear doth her young ones. — ROBERT BURTON, *Anatomy of Melancholy* [1621–1651], *Democritus to the Reader*

[8]Cum grano salis.
Pompey's antidote against poison was "to be taken fasting, a grain of salt being added."

[9]The god delights in an odd number. — VIRGIL, *Eclogues, VIII, 75*

[10]Magister artis ingenique largitor venter.
Necessity, mother of invention. — WILLIAM WYCHERLEY [c 1640–1716], *Love in a Wood* [1671], *act III, sc. iii*

Art imitates Nature, and necessity is the mother of invention. — RICHARD FRANCK [c. 1624–1708], *Northern Memoirs* [written 1658, published 1694]

Sheer necessity — the proper parent of an art so nearly allied to invention. — R. B. SHERIDAN, *The Critic* [1779], *act I, sc. ii*

1   Tell, priests, what is gold doing in a holy place?
Satires, II, l. 69

2   Let them look upon virtue and pine because they have lost her.   *Satires, III, l. 38*

3   Meet the disease at its first stage.[1]
Satires, III, l. 64

Gaius Petronius
[Petronius Arbiter]
d. A.D. c. 66

4   He has joined the great majority.[2]
Satyricon, sec. 42

5   A man who is always ready to believe what is told him will never do well.
Satyricon, 43

6   One good turn deserves another.
Satyricon, 45

7   A man must have his faults.
Satyricon, 45

8   Not worth his salt.
Satyricon, 57

9   My heart was in my mouth.
Satyricon, 62

10   Beauty and wisdom are rarely conjoined.
Satyricon, 94

11   The studied spontaneity of Horace.[3]
Satyricon, 118

12   Natural curls.[4]   *Satyricon, 126*

Quintilian
[Marcus Fabius Quintilianus]
A.D. c. 35–c. 100

13   We give to necessity the praise of virtue.[5]
De Institutione Oratoria, bk. I, 8, 14

14   A liar should have a good memory.[6]
De Institutione Oratoria, IV, 2, 91

15   Vain hopes are often like the dreams of those who wake.   *De Institutione Oratoria, VI, 2, 30*

16   For it is feeling and force of imagination that makes us eloquent.[7]
De Institutione Oratoria, X, 7, 15

17   Those who wish to appear wise among fools, among the wise seem foolish.[8]
De Institutione Oratoria, X, 7, 21

Flavius Josephus[9]
[Joseph ben Matthias]
A.D. 37–95?

18   Everyone ought to worship God according to his own inclinations, and not to be constrained by force.   *Life, ch. 23*

19   While I am alive I shall never be in such slavery as to forgo my own kindred, or forget the laws of our forefathers.   *The Wars of the Jews, bk. VI, ch. 8*

Eleazar ben Jair[9]
d. A.D. 73

20   Let us spare nothing but our provisions. For they will be a testimonial when we are dead, that we were not subdued for want of necessaries; but that, according to our original resolution, we have preferred death before slavery.
Speech at Masada. From JOSEPHUS, *The Wars of the Jews, bk. VII, ch. 8*

Nero
[Lucius Domitius Ahenobarbus]
A.D. 37–68

21   What an artist dies with me![10]
From SUETONIUS, *The Lives of the Caesars, Nero, sec. 49*

---

[1]Venienti occurrite morbo.
A stitch in time saves nine. — *Proverb*

[2]Abiit ad plures.

[3]Horatii curiosa felicitas.

[4]Crines ingenio suo flexi.

[5]Seize the opportunity, I beg, and make a virtue of necessity [fac de necessitate virtutem]. — SAINT JEROME, *Letter 54*
Thus maketh vertue of necessitee. — CHAUCER, *Troilus and Criseyde* [c. 1385], *bk. IV, l. 1586*
Make a virtue of necessity. — ROBERT BURTON, *Anatomy of Melancholy* [1621–1651], *pt. III, sec. 3, member 4, subsec. I*

[6]He who has not a good memory should never take upon him the trade of lying. — MONTAIGNE, *Essays* [1580–1595], *bk. I, ch. 9, Of Liars*
Il faut bonne mémoire, après qu'on a menti [You must have a good memory after you have lied]. — PIERRE CORNEILLE, *Le Menteur* [1642], *act IV, sc. v*
Liars ought to have good memories. — ALGERNON SIDNEY, *Discourses on Government* [1698], *ch. 2, sec. 15*

[7]Pectus est enim, quod disertos facit.

[8]A fool with judges, amongst fools a judge. — WILLIAM COWPER, *Conversation* [1782], *l. 298*

[9]Translated by WILLIAM WHISTON.

[10]Qualis artifex pereo!

Lucan

A.D. 39–65

1   If the victor had the gods on his side, the vanquished had Cato.[1]   *The Civil War, bk. I, l. 128*

2   There stands the shadow of a glorious name.[2]
The Civil War, I, l. 135

3   Keep to moderation, keep the end in view, follow nature.[3]   *The Civil War, II, l. 381*

4   Thinking nothing done while anything remained to be done.[4]   *The Civil War, II, l. 657*

5   More was lost than mere life and existence.[5]
The Civil War, VII, l. 639

6   We all praise fidelity; but the true friend pays the penalty when he supports those whom Fortune crushes.   *The Civil War, VIII, l. 485*

7   A name illustrious and revered by nations.[6]
The Civil War, IX, l. 203

8   Is the dwelling place of God anywhere but in the earth and sea, the air and sky, and virtue? Why seek we further for deities? Whatever you see, whatever you touch, that is Jupiter.   *The Civil War, IX, l. 578*

9   The very ruins have been destroyed.[7]
The Civil War, IX, l. 969

Longinus

First century A.D.

10   It frequently happens that where the second line is sublime, the third, in which he [Lucan] meant to rise still higher, is perfect bombast.
On the Sublime, sec. 3

11   Sublimity is the echo of a noble mind.
On the Sublime, 9

12   In the Odyssey one may liken Homer to the setting sun, of which the grandeur remains without the intensity.   *On the Sublime, 9*

Martial[8]
[Marcus Valerius Martialis]

A.D. c. 40–c. 104

13   My poems are naughty, but my life is pure.[9]
Epigrams, bk. I, poem 4, l.

14   Tomorrow's life is too late. Live today.
Epigrams, I, 15, l.

15   Some good, some so-so, and lots plain bad that's how a book of poems is made, my friend.
Epigrams, I, 16, l.

16   I don't like you, Sabidius, I can't say why; But can say this: I don't like you, Sabidius.[10]
Epigrams, I, 32, l.

17   Stop abusing my verses, or publish some of your own.   *Epigrams, I, 91, l.*

18   You complain, friend Swift, of the length of m epigrams, but you yourself write nothing. Yours ar shorter.   *Epigrams, I, 110, l.*

19   Conceal a flaw, and the world will imagine th worst.   *Epigrams, III, 42, l.*

20   The bee is enclosed, and shines preserved in am ber, so that it seems enshrined in its own nectar.[11]
Epigrams, IV, 32, l.

21   They praise those verses, yes, but read some thing else.   *Epigrams, IV, 49, l. 1*

22   You ask what a nice girl will do? She won't giv an inch, but she won't say no.
Epigrams, IV, 71, l.

23   Our days pass by, and are scored against us.[12]
Epigrams, V, 20, l. 1.

24   A man who lives everywhere lives nowhere.
Epigrams, VII, 73, l. (

25 You puff the poets of other days,
The living you deplore.
Spare me the accolade: your praise
Is not worth dying for.   *Epigrams, VIII, 69, l.*

26   Virtue extends our days: he lives two lives who relives his past with pleasure.

Epigrams, X, 23, l. 8

---

[1]Victrix causa deis placuit, sed victa Catoni.

[2]Stat magni nominis umbra.

[3]Servare modum, finemque tenere, / Naturamque sequi.

[4]The reference is to Caesar.

[5]Plus est quam vita salusque / Quod perit.

[6]Clarum et venerabile nomen / Gentibus.
Cato's tribute to the fallen Pompey.

[7]Etiam periere ruinae.
The reference is to Troy.

---

[8]Translated by DUDLEY FITTS.

[9]Lasciva est nobis pagina, vita proba.

[10]See Tom Brown, 286:25.

[11]Whence we see spiders, flies, or ants entombed preserved for ever in amber, a more than royal tomb. — FRANCIS BACON, *Histo ria Vitae et Mortis* [1623], *Sylva Sylvarum, cent. I, exper. 100*
I saw a fly within a bead / Of amber cleanly buried. — ROBER HERRICK, *On a Fly Buried in Amber*

[12]Nobis pereunt et imputantur.

1   Neither fear your death's day nor long for it.
Epigrams, X, 47, l. 13

2   You'll get no laurel crown for outrunning a burro.   *Epigrams, XII, 36, l. 13*

3   You're obstinate, pliant, merry, morose, all at once. For me there's no living with you, or without you.[1]   *Epigrams, XII, 46, l. 1*

4   The country in town.[2]   *Epigrams, XII, 57, l. 21*

5   I know these are nothing.[3]
Epigrams, XIII, 2, l. 8

Titus Vespasianus
A.D. c. 41–81

6   Friends, I have lost a day.[4]
From SUETONIUS, *The Lives of the Caesars, Titus, sec. 8*

Plutarch
A.D. 46–120

7   As geographers, Sosius, crowd into the edges of their maps parts of the world which they do not know about, adding notes in the margin to the effect that beyond this lies nothing but sandy deserts full of wild beasts, and unapproachable bogs.[5]
Lives, Aemilius Paulus, sec. 5

8   A Roman divorced from his wife, being highly blamed by his friends, who demanded, "Was she not chaste? Was she not fair? Was she not fruitful?" holding out his shoe, asked them whether it was not new and well made. "Yet," added he, "none of you can tell where it pinches me."[6]
Lives, Aemilius Paulus, 29

9   Where the lion's skin will not reach, you must patch it out with the fox's.[7]   *Lives, Lysander, sec. 7*

10   Perseverance is more prevailing than violence; and many things which cannot be overcome when they are together, yield themselves up when taken little by little.   *Lives, Sertorius, sec. 16*

11   Medicine, to produce health, has to examine disease; and music, to create harmony, must investigate discord.   *Lives, Demetrius, sec. 1*

12   The very spring and root of honesty and virtue lie in good education.
Morals. On the Training of Children

13   It is indeed desirable to be well descended, but the glory belongs to our ancestors.
Morals. On the Training of Children

14   It is wise to be silent when occasion requires, and better than to speak, though never so well.[8]
Morals. On the Training of Children

15   An old doting fool, with one foot already in the grave.   *Morals. On the Training of Children*

16   He is a fool who leaves things close at hand to follow what is out of reach.[9]
Morals. On Garrulity

17   All men whilst they are awake are in one common world; but each of them, when he is asleep, is in a world of his own.[10]
Morals. On Superstition

18   Spintharus, speaking in commendation of Epaminondas, says he scarce ever met with any man who knew more and spoke less.
Morals. On Hearing, sec. 6

19   Antiphanes said merrily that in a certain city the cold was so intense that words were congealed as soon as spoken, but that after some time they thawed and became audible; so that the words spoken in winter were articulated next summer.
Morals. On Man's Progress in Virtue

20   When the candles are out all women are fair.[11]
Morals. Conjugal Precepts

---

[1]Difficilis facilis iucundus acerbus es idem: / Nec tecum possum vivere nec sine te.

[2]Rus in urbe.

[3]Nos haec novimus esse nihil.
Said of his own poems. The phrase was used by John Gay as an epigraph for *The Beggar's Opera* [1728].

[4]Amici, diem perdidi.

[5]So geographers, in Afric maps, / With savage pictures fill their gaps, / And o'er unhabitable downs / Place elephants for want of towns. — JONATHAN SWIFT, *On Poetry, A Rhapsody* [1733]

[6]The wearer knows where the shoe wrings. — GEORGE HERBERT, *Jacula Prudentum* [1651]
I can tell where my own shoe pinches me. — CERVANTES, *Don Quixote, pt. I* [1605], *bk. IV, ch. 5*

[7]The prince must be a lion, but he must also know how to play the fox. — MACHIAVELLI, *The Prince* [1532]

---

[8]Closed lips hurt no one, speaking may. — CATO THE CENSOR, *On Agriculture, bk. I, distich 12*

[9]Better one bird in hand than ten in the wood. — JOHN HEYWOOD, *Proverbs* [1546], *pt. I, ch. 2*
One bird in the hand is worth two in the wood. — THOMAS LODGE, *Rosalynde* [1590]
A bird in hand is worth two in the bush. — CERVANTES, *Don Quixote, pt. I* [1605], *bk. IV, ch. 4*
A feather in hand is better than a bird in the air. — GEORGE HERBERT, *Jacula Prudentum* [1651]

[10]A saying attributed to Heraclitus.

[11]When all candles be out, all cats be gray. — JOHN HEYWOOD, *Proverbs* [1546], *pt. I, ch. 5*

1   Like watermen, who look astern while they row the boat ahead.[1]

> *Morals. Whether 'Twas Rightfully Said, Live Concealed*

2   The great god Pan is dead.

> *Morals. Why the Oracles Cease to Give Answers*

3   I am whatever was, or is, or will be; and my veil no mortal ever took up.[2]

> *Morals. On Isis and Osiris*

4   For to err in opinion, though it be not the part of wise men, is at least human.

> *Morals. Against Colotes*

5   Pythagoras, when he was asked what time was, answered that it was the soul of this world.

> *Morals. Platonic Questions*

Epictetus[3]
A.D. c. 55–135

6   When you close your doors, and make darkness within, remember never to say that you are alone, for you are not alone;[4] nay, God is within, and your genius is within. And what need have they of light to see what you are doing?

> *Discourses, bk. I, ch. 14*

7   No thing great is created suddenly, any more than a bunch of grapes or a fig. If you tell me that you desire a fig, I answer you that there must be time. Let it first blossom, then bear fruit, then ripen.

> *Discourses, I, 15*

8   Any one thing in the creation is sufficient to demonstrate a Providence to a humble and grateful mind.

> *Discourses, I, 16*

9   Were I a nightingale, I would sing like a nightingale; were I a swan, like a swan. But as it is, I am a rational being, therefore I must sing hymns of praise to God.

> *Discourses, I, 16*

10   Practice yourself, for heaven's sake, in little things; and thence proceed to greater.

> *Discourses, I, 18*

11   Appearances to the mind are of four kinds. Things either are what they appear to be; or they neither are, nor appear to be; or they are, and do not appear to be; or they are not, and yet appear to be. Rightly to aim in all these cases is the wise man's task.

> *Discourses, I, 27*

12   Only the educated are free.   *Discourses, II, 1*

13   Shall I show you the sinews of a philosopher? "What sinews are those?"—A will undisappointed; evils avoided; powers daily exercised; careful resolutions; unerring decisions.

> *Discourses, II, 8*

14   What is the first business of one who practices philosophy? To get rid of self-conceit. For it is impossible for anyone to begin to learn that which he thinks he already knows.

> *Discourses, II, 17*

15   Be not swept off your feet by the vividness of the impression, but say, "Impression, wait for me a little. Let me see what you are and what you represent. Let me try you."

> *Discourses, II, 18*

16   First say to yourself what you would be; and then do what you have to do.

> *Discourses, III, 23*

17   Remember that you ought to behave in life as you would at a banquet. As something is being passed around it comes to you; stretch out your hand, take a portion of it politely. It passes on; do not detain it. Or it has not come to you yet; do not project your desire to meet it, but wait until it comes in front of you. So act toward children, so toward a wife, so toward office, so toward wealth.

> *The Encheiridion, 15*

18   Where do you suppose he got that high brow?

> *The Encheiridion, 22*

19   Everything has two handles—by one of which it ought to be carried and by the other not.[5]

> *The Encheiridion, 43*

Juvenal [Decimus Junius Juvenalis]
A.D. c. 55–c. 130

20   It is hard not to write satire.[6]

> *Satires, I, l. 30*

21   Honesty is praised and starves.[7]

> *Satires, I, l. 74*

---

[1]Like rowers, who advance backward.—MONTAIGNE, *Essays* [1580–1595], *Of Profit and Honor, bk. III, ch. I*

Like the watermen that row one way and look another.—ROBERT BURTON, *Anatomy of Melancholy* [1621–1651], *Democritus to the Reader*

[2]I am the things that are, and those that are to be, and those that have been. No one ever lifted my skirts; the fruit which I bore was the sun.—PROCLUS [c. 411–485], *On Plato's Timaeus* (inscription in the temple of Neith at Sais, in Egypt)

[3]Translated by W. A. OLDFATHER (Loeb Classical Library).

[4]Though in a wilderness, a man is never alone.—THOMAS BROWNE, *Religio Medici* [1643], *p. 82* (Everyman edition)

[5]There is a right and wrong handle to everything.—RUDOLF ERICH RASPE, *Travels of Baron Munchausen* [1785], *ch. 30*

[6]Difficile est saturam non scribere.

Translated by G. G. RAMSAY (Loeb Classical Library).

[7]Probitas laudatur et alget.

1   If nature refuses, indignation will produce verses.[1]
Satires, I, l. 79

2   All the doings of mankind, their wishes, fears, anger, pleasures, joys, and varied pursuits, form the motley subject of my book.   *Satires, I, l. 85*

3   Censure pardons the raven, but is visited upon the dove.[2]   *Satires, II, l. 63*

4   No one becomes depraved in a moment.[3]
Satires, II, l. 83

5   Grammarian, rhetorician, geometrician, painter, trainer, soothsayer, rope-dancer, physician, magician — he knows everything. Tell the hungry little Greek to go to heaven; he'll go.
Satires, III, l. 76

6   Bitter poverty has no harder pang than that it makes men ridiculous.[4]   *Satires, III, l. 152*

7   It is not easy for men to rise whose qualities are thwarted by poverty.   *Satires, III, l. 164*

8   We all live in a state of ambitious poverty.
Satires, III, l. 182

9   A rare bird on earth, comparable to a black swan.[5]
Satires, VI, l. 165

10   I wish it, I command it. Let my will take the place of reason.[6]   *Satires, VI, l. 223*

11   We are now suffering the evils of a long peace. Luxury, more deadly than war, broods over the city, and avenges a conquered world.[7] *Satires, VI, l. 292*

12   But who is to guard the guards themselves?[8]
Satires, VI, l. 347

13   An inveterate and incurable itch for writing besets many, and grows old in their sick hearts.
Satires, VII, l. 51

14   Count it the greatest sin to prefer life to honor, and for the sake of living to lose what makes life worth having.[9]   *Satires, VIII, l. 83*

15   The people that once bestowed commands, consulships, legions, and all else, now concerns itself no more, and longs eagerly for just two things — bread and circuses![10]   *Satires, X, l. 79*

16   Put Hannibal in the scales.[11]   *Satires, X, l. 147*

17   You should pray for a sound mind in a sound body.[12]   *Satires, X, l. 356*

18   For revenge is always the delight of a mean spirit, of a weak and petty mind! You may immediately draw proof of this — that no one rejoices more in revenge than a woman.   *Satires, XIII, l. 189*

19   The greatest reverence is due the young.[13]
Satires, XIV, l. 47

Cornelius Tacitus
A.D. c. 56–c. 120

20   The images of the most illustrious families . . . were carried before it [the bier of Julia]. Those of Brutus and Cassius were not displayed; but for that reason they shone with preeminent luster.
Annals, bk. III, 76

21   He had talents equal to business, and aspired no higher.   *Annals, VI, 39*

22   What is today supported by precedents will hereafter become a precedent.   *Annals, XI, 24*

23   [Of Petronius:] Arbiter of taste.[14]
Annals, XVI, 18

24   It is the rare fortune of these days that one may think what one likes and say what one thinks.
Histories, bk. I, 1

25   [Of Servius Galba:] He seemed more important than a private citizen while he was a private citizen, and in the opinion of all he was capable of rule — if he had not ruled.   *Histories, I, 49*

26   The desire for glory clings even to the best men longer than any other passion.[15]   *Histories, IV, 6*

27   The gods are on the side of the stronger.[16]
Histories, IV, 17

28   Whatever is unknown is taken for marvelous;[17] but now the limits of Britain are laid bare.
Agricola, sec. 30

---

[1] Si natura negat, facit indignatio versum.

[2] Dat veniam corvis, vexat censura columbas.

[3] Nemo repente fuit turpissimus.
Translated by GILBERT HIGHET.

[4] Nil habet infelix paupertas durius in se / Quam quod ridiculos homines facit.

[5] Rara avis in terris nigroque simillima cycno.

[6] Hoc volo, sic iubeo, sit pro ratione voluntas.

[7] Nunc patimur longae pacis mala, saevior armis / Luxuria incubuit victumque ulciscitur orbem.

[8] Sed quis custodiet ipsos / Custodes?
What an absurd idea — a guardian to need a guardian! — PLATO, *The Republic, bk. III, 403–E*

[9] Summum crede nefas animam praeferre pudori, / Et propter vitam vivendi perdere causas.

---

[10] Panem et circenses.

[11] Expende Hannibalem.

[12] Mens sana in corpore sano.

[13] Maxima debetur puero reverentia.

[14] Elegantiae arbiter.

[15] See Milton, 261:19.

[16] Deos fortioribus adesse.

[17] Omne ignotum pro magnifico est.

1   Where they make a desert, they call it peace.[1]
Agricola, 30

2   Think of your forefathers and posterity.[2]
Agricola, 32

3   Fortune favored him . . . in the opportune moment of his death.   *Agricola, 45*

Pliny the Younger
[Gaius Plinius Caecilius Secundus]
A.D. c. 61–c. 112

4   Modestus said of Regulus that he was "the biggest rascal that walks upon two legs."
Letters, bk. I, letter 5

5   There is nothing to write about, you say. Well then, write and let me know just this—that there is nothing to write about; or tell me in the good old style if you are well. That's right. I am quite well.
Letters, I, 11

6   An object in possession seldom retains the same charm that it had in pursuit.[3]   *Letters, II, 15*

7   He [Pliny the Elder] used to say that "no book was so bad but some good might be got out of it."[4]
Letters, III, 5

8   This expression of ours, "Father of a family."[5]
Letters, V, 19

9   That indolent but agreeable condition of doing nothing.[6]   *Letters, VIII, 9*

10   His only fault is that he has no fault.[7]
Letters, IX, 26

Suetonius
[Gaius Suetonius Tranquillus]
A.D. c. 69–c. 140

11   Hail, Emperor, we who are about to die salute you.[8]   *Lives of the Caesars, Claudius, 21*

---

[1]Calgacus, addressing the Britons at the battle of the Grampians, referring to the Romans.

[2]Et maiores vestros et posteros cogitate.

[3]It has been a thousand times observed, and I must observe it once more, that the hours we pass with happy prospects in view are more pleasing than those crowned with fruition—OLIVER GOLDSMITH, *The Vicar of Wakefield* [1766], *ch. 10*

[4]"There is no book so bad," said the bachelor, "but something good may be found in it."—CERVANTES, *Don Quixote*, pt. II [1615], *ch. 3*

[5]Paterfamilias.

[6]Dolce far niente [Sweet doing-nothing].—*Italian proverb*

[7]The greatest of faults, I should say, is to be conscious of none.—THOMAS CARLYLE, *On Heroes and Hero Worship* [1841], *The Hero as Prophet*

[8]Ave, Caesar, morituri te salutamus.

Hadrian
[Publius Aelius Hadrianus]
A.D. 76–138

12   Little soul, wandering, gentle guest and companion of the body, into what places will you now go, pale, stiff, and naked, no longer sporting as you did![9]   *Ad Animam Suam*

Chang Heng[10]
A.D. 78–139

13   Heaven is like an egg, and the earth is like the yolk of the egg.   *Saying*

Lucius Annaeus Florus
fl. 125

14   Each year new consuls and proconsuls are made; but not every year is a king or a poet born.[11]
De Qualitate Vitae, fragment 8

Ptolemy [Claudius Ptolemaeus][12]
c. 100–178

15   Everything that is hard to attain is easily assailed by the generality of men.
Tetrabiblos, bk. I, sec. 1

16   The length of life takes the leading place among inquiries about events following birth.
Tetrabiblos, III, 10

17   As material fortune is associated with the properties of the body, so honor belongs to those of the soul.   *Tetrabiblos, IV, 1*

18   There are three classes of friendship and enmity, since men are so disposed to one another either by preference or by need or through pleasure and pain.
Tetrabiblos, IV, 7

---

[9]Animula vagula blandula, / Hospes comesque corporis, / Quae nunc abibis in loca / Pallidula rigida nudula, / Nec ut soles dabis iocosi.

Amelette Ronsardelette, / mignonelette doucelette, / très chère hostesse de mon corps, / tu descens là bas foibelette, / pasle, maigrelette, seulete, / dans le froid Royaulme des mors.—PIERRE DE RONSARD, *A son âme* [dictated on his deathbed, December 27, 1585]

[10]From *Sources of Chinese Tradition* [1960], edited by WILLIAM THEODORE DE BARY.

[11]From this derived the proverb: Poeta nascitur, non fit (The poet is born, not made).

[12]Translated by F. E. ROBBINS (Loeb Classical Library).

Marcus Aurelius Antoninus[1]
121–180

1 This Being of mine, whatever it really is, consists of a little flesh, a little breath, and the part which governs. *Meditations, II, 2*

2 You will find rest from vain fancies if you perform every act in life as though it were your last. *Meditations, II, 5*

3 Remember that no man loses other life than that which he lives, nor lives other than that which he loses. *Meditations, II, 14*

4 Each thing is of like form from everlasting and comes round again in its cycle. *Meditations, II, 14*

5 The longest-lived and the shortest-lived man, when they come to die, lose one and the same thing. *Meditations, II, 14*

6 As for life, it is a battle and a sojourning in a strange land; but the fame that comes after is oblivion. *Meditations, II, 17*

7 Never esteem anything as of advantage to you that will make you break your word or lose your self-respect. *Meditations, III, 7*

8 By a tranquil mind I mean nothing else than a mind well ordered. *Meditations, IV, 3*

9 The universe is change; our life is what our thoughts make it. *Meditations, IV, 3*

10 How much time he gains who does not look to see what his neighbor says or does or thinks, but only at what he does himself, to make it just and holy. *Meditations, IV, 18*

11 Whatever is in any way beautiful hath its source of beauty in itself, and is complete in itself; praise forms no part of it. So it is none the worse nor the better for being praised. *Meditations, IV, 20*

12 All that is harmony for you, my Universe, is in harmony with me as well. Nothing that comes at the right time for you is too early or too late for me. Everything is fruit to me that your seasons bring, Nature. All things come of you, have their being in you, and return to you. *Meditations, IV, 23*

13 "Let your occupations be few," says the sage,[2] "if you would lead a tranquil life." *Meditations, IV, 24*

14 Love the little trade which you have learned, and be content with it. *Meditations, IV, 31*

15 All is ephemeral—fame and the famous as well. *Meditations, IV, 35*

16 Search men's governing principles, and consider the wise, what they shun and what they cleave to. *Meditations, IV, 38*

17 Time is a sort of river of passing events, and strong is its current; no sooner is a thing brought to sight than it is swept by and another takes its place, and this too will be swept away. *Meditations, IV, 43*

18 All that happens is as usual and familiar as the rose in spring and the crop in summer. *Meditations, IV, 44*

19 Mark how fleeting and paltry is the estate of man—yesterday in embryo, tomorrow a mummy or ashes. So for the hairsbreadth of time assigned to thee, live rationally, and part with life cheerfully, as drops the ripe olive, extolling the season that bore it and the tree that matured it. *Meditations, IV, 48*

20 In the morning, when you are sluggish about getting up, let this thought be present: "I am rising to a man's work." *Meditations, V, 1*

21 A man makes no noise over a good deed, but passes on to another as a vine to bear grapes again in season. *Meditations, V, 6*

22 Nothing happens to anybody which he is not fitted by nature to bear. *Meditations, V, 18*

23 Live with the gods. *Meditations, V, 27*

24 The controlling intelligence understands its own nature, and what it does, and whereon it works. *Meditations, VI, 5*

25 What is not good for the swarm is not good for the bee. *Meditations, VI, 54*

26 One universe made up of all that is; and one God in it all, and one principle of being, and one law, the reason, shared by all thinking creatures, and one truth. *Meditations, VII, 9*

27 It is man's peculiar duty to love even those who wrong him. *Meditations, VII, 22*

28 Very little is needed to make a happy life. *Meditations, VII, 67*

29 To change your mind and to follow him who sets you right is to be nonetheless the free agent that you were before. *Meditations, VIII, 16*

30 Look to the essence of a thing, whether it be a point of doctrine, of practice, or of interpretation. *Meditations, VIII, 22*

---

[1]Translated by MORRIS HICKEY MORGAN, with some adaptations.

[2]Democritus, *Fragment 3;* also quoted by Seneca in *On Anger, III, 6,* and *On the Happy Life, 13.*

1 Be not careless in deeds, nor confused in words, nor rambling in thought.
Meditations, VIII, 51

2 Think not disdainfully of death, but look on it with favor; for even death is one of the things that Nature wills.
Meditations, IX, 3

3 A wrongdoer is often a man who has left something undone, not always one who has done something.
Meditations, IX, 5

4 Blot out vain pomp; check impulse; quench appetite; keep reason under its own control.
Meditations, IX, 7

5 Whatever may befall you, it was preordained for you from everlasting.
Meditations, X, 5

Galen
129–199

6 The chief merit of language is clearness, and we know that nothing detracts so much from this as do unfamiliar terms.
On the Natural Faculties,[1] *bk. I, sec. 2*

7 It was, of course, a grand and impressive thing to do, to mistrust the obvious, and to pin one's faith in things which could not be seen!
On the Natural Faculties, I, 13

8 Praxiteles and Phidias . . . were unable to . . . reach and handle all portions of the material. It is not so, however, with nature. Every part of a bone she makes bone, every part of the flesh she makes flesh, and so with fat and all the rest; there is no part she has not touched, elaborated, and embellished.
On the Natural Faculties, II, 3

9 That which *is* grows, while that which *is not* becomes.
On the Natural Faculties, II, 3

Diogenes Laertius
fl. c. 200

10 Time is the image of eternity.
Plato, 41

11 There is a written and an unwritten law. The one by which we regulate our constitutions in our cities is the written law; that which arises from custom is the unwritten law.
Plato, 51

Tertullian
[Quintus Septimius Tertullianus]
c. 160–240

12 O witness of the soul naturally Christian.
Apologeticus, 17

13 See how these Christians love one another.[2]
Apologeticus, 39

14 We multiply whenever we are mown down by you; the blood of Christians is seed.[3]
Apologeticus, 50

15 Man is one name belonging to every nation upon earth. In them all is one soul though many tongues. Every country has its own language, yet the subjects of which the untutored soul speaks are the same everywhere.
Testimony of the Soul

16 Mother Church.[4]
Ad Martyras, 1

17 Truth persuades by teaching, but does not teach by persuading.
Adversus Valentinianos, 1

18 Truth does not blush.[5]
Adversus Valentinianos, 3

19 It is to be believed because it is absurd.[6]
De Carne Christi, 5

20 It is certain because it is impossible.[7]
De Carne Christi, 5

21 Out of the frying pan into the fire.[8]
De Carne Christi, 6

---

[2]Tertullian is sarcastically repeating what the enemies of Christianity are saying.

[3]Plures efficimur, quoties metimur a vobis; semen est sanguis christianorum.

This is often rendered as: The blood of the martyrs is the seed of the Church.

The Church of Christ has been founded by shedding its own blood, not that of others; by enduring outrage, not by inflicting it. Persecutions have made it grow; martyrdoms have crowned it. — SAINT JEROME, *letter 82*

The blood of martyrs is the seed of Christians. — LAURENS BEYERLINCK [1578–1627], *Magnum Theatrum Vitae Humanorum* [1665]

The seed of the Church, I mean the blood of primitive martyrs. — THOMAS FULLER, *Church History of Britain* [1655], *pt. IV, bk. I*

[4]Domina mater ecclesia.

[5]Veritas non erubescit.

[6]Prorsus credibile est, quia ineptum est.

[7]Certum est, quia impossible est.

This is called Tertullian's rule of faith. It is sometimes rendered as: Credo quia impossible [I believe because it is impossible]. Saint Augustine expresses the same idea in *Confessions, VI, 5, 7.*

[8]De calcaria in carbonarium.

Leap out of the frying pan into the fire. — JOHN HEYWOOD, *Proverbs* [1546], *pt. II, ch. 5*

---

[1]Translated by ARTHUR J. BROCK (Loeb Classical Library).

1 One man's religion neither harms nor helps another man. *Ad Scapulam, 2*

2 It is certainly no part of religion to compel religion. *Ad Scapulam, 2*

3 I must dispel vanity with vanity. *Adversus Marcionem, IV, 30*

The Sayings of Jesus
Third century

4 Jesus saith, Wherever there are two, they are not without God, and wherever there is one alone, I say, I am with him. Raise the stone, and there thou shalt find Me, cleave the wood and there am I.
The Oxyrhynchus Papyri,[1] Part 1 [1898], no. I, ΛΟΓΙΑ ΙΗΣΟΥ [Logia Iesou], logion 5

5 Jesus saith, Ye ask who are those that draw us to the kingdom, if the kingdom is in Heaven? . . . The fowls of the air, and all beasts that are under the earth or upon the earth, and the fishes of the sea, these are they which draw you, and the kingdom of Heaven is within you.
Oxyrhynchus Papyri, IV [1904], no. 654, New Sayings of Jesus, second saying

Saint Cyprian
d. 258

6 He cannot have God for his father who has not the Church for his Mother.[2]
De Unitate Ecclesiae [251], ch. 6

7 There is no salvation outside the Church.[3]
Letter 73 [c. 256]

Plotinus
205–270

8 All things are filled full of signs, and it is a wise man who can learn about one thing from another.
Enneads,[4] bk. II, treatise iii, sec. 7

9 One principle must make the universe a single complex living creature, one from all.
Enneads, II, iii, 8

Longus
Third century?

10 There was never any yet that wholly could escape love, and never shall there be any, never so long as beauty shall be, never so long as eyes can see.
Daphnis and Chloe, proem, ch. 2

11 He is so poor that he could not keep a dog.
Daphnis and Chloe, 15

Constantine [Flavius Valerius Aurelius Constantinus]
c. 285–337

12 In this sign shalt thou conquer.[5]
From EUSEBIUS, Life of Constantine, I, 28

Ammianus Marcellinus
c. 330–395

13 Rose among thorns. *History, bk. XVI, ch. 17*

Julian [the Apostate] [Flavius Claudius Julianus][6]
332–363

14 You have conquered, Galilean.[7]
From THEODORET, Church History, III, 20

Saint Ambrose
c. 340–397

15 When you are at Rome live in the Roman style; when you are elsewhere live as they live elsewhere.[8]
Advice to Saint Augustine. From JEREMY TAYLOR, Ductor Dubitantium [1660], I, 1, 5

---

[1]Translated and edited by BERNARD P. GRENFELL and ARTHUR H. HUNT, who also discovered the papyri. The *Logia* were first published [1897] as ΛΟΓΙΑ ΙΗΣΟΥ: *Sayings of Our Lord.*

[2]Habere non potest deum patrem qui ecclesiam non habet matrem.

[3]Salus extra ecclesiam non est.
Quoted by Saint Augustine in *De Baptismo,* hence sometimes attributed to him.

[4]Translated by A. H. ARMSTRONG (Loeb Classical Library).

[5]In hoc signo vinces.
The alleged words of Constantine's vision before his battle with Maxentius at Saxa Rubra, near Rome [312].

[6]Known as Julian the Apostate.

[7]Vicisti, Galilaee.
The Latin translation of the alleged dying words of the emperor.

[8]Si fueris Romae, Romano vivito more; / Si fueris alibi, vivito sicut ibi.
My mother, having joined me at Milan, found that the church there did not fast on Saturdays as at Rome, and was at a loss what to do. I consulted Saint Ambrose, of holy memory, who replied, "When I am at Rome, I fast on a Saturday; when I am at Milan, I do not. Follow the custom of the church where you are." — SAINT AUGUSTINE, *Epistle to Januarius (Epistle 2), sec. 18. Also Epistle to Casualanus (Epistle 36), sec. 32*
When in Rome, do as the Romans do. — *Proverb*

Saint Jerome[1]

c. 342–420

1   The friendship that can cease has never been real. *Letter 3*

2   It is easier to mend neglect than to quicken love. *Letter 7*

3   Love knows nothing of order. *Letter 7*

4   The fact is that my native land is a prey to barbarism, that in it men's only God is their belly, that they live only for the present, and that the richer a man is the holier he is held to be. *Letter 7*

5   An unstable pilot steers a leaking ship, and the blind is leading the blind straight to the pit. The ruler is like the ruled. *Letter 7*

6   No athlete is crowned but in the sweat of his brow. *Letter 14*

7   If there is but little water in the stream, it is the fault, not of the channel, but of the source. *Letter 17*

8   You are a Ciceronian, not a Christian.[2] *Letter 22*

9   It is idle to play the lyre for an ass.[3] *Letter 27*

10   The line, often adopted by strong men in controversy, of justifying the means by the end. *Letter 48*

11   Do not let your deeds belie your words, lest when you speak in church someone may say to himself, "Why do you not practice what you preach?"[4] *Letter 48*

12   Avoid, as you would the plague, a clergyman who is also a man of business.[5] *Letter 52*

13   A fat paunch never breeds fine thoughts.[6] *Letter 52*

14   That clergyman soon becomes an object of contempt who being often asked out to dinner never refuses to go. *Letter 52*

15   The best almoner is he who keeps back nothing for himself. *Letter 52*

16   It is worse still to be ignorant of your ignorance. *Letter 53*

17   Even brute beasts and wandering birds do not fall into the same traps or nets twice.[5] *Letter 54*

18   Sometimes the character of the mistress is inferred from the dress of her maids. *Letter 54*

19   The face is the mirror of the mind, and eyes without speaking confess the secrets of the heart. *Letter 54*

20   The scars of others should teach us caution. *Letter 54*

21   I have always revered not crude verbosity but holy simplicity.[7] *Letter 57*

22   When the stomach is full, it is easy to talk of fasting. *Letter 58*

23   The Roman world is falling,[8] yet we hold our heads erect instead of bowing our necks. *Letter 60*

24   Every day we are changing, every day we are dying, and yet we fancy ourselves eternal. *Letter 60*

25   Early impressions are hard to eradicate from the mind. When once wool has been dyed purple, who can restore it to its previous whiteness? *Letter 107*

26   Christians are not born but made.[9] *Letter 107*

27   The tired ox treads with a firmer step.[10] *Letter 112*

28   For they wished to fill the winepress of eloquence not with the tendrils of mere words but with the rich grape juice of good sense. *Letter 125*

29   Preferring to store her money in the stomachs of the needy rather than hide it in a purse.[5] *Letter 127*

30   The privileges of a few do not make common law.[11] *Exposition on Jona*

---

[1] Translated by W. H. FREMANTLE.

[2] This was addressed to Jerome in a dream by Christ the Judge, censuring him for loving the classics more than the Fathers.

[3] A Greek proverb frequently quoted by Jerome.

[4] Cur ergo haec ipse non facis?

[5] Translated by F. A. WRIGHT (Loeb Classical Library).

[6] This is a Greek proverb.

Fat paunches have lean pates, and dainty bits / Make rich the ribs, but bankrupt quite the wits. — SHAKESPEARE, *Love's Labour's Lost*, act I, sc. i, l. 26

---

[7] Venerationi mihi semper fuit non verbosa rusticas sed sancta simplicitas.

[8] Romanus orbis ruit.

[9] Fiunt, non nascuntur Christiani.

[10] An old Roman proverb quoted by Saint Jerome to Saint Augustine.

[11] Privilegia paucorum non faciunt legem.

1   Never look a gift horse in the mouth.[1]
On the Epistle to the Ephesians

Saint John Chrysostom
c. 345–407

2   Hell is paved with priests' skulls.
De Sacerdotio [c. 390]

3   No one can harm the man who does himself no wrong.[2]
Letter to Olympia

Vegetius [Flavius Vegetius Renatus]
fl. c. 375

4   Let him who desires peace prepare for war.[3]
De Rei Militari, III, prologue

Saint Augustine
354–430

5   The weakness of little children's limbs is innocent, not their souls.
Confessions [397–401], I, 7

6   To Carthage I came, where all about me resounded a caldron of dissolute loves.
Confessions, III, 1

7   I was in love with loving.   *Confessions, III, 1*

8   In the usual course of study I had come to a book of a certain Cicero.   *Confessions, III, 4*

9   Give me chastity and continence, but not just now.
Confessions, VIII, 7

10   Take up, read! Take up, read![4]
Confessions, VIII, 12

11   Too late I loved you, O Beauty ever ancient and ever new! Too late I loved you! And, behold, you were within me, and I out of myself, and there I searched for you.   *Confessions, X, 27*

12   Give what you command, and command what you will.   *Confessions, X, 29*

13   Hear the other side.[5]
De Duabus Animabus, XIV, 2

14   I would not have believed the gospel had not the authority of the Church moved me.
Contra Epistulam Fundamenti [c. 410], ch. 5

15   Necessity has no law.
Soliloquiorum. Animae ad Deum [c. 410], 2

16   We make a ladder of our vices, if we trample those same vices underfoot.   *Sermones, 3*

17   Anger is a weed; hate is the tree.
Sermones, 58

18   The dove loves when it quarrels; the wolf hates when it flatters.   *Sermones, 64*

19   Rome has spoken; the case is closed.[6]
Sermones, 131

20   He who created you without you will not justify you without you.   *Sermones, 169*

21   The most glorious city of God.
De Civitate Dei [415], I, preface

22   Two cities have been formed by two loves: the earthly by the love of self, even to the contempt of God; the heavenly by the love of God, even to the contempt of self.   *De Civitate Dei, XIV, 28*

Saint Vincent of Lérins
d. c. 450

23   [That faith is catholic] which has been believed always, everywhere, and by all.[7]
Commonitorium, ch. 2

24   Every word [of Tertullian] almost was a sentence; every sentence a victory.
Commonitorium, 18

Saint Remy [Remigius]
c. 438–c. 533

25   Henceforward burn what thou hast worshipped, and worship what thou hast burned.
Said to Clovis at his baptism [496]

Clovis
466–511

26   God of Clotilda,[8] if you grant me victory I shall become a Christian.[9]
Legendary vow before battle

---

[1]Noli equi dentes inspicere donati.

[2]No one is injured save by himself. —ERASMUS, *Adagia*

[3]Qui desiderat pacem, praeparet bellum.

[4]Tolle lege, tolle lege.
What the bell seemed to say to Augustine at the moment of his conversion. When he opened the Bible, his eyes fell on *Romans 13:12–14*, 43:26.

[5]Audi partem alteram.

---

[6]Roma locuta est; causa finita est.

[7]Quod semper, quod ubique, quod ab omnibus creditum est.
The definition of the traditional articles of faith.

[8]Saint Clotilda, wife of Clovis.

[9]Clovis defeated the Alemanni in 496, and following his vow was baptized with three thousand followers by Saint Remy at Rheims.

Saint Benedict
480–543

1   We are therefore about to establish a school of the Lord's service in which we hope to introduce nothing harsh or burdensome.
Rule of Saint Benedict, prologue

Boethius
[Anicius Manlius Severinus]
480–524

2   In every adversity of fortune, to have been happy is the most unhappy kind of misfortune.
De Consolatione Philosophiae, bk. II, 4, 4

3   Who hath so entire happiness that he is not in some part offended with the condition of his estate?
De Consolatione Philosophiae, II, 4, 41

4   Nothing is miserable but what is thought so, and contrariwise, every estate is happy if he that bears it be content.
De Consolatione Philosophiae, II, 4, 64

5 From thee, great God, we spring, to thee we tend—
Path, motive, guide, original and end.[1]
De Consolatione Philosophiae, III, 9, 27

6   Who can give law to lovers? Love is a greater law to itself.
De Consolatione Philosophiae, III, 12, 47

Pope Gregory I
540–604

7   [They answered that they were called Angles.] It is well, for they have the faces of angels, and such should be the co-heirs of the angels in heaven.[2]
From Bede, *Ecclesiastical History of the English People, II, 1*

Talmud
compiled c. sixth century A.D.

8   The day is short, the labor long, the workers are idle, and reward is great, and the Master is urgent.
Mishna. The Wisdom of the Fathers

9   Whoever destroys a single life is as guilty as though he had destroyed the entire world; and whoever rescues a single life earns as much merit as though he had rescued the entire world.
Mishna. Sanhedrin

Ali ibn-Abi-Talib[3]
c. 602–661

10 He who has a thousand friends has not a friend to spare,
And he who has one enemy will meet him everywhere.
A Hundred Sayings

The Koran[4]

11   In the name of the most merciful God: Praise be to God, the Lord of all Being; the most merciful, the Master of the day of judgment. Thee do we worship, and of Thee do we beg assistance. Direct us in the right path, in the path of those to whom Thou hast been gracious; not of those against whom Thou art incensed, nor of those who go astray.
Chapter 1, verses 1–3

12   Do not veil the truth with falsehood, nor conceal the truth knowingly.
2:42

13   We believe in God, and in that which has been sent down on us and sent down on Abraham, Ishmael, Isaac and Jacob, and the Tribes, and that which was given to Moses and Jesus and the Prophets, of their Lord; we make no division between any of them, and to Him we surrender.[5]
2:135–136

14   A believing slave is better than an idolater, even though ye admire him.
2:221

15   God will not take you to task for vain words in your oaths, but He will take you to task for what your hearts have amassed.
2:225

---

[1]Translated by Samuel Johnson, and used as motto to *The Rambler, no. 7* [1750].

[2]Traditionally quoted "Non Angli sed angeli" (Not Angles but angels), these were the words of Pope Gregory when he beheld two English slaves in a Roman slave market.

[3]Ali ibn-Abi-Talib, son-in-law of Muhammad and fourth caliph, who was called the Lion of God, was murdered in 661.

[4]Also spelled Qur'an; Quran. Muslims believe that the Koran is of divine origin, revealed by God to the prophet Muhammad [c. 570–632].

The word Koran, derived from the verb *karaa, to read,* signifies properly in Arabic "the reading," or rather, "that which ought to be read." . . . The Koran is divided into 114 larger portions of very unequal length, which we call chapters, but the Arabians *sowar,* in the singular *sura,* a word rarely used on any other occasion.—
George Sale, *The Koran* [1734], *The Preliminary Discourse, sec. III*

Translations by George Sale [1734], E. H. Palmer [1900], J. M. Rodwell [1909], Richard Bell [1927], M. M. Pickthall [1953], and A. J. Arberry [1955], edited and adapted by Sari Nuseibah.

[5]"Surrender" is the literal translation of the word Islam.

1   I [Muhammad] have no power over benefit or hurt to myself except as God willeth . . . I am only a warner, and a bringer of good tidings to a people who believe.   *7:188*

2   God sufficeth me: there is no God but He. In Him I put my trust.   *9:129*

3   In the alternation of night and day, and what God has created in the heavens and the earth—surely there are signs for a god-fearing people.   *10:6*

4   Surely God wrongs not men, but themselves men wrong.   *10:44*

5   Not so much as the weight of an ant in earth or heaven escapes from the Lord, neither is aught smaller than that, or greater, but is clearly written in God's book.   *10:61*

6   God changes not what is in a people, until they change what is in themselves.   *13:11*

7   We [God] never sent a messenger save with the language of his folk, that he might make (the message)[1] clear for them.   *14:4*

8   Seest thou not how God hath coined a parable? A good word is like a good tree whose root is firmly fixed, and whose top is in the sky. And it produces its edible fruit every season, by the permission of its Lord. . . . And a corrupt word is like a corrupt tree which has been torn off the ground, and has no fixity. God makes those who believe stand firm in this life and the next by His firm Word.   *14:24–27*

9   Our [God's] word to a thing when We will it, is but to say, "Be," and it is.   *16:40*

10   Glory be to Him who carried His servant by night from the sacred temple of Mecca to the temple of Jerusalem that is more remote, whose precinct We have blessed, that We might show him of Our tokens.   *17:1*

11   Thy Lord hath decreed that ye worship none save Him, and (that ye show) kindness to parents. . . . Lower unto them the wing of submission through mercy, and say, "My Lord, have mercy on them both as they took care of me when I was little."   *17:23–24*

12   Walk not on the earth exultantly, for thou canst not cleave the earth, neither shalt thou reach to the mountains in height.   *17:37*

13   They will question thee concerning the soul. Say: "The soul is the concern of my Lord, and you have been given of knowledge but a little."   *17:85*

14   They say: "We will not believe thee till thou makest a spring to gush forth from the earth for us, or . . . bringest God and the angels as a surety." . . . And naught prevented men from believing when the guidance came to them, but that they said, "Has God sent forth a mortal as messenger?" Say: "Had there been in the earth angels walking at peace, We would have sent down upon them out of heaven an angel as messenger."   *17:90–95*

15   And do not say, regarding anything, "I am going to do that tomorrow," but only, "if God will."[2]   *18:23–24*

16   Wealth and children are the adornment of this present life: but good works, which are lasting, are better in the sight of thy Lord as to recompense, and better as to hope.   *18:46*

17   Man says: "How is it possible, when I am dead, that I shall then be brought forth alive?" Does he not remember that We have created him once, and that he was nothing then?   *19:66–67*

18   Do not the unbelievers see that the skies and the earth were both a solid mass, and that We clave them asunder, and that by means of water We give life to everything? Will they not then believe?   *21:30*

19   O men, if you are in doubt as to the Resurrection, surely We created you of dust, then of a sperm drop, then of a blood clot, then of a lump of flesh. . . . And thou beholdest the earth blackened; then, when We send down water upon it, it quivers, and swells, and puts forth herbs of every joyous kind.   *22:5*

20   We [God] charge not any soul save to its ability.   *23:62*

21   God is the light of the heavens and of the earth. His light is like a niche in which is a lamp—the lamp encased in glass—the glass, as it were, a glistening star. From a blessed tree it is lighted, the olive neither from the East nor of the West, whose oil would well nigh shine out, even though fire touched it not. It is light upon light. God guideth whom He will to His light, and God setteth forth parables to men.   *24:35*

22   As for the unbelievers, their works are as a mirage in a spacious plain which the man athirst supposes to be water, till, when he comes to it, he finds it is nothing; there indeed he finds God, and He pays him his account in full; and God is swift at the reckoning.

Or they are as shadows upon a sea obscure, covered by a billow above which is a billow, above

---

[1]Throughout the Koran, parentheses indicate additions to the Arabic.

[2]In Arabic: Inshallah.

which are clouds, shadows piled upon one another; when he puts forth his hand, wellnigh he cannot see it. And to whomsoever God assigns no light, no light has he.   *24:39–40*

1   Thou seest the mountains and thou deemest them affixed, (verily) they are as fleeting as the clouds.
27:88

2   Thou truly canst not guide whom thou lovest; but God guideth whom He will; and He best knoweth those who yield to guidance.   *28:55*

3   The present life is naught but a diversion and a sport; surely the Last Abode is Life, did they but know.   *29:64*

4   Whosoever surrenders his face to God and performs good deeds, he verily has grasped the surest handle, and unto God is the sequel of all things.
31:22

5   If whatever trees are in the earth were pens, and He should after that swell the seas into seven seas of ink, the Words of God would not be exhausted.
31:27

6   We offered this trust[1] to the heavens and the earth and the mountains, but they were humbled by it, and shrank from bearing it. Yet, man bore it. Truly he is ever in the darkness of injustice, and of ignorance.   *33:72*

7   He makes the night seep into the day, and makes the day seep into the night; He has subordinated the sun and the moon, making each of them journey towards a preordained time.   *35:13*

8   And on that day no soul shall be wronged at all, nor shall ye be rewarded for aught but that which ye have done.   *36:54*

9   They say: "We only have the life of this world. We die and we live, and nothing destroys us but time." Yet, not true knowledge have they of this; only belief.   *45:24*

10   O true believers, let not men laugh other men to scorn, who peradventure may be better than themselves. . . . Neither let the one of you speak ill of another in his absence.   *49:10–13*

11   The Arabs of the desert say, We believe. Answer, Ye do by no means believe; but say, We have embraced Islam: for the faith hath not yet entered into your hearts.   *49:14*

12   We [God] created Man, and We know what his soul whispereth within him; and We are nearer unto him than his jugular vein.   *50:16*

13   The heart of Muhammad did not falsely represent that which he saw. Will you therefore dispute with him concerning that which he saw?
53:11–12

14   O tribe of spirits and of men, if you are able to slip through the parameters of the skies and the earth, then do so. You shall not pass through them save with My [the Lord's] authority.   *55:33*

15   He is the first and the last, the manifest and the hidden: and He knoweth all things.   *57:3*

16   Let every soul look upon the morrow for the deed it has performed.   *59:18*

17   Is he, therefore, who goeth groveling upon his face, better directed than he who walketh upright in a straight way?   *67:22*

18   Man is a witness unto his deeds.   *75:14*

19   Recite: In the name of thy Lord who created, Created Man of a blood clot.
Recite: And thy Lord is the most Generous, who taught by the Pen, Taught Man that he knew not.   *96:1–5*

20   Whoso has done an atom's weight of good shall see it; and whoso has done an atom's weight of evil shall see it.   *99:7–8*

21   Say: "He is God, One God, the Everlasting Refuge, who has not begotten, and has not been begotten, and equal to Him is not anyone."
112

Anonymous: Early Miscellaneous

22   Whatever kind of word thou speakest the like shalt thou hear.
The Greek Anthology,[2] bk. IX, 382

23   Envy slays itself by its own arrows.
The Greek Anthology, X, 111

24   Give a sop to Cerberus.
Greek and Roman saying

25   Give me today, and take tomorrow.
Quoted, and condemned, by Saint Chrysostom

26   Keep a green tree in your heart and perhaps the singing bird will come.   *Chinese proverb*

27   On the day of victory no one is tired.
Arab proverb

28   Death is afraid of him because he has the heart of a lion.   *Arab proverb*

---

[1]The message conveyed in the Koran.

[2]Translated by W. R. PATON (Loeb Classical Library).

1   I came to the place of my birth, and cried, "The friends of my youth, where are they?" And echo answered, "Where are they?"   *Arab saying*

2   If you have two loaves of bread, sell one and buy a hyacinth.   *Persian saying*[1]

3 If only, when one heard
That Old Age was coming
One could bolt the door,
Answer "Not at home"
And refuse to meet him!
    Kokinshu (Collection of Ancient and Modern Poems) [905][2]

Anonymous: Latin

4   Ab urbe condita [Since the founding of the city (Rome)].   *Saying*

5   Absit omen [May it not be an omen].
    Saying

6   Acta est fabula [The play is over].
    Said at ancient dramatic performances and quoted by Augustus on his deathbed

7   Actus non facit reum, nisi mens sit rea [The act is not criminal unless the intent is criminal].
    Legal maxim

8   Ad astra per aspera [To the stars through hardships].   *Proverb*

9 Adeste, fideles,
Laeti triumphantes;
Venite, venite in Bethlehem.

[O come, all ye faithful,
Joyful and triumphant,
O come ye, O come ye to Bethlehem.]
    Hymn [18th century]

10   Anno aetatis suae . . . [In the year of his age].
    Phrase

11   Bis dat qui cito dat [He gives twice who gives promptly].   *Saying*

12   Cave ab homine unius libri [Beware the man of one book].
    Quoted by ISAAC D'ISRAELI in Curiosities of Literature [1791–1793]

13   Cave canem [Beware of the dog].   *Proverb*

14   Caveat emptor [Let the buyer beware].
    Proverb

15   Cras amet qui nunquam amavit quique amavit cras amet [Tomorrow let him love who has never loved and tomorrow let him who has loved love].
    Pervigilium Veneris [c. 350], refrain

16   Cucullus non facit monachum [The cowl does not make a monk].[3]   *Medieval proverb*

17   Cuius regio eius religio [He who controls the area controls the religion].   *Proverb*

18   De gustibus non disputandum [There is no accounting for tastes].   *Proverb*

19   De minimis non curat lex [The law is not concerned with trifles].   *Legal maxim*

20   Deus vult [God wills it].
    Motto of the Crusades [1095]

21   Dis manibus sacrum[4] [Sacred to the departed spirit(s)].   *Tombstone inscription*

22   Divide et impera [Divide and rule].
    Ancient political maxim cited by MACHIAVELLI

23   Errare humanum est [To err is human].
    Saying

24   Et in Arcadia ego [I too am in Arcadia].[5]
    Inscription on a tomb in a painting [c. 1623] by GUERCINO [1591–1666]

25   Ex ungue leonem (From his claw one can tell a lion].[6]   *Saying*

26   Fiat justitia ruat coelum [Let justice be done though heaven should fall].[7]
    Proverb, sometimes attributed to LUCIUS CALPURNIUS PISO CAESONINUS [d. 43 B.C.]

27   Finis coronat opus [The end crowns the work].
    Saying

28   Flagrante delicto ["Red-handed"].
    Saying

29   Fluctuat nec mergitur (It tosses but doesn't sink).
    Saying

30 Gaudeamus igitur,
Iuvenes dum sumus.

---

[1]Quoted also as a Chinese or Greek saying, and in various versions, including: If you have two pieces of silver, take one and buy a lily.

[2]Translated by ARTHUR WALEY in *Anthology of Japanese Literature* [1955], edited by DONALD KEENE.

[3]It takes more than a hood and sad eyes to make a monk. — *Albanian proverb*

[4]Abbreviated DMS.

[5]That is, Even in Arcadia there am I [Death].

[6]Literally: From the claw a lion.
See Herodotus, 71:18.

[7]Also familiar as: Fiat justitia et ruant coeli [Let justice be done though the heavens fall].
    And as: Fiat justitia et pereat mundus [Let justice be done though the world perish].

[Let us live then and be glad
While young life is before us.]

Students' song [c. 1267]

1   Habeas corpus [You are to produce the person[1]].
Legal phrase

2   Hannibal ad portas [Hannibal is at the gates]!
Saying

3   In vino veritas [In wine is truth].
Proverb quoted by PLATO, *Symposium 217*

4   Ipse dixit [He himself said it].   *Phrase of "proof"*

5   Ius est ars boni et aequi [Legal justice is the art of the good and the fair].   *Saying*

6   Mater artium necessitas [Necessity is the mother of invention].   *Saying*

7   Mors ultima ratio [Death is the final accounting].   *Saying*

8   Nemo me impune lacessit [No one provokes me with impunity].
Motto of the Crown of Scotland

9   Nihil nimis [Nothing in excess].[2]   *Saying*

10   Non multa sed multum [Not many but much].[3]
Proverb

11   Orate est laborare, laborare est orare [To pray is to work, to work is to pray].
Ancient motto of the Benedictine order

12   Parvis e glandibus quercus [Tall oaks from little acorns grow].   *Saying*

13   Pereant qui nostra ante nos dixerunt [May they perish who have used our words before us].
Saying

14   Piscem natare doces [You're teaching a fish to swim].   *Saying*

15   Post coitum omne animal triste [Every creature is sad after coitus].   *Saying*

16   Post hoc, ergo propter hoc [After this, therefore because of this].   *Definition of fallacy in logic*

17   Primus inter pares [First among equals].
Saying

18   Pro bono publico [For the public good].
Saying

19   Quos [or Quem] deus vult perdere prius dementat [Those whom God wishes to destroy, he first makes mad].   *Saying*

20   Requiescat in pace[4] [May he rest in peace; May she rest in peace].   *Saying*

21   Res iudicata pro veritate habetur [A matter that has been legally decided is considered true].
Legal maxim

22   Ruat coelum, fiat voluntas tua [Though heaven should fall, let thy will be done].   *Proverb*

23   Semper fidelis [Ever faithful].   *Saying*

24   Sic semper tyrannis[5] [Thus always to tyrants].
Saying

25   Sit tibi terra levis[6] [May the earth rest lightly on you].   *Tombstone inscription*

26   Summum ius summa iniuria [Extreme justice is extreme injustice].[7]
Legal maxim cited by CICERO *in De Officiis, I, 10, 33*

27   Tempora mutantur, nos et mutamur in illis [Times change, and we change with them too].[8]
From OWEN'S *Epigrammata [1615]*

28   Testis unus testis nullus [A single witness is no witness].   *Legal maxim*

29   Ubi bene ibi patria [Where one is happy, there's one's homeland].   *Saying*

30   Urbi et orbi [To the city[9] and to the world].
Apostolic blessing

31   Vade in pace [Go in peace].
End of confessional absolution

32   Vae victis [Woe to the conquered]!
From LIVY, *History, bk. V, sec. 48, as said by Brennus to the Romans*

33   Volenti non fit iniuria [To a person who consents no injustice is done].   *Legal maxim*

Bede [Venerable Bede]

c. 672–c. 735

34   No reptiles are found there [in Ireland], and no snake can live there; for, though often carried thither out of Britain, as soon as the ship comes near the shore, and the scent of the air reaches them, they die.
Ecclesiastical History of the English People, bk. I, ch. 1

---

[1]The person of the accused.

[2]Also quoted as: Ne quid nimis.

[3]I.e., Not quantity but quality.

[4]Abbreviated RIP.

[5]Motto of Virginia.

[6]Abbreviated STTL.

[7]I.e., Extreme legal justice.

[8]Translated by JOHN OWEN in *Epigrams* [1615]. Also quoted by RAPHAEL HOLINSHED in *Chronicles of England* [1578].

[9]Rome.

1   The present life of man, O king, seems to me, in comparison of that time which is unknown to us, like to the swift flight of a sparrow through the room wherein you sit at supper in winter, with your commanders and ministers, and a good fire in the midst, whilst the storms of rain and snow prevail abroad; the sparrow, I say, flying in at one door, and immediately out at another, whilst he is within, is safe from the wintry storm; but after a short space of fair weather, he immediately vanishes out of your sight, into the dark winter from which he had emerged. So this life of man appears for a short space, but of what went before, or what is to follow, we are utterly ignorant.

Ecclesiastical History of the English People,
II, 13

Saint John of Damascus
c. 675–c. 749

2   God is a sea of infinite substance.[1]

De Fide Orthodoxa, bk. I, ch. 9

Alcuin
c. 732–804

3   The voice of the people is the voice of God [Vox populi vox Dei].   *Letter to Charlemagne [A.D. 800]*

4 Here halt, I pray you, make a little stay,
O wayfarer, to read what I have writ,
And know by my fate what thy fate shall be.
What thou art now, wayfarer, world renowned,
I was: what I am now, so shall thou be.
The world's delight I followed with a heart
Unsatisfied: ashes am I, and dust.

His own epitaph[2]

5   Alcuin was my name: learning I loved.

His own epitaph

Ono no Komachi
Ninth century

6 The flowers withered,
Their color faded away,
While meaninglessly
I spent my days in the world
And the long rains were falling.

Kokinshu [905][3]

7 This night of no moon
There is no way to meet him.
I rise in longing—
My breast pounds, a leaping flame,
My heart is consumed in fire.   *Kokinshu*

Ching Hao
fl. 925

8   There are Six Essentials in painting. The first is called *spirit;* the second, *rhythm;* the third, *thought;* the fourth, *scenery;* the fifth, the *brush;* and the last is the *ink.*   *Notes on Brushwork[4]*

9   Resemblance reproduces the formal aspect of objects, but neglects their spirit; truth shows the spirit and substance in like perfection.

Notes on Brushwork

Murasaki Shikibu
c. 978–c. 1031

10   [The art of the novel] happens because the storyteller's own experience of men and things, whether for good or ill—not only what he has passed through himself, but even events which he has only witnessed or been told of—has moved him to an emotion so passionate that he can no longer keep it shut up in his heart.

The Tale of Genji [c. 1000][5]

11   Anything whatsoever may become the subject of a novel, provided only that it happens in this mundane life and not in some fairyland beyond our human ken.   *The Tale of Genji*

The Primary Chronicle[6]
1040–1118

12   The Chuds, the Slavs and the Krivchians then said to the peoples of Rus: "Our whole land is great and rich, but there is no order in it. Come to rule and reign over us."

Annal for the years 860–862: Invitation of the
Varangians to Novgorod

---

[4]From *The Spirit of the Brush,* translated by SHIO SAKANISHI [Wisdom of the East Series, 1957].

[5]Translated by ARTHUR WALEY.

[6]The earliest of the Russian chronicles or annals, begun in 1040 and continued through 1118 by various annalists, gives the record of Russian history since 852. It was copied several times and incorporated into later chronicles as the beginning. These quotations are from the Laurentian version, copied in 1377, translated by SAMUEL CROSS.

---

[1]This is the most frequently quoted definition of God in the Middle Ages. It is based on SAINT GREGORY OF NAZIANZUS [c. 330–390], *Oration 38.*

[2]Translated by HELEN WADDELL.

[3]Translated by DONALD KEENE in his *Anthology of Japanese Literature* [1955].

1   Then we went to Greece, and the Greeks led us to the edifices where they worship their God, and we knew not whether we were in heaven or on earth. For on earth there is no such splendor or such beauty, and we are at a loss how to describe it. We only know that God dwells there among men, and their service is fairer than the ceremonies of other nations.
Annal for the year 987: Vladimir's Christianization of Russia

2   It is the Russians' joy to drink; we cannot do without it.
Annal for the year 987: Vladimir's Christianization of Russia

Saint Anselm
c. 1033–1109

3   God is that, the greater than which cannot be conceived.[1]   *Proslogion, ch. 3*

Abu Muhammad al-Kasim al-Hariri
1054–1122

4 We praise Thee, O God,
For whatever perspicuity of language Thou hast taught us
And whatever eloquence Thou hast inspired us with.   *Makamat. Prayer*

Peter Abelard
1079–1142

5 O what their joy and their glory must be,
Those endless sabbaths the blessed ones see![2]
Hymnus Paraclitensis

6   Against the disease of writing one must take special precautions, since it is a dangerous and contagious disease.   *Letter 8, Abelard to Héloise*

Saint Bernard
1091–1153

7   You will find something more in woods than in books. Trees and stones will teach you that which you can never learn from masters.   *Epistle 106*

---

8   I have liberated my soul.[3]   *Epistle 371*

9   Hell is full of good intentions or desires.[4]
Attributed. From Saint Francis de Sales, *Letter 74*

Héloise
c. 1098–c. 1164

10   Riches and power are but gifts of blind fate, whereas goodness is the result of one's own merits.
Letter 2, Héloise to Abelard

Song of Roland
Eleventh century

11   Friend Roland, sound your horn.[5]
La Chanson de Roland, l. 1070

12   Roland is valorous and Oliver is wise.[6]
La Chanson de Roland, l. 1093

Poem of the Cid[7]
Twelfth century

13   Were his lord but worthy, God, how fine a vassal.
l. 20

14   Thus parted the one from the others as the nail from the flesh.   *l. 375*

15   Who serves a good lord lives always in luxury.
l. 850

16   One would grow poor staying in one place always.
l. 948

Frederick I [Barbarossa]
c. 1122–1190

17   An emperor is subject to no one but God and Justice.
From Julius Wilhelm Zincgref, *Apophthegmata, bk. I [1626]*

---

[1]This is commonly referred to as the ontological argument for the existence of God, and derives from Saint Augustine, *De Doctrina Christiana, bk. I, ch. 7.* It is also to be found in René Descartes, *Third Meditation.*

[2]O quanta qualia sunt illa sabbata, / Quae semper celebrat superna curia.
Translated by John Mason Neale [1884].

[3]Liberavi animam meam.

[4]Hell is full of good meanings and wishings. — George Herbert, *Jacula Prudentum* [1651], *no. 170*
Hell is paved with good intentions. — John Ray, *English Proverbs* [1670]
Hell is paved with good intentions, not with bad ones. — George Bernard Shaw, *Maxims for Revolutionists*

[5]Compagnon Roland, sonnez de votre oliphant.

[6]Roland est preux et Oliver est sage.
A Roland for an Oliver — i.e., a blow for a blow, tit for tat, referring to the drawn combat between Roland and Oliver.

[7]Translated by W. S. Merwin.

Averroës
1126–1198

1   Knowledge is the conformity of the object and the intellect.   *Destructio Destructionum*

Henry II
1133–1189

2   Who will free me from this turbulent priest?[1]
    Attributed

Maimonides
[Moses ben Maimon]
1135–1204

3   Anticipate charity by preventing poverty; assist the reduced fellowman, either by a considerable gift, or a sum of money, or by teaching him a trade, or by putting him in the way of business, so that he may earn an honest livelihood, and not be forced to the dreadful alternative of holding out his hand for charity. This is the highest step and the summit of charity's golden ladder.   *Charity's Eight Degrees*

4   Astrology is a disease, not a science.
    Laws of Repentance [1170–1180]

5   When I find the road narrow, and can see no other way of teaching a well-established truth except by pleasing one intelligent man and displeasing ten thousand fools—I prefer to address myself to the one man.[2]
    The Guide for the Perplexed [1190].
    Introduction

6   The spiritual perfection of man consists in his becoming an intelligent being—one who knows all that he is capable of learning.
    The Guide for the Perplexed, pt. I, ch. 3

7   In the realm of Nature there is nothing purposeless, trivial, or unnecessary.
    The Guide for the Perplexed, I, 15

8   The foundation of our faith is the belief that God created the Universe from nothing; that time did not exist previously, but was created.
    The Guide for the Perplexed, II, 30

9   Thou has endowed man with the wisdom to relieve the suffering of his brother, to recognize his disorders, to extract the healing substances, to discover their powers and to apply them to suit every ill.
    Attributed

Walter Map [Mapes]
c. 1140–c. 1210

10   I intend to die in a tavern; let the wine be placed near my dying mouth,[3] so that when the choirs of angels come, they may say, "God be merciful to this drinker!"   *De Nugis Curialium*

Alain de Lille [Alanus de Insulis]
d. 1202

11   Do not hold as gold all that shines as gold.[4]
    Parabolae

Kamo no Chōmei
1153–1216

12   The flow of the river is ceaseless and its water is never the same. The bubbles that float in the pools, now vanishing, now forming, are not of long duration: so in the world are man and his dwellings. . . . [People] die in the morning, they are born in the evening, like foam on the water.
    Hojoki (An Account of My Hut) [1212][5]

Walther von der Vogelweide
c. 1170–c. 1230

13   Now the summer came to pass
And flowers through the grass
Joyously sprang,
While all the tribes of birds sang.[6]
    Dream Song, st. 1

14   The sun no longer shows
His face; and treason sows
His secret seeds that no man can detect;
Fathers by their children are undone;
The brother would the brother cheat;

---

[3]Meum est propositum in taberna mori;/Vinum sit appositum morientis ori.

[4]Non teneas aurum totum quod splendet ut aurum.
    Hyt is not al gold that glareth.—CHAUCER, *The House of Fame* [1374–1385], *bk. I, l. 272*
    But al thyng which that shineth as the gold/Nis nat gold, as that I have herd it told.—CHAUCER, *The Canterbury Tales* [c. 1387], *The Canon's Yeoman's Tale, l. 962*
    All is not gold that outward showeth bright.—JOHN LYDGATE [c. 1370–c. 1451], *On the Mutability of Human Affairs*
    Non omne quod fulget est aurum.—GABRIEL BIEL [c. 1420–1495], *Expositio Canonis Messe, lecture 77,* derived from WILLIAM OF AUVERGNE [d. 1249]
    All that glisters is not gold—/Often have you heard that told.—SHAKESPEARE, *The Merchant of Venice, act II, sc. vii, l. 65*

[5]Translated by DONALD KEENE in his *Anthology of Japanese Literature* [1955].

[6]Dô der sumer komen was,/Und die blumen dur daz gras/Wünneclâchen sprungen,/Aedâ die vogele sungen.

---

[1]Thomas à Becket.

[2]Translated from the Arabic by M. FRIEDLANDER.

And the cowled monk is a deceit . . .
Might is right, and justice there is none.[1]

Millennium

Eike von Repkow
fl. c. 1220

1   He who comes first, eats first.[2]

Sachsenspiegel [1219–1233]

Saint Francis of Assisi[3]
c. 1181–1226

2 Praise to thee, my Lord, for all thy creatures,
Above all Brother Sun
Who brings us the day and lends us his light.

*The Song of Brother Sun and of All His
Creatures [1225]*

3 Love is he, radiant with great splendor,
And speaks to us of Thee, O Most High.

*The Song of Brother Sun and of All His
Creatures*

4   Where there is charity and wisdom, there is neither fear nor ignorance. Where there is patience and
humility, there is neither anger nor vexation. Where
there is poverty and joy, there is neither greed nor
avarice. Where there is peace and meditation, there
is neither anxiety nor doubt.

*The Counsels of the Holy Father Saint Francis.
Admonition 27*

5   Lord, make me an instrument of Your peace.
Where there is hatred let me sow love; where there
is injury, pardon; where there is doubt, faith; where
there is despair, hope; where there is darkness, light;
and where there is sadness, joy.

O divine Master, grant that I may not so much
seek to be consoled as to console; to be understood
as to understand; to be loved as to love. For it is in
giving that we receive; it is in pardoning that we are
pardoned; and it is in dying that we are born to
eternal life.

Attributed

6   I have sinned against my brother the ass.

Dying words

Jalal Al-Din Rumi
1207–1273

7 This poetry. I never know what I'm going to say.
I don't plan it.

When I'm outside the saying of it,
I get very quiet and rarely speak at all.

Who Says Words with My Mouth[4]

Magna Carta
1215

8   No freeman shall be taken, or imprisoned, or
outlawed, or exiled, or in any way harmed, nor will
we go upon him nor will we send upon him, except
by the legal judgment of his peers or by the law of
the land.

Clause 39

9   To none will we sell, to none deny or delay, right
or justice.

Clause 40

Saint Bonaventure
c. 1217–1274

10   An example from the monkey: The higher it
climbs, the more you see of its behind.[5]

Conferences on the Gospel of John

Roger Bacon
c. 1220–c. 1292

11   If in other sciences we should arrive at certainty
without doubt and truth without error, it behooves
us to place the foundations of knowledge in mathematics.

Opus Majus,[6] *bk. I, ch. 4*

Alfonso X [Alfonso the Wise]
1221–1284

12   Had I been present at the creation, I would have
given some useful hints for the better ordering of
the universe.

Attributed

Rutebeuf
d. 1285

13 What became of the friends I had
With whom I was always so close
And loved so dearly?

La Complainte Rutebeuf

---

[1]Translated by JETHRO BITHELL.

[2]Familiar as: First come first served.

[3]Translated by LEO SHERLEY-PRICE.

[4]Translated from the Persian by JOHN MOYNE and COLEMAN
BARKS.

[5]Exemplum de simia, quae, quanto plus ascendit, tanto plus apparent posteriora eius.
Translated by the REV. WALTER J. BURGHARDT, S.J.

[6]Translated by ROBERT BURKE.

1 Friendship is dead:
They were friends who go with the wind,
And the wind was blowing at my door.
La Complainte Rutebeuf

Saint Thomas Aquinas
c. 1225–1274

2 Sing, my tongue, the Savior's glory,
Of His Flesh the mystery sing;
Of the Blood, all price exceeding,
Shed by our immortal King.[1]
*Pange, Lingua (hymn for Vespers on the Feast
of Corpus Christi), st. 1*

3 Down in adoration falling,
Lo! the sacred Host we hail;
Lo! o'er ancient forms departing,
Newer rites of grace prevail;
Faith for all defects supplying,
Where the feeble senses fail.
Pange, Lingua, st. 5 (Tantum Ergo)

4 Thus Angels' Bread is made
The Bread of man today:
The Living Bread from Heaven
With figures doth away:
O wondrous gift indeed!
The poor and lowly may
Upon their Lord and Master feed.[2]
*Sacris Solemniis Juncta Sint Gaudia (Matins
hymn for Corpus Christi), st. 6 (Panis
Angelicus)*

5 O saving Victim, opening wide
The gate of heaven to man below,
Our foes press on from every side,
Thine aid supply, Thy strength bestow.[3]
*Verbum Supernum Prodiens (hymn for Lauds
on Corpus Christi), st. 5 (O Salutaris Hostia)*

6 Lord Jesu, blessed Pelican.
*Adoro Te Devote (hymn appointed for the
Thanksgiving after Mass), st. 6 (Pie Pellicane
Jesu Domine)*

7 Three things are necessary for the salvation of
man: to know what he ought to believe; to know
what he ought to desire; and to know what he
ought to do.   *Two Precepts of Charity [1273]*

8 Law: an ordinance of reason for the common
good, made by him who has care of the community.
Summa Theologica [1273]

9 Concerning perfect blessedness which consists in
a vision of God.[4]   *Summa Theologica*

10 Reason in man is rather like God in the world.
Opuscule 11, De Regno

Meister Eckhart
c. 1260–c. 1327

11 In silence man can most readily preserve his integrity.
Directions for the Contemplative Life

12 The more wise and powerful a master, the more
directly is his work created, and the simpler it is.
Of the Eternal Birth

13 One must not always think so much about what
one should do, but rather what one should be. Our
works do not ennoble us; but we must ennoble our
works.   *Work and Being*

Dante Alighieri
1265–1321

14 In that part of the book of my memory before
which is little that can be read, there is a rubric, saying, "Incipit Vita Nova [The new life begins]."
La Vita Nuova [1293][5]

15 Love hath so long possessed me for his own
And made his lordship so familiar.
La Vita Nuova

16 Love with delight discourses in my mind
Upon my lady's admirable gifts . . .
Beyond the range of human intellect.
Il Convito,[6] *Trattato Terzo, l. 1*

17 In the middle of the journey of our life I came to
myself within a dark wood where the straight way
was lost.[7]
The Divine Comedy [c. 1310–1321]. Inferno,[8]
canto I, l. 1

---

[1]Pange, lingua, gloriosi / Corporis mysterium / Sanguinisque
pretiosi, / Quem in mundi pretium / Fructus ventris generosi /
Rex effudit gentium.
Translated by EDWARD CASWALL.
Pange, lingua, gloriosi proelium certáminis [Sing, my tongue,
the glorious battle].—SAINT VENANTIUS FORTUNATUS [c. 530–
c. 610], bishop of Poitiers

[2]Translated by J. D. CHAMBERS.

[3]Translated by EDWARD CASWALL.

---

[4]Probably the origin of the phrase: beatific vision.

[5]Translated by DANTE GABRIEL ROSSETTI.

[6]Translated by CHARLES LYELL.
The first line is also in *The Divine Comedy, Purgatorio, canto II,
l. 112.*

[7]Nel mezzo del cammin di nostra vita / Mi ritrovai per una selva
oscura, / Che la diritta via era smarrita.

[8]Translated by JOHN D. SINCLAIR unless otherwise noted.

1   And as he, who with laboring breath has escaped from the deep to the shore, turns to the perilous waters and gazes.
The Divine Comedy. Inferno, I, l. 22

2   Thou [Virgil] art my master and my author, thou art he from whom alone I took the style whose beauty has done me honor.
The Divine Comedy. Inferno, I, l. 85

3   All hope abandon, ye who enter here![1]
The Divine Comedy. Inferno, III, l. 9

4   Here must all distrust be left behind; all cowardice must be ended.
The Divine Comedy. Inferno, III, l. 14

5   There sighs, lamentations and loud wailings resounded through the starless air, so that at first it made me weep; strange tongues, horrible language, words of pain, tones of anger, voices loud and hoarse, and with these the sound of hands, made a tumult which is whirling through that air forever dark, as sand eddies in a whirlwind.
The Divine Comedy. Inferno, III, l. 22

6   This miserable state is borne by the wretched souls of those who lived without disgrace and without praise.
The Divine Comedy. Inferno, III, l. 34

7   Let us not speak of them; but look, and pass on.[2]
The Divine Comedy. Inferno, III, l. 51

8   These wretches, who never were alive.
The Divine Comedy. Inferno, III, l. 64

9   Into the eternal darkness, into fire and into ice.[2]
The Divine Comedy. Inferno, III, l. 87

10   Without hope we live in desire.
The Divine Comedy. Inferno, IV, l. 42

11   I came into a place void of all light, which bellows like the sea in tempest, when it is combated by warring winds.[2]
The Divine Comedy. Inferno, V, l. 28

12   As in the cold season their wings bear the starlings along in a broad, dense flock, so does that blast the wicked spirits. Hither, thither, downward, upward, it drives them.[3]
The Divine Comedy. Inferno, V, l. 40

13   Love, which is quickly kindled in the gentle heart, seized this man for the fair form that was taken from me, and the manner still hurts me. Love, which absolves no beloved one from loving, seized me so strongly with his charm that, as thou seest, it does not leave me yet.
The Divine Comedy. Inferno, V, l. 100

14   What sweet thoughts, what longing led them to the woeful pass.[2]
The Divine Comedy. Inferno, V, l. 113

15   There is no greater sorrow
Than to be mindful of the happy time
In misery.[4]
The Divine Comedy. Inferno, V, l. 121

16   Galeotto was the book and he that wrote it; that day we read in it no farther.[5]
The Divine Comedy. Inferno, V, l. 137

17   I fell as a dead body falls.
The Divine Comedy. Inferno, V, last line

18   Pride, Envy, and Avarice are the three sparks that have set these hearts on fire.
The Divine Comedy. Inferno, VI, l. 74

19   But when thou shalt be in the sweet world, I pray thee bring me to men's memory.
The Divine Comedy. Inferno, VI, l. 88

20   Ye that are of good understanding, note the doctrine that is hidden under the veil of the strange verses!
The Divine Comedy. Inferno, IX, l. 61

21   Already I had fixed my look on his; and he rose upright with breast and countenance, as if he entertained great scorn of Hell.[2]
The Divine Comedy. Inferno, X, l. 34

22   Necessity brings him [Dante] here, not pleasure.
The Divine Comedy. Inferno, XII, l. 87

23   If thou follow thy star, thou canst not fail of a glorious haven.
The Divine Comedy. Inferno, XV, l. 55

24   So my conscience chide me not, I am ready for Fortune as she wills.
The Divine Comedy. Inferno, XV, l. 91

25   He listens well who takes notes.
The Divine Comedy. Inferno, XV, l. 99

---

[1]Lasciate ogni speranza, voi ch'entrate.
Traditional translation.

[2]Translated by JOHN AITKEN CARLYLE, *The Temple Classics* [1900].

[3]Di qua, di là, di giù, di su li mena.

[4]Nessun maggior dolore / Che ricordarsi del tempo felice / Nella miseria.
Translated by HENRY WADSWORTH LONGFELLOW.

[5]Galeotto fu il libro e chi lo scrisse: / Quel giorno più non vi leggemmo avante.

1   A fair request should be followed by the deed in silence.   *The Divine Comedy. Inferno, XXIV, l. 77*

2   Consider your origin; you were not born to live like brutes, but to follow virtue and knowledge.
The Divine Comedy. Inferno, XXVI, l. 118

3   If I thought my answer were to one who would ever return to the world, this flame should stay without another movement; but since none ever returned alive from this depth, if what I hear is true, I answer thee without fear of infamy.
The Divine Comedy. Inferno, XXVII, l. 60

4   And thence we came forth, to see again the stars.[1]
The Divine Comedy. Inferno, XXXIV, l. 139

5   To run over better waters the little vessel of my genius now hoists her sails, as she leaves behind her a sea so cruel.   *The Divine Comedy. Purgatorio,[2] I, l. 1*

6   He goes seeking liberty, which is so dear, as he knows who for it renounces life.
The Divine Comedy. Purgatorio, I, l. 71

7   O conscience, upright and stainless, how bitter a sting to thee is a little fault!
The Divine Comedy. Purgatorio, III, l. 8

8   For to lose time is most displeasing to him who knows most.
The Divine Comedy. Purgatorio, III, l. 78

9   The Infinite Goodness has such wide arms that it takes whatever turns to it.
The Divine Comedy. Purgatorio, III, l. 121

10   Unless, before then, the prayer assist me which rises from a heart that lives in grace: what avails the other, which is not heard in heaven?
The Divine Comedy. Purgatorio, IV, l. 133

11   "Why is thy mind so entangled," said the Master [Virgil], "that thou slackenest thy pace? What is it to thee what they whisper there? Come after me and let the people talk. Stand like a firm tower that never shakes its top for blast of wind."
The Divine Comedy. Purgatorio, V,[3] l. 10

12   Go right on and listen as thou goest.
The Divine Comedy. Purgatorio, V, l. 45

13   [Beatrice] who shall be a light between truth and intellect.
The Divine Comedy. Purgatorio, VI, l. 45

14   It was now the hour that turns back the longing of seafarers and melts their hearts, the day they have bidden dear friends farewell, and pierces the new traveler with love if he hears in the distance the bell that seems to mourn the dying day.[3]
The Divine Comedy. Purgatorio, VIII, l. 1

15   Give us this day the daily manna, without which, in this rough desert, he backward goes, who toils most to go on.
The Divine Comedy. Purgatorio, XI, l. 13

16   Worldly renown is naught but a breath of wind, which now comes this way and now comes that, and changes name because it changes quarter.
The Divine Comedy. Purgatorio, XI, l. 100

17   O human race, born to fly upward, wherefore at a little wind dost thou so fall?
The Divine Comedy. Purgatorio, XII, l. 95

18   To a greater force, and to a better nature, you, free, are subject, and that creates the mind in you, which the heavens have not in their charge. Therefore if the present world go astray, the cause is in you, in you it is to be sought.
The Divine Comedy. Purgatorio, XVI, l. 79

19   Everyone confusedly conceives of a good in which the mind may be at rest, and desires it; wherefore everyone strives to attain to it.
The Divine Comedy. Purgatorio, XVII, l. 127

20   Love kindled by virtue always kindles another, provided that its flame appear outwardly.
The Divine Comedy. Purgatorio, XXII, l. 10

21   Less than a drop of blood remains in me that does not tremble; I recognize the signals of the ancient flame.[4]
The Divine Comedy. Purgatorio, XXX, l. 46

22   But so much the more malign and wild does the ground become with bad seed and untilled, as it has the more of good earthly vigor.
The Divine Comedy. Purgatorio, XXX, l. 118

23   Pure and disposed to mount unto the stars.[5]
The Divine Comedy. Purgatorio, XXXIII, l. 145

24   The glory of Him who moves everything penetrates through the universe, and is resplendent in one part more and in another less.
The Divine Comedy. Paradiso,[3] I, l. 1

25   A great flame follows a little spark.
The Divine Comedy. Paradiso, I, l. 34

26   And in His will is our peace.[6]
The Divine Comedy. Paradiso, III, l. 85

---

[1]E quindi uscimmo a riveder le stelle.

[2]Translated [1902] by Charles Eliot Norton unless otherwise noted.

[3]Translated by John D. Sinclair.

[4]Men che dramma / Di sangue m'è rimaso, che no tremi; / Conosco i segni dell' antica fiamma.

[5]Puro e disposto a salire alle stelle.

[6]E'n la sua volontade e nostra pace.

1   The greatest gift that God in His bounty made in creation, and the most conformable to His goodness, and that which He prizes the most, was the freedom of the will, with which the creatures with intelligence, they all and they alone, were and are endowed.
The Divine Comedy. Paradiso, V, l. 19

2   Thou shalt prove how salt is the taste of another's bread and how hard is the way up and down another man's stairs.
The Divine Comedy. Paradiso, XVII, l. 58

3   Overcoming me with the light of a smile, she [Beatrice] said to me: "Turn and listen, for not only in my eyes is Paradise."
The Divine Comedy. Paradiso, XVIII, l. 19

4   Therefore the sight that is granted to your world penetrates within the Eternal Justice as the eye into the sea; for though from the shore it sees the bottom, in the open sea it does not, and yet the bottom is there but the depth conceals it.
The Divine Comedy. Paradiso, XIX, l. 73

5   The experience of this sweet life.[1]
The Divine Comedy. Paradiso, XX, l. 47

6   Like the lark that soars in the air, first singing, then silent, content with the last sweetness that satiates it, such seemed to me that image, the imprint of the Eternal Pleasure.
The Divine Comedy. Paradiso, XX, l. 73

7   The night that hides things from us.
The Divine Comedy. Paradiso, XXIII, l. 3

8   With the color that paints the morning and evening clouds that face the sun I saw then the whole heaven suffused.
The Divine Comedy. Paradiso, XXVII, l. 28

9   The Love that moves the sun and the other stars.[2]
The Divine Comedy. Paradiso, XXXIII, l. 145

William of Occam [Ockham]
c. 1285–c. 1349

10   Entities should not be multiplied unnecessarily.[3]
Quodlibeta Septem [c. 1320]

---

[1]L'esperienza di questa dolce vita.

[2]L'amor che muove il sole e l'altre stelle.

[3]Translated [seventeenth century] by JOHN PONCE of Cork. The axiom became known as Occam's Razor.

Philip VI [Philip of Valois]
1293–1350

11   He who loves me, let him follow me.[4]
Attributed

Petrarch [Francesco Petrarca]
1304–1374

12   Who overrefines his argument brings himself to grief.
To Laura in Life, canzone 11

13   A good death does honor to a whole life.
To Laura in Death, 16

14   To be able to say how much you love is to love but little.
To Laura in Death, 137

15   Rarely do great beauty and great virtue dwell together.
De Remediis, bk. II

Edward III
1312–1377

16   Honi soit qui mal y pense [Evil to him who evil thinks].
Motto of the Order of the Garter [1349]

17   Let the boy win his spurs.
Said of the Black Prince at the battle of Crécy [1345]

John Barbour
c. 1316–1395

18   Freedom all solace to man gives;
He lives at ease that freely lives.
The Bruce [c. 1375], l. 227

William of Wykeham
1324–1404

19   Manners maketh man.
Motto of his two foundations, Winchester College and New College, Oxford

William Langland
c. 1330–c. 1400

20   In a summer season when soft was the sun.
The Vision of Piers Plowman [1362–1390]

---

[4]Qui m'aime me suive.

1 A fair field full of folk found I there.
The Vision of Piers Plowman

2 Who will bell the cat?
The Vision of Piers Plowman

John Wycliffe
c. 1330–1384

3 I believe that in the end the truth will conquer.
To the Duke of Lancaster [1381]. From J. R. GREEN, A Short History of the English People [1874], ch. 5

Juliana of Norwich
c. 1342–after 1416

4 It behoved that there should be sin; but all shall be well, and all shall be well, and all manner of thing shall be well.[1]
Revelations of Divine Love [1373–c. 1393], ch. 27, The Thirteenth Revelation

5 He said not "Thou shalt not be tempested, thou shalt not be travailed, thou shalt not be dis-eased"; but he said, "Thou shalt not be overcome."
Revelations of Divine Love, 68

Geoffrey Chaucer[2]
c. 1343–1400

6 Soun ys noght but eyr ybroken,
And every speche that ys spoken,
Lowd or pryvee, foul or fair,
In his substaunce ys but air.
The House of Fame [1374–1385], bk. II, l. 765

7 Venus clerk, Ovide,
That hath ysowen wonder wide
The grete god of Loves name.
The House of Fame, III, l. 1487

8 Hard is the herte that loveth nought
In May.
The Romaunt of the Rose [c. 1380], l. 85

9 For nakid as a worm was she.
The Romaunt of the Rose, l. 454

10 As round as appil was his face.
The Romaunt of the Rose, l. 819

11 The lyf so short, the craft so long to lerne,
Th' assay so hard, so sharp the conquerynge.
The Parliament of Fowls [1380–1386], l. 1

12 For out of olde feldes, as men seyth,
Cometh al this newe corn fro yer to yere;[3]
And out of olde bokes, in good feyth,
Cometh al this newe science that men lere.
The Parliament of Fowls, l. 22

13 Nature, the vicaire of the almyghty lorde.
The Parliament of Fowls, l. 379

14 Now welcome, somer, with thy sonne softe,
That hast this wintres wedres overshake.
The Parliament of Fowls, l. 680

15 But the Troian gestes, as they felle,
In Omer, or in Dares, or in Dite,
Whoso that kan may rede hem as they write.
Troilus and Criseyde [c. 1385], bk. I, l. 145

16 If no love is, O God, what fele I so?
And if love is, what thing and which is he?
If love be good, from whennes cometh my woo?
Troilus and Criseyde, I, l. 400 (Canticus Troili)

17 Unknowe, unkist, and lost, that is unsought.
Troilus and Criseyde, I, l. 809

18 O wynd, o wynd, the weder gynneth clere.
Troilus and Criseyde, II, l. 2

19 Til crowes feet be growen under youre yë.
Troilus and Criseyde, II, l. 403

20 Lord, this is an huge rayn!
This were a weder for to slepen inne!
Troilus and Criseyde, III, l. 656

21 For I have seyn, of a ful misty morwe
Folowen ful often a myrie someris day.
Troilus and Criseyde, III, l. 1060

22 Right as an aspes leef she gan to quake.
Troilus and Criseyde, III, l. 1200

23 For of fortunes sharpe adversitee
The worste kynde of infortune is this,
A man to han ben in prosperitee,
And it remembren, whan it passed is.
Troilus and Criseyde, III, l. 1625

24 Oon ere it herde, at tothir out it wente.[4]
Troilus and Criseyde, IV, l. 434

---

[1]Sin is Behovely . . . —T. S. ELIOT, *Four Quartets. Little Gidding* [1942], *III*

[2]From the text of F. N. ROBINSON, *The Works of Geoffrey Chaucer, 2nd edition* [1957].

---

[3]John Bartlett quoted this line at the head of his preface to the ninth edition of *Bartlett's Familiar Quotations* [1891].

[4]Commonly quoted: In one ear and out the other.

1 But manly sette the world on six and sevene;[1]
And if thow deye a martyr, go to hevene!
Troilus and Criseyde, IV, l. 622

2 For tyme ylost may nought recovered be.
Troilus and Criseyde, IV, l. 1283

3   They take it wisly, faire, and softe.[2]
Troilus and Criseyde, V, l. 347

4 For he that naught n' assaieth, naught
    n' acheveth.   *Troilus and Criseyde, V, l. 784*

5 That Paradis stood formed in her yën.
Troilus and Criseyde, V, l. 817

6 Trewe as stiel.   *Troilus and Criseyde, V, l. 831*

7   This sodeyn Diomede.
Troilus and Criseyde, V, l. 1024

8 Ye, fare wel al the snow of ferne yere!
Troilus and Criseyde, V, l. 1176

9 Ek gret effect men write in place lite;
Th' entente is al, and nat the lettres space.
Troilus and Criseyde, V, l. 1629

10 Go, litel bok, go, litel myn tragedye.[3]
Troilus and Criseyde, V, l. 1786

11 O yonge, fresshe folkes, he or she,
In which that love up groweth with youre age,
Repeyreth hom fro worldly vanyte.
Troilus and Criseyde, V, l. 1835

12 O moral Gower, this book I directe
To the.   *Troilus and Criseyde, V, l. 1856*

13   Whan that the month of May
Is comen, and that I here the foules synge,
And that the floures gynnen for to sprynge,
Farewel my bok, and my devocioun!
The Legend of Good Women [c. 1386], l. 36

---

[1]All is uneven,/And everything is left at six and seven.—
SHAKESPEARE, *Richard II, act II, sc. ii, l. 120*

Things going on at sixes and sevens.—OLIVER GOLDSMITH, *The Good-Natur'd Man* [1768], *act I*

[2]The proverb is: Fair and softly goes far.

[3]Off with you down where you want to go.—HORACE, *Epistles, I, xx, 5*

Little book, you will go without me—I don't mind—to the city.—OVID, *Tristia, I, i, 1*

Vade salutatum pro me, liber [Go forth, my book, to bear my greetings].—MARTIAL, *Epigrams, I, 70*

Go now, my little book, to every place/Where my first pilgrim has but shown his face.—JOHN BUNYAN, *The Pilgrim's Progress* [1678], *Apology*

Go, little Book! From this my solitude/I cast thee on the Waters—go thy ways.—SOUTHEY, *Lay of the Laureate* [1815], *L'Envoi*

These lines of Southey's and the next two were quoted by BYRON in *Don Juan* [1818], *canto I, st. 222:* The four first rhymes are Southey's, every line:/For God's sake, reader! take them not for mine!

Go, little book, and wish to all/Flowers in the garden, meat in the hall.—R. L. STEVENSON, *Underwoods* [1887], *Envoy*

14 That, of al the floures in the mede,
Thanne love I most thise floures white and rede,
Swiche as men callen daysyes in our toun.
The Legend of Good Women, l. 41

15 Whan that Aprille with his shoures soote
The droghte of March hath perced to the roote.
The Canterbury Tales [c. 1387]. Prologue, l. 1

16 And smale foweles maken melodye,
That slepen al the nyght with open yë,
(So priketh hem nature in hit corages);
Thanne longen folk to goon on pilgrimages.
The Canterbury Tales. Prologue, l. 9

17 He was a verray, parfit gentil knyght.
The Canterbury Tales. Prologue, l. 72

18 He was as fressh as is the month of May.
The Canterbury Tales. Prologue, l. 92

19 He koude songes make and wel endyte.
The Canterbury Tales. Prologue, l. 95

20 Curteis he was, lowely, and servysable,
And carf biforn his fader at the table.
The Canterbury Tales. Prologue, l. 99

21 Ful weel she soong the service dyvyne,
Entuned in hir nose ful semely;
And Frenssh she spak ful faire and fetisly,
After the scole of Stratford atte Bowe
For Frenssh of Parys was to hir unknowe.
The Canterbury Tales. Prologue, l. 122

22 She wolde wepe, if that she saugh a mous
Kaught in a trappe, if it were deed or bledde.
The Canterbury Tales. Prologue, l. 144

23 And theron heng a brooch of gold ful sheene,
On which ther was first write a crowned *A*,
And after *Amor vincit omnia.*
The Canterbury Tales. Prologue, l. 160

24 His palfrey was as broun as is a berye.
The Canterbury Tales. Prologue, l. 207

25 A Frere ther was, a wantowne and a merye.
The Canterbury Tales. Prologue, l. 208

26 He knew the tavernes wel in every toun.
The Canterbury Tales. Prologue, l. 240

27 Somwhat he lipsed, for his wantownesse,
To make his Englissh sweete upon his tonge.
The Canterbury Tales. Prologue, l. 264

28 A Clerk ther was of Oxenford also.
The Canterbury Tales. Prologue, l. 285

29 As leene was his hors as is a rake.
The Canterbury Tales. Prologue, l. 287

30 For hym was levere have at his beddes heed
Twenty bookes, clad in blak or reed,
Of Aristotle and his philosophie,

Than robes riche, or fithele, or gay sautrie,
But al be that he was a philosophre,
Yet hadde he but litel gold in cofre.
The Canterbury Tales. Prologue, l. 293

1 And gladly wolde he lerne, and gladly teche.
The Canterbury Tales. Prologue, l. 308

2 Nowher so bisy a man as he ther nas,
And yet he semed bisier than he was.
The Canterbury Tales. Prologue, l. 321

3 For he was Epicurus owene sone.
The Canterbury Tales. Prologue, l. 336

4 It snewed in his hous of mete and drynke.
The Canterbury Tales. Prologue, l. 345

5　　　He was a good felawe.
The Canterbury Tales. Prologue, l. 395

6 His studie was but litel on the Bible.
The Canterbury Tales. Prologue, l. 438

7 For gold in phisik is a cordial,
Therefore he lovede gold in special.
The Canterbury Tales. Prologue, l. 443

8 She was a worthy womman al hit lyve,
Housbondes at chirche dore she hadde fyve.
The Canterbury Tales. Prologue, l. 459

9 This noble ensample to his sheep he yaf,
That first he wroghte, and afterward he taughte.
The Canterbury Tales. Prologue, l. 496

10 If gold ruste, what shal iren do?
The Canterbury Tales. Prologue, l. 500

11 But Cristes loore and his apostles twelve
He taughte, but first he folwed it hymselve.
The Canterbury Tales. Prologue, l. 527

12 And yet he hadde a thombe of gold.[1]
The Canterbury Tales. Prologue, l. 563

13 That hadde a fyr-reed cherubynnes face.
The Canterbury Tales. Prologue, l. 624

14 Wel loved he garleek, oynons, and eek lekes,
And for to drynken strong wyn, reed as blood.
The Canterbury Tales. Prologue, l. 634

15 And whan that he wel dronken hadde the wyn,
Than wolde he speke no word but Latyn.
The Canterbury Tales. Prologue, l. 637

16 Whoso shal telle a tale after a man,
He moot reherce as ny as evere he kan
Everich a word, if it be in his charge,
Al speke he never so rudeliche and large,
Or ellis he moot telle his tale untrewe,
Or feyne thyng, or fynde wordes new.
The Canterbury Tales. Prologue, l. 731

17 For May wol have no slogardie anyght.
The sesoun priketh every gentil herte,
And maketh hym out of his slep to sterte.
The Canterbury Tales. The Knight's Tale, l. 1042

18 Ech man for hymself.
The Canterbury Tales. The Knight's Tale, l. 1182

19 The bisy larke, messager of day.
The Canterbury Tales. The Knight's Tale, l. 1491

20 May, with alle thy floures and thy grene,
Welcome be thou, faire, fresshe May.
The Canterbury Tales. The Knight's Tale, l. 1510

21 That "feeld hath eyen, and the wode hath eres."[2]
The Canterbury Tales. The Knight's Tale, l. 1522

22 Now up, now doun, as boket in a welle.
The Canterbury Tales. The Knight's Tale, l. 1533

23 For pitee renneth soone in gentil herte.
The Canterbury Tales. The Knight's Tale, l. 1761

24　　　Cupido,
Upon his shuldres wynges hadde he two;
And blynd he was, as it is often seene;
A bowe he bar and arwes brighte and kene.
The Canterbury Tales. The Knight's Tale, l. 1963

25 The smylere with the knyf under the cloke.
The Canterbury Tales. The Knight's Tale, l. 1999

26 Up roos the sonne, and up roose Emelye.
The Canterbury Tales. The Knight's Tale, l. 2273

27 Myn be the travaille, and thyn be the glorie!
The Canterbury Tales. The Knight's Tale, l. 2406

28 And was al his chiere, as in his herte.
The Canterbury Tales. The Knight's Tale, l. 2683

---

[2]The proverb also occurs in the Latin form: Campus habet lumen, et habet nemus auris acumen [The field has sight, and the wood a sharp ear].
Wode has erys, felde has sigt. — *King Edward and the Shepherd, MS* [c. 1300]
Fields have eyes and woods have ears. — JOHN HEYWOOD, *Proverbs* [1546], *pt. II, ch. 5*
Walls have ears. — CERVANTES, *Don Quixote, pt. II* [1615], *ch. 48*
Woods have tongues / As walls have ears. — ALFRED, LORD TENNYSON, *Idylls of the King, Balin and Balan* [1885], *l. 522*

---

[1]In allusion to the proverb: An honest miller hath a golden thumb.

1 What is this world? what asketh men to have?
Now with his love, now in his colde grave
Allone, withouten any compaignye.
The Canterbury Tales. The Knight's Tale,
l. 2777

2 This world nys but a thurghfare ful of wo,
And we been pilgrymes, passing to and fro.
Deeth is an ende of every worldly soore.
The Canterbury Tales. The Knight's Tale,
l. 2847

3 Jhesu Crist, and seiynte Benedight,
Blesse this hous from every wikked wight.
The Canterbury Tales. The Miller's Tale,
l. 3483

4 And broghte of myghty ale a large quart.
The Canterbury Tales. The Miller's Tale,
l. 3497

5 "Tehee!" quod she, and clapte the wyndow to.
The Canterbury Tales. The Miller's Tale,
l. 3740

6 Yet in our asshen olde is fyr yreke.
The Canterbury Tales. The Reeve's Prologue,
l. 3882

7 The gretteste clerkes been noght the wisest men.
The Canterbury Tales. The Reeve's Tale,
l. 4054

8 Thurgh thikke and thurgh thenne.[1]
The Canterbury Tales. The Reeve's Tale,
l. 4066

9 So was hir joly whistle wel ywet.
The Canterbury Tales. The Reeve's Tale,
l. 4155

10 She is mirour of alle curteisye.[2]
The Canterbury Tales. The Man of Law's Tale,
l. 166

11 For in the sterres, clerer than is glas,
Is writen, God woot, whoso koude it rede,
The deeth of every man.
The Canterbury Tales. The Man of Law's Tale,
l. 194

12 Sathan, that evere us waiteth to bigile.
The Canterbury Tales. The Man of Law's Tale,
l. 582

13 But, Lord Crist! whan that it remembreth me
Upon my yowthe, and on my jolitee,

It tikleth me aboute myn herte roote.
Unto this day it dooth myn herte boote
That I have had my world as in my tyme.
The Canterbury Tales. The Wife of Bath's
Prologue, l. 469

14 In his owene grece I made hym frye.[3]
The Canterbury Tales. The Wife of Bath's
Prologue, l. 487

15 By God! in erthe I was his purgatorie,
For which I hope his Soule be in glorie.
The Canterbury Tales. The Wife of Bath's
Prologue, l. 489

16   What thyng we may nat lightly have,
Thereafter wol we crie al day and crave.
The Canterbury Tales. The Wife of Bath's
Prologue, l. 517

17 Greet prees at market maketh deere ware,
And to greet cheep is holde at litel prys.
The Canterbury Tales. The Wife of Bath's
Prologue, l. 522

18 But yet I hadde alwey a coltes tooth.
Gat-toothed I was, and that bicam me weel.
The Canterbury Tales. The Wife of Bath's
Prologue, l. 601

19   A womman cast hir shame away,
Whan she cast of hir smok.
The Canterbury Tales. The Wife of Bath's
Prologue, l. 782

20 As thikke as motes in the sonne-beem.
The Canterbury Tales. The Wife of Bath's Tale,
l. 868

21 "My lige lady, generally," quod he,
"Wommen desiren have sovereynetee
As well over hir housbond as hir love."
The Canterbury Tales. The Wife of Bath's
Tale, l. 1037

22 Looke who that is moost vertuous alway,
Pryvee and apert, and most entendeth ay
To do the gentil dedes that he kan;
Taak hym for the grettest gentil man.
The Canterbury Tales. The Wife of Bath's
Tale, l. 1113

23 That he is gentil that dooth gentil dedis.
The Canterbury Tales. The Wife of Bath's
Tale, l. 1170

---

[1]Through thick and thin. — DU BARTAS, *Divine Weeks and Works*
[1578], *Second Week, Fourth Day*

[2]Call him bounteous Buckingham, / The mirror of all
courtesy. — SHAKESPEARE, *Henry VIII, act II, sc. i, l. 52*

[3]Proverbial.
Fryeth in her own grease. — JOHN HEYWOOD, *Proverbs* [1546],
pt. I, ch. 11
    The best way were to entertain him with hope, till the wicked
fire of lust have melted him in his own grease. — SHAKESPEARE, *The*
Merry Wives of Windsor, act II, sc. i, l. 69

1 For thogh we slepe, or wake, or rome, or ryde,
   Ay fleeth the tyme, it nyl no man abyde.
   The Canterbury Tales. The Clerk's Tale, l. 118

2 Ye been oure lord, dooth with youre owene thyng
   Right as yow list.
   The Canterbury Tales. The Clerk's Tale, l. 652

3 Love is noght oold as whan that it is newe.
   The Canterbury Tales. The Clerk's Tale, l. 857

4   This flour of wyfly pacience.
   The Canterbury Tales. The Clerk's Tale, l. 919

5 O stormy peple! unsad and evere untrewe!
   *The Canterbury Tales. The Clerk's Tale,
   l. 995*

6 No wedded man so hardy be t'assaille
   His wyves pacience, in trust to fynde
   Grisildis, for in certein he shal faille!
   *The Canterbury Tales. The Clerk's Tale,
   l. 1180*

7   It is no childes pley
   To take a wyf withouten avysement.
   *The Canterbury Tales. The Merchant's Tale,
   l. 1530*

8 For love is blynd.[1]
   *The Canterbury Tales. The Merchant's Tale,
   l. 1598*

9   My wit is thynne.
   *The Canterbury Tales. The Merchant's Tale,
   l. 1682*

10 Ther nys no werkman, whatsoevere he be,
   Tha⁺ may bothe werke wel and hastily;
   This wol be doon at leyser parfitly.
   *The Canterbury Tales. The Merchant's Tale,
   l. 1832*

11 Therfore bihoveth hire a ful long spoon
   That shal ete with a feend.[2]
   *The Canterbury Tales. The Squire's Tale,
   l. 602*

12 Men loven of propre kynde newefangelnesse.
   *The Canterbury Tales. The Squire's Tale,
   l. 610*

13   Fy on possessioun
   But if a man be vertuous withal.
   *The Canterbury Tales. The Squire's Tale,
   l. 686*

14 Pacience is an heigh vertu, certeyn.
   *The Canterbury Tales. The Franklin's Tale,
   l. 773*

15 Servant in love and lord in marriage.
   *The Canterbury Tales. The Franklin's Tale,
   l. 793*

16 It is agayns the proces of nature.
   *The Canterbury Tales. The Franklin's Tale,
   l. 1345*

17 Trouthe is the hyeste thyng that men may kepe.
   *The Canterbury Tales. The Franklin's Tale,
   l. 1479*

18 For dronkenesse is verray sepulture
   Of mannes wit and his discrecioun.
   *The Canterbury Tales. The Pardoner's Tale,
   l. 558*

19 Mordre wol out, certeyn, it wol nat faille.[3]
   *The Canterbury Tales. The Prioress's Tale,
   l. 1766*

20 This may wel be rym dogerel.
   *The Canterbury Tales. Chaucer's Tale of Sir
   Thopas, l. 2115*

21 Ful wys is he that kan hymselven knowe!
   *The Canterbury Tales. The Monk's Tale,
   l. 3329*

22 He was of knyghthod and of fredom flour.
   *The Canterbury Tales. The Monk's Tale,
   l. 3832*

23 For whan a man hath over-greet a wit,
   Ful oft hym happeth to mysusen it.
   *The Canterbury Tales. The Canon Yeoman's
   Prologue, l. 648*

24 My sone, keep wel thy tonge, and keep thy freend.
   *The Canterbury Tales. The Manciple's Tale,
   l. 319*

25 Thing that is seyd is seyd; and forth it gooth.
   *The Canterbury Tales. The Manciple's Tale,
   l. 355*

---

[3]Proverbial.
   How easily murder is discovered! —SHAKESPEARE, *Titus Andronicus, act II, sc. iii, l. 287*
   Truth will come to light; murder cannot be hid long. —SHAKESPEARE, *The Merchant of Venice, act II, sc. ii, l. 86*
   Murder, though it have no tongue, will speak / With most miraculous organ. —SHAKESPEARE, *Hamlet, act II, sc. ii, l. 630*
   Murder will out. —CERVANTES, *Don Quixote, pt. I* [1605], *bk. III, ch. 8*
   Carcasses bleed at the sight of the murderer. —ROBERT BURTON, *Anatomy of Melancholy* [1621–1651], *pt. I, sec. I, member 2, subsec. 5*
   Other sins only speak; murder shrieks out. —JOHN WEBSTER, *The Duchess of Malfi* [1623], *act IV, sc. ii*

---

[1]Proverbial.

[2]Proverbial.
   He must have a long spoon that must eat with the devil. —SHAKESPEARE, *The Comedy of Errors, act IV, sc. iii, l. 64*

1 For the proverbe seith that "manye smale maken a
  greet."[1]
    The Canterbury Tales. The Parson's Tale,
    l. 361

2 Reule wel thyself, that other folk canst rede.
  And trouthe thee shal delivere, it is no drede.
    Truth [c. 1390], l. 6

3 The wrastling for this world axeth a fal.
    Truth, l. 16

John Huss [Jan Hus]
c. 1372–1415

4 O holy simplicity![2]   *Last words, at the stake*

Thomas à Kempis
1380–1471

5 Sic transit gloria mundi [So passes away the
glory of this world].[3]
    Imitation of Christ [c. 1420], bk. I, ch. 3

6 Be not angry that you cannot make others as
you wish them to be, since you cannot make yourself as you wish to be.   *Imitation of Christ, I, 16*

7 Man proposes, but God disposes.[4]
    Imitation of Christ, I, 19

8 What canst thou see elsewhere which thou canst
not see here? Behold the heaven and the earth and
all the elements; for of these are all things created.
    Imitation of Christ, I, 20

9 No man ruleth safely but he that is willingly
ruled.   *Imitation of Christ, I, 20*

10 And when he is out of sight, quickly also is he
out of mind.[5]   *Imitation of Christ, I, 23*

11 O that we had spent but one day in this worl[d]
thoroughly well!   *Imitation of Christ, I, 2[...]*

12 First keep the peace within yourself, then yo[u]
can also bring peace to others.
    Imitation of Christ, II,

13 Love is swift, sincere, pious, pleasant, gentl[e]
strong, patient, faithful, prudent, long-suffering
manly and never seeking her own; for wheresoever
man seeketh his own, there he falleth from love.
    Imitation of Christ, III,

Charles d'Orléans
1394–1465

14 I am dying of thirst by the side of the fountain.
    Ballades,

15 The season has shed its mantle of wind and chi[ll]
and rain.[7]   *Rondeaux, 6*

16 All by myself, wrapped in my thoughts,
  And building castles in Spain and in France.[8]
    Rondeaux, 10

John Fortescue
c. 1395–c. 1479

17 Much cry and no wool.[9]
    De Laudibus Legum Angliae [1471], ch. 1

18 Comparisons are odious.[10]
    De Laudibus Legum Angliae, 1

Sir Thomas Malory
d. 1471

19 The noble history of the Sangreal,[11] and of th[e]
most renowned Christian king . . . King Arthur.
    Le Morte d'Arthur [1485]. Preface by WILLIA[M]
    CAXTON [c. 1422–1491], the first English printer

---

[1]The proverb goes back to Saint Augustine.
Many small make a great. — JOHN HEYWOOD, *Proverbs* [1546],
pt. I, ch. 11

[2]O sancta simplicitas!

[3]These words are used in the crowning of the pope.

[4]Homo proponet et Deus disponit. — WILLIAM LANGLAND, *The
Vision of Piers Plowman, l. 13,994* [1550 edition]
Man appoints, and God disappoints. — CERVANTES, *Don
Quixote, pt. II* [1615], *bk. IV, ch. 55*

[5]Fer from eze, fer from herte, / Quoth Hendyng. — HENDYNG
[1272–1307], *Proverbs, MS*
Out of sight, out of mind. — BARNABE GOOGE [1540–1594],
Eglogs [1563]
And out of mind as soon as out of sight. — GREVILLE, *Sonnet 56*
I do perceive that the old proverbs be not always true, for I do
find that the absence of my Nath. doth breed in me the more continual remembrance of him. — LADY ANN BACON [1528–1610],
letter to Lady Jane Cornwallis

[6]Je meurs de soif auprès de la fontaine.

[7]Le temps a laissé son manteau / De vent, de froidure et de plui[e]

[8]Translated by NORBERT GUTERMAN.
Thou shalt make castels thanne in Spayne, / And dreme of joy[e]
all but in vayne. — JEAN DE MEUN [13th cent.], *The Romaunt [of]
the Rose* [c. 1277], *fragment B, l. 2573,* translated by CHAUCER

[9]A great cry, but little wool. — CERVANTES, *Don Quixote, pt. I*
[1615], *bk. III, ch. 13*
All cry and no wool. — SAMUEL BUTLER, *Hudibras, pt. I* [1663]
canto I, l. 852

[10]This was a well-known phrase in the fourteenth century, an[d]
has been repeated by many, including Lydgate, Shakespeare, an[d]
Swift.

[11]The Holy Grail.

1   Whoso pulleth out this sword of this stone and anvil, is rightwise king born of all England.
Le Morte d'Arthur, bk. I, ch. 5

2   And with that the king saw coming toward him the strangest beast that ever he saw or heard of; so the beast went to the well and drank, and the noise was in the beast's belly like unto the questing of thirty couple hounds; but all the while the beast drank there was no noise in the beast's belly: and therewith the beast departed with a great noise . . . Pellinore, that time king, followed the questing beast.
Le Morte d'Arthur, I, 19

3   In the midst of the lake Arthur was ware of an arm clothed in white samite, that held a fair sword in that hand.
Le Morte d'Arthur, I, 25

4   Always Sir Arthur lost so much blood that it was marvel he stood on his feet, but he was so full of knighthood that knightly he endured the pain.
Le Morte d'Arthur, IV, 9

5   What, nephew, said the king, is the wind in that door?
Le Morte d'Arthur, VII, 34

6   The joy of love is too short, and the sorrow thereof, and what cometh thereof, dureth over long.
Le Morte d'Arthur, X, 56

7   It is his day.
Le Morte d'Arthur, X, 70

8   The month of May was come, when every lusty heart beginneth to blossom, and to bring forth fruit; for like as herbs and trees bring forth fruit and flourish in May, in likewise every lusty heart that is in any manner a lover, springeth and flourisheth in lusty deeds. For it giveth unto all lovers courage, that lusty month of May.
Le Morte d'Arthur, XVIII, 25

9   All ye that be lovers call unto your remembrance the month of May, like as did Queen Guenever, for whom I make here a little mention, that while she lived she was a true lover, and therefore she had a good end.
Le Morte d'Arthur, XVIII, 25

10   Such a fellowship of good knights shall never be together in no company.
Le Morte d'Arthur, XX, 9

11   I shall curse you with book and bell and candle.[1]
Le Morte d'Arthur, XXI, 1

12   Through this man [Launcelot] and me [Guenever] hath all this war been wrought, and the death of the most noblest knights of the world; for through our love that we have loved together is my most noble lord slain.
Le Morte d'Arthur, XXI, 9

13   For as well as I have loved thee, mine heart will not serve me to see thee, for through thee and me is the flower of kings and knights destroyed.
Le Morte d'Arthur, XXI, 9

14   Thou were the meekest man and the gentlest that ever ate in hall among ladies. And thou were the sternest knight to thy mortal foe that ever put spear in the rest.
Le Morte d'Arthur, XXI, 13

15   Yet some men say in many parts of England that King Arthur is not dead, but had by the will of our Lord Jesu into another place. And men say that he shall come again and he shall win the Holy Cross. Yet I will not say that it shall be so, but rather I will say, Here in this world he changed his life. And many men say that there is written upon his tomb this verse: *Hic iacet Arthurus, rex quondam, rexque futurus.*[2]
Le Morte d'Arthur, XXXI, 7

Henry VI
1421–1471

16   Kingdoms are but cares,
State is devoid of stay;
Riches are ready snares,
And hasten to decay.
From SIR JOHN HARINGTON, *Nugae Antiquae [1769]*

François Villon
1431–c. 1465

17   Ah God! Had I but studied
In the days of my foolish youth.[3]
Le Grand Testament, 26

18   But where are the snows of yesteryear?[4]
Le Grand Testament. Ballade des Dames du Temps Jadis

19   In this faith I will to live and die.
Le Grand Testament. Ballade de l'Homage à Notre Dame

20   There's no good speech save in Paris.[5]
Le Grand Testament. Ballade des Femmes de Paris

21   But pray God that he absolve us all![6]
Codicile

---

[1]The reference is to the ceremony of excommunication, performed with bell, book, and candle.

[2]Here lies Arthur, the once and future king.

[3]Hé Dieu! si j'eusse étudié / Au temps de ma jeunesse folle.

[4]Mais où sont les neiges d'antan?
Translated by DANTE GABRIEL ROSSETTI.
See Chaucer, 134:8.

[5]Il n'est bon bec que de Paris.

[6]Mais priez Dieu que tous nous veuille absoudre.

1 I know all except myself.[1]

Ballade des Menus Propres

Aldus Manutius
1449–1515

2   Talk of nothing but business, and dispatch that business quickly.

Placard on the door of the Aldine Press, Venice, established about 1490

Christopher Columbus
1451–1506

3   Here the people could stand it no longer and complained of the long voyage; but the Admiral cheered them as best he could, holding out good hope of the advantages they would have. He added that it was useless to complain, he had come [to go] to the Indies, and so had to continue it until he found them, with the help of Our Lord.

Journal of the First Voyage,[2] October 10, 1492

4   At two hours after midnight appeared the land, at a distance of 2 leagues. They handed all sails and set the *treo,* which is the mainsail without bonnets, and lay-to waiting for daylight Friday, when they arrived at an island of the Bahamas that was called in the Indians' tongue Guanahaní [San Salvador].

Journal of the First Voyage, October 12, 1492

5   The two Christians met on the way many people who were going to their towns, women and men, with a firebrand in the hand, [and] herbs to drink the smoke thereof, as they are accustomed.[3]

Journal of the First Voyage, November 6, 1492

6   And I say that Your Highnesses ought not to consent that any foreigner does business or sets foot here, except Christian Catholics, since this was the end and the beginning of the enterprise, that it should be for the enhancement and glory of the Christian religion, nor should anyone who is not a good Christian come to these parts.

Journal of the First Voyage, November 27, 1492

7   And they know neither sect nor idolatry, with the exception that all believe that the source of all power and goodness is in the sky, and they believe very firmly that I, with these ships and people, came from the sky, and in this belief they everywhere received me, after they had overcome their fear.

Letter to the Sovereigns on the First Voyage, February 15–March 4, 1493[4]

8   I have always read that the world, both land and water, was spherical, as the authority and research of Ptolemy and all the others who have written on this subject demonstrate and prove, as do the eclipses of the moon and other experiments that are made from east to west, and the elevation of the North Star from north to south.

Letter to the Sovereigns on the Third Voyage, October 18, 1498[5]

9   I should be judged as a captain who went from Spain to the Indies to conquer a people numerous and warlike, whose manners and religion are very different from ours, who live in sierras and mountains, without fixed settlements, and where by divine will I have placed under the sovereignty of the King and Queen our Lords, an Other World, whereby Spain, which was reckoned poor, is become the richest of countries.

Letter to Doña Juana de Torres, October 1500[6]

10   I came to serve you at the age of 28 and now I have not a hair on me that is not white, and my body is infirm and exhausted. All that was left to me and my brothers has been taken away and sold, even to the cloak that I wore, without hearing or trial, to my great dishonor.

Lettera Rarissima to the Sovereigns, July 7, 1503 (Fourth Voyage)[7]

Leonardo da Vinci
1452–1519

11   Man and the animals are merely a passage and channel for food, a tomb for other animals, a haven for the dead, giving life by the death of others, a coffer full of corruption.

The Notebooks [1508–1518],[8] vol. I, ch. 1

12   Intellectual passion drives out sensuality.

The Notebooks, I, 1

---

[1]Je connais tout, fors moi-même.

[2]BARTOLOMÉ DE LAS CASAS [1474–1566] made an abstract of Columbus's *Journal of the First Voyage (El Libro de la Primera Navegación),* which is the nearest thing to an original journal that we have. Translated by SAMUEL ELIOT MORISON.

[3]The first certain reference in history to smoking tobacco.

[4]This letter, the first and rarest of all printed Americana, describes the scenery and the natives of Hispaniola.

[5]Translated by SAMUEL ELIOT MORISON and MILTON ANASTOS.

[6]Columbus is returning from the Indies as a prisoner.

[7]Translated by MILTON ANASTOS.

[8]Translated by EDWARD MacCURDY.

1 As a well-spent day brings happy sleep, so life well used brings happy death.
The Notebooks, I, 1

2 Life well spent is long. *The Notebooks, I, 1*

3 Shun those studies in which the work that results dies with the worker. *The Notebooks, I, 1*

4 Whoever in discussion adduces authority uses not intellect but rather memory.
The Notebooks, I, 2

5 Iron rusts from disuse; stagnant water loses its purity and in cold weather becomes frozen; even so does inaction sap the vigor of the mind.
The Notebooks, I, 2

6 Savage is he who saves himself.
The Notebooks, I, 2

7 It is easier to resist at the beginning than at the end. *The Notebooks, I, 2*

8 Necessity is the mistress and guardian of nature.
The Notebooks, I, 2

9 Human subtlety . . . will never devise an invention more beautiful, more simple or more direct than does nature, because in her inventions nothing is lacking, and nothing is superfluous.
The Notebooks, I, 3

10 Mechanics is the paradise of the mathematical sciences because by means of it one comes to the fruits of mathematics. *The Notebooks, I, 20*

11 O speculators about perpetual motion, how many vain chimeras have you created in the like quest? Go and take your place with the seekers after gold.
The Notebooks, II, 25

12 O neglectful Nature, wherefore art thou thus partial, becoming to some of thy children a tender and benignant mother, to others a most cruel and ruthless stepmother? I see thy children given into slavery to others without ever receiving any benefit, and in lieu of any reward for the services they have done for them they are repaid by the severest punishments. *The Notebooks, II, 45*

13 The Medici created and destroyed me.
The Notebooks, II, 46

Amerigo Vespucci
1454–1512

14 Those new regions [America] which we found and explored with the fleet . . . we may rightly call a New World . . . a continent more densely peopled and abounding in animals than our Europe or Asia or Africa; and, in addition, a climate milder than in any other region known to us.[1]
Letter called Mundus Novus [1503] to Lorenzo Pier Francesco de'Medici

Sebastian Brant
c. 1458–1521

15 The world wants to be deceived.
The Ship of Fools (Das Narrenschiff) [1494]

John Skelton
c. 1460–1529

16 I say, thou mad March hare.[2]
Replication Against Certain Young Scholars

17 He ruleth all the roost.[3]
Why Come Ye Not to Court, l. 198

18 The wolf from the door.[4]
Why Come Ye Not to Court, l. 1531

19 Old proverb says,
That bird is not honest
That filleth his own nest.[5]
Poems Against Garnesche

20 Maid, widow, or wife. *Philip Sparrow*

21 Vengeance I ask and cry,
By way of exclamation,
On the whole nation
Of cats wild and tame:
God send them sorrow and shame!
Philip Sparrow

22 Merry Margaret,
As midsummer flower,

---

[1]Translated by G. T. NORTHUP.

This, and a letter of Vespucci to his friend Pier Soderini [1504], led geography professor Martin Waldseemüller to credit Vespucci with discovering "a fourth part of the world" and to issue a map [1507] with a bold AMERICA on the continent now called South America. Vespucci had invented a voyage of 1497, a year before Columbus's Third Voyage to the mainland of South America.

[2]Mad as a March hare. — JOHN HEYWOOD, *Proverbs* [1546], *pt. II, ch. 5*

[3]Rule the rost. — JOHN HEYWOOD, *Proverbs* [1546], *pt. I, ch. 5*
Rules the roast. — JONSON, CHAPMAN, MARSTON, *Eastward Ho* [1605], *act II, sc. ii*
Her that ruled the rost. — THOMAS HEYWOOD, *History of Women* [ed. 1624]

[4]To keep the wolf from the door. — JOHN HEYWOOD, *Proverbs* [1546], *pt. II, ch. 7*

[5]It is a foul bird that filleth his own nest. — JOHN HEYWOOD, *Proverbs* [1546], *pt. II, ch. 5*

Gentle as falcon
Or hawk of the tower.

To Mistress Margaret Hussey

Giovanni Pico della Mirandola
1463–1494

1   We have made thee neither of heaven nor of earth, neither mortal nor immortal, so that with freedom of choice and with honor, as though the maker and molder of thyself, thou mayest fashion thyself in whatever shape thou shalt prefer. Thou shalt have the power to degenerate into the lower forms of life, which are brutish. Thou shalt have the power, out of thy soul's judgment, to be reborn into the highest forms, which are divine.[1]

On the Dignity of Man [1496]

William Dunbar
c. 1465–c. 1530

2 London, thou art the flower of Cities all.

London, refrain

3 Gem of all joy, jasper of jocundity.

London, st. 3

4 I that in heill wes and gladnes
Am trublit now with gret seiknes
And feblit with infermite:
Timor Mortis conturbat me.[2]

Lament for the Makers (Makaris)[3] [c. 1508], refrain

5 Our plesance here is all vain glory,
This false world is but transitory.

Lament for the Makers, st. 2

Desiderius Erasmus
c. 1466–1536

6   In the country of the blind the one-eyed man is king.[4]

Adagia [1500]

7   It is folly alone that stays the fugue of Youth and beats off louring Old Age.

The Praise of Folly [1509]

---

8   They may attack me with an army of six hundred syllogisms; and if I do not recant, they will proclaim me a heretic.   *The Praise of Folly*

Niccolò Machiavelli[5]
1469–1527

9   There is nothing more difficult to take in hand, more perilous to conduct, or more uncertain in its success, than to take the lead in the introduction of a new order of things.

The Prince [1532],[6] ch. 6

10   Since love and fear can hardly exist together, if we must choose between them, it is far safer to be feared than loved.   *The Prince, 8*

11   The chief foundations of all states, new as well as old or composite, are good laws and good arms; and as there cannot be good laws where the state is not well armed, it follows that where they are well armed they have good laws.   *The Prince, 12*

12   A prince should therefore have no other aim or thought, nor take up any other thing for his study, but war and its organization and discipline, for that is the only art that is necessary to one who commands.   *The Prince, 14*

13   Among other evils which being unarmed brings you, it causes you to be despised.

The Prince, 14

14   Many have imagined republics and principalities which have never been seen or known to exist in reality; for how we live is so far removed from how we ought to live, that he who abandons what is done for what ought to be done, will rather bring about his own ruin than his preservation.

The Prince, 15

15   A prince being thus obliged to know well how to act as a beast must imitate the fox and the lion, for the lion cannot protect himself from traps, and the fox cannot defend himself from wolves. One must therefore be a fox to recognize traps, and a lion to frighten wolves.   *The Prince, 17*

16   When neither their property nor their honor is touched, the majority of men live content.

The Prince, 19

17   There are three classes of intellects: one which comprehends by itself; another which appreciates

---

[1]Translated by ELIZABETH LIVERMORE FORBES.

[2]Fear of Death troubles me.

[3]Makers: poets.

[4]In regione caecorum rex est luscus.
    In the country of the blind the one-eyed man is king; I passed for a good teacher, because the rest in town were bad. —JEAN-JACQUES ROUSSEAU, *Confessions* [1781–1788], *pt. I, bk. 5*

[5]Every Country hath its Machiavel. —THOMAS BROWNE, *Religio Medici* [1643], *pt. I, sec. 20*
    Out of his surname they have coined an epithet for a knave, and out of his Christian name a synonym for the Devil. —THOMAS MACAULAY, *On Machiavelli* [1827]

[6]Translated by W. K. MARRIOTT.

what others comprehend; and a third which neither comprehends by itself nor by the showing of others; the first is the most excellent, the second is good, the third is useless. *The Prince, 22*

1 There is no other way of guarding oneself against flattery than by letting men understand that they will not offend you by speaking the truth; but when everyone can tell you the truth, you lose their respect. *The Prince, 23*

2 God is not willing to do everything, and thus take away our free will and that share of glory which belongs to us. *The Prince, 26*

3 Whoever desires to found a state and give it laws, must start with assuming that all men are bad and ever ready to display their vicious nature, whenever they may find occasion for it.
Discourse upon the First Ten Books of Livy, bk. I, ch. 3

4 The people resemble a wild beast, which, naturally fierce and accustomed to live in the woods, has been brought up, as it were, in a prison and in servitude, and having by accident got its liberty, not being accustomed to search for its food, and not knowing where to conceal itself, easily becomes the prey of the first who seeks to incarcerate it again.
Discourse upon the First Ten Books of Livy, I, 16

5 He who establishes a tyranny and does not kill Brutus, and he who establishes a democratic regime and does not kill the sons of Brutus, will not last long.[1]
Discourse upon the First Ten Books of Livy, III, 3

Charles VIII
1470–1498

6 This is our gracious will.[2]
Royal Order of March 12, 1497

Nicholas Copernicus
1473–1543

7 Finally we shall place the Sun himself at the center of the Universe. All this is suggested by the systematic procession of events and the harmony of the whole Universe, if only we face the facts, as they say, "with both eyes open."
De Revolutionibus Orbium Coelestium [1543][3]

Ludovico Ariosto
1474–1533

8 Nature made him, and then broke the mold.[4]
Orlando Furioso [1532], canto X, st. 84

Michelangelo [Buonarroti]
1475–1564

9 The more the marble wastes, the more the statue grows. *Sonnet*

10 If it be true that any beautiful thing raises the pure and just desire of man from earth to God, the eternal fount of all, such I believe my love.
Sonnet

11 The power of one fair face makes my love sublime, for it has weaned my heart from low desires.
Sonnet

12 I live and love in God's peculiar light.
Sonnet

Sir Thomas More[5]
1478–1535

13 They wonder much to hear that gold, which in itself is so useless a thing, should be everywhere so much esteemed, that even men for whom it was made, and by whom it has its value, should yet be thought of less value than it is.
Utopia [1516]. Of Jewels and Wealth

14 They have no lawyers among them, for they consider them as a sort of people whose profession it is to disguise matters. *Utopia. Of Law and Magistrates*

15 Plato by a goodly similitude declareth, why wise men refrain to meddle in the commonwealth. For when they see the people swarm into the streets, and daily wet to the skin with rain, and yet cannot persuade them to go out of the rain,[6] they do keep themselves within their houses, seeing they cannot remedy the folly of the people.
Utopia. Concerning the Best State of a Commonwealth

16 A little wanton money, which burned out the bottom of his purse. *Works [c. 1530]*

---

[1]Translated by Leslie J. Walker, S.J.
[2]Tel est notre bon plaisir.
[3]Translated by John F. Dobson.

[4]Natura il fece, e poi ruppe la stampa.
[5]Canonized [1935] by Pope Pius XI.
[6]In the modern phrase: Not sense enough to come in out of the rain.

1   This is a fair tale of a tub told of his election.[1]
Confutation of Tyndale's Answers [1532]

2   For men use, if they have an evil turn, to write it in marble: and whoso doth us a good turn we write it in dust.
Richard III and His Miserable End [1543]

3   See me safe up, and for my coming down let me shift for myself.
On ascending the scaffold. From WILLIAM ROPER, *Life of Sir Thomas More [1626]*

4   This hath not offended the king.
As he drew his beard aside upon placing his head on the block. From BACON, *Apothegms, no. 22*

Robert Whittinton
c. 1480–c. 1530

5   [Sir Thomas] More is a man of angel's wit and singular learning; I know not his fellow. For where is the man of that gentleness, lowliness and affability? And as time requireth, a man of marvelous mirth and pastimes; and sometimes of as sad a gravity; a man for all seasons.
Passage composed for schoolboys to put into Latin

Martin Luther
1483–1546

6   If it were an art to overcome heresy with fire, the executioners would be the most learned doctors on earth.
To the Christian Nobility of the German States [1520]

7   Here I stand; I can do no other. God help me. Amen.[2]
Speech at the Diet of Worms [April 18, 1521]

8   The mad mob does not ask how it could be better, only that it be different. And when it then becomes worse, it must change again. Thus they get bees for flies, and at last hornets for bees.
Whether Soldiers Can Also Be in a State of Grace [1526]

9 A mighty fortress is our God,
A bulwark never failing.

Our helper He amid the flood
Of mortal ills prevailing.[3]
Ein' Feste Burg [1529]

10   What can only be taught by the rod and wi[t] blows will not lead to much good; they will not re main pious any longer than the rod is behind them
The Great Catechism. Second Command [1529]

11   Peace is more important than all justice; an peace was not made for the sake of justice, but jus tice for the sake of peace.
On Marriage [1530]

12   Justice is a temporary thing that must at la[s] come to an end; but the conscience is eternal an will never die.   *On Marriag[e]*

13   Superstition, idolatry, and hypocrisy have amp[l] wages, but truth goes a-begging.
Table Talk [1569], 5.

14   For where God built a church, there the Dev would also build a chapel.[4] . . . Thus is the Dev ever God's ape.   *Table Talk, 6.*

15   The Mass is the greatest blasphemy of God, an the highest idolatry upon earth, an abomination th like of which has never been in Christendom sinc the time of the Apostles.   *Table Talk, 17*

16   There is no more lovely, friendly and charmin relationship, communion or company than a goo marriage.   *Table Talk, 29.*

17   A theologian is born by living, nay dying and be ing damned, not by thinking, reading, or speculat ing.   *Table Talk, 35.*

18   Reason is the greatest enemy that faith has: it neve comes to the aid of spiritual things, but — more fre quently than not — struggles against the divin Word, treating with contempt all that emanate from God.   *Table Talk, 35.*

19   If I had heard that as many devils would set o me in Worms as there are tiles on the roofs, I shoul nonetheless have ridden there.
Works [1745], XVI, 1

20   It makes a difference whose ox is gored.
Works [1854], LXI

---

[1]A tale of a tub is a cock-and-bull story. Jonson used it as the ti tle of a comedy [1633], and Swift as the title of a satire [1696].

[2]Hier stehe ich, ich kann nicht anders. Gott helfe mir. Amen. Inscribed on his monument at Worms.
    Also translated as: Here I stand, I cannot do otherwise. And: God helping me, I can do no other.

[3]Ein' feste burg is unser Gott, / ein gute wehr und waffen. / E hilft uns frei aus aller not, / die uns itzt hat betroffen.
    Translated by FREDERICK HENRY HEDGE.
    Great God! there is no safety here below; / Thou art my fortres thou that seem'st my foe. — FRANCIS QUARLES, *Divine Poems*

[4]Where God hath a temple, the Devil will have a chapel. — ROBERT BURTON, *Anatomy of Melancholy* [1621–1651], *pt. II sec. 4, member I, subsec. 1*
    No sooner is a temple built to God but the Devil builds a chap hard by. — GEORGE HERBERT, *Jacula Prudentum* [1651]

Hernán Cortés [Hernando Cortez]
1485–1547

1 [The Aztecs] said that by no means would they give themselves up, for as long as one of them was left he would die fighting, and that we would get nothing of theirs because they would burn everything or throw it into the water.

Third Dispatch [May 15, 1522]. To Charles V

Hugh Latimer
c. 1485–1555

2 Play the man, Master Ridley; we shall this day light such a candle, by God's grace, in England, as I trust shall never be put out.

To Nicholas Ridley [1500–1555] as they were being burned alive at Oxford for heresy [October 16, 1555]. From J. R. GREEN, A Short History of the English People [1874], ch. 7

Pope Julius III
1487–1555

3 Do you not know, my son, with what little understanding the world is ruled?[1]

To a Portuguese monk who sympathized with the pope's burdens of office

Jacques Cartier
1491–1557

4 I am rather inclined to believe that this is the land God gave to Cain.[2] *La Première Relation*

Saint Ignatius of Loyola
1491–1556

5 Teach us, good Lord, to serve Thee as Thou
    deservest:
To give and not to count the cost;
To fight and not to heed the wounds;
To toil and not to seek for rest;
To labor and not ask for any reward
Save that of knowing that we do Thy will.

Prayer for Generosity [1548]

Bernal Díaz del Castillo
c. 1492–c. 1581

6 To me it appears that the names of those[3] ought to be written in letters of gold, who died so cruel a death, for the service of God and His Majesty, to give light to those who were in darkness, and to procure wealth which all men desire.[4]

The True History of the Conquest of New Spain (Historia Verdadera de la Conquista de la Nueve España) [1800], pt. II, ch. 10

Philippus Aureolus Paracelsus
c. 1493–1541

7 Every experiment is like a weapon which must be used in its particular way—a spear to thrust, a club to strike. Experimenting requires a man who knows when to thrust and when to strike, each according to need and fashion.[5]

Surgeon's Book (Chirurgische Bucher) [1605]

Francis [François] I
1494–1547

8 All is lost save honor.[6]

Letter to his mother after his defeat at Pavia [February 23, 1525]

François Rabelais
c. 1494–1553

9 Break the bone and suck out the substantific marrow.

Gargantua and Pantagruel,[7] bk. I [1532], prologue

10 To laugh is proper to man.[8]

Gargantua and Pantagruel, I, Rabelais to the Reader

---

[3]The five hundred and fifty soldiers who came to Mexico with Cortés [1519], all but five of whom were dead at the time Díaz was writing [1568].

[4]Translated by MAURICE KEATINGE.

[5]Translated by HENRY M. PACHTER.

[6]Tout est perdu fors l'honneur.
The actual words written were: De toutes choses ne m'est demeuré que l'honneur et la vie qui est sauvé. The letter is in DULAURE, *Histoire Civile, Physique et Morale de Paris* [1821–1825].

[7]Translated by SIR THOMAS URQUHART and PETER ANTHONY MOTTEUX [1653–1694].

[8]Pour ce que rire est le propre de l'homme.

---

[1]An nescis, mi fili, quantilla prudentia mundus regatur?

[2]J'estime mieux que autrement, que c'est la terre que Dieu donna à Caïn.
Upon discovering the bleak shore of the Gulf of St. Lawrence, today's Labrador and Quebec [summer 1534].

1   Appetite comes with eating[1] . . . but the thirst goes away with drinking.

Gargantua and Pantagruel, I, ch. 5

2   War begun without good provision of money beforehand for going through with it is but as a breathing of strength and blast that will quickly pass away. Coin is the sinews of war.

Gargantua and Pantagruel, I, 46

3   How shall I be able to rule over others, that have not full power and command of myself?[2]

Gargantua and Pantagruel, I, 52

4   Do what thou wilt.[3]

Gargantua and Pantagruel, I, 57

5   Wisdom entereth not into a malicious mind, and science without conscience is but the ruin of the soul.

Gargantua and Pantagruel, II [1534], 8

6   Subject to a kind of disease, which at that time they called lack of money.

Gargantua and Pantagruel, II, 16

7   So much is a man worth as he esteems himself.

Gargantua and Pantagruel, II, 29

8   A good crier of green sauce.

Gargantua and Pantagruel, II, 31

9   This flea which I have in mine ear.

Gargantua and Pantagruel, III [1545], 31

10   Oh thrice and four times happy those who plant cabbages!

Gargantua and Pantagruel, IV [1548], 18

11   Which was performed to a T.[4]

Gargantua and Pantagruel, IV, 41

12   He that has patience may compass anything.

Gargantua and Pantagruel, IV, 48

13   We will take the good will for the deed.[5]

Gargantua and Pantagruel, IV, 49

14   Speak the truth and shame the Devil.[6]

Gargantua and Pantagruel, V [1552], author's prologue

15   Plain as a nose in a man's face.[7]

Gargantua and Pantagruel, V, author's prologue

16   Like hearts of oak.

Gargantua and Pantagruel, V, author's prologue

17   Go hang yourselves [critics] . . . you shall never want rope enough.[8]

Gargantua and Pantagruel, V, author's prologue

18   Looking as like . . . as one pea does like another.[9]

Gargantua and Pantagruel, V, 2

19   It is meat, drink, and cloth to us.

Gargantua and Pantagruel, V, 7

20   I am going to seek a grand perhaps; draw the curtain, the farce is played.[10]

Alleged last words. From MOTTEUX, *Life of Rabelais*

---

[1]My appetite comes to me while eating. — MONTAIGNE, *Essays* [1580–1595], *III, 9*

[2]He is most powerful who has power over himself. — SENECA, *Epistles, 90, 34*

[3]Fais ce que voudras.

[4]We could manage this matter to a T. — LAURENCE STERNE, *Tristram Shandy, bk. II* [1760], *ch. 5*

You see they'd have fitted him to a T. — SAMUEL JOHNSON; from BOSWELL, *Life of Johnson* [1791]

You will find it shall echo my speech to a T. — THOMAS MOORE, *Address for the Opening of the New Theatre of St. Stephen*

[5]The will for deed I do accept. — DU BARTAS, *Divine Weeks and Works* [1578], *Second Week, Third Day, pt. 2*

You must take the will for the deed. — JONATHAN SWIFT, *Polite Conversation* [1738], *Dialogue 2*

[6]While you live, tell truth and shame the devil! — SHAKESPEARE, *Henry IV, pt. I, act III, sc. i, l. 62*

I'd tell the truth, and shame the devil. — SAMUEL JOHNSON; from BOSWELL, *Life of Johnson* [1791], *vol. I, p. 460* (Everyman edition)

Truth being truth, / Tell it and shame the devil. — ROBERT BROWNING, *The Ring and the Book* [1868–1869], *III, The Other Half-Rome*

[7]As clear and as manifest as the nose in a man's face. — ROBERT BURTON, *Anatomy of Melancholy* [1621–1651], *pt. III, sec. 3, member 4, subsec. 1*

[8]They were suffered to have rope enough till they had haltered themselves. — THOMAS FULLER, *The Historie of the Holy Warre* [1639], *bk. 5, ch. 7*

Give a man enough rope and he'll hang himself. — *Proverb*

[9]As like as one pease is to another. — JOHN LYLY, *Euphues* [1579]

They say we are / Almost as like as eggs. — SHAKESPEARE, *The Winter's Tale, act I, sc. ii, l. 130*

As one egg is like another. — CERVANTES, *Don Quixote, pt. II* [1615], *bk. III, ch. 14*

[10]Je m'en vais chercher un grand peut-être; tirez le rideau, la farce est jouée.

His religion, at best, is an anxious wish; like that of Rabelais, "a great Perhaps." — THOMAS CARLYLE, *Essays, Burns* [1828]

The grand perhaps. — ROBERT BROWNING, *Bishop Blougram's Apology* [1855]

John Heywood[1]

c. 1497–c. 1580

1 All a green willow, willow, willow,
All a green willow is my garland.[2]

The Green Willow

2 The loss of wealth is loss of dirt,
As sages in all times assert;
The happy man's without a shirt.

Be Merry Friends

3 Let the world slide,[3] let the world go;
A fig for care, and a fig for woe!
If I can't pay, why I can owe,
And death makes equal the high and low.

Be Merry Friends

4 Haste maketh waste.[4]

Proverbs [1546], pt. I, ch. 2

5 Good to be merry and wise.   *Proverbs, I, 2*

6 Look ere ye leap.[5]   *Proverbs, I, 2*

7 While between two stools my tail go to the ground.[6]   *Proverbs, I, 2*

8 The fat is in the fire.   *Proverbs, I, 3*

9 When the sun shineth, make hay.

Proverbs, I, 3

10 The tide tarrieth no man.[7]

Proverbs, I, 3

11 And while I at length debate and beat the bush,
There shall step in other men and catch the birds.[8]

Proverbs, I, 3

12 Wedding is destiny,
And hanging likewise.[9]   *Proverbs, I, 3*

13 Happy man, happy dole.[10]   *Proverbs, I, 3*

14 God never send'th mouth but he sendeth meat.[11]   *Proverbs, I, 4*

15 A hard beginning maketh a good ending.

Proverbs, I, 4

16 Like will to like.   *Proverbs, I, 4*

17 More afraid than hurt.   *Proverbs, I, 4*

18 Nothing is impossible to a willing heart.

Proverbs, I, 5

19 Let the world wag, and take mine ease in mine inn.   *Proverbs, I, 5*

20 Hold their noses to grindstone.

Proverbs, I, 5

21 Cut my coat after my cloth.   *Proverbs, I, 8*

22 The nearer to the church, the further from God.[12]

Proverbs, I, 9

23 Now for good luck, cast an old shoe after me.

Proverbs, I, 9

24 Better is to bow than break.[13]

Proverbs, I, 9

25 It hurteth not the tongue to give fair words.[14]

Proverbs, I, 9

26 Two heads are better than one.

Proverbs, I, 9

27 A short horse is soon curried.

Proverbs, I, 10

---

[1]John Heywood's *Proverbs,* first printed in 1546, is the earliest collection of English colloquial sayings. The selection here given is from the edition of 1874 (a reprint of 1598), edited by JULIAN SHARMAN.

[2]The earliest known of the "willow" songs (see Shakespeare, 215:1).

[3]Let the world slide. — *Towneley Mysteries* [1420]
Let the world slide. — SHAKESPEARE, *The Taming of the Shrew, Induction, sc. i, l. 6*

[4]In wikked haste is no profit. — CHAUCER, *The Canterbury Tales* [c. 1387], *Melibee, 2240*

[5]Thou shouldst have looked before thou hadst leapt. — JONSON, CHAPMAN, MARSTON, *Eastward Ho* [1605], *act V, sc. i*

[6]Between two stools one sits on the ground. — *Les Proverbes del Vilain,* MS Bodleian [c. 1303]

[7]Time nor tide tarrieth no man. — ROBERT GREENE, *Disputations* [1592]
Hoist up sail while gale doth last, / Tide and wind stay no man's pleasure. — ROBERT SOUTHWELL, *St. Peter's Complaint* [1595]
Nae man can tether time or tide. — ROBERT BURNS, *Tam o' Shanter* [1791]

[8]It is this proverb which Henry V is reported to have uttered at the siege of Orléans: Shall I beat the bush and another take the bird?

[9]Hanging and wiving go by destiny. — *The Schole-hous for Women* [1541]
Marriage and hanging go by destiny; matches are made in heaven. — ROBERT BURTON, *Anatomy of Melancholy* [1621–1651], *pt. III, sec. 2, member 5, subsec. 5*

[10]Happy man be his dole. — SHAKESPEARE, *The Merry Wives of Windsor, act III, sc. iv, l. 68,* and *The Winter's Tale, act I, sc. ii, l. 163*

[11]God sendeth and giveth both mouth and the meat. — THOMAS TUSSER, *A Hundred Good Points of Husbandry* [1557]
God sends meat, and the Devil sends cooks. — JOHN TAYLOR [1580–1653], *Works* [1630], *vol. II, p. 85*
The holy prophet Zoroaster said, / The Lord who made thy teeth shall give thee bread. — *Persian couplet*

[12]Qui est près de l'église est souvent loin de Dieu [He who is near the Church is often far from God]. — *Les Proverbes Communs* [c. 1500]

[13]Rather to bow than break is profitable: / Humility is a thing commendable. — *The Moral Proverbs of Cristyne* [1390]

[14]Fair words never hurt the tongue. — JONSON, CHAPMAN, MARSTON, *Eastward Ho* [1605], *act IV, sc. i*

1　To tell tales out of school.

Proverbs, I, 10

2　To hold with the hare and run with the hound.

Proverbs, I, 10

3　Neither fish nor flesh, nor good red herring.

Proverbs, I, 10

4　All is well that ends well.[1]　*Proverbs, I, 10*

5　Of a good beginning cometh a good end.[2]

Proverbs, I, 10

6　When the steed is stolen, shut the stable door.[3]

Proverbs, I, 10

7　She looketh as butter would not melt in her mouth.　*Proverbs, I, 10*

8　Ill weed groweth fast.[4]　*Proverbs, I, 10*

9　Beggars should be no choosers.

Proverbs, I, 10

10　Merry as a cricket.　*Proverbs, I, 11*

11　To rob Peter and pay Paul.[5]　*Proverbs, I, 11*

12 A man may well bring a horse to the water,
But he cannot make him drink without he will.[6]

Proverbs, I, 11

13　Rome was not built in one day.

Proverbs, I, 11

14　Ye have many strings to your bow.[7]

Proverbs, I, 11

15　Children learn to creep ere they can learn to go.

Proverbs, I, 11

16　Better is half a loaf than no bread.

Proverbs, I, 11

17　Nought venture nought have.

Proverbs, I, 11

18　Children and fools cannot lie.[8]

Proverbs, I, 11

19　All is fish that cometh to net.[9]

Proverbs, I, 11

20　Who is worse shod than the shoemaker's wife?[10]

Proverbs, I, 11

21　One good turn asketh another.

Proverbs, I, 11

22　A dog hath a day.　*Proverbs, I, 11*

23　A hair of the dog that bit us.[11]　*Proverbs, I, 11*

24　　But in deed,
A friend is never known till a man have need.

Proverbs, I, 11

25　Burnt child fire dreadeth.[12]　*Proverbs, II, 2*

26　There is no fool to the old fool.[13]

Proverbs, II, 2

27　A woman hath nine lives like a cat.

Proverbs, II, 4

28　A penny for your thought.　*Proverbs, II, 4*

29　You cannot see the wood for the trees.

Proverbs, II, 4

30　You stand in your own light.　*Proverbs, II, 4*

31　Tit for tat.[14]　*Proverbs, II, 4*

32　Three may keep counsel, if two be away.[15]

Proverbs, II, 5

---

[1]Si finis bonus est, totum bonum erit [If the end is good, all will be good].— *Gesta Romanorum* [1472], *tale 67*

[2]Who that well his warke beginneth, / The rather a good end he winneth.— JOHN GOWER [c. 1325–1408], *Confessio Amantis* [c. 1386–1390]

[3]Quant le cheval est emblé dounke ferme fols l'estable [When the horse has been stolen, the fool shuts the stable].— *Les Proverbes del Vilain, MS Bodleian* [c. 1303]

[4]Ewyl weed ys sone y-growe.— *MS Harleian* [c. 1490]
Great weeds do grow apace.— SHAKESPEARE, *Richard III, act II, sc. iv, l. 13*
An ill weed grows apace.— GEORGE CHAPMAN, *An Humorous Day's Mirth* [1599]

[5]Give not Saint Peter so much, to leave Saint Paul nothing.— GEORGE HERBERT, *Jacula Prudentum* [1640]
"To rob Peter and pay Paul" is said to have had its origin in the reign of Edward VI when the lands of St. Peter at Westminster were appropriated to raise money for the repair of St. Paul's in London.
The French form of the proverb is: Découvrir saint Pierre pour couvrir saint Paul.

[6]You may bring a horse to the river, but he will drink when and what he pleaseth.— GEORGE HERBERT, *Jacula Prudentum* [1651]

[7]Two strings to his bow.— RICHARD HOOKER, *Laws of Ecclesiastical Polity, bk. V* [1597], *ch. 80*

[8]'Tis an old saw, children and fools speak true.— JOHN LYLY, *Endymion* [1591]

[9]All's fish they get that cometh to net.— THOMAS TUSSER, *A Hundred Good Points of Husbandry* [1557], *February Abstract*

[10]Him that makes shoes go barefoot himself.— ROBERT BURTON, *Anatomy of Melancholy* [1621–1651], *Democritus to the Reader*

[11]Old recipe books advised that an inebriate should drink sparingly in the morning some of the same kind of liquor which he had drunk to excess the night before.

[12]Brend child fur dredth, / Quoth Hendyng.— HENDYNG [1272–1307], *Proverbs, MS*

[13]There is no fool like an old fool.— JOHN LYLY, *Mother Bombie* [1590], *act IV, sc. ii*, and in frequent use thereafter

[14]This is a corruption of *Tant pour tant.*

[15]Two may keep counsel when the third's away.— SHAKESPEARE, *Titus Andronicus, act IV, sc. ii, l. 145*
Three can hold their peace if two be away.— GEORGE HERBERT, *Jacula Prudentum* [1651]

1 Small pitchers have wide ears.[1]
Proverbs, II, 5

2 Many hands make light work.
Proverbs, II, 5

3 Out of God's blessing into the warm sun.[2]
Proverbs, II, 5

4 There is no fire without some smoke.[3]
Proverbs, II, 5

5 A cat may look on a king.   *Proverbs, II, 5*

6 Much water goeth by the mill
That the miller knoweth not of.[4]
Proverbs, II, 5

7 He must needs go whom the devil doth drive.
Proverbs, II, 7

8 Set the cart before the horse.   *Proverbs, II, 7*

9 The more the merrier.   *Proverbs, II, 7*

10 Be the day never so long,
Evermore at last they ring to even-song.[5]
Proverbs, II, 7

11 The moon is made of a green cheese.[6]
Proverbs, II, 7

12 I know on which side my bread is buttered.
Proverbs, II, 7

13 The wrong sow by th' ear.   *Proverbs, II, 9*

14 An ill wind that bloweth no man to good.[7]
Proverbs, II, 9

15 For when I gave you an inch, you took an ell.[8]
Proverbs, II, 9

16 Would ye both eat your cake and have your
cake?[9]   *Proverbs, II, 9*

17 Every man for himself and God for us all.[10]
Proverbs, II, 9

18 Though he love not to buy the pig in the poke.[11]

Proverbs, II, 9

19 This hitteth the nail on the head.
Proverbs, II, 11

20 Enough is as good as a feast.
Proverbs, II, 11

Charles V
1500–1558

21 Iron hand in a velvet glove.
Attributed. From THOMAS CARLYLE, *Latter-Day
Pamphlets, 11*

22 I make war on the living, not on the dead.
*Said when advised to hang Luther's corpse on
the gallows [1546]*

23 I speak Spanish to God, Italian to women, French
to men, and German to my horse.[12]

Attributed

Pope Gregory XIII
1502–1585

24 To the greater glory of God.[13]
*From The Canons and Decrees of the Council
of Trent [1542–1560]*

Sir Thomas Wyatt
c. 1503–1542

25 Forget not yet the tried intent
Of such a truth as I have meant;

---

[1]Pitchers have ears.—SHAKESPEARE, *The Taming of the Shrew,
act IV, sc. iv, l. 52,* and *Richard III, act II, sc. iv, l. 37*
Little pitchers have wide ears.—GEORGE HERBERT, *Jacula Prudentum* [1640]

[2]Thou shalt come out of a warm sun into God's blessing.
—JOHN LYLY, *Euphues* [1579]
Thou out of Heaven's benediction com'st / To the warm sun.
—SHAKESPEARE, *King Lear, act II, sc. ii, l. 168*

[3]There can no great smoke arise, but there must be some fire.
—JOHN LYLY, *Euphues* [1579]

[4]More water glideth by the mill / Than wots the miller of.
—SHAKESPEARE, *Titus Andronicus, act II, sc. i, l. 85*
The miller sees not all the water that goes by his mill.—ROBERT
BURTON, *Anatomy of Melancholy* [1621–1651], *pt. III, sec. 3,
member 4, subsec. 1*

[5]Be the day short or never so long, / At length it ringeth to
evensong.—*Quoted at the stake by George Tankerfield* [1555].
From JOHN FOXE [1516–1587], *Actes and Monuments (The Book
of Martyrs)* [1563], *ch. 7*

[6]They would make me believe that the moon was made of green
cheese.—JOHN FRITH [1503–1533], *A Pistle to the Christian
Reader* [1529]

[7]Except wind stands as never it stood, / It is an ill wind turns
none to good.—TUSSER, *A Description of the Properties of Winds*
Falstaff. What wind blew you hither, Pistol?
Pistol. Not the ill wind which blows no man to good.—SHAKE-
SPEARE, *Henry IV, Part II, act V, sc. iii, l. 87*

[8]Give an inch, he'll take an ell.—JOHN WEBSTER, *Sir Thomas
Wyatt*

[9]Wouldst thou both eat thy cake and have it?—GEORGE HER-
BERT, *The Size* [1633]

[10]Every man for himself, his own ends, the Devil for all.—
ROBERT BURTON, *Anatomy of Melancholy* [1621–1651], *pt. III,
sec. 1, member 3*

[11]For buying or selling of pig in a poke.—THOMAS TUSSER, *A
Hundred Good Points of Husbandry* [1557], *September Abstract*

[12]Je parle espagnol à Dieu, italien aux femmes, français aux
hommes, et allemand à mon cheval.

[13]Ad maiorem Dei gloriam. Motto of the Society of Jesus.

My great travail so gladly spent,
Forget not yet!   *Forget Not Yet*

1 My lute, awake! perform the last
  Labor that thou and I shall waste,
  And end that I have now begun;
  For when this song is sung and past,
  My lute, be still, for I have done.
      *The Lover Complaineth the Unkindness of
      His Love*

2 They flee from me, that sometime did me seek
  With naked foot, stalking in my chamber.
      *The Lover Showeth How He Is Forsaken of
      Such as He Sometime Enjoyed*

3 And graven with diamonds in letters plain
  There is written her fair neck round about:
  Noli me tangere, for Caesar's I am,
  And wild for to hold, though I seem tame.
      Whoso List to Hunt

John Bradford
c. 1510–1555

4 The familiar story, that, on seeing evildoers taken
  to the place of execution, he was wont to exclaim:
  "But for the grace of God there goes John Bradford,"
  is a universal tradition, which has overcome the lapse
  of time.[1]
      *Biographical notice, Parker Society edition,
      The Writings of John Bradford [1853]*

Ambroise Paré
1510–1590

5 I treated him, God cured him.[2]
      His favorite saying

Sir Thomas Vaux
1510–1556

6 Companion none is like
  Unto the mind alone;
  For many have been harmed by speech,
  Through thinking, few or none.
      Of a Contented Mind [1557]

7 But age, with his stealing steps,
  Hath claw'd me in his clutch.[3]
      The Aged Lover Renounceth Love, st. 3

---

[1]There but for the grace of God goes God. — *Anonymous saying,*
attributed to ORSON WELLES, *among others*

[2]Je le soignay, Dieu le guérit.

[3]Quoted by First Clown in SHAKESPEARE, *Hamlet, act V, sc. i,*
l. 77.

Richard Grafton
c. 1513–1572

8 Thirty days hath November,
  April, June, and September,
  February hath twenty-eight alone,
  And all the rest have thirty-one.[4]
      Chronicles of England [1562]

John Knox
c. 1513–1572

9 The First Blast of the Trumpet Against the Mon
  strous Regiment [Regimen] of Women.
      Title of pamphlet [1558]

10 A man with God is always in the majority.[5]
      *Inscription on Reformation Monument,
      Geneva, Switzerland*

Mary Tudor [Mary I]
1516–1558

11 When I am dead and opened, you shall find
   "Calais" lying in my heart.
      From HOLINSHED, *Chronicles [1577], III, 1160*

Joachim du Bellay
1522–1560

12 Happy he who like Ulysses has made a glorious
   voyage.[6]   *Les Regrets [1559], XXXI*

Pierre de Ronsard
1524–1585

13 When you are old, at evening candlelit,
   Beside the fire bending to your wool,
   Read out my verse and murmur, "Ronsard writ
   This praise for me when I was beautiful."[7]
      Sonnets pour Hélène, I, 43

---

[4]Thirty days hath September, / April, June, and November; / All
the rest have thirty-one, / Excepting February alone, / Which hath
but twenty-eight, in fine, / Till leap year gives it twenty-nine.—
Common in the New England states
   Compare the old Latin class mnemonic:
   In March, July, October, May, / The Ides are on the fifteenth
day, / The Nones the seventh: all other months besides / Have two
days less for Nones and Ides.

[5]Un homme avec Dieu est toujours dans la majorité.

[6]Heureux qui, comme Ulysse, a fait un beau voyage.

[7]Quand vous serez bien vieille, au soir à la chandelle, / Assise
auprès du feu, dévidant et filant, / Direz, chantant mes vers, en vous
émerveillant: / "Ronsard me célébrait du temps que j'étais belle."
   Translated by HUMBERT WOLFE.
   See the adaptation by Yeats: When you are old and gray and full
of sleep, 637:4.

1 Live now, believe me, wait not till tomorrow;
  Gather the roses of life today.[1]
> *Sonnets pour Hélène, I, 43*

2 Sweetheart, come see if the rose
  Which at morning began to unclose
  Its damask gown to the sun
  Has not lost, now the day is done,
  The folds of its damasked gown
  And its colors so like your own.
> *Odes [1553]. À Cassandre*[2]

3 Harvest, oh! harvest your hour
  While life is abloom with youth!
  For age with bitter ruth
  Will fade your beauty's flower.[3]
> *Odes. À Cassandre, last lines*

Thomas Tusser
c. 1524–1580

4 At Christmas play and make good cheer,
  For Christmas comes but once a year.
> *A Hundred Good Points of Husbandry
> [1557]. The Farmer's Daily Diet*

5 Such mistress, such Nan,
  Such master, such man.[4]
> *A Hundred Good Points of Husbandry.
> April's Abstract*

6 Sweet April showers
  Do spring May flowers.
> *A Hundred Good Points of Husbandry.
> April's Husbandry*

7 'Tis merry in hall
  Where beards wag all.
> *A Hundred Good Points of Husbandry.
> August's Abstract*

Gabriel Meurier
1530–1601

8 He who excuses himself accuses himself.[5]
> *Trésor des Sentences*

William Stevenson
c. 1530–1575

9 I cannot eat but little meat,
  My stomach is not good;
  But sure I think that I can drink
  With him that wears a hood.
> *Gammer Gurton's Needle [1566], drinking
> song, act II*

10 Back and side go bare, go bare,
   Both foot and hand go cold;
   But, belly, God send thee good ale enough,
   Whether it be new or old.
> *Gammer Gurton's Needle, drinking song,
> refrain*

Henri Estienne
c. 1531–1598

11 Si jeunesse savait, si vieillesse pouvait [If youth
   but knew, if old age but could].
> *Les Prémices [1594]*

12 God tempers the wind to the shorn lamb.[6]
> *Les Prémices*

Elizabeth I
1533–1603

13 I know I have the body of a weak and feeble
   woman, but I have the heart and stomach of a king,
   and of a king of England too; and think foul scorn
   that Parma or Spain, or any prince of Europe,
   should dare to invade the borders of my realm.
> *Speech to the troops at Tilbury on the approach
> of the Armada [1588]*

14 I am your anointed Queen. I will never be by violence constrained to do anything. I thank God I
   am endued with such qualities that if I were turned
   out of the Realm in my petticoat I were able to live
   in any place in Christendom.
> *From* CHAMBERLIN, *Sayings of Queen Elizabeth*

15 I will make you shorter by the head.
> *From* CHAMBERLIN, *Sayings of Queen Elizabeth*

16 The daughter of debate, that eke discord doth
   sow.[7]
> *From* CHAMBERLIN, *Sayings of Queen Elizabeth*

17 [To the Countess of Nottingham] God may forgive you, but I never can.
> *From* HUME, *History of England Under the
> House of Tudor, vol. II, ch. 7*

---

[1] Vivez, si m'en croyez, n'attendez à demain: / Cueillez dès aujourd'hui les roses de la vie.

[2] Mignonne, allons voir si la rose / Qui, ce matin, avoit déclose / Sa robe de pourpre au soleil, / A point perdu, cette vesprée / Les plis de sa robe pourprée / Et son teint au vôtre pareil.
Translated by CURTIS HIDDEN PAGE.

[3] Cueillez, cueillez votre jeunesse: / Comme à cette fleur, la vieillesse / Fera ternir votre beauté.

[4] Tel maître, tel valet. — *Attributed to* PIERRE TERRÀIL, SEIGNEUR DE BAYARD [c. 1473–1524], *known as the* CHEVALIER BAYARD

[5] Qui s'excuse, s'accuse.

[6] Dieu mesure le froid à la brebis tondue.

[7] Mary, Queen of Scots.

1   Though God hath raised me high, yet this I count the glory of my crown: that I have reigned with your loves.   *The Golden Speech [1601]*

2   Semper eadem [Ever the same].   *Motto*

3   'Twas God the word that spake it,
He took the Bread and brake it;
And what the word did make it,
That I believe, and take it.[1]
    From S. CLARKE, Marrow of Ecclesiastical History [ed. 1675], pt. II, Life of Queen Elizabeth

4   Must! Is *must* a word to be addressed to princes? Little man, little man!
    On her deathbed, to Robert Cecil, her principal secretary [March 24, 1603]

Michel Eyquem de Montaigne[2]
1533–1592

5   I want to be seen here in my simple, natural, ordinary fashion, without straining or artifice; for it is myself that I portray. . . . I am myself the matter of my book.[3]
    Essays,[4] bk. I [1580], To the Reader

6   Truly man is a marvelously vain, diverse, and undulating object. It is hard to found any constant and uniform judgment on him.[5]
    Essays, I, ch. 1

7   The thing I fear most is fear.[6]
    Essays, I, 18

8   I want death to find me planting my cabbages.[7]
    Essays, I, 20

9   He who would teach men to die would teach them to live.[8]
    Essays, I, 20

10   Live as long as you please, you will strike nothing off the time you will have to spend dead.
    Essays, I, 20

11   Wherever your life ends, it is all there. The advantage of living is not measured by length, but by use; some men have lived long, and lived little; attend to it while you are in it. It lies in your will, not in the number of years, for you to have lived enough.
    Essays, I, 20

12   I do not speak the minds of others except to speak my own mind better.
    Essays, I, 26

13   Since I would rather make of him [the child] an able man than a learned man, I would also urge that care be taken to choose a guide [tutor] with a well-made rather than a well-filled head.[9]
    Essays, I, 26

14   If you press me to say why I loved him, I can say no more than it was because he was he and I was I.[10]
    Essays, I, 28

15   Nothing is so firmly believed as what is least known.
    Essays, I, 32

16   A man of understanding has lost nothing, if he has himself.[11]
    Essays, I, 39

17   We must reserve a back shop all our own,[12] entirely free, in which to establish our real liberty and our principal retreat and solitude.
    Essays, I, 39

18   The greatest thing in the world is to know how to belong to oneself.[13]   *Essays, I, 39*

19   It is a thorny undertaking, and more so than it seems, to follow a movement so wandering as that of our mind, to penetrate the opaque depths of its innermost folds, to pick out and immobilize the innumerable flutterings that agitate it.[14]
    Essays, II [1580], 6

20   My trade and my art is living.[15]
    Essays, II, 6

21   The easy, gentle, and sloping path . . . is not the path of true virtue. It demands a rough and thorny road.   *Essays, II, 11*

---

[1]Answer on being asked her opinion of Christ's presence in the Sacrament.

[2]Translated by DONALD M. FRAME unless otherwise noted.

[3]Je veux qu'on m'y voit en ma façon simple, naturelle, et ordinaire, sans étude et artifice; car c'est moi que je peins. . . . Je suis moi-même la matière de mon livre.

[4]Books I and II of the *Essays* were published in 1580; republished [1588] with the addition of book III and with many interpolations in books I and 11; the whole republished posthumously [1595], incorporating material based on Montaigne's marginal annotations in the 1588 edition.

[5]Certes, c'est un subject [sic] merveilleusement vain, divers, et ondoyant, que l'homme. Il est malaisé d'y fonder jugement constant et uniforme.

[6]C'est de quoi j'ai le plus de peur que la peur.

[7]Je veux que la mort me trouve plantant mes choux.

[8]I have taught you, my dear flock, for above thirty years how to live, and I will show you in a very short time how to die. —SIR EDWIN SANDYS [1561–1629], *Anglorum Speculum*
    Teach him how to live, / And, oh still harder lesson! how to die. —PORTEUS, *Death, l. 316*

[9]Plutôt la tête bien faite que bien pleine.

[10]Parce que c'était lui; parce que c'était moi.
    Translated by CHARLES COTTON, revised by HAZLETT and WIGHT.

[11]L'homme d'entendement n'a rien perdu, s'il a soi-même.

[12]Il se faut réserver une arrière boutique toute notre.

[13]La plus grande chose du monde, c'est de savoir être à soi.

[14]C'est une épineuse entreprise, et plus qu'il ne semble, de suivre une allure si vagabonde que celle de nôtre esprit; de pénétrer les profondeurs opaques de ses replis internes; de choisir et arrêter tant de menus de ses agitations.

[15]Mon métier et mon art, c'est vivre.

1   When I play with my cat, who knows if I am not a pastime to her more than she is to me?

Essays, II, 12

2   The souls of emperors and cobblers are cast in the same mold. . . . The same reason that makes us bicker with a neighbor creates a war between princes.

Essays, II, 12

3   Their [the Skeptics'] way of speaking is: "I settle nothing . . . I do not understand it . . . Nothing seems true that may not seem false." Their sacramental word is Επεχω, which is to say, I suspend my judgment.[1]

Essays, II, 12

4   This notion [skepticism] is more clearly understood by asking "What do I know?"[2]

Essays, II, 12

5   Man is certainly crazy. He could not make a mite, and he makes gods by the dozen.[3]

Essays, II, 12

6   What of a truth that is bounded by these mountains and is falsehood to the world that lives beyond?[4]

Essays, II, 12

7   Those who have compared our life to a dream were right. . . . We sleeping wake, and waking sleep.[5]

Essays, II, 12

8   How many valiant men we have seen to survive their own reputation!

Essays, II, 16

9   A man may be humble through vainglory.

Essays, II, 17

10   I find that the best goodness I have has some tincture of vice.

Essays, II, 20

11   Saying is one thing and doing is another.

Essays, II, 31

12   There were never in the world two opinions alike, any more than two hairs or two grains. Their most universal quality is diversity.

Essays, II, 37

13   I will follow the good side right to the fire, but not into it if I can help it.

Essays, III [1595], 1

14   I speak the truth, not my fill of it, but as much as I dare speak; and I dare to do so a little more as I grow old.

Essays, III, 1

15   Few men have been admired by their own households.

Essays, III, 1

16   Every man bears the whole stamp of the human condition.[6]

Essays, III, 1

17   It [marriage] happens as with cages: the birds without despair to get in, and those within despair of getting out.[7]

Essays, III, 5

18   Everyone recognizes me in my book, and my book in me.

Essays, III, 5

19   It takes so much to be a king that he exists only as such. That extraneous glare that surrounds him hides him and conceals him from us; our sight breaks and is dissipated by it, being filled and arrested by this strong light.

Essays, III, 7

20   Our wisdom and deliberation for the most part follow the lead of chance.[8]   *Essays, III, 8*

21   Not because Socrates said so, but because it is in truth my own disposition — and perchance to some excess — I look upon all men as my compatriots, and embrace a Pole as a Frenchman, making less account of the national than of the universal and common bond.[9]

Essays, III, 9

---

[1]Je suspends mon jugement.
Translated by E. J. TRECHMANN.
Greek word (*epecho*) inscribed on a bay in Montaigne's library. — MAURICE RAT, *Oeuvres Complètes de Montaigne, La Pléiade Edition* [1962], *note*
This is one of a dozen maxims from Sextus Empiricus, third-century Greek philosopher, which together with biblical and Latin quotations comprise the fifty-seven sentences painted on the roof bays of Montaigne's library. About two-thirds of the sentences are in *Apologie de Raimond Sebond* (chapter 12 of book II of the *Essays*).

[2]Que sais-je?
Translated by E. J. TRECHMANN.
This phrase appeared on a medal Montaigne had struck, which showed also his coat of arms and the collar of the order of Saint Michael, and on the reverse side a pair of scales in perfect balance, the date [1576], his age (forty-two), and the Skeptics' motto Επεχω (see Montaigne, 153:3).

[3]L'homme est bien insensé. Il ne saurait forger un ciron, et forge des Dieux à douzaines.

[4]Quelle vérité que ces montagnes bornent, qui est mensonge qui se tient au delà?

[5]Ceux qui ont apparié notre vie à un songe ont eu de la raison. . . . Nous veillons dormants et veillants dormons.
Translated by E. J. TRECHMANN.

[6]Chaque homme porte la forme, entière de l'humaîne condition.
Translated by CHARLES COTTON, revised by HAZLITT and WIGHT.

[7]Translated by CHARLES COTTON, revised by HAZLITT and WIGHT.
I myself have loved a lady and pursued her with a great deal of under-age protestation, whom some three or four gallants that have enjoyed would all with all their hearts have been glad to have been rid of. 'Tis just like a summer bird-cage in a garden: the birds that are without despair to get in, and the birds that are within despair and are in a consumption for fear they shall never get out. — JOHN WEBSTER, *The White Devil* [1612], act I, sc. ii
Wedlock, indeed, hath oft comparèd been / To public feasts, where meet a public rout — / Where they that are without would fain go in, / And they that are within would fain go out. — SIR JOHN DAVIES [1569–1626], *Contention Betwixt a Wife, etc.*

[8]Although men flatter themselves with their great actions, they are not so often the result of great design as of chance. — LA ROCHEFOUCAULD, *Maxim 57*

[9]Translated by CHARLES COTTON, revised by HAZLITT and WIGHT.

1   There is no man so good that if he placed all his actions and thoughts under the scrutiny of the laws, he would not deserve hanging ten times in his life.
Essays, III, 9

2   A man must be a little mad if he does not want to be even more stupid.   *Essays, III, 9*

3   I have seen no more evident monstrosity and miracle in the world than myself.
Essays, III, 11

4   I have here only made a nosegay of culled flowers, and have brought nothing of my own but the thread that ties them together.[1]   *Essays, III, 12*

5   It is more of a job to interpret the interpretations than to interpret the things, and there are more books about books than about any other subject: we do nothing but write glosses about each other.   *Essays, III, 13*

6   For truth itself does not have the privilege to be employed at any time and in every way; its use, noble as it is, has its circumscriptions and limits.
Essays, III, 13

7   No matter that we may mount on stilts, we still must walk on our own legs. And on the highest throne in the world, we still sit only on our own bottom.[2]   *Essays, III, 13*

8   Let us give Nature a chance; she knows her business better than we do.   *Essays, III, 13*

William I [William the Silent]
1533–1584

9   My God, have mercy on my soul and on my poor people.[3]
Last words as he fell under an assassin's bullets

William Butler
1535–1618

10   It is unseasonable and unwholesome in all months that have not an *r* in their name to eat an oyster.   *Dyet's Dry Dinner [1599]*

Sir Humphrey Gilbert
c. 1539–1583

11   We are as near to heaven by sea as by land![4]
From HAKLUYT, Voyages, vol. III [1600], p. 159

Saint John of the Cross [San Juan de la Cruz]
1542–1591

12   The Dark Night of the Soul.
Title of treatise [c. 1583] based on his poem Songs of the Soul Which Rejoices at Having Reached . . . Union with God by the Road of Spiritual Negation [c. 1578]

Mary Stuart [Mary, Queen of Scots]
1542–1587

13   In my end is my beginning.   *Motto*

14   O Lord my God, I have trusted in thee;
O Jesu my dearest one, now set me free.
In prison's oppression, in sorrow's obsession,
I weary for thee.
With sighing and crying bowed down as dying,
I adore thee, I implore thee, set me free![5]
Prayer written in her Book of Devotion before her execution

Jan Zamoyski
1542–1605

15   The king reigns, but does not govern.[6]
Speech in the Polish Parliament [1605], referring to King Sigismund III

---

[1]Translated by CHARLES COTTON, revised by HAZLITT and WIGHT. John Bartlett used this passage as an epigraph for the fourth edition of *Bartlett's Familiar Quotations* [1864].
I am but a gatherer and disposer of other men's stuff, at my best value. —SIR HENRY WOTTON, *The Elements of Architecture* [1624], *preface*

[2]Si, avons nous beau monter sur des échasses, car sur des échasses encore faut-il marcher de nos jambes. Et au plus élevé trône du monde, si ne sommes assis que sur notre cul.
Translated by WALTER KAISER.

[3]Mon Dieu, ayez pitié de mon âme et de mon pauvre peuple.

[4]The way to heaven out of all places is of like length and distance. —SIR THOMAS MORE, *Utopia* [1516]
Gilbert, on the last day of his life, was seen in his tiny pinnace *Squirrel* with a book in hand, probably More's *Utopia*, which inspired his last utterance. He was homeward bound from Newfoundland, which he had just taken possession of in the name of the queen [August 1583].
"Do not fear! Heaven is as near," / He said, "by water as by land!" —HENRY WADSWORTH LONGFELLOW, *Sir Humphrey Gilbert* [1849], *st. 6*

[5]O Domine Deus! speravi in te; / O care mi Jesu! nunc libera me. / In dura catena, in misera poena, / Disidero te. / Languendo, gemendo, et genuflectendo, / Adoro, imploro, ut liberes me!
Translated by ALGERNON CHARLES SWINBURNE.

[6]Adolphe Thiers adopted the epigram as the motto for his journal *Le National*.

Sir Edward Dyer
1543–1607

1 My mind to me a kingdom is;
  Such present joys therein I find
  That it excels all other bliss
  That earth affords or grows by kind:
  Though much I want which most would have,
  Yet still my mind forbids to crave.
  Rawlinson Poetry MS 85,[1] p. 17

Guillaume de Salluste, Seigneur Du Bartas
1544–1590

2 For where's the state beneath the firmament
  That doth excel the bees for government?
  Divine Weeks and Works [1578], First Week, Fifth Day, pt. 1

3 Or almost like a spider, who, confined
  In her web's center, shakt with every wind,
  Moves in an instant if the buzzing fly
  Stir but a string of her lawn canapie.[2]
  Divine Weeks and Works, First Week, Sixth Day

4 Living from hand to mouth.
  Divine Weeks and Works, Second Week, First Day, pt. 4

5 In the jaws of death.[3]
  Divine Weeks and Works, Second Week, First Day, pt. 4

6   Only that he may conform
  To tyrant custom.
  Divine Weeks and Works, Second Week, Third Day, pt. 2

7 Who well lives, long lives; for this age of ours
  Should not be numbered by years, days, and hours.
  Divine Weeks and Works, Second Week, Fourth Day, pt. 2

8   My lovely living boy,
  My hope, my hap, my love, my life, my joy.[4]
  Divine Weeks and Works, Second Week, Fourth Day, pt. 2

9 Out of the book of Nature's learned breast.[5]
  Divine Weeks and Works, Second Week, Fourth Day, pt. 2

10 Flesh of thy flesh, nor yet bone of thy bone.
  Divine Weeks and Works, Second Week, Fourth Day, pt. 2

William Gilbert
1544–1603

11   Philosophy is for the few.[6]
  De Magnete (On the Magnet) [1600]

12   In the discovery of secret things and in the investigation of hidden causes, stronger reasons are obtained from sure experiments and demonstrated arguments than from probable conjectures and the opinions of philosophical speculators of the common sort.[6]
  De Magnete

Miguel de Cervantes
1547–1616

13   You are a king by your own fireside, as much as any monarch in his throne.
  Don Quixote de la Mancha [1605–1615],[7] author's preface, p. xix

14   I was so free with him as not to mince the matter.
  Don Quixote, preface, p. xx

15   They can expect nothing but their labor for their pains.[8]
  Don Quixote, preface, p. xxiii

16   Time out of mind.[9]
  Don Quixote, pt. I [1605], bk. I, ch. 1, p. 4

---

[1]This poem became popular as a song, altered thus:
My mind to me a kingdom is; / Such perfect joy therein I find, / As far exceeds all earthly bliss / That God and Nature hath assigned. / Though much I want that most would have, / Yet still my mind forbids to crave. —WILLIAM BYRD [1543–1623], *Psalms, Sonnets, and Songs of Sadness and Piety* [1588]

[2]Much like a subtle spider which doth sit / In middle of her web, which spreadeth wide; / If aught do touch the utmost thread of it / She feels it instantly on every side. —SIR JOHN DAVIES [1569–1626], *The Immortality of the Soul* [1599]

Our souls sit close and silently within, / And their own webs from their own entrails spin; / And when eyes meet far off, our sense is such / That, spider-like, we feel the tenderest touch. —JOHN DRYDEN, *Marriage à la Mode* [1673], *act II, sc. i*

The spider's touch, how exquisitely fine! / Feels at each thread, and lives along the line. —ALEXANDER POPE, *An Essay on Man* [1733–1734], *epistle I, l. 217*

[3]Out of the jaws of death. —SHAKESPEARE, *Twelfth-Night, act III, sc. iv, l. 396*

[4]My fair son! / My life, my joy, my food, my all the world! —SHAKESPEARE, *King John, act III, sc. iv, l. 103*

[5]The book of Nature is that which the physician must read; and to do so he must walk over the leaves. —PARACELSUS. From *Encyclopaedia Britannica (11th edition), vol. XX, p. 749*

[6]Translated by P. F. MOTTELAY.

[7]Translated [1700–1703] by PETER ANTHONY MOTTEUX. Page numbers are those of the Modern Library Giant edition.

[8]Nothing is to be gotten without pains (labor). —*Proverb*

[9]Time out o' mind. —SHAKESPEARE, *Romeo and Juliet, act I, sc. iv, l. 70*

1　Which I have earned with the sweat of my brows.　*Don Quixote, pt. I, I, 4, p. 22*

2　By a small sample we may judge of the whole piece.　*Don Quixote, pt. I, I, 4, p. 25*

3　Put you in this pickle.[1]
　Don Quixote, pt. I, I, 5, p. 30

4　Can we ever have too much of a good thing?
　Don Quixote, pt. I, I, 6, p. 37

5　The charging of his enemy was but the work of a moment.[2]
　Don Quixote, pt. I, I, 8, p. 50

6　I don't know that ever I saw one in my born days.　*Don Quixote, pt. I, II, 2, p. 57*

7　Those two fatal words, Mine and Thine.
　Don Quixote, pt. I, II, 3, p. 63

8　The eyes those silent tongues of Love.
　Don Quixote, pt. I, II, 3, p. 65

9　And had a face like a benediction.
　Don Quixote, pt. I, II, 4, p. 69

10　There's not the least thing can be said or done, but people will talk and find fault.[3]
　Don Quixote, pt. I, II, 4, p. 70

11　Without a wink of sleep.
　Don Quixote, pt. I, II, 4, p. 72

12　Fortune leaves always some door open to come at a remedy.
　Don Quixote, pt. I, III, 1, p. 94

13　Thank you for nothing.
　Don Quixote, pt. I, III, 1, p. 94

14　No limits but the sky.[4]
　Don Quixote, pt. I, III, 3, p. 110

15　To give the devil his due.
　Don Quixote, pt. I, III, 3, p. 111

16　You're leaping over the hedge before you come to the stile.　*Don Quixote, pt. I, III, 4, p. 117*

17　Paid him in his own coin.
　Don Quixote, pt. I, III, 4, p. 119

18　The famous Don Quixote de la Mancha, otherwise called the Knight of the Sorrowful Countenance.[5]　*Don Quixote, pt. I, III, 5, p. 120*

19　You are come off now with a whole skin.
　Don Quixote, pt. I, III, 5, p. 127

20　Fear is sharp-sighted, and can see things underground, and much more in the skies.
　Don Quixote, pt. I, III, 6, p. 131

21　A finger in every pie.[6]
　Don Quixote, pt. I, III, 6, p. 133

22　No better than she should be.[7]
　Don Quixote, pt. I, III, 6, p. 133

23　That's the nature of women . . . not to love when we love them, and to love when we love them not.　*Don Quixote, pt. I, III, 6, p. 133*

24　You may go whistle for the rest.
　Don Quixote, pt. I, III, 6, p. 134

25　Ill luck, you know, seldom comes alone.
　Don Quixote, pt. I, III, 6, p. 135

26　Why do you lead me a wild-goose chase?
　Don Quixote, pt. I, III, 6, p. 136

27　Experience, the universal Mother of Sciences.
　Don Quixote, pt. I, III, 7, p. 140

28　Give me but that, and let the world rub, there I'll stick.　*Don Quixote, pt. I, III, 7, p. 148*

29　Sing away sorrow, cast away care.
　Don Quixote, pt. I, III, 8, p. 153

30　Of good natural parts, and of a liberal education.
　Don Quixote, pt. I, III, 8, p. 154

31　Let every man mind his own business.
　Don Quixote, pt. I, III, 8, p. 157

32　Those who'll play with cats must expect to be scratched.　*Don Quixote, pt. I, III, 8, p. 159*

33　Raise a hue and cry.
　Don Quixote, pt. I, III, 8, p. 159

34　'Tis the part of a wise man to keep himself today for tomorrow, and not venture all his eggs in one basket.　*Don Quixote, pt. I, III, 9, p. 162*

35　The ease of my burdens, the staff of my life.
　Don Quixote, pt. I, III, 9, p. 163

---

[1]How cam'st thou in this pickle? —Shakespeare, *The Tempest*, act V, sc. i, l. 281

[2]Don Quixote has mistaken windmills for giants, the "enemy," and attacks them. The expression "tilting at windmills" alludes to this incident.

[3]Do you think you could keep people from talking? —Molière, *Tartuffe* [1667], act I, sc. viii

Take wife, or cowl; ride you, or walk: / Doubt not but tongues will have their talk. —Jean de La Fontaine, *The Miller, His Son, and the Donkey* [1694]

[4]Modern saying: The sky's the limit.

---

[5]El Caballero de la Triste Figura.
Translated by Tobias Smollett.

[6]No pie was baked at Castlewood but her little finger was in it. —William Makepeace Thackeray, *The Virginians* [1857–1859], ch. 5

[7]An old proverb.
You are no better than you should be. —Beaumont and Fletcher, *The Coxcomb* [1647], act IV, sc. iii

1 Within a stone's throw of it.
Don Quixote, pt. I, III, 9, p. 170

2 The very remembrance of my former misfortune proves a new one to me.
Don Quixote, pt. I, III, 10, p. 174

3 Absence, that common cure of love.
Don Quixote, pt. I, III, 10, p. 177

4 From pro's and con's they fell to a warmer way of disputing.
Don Quixote, pt. I, III, 10, p. 181

5 Little said is soon amended.[1]
Don Quixote, pt. I, III, 10, p. 184

6 Thou hast seen nothing yet.
Don Quixote, pt. I, III, 11, p. 190

7 Between jest and earnest.
Don Quixote, pt. I, III, 11, p. 190

8 My love and hers have always been purely Platonic.   *Don Quixote, pt. I, III, 11, p. 192*

9 'Tis ill talking of halters in the house of a man that was hanged.
Don Quixote, pt. I, III, 11, p. 195

10 My memory is so bad that many times I forget my own name!   *Don Quixote, pt. I, III, 11, p. 195*

11 'Twill grieve me so to the heart that I shall cry my eyes out.
Don Quixote, pt. I, III, 11, p. 197

12 Ready to split his sides with laughing.
Don Quixote, pt. I, III, 13, p. 208

13 My honor is dearer to me than my life.
Don Quixote, pt. I, IV, 1, p. 226

14 On the word of a gentleman, and a Christian.
Don Quixote, pt. I, IV, 1, p. 236

15 Think before thou speakest.
Don Quixote, pt. I, IV, 3, p. 252

16 Let us forget and forgive injuries.
Don Quixote, pt. I, IV, 3, p. 254

17 I must speak the truth, and nothing but the truth.   *Don Quixote, pt. I, IV, 3, p. 255*

18 More knave than fool.
Don Quixote, pt. I, IV, 4, p. 261

19 Here's the devil-and-all to pay.
Don Quixote, pt. I, IV, 10, p. 319

20 I begin to smell a rat.
Don Quixote, pt. I, IV, 10, p. 319

21 The proof of the pudding is in the eating.
Don Quixote, pt. I, IV, 10, p. 322

22 Let none presume to tell me that the pen is preferable to the sword.
Don Quixote, pt. I, IV, 10, p. 325

23 There's no striving against the stream; and the weakest still goes to the wall.
Don Quixote, pt. I, IV, 20, p. 404

24 The bow cannot always stand bent, nor can human frailty subsist without some lawful recreation.
Don Quixote, pt. I, IV, 21, p. 412

25 It is not the hand but the understanding of a man that may be said to write.[2]
Don Quixote, pt. II [1615], III, author's preface, p. 441

26 When the head aches, all the members partake of the pains.[3]   *Don Quixote, pt. II, III, 2, p. 455*

27 Youngsters read it [Don Quixote's story], grown men understand it, and old people applaud it.
Don Quixote, pt. II, III, 3, p. 464

28 History is in a manner a sacred thing, so far as it contains truth; for where truth is, the supreme Father of it may also be said to be, at least, inasmuch as concerns truth.
Don Quixote, pt. II, III, 3, p. 465

29 Every man is as Heaven made him, and sometimes a great deal worse.
Don Quixote, pt. II, III, 4, p. 468

30 There's no sauce in the world like hunger.
Don Quixote, pt. II, III, 5, p. 473

31 He casts a sheep's eye at the wench.
Don Quixote, pt. II, III, 5, p. 474

32 I ever loved to see everything upon the square.
Don Quixote, pt. II, III, 5, p. 475

33 Neither will I make myself anybody's laughing-stock.   *Don Quixote, pt. II, III, 5, p. 475*

34 Journey over all the universe in a map, without the expense and fatigue of traveling, without suffering the inconveniences of heat, cold, hunger, and thirst.   *Don Quixote, pt. II, III, 6, p. 479*

35 Presume to put in her oar.
Don Quixote, pt. II, III, 6, p. 480

36 The fair sex.[4]
Don Quixote, pt. II, III, 6, p. 480

---

[1]Often rendered: Least said soonest mended.

[2]Cervantes's left hand was maimed for life by gunshot wounds in the battle of Lepanto.

[3]When the head is not sound, the rest cannot be well. —Du Bartas, *Divine Weeks and Works* [1578]

For let our finger ache, and it indues / Our other healthful members ev'n to that sense / Of pain. —Shakespeare, *Othello*, act III, sc. iv, l. 145

[4]That sex which is therefore called fair. —Sir Richard Steele, *The Spectator, no. 302* [February 15, 1712]

1   A little in one's own pocket is better than much in another man's purse. 'Tis good to keep a nest egg. Every little makes a mickle.

Don Quixote, pt. II, III, 7, p. 486

2   Remember the old saying, "Faint heart ne'er won fair lady."

Don Quixote, pt. II, III, 10, p. 501

3   Forewarned forearmed.

Don Quixote, pt. II, III, 10, p. 502

4   As well look for a needle in a bottle of hay.[1]

Don Quixote, pt. II, III, 10, p. 502

5   Are we to mark this day with a white or a black stone?   *Don Quixote, pt. II, III, 10, p. 502*

6   The very pink of courtesy.[2]

Don Quixote, pt. II, III, 13, p. 521

7   I'll turn over a new leaf.

Don Quixote, pt. II, III, 13, p. 524

8   He's [Don Quixote's] a muddled fool, full of lucid intervals.

Don Quixote, pt. II, III, 18, p. 556

9   Marriage is a noose.

Don Quixote, pt. II, III, 19, p. 564

10   There are only two families in the world, the Haves and the Have-Nots.

Don Quixote, pt. II, III, 20, p. 574

11   He preaches well that lives well, quoth Sancho; that's all the divinity I understand.

Don Quixote, pt. II, III, 20, p. 575

12   Love and War are the same thing, and stratagems and policy are as allowable in the one as in the other.   *Don Quixote, pt. II, III, 21, p. 580*

13   A private sin is not so prejudicial in this world as a public indecency.

Don Quixote, pt. II, III, 22, p. 582

14   There is no love lost, sir.

Don Quixote, pt. II, III, 22, p. 582

15   Come back sound, wind and limb.

Don Quixote, pt. II, III, 22, p. 587

16   Patience, and shuffle the cards.[3]

Don Quixote, pt. II, III, 23, p. 592

17   Tell me thy company, and I'll tell thee what thou art.   *Don Quixote, pt. II, III, 23, p. 594*

18   Tomorrow will be a new day.

Don Quixote, pt. II, III, 26, p. 618

19   I can see with half an eye.

Don Quixote, pt. II, III, 29, p. 632

20   Great persons are able to do great kindnesses.

Don Quixote, pt. II, III, 32, p. 662

21   Honesty's the best policy.[4]

Don Quixote, pt. II, III, 33, p. 666

22   An honest man's word is as good as his bond.

Don Quixote, pt. II, IV, 34, p. 674

23   A blot in thy scutcheon to all futurity.

Don Quixote, pt. II, IV, 35, p. 681

24   They had best not stir the rice, though it sticks to the pot.   *Don Quixote, pt. II, IV, 37, p. 691*

25   Good wits jump;[5] a word to the wise is enough.

Don Quixote, pt. II, IV, 37, p. 692

26   Diligence is the mother of good fortune.

Don Quixote, pt. II, IV, 38, p. 724

27   What a man has, so much he's sure of.

Don Quixote, pt. II, IV, 38, p. 725

28   The pot calls the kettle black.

Don Quixote, pt. II, IV, 38, p. 727

29   Mum's the word.[6]

Don Quixote, pt. II, IV, 44, p. 729

30   I shall be as secret as the grave.

Don Quixote, pt. II, IV, 62, p. 862

31   Now blessings light on him that first invented this same sleep! It covers a man all over, thoughts and all, like a cloak;[7] 'Tis meat for the hungry, drink for the thirsty, heat for the cold, and cold for the hot. 'Tis the current coin that purchases all the pleasures of the world cheap; and the balance that sets the king and the shepherd, the fool and the wise man even.

Don Quixote, pt. II, IV, 68, p. 898

32   The ass will carry his load, but not a double load; ride not a free horse to death.

Don Quixote, pt. II, IV, 71, p. 917

---

[1]A needle in a haystack.

[2]La mesma cortesía.

[3]But patience, cousin, and shuffle the cards, till our hand is a stronger one. —WALTER SCOTT, *Quentin Durward* [1823], *ch. 8*
Men disappoint me so, I disappoint myself so, yet courage, patience, shuffle the cards. —MARGARET FULLER, *letter to the Reverend W. H. Channing*

[4]I hold the maxim no less applicable to public than to private affairs, that honesty is always the best policy. —GEORGE WASHINGTON, *Farewell Address* [1796]

[5]Great wits jump. —LAURENCE STERNE, *Tristram Shandy, vol. III* [1761–1762], *ch. 9*

[6]Cry "mum." —SHAKESPEARE, *The Merry Wives of Windsor,* act V, sc. ii, l. 6

[7]"God's blessing," said Sancho Panza, "be upon the man who first invented this self-same thing called sleep; it covers a man all over like a cloak." —LAURENCE STERNE, *Tristram Shandy, vol. IV, ch. 15*

1   He . . . got the better of himself, and that's the best kind of victory one can wish for.
Don Quixote, pt. II, IV, 72, p. 924

2   Every man was not born with a silver spoon in his mouth.   *Don Quixote, pt. II, IV, 73, p. 926*

3   Ne'er look for birds of this year in the nests of the last.   *Don Quixote, pt. II, IV, 74, p. 933*

4   There is a strange charm in the thoughts of a good legacy, or the hopes of an estate, which wondrously alleviates the sorrow that men would otherwise feel for the death of friends.
Don Quixote, pt. II, IV, 74, p. 934

5 For if he like a madman lived,
At least he like a wise one died.
Don Quixote, pt. II, IV, 74, p. 935 (Don Quixote's epitaph)

6   Don't put too fine a point to your wit for fear it should get blunted.
The Little Gypsy (La Gitanilla)

7   My heart is wax molded as she pleases, but enduring as marble to retain.   *The Little Gypsy*

Giordano Bruno
1548–1600

8   Time takes all and gives all.
The Candle Bearer [1582],[1] *dedication*

9   It is Unity that doth enchant me. By her power I am free though thrall, happy in sorrow, rich in poverty, and quick even in death.
On the Infinite Universe and Worlds [1584],[2] *introductory epistle*

10   Our bodily eye findeth never an end, but is vanquished by the immensity of space.
On the Infinite Universe and Worlds, fifth dialogue

11   There is in the universe neither center nor circumference.
On the Infinite Universe and Worlds, fifth dialogue

Charles IX
1550–1574

12   Horses and poets should be fed, not overfed.[3]
Saying

---
[1]Translated by J. B. HALLE.

[2]Translated by DOROTHEA SINGER.

[3]Equi et poetae alendi, non saginandi.

William Camden
1551–1623

13 My friend, judge not me,
Thou seest I judge not thee.
Betwixt the stirrup and the ground
Mercy I asked, and mercy found.
Remains Concerning Britain [1605]. Epitaph for a man killed by falling from his horse

Sir Edward Coke
1552–1634

14   Reason is the life of the law; nay, the common law itself is nothing else but reason. . . . The law, which is perfection of reason.
First Institute [1628]

15   The gladsome light of jurisprudence.
First Institute, epilogue

16   For a man's house is his castle, *et domus sua cuique tutissimum refugium.*[4]
Third Institute [1644]

17   The house of everyone is to him as his castle and fortress, as well for his defense against injury and violence as for his repose.
Semayne's Case. 5 Report 91

18   They [corporations] cannot commit treason, nor be outlawed nor excommunicate, for they have no souls.   *Case of Sutton's Hospital. 10 Report 32*

19   Magna Carta is such a fellow that he will have no sovereign.
Debate in the Commons [May 17, 1628]

20 Six hours in sleep, in law's grave study six,
Four spend in prayer, the rest on Nature fix.[5]
Translation quoted by COKE. *From The Pandects (Digest of Justinian). De in Ius Vocando*

Sir Walter Ralegh
c. 1552–1618

21 Like to an hermit poor in place obscure,
I mean to spend my days of endless doubt,
To wail such woes as time cannot recure,
Where none but Love shall ever find me out.
The Phoenix Nest [1593]. Sonnet

---
[4]One's home is the safest refuge to everyone. — *Pandects* [533], *lib. II, tit. IV, De in Ius Vocando*

I in mine own house am an emperor / And will defend what's mine. — PHILIP MASSINGER, *The Roman Actor* [1629], act I, sc. ii

[5]Seven hours to law, to soothing slumber seven; / Ten to the world allot, and all to heaven. — SIR WILLIAM JONES [1746–1794]

1 As you came from the holy land
Of Walsinghame,
Met you not with my true Love
By the way as you came?
*As You Came from the Holy Land [c. 1599],
st. 1*

2 But true love is a durable fire,
In the mind ever burning,
Never sick, never old, never dead,
From itself never turning.
As You Came from the Holy Land, st. 11

3 If all the world and love were young,
And truth in every shepherd's tongue,
These pretty pleasures might me move
To live with thee, and be thy love.
The Nymph's Reply to the Passionate Shepherd[1]
(printed in England's Helicon) [1600], st. 1

4 Fain would I climb, yet fear I to fall.
Written on a windowpane[2]

5 Our passions are most like to floods and streams,
The shallow murmur, but the deep are dumb.[3]
Sir Walter Ralegh to the Queen [c. 1599], st. 1

6 Silence in love bewrays more woe
Than words, though ne'er so witty;
A beggar that is dumb, you know,
Deserveth double pity.
Sir Walter Ralegh to the Queen, st. 5

7 Go, Soul, the body's quest,
Upon a thankless arrant:
Fear not to touch the best,
The truth shall be thy warrant:
Go, since I needs must die,
And give the world the lie.
The Lie (printed in FRANCIS DAVISON,
*Poetical Rhapsody) [1608; manuscript copy
traced to 1595], st. 1*

8 Give me my scallop shell of quiet,
My staff of faith to walk upon,
My scrip of joy, immortal diet,
My bottle of salvation,

My gown of glory, hope's true gage
And thus I'll take my pilgrimage.
*Diaphantus [1604]. The Passionate Man's
Pilgrimage*

9 Methought I saw the grave where Laura lay.
Verses to Edmund Spenser

10 Shall I, like a hermit, dwell
On a rock or in a cell?   *Poem*

11 [History] hath triumphed over time, which besides it nothing but eternity hath triumphed over.
History of the World [1614], preface

12 Whosoever, in writing a modern history, shall follow truth too near the heels, it may haply strike out his teeth.   *History of the World, preface*

13 O eloquent, just, and mighty Death! whom none could advise, thou hast persuaded; what none hath dared, thou hast done; and whom all the world hath flattered, thou only hast cast out of the world and despised. Thou hast drawn together all the far-stretched greatness, all the pride, cruelty, and ambition of man, and covered it all over with these two narrow words, *Hic jacet!*
History of the World, bk. V, pt. I, ch. 6, conclusion

14 Even such is time, that takes in trust
Our youth, our joys, our all we have,
And pays us but with age and dust;
Who in the dark and silent grave,
When we have wandered all our ways,
Shuts up the story of our days.
And from which earth, and grave, and dust,
The Lord shall raise me up, I trust.
*A version of one of his earlier poems, found at
his death in his Bible in the Gatehouse at
Westminster*

Edmund Spenser
1552–1599

15 To kirk the nearer, from God more far,
Has been an old-said saw.
And he that strives to touch the stars,
Oft stumbles at a straw.
The Shepherd's Calendar [1579]. July, l. 97

16 Fierce wars and faithful loves shall moralize my
song.[4]
The Faerie Queene [1590], introduction, st. 1

17 A gentle knight was pricking on the plain.
The Faerie Queene, bk. I, canto 1, st. 1

18 A bold bad man.   *The Faerie Queene, I, 1, st. 37*

---

[1]An answer to CHRISTOPHER MARLOWE, *The Passionate Shepherd to His Love* (see 170:6).

[2]Under this Queen Elizabeth wrote, "If thy heart fails thee, climb not at all." —THOMAS FULLER, *Worthies of England* [1662]

[3]Altissima quaeque flumina minimo sono labi [The deepest rivers flow with the least sound].—QUINTUS CURTIUS [first century A.D.], *VII, 4, 13*

Where the stream runneth smoothest, the water is deepest.—JOHN LYLY, *Euphues and His England* [1580]

Smooth runs the water where the brook is deep.—SHAKESPEARE, *Henry VI, Part II, act III, sc. i, l. 53*

Take heed of still waters, the quick pass away. —GEORGE HERBERT, *Jacula Prudentum* [1651]

[4]And moralized his song.—ALEXANDER POPE, *Epistle to Dr. Arbuthnot* [1735], *l. 340*

1   Her angel's face
As the great eye of heaven shined bright,
And made a sunshine in the shady place.
The Faerie Queene, I, 3, st. 4

2 Ay me, how many perils do enfold
The righteous man, to make him daily fall.[1]
The Faerie Queene, I, 8, st. 1

3 Sleep after toil, port after stormy seas,
Ease after war, death after life does greatly please.[2]
The Faerie Queene, I, 9, st. 40

4 All for love, and nothing for reward.
The Faerie Queene, II, 8, st. 2

5 Gather therefore the Rose, whilst yet is prime,
For soon comes age, that will her pride deflower:
Gather the Rose of love, whilst yet is time.
The Faerie Queene, II, 12, st. 75

6 Her birth was of the womb of morning dew.[3]
The Faerie Queene, III, 6, st. 3

7   Roses red and violets blue,
And all the sweetest flowers, that in the forest grew.
The Faerie Queene, III, 6, st. 6

8 All that in this delightful garden grows,
Should happy be, and have immortal bliss.
The Faerie Queene, III, 6, st. 41

9 That Squire of Dames.
The Faerie Queene, III, 8, st. 44

10 And painful pleasure turns to pleasing pain.
The Faerie Queene, III, 10, st. 60

11 How over that same door was likewise writ,
Be bold, be bold, and everywhere *Be bold.*
The Faerie Queene, III, 11, st. 54

12 Another iron door, on which was writ,
Be not too bold.[4]
The Faerie Queene, III, 11, st. 54

13 Dan Chaucer, well of English undefiled,
On Fame's eternal beadroll worthy to be filed.
The Faerie Queene, IV [1596], 2, st. 32

---

[1]Ay me! what perils do environ / The man that meddles with cold iron! — SAMUEL BUTLER, *Hudibras, pt. 1* [1663], *canto III, l. 1*

[2]These lines are cut on Joseph Conrad's gravestone at Canterbury.

[3]The dew of thy birth is of the womb of the morning. — *Book of Common Prayer, Psalter, Psalm 110:3*

[4]Jockey of Norfolk, be not too bold, / For Dickon thy master is bought and sold. — SHAKESPEARE, *Richard III, act V, sc. iii, l. 305*
Forbear, said I: be not too bold. / Your fleece is white but 'Tis too cold. — RICHARD CRASHAW, *Hymn of the Nativity* [1652], *l. 50*
Write on your doors the saying wise and old, / "Be bold! be bold!" and everywhere — "Be bold; / Be not too bold!" — HENRY WADSWORTH LONGFELLOW, *Morituri Salutamus* [1875]

14 For all that nature by her mother wit
Could frame in earth.
The Faerie Queene, IV, 10, st. 21

15 Ill can he rule the great, that cannot reach the
small.   *The Faerie Queene, V, 2, st. 43*

16 Who will not mercy unto others show,
How can he mercy ever hope to have?
The Faerie Queene, VI, 1, st. 42

17 The gentle mind by gentle deeds is known.
For a man by nothing is so well bewrayed,
As by his manners.   *The Faerie Queene, VI, 3, st. 1*

18 That here on earth is no sure happiness.
The Faerie Queene, VI, 11, st. 1

19   The ever-whirling wheel
Of Change; the which all mortal things doth sway.
The Faerie Queene, VII, 6, st. 1

20 Wars and alarums unto nations wide.
The Faerie Queene, VII, 6, st. 3

21 But times do change and move continually.
The Faerie Queene, VII, 6, st. 47

22 For deeds do die, however nobly done,
And thoughts of men do as themselves decay,
But wise words taught in numbers for to run,
Recorded by the Muses, live for ay.
The Ruines of Time [1591], l. 400

23 Full little knowest thou that hast not tried,
What hell it is, in suing long to bide:
To lose good days, that might be better spent;
To waste long nights in pensive discontent;
To speed today, to be put back tomorrow;
To feed on hope, to pine with fear and sorrow.
Mother Hubberd's Tale [1591], l. 895

24 To fret thy soul with crosses and with cares;
To eat thy heart through comfortless despairs;
To fawn, to crouch, to wait, to ride, to run,
To spend, to give, to want, to be undone.
Unhappy wight, born to disastrous end,
That doth his life in so long tendance spend.
Mother Hubberd's Tale, l. 903

25 What more felicity can fall to creature,
Than to enjoy delight with liberty.
Muiopotmos; or, The Fate of the Butterfly
[1591], l. 209

26 I hate the day, because it lendeth light
To see all things, and not my love to see.
Daphnaida [1591], l. 407

27 Death slew not him, but he made death his ladder
to the skies.
An Epitaph upon Sir Philip Sidney [1591], l. 20

1 Though last not least.[1]
> *Colin Clouts Come Home Again [1595],*
> *l. 144*

2 Tell her the joyous time will not be stayed
Unlesse she do him by the forelock take.[2]
> *Amoretti [1595]. Sonnet 70*

3 The woods shall to me answer, and my Echo ring.
> *Epithalamion [1595], l. 18*

4 Ah! when will this long weary day have end,
And lend me leave to come unto my love?
> *Epithalamion, l. 278*

5 For of the soul the body form doth take:
For soul is form, and doth the body make.
> *Hymn in Honor of Beauty [1596], l. 132*

6 For all that fair is, is by nature good;
That is a sign to know the gentle blood.
> *Hymn in Honor of Beauty, l. 139*

7 Sweet Thames! run softly, till I end my Song.[3]
> *Prothalamion [1596], refrain*

8 I was promised on a time
To have reason for my rhyme;
From that time unto this season,
I received nor rhyme nor reason.
> *Lines on his promised pension. From* THOMAS
> FULLER, *Worthies of England [1662]*

John Florio
c. 1553–1625

9   England is the paradise of women, the purgatory of men, and the hell of horses.
> *Second Frutes [1591]*

10   Praise the sea; on shore remain.
> *Second Frutes*

Henri IV [Henry of Navarre]
1553–1610

11   I want there to be no peasant in my realm so poor that he will not have a chicken in his pot every Sunday.
> *Attributed*

12   Paris is well worth a Mass.[4]
> *Attributed*[5]

13   Hang yourself, brave Crillon; we fought at Arques and you were not there.[6]
> *Letter [1597]. From Lettres missives de Henri*
> *IV, Collection des Documents Inédits de*
> *l'Histoire de France, vol. IV [1847]*

14   The wisest fool in Christendom [James I of England].
> *Attributed*[5]

George Keith, Fifth Earl Marischal
c. 1553–1623

15   Thai half said. Quhat say thai? Let thame say.[7]
> *Family motto, Mitchell Tower, Marischal*
> *College, Aberdeen, Scotland [founded 1593]*

Fulke Greville, Lord Brooke
1554–1628

16 Oh wearisome condition of humanity!
Born under one law, to another bound.
> *Mustapha [1609], act V, sc. 4*

17   Fulke Greville, Servant to Queen Elizabeth, Councillor to King James, and Friend to Sir Philip Sidney.
> *Epitaph, on his monument in Warwick*

Richard Hooker
c. 1554–1600

18   Of Law there can be no less acknowledged than that her seat is the bosom of God, her voice the harmony of the world. All things in heaven and earth do her homage—the very least as feeling her care, and the greatest as not exempted from her power.
> *Laws of Ecclesiastical Polity [1593], bk. 1*

19   That to live by one man's will became the cause of all men's misery.
> *Laws of Ecclesiastical Polity, 1*

---

[1]The last, not least in honor or applause.—ALEXANDER POPE, *The Dunciad* [1728], *bk. IV, l. 577*

[2]Take Time by the forelock.—THALES [c. 640–c. 546 B.C.]

[3]Sweet Thames, run softly till I end my song, / Sweet Thames, run softly, for I speak not loud or long.—T. S. ELIOT, *The Waste Land* [1922], *pt. III*

[4]Paris vaut bien une messe.

[5]Attributed also to Henri's minister, Duc de Sully.

[6]Pends-toi, brave Crillon, nous avons combattu à Arques et tu n'y étais pas.

Louis de Balbes de Berton de Crillon [c. 1541–1615], French soldier of legendary courage, fought as captain under Henri IV in the battle of Ivry and the siege of Paris.

[7]They say. What say they? Let them say. — *Motto over the fireplace in George Bernard Shaw's home*

John Lyly

c. 1554–1606

1   Be valiant, but not too venturous. Let thy attire be comely, but not costly.

Euphues: The Anatomy of Wit [1579]. Arber's reprint, p. 39

2   The finest edge is made with the blunt whetstone.

Euphues: The Anatomy of Wit. Arber's reprint, p. 47

3   Delays breed dangers.[1]

Euphues: The Anatomy of Wit. Arber's reprint, p. 65

4   It seems to me (said she) that you are in some brown study.

Euphues: The Anatomy of Wit. Arber's reprint, p. 80

5   Many strokes overthrow the tallest oaks.[2]

Euphues: The Anatomy of Wit. Arber's reprint, p. 81

6   Let me stand to the main chance.

Euphues: The Anatomy of Wit. Arber's reprint, p. 104

7   It is a world to see.

Euphues: The Anatomy of Wit. Arber's reprint, p. 116

8   A clear conscience is a sure card.

Euphues: The Anatomy of Wit. Arber's reprint, p. 207

9   Go to bed with the lamb, and rise with the lark.[3]

Euphues and His England [1580], p. 229

10   A comely old man as busy as a bee.

Euphues and His England, p. 252

11   Maidens, be they never so foolish, yet being fair they are commonly fortunate.

Euphues and His England, p. 279

12   Your eyes are so sharp that you cannot only look through a millstone, but clean through the mind.

Euphues and His England, p. 289

13   I am glad that my Adonis hath a sweet tooth in his head.   *Euphues and His England, p. 308*

14   A rose is sweeter in the bud than full-blown.[4]

Euphues and His England, p. 314

15   Cupid and my Campaspe played
At cards for kisses: Cupid paid.

Alexander and Campaspe [1584], act III, sc. v

16   How at heaven's gates she claps her wings,
The morn not waking till she sings.

Alexander and Campaspe, V, i

17   Night hath a thousand eyes.

Maides Metamorphosis, III, 1

18   Marriages are made in heaven and consummated on earth.[5]   *Mother Bombie [1590], act IV, sc. i*

Sir Philip Sidney

1554–1586

19   High-erected thoughts seated in the heart of courtesy.   *Arcadia [written 1580], bk. I*

20   They are never alone that are accompanied with noble thoughts.[6]   *Arcadia, I*

21   My dear, my better half.   *Arcadia, III*

22   My true-love hath my heart, and I have his,
By just exchange one for the other given:
I hold his dear, and mine he cannot miss,
There never was a better bargain driven.

Arcadia, song

23   Ring out your bells! Let mourning shows be spread!
For Love is dead.   *Sonnet*

24   Leave me, O Love, which reachest but to dust,
And thou, my mind, aspire to higher things;
Grow rich in that which never taketh rust:
Whatever fades, but fading pleasure brings.   *Sonnet*

25   Sweet food of sweetly uttered knowledge.

The Defense of Poesy [written c. 1580]

26   He cometh unto you with a tale which holdeth children from play, and old men from the chimney corner.   *The Defense of Poesy*

27   I never heard the old song of Percy and Douglas that I found not my heart moved more than with a trumpet.   *The Defense of Poesy*

28   "Fool!" said my muse to me, "look in thy heart, and write."   *Astrophel and Stella [1591], I*

29   With how sad steps, O Moon, thou climb'st the skies!
How silently, and with how wan a face!

Astrophel and Stella, XXXI

---

[1]Periculum in mora. — *Latin proverb*

All delays are dangerous in war. — JOHN DRYDEN, *Tyrannic Love* [1669], *act I, sc. i*

[2]Many strokes, though with a little axe, / Hew down and fell the hardest-timber'd oak. — SHAKESPEARE, *Henry VI, pt. III, act II, sc. i, l. 54*

[3]To rise with the lark and go to bed with the lamb. — NICHOLAS BRETON [c. 1553–c. 1625], *Court and Country* [1618]

[4]The rose is fairest when 'tis budding new. — WALTER SCOTT, *The Lady of the Lake* [1810], *canto III, st. I*

[5]Les mariages se font au ciel, et se consomment sur la terre. — *French proverb*

If marriages / Are made in heaven, they should be happier. — THOMAS SOUTHERNE [1660–1746], *The Fatal Marriage* [1694]

[6]He never is alone that is accompanied with noble thoughts. — BEAUMONT AND FLETCHER, *Love's Cure* [1647], *act III, sc. iii*

1 Have I caught my heav'nly jewel.[1]
Astrophel and Stella, second song

2   Thy necessity[2] is yet greater than mine.
Said on the battlefield of Zutphen [September 22, 1586] on giving his water bottle to a dying soldier

François de Malherbe[3]
1555–1628

3   And a rose, she lived as roses do, the space of a morn.[4]
Consolation à Monsieur du Périer [1599]

4   And the fruits will outdo what the flowers have promised.[5]
Prière pour le roi Henri le Grand [1605]

5   What Malherbe writes will endure forever.
Sonnet à Louis XIII [1624]

Philip Nicolai
1556–1608

6 Wake, awake, for night is flying:
The watchmen on the heights are crying.[6]
Hymn [1597]

George Peele
1556–1596

7 Fair and fair, and twice so fair,
As fair as any may be.
The Arraignment of Paris [1584]

8 My merry, merry, merry roundelay
Concludes with Cupid's curse:
They that do change old love for new,
Pray gods, they change for worse!
The Arraignment of Paris

9 His golden locks time hath to silver turned;
O time too swift, O swiftness never ceasing!
His youth 'gainst time and age hath ever spurned,
But spurned in vain; youth waneth by increasing.
Polyhymnia [1590]. Farewell to Arms, st. 1

---

[1]Quoted by SHAKESPEARE in *The Merry Wives of Windsor, act III, sc. iii, l. 45.*

[2]More often quoted as: Thy need.

[3]See Boileau, 289:6.

[4]Et rose, elle a vécu ce que vivent les roses, / L'espace d'un matin.

[5]Et les fruits passeront la promesse des fleurs.

[6]Wachet auf, tuft uns die stimme.
Translated by CATHERINE WINKWORTH.

10 His helmet now shall make a hive for bees,
And lovers' sonnets turned to holy psalms,
A man-at-arms must now serve on his knees,
And feed on prayers, which are age his alms.
Polyhymnia. Farewell to Arms, st. 2

Thomas Kyd
1558–1594

11 What outcries call me from my naked bed?
The Spanish Tragedy [1594], act II, sc. v, l. 1

12 O eyes, no eyes, but fountains fraught with tears;
O life, no life, but lively form of death;
O world, no world, but mass of public wrongs,
Confused and filled with murder and misdeeds.
The Spanish Tragedy, III, ii, l.1

13 Hieronymo, beware: go by, go by.
The Spanish Tragedy, III, xii, l. 31

14 Why then I'll fit you, say no more.
When I was young, I gave my mind
And plied myself to fruitless poetry:
Which though it profit the professor naught
Yet it is passing pleasing to the world.
The Spanish Tragedy, IV, ii, l. 70

Thomas Lodge
c. 1558–1625

15 Love in my bosom like a bee
Doth suck his sweet.   *Rosalynde [1590]*

16   Devils are not so black as they are painted.
A Margarite of America [1596]

Chidiock Tichborne[7]
c. 1558–1586

17 My prime of youth is but a frost of cares;
My feast of joy is but a dish of pain;
My crop of corn is but a field of tares;
And all my good is but vain hope of gain:
The day is past, and yet I saw no sun;
And now I live, and now my life is done.
Tichborne's Elegy [1586]

George Chapman
c. 1559–1634

18 Promise is most given when the least is said.
Hero and Leander [1598]

19 Love calls to war;
Sighs his alarms,

---

[7]He was beheaded for an attempt on Queen Elizabeth's life.

Lips his swords are,
The field his arms.
> *Hero and Leander, Epithalamion Teratos,*
> *refrain*

1 Young men think old men are fools; but old men know young men are fools.
> *All Fools [1605], act V, sc. i*

2 Keep thy shop, and thy shop will keep thee. Light gains make heavy purses.[1]
> *Eastward Ho [1605],[2] act I, sc. i*

3 Why, do nothing, be like a gentleman, be idle. . . . Make ducks and drakes with shillings.
> *Eastward Ho, I, i*

4 I will neither yield to the song of the siren nor the voice of the hyena, the tears of the crocodile[3] nor the howling of the wolf.
> *Eastward Ho, V, i*

5 For one heat, all know, doth drive out another,
One passion doth expel another still.
> *Monsieur d'Olive [1606], act V, sc. i*

6 To put a girdle round about the world.
> *Bussy d'Ambois [1607], act I, sc. i*

7 Speed his plow.[4]
> *Bussy d'Ambois, I, i*

8 So our lives
In acts exemplary, not only win
Ourselves good names, but doth to others give
Matter for virtuous deeds, by which we live.
> *Bussy d'Ambois, I, i*

9 Who to himself is law no law doth need,
Offends no law, and is a king indeed.
> *Bussy d'Ambois, II, i*

10 Be free, all worthy spirits,
And stretch yourselves, for greatness and for height.
> *The Conspiracy of Charles, Duke of Byron [1608], act III, sc. i*

11 Give me a spirit that on this life's rough sea
Loves t' have his sails filled with a lusty wind,
Even till his sail-yards tremble, his masts crack,
And his rapt ship run on her side so low
That she drinks water, and her keel plows air.
> *The Conspiracy of Charles, Duke of Byron, III, i*

12 Danger, the spur of all great minds.
> *The Revenge of Bussy d'Ambois [1610], act V, sc. i*

13 We have watered our horses in Helicon.
> *May-Day [1611], act III, sc. iii*

Maximilien de Béthune, Duc de Sully
1559–1641

14 Tilling and grazing are the two breasts that feed France.[5]
> *Économies Royales, III*

15 The English take their pleasures sadly after the fashion of their country.[6]
> *Memoirs*

Robert Greene
c. 1560–1592

16 Sweet are the thoughts that savor of content;
The quiet mind is richer than a crown.
> *Farewell to Folly [1591], st. 1*

17 A mind content both crown and kingdom is.
> *Farewell to Folly, st. 2*

18 For there is an upstart crow, beautified with our feathers, that with his tiger's heart wrapped in a player's hide, supposes he is as well able to bumbast out a blank verse as the best of you; and being an absolute *Johannes fac totum,* is in his own conceit the only Shake-scene in a country.[7]
> *The Groatsworth of Wit [1592]*

19 Hangs in the uncertain balance of proud time.
> *Friar Bacon and Friar Bungay [acted 1594], act III*

20 Hell's broken loose.
> *Friar Bacon and Friar Bungay, IV*

Francis Bacon[8]
1561–1626

21 I have taken all knowledge to be my province.
> *Letter to Lord Burleigh [1592]*

22 The monuments of wit survive the monuments of power.
> *Essex's Device [1595]*

---

[1] Quoted by Benjamin Franklin in *Poor Richard's Almanac* [1735], *June.*

[2] By Chapman, Jonson, and Marston.

[3] These crocodile tears. — ROBERT BURTON, *Anatomy of Melancholy* [1621–1651], pt. III, sec. 2, member 2, subsec. 4
    She's false, false as the tears of crocodiles. — SIR JOHN SUCKLING, *The Sad One* [produced posthumously in 1659], act IV, sec. v

[4] Usually quoted: Speed the plow.

[5] Labourage et pâturage sont les deux mamelles dont la France est alimentée.

[6] Les anglais s'amusent tristement selon l'usage de leur pays.

[7] First known literary reference to Shakespeare.

[8] If parts allure thee, think how Bacon shined, / The wisest, brightest, meanest of mankind. — ALEXANDER POPE, *Essay on Man* [1733–1734], epistle IV, l. 281

1   Knowledge is power [*Nam et ipsa scientia potestas est*].[1]

Meditationes Sacrae [1597]. De Haeresibus

2   For all knowledge and wonder (which is the seed of knowledge) is an impression of pleasure in itself.

The Advancement of Learning [1605], bk. I, i, 3

3   Time, which is the author of authors.

The Advancement of Learning, I, iv, 12

4   If a man will begin with certainties, he shall end in doubts; but if he will be content to begin with doubts he shall end in certainties.

The Advancement of Learning, I, v, 8

5   *Antiquitas saeculi juventus mundi.*[2] These times are the ancient times, when the world is ancient, and not those which we account ancient *ordine retrogrado*, by a computation backward from ourselves.[3]

The Advancement of Learning, I, v, 8

6   [Knowledge] is a rich storehouse for the glory of the Creator and the relief of man's estate.

The Advancement of Learning, I, v, 11

7   It [Poesy] was ever thought to have some participation of divineness, because it doth raise and erect the mind by submitting the shows of things to the desires of the mind.

The Advancement of Learning, II, iv, 2

8   They are ill discoverers that think there is no land, when they can see nothing but sea.

The Advancement of Learning, II, vii, 5

9   But men must know that in this theater of man's life it is reserved only for God and angels to be lookers on.

The Advancement of Learning, II, xx, 8

10   We are much beholden to Machiavel and others, that write what men do, and not what they ought to do.

The Advancement of Learning, II, xxi, 9

---

[1]Knowledge is more than equivalent to force. —SAMUEL JOHNSON, *Rasselas* [1759], *ch. 13*

[2]The age of antiquity is the youth of the world.

[3]As in the little, so in the great world, reason will tell you that old age or antiquity is to be accounted by the farther distance from the beginning and the nearer approach to the end—the times wherein we now live being in propriety of speech the most ancient since the world's creation. —GEORGE HAKEWILL [1578–1649], *An Apologie or Declaration of the Power and Providence of God in the Government of the World* [1627]

For as old age is that period of life most remote from infancy, who does not see that old age in this universal man ought not to be sought in the times nearest his birth, but in those most remote from it? —BLAISE PASCAL, *Preface to the Treatise on Vacuum*

We are Ancients of the earth, / And in the morning of the times. —ALFRED, LORD TENNYSON, *The Day Dream* [1842], *L'Envoi*

11   All good moral philosophy is but the handmaid to religion.

The Advancement of Learning, II, xxii, 14

12   There are and can be only two ways of searching into and discovering truth. The one flies from the senses and particulars to the most general axioms . . . this way is now in fashion. The other derives axioms from the senses and particulars, rising by a gradual and unbroken ascent, so that it arrives at the most general axioms last of all. This is the true way, but as yet untried.

Novum Organum [1620]

13   There are four classes of Idols which beset men's minds. To these for distinction's sake I have assigned names—calling the first class, Idols of the Tribe; the second, Idols of the Cave; the third, Idols of the Market-Place; the fourth, Idols of the Theater.

Novum Organum, aphorism 39

14   The human understanding is like a false mirror, which, receiving rays irregularly, distorts and discolors the nature of things by mingling its own nature with it.   *Novum Organum, aphorism 41*

15   Nature, to be commanded, must be obeyed.

Novum Organum, aphorism 129

16   I do plainly and ingenuously confess that I am guilty of corruption, and do renounce all defense. I beseech your Lordships to be merciful to a broken reed.

On being charged by Parliament with corruption in office [1621]

17   Lucid intervals and happy pauses.

History of King Henry VII [1622], III

18   Nothing is terrible except fear itself.[4]

De Augmentis Scientiarum, bk. II, Fortitudo [1623]

19   Riches are a good handmaid, but the worst mistress.

De Augmentis Scientiarum, II, Antitheta

20   Hope is a good breakfast, but it is a bad supper.

Apothegms [1624], no. 36

21   Like strawberry wives, that laid two or three great strawberries at the mouth of their pot, and all the rest were little ones.   *Apothegms, 54*

22   Sir Amice Pawlet, when he saw too much haste made in any matter, was wont to say, "Stay a while, that we may make an end the sooner."

Apothegms, 76

---

[4]Nil terribile nisi ipse timor.

1   Alonso of Aragon was wont to say in commendation of age, that age appears to be best in four things—old wood best to burn, old wine to drink, old friends to trust, and old authors to read.
Apothegms, 97

2   Cosmus, Duke of Florence, was wont to say of perfidious friends, that "We read that we ought to forgive our enemies; but we do not read that we ought to forgive our friends."
Apothegms, 206

3   Cato said the best way to keep good acts in memory was to refresh them with new.
Apothegms, 247

4   My essays . . . come home to men's business and bosoms.   *Essays [1625],*[1] *dedication*

5   What is truth? said jesting Pilate, and would not stay for an answer.   *Essays. Of Truth*

6   No pleasure is comparable to the standing upon the vantage-ground of truth.   *Essays. Of Truth*

7   Men fear death as children fear to go in the dark; and as that natural fear in children is increased with tales, so is the other.   *Essays. Of Death*

8   Revenge is a kind of wild justice, which the more man's nature runs to, the more ought law to weed it out.   *Essays. Of Revenge*

9   It was a high speech of Seneca (after the manner of the Stoics), that "The good things which belong to prosperity are to be wished, but the good things that belong to adversity are to be admired."
Essays. Of Adversity

10   Prosperity is the blessing of the Old Testament; adversity is the blessing of the New.
Essays. Of Adversity

11   Prosperity is not without many fears and distastes; and adversity is not without comforts and hopes.   *Essays. Of Adversity*

12   Prosperity doth best discover vice, but adversity doth best discover virtue.   *Essays. Of Adversity*

13   Virtue is like precious odors—most fragrant when they are incensed or crushed.[2]
Essays. Of Adversity

14   He that hath wife and children hath given hostages to fortune; for they are impediments to great enterprises, either of virtue or mischief.
Essays. Of Marriage and Single Life

15   Wives are young men's mistresses, companions for middle age, and old men's nurses.
Essays. Of Marriage and Single Life

16   A good name is like a precious ointment; it filleth all around about, and will not easily away; for the odors of ointments are more durable than those of flowers.   *Essays. Of Praise*

17   In charity there is no excess.
Essays. Of Goodness and Goodness of Nature

18   If a man be gracious and courteous to strangers, it shows he is a citizen of the world, and that his heart is no island cut off from other lands, but a continent that joins to them.
Essays. Of Goodness and Goodness of Nature

19   The desire of power in excess caused the angels to fall; the desire of knowledge in excess caused man to fall.[3]
Essays. Of Goodness and Goodness of Nature

20   Money is like muck, not good except it be spread.   *Essays. Of Seditions and Troubles*

21   I had rather believe all the fables in the legends and the Talmud and the Alcoran, than that this universal frame is without a mind.
Essays. Of Atheism

22   A little philosophy inclineth man's mind to atheism, but depth in philosophy bringeth men's minds about to religion.[4]   *Essays. Of Atheism*

23   Travel, in the younger sort, is a part of education; in the elder, a part of experience. He that traveleth into a country before he hath some entrance into the language, goeth to school, and not to travel.   *Essays. Of Travel*

24   Princes are like to heavenly bodies, which cause good or evil times, and which have much veneration but no rest.   *Essays. Of Empire*

25   Fortune is like the market, where many times, if you can stay a little, the price will fall.
Essays. Of Delays

26   Nothing doth more hurt in a state than that cunning men pass for wise.
Essays. Of Cunning

---

[1]First edition, 1597; first complete edition, 1625.

[2]As aromatic plants bestow / No spicy fragrance while they grow; / But crushed or trodden to the ground, / Diffuse their balmy sweets around.—OLIVER GOLDSMITH, *The Captivity* [1764], *act I*

[3]Pride still is aiming at the blest abodes; / Men would be angels, angels would be gods. / Aspiring to be gods if angels fell, / Aspiring to be angels men rebel.—ALEXANDER POPE, *Essay on Man,* epistle I [1733], *l. 125*

[4]A little skill in antiquity inclines a man to Popery; but depth in that study brings him about again to our religion.—THOMAS FULLER, *The Holy State and the Profane State* [1642], *The True Church Antiquary*

1   Be so true to thyself, as thou be not false to others.   *Essays. Of Wisdom for a Man's Self*

2   It is the nature of extreme self-lovers, as they will set an house on fire, and it were but to roast their eggs.   *Essays. Of Wisdom for a Man's Self*

3   It is the wisdom of the crocodiles, that shed tears when they would devour.   *Essays. Of Wisdom for a Man's Self*

4   He that will not apply new remedies must expect new evils; for time is the greatest innovator.   *Essays. Of Innovations*

5   Cure the disease and kill the patient.   *Essays. Of Friendship*

6   Riches are for spending.   *Essays. Of Expense*

7   There is a wisdom in this beyond the rules of physic. A man's own observation, what he finds good of and what he finds hurt of, is the best physic to preserve health.   *Essays. Of Regimen of Health*

8   Intermingle . . . jest with earnest.   *Essays. Of Discourse*

9   Nature is often hidden; sometimes overcome; seldom extinguished.   *Essays. Of Nature in Men*

10   If a man look sharply and attentively, he shall see Fortune; for though she is blind, she is not invisible.[1]   *Essays. Of Fortune*

11   Chiefly the mold of a man's fortune is in his own hands.   *Essays. Of Fortune*

12   There is no excellent beauty that hath not some strangeness in the proportion.   *Essays. Of Beauty*

13   God Almighty first planted a garden.[2]   *Essays. Of Gardens*

14   He that commands the sea is at great liberty, and may take as much and as little of the war as he will.[3]   *Essays. Of the True Greatness of Kingdoms*

15   Some books are to be tasted, others to be swallowed, and some few to be chewed and digested.   *Essays. Of Studies*

16   Reading maketh a full man, conference a ready man, and writing an exact man.   *Essays. Of Studies*

17   Histories make men wise; poets, witty; the mathematics, subtile; natural philosophy, deep; moral, grave; logic and rhetoric, able to contend.   *Essays. Of Studies*

18   The greatest vicissitude of things amongst men is the vicissitude of sects and religions.   *Essays. Of Vicissitude of Things*

19   I bequeath my soul to God. . . . My body to be buried obscurely. For my name and memory, I leave it to men's charitable speeches, and to foreign nations, and the next age.   *From his will [1626]*

20   The world's a bubble, and the life of man
Less than a span.   *The World [1629]*

21   Who then to frail mortality shall trust
But limns on water, or but writes in dust.   *The World*

22   What then remains but that we still should cry
For being born, and, being born, to die?   *The World*

Sir John Harington
1561–1612

23   Treason doth never prosper: what's the reason?
For if it prosper, none dare call it treason.   *Epigrams. Of Treason*

24   The readers and the hearers like my books,
But yet some writers cannot them digest;
But what care I? for when I make a feast
I would my guests should praise it, not the cooks.   *Epigrams. Of Writers Who Carp at Other Men's Books*

Robert Southwell
c. 1561–1595

25   Times go by turns, and chances change by course,
From foul to fair, from better hap to worse.   *Times Go by Turns [c. 1595], st. 1*

26   As I in hoary winter night stood shivering in the snow,
Surprised was I with sudden heat which made my heart to glow;
And lifting up a fearful eye to view what fire was near
A pretty Babe all burning bright did in the air appear.   *The Burning Babe [written c. 1595]*

---

[1]Fortune is painted blind, with a muffler afore her eyes, to signify to you that Fortune is blind. — SHAKESPEARE, *King Henry V, act III, sc. vi, l. 31*

[2]Gardens were before gardeners, and but some hours after the earth. — THOMAS BROWNE, *The Garden of Cyrus* [1658], *ch. 1*

[3]He that is master of the sea, may, in some sort, be said to be Master of every country; at least such as are bordering on the sea. For he is at liberty to begin and end War, where, when, and on what terms he pleaseth, and extend his conquests even to the Antipodes. — JOSEPH GANDER [fl. c. 1703], *The Glory of Her Sacred Majesty Queen Anne in the Royal Navy* [1703]

1 With this he vanished out of sight, and swiftly
   shrunk away,
  And straight I called unto mind that it was
   Christmas Day.   *The Burning Babe*

Samuel Daniel
c. 1562–1619

2 Make me to say, when all my griefs are gone,
  "Happy the heart that sighed for such a one!"
      Sonnets to Delia [1592], XLIII

3 Care-charmer Sleep, son of the sable Night,
  Brother to Death, in silent darkness born.
      Sonnets to Delia, XLV

4 Let others sing of knights and paladins
  In aged accents and untimely words.
      Sonnets to Delia, XLVI

5 These are the arks, the trophies, I erect,
  That fortify thy name against old age.
      Sonnets to Delia, XLVI

6 And for the few that only lend their ear,
  That few is all the world.
      *Musophilus, or Defence of All Learning
      [1602–1603], st. 97*

7 This is the thing that I was born to do.
      Musophilus, st. 100

8 Unless above himself he can
  Erect himself, how poor a thing is man!
      *To the Lady Margaret, Countess of
      Cumberland [c. 1600], st. 12*

9 Love is a sickness full of woes,
  All remedies refusing.
      Hymen's Triumph [1615]

Lope de Vega
1562–1635

10 Harmony is pure love, for love is complete
agreement.
      Fuenteovejuna [c. 1613],[1] act I, l. 381

11 Except for God, the King's our only lord.
      Fuenteovejuna, I, l. 1701

Michael Drayton
1563–1631

12 Fair stood the wind for France.
      The Ballad of Agincourt [1606], st. 1

13 O, when shall Englishmen
  With such acts fill a pen,
  Or England breed again
  Such a King Harry?
      The Ballad of Agincourt, st. 15

14 Since there's no help, come let us kiss and part—
  Nay, I have done: you get no more of me,
  And I am glad, yea glad with all my heart,
  That thus so cleanly I myself can free.
  Shake hands forever, cancel all our vows,
  And when we meet at any time again,
  Be it not seen in either of our brows
  That we one jot of former love retain.
      Poems [1619]. Idea

15 The coast was clear.   *Nymphidia [1627]*

16 Had in him those brave translunary things
  That the first poets had.
      *Said of MARLOWE. To Henry Reynolds, Of
      Poets and Poesy [1627]*

17 For that fine madness still he did retain
  Which rightly should possess a poet's brain.
      *Said of MARLOWE. To Henry Reynolds, Of
      Poets and Poesy*

Galileo Galilei
1564–1642

18 Philosophy is written in this grand book—I mean the universe—which stands continually open to our gaze, but it cannot be understood unless one first learns to comprehend the language and interpret the characters in which it is written. It is written in the language of mathematics, and its characters are triangles, circles, and other geometrical figures, without which it is humanly impossible to understand a single word of it; without these, one is wandering about in a dark labyrinth.
      Il Saggiatore [1623][2]

19 But it does move![3]
      *Attributed. From ABBÉ IRAILH, Querelles
      littéraires [1761], vol. III, p. 49*

20 Facts which at first seem improbable will, even on scant explanation, drop the cloak which has hidden them and stand forth in naked and simple beauty.
      *Dialogues Concerning Two New Sciences
      [1638],[4] Day 1*

---

[1]Translated by ANGEL FLORES and MURIEL KITTEL.

[2]The Assayer in *The Controversy on the Comets of 1618* [1960], translated by STILLMAN DRAKE and C. D. O'MALLEY.

[3]E pur si muove!
Alleged to have been whispered by him after recanting before the Inquisition his claim that the earth revolved around the sun.

[4]Translated by HENRY CREW and ALFONSO DE SALVIO.

Christopher Marlowe
1564–1593

1 Our swords shall play the orators for us.
Tamburlaine the Great [c. 1587], pt. I, l. 328

2 Accurst be he that first invented war.
Tamburlaine the Great, I, l. 664

3 Is it not passing brave to be a king,
And ride in triumph through Persepolis?
Tamburlaine the Great, I, l. 758

4 Nature that framed us of four elements,
Warring within our breasts for regiment,
Doth teach us all to have aspiring minds:
Our souls, whose faculties can comprehend
The wondrous Architecture of the world:
And measure every wandering planet's course,
Still climbing after knowledge infinite,
And always moving as the restless Spheres,
Will us to wear ourselves and never rest,
Until we reach the ripest fruit of all,
That perfect bliss and sole felicity,
The sweet fruition of an earthly crown.
Tamburlaine the Great, I, l. 869

5 Tamburlaine, the Scourge of God, must die.
Tamburlaine the Great, I, l. 4641

6 Come live with me, and be my love;
And we will all the pleasures prove
That valleys, groves, hills, and fields,[1]
Woods or steepy mountain yields.
The Passionate Shepherd to His Love [c. 1589]

7 By shallow rivers, to whose falls
Melodious birds sing madrigals.[2]
The Passionate Shepherd to His Love

8 And I will make thee beds of roses
And a thousand fragrant posies.[2]
The Passionate Shepherd to His Love

9 I count religion but a childish toy,
And hold there is no sin but ignorance.
The Jew of Malta [c. 1589], prologue

10 Infinite riches in a little room.[3]
The Jew of Malta, act I, sc. i

11 Excess of wealth is cause of covetousness.
The Jew of Malta, I, ii

---

[1]Also given as: Hills and valleys, dales, and fields.

[2]To shallow rivers, to whose falls / Melodious birds sing madrigals; / There will we make our peds of roses, / And a thousand fragrant posies. —SHAKESPEARE, *The Merry Wives of Windsor, act III, sc. i, l. 17*

[3]Here lyeth muche rychnesse in lytell space. —JOHN HEYWOOD, *The Foure PP [1521–1525]*

---

12 Now will I show myself to have more of the serpent than the dove; that is, more knave than fool.
The Jew of Malta, II, iii

13 *Friar Barnadine:* Thou hast committed—
Barabas: Fornication—but that was in another country;
And besides, the wench is dead.
The Jew of Malta, IV, i

14 My men, like satyrs grazing on the lawns,
Shall with their goat feet dance the antic hay.
Edward II [1593], act I, sc. i

15 Who ever loved that loved not at first sight?[4]
Hero and Leander [1598]

16 Like untuned golden strings all women are,
Which long time lie untouched, will harshly jar.
Vessels of brass oft handled brightly shine.
Hero and Leander

17 Live and die in Aristotle's works.
The Tragical History of Doctor Faustus [1604], act I, sc. i

18 Unhappy spirits that fell with Lucifer,
Conspired against our God with Lucifer,
And are forever damned with Lucifer.
The Tragical History of Doctor Faustus, I, iii

19 Why this is hell, nor am I out of it:
Think'st thou that I who saw the face of God,
And tasted the eternal joys of Heaven,
Am not tormented with ten thousand hells,
In being deprived of everlasting bliss?
The Tragical History of Doctor Faustus, I, iii

20 Hell hath no limits, nor is circumscribed
In one self place; for where we are is hell,
And where hell is there must we ever be.
The Tragical History of Doctor Faustus, II, i

21 When all the world dissolves,
And every creature shall be purified,
All places shall be hell that is not Heaven.
The Tragical History of Doctor Faustus, II, i

22 Have not I made blind Homer sing to me?
The Tragical History of Doctor Faustus, II, ii

23 Was this the face that launched a thousand ships,
And burnt the topless towers of Ilium?[5]

---

[4]Quoted in SHAKESPEARE, *As You Like It, act III, sc. v, l. 82.*
None ever loved but at first sight they loved. —GEORGE CHAPMAN, *The Blind Beggar of Alexandria [1598]*

[5]Was this fair face the cause, quoth she, / Why the Grecians sacked Troy? —SHAKESPEARE, *All's Well That Ends Well, act I, sc. iii, l. 75*

Sweet Helen, make me immortal with a kiss.
Her lips suck forth my soul;[1] see, where it flies!
The Tragical History of Doctor Faustus, V, i

1 Oh, thou art fairer than the evening air
Clad in the beauty of a thousand stars.
The Tragical History of Doctor Faustus, V, i

2   Pray for me! and what noise soever ye hear,
come not unto me, for nothing can rescue me.
The Tragical History of Doctor Faustus, V, ii

3 Now hast thou but one bare hour to live,
And then thou must be damned perpetually!
Stand still, you ever-moving spheres of Heaven,
That time may cease, and midnight never come.
The Tragical History of Doctor Faustus, V, ii

4 *O lente, lente currite noctis equi:*[2]
The stars move still, time runs, the clock will strike,
The Devil will come, and Faustus must be damned.
O, I'll leap up to my God! Who pulls me down?
See, see where Christ's blood streams in the
firmament!
One drop would save my soul—half a drop: ah, my
Christ!
The Tragical History of Doctor Faustus, V, ii

5 O soul, be changed into little waterdrops,
And fall into the ocean—ne'er to be found.
My God! my God! look not so fierce on me!
The Tragical History of Doctor Faustus, V, ii

6 I'll burn my books!
The Tragical History of Doctor Faustus, V, ii

7 Cut is the branch that might have grown full
straight,
And burned is Apollo's laurel bough,
That sometime grew within this learned man.
The Tragical History of Doctor Faustus, V, iii

Matthew Roydon
c. 1564–c. 1622

8 You knew—who knew not Astrophil?
*The Phoenix Nest [1593]; An Elegy, or
Friend's Passion for His Astrophil (on the
death of Sir Philip Sidney)*

9 A sweet attractive kind of grace,
A full assurance given by looks,
Continual comfort in a face,
The lineaments of Gospel books;

I trow that countenance cannot lie.
Whose thoughts are legible in the eye.
The Phoenix Nest

10 Was never eye, did see that face,
Was never ear, did hear that tongue,
Was never mind, did mind his grace,
That ever thought the travel long,
But eyes, and ears, and ev'ry thought,
Were with his sweet perfections caught.
The Phoenix Nest

William Shakespeare[3]
1564–1616

11 Hung be the heavens with black, yield day to
night!
*King Henry the Sixth, Part I [1589–1590],
act I, sc. i, l. 1*

12 Fight till the last gasp.   *I, ii, 127*

13 Expect Saint Martin's summer, halcyon days.
I, ii, 131

14 Glory is like a circle in the water,
Which never ceaseth to enlarge itself,
Till by broad spreading it disperse to nought.
I, ii, 133

15   Unbidden guests
Are often welcomest when they are gone.
II, ii, 55

16 Between two hawks, which flies the higher pitch;
Between two dogs, which hath the deeper mouth;
Between two blades, which bears the better temper;
Between two horses, which doth bear him best;
Between two girls, which hath the merriest eye;
I have perhaps, some shallow spirit of judgment;
But in these nice sharp quillets of the law,
Good faith, I am no wiser than a daw.
II, iv, 12

17 I'll note you in my book of memory.
II, iv, 101

18 Just death, kind umpire of men's miseries.
II, v, 29

19 Chok'd with ambition of the meaner sort.
II, v, 123

20 Delays have dangerous ends.   *III, ii, 33*

---

[1]Once he drew / With one long kiss my whole soul through /
My lips. —ALFRED, LORD TENNYSON, *Fatima* [1833], *st. 3*

[2]Slowly, slowly run, O horses of the night.

[3]From the text of W. J. CRAIG, Oxford University Press [1935].
For the dating and sequence of the plays and poems see E. K.
CHAMBERS, *William Shakespeare* (1930), and JAMES G. McMAN-
AWAY, "Recent Studies in Shakespeare's Chronology," *Shakespeare
Survey*, III (1950).

1 Of all base passions, fear is most accurs'd.
King Henry VI, Pt. I, V, ii, 18

2 She's beautiful and therefore to be woo'd,
She is a woman, therefore to be won.   *V, iii, 78*

3 For what is wedlock forced, but a hell,
An age of discord and continual strife?
Whereas the contrary bringeth bliss,
And is a pattern of celestial peace.   *V, v, 62*

4 'Tis not my speeches that you do mislike,
But 'tis my presence that doth trouble ye.
Rancor will out.
*King Henry the Sixth, Part II [1590–1591],
act I, sc. i, l. 141*

5 Could I come near your beauty with my nails
I'd set my ten commandments in your face.
I, iii, 144

6 Blessed are the peacemakers on earth.
II, i, 34

7 Now, God be prais'd, that to believing souls
Gives light in darkness, comfort in despair!
II, i, 66

8 God defend the right!   *II, iii, 55*

9 Sometimes hath the brightest day a cloud;
And after summer evermore succeeds
Barren winter, with his wrathful nipping cold:
So cares and joys abound, as seasons fleet.
II, iv, 1

10 Now 'tis the spring, and weeds are shallow-rooted;
Suffer them now and they'll o'ergrow the garden.
III, i, 31

11   In thy face I see
The map of honor, truth, and loyalty.
III, i, 202

12 What stronger breastplate than a heart untainted!
Thrice is he arm'd that hath his quarrel just,
And he but naked, though lock'd up in steel,
Whose conscience with injustice is corrupted.
III, ii, 232

13 He dies, and makes no sign.   *III, iii, 29*

14 Forbear to judge, for we are sinners all.
Close up his eyes, and draw the curtain close;
And let us all to meditation.
III, iii, 31

15 The gaudy, blabbing, and remorseful day
Is crept into the bosom of the sea.   *IV, i, 1*

16 Small things make base men proud.   *IV, i, 106*

17 True nobility is exempt from fear.   *IV, i, 129*

18 I will make it felony to drink small beer.
IV, ii, 75

19 The first thing we do, let's kill all the lawyers.
IV, ii, 86

20 Is not this a lamentable thing, that of the skin of an innocent lamb should be made parchment? that parchment, being scribbled o'er, should undo a man?   *IV, ii, 88*

21 Adam was a gardener.   *IV, ii, 146*

22 Thou hast most traitorously corrupted the youth of the realm in erecting a grammar-school; and whereas, before, our forefathers had no other books but the score and the tally, thou hast caused printing to be used; and, contrary to the king, his crown, and dignity, thou hast built a paper-mill.
IV, vii, 35

23 Beggars mounted run their horse to death.[1]
*King Henry the Sixth, Part III [1590–1591],
act I, sc. iv, l. 127*

24 O tiger's heart wrapp'd in a woman's hide!
I, iv, 137

25 To weep is to make less the depth of grief.
II, i, 85

26 The smallest worm will turn being trodden on.
II, ii, 17

27   Didst thou never hear
That things ill got had ever bad success?
II, ii, 45

28 Thou [Death] setter up and plucker down of
kings.[2]   *II, iii, 37*

29 And what makes robbers bold but too much lenity?
II, vi, 22

30 My crown is in my heart, not on my head;
Not deck'd with diamonds and Indian stones,
Nor to be seen: my crown is call'd content;
A crown it is that seldom kings enjoy.   *III, i, 62*

31   'Tis a happy thing
To be the father unto many sons.   *III, ii, 104*

32 Like one that stands upon a promontory,
And spies a far-off shore where he would tread,
Wishing his foot were equal with his eye.
III, ii, 135

_____

[1]Set a beggar on horseback and he will ride a gallop. —Robert Burton, *Anatomy of Melancholy* [1621–1651], pt. II, sec. 2, member 2

Set a beggar on horseback, and he'll outride the Devil. —Henry George Bohn [1796–1884], *Foreign Proverbs, German* [1855]

[2]Proud setter up and puller down of kings. —*King Henry VI, Part III, act III, sc. iii, l. 157*

1   Yield not thy neck
To fortune's yoke, but let thy dauntless mind
Still ride in triumph over all mischance.
III, iii, 16

2 For how can tyrants safely govern home,
Unless abroad they purchase great alliance?
III, iii, 69

3 Having nothing, nothing can he lose.
III, iii, 152

4 Hasty marriage seldom proveth well.
IV, i, 18

5 What fates impose, that men must needs abide;
It boots not to resist both wind and tide.
IV, iii, 57

6 Now join your hands, and with your hands your
hearts.   *IV, vi, 39*

7 For many men that stumble at the threshold
Are well foretold that danger lurks within.
IV, vii, 11

8 A little fire is quickly trodden out,
Which, being suffer'd, rivers cannot quench.
IV, viii, 7

9   When the lion fawns upon the lamb,
The lamb will never cease to follow him.
IV, viii, 49

10   What is pomp, rule, reign, but earth and dust?
And, live we how we can, yet die we must.
V, ii, 27

11 For every cloud engenders not a storm.   *V, iii, 13*

12 What though the mast be now blown overboard,
The cable broke, the holding anchor lost,
And half our sailors swallow'd in the flood?
Yet lives our pilot still.   *V, iv, 3*

13 So part we sadly in this troublous world,
To meet with joy in sweet Jerusalem.   *V, v, 7*

14 Men ne'er spend their fury on a child.   *V, v, 57*

15 He's sudden if a thing comes in his head.
V, v, 86

16 Suspicion always haunts the guilty mind;
The thief doth fear each bush an officer.
V, vi, 11

17 This word "love," which greybeards call divine.
V, vi, 81

18 Bid me discourse, I will enchant thine ear.
Venus and Adonis [1592], l. 145

19 Love is a spirit all compact of fire,
Not gross to sink, but light, and will aspire.
l. 149

20 "Fondling," she saith, "since I have hemm'd thee
here
Within the circuit of this ivory pale,
I'll be a park, and thou shalt be my deer;
Feed where thou wilt, on mountain, or in dale:
Graze on my lips, and if those hills be dry,
Stray lower, where the pleasant fountains lie."
l. 229

21 O! what a war of looks was then between them.
l. 355

22 Like a red morn, that ever yet betoken'd
Wrack to the seaman, tempest to the field.   *l. 453*

23 The owl, night's herald.   *l. 531*

24 Love comforteth like sunshine after rain.   *l. 799*

25 The text is old, the orator too green.   *l. 806*

26 For he being dead, with him is beauty slain,
And, beauty dead, black chaos comes again.
l. 1019

27 The grass stoops not, she treads on it so light.
l. 1028

28 Now is the winter of our discontent
Made glorious summer by this sun of York.
*King Richard the Third [1592–1593], act I,
sc. i, l. 1*

29 Grim-visag'd war hath smooth'd his wrinkled front.
I, i, 9

30 He capers nimbly in a lady's chamber
To the lascivious pleasing of a lute.   *I, i, 12*

31 This weak piping time of peace.   *I, i, 24*

32 No beast so fierce but knows some touch of pity.
I, ii, 71

33 Look, how my ring encompasseth thy finger,
Even so thy breast encloseth my poor heart;
Wear both of them, for both of them are thine.
I, ii, 204

34 Was ever woman in this humor woo'd?
Was ever woman in this humor won?   *I, ii, 229*

35   The world is grown so bad
That wrens make prey where eagles dare not perch.
I, iii, 70

36 The day will come that thou shalt wish for me
To help thee curse this pois'nous bunch-back'd
toad.   *I, iii, 245*

37 And thus I clothe my naked villany
With odd old ends stol'n forth of holy writ,
And seem a saint when most I play the devil.
I, iii, 336

1 Talkers are no good doers.
King Richard III, I, iii, 351

2 O, I have pass'd a miserable night,
  So full of ugly sights, of ghastly dreams,
  That, as I am a Christian faithful man,
  I would not spend another such a night,
  Though 'twere to buy a world of happy days.
I, iv, 2

3 Lord, Lord! methought what pain it was to drown:
  What dreadful noise of water in mine ears!
  What sights of ugly death within mine eyes!
  Methought I saw a thousand fearful wracks;
  A thousand men that fishes gnaw'd upon.
I, iv, 21

4 The kingdom of perpetual night.   *I, iv, 47*

5 Sorrow breaks seasons and reposing hours,
  Makes the night morning, and the noontide night.
I, iv, 76

6 A parlous boy.   *II, iv, 35*

7 So wise so young, they say, do never live long.[1]
III, i, 79

8 Off with his head!   *III, iv, 75*

9 Lives like a drunken sailor on a mast;
  Ready with every nod to tumble down
  Into the fatal bowels of the deep.   *III, iv, 98*

10 I am not in the giving vein today.   *IV, ii, 115*

11 The sons of Edward sleep in Abraham's bosom.
IV, iii, 38

12 A grievous burden was thy birth to me;
  Tetchy and wayward was thy infancy.   *IV, iv, 168*

13 An honest tale speeds best being plainly told.
IV, iv, 359

14 Harp not on that string.   *IV, iv, 365*

15 Relenting fool, and shallow changing woman!
IV, iv, 432

16 Is the chair empty? is the sword unsway'd?
  Is the king dead? the empire unpossess'd?
IV, iv, 470

17 True hope is swift, and flies with swallow's wings;
  Kings it makes gods, and meaner creatures kings.
V, ii, 23

18 The king's name is a tower of strength.   *V, iii, 12*

19 Give me another horse! bind up my wounds!
V, iii, 178

20 O coward conscience, how dost thou afflict me!
V, iii, 180

21 My conscience hath a thousand several tongues,
  And every tongue brings in a several tale,
  And every tale condemns me for a villain.
V, iii, 194

22 Conscience is but a word that cowards use,
  Devis'd at first to keep the strong in awe.
V, iii, 310

23 A horse! a horse! my kingdom for a horse!
V, iv, 7

24   I have set my life upon a cast,
  And I will stand the hazard of the die.
  I think there be six Richmonds in the field.
V, iv, 9

25 The pleasing punishment that women bear.
  *The Comedy of Errors [1592–1594], act I, sc.
  i, l. 46*

26 For we may pity, though not pardon thee.
I, i, 97

27 Why, headstrong liberty is lash'd with woe.
  There's nothing situate under heaven's eye
  But hath his bound, in earth, in sea, in sky.
II, i, 15

28   Every why hath a wherefore.[2]   *II, ii, 45*

29   There's no time for a man to recover his hair
  that grows bald by nature.   *II, ii, 74*

30   What he hath scanted men in hair, he hath given
  them in wit.   *II, ii, 83*

31   Small cheer and great welcome makes a merry
  feast.   *III, i, 26*

32 There is something in the wind.   *III, i, 69*

33 We'll pluck a crow together.   *III, i, 83*

34 For slander lives upon succession,
  Forever housed where it gets possession.
III, i, 105

35 Be not thy tongue thy own shame's orator.
III, ii, 10

36 Ill deeds are doubled with an evil word.   *III, ii, 20*

37 A back-friend, a shoulder-clapper.   *IV, ii, 37*

38 The venom clamors of a jealous woman
  Poison more deadly than a mad dog's tooth.
V, i, 69

39 Unquiet meals make ill digestions.   *V, i, 74*

---

[1]A little too wise, they say, do ne'er live long.—THOMAS MIDDLE-
TON, *The Phoenix, act I, sc. i*

[2]For every why he had a wherefore.—SAMUEL BUTLER, *Hudibras, pt. I* [1663], *canto 1, l. 132*

1   One Pinch, a hungry lean-fac'd villain,
A mere anatomy, a mountebank,
A threadbare juggler, and a fortune-teller,
A needy, hollow-ey'd, sharp-looking wretch,
A living-dead man.   *V, i, 238*

2 Beauty itself doth of itself persuade
The eyes of men without an orator.
      The Rape of Lucrece [1593–1594], l. 29

3 This silent war of lilies and of roses,
Which Tarquin view'd in her fair face's field.
      l. 71

4 One for all, or all for one we gage.   *l. 144*

5 Who buys a minute's mirth to wail a week?
Or sells eternity to get a toy?
For one sweet grape who will the vine destroy?
      l. 213

6 Extreme fear can neither fight nor fly.   *l. 230*

7 All orators are dumb when beauty pleadeth.
      l. 268

8 Time's glory is to calm contending kings,
To unmask falsehood and bring truth to light.
      l. 939

9 For greatest scandal waits on greatest state.
      l. 1006

10 To see sad sights moves more than hear them told.
      l. 1324

11 Cloud-kissing Ilion.   *l. 1370*

12 Lucrece swears he did her wrong.[1]   *l. 1462*

13 Sweet mercy is nobility's true badge.
      Titus Andronicus [1593–1594], act I, sc. i, l. 119

14 These words are razors to my wounded heart.
      I, i, 314

15 He lives in fame that died in virtue's cause.
      I, i, 390

16 These dreary dumps.[2]   *I, i, 391*

17 The eagle suffers little birds to sing,
And is not careful what they mean thereby.
      IV, iv, 82

18 Tut! I have done a thousand dreadful things
As willingly as one would kill a fly.   *V, i, 141*

19   I'll not budge an inch.
      The Taming of the Shrew [1593–1594], Induction, sc. i, l. 13

20 And if the boy have not a woman's gift
To rain a shower of commanded tears,
An onion will do well for such a shift.   *i, 124*

21 No profit grows where is no pleasure ta'en;
In brief, sir, study what you most affect.
      Act I, sc. i, l. 39

22   There's small choice in rotten apples.
      I, i, 137

23 To seek their fortunes further than at home,
Where small experience grows.   *I, ii, 51*

24 I come to wive it wealthily in Padua.   *I, ii, 75*

25   Nothing comes amiss, so money comes withal.
      I, ii, 82

26 And do as adversaries do in law,
Strive mightily, but eat and drink as friends.
      I, ii, 281

27 I must dance barefoot on her wedding day,
And, for your love to her, lead apes in hell.
      II, i, 33

28 Asses are made to bear, and so are you.
      II, i, 200

29 Kiss me, Kate, we will be married o' Sunday.
      II, i, 318

30 Old fashions please me best.   *III, i, 81*

31 Who woo'd in haste and means to wed at leisure.
      III, ii, 11

32 Such an injury would vex a very saint.
      III, ii, 28

33   A little pot and soon hot.   *IV, i, 6*

34 Sits as one new-risen from a dream.   *IV, i, 189*

35 This is a way to kill a wife with kindness.
      IV, i, 211

36 Kindness in women, not their beauteous looks,
Shall win my love.   *IV, ii, 41*

37 Our purses shall be proud, our garments poor:
For 'tis the mind that makes the body rich;
And as the sun breaks through the darkest clouds,
So honor peereth in the meanest habit.
      IV, iii, 173

38 Forward, I pray, since we have come so far,
And be it moon, or sun, or what you please.
An if you please to call it a rush-candle,
Henceforth I vow it shall be so for me.
      IV, v, 12

39 He that is giddy thinks the world turns round.
      V, ii, 20

---

[1] Some villain hath done me wrong. — *King Lear*, act I, sc. ii, l. 186

[2] And doleful dumps the mind oppress. — *Romeo and Juliet*, act IV, sc. v, l. 130

1 A woman mov'd is like a fountain troubled,
Muddy, ill-seeming, thick, bereft of beauty.
The Taming of the Shrew, V, ii, 143

2 Such duty as the subject owes the prince,
Even such a woman oweth to her husband.
V, ii, 156

3 Home-keeping youth have ever homely wits.
The Two Gentlemen of Verona [1594], act I, sc. i, l. 2

4 I have no other but a woman's reason:
I think him so, because I think him so.
I, ii, 23

5 *Julia:* They do not love that do not show their love.
Lucetta: O! they love least that let men know their love.   *I, ii, 31*

6 O! how this spring of love resembleth
The uncertain glory of an April day!   *I, iii, 84*

7 O jest unseen, inscrutable, invisible,
As a nose on a man's face, or a weathercock on a steeple!   *II, i, 145*

8 He makes sweet music with th' enamell'd stones.
II, vii, 28

9 That man that hath a tongue, I say, is no man,
If with his tongue he cannot win a woman.
III, i, 104

10 Except I be by Silvia in the night,
There is no music in the nightingale.
III, i, 178

11 Much is the force of heaven-bred poesy.
III, ii, 72

12 Who is Silvia? what is she,
That all our swains commend her?
Holy, fair, and wise is she;
The heaven such grace did lend her,
That she might admired be.   *IV, ii, 40*

13 Alas, how love can trifle with itself!   *IV, iv, 190*

14 Black men are pearls in beauteous ladies' eyes.
V, ii, 12

15 How use doth breed a habit in a man!   *V, iv, 1*

16 Spite of cormorant devouring Time.
Love's Labour's Lost [1594–1595], act I, sc. i, l. 4

17 Make us heirs of all eternity.   *I, i, 7*

18 Why, all delights are vain; but that most vain
Which, with pain purchas'd doth inherit pain.
I, i, 72

19 Light seeking light doth light of light beguile.
I, i, 77

20 Study is like the heaven's glorious sun,
That will not be deep-search'd with saucy looks;
Small have continual plodders ever won,
Save base authority from others' books.
These earthly godfathers of heaven's lights
That give a name to every fixed star,
Have no more profit of their shining nights
Than those that walk and wot not what they are.
I, i, 84

21 At Christmas I no more desire a rose
Than wish a snow in May's newfangled mirth;
But like of each thing that in season grows.
I, i, 105

22   And men sit down to that nourishment which is called supper.   *I, i, 237*

23   That unlettered small-knowing soul.
I, i, 251

24   A child of our grandmother Eve, a female; or, for thy more sweet understanding, a woman.
I, i, 263

25   Affliction may one day smile again; and till then, sit thee down, sorrow!   *I, i, 312*

26   Devise, wit; write, pen; for I am for whole volumes in folio.   *I, ii, 194*

27 Beauty is bought by judgment of the eye,
Not utter'd by base sale of chapmen's tongues.
II, i, 15

28   A merrier man,
Within the limit of becoming mirth,
I never spent an hour's talk withal.   *II, i, 66*

29 Your wit's too hot, it speeds too fast, 'twill tire.
II, i, 119

30   Warble, child; make passionate my sense of hearing.   *III, i, 1*

31   Remuneration! O! that's the Latin word for three farthings.   *III, i, 143*

32 A very beadle to a humorous sigh.   *III, i, 185*

33 This wimpled, whining, purblind, wayward boy,
This senior-junior, giant-dwarf, Dan Cupid;
Regent of love-rimes, lord of folded arms,
The anointed sovereign of sighs and groans,
Liege of all loiters and malcontents.
III, i, 189

34   He hath not fed of the dainties that are bred of a book; he hath not eat paper, as it were; he hath not drunk ink.   *IV, ii, 25*

35 Many can brook the weather that love not the wind.   *IV, ii, 34*

36   You two are book-men.   *IV, ii, 35*

1 These are begot in the ventricle of memory, nourished in the womb of pia mater, and delivered upon the mellowing of occasion. *IV, ii, 70*

2 By heaven, I do love, and it hath taught me to rime, and to be melancholy. *IV, iii, 13*

3 The heavenly rhetoric of thine eye. *IV, iii, 60*

4 For where is any author in the world
Teaches such beauty as a woman's eye?
Learning is but an adjunct to ourself.
IV, iii, 312

5 But love, first learned in a lady's eyes,
Lives not alone immured in the brain.
IV, iii, 327

6 It adds a precious seeing to the eye.
IV, iii, 333

7   As sweet and musical
As bright Apollo's lute, strung with his hair;
And when Love speaks, the voice of all the gods
Makes heaven drowsy with the harmony.
IV, iii, 342

8 From women's eyes this doctrine I derive:
They sparkle still the right Promethean fire;
They are the books, the arts, the academes,
That show, contain, and nourish all the world.
IV, iii, 350

9   He draweth out the thread of his verbosity finer than the staple of his argument. *V, i, 18*

10 *Moth:* They have been at a great feast of languages, and stolen the scraps.
Costard: O! they have lived long on the alms-basket of words. I marvel thy master hath not eaten thee for a word; for thou art not so long by the head as *honorificabilitudinitatibus:* thou art easier swallowed than a flap-dragon. *V, i, 39*

11   In the posteriors of this day, which the rude multitude call the afternoon. *V, i, 96*

12 Taffeta phrases, silken terms precise,
Three-pil'd hyperboles, spruce affectation,
Figures pedantical. *V, ii, 407*

13   Let me take you a button-hole lower.
V, ii, 705

14   The naked truth of it is, I have no shirt.
V, ii, 715

15 A jest's prosperity lies in the ear
Of him that hears it, never in the tongue
Of him that makes it. *V, ii, 869*

16 When daisies pied and violets blue,
And lady-smocks all silver-white,
And cuckoo-buds of yellow hue
Do paint the meadows with delight,

The cuckoo then, on every tree,
Mocks married men; for thus sings he,
        Cuckoo;
Cuckoo, cuckoo: O word of fear,
Unpleasing to a married ear! *V, ii, 902*

17 When icicles hang by the wall,
And Dick the shepherd blows his nail,
And Tom bears logs into the hall,
And milk comes frozen home in pail,
When blood is nipp'd and ways be foul,
Then nightly sings the staring owl,
        Tu-who;
Tu-whit, tu-who — a merry note,
While greasy Joan doth keel the pot.
V, ii, 920

18 When all aloud the wind doth blow,
And coughing drowns the parson's saw,
And birds sit brooding in the snow,
And Marian's nose looks red and raw,
When roasted crabs hiss in the bowl.
V, ii, 929

19   The words of Mercury are harsh after the songs of Apollo. *V, ii, 938*

20 For new-made honor doth forget men's names.
King John [1594–1596], act I, sc. i, l. 187

21 Sweet, sweet, sweet poison for the age's tooth.
I, i, 213

22 Bearing their birthrights proudly on their backs,
To make a hazard of new fortunes here.
II, i, 70

23 For courage mounteth with occasion.
II, i, 82

24   The hare of whom the proverb goes,
Whose valor plucks dead lions by the beard.[1]
II, i, 137

25 A woman's will. *II, i, 194*

26 Saint George, that swing'd the dragon, and e'er since
Sits on his horse back at mine hostess' door.
II, i, 288

27 He is the half part of a blessed man,
Left to be finished by such a she;
And she a fair divided excellence,
Whose fullness of perfection lies in him.
II, i, 437

28 'Zounds! I was never so bethump'd with words
Since I first call'd my brother's father dad.
II, i, 466

---

[1]So hares may pull dead lions by the beard. —THOMAS KYD, *The Spanish Tragedy* [1594], *act I, sc. ii, l. 172*

1 Mad world! mad kings, mad composition!
King John, II, i, 561

2 That smooth-fac'd gentleman, tickling
    Commodity,
Commodity, the bias of the world.   *II, i, 573*

3 I will instruct my sorrows to be proud;
  For grief is proud and makes his owner stoop.
III, i, 68

4 Thou wear a lion's hide! doff it for shame,
  And hang a calf's-skin on those recreant limbs.
III, i, 128

5 The sun's o'ercast with blood: fair day, adieu!
  Which is the side that I must go withal?
  I am with both: each army hath a hand;
  And in their rage, I having hold of both,
  They whirl asunder and dismember me.
III, i, 326

6 Bell, book, and candle shall not drive me back.
III, iii, 12

7 Look, who comes here! a grave unto a soul.
III, iv, 17

8 Death, death: O, amiable lovely death!
III, iv, 25

9 Grief fills the room up of my absent child,
  Lies in his bed, walks up and down with me,
  Puts on his pretty looks, repeats his words,
  Remembers me of all his gracious parts,
  Stuffs out his vacant garments with his form.
III, iv, 93

10 Life is as tedious as a twice-told tale,
  Vexing the dull ear of a drowsy man.
III, iv, 108

11 When Fortune means to men most good,
  She looks upon them with a threatening eye.
III, iv, 119

12 A scepter snatch'd with an unruly hand
  Must be as boisterously maintain'd as gain'd;
  And he that stands upon a slippery place
  Makes nice of no vile hold to stay him up.
III, iv, 135

13 As quiet as a lamb.   *IV, i, 80*

14 To gild refined gold, to paint the lily,
  To throw a perfume on the violet,
  To smooth the ice, or add another hue
  Unto the rainbow, or with taper-light
  To seek the beauteous eye of heaven to garnish,
  Is wasteful and ridiculous excess.   *IV, ii, 11*

15 And oftentimes excusing of a fault
  Doth make the fault the worse by the excuse.
IV, ii, 30

16 We cannot hold mortality's strong hand.
IV, ii, 82

17 There is no sure foundation set on blood,
  No certain life achiev'd by others' death.
IV, ii, 104

18 Make haste; the better foot before.
IV, ii, 170

19 Another lean unwash'd artificer.   *IV, ii, 201*

20 How oft the sight of means to do ill deeds
  Makes ill deeds done!   *IV, ii, 219*

21 Heaven take my soul, and England keep my bones!
IV, iii, 10

22 I am amaz'd, methinks, and lose my way
  Among the thorns and dangers of this world.
IV, iii, 140

23 Unthread the rude eye of rebellion,
  And welcome home again discarded faith.
V, iv, 11

24 The day shall not be up so soon as I,
  To try the fair adventure of tomorrow.
V, v, 21

25   'Tis strange that death should sing.
  I am the cygnet to this pale faint swan,
  Who chants a doleful hymn to his own death.
V, vii, 20

26 Now my soul hath elbow-room.   *V, vii, 28*

27   I do not ask you much:
  I beg cold comfort.   *V, vii, 41*

28 This England never did, nor never shall,
  Lie at the proud foot of a conqueror.
V, vii, 112

29 Come the three corners of the world in arms,
  And we shall shock them. Nought shall make us
    rue,
  If England to itself do rest but true.
V, vii, 116

30 The purest treasure mortal times afford
  Is spotless reputation.
    King Richard the Second [1595], act I, sc. i, l.
    177

31 Mine honor is my life; both grow in one;
  Take honor from me, and my life is done.
I, i, 182

32 We were not born to sue, but to command.
I, i, 196

33 The daintiest last, to make the end most sweet.
I, iii, 68

34 Truth hath a quiet breast.   *I, iii, 96*

1 How long a time lies in one little word!
I, iii, 213

2 Things sweet to taste prove in digestion sour.
I, iii, 236

3 Must I not serve a long apprenticehood
To foreign passages, and in the end,
Having my freedom, boast of nothing else
But that I was a journeyman to grief?
I, iii, 271

4 All places that the eye of heaven visits
Are to a wise man ports and happy havens.
Teach thy necessity to reason thus;
There is no virtue like necessity.
Think not the king did banish thee,
But thou the king.
I, iii, 275

5 For gnarling sorrow hath less power to bite
The man that mocks at it and sets it light.
I, iii, 292

6 O! who can hold a fire in his hand
By thinking on the frosty Caucasus?
Or cloy the hungry edge of appetite
By bare imagination of a feast?
Or wallow naked in December snow
By thinking on fantastic summer's heat?
O, no! the apprehension of the good
Gives but the greater feeling to the worse.
I, iii, 294

7 Where'er I wander, boast of this I can,
Though banish'd, yet a true-born Englishman.
I, iii, 308

8   The tongues of dying men
Enforce attention like deep harmony.
II, i, 5

9 The setting sun, and music at the close,
As the last taste of sweets, is sweetest last,
Writ in remembrance more than things long past.
II, i, 12

10 Report of fashions in proud Italy,
Whose manners still our tardy apish nation
Limps after in base imitation.   *II, i, 21*

11 For violent fires soon burn out themselves;
Small showers last long, but sudden storms are
      short.   *II, i, 34*

12 This royal throne of kings, this scepter'd isle,
This earth of majesty, this seat of Mars,
This other Eden, demi-paradise,
This fortress built by Nature for herself
Against infection and the hand of war,
This happy breed of men, this little world,
This precious stone set in the silver sea,
Which serves it in the office of a wall,

Or as a moat defensive to a house,
Against the envy of less happier lands,
This blessed plot, this earth, this realm, this
      England,
This nurse, this teeming womb of royal kings,
Fear'd by their breed and famous by their birth.
II, i, 40

13 England, bound in with the triumphant sea,
Whose rocky shore beats back the envious siege
Of watery Neptune.   *II, i, 61*

14 That England, that was wont to conquer others,
Hath made a shameful conquest of itself.
II, i, 65

15 The ripest fruit first falls.   *II, i, 154*

16 Each substance of a grief hath twenty shadows.
II, ii, 14

17 I count myself in nothing else so happy
As in a soul remembering my good friends.
II, iii, 46

18 Evermore thanks, the exchequer of the poor.
II, iii, 65

19 Grace me no grace, nor uncle me no uncle.
II, iii, 87

20 The caterpillars of the commonwealth,
Which I have sworn to weed and pluck away.
II, iii, 166

21 Things past redress are now with me past care.
II, iii, 171

22 I see thy glory like a shooting star
Fall to the base earth from the firmament.
II, iv, 19

23 Eating the bitter bread of banishment.
III, i, 21

24 Not all the water in the rough rude sea
Can wash the balm from an anointed king.
III, ii, 54

25 O! call back yesterday, bid time return.
III, ii, 69

26 The worst is death, and death will have his day.
III, ii, 103

27   Of comfort no man speak:
Let's talk of graves, of worms, and epitaphs;
Make dust our paper, and with rainy eyes
Write sorrow on the bosom of the earth;
Let's choose executors and talk of wills.
III, ii, 144

28 And nothing can we call our own but death,
And that small model of the barren earth

Which serves as paste and cover to our bones.
For God's sake, let us sit upon the ground
And tell sad stories of the death of kings:
How some have been depos'd, some slain in war,
Some haunted by the ghosts they have depos'd,
Some poison'd by their wives, some sleeping kill'd;
All murder'd: for within the hollow crown
That rounds the mortal temples of a king
Keeps Death his court.
King Richard II, III, ii, 152

1 Comes at the last, and with a little pin
Bores through his castle wall, and farewell king!
III, ii, 169

2   He is come to open
The purple testament of bleeding war. *III, iii, 93*

3   O! that I were as great
As is my grief, or lesser than my name,
Or that I could forget what I have been,
Or not remember what I must be now.
III, iii, 136

4 I'll give my jewels for a set of beads,
My gorgeous palace for a hermitage,
My gay apparel for an almsman's gown.
III, iii, 147

5 And my large kingdom for a little grave,
A little little grave, an obscure grave. *III, iii, 153*

6   And there at Venice gave
His body to that pleasant country's earth,
And his pure soul unto his captain Christ,
Under whose colors he had fought so long.
IV, i, 97

7 Peace shall go sleep with Turks and infidels.
IV, i, 139

8 So Judas did to Christ: but he, in twelve,
Found truth in all but one; I, in twelve thousand,
    none.
God save the king! Will no man say, amen?
IV, i, 170

9 Now is this golden crown like a deep well
That owes two buckets filling one another;
The emptier ever dancing in the air,
The other down, unseen and full of water:
That bucket down and full of tears am I,
Drinking my griefs, whilst you mount up on high.
IV, i, 184

10 You may my glories and my state depose,
But not my griefs; still am I king of those.
IV, i, 192

11   Some of you with Pilate wash your hands,
Showing an outward pity. *IV, i, 239*

12 A mockery king of snow. *IV, i, 260*

13 As in a theater, the eyes of men,
After a well-grac'd actor leaves the stage,
Are idly bent on him that enters next,
Thinking his prattle to be tedious. *V, ii, 23*

14   How sour sweet music is
When time is broke and no proportion kept!
So is it in the music of men's lives. *V, v, 42*

15 I wasted time, and now doth time waste me;
For now hath time made me his numbering clock:
My thoughts are minutes. *V, v, 49*

16 This music mads me: let it sound no more.
V, v, 61

17 Mount, mount, my soul! thy seat is up on high,
Whilst my gross flesh sinks downward, here to die.
V, v, 112

18 To live a barren sister all your life,
Chanting faint hymns to the cold fruitless moon.
*A Midsummer-Night's Dream [1595–1596],
act I, sc. i, l. 72*

19   For aught that I could ever read,
Could ever hear by tale or history,
The course of true love never did run smooth.
I, i, 132

20 Swift as a shadow, short as any dream,
Brief as the lightning in the collied night,
That, in a spleen, unfolds both heaven and earth,
And ere a man hath power to say, "Behold!"
The jaws of darkness do devour it up:
So quick bright things come to confusion.
I, i, 144

21 Love looks not with the eyes, but with the mind,
And therefore is wing'd Cupid painted blind.[1]
I, i, 234

22   The most lamentable comedy, and most cruel
death of Pyramus and Thisby. *I, ii, 11*

23   Masters, spread yourselves. *I, ii, 16*

24   This is Ercles' vein, a tyrant's vein.
I, ii, 43

25   I'll speak in a monstrous little voice.
I, ii, 55

26   I am slow of study. *I, ii, 70*

27   That would hang us, every mother's son.
I, ii, 81

[1] I have heard of reasons manifold / Why Love must needs be blind, / But this the best of all I hold / His eyes are in his mind. — SAMUEL TAYLOR COLERIDGE, *Reason for Love's Blindness* [1828]

1   I will aggravate my voice so that I will roar you
as gently as any sucking dove; I will roar you as
'twere any nightingale.   *I, ii, 85*

2   A proper man, as one shall see in a summer's
day; a most lovely, gentleman-like man.
                       I, ii, 89

3 Over hill, over dale,
  Thorough bush, thorough brier,
  Over park, over pale,
  Thorough flood, thorough fire.   *II, i, 2*

4 I must go seek some dew drops here,
  And hang a pearl in every cowslip's ear.
                       II, i, 14

5 I am that merry wanderer of the night.
  I jest to Oberon, and make him smile
  When I a fat and bean-fed horse beguile,
  Neighing in likeness of a filly foal:
  And sometimes lurk I in a gossip's bowl,
  In very likeness of a roasted crab.   *II, i, 43*

6 Ill met by moonlight, proud Titania.
                       II, i, 60

7 These are the forgeries of jealousy.   *II, i, 81*

8 Since once I sat upon a promontory,
  And heard a mermaid on a dolphin's back
  Uttering such dulcet and harmonious breath,
  That the rude sea grew civil at her song,
  And certain stars shot madly from their spheres
  To hear the sea-maid's music.   *II, i, 149*

9 And the imperial votaress passed on,
  In maiden meditation, fancy-free.
  Yet mark'd I where the bolt of Cupid fell:
  It fell upon a little western flower,
  Before milk-white, now purple with love's wound,
  And maidens call it, Love-in-idleness.
                       II, i, 163

10 I'll put a girdle round about the earth
  In forty minutes.   *II, i, 175*

11 For you in my respect are all the world:
  Then how can it be said I am alone,
  When all the world is here to look on me?
                       II, i, 224

12 I know a bank whereon the wild thyme blows,
  Where oxlips and the nodding violet grows
  Quite over-canopied with luscious woodbine,
  With sweet musk-roses, and with eglantine:
  There sleeps Titania some time of the night,
  Lull'd in these flowers with dances and delight;
  And there the snake throws her enamell'd skin,
  Weed wide enough to wrap a fairy in.
                       II, i, 249

13 Some to kill cankers in the musk-rose buds,
  Some war with rere-mice for their leathern wings,
  To make my small elves coats.   *II, ii, 3*

14 The clamorous owl, that nightly hoots, and
    wonders
  At our quaint spirits.   *II, ii, 6*

15 You spotted snakes with double tongue,
  Thorny hedge-hogs, be not seen;
  Newts, and blind-worms, do no wrong;
  Come not near our fairy queen.   *II, ii, 9*

16 Night and silence! who is here?
  Weeds of Athens he doth wear.   *II, ii, 70*

17 As a surfeit of the sweetest things
  The deepest loathing to the stomach brings.
                     II, ii, 137

18   To bring in—God shield us!—a lion among
ladies, is a most dreadful thing; for there is not a
more fearful wild-fowl than your lion living.
                     III, i, 32

19   A calendar, a calendar! look in the almanack; find
out moonshine.   *III, i, 55*

20   Bless thee, Bottom! bless thee! thou art translated.   *III, i, 124*

21 Lord, what fools these mortals be!
                     III, ii, 115

22   So we grew together,
  Like to a double cherry, seeming parted,
  But yet an union in partition;
  Two lovely berries molded on one stem.
                   III, ii, 208

23 Though she be but little, she is fierce.
                   III, ii, 325

24   I have a reasonable good ear in music: let us
have the tongs and the bones.   *IV, i, 32*

25   Truly, a peck of provender: I could munch your
good dry oats. Methinks I have a great desire to a
bottle of hay: good hay, sweet hay, hath no fellow.
                    IV, i, 36

26   I have an exposition of sleep come upon me.
                    IV, i, 44

27 My Oberon! what visions have I seen!
  Methought I was enamor'd of an ass.
                    IV, i, 82

28   I never heard
  So musical a discord, such sweet thunder.
                    IV, i, 123

29   I have had a dream, past the wit of man to say
what dream it was.   *IV, i, 211*

1   The eye of man hath not heard, the ear of man hath not seen, man's hand is not able to taste, his tongue to conceive, nor his heart to report, what my dream was.

A Midsummer-Night's Dream, IV, i, 218

2   Eat no onions nor garlic, for we are to utter sweet breath.   *IV, ii, 44*

3 The lunatic, the lover, and the poet,
Are of imagination all compact:
One sees more devils than vast hell can hold,
That is, the madman; the lover, all as frantic,
Sees Helen's beauty in a brow of Egypt:
The poet's eye, in a fine frenzy rolling,
Doth glance from heaven to earth, from earth to
heaven;
And, as imagination bodies forth
The forms of things unknown, the poet's pen
Turns them to shapes, and gives to airy nothing
A local habitation and a name.
Such tricks hath strong imagination,
That, if it would but apprehend some joy,
It comprehends some bringer of that joy;
Or in the night, imagining some fear,
How easy is a bush suppos'd a bear!   *V, i, 7*

4 But all the story of the night told over,
And all their minds transfigur'd so together,
More witnesseth than fancy's images,
And grows to something of great constancy,
But, howsoever, strange and admirable.

V, i, 23

5 Very tragical mirth.   *V, i, 57*

6 The true beginning of our end.[1]   *V, i, 111*

7   The best in this kind are but shadows.

V, i, 215

8   A very gentle beast, and of a good conscience.

V, i, 232

9   All that I have to say, is, to tell you that the lanthorn is the moon; I, the man in the moon; this thorn-bush, my thorn-bush; and this dog, my dog.

V, i, 263

10   Well roared, Lion.   *V, i, 272*

11   This passion, and the death of a dear friend, would go near to make a man look sad.

V, i, 295

12   With the help of a surgeon, he might yet recover, and prove an ass.   *V, i, 318*

13   No epilogue, I pray you, for your play needs no excuse. Never excuse.   *V, i, 363*

14 The iron tongue of midnight hath told twelve;
Lovers, to bed; 'tis almost fairy time.

V, i, 372

15 If we shadows have offended,
Think but this, and all is mended,
That you have but slumber'd here
While these visions did appear.   *V, ii, 54*

16 A pair of star-cross'd lovers.
Romeo and Juliet [1595–1596], prologue, l. 6

17 Saint-seducing gold.   *Act I, sc. i, l. 220*

18   One fire burns out another's burning,
One pain is lessen'd by another's anguish.

I, ii, 47

19 I will make thee think thy swan a crow.

I, ii, 92

20 For I am proverb'd with a grandsire phrase.

I, iv, 37

21 We burn daylight.   *I, iv, 43*

22 O! then, I see, Queen Mab hath been with
you! . . .
She is the fairies' midwife, and she comes
In shape no bigger than an agate-stone
On the forefinger of an alderman,
Drawn with a team of little atomies
Athwart men's noses as they lie asleep.

I, iv, 53

23   True, I talk of dreams,
Which are the children of an idle brain,
Begot of nothing but vain fantasy.   *I, iv, 97*

24 For you and I are past our dancing days.[2]

I, v, 35

25 It seems she hangs upon the cheek of night
Like a rich jewel in an Ethiop's ear;
Beauty too rich for use, for earth too dear!

I, v, 49

26 My only love sprung from my only hate!
Too early seen unknown, and known too late!

I, v, 142

27 Young Adam Cupid, he that shot so trim
When King Cophetua lov'd the beggarmaid.

II, i, 13

28 He jests at scars, that never felt a wound.
But, soft! what light through yonder window
breaks?
It is the east, and Juliet is the sun!   *II, ii, 1*

29 She speaks, yet she says nothing.   *II, ii, 12*

---

[1]I see the beginning of my end. — PHILIP MASSINGER, *The Virgin Martyr* [1622], act III, sc. iii

[2]My dancing days are done. — BEAUMONT AND FLETCHER, *The Scornful Lady* [1616], act V, sc. iii

1 See! how she leans her cheek upon her hand:
O! that I were a glove upon that hand,
That I might touch that cheek.   *II, ii, 23*

2 O Romeo, Romeo! wherefore art thou Romeo?[1]
Deny thy father, and refuse thy name;
Or, if thou wilt not, be but sworn my love,
And I'll no longer be a Capulet.   *II, ii, 33*

3 What's in a name? that which we call a rose
By any other name would smell as sweet.
                                    II, ii, 43

4 For stony limits cannot hold love out.
                                    II, ii, 67

5   At lovers' perjuries,
They say, Jove laughs.   *II, ii, 92*

6 In truth, fair Montague, I am too fond.
                                    II, ii, 98

7   I'll prove more true
Than those that have more cunning to be strange.
                                    II, ii, 100

8 *Romeo:* Lady, by yonder blessed moon I swear
That tips with silver all these fruit-tree tops —
Juliet: O! swear not by the moon, the inconstant
    moon,
That monthly changes in her circled orb,
Lest that thy love prove likewise variable.
                                    II, ii, 107

9   Do not swear at all;
Or, if thou wilt, swear by thy gracious self,
Which is the god of my idolatry.   *II, ii, 112*

10 It is too rash, too unadvis'd, too sudden;
Too like the lightning, which doth cease to be
Ere one can say it lightens.   *II, ii, 118*

11 This bud of love, by summer's ripening breath,
May prove a beauteous flower when next we meet.
                                    II, ii, 121

12 Love goes toward love, as schoolboys from their
    books;
But love from love, toward school with heavy
    looks.   *II, ii, 156*

13   O! for a falconer's voice,
To lure this tassel-gentle back again.   *II, ii, 158*

14 How silver-sweet sound lovers' tongues by night,
Like softest music to attending ears!   *II, ii, 165*

15   I would have thee gone;
And yet no further than a wanton's bird,
Who lets it hop a little from her hand,

Like a poor prisoner in his twisted gyves,
And with a silk thread plucks it back again,
So loving-jealous of his liberty.   *II, ii, 176*

16 Good night, good night! parting is such sweet
    sorrow,
That I shall say good night till it be morrow.
                                    II, ii, 184

17 Virtue itself turns vice, being misapplied;
And vice sometime's by action dignified.
                                    II, iii, 21

18 Care keeps his watch in every old man's eye,
And where care lodges, sleep will never lie.
                                    II, iii, 35

19 Wisely and slow; they stumble that run fast.
                                    II, iii, 94

20   One, two, and the third in your bosom.
                                    II, iv, 24

21   O flesh, flesh, how art thou fishified!
                                    II, iv, 41

22   The very pink of courtesy.   *II, iv, 63*

23   A gentleman, nurse, that loves to hear himself
talk, and will speak more in a minute than he will
stand to in a month.   *II, iv, 156*

24 These violent delights have violent ends.
                                    II, vi, 9

25 Therefore love moderately; long love doth so;
Too swift arrives as tardy as too slow.
                                    II, vi, 14

26   Thy head is as full of quarrels as an egg is full of
meat.[2]   *III, i, 23*

27   A word and a blow.   *III, i, 44*

28   No, 'tis not so deep as a well, nor so wide as a
church door; but 'tis enough, 'twill serve: ask for
me tomorrow, and you shall find me a grave man.
                                    III, i, 101

29   A plague o' both your houses!
They have made worms' meat of me.
                                    III, i, 112

30 O! I am Fortune's fool.   *III, i, 142*

31 Gallop apace, you fiery-footed steeds,
Towards Phoebus' lodging.   *III, ii, 1*

32   When he shall die,
Take him and cut him out in little stars,
And he will make the face of heaven so fine

---

[1] *Huncamunca:* O Tom Thumb! Tom Thumb! wherefore art
thou Tom Thumb? — HENRY FIELDING, *Tom Thumb* [1730], *act
II, sc. iii*

---

[2] It's as full of good-nature as an egg's full of meat. — RICHARD
BRINSLEY SHERIDAN, *A Trip to Scarborough* [1777], *act III, sc. iv*

That all the world will be in love with night,
And pay no worship to the garish sun.
Romeo and Juliet, III, ii, 21

1   He was not born to shame:
Upon his brow shame is asham'd to sit.
III, ii, 91

2 Adversity's sweet milk, philosophy.
III, iii, 54

3   Hang up philosophy!
Unless philosophy can make a Juliet.
III, iii, 56

4 The lark, the herald of the morn.
III, v, 6

5 Night's candles are burnt out, and jocund day
Stands tiptoe on the misty mountaintops.
III, v, 9

6 Thank me no thankings, nor proud me no prouds.
III, v, 153

7 Is there no pity sitting in the clouds,
That sees into the bottom of my grief?
III, v, 198

8 Past hope, past cure, past help!   *IV, i, 45*

9   'Tis an ill cook that cannot lick his own fingers.
IV, ii, 6

10 *Apothecary:* My poverty, but not my will, consents.
Romeo: I pay thy poverty, and not thy will.
V, i, 75

11   The strength
Of twenty men.   *V, i, 78*

12 The time and my intents are savage-wild,
More fierce and more inexorable far
Than empty tigers or the roaring sea.   *V, iii, 39*

13 Tempt not a desperate man.   *V, iii, 59*

14 One writ with me in sour misfortune's book.
V, iii, 82

15 How oft when men are at the point of death
Have they been merry!   *V, iii, 88*

16   Beauty's ensign yet
Is crimson in thy lips and in thy cheeks,
And death's pale flag is not advanced there.
V, iii, 94

17   O! here
Will I set up my everlasting rest,
And shake the yoke of inauspicious stars
From this world-wearied flesh. Eyes, look your last!
Arms, take your last embrace!   *V, iii, 109*

18   O true apothecary!
Thy drugs are quick.   *V, iii, 119*

19 See what a scourge is laid upon your hate,
That heaven finds means to kill your joys with love.
V, iii, 292

20 For never was a story of more woe
Than this of Juliet and her Romeo.
V, iii, 309

21 So shaken as we are, so wan with care.
*King Henry the Fourth, Part I [1596–1597],
act I, sc. i, l. 1*

22   In those holy fields
Over whose acres walk'd those blessed feet
Which fourteen hundred years ago were nail'd
For our advantage on the bitter cross.
I, i, 24

23   Unless hours were cups of sack, and minutes
capons, and clocks the tongues of bawds, and dials
the signs of leaping-houses, and the blessed sun
himself a fair hot wench in flame-color'd taffeta, I
see no reason why thou shouldst be so superfluous
to demand the time of the day.   *I, ii, 7*

24   Diana's foresters, gentlemen of the shade, minions of the moon.   *I, ii, 29*

25   A purse of gold most resolutely snatched on
Monday night and most dissolutely spent on
Tuesday morning.   *I, ii, 38*

26   Thy quips and thy quiddities.   *I, ii, 51*

27   So far as my coin would stretch; and where it
would not, I have used my credit.
I, ii, 61

28   Old father antick the law.   *I, ii, 69*

29   I am as melancholy as a gib cat, or a lugged bear.
I, ii, 82

30   I would to God thou and I knew where a commodity of good names were to be bought.
I, ii, 92

31   O! thou hast damnable iteration, and art indeed
able to corrupt a saint.   *I, ii, 101*

32   Now am I, if a man should speak truly, little better than one of the wicked.   *I, ii, 105*

33   'Tis my vocation, Hal; 'tis no sin for a man to labor in his vocation.   *I, ii, 116*

34   There's neither honesty, manhood, nor good fellowship in thee.   *I, ii, 154*

35   Well then, once in my days I'll be a madcap.
I, ii, 158

36 I know you all, and will a while uphold
The unyok'd humor of your idleness:
Yet herein will I imitate the sun,
Who doth permit the base contagious clouds

To smother up his beauty from the world,
That when he please again to be himself,
Being wanted, he may be more wonder'd at,
By breaking through the foul and ugly mists
Of vapors that did seem to strangle him.
If all the year were playing holidays,
To sport would be as tedious as to work.

I, ii, 217

1 You tread upon my patience. *I, iii, 4*

2 Came there a certain lord, neat, and trimly dress'd,
Fresh as a bridegroom; and his chin new-reap'd,
Show'd like a stubble-land at harvest-home:
He was perfumed like a milliner,
And 'twixt his finger and his thumb he held
A pouncet-box, which ever and anon
He gave his nose and took 't away again.

I, iii, 33

3 And as the soldiers bore dead bodies by,
He call'd them untaught knaves, unmannerly,
To bring a slovenly unhandsome corpse
Betwixt the wind and his nobility. *I, iii, 42*

4 So pester'd with a popinjay. *I, iii, 50*

5 God save the mark! *I, iii, 56*

6 To put down Richard, that sweet lovely rose,
And plant this thorn, this canker, Bolingbroke.

I, iii, 176

7 Or sink or swim. *I, iii, 194*

8 O! the blood more stirs
To rouse a lion than to start a hare!

I, iii, 197

9 By heaven methinks it were an easy leap
To pluck bright honor from the pale-fac'd moon,
Or dive into the bottom of the deep,
Where fathom-line could never touch the
ground,
And pluck up drowned honor by the locks.

I, iii, 201

10 Why, what a candy deal of courtesy
This fawning greyhound then did proffer me!

I, iii, 251

11 I know a trick worth two of that.

II, i, 40

12 If the rascal have not given me medicines to
make me love him, I'll be hanged.

II, ii, 20

13 I'll starve ere I'll rob a foot further.

II, ii, 24

14 It would be argument for a week, laughter for a
month, and a good jest forever. *II, ii, 104*

15 Falstaff sweats to death
And lards the lean earth as he walks along.

II, ii, 119

16 Out of this nettle, danger, we pluck this flower,
safety. *II, iii, 11*

17 I could brain him with his lady's fan. *II, iii, 26*

18 Constant you are,
But yet a woman: and for secrecy,
No lady closer; for I well believe
Thou wilt not utter what thou dost not know;
And so far will I trust thee, gentle Kate.

II, iii, 113

19 A Corinthian, a lad of mettle, a good boy.

II, iv, 13

20 I am not yet of Percy's mind, the Hotspur of the
North; he that kills me some six or seven dozen of
Scots at a breakfast, washes his hands, and says to
his wife, "Fie upon this quiet life! I want work."

II, iv, 116

21 A plague of all cowards, I say. *II, iv, 129*

22 There live not three good men unhanged in
England, and one of them is fat and grows old.

II, iv, 146

23 You care not who sees your back: call you that
backing of your friends? A plague upon such
backing! *II, iv, 168*

24 I have peppered two of them. . . . I tell thee
what, Hal, if I tell thee a lie, spit in my face, call me
horse. *II, iv, 216*

25 Give you a reason on compulsion! if reasons
were as plenty as blackberries, I would give no man
a reason upon compulsion, I. *II, iv, 267*

26 Mark now, how a plain tale shall put you down.

II, iv, 285

27 What doth gravity out of his bed at midnight?

II, iv, 328

28 A plague of sighing and grief! it blows a man up
like a bladder. *II, iv, 370*

29 I must speak in passion, and I will do it in King
Cambyses' vein. *II, iv, 429*

30 That reverend vice, that gray iniquity, that father
ruffian, that vanity in years. *II, iv, 505*

31 If sack and sugar be a fault, God help the wicked!
If to be old and merry be a sin, then many an old
host that I know is damned: if to be fat be to be
hated, then Pharaoh's lean kine are to be loved.

II, iv, 524

32 Banish plump Jack, and banish all the world.

II, iv, 534

1   Play out the play.

King Henry IV, Pt. I, II, iv, 539

2   O, monstrous! but one half-penny-worth of bread to this intolerable deal of sack!

II, iv, 597

3 Diseased nature oftentimes breaks forth
In strange eruptions.   *III, i, 27*

4 I am not in the roll of common men.   *III, i, 43*

5 *Glendower:* I can call spirits from the vasty deep.
Hotspur: Why, so can I, or so can any man;
But will they come when you do call for them?

III, i, 53

6 I had rather be a kitten and cry mew,
Than one of these same meter ballad-mongers.

III, i, 128

7   Mincing poetry:
'Tis like the forc'd gait of a shuffling nag.

III, i, 133

8 But in the way of bargain, mark you me,
I'll cavil on the ninth part of a hair.   *III, i, 138*

9 A deal of skimble-skamble stuff.   *III, i, 153*

10 I understand thy kisses and thou mine,
And that's a feeling disputation.   *III, i, 204*

11   *Lady Percy:* . . . Lie still, ye thief, and hear the lady sing in Welsh.
Hotspur: I had rather hear Lady, my brach, howl in Irish.   *III, i, 238*

12 A good mouth-filling oath.   *III, i, 258*

13 They surfeited with honey and began
To loathe the taste of sweetness, whereof a little
More than a little is by much too much.

III, ii, 71

14 He was but as the cuckoo is in June,
Heard, not regarded.   *III, ii, 75*

15 My near'st and dearest enemy.   *III, ii, 123*

16 The end of life cancels all bands.   *III, ii, 157*

17   An I have not forgotten what the inside of a church is made of, I am a peppercorn, a brewer's horse.   *III, iii, 8*

18   Company, villanous company, hath been the spoil of me.   *III, iii, 10*

19   I have more flesh than another man, and therefore more frailty.   *III, iii, 187*

20 The very life-blood of our enterprise.

IV, i, 28

21   Were it good
To set the exact wealth of all our states
All at one cast? to set so rich a main
On the nice hazard of one doubtful hour?

IV, i, 45

22 Baited like eagles having lately bath'd . . .
As full of spirit as the month of May,
And gorgeous as the sun at midsummer.

IV, i, 99

23 I saw young Harry, with his beaver on.

IV, i, 104

24 To turn and wind a fiery Pegasus
And witch the world with noble horsemanship.

IV, i, 109

25   Worse than the sun in March
This praise doth nourish agues.   *IV, i, 111*

26 Doomsday is near; die all, die merrily.

IV, i, 134

27   The cankers of a calm world and a long peace.

IV, ii, 32

28   Tut, tut, good enough to toss; food for powder, food for powder; they'll fill a pit as well as better.

IV, ii, 72

29 To the latter end of a fray and the beginning of a feast
Fits a dull fighter and a keen guest.   *IV, ii, 86*

30 Greatness knows itself.   *IV, iii, 74*

31   I could be well content
To entertain the lag-end of my life
With quiet hours.   *V, i, 23*

32 Rebellion lay in his way, and he found it.

V, i, 28

33   Never yet did insurrection want
Such water-colors to impaint his cause.

V, i, 79

34   I would it were bed-time, Hal, and all well.

V, i, 126

35   Honor pricks me on. Yea, but how if honor prick me off when I come on? how then? Can honor set to a leg? No. Or an arm? No. Or take away the grief of a wound? No. Honor hath no skill in surgery then? No. What is honor? a word. What is that word, honor? Air. A trim reckoning! Who hath it? he that died o' Wednesday. Doth he feel it? No. Doth he hear it? No. It is insensible then? Yea, to the dead. But will it not live with the living? No. Why? Detraction will not suffer it. Therefore I'll none of it: honor is a mere scutcheon; and so ends my catechism.

V, i, 131

1 Suspicion all our lives shall be stuck full of eyes;
    For treason is but trusted like the fox.
                                        V, ii, 8

2 Let me tell the world.[1]   *V, ii, 65*

3   The time of life is short;
    To spend that shortness basely were too long.
                                        V, ii, 81

4 Two stars keep not their motion in one sphere.
                                        V, iv, 65

5 But thought's the slave of life, and life time's fool;
    And time, that takes survey of all the world,
    Must have a stop. O! I could prophesy,
    But that the earthy and cold hand of death
    Lies on my tongue.   *V, iv, 81*

6   This earth, that bears thee dead,
    Bears not alive so stout a gentleman.   *V, iv, 92*

7 Thy ignominy sleep with thee in the grave,
    But not remember'd in thy epitaph!
                                        V, iv, 100

8 I could have better spar'd a better man.
                                        V, iv, 104

9   The better part of valor is discretion.[2]
                                        V, iv, 120

10   Full bravely hast thou flesh'd
    Thy maiden sword.   *V, iv, 132*

11   Lord, Lord, how this world is given to lying!
                                        V, iv, 148

12   I'll purge, and leave sack, and live cleanly.
                                        V, iv, 168

13 Your mind is tossing on the ocean.
    The Merchant of Venice [1596–1597], act I,
    sc. i, l. 8

14 My ventures are not in one bottom trusted,
    Nor to one place.   *I, i, 42*

15 Nature hath fram'd strange fellows in her time.
                                        I, i, 51

16 You have too much respect upon the world:
    They lose it that do buy it with much care.
                                        I, i, 74

17 I hold the world but as the world, Gratiano;
    A stage where every man must play a part,
    And mine a sad one.   *I, i, 77*

18 Why should a man, whose blood is warm within,
    Sit like his grandsire cut in alabaster?   *I, i, 83*

19 There are a sort of men whose visages
    Do cream and mantle like a standing pond.
                                        I, i, 88

20   I am Sir Oracle,
    And when I ope my lips let no dog bark!
                                        I, i, 93

21   I do know of these,
    That therefore only are reputed wise
    For saying nothing.   *I, i, 95*

22 Fish not, with this melancholy bait,
    For this fool-gudgeon, this opinion.
                                        I, i, 101

23   Gratiano speaks an infinite deal of nothing, more
    than any man in all Venice. His reasons are as two
    grains of wheat hid in two bushels of chaff: you
    shall seek all day ere you find them, and, when you
    have them, they are not worth the search.
                                        I, i, 114

24 In my school-days, when I had lost one shaft,
    I shot his fellow of the selfsame flight
    The selfsame way with more advised watch,
    To find the other forth, and by adventuring both,
    I oft found both.   *I, i, 141*

25   They are as sick that surfeit with too much as
    they that starve with nothing.   *I, ii, 5*

26   Superfluity comes sooner by white hairs, but
    competency lives longer.   *I, ii, 9*

27   If to do were as easy as to know what were good
    to do, chapels had been churches, and poor men's
    cottages princes' palaces.
                                        I, ii, 13

28   The brain may devise laws for the blood, but a
    hot temper leaps o'er a cold decree.
                                        I, ii, 19

29   He doth nothing but talk of his horse.
                                        I, ii, 43

30   I fear he will prove the weeping philosopher
    when he grows old, being so full of unmannerly
    sadness in his youth.   *I, ii, 51*

31   God made him, and therefore let him pass for a
    man.   *I, ii, 59*

32   When he is best, he is a little worse than a man,
    and when he is worst, he is little better than a beast.
                                        I, ii, 93

33   I dote on his very absence.   *I, ii, 118*

---

[1]I'll tell the world. — *Measure for Measure, act II, sc. iv, l.* 154
    Ay, tell the world! — ROBERT BROWNING, *Paracelsus* [1835], *pt.* II

[2]It showed discretion the best part of valor. — BEAUMONT AND
FLETCHER, *A King and No King* [1619], *act II, sc. iii*

1   Ships are but boards, sailors but men: there be land-rats and water-rats, land-thieves and water-thieves.   *The Merchant of Venice, I, iii, 22*

2   Yes, to smell pork; to eat of the habitation which your prophet the Nazarite[1] conjured the devil into. I will buy with you, sell with you, talk with you, walk with you, and so following; but I will not eat with you, drink with you, nor pray with you. What news on the Rialto?   *I, iii, 34*

3   How like a fawning publican he looks!
I hate him for he is a Christian.   *I, iii, 42*

4   If I can catch him once upon the hip,
I will feed fat the ancient grudge I bear him.
    I, iii, 47

5   Cursed be my tribe,
If I forgive him!   *I, iii, 52*

6   The devil can cite Scripture for his purpose.
    I, iii, 99

7   A goodly apple rotten at the heart.
O, what a goodly outside falsehood hath!
    I, iii, 102

8   For sufferance is the badge of all our tribe.
You call me misbeliever, cut-throat dog,
And spet upon my Jewish gaberdine.
    I, iii, 111

9   Shall I bend low, and in a bondman's key,
With bated breath, and whispering humbleness,
Say this.   *I, iii, 124*

10   I'll seal to such a bond,
And say there is much kindness in the Jew.
    I, iii, 153

11   O father Abram! what these Christians are,
Whose own hard dealing teaches them suspect
The thoughts of others.   *I, iii, 161*

12   I like not fair terms and a villain's mind.
    I, iii, 180

13   Mislike me not for my complexion,
The shadow'd livery of the burnish'd sun.   *II, i, 1*

14   O heavens! this is my true-begotten father.
    II, ii, 36

15   An honest, exceeding poor man.
    II, ii, 54

16   The very staff of my age, my very prop.
    II, ii, 71

17   It is a wise father that knows his own child.
    II, ii, 8.

18   And the vile squealing of the wry-neck'd fife.
    II, v, 3

19   Who riseth from a feast
With that keen appetite that he sits down?
    II, vi, 8

20   But love is blind, and lovers cannot see
The pretty follies that themselves commit.
    II, vi, 3

21   Must I hold a candle to my shames?
    II, vi, 41

22   Men that hazard all
Do it in hope of fair advantages:
A golden mind stoops not to shows of dross.
    II, vii, 18

23   Young in limbs, in judgment old.   *II, vii, 71*

24   My daughter! O my ducats! O my daughter!
Fled with a Christian! O my Christian ducats!
Justice! the law! my ducats, and my daughter!
A sealed bag, two sealed bags of ducats,
Of double ducats, stol'n from me by my daughter!
    II, viii, 15

25   The fool multitude, that choose by show.
    II, ix, 26

26   I will not jump with common spirits
And rank me with the barbarous multitude.
    II, ix, 32

27   Let none presume
To wear an undeserved dignity.
O! that estates, degrees, and offices
Were not deriv'd corruptly, and that clear honor
Were purchas'd by the merit of the wearer.
    II, ix, 39

28   Some there be that shadows kiss;
Such have but a shadow's bliss.   *II, ix, 66*

29   Let him look to his bond.   *III, i, 49*

30   I am a Jew. Hath not a Jew eyes? hath not a Jew hands, organs, dimensions, senses, affections, passions?   *III, i, 62*

31   If you prick us, do we not bleed? if you tickle us, do we not laugh? if you poison us, do we not die? and if you wrong us, shall we not revenge?
    III, i, 65

32   The villainy you teach me I will execute, and it shall go hard but I will better the instruction.
    III, i, 76

33   I would not have given it for a wilderness of monkeys.   *III, i, 130*

---

[1]That hee shall be called a Nazarite. — *The Geneva Bible* [1557–1560], *Matthew 2:23*
The Geneva version of the Bible is the one Shakespeare was familiar with.

1 There's something tells me, but it is not love,
   I would not lose you; and you know yourself,
   Hate counsels not in such a quality.   *III, ii, 4*

2   Makes a swanlike end,
   Fading in music.   *III, ii, 44*

3 Tell me where is fancy bred,
   Or in the heart or in the head?
   How begot, how nourished?
      Reply, reply.   *III, ii, 63*

4 In law, what plea so tainted and corrupt
   But, being season'd with a gracious voice,
   Obscures the show of evil?   *III, ii, 75*

5 There is no vice so simple but assumes
   Some mark of virtue on his outward parts.
                                                 III, ii, 81

6 The seeming truth which cunning times put on
   To entrap the wisest.   *III, ii, 100*

7 How all the other passions fleet to air,
   As doubtful thoughts, and rash-embrac'd despair,
   And shuddering fear, and green-ey'd jealousy.
                                                 III, ii, 108

8 An unlesson'd girl, unschool'd, unpractic'd;
   Happy in this, she is not yet so old
   But she may learn.   *III, ii, 160*

9 Here are a few of the unpleasant'st words
   That ever blotted paper.   *III, ii, 252*

10 Thou call'dst me dog before thou hadst a cause,
   But, since I am a dog, beware my fangs.
                                                 III, iii, 6

11   Thus when I shun Scylla, your father, I fall into
   Charybdis, your mother.[1]   *III, v, 17*

12 Some men there are love not a gaping pig;
   Some, that are mad if they behold a cat.
                                                 IV, i, 47

13 A harmless necessary cat.   *IV, i, 55*

14 *Bassanio:* Do all men kill the things they do not
         love?
   Shylock: Hates any man the thing he would not kill?
                                                 IV, i, 66

15 What! wouldst thou have a serpent sting thee
         twice?   *IV, i, 69*

16   The weakest kind of fruit
   Drops earliest to the ground.   *IV, i, 115*

17 To hold opinion with Pythagoras,
   That souls of animals infuse themselves
   Into the trunks of men.[2]   *IV, i, 131*

18   I never knew so young a body with so old a
   head.[3]   *IV, i, 163*

19 The quality of mercy is not strain'd,
   It droppeth as the gentle rain from heaven
   Upon the place beneath: it is twice bless'd;
   It blesseth him that gives and him that takes:
   'Tis mightiest in the mightiest; it becomes
   The throned monarch better than his crown;
   His scepter shows the force of temporal power,
   The attribute to awe and majesty,
   Wherein doth sit the dread and fear of kings;
   But mercy is above this sceptered sway,
   It is enthroned in the hearts of kings,
   It is an attribute to God himself,
   And earthly power doth then show likest God's
   When mercy seasons justice. Therefore, Jew,
   Though justice be thy plea, consider this,
   That in the course of justice none of us
   Should see salvation: we do pray for mercy,
   And that same prayer doth teach us all to render
   The deeds of mercy.   *IV, i, 184*

20 To do a great right, do a little wrong.
                                                 IV, i, 216

21 A Daniel come to judgment! yea, a Daniel!
                                                 IV, i, 223

22 How much more elder art thou than thy looks!
                                                 IV, i, 251

23 Is it so nominated in the bond?   *IV, i, 260*

24 'Tis not in the bond.   *IV, i, 263*

25 For herein Fortune shows herself more kind
   Than is her custom: it is still her use
   To let the wretched man outlive his wealth,
   To view with hollow eye and wrinkled brow
   An age of poverty.   *IV, i, 268*

26   I have a daughter;
   Would any of the stock of Barabbas
   Had been her husband rather than a Christian!
                                                 IV, i, 296

27 An upright judge, a learned judge!
                                                 IV, i, 324

28 Now, infidel, I have thee on the hip.
                                                 IV, i, 334

---

[1]Scylla to port, and on our starboard beam Charybdis, dire gorge of the salt sea tide. — HOMER, *Odyssey*, bk. XII, l. 232

Scylla guards the right side; implacable Charybdis the left. — VIRGIL, *Aeneid*, bk. III, l. 420

Incidis in Scyllam cupiens vitare Charybdim [You fall into Scylla in seeking to avoid Charybdis]. — PHILIPPE GUALTIER [fl. c. 1300], *Alexandreis* [c. 1300], bk. V, l. 301

[2]*Clown:* What is the opinion of Pythagoras concerning wild fowl? / *Malvolio:* That the soul of our grandam might haply inhabit a bird. — *Twelfth-Night*, act IV, sc. ii, l. 55

[3]He is young, but take it from me, a very staid head. — THOMAS WENTWORTH, EARL OF STRAFFORD [1593–1641], *letter commending the Earl of Ormond to Charles I for appointment as councilor*

1 A Daniel, still say I; a second Daniel!
I thank thee, Jew, for teaching me that word.
The Merchant of Venice, IV, i, 341

2 You take my house when you do take the prop
That doth sustain my house; you take my life
When you do take the means whereby I live.
IV, i, 376

3 He is well paid that is well satisfied.   *IV, i, 416*

4 *Lorenzo:* The moon shines bright: in such a night as
    this . . .
Troilus methinks mounted the Troyan walls,
And sigh'd his soul toward the Grecian tents,
Where Cressid lay that night.
Jessica: In such a night
Did Thisbe fearfully o'ertrip the dew,
And saw the lion's shadow ere himself,
And ran dismay'd away.
Lorenzo: In such a night
Stood Dido with a willow in her hand
Upon the wild sea-banks, and waft her love
To come again to Carthage.
Jessica: In such a night
Medea gather'd the enchanted herbs
That did renew old Aeson.   *V, i, 1*

5 How sweet the moonlight sleeps upon this bank!
Here we will sit, and let the sounds of music
Creep in our ears: soft stillness and the night
Become the touches of sweet harmony.
Sit, Jessica: look, how the floor of heaven
Is thick inlaid with patines of bright gold:
There's not the smallest orb which thou behold'st
But in his motion like an angel sings,
Still quiring to the young-eyed cherubins.
Such harmony is in immortal souls;
But, whilst this muddy vesture of decay
Doth grossly close it in, we cannot hear it.
V, i, 54

6 I am never merry when I hear sweet music.
V, i, 69

7 The man that hath no music in himself,
Nor is not mov'd with concord of sweet sounds,
Is fit for treasons, stratagems, and spoils;
The motions of his spirit are dull as night,
And his affections dark as Erebus:
Let no such man be trusted.   *V, i, 83*

8 How far that little candle throws his beams!
So shines a good deed in a naughty world.
V, i, 90

9 How many things by season season'd are
To their right praise and true perfection!
V, i, 107

10 This night methinks is but the daylight sick.
V, i, 124

11 A light wife doth make a heavy husband.
V, i, 130

12 These blessed candles of the night.   *V, i, 220*

13   I will make a Star Chamber matter of it.
*The Merry Wives of Windsor [1597; revised
    1600–1601], act I, sc. i, l. 2*

14   She has brown hair, and speaks small like a
woman.   *I, i, 48*

15   Seven hundred pounds and possibilities is good
gifts.   *I, i, 65*

16   I had rather than forty shillings I had my Book
of Songs and Sonnets here.   *I, i, 205*

17   "Convey," the wise it call. "Steal'" foh! a fico for
the phrase!   *I, iii, 30*

18   I am almost out at heels.   *I, iii, 32*

19   Thou art the Mars of malcontents.
I, iii, 111

20   Here will be an old abusing of God's patience
and the king's English.   *I, iv, 5*

21   Dispense with trifles.   *II, i, 47*

22   Faith, thou hast some crotchets in thy head now.
II, i, 158

23 Why, then the world's mine oyster,
Which I with sword will open.   *II, ii, 2*

24   This is the short and the long of it.
II, ii, 62

25   Like a fair house built upon another man's
ground.   *II, ii, 229*

26   Better three hours too soon than a minute too
late.   *II, ii, 332*

27   I cannot tell what the dickens his name is.
III, ii, 20

28   He capers, he dances, he has eyes of youth, he
writes verses, he speaks holiday, he smells April and
May.   *III, ii, 71*

29 O, what a world of vile ill-favor'd faults
Looks handsome in three hundred pounds a year!
III, iv, 32

30   A woman would run through fire and water for
such a kind heart.   *III, iv, 106*

31   I have a kind of alacrity in sinking.
III, v, 13

32   As good luck would have it.[1]   *III, v, 86*

---

[1]As ill luck would have it.—CERVANTES, *Don Quixote, pt. I*
[1605], bk. I, ch. 2

1   A man of my kidney.   *III, v, 119*

2   [He] curses all Eve's daughters, of what complexion soever.   *IV, ii, 24*

3   Wives may be merry, and yet honest too.   *IV, ii, 110*

4   This is the third time; I hope good luck lies in odd numbers. . . . There is divinity in odd numbers, either in nativity, chance or death.   *V, i, 2*

5   Better a little chiding than a great deal of heartbreak.   *V, iii, 10*

6   Rumor is a pipe
Blown by surmises, jealousies, conjectures,
And of so easy and so plain a stop
That the blunt monster with uncounted heads,
The still-discordant wavering multitude,
Can play upon it.
    King Henry the Fourth, Part II [1598], Induction, l. 15

7   Even such a man, so faint, so spiritless,
So dull, so dead in look, so woe-begone,
Drew Priam's curtain in the dead of night,
And would have told him half his Troy was burn'd.
    Act I, sc. i, l. 70

8   Yet the first bringer of unwelcome news
Hath but a losing office, and his tongue
Sounds ever after as a sullen bell,
Remember'd knolling a departing friend.
    I, i, 100

9   I am not only witty in myself, but the cause that wit is in other men.   *I, ii, 10*

10   A rascally yea-forsooth knave.   *I, ii, 40*

11   You lie in your throat.   *I, ii, 97*

12   Your lordship, though not clean past your youth, hath yet some smack of age in you, some relish of the saltness of time.   *I, ii, 112*

13   It is the disease of not listening, the malady of not marking, that I am troubled withal.   *I, ii, 139*

14   I am as poor as Job, my lord, but not so patient.   *I, ii, 145*

15   We that are in the vaward of our youth.   *I, ii, 201*

16   Have you not a moist eye, a dry hand, a yellow cheek, a white beard, a decreasing leg, an increasing belly?   *I, ii, 206*

17   Every part about you blasted with antiquity.   *I, ii, 210*

18   For my voice, I have lost it with hollaing and singing of anthems.   *I, ii, 215*

19   It was always yet the trick of our English nation, if they have a good thing, to make it too common.   *I, ii, 244*

20   I were better to be eaten to death with rust than to be scoured to nothing with perpetual motion.   *I, ii, 249*

21   I can get no remedy against this consumption of the purse: borrowing only lingers and lingers it out, but the disease is incurable.   *I, ii, 267*

22   Who lin'd himself with hope,
Eating the air on promise of supply.   *I, iii, 27*

23 A habitation giddy and unsure
Hath he that buildeth on the vulgar heart.   *I, iii, 89*

24 Past and to come seem best; things present worst.   *I, iii, 108*

25   A poor lone woman.   *II, i, 37*

26   Away, you scullion! you rampallian! you fustilarian! I'll tickle your catastrophe.   *II, i, 67*

27   He hath eaten me out of house and home.   *II, i, 82*

28   Let the end try the man.   *II, ii, 52*

29   Thus we play the fools with the time, and the spirits of the wise sit in the clouds and mock us.   *II, ii, 155*

30   He was indeed the glass
Wherein the noble youth did dress themselves.   *II, iii, 21*

31 And let the welkin roar.   *II, iv, 181*

32   Is it not strange that desire should so many years outlive performance?   *II, iv, 283*

33   O sleep! O gentle sleep![1]
Nature's soft nurse, how have I frighted thee,
That thou no more wilt weigh my eyelids down
And steep my senses in forgetfulness?   *III, i, 5*

34 With all appliances and means to boot.   *III, i, 29*

35   Uneasy lies the head that wears a crown.   *III, i, 31*

36 O God! that one might read the book of fate.   *III, i, 45*

37 There is a history in all men's lives.   *III, i, 80*

38   Death, as the Psalmist saith, is certain to all; all shall die.   *III, ii, 41*

---

[1]Sleep, most gentle sleep. —OVID, *Metamorphoses, bk. II, l.* 624

1   We have heard the chimes at midnight.
King Henry IV, Pt. II, III, ii, 231

2   A man can die but once; we owe God a death.
III, ii, 253

3 We see which way the stream of time doth run
And are enforc'd from our most quiet sphere
By the rough torrent of occasion.   *IV, i, 70*

4   We ready are to try our fortunes
To the last man.   *IV, ii, 43*

5   I may justly say with the hook-nosed fellow of
Rome, "I came, saw, and overcame."   *IV, iii, 44*

6 O polish'd perturbation! golden care!
That keep'st the ports of slumber open wide
To many a watchful night!   *IV, v, 22*

7   See, sons, what things you are!
How quickly nature falls into revolt
When gold becomes her object!   *IV, v, 63*

8 Thy wish was father, Harry, to that thought!
IV, v, 91

9 Before thy hour be ripe.   *IV, v, 95*

10   Commit
The oldest sins the newest kind of ways.
IV, v, 124

11 His cares are now all ended.   *V, ii, 3*

12 This is the English, not the Turkish court;
Not Amurath an Amurath succeeds,
But Harry Harry.   *V, ii, 47*

13 I know thee not, old man: fall to thy prayers;
How ill white hairs become a fool and jester!
V, v, 52

14   Master Shallow, I owe you a thousand pound.
V, v, 78

15 O! for a Muse of fire, that would ascend
The brightest heaven of invention!
*King Henry the Fifth [1598–1599], Chorus,
l. 1*

    Or may we cram
16 Within this wooden O the very casques
That did affright the air at Agincourt?
Chorus, l. 12

17 Consideration like an angel came,
And whipp'd the offending Adam out of him.
Act I, sc. i, l. 28

18 Hear him debate of commonwealth affairs,
You would say it hath been all in all his study.
I, i, 41

19 Turn him to any cause of policy,
The Gordian knot of it he will unloose,

Familiar as his garter; that, when he speaks,
The air, a charter'd libertine, is still.   *I, i, 4*

20   Therefore doth heaven divide
The state of man in divers functions,
Setting endeavor in continual motion;
To which is fixed, as an aim or butt,
Obedience: for so work the honeybees,
Creatures that by a rule in nature teach
The act of order to a peopled kingdom.
I, ii, 18.

21 The singing masons building roofs of gold.
I, ii, 198

22   Many things, having full reference
To one consent, may work contrariously;
As many arrows, loosed several ways,
Fly to one mark; as many ways meet in one town;
As many fresh streams meet in one salt sea;
As many lines close in the dial's center;
So may a thousand actions, once afoot,
End in one purpose, and be all well borne
Without defeat.   *I, ii, 205*

23   'Tis ever common
That men are merriest when they are from home.
I, ii, 271

24 Now all the youth of England are on fire,
And silken dalliance in the wardrobe lies.
II, Chorus, 1

25 O England! model to thy inward greatness,
Like little body with a mighty heart,
What mightst thou do, that honor would thee do,
Were all thy children kind and natural!
II, Chorus, 16

26 That's the humor of it.   *II, i, 63*

27   He's [Falstaff's] in Arthur's bosom, if ever man
went to Arthur's bosom. A' made a finer end and
went away an it had been any christom child; a'
parted even just between twelve and one, even at
the turning o' the tide: for after I saw him fumble
with the sheets and play with flowers and smile
upon his fingers' ends, I knew there was but one
way; for his nose was as sharp as a pen, and a' babbled of green fields.   *II, iii, 11*

28   As cold as any stone.   *II, iii, 26*

29 Trust none;
For oaths are straws, men's faiths are wafer-cakes,
And hold-fast is the only dog, my duck.
II, iii, 53

30 Once more unto the breach, dear friends, once
more;
Or close the wall up with our English dead!
In peace there's nothing so becomes a man

As modest stillness and humility:
But when the blast of war blows in our ears,
Then imitate the action of the tiger;
Stiffen the sinews, summon up the blood,
Disguise fair nature with hard-favor'd rage;
Then lend the eye a terrible aspect.   *III, i, 1*

1 And sheath'd their swords for lack of argument.
    III, i, 21

2 I see you stand like greyhounds in the slips,
Straining upon the start. The game's afoot:
Follow your spirit; and, upon this charge
Cry "God for Harry! England and Saint George!"
    III, i, 31

3   I would give all my fame for a pot of ale, and
safety.   *III, ii, 14*

4   Men of few words are the best men.
    III, ii, 40

5   He will maintain his argument as well as any military man in the world.   *III, ii, 89*

6   I know the disciplines of wars.   *III, ii, 156*

7 I thought upon one pair of English legs
Did march three Frenchmen.   *III, vi, 161*

8 We are in God's hand.   *III, vi, 181*

9   That island of England breeds very valiant creatures: their mastiffs are of unmatchable courage.
    III, vii, 155

10   Give them great meals of beef and iron and steel,
they will eat like wolves and fight like devils.
    III, vii, 166

11 The hum of either army stilly sounds,
That the fix'd sentinels almost receive
The secret whispers of each other's watch:
Fire answers fire, and through their paly flames
Each battle sees the other's umber'd face:
Steed threatens steed, in high and boastful neighs
Piercing the night's dull ear; and from the tents
The armorers, accomplishing the knights,
With busy hammers closing rivets up,
Give dreadful note of preparation.
    IV, Chorus, 5

12 A little touch of Harry in the night.
    IV, Chorus, 47

13 There is some soul of goodness in things evil,
Would men observingly distill it out.
    IV, i, 4

14   Every subject's duty is the king's; but every subject's soul is his own.   *IV, i, 189*

15   What infinite heart's ease
Must kings neglect that private men enjoy!
And what have kings that privates have not too,

Save ceremony, save general ceremony?
And what art thou, thou idol[1] ceremony?
What kind of god art thou, that suffer'st more
Of mortal griefs than do thy worshippers?
What are thy rents? what are thy comings-in?
O ceremony! show me but thy worth.
    IV, i, 256

16 'Tis not the balm, the scepter and the ball,
The sword, the mace, the crown imperial,
The intertissued robe of gold and pearl,
The farced title running 'fore the king,
The throne he sits on, nor the tide of pomp
That beats upon the high shore of this world,
No, not all these, thrice-gorgeous ceremony,
Not all these, laid in bed majestical,
Can sleep so soundly as the wretched slave,
Who with a body fill'd and vacant mind
Gets him to rest, cramm'd with distressful bread.
    IV, i, 280

17 O God of battles! steel my soldiers' hearts;
Possess them not with fear; take from them now
The sense of reckoning, if the opposed numbers
Pluck their hearts from them.   *IV, i, 309*

18 But if it be a sin to covet honor,
I am the most offending soul alive.   *IV, iii, 28*

19 This day is call'd the feast of Crispian:
He that outlives this day, and comes safe home,
Will stand a tip-toe when this day is nam'd.
And rouse him at the name of Crispian.
    IV, iii, 40

20 We few, we happy few, we band of brothers;
For he today that sheds his blood with me
Shall be my brother.   *IV, iii, 60*

21   The saying is true, "The empty vessel makes the
greatest sound."   *IV, iv, 72*

22   There is occasions and causes why and wherefore
in all things.   *V, i, 3*

23   By this leek, I will most horribly revenge. I eat
and eat, I swear.   *V, i, 49*

24   All hell shall stir for this.   *V, i, 72*

25   The naked, poor, and mangled Peace,
Dear nurse of arts, plenties, and joyful births.
    V, ii, 34

26   Grow like savages—as soldiers will,
That nothing do but meditate on blood.
    V, ii, 59

27   For these fellows of infinite tongue, that can
rime themselves into ladies' favors, they do always
reason themselves out again.   *V, ii, 162*

---

[1]Sometimes rendered: idle.

1   My comfort is, that old age, that ill layer-up of beauty, can do no more spoil upon my face.
            King Henry V, V, ii, 246

2   O Kate! nice customs curtsy to great kings.
            V, ii, 291

3   He hath indeed better bettered expectation than you must expect of me to tell you how.
            Much Ado About Nothing [1598–1600], act I, sc. i, l. 15

4   How much better is it to weep at joy than to joy at weeping!
            I, i, 28

5   A very valiant trencher-man.
            I, i, 52

6   There's a skirmish of wit between them.
            I, i, 64

7   He wears his faith but as the fashion of his hat.
            I, i, 76

8   I see, lady, the gentleman is not in your books.
            I, i, 79

9   What! my dear Lady Disdain, are you yet living?
            I, i, 123

10 Shall I never see a bachelor of threescore again?
            I, i, 209

11 In time the savage bull doth bear the yoke.
            I, i, 271

12 Benedick the married man.
            I, i, 278

13 I could not endure a husband with a beard on his face: I had rather lie in the woollen.
            II, i, 31

14 As merry as the day is long.
            II, i, 52

15 Would it not grieve a woman to be over-mastered with a piece of valiant dust? to make an account of her life to a clod of wayward marl?
            II, i, 64

16 I have a good eye, uncle: I can see a church by daylight.
            II, i, 86

17 Speak low, if you speak love.
            II, i, 104

18 Friendship is constant in all other things
    Save in the office and affairs of love:
    Therefore all hearts in love use their own tongues;
    Let every eye negotiate for itself
    And trust no agent.
            II, i, 184

19 She speaks poniards, and every word stabs: if her breath were as terrible as her terminations, there were no living near her; she would infect to the north star.
            II, i, 257

20 Silence is the perfectest herald of joy: I were but little happy, if I could say how much.
            II, i, 319

21 It keeps on the windy side of care.[1]
            II, i, 32[8]

22 There was a star danced, and under that was [I] born.
            II, i, 35[1]

23 I will tell you my drift.[2]
            II, i, 406

24 He was wont to speak plain and to the purpose.
            II, iii, 1[9]

25 Sigh no more, ladies, sigh no more.
    Men were deceivers ever;
    One foot in sea, and one on shore,
    To one thing constant never.
            II, iii, 65

26 Sits the wind in that corner?
            II, iii, 108

27 Bait the hook well: this fish will bite.
            II, iii, 121

28 Shall quips and sentences and these paper bullets of the brain awe a man from the career of his humor? No; the world must be peopled. When I said I would die a bachelor, I did not think I should live till I were married.
            II, iii, 260

29 From the crown of his head to the sole of his foot, he is all mirth.
            III, ii, 9

30 He hath a heart as sound as a bell, and his tongue is the clapper; for what his heart thinks his tongue speaks.
            III, ii, 12

31 Everyone can master a grief but he that has it.
            III, ii, 28

32 Are you good men and true?
            III, iii, 1

33 To be a well-favored man is the gift of fortune; but to write and read comes by nature.
            III, iii, 14

34 If they make you not then the better answer, you may say they are not the men you took them for.
            III, iii, 49

35 The fashion wears out more apparel than the man.
            III, iii, 147

36 A good old man, sir; he will be talking: as they say, When the age is in, the wit is out.
            III, v, 36

37 Of what men dare do! what men may do! what men daily do, not knowing what they do!
            IV, i, 19

38 O! what authority and show of truth
    Can cunning sin cover itself withal.
            IV, i, 35

39 For it so falls out
    That what we have we prize not to the worth
    Whiles we enjoy it, but being lack'd and lost,

---

[1]The windy side of the law. — *Twelfth-Night, act III, sc. iv, l. 183*
[2]We know your drift. — *Coriolanus, act III, sc. iii, l. 114*

Why, then we rack the value, then we find
The virtue that possession would not show us
Whiles it was ours.   *IV, i, 219*

1   Masters, it is proved already that you are little better than false knaves, and it will go near to be thought so shortly.   *IV, ii, 23*

2   Flat burglary as ever was committed.
                    IV, ii, 54

3   Thou wilt be condemned into everlasting redemption for this.   *IV, ii, 60*

4   O that he were here to write me down an ass!
                    IV, ii, 80

5 Patch griefs with proverbs.   *V, i, 17*

6 Charm ache with air and agony with words.
                    V, i, 26

7 For there was never yet philosopher
That could endure the toothache patiently.
                    V, i, 35

8 Some of us will smart for it.   *V, i, 108*

9   What though care killed a cat,[1] thou hast mettle enough in thee to kill care.   *V, i, 135*

10   I was not born under a riming planet.
                    V, ii, 40

11   The trumpet of his own virtues.   *V, ii, 91*

12 Done to death by slanderous tongues.   *V, iii, 3*

13   A surgeon to old shoes.
                    Julius Caesar [1599], act I, sc. i, l. 26

14   As proper men as ever trod upon neat's leather.
                    I, i, 27

15 Have you not made a universal shout,
That Tiber trembled underneath her banks,
To hear the replication of your sounds
Made in her concave shores?   *I, i, 48*

16 Beware the ides of March.   *I, ii, 18*

17 Set honor in one eye and death i' the other,
And I will look on both indifferently.   *I, ii, 86*

18 Well, honor is the subject of my story.
I cannot tell what you and other men
Think of this life; but, for my single self,
I had as lief not be as live to be
In awe of such a thing as I myself.   *I, ii, 92*

19 Stemming it with hearts of controversy.
                    I, ii, 109

20 Why, man, he doth bestride the narrow world
Like a Colossus; and we petty men
Walk under his huge legs, and peep about
To find ourselves dishonorable graves.
Men at some time are masters of their fates:
The fault, dear Brutus, is not in our stars,
But in ourselves, that we are underlings.
                    I, ii, 134

21 Upon what meat doth this our Caesar feed,
That he is grown so great?   *I, ii, 148*

22 Let me have men about me that are fat;
Sleek-headed men and such as sleep o' nights.
Yond Cassius has a lean and hungry look;
He thinks too much: such men are dangerous.
                    I, ii, 191

23   He reads much;
He is a great observer, and he looks
Quite through the deeds of men.   *I, ii, 200*

24 Seldom he smiles, and smiles in such a sort
As if he mock'd himself, and scorn'd his spirit
That could be mov'd to smile at anything.
                    I, ii, 204

25 But, for my own part, it was Greek to me.[2]
                    I, ii, 288

26   Yesterday the bird of night did sit,
Even at noonday, upon the marketplace,
Hooting and shrieking.   *I, iii, 26*

27 So every bondman in his own hand bears
The power to cancel his captivity.   *I, iii, 101*

28 O! he sits high in all the people's hearts:
And that which would appear offense in us,
His countenance, like richest alchemy,
Will change to virtue and to worthiness.
                    I, iii, 157

29 The abuse of greatness is when it disjoins
Remorse from power.   *II, i, 18*

30   'Tis a common proof,
That lowliness is young ambition's ladder,
Whereto the climber-upward turns his face;
But when he once attains the upmost round,
He then unto the ladder turns his back,
Looks in the clouds, scorning the base degrees
By which he did ascend.   *II, i, 21*

31 Therefore think him as a serpent's egg
Which, hatch'd, would, as his kind, grow
    mischievous,
And kill him in the shell.   *II, i, 32*

---

[1]Let care kill a cat, / We'll laugh and grow fat. — *Shirburn Ballads* [1585], *91*
    Hang sorrow, care'll kill a cat. — BEN JONSON, *Every Man in His Humour* [1598], *act I, sc. i*

[2]This geare is Greeke to me. — GEORGE GASCOIGNE [c. 1525–1577], *Supposes, I* [1573]

1 Between the acting of a dreadful thing
And the first motion, all the interim is
Like a phantasma, or a hideous dream:
The genius and the mortal instruments
Are then in council; and the state of man,
Like to a little kingdom, suffers then
The nature of an insurrection.

Julius Caesar, II, i, 63

2   O conspiracy!
Sham'st thou to show thy dangerous brow by
    night,
When evils are most free?   *II, i, 77*

3 Let's carve him as a dish fit for the gods,
Not hew him as a carcass fit for hounds.

II, i, 173

4 But when I tell him he hates flatterers,
He says he does, being then most flattered.

II, i, 207

5 Enjoy the honey-heavy dew of slumber.

II, i, 230

6   Dwell I but in the suburbs
Of your good pleasure?   *II, i, 285*

7 You are my true and honorable wife,
As dear to me as are the ruddy drops
That visit my sad heart.   *II, i, 288*

8 Think you I am no stronger than my sex,
Being so father'd and so husbanded?   *II, i, 296*

9 When beggars die there are no comets seen;
The heavens themselves blaze forth the death of
    princes.   *II, ii, 30*

10 Cowards die many times before their deaths;
The valiant never taste of death but once.
Of all the wonders that I yet have heard,
It seems to me most strange that men should fear;
Seeing that death, a necessary end,
Will come when it will come.   *II, ii, 32*

11 Antony, that revels long o' nights.

II, ii, 116

12 How hard it is for women to keep counsel!

II, iv, 9

13 But I am constant as the northern star,
Of whose true-fix'd and resting quality
There is no fellow in the firmament.

III, i, 60

14 Speak, hands, for me!   *III, i, 76*

15 Et tu, Brute?   *III, i, 77*

16 Some to the common pulpits, and cry out,
"Liberty, freedom, and enfranchisement!"

III, i, 79

17   How many ages hence
Shall this our lofty scene be acted o'er,
In states unborn and accents yet unknown!

III, i, 11.

18 O mighty Caesar! dost thou lie so low?
Are all thy conquests, glories, triumphs, spoils,
Shrunk to this little measure?   *III, i, 14*

19 The choice and master spirits of this age.

III, i, 16.

20 Though last, not least in love.   *III, i, 18*

21 O! pardon me, thou bleeding piece of earth,
That I am meek and gentle with these butchers;
Thou art the ruins of the noblest man
That ever lived in the tide of times.   *III, i, 25*

22 Cry "Havoc!" and let slip the dogs of war.

III, i, 27.

23   Romans, countrymen, and lovers! hear me fo
my cause; and be silent, that you may hear.

III, ii, 1.

24   Not that I loved Caesar less, but that I love
Rome more.   *III, ii, 2.*

25   As he was valiant, I honor him; but, as he wa
ambitious, I slew him.   *III, ii, 2.*

26   If any, speak; for him have I offended. I paus
for a reply.   *III, ii, 3*

27 Friends, Romans, countrymen, lend me your ears;
I come to bury Caesar, not to praise him.
The evil that men do lives after them,
The good is oft interred with their bones.

III, ii, 7

28 For Brutus is an honorable man;
So are they all, all honorable men.

III, ii, 88

29 When that the poor have cried, Caesar hath wept;
Ambition should be made of sterner stuff.

III, ii, 9

30 O judgment! thou art fled to brutish beasts,
And men have lost their reason.   *III, ii, 11*

31 But yesterday the word of Caesar might
Have stood against the world; now lies he there,
And none so poor to do him reverence.

III, ii, 12

32 If you have tears, prepare to shed them now.

III, ii, 17

33 See what a rent the envious Casca made.

III, ii, 18

34 This was the most unkindest cut of all.

III, ii, 18

1   Great Caesar fell.
O! what a fall was there, my countrymen;
Then I, and you, and all of us fell down,
Whilst bloody treason flourish'd over us.
III, ii, 194

2 What private griefs they have, alas! I know not.
III, ii, 217

3 I come not, friends, to steal away your hearts:
I am no orator, as Brutus is;
But, as you know me all, a plain blunt man.
III, ii, 220

4 For I have neither wit, nor words, nor worth,
Action, nor utterance, nor the power of speech,
To stir men's blood: I only speak right on.
III, ii, 225

5   Put a tongue
In every wound of Caesar, that should move
The stones of Rome to rise and mutiny.
III, ii, 232

6 When love begins to sicken and decay,
It useth an enforced ceremony.
There are no tricks in plain and simple faith.
IV, ii, 20

7 An itching palm.   *IV, iii, 10*

8 I had rather be a dog, and bay the moon,
Than such a Roman.   *IV, iii, 27*

9 I'll use you for my mirth, yea, for my laughter,
When you are waspish.   *IV, iii, 49*

10 There is no terror, Cassius, in your threats;
For I am arm'd so strong in honesty
That they pass by me as the idle wind,
Which I respect not.   *IV, iii, 66*

11 A friend should bear his friend's infirmities,
But Brutus makes mine greater than they are.
IV, iii, 85

12   All his faults observ'd,
Set in a notebook, learn'd, and conn'd by rote.
IV, iii, 96

13 There is a tide in the affairs of men,
Which, taken at the flood, leads on to fortune;
Omitted, all the voyage of their life
Is bound in shallows and in miseries.
IV, iii, 217

14 We must take the current when it serves,
Or lose our ventures.   *IV, iii, 222*

15 The deep of night is crept upon our talk,
And nature must obey necessity.   *IV, iii, 225*

16 But for your words, they rob the Hybla bees,
And leave them honeyless.   *V, i, 34*

17 Forever, and forever, farewell, Cassius!
If we do meet again, why, we shall smile;
If not, why then, this parting was well made.
V, i, 117

18   O! that a man might know
The end of this day's business, ere it come.
V, i, 123

19 O Julius Caesar! thou art mighty yet!
Thy spirit walks abroad, and turns our swords
In our own proper entrails.   *V, iii, 94*

20 The last of all the Romans, fare thee well!
V, iii, 99

21 This was the noblest Roman of them all.
V, v, 68

22 His life was gentle, and the elements
So mix'd in him that Nature might stand up
And say to all the world, "This was a man!"
V, v, 73

23   What's the new news at the new court?
As You Like It [1599–1600], act I, sc. i, l. 103

24   Fleet the time carelessly, as they did in the
golden world.   *I, i, 126*

25   Always the dullness of the fool is the whetstone
of the wits.   *I, ii, 59*

26   The little foolery that wise men have makes a
great show.   *I, ii, 97*

27   Well said: that was laid on with a trowel.
I, ii, 113

28   Your heart's desires be with you!   *I, ii, 214*

29 One out of suits with fortune.   *I, ii, 263*

30 My pride fell with my fortunes.   *I, ii, 269*

31 Hereafter, in a better world than this,
I shall desire more love and knowledge of you.
I, ii, 301

32 Heavenly Rosalind!   *I, ii, 306*

33   O, how full of briers is this working-day world!
I, iii, 12

34 Beauty provoketh thieves sooner than gold.
I, iii, 113

35 We'll have a swashing and a martial outside,
As many other mannish cowards have.   *I, iii, 123*

36 Hath not old custom made this life more sweet
Than that of painted pomp? Are not these woods
More free from peril than the envious court?
II, i, 2

37 Sweet are the uses of adversity,
Which, like the toad, ugly and venomous,

Wears yet a precious jewel in his head;
And this our life exempt from public haunt,
Finds tongues in trees, books in the running brooks,
Sermons in stones, and good in everything.

As You Like It, II, i, 12

1   The big round tears
Cours'd one another down his innocent nose
In piteous chase.   *II, i, 38*

2 Sweep on, you fat and greasy citizens.   *II, i, 55*

3   And He that doth the ravens feed,
Yea, providently caters for the sparrow,
Be comfort to my age!   *II, iii, 43*

4 Though I look old, yet I am strong and lusty;
For in my youth I never did apply
Hot and rebellious liquors in my blood.
                                                    II, iii, 47

5 Therefore my age is as a lusty winter,
Frosty, but kindly.   *II, iii, 52*

6 Thou art not for the fashion of these times,
Where none will sweat but for promotion.
                                                    II, iii, 59

7   Ay, now am I in Arden; the more fool I: when I
was at home, I was in a better place: but travelers
must be content.   *II, iv, 16*

8 If you remember'st not the slightest folly
That ever love did make thee run into,
Thou hast not lov'd.   *II, iv, 34*

9   We that are true lovers run into strange capers.
                                                    II, iv, 53

10   I shall ne'er be ware of mine own wit, till I break
my shins against it.   *II, iv, 59*

11 Under the greenwood tree
Who loves to lie with me,
And turn his merry note
Unto the sweet bird's throat,
Come hither, come hither, come hither:
Here shall he see
No enemy
But winter and rough weather.   *II, v, 1*

12   I can suck melancholy out of a song as a weasel
sucks eggs.   *II, v, 12*

13 Who doth ambition shun,
And loves to live i' the sun,
Seeking the food he eats,
And pleas'd with what he gets.   *II, v, 38*

14   I met a fool i' the forest,
A motley fool.   *II, vii, 12*

15 And then he drew a dial from his poke,
And, looking on it with lack-luster eye,

Says very wisely, "It is ten o'clock;
Thus may we see," quoth he, "how the world
wags."[1]   *II, vii, 2*

16 And so, from hour to hour we ripe and ripe,
And then from hour to hour we rot and rot,
And thereby hangs a tale.
                                                    II, vii, 20

17 My lungs began to crow like chanticleer,
That fools should be so deep-contemplative,
And I did laugh sans intermission
An hour by his dial.   *II, vii, 30*

18 Motley's the only wear.   *II, vii, 34*

19   If ladies be but young and fair,
They have the gift to know it.
                                                    II, vii, 37

20   I must have liberty
Withal, as large a charter as the wind,
To blow on whom I please.   *II, vii, 47*

21 The "why" is plain as way to parish church.
                                                    II, vii, 52

22   But whate'er you are
That in this desert inaccessible,
Under the shade of melancholy boughs,
Lose and neglect the creeping hours of time;
If ever you have look'd on better days,
If ever been where bells have knoll'd to church,
If ever sat at any good man's feast,
If ever from your eyelids wip'd a tear,
And know what 'tis to pity, and be pitied,
Let gentleness my strong enforcement be.
                                                    II, vii, 109

23 True is it that we have seen better days.
                                                    II, vii, 120

24 Oppress'd with two weak evils, age and hunger.
                                                    II, vii, 132

25   All the world's a stage,[2]
And all the men and women merely players:
They have their exits and their entrances;
And one man in his time plays many parts,
His acts being seven ages. At first the infant,
Mewling and puking in the nurse's arms.
And then the whining school-boy, with his satchel,
And shining morning face, creeping like snail
Unwillingly to school. And then the lover,

---

[1]So wags the world. —WALTER SCOTT, *Ivanhoe* [1819], *ch. 37*

[2]The world's a theater, the earth a stage, / Which God and Nature
do with actors fill. —THOMAS HEYWOOD, *Apology for Actors* [1612]

The world's a stage on which all the parts are played. —THOMAS
MIDDLETON, *A Game of Chess* [1624], *act V, sc. i*

Sighing like furnace, with a woful ballad
Made to his mistress' eyebrow. Then a soldier,
Full of strange oaths, and bearded like the pard,
Jealous in honor, sudden and quick in quarrel,
Seeking the bubble reputation
Even in the cannon's mouth. And then the justice,
In fair round belly with good capon lin'd,
With eyes severe, and beard of formal cut,
Full of wise saws and modern instances;
And so he plays his part. The sixth age shifts
Into the lean and slipper'd pantaloon,
With spectacles on nose and pouch on side,
His youthful hose well sav'd, a world too wide
For his shrunk shank; and his big manly voice,
Turning again toward childish treble, pipes
And whistles in his sound. Last scene of all,
That ends this strange eventful history,
Is second childishness and mere oblivion,
Sans teeth, sans eyes, sans taste, sans everything.
II, vii, 139

1 Blow, blow, thou winter wind,
  Thou art not so unkind
  As man's ingratitude.   *II, vii, 174*

2 These trees shall be my books.   *III, ii, 5*

3 The fair, the chaste, and unexpressive she.
III, ii, 10

4   It goes much against my stomach. Hast any philosophy in thee, shepherd?   *III, ii, 21*

5   He that wants money, means, and content, is
without three good friends.   *III, ii, 25*

6   I am a true laborer: I earn that I eat, get that I
wear, owe no man hate, envy no man's happiness,
glad of other men's good, content with my harm.
III, ii, 78

7 From the east to western Ind,
  No jewel is like Rosalind.   *III, ii, 94*

8   This is the very false gallop of verses.
III, ii, 120

9   Let us make an honorable retreat; though not
with bag and baggage, yet with scrip and scrippage.
III, ii, 170

10   O, wonderful, wonderful, and most wonderful,
wonderful! and yet again wonderful! and after that,
out of all whooping.   *III, ii, 202*

11   Answer me in one word.   *III, ii, 238*

12   Do you not know I am a woman? when I think,
I must speak.   *III, ii, 265*

13   I do desire we may be better strangers.
III, ii, 276

14   *Jaques:* What stature is she of?
  Orlando: Just as high as my heart.
III, ii, 286

15   Time travels in divers paces with divers persons.
I'll tell you who Time ambles withal, who Time
trots withal, who Time gallops withal, and who he
stands still withal.   *III, ii, 328*

16   Every one fault seeming monstrous till his fellow
fault came to match it.   *III, ii, 377*

17   Everything about you demonstrating a careless
desolation.   *III, ii, 405*

18   Truly, I would the gods had made thee poetical.
III, iii, 16

19   The wounds invisible
That love's keen arrows make.   *III, v, 30*

20   Down on your knees,
And thank heaven, fasting, for a good man's love.
III, v, 57

21 Sell when you can, you are not for all markets.
III, v, 60

22 I am falser than vows made in wine.   *III, v, 73*

23   It is a melancholy of mine own, compounded of
many simples, extracted from many objects, and indeed the sundry contemplation of my travels, which,
by often rumination, wraps me in a most humorous
sadness.   *IV, i, 16*

24   I had rather have a fool to make me merry than
experience to make me sad.   *IV, i, 28*

25   Farewell, Monsieur Traveler: look you lisp, and
wear strange suits, disable all the benefits of your
own country, be out of love with your nativity, and
almost chide God for making you that countenance
you are; or I will scarce think you have swam in a
gondola.   *IV, i, 35*

26   I'll warrant him heart-whole.   *IV, i, 51*

27   Men have died from time to time, and worms
have eaten them, but not for love.   *IV, i, 110*

28   Forever and a day.   *IV, i, 151*

29   Men are April when they woo, December when
they wed: maids are May when they are maids, but
the sky changes when they are wives.   *IV, i, 153*

30   My affection hath an unknown bottom, like the
bay of Portugal.   *IV, i, 219*

31 The horn, the horn, the lusty horn
Is not a thing to laugh to scorn.   *IV, ii, 17*

32 Chewing the food of sweet and bitter fancy.
IV, iii, 103

1   "So so," is good, very good, very excellent good: and yet it is not; it is but so so.

As You Like It, V, i, 30

2   The fool doth think he is wise, but the wise man knows himself to be a fool.   *V, i, 35*

3   No sooner met, but they looked; no sooner looked but they loved; no sooner loved but they sighed; no sooner sighed but they asked one another the reason; no sooner knew the reason but they sought the remedy.   *V, ii, 37*

4   But, O! how bitter a thing it is to look into happiness through another man's eyes!   *V, ii, 48*

5   It was a lover and his lass,
With a hey, and a ho, and a hey nonino,
That o'er the green corn-field did pass,
In the spring time, the only pretty ring time,
When birds do sing, hey ding a ding, ding;
Sweet lovers love the spring.   *V, iii, 18*

6   Here comes a pair of very strange beasts, which in all tongues are called fools.   *V, iv, 36*

7   An ill-favored thing, sir, but mine own.[1]
V, iv, 60

8   Rich honesty dwells like a miser, sir, in a poor house, as your pearl in your foul oyster.
V, iv, 62

9   "The retort courteous." . . . "the quip modest." . . . "the reply churlish." . . . "the reproof valiant . . . "the countercheck quarrelsome." . . . "the lie circumstantial," and "the lie direct."
V, iv, 75

10   Your "if" is the only peacemaker; much virtue in "if."   *V, iv, 108*

11   He uses his folly like a stalking horse, and under the presentation of that he shoots his wit.
V, iv, 112

12   For this relief much thanks; 'tis bitter cold,
And I am sick at heart.
Hamlet [1600–1601], act I, sc. i, l. 8

13   Not a mouse stirring.   *I, i, 10*

14   Thou art a scholar; speak to it, Horatio.   *I, i, 42*

15   But in the gross and scope of my opinion,
This bodes some strange eruption to our state.
I, i, 68

16   Whose sore task
Does not divide the Sunday from the week.
I, i, 75

17   This sweaty haste
Doth make the night joint-laborer with the day.
I, i, 77

18   In the most high and palmy state of Rome,
A little ere the mightiest Julius fell,
The graves stood tenantless and the sheeted dead
Did squeak and gibber in the Roman streets.
I, i, 113

19   And then it started like a guilty thing
Upon a fearful summons.   *I, i, 148*

20   The cock, that is the trumpet to the morn.
I, i, 150

21   Whether in sea or fire, in earth or air,
The extravagant and erring spirit hies
To his confine.   *I, i, 153*

22   It faded on the crowing of the cock.
Some say that ever 'gainst that season comes
Wherein our Savior's birth is celebrated,
The bird of dawning singeth all night long;
And then, they say, no spirit can walk abroad;
The nights are wholesome; then no planets strike,
No fairy takes, nor witch hath power to charm,
So hallow'd and so gracious is the time.
I, i, 157

23   But, look, the morn in russet mantle clad,
Walks o'er the dew of yon high eastern hill.
I, i, 166

24   The memory be green.   *I, ii, 2*

25   With one auspicious and one dropping eye,
With mirth in funeral and with dirge in marriage,
In equal scale weighing delight and dole.
I, ii, 11

26   So much for him.   *I, ii, 25*

27   A little more than kin, and less than kind.
I, ii, 65

28   Thou know'st 'tis common; all that live must die,
Passing through nature to eternity.   *I, ii, 72*

29   Seems, madam! Nay, it is; I know not "seems."
'Tis not alone my inky cloak, good mother,
Nor customary suits of solemn black.   *I, ii, 76*

30   But I have that within which passeth show;
These but the trappings and the suits of woe.
I, ii, 85

31   To persever
In obstinate condolement is a course
Of impious stubbornness; 'tis unmanly grief:
It shows a will most incorrect to heaven,
A heart unfortified, a mind impatient.
I, ii, 92

---

[1]"A poor thing but mine own" is the popular version.

1 O! that this too too solid[1] flesh would melt,
Thaw and resolve itself into a dew;
Or that the Everlasting had not fix'd
His canon 'gainst self-slaughter! O God! O God!
How weary, stale, flat, and unprofitable
Seem to me all the uses of this world.
I, ii, 129

2   Things rank and gross in nature
Possess it merely. That it should come to this!
I, ii, 136

3 So excellent a king; that was, to this,
Hyperion to a satyr; so loving to my mother
That he might not beteem the winds of heaven
Visit her face too roughly.
I, ii, 139

4   Why, she would hang on him,
As if increase of appetite had grown
By what it fed on.
I, ii, 143

5 Frailty, thy name is woman!
I, ii, 146

6 Like Niobe, all tears.
I, ii, 149

7 A beast, that wants discourse of reason.
I, ii, 150

8 It is not nor it cannot come to good.
I, ii, 158

9 A truant disposition.
I, ii, 169

10 Thrift, thrift, Horatio! the funeral bak'd meats
Did coldly furnish forth the marriage tables.
Would I had met my dearest foe in heaven
Ere I had ever seen that day.
I, ii, 180

11 In my mind's eye, Horatio.
I, ii, 185

12 He was a man, take him for all in all,
I shall not look upon his like again.
I, ii, 187

13 Season your admiration for a while.
I, ii, 192

14 In the dead vast and middle of the night.
I, ii, 198

15 Armed at points exactly, cap-a-pe.
I, ii, 200

16   Distill'd
Almost to jelly with the act of fear.
I, ii, 204

17 A countenance more in sorrow than in anger.
I, ii, 231

18 *Hamlet:*   His beard was grizzled, no?
Horatio: It was, as I have seen it in his life,
A sable silver'd.
I, ii, 239

19 Give it an understanding, but no tongue.
I, ii, 249

20   All is not well;
I doubt some foul play.
I, ii, 254

21   Foul deeds will rise,
Though all the earth o'erwhelm them, to men's
eyes.
I, ii, 256

22 The chariest maid is prodigal enough
If she unmask her beauty to the moon;
Virtue itself 'scapes not calumnious strokes;
The canker galls the infants of the spring
Too oft before their buttons be disclos'd,
And in the morn and liquid dew of youth
Contagious blastments are most imminent.
I, iii, 36

23 Do not, as some ungracious pastors do,
Show me the steep and thorny way to heaven,
Whiles, like a puff'd and reckless libertine,
Himself the primrose path of dalliance treads,
And recks not his own rede.[2]
I, iii, 47

24 Give thy thoughts no tongue.
I, iii, 59

25 Be thou familiar, but by no means vulgar;
Those friends thou hast, and their adoption tried,
Grapple them to thy soul with hoops of steel.
I, iii, 61

26   Beware
Of entrance to a quarrel, but, being in,
Bear 't that th' opposed may beware of thee.
Give every man thy ear, but few thy voice;
Take each man's censure, but reserve thy
judgment.
Costly thy habit as thy purse can buy,
But not express'd in fancy; rich, not gaudy;
For the apparel oft proclaims the man.
I, iii, 65

27 Neither a borrower, nor a lender be;
For loan oft loses both itself and friend,
And borrowing dulls the edge of husbandry.
This above all: to thine own self be true,
And it must follow, as the night the day,
Thou canst not then be false to any man.
I, iii, 75

28   'Tis in my memory lock'd,
And you yourself shall keep the key of it.
I, iii, 85

29   You speak like a green girl,
Unsifted in such perilous circumstance.
I, iii, 101

30 Springes to catch woodcocks.
I, iii, 115

31 When the blood burns, how prodigal the soul
Lends the tongue vows.
I, iii, 116

---

[1]Alternative readings are "sallied" and "sullied."

[2]Wel oghte a preest ensample for to yive. / By his clennesse, how that his sheep shold live. — GEOFFREY CHAUCER, *The Canterbury Tales* [c. 1387], *prologue, l. 504*
And may ye better reck the rede, / Than ever did th' adviser. — ROBERT BURNS, *Epistle to a Young Friend* [1786]

1 Be somewhat scanter of your maiden presence.

Hamlet, I, iii, 121

2 The air bites shrewdly. *I, iv, 1*

3 But to my mind,—though I am native here
And to the manner born—it is a custom
More honor'd in the breach than the observance.

I, iv, 14

4 Angels and ministers of grace defend us!

I, iv, 39

5 Be thy intents wicked or charitable,
Thou com'st in such a questionable shape
That I will speak to thee. *I, iv, 42*

6   What may this mean,
That thou, dead corse, again in complete steel
Revisit'st thus the glimpses of the moon,
Making night hideous;[1] and we fools of nature
So horridly to shake our disposition
With thoughts beyond the reaches of our souls?

I, iv, 51

7 I do not set my life at a pin's fee. *I, iv, 65*

8   The dreadful summit of the cliff
That beetles o'er his base into the sea.

I, iv, 70

9   My fate cries out,
And makes each petty artery in this body
As hardy as the Nemean lion's nerve.

I, iv, 81

10   Unhand me, gentlemen,
By heaven! I'll make a ghost of him that lets me.

I, iv, 84

11 Something is rotten in the state of Denmark.

I, iv, 90

12 I could a tale unfold whose lightest word
Would harrow up thy soul, freeze thy young blood,
Make thy two eyes, like stars, start from their
     spheres,
Thy knotted and combined locks to part,
And each particular hair to stand an end,
Like quills upon the fretful porpentine.

I, v, 15

13 Murder most foul, as in the best it is. *I, v, 27*

14 And duller shouldst thou be than the fat weed
That rots itself in ease on Lethe wharf.

I, v, 32

15   O my prophetic soul!
My uncle! *I, v, 40*

16 O Hamlet! what a falling-off was there.

I, v, 47

17 But virtue, as it never will be mov'd,
Though lewdness court it in a shape of heaven,
So lust, though to a radiant angel link'd,
Will sate itself in a celestial bed,
And prey on garbage. *I, v, 5_*

18 In the porches of mine ears. *I, v, 6_*

19 Cut off even in the blossoms of my sin,
Unhousel'd, disappointed, unanel'd,
No reckoning made, but sent to my account
With all my imperfections on my head.

I, v, 76

20   Leave her to heaven,
And to those thorns that in her bosom lodge,
To prick and sting her. *I, v, 86*

21 The glowworm shows the matin to be near,
And 'gins to pale his uneffectual fire.

I, v, 89

22   While memory holds a seat
In this distracted globe. Remember thee!
Yea, from the table of my memory
I'll wipe away all trivial fond records. *I, v, 96*

23 Within the book and volume of my brain.

I, v, 103

24 O villain, villain, smiling, damned villain!
My tables—meet it is I set it down,
That one may smile, and smile, and be a villain;
At least I'm sure it may be so in Denmark.

I, v, 106

25 There's ne'er a villain dwelling in all Denmark,
But he's an arrant knave. *I, v, 123*

26 There are more things in heaven and earth,
     Horatio,
Than are dreamt of in your philosophy.

I, v, 166

27 To put an antic disposition on. *I, v, 172*

28 Rest, rest, perturbed spirit! *I, v, 182*

29 The time is out of joint; O cursed spite,
That ever I was born to set it right!

I, v, 188

30 Your bait of falsehood takes this carp of truth;
And thus do we of wisdom and of reach,
With windlasses and with assays of bias,
By indirections find directions out.

II, i, 63

31 Ungarter'd, and down-gyved to his ankle.

II, i, 80

32 This is the very ecstasy of love. *II, i, 102*

33 Brevity is the soul of wit. *II, ii, 90*

34 More matter, with less art. *II, ii, 95*

---

[1]And makes night hideous.—ALEXANDER POPE, *The Dunciad,*
bk. III [1728], *l. 166*

1 That he is mad, 'tis true; 'tis true 'tis pity;
And pity 'tis 'tis true. *II, ii, 97*

2   Find out the cause of this effect,
Or rather say, the cause of this defect,
For this effect defective comes by cause.
    II, ii, 101

3 Doubt thou the stars are fire;
Doubt that the sun doth move;
Doubt truth to be a liar;
But never doubt I love. *II, ii, 115*

4 *Polonius:* Do you know me, my lord?
Hamlet: Excellent well; you are a fishmonger.
    II, ii, 173

5   To be honest, as this world goes, is to be one
man picked out of ten thousand.   *II, ii, 179*

6   *Hamlet:* For if the sun breed maggots in a dead
dog, being a god[1] kissing carrion,—Have you a
daughter?
    Polonius: I have, my lord.
    Hamlet: Let her not walk i' the sun.
    II, ii, 183

7   Still harping on my daughter. *II, ii, 190*

8   *Polonius:* What do you read, my lord?
    Hamlet: Words, words, words. *II, ii, 195*

9   They have a plentiful lack of wit.
    II, ii, 204

10   Though this be madness, yet there is method
in 't. *II, ii, 211*

11   These tedious old fools! *II, ii, 227*

12   The indifferent children of the earth.
    II, ii, 235

13   Happy in that we are not over happy.
    II, ii, 236

14   There is nothing either good or bad, but thinking makes it so. *II, ii, 259*

15   O God! I could be bounded in a nutshell, and
count myself a king of infinite space, were it not
that I have bad dreams. *II, ii, 263*

16   Beggar that I am, I am even poor in thanks.
    II, ii, 286

17   This goodly frame, the earth, seems to me a sterile
promontory; this most excellent canopy, the air, look
you, this brave o'erhanging firmament, this majestical roof fretted with golden fire, why, it appears no
other thing to me but a foul and pestilent congregation of vapors. What a piece of work is a man! How
noble in reason! how infinite in faculty! in form, in

moving, how express and admirable! in action how
like an angel! in apprehension how like a god!
    II, ii, 317

18   And yet, to me, what is this quintessence of dust?
man delights not me; no, nor woman neither.
    II, ii, 328

19   There is something in this more than natural, if
philosophy could find it out. *II, ii, 392*

20   I am but mad north-northwest: when the wind
is southerly I know a hawk from a handsaw.[2]
    II, ii, 405

21   They say an old man is twice a child.
    II, ii, 413

22 One fair daughter and no more,
The which he loved passing well. *II, ii, 435*

23   Come, give us a taste of your quality.
    II, ii, 460

24   The play, I remember, pleased not the million;
'twas caviare to the general. *II, ii, 465*

25   They are the abstracts and brief chronicles of the
time: after your death you were better have a bad
epitaph than their ill report while you live.
    II, ii, 555

26   Use every man after his desert, and who should
'scape whipping? *II, ii, 561*

27 O! what a rogue and peasant slave am I.
    II, ii, 584

28 What's Hecuba to him or he to Hecuba,
That he should weep for her? *II, ii, 593*

29 Who calls me villain? breaks my pate across?
Plucks off my beard and blows it in my face?
    II, ii, 607

30 But I am pigeon-liver'd, and lack gall
To make oppression bitter. *II, ii, 613*

31   The play's the thing
Wherein I'll catch the conscience of the king.
    II, ii, 641

32   With devotion's visage
And pious action we do sugar o'er
The devil himself. *III, i, 47*

33 To be, or not to be: that is the question:
Whether 'tis nobler in the mind to suffer
The slings and arrows of outrageous fortune,

---

[2]The *hawk* was a basic tool of the plasterer and the *handsaw* a
basic tool of the carpenter. . . . The tools are quite easy to distinguish. I know that *heronshaw* [a young heron] is the classic answer
but why go all round Robin Hood's barn for an answer to a simple
comparison of common tools? — *Morris Dictionary of Word and
Phrase Origins* [1977], quoting FRANCIS W. SHERIDAN

---

[1]In some editions: good.

Or to take arms against a sea of troubles,
And by opposing end them? To die: to sleep;
No more; and, by a sleep to say we end
The heartache and the thousand natural shocks
That flesh is heir to, 'tis a consummation
Devoutly to be wish'd. To die, to sleep;
To sleep: perchance to dream: ay, there's the rub;
For in that sleep of death what dreams may come
When we have shuffled off this mortal coil,
Must give us pause. There's the respect
That makes calamity of so long life;
For who would bear the whips and scorns of time,
The oppressor's wrong, the proud man's
    contumely,
The pangs of dispriz'd love, the law's delay,
The insolence of office, and the spurns
That patient merit of the unworthy takes,
When he himself might his quietus make
With a bare bodkin? who would fardels bear,
To grunt and sweat under a weary life,
But that the dread of something after death,
The undiscover'd country from whose bourn
No traveler returns, puzzles the will,
And makes us rather bear those ills we have
Than fly to others that we know not of?
Thus conscience does make cowards of us all;
And thus the native hue of resolution
Is sicklied o'er with the pale cast of thought,
And enterprises of great pith and moment
With this regard their currents turn awry,
And lose the name of action.   *Hamlet, III, i, 56*

1   Nymph, in thy orisons
Be all my sins remember'd.   *III, i, 89*

2   To the noble mind
Rich gifts wax poor when givers prove unkind.
    III, i, 100

3   Get thee to a nunnery.   *III, i, 124*

4   What should such fellows as I do crawling between heaven and earth? We are arrant knaves, all.
    III, i, 128

5   Be thou as chaste as ice, as pure as snow, thou
shalt not escape calumny.   *III, i, 142*

6   I have heard of your paintings too, well enough;
God has given you one face, and you make yourselves another.   *III, i, 150*

7 O! what a noble mind is here o'erthrown:
The courtier's, soldier's, scholar's, eye, tongue,
    sword.   *III, i, 159*

8 The glass of fashion and the mould of form,
The observ'd of all observers!   *III, i, 162*

9 Now see that noble and most sovereign reason,
Like sweet bells jangled, out of tune and harsh.
    III, i, 166

10   O! woe is me,
To have seen what I have seen, see what I see!
    III, i, 16

11   Speak the speech, I pray you, as I pronounced
to you, trippingly on the tongue; but if you mouth
it, as many of your players do, I had as lief the town
crier spoke my lines. Nor do not saw the air too
much with your hand, thus; but use all gently: for
in the very torrent, tempest, and—as I may say—
whirlwind of passion, you must acquire and beget a
temperance, that may give it smoothness. O! it offends me to the soul to hear a robustious periwig-
pated fellow tear a passion to tatters, to very rags, to
split the ears of the groundlings, who for the most
part are capable of nothing but inexplicable dumbshows and noise: I would have such a fellow
whipped for o'erdoing Termagant; it out-herods
Herod.
    III, ii, 1

12   Suit the action to the word, the word to the action; with this special observance, that you o'erstep
not the modesty of nature.   *III, ii, 20*

13   To hold, as 'twere, the mirror up to nature; to
show virtue her own feature, scorn her own image,
and the very age and body of the time his form and
pressure.   *III, ii, 25*

14   I have thought some of nature's journeymen had
made men and not made them well, they imitated
humanity so abominably.   *III, ii, 38*

15 No; let the candied tongue lick absurd pomp,
And crook the pregnant hinges of the knee
Where thrift may follow fawning.   *III, ii, 65*

16 A man that fortune's buffets and rewards
Hast ta'en with equal thanks.   *III, ii, 72*

17 They are not a pipe for fortune's finger
To sound what stop she please. Give me that man
That is not passion's slave, and I will wear him
In my heart's core, ay, in my heart of heart,
As I do thee. Something too much of this.
    III, ii, 75

18   My imaginations are as foul
As Vulcan's stithy.   *III, ii, 88*

19 The chameleon's dish: I eat the air, promise-
crammed; you cannot feed capons so.
    III, ii, 98

20   Nay, then, let the devil wear black, for I'll have a
suit of sables.   *III, ii, 138*

21   There's hope a great man's memory may outlive
his life half a year.   *III, ii, 141*

22   Marry, this is miching mallecho; it means mischief.   *III, ii, 148*

1 *Ophelia:* 'Tis brief, my lord.
   Hamlet: As woman's love. *III, ii, 165*

2 Where love is great, the littlest doubts are fear;
   When little fears grow great, great love grows
   there. *III, ii, 183*

3 Wormwood, wormwood. *III, ii, 193*

4 The lady doth protest too much, methinks.
   III, ii, 242

5 Let the galled jade wince, our withers are unwrung. *III, ii, 256*

6 Why, let the stricken deer go weep,
   The hart ungalled play;
   For some must watch, while some must sleep:
   So runs the world away. *III, ii, 287*

7 You would pluck out the heart of my mystery.
   III, ii, 389

8 Do you think I am easier to be played on than a
   pipe? *III, ii, 393*

9 *Hamlet:* Do you see yonder cloud that's almost
   in shape of a camel?
   Polonius: By the mass, and 'tis like a camel, in-
   deed.
   Hamlet: Methinks it is like a weasel.
   Polonius: It is backed like a weasel.
   Hamlet: Or like a whale?
   Polonius: Very like a whale. *III, ii, 400*

10 They fool me to the top of my bent.
    III, ii, 408

11 By and by is easily said. *III, ii, 411*

12 'Tis now the very witching time of night,
    When churchyards yawn and hell itself breathes out
    Contagion to this world. *III, ii, 413*

13 I will speak daggers to her, but use none.
    III, ii, 421

14 O! my offense is rank, it smells to heaven;
    It hath the primal eldest curse upon 't;
    A brother's murder! *III, iii, 36*

15 Now might I do it pat, now he is praying;
    And now I'll do 't: and so he goes to heaven;
    And so I am reveng'd. *III, iii, 73*

16 With all his crimes broad blown, as flush as May.
    III, iii, 81

17 My words fly up, my thoughts remain below:
    Words without thoughts never to heaven go.
    III, iii, 97

18 How now! a rat? Dead, for a ducat, dead!
    III, iv, 23

19 False as dicers' oaths. *III, iv, 45*

20 A rhapsody of words. *III, iv, 48*

21 See, what a grace was seated on this brow;
    Hyperion's curls, the front of Jove himself,
    An eye like Mars, to threaten and command,
    A station like the herald Mercury
    New-lighted on a heaven-kissing hill,
    A combination and a form indeed,
    Where every god did seem to set his seal,
    To give the world assurance of a man. *III, iv, 55*

22 At your age
    The heyday in the blood is tame, it's humble.
    III, iv, 68

23 O shame! where is thy blush? Rebellious hell,
    If thou canst mutine in a matron's bones,
    To flaming youth let virtue be as wax,
    And melt in her own fire: proclaim no shame
    When the compulsive ardor gives the charge,
    Since frost itself as actively doth burn,
    And reason panders will. *III, iv, 82*

24 A king of shreds and patches. *III, iv, 102*

25 Lay not that flattering unction to your soul.
    III, iv, 145

26 Confess yourself to heaven;
    Repent what's past; avoid what is to come.
    III, iv, 149

27 For in the fatness of these pursy times
    Virtue itself of vice must pardon beg.
    III, iv, 153

28 Assume a virtue, if you have it not. *III, iv, 160*

29 Refrain tonight;
    And that shall lend a kind of easiness
    To the next abstinence: the next more easy;
    For use almost can change the stamp of nature.
    III, iv, 165

30 I must be cruel only to be kind. *III, iv, 178*

31 For 'tis the sport to have the enginer
    Hoist with his own petar. *III, iv, 206*

32 Diseases desperate grown
    By desperate appliance are relieved,
    Or not at all. *IV, iii, 9*

33 A man may fish with the worm that hath eat of a
    king, and eat of the fish that hath fed of that worm.
    IV, iii, 29

34 We go to gain a little patch of ground
    That hath in it no profit but the name.
    IV, iv, 18

35 How all occasions do inform against me,
    And spur my dull revenge! What is a man,
    If his chief good and market of his time
    Be but to sleep and feed? a beast, no more.

Sure he that made us with such large discourse,
Looking before and after, gave us not
That capability and godlike reason
To fust in us unus'd.   *Hamlet, IV, iv, 32*

1   Some craven scruple
Of thinking too precisely on the event.
                              IV, iv, 40

2   Rightly to be great
Is not to stir without great argument,
But greatly to find quarrel in a straw
When honor's at the stake.   *IV, iv, 53*

3 So full of artless jealousy is guilt,
It spills itself in fearing to be spilt.   *IV, v, 19*

4 How should I your true love know
From another one?
By his cockle hat and staff,
And his sandal shoon.[1]   *IV, v, 23*

5 He is dead and gone, lady,
He is dead and gone;
At his head a grass-green turf
At his heels a stone.   *IV, v, 29*

6   We know what we are, but know not what we
may be.   *IV, v, 43*

7   Come, my coach! Good night, ladies; good
night, sweet ladies; good night, good night.
                              IV, v, 72

8 When sorrows come, they come not single spies,
But in battalions.[2]   *IV, v, 78*

9   We have done but greenly,
In hugger-mugger to inter him.   *IV, v, 84*

10 There's such divinity doth hedge a king,
That treason can but peep to what it would.
                              IV, v, 123

11   There's rosemary, that's for remembrance . . .
and there is pansies, that's for thoughts.
                              IV, v, 174

12   O! you must wear your rue with a difference.
There's a daisy; I would give you some violets, but
they withered all when my father died.
                              IV, v, 181

13 A very riband in the cap of youth.   *IV, vii, 77*

14   Nature her custom holds,
Let shame say what it will.   *IV, vii, 188*

_____
[1]Ophelia is quoting a version of a poem by Walter Ralegh.

[2]One woe doth tread upon another's heel, / So fast they
follow. — *Hamlet, act IV, sc. vii, l. 164*

Thus woe succeeds a woe, as wave a wave. — ROBERT HERRICK,
Sorrows Succeed [1648]

Woes cluster; rare are solitary woes; / They love a train, they
tread each other's heel. — EDWARD YOUNG, *Night Thoughts* [1742–
1745], *Night III, l. 63*

15   There is no ancient gentlemen but gardeners,
ditchers, and grave-makers; they hold up Adam's
profession.   *V, i, 32*

16   Cudgel thy brains no more about it.
                              V, i, 61

17   Has this fellow no feeling of his business, that he
sings at grave-making?   *V, i, 71*

18   Custom hath made it in him a property of easiness.   *V, i, 73*

19   A politician . . . one that would circumvent God.
                              V, i, 84

20   Why may not that be the skull of a lawyer?
Where be his quiddities now, his quillets, his cases,
his tenures, and his tricks?   *V, i, 104*

21   One that was a woman, sir; but, rest her soul,
she's dead.   *V, i, 145*

22   How absolute the knave is! we must speak by the
card, or equivocation will undo us.
                              V, i, 147

23   The age is grown so picked that the toe of the
peasant comes so near the heel of the courtier, he
galls his kibe.   *V, i, 150*

24   Alas! poor Yorick. I knew him, Horatio; a fellow
of infinite jest, of most excellent fancy; he hath
borne me on his back a thousand times; and now,
how abhorred in my imagination it is! my gorge
rises at it. Here hung those lips that I have kissed I
know not how oft. Where be your gibes now? your
gambols? your songs? your flashes of merriment,
that were wont to set the table on a roar? Not one
now, to mock your own grinning? quite chapfallen?
Now get you to my lady's chamber, and tell her, let
her paint an inch thick, to this favor she must come;
make her laugh at that.   *V, i, 201*

25   To what base uses we may return, Horatio! Why
may not imagination trace the noble dust of Alexander, till he find it stopping a bung-hole?
                              V, i, 222

26 Imperious Caesar, dead and turn'd to clay,
Might stop a hole to keep the wind away.
                              V, i, 235

27   Lay her i' the earth;
And from her fair and unpolluted flesh
May violets spring!   *V, i, 260*

28 A ministering angel shall my sister be.   *V, i, 263*

29 Sweets to the sweet: farewell!   *V, i, 265*

30 I thought thy bride-bed to have deck'd, sweet
maid,
And not have strew'd thy grave.   *V, i, 267*

1 Though I am not splenetive and rash
Yet have I in me something dangerous.
V, i, 283

2 I lov'd Ophelia: forty thousand brothers
Could not, with all their quantity of love,
Make up my sum.
V, i, 291

3   Nay, an thou'lt mouth,
I'll rant as well as thou.
V, i, 305

4 Let Hercules himself do what he may,
The cat will mew and dog will have his day.
V, i, 313

5 There's a divinity that shapes our ends,
Rough-hew them how we will.
V, ii, 10

6 I once did hold it, as our statists do,
A baseness to write fair.
V, ii, 33

7 It did me yeoman's service.
V, ii, 36

8   Not a whit, we defy augury; there's a special
providence in the fall of a sparrow. If it be now, 'tis
not to come; if it be not to come, it will be now; if it
be not now, yet it will come: the readiness is all.
V, ii, 232

9 A hit, a very palpable hit.
V, ii, 295

10   This fell sergeant, death,
Is strict in his arrest.
V, ii, 350

11 Report me and my cause aright.
V, ii, 353

12 I am more an antique Roman than a Dane.
V, ii, 355

13 O God! Horatio, what a wounded name,
Things standing thus unknown, shall live behind me.
If thou didst ever hold me in thy heart,
Absent thee from felicity awhile,
And in this harsh world draw thy breath in pain,
To tell my story.
V, ii, 358

14 The rest is silence.
V, ii, 372

15 Now cracks a noble heart. Good night, sweet
prince,
And flights of angels sing thee to thy rest!
V, ii, 373

16   O proud death!
What feast is toward in thine eternal cell?
V, ii, 378

17 Property was thus appall'd,
That the self was not the same;
Single nature's double name
Neither two nor one was call'd.
The Phoenix and the Turtle [1601], l. 37

18 Reason, in itself confounded,
Saw division grow together.
l. 41

19 The chance of war.
*Troilus and Cressida [1601–1602], prologue,
l. 31*

20   I have had my labor for my travail.
Act I, sc. i, l. 73

21   Women are angels, wooing:
Things won are done; joy's soul lies in the doing.
I, ii, 310

22 Men prize the thing ungain'd more than it is.
I, ii, 313

23   The sea being smooth,
How many shallow bauble boats dare sail
Upon her patient breast.
I, iii, 34

24 The heavens themselves, the planets, and this
center
Observe degree, priority, and place,
Insisture, course, proportion, season, form,
Office, and custom, in all line of order.
I, iii, 85

25   O! when degree is shaked,
Which is the ladder to all high designs,
The enterprise is sick.
I, iii, 101

26 Take but degree away, untune that string,
And, hark! what discord follows; each thing meets
In mere oppugnancy: the bounded waters
Should lift their bosoms higher than the shores,
And make a sop of all this solid globe.
I, iii, 109

27 Then everything includes itself in power,
Power into will, will into appetite;
And appetite, a universal wolf,
So doubly seconded with will and power,
Must make perforce a universal prey,
And last eat up himself.
I, iii, 119

28 Like a strutting player, whose conceit
Lies in his hamstring, and doth think it rich
To hear the wooden dialogue and sound
'Twixt his stretch'd footing and the scaffoldage.
I, iii, 153

29 And in such indexes, although small pricks
To their subsequent volumes, there is seen
The baby figure of the giant mass
Of things to come.
I, iii, 343

30   Who wears his wit in his belly, and his guts in his
head.
II, i, 78

31   Modest doubt is call'd
The beacon of the wise, the tent that searches
To the bottom of the worst.
II, ii, 15

32   'Tis mad idolatry
To make the service greater than the god.
II, ii, 56

1   He that is proud eats up himself; pride is his own glass, his own trumpet, his own chronicle.

Troilus and Cressida, II, iii, 165

2 I am giddy, expectation whirls me round.
The imaginary relish is so sweet
That it enchants my sense.   *III, ii, 17*

3   Words pay no debts.   *III, ii, 56*

4   To fear the worst oft cures the worse.

III, ii, 77

5   All lovers swear more performance than they are able, and yet reserve an ability that they never perform; vowing more than the perfection of ten and discharging less than the tenth part of one.

III, ii, 89

6   For to be wise, and love,
Exceeds man's might; that dwells with gods above.

III, ii, 163

7 If I be false, or swerve a hair from truth,
When time is old and hath forgot itself,
When waterdrops have worn the stones of Troy,
And blind oblivion swallow'd cities up.
And mighty states characterless are grated
To dusty nothing, yet let memory,
From false to false, among false maids in love
Upbraid my falsehood! when they have said "as false
As air, as water, wind, or sandy earth,
As fox to lamb, as wolf to heifer's calf,
Pard to the hind, or stepdame to her son";
Yea, let them say, to stick the heart of falsehood,
"As false as Cressid."   *III, ii, 191*

8 Time hath, my lord, a wallet at his back,
Wherein he puts alms for oblivion.   *III, iii, 145*

9   Perseverance, dear my lord,
Keeps honor bright: to have done, is to hang
Quite out of fashion, like a rusty mail
In monumental mockery.   *III, iii, 150*

10 For honor travels in a strait so narrow
Where one but goes abreast.   *III, iii, 154*

11   Time is like a fashionable host,
That slightly shakes his parting guest by the hand,
And with his arms outstretch'd, as he would fly,
Grasps in the comer: welcome ever smiles,
And farewell goes out sighing.   *III, iii, 168*

12   Beauty, wit,
High birth, vigor of bone, desert in service,
Love, friendship, charity, are subjects all
To envious and calumniating time.
One touch of nature makes the whole world kin.

III, iii, 171

13 And give to dust that is a little gilt
More laud than gilt o'er-dusted.   *III, iii, 178*

14 My mind is troubled, like a fountain stirr'd;
And I myself see not the bottom of it.

III, iii, 31

15   You do as chapmen do,
Dispraise the thing that you desire to buy.

IV, i, 7

16 As many farewells as be stars in heaven.

IV, iv, 4

17 And sometimes we are devils to ourselves
When we will tempt the frailty of our powers,
Presuming on their changeful potency.

IV, iv, 95

18 The kiss you take is better than you give.

IV, v, 38

19   Fie, fie upon her!
There's language in her eye, her cheek, her lip,
Nay, her foot speaks; her wanton spirits look out
At every joint and motive of her body.

IV, v, 54

20 What's past and what's to come is strew'd with husks
And formless ruin of oblivion.   *IV, v, 165*

21   The end crowns all,
And that old common arbitrator, Time,
Will one day end it.   *IV, v, 223*

22 Words, words, mere words, no matter from the heart.   *V, iii, 109*

23 Hector is dead; there is no more to say.

V, x, 22

24   O world! world! world! thus is the poor agent despised.   *V, x, 36*

25 If music be the food of love,[1] play on;
Give me excess of it, that, surfeiting,
The appetite may sicken, and so die.
That strain again! it had a dying fall:
O! it came o'er my ear like the sweet sound
That breathes upon a bank of violets,
Stealing and giving odor!

Twelfth-Night [1601–1602], act I, sc. i, l. 1

26 O spirit of love! how quick and fresh art thou,
That, notwithstanding thy capacity
Receiveth as the sea, nought enters there,
Of what validity and pitch soe'er,
But falls into abatement and low price,
Even in a minute: so full of shapes is fancy,
That it alone is high fantastical.   *I, i, 9*

27 When my tongue blabs, then let mine eyes not see.

I, ii, 61

---

[1]Is not music the food of love? — RICHARD BRINSLEY SHERIDAN, *The Rivals* [1775], *act II, sc. i*

1   I am sure care's an enemy to life. *I, iii, 2*

2   Let them hang themselves in their own straps. *I, iii, 13*

3   I am a great eater of beef, and I believe that does harm to my wit. *I, iii, 92*

4   Wherefore are these things hid? *I, iii, 135*

5   Is it a world to hide virtues in? *I, iii, 142*

6   God give them wisdom that have it; and those that are fools, let them use their talents. *I, v, 14*

7   One draught above heat makes him a fool, the second mads him, and a third drowns him. *I, v, 139*

8   'Tis beauty truly blent, whose red and white
Nature's own sweet and cunning hand laid on:
Lady, you are the cruel'st she alive,
If you will lead these graces to the grave
And leave the world no copy. *I, v, 259*

9   Make me a willow cabin at your gate,
And call upon my soul within the house. *I, v, 289*

10 Holla your name to the reverberate hills,
And make the babbling gossip of the air
Cry out, "Olivia!" *I, v, 293*

11 Farewell, fair cruelty. *I, v, 309*

12 O mistress mine! where are you roaming? *II, iii, 42*

13 Journeys end in lovers meeting,
Every wise man's son doth know. *II, iii, 46*

14 What is love? 'tis not hereafter;
Present mirth hath present laughter.
What's to come is still unsure:
In delay there lies no plenty;
Then come kiss me, sweet and twenty,
Youth's a stuff will not endure. *II, iii, 50*

15 He does it with a better grace, but I do it more natural. *II, iii, 91*

16 Is there no respect of place, persons, nor time, in you? *II, iii, 100*

17 *Sir Toby:* Dost thou think, because thou art virtuous, there shall be no more cakes and ale?
Clown: Yes, by Saint Anne; and ginger shall be hot i' the mouth too. *II, iii, 124*

18 The devil a puritan that he is, or anything constantly but a time-pleaser; an affectioned ass. *II, iii, 161*

19 My purpose is, indeed, a horse of that color.[1] *II, iii, 184*

---

[1]A play on "a horse of a different color."

20 These most brisk and giddy-paced times. *II, iv, 6*

21 If ever thou shalt love,
In the sweet pangs of it remember me;
For such as I am all true lovers are:
Unstaid and skittish in all motions else
Save in the constant image of the creature
That is belov'd. *II, iv, 15*

22 Let still the woman take
An elder than herself, so wears she to him,
So sways she level in her husband's heart:
For, boy, however we do praise ourselves,
Our fancies are more giddy and unfirm,
More longing, wavering, sooner lost and worn,
Than women's are. *II, iv, 29*

23 Then, let thy love be younger than thyself,
Or thy affection cannot hold the bent;
For women are as roses, whose fair flower
Being once display'd, doth fall that very hour. *II, iv, 36*

24 The spinsters and the knitters in the sun,
And the free maids that weave their thread with bones,
Do use to chant it: it is silly sooth,
And dallies with the innocence of love,
Like the old age. *II, iv, 44*

25 Come away, come away, death,
And in sad cypress let me be laid;
Fly away, fly away, breath;
I am slain by a fair cruel maid. *II, iv, 51*

26 *Duke:*   And what's her history?
Viola: A blank, my lord. She never told her love,
But let concealment, like a worm i' the bud,
Feed on her damask cheek: she pin'd in thought,
And with a green and yellow melancholy,
She sat like Patience on a monument,
Smiling at grief. *II, iv, 112*

27 I am all the daughters of my father's house,
And all the brothers too. *II, iv, 122*

28 Here comes the trout that must be caught with tickling. *II, v, 25*

29 I may command where I adore. *II, v, 116*

30 Be not afraid of greatness: some are born great, some achieve greatness, and some have greatness thrust upon them. *II, v, 159*

31 Remember who commended thy yellow stockings, and wished to see thee ever cross-gartered. *II, v, 168*

32 Foolery, sir, does walk about the orb like the sun; it shines everywhere. *III, i, 44*

1 This fellow's wise enough to play the fool,
And to do that well craves a kind of wit.
Twelfth-Night, III, i, 68

2 Music from the spheres.[1] *III, i, 122*

3 How apt the poor are to be proud. *III, i, 141*

4 Then westward-ho! *III, i, 148*

5 O! what a deal of scorn looks beautiful
In the contempt and anger of his lip.
III, i, 159

6 Love sought is good, but giv'n unsought is better.
III, i, 170

7 You will hang like an icicle on a Dutchman's beard. *III, ii, 30*

8 Let there be gall enough in thy ink.
III, ii, 54

9 Laugh yourselves into stitches. *III, ii, 75*

10 I think we do know the sweet Roman hand.
III, iv, 31

11 This is very midsummer madness.
III, iv, 62

12 More matter for a May morning.
III, iv, 158

13 He's a very devil. *III, iv, 304*

14 Out of my lean and low ability
I'll lend you something. *III, iv, 380*

15 I hate ingratitude more in a man
Than lying, vainness, babbling drunkenness,
Or any taint of vice whose strong corruption
Inhabits our frail blood. *III, iv, 390*

16 As the old hermit of Prague, that never saw pen
and ink, very wittily said to a niece of King Gorboduc, "That, that is, is." *IV, ii, 14*

17 I say there is no darkness but ignorance, in
which thou art more puzzled than the Egyptians in
their fog. *IV, ii, 47*

18 Thus the whirligig of time brings in his revenges.
V, i, 388

19 When that I was and a little tiny boy,
With hey, ho, the wind and the rain;
A foolish thing was but a toy,
For the rain it raineth every day.[2]
V, i, 404

20 Love all, trust a few,
Do wrong to none: be able for thine enemy
Rather in power than use, and keep thy friend
Under thy own life's key: be check'd for silence,
But never tax'd for speech.
*All's Well That Ends Well [1602–1604], act I,
sc. i, l. 74*

21 It were all one
That I should love a bright particular star
And think to wed it, he is so above me.
I, i, 97

22 The hind that would be mated by the lion
Must die for love. *I, i, 103*

23 My friends were poor, but honest.[3]
I, iii, 203

24 Oft expectation fails, and most oft there
Where most it promises. *II, i, 145*

25 They say miracles are past. *II, iii, 1*

26 A young man married is a man that's marr'd.
II, iii, 315

27 The web of our life is of a mingled yarn, good
and ill together. *IV, iii, 83*

28 There's place and means for every man alive.
IV, iii, 379

29 All's well that ends well: still the fine's the crown;
Whate'er the course, the end is the renown.
IV, iv, 35

30 I am a man whom Fortune hath cruelly scratched.
V, ii, 28

31 Praising what is lost
Makes the remembrance dear. *V, iii, 19*

32 The inaudible and noiseless foot of time.
V, iii, 41

33 Love that comes too late,
Like a remorseful pardon slowly carried.
V, iii, 57

34 All impediments in fancy's course
Are motives of more fancy. *V, iii, 216*

35 Good counselors lack no clients.
Measure for Measure [1604], act I, sc. ii, l. 115

36 And liberty plucks justice by the nose.
I, iii, 29

37 I hold you as a thing ensky'd and sainted.
I, iv, 34

---

[1]The music of the spheres. — *Pericles, act V, sc. i, l. 231*
A phrase that stems from the Pythagorean Theory (sixth century
B.C.) of the music or harmony of the spheres.

[2]Parodied by the Fool in *King Lear*, 216:25.

---

[3]Though I be poor, I'm honest. — Thomas Middleton, *The
Witch* [c. 1627], *III, 2*

1　　　A man whose blood
Is very snow-broth; one who never feels
The wanton stings and motions of the sense.
I, iv, 57

2　　　Our doubts are traitors,
And make us lose the good we oft might win,
By fearing to attempt.
I, iv, 78

3 We must not make a scarecrow of the law,
Setting it up to fear the birds of prey,
And let it keep one shape, till custom make it
Their perch and not their terror.
II, i, 1

4 The jury, passing on the prisoner's life,
May in the sworn twelve have a thief or two
Guiltier than him they try.
II, i, 19

5 Some rise by sin, and some by virtue fall.
II, i, 38

6　　Great with child, and longing . . . for stewed
prunes.
II, i, 94

7 This will last out a night in Russia,
When nights are longest there.
II, i, 144

8　　His face is the worst thing about him.
II, i, 167

9 Condemn the fault, and not the actor of it?
II, ii, 37

10 No ceremony that to great ones 'longs,
Not the king's crown, nor the deputed sword,
The marshal's truncheon, nor the judge's robe,
Become them with one half so good a grace
As mercy does.
II, ii, 59

11 The law hath not been dead, though it hath slept
II, ii, 90

12　　O! it is excellent
To have a giant's strength, but it is tyrannous
To use it like a giant.
II, ii, 107

13　　But man, proud man,
Drest in a little brief authority,
Most ignorant of what he's most assur'd,
His glassy essence, like an angry ape,
Plays such fantastic tricks before high heaven
As make the angels weep.
II, ii, 117

14 That in the captain's but a choleric word,
Which in the soldier is flat blasphemy.
II, ii, 130

15　　It oft falls out,
To have what we would have, we speak not what
we mean.
II, iv, 118

16 The miserable have no other medicine
But only hope.
III, i, 2

17 Be absolute for death.
III, i, 5

18　　A breath thou art,
Servile to all the skyey influences.
III, i, 8

19　　Thou hast nor youth nor age;
But, as it were, an after-dinner's sleep,
Dreaming on both; for all thy blessed youth
Becomes as aged, and doth beg the alms
Of palsied eld; and when thou art old and rich,
Thou hast neither heat, affection, limb, nor beauty,
To make thy riches pleasant.
III, i, 32

20 The sense of death is most in apprehension,
And the poor beetle, that we tread upon,
In corporal sufferance finds a pang as great
As when a giant dies.
III, i, 76

21　　If I must die,
I will encounter darkness as a bride,
And hug it in my arms.
III, i, 81

22 The cunning livery of hell.
III, i, 93

23 Ay, but to die, and go we know not where;
To lie in cold obstruction and to rot;
This sensible warm motion to become
A kneaded clod; and the delighted spirit
To bathe in fiery floods, or to reside
In thrilling region of thick-ribbed ice;
To be imprison'd in the viewless winds,
And blown with restless violence round about
The pendant world.
III, i, 116

24 The weariest and most loathed worldly life
That age, ache, penury, and imprisonment
Can lay on nature is a paradise
To what we fear of death.
III, i, 127

25　　The hand that hath made you fair hath made
you good.
III, i, 182

26　　Virtue is bold, and goodness never fearful.
III, i, 214

27　　There, at the moated grange, resides this dejected Mariana.[1]
III, i, 279

28　　This news is old enough, yet it is every day's
news.
III, ii, 249

29 He, who the sword of heaven will bear
Should be as holy as severe.
III, ii, 283

30 O, what may man within him hide,
Though angel on the outward side!
III, ii, 293

31 Take, O take those lips away,
That so sweetly were forsworn;
And those eyes, the break of day,

---

[1]"Mariana in the moated grange." — *Motto used by* TENNYSON
for the poem Mariana [1830]

Lights that do mislead the morn:
But my kisses bring again, bring again,
Seals of love, but seal'd in vain, seal'd in vain.[1]
Measure for Measure, IV, i, 1

1   Music oft hath such a charm
To make bad good, and good provoke to harm.
IV, i, 16

2   Every true man's apparel fits your thief.
IV, ii, 46

3   The old fantastical duke of dark corners.
IV, iii, 167

4   I am a kind of burr; I shall stick.
IV, iii, 193

5 We would, and we would not.   *IV, iv, 37*

6 A forted residence 'gainst the tooth of time
And razure of oblivion.   *V, i, 12*

7   Truth is truth
To the end of reckoning.   *V, i, 45*

8 Neither maid, widow, nor wife.   *V, i, 173*

9 Haste still pays haste, and leisure answers leisure,
Like doth quit like, and Measure still for Measure.
V, i, 411

10 They say best men are molded out of faults,
And, for the most, become much more the better
For being a little bad.   *V, i, 440*

11 What's mine is yours, and what is yours is mine.
V, i, 539

12 Horribly stuff'd with epithets of war.
Othello [1604–1605], act I, sc. i, l. 14

13 A fellow almost damn'd in a fair wife.   *I, i, 21*

14 The bookish theoric.   *I, i, 24*

15 We cannot all be masters.   *I, i, 43*

16 And when he's old, cashier'd.   *I, i, 48*

17 In following him, I follow but myself.   *I, i, 58*

18 But I will wear my heart upon my sleeve
For daws to peck at.   *I, i, 64*

19   An old black ram
Is tupping your white ewe.   *I, i, 88*

20   You are one of those that will not serve God if
the devil bid you.   *I, i, 108*

21   Your daughter and the Moor are now making
the beast with two backs.   *I, i, 117*

22 Keep up your bright swords, for the dew will rust
them.   *I, ii, 59*

23 The wealthy curled darlings of our nation.
I, ii, 68

24   The bloody book of law
You shall yourself read in the bitter letter
After your own sense.   *I, iii, 67*

25   Rude am I in my speech,
And little bless'd with the soft phrase of peace.
I, iii, 81

26   Little shall I grace my cause
In speaking for myself. Yet, by your gracious patience,
I will a round unvarnish'd tale deliver
Of my whole course of love.   *I, iii, 88*

27   A maiden never bold;
Of spirit so still and quiet, that her motion
Blush'd at herself.   *I, iii, 94*

28 Still question'd me the story of my life
From year to year, the battles, sieges, fortunes
That I have pass'd.   *I, iii, 129*

29 Wherein I spake of most disastrous chances,
Of moving accidents by flood and field,
Of hair-breadth 'scapes i' the imminent deadly
breach.   *I, iii, 134*

30 Hills whose heads touch heaven.   *I, iii, 141*

31 And of the Cannibals that each other eat,
The Anthropophagi, and men whose heads
Do grow beneath their shoulders.   *I, iii, 143*

32   My story being done,
She gave me for my pains a world of sighs:
She swore, in faith, 'twas strange, 'twas passing
strange;
'Twas pitiful, 'twas wondrous pitiful:
She wish'd she had not heard it, yet she wish'd
That heaven had made her such a man; she
thank'd me,
And bade me, if I had a friend that lov'd her,
I should but teach him how to tell my story,
And that would woo her. Upon this hint I spake:
She lov'd me for the dangers I had pass'd,
And I lov'd her that she did pity them.
This only is the witchcraft I have us'd.
I, iii, 158

33 I do perceive here a divided duty.   *I, iii, 181*

34 To mourn a mischief that is past and gone
Is the next way to draw new mischief on.
I, iii, 204

---

[1]This song occurs in act V, sc. ii, of JOHN FLETCHER'S *Bloody Brother* [c. 1616], with an additional stanza:
Hide, O hide those hills of snow, / Which thy frozen bosom bears, / On whose tops the pinks that grow / Are of those that April wears! / But first set my poor heart free, / Bound in those icy chains by thee.

1 The robb'd that smiles steals something from the thief. *I, iii, 208*

2 Our bodies are our gardens, to the which our wills are gardeners. *I, iii, 324*

3 Put money in thy purse. *I, iii, 345*

4 The food that to him now is as luscious as locusts, shall be to him shortly as bitter as coloquintida. *I, iii, 354*

5 Framed to make women false. *I, iii, 404*

6 The enchafed flood. *II, i, 17*

7 One that excels the quirks of blazoning pens. *II, i, 63*

8 You are pictures out of doors,
Bells in your parlors, wildcats in your kitchens,
Saints in your injuries, devils being offended,
Players in your housewifery, and housewives in your beds. *II, i, 109*

9 For I am nothing if not critical. *II, i, 119*

10 I am not merry, but I do beguile
The thing I am by seeming otherwise. *II, i, 122*

11 She that was ever fair and never proud,
Had tongue at will and yet was never loud. *II, i, 148*

12 *Iago:* To suckle fools and chronicle small beer.
Desdemona: O most lame and impotent conclusion! *II, i, 160*

13 You may relish him more in the soldier than in the scholar. *II, i, 165*

14 If it were now to die,
'Twere now to be most happy. *II, i, 192*

15 Base men being in love have then a nobility in their natures more than is native to them. *II, i, 218*

16 Egregiously an ass. *II, i, 321*

17 I have very poor and unhappy brains for drinking. *II, iii, 34*

18 Potations pottle deep. *II, iii, 57*

19 Well, God's above all; and there be souls must be saved, and there be souls must not be saved. *II, iii, 106*

20 Silence that dreadful bell! it frights the isle
From her propriety. *II, iii, 177*

21 But men are men; the best sometimes forget. *II, iii, 243*

22 Thy honesty and love doth mince this matter. *II, iii, 249*

23 Reputation, reputation, reputation! O! I have lost my reputation. I have lost the immortal part of myself, and what remains is bestial. *II, iii, 264*

24 Reputation is an idle and most false imposition; oft got without merit, and lost without deserving. *II, iii, 270*

25 O thou invisible spirit of wine! if thou hast no name to be known by, let us call thee devil! *II, iii, 285*

26 O God! that men should put an enemy in their mouths to steal away their brains; that we should, with joy, pleasance, revel, and applause, transform ourselves into beasts. *II, iii, 293*

27 Good wine is a good familiar creature if it be well used. *II, iii, 315*

28 Play the villain. *II, iii, 345*

29 How poor are they that have not patience!
What wound did ever heal but by degrees? *II, iii, 379*

30 Excellent wretch! Perdition catch my soul
But I do love thee! and when I love thee not,
Chaos is come again. *III, iii, 90*

31 Men should be what they seem. *III, iii, 126*

32 Speak to me as to thy thinkings,
As thou dost ruminate, and give thy worst of thoughts
The worst of words. *III, iii, 131*

33 Good name in man and woman, dear my lord,
Is the immediate jewel of their souls:
Who steals my purse steals trash; 'tis something, nothing;
'Twas mine, 'tis his, and has been slave to thousands;
But he that filches from me my good name
Robs me of that which not enriches him,
And makes me poor indeed. *III, iii, 155*

34 O! beware, my lord, of jealousy;
It is the green-ey'd monster which doth mock
The meat it feeds on; that cuckold lives in bliss
Who, certain of his fate, loves not his wronger;
But, O! what damned minutes tells he o'er
Who dotes, yet doubts; suspects, yet soundly loves! *III, iii, 165*

35 Poor and content is rich, and rich enough. *III, iii, 172*

36 Think'st thou I'd make a life of jealousy,
To follow still the changes of the moon
With fresh suspicions? No; to be once in doubt
Is once to be resolved. *III, iii, 177*

1 I humbly do beseech you of your pardon
For too much loving you.   *Othello, III, iii, 212*

2   If I do prove her haggard,
Though that her jesses were my dear heart-strings,
I'd whistle her off and let her down the wind,
To prey at fortune.   *III, iii, 260*

3   I am declin'd
Into the vale of years.   *III, iii, 265*

4   O curse of marriage!
That we can call these delicate creatures ours,
And not their appetites. I had rather be a toad,
And live upon the vapor of a dungeon,
Than keep a corner in the thing I love
For others' uses.   *III, iii, 268*

5   Trifles light as air
Are to the jealous confirmations strong
As proofs of holy writ.   *III, iii, 323*

6   Not poppy, nor mandragora,
Nor all the drowsy syrups of the world,
Shall ever medicine thee to that sweet sleep
Which thou ow'dst yesterday.   *III, iii, 331*

7 He that is robb'd, not wanting what is stol'n,
Let him not know 't and he's not robb'd at all.
        III, iii, 343

8   O! now, forever
Farewell the tranquil mind; farewell content!
Farewell the plumed troop and the big wars
That make ambition virtue! O, farewell!
Farewell the neighing steed, and the shrill trump,
The spirit-stirring drum, the ear-piercing fife,
The royal banner, and all quality,
Pride, pomp, and circumstance of glorious war!
And, O you mortal engines, whose rude throats
The immortal Jove's dread clamors counterfeit,
Farewell! Othello's occupation's gone!
        III, iii, 348

9 Be sure of it; give me the ocular proof.
        III, iii, 361

10   No hinge nor loop
To hang a doubt on.   *III, iii, 366*

11 On horror's head horrors accumulate.
        III, iii, 371

12   Take note, take note, O world!
To be direct and honest is not safe.
        III, iii, 378

13 But this denoted a foregone conclusion.
        III, iii, 429

14   Swell, bosom, with thy fraught,
For 'tis of aspics' tongues!   *III, iii, 450*

15   Like to the Pontick sea,
Whose icy current and compulsive course

Ne'er feels retiring ebb, but keeps due on
To the Propontic and the Hellespont,
Even so my bloody thoughts, with violent pace,
Shall ne'er look back, ne'er ebb to humble love,
Till that a capable and wide revenge
Swallow them up.   *III, iii, 454*

16 Our new heraldry is hands not hearts.
        III, iv, 48

17 But jealous souls will not be answer'd so;
They are not ever jealous for the cause,
But jealous for they are jealous; 'tis a monster
Begot upon itself, born on itself.
        III, iv, 158

18   'Tis the strumpet's plague
To beguile many and be beguil'd by one.
        IV, i, 97

19   They laugh that win.   *IV, i, 123*

20   My heart is turned to stone; I strike it, and it
hurts my hand. O! the world hath not a sweeter
creature; she might lie by an emperor's side and
command him tasks.   *IV, i, 190*

21   O, she will sing the savageness out of a bear.
        IV, i, 198

22   But yet the pity of it, Iago! O! Iago, the pity of
it, Iago!   *IV, i, 205*

23   Is this the noble nature
Whom passion could not shake? whose solid virtue
The shot of accident nor dart of chance
Could neither graze nor pierce?   *IV, i, 276*

24 I understand a fury in your words,
But not the words.   *IV, ii, 31*

25 Steep'd me in poverty to the very lips.
        IV, ii, 49

26   But, alas! to make me
A fixed figure for the time of scorn
To point his slow and moving finger at.
        IV, ii, 52

27 Patience, thou young and rose-lipp'd cherubin.
        IV, ii, 62

28   O thou weed!
Who art so lovely fair and smell'st so sweet
That the sense aches at thee, would thou hadst
        ne'er been born.   *IV, ii, 66*

29 O heaven! that such companions thou'dst unfold,
And put in every honest hand a whip
To lash the rascals naked through the world.
        IV, ii, 141

30   Unkindness may do much;
And his unkindness may defeat my life,
But never taint my love.   *IV, ii, 159*

1 The poor soul sat sighing by a sycamore tree,
   Sing all a green willow;
   Her hand on her bosom, her head on her knee,
   Sing willow, willow, willow.   *IV, iii, 41*

2 It makes us, or it mars us.   *V, i, 4*

3 Every way makes my gain.   *V, i, 14*

4 He hath a daily beauty in his life.   *V, i, 19*

5   This is the night
   That either makes me or fordoes me quite.
                                    V, i, 128

6 And smooth as monumental alabaster.   *V, ii, 5*

7 Put out the light, and then put out the light:
   If I quench thee, thou flaming minister,
   I can again thy former light restore,
   Should I repent me; but once put out thy light,
   Thou cunning'st pattern of excelling nature,
   I know not where is that Promethean heat
   That can thy light relume.   *V, ii, 7*

8 It is the very error of the moon;
   She comes more near the earth than she was wont,
   And makes men mad.   *V, ii, 107*

9 She was as false as water.   *V, ii, 132*

10 Curse his better angel from his side,
   And fall to reprobation.   *V, ii, 206*

11 Here is my journey's end, here is my butt,
   And very sea-mark of my utmost sail.   *V, ii, 266*

12 An honorable murderer, if you will;
   For nought I did in hate, but all in honor.
                                    V, ii, 293

13 I have done the state some service, and they know 't;
   No more of that. I pray you, in your letters,
   When you shall these unlucky deeds relate,
   Speak of me as I am; nothing extenuate,
   Nor set down aught in malice: then, must you speak
   Of one that lov'd not wisely but too well;
   Of one not easily jealous, but, being wrought,
   Perplex'd in the extreme; of one whose hand,
   Like the base Indian, threw a pearl away
   Richer than all his tribe; of one whose subdu'd eyes
   Albeit unused to the melting mood,
   Drop tears as fast as the Arabian trees
   Their med'cinable gum.   *V, ii, 338*

14   In Aleppo once,
   Where a malignant and a turban'd Turk
   Beat a Venetian and traduc'd the state,
   I took by the throat the circumcised dog,
   And smote him thus.   *V, ii, 354*

15   My love's
   More richer than my tongue.
                    King Lear [1605], act I, sc. i, l. 79

16   Now, our joy,
   Although our last, not least.   *I, i, 84*

17 Nothing will come of nothing.   *I, i, 92*

18   Mend your speech a little,
   Lest you may mar your fortunes.   *I, i, 96*

19 *Lear:* So young, and so untender?
   Cordelia: So young, my lord, and true.   *I, i, 108*

20 Come not between the dragon and his wrath.
                                    I, i, 124

21 Kill thy physician, and the fee bestow
   Upon the foul disease.   *I, i, 166*

22   I want that glib and oily art
   To speak and purpose not.   *I, i, 227*

23 A still-soliciting eye.   *I, i, 234*

24 Time shall unfold what plighted cunning hides;
   Who covers faults, at last shame them derides.
                                    I, i, 282

25   The infirmity of his age.   *I, i, 296*

26 Who in the lusty stealth of nature take
   More composition and fierce quality
   Than doth, within a dull, stale, tired bed,
   Go to the creating a whole tribe of fops.
                                    I, ii, 11

27 Now, gods, stand up for bastards!   *I, ii, 22*

28   We have seen the best of our time: machinations,
   hollowness, treachery, and all ruinous disorders, follow us disquietly to our graves.   *I, ii, 125*

29   This is the excellent foppery of the world, that,
   when we are sick in fortune,—often the surfeit of
   our own behavior,—we make guilty of our disasters
   the sun, the moon, and the stars; as if we were villains
   by necessity, fools by heavenly compulsion, knaves,
   thieves, and treachers by spherical predominance,
   drunkards, liars, and adulterers by an enforced obedience of planetary influence.   *I, ii, 129*

30   Edgar—

       [Enter Edgar]
   and pat he comes, like the catastrophe of the old
   comedy: my cue is villainous melancholy, with a sigh
   like Tom o' Bedlam.   *I, ii, 149*

31 *Lear:* Dost thou know me, fellow?
   Kent: No, sir, but you have that in your counte-
   nance which I would fain call master.
   Lear: What's that?
   Kent: Authority.   *I, iv, 28*

32   That which ordinary men are fit for, I am qualified in, and the best of me is diligence.
                                    I, iv, 36

1   Truth's a dog must to kennel; he must be whipped out when Lady the brach may stand by the fire and stink.   *King Lear, I, iv, 125*

2 Have more than thou showest,
Speak less than thou knowest,
Lend less than thou owest.   *I, iv, 132*

3   Can you make no use of nothing, nuncle?   *I, iv, 144*

4 Ingratitude, thou marble-hearted fiend,
More hideous, when thou show'st thee in a child,
Than the sea-monster.   *I, iv, 283*

5 How sharper than a serpent's tooth it is
To have a thankless child!   *I, iv, 312*

6 Striving to better, oft we mar what's well.   *I, iv, 371*

7   The son and heir of a mongrel bitch.   *II, ii, 23*

8 I have seen better faces in my time
Than stands on any shoulder that I see
Before me at this instant.   *II, ii, 99*

9 A good man's fortune may grow out at heels.   *II, ii, 164*

10 Fortune, good night, smile once more; turn thy wheel!   *II, ii, 180*

11 *Hysterica passio!* down, thou climbing sorrow!
Thy element's below.   *II, iv, 57*

12 That sir which serves and seeks for gain,
And follows but for form,
Will pack when it begins to rain,
And leave thee in the storm.   *II, iv, 79*

13 Nature in you stands on the very verge
Of her confine.   *II, iv, 149*

14 Necessity's sharp pinch!   *II, iv, 214*

15   Our basest beggars
Are in the poorest thing superfluous:
Allow not nature more than nature needs,
Man's life is cheap as beast's.   *II, iv, 267*

16 Let not women's weapons, waterdrops,
Stain my man's cheeks!   *II, iv, 280*

17 I have full cause of weeping, but this heart
Shall break into a hundred thousand flaws
Or ere I'll weep. O fool! I shall go mad.   *II, iv, 287*

18 Blow, winds, and crack your cheeks! rage! blow!
You cataracts and hurricanoes, spout
Till you have drench'd our steeples, drown'd the cocks!
You sulphurous and thought-executing fires,

Vaunt-couriers to oak-cleaving thunderbolts,
Singe my white head! And thou, all-shaking thunder,
Strike flat the thick rotundity o' the world!
Crack nature's molds, all germens spill at once
That make ingrateful man!   *III, ii, 1*

19 I tax not you, you elements, with unkindness.   *III, ii, 16*

20 A poor, infirm, weak, and despis'd old man.   *III, ii, 20*

21   There was never yet fair woman but she made mouths in a glass.   *III, ii, 35*

22 I will be the pattern of all patience.   *III, ii, 37*

23   I am a man
More sinn'd against than sinning.   *III, ii, 59*

24 The art of our necessities is strange,
That can make vile things precious.   *III, ii, 70*

25 He that has and a little tiny wit,
With hey, ho, the wind and the rain,
Must make content with his fortunes fit,
Though the rain it raineth every day.   *III, ii, 76*

26 O! that way madness lies; let me shun that.   *III, iv, 21*

27 Poor naked wretches, wheresoe'er you are,
That bide the pelting of this pitiless storm,
How shall your houseless heads and unfed sides,
Your loop'd and window'd raggedness, defend you
From seasons such as these? O! I have ta'en
Too little care of this. Take physic, pomp;
Expose thyself to feel what wretches feel,
That thou mayst shake the superflux to them,
And show the heavens more just.   *III, iv, 28*

28 Pillicock sat on Pillicock-hill:
Halloo, halloo, loo, loo!   *III, iv, 75*

29   Out-paramoured the Turk.   *III, iv, 91*

30   Is man no more than this? Consider him well. Thou owest the worm no silk, the beast no hide, the sheep no wool, the cat no perfume. Ha! here's three on 's are sophisticated; thou art the thing itself; unaccommodated man is no more but such a poor, bare, forked animal as thou art. Off, off, you lendings! Come; unbutton here.   *III, iv, 105*

31   'Tis a naughty night to swim in.   *III, iv, 113*

32   The green mantle of the standing pool.   *III, iv, 137*

33 But mice and rats and such small deer
Have been Tom's food for seven long year.   *III, iv, 142*

1 The prince of darkness is a gentleman.[1]

III, iv, 147

2 Poor Tom's a-cold.   *III, iv, 151*

3 Child Rowland to the dark tower came,[2]
His word was still, Fie, foh, and fum,
I smell the blood of a British man.

III, iv, 185

4   He's mad that trusts in the tameness of a wolf, a
horse's health, a boy's love, or a whore's oath.

III, vi, 20

5   The little dogs and all,
Tray, Blanch, and Sweetheart, see, they bark at me.

III, vi, 65

6   Is there any cause in nature that makes these
hard hearts?   *III, vi, 81*

7 I am tied to the stake, and I must stand the course.

III, vii, 54

8 Out, vile jelly!   *III, vii, 83*

9 The lowest and most dejected thing of fortune.

IV, i, 3

10   The worst is not,
So long as we can say, "This is the worst."

IV, i, 27

11 As flies to wanton boys, are we to the gods;
They kill us for their sport.   *IV, i, 36*

12 You are not worth the dust which the rude wind
Blows in your face.   *IV, ii, 30*

13 She that herself will sliver and disbranch
From her material sap, perforce must wither
And come to deadly use.   *IV, ii, 34*

14 Wisdom and goodness to the vile seem vile;
Filths savor but themselves.   *IV, ii, 38*

15 Tigers, not daughters.   *IV, ii, 39*

16   It is the stars,
The stars above us, govern our conditions.

IV, iii, 34

17 Our foster-nurse of nature is repose.   *IV, iv, 12*

18   How fearful
And dizzy 'tis to cast one's eyes so low!
The crows and choughs that wing the midway air
Show scarce so gross as beetles; halfway down

---

[1]The Devil is a gentleman.—PERCY BYSSHE SHELLEY, *Peter Bell the Third* [1819], *pt. II, st. 2*

[2]Child Roland to the dark tower came.—SIR WALTER SCOTT, *The Bridal of Triermain* [1813]
Dauntless the slug-horn to my lips I set, / And blew. *"Childe Roland to the Dark Tower came."*—ROBERT BROWNING, *Child Roland to the Dark Tower Came* [1855], *st. 34*

Hangs one that gathers samphire, dreadful trade!
Methinks he seems no bigger than his head.
The fishermen that walk upon the beach
Appear like mice, and yond tall anchoring bark
Diminish'd to her cock, her cock a buoy
Almost too small for sight. The murmuring surge,
That on the unnumber'd idle pebbles chafes,
Cannot be heard so high.   *IV, vi, 12*

19   Nature's above art in that respect.

IV, vi, 87

20 Ay, every inch a king.   *IV, vi, 110*

21 The wren goes to 't, and the small gilded fly
Does lecher in my sight.
Let copulation thrive.   *IV, vi, 115*

22   Give me an ounce of civet, good apothecary, to
sweeten my imagination.   *IV, vi, 133*

23   A man may see how this world goes with no eyes.
Look with thine ears: see how yond justice rails upon
yon simple thief. Hark, in thine ear: change places;
and, handy-dandy, which is the justice, which is the
thief?   *IV, vi, 154*

24 Through tatter'd clothes small vices do appear;
Robes and furr'd gowns hide all. Plate sin with
gold,
And the strong lance of justice hurtless breaks;
Arm it in rags, a pigmy's straw does pierce it.

IV, vi, 169

25   Get thee glass eyes;
And, like a scurvy politician, seem
To see the things thou dost not.   *IV, vi, 175*

26 When we are born, we cry that we are come
To this great stage of fools.   *IV, vi, 187*

27 Then, kill, kill, kill, kill, kill, kill!   *IV, vi, 192*

28   Mine enemy's dog,
Though he had bit me, should have stood that
night
Against my fire.   *IV, vii, 36*

29 Thou art a soul in bliss; but I am bound
Upon a wheel of fire, that mine own tears
Do scald like molten lead.   *IV, vii, 46*

30 I am a very foolish fond old man,
Fourscore and upward, not an hour more or less;
And, to deal plainly,
I fear I am not in my perfect mind.

IV, vii, 60

31 Pray you now, forget and forgive.

IV, vii, 84

32   Men must endure
Their going hence, even as their coming hither:
Ripeness is all.   *V, ii, 9*

1 Come, let's away to prison;
We two alone will sing like birds i' the cage:
When thou dost ask me blessing, I'll kneel down,
And ask of thee forgiveness: so we'll live,
And pray, and sing, and tell old tales, and laugh
At gilded butterflies, and hear poor rogues
Talk of court news; and we'll talk with them too,
Who loses and who wins; who's in, who's out;
And take upon's the mystery of things,
As if we were God's spies: and we'll wear out,
In a wall'd prison, packs and sets of great ones
That ebb and flow by the moon.
        King Lear, V, iii, 8

2 Upon such sacrifices, my Cordelia,
The gods themselves throw incense. *V, iii, 20*

3 The gods are just, and of our pleasant vices
Make instruments to plague us. *V, iii, 172*

4 The wheel is come full circle. *V, iii, 176*

5 Howl, howl, howl, howl! O! you are men of stones:
Had I your tongues and eyes, I'd use them so
That heaven's vaults should crack. She's gone
  forever.   *V, iii, 259*

6 Her voice was ever soft,
Gentle and low, an excellent thing in woman.
         V, iii, 274

7 And my poor fool is hang'd! No, no, no life!
Why should a dog, a horse, a rat, have life,
And thou no breath at all? Thou'lt come no more,
Never, never, never, never, never!
Pray you, undo this button. *V, iii, 307*

8 Vex not his ghost: O! let him pass; he hates him
That would upon the rack of this tough world
Stretch him out longer. *V, iii, 315*

9 The weight of this sad time we must obey;
Speak what we feel, not what we ought to say.
The oldest hath borne most: we that are young,
Shall never see so much, nor live so long.
         V, iii, 325

10 'Tis not enough to help the feeble up,
But to support him after.
  *Timon of Athens [1605–1608], act I, sc. i, l.
  108*

11 I call the gods to witness. *I, i, 138*

12 I wonder men dare trust themselves with men.
         I, ii, 45

13 Here's that which is too weak to be a sinner,
Honest water, which ne'er left man i' the mire.[1]
         I, ii, 60

---

[1]Inscribed on the drinking fountain in the market square of Stratford-on-Avon.

14 Immortal gods, I crave no pelf;
I pray for no man but myself:
Grant I may never prove so fond,
To trust man on his oath or bond. *I, ii, 64*

15 Men shut their doors against a setting sun.
         I, ii, 152

16 Every man has his fault, and honesty is his.
         III, i, 30

17 Nothing emboldens sin so much as mercy.
         III, v, 3

18 You fools of fortune, trencher-friends, time's flies.
         III, vi, 107

19 We have seen better days. *IV, ii, 27*

20 O! the fierce wretchedness that glory brings us.
         IV, ii, 30

21 I am Misanthropos, and hate mankind.
         IV, iii, 53

22 Life's uncertain voyage. *V, i, 207*

23 *First Witch:* When shall we three meet again
In thunder, lightning, or in rain?
Second Witch: When the hurlyburly's done,
When the battle's lost and won.
    Macbeth [1606], act 1, sc. i, l. 1

24 Fair is foul, and foul is fair:
Hover through the fog and filthy air. *I, i, 12*

25 Banners flout the sky. *I, ii, 50*

26 A sailor's wife had chestnuts in her lap,
And munch'd, and munch'd, and munch'd: "Give
  me," quoth I:
"Aroint thee, witch!" the rump-fed ronyon cries.
         I, iii, 4

27 Sleep shall neither night nor day
Hang upon his pent-house lid. *I, iii, 19*

28 Dwindle, peak, and pine. *I, iii, 23*

29 The weird sisters, hand in hand,
Posters of the sea and land,
Thus do go about, about:
Thrice to thine, and thrice to mine,
And thrice again, to make up nine.
Peace! The charm's wound up. *I, iii, 32*

30 So foul and fair a day I have not seen. *I, iii, 38*

31 If you can look into the seeds of time,
And say which grain will grow and which will not,
Speak.   *I, iii, 58*

32 And to be king
Stands not within the prospect of belief.
         I, iii, 73

1 The earth hath bubbles, as the water has,
And these are of them. *I, iii, 79*

2 Or have we eaten on the insane root
That takes the reason prisoner? *I, iii, 84*

3 And oftentimes, to win us to our harm,
The instruments of darkness tell us truths,
Win us with honest trifles, to betray 's
In deepest consequence. *I, iii, 123*

4 As happy prologues to the swelling act
Of the imperial theme. *I, iii, 128*

5   I am Thane of Cawdor:
If good, why do I yield to that suggestion
Whose horrid image doth unfix my hair
And make my seated heart knock at my ribs,
Against the use of nature? Present fears
Are less than horrible imaginings. *I, iii, 134*

6 If chance will have me king, why, chance may
      crown me,
Without my stir. *I, iii, 143*

7   Come what come may,
Time and the hour runs through the roughest day.
I, iii, 146

8   Nothing in his life
Became him like the leaving it; he died
As one that had been studied in his death
To throw away the dearest thing he ow'd,
As 'twere a careless trifle. *I, iv, 7*

9   There's no art
To find the mind's construction in the face:
He was a gentleman on whom I built
An absolute trust. *I, iv, 11*

10 Glamis thou art, and Cawdor; and shalt be
What thou art promis'd. Yet do I fear thy nature;
It is too full o' the milk of human kindness[1]
To catch the nearest way. *I, v, 16*

11   The raven himself is hoarse
That croaks the fatal entrance of Duncan
Under my battlements. Come, you spirits
That tend on mortal thoughts! unsex me here,
And fill me from the crown to the toe top full
Of direst cruelty; make thick my blood,
Stop up the access and passage to remorse,
That no compunctious visitings of nature
Shake my fell purpose, nor keep peace between
The effect and it! Come to my woman's breasts,
And take my milk for gall, you murdering
      ministers. *I, v, 38*

---

[1]The thunder of your words has soured the milk of human kindness in my heart.—RICHARD BRINSLEY SHERIDAN, *The Rivals* [1775], *act III, sc. iv*

12 Nor heaven peep through the blanket of the dark,
To cry, "Hold, hold!" *I, v, 54*

13 Your face, my thane, is as a book where men
May read strange matters. *I, v, 63*

14   Look like the innocent flower,
But be the serpent under 't. *I, v, 66*

15 *Duncan:* This castle hath a pleasant seat; the air
Nimbly and sweetly recommends itself
Unto our gentle senses.
Banquo: This guest of summer,
The temple-haunting martlet, does approve
By his lov'd mansionry that the heaven's breath
Smells wooingly here: no jutty, frieze,
Buttress, nor coign of vantage, but this bird
Hath made his pendent bed and procreant cradle:
Where they most breed and haunt, I have observ'd
The air is delicate. *I, vi, 1*

16 If it were done when 'tis done, then 'twere well
It were done quickly; if the assassination
Could trammel up the consequence, and catch
With his surcease success; that but this blow
Might be the be-all and the end-all here,
But here, upon this bank and shoal of time,
We'd jump the life to come. *I, vii, 1*

17 This even-handed justice. *I, vii, 10*

18   Besides, this Duncan
Hath borne his faculties so meek, hath been
So clear in his great office, that his virtues
Will plead like angels trumpet-tongu'd against
The deep damnation of his taking-off;
And pity, like a naked new-born babe,
Striding the blast, or heaven's cherubin, hors'd
Upon the sightless couriers of the air,
Shall blow the horrid deed in every eye,
That tears shall drown the wind. I have no spur
To prick the sides of my intent, but only
Vaulting ambition, which o'erleaps itself
And falls on the other. *I, vii, 16*

19   I have bought
Golden opinions from all sorts of people.
I, vii, 32

20 Letting "I dare not" wait upon "I would,"
Like the poor cat i' the adage. *I, vii, 44*

21 I dare do all that may become a man;
Who dares do more is none. *I, vii, 46*

22   Nor time nor place
Did then adhere. *I, vii, 51*

23   I have given suck, and know
How tender 'tis to love the babe that milks me:
I would, while it was smiling in my face,
Have pluck'd my nipple from his boneless gums,

And dash'd the brains out, had I so sworn as you
Have done to this.   *Macbeth, I, vii, 54*

1 *Macbeth:* If we should fail—
  Lady Macbeth: We fail!
But screw your courage to the sticking-place,
And we'll not fail.   *I, vii, 59*

2 Memory, the warder of the brain.   *I, vii, 65*

3 Away, and mock the time with fairest show:
False face must hide what the false heart doth
              know.   *I, vii, 81*

4 The moon is down.   *III i, 2*

5   There's husbandry in heaven;
Their candles are all out.   *II, i, 4*

6   Merciful powers!
Restrain in me the cursed thoughts that nature
Gives way to in repose.   *II, i, 7*

7   Shut up
In measureless content.   *II, i, 16*

8 Is this a dagger which I see before me,
The handle toward my hand? Come, let me clutch
              thee:
I have thee not, and yet I see thee still.
Art thou not, fatal vision, sensible
To feeling as to sight? or art thou but
A dagger of the mind, a false creation,
Proceeding from the heat-oppressed brain?
                                    II, i, 33

9   Now o'er the one half-world
Nature seems dead, and wicked dreams abuse
The curtain'd sleep; witchcraft celebrates
Pale Hecate's offerings.   *II, i, 49*

10   Thou sure and firm-set earth,
Hear not my steps, which way they walk, for fear
The very stones prate of my whereabout.
                                    II, i, 56

11   The bell invites me.
Hear it not, Duncan; for it is a knell
That summons thee to heaven or to hell.
                                    II, i, 62

12 It was the owl that shriek'd, the fatal bellman,
Which gives the stern'st good-night. *II, ii, 4*

13   The attempt and not the deed
Confounds us.   *II, ii, 12*

14   Had he not resembled
My father as he slept I had done 't. *II, ii, 14*

15 I had most need of blessing, and "Amen"
Stuck in my throat.   *II, ii, 33*

16 Methought I heard a voice cry "Sleep no more!
Macbeth does murder sleep," the innocent sleep,

Sleep that knits up the ravell'd sleave of care,
The death of each day's life, sore labor's bath,
Balm of hurt minds, great nature's second course,
Chief nourisher in life's feast.
                                    II, ii, 36

17 Glamis hath murder'd sleep, and therefore Cawdor
Shall sleep no more, Macbeth shall sleep no more!
                                    II, ii, 43

18   Infirm of purpose!
Give me the daggers. The sleeping and the dead
Are but as pictures; 'tis the eye of childhood
That fears a painted devil.   *II, ii, 53*

19 Will all great Neptune's ocean wash this blood
Clean from my hand? No, this my hand will rather
The multitudinous seas incarnadine,
Making the green one red.   *II, ii, 61*

20   The primrose way to the everlasting bonfire.
                                    II, iii, 22

21   It [drink] provokes the desire, but it takes away
the performance.   *II, iii, 34*

22 The labor we delight in physics pain.
                                    II, iii, 56

23 Confusion now hath made his masterpiece!
Most sacrilegious murder hath broke ope
The Lord's anointed temple, and stole thence
The life o' the building!   *II, iii, 72*

24 Shake off this downy sleep, death's counterfeit.
                                    II, iii, 83

25 Had I but died an hour before this chance
I had liv'd a blessed time; for, from this instant,
There's nothing serious in mortality,
All is but toys; renown and grace is dead,
The wine of life is drawn, and the mere lees
Is left this vault to brag of.   *II, iii, 98*

26 Who can be wise, amaz'd, temperate and furious,
Loyal and neutral, in a moment? No man.
                                    II, iii, 115

27 To show an unfelt sorrow is an office
Which the false man does easy.   *II, iii, 143*

28 A falcon, towering in her pride of place,
Was by a mousing owl hawk'd at and kill'd.
                                    II, iv, 12

29 I must become a borrower of the night
For a dark hour or twain.   *III, i, 27*

30   To be thus is nothing;
But to be safely thus.   *III, i, 48*

31 *Murderer:*   We are men, my liege.
Macbeth: Ay, in the catalogue ye go for men.
                                    III, i, 91

1   I am one, my liege,
Whom the vile blows and buffets of the world
Have so incens'd that I am reckless what
I do to spite the world.   *III, i, 108*

2 So weary with disasters, tugg'd with fortune,
That I would set my life on any chance,
To mend it or be rid on 't.   *III, i, 112*

3   Things without all remedy
Should be without regard: what's done is done.
      III, ii, 11

4 We have scotch'd the snake, not kill'd it.
      III, ii, 13

5   Duncan is in his grave;
After life's fitful fever he sleeps well;
Treason has done his worst: nor steel, nor poison,
Malice domestic, foreign levy, nothing
Can touch him further.   *III, ii, 22*

6 Then be thou jocund. Ere the bat hath flown
His cloister'd flight, ere, to black Hecate's
      summons
The shard-borne beetle with his drowsy hums
Hath rung night's yawning peal, there shall be
      done
A deed of dreadful note.   *III, ii, 40*

7   Come, seeling night,
Scarf up the tender eye of pitiful day,
And with thy bloody and invisible hand
Cancel and tear to pieces that great bond
Which keeps me pale! Light thickens, and the crow
Makes wing to the rooky wood.   *III, ii, 46*

8 Now spurs the lated traveler apace
To gain the timely inn.   *III, iii, 6*

9 But now I am cabin'd, cribb'd, confin'd, bound in
To saucy doubts and fears.   *III, iv, 24*

10 Now good digestion wait on appetite,
And health on both!   *III, iv, 38*

11 Thou canst not say I did it: never shake
Thy gory locks at me.   *III, iv, 50*

12 The air-drawn dagger.   *III, iv, 62*

13 I drink to the general joy of the whole table.
      III, iv, 89

14   What man dare, I dare:
Approach thou like the rugged Russian bear,
The arm'd rhinoceros, or the Hyrcan tiger;
Take any shape but that, and my firm nerves
Shall never tremble.   *III, iv, 99*

15   Hence, horrible shadow!
Unreal mockery, hence!   *III, iv, 106*

16 Stand not upon the order of your going,
But go at once.   *III, iv, 119*

17 It will have blood, they say; blood will have blood:
Stones have been known to move and trees to
      speak.   *III, iv, 122*

18 *Macbeth:*   What is the night?
Lady Macbeth: Almost at odds with morning, which
      is which.   *III, iv, 126*

19   I am in blood
Stepp'd in so far, that, should I wade no more,
Returning were as tedious as go o'er.
      III, iv, 136

20 Double, double toil and trouble;
Fire burn and cauldron bubble.   *IV, i, 10*

21 Eye of newt, and toe of frog,
Wool of bat, and tongue of dog.   *IV, i, 14*

22 Finger of birth-strangled babe,
Ditch-deliver'd by a drab.   *IV, i, 30*

23 By the pricking of my thumbs,
Something wicked this way comes.
Open, locks,
Whoever knocks!   *IV, i, 44*

24 How now, you secret, black, and midnight hags!
      IV, i, 48

25 A deed without a name.   *IV, i, 49*

26 Be bloody, bold, and resolute; laugh to scorn
The power of man, for none of woman born
Shall harm Macbeth.   *IV, i, 79*

27 But yet I'll make assurance double sure,
And take a bond of fate.   *IV, i, 83*

28 Macbeth shall never vanquish'd be until
Great Birnam wood to high Dunsinane hill
Shall come against him.[1]   *IV, i, 92*

29 Show his eyes, and grieve his heart;
Come like shadows, so depart.   *IV, i, 110*

30 What! will the line stretch out to the crack of
      doom?   *IV, i, 117*

31   When our actions do not,
Our fears do make us traitors.   *IV, ii, 3*

32 He wants the natural touch.   *IV, ii, 9*

33 Angels are bright still, though the brightest fell.
      IV, iii, 22

34 Pour the sweet milk of concord into hell,
Uproar the universal peace, confound
All unity on earth.   *IV, iii, 98*

35 Give sorrow words; the grief that does not speak
Whispers the o'er-fraught heart and bids it break.
      IV, iii, 209

---

[1]Till Birnam wood remove to Dunsinane / I cannot taint with
fear. — *Macbeth, act V, sc. iii, l. 2*

1   All my pretty ones?
Did you say all? O hell-kite! All?
What! all my pretty chickens and their dam
At one fell swoop?   *Macbeth, IV, iii, 216*

2 *Malcolm:* Dispute it like a man.
Macduff: I shall do so;
But I must also feel it as a man:
I cannot but remember such things were,
That were most precious to me.   *IV, iii, 219*

3   Out, damned spot! out, I say!   *V, i, 38*

4   Fie, my lord, fie! a soldier, and afeard?   *V, i, 40*

5   Who would have thought the old man to have
had so much blood in him?   *V, i, 42*

6   The Thane of Fife had a wife: where is she now?
                                    V, i, 46

7   All the perfumes of Arabia will not sweeten this
little hand.   *V, i, 56*

8 Those he commands move only in command,
Nothing in love; now does he feel his title
Hang loose about him, like a giant's robe
Upon a dwarfish thief.   *V, ii, 19*

9 The devil damn thee black, thou cream-fac'd loon!
Where gott'st thou that goose look?   *V, iii, 11*

10 Thou lily-liver'd boy.   *V, iii, 15*

11 I have liv'd long enough: my way of life
Is fall'n into the sere, the yellow leaf;
And that which should accompany old age,
As honor, love, obedience, troops of friends,
I must not look to have; but, in their stead,
Curses, not loud but deep, mouth-honor, breath,
Which the poor heart would fain deny, and dare
        not.   *V, iii, 22*

12 *Macbeth:* Canst thou not minister to a mind diseas'd,
Pluck from the memory a rooted sorrow,
Raze out the written troubles of the brain,
And with some sweet oblivious antidote
Cleanse the stuff'd bosom of that perilous stuff
Which weighs upon the heart?
Doctor: Therein the patient
Must minister to himself.
Macbeth: Throw physic to the dogs; I'll none of it.
                                    V, iii, 40

13 I would applaud thee to the very echo,
That should applaud again.   *V, iii, 53*

14 Hang out our banners on the outward walls;
The cry is still, "They come"; our castle's strength
Will laugh a siege to scorn.   *V, v, 1*

15   My fell of hair
Would at a dismal treatise rouse and stir
As life were in 't. I have supp'd full with horrors.
                                    V, v, 11

16   She should have died hereafter;
There would have been a time for such a word.
Tomorrow, and tomorrow, and tomorrow,
Creeps in this petty pace from day to day,
To the last syllable of recorded time;
And all our yesterdays have lighted fools
The way to dusty death. Out, out, brief candle!
Life's but a walking shadow, a poor player
That struts and frets his hour upon the stage,
And then is heard no more; it is a tale
Told by an idiot, full of sound and fury,
Signifying nothing.   *V, v, 17*

17 I 'gin to be aweary of the sun,
And wish the estate o' the world were now
        undone.   *V, v, 49*

18   Blow, wind! come, wrack!
At least we'll die with harness on our back.
                                    V, v, 51

19 Why should I play the Roman fool; and die
On mine own sword?
                                    V, vii, 30

20 I bear a charmed life.
                                    V, vii, 41

21   Macduff was from his mother's womb
Untimely ripp'd.   *V, vii, 44*

22 And be these juggling fiends no more believ'd,
That palter with us in a double sense;
That keep the word of promise to our ear
And break it to our hope.   *V, vii, 48*

23 Live to be the show and gaze o' the time.
                                    V, vii, 53

24   Lay on, Macduff,
And damn'd be him that first cries, "Hold,
        enough!"   *V, vii, 62*

25   You shall see in him
The triple pillar of the world transform'd
Into a strumpet's fool.
    *Antony and Cleopatra [1606–1607], act 1, sc.
    i, l. 12*

26 There's beggary in the love that can be reckon'd.
                                    I, i, 15

27 Let Rome in Tiber melt, and the wide arch
Of the rang'd empire fall! Here is my space.
Kingdoms are clay.   *I, i, 33*

28 In nature's infinite book of secrecy
A little I can read.   *I, ii, 11*

29 I love long life better than figs.   *I, ii, 34*

30   On the sudden
A Roman thought hath struck him.
                                    I, ii, 90

1 Eternity was in our lips and eyes,
  Bliss in our brows bent.   *I, iii, 35*

2   Good now, play one scene
  Of excellent dissembling, and let it look
  Like perfect honor.   *I, iii, 78*

3 O! my oblivion is a very Antony,
  And I am all forgotten.   *I, iii, 90*

4 Give me to drink mandragora. . . .
  That I might sleep out this great gap of time
  My Antony is away.   *I, v, 4*

5 O happy horse, to bear the weight of Antony!
                                                       I, v, 21

6 The demi-Atlas of this earth, the arm
  And burgonet of men.   *I, v, 23*

7 Where's my serpent of old Nile?   *I, v, 25*

8 A morsel for a monarch.   *I, v, 31*

9 My man of men.   *I, v, 71*

10   My salad days,
  When I was green in judgment.   *I, v, 73*

11   We, ignorant of ourselves,
  Beg often our own harms, which the wise powers
  Deny us for our good; so find we profit
  By losing of our prayers.   *II, i, 5*

12   Epicurean cooks
  Sharpen with cloyless sauce his appetite.   *II, i, 24*

13 No worse a husband than the best of men.
                                                       II, ii, 135

14 The barge she sat in, like a burnish'd throne,
  Burn'd on the water; the poop was beaten gold,
  Purple the sails, and so perfumed, that
  The winds were love-sick with them; the oars were
      silver,
  Which to the tune of flutes kept stroke, and made
  The water which they beat to follow faster,
  As amorous of their strokes. For her own person,
  It beggar'd all description.   *II, ii, 199*

15 Age cannot wither her, nor custom stale
  Her infinite variety; other women cloy
  The appetites they feed, but she makes hungry
  Where most she satisfies; for vilest things
  Become themselves in her, that the holy priests
  Bless her when she is riggish.   *II, ii, 243*

16 I have not kept my square, but that to come
  Shall all be done by the rule.   *II, iii, 6*

17   I will to Egypt
  And though I make this marriage for my peace,
  I' the East my pleasure lies.   *II, iii, 38*

18   Music, moody food
  Of us that trade in love.   *II, v, 1*

19 Though it be honest, it is never good
  To bring bad news.   *II, v, 85*

20 He will to his Egyptian dish again.   *II, vi, 133*

21 Come, thou monarch of the vine,
  Plumpy Bacchus, with pink eyne!
                                          II, vii, 120

22   Ambition,
  The soldier's virtue.   *III, i, 22*

23 Celerity is never more admir'd
  Than by the negligent.   *III, vii, 24*

24   We have kiss'd away
  Kingdoms and provinces.   *III, viii, 17*

25   He wears the rose
  Of youth upon him.   *III, xi, 20*

26   Men's judgments are
  A parcel of their fortunes, and things outward
  Do draw the inward quality after them,
  To suffer all alike.   *III, xi, 31*

27 I found you as a morsel, cold upon
  Dead Caesar's trencher.   *III, xi, 116*

28 Let's have one other gaudy night.
                                          III, xi, 182

29 Now he'll outstare the lightning. To be furious
  Is to be frighted out of fear.   *III, xi, 194*

30 To business that we love we rise betime,
  And go to 't with delight.   *IV, iv, 20*

31 O infinite virtue! com'st thou smiling from
  The world's great snare uncaught?
                                          IV, viii, 17

32 The shirt of Nessus is upon me.   *IV, x, 56*

33 Sometimes we see a cloud that's dragonish;
  A vapor sometime like a bear or lion,
  A tower'd citadel, a pendant rock,
  A forked mountain, or blue promontory
  With trees upon 't.   *IV, xii, 2*

34 Unarm, Eros; the long day's task is done,
  And we must sleep.   *IV, xii, 35*

35   But I will be
  A bridegroom in my death, and run into 't
  As to a lover's bed.   *IV, xii, 99*

36   O sun!
  Burn the great sphere thou mov'st in; darkling
      stand
  The varying shore o' the world.   *IV, xiii, 10*

37 I am dying, Egypt, dying; only
  I here importune death awhile, until
  Of many thousand kisses the poor last
  I lay upon thy lips.   *IV, xiii, 18*

1 O! wither'd is the garland of the war,
  The soldier's pole is fall'n; young boys and girls
  Are level now with men; the odds is gone,
  And there is nothing left remarkable
  Beneath the visiting moon.

  Antony and Cleopatra, IV, xiii, 64

2 Let's do it after the high Roman fashion,
  And make death proud to take us.   *IV, xiii, 87*

3   And it is great
  To do that thing that ends all other deeds,
  Which shackles accidents, and bolts up change.

  V, ii, 4

4 His legs bestrid the ocean; his rear'd arm
  Crested the world; his voice was propertied
  As all the tuned spheres, and that to friends;
  But when he meant to quail and shake the orb,
  He was as rattling thunder. For his bounty,
  There was no winter in 't, an autumn 'twas
  That grew the more by reaping; his delights
  Were dolphin-like, they show'd his back above
  The element they liv'd in; in his livery
  Walk'd crowns and crownets, realms and islands
    were
  As plates dropp'd from his pocket.

  V, ii, 82

5   The bright day is done,
  And we are for the dark.   *V, ii, 192*

6   The quick comedians
  Extemporally will stage us, and present
  Our Alexandrian revels. Antony
  Shall be brought drunken forth, and I shall see
  Some squeaking Cleopatra boy my greatness
  I' the posture of a whore.

  V, ii, 215

7   A woman is a dish for the gods, if the devil dress
  her not.   *V, ii, 274*

8   I wish you joy of the worm.   *V, ii, 280*

9   I have
  Immortal longings in me.   *V, ii, 282*

10 Husband, I come.   *V, ii, 289*

11 If thou and nature can so gently part,
  The stroke of death is as a lover's pinch,
  Which hurts, and is desir'd.

  V, ii, 296

12 Dost thou not see my baby at my breast,
  That sucks the nurse asleep?

  V, ii, 311

13 Now boast thee, death, in thy possession lies
  A lass unparallel'd.   *V, ii, 317*

14 *First Guard:* . . . Charmian, is this well done?
  Charmian: It is well done, and fitting for a princess
  Descended of so many royal kings.[1]   *V, ii, 327*

15 As she would catch another Antony
  In her strong toil of grace.   *V, ii, 348*

16   The gods sent not
  Corn for the rich men only.

  Coriolanus [1607–1608], act 1, sc. i, l. 213

17   They threw their caps
  As they would hang them on the horns o' the
    moon,
  Shouting their emulation.   *I, i, 218*

18   All the yarn she spun in Ulysses' absence did but
  fill Ithaca full of moths.   *I, iii, 93*

19   Nature teaches beasts to know their friends.

  II, i, 6

20   A cup of hot wine with not a drop of allaying
  Tiber in 't.   *II, i, 52*

21 My gracious silence, hail!   *II, i, 194*

22   He himself stuck not to call us the many-headed
  multitude.   *II, iii, 18*

23   Bid them wash their faces,
  And keep their teeth clean.   *II, iii, 65*

24 I thank you for your voices, thank you,
  Your most sweet voices.   *II, iii, 179*

25 The mutable, rank-scented many.   *III, i, 65*

26 Hear you this Triton of the minnows? mark you
  His absolute "shall"?   *III, i, 88*

27 What is the city but the people?   *III, i, 198*

28 His nature is too noble for the world:
  He would not flatter Neptune for his trident,
  Or Jove for 's power to thunder. His heart's his
    mouth:
  What his breast forges, that his tongue must vent.

  III, i, 254

29   The beast
  With many heads butts me away.   *IV, i, 1*

30   O! a kiss
  Long as my exile, sweet as my revenge!   *V, iii, 44*

31   Chaste as the icicle
  That's curdied by the frost from purest snow,
  And hangs on Dian's temple.   *V, iii, 65*

---

[1]One of the soldiers seeing her, angrily said unto her: is that well
done Charmian? Very well said she again, and meet for a princess
descended of so many noble kings. — PLUTARCH, *Lives;* translated
[1579] by THOMAS NORTH

1 He wants nothing of a god but eternity and a heaven to throne in. *V, iv, 25*

2 They'll give him death by inches. *V, iv, 43*

3 If you have writ your annals true, 'tis there,
That, like an eagle in a dovecote, I
Flutter'd your Volscians in Corioli:
Alone I did it. *V, v, 114*

4 Thou hast done a deed whereat valor will weep.
V, v, 135

5 He shall have a noble memory. *V, v, 155*

6 See, where she comes apparell'd like the spring.
Pericles [1608–1609], act I, sc. i, l. 12

7 Few love to hear the sins they love to act.
I, i, 92

8 The sad companion, dull-ey'd melancholy.
I, ii, 2

9 *Third Fisherman:* . . . Master, I marvel how the fishes live in the sea.
First Fisherman: Why, as men do a-land; the great ones eat up the little ones.[1] *II, i, 29*

10 Lest the bargain should catch cold and starve.
Cymbeline [1609–1610], act I, sc. iv, l. 186

11 Hath his bellyful of fighting.
II, i, 24

12 Hark! hark! the lark at heaven's gate sings,
And Phoebus 'gins arise,
His steeds to water at those springs
On chalic'd flowers that lies;
And winking Mary-buds begin
To ope their golden eyes:
With everything that pretty is,
My lady sweet, arise. *II, iii, 22*

13 As chaste as unsunn'd snow. *II, v, 13*

14 Some griefs are med'cinable. *III, ii, 33*

15 O! for a horse with wings! *III, ii, 49*

16 The game is up. *III, iii, 107*

17 Slander,
Whose edge is sharper than the sword, whose tongue
Outvenoms all the worms of Nile, whose breath
Rides on the posting winds and doth belie
All corners of the world. *III, iv, 35*

18 I have not slept one wink. *III, iv, 103*

19 Weariness
Can snore upon the flint when resty sloth
Finds the down pillow hard. *III, vi, 33*

20 An angel! or, if not,
An earthly paragon! *III, vi, 42*

21 Society is no comfort
To one not sociable. *IV, ii, 12*

22 I wear not
My dagger in my mouth. *IV, ii, 78*

23 Fear no more the heat o' the sun,
Nor the furious winter's rages;
Thou thy worldly task hast done,
Home art gone, and ta'en thy wages;
Golden lads and girls all must,
As chimney-sweepers, come to dust.
IV, ii, 258

24 Quiet consummation have;
And renowned be thy grave! *IV, ii, 280*

25 Fortune brings in some boats that are not steer'd.
IV, iii, 46

26 Hang there like fruit, my soul,
Till the tree die! *V, v, 264*

27 From fairest creatures we desire increase,
That thereby beauty's rose might never die.
Sonnets[2] [1609], 1, l. 1

28 When forty winters shall besiege thy brow,
And dig deep trenches in thy beauty's field.
Sonnet 2, l. 1

29 Thou art thy mother's glass, and she in thee
Calls back the lovely April of her prime.
Sonnet 3, l. 9

30 Music to hear, why hear'st thou music sadly?
Sweets with sweet war not, joy delights in joy.
Sonnet 8, l. 1

---

[2]Most of the sonnets were written before 1598, according to the *Palladis Tamia* [1598] of Francis Meres [1565–1647]. They were published [1609] by THOMAS THORPE, who wrote the dedication:

TO THE ONLIE BEGETTER OF
THESE INSUING SONNETS
MR. W. H., ALL HAPPINESSE
AND THAT ETERNITIE
PROMISED
BY
OUR EVER-LIVING POET
WISHETH
THE WELL-WISHING
ADVENTURER IN
SETTING
FORTH
T.T.

---

[1]Men lived like fishes; the great ones devoured the small. —
ALGERNON SIDNEY, *Discourses on Government* [1698], ch. 2, sec. 18

1   Everything that grows
      Holds in perfection but a little moment.

Sonnet 15, l. 1

2 Shall I compare thee to a summer's day?
  Thou art more lovely and more temperate:
  Rough winds do shake the darling buds of May,
  And summer's lease hath all too short a date.

Sonnet 18, l. 1

3 But thy eternal summer shall not fade.

Sonnet 18, l. 9

4 The painful warrior famoused for fight,
  After a thousand victories, once foil'd,
  Is from the books of honor razed quite,
  And all the rest forgot for which he toil'd.

Sonnet 25, l. 9

5 When in disgrace with fortune and men's eyes
  I all alone beweep my outcast state,
  And trouble deaf heaven with my bootless cries.

Sonnet 29, l. 1

6 Desiring this man's art, and that man's scope,
  With what I most enjoy contented least;
  Yet in these thoughts myself almost despising,
  Haply I think on thee.   *Sonnet 29, l. 7*

7 For thy sweet love remember'd such wealth brings
  That then I scorn to change my state with kings.

Sonnet 29, l. 13

8 When to the sessions of sweet silent thought
  I summon up remembrance of things past,
  I sigh the lack of many a thing I sought,
  And with old woes new wail my dear times' waste.

Sonnet 30, l. 1

9 But if the while I think on thee, dear friend,
  All losses are restor'd and sorrows end.

Sonnet 30, l. 13

10 Full many a glorious morning have I seen.

Sonnet 33, l. 1

11 Roses have thorns, and silver fountains mud;
   Clouds and eclipses stain both moon and sun,
   And loathsome canker lives in sweetest bud.
   All men make faults.   *Sonnet 35, l. 2*

12 Be thou the tenth Muse.   *Sonnet 38, l. 9*

13 For nimble thought can jump both sea and land.

Sonnet 44, l. 7

14 Against that time when thou shalt strangely pass,
   And scarcely greet me with that sun, thine eye,
   When love, converted from the thing it was,
   Shall reasons find of settled gravity.

Sonnet 49, l. 5

15 Not marble, nor the gilded monuments
   Of princes, shall outlive this powerful rime.

Sonnet 55, l. 1

16 Like as the waves make towards the pebbled shore,
   So do our minutes hasten to their end.

Sonnet 60, l. 1

17 Time doth transfix the flourish set on youth
   And delves the parallels in beauty's brow.

Sonnet 60, l. 9

18 When I have seen by Time's fell hand defaced
   The rich proud cost of outworn buried age,
   When sometime lofty towers I see down-rased
   And brass eternal slave to mortal rage;
   When I have seen the hungry ocean gain
   Advantage on the kingdom of the shore,
   And the firm soil win of the wat'ry main,
   Increasing store with loss and loss with store.

Sonnet 64, l. 1

19 Ruin hath taught me thus to ruminate,
   That Time will come and take my love away.
   This thought is as a death, which cannot choose
   But weep to have that which it fears to lose.

Sonnet 64, l. 11

20 Tir'd with all these, for restful death I cry.

Sonnet 66, l. 1

21 And art made tongue-tied by authority.

Sonnet 66, l. 9

22 And simple truth miscall'd simplicity,
   And captive good attending captain ill.

Sonnet 66, l. 11

23 No longer mourn for me when I am dead
   Than you shall hear the surly sullen bell
   Give warning to the world that I am fled
   From this vile world, with vilest worms to dwell.

Sonnet 71, l. 1

24 That time of year thou mayst in me behold
   When yellow leaves, or none, or few, do hang
   Upon those boughs which shake against
       the cold,
   Bare ruin'd choirs, where late the sweet
       birds sang.

Sonnet 73, l. 1

25 Clean starved for a look.   *Sonnet 75, l. 10*

26 Who is it that says most? which can say more
   Than this rich praise,—that you alone are you?

Sonnet 84, l. 1

27 Farewell! thou art too dear for my possessing,
   And like enough thou know'st thy estimate.

Sonnet 87, l. 1

1 In sleep a king, but, waking, no such matter.
Sonnet 87, l. 14

2 Ah! do not, when my heart hath 'scap'd this sor-
    row,
  Come in the rearward of a conquer'd woe;
  Give not a windy night a rainy morrow,
  To linger out a purpos'd overthrow.
Sonnet 90, l. 5

3 They that have power to hurt and will do none,
  That do not do the thing they most do show,
  Who, moving others, are themselves as stone,
  Unmoved, cold, and to temptation slow.
Sonnet 94, l. 1

4 They are the lords and owners of their faces,
  Others but stewards of their excellence.
  The summer's flower is to the summer sweet,
  Though to itself it only live and die.
Sonnet 94, l. 7

5 Lilies that fester smell far worse than weeds.[1]
Sonnet 94, l. 14

6 The hardest knife ill-used doth lose his edge.
Sonnet 95, l. 14

7 How like a winter hath my absence been.
Sonnet 97, l. 1

8 From you have I been absent in the spring,
  When proud-pied April, dress'd in all his trim,
  Hath put a spirit of youth in everything.
Sonnet 98, l. 1

9 Sweets grown common lose their dear delight.
Sonnet 102, l. 12

10 To me, fair friend, you never can be old,
  For as you were when first your eye I ey'd,
  Such seems your beauty still.   *Sonnet 104, l. 1*

11 When in the chronicle of wasted time
  I see descriptions of the fairest wights,
  And beauty making beautiful old rime,
  In praise of ladies dead and lovely knights,
  Then, in the blazon of sweet beauty's best,
  Of hand, of foot, of lip, of eye, of brow,
  I see their antique pen would have express'd
  Even such a beauty as you master now.
Sonnet 106, l. 1

12 Not mine own fears, nor the prophetic soul
  Of the wide world dreaming on things to come,

---

[1] As in the nature of things, those which most admirably flourish, most swiftly fester or putrefy, as roses, lilies, violets, while others last: so in the lives of men, those that are most blooming, are soonest turned into the opposite. —PLINY THE ELDER, *Natural History*, bk. XVI, ch. 15

Can yet the lease of my true love control,
Suppos'd as forfeit to a confin'd doom.
The mortal moon hath her eclipse endur'd,
And the sad augurs mock their own presage;
Incertainties now crown themselves assur'd,
And peace proclaims olives of endless age.
Sonnet 107, l. 1

13 O! never say that I was false of heart,
  Though absence seem'd my flame to qualify.
Sonnet 109, l. 1

14 That is my home of love: if I have rang'd,
  Like him that travels, I return again.
Sonnet 109, l. 5

15 Alas! 'tis true I have gone here and there,
  And made myself a motley to the view,
  Gor'd mine own thoughts, sold cheap what is
    most dear,
  Made old offenses of affections new.
Sonnet 110, l. 1

16   My nature is subdu'd
  To what it works in, like the dyer's hand.
Sonnet 111, l. 6

17 Let me not to the marriage of true minds
  Admit impediments. Love is not love
  Which alters when it alteration finds,
  Or bends with the remover to remove:
  O, no! it is an ever-fixed mark,
  That looks on tempests and is never shaken;
  It is the star to every wandering bark,
  Whose worth's unknown, although his height be
    taken.
  Love's not Time's fool, though rosy lips and cheeks
  Within his bending sickle's compass come;
  Love alters not with his brief hours and weeks,
  But bears it out even to the edge of doom.
  If this be error, and upon me prov'd,
  I never writ, nor no man ever lov'd.
Sonnet 116

18 What potions have I drunk of Siren tears,
  Distill'd from limbecks foul as hell within.
Sonnet 119, l. 1

19 O benefit of ill!   *Sonnet 119, l. 9*

20 And ruin'd love, when it is built anew,
  Grows fairer than at first, more strong, far greater.
Sonnet 119, l. 11

21 'Tis better to be vile than vile esteem'd,
  When not to be receives reproach of being.
Sonnet 121, l. 1

22 The expense of spirit in a waste of shame
  Is lust in action; and till action, lust

Is perjur'd, murderous, bloody, full of blame,
Savage, extreme, rude, cruel, not to trust;
Enjoy'd no sooner but despised straight;
Past reason hunted; and no sooner had,
Past reason hated, as a swallow'd bait,
On purpose laid to make the taker mad:
Mad in pursuit, and in possession so;
Had, having, and in quest to have, extreme;
A bliss in proof,—and prov'd, a very woe;
Before, a joy propos'd; behind, a dream.
All this the world well knows; yet none knows well
To shun the heaven that leads men to this hell.
Sonnet 129

1 My mistress' eyes are nothing like the sun;
Coral is far more red than her lips' red:
If snow be white, why then her breasts are dun;
If hairs be wires, black wires grow on her head.
Sonnet 130, l. 1

2 When my love swears that she is made of truth,
I do believe her, though I know she lies.
Sonnet 138, l. 1

3 Two loves I have of comfort and despair,
Which like two spirits do suggest me still.
Sonnet 144, l. 1

4 Poor soul, the center of my sinful earth.
Sonnet 146, l. 1

5 So shalt thou feed on Death, that feeds on men,
And Death once dead, there's no more dying then.
Sonnet 146, l. 13

6 Past cure I am, now Reason is past care,
And frantic-mad with evermore unrest.
Sonnet 147, l. 9

7 For I have sworn thee fair, and thought thee
bright,
Who art as black as hell, as dark as night.
Sonnet 147, l. 13

8 You pay a great deal too dear for what's given
freely.
The Winter's Tale [1610–1611], act I, sc. i, l. 18

9 Two lads that thought there was no more behind
But such a day tomorrow as today,
And to be boy eternal. *I, ii, 63*

10 We were as twinn'd lambs that did frisk i' the sun,
And bleat the one at the other: what we chang'd
Was innocence for innocence. *I, ii, 67*

11 Paddling palms and pinching fingers. *I, ii, 116*

12 Affection! thy intention stabs the center:
Thou dost make possible things not so held,
Communicat'st with dreams. *I, ii, 139*

13 He makes a July's day short as December.
I, ii, 169

14   A sad tale's best for winter.
I have one of sprites and goblins. *II, i, 24*

15 The silence often of pure innocence
Persuades when speaking fails. *II, ii, 41*

16 It is a heretic that makes the fire,
Not she which burns in 't. *II, iii, 115*

17 I am a feather for each wind that blows.
II, iii, 153

18   What's gone and what's past help
Should be past grief. *III, ii, 223*

19   Exit, pursued by a bear.[1] *III, iii, 57*

20   This is fairy gold, boy, and 'twill prove so.
III, iii, 127

21 Then comes in the sweet o' the year. *IV, ii, 3*

22   A snapper-up of unconsidered trifles.
IV, ii, 26

23   For the life to come, I sleep out the thought of it.
IV, ii, 30

24 Jog on, jog on, the footpath way,
And merrily hent the stile-a:
A merry heart goes all the day,
Your sad tires in a mile-a. *IV, ii, 133*

25 For you there's rosemary and rue; these keep
Seeming and savor all the winter long.
IV, iii, 74

26   Here's flowers for you:
Hot lavender, mints, savory, marjoram,
The marigold, that goes to bed wi' the sun,
And with him rises weeping: these are flowers
Of middle summer, and I think they are given
To men of middle age. *IV, iii, 103*

27   Daffodils,
That come before the swallow dares, and take
The winds of March with beauty. *IV, iii, 118*

28   What you do
Still betters what is done. *IV, iii, 135*

29   When you do dance, I wish you
A wave o' the sea, that you might ever do
Nothing but that. *IV, iii, 140*

30 Lawn as white as driven snow. *IV, iii, 220*

31   I love a ballad in print, a-life, for then we are sure
they are true. *IV, iii, 262*

---

[1]Perhaps the most famous stage direction in English.

The self-same sun that shines upon his court
Hides not his visage from our cottage, but
Looks on alike.   *IV, iii, 457*

I'll queen it no inch further,
But milk my ewes and weep.   *IV, iii, 462*

Prosperity's the very bond of love,
Whose fresh complexion and whose heart together
Affliction alters.   *IV, iii, 586*

Let me have no lying; it becomes none but
tradesmen.   *IV, iii, 747*

To purge melancholy.   *IV, iii, 792*

There's time enough for that.   *V, iii, 128*

He hath no drowning mark upon him; his complexion is perfect gallows.
The Tempest [1611–1612], act I, sc. i, l. 33

Now would I give a thousand furlongs of sea for
an acre of barren ground.   *I, i, 70*

I would fain die a dry death.   *I, i, 73*

What seest thou else
In the dark backward and abysm of time?
                                    I, ii, 49

By telling of it,
Made such a sinner of his memory,
To credit his own lie.   *I, ii, 100*

Your tale, sir, would cure deafness. *I, ii, 106*

My library
Was dukedom large enough.   *I, ii, 109*

The very rats
Instinctively have quit it.   *I, ii, 147*

Knowing I lov'd my books, he furnish'd me,
From mine own library with volumes that
I prize above my dukedom.   *I, ii, 166*

I [Ariel] will be correspondent to command,
And do my spiriting gently.   *I, ii, 297*

You taught me language; and my profit on 't
Is, I know how to curse: the red plague rid you,
For learning me your language!   *I, ii, 363*

Come unto these yellow sands,
And then take hands:
Curtsied when you have, and kiss'd—
The wild waves whist,—
Foot it featly here and there.   *I, ii, 375*

This music crept by me upon the waters,
Allaying both their fury, and my passion,
With its sweet air.   *I, ii, 389*

Full fathom five thy father lies;
Of his bones are coral made:
Those are pearls that were his eyes:
Nothing of him that doth fade,
But doth suffer a sea-change
Into something rich and strange.[1]   *I, ii, 394*

The fringed curtains of thine eye advance.
                                    I, ii, 405

Lest too light winning
Make the prize light.   *I, ii, 448*

There's nothing ill can dwell in such a temple:
If the ill spirit have so fair a house,
Good things will strive to dwell with 't.
                                    I, ii, 454

He receives comfort like cold porridge.
                                    II, i, 10

I' the commonwealth I would by contraries
Execute all things; for no kind of traffic
Would I admit; no name of magistrate;
Letters should not be known; riches, poverty,
And use of service, none; contract, succession,
Bourn, bound of land, tilth, vineyard, none;
No use of metal, corn, or wine, or oil;
No occupation; all men idle, all;
And women too, but innocent and pure.[2]
                                    II, i, 154

What's past is prologue.   *II, i, 261*

Open-ey'd Conspiracy
His time doth take.   *II, i, 309*

A very ancient and fish-like smell. *II, ii, 27*

Misery acquaints a man with strange bedfellows.
                                    II, ii, 42

How cam'st thou to be the siege of this mooncalf?   *II, ii, 115*

I shall laugh myself to death.   *II, ii, 167*

'Ban, 'Ban, Ca—Caliban,
Has a new master—Get a new man.
                                    II, ii, 197

For several virtues
Have I lik'd several women.   *III, i, 42*

---

[1]The last three lines are inscribed on Shelley's gravestone.

[2]It is a nation, would I answer Plato, that hath no kind of traffic, no knowledge of letters, no intelligence of numbers, no name of magistrate, nor of politic superiority; no use of service, of riches or poverty, no contracts, no successions, no partitions, no occupation but idle; no respect of kindred, but common, no apparel but natural, no manuring of lands, no use of wine, corn, or metal.—MONTAIGNE, *Essays*, bk. *I* [1580], *ch. 30, Of the Cannibals*

1 *Ferdinand:* . . . Here's my hand.
Miranda: And mine, with my heart in't.
The Tempest, III, i, 89

2   Thou deboshed fish thou.   *III, ii, 30*

3   Keep a good tongue in your head.   *III, ii, 41*

4 Flout 'em, and scout 'em; and scout 'em, and
    flout 'em;
Thought is free.[1]   *III, ii, 133*

5   He that dies pays all debts.   *III, ii, 143*

6   The isle is full of noises,
Sounds and sweet airs, that give delight, and hurt
    not.
Sometimes a thousand twangling instruments
Will hum about mine ears; and sometimes voices,
That, if I then had wak'd after long sleep,
Will make me sleep again.   *III, ii, 146*

7   A kind
Of excellent dumb discourse.   *III, iii, 38*

8   Do not give dalliance
Too much the rein.   *IV, i, 51*

9 Our revels now are ended. These our actors,
As I foretold you, were all spirits and
Are melted into air, into thin air:
And, like the baseless fabric of this vision,
The cloud-capp'd towers, the gorgeous palaces,
The solemn temples, the great globe itself,
Yea, all which it inherit, shall dissolve
And, like this insubstantial pageant faded,
Leave not a rack behind. We are such stuff
As dreams are made on, and our little life
Is rounded with a sleep.   *IV, i, 148*

10 With foreheads villainous low.   *IV, i, 252*

11   But this rough magic
I here abjure.   *V, i, 50*

12   I'll break my staff,
Bury it certain fathoms in the earth,
And, deeper than did ever plummet sound,
I'll drown my book.   *V, i, 54*

13 Where the bee sucks, there suck I
In a cowslip's bell I lie;
There I couch when owls do cry.
On the bat's back I do fly
After summer merrily:
Merrily, merrily shall I live now
Under the blossom that hangs on the bough.
V, i, 88

14   O brave new world,
That has such people in't!   *V, i, 183*

15 Let us not burden our remembrances
With a heaviness that's gone.   *V, i, 1*

16   This thing of darkness I
Acknowledge mine.   *V, i, 2*

17 And my ending is despair,
Unless I be reliev'd by prayer,
Which pierces so that it assaults
Mercy itself and frees all faults.   *Epilogue, l.*

18   No man's pie is freed
From his ambitious finger.
King Henry the Eighth [1613],[2] act I, sc. i, l. 5

19 The force of his own merit makes his way.
I, i,

20 Heat not a furnace for your foe so hot
That it do singe yourself.   *I, i,*

21 If I chance to talk a little wild, forgive me;
I had it from my father.   *I, iv,*

22 The mirror of all courtesy.   *II, i,*

23 Go with me, like good angels, to my end;
And, as the long divorce of steel falls on me,
Make of your prayers one sweet sacrifice,
And lift my soul to heaven.   *II, i,*

24 This bold bad man.   *II, ii,*

25   'Tis better to be lowly born,
And range with humble livers in content,
Than to be perk'd up in a glist'ring grief
And wear a golden sorrow.   *II, iii,*

26   I would not be a queen
For all the world.   *II, iii,*

27 Orpheus with his lute made trees,
And the mountain-tops that freeze,
Bow themselves, when he did sing.   *III, i,*

28 Heaven is above all yet; there sits a judge
That no king can corrupt.   *III, i,*

29   'Tis well said again;
And 'tis a kind of good deed to say well:
And yet words are no deeds.   *III, ii, 1*

30   And then to breakfast with
What appetite you have.   *III, ii, 2*

31 I have touch'd the highest point of all my
    greatness;
And from that full meridian of my glory,
I haste now to my setting: I shall fall
Like a bright exhalation in the evening,
And no man see me more.   *III, ii, 22*

---

[1]Thought is free. — *Twelfth-Night, act I, sc. iii, l. 73*

[2]Written by Shakespeare and John Fletcher; see 242 and 245.

1 Press not a falling man too far.[1]   *III, ii, 334*

2 Farewell! a long farewell, to all my greatness!
  This is the state of man: today he puts forth
  The tender leaves of hopes; tomorrow blossoms,
  And bears his blushing honors thick upon him;
  The third day comes a frost, a killing frost;
  And, when he thinks, good easy man, full surely
  His greatness is a-ripening, nips his root,
  And then he falls, as I do. I have ventur'd,
  Like little wanton boys that swim on bladders,
  This many summers in a sea of glory,
  But far beyond my depth: my high-blown pride
  At length broke under me, and now has left me,
  Weary and old with service, to the mercy
  Of a rude stream, that must forever hide me.
  Vain pomp and glory of this world, I hate ye:
  I feel my heart new open'd. O! how wretched
  Is that poor man that hangs on princes' favors!
  There is, betwixt that smile we would aspire to,
  That sweet aspect of princes, and their ruin,
  More pangs and fears than wars or women have;
  And when he falls, he falls like Lucifer,
  Never to hope again.   *III, ii, 352*

3 A peace above all earthly dignities,
  A still and quiet conscience.   *III, ii, 380*

4 A load would sink a navy.   *III, ii, 384*

5 And sleep in dull cold marble.   *III, ii, 434*

6 Cromwell, I charge thee, fling away ambition:
  By that sin fell the angels.   *III, ii, 441*

7 Love thyself last: cherish those hearts that hate
    thee;
  Corruption wins not more than honesty.
  Still in thy right hand carry gentle peace,
  To silence envious tongues: be just, and fear not.
  Let all the ends thou aim'st at be thy country's,
  Thy God's, and truth's; then if thou fall'st, O
    Cromwell!
  Thou fall'st a blessed martyr!   *III, ii, 444*

8 Had I but serv'd my God with half the zeal[2]
  I serv'd my king, he would not in mine age
  Have left me naked to mine enemies.
                                        III, ii, 456

9 An old man, broken with the storms of state,
  Is come to lay his weary bones among ye;
  Give him a little earth for charity.
                                        IV, ii, 21

10 He gave his honors to the world again,
   His blessed part to heaven, and slept in peace.
                                        IV, ii, 29

11 So may he rest; his faults lie gently on him!
                                        IV, ii, 31

12   He was a man
   Of an unbounded stomach.   *IV, ii, 33*

13 Men's evil manners live in brass; their virtues
   We write in water.   *IV, ii, 45*

14 He was a scholar, and a ripe and good one;
   Exceeding wise, fair-spoken, and persuading;
   Lofty and sour to them that lov'd him not;
   But, to those men that sought him sweet as
       summer.   *IV, ii, 51*

15 To dance attendance on their lordships' pleasures.
                                        V, ii, 30

16 Nor shall this peace sleep with her; but as when
   The bird of wonder dies, the maiden phoenix,
   Her ashes new-create another heir
   As great in admiration as herself.   *V, v, 40*

17 Wherever the bright sun of heaven shall shine,
   His honor and the greatness of his name
   Shall be, and make new nations.   *V, v, 51*

18   Some come to take their ease
   And sleep an act or two.   *Epilogue, l. 2*

19 Good friend, for Jesus' sake forbear
   To dig the dust enclosed here;
   Blest be the man that spares these stones,
   And curst be he that moves my bones.
                                Shakespeare's epitaph

John Davies of Hereford
c. 1565–1618

20 Beauty's but skin deep.
   *A Select Second Husband for Sir Thomas
   Overburie's Wife [1616], st. 13*

Thomas Campion
1567–1620

21 My sweetest Lesbia, let us live and love,
   And though the sager sort our deeds reprove,
   Let us not weigh them. Heaven's great lamps do
     dive
   Into their west, and straight again revive,
   But soon as once set is our little light,
   Then must we sleep one ever-during night.
                       A Book of Airs [1601], I

---

[1]'Tis a cruelty / To load a falling man. — *King Henry VIII, act V, sc. iii, l. 76*

[2]Had I served God as well in every part / As I did serve my king and master still, / My scope had not this season been so short, / Nor would have had the power to do me ill. — THOMAS CHURCHYARD [c. 1520–1604], *Death of Morton* [1593]

1 Then wilt thou speak of banqueting delights,
Of masks and revels which sweet youth did make.
A Book of Airs, XX

2 Rose-cheeked Laura, come;
Sing thou smoothly with thy beauty's
Silent music, either other
Sweetly gracing.
*Observations on the Art of English Poesie
[1602], ch. 8*

3 The summer hath his joys,
And winter his delights;
Though love and all his pleasures are but toys,
They shorten tedious nights.
Third Book of Airs [1617], XII

4 Never love unless you can
Bear with all the faults of man.
Third Book of Airs, XXVII

5 There is a garden in her face
Where roses and white lilies grow;
A heavenly paradise is that place
Wherein all pleasant fruits do flow.
There cherries grow which none may buy,
Till "cherry-ripe"[1] themselves do cry.
Fourth Book of Airs [1617], VII, st. 1

6 Those cherries fairly do enclose
Of orient pearl a double row,
Which when her lovely laughter shows,
They look like rosebuds filled with snow.
Fourth Book of Airs, VII, st. 2

Thomas Nashe
1567–1601

7 Spring, the sweet spring, is the year's pleasant king;
Then blooms each thing, then maids dance in a
ring,
Cold doth not sting, the pretty birds do sing.
Cuckoo, jug-jug, pu-we, to-witta-woo!
*Summer's Last Will and Testament [1600].
Spring, st. 1*

8 From winter, plague and pestilence, good Lord,
deliver us!
*Summer's Last Will and Testament. Autumn,
refrain*

9 Brightness falls from the air;
Queens have died young and fair;
Dust hath closed Helen's eye.
I am sick, I must die.
Lord, have mercy on us!
*Summer's Last Will and Testament. Adieu!
Farewell Earth's Bliss!*

Tommaso Campanella
1568–1639

10   Now that they are called masters, [they] ar
ashamed again to become disciples.
The Defense of Galileo

11   The new philosophy proceeds from the world
the book of God.
The Defense of Galile

Sir Henry Wotton
1568–1639

12 Love lodged in a woman's breast
Is but a guest.   *A Woman's Heart [1651*

13 How happy is he born and taught,
That serveth not another's will;
Whose armor is his honest thought,
And simple truth his utmost skill!
*The Character of a Happy Life
[1614], st. 1*

14 Who God doth late and early pray,
More of his grace than gifts to send,
And entertains the harmless day
With a well-chosen book or friend.
The Character of a Happy Life, st.

15 Lord of himself, though not of lands;
And having nothing, yet hath all.
The Character of a Happy Life, st.

16 You meaner beauties of the night,
That poorly satisfy our eyes
More by your number than your light;
You common people of the skies,
What are you when the sun shall rise?
*On His Mistress, the Queen of Bohemia,
st. 1*

17 He first deceased; she for a little tried
To live without him, liked it not, and died.
*Upon the Death of Sir Albert Morton's Wife
[1651]*

18 Hanging was the worst use a man could be put to.
*The Disparity Between Buckingham and Essex
[1651]*

19   An ambassador is an honest man sent to li
abroad for the commonwealth.[3]
Reliquiae Wottonianae [1651

---

1 "Cherry-ripe" was a familiar street cry of the time. See Herrick, 247:17.

[2] Translated by GRANT McCOLLEY.

[3] In a letter to Velserus [1612], Wotton says that this "merry def
inition of an ambassador . . . I had chanced to set down at m
friend's, Mr. Christopher Fleckmore, in his Album."

1   The ⸱⸱⸱ of disputing will prove the scab of churches.[1]   *A Panegyric to King Charles [1651]*

Sir John Davies
1569–1626

2   I know my soul hath power to know all things,
Yet is she blind and ignorant in all:
I know I'm one of Nature's little kings,
Yet to the least and vilest things am thrall.
Nosce Teipsum [1599], st. 44

3   I know my life's a pain, and but a span;
I know my sense is mocked in ev'ry thing:
And to conclude, I know myself a man,
Which is a proud, and yet a wretched thing.
Nosce Teipsum, st. 45

Johannes Kepler
1571–1630

4   So long as the mother, Ignorance, lives, it is not safe for Science, the offspring, to divulge the hidden causes of things.   *Somnium [1634][2]*

Thomas Dekker
1572–1632

5   This age thinks better of a gilded fool
Than of a threadbare saint in wisdom's school.
Old Fortunatus [1600], act I, sc. i

6   Honest labor bears a lovely face.
Patient Grissell [1603], act II, sc. i

7   The best of men
That e'er wore earth about him, was a sufferer,
A soft, meek, patient, humble, tranquil spirit,
The first true gentleman that ever breathed.
The Honest Whore, pt. I [1604] (in collaboration with THOMAS MIDDLETON*), act I, sc. ii*

8   We are ne'er like angels till our passion dies.
The Honest Whore, pt. II [1630], I, ii

9   Cast away care, he that loves sorrow
Lengthens not a day, nor can buy tomorrow;
Money is trash, and he that will spend it,
Let him drink merrily, fortune will send it.
The Sun's Darling [1656] (in collaboration with JOHN FORD*)*

John Donne[3]
1572–1631

10   I wonder by my troth, what thou, and I
Did, till we lov'd? were we not wean'd till then
But suck'd on country pleasures, childishly?
Or snorted we in the seven sleepers' den?
The Good Morrow, st. 1[4]

11   And now good morrow to our waking souls,
Which watch not one another out of fear;
For love, all love of other sights controls,
And makes one little room, an everywhere.
Let sea-discoverers to new worlds have gone,
Let maps to other, worlds on worlds have shown,
Let us possess one world, each hath one, and is one.   *The Good Morrow, st. 2*

12   My face in thine eye, thine in mine appears,
And true plain hearts do in the faces rest,
Where can we find two better hemispheres
Without sharp North, without declining West?
The Good Morrow, st. 3

13   Go, and catch a falling star,
Get with child a mandrake root,
Tell me, where all past years are,
Or who cleft the Devil's foot.
Teach me to hear mermaids singing.
Song (Go and Catch a Falling Star), st. 1

14   And swear
No where
Lives a woman true, and fair.
Song (Go and Catch a Falling Star), st. 2

15   Though she were true, when you met her,
And last, till you write your letter,
Yet she
Will be
False, ere I come, to two, or three.
Song (Go and Catch a Falling Star), st. 3

16   I have done one braver thing
Than all the Worthies did;
And yet a braver thence doth spring,
Which is, to keep that hid.
The Undertaking, st. 1

17   But he who loveliness within
Hath found, all outward loathes,

---

[1]He directed that the stone over his grave be inscribed: Hic jacet hujus sententiae primus auctor: DISPUTANDI PRURITUS ECCLE-SIARUM SCABIES. Nomen alias quaere [Here lies the author of this phrase: "The itch for disputing is the sore of churches." Seek his name elsewhere]. — IZAAK WALTON, *Life of Wotton* [1651]

[2]Translated by PATRICIA KIRKWOOD.

[3]John Donne, Anne Donne, Un-done. — *Letter to his wife* [1602], quoted in IZAAK WALTON, *The Life of Dr. John Donne* [1675 edition]

[4]The poems we quote from were published, for the first time unless otherwise noted, in Donne's posthumous *Poems* [1633; further editions 1635–1669]. The general composition dates are: Songs and Sonnets (through *Farewell to Love,* 235:13) about 1593–1601, with some considerably later; Elegies about 1593–1598; and Holy Sonnets about 1609–1611, 1615–1617.

For he who color loves, and skin,
Loves but their oldest clothes.
The Undertaking, st. 4

1 And dare love that, and say so too,
And forget the He and She.
The Undertaking, st. 5

2   Busy old fool, unruly Sun,
        Why dost thou thus,
Through windows, and through curtains call on us?
Must to thy motions lovers' seasons run?
The Sun Rising, st. 1

3 Love, all alike, no season knows, nor clime,
Nor hours, days, months, which are the rags of
        time.   *The Sun Rising, st. 1*

4 She is all states, and all princes, I,
Nothing else is.   *The Sun Rising, st. 3*

5 For God sake hold your tongue, and let me love.
The Canonization, st. 1

6 The Phoenix riddle hath more wit
By us, we two being one, are it.
So to one neutral thing both sexes fit,
We die and rise the same, and prove
Mysterious by this love.
The Canonization, st. 3

7 As well a well-wrought urn becomes
The greatest ashes, as half-acre tombs.
The Canonization, st. 4

8 I am two fools, I know,
For loving, and for saying so
In whining poetry.   *The Triple Fool, st. 1*

9 Who are a little wise, the best fools be.
The Triple Fool, st. 2

10 Sweetest love, I do not go,
    For weariness of thee,
Nor in hope the world can show
A fitter love for me;
        But since that I
    Must die at last, 'tis best,
    To use my self in jest
        Thus by feign'd deaths to die.
Song (Sweetest Love, I Do Not Go), st. 1

11 Yesternight the sun went hence,
And yet is here today.
Song (Sweetest Love, I Do Not Go), st. 2

12 But think that we
Are but turn'd aside to sleep.
Song (Sweetest Love, I Do Not Go), st. 5

13 When I died last, and dear, I die
As often as from thee I go.   *The Legacy, st. 1*

14 Oh do not die, for I shall hate
All women so, when thou art gone.   *A Fever, st.*

15 Twice or thrice had I loved thee,
Before I knew thy face or name.
Air and Angels, st.

16 'Tis true, 'tis day; what though it be?
O wilt thou therefore rise from me?
Why should we rise, because 'tis light?
Did we lie down, because 'twas night?
Love which in spite of darkness brought us hither
Should in despite of light keep us together.
Break of Day, st.

17 All Kings, and all their favorites,
All glory of honors, beauties, wits,
The sun itself, which makes times, as they pass,
Is elder by a year, now, than it was
When thou and I first one another saw:
All other things, to their destruction draw,
Only our love hath no decay;
This, no tomorrow hath, nor yesterday,
Running, it never runs from us away,
But truly keeps his first, last, everlasting day.
The Anniversary, st.

18 Send home my long strayed eyes to me,
Which (Oh) too long have dwelt on thee.
The Message, st.

19 'Tis the year's midnight, and it is the day's.
*A Nocturnal upon St. Lucy's Day, being the
shortest day, st. 1*

20 The world's whole sap is sunk:
The general balm th' hydroptic earth hath drunk,
Whither, as to the bed's-feet, life is shrunk,
Dead and interr'd; yet all these seem to laugh,
Compared with me, who am their epitaph.
A Nocturnal upon St. Lucy's Day, st.

21 For I am every dead thing,
In whom love wrought new alchemy.
For his art did express
A quintessence even from nothingness,
From dull privations, and lean emptiness
He ruin'd me, and I am re-begot
Of absence, darkness, death; things which are not.
A Nocturnal upon St. Lucy's Day, st.

22 Come live with me, and be my love,
And we will some new pleasures prove
Of golden sands, and crystal brooks,
With silken lines, and silver hooks.
The Bait,[1] *st.*

----

[1]Included by Izaak Walton in *The Compleat Angler* [1676], *c*
12, as "made by Dr. Donne, and made to shew the world that h
could make soft and smooth verses, when he thought smoothnes
worth his labor."

1 Dull sublunary lovers' love
  (Whose soul is sense) cannot admit
  Absence, because it doth remove
  Those things which elemented it.
  A Valediction Forbidding Mourning, st. 4

2 Our two souls therefore which are one,
  Though I must go, endure not yet
  A breach, but an expansion,
  Like gold to airy thinness beat.
  A Valediction Forbidding Mourning, st. 6

3 If they be two, they are two so
  As stiff twin compasses are two,
  Thy soul the fixt foot, makes no show
  To move, but doth, if the other do.
  A Valediction Forbidding Mourning, st. 7

4 Our eye-beams twisted, and did thread
  Our eyes, upon one double string;
  So to entergraft our hands, as yet
  Was all the means to make us one,
  And pictures in our eyes to get
  Was all our propagation.   *The Extasy, l. 7*

5 That subtle knot which makes us man:
  So must pure lovers' souls descend
  T' affections, and to faculties,
  Which sense may reach and apprehend,
  Else a great Prince in prison lies.
  The Extasy, l. 64

6 Love's mysteries in souls do grow,
  But yet the body is his book.   *The Extasy, l. 71*

7 I long to talk with some old lover's ghost,
  Who died before the god of love was born.
  Love's Deity, st. 1

8 To rage, to lust, to write to, to commend,
  All is the purlieu of the god of love.
  Love's Deity, st. 3

9 Who ever comes to shroud me, do not harm
       Nor question much
  That subtle wreath of hair, which crowns my arm;
  The mystery, the sign you must not touch,
       For 'tis my outward soul,
  Viceroy to that, which then to heaven being gone,
       Will leave this to control,
  And keep these limbs, her provinces, from dissolu-
       tion.   *The Funeral, st. 1*

10 A bracelet of bright hair about the bone.
   The Relic, st. 1

11 Take heed of loving me.   *The Prohibition, st. 1*

12 So, so, break off this last lamenting kiss,
   Which sucks two souls, and vapors both away.
   The Expiration, st. 1

13   Ah cannot we
   As well as cocks and lions jocund be,
   After such pleasures?
   Farewell to Love, st. 3

14 Love built on beauty, soon as beauty, dies.
   Elegies, no. 2, The Anagram, l. 27

15 Nature's lay idiot, I taught thee to love.
   Elegies, 7, Nature's Lay Idiot, l. 1

16   The Alphabet
   Of flowers.   *Elegies, 7, Nature's Lay Idiot, l. 9*

17 She, and comparisons are odious.
   Elegies, 8, The Comparison, l. 54

18 No spring, nor summer beauty hath such grace,
   As I have seen in one autumnal face.
   Elegies, 9, The Autumnal, l. 1

19 The heavens rejoice in motion, why should I
   Abjure my so much lov'd variety.
   Elegies, 17, Variety, l. 1

20 Who ever loves, if he do not propose
   The right true end of love, he's one that goes
   To sea for nothing but to make him sick.
   Elegies, 18, Love's Progress, l. 1

21 The Sestos and Abydos of her breasts
   Not of two lovers, but two loves the nests.
   Elegies, 18, Love's Progress, l. 61

22 Those set our hairs, but these our flesh upright.
   *Elegies, 19, To His Mistress Going
   to Bed, l. 24*

23 O my America! my new-found land.
   *Elegies, 19, To His Mistress Going
   to Bed, l. 27*

24 Full nakedness! All joys are due to thee,
   As souls unbodied, bodies unclothed must be,
   To taste whole joys.
   *Elegies, 19, To His Mistress Going
   to Bed, l. 33*

25 Sir, more than kisses, letters mingle souls;
   For, thus friends absent speak.
   *Verse Letter to Sir Henry Wotton, written
   before April 1598, l. 1*

26 And new philosophy calls all in doubt,
   The element of fire is quite put out;
   The sun is lost, and the earth, and no man's wit
   Can well direct him where to look for it.
   And freely men confess that this world's spent,
   When in the planets, and the firmament
   They seek so many new; then see that this
   Is crumbled out again to his atomies.
   'Tis all in pieces, all coherence gone;

All just supply, and all relation:
Prince, subject, Father, Son, are things forgot.
  *An Anatomy of the World. The First
  Anniversary [first published 1611],*[1] *l. 205*

1   Her pure, and eloquent blood
Spoke in her cheeks, and so distinctly wrought,
That one might almost say, her body thought.
  *Of the Progress of the Soul. The Second
  Anniversary [first published 1612],*[2] *l. 244*

2 Nature's great masterpiece, an Elephant,
The only harmless great thing; the giant
Of beasts.   *On the Progress of the Soul, st. 39*

3 I am a little world made cunningly
Of elements, and an angelic sprite.
  Holy Sonnets, no. 5, l. 1

4 At the round earth's imagin'd corners, blow
Your trumpets, angels, and arise, arise
From death, you numberless infinities
Of souls.   *Holy Sonnets, 7, l. 1*

5 All whom war, dearth, age, agues, tyrannies,
Despair, law, chance, hath slain.
  Holy Sonnets, 7, l. 6

6 If poisonous minerals, and if that tree,
Whose fruit threw death on else immortal us,
If lecherous goats, if serpents envious
Cannot be damn'd; alas; why should I be?
  Holy Sonnets, 9, l. 1

7 Death be not proud, though some have called thee
Mighty and dreadful, for thou art not so,
For those whom thou think'st thou dost over-
  throw,
Die not, poor death, nor yet canst thou kill me.
  Holy Sonnets, 10, l. 1

8 Thou art slave to fate, chance, kings, and desperate
  men.   *Holy Sonnets, 10, l. 9*

9 One short sleep past, we wake eternally,
And death shall be no more; death, thou shalt die.
  Holy Sonnets, 10, l. 13

10 What if this present were the world's last night?
  Holy Sonnets, 13, l. 1

11 Batter my heart, three-person'd God; for you
As yet but knock, breathe, shine, and seek to
  mend.   *Holy Sonnets, 14, l. 1*

12 Show me, dear Christ, Thy spouse, so bright and
  clear.   *Holy Sonnets, 18,*[2] *l. 1*

13 Since I am coming to that holy room,
Where, with thy choir of saints forevermore,
I shall be made thy music; as I come

---

[1]"Anniversary" of the death of Elizabeth Drury [c. 1595–1610].

[2]First published in 1899.

I tune the instrument here at the door,
And what I must do then, think here before.
  *Hymn to God My God, in My Sickness
  [written c. 1623 or 1631], st. 1*

14 Whilst my physicians by their love are grown
Cosmographers, and I their map, who lie
Flat on this bed.   *Hymn to God My God, st. 2*

15 Wilt thou forgive that sin where I begun,
Which was my sin, though it were done before?
Wilt thou forgive that sin; through which I run,
And do run still: though still I do deplore?
When thou hast done, thou hast not done,
For, I have more.
  *A Hymn to God the Father [first published
  1633]*

16   I observe the physician with the same diligence
as he the disease.
  Devotions upon Emergent Occasions [1624], no. 6

17   I do nothing upon myself, and yet am mine own
executioner.
  Devotions upon Emergent Occasions, 12

18   The flea, though he kill none, he does all the
harm he can.
  Devotions upon Emergent Occasions, 12

19   No man is an island, entire of itself; every man is
a piece of the continent, a part of the main; if a clod
be washed away by the sea, Europe is the less, as
well as if a promontory were, as well as if a manor of
thy friends or of thine own were; any man's death
diminishes me, because I am involved in mankind;
and therefore never send to know for whom the bell
tolls; it tolls for thee.
  Devotions upon Emergent Occasions, 17

20   What gnashing is not a comfort, what gnawing
of the worm is not a tickling, what torment is not a
marriage bed to this damnation, to be secluded
eternally, eternally, eternally from the sight of God?
  *LXXX Sermons [1640], no. 76, preached to
  the Earl of Carlisle, c. autumn 1622*

21   Now God comes to thee, not as in the dawning
of the day, not as in the bud of the spring, but as
the sun at noon to illustrate all shadows, as the
sheaves in harvest, to fill all penuries, all occasions
invite his mercies, and all times are his seasons.
  *LXXX Sermons, 3, preached on Christmas
  Day, 1625*

22   I throw myself down in my chamber, and I call
in and invite God and his angels thither, and when
they are there, I neglect God and his angels, for the
noise of a fly, for the rattling of a coach, for the
whining of a door.
  *LXXX Sermons, 80, preached at the funeral of
  Sir William Cokayne, December 12, 1626*

1   And what is so intricate, so entangling as death?
Who ever got out of a winding sheet?
> *LXXX Sermons, 54, preached to the King at*
> *Whitehall, April 5, 1628*

2   Poor intricated soul! Riddling, perplexed, labyrinthical soul!
> *LXXX Sermons, 48, preached upon the Day of*
> *St. Paul's Conversion, January 25, 1629*

3   When my mouth shall be filled with dust, and
the worm shall feed, and feed sweetly upon me,
when the ambitious man shall have no satisfaction if
the poorest alive tread upon him, nor the poorest
receive any contentment in being made equal to
princes, for they shall be equal but in dust.
> *XXVI Sermons [1661], no. 26, Death's Duel,*
> *last sermon, February 15, 1631*[1]

Ben Jonson[2]
c. 1573–1637

4 As sure as death.
> *Every Man in His Humour [1598], act II, sc. i*

5 As he brews, so shall he drink.
> *Every Man in His Humour, II, i*

6 It must be done like lightning.
> *Every Man in His Humour, IV, 5*

7 Art hath an enemy called Ignorance.
> *Every Man out of His Humour [1599], act I, sc. i*

8 There shall be no love lost.
> *Every Man out of His Humour, II, i*

9   True happiness
Consists not in the multitude of friends,
But in the worth and choice.
> *Cynthia's Revels [1600], act III, sc. ii*

10 Queen and huntress, chaste and fair,
Now the sun is laid to sleep,
Seated in thy silver chair,
State in wonted manner keep:
   Hesperus entreats thy light,
   Goddess, excellently bright.
> *Cynthia's Revels, V, iii*

11 That old bald cheater, Time.
> *The Poetaster [1601], act I, sc. i*

12   Of all wild beasts preserve me from a tyrant; and
of all tame, a flatterer.   *Sejanus [1603], act I*

13 Calumnies are answered best with silence.
> *Volpone [1606], act II, sc. ii*

14 Come my Celia, let us prove,
While we can, the sports of love;
Time will not be ours forever,
He at length our good will sever.
Spend not then his gifts in vain;
Suns that set may rise again,
But if once we lose this light,
'Tis with us perpetual night.
> *Song, To Celia [1607]*

15 Still to be neat, still to be drest,
As you were going to a feast.
> *Epicene; or, The Silent Woman [1609],*
> *act I, sc. i*

16 Give me a look, give me a face,
That makes simplicity a grace;
Robes loosely flowing, hair as free,
Such sweet neglect more taketh me
Than all the adulteries of art:
They strike mine eyes, but not my heart.
> *Epicene; or, The Silent Woman, I, i*

17 The dignity of truth is lost with much protesting.
> *Catiline's Conspiracy [1611], act III, sc. ii*

18 Truth is the trial of itself
And needs no other touch,
And purer than the purest gold,
Refine it ne'er so much.
> *On Truth [1616], st. 1*

19   Preserving the sweetness of proportion and expressing itself beyond expression.
> *The Masque of Hymen [1616]*

20 Farewell, thou child of my right hand, and joy!
My sin was too much hope of thee, loved boy.
> *Epigrams [1616]. On My First Son [written*
> *c. 1603]*

21 Rest in soft peace, and, asked, say here doth lie
Ben Jonson his best piece of poetry:
For whose sake, henceforth, all his vows be such,
As what he loves may never like too much.
> *Epigrams. On My First Son*

22 Underneath this stone doth lie
As much beauty as could die;
Which in life did harbor give
To more virtue than doth live.
> *Epigrams. Epitaph on*
> *Elizabeth, Lady H——*

23 Follow a shadow, it still flies you;
Seem to fly it, it will pursue:
So court a mistress, she denies you;
Let her alone, she will court you.
> *The Forest [1616]. Follow a Shadow, st. 1*

---

[1]Called by His Majesty's household the Doctor's Own Funeral
Sermon. — *Preface to the first edition* [1632]

[2]O rare Ben Jonson! —JOHN YOUNG, *Epitaph*
Which was done at the charge of Jack Young, who, walking
there when the grave was covering, gave the fellow 18 pence to cut
it. —JOHN AUBREY, *Brief Lives*

1 Whilst that for which all virtue now is sold,
And almost every vice—almighty gold.
The Forest. Epistle to Elizabeth, Countess of
Rutland

2 Drink to me only with thine eyes,
And I will pledge with mine;
Or leave a kiss but in the cup
And I'll not look for wine.[1]
The thirst that from the soul doth rise
Doth ask a drink divine;
But might I of Jove's nectar sup,
I would not change for thine.
The Forest. To Celia, st. 1

3 I sent thee late a rosy wreath,
Not so much honoring thee
As giving it a hope that there
It could not wither'd be.
But thou thereon didst only breathe,
And sent'st it back to me;
Since when it grows and smells, I swear,
Not of itself, but thee.
The Forest. To Celia, st. 2

4   Reader, look,
Not at his picture, but his book.
On the portrait of Shakespeare prefixed to the
First Folio [1623]

5   Soul of the age!
The applause, delight, the wonder of our stage!
My Shakespeare, rise; I will not lodge thee by
Chaucer or Spenser, or bid Beaumont lie
A little further, to make thee a room;
Thou art a monument, without a tomb,
And art alive still, while thy book doth live,
And we have wits to read, and praise to give.
To the Memory of My Beloved, the Author,
Mr. William Shakespeare [1623]

6 Marlowe's mighty line.
To the Memory of My Beloved, the Author,
Mr. William Shakespeare

7 And though thou hadst small Latin and less Greek.
To the Memory of My Beloved, the Author,
Mr. William Shakespeare

8 Call forth thundering Aeschylus.
To the Memory of My Beloved, the Author,
Mr. William Shakespeare

9 He was not of an age but for all time.
To the Memory of My Beloved, the Author,
Mr. William Shakespeare

10 Who casts to write a living line, must sweat.
To the Memory of My Beloved, the Author,
Mr. William Shakespeare

11 For a good poet's made, as well as born.
To the Memory of My Beloved, the Author,
Mr. William Shakespeare

12 Sweet Swan of Avon!
To the Memory of My Beloved, the Author,
Mr. William Shakespeare

13 Those that merely talk and never think,
That live in the wild anarchy of drink.[2]
Underwoods [1640]. An Epistle, Answering
to One That Asked to Be Sealed of the Tribe
of Ben

14 In small proportions we just beauties see,
And in short measures life may perfect be.
Underwoods. To the Immortal Memory
of Sir Lucius Cary and Sir Henry Morison

15   The players have often mentioned it as an honor
to Shakespeare that in his writing (whatsoever he
penned) he never blotted out a line. My answer
hath been, "Would he had blotted a thousand."
Timber; or, Discoveries Made upon Men
and Matter [1640]

16   I loved the man [Shakespeare] and do honor his
memory, on this side idolatry, as much as any.
Timber; or, Discoveries Made upon Men
and Matter

17   Greatness of name in the father oft-times overwhelms the son; they stand too near one another.
The shadow kills the growth: so much, that we see
the grandchild come more and oftener to be heir of
the first.
Timber; or, Discoveries Made upon Men
and Matter

18   Though the most be players, some must be spectators.
Timber; or, Discoveries Made upon Men
and Matter

19   Talking and eloquence are not the same: to
speak, and to speak well, are two things. A fool may
talk, but a wise man speaks.
Timber; or, Discoveries Made upon Men
and Matter

---

[1]Drink to me with your eyes alone. . . . And if you will, take the
cup to your lips and fill it with kisses, and give it so to me.—
Philostratus [c. 181–250], *Letter 24*

---

[2]They never taste who always drink;/They always talk who
never think.—Prior, *Upon a Passage in the Scaligerana*

Richard Barnfield
1574–1627

1 The waters were his winding sheet, the sea was
    made for his tomb;
  Yet for his fame the ocean sea, was not sufficient
    room.   *Epitaph on Hawkins*[1] *[1595]*

2 As it fell upon a day
  In the merry month of May,
  Sitting in a pleasant shade
  Which a grove of myrtles made.
        Poems: In Divers Humours [1598]. Ode

3 Every one that flatters thee
  Is no friend in misery.
  Words are easy, like the wind;
  Faithful friends are hard to find.
  Every man will be thy friend
  Whilst thou hast wherewith to spend;
  But if store of crowns be scant,
  No man will supply thy want.
        Poems: In Divers Humours. Ode

4 If music and sweet poetry agree.
        Poems: To His Friend, Mr. R. L.

Joseph Hall
1574–1656

5 So little in his purse, so much upon his back.
        Portrait of a Poor Gallant

6 'Mongst all these stirs of discontented strife,
  O, let me lead an academic life;
  To know much, and to think for nothing, know
  Nothing to have, yet think we have enow.
      Discontent of Men with Their Condition

7   Death borders upon our birth, and our cradle
stands in the grave.
      Epistles [1608–1611]. Decade III, epistle 2

Thomas Heywood
c. 1574–c. 1641

8 Within the red-leaved table of my heart.
      A Woman Killed with Kindness [1607], sc. vi

9 I will walk on eggs.
      A Woman Killed with Kindness, xiii

10 O God! O God! that it were possible
  To undo things done; to call back yesterday!

That Time could turn up his swift sandy glass,
  To untell the days, and to redeem these hours.
      A Woman Killed with Kindness, xiii

11 Pack clouds away, and welcome day,
  With night we banish sorrow.
      Pack Clouds Away [1630], st. 1

12 I hold he loves me best that calls me Tom.
      Hierarchie of the Blessed Angels [1635]

13 Seven cities warr'd for Homer being dead,
  Who living had no roof to shroud his head.[2]
      Hierarchie of the Blessed Angels

John Marston
c. 1575–c. 1634

14 Oblivioni sacrum [Sacred to oblivion].   *Epitaph*

Cyril Tourneur
1575–1626

15 Does the silkworm expend her yellow labors
  For thee? For thee does she undo herself?
  Are lordships sold to maintain ladyships,
  For the poor benefit of a bewildering minute?
      The Revenger's Tragedy [1607], act III, sc. iv

Henry Peacham
c. 1576–c. 1643

16   Affect not as some do that bookish ambition to
be stored with books and have well-furnished libraries, yet keep their heads empty of knowledge; to
desire to have many books, and never to use them,
is like a child that will have a candle burning by him
all the while he is sleeping.
      The Compleat Gentleman [1622]

Robert Burton
1577–1640

17 All my joys to this are folly,
  Naught so sweet as melancholy.
      The Anatomy of Melancholy [1621–1651].
      The Author's Abstract

---

[1]Sir John Hawkins [1532–1595], second in command to Drake on the expedition to the West Indies, died at sea off Puerto Rico.

[2]Seven cities strive for the learned root of Homer: / Smyrna, Chios, Colophon, Ithaca, Pylos, Argos, Athens. — ANONYMOUS; *from The Greek Anthology* [1906], *ed.* J. W. MACKAIL, *bk. VI, epigram 298*
  Seven wealthy towns contend for Homer dead, / Through which the living Homer begged his bread. — THOMAS SEWARD [1708–1790], *On Homer*

1 I would help others, out of a fellow-feeling.[1]
The Anatomy of Melancholy. Democritus to the Reader

2 They lard their lean books with the fat of others' works.
The Anatomy of Melancholy. Democritus to the Reader

3 We can say nothing but what hath been said. Our poets steal from Homer. . . . Our story-dressers do as much; he that comes last is commonly best.
The Anatomy of Melancholy. Democritus to the Reader

4 A dwarf standing on the shoulders of a giant may see farther than a giant himself.
The Anatomy of Melancholy. Democritus to the Reader

5 It is most true, *stilus virum arguit*—our style betrays us.[2]
The Anatomy of Melancholy. Democritus to the Reader

6 Old friends become bitter enemies on a sudden for toys and small offenses.
The Anatomy of Melancholy. Democritus to the Reader

7 Penny wise, pound foolish.
The Anatomy of Melancholy. Democritus to the Reader

8 Women wear the breeches . . . in a word, the world turned upside downward.
The Anatomy of Melancholy. Democritus to the Reader

9 Like Aesop's fox, when he had lost his tail, would have all his fellow foxes cut off theirs.
The Anatomy of Melancholy. Democritus to the Reader

10 All poets are mad.
The Anatomy of Melancholy. Democritus to the Reader

11 Every man hath a good and a bad angel attending on him in particular, all his life long.
The Anatomy of Melancholy, pt. I, sec. 2, member 1, subsec. 2

12 That which Pythagoras said to his scholars of old, may be forever applied to melancholy men, *A fabis abstinete*, eat no beans.
The Anatomy of Melancholy, pt. I, sec. 2, member 2, subsec. 1

13 Cookery is become an art, a noble science; cook are gentlemen.
The Anatomy of Melancholy, pt. I, sec. 2, member 2, subsec. 2

14 No rule is so general, which admits not some ex ception.[3]
The Anatomy of Melancholy, pt. I, sec. 2, member 2, subsec. 3

15 Idleness is an appendix to nobility.
The Anatomy of Melancholy, pt. I, sec. 2, member 2, subsec. 6

16 Why doth one man's yawning make anothe yawn?
The Anatomy of Melancholy, pt. I, sec. 2, member 3, subsec. 2

17 They do not live but linger.
The Anatomy of Melancholy, pt. I, sec. 2, member 3, subsec. 10

18 [Desire is] a perpetual rack, or horsemill, accord ing to Austin [Saint Augustine], still going round a in a ring.
The Anatomy of Melancholy, pt. I, sec. 2, member 3, subsec. 11

19 [The rich] are indeed rather possessed by thei money than possessors.
The Anatomy of Melancholy, pt. I, sec. 2, member 3, subsec. 12

20 Were it not that they are loath to lay out mone on a rope, they would be hanged forthwith, an sometimes die to save charges.
The Anatomy of Melancholy, pt. I, sec. 2, member 3, subsec. 12

21 A mere madness, to live like a wretch and die rich
The Anatomy of Melancholy, pt. I, sec. 2, member 3, subsec. 12

22 I may not here omit those two main plagues an common dotages of human kind, wine and women which have infatuated and besotted myriads of peo ple; they go commonly together.
The Anatomy of Melancholy, pt. I, sec. 2, member 3, subsec. 13

23 All our geese are swans.[4]
The Anatomy of Melancholy, pt. I, sec. 2, member 3, subsec. 14

24 They are proud in humility; proud in that the are not proud.
The Anatomy of Melancholy, pt. I, sec. 2, member 3, subsec. 14

---

[1]A fellow-feeling makes one wondrous kind. — DAVID GARRICK, *Prologue on Quitting the Stage* [1776]

[2]Latin proverb.

[3]The exception proves the rule. — *Proverb*

[4]Every man thinks his own geese swans. — CHARLES DICKENS, *T Cricket on the Hearth* [1845], *Chirp the Second*

1   We can make mayors and officers every year, but not scholars.
> *The Anatomy of Melancholy, pt. I, sec. 2, member 3, subsec. 15*

2   *Hinc quam sic calamus saevior ense, patet.* The pen worse than the sword.
> *The Anatomy of Melancholy, pt. I, sec. 2, member 4, subsec. 4*

3   See one promontory (said Socrates of old), one mountain, one sea, one river, and see all.[1]
> *The Anatomy of Melancholy, pt. I, sec. 2, member 4, subsec. 7*

4   One was never married, and that's his hell; another is, and that's his plague.
> *The Anatomy of Melancholy, pt. I, sec. 2, member 4, subsec. 7*

5   Aristotle said melancholy men of all others are most witty.
> *The Anatomy of Melancholy, pt. I, sec. 3, member 1, subsec. 3*

6   Seneca thinks the gods are well pleased when they see great men contending with adversity.
> *The Anatomy of Melancholy, pt. II, sec. 2, member 1, subsec. 1*

7   Machiavel says virtue and riches seldom settle on one man.
> *The Anatomy of Melancholy, pt. II, sec. 2, member 2*

8   As he said in Machiavel, *omnes eodem patre nati,* Adam's sons, conceived all and born in sin, etc. "We are by nature all as one, all alike, if you see us naked; let us wear theirs and they our clothes, and what is the difference?"
> *The Anatomy of Melancholy, pt. II, sec. 2, member 2*

9   Who cannot give good counsel? 'Tis cheap, it costs them nothing.
> *The Anatomy of Melancholy, pt. II, sec. 2, member 3*

10   Many things happen between the cup and the lip.[2]
> *The Anatomy of Melancholy, pt. II, sec. 2, member 3*

11   All places are distant from heaven alike.
> *The Anatomy of Melancholy, pt. II, sec. 2, member 4*

12   The commonwealth of Venice in their armory have this inscription: "Happy is that city which in time of peace thinks of war."
> *The Anatomy of Melancholy, pt. II, sec. 2, member 6*

13   Every man, as the saying is, can tame a shrew but he that hath her.
> *The Anatomy of Melancholy, pt. II, sec. 2, member 6*

14   Tobacco, divine, rare, superexcellent tobacco, which goes far beyond all the panaceas, potable gold, and philosopher's stones, a sovereign remedy to all diseases . . . but as it is commonly abused by most men, which take it as tinkers do ale, 'tis a plague, a mischief, a violent purger of goods, lands, health, hellish, devilish and damned tobacco, the ruin and overthrow of body and soul.
> *The Anatomy of Melancholy, pt. II, sec. 4, member 2, subsec. 2*

15   "Let me not live," said Aretine's Antonia, "if I had not rather hear thy discourse than see a play."
> *The Anatomy of Melancholy, pt. III, sec. 1, member 1, subsec. 1*

16   Birds of a feather will gather together.
> *The Anatomy of Melancholy, pt. III, sec. 1, member 1, subsec. 2*

17   No cord nor cable can so forcibly draw, or hold so fast, as love can do with a twined thread.[3]
> *The Anatomy of Melancholy, pt. III, sec. 2, member 1, subsec. 2*

18   To enlarge or illustrate this power and effect of love is to set a candle in the sun.[4]
> *The Anatomy of Melancholy, pt. III, sec. 2, member 1, subsec. 2*

19   [Quoting Seneca:] Cornelia kept her in talk till her children came from school, "and these," said she, "are my jewels."
> *The Anatomy of Melancholy, pt. III, sec. 2, member 2, subsec. 3*

20   Diogenes struck the father when the son swore.
> *The Anatomy of Melancholy, pt. III, sec. 2, member 2, subsec. 5*

---

[1]A blade of grass is always a blade of grass, whether in one country or another. — SAMUEL JOHNSON, in Hester Piozzi, *Anecdotes of Samuel Johnson* [1786]

[2]A very ancient proverb, sometimes attributed to Homer.
There is many a slip 'twixt the cup and the lip. — PALLADAS [fl. 400], in *The Greek Anthology* [1906], ed. J. W. MACKAIL, *bk. X, epigram 32*
Though men determine, the gods do dispose; and ofttimes many things fall out between the cup and the lip. — ROBERT GREENE, *Perimedes the Blacksmith* [1588]

[3]One hair of a woman can draw more than a hundred pair of oxen. — JAMES HOWELL, *Letters* [1645–1655], *bk. II, 4*
She knows her man, and when you rant and swear, / Can draw you to her with a single hair. — JOHN DRYDEN, *Persius* [1693], *satire V, l. 246*

[4]And hold their farthing candle to the sun. — EDWARD YOUNG, *Love of Fame* [1725–1728], *Satire VII, l. 99*
And hold their glimmering tapers to the sun. — GEORGE CRABBE, *The Parish Register* [1807], *pt. I, introduction*

1   For "ignorance is the mother of devotion," as all the world knows.

> *The Anatomy of Melancholy, pt. III, sec. 4, member 1, subsec. 2*

2   The fear of some divine and supreme powers keeps men in obedience.[1]

> *The Anatomy of Melancholy, pt. III, sec. 4, member 1, subsec. 2*

3   One religion is as true as another.

> *The Anatomy of Melancholy, pt. III, sec. 4, member 2, subsec. 1*

4   Melancholy and despair, though often, do not always concur; there is much difference: melancholy fears without a cause, this upon great occasion; melancholy is caused by fear and grief, but this torment procures them and all extremity of bitterness.

> *The Anatomy of Melancholy, pt. III, sec. 4, member 2, subsec. 3*

5   A good conscience is a continual feast.

> *The Anatomy of Melancholy, pt. III, sec. 4, member 2, subsec. 3*

6   Our conscience, which is a great ledger book, wherein are written all our offenses . . . grinds our souls with the remembrance of some precedent sins, makes us reflect upon, accuse and condemn ourselves.

> *The Anatomy of Melancholy, pt. III, sec. 4, member 2, subsec. 3*

7   What physic, what chirurgery, what wealth, favor, authority can relieve, bear out, assuage, or expel a troubled conscience? A quiet mind cureth all.

> *The Anatomy of Melancholy, pt. III, sec. 4, member 2, subsec. 5*

8   Be not solitary, be not idle.

> *The Anatomy of Melancholy, pt. III, sec. 4, member 2, subsec. 6*

William Harvey
1578–1657

9   The heart of animals is the foundation of their life, the sovereign of everything within them, the sun of their microcosm.

> *De Motu Cordis et Sanguinis [1628],[2] dedication to King Charles*

10   All we know is still infinitely less than all that still remains unknown.

> *De Motu Cordis et Sanguinis, dedication to Dr. Argent and Other Learned Physicians*

11   I profess both to learn and to teach anatomy, not from books but from dissections; not from positions of philosophers but from the fabric of nature.

> *De Motu Cordis et Sanguinis, dedication to Dr. Argent and Other Learned Physicians*

12   I appeal to your own eyes as my witness and judge

> *De Generatione Animalium (On the Generation of Animals) [1651],[3] introduction*

John Fletcher
1579–1625

13 Drink today, and drown all sorrow;
You shall perhaps not do 't tomorrow.

> *Rollo, Duke of Normandy [1639] (in collaboration with JONSON and others), act II, sc. ii*

14 And he that will to bed go sober
Falls with the leaf in October.[4]

> *Rollo, Duke of Normandy, II, ii*

15 Three merry boys, and three merry boys,
And three merry boys are we.[5]
As ever did sing in a hempen string
Under the gallows tree.

> *Rollo, Duke of Normandy, III, ii*

16 O woman, perfect woman! what distraction
Was meant to mankind when thou wast made a devil!

> *Monsieur Thomas [1639], act III, sc. i*

17   That soul that can
Be honest is the only perfect man.

> *The Honest Man's Fortune [1647] (in collaboration with three other authors), epilogue*

18 Weep no more, nor sigh, nor groan,
Sorrow calls no time that's gone;
Violets plucked, the sweetest rain
Makes not fresh nor grow again.

> *The Queen of Corinth [1647] (in collaboration with MASSINGER and a third author), act III, sc. ii*

---

[1]The fear o' hell's a hangman's whip / To haud the wretch in order. — ROBERT BURNS, *Epistle to a Young Friend*

[2]*An Anatomical Disquisition on the Motion of the Heart and Blood in Animals.* Translated by ROBERT WILLIS.

[3]Translated by ROBERT WILLIS.

[4]The following well-known catch, or glee, is formed on this song:
He who goes to bed, and goes to bed sober, / Falls as the leaves do, and dies in October; / But he who goes to bed, and goes to bed mellow, / Lives as he ought to do, and dies an honest fellow.

[5]Three merry men be we. — GEORGE PEELE, *Old Wives' Tale* [1595]

1 Of all the paths lead to a woman's love
  Pity's the straightest.
    The Knight of Malta [1647] (in collaboration with MASSINGER), act I, sc. i

2 Go to grass.
    The Little French Lawyer [1647] (in collaboration with MASSINGER), act IV, sc. vii

3 There is no jesting with edge tools.
    The Little French Lawyer, IV, vii

4 Let's meet, and either do or die.[1]
    The Island Princess [1647], act II, sc. ii

5 Hence, all you vain delights,
  As short as are the nights
  Wherein you spend your folly!
  There's naught in this life sweet
  But only melancholy;
  O sweetest melancholy!
    The Nice Valor [1647]. Melancholy[2]

Thomas Middleton
1580–1627

6 Better the day, better the deed.[3]
    Michaelmas Term [1607], act III, sc. i

7 Since the worst comes to the worst.[4]
    Michaelmas Term, III, iv

8 What is got over the Devil's back (that's by knavery), is spent under the belly (that's by lechery).[5]
    Michaelmas Term, IV, i

9 As true as I live.
    The Family of Love [1608], act V, sc. iii

10 Have you summoned your wits from woolgathering?[6]
    The Family of Love, V, iii

11 By my faith the fool has feathered his nest well.[7]
    The Roaring Girl [1611], act I, sc. i

12 That disease of which all old men sicken—avarice.[8]
    The Roaring Girl, I, i

13 I that am of your blood was taken from you
  For your better health; look no more upon't,
  But cast it to the ground regardlessly,
  Let the common sewer take it from distinction.
    The Changeling [written 1622], act V, sc. iii

14 As the case stands.
    The Old Law [1656], act II, sc. i

15 On his last legs.
    The Old Law, V, i

16 'Tis a stinger.
    More Dissemblers Besides Women [1657], act III, sc. ii

17 How many honest words have suffered corruption since Chaucer's days!
    No Wit, No Help, Like a Woman's [1657], act II, sc. i

18 By many a happy accident.
    No Wit, No Help, Like a Woman's, IV, i

19 Anything for a Quiet Life.
    Title of play [1662] (in collaboration with WEBSTER)

20 This was a good week's labor.
    Anything for a Quiet Life, act V, sc. ii

21 There's no hate lost between us.
    The Witch [written c. 1627], act IV, sc. iii

22 Black spirits and white, red spirits and gray,
  Mingle, mingle, mingle, you that mingle may.[9]
    The Witch, V, ii

Richard Rich
fl. 1610

23 God will not let us fall . . .
  For . . . our work is good,
  We hope to plant a nation,
  Where none before hath stood.
    Newes from Virginia: The Flock Triumphant [1610][10]

---

[1]This expression is a kind of common property, being the motto, we believe, of a Scottish family. —SIR WALTER SCOTT, review of Thomas Campbell's *Gertrude of Wyoming* [1809], where it appears (*pt. III, l. 37*): Tomorrow let us do or die!

[2]This poem is frequently and with some likelihood attributed to WILLIAM STRODE (1602–1645).

[3]The better the day, the worse deed. —MATTHEW HENRY, *Commentaries, Genesis 3*

[4]If the worst comes to the worst. —*Discovery of the Knights of the Poste* [1597]

[5]What is got over the Devil's back is spent under the belly. —FRANÇOIS RABELAIS, *Works, bk. V* [1552], *ch. 11*
  Isocrates was in the right to insinuate that what is got over the Devil's back is spent under his belly. —ALAIN RENÉ LESAGE, *Gil Blas* [1715–1735], *bk. VIII, ch. 9*

[6]My understanding has forsook me, and is gone a-woolgathering. —CERVANTES, *Don Quixote, pt. II* [1605–1615], *bk. IV, ch. 38*

[7]We will feather our nests ere time may us espy. —*A Merry Interlude Entitled Respublica* [1553], *act III, sc. vi*

[8]So for a good old-gentlemanly vice / I think I must take up with avarice. —LORD BYRON, *Don Juan* [1818–1824], *canto I, st. 216*

[9]These lines are introduced into *Macbeth, act IV, sc. i.*

[10]Narrative poem about Rich's voyage to Virginia [1609] with Captain Christopher Newport. Its account of a shipwreck on the Bermudas may have been a source for scenes in Shakespeare's *The Tempest.*

John Webster
c. 1580–c. 1625

1   Is not old wine wholesomest, old pippins toothsome, old wood burn brightest, old linen wash whitest? Old soldiers, sweethearts, are surest, and old lovers are soundest.
> *Westward Hoe [1607] (in collaboration with* Dekker*), act II, sc. ii*

2   I saw him now going the way of all flesh.
> *Westward Hoe, II, ii*

3 Call for the robin redbreast and the wren,
Since o'er shady groves they hover,
And with leaves and flowers do cover
The friendless bodies of unburied men.
> *The White Devil [1612], act V, sc. iv*

4 But keep the wolf far thence, that's foe to men,
For with his nails he'll dig them up again.
> *The White Devil, V, iv*

5 Prosperity doth bewitch men, seeming clear;
But seas do laugh, show white, when rocks are
      near.   *The White Devil, V, vi*

6 I am Duchess of Malfi still.
> *Duchess of Malfi [1623], act IV, sc. ii*

7 I know death hath ten thousand several doors
For men to take their exits.[1]
> *Duchess of Malfi, IV, ii*

8 Heaven-gates are not so highly arch'd
As princes' palaces; they that enter there
Must go upon their knees.
> *Duchess of Malfi, IV, ii*

9 *Ferdinand:* Cover her face; mine eyes dazzle; she
      died young.
Bosola: I think not so; her infelicity
      Seemed to have years too many.
> *Duchess of Malfi, IV, ii*

10 Vain the ambition of kings
Who seek by trophies and dead things
To leave a living name behind,
And weave but nets to catch the wind.[2]
> *The Devil's Law Case [1623], song*

---

[1]The thousand doors that lead to death. — Thomas Browne, *Religio Medici* [1643], *pt. I, sec. 44*
   Death hath so many doors to let out life. — John Fletcher and Philip Massinger, *The Custom of the Country* [1647], *act II, sc. ii*
   Death hath a thousand doors to let out life. — Philip Massinger, *A Very Woman* [1665], *act V, sc. iv*

[2]Since in a net I seek to hold the wind. — Sir Thomas Wyatt, *Sonnet, Whoso List to Hunt*

Sir Thomas Overbury
1581–1613

11 Give me, next good, an understanding wife,
By nature wise, not learned much by art.
> *A Wife [1614*

12   He disdains all things above his reach, and preferreth all countries before his own.
> *An Affectate Traveller [1614*

James Ussher
1581–1656

13   According to our chronology, [the creation of the world] fell upon the entrance of the night preceding the twenty third day of October in the year of the Julian Calendar, 710 [4004 B.C.].
> *The Annals of the World [1658]*

Richard Corbet
1582–1635

14 Farewell, rewards and fairies,
Good housewives now may say.
> *The Fairies Farewell, st. 1*

15   Who of late for cleanliness,
Finds sixpence in her shoe?
> *The Fairies Farewell, st. 1*

16 Nor too much wealth nor wit come to thee,
So much of either may undo thee.
> *To His Son, Vincent Corbet*

Jacques du Laurens
1583–1650

17   I do not attack fools, but foolishness.
> *Satires [1624]*

Philip Massinger
1583–1640

18   Be wise;
Soar not too high to fall; but stoop to rise.
> *Duke of Milan [1623], act I, sc. ii*

19 He that would govern others, first should be
The master of himself.
> *The Bondman [1624], act I, sc. iii*

20   To be nobly born
Is now a crime.
> *The Roman Actor [1629], act I, sc. i*

Whose wealth
Arithmetic cannot number.
The Roman Actor, I, iii

2 Grim death. *The Roman Actor, IV, ii*

3 A New Way to Pay Old Debts.
Title of play [1632]

Francis Beaumont
c. 1584–1616

4 What things have we seen
Done at the Mermaid! heard words that have been
So nimble, and so full of subtle flame,
As if that everyone from whence they came,
Had meant to put his whole wit in a jest,
And resolv'd to live a fool, the rest
Of his dull life. *Letter to Ben Jonson [1640]*

Beaumont and Fletcher[1]
[Francis Beaumont c. 1584–1616]
[John Fletcher 1579–1625]

5 It is always good
When a man has two irons in the fire.
The Faithful Friends [c. 1608], act I, sc. ii

6 As cold as cucumbers.
Cupid's Revenge [1615], act I, sc. i

7 Kiss till the cow comes home.[2]
The Scornful Lady [1616], act III, sc. i

8 There is a method in man's wickedness—
It grows up by degrees.
A King and No King [1619], act V, sc. iv

9 Upon my buried body lie lightly, gentle earth.
The Maid's Tragedy [1619], act II, sc. ii

10 The devil take the hindmost!
Philaster [1620], act V, sc. iii

11 Whistle, and she'll come to you.
Wit Without Money [1639], act IV, sc. iv

12 Calamity is man's true touchstone.
Four Plays in One. The Triumph of Honour [1647], sc. i

13 Though I say it that should not say it.
Wit at Several Weapons (probably in collaboration with WILLIAM ROWLEY [c. 1585–c. 1642]), act II, sc. ii

John Selden
1584–1654

14 *Scrutamini scripturas* [Let us look at the scriptures]. These two words have undone the world.
Table Talk [1689]. Bible, Scripture

15 Old friends are best. King James used to call for his old shoes; they were easiest for his feet.
Table Talk. Friends

16 Humility is a virtue all preach, none practice; and yet everybody is content to hear.
Table Talk. Humility

17 Tis not the drinking that is to be blamed, but the excess. *Table Talk. Humility*

18 Ignorance of the law excuses no man; not that all men know the law, but because 'tis an excuse every man will plead, and no man can tell how to refute him. *Table Talk. Law*

19 Wit and wisdom are born with a man.
Table Talk. Learning

20 Few men make themselves masters of the things they write or speak. *Table Talk. Learning*

21 Take a straw and throw it up into the air—you shall see by that which way the wind is.
Table Talk. Libels

22 Marriage is a desperate thing.
Table Talk. Marriage

23 Pleasure is nothing else but the intermission of pain. *Table Talk. Pleasure*

24 Thou little thinkest what a little foolery governs the whole world.[3] *Table Talk. Pope*

25 They that govern most make the least noise.
Table Talk. Power

26 Syllables govern the world.
Table Talk. Power

27 Wise men say nothing in dangerous times.
Table Talk. Wisdom

28 Preachers say, Do as I say, not as I do.
Table Talk. Preaching

---

[1]Of whose partnership John Aubrey said: "There was a wonderful consimility of fancy. They lived together not far from the playhouse, had one wench in the house between them, the same clothes and cloak, &c."

[2]Also familiar as: Till the cows come home.

[3]Behold, my son, with how little wisdom the world is governed.—AXEL OXENSTIERN [1583–1654]

1 A king is a thing men have made for their own sakes, for quietness' sake. Just as in a family one man is appointed to buy the meat.

Table Talk. Of a King

Tirso de Molina [Gabriel Téllez]
c. 1584–1648

2 Through his honor I conquered him. For these peasants carry their honor in their hands so that they may constantly consult it; this same honor that once felt so much at home in the city but now has taken refuge in a more rural setting.

El Burlador de Sevilla (The Rogue of Seville) [1630],[1] *act III, sc. iii*

John Ford
c. 1586–1639

3 Diamond cut diamond.

The Lover's Melancholy [1629], act I, sc. i

4 Remember
When we last gathered roses in the garden,
I found my wits; but truly you lost yours.

The Broken Heart [1629], act IV, sc. ii

5 'Tis Pity She's a Whore.   *Title of play [1633]*

Thomas Rainsborough
d. 1648

6 The poorest he that is in England hath a life to live as the greatest he.

In the army debates at Putney [October 29, 1647]

Thomas Hobbes
1588–1679

7 Words are wise men's counters, they do but reckon with them, but they are the money of fools.

Leviathan [1651], pt. I, ch. 4

8 The privilege of absurdity; to which no living creature is subject but man only.

Leviathan, I, 5

9 Sudden glory is the passion which maketh those grimaces called laughter.   *Leviathan, I, 6*

10 The secret thoughts of a man run over all things, holy, profane, clean, obscene, grave, and light, without shame or blame.   *Leviathan, I, 8*

---

[1]Translated by ROBERT O'BRIEN.
This is the original Don Juan play.

11 During the time men live without a commo power to keep them all in awe, they are in that co dition which is called *war;* and such a war, as is every man, against every man.

Leviathan, I,

12 [In a state of nature] No arts; no letters; no so ety; and which is worst of all, continual fear ar danger of violent death; and the life of man, so tary, poor, nasty, brutish, and short.

Leviathan, I,

13 The Papacy is not other than the Ghost of t deceased Roman Empire, sitting crowned upon t grave thereof.   *Leviathan, IV, ch.*

14 The praise of ancient authors proceeds not fro the reverence of the dead, but from the competiti and mutual envy of the living.

Leviathan, A Review and Conclusi

15 Such truth as opposeth no man's profit n pleasure is to all men welcome.

Leviathan, A Review and Conclusi

16 I am about to take my last voyage, a great leap the dark.   *Last wor*

John Winthrop
1588–1649

17 For we must consider that we shall be as a ci upon a hill. The eyes of all people are upon us, that if we shall deal falsely with our God in th work we have undertaken, and so cause Him withdraw His present help from us, we shall made a story and a byword through the world.

A Model of Christian Charity [1630], a sermon delivered on board the Arbella

George Wither
1588–1667

18 Shall I wasting in despair
Die because a woman's fair?
Or make pale my cheeks with care
'Cause another's rosy are?
Be she fairer than the day,
Or the flow'ry meads in May,
If she be not so to me,
What care I how fair she be?

Fair Virtue [1622]. Sonnet 4, st.

19 'Twas I that beat the bush,
The bird to others flew.

A Love Sonnet [1622], st.

1 Though I am young, I scorn to flit
On the wings of borrowed wit.
The Shepherd's Hunting [1622]. *Eclogue 4*

Honorat de Bueil, Marquis de Racan
1589–1670

2 Nothing in the world lasts
Save eternal change.[1]
Odes. The Coming of Spring

3 The good effect of Fortune may be short-lived.
To build on it is to build on sand.[2]
Poésies Diverses

William Bradford
1590–1657

4 They knew they were pilgrims.[3]
Of Plymouth Plantation [1620–1647], *ch. 7*

5 So they committed themselves to the will of God and resolved to proceed.
Of Plymouth Plantation, 9

6 Being thus arrived in a good harbor, and brought safe to land, they fell upon their knees and blessed the God of Heaven, who had brought them over the vast and furious ocean, and delivered them from all the perils and miseries thereof, again to set their feet on the firm and stable earth, their proper element.
Of Plymouth Plantation, 9

7 And for the season it was winter, and they that know the winters of that country know them to be sharp and violent, and subject to cruel and fierce storms, dangerous to travel to known places, much more to search an unknown coast. . . . For summer being done, all things stand upon them with a weather-beaten face, and the whole country, full of woods and thickets, represented a wild and savage hue.
Of Plymouth Plantation, 9

8 But it pleased God to visit us then with death daily, and with so general a disease that the living were scarce able to bury the dead.
Of Plymouth Plantation, 12

9 Behold, now, another providence of God. A ship comes into the harbor.
Of Plymouth Plantation, 13

10 Thus out of small beginnings greater things have been produced by His hand that made all things of nothing, and gives being to all things that are; and, as one small candle may light a thousand, so the light here kindled hath shone unto many, yea in some sort to our whole nation.
Of Plymouth Plantation, 21

William Basse
d. c. 1653

11 Renowned Spenser, lie a thought more nigh
To learned Chaucer; and rare Beaumont, lie
A little nearer Spenser; to make room
For Shakespeare in your threefold fourfold tomb.
On Mr. Wm. Shakespeare [c. 1616]

William Browne
1591–c. 1645

12 Underneath this sable hearse
Lies the subject of all verse:
Sidney's sister, Pembroke's mother.
Death, ere thou hast slain another
Fair and learned and good as she,
Time shall throw a dart at thee.
Epitaph on the Countess of Pembroke [1621]

13 There is no season such delight can bring,
As summer, autumn, winter, and the spring.
Variety

Robert Herrick
1591–1674

14 I sing of brooks, of blossoms, birds, and bowers:
Of April, May, of June, and July flowers.
I sing of Maypoles, Hock-carts, wassails, wakes,
Of bridegrooms, brides, and of their bridal cakes.
Hesperides [1648]. *Argument of His Book*

15 What is a kiss? Why this, as some approve:
The sure, sweet cement, glue, and lime of love.
Hesperides. A Kiss

16 Bid me to live, and I will live
Thy Protestant to be,
Or bid me love, and I will give
A loving heart to thee.
Hesperides. To Anthea, Who May Command Him Any Thing

17 Cherry ripe, ripe, ripe, I cry,
Full and fair ones; come and buy!
If so be you ask me where

---

[1] Rien au monde ne dure / Qu'un éternel changement.

[2] Le bien de la fortune est un bien périssable; quand on bâtit sur elle, on bâtit sur le sable.

[3] It was owing to this passage, first printed in 1669, that the *Mayflower*'s company came eventually to be called the Pilgrim Fathers.

They do grow, I answer, there,
Where my Julia's lips do smile;
There's the land, or cherry-isle.
Hesperides. Cherry Ripe

1 It is the end that crowns us, not the fight.
Hesperides. The End

2 Some asked how pearls did grow, and where?
Then spoke I to my girl
To part her lips, and showed them there
The quarelets of pearl.
*Hesperides. The Rock of Rubies, and the
Quarrie of Pearls*

3 A sweet disorder in the dress
Kindles in clothes a wantonness.
Hesperides. Delight in Disorder

4 A winning wave, deserving note,
In the tempestuous petticoat,
A careless shoestring, in whose tie
I see a wild civility,
Do more bewitch me than when art
Is too precise in every part.
Hesperides. Delight in Disorder

5 You say to me-wards your affection's strong;
Pray love me little, so you love me long.
Hesperides. Love Me Little, Love Me Long

6 Night makes no difference 'twixt the Priest and
Clerk;
Joan as my Lady is as good i' the dark.
Hesperides. No Difference i' th' Dark

7 Give me a kiss, and to that kiss a score;
Then to that twenty, add a hundred more:
A thousand to that hundred: so kiss on,
To make that thousand up a million.
Treble that million, and when that is done,
Let's kiss afresh, as when we first begun.
Hesperides. To Anthea: Ah, My Anthea!

8 Gather ye rosebuds while ye may,
Old Time is still a-flying,
And this same flower that smiles today
Tomorrow will be dying.
*Hesperides. To the Virgins to Make Much
of Time*

9 Fair daffodils, we weep to see
You haste away so soon.
Hesperides. To Daffodils

10 Her pretty feet, like snails, did creep
A little out, and then,
As if they played at bo-peep,
Did soon draw in again.
*Hesperides. To Mistress Susanna Southwell:
Upon Her Feet*

11 Her eyes the glowworm lend thee,
The shooting stars attend thee;
And the elves also,
Whose little eyes glow
Like the sparks of fire, befriend thee.
Hesperides. The Night Piece to Julia

12 Thus times do shift, each thing his turn does hold;
New things succeed, as former things grow old.
Hesperides. Ceremonies for Candlemas Eve

13 Made us nobly wild, not mad.
Hesperides. Ode for Ben Jonson

14 Outdid the meat, outdid the frolic wine.
Hesperides. Ode for Ben Jonson

15 Attempt the end, and never stand to doubt;
Nothing's so hard but search will find it out.
Hesperides. Seek and Find

16 Get up, sweet Slug-a-bed, and see
The dew bespangling herb and tree.
Hesperides. Corinna's Going A-Maying

17 'Tis sin,
Nay, profanation to keep in.
Hesperides. Corinna's Going A-Maying

18 So when or you or I are made
A fable, song, or fleeting shade,
All love, all liking, all delight
Lies drowned with us in endless night.
Hesperides. Corinna's Going A-Maying

19 Whenas in silks my Julia goes,
Then, then (methinks) how sweetly flows
That liquefaction of her clothes.

Next, when I cast mine eyes and see
That brave vibration each way free;
Oh how that glittering taketh me!
Hesperides. Upon Julia's Clothes

20 Here a little child I stand
Heaving up my either hand.
Cold as paddocks though they be,
Here I lift them up to Thee,
For a benison to fall
On our meat, and on us all.
*His Noble Numbers [1648]. Another Grace
for a Child*

Henry King
1592–1669

21 Thou art the book,
The library whereon I look.   *The Exequy [1657]*

22 Then we shall rise
And view ourselves with clearer eyes

In that calm region where no night
Can hide us from each other's sight.
The Exequy

1 Sleep on, my Love, in thy cold bed,
Never to be disquieted!
My last good-night! Thou wilt not wake,
Till I thy fate shall overtake;
Till age, or grief, or sickness, must
Marry my body to that dust
It so much loves, and fill the room
My heart keeps empty in thy tomb.
Stay for me there; I will not fail
To meet thee in that hollow vale.   *The Exequy*

2 But hark! my pulse like a soft drum
Beats my approach, tells thee I come.
The Exequy

3 We that did nothing study but the way
To love each other, with which thoughts the day
Rose with delight to us, and with them set,
Must learn the hateful art, how to forget.
The Surrender

Francis Quarles
1592–1644

4 No man is born unto himself alone;
Who lives unto himself, he lives to none.
Esther [1621], sec. 1, Meditation 1

5 The way to bliss lies not on beds of down,
And he that had no cross deserves no crown.
Esther, sec. 9, Meditation 9

6 We spend our midday sweat, our midnight oil;
We tire the night in thought, the day in toil.
Emblems [1635], bk. II, no. 2

7 Be wisely worldly, be not worldly wise.
Emblems, II, 2

8 This house is to be let for life or years;
Her rent is sorrow, and her income tears.
Cupid, 't has long stood void; her bills make
known,
She must be dearly let, or let alone.
Emblems, II, 10, Epigram

9 The slender debt to Nature's quickly paid,[1]
Discharged, perchance, with greater ease than
made.   *Emblems, II, 13*

10 The road to resolution lies by doubt:
The next way home's the farthest way about.[2]
Emblems, IV, 2, Epigram

---

11 It is the lot of man but once to die.
Emblems, V, 7

12 My soul, sit thou a patient looker-on;
Judge not the play before the play is done:
Her plot hath many changes; every day
Speaks a new scene; the last act crowns the play.
Epigram. Respice Finem

13 And what's a life? — a weary pilgrimage,
Whose glory in one day doth fill the stage
With childhood, manhood, and decrepit age.
What Is Life?

14 Let all thy joys be as the month of May,
And all thy days be as a marriage day:
Let sorrow, sickness, and a troubled mind
Be stranger to thee.   *To a Bride*

Thomas Ravenscroft
c. 1592–c. 1635

15 Nose, nose, nose, nose!
And who gave thee this jolly red nose?
Nutmegs and ginger, cinnamon and cloves,
And they gave me this jolly red nose.
Deuteromelia [1609]. Song no. 7[3]

George Herbert
1593–1633

16 A verse may find him who a sermon flies.[4]
The Temple [1633]. The Church Porch, st. 1

17 Drink not the third glass, which thou canst not
tame
When once it is within thee.
The Temple. The Church Porch, st. 5

18 Dare to be true: nothing can need a lie:
A fault, which needs it most, grows two thereby.[5]
The Temple. The Church Porch, st. 13

19 By all means use sometimes to be alone.
The Temple. The Church Porch, st. 25

20 By no means run in debt: take thine own measure.
Who cannot live on twenty pound a year,
Cannot on forty.
The Temple. The Church Porch, st. 30

---

[3]Quoted by Beaumont and Fletcher, *The Knight of the Burning Pestle* [1613], *act I, sc. iii.* Ravenscroft's *Deuteromelia* was a supplement to his *Pammelia*, which was the earliest collection of rounds, catches, and canons printed in England.

[4]That many people read a song / Who will not read a sermon. — WINTHROP MACKWORTH PRAED [1802–1839], *The Chant of the Brazenhead, st. 1*

[5]And he that does one fault at first, / And lies to hide it, makes it two. — ISAAC WATTS, *Song 15*

---

[1]To die is a debt we must all of us discharge. — EURIPIDES, *Alcestis, l. 418*

[2]The longest way round is the shortest way home. — *Proverb*

1 Wit's an unruly engine, wildly striking
Sometimes a friend, sometimes the engineer.
The Temple. The Church Porch, st. 41

2 Be useful where thou livest.
The Temple. The Church Porch, st. 55

3 Man is God's image; but a poor man is
Christ's stamp to boot: both images regard.
The Temple. The Church Porch, st. 64

4 Was ever grief like mine?
The Temple. The Church. The Sacrifice, refrain

5 For thirty pence he did my death devise,
Who at three hundred did the ointment prize.
The Temple. The Church. The Sacrifice, st. 3

6 Man stole the fruit, but I must climb the tree.
The Temple. The Church. The Sacrifice, st. 49

7 I got me flowers to strew Thy way,
I got me boughs off many a tree:
But Thou wast up by break of day,
And brought'st Thy sweets along with Thee.
The Temple. The Church. Easter, st. 4

8 Who says that fictions only and false hair
Become a verse? Is there in truth no beauty?
The Temple. The Church. Jordan, st. 1

9 Sweet day, so cool, so calm, so bright,
The bridal of the earth and sky.
The Temple. The Church. Virtue, st. 1

10 Sweet spring, full of sweet days and roses,
A box where sweets compacted lie.
The Temple. The Church. Virtue, st. 3

11 Only a sweet and virtuous soul,
Like season'd timber, never gives.
The Temple. The Church. Virtue, st. 4

12 Who goes to bed and does not pray,
Maketh two nights to every day.
*The Temple. The Church. Charms and Knots,
st. 4*

13 Nothing wears clothes, but Man; nothing doth need
But he to wear them.
The Temple. The Church. Providence, st. 28

14 Most things move th' under-jaw, the crocodile
not.[1]
Most things sleep lying, th' elephant leans or
stands.[2]
The Temple. The Church. Providence, st. 35

---

[1]The crocodile does not move the lower jaw, but is the only animal that brings down its upper jaw to the under one. —HERODOTUS, *Customs of the Egyptians*

[2]Leans the huge elephant. —JAMES THOMSON, *The Seasons, Summer* [1727], *l. 725*

15 I struck the board, and cried, No more:
I will abroad.
What? shall I ever sigh and pine?
My lines and life are free; free as the road,
Loose as the wind, as large as store.
Shall I be still in suit?
Have I no harvest but a thorn
To let me blood, and not restore
What I have lost with cordial fruit?
Sure there was wine
Before my sighs did dry it; there was corn
Before my tears did drown it;
Is the year only lost to me?
Have I no bays to crown it?
The Temple. The Church. The Collar

16 Call in thy death's head there: tie up thy fears.
The Temple. The Church. The Collar

17 But as I rav'd and grew more fierce and wild
At every word,
Methought I heard one calling, *Child!*
And I replied, *My Lord.*
The Temple. The Church. The Collar

18 He would adore my gifts instead of me,
And rest in Nature, not the God of Nature:
So both should losers be.
The Temple. The Church. The Pulley, st. 3

19 Let him be rich and weary, that at least,
If goodness lead him not, yet weariness
May toss him to my breast.
The Temple. The Church. The Pulley, st. 4

20   Grief melts away
Like snow in May,
As if there were no such cold thing.
The Temple. The Church. The Flower, st. 1

21 Who would have thought my shrivel'd heart
Could have recovered greenness?
The Temple. The Church. The Flower, st. 2

22 And now in age I bud again,
After so many deaths I live and write;
I once more smell the dew and rain,
And relish versing: O my only light,
It cannot be
That I am he
On whom thy tempests fell all night.
The Temple. The Church. The Flower, st. 6

23 The harbingers are come. See, see their mark;
White is their color, and behold my head.
*The Temple. The Church. The Forerunners,
st. 1*

24 Teach me, my God and King,
In all things thee to see

And what I do in any thing,
To do it as for thee.
The Temple. The Church. The Elixir, st. 1

1 A servant with this clause
Makes drudgery divine:
Who sweeps a room, as for thy laws,
Makes that and th' action fine.
The Temple. The Church. The Elixir, st. 5

2 Love bade me welcome: yet my soul drew back,
Guilty of dust and sin.
But quick-ey'd Love, observing me grow slack
From my first entrance in,
Drew nearer to me, sweetly questioning,
If I lack'd anything.
The Temple. The Church. Love, st. 1

3 You must sit down, says Love, and taste my meat:
So I did sit and eat.
The Temple. The Church. Love, st. 3

4 Religion stands on tiptoe in our land,
Ready to pass to the American strand.
The Church Militant [1633], l. 235

5 Love, and a cough, cannot be hid.
Jacula Prudentum [1651], no. 49

6 Ill ware is never cheap. Pleasing ware is half sold.
Jacula Prudentum, 61

7 When a dog is drowning, everyone offers him drink.
Jacula Prudentum, 77

8 Deceive not thy physician, confessor, nor lawyer.
Jacula Prudentum, 105

9 Who would do ill ne'er wants occasion.
Jacula Prudentum, 116

10 A snow year, a rich year.
Jacula Prudentum, 125

11 Well may he smell fire, whose gown burns.
Jacula Prudentum, 138

12 Love your neighbor, yet pull not down your hedge.
Jacula Prudentum, 141

13 Marry your son when you will; your daughter when you can.
Jacula Prudentum, 149

14 The mill cannot grind with the water that's past.
Jacula Prudentum, 153

15 Good words are worth much, and cost little.
Jacula Prudentum, 155

16 Hell is full of good meanings and wishings.[1]
Jacula Prudentum, 170

17 Where the drink goes in, there the wit goes out.
Jacula Prudentum, 187

18 Whose house is of glass, must not throw stones at another.[2]
Jacula Prudentum, 196

19 By suppers more have been killed than Galen ever cured.
Jacula Prudentum, 272

20 The lion is not so fierce as they paint him.[3]
Jacula Prudentum, 289

21 Go not for every grief to the physician, nor for every quarrel to the lawyer, nor for every thirst to the pot.
Jacula Prudentum, 290

22 The best mirror is an old friend.
Jacula Prudentum, 296

23 When you are an anvil, hold you still; when you are a hammer, strike your fill.[4]
Jacula Prudentum, 338

24 He that lies with the dogs, riseth with fleas.
Jacula Prudentum, 343

25 He that is not handsome at twenty, nor strong at thirty, nor rich at forty, nor wise at fifty, will never be handsome, strong, rich, or wise.
Jacula Prudentum, 349

26 The buyer needs a hundred eyes, the seller not one.
Jacula Prudentum, 390

27 My house, my house, though thou art small, thou art to me the Escurial.
Jacula Prudentum, 413

28 Trust not one night's ice.
Jacula Prudentum, 453

29 For want of a nail the shoe is lost, for want of a shoe the horse is lost, for want of a horse the rider is lost.
Jacula Prudentum, 499

30 Pension never enriched young man.
Jacula Prudentum, 515

31 One enemy is too much.
Jacula Prudentum, 523

32 Living well is the best revenge.
Jacula Prudentum, 524

33 Thursday come, and the week is gone.
Jacula Prudentum, 587

34 Time is the rider that breaks youth.
Jacula Prudentum, 615

---

[2]People in glass houses shouldn't throw stones. — *Proverb*

[3]The lion is not so fierce as painted. — THOMAS FULLER, *Expecting Preferment*

[4]Stand like an anvil when it is beaten upon. — SAINT IGNATIUS THEOPHORUS, bishop of Antioch [fl. c. 100]
When you are the anvil, bear— /When you are the hammer, strike. — EDWIN MARKHAM, *Preparedness*

---

[1]Sir, Hell is paved with good intentions. — SAMUEL JOHNSON [1775]; from BOSWELL, *Life of Johnson [1791], vol. I, p. 555* (Everyman edition)

1   Show me a liar, and I'll show thee a thief.
Jacula Prudentum, 652

2   One father is more than a hundred schoolmasters.
Jacula Prudentum, 686

3   Reason lies between the spur and the bridle.
Jacula Prudentum, 711

4   One sword keeps another in the sheath.
Jacula Prudentum, 723

5   God's mill grinds slow, but sure.
Jacula Prudentum, 747

6   He that lends, gives.
Jacula Prudentum, 787

7   Words are women, deeds are men.[1]
Jacula Prudentum, 843

8   Poverty is no sin.   *Jacula Prudentum, 844*

9   None knows the weight of another's burthen.
Jacula Prudentum, 880

10   One hour's sleep before midnight is worth three after.   *Jacula Prudentum, 882*

11   He hath no leisure who useth it not.
Jacula Prudentum, 897

12   Half the world knows not how the other half lives.   *Jacula Prudentum, 907*

13   Life is half spent before we know what it is.
Jacula Prudentum, 917

14   Every mile is two in winter.
Jacula Prudentum, 949

15   The eye is bigger than the belly.
Jacula Prudentum, 1018

16   His bark is worse than his bite.
Jacula Prudentum, 1090

17   There is an hour wherein a man might be happy all his life, could he find it.
Jacula Prudentum, 1143

18   Woe be to him that reads but one book.
Jacula Prudentum, 1146

Izaak Walton
1593–1683

19   But God, who is able to prevail, wrestled with him, as the Angel did with Jacob, and marked him; marked him for his own.   *Life of Donne [1640]*

20   I have laid aside business, and gone a-fishing.
The Compleat Angler [1653–1655]. Epistle to the Reader

21   Angling may be said to be so like the mathematics that it can never be fully learnt.
The Compleat Angler. Epistle to the Reader

22   As no man is born an artist, so no man is born an angler.
The Compleat Angler. Epistle to the Reader

23   I shall stay him no longer than to wish him a rainy evening to read this following discourse; and that if he be an honest angler, the east wind may never blow when he goes a-fishing.
The Compleat Angler. Epistle to the Reader

24   I am, Sir, a brother of the Angle.
The Compleat Angler, pt. I, ch. I

25   Doubt not but angling will prove to be so pleasant that it will prove to be, like virtue, a reward to itself.[2]

Sir Henry Wotton . . . was a most dear lover, and a frequent practicer of the art of angling; of which he would say, "it was an employment for his idle time, which was then not idly spent . . . a rest to his mind, a cheerer of his spirits, a diverter of sadness, a calmer of unquiet thoughts, a moderator of passions, a procurer of contentedness; and that it begat habits of peace and patience in those that professed and practiced it."   *The Compleat Angler, I, 1*

26   You will find angling to be like the virtue of humility, which has a calmness of spirit and a world of other blessings attending upon it.[3]
The Compleat Angler, I, 1

27   I remember that a wise friend of mine did usually say, "That which is everybody's business is nobody's business."   *The Compleat Angler, I, 2*

28   Good company and good discourse are the very sinews of virtue.   *The Compleat Angler, I, 2*

29   An honest ale-house where we shall find a cleanly room, lavender in the windows, and twenty ballads stuck about the wall.
The Compleat Angler, I, 2

---

[1] Fatti maschii parole femine [Manly deeds, womanly words]. — *Motto of Maryland*

---

[2] Ipsa quidem virtus sibimet pulcherrima merces [Virtue herself is her own fairest reward]. — Silius Italicus [A.D. c. 25–99], *Punica, bk. XIII, l. 663*

Virtue was sufficient of herself for happiness. — Diogenes Laertius, *Lives of Eminent Philosophers, XLII, Plato*

That virtue is her own reward, is but a cold principle. — Thomas Browne, *Religio Medici* [1643], *pt. I, sec. 47*

Virtue is its own reward. — Prior, *Imitations of Horace, bk. III, ode 2*

I think mankind by thee would be less bored / If only thou wert not thine own reward. — John Kendrick Bangs [1862–1922], *A Hint to Virtue*

[3] There is certainly something in angling . . . that tends to produce a gentleness of spirit, and a pure serenity of mind. — Washington Irving, *The Sketch-Book* [1819–1820], *The Angler*

1   An excellent angler, and now with God.
The Compleat Angler, I, 4

2   Old-fashioned poetry, but choicely good.
The Compleat Angler, I, 4

3   I love such mirth as does not make friends ashamed to look upon one another next morning.
The Compleat Angler, I, 5

4   No man can lose what he never had.
The Compleat Angler, I, 5

5   We may say of angling as Dr. Boteler[1] said of strawberries: "Doubtless God could have made a better berry, but doubtless God never did"; and so, if I might be judge, God never did make a more calm, quiet, innocent recreation than angling.
The Compleat Angler, I, 5

6   Thus use your frog. . . . Put your hook through his mouth, and out at his gills; . . . and then with a fine needle and silk sew the upper part of his leg, with only one stitch, to the arming-wire of your hook; or tie the frog's leg, above the upper joint, to the armed-wire; and in so doing use him as though you loved him.   *The Compleat Angler, I, 8*

7   This dish of meat is too good for any but anglers, or very honest men.
The Compleat Angler, I, 8

8   Look to your health; and if you have it, praise God, and value it next to a good conscience; for health is the second blessing that we mortals are capable of; a blessing that money cannot buy.
The Compleat Angler, I, 21

9   Let the blessing of Saint Peter's Master be . . . upon all that are lovers of virtue, and dare trust in his Providence, and be quiet and go a-angling.
The Compleat Angler, I, 21

10   The great secretary of Nature and all learning, Sir Francis Bacon.   *Life of Herbert [1670]*

James Howell
c. 1594–1666

11   All work and no play makes Jack a dull boy.
Proverbs [1659]

Thomas Carew
c. 1595–c. 1639

12 Here lies a King that rul'd, as he thought fit
The universal monarchy of wit;

Here lies two flamens, and both those the best:
Apollo's first, at last the true God's priest.
An Elegy upon the Death of Dr. Donne [1633]

13 Ask me no more where Jove bestows,
When June is past, the fading rose;
For in your beauty's orient deep
These flowers, as in their causes, sleep.
Poems [1640]. To Celia, st. 1

14 Ask me no more whither doth haste
The nightingale when May is past;
For in your sweet dividing throat
She winters and keeps warm her note.
Poems. To Celia, st. 3

15 Ask me no more if east or west
The Phoenix builds her spicy nest;
For unto you at last she flies,
And in your fragrant bosom dies.
Poems. To Celia, st. 5

16 Give me more love or more disdain;
The torrid or the frozen zone:
Bring equal ease unto my pain;
The temperate affords me none.
Poems. Mediocrity in Love Rejected, st. 1

17 Thou shalt confess the vain pursuit
Of human glory yields no fruit
  But an untimely grave.
Poems. On the Duke of Buckingham

18 He that loves a rosy cheek,
Or a coral lip admires,
Or, from starlike eyes, doth seek
Fuel to maintain his fires;
As old Time makes these decay,
So his flames must waste away.
Poems. Disdain Returned, st. 1

19 The firstling of the infant year.   *Poems. The Primrose*

20 Then fly betimes, for only they
Conquer Love that run away.
Poems. Conquest by Flight

21 The magic of a face.
Poems. Epitaph on the Lady S——

René Descartes
1596–1650

22   Good sense is of all things in the world the most equally distributed, for everybody thinks he is so well supplied with it, that even those most difficult to please in all other matters never desire more of it than they already possess.
Le Discours de la Méthode [1637], I

23   It is not enough to have a good mind. The main thing is to use it well.   *Le Discours de la Méthode, I*

---

[1]This praise of the strawberry first appeared in the second edition of *The Angler* [1655].

1   The greatest minds are capable of the greatest vices as well as of the greatest virtues.
Le Discours de la Méthode, I

2   The first precept was never to accept a thing as true until I knew it as such without a single doubt.
Le Discours de la Méthode, I

3   One cannot conceive anything so strange and so implausible that it has not already been said by one philosopher or another.
Le Discours de la Méthode, II

4   I think, therefore I am [Cogito, ergo sum; Je pense, donc je suis].
Le Discours de la Méthode, IV

James Shirley
1596–1666

5   How little room
Do we take up in death that, living, know
No bounds!   *The Wedding [1626], act IV, sc. iv*

6   I presume you're mortal, and may err.
The Lady of Pleasure [1635]

7   Only the actions of the just
Smell sweet and blossom in their dust.
The Lady of Pleasure

8   Death calls ye to the crowd of common men.
Cupid and Death [1653]

9   The glories of our blood and state
Are shadows, not substantial things;
There is no armor against fate;
Death lays his icy hand on kings.
Contention of Ajax and Ulysses [1659], sc. iii

Oliver Cromwell
1599–1658

10   A few honest men are better than numbers.
Letter to Sir W. Spring [September 1643]

11   The State, in choosing men to serve it, takes no notice of their opinions. If they be willing faithfully to serve it, that satisfies.
Before the battle of Marston Moor [July 2, 1644]

12   I beseech you, in the bowels of Christ, think it possible you may be mistaken.
Letter to the General Assembly of the Church of Scotland [August 3, 1650]

13   You have sat too long here for any good you have been doing lately. . . . Depart, I say; and let us have done with you. In the name of God, go!
To the Rump Parliament [April 20, 1653]

14   Necessity hath no law. Feigned necessities, imaginary necessities . . . are the greatest cozenage that men can put upon the Providence of God, and make pretenses to break known rules by.
To Parliament [September 12, 1654]

15   I would have been glad to have lived under my woodside, and to have kept a flock of sheep, rather than to have undertaken this government.
To Parliament [1658]

16   Mr. Lely, I desire you would use all your skill to paint my picture truly like me, and not flatter me at all; but remark all these roughnesses, pimples, warts, and everything as you see me, otherwise I will never pay a farthing for it.[1]
From Horace Walpole, Anecdotes of Painting in England [1762–1771]

17   It is not my design to drink or to sleep, but my design is to make what haste I can to be gone.
Dying words

Pedro Calderón de la Barca
1600–1681

18   What is life? A madness. What is life? An illusion, a shadow, a story. And the greatest good is little enough: for all life is a dream, and dreams themselves are only dreams.[2]
Life Is a Dream, act II, l. 1195

19   But whether it be dream or truth, to do well is what matters. If it be truth, for truth's sake. If not, then to gain friends for the time when we awaken.
Life Is a Dream, III, l. 236

20   The treason past, the traitor is no longer needed.
Life Is a Dream, III, l. 1109

21   What surprises you, if a dream taught me this wisdom, and if I still fear I may wake up and find myself once more confined in prison? And even if this should not happen, merely to dream it is enough. For this I have come to know, that all human happiness finally ceases, like a dream.
Life Is a Dream, III, l. 1114

Martin Parker
c. 1600–c. 1656

22   Ye gentlemen of England
That live at home at ease,

---

[1]Warts and all. — *Saying*

[2]Que es la pequeño: / Que toda la vida es sueño, / y los sueños sueños son.
Translated by Edward and Elizabeth Huberman.

Ah! little do you think upon
The dangers of the seas.   *Song*

Pierre de Fermat
1601–1665

1   I have discovered a truly marvellous demonstration [of this general theorem[1]] which this margin is too narrow to contain.
   Note [Fermat's Last Theorem] [c. 1637] in his copy of CLAUDE BACHET, *Diophanti Alexandrini Arithmeticorum*

Jules Cardinal Mazarin
1602–1661

2   I must leave all that! Farewell, dear paintings that I have loved so much and which have cost me so much.[2]   *Remark shortly before his death*

Roger Williams
c. 1603–1683

3   There goes many a ship to sea, with many hundred souls in one ship, whose weal and woe is common, and is a true picture of a commonwealth or a human combination or society. It hath fallen out sometimes that both Papists and Protestants, Jews and Turks may be embarked in one ship; upon which supposal I affirm that all the liberty of conscience that ever I pleaded for turns upon these two hinges — that none of the papists, Protestants, Jews or Turks be forced to come to the ship's prayers or worship, nor compelled from their own particular prayers or worship, if they practice any.
   Letter to the Town of Providence [January 1655]

Friedrich von Logau
1604–1655

4 Armed peace.
   Poetic Aphorisms (Sinngedichten) [1654]

5 Though the mills of God grind slowly, yet they grind exceeding small.[3]
   Poetic Aphorisms. Retribution

---

[1]Restated in modern terms: The equation $x^n + y^n = z^n$, where x, y, and z are nonzero integers, has no solution for n greater than 2. Mathematician Andrew Wiles (1953–) proved Fermat's theorem in 1994.

[2]Il faut quitter tout cela! Adieu, chers tableaux que j'ai tant aimés et qui m'ont tant coûté.

[3]Translated by HENRY WADSWORTH LONGFELLOW.

Sir Thomas Browne
1605–1682

6   I dare, without usurpation, assume the honorable style of a Christian.
   Religio Medici [1643], pt. I, sec. 1

7   I could never divide myself from any man upon the difference of an opinion, or be angry with his judgment for not agreeing with me in that from which perhaps within a few days I should dissent myself.   *Religio Medici, I, 6*

8   Many . . . have too rashly charged the troops of error, and remain as trophies unto the enemies of truth.   *Religio Medici, I, 6*

9   A man may be in as just possession of truth as of a city, and yet be forced to surrender.
   Religio Medici, I, 6

10   As for those wingy mysteries in divinity, and airy subtleties in religion, which have unhinged the brains of better heads, they never stretched the *pia mater* of mine.   *Religio Medici, I, 9*

11   I love to lose myself in a mystery, to pursue my Reason to an *O altitudo!*   *Religio Medici, I, 9*

12   Rich with the spoils of Nature.
   Religio Medici, I, 13

13   We carry with us the wonders we seek without us: There is all Africa and her prodigies in us.
   Religio Medici, I, 15

14   All things are artificial, for nature is the art of God.[4]   *Religio Medici, I, 16*

15   Obstinacy in a bad cause is but constancy in a good.   *Religio Medici, I, 25*

16   Persecution is a bad and indirect way to plant religion.   *Religio Medici, I, 25*

17   Thus is man that great and true *Amphibium*, whose nature is disposed to live . . . in divided and distinguished worlds; for though there be but one [world] to sense, there are two to reason; the one visible; the other invisible.
   Religio Medici, I, 34

18   Not picked from the leaves of any author, but bred amongst the weeds and tares of mine own brain.   *Religio Medici, I, 36*

19   This reasonable moderator, and equal piece of justice, Death.   *Religio Medici, I, 38*

20   I am not so much afraid of death, as ashamed thereof. 'Tis the very disgrace and ignominy of our

---

[4]The course of Nature is the art of God. — EDWARD YOUNG, *Night Thoughts* [1742–1745], *Night IX, l. 1267*

natures, that in a moment can so disfigure us, that our nearest friends, wife, and children, stand afraid and start at us.   *Religio Medici, I, 40*

1   How shall the dead arise, is no question of my faith; to believe only possibilities, is not faith, but mere philosophy.   *Religio Medici, I, 48*

2   The heart of man is the place the devil dwells in: I feel sometimes a hell within myself.

Religio Medici, I, 51

3   There is no road or ready way to virtue.

Religio Medici, I, 55

4   All places, all airs make unto me one country; I am in England, everywhere, and under any meridian.   *Religio Medici, II, 1*

5   But how shall we expect charity towards others, when we are uncharitable to ourselves? Charity begins at home, is the voice of the world; yet is every man his greatest enemy, and, as it were, his own executioner.   *Religio Medici, II, 4*

6   I could be content that we might procreate like trees, without conjunction, or that there were any way to perpetuate the World without this trivial and vulgar way of coition.   *Religio Medici, II, 9*

7   Sure there is music even in the beauty, and the silent note which Cupid strikes, far sweeter than the sound of an instrument. For there is a music wherever there is a harmony, order, or proportion; and thus far we may maintain the music of the spheres.

Religio Medici, II, 9

8   For the world, I count it not an inn, but a hospital; and a place not to live, but to die in.

Religio Medici, II, 11

9   There is surely a piece of divinity in us, something that was before the elements, and owes no homage unto the sun.   *Religio Medici, II, 11*

10   When we desire to confine our words, we commonly say they are spoken under the rose.[1]

Vulgar Errors [1645]

11   An old and gray-headed error.

Vulgar Errors

---

[1]Sub rosa.

In strict confidence. The origin of the phrase is obscure but the story is that Cupid gave Harpocrates (the god of silence) a rose, to bribe him not to betray the amours of Venus. Hence the flower became the emblem of silence and was sculptured on the ceilings of banquet-rooms, to remind the guests that what was spoken *sub vino* was not to be repeated *sub divo*. In the sixteenth century it was placed over confessionals. — *Brewer's Dictionary of Phrase and Fable, 14th ed.* [1989]

12   Times before you, when even living men were antiquities; when the living might exceed the dead, and to depart this world could not be properly said to go unto the greater number.

Urn-Burial; or, Hydriotaphia [1658].
Dedication

13   With rich flames, and hired tears, they solemnized their obsequies.   *Urn-Burial, ch. 3*

14   Were the happiness of the next world as closely apprehended as the felicities of this, it were a martyrdom to live.   *Urn-Burial, 4*

15   These dead bones have . . . quietly rested under the drums and tramplings of three conquests.

Urn-Burial, 5

16   Time which antiquates antiquities, and hath an art to make dust of all things.

Urn-Burial, 5

17   What song the Sirens sang, or what name Achilles assumed when he hid himself among women, though puzzling questions, are not beyond all conjecture.

Urn-Burial, 5

18   The long habit of living indisposeth us for dying.

Urn-Burial, 5

19   The iniquity of oblivion blindly scattereth her poppy, and deals with the memory of men without distinction to merit of perpetuity.

Urn-Burial, 5

20   Oblivion is not to be hired: the greater part must be content to be as though they had not been, to be found in the register of God, not in the record of man.   *Urn-Burial, 5*

21   The night of time far surpasseth the day, and who knows when was the equinox?

Urn-Burial, 5

22   Man is a noble animal, splendid in ashes, and pompous in the grave.

Urn-Burial, 5

23   That unextinguishable laugh in heaven.

The Garden of Cyrus [1658], ch. 2

24   Life itself is but the shadow of death, and souls departed but the shadows of the living. All things fall under this name. The sun itself is but the dark simulacrum, and light but the shadow of God.

The Garden of Cyrus, 4

25   To keep our eyes open longer were but to act our Antipodes. The huntsmen are up in America, and they are already past their first sleep in Persia. But who can be drowsy at that hour which freed us from

everlasting sleep? or have slumbering thoughts at that time, when sleep itself must end, and, as some conjecture, all shall awake again?

The Garden of Cyrus, 5

Anne Bigot Cornuel
1605–1694

1 No man is a hero to his valet.[1] *Attributed*

Pierre Corneille
1606–1684

2 To conquer without risk is to triumph without glory. *Le Cid [1636], act II, sc. ii*

3 Brave men are brave from the very first.

Le Cid, II, iii

4 And the combat ceased for want of combatants.

Le Cid, IV, iii

5 Do your duty, and leave the rest to heaven.

Horace [1639], act II, sc. viii

6 All evils are equal when they are extreme.

Horace, III, iv

7 The worst of all states is the people's state.

Cinna [1640], act II, sc. i

8 Who is all-powerful should fear everything.

Cinna, IV, ii

9 By speaking of our misfortunes we often relieve them. *Polyeucte [1640], act I, sc. iii*

10 The manner of giving is worth more than the gift. *Le Menteur [1642], act I, sc. i*

11 A liar is always lavish of oaths.

Le Menteur, III, v

12 The fire which seems extinguished often slumbers beneath the ashes.

Rodogune [1644], act III, sc. iv

13 Guess if you can, choose if you dare.

Héraclius [1646], act IV, sc. iv

14 A service beyond all recompense
Weighs so heavy that it almost gives offense.

Suréna [1674], act III, sc. i

15 I owe my fame only to myself.

Poésies Diverses, 23

---

[1] Il n'y avoit point de héros pour les valets de chambre.

Sir William Davenant
1606–1668

16 The lark now leaves his wat'ry nest
And, climbing, shakes his dewy wings.

Song [1638], st. 1

17 I shall ask leave to desist, when I am interrupted by so great an experiment as dying.

His apology, in illness, for not having finished Gondibert

18 How much pleasure they lose (and even the pleasures of heroic poesy are not unprofitable) who take away the liberty of a poet, and fetter his feet in the shackles of a historian.

Prefatory letter to Thomas Hobbes. From S. T. COLERIDGE, Biographia Literaria [1817], ch. 22

Edmund Waller
1606–1687

19 Illustrious acts high raptures do infuse,
And every conqueror creates a muse.

Panegyric to My Lord Protector

20 Guarded with ships, and all our sea our own.

To My Lord of Falkland

21 To man, that was in th' evening made,
Stars gave the first delight;
Admiring, in the gloomy shade,
Those little drops of light.

An Apology for Having Loved Before [1664]

22 That which her slender waist confin'd
Shall now my joyful temples bind;
No monarch but would give his crown
His arms might do what this has done.

On a Girdle [1664]

23 My joy, my grief, my hope, my love,
Did all within this circle move! *On a Girdle*

24 Go, lovely rose!
Tell her that wastes her time and me
That now she knows,
When I resemble her to thee,
How sweet and fair she seems to be.

Go, Lovely Rose [1664]

25 So all we know
Of what they do above
Is that they happy are, and that they love.

Upon the Death of My Lady Rich [1664]

26 Poets that lasting marble seek
Must carve in Latin or in Greek.

Of English Verse [1668]

1 And keeps the palace of the soul.   *Of Tea*

2 Poets lose half the praise they should have got,
Could it be known what they discreetly blot.
Upon Roscommon's Translation of HORACE,
De Arte Poetica

3 The soul's dark cottage, batter'd and decay'd,
Lets in new light through chinks that Time has
made;
Stronger by weakness, wiser, men become
As they draw near to their eternal home.
Leaving the old, both worlds at once they view,
That stand upon the threshold of the new.
On the Divine Poems [1686]

Paul Gerhardt
1607–1676

4 O sacred head, now wounded,
With grief and shame bowed down;
Now scornfully surrounded
With thorns, thy only crown.[1]
*Passion Chorale [1656], based on twelfth-
century Latin hymn, st. 1*

Thomas Fuller
1608–1661

5   Drawing near her death, she sent most pious
thoughts as harbingers to heaven; and her soul saw
a glimpse of happiness through the chinks of her
sickness-broken body.   *Life of Monica [1642]*

6   He was one of a lean body and visage, as if his
eager soul, biting for anger at the clog of his body,
desired to fret a passage through it.
Life of the Duke of Alva [1642]

7   He knows little who will tell his wife all he
knows.
*The Holy State and the Profane State [1642].
The Good Husband*

8   One that will not plead that cause wherein his
tongue must be confuted by his conscience.
*The Holy State and the Profane State. The
Good Advocate*

9   Light, God's eldest daughter, is a principal
beauty in a building.
*The Holy State and the Profane State.
Of Building*

10   Learning hath gained most by those books by
which the printers have lost.
*The Holy State and the Profane State.
Of Books*

11   Deceive not thyself by overexpecting happiness
in the married estate. . . . Remember the nightingales which sing only some months in the spring,
but commonly are silent when they have hatched
their eggs.
*The Holy State and the Profane State.
Of Marriage*

12   They that marry ancient people, merely in expectation to bury them, hang themselves in hope
that one will come and cut the halter.
*The Holy State and the Profane State.
Of Marriage*

13   Fame sometimes hath created something of
nothing.
The Holy State and the Profane State. Fame

14   Anger is one of the sinews of the soul; he that
wants it hath a maimed mind.
*The Holy State and the Profane State.
Of Anger*

15   It is always darkest just before the day dawneth.
Pisgah Sight [1650], bk. II, ch. 2

John Milton
1608–1674

16 This is the month, and this the happy morn,
Wherein the Son of Heav'n's eternal King,
Of wedded maid and virgin mother born,
Our great redemption from above did bring;
For so the holy sages once did sing,
That He our deadly forfeit should release,
And with His Father work us a perpetual peace.
*On the Morning of Christ's Nativity [1629],
st. 1, l. 1*

17 It was the winter wild
While the Heav'n-born child
All meanly wrapt in the rude manger lies.
*On the Morning of Christ's Nativity. The
Hymn, st. 1, l. 29*

18 No war, or battle's sound
Was heard the world around.
The idle spear and shield were high up hung.
*On the Morning of Christ's Nativity. The
Hymn, st. 4, l. 53*

19 Time will run back and fetch the Age of Gold.
*On the Morning of Christ's Nativity. The
Hymn, st. 14, l. 135*

---

[1]O Haupt vol Blut und Wunden / Vol Schmerz und voller Hohn! /
O Haupt zum Spott gebunden / Mit einer Dornen Krohn!
Translated by JAMES WADDELL ALEXANDER.

1 The Oracles are dumb.
> *On the Morning of Christ's Nativity. The
> Hymn, st. 19, l. 173*

2 Peor and Baalim
  Forsake their temples dim.
> *On the Morning of Christ's Nativity. The
> Hymn, st. 22, l. 197*

3 What needs my Shakespeare for his honor'd bones,
  The labor of an age in piled stones,
  Or that his hallow'd relics should be hid
  Under a star-y-pointing pyramid?
  Dear son of memory, great heir of fame,
  What need'st thou such weak witness of thy name?
> *On Shakespeare [1630]*

4 How soon hath Time, the subtle thief of youth,
  Stol'n on his wing my three-and-twentieth year.
> *On His Having Arrived at the Age of
> Twenty-three [1631]*

5 As ever in my great Taskmaster's eye.
> *On His Having Arrived at the Age of
> Twenty-three*

6 Such sweet compulsion doth in music lie.
> *Arcades [1630–1634], l. 68*

7 Hence, loathed Melancholy,
  Of Cerberus and blackest Midnight born,
  In Stygian cave forlorn,
  'Mongst horrid shapes, and shrieks, and sights
    unholy.   *L'Allegro [1631], l. 1*

8 So buxom, blithe, and debonair.   *L'Allegro, l. 24*

9 Haste thee, Nymph, and bring with thee
  Jest, and youthful jollity,
  Quips and cranks and wanton wiles,
  Nods and becks and wreathed smiles.
> *L'Allegro, l. 25*

10 Sport, that wrinkled Care derides,
   And Laughter, holding both his sides.
   Come, and trip it, as you go,
   On the light fantastic toe.   *L'Allegro, l. 31*

11 The mountain nymph, sweet liberty.
> *L'Allegro, l. 36*

12 Mirth, admit me of thy crew,
   To live with her, and live with thee,
   In unreproved pleasures free.   *L'Allegro, l. 38*

13 While the cock with lively din
   Scatters the rear of darkness thin,
   And to the stack, or the barn door,
   Stoutly struts his dames before,
   Oft list'ning how the hounds and horn
   Cheerly rouse the slumb'ring morn.
> *L'Allegro, l. 49*

14 And every shepherd tells his tale
   Under the hawthorn in the dale.
> *L'Allegro, l. 67*

15 Meadows trim, with daisies pied,
   Shallow brooks, and rivers wide;
   Towers and battlements it sees
   Bosom'd high in tufted trees,
   Where perhaps some beauty lies,
   The cynosure of neighboring eyes.
> *L'Allegro, l. 75*

16 And the jocund rebecks sound
   To many a youth, and many a maid,
   Dancing in the checkered shade.
   And young and old come forth to play
   On a sunshine holiday.   *L'Allegro, l. 94*

17 Then to the spicy nut-brown ale.
> *L'Allegro, l. 100*

18 Tower'd cities please us then,
   And the busy hum of men.   *L'Allegro, l. 117*

19   Ladies, whose bright eyes
   Rain influence, and judge the prize.
> *L'Allegro, l. 121*

20 And pomp, and feast, and revelry,
   With mask, and antique pageantry,
   Such sights as youthful poets dream
   On summer eves by haunted stream.
   Then to the well-trod stage anon,
   If Jonson's learned sock be on,
   Or sweetest Shakespeare, Fancy's child,
   Warble his native wood-notes wild,
   And ever, against eating cares,
   Lap me in soft Lydian airs,
   Married to immortal verse
   Such as the meeting soul may pierce,
   In notes with many a winding bout
   Of linked sweetness long drawn out.
> *L'Allegro, l. 127*

21 Such strains as would have won the ear
   Of Pluto, to have quite set free
   His half-regain'd Eurydice.
   These delights, if thou canst give,
   Mirth, with thee, I mean to live.
> *L'Allegro, l. 148*

22 Hence vain deluding Joys,
   The brood of Folly without father bred!
> *Il Penseroso [1631], l. 1*

23 Hail divinest Melancholy.   *Il Penseroso, l. 12*

24 Sober, steadfast, and demure.   *Il Penseroso, l. 32*

25 And looks commercing with the skies,
   Thy rapt soul sitting in thine eyes.
> *Il Penseroso, l. 39*

1 And add to these retired Leisure,
 That in trim gardens takes his pleasure.
                           Il Penseroso, l. 49

2 Sweet bird, that shunn'st the noise of folly,
 Most musical, most melancholy!
                           Il Penseroso, l. 61

3   I walk unseen
 On the dry smooth-shaven green,
 To behold the wandering moon,
 Riding near her highest noon,
 Like one that had been led astray
 Through the heav'n's wide pathless way,
 And oft, as if her head she bow'd,
 Stooping through a fleecy cloud.
                           Il Penseroso, l. 65

4 Oft, on a plat of rising ground,
 I hear the far-off curfew sound
 Over some wide-watered shore,
 Swinging low with sullen roar.
                           Il Penseroso, l. 73

5 Where glowing embers through the room
 Teach light to counterfeit a gloom,
 Far from all resort of mirth,
 Save the cricket on the hearth.
                           Il Penseroso, l. 79

6 Sometime let gorgeous Tragedy
 In sceptered pall come sweeping by,
 Presenting Thebes, or Pelops' line,
 Or the tale of Troy divine.   *Il Penseroso, l. 97*

7 Or bid the soul of Orpheus sing
 Such notes as, warbled to the string,
 Drew iron tears down Pluto's cheek.
                           Il Penseroso, l. 105

8 Or call up him that left half told
 The story of Cambuscan bold.
                           Il Penseroso, l. 109

9 Where more is meant than meets the ear.
                           Il Penseroso, l. 120

10 And storied windows richly dight,
 Casting a dim religious light.
 There let the pealing organ blow,
 To the full-voiced choir below,
 In service high, and anthems clear
 As may, with sweetness, through mine ear
 Dissolve me into ecstasies,
 And bring all Heaven before mine eyes.
                           Il Penseroso, l. 159

11 Before the starry threshold of Jove's Court
 My mansion is.   *Comus [1634], l. 1*

12 Above the smoke and stir of this dim spot
 Which men call earth.   *Comus, l. 5*

13 Yet some there be that by due steps aspire
 To lay their just hands on that golden key
 That opes the palace of Eternity.   *Comus, l. 12*

14 An old, and haughty nation proud in arms.
                           Comus, l. 33

15 What never yet was heard in tale or song,
 From old or modern bard, in hall or bower.
                           Comus, l. 44

16 Bacchus, that first from out the purple grape
 Crush'd the sweet poison of misused wine.
                           Comus, l. 46

17 These my sky-robes, spun out of Iris' woof.
                           Comus, l. 83

18 The star that bids the shepherd fold.
                           Comus, l. 93

19 And the gilded car of day,
 His glowing axle doth allay
 In the steep Atlantic stream.   *Comus, l. 95*

20 Midnight shout and revelry,
 Tipsy dance and jollity.   *Comus, l. 103*

21 What hath night to do with sleep?   *Comus, l. 122*

22 Ere the blabbing eastern scout,
 The nice morn on th' Indian steep,
 From her cabin'd loophole peep.   *Comus, l. 138*

23 Come, knit hands, and beat the ground,
 In a light fantastic round.   *Comus, l. 143*

24   A thousand fantasies
 Begin to throng into my memory,
 Of calling shapes, and beck'ning shadows dire,
 And airy tongues that syllable men's names
 On sands and shores and desert wildernesses.
                           Comus, l. 205

25 Was I deceiv'd or did a sable cloud
 Turn forth her silver lining on the night?
                           Comus, l. 221

26 Sweet Echo, sweetest nymph, that liv'st unseen
 Within thy airy shell
 By slow Meander's margent green,
 And in the violet-embroider'd vale.
                           Comus, l. 230

27 How sweetly did they float upon the wings
 Of silence, through the empty-vaulted night,
 At every fall smoothing the raven down
 Of darkness till it smil'd!   *Comus, l. 249*

28 Such sober certainty of waking bliss.
                           Comus, l. 263

29 Virtue could see to do what Virtue would
 By her own radiant light, though sun and moon

Were in the flat sea sunk. And Wisdom's self
Oft seeks to sweet retired solitude,
Where, with her best nurse Contemplation,
She plumes her feathers, and lets grow her wings.
Comus, l. 373

1   The unsunn'd heaps
Of miser's treasure.   *Comus, l. 398*

2 Tis Chastity, my brother, Chastity:
She that has that, is clad in complete steel.
Comus, l. 420

3 How charming is divine philosophy!
Not harsh and crabbed, as dull fools suppose,
But musical as is Apollo's lute,
And a perpetual feast of nectar'd sweets
Where no crude surfeit reigns.   *Comus, l. 476*

4 Fill'd the air with barbarous dissonance.
Comus, l. 550

5   I was all ear,
And took in strains that might create a soul
Under the ribs of Death.   *Comus, l. 560*

6   That power
Which erring men call Chance.   *Comus, l. 587*

7 Praising the lean and sallow abstinence.
Comus, l. 709

8 Beauty is Nature's coin, must not be hoarded,
But must be current, and the good thereof
Consists in mutual and partaken bliss.
Comus, l. 739

9 Beauty is Nature's brag, and must be shown
In courts, at feasts, and high solemnities,
Where most may wonder at the workmanship;
It is for homely features to keep home—
They had their name thence; coarse complexions
And cheeks of sorry grain will serve to ply
The sampler, and to tease the huswife's wool.
What need a vermeil-tinctur'd lip for that,
Love-darting eyes, or tresses like the morn?
Comus, l. 745

10 Sabrina fair,
Listen where thou art sitting
Under the glassy, cool, translucent wave,
In twisted braids of lilies knitting
The loose train of thy amber-dropping hair;
Listen for dear honor's sake,
Goddess of the silver lake,
     Listen and save.   *Comus, l. 859*

11 But now my task is smoothly done:
I can fly, or I can run.   *Comus, l. 1012*

12 Love Virtue, she alone is free,
She can teach ye how to climb

Higher than the sphery chime;
Or, if Virtue feeble were,
Heav'n itself would stoop to her.
Comus, l. 1019

13 Yet once more, O ye laurels, and once more
Ye myrtles brown, with ivy never sere,
I come to pluck your berries harsh and crude,
And with forc'd fingers rude
Shatter your leaves before the mellowing year.
Lycidas [1637], l. 1

14   He knew
Himself to sing, and build the lofty rhyme.
Lycidas, l. 10

15 Hence with denial vain, and coy excuse.
Lycidas, l. 18

16 Under the opening eyelids of the morn,
We drove afield; and both together heard
What time the gray-fly winds her sultry horn,
Batt'ning our flocks with the fresh dews of night.
Lycidas, l. 26

17 But O the heavy change, now thou art gone,
Now thou art gone and never must return!
Lycidas, l. 37

18 As killing as the canker to the rose.
Lycidas, l. 45

19 Alas! what boots it with incessant care
To tend the homely slighted shepherd's trade,
And strictly meditate the thankless Muse?
Were it not better done as others use,
To sport with Amaryllis in the shade,
Or with the tangles of Neaera's hair?
Fame is the spur that the clear spirit doth raise
(That last infirmity of noble mind)[1]
To scorn delights, and live laborious days;
But the fair guerdon when we hope to find,
And think to burst out into sudden blaze,
Comes the blind Fury with th' abhorred shears,
And slits the thin-spun life.   *Lycidas, l. 64*

20 Fame is no plant that grows on mortal soil.
Lycidas, l. 78

21 It was that fatal and perfidious bark,
Built in th' eclipse, and rigg'd with curses dark,
That sunk so low that sacred head of thine.
Lycidas, l. 100

22 Last came, and last did go,
The Pilot of the Galilean lake;

---

[1] That thirst [for applause], if the last infirmity of noble minds, is also the first infirmity of weak ones; and on the whole, the strongest impulsive influence of average humanity.—JOHN RUSKIN, *Sesame and Lilies* [1865], *Of Kings' Treasuries, sec. 3*

Two massy keys he bore of metals twain,
(The golden opes, the iron shuts amain).
                                    Lycidas, l. 108

1 Blind mouths! That scarce themselves know how to
        hold
   A sheep-hook.   *Lycidas, l. 119*

2 The hungry sheep look up, and are not fed,
   But swoln with wind and the rank mist they draw,
   Rot inwardly, and foul contagion spread:
   Besides what the grim wolf with privy paw
   Daily devours apace, and nothing said;
   But that two-handed engine at the door
   Stands ready to smite once, and smite no more.
                                    Lycidas, l. 123

3 Whether beyond the stormy Hebrides,
   Where thou perhaps under the whelming tide
   Visit'st the bottom of the monstrous world.
                                    Lycidas, l. 156

4 Look homeward, Angel, now, and melt with ruth.
                                    Lycidas, l. 163

5 For Lycidas your sorrow is not dead,
   Sunk though he be beneath the watery floor;
   So sinks the day-star in the ocean bed;
   And yet anon repairs his drooping head,
   And tricks his beams, and with new-spangled ore
   Flames in the forehead of the morning sky.
   So Lycidas sunk low, but mounted high,
   Through the dear might of him that walk'd the
        waves.   *Lycidas, l. 166*

6 At last he rose, and twitch'd his mantle blue:
   Tomorrow to fresh woods and pastures new.
                                    Lycidas, l. 192

7 O nightingale, that on yon bloomy spray
   Warbl'st at eve, when all the woods are still.
                        Sonnet. To the Nightingale [c. 1637], l. 1

8 Thy liquid notes that close the eye of day.
                        Sonnet. To the Nightingale, l. 5

9 Where the bright seraphim in burning row
   Their loud uplifted angel trumpets blow.
                        At a Solemn Music [c. 1637], l. 10

10   A poet soaring in the high region of his fancies,
     with his garland and singing robes about him.
                        *The Reason of Church Government [1641],
                        bk. II, introduction*

11   By labor and intent study (which I take to be my
     portion in this life), joined with the strong propen-
     sity of nature, I might perhaps leave something so
     written to after-times, as they should not willingly
     let it die.
                        *The Reason of Church Government, II,
                        introduction*

12   Beholding the bright countenance of truth in
     the quiet and still air of delightful studies.
                        *The Reason of Church Government, II,
                        introduction*

13   He who would not be frustrate of his hope to
     write well hereafter in laudable things ought himself
     to be a true poem.
                        Apology for Smectymnuus [1642]

14   His words . . . like so many nimble and air[y]
     servitors trip about him at command.
                        Apology for Smectymnu[us]

15   Truth . . . never comes into the world but like [a]
     bastard, to the ignominy of him that brought h[er]
     forth.[1]
                        *The Doctrine and Discipline of Divorce
                        [1643], introduction*

16   Let not England forget her precedence of teach[-]
     ing nations how to live.
                        *The Doctrine and Discipline of Divorce,
                        introduction*

17   Litigious terms, fat contentions, and flowing fee[s.]
                        Tractate of Education [1644]

18   Inflamed with the study of learning and the a[d-]
     miration of virtue; stirred up with high hopes of li[v-]
     ing to be brave men and worthy patriots, dear t[o]
     God, and famous to all ages.
                        Tractate of Educatio[n]

19   Ornate rhetoric taught out of the rule [of]
     Plato. . . . To which poetry would be made subs[e-]
     quent, or indeed rather precedent, as being less su[b-]
     tle and fine, but more simple, sensuous, an[d]
     passionate.   *Tractate of Educatio[n]*

20   In those vernal seasons of the year, when the a[ir]
     is calm and pleasant, it were an injury and sullenne[ss]
     against Nature not to go out, and see her riche[s,]
     and partake in her rejoicing with heaven and earth.
                        Tractate of Educatio[n]

21   As good almost kill a man as kill a good boo[k;]
     who kills a man kills a reasonable creature, God[']
     image; but he who destroys a good book kills re[a-]
     son itself.   *Areopagitica [1644]*

22   A good book is the precious lifeblood of a ma[s-]
     ter spirit, embalmed and treasured up on purpose t[o]
     a life beyond life.   *Areopagiti[ca]*

23   I cannot praise a fugitive and cloistered virtu[e]
     unexercised and unbreathed, that never sallies o[ut]

───────────

[1]Still rule those minds on earth / At whom sage Milton's wor[d-]
wood words were hurled:/ "Truth like a bastard comes into th[e]
world / Never without ill-fame to him who gives her birth"?—
THOMAS HARDY, *Lausanne* [1897]

and sees her adversary, but slinks out of the race, where that immortal garland is to be run for, not without dust and heat.   *Areopagitica*

1   Where there is much desire to learn, there of necessity will be much arguing, much writing, many opinions; for opinion in good men is but knowledge in the making.   *Areopagitica*

2   God is decreeing to begin some new and great period in His Church, even to the reforming of Reformation itself: what does He then but reveal Himself to His servants, and as His manner is, first to His Englishmen?   *Areopagitica*

3   Methinks I see in my mind a noble and puissant nation rousing herself like a strong man after sleep, and shaking her invincible locks. Methinks I see her as an eagle mewing her mighty youth, and kindling her undazzled eyes at the full midday beam.   *Areopagitica*

4   Give me the liberty to know, to utter, and to argue freely according to conscience, above all liberties.   *Areopagitica*

5   Though all the winds of doctrine were let loose to play upon the earth, so Truth be in the field, we do injuriously, by licensing and prohibiting, to misdoubt her strength. Let her and Falsehood grapple; who ever knew Truth put to the worse, in a free and open encounter?   *Areopagitica*

6   Men of most renowned virtue have sometimes by transgressing most truly kept the law.
    Tetrachordon [1644–1645]

7   That would have made Quintilian stare and gasp.
    On the Detraction Which Followed upon My Writing Certain Treatises [1645]

8   For such kind of borrowing as this, if it be not bettered by the borrower, among good authors is accounted Plagiarè.   *Eikonoklastes [1649], ch. 23*

9   None can love freedom heartily, but good men; the rest love not freedom, but license.
    Tenure of Kings and Magistrates [1649]

10   No man who knows aught, can be so stupid to deny that all men naturally were born free.
    Tenure of Kings and Magistrates

11   Peace hath her victories
No less renown'd than war.
    To the Lord General Cromwell [1652]

12   When I consider how my light is spent,
Ere half my days, in this dark world and wide,
And that one talent which is death to hide
Lodg'd with me useless.
    On His Blindness [1652]

13   Doth God exact day-labor, light denied?
    On His Blindness

14   Who best
Bear his mild yoke, they serve him best: his state
Is kingly; thousands at his bidding speed,
And post o'er land and ocean without rest;
They also serve who only stand and wait.
    On His Blindness

15   Avenge, O Lord, thy slaughter'd saints, whose bones
Lie scatter'd on the Alpine mountains cold;
Ev'n them who kept thy truth so pure of old
When all our fathers worshipp'd stocks and stones
Forget not.
    On the Late Massacre in Piedmont [1655]

16   Yet I argue not
Against Heav'n's hand or will, nor bate one jot
Of heart or hope; but still bear up, and steer
Right onward.
    To Cyriack Skinner, upon His Blindness [c. 1655]

17   Methought I saw my late espoused saint
Brought to me like Alcestis from the grave.
    On His Deceased Wife [c. 1658]

18   But oh! as to embrace me she inclin'd,
I wak'd, she fled, and day brought back my night.
    On His Deceased Wife

19   Of Man's first disobedience, and the fruit
Of that forbidden tree whose mortal taste
Brought death into the world, and all our woe,
With loss of Eden.
    Paradise Lost [1667], bk. I, l. 1

20   Things unattempted yet in prose or rhyme.
    Paradise Lost, l. 16

21   What in me is dark
Illumine, what is low raise and support;
That to the height of this great argument
I may assert eternal Providence,
And justify the ways of God to men.
    Paradise Lost, I, l. 22

22   The infernal serpent; he it was, whose guile,
Stirr'd up with envy and revenge, deceiv'd
The mother of mankind.
    Paradise Lost, I, l. 34

23   Him the Almighty Power
Hurl'd headlong flaming from th' ethereal sky
With hideous ruin and combustion down
To bottomless perdition, there to dwell
In adamantine chains and penal fire,
Who durst defy th' Omnipotent to arms.
    Paradise Lost, I, l. 44

1 No light, but rather darkness visible.
Paradise Lost, I, l. 63

2 Regions of sorrow, doleful shades, where peace
And rest can never dwell, hope never comes
That comes to all.   *Paradise Lost, I, l. 65*

3   What though the field be lost?
All is not lost; th' unconquerable will,
And study of revenge, immortal hate,
And courage never to submit or yield.
Paradise Lost, I, l. 105

4   To be weak is miserable,
Doing or suffering.   *Paradise Lost, I, l. 157*

5 And out of good still to find means of evil.
Paradise Lost, I, l. 165

6 The seat of desolation, void of light.
Paradise Lost, I, l. 181

7 A mind not to be chang'd by place or time.
The mind is its own place, and in itself
Can make a heav'n of hell, a hell of heav'n.
Paradise Lost, I, l. 253

8 To reign is worth ambition though in hell:
Better to reign in hell than serve in heav'n.
Paradise Lost, I, l. 262

9 His spear, to equal which the tallest pine
Hewn on Norwegian hills, to be the mast
Of some great ammiral, were but a wand,
He walk'd with, to support uneasy steps
Over the burning marle.
Paradise Lost, I, l. 292

10 Thick as autumnal leaves that strow the brooks
In Vallombrosa.   *Paradise Lost, I, l. 302*

11 Awake, arise, or be forever fallen!
Paradise Lost, I, l. 330

12   Spirits, when they please,
Can either sex assume, or both.
Paradise Lost, I, l. 423

13   When night
Darkens the streets, then wander forth the sons
Of Belial, flown with insolence and wine.
Paradise Lost, I, l. 500

14 Th' imperial ensign, which, full high advanc'd,
Shone like a meteor, streaming to the wind.[1]
Paradise Lost, I, l. 536

15 Sonorous metal blowing martial sounds:
At which the universal host up sent
A shout that tore hell's concave, and beyond
Frighted the reign of Chaos and old Night.
Paradise Lost, I, l. 540

16   Anon they move
In perfect phalanx, to the Dorian mood
Of flutes and soft recorders.
Paradise Lost, I, l. 549

17   His form had yet not lost
All her original brightness, nor appear'd
Less than archangel ruin'd, and th' excess
Of glory obscur'd.   *Paradise Lost, I, l. 591*

18   The sun . . .
In dim eclipse, disastrous twilight sheds
On half the nations, and with fear of change
Perplexes monarchs.   *Paradise Lost, I, l. 594*

19   Care
Sat on his faded cheek, but under brows
Of dauntless courage.   *Paradise Lost, I, l. 601*

20 Thrice he assay'd, and thrice, in spite of scorn,
Tears, such as angels weep, burst forth.
Paradise Lost, I, l. 619

21   Who overcomes
By force hath overcome but half his foe.
Paradise Lost, I, l. 648

22 Mammon, the least erected spirit that fell
From heaven; for ev'n in heaven his looks and
thoughts
Were always downward bent, admiring more
The riches of heaven's pavement, trodden gold,
Than aught divine or holy else enjoyed
In vision beatific.   *Paradise Lost, I, l. 679*

23   Let none admire
That riches grow in hell; that soil may best
Deserve the precious bane.
Paradise Lost, I, l. 690

24   From morn
To noon he fell, from noon to dewy eve,
A summer's day; and with the setting sun
Dropp'd from the zenith like a falling star.
Paradise Lost, I, l. 742

25 High on a throne of royal state, which far
Outshone the wealth of Ormus and of Ind,
Or where the gorgeous East with richest hand
Showers on her kings barbaric pearl and gold,
Satan exalted sat, by merit rais'd
To that bad eminence; and from despair
Thus high uplifted beyond hope, aspires
Beyond thus high, insatiate to pursue
Vain war with heav'n.   *Paradise Lost, II, l. 1*

26   Moloch, scepter'd king,
Stood up, the strongest and the fiercest spirit
That fought in heav'n; now fiercer by despair.
Paradise Lost, II, l. 44

27   Rather than be less
Car'd not to be at all.   *Paradise Lost, II, l. 47*

---

[1]Streamed like a meteor to the troubled air. — THOMAS GRAY,
The Bard [1757], *sec. I, st. 2, l. 6*

1 My sentence is for open war.
Paradise Lost, II, l. 51

2 Which if not victory is yet revenge.
Paradise Lost, II, l. 105

3 But all was false and hollow; through his tongue
Dropp'd manna, and could make the worse appear
The better reason.
Paradise Lost, II, l. 112

4   For who would lose,
Though full of pain, this intellectual being,
Those thoughts that wander through eternity,
To perish rather, swallow'd up and lost
In the wide womb of uncreated night,
Devoid of sense and motion?
Paradise Lost, II, l. 146

5 Unrespited, unpitied, unrepriev'd.
Paradise Lost, II, l. 185

6   The never-ending flight
Of future days.   *Paradise Lost, II, l. 221*

7 Thus Belial with words cloth'd in reason's garb
Counsel'd ignoble ease, and peaceful sloth,
Not peace.   *Paradise Lost, II, l. 226*

8   With grave
Aspect he rose, and in his rising seem'd
A pillar of state; deep on his front engraven
Deliberation sat and public care;
And princely counsel in his face yet shone,
Majestic though in ruin.
Paradise Lost, II, l. 300

9   To sit in darkness here
Hatching vain empires.   *Paradise Lost, II, l. 377*

10 The palpable obscure.   *Paradise Lost, II, l. 406*

11   Long is the way
And hard, that out of hell leads up to light.
Paradise Lost, II, l. 432

12 Their rising all at once was as the sound
Of thunder heard remote.
Paradise Lost, II, l. 476

13 Others apart sat on a hill retir'd,
In thoughts more elevate, and reason'd high
Of Providence, foreknowledge, will, and fate,
Fix'd fate, free will, foreknowledge absolute,
And found no end, in wand'ring mazes lost.
Paradise Lost, II, l. 557

14 Vain wisdom all, and false philosophy.
Paradise Lost, II, l. 565

15   Arm th' obdur'd breast
With stubborn patience as with triple steel.
Paradise Lost, II, l. 568

16 Far off from these a slow and silent stream,
Lethe the river of oblivion rolls.
Paradise Lost, II, l. 582

17 At certain revolutions all the damn'd
Are brought: and feel by turns the bitter change
Of fierce extremes, extremes by change more fierce.
Paradise Lost, II, l. 597

18 Whence and what art thou, execrable shape?
Paradise Lost, II, l. 681

19 Before mine eyes in opposition sits
Grim Death my son and foe.
Paradise Lost, II, l. 803

20 Hot, cold, moist, and dry, four champions fierce,[1]
Strive here for mast'ry.   *Paradise Lost, II, l. 898*

21   To compare
Great things with small.   *Paradise Lost, II, l. 921*

22 With ruin upon ruin, rout on rout,
Confusion worse confounded.
Paradise Lost, II, l. 995

23 And fast by hanging in a golden chain,
This pendent world, in bigness as a star
Of smallest magnitude close by the moon.
Paradise Lost, II, l. 1051

24 Hail, holy light! offspring of heav'n firstborn.[2]
Paradise Lost, III, l. 1

25   Thus with the year
Seasons return; but not to me returns
Day, or the sweet approach of ev'n or morn,
Or sight of vernal bloom, or summer's rose,
Or flocks, or herds, or human face divine;
But cloud instead, and ever-during dark
Surrounds me, from the cheerful ways of men
Cut off, and for the book of knowledge fair
Presented with a universal blank
Of Nature's works to me expung'd and raz'd,
And wisdom at one entrance quite shut out.
Paradise Lost, III, l. 40

26 See golden days, fruitful of golden deeds,
With Joy and Love triumphing.
Paradise Lost, III, l. 337

27 Dark with excessive bright.
Paradise Lost, III, l. 380

28 Into a limbo large and broad, since called
The Paradise of Fools, to few unknown.
Paradise Lost, III, l. 495

---

[1]Hot and cold, and moist and dry. — Du Bartas, *Divine Weeks and Works* [1578], *Second Day*

[2]God's first creature, which was light. — Francis Bacon, *The New Atlantis* [1626]

Light, the prime work of God. — John Milton, *Samson Agonistes* [1671], *l. 70*

1 The hell within him.   *Paradise Lost, IV, l. 20*

2   At whose sight all the stars
Hide their diminish'd heads.[1]
Paradise Lost, IV, l. 34

3 Me miserable! which way shall I fly
Infinite wrath, and infinite despair?
Which way I fly is hell; myself am hell;
And in the lowest deep a lower deep,
Still threat'ning to devour me, opens wide,
To which the hell I suffer seems a heaven.
Paradise Lost, IV, l. 73

4 So farewell hope, and with hope farewell fear,
Farewell remorse: all good to me is lost;
Evil, be thou my good.   *Paradise Lost, IV, l. 108*

5   And on the Tree of Life,
The middle tree and highest there that grew,
Sat like a cormorant.   *Paradise Lost, IV, l. 194*

6 A heaven on earth.   *Paradise Lost, IV, l. 208*

7 Flowers of all hue, and without thorn the rose.
Paradise Lost, IV, l. 256

8   Not that fair field
Of Enna, where Proserpin gathering flowers
Herself a fairer flower by gloomy Dis
Was gathered, which cost Ceres all that pain
To seek her through the world.
Paradise Lost, IV, l. 268

9 Two of far nobler shape erect and tall,
Godlike erect, with native honor clad
In naked majesty seem'd lords of all.
Paradise Lost, IV, l. 288

10 For contemplation he and valor form'd,
For softness she and sweet attractive grace;
He for God only, she for God in him.
Paradise Lost, IV, l. 297

11   Implied
Subjection, but requir'd with gentle sway,
And by her yielded, by him best receiv'd,
Yielded with coy submission, modest pride,
And sweet reluctant amorous delay.
Paradise Lost, IV, l. 307

12 Adam the goodliest man of men since born
His sons, the fairest of her daughters Eve.
Paradise Lost, IV, l. 323

13 Imparadis'd in one another's arms.
Paradise Lost, IV, l. 506

14   Live while ye may,
Yet happy pair.   *Paradise Lost, IV, l. 533*

15 Now came still evening on, and twilight gray
Had in her sober livery all things clad.
Paradise Lost, IV, l. 59

16   The wakeful nightingale,
She all night long her amorous descant sung;
Silence was pleas'd: now glow'd the firmament
With living sapphires: Hesperus, that led
The starry host, rode brightest, till the moon,
Rising in clouded majesty, at length
Apparent queen unveil'd her peerless light,
And o'er the dark her silver mantle threw.
Paradise Lost, IV, l. 60

17 With thee conversing I forget all time,
All seasons, and their change; all please alike.
Sweet is the breath of morn, her rising sweet,
With charm of earliest birds.
Paradise Lost, IV, l. 63

18   Sweet the coming on
Of grateful ev'ning mild, then silent night
With this her solemn bird, and this fair moon,
And these the gems of heaven, her starry train.
Paradise Lost, IV, l. 64

19 Millions of spiritual creatures walk the earth
Unseen, both when we wake, and when we sleep.
Paradise Lost, IV, l. 67

20   In naked beauty more adorn'd,
More lovely, than Pandora.
Paradise Lost, IV, l. 71

21   Eas'd the putting off
These troublesome disguises which we wear.
Paradise Lost, IV, l. 73

22 Hail wedded love, mysterious law, true source
Of human offspring.   *Paradise Lost, IV, l. 75*

23 Squat like a toad, close at the ear of Eve.
Paradise Lost, IV, l. 80

24 Not to know me argues yourselves unknown.
Paradise Lost, IV, l. 83

25   Abash'd the Devil stood,
And felt how awful goodness is, and saw
Virtue in her shape how lovely.
Paradise Lost, IV, l. 84

26 All hell broke loose.   *Paradise Lost, IV, l. 91*

27 Like Teneriff or Atlas unremoved.
Paradise Lost, IV, l. 98

28   The starry cope
Of heaven.   *Paradise Lost, IV, l. 99*

29   His sleep
Was airy light from pure digestion bred.
Paradise Lost, V, l.

---

[1]Ye little stars! hide your diminished rays. —ALEXANDER POPE, *Moral Essays* [1731–1735], *Epistle III, l. 282*

1   My latest found,
 Heaven's last, best gift, my ever new delight!
     Paradise Lost, V, l. 18

2 These are thy glorious works, Parent of good.
     Paradise Lost, V, l. 153

3 Him first, him last, him midst, and without end.
     Paradise Lost, V, l. 165

4 A wilderness of sweets. *Paradise Lost, V, l. 294*

5 So saying, with dispatchful looks in haste
 She turns, on hospitable thoughts intent.
     Paradise Lost, V, l. 331

6   Freely we serve,
 Because we freely love, as in our will
 To love or not; in this we stand or fall.
     Paradise Lost, V, l. 538

7   What if earth
 Be but the shadow of heaven, and things therein
 Each to other like, more than on earth is thought?
     Paradise Lost, V, l. 574

8 Hear all ye Angels, progeny of light,
 Thrones, Dominations, Princedoms, Virtues,
   Powers. *Paradise Lost, V, l. 600*

9 Among the faithless, faithful only he.
     Paradise Lost, V, l. 897

10   Morn,
 Wak'd by the circling hours, with rosy hand
 Unbarr'd the gates of light.
     Paradise Lost, VI, l. 2

11 Servant of God, well done, well hast thou fought
 The better fight, who single hast maintained
 Against revolted multitudes the cause
 Of truth, in word mightier than they in arms.
     Paradise Lost, VI, l. 29

12 He onward came; far off his coming shone.
     Paradise Lost, VI, l. 768

13 More safe I sing with mortal voice, unchang'd
 To hoarse or mute, though fall'n on evil days,
 On evil days though fall'n, and evil tongues;
 In darkness, and with dangers compass'd round,
 And solitude. *Paradise Lost, VII, l. 24*

14   Out of one man a race
 Of men innumerable. *Paradise Lost, VII, l. 155*

15   There Leviathan
 Hugest of living creatures, on the deep
 Stretch'd like a promontory sleeps or swims,
 And seems a moving land, and at his gills
 Draws in, and at his trunk spouts out a sea.
     Paradise Lost, VII, l. 412

16 The planets in their stations list'ning stood,
 While the bright pomp ascended jubilant.
 Open, ye everlasting gates, they sung,
 Open, ye heavens, your living doors; let in
 The great Creator from his work return'd
 Magnificent, his six days' work, a world.
     Paradise Lost, VII, l. 563

17 The angel ended, and in Adam's ear
 So charming left his voice that he awhile
 Thought him still speaking, still stood fix'd to hear.
     Paradise Lost, VIII, l. 1

18 Liquid lapse of murmuring streams.
     Paradise Lost, VIII, l. 263

19 And feel that I am happier than I know.
     Paradise Lost, VIII, l. 282

20 Her virtue and the conscience of her worth,
 That would be woo'd, and not unsought be won.
     Paradise Lost, VIII, l. 502

21 The sum of earthly bliss.
     Paradise Lost, VIII, l. 522

22   So absolute she seems
 And in herself complete, so well to know
 Her own, that what she wills to do or say,
 Seems wisest, virtuousest, discreetest, best.
     Paradise Lost, VIII, l. 547

23 Accuse not Nature, she hath done her part;
 Do thou but thine. *Paradise Lost, VIII, l. 561*

24 My unpremeditated verse.
     Paradise Lost, IX, l. 24

25   Unless an age too late, or cold
 Climate, or years damp my intended wing.
     Paradise Lost, IX, l. 44

26 The serpent subtlest beast of all the field.
     Paradise Lost, IX, l. 86

27 For solitude sometimes is best society,
 And short retirement urges sweet return.
     Paradise Lost, IX, l. 249

28 As one who long in populous city pent.
     Paradise Lost, IX, l. 445

29 God so commanded, and left that command
 Sole daughter of his voice; the rest, we live
 Law to ourselves, our reason is our law.
     Paradise Lost, IX, l. 652

30   Her rash hand in evil hour
 Forth reaching to the fruit, she pluck'd, she eat:
 Earth felt the wound, and Nature from her seat,
 Sighing through all her works, gave signs of woe
 That all was lost. *Paradise Lost, IX, l. 780*

1 So dear I love him, that with him all deaths
I could endure, without him live no life.
Paradise Lost, IX, l. 832

2   In her face excuse
Came prologue, and apology too prompt.
Paradise Lost, IX, l. 853

3 O fairest of creation! last and best
Of all God's works! creature in whom excell'd
Whatever can to sight or thought be form'd,
Holy, divine, good, amiable, or sweet!
How art thou lost, how on a sudden lost,
Defac'd, deflower'd, and now to Death devote?
Paradise Lost, IX, l. 896

4   I feel
The link of nature draw me: flesh of flesh,
Bone of my bone thou art, and from thy state
Mine never shall be parted, bliss or woe.
Paradise Lost, IX, l. 913

5 Our state cannot be sever'd; we are one,
One flesh; to lose thee were to lose myself.
Paradise Lost, IX, l. 958

6   I shall temper so
Justice with mercy.   *Paradise Lost, X, l. 77*

7 Pandemonium, city and proud seat
Of Lucifer.   *Paradise Lost, X, l. 424*

8 A dismal universal hiss, the sound
Of public scorn.   *Paradise Lost, X, l. 508*

9 Death . . . on his pale horse.
Paradise Lost, X, l. 588

10 Demoniac frenzy, moping melancholy,
And moon-struck madness.
Paradise Lost, XI, l. 485

11 Nor love thy life, nor hate; but what thou liv'st
Live well; how long or short permit to Heaven.
Paradise Lost, XI, l. 553

12 A bevy of fair women.   *Paradise Lost, XI, l. 582*

13   The evening star,
Love's harbinger.   *Paradise Lost, XI, l. 588*

14 The brazen throat of war.
Paradise Lost, XI, l. 713

15   For now I see
Peace to corrupt no less than war to waste.
Paradise Lost, XI, l. 783

16 An olive leaf he brings, pacific sign.
Paradise Lost, XI, l. 860

17 The world was all before them, where to choose
Their place of rest, and Providence their guide:

They hand in hand with wand'ring steps and slow
Through Eden took their solitary way.
Paradise Lost, XII, l. 64

18   Most men admire
Virtue who follow not her lore.
Paradise Regained [1671], bk. I, l. 48

19 Skill'd to retire, and in retiring draw
Hearts after them tangled in amorous nets.
Paradise Regained, II, l. 16

20   Beauty stands
In the admiration only of weak minds
Led captive.   *Paradise Regained, II, l. 22*

21 Of whom to be disprais'd were no small praise.
Paradise Regained, III, l. 5

22 Elephants endorsed with towers.
Paradise Regained, III, l. 32

23 Dusk faces with white silken turbans wreath'd.
Paradise Regained, IV, l. 7

24   The childhood shows the man,
As morning shows the day.
Paradise Regained, IV, l. 22

25 Athens, the eye of Greece, mother of arts
And eloquence.   *Paradise Regained, IV, l. 24*

26   The olive grove of Academe,
Plato's retirement, where the Attic bird
Trills her thick-warbled notes the summer long.
Paradise Regained, IV, l. 24

27   Socrates . . .
Whom well inspir'd the oracle pronounc'd
Wisest of men.   *Paradise Regained, IV, l. 27*

28 The first and wisest of them all professed
To know this only, that he nothing knew.
Paradise Regained, IV, l. 29

29 Deep vers'd in books and shallow in himself.
Paradise Regained, IV, l. 32

30   Till morning fair
Came forth with pilgrim steps, in amice gray.
Paradise Regained, IV, l. 42

31 Eyeless in Gaza, at the mill with slaves.
Samson Agonistes [1671], l. 4

32 O dark, dark, dark, amid the blaze of noon,
Irrecoverably dark, total eclipse
Without all hope of day!   *Samson Agonistes, l. 8*

33 The sun to me is dark
And silent as the moon,
When she deserts the night,
Hid in her vacant interlunar cave.
Samson Agonistes, l. 8

1 To live a life half dead, a living death.
    Samson Agonistes, l. 100

2   Apt words have power to suage
  The tumors of a troubled mind.
    Samson Agonistes, l. 184

3 Just are the ways of God,
  And justifiable to men;
  Unless there be who think not God at all.
    Samson Agonistes, l. 293

4 What boots it at one gate to make defense,
  And at another to let in the foe?
    Samson Agonistes, l. 560

5 My race of glory run, and race of shame,
  And I shall shortly be with them at rest.
    Samson Agonistes, l. 597

6 But who is this, what thing of sea or land?
  Female of sex it seems,
  That so bedeck'd, ornate, and gay,
  Comes this way sailing
  Like a stately ship
  Of Tarsus, bound for th' isles
  Of Javan or Gadire,
  With all her bravery on, and tackle trim,
  Sails fill'd, and streamers waving,
  Courted by all the winds that hold them play;
  An amber scent of odorous perfume
  Her harbinger?
    Samson Agonistes, l. 710

7 *Dalila:* In argument with men a woman ever
  Goes by the worse, whatever be her cause.
  Samson: For want of words, no doubt, or lack of
    breath!   *Samson Agonistes, l. 903*

8 Fame, if not double-faced, is double-mouthed,
  And with contrary blast proclaims most deeds;
  On both his wings, one black, the other white,
  Bears greatest names in his wild airy flight.
    Samson Agonistes, l. 971

9 Yet beauty, though injurious, hath strange power,
  After offense returning, to regain
  Love once possess'd.
    Samson Agonistes, l. 1003

10 Love-quarrels oft in pleasing concord end;
  Not wedlock-treachery.
    Samson Agonistes, l. 1008

11 Boast not of what thou would'st have done, but do
  What then thou would'st.
    Samson Agonistes, l. 1104

12 He's gone; and who knows how he may report
  Thy words by adding fuel to the flame?
    Samson Agonistes, l. 1350

13 For evil news rides post, while good news baits.
    Samson Agonistes, l. 1538

14 Suspense in news is torture.
    Samson Agonistes, l. 1569

15 Nothing is here for tears, nothing to wail
  Or knock the breast, no weakness, no contempt,
  Dispraise, or blame, nothing but well and fair,
  And what may quiet us in a death so noble.
    Samson Agonistes, l. 1721

16 All is best, though we oft doubt,
  What the unsearchable dispose
  Of highest Wisdom brings about.
    Samson Agonistes, l. 1745

17 Calm of mind, all passion spent.
    Samson Agonistes, l. 1758

18   Such bickerings to recount, met often in these
our writers, what more worth is it than to chronicle
the wars of kites or crows flocking and fighting in
the air?   *The History of England [1670], bk. IV*

Edward Hyde, Earl of Clarendon
1609–1674

19   He [Hampden] had a head to contrive, a tongue
to persuade, and a hand to execute any mischief.
    *History of the Rebellion [1702–1704], vol. III,
bk. VII, sec. 84*

Sir John Suckling
1609–1642

20 Why so pale and wan, fond lover?
  Prithee, why so pale?
  Will, when looking well can't move her,
  Looking ill prevail?   *Aglaura [1638]. Song, st. 1*

21 Quit, quit, for shame, this will not move,
  This cannot take her.
  If of herself she will not love,
  Nothing can make her.
  The devil take her!   *Aglaura. Song, st. 3*

22 High characters (cries one), and he would see
  Things that ne'er were, nor are, nor ne'er will be.[1]
    The Goblins [1639], epilogue

23 Her feet beneath her petticoat
  Like little mice, stole in and out,
  As if they feared the light;
  But oh, she dances such a way!

---

[1]There's no such thing in Nature, and you'll draw / A faultless monster which the world ne'er saw. —JOHN SHEFFIELD, DUKE OF BUCKINGHAM AND NORMANBY, *Essay on Poetry*

No sun upon an Easter-day
Is half so fine a sight.
A Ballad upon a Wedding [1641], st. 8

1 Her lips were red, and one was thin,
Compared to that was next her chin,
Some bee had stung it newly.
A Ballad upon a Wedding, st. 11

2 I prithee send me back my heart,
Since I cannot have thine;
For if from yours you will not part,
Why then shouldst thou have mine?
Fragmenta Aurea [1646]. Song, st. 1

3 'Tis not the meat, but 'tis the appetite
Makes eating a delight.
Fragmenta Aurea. Of Thee, Kind Boy, st. 3

4 Out upon it, I have loved
Three whole days together;
And am like to love three more,
If it prove fair weather.
Fragmenta Aurea. A Poem with the Answer, st. 1

5 'Tis expectation makes a blessing dear,
Heaven were not heaven, if we knew what it were.
Fragmenta Aurea. Against Fruition, st. 4

Anne Bradstreet
c. 1612–1672

6   Let Greeks be Greeks, and Women what they are.
The Prologue [1650]

7   Youth is the time of getting, middle age of improving, and old age of spending.
Meditations Divine and Moral [1664], 3

8   Authority without wisdom is like a heavy axe without an edge, fitter to bruise than polish.
Meditations Divine and Moral, 12

9   If we had no winter, the spring would not be so pleasant: if we did not sometimes taste of adversity, prosperity would not be so welcome.
Meditations Divine and Moral, 14

10   Sore laborers have hard hands and old sinners have brawny consciences.
Meditations Divine and Moral, 36

11 If ever two were one, then surely we.
If ever man were loved by wife, then thee;
If ever wife was happy in a man,
Compare with me ye women if you can.
To My Dear and Loving Husband [1678]

12   After a short time I changed my condition and was married, and came into this country, where I found a new world and new manners, at which my heart rose. But after I was convinced it was the way of God, I submitted to it and joined the church at Boston.
To My Dear Children [1867]

Samuel Butler
1612–1680

13 When civil fury first grew high,
And men fell out they knew not why.
Hudibras, pt. I [1663], canto I, l. 1

14 And pulpit, drum ecclesiastic,[1]
Was beat with fist, instead of a stick.
Hudibras, pt. I, canto I, l. 11

15 Beside, 'tis known he could speak Greek
As naturally as pigs squeak:[2]
That Latin was no more difficile
Than to a blackbird 'tis to whistle.
Hudibras, pt. I, canto I, l. 51

16 He could distinguish and divide
A hair 'twixt south and southwest side,
On either which he would dispute,
Confute, change hands, and still confute.
Hudibras, pt. I, canto I, l. 67

17 He'd run in debt by disputation,
And pay with ratiocination.
Hudibras, pt. I, canto I, l. 77

18 For rhetoric, he could not ope
His mouth, but out there flew a trope.
Hudibras, pt. I, canto I, l. 81

19 For all a rhetorician's rules
Teach nothing but to name his tools.
Hudibras, pt. I, canto I, l. 89

20 A Babylonish dialect
Which learned pedants much affect.
Hudibras, pt. I, canto I, l. 93

21 For he by geometric scale,
Could take the size of pots of ale.
Hudibras, pt. I, canto I, l. 121

22 And wisely tell what hour o' th' day
The clock doth strike, by algebra.
Hudibras, pt. I, canto I, l. 125

23 Where entity and quiddity,
The ghosts of defunct bodies, fly.
Hudibras, pt. I, canto I, l. 145

---

[1]This is the first we hear of the "drum ecclesiastic" beating up for recruits in worldly warfare in our country. —WASHINGTON IRVING, *Knickerbocker's History of New York* [1809], *bk. V, ch. 7*

[2]He Greek and Latin speaks with greater ease / Than hogs eat acorns, and tame pigeons peas. —LIONEL CRANFIELD, EARL OF MIDDLESEX [1575–1645], *Panegyric on Tom Coriate*

1 'Twas Presbyterian true blue.
Hudibras, pt. I, canto I, l. 191

2 Such as do build their faith upon
The holy text of pike and gun.
Hudibras, pt. I, canto I, l. 195

3 And prove their doctrine orthodox,
By apostolic blows and knocks.
Hudibras, pt. I, canto I, l. 199

4 Compound for sins they are inclin'd to,
By damning those they have no mind to.
Hudibras, pt. I, canto I, l. 215

5 The trenchant blade, Toledo trusty,
For want of fighting was grown rusty,
And ate into itself, for lack
Of somebody to hew and hack.
Hudibras, pt. I, canto I, l. 357

6 For rhyme the rudder is of verses,
With which like ships they steer their courses.
Hudibras, pt. I, canto I, l. 463

7 And force them, though it was in spite
Of Nature and their stars, to write.
Hudibras, pt. I, canto I, l. 647

8 Great actions are not always true sons
Of great and mighty resolutions.
Hudibras, pt. I, canto I, l. 885

9   I'll make the fur
Fly 'bout the ears of the old cur.
Hudibras, pt. I, canto III, l. 277

10 These reasons made his mouth to water.
Hudibras, pt. I, canto III, l. 379

11 I am not now in fortune's power:
He that is down can fall no lower.
Hudibras, pt. I, canto III, l. 877

12 Cheer'd up himself with ends of verse,
And sayings of philosophers.
Hudibras, pt. I, canto III, l. 1011

13 Cleric before, and Lay behind;
A lawless linsey-woolsey brother,
Half of one order, half another.
Hudibras, pt. I, canto III, l. 1226

14 Some have been beaten till they know
What wood a cudgel's of by th' blow;
Some kick'd, until they can feel whether
A shoe be Spanish or neat's leather.
*Hudibras, pt. II [1664], canto I,
l. 221*

15 For what is worth in anything
But so much money as 'twill bring?
Hudibras, pt. II, canto I, l. 465

16 She that with poetry is won
Is but a desk to write upon.
Hudibras, pt. II, canto I, l. 591

17 Love is a boy by poets styled;
Then spare the rod, and spoil the child.
Hudibras, pt. II, canto I, l. 843

18 Oaths are but words, and words but wind.
Hudibras, pt. II, canto II, l. 107

19 For truth is precious and divine—
Too rich a pearl for carnal swine.
Hudibras, pt. II, canto II, l. 257

20 He that imposes an oath makes it,
Not he that for convenience takes it;
Then how can any man be said
To break an oath he never made?
Hudibras, pt. II, canto II, l. 377

21   As the ancients
Say wisely, have a care o' th' main chance,
And look before you ere you leap;
For as you sow, ye are like to reap.
Hudibras, pt. II, canto II, l. 501

22 Doubtless the pleasure is as great
Of being cheated as to cheat.
Hudibras, pt. II, canto III, l. 1

23 He made an instrument to know
If the moon shine at full or no.
Hudibras, pt. II, canto III, l. 261

24 As men of inward light are wont
To turn their optics in upon 't.
Hudibras, pt. III [1678], canto I, l. 481

25 What makes all doctrines plain and clear?
About two hundred pounds a year.
And that which was proved true before,
Prove false again? Two hundred more.
Hudibras, pt. III, canto I, l. 1277

26 Nick Machiavel had ne'er a trick,
Though he gave his name to our Old Nick.
Hudibras, pt. III, canto I, l. 1313

27 True as the dial to the sun,[1]
Although it be not shined upon.
Hudibras, pt. III, canto II, l. 175

28 He that complies against his will
Is of his own opinion still.
Hudibras, pt. III, canto III, l. 547

29 Neither have the hearts to stay,
Nor wit enough to run away.
Hudibras, pt. III, canto III, l. 569

---

[1]True as the needle to the pole, / Or as the dial to the sun.—
BARTON BOOTH [1681–1733], *Song*

1 And poets by their sufferings grow,
  As if there were no more to do,
  To make a poet excellent,
  But only want and discontent.   *Fragments*

James Graham,
Marquess of Montrose
1612–1650

2 He either fears his fate too much,
  Or his deserts are small,
  That puts it not unto the touch
  To win or lose it all.
                    My Dear and Only Love, st. 2

3 I'll make thee glorious by my pen,
  And famous by my sword.[1]
                    My Dear and Only Love, st. 5

Richard Crashaw
c. 1613–1649

4 The conscious water saw its God, and blushed.[2]
     *Epigrammata Sacra [1634]. Aquae in
     Vinum Versae*

5 Two went to pray? Oh, rather say
  One went to brag, the other to pray.
     *Steps to the Temple [1648]. Two Went Up into
     the Temple to Pray*

6 Whoe'er she be,
  That not impossible she
  That shall command my heart and me.
     *Steps to the Temple. Wishes to His Supposed
     Mistress, l. 1*

7 Where'er she lie,
  Locked up from mortal eye,
  In shady leaves of destiny.
     *Steps to the Temple. Wishes to His Supposed
     Mistress, l. 4*

8 Life that dares send
  A challenge to his end,
  And when it comes, say, Welcome, friend!
     *Steps to the Temple. Wishes to His Supposed
     Mistress, l. 85*

9 Sidnaeian showers
  Of sweet discourse, whose powers
  Can crown old Winter's head with flowers.
     *Steps to the Temple. Wishes to His Supposed
     Mistress, l. 88*

10 I would be married, but I'd have no wife,
   I would be married to a single life.
                    Steps to the Temple. On Marriage

11 All is Caesar's, and what odds
   So long as Caesar's self is God's?
                    Steps to the Temple. Mark XII

12 All those fair and flagrant things.
     *The Flaming Heart upon the Book of Saint
     Teresa [1652], l. 34*

13 Love's passives are his activ'st part.
   The wounded is the wounding heart.
     *The Flaming Heart upon the Book of Saint
     Teresa, l. 73*

14 O thou undaunted daughter of desires!
     *The Flaming Heart upon the Book of Saint
     Teresa, l. 93*

15 By all the eagle in thee, all the dove.
     *The Flaming Heart upon the Book of Saint
     Teresa, l. 95*

16 Poor world (said I) what wilt thou do
   To entertain this starry stranger?
   Is this the best thou canst bestow?
   A cold, and not too cleanly, manger?
   Contend, ye powers of heav'n and earth,
   To fit a bed for this huge birth.
                    Hymn of the Nativity [1652], st. 6

17 Proud world, said I, cease your contest,
   And let the mighty babe alone.
   The phoenix builds the phoenix' nest.
   Love's architecture is his own.
   The babe whose birth embraves this morn,
   Made his own bed ere he was born.
                    Hymn of the Nativity, st. 7

18 Welcome, all wonders in one sight!
   Eternity shut in a span.
                    Hymn of the Nativity, Full Chorus

19 The modest front of this small floor,
   Believe me, reader, can say more
   Than many a braver marble can—
   "Here lies a truly honest man!"

                    Epitaph upon Mr. Ashton

---

[1] I'll make thee famous by my pen, / And glorious by my sword. — Sir Walter Scott, *The Legend of Montrose* [1819], *ch. 15*

[2] Nympha pudica Deum vidit, et erubuit. — Quoted by Samuel Johnson [1778]; from Boswell, *Life of Johnson* [1791], *vol. II, p. 218* (Everyman edition).

The bashful stream hath seen its God and blushed. — Aaron Hill

The water hears thy faintest word, / And blushes into wine. — John Samuel Bewley Monsell [1811–1875], *Mysterious Is Thy Presence, Lord, st. 1*

François, Duc de La Rochefoucauld
1613–1680

1 Self-love is the greatest of all flatterers.
Reflections; or, Sentences and Moral Maxims
[1678], maxim 2

2 We all have strength enough to endure the misfortunes of others.
Reflections, maxim 19

3 Philosophy triumphs easily over past evils and future evils; but present evils triumph over it.
Reflections, maxim 22

4 We need greater virtues to sustain good fortune
than bad. *Reflections, maxim 25*

5 If we had no faults of our own, we would not
take so much pleasure in noticing those of others.
Reflections, maxim 31

6 Jealousy feeds upon suspicion, and it turns into
fury or it ends as soon as we pass from suspicion to
certainty. *Reflections, maxim 32*

7 Self-interest speaks all sorts of tongues, and plays
all sorts of roles, even that of disinterestedness.
Reflections, maxim 39

8 We are never so happy nor so unhappy as we
imagine. *Reflections, maxim 49*

9 To succeed in the world, we do everything we
can to appear successful. *Reflections, maxim 56*

10 There is no disguise which can for long conceal
love where it exists or simulate it where it does not.
Reflections, maxim 70

11 There are very few people who are not ashamed
of having been in love when they no longer love
each other. *Reflections, maxim 71*

12 True love is like ghosts, which everybody talks
about and few have seen. *Reflections, maxim 76*

13 The love of justice in most men is simply the fear
of suffering injustice. *Reflections, maxim 78*

14 Silence is the best tactic for him who distrusts
himself. *Reflections, maxim 79*

15 It is more ignominious to mistrust our friends
than to be deceived by them.
Reflections, maxim 84

16 Everyone complains of his memory, and no one
complains of his judgment.
Reflections, maxim 89

17 Old people like to give good advice, as solace for
no longer being able to provide bad examples.
Reflections, maxim 93

18 A man who is ungrateful is sometimes less to
blame for it than his benefactor.
Reflections, maxim 96

19 The mind is always the dupe of the heart.[1]
Reflections, maxim 102

20 Nothing is given so profusely as advice.
Reflections, maxim 110

21 The true way to be deceived is to think oneself
more clever than others. *Reflections, maxim 127*

22 We would rather speak ill of ourselves than not
talk about ourselves at all.
Reflections, maxim 138

23 Usually we praise only to be praised.
Reflections, maxim 146

24 Our repentance is not so much regret for the ill
we have done as fear of the ill that may happen to us
in consequence. *Reflections, maxim 180*

25 Who lives without folly is not so wise as he
thinks. *Reflections, maxim 209*

26 Most people judge men only by their success or
their good fortune. *Reflections, maxim 212*

27 Hypocrisy is the homage that vice pays to virtue.
Reflections, maxim 218

28 Too great haste in paying off an obligation is a
kind of ingratitude. *Reflections, maxim 226*

29 There is great skill in knowing how to conceal
one's skill. *Reflections, maxim 245*

30 The pleasure of love is in loving. We are happier
in the passion we feel than in that we arouse.
Reflections, maxim 259

31 Absence diminishes mediocre passions and increases great ones, as the wind blows out candles
and fans fire. *Reflections, maxim 276*

32 We always like those who admire us; we do not
always like those whom we admire.
Reflections, maxim 294

33 The gratitude of most men is merely a secret desire to receive greater benefits.[2]
Reflections, maxim 298

34 We frequently forgive those who bore us, but
cannot forgive those whom we bore.
Reflections, maxim 304

---

[1]The Mind lives on the Heart / Like any Parasite. — EMILY
DICKINSON, *The Mind Lives on the Heart* [c. 1876]

[2]A lively sense of future favors. — ROBERT WALPOLE, *definition
of the gratitude of place-expectants;* from WILLIAM HAZLITT, *English Comic Writers* [1819], *Wit and Humor*

1   Lovers never get tired of each other, because they are always talking about themselves.
Reflections, maxim 312

2   In jealousy there is more self-love than love.
Reflections, maxim 324

3   We confess to little faults only to persuade ourselves that we have no great ones.
Reflections, maxim 327

4   We pardon to the extent that we love.
Reflections, maxim 330

5   We rarely find that people have good sense unless they agree with us.[1]
Reflections, maxim 347

6   Jealousy is always born together with love, but it does not always die when love dies.
Reflections, maxim 361

7   Mediocre minds usually dismiss anything which reaches beyond their own understanding.
Reflections, maxim 375

8   The greatest fault of a penetrating wit is to go beyond the mark.   *Reflections, maxim 377*

9   We may give advice, but we do not inspire conduct.   *Reflections, maxim 378*

10   The veracity which increases with old age is not far from folly.   *Reflections, maxim 416*

11   Few people know how to be old.
Reflections, maxim 423

12   Nothing prevents our being natural so much as the desire to appear so.   *Reflections, maxim 431*

13   In their first passion women love their lovers, in the others they love love.   *Reflections, maxim 471*

14   Quarrels would not last long if the fault were only on one side.   *Reflections, maxim 496*

15   In the misfortune of our best friends we often find something that is not displeasing.[2]
Reflections, maxim 583

Jeremy Taylor
1613–1667

16   Too quick a sense of constant infelicity.
Holy Dying [1650–1651]

17   Every schoolboy knows it.
On the Real Presence, ▮

18   The union of hands and hearts.
Sermons [1653], The Marriage Ring, pt. ▮

19   No man ever repented that he arose from th▮ table sober, healthful, and with his wits about him.
Sermons, The Marriage Ring, pt. ▮

Thomas Ady
fl. 1655

20 Matthew, Mark, Luke, and John,
The bed be blest that I lie on.
Four angels to my bed,
Four angels round my head,[3]
One to watch, and one to pray,
And two to bear my soul away.
A Candle in the Dark [1655

Richard Baxter
1615–1691

21 I preached as never sure to preach again,
And as a dying man to dying men.
Poetical Fragments [1681]. Love Breathing
Thanks and Praise

22   In necessary things, unity; in doubtful thing▮ liberty; in all things, charity.[4]   *Mott▮*

Sir John Denham
1615–1669

23 Oh, could I flow like thee,[5] and make thy stream
My great example, as it is my theme!
Though deep yet clear, though gentle yet not dull;
Strong without rage, without o'erflowing full.
Cooper's Hill [1642], l. 18▮

Sir Roger L'Estrange
1616–1704

24   Though this may be play to you, 'tis death to u▮
Fables [1692]. Fable 398, Boys and Fro▮

---

[1]"That was excellently observed," say I when I read a passage in another where his opinion agrees with mine. When we differ, then I pronounce him to be mistaken. —JONATHAN SWIFT, *Thoughts on Various Subjects*

[2]*Maxim 583* is one of the "maximes supprimées" discarded before the 1678 edition.
In all distresses of our friends / We first consult our private ends; / While Nature, kindly bent to ease us, / Points out some circumstance to please us. —SWIFT, *A Paraphrase of Rochefoucauld's Maxim*

---

[3]Usual version: Bless the bed that I lie on. / Four corners to n▮ bed, / Four angels round my head.
[4]In necessariis unitas; in dubiis libertas; in omnibus caritas.
[5]The river Thames.

Roger de Bussy-Rabutin
1618–1693

1   God is usually on the side of the big squadrons and against the small ones.[1]
> *Letter to the Comte de Limoges [October 18, 1677]*

Abraham Cowley
1618–1667

2 What shall I do to be forever known,
And make the age to come my own?   *The Motto*

3 This only grant me, that my means may lie
Too low for envy, for contempt too high.
> *A Vote [1636]*

4 Well then; I now do plainly see
This busy world and I shall ne'er agree;
The very honey of all earthly joy
Does of all meats the soonest cloy,
And they (methinks) deserve my pity,
Who for it can endure the stings,
The crowd, and buzz and murmurings,
Of this great hive, the city.   *The Wish [1647]*

5 Ah yet, ere I descend to the grave
May I a small house and large garden have;
And a few friends, and many books, both true,
Both wise, and both delightful too!   *The Wish*

6 A mistress moderately fair.   *The Wish*

7 The world's a scene of changes, and to be
Constant, in Nature were inconstancy.
> *Inconstancy [1647]*

8 The thirsty earth soaks up the rain,
And drinks, and gapes for drink again.
The plants suck in the earth, and are
With constant drinking fresh and fair.
> *Anacreon [1656], II, Drinking*

9 Fill all the glasses there, for why
Should every creature drink but I,
Why, man of morals, tell me why?
> *Anacreon, II, Drinking*

10 A mighty pain to love it is,
And 'tis a pain that pain to miss;
But of all pains, the greatest pain
It is to love, but love in vain.
> *Anacreon, VII, Gold*

11 His time is forever, everywhere his place.
> *Friendship in Absence*

12 Nothing is there to come, and nothing past,
But an eternal now does always last.
> *Davideis [1656], bk. I, l. 361*

13 Life is an incurable disease.
> *To Dr. Scarborough [1656]*

14 Ye fields of Cambridge, our dear Cambridge, say,
Have ye not seen us walking every day?
Was there a tree about which did not know
The love betwixt us two?
> *On the Death of Mr. William Harvey [1657][2]*

15 God the first garden made, and the first city.
> *The Garden [1664], essay 5*

16 Hence ye profane! I hate ye all,
Both the great vulgar and the small.[3]
> *Horace, bk. III, ode 1*

17 Charm'd with the foolish whistlings of a name.
> *Virgil, Georgics, bk. II, l. 72*

18 Words that weep and tears that speak.
> *The Prophet*

19 Poet and Saint! to thee alone are given
The two most sacred names of earth and Heaven.
> *On the Death of Mr. Crashaw[4] [1668]*

20 His faith, perhaps, in some nice tenets might
Be wrong; his life, I'm sure, was in the right.
> *On the Death of Mr. Crashaw*

Richard Lovelace
1618–1658

21 Oh, could you view the melody
    Of every grace
    And music of her face,[5]
You'd drop a tear;
    Seeing more harmony
    In her bright eye
Than now you hear.
> *Lucasta [1649]. Orpheus to Beasts*

22 Tell me not, sweet, I am unkind,
That from the nunnery
Of thy chaste breast and quiet mind,
To war and arms I fly.
> *Lucasta. To Lucasta: Going to the Wars, st. 1*

---

[1]It is said that God is always for the big battalions. —VOLTAIRE, *letter to M. le Riche* [February 6, 1770]

Providence is always on the side of the last reserve. —*Attributed to* NAPOLEON

[2]See Harvey, 242.

[3]Odi profanum vulgus.

[4]See Crashaw, 272.

[5]The mind, the music breathing from her face. —LORD BYRON, *The Bride of Abydos* [1813], canto I, st. 6

1 I could not love thee, dear, so much,
Lov'd I not honor more.
Lucasta. To Lucasta: Going to the Wars, st. 3

2 When I lie tangled in her hair,
And fettered to her eye,
The gods that wanton in the air
Know no such liberty.
Lucasta. To Althea: From Prison, st. 1

3 When flowing cups run swiftly round
With no allaying Thames.
Lucasta. To Althea: From Prison, st. 2

4 Stone walls do not a prison make,[1]
Nor iron bars a cage;
Minds innocent and quiet take
That for an hermitage;
If I have freedom in my love,
And in my soul am free,
Angels alone that soar above
Enjoy such liberty.
Lucasta. To Althea: From Prison, st. 4

5 If to be absent were to be
Away from thee;
Or that when I am gone,
You and I were alone;
Then, my Lucasta, might I crave
Pity from blust'ring wind, or swallowing wave.
*Lucasta. To Lucasta: Going Beyond the Seas,
st. 1*

Ninon de L'Enclos
1620–1705

6 Old age is woman's hell.[2]   *Attributed*

Jean de La Fontaine
1621–1695

7 We believe no evil till the evil's done.
Fables, bk. I [1668], fable 8

8 We heed no instincts but our own.
Fables, I, 8

9 The opinion of the strongest is always the best.
Fables, I, 10

10 Better to suffer than to die: that is mankind's
motto.   *Fables, I, 16*

11 By the work one knows the workman.
Fables, I, 2

12 I bend but do not break.   *Fables, I, 2*

13 It is a double pleasure to deceive the deceiver.
Fables, II [1668], 1

14 It is impossible to please all the world and one
father.   *Fables, III [1668],*

15 In everything one must consider the end.
Fables, III,

16 Beware, as long as you live, of judging people b
appearances.   *Fables, VI [1668],*

17 On the wings of Time grief flies away.
Fables, VI, 2

18 The sign brings customers.
Fables, VII [1678–1679], 1

19 People who make no noise are dangerous.
Fables, VIII [1678–1679], 2

20 He knows the universe, and himself he does no
know.   *Fables, VIII, 2*

21 A hungry stomach cannot hear.[3]
Fables, IX [1678–1679], 1

Andrew Marvell
1621–1678

22 The inglorious arts of peace.
Upon Cromwell's Return from Ireland [1650

23 He[4] nothing common did or mean
Upon that memorable scene,
But with his keener eye
The axe's edge did try.
Upon Cromwell's Return from Irelan

24 But bowed his comely head
Down as upon a bed.
Upon Cromwell's Return from Irelan

25 So much one man can do,
That does both act and know.
Upon Cromwell's Return from Irelan

26 Had we but world enough, and time,
This coyness, lady, were no crime.
To His Coy Mistress [1650–1652

27 I would
Love you ten years before the Flood,

---

[1]Stone walls a prisoner make, but not a slave. —WILLIAM
WORDSWORTH, *Humanity*

[2]La vieillesse est l'enfer des femmes.

[3]Ventre affamé n'a point d'oreilles.

[4]King Charles I.

And you should, if you please, refuse
Till the conversion of the Jews.
My vegetable love should grow
Vaster than empires, and more slow.
                              To His Coy Mistress

1 But at my back I always hear
Time's winged chariot hurrying near;
And yonder all before us lie
Deserts of vast eternity.   *To His Coy Mistress*

2   Then worms shall try
That long preserved virginity,
And your quaint honor turn to dust,
And into ashes all my lust.
The grave's a fine and private place,
But none, I think, do there embrace.
                              To His Coy Mistress

3 Thus, though we cannot make our sun
Stand still, yet we will make him run.
                              To His Coy Mistress

4 Annihilating all that's made
To a green thought in a green shade.
                              The Garden [1650–1652]

5 Casting the body's vest aside,
My soul into the boughs does glide.   *The Garden*

6 The world in all doth but two nations bear —
The good, the bad; and these mixed everywhere.
                              The Loyal Scot [1650–1652]

7 My love is of a birth as rare
As 'tis for object strange and high;
It was begotten by despair
Upon impossibility.
            The Definition of Love [1650–1652], st. 1

8 As lines, so loves oblique, may well
Themselves in every angle greet;
But ours, so truly parallel,
Though infinite, can never meet.

Therefore the love which us doth bind
But fate so enviously debars,
Is the conjunction of the mind,
And opposition of the stars.
                   The Definition of Love, st. 7, 8

9 Where the remote Bermudas ride,
In th' ocean's bosom unespied.
                              Bermudas [1657]

10 He hangs in shades the orange bright,
Like golden lamps in a green night.   *Bermudas*

11 And all the way, to guide their chime,
With falling oars they kept the time.   *Bermudas*

Anthony Ashley Cooper, 1st Earl of Shaftesbury
1621–1683

12   "People differ in their discourse and profession about these matters, but men of sense are really but of one religion." Upon which says the lady of a sudden, "Pray, my lord, what religion is that which men of sense agree in?" "Madam," says the earl immediately, "men of sense never tell it."[1]
       Gilbert Burnet. History of My Own Time [1724], book II, ch. 1n

Molière [Jean-Baptiste Poquelin]
1622–1673

13   To pull the chestnuts out of the fire with the cat's paw.[2]   *L'Étourdi [1655], act III, sc. vi*

14   We die only once, and for such a long time!
                   Le Dépit Amoureux [1656], act V, sc. iii

15   I always make the first verse well, but I have trouble making the others.
              Les Précieuses Ridicules [1659], act I, sc. xi

16   The world, dear Agnes, is a strange affair.
              L'École des Femmes [1662], act II, sc. vi

17   There is no rampart that will hold out against malice.   *Tartuffe [1664], act I, sc. i*

18   Those whose conduct gives room for talk are always the first to attack their neighbors.
                              Tartuffe, I, i

19   You are an ass in three letters, my son.[3]
                              Tartuffe, I, i

20   She is laughing up her sleeve at you.
                              Tartuffe, I, vi

21   A woman always has her revenge ready.
                              Tartuffe, II, ii

22   Cover that bosom that I must not see: souls are wounded by such things.[4]   *Tartuffe, III, ii*

23   Although I am a pious man, I am not the less a man.   *Tartuffe, III, iii*

24   To create a public scandal is what's wicked; to sin in private is not a sin.   *Tartuffe, IV, v*

---

[1]See Disraeli, 459:26.

[2]Tirer les marrons du feu avec la patte du chat. — *Proverb in many languages*

[3]Vous êtes un sot en trois lettres, mon fils.

[4]Couvrez ce sein que je ne saurais voir: / Par de pareils objets les âmes sont blessées.

1   I saw him, I say, saw him with my own eyes.
    Tartuffe, V, iii

2   We have changed all that.[1]
    Le Médecin Malgré Lui [1666], act II, sc. vi

3   On some preference esteem is based; to esteem everything is to esteem nothing.
    Le Misanthrope [1666], act I, sc. i

4   He's a wonderful talker, who has the art of telling you nothing in a great harangue.
    Le Misanthrope, II, v

5   He makes his cook his merit, and the world visits his dinners and not him.   *Le Misanthrope, II, v*

6   You see him laboring to produce *bons mots*.
    Le Misanthrope, II, v

7   The more we love our friends, the less we flatter them; it is by excusing nothing that pure love shows itself.   *Le Misanthrope, II, v*

8   Doubts are more cruel than the worst of truths.
    Le Misanthrope, III, vii

9   Anyone may be an honorable man, and yet write verse badly.   *Le Misanthrope, IV, i*

10   If everyone were clothed with integrity, if every heart were just, frank, kindly, the other virtues would be well-nigh useless, since their chief purpose is to make us bear with patience the injustice of our fellows.   *Le Misanthrope, V, i*

11   It is a wonderful seasoning of all enjoyments to think of those we love.   *Le Misanthrope, V, iv*

12   I prefer an accommodating vice to an obstinate virtue.   *Amphitryon [1666], act I, sc. iv*

13   One must eat to live, and not live to eat.
    Amphitryon, III, i

14   The true Amphitryon is the Amphitryon who gives dinners.[2]   *Amphitryon, III, v*

15   My Lord Jupiter knows how to sugarcoat the pill.   *Amphitryon, III, x*

16   You've asked for it, Georges Dandin, you've asked for it.[3]   *Georges Dandin [1668], act I, sc. ix*

17   Good Heavens! For more than forty years I have been speaking prose without knowing it.
    Le Bourgeois Gentilhomme [1670], act II, sc. iv

18   All that is not prose is verse; and all that is not verse is prose.   *Le Bourgeois Gentilhomme, II, iv*

19   My fair one, let us swear an eternal friendship.[4]
    Le Bourgeois Gentilhomme, IV,

20   I will maintain it before the whole world.
    Le Bourgeois Gentilhomme, IV,

21   What the devil was he doing in that galley?[5]
    Les Fourberies de Scapin [1671], act II, sc. x

22   Grammar, which knows how to control even kings.[6]   *Les Femmes Savantes [1672], act II, sc.*

23   It is seasoned throughout with Attic salt.
    Les Femmes Savantes, III, i

24   A learned fool is more foolish than an ignorant one.   *Les Femmes Savantes, IV, ii*

25   Ah, there are no longer any children!
    Le Malade Imaginaire [1673], act II, sc. x

26   Nearly all men die of their remedies, and not of their illnesses.   *Le Malade Imaginaire, III, ii*

Algernon Sidney
1622–1683

27   This hand, unfriendly to tyrants,
    Seeks with the sword placid repose under liberty.[7]
    Life and Memoirs of Algernon Sidney

28   It is not necessary to light a candle to the sun.
    Discourses on Government [1698], ch. 2, sec. 23

Henry Vaughan
1622–1695

29   Dear Night! this world's defeat;
    The stop to busy fools; care's check and curb;
    The day of spirits; my soul's calm retreat

---

[1]Nous avons changé tout cela.

[2]Le véritable Amphitryon est l'Amphitryon où l'on dine.

[3]Vous l'avez voulu, Georges Dandin, vous l'avez voulu.

[4]Madam, I have been looking for a person who disliked gravy all my life; let us swear eternal friendship.—SYDNEY SMITH, *Lady Holland's Memoir* [1855], *vol. I, ch. 9*

[5]Que diable allait-il faire dans cette galère?
Que diable aller faire aussi dans la galère d'un Turc? d'un Turc! [What the deuce did he want on board a Turk's galley? A Turk!]—CYRANO DE BERGERAC [1619–1655], *Le Pédant Joué* [1654], *act II, sc. iv*
The saying of Molière came into his head: "But what the devil was he doing in that galley?" and he laughed at himself.—LEO TOLSTOI, *War and Peace* [1865–1872], *bk. IV, ch. 6*

[6]SIGISMUND [1368–1437], Holy Roman emperor, at the Council of Constance [1414] said to a prelate who had objected to His Majesty's grammar: Ego sum rex Romanus, et supra grammaticam [I am the Roman king, and am above grammar].

[7]Manus haec, inimica tyrannis, / Ense petit placidam sub libertate quietem.
The second line is the motto of the Commonwealth of Massachusetts: By the sword we seek peace, but peace only under liberty.

Which none disturb!
Christ's progress, and His prayer-time;
The hours to which high Heaven doth chime.
  Silex Scintillans, pt. I [1650]. The Night, l. 25

1 There is in God, some say,
A deep but dazzling darkness.
  Silex Scintillans, pt. I. The Night, l. 49

2 Happy those early days, when I
Shin'd in my angel-infancy!
Before I understood this place
Appointed for my second race.
  Silex Scintillans, pt. I. The Retreat, l. 1

3 But felt through all this fleshly dress
Bright shoots of everlastingness.
  Silex Scintillans, pt. I. The Retreat, l. 19

4 Some men a forward motion love,
But I by backward steps would move.
  Silex Scintillans, pt. I. The Retreat, l. 29

5 I saw Eternity the other night
Like a great ring of pure and endless light.
    All calm, as it was bright;
And round beneath it, Time in hours, days, years,
    Driv'n by the spheres
Like a vast shadow mov'd; in which the world
    And all her train were hurl'd.
  Silex Scintillans, pt. I. The World

6 My soul, there is a country
    Far beyond the stars
Where stands a winged sentry
    All skillful in the wars:
There, above noise and danger,
Sweet Peace is crown'd with smiles,
And One born in a manger
Commands the beauteous files.
  Silex Scintillans, pt. I. Peace, st. 1

7 They are all gone into the world of light!
And I alone sit lingering here;
Their very memory is fair and bright,
And my sad thoughts doth clear.
  *Silex Scintillans, pt. II [1655]. They Are All
  Gone, st. 1*

8 I see them walking in an air of glory
Whose light doth trample on my days,
My days, which are at best but dull and hoary,
Mere glimmering and decays.
  *Silex Scintillans, pt. II. They Are All Gone,
  st. 3*

9 Dear, beauteous death, the jewel of the just!
Shining nowhere but in the dark;
What mysteries do lie beyond thy dust,
Could man outlook that mark!
  *Silex Scintillans, pt. II. They Are All Gone,
  st. 5*

10 I cannot reach it, and my striving eye
Dazzles at it, as at eternity.
  Silex Scintillans, pt. II. Childhood

Blaise Pascal
1623–1662

11 Things are always at their best in their beginning.
  Lettres Provinciales [1656–1657], no. 4

12 I have made this letter longer than usual, because
I lack the time to make it short.[1]
  Lettres Provinciales, 16

13 True eloquence takes no heed of eloquence, true
morality takes no heed of morality.
  Pensées [1670], no. 4

14 Do you wish people to think well of you? Don't
speak well of yourself.   *Pensées, 44*

15 Physical science will not console me for the ignorance of morality in the time of affliction.
  Pensées, 67

16 What is man in nature? Nothing in relation to
the infinite, everything in relation to nothing, a
mean between nothing and everything.[2]
  Pensées, 72

17 I lay it down as a fact that if all men knew what
others say of them, there would not be four friends
in the world.   *Pensées, 101*

18 The state of man: inconstancy, boredom, anxiety.[3]
  Pensées, 127

19 I have discovered that all human evil comes from
this, man's being unable to sit still in a room.
  Pensées, 139

20 Cleopatra's nose, had it been shorter, the whole
face of the world would have been changed.
  Pensées, 162

21 The eternal silence of these infinite spaces terrifies me.[4]   *Pensées, 206*

22 We shall die alone.[5]   *Pensées, 211*

23 "God is, or He is not." But to which side shall
we incline? Reason can decide nothing here. There
is an infinite chaos which separated us. A game is

---

[1]Je n'ai fait celle-ci plus longue parceque je n'ai pas eu le loisir de
la faire plus courte.
  Not that the story need be long, but it will take a long while to
make it short. — THOREAU, *Letter to Mr. B* [November 16, 1857]
[2]Qu'est-ce que l'homme dans la nature? Un néant à l'égard de
l'infini, un tout à l'égard du néant, un milieu entre rien et tout.
[3]Condition de l'homme: inconstance, ennui, inquiétude.
[4]Le silence éternel de ces espaces infinis m'effraie.
[5]On mourra seul.

being played at the extremity of this infinite distance where heads or tails will turn up. What will you wager? . . . If you win, you win everything; if you lose, you lose nothing. Wager, then, without hesitation that He is.   *Pensées, 233*

1   The heart has its reasons which reason knows nothing of.[1]   *Pensées, 277*

2   We know the truth, not only by the reason, but by the heart.   *Pensées, 282*

3   Justice without strength is helpless, strength without justice is tyrannical. . . . Unable to make what is just strong, we have made what is strong just.   *Pensées, 298*

4   Man is but a reed, the weakest in nature, but he is a thinking reed.[2]   *Pensées, 347*

5   Man is neither angel nor beast; and the misfortune is that he who would act the angel acts the beast.[3]   *Pensées, 358*

6   Evil is easy, and has infinite forms.
    Pensées, 408

7   To ridicule philosophy is really to philosophize.[4]
    Pensées, 430

8   What a chimera then is man! What a novelty! What a monster, what a chaos, what a contradiction, what a prodigy! Judge of all things, feeble earthworm, depository of truth, a sink of uncertainty and error, the glory and the shame of the universe.   *Pensées, 434*

9   Self is hateful.[5]   *Pensées, 455*

10   Men blaspheme what they do not know.
    Pensées, 556

11   Men never do evil so completely and cheerfully as when they do it from religious conviction.
    Pensées, 894

12   "The God of Abraham, the God of Isaac, the God of Jacob," not of philosophers and scholars.
    Writing found in Pascal's effects after his death

George Fox[6]
1624–1691

13   The Lord showed me, so that I did see clearly, that he did not dwell in these temples which men

---

had commanded and set up, but in people's hearts . . his people were his temple, and he dwelt in them.
    Journal [169-

14   When the Lord sent me forth into the world, H forbade me to put off my hat to any, high or low.
    Journ

15   [It was] Justice Bennet of Derby, who was th first that called us Quakers, because we bid the tremble at the word of the Lord. This was in th year 1650.   *Journ*

16   He [Oliver Cromwell] said: "I see there is a pe ple risen and come up that I cannot win either wi gifts, honors, offices or places; but all other se and people I can."   *Journ*

Thomas Sydenham
1624–1689

17   Fever itself is Nature's instrument.
    Quoted in Bulletin of the New York Academy of Medicine, vol. IV [1928], p. 922

18   Gout, unlike any other disease, kills more ri men than poor, more wise men than simple.
    Quoted in Bulletin of the New York Academy of Medicine, IV, 993

19   A man is as old as his arteries.
    Quoted in Bulletin of the New York Academy of Medicine, IV, 993

John Aubrey
1626–1697

20   I have heard him [William Harvey] say, that aft his book of the circulation of the blood came o that he fell mightily in his practice, and that 'tw believed by the vulgar that he was crack-braine and all the physicians were against his opinion.
    Brief Lives [1690]. William Harv

21   He [Thomas Hobbes] had read much, if o considers his long life; but his contemplation w more than his reading. He was wont to say that he had read as much as other men, he should ha known no more than other men.
    Brief Lives. Thomas Hobb

22   He [John Milton] was so fair that they call him *the Lady of Christ's College.*
    Brief Lives. John Milt

23   Mr. William Shakespeare was born at Stratfo upon Avon in the County of Warwick. His fath was a butcher, and I have been told heretofore l some of the neighbors, that when he was a boy l

---

[1] Le coeur a ses raisons que la raison ne connaît point.

[2] L'homme n'est qu'un roseau, le plus faible de la nature, mais c'est un roseau pensant.

[3] L'homme n'est ni ange ni bête; et le malheur veut que qui veut faire l'ange fait la bête.

[4] Se moquer de la philosophie, c'est vraiment philosopher.

[5] Le moi est haïssable.

[6] Founder of the Society of Friends (Quakers).

exercised his father's trade, but when he killed a calf he would do it in a high style and make a speech.
Brief Lives. William Shakespeare

Marie de Rabutin-Chantal, Marquise de Sévigné
1626–1696

1   True friendship is never serene.
Lettres. À Madame de Grignan [September 10, 1671]

2   Racine will go out of style like coffee.
Attributed

Jacques Bénigne Bossuet
1627–1704

3   The greatest weakness of all weaknesses is to fear too much to appear weak.
Politique Tirée de l'Écriture Sainte

4   The inexorable boredom that is at the core of life.
From M. A. COUTURIER, Se Garder Libre

Robert Boyle
1627–1691

5   I am not ambitious to appear a man of letters: I could be content the world should think I had scarce looked upon any other book than that of nature.
The Philosophical Works of Robert Boyle [1738], vol. I, preliminary discourse

John Ray
1627–1705

6   In a calm sea every man is a pilot.
English Proverbs [1670]

7   If wishes were horses, beggars might ride.
English Proverbs

8   Money begets money.   *English Proverbs*

9   Blood is thicker than water.   *English Proverbs*

10   Misery loves company.   *English Proverbs*

11   To go like a cat upon a hot bakestone.[1]
English Proverbs

John Bunyan
1628–1688

12   Some said, "John, print it"; others said, "Not so."
Some said, "It might do good"; others said, "No."
The Pilgrim's Progress [1678]. Apology for His Book

13   As I walked through the wilderness of this world.   *The Pilgrim's Progress, pt. I*

14   I saw a man clothed with rags . . . a book in his hand, and a great burden upon his back.
The Pilgrim's Progress, I

15   The name of the one was Obstinate and the name of the other Pliable.
The Pilgrim's Progress, I

16   The name of the slough was Despond.
The Pilgrim's Progress, I

17   Every fat [vat] must stand upon his bottom.[2]
The Pilgrim's Progress, I

18   The gentleman's name was Mr. Worldly-Wise-Man.   *The Pilgrim's Progress, I*

19   A very stately palace before him, the name of which was Beautiful.   *The Pilgrim's Progress, I*

20   The valley of Humiliation.
The Pilgrim's Progress, I

21   A foul Fiend coming over the field to meet him; his name is Apollyon.   *The Pilgrim's Progress, I*

22   I will talk of things heavenly, or things earthly; things moral, or things evangelical; things sacred, or things profane; things past, or things to come; things foreign, or things at home; things more essential, or things circumstantial.   *The Pilgrim's Progress, I*

23   It beareth the name of Vanity Fair, because the town where 'tis kept is lighter than vanity.
The Pilgrim's Progress, I

24   Hanging is too good for him, said Mr. Cruelty.
The Pilgrim's Progress, I

25   My great-grandfather was but a water-man, looking one way, and rowing another.
The Pilgrim's Progress, I

26   A castle called Doubting Castle, the owner whereof was Giant Despair.
The Pilgrim's Progress, I

27   They came to the Delectable Mountains.
The Pilgrim's Progress, I

28   A great horror and darkness fell upon Christian.
The Pilgrim's Progress, I

---

[1] *Cat on a Hot Tin Roof*—TENNESSEE WILLIAMS, *title of play* [1955]

[2] Every tub must stand upon its bottom.—CHARLES MACKLIN, *The Man of the World* [1781], *act I, sc. ii*

1   So I awoke, and behold it was a dream.
The Pilgrim's Progress, I

2   A man that could look no way but downwards
with a muckrake in his hand.[1]
The Pilgrim's Progress, pt. II

3 He that is down, needs fear no fall,
He that is low, no pride.
The Pilgrim's Progress. Shepherd Boy's Song

4 Who would true valor see,
Let him come hither;
One here will constant be,
Come wind, come weather.
There's no discouragement
Shall make him once relent
His first avow'd intent
To be a pilgrim.
The Pilgrim's Progress. Shepherd Boy's Song

5   My sword I give to him that shall succeed me in
my pilgrimage, and my courage and skill to him that
can get it. My marks and scars I carry with me, to
be a witness for me, that I have fought His battles
who now will be my rewarder.
The Pilgrim's Progress. Shepherd Boy's Song

6   So he passed over, and all the trumpets sounded
for him on the other side.
The Pilgrim's Progress. Shepherd Boy's Song

7   The captain of all these men of death that came
against him to take him away, was the Consumption, for it was that that brought him down to the
grave.   *The Life and Death of Mr. Badman [1680]*

Sir William Temple
1628–1699

8   Books, like proverbs, receive their chief value
from the stamp and esteem of ages through which
they have passed.
*Miscellanea, pt. II [1690]. Ancient and
Modern Learning*

9   When all is done, human life is, at the greatest
and the best, but like a froward child, that must be
played with and humored a little to keep it quiet till
it falls asleep, and then the care is over.
Miscellanea, pt. II. Of Poetry

George Villiers, Duke of Buckingham
1628–1687

10   Ay, now the plot thickens very much upon us.
*The Rehearsal [written 1663, performed
1671], act III, sc. ii*

Charles II
1630–1685

11   This is very true: for my words are my own, an[d]
my actions are my ministers'.
Reply to John Wilmot, Earl of Rocheste[r]

12   Let not poor Nelly starve.
*On his deathbed. From GILBERT BURNET, The
History of My Own Times [1724–1734], vol.
bk. 2, ch. 17*

13   He had been, he said, an unconscionable tim[e]
dying; he hoped that they would excuse it.
*From MACAULAY, History of England [1849]
vol. I, ch. 4*

Richard Cumberland
1631–1718

14   It is better to wear out than to rust out.
*From BISHOP GEORGE HORNE [1730–1792],
Sermon on the Duty of Contending for the Trut[h]*

John Dryden
1631–1700

15 By viewing Nature, Nature's handmaid Art,
Makes mighty things from small beginnings grow.
Annus Mirabilis [1667], st. 155

16   He [Shakespeare] was the man who of all modern, and perhaps ancient poets, had the largest an[d]
most comprehensive soul.
Essay of Dramatic Poesy [1668]

17   He was naturally learned; he needed not the spectacles of books to read Nature; he looked inwards,
and found her there.   *Essay of Dramatic Poesy*

18 Pains of love be sweeter far
Than all other pleasures are.
Tyrannic Love [1669], act IV, sc. i

19 I am as free as Nature first made man,
Ere the base laws of servitude began,
When wild in woods the noble savage ran.
*The Conquest of Granada [1669–1670], pt. I,
act I, sc. i*

20 Death in itself is nothing; but we fear
To be we know not what, we know not where.
Aureng-Zebe [1676], act IV, sc. i

21 When I consider life, 'tis all a cheat;
Yet, fool'd with hope, men favor the deceit;
Trust on, and think tomorrow will repay.
Tomorrow's falser than the former day.
Aureng-Zebe, IV, i

---

[1]See Theodore Roosevelt, 615:8.

[2]See Rochester, 292:24.

1 The wretched have no friends.
All for Love [1678], act III, sc. i

2 Your Cleopatra; Dolabella's Cleopatra; every man's
Cleopatra. *All for Love, IV, i*

3 With how much ease believe we what we wish!
Whatever is, is in its causes just.
*Oedipus [1679] (with NATHANIEL LEE), act
III, sc. i*

4 His hair just grizzled,
As in a green old age.[1] *Oedipus, III, i*

5 Of no distemper, of no blast he died,
But fell like autumn fruit that mellow'd long —
Even wondered at, because he dropp'd no
sooner.
Fate seem'd to wind him up for fourscore years,
Yet freshly ran he on ten winters more;
Till like a clock worn out with eating time,
The wheels of weary life at last stood still.
Oedipus, IV, i

6 In pious times, ere priestcraft did begin,
Before polygamy was made a sin.
Absalom and Achitophel, pt. I [1680], l. 1

7 Whate'er he did was done with so much ease,
In him alone, 'twas natural to please.
Absalom and Achitophel, I, l. 27

8 Of these the false Achitophel was first,
A name to all succeeding ages curs'd.
For close designs and crooked counsels fit,
Sagacious, bold, and turbulent of wit,
Restless, unfix'd in principles and place,
In power unpleas'd, impatient of disgrace;
A fiery soul, which working out its way,
Fretted the pygmy-body to decay:
And o'er-inform'd the tenement of clay.
A daring pilot in extremity;
Pleased with the danger, when the waves
went high
He sought the storms; but for a calm unfit,
Would steer too nigh the sands to boast his wit.
Great wits are sure to madness near allied,
And thin partitions do their bounds divide.[2]
Absalom and Achitophel, I, l. 150

9 Bankrupt of life, yet prodigal of ease.
Absalom and Achitophel, I, l. 168

10 And all to leave what with his toil he won
To that unfeather'd two-legg'd thing, a son.
Absalom and Achitophel, I, l. 169

11 In friendship false, implacable in hate,
Resolved to ruin or to rule the state.
Absalom and Achitophel, I, l. 173

12 All empire is no more than power in trust.
Absalom and Achitophel, I, l. 411

13 Better one suffer, than a nation grieve.
Absalom and Achitophel, I, l. 416

14 Who think too little, and who talk too much.
Absalom and Achitophel, I, l. 534

15 A man so various that he seem'd to be
Not one, but all mankind's epitome:
Stiff in opinions, always in the wrong;
Was everything by starts, and nothing long:
But, in the course of one revolving moon,
Was chemist, fiddler, statesman, and buffoon.
Absalom and Achitophel, I, l. 545

16 So over violent, or over civil,
That every man with him was God or Devil.
Absalom and Achitophel, I, l. 557

17 His tribe were God Almighty's gentlemen.
Absalom and Achitophel, I, l. 645

18 Nor is the people's judgment always true:
The most may err as grossly as the few.
Absalom and Achitophel, I, l. 781

19 Of ancient race by birth, but nobler yet
In his own worth.
Absalom and Achitophel, I, l. 900

20 Made still a blund'ring kind of melody;
Spurr'd boldly on, and dash'd through thick and
thin,
Through sense and nonsense, never out nor in.
Free from all meaning, whether good or bad,
And in one word, heroically mad.
Absalom and Achitophel, pt. II [1682],[3] l. 413

21 For every inch that is not fool is rogue.
Absalom and Achitophel, pt. II, l. 463

22 There is a pleasure sure
In being mad which none but madmen know.[4]
The Spanish Friar [1681], act II, sc. i

23 And, dying, bless the hand that gave the blow.
The Spanish Friar, II, i

24 He's a sure card. *The Spanish Friar, II, iii*

25 They say everything in the world is good for
something. *The Spanish Friar, III, ii*

26 Dead men tell no tales.[5] *The Spanish Friar, IV, ii*

---

[1]A green old age, unconscious of decays. —ALEXANDER POPE,
Translation of the Iliad [1715], *bk. XXIII, l. 929*

[2]Remembrance and reflection how allied! / What thin partitions
sense from thought divide! —ALEXANDER POPE, *An Essay on Man*
[1733–1734], *epistle I, l. 225*

[3]In collaboration with NAHUM TATE. See 294.

[4]There is a pleasure in poetic pains / Which only poets know. —
WILLIAM COWPER, *The Task* [1785], *II, The Timepiece, l. 285*

[5]Cited in the play text as a proverb.

1 Or break the eternal Sabbath of his rest.
The Spanish Friar, V, ii

2 All human things are subject to decay,
And, when fate summons, monarchs must obey.
Mac Flecknoe [1682], l. 1

3 The rest to some faint meaning make pretense,
But Shadwell[1] never deviates into sense.
Some beams of wit on other souls may fall,
Strike through and make a lucid interval;
But Shadwell's genuine night admits no ray,
His rising fogs prevail upon the day.
Mac Flecknoe, l. 19

4 And torture one poor word ten thousand ways.
Mac Flecknoe, l. 208

5   Wit will shine
Through the harsh cadence of a rugged line.
To the Memory of Mr. Oldham [1684], l. 15

6 Happy the man, and happy he alone,
He who can call today his own;
He who, secure within, can say,
Tomorrow, do thy worst, for I have liv'd today.
Imitation of Horace, bk. III, ode 29 [1685], l. 65

7 Not heaven itself upon the past has power;
But what has been, has been, and I have had my
hour.   *Imitation of Horace, III, 29, l. 71*

8 I can enjoy her [Fortune] while she's kind;
But when she dances in the wind,
And shakes the wings and will not stay,
I puff the prostitute away.
Imitation of Horace, III, 29, l. 81

9 And virtue, though in rags, will keep me warm.
Imitation of Horace, III, 29, l. 87

10 Since heaven's eternal year is thine.
To the Pious Memory of Mrs. Anne Killegrew [1686], l. 15

11 O gracious God! how far have we
Profaned thy heavenly gift of poesy!
To the Pious Memory of Mrs. Anne Killegrew, l. 56

12 Her wit was more than man, her innocence a child.
To the Pious Memory of Mrs. Anne Killegrew, l. 70

13 Then cold, and hot, and moist, and dry,
In order to their stations leap,
And Music's power obey.
From harmony, from heavenly harmony,
This universal frame began:
From harmony to harmony

Through all the compass of the notes it ran,
The diapason closing full in Man.
A Song for Saint Cecilia's Day, 1687, st.

14 What passion cannot Music raise and quell?
A Song for Saint Cecilia's Day, 1687, st.

15 The trumpet's loud clangor
Excites us to arms.
A Song for Saint Cecilia's Day, 1687, st.

16 The soft complaining flute,
In dying notes, discovers
The woes of hopeless lovers.
A Song for Saint Cecilia's Day, 1687, st.

17 The trumpet shall be heard on high
The dead shall live, the living die,
And Music shall untune the sky!
A Song for Saint Cecilia's Day, 1687, Grand Chorus

18 She fear'd no danger, for she knew no sin.
The Hind and the Panther [1687], pt. I, l.

19 Of all the tyrannies on human kind
The worst is that which persecutes the mind.
The Hind and the Panther, I, l. 239

20 And kind as kings upon their coronation day.
The Hind and the Panther, I, l. 271

21 All have not the gift of martyrdom.
The Hind and the Panther, II, l. 59

22 War seldom enters but where wealth allures.
The Hind and the Panther, II, l. 706

23 Much malice mingled with a little wit.
The Hind and the Panther, III, l. 1

24 For present joys are more to flesh and blood
Than a dull prospect of a distant good.
The Hind and the Panther, III, l. 364

25 T' abhor the makers, and their laws approve,
Is to hate traitors and the treason love.
The Hind and the Panther, III, l. 706

26 Possess your soul with patience.
The Hind and the Panther, III, l. 839

27 Three poets, in three distant ages born,
Greece, Italy, and England did adorn.
The first in loftiness of thought surpass'd;
The next, in majesty; in both the last.
The force of Nature could no further go.
To make a third, she joined the former two.
Under Mr. Milton's Picture [1688]

28 This is the porcelain clay of humankind.[2]
Don Sebastian [1690], act I, sc. i

---

[1]See Shadwell, 291.

[2]The precious porcelain of human clay. —LORD BYRON, *Don Juan* [1818–1824], *canto IV, st. 11*

1 A knockdown argument: 'tis but a word and a blow. *Amphitryon [1690], act I, sc. i*

2 Whistling to keep myself from being afraid.[1]
Amphitryon, III, i

3 I am the true Amphitryon. *Amphitryon, V, i*

4 Theirs was the giant race, before the flood.
Epistle to Congreve [1693], l. 5

5 Genius must be born, and never can be taught.
Epistle to Congreve, l. 60

6 Arms, and the man I sing,[2] who, forced by fate,
And haughty Juno's unrelenting hate.
Virgil, Aeneid [1697], bk. I, l. 1

7 None but the brave deserves the fair.
Alexander's Feast [1697], l. 15

8   With ravish'd ears
The monarch hears;
Assumes the god,
Affects to nod,
And seems to shake the spheres.
Alexander's Feast, l. 37

9 Sound the trumpets; beat the drums . . .
Now give the hautboys breath; he comes, he
comes. *Alexander's Feast, l. 50*

10 Bacchus, ever fair and ever young.
Alexander's Feast, l. 54

11   Rich the treasure,
Sweet the pleasure —
Sweet is pleasure after pain.
Alexander's Feast, l. 58

12 Fallen, fallen, fallen, fallen,
Fallen from his high estate,
And welt'ring in his blood;
Deserted, at his utmost need,
By those his former bounty fed,
On the bare earth expos'd he lies,
With not a friend to close his eyes.
Alexander's Feast, l. 77

13 Sigh'd and look'd, and sigh'd again.
Alexander's Feast, l. 120

14 And, like another Helen, fir'd another Troy.
Alexander's Feast, l. 154

15 Could swell the soul to rage, or kindle soft desire.
Alexander's Feast, l. 160

16 He rais'd a mortal to the skies,
She drew an angel down.
Alexander's Feast, l. 169

17 Words, once my stock, are wanting to commend
So great a poet and so good a friend.
To My Friend Mr. Motteux [1698], l. 54

18 Lord of yourself, uncumber'd with a wife.
*Epistle to John Driden of Chesterton [1700],
l. 18*

19 Better to hunt in fields, for health unbought,
Than fee the doctor for a nauseous draught.
The wise, for cure, on exercise depend;
God never made his work for man to mend.
Epistle to John Driden of Chesterton, l. 92

20 A very merry, dancing, drinking,
Laughing, quaffing, and unthinking time.
The Secular Masque [1700], l. 39

21 The sword within the scabbard keep,
And let mankind agree.
The Secular Masque, l. 69

22 All, all of a piece throughout:
Thy chase had a beast in view;
Thy wars brought nothing about;
Thy lovers were all untrue.
'Tis well an old age is out,
And time to begin a new.
The Secular Masque, l. 96

23 Ill habits gather by unseen degrees —
As brooks make rivers, rivers run to seas.
*Ovid, Metamorphoses [1700], bk. XV, The
Worship of Aesculapius, l. 155*

24   [Of Chaucer's *Canterbury Tales:*] Here is God's
plenty.
Fables Ancient and Modern [1700], preface

25 For Art may err, but Nature cannot miss.
*Fables Ancient and Modern. The Cock and the
Fox, l. 452*

26 She hugg'd the offender, and forgave the offense:
Sex to the last.[3]
*Fables Ancient and Modern. Cymon and
Iphigenia, l. 367*

27 He was exhal'd; his great Creator drew
His spirit, as the sun the morning dew.[4]
*On the Death of a Very Young Gentleman
[1700]*

28 Here lies my wife: here let her lie!
Now she's at rest, and so am I.
Epitaph intended for his wife

---

[1] Whistling aloud to bear his courage up. — ROBERT BLAIR [1699–1746], *The Grave* [1743], *l. 58*

[2] See Virgil, 96:23.

[3] And love the offender, yet detest the offense. — ALEXANDER POPE, *Eloisa to Abelard* [1717], *l. 192*

[4] Early, bright, transient, chaste as morning dew, / She sparkled, was exhaled, and went to heaven. — EDWARD YOUNG, *Night Thoughts* [1742–1745], *Night V, l. 600*

William Stoughton
1631–1701

1 God hath sifted a nation that he might send choice grain into this wilderness.[1]
Election sermon at Boston [April 29, 1669]

Anton van Leeuwenhoek
1632–1723

2 We cannot in any better manner glorify the Lord and Creator of the universe than that in all things, how small soever they appear to our naked eyes, but which have yet received the gift of life and power of increase, we contemplate the display of his omnificence and perfections with the utmost admiration.
The Select Works of Anthony van Leeuwenhoek [1798][2]

John Locke
1632–1704

3 New opinions are always suspected, and usually opposed, without any other reason but because they are not already common.
Essay Concerning Human Understanding [1690], dedicatory epistle

4 No man's knowledge here can go beyond his experience.
Essay Concerning Human Understanding, bk. II, ch. 1, sec. 19

5 It is one thing to show a man that he is in an error, and another to put him in possession of truth.
Essay Concerning Human Understanding, IV, 7, 11

6 All men are liable to error; and most men are, in many points, by passion or interest, under temptation to it.
Essay Concerning Human Understanding, IV, 20, 17

7 Wherever Law ends, Tyranny begins.
Second Treatise of Government [1690], sec. 202

8 A sound mind in a sound body, is a short but full description of a happy state in this world.
Some Thoughts Concerning Education [1693], sec. 1

9 Good and evil, reward and punishment, are the only motives to a rational creature: these are the spur and reins whereby all mankind are set on work and guided.[3]
Some Thoughts Concerning Education, 5

10 He that will have his son have a respect for him and his orders, must himself have a great reverence for his son.
Some Thoughts Concerning Education, 6

11 Virtue is harder to be got than a knowledge of the world; and, if lost in a young man, is seldom recovered.
Some Thoughts Concerning Education, 7

12 The only fence against the world is a thorough knowledge of it.
Some Thoughts Concerning Education, 8

Benedict [or Baruch] Spinoza[4]
1632–1677

13 Peace is not an absence of war, it is a virtue, a state of mind, a disposition for benevolence, confidence, justice.
Theological-Political Treatise [1670]

14 Nature abhors a vacuum.
Ethics [1677],[5] pt. I, proposition 15: note

15 God and all the attributes of God are eternal.
Ethics, I, proposition 19

16 Nothing exists from whose nature some effect does not follow.
Ethics, I, proposition 36

17 He who would distinguish the true from the false must have an adequate idea of what is true and false.
Ethics, II, proposition 42: proof

18 Will and Intellect are one and the same thing.
Ethics, II, proposition 49: corollary

19 He that can carp in the most eloquent or acute manner at the weakness of the human mind is held by his fellows as almost divine.
Ethics, III: preface

---

[3]By education, then, I mean goodness in the form in which it is first acquired by a child . . . the rightly disciplined state of pleasures and pains whereby a man from his first beginnings on will abhor what he should abhor and relish what he should relish. —PLATO, *Laws, bk. II*

In educating the young we use pleasure and pain as rudders to steer their course. —ARISTOTLE, *Nicomachean Ethics, bk. X*

[4]Ein Gottbetrunkener Mensch [A God-intoxicated man].— NOVALIS (FRIEDRICH VON HARDENBERG)

The Lord blot out his name under heaven. The Lord set him apart for destruction from all the tribes of Israel, with all the curses of the firmament which are written in the Book of the Law. . . . There shall no man speak to him, no man write to him, no man show him any kindness, no man stay under the same roof with him, no man come nigh him. —*Amsterdam synagogue's curse on Spinoza [1656]*

[5]Translated by ANDREW BOYLE.

---

[1]God had sifted three kingdoms to find the wheat for this planting. —LONGFELLOW, *The Courtship of Miles Standish [1858], IV*

[2]Translated by SAMUEL HOOLE.

1   Surely human affairs would be far happier if the power in men to be silent were the same as that to speak. But experience more than sufficiently teaches that men govern nothing with more difficulty than their tongues.

Ethics, III, proposition 2: note

2   Pride is therefore pleasure arising from a man's thinking too highly of himself.

Ethics, III, proposition 26: note

3   It may easily come to pass that a vain man may become proud and imagine himself pleasing to all when he is in reality a universal nuisance.

Ethics, III, proposition 30: note

4   Self-complacency is pleasure accompanied by the idea of oneself as cause.

Ethics, III, proposition 51: note

5   It therefore comes to pass that everyone is fond of relating his own exploits and displaying the strength both of his body and his mind, and that men are on this account a nuisance one to the other.   *Ethics, III, proposition 54: note*

6   I refer those actions which work out the good of the agent to courage, and those which work out the good of others to nobility. Therefore temperance, sobriety, and presence of mind in danger, etc., are species of courage; but modesty, clemency, etc., are species of nobility.   *Ethics, III, proposition 59: note*

7   Fear cannot be without hope nor hope without fear.   *Ethics, III, definition 13: explanation*

8   Those who are believed to be most abject and humble are usually most ambitious and envious.

Ethics, III, definition 29: explanation

9   One and the same thing can at the same time be good, bad, and indifferent, e.g., music is good to the melancholy, bad to those who mourn, and neither good nor bad to the deaf.   *Ethics, IV: preface*

10   Man is a social animal.

Ethics, IV, proposition 35: note

11   Men will find that they can prepare with mutual aid far more easily what they need, and avoid far more easily the perils which beset them on all sides, by united forces.   *Ethics, IV, proposition 35: note*

12   Avarice, ambition, lust, etc., are nothing but species of madness.[1]   *Ethics, IV, proposition 44: note*

13   He whose honor depends on the opinion of the mob must day by day strive with the greatest anxiety, act and scheme in order to retain his reputation.

For the mob is varied and inconstant, and therefore if a reputation is not carefully preserved it dies quickly.   *Ethics, IV, proposition 58: note*

14   In refusing benefits caution must be used lest we seem to despise or to refuse them for fear of having to repay them in kind.

Ethics, IV, proposition 70: note

15   To give aid to every poor man is far beyond the reach and power of every man. . . . Care of the poor is incumbent on society as a whole.

Ethics, IV, appendix, 17

16   We feel and know that we are eternal.

Ethics, V, proposition 23: note

17   All excellent things are as difficult as they are rare.   *Ethics, V, proposition 42: note*

18   The things which . . . are esteemed as the greatest good of all . . . can be reduced to these three headings: to wit, Riches, Fame, and Pleasure. With these three the mind is so engrossed that it cannot scarcely think of any other good.

Tractatus de Intellectus Emendatione [1677], I, 3

Sir Christopher Wren[2]
1632–1723

19   Si monumentum requiris circumspice [If you would see the man's monument, look around].

Inscription in St. Paul's Cathedral, London. Written by Wren's son

Wentworth Dillon, Earl of Roscommon
c. 1633–1685

20 Choose an author as you choose a friend.

Essay on Translated Verse [1684], l. 96

21 Immodest words admit of no defense,
For want of decency is want of sense.

Essay on Translated Verse, l. 113

22 The multitude is always in the wrong.

Essay on Translated Verse, l. 183

Samuel Pepys
1633–1703

23   I pray God to keep me from being proud.

Diary, March 22, 1660

---

[1]To me, avarice seems not so much a vice, as a deplorable piece of madness. —THOMAS BROWNE, *Religio Medici* [1643]

[2]See E. C. Bentley, 674:4.

1   This morning came home my fine camlet cloak, with gold buttons, and a silk suit, which cost me much money, and I pray God to make me able to pay for it.   *Diary, July 1, 1660*

2   And so to bed.   *Diary, July 22, 1660, passim*

3   I am unwilling to mix my fortune with him that is going down the wind.
    Diary, September 6, 1660

4   I went out to Charing Cross, to see Major-General Harrison hanged, drawn, and quartered; which was done there, he looking as cheerful as any man could do in that condition.   *Diary, October 13, 1660*

5   A good honest and painful sermon.
    Diary, March 17, 1661

6   One, by his own confession to me, that can put on two several faces, and look his enemies in the face with as much love as his friends. But, good God! what an age is this, and what a world is this! that a man cannot live without playing the knave and dissimulation.   *Diary, September 1, 1661*

7   Though he be a fool, yet he keeps much company, and will tell all he sees or hears, and so a man may understand what the common talk of the town is.
    Diary, September 2, 1661

8   My wife, poor wretch.
    Diary, September 18, 1661, passim

9   Thanks be to God, since my leaving drinking of wine, I do find myself much better, and do mind my business better, and do spend less money, and less time lost in idle company.
    Diary, January 26, 1662

10   As happy a man as any in the world, for the whole world seems to smile upon me.
    Diary, October 31, 1662

11   To the Trinity House, where a very good dinner among the old soakers.   *Diary, February 15, 1665*

12   But Lord! how everybody's looks, and discourse in the street, is of death, and nothing else; and few people going up and down, that the town is like a place distressed and forsaken.[1]
    Diary, August 30, 1665

13   Strange to see how a good dinner and feasting reconciles everybody.   *Diary, November 9, 1665*

14   Saw a wedding in the church . . . and strange to see what delight we married people have to see these poor fools decoyed into our condition.
    Diary, December 25, 1665

15   Musick and women I cannot but give way to, whatever my business is.   *Diary, March 9, 1666*

16   Home, and, being washing-day, dined upon col meat.   *Diary, April 4, 166*

17   Musick is the thing of the world that I lov most.   *Diary, July 30, 166*

18   Did satisfy myself mighty fair in the truth of th saying that the world do not grow old at all, but in as good condition in all respects as ever it was.
    Diary, February 3, 166

19   This day I am, by the blessing of God, 34 year old, in very good health and mind's content, and i condition of estate much beyond whatever m friends could expect of a child of theirs, this day 3 years. The Lord's name be praised! and may I b ever thankful for it.   *Diary, February 23, 166*

20   But it is pretty to see what money will do.
    Diary, March 21, 166

21   To church; and with my mourning, very hand some, and new periwig, make a great show.
    Diary, March 31, 166

22   But to think of the clatter they make with hi coach, and his own fine clothes, and yet how meanly they live within doors, and nastily, and borrowing everything of neighbors.   *Diary, April 1, 166*

23   Whose red nose makes me ashamed to be seer with him.   *Diary, May 3, 1667*

24   Gives me some kind of content to remember how painful it is sometimes to keep money, as well as to get it.   *Diary, October 11, 1667*

25   I find my wife hath something in her gizzard. that only waits an opportunity of being provoked to bring up; but I will not, for my content-sake, give it.
    Diary, June 17, 1668

26   In appearance, at least, he being on all occasions glad to be at friendship with me, though we hate one another, and know it on both sides.
    Diary, September 22, 1668

27   I do hate to be unquiet at home.
    Diary, January 21, 1669

28   And so I betake myself to that course, which is almost as much as to see myself go into my grave; for which, and all the discomforts that will accompany my being blind, the good God prepare me!
    Diary, May 31, 1669 (final entry)

George Savile, Marquess of Halifax
1633–1695

29   Children and fools want everything, because they want wit to distinguish; there is no stronger evidence

---

[1]The time of the Great Plague.

of a crazy understanding than the making too large a catalogue of things necessary.

Advice to a Daughter [1688]

1 Popularity is a crime from the moment it is sought; it is only a virtue where men have it whether they will or no.

Political, Moral, and Miscellaneous Reflections [1750]

2 Misspending a man's time is a kind of self-homicide.

Political, Moral, and Miscellaneous Reflections

3 Men are not hanged for stealing horses, but that horses may not be stolen.

Political, Moral, and Miscellaneous Reflections

Robert Hooke
1635–1703

4 The truth is, the science of Nature has been already too long made only a work of the brain and the fancy: It is now high time that it should return to the plainness and soundness of observations on material and obvious things. *Micrographia [1665]*

Nicolas Boileau-Despréaux
1636–1711

5 Happy who in his verse can gently steer
From grave to light, from pleasant to severe.[1]

The Art of Poetry [1674], canto I, l. 75

6 At last comes Malherbe[2] and, the first to do so in France, brings to his verse a smooth cadence.

The Art of Poetry, I, l. 131

7 Whate'er is well conceived is clearly said,
And the words to say it flow with ease.

The Art of Poetry, I, l. 153

8 Every age has its pleasures, its style of wit, and its own ways. *The Art of Poetry, III, l. 374*

9 The wisest man is he who does not fancy that he is so at all. *Satire 1, l. 46*

10 A Cat's a cat, and Rolet is a knave. *Satire 1, l. 52*

11 He [Molière] pleases all the world, but cannot please himself. *Satire 1, l. 94*

12 In spite of every sage whom Greece can show,
Unerring wisdom never dwelt below;
Folly in all of every age we see,
The only difference lies in the degree.

Satire 4, l. 37

13 Greatest fools are oft most satisfied.

Satire 4, l. 128

14 If your descent is from heroic sires,
Show in your life a remnant of their fires.

Satire 5, l. 43

15 Of all the creatures that creep, swim, or fly,
Peopling the earth, the waters, and the sky,
From Rome to Iceland, Paris to Japan,
I really think the greatest fool is man.

Satire 8, l. 1

16 But satire, ever moral, ever new,
Delights the reader and instructs him, too.
She, if good sense refine her sterling page,
Oft shakes some rooted folly of the age.

Satire 8, l. 257

17 Honor is like an island, rugged and without a beach; once we have left it, we can never return.

Satire 10, l. 167

18 Now two punctilious envoys, Thine and Mine,
Embroil the earth about a fancied line;
And, dwelling much on right and much on wrong,
Prove how the right is chiefly with the strong.

Satire 11, l. 141

19 Nothing but truth is lovely, nothing fair.

Epistle 9

20 The terrible burden of having nothing to do.

Epistle 11

Thomas Ken
1637–1711

21 Awake, my soul, and with the sun
Thy daily stage of duty run.

Morning Hymn [1695]

22 Praise God, from whom all blessings flow!
Praise Him, all creatures here below!
Praise Him above, ye heavenly host!
Praise Father, Son, and Holy Ghost!

Doxology [1709]

Mary Rowlandson
c. 1637–c. 1710/11

23 The portion of some is to have their Affliction by drops, now one drop and then another; but the dregs of the Cup, the wine of astonishment, like a sweeping rain that leaveth no food, did the Lord prepare to be my portion.

A Narrative of the Captivity and Restoration of Mrs. Mary Rowlandson [1682]

---

[1]Translated by JOHN DRYDEN.

[2]Enfin Malherbe vint.

Thomas Traherne

c. 1637–1674

1   You never enjoy the world aright, till the sea it-self floweth in your veins, till you are clothed with the heavens, and crowned with the stars: and per-ceive yourself to be the sole heir of the whole world.
Centuries of Meditations [1908], Century I, sec. 29

2   The corn was orient and immortal wheat, which never should be reaped, nor was ever sown. I thought it had stood from everlasting to everlasting.
Centuries of Meditations, III, 3

3 How like an angel came I down!
Wonder [1910], st. 1

4   I within did flow
With seas of life like wine.   *Wonder, st. 3*

Louis XIV

1638–1715

5   I am the state.[1]
Attributed remark before the parliament in 1651

6   Has God forgotten all I have done for him?[2]
Attributed remark upon hearing the news of the French defeat at Malplaquet [1709]

7   I almost had to wait.[3]
Attributed remark when a coach he had ordered arrived just in time

Jean Racine

1639–1699

8   I loved him too much not to hate him at all!
Andromaque [1667], act II

9   You are Emperor, my lord, and yet you weep?
Bérénice [1670], act IV, sc. v

10   My only hope lies in my despair.
Bajazet [1672], act I, sc. iv

11   You have named him, not I.[4]
Phèdre [1677], act I, sc. iii

12   It is no longer a passion hidden in my heart: it is Venus herself fastened to her prey.[5]   *Phèdre, I, iii*

13   Innocence has nothing to dread.
Phèdre, III, vi

---

[1]L'état c'est moi.

[2]Dieu a donc oublié tout ce que j'ai fait pour lui?

[3]J'ai failli attendre.

[4]C'est toi qui l'a nommé.

[5]Ce n'est plus une ardeur dans mes veines cachée: / C'est Vénus toute entière à sa proie attachée.

14   Crime like virtue has its degrees; and timid inno-cence was never known to blossom suddenly into extreme license.   *Phèdre, IV,*

15   To repair the irreparable ravages of time.
Athalie [1691], act II, sc.

Sir Charles Sedley

c. 1639–1701

16 Phyllis is my only joy,
Faithless as the winds or seas;
Sometimes coming, sometimes coy,
Yet she never fails to please.   *Song [1702], st.*

Aphra Behn

1640–1689

17   A brave world, sir, full of religion, knavery, and change: we shall shortly see better days.
The Roundheads [1677,

18   Variety is the soul of pleasure.
The Rover, pt. II [1680], act

19   Come away; poverty's catching.
The Rover, pt. II, act

20   Money speaks sense in a language all nations un-derstand.   *The Rover, pt. II, act III, sc.*

21   Beauty unadorned.
The Rover, pt. II, act IV, sc. i

22   Faith, sir, we are here today, and gone tomor-row.   *The Lucky Chance [1686–1687], act IV*

23   Oh, what a dear ravishing thing is the beginning of an Amour!
The Emperor of the Moon [1687], act I, sc. i

William Wycherley

1641–1715

24   A mistress should be like a little country retreat near the town, not to dwell in constantly, but only for a night and away.
The Country Wife [1675], act I, sc. i

Sir Isaac Newton

1642–1727

25   If I have seen further it is by standing on the shoulders of Giants.
Letter to Robert Hooke, February 5, 1675/1676

26   I frame no hypotheses; for whatever is not de-duced from the phenomena is to be called an hy-

pothesis; and hypotheses, whether metaphysical or physical, whether of occult qualities or mechanical, have no place in experimental philosophy.
Letter to Robert Hooke, February 5, 1675/1676

1   Errors are not in the art but in the artificers.
Philosophiae Naturalis Principia Mathematica [1687],[1] *preface*

2   Every body continues in its state of rest, or of uniform motion in a right line, unless it is compelled to change that state by forces impressed upon it.
Principia Mathematica. Laws of Motion, I

3   The change of motion is proportional to the motive force impressed; and is made in the direction of the right line in which that force is impressed.[2]
Principia Mathematica. Laws of Motion, II

4   To every action there is always opposed an equal reaction: or, the mutual actions of two bodies upon each other are always equal, and directed to contrary parts.
Principia Mathematica. Laws of Motion, III

5   God in the beginning formed matter in solid, massy, hard, impenetrable, movable particles, of such sizes and figures, and with such other properties, and in such proportion to space, as most conduced to the end for which he formed them.
Optics [1704]

6   I do not know what I may appear to the world; but to myself I seem to have been only like a boy playing on the seashore, and diverting myself in now and then finding a smoother pebble or a prettier shell than ordinary, whilst the great ocean of truth lay all undiscovered before me.
From BREWSTER, *Memoirs of Newton [1855], vol. II, ch. 27*

7   O Diamond! Diamond! thou little knowest the mischief done!
Said to a pet dog who knocked over a candle and set fire to his papers

Thomas Shadwell[3]
c. 1642–1692

8   And wit's the noblest frailty of the mind.
A True Widow [1679], act II, sc. i

9   The haste of a fool is the slowest thing in the world.
A True Widow, III, i

10   I am, out of the ladies' company, like a fish out of the water.
A True Widow, III, i

11   Every man loves what he is good at.
A True Widow, V, i

Bashō [Matsuo Bashō]
1644–1694

12   The months and days are the travelers of eternity. The years that come and go are also voyagers. . . . I too for years past have been stirred by the sight of a solitary cloud drifting with the wind to ceaseless thoughts of roaming.
The Narrow Road of Oku (Oku no Hosomichi)[4]

13 Such stillness —
The cries of the cicadas
Sink into the rocks.   *The Narrow Road of Oku*

14 The white chrysanthemum
Even when lifted to the eye
Remains immaculate.[5]
Conversations with Bashō. From the collection Kyoraisho Hyokai

15 Clear cascades!
Into the waves scatter
Blue pine needles.   *Conversations with Bashō*

16 An old pond —
A frog leaping in —
The sound of water.[6]   *Poem*

17 A rough sea!
Stretched out over Sado
The Milky Way.[6]   *Poem*

William Penn
1644–1718

18   No Cross, No Crown.
Title of pamphlet [1669]

19   Any government is free to the people under it where the laws rule and the people are a party to the laws.   *Frame of Government [1682]*

20   Truth often suffers more by the heat of its defenders than from the arguments of its opposers.
Some Fruits of Solitude [1693]

21   It is a reproach to religion and government to suffer so much poverty and excess.
Some Fruits of Solitude, 52

---

[1]*Mathematical Principles of Natural Philosophy [1729],* translated by ANDREW MOTTE.

[2]In modern terms, acceleration is directly proportional to applied force.

[3]See Dryden, 284:3.

[4]From *Anthology of Japanese Literature* [1955], edited by DONALD KEENE.

[5]From *Sources of Japanese Tradition* [1960], edited by WILLIAM THEODORE DE BARY.

[6]Translated by DANA B. YOUNG.

1   They that love beyond the world cannot be separated by it. Death is but crossing the world, as friends do the seas; they live in one another still.
Some Fruits of Solitude, 52

2   Men are generally more careful of the breed of their horses and dogs than of their children.
Some Fruits of Solitude, 85

3   It were endless to dispute upon everything that is disputable.   *Some Fruits of Solitude, 184*

4   Have a care therefore where there is more sail than ballast.   *Some Fruits of Solitude, 260*

5   Passion is a sort of fever in the mind, which ever leaves us weaker than it found us.
Some Fruits of Solitude, 279

6   The public must and will be served.
Some Fruits of Solitude, 279

Edward Taylor
c. 1644–1729

7 Who spread its canopy? Or curtains spun?
Who in this bowling alley bowled the sun?
Poetical Works [1939]. God's Determinations Touching His Elect, preface

8 For in Christ's coach saints sweetly sing
As they to glory ride therein.
Poetical Works. The Joy of Church Fellowship Rightly Attended

9 Make me, O Lord, thy spinning-wheel complete.
Poetical Works. Housewifery

10 It's food too fine for angels; yet come, take
And eat thy fill! It's Heaven's sugar cake.
Poetical Works. Sacramental Meditations, 8

11 This bread of life dropped in thy mouth doth cry:
Eat, eat me, soul, and thou shalt never die.
Poetical Works. Sacramental Meditations, 8

12 Is Christ thy advocate to plead thy cause?
Art thou his client? Such shall never slide.
He never lost his case.
Poetical Works. Sacramental Meditations, 38

13 My case is bad. Lord, be my advocate.
My sin is red: I'm under God's arrest.
Poetical Works. Sacramental Meditations, 38

Jean de La Bruyère
1645–1696

14   We come too late to say anything which has not been said already.
Les Caractères [1688]. Des Ouvrages de l'Esprit

15   Liberality consists less in giving a great deal th₃ in gifts well timed.   *Les Caractères. Du Coer*

16   Time, which strengthens friendship, weake₃ love.   *Les Caractères. Du Coer*

17   We must laugh before we are happy, for fear v die before we laugh at all.
Les Caractères. Du Coer

18   To laugh at men of sense is the privilege of fool
Les Caractères. De la Socie

19   There are but three events in a man's life: birt₃ life and death. He is not conscious of being bor₃ he dies in pain, and he forgets to live.
Les Caractères. De l'Homm

20   Most men make use of the first part of their li₃ to render the last part miserable.
Les Caractères. De l'Homm

21   Women run to extremes; they are either bett₃ or worse than men.   *Les Caractères. Des Femm*

Baron Gottfried Wilhelm von Leibni₃
1646–1716

22   I often say a great doctor kills more people th₃ a great general.
Quoted in Bulletin of the New York Academy of Medicine, vol. V [1929], p. 152

Henry Aldrich
1647–1710

23 If all be true that I do think,
There are five reasons we should drink:
Good wine — a friend — or being dry —
Or lest we should be by and by —
Or any other reason why.
Five Reasons for Drinkin₃

John Wilmot, Earl of Rochester
1647–1680

24 Here lies our sovereign lord the King,
Whose promise none relies on;
He never said a foolish thing,
Nor ever did a wise one.
Written on the bedchamber door of Charles I₃

25 For pointed satire I would Buckhurst choose,
The best good man with the worst-natured muse.₃
An Allusion to Horace, bk. I, satire ₃

---

[1]See Charles II, 282.

[2]Thou best-humored man with the worst-humored muse!
Oliver Goldsmith, *Retaliation* [1774], Postscript

1 A merry monarch, scandalous and poor.
A Satire on King Charles II

2 There's not a thing on earth that I can name,
So foolish, and so false, as common fame.
Did E'er This Saucy World

3 Reason, which fifty times for one does err,
Reason, an ignis fatuus of the mind.
A Satire Against Mankind [1675], l. 11

4 Books bear him up a while, and make him try
To swim with bladders of philosophy.
A Satire Against Mankind, l. 20

5 Then Old Age and Experience, hand in hand,
Lead him to death, and make him understand,
After a search so painful and so long,
That all his life he has been in the wrong.
A Satire Against Mankind, l. 25

6 Dead, we become the lumber of the world.
Seneca's Troas, act 2, chorus

John Sheffield,
Duke of Buckingham and Normanby
1648–1721

7 Of all those arts in which the wise excel,
Nature's chief masterpiece is writing well.
Essay on Poetry [1682]

8 Read Homer once, and you can read no more;
For all books else appear so mean, so poor,
Verse will seem prose; but still persist to read,
And Homer will be all the books you need.
Essay on Poetry

9 And when I feigned an angry look,
Alas! I loved you best.　*The Reconcilement [1701]*

William III, Prince of Orange
1650–1702

10　There is one certain means by which I can be sure never to see my country's ruin: I will die in the last ditch.
*From HUME, History of England
[1754–1757], ch. 65*

11　Every bullet has its billet.
From JOHN WESLEY, Journal [June 6, 1765]

Juana Inés de la Cruz
1651–1695

12 Foolish men who accuse
a woman mindlessly —

you cannot even see
you cause what you abuse.
Hombres Necios (Foolish Men),[1] st. 1

13 Has anyone ever seen
a stranger moral fervor?
You who dirty the mirror
cry that it isn't clean.　*Hombres Necios, st. 6*

14　I became a nun, because although I recognized it as having many ramifications . . . foreign to my temperament, still, given my completely negative feelings about marriage, it was the least disproportionate and most fitting thing I could do.
Reply to Sor Filotea de la Cruz[2] [1691]

15　Since I first gained the use of reason my inclination towards learning has been so violent and strong that neither the scoldings of other people . . . nor my own reflections . . . have been able to stop me from following this natural impulse that God gave me. He alone must know why; and He knows too that I have begged Him to take away the light of my understanding, leaving only enough for me to keep His law, for anything else is excessive in a woman, according to some people, and others say it is even harmful.　*Reply to Sor Filotea de la Cruz*

François de Salignac
de la Mothe Fénelon
1651–1715

16　Do not men die fast enough without being destroyed by each other? Can any man be insensible of the brevity of life? and can he who knows it, think life too long?　*Télémaque [1699], bk. VII*

17　To be always ready for war, said Mentor, is the surest way to avoid it.　*Télémaque, X*

18　Some of the most dreadful mischiefs that afflict mankind proceed from wine; it is the cause of disease, quarrels, sedition, idleness, aversion to labor, and every species of domestic disorder.　*Télémaque, X*

19　Mankind, by the perverse depravity of their nature, esteem that which they have most desired as of no value the moment it is possessed, and torment themselves with fruitless wishes for that which is beyond their reach.　*Télémaque, XVIII*

Thomas Otway
1652–1685

20 What mighty ills have not been done by woman!
Who was 't betrayed the Capitol? — A woman!

---

[1]Translated by WILLIS and ALICKI BARNSTONE.
[2]Translated by RACHEL PHILLIPS.

Who lost Mark Antony the world? — A woman!
Who was the cause of a long ten years' war,
And laid at last old Troy in ashes? — Woman!
Destructive, damnable, deceitful woman!
                    The Orphan [1680], act III, sc. i

1   Let us embrace, and from this very moment vow
an eternal misery together.   *The Orphan, IV, ii*

2 O woman! lovely woman! Nature made thee
To temper man: we had been brutes without you;
Angels are painted fair, to look like you.
                    Venice Preserved [1682], act I, sc. i

Nahum Tate
1652–1715

3 When I am laid in earth.
                    Dido and Aeneas [c. 1690][1]

4 While shepherds watch'd their flocks by night,
All seated on the ground,
The angel of the Lord came down,
And glory shone around.
                    Christmas Hymn [1700], st. 1

5 Glad tidings of great joy I bring
To you and all mankind.
                    Christmas Hymn, st. 1

Nahum Tate
1652–1715
and Nicholas Brady
1659–1726

6 Through all the changing scenes of life,
In trouble and in joy.
                    *New Version of the Psalms of David [1696],
                    Psalm 34*

7 As pants the hart for cooling streams
When heated in the chase.
                    New Version of the Psalms of David, Psalm 42

8 Jesus Christ is risen today,
Alleluia!
                    *Easter Hymn [1698], translated from the
                    Latin [fourteenth century]*

Nathaniel Lee
c. 1653–1692

9 Then he will talk — good gods! how he will talk!
                    *The Rival Queens; or, The Death of Alexander
                    the Great [1677], act I, sc. iii*

10 When Greeks joined Greeks, then was the tug of
war.
                    *The Rival Queens; or, The Death of Alexander
                    the Great, IV, ii*

11 'Tis beauty calls, and glory shows the way.
                    *The Rival Queens; or, The Death of Alexander
                    the Great, IV, ii*

12 Man, false man, smiling, destructive man!
                    Theodosius [1680], act III, sc. i

Andrew Fletcher of Saltoun
1655–1716

13   If a man were permitted to make all the ballads
he need not care who should make the laws of a
nation.
                    *Conversation Concerning a Right Regulation
                    of Governments for the Common Good of
                    Mankind [1704]*

John Dennis
1657–1734

14   A man who could make so vile a pun would not
scruple to pick a pocket.
                    *The Gentleman's Magazine, vol. LI [1781],
                    p. 324*

15   They will not let my play run, and yet they steal
my thunder![2]   *Remark*

Daniel Defoe
1660–1731

16 Wherever God erects a house of prayer,
The Devil always builds a chapel there;
And 'twill be found, upon examination,
The latter has the largest congregation.
                    The True-Born Englishman [1701], pt. I, l. 1

17 From this amphibious ill-born mob began
That vain, ill-natur'd thing, an Englishman.
                    The True-Born Englishman, I, l. 132

---

[1]Libretto for the opera by Henry Purcell.

[2]For his play *Appius and Virginia* [1709], Dennis had invented
a new species of thunder. "The tragedy however was coldly received, notwithstanding such assistance, and was acted but a short
time. Some nights after, Mr. Dennis, being in the pit at the representation of *Macbeth*, heard his own thunder made use of; upon
which he rose in a violent passion, and exclaimed, with an oath,
that it was his thunder. 'See,' said he, 'how the rascals use me!
They will not let my play run, and yet they steal my thunder!'" —
Biographia Britannica, vol. V, p. 103

1 Great families of yesterday we show,
And lords whose parents were the Lord knows
who.
The True-Born Englishman, I, l. 374

2 In their religion they are so uneven,
That each man goes his own byway to heaven.
The True-Born Englishman, II, l. 104

3 And of all plagues with which mankind are curs'd,
Ecclesiastic tyranny's the worst.
The True-Born Englishman, II, l. 299

4 When kings the sword of justice first lay down,
They are no kings, though they possess the crown.
Titles are shadows, crowns are empty things,
The good of subjects is the end of kings.
The True-Born Englishman, II, l. 313

5 All men would be tyrants if they could.
The Kentish Petition [1712–1713]

6 The best of men cannot suspend their fate:
The good die early, and the bad die late.
Character of the Late Dr. S. Annesley [1715]

7 He bid me [Robinson Crusoe] observe it, and I
should always find that the calamities of life were
shared among the upper and lower part of mankind; but that the middle station had the fewest disasters.   *Robinson Crusoe*[1] *[1719]*

8 One day, about noon, going towards my boat, I
was exceedingly surprised with the print of a man's
naked foot on the shore, which was very plain to be
seen in the sand.   *Robinson Crusoe*

9 My man Friday.   *Robinson Crusoe*

Sir Samuel Garth
1661–1719

10 A barren superfluity of words.
The Dispensary [1699], canto II, l. 95

11 Hard was their lodging, homely was their food;
For all their luxury was doing good.[2]
Claremont, l. 148

Richard Bentley
1662–1742

12 No man was ever written out of reputation but
by himself.
From J. H. MONK, Life of Bentley [1831]

---

[1]See Rousseau, 331:10.

[2]And learn the luxury of doing good. — OLIVER GOLDSMITH, *The
Traveller* [1764], *l. 22*

13 It is a pretty poem, Mr. Pope, but you must not
call it Homer.[3]   *From JOHNSON, Life of Pope*

Matthew Henry
1662–1714

14 He rolls it under his tongue as a sweet morsel.
Commentaries [1708–1710], Psalm 36

15 Our creature comforts.
Commentaries, Psalm 37

16 They that die by famine die by inches.
Commentaries, Psalm 59

17 To fish in troubled waters.
Commentaries, Psalm 60

18 Here is bread, which strengthens man's heart,
and therefore called the staff of life.[4]
Commentaries, Psalm 104

19 Hearkeners, we say, seldom hear good of themselves.   *Commentaries, Ecclesiastes 7*

20 It was a common saying among the Puritans,
"Brown bread and the Gospel is good fare."
Commentaries, Isaiah 30

21 None so blind as those that will not see.
Commentaries, Jeremiah 20

22 Judas had given them the slip.
Commentaries, Luke 22

23 After a storm comes a calm.
Commentaries, Acts 9

24 Men of polite learning and a liberal education.
Commentaries, Acts 10

25 It is good news, worthy of all acceptation! and
yet not too good to be true.
Commentaries, Timothy 1

26 All this and heaven too.   *Life of Philip Henry*

Samuel Wesley
1662–1735

27 Style is the dress of thought; a modest dress,
Neat, but not gaudy, will true critics please.
*An Epistle to a Friend Concerning Poetry
[1700]*

---

[3]The reference is to Pope's translation of the *Iliad*.

[4]Bread is the staff of life. — JONATHAN SWIFT, *A Tale of a Tub*
[1704]

Corn, which is the staff of life. — EDWARD WINSLOW [1595–
1655], *Good News from New England* [1624]

Thomas [Tom] Brown
1663–1704

1 I do not love thee, Doctor Fell.
The reason why I cannot tell;
But this alone I know full well,
I do not love thee, Doctor Fell.[1]
Written while a student at Christ Church, Oxford

2   To treat a poor wretch with a bottle of Burgundy, and fill his snuffbox, is like giving a pair of laced ruffles to a man that has never a shirt on his back.
Laconics [1707]

Mary de la Rivière Manley
1663–1724

3   No time like the present.
The Lost Lover [1696], act IV, sc. i

Cotton Mather
1663–1728

4   I write the wonders of the Christian religion, flying from the depravations of Europe, to the American strand: and, assisted by the Holy Author of that religion, I do, with all conscience of truth, required therein by Him, who is the Truth itself, report the wonderful displays of His infinite power, wisdom, goodness, and faithfulness, wherewith his Divine Providence hath irradiated an Indian wilderness.
Magnalia Christi Americana [1702], introduction

William Walsh
1663–1708

5 Of all the plagues a lover bears,
Sure rivals are the worst.   *Song, st. 1*

6 I can endure my own despair,
But not another's hope.   *Song, st. 2*

The New England Primer[2]

7 In Adam's fall
We sinned all.

8 My book and heart
Must never part.

9 Young Obadias,
David, Josias—
All were pious.

10 Peter denied
His Lord, and cried.

11 Young Timothy
Learnt sin to fly.

12 Xerxes did die,
And so must I.

13 Zaccheus he
Did climb the tree
Our Lord to see.

14 Our days begin with trouble here,
Our life is but a span,
And cruel death is always near,
So frail a thing is man.

15 Now I lay me down to sleep,[3]
I pray the Lord my soul to keep;
If I should die before I wake,
I pray the Lord my soul to take.

Matthew Prior
1664–1721

16 All jargon of the schools.
I Am That I Am, An Ode [168█

17 Our hopes, like towering falcons, aim
At objects in an airy height;
The little pleasure of the game
Is from afar to view the flight.
To the Honorable Charles Montague [169█

18 The end must justify the means.
Hans Carvel [170█

19 Be to her virtues very kind;
Be to her faults a little blind;
Let all her ways be unconfin'd;
And clap your padlock—on her mind!
An English Padlock [170█

20 And thought the nation ne'er would thrive
Till all the whores were burnt alive.
Paulo Purganti and His Wife [170█

21 He rang'd his tropes, and preach'd up patience;
Back'd his opinion with quotations.
Paulo Purganti and His W█

---

[1]Je ne vous aime pas, Hylas;／Je n'en saurois dire la cause,／Je sais seulement une chose;／C'est que je ne vous aime pas.—ROGER DE BUSSY-RABUTIN
    See Martial, 110:16.

[2]As early as 1691, Benjamin Harris of Boston advertised the forthcoming second impression of the *New England Primer.* The oldest known copy extant is dated 1737.

[3]The first record of this prayer is found in the *Enchiridion Leon* [1160]. The early editions of the *Primer* give the first line of t█ prayer as: Now I lay me down to take my sleep. The familiar ve█ sion of the line appeared in the edition of 1784. In the edition 1814 the second line reads: I pray thee, Lord, my soul to keep.

1 Cured yesterday of my disease,
  I died last night of my physician.
  The Remedy Worse than the Disease [1714]

2 And often took leave, but was loth to depart.
  The Thief and the Cordelier [1718]

3 His noble negligences teach
  What others' toils despair to reach.
  Alma [1718], canto II, l. 7

4 Till their own dreams at length deceive 'em,
  And oft repeating, they believe 'em.
  Alma, III, l. 13

5 To John I ow'd great obligation;
  But John, unhappily, thought fit
  To publish it to all the nation:
  Sure John and I are more than quit.
  Epigram [1718]

6 Venus, take my votive glass;
  Since I am not what I was,
  What from this day I shall be,
  Venus, let me never see.
  *The Lady Who Offers Her Looking-Glass to
  Venus [1718]*

7 Nobles and heralds, by your leave,
  Here lies what once was Matthew Prior;
  The son of Adam and of Eve:
  Can Bourbon or Nassau go higher?
  Epitaph [1721]

Sir John Vanbrugh[1]
1664–1726

8 Once a woman has given you her heart you can
  never get rid of the rest of her.
  The Relapse [1697], act III, sc. i

9 No man worth having is true to his wife, or can
  be true to his wife, or ever was, or ever will be so.
  The Relapse, III, ii

10 *Belinda:* Ay, but you know we must return good
   for evil.
   Lady Brute: That may be a mistake in the translation.   *The Provok'd Wife [1698], act I, sc. i*

11 He laughs best who laughs last.[2]
   The Country House [1706], act II, sc. v

12 Much of a muchness.
   *The Provok'd Husband [1728] (completed by
   Colley Cibber), act I, sc. i*

Susannah Centlivre
c. 1667–1723

13 The real Simon Pure.
   A Bold Stroke for a Wife [1718], act V, sc. i

John Pomfret
1667–1702

14 We live and learn, but not the wiser grow.[3]
   Reason, l. 112

Jonathan Swift
1667–1745

15 Books, like men their authors, have no more than
   one way of coming into the world, but there are ten
   thousand to go out of it, and return no more.
   A Tale of a Tub [1704], dedication

16 Books, the children of the brain.
   A Tale of a Tub, sec. 1

17 As boys do sparrows, with flinging salt upon their
   tails.   *A Tale of a Tub, 7*

18 Satire is a sort of glass, wherein beholders do
   generally discover everybody's face but their own.
   The Battle of the Books [1704]

19 Instead of dirt and poison we have rather chosen
   to fill our hives with honey and wax; thus furnishing
   mankind with the two noblest of things, which are
   sweetness and light.   *The Battle of the Books*

20 Laws are like cobwebs, which may catch small flies,
   but let wasps and hornets break through.
   *A Critical Essay upon the Faculties of the
   Mind [1707]*

21 There is nothing in this world constant, but
   inconstancy.
   *A Critical Essay upon the Faculties of the
   Mind*

22 'Tis very warm weather when one's in bed.
   Journal to Stella [November 8, 1710]

23 With my own fair hands.
   Journal to Stella [January 4, 1711]

24 We are so fond of one another, because our ailments are the same.
   Journal to Stella [February 1, 1711]

---

[1]Under this stone, Reader, survey / Dead Sir John Vanbrugh's
house of clay. / Lie heavy on him, Earth! for he / Laid many heavy
loads on thee! — ABEL EVANS [1679–1737]. Vanbrugh was the architect of Blenheim Palace.

[2]Better the last smile than the first laughter. — JOHN RAY, *Proverbs*
[1670]

---

[3]It is good to live and learn. — CERVANTES, *Don Quixote, pt. II*
[1615], *ch. 32*

  Live and learn, / Not first learn and then live. — ROBERT BROWN-
ING, *Parleyings with Certain People, With Christopher Smart* [1887],
IX

1   I love good creditable acquaintance; I love to be the worst of the company.
Journal to Stella [May 17, 1711]

2   We were to do more business after dinner; but after dinner is after dinner—an old saying and a true, "much drinking, little thinking."
Journal to Stella [February 26, 1712]

3   We have just religion enough to make us hate, but not enough to make us love one another.
Thoughts on Various Subjects; from Miscellanies [1711]

4   When a true Genius appears in the World, you may know him by this Sign, that the Dunces are all in confederacy against him.
Thoughts on Various Subjects; from Miscellanies

5   Censure is the tax a man pays to the public for being eminent.
Thoughts on Various Subjects; from Miscellanies

6   Every man desires to live long, but no man would be old.
Thoughts on Various Subjects; from Miscellanies

7   A nice man is a man of nasty ideas.
Thoughts on Various Subjects; from Miscellanies

8   Vision is the art of seeing things invisible.
Thoughts on Various Subjects; from Miscellanies [1726]

9 'Tis an old maxim in the schools,
That flattery's[1] the food of fools;
Yet now and then your men of wit
Will condescend to take a bit.
Cadenus and Vanessa [1713][2]

10   Proper words in proper places, make the true definition of a style.
Letter to a Young Clergyman [January 9, 1720]

11   If Heaven had looked upon riches to be a valuable thing, it would not have given them to such a scoundrel.
Letter to Miss Vanhomrigh [August 12, 1720]

[1]"Vanity's" in some texts.

[2]When the poem of "Cadenus and Vanessa" was the general topic of conversation, someone said, "Surely that Vanessa must be an extraordinary woman that could inspire the Dean to write so finely upon her." Mrs. Johnson smiled, and answered that "she thought that point not quite so clear; for it was well known the Dean could write finely upon a broomstick."—SAMUEL JOHNSON, *Lives of the Poets* [1779–1781], *Life of Swift*

12   He [the Emperor] is taller by almost the bread[t] of my nail, than any of his court, which alone [is] enough to strike an awe into the beholders.
Gulliver's Travels [1726]. Voyage to Lilliput, ch. 2

13   *All true believers shall break their eggs at the con venient end:* and which is the convenient end seems, in my humble opinion, to be left to ever man's conscience.
Gulliver's Travels. Voyage to Lilliput,

14   I cannot but conclude the bulk of your nativ[e] to be the most pernicious race of little odious ve min that nature ever suffered to crawl upon the su face of the earth.
Gulliver's Travels. Voyage to Brobdingnag, ch. 6

15   And he gave it for his opinion, that whoever coul make two ears of corn or two blades of grass t grow upon a spot of ground where only one gre before, would deserve better of mankind, and d more essential service to his country, than the whol race of politicians put together.[3]
Gulliver's Travels. Voyage to Brobdingnag,

16   He had been eight years upon a project for ex tracting sunbeams out of cucumbers, which were t be put in vials hermetically sealed, and let out t warm the air in raw inclement summers.
Gulliver's Travels. Voyage to Laputa, ch.

17   I said the thing which was not. (For they have n word in their language to express lying or falsehood
Gulliver's Travels. Voyage to the Houyhnhnms ch. 3

18   I told him . . . that we ate when we were not hun gry, and drank without the provocation of thirst.
Gulliver's Travels. Voyage to the Houyhnhnms, 6

19 A set of phrases learnt by rote;
A passion for a scarlet coat;
When at a play to laugh, or cry,
Yet cannot tell the reason why:
Never to hold her tongue a minute;
While all she prates has nothing in it.
The Furniture of a Woman's Mind [1727

20 For conversation well endu'd;
She calls it witty to be rude;
And, placing raillery in railing,
Will tell aloud your greatest failing.
The Furniture of a Woman's Min[d]

[3]He who makes two blades of grass grow in place of one rende[rs] a service to the state.—VOLTAIRE, *Letter to M. Moreau* [1765]

1 Not die here in a rage, like a poisoned rat in a hole.   *Letter to Bolingbroke [March 21, 1729]*

2 Yet malice never was his aim;
He lash'd the vice but spar'd the name.
No individual could resent,
Where thousands equally were meant.
His satire points at no defect
But what all mortals may correct;
For he abhorr'd that senseless tribe
Who call it humor when they gibe.
    Verses on the Death of Dr. Swift [1731], l. 459

3 Hobbes clearly proves that every creature
Lives in a state of war by nature.
    On Poetry. A Rhapsody [1733]

4 So, naturalists observe, a flea
Hath smaller fleas that on him prey;
And these have smaller still to bite 'em;
And so proceed *ad infinitum.*
Thus every poet, in his kind,
Is bit by him that comes behind.
    On Poetry. A Rhapsody

5 Conversation is but carving!
Give no more to every guest
Than he's able to digest.
Give him always of the prime,
And but little at a time.
Carve to all but just enough,
Let them neither starve nor stuff,
And that you may have your due,
Let your neighbor carve for you.
    Conversation

6 Under an oak, in stormy weather,
I joined this rogue and whore together;
And none but he who rules the thunder
Can put this rogue and whore asunder.
    Marriage certificate. From The Oxford Book of Literary Anecdotes, JAMES SUTHERLAND, *ed. [1975], no. 77*

7 The sight of you is good for sore eyes.[1]
    Polite Conversation [1738], dialogue 1

8 'Tis as cheap sitting as standing.
    Polite Conversation, 1

9 I hate nobody: I am in charity with all the world.
    Polite Conversation, 1

10 You were half seas over.
    Polite Conversation, 1

11 I won't quarrel with my bread and butter.
    Polite Conversation, 1

12 She's no chicken; she's on the wrong side of thirty, if she be a day.   *Polite Conversation, 1*

13 She wears her clothes, as if they were thrown on her with a pitchfork.   *Polite Conversation, 1*

14 He was a bold man that first eat an oyster.
    Polite Conversation, 2

15 That's as well said, as if I had said it myself.
    Polite Conversation, 2

16 Fingers were made before forks, and hands before knives.   *Polite Conversation, 2*

17 She has more goodness in her little finger, than he has in his whole body.   *Polite Conversation, 2*

18 Lord, I wonder what fool it was that first invented kissing!   *Polite Conversation, 2*

19 The best doctors in the world are Doctor Diet, Doctor Quiet, and Doctor Merryman.
    Polite Conversation, 2

20 May you live all the days of your life.
    Polite Conversation, 2

21 I always love to begin a journey on Sundays, because I shall have the prayers of the church to preserve all that travel by land, or by water.
    Polite Conversation, 2

22 I thought you and he had been hand-and-glove.
    Polite Conversation, 2

23 She watches him, as a cat would watch a mouse.
    Polite Conversation, 3

24 She pays him in his own coin.
    Polite Conversation, 3

25 There was all the world and his wife.
    Polite Conversation, 3

26 Hail, fellow, well met,
All dirty and wet:
Find out if you can,
Who's master, who's man.
    My Lady's Lamentation [1765], l. 171

27 I shall be like that tree, I shall die at the top.
    From SIR WALTER SCOTT, *Life of Swift [1814]*

28 Good God! What a genius I had when I wrote that book *[A Tale of a Tub].*
    From SIR WALTER SCOTT, *Life of Swift*

29 Ubi saeva indignatio ulterius cor lacerare nequit [Where savage indignation can lacerate his heart no more].[2]
    Epitaph. Inscribed on Swift's grave, Saint Patrick's, Dublin

---

[1]What a sight for sore eyes that would be!—WILLIAM HAZLITT, *Of Persons One Would Have Seen*

[2]See Yeats, 641:3.

Alain René Lesage
1668–1747

1   It may be said that his wit shines at the expense of his memory.
Gil Blas [1715–1735], bk. III, ch. 11

2   A flatterer can risk everything with great personages.
Gil Blas, IV, 7

3   Pride and conceit were the original sin of man.
Gil Blas, VII, 3

4   I wish you all sorts of prosperity with a little more taste.
Gil Blas, VII, 4

5   The pleasure of talking is the inextinguishable passion of a woman, coeval with the act of breathing.
Gil Blas, VII, 7

6   Facts are stubborn things.
Gil Blas, X, 1

Giovanni Battista [Giambattista] Vico
1668–1744

7   The nature of things is nothing other than that they come into being at certain times and in certain ways. Wherever the same circumstances are present, the same phenomena arise and no others.
Scienza Nuova [1725][1]

8   In that dark night which shrouds from our eyes the most remote antiquity, a light appears which cannot lead us astray; I speak of this incontestable truth: the social world is certainly the work of man.
Scienza Nuova

9   Governments must be conformable to the nature of the governed; governments are even a result of that nature.
Scienza Nuova

William Congreve
1670–1729

10   Eternity was in that moment.
The Old Bachelor [1693], act IV, sc. vii

11   Married in haste, we may repent at leisure.
The Old Bachelor, V, viii

12   It is the business of a comic poet to paint the vices and follies of human kind.
The Double Dealer [1694], epistle dedicatory

13   Retired to their tea and scandal, according to their ancient custom.
The Double Dealer, act I, sc. i

14   Though marriage makes man and wife one flesh, it leaves 'em still two fools.
The Double Dealer, II, iii

15   No mask like open truth to cover lies,
As to go naked is the best disguise.
The Double Dealer, V,

16   Thou liar of the first magnitude.
Love for Love [1695], act II, sc.

17   I warrant you, if he danced till doomsday, thought I was to pay the piper.[2]
Love for Love, II

18   O fie, miss, you must not kiss and tell.
Love for Love, II

19   Women are like tricks by sleight of hand,
Which, to admire, we should not understand.
Love for Love, IV,

20   Music has charms to soothe a savage breast,
To soften rocks, or bend a knotted oak.
The Mourning Bride [1697], act I, sc

21   By magic numbers and persuasive sound.
The Mourning Bride, I

22   Heaven has no rage like love to hatred turned,
Nor hell a fury like a woman scorned.
The Mourning Bride, III, v

23   Here she comes i' faith full sail, with her f spread and streamers out, and a shoal of fools tenders. — Ha, no, I cry her mercy!
The Way of the World [1700], act II, sc.

24   I nauseate walking; 'tis a country diversion, loathe the country.
The Way of the World, IV,

25   Let us be very strange and well-bred: Let us as strange as if we had been married a great wh and as well-bred as if we were not married at all.
The Way of the World, IV,

26   If I continue to endure you a little longer, I m by degrees dwindle into a wife.
The Way of the World, IV,

27   Thou art a retailer of phrases, and dost deal remnants of remnants.
The Way of the World, IV,

28   O, she is the antidote to desire.
The Way of the World, IV, x

29   Careless she is with artful care,
Affecting to seem unaffected.
Amor

Colley Cibber
1671–1757

30   As good be out of the world as out of the fas ion.
Love's Last Shift [1696], act

---

[1] Translated by JULES MICHELET.

[2] Pay the piper: phrase for settling the score. He who pays piper calls the tune. — *Proverb*

1 Possession is eleven points in the law.
Woman's Wit [1697], act I

2 Words are but empty thanks.   *Woman's Wit, V*

3 Off with his head — so much for Buckingham.
Richard III (altered) [1700], act IV, sc. iii

4 Perish the thought!
Richard III (altered), V, v

5 This business will never hold water.
She Wou'd and She Wou'd Not [1703], act IV

6 Old houses mended,
Cost little less than new before they're ended.
The Double Gallant [1707], prologue

7 Oh, how many torments lie in the small circle of
a wedding ring!
The Double Gallant, act I, sc. ii

8 Stolen sweets are best.
The Rival Fools [1709], act I

Anthony Ashley Cooper, 3rd Earl of Shaftesbury
1671–1713

9 How comes it to pass, then, that we appear such
cowards in reasoning, and are so afraid to stand the
test of ridicule?
A Letter Concerning Enthusiasm [1708], sec. 2

10 Truth, 'tis supposed, may bear all lights; and one
of those principal lights or natural mediums by
which things are to be viewed in order to a thorough recognition is ridicule itself.
*Essay on the Freedom of Wit and Humor
[1709], pt. I, sec. 1*

Joseph Addison
1672–1719

11 For wheresoe'er I turn my ravish'd eyes,
Gay gilded scenes and shining prospects rise,
Poetic fields encompass me around,
And still I seem to tread on classic ground.
A Letter from Italy [1703]

12 And, pleas'd the Almighty's orders to perform,
Rides in the whirlwind and directs the storm.
The Campaign [1704], l. 91

13 Reading is to the mind what exercise is to the
body.   *Tatler [1709–1711], no. 147*

14 The spacious firmament on high,
With all the blue ethereal sky,
And spangled heavens, a shining frame,
Their great Original proclaim.
*Ode [in The Spectator, no. 465, August 23,
1712]*

15 Soon as the evening shades prevail,
The moon takes up the wondrous tale,
And nightly to the listening earth
Repeats the story of her birth;
While all the stars that round her burn,
And all the planets in their turn,
Confirm the tidings as they roll,
And spread the truth from pole to pole.   *Ode*

16 Should the whole frame of Nature round him break,
In ruin and confusion hurled,
He, unconcerned, would hear the mighty crack,
And stand secure amidst a falling world.
Horace, Odes, bk. III, ode iii

17 'Tis not in mortals to command success,
But we'll do more, Sempronius; we'll deserve it.
Cato [1713], act I, sc. ii

18 Blesses his stars and thinks it luxury.   *Cato, I, iv*

19 'Tis pride, rank pride, and haughtiness of soul;
I think the Romans call it stoicism.   *Cato, I, iv*

20 Beauty soon grows familiar to the lover,
Fades in his eye, and palls upon the sense.
Cato, I, iv

21 My voice is still for war.
Gods! can a Roman senate long debate
Which of the two to choose, slavery or death?
Cato, II, i

22 The woman that deliberates is lost.   *Cato, IV, i*

23 Curse on his virtues! they've undone his country.
Cato, IV, iv

24 What pity is it
That we can die but once to serve our country!
Cato, IV, iv

25 When vice prevails, and impious men bear sway,
The post of honor is a private station.[1]
Cato, IV, iv

26 It must be so — Plato, thou reasonest well!
Else whence this pleasing hope, this fond desire,
This longing after immortality?
Or whence this secret dread, and inward horror,
Of falling into naught? Why shrinks the soul
Back on herself, and startles at destruction?
'Tis the divinity that stirs within us;
'Tis heaven itself, that points out an hereafter,

---

[1] Give me, kind Heaven, a mind serene for
contemplation! / Title and profit I resign; / The post of honor
shall be mine. — JOHN GAY, *Fables, pt. II [1738], The Vulture, the
Sparrow, and Other Birds*

And intimates eternity to man.
Eternity! thou pleasing, dreadful thought!

Cato, V, i

1 Sweet are the slumbers of the virtuous man.

Cato, V, iv

2 From hence, let fierce contending nations know
What dire effects from civil discord flow.

Cato, V, iv

3 Round-heads and Wooden-shoes are standing jokes.

The Drummer [1716], prologue, l. 8

4 Thus I live in the world rather as a spectator of mankind than as one of the species.

The Spectator, no. 1 [March 1, 1711]

5 If I can any way contribute to the diversion or improvement of the country in which I live, I shall leave it, when I am summoned out of it, with the secret satisfaction of thinking that I have not lived in vain. *The Spectator, 1*

6 I shall endeavor to enliven morality with wit, and to temper wit with morality.

The Spectator, 10 [March 12, 1711]

7 True happiness is of a retired nature, and an enemy to pomp and noise; it arises, in the first place, from the enjoyment of one's self; and, in the next, from the friendship and conversation of a few select companions.

The Spectator, 15 [March 17, 1711]

8 There is not a more unhappy being than a superannuated idol.

The Spectator, 73 [May 24, 1711]

9 A man that has a taste of music, painting, or architecture, is like one that has another sense, when compared with such as have no relish of those arts.

The Spectator, 93 [June 16, 1711]

10 There is no defense against reproach but obscurity. *The Spectator, 101 [June 26, 1711]*

11 Much might be said on both sides.

The Spectator, 122 [July 20, 1711]

12 Authors have established it as a kind of rule, that a man ought to be dull sometimes; as the most severe reader makes allowances for many rests and nodding places in a voluminous writer.

The Spectator, 124 [July 23, 1711]

13 Books are the legacies that a great genius leaves to mankind, which are delivered down from generation to generation, as presents to the posterity of those who are yet unborn.

The Spectator, 166 [September 10, 1711]

14 Good nature is more agreeable in conversation than wit, and gives a certain air to the countenance which is more amiable than beauty.

The Spectator, 169 [September 13, 1711]

15 Were I to prescribe a rule for drinking, it should be formed upon a saying quoted by Sir William Temple: the first glass for myself, the second for my friends, the third for good humor, and the fourth for mine enemies.

The Spectator, 195 [October 13, 1711]

16 A true critic ought to dwell rather upon excellencies than imperfections, to discover the concealed beauties of a writer, and communicate to the world such things as are worth their observation.

The Spectator, 291 [February 2, 1712]

17 These widows, sir, are the most perverse creatures in the world. *The Spectator, 335 [March 25, 1712]*

18 Mirth is like a flash of lightning, that breaks through a gloom of clouds, and glitters for a moment; cheerfulness keeps up a kind of daylight in the mind, and fills it with a steady and perpetual serenity. *The Spectator, 381 [May 17, 1712]*

19 [Sir Roger] made several reflections on the greatness of the British Nation; as, that one Englishman could beat three Frenchmen; that we could never be in danger of Popery so long as we took care of our fleet; that the Thames was the noblest river in Europe . . . with many other honest prejudices which naturally cleave to the heart of a true Englishman.

The Spectator, 383 [May 20, 1712]

20 Our disputants put me in mind of the skuttle fish, that when he is unable to extricate himself blackens all the water about him, till he becomes invisible.

The Spectator, 476 [September 5, 1712]

21 The fraternity of the henpecked.

The Spectator, 482 [September 12, 1712]

22 A man should always consider how much he has more than he wants; and secondly, how much more unhappy he might be than he really is.

The Spectator, 574 [July 30, 1714]

23 We are always doing, says he, something for Posterity, but I would fain see Posterity do something for us.

The Spectator, 583 [August 20, 1714]

24 See in what peace a Christian can die.

Dying words [1719]. From EDWARD
YOUNG, *Conjectures on Original
Composition* [1759]

Edmond Hoyle[1]
1672–1769

1   When in doubt, win the trick.
Twenty-four Rules for Learners, rule 12

Sir Richard Steele
1672–1729

2   I am come to a tavern alone to eat a steak, after which I shall return to the office.
Letters to His Wife [October 28, 1707]

3   I was going home two hours ago, but was met by Mr. Griffith, who has kept me ever since. . . . I will come within a pint of wine.
Letters to His Wife [Eleven at night, January 5, 1708]

4   A little in drink, but at all times yr faithful husband.
Letters to His Wife [September 27, 1708]

5   The finest woman in nature should not detain me an hour from you; but you must sometimes suffer the rivalship of the wisest men.
Letters to His Wife [September 17, 1712]

6   Though her mien carries much more invitation than command, to behold her is an immediate check to loose behavior; and to love her is a liberal education.[2]   *Tatler [1709–1711], no. 49*

7   When you fall into a man's conversation, the first thing you should consider is, whether he has a greater inclination to hear you, or that you should hear him.
The Spectator, no. 49 [April 26, 1711]

8   Of all the affections which attend human life, the love of glory is the most ardent.
The Spectator, 139 [August 9, 1711]

9   Age in a virtuous person, of either sex, carries in it an authority which makes it preferable to all the pleasures of youth.
The Spectator, 153 [August 25, 1711]

10   Among all the diseases of the mind there is not one more epidemical or more pernicious than the love of flattery.
The Spectator, 238 [December 3, 1711]

11   Will Honeycomb calls these over-offended ladies the outrageously virtuous.
The Spectator, 266 [January 4, 1712]

François Goyot de Pitavals
1673–1743

12   Causes Célèbres.
Title of book recounting famous trials and judgments

Nicholas Rowe
1674–1718

13   As if Misfortune made the throne her seat,
And none could be unhappy but the great.[3]
The Fair Penitent [1703], prologue

14   At length the morn and cold indifference came.
The Fair Penitent, act I, sc. i

15   Is this that haughty gallant, gay Lothario?
The Fair Penitent, V, i

Isaac Watts
1674–1748

16   Were I so tall to reach the pole,
Or grasp the ocean with my span,
I must be measured by my soul;
The mind's the standard of the man.
Horae Lyricae [1706], bk. II, False Greatness

17   Let dogs delight to bark and bite,
For God hath made them so.
Divine Songs [1715], 16, Against Quarreling and Fighting

18   But, children, you should never let
Such angry passions rise;
Your little hands were never made
To tear each other's eyes.
Divine Songs, 16, Against Quarreling and Fighting

19   Birds in their little nests agree;
And 'tis a shameful sight,
When children of one family
Fall out, and chide, and fight.
Divine Songs, 17, Love Between Brothers and Sisters

---

[1]Hoyle published a *Short Treatise on Whist* [1742], which in subsequent editions added rules for playing piquet, backgammon, chess, and other games. His *Laws* [1760] ruled whist playing until 1864; hence the saying, "according to Hoyle."

[2]Lady Elizabeth Hastings [1682–1739].

[3]None think the great unhappy, but the great. — EDWARD YOUNG, *Love of Fame* [1725–1728], *satire I, l. 238*

1 How doth the little busy bee
 Improve each shining hour,[1]
 And gather honey all the day
 From every opening flower!
     Divine Songs, 20, Against Idleness and Mischief

2 For Satan finds some mischief still
 For idle hands to do.
     Divine Songs, 20, Against Idleness and Mischief

3 Let me be dress'd fine as I will,
 Flies, worms, and flowers, exceed me still.
     Divine Songs, 22, Against Pride in Clothes

4 Hush! my dear, lie still and slumber,
 Holy angels guard thy bed!
 Heavenly blessings without number
 Gently falling on thy head.
     Divine Songs, 35, A Cradle Hymn

5 'Tis the voice of the sluggard; I heard him com-
    plain,
 "You have wak'd me too soon, I must slumber
    again."[2]   *Divine Songs, 39, The Sluggard*

6 O God, our help in ages past,
 Our hope for years to come,
 Our shelter from the stormy blast,
 And our eternal home.   *Psalm 90 [1719], st. 1*

7 A thousand ages in Thy sight
 Are like an evening gone;
 Short as the watch that ends the night
 Before the rising sun.   *Psalm 90, st. 4*

8 Time, like an ever-rolling stream,
 Bears all its sons away;
 They fly forgotten, as a dream
 Dies at the opening day.   *Psalm 90, st. 5*

9 Joy to the world! the Lord is come;
 Let earth receive her King.
 Let ev'ry heart prepare Him room,
 And heav'n and nature sing.
     Psalm 98 [1719], st. 1

10 When I can read my title clear
 To mansions in the skies,
 I'll bid farewell to every fear,
 And wipe my weeping eyes.
     Hymns and Spiritual Songs, bk. II, hymn 65

11 There is a land of pure delight,
 Where saints immortal reign;
 Infinite day excludes the night,
 And pleasures banish pain.
     Hymns and Spiritual Songs, II, 66

William Somerville[3]
1675–1742

12 Let all the learned say what they can,
 'Tis ready money makes the man.
     Ready Money [1727]

13 There is something in a face,
 An air, and a peculiar grace,
 Which boldest painters cannot trace.
     The Lucky Hit [1727]

14   The chase, the sport of kings;
 Image of war, without its guilt.
     The Chase [1735], bk. I, l. 13

John Philips
1676–1709

15 Happy the man who, void of cares and strife,
 In silken or in leathern purse retains
 A Splendid Shilling.
     The Splendid Shilling [1701], l. 1

Sir Robert Walpole
1676–1745

16   The balance of power.
     Speech in the House of Commons [February 13, 1741]

17   All those men have their price.
     From WILLIAM COXE, Memoirs of Walpole [1798], vol. IV, p. 369

18   Anything but history, for history must be false.
     Walpoliana, no. 141

Henry St. John, Viscount Bolingbroke
1678–1751

19   Truth lies within a little and certain compass, but error is immense.   *Reflections upon Exile [1716]*

20   Nations, like men, have their infancy.
     On the Study and Use of History [1752], letter 4

21   They [Thucydides and Xenophon] maintained the dignity of history.
     On the Study and Use of History, 5

---

[1]See Carroll, 549:13.
[2]See Carroll, 551:3.

[3]Of whom Samuel Johnson, in *Lives of the Poets,* made the famous remark, "He writes very well for a gentleman." See Samuel Johnson, 329:8.

1   It is the modest, not the presumptuous, inquirer who makes a real and safe progress in the discovery of divine truths. One follows Nature and Nature's God; that is, he follows God in his works and in his word.   *Letter to Alexander Pope*

George Farquhar
1678–1707

2   Reason still keeps its throne, but it nods a little, that's all.
The Recruiting Officer [1706], act III, sc. ii

3   I have fed purely upon ale; I have eat my ale, and I always sleep upon ale.
The Beaux' Stratagem [1707], act I, sc. i

4   My Lady Bountiful.   *The Beaux' Stratagem, I, i*

5   I believe they talked of me, for they laughed consumedly.   *The Beaux' Stratagem, III, i*

6   'Twas for the good of my country that I should be abroad.[1]—Anything for the good of one's country—I'm a Roman for that.
The Beaux' Stratagem, III, ii

7   How a little love and good company improves a woman!   *The Beaux' Stratagem, IV, i*

8   Spare all I have, and take my life.
The Beaux' Stratagem, V, ii

Thomas Parnell
1679–1718

9   My days have been so wondrous free,
The little birds that fly
With careless ease from tree to tree,
Were but as bless'd as I.
Song [1714],[2] st. 1

10   Still an angel appear to each lover beside,
But still be a woman to you.
When Thy Beauty Appears [1722], st. 3

11   We call it only pretty Fanny's way.
An Elegy to an Old Beauty [1722], st. 4

---

[1]Leaving his country for his country's sake. —Charles Fitz-Geffrey [c. 1575–1638], *The Life and Death of Sir Francis Drake* [1596], *st. 213*

True patriots all; for, be it understood, / We left our country for our country's good. — *Prologue for opening of playhouse at New South Wales* [January 16, 1796]; attributed to the famous pickpocket known as George Barrington [1755–c. 1840]

[2]Set to music by Francis Hopkinson; one of the earliest American songs.

12 Let those love now who never loved before;
Let those who always loved, now love the more.
Translation of the Pervigilium Veneris

Philippe Destouches [Philippe Néricault]
1680–1754

13   Those not present are always wrong.[3]
L'Obstacle Imprévu [1717], act I, sc. vi

14   Criticism is easy, art is difficult.
Le Glorieux [1732], act II, sc. v

Edward Young
1683–1765

15 The love of praise, howe'er conceal'd by art,
Reigns more or less, and glows in ev'ry heart.
Love of Fame [1725–1728], satire I, l. 51

16 Some for renown, on scraps of learning dote,
And think they grow immortal as they quote.
Love of Fame, I, l. 89

17   Be wise with speed;
A fool at forty is a fool indeed.
Love of Fame, II, l. 282

18 Forever most divinely in the wrong.
Love of Fame, VI, l. 105

19 For her own breakfast she'll project a scheme,
Nor take her tea without a stratagem.
Love of Fame, VI, l. 187

20 One to destroy, is murder by the law;
And gibbets keep the lifted hand in awe;
To murder thousands takes a specious name,
War's glorious art, and gives immortal fame.
Love of Fame, VII, l. 55

21 The man that makes a character makes foes.
To Mr. Pope, epistle I, l. 28

22 In records that defy the tooth of time.
The Statesman's Creed

23 Tired nature's sweet restorer, balmy sleep!
Night Thoughts [1742–1745]. Night I, l. 1

24 Night, sable goddess! from her ebon throne,
In rayless majesty, now stretches forth
Her leaden scepter o'er a slumbering world.
Night Thoughts. Night I, l. 18

---

[3]Les absents ont toujours tort.

1 Creation sleeps! 'Tis as the general pulse
Of life stood still, and Nature made a pause;
An awful pause! prophetic of her end.
Night Thoughts. Night I, l. 23

2 The bell strikes one. We take no note of time
But from its loss.
Night Thoughts. Night I, l. 55

3 Be wise today; 'tis madness to defer.
Night Thoughts. Night I, l. 390

4 Procrastination is the thief of time.
Night Thoughts. Night I, l. 393

5 At thirty, a man suspects himself a fool;
Knows it at forty, and reforms his plan;
At fifty chides his infamous delay,
Pushes his prudent purpose to resolve;
In all the magnanimity of thought
Resolves, and re-resolves; then dies the same.
Night Thoughts. Night I, l. 417

6 All men think all men mortal but themselves.
Night Thoughts. Night I, l. 424

7 Man wants but little, nor that little long.
Night Thoughts. Night IV, l. 118

8 A God all mercy is a God unjust.
Night Thoughts. Night IV, l. 233

9 By night an atheist half believes a God.
Night Thoughts. Night V, l. 177

10   Like our shadows,
Our wishes lengthen as our sun declines.
Night Thoughts. Night V, l. 661

11 Death loves a shining mark, a signal blow.
Night Thoughts. Night V, l. 1011

12 Too low they build, who build beneath the stars.
Night Thoughts. Night VIII, l. 215

13   Final Ruin fiercely drives
Her plowshare o'er creation.
Night Thoughts. Night IX, l. 167

14 An undevout astronomer is mad.
Night Thoughts. Night IX, l. 771

Sir William Pulteney, Earl of Bath
1684–1764

15 Since twelve honest men have decided the cause,
And were judges of facts, though not judges of
laws.   *The Honest Jury [1731], III*

George Berkeley
1685–1753

16   And what are these fluxions? The velocities o[f]
evanescent increments. And what are these sam[e]
evanescent increments? They are neither finite quan[-]
tities, nor quantities infinitely small, nor yet nothing[.]
May we not call them ghosts of departed quantities?
The Analyst [1734], sec. 3[5]

17   [Tar water] is of a nature so mild and benign an[d]
proportioned to the human constitution, as t[o]
warm without heating, to cheer but not inebriate.
Siris [1744], par. 217

18   He who says there is no such thing as an hones[t]
man, you may be sure is himself a knave.
Maxims Concerning Patriotism

19 Westward the course of empire takes its way;[1]
The four first acts already past,
A fifth shall close the drama with the day:
Time's noblest offspring is the last.
*On the Prospect of Planting Arts and
Learning in America [1752], st. 6*

Jane Brereton
1685–1740

20 The picture placed the busts between,
Adds to the thought much strength,
Wisdom, and Wit are little seen,
But Folly's at full length.
*On Beau Nash's Picture at Full Length
Between the Busts of Sir Isaac Newton and
Mr. Pope*[2]

John Gay[3]
1685–1732

21 'Twas when the seas were roaring
With hollow blasts of wind,
A damsel lay deploring,
All on a rock reclin'd.
The What D'ye Call It [1715], act II, sc. viii

22 All in the Downs the fleet was moor'd.
*Sweet William's Farewell to Black-eyed Susan
[1720]*

---

[1]Westward the star of empire takes its way. —JOHN QUINCY ADAMS, *Oration at Plymouth* [1802]

[2]In ALEXANDER DYCE [1798–1869], *Specimens of British Poetesses.* This epigram is often ascribed to CHESTERFIELD.

[3]See Pope's *Epitaph on Gay*, 310:19.

1 Adieu! she cries; and waved her lily hand.
Sweet William's Farewell to Black-eyed Susan

2 My lodging is on the cold ground,
And hard, very hard, is my fare,
But that which grieves me more
Is the coldness of my dear.
My Lodging Is on the Cold Ground [1720], st. 1

3 Whence is thy learning? Hath thy toil
O'er books consumed the midnight oil?
*Fables, pt. I [1727]. The Shepherd and the
Philosopher*

4 Where yet was ever found a mother
Who'd give her booby for another?
Fables, I. The Mother, the Nurse, and the Fairy

5 When we risk no contradiction,
It prompts the tongue to deal in fiction.
Fables, I. The Elephant and the Bookseller

6 In every age and clime we see
Two of a trade can never agree.
Fables, I. The Rat-catcher and Cats

7 Those who in quarrels interpose
Must often wipe a bloody nose.
Fables, I. The Mastiffs

8 I hate the man who builds his name
On ruins of another's fame.
Fables, I. The Poet and the Rose

9 And when a lady's in the case,
You know all other things give place.
Fables, I. The Hare and Many Friends

10 From wine what sudden friendship springs!
Fables, II [1738]. The Squire and His Cur

11 O Polly, you might have toy'd and kiss'd,
By keeping men off, you keep them on.
The Beggar's Opera [1728], act I, sc. viii, air 9

12 If with me you'd fondly stray.
Over the hills and far away.[1]
The Beggar's Opera, I, xiii, air 16

13 Fill ev'ry glass, for wine inspires us,
And fires us
With courage, love and joy.
Women and wine should life employ.
Is there ought else on earth desirous?
The Beggar's Opera, II, i, air 19

14 If the heart of a man is depress'd with cares,
The mist is dispelled when a woman appears.
The Beggar's Opera, II, iii, air 21

15 Youth's the season made for joys,
Love is then our duty.
The Beggar's Opera, II, iv, air 22

16 Man may escape from rope and gun;
Nay, some have outliv'd the doctor's pill:
Who takes a woman must be undone,
That basilisk is sure to kill.
The fly that sips treacle is lost in the sweets,
So he that tastes woman, woman, woman,
He that tastes woman, ruin meets.
The Beggar's Opera, II, viii, air 26

17 How happy could I be with either,
Were t'other dear charmer away!
The Beggar's Opera, II, xiii, air 35

18 The charge is prepar'd; the lawyers are met;
The Judges all ranged (a terrible show!)
The Beggar's Opera, III, xi, air 57

19 Life is a jest; and all things show it.
I thought so once; but now I know it.
My Own Epitaph

Aaron Hill
1685–1750

20 Tender-handed stroke a nettle,
And it stings you for your pains;
Grasp it like a man of mettle,
And it soft as silk remains.
Verses Written on a Window in Scotland

Samuel Madden
1686–1765

21 In an orchard there should be enough to eat,
enough to lay up, enough to be stolen, and enough
to rot upon the ground.
*Quoted by SAMUEL JOHNSON [1783]. From
BOSWELL, Life of Johnson [1791], vol. II, p.
457 (Everyman edition)*

Henry Carey
c. 1687–1743

22 Namby Pamby's little rhymes,
Little jingle, little chimes.
Namby Pamby[2]

23 Of all the girls that are so smart,
There's none like pretty Sally.

---

[1]O'er the hills and far away.—THOMAS D'URFEY [1653–1723], *Pills to Purge Melancholy* [1719]

[2]Ambrose Phillips . . . who had the honor of bringing into fashion a species of composition which has been called, after his name, Namby Pamby.—THOMAS MACAULAY, *Review of Aikin's Life of Addison* [1843]

She is the darling of my heart,
And she lives in our alley.
                    Sally in Our Alley [1729], st. 1

1 God save our gracious king!
Long live our noble king!
God save the king!
                    God Save the King [c. 1740]

Pierre Carlet de Chamblain de Marivaux
1688–1763

2   In this world, you must be a bit too kind in order to be kind enough.
                    Le Jeu de l'Amour et du Hasard [1730], act I, sc. ii

Alexander Pope
1688–1744

3 Happy the man whose wish and care
A few paternal acres bound,
Content to breathe his native air
In his own ground.
                    Ode on Solitude [c. 1700], st. 1

4 Thus let me live, unseen, unknown,
Thus unlamented let me die,
Steal from the world, and not a stone
Tell where I lie.
                    Ode on Solitude, st. 5

5 Where'er you walk, cool gales shall fan the glade,
Trees, where you sit, shall crowd into a shade:
Where'er you tread, the blushing flow'rs shall rise,
And all things flourish where you turn your eyes.
                    Pastorals [written 1704]. Summer, l. 73

6 Nor Fame I slight, nor for her favors call;
She comes unlook'd for, if she comes at all.
                    The Temple of Fame [1711], l. 513

7 'Tis with our judgments as our watches, none
Go just alike, yet each believes his own.
                    An Essay on Criticism [1711], pt. I, l. 9

8 Let such teach others who themselves excel,
And censure freely who have written well.
                    An Essay on Criticism, I, l. 15

9 Some are bewilder'd in the maze of schools,
And some made coxcombs nature meant but fools.
                    An Essay on Criticism, I, l. 26

10 Those oft are stratagems which errors seem,
Nor is it Homer nods, but we that dream.
                    An Essay on Criticism, I, l. 179

11 A little learning is a dangerous thing;
Drink deep, or taste not the Pierian spring:

There shallow draughts intoxicate the brain,
And drinking largely sobers us again.
                    An Essay on Criticism, II, l. 15

12 True wit is nature to advantage dress'd,
What oft was thought, but ne'er so well express'd.
                    An Essay on Criticism, II, l. 97

13 Words are like leaves; and where they most abound,
Much fruit of sense beneath is rarely found.
                    An Essay on Criticism, II, l. 109

14 Such labored nothings, in so strange a style,
Amaze th' unlearn'd, and make the learned smile.
                    An Essay on Criticism, II, l. 126

15 Be not the first by whom the new are tried,
Nor yet the last to lay the old aside.
                    An Essay on Criticism, II, l. 135

16   As some to church repair,
Not for the doctrine, but the music there.
These equal syllables alone require,
Though oft the ear the open vowels tire;
While expletives their feeble aid do join,
And ten low words oft creep in one dull line.
                    An Essay on Criticism, II, l. 142

17 Then, at the last and only couplet fraught
With some unmeaning thing they call a thought,
A needless Alexandrine ends the song,
That, like a wounded snake, drags its slow length
     along.   *An Essay on Criticism, II, l. 154*

18 True ease in writing comes from art, not chance,
As those move easiest who have learn'd to dance.
'Tis not enough no harshness gives offense;
The sound must seem an echo to the sense.
                    An Essay on Criticism, II, l. 162

19 At ev'ry trifle scorn to take offense.
                    An Essay on Criticism, II, l. 186

20 Some judge of authors' names, not works, and then
Nor praise nor blame the writings, but the men.
                    An Essay on Criticism, II, l. 212

21 What woeful stuff this madrigal would be,
In some starv'd hackney sonneteer, or me!
But let a lord once own the happy lines,
How the wit brightens! how the style refines!
                    An Essay on Criticism, II, l. 218

22 Some praise at morning what they blame at night,
But always think the last opinion right.
                    An Essay on Criticism, II, l. 230

23 To err is human, to forgive divine.
                    An Essay on Criticism, II, l. 325

24 All seems infected that th' infected spy,
As all looks yellow to the jaundic'd eye.
                    An Essay on Criticism, II, l. 358

1 For fools rush in where angels fear to tread.
      An Essay on Criticism, III, l. 65

2 But where's the man who counsel can bestow,
   Still pleas'd to teach, and yet not proud to know?
      An Essay on Criticism, III, l. 71

3 Vital spark of heav'nly flame!
   Quit, oh quit, this mortal frame:
   Trembling, hoping, ling'ring, flying,
   Oh the pain, the bliss of dying!
      The Dying Christian to His Soul [1712], st. 1

4 What dire offense from amorous causes springs,
   What mighty contests rise from trivial things!
      The Rape of the Lock [1712], canto I, l. 1

5 On her white breast a sparkling cross she wore,
   Which Jews might kiss, and infidels adore.
      The Rape of the Lock, II, l. 7

6 If to her share some female errors fall,
   Look on her face, and you'll forget 'em all.
      The Rape of the Lock, II, l. 17

7 Fair tresses man's imperial race ensnare,
   And beauty draws us with a single hair.
      The Rape of the Lock, II, l. 27

8 Here thou, great Anna![1] whom three realms obey,
   Dost sometimes counsel take—and sometimes tea.
      The Rape of the Lock, III, l. 7

9 At every word a reputation dies.
      The Rape of the Lock, III, l. 16

10 The hungry judges soon the sentence sign,
   And wretches hang that jurymen may dine.
      The Rape of the Lock, III, l. 21

11 Let spades be trumps! she said, and trumps they
   were.   *The Rape of the Lock, III, l. 46*

12 But when to mischief mortals bend their will,
   How soon they find fit instruments of ill!
      The Rape of the Lock, III, l. 125

13 The meeting points the sacred hair dissever
   From the fair head, forever, and forever!
   Then flash'd the living lightning from her eyes,
   And screams of horror rend th' affrighted skies.
      The Rape of the Lock, III, l. 153

14 To wake the soul by tender strokes of art,
   To raise the genius, and to mend the heart;
   To make mankind, in conscious virtue bold,
   Live o'er each scene, and be what they behold:
   For this the Tragic Muse first trod the stage.
      Prologue to Mr. Addison's Cato [1713], l. 1

15 Ignobly vain, and impotently great.
      Prologue to Mr. Addison's Cato, l. 29

16 Here hills and vales, the woodland and the plain,
   Here earth and water seem to strive again,
   Not chaos-like together crush'd and bruis'd,
   But, as the world, harmoniously confus'd:
   Where order in variety we see,
   And where, though all things differ, all agree.
      Windsor Forest [1713], l. 11

17   Party-spirit, which at best is but the madness of
   many for the gain of a few.
      Letter to E. Blount [August 27, 1714]

18 The wrath of Peleus' son, the direful spring
   Of all the Grecian woes, O goddess sing!
      Translation of the Iliad [1715], bk. I, l. 1

19 She moves a goddess, and she looks a queen.
      Translation of the Iliad, III, l. 208

20 Tell me, Muse, of the man of many wiles.
      *Translation of the Odyssey [1725–1756],
      bk. I, l. 1*

21 True friendship's laws are by this rule express'd,
   Welcome the coming, speed the parting guest.
      Translation of the Odyssey, XV, l. 83

22 Dear, damn'd, distracting town, farewell!
      Thy fools no more I'll tease:
   This year in peace, ye critics, dwell,
      Ye harlots, sleep at ease!
      A Farewell to London [1715], st. 1

23 Luxurious lobster-nights, farewell,
   For sober, studious days!
      A Farewell to London, st. 12

24 Oh name forever sad! forever dear!
   Still breath'd in sighs, still usher'd with a tear.
      Eloisa to Abelard [1717], l. 31

25 Now warm in love, now with'ring in my bloom,
   Lost in a convent's solitary gloom!
      Eloisa to Abelard, l. 37

26 How happy is the blameless vestal's lot!
   The world forgetting, by the world forgot.
      Eloisa to Abelard, l. 207

27 What beck'ning ghost, along the moonlight shade
   Invites my steps, and points to yonder glade?
      *Elegy to the Memory of an Unfortunate Lady
      [1717], l. 1*

28 Is it, in Heav'n, a crime to love too well?
   To bear too tender, or too firm a heart,
   To act a lover's or a Roman's part?
   Is there no bright reversion in the sky,
   For those who greatly think, or bravely die?
      *Elegy to the Memory of an Unfortunate Lady,
      l. 6*

29 How lov'd, how honor'd once, avails thee not,
   To whom related, or by whom begot;

---

[1]Queen Anne [1665–1714].

A heap of dust alone remains of thee;
'Tis all thou art, and all the proud shall be!
> *Elegy to the Memory of an Unfortunate Lady,*
> *l. 71*

1 And yet the fate of all extremes is such,
Men may be read, as well as books, too much.
To observations which ourselves we make,
We grow more partial for th' observer's sake.
> *Moral Essays [1731–1735]. Epistle I, To Lord*
> *Cobham [1734], l. 9*

2 Not always actions show the man: we find
Who does a kindness is not therefore kind.
> *Moral Essays. Epistle I, To Lord Cobham, l. 109*

3 'Tis education forms the common mind:
Just as the twig is bent, the tree's inclin'd.
> *Moral Essays. Epistle I, To Lord Cobham, l. 149*

4 Most women have no characters at all.
> *Moral Essays. Epistle II, To Mrs. M. Blount*
> *[1735], l. 2*

5 Chaste to her husband, frank to all beside,
A teeming mistress, but a barren bride.
> *Moral Essays. Epistle II, To Mrs. M. Blount,*
> *l. 71*

6 Wise wretch! with pleasures too refin'd to please;
With too much spirit to be e'er at ease;
With too much quickness ever to be taught;
With too much thinking to have common thought.
You purchase pain with all that joy can give,
And die of nothing but a rage to live.
> *Moral Essays. Epistle II, To Mrs. M. Blount,*
> *l. 95*

7 In men, we various ruling passions find;
In women, two almost divide the kind;
Those, only fix'd, they first or last obey,
The love of pleasure, and the love of sway.
> *Moral Essays. Epistle II, To Mrs. M. Blount,*
> *l. 207*

8 Men, some to business, some to pleasure take;
But ev'ry woman is at heart a rake.
> *Moral Essays. Epistle II, To Mrs. M. Blount,*
> *l. 215*

9 She who ne'er answers till a husband cools,
Or, if she rules him, never shows she rules;
Charms by accepting, by submitting, sways,
Yet has her humor most, when she obeys.
> *Moral Essays. Epistle II, To Mrs. M. Blount,*
> *l. 261*

10 And mistress of herself, though china fall.
> *Moral Essays. Epistle II, To Mrs. M. Blount,*
> *l. 268*

11 Woman's at best a contradiction still.
> *Moral Essays. Epistle II, To Mrs. M. Blount,*
> *l. 270*

12 Who shall decide when doctors disagree?[1]
> *Moral Essays. Epistle III, To Lord Bathurst*
> *[1732], l. 1*

13 But thousands die, without or this or that,
Die, and endow a college, or a cat.
> *Moral Essays. Epistle III, To Lord Bathurst,*
> *l. 95*

14 The ruling passion, be it what it will,
The ruling passion conquers reason still.
> *Moral Essays. Epistle III, To Lord Bathurst,*
> *l. 153*

15 Statesman, yet friend to truth! of soul sincere,
In action faithful, and in honor clear;
Who broke no promise, served no private end,
Who gain'd no title, and who lost no friend.
> *Moral Essays. Epistle V, To Mr. Addison*
> *[written 1720], l. 67*

16   "Blessed is the man who expects nothing, for he
shall never be disappointed" was the ninth beatitude.
> *Letter to Fortescue [September 23, 1725]*

17 You beat your pate, and fancy wit will come:
Knock as you please, there's nobody at home.
> *Epigram: An Empty House [1727]*

18 Ye Gods! annihilate but space and time,
And make two lovers happy.
> *Martinus Scriblerus on the Art of Sinking in*
> *Poetry [1728], ch. 11*

19 In wit a man, simplicity a child.
> *Epitaph on Gay [1732][2]*

20 Awake, my St. John![3] leave all meaner things
To low ambition, and the pride of kings.
Let us, since life can little more supply
Than just to look about us, and to die,
Expatiate free o'er all this scene of man;
A mighty maze! but not without a plan.
> *An Essay on Man [1733–1734].*
> *Epistle I, l. 1*

21 Eye Nature's walks, shoot folly as it flies,
And catch the manners living as they rise:
Laugh where we must, be candid where we can;
But vindicate the ways of God to man.
> *An Essay on Man. Epistle I, l. 13*

---

[1]When doctors differ who decides amid the milliard-headed throng? — RICHARD FRANCIS BURTON, *The Kasîdah of Hajî Abdú El-Yazdi, VIII, 29*

[2]See Gay, 306.

[3]Bolingbroke.

1 Say first, of God above or man below,
  What can we reason but from what we know?
  An Essay on Man. Epistle I, l. 17

2 Pleased to the last, he crops the flowery food,
  And licks the hand just rais'd to shed his blood.
  An Essay on Man. Epistle I, l. 83

3 Who sees with equal eye, as God of all,
  A hero perish or a sparrow fall,
  Atoms or systems into ruin hurl'd,
  And now a bubble burst, and now a world.
  An Essay on Man. Epistle I, l. 87

4 Hope springs eternal in the human breast:
  Man never is, but always to be blest.
  An Essay on Man. Epistle I, l. 95

5 Lo, the poor Indian! whose untutor'd mind
  Sees God in clouds, or hears him in the wind;
  His soul proud Science never taught to stray
  Far as the solar walk or milky way;
  Yet simple nature to his hope has giv'n,
  Behind the cloud-topp'd hill, an humbler heav'n.
  An Essay on Man. Epistle I, l. 99

6 Die of a rose in aromatic pain?
  An Essay on Man. Epistle I, l. 200

7 All are but parts of one stupendous whole,
  Whose body Nature is, and God the soul.
  An Essay on Man. Epistle I, l. 267

8 All nature is but art, unknown to thee;
  All chance, direction which thou canst not see;
  All discord, harmony not understood;
  All partial evil, universal good;
  And, spite of pride, in erring reason's spite,
  One truth is clear, Whatever is, is right.
  An Essay on Man. Epistle I, l. 289

9 Know then thyself, presume not God to scan;
  The proper study of mankind is man.[1]
  Placed on this isthmus of a middle state,
  A being darkly wise and rudely great:
  With too much knowledge for the skeptic side,
  With too much weakness for the stoic's pride,
  He hangs between; in doubt to act or rest;
  In doubt to deem himself a god, or beast;
  In doubt his mind or body to prefer;
  Born but to die, and reas'ning but to err;

Alike in ignorance, his reason such,
  Whether he thinks too little or too much;
  Chaos of thought and passion, all confus'd;
  Still by himself abus'd, or disabus'd;
  Created half to rise, and half to fall;
  Great lord of all things, yet a prey to all;
  Sole judge of truth, in endless error hurl'd;
  The glory, jest, and riddle of the world!
  An Essay on Man. Epistle II, l. 1

10 Vice is a monster of so frightful mien,
  As to be hated needs but to be seen;
  Yet seen too oft, familiar with her face,
  We first endure, then pity, then embrace.
  An Essay on Man. Epistle II, l. 217

11 Behold the child, by Nature's kindly law,
  Pleas'd with a rattle, tickled with a straw:
  Some livelier plaything gives his youth delight,
  A little louder, but as empty quite:
  Scarfs, garters, gold, amuse his riper stage,
  And beads and prayer books are the toys of age!
  Pleas'd with this bauble still, as that before;
  Till tir'd he sleeps, and life's poor play is o'er.
  An Essay on Man. Epistle II, l. 275

12 Worth makes the man, and want of it the fellow;
  The rest is all but leather or prunella.
  An Essay on Man. Epistle IV, l. 203

13 A wit's a feather, and a chief a rod;
  An honest man's the noblest work of God.
  An Essay on Man. Epistle IV, l. 247

14 Slave to no sect, who takes no private road,
  But looks through Nature up to Nature's God.
  An Essay on Man. Epistle IV, l. 331

15 Form'd by thy converse, happily to steer
  From grave to gay, from lively to severe.
  An Essay on Man. Epistle IV, l. 379

16 Say, shall my little bark attendant sail,
  Pursue the triumph and partake the gale?
  An Essay on Man. Epistle IV, l. 385

17 Thou wert my guide, philosopher, and friend.[2]
  An Essay on Man. Epistle IV, l. 390

18 That true self-love and social are the same.
  An Essay on Man. Epistle IV, l. 396

19 Shut, shut the door, good John! fatigu'd, I said;
  Tie up the knocker! say I'm sick, I'm dead.
  The Dog-star rages!
  *Epistle to Dr. Arbuthnot [1734]. Prologue to
  Imitations of Horace, l. 1*

---

[1] Trees and fields tell me nothing: men are my teachers. —PLATO, *Phaedrus*

La vraie science et la vraie étude de l'homme, c'est l'homme [The true science and the true study of man is man]. —PIERRE CHARRON [1541–1603], *Traité de la Sagesse* [1601], *bk. I, preface*

Das eigentliche Studium der Menschheit ist der Mensch [The proper study of mankind is man]. —JOHANN WOLFGANG VON GOETHE, *Elective Affinities* [1808], *bk. II, ch. 7*

---

[2] Is this my guide, philosopher, and friend? —POPE, *Imitations of Horace* [1733–1738], *epistle I, bk. I, l. 177*

1 As yet a child, nor yet a fool to fame,
  I lisp'd in numbers, for the numbers came.
  Epistle to Dr. Arbuthnot. Prologue to
  Imitations of Horace, l. 127

2 This long disease, my life.
  Epistle to Dr. Arbuthnot. Prologue to
  Imitations of Horace, l. 132

3 Means not, but blunders round about a
      meaning;
  And he whose fustian's so sublimely bad,
  It is not poetry, but prose run mad.
  Epistle to Dr. Arbuthnot. Prologue to
  Imitations of Horace, l. 186

4   Were there one whose fires
  True Genius kindles, and fair Fame inspires,
  Bless'd with each talent, and each art to please,
  And born to write, converse, and live with ease;
  Should such a man, too fond to rule alone,
  Bear, like the Turk, no brother near the throne;
  View him with scornful, yet with jealous eyes,
  And hate for arts that caus'd himself to rise;
  Damn with faint praise, assent with civil leer,
  And, without sneering, teach the rest to sneer;
  Willing to wound, and yet afraid to strike,
  Just hint a fault, and hesitate dislike;
  Alike reserv'd to blame or to commend,
  A tim'rous foe, and a suspicious friend;
  Dreading e'en fools, by flatterers besieged,
  And so obliging that he ne'er oblig'd;
  Like Cato, give his little Senate laws,
  And sit attentive to his own applause.
  Epistle to Dr. Arbuthnot. Prologue to
  Imitations of Horace, l. 193

5 Who but must laugh, if such a man there be?
  Who would not weep, if Atticus were he!
  Epistle to Dr. Arbuthnot. Prologue to
  Imitations of Horace, l. 213

6 Curs'd be the verse, how well soe'er it flow,
  That tends to make one worthy man my foe.
  Epistle to Dr. Arbuthnot. Prologue to
  Imitations of Horace, l. 283

7 Let Sporus tremble — "What? that thing of silk,
  Sporus, that mere white curd of ass's milk?
  Satire or sense, alas! can Sporus feel?
  Who breaks a butterfly upon a wheel?"
  Epistle to Dr. Arbuthnot. Prologue to
  Imitations of Horace, l. 305

8 Yet let me flap this bug with gilded wings,
  This painted child of dirt, that stinks and stings;
  Whose buzz the witty and the fair annoys,
  Yet wit ne'er tastes, and beauty ne'er enjoys.
  Epistle to Dr. Arbuthnot. Prologue to
  Imitations of Horace, l. 309

9 And he himself one vile antithesis.
  Epistle to Dr. Arbuthnot. Prologue to
  Imitations of Horace, l. 325

10 Wit that can creep, and pride that licks the dust.
  Epistle to Dr. Arbuthnot. Prologue to
  Imitations of Horace, l. 333

11 Unlearn'd, he knew no schoolman's subtle art,
  No language, but the language of the heart.
  Epistle to Dr. Arbuthnot. Prologue to
  Imitations of Horace, l. 398

12 I cannot sleep a wink.
  Imitations of Horace [1733–1738], satire I,
  bk. II, l. 12

13 Satire's my weapon, but I'm too discreet
  To run amuck, and tilt at all I meet.
  Imitations of Horace, I, II, l. 69

14 There St. John mingles with my friendly bowl
  The feast of reason and the flow of soul.
  Imitations of Horace, I, II, l. 127

15 For I, who hold sage Homer's rule the best,
  Welcome the coming, speed the going guest.
  Imitations of Horace, II, II, l. 159

16 I've often wish'd that I had clear,
  For life, six hundred pounds a year;
  A handsome house to lodge a friend,
  A river at my garden's end,
  A terrace walk, and half a rood
  Of land set out to plant a wood.
  Imitations of Horace, VI, II, l. 1

17 Give me again my hollow tree,
  A crust of bread, and liberty.
  Imitations of Horace, VI, II, l. 220

18 A patriot is a fool in ev'ry age.
  Imitations of Horace, epilogue to the Satires,
  Dialogue I, l. 41

19 Never gallop Pegasus to death.
  Imitations of Horace, epistle I, bk. I, l. 14

20 Not to go back is somewhat to advance,
  And men must walk, at least, before they dance.
  Imitations of Horace, I, I, l. 53

21 Get place and wealth, if possible with grace;
  If not, by any means get wealth and place.
  Imitations of Horace, I, I, l. 103

22   The people's voice is odd,
  It is, and it is not, the voice of God.
  Imitations of Horace, I, II, l. 89

23 In quibbles angel and archangel join,
  And God the Father turns a school-divine.
  Imitations of Horace, I, II, l. 101 (on
  Paradise Lost)

1 The mob of gentlemen who wrote with ease.
> *Imitations of Horace, I, II, l. 108*

2 One simile that solitary shines
  In the dry desert of a thousand lines.
> *Imitations of Horace, I, II, l. 111*

3 Ev'n copious Dryden wanted, or forgot,
  The last and greatest art—the art to blot.
> *Imitations of Horace, I, II, l. 280*

4 There still remains, to mortify a wit,
  The many-headed monster of the pit.
> *Imitations of Horace, I, II, l. 304*

5 We poets are (upon a poet's word)
  Of all mankind the creatures most absurd:
  The season when to come, and when to go,
  To sing, or cease to sing, we never know.
> *Imitations of Horace, I, II, l. 358*

6 Vain was the chief's, the sage's pride!
  They had no poet, and they died.
> *Imitations of Horace, odes, bk. IV, ode 9, st. 4*

7 Father of all! in every age,
  In every clime ador'd,
  By saint, by savage, and by sage,
  Jehovah, Jove, or Lord!
> *The Universal Prayer [1738], st. 1*

8 And binding Nature fast in fate,
  Left free the human will.
> *The Universal Prayer, st. 3*

9 I am his Highness'[1] dog at Kew;
  Pray tell me, sir, whose dog are you?
> *On the collar of a dog*

10 Nature and Nature's laws lay hid in night:
  God said, Let Newton be! and all was light.
> *Epitaph intended for Sir Isaac Newton*

11 This is the Jew
  That Shakespeare drew.
> *Of Macklin's performance in 1741 of
> Shylock in The Merchant of Venice
> (attributed to Pope)*

12 I never knew any man in my life who could not
  bear another's misfortunes perfectly like a Christian.
> *Thoughts on Various Subjects; published in
> Swift's Miscellanies [1727]*

13 It is with narrow-souled people as with narrow-
  necked bottles; the less they have in them the more
  noise they make in pouring out.
> *Thoughts on Various Subjects; published in
> Swift's Miscellanies*

14 Party is the madness of many, for the gain of a
  few.
> *Thoughts on Various Subjects; published in
> Swift's Miscellanies*

15 Whether thou choose Cervantes' serious air,
  Or laugh and shake in Rabelais' easy chair.
> *The Dunciad [1728–1743], bk. I, l. 21*

16 Poetic Justice, with her lifted scale,
  Where, in nice balance, truth with gold she weighs,
  And solid pudding against empty praise.
> *The Dunciad, I, l. 52*

17 Next o'er his books his eyes began to roll,
  In pleasing memory of all he stole.
> *The Dunciad, I, l. 127*

18 A brain of feathers, and a heart of lead.
> *The Dunciad, II, l. 44*

19 Peel'd, patch'd, and piebald, linsey-woolsey
     brothers,
  Grave mummers! sleeveless some, and shirtless
     others.
  That once was Britain.   *The Dunciad, III, l. 115*

20 And proud his mistress' orders to perform,
  Rides in the whirlwind and directs the storm.
> *The Dunciad, III, l. 263*

21 A wit with dunces, and a dunce with wits.
> *The Dunciad, IV, l. 90*

22 The Right Divine of Kings to govern wrong.
> *The Dunciad, IV, l. 188*

23   Stuff the head
  With all such reading as was never read:
  For thee explain a thing till all men doubt it,
  And write about it, Goddess, and about it.
> *The Dunciad, IV, l. 249*

24 To happy convents, bosom'd deep in vines,
  Where slumber abbots, purple as their wines.
> *The Dunciad, IV, l. 301*

25 Religion blushing veils her sacred fires,
  And unawares Morality expires.
  Nor public flame, nor private, dares to shine;
  Nor human spark is left, nor glimpse divine!
  Lo! thy dread empire Chaos! is restor'd:
  Light dies before thy uncreating word;
  Thy hand, great Anarch! lets the curtain fall,
  And universal darkness buries all.
> *The Dunciad, IV, l. 649*

---

[1] Frederick, Prince of Wales.

Lady Mary Wortley Montagu
1689–1762

1 And we meet, with champagne and a chicken,
    at last.   *The Lover [1748]*

2 Be plain in dress, and sober in your diet;
    In short, my deary, kiss me, and be quiet.
                    A Summary of Lord Lyttelton's Advice

3 Satire should, like a polished razor keen,
    Wound with a touch that's scarcely felt or seen.
                    To the Imitator of the First Satire of Horace,
                    bk. II

4 But the fruit that can fall without shaking
    Indeed is too mellow for me.
                    Letters and Works [1837]. The Answer

Charles de Secondat, Baron de Montesquieu[1]
1689–1755

5   How can anyone be Persian?
                    Lettres Persanes [1721], no. 30

6   A man should be mourned at his birth, not at his
death.   *Lettres Persanes, 40*

7   If triangles had a god, he would have three sides.
                    Lettres Persanes, 59

8   Liberty is the right of doing whatever the laws
permit.   *De l'Esprit des Lois [1748], XI, 3*

9   Useless laws weaken the necessary laws.
                    De l'Esprit des Lois, XXIX, 16

10   If I knew of something that could serve my nation but would ruin another, I would not propose it
to my prince, for I am first a man and only then a
Frenchman . . . because I am necessarily a man, and
only accidentally am I French.
                    Pensées et Fragments Inédits de Montesquieu
                    [1899], I

11   You have to study a great deal to know a little.
                    Pensées et Fragments Inédits de Montesquieu, I

John Byrom
1692–1763

12 God bless the King, I mean the Faith's Defender;
    God bless—no harm in blessing—the Pretender;
    But who Pretender is, or who is King,
    God bless us all—that's quite another thing.
                    Miscellaneous Poems [1773]. To an Officer in
                    the Army, Extempore; Intended to Allay the
                    Violence of Party Spirit

---

[1]See Thomas Carlyle, 435:11.

13 Some say, that Signor Bononcini,
    Compared to Handel's a mere ninny;
    Others aver, to him, that Handel
    Is scarcely fit to hold a candle.
    Strange! that such high dispute should be
    'Twixt Tweedledum and Tweedledee.
                    Miscellaneous Poems. On the Feuds Between
                    Handel and Bononcini

14 As clear as a whistle.   *Epistle to Lloyd*

Philip Dormer Stanhope, Earl of Chesterfield
1694–1773

15   Measures not men.
                    Letters to His Son [1774]. March 6, 1742

16   Whatever is worth doing at all, is worth doing
well.   *Letters to His Son. March 10, 1746*

17   The knowledge of the world is only to be acquired in the world, and not in a closet.
                    Letters to His Son. October 4, 1746

18   An injury is much sooner forgotten than an insult.   *Letters to His Son. October 9, 1746*

19   Do as you would be done by, is the surest method
that I know of pleasing.[2]
                    Letters to His Son. October 16, 1747

20   Take the tone of the company that you are in.
                    Letters to His Son. October 16, 1747

21   I knew once a very covetous, sordid fellow,[3] who
used frequently to say, "Take care of the pence, for
the pounds will take care of themselves."
                    Letters to His Son. November 6, 1747

22   Advice is seldom welcome; and those who want
it the most always like it the least.
                    Letters to His Son. January 29, 1748

23   Speak of the moderns without contempt, and of
the ancients without idolatry.
                    Letters to His Son. February 22, 1748

24   Wear your learning, like your watch, in a private
pocket: and do not pull it out and strike it, merely
to show that you have one.
                    Letters to His Son. February 22, 1748

25   Manners must adorn knowledge, and smooth its
way through the world. Like a great rough dia-

---

[2]See *Matthew 7:12*, 35:5; Confucius, 63:21; Aristotle, 79:16;
and Hillel, 106:1.

[3]William Lowndes [1652–1724], Secretary of the Treasury in
the reigns of William III, Queen Anne, and George I.
See Carroll, 550:17.

mond, it may do very well in a closet by way of curiosity, and also for its intrinsic value.
Letters to His Son, July 1, 1748

1 Women, then, are only children of a larger growth.
Letters to His Son, September 5, 1748

2 Women who are either indisputably beautiful, or indisputably ugly, are best flattered upon the score of their understandings; but those who are in a state of mediocrity are best flattered upòn their beauty, or at least their graces; for every woman who is not absolutely ugly thinks herself handsome.
Letters to His Son, September 5, 1748

3 Without some dissimulation no business can be carried on at all.
Letters to His Son, May 22, 1749

4 Idleness is only the refuge of weak minds.
Letters to His Son, July 20, 1749

5 Style is the dress of thoughts.
Letters to His Son, November 24, 1749

6 Dispatch is the soul of business.
Letters to His Son, February 5, 1750

7 Knowledge may give weight, but accomplishments give luster, and many more people see than weigh.
Letters to His Son, May 8, 1750

8 Let blockheads read what blockheads wrote.
Letters to His Son, November 1, 1750

9 Every woman is infallibly to be gained by every sort of flattery, and every man by one sort or other.
Letters to His Son, March 16, 1752

10 The chapter of knowledge is a very short, but the chapter of accidents is a very long one.
To Solomon Dayrolles, February 16, 1753

11 I assisted at the birth of that most significant word "flirtation," which dropped from the most beautiful mouth in the world.
The World [December 5, 1754], no. 101

12 Unlike my subject will I frame my song,
It shall be witty, and it shan't be long.
Epigram on ("Long") Sir Thomas Robinson

13 The dews of the evening most carefully shun —
Those tears of the sky for the loss of the sun.
Advice to a Lady in Autumn

14 Give Dayrolles a chair.   *Last words*

Francis Hutcheson
1694–1746

15 That action is best which procures the greatest happiness for the greatest numbers.[1]
Inquiry Concerning Moral Good and Evil [1720], sec. 3

François Quesnay
1694–1774

16 Laissez faire, laissez passer.[2]   *Attributed*

Voltaire
[François Marie Arouet]
1694–1778

17 Virtue debases itself in justifying itself.
Oedipe [1718], act I, sc. iv

18 O what fine times, this age of iron!
Le Mondain [1736]

19 Paradise is where I am.   *Le Mondain*

20 The superfluous, a very necessary thing.
Le Mondain

21 The secret of being a bore is to tell everything.
Sept Discours en Vers sur l'Homme [1738]

22 Love truth, but pardon error.
Sept Discours en Vers sur l'Homme

23 He who is merely just is severe.
Letter to Frederick the Great [1740]

24 The first who was king was a fortunate soldier: Who serves his country well has no need of ancestors.[3]   *Mérope [1743], act I, sc. iii*

25 It is better to risk saving a guilty person than to condemn an innocent one.   *Zadig [1747], ch. 6*

26 They squeeze the orange and throw away the skin.
Letter to Madame Denis [September 2, 1751] referring to his quarrel with Frederick the Great

---

[1] The greatest happiness of the greatest number is the foundation of morals and legislation. — JEREMY BENTHAM [1748–1832], *Works, vol. X, p. 142*

[2] Let it be, let it pass.
The phrase is not readily translatable, and also appears as: Laissez faire, laissez aller. It has also been attributed to PIERRE LE PESANT BOISGUILLEBERT [1646–1714] and JEAN CLAUDE GOURNAY [1712–1759]. It was widely used by the Physiocrats in urging freedom from government interference, and was adopted by Adam Smith [1723–1790].

[3] What can they see in the longest kingly line in Europe, save that it runs back to a successful soldier? — SIR WALTER SCOTT, *Woodstock* [1826], *ch. 37*

1　This agglomeration which was called and which still calls itself the Holy Roman Empire is neither holy, nor Roman, nor an Empire.
Essai sur les Moeurs [1756]

2　In this best of all possible worlds . . . everything is for the best.[1]　*Candide [1759],[2] ch. 1*

3　If this is the best of all possible worlds, what are the others like?　*Candide, 6*

4　[Optimism] is a mania for saying things are well when one is in hell.　*Candide, 19*

5　You know that these two nations [France and England] have been at war over a few acres of snow near Canada, and that they are spending on this fine struggle more than Canada itself is worth.
Candide, 23

6　In this country [England] it is useful from time to time to kill one admiral in order to encourage the others.[3]　*Candide, 23*

7　This is the happiest of all men, for he is superior to everything he possesses.　*Candide, 25*

8　Work keeps us from three great evils, boredom, vice, and poverty.[4]　*Candide, 30*

9　We must cultivate our garden.[5]　*Candide, 30*

10　There are truths which are not for all men, nor for all times.
Letter to Cardinal de Bernis [April 23, 1761]

11　One feels like crawling on all fours after reading your work.
Letter to Rousseau [August 31, 1761]

12　Whatever you do, crush the infamous thing [superstition], and love those who love you.[6]
Letter to d'Alembert [November 28, 1762]

13　Common sense is not so common.
Dictionnaire Philosophique [1764]. Common Sense

14　In general, the art of government consists in taking as much money as possible from one class of citizens to give to the other.
Dictionnaire Philosophique. Money

15　We have a natural right to make use of our pen as of our tongue, at our peril, risk and hazard.
Dictionnaire Philosophique. Liberty of the Pres

16　The best is the enemy of the good.[7]
Dictionnaire Philosophique. Dramatic Ar

17　Very learned women are to be found, in the same manner as female warriors; but they are seldom o never inventors.
Dictionnaire Philosophique. Women

18　Men use thought only to justify their wrongdoings, and speech only to conceal their thoughts.
Dialogue 14. Le Chapon et la Poularde [1766]

19　I have never made but one prayer to God, a very short one: "O Lord, make my enemies ridiculous." And God granted it.
Letter to M. Damilaville [May 16, 1767]

20　History is no more than the portrayal of crimes and misfortunes.[8]
L'Ingénu [1767], ch. 10

21　Thought depends absolutely on the stomach, but in spite of that, those who have the best stomachs are not the best thinkers.
Letter to d'Alembert [August 20, 1770]

22　If God did not exist, it would be necessary to invent him.
Épître à l'Auteur du Livre des Trois Imposteurs [November 10, 1770]

23　Change everything, except your loves.
Sur l'Usage de la Vie

24　I am very fond of truth, but not at all of martyrdom.　*Letter to d'Alembert [February 1776]*

25　The embarrassment of riches.[9]
Le Droit du Seigneur, act II, sc. vi

26　Who has not the spirit of his age,
Of his age has all the unhappiness.[10]
Letter to Madame du Châtelet

27　I advise you to go on living solely to enrage those who are paying your annuities. It is the only pleasure I have left.
Letter to Madame du Deffand

28　Liberty of thought is the life of the soul.
Essay on Epic Poetry (written in English)

---

[1]Dans ce meilleur des mondes possibles . . . tout est au mieux.
Often quoted: All is for the best in the best of all possible worlds.

[2]Translated by ROBERT M. ADAMS.

[3]Pour encourager les autres.
The reference is to Admiral John Byng, who was executed in 1757 for failing to relieve Minorca.

[4]Le travail éloigne de nous trois grands maux, l'ennui, le vice, et le besoin.

[5]Il faut cultiver notre jardin.

[6]Quoi que vous fassiez, écrasez l'infâme, et aimez qui vous aime.

---

[7]Le mieux est l'ennemi du bien.

[8]L'histoire n'est que le tableau des crimes et des malheurs.

[9]L'embarras des richesses.—ABBÉ D'ALLAINVAL [1700–1753], *title of play* [1726]

[10]Qui n'a pas l'esprit de son âge, / De son âge a tout le malheur.

1 Whoever you are, behold your master,
He is, or was, or has to be.[1]
On a statuette of Cupid in the Cirey Gardens

2   I disapprove of what you say, but I will defend to
the death your right to say it.   *Attributed*[2]

3   I die adoring God, loving my friends, not hating
my enemies, and detesting superstition.
Written February 28, 1778

Matthew Green
1696–1737

4 They politics like ours profess,
The greater prey upon the less.   *The Grotto, l. 69*

5 Fling but a stone, the giant dies.
Laugh and be well.   *The Spleen [1737], l. 92*

6 By happy alchemy of mind
They turn to pleasure all they find.
The Spleen, l. 610

William Oldys
1696–1761

7 Busy, curious, thirsty fly,
Drink with me, and drink as I.
On a Fly Drinking out of a Cup of Ale, st. 1

Marie de Vichy-Chamrond, Marquise du Deffand
1697–1780

8   [Of Voltaire:] He has invented history.
From FOURNIER, L'Esprit dans l'Histoire
[1857]

9   The first step is the hardest.[3]
Letter to d'Alembert [July 7, 1763]

---

[1]Qui que tu sois, voici ton maître; / Il l'est—le fut—ou le doit
être.

[2]This sentence is not Voltaire's, but was first used in quoting a
letter from Voltaire to Helvétius in *The Friends of Voltaire* [1906]
by S. G. Tallentyre (E. Beatrice Hall). She claims it was a paraphrase of Voltaire's words in the *Essay on Tolerance:* Think for
yourselves and let others enjoy the privilege to do so too.
   Norbert Guterman, in *A Book of French Quotations* [1963], suggests that the probable source for the quotation is a line in a letter
to M. le Riche [February 6, 1770]: "Monsieur l'abbé, I detest
what you write, but I would give my life to make it possible for
you to continue to write."

[3]This remark refers to the legend that Saint Denis, carrying his
head in his hands, walked from Montmartre to St. Denis, a few
miles north of Paris. Voltaire wrote to Madame du Deffand [Janu-
ary 1764] that one of her bons mots was quoted in the notes of
La Pucelle, canto 1: Il n'y a que le premier pas qui coûte.

Charles Macklin
c. 1697–1797

10   The law is a sort of hocus-pocus science.[4]
Love à la Mode [1759], act II, sc. i

William Warburton
1698–1779

11   Orthodoxy is my doxy; heterodoxy is another
man's doxy.[5]
From JOSEPH PRIESTLEY [1733–1804],
Memoirs, vol. I, p. 572

John Dyer
1699–1757

12 A little rule, a little sway,
A sunbeam in a winter's day,
Is all the proud and mighty have
Between the cradle and the grave.
Grongar Hill [1726], l. 89

James Thomson
1700–1748

13 See, Winter comes to rule the varied year,
Sullen and sad.   *The Seasons. Winter [1726], l. 1*

14   Welcome, kindred glooms!
Congenial horrors, hail!
The Seasons. Winter, l. 5

15 Cruel as death, and hungry as the grave.
The Seasons. Winter, l. 393

16   There studious let me sit,
And hold high converse with the mighty dead.
The Seasons. Winter, l. 431

17 Ships dim-discover'd dropping from the clouds.
The Seasons. Summer [1727], l. 946

18 Sigh'd and look'd unutterable things.
The Seasons. Summer, l. 1188

19 Come, gentle Spring! ethereal mildness, come.
The Seasons. Spring [1728], l. 1

---

[4]Hocus was an old cunning attorney.—DR. JOHN ARBUTHNOT
[1667–1735], *Law Is a Bottomless Pit; or, History of John Bull*
[1712], *ch. 5*
   The words of consecration, "Hoc est corpus," were travestied
into a nickname for jugglery, as "Hocus-pocus."—JOHN RICHARD
GREEN [1837–1883], *A Short History of the English People* [1874],
ch. 7

[5]Priestley relates that in a debate on the Test Laws, Lord Sandwich said, "I have heard frequent use of the words 'orthodoxy' and
'heterodoxy' but I confess myself at a loss to know precisely what
they mean." Bishop Warburton whispered his definition to him.

1 Delightful task! to rear the tender thought,
To teach the young idea how to shoot.
The Seasons. Spring, l. 1152

2 An elegant sufficiency, content,
Retirement, rural quiet, friendship, books.
The Seasons. Spring, l. 1161

3 Crown'd with the sickle, and the wheaten sheaf,
While Autumn, nodding o'er the yellow plain,
Comes jovial on.
The Seasons. Autumn [1730], l. 1

4   For loveliness
Needs not the foreign aid of ornament,
But is when unadorned adorned the most.
The Seasons. Autumn, l. 204

5 Or where the Northern ocean, in vast whirls,
Boils round the naked melancholy isles
Of farthest Thulè, and th' Atlantic surge
Pours in among the stormy Hebrides.
The Seasons. Autumn, l. 862

6 Come then, expressive silence, muse His praise.
A Hymn [1730], l. 118

7 Forever, Fortune, wilt thou prove
An unrelenting foe to love,
And, when we meet a mutual heart,
Come in between and bid us part?
Song. Forever, Fortune

8 When Britain first, at Heaven's command,
Arose from out the azure main,
This was the charter of the land,
And guardian angels sung this strain:
Rule, Britannia, rule the waves;
Britons never will be slaves.
Alfred [1740], act II, sc. v

9 A pleasing land of drowsyhead it was.
The Castle of Indolence [1748], canto I, st. 6

10 A bard here dwelt, more fat than bard beseems,
Who, void of envy, guile, and lust of gain,
On virtue still, and nature's pleasing themes,
Poured forth his unpremeditated strain.
The Castle of Indolence, I, st. 68

11 A little round, fat, oily man of God.
The Castle of Indolence, I, st. 69

Philip Doddridge
1702–1751

12 Awake my soul! stretch every nerve,
And press with vigor on;
A heavenly race demands thy zeal,
And an immortal crown.
Hymns [1755]. Zeal and Vigor in the Christian Race, st. 1

Jonathan Edwards
1703–1758

13   Resolved, never to do anything which I should
be afraid to do if it were the last hour of my life.
Seventy Resolution

14   Intend to live in continual mortification, and
never to expect or desire any worldly ease or pleasure.
Diary [1723]

15   A little, wretched, despicable creature; a worm, a
mere nothing, and less than nothing; a vile insect
that has risen up in contempt against the majesty of
Heaven and earth.
The Justice of God in the Damnation of Sinners [1734]

16   The God that holds you over the pit of hell,
much as one holds a spider, or some loathsome insect over the fire, abhors you, and is dreadfully provoked: his wrath towards you burns like fire; he
looks upon you as worthy of nothing else, but to be
cast into the fire.
Sinners in the Hands of an Angry God [1741][1]

17   I assert that nothing ever comes to pass without
a cause.
Freedom of Will [1754], sec. 3

18   This dictate of common sense.
Freedom of Will, 3

Thomas Morell
1703–1784

19 See, the conquering hero comes!
Sound the trumpet, beat the drums![2]
Joshua [1748], pt. III

John Wesley
1703–1791

20   I look upon the world as my parish.
Journal [1909–1916]. June 11, 1739

21   That execrable sum of all villainies, commonly
called the Slave Trade.
Journal. February 12, 1772

22   Though I am always in haste, I am never in a
hurry.   *Letters [1831]. December 10, 1777*

23   Let it be observed, that slovenliness is no part of
religion; that neither this nor any text of Scripture,

---

[1] See Robert Lowell, 800:11 and note.

[2] Handel used this in his oratorios *Judas Maccabaeus* [April 1, 1747] and *Joshua* [March 9, 1748], the libretti of which were written by Morell.

condemns neatness of apparel. Certainly this is a duty, not a sin. "Cleanliness is, indeed, next to godliness."   *Sermon 93, On Dress*

1 Do all the good you can,
   By all the means you can,
   In all the ways you can,
   In all the places you can,
   At all the times you can,
   To all the people you can,
   As long as ever you can.   *John Wesley's Rule*

Benjamin Franklin[1]
1706–1790

2 The body of Benjamin Franklin, Printer (like the cover of an old book, its contents torn out and stripped of its lettering and gilding), lies here, food for worms; but the work shall not be lost, for it will (as he believed) appear once more in a new and more elegant edition, revised and corrected by the Author.   *Epitaph on Himself [composed in 1728]*

3 Eat to live, and not live to eat.
                 Poor Richard's Almanac [1733]. May

4 After three days men grow weary, of a wench, a guest, and weather rainy.
                      Poor Richard's Almanac. June

5 There is no little enemy.
                 Poor Richard's Almanac. September

6 Without justice, courage is weak.
                 Poor Richard's Almanac [1734]. January

7 Blame-all and Praise-all are two blockheads.
                  Poor Richard's Almanac. February

8 Where there's marriage without love, there will be love without marriage.
                       Poor Richard's Almanac. May

9 Avarice and happiness never saw each other, how then should they become acquainted.
                   Poor Richard's Almanac. November

10 A little house well filled, a little field well tilled, and a little wife well willed, are great riches.
                 Poor Richard's Almanac [1735]. February

11 Necessity never made a good bargain.
                    Poor Richard's Almanac. April

12 Three may keep a secret, if two of them are dead.   *Poor Richard's Almanac. July*

13 Opportunity is the great bawd.
                 Poor Richard's Almanac. September

14 Early to bed and early to rise, makes a man healthy, wealthy, and wise.
                   Poor Richard's Almanac. October

15 Here comes the orator! with his flood of words, and his drop of reason.
                   Poor Richard's Almanac. October

16 Some are weatherwise, some are otherwise.
                  Poor Richard's Almanac. December

17 God helps them that help themselves.
                Poor Richard's Almanac [1736]. June

18 Don't throw stones at your neighbors', if your own windows are glass.
                  Poor Richard's Almanac. August

19 There are three faithful friends—an old wife, an old dog, and ready money.
                Poor Richard's Almanac [1738]. January

20 If you would not be forgotten,
    As soon as you are dead and rotten,
    Either write things worthy reading,
    Or do things worth the writing.
                     Poor Richard's Almanac. May

21 Keep your eyes wide open before marriage, half shut afterwards.   *Poor Richard's Almanac. June*

22 None but the well-bred man knows how to confess a fault, or acknowledge himself in an error.
                  Poor Richard's Almanac. November

23 An empty bag cannot stand upright.
                Poor Richard's Almanac [1740]. January

24 He that riseth late, must trot all day, and shall scarce overtake his business at night.
                 Poor Richard's Almanac [1742]. August

25 Experience keeps a dear school, but fools will learn in no other.
                Poor Richard's Almanac [1743]. December

26 The used key is always bright.
                 Poor Richard's Almanac [1744]. July

27 When the well's dry, we know the worth of water.[2]
                Poor Richard's Almanac [1746]. January

---

[1]Eripuit coelo fulmen mox sceptra tyrannis [He snatched the thunderbolt from heaven, then the scepter from tyrants].—*Attributed to* TURGOT
  This line was inscribed on Houdon's bust of Franklin in 1778.
  Antiquity would have raised altars to this mighty genius, who, to the advantage of mankind, compassing in his mind the heavens and the earth, was able to restrain alike thunderbolts and tyrants.—MIRABEAU, *Address upon the Death of Franklin*
  I succeed him; no one could replace him.—THOMAS JEFFERSON (to Charles Gravier, Comte de Vergennes, who had remarked, "You replace Mr. Franklin" as envoy to France)

---

[2]Do not let your chances like sunbeams pass you by, / For you never miss the water till the well runs dry.—ROWLAND HOWARD [fl. 1876], *You Never Miss the Water* [1876]

1   Dost thou love life? Then do not squander time; for that's the stuff life is made of.
Poor Richard's Almanac. June

2   Lost time is never found again.
Poor Richard's Almanac [1748]. January

3   He that's secure is not safe.
Poor Richard's Almanac. August

4   Little strokes,
Fell great oaks.
Poor Richard's Almanac [1750]. August

5   The cat in gloves catches no mice.
Poor Richard's Almanac [1754]. February

6   Work as if you were to live a hundred years,
Pray as if you were to die tomorrow.
Poor Richard's Almanac [1757]. May

7   A word to the wise is enough, and many words won't fill a bushel.
Poor Richard's Almanac [1758]. Preface: Courteous Reader

8   He that lives upon hope will die fasting.
Poor Richard's Almanac. Preface: Courteous Reader

9   Three removes is as bad as a fire.
Poor Richard's Almanac. Preface: Courteous Reader

10   A little neglect may breed great mischief . . . for want of a nail the shoe was lost; for want of a shoe the horse was lost; and for want of a horse the rider was lost.
Poor Richard's Almanac. Preface: Courteous Reader

11   Eighth and lastly. They are so grateful!!
Reasons for Preferring an Elderly Mistress [1745]

12   Remember that time is money.[1]
Advice to a Young Tradesman [1748]

13   They that can give up essential liberty to obtain a little temporary safety deserve neither liberty nor safety.
Historical Review of Pennsylvania [1759]

14   Idleness and pride tax with a heavier hand than kings and parliaments. If we can get rid of the former, we may easily bear the latter.
Letter on the Stamp Act [July 11, 1765]

15   The grand leap of the whale up the Fall of Niagara is esteemed, by all who have seen it, as one of the finest spectacles in nature.
To the editor of a London newspaper [1765], intended to chaff the English for their ignorance of America

16   Here Skugg lies snug
As a bug in a rug.
Letter to Miss Georgiana Shipley [September 1772]

17   You and I were long friends: you are now my enemy, and I am
Yours.
B. Franklin
Letter to William Strahan [July 5, 1775]

18   We must all hang together, or assuredly we shall all hang separately.
At the signing of the Declaration of Independence [July 4, 1776]

19   Poor man, said I, you pay too much for your whistle.
The Whistle [1779]

20   Here you would know and enjoy what posterity will say of Washington. For a thousand leagues have nearly the same effect with a thousand years.
Letter to George Washington [March 5, 1780]

21   George Washington, Commander of the American armies, who, like Joshua of old, commanded the sun and the moon to stand still, and they obeyed him.
A toast at a dinner in Versailles[2]

22   No nation was ever ruined by trade.
Thoughts on Commercial Subjects

23   There never was a good war or a bad peace.[3]
Letter to Josiah Quincy [September 11, 1783]

24   I wish the bald eagle had not been chosen as the representative of our country; he is a bird of bad moral character . . . like those among men who live by sharping and robbing, he is generally poor, and often very lousy . . .

The turkey . . . is a much more respectable bird, and withal a true original native of America.
Letter to Sarah Bache [January 26, 1784]

---

[1]We reckon hours and minutes to be dollars and cents. —SAM SLICK [T. C. HALIBURTON], *The Clockmaker*

[2]The British minister had proposed a toast to George III, in which he likened him to the sun, and the French minister had toasted Louis XVI, comparing him with the moon.

[3]I cease not to advocate peace; even though unjust it is better than the most just war. —CICERO, *Epistolae ad Atticum, bk. VII, epistle 14*

It hath been said that an unjust peace is to be preferred before a just war. —SAMUEL BUTLER [1612–1680], *Butler's Remains* [1759], *Speeches in the Rump Parliament*

1   He [the sun] gives light as soon as he rises.
An Economical Project [1784][1]

2   A republic, if you can keep it.[2]
Response [September 18, 1787]

3   Our new Constitution is now established, and has an appearance that promises permanency; but in this world nothing can be said to be certain, except death and taxes.
Letter to Jean-Baptiste Leroy [November 13, 1789]

4   The next thing most like living one's life over again seems to be a recollection of that life, and to make that recollection as durable as possible by putting it down in writing.
Autobiography [1731–1759],[3] *ch. 1*

5   Eat not to dullness; drink not to elevation.
Autobiography, 6

6   I shall never ask, never refuse, nor ever resign an office.   *Autobiography, 8*

7   Human felicity is produced not so much by great pieces of good fortune that seldom happen, as by little advantages that occur every day.
Autobiography, 9

8   When men are employed, they are best contented; for on the days they worked they were good-natured and cheerful, and, with the consciousness of having done a good day's work, they spent the evening jollily; but on our idle days they were mutinous and quarrelsome.   *Autobiography, 10*

Georges Louis Leclerc de Buffon
1707–1788

9   [Of the horse:] The noblest conquest man has ever made.
L'Histoire des Mammifères. Le Cheval

10   The style is the man himself.[4]
Discourse (on his admission to the French Academy [1753])

11   Genius is nothing but a greater aptitude for patience.   *Attributed*[5]

Henry Fielding
1707–1754

12 All Nature wears one universal grin.
Tom Thumb [1730], act I, sc. i

13 Today it is our pleasure to be drunk;
And this our queen shall be as drunk as we.
Tom Thumb, I, ii

14 When I'm not thanked at all, I'm thanked enough;
I've done my duty, and I've done no more.
Tom Thumb, I, iii

15 Oh, the roast beef of England,
And old England's roast beef![6]
The Grub Street Opera [1731], act III, sc. iii

16 I am as sober as a judge.
Don Quixote in England [1734], act III, sc. xiv

17 This story will never go down.
Tumble-Down Dick

18 The dusky night rides down the sky,
And ushers in the morn;
The hounds all join in glorious cry,
The huntsman winds his horn,
And a-hunting we will go.[7]
A-Hunting We Will Go [1734], st. 1

19   To whom nothing is given, of him can nothing be required.
Joseph Andrews [1742], bk. II, ch. 8

20   I describe not men, but manners; not an individual, but a species.   *Joseph Andrews, III, 1*

21   They are the affectation of affectation.
Joseph Andrews, III, 3

---

[1]Letter to the *Journal de Paris* advocating Daylight Saving Time.

[2]In Philadelphia, a Mrs. Powel "asked Dr. Franklin, Well, Doctor, what have we got a republic or a monarchy? A republic, replied the Doctor, if you can keep it." Recorded by James McHenry, one of Washington's aides, in his diary; published in the *American Historical Review, XI* [1906], 618.

[3]The *Autobiography,* begun in 1771, was first published (unauthorized, mangled, and in French) in 1791, and in complete form in 1868.

[4]Le style c'est l'homme même.

[5]Le génie n'est qu'une plus grande aptitude à la patience.
Hérault de Séchelles, in *Voyage à Montbard,* first attributed this to Buffon. It is quoted by Matthew Arnold in "A French Coleridge" [*Essays in Criticism,* 1865]. There is also a popular proverb: Genius is patience. Charles Thomson, Baron Sydenham [1799–1841], defined genius as a consummate sense of proportion.
Genius is an intuitive talent for labor. —JOHANNES WALAEUS [JAN VAN WALE] [1604–1699]
Patience is a necessary ingredient of genius. —BENJAMIN DISRAELI, *The Young Duke* [1831]
Genius is capacity for taking trouble. —LESLIE STEPHEN [1832–1904]

[6]The Roast Beef of Old England. —RICHARD LEVERIDGE [c. 1670–1758], *title of poem*

[7]It's of three jovial huntsmen, and a-hunting they did go; / And they hunted, and they holloed, and they blew their horns also; / Look ye there! — *The Three Jovial Huntsmen* (old English ballad), *st. 1*

1   Public schools are the nurseries of all vice and immorality.   *Joseph Andrews, III, 5*

2   Some folks rail against other folks, because other folks have what some folks would be glad of.
Joseph Andrews, IV, 6

3   Love and scandal are the best sweeteners of tea.
Love in Several Masques [1743]

4   Every physician almost hath his favorite disease.
Tom Jones [1749], bk. II, ch. 9

5   When I mention religion I mean the Christian religion; and not only the Christian religion, but the Protestant religion; and not only the Protestant religion, but the Church of England.   *Tom Jones, III, 3*

6   Thwackum was for doing justice, and leaving mercy to heaven.   *Tom Jones, III, 10*

7   Can any man have a higher notion of the rule of right and the eternal fitness of things?
Tom Jones, IV, 4

8   Distinction without a difference.
Tom Jones, VI, 13

9   O! more than Gothic ignorance.
Tom Jones, VII, 3

10   An amiable weakness.[1]   *Tom Jones, X, 8*

11   His designs were strictly honorable, as the phrase is; that is, to rob a lady of her fortune by way of marriage.   *Tom Jones, XI, 4*

12   Hairbreadth missings of happiness look like the insults of Fortune.   *Tom Jones, XIII, 2*

13   The republic of letters.   *Tom Jones, XIV, 1*

14   It hath been often said, that it is not death, but dying which is terrible.
Amelia [1751], bk. III, ch. 4

15   When widows exclaim loudly against second marriages, I would always lay a wager that the man, if not the wedding day, is absolutely fixed on.
Amelia, VI, 8

16   There is not in the universe a more ridiculous, nor a more contemptible animal, than a proud clergyman.   *Amelia, VI, 10*

17   One of my illustrious predecessors.[2]
Covent Garden Journal [January 11, 1752]

---

[1]Amiable weaknesses of human nature.—Gibbon, *The History of the Decline and Fall of the Roman Empire* [1776–1788], bk. I, ch. 14
It was an amiable weakness.—Richard Brinsley Sheridan, *The School for Scandal* [1777]

[2]Illustrious predecessor.—Edmund Burke, *The Present Discontents* [1770]
I tread in the footsteps of illustrious men. . . . In receiving from the people the sacred trust twice confined to my illustrious predecessor [Andrew Jackson].—Martin Van Buren [1782–1862], *Inaugural Address* [March 4, 1837]

Linnaeus [Carl von Linné]
1707–1778

18   To live by medicine is to live horribly.
Diaeta Naturalis, introductio

19   Nature does not proceed by leaps.[3]
Philosophia Botanica [1750], sec. 7

20   A professor can never better distinguish himself in his work than by encouraging a clever pupil, for the true discoverers are among them, as comets amongst the stars.
From biography by Theodor Magnus Fries, trans. Benjamin Daydon Jackson, ch. 9

21   Live innocently; God is here.
From biography by Theodor Magnus Fries, trans. Benjamin Daydon Jackson, 15 (inscribed over the door of Linnaeus's bedchamber)

22   If a tree dies, plant another in its place.
From biography by Theodor Magnus Fries, trans. Benjamin Daydon Jackson, 15

Charles Wesley
1707–1788

23   "Christ, the Lord, is risen today,"
Sons of men and angels say,
Raise your joys and triumphs high,
Sing, ye heavens, and earth reply.
Hymns and Sacred Poems [1739]. Christ, the Lord, Is Risen Today

24   Jesus, lover of my soul,
Let me to Thy bosom fly,
While the waters nearer roll,
While the tempest still is high;
Hide me, O my Savior, hide,
Till the storm of life is past;
Safe into the haven glide,
O receive my soul at last.
Hymns and Sacred Poems [1740]. Jesus, Lover of My Soul

25   Gentle Jesus, meek and mild,
Look upon a little child;
Pity my simplicity,
Suffer me to come to thee.
Hymns and Sacred Poems [1742]. Gentle Jesus, Meek and Mild

26   Soldiers of Christ, arise,
And put your armor on.
Hymns and Sacred Poems [1749]. Soldiers of Christ, Arise

---

[3]Natura non facit saltus.

1 Hark! the herald angels sing
Glory to the newborn King;
Peace on earth, and mercy mild,
God and sinners reconciled!
Joyful all ye nations rise,
Join the triumph of the skies;
With th' angelic host proclaim
Christ is born in Bethlehem.[1]
> *Hymns and Sacred Poems [1753]. Christmas*
> *Hymn: Hark! the Herald Angels Sing*

William Pitt, Earl of Chatham
1708–1778

2 The atrocious crime of being a young man, which the honorable gentleman [Walpole] has with such spirit and decency charged upon me, I shall neither attempt to palliate nor deny; but content myself with wishing that I may be one of those whose follies may cease with their youth, and not of that number who are ignorant in spite of experience.
> *Speech in the House of Commons [March 6, 1741][2]*

3 The poorest man may in his cottage bid defiance to all the forces of the Crown. It may be frail — its roof may shake — the wind may blow through it — the storm may enter — the rain may enter — but the King of England cannot enter — all his force dares not cross the threshold of the ruined tenement!
> *Speech in the House of Commons [1763]*

4 I rejoice that America has resisted. Three millions of people, so dead to all the feelings of liberty, as voluntarily to submit to be slaves, would have been fit instruments to make slaves of the rest.
> *Speech in the House of Commons [January 14, 1766]*

5 Confidence is a plant of slow growth in an aged bosom; youth is the season of credulity.
> *Speech in the House of Commons [January 14, 1766]*

6 Unlimited power is apt to corrupt the minds of those who possess it; and this I know, my lords, that where laws end, tyranny begins.
> *Case of Wilkes. Speech [January 9, 1770]*

7 There is something behind the throne greater than the King himself.
> *Speech in the House of Lords*
> *[March 2, 1770]*

8 I love the Americans because they love liberty, and I love them for the noble efforts they made in the last war.
> *Speech in the House of Lords*
> *[March 2, 1770]*

9 Reparation for our rights at home, and security against the like future violations.[3]
> *Letter to the Earl of Shelburne [September 29, 1770]*

10 If I were an American, as I am an Englishman, while a foreign troop was landed in my country, I never would lay down my arms — never — never — never! You cannot conquer America.
> *Speech [November 18, 1777]*

11 I invoke the genius of the Constitution.
> *Speech [November 18, 1777]*

Samuel Johnson
1709–1784

12 Of all the griefs that harass the distrest,
Sure the most bitter is a scornful jest.
> *London [1738] (an imitation of the Third*
> *Satire of Juvenal), l. 166*

13 This mournful truth is ev'rywhere confessed —
Slow rises worth, by poverty depress'd.[4]
> *London, l. 176*

14 When learning's triumph o'er her barb'rous
foes
First rear'd the stage, immortal Shakespeare
rose;
Each change of many-color'd life he drew,
Exhausted worlds, and then imagin'd new:
Existence saw him spurn her bounded reign,
And panting Time toil'd after him in vain.
> *Prologue at the Opening of Drury Lane*
> *Theatre [1747]*

15 Cold approbation gave the ling'ring bays,
For those who durst not censure, scarce could
praise.
> *Prologue at the Opening of Drury Lane*
> *Theatre*

---

[1] GEORGE WHITEFIELD [1714–1770] altered lines 1 and 2, 7 and 8, from Wesley's original:
Hark, how all the welkin rings, / "Glory to the King of kings." . . . / Universal nature say, / "Christ the Lord is born to-day."

[2] This is the composition of Johnson, founded on some note or statement of the actual speech. Johnson said, "That speech I wrote in a garret, in Exeter Street." — BOSWELL, *Life of Johnson* [1791]

[3] Indemnity for the past and security for the future. — JOHN RUSSELL, *Life and Times of Charles James Fox* [1859–1860], *vol. III, p. 345,* letter to the Honorable T. Maitland

[4] Three years later Johnson wrote, "Mere unassisted merit advances slowly, if — what is not very common — it advances at all."

1 Declamation roar'd, while Passion slept.
Prologue at the Opening of Drury Lane Theatre

2 The wild vicissitudes of taste.
Prologue at the Opening of Drury Lane Theatre

3 For we that live to please must please to live.
Prologue at the Opening of Drury Lane Theatre

4 Studious to please, yet not ashamed to fail.
Prologue to the Tragedy of Irene [1749]

5 Let observation with extensive view
Survey mankind, from China to Peru.[1]
Vanity of Human Wishes [1749], l. 1

6 Deign on the passing world to turn thine eyes,
And pause a while from learning to be wise.
There mark what ills the scholar's life assail—
Toil, envy, want, the patron, and the jail.
Vanity of Human Wishes, l. 157

7 He left the name at which the world grew pale,
To point a moral, or adorn a tale.
Vanity of Human Wishes, l. 221

8 "Enlarge my life with multitude of days!"
In health, in sickness, thus the suppliant prays:
Hides from himself his state, and shuns to know
That life protracted is protracted woe.
Vanity of Human Wishes, l. 255

9 Must helpless man, in ignorance sedate,
Roll darkling down the torrent of his fate?
Vanity of Human Wishes, l. 345

10 Secure, whate'er he gives, he gives the best.
Vanity of Human Wishes, l. 356

11 With these celestial Wisdom calms the mind,
And makes the happiness she does not find.
Vanity of Human Wishes, l. 367

12 Curiosity is one of the permanent and certain characteristics of a vigorous mind.
The Rambler[2] [March 12, 1751]

13 No place affords a more striking conviction of the vanity of human hopes than a public library.
The Rambler [March 23, 1751]

14 I am not yet so lost in lexicography as to forget that words are the daughters of earth, and that things are the sons of heaven.
Dictionary [1755], preface

15 CLUB—An assembly of good fellows, meeting under certain conditions.   *Dictionary*

16 ESSAY—A loose sally of the mind; an irregular indigested piece; not a regular and orderly composition.   *Dictionary*

17 EXCISE—A hateful tax levied upon commodities, and adjudged not by the common judges of property, but wretches hired by those to whom excise is paid.   *Dictionary*

18 GRUBSTREET—The name of a street near Moorfield, London, much inhabited by writers of small histories, dictionaries, and temporary poems.
Dictionary

19 LEXICOGRAPHER—A writer of dictionaries, a harmless drudge.   *Dictionary*

20 OATS—A grain which in England is generally given to horses, but in Scotland supports the people.[3]   *Dictionary*

21 Among the calamities of war, may be justly numbered the diminution of the love of truth, by the falsehoods which interest dictates, and credulity encourages.[4]   *The Idler [1758–1760], no. 3*

22 The joy of life is variety; the tenderest love requires to be rekindled by intervals of absence.
The Idler, 3

23 He is no wise man who will quit a certainty for an uncertainty.   *The Idler, 5*

24 Ye who listen with credulity to the whispers of fancy, and pursue with eagerness the phantoms of hope; who expect that age will perform the promises of youth, and that the deficiencies of the present day will be supplied by the morrow; attend to the history of Rasselas, Prince of Abyssinia.
Rasselas [1759], ch.

25 To a poet nothing can be useless.
Rasselas,

26 Human life is everywhere a state in which much is to be endured and little to be enjoyed.
Rasselas,

27 Marriage has many pains, but celibacy has no pleasures.   *Rasselas,*

---

[1] De Quincey quotes with approval, but without naming him, the criticism of a writer who contends that this couplet amounts in effect to this: "Let observation with extensive observation observe mankind extensively." — *Rhetoric* [1828]

[2] For the *Rambler* motto, see Johnson's translation of BOETHIUS, *De Consolatione Philosophiae, III, 9, 27, 120:5.*

[3] It was pleasant to me to find, that "oats," the "food of horses," were so much used as the food of the people in Dr. Johnson's own town. — BOSWELL, *Life of Johnson* [1791], *vol. I, p. 628* (Everyman edition)

I own that by my definition of *oats* I meant to vex them [the Scots]. — JOHNSON, in BOSWELL, *Life of Johnson* [1791], *vol. II, 434* (Everyman edition)

[4] The first casualty when war comes is truth — HIRAM WARREN JOHNSON [1866–1945], *remark in U.S. Senate* [1918]. *Attribut*

1   Example is always more efficacious than precept.
Rasselas, 30

2   The endearing elegance of female friendship.
Rasselas, 46

3   How small, of all that human hearts endure,
That part which laws or kings can cause or cure!
Still to ourselves in every place consign'd,
Our own felicity we make or find.
Lines added to OLIVER GOLDSMITH, *The Traveller [1763–1764]*

4   That man is little to be envied whose patriotism would not gain force upon the plain of Marathon, or whose piety would not grow warmer among the ruins of Iona.
Journey to the Western Islands [1775]. Inch Kenneth

5   Whoever wishes to attain an English style, familiar but not coarse, and elegant but not ostentatious, must give his days and nights to the volumes of Addison.
Lives of the Poets [1779–1781]. Addison

6   To be of no church is dangerous. Religion, of which the rewards are distant, and which is animated only by faith and hope, will glide by degrees out of the mind unless it be invigorated and reimpressed by external ordinances, by stated calls to worship, and the salutary influence of example.
Lives of the Poets. Milton

7   The father of English criticism.
Lives of the Poets. Dryden

8   He delighted to tread upon the brink of meaning.
Lives of the Poets. Dryden

9   The *Churchyard* abounds with images which find a mirror in every mind, and with sentiments to which every bosom returns an echo.
Lives of the Poets. Gray

10   I am disappointed by that stroke of death [Garrick's], which has eclipsed the gaiety of nations, and impoverished the public stock of harmless pleasure.
Lives of the Poets. Edmund Smith

11   New things are made familiar, and familiar things are made new.
Lives of the Poets. Pope

12   Tomorrow I purpose to regulate my room.
Prayers and Meditations [1785]. 1764

13   Preserve me from unseasonable and immoderate sleep.
Prayers and Meditations. 1767

14   Every man naturally persuades himself that he can keep his resolutions, nor is he convinced of his imbecility but by length of time and frequency of experiment.
Prayers and Meditations. 1770

15   This world, where much is to be done and little to be known.
Prayers and Meditations. 1770. Against Inquisitive and Perplexing Thoughts

16   [Sunday] should be different from another day. People may walk, but not throw stones at birds. There may be relaxation, but there should be no levity.
From BOSWELL, *Journal of a Tour to the Hebrides [1785]. August 20, 1773*

17   I have, all my life long, been lying till noon; yet I tell all young men, and tell them with great sincerity, that nobody who does not rise early will ever do any good.
From BOSWELL, *Journal of a Tour to the Hebrides. September 14, 1773*

18   Gratitude is a fruit of great cultivation; you do not find it among gross people.
From BOSWELL, *Journal of a Tour to the Hebrides. September 20, 1773*

19   Here closed in death th' attentive eyes
That saw the manners in the face.
Epitaph on Hogarth [1786]

20   When the hoary Sage replied,
"Come, my lad, and drink some beer."
From MRS. PIOZZI, *Anecdotes of Samuel Johnson [1786]*

21   If the man who turnips cries,
Cry not when his father dies,
'Tis a proof that he had rather
Have a turnip than his father.
From MRS. PIOZZI, *Anecdotes of Samuel Johnson*

22   He was a very good hater.
From MRS. PIOZZI, *Anecdotes of Samuel Johnson*

23   The law is the last result of human wisdom acting upon human experience for the benefit of the public.
From MRS. PIOZZI, *Anecdotes of Samuel Johnson*

24   The use of traveling is to regulate imagination by reality, and instead of thinking how things may be, to see them as they are.
From MRS. PIOZZI, *Anecdotes of Samuel Johnson*

1   Dictionaries are like watches; the worst is better than none, and the best cannot be expected to go quite true.

From Mrs. Piozzi, *Anecdotes of Samuel Johnson*

2   Books that you may carry to the fire, and hold readily in your hand, are the most useful after all.

From Sir John Hawkins, *Life of Johnson [1787]. Apothegms*

3   As with my hat[1] upon my head
I walk'd along the Strand,
I there did meet another man
With his hat in his hand.[2]

Anecdotes of Johnson by George Steevens

4   Abstinence is as easy to me as temperance would be difficult.

Anecdotes of Johnson by Hannah More

5   *Boswell:* That, sir, was great fortitude of mind.
Johnson: No, sir; stark insensibility.

From James Boswell, *Life of Johnson*[3] *[1791], November 5, 1728*

6   [Of Pembroke College:] Sir, we are a nest of singing birds.

From James Boswell, *Life of Johnson, 1730*

7   I'll come no more behind your scenes, David [Garrick]; for the silk stockings and white bosoms of your actresses excite my amorous propensities.

From James Boswell, *Life of Johnson, 1749*

8   A man may write at any time, if he will set himself doggedly to it.

From James Boswell, *Life of Johnson, March 1750*

9   Wretched un-idea'd girls.

From James Boswell, *Life of Johnson, 1753*

10   Is not a patron, my lord, one who looks with unconcern on a man struggling for life in the water, and when he has reached ground encumbers him with help? The notice which you have been pleased to take of my labors, had it been early, had been kind; but it has been delayed till I am indifferent, and cannot enjoy it; till I am solitary, and cannot impart it; till I am known, and do not want it.

From James Boswell, *Life of Johnson, February 7, 1754 (Letter to Lord Chesterfield)*

11   [Of Lord Chesterfield:] This man, I thought, had been a Lord among wits; but, I find, he is only a wit among Lords!

From James Boswell, *Life of Johnson, 1754*

12   Sir, he [Bolingbroke] was a scoundrel, and coward: a scoundrel, for charging a blunderbuss against religion and morality; a coward, because he had not resolution to fire it off himself, but left half a crown to a beggarly Scotchman, to draw the trigger after his death.

From James Boswell, *Life of Johnson, March 6, 1754*

13   Ignorance, madame, pure ignorance.[4]

From James Boswell, *Life of Johnson, 1755*

14   If a man does not make new acquaintances as he advances through life, he will soon find himself left alone. A man, sir, should keep his friendship in a constant repair.[5]

From James Boswell, *Life of Johnson, 1755*

15   Towering in the confidence of twenty-one.

From James Boswell, *Life of Johnson, January 9, 1758*

16   Being in a ship is being in a jail, with the chance of being drowned.

From James Boswell, *Life of Johnson, March 1759*

17   Sir, I think all Christians, whether Papists or Protestants, agree in the essential articles, and that their differences are trivial, and rather political than religious.[6]

From James Boswell, *Life of Johnson, 1763*

18   The noblest prospect which a Scotchman ever sees is the high road that leads him to England!

From James Boswell, *Life of Johnson, July 6, 1763*

19   A man ought to read just as inclination leads him; for what he reads as a task will do him little good.

From James Boswell, *Life of Johnson, July 14, 1763*

20   If he does really think that there is no distinction between virtue and vice, why, sir, when he leaves our houses let us count our spoons.

From James Boswell, *Life of Johnson, July 14, 1763*

---

[4]When asked by a lady why he defined "pastern" as the "knee" of a horse in his Dictionary.

[5]Keep your friendships in repair. — Ralph Waldo Emerson, *Uncollected Lectures: Table-Talk* [1864].

[6]I do not find that the age or country makes the least difference; no, nor the language the actor spoke, nor the religion which they professed — whether Arab in the desert, or Frenchman in the Academy. I see that sensible men and conscientious men all over the world were of one religion of well-doing and daring. — Ralph Waldo Emerson, *Lectures and Biographical Sketches* [1883], *The Preacher*

---

[1]Elsewhere found: I put my hat.

[2]A parody on Thomas Percy's ballad *The Hermit of Warkworth.*

[3]Edited by G. B. Hill and revised by L. F. Powell [1934].

1   Sir, your levelers wish to level *down* as far as themselves; but they cannot bear leveling *up* to themselves.

From BOSWELL, *Life of Johnson, July 21, 1763*

2   Sherry[1] is dull, naturally dull; but it must have taken him a great deal of pains to become what we now see him. Such an excess of stupidity, sir, is not in Nature.

From BOSWELL, *Life of Johnson, July 28, 1763*

3   Sir, a woman preaching is like a dog's walking on his hinder legs. It is not done well; but you are surprised to find it done at all.

From BOSWELL, *Life of Johnson, July 31, 1763*

4   This was a good dinner enough, to be sure, but it was not a dinner to *ask* a man to.

From BOSWELL, *Life of Johnson, July 31, 1763*

5   [Of Sir John Hawkins:] A very unclubable man.

From BOSWELL, *Life of Johnson, 1764*

6   It matters not how a man dies, but how he lives.

From BOSWELL, *Life of Johnson, October 26, 1769*

7   That fellow seems to me to possess but one idea, and that is a wrong one.

From BOSWELL, *Life of Johnson, 1770*

8   A gentleman who had been very unhappy in marriage, married immediately after his wife died: Johnson said, it was the triumph of hope over experience.

From BOSWELL, *Life of Johnson, 1770*

9   A decent provision for the poor is the true test of civilization.

From BOSWELL, *Life of Johnson, 1770*

10   All denominations of Christians have really little difference in point of doctrine, though they may differ widely in external forms.

From BOSWELL, *Life of Johnson, 1772*

11   Nobody can write the life of a man, but those who have eat and drunk and lived in social intercourse with him.

From BOSWELL, *Life of Johnson, March 31, 1772*

12   I am a great friend to public amusements; for they keep people from vice.

From BOSWELL, *Life of Johnson, March 31, 1772*

13   There is more knowledge of the heart in one letter of Richardson's than in all *Tom Jones*.

From BOSWELL, *Life of Johnson, April 6, 1772*

14   Why, sir, if you were to read Richardson for the story, your impatience would be so much fretted that you would hang yourself. But you must read him for the sentiment, and consider the story as only giving occasion to the sentiment.

From BOSWELL, *Life of Johnson, April 6, 1772*

15   A cow is a very good animal in the field; but we turn her out of a garden.

From BOSWELL, *Life of Johnson, April 15, 1772*

16   Much may be made of a Scotchman if he be *caught* young.[2]

From BOSWELL, *Life of Johnson, Spring 1772*

17   It is a foolish thing well done.[3]

From BOSWELL, *Life of Johnson, April 3, 1773*

18   No, sir, do *you* read books *through*?[4]

From BOSWELL, *Life of Johnson, April 19, 1773*

19   An old tutor of a college said to one of his pupils: Read over your compositions, and wherever you meet with a passage which you think is particularly fine, strike it out.

From BOSWELL, *Life of Johnson, April 30, 1773*

20   You are the most unscottified of your countrymen.

From BOSWELL, *Life of Johnson, May 1, 1773*

21   The woman's a whore, and there's an end on 't.[5]

From BOSWELL, *Life of Johnson, May 7, 1773*

22   Attack is the reaction; I never think I have hit hard unless it rebounds.

From BOSWELL, *Life of Johnson, April 2, 1775*

23   Most vices may be committed very genteelly: a man may debauch his friend's wife genteelly: he may cheat at cards genteelly.

From BOSWELL, *Life of Johnson, April 6, 1775*

24   A man will turn over half a library to make one book.

From BOSWELL, *Life of Johnson, April 6, 1775*

25   Patriotism is the last refuge of a scoundrel.

From BOSWELL, *Life of Johnson, April 7, 1775*

26   Knowledge is of two kinds. We know a subject ourselves, or we know where we can find information upon it.

From BOSWELL, *Life of Johnson, April 18, 1775*

---

[1]Thomas Sheridan [1719–1788], actor, lecturer, and author.

[2]Of Lord Mansfield, educated in England.

[3]Of Goldsmith's apology in the *London Chronicle* for beating Evans the bookseller.

[4]Upon being asked by Elphinstone if he had read a new book through.

[5]Of Lady Diana Beauclerk, divorced.

Theodore Tronchin
1709–1781

1   In medicine, sins of commission are mortal, sins of omission venial.
Quoted in Bulletin of New York Academy of Medicine, V [1929], 151

Oliver Edwards
1711–1791

2   I have tried too in my time to be a philosopher; but I don't know how, cheerfulness was always breaking in.
From JAMES BOSWELL, Life of Johnson [1791], April 17, 1778

David Hume
1711–1776

3   Generally speaking, the errors in religion are dangerous; those in philosophy only ridiculous.
A Treatise of Human Nature [1739], bk. I, pt. iv, sec. vii

4   Avarice, the spur of industry.
Essays [1741–1742]. Of Civil Liberty

5   Beauty in things exists in the mind which contemplates them.
Essays. Of Tragedy

6   Custom, then, is the great guide of human life.
An Enquiry Concerning Human Understanding [1748], pt. 1

7   No testimony is sufficient to establish a miracle, unless the testimony be of such a kind that its falsehood would be more miraculous than the fact which it endeavors to establish.
An Enquiry Concerning Human Understanding. Of Miracles

8   Opposing one species of superstition to another, set them a-quarreling; while we ourselves, during their fury and contention, happily make our escape into the calm, though obscure, regions of philosophy.
The Natural History of Religion [1757]

9   Never literary attempt was more unfortunate than my Treatise of Human Nature. It fell deadborn from the press.
My Own Life [1777], ch. 1

Frederick the Great
1712–1786

10   By push of bayonets, no firing till you see the whites of their eyes.[1]
At Prague [May 6, 1757]

---

11   Rascals, would you live forever?[2]
When the Guards hesitated at Kolin [June 1, 1757]

12   The prince is the first servant of his state.
Memoirs of the House of Brandenburg [175...

13   God is always with the strongest battalions.
Letter to the Duchess Luise Dorothea von Gotha [May 8, 1760]

14   I am tired of ruling over slaves.
Last words [April 1, 178...

Edward Moore
1712–1757

15   This is adding insult to injury.
The Foundling [1748], act V, sc.

16   I am rich beyond the dreams of avarice.
The Gamester [1753], act II, sc.

Jean-Jacques Rousseau
1712–1778

17   The first man who, having fenced in a piece ... land, said, "This is mine," and found people naï... enough to believe him, that man was the tru... founder of civil society.
Discourse upon the Origin and Foundation o... the Inequality Among Mankind [1754]

18   Never exceed your rights, and they will soon b... come unlimited.
Discourse upon the Origin and Foundation o... the Inequality Among Mankind

19   Money is the seed of money, and the first guin... is sometimes more difficult to acquire than the se... ond million.
Discourse upon the Origin and Foundation o... the Inequality Among Mankind

20   Man is born free, and everywhere he is in chains...
The Social Contract [1762], I, ch.

21   The strongest is never strong enough to be a... ways the master, unless he transforms his streng... into right, and obedience into duty.
The Social Contract, I,

---

[2]Ihr Racker, wollt ihr ewig leben?
Come on, you sons of bitches! Do you want to live forever? World War I American battle cry attributed to Marine Serge... DANIEL DALY [1874–1937] at the battle of Belleau Wood, Ju... 1918.

[3]L'homme est né libre, et partout il est dans les fers.

[1]See William Prescott, 340:5.

1 The right of conquest has no foundation other than the right of the strongest.
The Social Contract, I, 4

2 In the strict sense of the term, a true democracy has never existed, and never will exist.
The Social Contract, III, 4

3 The body politic, like the human body, begins to die from its birth, and bears in itself the causes of its destruction. *The Social Contract, III, 11*

4 Good laws lead to the making of better ones; bad ones bring about worse.
The Social Contract, III, 15

5 Everything is good when it leaves the hands of the Creator; everything degenerates in the hands of man. *Emile; or, On Education [1762], I*

6 I shall always maintain that whoso says in his heart, "There is no God," while he takes the name of God upon his lips, is either a liar or a madman.
Emile; or, On Education, I

7 People who know little are usually great talkers, while men who know much say little.
Emile; or, On Education, I

8 What wisdom can you find that is greater than kindness? *Emile; or, On Education, II*

9 Nature never deceives us; it is always we who deceive ourselves. *Emile; or, On Education, III*

10 There exists one book, which, to my taste, furnishes the happiest treatise of natural education. What then is this marvelous book? Is it Aristotle? Is it Pliny, is it Buffon? No—it is *Robinson Crusoe*.
Emile; or, On Education, III

11 Self-love makes more libertines than love.
Emile; or, On Education, IV

12 Provided a man is not mad, he can be cured of every folly but vanity.
Emile; or, On Education, IV

13 A man says what he knows, a woman says what will please. *Emile; or, On Education, V*

14 Where is the man who owes nothing to the land in which he lives? Whatever that land may be, he owes to it the most precious thing possessed by man, the morality of his actions and the love of virtue. *Emile; or, On Education, V*

15 I have entered on an enterprise which is without precedent, and will have no imitator. I propose to show my fellows a man as nature made him, and this man shall be myself.
Confessions [1781–1788], I

16 Remorse sleeps during a prosperous period but wakes up in adversity. *Confessions, II*

17 It is too difficult to think nobly when one only thinks to get a living. *Confessions, II*

18 Hatred, as well as love, renders its votaries credulous. *Confessions, V*

19 At length I recollected the thoughtless saying of a great princess, who, on being informed that the country people had no bread, replied, "Let them eat cake."[1] *Confessions, VI*

20 The thirst after happiness is never extinguished in the heart of man. *Confessions, IX*

21 He[2] thinks like a philosopher, but governs like a king. *Confessions, XII*

Josiah Tucker
1712–1799

22 What is true of a shopkeeper is true of a shopkeeping nation.
Tract Against Going to War for the Sake of Trade [1763]

Denis Diderot
1713–1784

23 My thoughts are my trollops.
Rameau's Nephew[3]

24 If your little savage were left to himself and to his native blindness, he would in time join the infant's reasoning to the grown man's passion—he would strangle his father and sleep with his mother. *Rameau's Nephew*

25 I can be expected to look for truth but not to find it. *Pensées Philosophiques [1746], no. 29*

26 L'esprit de l'escalier [staircase wit].[4]
Paradoxe sur le Comédien

27 From fanaticism to barbarism is only one step.
Essai sur le Mérite de la Vertu

---

[1] Qu'ils mangent de la brioche.
This remark is usually attributed to Marie Antoinette, after her arrival in France in 1770, but the sixth book of the *Confessions* was written two or three years earlier.

[2] Frederick the Great.

[3] Translated by JACQUES BARZUN and RALPH H. BOWEN.

[4] The witty retort thought of only after the conversation is finished and one is on one's way downstairs.

Laurence Sterne
1713–1768

1   Only the brave know how to forgive. . . . A coward never forgave; it is not in his nature.
Sermons, vol. I [1760], no. 12

2   This sad vicissitude of things.   *Sermons, I, 15*

3   I wish either my father or my mother, or indeed both of them, as they were in duty both equally bound to it, had minded what they were about when they begot me.
Tristram Shandy, bk. I [1760], ch. 1

4   "Pray, my dear," quoth my mother, "have you not forgot to wind up the clock?"—"Good G—!" cried my father, making an exclamation, but taking care to moderate his voice at the same time—"Did ever woman, since the creation of the world, interrupt a man with such a silly question?"
Tristram Shandy, I, 1

5   So long as a man rides his hobbyhorse peaceably and quietly along the king's highway, and neither compels you or me to get up behind him—pray, sir, what have either you or I to do with it?
Tristram Shandy, I, 7

6   For every ten jokes, thou hast got an hundred enemies.   *Tristram Shandy, I, 12*

7   He was within a few hours of giving his enemies the slip forever.   *Tristram Shandy, I, 12*

8   Whistled up to London, upon a Tom Fool's errand.   *Tristram Shandy, I, 16*

9   'Tis known by the name of perseverance in a good cause—and of obstinacy in a bad one.
Tristram Shandy, I, 17

10   There was a strange kind of magick bias, which good or bad names, as he called them, irresistibly impressed upon our characters and conduct. . . . How many Caesars and Pompeys, he would say, by mere inspiration of the names, have been rendered worthy of them?   *Tristram Shandy, I, 19*

11   Persuasion hung upon his lips.
Tristram Shandy, I, 19

12   Digressions, incontestably, are the sunshine—they are the life, the soul of reading; take them out of this book for instance—you might as well take the book along with them.
Tristram Shandy, I, 22

13   The history of a soldier's wound beguiles the pain of it.   *Tristram Shandy, I, 25*

14   But desire of knowledge, like the thirst of riches, increases ever with the acquisition of it.
Tristram Shandy, II [1760], ch. 3

15   Writing, when properly managed (as you may be sure I think mine is), is but a different name for conversation.   *Tristram Shandy, II,*

16   Go, poor devil, get thee gone! Why should I hurt thee? This world surely is wide enough to hold both thee and me.
Tristram Shandy, II, 12 (Uncle Toby to the fly

17   That's another story,[1] replied my father.
Tristram Shandy, II, 1

18   Trust that man in nothing who has not a conscience in everything.   *Tristram Shandy, II, 1*

19   It is in the nature of an hypothesis, when once a man has conceived it, that it assimilates every thing to itself, as proper nourishment; and, from the first moment of your begetting it, it generally grows the stronger by every thing you see, hear, read, or understand.   *Tristram Shandy, II, 1*

20   Good—bad—indifferent.
Tristram Shandy, III [1761–1762], ch.

21   "Our armies swore terribly in Flanders," cried my uncle Toby—"but nothing to this."
Tristram Shandy, III, 1

22   Of all the cants which are canted in this canting world, though the cant of hypocrites may be the worst, the cant of criticism is the most tormenting!
Tristram Shandy, III, 1

23   'Twould be as much as my life was worth.
Tristram Shandy, III, 2

24   One of the two horns of my dilemma.
Tristram Shandy, IV [1761–1762], ch. 20

25   The feather put into his cap of having been abroad.   *Tristram Shandy, IV, 31*

26   Now or never was the time.
Tristram Shandy, IV, 31

27   There is a Northwest Passage to the intellectual world.   *Tristram Shandy, V [1761–1762], ch. 42*

28   The Accusing Spirit, which flew up to heaven's chancery with the oath, blushed as he gave it in; and the Recording Angel, as he wrote it down, dropped a tear upon the word and blotted it out forever.[2]
Tristram Shandy, VI [1761–1762], ch. 8

29   A man should know something of his own country, too, before he goes abroad.
Tristram Shandy, VII [1765], ch. 2

---

[1]But that is another story.—RUDYARD KIPLING, *Plain Tales from the Hills* [1888], *Three and—An Extra*

[2]But sad as angels for the good man's sin, / Weep to record, and blush to give it in.—THOMAS CAMPBELL, *Pleasures of Hope* [1799], *pt. II, l. 357*

1   Ho! 'tis the time of salads.
Tristram Shandy, VII, 17

2   L—d! said my mother, what is all this story about?—A Cock and a Bull, said Yorick.
Tristram Shandy, IX [1767], ch. 33

3   They order, said I, this matter better in France.
A Sentimental Journey [1768], l. 1

4   I pity the man who can travel from Dan to Beersheba and cry, 'Tis all barren!
A Sentimental Journey. In the Street, Calais

5   *Tant pis* and *tant mieux*, being two of the great hinges in French conversation, a stranger would do well to set himself right in the use of them before he gets to Paris.
A Sentimental Journey. Montreuil

6   Hail, ye small, sweet courtesies of life! for smooth do ye make the road of it.
A Sentimental Journey. The Pulse, Paris

7   God tempers the wind, said Maria, to the shorn lamb.   *A Sentimental Journey. Maria*

Étienne Bonnot de Condillac
[L'Abbé de Condillac]
1715–1780

8   We cannot recollect the ignorance in which we were born.
Traité des Sensations [1754], dedication

9   The statue is therefore nothing but the sum of all it has acquired. May not this be the same with man?   *Traité des Sensations, conclusion*

Claude Adrien Helvétius
1715–1771

10   Truth is a torch that gleams through the fog without dispelling it.
De l'Esprit [1758],[1] preface

11   What makes men happy is liking what they have to do. This is a principle on which society is not founded.   *De l'Esprit, preface*

12   We don't call a man mad who believes that he eats God, but we do the one who says he is Jesus Christ.   *De l'Esprit, preface*

---

[1]Voltaire, when he read *De l'Esprit*, wrote the author: "Your book is dictated by the soundest reason. You had better get out of France as quickly as you can." The book was condemned by the *parlement* and burned.

Luc de Clapiers,
Marquis de Vauvenargues
1715–1747

13   Great thoughts come from the heart.
Réflexions et Maximes [c. 1747], no. 127

14   Lazy people are always looking for something to do.   *Réflexions et Maximes, 458*

15   The things we know best are those we have not learned.   *Réflexions et Maximes, 479*

William Whitehead
1715–1785

16   Yes, I'm in love, I feel it now
And Caelia has undone me;
And yet I swear I can't tell how
The pleasing plague stole on me.
The Je ne sçay quoi song

17   An old tale which every schoolboy knows.
The Roman Father, prologue

Thomas Gray
1716–1771

18   Ye distant spires, ye antique towers,
That crown the wat'ry glade.
On a Distant Prospect of Eton College [1742], st. 1

19   Still as they run they look behind,
They hear a voice in every wind,
And snatch a fearful joy.
On a Distant Prospect of Eton College, st. 4

20   Alas, regardless of their doom,
The little victims play!
No sense have they of ills to come,
Nor care beyond today.
On a Distant Prospect of Eton College, st. 6

21   Grim-visag'd comfortless Despair.
On a Distant Prospect of Eton College, st. 7

22   To each his suff'rings: all are men,
Condemn'd alike to groan,
The tender for another's pain,
Th' unfeeling for his own.
Yet ah! why should they know their fate,
Since sorrow never comes too late,
And happiness too swiftly flies?
Thought would destroy their paradise.
No more; where ignorance is bliss,
'Tis folly to be wise.
On a Distant Prospect of Eton College, st. 10

1 Daughter of Jove, relentless power,
  Thou tamer of the human breast,
  Whose iron scourge and tort'ring hour
  The bad affright, afflict the best!
                    Hymn to Adversity [1742], st. 1

2 What sorrow was, thou bad'st her know,
  And from her own she learn'd to melt at others'
                    woe.   *Hymn to Adversity, st. 2*

3 What female heart can gold despise?
  What cat's averse to fish?
                    On the Death of a Favorite Cat [1747], st. 4

4 A fav'rite has no friend!
                    On the Death of a Favorite Cat, st. 6

5 As sickly plants betray a niggard earth,
  Whose barren bosom starves her gen'rous birth.
                    *The Alliance of Education and Government
                    [c. 1748], l. 1*

6 The social smile, the sympathetic tear.
                    *The Alliance of Education and Government,
                    l. 37*

7 When love could teach a monarch to be wise,
  And gospel-light first dawn'd from Bullen's eyes.[1]
                    *The Alliance of Education and Government,
                    l. 108*

8 The curfew tolls the knell of parting day,
  The lowing herd wind slowly o'er the lea,
  The plowman homeward plods his weary way,
  And leaves the world to darkness and to me.
                    *Elegy Written in a Country Churchyard
                    [1750], st. 1*

9 Now fades the glimmering landscape on the sight,
  And all the air a solemn stillness holds,
  Save where the beetle wheels his droning flight,
  And drowsy tinklings lull the distant folds.
                    Elegy Written in a Country Churchyard, st. 2

10 Save that from yonder ivy-mantled tow'r
   The moping owl does to the moon complain.
                    Elegy Written in a Country Churchyard, st. 3

11 Each in his narrow cell forever laid,
   The rude forefathers of the hamlet sleep.
                    Elegy Written in a Country Churchyard, st. 4

12 The breezy call of incense-breathing Morn.
                    Elegy Written in a Country Churchyard, st. 5

13 For them no more the blazing hearth shall burn,
   Or busy housewife ply her evening care.
                    Elegy Written in a Country Churchyard, st. 6

14 Let not ambition mock their useful toil,
   Their homely joys, and destiny obscure;

---
[1]The monarch is Henry VIII; Anne Boleyn's name is here
spelled (as it is in Shakespeare's *Henry VIII*) as it is pronounced.

Nor grandeur hear with a disdainful smile,
The short and simple annals of the poor.
                    Elegy Written in a Country Churchyard, st.

15 The boast of heraldry, the pomp of pow'r,
   And all that beauty, all that wealth e'er gave,
   Awaits alike the inevitable hour:
   The paths of glory lead but to the grave.
                    Elegy Written in a Country Churchyard, st.

16 Where through the long-drawn aisle and fretted
                    vault
   The pealing anthem swells the note of praise.
                    Elegy Written in a Country Churchyard, st. 1

17 Can storied urn, or animated bust
   Back to its mansion call the fleeting breath?
   Can honor's voice provoke the silent dust,
   Or flatt'ry soothe the dull cold ear of death?
                    Elegy Written in a Country Churchyard, st. 1

18 Hands, that the rod of empire might have sway'd,
   Or wak'd to ecstasy the living lyre.
                    Elegy Written in a Country Churchyard, st. 1

19 But knowledge to their eyes her ample page
   Rich with the spoils of time did ne'er unroll;
   Chill penury repress'd their noble rage,
   And froze the genial current of the soul.
                    Elegy Written in a Country Churchyard, st. 1

20 Full many a gem of purest ray serene,
   The dark unfathom'd caves of ocean bear:
   Full many a flower is born to blush unseen,
   And waste its sweetness on the desert air.
                    Elegy Written in a Country Churchyard, st. 1

21 Some village Hampden, that with dauntless breast
   The little tyrant of his fields withstood;
   Some mute inglorious Milton here may rest,
   Some Cromwell guiltless of his country's blood.
                    Elegy Written in a Country Churchyard, st. 1

22 To scatter plenty o'er a smiling land,
   And read their hist'ry in a nation's eyes.
                    Elegy Written in a Country Churchyard, st. 1

23 Far from the madding crowd's ignoble strife,
   Their sober wishes never learn'd to stray;
   Along the cool sequester'd vale of life
   They kept the noiseless tenor of their way.
                    Elegy Written in a Country Churchyard, st. 1

24 For who to dumb forgetfulness a prey,
   This pleasing anxious being e'er resign'd,
   Left the warm precincts of the cheerful day,
   Nor cast one longing ling'ring look behind?
                    Elegy Written in a Country Churchyard, st. 2

25 E'en from the tomb the voice of nature cries,
   E'en in our ashes live their wonted fires.
                    Elegy Written in a Country Churchyard, st. 2

1 Mindful of th' unhonor'd dead.
Elegy Written in a Country Churchyard, st. 24

2 Here rests his head upon the lap of Earth
A youth to fortune and to fame unknown.
Fair Science frown'd not on his humble birth,
And Melancholy mark'd him for her own.
*Elegy Written in a Country Churchyard. The
Epitaph, st. 1*

3 Large was his bounty, and his soul sincere,
Heav'n did a recompense as largely send:
He gave to mis'ry all he had, a tear,
He gain'd from Heav'n ('twas all he wish'd) a
friend.
*Elegy Written in a Country Churchyard. The
Epitaph, st. 2*

4 No farther seek his merits to disclose,
Or draw his frailties from their dread abode,
(There they alike in trembling hope repose,)
The bosom of his Father and his God.
*Elegy Written in a Country Churchyard. The
Epitaph, st. 3*

5 The meanest floweret of the vale,
The simplest note that swells the gale,
The common sun, the air, the skies,
To him are opening paradise.
*Ode on the Pleasure Arising from Vicissitude
[1754], l. 49*

6 O'er her warm cheek and rising bosom move
The bloom of young Desire and purple light of
Love.
The Progress of Poesy [1754], I. 3, l. 16

7 Far from the sun and summer-gale,
In thy green lap was Nature's Darling[1] laid.
The Progress of Poesy, III. 1, l. 1

8 Or ope the sacred source of sympathetic tears.
The Progress of Poesy, III. 1, l. 12

9 He[2] pass'd the flaming bounds of place and time:
The living throne, the sapphire-blaze,
Where angels tremble, while they gaze,
He saw; but blasted with excess of light,
Closed his eyes in endless night.
The Progress of Poesy, III. 2, l. 4

10 Thoughts that breathe, and words that burn.
The Progress of Poesy, III. 3, l. 4

11 Ruin seize thee, ruthless King!
Confusion on thy banners wait,
Though fann'd by Conquest's crimson wing
They mock the air with idle state.
The Bard [1757], I. 1, l. 1

12 Weave the warp, and weave the woof,
The winding sheet of Edward's race.
Give ample room and verge enough,
The characters of hell to trace.
The Bard, II. 1, l. 1

13 Fair laughs the morn, and soft the zephyr blows,
While proudly riding o'er the azure realm
In gallant trim the gilded vessel goes;
Youth on the prow, and Pleasure at the helm;
Regardless of the sweeping whirlwind's sway,
That, hush'd in grim repose, expects his evening
prey.   *The Bard, II. 2, l. 9*

14 Visions of glory, spare my aching sight,
Ye unborn ages, crowd not on my soul!
The Bard, III. 1, l. 11

15 And truth severe, by fairy fiction drest.
The Bard, III. 3, l. 3

16 Now my weary lips I close;
Leave me, leave me to repose!
The Descent of Odin [1761], l. 71

17 Iron sleet of arrowy shower
Hurtles in the darken'd air.
The Fatal Sisters [1761], l. 3

18 Too poor for a bribe, and too proud to importune,
He had not the method of making a fortune.
On His Own Character [1761]

19 I shall be but a shrimp of an author.
Letter to Horace Walpole [February 25, 1768]

20 Sweet is the breath of vernal shower,
The bee's collected treasures sweet,
Sweet music's melting fall, but sweeter yet
The still small voice of gratitude.
Ode for Music [1769], l. 61

David Garrick
1717–1779

21 Let others hail the rising sun:
I bow to that whose course is run.
On the Death of Mr. Pelham

22 Heart of oak are our ships,
Heart of oak are our men:
We always are ready;
Steady, boys, steady;
We'll fight, and we'll conquer again and again.
Heart of Oak [c. 1770]

23 Here lies Nolly Goldsmith, for shortness called
Noll,
Who wrote like an angel, but talked like poor Poll.
Impromptu epitaph on Oliver Goldsmith

---

[1]Shakespeare.

[2]Milton.

Horace Walpole
1717–1797

1   Our supreme governors, the mob.
Letters. To Sir Horace Mann [September 7, 1743]

2   Every drop of ink in my pen ran cold.
Letters. To George Montagu [July 20, 1752]

3   *Serendipity* . . . you will understand it better by the derivation than by the definition. I once read a silly fairy tale, called *The Three Princes of Serendip*: as their highnesses traveled, they were always making discoveries, by accidents and sagacity, of things they were not in quest of. . . . Now do you understand *serendipity*?
Letters. To Sir Horace Mann [January 28, 1754]

4   It is charming to totter into vogue.
Letters. To G. A. Selwyn [December 2, 1765]

5   The next Augustan age will dawn on the other side of the Atlantic. There will, perhaps, be a Thucydides at Boston, a Xenophon at New York, and, in time, a Virgil at Mexico, and a Newton at Peru. At last, some curious traveler from Lima will visit England and give a description of the ruins of St. Paul's, like the editions of Balbec and Palmyra.[1]
Letters. To Sir Horace Mann [November 24, 1774]

6   This world is a comedy to those that think, a tragedy to those that feel.
Letters. To the Countess of Upper Ossory [August 16, 1776]

7   Prognostics do not always prove prophecies—at least the wisest prophets make sure of the event first.
Letters. To Thomas Walpole [February 19, 1785]

8   All his [Sir Joshua Reynolds's] own geese are swans, as the swans of others are geese.
Letters. To Thomas Walpole [December 1, 1786]

Samuel Foote
1720–1777

9   Born in a cellar . . . and living in a garret.[2]
The Author [1757], act II

10   Matt Minikin won't set fire to the Thames though he lives near the Bridge.
Trip to Calais [1776]

---

[1]See Macaulay, 448:7.

[2]Born in the garret, in the kitchen bred.—LORD BYRON, *A Sketch* [1816]

11   He is not only dull himself, but the cause dullness in others.
From JAMES BOSWELL, Life of Johnson [1791] 1783

12   So she went into the garden to cut a cabbage le to make an apple pie; and at the same time a gre she-bear, coming up the street, pops its head int the shop. "What! no soap?" So he died, and sh very imprudently married the barber; and ther were present the Picninnies, and the Joblillies, an the Garyalies, and the grand Panjandrum himsel with the little round button at top, and they all fe to playing the game of catch as catch can, till th gunpowder ran out at the heels of their boots.
Nonsense written to test the boasted memory o Charles Macklin, The Quarterly Review [1854]. Credited to Foote by MARIA EDGEWORTH, Harry and Lucy Concluded [1825], vol. II

Dennis O'Kelly
1720–1787

13   It will be Eclipse first, the rest nowhere.
Declaration at Epsom [May 3, 1769], when the great racehorse Eclipse was to run his first race. Annals of Sporting, vol. II, p. 271

John Woolman
1720–1772

14   Though I felt uneasy at the thought of writing an instrument of slavery . . . through weakness gave way and wrote it; but . . . said before my master and the Friend that I believed slavekeeping to be a practice inconsistent with the Christian religion. This, in some degree, abated my uneasiness; yet . . . I should have been clearer if I had desired to be excused from it, as a thing against my conscience.
Journal [1774]

William Collins
1721–1759

15 How sleep the brave, who sink to rest,
By all their country's wishes bless'd!
Ode Written in the Beginning of the Year 1746, st. 1

16 By fairy hands their knell is rung,
By forms unseen their dirge is sung;
There Honor comes, a pilgrim gray,
To bless the turf that wraps their clay,

And Freedom shall awhile repair,
To dwell a weeping hermit there!
*Ode Written in the Beginning of the Year
1746, st. 2*

1 If aught of oaten stop or pastoral song
May hope, O pensive Eve, to soothe thine ear.
Ode to Evening [1747], l. 1

2 Now air is hush'd, save where the weak-ey'd bat,
With short shrill shriek flits by on leathern wing,
Or where the beetle winds
His small but sullen horn.   *Ode to Evening, l. 9*

3 'Twas sad by fits, by starts 'twas wild.
The Passions [1747], l. 28

4 With eyes uprais'd, as one inspir'd,
Pale Melancholy sate retir'd,
And from her wild sequester'd seat,
In notes by distance made more sweet,
Pour'd through the mellow horn her pensive soul.
The Passions, l. 57

5 In hollow murmurs died away.
The Passions, l. 68

Jeanne Antoinette Poisson, Marquise de Pompadour
1721–1764

6 Après nous le déluge [After us the deluge].[1]
*Reputed reply to Louis XV [November 5,
1757] after the defeat of the French and
Austrian armies by Frederick the Great in the
battle of Rossbach*

Tobias Smollett
1721–1771

7 He was formed for the ruin of our sex.
*The Adventures of Roderick Random [1748],
ch. 22*

8 That great Cham of literature, Samuel Johnson.
Letter to John Wilkes [March 16, 1759]

9 8 June. At London. I am pent up in frowsy lodgings, where there is not room enough to swing a
cat.
*The Expedition of Humphry Clinker [1771],
vol. II*

---

[1]The attribution to Madame de Pompadour is made by Desprès
(*Mémoires de Madame de Hausset*); also by Sainte-Beuve and La
Tour. Larousse (*Fleurs Historiques*) attributes the saying to the
king. It was original with neither, for it is an old French proverb.

Samuel Adams
1722–1803

10   Let us contemplate our forefathers, and posterity, and resolve to maintain the rights bequeathed to us from the former, for the sake of the latter. The necessity of the times, more than ever, calls for our utmost circumspection, deliberation, fortitude and perseverance. Let us remember that "if we suffer tamely a lawless attack upon our liberty, we encourage it, and involve others in our doom." It is a very serious consideration . . . that millions yet unborn may be the miserable sharers of the event.
Speech [1771]

11   What a glorious morning for America![2]
*Upon hearing the gunfire at Lexington,
Massachusetts [April 19, 1775]*

12   Driven from every other corner of the earth, freedom of thought and the right of private judgment in matters of conscience direct their course to this happy country as their last asylum.
Speech, Philadelphia [August 1, 1776]

John Home
1722–1808

13 I'll woo her as the lion woos his brides.
Douglas [1756], act I, sc. i

14 My name is Norval; on the Grampian hills
My father feeds his flocks; a frugal swain,
Whose constant cares were to increase his store,
And keep his only son, myself, at home.
Douglas, III, i

15 Like Douglas conquer, or like Douglas, die.
Douglas, V, i

Christopher Smart
1722–1771

16 Tell them I Am, Jehovah said
To Moses; while earth heard in dread,
And smitten to the heart,
At once above, beneath, around,
All nature, without voice or sound,
Replied, O Lord, Thou art.
A Song to David [1763], st. 40

17 For adoration all the ranks
Of angels yield eternal thanks,
And David in the midst.
A Song to David, st. 51

---

[2]The phrase was adopted by the town of Lexington as a legend
for the town seal.

1 Where ask is have, where seek is find,
Where knock is open wide.   *A Song to David, st. 77*

2 And now the matchless deed's achiev'd,
Determin'd, dar'd, and done.
                    A Song to David, st. 86

3 For I bless God in the libraries of the learned and
for all the booksellers in the world.
                    Jubilate Agno, frag. B1, l. 79

4 Let James rejoice with the Skuttle-Fish who foils
his foe by the effusion of his ink.
                    Jubilate Agno, l. 125

5 For the Mouse (mus) prevails in the Latin.
For Edi-mus, bibi-mus, vivi-mus, oremus.
                    Jubilate Agno, frag. B2, l. 636

6 For I will consider my Cat Jeoffrey,
For he is the servant of the Living God, duly and
daily serving him.
                    Jubilate Agno, frag. B2, l. 695

7 For he counteracts the Devil, who is Death, by
brisking about the life.
                    Jubilate Agno, frag. B2, l. 720

Sir William Blackstone
1723–1780

8   Man was formed for society.
                Commentaries [1765–1769], introduction

9   The royal navy of England hath ever been its
greatest defense and ornament; it is its ancient and
natural strength; the floating bulwark of our island.
                Commentaries, bk. I, ch. 13

10   Time whereof the memory of man runneth not
to the contrary.[1]   *Commentaries, I, 18*

11   That the king can do no wrong is a necessary and
fundamental principle of the English constitution.
                Commentaries, III, 17

12   It is better that ten guilty persons escape than
one innocent suffer.   *Commentaries, IV, 27*

Adam Smith
1723–1790

13   It is not from the benevolence of the butcher, the
brewer, or the baker that we expect our dinner, but
from their regard to their own interest. We address
ourselves, not to their humanity but to their self-love.
                *An Inquiry into the Nature and Causes of the
                Wealth of Nations [1776], vol. I, bk. I, ch. 2*

14   A monopoly granted either to an individual or
a trading company has the same effect as a secret in
trade or manufactures.
                *An Inquiry into the Nature and Causes of the
                Wealth of Nations, I, I, 7*

15   People of the same trade seldom meet together
even for merriment and diversion, but the conversation ends in a conspiracy against the public, or in
some contrivance to raise prices.
                *An Inquiry into the Nature and Causes of the
                Wealth of Nations, I, I, 10, pt. 2*

16   With the greater part of rich people, the chief
enjoyment of riches consists in the parade of riches,
which in their eyes is never so complete as when
they appear to possess those decisive marks of opu-
lence which nobody can possess but themselves.
                *An Inquiry into the Nature and Causes of the
                Wealth of Nations, I, I, 11, pt. 2*

17   It is the highest impertinence and presumption,
therefore, in kings and ministers to pretend to
watch over the economy of private people, and
to restrain their expense. . . . They are themselves
always, and without any exception, the greatest
spendthrifts in the society.
                *An Inquiry into the Nature and Causes of the
                Wealth of Nations, I, II, 3*

18   Every individual necessarily labors to render the
annual revenue of the society as great as he can. He
generally indeed neither intends to promote the
public interest, nor knows how much he is promoting it. . . . He intends only his own gain, and he is
in this, as in many other cases, led by an invisible
hand to promote an end which was no part of his
intention. . . . By pursuing his own interest he frequently promotes that of the society more effectually than when he really intends to promote it. I
have never known much good done by those who
affected to trade for the public good.
                *An Inquiry into the Nature and Causes of the
                Wealth of Nations, I, IV, 2*

19   To found a great empire for the sole purpose of
raising up a people of customers, may at first sight
appear a project fit only for a nation of shopkeepers.
It is, however, a project altogether unfit for a nation
of shopkeepers; but extremely fit for a nation whose
government is influenced by shopkeepers.[2]
                *An Inquiry into the Nature and Causes of the
                Wealth of Nations, II, IV, 7, pt. 3*

---

[1]The favorite phrase of their law is "a custom whereof the memory of man runneth not back to the contrary." — RALPH WALDO
EMERSON, *English Traits* [1856]

[2]Let Pitt then boast of his victory to his nation of shopkeepers. — BERTRAND BARÈRE [1755–1841], *Speech* [June 11, 1794]
    But it may be said as a rule, that every Englishman in the Duke
of Wellington's army paid his way. The remembrance of such a fact
surely becomes a nation of shopkeepers. — WILLIAM MAKEPEACE
THACKERAY, *Vanity Fair* [1847–1848], *vol. I, ch. 28*
    See Josiah Tucker, 331:22.

Consumption is the sole end and purpose of all production; and the interest of the producer ought to be attended to only so far as it may be necessary for promoting that of the consumer.
An Inquiry into the Nature and Causes of the Wealth of Nations, II, IV, 8

2 All systems either of preference or of restraint, therefore, being thus completely taken away, the obvious and simple system of natural liberty establishes itself of its own accord. Every man, as long as he does not violate the laws of justice, is left perfectly free to pursue his own interest his own way, and to bring both his industry and capital into competition with those of any other man or order of men.
An Inquiry into the Nature and Causes of the Wealth of Nations, II, IV, 9

Immanuel Kant
1724–1804

3 Out of wood so crooked and perverse as that which man is made of, nothing absolutely straight can ever be wrought.
The Idea of a Universal History [1784]. Proposition 6[1]

4 Two things fill the mind with ever-increasing wonder and awe, the more often and the more intensely the mind of thought is drawn to them: the starry heavens above me and the moral law within me.
Critique of Practical Reason [1788]

5 Morality is not properly the doctrine of how we may make ourselves happy, but how we may make ourselves worthy of happiness.
Critique of Practical Reason

6 There is . . . only a single categorical imperative and it is this: Act only on that maxim through which you can at the same time will that it should become a universal law.
The Metaphysic of Morals [1797],[2] *ch. 11*

Robert, Lord Clive
1725–1774

7 By God, Mr. Chairman, at this moment I stand astonished at my own moderation!
Reply During Parliamentary Inquiry [1773]

Logan[3]
1725–1780

8 I appeal to any white man to say if he ever entered Logan's cabin hungry and he gave him not meat; if ever he came cold and naked and he clothed him not?
Message to Lord Dunmore, governor of Virginia [November 11, 1774]. From THOMAS JEFFERSON, *Notes on Virginia [1784–1785]*

George Mason
1725–1792

9 That all men are by nature equally free and independent, and have certain inherent rights, of which, when they enter into a state of society, they cannot by any compact deprive or divest their posterity; namely, the enjoyment of life and liberty, with the means of acquiring and possessing property, and pursuing and obtaining happiness and safety.
Virginia Bill of Rights[4] *[June 12, 1776], article 1*

10 Government is, or ought to be instituted for the common benefit, protection, and security of the people, nation, or community; of all the various modes and forms of government, that is best which is capable of producing the greatest degree of happiness and safety, and is most effectually secured against the danger of maladministration.
Virginia Bill of Rights, 3

11 The freedom of the press is one of the greatest bulwarks of liberty, and can never be restrained but by despotic governments.
Virginia Bill of Rights, 12

John Newton[5]
1725–1807

12 Amazing grace! How sweet the sound
That saved a wretch like me!
I once was lost, but now am found,
Was blind, but now I see.
Olney Hymns [1779]. Amazing Grace

13 Glorious things of thee are spoken,
Zion, city of our God.
Olney Hymns. Glorious Things

---

[3]Tah-gah-jute. Leader of the Mingo Indians.

[4]See Patrick Henry, 353:4. Henry drafted Article 16, on religious freedom.

[5]Newton wrote his own epitaph: John Newton, clerk, once an infidel and libertine, a servant of slaves in Africa, was by the rich mercy of our Lord and Savior Jesus Christ preserved, restored, pardoned, and appointed to preach the Faith he had long labored to destroy.

---

[1]Translated by THOMAS DE QUINCEY.

[2]Translated by A. D. LINDSAY.

James Otis[1]
1725–1783

1   An act against the Constitution is void; an act against natural equity is void.
Argument Against the Writs of Assistance [1761]

2   Taxation without representation is tyranny.[2]
Attributed [1763]

3   Ubi libertas ibi patria [Where liberty is, there is my country].   *His motto*

James Hutton
1726–1797

4   The result, therefore, of this physical inquiry [into the age of the earth] is, that we find no vestige of a beginning — no prospect of an end.
The Theory of the Earth [1795]

William Prescott
1726–1795

5   Don't one of you fire until you see the whites of their eyes.[3]   *At Bunker Hill [June 17, 1775]*

Jane Elliot
1727–1805

6 I've heard them lilting, at the ewe milking,
Lasses a' lilting, before dawn of day;
But now they are moaning, on ilka green loaning;
The flowers of the forest are a' wede away.
The Flowers of the Forest[4]

---

[1][Otis arguing] was a flame of fire . . . the seeds of patriots and heroes were then and there sown.—JOHN ADAMS, *Works* [1850–1856], *vol. II, p. 522*

[2]This maxim was the guide and watchword of all the friends of liberty. Otis actually said: No parts of His Majesty's dominions can be taxed without their consent.—OTIS, *Rights of the Colonies* [1764], *p. 64*

[3]Also attributed to ISRAEL PUTNAM [1718–1790].
Silent till you see the whites of their eyes.—PRINCE CHARLES OF PRUSSIA [fl. c. 1745], *at Jagerndorf* [May 23, 1745]
See Frederick the Great, 330:10.

[4]Sir Walter Scott in *Minstrelsy of the Scottish Border* says that *The Flowers of the Forest* was written to an ancient tune and that the last line, the refrain, is indisputably ancient. The air was also used for verses by Alison Cockburn [1713–1794].

Anne Robert Jacques Turgot, Baron de l'Aulne
1727–1781

7   They [the Americans] are the hope of this wor[l]
They may become its model.
Letter to Dr. Richard Price [March 22, 177

John Wilkes
1727–1797

8   *Earl of Sandwich:* 'Pon my honor, Wilkes, don't know whether you'll die on the gallows or the pox.
Wilkes: That must depend, my Lord, up[on] whether I first embrace your Lordship's principl[es] or your Lordship's mistresses.
From SIR CHARLES PETRIE, *The Four George[s] [1935]*

Oliver Goldsmith
c. 1728–1774

9   One writer excels at a plan or a title page, a[n] other works away the body of the book, and a thi[rd] is a dab at an index.
The Bee [1759], no.

10 Good people all, with one accord,
Lament for Madame Blaize,
Who never wanted a good word —
From those who spoke her praise.
The Bee, 4. Elegy on Mrs. Mary Blaize [1759
st. 1

11   As writers become more numerous, it is natu[ral] for readers to become more indolent.
The Bee, 5. Upon Unfortunate Me[n

12 To the last moment of his breath
On hope the wretch relies;
And e'en the pang preceding death
Bids expectation rise.
The Captivity, An Oratorio [1764], act

13 Hope, like the gleaming taper's light,
Adorns and cheers our way;
And still, as darker grows the night,
Emits a brighter ray.
The Captivity, An Oratorio,

14 Remote, unfriended, melancholy, slow,
Or by the lazy Scheldt, or wandering Po.
The Traveller [1764], l.

15 Where'er I roam, whatever realms to see,
My heart untravel'd fondly turns to thee;

Still to my brother turns with ceaseless pain,
And drags at each remove a lengthening chain.
The Traveller, l. 7

1 Such is the patriot's boast, where'er we roam,
His first, best country ever is, at home.
The Traveller, l. 73

2 Where wealth and freedom reign contentment fails,
And honor sinks where commerce long prevails.
The Traveller, l. 91

3 They please, are pleas'd, they give to get esteem,
Till, seeming blest, they grow to what they seem.[1]
The Traveller, l. 265

4 To men of other minds my fancy flies,
Embosom'd in the deep where Holland lies.
Methinks her patient sons before me stand,
Where the broad ocean leans against the land.
The Traveller, l. 281

5 Pride in their port, defiance in their eye,
I see the lords of humankind[2] pass by.
The Traveller, l. 327

6 The land of scholars, and the nurse of arms.[3]
The Traveller, l. 356

7 For just experience tells; in every soil,
That those that think must govern those that toil.
The Traveller, l. 371

8 Laws grind the poor, and rich men rule the law.
The Traveller, l. 386

9 A book may be very amusing with numerous errors, or it may be very dull without a single absurdity.
The Vicar of Wakefield [1766], preface

10 I . . . chose my wife, as she did her wedding gown, not for a fine glossy surface, but such qualities as would wear well.
The Vicar of Wakefield, ch. 1

11 Handsome is that handsome does.
The Vicar of Wakefield, 1

12 I find you want me to furnish you with argument and intellects too.
The Vicar of Wakefield, 7

13 Man wants but little here below,
Nor wants that little long.
*The Vicar of Wakefield, 8 [The Hermit
(Edwin and Angelina), st. 8]*

14 She was all of a muck of sweat.
The Vicar of Wakefield, 9

15 They would talk of nothing but high life, and high-lived company, with other fashionable topics, such as pictures, taste, Shakespeare, and the musical glasses. *The Vicar of Wakefield, 9*

16 The naked every day he clad
When he put on his clothes.
*The Vicar of Wakefield, 17 [An Elegy on the
Death of a Mad Dog, st. 3]*

17 And in that town a dog was found,
As many dogs there be,
Both mongrel, puppy, whelp, and hound,
And curs of low degree.
The Vicar of Wakefield, 17, st. 4

18 The dog, to gain some private ends,
Went mad, and bit the man.
The Vicar of Wakefield, 17, st. 5

19 The man recover'd of the bite,
The dog it was that died.
The Vicar of Wakefield, 17, st. 8

20 When lovely woman stoops to folly,
And finds too late that men betray,
What charm can soothe her melancholy?
What art can wash her guilt away?
The Vicar of Wakefield, 24. Song, st. 1

21 The only art her guilt to cover,
To hide her shame from every eye,
To give repentance to her lover,
And wring his bosom, is — to die.
The Vicar of Wakefield, 24. Song, st. 2

22 This same philosophy is a good horse in the stable, but an arrant jade on a journey.
The Good-Natur'd Man [1768], act I

23 He calls his extravagance, generosity; and his trusting everybody, universal benevolence.
The Good-Natur'd Man, I

24 All his faults are such that one loves him still the better for them. *The Good-Natur'd Man, I*

25 Friendship is a disinterested commerce between equals; love, an abject intercourse between tyrants and slaves. *The Good-Natur'd Man, I*

26 Silence gives consent.
The Good-Natur'd Man, II

27 Measures, not men, have always been my mark.
The Good-Natur'd Man, II

28 Sweet Auburn! loveliest village of the plain.
The Deserted Village [1770], l. 1

29 Ill fares the land, to hastening ills a prey,
Where wealth accumulates, and men decay;

---

[1]The character of the French.

[2]The British.

[3]England.

Princes and lords may flourish, or may fade;
A breath can make them, as a breath has made;
But a bold peasantry, their country's pride,
When once destroy'd, can never be supplied.

The Deserted Village, l. 51

1 His best companions, innocence and health;
And his best riches, ignorance of wealth.

The Deserted Village, l. 61

2 How happy he who crowns in shades like these,
A youth of labor with an age of ease.

The Deserted Village, l. 99

3 The watchdog's voice that bay'd the whispering
   wind,
And the loud laugh that spoke the vacant mind.[1]

The Deserted Village, l. 121

4 A man he was to all the country dear,
And passing rich with forty pounds a year.

The Deserted Village, l. 141

5 Careless their merits or their faults to scan,
His pity gave ere charity began.
Thus to relieve the wretched was his pride,
And e'en his failings leaned to Virtue's side.

The Deserted Village, l. 161

6 And, as a bird each fond endearment tries
To tempt its new-fledg'd offspring to the skies,
He tried each art, reprov'd each dull delay,
Allur'd to brighter worlds, and led the way.

The Deserted Village, l. 167

7 Truth from his lips prevail'd with double sway,
And fools, who came to scoff, remain'd to pray.

The Deserted Village, l. 179

8 A man severe he was, and stern to view;
I knew him well, and every truant knew:
Well had the boding tremblers learned to trace
The day's disasters in his morning face;
Full well they laugh'd with counterfeited glee,
At all his jokes, for many a joke had he;
Full well the busy whisper, circling round,
Convey'd the dismal tidings when he frown'd;
Yet he was kind; or if severe in aught,
The love he bore to learning was in fault;
The village all declar'd how much he knew;
'Twas certain he could write, and cipher too.

The Deserted Village, l. 197

9 In arguing too, the parson own'd his skill,
For e'en though vanquish'd, he could argue still;

While words of learned length, and thundering
   sound
Amaz'd the gazing rustics rang'd around;
And still they gaz'd, and still the wonder grew,
That one small head could carry all he knew.

The Deserted Village, l. 21

10 The whitewash'd wall, the nicely sanded floor,
The varnish'd clock that click'd behind the door;
The chest contriv'd a double debt to pay,
A bed by night, a chest of drawers by day.

The Deserted Village, l. 22

11 To me more dear, congenial to my heart,
One native charm, than all the gloss of art.

The Deserted Village, l. 25.

12 Her modest looks the cottage might adorn,
Sweet as the primrose peeps beneath the thorn.

The Deserted Village, l. 32

13 Thou source of all my bliss, and all my woe,
That found'st me poor at first, and keep'st me so.

The Deserted Village, l. 41

14   In my time, the follies of the town crept slowly
among us, but now they travel faster than a stage
coach.   *She Stoops to Conquer [1773], act*

15   I love everything that's old: old friends, old
times, old manners, old books, old wines.

She Stoops to Conquer,

16   The very pink of perfection.

She Stoops to Conquer,

17 Let schoolmasters puzzle their brain,
   With grammar, and nonsense, and learning;
Good liquor, I stoutly maintain,
   Gives genius a better discerning.

She Stoops to Conquer, I

18   I'll be with you in the squeezing of a lemon.

She Stoops to Conquer, I

19   A modest woman, dressed out in all her finery, is
the most tremendous object of the whole creation.

She Stoops to Conquer, II

20   This is Liberty Hall, gentlemen.

She Stoops to Conquer, II

21   The first blow is half the battle.

She Stoops to Conquer, II

22   They liked the book the better the more it made
them cry.   *She Stoops to Conquer, II*

23   Ask me no questions, and I'll tell you no fibs.[2]

She Stoops to Conquer, III

---

[1] Frequent and loud laughter is the characteristic of folly and ill
manners: it is the manner in which the mob express their silly joy at
silly things, and they call it being merry. In my mind there is nothing
so illiberal and so ill-bred as audible laughter. — EARL OF CHESTER-
FIELD, *Letters* [March 9, 1748]

---

[2] Them that asks no questions isn't told a lie. — RUDYARD KIPLING,
A Smuggler's Song, st. 6

Our Garrick's a salad; for in him we see
Oil, vinegar, sugar, and saltness agree!
Retaliation [1774], l. 11

Here lies our good Edmund,[1] whose genius was
    such,
We scarcely can praise it, or blame it too much;
Who, born for the universe, narrow'd his mind,
And to party gave up what was meant for
    mankind . . .
Who, too deep for his hearers, still went on
    refining,
And thought of convincing, while they thought of
    dining;
Though equal to all things, for all things unfit;
Too nice for a statesman, too proud for a wit.
Retaliation, l. 29

His conduct still right, with his argument wrong.
Retaliation, l. 46

On the stage he was natural, simple, affecting;
'Twas only that when he was off he was acting.
Retaliation, l. 101

He cast off his friends as a huntsman his pack,
For he knew when he pleas'd he could whistle
    them back.   *Retaliation, l. 107*

When they talk'd of their Raphaels, Correggios,
    and stuff,
He shifted his trumpet and only took snuff.[2]
Retaliation, l. 145

Such dainties to them, their health it might hurt;
It's like sending them ruffles, when wanting a shirt.
The Haunch of Venison [1776], l. 33

There is no arguing with Johnson: for if his pistol misses fire, he knocks you down with the butt end of it.
*From JAMES BOSWELL, Life of Johnson [1791].
October 26, 1769*

[To Dr. Johnson:] If you were to make little fishes talk, they would talk like whales.
*From BOSWELL, Life of Johnson, April 27,
1773*

You may all go to pot.
*Verses in reply to an invitation to dine at Dr.
Baker's*

John Stark
1728–1822

My men, yonder are the Hessians. They were bought for seven pounds and ten pence a man. Are you worth more? Prove it. Tonight, the American flag floats from yonder hill or Molly Stark sleeps a widow!
*Before the battle of Bennington [August 16,
1777]*

Edmund Burke[3]
1729–1797

12   Custom reconciles us to everything.
    *On the Sublime and Beautiful [1756],
    sec. 18*

13   There is, however, a limit at which forbearance ceases to be a virtue.
    *Observations on a Late Publication on the
    Present State of the Nation [1769]*

14   The wisdom of our ancestors.[4]
    *Observations on a Late Publication on the
    Present State of the Nation*

15   When bad men combine, the good must associate; else they will fall one by one, an unpitied sacrifice in a contemptible struggle.
    *Thoughts on the Cause of the Present
    Discontents [April 23, 1770]*

16   Of this stamp is the cant of, Not men, but measures; a sort of charm by which many people get loose from every honorable engagement.
    *Thoughts on the Cause of the Present
    Discontents*

17   So to be patriots as not to forget we are gentlemen.
    *Thoughts on the Cause of the Present
    Discontents*

18   Public life is a situation of power and energy; he trespasses against his duty who sleeps upon his watch, as well as he that goes over to the enemy.
    *Thoughts on the Cause of the Present
    Discontents*

19   Reflect how you are to govern a people who think they ought to be free, and think they are not. Your scheme yields no revenue; it yields nothing but discontent, disorder, disobedience; and such is the

---

[1]Edmund Burke.

[2]Sir Joshua Reynolds, who was exceedingly deaf.

[3]You could not stand five minutes with that man [Burke] beneath a shed while it rained, but you must be convinced you had been standing with the greatest man you had ever seen. — SAMUEL JOHNSON, *Johnsonian Miscellanies* [1897], *edited by* G. B. HILL, *vol. I, p. 290*

[4]*De Sapienta Veterum [The Wisdom of the Ancients].* — FRANCIS BACON [1609], *title of work*

The phrase is also in Burke, *Discussion on the Traitorous Correspondence Bill* [1793].

state of America, that after wading up to your eyes in blood, you could only end just where you begun; that is, to tax where no revenue is to be found, to— my voice fails me; my inclination indeed carries me no farther—all is confusion beyond it.

First Speech on the Conciliation with America. American Taxation [April 19, 1774]

1   Your representative owes you, not his industry only, but his judgment; and he betrays instead of serving you if he sacrifices it to your opinion.

Speech to the Electors of Bristol [November 3, 1774]

2   I have in general no very exalted opinion of the virtue of paper government.

Second Speech on Conciliation with America. The Thirteen Resolutions [March 22, 1775]

3   Young man, there is America—which at this day serves for little more than to amuse you with stories of savage men and uncouth manners; yet shall, before you taste of death, show itself equal to the whole of that commerce which now attracts the envy of the world.

Second Speech on Conciliation with America. The Thirteen Resolutions

4   When we speak of the commerce with our colonies, fiction lags after truth; invention is unfruitful, and imagination cold and barren.

Second Speech on Conciliation with America. The Thirteen Resolutions

5   A people who are still, as it were, but in the gristle, and not yet hardened into the bone of manhood.

Second Speech on Conciliation with America. The Thirteen Resolutions

6   Through a wise and salutary neglect [of the colonies], a generous nature has been suffered to take her own way to perfection; when I reflect upon these effects, when I see how profitable they have been to us, I feel all the pride of power sink and all presumption in the wisdom of human contrivances melt and die away within me. My rigor relents. I pardon something to the spirit of liberty.

Second Speech on Conciliation with America. The Thirteen Resolutions

7   The use of force alone is but *temporary*. It may subdue for a moment; but it does not remove the necessity of subduing again: and a nation is not governed, which is perpetually to be conquered.

Second Speech on Conciliation with America. The Thirteen Resolutions

8   Nothing less will content me, than *whole Ameri*

Second Speech on Conciliation with America The Thirteen Resolutions

9   Abstract liberty, like other mere abstractions, not to be found.

Second Speech on Conciliation with America The Thirteen Resolutions

10   In no country perhaps in the world is law general a study [as in America]. . . . This study re ders men acute, inquisitive, dexterous, prompt attack, ready in defense, full of resources. . . . Th augur misgovernment at a distance, and snuff t approach of tyranny in every tainted breeze.

Second Speech on Conciliation with America The Thirteen Resolutions

11   I do not know the method of drawing up an dictment against an whole people.

Second Speech on Conciliation with America The Thirteen Resolutions

12   It is not, what a lawyer tells me I *may* do; b what humanity, reason, and justice, tell me I oug to do.

Second Speech on Conciliation with America The Thirteen Resolutions

13   The march of the human mind is slow.

Second Speech on Conciliation with America The Thirteen Resolutions

14   All government—indeed, every human bene and enjoyment, every virtue and every prude act—is founded on compromise and barter.

Second Speech on Conciliation with America The Thirteen Resolutions

15   Slavery they can have anywhere. It is a weed tl grows in every soil.

Second Speech on Conciliation with America The Thirteen Resolutions

16   Deny them [the colonies] this participation freedom, and you break that sole bond, which ori inally made, and must still preserve the unity of t empire.

Second Speech on Conciliation with America The Thirteen Resolutions

17   It is the love of the [British] people; it is their tachment to their government, from the sense the deep stake they have in such a glorious instit tion, which gives you both your army and yo navy, and infuses into both that liberal obedien without which your army would be a base rabb and your navy nothing but rotten timber.

Second Speech on Conciliation with America The Thirteen Resolutions

1 Magnanimity in politics is not seldom the truest wisdom; and a great empire and little minds go ill together.

Second Speech on Conciliation with America. The Thirteen Resolutions

2 By adverting to the dignity of this high calling our ancestors have turned a savage wilderness into a glorious empire: and have made the most extensive, and the only honorable conquests, not by destroying, but by promoting the wealth, the number, the happiness of the human race.

Second Speech on Conciliation with America. The Thirteen Resolutions

3 Corrupt influence, which is itself the perennial spring of all prodigality, and of all disorder; which loads us, more than millions of debt; which takes away vigor from our arms, wisdom from our councils, and every shadow of authority and credit from the most venerable parts of our constitution.

Speech on the Economical Reform [1780]

4 He was not merely a chip of the old block, but the old block itself.

On Pitt's first speech [February 26, 1781]

5 A rapacious and licentious soldiery.

Speech on Fox's East India Bill [1783]

6 There never was a bad man that had ability for good service.

Impeachment of Warren Hastings [February 15, 1788]

7 An event has happened, upon which it is difficult to speak, and impossible to be silent.

Impeachment of Warren Hastings [May 5, 1789]

8 Resolved to die in the last dike of prevarication.

Impeachment of Warren Hastings [May 7, 1789]

9 There is but one law for all, namely, that law which governs all law, the law of our Creator, the law of humanity, justice, equity — the law of nature, and of nations.

Impeachment of Warren Hastings [May 28, 1794]

10 They made and recorded a sort of institute and digest of anarchy, called the Rights of Man.

On the Army Estimates [1790]

11 People will not look forward to posterity who never look backward to their ancestors.

Reflections on the Revolution in France [1790]

12 Government is a contrivance of human wisdom to provide for human wants. Men have a right that these wants should be provided for by this wisdom.

Reflections on the Revolution in France

13 The age of chivalry has gone. That of sophisters, economists, and calculators has succeeded, and the glory of Europe is extinguished forever.

Reflections on the Revolution in France

14 Kings will be tyrants from policy, when subjects are rebels from principle.

Reflections on the Revolution in France

15 Learning will be cast into the mire, and trodden down under the hoofs of a swinish multitude.

Reflections on the Revolution in France

16 Because half a dozen grasshoppers under a fern make the field ring with their importunate chink, whilst thousands of great cattle, reposed beneath the shadow of the British oak, chew the cud and are silent, pray do not imagine that those who make the noise are the only inhabitants of the field; that, of course, they are many in number; or that, after all, they are other than the little shriveled, meager, hopping, though loud and troublesome *insects* of the hour.

Reflections on the Revolution in France

17 Superstition is the religion of feeble minds.

Reflections on the Revolution in France

18 You can never plan the future by the past.

Letter to a member of the National Assembly [1791]

19 Old religious factions are volcanoes burnt out.

Speech on the Petition of the Unitarians [1792]

20 The cold neutrality of an impartial judge.

Preface to Brissot's Address [1794]

21 All men that are ruined, are ruined on the side of their natural propensities.

Letters on a Regicide Peace [1796], no. 1

22 Example is the school of mankind, and they will learn at no other.

Letters on a Regicide Peace, 1

23 Mere parsimony is not economy. . . . Expense, and great expense, may be an essential part of true economy.

Letter to a Noble Lord [1796]

24 Economy is a distributive virtue, and consists not in saving but selection. Parsimony requires no providence, no sagacity, no powers of combination, no comparison, no judgment.

Letter to a Noble Lord

1   And having looked to Government for bread, on the very first scarcity they will turn and bite the hand that fed them.
Thoughts and Details on Scarcity [1800]

2   The only thing necessary for the triumph of evil is for good men to do nothing.   *Attributed*[1]

Gotthold Ephraim Lessing
1729–1781

3   He who doesn't lose his wits over certain things has no wits to lose.
Emilia Galotti [1772], act IV, sc. vii

4   No person must have to.
Nathan der Weise [1779], act I, sc. iii

5   People are not always what they seem.
Nathan der Weise, I, vi

6   The true beggar is the true king.
Nathan der Weise, II, end

7   Not all are free who scorn their chains.
Nathan der Weise, IV, iv

8   One can drink too much, but one never drinks enough.   *Lieder*

John Parker
1729–1775

9   Stand your ground. Don't fire unless fired upon, but if they mean to have a war let it begin here!
To his Minute Men at Lexington, Massachusetts [April 19, 1775]

Speckled Snake[2]
c. 1729–1829

10   When the white man had warmed himself before the Indians' fire and filled himself with their hominy, he became very large. With a step he bestrode the mountains, and his feet covered the plains and the valleys. His hand grasped the eastern and the western sea, and his head rested on the moon.
Statement when President Andrew Jackson recommended that the Cherokees, Chickasaws, Choctaws, Creeks, and Seminoles move west beyond the Mississippi [1829]

11   Brothers, I have listened to a great many talks from our great father.[3] But they always began and ended in this: "Get a little further; you are too near me."
Statement when President Andrew Jackson recommended that the Cherokees, Chickasaws, Choctaws, Creeks, and Seminoles move west beyond the Mississippi

Thomas Osbert Mordaunt
1730–1809

12   One crowded hour of glorious life
Is worth an age without a name.
Verses Written During the War [1756–1763]. From the Bee [October 12, 1791]

Josiah Wedgwood
1730–1795

13   Am I not a man and a brother?
On a medallion[4] *[1787*

Charles Churchill
1731–1764

14   Genius is of no country.
The Rosciad [1761], l. 20

15   Learn'd without sense, and venerably dull.
The Rosciad, l. 59

16   Those who would make us feel—must feel themselves.   *The Rosciad, l. 96*

17   Apt alliteration's artful aid.
The Prophecy of Famine [1763], l. 8

18   Fame
Is nothing but an empty name.
The Ghost [1763], bk. I, l. 22

19   Just to the windward of the law.
The Ghost, III, l. 5

20   Though by whim, envy, or resentment led,
They damn those authors whom they never read.
The Candidate [1764], l. 5

21   Be England what she will,
With all her faults she is my country still.[5]
The Farewell, l. 2

---

[1] Vigorous searches by many people have failed to locate this quotation anywhere in Burke's writings. In her preface to the fifteenth edition of *Bartlett's* [1980, p. ix] Emily Morison Beck suggests that it may be "a twentieth-century paraphrase" of Burke, 343:15.

[2] A Creek.

[3] President Jackson.

[4] Representing a black man in chains, with one knee on the ground and both hands lifted up to heaven. This was adopted as seal by the Anti-Slavery Society of London.

[5] England, with all thy faults I love thee still, / My country!—WILLIAM COWPER, *The Task* [1785], *bk. II, The Timepiece, l. 206*

William Cowper
1731–1800

1 Oh! for a closer walk with God.
> *Olney Hymns [1779], no. 1, Walking with God*

2 What peaceful hours I once enjoy'd!
> How sweet their memory still!
> But they have left an aching void
> The world can never fill.
> *Olney Hymns, 1, Walking with God*

3 God moves in a mysterious way
> His wonders to perform;
> He plants his footsteps in the sea
> And rides upon the storm.
> *Olney Hymns, 35, Light Shining out of*
> *Darkness*

4 Behind a frowning providence
> He hides a smiling face.
> *Olney Hymns, 35, Light Shining out of*
> *Darkness*

5 Thus happiness depends, as Nature shows,
> Less on exterior things than most suppose.
> *Table Talk [1782], l. 246*

6 Freedom has a thousand charms to show,
> That slaves, howe'er contented, never know.
> *Table Talk, l. 260*

7 Manner is all in all, whate'er is writ,
> The substitute for genius, sense, and wit.
> *Table Talk, l. 542*

8 [Pope] Made poetry a mere mechanic art.
> *Table Talk, l. 656*

9 Lights of the world, and stars of human race.
> *The Progress of Error [1782], l. 97*

10 How much a dunce that has been sent to roam
> Excels a dunce that has been kept at home!
> *The Progress of Error, l. 415*

11 A fool must now and then be right, by chance.
> *Conversation [1782], l. 96*

12 He would not, with a peremptory tone,
> Assert the nose upon his face his own.
> *Conversation, l. 121*

13 I cannot talk with civet in the room,
> A fine puss-gentleman that's all perfume.
> *Conversation, l. 283*

14 His wit invites you by his looks to come,
> But when you knock it never is at home.
> *Conversation, l. 303*

15 A business with an income at its heels
> Furnishes always oil for its own wheels.
> *Retirement [1782], l. 615*

16 Absence of occupation is not rest,
> A mind quite vacant is a mind distress'd.
> *Retirement, l. 623*

17 Built God a church, and laugh'd His word to
> scorn.[1]
> *Retirement, l. 688*

18   Philologists, who chase
> A panting syllable through time and space,
> Start it at home, and hunt it in the dark
> To Gaul, to Greece, and into Noah's ark.
> *Retirement, l. 691*

19 I praise the Frenchman,[2] his remark was shrewd—
> How sweet, how passing sweet, is solitude!
> But grant me still a friend in my retreat
> Whom I may whisper—solitude is sweet.
> *Retirement, l. 739*

20 I am monarch of all I survey,
> My right there is none to dispute.
> *Verses Supposed to Be Written by Alexander*
> *Selkirk [1782], st. 1*

21 O Solitude! where are the charms
> That sages have seen in thy face?
> *Verses Supposed to Be Written by Alexander*
> *Selkirk*

22   Though on pleasure she was bent,
> She had a frugal mind.
> *History of John Gilpin [1785], st. 8*

23 A hat not much the worse for wear.
> *History of John Gilpin, st. 46*

24 Now let us sing—Long live the king,
> And Gilpin, long live he;
> And, when he next doth ride abroad,
> May I be there to see!
> *History of John Gilpin, st. 63*

25 God made the country, and man made the town.
> *The Task [1785], bk. I, The Sofa, l. 749*

26 Oh for a lodge in some vast wilderness,
> Some boundless contiguity of shade,
> Where rumor of oppression and deceit,
> Of unsuccessful or successful war,
> Might never reach me more.
> *The Task, II, The Timepiece, l. 1*

27 Slaves cannot breathe in England; if their lungs
> Receive our air, that moment they are free!
> They touch our country, and their shackles fall.
> *The Task, II, The Timepiece, l. 40*

---

[1]Voltaire, who built a church at Ferney [1760–1761], with the inscription *Deo erexit Voltaire.*

[2]La Bruyère.

1 Variety's the very spice of life.
        The Task, II, The Timepiece, l. 606

2 From reveries so airy, from the toil
  Of dropping buckets into empty wells,
  And growing old in drawing nothing up.
        The Task, III, The Garden, l. 188

3 Who loves a garden loves a greenhouse too.
        The Task, III, The Garden, l. 566

4 Now stir the fire, and close the shutters fast,
  Let fall the curtains, wheel the sofa round,
  And, while the bubbling and loud-hissing urn
  Throws up a steamy column, and the cups,
  That cheer but not inebriate, wait on each,
  So let us welcome peaceful evening in.
        The Task, IV, The Winter Evening, l. 36

5 'Tis pleasant, through the loopholes of retreat,
  To peep at such a world; to see the stir
  Of the great Babel, and not feel the crowd.
        The Task, IV, The Winter Evening, l. 88

6 With spots quadrangular of diamond form,
  Ensanguin'd hearts, clubs typical of strife,
  And spades, the emblems of untimely graves.
        The Task, IV, The Winter Evening, l. 217

7 All learned, and all drunk!
        The Task, IV, The Winter Evening, l. 478

8 Gloriously drunk, obey th' important call.
        The Task, IV, The Winter Evening, l. 510

9 But war's a game, which, were their subjects wise,
  Kings would not play at.
        The Task, V, The Winter Morning Walk, l. 187

10 There is in souls a sympathy with sounds;
   And as the mind is pitch'd the ear is pleas'd
   With melting airs or martial, brisk, or grave:
   Some chord in unison with what we hear
   Is touch'd within us, and the heart replies.
        The Task, VI, Winter Walk at Noon, l. 1

11   Here the heart
   May give a useful lesson to the head,
   And Learning wiser grow without his books.
        The Task, VI, Winter Walk at Noon, l. 85

12 Knowledge is proud that he has learn'd so much;
   Wisdom is humble that he knows no more.
        The Task, VI, Winter Walk at Noon, l. 96

13 Nature is but a name for an effect,
   Whose cause is God.
        The Task, VI, Winter Walk at Noon, l. 223

14 An honest man, close-button'd to the chin,
   Broadcloth without, and a warm heart within.
        Epistle to Joseph Hill [1785], l. 62

15 Shine by the side of every path we tread
   With such a luster, he that runs may read.
        Tirocinium [1785], l. 7

16 Toll for the brave —
   The brave! that are no more;
   All sunk beneath the wave,
   Fast by their native shore!
        On the Loss of the Royal George[1] *[1791], st.*

17 And still to love, though prest with ill,
   In wintry age to feel no chill,
   With me is to be lovely still,
     My Mary!   *To Mary [1791], st. 1*

18 Beware of desp'rate steps! The darkest day
   (Live till tomorrow) will have pass'd away.
        The Needless Alarm [1794]. Mora

19 I shall not ask Jean Jacques Rousseau
   If birds confabulate or no.
        Pairing Time Anticipated [c. 1794

20 Misses! the tale that I relate
   This lesson seems to carry —
   Choose not alone a proper mate,
   But proper time to marry.
        Pairing Time Anticipated. Mora

21   Misery still delights to trace
   Its semblance in another's case.
        The Castaway [1799], l. 5

22 No voice divine the storm allayed,
       No light propitious shone;
   When, snatched from all effectual aid,
       We perished, each alone:
   But I beneath a rougher sea,
   And whelmed in deeper gulfs than he.
        The Castaway, l. 6

Erasmus Darwin
1731–1802

23 Soon shall thy arm, unconquer'd steam! afar
   Drag the slow barge, or drive the rapid car;
   Or on wide-waving wings expanded bear
   The flying-chariot through the fields of air.
        The Botanic Garden, pt. I [1789], l. 28

24   Would it be too bold to imagine, that in th
   great length of time, since the earth began to exist
   perhaps millions of ages before the commencemen
   of the history of mankind, would it be too bold t

---

[1]The *Royal George* was an English man-of-war of 108 gun
which suddenly heeled over, under the strain caused by the shiftin
of her guns, while being refitted at Spithead, August 29, 178
The commander, Admiral Kempenfeldt, and eight hundred of th
sailors, marines, and visitors on board were drowned.

imagine, that all warm-blooded animals have arisen from one living filament which the Great First Cause endued with animality . . . and thus possessing the faculty of continuing to improve by its own inherent activity, and of delivering down those improvements by generation to its posterity, world without end![1]
Zoonomia [1794]

Charles Lee
1731–1782

Beware that your Northern laurels do not change to Southern willows.[2]
To General Horatio Gates after the surrender of Burgoyne at Saratoga [October 17, 1777]

Beilby Porteus
1731–1808

One murder made a villain,
Millions, a hero.   *Death [1759], l. 154*

War its thousands slays, Peace, its ten thousands.
Death, l. 178

Pierre de Beaumarchais
1732–1799

Judging by the virtues expected of a servant, does your Excellency know many masters who would be worthy valets?
Le Barbier de Séville [1775], act I, sc. ii

I quickly laugh at everything, for fear of having to cry.[3]   *Le Barbier de Séville, I, ii*

If you assure me that your intentions are honorable.   *Le Barbier de Séville, IV, vi*

If you are mediocre and you grovel, you shall succeed.
Le Mariage de Figaro [1784], act III, sc. iii

You went to some trouble to be born, and that's all.[4]   *Le Mariage de Figaro, V, iii*

If censorship reigns there cannot be sincere flattery, and only small men are afraid of small writings.
Le Mariage de Figaro, V, iii

John Dickinson
1732–1808

10 Then join hand in hand, brave Americans all!
By uniting we stand, by dividing we fall.[5]
The Liberty Song [1768]

Richard Henry Lee
1732–1794

11 That these united colonies are, and of right ought to be, free and independent states; that they are absolved from all allegiance to the British crown; and that all political connection between them and the State of Great Britain is, and ought to be, totally dissolved.
Resolution moved at the Continental Congress [June 7, 1776; adopted July 2][6]

George Washington[7]
1732–1799

12 Discipline is the soul of an army. It makes small numbers formidable; procures success to the weak, and esteem to all.
Letter of Instructions to the Captains of the Virginia Regiments [July 29, 1759]

13 Let us therefore animate and encourage each other, and show the whole world that a Freeman, contending for liberty on his own ground, is superior to any slavish mercenary on earth.
General Orders, Headquarters, New York [July 2, 1776]

14 The time is now near at hand which must probably determine whether Americans are to be freemen or slaves; whether they are to have any property they can call their own; whether their houses and farms are to be pillaged and destroyed, and themselves consigned to a state of wretchedness from which no human efforts will deliver them. The fate of unborn millions will now depend, under God, on the courage and conduct of this army. Our cruel and unrelenting enemy leaves us only the choice of brave resistance, or the most abject submission. We have, therefore, to resolve to conquer or die.
Address to the Continental Army before the battle of Long Island [August 27, 1776]

---

[1]Here the grandfather of Charles Darwin announces his own early theory of organic evolution.

[2]Gates was later defeated by Cornwallis at Camden, South Carolina [August 16, 1780], and was relieved of his command.

[3]Je me presse de rire de tout, de peur d'être obligé d'en pleurer.

[4]Vous vous êtes donné la peine de naître, et rien de plus.

[5]United we stand, divided we fall.—*A watchword of the American Revolution*

[6]See John Adams, 351:8.

[7]The Father of your Country.—HENRY KNOX [1750–1806], *Letter to Washington* [March 19, 1787]
I can't tell a lie. I did cut it [the cherry tree] with my hatchet.—*Attributed to Washington as a child;* MASON LOCKE WEEMS [1759–1825], *The Life of George Washington* [1800]

1   There is nothing that gives a man consequence, and renders him fit for command, like a support that renders him independent of everybody but the State he serves.
Letter to the president of Congress, Heights of Harlem [September 24, 1776]

2   To place any dependence upon militia, is, assuredly, resting upon a broken staff.
Letter to the president of Congress, Heights of Harlem

3   Without a decisive naval force we can do nothing definitive. And with it, everything honorable and glorious.
To Lafayette [November 15, 1781]

4   If men are to be precluded from offering their sentiments on a matter which may involve the most serious and alarming consequences that can invite the consideration of mankind, reason is of no use to us; the freedom of speech may be taken away, and dumb and silent we may be led, like sheep to the slaughter.
Address to officers of the Army [March 15, 1783]

5   The preservation of the sacred fire of liberty, and the destiny of the republican model of government, are justly considered as deeply, perhaps as finally staked, on the experiment entrusted to the hands of the American people.
First Inaugural Address [April 30, 1789]

6   Happily the Government of the United States, which gives to bigotry no sanction, to persecution no assistance, requires only that they who live under its protection should demean themselves as good citizens in giving it on all occasions their effectual support.
Letter to the Jewish congregation of Newport, Rhode Island [1790]

7   To be prepared for war is one of the most effectual means of preserving peace.
First Annual Address [to both houses of Congress, January 8, 1790]

8   The basis of our political systems is the right of the people to make and to alter their constitutions of government.
Farewell Address [September 17, 1796]

9   Let me now . . . warn you in the most solemn manner against the baneful effects of the spirit of party.   *Farewell Address*

10   Observe good faith and justice toward all nations. Cultivate peace and harmony with all. . . . The Nation which indulges toward another an habitual hatred or an habitual fondness is in some de-

gree a slave. It is a slave to its animosity or to its affection, either of which is sufficient to lead it astr from its duty and its interest.
Farewell Addr

11   'Tis our true policy to steer clear of permane alliances, with any portion of the foreign world.
Farewell Addr

12   There can be no greater error than to expect calculate upon real favors from nation to nation.
Farewell Addr

13   It is well, I die hard, but I am not afraid to go.
Last words [December 14, 179

John Adams[1]
1735–1826

14   Now to what higher object, to what great character, can any mortal aspire than to be po sessed of all this knowledge, well digested and rea at command, to assist the feeble and friendless, discountenance the haughty and lawless, to procu redress of wrongs, the advancement of right, to a sert and maintain liberty and virtue, to discoura and abolish tyranny and vice?
Letter to Jonathan Sewall [October 175

15   A pen is certainly an excellent instrument to fi man's attention and to inflame his ambition.
Diary [November 14, 176

16   I always consider the settlement of America wi reverence and wonder, as the opening of a gra scene and design in providence, for the illuminatio of the ignorant and the emancipation of the slavi part of mankind all over the earth.
Notes for "A Dissertation on the Canon and Feudal Law" [1765]

17   Liberty cannot be preserved without a gener knowledge among the people, who have a right . and a desire to know; but besides this, they have right, an indisputable, unalienable, indefeasible, vine right to that most dreaded and envied kind knowledge, I mean of the characters and conduct their rulers.
A Dissertation on the Canon and Feudal La [1765]

18   Let every sluice of knowledge be opened and s a-flowing.
A Dissertation on the Canon and Feudal La

---

[1]He is as disinterested as the being who made him: he is p found in his view; and accurate in his judgment, except wh knowledge of the world is necessary to form a judgment. THOMAS JEFFERSON [January 30, 1787]

1 Facts are stubborn things; and whatever may be our wishes, our inclinations, or the dictates of our passions, they cannot alter the state of facts and evidence.

Argument in Defense of the [British] Soldiers in the Boston Massacre Trials [December 1770]

2 There is danger from all men. The only maxim of a free government ought to be to trust no man living with power to endanger the public liberty.

Notes for an Oration at Braintree, Massachusetts [Spring 1772]

3 This is the most magnificent movement of all! There is a dignity, a majesty, a sublimity, in this last effort of the patriots that I greatly admire. The people should never rise without doing something to be remembered—something notable and striking. This destruction of the tea is so bold, so daring, so firm, intrepid and inflexible, and it must have so important consequences, and so lasting, that I can't but consider it as an epocha in history!

Diary [on the Boston Tea Party, December 17, 1773]

4 A government of laws, and not of men.[1]

"Novanglus" papers, Boston Gazette [1774], no. 7. Incorporated [1780] in the Massachusetts Constitution

5 Metaphysicians and politicians may dispute forever, but they will never find any other moral principle or foundation of rule or obedience, than the consent of governors and governed.

"Novanglus" papers, Boston Gazette, no. 7

6 I agree with you that in politics the middle way is none at all.

Letter to Horatio Gates [March 23, 1776]

7 You bid me burn your letters. But I must forget you first.

Letter to Abigail Adams [April 28, 1776]

8 Yesterday, the greatest question was decided which ever was debated in America, and a greater perhaps never was nor will be decided among men. A resolution was passed without one dissenting colony, "that these United Colonies are, and of right ought to be, free and independent States."[2]

Letter to Abigail Adams [July 3, 1776]

9 The second day of July, 1776,[3] will be the most memorable epoch in the history of America. I am apt to believe that it will be celebrated by succeeding generations as the great anniversary festival. It ought to be commemorated as the day of deliverance, by solemn acts of devotion to God Almighty. It ought to be solemnized with pomp and parade, with shows, games, sports, guns, bells, bonfires, and illuminations, from one end of this continent to the other, from this time forward forevermore.

Second Letter to Abigail Adams [July 3, 1776]

10 The happiness of society is the end of government. *Thoughts on Government [1776]*

11 The judicial power ought to be distinct from both the legislative and executive, and independent upon both, that so it may be a check upon both, as both should be checks upon that.

Thoughts on Government

12 Virtue is not always amiable.

Diary [February 9, 1779]

13 By my physical constitution I am but an ordinary man. . . . Yet some great events, some cutting expressions, some mean hypocrisies, have at times thrown this assemblage of sloth, sleep, and littleness into rage like a lion. *Diary [April 26, 1779]*

14 I must study politics and war that my sons may have liberty to study mathematics and philosophy. My sons ought to study mathematics and philosophy, geography, natural history, naval architecture, navigation, commerce, and agriculture, in order to give their children a right to study painting, poetry, music, architecture, statuary, tapestry, and porcelain. *Letter to Abigail Adams [May 12, 1780]*

15 You will never be alone with a poet in your pocket.

Letter to John Quincy Adams [May 14, 1781]

16 My country has in its wisdom contrived for me the most insignificant office [the vice-presidency] that ever the invention of man contrived or his imagination conceived; and as I can do neither good nor evil, I must be borne away by others and meet the common fate.

Letter to Abigail Adams [December 19, 1793]

17 I pray Heaven to bestow the best of blessings on this house and all that shall hereafter inhabit it.

---

[1]Adams credits this formulation to James Harrington [1611–1677], with whose work *The Commonwealth of Oceana* [1656] he was familiar. Adams's use of the phrase gave it wide circulation in America.

[2]See Richard Henry Lee, 349:11.

[3]On July 2, 1776, the resolution for independence, drafted by Richard Henry Lee of Virginia, was adopted by a committee including John Adams. On July 4 the Declaration of Independence was agreed to, engrossed, signed by John Hancock, and sent to the legislatures of the States.

May none but honest and wise men ever rule under this roof.[1]

Letter to Abigail Adams [November 2, 1800]

1   I had heard my father say that he never knew a piece of land [to] run away or break.

Autobiography [1802–1807]

2   You and I ought not to die before we have explained ourselves to each other.

Letter to Thomas Jefferson [July 15, 1813]

3   The fundamental article of my political creed is that despotism, or unlimited sovereignty, or absolute power, is the same in a majority of a popular assembly, an aristocratical council, an oligarchical junto, and a single emperor.

Letter to Thomas Jefferson [November 13, 1815]

4   Thomas — Jefferson — still surv —[2]

Last words [July 4, 1826]

Isaac Bickerstaffe
c. 1735–c. 1812

5 There was a jolly miller once
Lived on the River Dee;
He worked and sang from morn till night
No lark more blithe than he.

Love in a Village [1762], act I, sc. ii

6 And this the burthen of his song
Forever used to be,
"I care for nobody, not I,
If no one cares for me."[3]   *Love in a Village, I, ii*

Michel Guillaume Jean de Crèvecoeur [J. Hector St. John]
1735–1813

7   What then is the American, this new man? He is either an European, or the descendant of an European, hence that strange mixture of blood, which you will find in no other country. . . . Here individuals of all nations are melted into a new race of men, whose labors and posterity will one day cause great changes in the world.

Letters from an American Farmer [1782], III

---

[1]Written the day after Adams moved into the new White House. President Franklin D. Roosevelt had it inscribed on the mantelpiece of the State Dining Room.

[2]Jefferson at Monticello died the same day — the fiftieth anniversary of the adoption of the Declaration of Independence.

[3]Naebody cares for me, / I care for naebody. — ROBERT BURNS, *I Hae a Wife o' My Ain, st. 4*

Charles Joseph, Prince de Ligne
1735–1814

8   The Congress doesn't run — it waltzes.[4]

Comment to Comte Auguste de La Garde–Chambonas [1814]

Paul Revere
1735–1818

9   To the memory of the glorious Ninety-two members of the Honorable House of Representative of the Massachusetts Bay who, undaunted by th insolent menaces of villains in power, from a stri regard to conscience and the liberties of their con stituents on the 30th of June 1768 voted NOT T RESCIND.

Inscription on Revere's silver "Liberty" bowl [1768]

10   If the British went out by water, to show tw lanterns in the North Church steeple; and if b land, one as a signal, for we were apprehensive would be difficult to cross the Charles River or g over Boston Neck.[5]

Signal code arranged with Colonel Conant of the Charlestown Committee of Safety [April 16, 1775]. Letter to Dr. Jeremy Belknap

Patrick Henry
1736–1799

11   Caesar had his Brutus; Charles the First h Cromwell; and George the Third ["Treason!" crie the Speaker] — *may profit by their example. If this b treason, make the most of it.*

Speech on the Stamp Act, House of Burgesses, Williamsburg, Virginia [May 29, 1765]

12   I am not a Virginian, but an American.

Speech in the First Continental Congress, Philadelphia [October 14, 1774]

13   It is natural for man to indulge in the illusions hope. We are apt to shut our eyes against a painf truth, and listen to the song of that siren till sh transforms us into beasts. Is this the part of wis men, engaged in a great and arduous struggle f liberty? Are we disposed to be the number of thos

---

[4]Le Congrès ne marche pas, il danse [said of the Congress of V enna].

[5]See Longfellow, 467:15.

who, having eyes, see not, and having ears, hear not, the things which so nearly concern their temporal salvation? For my part, whatever anguish of spirit it may cost, I am willing to know the whole truth; to know the worst, and to provide for it.
Speech in Virginia Convention, Richmond [March 23, 1775]

1   I have but one lamp by which my feet are guided, and that is the lamp of experience. I know no way of judging of the future but by the past.
Speech in Virginia Convention, Richmond

2   We are not weak if we make a proper use of those means which the God of Nature has placed in our power. . . . The battle, sir, is not to the strong alone; it is to the vigilant, the active, the brave.
Speech in Virginia Convention, Richmond

3   It is vain, sir, to extenuate the matter. The gentlemen may cry, Peace, peace! but there is no peace. The war has actually begun! The next gale that sweeps from the north will bring to our ears the clash of resounding arms! Our brethren are already in the field! Why stand we here idle? What is it that the gentlemen wish? What would they have? Is life so dear or peace so sweet as to be purchased at the price of chains and slavery? Forbid it, Almighty God. I know not what course others may take, but as for me, give me liberty or give me death!
Speech in Virginia Convention, Richmond

4   That religion, or the duty which we owe to our Creator, and the manner of discharging it, can be directed only by reason and conviction, not by force or violence; and therefore all men are equally entitled to the free exercise of religion, according to the dictates of conscience; and that it is the mutual duty of all to practice Christian forbearance, love, and charity towards each other.
Virginia Bill of Rights [June 12, 1776],[1] article 16

Edward Gibbon
1737–1794

5   The various modes of worship, which prevailed in the Roman world, were all considered by the people, as equally true; by the philosopher, as equally false; and by the magistrate, as equally useful.
The History of the Decline and Fall of the Roman Empire [1776–1788], ch. 2

6   The principles of a free constitution are irrevocably lost, when the legislative power is nominated by the executive.
The History of the Decline and Fall of the Roman Empire, 3

7   Their united reigns [the Antonines'] are possibly the only period of history in which the happiness of a great people was the sole object of government.[2]
The History of the Decline and Fall of the Roman Empire, 3

8   History . . . is indeed little more than the register of the crimes, follies, and misfortunes of mankind.
The History of the Decline and Fall of the Roman Empire, 3

9   Corruption, the most infallible symptom of constitutional liberty.
The History of the Decline and Fall of the Roman Empire, 21

10   Our sympathy is cold to the relation of distant misery.
The History of the Decline and Fall of the Roman Empire, 49

11   The winds and waves are always on the side of the ablest navigators.
The History of the Decline and Fall of the Roman Empire, 68

12   Vicissitudes of fortune, which spares neither man nor the proudest of his works, which buries empires and cities in a common grave.
The History of the Decline and Fall of the Roman Empire, 71

13   All that is human must retrograde if it do not advance.
The History of the Decline and Fall of the Roman Empire, 71

14   The successors of Charles the Fifth may disdain their brethren of England; but the romance of *Tom Jones,* that exquisite picture of human manners, will outlive the palace of the Escurial and the imperial eagle of the house of Austria.
Memoirs (Autobiography) [1796]

15   Decent easy men, who supinely enjoyed the gifts of the founder.   *Memoirs*

16   It was here [at the age of seventeen] that I suspended my religious inquiries.   *Memoirs*

17   I saw and loved.   *Memoirs*

---

[1]See George Mason, 339:*n*4. Mason drafted Articles 1, 3, and 12.

[2]Ah, might we read in America's signs / The Age restored of the Antonines. —HERMAN MELVILLE, *Timoleon* [1891], *The Age of the Antonines,* st. 3

1   I sighed as a lover, I obeyed as a son.
Memoirs

2   [Of London:] Crowds without company, and dissipation without pleasure.   *Memoirs*

3   The captain of the Hampshire grenadiers[1] . . . has not been useless to the historian of the Roman Empire.   *Memoirs*

4   It was at Rome, on the fifteenth of October 1764, as I sat musing amidst the ruins of the Capitol, while the barefoot friars were singing vespers in the Temple of Jupiter, that the idea of writing the decline and fall of the city first started to my mind.
Memoirs

Thomas Paine
1737–1809

5 From the east to the west blow the trumpet to
      arms!
Through the land let the sound of it flee;
Let the far and the near all unite, with a cheer,
In defense of our Liberty Tree.
The Liberty Tree [July 1775], st. 4

6   Society in every state is a blessing, but Government, even in its best state, is but a necessary evil; in its worst state, an intolerable one.
Common Sense [1776]

7   Suspicion is the companion of mean souls, and the bane of all good society.   *Common Sense*

8   When we are planning for posterity, we ought to remember that virtue is not hereditary.
Common Sense

9   O! ye that love mankind! Ye that dare oppose not only the tyranny but the tyrant, stand forth! Every spot of the Old World is overrun with oppression. Freedom hath been hunted round the globe. Asia and Africa have long expelled her. Europe regards her like a stranger and England hath given her warning to depart. O! receive the fugitive and prepare in time an asylum for mankind.
Common Sense

10   These are the times that try men's souls. The summer soldier and the sunshine patriot will, in this crisis, shrink from the service of their country; but he that stands it *now,* deserves the love and thanks of man and woman. Tyranny, like hell, is not easily conquered; yet we have this consolation with us,

that the harder the conflict, the more glorious the triumph. What we obtain too cheap, we esteem too lightly; it is dearness only that gives everything its value. Heaven knows how to put a proper price upon its goods; and it would be strange indeed, if so celestial an article as *Freedom* should not be highly rated.
The American Crisis, no. 1 [December 23, 1776]

11   Panics, in some cases, have their uses; they produce as much good as hurt. Their duration is always short; the mind soon grows through them and acquires a firmer habit than before. But their peculiar advantage is, that they are the touchstones of sincerity and hypocrisy, and bring things and men to light, which might otherwise have lain forever undiscovered.
The American Crisis, 1

12   Not a place upon earth might be so happy as America. Her situation is remote from all the wrangling world, and she has nothing to do but to trade with them.   *The American Crisis, 1*

13   A bad cause will ever be supported by bad means and bad men.
The American Crisis, 2 [January 13, 1777]

14   Those who expect to reap the blessings of freedom must, like men, undergo the fatigue of supporting it.
The American Crisis, 4 [September 12, 1777]

15   It is not a field of a few acres of ground, but a cause, that we are defending, and whether we defeat the enemy in one battle, or by degrees, the consequences will be the same.
The American Crisis, 4

16   We fight not to enslave, but to set a country free, and to make room upon the earth for honest men to live in.   *The American Crisis, 4*

17   It is the object only of war that makes it honorable. And if there was ever a *just* war since the world began, it is this in which America is now engaged.
The American Crisis, 5 [March 21, 1778]

18   War involves in its progress such a train of unforeseen and unsupposed circumstances . . . that no human wisdom can calculate the end. It has but one thing certain, and that is to increase taxes.
Prospects on the Rubicon [1787]

19   [Burke] is not affected by the reality of distress touching his heart, but by the showy resemblance of it striking his imagination. He pities the plumage, but forgets the dying bird.
The Rights of Man, pt. I [1791]

---

[1]Gibbon was a captain in the Hampshire militia from June 12, 1759, to December 23, 1762.

1 My country is the world and my religion is to do good. *The Rights of Man, II [1792], ch. 5*

2 A thing moderately good is not so good as it ought to be. Moderation in temper is always a virtue; but moderation in principle is always a vice.[1] *The Rights of Man, II, 5*

3 I believe in one God and no more, and I hope for happiness beyond this life. I believe in the equality of man; and I believe that religious duties consist in doing justice, loving mercy, and endeavoring to make our fellow creatures happy. *The Age of Reason [1793], pt. I*

4 It is with a pious fraud as with a bad action; it begets a calamitous necessity of going on. *The Age of Reason, I*

5 When authors and critics talk of the sublime, they see not how nearly it borders on the ridiculous. *The Age of Reason, II, note*

Rudolf Erich Raspe
1737–1794

6 His tunes were frozen up in the horn, and came out now by thawing. *Travels of Baron Munchausen [1785], ch. 6*

7 If any of the company entertain a doubt of my veracity, I shall only say to such, I pity their want of faith. *Travels of Baron Munchausen, 6*

8 A traveler has a right to relate and embellish his adventures as he pleases, and it is very impolite to refuse that deference and applause they deserve. *Travels of Baron Munchausen, 21*

Ethan Allen
1738–1789

9 [Captain Delaplace[2]] gazed at Allen in bewildered astonishment. "By whose authority do you act?" exclaimed he. "In the name of the great Jehovah, and the Continental Congress!" replied Allen. *From* WASHINGTON IRVING, *Life of Washington [1855–1859], vol. I, ch. 38*

Jacques Delille
1738–1813

10 Fate chooses our relatives, we choose our friends.[3] *Malheur et Pitié [1803], canto I*

John Wolcot [Peter Pindar]
1738–1819

11 What rage for fame attends both great and small! Better be damned than mentioned not at all! *To the Royal Academicians [1782–1785]*

Daniel Bliss
1740–1806

12 God wills us free, man wills us slaves, I will as God wills, God's will be done. *Epitaph on gravestone of John Jack, "A Native of Africa, who died March 1773, aged about 60 years. Tho' born in a land of slavery he was born free."*

James Boswell[4]
1740–1795

13 That favorite subject, Myself. *Letter to Temple [July 26, 1763]*

14 He who praises everybody, praises nobody. *Life of Johnson [1791], footnote [March 30, 1778]*

15 We cannot tell the precise moment when friendship is formed. As in filling a vessel drop by drop, there is at last a drop which makes it run over; so in a series of kindnesses there is at last one which makes the heart run over. *Life of Johnson [September 1777]*

16 I think no innocent species of wit or pleasantry should be suppressed; and that a good pun may be admitted among the smaller excellencies of lively conversation. *Life of Johnson [June 1784]*

---

[1]Extremism in the defense of liberty is no vice. And . . . moderation in the pursuit of justice is no virtue.—BARRY GOLDWATER [1909–1998], *Acceptance speech, Republican presidential nomination* [July 16, 1964]

[2]Commandant at Fort Ticonderoga, New York [May 10, 1775].

[3]Le sort fait les parents, le choix fait les amis.

[4]See also excerpts from BOSWELL, *Life of Johnson* [1791], 326:5–329:20.

Louis Sébastien Mercier
1740–1814

1   Extremes Meet.[1]
Tableaux de Paris [1782], vol. IV, ch. 348, title

Augustus Montague Toplady
1740–1778

2   Rock of Ages, cleft for me,
Let me hide myself in thee.
Rock of Ages [1775],[2] st.1

Sébastien Roch Nicolas Chamfort
1741–1794

3   The most wasted day of all is that on which we
have not laughed.   *Maxims and Thoughts, 1*

4   Chance is a nickname for Providence.
Maxims and Thoughts, 62

5   Be my brother, or I will kill you.[3]
From CARLYLE, *French Revolution [1837],
vol. II, pt. 1, ch. 12*

Johann Kaspar Lavater
1741–1801

6   Say not you know another entirely, till you have
divided an inheritance with him.
Aphorisms on Man [c. 1788], no. 157

7   Trust not him with your secrets, who, when left
alone in your room, turns over your papers.
Aphorisms on Man, 449

8   The public seldom forgive twice.
Aphorisms on Man, 606

Hester Lynch Thrale Piozzi
[Mrs. Thrale]
1741–1821

9   Johnson's conversation was by much too strong
for a person accustomed to obsequiousness and flattery; it was *mustard in a young child's mouth!*
From JAMES BOSWELL, *Life of Johnson [1791].
May 1781*

---

[1] "Extremes meet," as the whiting said with its tail in its mouth. —
THOMAS HOOD [1799–1845], *The Doves and the Crows*

[2] Music by THOMAS HASTINGS [1784–1872].

[3] Sois mon frère on je te tue.
A paraphrase of the revolutionary watchword: Fraternity or death.

Gebhard Leberecht von Blücher
1742–1819

10   Ever forward, but slowly.
*While leading the Russians at Leipzig
[October 19, 1813]*

11   May the pens of the diplomats not ruin again
what the people have attained with such exertions.
After the battle of Waterloo [1815]

Georg Christoph Lichtenberg
1742–1799

12   A knife without a blade, for which the handle is
missing.
*Göttingen Pocket Calendar [1798], describing
an impossible existence*

13   Nothing contributes more to peace of soul than
having no opinion at all.   *Aphorisms*

14   To do just the opposite is also a form of imitation.   *Aphorisms*

15   A donkey appears to me like a horse translated
into Dutch.   *Aphorisms*

16   I am always grieved when a man of real talent
dies. The world needs such men more than Heaven
does.   *Aphorisms*

17   Soothsayers make a better living in the world
than truthsayers.   *Aphorisms*

18   It may not be natural for man to walk on two
legs, but it was a noble invention.   *Aphorisms*

19   The thing that astonished him was that cats
should have two holes cut in their coat exactly at
the place where their eyes are.   *Aphorisms*

William Henry, Duke of Gloucester
1743–1805

20   Another damned, thick, square book! Always
scribble, scribble, scribble! Eh! Mr. Gibbon?
Upon receiving from EDWARD GIBBON *volume
II of the History of the Decline and Fall of the
Roman Empire [1781]. From Best's Literary
Memorials*

Thomas Jefferson
1743–1826

21   A lively and lasting sense of filial duty is more effectually impressed on the mind of a son or daugh-

ter by reading *King Lear,* than by all the dry volumes of ethics, and divinity, that ever were written.
Letter to Robert Skipwith [August 3, 1771]

1   The God who gave us life, gave us liberty at the same time.
Summary View of the Rights of British America [1774]

2   When, in the course of human events, it becomes necessary for one people to dissolve the political bands which have connected them with another, and to assume among the powers of the earth the separate and equal station to which the laws of nature and of nature's God entitle them, a decent respect to the opinions of mankind requires that they should declare the causes which impel them to the separation. We hold these truths to be self-evident; that all men are created equal; that they are endowed by their creator with certain unalienable[1] rights; that among these are life, liberty, and the pursuit of happiness; that to secure these rights, governments are instituted among men, deriving their just powers from the consent of the governed; that whenever any form of government becomes destructive of these ends, it is the right of the people to alter or to abolish it, and to institute new government, laying its foundation on such principles, and organizing its powers in such form, as to them shall seem most likely to effect their safety and happiness.
Declaration of Independence [July 4, 1776]

3   We must therefore . . . hold them [the British] as we hold the rest of mankind, enemies in war, in peace friends.   *Declaration of Independence*

4   And for the support of this declaration, with a firm reliance on the protection of divine providence, we mutually pledge to each other our lives, our fortunes, and our sacred honor.
Declaration of Independence

5   Ignorance is preferable to error; and he is less remote from the truth who believes nothing, than he who believes what is wrong.
Notes on the State of Virginia [1781–1785], query 6

6   The Newtonian principle of gravitation is now more firmly established, on the basis of reason, than it would be were the government to step in, and to make it an article of necessary faith. Reason and experiment have been indulged, and error has fled before them.   *Notes on the State of Virginia, 17*

7   Subject opinion to coercion: whom will you make your inquisitors? Fallible men; men governed by bad passions, by private as well as public reasons.
Notes on the State of Virginia, 17

8   Is uniformity [of opinion] attainable? Millions of innocent men, women, and children, since the introduction of Christianity, have been burnt, tortured, fined, imprisoned; yet we have not advanced one inch towards uniformity. What has been the effect of coercion? To make one half the world fools, and the other half hypocrites.
Notes on the State of Virginia, 17

9   Indeed, I tremble for my country when I reflect that God is just.
Notes on the State of Virginia, 18

10   Those who labor in the earth are the chosen people of God, if ever He had a chosen people, whose breasts He has made His peculiar deposit for substantial and genuine virtue.
Notes on the State of Virginia, 19

11   He who permits himself to tell a lie once, finds it much easier to do it a second and third time, till at length it becomes habitual; he tells lies without attending to it, and truths without the world's believing him. This falsehood of the tongue leads to that of the heart, and in time depraves all its good dispositions.   *Letter to Peter Carr [August 19, 1785]*

12   The basis of our government being the opinion of the people, the very first object should be to keep that right; and were it left to me to decide whether we should have a government without newspapers, or newspapers without a government, I should not hesitate a moment to prefer the latter.
Letter to Colonel Edward Carrington [January 16, 1787]

13   Experience declares that man is the only animal which devours his own kind; for I can apply no milder term to the governments of Europe, and to the general prey of the rich on the poor.
Letter to Colonel Edward Carrington [January 16, 1787]

14   I hold it, that a little rebellion, now and then, is a good thing, and as necessary in the political world as storms in the physical.
Letter to James Madison [January 30, 1787]

15   What country before ever existed a century and a half without a rebellion? . . . The tree of liberty must be refreshed from time to time with the blood of patriots and tyrants. It is its natural manure.
Letter to William Stevens Smith [November 13, 1787]

---

[1]Frequently quoted as "inalienable."
All men are born free and equal, and have certain natural, essential and unalienable rights. — *Constitution of Massachusetts* [1780]

1   The republican is the only form of government which is not eternally at open or secret war with the rights of mankind.
Letter to William Hunter [March 11, 1790]

2   We are not to expect to be translated from despotism to liberty in a featherbed.
Letter to Lafayette [April 2, 1790]

3   Let what will be said or done, preserve your *sangfroid* immovably, and to every obstacle, oppose patience, perseverance, and soothing language.
Letter to William Short [March 18, 1792]

4   Delay is preferable to error.
Letter to George Washington [May 16, 1792]

5   We confide in our strength, without boasting of it; we respect that of others, without fearing it.
Letter to William Carmichael and William Short [June 30, 1793]

6   The second office of the government is honorable and easy, the first is but a splendid misery.
Letter to Elbridge Gerry [May 13, 1797]

7   Offices are as acceptable here as elsewhere, and whenever a man has cast a longing eye on them, a rottenness begins in his conduct.
Letter to Tench Coxe [May 21, 1799]

8   I have sworn upon the altar of God, eternal hostility against every form of tyranny over the mind of man.
Letter to Dr. Benjamin Rush [September 23, 1800]

9   We are all Republicans—we are all Federalists. If there be any among us who would wish to dissolve this Union or to change its republican form, let them stand undisturbed as monuments of the safety with which error of opinion may be tolerated where reason is left free to combat it.
First Inaugural Address [March 4, 1801]

10   But would the honest patriot, in the full tide of successful experiment, abandon a government which has so far kept us free and firm, on the theoretic and visionary fear that this government, the world's best hope, may by possibility want energy to preserve itself?
First Inaugural Address

11   Sometimes it is said that man cannot be trusted with the government of himself. Can he, then, be trusted with the government of others? Or have we found angels in the forms of kings to govern him? Let history answer this question.
First Inaugural Address

12   Still one thing more, fellow citizens—a wise and frugal government, which shall restrain men from injuring one another, which shall leave them otherwise free to regulate their own pursuits of industry and improvement, and shall not take from the mouth of labor the bread it has earned. This is the sum of good government, and this is necessary to close the circle of our felicities.
First Inaugural Address

13   Equal and exact justice to all men, of whatever state or persuasion, religious or political; peace, commerce, and honest friendship with all nations, entangling alliances with none. . . . Freedom of religion; freedom of the press, and freedom of person under the protection of the *habeas corpus,* and trial by juries impartially selected. These principles form the bright constellation which has gone before us, and guided our steps through an age of revolution and reformation. The wisdom of our sages and the blood of our heroes have been devoted to their attainment. They should be the creed of our political faith, the text of civil instruction, the touchstone by which to try the services of those we trust; and should we wander from them in moments of error or alarm, let us hasten to retrace our steps and to regain the road which alone leads to peace, liberty, and safety.
First Inaugural Address

14   Whensoever hostile aggressions . . . require a resort to war, we must meet our duty and convince the world that we are just friends and brave enemies.
Letter to Andrew Jackson [December 3, 1806]

15   The care of human life and happiness, and not their destruction, is the first and only legitimate object of good government.
To the Republican Citizens of Washington County, Maryland [March 31, 1809]

16   Politics, like religion, hold up the torches of martyrdom to the reformers of error.
Letter to James Ogilvie [August 4, 1811]

17   But though an old man, I am but a young gardener.
Letter to Charles Willson Peale [August 20, 1811]

18   The earth belongs to the living, not to the dead.
Letter to John W. Eppes [June 24, 1813]

19   I agree with you that there is a natural aristocracy among men. The grounds of this are virtue and talents.
Letter to John Adams [October 28, 1813]

20   Merchants have no country. The mere spot they stand on does not constitute so strong an attachment as that from which they draw their gains.
Letter to Horatio G. Spafford [March 17, 1814]

1   I cannot live without books.
        Letter to John Adams [June 10, 1815]

2   If a nation expects to be ignorant and free, in a state of civilization, it expects what never was and never will be.
        Letter to Colonel Charles Yancey [January 6, 1816]

3   Enlighten the people generally, and tyranny and oppressions of body and mind will vanish like evil spirits at the dawn of day.
        Letter to Du Pont de Nemours [April 24, 1816]

4   I have the consolation to reflect that during the period of my administration not a drop of the blood of a single fellow citizen was shed by the sword of war or of the law.
        Letter to papal nuncio Count Dugnani [February 14, 1818]

5   But this momentous question [the Missouri Compromise], like a firebell in the night awakened and filled me with terror. I considered it the knell of the Union.
        Letter to John Holmes [April 22, 1820]

6   I know no safe depository of the ultimate powers of the society but the people themselves; and if we think them not enlightened enough to exercise their control with a wholesome discretion, the remedy is not to take it from them, but to inform their discretion.
        Letter to William Charles Jarvis [September 28, 1820]

7   We are not afraid to follow truth wherever it may lead, nor to tolerate any error so long as reason is left free to combat it.
        Letter to William Roscoe [December 27, 1820]

8   That one hundred and fifty lawyers should do business together ought not to be expected.
        Autobiography [January 6, 1821], on the United States Congress

9   And even should the cloud of barbarism and despotism again obscure the science and liberties of Europe, this country remains to preserve and restore light and liberty to them. In short, the flames kindled on the fourth of July, 1776, have spread over too much of the globe to be extinguished by the feeble engines of despotism; on the contrary, they will consume these engines and all who work them.
        Letter to John Adams [September 12, 1821]

10   Men by their constitutions are naturally divided into two parties: (1) Those who fear and distrust the people, and wish to draw all powers from them into the hands of the higher classes. (2) Those who identify themselves with the people, have confidence in them, cherish and consider them as the most honest and safe, although not the most wise depository of the public interests. In every country these two parties exist; and in every one where they are free to think, speak, and write, they will declare themselves.
        Letter to Henry Lee [August 10, 1824]

11   Never buy what you do not want, because it is cheap; it will be dear to you.
        A Decalogue of Canons for Observation in Practical Life [February 21, 1825]

12   When angry, count ten before you speak; if very angry, an hundred.
        A Decalogue of Canons for Observation in Practical Life

13   The good old Dominion, the blessed mother of us all.   *Thoughts on Lotteries [1826]*

14   This is the Fourth?
        Last words [July 4, 1826][1]

Antoine Laurent Lavoisier
1743–1794

15   It is impossible to dissociate language from science or science from language, because every natural science always involves three things: the sequence of phenomena on which the science is based; the abstract concepts which call these phenomena to mind; and the words in which the concepts are expressed. To call forth a concept a word is needed; to portray a phenomenon, a concept is needed. All three mirror one and the same reality.[2]
        Traité Elémentaire de Chimie [1789]

16   If, by the term *elements,* we mean to express the simple and indivisible molecules that compose bodies, it is probable that we know nothing about them; but if, on the contrary, we express by the term *elements* or *principles of bodies* the idea of the last point reached by analysis, all substances that we have not yet been able to decompose by any means are elements to us.[3]
        Traité Elémentaire de Chimie

---

[1] John Adams died the same day. See 352:4.
[2] Translated by J. Lipetz, D. E. Gershenson, and D. A. Greenberg.
[3] Translated by D. McKie.

William Paley
1743–1805

1   Who can refute a sneer?
Moral Philosophy [1785], vol. II, bk. V, ch. 9

The Letters of Junius[1]
1769–1771

2   One precedent creates another. They soon accumulate and constitute law. What yesterday was fact, today is doctrine.
Dedication to the English Nation

3   The liberty of the press is the palladium of all the civil, political, and religious rights of an Englishman.
Dedication to the English Nation

4   I believe there is yet a spirit of resistance in this country, which will not submit to be oppressed; but I am sure there is a fund of good sense in this country, which cannot be deceived.
No. 16, to the Printer of the Public Advertiser (H. S. Woodfall) [July 19, 1769]

5   We owe it to our ancestors to preserve entire those rights, which they have delivered to our care: we owe it to our posterity, not to suffer their dearest inheritance to be destroyed.
No. 20, to the Printer of the Public Advertiser [August 8, 1769]

6   When the constitution is openly invaded, when the first original right of the people, from which all laws derive their authority, is directly attacked, inferior grievances naturally lose their force, and are suffered to pass by without punishment or observation.
No. 30, to the Printer of the Public Advertiser [October 17, 1769]

7   There is a moment of difficulty and danger at which flattery and falsehood can no longer deceive, and simplicity itself can no longer be misled.
No. 35,[2] to the Printer of the Public Advertiser [December 19, 1769]

8   They [the Americans] equally detest the pageantry of a king, and the supercilious hypocrisy of a bishop.
No. 35,[2] to the Printer of the Public Advertiser [December 19, 1769]

9   The least considerable man among us has an interest equal to the proudest nobleman, in the law and constitution of his country, and is equally called upon to make a generous contribution in support of them—whether it be the heart to conceive, the understanding to direct, or the hand to execute.
No. 37, to the Printer of the Public Advertiser [March 19, 1770]

10   We lament the mistakes of a good man, and do not begin to detest him until he affects to renounce his principles.
No. 41, to Lord Mansfield [November 14, 1770]

11   The injustice done to an individual is sometimes of service to the public. Facts are apt to alarm us more than the most dangerous principles.
No. 41, to Lord Mansfield [November 14, 1770]

12   If individuals have no virtues, their vices may be of use to us.
No. 59, to the Printer of the Public Advertiser [October 5, 1771]

Constitution of the United States
1787

13   We the people of the United States, in order to form a more perfect Union, establish justice, insure domestic tranquillity, provide for the common defense, promote the general welfare, and secure the blessings of liberty to ourselves and our posterity do ordain and establish this Constitution for the United States of America.   *Preamble*

14   The President, Vice-President, and all civil officers of the United States, shall be removed from office on impeachment for, and conviction of, treason, bribery, or other high crimes and misdemeanors.
Article II, sec. 4

15   Treason against the United States, shall consist only in levying war against them, or in adhering to their enemies, giving them aid and comfort. No person shall be convicted of treason unless on the testimony of two witnesses to the same overt act, or on confession in open court.
Article III, sec. 3

16   This Constitution, and the laws of the United States, which shall be made in pursuance thereof; and all treaties made, or which shall be made, under the authority of the United States, shall be the Supreme Law of the land; and the judges in every State shall be bound thereby, any thing in the Constitution or laws of any State to the contrary notwithstanding.   *Article VI, sec. 2*

---

[1]Pseudonym of the author of a series of letters [1769–1771] in the London *Public Advertiser* (published in book form, 1772). They have been attributed to, among others, Sir Philip Francis, Lord Shelburne, Lord George Sackville, and Lord Temple.

[2]This letter is of great significance in the history of freedom of the press. The publisher was prosecuted for seditious libel, and the jury brought in a verdict of "guilty of printing and publishing only." After a second trial, Woodfall was freed on payment of costs.

1 Congress shall make no law respecting an establishment of religion, or prohibiting the free exercise thereof; or abridging the freedom of speech, or of the press; or the right of the people peaceably to assemble, and to petition the government for a redress of grievances.
First Amendment [1791][1]

2 A well-regulated militia, being necessary to the security of a free State, the right of the people to keep and bear arms, shall not be infringed.
Second Amendment [1791]

3 The right of the people to be secure . . . against unreasonable searches and seizures, shall not be violated, and no warrants shall issue, but upon probable cause. *Fourth Amendment [1791]*

4 Nor shall any person be subject for the same offense to be twice put in jeopardy of life or limb; nor shall be compelled in any criminal case to be a witness against himself, nor be deprived of life, liberty, or property, without due process of law.
Fifth Amendment [1791]

5 In all criminal prosecutions, the accused shall enjoy the right to a speedy and public trial, by an impartial jury of the State and district wherein the crime shall have been committed.
Sixth Amendment [1791]

6 The right of trial by jury shall be preserved.
Seventh Amendment [1791]

7 Excessive bail shall not be required, nor excessive fines imposed, nor cruel and unusual punishment inflicted.
Eighth Amendment [1791]

8 All persons born or naturalized in the United States, and subject to the jurisdiction thereof, are citizens of the United States and of the State wherein they reside. No State shall . . . abridge the privileges or immunities of citizens of the United States; nor shall any State deprive any person of life, liberty, or property, without due process of law; nor deny to any person within its jurisdiction the equal protection of the laws.
Fourteenth Amendment [1868], sec. 1

9 The right of citizens of the United States to vote shall not be denied or abridged . . . on account of race, color, or previous condition of servitude.
Fifteenth Amendment [1870], sec. 1

10 The right of citizens of the United States to vote shall not be denied or abridged . . . on account of sex. *Nineteenth Amendment [1920], sec. 1*

Abigail Adams[2]
1744–1818

11 In the new code of laws which I suppose it will be necessary for you to make I desire you would remember the ladies, and be more generous and favorable to them than your ancestors. Do not put such unlimited power into the hands of the husbands. Remember all men would be tyrants if they could. If particular care and attention is not paid to the ladies we are determined to foment a rebellion, and will not hold ourselves bound by any laws in which we have no voice, or representation.
Letter to John Adams [March 31, 1776]

12 Whilst you are proclaiming peace and good will to men, emancipating all nations, you insist upon retaining an absolute power over wives. But you must remember that arbitrary power is like most other things which are very hard, very liable to be broken — and notwithstanding all your wise laws and maxims we have it in our power not only to free ourselves but to subdue our masters, and without violence throw both your natural and legal authority at our feet.
Letter to John Adams [May 7, 1776]

13 Deliver me from your cold phlegmatic preachers, politicians, friends, lovers and husbands.
Letter to John Adams [August 5, 1776]

14 If we mean to have heroes, statesmen and philosophers, we should have learned women. . . . If much depends as is allowed upon the early education of youth and the first principles which are instilled take the deepest root, great benefit must arise from literary accomplishments in women.
Letter to John Adams [August 14, 1776]

15 It is really mortifying, sir, when a woman possessed of a common share of understanding considers the difference of education between the male and female sex, even in those families where education is attended to. . . . Nay why should your sex wish for such a disparity in those whom they one day intend for companions and associates. Pardon me, sir, if I cannot help sometimes suspecting that this neglect arises in some measure from an ungenerous jealousy of rivals near the throne.
Letter to John Thaxter [February 15, 1778]

16 I regret the trifling narrow contracted education of the females of my own country.
Letter to John Adams [June 30, 1778]

[2]Had she lived to the age of the Patriarchs . . . every day of her life would have been filled with clouds of goodness and love. — JOHN QUINCY ADAMS, *Memoirs, vol. IV, 157–158, 202*

[1]The first ten amendments are known as the Bill of Rights.

1   If we do not lay out ourselves in the service of mankind whom should we serve?
Letter to John Thaxter [September 29, 1778]

2   These are times in which a genius would wish to live. It is not in the still calm of life, or in the repose of a pacific station, that great characters are formed. . . . Great necessities call out great virtues.
Letter to John Quincy Adams [January 19, 1780]

3   A little of what you call frippery is very necessary towards looking like the rest of the world.
Letter to John Adams [May 1, 1780]

4   Learning is not attained by chance, it must be sought for with ardor and attended to with diligence.
Letter to John Quincy Adams [May 8, 1780]

5   Patriotism in the female sex is the most disinterested of all virtues. Excluded from honors and from offices, we cannot attach ourselves to the State or Government from having held a place of eminence. Even in the freest countries our property is subject to the control and disposal of our partners, to whom the laws have given a sovereign authority. Deprived of a voice in legislation, obliged to submit to those laws which are imposed upon us, is it not sufficient to make us indifferent to the public welfare? Yet all history and every age exhibit instances of patriotic virtue in the female sex; which considering our situation equals the most heroic of yours.
Letter to John Adams [June 17, 1782]

Rowland Hill
1744–1833

6   He did not see any reason why the devil should have all the good tunes.
Sermons. From E. W. BROOME, The Reverend Rowland Hill, p. 93

Jean Baptiste Lamarck
1744–1829

7   FIRST LAW. In every animal . . . a more frequent and continuous use of any organ gradually strengthens, develops and enlarges that organ . . . while the permanent disuse of any organ imperceptibly weakens and deteriorates it, and progressively diminishes its functional capacity, until it finally disappears.
SECOND LAW. All the acquisitions or losses wrought by nature in individuals . . . are preserved by reproduction to the new individuals which arise.
Philosophie Zoologique [1809],[1] pt. II, ch. 7

8   Habits form a second nature.[2]
Philosophie Zoologique, II, 7

Josiah Quincy
1744–1775

9   Blandishments will not fascinate us, nor wil threats of a "halter" intimidate. For, under God, we are determined that wheresoever, whensoever, o howsoever we shall be called to make our exit, we will die free men.
Observations on the Boston Port Bill [1774]

Charles Dibdin
1745–1814

10   Did you ever hear of Captain Wattle?
He was all for love, and a little for the bottle.
Captain Wattle and Miss Ro

11   Here, a sheer hulk, lies poor Tom Bowling,
The darling of our crew;
No more he'll hear the tempest howling,
For death has broach'd him to.   *Tom Bowling*

William Scott, Lord Stowell
1745–1836

12   A dinner lubricates business.
From BOSWELL, Life of Johnson [1791]

13   The elegant simplicity of the three per cents.
From CAMPBELL, Lives of the Lord Chancellors [1857], vol. X, ch. 212

Francisco José de Goya y Lucientes
1746–1828

14   The sleep of reason produces monsters [El sueñ de la razón produce monstruos].
Los Caprichos [1799]. Plate 43

---

[1]Translated by HUGH ELLIOT.

[2]Habit is a second nature and it destroys the first. — BLAIS PASCAL, *Pensées* [1670], *no. 376*

[3]Translated by HILDA HARRIS.
In plate 43 the artist rests, his head in his arms, on a desk in scribed with the Spanish line. Behind him hover monstrous owls bats, and a great cat. Goya's text for the plate:
Imagination abandoned by Reason produces impossible mon sters: united with her, she is the mother of the arts and the source of their wonders.

John Paul Jones
1747–1792

1   I wish to have no connection with any ship that does not sail *fast;* for I intend to go *in harm's way.*
Letter [November 16, 1778]

2   I have not yet begun to fight.
Attributed. Aboard the Bonhomme Richard [September 23, 1779]

François Alexandre Frédéric, Duc de La Rochefoucauld–Liancourt
1747–1827

3   *Louis XVI:* Is it a revolt?
La Rochefoucauld–Liancourt: No, Sire, it is a revolution.
Upon learning at Versailles of the fall of the Bastille [1789]

John O'Keeffe
1747–1833

4 Amo, amas,
I love a lass,
As a cedar tall and slender;
Sweet cowslip's grace
Is her nominative case,
And she's of the feminine gender!
The Agreeable Surprise [1783], act II, sc. ii. Song

5   You should always except the present company.
The London Hermit; or, Rambles in Dorsetshire [1793]

6   Fat, fair and forty[1] were all the toasts of the young men.
The Irish Mimic; or, Blunders at Brighton [1795]

Emmanuel Joseph Sieyès
1748–1836

7   I survived [J'ai vécu].
Upon being asked what he had done during the French Revolutionary Reign of Terror

---

[1] I am resolved to grow fat, and look young till forty! — JOHN DRYDEN, *Secret Love; or, The Maiden Queen* [1667], *act III, sc. i*

Charles James Fox
1749–1806

8   [On the fall of the Bastille:] How much the greatest event it is that ever happened in the world! and how much the best!
Letter to Richard Fitzpatrick [July 30, 1789]. From LORD JOHN RUSSELL, *Life and Times of C. J. Fox [1859–1866], vol. II, p. 361*

Johann Wolfgang von Goethe
1749–1832

9 There is strong shadow where there is much light.
Götz von Berlichingen [1773], act I

10 One lives but once in the world.
Clavigo [1774], act I, sc. i

11 If you inquire what the people are like here,
I must answer, "The same as everywhere!"
The Sorrows of Young Werther[2] *[1774–1787]. May 17*

12 Getting along with women,
Knocking around with men,
Having more credit than money,
Thus one goes through the world.
Claudine von Villa Bella [1776]

13 Noble be man,
Helpful and good!
For that alone
Sets him apart
From every other creature
On earth.   *The Divine [1783]*

14 I sing as the bird sings
That lives in the boughs.[3]
Wilhelm Meister's Apprenticeship [1786–1830], bk. II, ch. 11

15 Who ne'er his bread in sorrow ate,
Who ne'er the mournful midnight hours
Weeping upon his bed has sate,
He knows you not, ye Heavenly Powers.[4]
Wilhelm Meister's Apprenticeship, II, 13

16 Knowst thou the land where the lemon trees bloom,[5]
Where the gold orange glows in the deep thicket's gloom,

---

[2] See Thackeray, 490:18.

[3] Ich singe, wie der Vogel singt / Der in den Zweigen wohnet.

[4] Wer nie sein Brod mit Tränen ass, / Wer nie die kummervollen Nächte / Auf seinem Bette weinend sass, / Der kennt euch nicht, ihr himmlischen Mächte.
Translated by HENRY WADSWORTH LONGFELLOW as motto for book I of *Hyperion* [1839].

[5] Kennst du das Land, wo die Zitronen blühn?

Where a wind ever soft from the blue heaven
  blows,
And the groves are of laurel and myrtle and rose?
          Wilhelm Meister's Apprenticeship, III, 1

1 If I love you, what business is it of yours?
          Wilhelm Meister's Apprenticeship, IV, 9

2   One ought, every day at least, to hear a little
song, read a good poem, see a fine picture, and, if it
were possible, to speak a few reasonable words.
          Wilhelm Meister's Apprenticeship, V, 1

3   To know of someone here and there whom we
accord with, who is living on with us, even in silence—this makes our earthly ball a peopled garden.   *Wilhelm Meister's Apprenticeship, VII, 5*

4   Art is long, life short; judgment difficult, opportunity transient.
          Wilhelm Meister's Apprenticeship, VII, 9

5 Seeking with the soul the land of the Greeks.
          Iphigenia in Tauris [1787], act I, sc. i

6 A useless life is an early death.
          Iphigenia in Tauris, I, ii

7 One says a lot in vain, refusing;
The other mainly hears the "No."
          Iphigenia in Tauris, I, iii

8   Pleasure and love are the pinions of great deeds.
          Iphigenia in Tauris, II, i

9   Life teaches us to be less harsh with ourselves
and with others.   *Iphigenia in Tauris, IV, iv*

10   In art the best is good enough.[1]
          Italian Journey. March 3, 1787

11   A noble person attracts noble people, and knows
how to hold on to them.
          Torquato Tasso [1790], act I, sc. i

12   A talent is formed in stillness, a character in the
world's torrent.   *Torquato Tasso, I, ii*

13   We can't form our children on our own concepts; we must take them and love them as God
gives them to us.
          Hermann and Dorothea [1797]

14 The spirits that I summoned up
I now can't rid myself of.
          The Sorcerer's Apprentice [1797]

15   Three things are to be looked to in a building:
that it stand on the right spot; that it be securely
founded; that it be successfully executed.
          Elective Affinities[2] [1808], bk. I, ch. 9

16   The sum which two married people owe to one
another defies calculation. It is an infinite debt
which can only be discharged through all eternity.
          Elective Affinities, I, 9

17   One is never satisfied with a portrait of a person
that one knows.   *Elective Affinities, II, 2*

18   Time does not relinquish its rights, either over
human beings or over monuments.
          Elective Affinities, II, 2

19   The fate of the architect is the strangest of all.
How often he expends his whole soul, his whole
heart and passion, to produce buildings into which
he himself may never enter.
          Elective Affinities, II, 3

20   Let us live in as small a circle as we will, we are
either debtors or creditors before we have had time
to look round.   *Elective Affinities, II, 4*

21   No one would talk much in society, if he knew
how often he misunderstands others.
          Elective Affinities, II, 4

22   A teacher who can arouse a feeling for one single
good action, for one single good poem, accomplishes
more than he who fills our memory with rows on
rows of natural objects, classified with name and
form.   *Elective Affinities, II, 7*

23   One never goes so far as when one doesn't know
where one is going.
          *Letter to Karl Friedrich Zelter [December 3,
          1812]*

24 Who wants to understand the poem
Must go to the land of poetry;
Who wishes to understand the poet
Must go to the poet's land.
          Divan of East and West [1819], motto

25   For I have been a man, and that means to have
been a fighter.
          Divan of East and West. Book of Paradise

26   One must *be* something to be able to *do* something.
          *Conversation with Johann Peter Eckermann
          [October 20, 1828]*

27   If I work incessantly to the last, nature owes me
another form of existence when the present one col-
lapses.
          Letter to Eckermann [February 4, 1829]

28   I call architecture frozen music.[3]
          Letter to Eckermann [March 23, 1829]

---

[1]In der Kunst ist das Beste gut genug.

[2]Translated by JAMES ANTHONY FROUDE.

[3]Ich die Baukunst eine erstarrte Musik nenne.
    Since it [architecture] is music in space, as it were a frozen mu-
sic.—FRIEDRICH VON SCHELLING [1775–1854], *Philosophie der
Kunst, p. 576*

1 The artist may be well advised to keep his work to himself till it is completed, because no one can readily help him or advise him with it . . . but the scientist is wiser not to withhold a single finding or a single conjecture from publicity.
> *Essay on Experimentation*

2 Age does not make us childish, as they say.
It only finds us true children still.
> *Faust [1808–1832]. The First Part. Prelude on the Stage*

3 Man errs as long as he strives.[1]
> *Faust. The First Part. Prologue in Heaven*

4 And here, poor fool! with all my lore
I stand! no wiser than before.[2]
> *Faust. The First Part. Night, Faust in His Study*

5 Am I a god? I see so clearly!
> *Faust. The First Part. Night, Faust in His Study*

6 Two souls alas! dwell in my breast.
> *Faust. The First Part. Outside the Gate of the Town*

7 I am the Spirit that always denies![3]
> *Faust. The First Part. Faust's Study*

8 Dear friend, all theory is gray,
And green the golden tree of life.
> *Faust. The First Part. Mephistopheles and the Student*

9 Just trust yourself, then you will know how to live.
> *Faust. The First Part. Mephistopheles and the Student*

10 A true German can't stand the French,
Yet willingly he drinks their wines.
> *Faust. The First Part. Auerbach's Cellar*

11 He who maintains he's right—if his the gift of tongues—
Will have the last word certainly.[4]
> *Faust. The First Part. Faust and Gretchen. A Street*

12 My peace is gone,
My heart is heavy.[5]
> *Faust. The First Part. Gretchen's Room*

13 Fair I was also, and that was my ruin.[6]
> *Faust. The First Part. A Prison*

14 Law is mighty, mightier necessity.
> *Faust. The Second Part, act I, A Spacious Hall*

15 Once a man's thirty, he's already old,
He is indeed as good as dead.
It's best to kill him right away.
> *Faust. The Second Part, II, The Gothic Chamber*

16 What wise or stupid thing can man conceive
That was not thought of in ages long ago?
> *Faust. The Second Part, II, The Gothic Chamber*

17 I love those who yearn for the impossible.
> *Faust. The Second Part, II, Classical Walpurgis Night*

18 The deed is everything, the glory nothing.
> *Faust. The Second Part, IV, A High Mountain Range*

19 Of freedom and of life he only is deserving
Who every day must conquer them anew.[7]
> *Faust. The Second Part, V, Court of the Palace*

20 Who strives always to the utmost,
For him there is salvation.[8]
> *Faust. The Second Part, V, Mountain Gorges*

21 The Eternal Feminine draws us on.[9]
> *Faust. The Second Part, V, Heaven, last line*

22 Do you wish to roam farther and farther?
See! The Good lies so near.
Only learn to seize good fortune,
For good fortune's always here.   *Remembrance*

23 In limitations he first shows himself the master,
And the law can only bring us freedom.
> *What We Bring [1802]*

24 Create, artist! Do not talk!   *Saying*

25 O'er all the hilltops
Is quiet now,
In all the treetops
Hearest thou
Hardly a breath;
The birds are asleep in the trees:
Wait; soon like these
Thou too shalt rest.[10]   *Wanderer's Nightsong*

26 Individuality of expression is the beginning and end of all art.   *Proverbs in Prose*

---

[1] Es irrt der Mensch, so lang er strebt.

[2] Da stehe ich nun, ich armer Thor! / Und bin so klug als wie zuvor.
Translated by BAYARD TAYLOR.

[3] Ich bin der Geist der stets verneint.

[4] Translated by GEORGE MADISON PRIEST.

[5] Meine Ruh' ist hin, / Mein Herz ist schwer.

[6] Schön war ich auch, und das war mein Verderben.

[7] Nur der verdient sich Freiheit wie das Leben der täglich sie erobern muss.

[8] Wer immer strebend sich bemüht, / Den können wir erlösen.

[9] Das Ewig-Weibliche zieht uns hinan.

[10] Translated by LONGFELLOW.

1   Nothing is more damaging to a new truth than an old error.   *Proverbs in Prose*

2   Doubt grows with knowledge.   *Proverbs in Prose*

3   The greatest happiness for the thinking man is to have fathomed the fathomable, and to quietly revere the unfathomable.   *Proverbs in Prose*

4   First and last, what is demanded of genius is love of truth.   *Proverbs in Prose*

5   A man's manners are a mirror in which he shows his portrait.   *Proverbs in Prose*

6   All intelligent thoughts have already been thought; what is necessary is only to try to think them again.[1]   *Proverbs in Prose*

7   Nothing is more terrible than ignorance in action.[1]   *Proverbs in Prose*

8   Of all peoples the Greeks have dreamt the dream of life best.[2]   *Proverbs in Prose*

9   Everything that emancipates the spirit without giving us control over ourselves is harmful.   *Proverbs in Prose*

10   America, you have it better than our continent, the old one.[3]   *Almanac for the Muses [1831]*

11   Without haste, but without rest.   *Motto*

12   More light![4]   *Last words*

Pierre Simon de Laplace
1749–1827

13   Given for one instant an intelligence which could comprehend all the forces by which nature is animated and the respective positions of the beings which compose it, if moreover this intelligence were vast enough to submit these data to analysis, it would embrace in the same formula both the movements of the largest bodies in the universe and those of the lightest atom; to it nothing would be uncertain, and the future as the past would be present to its eyes.
     Oeuvres, vol. VII, Théorie Analytique des Probabilités [1812–1820], introduction

14   The theory of probabilities is at bottom nothing but common sense reduced to calculus.
     Oeuvres, VII, Théorie Analytique des Probabilités, introduction

15   Sire, I have no need of that hypothesis.[5]
     From ERIC TEMPLE BELL, *Men of Mathematics* [1937]

Honoré Gabriel Riqueti, Comte de Mirabeau
1749–1791

16   Go and tell those who have sent you that we are here by the will of the nation and that we shall not leave save at the point of bayonets.
     Speech in the States-General [June 23, 1789]

John Philpot Curran
1750–1817

17   The condition upon which God hath given liberty to man is eternal vigilance;[6] which condition if he break, servitude is at once the consequence of his crime and the punishment of his guilt.
     Speech upon the Right of Election of the Lord Mayor of Dublin [July 10, 1790]

James Madison
1751–1836

18   By a faction, understand a number of citizens, whether amounting to a majority or minority of the whole, who are united and actuated by some common impulse of passion, or of interest, adverse to the rights of other citizens, or to the permanent and aggregate interests of the community.
     The Federalist [1787], no. 10

19   A zeal for different opinions concerning religion, concerning government, and many other points, as well of speculation as of practice; an attachment to different leaders ambitiously contending for preeminence and power; or to persons of other descriptions whose fortunes have been interesting to the human passions, have, in turn, divided mankind into parties, inflamed them with mutual animosity, and rendered them much more disposed to vex and oppress each other than to cooperate for their com-

---

[1]Translated by NORBERT GUTERMAN.

[2]Translated by BAILEY SAUNDERS.

[3]Amerika, du hast es besser—als unser Kontinent, das alte.

[4]Someday perhaps the inner light will shine forth from us, and then we shall need no other light.—*Elective Affinities, pt. II, ch. 3*

[5]Reply to Napoleon Bonaparte's remark upon receiving a copy of Laplace's *Mécanique Céleste:* You have written this huge book on the system of the world without once mentioning the author of the universe.

[6]Attributed also to JEFFERSON.
Commonly quoted: Eternal vigilance is the price of liberty.
There is one safeguard known generally to the wise, which is an advantage and security to all, but especially to democracies as against despots. What is it? Distrust.—DEMOSTHENES, *Philippic 2, sec. 24*

mon good. . . . But the most common and durable source of factions has been the various and unequal distribution of property.   *The Federalist, no. 10*

1   To secure the public good, and private rights, against the danger of . . . faction, and at the same time to preserve the spirit and form of popular government, is then the great object to which our inquiries are directed.   *The Federalist, no. 10*

2   I believe there are more instances of the abridgment of the freedom of the people by gradual and silent encroachments of those in power than by violent and sudden usurpations.
    Speech in the Virginia Convention [June 16, 1788]

Richard Brinsley Sheridan
1751–1816

3   *Mrs. Malaprop:* Illiterate him, I say, quite from your memory.   *The Rivals [1775], act I, sc. ii*

4   'Tis safest in matrimony to begin with a little aversion.   *The Rivals, I, ii*

5   A progeny of learning.   *The Rivals, I, ii*

6   Never say more than is necessary.
    The Rivals, II, i

7   I know you are laughing in your sleeve.
    The Rivals, II, i

8   He is the very pineapple of politeness!
    The Rivals, III, iii

9   If I reprehend anything in this world, it is the use of my oracular tongue, and a nice derangement of epitaphs!   *The Rivals, III, iii*

10   As headstrong as an allegory on the banks of the Nile.   *The Rivals, III, iii*

11   Too civil by half.   *The Rivals, III, iv*

12   Our ancestors are very good kind of folks; but they are the last people I should choose to have a visiting acquaintance with.   *The Rivals, IV, i*

13   No caparisons, miss, if you please. Caparisons don't become a young woman.
    The Rivals, IV, ii

14   You are not like Cerberus, three gentlemen at once, are you?   *The Rivals, IV, ii*

15   The quarrel is a very pretty quarrel as it stands; we should only spoil it by trying to explain it.
    The Rivals, IV, iii

16   My valor is certainly going! — it is sneaking off! I feel it oozing out, as it were, at the palm of my hands!   *The Rivals, V, iii*

17   I own the soft impeachment.
    The Rivals, V, iii

18   Through all the drama — whether damned or not —
Love gilds the scene, and women guide the plot.
    The Rivals, epilogue

19   An apothecary should never be out of spirits.
    St. Patrick's Day [1775], act I, sc. i

20   Death's a debt; his mandamus binds all alike — no bail, no demurrer.   *St. Patrick's Day, II, iv*

21   I ne'er could any luster see
In eyes that would not look on me.
    The Duenna [1775], act I, sc. ii

22   I loved him for himself alone.
    The Duenna, I, iii

23   I was struck all on a heap.
    The Duenna, II, ii

24   A bumper of good liquor
Will end a contest quicker
Than justice, judge, or vicar.
    The Duenna, II, iii

25   Conscience has no more to do with gallantry than it has with politics.   *The Duenna, II, iv*

26   Tale-bearers are as bad as the tale-makers.
    The School for Scandal [1777], act I, sc. i

27   You shall see them on a beautiful quarto page, where a neat rivulet of text shall meander through a meadow of margin.   *The School for Scandal, I, i*

28   You had no taste when you married me.
    The School for Scandal, I, ii

29   Here's to the maiden of bashful fifteen;
Here's to the widow of fifty;
Here's to the flaunting, extravagant quean,
And here's to the housewife that's thrifty.
        Let the toast pass —
        Drink to the lass;
I'll warrant she'll prove an excuse for the glass.
    The School for Scandal, III, iii

30   An unforgiving eye, and a damned disinheriting countenance.   *The School for Scandal, IV, i*

31   Be just before you're generous.
    The School for Scandal, IV, i

32   There is not a passion so strongly rooted in the human heart as envy.
    The Critic [1779], act I, sc. i

33   The newspapers! Sir, they are the most villainous — licentious — abominable — infernal — Not that I ever read them — no — I make it a rule never to look into a newspaper.   *The Critic, I, i*

1   Egad, I think the interpreter is the hardest to be understood of the two!

The Critic, I, ii

2   A practitioner in panegyric, or, to speak more plainly, a professor of the art of puffing.

The Critic, I, ii

3   The number of those who undergo the fatigue of judging for themselves is very small indeed.

The Critic, I, ii

4   Certainly nothing is unnatural that is not physically impossible.   *The Critic, II, i*

5   I wish, sir, you would practice this without me. I can't stay dying here all night.

The Critic, III, i

6   You write with ease to show your breeding,
But easy writing's curst hard reading.

Clio's Protest [1819]

7   An oyster may be crossed in love.[1]

Clio's Protest

8   The right honorable gentleman is indebted to his memory for his jests, and to his imagination for his facts.

Sheridaniana. Speech in Reply to Mr. Dundas

Johann Heinrich Voss
1751–1826

9   Who does not love wine, women, and song
Remains a fool his whole life long.[2]

Attributed

Thomas Chatterton[3]
1752–1770

10   Mie love ys dedde,
Gon to hys death-bedde,
Al under the wyllowe-tree.   *Mynstrelles Songe[4]*

1From the interpolated tragedy, *The Spanish Armada*.

2Wer nicht liebt Wein, Weib und Gesang, / Der bleibt ein Narr sein Leben lang.

The couplet has also been attributed to Luther, apparently on no better authority than an eighteenth-century jingle in which "Luther" is needed to rhyme with "Futter."

3See William Wordsworth, 392:9.

4This is from the poems of "Thomas Rowley," an imaginary fifteenth-century Bristol poet invented by Chatterton. Editions of the poems appeared in 1778 and 1782, and were exposed [1777–1778] by Thomas Tyrwhitt.

Philip Freneau
1752–1832

11   Then rushed to meet the insulting foe;
They took the spear—but left the shield.[5]

To the Memory of the Brave Americans Who Fell at Eutaw Springs, S.C., September 8, 1781 [1786], st. 5

12   O come the time, and haste the day,
When man shall man no longer crush,
When Reason shall enforce her sway,
Nor these fair regions raise our blush,
Where still the African complains,
And mourns his yet unbroken chains.

On the Emigration to America and Peopling the Western Country [1786]

13   An age employed in edging steel
Can no poetic raptures feel . . .
No shaded stream, no quiet grove
Can this fantastic century move.

Poems [1795]. To an Author, st. 6

Friedrich Maximilian von Klinger
1752–1831

14   Sturm und Drang [Storm and Stress].

Title of play [1776]

Leonard MacNally
1752–1820

15   On Richmond Hill there lives a lass
More bright than Mayday morn;
Whose charms all other maids' surpass—
A rose without a thorn.

The Lass of Richmond Hill,[6] st.

Joseph de Maistre
1753–1821

16   Every nation has the government it deserves.

Letter to X [1811]

17   The sword of justice has no scabbard.

Les Soirées de Saint-Pétersbourg [1821]. Premier Entretien

5When Prussia hurried to the field, / And snatched the spear, but left the shield. —SIR WALTER SCOTT, *Marmion* [1808], *canto II. introduction*

6Also attributed to JAMES UPTON [1670–1749] and W. HUDSON

Antoine de Rivarol
1753–1801

1 What is not clear is not French.
Discours sur l'Universalité de la Langue Française [1784]

Joel Barlow
1754–1812

2 My morning incense, and my evening meal—
The sweets of Hasty Pudding.
The Hasty Pudding [1792], canto I

George Crabbe
1754–1832

3 Habit with him was all the test of truth,
"It must be right: I've done it from my youth."
The Borough [1810]. Letter 3, The Vicar

4 In idle wishes fools supinely stay;
Be there a will, and wisdom finds a way.
The Birth of Flattery [1807]

5 Cut and came again.
Tales [1812]. VII, The Widow's Tale

6 The ring, so worn as you behold,
So thin, so pale, is yet of gold.
His Mother's Wedding Ring

William Drennan
1754–1820

7 Nor one feeling of vengeance presume to defile
The cause, or the men, of the Emerald Isle.[1]
Erin [1795], st. 3

Jeanne Manon Phlipon Roland de la Platière [Madame Roland]
1754–1793

8 O liberty! O liberty! What crimes are committed in thy name!
Last words, before her death on the guillotine. From LAMARTINE, Histoire des Girondins [1847]

Charles Maurice de Talleyrand-Périgord
1754–1838

9 Black as the devil,
Hot as hell,
Pure as an angel,
Sweet as love.[2]
Recipe for coffee

10 [Of the Bourbons:] They have learned nothing, and forgotten nothing.[3]
From CHEVALIER DE PANAT, letter to Mallet du Pan [January 1796]

11 [Of the battle of Borodino, 1812:] It is the beginning of the end.[4]
From EDOUARD FOURNIER, L'Esprit dans l'Histoire [1857]

12 The United States has thirty-two religions but only one dish.
Attributed

13 Women sometimes forgive a man who forces the opportunity, but never a man who misses one.
Attributed

14 [To a young diplomat:] Don't be eager![5]
From CHARLES AUGUSTIN SAINTE-BEUVE, Portraits de Femmes [1858]. Madame de Staël

15 War is much too serious a matter to be entrusted to the military.[6]
Attributed. Quoted by Briand to Lloyd George during World War I. Also attributed to Clemenceau

Benjamin Waterhouse
1754–1846

16 Tobacco is a filthy weed,
That from the devil does proceed;
It drains your purse, it burns your clothes,
And makes a chimney of your nose.
From OLIVER WENDELL HOLMES [1809–1894], who was vaccinated by Dr. Waterhouse

---

[1]The first known use of this term for Ireland.

[2]Noir comme le diable, / Chaud comme l'enfer, / Pur comme un ange, / Doux comme l'amour.
This appears as an inscription on many old coffeepots.

[3]Ils n'ont rien appris, ni rien oublié.

[4]Voilà le commencement de la fin.

[5]Pas de zèle!

[6]La guerre! C'est une chose trop grave pour la confier à des militaires. Sometimes quoted as: War is much too serious to leave to the generals.

Bertrand Barère de Vieuzac
1755–1841

1   The tree of liberty only grows when watered by the blood of tyrants.
Speech in the National Convention [January 16, 1793]

2   It is only the dead who do not return.
Speech [1794]

Anthelme Brillat-Savarin
1755–1826

3   Animals feed themselves, men eat; but only wise men know the art of eating.
La Physiologie du Goût (The Physiology of Taste) [1825].[1] Aphorisms

4   Tell me what you eat, and I shall tell you what you are.   *La Physiologie du Goût. Aphorisms*

5   The discovery of a new dish does more for human happiness than the discovery of a star.
La Physiologie du Goût. Aphorisms

Nathan Hale
1755–1776

6   I only regret that I have but one life to lose for my country.
Last words, before being hanged by the British as a spy [September 22, 1776]

Alexander Hamilton
1755–1804

7   A national debt, if it is not excessive, will be to us a national blessing.[2]
Letter to Robert Morris [April 30, 1781]

8   I believe the British government forms the best model the world ever produced. . . . This government has for its object public strength and individual security.
Debates of the Federal Convention [May 14–September 17, 1787].[3] June 18, 1787

9   All communities divide themselves into the few and the many. The first are the rich and wellborn, the other the mass of the people. . . . The people are turbulent and changing; they seldom judge or determine right. Give therefore to the first class a distinct, permanent share in the government. They will check the unsteadiness of the second, and as they cannot receive any advantage by a change, they therefore will ever maintain good government.
Debates of the Federal Convention. June 18, 1787

10   We are now forming a republican government. Real liberty is neither found in despotism or the extremes of democracy, but in moderate governments.
Debates of the Federal Convention. June 26, 1787

11   Let Americans disdain to be the instruments of European greatness. Let the thirteen States, bound together in a strict and indissoluble Union, concur in erecting one great American system, superior to the control of all transatlantic force or influence and able to dictate the terms of the connection between the old and the new world!
The Federalist [1787–1788], no. 1

12   Government implies the power of making laws. It is essential to the idea of a law, that it be attended with a sanction; or, in other words, a penalty or punishment for disobedience.
The Federalist, 1

13   Why has government been instituted at all? Because the passions of men will not conform to the dictates of reason and justice, without constraint.
The Federalist, 1

14   Every power vested in a government is in its nature sovereign, and includes by force of the term a right to employ all the means requisite . . . to the attainment of the ends of such power.
Opinion on the Constitutionality of the Bank [February 23, 1791]

15   If the end be clearly comprehended within any of the specified powers, and if the measure have an obvious relation to that end, and is not forbidden by any particular provision of the Constitution, it may safely be deemed to come within the compass of the national authority.
Opinion on the Constitutionality of the Bank.

Louis XVIII
1755–1824

16   Punctuality is the politeness of kings.[4]
A favorite saying

---

[1]Translated by M. F. K. FISHER.

[2]At the time we were funding our national debt, we heard much about "a public debt being a public blessing." —THOMAS JEFFERSON, *Letter to John W. Epps* [November 6, 1813]

[3]At which the Constitution was written.

[4]L'exactitude est la politesse des rois.

John Marshall
1755–1835

1 It is emphatically the province and duty of the judicial department to say what the law is. . . . If two laws conflict with each other, the courts must decide on the operation of each. . . . This is of the very essence of judicial duty.
> *Marbury v. Madison, 1 Cranch 1317 [1803]*

2 We must never forget that it is a *constitution* we are expounding.
> *McCulloch v. Maryland, 4 Wheaton 316, 407 [1819]*

3 This provision is made in a constitution, intended to endure for ages to come, and consequently, to be adapted to the various *crises* of human affairs.
> *McCulloch v. Maryland, 4 Wheaton 316, 415*

4 Let the end be legitimate, let it be within the scope of the constitution, and all means which are appropriate, which are plainly adapted to that end, which are not prohibited, but consistent with the letter and spirit of the constitution, are constitutional.
> *McCulloch v. Maryland, 4 Wheaton 316, 421*

5 The power to tax involves the power to destroy.
> *McCulloch v. Maryland, 4 Wheaton 316, 431*

6 The people made the Constitution, and the people can unmake it. It is the creature of their own will, and lives only by their will.
> *Cohens v. Virginia, 6 Wheaton (19 U.S.) 264, 389 [1821]*

Martin Joseph Routh
1755–1854

7 You will find it a very good practice always to verify your references, sir.
> *From J. W. Burgon, Memoir of Dr. Routh, Quarterly Review [July 1878]*

Henry [Light-Horse Harry] Lee
1756–1818

8 To the memory of the Man, first in war, first in peace, and first in the hearts of his countrymen.
> *Eulogy on the death of Washington [December 1799][1]*

---

[1]Based on resolutions presented to the House of Representatives a week earlier. In the resolutions, the statement ends with "fellow-citizens."

William Blake
1757–1827

9 How sweet I roam'd from field to field,
And tasted all the summer's pride,
Till I the prince of love beheld,
Who in the sunny beams did glide!
> *Poetical Sketches [1783]. Song (How Sweet I Roamed), st. 1*

10 He loves to sit and hear me sing,
Then, laughing, sports and plays with me;
Then stretches out my golden wing,
And mocks my loss of liberty.
> *Poetical Sketches. Song (How Sweet I Roamed), st. 4*

11 Like a fiend in a cloud,
With howling woe,
After night I do crowd,
And with night will go.
> *Poetical Sketches. Mad Song, st. 3*

12 The languid strings do scarcely move!
The sound is forced, the notes are few!
> *Poetical Sketches. To the Muses, st. 4*

13 Piping down the valleys wild,
Piping songs of pleasant glee,
On a cloud I saw a child,
And he laughing said to me:

"Pipe a song about a Lamb."
So I piped with merry cheer;
"Piper, pipe that song again."
So I piped; he wept to hear.
> *Songs of Innocence [1789–1790]. Introduction, st. 1, 2*

14 And I made a rural pen,
And I stain'd the water clear,
And I wrote my happy songs
Every child may joy to hear.
> *Songs of Innocence. Introduction, st. 5*

15 Little Lamb, who made thee?
Dost thou know who made thee?
Gave thee life and bid thee feed
By the stream and o'er the mead;
Gave thee clothing of delight,
Softest clothing, woolly, bright.
> *Songs of Innocence. The Lamb, st. 1*

16 Little Lamb, I'll tell thee,
Little Lamb, I'll tell thee:
He is called by thy name,
For he calls himself a Lamb.
He is meek and he is mild;
He became a little child.
I a child, and thou a lamb,
We are called by his name.

Little Lamb, God bless thee!
Little Lamb, God bless thee!
> *Songs of Innocence. The Lamb, st. 2*

1 My mother bore me in the southern wild,
And I am black, but O! my soul is white;
White as an angel is the English child,
But I am black as if bereav'd of light.
> *Songs of Innocence. The Little Black Boy, st. 1*

2 And we are put on earth a little space,
That we may learn to bear the beams of love,
And these black bodies and this sunburnt face
Is but a cloud, and like a shady grove.
> *Songs of Innocence. The Little Black Boy, st. 4*

3 I'll shade him from the heat till he can bear
To lean in joy upon our Father's knee;
And then I'll stand and stroke his silver hair,
And be like him and he will then love me.
> *Songs of Innocence. The Little Black Boy, st. 7*

4 When my mother died I was very young,
And my father sold me while yet my tongue
Could scarcely cry 'weep! 'weep! 'weep! 'weep!
So your chimneys I sweep, and in soot I sleep.
> *Songs of Innocence. The Chimney*
> *Sweeper, st. 1*

5 To Mercy, Pity, Peace, and Love
All pray in their distress;
And to these virtues of delight
Return their thankfulness.
> *Songs of Innocence. The Divine*
> *Image, st. 1*

6 For Mercy has a human heart,
Pity, a human face,
And Love, the human form divine,
And Peace, the human dress.
> *Songs of Innocence. The Divine*
> *Image, st. 3*

7 And all must love the human form,
In heathen, turk, or jew;
Where Mercy, Love, & Pity dwell
There God is dwelling too.
> *Songs of Innocence. The Divine*
> *Image, st. 5*

8 The moon like a flower
In heaven's high bower,
With silent delight,
Sits and smiles on the night.
> *Songs of Innocence. Night, st. 1*

9 And there the lion's ruddy eyes
Shall flow with tears of gold,
And pitying the tender cries,
And walking round the fold,
Saying: "Wrath by his meekness,

And by his health, sickness,
Is driven away
From our immortal day."
> *Songs of Innocence. Night, st. 5*

10 When the voices of children are heard on the green
And laughing is heard on the hill,
My heart is at rest within my breast
And everything else is still.
> *Songs of Innocence. Nurse's Song, st. 1*

11 Can I see another's woe,
And not be in sorrow too?
Can I see another's grief,
And not seek for kind relief?
> *Songs of Innocence. On Another's Sorrow, st. 1*

12 Does the Eagle know what is in the pit?
Or wilt thou go ask the Mole?
Can Wisdom be put in a silver rod?
Or Love in a golden bowl?
> *The Book of Thel [1789–1792]. Thel's Motto*

13   The reason Milton wrote in fetters when he wrote
of Angels and God, and at liberty when of Devils
and Hell, is because he was a true poet and of the
Devil's party without knowing it.
> *The Marriage of Heaven and Hell*
> *[1790–1793]. Note to The Voice of the Devil*

14 The road of excess leads to the palace of wisdom.
> *The Marriage of Heaven and Hell. Proverbs of*
> *Hell, l. 3.*

15 Eternity is in love with the production of time.
> *The Marriage of Heaven and Hell. Proverbs of*
> *Hell, l. 10*

16 No bird soars too high, if he soars with his own wings.
> *The Marriage of Heaven and Hell. Proverbs of*
> *Hell, l. 15*

17 The pride of the peacock is the glory of God.
The lust of the goat is the bounty of God.
The wrath of the lion is the wisdom of God.
The nakedness of woman is the work of God.
> *The Marriage of Heaven and Hell. Proverbs of*
> *Hell, l. 22*

18 The cistern contains: the fountain overflows.
> *The Marriage of Heaven and Hell. Proverbs of*
> *Hell, l. 35*

19 Think in the morning. Act in the noon. Eat in the
evening. Sleep in the night.
> *The Marriage of Heaven and Hell. Proverbs of*
> *Hell, l. 41*

20 The tygers of wrath are wiser than the horses of instruction.
> *The Marriage of Heaven and Hell. Proverbs of*
> *Hell, l. 44*

1 You never know what is enough unless you know
what is more than enough.
*The Marriage of Heaven and Hell. Proverbs of
Hell, l. 46*

2 Improvement makes straight roads; but the
crooked roads without improvement are roads
of genius.
*The Marriage of Heaven and Hell. Proverbs of
Hell, l. 66*

3 Sooner murder an infant in its cradle than nurse
unacted desires.
*The Marriage of Heaven and Hell. Proverbs of
Hell, l. 67*

4 Truth can never be told so as to be understood,
and not be believ'd.
*The Marriage of Heaven and Hell. Proverbs of
Hell, l. 69*

5 Enough! or too much.
*The Marriage of Heaven and Hell. Proverbs of
Hell, l. 70*

6 One Law for the Lion & Ox is Oppression.
*The Marriage of Heaven and Hell. A
Memorable Fancy*

7 For every thing that lives is Holy.
*The Marriage of Heaven and Hell. A Song
of Liberty*

8 Never seek to tell thy love
Love that never told can be;
For the gentle wind does move
Silently, invisibly.

I told my love, I told my love,
I told her all my heart;
Trembling, cold, in ghastly fears—
Ah, she doth depart.

Soon as she was gone from me
A traveler came by
Silently, invisibly—
Oh, was no deny.
*Poems [written c. 1791–1792] from Blake's
Notebook. Never Seek to Tell*

9 I ask'd a thief to steal me a peach:
He turned up his eyes.
I ask'd a lithe lady to lie her down:
Holy and meek, she cries.

As soon as I went
An angel came.
He wink'd at the thief
And smil'd at the dame—

And without one word said
Had a peach from the tree,

And still as a maid
Enjoy'd the lady.
*Poems [c. 1791–1792] from Blake's Notebook.
I Asked a Thief*

10 Love to faults is always blind,
Always is to joy inclin'd,
Lawless, wing'd, and unconfin'd,
And breaks all chains from every mind.
*Poems [c. 1791–1792] from Blake's Notebook.
Love to Faults*

11 Abstinence sows sand all over
The ruddy limbs and flaming hair,
But Desire gratified
Plants fruits of life and beauty there.
*Poems [c. 1791–1792] from Blake's Notebook.
Abstinence Sows Sand*

12 If you trap the moment before it's ripe,
The tears of repentance you'll certainly wipe;
But if once you let the ripe moment go
You can never wipe off the tears of woe.
*Poems [c. 1791–1792] from Blake's Notebook.
If You Trap the Moment*

13 He who binds to himself a joy
Does the winged life destroy;
But he who kisses the joy as it flies
Lives in eternity's sunrise.
*Poems [c. 1791–1792] from Blake's Notebook.
Several Questions Answered, no. 1, He Who
Binds*

14 The look of love alarms
Because 'tis fill'd with fire;
But the look of soft deceit
Shall win the lover's hire.
*Poems [c. 1791–1792] from Blake's Notebook.
Several Questions Answered, 2, The Look of
Love*

15 What is it men in women do require?
The lineaments of Gratified Desire.
What is it women do in men require?
The lineaments of Gratified Desire.
*Poems [c. 1791–1792] from Blake's Notebook.
Several Questions Answered, 4, What Is It*

16 Hear the voice of the Bard!
Who Present, Past, and Future sees,
Whose ears have heard
The Holy Word
That walk'd among the ancient trees.
*Songs of Experience [1794].
Introduction, st. 1*

17 Turn away no more.
Why wilt thou turn away?
The starry floor,

The wat'ry shore
Is giv'n thee till the break of day.
Songs of Experience. Introduction, st. 4

1 Love seeketh not itself to please,
Nor for itself hath any care,
But for another gives its ease,
And builds a Heaven in Hell's despair.
*Songs of Experience. The Clod and the Pebble,
st. 1*

2 Love seeketh only self to please,
To bind another to its delight,
Joys in another's loss of ease,
And builds a Hell in Heaven's despite.
*Songs of Experience. The Clod and the Pebble,
st. 3*

3 O Rose, thou art sick.
The invisible worm
That flies in the night,
In the howling storm,

Has found out thy bed
Of crimson joy,
And his dark secret love
Does thy life destroy.
Songs of Experience. The Sick Rose

4 Little Fly,
Thy summer's play
My thoughtless hand
Has brushed away.

Am not I
A fly like thee?
Or art not thou
A man like me?

For I dance
And drink and sing,
Till some blind hand
Shall brush my wing.
Songs of Experience. The Fly, st. 1–3

5 Tyger! Tyger! burning bright
In the forests of the night,
What immortal hand or eye
Could frame thy fearful symmetry?

In what distant deeps or skies
Burnt the fire of thine eyes?
On what wings dare he aspire?
What the hand dare seize the fire?
Songs of Experience. The Tyger, st. 1, 2

6 What the hammer? what the chain?
In what furnace was thy brain?
What the anvil? what dread grasp
Dare its deadly terrors clasp?

When the stars threw down their spears
And water'd heaven with their tears,

Did he smile his work to see?
Did he who made the Lamb make thee?
Songs of Experience. The Tyger, st. 4,

7 In every cry of every man,
In every infant's cry of fear,
In every voice, in every ban,
The mind-forg'd manacles I hear.
Songs of Experience. London, st.

8 But most through midnight streets I hear
How the youthful harlot's curse
Blasts the newborn infant's tear
And blights with plagues the marriage hearse.
Songs of Experience. London, st.

9 Pity would be no more,
If we did not make somebody poor;
And Mercy no more could be,
If all were as happy as we.
*Songs of Experience. The Human Abstract,
st. 1*

10 My mother groan'd! my father wept.
Into the dangerous world I leapt:
Helpless, naked, piping loud,
Like a fiend hid in a cloud.
Songs of Experience. Infant Sorrow, st.

11 I was angry with my friend;
I told my wrath, my wrath did end.
I was angry with my foe;
I told it not, my wrath did grow.
Songs of Experience. A Poison Tree, st.

12 Cruelty has a human heart,
And Jealousy a human face;
Terror, the human form divine,
And Secrecy, the human dress.
A Divine Image,[1] st.

13 Degrade first the arts if you'd mankind degrade,
Hire idiots to paint with cold light and hot shade.
*Annotations [c. 1798–1809] to Sir Joshua
Reynolds's Discourses,[2] title page*

14　To generalize is to be an idiot. To particularize
the alone distinction of merit—general knowledge
are those knowledges that idiots possess.
*Annotations to Sir Joshua Reynolds's
Discourses, pp. xcvii–xcviii*

15 My specter around me night and day
Like a wild beast guards my way.

---

[1]This poem was written and etched by Blake [1790–1791] as
"Song of Experience" linked with *The Divine Image* in *Songs of Innocence* (see 372:5, 372:6, and 372:7), but in the published *Song
of Experience* it was replaced by *The Human Abstract* (374:9).

[2]Volume I of Reynolds's *Works*, edited by EDMOND MALON
[second edition, 1798].

My emanation far within
Weeps incessantly for my sin.
> *Poems [written c. 1804] from Blake's*
> *Notebook. My Specter, st. 1*

1 And throughout all eternity
I forgive you, you forgive me.
> *Poems [c. 1804] from Blake's Notebook. My*
> *Specter, st. 14*

2 Mock on, mock on, Voltaire, Rousseau.
Mock on, mock on—'tis all in vain!
You throw the sand against the wind,
And the wind blows it back again.
> *Poems [c. 1804] from Blake's Notebook. Mock*
> *On, st. 1*

3 There is a smile of love,
And there is a smile of deceit,
And there is a smile of smiles
In which these two smiles meet.
> *Poems from the Pickering Manuscript*
> *[c. 1805]. The Smile, st. 1*

4 For a tear is an intellectual thing,
And a sigh is the sword of an Angel King,
And the bitter groan of the martyr's woe
Is an arrow from the Almighty's bow.
> *Poems from the Pickering Manuscript. The*
> *Gray Monk, st. 8*

5 To see a world in a grain of sand
And a heaven in a wild flower,
Hold infinity in the palm of your hand
And eternity in an hour.
> *Poems from the Pickering Manuscript.*
> *Auguries of Innocence, l. 1*

6 A robin redbreast in a cage
Puts all Heaven in a rage.
> *Poems from the Pickering Manuscript.*
> *Auguries of Innocence, l. 5*

7 A dog starv'd at his master's gate
Predicts the ruin of the state.
> *Poems from the Pickering Manuscript.*
> *Auguries of Innocence, l. 9*

8 He who shall hurt the little wren
Shall never be belov'd by men.
> *Poems from the Pickering Manuscript.*
> *Auguries of Innocence, l. 29*

9 A truth that's told with bad intent
Beats all the lies you can invent.
> *Poems from the Pickering Manuscript.*
> *Auguries of Innocence, l. 53*

10 Man was made for joy and woe,
And when this we rightly know
Through the world we safely go.
> *Poems from the Pickering Manuscript.*
> *Auguries of Innocence, l. 56*

11 He who shall teach the child to doubt
The rotting grave shall ne'er get out.
> *Poems from the Pickering Manuscript.*
> *Auguries of Innocence, l. 87*

12 The Questioner, who sits so sly,
Shall never know how to Reply.
> *Poems from the Pickering Manuscript.*
> *Auguries of Innocence, l. 93*

13 The strongest poison ever known
Came from Caesar's laurel crown.
> *Poems from the Pickering Manuscript.*
> *Auguries of Innocence, l. 97*

14 He who doubts from what he sees
Will ne'er believe, do what you please.
If the sun and moon should doubt
They'd immediately go out.
> *Poems from the Pickering Manuscript.*
> *Auguries of Innocence, l. 107*

15 The harlot's cry from street to street
Shall weave old England's winding sheet.
> *Poems from the Pickering Manuscript.*
> *Auguries of Innocence, l. 115*

16 God Appears and God is Light
To those poor Souls who dwell in Night,
But does a Human Form Display
To those who Dwell in Realms of day.
> *Poems from the Pickering Manuscript.*
> *Auguries of Innocence, l. 129*

17 And did those feet in ancient time
Walk upon England's mountains green?
And was the holy Lamb of God
On England's pleasant pastures seen?

And did the Countenance Divine
Shine forth upon our clouded hills?
And was Jerusalem builded here
Among these dark Satanic mills?

Bring me my bow of burning gold,
Bring me my arrows of desire,
Bring me my spear—O clouds, unfold!
Bring me my chariot of fire!

I will not cease from mental fight,
Nor shall my sword sleep in my hand,
Till we have built Jerusalem
In England's green and pleasant land.
> *Milton [c. 1809], prefatory poem*

18 Great things are done when men and mountains
meet;
This is not done by jostling in the street.
> *Poems [written c. 1807–1809] from*
> *Blake's Notebook. Great Things*
> *Are Done*

1 If you have form'd a circle to go into,
Go into it yourself and see how you would do.
*Poems [c. 1807–1809] from Blake's Notebook.
To God*

2 The Angel that presided o'er my birth
Said, "Little creature, formed of joy and mirth,
Go love without the help of any thing on earth."
*Poems [c. 1807–1809] from Blake's Notebook.
The Angel That Presided*

3 Grown old in love from seven till seven times
seven,
I oft have wish'd for Hell for ease from Heaven.
*Poems [c. 1807–1809] from Blake's Notebook.
Grown Old in Love*

4   Poetry fettered fetters the human race. Nations
are destroyed, or flourish, in proportion as their poetry, painting, and music are destroyed or flourish!
*Jerusalem [c. 1818–1820]. To the Public,
plate 1*

5 He who would do good to another must do it in
minute particulars;
General good is the plea of the scoundrel,
hypocrite, and flatterer:
For art and science cannot exist but in minutely
organized particulars.
Jerusalem, ch. 3, plate 55, l. 60

6 England! awake! awake! awake!
Jerusalem thy sister calls!
Why wilt thou sleep the sleep of death
And close her from thy ancient walls?
*Jerusalem, 4, prefatory poem,
plate 77, st. 1*

7 The vision of Christ that thou dost see
Is my vision's greatest enemy.
*The Everlasting Gospel [written c. 1818], sec.
4, l. 1*

8 Both read the Bible day and night,
But thou read'st black where I read white.
The Everlasting Gospel, 4, l. 13

9 This life's dim windows of the soul
Distorts the heavens from pole to pole
And leads you to believe a lie
When you see with, not through, the eye.[1]
The Everlasting Gospel, 5, l. 101

10 I am sure this Jesus will not do
Either for Englishman or Jew.
The Everlasting Gospel, 8

James Gillray
c. 1757–1815

11   The Old Lady of Threadneedle Street.[2]
Title of cartoon [1797

John Philip Kemble
1757–1823

12 Perhaps it was right to dissemble your love,
But—why did you kick me down stairs?
The Panel, act I, sc. ?

Fisher Ames
1758–1808

13   A monarchy is a merchantman which sails well,
but will sometimes strike on a rock, and go to the
bottom; a republic is a raft which will never sink,
but then your feet are always in the water.
Speech in the House of Representatives [1795]

John Heath
1758–1810

14   Love of wisdom [philosophy] the guide of life.[3]
*Greek phrase for Phi Beta Kappa, society
founded at the College of William and Mary
[December 5, 1776]*

James Monroe
1758–1831

15   National honor is national property of the highest value.
First Inaugural Address [March 4, 1817]

16   The American continents . . . are henceforth not
to be considered as subjects for future colonization
by any European powers.
*Annual Message to Congress [December 2,
1823]. The Monroe Doctrine*

17   In the wars of the European powers in matters
relating to themselves we have never taken any part,
nor does it comport with our policy so to do.
*Annual Message to Congress. The Monroe
Doctrine*

---

[1]We are led to believe a lie / When we see not through the
eye.—WILLIAM BLAKE, *Auguries of Innocence, l. 125*

[2]The Bank of England.

[3]Philosophia biou kybernetes. The name Phi Beta Kappa is from
the Greek initial letters in the phrase.

1   We owe it, therefore, to candor, and to the amicable relations existing between the United States and those powers to declare that we should consider any attempt on their part to extend their system to any portion of this hemisphere as dangerous to our peace and safety. With the existing colonies or dependencies of any European power we . . . shall not interfere. But with the governments . . . whose independence we have . . . acknowledged, we could not view any interposition for the purpose of oppressing them, or controlling, in any other manner, their destiny, by any European power, in any other light than as a manifestation of an unfriendly disposition toward the United States.

Annual Message to Congress. The Monroe Doctrine

Horatio Nelson, Viscount Nelson
1758–1805

2   Westminster Abbey, or victory!

At the battle of Cape St. Vincent [February 14, 1797]. From ROBERT SOUTHEY, *Life of Nelson [1813], ch. 4*

3   I have only one eye, I have a right to be blind sometimes. . . . I really do not see the signal.

At the battle of Copenhagen [1801]. From ROBERT SOUTHEY, *Life of Nelson, 9*

4   Something must be left to chance; nothing is sure in a sea fight beyond all others.

Memorandum to the fleet, off Cadiz [October 9, 1805]

5   But, in case signals can neither be seen or perfectly understood, no captain can do very wrong if he places his ship alongside that of the enemy.

Memorandum to the fleet, off Cadiz

6   England expects every man will do his duty.[1]

At the battle of Trafalgar [October 21, 1805]. From ROBERT SOUTHEY, *Life of Nelson [1813], ch. 9*

7   Thank God, I have done my duty.

At the battle of Trafalgar. From ROBERT SOUTHEY, *Life of Nelson, 9*

8   Kiss me, Hardy.

At the battle of Trafalgar. From ROBERT SOUTHEY, *Life of Nelson, 9*

---

[1]This famous sentence is thus first reported: Say to the fleet, England confides that every man will do his duty. Captain Pasco, Nelson's flag lieutenant, suggested substituting "expects" for "confides," which was adopted. Captain Blackwood, who commanded the *Euryalus*, says that the correction suggested was from "Nelson expects" to "England expects."

Red Jacket [Sagoyewatha][2]
c. 1758–1830

9   We first knew you a feeble plant which wanted a little earth whereon to grow. We gave it to you; and afterward, when we could have trod you under our feet, we watered and protected you; and now you have grown to be a mighty tree, whose top reaches the clouds, and whose branches overspread the whole land, whilst we, who were the tall pine of the forest, have become a feeble plant and need your protection.

Statement [c. 1792]

Robert Burns
1759–1796

10 Wee, sleekit, cow'rin, tim'rous beastie,
  O, what a panic's in thy breastie!
  Thou need na start awa sae hasty,
    Wi' bickering brattle!

To a Mouse [1785], st. 1

11 I'm truly sorry man's dominion
  Has broken Nature's social union.

To a Mouse, st. 2

12 The best laid schemes o' mice and men
  Gang aft a-gley.   *To a Mouse, st. 7*

13   Nature's law,
  That man was made to mourn.

Man Was Made to Mourn [1786], st. 4

14 Man's inhumanity to man.
  Makes countless thousands mourn!

Man Was Made to Mourn, st. 7

15 He wales a portion with judicious care;
  And "Let us worship God" he says, with solemn air.

The Cotter's Saturday Night [1786], st. 12

16 From scenes like these, old Scotia's grandeur
    springs,
  That makes her loved at home, revered abroad:
  Princes and lords are but the breath of kings,
  "An honest man's the noblest work of God."

The Cotter's Saturday Night, st. 19

17 Gie me ae spark o' Nature's fire,
  That's a' the learning I desire.

First Epistle to J. Lapraik [1786], st. 13

18 The social, friendly, honest man,
  Whate'er he be,

---

[2]Seneca chief.

'Tis he fulfills great Nature's plan,
And none but he!
Second Epistle to J. Lapraik [1786], st. 15

1 On ev'ry hand it will allow'd be,
He's just—nae better than he should be.
A Dedication to Gavin Hamilton [1786]

2 It's hardly in a body's pow'r,
To keep, at times, frae being sour.
Epistle to Davie [1786], st. 2

3 Misled by fancy's meteor ray,
By passion driven;
But yet the light that led astray
Was light from heaven.
The Vision [1786], II, st. 18

4 His locked, lettered, braw brass collar
Showed him the gentleman an' scholar.
The Twa Dogs [1786], st. 3

5 An' there began a lang digression
About the lords o' the creation.
The Twa Dogs, st. 6

6 Oh wad some power the giftie gie us
To see oursels as ithers see us!
It wad frae monie a blunder free us,
An' foolish notion.   *To a Louse [1786], st. 8*

7 Wee, modest, crimson-tipped flow'r,
Thou's met me in an evil hour;
For I maun crush amang the stoure
Thy slender stem:
To spare thee now is past my pow'r,
Thou bonie gem.
To a Mountain Daisy [1786], st. 1

8 Stern Ruin's plowshare drives elate,
Full on thy bloom.   *To a Mountain Daisy, st. 9*

9 Perhaps it may turn out a sang,
Perhaps turn out a sermon.
Epistle to a Young Friend [1786], st. 1

10 I waive the quantum o' the sin,
The hazard of concealing:
But, och! it hardens a' within,
And petrifies the feeling!
Epistle to a Young Friend, st. 6

11 An atheist-laugh's a poor exchange
For Deity offended.
Epistle to a Young Friend, st. 9

12 There's nought but care on ev'ry han',
In every hour that passes, O:
What signifies the life o' man,
An' 't were nae for the lasses, O.
Green Grow the Rashes, O [1787], st. 1

13 Auld Nature swears, the lovely dears
Her noblest work she classes, O:

Her prentice han' she tried on man,
An' then she made the lasses, O.
Green Grow the Rashes, O, st.

14 Green grow the rashes, O;
Green grow the rashes, O;
The sweetest hours that e'er I spend
Are spent among the lasses, O.
Green Grow the Rashes, O, chor

15 I wasna fou, but just had plenty.
Death and Dr. Hornbook [1787], st.

16 John Barleycorn got up again,
And sore surprised them all.
John Barleycorn [1787], st.

17 The heart benevolent and kind
The most resembles God.
A Winter Night [1787

18 Then gently scan your brother man,
Still gentler sister woman;
Tho' they may gang a kennin wrang,
To step aside is human.
Address to the Unco Guid [1787], st.

19 O, my Luve is like a red, red rose,
That's newly sprung in June.
O, my Luve is like the melodie,
That's sweetly played in tune.
*Johnson's Musical Museum [1787–1796]. A
Red, Red Rose, st. 1*

20 Contented wi' little and cantie wi' mair.
*Johnson's Musical Museum. Contented wi'
Little, st. 1*

21 Ye banks and braes o' bonny Doon,
How can ye bloom sae fresh and fair?
How can ye chant, ye little birds,
And I sae weary fu' o' care!
Thou'll break my heart, thou warbling bird,
That wantons thro' the flowering thorn!
Thou minds me o' departed joys,
Departed never to return.
*Johnson's Musical Museum. The Banks o'
Doon, st. 1*

22 Chords that vibrate sweetest pleasure
Thrill the deepest notes of woe.
*Johnson's Musical Museum. Sensibility How
Charming, st. 4*

23 Ae fond kiss, and then we sever;
Ae farewell and then forever!
Johnson's Musical Museum. Ae Fond Kiss, st. 1

24 But to see her was to love her,
Love but her, and love forever.
Had we never lov'd sae kindly,
Had we never lov'd sae blindly,

Never met—or never parted—
We had ne'er been brokenhearted.
Johnson's Musical Museum. Ae Fond
Kiss, st. 2

1 It was a' for our rightfu' King
We left fair Scotland's strand.
Johnson's Musical Museum. It Was A' for Our
Rightfu' King, st. 1

2 Now a' is done that men can do,
And a' is done in vain.
Johnson's Musical Museum. It Was A' for Our
Rightfu' King, st. 2

3 He turn'd him right and round about
Upon the Irish shore;
And gae his bridle reins a shake,
With adieu forevermore,
    My dear—
And adieu forevermore!
Johnson's Musical Museum. It Was A' for Our
Rightfu' King, st. 3

4 John Anderson my jo, John,
When we were first acquent,
Your locks were like the raven,
Your bonie brow was brent;
But now your brow is beld, John,
Your locks are like the snaw,
But blessings on your frosty pow,
John Anderson my jo!
Johnson's Musical Museum. John Anderson My
Jo, st. 1

5 Farewell to the Highlands, farewell to the North,
The birthplace of valor, the country of worth!
Wherever I wander, wherever I rove,
The hills of the Highlands for ever I love.
Johnson's Musical Museum. My Heart's in the
Highlands, st. 1

6 My heart's in the Highlands, my heart is not here,
My heart's in the Highlands a-chasing the deer;
A-chasing the wild deer, and following the roe,
My heart's in the Highlands wherever I go.
Johnson's Musical Museum. My Heart's in the
Highlands, chorus

7 O whistle, and I'll come to you, my lad:
Tho' father and mither and a' should gae mad.
Whistle, and I'll Come to You, My Lad

8 Should auld acquaintance be forgot,
And never brought to min'?
Should auld acquaintance be forgot,
And days o' auld lang syne?
Auld Lang Syne [1788], st. 1

9 For auld lang syne, my dear,
For auld lang syne,

We'll tak a cup o' kindness yet
For auld lang syne!   *Auld Lang Syne, chorus*

10 Flow gently, sweet Afton, among thy green braes,
Flow gently, I'll sing thee a song in thy praise.
My Mary's asleep by thy murmuring stream,
Flow gently, sweet Afton, disturb not her dream.
Afton Water [1789], st. 1

11 This day Time winds th' exhausted chain,
To run the twelvemonth's length again.
New Year's Day [1791], st. 1

12 The voice of Nature loudly cries,
And many a message from the skies,
That something in us never dies.
New Year's Day, st. 3

13 When Nature her great masterpiece design'd,
And fram'd her last, best work, the human mind,
Her eye intent on all the mazy plan,
She form'd of various stuff the various Man.
To Robert Graham [1791], st. 1

14 Whare sits our sulky, sullen dame,
Gathering her brows like gathering storm,
Nursing her wrath to keep it warm.
Tam o' Shanter [1791], l. 10

15 Ah, gentle dames! it gars me greet
To think how monie counsels sweet,
How monie lengthened, sage advices,
The husband frae the wife despises.
Tam o' Shanter, l. 33

16 His ancient, trusty, drouthy crony;
Tam lo'ed him like a vera brither—
They had been fou for weeks thegither.
Tam o' Shanter, l. 43

17 Kings may be blest, but Tam was glorious,
O'er a' the ills o' life victorious.
Tam o' Shanter, l. 57

18 But pleasures are like poppies spread—
You seize the flow'r, its bloom is shed;
Or like the snow falls in the river—
A moment white—then melts forever.
Tam o' Shanter, l. 59

19 Inspiring bold John Barleycorn!
What dangers thou canst make us scorn!
Wi' tippenny, we fear nae evil;
Wi' usquebae, we'll face the devil!
Tam o' Shanter, l. 105

20 As Tammie glow'red, amazed, and curious,
The mirth and fun grew fast and furious.
Tam o' Shanter, l. 143

21 Her cutty sark, o' Paisley harn,
That while a lassie she had worn,

In longitude tho' sorely scanty,
It was her best, and she was vauntie.
Tam o' Shanter, l. 171

1 "Weel done, Cutty Sark!"[1]
Tam o' Shanter, l. 189

2 Ah, Tam! Ah! Tam! Thou'll get thy fairin!
In hell they'll roast you like a herrin!
Tam o' Shanter, l. 201

3 She is a winsome wee thing,
She is a handsome wee thing,
She is a lo'esome wee thing,
    This sweet wee wife o' mine.
My Wife's a Winsome Wee Thing [1792],
chorus

4 The golden hours on angel wings
Flew o'er me and my dearie;
For dear to me as light and life
Was my sweet Highland Mary.
Highland Mary [1792], st. 2

5 But, oh! fell death's untimely frost,
That nipt my flower sae early.
Highland Mary, st. 3

6 If there's a hole in a' your coats,
I rede you tent it;
A chield's amang you takin' notes,
And faith he'll prent it.
On the Late Captain Grose's Peregrinations
Thro' Scotland [1793], st. 1

7 Some hae meat and canna eat,
And some wad eat that want it;
But we hae meat, and we can eat,
And sae the Lord be thankit.
The Selkirk Grace [1793] (attributed)

8 O Mary, at thy window be!
It is the wish'd, the trysted hour.
Mary Morison [1793], st. 1

9 The lovely Mary Morison!   *Mary Morison, st. 1*

10 Scots wha hae wi' Wallace bled,
Scots wham Bruce has aften led,
Welcome to your gory bed
    Or to victorie.

Now's the day, and now's the hour;
See the front o' battle lour!
See approach proud Edward's power—
    Chains and slaverie!
Scots Wha Hae [1794], st. 1, 2

11 Lay the proud usurpers low!
Tyrants fall in every foe!
Liberty's in every blow!
Let us do or die!
Scots Wha Hae, st.

12 The rank is but the guinea's stamp,
The man's the gowd for a' that.
For A' That and A' That [1795], st.

13 A prince can mak a belted knight,
A marquis, duke, and a' that;
But an honest man's aboon his might,
Guid faith, he mauna fa' that.
For A' That and A' That, st.

14 For a' that and a' that,
It's coming yet, for a' that,
That man to man the world o'er
Shall brothers be for a' that.
For A' That and A' That, st.

15 For a' that, and a' that,
An' twice as muckle 's a' that,
I've lost but ane, I've twa behin',
I've wife eneugh for a' that.
Posthumous Pieces [1799]. The Jolly Beggars,
chorus

16 God knows, I'm no the thing I should be,
Nor am I even the thing I could be.
Posthumous Pieces. To the Reverend John
M'Math, st. 8

17 If there's another world, he lives in bliss;
If there is none, he made the best of this.
Posthumous Pieces. Epitaph on
William Muir

18 In durance vile here must I wake and weep,
And all my frowsy couch in sorrow steep.
Posthumous Pieces. Epistle from Esopus to
Maria

19 It's guid to be merry and wise,
It's guid to be honest and true,
It's guid to support Caledonia's cause
And bide by the buff and the blue.
Posthumous Pieces. Here's a Health to Them
That's Awa', st. 1

Georges Jacques Danton
1759–1794

20   Everything belongs to the fatherland when the
fatherland is in danger.
Speech to the Legislative Assembly [August 28,
1792]

---

[1]The famous tea clipper *Cutty Sark*, designed by Hercules Linton and built in 1869, had the story of Tam o' Shanter carved upon her bow and counter. Nannie, with flying locks and scanty shift, was the figurehead.

1. Audacity, more audacity, always audacity.[1]
   Speech to the Legislative Assembly [September 2, 1792]

2. Show my head to the people, it is worth seeing.
   Last words, addressed to the executioner

Joseph Fouché
1759–1820

3. Death is an eternal sleep.
   Inscription placed by his orders on cemetery gates [1794]

William Pitt
1759–1806

4. Necessity is the plea for every infringement of human freedom. It is the argument of tyrants; it is the creed of slaves.
   Speech in the House of Commons [November 18, 1783]

Johann [Christoph] Friedrich von Schiller
1759–1805

5. I feel an army in my fist.
   The Robbers [1781], act II, end

6. The joke loses everything when the joker laughs himself.
   The Conspiracy of Fiesco [1783], act I, sc. vii

7. Did you think the lion was sleeping because he didn't roar?   *The Conspiracy of Fiesco, I, xviii*

8. Joy, thou spark from Heav'n immortal,
   Daughter of Elysium!
   Drunk with fire, toward Heaven advancing
   Goddess, to thy shrine we come.
   Thy sweet magic brings together
   What stern Custom spreads afar;
   All men become brothers
   Where thy happy wing-beats are.[2]
   Ode to Joy [1785], st. 1

9. There are three lessons I would write,
   Three words as with a burning pen,
   In tracings of eternal light
   Upon the hearts of men.
   Hope, Faith, and Love [c. 1786], st. 1

10. World history is the world's court.[3]
    Resignation [1786]

11. What one refuses in a minute
    No eternity will return.   *Resignation*

12. O who knows what slumbers in the background of the times?   *Don Carlos [1787], act I, sc. i*

13. O the idea was childish, but divinely beautiful.
    Don Carlos, I, ii

14. Great souls suffer in silence.   *Don Carlos, I, iv*

15. The richest monarch in the Christian world;
    The sun in my own dominions never sets.[4]
    Don Carlos, I, vi

16. If you want to know yourself,
    Just look how others do it;
    If you want to understand others,
    Look into your own heart.
    Tabulae Votivae [1797]

17. Posterity weaves no garlands for imitators.
    Wallenstein's Camp [1798], prologue

18. He who has done his best for his own time has lived for all times.
    Wallenstein's Camp, prologue

19. Life is earnest, art is gay.
    Wallenstein's Camp, prologue

20. Whatever is not forbidden is permitted.
    Wallenstein's Camp, sc. vi

21. Man is made of ordinary things, and habit is his nurse.
    The Death of Wallenstein [1798], act I, sc. iv

22. Many a crown shines spotless now
    That yet was deeply sullied in the winning.[5]
    The Death of Wallenstein, II, ii

23. There's no such thing as chance;
    And what to us seems merest accident
    Springs from the deepest source of destiny.[5]
    The Death of Wallenstein, II, iii

---

[3]Die Weltgeschichte ist das Weltgericht.

[4]Why should the brave Spanish soldier brag the sun never sets in the Spanish dominions, but ever shineth on one part or other we have conquered for our king?— JOHN SMITH [1580–1631], *Advertisements for the Unexperienced, etc.* [1631]

It may be said of them [the Hollanders] as of the Spaniards, that the sun never sets on their dominions. — THOMAS GAGE [d. 1656], *New Survey of the West Indies* [1648], *Epistle Dedicatory*

The sun never sets on the immense empire of Charles V. — SIR WALTER SCOTT, *Life of Napoleon* [1827]

His Majesty's dominions, on which the sun never sets. — JOHN WILSON [CHRISTOPHER NORTH, 1785–1854], *Noctes Ambrosianae, no. 20* [April 1829]

[5]Translated by SAMUEL TAYLOR COLERIDGE.

---

[1]Il nous faut de l'audace, encore de l'audace, toujours de l'audace.

[2]Alle Menschen werden Brüder, / Wo dein sanfter Flügel weilt.
Translated by THEODORE SPENCER (adapted).
Music by LUDWIG VAN BEETHOVEN.

1   Time is man's angel.
The Death of Wallenstein, V, xi

2   What is the short meaning of the long speech?
The Piccolomini [1799], act I, sc. ii

3   War nourishes war.[1]   *The Piccolomini, I, ii*

4   In thy breast are the stars of thy fate.
The Piccolomini, II, vi

5   You say it as you understand it.
The Piccolomini, II, vi

6   When the wine goes in, strange things come out.
The Piccolomini, II, xii

7 O tender yearning, sweet hoping!
The golden time of first love!
The eye sees the open heaven,
The heart is intoxicated with bliss;
O that the beautiful time of young love
Could remain green forever.
The Song of the Bell [1799]

8 Appearance should never attain reality,
And if nature conquers, then must art retire.
To Goethe, when he put Voltaire's Mahomet on the stage [1800]

9 Life is only error,
And death is knowledge.   *Cassandra [1802]*

10 I am better than my reputation.
Mary Stuart [1801], act III, sc. iv

11 For this should the singer accompany the king:
Both dwell on the heights of mankind.
The Maid of Orleans [1801], act I, sc. ii

12 Against stupidity the very gods
Themselves contend in vain.[2]
The Maid of Orleans, III, vi

13 Pain is short, and joy is eternal.
The Maid of Orleans, last lines

14 On the mountains there is freedom!
The world is perfect everywhere,
Save where man comes with his torment.
The Bride of Messina [1803], act IV, sc. vii

15 The mountain cannot frighten one who was born
on it.   *Wilhelm Tell [1804], act III, sc. i*

16 Who reflects too much will accomplish little.
Wilhelm Tell, III, i

17 You saw his weakness, and he will never forgive
you.   *Wilhelm Tell, III, i*

18 This feat of Tell, the archer, will be told
While yonder mountains stand upon their base.

---

[1]Der Krieg ernährt den Krieg.

[2]Against boredom even the gods themselves struggle in vain. —
Friedrich Nietzsche, *The Antichrist* [1888], 48

By heaven! The apple's cleft right through the core.
Wilhelm Tell, III, i

Mary Wollstonecraft [Godwin]
1759–1797

19   Nothing, I am sure, calls forth the faculties
much as the being obliged to struggle with th
world.
Thoughts on the Education of Daughters [1787]. Matrimony

20   No man chooses evil because it is evil; he on
mistakes it for happiness, the good he seeks.
A Vindication of the Rights of Men [1790

21   Virtue can only flourish amongst equals.
A Vindication of the Rights of Me

22   Till women are more rationally educated, the pro
ress in human virtue and improvement in know
edge must receive continual checks.
*A Vindication of the Rights of Woman [1792
ch. 3*

23   If women be educated for dependence; that i
to act according to the will of another fallible bein
and submit, right or wrong, to power, where are w
to stop?
A Vindication of the Rights of Woman,

24   How can a rational being be ennobled by an
thing that is not obtained by its own exertions?
A Vindication of the Rights of Woman,

25   Women are systematically degraded by receivir
the trivial attentions which men think it manly
pay to the sex, when, in fact, men are insulting
supporting their own superiority.
A Vindication of the Rights of Woman,

26   It would be an endless task to trace the variety
meannesses, cares, and sorrows into which wom
are plunged by the prevailing opinion that the
were created rather to feel than reason, and that
the power they obtain must be obtained by the
charms and weakness.
A Vindication of the Rights of Woman,

27   It is justice, not charity, that is wanting in th
world.
A Vindication of the Rights of Woman,

28   Women ought to have representatives, instead
being arbitrarily governed without any direct sha
allowed them in the deliberations of government.
A Vindication of the Rights of Woman,

29   Till society is very differently constituted, pa
ents, I fear, will still insist on being obeyed becau
they will be obeyed, and constantly endeavor to se

tle that power on a divine right which will not bear the investigation of reason.
A Vindication of the Rights of Woman, 11

1   Every political good carried to the extreme must be productive of evil.
The French Revolution [1794], bk. V, ch. 4

2   Executions, far from being useful examples to the survivors, have, I am persuaded, a quite contrary effect, by hardening the heart they ought to terrify. Besides, the fear of an ignominious death, I believe, never deterred anyone from the commission of a crime, because in committing it the mind is roused to activity about present circumstances.
Letters Written During a Short Residence in Sweden, Norway, and Denmark [1796], letter 19

3   The same energy of character which renders a man a daring villain would have rendered him useful to society, had that society been well organized.
Letters Written During a Short Residence in Sweden, Norway, and Denmark, 19

4   We reason deeply, when we forcibly feel.
Letters Written During a Short Residence in Sweden, Norway, and Denmark, 19

5   It is the preservation of the species, not of individuals, which appears to be the design of Deity throughout the whole of nature.
Letters Written During a Short Residence in Sweden, Norway, and Denmark, 22

François Noël Babeuf [Gracchus]
1760–1797

6   Let the revolting distinction of rich and poor disappear once and for all, the distinction of great and small, of masters and valets, of governors and governed. Let there be no other difference between human beings than those of age and sex. Since all have the same needs and the same faculties, let there be one education for all, one food for all.
Manifesto of the Equals [c. 1795]

7   We aim at something more sublime and more equitable — the common good, or the community of goods. . . . We demand, we would have, the communal enjoyment of the fruits of the earth, fruits which are for everyone.
Manifesto of the Equals

[Claude] Joseph Rouget de Lisle
1760–1836

8 Allons, enfants de la patrie,
Le jour de gloire est arrivé! . . .

Aux armes, citoyens!
Formez vos bataillons!
Marchons! Marchons! Qu'un sang impur
Abreuve nos sillons!   *The Marseillaise [1792]*[1]

Antoine [Jacques Claude Joseph] Boulay de la Meurthe
1761–1840

9   It is worse than a crime, it is a blunder [C'est pire qu'un crime, c'est une faute].[2]
On the execution of the Duc d'Enghien [1804]

August Friedrich Ferdinand von Kotzebue
1761–1819

10 There is another and a better world.
The Stranger [1798], act I, sc. i

William Lisle Bowles
1762–1850

11 The cause of Freedom is the cause of God!
The Right Honorable Edmund Burke [1791], l. 78

George Colman the Younger
1762–1836

12   Tell 'em Queen Anne's dead.[3]
The Heir-at-Law [1797], act I, sc. i

13   Not to be sneezed at.   *The Heir-at-Law, II, i*

14 When taken,
To be well shaken.
Broad Grins [1802]. The Newcastle Apothecary

15   John Bull;[4] or, The Englishman's Fireside.
Title of play [1803]

16   His heart runs away with his head.
Who Wants a Guinea? [1805], act I, sc. i

---

[1]Forward, sons of France, the day of glory has come! . . . To arms, citizens! Line up in battalions! Let us march on! And let the impure blood [of our enemies] drench our fields.

Composed in the garrison at Strasbourg and originally called *Chant de guerre de l'armée du Rhin*, the *Marseillaise* took its name from the patriots of Marseilles, who first made it known in Paris.

[2]Attributed also to TALLEYRAND and FOUCHÉ. Sainte-Beuve attributed it to BOULAY DE LA MEURTHE.

[3]The phrase became proverbial for telling what everybody knows.

[4]The origin of the supposed type of the British character.

1   O Miss Bailey!
Unfortunate Miss Bailey!
Love Laughs at Locksmiths [1806], act II, song

2 Says he, "I am a handsome man, but I'm a gay
    deceiver."
Love Laughs at Locksmiths, II, song

Dorothea Jordan
1762–1816

3 "Oh where, and Oh! where is your Highland
    laddie gone?"
"He's gone to fight the French, for King George
    upon the throne,
And it's Oh! in my heart, how I wish him safe at
    home!"   *The Blue Bells of Scotland*

Johann Paul Friedrich Richter
[Jean Paul]
1763–1825

4 Weltschmerz.[1]
Selina; or, Above Immortality [1827], 2

Samuel Rogers
1763–1855

5 Think nothing done while aught remains to do.
Human Life [1819], l. 49

6 Never less alone than when alone.
Human Life, l. 756

7 By many a temple half as old as Time.
Italy. A Farewell

8 Go! you may call it madness, folly;
You shall not chase my gloom away!
There's such a charm in melancholy
I would not if I could be gay.
To——— [1814], st. 1

9   It doesn't much signify whom one marries, for
one is sure to find next morning that it was someone else.   *Table Talk*

Robert Hall
1764–1831

10   Call things by their right names. . . . Glass of
brandy and water! That is the current but not the
appropriate name: ask for a glass of liquid fire and
distilled damnation.
*From OLINTHUS GREGORY, Brief Memoir of
the Life of Hall*

Gaston Pierre Marc,
Duc de Lévis
1764–1830

11   Noblesse oblige [Rank has its obligations].
Maxims and Reflections [1808

Thomas Morton
1764–1838

12   Push on—keep moving.
A Cure for the Heartache [1797], act II, sc.

13   Approbation from Sir Hubert Stanley is prais
indeed.   *A Cure for the Heartache, V, ?*

14   What will Mrs. Grundy say? What will Mrs
Grundy think?
Speed the Plow [1798], act I, sc.

Ann Radcliffe
1764–1823

15 Fate sits on these dark battlements and frowns,
And as the portal opens to receive me,
A voice in hollow murmurs through the courts
Tells of a nameless deed.
The Mysteries of Udolpho [1794], mott

Robert Goodloe Harper
1765–1825

16   Millions for defense, but not one cent for tribute.
*Toast at banquet for John Marshall [June 18,
1798]*

Sir James Mackintosh
1765–1832

17   Diffused knowledge immortalizes itself.
Vindiciae Gallicae [1791

18   The Commons, faithful to their system, re
mained in a wise and masterly inactivity.
Vindiciae Gallica

19   The frivolous work of polished idleness.
*Dissertation on Ethical Philosophy [1830].
Remarks on Thomas Brown*

---

[1]Literally, world pain.

[2]In 1797 a secret agent from Talleyrand told Charles Cotesworth
Pinckney, minister to the French republic, that the American com
missioners in Paris to protest French attacks on U.S. shippin
would be received only if they paid a $50,000 bribe and made
large loan to the French government. Pinckney's reply was: "Not
sixpence, sir." Later, Harper's remark was attributed to him.

1   Disciplined inaction.
History of the Revolution in England in 1688
[1834], ch. 7

James Smithson
1765–1829

2   To found at Washington, under the name of the Smithsonian Institution, an establishment for the increase and diffusion of knowledge among men.[1]
Bequest [1829] with which the Smithsonian Institution was established [1846]

Isaac D'Israeli
1766–1848

3   Whatever is felicitously expressed risks being worse expressed: it is a wretched taste to be gratified with mediocrity when the excellent lies before us.
Curiosities of Literature [1834]. On Quotation

Thomas Robert Malthus
1766–1834

4   Population, when unchecked, increases in a geometrical ratio. Subsistence increases only in an arithmetical ratio. A slight acquaintance with numbers will show the immensity of the first power in comparison of the second.
An Essay on the Principle of Population [1798]

Ernst Friedrich Herbert von Münster
1766–1839

5   Absolutism tempered by assassination.
Description of the Russian Constitution

Carolina Oliphant, Baroness Nairne
1766–1845

6 Better lo'ed ye canna be,
Will ye no come back again?
Life and Songs [1869]. Bonnie Charlie's Now Awa'[2]

7 Charlie is my darling, the young Chevalier.
Life and Songs. Charlie Is My Darling[2]

8 We'll up an' gie them a blaw, a blaw,
Wi' a hundred pipers an' a', an' a'.
Life and Songs. The Hundred Pipers

9 Gude nicht, and joy be wi' you a'.
Life and Songs. Gude Nicht

10 A penniless lass wi' a lang pedigree.
Life and Songs. The Laird o' Cockpen

11 I'm wearin' awa'
To the land o' the leal.
Life and Songs. The Land o' the Leal

Germaine de Staël
[Anna Louise Germaine Necker, Baronne de Staël-Holstein]
1766–1817

12   Love is the whole history of a woman's life, it is but an episode in a man's.[3]
De l'Influence des Passions [1796]

13   A man must know how to defy opinion; a woman how to submit to it.   *Delphine [1802]*

14   To understand everything makes one tolerant.[4]
Corinne [1807], bk. XVIII, ch. 5

15   I would gladly give half of the wit with which I am credited for half of the beauty you possess.
Letter to Juliette Récamier

John Quincy Adams
1767–1848

16   I can never join with my voice in the toast which I see in the papers attributed to one of our gallant naval heroes. I cannot ask of heaven success, even for my country, in a cause where she should be in the wrong. *Fiat justitia, pereat coelum.*[5] My toast would be, may our country be always successful, but whether successful or otherwise, always right.
Letter to John Adams [August 1, 1816]

17   America, with the same voice which spoke herself into existence as a nation, proclaimed to mankind the inextinguishable rights of human nature, and the only lawful foundations of government.
Address [July 4, 1821]

18   America . . . well knows that by once enlisting under other banners than her own, were they even the banners of foreign independence, she would in-

---

[1]Quoted by John Quincy Adams in the *Committee Report on the Smithson Bequest* [March 5, 1840].

[2]Also attributed to James Hogg.

[3]L'amour est l'histoire de la vie des femmes, c'est un épisode dans celle des hommes.

[4]Tout comprendre rend très indulgent.
Attributed to Germaine de Staël are similar phrases: Comprendre c'est pardonner [To understand is to forgive]. Tout comprendre c'est tout pardonner [To know everything is to forgive everything].

[5]Let justice be done though heaven may perish.

volve herself beyond the power of extraction, in all the wars of interest and intrigue, of individual avarice, envy, and ambition, which assume the colors and usurp the standard of freedom. The fundamental maxims of her policy would insensibly change from liberty to force. . . . She might become dictatress of the world. She would be no longer the ruler of her own spirit.   *Address [July 4, 1821]*

1   Individual liberty is individual power, and as the power of a community is a mass compounded of individual powers, the nation which enjoys the most freedom must necessarily be in proportion to its numbers the most powerful nation.
Letter to James Lloyd [October 1, 1822]

2 Who but shall learn that freedom is the prize
Man still is bound to rescue or maintain;
That nature's God commands the slave to rise,
And on the oppressor's head to break the chain.
Roll, years of promise, rapidly roll round,
Till not a slave shall on this earth be found.
Poem

3   This house will bear witness to his piety; this town, his birthplace, to his munificence; history to his patriotism; posterity to the depth and compass of his mind.
From his epitaph for John Adams [1829][1]

4   In charity to all mankind, bearing no malice or ill will to any human being, and even compassionating those who hold in bondage their fellow men, not knowing what they do.
Letter to A. Bronson [July 30, 1838]

5   The great problem of legislation is, so to organize the civil government of a community . . . that in the operation of human institutions upon social action, self-love and social may be made the same.
Society and Civilization; in the American Review [July 1845]

6   To furnish the means of acquiring knowledge is . . . the greatest benefit that can be conferred upon mankind. It prolongs life itself and enlarges the sphere of existence.
Report on the establishment of the Smithsonian Institution [c. 1846]

7   This is the last of earth! I am content.
Last words [February 21, 1848]

Black Hawk[2]
1767–1838

8   I saw my evil day at hand. The sun rose dim on us in the morning, and at night it sank in a dark cloud, and looked like a ball of fire. That was the last sun that shone on Black Hawk. His heart is dead. . . . He is now a prisoner to the white man.
Speech upon surrender, Prairie du Chien, Wisconsin [August 27, 1832]

9   [Black Hawk] has done nothing for which an Indian ought to be ashamed. He has fought for his countrymen, the squaws and papooses, against white men, who came year after year, to cheat them and take away their lands. You know the cause of our making war.[3] It is known to all white men. They ought to be ashamed of it.
Speech upon surrender, Prairie du Chien, Wisconsin [August 27, 1832]

Andrew Jackson
1767–1845

10   The individual who refuses to defend his rights when called by his Government, deserves to be a slave, and must be punished as an enemy of his country and friend to her foe.
Proclamation to the people of Louisiana from Mobile [September 21, 1814]

11   The brave man inattentive to his duty, is worth little more to his country, than the coward who deserts her in the hour of danger.
To troops who had abandoned their lines during the battle of New Orleans [January 8, 1815]

12   Our Federal Union! it must be preserved!
Toast at Jefferson Birthday Celebration [1830]

13   Every man is equally entitled to protection by law; but when the laws undertake to add . . . artificial distinctions, to grant titles, gratuities, and exclusive privileges, to make the rich richer and the potent more powerful, the humble members of society — the farmers, mechanics, and laborers — who have neither the time nor the means of securing like favors to themselves, have a right to complain of the injustice of their government.
Veto of the Bank Bill [July 10, 1832]

14   There are no necessary evils in government. Its evils exist only in its abuses. If it would confine itsel

---

[1]Inscribed on one of the portals of the United First Parish Church Unitarian (Church of the Presidents), Quincy, Massachusetts.

[2]Ma-ke-tai-me-she-kia-kiak.
Chief of the Sauk and Fox Indians.
[3]The Black Hawk War [1832].

to equal protection, and, as Heaven does its rains, shower its favors alike on the high and the low, the rich and the poor, it would be an unqualified blessing.
Veto of the Bank Bill

1   One man with courage makes a majority.
Attributed

Jean-Baptiste Say
1767–1832

2   It is production which opens a demand for products. . . . A product is no sooner created, than it, from that instant, affords a market for other products to the full extent of its own value.[1]
A Treatise on Political Economy [1803]

François René de Chateaubriand
1768–1848

3   [On his conversion to Christianity:] I wept and I believed.[2]   *Le Génie du Christianisme [1802]*

4   The original writer is not one who imitates nobody, but one whom nobody can imitate.[3]
Le Génie du Christianisme

5   Achilles exists only through Homer. Take away the art of writing from this world, and you will probably take away its glory.
Les Natchez [1826], preface

Tecumseh[4]
1768–1813

6   These lands are ours. No one has a right to remove us, because we were the first owners. The Great Spirit above has appointed this place for us, on which to light our fires, and here we will remain. As to boundaries, the Great Spirit knows no boundaries, nor will his red children acknowledge any.[5]
To Joseph Barron, messenger of President James Madison [1810]

---

[1]Say's so-called law of markets, popularly rephrased as "Supply creates its own demand."

[2]J'ai pleuré et j'ai cru.

[3]L'écrivain original n'est pas celui qui n'imite personne, mais celui que personne ne peut imiter.

[4]Chief of the Shawnees.

[5]He remembered the belligerent ants, who claimed their boundaries, and the pacific geese, who did not. . . . All those puffins, razorbills, guillemots and kittiwakes had lived together peacefully, preserving their own kinds of civilization without war—because they claimed no boundaries.—T. H. WHITE [1906–1964], *The Once and Future King* [1939], *bk. IV, ch. 14*

7   My father! The Great Spirit is my father! The earth is my mother—and on her bosom I will recline.
Council at Vincennes, Indiana Territory [August 14, 1810]. Answer to request to sit at "his father's" (Governor William Henry Harrison's) side

8   I am a Shawnee. My forefathers were warriors. Their son is a warrior. From them I take only my existence. From my tribe I take nothing. I am the maker of my own fortune. And oh, that I might make the fortunes of my red people, and of my country, as great as the conceptions of my mind, when I think of the Great Spirit that rules this universe.
Council at Vincennes, Indiana Territory [August 14, 1810]. Speech to Harrison

9   Once they were a happy race. Now they are made miserable by the white people, who are never contented but are always encroaching.
Council at Vincennes, Indiana Territory [August 14, 1810]. Speech to Harrison

10   Sell a country! Why not sell the air, the clouds and the great sea, as well as the earth? Did not the Great Spirit make them all for the use of his children?
Council at Vincennes, Indiana Territory [August 14, 1810]. Speech to Harrison

11   Our lives are in the hands of the Great Spirit. He gave to our ancestors the lands which we possess. We are determined to defend them, and if it is His will, our bones shall whiten on them, but we will never give them up.[6]
Speech to Major General Henry Procter, British commander, Fort Malden [September 1813]

Napoleon I [Napoleon Bonaparte]
1769–1821

12   Soldiers, from the summit of yonder pyramids forty centuries look down upon you.
In Egypt [July 21, 1798]

13   Go, sir, gallop, and don't forget that the world was made in six days. You can ask me for anything you like, except time.
To an aide [1803]. From R. M. JOHNSTON, The Corsican

---

[6]Tecumseh was killed in the battle of the Thames River [October 5, 1813].

1   A form of government that is not the result of a long sequence of shared experiences, efforts, and endeavors can never take root.

> *[1803]. From J.* CHRISTOPHER HEROLD, *The Mind of Napoleon [1955]*

2   From the sublime to the ridiculous is but a step.[1]

> *To the Abbé du Pradt, on the return from Russia [1812], referring to the retreat from Moscow*

3   You write to me that it's impossible; the word is not French.

> *Letter to General Lemarois [July 9, 1813]*

4   What is the throne? — a bit of wood gilded and covered with velvet. I am the state — I alone am here the representative of the people. Even if I had done wrong you should not have reproached me in public — people wash their dirty linen at home.[2] France has more need of me than I of France.

> *To the Senate [1814]*

5   France is invaded; I am leaving to take command of my troops, and, with God's help and their valor, I hope soon to drive the enemy beyond the frontier.

> *At Paris [January 23, 1814]*

6   The bullet that will kill me is not yet cast.

> *At Montereau [February 17, 1814]*

7   The Allied Powers having proclaimed that the Emperor Napoleon is the sole obstacle to the reestablishment of peace in Europe, he, faithful to his oath, declares that he is ready to descend from the throne, to quit France, and even to relinquish life, for the good of his country.

> *Act of Abdication [April 4, 1814]*

8   Unite for the public safety, if you would remain an independent nation.

> *Proclamation to the French People [June 22, 1815]*

9   Wherever wood can swim, there I am sure to find this flag of England.

> *At Rochefort [July 1815]*

10   Whatever shall we do in that remote spot? Well, we will write our memoirs. Work is the scythe of time.

> *On board H.M.S. Bellerophon [August 1815]*

11   [Of his relations with the Empress Josephine:] I generally had to give in.

> *On St. Helena [May 19, 1816]*

12   My maxim was, *la carrière est ouverte aux talents,* without distinction of birth or fortune.

> *On St. Helena [March 3, 1817]*

13   Our hour is marked, and no one can claim a moment of life beyond what fate has predestined.

> *To Dr. Arnott [April 1821]*

14   Two o'clock in the morning courage: I mean unprepared courage.[3]

> *[December 4, 5, 1815]. From* LAS CASES, *Mémorial de Ste-Hélène [1823]*

15   Madame Montholon having inquired what troops he considered the best, "Those which are victorious, Madame," replied the Emperor.

> *From* BOURRIENNE, *Memoirs [1829]*

16   A silk stocking filled with mud.

> *Description of Talleyrand*

17   An army marches on its stomach.[5]

> *Attributed*

18   Every French soldier carries a marshal's baton in his knapsack.[6]

> *Attributed*

19   Perfidious Albion.[7]

> *Attributed*

20   Chief of the Army.[8]

> *Last words*

Arthur Wellesley, Duke of Wellington
1769–1852

21   Nothing except a battle lost can be half so melancholy as a battle won.

> *Dispatch from the field of Waterloo [June 1815]*

22   I used to say of him [Napoleon] that his presence on the field made the difference of forty thousand men.

> *[November 2, 1831]. From* PHILIP HENRY, EARL OF STANHOPE, *Notes of Conversations with the Duke of Wellington [1888]*

23   The only thing I am afraid of is fear.

> *[November 3, 1831]. From* PHILIP HENRY, EARL OF STANHOPE, *Notes of Conversations with the Duke of Wellington*

---

[1]Du sublime au ridicule il n'y a qu'un pas.
The saying has been attributed also to TALLEYRAND.

[2]Il faut laver son linge sale en famille [One should wash one's dirty linen at home]. — *Saying current since about 1720*

[3]Le courage de l'improviste.

[4]Attributed by SAINTE-BEUVE.

[5]No man can be a patriot on an empty stomach. — WILLIAM COWPER BRANN, *The Iconoclast, Old Glory* [July 4, 1893]

[6]Tout soldat français porte dans sa giberne le bâton de maréchal de France.

[7]L'Angleterre, ah! la perfide Angleterre. — JACQUES BÉNIGNE BOSSUET, *Sermon sur la Circoncision*

[8]Tête d'armée.

1 Ours [our army] is composed of the scum of the earth—the mere scum of the earth.
[November 4, 1831]. From PHILIP HENRY, EARL OF STANHOPE, Notes of Conversations with the Duke of Wellington

2 My rule always was to do the business of the day in the day.
[November 2, 1835]. From PHILIP HENRY, EARL OF STANHOPE, Notes of Conversations with the Duke of Wellington

3 They wanted this iron fist to command them.
[November 8, 1840]. From PHILIP HENRY, EARL OF STANHOPE, Notes of Conversations with the Duke of Wellington; of troops sent by Wellington to the Canadian frontier in the war with America

4 There is no mistake; there has been no mistake; and there shall be no mistake.
Wellingtoniana [1832], p. 78

5 I don't care a twopenny damn what becomes of the ashes of Napoleon Bonaparte.
Attributed

6 The battle of Waterloo was won on the playing fields of Eton.
From SIR WILLIAM FRASER, Words on Wellington [1889]

7 Publish and be damned.
Attributed; when the courtesan Harriette Wilson threatened to publish her memoirs and his letters

Ludwig van Beethoven
1770–1827

8 I want to seize fate by the throat.
Letter to Dr. Franz Wegeler [November 16, 1801]

9 Art! Who comprehends her? With whom can one consult concerning this great goddess?
Letter to Bettina von Arnim [August 11, 1810]

10 The world is a king, and, like a king, desires flattery in return for favor; but true art is selfish and perverse—it will not submit to the mold of flattery.
Conversations [March 1820]

Pierre Jacques Étienne, Count Cambronne
1770–1842

11 The Guards die, but never surrender.[1]
Attributed. Reply to surrender demand at Waterloo [1815]

George Canning
1770–1827

12 I give thee sixpence! I will see thee damned first.
The Anti-Jacobin, no. 11 [1797]. The Friend of Humanity and the Knife-Grinder, st. 9

13 I think of those companions true
Who studied with me at the U-
niversity of Göttingen.
The Anti-Jacobin, no. 30 [1798]. The Rovers, song, st. 1

14 A steady patriot of the world alone,
The friend of every country but his own.
The Anti-Jacobin, no. 36 [1798]. New Morality, l. 113

15 And finds, with keen, discriminating sight,
Black's not so black—nor white so *very* white.
The Anti-Jacobin, no. 36. New Morality, l. 199

16 Give me th'avowed, th'erect, the manly foe,
Bold I can meet—perhaps may turn his blow;
But of all plagues, good Heav'n, thy wrath can send,
Save, save, oh! save me from the Candid Friend![2]
The Anti-Jacobin, no. 36. New Morality, l. 207

17 When our perils are past, shall our gratitude sleep?
No—here's to the pilot that weathered the storm.
Song for the Inauguration of the Pitt Club [May 25, 1802]

18 In matters of commerce the fault of the Dutch
Is offering too little and asking too much.
Dispatch to Sir Charles Bagot, British minister at The Hague [January 31, 1826]

---

[1]La Garde meurt, mais ne se rend pas.
Probably the invention of a French journalist; Cambronne denied ever having said it. "Merde!," a more likely reply also attributed to him, has been euphemized as "Le mot de Cambronne."
The finest word, perhaps, that a Frenchman ever uttered. . . . To speak that word, and then to die, what could be more grand! for to accept death is to die, and it is not the fault of this man, if, in the storm of grape, he survived.—VICTOR HUGO, *Les Misérables* [1862], *Cosette, bk. I. Waterloo, ch. 15, translated by* CHARLES E. WILBOUR

[2]Defend me from my friends; I can defend myself from my enemies.—*Attributed to* CLAUDE LOUIS HECTOR, DUC DE VILLARS [1653–1734], *when taking leave of Louis XIV*

1   I called the New World into existence to redress the balance of the Old.
The King's Message [December 12, 1826]

Georg Wilhelm Friedrich Hegel
1770–1831

2   What is reasonable is real; that which is real is reasonable.   *Philosophy of Right [1821]*

3   The owl of Minerva spreads its wings only with the falling of dusk.[1]   *Philosophy of Right*

4   What experience and history teach is this — that people and governments never have learned anything from history, or acted on principles deduced from it.
Philosophy of History [1832],[2] introduction

5   Amid the pressure of great events, a general principle gives no help.
Philosophy of History, introduction

6   To him who looks upon the world rationally, the world in its turn presents a rational aspect. The relation is mutual.
Philosophy of History, introduction

7   The history of the world is none other than the progress of the consciousness of freedom.
Philosophy of History, introduction

8   We may affirm absolutely that nothing great in the world has been accomplished without passion.
Philosophy of History, introduction

9   It is easier to discover a deficiency in individuals, in states, and in Providence, than to see their real import and value.
Philosophy of History, introduction

10   Serious occupation is labor that has reference to some want.   *Philosophy of History, pt. I, sec. 2, ch. 1*

11   It is a matter of perfect indifference where a thing originated; the only question is: "Is it true in and for itself?"
Philosophy of History, III, 3, 2

James Hogg
1770–1835

12   We'll o'er the water, we'll o'er the sea,
We'll o'er the water to Charlie;

Come weal, come woe, we'll gather and go,
And live and die wi' Charlie.
O'er the Water to Charlie

Joseph Hopkinson
1770–1842

13   Hail, Columbia! happy land!
Hail, ye heroes! heaven-born band!
Who fought and bled in Freedom's cause.
Hail, Columbia [1798],[3] st.

William Wordsworth
1770–1850

14   And homeless near a thousand homes I stood,
And near a thousand tables pined and wanted food.
Guilt and Sorrow [written 1791–1794],[4] st. 4

15   ——A simple child,[5]
That lightly draws its breath,
And feels its life in every limb,
What should it know of death?
We Are Seven [1798], st.

16   Have I not reason to lament
What man has made of man?
Lines Written in Early Spring [1798], st.

17   Nor less I deem that there are Powers
Which of themselves our minds impress;
That we can feed this mind of ours
In a wise passiveness.
Expostulation and Reply [1798], st.

18   Come forth into the light of things,
Let Nature be your teacher.
The Tables Turned [1798], st.

19   One impulse from a vernal wood
May teach you more of man,
Of moral evil and of good,
Than all the sages can.   *The Tables Turned, st.*

20   That best portion of a good man's life,
His little, nameless, unremembered acts
Of kindness and of love.
Lines Composed a Few Miles Above Tintern Abbey [1798], l. 33

---

[3]The music, generally attributed to PHILIP PHILE, was Washington's inaugural march. Hopkinson supplied verses at a singer's request, and the song won instant acclaim.

[4]Published 1842.

[5]In the first edition the line is: A simple child, dear brother Jim. It was reduced to the current text in the 1815 edition of Wordsworth's poems.

---

[1]Translated by T. M. KNOX.

[2]Translated by J. SIBREE.
Quoted by G. B. Shaw in *The Revolutionist's Handbook.*

1   Blessed mood,
In which the burthen of the mystery,
In which the heavy and the weary weight
Of all this unintelligible world,
Is lightened.
    Lines Composed a Few Miles Above Tintern
    Abbey, l. 37

2 While with an eye made quiet by the power
Of harmony, and the deep power of joy,
We see into the life of things.
    Lines Composed a Few Miles Above Tintern
    Abbey, l. 47

3   The sounding cataract
Haunted me like a passion: the tall rock,
The mountain, and the deep and gloomy wood,
Their colors and their forms, were then to me
An appetite; a feeling and a love,
That had no need of a remoter charm,
By thought supplied, nor any interest
Unborrowed from the eye.
    Lines Composed a Few Miles Above Tintern
    Abbey, l. 76

4   I have learned
To look on nature, not as in the hour
Of thoughtless youth; but hearing oftentimes
The still, sad music of humanity,
Nor harsh nor grating, though of ample power
To chasten and subdue. And I have felt
A presence that disturbs me with the joy
Of elevated thoughts; a sense sublime
Of something far more deeply interfused,
Whose dwelling is the light of setting suns,
And the round ocean and the living air,
And the blue sky, and in the mind of man:
A motion and a spirit, that impels
All thinking things, all objects of all thought,
And rolls through all things.
    Lines Composed a Few Miles Above Tintern
    Abbey, l. 88

5 Knowing that Nature never did betray
The heart that loved her.
    Lines Composed a Few Miles Above Tintern
    Abbey, l. 122

6 Fair seedtime had my soul, and I grew up
Fostered alike by beauty and by fear.
    The Prelude [written 1799–1805],[1] *bk. I, l. 301*

7 Dust as we are, the immortal spirit grows
Like harmony in music; there is a dark
Inscrutable workmanship that reconciles
Discordant elements, makes them cling together
In one society.   *The Prelude, I, l. 340*

8   The grim shape
Towered up between me and the stars, and still,
For so it seemed, with purpose of its own
And measured motion like a living thing,
Strode after me.   *The Prelude, I, l. 381*

9   Where the statue stood
Of Newton with his prism and silent face,
The marble index of a mind forever
Voyaging through strange seas of thought, alone.
    The Prelude, III, l. 60

10 But Europe at that time was thrilled with joy,
France standing on the top of golden hours,
And human nature seeming born again.
    The Prelude, VI, l. 339

11 Bliss was it in that dawn to be alive,
But to be young was very heaven!
    The Prelude, XI, l. 108

12   There is
One great society alone on earth:
The noble Living and the noble Dead.
    The Prelude, XI, l. 393

13 Prophets of Nature, we to them will speak
A lasting inspiration, sanctified
By reason, blest by faith: what we have loved,
Others will love, and we will teach them how;
Instruct them how the mind of man becomes
A thousand times more beautiful than the earth
On which he dwells.   *The Prelude, XIV, l. 444*

14   Poetry is the breath and finer spirit of all knowledge; it is the impassioned expression which is in
the countenance of all Science.
    Lyrical Ballads [2nd ed., 1800]. Preface

15   In spite of difference of soil and climate, of language and manners, of laws and customs — in spite
of things silently gone out of mind, and things violently destroyed, the Poet binds together by passion
and knowledge the vast empire of human society, as
it is spread over the whole earth, and over all time.
    Lyrical Ballads. Preface

16   I have said that poetry is the spontaneous overflow of powerful feelings: it takes its origin from
emotion recollected in tranquillity.
    Lyrical Ballads. Preface

17 What fond and wayward thoughts will slide
Into a lover's head!
"O mercy!" to myself I cried,
"If Lucy should be dead!"
    Strange Fits of Passion Have I Known [1800],
    st. 7

18 She dwelt among the untrodden ways
Beside the springs of Dove,

---
[1]Published 1850.

A maid whom there were none to praise
And very few to love:[1]

A violet by a mossy stone
Half hidden from the eye!
—Fair as a star, when only one
Is shining in the sky.

She lived unknown, and few could know
When Lucy ceased to be;
But she is in her grave, and, oh,
The difference to me!
She Dwelt Among the Untrodden Ways [1800]

1 A slumber did my spirit seal;
I had no human fears:
She seemed a thing that could not feel
The touch of earthly years.

No motion has she now, no force;
She neither hears nor sees;
Rolled round in earth's diurnal course,
With rocks, and stones, and trees.
A Slumber Did My Spirit Seal [1800]

2   A fingering slave,
One that would peep and botanize
Upon his mother's grave?
A Poet's Epitaph [1800], st. 5

3 A reasoning, self-sufficing thing,
An intellectual All-in-all!
A Poet's Epitaph, st. 8

4 The harvest of a quiet eye.
A Poet's Epitaph, st. 13

5 Something between a hindrance and a help.
Michael [1800], l. 189

6 I traveled among unknown men,
In lands beyond the sea;
Nor, England! did I know till then
What love I bore to thee.
*I Traveled Among Unknown Men [1807],
st. 1*

7 My heart leaps up when I behold
A rainbow in the sky:
So was it when my life began;
So is it now I am a man;
So be it when I shall grow old,
Or let me die!
The child is father of the man;

And I could wish my days to be
Bound each to each by natural piety.
My Heart Leaps Up [1807]

8 Sweet childish days, that were as long
As twenty days are now.
*To a Butterfly (I've Watched You Now a Full
Half-Hour) [1807], st. 2*

9 I thought of Chatterton, the marvelous boy,
The sleepless soul that perished in his pride;
Of him[3] who walked in glory and in joy
Following his plow, along the mountainside:
By our own spirits are we deified:
We Poets in our youth begin in gladness;
But thereof come in the end despondency and
madness.
Resolution and Independence [1807], st. ?

10 Choice word and measured phrase, above the reach
Of ordinary men.
Resolution and Independence, st. 1

11 And mighty poets in their misery dead.
Resolution and Independence, st. 1?

12 Earth has not anything to show more fair:
Dull would he be of soul who could pass by
A sight so touching in its majesty.
*Composed upon Westminster Bridge,
September 3, 1802 [1807], l. 1*

13 Ne'er saw I, never felt, a calm so deep!
The river glideth at his own sweet will!
Dear God! the very houses seem asleep;
And all that mighty heart is lying still!
*Composed upon Westminster Bridge,
September 3, 1802, l. 11*

14 Plain living and high thinking are no more:
The homely beauty of the good old cause
Is gone; our peace, our fearful innocence,
And pure religion breathing household laws.
*Written in London, September 1802
[1807]*

15 It is a beauteous evening, calm and free,
The holy time is quiet as a nun
Breathless with adoration.
It Is a Beauteous Evening [1807], l. ?

16 Thou liest in Abraham's bosom all the year;
And worship'st at the Temple's inner shrine,
God being with thee when we know it not.
It Is a Beauteous Evening, l. 1?

---

[1]He lived amidst th' untrodden ways / To Rydal Lake that lead; / A bard whom there were none to praise, / And very few to read; / Unread his works—his "Milk White Doe" / With dust is dark and dim; / It's still in Longmans' shop, and oh! / The difference to him! — *Parody by* HARTLEY COLERIDGE

---

[2]The last three lines are the epigraph for *Intimations of Immortality,* 393:7.

[3]Robert Burns.

1 Once did she hold the gorgeous east in fee:
And was the safeguard of the west.
On the Extinction of the Venetian Republic
[1807], l. 1

2   Thou hast great allies;
Thy friends are exultations, agonies,
And love, and man's unconquerable mind.
To Toussaint L'Ouverture [1807], l. 12

3 Milton! thou shouldst be living at this hour:
England hath need of thee: she is a fen
Of stagnant waters.
London, 1802 [1807], l. 1

4 Thy soul was like a star, and dwelt apart;
Thou hadst a voice whose sound was like the sea:
Pure as the naked heavens, majestic, free,
So didst thou travel on life's common way,
In cheerful godliness.
London, 1802, l. 9

5 We must be free or die, who speak the tongue
That Shakespeare spake; the faith and morals hold
Which Milton held.
It Is Not to Be Thought Of [1807], l. 11

6 The music in my heart I bore
Long after it was heard no more.
The Solitary Reaper [1807], st. 4

7 There was a time when meadow, grove, and
    stream,
The earth, and every common sight,
    To me did seem
    Appareled in celestial light,
The glory and the freshness of a dream.
It is not now as it hath been of yore —
    Turn wheresoe'er I may,
    By night or day,
The things which I have seen I now can see no
    more.
Ode. Intimations of Immortality from
Recollections of Early Childhood [1807], st. 1

8 The Rainbow comes and goes,
And lovely is the Rose.
Ode. Intimations of Immortality from
Recollections of Early Childhood, st. 2

9   The sunshine is a glorious birth;
    But yet I know, where'er I go,
That there hath passed away a glory from the earth.
Ode. Intimations of Immortality from
Recollections of Early Childhood, st. 2

10 Whither is fled the visionary gleam?
Where is it now, the glory and the dream?
Ode. Intimations of Immortality from
Recollections of Early Childhood, st. 4

11 Our birth is but a sleep and a forgetting:
The soul that rises with us, our life's star,
    Hath had elsewhere its setting,
    And cometh from afar:
Not in entire forgetfulness,
And not in utter nakedness,
But trailing clouds of glory do we come
    From God, who is our home:
Heaven lies about us in our infancy!
Shades of the prison-house begin to close
    Upon the growing boy.
Ode. Intimations of Immortality from
Recollections of Early Childhood, st. 5

12 The youth, who daily farther from the east
    Must travel, still is Nature's priest,
    And by the vision splendid
    Is on his way attended;
At length the man perceives it die away,
And fade into the light of common day.
Ode. Intimations of Immortality from
Recollections of Early Childhood, st. 5

13 As if his whole vocation
Were endless imitation.
Ode. Intimations of Immortality from
Recollections of Early Childhood, st. 7

14 O joy! that in our embers
Is something that doth live,
That nature yet remembers
What was so fugitive!
Ode. Intimations of Immortality from
Recollections of Early Childhood, st. 9

15 High instincts before which our mortal nature
Did tremble like a guilty thing surprised.
Ode. Intimations of Immortality from
Recollections of Early Childhood, st. 9

16   Truths that wake,
To perish never.
Ode. Intimations of Immortality from
Recollections of Early Childhood, st. 9

17   Though inland far we be,
Our souls have sight of that immortal sea
    Which brought us hither.
Ode. Intimations of Immortality from
Recollections of Early Childhood, st. 9

18 Though nothing can bring back the hour
Of splendor in the grass, of glory in the flower.
Ode. Intimations of Immortality from
Recollections of Early Childhood, st. 10

19 The clouds that gather round the setting sun
Do take a sober coloring from an eye
That hath kept watch o'er man's mortality;

Another race hath been, and other palms are won.
Thanks to the human heart by which we live,
Thanks to its tenderness, its joys, and fears,
To me the meanest flower that blows can give
Thoughts that do often lie too deep for tears.
Ode. Intimations of Immortality from
Recollections of Early Childhood, st. 11

1 She was a phantom of delight
When first she gleamed upon my sight;
A lovely apparition, sent
To be a moment's ornament.
She Was a Phantom of Delight [1807], st. 1

2 And now I see with eye serene
The very pulse of the machine.
She Was a Phantom of Delight, st. 3

3 A perfect woman, nobly planned,
To warn, to comfort, and command.
And yet a Spirit still, and bright
With something of angelic light.
She Was a Phantom of Delight, st. 3

4 I wandered lonely as a cloud
That floats on high o'er vales and hills,
When all at once I saw a crowd,
A host, of golden daffodils.[1]
I Wandered Lonely as a Cloud [1807], st. 1

5 Continuous as the stars that shine
And twinkle on the milky way.
I Wandered Lonely as a Cloud, st. 2

6 Ten thousand saw I at a glance,
Tossing their heads in sprightly dance.
I Wandered Lonely as a Cloud, st. 2

7 A poet could not but be gay,
In such a jocund company.
I Wandered Lonely as a Cloud, st. 3

8   That inward eye
Which is the bliss of solitude.
I Wandered Lonely as a Cloud, st. 4

9 Stern daughter of the voice of God!
O Duty!   *Ode to Duty [1807], st. 1*

10   A light to guide, a rod
To check the erring, and reprove.
Ode to Duty, st. 1

11 Me this unchartered freedom tires;
I feel the weight of chance desires;
My hopes no more must change their name,
I long for a repose that ever is the same.
Ode to Duty, st. 5

12 Thou dost preserve the stars from wrong;
And the most ancient heavens, through Thee, are
    fresh and strong.   *Ode to Duty, st. 7*

---

[1]See Larkin, 810:10.

13 The light that never was, on sea or land,
The consecration, and the poet's dream.
Elegiac Stanzas. Suggested by a Picture of
Peele Castle in a Storm [1807], st. 4

14   A deep distress hath humanized my Soul.
Elegiac Stanzas. Suggested by a Picture of
Peele Castle in a Storm, st. 9

15 Who is the happy Warrior? Who is he
That every man in arms should wish to be?
Character of the Happy Warrior [1807], l. 1

16 Who, doomed to go in company with pain,
And fear, and bloodshed, miserable train!
Turns his necessity to glorious gain.
Character of the Happy Warrior, l. 12

17 Nuns fret not at their convent's narrow room.
Nuns Fret Not [1807], l. 1

18 The world is too much with us; late and soon,
Getting and spending, we lay waste our powers:
Little we see in Nature that is ours;
We have given our hearts away, a sordid boon!
The World Is Too Much with Us [1807], l. 1

19   Great God! I'd rather be
A pagan suckled in a creed outworn;
So might I, standing on this pleasant lea,
Have glimpses that would make me less forlorn;
Have sight of Proteus rising from the sea;
Or hear old Triton blow his wreathèd horn.
The World Is Too Much with Us, l. 9

20 Where lies the land to which yon ship must go?
Fresh as a lark mounting at break of day,
Festively she puts forth in trim array.
Where Lies the Land [1807], l. 1

21 Dreams, books, are each a world; and books, we
    know,
Are a substantial world, both pure and good:
Round these, with tendrils strong as flesh and
    blood,
Our pastime and our happiness will grow.
Personal Talk [1807], sonnet 3

22 A power is passing from the earth.
Lines on the Expected Dissolution of Mr. Fox
[1807], st. 5

23 Two voices are there: one is of the sea,[2]
One of the mountains; each a mighty voice.
Thought of a Briton on the Subjugation of
Switzerland [1807], l. 1

---

[2]Two voices are there: one is of the deep; . . . / And one is of an
old half-witted sheep / Which bleats articulate monotony, / And
indicates that two and one are three. . . . / And, Wordsworth,
both art thine. —JAMES KENNETH STEPHEN [1859–1892], *Sonnet,*
Wordsworth [1891]

1 The silence that is in the starry sky,
The sleep that is among the lonely hills.
Song at the Feast of Brougham Castle [1807],
l. 163

2 Every great and original writer, in proportion as
he is great or original, must himself create the taste
by which he is to be relished.
Letter to Lady Beaumont [May 21, 1807]

3 Strongest minds
Are often those of whom the noisy world
Hears least. *The Excursion [1814],*[1] *bk. I, l. 91*

4 The good die first,
And they whose hearts are dry as summer dust
Burn to the socket. *The Excursion, I, l. 500*

5 I have seen
A curious child, who dwelt upon a tract
Of inland ground, applying to his ear
The convolutions of a smooth-lipped shell,
To which, in silence hushed, his very soul
Listened intensely; and his countenance soon
Brightened with joy, for from within were heard
Murmurings, whereby the monitor expressed
Mysterious union with its native sea.
Even such a shell the universe itself
Is to the ear of Faith; and there are times,
I doubt not, when to you it doth impart
Authentic tidings of invisible things;
Of ebb and flow, and ever-during power;
And central peace, subsisting at the heart
Of endless agitation. *The Excursion, IV, l. 1132*

6 One in whom persuasion and belief
Had ripened into faith, and faith become
A passionate intuition.
The Excursion, IV, l. 1293

7 Spires whose "silent finger points to heaven."[2]
The Excursion, VI, l. 19

8 A man he seems of cheerful yesterdays
And confident tomorrows.
The Excursion, VII, l. 557

9 Surprised by joy—impatient as the wind.
Surprised by Joy [1815], l. 1

10 The gods approve
The depth, and not the tumult, of the soul.
Laodamia [1815], st. 13

11 An ampler ether, a diviner air. *Laodamia, st. 18*

12 Enough, if something from our hands have power
To live, and act, and serve the future hour.
The River Duddon [1820], sonnet 34,
Afterthought, l. 10

13 We feel that we are greater than we know.
The River Duddon, 34, Afterthought, l. 14

14 The feather, whence the pen
Was shaped that traced the lives of these good men,
Dropped from an angel's wing.[3]
Ecclesiastical Sonnets [1822], pt. III, sonnet 5.
Walton's Book of Lives, l. 2

15 The unimaginable touch of Time.
Ecclesiastical Sonnets, III, 34. Mutability

16 Give all thou canst; high Heaven rejects the lore
Of nicely calculated less or more.
Ecclesiastical Sonnets, III, 43. Inside of King's
College Chapel, Cambridge, l. 6

17 But hushed be every thought that springs
From out the bitterness of things.
Elegiac Stanzas. Addressed to Sir G. H. B.
[1827], st. 7

18 Type of the wise who soar, but never roam,
True to the kindred points of heaven and home!
To a Skylark [1827]

19 Scorn not the sonnet; Critic, you have frowned,
Mindless of its just honors; with this key
Shakespeare unlocked his heart.
Scorn Not the Sonnet [1827], l. 1

20 Small service is true service while it lasts:
Of humblest friends, bright creature! scorn not
one:
The daisy, by the shadow that it casts,
Protects the lingering dewdrop from the sun.
To a Child. Written in Her Album [1835]

Thomas John Dibdin
1771–1841

21 Oh, it's a snug little island!
A right little, tight little island.
The Snug Little Island

James Montgomery
1771–1854

22 Give me the hand that is honest and hearty,
Free as the breeze and unshackled by party.
Give Me Thy Hand, st. 2

---

[1]This will never do.—FRANCIS JEFFREY [1773–1850], *opening sentence, review of* WORDSWORTH, *Excursion, Edinburgh Review* [1814]

[2]An instinctive taste teaches men to build their churches in flat countries with spire steeples, which, as they cannot be referred to any other object, point as with silent finger to the sky and stars.— SAMUEL TAYLOR COLERIDGE, *The Friend* [1809], *no. 14*

---

[3]The pen wherewith thou dost so heavenly sing / Made of a quill from an angel's wing.—HENRY CONSTABLE [1562–1613], *Sonnet*

1 Here in the body pent,
   Absent from Him I roam,
   Yet nightly pitch my moving tent
   A day's march nearer home.
                              At Home in Heaven

2 Prayer is the soul's sincere desire,
   Uttered or unexpressed;
   The motion of a hidden fire
   That trembles in the breast.
                              What Is Prayer? st. 1

Sir Walter Scott
1771–1832

3 The way was long, the wind was cold,
   The Minstrel was infirm and old;
   His withered cheek, and tresses gray,
   Seem'd to have known a better day.
         The Lay of the Last Minstrel [1805],
         introduction

4 The unpremeditated lay.
         The Lay of the Last Minstrel, introduction

5 Such is the custom of Branksome Hall.
         The Lay of the Last Minstrel, canto I, st. 7

6 Steady of heart, and stout of hand.
         The Lay of the Last Minstrel, canto I, st. 21

7 If thou would'st view fair Melrose aright,
   Go visit it by the pale moonlight.
         The Lay of the Last Minstrel, II, st. 1

8 I cannot tell how the truth may be;
   I say the tale as 'twas said to me.
         The Lay of the Last Minstrel, II, st. 22

9 In peace, Love tunes the shepherd's reed;
   In war, he mounts the warrior's steed;
   In halls, in gay attire is seen;
   In hamlets, dances on the green.
   Love rules the court, the camp, the grove,
   And men below, and saints above;
   For love is heaven, and heaven is love.
         The Lay of the Last Minstrel, III, st. 2

10   For ne'er
   Was flattery lost on poet's ear:
   A simple race! they waste their toil
   For the vain tribute of a smile.
         The Lay of the Last Minstrel, IV, conclusion

   Breathes there the man, with soul so dead,
11 Who never to himself hath said,
   This is my own, my native land!
   Whose heart hath ne'er within him burn'd
   As home his footsteps he hath turn'd
   From wandering on a foreign strand!

If such there breathe, go, mark him well;
For him no Minstrel raptures swell;
High though his titles, proud his name,
Boundless his wealth as wish can claim;
Despite those titles, power, and pelf,
The wretch, concentered all in self,
Living, shall forfeit fair renown,
And, doubly dying, shall go down
To the vile dust, from whence he sprung,
Unwept, unhonor'd, and unsung.
         The Lay of the Last Minstrel, VI, st. 1

12 O Caledonia! stern and wild,
   Meet nurse for a poetic child!
   Land of brown heath and shaggy wood;
   Land of the mountain and the flood!
         The Lay of the Last Minstrel, VI, st. 2

13 November's sky is chill and drear,
   November's leaf is red and sear.
         Marmion [1808], canto I, introduction, st. 1

14 Stood for his country's glory fast,
   And nail'd her colors to the mast!
         Marmion, I, introduction, st. 10

15 But search the land of living men,
   Where wilt thou find their like again?
         Marmion, I, introduction, st. 11

16 And come he slow, or come he fast,
   It is but Death who comes at last.
         Marmion, II, st. 30

17 Oh, young Lochinvar is come out of the West,
   Through all the wide Border his steed was the best
         Marmion, V, st. 12 [Lochinvar, st. 1]

18 So faithful in love, and so dauntless in war,
   There never was knight like the young Lochinvar.
         Marmion, V, st. 12 [Lochinvar, st. 1]

19 For a laggard in love, and a dastard in war,
   Was to wed the fair Ellen of brave Lochinvar.
         Marmion, V, st. 12 [Lochinvar, st. 2]

20 With a smile on her lips, and a tear in her eye.
         Marmion, V, st. 12 [Lochinvar, st. 5]

21 Heap on more wood! — the wind is chill;
   But let it whistle as it will,
   We'll keep our Christmas merry still.
         Marmion, VI, introduction, st. 1

22   And dar'st thou, then,
   To beard the lion in his den,
   The Douglas in his hall?
         Marmion, VI, introduction, st. 14

23 Oh, what a tangled web we weave,
   When first we practice to deceive!
         Marmion, VI, introduction, st. 17

1 O Woman! in our hours of ease,
  Uncertain, coy, and hard to please,
  And variable as the shade
  By the light quivering aspen made;
  When pain and anguish wring the brow,
  A ministering angel thou!   *Marmion, VI, st. 30*

2 "Charge, Chester, charge! On, Stanley, on!"
  Were the last words of Marmion.
                                Marmion, VI, st. 32

3 To all, to each, a fair goodnight,
  And pleasing dreams, and slumbers light!
                                Marmion, L'Envoy

4 The stag at eve had drunk his fill,
  Where danced the moon on Monan's rill,
  And deep his midnight lair had made
  In lone Glenartney's hazel shade.
       The Lady of the Lake [1810], canto I, st. 1

5 In listening mood she seemed to stand,
  The guardian Naiad of the strand.
                     The Lady of the Lake, I, st. 17

6 The will to do, the soul to dare.
                     The Lady of the Lake, I, st. 21

7 Soldier, rest! thy warfare o'er,
  Sleep the sleep that knows not breaking,
  Dream of battled fields no more,
  Days of danger, nights of waking.
                     The Lady of the Lake, I, st. 31

8 Hail to the Chief who in triumph advances![1]
                    The Lady of the Lake, II, st. 19

9 Like the dew on the mountain,
  Like the foam on the river,
  Like the bubble on the fountain,
  Thou art gone, and forever!
       *The Lady of the Lake, III, st. 16 [Coronach,
       st. 3]*

10 And, Saxon—I am Roderick Dhu!
                      The Lady of the Lake, V, st. 9

11 Come one, come all! this rock shall fly
   From its firm base as soon as I.
                     The Lady of the Lake, V, st. 10

12 Respect was mingled with surprise,
   And the stern joy which warriors feel
   In foemen worthy of their steel.
                     The Lady of the Lake, V, st. 10

13 Where, where was Roderick then!
   One blast upon his bugle horn
   Were worth a thousand men!
                    The Lady of the Lake, VI, st. 18

14 Still are the thoughts to memory dear.
                       Rokeby [1813], canto I, st. 33

15 A mother's pride, a father's joy.
                                Rokeby, III, st. 15

16 Oh, Brignal banks are wild and fair,
   And Greta woods are green,
   And you may gather garlands there
   Would grace a summer queen.
                                Rokeby, III, st. 16

17 O! many a shaft at random sent
   Finds mark the archer little meant!
   And many a word, at random spoken,
   May soothe or wound a heart that's broken!
           The Lord of the Isles [1815], canto V, st. 18

18 Randolph, thy wreath has lost a rose.[2]
                       The Lord of the Isles, VI, st. 18

19   A lawyer without history or literature is a mechanic, a mere working mason; if he possesses some
knowledge of these, he may venture to call himself
an architect.   *Guy Mannering [1815], ch. 37*

20   It's no fish ye're buying, it's men's lives.
                        The Antiquary [1816], ch. 11

21 Come as the winds come, when
   Forests are rended,
   Come as the waves come, when
   Navies are stranded.
                    Pibroch of Donald Dhu [1816], st. 4

22 Time will rust the sharpest sword,
   Time will consume the strongest cord;
   That which molders hemp and steel,
   Mortal arm and nerve must feel.
            Harold the Dauntless [1817], canto I, st. 4

23   Sea of upturned faces.   *Rob Roy [1817], ch. 20*

24   There's a gude time coming.   *Rob Roy, 32*

25   My foot is on my native heath, and my name is
MacGregor.   *Rob Roy, 34*

26   Jock, when ye hae naething else to do, ye may be
ay sticking in a tree; it will be growing, Jock, when
ye're sleeping.
                 The Heart of Midlothian [1818], ch. 8

27 Vacant heart, and hand, and eye,
   Easy live and quiet die.
        *The Bride of Lammermoor [1819], ch. 3. Lucy
        Ashton's Song*

28   There is a southern proverb—fine words butter
no parsnips.
                 The Legend of Montrose [1819], ch. 3

---

[1]The verses beginning with this line were set to music by JAMES
SANDERSON [1769–c. 1841]. The march has become traditionally
attached to the President of the United States.

[2]Robert Bruce's censure of Randolph for permitting a body of
English cavalry to pass his flank on the day before the battle of
Bannockburn [June 24, 1314].

1   The happy combination of fortuitous circumstances.

The Monastery [1820]. Answer of the Author of Waverley to the Letter of Captain Clutterbuck

2   As old as the hills.   *The Monastery, ch. 9*

3   And better had they ne'er been born,
Who read to doubt, or read to scorn.
The Monastery, 12

4   Spur not an unbroken horse; put not your plowshare too deep into new land.   *The Monastery, 25*

5   Oh, poverty parts good company.
The Abbot [1820], ch. 7

6   Tell that to the marines — the sailors won't believe it.[1]   *Redgauntlet [1824], vol. II, ch. 7*

7   Rouse the lion from his lair.
The Talisman [1825], heading, ch. 6

8   Recollect that the Almighty, who gave the dog to be companion of our pleasures and our toils, hath invested him with a nature noble and incapable of deceit.   *The Talisman, 24*

9   A miss is as good as a mile.
Journal [December 3, 1825]

10   If you keep a thing seven years, you are sure to find a use for it.   *Woodstock [1826], ch. 28*

11   Come fill up my cup, come fill up my can,
Come saddle your horses, and call up your men;
Come open the West Port, and let me gang free,
And it's room for the bonnets of Bonny Dundee!
The Doom of Devorgoil [1830]. Bonny Dundee, chorus

Sydney Smith
1771–1845

12   In the four quarters of the globe, who reads an American book, or goes to an American play, or looks at an American picture or statue? . . . Under which of the old tyrannical governments of Europe is every sixth man a slave, whom his fellow-creatures may buy, and sell, and torture?
In Edinburgh Review [January–May 1820]

13   If you choose to represent the various parts in life by holes upon a table, of different shapes — some circular, some triangular, some square, some oblong — and the persons acting these parts by bits of wood of similar shapes, we shall generally find that the triangular person has got into the square hole, the oblong into the triangular, and a square person has squeezed himself into the round hole.[2]
Sketches of Moral Philosophy [1850]

14   That knuckle-end of England — that land of Calvin, oatcakes, and sulphur.
Lady Holland's Memoir [1855], vol. I, ch. 2

15   Preaching has become a byword for long and dull conversation of any kind; and whoever wishes to imply, in any piece of writing, the absence of everything agreeable and inviting, calls it a sermon.
Lady Holland's Memoir, I, 3

16   Avoid shame, but do not seek glory — nothing so expensive as glory.   *Lady Holland's Memoir, I, 4*

17   Take short views, hope for the best, and trust in God.   *Lady Holland's Memoir, I, 6*

18   Looked as if she had walked straight out of the ark.   *Lady Holland's Memoir, I, 7*

19   Not body enough to cover his mind decently with; his intellect is improperly exposed.
Lady Holland's Memoir, I, 9

20   He has spent all his life in letting down empty buckets into empty wells; and he is frittering away his age in trying to draw them up again.
Lady Holland's Memoir, I, 9

21   Ah, you flavor everything; you are the vanilla of society.   *Lady Holland's Memoir, I, 9*

22   As the French say, there are three sexes — men, women, and clergymen.
Lady Holland's Memoir, I, 9

23   My living in Yorkshire was so far out of the way, that it was actually twelve miles from a lemon.
Lady Holland's Memoir, I, 9

24   Daniel Webster struck me much like a steam engine in trousers.   *Lady Holland's Memoir, I, 9*

25   Live always in the best company when you read.
Lady Holland's Memoir, I, 10

26   Never give way to melancholy; resist it steadily, for the habit will encroach.
Lady Holland's Memoir, I, 10

27   He was a one-book man. Some men have only one book in them; others, a library.
Lady Holland's Memoir, I, 11

28   Marriage resembles a pair of shears, so joined that they can not be separated; often moving in op-

---

[1]"Right," quoth Ben, "that will do for the marines." — LORD BYRON, *The Island* [1823], *canto II, last line*
"That will do for the marines, but the sailors won't believe it" is an old saying.

[2]Generally accepted as the origin of the phrase: A square peg in a round hole.

posite directions, yet always punishing anyone who comes between them.[1]
Lady Holland's Memoir, I, 11

1 Macaulay is like a book in breeches. . . . He has occasional flashes of silence, that make his conversation perfectly delightful.
Lady Holland's Memoir, I, 11

2 Let onion atoms lurk within the bowl
And, scarce suspected, animate the whole.
Lady Holland's Memoir, I, 11, Recipe for Salad

3 Serenely full, the epicure would say,
Fate cannot harm me, I have dined today.
Lady Holland's Memoir, I, 11

4 What you don't know would make a great book.
Lady Holland's Memoir, I, 11

5 In composing, as a general rule, run your pen through every other word you have written; you have no idea what vigor it will give your style.
Lady Holland's Memoir, I, 11

6 Thank God for tea! What would the world do without tea? — how did it exist? I am glad I was not born before tea. *Lady Holland's Memoir, I, 11*

7 That sign of old age, extolling the past at the expense of the present.
Lady Holland's Memoir, I, 11

8 We know nothing of tomorrow; our business is to be good and happy today.
Lady Holland's Memoir, I, 12

Samuel Taylor Coleridge
1772–1834

9 O the one life within us and abroad,
Which meets all motion and becomes its soul,
A light in sound, a sound-like power in light,
Rhythm in all thought, and joyance everywhere —
Methinks, it should have been impossible
Not to love all things in a world so filled.
The Eolian Harp [1795], l. 26

10 And what if all of animated nature
Be but organic harps diversely fram'd,
That tremble into thought, as o'er them sweeps
Plastic and vast, one intellectual breeze,
At once the Soul of each, and God of All?
The Eolian Harp, l. 44

11 It is an ancient Mariner,
And he stoppeth one of three.

---

[1]We are the two halves of a pair of scissors, when apart, Pecksniff, but together we are something. — CHARLES DICKENS, *Martin Chuzzlewit* [1843–1844], *ch. 11*

"By thy long gray beard and glittering eye,
Now wherefore stopp'st thou me?"
The Rime of the Ancient Mariner [1798], pt. I, st. 1

12 The guests are met, the feast is set:
May'st hear the merry din.
The Rime of the Ancient Mariner, I, st. 2

13 He holds him with his glittering eye —
The Wedding Guest stood still,
And listens like a three years' child:
The Mariner hath his will.
The Rime of the Ancient Mariner, I, st. 4

14 The ship was cheered, the harbor cleared,
Merrily did we drop
Below the kirk, below the hill,
Below the lighthouse top.
The Rime of the Ancient Mariner, I, st. 6

15 The Wedding Guest here beat his breast,
For he heard the loud bassoon.
The Rime of the Ancient Mariner, I, st. 8

16 The bride hath paced into the hall,
Red as a rose is she.
The Rime of the Ancient Mariner, I, st. 9

17 And now there came both mist and snow,
And it grew wondrous cold:
And ice, mast-high, came floating by,
As green as emerald.
The Rime of the Ancient Mariner, I, st. 13

18 The ice was here, the ice was there,
The ice was all around:
It cracked and growled, and roared and howled,
Like noises in a swound!
The Rime of the Ancient Mariner, I, st. 15

19 "God save thee, ancient Mariner!
From the fiends, that plague thee thus! —
Why look'st thou so?" — "With my crossbow
I shot the Albatross."
The Rime of the Ancient Mariner, I, st. 20

20 The fair breeze blew, the white foam flew,
The furrow followed free;
We were the first that ever burst
Into that silent sea.
The Rime of the Ancient Mariner, II, st. 5

21 As idle as a painted ship
Upon a painted ocean.
The Rime of the Ancient Mariner, II, st. 8

22 Water, water, everywhere,
Nor any drop to drink.
The Rime of the Ancient Mariner, II, st. 9

23 The very deep did rot: O Christ!
That ever this should be!

Yea, slimy things did crawl with legs
Upon the slimy sea.
The Rime of the Ancient Mariner, II, st. 10

1 About, about, in reel and rout
The death fires danced at night.
The Rime of the Ancient Mariner, II, st. 11

2 I bit my arm, I sucked the blood,
And cried, A sail! a sail!
The Rime of the Ancient Mariner, III, st. 4

3 Her lips were red, her looks were free,
Her locks were yellow as gold:
Her skin was white as leprosy,
The nightmare Life-in-Death was she,
Who thicks man's blood with cold.
The Rime of the Ancient Mariner, III, st. 11

4 "The game is done! I've won, I've won!"
Quoth she, and whistles thrice.
The Rime of the Ancient Mariner, III, st. 12

5 The sun's rim dips, the stars rush out:
At one stride comes the dark;
With far-heard whisper o'er the sea
Off shot the specter bark.
The Rime of the Ancient Mariner, III, st. 13

6 We listened and looked sideways up!
Fear at my heart, as at a cup,
My lifeblood seemed to sip.
The Rime of the Ancient Mariner, III, st. 14

7 The hornèd Moon, with one bright star
Within the nether tip.
The Rime of the Ancient Mariner, III, st. 14

8 Each turned his face with a ghastly pang,
And cursed me with his eye.
The Rime of the Ancient Mariner, III, st. 15

9 I fear thee, ancient Mariner!
I fear thy skinny hand!
And thou art long, and lank, and brown,
As is the ribbed sea-sand.[1]
The Rime of the Ancient Mariner, IV, st. 1

10 Alone, alone, all, all alone;
Alone on a wide, wide sea.
The Rime of the Ancient Mariner, IV, st. 3

11 The moving moon went up the sky,
And nowhere did abide;
Softly she was going up,
And a star or two beside.
The Rime of the Ancient Mariner, IV, st. 10

12 Her beams bemocked the sultry main,
Like April hoarfrost spread;

---
[1]A note by Coleridge in *Sibylline Leaves* [1817] says: "For [these] lines I am indebted to Mr. Wordsworth."

But where the ship's huge shadow lay,
The charmed water burnt alway
A still and awful red.
The Rime of the Ancient Mariner, IV, st. 11

13 O happy living things! no tongue
Their beauty might declare:
A spring of love gushed from my heart,
And I blessed them unaware.
The Rime of the Ancient Mariner, IV, st. 14

14 Oh sleep! it is a gentle thing,
Beloved from pole to pole.
The Rime of the Ancient Mariner, V, st. 1

15 A noise like of a hidden brook
In the leafy month of June,
That to the sleeping woods all night
Singeth a quiet tune.
The Rime of the Ancient Mariner, V, st. 18

16   The man hath penance done,
And penance more will do.
The Rime of the Ancient Mariner, V, st. 26

17 Like one that on a lonesome road
Doth walk in fear and dread,
And having once turned round walks on,
And turns no more his head;
Because he knows a frightful fiend
Doth close behind him tread.
The Rime of the Ancient Mariner, VI, st. 10

18 Is this the hill? is this the kirk?
Is this mine own countree?
The Rime of the Ancient Mariner, VI, st. 14

19 No voice; but oh! the silence sank
Like music on my heart.
The Rime of the Ancient Mariner, VI, st. 22

20 And the owlet whoops to the wolf below,
That eats the she-wolf's young.
The Rime of the Ancient Mariner, VII, st. 5

21 "Ha! ha!" quoth he, "full plain I see,
The Devil knows how to row."
The Rime of the Ancient Mariner, VII, st. 12

22 I pass, like night, from land to land;
I have strange power of speech;
That moment that his face I see,
I know the man that must hear me:
To him my tale I teach.
The Rime of the Ancient Mariner, VII, st. 17

23 O Wedding Guest! This soul hath been
Alone on a wide wide sea:
So lonely 'twas, that God himself
Scarce seemèd there to be.
*The Rime of the Ancient Mariner,
VII, st. 19*

1 He prayeth well who loveth well
  Both man and bird and beast.
    The Rime of the Ancient Mariner, VII, st. 22

2 He prayeth best who loveth best
  All things both great and small;
  For the dear God who loveth us,
  He made and loveth all.
    The Rime of the Ancient Mariner, VII, st. 23

3 A sadder and a wiser man
  He rose the morrow morn.
    The Rime of the Ancient Mariner, VII, st. 25

4 'Tis a month before the month of May,
  And the Spring comes slowly up this way.
    Christabel [1797–1800], pt. I, l. 21

5 The one red leaf, the last of its clan,
  That dances as often as dance it can.
    Christabel, I, l. 49

6 Her gentle limbs did she undress,
  And lay down in her loveliness.
    Christabel, I, l. 237

7 A sight to dream of, not to tell!
    Christabel, I, l. 252

8 That saints will aid if men will call:
  For the blue sky bends over all!
    Christabel, I, l. 330

9 Alas! they had been friends in youth;
  But whispering tongues can poison truth;
  And constancy lives in realms above;
  And life is thorny; and youth is vain;
  And to be wroth with one we love
  Doth work like madness in the brain.
    Christabel, II, l. 408

10 The frost performs its secret ministry,
   Unhelped by any wind.
    Frost at Midnight [1798], l. 1

11   Therefore all seasons shall be sweet to thee,
   Whether the summer clothe the general earth
   With greenness, or the redbreast sit and sing
   Betwixt the tufts of snow on the bare branch
   Of mossy apple-tree, while the nigh thatch
   Smokes in the sun-thaw; whether the eave-drops
     fall
   Heard only in the trances of the blast,
   Or if the secret ministry of frost
   Shall hang them up in silent icicles,
   Quietly shining to the quiet moon.
    Frost at Midnight, l. 65

12 Forth from his dark and lonely hiding place
   (Portentous sight!) the owlet Atheism,
   Sailing on obscene wings athwart the noon,
   Drops his blue-fringèd lids, and holds them close,

And hooting at the glorious sun in Heaven,
  Cries out, "Where is it?"
    Fears in Solitude [1798], l. 81

13 In Xanadu did Kubla Khan
   A stately pleasure dome decree:
   Where Alph, the sacred river, ran
   Through caverns measureless to man
   Down to a sunless sea.
   So twice five miles of fertile ground
   With walls and towers were girdled round.
    Kubla Khan [1798], l. 1

14 A savage place! as holy and enchanted
   As e'er beneath a waning moon was haunted
   By woman wailing for her demon-lover!
    Kubla Khan, l. 14

15 Five miles meandering with a mazy motion.
    Kubla Khan, l. 25

16 Ancestral voices prophesying war!
    Kubla Khan, l. 30

17 It was a miracle of rare device,
   A sunny pleasure dome with caves of ice!
    Kubla Khan, l. 35

18 A damsel with a dulcimer
   In a vision once I saw:
   It was an Abyssinian maid,
   And on her dulcimer she played,
   Singing of Mount Abora.   *Kubla Khan, l. 37*

19 Could I revive within me
   Her symphony and song,
   To such a deep delight 'twould win me,
   That with music loud and long,
   I would build that dome in air,
   That sunny dome! those caves of ice!
   And all who heard should see them there,
   And all should cry, Beware! Beware!
   His flashing eyes, his floating hair!
   Weave a circle round him thrice,
   And close your eyes with holy dread,
   For he on honeydew hath fed,
   And drunk the milk of Paradise.   *Kubla Khan, l. 42*

20 Strongly it bears us along in swelling and limitless
     billows,
   Nothing before and nothing behind but the sky
     and the ocean.
    The Homeric Hexameter (translated from
    SCHILLER) [1799?]

21 In the hexameter rises the fountain's silvery column;
   In the pentameter aye falling in melody back.
    The Ovidian Elegiac Metre (translated from
    SCHILLER) [1799]

22 All thoughts, all passions, all delights,
   Whatever stirs this mortal frame,

All are but ministers of Love,
And feed his sacred flame.   *Love [1799], st. 1*

1 Earth, with her thousand voices, praises God.
   Hymn Before Sunrise, in the Vale of
   Chamouni [1802], last line

2 What is an epigram? A dwarfish whole,
   Its body brevity, and wit its soul.
                                  An Epigram [1802]

3 I see, not feel, how beautiful they are!
                          Dejection: An Ode [1802], st. 2

4   It were a vain endeavor,
         Though I should gaze forever
   On that green light that lingers in the west:
   I may not hope from outward forms to win
   The passion and the life, whose fountains are
         within.   *Dejection: An Ode, st. 3*

5 O lady! we receive but what we give
   And in our life alone does Nature live.
                              Dejection: An Ode, st. 4

6 A light, a glory, a fair luminous cloud
   Enveloping the earth.   *Dejection: An Ode, st. 4*

7 Joy is the sweet voice, joy the luminous cloud —
   We in ourselves rejoice!
   And thence flows all that charms or ear or sight,
   All melodies the echoes of that voice,
   All colors a suffusion from that light.
                              Dejection: An Ode, st. 5

8 Trochee trips from long to short;
   From long to long in solemn sort
   Slow Spondee stalks.   *Metrical Feet [1806]*

9 With Donne, whose muse on dromedary trots,
   Wreathe iron pokers into true-love knots.
                          On Donne's Poetry [c. 1818]

10 Flowers are lovely; love is flower-like;
    Friendship is a sheltering tree.
                      Youth and Age [1823–1832], st. 2

11 All Nature seems at work. Slugs leave their lair —
    The bees are stirring — birds are on the wing —
    And Winter slumbering in the open air,
    Wears on his smiling face a dream of Spring!
    And I the while, the sole unbusy thing,
    Nor honey make, nor pair, nor build, nor sing.
              Work Without Hope [February 21, 1825], l. 1

12 Work without Hope draws nectar in a sieve,
    And Hope without an object cannot live.
                          Work Without Hope, l. 13

13 I counted two and seventy stenches,
    All well defined, and several stinks.
                              Cologne [1828]

14 In looking at objects of Nature while I am think-
    ing, as at yonder moon dim-glimmering through
    the dewy window-pane, I seem rather to be seeking,
    as it were *asking* for, a symbolical language for
    something within me that already and forever exists,
    than observing anything new.
                          Anima Poetae [1805], ch. 4

15 Poetry is not the proper antithesis to prose, but
    to science. Poetry is opposed to science, and prose
    to metre. The proper and immediate object of sci-
    ence is the acquirement, or communication, of truth;
    the proper and immediate object of poetry is the
    communication of immediate pleasure.
                          Definitions of Poetry [1811]

16 Reviewers are usually people who would have
    been poets, historians, biographers, etc., if they
    could; they have tried their talents at one or at the
    other, and have failed; therefore they turn critics.
    Lectures on Shakespeare and Milton
    [1811–1812]

17 The last speech [Iago's soliloquy], the motive
    hunting of a motiveless malignity — how awful!
                          Notes on Shakespeare [c. 1812]

18 The most general definition of beauty . . . Multeity
    in Unity.
              On the Principles of Genial Criticism [1814]

19 The Good consists in the congruity of a thing
    with the laws of the reason and the nature of the
    will, and in its fitness to determine the latter to ac-
    tualize the former: and it is always discursive. The
    Beautiful arises from the perceived harmony of an
    object, whether sight or sound, with the inborn and
    constitutive rules of the judgment and imagination:
    and it is always intuitive.
              On the Principles of Genial Criticism

20 The imagination . . . that reconciling and media-
    tory power, which incorporating the reason in im-
    ages of the sense and organizing (as it were) the flux
    of the senses by the permanence and self-circling
    energies of the reason, gives birth to a system of
    symbols, harmonious in themselves, and consub-
    stantial with the truths of which they are the con-
    ductors.
                          The Statesman's Manual [1816]

21 Not the poem which we have *read,* but that to
    which we *return,* with the greatest pleasure, pos-
    sesses the genuine power, and claims the name of *es-*
    sential poetry.
                      Biographia Literaria [1817], ch. 1

22 Every reform, however necessary, will by weak
    minds be carried to an excess, that itself will need
    reforming.   *Biographia Literaria, 1*

1   Until you understand a writer's ignorance, presume yourself ignorant of his understanding.
Biographia Literaria, 12

2   During the act of knowledge itself, the objective and subjective are so instantly united, that we cannot determine to which of the two the priority belongs.
Biographia Literaria, 12

3   The primary imagination I hold to be the living power and prime agent of all human perception, and as a repetition in the finite mind of the eternal act of creation in the infinite I Am.
Biographia Literaria, 13

4   The secondary [imagination] . . . dissolves, diffuses, dissipates, in order to re-create; or where this process is rendered impossible, yet still at all events it struggles to idealize and to unify. It is essentially vital, even as all objects (*as* objects) are essentially fixed and dead.   *Biographia Literaria, 13*

5   The fancy is indeed no other than a mode of memory emancipated from the order of time and space.   *Biographia Literaria, 13*

6   The two cardinal points of poetry, the power of exciting the sympathy of the reader by a faithful adherence to the truth of nature, and the power of giving the interest of novelty by the modifying colors of imagination.   *Biographia Literaria, 14*

7   That willing suspension of disbelief for the moment, which constitutes poetic faith.
Biographia Literaria, 14

8   A poem is that species of composition, which is opposed to works of science, by proposing for its immediate object pleasure, not truth; and from all other species (having this object in common with it) it is discriminated by proposing to itself such delight from the whole, as is compatible with a distinct gratification from each component part.
Biographia Literaria, 14

9   A poem of any length neither can be, or ought to be, all poetry.   *Biographia Literaria, 14*

10   The poet, described in *ideal* perfection, brings the whole soul of man into activity, with the subordination of its faculties to each other, according to their relative worth and dignity. He diffuses a tone and spirit of unity, that blends, and (as it were) *fuses,* each into each, by that synthetic and magical power . . . imagination.
Biographia Literaria, 14

11   [Imagination] reveals itself in the balance or reconciliation of opposite or discordant qualities: of sameness, with difference; of the general, with the concrete; the idea, with the image; the individual, with the representative; the sense of novelty and freshness, with old and familiar objects; a more than usual state of emotion, with more than usual order; judgment ever awake and steady self-possession, with enthusiasm and feeling profound or vehement; and while it blends and harmonizes the natural and the artificial, still subordinates art to nature; the manner to the matter; and our admiration of the poet to our sympathy with the poetry.
Biographia Literaria, 14

12   No man was ever yet a great poet, without being at the same time a profound philosopher.
Biographia Literaria, 15

13   While [Shakespeare] darts himself forth and passes into all the forms of human character and passion, the one Proteus of the fire and the flood, [Milton] attracts all forms and things to himself, into the unity of his own *Ideal.* All things and modes of action shape themselves anew in the being of Milton; while Shakespeare becomes all things, yet for ever remaining himself.
Biographia Literaria, 15

14   Our myriad-minded Shakespeare.[1]
Biographia Literaria, 15

15   The best part of human language, properly so called, is derived from reflection on the acts of the mind itself.[2]   *Biographia Literaria, 17*

16   Now Art, used collectively for painting, sculpture, architecture and music, is the mediatress between, and reconciler of, nature and man. It is, therefore, the power of humanizing nature, of infusing the thoughts and passions of man into everything which is the object of his contemplation.
On Poesy or Art [1818]

17   The artist must imitate that which is within the thing, that which is active through form and figure, and discourses to us by symbols.
On Poesy or Art

18   The heart should have fed upon the truth, as insects on a leaf, till it be tinged with the color, and show its food in every . . . minutest fiber.
On Poesy or Art

19   Schiller has the material sublime.
Table Talk [December 29, 1822]

20   I wish our clever young poets would remember my homely definitions of prose and poetry; that is,

---

[1]A phrase which I have borrowed from a Greek monk, who applies it to a patriarch of Constantinople. —COLERIDGE'S *footnote*

[2]The poem of the act of the mind. —WALLACE STEVENS, *Of Modern Poetry*

prose = words in their best order; poetry = the best words in their best order.

Table Talk [July 12, 1827]

1   The man's desire is for the woman; but the woman's desire is rarely other than for the desire of the man.   *Table Talk [July 23, 1827]*

2   That passage is what I call the sublime dashed to pieces by cutting too close with the fiery four-in-hand round the corner of nonsense.

Table Talk [July 23, 1827]

3   The happiness of life is made up of minute fractions — the little soon forgotten charities of a kiss or smile, a kind look, a heartfelt compliment, and the countless infinitesimals of pleasurable and genial feeling.   *The Friend. The Improvisatore [1828]*

4   Beneath this sod
A poet lies, or that which once seemed he —
Oh, lift a thought in prayer for S.T.C.!
That he, who many a year, with toil of breath,
Found death in life, may here find life in death.

Epitaph written for himself [1833]

Novalis
[Baron Friedrich von Hardenberg]
1772–1801

5   We are near awakening when we dream that we dream.   *Pollen [1798]*

Josiah Quincy, Jr.
1772–1864

6   If this bill [for the admission of Orleans Territory as a State] passes, I am compelled to declare it as my deliberate opinion that the bonds of this Union are virtually dissolved; that the States which compose it are free from their moral obligations; and that, as it will be the right of all, so it will be the duty of some, to prepare definitely for a separation — amicably if they can; violently if they must.[1]

Speech in the House of Representatives [January 14, 1811]

William Barnes Rhodes
1772–1826

7   *Bombastes:* So have I heard on Afric's burning shore
A hungry lion give a grievous roar;
The grievous roar echoed along the shore.

Artaxaminous: So have I heard on Afric's burning shore
Another lion give a grievous roar;
And the first lion thought the last a bore.

Bombastes Furioso [1810], act I, sc. i

David Ricardo
1772–1823

8   Labor, like all other things which are purchased and sold, and which may be increased or diminished in quantity, has its natural and its market price. The natural price of labor is that price which is necessary to enable the laborers, one with another, to subsist and perpetuate their race, without either increase or diminution.

On the Principles of Political Economy and Taxation [1817], ch. 5

9   There is no way of keeping profits up but by keeping wages down.

On Protection to Agriculture [1820], sec. 6

Friedrich von Schlegel
1772–1829

10   The historian is a prophet in reverse.

Athenaeum [1798–1800]

William Henry Harrison[2]
1773–1841

11   We admit of no government by divine right . . . the only legitimate right to govern is an express grant of power from the governed.

Inaugural Address [March 4, 1841]

12   A decent and manly examination of the acts of government should be not only tolerated, but encouraged.

Inaugural Address [March 4, 1841]

John Randolph
1773–1833

13   The surest way to prevent war is not to fear it.
Speech in the House of Representatives [March 5, 1806]

---

[1]The gentleman [Quincy] cannot have forgotten his own sentiment, uttered even on the floor of this House, "Peaceably if we can, forcibly if we must." —HENRY CLAY, *Speech* [January 8, 1813]

---

[2]Tippecanoe and Tyler, Too. —A. C. ROSS [fl. c. 1840], *Presidential campaign song* [1840]
The iron-armed soldier, the true-hearted soldier, / The gallant old soldier of Tippecanoe. —GEORGE POPE MORRIS, *campaign song for Harrison* [1840], *sung to the tune of The Old Oaken Bucket*

1 Never were abilities so much below mediocrity so well rewarded; no, not when Caligula's horse was made Consul.[1]   *Speech [February 1, 1828]*

2 [Of Edward Livingston:] He is a man of splendid abilities, but utterly corrupt. He shines and stinks like rotten mackerel by moonlight.
From W. CABELL BRUCE, John Randolph of Roanoke [1923], vol. II, p. 197

3 [Of Martin Van Buren:] He rowed to his object with muffled oars.
From W. CABELL BRUCE, John Randolph of Roanoke, II, p. 203

Robert Southey
1774–1843

4 It was a summer evening;
Old Kaspar's work was done,
And he before his cottage door
Was sitting in the sun;
And by him sported on the green
His little grandchild Wilhelmine.
The Battle of Blenheim [1798], st. 1

5 He came to ask what he had found,
That was so large, and smooth, and round.
The Battle of Blenheim, st. 2

6 "'Tis some poor fellow's skull," said he,
"Who fell in the great victory."
The Battle of Blenheim, st. 3

7 But what they fought each other for,
I could not well make out.
The Battle of Blenheim, st. 6

8 "And everybody praised the duke,
Who this great fight did win."
"But what good came of it at last?"
Quoth little Peterkin.
"Why, that I cannot tell," said he;
"But 'twas a famous victory."
The Battle of Blenheim, st. 11

9 "You are old, Father William," the young man cried,
"The few locks which are left you are gray;
You are hale, Father William—a hearty old man:
Now tell me the reason, I pray."
The Old Man's Comforts and How He Gained Them [1799],[2] st. 1

10 "In the days of my youth, I remembered my God,
And he hath not forgotten my age."
The Old Man's Comforts and How He Gained Them, st. 6

11 And then they knew the perilous rock,
And blessed the Abbot of Aberbrothok.
The Inchcape Rock [1802],[3] st. 4

12 Till the vessel strikes with a shivering shock—
"O Christ! It is the Inchcape Rock."
The Inchcape Rock, st. 15

13 Curses are like young chickens, they always come home to roost.
The Curse of Kehama [1810], motto

14 They sin who tell us love can die;
With life all other passions fly,
All others are but vanity.
The Curse of Kehama, canto X, st. 10

15 Thou hast been called, O sleep! the friend of woe;
But 'tis the happy that have called thee so.
The Curse of Kehama, XV, st. 12

16 My days among the dead are past;
Around me I behold,
Where'er these casual eyes are cast,
The mighty minds of old.
My Days Among the Dead Are Past [1818], st. 1

17 Yet leaving here a name, I trust,
That will not perish in the dust.
My Days Among the Dead Are Past, st. 4

18 Agreed to differ.   *Life of Wesley [1820]*

19 The Satanic school.
Vision of Judgment [1821], original preface

20 The arts babblative and scribblative.
Colloquies on the Progress and Prospects of Society [1829], no. 1, pt. 2

21 The march of intellect.
Colloquies on the Progress and Prospects of Society, 1, 14

22 From his brimstone bed, at break of day,
A-walking the Devil is gone,
To look at his little snug farm of the world,
And see how his stock went on.
The Devil's Walk [1830], st. 1

23 His coat was red, and his breeches were blue,
And there was a hole where his tail came through.
The Devil's Walk, st. 3

---

[1] Referring to President John Quincy Adams's appointment of Richard Rush as Secretary of the Treasury. According to Suetonius, Emperor Gaius Caligula (see 107) was said to have intended awarding his horse Incitatus a consulship.

[2] Of several parodies of this poem, the one by Lewis Carroll is probably better known than the original. See 550:1–550:3.

[3] A rock in the North Sea, off the Firth of Tay, Scotland, dangerous to navigators because it is covered with every tide. There is a tradition that a warning bell was fixed on the rock by the Abbot of Aberbrothok, which was stolen by a sea pirate, who perished on the rock a year later.

Jane Austen[1]
1775–1817

1   An annuity is a very serious business; it comes over and over every year, and there is no getting rid of it.   *Sense and Sensibility [1811], bk. I, ch. 2*

2   It is not time or opportunity that is to determine intimacy;—it is disposition alone. Seven years would be insufficient to make some people acquainted with each other, and seven days are more than enough for others.
Sense and Sensibility, I, 12

3   It is a truth universally acknowledged, that a single man in possession of a good fortune, must be in want of a wife.
Pride and Prejudice [1813], ch. 1

4   She [Mrs. Bennet] was a woman of mean understanding, little information, and uncertain temper.
Pride and Prejudice, 1

5   A lady's imagination is very rapid; it jumps from admiration to love, from love to matrimony in a moment.   *Pride and Prejudice, 6*

6   May I ask whether these pleasing attentions proceed from the impulse of the moment, or are the result of previous study?   *Pride and Prejudice, 14*

7   Mr. Collins had only to change from Jane to Elizabeth—and it was soon done—done while Mrs. Bennet was stirring the fire.
Pride and Prejudice, 15

8   You have delighted us long enough.
Pride and Prejudice, 18

9   Without thinking highly either of men or of matrimony, marriage had always been her object; it was the only honorable provision for well-educated young women of small fortune, and however uncertain of giving happiness, must be their pleasantest preservative from want.
Pride and Prejudice, 22

10   Mrs. Bennet was restored to her usual querulous serenity.   *Pride and Prejudice, 42*

11   You ought certainly to forgive them, as a Christian, but never to admit them in your sight, or allow their names to be mentioned in your hearing.
Pride and Prejudice, 57

12   For what do we live, but to make sport for our neighbors, and laugh at them in our turn?
Pride and Prejudice, 5?

13   I have been a selfish being all my life, in practice though not in principle.   *Pride and Prejudice, 58*

14   A large income is the best recipe for happiness I ever heard of. It certainly may secure all the myrtle and turkey part of it.
Mansfield Park [1814], bk. II, ch. 4

15   One half of the world cannot understand the pleasures of the other.   *Emma [1815], ch. 9*

16   It was a delightful visit—perfect, in being much too short.   *Emma, 13*

17   With men he can be rational and unaffected, but when he has ladies to please every feature works.
Emma, 13

18   Nobody who has not been in the interior of a family can say what the difficulties of any individual of that family may be.   *Emma, 18*

19   The sooner every party breaks up, the better.
Emma, 25

20   Business, you know, may bring money, but friendship hardly ever does.   *Emma, 34*

21   "Only a novel" . . . in short, only some work in which the greatest powers of the mind are displayed, in which the most thorough knowledge of human nature, the happiest delineation of its varieties, the liveliest effusions of wit and humor are conveyed to the world in the best chosen language.
Northanger Abbey [1818], ch. 5

22   She had been forced into prudence in her youth, she learned romance as she grew older—the natural sequence of an unnatural beginning.
Persuasion [1818], ch. 4

23   I do not want people to be very agreeable, as it saves me the trouble of liking them a great deal.
Letters. To her sister Cassandra [December 24, 1798]

24   We met a gentleman in a buggy, who, on minute examination, turned out to be Dr. Hall—and Dr. Hall in such very deep mourning that either his mother, his wife, or himself must be dead.
Letters. To her sister Cassandra [May 17, 1799]

25   The little bit (two inches wide) of ivory on which I work with so fine a brush as produces little effect after much labor.
Letters. To J. Edward Austen [December 16, 1816]

---

[1][Miss Austen] had a talent for describing the involvements and feelings and characters of ordinary life which is to me the most wonderful I ever met with. The Big Bow-Wow strain I can do myself like any now going; but the exquisite touch, which renders ordinary commonplace things and characters interesting, from the truth of the description and the sentiment, is denied to me.— SIR WALTER SCOTT, *Journal* [March 14, 1826]

Charles Lamb
1775–1834

1 I have had playmates, I have had companions,
In my days of childhood, in my joyful school days—
All, all are gone, the old familiar faces.
Old Familiar Faces [1798]

2 For God's sake (I never was more serious) don't make me ridiculous any more by terming me gentle-hearted in print[1] . . . substitute drunken dog, ragged head, seld-shaven, odd-eyed, stuttering, or any other epithet which truly and properly belongs to the gentleman in question.
Letter to Samuel Taylor Coleridge [August 1800]

3 Separate from the pleasure of your company, I don't much care if I never see a mountain in my life.
Letter to William Wordsworth [1801]

4 The man must have a rare recipe for melancholy, who can be dull in Fleet Street.
Letter to Thomas Manning [February 15, 1802]

5 Gone before
To that unknown and silent shore.
Hester [1803], st. 7

6 A good-natured woman, though, which is as much as you can expect from a friend's wife, whom you got acquainted with a bachelor.
Letter to William Hazlitt [1805]

7 This very night I am going to leave off tobacco! Surely there must be some other world in which this unconquerable purpose shall be realized.
Letter to Thomas Manning [1815]

8 Anything awful makes me laugh. I misbehaved once at a funeral. *Letter to Robert Southey [1815]*

9 [Of Coleridge:] An archangel a little damaged.
Letter to William Wordsworth [1816]

10 The red-letter days, now become, to all intents and purposes, dead-letter days.
Essays of Elia [1823]. Oxford in the Vacation

11 The human species, according to the best theory I can form of it, is composed of two distinct races, the men who borrow, and the men who lend.
Essays of Elia. The Two Races of Men

12 Your borrowers of books—those mutilators of collections, spoilers of the symmetry of shelves, and creators of odd volumes.
Essays of Elia. The Two Races of Men

13 A clear fire, a clean hearth, and the rigor of the game.
Essays of Elia. Mrs. Battle's Opinions on Whist

14 I have no ear.
Essays of Elia. A Chapter on Ears

15 Sentimentally I am disposed to harmony; but organically I am incapable of a tune.
Essays of Elia. A Chapter on Ears

16 Credulity is the man's weakness, but the child's strength.
Essays of Elia. Witches, and Other Night Fears

17 Not many sounds in life, and I include all urban and all rural sounds, exceed in interest a knock at the door. *Essays of Elia. Valentine's Day*

18 It is good to love the unknown.
Essays of Elia. Valentine's Day

19 Presents, I often say, endear absents.
Essays of Elia. A Dissertation upon Roast Pig

20 I came home forever!
Letter to Bernard Barton [1825], on leaving his "33 years' desk" at the East India House

21 Who first invented work, and bound the free
And holiday-rejoicing spirit down? *Work*

22 Some cry up Haydn, some Mozart,
Just as the whim bites. For my part,
I do not care a farthing candle
For either of them, nor for Handel.
Letter to Mrs. William Hazlitt [1830]

23 For thy sake, Tobacco, I
Would do anything but die. *A Farewell to Tobacco*

24 A poor relation—is the most irrelevant thing in nature. *Last Essays of Elia [1833]. Poor Relations*

25 I love to lose myself in other men's minds.
Last Essays of Elia. Detached Thoughts on Books and Reading

26 Books think for me.
Last Essays of Elia. Detached Thoughts on Books and Reading

27 How sickness enlarges the dimensions of a man's self to himself.
Last Essays of Elia. The Convalescent

28 Your absence of mind we have borne, till your presence of body came to be called in question by it.
Last Essays of Elia. Amicus Redivivus

29 A pun is a pistol let off at the ear; not a feather to tickle the intellect.
Last Essays of Elia. Popular Fallacies: IX, That the Worst Puns Are the Best

[1] For thee, my gentlehearted Charles, to whom / No sound is dissonant which tells of life.—SAMUEL TAYLOR COLERIDGE, *This Lime Tree Bower My Prison* [1797]

1   A presentation copy . . . is a copy of a book which does not sell, sent you by the author, with his foolish autograph at the beginning of it; for which, if a stranger, he only demands your friendship; if a brother author, he expects from you a book of yours, which does not sell, in return.
Last Essays of Elia. Popular Fallacies: XI, That We Must Not Look a Gift Horse in the Mouth

2   The good things of life are not to be had singly, but come to us with a mixture.
Last Essays of Elia. Popular Fallacies: XIII, That You Must Love Me and Love My Dog

3   The greatest pleasure I know is to do a good action by stealth, and to have it found out by accident.   *Table Talk. In the Athenaeum [1834]*

Walter Savage Landor
1775–1864

4 Ah what avails the sceptred race,
Ah what the form divine!   *Rose Aylmer [1806]*

5 Rose Aylmer, whom these wakeful eyes
May weep, but never see,
A night of memories and of sighs
I consecrate to thee.   *Rose Aylmer*

6   Of all failures, to fail in a witticism is the worst, and the mishap is the more calamitous in a drawn-out and detailed one.
Imaginary Conversations [1824–1829]. Chesterfield and Chatham

7   ’Tis verse that gives
Immortal youth to mortal maids.   *Verse*

8 When we play the fool, how wide
The theatre expands! beside,
How long the audience sits before us!
How many prompters! what a chorus!
Plays [1846], st. 2

9 Mother, I cannot mind my wheel;
My fingers ache, my lips are dry:
Oh, if you felt the pain I feel!
But Oh, who ever felt as I?

No longer could I doubt him true —
All other men may use deceit;
He always said my eyes were blue,
And often swore my lips were sweet.
Mother, I Cannot Mind My Wheel [1846]

10 There is delight in singing, though none hear
Beside the singer.   *To Robert Browning [1846]*

11 I strove with none, for none was worth my strife;
Nature I loved; and next to Nature, Art.

I warm’d both hands before the fire of life;
It sinks, and I am ready to depart.
I Strove with None [1853]

Thomas Campbell
1777–1844

12 ’Tis distance lends enchantment to the view,
And robes the mountain in its azure hue.[1]
Pleasures of Hope [1799], pt. I, l. ?

13 Hope, for a season, bade the world farewell,
And Freedom shriek’d — as Kosciusko fell!
Pleasures of Hope, I, l. 38?

14 And muse on Nature with a poet’s eye.
Pleasures of Hope, II, l. 98?

15 On the green banks of Shannon, when Sheelah was nigh,
No blithe Irish lad was so happy as I;
No harp like my own could so cheerily play,
And wherever I went was my poor dog Tray.[2]
The Harper [1799], st. ?

16 Ye mariners of England,
That guard our native seas;
Whose flag has braved, a thousand years,
The battle and the breeze!
Ye Mariners of England [1800], st. ?

17 Britannia needs no bulwarks,
No towers along the steep;
Her march is o’er the mountain waves,
Her home is on the deep.
Ye Mariners of England, st. 3

18 The meteor flag of England
Shall yet terrific burn,
Till danger’s troubled night depart,
And the star of peace return.
Ye Mariners of England, st. 4

19 ’Tis the sunset of life gives me mystical lore,
And coming events cast their shadows before.[3]
Lochiel’s Warning [1802]

20 The combat deepens. On, ye brave,
Who rush to glory or the grave!
Wave, Munich! all thy banners wave,
And charge with all thy chivalry!
Hohenlinden [1802], st. ?

---

[1]The mountains too, at a distance, appear airy masses and smooth, but seen near at hand they are rough. — DIOGENES LAERTIUS, *Pyrrho, sec. 9*

[2]My Old Dog Tray. — STEPHEN C. FOSTER, *title of song*

[3]Often do the spirits / Of great events stride on before the events, / And in today already walks tomorrow. — JOHANN FRIEDRICH VON SCHILLER, *Wallenstein* [1799–1800], *pt. II, act V, sc. i* Translated by SAMUEL TAYLOR COLERIDGE.

1 There was silence deep as death,
And the boldest held his breath,
For a time.   *Battle of the Baltic [1805], st. 2*

2 Ye are brothers! ye are men!
And we conquer but to save.
              Battle of the Baltic, st. 5

3 Oh, how hard it is to find
The one just suited to our mind!
              Song, st. 1

4 Oh leave this barren spot to me!
Spare, woodman, spare the beechen tree!
              The Beech Tree's Petition, st. 1

5 A stoic of the woods — a man without a tear.
              Gertrude of Wyoming [1809], pt. I, st. 23

6 Oh! once the harp of Innisfail
Was strung full high to notes of gladness;
But yet it often told a tale
Of more prevailing sadness.
              O'Connor's Child [1810], st. 1

Henry Clay
1777–1852

7 How often are we forced to charge fortune with partiality towards the unjust!
              Letter [December 4, 1801]

8 If you wish to avoid foreign collision, you had better abandon the ocean.
              Speech in the House of Representatives [January 22, 1812]

9 Government is a trust, and the officers of the government are trustees; and both the trust and the trustees are created for the benefit of the people.
              Speech at Ashland, Kentucky [March 1829]

10 The arts of power and its minions are the same in all countries and in all ages. It marks its victim; denounces it; and excites the public odium and the public hatred, to conceal its own abuses and encroachments.
              Speech in the Senate [March 14, 1834]

11 I have heard something said about allegiance to the South. I know no South, no North, no East, no West, to which I owe any allegiance. . . . The Union, sir, is my country.
              Speech in the Senate [1848]

12 The Constitution of the United States was made not merely for the generation that then existed, but for posterity — unlimited, undefined, endless, perpetual posterity.
              Speech in the Senate [January 29, 1850]

13 I would rather be right than be President.[1]
              Speech in the Senate [1850]

Lorenzo Dow
1777–1834

14 You will be damned if you do. — And you will be damned if you don't [definition of Calvinism].
              Reflections on the Love of God

Carl Friedrich Gauss
1777–1855

15 Mathematics is the queen of the sciences.
              From SARTORIUS VON WALTERSHAUSEN, Gauss zum Gedächtniss [1856]

Valentine Blacker
1778–1823

16 Put your trust in God, my boys, and keep your powder dry!
              From EDWARD HAYES, Ballads of Ireland [1856]. Oliver's Advice, An Orange Ballad

Henry Peter Brougham, Baron Brougham and Vaux
1778–1868

17 What is valuable is not new, and what is new is not valuable.
              From The Edinburgh Review [c. 1802], The Work of Thomas Young

18 The schoolmaster is abroad,[2] and I trust to him, armed with his primer, against the soldier in full military array.
              Speech, Opening of Parliament [January 29, 1828]

19 In my mind, he was guilty of no error — he was chargeable with no exaggeration — he was betrayed by his fancy into no metaphor, who once said that all we see about us, Kings, Lords, and Commons, the whole machinery of the State, all the apparatus

---

[1] Said when told that his defense of the Compromise of 1850 would endanger his chances for the presidency.

[2] At the first meeting of the London Mechanics' Institution [1825], John Reynolds, head of a school in Clerkenwell, acted as secretary of the meeting. Lord Brougham, who spoke at this meeting, said in the course of his remarks, "Look out, gentlemen, the schoolmaster is abroad." The phrase attracted little attention at that time, but when used in a speech three years later, it at once became popular.

of the system, and its varied workings, end in simply bringing twelve good men into a box.

Present State of the Law [February 7, 1828]

1   Pursuit of Knowledge Under Difficulties.

Title of book [1830]

2   Education makes a people easy to lead, but difficult to drive; easy to govern but impossible to enslave. *Attributed*

3   The great unwashed. *Attributed*

William Hazlitt
1778–1830

4   One has no notion of him [William Cobbett] as making use of a fine pen, but a great mutton-fist; his style stuns readers. . . . He is too much for any single newspaper antagonist; "lays waste" a city orator or Member of Parliament, and bears hard upon the government itself. He is a kind of *fourth estate* in the politics of the country.

Table Talk [1821–1822]. Character of Cobbett

5   It is better to be able neither to read nor write than to be able to do nothing else.

Table Talk. On the Ignorance of the Learned

6   What I mean by living to one's self is living in the world, as in it, not of it. . . . It is to be a silent spectator of the mighty scene of things; . . . to take a thoughtful, anxious interest in what is passing in the world, but not to feel the slightest inclination to make or meddle with it.

Table Talk. On Living to One's Self

7   Even in the common affairs of life, in love, friendship, and marriage, how little security have we when we trust our happiness in the hands of others!

Table Talk. On Living to One's Self

8   There is not a more mean, stupid, dastardly, pitiful, selfish, spiteful, envious, ungrateful animal than the Public. It is the greatest of cowards, for it is afraid of itself.

Table Talk. On Living to One's Self

9   When a man is dead, they put money in his coffin, erect monuments to his memory, and celebrate the anniversary of his birthday in set speeches. Would they take any notice of him if he were living? No!   *Table Talk. On Living to One's Self*

10   One of the pleasantest things in the world is going a journey; but I like to go by myself.

Table Talk. On Going a Journey

11   When I am in the country I wish to vegetate like the country.   *Table Talk. On Going a Journey*

12   The soul of a journey is liberty, perfect liberty, to think, feel, do just as one pleases.

Table Talk. On Going a Journey

13   Give me the clear blue sky over my head, and the green turf beneath my feet, a winding road before me, and a three hours' march to dinner — and then to thinking! It is hard if I cannot start some game on these lone heaths.

Table Talk. On Going a Journey

14   No young man ever thinks he shall die.

Table Talk. On the Fear of Death

15   *Horas non numero nisi serenas*[1] is the motto of a sundial near Venice. There is a softness and a harmony in the words and in the thought unparalleled.

Table Talk. Of a Sundial in Venice

16   The love of liberty is the love of others; the love of power is the love of ourselves.

Political Essays. The Times Newspaper

17   We never do anything well till we cease to think about the manner of doing it.

Sketches and Essay. On Prejudice

18   Men of genius do not excel in any profession because they labor in it, but they labor in it because they excel.   *Characteristics, no. 416 [c. 1821]*

19   We are not hypocrites in our sleep.

On Dreams

Stephen Decatur
1779–1820

20   Our country! In her intercourse with foreign nations may she always be in the right; but our country, right or wrong.[2]

Toast given at Norfolk [April 1816]. From Alexander Slidell Mackenzie, *Life of Stephen Decatur [1848]*[3]

Thomas, Lord Denman
1779–1854

21   Trial by jury, instead of being a security to persons who are accused, will be a delusion, a mockery, and a snare.

O'Connell v. The Queen [September 4, 1844]

---

[1] I count only the hours that are serene. — *Proverb*
Also quoted as: I count only the sunny hours.

[2] I hope to find my country in the right: however, I will stand by her, right or wrong. — John Jordan Crittenden [1787–1863], *On the Mexican War*

[3] *Niles' Weekly Register* [Baltimore; April 20, 1816] gives a slightly different reading: *Our Country* — In her intercourse with foreign nations may she always be in the *right,* and always *successful, right* or *wrong.*

Francis Scott Key
1779–1843

1 Oh, say, can you see by the dawn's early light,
What so proudly we hailed at the twilight's last
    gleaming?
Whose broad stripes and bright stars, through the
    perilous fight,
O'er the ramparts we watched were so gallantly
    streaming?
And the rockets' red glare, the bombs bursting in
    air,
Gave proof through the night that our flag was still
    there.
Oh, say, does that star-spangled banner yet wave
O'er the land of the free and the home of the
    brave?
> *The Star-Spangled Banner [September 14,
> 1814], st. 1*

2 Blessed with victory and peace, may the Heaven-
    rescued land
Praise the Power that hath made and preserved us a
    nation.
Then conquer we must, when our cause it is just,
And this be our motto, "In God is our trust."
> *The Star-Spangled Banner, st. 4*

William Lamb, Viscount Melbourne
1779–1848

3 I wish I was as cocksure of anything as Tom
Macaulay is of everything.
> *From Melbourne's Papers [1889]. Preface by*
> EARL COWPER

4 Things have come to a pretty pass when religion
is allowed to invade the sphere of private life.
> *From G. W. E. RUSSELL, Collections and
> Recollections [1898]*

Clement Clarke Moore[1]
1779–1863

5 'Twas the night before Christmas, when all
    through the house
Not a creature was stirring—not even a mouse;
The stockings were hung by the chimney with care,
In hopes that St. Nicholas soon would be there.
> *A Visit from St. Nicholas [December 1823]*

---

[1]Don Foster's study *Author Unknown* (2000) argues that the
author of *A Visit from St. Nicholas* was not Moore but probably
Major Henry Livingston, Jr. (1748–1828).

6 "Happy Christmas to all, and to all a goodnight!"
> *A Visit from St. Nicholas*

Thomas Moore
1779–1852

7 Faintly as tolls the evening chime,
Our voices keep tune and our oars keep time.
> *Poems Relating to America. A Canadian
> Boat Song, st. 1*

8 Go where glory waits thee!
But while fame elates thee,
Oh, still remember me!
> *Irish Melodies [1807–1834]. Go Where Glory
> Waits Thee, st. 1*

9 Oh, breathe not his name! let it sleep in the
    shade,
Where cold and unhonor'd his relics are laid.
> *Irish Melodies. Oh, Breathe Not His Name, st. 1*

10 And the tear that we shed, though in secret it rolls,
Shall long keep his memory green in our souls.
> *Irish Melodies. Oh, Breathe Not His Name, st. 2*

11 The harp that once through Tara's halls
The soul of music shed,
Now hangs as mute on Tara's walls
As if that soul were fled.
> *Irish Melodies. The Harp That Once Through
> Tara's Halls, st. 1*

12 Believe me, if all those endearing young charms
Which I gaze on so fondly today,
Were to change by tomorrow and fleet in my arms,
Like fairy gifts fading away,
Thou would'st still be ador'd as this moment thou
    art,
Let thy loveliness fade as it will,
And around the dear ruin each wish of my heart
Would entwine itself verdantly still.
> *Irish Melodies. Believe Me, If All Those
> Endearing Young Charms, st. 1*

13 But there's nothing half so sweet in life
As love's young dream.
> *Irish Melodies. Love's Young Dream, st. 1*

14 Eyes of unholy blue.
> *Irish Melodies. By That Lake Whose Gloomy
> Shore, st. 2*

15 'Tis the last rose of summer,
Left blooming alone;
All her lovely companions
Are faded and gone.
> *Irish Melodies. The Last Rose of Summer, st. 1*

16 The Minstrel Boy to the war is gone,
In the ranks of death you'll find him.

His father's sword he has girded on,
And his wild harp slung behind him.
Irish Melodies. The Minstrel Boy, st. 1

1   And the best of all ways
To lengthen our days
Is to steal a few hours from the night, my dear.
Irish Melodies. The Young May Moon, st. 1

2 You may break, you may shatter the vase, if you will,
But the scent of the roses will hang round it still.[1]
Irish Melodies. Farewell! But Whenever, st. 3

3 No eye to watch, and no tongue to wound us,
All earth forgot, and all heaven around us.
Irish Melodies. Come O'er the Sea, st. 2

4 The light that lies
In woman's eyes,
Has been my heart's undoing.
Irish Melodies. The Time I've Lost in Wooing, st. 1

5   My only books
Were woman's looks,
And folly's all they've taught me.
Irish Melodies. The Time I've Lost in Wooing, st. 1

6 A Persian's heaven is easily made:
'Tis but black eyes and lemonade.
Intercepted Letters; or, The Two Penny Post Bag [1813], VI

7 Oft in the stilly night,
Ere Slumber's chain has bound me,
Fond Memory brings the light
Of other days around me;
The smiles, the tears,
Of boyhood's years,
The words of love then spoken;
The eyes that shone
Now dimmed and gone,
The cheerful hearts now broken.
National Airs [1815]. Oft in the Stilly Night, st. 1

8   I feel like one,
Who treads alone
Some banquet hall deserted,
Whose lights are fled,
Whose garlands dead,
And all but he departed.
National Airs. Oft in the Stilly Night, st. 2

9 What though youth gave love and roses,
Age still leaves us friends and wine.
National Airs. Spring and Autumn, st.

10 Oh, call it by some better name,
For friendship sounds too cold.
Ballads and Songs. Oh, Call It by Some Better Name, st. 1

11 There's a bower of roses by Bendemeer's stream,
And the nightingale sings round it all the day long.
Lalla Rookh [1817], pt. I.

12 Some flow'rets of Eden ye still inherit,
But the trail of the serpent is over them all.
Lalla Rookh, I.

13 Oh! ever thus, from childhood's hour,
I've seen my fondest hope decay;
I never loved a tree or flower,
But 'twas the first to fade away.
I never nurs'd a dear gazelle
To glad me with its soft black eye,
But when it came to know me well,
And love me, it was sure to die.   *Lalla Rookh, V*

14 Like Dead Sea fruits, that tempt the eye,
But turn to ashes on the lips.   *Lalla Rookh, V*

15   Paradise itself were dim
And joyless, if not shared with him!
Lalla Rookh, VI

Joseph Story
1779–1845

16   [The law] is a jealous mistress, and requires a long and constant courtship. It is not to be won by trifling favors, but by lavish homage.
The Value and Importance of Legal Studies [August 5, 1829]

William Ellery Channing
1780–1842

17   We do, then, with all earnestness, though without reproaching our brethren, protest against the irrational and unscriptural doctrine of the Trinity. "To us," as to the Apostle and the primitive Christians, "there is one God, even the Father." With Jesus, we worship the Father, as the only living and true God. We are astonished, that any man can read the New Testament, and avoid the conviction, that the Father alone is God.
Unitarian Christianity [Baltimore, 1819]

18   I see the marks of God in the heavens and the earth, but how much more in a liberal intellect, in

---

[1]The jar will long keep the fragrance of what it was once steeped in when new. —HORACE, *Epistles, I, ii, 69*
    That flavor, absorbed when new, remains. —QUINTILIAN
    But, somehow or other, though you fill it with water, the jar retains the odor which it acquired when first used. —SAINT JEROME
    The image was frequently used in the classical period; unglazed ware is more absorbent than glazed.

magnanimity, in unconquerable rectitude, in a philanthropy which forgives every wrong, and which never despairs of the cause of Christ and human virtue! I do and I must reverence human nature. . . . I thank God that my own lot is bound up with that of the human race.

Likeness to God [Providence, Rhode Island, 1828]

1 There are seasons, in human affairs, of inward and outward revolution, when new depths seem to be broken up in the soul, when new wants are unfolded in multitudes, and a new and undefined good is thirsted for. These are periods when . . . *to dare* is the highest wisdom.

Complete Works [1879]. The Union [1829]

2 I call that mind free which jealously guards its intellectual rights and powers, which calls no man master, which does not content itself with a passive or hereditary faith, which opens itself to light whencesoever it may come, which receives new truth as an angel from Heaven.

Spiritual Freedom

Karl von Clausewitz
1780–1831

3 War is not merely a political act, but also a political instrument, a continuation of political relations, a carrying out of the same by other means.[1]

Vom Kriege (On War) [1833]

Charles Caleb Colton
1780–1832

4 When you have nothing to say, say nothing.

Lacon [1820–1822], vol. I, no. 183

5 Imitation is the sincerest of flattery.

Lacon, I, 217

6 That debt which cancels all others.

Lacon, II, 66

Philip Hone
1780–1851

7 By and by we shall have balloons and pass over to Europe between sun and sun. Oh, for the good old days of heavy post-coaches and speed at the rate of six miles an hour! *Diary [November 28, 1844]*

Charles Miner
1780–1865

8 When I see a merchant overpolite to his customers, begging them to taste a little brandy and throwing half his goods on the counter—thinks I, that man has an ax to grind.

Essays from the Desk of Poor Robert the Scribe [1815]. Who'll Turn Grindstones[2]

Frances [Milton] Trollope
1780–1863

9 Let no one who wishes to receive agreeable impressions of American manners, commence their travels in a Mississippi steamboat.

Domestic Manners of the Americans [1832]

Ebenezer Elliott
1781–1849

10 Not kings and lords, but nations!
Not thrones and crowns, but men!

Corn Law Rhymes [1828]. When Wilt Thou Save the People?, st. 1

11 God save the people!

Corn Law Rhymes. When Wilt Thou Save the People?, st. 1

12 What is a communist? One who hath yearnings
For equal division of unequal earnings.

Poetical Works [1846]. Epigram

James Lawrence
1781–1813

13 Tell the men to fire faster and not to give up the ship; fight her till she sinks.[3]

On board the U.S. frigate Chesapeake [June 1, 1813]

John C[aldwell] Calhoun
1782–1850

14 The very essence of a free government consists in considering offices as public trusts, bestowed for

---

[1]Der Krieg ist nichts anderes als die Fortsetzung der Politik mit anderen Mitteln.

[2]First published in *Luzerne Federalist* [September 7, 1810]. Because of the similarity of the title to *Poor Richard,* the phrase "an ax to grind" has often been attributed to BENJAMIN FRANKLIN.

[3]Usually quoted as "Don't give up the ship"; Captain Lawrence's final order as he was carried below, fatally wounded, before the capture of his ship by the British frigate *Shannon.*

the good of the country, and not for the benefit of an individual or a party.

Speech [February 13, 1835]

1   A power has risen up in the government greater than the people themselves, consisting of many and various and powerful interests, combined into one mass, and held together by the cohesive power of the vast surplus in the banks.[1]

Speech [May 27, 1836]

2   The surrender of life is nothing to sinking down into acknowledgment of inferiority.

Speech in the Senate [February 19, 1847]

Thomas H. Palmer
1782–1861

3   'Tis a lesson you should heed,
Try, try again.
If at first you don't succeed,
Try, try again.   *Teacher's Manual [1840][2]*

Ann Taylor
1782–1866

Jane Taylor
1783–1824

4   Who ran to help me when I fell,
And would some pretty story tell,
Or kiss the place to make it well?
      My mother.
      Original Poems for Infant Minds [1804]. My Mother [by Ann Taylor*], st. 6*

5   Twinkle, twinkle, little star,
How I wonder what you are,
Up above the world so high,
Like a diamond in the sky![3]
      Rhymes for the Nursery [1806]. The Star, st. 1

6   I like little pussy, her coat is so warm;
And if I don't hurt her she'll do me no harm.
      Rhymes for the Nursery. I Like Little Pussy [by Jane Taylor*], st. 1*

7   Oh, that it were my chief delight
To do the things I ought!
Then let me try with all my might
To mind what I am taught.
      Hymns for Infant Minds [1810]. For a Very Little Child

Daniel Webster
1782–1852

8   It is, sir, as I have said, a small college, and ye there are those who love it.

Dartmouth College Case [1818

9   Whatever makes men good Christians, make them good citizens.

Speech at Plymouth, Massachusetts [December 22, 1820]

10   Labor in this country is independent and proud It has not to ask the patronage of capital, but capita solicits the aid of labor.   *Speech [April 2, 1824*

11   We wish that this column, rising towards heave among the pointed spires of so many temples dedi cated to God, may contribute also to produce in a minds a pious feeling of dependence and gratitude We wish, finally, that the last object to the sight c him who leaves his native shore, and the first t gladden his who revisits it, may be something whic shall remind him of the liberty and the glory of h country.

Address on Laying the Cornerstone of the Bunker Hill Monument [June 17, 1825]

12   Sink or swim, live or die, survive or perish, I giv my hand and my heart to this vote.[4]

Discourse in Commemoration of Adams and Jefferson, Faneuil Hall, Boston [August 2, 1826]

13   It is my living sentiment, and by the blessing c God it shall be my dying sentiment— Independenc now and Independence forever.[5]

Discourse in Commemoration of Adams and Jefferson, Faneuil Hall, Boston [August 2, 1826]

14   Washington is in the clear upper sky.

Discourse in Commemoration of Adams and Jefferson, Faneuil Hall, Boston [August 2, 1826]

15   The gentleman has not seen how to reply to thi otherwise than by supposing me to have advance the doctrine that a national debt is a national blessing

Second Speech on Foote's Resolution [January 26, 1830]

16   I shall enter on no encomium upon Massachu setts; she needs none. There she is.[6] Behold her, an

---

[1]From this speech comes the phrase: Cohesive power of public plunder.

[2]Later popularized by Edward Hickson [1803–1870] in his *Moral Songs* [1857] and often attributed to him or cited as a proverb.

[3]See Carroll, 550:12.

[4]Live or die, sink or swim. — George Peele, *Edward I* [c. 1584

[5]On the day of his [John Adams's] death, hearing the noise bells and cannon, he asked the occasion. On being reminded tha it was "Independent Day," he replied, "Independence forever." - Daniel Webster, *Works* [1903], *vol. I, p. 150*

[6]Generally misquoted as "Massachusetts, there she stands."

judge for yourselves. There is her history; the world knows it by heart. The past, at least, is secure. There is Boston and Concord and Lexington and Bunker Hill; and there they will remain forever.
Second Speech on Foote's Resolution [January 26, 1830]

1 The people's government, made for the people, made by the people, and answerable to the people.[1]
Second Speech on Foote's Resolution [January 26, 1830]

2 When my eyes shall be turned to behold for the last time the sun in heaven, may I not see him shining on the broken and dishonored fragments of a once glorious Union; on States dissevered, discordant, belligerent; on a land rent with civil feuds, or drenched, it may be, in fraternal blood.
Second Speech on Foote's Resolution [January 26, 1830]

3 Liberty and Union, now and forever, one and inseparable.
Second Speech on Foote's Resolution [January 26, 1830]

4 There is no refuge from confession but suicide; and suicide is confession.
Argument on the murder of Captain White [April 6, 1830]

5 He smote the rock of the national resources, and abundant streams of revenue gushed forth. He touched the dead corpse of the Public Credit, and it sprung upon its feet.
Speech on Hamilton [March 10, 1831]

6 On this question of principle, while actual suffering was yet afar off, they [the Colonies] raised their flag against a power, to which, for purposes of foreign conquest and subjugation, Rome in the height of her glory is not to be compared — a power which has dotted over the surface of the whole globe with her possessions and military posts, whose morning drumbeat, following the sun, and keeping company with the hours, circles the earth with one continuous and unbroken strain of the martial airs of England.
Speech [May 7, 1834]

7 God grants liberty only to those who love it, and are always ready to guard and defend it.
Speech [June 3, 1834]

8 One country, one constitution, one destiny.
Speech [March 15, 1837]

9 When tillage begins, other arts follow. The farmers therefore are the founders of human civilization.
On Agriculture [January 13, 1840]

10 America has furnished to the world the character of Washington. And if our American institutions had done nothing else, that alone would have entitled them to the respect of mankind.
On the Completion of the Bunker Hill Monument [June 17, 1843]

11 Justice, sir, is the great interest of man on earth.
On Mr. Justice Story [September 12, 1845]

12 Inconsistencies of opinion, arising from changes of circumstances, are often justifiable.
Speech [July 25 and 27, 1846]

13 Liberty exists in proportion to wholesome restraint.
Speech at the Charleston Bar Dinner [May 10, 1847]

14 The law: It has honored us; may we honor it.
Speech at the Charleston Bar Dinner [May 10, 1847]

15 I was born an American; I will live an American; I shall die an American.   *Speech [July 17, 1850]*

16 Faneuil Hall, the cradle of American liberty.
Letter [April 1851]

17 Men hang out their signs indicative of their respective trades: shoemakers hang out a gigantic shoe; jewelers, a monster watch; and the dentist hangs out a gold tooth; but up in the mountains of New Hampshire, God Almighty has hung out a sign to show that there He makes men.
On the Old Man of the Mountain;[2] attributed

18 I still live.   *Last words [October 24, 1852]*

Simón Bolívar
1783–1830

19 A state too extensive in itself, or by virtue of its dependencies, ultimately falls into decay; its free government is transformed into a tyranny; it disregards the principles which it should preserve, and finally degenerates into despotism. The distinguishing characteristic of small republics is stability: the character of large republics is mutability.
Letter from Jamaica [Summer 1815]

20 Those who have served the cause of the revolution have plowed the sea.   *Attributed*

21 The three greatest dolts in the world: Jesus Christ, Don Quixote, and I.   *Attributed*

---

[1]Our sovereign, the people. — CHARLES JAMES FOX, *toast* [1798], *for which his name was erased from the Privy Council*

[2]Natural rock formation in the shape of a human profile, in the Presidential Range of the White Mountains. It gave Nathaniel Hawthorne the theme of his story *The Great Stone Face.*

Reginald Heber
1783–1826

1 Brightest and best of the sons of the morning,
Dawn on our darkness, and lend us thine aid.
Hymns. Epiphany [1811], st. 1

2 The Son of God goes forth to war,
A kingly crown to gain;
His blood-red banner streams afar;
Who follows in His train?
*Hymns. The Son of God Goes Forth to War
[1812], st. 1*

3 From Greenland's icy mountains,
From India's coral strand,
Where Afric's sunny fountains
Roll down their golden sand.
Hymns. Missionary Hymn [1819], st. 1

4 Though every prospect pleases,
And only man is vile.
Hymns. Missionary Hymn, st. 2

5 The heathen in his blindness
Bows down to wood and stone.
Hymns. Missionary Hymn, st. 2

6 Holy, Holy, Holy! Lord God Almighty!
Early in the morning our song shall rise to Thee:
Holy, Holy, Holy! Merciful and Mighty!
God in Three Persons, Blessed Trinity.
Hymns. Holy, Holy, Holy! [1827]

Washington Irving
1783–1859

7 How convenient it would be to many of our
great men and great families of doubtful origin,
could they have the privilege of the heroes of yore,
who, whenever their origin was involved in obscurity, modestly announced themselves descended
from a god.
*Knickerbocker's History of New York [1809],
bk. II, ch. 3*

8 His wife "ruled the roast," and in governing the
governor, governed the province, which might thus
be said to be under petticoat government.
Knickerbocker's History of New York, IV, 4

9 They claim to be the first inventors of those re-
condite beverages, cocktail, stonefence, and sherry
cobbler.
Knickerbocker's History of New York, IV, 241

10 There is in every true woman's heart a spark of
heavenly fire, which lies dormant in the broad daylight of prosperity; but which kindles up, and beam[s]
and blazes in the dark hour of adversity.
The Sketch-Book [1819–1820]. The Wi[fe]

11 Those men are most apt to be obsequious an[d]
conciliating abroad, who are under the discipline [of]
shrews at home. *The Sketch-Book. Rip Van Winkl[e]*

12 A sharp tongue is the only edged tool that grow[s]
keener with constant use.
The Sketch-Book. Rip Van Winkl[e]

13 That happy age when a man can be idle with im[-]
punity. *The Sketch-Book. Rip Van Winkl[e]*

14 A woman's whole life is a history of the affec[-]
tions. *The Sketch-Book. The Broken Hear[t]*

15 His [the author's] renown . . . has been pur[-]
chased, not by deeds of violence and blood, but b[y]
the diligent dispensation of pleasure.
*The Sketch-Book. Westminster Abbey [The
Poets' Corner]*

16 Whenever a man's friends begin to complimen[t]
him about looking young, he may be sure that the[y]
think he is growing old.
Bracebridge Hall [1822]. Bachelor[s]

17 I am always at a loss to know how much to be[-]
lieve of my own stories.
Tales of a Traveler [1824]. To the Reade[r]

18 The almighty dollar, that great object of univer[-]
sal devotion throughout our land.
Wolfert's Roost [1855]. The Creole Villag[e]

Stendhal [Henri Beyle]
1783–1842

19 Almost all our misfortunes in life come from th[e]
wrong notions we have about the things that hap[-]
pen to us. To know men thoroughly, to judge event[s]
sanely is, therefore, a great step towards happiness.
Journal [December 10, 1801]

20 I call "crystallization" that action of the mind
that discovers fresh perfections in its beloved a[t]
every turn of events. *De l'Amour [1822], ch. 1[2]*

21 A wise woman never yields by appointment. It
should always be an unforeseen happiness.
De l'Amour, 60

22 Prudery is a kind of avarice, the worst of all.
De l'Amour, fragments

23 In matters of sentiment, the public has very
crude ideas; and the most shocking fault of women
is that they make the public the supreme judge of
their lives. *De l'Amour, fragments*

1   A novel is a mirror that strolls along a highway. Now it reflects the blue of the skies, now the mud puddles underfoot.
Le Rouge et le Noir (The Red and the Black)[1]
[1830]

2   There is no such thing as "natural law": this expression is nothing but old nonsense. Prior to laws, what is natural is only the strength of the lion, or the need of the creature suffering from hunger or cold, in short, need.   *Le Rouge et le Noir*

3   I see but one rule: to be clear. If I am not clear, all my world crumbles to nothing.
Reply to Balzac [October 30, 1840]

4   Wit lasts no more than two centuries.
Reply to Balzac

5   It is the nobility of their style which will make our writers of 1840 unreadable forty years from now.   *Manuscript note [1840]*

6   Love has always been the most important business in my life, I should say the only one.
La Vie d'Henri Brulard [1890]

Allan Cunningham
1784–1842

7 A wet sheet and a flowing sea,
A wind that follows fast,
And fills the white and rustling sail,
And bends the gallant mast.
The Songs of Scotland [1825]. A Wet Sheet and a Flowing Sea, st. 1

[James Henry] Leigh Hunt
1784–1859

8   This Adonis in loveliness was a corpulent man of fifty.[2]   *The Examiner [March 22, 1812]*

9 Where the light woods go seaward from the town.
The Story of Rimini [1816], canto I, l. 18

10 Green little vaulter in the sunny grass.
To the Grasshopper and the Cricket [1817]

11 There lived a knight, when knighthood was in flow'r,
Who charmed alike the tilt-yard and the bower.
The Gentle Armour [1832], canto I

12 Abou Ben Adhem (may his tribe increase!)
Awoke one night from a deep dream of peace.
Abou Ben Adhem [1838]

13 An angel writing in a book of gold.
Abou Ben Adhem

14 Write me as one that loves his fellow men.
Abou Ben Adhem

15 And showed the names whom love of God had bless'd,
And lo! Ben Adhem's name led all the rest.
Abou Ben Adhem

16 Jenny kissed me when we met,
Jumping from the chair she sat in;
Time, you thief, who love to get
Sweets into your list, put that in:
Say I'm weary, say I'm sad,
Say that health and wealth have missed me,
Say I'm growing old, but add,
Jenny kissed me.[3]   *Rondeau [1838]*

17 A Venus grown fat!   *Blue-Stocking Revels*

18 "No love," quoth he, "but vanity, sets love a task like that."   *The Glove and the Lions, st. 4*

19   A pleasure so exquisite as almost to amount to pain.   *Letter to Alexander Ireland [June 2, 1848]*

Henry John Temple, Viscount Palmerston
1784–1865

20   We have no eternal allies and we have no perpetual enemies. Our interests are eternal and perpetual, and these interests it is our duty to follow.
Speech in the House of Commons on foreign policy [March 1, 1848]

Zachary Taylor
1784–1850

21   Hurrah for Old Kentuck! That's the way to do it. Give 'em hell, damn 'em.
Shouted to the 2nd Kentucky Regiment on seeing them rally in battle [Buena Vista, Mexico, February 23, 1847]

22   A little more grape, Captain Bragg.
Attributed [Buena Vista, Mexico, February 23, 1847]

23   Tell him to go to hell.
Reply to Santa Anna's demand for surrender [Buena Vista, Mexico, February 23, 1847]

---

[1]Translated by NORBERT GUTERMAN.

[2]For this reference to the Prince Regent, Hunt was imprisoned.

[3]Jenny was Jane Welsh Carlyle, who kissed Hunt when he brought Carlyle good news.

Thomas De Quincey
1785–1859

1   The burden of the incommunicable.
*Confessions of an English Opium Eater
[1822–1856], pt. I*

2   So, then, Oxford Street, stonyhearted step-mother, thou that listenest to the sighs of orphans, and drinkest the tears of children, at length I was dismissed from thee.
Confessions of an English Opium Eater, I

3   Thou only givest these gifts to man, and thou hast the keys of Paradise, O just, subtle, and mighty opium!   *Confessions of an English Opium Eater, II*

4   Everlasting farewells! and again, and yet again reverberated — everlasting farewells!
Confessions of an English Opium Eater, III

5   Dyspepsy is the ruin of most things: empires, expeditions, and everything else.
Letter to James Hessey [1823]

6   If once a man indulges himself in murder, very soon he comes to think little of robbing; and from robbing he comes next to drinking and Sabbath-breaking, and from that to incivility and procrastination.
Murder Considered as One of the Fine Arts [1827]

Lady Caroline Lamb
1785–1828

7   [Of Byron:] Mad, bad, and dangerous to know.
Journal [March 1812]

Thomas Love Peacock
1785–1866

8 Not drunk is he who from the floor
Can rise alone and still drink more;
But drunk is he who prostrate lies,
Without the power to drink or rise.
*The Misfortunes of Elphin [1829], ch. 3,
heading (translated from the Welsh)*

9 The mountain sheep are sweeter,
But the valley sheep are fatter;
We therefore deemed it meeter
To carry off the latter.
The Misfortunes of Elphin, 11

10   Ancient sculpture is the true school of modesty. But where the Greeks had modesty, we have cant; where they had poetry, we have cant; where they had patriotism, we have cant; where they had anything that exalts, delights, or adorns humanity, we have nothing but cant, cant, cant.
Crotchet Castle [1831], ch. .

11   A book that furnishes no quotations is, *me ju dice*, no book — it is a plaything.
Crotchet Castle, .

Oliver Hazard Perry
1785–1819

12   We have met the enemy, and they are ours.[1]
*Dispatch from U.S. brig Niagara to General
William Henry Harrison, announcing his
victory at the battle of Lake Erie [September
10, 1813]*

Samuel Woodworth
1785–1842

13 How dear to this heart are the scenes of my childhood,
When fond recollection presents them to view!
The Old Oaken Bucket

14 The old oaken bucket, the iron-bound bucket,
The moss-covered bucket which hung in the well.
The Old Oaken Bucket

David Crockett
1786–1836

15 I leave this rule for others when I'm dead,
Be always sure you're right — then go ahead.[2]
*Narrative of the Life of Colonel Crockett
[1834]*

16   My love was so hot as mighty nigh to burst my boilers.
Narrative of the Life of Colonel Crockett

17   If I could rest anywhere it would be in Arkansaw where the men are of the real half-horse, half-alligator breed such as grows nowhere else on the face of the earth.
Narrative of the Life of Colonel Crockett

---

[1]We have met the enemy and he is us. — WALT KELLY [1913–1973], 1970 *Pogo* cartoon, used in 1971 Earth Day poster. In its original form: We shall meet the enemy, and not only may he be ours, he may be us. — *The Pogo Papers* [1953], *introduction*

[2]Crockett's motto in the War of 1812.

1 Don't shoot, Colonel, I'll come down: I know I'm a gone coon.[1]

Story told by Crockett of a treed raccoon

William Learned Marcy
1786–1857

2 They see nothing wrong in the rule that to the victor belong the spoils of the enemy.

Speech in the Senate [January 1832]

Winfield Scott
1786–1866

3 The enemy say that Americans are good at a long shot, but cannot stand the cold iron. I call upon you instantly to give a lie to the slander. Charge!

Address to the 11th Infantry Regiment [Chippewa, Canada, June 5, 1814]

4 Say to the seceded States, "Wayward sisters, depart in peace."

Letter to W. H. Seward [March 3, 1861]

Seattle[2]
c. 1786–1866

5 When the last red man has vanished from this earth, and his memory is only a story among the whites, these shores will still swarm with the invisible dead of my people. And when your children's children think they are alone in the fields, the forests, the shops, the highways, or the quiet of the woods, they will not be alone. There is no place in this country where a man can be alone. At night when the streets of your town and cities are quiet, and you think they are empty, they will throng with the returning spirits that once thronged them, and that still love these places. The white man will never be alone. Let him be just and deal kindly with my people, for the dead are not powerless.

Speech to governor of Washington Territory [c. 1855]

---

[1]A humorous Revolutionary War expression referring to a story about a backwoods spy dressed in raccoon skins who said to the British soldiers who discovered him, "I'm a gone coon." — STUART BERG FLEXNER, *I Hear America Talking* (1976)

[2]Chief of the Suquamish and Dowamish tribes of Puget Sound. The city of Seattle was named after him. A popular picture book, *Brother Eagle, Sister Sky: A Message from Chief Seattle* [1991], and other sources conflate Seattle's statement with modern-day material from a 1971–1972 television documentary on ecology written by Ted Perry. In the embellished, environmentally sensitive version, Seattle refers to seeing buffalo herds and railroad trains, neither of which in his lifetime existed within six hundred miles of the tribal territories.

François Guizot
1787–1874

6 Enrich yourselves![3]   *Speech [March 1, 1843]*

Emma Willard
1787–1870

7 Rocked in the cradle of the deep.

The Cradle of the Deep [1831]

George Noel Gordon, Lord Byron
1788–1824

8 "Friendship is Love without his wings!"

L'Amitié Est l'Amour sans Ailes[4] [written 1806]

9 I only know we loved in vain;
I only feel — farewell! farewell!

Farewell! If Ever Fondest Prayer [1808], st. 2

10 Near this spot are deposited the remains of one who possessed beauty without vanity, strength without insolence, courage without ferocity, and all the virtues of Man, without his vices. This praise, which would be unmeaning flattery if inscribed over human ashes, is but a just tribute to the memory of Boatswain, a dog.

Inscription on the monument of a Newfoundland dog [1808]

11 The poor dog, in life the firmest friend,
The first to welcome, foremost to defend.

Inscription on the monument of a Newfoundland dog

12 I'll publish right or wrong:
Fools are my theme, let satire be my song.

English Bards and Scotch Reviewers [1809], l. 5

13 'Tis pleasant, sure, to see one's name in print;
A book's a book, although there's nothing in 't.

English Bards and Scotch Reviewers, l. 51

14 A man must serve his time to every trade
Save censure — critics all are ready-made.

English Bards and Scotch Reviewers, l. 63

15 With just enough of learning to misquote.

English Bards and Scotch Reviewers, l. 66

16 As soon
Seek roses in December, ice in June;
Hope constancy in wind, or corn in chaff;

---

[3]Enrichissez-vous!

[4]A French proverb.

Believe a woman or an epitaph,
Or any other thing that's false, before
You trust in critics.
English Bards and Scotch Reviewers, l. 75

1 Better to err with Pope, than shine with Pye.
English Bards and Scotch Reviewers, l. 102

2 Maid of Athens, ere we part,
Give, oh give me back my heart!
Maid of Athens [1810], st. 1

3 Vex'd with mirth the drowsy ear of night.
Childe Harold's Pilgrimage, canto I [1812],
st. 2

4 Had sigh'd to many, though he loved but one.
Childe Harold's Pilgrimage, I, st. 5

5 Maidens, like moths, are ever caught by glare,
And Mammon wins his way where seraphs might
despair.   *Childe Harold's Pilgrimage, I, st. 9*

6 Might shake the saintship of an anchorite.[1]
Childe Harold's Pilgrimage, I, st. 11

7 War, war is still the cry, "War even to the knife!"[2]
Childe Harold's Pilgrimage, I, st. 86

8 Gone—glimmering through the dream of things
that were.
Childe Harold's Pilgrimage, II [1812], st. 2

9 A schoolboy's tale, the wonder of an hour!
Childe Harold's Pilgrimage, II, st. 2

10 Who would be free themselves must strike the
blow.   *Childe Harold's Pilgrimage, II, st. 76*

11 Where'er we tread 'tis haunted, holy ground.
Childe Harold's Pilgrimage, II, st. 88

12 What is the worst of woes that wait on age?
What stamps the wrinkle deeper on the brow?
To view each loved one blotted from life's page,
And be alone on earth, as I am now.
Childe Harold's Pilgrimage, II, st. 98

13 Once more upon the waters, yet once more!
And the waves bound beneath me as a steed
That knows his rider!
Childe Harold's Pilgrimage, III [1816], st. 2

14   Years steal
Fire from the mind as vigor from the limb;
And life's enchanted cup but sparkles near the
brim.   *Childe Harold's Pilgrimage, III, st. 8*

15 And Harold stands upon this place of skulls.
Childe Harold's Pilgrimage, III, st. 1

16 There was a sound of revelry by night,
And Belgium's capital had gather'd then
Her beauty and her chivalry, and bright
The lamps shone o'er fair women and brave men.
A thousand hearts beat happily; and when
Music arose with its voluptuous swell,
Soft eyes look'd love to eyes which spake again,
And all went merry as a marriage bell.
But hush! hark! a deep sound strikes like a rising
knell!   *Childe Harold's Pilgrimage, III, st. 2*

17 Did ye not hear it?—No! 'twas but the wind,
Or the car rattling o'er the stony street.
On with the dance! let joy be unconfined;
No sleep till morn, when Youth and Pleasure meet
To chase the glowing hours with flying feet.
Childe Harold's Pilgrimage, III, st. 2

18 Like to the apples on the Dead Sea's shore,
All ashes to the taste.
Childe Harold's Pilgrimage, III, st. 3

19   Thou fatal Waterloo.
Millions of tongues record thee, and anew
Their children's lips shall echo them, and say—
"Here, where the sword united nations drew,
Our countrymen were warring on that day!"
And this is much, and all which will not pass away.
Childe Harold's Pilgrimage, III, st. 3

20 He who ascends to mountaintops, shall find
The loftiest peaks most wrapt in clouds and snow;
He who surpasses or subdues mankind
Must look down on the hate of those below.
Childe Harold's Pilgrimage, III, st. 4

21 All tenantless, save to the crannying wind.
Childe Harold's Pilgrimage, III, st. 4

22 History's purchased page to call them great.
Childe Harold's Pilgrimage, III, st. 4

23 The castled crag of Drachenfels
Frowns o'er the wide and winding Rhine.
Childe Harold's Pilgrimage, III, st. 5

24 To fly from, need not be to hate, mankind.
Childe Harold's Pilgrimage, III, st. 6

25 By the blue rushing of the arrowy Rhone.
Childe Harold's Pilgrimage, III, st. 7

26 I live not in myself, but I become
Portion of that around me: and to me

---

[1]Such lips would tempt a saint; such hands as those / Would make an anchorite lascivious. —JOHN FORD, *'Tis Pity She's a Whore* [1633], *act* I, *sc. iii, l.* 196

[2]War even to the knife! —JOSÉ DE PALAFOX Y MELZI [1775–1847] Palafox, governor of Saragossa, had been summoned by the besieging French to surrender the city [1808].

---

[3]This was the passage Sir Winston Churchill quoted to Preside Franklin D. Roosevelt when both agreed to substitute the ter United Nations for Associated Powers in the pact that the tw leaders wished all the free nations to sign. [In a conference at th White House, January 1942]

High mountains are a feeling, but the hum
Of human cities torture.
Childe Harold's Pilgrimage, III, st. 72

1 Sapping a solemn creed with solemn sneer.
Childe Harold's Pilgrimage, III, st. 107

2 Fame is the thirst of youth.
Childe Harold's Pilgrimage, III, st. 112

3 I have not loved the world, nor the world me;
I have not flatter'd its rank breath, nor bow'd
To its idolatries a patient knee.
Childe Harold's Pilgrimage, III, st. 113

4   I stood
Among them, but not of them; in a shroud
Of thoughts which were not their thoughts.
Childe Harold's Pilgrimage, III, st. 113

5 I stood in Venice on the Bridge of Sighs,
A palace and a prison on each hand.
Childe Harold's Pilgrimage, IV [1818], st. 1

6 Where Venice sate in state, throned on her hundred
      isles.
Childe Harold's Pilgrimage, IV, st. 1

7 She looks a sea Cybele, fresh from ocean,
Rising with her tiara of proud towers
At airy distance, with majestic motion,
A ruler of the waters and their powers.
Childe Harold's Pilgrimage, IV, st. 2

8 The beings of the mind are not of clay;
Essentially immortal, they create
And multiply in us a brighter ray
And more beloved existence.
Childe Harold's Pilgrimage, IV, st. 5

9 'Tis solitude should teach us how to die;
It hath no flatterers; vanity can give
No hollow aid; alone—man with his God must
      strive.
Childe Harold's Pilgrimage, IV, st. 33

10 The Ariosto of the North.[1]
Childe Harold's Pilgrimage, IV, st. 40

11 Italia! O Italia! thou who hast
The fatal gift of beauty.
Childe Harold's Pilgrimage, IV, st. 42

12 Let these describe the undescribable.
Childe Harold's Pilgrimage, IV, st. 53

13 The starry Galileo, with his woes.
Childe Harold's Pilgrimage, IV, st. 54

14 The poetry of speech.
Childe Harold's Pilgrimage, IV, st. 58

15 Then farewell, Horace; whom I hated so,
Not for thy faults, but mine.
Childe Harold's Pilgrimage, IV, st. 77

16 O Rome! my country! city of the soul!
Childe Harold's Pilgrimage, IV, st. 78

17 The Niobe of nations! there she stands,
Childless and crownless, in her voiceless woe.
Childe Harold's Pilgrimage, IV, st. 79

18 Yet, Freedom! yet thy banner, torn, but flying,
Streams like the thunderstorm *against* the wind.
Childe Harold's Pilgrimage, IV, st. 98

19 Alas! our young affections run to waste,
Or water but the desert.
Childe Harold's Pilgrimage, IV, st. 120

20 Of its own beauty is the mind diseased.
Childe Harold's Pilgrimage, IV, st. 122

21 Time, the avenger! unto thee I lift
My hands, and eyes, and heart, and crave of thee
      a gift.   *Childe Harold's Pilgrimage, IV, st. 130*

22 Butcher'd to make a Roman holiday!
Childe Harold's Pilgrimage, IV, st. 141

23 "While stands the Coliseum, Rome shall stand;
When falls the Coliseum, Rome shall fall;
And when Rome falls—the world."[2]
Childe Harold's Pilgrimage, IV, st. 145

24 Oh! that the desert were my dwelling place.
Childe Harold's Pilgrimage, IV, st. 177

25 There is a pleasure in the pathless woods,
There is a rapture on the lonely shore,
There is society, where none intrudes,
By the deep sea, and music in its roar:
I love not man the less, but Nature more.
Childe Harold's Pilgrimage, IV, st. 178

26 Roll on, thou deep and dark blue ocean—roll!
Ten thousand fleets sweep over thee in vain;
Man marks the earth with ruin—his control
Stops with the shore.
Childe Harold's Pilgrimage, IV, st. 179

27 He sinks into thy depths with bubbling
      groan,
Without a grave, unknell'd, uncoffin'd, and
      unknown.
Childe Harold's Pilgrimage, IV, st. 179

28 Time writes no wrinkle on thine azure brow—
Such as creation's dawn beheld, thou rollest now.
Childe Harold's Pilgrimage, IV, st. 182

---

[1]Walter Scott.

[2]The saying of the ancient pilgrims, quoted from Bede by Gibbon in *Decline and Fall of the Roman Empire* [1776–1788], *ch. 71.*

1 Thou glorious mirror, where the Almighty's form
   Glasses itself in tempests.
   Childe Harold's Pilgrimage, IV, st. 183

2 Dark-heaving—boundless, endless, and sublime—
   The image of Eternity.
   Childe Harold's Pilgrimage, IV, st. 183

3 And I have loved thee, Ocean! and my joy
   Of youthful sports was on thy breast to be
   Borne, like thy bubbles, onward: from a boy
   I wanton'd with thy breakers.
   Childe Harold's Pilgrimage, IV, st. 184

4 And trusted to thy billows far and near,
   And laid my hand upon thy mane—as I do here.
   Childe Harold's Pilgrimage, IV, st. 184

5   I awoke one morning and found myself famous.
   *Entry in Memoranda after publication of first
   two cantos of Childe Harold's Pilgrimage.
   From* THOMAS MOORE, *Life of Byron [1830],
   ch. 14*

6 Clime of the unforgotten brave!
   The Giaour [1813], l. 103

7 I die—but first I have possess'd,
   And come what may, I have been bless'd.
   The Giaour, l. 1114

8 Mark! where his carnage and his conquests cease!
   He makes a solitude, and calls it—peace!
   The Bride of Abydos [1813], canto II, st. 20

9   The fatal facility of the octosyllabic verse.
   The Corsair [1814]. Dedication

10 Such hath it been—shall be—beneath the sun
   The many still must labor for the one.
   The Corsair, canto I, st. 8

11 The Cincinnatus of the West,
   Whom envy dared not hate,
   Bequeathed the name of Washington
   To make man blush there was but one!
   Ode to Napoleon Bonaparte [1814], st. 19

12 Lord of himself—that heritage of woe.
   Lara [1814], canto I, st. 2

13 She walks in beauty, like the night
   Of cloudless climes and starry skies;
   And all that's best of dark and bright
   Meet in her aspect and her eyes:
   Thus mellow'd to that tender light
   Which heaven to gaudy day denies.
   *Hebrew Melodies [1815]. She Walks in Beauty,
   st. 1*

14 The Assyrian came down like the wolf on the fold,
   And his cohorts were gleaming in purple and gold;

And the sheen of their spears was like stars on the
   sea,
   When the blue wave rolls nightly on deep Galilee.
   *Hebrew Melodies. The Destruction of
   Sennacherib, st. 1*

15 And the might of the Gentile, unsmote by the
   sword,
   Hath melted like snow in the glance of the Lord!
   *Hebrew Melodies. The Destruction of
   Sennacherib, st. 6*

16 There's not a joy the world can give like that it
   takes away,
   When the glow of early thought declines in
   feeling's dull decay.
   Stanzas for Music [1815], st.

17 The glory and the nothing of a name.
   Churchill's Grave, l. 4

18 For years fleet away with the wings of the dove.
   The First Kiss of Love, st.

19 Fare thee well! and if forever,
   Still forever, fare thee well.
   Fare Thee Well [1816], st.

20 Sighing that Nature form'd but one such man,
   And broke the die, in molding Sheridan.
   *Monody on the Death of Sheridan [1816],
   l. 117*

21 Eternal Spirit of the chainless Mind!
   Brightest in dungeons, Liberty! thou art.
   *The Prisoner of Chillon [1816]. Sonnet on
   Chillon, l. 1*

22 A light broke in upon my brain—
   It was the carol of a bird;
   It ceased, and then it came again,
   The sweetest song ear ever heard.
   *The Prisoner of Chillon. Sonnet on Chillon,
   st. 10*

23 There be none of Beauty's daughters
   With a magic like thee;
   And like music on the waters
   Is thy sweet voice to me.
   Stanzas for Music [1816], st.

24 I had a dream which was not all a dream.
   Darkness [181

25 Though the day of my destiny's over,
   And the star of my fate hath declined.
   Stanzas to Augusta [1816], st.

26 My boat is on the shore,
   And my bark is on the sea;
   But, before I go, Tom Moore,
   Here's a double health to thee!

Here's a sigh to those who love me,
And a smile to those who hate;
And, whatever sky's above me,
Here's a heart for every fate.
To Thomas Moore [1817], st. 1, 2

1 So we'll go no more a-roving
So late into the night,
Though the heart be still as loving,
And the moon be still as bright.

For the sword outwears its sheath,
And the soul wears out the breast,
And the heart must pause to breathe,
And love itself have rest.

Though the night was made for loving,
And the day returns too soon,
Yet we'll go no more a-roving
By the light of the moon.
So We'll Go No More A-Roving [1817]

2 Sorrow is knowledge: they who know the most
Must mourn the deepest o'er the fatal truth,
The Tree of Knowledge is not that of Life.
Manfred [1817], act I, sc. i

3 His heart was one of those which most enamor us,
Wax to receive, and marble to retain.
Beppo [1818], st. 34

4 I love the language, that soft bastard Latin,
Which melts like kisses from a female mouth.
Beppo, st. 44

5 I wish he[1] would explain his explanation.
Don Juan. Dedication [written 1818], st. 2

6 But—Oh! ye lords of ladies intellectual,
Inform us truly, have they not henpeck'd
you all?   *Don Juan, canto I, st. 22*

7 Her stature tall—I hate a dumpy woman.
Don Juan, I, st. 61

8 What men call gallantry, and gods adultery,
Is much more common where the climate's sultry.
Don Juan, I, st. 63

9 Christians have burnt each other, quite persuaded
That all the Apostles would have done as they did.
Don Juan, I, st. 83

10 A little still she strove, and much repented,
And whispering "I will ne'er consent"—
consented.
Don Juan, I, st. 117

11 'Tis sweet to hear the watchdog's honest bark
Bay deep-mouth'd welcome as we draw near home;

'Tis sweet to know there is an eye will mark
Our coming, and look brighter when we come.
Don Juan, I, st. 123

12 Sweet is revenge—especially to women.
Don Juan, I, st. 124

13 Pleasure's a sin, and sometimes sin's a pleasure.
Don Juan, I, st. 133

14 Man's love is of man's life a thing apart,
'Tis woman's whole existence.   *Don Juan, I, st. 194*

15 What is the end of fame? 'tis but to fill
A certain portion of uncertain paper:
Some liken it to climbing up a hill,
Whose summit, like all hills, is lost in vapor.
Don Juan, I, st. 218

16 There's nought, no doubt, so much the spirit calms
As rum and true religion.
Don Juan, II [1819], st. 34

17 A solitary shriek, the bubbling cry
Of some strong swimmer in his agony.
Don Juan, II, st. 53

18 Let us have wine and women, mirth and laughter,
Sermons and soda water the day after.
Don Juan, II, st. 178

19 Man, being reasonable, must get drunk;
The best of life is but intoxication.
Don Juan, II, st. 179

20   For man, to man so oft unjust,
Is always so to women; one sole bond
Awaits them, treachery is all their trust;
Taught to conceal, their bursting hearts despond
Over their idol, till some wealthier lust
Buys them in marriage—and what rests beyond?
A thankless husband, next a faithless lover,
Then dressing, nursing, praying, and all's over.
Don Juan, II, st. 200

21 In her first passion woman loves her lover,
In all the others, all she loves is love.
Don Juan, III [1821], st. 3

22 Think you, if Laura had been Petrarch's wife,
He would have written sonnets all his life?
Don Juan, III, st. 8

23 Even good men like to make the public stare.
Don Juan, III, st. 81

24 The isles of Greece, the isles of Greece![2]
Where burning Sappho loved and sung.
Don Juan, III, st. 86 [song, st. 1]

---

[1]Samuel Taylor Coleridge.

[2]From isles of Greece / The princes orgulous, their high blood
chaf'd, / Have to the port of Athens sent their ships.—WILLIAM
SHAKESPEARE, *Troilus and Cressida, prologue*

1 Eternal summer gilds them yet,
   But all, except their sun, is set.
                  Don Juan, III, st. 86 [song, st. 1]

2 The mountains look on Marathon,
   And Marathon looks on the sea;
   And musing there an hour alone,
   I dreamed that Greece might still be free.
                  Don Juan, III, st. 86 [song, st. 3]

3 Earth! render back from out thy breast
   A remnant of our Spartan dead!
   Of the three hundred grant but three,
   To make a new Thermopylae.
                  Don Juan, III, st. 86 [song, st. 7]

4 What, silent still? and silent all?
   Ah! no;—the voices of the dead
   Sound like a distant torrent's fall.
                  Don Juan, III, st. 86 [song, st. 8]

5 And if I laugh at any mortal thing,
   'Tis that I may not weep.
                  Don Juan, IV [1821], st. 4

6   These two hated with a hate
   Found only on the stage.   *Don Juan, IV, st. 93*

7   I've stood upon Achilles' tomb,
   And heard Troy doubted; time will doubt of
            Rome.   *Don Juan, IV, st. 101*

8 There's not a sea the passenger e'er pukes in,
   Turns up more dangerous breakers than the
            Euxine.   *Don Juan, V [1821], st. 5*

9 And put himself upon his good behavior.
                  Don Juan, V, st. 47

10 The women pardon'd all except her face.
                  Don Juan, V, st. 113

11 A lady of "a certain age," which means
    Certainly aged.   *Don Juan, VI [1823], st. 69*

12 Not so Leonidas and Washington,
    Whose every battlefield is holy ground,
    Which breathes of nations saved, not worlds un-
            done.   *Don Juan, VIII [1823], st. 5*

13 "Gentlemen farmers"—a race worn out quite.
                  Don Juan, IX [1823], st. 32

14 When Bishop Berkeley said "there was no matter,"
    And proved it—'twas no matter what he said.
                  Don Juan, XI [1823], st. 1

15 And, after all, what is a lie? 'Tis but
    The truth in masquerade.   *Don Juan, XI, st. 37*

16 'Tis strange the mind, that very fiery particle,
    Should let itself be snuff'd out by an article.
                  Don Juan, XI, st. 60 (of John Keats)

17 Ready money is Aladdin's lamp.
                  Don Juan, XII [1823], st. 1

18 Cervantes smil'd Spain's chivalry away.
                  Don Juan, XIII [1823], st. 1

19 The English winter—ending in July,
    To recommence in August.
                  Don Juan, XIII, st. 4

20 Society is now one polish'd horde,
    Formed of two mighty tribes, the *Bores* and *Bored.*
                  Don Juan, XIII, st. 9

21   All human history attests
    That happiness for man—the hungry sinner!—
    Since Eve ate apples, much depends on dinner.
                  Don Juan, XIII, st. 9

22 Of all the horrid, hideous notes of woe,
    Sadder than owl songs or the midnight blast,
    Is that portentous phrase, "I told you so."
                  Don Juan, XIV [1823], st. 5

23 'Tis strange—but true; for truth is always strange;
    Stranger than fiction.[1]   *Don Juan, XIV, st. 10*

24 The Devil hath not, in all his quiver's choice,
    An arrow for the heart like a sweet voice.
                  Don Juan, XV [1824], st. 13

25 The antique Persians taught three useful things—
    To draw the bow, to ride, and speak the truth.
                  Don Juan, XVI [1824], st. 1

26 Oh, talk not to me of a name great in story;
    The days of our youth are the days of our glory;
    And the myrtle and ivy of sweet two-and-twenty
    Are worth all your laurels, though ever so plenty.
                  *Stanzas Written on the Road Between Florence
                  and Pisa [1821], st. 1*

27 All farewells should be sudden.
                  Sardanapalus [1821], act V

28   The best of prophets of the future is the past.
                  Journal [January 28, 1821]

29 The world is a bundle of hay,
    Mankind are the asses that pull,
    Each tugs in a different way—
    And the greatest of all is John Bull!
                  Letter to Thomas Moore [June 22, 1821]

30   Because
    He is all-powerful, must all-good, too, follow?
    I judge but by the fruits—and they are bitter—
    Which I must feed on for a fault not mine.
                  Cain [1821], act I, sc. i

---

[1] Le vrai peut quelquefois n'être pas vraisemblable [Truth may sometimes be improbable].—BOILEAU, *L'Art Poétique, III, l. 48*
Truth is stranger than fiction, but not so popular.—*Anonymous*

◄ Who killed John Keats?
"I," says the Quarterly,
So savage and Tartarly;
" 'Twas one of my feats."   *John Keats [c. 1821]*

2   He seems
To have seen better days, as who has not
Who has seen yesterday?
          Werner [1822], act I, sc. i

3 The "good old times" — all times when old are
          good —
Are gone.   *The Age of Bronze [1823], st. 1*

4 Whose[1] game was empires and whose stakes were
          thrones,
Whose table earth — whose dice were human
          bones.
          The Age of Bronze, st. 3

5 While Franklin's quiet memory climbs to heaven,
Calming the lightning which he thence had riven,
Or drawing from the no less kindled earth
Freedom and peace to that which boasts his birth;
While Washington's a watchword, such as ne'er
Shall sink while there's an echo left to air.
          The Age of Bronze, st. 5

6 Sublime tobacco! which from east to west
Cheers the tar's labor or the Turkman's rest.[2]
          The Island [1823], canto II, st. 19

7   What's drinking?
A mere pause from thinking!
          *The Deformed Transformed [1824], act III,
          sc. i*

8 My days are in the yellow leaf;
The flowers and fruits of love are gone;
The worm, the canker, and the grief
Are mine alone!
          On My Thirty-sixth Year [1824], st. 2

9 Seek out — less often sought than found —
A soldier's grave, for thee the best;
Then look around, and choose thy ground,
And take thy rest.
          On My Thirty-sixth Year, st. 10

10   Now Barabbas was a publisher.
          Alleged alteration in the Bible, John 18:40[3]

---

[1]Napoleon.

[2]Let Aristotle and all your philosophers say what they like, there is nothing to be compared with tobacco. — MOLIÈRE, *Dom Juan; ou Le Festin de Pierre* [1665], *act I, sc. i*
Translated by CURTIS HIDDEN PAGE.

[3]The publisher John Murray sent Byron a Bible in acknowledgment of a favor, and the poet returned it with the word "robber" changed to "publisher."

Sarah Josepha Hale
1788–1879

11 Mary had a little lamb,
Its fleece was white as snow,
And everywhere that Mary went,
The lamb was sure to go.
          Mary's Lamb,[4] *st. 1. From The Juvenile
          Miscellany [September 1830]*

Arthur Schopenhauer
1788–1860

12   To marry is to halve your rights and double your
duties.
          The World as Will and Idea [1819], vol. II

13   Hatred comes from the heart; contempt from
the head; and neither feeling is quite within our
control.
          Studies in Pessimism [1851].[5] *Psychological
          Observations*

14   Every man takes the limits of his own field of vision for the limits of the world.
          Studies in Pessimism. Psychological Observations

15   Every parting gives a foretaste of death; every coming together again a foretaste of the resurrection.
          Studies in Pessimism. Psychological Observations

16   Dissimulation is innate in woman, and almost as
much a quality of the stupid as of the clever.
          Studies in Pessimism. On Women

17   The two foes of human happiness are pain and
boredom.   *Essays. Personality; or, What a Man Is*

18   A man who has no mental needs, because his intellect is of the narrow and normal amount, is, in the
strict sense of the word, what is called a philistine.
          Essays. Personality; or, What a Man Is

19   Intellect is invisible to the man who has none.
          Essays. Our Relation to Others, sec. 23

20   There is no more mistaken path to happiness
than worldliness, revelry, high life.
          Essays. Our Relation to Ourselves, sec. 24

21   Do not shorten the morning by getting up late;
look upon it as the quintessence of life, as to a certain extent sacred.
          Counsels and Maxims, ch. 2

---

[4]According to *The Story of Mary's Little Lamb* [1928], the first three stanzas of the poem are by John Roulstone [1805–1822]; Sarah Josepha Hale's "genius completed the poem in its present form" (six stanzas); "Mary" was Mary Elizabeth Sawyer [1806–1889] of Sterling, Massachusetts; and the events of the poem are true.

[5]Translated by T. BAILEY SAUNDERS.

James Fenimore Cooper
1789–1851

1   Few men exhibit greater diversity, or, if we may so express it, greater antithesis of character than the native warrior of North America. In war, he is daring, boastful, cunning, ruthless, self-denying, and self-devoted; in peace, just, generous, hospitable, revengeful, superstitious, modest, and commonly chaste.

The Last of the Mohicans [1826]

2   'Tis grand! 'tis solemn! 'tis an education of itself to look upon!

The Deerslayer [1841], ch. 2

3   Those families, you know, are our upper crust — not upper ten thousand.

The Ways of the Hour [1850], ch. 6

Astolphe Louis Léonard, Marquis de Custine
1790–1857

4   This empire [Russia], vast as it is, is only a prison to which the emperor holds the key.

La Russie en 1839.[1] *Peterhof, July 23, 1839*

5   Whoever has really seen Russia will find himself content to live anywhere else. It is always good to know that a society exists where no happiness is possible because, by a law of nature, man cannot be happy unless he is free.

La Russie en 1839. Conclusion

Fitz-Greene Halleck
1790–1867

6 Green be the turf above thee,
Friend of my better days!
None knew thee but to love thee,
Nor named thee but to praise.

On the Death of Joseph Rodman Drake [1820], st. 1

7 One of the few, the immortal names
That were not born to die.

Marco Bozzaris [1855], st. 7

Alphonse de Lamartine
1790–1869

8   O time, arrest your flight! and you, propitio[us] hours, arrest your course! Let us savor the fleeti[ng] delights of our most beautiful days![2]

The Lake [1820], st.

9   I say to this night: "Pass more slowly"; and t[he] dawn will come to dispel the night.[3]

The Lake, st.

10   Limited in his nature, infinite in his desires, ma[n] is a fallen god who remembers the heavens.

Méditations Poétiques [1820]. Sermon

11   What is our life but a succession of preludes t[o] that unknown song whose first solemn note [is] sounded by death?[4]

Méditations Poétiques, 2nd series. Sermon 1

12   The more I see of the representatives of the peo[ple], the more I admire my dogs.

From A. G. G. D'ORSAY, Letter to John Forste[r] [1850]

Samuel Gilman
1791–1858

13 Fair Harvard! Thy sons to thy Jubilee throng.

Ode, Bicentennial, Harvard University [September 8, 1836], st. 1

14 First flower of their wilderness, star of their night,
Calm rising through change and through storm.

Ode, Bicentennial, Harvard University, st.

John Howard Payne
1791–1852

15 'Mid pleasures and palaces though we may roam,
Be it ever so humble, there's no place like home.[5]

Home, Sweet Home. From the opera Clari, the Maid of Milan [1823]

---

[1]Translated by PHYLLIS PENN KOHLER.

[2]O temps, suspends ton vol! et vous, heures propices, / Suspendez votre cours! / Laissez-nous savourer les rapides délices / Des plus beaux de nos jours!

[3]Je dis à cette nuit: "Sois plus lente"; et l'aurore / Va dissiper la nuit.

[4]This passage was used by Franz Liszt as a heading for his tone poem *Les Préludes.*

[5]Home is home, be it never so homely. — *English proverb* [c. 1300]

Charles Wolfe
1791–1823

1 Not a drum was heard, not a funeral note,
  As his corse to the rampart we hurried.
*The Burial of Sir John Moore at Corunna
[1817], st. 1*

2 But he lay like a warrior taking his rest,
  With his martial cloak around him.
The Burial of Sir John Moore at Corunna, st. 3

3 We carved not a line, and we raised not a stone —
  But we left him alone with his glory.
The Burial of Sir John Moore at Corunna, st. 8

Victor Cousin
1792–1867

4   We need religion for religion's sake, morality for
morality's sake, art for art's sake.
Cours de Philosophie [1818]

John Keble
1792–1866

5 The voice that breathed o'er Eden
  That earliest wedding day.
Poems [1869]. Holy Matrimony, st. 1

Frederick Marryat
1792–1848

6   All zeal, Mr. Easy.
Midshipman Easy [1836], ch. 9

7   I haven't the gift of the gab, my sons — because
  I'm bred to the sea.   *The Old Navy, st. 1*

8   It's just six of one and half a dozen of the other.
The Pirate, ch. 4

9   Every man paddle his own canoe.
Settlers in Canada [1844], ch. 8

Joseph Mohr
1792–1848

10 Silent night! Holy night![1]
  All is calm, all is bright.   *Holy Night [1818]*

---

[1] Stille Nacht! Heilige Nacht!
Music by FRANZ GRÜBER [1787–1863].

Lord John Russell
1792–1878

11   If peace cannot be maintained with honor, it is
no longer peace.
Speech at Greenock [September 19, 1853]

12   Among the defects of the bill, which were numerous, one provision was conspicuous by its presence
and another by its absence.
*Speech to the electors of the City of London
[April 1859]*

Percy Bysshe Shelley
1792–1822

13 Power, like a desolating pestilence,
  Pollutes whate'er it touches; and obedience,
  Bane of all genius, virtue, freedom, truth,
  Makes slaves of men, and, of the human frame,
  A mechanized automaton.
Queen Mab [1813], pt. III

14 The awful shadow of some unseen Power
  Floats though unseen among us — visiting
  This various world with as inconstant wing
  As summer winds that creep from flower
    to flower.
Hymn to Intellectual Beauty [1816], st. 1

15 Spirit of Beauty, that dost consecrate
  With thine own hues all thou dost shine upon
  Of human thought or form.
Hymn to Intellectual Beauty, st. 2

16 Some say that gleams of a remoter world
  Visit the soul in sleep — that death is slumber,
  And that its shapes the busy thoughts outnumber
  Of those who wake and live.
Mont Blanc [1816], st. 3

17 Man's yesterday may ne'er be like his morrow;
  Nought may endure but Mutability.
Mutability [1816], st. 4

18 I met a traveler from an antique land
  Who said: Two vast and trunkless legs of stone
  Stand in the desert. Near them, on the sand,
  Half sunk, a shattered visage lies, whose frown,
  And wrinkled lip, and sneer of cold command,
  Tell that its sculptor well those passions read.
  Which yet survive, stamped on these lifeless things,
  The hand that mocked them and the heart that fed:
  And on the pedestal these words appear:
  "My name is Ozymandias, king of kings:
  Look on my works, ye Mighty, and despair!"
  Nothing beside remains. Round the decay

Of that colossal wreck, boundless and bare,
The lone and level sands stretch far away.

Ozymandias [1817]

1 With hue like that when some great painter dips
His pencil in the gloom of earthquake and eclipse.

The Revolt of Islam [1817], canto V, st. 23

2 I could lie down like a tired child,
And weep away the life of care
Which I have borne and yet must bear,
Till death like sleep might steal on me.

*Stanzas Written in Dejection near Naples
[1818], st. 4*

3   Ere Babylon was dust,
The Magus Zoroaster, my dead child,
Met his own image walking in the garden,
That apparition, sole of men, he saw.

*Prometheus Unbound [1818–1819], act I,
l. 191*

4 The good want power, but to weep barren tears.
The powerful goodness want: worse need for them.
The wise want love; and those who love want
        wisdom;
And all best things are thus confused with ill.

Prometheus Unbound, I, l. 625

5 Peace is in the grave.
The grave hides all things beautiful and good:
I am a God and cannot find it there.

Prometheus Unbound, I, l. 638

6 From the dust of creeds outworn.

Prometheus Unbound, I, l. 697

7 Forms more real than living man,
Nurslings of immortality!

Prometheus Unbound, I, l. 748

8 To know nor faith, nor love nor law; to be
Omnipotent but friendless is to reign.

Prometheus Unbound, II, sc. iv, l. 47

9   All love is sweet,
Given or returned. Common as light is love,
And its familiar voice wearies not ever. . . .
They who inspire it most are fortunate,
As I am now; but those who feel it most
Are happier still.

Prometheus Unbound, II, v, 39

10 Death is the veil which those who live call life:
They sleep, and it is lifted.[1]

Prometheus Unbound, III, iii, 113

11 Nor yet exempt, though ruling them like slaves,
From chance, and death, and mutability,

_____
[1]Lift not the painted veil which those who live / Call Life.—
PERCY BYSSHE SHELLEY, *Sonnet* [1818]

The clogs of that which else might overscar
The loftiest star of unascended heaven,
Pinnacled dim in the intense inane.

Prometheus Unbound, III, iv, 20

12 Familiar acts are beautiful through love.

Prometheus Unbound, IV, l. 40

13 Man, who wert once a despot and a slave;
A dupe and a deceiver; a decay;
A traveler from the cradle to the grave
Through the dim light of this immortal day.

Prometheus Unbound, IV, l. 54

14 To suffer woes which Hope thinks infinite;
To forgive wrongs darker than death or night;
To defy Power, which seems omnipotent;
To love, and bear; to hope till Hope creates
From its own wreck the thing it contemplates;
Neither to change, nor falter, nor repent;
This, like thy glory, Titan, is to be
Good, great and joyous, beautiful and free;
This is alone Life, Joy, Empire, and Victory.

Prometheus Unbound, IV, l. 57

15   I love all waste
And solitary places; where we taste
The pleasure of believing what we see
Is boundless, as we wish our souls to be.

Julian and Maddalo [1819], l. 14

16 Thou Paradise of exiles, Italy!

Julian and Maddalo, l. 57

17   It is our will
That thus enchains us to permitted ill—
We might be otherwise—we might be all
We dream of happy, high majestical.
Where is the love, beauty and truth we seek,
But in our mind? *Julian and Maddalo, l. 170*

18 *Me*—who am as a nerve o'er which do creep
The else unfelt oppressions of this earth.

Julian and Maddalo, l. 449

19   Most wretched men
Are cradled into poetry by wrong;
They learn in suffering what they teach in song.

Julian and Maddalo, l. 543

20 Chameleons feed on light and air:
Poets' food is love and fame.

An Exhortation [1819], st. 1

21 O wild West Wind, thou breath of Autumn's
        being,
Thou, from whose unseen presence the leaves dead
Are driven, like ghosts from an enchanter fleeing,
Yellow, and black, and pale, and hectic red,
Pestilence-stricken multitudes.

Ode to the West Wind [1819], l. 1

1 Wild Spirit, which art moving everywhere;
Destroyer and preserver; hear, oh, hear!
Ode to the West Wind, l. 13

2   Thou dirge
Of the dying year, to which this closing night
Will be the dome of a vast sepulcher.
Ode to the West Wind, l. 23

3 Oh, lift me as a wave, a leaf, a cloud!
I fall upon the thorns of life! I bleed!
Ode to the West Wind, l. 44

4 Make me thy lyre, even as the forest is:
What if my leaves are falling like its own!
The tumult of thy mighty harmonies
Will take from both a deep, autumnal tone,
Sweet though in sadness. Be thou, Spirit fierce,
My spirit! Be thou me, impetuous one!
Ode to the West Wind, l. 57

5 The trumpet of a prophecy! O Wind,
If winter comes, can spring be far behind?
Ode to the West Wind, l. 68

6 Men of England, wherefore plow
For the lords who lay ye low?
Song to the Men of England [1819], st. 1

7 Nothing in the world is single,
All things by a law divine
In one spirit meet and mingle.
Love's Philosophy [1819], st. 1

8 I arise from dreams of thee
In the first sweet sleep of night,
When the winds are breathing low,
And the stars are shining bright.
The Indian Serenade [1819], st. 1

9 Hell is a city much like London—
A populous and smoky city.
Peter Bell the Third [1819], pt. III, st. 1

10   Teas,
Where small talk dies in agonies.
Peter Bell the Third, III, st. 12

11 An old, mad, blind, despised and dying king.[1]
England in 1819 [written 1819], l. 1

12 I met Murder on the way—
He had a mask like Castlereagh.
The Mask of Anarchy [written 1819], st. 2

13   One by one, and two by two,
He tossed them human hearts to chew.
The Mask of Anarchy, st. 3

14 Rise like Lions after slumber
In unvanquishable number—
Shake your chains to earth like dew

---
[1]George III.

Which in sleep had fallen on you—
Ye are many—they are few.
The Mask of Anarchy, st. 38, 91

15 A lovely lady, garmented in light
From her own beauty.
The Witch of Atlas [1820], st. 5

16 Hail to thee, blithe spirit!
Bird thou never wert,
That from Heaven, or near it,
Pourest thy full heart
In profuse strains of unpremeditated art.
To a Skylark [1821], st. 1

17 And singing still dost soar, and soaring ever singest.
To a Skylark, st. 2

18 Thou art unseen—but yet I hear thy shrill delight.
To a Skylark, st. 4

19 We look before and after,
And pine for what is not;
Our sincerest laughter
With some pain is fraught;
Our sweetest songs are those that tell of saddest
        thought.   *To a Skylark, st. 18*

20 Teach me half the gladness
That thy brain must know,
Such harmonious madness,
From my lips would flow,
The world should listen then, as I am listening
        now.   *To a Skylark, st. 21*

21 Kings are like stars—they rise and set, they have
The worship of the world, but no repose.
Hellas [1821], l. 195

22 The world's great age begins anew,
The golden years return,
The earth doth like a snake renew
Her winter weeds outworn.   *Hellas, l. 1060*

23 The world is weary of the past,
Oh, might it die or rest at last!
Hellas, final chorus

24 What! alive, and so bold, O earth?
*Written on Hearing the News of the Death of
Napoleon [1821], st. 1*

25 I never was attached to that great sect,
Whose doctrine is, that each one should select
Out of the crowd a mistress or a friend,
And all the rest, though fair and wise, commend
To cold oblivion, though 'tis in the code
Of modern morals, and the beaten road
Which those poor slaves with weary footsteps tread
Who travel to their home among the dead
By the broad highway of the world, and so
With one chained friend, perhaps a jealous foe,

The dreariest and the longest journey go.
True love in this differs from gold and clay,
That to divide is not to take away.
Epipsychidion [1821], l. 149

1 I weep for Adonais[1] — he is dead!
Oh, weep for Adonais! though our tears
Thaw not the frost which binds so dear a head!
Adonais [1821], st. 1

2   Till the Future dares
Forget the Past, his fate and fame shall be
An echo and a light unto eternity!
Adonais, st. 1

3 To that high capital, where kingly Death
Keeps his pale court in beauty and decay,
He came.   *Adonais, st. 7*

4 Lost Angel of a ruined Paradise!   *Adonais, st. 10*

5 Ah woe is me! Winter is come and gone,
But grief returns with the revolving year.
Adonais, st. 18

6   The intense atom glows
A moment, then is quenched in a most cold repose.
Adonais, st. 20

7 Alas! that all we loved of him should be,
But for our grief, as if it had not been,
And grief itself be mortal!   *Adonais, st. 21*

8 As long as skies are blue, and fields are green,
Evening must usher night, night urge the morrow,
Month follow month with woe, and year wake year
to sorrow.   *Adonais, st. 21*

9 The Pilgrim of Eternity,[2] whose fame
Over his living head like heaven is bent,
An early but enduring monument,
Came, veiling all the lightnings of his song
In sorrow.   *Adonais, st. 30*

10 A pardlike spirit, beautiful and swift.
Adonais, st. 32

11 In mockery of monumental stone.
Adonais, st. 35

12 He hath awakened from the dream of life.
Adonais, st. 39

13 He has outsoared the shadow of our night;
Envy and calumny and hate and pain,
And that unrest which men miscall delight
Can touch him not and torture not again;

From the contagion of the world's slow stain
He is secure, and now can never mourn
A heart grown cold, a head grown gray in vain.
Adonais, st. 4

14 He lives, he wakes — 'tis Death is dead, not he.
Adonais, st. 4

15 He is made one with Nature: there is heard
His voice in all her music, from the moan
Of thunder to the song of night's sweet bird.
Adonais, st. 4

16 He is a portion of the loveliness
Which once he made more lovely.   *Adonais, st. 4*

17 The One remains, the many change and pass;
Heaven's light forever shines, earth's shadows fly;
Life, like a dome of many-colored glass,
Stains the white radiance of eternity,
Until Death tramples it to fragments — Die,
If thou wouldst be with that which thou dost seek!
Adonais, st. 52

18 The soul of Adonais, like a star,
Beacons from the abode where the Eternal are.
Adonais, st. 55

19 Music, when soft voices die,
Vibrates in the memory;
Odors, when sweet violets sicken,
Live within the sense they quicken.

Rose leaves, when the rose is dead,
Are heaped for the beloved's bed;
And so thy thoughts, when thou art gone,
Love itself shall slumber on.
To ——: Music, When Soft Voices Die [1821]

20 One word is too often profaned
For me to profane it,
One feeling too falsely disdained
For thee to disdain it.
*To ——: One Word Is Too Often Profaned
[1821], st. 1*

21 The desire of the moth for the star,
Of the night for the morrow,
The devotion to something afar
From the sphere of our sorrow.
To ——: One Word Is Too Often Profaned, st. 2

22 Swiftly walk o'er the western wave, Spirit of Night!
To Night [1821], st. 1

23 I ask of thee, beloved Night —
Swift be thine approaching flight,
Come soon, soon!   *To Night, st. 5*

24 Rarely, rarely, comest thou,
Spirit of Delight!
Song: Rarely, Rarely, Comest Thou [1821], st. 1

---

[1]John Keats.
    Morning star, you shone among the living; and now in death you shine, evening star, on the dead. — PLATO, *Aster (Star)*, epigraph (in Greek) for Shelley's Adonais
    [2]Byron.

1 Let me set my mournful ditty
  To a merry measure;
  Thou wilt never come for pity,
  Thou wilt come for pleasure.
      Song: Rarely, Rarely, Comest Thou, st. 4

2 I love tranquil solitude
  And such society
  As is quiet, wise, and good.
      Song: Rarely, Rarely, Comest Thou, st. 7

3 There is no sport in hate when all the rage
  Is on one side.   *Lines to a Reviewer [1821]*

4 When the lamp is shattered
  The light in the dust lies dead —
  When the cloud is scattered
  The rainbow's glory is shed.
      When the Lamp Is Shattered [1822], st. 1

5 Best and brightest, come away!
      To Jane: The Invitation [1822], l. 1

6 Away, away, from men and towns,
  To the wild wood and the downs.
      To Jane: The Invitation, l. 21

7 I am gone into the fields
  To take what this sweet hour yields —
  Reflection, you may come tomorrow,
  Sit by the fireside with Sorrow. —
  You with the unpaid bill, Despair —
  You, tiresome verse-reciter, Care —
  I will pay you in the grave.
      To Jane: The Invitation, l. 31

8   A tone
    Of some world far from ours,
  Where music and moonlight and feeling
    Are one.
      *To Jane: The Keen Stars Were Twinkling
      [1822], st. 4*

9   The great secret of morals is love; or a going out
  of our own nature, and an identification of ourselves
  with the beautiful which exists in thought, action,
  or person not our own. . . . The great instrument of
  moral good is the imagination; and poetry adminis-
  ters to the effect by acting upon the cause.
      A Defense of Poetry [1821]

0   Poetry is the record of the best and happiest moments of the happiest and best minds.
      A Defense of Poetry

1   Poets are the hierophants of an unapprehended
  inspiration; the mirrors of the gigantic shadows which
  futurity casts upon the present.
      A Defense of Poetry

2   Poets are the unacknowledged legislators of the
  world.   *A Defense of Poetry*

Thaddeus Stevens
1792–1868

13   Though the President is Commander-in-Chief,
Congress is his commander; and, God willing, he
shall obey. He and his minions shall learn that this is
not a Government of kings and satraps, but a Government of the people, and that Congress is the people.
      *Speech in House of Representatives
      [January 3, 1867]*

John Clare
1793–1864

14 I am! yet what I am who cares, or knows?
  My friends forsake me like a memory lost.
      I Am, l. 1

15 Untroubling and untroubled where I lie —
  The grass below — above the vaulted sky.
      I Am, l. 17

16 The wind and clouds, now here, now there,
  Hold no such strange dominion
  As woman's cold, perverted will,
  And soon estranged opinion.   *When Lovers Part*

17 Till kicked and torn and beaten out he lies
  And leaves his hold and cackles, groans, and dies.
      Badger

18   If life had a second edition, how I would correct
the proofs.
      *Letter to a friend. From J. W. AND ANNE
      TIBBLE, John Clare: A Life [1932]*

Felicia [Dorothea] Hemans
1793–1835

19 The stately homes of England!
  How beautiful they stand,
  Amidst their tall ancestral trees,
  O'er all the pleasant land![1]
      The Homes of England, st. 1

20 The breaking waves dashed high
  On a stern and rock-bound coast,
  And the woods, against a stormy sky,
  Their giant branches tossed.
      The Landing of the Pilgrim Fathers, st. 1

21 A band of exiles moored their bark
  On a wild New England shore.
      The Landing of the Pilgrim Fathers, st. 2

---

[1]The stately homes of England, / How beautiful they stood / Before their recent owners / Relinquished them for good. — E. V.
KNOX [1881–1971], *The Stately Homes*

    I became one of the stately homos of England. — QUENTIN
CRISP [1908–1999], *The Naked Civil Servant*

    See Woolf, 700:1.

1 The boy[1] stood on the burning deck,
Whence all but he had fled.   *Casabianca, st. 1*

2 The flames rolled on; he would not go
Without his father's word.   *Casabianca, st. 3*

3 In the busy haunts of men.
Tale of the Secret Tribunal, pt. I

4 He Never Smiled Again.
Title and refrain of poem

Henry Francis Lyte
1793–1847

5 Abide with me: fast falls the eventide;
The darkness deepens; Lord, with me abide:
When other helpers fail, and comforts flee,
Help of the helpless, O abide with me.
Eventide [1847], st. 1

Lucretia [Coffin] Mott
1793–1880

6   Let woman then go on — not asking favors, but
claiming as a right the removal of all hindrances to
her elevation in the scale of being — let her receive
encouragement for the proper cultivation of all her
powers, so that she may enter profitably into the active business of life . . . Then in the marriage union,
the independence of the husband and wife will be
equal, their dependence mutual, and their obligations reciprocal.
*Discourse on Woman [delivered December 17,
1849], last paragraph*

William Cullen Bryant
1794–1878

7 To him who in the love of Nature holds
Communion with her visible forms, she speaks
A various language.   *Thanatopsis [1817–1821], l. 1*

8 Go forth, under the open sky, and list
To Nature's teachings.   *Thanatopsis, l. 14*

9   The hills,
Rock-ribbed, and ancient as the sun.
Thanatopsis, l. 37

10 So live, that when thy summons comes to join
The innumerable caravan which moves
To that mysterious realm, where each shall take
His chamber in the silent halls of death,

---

[1]Giacomo Casabianca, whose father, Louis, at the battle of the
Nile [1798], commanded the flagship *Orient*. It took fire and blew
up, the commander was mortally wounded, and when most of the
crew fled, Giacomo remained aboard, in an effort to help his father.

Thou go not, like the quarry-slave at night,
Scourged to his dungeon, but, sustained and
soothed
By an unfaltering trust, approach thy grave,
Like one that wraps the drapery of his couch
About him, and lies down to pleasant dreams.
Thanatopsis, l. 7

11 He who, from zone to zone,
Guides through the boundless sky thy certain
flight,
In the long way that I must tread alone,
Will lead my steps aright.
To a Waterfowl [1818], st.

12 The groves were God's first temples.
A Forest Hymn [182

13 Loveliest of lovely things are they,
On earth, that soonest pass away.
The rose that lives its little hour
Is prized beyond the sculptured flower.
*A Scene on the Banks of the Hudson [1828],
st. 3*

14 The melancholy days are come, the saddest of the
year,
Of wailing winds, and naked woods, and meadows
brown and sere.   *The Death of the Flowers [1832], st.*

15 These are the gardens of the desert, these
The unshorn fields, boundless and beautiful,
For which the speech of England has no name —
The prairies.   *The Prairies [1833*

16 Truth, crushed to earth, shall rise again.
The Battlefield [1839], st.

Cornelius Vanderbilt
1794–1877

17   You have undertaken to cheat me. I won't su
you, for the law is too slow. I'll ruin you.
Letter to former business associates [1853

William Whewell
1794–1866

18   And so no force however great can stretch a co
however fine into an horizontal line which is accu
rately straight.
*Elementary Treatise on Mechanics [1819].
The Equilibrium of Forces on a Point*

19   Man is the interpreter of nature, science the rig
interpretation.
*Philosophy of the Inductive Sciences [1840],
aphorism 17*

1 It is a test of true theories not only to account for but to predict phenomena.
Philosophy of the Inductive Sciences, aphorism 39

Narcisse Achille, Comte de Salvandy
1795–1856

2 We are dancing on a volcano.
At a fête given by the Duc d'Orléans for the King of Naples [1830]

Thomas Carlyle
1795–1881

3 Aesop's Fly, sitting on the axle of the chariot, has been much laughed at for exclaiming: What a dust I do raise! *On Boswell's Life of Johnson [1832]*

4 Whoso belongs only to his own age, and reverences only its gilt Popinjays or soot-smeared Mumbo-jumbos, must needs die with it.
On Boswell's Life of Johnson

5 The stupendous Fourth Estate, whose wide world-embracing influences what eye can take in?[1]
On Boswell's Life of Johnson

6 All work is as seed sown; it grows and spreads, and sows itself anew.
On Boswell's Life of Johnson

7 The courage we desire and prize is not the courage to die decently, but to live manfully.
On Boswell's Life of Johnson

8 No man who has once heartily and wholly laughed can be altogether irreclaimably bad.
Sartor Resartus [1833–1834], bk. I, ch. 4

9 He who first shortened the labor of copyists by device of movable types was disbanding hired armies, and cashiering most kings and senates, and creating a whole new democratic world: he had invented the art of printing. *Sartor Resartus, I, 5*

10 Man is a tool-using animal. . . . Without tools he is nothing, with tools he is all.
Sartor Resartus, I, 5

11 Be not the slave of Words.
Sartor Resartus, I, 8

12 What you see, yet can not see over, is as good as infinite. *Sartor Resartus, II, 1*

13 Sarcasm I now see to be, in general, the language of the Devil; for which reason I have long since as good as renounced it.
Sartor Resartus, II, 4

14 The Everlasting No.
Sartor Resartus, II, 7 (chapter title)

15 With stupidity and sound digestion man may front much. *Sartor Resartus, II, 7*

16 Great men are the inspired (speaking and acting) texts of that divine Book of Revelations, whereof a chapter is completed from epoch to epoch, and by some named History.
Sartor Resartus, II, 8

17 The Everlasting Yea.
Sartor Resartus, II, 9 (chapter title)

18 Man's unhappiness, as I construe, comes of his greatness; it is because there is an Infinite in him, which with all his cunning he cannot quite bury under the Finite.
Sartor Resartus, II, 9

19 Close thy Byron; open thy Goethe.
Sartor Resartus, II, 9

20 Love not Pleasure; love God.
Sartor Resartus, II, 9

21 As the Swiss inscription says: *Sprechen ist silbern, Schweigen ist golden*— "Speech is silvern, Silence is golden"; or, as I might rather express it, speech is of time, silence is of eternity.[2]
Sartor Resartus, III, 3

22 It is now almost my sole rule of life to clear myself of cants and formulas, as of poisonous Nessus shirts. *Letter to His Wife [1835]*

23 France was long a despotism tempered by epigrams.
History of the French Revolution [1837], pt. I, bk. I, ch. 1

24 No lie you can speak or act but it will come, after longer or shorter circulation, like a bill drawn on Nature's Reality, and be presented there for payment—with the answer, No effects.
History of the French Revolution, I, III, 1

25 To a shower of gold most things are penetrable.
History of the French Revolution, I, III, 7

26 A whiff of grapeshot.
History of the French Revolution, I, V, 3

---

[1] [Edmund] Burke said there were Three Estates in Parliament; but, in the Reporters' Gallery yonder, there sat a Fourth Estate more important far than they all.—CARLYLE, *On Heroes and Hero Worship* [1841], *The Hero as Man of Letters*

[2] Silence is deep as Eternity; speech is shallow as Time.—CARLYLE, *Critical and Miscellaneous Essays. Sir Walter Scott* [1838]
  [Carlyle] loves silence somewhat platonically. — GIUSEPPI MAZZINI [1805–1872]; *from* JANE WELSH CARLYLE, *Letter to Mrs. Stirling* [October 1843]

1   O poor mortals, how ye make this earth bitter for each other.
History of the French Revolution, I, V, 5

2   Battles, in these ages, are transacted by mechanism; with the slightest possible development of human individuality or spontaneity; men now even die, and kill one another, in an artificial manner.
History of the French Revolution, I, VII, 4

3   History a distillation of rumor.
History of the French Revolution, I, VII, 5

4   The difference between Orthodoxy or My-doxy and Heterodoxy or Thy-doxy.
History of the French Revolution, II, IV, 2

5   The sea-green Incorruptible [Robespierre].
History of the French Revolution, II, VI, 7

6   Aristocracy of the Moneybag.
History of the French Revolution, II, VII, 7

7   Democracy is, by the nature of it, a self-canceling business; and gives in the long run a net result of zero.   *Chartism [1839], ch. 6, Laissez-Faire*

8   A well-written Life is almost as rare as a well-spent one.
Critical and Miscellaneous Essays [1839–1857]. Richter

9   The great law of culture is: Let each become all that he was created capable of being.
Critical and Miscellaneous Essays. Richter

10   The three great elements of modern civilization, gunpowder, printing, and the Protestant religion.
Critical and Miscellaneous Essays. The State of German Literature

11   In every man's writings, the character of the writer must lie recorded.
Critical and Miscellaneous Essays. Goethe

12   There is no heroic poem in the world but is at bottom a biography, the life of a man; also, it may be said, there is no life of a man, faithfully recorded, but is a heroic poem of its sort, rhymed or unrhymed.
Critical and Miscellaneous Essays. Sir Walter Scott

13   No man lives without jostling and being jostled; in all ways he has to elbow himself through the world, giving and receiving offense.
Critical and Miscellaneous Essays. Sir Walter Scott

14   The uttered part of a man's life, let us always repeat, bears to the unuttered, unconscious part a small unknown proportion. He himself never knows it, much less do others.
Critical and Miscellaneous Essays. Sir Walter Scott

15   Nothing that was worthy in the past departs; no truth or goodness realized by man ever dies, or can die.
Critical and Miscellaneous Essays. Sir Walter Scott

16   No sadder proof can be given by a man of his own littleness than disbelief in great men.
On Heroes and Hero Worship [1841]. The Hero as Divinity

17   The history of the world is but the biography of great men.[1]
On Heroes and Hero Worship. The Hero as Divinity

18   A vein of poetry exists in the hearts of all men.
On Heroes and Hero Worship. The Hero as Poet

19   The Age of Miracles is forever here!
On Heroes and Hero Worship. The Hero as Priest

20   All that mankind has done, thought, gained or been: it is lying as in magic preservation in the pages of books.
On Heroes and Hero Worship. The Hero as Man of Letters

21   The true university of these days is a collection of books.
On Heroes and Hero Worship. The Hero as Man of Letters

22   The suffering man ought really to consume his own smoke; there is no good in emitting smoke till you have made it into fire.[2]
On Heroes and Hero Worship. The Hero as Man of Letters

23   Adversity is sometimes hard upon a man; but for one man who can stand prosperity, there are a hundred that will stand adversity.
On Heroes and Hero Worship. The Hero as Man of Letters

24   "A fair day's wages for a fair day's work": it is as just a demand as governed men ever made of governing. It is the everlasting right of man.
Past and Present [1843], bk. I, ch.

25   Fire is the best of servants; but what a master![3]
Past and Present, II,

---

[1] History is the essence of innumerable biographies. — CARLYLE, *On History* [1830]

[2] Would that he consumed his own smoke. — HERMAN MELVILLE, *Moby-Dick* [1851], ch. 96
Consume your own smoke. — ROBERT BROWNING, *Pacchiarotto* [1876], 25

[3] Mammon is like fire: the usefulest of all servants, if the frightfulest of all masters! — CARLYLE, *Past and Present, IV, 7*

1 All work, even cotton spinning, is noble; work is alone noble. . . . A life of ease is not for any man, nor for any god. *Past and Present, III, 4*

2 Every noble crown is, and on earth will forever be, a crown of thorns. *Past and Present, III, 8*

3 He who takes not counsel of the Unseen and Silent, from him will never come real visibility and speech. *Past and Present, III, 12*

4 Captains of Industry.
Past and Present, IV, 4 (chapter title)

5 There is endless merit in a man's knowing when to have done. *Francia [1845]*

6 He that works and *does* some Poem, not he that merely *says* one, is worthy of the name of Poet.
Introduction to Cromwell's Letters and Speeches [1845]

7 Respectable Professors of the Dismal Science.[1]
Latter Day Pamphlets, no. 1 [1850]

8 A Parliament speaking through reporters to Buncombe and the twenty-seven millions, mostly fools.
Latter Day Pamphlets, 6

9 A healthy hatred of scoundrels.
Latter Day Pamphlets, 12

10 "Genius" (which means transcendent capacity of taking trouble, first of all).
Life of Frederick the Great [1858–1865], bk. IV, ch. 3

11 Happy the people whose annals are blank in history books![2] *Life of Frederick the Great, XVI, 1*

12 So here hath been dawning
Another blue day:
Think, wilt thou let it
Slip useless away? *Today*

13 Lord Bacon could as easily have created the planets as he could have written Hamlet.
Remark in discussion

Joseph Rodman Drake
1795–1820

14 When Freedom from her mountain height,
Unfurled her standard to the air,
She tore the azure robe of night,
And set the stars of glory there.
The American Flag [1819], st. 1

John Woodcock Graves
1795–1886

15 D' ye ken John Peel with his coat so gay?
D' ye ken John Peel at the break of day?
D' ye ken John Peel when he's far far away
With his hounds and his horn in the morning?

'Twas the sound of his horn brought me from my bed,
And the cry of his hounds, has me ofttimes led;
For Peel's view-hollo would waken the dead,
Or the fox from his lair in the morning.
John Peel [1832]

John Keats
1795–1821

16 How many bards gild the lapses of time!
Poems [1817]. Sonnet. How Many Bards Gild the Lapses of Time

17 To one who has been long in city pent,
'Tis very sweet to look into the fair
And open face of heaven.
Poems. Sonnet. To One Who Has Been Long in City Pent

18 He mourns that day so soon has glided by:
E'en like the passage of an angel's tear
That falls through the clear ether silently.
Poems. Sonnet. To One Who Has Been Long in City Pent

19 Much have I travel'd in the realms of gold,
And many goodly states and kingdoms seen;
Round many western islands have I been
Which bards in fealty to Apollo hold.
Oft of one wide expanse had I been told
That deep-brow'd Homer ruled as his demesne;
Yet did I never breathe its pure serene
Till I heard Chapman speak out loud and bold:
Then felt I like some watcher of the skies
When a new planet swims into his ken;
Or like stout Cortez when with eagle eyes
He star'd at the Pacific—and all his men
Look'd at each other with a wild surmise—
Silent, upon a peak in Darien.
Poems [1817]. Sonnet. On First Looking into Chapman's Homer

20 And other spirits there are standing apart
Upon the forehead of the age to come;
These, these will give the world another heart,
And other pulses. Hear ye not the hum
Of mighty workings —— ?
Listen awhile, ye nations, and be dumb.
Poems. Sonnet. Addressed to the Same (Benjamin Robert Haydon)

[1]Referring to political economy and social science, Carlyle also in his *Occasional Discourse on the Negro Question* [1849] speaks of: What we might call, by way of eminence, the Dismal Science.

[2]Carlyle identifies this as "Montesquieu's aphorism."

1 The poetry of earth is never dead.
Poems. Sonnet. On the Grasshopper and the Cricket

2 O for ten years, that I may overwhelm
Myself in poesy; so I may do the deed
That my own soul has to itself decreed.
Poems. Sleep and Poetry, l. 96

3 And can I ever bid these joys farewell?
Yes, I must pass them for a nobler life,
Where I may find the agonies, the strife
Of human hearts.
Poems. Sleep and Poetry, l. 122

4   A drainless shower
Of light is poesy; 'tis the supreme of power;
'Tis might half slumb'ring on its own right arm.
Poems. Sleep and Poetry, l. 235

5 But strength alone though of the Muses born
Is like a fallen angel: trees uptorn,
Darkness, and worms, and shrouds, and sepulchers
Delight it; for it feeds upon the burrs
And thorns of life; forgetting the great end
Of poesy, that it should be a friend
To soothe the cares, and lift the thoughts of man.
Poems. Sleep and Poetry, l. 241

6   There is not a fiercer hell than the failure in a great object.   *Endymion [1818], preface*

7   The imagination of a boy is healthy, and the mature imagination of a man is healthy; but there is a space of life between, in which the soul is in a ferment, the character undecided, the way of life uncertain, the ambition thicksighted: thence proceeds mawkishness, and the thousand bitters which those men I speak of must necessarily taste in going over the following pages.   *Endymion, preface*

8 A thing of beauty is a joy forever:
Its loveliness increases; it will never
Pass into nothingness; but still will keep
A bower quiet for us, and a sleep
Full of sweet dreams, and health, and quiet
breathing.   *Endymion, bk. I, l. 1*

9   The grandeur of the dooms
We have imagined for the mighty dead.
Endymion, I, l. 20

10 Wherein lies happiness? In that which becks
Our ready minds to fellowship divine,
A fellowship with essence; till we shine,
Full alchemiz'd, and free of space. Behold
The clear religion of heaven!   *Endymion, I, l. 777*

11   The crown of these
Is made of love and friendship, and sits high
Upon the forehead of humanity.
Endymion, I, l. 800

12 A hope beyond the shadow of a dream.
Endymion, I, l. 85

13   'Tis the pest
Of love, that fairest joys give most unrest.
Endymion, II, l. 36.

14 A virgin purest lipp'd, yet in the lore
Of love deep learned to the red heart's core.
Poems [1820]. Lamia, pt. I, l. 18

15 Let the mad poets say whate'er they please
Of the sweets of Fairies, Peris, Goddesses,
Haunters of cavern, lake, and waterfall,
As a real woman, lineal indeed
From Pyrrha's pebbles or old Adam's seed.
Poems. Lamia, I, l. 32.

16 Love in a hut, with water and a crust,
Is—Love, forgive us!—cinders, ashes, dust.
Poems. Lamia, II, l.

17 Do not all charms fly
At the mere touch of cold philosophy?
Poems. Lamia, II, l. 22.

18 Philosophy will clip an angel's wings.
Poems. Lamia, II, l. 23.

19 For them the Ceylon diver held his breath,
And went all naked to the hungry shark;
For them his ears gush'd blood; for them in death
The seal on the cold ice with piteous bark
Lay full of darts; for them alone did seethe
A thousand men in troubles wide and dark:
Half-ignorant, they turn'd an easy wheel,
That set sharp racks at work, to pinch and peel.
Poems. Isabella; or, The Pot of Basil, st. 1.

20 St. Agnes' Eve—Ah, bitter chill it was!
The owl, for all his feathers, was a-cold.
The hare limp'd trembling through the frozen grass,
And silent was the flock in woolly fold.
Poems. The Eve of St. Agnes, st.

21 The silver, snarling trumpets 'gan to chide.
Poems. The Eve of St. Agnes, st.

22 The music, yearning like a God in pain.
Poems. The Eve of St. Agnes, st.

23 Asleep in lap of legends old.
Poems. The Eve of St. Agnes, st. 1.

24 Sudden a thought came like a full-blown rose,
Flushing his brow, and in his pained heart
Made purple riot.
Poems. The Eve of St. Agnes, st. 1.

25 Full on this casement shone the wintry moon,
And threw warm gules on Madeline's fair breast.
Poems. The Eve of St. Agnes, st. 2.

1 Unclasps her warmed jewels one by one;
Loosens her fragrant bodice; by degrees
Her rich attire creeps rustling to her knees.
    Poems. The Eve of St. Agnes, st. 26

2 And still she slept an azure-lidded sleep,
In blanched linen, smooth, and lavender'd,
While he from forth the closet brought a heap
Of candied apple, quince, and plum, and gourd;
With jellies soother than the creamy curd,
And lucent syrops, tinct with cinnamon;
Manna and dates, in argosy transferr'd
From Fez; and spiced dainties, every one,
From silken Samarcand to cedar'd Lebanon.
    Poems. The Eve of St. Agnes, st. 30

3 Beyond a mortal man impassion'd far
At these voluptuous accents, he arose,
Ethereal, flush'd, and like a throbbing star
Seen mid the sapphire heaven's deep repose;
Into her dream he melted, as the rose,
Blendeth its odour with the violet,—
Solution sweet: meantime the frost-wind blows
Like Love's alarum pattering the sharp sleet
Against the window-panes; St. Agnes' moon
    hath set.   *Poems. The Eve of St. Agnes, st. 36*

4 And they are gone: aye, ages long ago
These lovers fled away into the storm.
    Poems. The Eve of St. Agnes, st. 42

5 My heart aches, and a drowsy numbness pains
My sense, as though of hemlock I had drunk,
Or emptied some dull opiate to the drains
One minute past, and Lethe-wards had sunk.
    Poems. Ode to a Nightingale, st. 1

6 That thou, light-winged Dryad of the trees,
    In some melodious plot
Of beechen green, and shadows numberless,
Singest of summer in full-throated ease.
    Poems. Ode to a Nightingale, st. 1

7 O, for a draught of vintage! that hath been
Cool'd a long age in the deep-delved earth,
Tasting of Flora and the country green,
Dance, and Provençal song, and sunburnt
    mirth!
O, for a beaker full of the warm South,
Full of the true, the blushful Hippocrene,
With beaded bubbles winking at the brim,
    And purple-stained mouth.
    Poems. Ode to a Nightingale, st. 2

8 Fade far away, dissolve, and quite forget
What thou among the leaves hast never known,
The weariness, the fever, and the fret
Here, where men sit and hear each other groan;
Where palsy shakes a few, sad, last gray hairs,
Where youth grows pale, and specter-thin,
    and dies;

Where but to think is to be full of sorrow
    And leaden-eyed despairs.
    Poems. Ode to a Nightingale, st. 3

9 Already with thee! tender is the night.
    Poems. Ode to a Nightingale, st. 4

10 I cannot see what flowers are at my feet,
Nor what soft incense hangs upon the boughs,
But, in embalmed darkness, guess each sweet.
    Poems. Ode to a Nightingale, st. 5

11 The murmurous haunt of flies on summer eves.
    Poems. Ode to a Nightingale, st. 5

12 Darkling I listen; and, for many a time
I have been half in love with easeful Death,
Call'd him soft names in many a mused rhyme,
To take into the air my quiet breath;
Now more than ever seems it rich to die,
To cease upon the midnight with no pain,
While thou art pouring forth thy soul abroad
    In such an ecstasy!
Still wouldst thou sing, and I have ears in vain—
To thy high requiem become a sod.
    Poems. Ode to a Nightingale, st. 6

13 Thou wast not born for death, immortal Bird!
No hungry generations tread thee down;
The voice I hear this passing night was heard
In ancient days by emperor and clown:
Perhaps the self-same song that found a path
Through the sad heart of Ruth, when, sick for
    home,
She stood in tears amid the alien corn;
The same that oft-times hath
Charm'd magic casements, opening on the foam
Of perilous seas, in faery lands forlorn.
    Poems. Ode to a Nightingale, st. 7

14 Forlorn! the very word is like a bell
To toll me back from thee to my sole self!
    Poems. Ode to a Nightingale, st. 8

15 Was it a vision, or a waking dream?
Fled is that music:—Do I wake or sleep?
    Poems. Ode to a Nightingale, st. 8

16 Thou still unravish'd bride of quietness,
Thou foster-child of silence and slow time,
Sylvan historian, who canst thus express
A flowery tale more sweetly than our rhyme:
What leaf-fring'd legend haunts about thy shape?
    Poems. Ode on a Grecian Urn, st. 1

17 What men or gods are these? What maidens loth?
What mad pursuit? What struggle to escape?
What pipes and timbrels? What wild ecstasy?
    Poems. Ode on a Grecian Urn, st. 1

18 Heard melodies are sweet, but those unheard
Are sweeter.   *Poems. Ode on a Grecian Urn, st. 2*

1 Forever wilt thou love, and she be fair!
Poems. Ode on a Grecian Urn, st. 2

2 Forever piping songs forever new.
Poems. Ode on a Grecian Urn, st. 3

3 Who are these coming to the sacrifice?
To what green altar, O mysterious priest,
Lead'st thou that heifer lowing at the skies,
And all her silken flanks with garlands drest?
Poems. Ode on a Grecian Urn, st. 4

4 O Attic shape! Fair attitude!
Poems. Ode on a Grecian Urn, st. 5

5 When old age shall this generation waste,
Thou shalt remain, in midst of other woe
Than ours, a friend to man, to whom thou say'st,
"Beauty is truth, truth beauty,"[1]—that is all
Ye know on earth, and all ye need to know.
Poems. Ode on a Grecian Urn, st. 5

6   To make delicious moan
Upon the midnight hours.
Poems. Ode to Psyche, st. 3

7 A bright torch, and a casement ope at night,
To let the warm Love in!
Poems. Ode to Psyche, st. 5

8 Ever let the fancy roam,
Pleasure never is at home.   *Poems. Fancy, l. 1*

9 Bards of Passion and of Mirth,
Ye have left your souls on earth!
Have ye souls in heaven too,
Double-lived in regions new?
Poems. Ode written on the blank page before
BEAUMONT AND FLETCHER, *The Fair Maid of*
the Inn

10 Souls of Poets dead and gone,
What Elysium have ye known,
Happy field or mossy cavern,
Choicer than the Mermaid Tavern?
Have ye tippled drink more fine
Than mine host's Canary wine?
Poems. Lines on the Mermaid Tavern

11 Season of mists and mellow fruitfulness,
Close bosom-friend of the maturing sun.
Poems. To Autumn, st. 1

---

[1]If asked who said "Beauty is truth, truth beauty!" a great many
readers would answer "Keats." But Keats said nothing of the sort.
It is what he said the Grecian Urn said, his description and criticism of a certain kind of work of art, the kind from which the evils
and problems of this life, the "heart high sorrowful and cloyed,"
are deliberately excluded. The Urn, for example, depicts, among
other beautiful sights, the citadel of a hill town; it does not depict
warfare, the evil which makes the citadel necessary.—W. H. AUDEN,
The Dyer's Hand [1962], *Robert Frost*
See George Herbert, 250:8.

12 Who hath not seen thee oft amid thy store?
Sometimes whoever seeks abroad may find
Thee sitting careless on a granary floor,
Thy hair soft-lifted by the winnowing wind;
Or on a half-reap'd furrow sound asleep,
Drows'd with the fume of poppies while thy hook
Spares the next swath and all its twined flowers.
Poems. To Autumn, st.

13 Where are the songs of Spring? Ay, where are they?
Think not of them, thou hast thy music too,—
While barred clouds bloom the soft-dying day,
And touch the stubble-plains with rosy hue;
Then in a wailful choir the small gnats mourn
Among the river sallows, borne aloft
Or sinking as the light wind lives or dies;
And full-grown lambs loud bleat from hilly bourn;
Hedge-crickets sing; and now with treble soft
The red-breast whistles from a garden-croft;
And gathering swallows twitter in the skies.
Poems. To Autumn, st.

14 No, no, go not to Lethe, neither twist
Wolf's-bane, tight-rooted, for its poisonous wine.
Poems. Ode on Melancholy, st.

15 Then glut thy sorrow on a morning rose.
Poems. Ode on Melancholy, st.

16 She dwells with Beauty—Beauty that must die;
And Joy, whose hand is ever at his lips
Bidding adieu; and aching Pleasure nigh,
Turning to poison while the bee-mouth sips:
Ay, in the very temple of Delight
Veil'd Melancholy has her sovran shrine,
Though seen of none save him whose strenuous
        tongue
Can burst Joy's grape against his palate fine;
His soul shall taste the sadness of her might,
And be among her cloudy trophies hung.
Poems. Ode on Melancholy, st.

17 Deep in the shady sadness of a vale
Far sunken from the healthy breath of morn,
Far from the fiery noon, and eve's one star,
Sat gray-hair'd Saturn, quiet as a stone.
Poems. Hyperion: A Fragment, bk. I, l.

18 How beautiful, if sorrow had not made
Sorrow more beautiful than Beauty's self.
Poems. Hyperion: A Fragment, I, l. 3

19 For to bear all naked truths,
And to envisage circumstance, all calm,
That is the top of sovereignty.
Poems. Hyperion: A Fragment, II, l. 20

20 Knowledge enormous makes a God of me.
Names, deeds, gray legends, dire events, rebellions,
Majesties, sovran voices, agonies,
Creations and destroyings, all at once

Pour into the wide hollows of my brain,
And deify me, as if some blithe wine
Or bright elixir peerless I had drunk,
And so become immortal.
> *Poems. Hyperion: A Fragment, III, l. 113*

1 My spirit is too weak — mortality
Weighs heavily on me like unwilling sleep,
And each imagin'd pinnacle and steep
Of godlike hardship, tells me I must die
Like a sick Eagle looking at the sky.[1]
> *Life, Letters and Literary Remains of John Keats, edited by* RICHARD MONCKTON MILNES *[1848]. On Seeing the Elgin Marbles*

2 This living hand, now warm and capable
Of earnest grasping, would, if it were cold
And in the icy silence of the tomb,
So haunt thy days and chill thy dreaming nights
That thou would wish thine own heart dry of blood
So in my veins red life might stream again,
And thou be conscience-calm'd — see here it is —
I hold it towards you.
> *Life, Letters and Literary Remains of John Keats, edited by* RICHARD MONCKTON MILNES. *Fragment: This Living Hand*

3 O, what can ail thee, knight-at-arms,
Alone and palely loitering?
The sedge has withered from the lake,
And no birds sing!
> *Life, Letters and Literary Remains of John Keats, edited by* RICHARD MONCKTON MILNES. *La Belle Dame Sans Merci,*[2] *st. 1*

4 I met a lady in the meads
Full beautiful, a faery's child;
Her hair was long, her foot was light,
And her eyes were wild.
> *Life, Letters and Literary Remains of John Keats, edited by* RICHARD MONCKTON MILNES. *La Belle Dame Sans Merci, st. 4*

5 She looked at me as she did love,
And made sweet moan.
> *Life, Letters and Literary Remains of John Keats, edited by* RICHARD MONCKTON MILNES. *La Belle Dame Sans Merci, st. 5*

6 I saw pale kings and princes too,
Pale warriors, death-pale were they all;
They cried — "La Belle Dame sans Merci
Hath thee in thrall!"
> *Life, Letters and Literary Remains of John Keats, edited by* RICHARD MONCKTON MILNES. *La Belle Dame Sans Merci, st. 10*

---

[1]Printed in the *Examiner* [February 23, 1817].

[2]Title of a French poem by ALAIN CHARTIER [c. 1385–c. 1433]. First printed by Leigh Hunt in the *Indicator* [May 10, 1820].

7 It keeps eternal whisperings around
Desolate shores, and with its mighty swell
Gluts twice ten thousand caverns.
> *Life, Letters and Literary Remains of John Keats, edited by* RICHARD MONCKTON MILNES. *La Belle Dame Sans Merci, On the Sea*[3]

8 When I have fears that I may cease to be
Before my pen has glean'd my teeming brain.
> *Life, Letters and Literary Remains of John Keats, edited by* RICHARD MONCKTON MILNES. *Sonnet. When I Have Fears*

9 When I behold, upon the night's starr'd face,
Huge cloudy symbols of a high romance.
> *Life, Letters and Literary Remains of John Keats, edited by* RICHARD MONCKTON MILNES. *Sonnet. When I Have Fears*

10   Then on the shore
Of the wide world I stand alone, and think
Till love and fame to nothingness do sink.
> *Life, Letters and Literary Remains of John Keats, edited by* RICHARD MONCKTON MILNES. *Sonnet. When I Have Fears*

11 Bright star, would I were steadfast as thou art —
Not in lone splendor hung aloft the night
And watching, with eternal lids apart,
Like nature's patient, sleepless Eremite,
The moving waters at their priestlike task
Of pure ablution round earth's human shores.
> *Life, Letters and Literary Remains of John Keats, edited by* RICHARD MONCKTON MILNES. *Sonnet. Bright Star*[4]

12 None can usurp this height . . .
But those to whom the miseries of the world
Are misery, and will not let them rest.
> *The Fall of Hyperion: A Dream, canto I, l. 147*

13   I am certain of nothing but of the holiness of the Heart's affections and the truth of Imagination — What the imagination seizes as Beauty must be truth — whether it existed before or not.
> *Letter to Benjamin Bailey [November 22, 1817]*

14   The Imagination may be compared to Adam's dream — he awoke and found it truth.
> *Letter to Benjamin Bailey [November 22, 1817]*

---

[3]From want of regular rests, I have been rather *narvus,* and the passage in *Lear* — "Do you not hear the sea?" — has haunted me intensely. — JOHN KEATS, *Letter to John Hamilton Reynolds* [April 17, 1817]

Edgar: . . . Hark! do you hear the sea? — WILLIAM SHAKESPEARE, *King Lear, act IV, sc. vi, l. 4*

[4]Written on a blank page in Shakespeare's *Poems.*

1   O for a Life of Sensations rather than of Thoughts!
Letter to Benjamin Bailey [November 22, 1817]

2   I scarcely remember counting upon any Happiness—I look not for it if it be not in the present hour—nothing startles me beyond the Moment. The setting sun will always set me to rights—or if a Sparrow come before my Window I take part in its existence and pick about the Gravel.
Letter to Benjamin Bailey [November 22, 1817]

3   At once it struck me, what quality went to form a Man of Achievement especially in Literature & which Shakespeare possessed so enormously—I mean *Negative Capability*, that is, when man is capable of being in uncertainties, Mysteries, doubts, without any irritable reaching after fact & reason.
Letter to George and Thomas Keats [December 22, 1817]

4   We hate poetry that has a palpable design upon us—and if we do not agree, seems to put its hand in its breeches pocket. Poetry should be great & unobtrusive, a thing which enters into one's soul, and does not startle it or amaze it with itself, but with its subject.
Letter to John Hamilton Reynolds [February 3, 1818]

5   Poetry should surprise by a fine excess and not by Singularity—it should strike the Reader as a wording of his own highest thoughts, and appear almost a Remembrance.
Letter to John Taylor [February 27, 1818]

6   If poetry comes not as naturally as the Leaves to a tree it had better not come at all.
Letter to John Taylor [February 27, 1818]

7   Scenery is fine—but human nature is finer.
Letter to Benjamin Bailey [March 13, 1818]

8   Axioms in philosophy are not axioms until they are proved upon our pulses: We read fine—things but never feel them to the full until we have gone the same steps as the Author.
Letter to John Hamilton Reynolds [May 3, 1818]

9   I compare human life to a large Mansion of Many Apartments, two of which I can only describe, the doors of the rest being as yet shut upon me.
Letter to John Hamilton Reynolds [May 3, 1818]

10   I begin to get a little acquainted with my own strength and weakness.—Praise or blame has but a momentary effect on the man whose love of beauty in the abstract makes him a severe critic on his own Works.   *Letter to James Hessey [October 8, 1818]*

11   The Genius of Poetry must work out its own salvation in a man: It cannot be matured by law & precept, but by sensation & watchfulness in itself—That which is creative must create itself—In Endymion, I leaped headlong into the Sea, and thereby have become better acquainted with the Soundings the quicksands, & the rocks, than if I had stayed upon the green shore, and piped a silly pipe, and took tea & comfortable advice.—I was never afraid of failure; for I would sooner fail than not be among the greatest.
Letter to James Hessey [October 8, 1818]

12   I think I shall be among the English Poets after my death.
Letter to George and Georgiana Keats [October 14, 1818]

13   As to the poetical character itself . . . it is not itself—it has no self—it is every thing and nothing. . . . It has as much delight in conceiving an Iago as an Imogen.
Letter to Richard Woodhouse [October 27, 1818]

14   A Poet is the most unpoetical of anything in existence; because he has no Identity—he is continually infor[ming]—and filling some other Body.
Letter to Richard Woodhouse [October 27, 1818]

15   A Man's life of any worth is a continual allegory—and very few eyes can see the Mystery of his life—a life like the scriptures, figurative. . . . Lord Byron cuts a figure, but he is not figurative—Shakespeare led a life of Allegory: his works are the comments on it.
Letter to George and Georgiana Keats [February 14–May 3, 1819]

16   I myself am pursuing the same instinctive course as the veriest human animal you can think of—I am however young writing at random—straining at particles of light in the midst of a great darkness—without knowing the bearing of any one assertion of any one opinion. Yet may I not in this be free from sin?
Letter to George and Georgiana Keats [March 19, 1819]

17   Though a quarrel in the streets is a thing to be hated, the energies displayed in it are fine; the commonest Man shows a grace in his quarrel.
Letter to George and Georgiana Keats [March 19, 1819]

18   Nothing ever becomes real till it is experienced—Even a proverb is no Proverb to you till your Life has illustrated it.
Letter to George and Georgiana Keats [March 19, 1819]

1 Call the world if you Please "The vale of Soul-making."
Letter to George and Georgiana Keats
[April 21, 1819]

2 Do you not see how necessary a World of Pains and troubles is to School an Intelligence and make it a soul? A Place where the heart must feel and suffer in a thousand diverse ways!
Letter to George and Georgiana Keats
[April 21, 1819]

3 I have two luxuries to brood over in my walks, your Loveliness and the hour of my death. O that I could have possession of them both in the same minute. *To Fanny Brawne [July 25, 1819]*

4 "If I should die," said I to myself, "I have left no immortal work behind me—nothing to make my friends proud of my memory—but I have lov'd the principle of beauty in all things, and if I had had time I would have made myself remember'd."
To Fanny Brawne [c. February 1820]

5 You might curb your magnanimity and be more of an artist, and "load every rift"[1] of your subject with ore. *Letter to Shelley [August 16, 1820]*

6 I can scarcely bid you good bye even in a letter. I always made an awkward bow. God bless you!
Letter to Charles Armitage Brown; Keats's
last letter [November 30, 1820]

7 Here lies one whose name was writ in water.[2]
Epitaph for himself [1821]

Leopold von Ranke
1795–1886

8 You have reckoned that history ought to judge the past and to instruct the contemporary world as to the future. The present attempt does not yield to that high office. It only wants to show what actually happened.[3]
Geschichten der Romanischen und
Germanischen Volker von 1492 bis 1535
(History of the Romance and Germanic
Peoples, 1492–1535) [1824], preface

---

[1]Keats is quoting Spenser, *The Faerie Queene, bk. II, canto 7, st. 28.*

[2]Among the many things he has requested of me tonight, this is the principal—that on his gravestone shall be this inscription.— *Letter from* Joseph Severn [1793–1879], *in* Richard Monckton Milnes, *Life, Letters and Literary Remains of John Keats* [1848]

[3]Wie es eigentlich gewesen ist.

Alfred Bunn
1796–1860

9 I dreamt that I dwelt in marble halls,
With vassals and serfs at my side.
The Bohemian Girl [1843], act II, song

[David] Hartley Coleridge
1796–1849

10 The soul of man is larger than the sky,
Deeper than ocean, or the abysmal dark
Of the unfathomed center. *To Shakespeare*

11 But what is Freedom? Rightly understood,
A universal license to be good. *Liberty [1833]*

Horace Mann
1796–1859

12 Lost, yesterday, somewhere between sunrise and sunset, two golden hours, each set with sixty diamond minutes. No reward is offered, for they are gone forever. *Aphorism*

13 Be ashamed to die until you have won some victory for humanity.
Commencement Address, Antioch College
[1859]

James Robinson Planché
1796–1880

14 It would have made a cat laugh.
The Queen of the Frogs [1879], act I, sc. iv

William Hickling Prescott
1796–1859

15 What, then, must have been the emotions of the Spaniards, when, after working their toilsome way into the upper air, the cloudy tabernacle parted before their eyes, and they beheld these fair scenes in all their pristine magnificence and beauty![4] It was like the spectacle which greeted the eyes of Moses from the summit of Pisgah, and, in the warm glow of their feelings, they cried out, "It is the promised land!"
The Conquest of Mexico [1843], bk. III, ch. 8

---

[4]From this summit [Popocatépetl, 17,887 feet] could be seen the great city of Mexico, and the whole of the lake, and all the towns which were built in it.— Díaz del Castillo, *Historia Verdadera de la Conquista de la Nueva España, pt. IV, ch. 53*

1   Drawing his sword he [Pizarro] traced a line with it on the sand from East to West. Then, turning towards the South, "Friends and comrades!" he said, "on that side are toil, hunger, nakedness, the drenching storm, desertion, and death; on this side ease and pleasure. There lies Peru with its riches; here, Panama and its poverty. Choose, each man, what best becomes a brave Castilian. For my part, I go to the South." So saying, he stepped across the line.

The Conquest of Peru [1847], II, 4

Sam Slick
[Thomas Chandler Haliburton]
1796–1865

2   I want you to see Peel, Stanley, Graham, Shiel, Russell, Macaulay, Old Joe, and so on. These men are all upper crust here.

Sam Slick in England [1843–1844],[1] *ch. 24*

3   Circumstances alter cases.

The Old Judge [1849], ch. 15

T[homas] H[aynes] Bayly
1797–1839

4 Tell me the tales that to me were so dear,
Long, long ago, long, long ago.

Long, Long Ago

Heinrich Heine
1797–1856

5 On wings of song, my dearest,
I will carry you off.   *Auf Flügeln des Gesanges*[2]

6 I will not mourn, although my heart is torn,
Oh, love forever lost! I will not mourn.

Ich grolle nicht[3]

7 I cannot tell why this imagined
Despair has fallen upon me;
The ghost of an ancient legend
That will not let me be.   *Lorelei*[4]

8 Child, you are like a flower,
So sweet and pure and fair.
I look at you, and sadness
Touches me with a prayer.

Du bist wie eine Blume

9   A knight of the holy spirit.   *Harzreis*

10   Wherever they burn books they will also, in th end, burn human beings.

Almansor: A Tragedy [1823

11   Every woman is the gift of a world to me.

Ideas: The Book Le Grand [1826

12   Don't send a poet to London.

English Fragments [1828], ch. 2, London

13   Christianity is an idea, and as such is indestructible and immortal, like every idea.

History of Religion and Philosophy in Germany [1834], vol. I

14   Mark this well, you proud men of action: You are nothing but the unwitting agents of the men o thought who often, in quiet self-effacement, mark out most exactly all your doings in advance.

History of Religion and Philosophy in Germany, III

15   People in those old times had convictions; we moderns only have opinions. And it needs more than a mere opinion to erect a Gothic cathedral.

The French Stage [1837], ch. 9

16   Wild, dark times are rumbling toward us, and the prophet who wishes to write a new apocalypse will have to invent entirely new beasts, and beasts so terrible that the ancient animal symbols of Saint John will seem like cooing doves and cupids in comparison.

Lutetia; or, Paris [1842]. From the Augsberg Gazette, 12, VII

17   The future smells of Russian leather, of blood, of godlessness and of much whipping. I advise our grandchildren to come into the world with very thick skin on their backs.

Lutetia; or, Paris. From the Augsberg Gazette, 12, VII

18   Ordinarily he is insane, but he has lucid moments when he is only stupid.

Of Savoye, appointed ambassador to Frankfurt by Lamartine [1848]

19 So we keep asking, over and over,
Until a handful of earth

---

[1]The "Sam Slick" papers first appeared in a weekly paper in Nova Scotia [1836].

[2]Auf Flügeln des Gesanges, / Herzliebchen, trag ich dich fort. Translated by LOUIS UNTERMEYER.

[3]Ich grolle nicht, und wenn das Herz auch bricht, / Ewig verlornes Lieb! Ich grolle nicht. Translated by LOUIS UNTERMEYER.

[4]Ich weiss nicht, was soll es bedeuten, / Dass ich so traurig bin; / Ein Märchen aus alten Zeiten, / Das kommt mir nicht aus dem Sinn. Translated by LOUIS UNTERMEYER.

[5]Du bist wie eine Blume, / So hold und schön und rein; / Ich schau dich an, und Wehmut / Schleicht mir ins Herz hinein. Translated by LOUIS UNTERMEYER.

Stops our mouths—
But is that an answer?   *Lazarus, I [1854]*

1   Of course he [God] will forgive me; that's his business.[1]   *Last words [1856]*

2   No author is a man of genius to his publisher.
    Attributed

Samuel Lover
1797–1868

3   Reproof on her lip, but a smile in her eye.
    Rory O'More [1836], st. 1

4   "For there's luck in odd numbers," says Rory
    O'More.   *Rory O'More, st. 3*

Sir Charles Lyell
1797–1875

5   Although we are mere sojourners on the surface
of the planet, chained to a mere point in space, enduring but for a moment of time, the human mind
is not only enabled to number worlds beyond the
unassisted ken of mortal eye, but to trace the events
of indefinite ages before the creation of our race,
and is not even withheld from penetrating into the
dark secrets of the ocean, or the interior of the solid
globe; free, like the spirit which the poet described
as animating the universe.
    Principles of Geology, vol. I [1830], ch. 13

6   It may be said that, so far from having a materi-
alistic tendency, the supposed introduction into the
earth at successive geological periods of life—sensation, instinct, the intelligence of the higher mammalia
bordering on reason, and lastly, the improvable reason of Man himself—presents us with a picture of
the ever-increasing dominion of mind over matter.
    *The Geological Evidences of the Antiquity of
    Man [1863]*

Mary [Wollstonecraft] Shelley
1797–1851

7   Nothing contributes so much to tranquilize the
mind as a steady purpose—a point on which the
soul may fix its intellectual eye.
    Frankenstein [1818], Letter I

8   I beheld the wretch—the miserable monster
whom I had created.   *Frankenstein, ch. 5*

Sojourner Truth
[Isabella Van Wagener]
c. 1797–1883

9   Frederick, is God dead?
    Question to speaker FREDERICK DOUGLASS
    [c. 1850]

10   That man . . . says that women need to be helped
into carriages, and lifted over ditches, and to have
the best place everywhere. Nobody ever helps me
into carriages, or over mud puddles, or gives me any
best place, and aren't I a woman? . . . I have plowed,
and planted, and gathered into barns, and no man
could head me—and aren't I a woman? I could
work as much and eat as much as a man (when I
could get it), and bear the lash as well—and aren't
I a woman? I have borne thirteen children and seen
them most all sold off into slavery, and when I cried
out with a mother's grief, none but Jesus heard—
and aren't I a woman?
    *Speech at Woman's Rights Convention, Akron,
    Ohio [1851]*

11   That . . . man . . . says women can't have as much
rights as man, cause Christ wasn't a woman. Where
did your Christ come from? . . . From God and a
woman. Man had nothing to do with him.
    *Speech at Woman's Rights Convention, Akron,
    Ohio*

12   The rich rob the poor and the poor rob one another.   *Saying*

Alfred de Vigny
1797–1863

13   I love the sound of the horn, at night, in the
depth of the woods.[2]
    Le Cor [1826]

14   God! how sad is the sound of the horn deep in
the woods![3]   *Le Cor*

15   I [Nature] am called a mother, but I am a grave.
    La Maison du Berger [1864]

16   Love that which will never be seen twice.
    La Maison du Berger

17   Silence alone is great; all else is weakness.
    La Mort du Loup [1864]

---

[1]Bien sûr, il me pardonnera; c'est son métier.

[2]J'aime le son du cor, le soir, au fond des bois.

[3]Dieu! que le son du cor est triste au fond des bois!

Auguste Comte
1798–1857

1   Love our principle, order our foundation, progress our goal.

Système de Politique Positive [1851–1854]

2   Nothing at bottom is real except humanity.[1]

Système de Politique Positive

3   The dead govern the living.

Catéchisme Positiviste [1852]

Eugène Delacroix
1798–1863

4   O young artist, you search for a subject—everything is a subject. Your subject is yourself, your impressions, your emotions in the presence of nature.

Oeuvres Littéraires

5   The first virtue of a painting is to be a feast for the eyes.   *Journal [1893–1895]*

6   Painting is only a bridge linking the painter's mind with that of the viewer.

Journal

August Heinrich Hoffmann [Hoffmann von Fallersleben]
1798–1874

7   Deutschland, Deutschland über Alles.[2]

Title of poem [September 1, 1841]

Jules Michelet
1798–1874

8   England is an empire, Germany is a nation, a race, France is a person.

Histoire de France [1833–1867]

9   What is the first part of politics? Education. The second? Education. And the third? Education.

Le Peuple [1846]

David Macbeth Moir
1798–1851

10   From the lone sheiling of the misty island
Mountains divide us, and the waste of seas—

---

[1]Il n'y a, au fond, de réel que l'humanité.
[2]Germany before everything.

Yet still the blood is strong, the heart is Highland,
And we in dreams behold the Hebrides.[3]

The Lone Sheiling [Canadian Boat Song, 1829

Dionysios Solomos
1798–1857

11 We knew thee of old,
O divinely restored,
By the light of thine eyes
And the light of thy sword.

From the graves of our slain
Shall thy valor prevail
As we greet thee again—
Hail, Liberty! Hail!

Hymn to Liberty [1823][4] st. 1,

12 On the blackened spine of Psara,
Glory, pacing alone,
Broods on her shining heroes;
She crowns her hair with a band
Born from the spare, few grasses
That are left in the ruined land.

The Destruction of Psara [1825]

13   Enclose in your soul Greece (or something equal) and you shall feel every kind of grandeur.

Note to "Free Besieged" [c. 1833][

[Amos] Bronson Alcott
1799–1888

14   The true teacher defends his pupils against his own personal influence. He inspires self-trust. He guides their eyes from himself to the spirit that quickens him. He will have no disciple.

*Orphic Sayings. From The Dial [July 1840].
The Teacher*

15 Who loves a garden still his Eden keeps,
Perennial pleasures plants, and wholesome
    harvests reaps.   *Tablets [1868]*

16   One must be a wise reader to quote wisely and well.   *Table Talk [1877]. Quotation*

---

[3]This poem, entitled *Canadian Boat Song,* appeared [September 1829] anonymously in the *Noctes Ambrosianae* series in *Blackwood's Edinburgh Magazine.* It has been attributed to (among others) John Wilson ("Christopher North"), John Galt, John Lockhart, Sir Walter Scott, and to David Macbeth Moir, who is now generally accepted as the author.

[4]Translated by RUDYARD KIPLING.
Out of a total of 158 stanzas in the hymn, the first four have been adopted as the Greek national anthem.

[5]Translated by CEDRIC WHITMAN.

[6]Translated by GEORGE SAVIDIS.

1   To be ignorant of one's ignorance is the malady of the ignorant.   *Table Talk. Discourse*

2 I press thee to my heart as Duty's faithful child.
    Sonnet to Louisa May Alcott [1882]

Honoré de Balzac
1799–1850

3   It is easier to be a lover than a husband for the simple reason that it is more difficult to be witty every day than to say pretty things from time to time.   *Physiologie du Mariage [1829]*

4   I am a galley slave to pen and ink.   *Lettres [1832]*

5   Fame is the sun of the dead.   *La Recherche de l'Absolu [1834]*

6   Our heart is a treasury; if you spend all its wealth at once you are ruined. We find it as difficult to forgive a person for displaying his feeling in all its nakedness as we do to forgive a man for being penniless.   *Le Père Goriot [1835]*[1]

7   Man is no angel. He is sometimes more of a hypocrite and sometimes less, and then fools say that he has or has not principles.   *Le Père Goriot*

8   "Temptations can be got rid of." "How?" "By yielding to them."   *Le Père Goriot*

9   I believe in the incomprehensibility of God.   *Letter to Éveline Hanska [1837]*

10   Those sweetly smiling angels with pensive looks, innocent faces, and cash-boxes for hearts.   *La Cousine Bette [1846], ch. 15*

Simon Cameron
1799–1889

11   An honest politician is one who when he's bought stays bought.   *Attributed*

Rufus Choate
1799–1859

12   The courage of New England was the "courage of conscience." It did not rise to that insane and awful passion, the love of war for itself.
    Address at Ipswich, Massachusetts, Centennial [1834]

---
[1]Translated by MARION AYTON CRAWFORD.

13   We join ourselves to no party that does not carry the flag and keep step to the music of the Union.
    Letter to the Whig Convention, Worcester, Massachusetts [October 1, 1855]

Thomas Hood
1799–1845

14 They went and told the sexton, and
    The sexton tolled the bell.
    Faithless Sally Brown [1826], st. 17

15 I remember, I remember
    The house where I was born,
    The little window where the sun
    Came peeping in at morn.
    I Remember, I Remember [1827], st. 1

16   Now 'tis little joy
    To know I'm farther off from heaven
    Than when I was a boy.
    I Remember, I Remember, st. 4

17 And there is even a happiness
    That makes the heart afraid.
    Ode to Melancholy [1827]

18 There's not a string attuned to mirth
    But has its chord in melancholy.
    Ode to Melancholy

19 But evil is wrought by want of thought,
    As well as want of heart.
    The Lady's Dream [1827], st. 16

20 I saw old Autumn in the misty morn
    Stand shadowless like silence, listening
    To silence.   *Ode: Autumn [1827], st. 1*

21 Straight down the Crooked Lane,
    And all round the Square.
    A Plain Direction, st. 1

22 Never go to France
    Unless you know the lingo,
    If you do, like me,
    You will repent, by jingo.
    French and English [1839], st. 1

23 No warmth, no cheerfulness, no healthful ease,
    No comfortable feel in any member—
    No shade, no shine, no butterflies, no bees,
    No fruits, no flowers, no leaves, no birds,
    November!   *No!*

24 Seem'd washing his hands with invisible soap
    In imperceptible water.
    Miss Kilmansegg and Her Precious Leg [1841–1843]. Her Christening, st. 10

1 O bed! O bed! delicious bed!
That heaven upon earth to the weary head.
Miss Kilmansegg and Her Precious Leg.
Her Dream, st. 8

2 With fingers weary and worn,
With eyelids heavy and red,
A woman sat in unwomanly rags
Plying her needle and thread—
Stitch! stitch! stitch!
In poverty, hunger, and dirt.
The Song of the Shirt [1843], st. 1

3 She sang the Song of the Shirt.
The Song of the Shirt, st. 1

4 Work! work! work!   *The Song of the Shirt, st. 2*

5 O men, with sisters dear!
O men, with mothers and wives!
It is not linen you're wearing out,
But human creatures' lives!
The Song of the Shirt, st. 4

6 O God! that bread should be so dear,
And flesh and blood so cheap!
The Song of the Shirt, st. 5

7 One more unfortunate,
Weary of breath,
Rashly importunate,
Gone to her death!

Take her up tenderly,
Lift her with care;
Fashioned so slenderly,
Young, and so fair!
The Bridge of Sighs [1844], st. 1, 2

8 Alas for the rarity
Of Christian charity
Under the sun!   *The Bridge of Sighs, st. 9*

Mary Howitt
1799–1888

9 "Will you walk into my parlor?" said the Spider to
the Fly;
"'Tis the prettiest little parlor that ever you
did spy."   *The Spider and the Fly [1844]*

Thomas Noel
1799–1861

10 Rattle his bones over the stones!
He's only a pauper, whom nobody owns!
The Pauper's Drive, st. 1

Alexander Sergeevich Pushkin
1799–1837

11   Reason's icy intimations,
and records of a heart in pain.
Eugene Onegin [1823],[1] dedication

12 Unforced, as conversation passed,
he had the talent of saluting
felicitously every theme,
of listening like a judge supreme
while serious topics were disputing,
or, with an epigram-surprise,
of kindling smiles in ladies' eyes.
Eugene Onegin, ch. 1, st. 5

13 Always contented with his life,
and with his dinner, and his wife.
Eugene Onegin, 1, st. 12

14 Why fight what's known to be decisive?
Custom is despot of mankind.
Eugene Onegin, 1, st. 25

15 The illness with which he'd been smitten
should have been analyzed when caught,
something like *spleen*, that scourge of Britain,
or Russia's *chondria*, for short.
Eugene Onegin, 1, st. 38

16 Habit is Heaven's own redress:
it takes the place of happiness.
Eugene Onegin, 2, st. 31

17 Love passed, the muse appeared, the weather
of mind got clarity newfound;
now free, I once more weave together
emotion, thought, and magic sound.
Eugene Onegin, 2, st. 59

18 *Pimen [writing by lamplight]*: One more, the final
record, and my annals
Are ended, and fulfilled the duty laid
By God on me, a sinner. Not in vain
Hath God appointed me for many years
A witness, teaching me the art of letters;
A day will come when some laborious monk
Will bring to light my zealous, nameless toil,
Kindle, as I, his lamp, and from the parchment
Shaking the dust of ages, will transcribe
My chronicles.   *Boris Godunov [written 1825][2]*

19 Like to some magistrate grown gray in office
Calmly he contemplates alike the just
And unjust, with indifference he notes
Evil and good, and knows not wrath nor pity.
Boris Godunov

[1]Translated by CHARLES JOHNSTON.
[2]Translated by ALFRED HAYES.

1   *Mosalsky:* Good folk! Maria Godunov and her son Feodor have poisoned themselves. We have seen their dead bodies. [*The people are silent with horror.*] Why are you silent? Cry, Long live Czar Dimitri Ivanovich! [*The people are speechless.*]

Boris Godunov

2   And thus he[1] mused: "From here, indeed
Shall we strike terror in the Swede;
And here a city, by our labor
Founded, shall gall our haughty neighbor;
'Here cut'—so Nature gives command—
'Your window through on Europe: stand
Firm-footed by the sea, unchanging!' "

The Bronze Horseman [written 1833][2]

John Brown
1800–1859

3   Had I so interfered in behalf of the rich, the powerful, the intelligent, the so-called great, or in behalf of any of their friends . . . every man in this court would have deemed it an act worthy of reward rather than punishment.

Last speech to the court [November 2, 1859]

4   I am yet too young to understand that God is any respecter of persons. I believe that to have interfered as I have done . . . in behalf of His despised poor, was not wrong, but right. Now, if it is deemed necessary that I should forfeit my life for the furtherance of the ends of justice, and mingle my blood further with the blood of my children, and with the blood of millions in this slave country whose rights are disregarded by wicked, cruel, and unjust enactments, I submit: so let it be done!

Last speech to the court [November 2, 1859]

5   This *is* a beautiful country.

Remark as he rode to the gallows, seated on his coffin [December 2, 1859]

Julia Crawford
1800–1885

6   Kathleen Mavourneen! the gray dawn is breaking,
The horn of the hunter is heard on the hill.

Kathleen Mavourneen [1835], st. 1

7   Oh! hast thou forgotten this day we must part?
It may be for years, and it may be forever;
Then why art thou silent, thou voice of my heart?

Kathleen Mavourneen, st. 1

---

[1]Peter I (the Great) [1672–1725].

[2]Translated by OLIVER ELTON.

Thomas Babington, Lord Macaulay
1800–1859

8   That is the best government which desires to make the people happy, and knows how to make them happy.

Essay on Mitford's History of Greece [1824]

9   Free trade, one of the greatest blessings which a government can confer on a people, is in almost every country unpopular.

Essay on Mitford's History of Greece

10   Nobles by the right of an earlier creation, and priests by the imposition of a mightier hand.

On Milton [1825]

11   The dust and silence of the upper shelf.

On Milton

12   As civilization advances, poetry almost necessarily declines.

On Milton

13   Perhaps no person can be a poet, or can even enjoy poetry, without a certain unsoundness of mind.

On Milton

14   There is only one cure for the evils which newly acquired freedom produces, and that cure is freedom.

On Milton

15   Nothing is so useless as a general maxim.

On Machiavelli [1827]

16   The gallery in which the reporters sit has become a fourth estate of the realm.

On Hallam's Constitutional History [1828]

17   The English Bible—a book which if everything else in our language should perish, would alone suffice to show the whole extent of its beauty and power.   *On John Dryden [1828]*

18   His imagination resembled the wings of an ostrich. It enabled him to run, though not to soar.

On John Dryden

19   Men are never so likely to settle a question rightly as when they discuss it freely.

Southey's Colloquies on Society [1830]

20   That wonderful book, while it obtains admiration from the most fastidious critics, is loved by those who are too simple to admire it.

On Southey's edition of Bunyan's Pilgrim's Progress [1830]

21   We know no spectacle so ridiculous as the British public in one of its periodical fits of morality.

On Moore's Life of Lord Byron [1831]

22   From the poetry of Lord Byron they drew a system of ethics compounded of misanthropy and volup-

tuousness—a system in which the two great commandments were to hate your neighbor and to love your neighbor's wife.

On Moore's Life of Lord Byron

1   Reform, that you may preserve.

Debate on the First Reform Bill [March 2, 1831]

2 Ye diners-out from whom we guard our spoons.[1]

Political Georgics

3   The conformation of his mind was such that whatever was little seemed to him great, and whatever was great seemed to him little.

On Horace Walpole [1833]

4 Such night in England ne'er had been, nor ne'er again shall be.   *The Armada [1833], l. 34*

5   An acre in Middlesex is better than a principality in Utopia.   *On Lord Bacon [1837]*

6   Every schoolboy knows who imprisoned Montezuma, and who strangled Atahualpa.

On Lord Clive [1840]

7   She [the Roman Catholic Church] may still exist in undiminished vigor when some traveler from New Zealand shall, in the midst of a vast solitude, take his stand on a broken arch of London Bridge to sketch the ruins of St. Paul's.[2]

On Leopold von Ranke's History of the Popes [1840]

8   She [the Catholic Church] thoroughly understands what no other Church has ever understood, how to deal with enthusiasts.

On Leopold von Ranke's History of the Popes

9   The Chief Justice was rich, quiet, and infamous.

On Warren Hastings [1841]

10   I shall not be satisfied unless I produce something which shall for a few days supersede the last fashionable novel on the tables of young ladies.

Letter to Macvey Napier [November 5, 1841]

11   In order that he might rob a neighbor whom he had promised to defend, black men fought on the coast of Coromandel and red men scalped each other by the great lakes of North America.

On Frederick the Great [1842]

---

[1]The louder he talked of his honor, the faster we counted our spoons. — EMERSON, *The Conduct of Life* [1860], *Worship*

[2]Who knows but that hereafter some traveler like myself will sit down upon the banks of the Seine, the Thames, or the Zuyder Zee, where now, in the tumult of enjoyment, the heart and the eyes are too slow to take in the multitude of sensations? Who knows but he will sit down solitary amid silent ruins, and weep a people inurned and their greatness changed into an empty name? — CONSTANTIN DE VOLNEY [1757–1820], *Ruins, ch. 11*

See Horace Walpole, 336:5.

12   We hardly know an instance of the strength and weakness of human nature so striking and so grotesque as the character of this haughty, vigilant, resolute, sagacious blue-stocking, half Mithridate and half Trissotin, bearing up against a world in arms, with an ounce of poison in one pocket and a quire of bad verses in the other.

On Frederick the Great

13 Lars Porsena of Clusium
By the Nine Gods he swore
That the great house of Tarquin
Should suffer wrong no more.
By the Nine Gods he swore it,
And named a trysting day,
And bade his messengers ride forth
East and west and south and north,
To summon his array.

Lays of Ancient Rome [1842]. Horatius, st. 1

14 To every man upon this earth
Death cometh soon or late;
And how can man die better
Than facing fearful odds
For the ashes of his fathers,
And the temples of his gods?

Lays of Ancient Rome. Horatius, st. 27

15   He [Richard Steele] was a rake among scholars, and a scholar among rakes.

Review of Lucy Aikin's Life and Writings of Addison [1843]

16   A man who has never looked on Niagara has but a faint idea of a cataract; and he who has not read Barère's *Memoirs* may be said not to know what it is to lie.

On Mémoires de Bertrand Barère [1844]

17   Those who compare the age in which their lot has fallen with a golden age which exists only in imagination, may talk of degeneracy and decay; but no man who is correctly informed as to the past will be disposed to take a morose or desponding view of the present.

History of England [1849–1861], vol. I, ch. 1

18   The Puritan hated bear-baiting, not because it gave pain to the bear, but because it gave pleasure to the spectators.   *History of England, I, 2*

19   There were gentlemen and there were seamen in the navy of Charles II. But the seamen were not gentlemen, and the gentlemen were not seamen.

History of England, I, 3

20   He [Richard Rumbold, c. 1622–1685] never would believe that Providence had sent a few men into the world ready booted and spurred to ride, and millions ready saddled and bridled to be ridden.

History of England, I, 5

1 The ambassador [of Russia] and the grandees who accompanied him were so gorgeous that all London crowded to stare at them, and so filthy that nobody dared to touch them. They came to the court balls dropping pearls and vermin.
History of England, V, 23

2 Your Constitution is all sail and no anchor.
Letter to H. S. Randall, author of a Life of Thomas Jefferson [May 23, 1857]

Helmuth von Moltke
1800–1891

3 First ponder, then dare.[1]   *Attributed*

4 The fate of every nation rests in its own power.
To the German Reichstag [March 1, 1880]

5 A war, even the most victorious, is a national misfortune.   *Letter [1880]*

Richard Bethell, Lord Westbury
1800–1873

6 Take a note of that; his Lordship says he will turn it over in what he is pleased to call his mind.
Attributed[2]

Jane [Baillie] Welsh Carlyle
1801–1866

7 A positive engagement to marry a certain person at a certain time, at all haps and hazards, I have always considered the most ridiculous thing on earth.
To Thomas Carlyle [January 1825]

8 In spite of the honestest efforts to annihilate my *I-ity,* or merge it in what the world doubtless considers my better half, I still find myself a self-subsisting and alas! self-seeking *me.*
To John Sterling [June 4, 1835]

9 Oh Lord! If you but knew what a brimstone of a creature I am behind all this beautiful amiability!
To Eliza Stodart [February 29, 1836]

10 Instead of boiling up individuals into the species, I would draw a chalk circle round every individuality, and preach to it to keep within that, and preserve and cultivate its identity.
To John Sterling [August 5, 1845]

11 I can see that the Lady has a genius for ruling, whilst I have a genius for *not being ruled.*
To Thomas Carlyle [September 28, 1845]

12 The surest way to get a thing in this life is to be prepared for doing without it, to the exclusion even of hope.   *Journal, August 1849*

13 Not a hundredth part of the thoughts in my head have ever been or ever will be spoken or written — as long as I keep my senses, at least.
Journal, July 16, 1858

14 The triumphal procession air which, in our manners and customs, is given to marriage at the outset — that singing of *Te Deum* before the battle has begun.   *To Miss Barnes [August 24, 1859]*

Thomas Cole
1801–1848

15 Over all, rocks, wood, and water, brooded the spirit of repose, and the silent energy of nature stirred the soul to its inmost depths.
Essay on American Scenery [1835]

David Glasgow Farragut
1801–1870

16 Damn the torpedoes — full speed ahead!
At the battle of Mobile Bay [August 5, 1864]

John Henry Cardinal Newman
1801–1890

17 Time hath a taming hand.
Persecution [1832], st. 3

18 Lead, kindly Light, amid the encircling gloom;
Lead thou me on!
The night is dark, and I am far from home;
Lead thou me on!
Keep thou my feet: I do not ask to see
The distant scene; one step enough for me.
The Pillar of Cloud [1833]. Lead Kindly Light, st. 1

19 Growth is the only evidence of life.
Apologia pro Vita Sua [1864]

20 It is thy very energy of thought
Which keeps thee from thy God.
Dream of Gerontius [1866], pt. III

21 Living Nature, not dull Art
Shall plan my ways and rule my heart.
Nature and Art [1868], st. 12

---

[1]Erst wägen, dann wagen.

[2]Reportedly an audible aside from the barristers' table in reference to a presiding judge. According to T. A. Nash, *Life of Lord Westbury* [1888], *vol. I, p. 158,* Westbury disclaimed invention of the mot.

1   O Lord, support us all the day long, until the shadows lengthen and the evening comes, and the busy world is hushed, and the fever of life is over, and our work is done. Then in thy mercy grant us a safe lodging, and a holy rest, and peace at the last.
Sermon [1834]. Included in the Book of Common Prayer

2   There is a knowledge which is desirable, though nothing come of it, as being of itself a treasure, and a sufficient remuneration of years of labor.
The Idea of a University [1873]. Discourse V, pt. 6

3   It is almost a definition of a gentleman to say that he is one who never inflicts pain.
The Idea of a University. Discourse VIII

4   The world is content with setting right the surface of things.
The Idea of a University. Discourse VIII

5   Ex umbris et imaginibus in veritatem [From shadows and symbols into the truth]!
His own epitaph at Edgbaston

William Henry Seward
1801–1872

6   Shall I tell you what this collision [of free and slave labor] means? . . . It is an irrepressible conflict between opposing and enduring forces, and it means that the United States must and will, sooner or later, become entirely a slave-holding nation or entirely a free-labor nation.
Speech at Rochester, New York [October 25, 1858]

7   I know, and all the world knows, that revolutions never go backward.
Speech at Rochester, New York [October 25, 1858]

Brigham Young
1801–1877

8   This is the place!
On first seeing the valley of the Great Salt Lake [July 24, 1847]

Lydia Maria Child
1802–1880

9   We first crush people to the earth, and then claim the right of trampling on them forever, because they are prostrate.
An Appeal on Behalf of That Class of Americans Called Africans [1833]

10   They [the slaves] have stabbed themselves for freedom—jumped into the waves for freedom—starved for freedom—fought like very tigers for freedom! But they have been hung, and burned, and shot—and their tyrants have been their historians!
An Appeal on Behalf of That Class of Americans Called Africans

11   Over the river and through the wood,
To grandfather's house we go;
    The horse knows the way
    To carry the sleigh,
Through the white and drifted snow.
Flowers for Children [1844–1846]. Thanksgiving Day, st. 1

12   Woman stock is rising in the market. I shall not live to see women vote, but I'll come and rap at the ballot box.
Letter to Sarah Shaw [August 3, 1856]

13   The United States is . . . a warning rather than an example to the world.
To the twenty-fifth-anniversary meeting of the Massachusetts Anti-Slavery Society [1857]

14   Yours for the unshackled exercise of every faculty by every human being.
Message to woman suffrage supporters [c. 1875]

David Christy
1802–c. 1868

15   Cotton Is King; or, The Economical Relations of Slavery.   *Title of book [1855]*

Alexandre Dumas the Elder
1802–1870

16   All for one, one for all, that is our motto.
The Three Musketeers [1844], ch. 9

17   Nothing succeeds like success.[2]
Ange Pitou [1854], vol. I

18   Let us look for the woman.[3]
The Mohicans of Paris [1854–1855], vol. III, ch. 10, 11

---

[1]Take away *time is money*, and what is left of England? take away *cotton is king*, and what is left of America? — HUGO, *Les Misérables* [1862], Marius, bk. IV, ch. 4

[2]Rien ne réussit comme le succès. — *French proverb*

[3]The phrase "Cherchez la femme" is attributed to JOSEPH FOUCHÉ [1759–1820].

Victor Hugo
1802–1885

1 These two halves of God, the Pope and the emperor. *Hernani [1830], act IV, sc. ii*

2 God became a man, granted. The devil became a woman.[1] *Ruy Blas [1838], act II, sc. v*

3 Popularity? It is glory's small change. *Ruy Blas, III, v*

4 An invasion of armies can be resisted, but not an idea whose time has come.[2] *Histoire d'un Crime [written 1852], conclusion*

5 Waterloo! Waterloo! Waterloo! Dismal plain![3] *Les Châtiments [1853]. L'Expiation*

6 You have created a new thrill.[4] *Letter to Baudelaire [October 6, 1859]*

7 The supreme happiness of life is the conviction that we are loved. *Les Misérables [1862].[5] Fantine, bk. V, ch. 4*

8 Great grief is a divine and terrible radiance which transfigures the wretched. *Les Misérables. Fantine, V, 13*

9 Napoleon . . . mighty somnambulist of a vanished dream. *Les Misérables. Cosette, bk. I, ch. 13*

10 Waterloo is a battle of the first rank won by a captain of the second. *Les Misérables. Cosette, I, 16*

11 Would you realize what Revolution is, call it Progress; and would you realize what Progress is, call it Tomorrow. *Les Misérables. Cosette, I, 17*

12 Great blunders are often made, like large ropes, of a multitude of fibers. *Les Misérables. Cosette, V, 10*

13 Upon the first goblet he read this inscription, *monkey wine;* upon the second, *lion wine;* upon the third, *sheep wine;* upon the fourth, *swine wine.* These four inscriptions expressed the four descending degrees of drunkenness: the first, that which enlivens; the second, that which irritates; the third, that which stupefies; finally the last, that which brutalizes. *Les Misérables. Cosette, VI, 9*

14 A man is not idle because he is absorbed in thought. There is a visible labor and there is an invisible labor. *Les Misérables. Cosette, VII, 8*

15 No one ever keeps a secret so well as a child. *Les Misérables. Cosette, VIII, 8*

16 Social prosperity means man happy, the citizen free, the nation great. *Les Misérables. Saint Denis, bk. I, ch. 4*

17 Where the telescope ends, the microscope begins. Which of the two has the grander view? *Les Misérables. Saint Denis, III, 3*

18 To rise at six, to dine at ten,
To sup at six, to sleep at ten,
Makes a man live for ten times ten. *Inscription over the door of Hugo's study*

19 I represent a party which does not yet exist: the party of revolution, civilization.
This party will make the twentieth century.
There will issue from it first the United States of Europe, then the United States of the World. *On the wall of the room in which Hugo died, Place des Vosges, Paris*

Letitia Elizabeth Landon
1802–1838

20 Few, save the poor, feel for the poor. *The Poor*

21 Were it not better to forget
Than but remember and regret? *Despondency*

George Pope Morris
1802–1864

22 Woodman, spare that tree!
Touch not a single bough!
In youth it sheltered me,
And I'll protect it now. *Woodman, Spare That Tree [1830], st. 1*

23 The union of hearts—the union of hands—
And the flag of our Union forever! *The Flag of Our Union [1851]*

William Allen
1803–1879

24 Fifty-four forty, or fight![6] *Speech in the Senate [1844]*

---

[1]Dieu s'est fait homme; soit. Le diable s'est fait femme.

[2]On résiste à l'invasion des armées; on ne résiste pas à l'invasion des idées. (Literally, one can resist the invasion of armies, but not the invasion of ideas.)

[3]Waterloo! Waterloo! Waterloo! Morne plaine!

[4]Vous créez un frisson nouveau.

[5]Translated by CHARLES E. WILBOUR.

---

[6]Slogan of expansionist Democrats in the 1844 presidential campaign, in which the Oregon boundary definition was a pressing issue. The new Democratic President, James K. Polk, compromised [1846] with Great Britain on the 49th parallel.

Thomas Lovell Beddoes
1803–1849

1 The anchor heaves, the ship swings free,
The sails swell full. To sea, to sea!
*Death's Jest-Book [1850]. Song from the Ship,
st. 2*

2 If there were dreams to sell,
What would you buy?
Some cost a passing-bell;
Some a light sigh.   *Dream Pedlary*

George Borrow
1803–1881

3 There's night and day, brother, both sweet things;
sun, moon, and stars, brother, all sweet things; there's
likewise a wind on the heath. Life is very sweet,
brother; who would wish to die?
Lavengro [1851], ch. 25

4 I learned . . . to fear God, and to take my own
part.   *Lavengro, 86*

5 Youth will be served, every dog has his day, and
mine has been a fine one.   *Lavengro, 92*

6 Youth is the only season for enjoyment, and the
first twenty-five years of one's life are worth all the
rest of the longest life of man, even though those
five-and-twenty be spent in penury and contempt,
and the rest in the possession of wealth, honors, re-
spectability.   *The Romany Rye [1857], ch. 30*

Edward Bulwer-Lytton,
Baron Lytton
1803–1873

7 In other countries poverty is a misfortune—with
us it is a crime.
England and the English [1833]

8 Rank is a great beautifier.
The Lady of Lyons [1838], act II, sc. i

9 Love, like Death,
Levels all ranks, and lays the shepherd's crook
Beside the scepter.   *The Lady of Lyons, III, ii*

10 Beneath the rule of men entirely great,
The pen is mightier than the sword.
Richelieu [1839], act II, sc. ii

11 In the lexicon of youth, which fate reserves
For a bright manhood, there is no such word
As—*fail.*   *Richelieu, II, ii*

12 It was a dark and stormy night.[1]
Paul Clifford [1840], opening word

13 [Tennyson:] Out-babying Wordsworth and outglittering Keats.
The New Timon [1846], pt.

William Driver
1803–1886

14 I name thee Old Glory.
*As the flag was hoisted to the masthead of his
brig*[2]

Ralph Waldo Emerson
1803–1882

15 Good-bye, proud world! I'm going home;
Thou art not my friend and I'm not thine.
Poems [1847]. Good-bye, st. 1

16 Nor knowest thou what argument
Thy life to thy neighbor's creed has lent.
All are needed by each one;
Nothing is fair or good alone.
Poems. Each and All, st. 1

17 I wiped away the weeds and foam,
I fetched my sea-born treasures home;
But the poor, unsightly, noisome things
Had left their beauty on the shore,
With the sun and the sand and the wild uproar.
Poems. Each and All, st. 3

18 I like a church; I like a cowl;
I love a prophet of the soul;
And on my heart monastic aisles
Fall like sweet strains or pensive smiles;
Yet not for all his faith can see
Would I that cowlèd churchman be.
Poems. The Problem, st. 1

19 The hand that rounded Peter's dome,
And groined the aisles of Christian Rome,
Wrought in a sad sincerity;
Himself from God he could not free;
He builded better than he knew—
The conscious stone to beauty grew.
Poems. The Problem, st. 2

20 Line in nature is not found;
Unit and universe are round;

---

[1] See Schulz, 811:2.

[2] On August 10, 1831, a large American flag was presented to
Driver, captain of the *Charles Doggett*, by a band of women in
recognition of his bringing the British mutineers of the ship
Bounty from Tahiti back to their former home, Pitcairn Island.

In vain produced, all rays return;
Evil will bless, and ice will burn.   *Poems. Uriel, st. 2*

1 Announced by all the trumpets of the sky,
  Arrives the snow.   *Poems. The Snowstorm, l. 1*

Enclosed
2 In a tumultuous privacy of storm.
     Poems. The Snowstorm, l. 8

3 In May, when sea winds pierced our solitudes,
  I found the fresh Rhodora in the woods.
     Poems. The Rhodora, l .1

4 Rhodora! if the sages ask thee why
  This charm is wasted on the earth and sky,
  Tell them, dear, that if eyes were made for seeing,
  Then Beauty is its own excuse for being.
     Poems. The Rhodora, l. 9

5 Things are of the snake.
     Poems. Ode Inscribed to W. H. Channing, st. 6

6 Things are in the saddle,
  And ride mankind.
     Poems. Ode Inscribed to W. H. Channing, st. 6

7 There are two laws discrete,
  Not reconciled —
  Law for man, and law for thing.
     Poems. Ode Inscribed to W. H. Channing, st. 7

8 Give all to love;
  Obey thy heart;
  Friends, kindred, days,
  Estate, good fame,
  Plans, credit and the Muse,
  Nothing refuse.   *Poems. Give All to Love, st. 1*

9 Heartily know,
  When half-gods go,
  The gods arrive.   *Poems. Give All to Love, st. 6*

10 Love not the flower they pluck, and know it not,
   And all their botany is Latin names.   *Poems. Blight*

11 By the rude bridge that arched the flood,
   Their flag to April's breeze unfurled,
   Here once the embattled farmers stood,
   And fired the shot heard round the world.
     *Poems. Hymn Sung at the Completion of the
     Battle Monument, Concord, Massachusetts
     [July 4, 1837], st. 1*

12 "Pass in, pass in," the angels say,
   "In to the upper doors,
   Nor count compartments of the floors,
   But mount to paradise
   By the stairway of surprise."   *Poems. Merlin I*

13 God said, I am tired of kings,
   I suffer them no more;

Up to my ear the morning brings
The outrage of the poor.
     *May-Day and Other Pieces [1867]. Boston
     Hymn, st. 2*

14 Today unbind the captive,
   So only are ye unbound;
   Lift up a people from the dust,
   Trump of their rescue, sound!
     *May-Day and Other Pieces. Boston Hymn,
     st. 17*

15 I think no virtue goes with size.
     May-Day and Other Pieces. The Titmouse

16 So nigh is grandeur to our dust,
   So near is God to man,
   When Duty whispers low, *Thou must,*
   The youth replies, *I can.*
     May-Day and Other Pieces. Voluntaries, III

17 Wilt thou seal up the avenues of ill?
   Pay every debt, as if God wrote the bill.
     May-Day and Other Pieces. "Suum Cuique"

18 Daughters of Time, the hypocritic Days,
   Muffled and dumb like barefoot dervishes,
   And marching single in an endless file,
   Bring diadems and fagots in their hands.
     May-Day and Other Pieces. Days

19   I, too late,
   Under her solemn fillet saw the scorn.
     May-Day and Other Pieces. Days

20 It is time to be old,
   To take in sail.
     May-Day and Other Pieces. Terminus

21 Obey the voice at eve obeyed at prime.
     May-Day and Other Pieces. Terminus

22 If the red slayer think he slays,
   Or if the slain think he is slain,
   They know not well the subtle ways
   I keep, and pass, and turn again.[1]
     May-Day and Other Pieces. Brahma

23 They reckon ill who leave me out;
   When me they fly, I am the wings;
   I am the doubter and the doubt,
   And I the hymn the Brahmin sings.
     May-Day and Other Pieces. Brahma

24 I am the owner of the sphere,
   Of the seven stars and the solar year,
   Of Caesar's hand, and Plato's brain,
   Of Lord Christ's heart, and Shakespeare's strain.
     May-Day and Other Pieces. History

---

[1]See *The Upanishads,* 51:24.

1   To different minds, the same world is a hell, and a heaven.   *Journal. December 20, 1822*

2   Four snakes gliding up and down a hollow for no purpose that I could see—not to eat, not for love, but only gliding.   *Journal. April 11, 1834*

3   I wish to write such rhymes as shall not suggest a restraint, but contrariwise the wildest freedom.   *Journal. June 27, 1839*

4   You shall have joy, or you shall have power, said God; you shall not have both.   *Journal. October 1842*

5   The sky is the daily bread of the eyes.   *Journal. May 25, 1843*

6   Poetry must be as new as foam, and as old as the rock.   *Journal. March 1845*

7   *Immortality.* I notice that as soon as writers broach this question they begin to quote. I hate quotation. Tell me what you know.   *Journal. May 1849*

8   Blessed are those who have no talent!   *Journal. February 1850*

9   The word *liberty* in the mouth of Mr. Webster sounds like the word *love* in the mouth of a courtesan.   *Journal. February 12 (?), 1851*

10   I trust a good deal to common fame, as we all must. If a man has good corn, or wood, or boards, or pigs, to sell, or can make better chairs or knives, crucibles or church organs, than anybody else, you will find a broad hard-beaten road to his house, though it be in the woods.[1]   *Journal. February 1855*

11   The blazing evidence of immortality is our dissatisfaction with any other solution.   *Journal. July 1855*

12   The foregoing generations beheld God and nature face to face; we, through their eyes. Why should not we also enjoy an original relation to the universe?   *Nature [1836, 1849]. Introduction*

13   Undoubtedly we have no questions to ask which are unanswerable. We must trust the perfection of the creation so far, as to believe that whatever curiosity the order of things has awakened in our minds, the order of things can satisfy.   *Nature. Introduction*

14   Crossing a bare common, in snow puddles, a twilight, under a clouded sky, without having in m thoughts any occurrence of special good fortune, have enjoyed a perfect exhilaration. I am glad to th brink of fear.   *Nature, sec.*

15   Standing on the bare ground . . . all mean ego tism vanishes. I become a transparent eyeball; I ar nothing; I see all; the currents of the Universa Being circulate through me; I am part or particle c God.   *Nature,*

16   Give me health and a day, and I will make th pomp of emperors ridiculous.   *Nature,*

17   Every natural fact is a symbol of some spiritua fact.   *Nature,*

18   A man is a god in ruins.   *Nature,*

19   All that Adam had, all that Caesar could, yo have and can do. . . . Build, therefore, your ow world.   *Nature,*

20   The scholar is the delegated intellect. In th right state he is *Man Thinking*.   *The American Scholar [1837], introductio*

21   Meek young men grow up in libraries, believin it their duty to accept the views which Cicero which Locke, which Bacon have given, forgetfu that Cicero, Locke and Bacon were only youn, men in libraries when they wrote these books.   *The American Scholar, sec.*

22   There is then creative reading as well as creativ writing.   *The American Scholar,*

23   Character is higher than intellect.   *The American Scholar,*

24   In self-trust all the virtues are comprehended.   *The American Scholar,*

25   Wherever Macdonald[2] sits, there is the head c the table.   *The American Scholar,*

26   This time, like all times, is a very good one, if w but know what to do with it.   *The American Scholar,*

27   I embrace the common, I explore and sit at th feet of the familiar, the low. Give me insight into to day, and you may have the antique and futur worlds. What would we really know the meanin of? The meal in the firkin; the milk in the pan; th ballad in the street; the news of the boat.   *The American Scholar,*

---

[1]If a man can write a better book, preach a better sermon, or make a better mousetrap than his neighbor, though he builds his house in the woods the world will make a beaten path to his door.—*Attributed to* EMERSON *(in a lecture) by* SARAH S. B. YULE *and* MARY S. KEENE, *Borrowings* [1889]. Often cited as: Build a better mousetrap and the world will beat a path to your door.

[2]Often quoted as "Macgregor."

1   If the single man plant himself indomitably on his instincts, and there abide, the huge world will come round to him.[1]   *The American Scholar, 3*

2   If utterance is denied, the thought lies like a burden on the man. Always the seer is a sayer.
Divinity School Address [1838]

3   Men grind and grind in the mill of a truism, and nothing comes out but what was put in. But the moment they desert the tradition for a spontaneous thought, then poetry, wit, hope, virtue, learning, anecdote, all flock to their aid.
Literary Ethics [1838]

4   I have no expectation that any man will read history aright who thinks that what was done in a remote age, by men whose names have resounded far, has any deeper sense than what he is doing today.
Essays: First Series [1841]. History

5   We are always coming up with the emphatic facts of history in our private experience and verifying them here. All history becomes subjective; in other words, there is properly no history; only biography.
Essays: First Series. History

6   It is the fault of our rhetoric that we cannot strongly state one fact without seeming to belie some other.   *Essays: First Series. History*

7   To believe your own thought, to believe that what is true for you in your private heart is true for all men—that is genius.
Essays: First Series. Self-Reliance

8   Society everywhere is in conspiracy against the manhood of every one of its members. . . . The virtue in most request is conformity. Self-reliance is its aversion. It loves not realities and creators, but names and customs.   *Essays: First Series. Self-Reliance*

9   Whoso would be a man must be a nonconformist.   *Essays: First Series. Self-Reliance*

10   It is easy in the world to live after the world's opinion; it is easy in solitude to live after our own; but the great man is he who in the midst of the crowd keeps with perfect sweetness the independence of solitude.
Essays: First Series. Self-Reliance

11   A foolish consistency is the hobgoblin of little minds, adored by little statesmen and philosophers and divines. With consistency a great soul has simply nothing to do.
Essays: First Series. Self-Reliance

12   To be great is to be misunderstood.
Essays: First Series. Self-Reliance

13   An institution is the lengthened shadow of one man.   *Essays: First Series. Self-Reliance*

14   I like the silent church before the service begins, better than any preaching.
Essays: First Series. Self-Reliance

15   Discontent is the want of self-reliance: it is infirmity of will.   *Essays: First Series. Self-Reliance*

16   For every Stoic was a Stoic; but in Christendom where is the Christian?
Essays: First Series. Self-Reliance

17   Nothing can bring you peace but yourself.
Essays: First Series. Self-Reliance

18   Every sweet hath its sour; every evil its good.
Essays: First Series. Compensation

19   For everything you have missed, you have gained something else; and for everything you gain, you lose something.
Essays: First Series. Compensation

20   Everything in Nature contains all the powers of Nature. Everything is made of one hidden stuff.
Essays: First Series. Compensation

21   All mankind love a lover.
Essays: First Series. Love

22   Thou art to me a delicious torment.
Essays: First Series. Friendship

23   Almost all people descend to meet.
Essays: First Series. Friendship

24   Happy is the house that shelters a friend.
Essays: First Series. Friendship

25   A friend is a person with whom I may be sincere. Before him, I may think aloud.
Essays: First Series. Friendship

26   A friend may well be reckoned the masterpiece of Nature.   *Essays: First Series. Friendship*

27   Two may talk and one may hear, but three cannot take part in a conversation of the most sincere and searching sort.
Essays: First Series. Friendship

28   The only reward of virtue is virtue; the only way to have a friend is to be one.
Essays: First Series. Friendship

29   I do then with my friends as I do with my books. I would have them where I can find them, but I seldom use them.   *Essays: First Series. Friendship*

30   In skating over thin ice our safety is in our speed.
Essays: First Series. Prudence

31   Heroism feels and never reasons and therefore is always right.   *Essays: First Series. Heroism*

---

[1]All things come round to him who will but wait.—H. W. LONGFELLOW, *Tales of a Wayside Inn, The Student's Tale* [1863]

1   Beware when the great God lets loose a thinker on this planet.   *Essays: First Series. Circles*

2   One man's justice is another's injustice; one man's beauty another's ugliness; one man's wisdom another's folly.   *Essays: First Series. Circles*

3   Nature abhors the old, and old age seems the only disease;[1] all others run into this one.
    Essays: First Series. Circles

4   Nothing great was ever achieved without enthusiasm.   *Essays: First Series. Circles*

5   Nothing astonishes men so much as common sense and plain dealing.   *Essays: First Series. Art*

6   A man may love a paradox without either losing his wit or his honesty.
    Walter Savage Landor. From The Dial [1841], XII

7   There is always a certain meanness in the argument of conservatism, joined with a certain superiority in its fact.   *The Conservative [1842]*

8   For it is not meters, but a metermaking argument that makes a poem—a thought so passionate and alive that like the spirit of a plant or an animal it has an architecture of its own, and adorns nature with a new thing.
    Essays: Second Series [1844]. The Poet

9   Language is the archives of history. . . . Language is fossil poetry.
    Essays: Second Series. The Poet

10   Nature and books belong to the eyes that see them.   *Essays: Second Series. Experience*

11   The less government we have, the better—the fewer laws, and the less confided power.
    Essays: Second Series. Politics

12   Money, which represents the prose of life, and which is hardly spoken of in parlors without an apology, is, in its effects and laws, as beautiful as roses.
    Essays: Second Series. Nominalist and Realist

13   Every man is wanted, and no man is wanted much.
    Essays: Second Series. Nominalist and Realist

14   The reward of a thing well done, is to have done it.   *Essays: Second Series. Nominalist and Realist*

15   As to what are called the masses, and common men—there are no common men. All men are at last of a size.
    Representative Men [1850]. The Uses of Great Men

16   He is great who is what he is from Nature, and who never reminds us of others.
    Representative Men. The Uses of Great Men

17   Every hero becomes a bore at last.
    Representative Men. The Uses of Great Men

18   Great geniuses have the shortest biographies.
    Representative Men. Plato; or, The Philosopher

19   Things added to things, as statistics, civil history, are inventories. Things used as language are inexhaustibly attractive.
    Representative Men. Plato; or, The Philosopher

20   Keep cool: it will be all one a hundred years hence.[2]
    Representative Men. Montaigne; or, The Skeptic

21   Is not marriage an open question, when it is alleged, from the beginning of the world, that such as are in the institution wish to get out, and such as are out wish to get in?
    Representative Men. Montaigne; or, The Skeptic

22   Self-reliance, the height and perfection of man, is reliance on God.
    The Fugitive Slave Law [1854]

23   Great men, great nations, have not been boasters and buffoons, but perceivers of the terror of life, and have manned themselves to face it.
    The Conduct of Life [1860]. Fate

24   Men are what their mothers made them.
    The Conduct of Life. Fate

25   Coal is a portable climate.
    The Conduct of Life. Wealth

26   The world is his, who has money to go over it.
    The Conduct of Life. Wealth

27   Art is a jealous mistress.
    The Conduct of Life. Wealth

28   Solitude, the safeguard of mediocrity, is to genius the stern friend.
    The Conduct of Life. Culture

29   There is always a best way of doing everything, if it be to boil an egg. Manners are the happy ways of doing things.   *The Conduct of Life. Behavior*

30   Fine manners need the support of fine manners in others.   *The Conduct of Life. Behavior*

31   I wish that life should not be cheap, but sacred. I wish the days to be as centuries, loaded, fragrant.
    The Conduct of Life. Considerations by the Way

---

[1] Old age is an incurable disease (senectus enim insanabilis morbus est).—SENECA, *Epistulae Morales ad Lucilium, no. 108, sec. 28*

[2] What matters what anybody thinks? "It will be all the same hundred years hence." That is the most sensible proverb ever invented.—GEORGE DU MAURIER, *Peter Ibbetson* [1891]

1   Our chief want in life is somebody who shall make us do what we can.
The Conduct of Life. Considerations by the Way

2   Make yourself necessary to somebody.
The Conduct of Life. Considerations by the Way

3   Beauty without grace is the hook without the bait.   *The Conduct of Life. Beauty*

4   Never read any book that is not a year old.
The Conduct of Life. In Praise of Books

5   There are always two parties, the party of the Past and the party of the Future; the Establishment and the Movement.
Historic Notes of Life and Letters in New England [1867]

6   The key to the period appeared to be that the mind had become aware of itself. . . . The young men were born with knives in their brain, a tendency to introversion, self-dissection, anatomizing of motives.
Historic Notes of Life and Letters in New England

7   Hitch your wagon to a star.
Society and Solitude [1870]. Civilization

8   The true test of civilization is, not the census, nor the size of cities, nor the crops—no, but the kind of man the country turns out.
Society and Solitude. Civilization

9   Every genuine work of art has as much reason for being as the earth and the sun.
Society and Solitude. Art

10   A masterpiece of art has in the mind a fixed place in the chain of being, as much as a plant or a crystal.
Society and Solitude. Art

11   We boil at different degrees.
Society and Solitude. Eloquence

12   The ornament of a house is the friends who frequent it.   *Society and Solitude. Domestic Life*

13   Can anybody remember when the times were not hard and money not scarce?
Society and Solitude. Works and Days

14   'Tis the good reader that makes the good book; . . . in every book he finds passages which seem confidences or asides hidden from all else and unmistakably meant for his ear.
Society and Solitude. Success

15   We do not count a man's years until he has nothing else to count.   *Society and Solitude. Old Age*

16   A mollusk is a cheap edition [of man] with a suppression of the costlier illustrations, designed for dingy circulation, for shelving in an oyster-bank or among the seaweed.
Power and Laws of Thought [c. 1870]

17   Life is not so short but that there is always time enough for courtesy.
Letters and Social Aims [1876]. Social Aims

18   I have heard with admiring submission the experience of the lady who declared that the sense of being perfectly well-dressed gives a feeling of inward tranquillity which religion is powerless to bestow.
Letters and Social Aims. Social Aims

19   Great men are they who see that spiritual is stronger than any material force, that thoughts rule the world.
Letters and Social Aims. Progress and Culture, Phi Beta Kappa Address [July 18, 1876]

20   Next to the originator of a good sentence is the first quoter of it.[1]
Letters and Social Aims. Quotation and Originality

21   When Shakespeare is charged with debts to his authors, Landor replies, "Yet he was more original than his originals. He breathed upon dead bodies and brought them into life."
Letters and Social Aims. Quotation and Originality

22   By necessity, by proclivity, and by delight, we all quote.
Letters and Social Aims. Quotation and Originality

23   Wit makes its own welcome, and levels all distinctions.
Letters and Social Aims. The Comic

24   The perception of the comic is a tie of sympathy with other men.
Letters and Social Aims. The Comic

25   What is a weed? A plant whose virtues have not yet been discovered.
Fortune of the Republic [1878]

26   To live without duties is obscene.
Lectures and Biographical Sketches [1883]. Aristocracy

27   Speak the affirmative; emphasize your choice by utter ignoring of all that you reject.
Lectures and Biographical Sketches. The Preacher

---

[1]There is not less wit nor less invention in applying rightly a thought one finds in a book, than in being the first author of that thought. — PIERRE BAYLE [1647–1706], *Dictionnaire Historique et Critique* [1697–1702]

1   Genius has no taste for weaving sand.
     Lectures and Biographical Sketches.
     The Scholar

2   This world we live in is but thickened light.
     Lectures and Biographical Sketches.
     The Scholar

3   All the thoughts of a turtle are turtles, and of a
     rabbit, rabbits.
     The Natural History of Intellect [1893]

4   When you strike at a king, you must kill him.
     Recollected by OLIVER WENDELL HOLMES, JR.
     From MAX LERNER, *The Mind and Faith of
     Justice Holmes [1943]*

Robert Stephen Hawker
1803–1875

5 And shall Trelawny die?
  Here's twenty thousand Cornish men
  Will know the reason why.
     The Song of the Western Men [1825],[1] *st. 1*

Richard Henry Hengist Horne
1803–1884

6 'Tis always morning somewhere in the world.
     Orion [1843], bk. III, canto 2

Douglas Jerrold
1803–1857

7   Dogmatism is puppyism come to its full growth.
     Wit and Opinions of Douglas Jerrold [1859]

8   That fellow would vulgarize the day of judgment.
     Wit and Opinions of Douglas Jerrold.
     A Comic Author

9   Some people are so fond of ill luck that they run
     halfway to meet it.
     Wit and Opinions of Douglas Jerrold.
     Meeting Troubles Halfway

10   Talk to him of Jacob's ladder, and he would ask
     the number of the steps.
     Wit and Opinions of Douglas Jerrold.
     A Matter-of-fact Man

---

[1]"And shall Trelawny die?" has been a popular phrase throughout Cornwall since the imprisonment in the Tower of London [1688] of Sir Jonathan Trelawny [1650–1721] with six other prelates for refusing to recognize the Declaration of Indulgence issued by James II.

Robert Smith Surtees
1803–1864

11   Jorrocks' Jaunts and Jollities.
     Title of novel [1838]

12   Full o' beans and benevolence.
     Handley Cross [1843], ch. 27

13   Three things I never lends—my 'oss, my wife
     and my name.
     Hillingdon Hall [1845], ch. 33

14   More people are flattered into virtue than bullied out of vice.
     *The Analysis of the Hunting Field [1846],
     ch. 1*

15   Better be killed than frightened to death.
     Mr. Facey Romford's Hounds [1864], ch. 32

Fëdor Tiutchev
1803–1873

16   A thought, once uttered, is a lie.
     Silentium [1830]

17   Like first love, the heart of Russia will not forget
     you.   *Tribute to Pushkin [January 29, 1837]*

18   Homeland of patience, land of the Russian
     people.   *These Poor Villages [1855]*

Benjamin Disraeli,
Earl of Beaconsfield
1804–1881

19   The microcosm of a public school.
     Vivian Grey [1826], bk. I, ch. 2

20   I hate definitions.
     Vivian Grey, II, 6

21   Variety is the mother of Enjoyment.
     Vivian Grey, V, 4

22   I repeat . . . that all power is a trust; that we are
     accountable for its exercise; that, from the people,
     and for the people, all springs, and all must exist.
     Vivian Grey, VI, 7

23   A *dark* horse, which had never been thought of,
     and which the careless St. James had never even observed in the list, rushed past the grandstand in
     sweeping triumph.
     The Young Duke [1831], bk. II, ch. 5

24   Yes, I am a Jew, and when the ancestors of the
     right honorable gentleman were brutal savages in

an unknown island, mine were priests in the temple of Solomon.[1]

Reply to a taunt by Daniel O'Connell

1 What we anticipate seldom occurs; what we least expected generally happens.

Henrietta Temple [1837], bk. II, ch. 4

2 Though I sit down now, the time will come when you will hear me.

Maiden speech in the House of Commons [1837]

3 A government of statesmen or of clerks? Of Humbug or Humdrum?

Coningsby [1844], bk. II, ch. 4

4 I rather like bad wine . . . one gets so bored with good wine.

Sybil; or, The Two Nations [1845], bk. I, ch. 1

5 Two nations, between whom there is no intercourse and no sympathy; who are as ignorant of each other's habits, thoughts, and feelings as if they were dwellers in different zones, or inhabitants of different planets; who are formed by a different breeding, are fed by a different food, are ordered by different manners, and are not governed by the same laws . . . *the rich and the poor.*

Sybil; or, The Two Nations, II, 5

6 Property has its duties as well as its rights.[2]

Sybil; or, The Two Nations, 11

7 Little things affect little minds.

Sybil; or, The Two Nations, III, 2

8 The right honorable gentleman [Sir Robert Peel] caught the Whigs bathing and walked away with their clothes.

Speech in the House of Commons [February 28, 1845]

9 He was fresh and full of faith that "something would turn up."

Tancred [1847], bk. III, ch. 6

10 A precedent embalms a principle.

Speech on the expenditures of the country [February 22, 1848]

11 How much easier it is to be critical than to be correct.   *Speech [January 24, 1860]*

12 Is man an ape or an angel? I, my lord, I am on the side of the angels. I repudiate with indignation and abhorrence those newfangled theories.

Speech at Oxford Diocesan Conference [November 25, 1864]

13 I have climbed to the top of the greasy pole.

To friends, on being made prime minister [1868]

14 When a man fell into his anecdotage, it was a sign for him to retire.   *Lothair [1870], ch. 28*

15 Every woman should marry — and no man.

Lothair, 30

16 You know who the critics are? The men who have failed in literature and art.   *Lothair, 35*

17 "My idea of an agreeable person," said Hugo Bohun, "is a person who agrees with me."

Lothair, 41

18 Increased means and increased leisure are the two civilizers of man.

Speech to the Conservatives of Manchester [April 3, 1872]

19 The secret of success is constancy to purpose.

Speech [June 24, 1872]

20 The health of the people is really the foundation upon which all their happiness and all their powers as a state depend.   *Speech [July 24, 1877]*

21 Lord Salisbury and myself have brought you back peace — but a peace I hope with honor.

Speech in the House of Commons [July 16, 1878]

22 A series of congratulatory regrets.

Speech at Knightsbridge [July 27, 1878]

23 A sophistical rhetorician [Gladstone], inebriated with the exuberance of his own verbosity, and gifted with an egotistical imagination that can at all times command an interminable and inconsistent series of arguments to malign an opponent and to glorify himself.   *Speech at Knightsbridge [July 27, 1878]*

24 The harebrained chatter of irresponsible frivolity.

Speech at the Guildhall, London [November 9, 1878]

25 The Athanasian Creed is the most splendid ecclesiastical lyric ever poured forth by the genius of man.   *Endymion [1880], ch. 52*

26 "As for that," said Waldershare, "sensible men are all of the same religion." "And pray, what is that?" inquired the prince. "Sensible men never tell."[3]

Endymion, 81

---

[1]The gentleman will please remember that when his half-civilized ancestors were hunting the wild boar in the forests of Silesia, mine were the princes of the earth. — JUDAH P. BENJAMIN [1811–1884], *reply to a senator; from* BEN PERLEY POORE, *Reminiscences of Sixty Years in the National Metropolis* [1886]

[2]Property has its duties as well as its rights. — THOMAS DRUMMOND [1797–1840; inventor of the Drummond light], *Letter to the Landlords of Tipperary* [May 22, 1838]

[3]See Shaftesbury, 277:12

1 No, it is better not. She would only ask me to take a message to Albert.
On his deathbed, declining a visit from Queen Victoria

Gavarni
[Sulpice Guillaume Chevalier]
1804–1866

2 Les Enfants Terribles [The Terrible Children].
Title of series of prints [1865]

Nathaniel Hawthorne
1804–1864

3 By the sympathy of your human hearts for sin ye shall scent out all the places—whether in church, bedchamber, street, field, or forest—where crime has been committed, and shall exult to behold the whole earth one stain of guilt, one mighty blood spot. *Young Goodman Brown [1835]*

4 As the moral gloom of the world overpowers all systematic gaiety, even so was their home of wild mirth made desolate amid the sad forest.
The Maypole of Merrymount [1836]

5 If a man, sitting all alone, cannot dream strange things, and make them look like truth, he need never try to write romances.
The Scarlet Letter [1850]. The Custom-House

6 On the breast of her gown, in fine red cloth, surrounded with an elaborate embroidery and fantastic flourishes of gold thread, appeared the letter A.
The Scarlet Letter, ch. 2

7 My heart was a habitation large enough for many guests, but lonely and chill, and without a household fire. I longed to kindle one! It seemed not so wild a dream. *The Scarlet Letter, 4*

8 There is a fatality, a feeling so irresistible and inevitable that it has the force of doom, which almost invariably compels human beings to linger around and haunt, ghostlike, the spot where some great and marked event has given the color to their lifetime; and still the more irresistibly, the darker the tinge that saddens it. *The Scarlet Letter, 5*

9 Let the black flower blossom as it may!
The Scarlet Letter, 14

10 Let men tremble to win the hand of woman, unless they win along with it the utmost passion of her heart. *The Scarlet Letter, 15*

11 "Never, never!" whispered she. "What we did had a consecration of its own."
The Scarlet Letter, 17

12 The scarlet letter was her passport into region where other women dared not tread. Shame, Despai Solitude! These had been her teachers—stern an wild ones—and they had made her strong, bu taught her much amiss.
The Scarlet Letter, 1

13 At some brighter period, when the world shoul have grown ripe for it, in Heaven's own time, a ne truth would be revealed, in order to establish th whole relation between man and woman on a sure ground of mutual happiness.
The Scarlet Letter, 2

14 The book, if you would see anything in it, re quires to be read in the clear, brown, twilight at mosphere in which it was written; if opened in th sunshine, it is apt to look exceedingly like a volum of blank pages. *Twice-Told Tales [1851], prefac*

15 Not to be deficient in this particular, the autho has provided himself with a moral—the truth namely, that the wrongdoing of one generatio lives into the successive ones.
The House of the Seven Gables [1851], prefac

16 God will give him blood to drink!
The House of the Seven Gables, ch.

17 Life is made up of marble and mud.
The House of the Seven Gables,

18 What other dungeon is so dark as one's ow heart! What jailer so inexorable as one's self!
The House of the Seven Gables, 1

19 Of all the events which constitute a person's bi ography, there is scarcely one . . . to which th world so easily reconciles itself as to his death.
The House of the Seven Gables, 2

20 The greatest obstacle to being heroic is th doubt whether one may not be going to prov one's self a fool; the truest heroism is, to resist th doubt; and the profoundest wisdom, to know whe it ought to be resisted, and when to be obeyed.
The Blithedale Romance [1852], ch.

21 In youth men are apt to write more wisely tha they really know or feel; and the remainder of lif may be not idly spent in realizing and convincin themselves of the wisdom which they uttered lon ago. *The Snow Image [1852], prefac*

22 No author, without a trial, can conceive of th difficulty of writing a romance about a countr where there is no shadow, no antiquity, no myster no picturesque and gloomy wrong, nor anythin but a commonplace prosperity, in broad and simpl daylight, as is happily the case with my dear nativ land. *The Marble Faun [1860], prefac*

1   Mountains are earth's undecaying monuments.
Sketches from Memory [1868]. The Notch of the White Mountains

Charles-Augustin Sainte-Beuve
1804–1869

2   Vigny, more secret,
As if in his tower of ivory, retired before noon.[1]
Pensées d'Août, à M. Villemain [1837], st. 3

3   Silence is the sovereign contempt.[2]
Mes Poisons

George Sand
[Amandine Aurore Lucile Dupin, Baronne Dudevant]
1804–1876

4   Love, bumping his head blindly against all the obstacles of civilization.   *Indiana [1832], preface*

5   No human creature can give orders to love.
Jacques [1834]

6   Deliberately, women are given a deplorable education. . . . While man frees himself from constraining civil and religious bonds, he is only too glad to have woman hold tightly to the Christian principle of suffering and keeping her silence.
Letters to Marcie [1837]

7   We cannot tear out a single page of our life, but we can throw the whole book in the fire.
Mauprat [1837]

8   Charity degrades those who receive it and hardens those who dispense it.   *Consuelo [1842]*

9   They [the peasants] were born kings of the earth far more truly than those who possess it only from having bought it.   *The Haunted Pool [1851]*

10   Life in common among people who love each other is the ideal of happiness.
Histoire de Ma Vie [1856]

11   In our wholly factitious society, to have no cash at all means frightful want or absolute powerlessness.   *Histoire de Ma Vie*

12   Revolutions . . . have put one half of France in mourning for the other.   *Histoire de Ma Vie*

13   There is only one happiness in life, to love and be loved.
Letter to Lina Calamatta [March 31, 1862]

14   Faith is an excitement and an enthusiasm: it is a condition of intellectual magnificence to which we must cling as to a treasure, and not squander . . . in the small coin of empty words, or in exact and priggish argument.
Letter to Des Planches [May 25, 1866]

15   The whole secret of the study of nature lies in learning how to use one's eyes.
Nouvelles Lettres d'un Voyageur [1869]

16   Art for art's sake is an empty phrase. Art for the sake of the true, art for the sake of the good and the beautiful, that is the faith I am searching for.
Letter to Alexandre Saint-Jean [1872]

17   I would rather believe that God did not exist than believe that He was indifferent.
Impressions et Souvenirs [1896]

Sarah Flower Adams
1805–1848

18   E'en though it be a cross
That raiseth me;
Still all my song would be,
Nearer, My God, to Thee,
Nearer, My God, to Thee,
Nearer to Thee.   *Nearer, My God, to Thee, st. 1*

Hans Christian Andersen
1805–1875

19   They could see she was a real princess and no question about it, now that she had felt one pea all the way through twenty mattresses and twenty more feather beds. Nobody but a princess could be so delicate.
Fairy Tales [1835].[3] The Princess and the Pea

20   Many, many steeples would have to be stacked one on top of another to reach from the bottom to the surface of the sea. It is down there that the sea folk live.   *Fairy Tales. The Little Mermaid*

21   We [sea folk] can live to be three hundred years old, but when we perish we turn into mere foam on the sea.   *Fairy Tales. The Little Mermaid*

22   "But he hasn't got anything on," a little child said.   *Fairy Tales. The Emperor's New Clothes*

23   The little live nightingale . . . had come to sing of comfort and hope. As he sang, the phantoms grew

---

[1]Vigny, plus secret, / Comme en sa tour d'ivoire, avant midi, rentrait.
  The poet, retired in his Tower of Ivory, isolated, according to his desire, from the world of man, resembles, whether he so wishes or not, another solitary figure, the watcher enclosed for months at a time in a lighthouse at the head of a cliff. — JULES DE GAULTIER [b. 1858], *La Guerre et les Destinées de l'Art*

[2]Le silence seul est le souverain mépris.

[3]Translated by JEAN HERSHOLT.

pale, and still more pale, and the blood flowed quicker and quicker through the Emperor's feeble body. Even Death listened, and said, "Go on, little nightingale, go on!"
Fairy Tales. The Nightingale

1   His own image . . . was no longer the reflection of a clumsy, dirty, gray bird, ugly and offensive. He himself was a swan! Being born in a duck yard does not matter, if only you are hatched from a swan's egg.
Fairy Tales. The Ugly Duckling

William Lloyd Garrison
1805–1879

2   Our country is the world — our countrymen are all mankind.
Motto of The Liberator [1831]

3   Let Southern oppressors tremble — let their secret abettors tremble — let their Northern apologists tremble — let all the enemies of the persecuted blacks tremble.
The Liberator, no. 1 [January 1, 1831]

4   I will be as harsh as truth and as uncompromising as justice. On this subject I do not wish to think, or speak, or write, with moderation. No! No! Tell a man whose house is on fire to give a moderate alarm; tell him to moderately rescue his wife from the hands of the ravisher; tell the mother to gradually extricate her babe from the fire into which it has fallen; but urge me not to use moderation.
The Liberator, 1

5   I am in earnest — I will not equivocate — I will not excuse — I will not retreat a single inch; and I will be heard!
The Liberator, 1

6   The compact which exists between the North and the South is a covenant with death and an agreement with hell.
Resolution adopted by the Anti-Slavery Society [January 27, 1843]

7   With reasonable men, I will reason; with humane men I will plead; but to tyrants I will give no quarter, nor waste arguments where they will certainly be lost.
W. P. and F. J. T. GARRISON, William Lloyd Garrison [1885–1889], vol. I, p. 188

8   Wherever there is a human being, I see God-given rights inherent in that being, whatever may be the sex or complexion.
W. P. and F. J. T. GARRISON, William Lloyd Garrison, III, p. 390

9   You cannot possibly have a broader basis for any government than that which includes all the people with all their rights in their hands, and with an equal power to maintain their rights.
W. P. and F. J. T. GARRISON, William Lloyd Garrison, IV, p. 224

Sidney Sherman
1805–1873

10   Remember the Alamo![1]
Battle cry, San Jacinto [April 21, 1836]; attributed

Alexis de Tocqueville
1805–1859

11   I know of no country, indeed, where the love of money has taken stronger hold on the affections of men and where a profounder contempt is expressed for the theory of the permanent equality of property.
Democracy in America,[2] pt. I [1835], ch. 3

12   Within these limits the power vested in the American courts of justice of pronouncing a statute to be unconstitutional forms one of the most powerful barriers that have ever been devised against the tyranny of political assemblies.
Democracy in America, I, 6

13   I have never been more struck by the good sense and the practical judgment of the Americans than in the manner in which they elude the numberless difficulties resulting from their Federal Constitution.
Democracy in America, I, 8

14   In order to enjoy the inestimable benefits that the liberty of the press ensures, it is necessary to submit to the inevitable evils that it creates.
Democracy in America, I, 9

15   They [the Americans] have all a lively faith in the perfectibility of man, they judge that the diffusion of knowledge must necessarily be advantageous, and the consequences of ignorance fatal; they all consider society as a body in a state of improvement, humanity as a changing scene, in which noth-

---

[1]On March 6, 1836, five days after Texas declared her independence from Mexico, President Antonio López de Santa Anna attacked the Alamo, the fortified mission at San Antonio; captured it after every Texan had been killed or wounded; and put the wounded to death. He was defeated and captured at San Jacinto [April 21, 1836] by the Texas army under Commander in Chief Samuel Houston. Sidney Sherman was a colonel in the army.

[2]The Henry Reeve text, as revised by Francis Bowen, corrected and edited by Phillips Bradley [1945].

ing is, or ought to be, permanent; and they admit that what appears to them today to be good, may be superseded by something better tomorrow.

Democracy in America, I, 18

1   America is a land of wonders, in which everything is in constant motion and every change seems an improvement. The idea of novelty is there indissolubly connected with the idea of amelioration.

Democracy in America, I, 18

2   There are at the present time two great nations in the world. . . . I allude to the Russians and the Americans. . . . Their starting-point is different and their courses are not the same; yet each of them seems marked out by the will of Heaven to sway the destinies of half the globe.

Democracy in America, I, 18

3   Democratic nations care but little for what has been, but they are haunted by visions of what will be; in this direction their unbounded imagination grows and dilates beyond all measure. . . . Democracy, which shuts the past against the poet, opens the future before him.

Democracy in America, pt. II [1840], bk. I, ch. 17

4   Thus not only does democracy make every man forget his ancestors, but it hides his descendants and separates his contemporaries from him; it throws him back forever upon himself alone and threatens in the end to confine him entirely within the solitude of his own heart.

Democracy in America, II, II, 2

5   If I were asked . . . to what the singular prosperity and growing strength of that people [the Americans] ought mainly to be attributed, I should reply: To the superiority of their women.

Democracy in America, II, III, 12

6   The love of wealth is therefore to be traced, as either a principal or accessory motive, at the bottom of all that the Americans do; this gives to all their passions a sort of family likeness.

Democracy in America, II, III, 17

7   Never was any such event [the French Revolution], stemming from factors so far back in the past, so inevitable yet so completely unforeseen.

The Old Regime and the French Revolution [1856],[1] pt. I, ch. 1

8   When a people which has put up with an oppressive rule over a long period without protest suddenly finds the government relaxing its pressure, it takes up arms against it.

The Old Regime and the French Revolution, III

Elizabeth Barrett Browning
1806–1861

9 Thou large-brained woman and large-hearted man.

To George Sand, A Desire [1844]

10 Knowledge by suffering entereth,
And life is perfected by death.

A Vision of Poets [1844], last lines

11 Do ye hear the children weeping, O my brothers,
Ere the sorrow comes with years?

The Cry of the Children [1844], st. 1

12 I tell you hopeless grief is passionless.

Grief [1844], l. 1

13 Therefore to this dog will I,
Tenderly not scornfully,
Render praise and favor.

To Flush, My Dog [1844], st. 14

14 "Yes," I answered you last night;
"No," this morning, sir, I say:
Colors seen by candlelight
Will not look the same by day.

The Lady's "Yes" [1844], st. 1

15 "Guess now who holds thee?" — "Death," I said.
    But there
The silver answer rang — "Not Death, but Love."

Sonnets from the Portuguese [1850], no. 1

16 Because God's gifts put man's best dreams to
    shame.

Sonnets from the Portuguese, 26

17 How do I love thee? Let me count the ways.
I love thee to the depth and breadth and height
My soul can reach, when feeling out of sight
For the ends of Being and ideal Grace.

Sonnets from the Portuguese, 43

18   I love thee with the breath,
Smiles, tears, of all my life! — and, if God choose,
I shall but love thee better after death.

Sonnets from the Portuguese, 43

19   Life, struck sharp on death,
Makes awful lightning.

Aurora Leigh[2] [1857], bk. I, l. 210

---

[1]Translated by Stuart Gilbert.

[2]See Edward FitzGerald, 472:8.

1 I should not dare to call my soul my own.
Aurora Leigh, II, l. 786

2 God answers sharp and sudden on some prayers,
And thrusts the thing we have prayed for in our
face,
A gauntlet with a gift in 't.
Aurora Leigh, II, l. 952

3 A little sunburnt by the glare of life.
Aurora Leigh, IV, l. 1140

4 Since when was genius found respectable?
Aurora Leigh, VI, l. 275

5 Earth's crammed with heaven,
And every common bush afire with God.
Aurora Leigh, VII, l. 820

6 What was he doing, the great god Pan,
Down in the reeds by the river?
Spreading ruin and scattering ban,
Splashing and paddling with hoofs of a goat,
And breaking the golden lilies afloat
With the dragonfly on the river.
A Musical Instrument [1860]

Friedrich Halm
[Eligius Franz Josef von Münch-Bellinghausen]
1806–1871

7 Two souls with but a single thought,
Two hearts that beat as one.[1]
Der Sohn der Wildness [1842], act II

Matthew Fontaine Maury
1806–1873

8 There is a river in the ocean: in the severest
droughts it never fails, and in the mightiest floods it
never overflows; its banks and its bottom are of cold
water, while its current is of warm; the Gulf of
Mexico is its fountain, and its mouth is the Arctic
Seas. It is the Gulf Stream. There is in the world no
other such majestic flow of waters.
*The Physical Geography of the Sea and Its
Meteorology [1855], ch. 2*

John Stuart Mill
1806–1873

9 The sole end for which mankind are warranted
individually or collectively, in interfering with the
liberty of action of any of their number is self
protection. *On Liberty [1859], introduction*

10 If all mankind minus one were of one opinion,
and only one person were of the contrary opinion,
mankind would be no more justified in silencing
that one person than he, if he had the power, would
be justified in silencing mankind.
On Liberty, ch. 2

11 There is no such thing as absolute certainty, but
there is assurance sufficient for the purposes of human
life. *On Liberty, 2*

12 He who knows only his own side of the case
knows little of that. *On Liberty, 2*

13 The fatal tendency of mankind to leave off thinking
about a thing when it is no longer doubtful is
the cause of half their errors. *On Liberty, 2*

14 We can never be sure that the opinion we are endeavoring
to stifle is a false opinion; and if we were
sure, stifling it would be an evil still.
On Liberty, 2

15 The liberty of the individual must be thus far
limited; he must not make himself a nuisance to
other people. *On Liberty, 3*

16 All good things which exist are the fruits of originality.
On Liberty, 3

17 Whatever crushes individuality is despotism, by
whatever name it may be called. *On Liberty, 3*

18 Everyone who receives the protection of society
owes a return for the benefit. *On Liberty, 4*

19 The individual is not accountable to society for
his actions, insofar as these concern the interests of
no person but himself. *On Liberty, 5*

20 The worth of a state, in the long run, is the
worth of the individuals composing it.
On Liberty, 5

21 Liberty consists in doing what one desires.
On Liberty, 5

22 Unearned increment.
Dissertations and Discussions [1859]

23 Instead of the function of governing, for which
it is radically unfit, the proper office of a representative
assembly is to watch and control the government.
Dissertations and Discussions

---

[1]Zwei Sellen und en Gedanke, / Zwei Herzen und ein Schlag!
Translated by MARIA LOVELL.

1   The creed which accepts as the foundation of morals Utility, or the Greatest Happiness Principle, holds that actions are right in proportion as they tend to promote happiness, wrong as they tend to produce the reverse of happiness.
Utilitarianism [1863], ch. 2

2   It is better to be a human being dissatisfied than a pig satisfied; better to be Socrates dissatisfied than a fool satisfied.   *Utilitarianism, 2*

3   The social state is at once so natural, so necessary, and so habitual to man, that . . . he never conceives himself otherwise than as a member of a body.   *Utilitarianism, 3*

4   It is only a man here and there who has any tolerable knowledge of the character even of the women of his own family.
The Subjection of Women [1869], ch. 1

5   The generality of the male sex cannot yet tolerate the idea of living with an equal.
The Subjection of Women, 2

6   Marriage is the only actual bondage known to our law. There remain no legal slaves, except the mistress of every house.
The Subjection of Women, 4

7   The moral regeneration of mankind will only really commence, when the most fundamental of the social relations [marriage] is placed under the rule of equal justice, and when human beings learn to cultivate their strongest sympathy with an equal in rights and in cultivation.
The Subjection of Women, 4

8   Ask yourself whether you are happy, and you cease to be so.   *Autobiography [1873], ch. 5*

Johann Bernhard, Graf von Rechberg
1806–1899

9   Guarantees which are not worth the paper they are written on.
In a dispatch concerning the recognition of Italy [1861]

Charles Francis Adams
1807–1886

10   It would be superfluous in me to point out to your Lordship that this is war.
Dispatch to Earl Russell [September 5, 1863]

Jean Louis Rodolphe Agassiz
1807–1873

11   The eye of the trilobite tells us that the sun shone on the old beach where he lived; for there is nothing in nature without a purpose, and when so complicated an organ was made to receive the light, there must have been light to enter it.
Geological Sketches [1870], ch. 2

12   The world has arisen in some way or another. How it originated is the great question, and Darwin's theory, like all other attempts to explain the origin of life, is thus far merely conjectural. I believe he has not even made the best conjecture possible in the present state of our knowledge.
Evolution and Permanence of Type [1874]

Giuseppe Garibaldi
1807–1882

13   I offer neither pay, nor quarters, nor provisions; I offer hunger, thirst, forced marches, battles and death. Let him who loves his country in his heart, and not with his lips only, follow me.
From G. M. Trevelyan, Garibaldi's Defense of the Roman Republic [1907–1911]

Robert E[dward] Lee
1807–1870

14   It is well that war is so terrible, or we should grow too fond of it.
On seeing a Federal charge repulsed at Fredericksburg [December 1862]

15   Strike the tent.   *Last words [October 12, 1870]*

Henry Wadsworth Longfellow
1807–1882

16 I heard the trailing garments of the Night
Sweep through her marble halls.
Hymn to Night [1839], st. 1

17 Tell me not, in mournful numbers,
Life is but an empty dream!
For the soul is dead that slumbers,
And things are not what they seem.

Life is real! Life is earnest!
And the grave is not its goal;
Dust thou art, to dust returnest,
Was not spoken of the soul.
A Psalm of Life [1839], st. 1, 2

1 Art is long, and Time is fleeting,
    And our hearts, though stout and brave,
    Still, like muffled drums, are beating
    Funeral marches to the grave.
                    A Psalm of Life, st. 4

2 Lives of great men all remind us
    We can make our lives sublime.
    And, departing, leave behind us
    Footprints on the sands of time.
                    A Psalm of Life, st. 7

3 Let us, then, be up and doing,
    With a heart for any fate;
    Still achieving, still pursuing,
    Learn to labor and to wait.
                    A Psalm of Life, st. 9

4 It was the schooner Hesperus,
    That sailed the wintry sea;
    And the skipper had taken his little daughter,
    To bear him company.
                The Wreck of the Hesperus [1842], st. 1

5 But the father answered never a word,
    A frozen corpse was he.
                The Wreck of the Hesperus, st. 12

6 Christ save us all from a death like this,
    On the reef of Norman's Woe!
                The Wreck of the Hesperus, st. 22

7 Under the spreading chestnut tree
    The village smithy stands;
    The smith a mighty man is he
    With large and sinewy hands.
    And the muscles of his brawny arms
    Are strong as iron bands.
                The Village Blacksmith [1842], st. 1

8 His brow is wet with honest sweat,
    He earns whate'er he can,
    And looks the whole world in the face,
    For he owes not any man.
                The Village Blacksmith, st. 2

9 Something attempted, something done,
    Has earned a night's repose.
                The Village Blacksmith, st. 7

10 Into each life some rain must fall,
    Some days must be dark and dreary.
                The Rainy Day [1842], st. 3

11 A banner with the strange device,
    Excelsior!   *Excelsior [1842], st. 1*

12 The day is done, and the darkness
    Falls from the wings of Night,
    As a feather is wafted downward
    From an eagle in his flight.
                The Day Is Done [1845], st. 1

13   The bards sublime,
    Whose distant footsteps echo
    Through the corridors of Time.
                    The Day Is Done, st.

14 And the night shall be filled with music,
    And the cares, that infest the day,
    Shall fold their tents, like the Arabs,
    And as silently steal away.
                    The Day Is Done, st. 1

15 I shot an arrow into the air,
    It fell to earth, I knew not where.
                The Arrow and the Song [1845], st.

16 This is the forest primeval. The murmuring pines
        and the hemlocks . . .
    Stand like Druids of old.
                    Evangeline [1847], l.

17 Build me straight, O worthy Master!
    Staunch and strong, a goodly vessel.
                The Building of the Ship [1849], l.

18 And see! she stirs!
    She starts — she moves — she seems to feel
    The thrill of life along her keel.
                The Building of the Ship, l. 34

19   Sail on, O Ship of State!
    Sail on, O Union, strong and great!
    Humanity with all its fears,
    With all the hopes of future years,
    Is hanging breathless on thy fate!
                The Building of the Ship, l. 37

20 Our hearts, our hopes, our prayers, our tears,
    Our faith triumphant o'er our fears,
    Are all with thee — are all with thee!
                The Building of the Ship, l. 39

21 God sent his Singers upon earth
    With songs of sadness and of mirth.
                    The Singers [1849], st.

22 But the great Master said, "I see
    No best in kind, but in degree;
    I gave a various gift to each,
    To charm, to strengthen, and to teach."
                    The Singers, st.

23 All your strength is in your union.
    All your danger is in discord;
    Therefore be at peace henceforward,
    And as brothers live together.
                The Song of Hiawatha [1855], pt.

24 By the shores of Gitche Gumee,
    By the shining Big-Sea-Water,
    Stood the wigwam of Nokomis,
    Daughter of the Moon, Nokomis.
                    The Song of Hiawatha, II

1 From the waterfall he named her,
  Minnehaha, Laughing Water.
                    The Song of Hiawatha, IV

2 As unto the bow the cord is,
  So unto the man is woman,
  Though she bends him, she obeys him,
  Though she draws him, yet she follows,
  Useless each without the other!
                    The Song of Hiawatha, X

3   If we could read the secret history of our enemies, we should find in each man's life sorrow and
  suffering enough to disarm all hostility.
                    Driftwood [1857]

4 If I am not worth the wooing, I surely am not
      worth the winning.
      The Courtship of Miles Standish [1858], pt. III

5 "Why don't you speak for yourself, John?"
                    The Courtship of Miles Standish, III

6 The long mysterious Exodus of death.
      The Jewish Cemetery at Newport [1858], st. 1

7   A boy's will is the wind's will,
  And the thoughts of youth are long, long
      thoughts.   *My Lost Youth [1858], refrain*

8 I remember the black wharves and the slips,
  And the sea-tides tossing free;
  And Spanish sailors with bearded lips,
  And the beauty and majesty of the ships,
  And the magic of the sea.   *My Lost Youth, st. 3*

9 A Lady with a Lamp[1] shall stand
  In the great history of the land,
  A noble type of good,
  Heroic womanhood.
                    Santa Filomena [1858], st. 10

10 Between the dark and the daylight,
  When the night is beginning to lower,
  Comes a pause in the day's occupations,
  That is known as the Children's Hour.
                    The Children's Hour [1860], st. 1

11 I hear in the chamber above me
  The patter of little feet.
                    The Children's Hour, st. 2

12 Grave Alice, and laughing Allegra,
  And Edith with golden hair.
                    The Children's Hour, st. 3

13   A solid man of Boston.
  A comfortable man with dividends,
  And the first salmon and the first green peas.
      *The New England Tragedies [1868]. John
      Endicott, act IV, sc. 1*

---

[1]Florence Nightingale [1820–1910].

14 Listen, my children, and you shall hear,
  Of the midnight ride of Paul Revere,
  On the eighteenth of April, in Seventy-five;
  Hardly a man is now alive
  Who remembers that famous day and year.
      *Tales of a Wayside Inn [1863–1874], pt. I,
      The Landlord's Tale: Paul Revere's Ride, st. 1*

15 One if by land, and two if by sea;[2]
  And I on the opposite shore will be,
  Ready to ride and spread the alarm
  Through every Middlesex village and farm.
      *Tales of a Wayside Inn, I, The Landlord's
      Tale: Paul Revere's Ride, st. 2*

16 The fate of a nation was riding that night.
      *Tales of a Wayside Inn, I, The Landlord's
      Tale: Paul Revere's Ride, st. 8*

17 He seemed the incarnate "Well, I told you so!"
      *Tales of a Wayside Inn, I, The Poet's Tale:
      The Birds of Killingworth, st. 9*

18 Ships that pass in the night, and speak each other in
      passing,
  Only a signal shown and a distant voice in the
      darkness;
  So on the ocean of life we pass and speak one
      another,[3]
  Only a look and a voice; then darkness again and a
      silence.
      *Tales of a Wayside Inn, III, The Theologian's
      Tale: Elizabeth, IV*

19   Time has laid his hand
  Upon my heart, gently, not smiting it,
  But as a harper lays his open palm
  Upon his harp to deaden its vibrations.
      *The Golden Legend [1872], pt. IV,
      The Cloisters*

20 Let him not boast who puts his armor on
  As he who puts it off, the battle done.
                    Morituri Salutamus [1875], st. 9

21 The love of learning, the sequestered nooks,
  And all the sweet serenity of books.
                    Morituri Salutamus, st. 21

22 Not in the clamor of the crowded street,
  Not in the shouts and plaudits of the throng,
  But in ourselves, are triumph and defeat.
                    The Poets

---

[2]See Revere, 352:10.

[3]Two lives that once part are as ships that divide. —EDWARD
ROBERT BULWER-LYTTON, *A Lament*

  As vessels starting from ports thousands of miles apart pass close
to each other in the naked breadths of the ocean, nay, sometimes
even touch in the dark. —OLIVER WENDELL HOLMES, *Professor at
the Breakfast-Table* [1860]

1 Three silences there are: the first of speech,
The second of desire, the third of thought.
The Three Silences of Molinos

2 In the long, sleepless watches of the night.
The Cross of Snow [1879]

3 The holiest of all holidays are those
Kept by ourselves in silence and apart;
The secret anniversaries of the heart.   *Holidays*

4 There was a little girl
Who had a little curl
Right in the middle of her forehead;
And when she was good
She was very, very good,
But when she was bad she was horrid.
There Was a Little Girl

John Greenleaf Whittier
1807–1892

5 No fetters in the Bay State — no slave upon our
land!
Massachusetts to Virginia [1843], st. 24

6 The Night is mother of the Day,
The Winter of the Spring,
And ever upon old Decay
The greenest mosses cling.
A Dream of Summer [1847], st. 4

7 So fallen! so lost! the light withdrawn
Which once he wore!
The glory from his gray hairs gone
Forevermore!   *Ichabod [1850],[1] st. 1*

8   From those great eyes
The soul has fled:
When faith is lost, when honor dies,
The man is dead!   *Ichabod, st. 8*

9 Blessings on thee, little man,
Barefoot boy, with cheek of tan!
The Barefoot Boy [1856], st. 1

10 Health that mocks the doctor's rules,
Knowledge never learned of schools.
The Barefoot Boy, st. 2

11 The age is dull and mean. Men creep,
Not walk.
*Lines Inscribed to Friends under Arrest for
Treason Against the Slave Power [1856], st. 1*

12 For of all sad words of tongue or pen,
The saddest are these: "It might have been!"[2]
Maud Muller [1856], st. 5

13 Up from the meadows rich with corn,
Clear in the cool September morn.
Barbara Frietchie [1864], st.

14 The clustered spires of Frederick stand
Green-walled by the hills of Maryland.
Barbara Frietchie, st.

15 "Shoot, if you must, this old gray head,
But spare your country's flag," she said.
Barbara Frietchie, st. 1

16 "Who touches a hair of yon gray head
Dies like a dog! March on!" he said.
Barbara Frietchie, st. 2

17 The sun that brief December day
Rose cheerless over hills of gray,
And, darkly circled, gave at noon
A sadder light than waning moon.
Snowbound [1866], l. 1

18 Shut in from all the world without,
We sat the clean-winged hearth about.
Snowbound, l. 155

19 Angel of the backward look.   *Snowbound, l. 714*

20 God is and all is well.   *My Birthday [1871], st. 2*

21 Dear Lord and Father of mankind,
Forgive our foolish ways!
Reclothe us in our rightful mind,
In purer lives Thy service find,
In deeper reverence, praise.
The Brewing of Soma [1872]

Salmon P[ortland] Chase
1808–1873

22   The Constitution, in all its provisions, looks to
an indestructible Union composed of indestructible
States.
*Decision in Texas v. White, 7 Wallace 725
[1868]*

Alphonse Karr
1808–1890

23   The more things change, the more they remain
the same.[3]   *Les Guêpes [January 1849]*

---

[1]This poem was the outcome of the surprise and grief and forecast of evil consequences which I felt on reading the seventh of
March speech of Daniel Webster in support of the "compromise,"
and the Fugitive Slave Law. No partisan or personal enmity dictated it. —Whittier's *Note*

---

[2]See Guiterman, 656:9.

[3]Plus ça change, plus c'est la même chose. A modern variant:
Plus ça change, plus c'est things go downhill.

Marie Edme Patrice Maurice, Comte de Mac-Mahon
1808–1893

1 Here I am, and here I stay.[1]

At Sevastopol [September 1855]

Gérard de Nerval [Gérard Labrunie]
1808–1855

2 Despair and suicide are the result of certain fatal situations for those who have no faith in immortality, its joys and sorrows. *Le Rêve et la Vie, II*

3 The jailer is another kind of captive—is the jailer envious of his prisoner's dreams?

Fragments de Faust

4 I am the somber one, the unconsoled widower,
The Prince of Aquitaine whose tower was
destroyed.[2]
My only star is dead, and my star-studded lute
Wears the black sun of Melancholy.

Les Chimères [1854]. El Desdichado

5 In what way is a lobster more ridiculous than a dog, a cat, a gazelle, a lion, or any other animal you take for a walk? I'm fond of lobsters. They're peaceful, serious, know the secrets of the deep, don't bark, and don't invade our privacy like dogs.

On walking with a leashed lobster in the Palais-Royal gardens. From Théophile Gautier, Portraits et Souvenirs Littéraires [1875]

Caroline Sheridan Norton
1808–1877

6 A soldier of the Legion lay dying in Algiers.
Bingen on the Rhine, st. 1

George Washington Patten
c. 1808–1882

7 If we must perish in the fight,
Oh! let us die like men.

Oh! Let Us Die Like Men, st. 4

Samuel Francis Smith
1808–1895

8 My country, 'tis of thee,
Sweet land of liberty,
Of thee I sing:
Land where my fathers died,
Land of the pilgrims' pride,
From every mountainside
Let freedom ring. *America [1831], st. 1*

9 Long may our land be bright
With freedom's holy light;
Protect us by thy might,
Great God, our King! *America, st. 4*

Charles Robert Darwin
1809–1882

10 Both in space and time, we seem to be brought somewhat near to that great fact—the mystery of mysteries—the first appearance of new beings on this earth.
The Voyage of the Beagle [1845], ch. 17. Galapagos Archipelago

11 I never dreamed that islands, about fifty or sixty miles apart, and most of them in sight of each other, formed of precisely the same rocks, placed under a quite similar climate, would have been differently tenanted.
The Voyage of the Beagle, 18. Galapagos Archipelago

12 I have called this principle, by which each slight variation, if useful, is preserved, by the term Natural Selection. *On the Origin of Species [1859], ch. 3*

13 The expression often used by Mr. Herbert Spencer, of the Survival of the Fittest, is more accurate, and is sometimes equally convenient.[3]
On the Origin of Species, 3

14 We will now discuss in a little more detail the Struggle for Existence.[4]
On the Origin of Species, 3

15 All we can do, is to keep steadily in mind that each organic being is striving to increase in a geometrical ratio; that each at some period of its life, during some season of the year, during each generation or at intervals, has to struggle for life and to suffer great destruction. When we reflect on this struggle, we may console ourselves with the full belief, that the war of nature is not incessant, that no

---

[1]J'y suis, j'y reste.

[2]Je suis le ténébreux, le veuf, l'inconsolé, / Le Prince d'Aquitaine à la tour abolie.

T. S. Eliot quotes the second line in *The Waste Land* [1922], *l. 429.*

[3]See Spencer, 523:13.

[4]The perpetual struggle for room and food.—MALTHUS, *On Population* [1798], *ch. 3*

fear is felt, that death is generally prompt, and that the vigorous, the healthy, and the happy survive and multiply.   *On the Origin of Species, 3*

1   When the views advanced by me in this volume, and by Mr. Wallace, and when analogous views on the origin of species are generally admitted, we can dimly foresee that there will be a considerable revolution in natural history.
On the Origin of Species, 3

2   It is interesting to contemplate an entangled bank, clothed with many plants of many kinds, with birds singing on the bushes, with various insects flitting about, and with worms crawling through the damp earth, and to reflect that these elaborately constructed forms, so different from each other, and dependent on each other in so complex a manner, have all been produced by laws acting around us.
On the Origin of Species, 3

3   From the war of nature, from famine and death, the most exalted object which we are capable of conceiving, namely, the production of the higher animals, directly follows. There is grandeur in this view of life, with its several powers, having been originally breathed by the Creator into a few forms or into one, and that whilst this planet has gone cycling on according to the fixed law of gravity, from so simple a beginning endless forms most beautiful and most wonderful have been and are being evolved.
On the Origin of Species, 15

4   The Simiadae then branched off into two great stems, the New World and Old World monkeys; and from the latter at a remote period, Man, the wonder and the glory of the universe, proceeded.[1]
The Descent of Man [1871], ch. 6

5   A hairy quadruped, furnished with a tail and pointed ears, probably arboreal in its habits.
The Descent of Man, 21

6   For my own part I would as soon be descended from that heroic little monkey, who braved his dreaded enemy in order to save the life of his keeper; or from that old baboon, who, descending from the mountains, carried away in triumph his young comrade from a crowd of astonished dogs — as from a savage who delights to torture his enemies, offers up bloody sacrifices, practices infanticide without remorse, treats his wives like slaves, knows no decency, and is haunted by the grossest superstitions.   *The Descent of Man, 21*

7   Man with all his noble qualities . . . with his godlike intellect which has penetrated into the move-

ments and constitution of the solar system . . . sti bears in his bodily frame the indelible stamp of hi lowly origin.   *The Descent of Man, 2*

8   The plow is one of the most ancient and mos valuable of man's inventions; but long before he ex isted the land was in fact regularly plowed, and sti continues to be thus plowed by earthworms. It ma be doubted whether there are many other anima which have played so important a part in the histor of the world, as have these lowly organized crea tures.
The Formation of Vegetable Mold Through the Action of Worms [1881], ch. 7

9   As for a future life, every man must judge fo himself between conflicting vague probabilities.
From Life and Letters of Charles Darwin [1887], edited by FRANCIS DARWIN

10   I love fools' experiments. I am always makin them.
From Life and Letters of Charles Darwin [1887], edited by FRANCIS DARWIN

11   My mind seems to have become a kind of ma chine for grinding general laws out of large collec tions of facts.   *Autobiography [1892], ch.*

12   I am inclined to look at everything as resultin from designed laws, with the details, whether goo or bad, left to the working out of what we may ca chance. Not that this notion at *all* satisfies me. I fee most deeply that the whole subject is too profoun for the human intellect. A dog might as well specu late on the mind of Newton. Let each man hop and believe what he can.
Letter to Asa Gray [May 22, 1860

Edward FitzGerald
1809–1883

13   Wake! For the Sun who scatter'd into flight
The Stars before him from the Field of night,
Drives Night along with them from Heav'n and strikes
The Sultan's Turret with a Shaft of Light.
The Rubáiyát of Omar Khayyám,[2] *st.*

14   Awake! for Morning in the Bowl of Night
Has flung the Stone that puts the Stars to flight:
And Lo! the Hunter of the East has caught
The Sultan's Turret in a Noose of Light.
The Rubáiyát of Omar Khayyám, st. 1 [first edition]

---

[1]I confess freely to you, I could never look long upon a monkey, without very mortifying reflections. —WILLIAM CONGREVE, *Letter to Dennis* [1695]

[2]Translated from the Persian of OMAR KHAYYÁM [died c. 113. in four editions, 1859, 1868, 1872, and 1879. The fourth editic is used here, unless otherwise stated.

1 Now the New Year reviving old Desires,
   The thoughtful Soul to Solitude retires.
   The Rubáiyát of Omar Khayyám, st. 4

2 Come, fill the Cup, and in the fire of Spring
   The Winter garment of Repentance fling:
   The Bird of Time has but a little way
   To fly — and Lo! the Bird is on the Wing.
   *The Rubáiyát of Omar Khayyám, st. 7 [first
   edition]*

3 The Leaves of Life keep falling one by one.
   The Rubáiyát of Omar Khayyám, st. 8

4 Each Morn a thousand Roses brings, you say:
   Yes, but where leaves the Rose of Yesterday?
   The Rubáiyát of Omar Khayyám, st. 9

5 A Book of Verses underneath the Bough,
   A Jug of Wine, a Loaf of Bread — and Thou
   Beside me singing in the Wilderness —
   Oh, Wilderness were Paradise enow!
   The Rubáiyát of Omar Khayyám, st. 12

6 Ah, take the Cash, and let the Credit go,
   Nor heed the rumble of a distant Drum!
   The Rubáiyát of Omar Khayyám, st. 13

7 Think, in this batter'd Caravanserai
   Whose Portals are alternate Night and Day,
   How Sultan after Sultan with his Pomp
   Abode his destin'd Hour, and went his way.
   The Rubáiyát of Omar Khayyám, st. 17

8 They say the Lion and the Lizard keep
   The Courts where Jamshyd gloried and drank
       deep:
   And Bahram, that great Hunter — the Wild Ass
   Stamps o'er his Head, but cannot break his sleep.
   The Rubáiyát of Omar Khayyám, st. 18

9 I sometimes think that never blows so red
   The Rose as where some buried Caesar bled;
   That every Hyacinth the Garden wears
   Dropt in her Lap from some once lovely Head.
   The Rubáiyát of Omar Khayyám, st. 19

10 Ah, my Belovèd, fill the Cup that clears
   Today of past Regrets and future Fears:
   Tomorrow! — Why, Tomorrow I may be
   Myself with Yesterday's Sev'n thousand Years.
   The Rubáiyát of Omar Khayyám, st. 21

11 For some we loved, the loveliest and the best
   That from his Vintage rolling Time hath prest.
   The Rubáiyát of Omar Khayyám, st. 22

12 Ah, make the most of what we yet may spend,
   Before we too into the Dust descend;
   Dust into Dust, and under Dust, to lie,
   Sans Wine, sans Song, sans Singer, and — sans End!
   The Rubáiyát of Omar Khayyám, st. 24

13 Myself when young did eagerly frequent
   Doctor and Saint, and heard great argument
   About it and about: but evermore
   Came out by the same door wherein I went.
   The Rubáiyát of Omar Khayyám, st. 27

14 And this was all the Harvest that I reap'd —
   "I came like Water, and like Wind I go."
   The Rubáiyát of Omar Khayyám, st. 28

15 There was the Door to which I found no Key;
   There was the Veil through which I might not see.
   Some little talk awhile of Me and Thee
   There was — and then no more of Thee and Me.
   The Rubáiyát of Omar Khayyám, st. 32

16   "While you live,
   Drink! — for, once dead, you never shall return."
   The Rubáiyát of Omar Khayyám, st. 35

17 For I remember stopping by the way
   To watch a Potter thumping his wet Clay:
   And with its all-obliterated Tongue
   It murmured — "Gently, Brother, gently, pray!"
   The Rubáiyát of Omar Khayyám, st. 37

18 And fear not lest Existence closing your
   Account, and mine, should know the like no
       more;
   The Eternal Saki from that Bowl has pour'd
   Millions of Bubbles like us, and will pour.
   The Rubáiyát of Omar Khayyám, st. 46

19 'Tis all a Checkerboard of Nights and Days
   Where Destiny with Men for Pieces plays:
   Hither and thither moves, and mates, and slays,
   And one by one back in the Closet lays.
   *The Rubáiyát of Omar Khayyám, st. 49
   [first edition]*

20   Striking from the Calendar
   Unborn Tomorrow and dead Yesterday.
   The Rubáiyát of Omar Khayyám, st. 57

21 The Moving Finger writes; and, having writ,
   Moves on: nor all your Piety nor Wit
   Shall lure it back to cancel half a Line,
   Nor all your Tears wash out a Word of it.
   The Rubáiyát of Omar Khayyám, st. 71

22   That inverted Bowl we call The Sky,
   Whereunder crawling coop'd we live and die.
   *The Rubáiyát of Omar Khayyám, st. 72
   [first edition]*

23 Ah, Moon of my Delight who know'st no wane.
   *The Rubáiyát of Omar Khayyám, st. 74
   [first edition]*

24 And He that with his hand the Vessel made
   Will surely not in after Wrath destroy.
   The Rubáiyát of Omar Khayyám, st. 85

1 After a momentary silence spake
Some Vessel of a more ungainly Make;
"They sneer at me for leaning all awry:
What! did the Hand then of the Potter shake?"
The Rubáiyát of Omar Khayyám, st. 86

2 Who *is* the Potter, pray, and who the Pot?
The Rubáiyát of Omar Khayyám, st. 87

3 Indeed the Idols I have loved so long
Have done my credit in this World much wrong:
Have drown'd my Glory in a shallow Cup,
And sold my Reputation for a Song.
The Rubáiyát of Omar Khayyám, st. 93

4 I wonder often what the Vintners buy
One half so precious as the stuff they sell.
The Rubáiyát of Omar Khayyám, st. 95

5 Ah Love! could you and I with Him conspire
To grasp this Sorry Scheme of Things entire,
Would not we shatter it to bits — and then
Remold it nearer to the Heart's Desire!
The Rubáiyát of Omar Khayyám, st. 99

6 And when like her, O Saki, you shall pass
Among the Guests Star-scatter'd on the Grass,
And in your joyous errand reach the spot
Where I made One — turn down an empty Glass!
The Rubáiyát of Omar Khayyám, st. 101

7 The King in a carriage may ride,
And the Beggar may crawl at his side;
But in the general race,
They are traveling all the same pace.
Chronomoros

8 Mrs. Browning's death was rather a relief to me,
I must say; no more Aurora Leighs, thank God!
Letter [July 15, 1861][1]

William Ewart Gladstone
1809–1898

9 Decision by majorities is as much an expedient as lighting by gas.
Speech in the House of Commons [1858]

10 You cannot fight against the future. Time is on our side.   *Speech on the Reform Bill [1866]*

11 Out of the range of practical politics.
Speech at Dalkeith [November 26, 1879]

12 The resources of civilization are not yet exhausted.   *Speech at Leeds [October 7, 1881]*

13 All the world over, I will back the masses against the classes.   *Speech at Liverpool [June 28, 1886]*

14 I have always regarded that Constitution as the most remarkable work known to me in modern times to have been produced by the human intellect, at a single stroke (so to speak), in its application to political affairs.
Letter to the committee in charge of the celebration of the centennial of the American Constitution [July 20, 1887]

15 Justice delayed is justice denied.   *Attributed*

Nikolai Vasilievich Gogol
1809–1852

16 It is no use to blame the looking glass if your face is awry.
The Inspector-General [1836], epigraph

17 Of course, Alexander the Great was a hero, but why smash the chairs?
The Inspector-General, epigraph

18 The more destruction there is everywhere, the more it shows the activity of town authorities.
The Inspector-General, act I, sc.

19 I tell everyone very plainly that I take bribes, but what kind of bribes? Why, greyhound puppies. That's a totally different matter.
The Inspector-General, I,

20 The sergeant's widow told you a lie when she said I flogged her. I never flogged her. She flogged herself.   *The Inspector-General, IV, x*

21 What are you laughing at? You are laughing at yourselves!   *The Inspector-General, V, vii*

22 And for a long time yet, led by some wondrous power, I am fated to journey hand in hand with my strange heroes and to survey the surging immensity of life, to survey it through the laughter that all can see and through the tears unseen and unknown by anyone.   *Dead Souls [1842], vol. I, ch. 7*

23 Rus! Rus! I see you, from my lovely enchanted remoteness I see you: a country of dinginess, and bleakness and dispersal; no arrogant wonders of nature crowned by the arrogant wonders of art appear within you to delight or terrify the eyes. . . . So what is the incomprehensible secret force driving me towards you? Why do I constantly hear the echo of your mournful song as it is carried from sea to sea through your entire expanse? . . . And since you are without end yourself, is it not within you that boundless thought will be born?[2]
Dead Souls, II, 1

24 Oh troika, winged troika, tell me who invented you? Surely, nowhere but among a nimble nation could you have been born: in a country which has

---

[1] See Elizabeth Barrett Browning, 463:19.

[2] Translated by Vladimir Nabokov.

taken itself in earnest and has evenly spread far and wide over half of the globe, so that once you start counting the milestones you may count on till a speckled haze dances before your eyes. . . .

Rus, are you not similar in your headlong motion to one of those nimble troikas that none can overtake? The flying road turns into smoke under you, bridges thunder and pass, all falls back and is left behind! . . . And what does this awesome motion mean? What is the passing strange force contained in these passing strange steeds? Steeds, steeds, what steeds! Has the whirlwind a home in your manes? . . . Rus, whither are you speeding so? Answer me. No answer. The middle bell trills out in a dream its liquid soliloquy; the roaring air is torn to pieces and becomes wind; all things on earth fly by and other nations and states gaze askance as they step aside and give her the right of way.[1]

Dead Souls, II, concluding paragraphs

1   In the course of the reading he [Pushkin] became more and more melancholy and finally became completely gloomy. When the reading was over he uttered in a voice full of sorrow: "Goodness, how sad is our Russia!"

Four Letters Concerning Dead Souls [1843]

2   I shall laugh my bitter laugh.

Epitaph on Gogol's tombstone

Oliver Wendell Holmes
1809–1894

3 Ay, tear her tattered ensign down!
Long has it waved on high,
And many an eye has danced to see
That banner in the sky;
Beneath it rung the battle shout,
And burst the cannon's roar —
The meteor of the ocean air
Shall sweep the clouds no more.

Old Ironsides [1830],[2] st. 1

4 And silence, like a poultice, comes
To heal the blows of sound.

The Music Grinders, st. 10

5 There is no time like the old time, when you and I
were young.

No Time Like the Old Time, st. 1

6   A thought is often original, though you have uttered it a hundred times.

The Autocrat of the Breakfast-Table [1858], ch. 1

7   Insanity is often the logic of an accurate mind overtasked.

The Autocrat of the Breakfast-Table, 2

8   Man has his will — but woman has her way!

The Autocrat of the Breakfast-Table, 2

9   Put not your trust in money, but put your money in trust.

The Autocrat of the Breakfast-Table, 2

10   I find the great thing in this world is not so much where we stand, as in what direction we are moving: To reach the port of heaven, we must sail sometimes with the wind and sometimes against it — but we must sail, and not drift, nor lie at anchor.   *The Autocrat of the Breakfast-Table, 4*

11 Build thee more stately mansions, O my soul,
As the swift seasons roll!
Leave thy low-vaulted past!

The Autocrat of the Breakfast-Table, 4
[The Chambered Nautilus, st. 5]

12   Sin has many tools, but a lie is the handle which fits them all.

The Autocrat of the Breakfast-Table, 6

13   Boston State-House is the hub of the solar system. You couldn't pry that out of a Boston man, if you had the tire of all creation straightened out for a crowbar.

The Autocrat of the Breakfast-Table, 6

14   The axis of the earth sticks out visibly through the center of each and every town or city.

The Autocrat of the Breakfast-Table, 6

15 Have you heard of the wonderful one-hoss shay,
That was built in such a logical way
It ran a hundred years to a day?

The Autocrat of the Breakfast-Table, 11
[The Deacon's Masterpiece, st. 1]

16 End of the wonderful one-hoss shay.
Logic is logic. That's all I say.

The Autocrat of the Breakfast-Table, 11
[The Deacon's Masterpiece, st. 12]

17   He comes of the Brahmin caste of New England. This is the harmless, inoffensive, untitled aristocracy.

The Brahmin Caste of New England [1860]

18   Science is a first-rate piece of furniture for a man's upper chamber, if he has common sense on the ground floor.

The Poet at the Breakfast-Table [1872], ch. 5

19 And if I should live to be
The last leaf upon the tree
In the spring,
Let them smile, as I do now,
At the old forsaken bough
Where I cling.   *The Last Leaf [1831], st. 8*

---

[1] Translated by VLADIMIR NABOKOV.

[2] This poem roused such popular feeling that it is generally credited with saving the frigate *Constitution* from being dismantled as unfit for service.

Abraham Lincoln
1809–1865

1   If the good people, in their wisdom, shall see fit to keep me in the background, I have been too familiar with disappointments to be very much chagrined.
>   *Address at New Salem, Illinois [March 9, 1832]*

2   Politicians [are] a set of men who have interests aside from the interests of the people, and who, to say the most of them, are, taken as a mass, at least one long step removed from honest men. I say this with the greater freedom because, being a politician myself, none can regard it as personal.
>   *Speech in the Illinois Legislature [January 11, 1837]*

3   If destruction be our lot we must ourselves be its author and finisher. As a nation of freemen we must live through all time, or die by suicide.
>   *Address at the Young Men's Lyceum, Springfield, Illinois [January 27, 1838]*

4   There is no grievance that is a fit object of redress by mob law.
>   *Address at the Young Men's Lyceum, Springfield, Illinois [January 27, 1838]*

5   Any people anywhere, being inclined and having the power, have the *right* to rise up, and shake off the existing government, and form a new one that suits them better.
>   *Speech in the House of Representatives [January 12, 1848]*

6   No man is good enough to govern another man without that other's consent.
>   *Speech at Peoria, Illinois [October 16, 1854]*

7   I hate [slavery] because it deprives the republican example of its just influence in the world—enables the enemies of free institutions, with plausibility, to taunt us as hypocrites—causes the real friends of freedom to doubt our sincerity.
>   *Speech at Peoria, Illinois [October 16, 1854]*

8   The ballot is stronger than the bullet.
>   *Speech at Bloomington, Illinois [May 19, 1856]*

9   "A house divided against itself cannot stand." I believe this government cannot endure permanently half slave and half free. I do not expect the Union to be dissolved—I do not expect the house to fall—but I do expect it will cease to be divided. It will become all one thing, or all the other.
>   *Speech at the Republican State Convention, Springfield, Illinois [June 16, 1858]*

10   Nobody has ever expected me to be President. In my poor, lean, lank face nobody has ever seen that any cabbages were sprouting out.[1]
>   *Second campaign speech against Douglas, Springfield, Illinois [July 17, 1858]*

11   As I would not be a *slave*, so I would not be a *master*. This expresses my idea of democracy. Whatever differs from this, to the extent of the difference is no democracy.
>   *Fragment [August 1, 1858?]. From ROY P. BASLER, The Collected Works of Abraham Lincoln [1953], vol. II, p. 532*

12   When . . . you have succeeded in dehumanizing the Negro; when you have put him down and made it forever impossible for him to be but as the beast of the field; when you have extinguished his soul and placed him where the ray of hope is blown out in darkness like that which broods over the spirits of the damned, are you quite sure that the demon you have roused will not turn and rend you?
>   *Speech at Edwardsville, Illinois [September 11, 1858]*

13   That is the issue that will continue in this country when these poor tongues of Judge Douglas and myself shall be silent. It is the eternal struggle between these two principles—right and wrong—throughout the world. They are the two principles that have stood face to face from the beginning of time; and will ever continue to struggle. The one is the common right of humanity, and the other the divine right of kings. It is the same principle in whatever shape it develops itself.
>   *Reply, seventh and last joint debate, Alton, Illinois [October 15, 1858]*

14   This is a world of compensations; and he who would be no slave must consent to have no slave. Those who deny freedom to others deserve it not for themselves, and, under a just God, cannot long retain it.
>   *Letter to H. L. Pierce and others [April 6, 1859]*

15   Public opinion in this country is everything.
>   *Speech at Columbus, Ohio [September 16, 1859]*

16   It is said an Eastern monarch once charged his wise men to invent him a sentence, to be ever in view, and which should be true and appropriate in all times and situations. They presented him the words: "And this, too, shall pass away." How much

---

[1]They have seen in his [Douglas's] round, jolly, fruitful face, post offices, land offices, marshalships and cabinet appointments, chargeships and foreign missions, bursting and sprouting out in wonderful exuberance, ready to be laid hold of by their greedy hands.—LINCOLN, *Second campaign speech against Douglas, Springfield, Illinois* [July 17, 1858]

it expresses! How chastening in the hour of pride! How consoling in the depths of affliction!

Address to the Wisconsin State Agricultural Society, Milwaukee [September 30, 1859]

1   Let us have faith that right makes might, and in that faith let us to the end dare to do our duty as we understand it.

Address at Cooper Union, New York [February 27, 1860]

2   No one, not in my situation, can appreciate my feeling of sadness at this parting. To this place, and the kindness of these people, I owe everything. Here I have lived a quarter of a century, and have passed from a young to an old man. Here my children have been born, and one is buried. I now leave, not knowing when or whether ever I may return, with a task before me greater than that which rested upon Washington. Without the assistance of that Divine Being who ever attended him, I cannot succeed. With that assistance I cannot fail. Trusting in Him who can go with me, and remain with you, and be everywhere for good, let us confidently hope that all will yet be well.

Farewell Address, Springfield, Illinois [February 11, 1861]

3   If we do not make common cause to save the good old ship of the Union on this voyage, nobody will have a chance to pilot her on another voyage.

Address at Cleveland, Ohio [February 15, 1861]

4   It is safe to assert that no government proper ever had a provision in its organic law for its own termination.

First Inaugural Address [March 4, 1861]

5   If by the mere force of numbers a majority should deprive a minority of any clearly written constitutional right, it might, in a moral point of view, justify revolution—certainly would if such a right were a vital one.

First Inaugural Address [March 4, 1861]

6   This country, with its institutions, belongs to the people who inhabit it. Whenever they shall grow weary of the existing government, they can exercise their constitutional right of amending it, or their revolutionary right to dismember or overthrow it.

First Inaugural Address [March 4, 1861]

7   Why should there not be a patient confidence in the ultimate justice of the people? Is there any better or equal hope in the world?

First Inaugural Address [March 4, 1861]

8   While the people retain their virtue and vigilance, no administration, by any extreme of wickedness or folly, can very seriously injure the government in the short space of four years.

First Inaugural Address [March 4, 1861]

9   I think the necessity of being *ready* increases. Look to it.

Letter (this is the whole message) to Governor Andrew G. Curtin of Pennsylvania [April 8, 1861]

10   This is essentially a people's contest. . . . It is a struggle for maintaining in the world that form and substance of government whose leading object is to elevate the condition of men—to lift artificial weights from all shoulders—to clear the paths of laudable pursuit for all—to afford all an unfettered start, and a fair chance, in the race of life.

Message to Congress in Special Session [July 4, 1861]

11   Labor is prior to, and independent of, capital. Capital is only the fruit of labor, and could never have existed if labor had not first existed. Labor is the superior of capital, and deserves much the higher consideration. Capital has its rights, which are as worthy of protection as any other rights.

First Annual Message to Congress [December 3, 1861]

12   It is called the Army of the Potomac but it is only McClellan's bodyguard. . . . If McClellan is not using the army, I should like to borrow it for a while.

Speech at Washington, D.C. [April 9, 1862]

13   My paramount object in this struggle is to save the Union, and is not either to save or to destroy slavery. If I could save the Union without freeing any slave, I would do it; and if I could save it by freeing all the slaves, I would do it; and if I could do it by freeing some and leaving others alone, I would also do that.

Letter to Horace Greeley [August 22, 1862]

14   I shall try to correct errors when shown to be errors; and I shall adopt new views so fast as they shall appear to be true views. . . . I intend no modification of my oft-expressed personal wish that all men, everywhere, could be free.

Letter to Horace Greeley [August 22, 1862]

15   On the first day of January in the year of our Lord, one thousand eight hundred and sixty-three, all persons held as slaves within any state, or designated part of a state, the people whereof shall then be in rebellion against the United States shall be then, thenceforward, and forever free.

Preliminary Emancipation Proclamation [September 22, 1862][1]

---

[1]The Emancipation Proclamation was issued one hundred days later [January 1, 1863].

1   [I feel] somewhat like the boy in Kentucky who stubbed his toe while running to see his sweetheart. The boy said he was too big to cry, and far too badly hurt to laugh.
Reply as to how he felt about the New York elections. From Frank Leslie's Illustrated Weekly [November 22, 1862]

2   If there ever could be a proper time for mere catch arguments, that time surely is not now. In times like the present, men should utter nothing for which they would not willingly be responsible through time and in eternity.
Second Annual Message to Congress [December 1, 1862]

3   Fellow citizens, we cannot escape history. We of this Congress and this administration will be remembered in spite of ourselves. No personal significance or insignificance can spare one or another of us. The fiery trial through which we pass will light us down in honor or dishonor to the last generation. We say we are for the Union. The world will not forget that we say this. We know how to save the Union. The world knows we do know how to save it. We, even we here, hold the power and bear the responsibility. In giving freedom to the slave, we assure freedom to the free—honorable alike in what we give and what we preserve. We shall nobly save or meanly lose the last, best hope of earth. Other means may succeed; this could not fail. The way is plain, peaceful, generous, just—a way which if followed the world will forever applaud and God must forever bless.
Second Annual Message to Congress [December 1, 1862]

4   Beware of rashness, but with energy and sleepless vigilance go forward and give us victories.
Letter to Major General Joseph Hooker [January 26, 1863]

5   The Father of Waters again goes unvexed to the sea.
Letter to James C. Conkling [August 26, 1863]

6   I have endured a great deal of ridicule without much malice; and have received a great deal of kindness, not quite free from ridicule. I am used to it.
Letter to James H. Hackett [November 2, 1863]

7   Fourscore and seven years ago our fathers brought forth on this continent, a new nation, conceived in Liberty, and dedicated to the proposition that all men are created equal.

Now we are engaged in a great civil war, testing whether that nation or any nation so conceived and so dedicated can long endure. We are met on a great battlefield of that war. We have come to dedicate a portion of that field, as a final resting place for those who here gave their lives that that nation might live. It is altogether fitting and proper that we should do this.

But, in a larger sense, we cannot dedicate—we cannot consecrate—we cannot hallow—this ground. The brave men, living and dead, who struggled here have consecrated it far above our poor power to add or detract. The world will little note nor long remember what we say here, but it can never forget what they did here. It is for us, the living, rather to be dedicated here to the unfinished work which they who fought here have thus far so nobly advanced. It is rather for us to be here dedicated to the great task remaining before us—that from these honored dead we take increased devotion to that cause for which they gave the last full measure of devotion; that we here highly resolve that these dead shall not have died in vain; that this nation, under God, shall have a new birth of freedom; and that government of the people, by the people, for the people, shall not perish from the earth.
Address at Gettysburg [November 19, 1863]

8   The President last night had a dream. He was in a party of plain people and as it became known who he was they began to comment on his appearance. One of them said, "He is a common-looking man." The President replied, "Common-looking people are the best in the world: that is the reason the Lord makes so many of them."
From Letters of John Hay and Extracts from His Diary, edited by C. L. HAY [December 23, 1863]

9   I claim not to have controlled events, but confess plainly that events have controlled me.
Letter to A. G. Hodges [April 4, 1864]

10   I do not allow myself to suppose that either the convention or the League have concluded to decide that I am either the greatest or best man in America, but rather they have concluded that it is not best to swap horses while crossing the river, and have further concluded that I am not so poor a horse that they might not make a botch of it in trying to swap.
Reply to the National Union League [June 9, 1864]

11   Truth is generally the best vindication against slander.
Letter to Secretary Stanton, refusing to dismiss Postmaster-General Montgomery Blair [July 18, 1864]

12   It has long been a grave question whether any government, not too strong for the liberties of its people, can be strong enough to maintain its existence in great emergencies.
Response to a serenade [November 10, 1864]

1 I desire so to conduct the affairs of this administration that if at the end, when I come to lay down the reins of power, I have lost every other friend on earth, I shall at least have one friend left, and that friend shall be down inside me.
Reply to the Missouri Committee of Seventy [1864]

2 Dear Madam, I have been shown in the files of the War Department a statement of the Adjutant-General of Massachusetts that you are the mother of five sons who have died gloriously on the field of battle. I feel how weak and fruitless must be any words of mine which should attempt to beguile you from the grief of a loss so overwhelming. But I cannot refrain from tendering to you the consolation that may be found in the thanks of the Republic they died to save. I pray that our heavenly Father may assuage the anguish of your bereavement, and leave you only the cherished memory of the loved and lost, and the solemn pride that must be yours to have laid so costly a sacrifice upon the altar of freedom.
Letter to Mrs. Bixby [November 21, 1864]

3 It may seem strange that any men should dare to ask a just God's assistance in wringing their bread from the sweat of other men's faces, but let us judge not, that we be not judged.
Second Inaugural Address [March 4, 1865]

4 Fondly do we hope, fervently do we pray, that this mighty scourge of war may speedily pass away. Yet, if God wills that it continue until all the wealth piled by the bondsman's two hundred and fifty years of unrequited toil shall be sunk, and until every drop of blood drawn with the lash shall be paid by another drawn with the sword, as was said three thousand years ago, so still it must be said, "The judgments of the Lord are true and righteous altogether."

With malice toward none, with charity for all, with firmness in the right as God gives us to see the right, let us strive on to finish the work we are in, to bind up the nation's wounds, to care for him who shall have borne the battle and for his widow and his orphan, to do all which may achieve and cherish a just and lasting peace among ourselves and with all nations.
Second Inaugural Address [March 4, 1865]

5 I have always thought that all men should be free; but if any should be slaves, it should be first those who desire it for themselves, and secondly those who desire it for others. Whenever I hear anyone arguing for slavery, I feel a strong impulse to see it tried on him personally.
Address to an Indiana Regiment [March 17, 1865]

6 Important principles may and must be inflexible.
Last public address, Washington, D.C. [April 11, 1865]

7 If you once forfeit the confidence of your fellow citizens, you can never regain their respect and esteem. It is true that you may fool all the people some of the time; you can even fool some of the people all the time; but you can't fool all of the people all the time.
To a caller at the White House. From ALEXANDER K. MCCLURE, *Lincoln's Yarns and Stories [1904]*

8 If I were to try to read, much less answer, all the attacks made on me, this shop might as well be closed for any other business. I do the very best I know how—the very best I can; and I mean to keep doing so until the end. If the end brings me out all right, what is said against me won't amount to anything. If the end brings me out wrong, ten angels swearing I was right would make no difference.
Conversation at the White House. From FRANCIS B. CARPENTER, *Six Months at the White House with Abraham Lincoln [1866]*

Benjamin Peirce
1809–1880

9 Mathematics is the science which draws necessary conclusions.
Linear Associative Algebra [1870], first sentence

Edgar Allan Poe
1809–1849

10 O, human love! thou spirit given,
On Earth, of all we hope in Heaven!
Tamerlane [1827], l. 177

11 All that we see or seem
Is but a dream within a dream.
A Dream Within a Dream [1827, revised 1849], l. 10

12 The happiest day—the happiest hour
My sear'd and blighted heart hath known,
The highest hope of pride and power,
I feel hath flown.   *The Happiest Day [1827], st. 1*

13 From childhood's hour I have not been
As others were—I have not seen
As others saw.
Alone [written 1829, published 1875], l. 1

14 Hast thou not torn the Naiad from her flood,
The Elfin from the green grass, and from me
The summer dream beneath the tamarind tree?
Sonnet. To Science [1829], l. 12

1   It is with literature as with law or empire—an established name is an estate in tenure, or a throne in possession.
Poems [1831]. Preface, Letter to Mr. B——

2 Helen, thy beauty is to me
Like those Nicean barks of yore,
That gently, o'er a perfumed sea,
The weary, wayworn wanderer bore
To his own native shore.

On desperate seas long wont to roam,
Thy hyacinth hair, thy classic face,
Thy Naiad airs have brought me home
To the glory that was Greece,
And the grandeur that was Rome.
To Helen [1831], st. 1, 2

3 If I could dwell
Where Israfel[1]
Hath dwelt, and he where I,
He might not sing so wildly well
A mortal melody,
While a bolder note than this might swell
From my lyre within the sky.
Israfel [1831], st. 8

4 Lo! Death has reared himself a throne
In a strange city, lying alone
Far down within the dim West,
Where the good and the bad and the worst and the best
Have gone to their eternal rest.
The City in the Sea [1831], st. 1

5 The viol, the violet, and the vine.
The City in the Sea, st. 2

6 While from a proud tower in the town
Death looks gigantically down.
The City in the Sea, st. 3

7 And when, amid no earthly moans,
Down, down that town shall settle hence,
Hell, rising from a thousand thrones,
Shall do it reverence.   *The City in the Sea, st. 5*

8 A dirge for the most lovely dead
That ever died so young!   *Lenore [1831], st. 1*

9 Thou wast that all to me, love,
For which my soul did pine—
A green isle in the sea, love,
A fountain and a shrine,
All wreathed with fairy fruits and flowers,
And all the flowers were mine.
To One in Paradise [1834], st. 1

10 And all my days are trances,
And all my nightly dreams
Are where thy gray eye glances,
And where thy footstep gleams—
In what ethereal dances,
By what eternal streams.
To One in Paradise, st.

11   During the whole of a dull, dark, and soundless day in the autumn of the year, when the clouds hung oppressively low in the heavens, I had been passing alone, on horseback, through a singularly dreary tract of country, and at length found myself as the shades of the evening drew on, within view of the melancholy House of Usher.
The Fall of the House of Usher [1839]

12 In the greenest of our valleys
By good angels tenanted,
Once a fair and stately palace—
Radiant palace—reared its head.
The Haunted Palace [1839], st.

13   They who dream by day are cognizant of many things which escape those who dream only by night.
Eleonora [1841]

14 And much of Madness, and more of Sin,
And Horror the soul of the plot.
The Conqueror Worm [1843], st.

15 While the angels, all pallid and wan,
Uprising, unveiling, affirm
That the play is the tragedy, "Man,"
And its hero the Conqueror Worm.
The Conqueror Worm, st.

16   There is something in the unselfish and self-sacrificing love of a brute, which goes directly to the heart of him who has had frequent occasion to test the paltry friendship and gossamer fidelity of mere Man.   *The Black Cat [1843]*

17   The boundaries which divide Life from Death are at best shadowy and vague. Who shall say where the one ends, and where the other begins?
The Premature Burial [1844]

18 From a wild weird clime that lieth, sublime,
Out of Space—out of Time.
Dreamland [1845], st.

19   With me poetry has been not a purpose, but a passion; and the passions should be held in reverence: they must not—they cannot at will be excited, with an eye to the paltry compensations, or the more paltry commendations, of mankind.
The Raven and Other Poems [1845], preface

20 Once upon a midnight dreary, while I pondered, weak and weary,

---

[1]Poe's epigraph for the poem: And the angel Israfel, whose heartstrings are a lute, and who has the sweetest voice of all God's creatures.—*Koran*

Over many a quaint and curious volume of
    forgotten lore —
While I nodded, nearly napping, suddenly there
    came a tapping,
As of someone gently rapping, rapping at my
    chamber door.   *The Raven [1845], st. 1*

1 Ah, distinctly I remember it was in the bleak
    December;
And each separate dying ember wrought its ghost
    upon the floor.   *The Raven, st. 2*

2   Sorrow for the lost Lenore —
For the rare and radiant maiden whom the angels
    name Lenore —
Nameless *here* for evermore.   *The Raven, st. 2*

3 The silken, sad, uncertain rustling of each purple
    curtain.   *The Raven, st. 3*

4 Deep into that darkness peering, long I stood there
    wondering, fearing,
Doubting, dreaming dreams no mortal ever dared
    to dream before.   *The Raven, st. 5*

5 "Ghastly grim and ancient Raven wandering from
    the Nightly shore —
Tell me what thy lordly name is on the Night's
    Plutonian shore!"
Quoth the Raven, "Nevermore."
        The Raven, st. 8

6 "Prophet!" said I, "thing of evil! — prophet still, if
    bird or devil!"   *The Raven, st. 15*

7 "Take thy beak from out my heart, and take thy
    form from off my door!"
Quoth the Raven, "Nevermore."
        The Raven, st. 17

8 And the Raven, never flitting, still is sitting, *still* is
    sitting
On the pallid bust of Pallas just above my chamber
    door.   *The Raven, st. 18*

9 And my soul from out that shadow that lies
    floating on the floor
Shall be lifted — nevermore!   *The Raven, st. 18*

10   The Imp of the Perverse.[1]
        Title of story [1845]

11 The skies they were ashen and sober;
The leaves they were crispèd and sere —
The leaves they were withering and sere:
It was night in the lonesome October
Of my most immemorial year.
        Ulalume [1847], st. 1

12 It was down by the dank tarn of Auber,
In the ghoul-haunted woodland of Weir.
        Ulalume, st. 1

13 Here once, through an alley Titanic,
Of cypress, I roamed with my Soul —
Of cypress, with Psyche, my Soul.
        Ulalume, st. 2

14 Thus I pacified Psyche and kissed her,
And tempted her out of her gloom.
        Ulalume, st. 8

15 "Over the Mountains
    Of the Moon,
Down the Valley of the Shadow,
    Ride, boldly ride,"
The shade replied —
    "If you seek for Eldorado!"
        Eldorado [1849], st. 4

16 And the fever called "Living"
Is conquered at last.   *For Annie [1849], st. 1*

17 And this maiden she lived with no other thought
Than to love and be loved by me.
        Annabel Lee [1849], st. 1

18 *I* was a child and *she* was a child,
In this kingdom by the sea,
But we loved with a love that was more than
    love —
I and my Annabel Lee —
With a love that the wingèd seraphs of Heaven
Coveted her and me.   *Annabel Lee, st. 2*

19 And neither the angels in Heaven above
Nor the demons down under the sea,
Can ever dissever my soul from the soul
Of the beautiful Annabel Lee.
        Annabel Lee, st. 5

20 In her sepulcher there by the sea —
In her tomb by the sounding sea.
        Annabel Lee, st. 6

21 Keeping time, time, time,
In a sort of Runic rhyme,
To the tintinnabulation that so musically wells
From the bells, bells, bells, bells,
Bells, bells, bells.   *The Bells [1849], st. 1*

22   I hold that a long poem does not exist. I maintain that the phrase "a long poem" is simply a flat
contradiction in terms.
        The Poetic Principle [1850]

23   There neither exists nor can exist any work more
thoroughly dignified — more supremely noble than
this very poem — this poem *per se* — this poem which
is a poem and nothing more — this poem written
solely for the poem's sake.   *The Poetic Principle*

---

[1]Perverseness is one of the primitive impulses of the human
heart. — POE, *The Black Cat* [1843]

1   I would define, in brief, the poetry of words as the rhythmical creation of Beauty. Its sole arbiter is taste. With the intellect or with the conscience, it has only collateral relations. Unless incidentally, it has no concern whatever either with duty or with truth.   *The Poetic Principle*

Pierre Joseph Proudhon
1809–1865

2   Property is theft [La propriété c'est le vol]!
Qu'est-ce que la Propriété? [1840], ch. 1

Alfred, Lord Tennyson
1809–1892

3 Weeded and worn the ancient thatch
Upon the lonely moated grange.
Mariana [1830], st. 1

4 She said, "I am aweary, aweary,
I would that I were dead!"
Mariana, refrain

5 A still small voice spake unto me,
"Thou art so full of misery,
Were it not better not to be?"
The Two Voices [1832], st. 1

6 Though thou wert scattered to the wind,
Yet is there plenty of the kind.
The Two Voices, st. 11

7 I know that age to age succeeds,
Blowing a noise of tongues and deeds,
A dust of systems and of creeds.
The Two Voices, st. 69

8 Like glimpses of forgotten dreams.
The Two Voices, st. 127

9 No life that breathes with human breath
Has ever truly longed for death.
The Two Voices, st. 132

10   In after-dinner talk,
Across the walnuts and the wine.
The Miller's Daughter [1832], st. 4

11 Self-reverence, self-knowledge, self-control,
These three alone lead life to sovereign power.
Oenone [1832], l. 142

12 The lion on your old stone gates
Is not more cold to you than I.
Lady Clara Vere de Vere, st. 3

13 The gardener Adam and his wife
Smile at the claims of long descent.
Lady Clara Vere de Vere, st. 7

14 'Tis only noble to be good.
Kind hearts are more than coronets,
And simple faith than Norman blood.
Lady Clara Vere de Vere, st.

15 You must wake and call me early, call me early, mother dear;
Tomorrow 'ill be the happiest time of all the glad New Year;
Of all the glad New Year, mother, the maddest, merriest day;
For I'm to be Queen o' the May, mother, I'm to be Queen o' the May.
The May Queen [1832], st.

16 In the afternoon they came unto a land
In which it seemed always afternoon.
The Lotos-Eaters [1832], st.

17 Music that gentlier on the spirit lies,
Than tir'd eyelids upon tir'd eyes.
The Lotos-Eaters. Choric Song, st.

18   Ah, why
Should life all labor be?
The Lotos-Eaters. Choric Song, st.

19 Let us alone. Time driveth onward fast,
And in a little while our lips are dumb.
Let us alone. What is it that will last?
All things are taken from us, and become
Portions and parcels of the dreadful Past.
The Lotos-Eaters. Choric Song, st.

20 Give us long rest or death, dark death or dreamful ease.   *The Lotos-Eaters. Choric Song, st.*

21 Surely, surely, slumber is more sweet than toil, the shore
Than labor in the deep mid-ocean, wind and wave and oar;
Oh rest ye, brother mariners, we will not wander more.
The Lotos-Eaters. Choric Song, last line

22 Dan Chaucer, the first warbler, whose sweet breath
Preluded those melodious bursts that fill
The spacious times of great Elizabeth
With sounds that echo still.
A Dream of Fair Women [1832], st.

23 A daughter of the gods, divinely tall,
And most divinely fair.
A Dream of Fair Women, st. 2

24 Many-tower'd Camelot.
The Lady of Shalott [1832], pt. I, st.

25 "Tirra lirra," by the river
Sang Sir Lancelot.   *The Lady of Shalott, III, st.*

26 She left the web, she left the loom,
She made three paces thro' the room,

She saw the water lily bloom,
She saw the helmet and the plume,
 She look'd down to Camelot.
Out flew the web and floated wide;
The mirror cracked from side to side.
"The curse has come upon me," cried
 The Lady of Shalott.
 The Lady of Shalott, III, st. 5

1 But Lancelot mused a little space;
 He said, "She has a lovely face;
 God in his mercy lend her grace,
 The Lady of Shalott."
 The Lady of Shalott, IV, st. 6

2 The great brand
 Made lightnings in the splendor of the moon,
 And flashing round and round, and whirled in an
  arch,
 Shot like a streamer of the northern morn,
 Seen where the moving isles of winter shock
 By night, with noises of the northern sea,
 So flashed and fell the brand Excalibur.
 Morte d'Arthur [1842], l. 136

3 Half light, half shade,
 She stood, a sight to make an old man young.
 The Gardener's Daughter [1842], l. 139

4 The long mechanic pacings to and fro,
 The set gray life, and apathetic end.
 Love and Duty [1842], l. 17

5 Meet is it changes should control
 Our being, lest we rest in ease.
 Love Thou Thy Land [1842], st. 11

6 Ah! when shall all men's good
 Be each man's rule, and universal peace
 Lie like a shaft of light across the land,
 And like a lane of beams athwart the sea,
 Through all the circle of the golden year?
 The Golden Year [1842], l. 47

7 It little profits that an idle king,
 By this still hearth, among these barren crags,
 Match'd with an aged wife, I mete and dole
 Unequal laws unto a savage race.
 Ulysses [1842], l. 1

8 I will drink
 Life to the lees. *Ulysses, l. 6*

9 Much have I seen and known; cities of men
 And manners, climates, councils, governments,
 Myself not least, but honor'd of them all;
 And drunk delight of battle with my peers,
 Far on the ringing plains of windy Troy.
 I am a part of all that I have met;
 Yet all experience is an arch wherethrough
 Gleams that untravel'd world. *Ulysses, l. 13*

10 How dull it is to pause, to make an end,
 To rust unburnished, not to shine in use,
 As though to breathe were life! *Ulysses, l. 22*

11 And this gray spirit yearning in desire
 To follow knowledge like a sinking star,
 Beyond the utmost bound of human thought.
 Ulysses, l. 30

12 This is my son, mine own Telemachus.
 Ulysses, l. 33

13 Death closes all: but something ere the end,
 Some work of noble note, may yet be done,
 Not unbecoming men that strove with gods.
 Ulysses, l. 51

14 The deep
 Moans round with many voices. Come, my friends,
 'Tis not too late to seek a newer world.
 Push off, and sitting well in order smite
 The sounding furrows, for my purpose holds
 To sail beyond the sunset, and the baths
 Of all the western stars, until I die.
 It may be that the gulfs will wash us down;
 It may be we shall touch the Happy Isles,
 And see the great Achilles, whom we knew.
 Ulysses, l. 55

15 To strive, to seek, to find, and not to yield.
 Ulysses, l. 70

16 Comrades, leave me here a little, while as yet 'tis
  early morn:
 Leave me here, and when you want me, sound
  upon the bugle horn.
 Locksley Hall [1842], l. 1

17 In the spring a young man's fancy lightly turns to
  thoughts of love. *Locksley Hall, l. 20*

18 He will hold thee, when his passion shall have
  spent its novel force,
 Something better than his dog, a little dearer than
  his horse. *Locksley Hall, l. 49*

19 This is the truth the poet sings,
 That a sorrow's crown of sorrow is remembering
  happier things. *Locksley Hall, l. 75*

20 Like a dog, he hunts in dreams.
 Locksley Hall, l. 79

21 With a little hoard of maxims preaching down a
  daughter's heart. *Locksley Hall, l. 94*

22 But the jingling of the guinea helps the hurt that
  Honor feels. *Locksley Hall, l. 105*

23 For I dipp'd into the future, far as human eye
  could see,
 Saw the Vision of the world, and all the wonder
  that would be;

Saw the heavens fill with commerce, argosies of
   magic sails,
Pilots of the purple twilight, dropping down with
   costly bales;
Heard the heavens fill with shouting, and there
   rain'd a ghastly dew
From the nations' airy navies grappling in the
   central blue.   *Locksley Hall, l. 119*

1 Till the war drum throbbed no longer and the
   battle flags were furled
In the Parliament of man, the Federation of the
   world.   *Locksley Hall, l. 127*

2 And the kindly earth shall slumber, lapp'd in
   universal law.   *Locksley Hall, l. 130*

3 Yet I doubt not through the ages one increasing
   purpose runs,
And the thoughts of men are widened with the
   process of the suns.   *Locksley Hall, l. 137*

4 Knowledge comes, but wisdom lingers.
    Locksley Hall, l. 141

5 Woman is the lesser man, and all thy passions,
   match'd with mine,
Are as moonlight unto sunlight, and as water unto
   wine.   *Locksley Hall, l. 151*

6 I will take some savage woman, she shall rear my
   dusky race.   *Locksley Hall, l. 168*

7 I the heir of all the ages, in the foremost files of time.
    Locksley Hall, l. 178

8 Let the great world spin forever down the ringing
   grooves of change.   *Locksley Hall, l. 182*

9 Better fifty years of Europe than a cycle of Cathay.
    Locksley Hall, l. 184

10 And o'er the hills and far away
   Beyond their utmost purple rim,
   Beyond the night, across the day,
   Through all the world she followed him.
    The Day Dream [1842]. The Departure, st. 4

11 My strength is as the strength of ten,
   Because my heart is pure.
    Sir Galahad [1842], st. 1

12 Or that eternal lack of pence,
   Which vexes public men.
    Will Waterproof's Lyrical Monologue [1842],
    st. 6

13 Cophetua sware a royal oath;
   "This beggar maid shall be my queen!"
    The Beggar Maid [1842], st. 2

14 A little grain of conscience made him sour.
    The Vision of Sin [1842], sec. 5

15 Break, break, break,
   On thy cold gray stones, O Sea!
   And I would that my tongue could utter
   The thoughts that arise in me.

O, well for the fisherman's boy,
   That he shouts with his sister at play!
O, well for the sailor lad,
   That he sings in his boat on the bay!

And the stately ships go on
   To their haven under the hill;
But O, for the touch of a vanish'd hand,
   And the sound of a voice that is still!
    Break, Break, Break [1842], st. 1–3

16 But the tender grace of a day that is dead
   Will never come back to me.
    Break, Break, Break, st. 4

17 And quoted odes, and jewels five-words-long
   That on the stretched forefinger of all Time
   Sparkle forever.
    The Princess [1847], pt. II, l. 355

18
Sweet and low, sweet and low,
   Wind of the western sea,
Low, low, breathe and blow,
   Wind of the western sea!
Over the rolling waters go,
Come from the dying moon, and blow,
   Blow him again to me;
While my little one, while my pretty one, sleeps.
    The Princess, III [song, Sweet and Low, st. 1]

19
The splendor falls on castle walls
   And snowy summits old in story:
The long light shakes across the lakes,
   And the wild cataract leaps in glory.
Blow, bugle, blow, set the wild echoes flying,
Blow, bugle; answer, echoes, dying, dying, dying.
    The Princess, IV [song, The Splendor Falls, st. 1]

20 The horns of Elfland faintly blowing.
    The Princess, IV [song, The Splendor Falls, st. 2]

21 Tears, idle tears, I know not what they mean,
   Tears from the depth of some divine despair
Rise in the heart, and gather to the eyes,
In looking on the happy autumn fields,
And thinking of the days that are no more.
    The Princess, IV [song, Tears, Idle
    Tears, st. 1]

22 Dear as remember'd kisses after death,
   And sweet as those by hopeless fancy feign'd
On lips that are for others; deep as love,
Deep as first love, and wild with all regret;
O Death in Life, the days that are no more.
    The Princess, IV [song, Tears, Idle
    Tears, st. 4]

1 O Swallow, Swallow, flying, flying South,
  Fly to her, and fall upon her gilded eaves,
  And tell her, tell her, what I tell to thee.
      *The Princess, IV [song, O Swallow,
      Swallow, st. 1]*

2 Man is the hunter; woman is his game.
      The Princess, V, l. 147

3 Man for the field and woman for the hearth:
  Man for the sword and for the needle she:
  Man with the head and woman with the heart:
  Man to command and woman to obey;
  All else confusion.
      The Princess, V, l. 437

4 Home they brought her warrior dead.
  She nor swoon'd nor utter'd cry:
  All her maidens, watching, said,
  "She must weep or she will die."
      *The Princess, VI [song, Home They Brought
      Her Warrior, st. 1]*

5 Ask me no more: thy fate and mine are seal'd:
  I strove against the stream and all in vain:
  Let the great river take me to the main:
  No more, dear love, for at a touch I yield;
  Ask me no more.
      *The Princess, VII [song, Ask Me No More,
      st. 3]*

6 Now sleeps the crimson petal, now the white;
  Nor waves the cypress in the palace walk;
  Nor winks the gold fin in the porphyry font:
  The firefly wakens: waken thou with me.
      *The Princess, VII [song, Now Sleeps the
      Crimson Petal, st. 1]*

7 Now lies the Earth all Danaë to the stars,
  And all thy heart lies open unto me.
      *The Princess, VII [song, Now Sleeps the
      Crimson Petal, st. 3]*

8   Sweet is every sound,
  Sweeter thy voice, but every sound is sweet;
  Myriads of rivulets hurrying through the lawn,
  The moan of doves in immemorial elms,
  And murmuring of innumerable bees.
      The Princess, VII, l. 203

9 Some sense of duty, something of a faith,
  Some reverence for the laws ourselves have made,
  Some patient force to change them when we will,
  Some civic manhood firm against the crowd.
      The Princess, VII, conclusion, l. 54

10 Believing where we cannot prove.
      In Memoriam[1] [1850]. Prologue, st. 1

11 Our little systems have their day.
      In Memoriam. Prologue, st. 5

12 Let knowledge grow from more to more,
   But more of reverence in us dwell;
   That mind and soul, according well,
   May make one music as before.
      In Memoriam. Prologue, st. 7

13 I held it truth, with him who sings[2]
   To one clear harp in divers tones,
   That men may rise on stepping-stones
   Of their dead selves to higher things.
      In Memoriam, 1, st. 1

14 I sometimes hold it half a sin
   To put in words the grief I feel;
   For words, like Nature, half reveal
   And half conceal the Soul within.
      In Memoriam, 5, st. 1

15 But, for the unquiet heart and brain
   A use in measured language lies;
   The sad mechanic exercise,
   Like dull narcotics numbing pain.
      In Memoriam, 5, st. 2

16 And from his ashes may be made
   The violet of his native land.
      In Memoriam, 18, st. 1

17 I do but sing because I must,
   And pipe but as the linnets sing.
      In Memoriam, 21, st. 6

18 And Thought leap'd out to wed with Thought
   Ere Thought could wed itself with Speech.
      In Memoriam, 23, st. 4

19 'Tis better to have loved and lost
   Than never to have loved at all.[3]
      In Memoriam, 27, st. 4

20 How fares it with the happy dead?
      In Memoriam, 44, st. 1

21 Be near me when my light is low.
      In Memoriam, 50, st. 1

22 And Time, a maniac scattering dust,
   And Life, a Fury slinging flame.
      In Memoriam, 50, st. 2

23 Do we indeed desire the dead
   Should still be near us at our side?
      In Memoriam, 51, st. 1

---

[2]Goethe.

[3]Say what you will, 'tis better to be left than never to have been loved. —W. CONGREVE, *The Way of the World* [1700], *act II, sc. vi*
Better to love amiss than nothing to have loved. —GEORGE CRABBE, *Tales* [1812], *XIV, The Struggles of Conscience*
'Tis better to have fought and lost / Than never to have fought at all. —ARTHUR HUGH CLOUGH, *Peschiera*

---

[1]In memory of Arthur Henry Hallam [1811–1833].

1 Hold thou the good; define it well;
    For fear divine Philosophy
    Should push beyond her mark, and be
    Procuress to the Lords of Hell.

In Memoriam, 53, st. 4

2 Oh yet we trust that somehow good
    Will be the final goal of ill.

In Memoriam, 54, st. 1

3   But what am I?
    An infant crying in the night:
    An infant crying for the light:
    And with no language but a cry.

In Memoriam, 54, st. 5

4 So careful of the type she seems,
    So careless of the single life.

In Memoriam, 55, st. 2

5   The great world's altar-stairs,
    That slope through darkness up to God.

In Memoriam, 55, st. 4

6 Nature, red in tooth and claw.

In Memoriam, 56, st. 4

7 O Sorrow, wilt Thou live with me
    No casual mistress, but a wife.

In Memoriam, 59, st. 1

8 So many worlds, so much to do,
    So little done, such things to be.

In Memoriam, 73, st. 1

9 God's finger touch'd him, and he slept.

In Memoriam, 85, st. 5

10   Fresh from brawling courts
    And dusty purlieus of the law.

In Memoriam, 89, st. 3

11 There lives more faith in honest doubt,
    Believe me, than in half the creeds.

In Memoriam, 96, st. 3

12 He seems so near, and yet so far.

In Memoriam, 97, st. 6

13 Ring out, wild bells, to the wild sky!

In Memoriam, 106, st. 1

14 Ring out the old, ring in the new,
    Ring, happy bells, across the snow:
    The year is going, let him go;
    Ring out the false, ring in the true.

In Memoriam, 106, st. 2

15 Ring out old shapes of foul disease,
    Ring out the narrowing lust of gold;
    Ring out the thousand wars of old,
    Ring in the thousand years of peace.

In Memoriam, 106, st. 7

16 Love is and was my lord and king.

In Memoriam, 126, st.

17   Wearing all that weight
    Of learning lightly like a flower.

In Memoriam, epilogue, st. 1

18 One God, one law, one element,
    And one far-off divine event,
    To which the whole creation moves.

In Memoriam, epilogue, st. 3

19 He clasps the crag with crooked hands;
    Close to the sun in lonely lands,
    Ring'd with the azure world he stands.

The wrinkled sea beneath him crawls;
    He watches from his mountain walls,
    And like a thunderbolt he falls.

The Eagle [1851]

20 Bury the Great Duke
    With an empire's lamentation.

*Ode on the Death of the Duke of Wellington
    [1852], st. 1*

21 The last great Englishman is low.

*Ode on the Death of the Duke of Wellington,
    st. 3*

22 O iron nerve to true occasion true,
    O fall'n at length, that tower of strength
    Which stood four-square to all the winds that blew.

*Ode on the Death of the Duke of Wellington,
    st. 4*

23 Speak no more of his renown.
    Lay your earthly fancies down,
    And in the vast cathedral leave him.
    God accept him, Christ receive him.

*Ode on the Death of the Duke of Wellington,
    st. 9*

24 Half a league, half a league,
    Half a league onward,
    All in the valley of death
    Rode the six hundred.

The Charge of the Light Brigade [1854],[1] *st. 1*

25 "Forward, the Light Brigade!"
    Was there a man dismay'd?

The Charge of the Light Brigade, st. 2

26 Someone had blundered.

The Charge of the Light Brigade, st. 2

27 Theirs not to make reply,
    Theirs not to reason why,
    Theirs but to do and die.

The Charge of the Light Brigade, st. 2

---

[1]See Bosquet, 487:9.

1 Cannon to right of them,
Cannon to left of them,
Cannon in front of them
Volley'd and thunder'd.
The Charge of the Light Brigade, st. 3

2 Into the jaws of death,
Into the mouth of hell
Rode the six hundred.
The Charge of the Light Brigade, st. 3

3 I come from haunts of coot and hern,
I make a sudden sally
And sparkle out among the fern,
To bicker down a valley.
The Brook [1855], song, st. 1

4 For men may come and men may go,
But I go on forever.   *The Brook, song, st. 6*

5 Faultily faultless, icily regular, splendidly null,
Dead perfection, no more.
Maud [1855], pt. I, sec. ii, l. 6

6 And ah for a man to arise in me,
That the man I am may cease to be!
Maud, I, x, st. 6

7 Gorgonized me from head to foot,
With a stony British stare.   *Maud, I, xiii, st. 2*

8 Come into the garden, Maud,
For the black bat, night, has flown,
Come into the garden, Maud,
I am here at the gate alone.   *Maud, I, xxii, st. 1*

9 For a breeze of morning moves,
And the planet of Love is on high,
Beginning to faint in the light that she loves
On a bed of daffodil sky.   *Maud, I, xxii, st. 2*

10 All night have the roses heard
The flute, violin, bassoon;
All night has the casement jessamine stirr'd
To the dancers dancing in tune;
Till a silence fell with the waking bird,
And a hush with the setting moon.
Maud, I, xxii, st. 3

11 There has fallen a splendid tear
From the passion-flower at the gate.
Maud, I, xxii, st. 10

12 She is coming, my own, my sweet;
Were it ever so airy a tread,
My heart would hear her and beat,
Were it earth in an earthy bed;
My dust would hear her and beat,
Had I lain for a century dead;
Would start and tremble under her feet,
And blossom in purple and red.
Maud, I, xxii, st. 11

13 Ah Christ, that it were possible
For one short hour to see
The souls we loved, that they might tell us
What and where they be.
Maud, II, iv, st. 3

14 The woods decay, the woods decay and fall,
The vapors weep their burthen to the ground,
Man comes and tills the field and lies beneath,
And after many a summer dies the swan.
Tithonus [1860], l. 1

15 Here at the quiet limit of the world.
Tithonus, l. 7

16 Wearing the white flower of a blameless life,
Before a thousand peering littlenesses,
In that fierce light which beats upon a throne,
And blackens every blot.
Idylls of the King [1859–1885], dedication, l. 24

17 Man's word is God in man.
Idylls of the King. The Coming of Arthur, l. 132

18 Large, divine, and comfortable words.
Idylls of the King. The Coming of Arthur, l. 267

19 Clothed in white samite, mystic, wonderful.
Idylls of the King. The Coming of Arthur, l. 284

20 Live pure, speak true, right wrong, follow the
King—
Else, wherefore born?
Idylls of the King. Gareth and Lynette, l. 117

21 Our hoard is little, but our hearts are great.
Idylls of the King. The Marriage of Geraint, l. 352

22 For man is man and master of his fate.
Idylls of the King. The Marriage of Geraint, l. 355

23 It is the little rift within the lute,
That by and by will make the music mute,
And ever widening slowly silence all.
Idylls of the King. Merlin and Vivien, l. 388

24   Blind and naked Ignorance
Delivers brawling judgments, unashamed,
On all things all day long.
Idylls of the King. Merlin and Vivien, l. 662

25 Elaine the fair, Elaine the lovable,
Elaine, the lily maid of Astolat.
Idylls of the King. Lancelot and Elaine, l. 1

1
    But, friend, to me
He is all fault who hath no fault at all.
For who loves me must have a touch of earth.
      Idylls of the King. Lancelot and Elaine, l. 131

2
    In me there dwells
No greatness, save it be some far-off touch
Of greatness to know well I am not great.
      Idylls of the King. Lancelot and Elaine, l. 447

3 The shackles of an old love straitened him,
His honor rooted in dishonor stood,
And faith unfaithful kept him falsely true.
      Idylls of the King. Lancelot and Elaine, l. 870

4 He makes no friend who never made a foe.
      *Idylls of the King. Lancelot and Elaine,
l. 1082*

5 The greater man the greater courtesy.
      *Idylls of the King. The Last Tournament,
l. 628*

6 The vow that binds too strictly snaps itself.
      *Idylls of the King. The Last Tournament,
l. 652*

7 For manners are not idle, but the fruit
Of loyal nature and of noble mind.
      Idylls of the King. Guinevere, l. 333

8
    No more subtle master under Heaven
Than is the maiden passion for a maid,
Not only to keep down the base in man,
But teach high thought, and amiable words
And courtliness, and the desire of fame,
And love of truth, and all that makes a man.
      Idylls of the King. Guinevere, l. 475

9 The days will grow to weeks, the weeks to months,
The months will add themselves and make the years,
The years will roll into the centuries,
And mine will ever be a name of scorn.
      Idylls of the King. Guinevere, l. 619

10 I found Him in the shining of the stars,
I mark'd Him in the flowering of His fields,
But in His ways with men I find Him not.
      Idylls of the King. The Passing of Arthur, l. 9

11 So all day long the noise of battle roll'd
Among the mountains by the winter sea.
      *Idylls of the King. The Passing of Arthur,
l. 170*

12 And slowly answer'd Arthur from the barge:
The old order changeth, yielding place to new;
And God fulfills himself in many ways,
Lest one good custom should corrupt the world.
      *Idylls of the King. The Passing of Arthur,
l. 407*

13
    More things are wrought by prayer
Than this world dreams of. Wherefore, let thy voic
Rise like a fountain for me night and day.
      *Idylls of the King. The Passing of Arthur,
l. 415*

14 From the great deep to the great deep he goes.
      *Idylls of the King. The Passing of Arthur,
l. 445*

15 Cast all your cares on God; that anchor holds.
      Enoch Arden [1864], l. 22

16 Insipid as the queen upon a card.
      Aylmer's Field [1864], l. 2

17 The worst is yet to come.
      Sea Dreams [1864], l. 30

18
    He said likewise
That a lie which is half a truth is ever the blackest
of lies,
That a lie which is all a lie may be met and fought
with outright,
But a lie which is part a truth is a harder matter to
fight.   *The Grandmother [1864], st.*

19 Dosn't thou 'ear my 'erse's legs, as they canters
awaäy?
Proputty, proputty, proputty—that's what I 'ears
'em saäy.
      Northern Farmer: New Style [1869], st.

20 Doänt thou marry for munny, but goä wheer
munny is!
      Northern Farmer: New Style, st.

21 Flower in the crannied wall,
I pluck you out of the crannies,
I hold you here, root and all, in my hand,
Little flower—but *if* I could understand
What you are, root and all, and all in all,
I should know what God and man is.
      Flower in the Crannied Wall [1869

22 At Flores in the Azores Sir Richard Grenville lay,
And a pinnace, like a flutter'd bird, came flying
from far away;
"Spanish ships of war at sea! we have sighted fifty-
three!"   *The Revenge [1878], st.*

23 All the charm of all the Muses often flowering in a
lonely word.
      To Virgil [1882], st.

24 Cleave ever to the sunnier side of doubt.
      The Ancient Sage [1885], l. 6

25 That man's the best Cosmopolite
Who loves his native country best.
      Hands All Round [1885], l.

1 I am Merlin
Who follow the Gleam.
Merlin and the Gleam [1889], st. 1

2 Sunset and evening star,
And one clear call for me!
And may there be no moaning of the bar,
When I put out to sea,

But such a tide as moving seems asleep,
Too full for sound and foam,
When that which drew from out the boundless
    deep
Turns again home.
Crossing the Bar [1889], st. 1, 2

3 Twilight and evening bell,
And after that the dark.   *Crossing the Bar, st. 3*

4 I hope to see my Pilot face to face
When I have crossed the bar.
Crossing the Bar, st. 4

Robert Charles Winthrop
1809–1894

5   Our Country—whether bounded by the St.
John's and the Sabine, or however otherwise
bounded[1] or described, and be the measurements
more or less—still our Country, to be cherished in
all our hearts, to be defended by all our hands.
Toast at Faneuil Hall [Fourth of July, 1845]

6   A star for every State, and a State for every star.
Address on Boston Common [1862]

Henry Alford
1810–1871

7 Come, ye thankful people, come,
Raise the song of harvest-home;
All is safely gathered in,
Ere the winter storms begin.
Come, Ye Thankful People, Come [1844]

8 Ten thousand times ten thousand
In sparkling raiment bright,
The armies of the ransomed saints
Throng up the steeps of light:
'Tis finished! all is finished,
Their fight with death and sin:

---

[1]The United States—bounded on the north by the Aurora Bo-
realis, on the south by the precession of the equinoxes, on the east
by the primeval chaos, and on the west by the Day of Judgment.—
JOHN FISKE [1842–1901], *Bounding the United States*

Fling open wide the golden gates,
And let the victors in.   *Hymn [1867], st. 1*

Pierre [Jean François Joseph] Bosquet
1810–1861

9   It is magnificent, but it is not war.[2]
*On the charge of the Light Brigade at
Balaklava [October 25, 1854]*

Sir Francis Hastings Doyle
1810–1888

10 Last night, among his fellow roughs,
He jested, quaffed, and swore;
A drunken private of the Buffs,
Who never looked before.
Today, beneath the foeman's frown,
He stands in Elgin's place,
Ambassador from Britain's crown,
And type of all her race.
The Private of the Buffs, st. 1

Margaret Fuller
1810–1850

11   I myself am more divine than any I see.
Letter to Emerson [March 1, 1838]

12   It does not follow because many books are written by persons born in America that there exists an
American literature. Books which imitate or represent the thoughts and life of Europe do not constitute an American literature. Before such can exist,
an original idea must animate this nation and fresh
currents of life must call into life fresh thoughts
along its shores.
Papers on Literature and Art [1846]

13   I now know all the people worth knowing in
America, and I find no intellect comparable to my
own.
*Memoirs of Margaret Fuller Ossoli [1852],
vol. I, pt. 4*

14   For precocity some great price is always demanded
sooner or later in life.
Diary. From THOMAS WENTWORTH
HIGGINSON, *Life of Margaret Fuller Ossoli
[1884], ch. 18*

---

[2]C'est magnifique, mais ce n'est pas la guerre.
See Tennyson, 484:24.

1   Genius will live and thrive without training, but it does not the less reward the watering pot and pruning knife.
> *Diary. From* THOMAS WENTWORTH HIGGINSON, *Life of Margaret Fuller Ossoli, 18*

2   I accept the universe.[1]   *Attributed*

Elizabeth Cleghorn Gaskell
1810–1865

3   A man is *so* in the way in the house.
> *Cranford [1851–1853], ch. 1*

4   A little credulity helps one on through life very smoothly.   *Cranford, 11*

5   I'll not listen to reason. . . . Reason always means what someone else has got to say.
> *Cranford, 14*

James Sloan Gibbons
1810–1892

6 We are coming, Father Abraham, three hundred thousand more.
> *Three Hundred Thousand More [1862],[2] st. 1*

William Miller
1810–1872

7 Wee Willie Winkie rins through the town,
Upstairs and downstairs, in his nichtgown,
Tirlin' at the window, cryin' at the lock,
"Are the weans in their bed? for it's now ten o'clock."   *Willie Winkie*

Alfred de Musset
1810–1857

8 I have come too late into a world too old.[3]
> *Rolla [1833]*

9   Do Not Trifle with Love.[4]
> *Title of a comedy [1834]*

10 The most despairing songs are the loveliest of all,
I know immortal ones composed only of tears.
> *Poésies Nouvelles. La Nuit de Mai [1835]*

11   How glorious it is, but how painful it is also, to be exceptional in this world!
> *La Merle Blanc [1842]*

Theodore Parker
1810–1860

12   Truth never yet fell dead in the streets; it has such affinity with the soul of man, the seed however broadcast will catch somewhere and produce its hundredfold.
> *A Discourse of Matters Pertaining to Religion [1842]*

13   A democracy—that is a government of all the people, by all the people, for all the people;[5] of course, a government of the principles of eternal justice, the unchanging law of God; for shortness' sake I will call it the idea of Freedom.
> *The American Idea [May 29, 1850][6]*

Robert [Alexander] Schumann
1810–1856

14   Hats off, gentlemen—a genius!
> *On first hearing Frédéric Chopin's music [1831]*

Edmund Hamilton Sears
1810–1876

15 It came upon the midnight clear,
That glorious song of old,
From angels bending near the earth
To touch their harps of gold:
"Peace on the earth, good will to men
From heav'n's all-gracious King."
The world in solemn stillness lay
To hear the angels sing.
> *The Angel's Song [1850], st. 1*

Martin Farquhar Tupper
1810–1889

16 Error is a hardy plant: it flourisheth in every soil.
> *Proverbial Philosophy [1838–1842]. Of Truth in Things False*

---

[1]By God! she'd better. — *Thomas Carlyle's reported comment*

[2]Song to help raise volunteers for the Union Army.

[3]Je suis venu trop tard dans un monde trop vieux.

[4]On Ne Badine Pas avec l'Amour.

[5]Parker used the same phrase in a speech delivered in Boston [May 31, 1854] and in a sermon in the Music Hall, Boston [July 4, 1858]. William H. Herndon visited Boston and on his return to Springfield, Illinois, took with him some of Parker's sermons and addresses. In his *Abraham Lincoln, vol. II, p. 65,* Herndon says that Lincoln marked with pencil the portion of the Music Hall address, "Democracy is direct self-government, over all the people, by all the people, for all the people."

[6]Speech at the New England Anti-Slavery Convention, Boston.

1 Well-timed silence hath more eloquence than speech.
Proverbial Philosophy. Of Discretion

2 A good book is the best of friends, the same today and forever.
Proverbial Philosophy. Of Reading

3 Nature's own Nobleman, friendly and frank,
Is a man with his heart in his hand!
Nature's Nobleman [1844], st. 1

John Bright
1811–1889

4 Force is not a remedy.
Speech at Birmingham [November 16, 1880]

5 My opinion is that the Northern States will manage somehow to muddle through.
Said during the American Civil War. From JUSTIN MCCARTHY, *Reminiscences [1899]*

6 He [Benjamin Disraeli] is a self-made man and worships his creator.   *Attributed*

Fanny Fern
[Sara Payson Parton]
1811–1872

7 The way to a man's heart is through his stomach.   *Fern Leaves [1853]*

Théophile Gautier
1811–1872

8 Everything passes — Robust art
Alone is eternal.
The bust
Survives the city.[1]   *L'Art [1832]*

Horace Greeley
1811–1872

9 The best business you can go into you will find on your father's farm or in his workshop. If you have no family or friends to aid you, and no prospect opened to you there, turn your face to the great West,[2] and there build up a home and fortune.
From JAMES PARTON, *Life of Horace Greeley [1855]. To Aspiring Young Men*

10 The illusion that times that were are better than those that are, has probably pervaded all ages.
The American Conflict [1864–1866]

11 I never said all Democrats were saloon keepers. What I said was that all saloon keepers were Democrats.   *Attributed*

Wendell Phillips
1811–1884

12 Revolutions are not made; they come. A revolution is as natural a growth as an oak. It comes out of the past. Its foundations are laid far back.
Speech [January 8, 1852]

13 The best use of laws is to teach men to trample bad laws under their feet.
Speech [April 12, 1852]

14 One on God's side is a majority.[3]
Speech [November 1, 1859]

15 Every man meets his Waterloo at last.
Speech [November 1, 1859]

16 Whether in chains or in laurels, Liberty knows nothing but victories.
Speech [November 1, 1859]

17 Truth is one forever absolute, but opinion is truth filtered through the moods, the blood, the disposition of the spectator.
Idols [October 4, 1859]

Harriet Beecher Stowe[4]
1811–1896

18 Eliza made her desperate retreat across the river just in the dusk of twilight. The gray mist of evening, rising slowly from the river, enveloped her as she disappeared up the bank, and the swollen current and floundering masses of ice presented a hopeless barrier between her and her pursuer.
Uncle Tom's Cabin [1852], ch. 8

19 I [Topsy] 'spect I growed. Don't think nobody never made me.   *Uncle Tom's Cabin, 20*

20 My soul an't yours, Mas'r! You haven't bought it, — ye can't buy it! It's been bought and paid for, by one that is able to keep it.
Uncle Tom's Cabin, 33

21 I did not write it. God wrote it. I merely did His dictation.
Uncle Tom's Cabin [1879], Introduction

---

[1] Tout passe — L'art robuste / Seul a l'éternité; / Le buste / Survit à la cité.

[2] See Soule, 503:4.

[3] See John Knox, 150:10.

[4] So you're the little woman who wrote the book that made this great war! — ABRAHAM LINCOLN, *on meeting the author of Uncle Tom's Cabin. Attributed*

Charles Sumner
1811–1874

1   Where Slavery is, there Liberty cannot be; and where Liberty is, there Slavery cannot be.

Slavery and the Rebellion; speech at Cooper Institute [November 5, 1864]

2   There is the National flag. He must be cold, indeed, who can look upon its folds rippling in the breeze without pride of country. If in a foreign land, the flag is companionship, and country itself, with all its endearments.

Are We a Nation? [November 19, 1867]

William Makepeace Thackeray
1811–1863

3   This I set down as a positive truth. A woman with fair opportunities, and without a positive hump, may marry whom she likes.[1]

Vanity Fair [1847–1848], vol. I, ch. 4

4   Them's my sentiments.   *Vanity Fair, I, 21*

5   Everybody in Vanity Fair must have remarked how well those live who are comfortably and thoroughly in debt; how they deny themselves nothing; how jolly and easy they are in their minds.

Vanity Fair, I, 22

6   How to Live Well on Nothing a Year.

Vanity Fair, I, 36 (title)

7   I think I could be a good woman if I had five thousand a year.   *Vanity Fair, II, 1*

8   Ah! *Vanitas vanitatum!* Which of us is happy in this world? Which of us has his desire? or, having it, is satisfied? — Come, children, let us shut up the box and the puppets, for our play is played out.

Vanity Fair, II, 27

9   He who meanly admires mean things is a Snob.

The Book of Snobs [1848], ch. 2

10   Rake's Progress.[2]

Pendennis [1848–1850], ch. 19 (title)

11   Yes, I am a fatal man, Madame Fribsbi. To inspire hopeless passion is my destiny.

Pendennis, 23

---

[1]I should like to see any kind of a man, distinguishable from a gorilla, that some good and even pretty woman could not shape a husband out of. — OLIVER WENDELL HOLMES, *The Professor at the Breakfast-Table* [1860]

The whole world is strewn with snares, traps, gins and pitfalls for the capture of men by women. — GEORGE BERNARD SHAW, *Man and Superman* [1903], Epistle Dedicatory

[2]The Rake's Progress. — WILLIAM HOGARTH [1697–1764], *title of series of paintings and engravings* [1735]

12   Remember, it's as easy to marry a rich woman a a poor woman.   *Pendennis, 2*

13   Of the Corporation of the Goosequill — of th Press . . . of the fourth estate. . . . There she is — the great engine — she never sleeps. She has her am bassadors in every quarter of the world — her couri ers upon every road. Her officers march along wit armies, and her envoys walk into statesmen's cabi nets. They are ubiquitous.   *Pendennis, 3*

14   'Tis not the dying for a faith that's so hard Master Harry — every man of every nation has don that — 'tis the living up to it that's difficult.

Henry Esmond [1852], bk. I, ch.

15   'Tis strange what a man may do, and a woma yet think him an angel.   *Henry Esmond, I,*

16   The wicked are wicked, no doubt, and they g astray and they fall, and they come by their deserts but who can tell the mischief which the very virtu ous do?   *The Newcomes [1853–1855], ch. 2*

17 This Bouillabaisse a noble dish is —
A sort of soup, or broth, or brew.

Ballads [1855]. The Ballad of Bouillabaisse, st. 2

18 Charlotte, having seen his body
Borne before her on a shutter,
Like a well-conducted person,
Went on cutting bread and butter.

Ballads. Sorrows of Werther

19   A pedigree reaching as far back as the Deluge.

The Rose and the Ring [1855], ch.

20   The book of female logic is blotted all over wit tears, and Justice in their courts is forever in a pas sion.   *The Virginians [1857–1859], ch.*

21   Women like not only to conquer, but to be con quered.   *The Virginians,*

22   Next to the very young, I suppose the very ol are the most selfish.   *The Virginians, 6*

23   To endure is greater than to dare; to tire ou hostile fortune; to be daunted by no difficulty; t keep heart when all have lost it; to go through in trigue spotless; to forgo even ambition when th end is gained — who can say this is not greatness?

The Virginians, 9

24   Bravery never goes out of fashion.

The Four Georges [1860]. George I

25   It is to the middle class we must look for th safety of England.

The Four Georges. George II

---

[3]See Goethe, 363:11.

1 George, be a King!
The Four Georges. Princess Augusta to her son
George III

Robert Browning
1812–1889

2 The year's at the spring
And day's at the morn;
Morning's at seven;
The hillside's dew-pearled;
The lark's on the wing;
The snail's on the thorn:
God's in his heaven—
All's right with the world.
Pippa Passes [1841], pt. I

3 Speak to me—not of me!   *Pippa Passes, I*

4 Some unsuspected isle in far-off seas.
Pippa Passes, II

5 In the morning of the world,
When earth was nigher heaven than now.
Pippa Passes, III

6 All service ranks the same with God:
With God, whose puppets, best and worst,
Are we; there is no last nor first.
Pippa Passes, IV

7 You know, we French stormed Ratisbon.
Incident of the French Camp [1842], st. 1

8 "You're wounded!" "Nay," the soldier's pride
Touched to the quick, he said:
"I'm killed, Sire!" And his chief beside,
Smiling the boy fell dead.
Incident of the French Camp, st. 5

9 That's my last Duchess painted on the wall,
Looking as if she were alive.
My Last Duchess [1842], l. 1

10   She had
A heart—how shall I say?—too soon made glad.
My Last Duchess, l. 21

11   I gave commands;
Then all smiles stopped together.
My Last Duchess, l. 45

12 Marching along, fifty-score strong,
Great-hearted gentlemen, singing this song.
Cavalier Tunes [1842]. Marching Along, st. 1

13 Boot, saddle, to horse, and away!
Cavalier Tunes. Boot and Saddle, refrain

14   Just my vengeance complete,
The man sprang to his feet,

Stood erect, caught at God's skirts, and prayed!
—So, *I* was afraid!
Instans Tyrannus [1845], st. 7

15 Hamelin Town's in Brunswick,
By famous Hanover city.
The Pied Piper of Hamelin [1845], st. 1

16   Rats!
They fought the dogs and killed the cats,
And bit the babies in the cradles,
And ate the cheeses out of the vats,
And licked the soup from the cooks' own ladles.
The Pied Piper of Hamelin, st. 2

17 And out of the houses the rats came tumbling.
Great rats, small rats, lean rats, brawny rats,
Brown rats, black rats, gray rats, tawny rats.
Grave old plodders, gay young friskers,
Fathers, mothers, uncles, cousins,
Cocking tails and pricking whiskers,
Families by tens and dozens,
Brothers, sisters, husbands, wives—
Followed the Piper for their lives.
The Pied Piper of Hamelin, st. 7

18 When the liquor's out, why clink the cannikin?
The Flight of the Duchess [1845], st. 16

19 It's a long lane that knows no turnings.
The Flight of the Duchess, st. 17

20 Just for a handful of silver he left us,
Just for a riband to stick in his coat.
The Lost Leader[1] [1845], st. 1

21 We that had loved him so, followed him, honored
him,
Lived in his mild and magnificent eye,
Learned his great language, caught his clear
accents,
Made him our pattern to live and to die!
The Lost Leader, st. 1

22 Shakespeare was of us, Milton was for us,
Burns, Shelley, were with us—they watch from
their graves!
The Lost Leader, st. 1

23 One more devils'-triumph and sorrow for angels,
One more wrong to man, one more insult to God!
The Lost Leader, st. 2

24   Let him never come back to us!
There would be doubt, hesitation and pain,
Forced praise on our part—the glimmer of
twilight,
Never glad confident morning again!
The Lost Leader, st. 2

---

[1]Often assumed to refer to Wordsworth.

1 It was roses, roses all the way.

> *The Patriot [1845], st. 1*

2 I sprang to the stirrup, and Joris, and he;
I galloped, Dirck galloped, we galloped all three.

> *How They Brought the Good News from Ghent
> to Aix [1845], st. 1*

3 Round the cape of a sudden came the sea,
And the sun looked over the mountain's rim:
And straight was a path of gold for him,
And the need of a world of men for me.

> *Parting at Morning [1845]*

4 Oh, to be in England now that April's there,
And whoever wakes in England sees, some morn-
ing, unaware,
That the lowest boughs and the brushwood sheaf
Round the elm tree bole are in tiny leaf,
While the chaffinch sings on the orchard bough
In England—now!

> *Home Thoughts, from Abroad [1845], l. 1*

5 That's the wise thrush; he sings each song twice
over,
Lest you should think he never could recapture
The first fine careless rapture!

> *Home Thoughts, from Abroad, l. 14*

6 Nobly, nobly Cape Saint Vincent to the northwest
died away;
Sunset ran, one glorious blood-red, reeking into
Cadiz Bay.

> *Home Thoughts, from the Sea [1845], l. 1*

7 The Savior at his sermon on the mount,
Saint Praxed in a glory, and one Pan
Ready to twitch the Nymph's last garment off.

> *The Bishop Orders His Tomb at Saint Praxed's
> Church [1845], l. 59*

8 And then how I shall lie through centuries,
And hear the blessed mutter of the mass,
And see God made and eaten all day long,
And feel the steady candle flame, and taste
Good strong thick stupefying incense smoke!

> *The Bishop Orders His Tomb at Saint Praxed's
> Church, l. 80*

9 Let's contend no more, Love,
Strive nor weep:
All be as before, Love,
—Only sleep!

> *A Woman's Last Word [1855], st. 1*

10 Where the quiet-colored end of evening smiles.

> *Love Among the Ruins [1855], st. 1*

11 Oh heart! oh blood that freezes, blood that burns!
Earth's returns
For whole centuries of folly, noise and sin!
Shut them in,

With their triumphs and their glories and the rest!
Love is best!   *Love Among the Ruins, st.*

12 Your ghost will walk, you lover of trees,
(If our loves remain)
In an English lane.   *De Gustibus [1855], st.*

13 Open my heart, and you will see
Graved inside of it, "Italy."

> *De Gustibus, st.*

14   Only I discern
Infinite passion, and the pain
Of finite hearts that yearn.

> *Two in the Campagna [1855], st. 12*

15 Escape me?
Never—
Beloved!
While I am I, and you are you.

> *Life in a Love [1855], l.*

16 To dry one's eyes and laugh at a fall,
And baffled, get up and begin again.

> *Life in a Love, l. 13*

17 Ah, did you once see Shelley plain,
And did he stop and speak to you,
And did you speak to him again?
How strange it seems, and new![1]

> *Memorabilia [1855], st. 1*

18 What's become of Waring
Since he gave us all the slip?

> *Waring [1855], pt. I, st. 1*

19 In Vishnu-land what Avatar?

> *Waring, I, st. 6*

20 Who knows but the world may end tonight?

> *The Last Ride Together [1855], st. 2*

21 The instant made eternity—
And heaven just prove that I and she
Ride, ride together, forever ride?

> *The Last Ride Together, st. 10*

22 He said, "What's time? Leave Now for dogs and
apes!
Man has Forever."

> *A Grammarian's Funeral [1855], l. 81*

23 He ventured neck or nothing—heaven's success
Found, or earth's failure.

> *A Grammarian's Funeral, l. 109*

24 That low man seeks a little thing to do,
Sees it and does it;
This high man, with a great thing to pursue,

---

[1] And did you once find Browning plain? / And did he really
seem quite clear? / And did you read the book again? / How
strange it seems, and queer.—CHARLES WILLIAM STUBBS [1845–
1912], *Parody*

Dies ere he knows it.
That low man goes on adding one to one,
His hundred's soon hit;
This high man, aiming at a million,
Misses an unit.
That, has the world here — should he need the
      next,
Let the world mind him!
This, throws himself on God, and unperplexed
Seeking shall find Him.
> *A Grammarian's Funeral, l. 113*

1 A common grayness silvers everything.
> *Andrea del Sarto [1855], l. 35*

2   Days decrease,
And autumn grows, autumn in everything.
> *Andrea del Sarto, l. 44*

3 Less is more.[1]   *Andrea del Sarto, l. 78*

4 Ah, but a man's reach should exceed his grasp,
Or what's a heaven for?
> *Andrea del Sarto, l. 97*

5 I am grown peaceful as old age tonight.
> *Andrea del Sarto, l. 244*

6   Truth that peeps
Over the glasses' edge when dinner's done.
> *Bishop Blougram's Apology [1855], l. 17*

7 The common problem, yours, mine, everyone's,
Is — not to fancy what were fair in life
Provided it could be — but, finding first
What may be, then find how to make it fair
Up to our means.
> *Bishop Blougram's Apology, l. 87*

8 Just when we are safest, there's a sunset touch,
A fancy from a flower bell, someone's death,
A chorus ending from Euripides.
> *Bishop Blougram's Apology, l. 183*

9 Our interest's on the dangerous edge of things.
The honest thief, the tender murderer,
The superstitious atheist, demirep
That loves and saves her soul in new French books.
> *Bishop Blougram's Apology, l. 396*

10   You call for faith:
I show you doubt, to prove that faith exists.
The more of doubt, the stronger faith, I say,
If faith o'ercomes doubt.
> *Bishop Blougram's Apology, l. 601*

11 No, when the fight begins within himself,
A man's worth something.
> *Bishop Blougram's Apology, l. 693*

---

[1] A popular aphorism with the architect Ludwig Mies van der Rohe.

12 While you sat and played toccatas, stately at the
      clavichord.
> *A Toccata of Galuppi's [1855], st. 6*

13 What of soul was left, I wonder, when the kissing
      had to stop?
> *A Toccata of Galuppi's, st. 14*

14 Dear dead women, with such hair, too — what's be-
      come of all the gold
Used to hang and brush their bosoms? I feel chilly
      and grown old.
> *A Toccata of Galuppi's, st. 15*

15 Stake your counter as boldly every whit,
Venture as warily, use the same skill,
Do your best, whether winning or losing it,
If you choose to play!
> *The Statue and the Bust [1855], l. 238*

16 How good is man's life, the mere living! how fit to
      employ
All the heart and the soul and the senses forever in
      joy!   *Saul [1855], st. 9*

17 Death was past, life not come: so he waited.
> *Saul, st. 10*

18   God is seen God
In the star, in the stone, in the flesh, in the soul
      and the clod.   *Saul, st. 17*

19 Do I find love so full in my nature, God's ultimate
      gift,
That I doubt his own love can compete with it?
      Here, the parts shift?
> *Saul, st. 17*

20 'Tis not what man does which exalts him, but what
      man would do!   *Saul, st. 18*

21 Thou shalt love and be loved by, forever: a Hand
      like this hand
Shall throw open the gates of new life to thee! See
      the Christ stand!   *Saul, st. 18*

22 Why stay we on the earth except to grow?
> *Cleon [1855], l. 114*

23   We're made so that we love
First when we see them painted, things we have
      passed
Perhaps a hundred times nor cared to see;
And so they are better, painted — better to us,
Which is the same thing. Art was given for that.
> *Fra Lippo Lippi [1855], l. 300*

24 Rafael made a century of sonnets.
> *One Word More [1855], pt. 2*

25 Does he paint? he fain would write a poem —
Does he write? he fain would paint a picture.
> *One Word More, 8*

1 Where my heart lies, let my brain lie also.
    One Word More, 14

2 Oh, their Rafael of the dear Madonnas,
    Oh, their Dante of the dread Inferno,
    Wrote one song—and in my brain I sing it,
    Drew one angel—borne, see, on my bosom!
    One Word More, 19

3 That out of three sounds he frame, not a fourth
    sound, but a star.   *Abt Vogler [1864], st. 7*

4 On the earth the broken arcs; in the heaven, a
    perfect round.   *Abt Vogler, st. 9*

5 The high that proved too high, the heroic for earth
    too hard,
    The passion that left the ground to lose itself in the
    sky,
    Are music sent up to God by the lover and the
    bard.   *Abt Vogler, st. 10*

6 The C Major of this life.   *Abt Vogler, st. 12*

7 Grow old along with me!
    The best is yet to be,
    The last of life, for which the first was made.
    Our times are in his hand.
    Rabbi Ben Ezra [1864], st. 1

8 Irks care the crop-full bird? Frets doubt the maw-
    crammed beast?   *Rabbi Ben Ezra, st. 4*

9 Then welcome each rebuff
    That turns earth's smoothness rough,
    Each sting that bids nor sit nor stand, but go!
    Be our joys three parts pain!
    Strive, and hold cheap the strain;
    Learn, nor account the pang; dare, never grudge
    the throe!   *Rabbi Ben Ezra, st. 6*

10 What I aspired to be,
    And was not, comforts me.
    Rabbi Ben Ezra, st. 7

11 Therefore I summon age
    To grant youth's heritage.
    Rabbi Ben Ezra, st. 13

12 Look not thou down but up!
    Rabbi Ben Ezra, st. 30

13 Such ever was love's way: to rise, it stoops.
    A Death in the Desert [1864], l. 134

14 Progress, man's distinctive mark alone,
    Not God's, and not the beasts': God is, they are;
    Man partly is, and wholly hopes to be.
    A Death in the Desert, l. 586

15 Setebos, Setebos, and Setebos!
    'Thinketh, He dwelleth i' the cold o' the moon.
    Caliban upon Setebos [1864], l. 24

16 The best way to escape His ire
    Is, not to seem too happy.
    Caliban upon Setebos, l. 256

17 How sad and bad and mad it was—
    But then, how it was sweet!
    Confessions [1864], st. 9

18 Fear death?—to feel the fog in my throat,
    The mist in my face.   *Prospice [1864], l. 1*

19 No! let me taste the whole of it, fare like my peers,
    The heroes of old,
    Bear the brunt, in a minute pay glad life's arrears
    Of pain, darkness, and cold.   *Prospice, l. 17*

20 This could but have happened once—
    And we missed it, lost it forever.
    Youth and Art [1864], st. 17

21 We find great things are made of little things,
    And little things go lessening till at last
    Comes God behind them.
    Mr. Sludge, "The Medium" [1864], l. 1112

22 'Tis because stiffish cock-tail, taken in time,
    Is better for a bruise than arnica.
    Mr. Sludge, "The Medium," l. 1478

23 O Lyric Love, half angel and half bird,
    And all a wonder and a wild desire.
    *The Ring and the Book [1868–1869], bk. I,
    l. 1391*

24 That's all we may expect of man, this side
    The grave: his good is—knowing he is bad.
    *The Ring and the Book, VI, Giuseppe
    Caponsacchi, l. 142*

25 'Twas a thief said the last kind word to Christ:
    Christ took the kindness and forgave the theft.
    *The Ring and the Book, VI, Giuseppe
    Caponsacchi, l. 869*

26 All poetry is difficult to read,
    —The sense of it is, anyhow.
    The Ring and the Book, VII, Pompilia, l. 1154

27   Through such souls alone
    God stooping shows sufficient of His light
    For us i' the dark to rise by. And I rise.
    The Ring and the Book, VII, Pompilia, l. 1843

28 Faultless to a fault.
    *The Ring and the Book, IX, Juris Doctor
    Johannes-Baptista Bottinius, l. 1175*

29   The curious crime, the fine
    Felicity and flower of wickedness.
    The Ring and the Book, X, The Pope, l. 589

30   What I call God,
    And fools call Nature.
    The Ring and the Book, X, The Pope, l. 1072

1 Why comes temptation, but for man to meet
  And master and make crouch beneath his foot,
  And so be pedestaled in triumph?
  The Ring and the Book, X, The Pope, l. 1184

2 White shall not neutralize the black, nor good
  Compensate bad in man, absolve him so:
  Life's business being just the terrible choice.
  The Ring and the Book, X, The Pope, l. 1235

3 You never know what life means till you die:
  Even throughout life, 'tis death that makes life live,
  Gives it whatever the significance.
  The Ring and the Book, XI, Guido, l. 2373

4 Save the squadron, honor France, love thy wife the
  Belle Aurore!   *Hervé Riel [1871], st. 11*

5 A man in armor is his armor's slave.
  Herakles [1871]

6 So absolutely good is truth, truth never hurts
  The teller.   *Fifine at the Fair [1872], st. 32*

7   That far land we dream about,
  Where every man is his own architect.
  Red Cotton Nightcap Country [1873], pt. II

8   A secret's safe
  'Twixt you, me, and the gatepost!
  The Inn Album [1875], II

9 Ignorance is not innocence but sin.
  The Inn Album, V

10 Have you found your life distasteful?
  My life did and does smack sweet.
  Was your youth of pleasure wasteful?
  Mine I saved and hold complete.
  Do your joys with age diminish?
  When mine fail me, I'll complain.
  Must in death your daylight finish?
  My sun sets to rise again.
  At the "Mermaid" [1876], st. 10

11 Out of the wreck I rise.   *Ixion [1883], l. 121*

12 Never the time and the place
  And the loved one all together!
  Never the Time and the Place [1883]

13 But little do or can the best of us:
  That little is achieved through Liberty.
  Why I Am a Liberal [1885], l. 9

14 A minute's success pays the failure of years.
  Apollo and the Fates [1886], st. 42

15 One who never turned his back but marched breast
    forward,
  Never doubted clouds would break,
  Never dreamed though right were worsted, wrong
    would triumph,

Held we fall to rise, are baffled to fight better,
Sleep to wake.   *Asolando [1889]. Epilogue, st. 3*

Samuel Dickinson Burchard
1812–1891

16   We are Republicans, and don't propose to leave
our party and identify ourselves with the party
whose antecedents have been Rum, Romanism, and
Rebellion.
  Speaking for a deputation of clergymen calling
  upon James G. Blaine, the Republican
  presidential candidate, in New York [October
  29, 1884]

Charles Dickens
1812–1870

17   A smattering of everything, and a knowledge of
nothing.   *Sketches by Boz [1836–1837]. Tales, ch. 3*

18   He had used the word [humbug] in its Pickwickian sense.
  Pickwick Papers [1836–1837], ch. 1

19   "An observer of human nature, sir," said Mr.
Pickwick.   *Pickwick Papers, 2*

20   "It wasn't the wine," murmured Mr. Snodgrass,
in a broken voice. "It was the salmon."
  Pickwick Papers, 8

21   I wants to make your flesh creep.
  Pickwick Papers, 8

22   Tongue; well that's a wery good thing when it
an't a woman's.   *Pickwick Papers, 19*

23   Be wery careful o' widders all your life.
  Pickwick Papers, 20

24   I took a good deal o' pains with his eddication,
sir; let him run in the streets when he was very
young, and shift for hisself. It's the only way to
make a boy sharp, sir.   *Pickwick Papers, 20*

25   The wictim o' connubiality, as Blue Beard's domestic chaplain said, with a tear of pity, ven he
buried him.   *Pickwick Papers, 20*

26   Dumb as a drum vith a hole in it, sir.
  Pickwick Papers, 25

27   Eccentricities of genius.   *Pickwick Papers, 30*

28   Keep yourself *to* yourself.   *Pickwick Papers, 32*

29   Poetry's unnat'ral; no man ever talked poetry
'cept a beadle on Boxin' Day.
  Pickwick Papers, 33

1   She'll wish there was more, and that's the great art o' letter-writin'.   *Pickwick Papers, 33*

2   Never mind the character, and stick to the alleybi.   *Pickwick Papers, 33*

3   She knows wot's wot, she does.   *Pickwick Papers, 37*

4   *They* don't mind it; it's a regular holiday to them—all porter and skittles.[1]   *Pickwick Papers, 41*

5   Anythin' for a quiet life, as the man said wen he took the sitivation at the lighthouse.   *Pickwick Papers, 43*

6   Right as a trivet.   *Pickwick Papers, 50*

7   Oliver Twist has asked for more!   *Oliver Twist [1837–1838], ch. 2*

8   "The artful Dodger."   *Oliver Twist, 8*

9   "Hard," replied the Dodger. "As nails," added Charley Bates.   *Oliver Twist, 9*

10   There is a passion for hunting something deeply implanted in the human breast.   *Oliver Twist, 10*

11   I'll eat my head.   *Oliver Twist, 10*

12   I only know two sorts of boys. Mealy boys, and beef-faced boys.   *Oliver Twist, 10*

13   There's light enough for wot I've got to do.   *Oliver Twist, 47*

14   "If the law supposes that," said Mr. Bumble . . . "the law is a ass, a idiot."   *Oliver Twist, 51*

15   He had but one eye, and the popular prejudice runs in favor of two.   *Nicholas Nickleby [1838–1839], ch. 4*

16   Subdue your appetites, my dears, and you've conquered human natur.   *Nicholas Nickleby, 5*

17   There are only two styles of portrait painting; the serious and the smirk.   *Nicholas Nickleby, 10*

18   Oh! they're too beautiful to live, much too beautiful!   *Nicholas Nickleby, 14*

19   I pity his ignorance and despise him.   *Nicholas Nickleby, 15*

20   The infant phenomenon.   *Nicholas Nickleby, 23*

21   The unities, sir . . . are a completeness—a kind of universal dove-tailedness with regard to place and time.   *Nicholas Nickleby, 24*

22   The two countesses had no outlines at all, and the dowager's was a demd outline.   *Nicholas Nickleby, 34*

23   A demd, damp, moist, unpleasant body!   *Nicholas Nickleby, 34*

24   Bring in the bottled lightning, a clean tumbler, and a corkscrew.   *Nicholas Nickleby, 49*

25   All is gas and gaiters.   *Nicholas Nickleby, 49*

26   My life is one demd horrid grind.   *Nicholas Nickleby, 64*

27   He has gone to the demnition bowwows.   *Nicholas Nickleby, 64*

28   What is the odds so long as the fire of soul is kindled at the taper of conwiviality, and the wing of friendship never moults a feather!   *The Old Curiosity Shop [1841], ch. 2*

29   She's the ornament of her sex.   *The Old Curiosity Shop, 5*

30   In love of home, the love of country has its rise.   *The Old Curiosity Shop, 38*

31   That vague kind of penitence which holidays awaken next morning.   *The Old Curiosity Shop, 40*

32   "Did you ever taste beer?" "I had a sip of it once," said the small servant. "Here's a state of things!" cried Mr. Swiveller. . . . "She *never* tasted it—it can't be tasted in a sip!"   *The Old Curiosity Shop, 57*

33   It was a maxim with Foxey—our revered father, gentlemen—"Always suspect everybody."   *The Old Curiosity Shop, 66*

34   Rather a tough customer in argyment.   *Barnaby Rudge [1841], ch. 1*

35   "There are strings," said Mr. Tappertit, ". . . in the human heart that had better not be wibrated."   *Barnaby Rudge, 22*

36   Oh gracious, why wasn't I born old and ugly?   *Barnaby Rudge, 70*

37   Any man may be in good spirits and good temper when he's well dressed. There ain't much credit in that.   *Martin Chuzzlewit [1843–1844], ch. 5*

38   With affection beaming in one eye, and calculation shining out of the other.   *Martin Chuzzlewit, 8*

39   "Do not repine, my friends," said Mr. Pecksniff tenderly. "Do not weep for me. It is chronic."   *Martin Chuzzlewit, 9*

40   Keep up appearances whatever you do.   *Martin Chuzzlewit, 11*

---

[1]Life is with such all beer and skittles; / They are not difficult to please / About their victuals.—CHARLES STUART CALVERLEY [1831–1884], *Contentment*

Life ain't all beer and skittles, and more's the pity. — GEORGE DU MAURIER, *Trilby* [1894], *pt. I*

1 "Do other men for they would do you." That's the true business precept.

Martin Chuzzlewit, 11

2 Buy an annuity cheap, and make your life interesting to yourself and everybody else that watches the speculation. *Martin Chuzzlewit, 18*

3 Leave the bottle on the chimleypiece, and don't ask me to take none, but let me put my lips to it when I am so dispoged. *Martin Chuzzlewit, 19*

4 Rich folks may ride on camels, but it a'n't so easy for 'em to see out of a needle's eye [Sairey Gamp]. *Martin Chuzzlewit, 25*

5 "She's the sort of woman now," said Mould . . . "one would almost feel disposed to bury for nothing: and do it neatly, too!"

Martin Chuzzlewit, 25

6 He'd make a lovely corpse.

Martin Chuzzlewit, 25

7 Gamp is my name, and Gamp my nater.

Martin Chuzzlewit, 26

8 Our fellow-countryman is a model of a man, quite fresh from Natur's mold!

Martin Chuzzlewit, 34

9 Oh Sairey, Sairey, little do we know wot lays afore us! *Martin Chuzzlewit, 40*

10 I don't believe there's no sich a person!

Martin Chuzzlewit, 49

11 The words she spoke of Mrs. Harris, lambs could not forgive . . . nor worms forget.

Martin Chuzzlewit, 49

12 Oh, but he was a tightfisted hand at the grindstone. Scrooge! a squeezing, wrenching, grasping, scraping, clutching, covetous old sinner! Hard and sharp as flint, from which no steel had ever struck out generous fire; secret, and self-contained, and solitary as an oyster.

A Christmas Carol [1843], stave 1

13 "Bah," said Scrooge. "Humbug!"

A Christmas Carol, 1

14 I wear the chain I forged in life [Marley's Ghost].

A Christmas Carol, 1

15 "I am the Ghost of Christmas Past." "Long past?" inquired Scrooge. . . . "No. Your past."

A Christmas Carol, 2

16 In came a fiddler . . . and tuned like fifty stomachaches. In came Mrs. Fezziwig, one vast substantial smile. *A Christmas Carol, 2*

17 I am the Ghost of Christmas Present.

A Christmas Carol, 3

18 As good as gold [Tiny Tim].

A Christmas Carol, 3

19 "God bless us every one!" said Tiny Tim, the last of all. *A Christmas Carol, 3*

20 "I am in the presence of the Ghost of Christmas Yet to Come?" said Scrooge.

A Christmas Carol, 4

21 I will honor Christmas in my heart, and try to keep it all the year. *A Christmas Carol, 4*

22 It *was* a turkey! He could never have stood upon his legs, that bird! He would have snapped 'em off short in a minute, like sticks of sealing wax.

A Christmas Carol, 5

23 Oh let us love our occupations,
Bless the squire and his relations,
Live upon our daily rations,
And always know our proper stations.
The Chimes [1844], second quarter

24 He's tough, ma'am, tough, is J.B. Tough and devilish sly! *Dombey and Son [1848], ch. 7*

25 "Wal'r, my boy," replied the Captain, "in the Proverbs of Solomon you will find the following words, 'May we never want a friend in need, nor a bottle to give him!' When found, make a note of."

Dombey and Son, 15

26 Cows are my passion. *Dombey and Son, 21*

27 The bearings of this observation lays in the application on it. *Dombey and Son, 23*

28 You'll find us rough, sir, but you'll find us ready.
David Copperfield [1849–1850], ch. 3

29 I am a lone lorn creetur . . . and everythink goes contrariy with me. *David Copperfield, 3*

30 Barkis is willin'. *David Copperfield, 5*

31 Experientia does it[1] — as Papa used to say.

David Copperfield, 11

32 "In case anything turned up," which was his [Mr. Micawber's] favorite expression.

David Copperfield, 11

33 I never will desert Mr. Micawber.

David Copperfield, 12

34 Annual income twenty pounds, annual expenditure nineteen nineteen six, result happiness. Annual income twenty pounds, annual expenditure twenty pounds ought and six, result misery.

David Copperfield, 12

35 It's a mad world. Mad as Bedlam.

David Copperfield, 14

---

[1]Experientia docet [Experience teaches].—TACITUS, *History, bk. V, ch. 6*

1   Never . . . be mean in anything; never be false; never be cruel.   *David Copperfield, 15*

2   I'm a very umble person.[1]

David Copperfield, 16

3   The mistake was made of putting some of the trouble out of King Charles's head into my head.[2]

David Copperfield, 17

4   It was as true . . . as turnips is. It was as true . . . as taxes is. And nothing's truer than them.

David Copperfield, 21

5   What a world of gammon and spinnage it is, though, ain't it!   *David Copperfield, 22*

6   Nobody's enemy but his own.

David Copperfield, 25

7   Accidents will occur in the best-regulated families.   *David Copperfield, 28*

8   Ride on! Rough-shod if need be, smooth-shod if that will do, but ride on! Ride on over all obstacles, and win the race!   *David Copperfield, 28*

9   A long pull, and a strong pull, and a pull all together.   *David Copperfield, 30*

10   He's a-going out with the tide.

David Copperfield, 30

11   I ate umble pie with an appetite.

David Copperfield, 39

12   Let sleeping dogs lie — who wants to rouse 'em?

David Copperfield, 39

13   Skewered through and through with office pens, and bound hand and foot with red tape.

David Copperfield, 43

14   It's only my child-wife.

David Copperfield, 44

15   There can be no disparity in marriage like unsuitability of mind and purpose.

David Copperfield, 45

16   A man must take the fat with the lean.

David Copperfield, 51

17   Trifles make the sum of life.

David Copperfield, 53

18   The seamen said it blew great guns.

David Copperfield, 55

---

[1]Not only humble but umble, which I look upon to be the comparative, or, indeed, superlative degree. — ANTHONY TROLLOPE, *Doctor Thorne* [1858], *ch. 4*

[2]"King Charles's head" has passed into common use in the English language as a phrase meaning some whimsical obsession. — G. B. STERN [1890–1973], *Monogram* [1936]

19   He is an honorable, obstinate, truthful, high spirited, intensely prejudiced, perfectly unreasonabl man.   *Bleak House [1852–1858], ch. :*

20   This is a London particular. . . . A fog, miss.

Bleak House, :

21   Not to put too fine a point upon it.

Bleak House, 1:

22   [Old Mr. Turveydrop] was not like anything ir the world but a model of Deportment.

Bleak House, 14

23   Now, what I want is Facts. Teach these boys anc girls nothing but Facts. Facts alone are wanted ir life. Plant nothing else, and root out everything else

Hard Times [1854], bk. I, ch. I

24   There is a wisdom of the head, and . . . a wisdom of the heart.   *Hard Times, III, I*

25   I am the only child of parents who weighed, measured, and priced everything; for whom what could not be weighed, measured, and priced had no existence.   *Little Dorrit [1857–1858], bk. I, ch. 2*

26   Whatever was required to be done, the Circumlocution Office was beforehand with all the public departments in the art of perceiving — HOW NOT TO DO IT.   *Little Dorrit, I, 10*

27   Papa, potatoes, poultry, prunes, and prism, are all very good words for the lips: especially prunes and prism.

Little Dorrit, II, 5

28   Once a gentleman, and always a gentleman.

Little Dorrit, II, 28

29   It was the best of times, it was the worst of times.

A Tale of Two Cities [1859], bk. I, ch. 1

30   A wonderful fact to reflect upon, that every human creature is constituted to be that profound secret and mystery to every other.

A Tale of Two Cities, I, 3

31   It is a far, far better thing that I do, than I have ever done; it is a far, far better rest that I go to, than I have ever known.

A Tale of Two Cities, III, 15

32   In the little world in which children have their existence, whosoever brings them up, there is nothing so finely perceived and so finely felt, as injustice.

Great Expectations [1860–1861], ch. 8

33   Ever been the best of friends!

Great Expectations, 18

34   My guiding star always is, Get hold of portable property.   *Great Expectations, 24*

1 Take nothing on its looks; take everything on evidence. There's no better rule.
Great Expectations, 40

2 Money and goods are certainly the best of references.
Our Mutual Friend [1864–1865], bk. I, ch. 4

3 People now call him the Golden Dustman [Mr. Boffin].
Our Mutual Friend, I, 11

4 I want to be something so much worthier than the doll in the doll's house.
Our Mutual Friend, I, 55

5 I don't care whether I am a Minx or a Sphinx [Lavvy].
Our Mutual Friend, II, 8

6 That's the state to live and die in! . . . R-r-rich!
Our Mutual Friend, III, 5

7 We must scrunch or be scrunched.
Our Mutual Friend, III, 5

Ivan Aleksandrovich Goncharov
1812–1891

8 "And he was as intelligent as other people, his soul was pure and clear as crystal; he was noble and affectionate — and yet he did nothing!"
"But why? What was the reason?"
"The reason . . . what reason was there? Oblomovism!"
Oblomov [1859], pt. IV, ch. 12

Alexander Ivanovich Herzen
1812–1870

9 Communism is a Russian autocracy turned upside down.
The Development of Revolutionary Ideas in Russia [1851]

10 Russia's future will be a great danger for Europe and a great misfortune for Russia if there is no emancipation of the individual. One more century of present despotism will destroy all the good qualities of the Russian people.
The Development of Revolutionary Ideas in Russia

Edward Lear
1812–1888

11 There was an Old Man with a beard,
Who said: "It is just as I feared!
Two owls and a hen,

Four larks and a wren
Have all built their nests in my beard."
Book of Nonsense [1846]. Limerick

12 How pleasant to know Mr. Lear![1]
Who has written such volumes of stuff!
Some think him ill-tempered and queer,
But a few think him pleasant enough.
Nonsense Songs [1871]. Preface, st. 1

13 He has ears, and two eyes, and ten fingers,
Leastways if you reckon two thumbs;
Long ago he was one of the singers,
But now he is one of the dumbs.
Nonsense Songs. Preface, st. 3

14 His body is perfectly spherical,
He weareth a runcible hat.
Nonsense Songs. Preface, st. 5

15 The Owl and the Pussycat went to sea
In a beautiful pea-green boat,
They took some honey, and plenty of money,
Wrapped up in a five-pound note.
The Owl looked up to the stars above,
And sang to a small guitar,
"O lovely Pussy! O Pussy, my love,
What a beautiful Pussy you are."
The Owl and the Pussycat [1871], st. 1

16 Pussy said to the Owl, "You elegant fowl!
How charmingly sweet you sing!
O let us be married! too long we have tarried:
But what shall we do for a ring?"
They sailed away, for a year and a day,
To the land where the Bong-tree grows
And there in a wood a Piggy-wig stood
With a ring at the end of his nose.
The Owl and the Pussycat, st. 2

17 "Dear Pig, are you willing to sell for one shilling
Your ring?" Said the Piggy, "I will."
The Owl and the Pussycat, st. 3

18 They dined on mince, and slices of quince,
Which they ate with a runcible spoon;
And hand in hand, on the edge of the sand,
They danced by the light of the moon.
The Owl and the Pussycat, st. 3

19 Far and few, far and few,
Are the lands where the Jumblies live;
Their heads are green, and their hands are blue,
And they went to sea in a sieve.
The Jumblies [1871], st. 1

20 Calico Pie,
The little Birds fly
Down to the calico tree,
Their wings were blue,

---

[1]See T. S. Eliot, 720:1.

And they sang "Tilly-loo!"
Till away they flew —
And they never came back to me!
Calico Pie [1871], st. 1

1   Calico Jam,
The little Fish swam,
Over the syllabub sea.   *Calico Pie, st. 2*

2 Who, or why, or which, or what,
Is the Akond of Swat?
The Akond of Swat[1] [1877], l. 1

3 On the top of the Crumpetty Tree
The Quangle Wangle sat,
But his face you could not see,
On account of his Beaver Hat.
The Quangle Wangle's Hat [1877], st. 1

4 On the coast of Coromandel
Where the early pumpkins blow,
In the middle of the woods
Lived the Yonghy-Bonghy-Bò.
Two old chairs, and half a candle,
One old jug without a handle —
These were all his worldly goods.
*The Courtship of the Yonghy-Bonghy-Bò
[1877], st. 1*

5 There he heard a Lady talking,
To some milk-white Hens of Dorking —
"'Tis the Lady Jingly Jones!"
The Courtship of the Yonghy-Bonghy-Bò, st. 2

6 "I would be your wife most gladly!"
(Here she twirled her fingers madly),
"But in England I've a mate!"
The Courtship of the Yonghy-Bonghy-Bò, st. 5

7 When awful darkness and silence reign
Over the great Gromboolian plain,
Through the long, long wintry nights.
The Dong with the Luminous Nose [1877], st. 1

8 When storm-clouds brood on the towering heights
Of the hills of the Chankly Bore.
The Dong with the Luminous Nose, st. 1

9 The Pobble who has no toes
Had once as many as we;
When they said, "Some day you may lose them all" —
He replied, "Fish fiddle-de-dee!"
The Pobble Who Has No Toes [1877], st. 1

10 It's a fact the whole world knows,
That Pobbles are happier without their toes.
The Pobble Who Has No Toes, st. 6

11 Ploffskin, Pluffskin, Pelican jee!
We think no Birds so happy as we!

Plumpskin, Ploshkin, Pelican jill!
We think so then, and we thought so still.
The Pelican Chorus [1877], choru

Samuel Smiles
1812–1904

12   The spirit of self-help is the root of all genuine
growth in the individual; and, exhibited in the lives
of many, it constitutes the true source of national
vigor and strength.   *Self-Help [1859]*

Henry Ward Beecher
1813–1887

13   Where is human nature so weak as in the bookstore!
Star Papers [1855]. Subtleties of Book Buyers

14   A thoughtful mind, when it sees a nation's flag,
sees not the flag only, but the nation itself; and
whatever may be its symbols, its insignia, he reads
chiefly in the flag the government, the principles,
the truths, the history which belongs to the nation
that sets it forth.   *The National Flag [1861]*

15   Now comes the mystery.
Last words [March 8, 1887]

Claude Bernard
1813–1878

16   Observation is a passive science, experimentation
an active science.
*Introduction à l'Étude de la Médecine
Expérimentale [1865][2]*

17   The science of life . . . is a superb and dazzlingly
lighted hall which may be reached only by passing
through a long and ghastly kitchen.
*Introduction à l'Étude de la Médecine
Expérimentale*

18   Our ideas are only intellectual instruments which
we use to break into phenomena; we must change
them when they have served their purpose, as we
change a blunt lancet that we have used long enough.
*Introduction à l'Étude de la Médecine
Expérimentale*

19   A contemporary poet has characterized this
sense of the personality of art and of the impersonality of science in these words — "Art is myself; science is ourselves."
*Introduction à l'Étude de la Médecine
Expérimentale*

---

[1]Pray tell me, good reader, if tell me you can, / What's the
Ahkoond of Swat to you folks or to me? — EUGENE FIELD, *The
Ahkoond of Swat* [1884]

---

[2]*An Introduction to the Study of Experimental Medicine*, translated by HENRY COPLEY GREENE.

1 The stability of the *internal medium* is a primary condition for the freedom and independence of certain living bodies in relation to the environment surrounding them.

Leçons sur les Phénomènes de la Vie Communs aux Animaux et aux Végétaux [1878–1879][1]

2 All the vital mechanisms, varied as they are, have only one object, that of preserving constant the conditions of life in the internal environment.

Leçons sur les Phénomènes de la Vie Communs aux Animaux et aux Végétaux

3 The mental never influences the physical. It is always the physical that modifies the mental, and when we think that the mind is diseased, it is always an illusion.   *Pensées [1937]*

Georg Büchner
1813–1837

4 The Revolution is like Saturn — it eats its own children.   *Danton's Death [1835]*

John William Burgon
1813–1888

5 A rose-red city half as old as time.   *Petra [1845]*

Harriet Ann Jacobs
1813–1897

6 Notwithstanding my grandmother's long and faithful service to her owners, not one of her children escaped the auction block. These God-breathing machines are no more, in the sight of their masters, than the cotton they plant, or the horses they tend.
Incidents in the Life of a Slave-Girl [1861], ch. 1

7 Reader, my story ends with freedom; not in the usual way, with marriage. I and my children are now free.   *Incidents in the Life of a Slave-Girl, 4*

Sören Kierkegaard
1813–1855

8 Philosophy is perfectly right in saying that life must be understood backward. But then one forgets the other clause — that it must be lived forward.   *Journals and Papers [1843]*,[2] *vol. I*

9 The absurd . . . the fact that with God all things are possible. The absurd is not one of the factors which can be discriminated within the proper compass of the understanding: it is not identical with the improbable, the unexpected, the unforeseen.
Fear and Trembling [1843]. Problemata: Preliminary Expectoration

10 All essential knowledge relates to existence, or only such knowledge as has an essential relationship to existence is essential knowledge.
Concluding Unscientific Postscript [1846]

John Louis O'Sullivan
1813–1895

11 Our manifest destiny is to overspread the continent allotted by Providence for the free development of our yearly multiplying millions.
United States Magazine and Democratic Review [July–August 1845]

Richard Wagner
1813–1883

12 O thou, my gracious evening star.
Tannhäuser [1845]

13 To be German means to carry on a matter for its own sake.
Deutsche Kunst und Deutsche Politik [1867]

14 Ride of the Valkyries.   *Die Walküre [1876]*

Thomas Osborne Davis
1814–1845

15 Come in the evening, or come in the morning,
Come when you're looked for, or come without warning.   *The Welcome, st. 1*

Frederick William Faber
1814–1863

16 Faith of our fathers! holy faith!
We will be true to thee till death.
A Pledge of Faithfulness [1849]

17 Hark! Hark! my soul, angelic songs are swelling
O'er earth's green fields, and ocean's wave-beat shore;
How sweet the truth those blessed strains are telling
Of that new life when sin shall be no more!
Pilgrims of the Night [1854][3]

---

[1] *Lessons on Reactions Common to Animals and Plants*, translated by J. M. D. Olmstead.

[2] Translated by Howard V. Hong and Edna H. Hong.

---

[3] Music by Henry T. Smart [1813–1879].

Mikhail Yurievich Lermontov
1814–1841

1   *A Hero of Our Time,* gentlemen, is indeed a portrait, but not of a single individual; it is a portrait composed of all the vices of our generation in the fullness of their development.
> *A Hero of Our Time [1840]. Author's introduction*

2 A solitary sail that rises
White in the blue mist on the foam—
What is it in far lands it prizes?
What does it leave behind at home?
> *A Sail [1841],*[1] *st. 1*

3 Beneath, the azure current floweth,
Above, the golden sunlight glows.
Rebellious, the storms it wooeth,
As if the storms could give repose.   *A Sail, st. 3*

Charles Mackay
1814–1889

4 There's a good time coming, boys!
A good time coming.
> *The Good Time Coming, st. 1*

John Lothrop Motley
1814–1877

5   As long as he [William of Orange] lived, he was the guiding-star of a whole brave nation, and when he died the little children cried in the streets.
> *The Rise of the Dutch Republic [1856], pt. VI, ch. 7*

6   Give us the luxuries of life, and we will dispense with its necessaries.
> *Quoted in* OLIVER WENDELL HOLMES, *The Autocrat of the Breakfast-Table [1858], ch. 6*

Edwin McMasters Stanton
1814–1869

7   Now he [Lincoln] belongs to the ages.
> *On the death of Lincoln [April 15, 1865]*

Otto von Bismarck
1815–1898

8   The great questions of the time are not decided by speeches and majority decisions—that was the error of 1848 and 1849—but by iron and blood.[2]
> *Speech to the Prussian Diet [September 30, 1862]*

9   Only a completely ready state can permit the luxury of a liberal government.   *Speech [1866]*

10   Let us put Germany in the saddle, so to speak—it already knows how to ride.
> *Speech to the North German Reichstag [March 11, 1867]*

11   Politics is the art of the possible.[3]
> *Remark [August 11, 1867]*

12   A conquering army on the border will not be halted by the power of eloquence.
> *Speech to the North German Reichstag [September 24, 1867]*

13   The luxury of one's own opinion.
> *Speech to the Prussian Diet [December 17, 1873]*

14   The right people in the right jobs.
> *Speech to the North German Reichstag [1875]*

15   We Germans fear God, but nothing else in the world.
> *Speech to the Reichstag [February 6, 1888]*

Richard Henry Dana
1815–1882

16 Six days shalt thou labor and do all thou art able,
And on the seventh—holystone the decks and
scrape the cable.
> *Two Years Before the Mast [1840], ch. 3*

17   If California ever becomes a prosperous country, this bay [San Francisco] will be the center of its prosperity.   *Two Years Before the Mast, 26*

David Davis
1815–1886

18   The Constitution of the United States is a law for rulers and people, equally in war and in peace, and covers with the shield of its protection all classes of men, at all times, and under all circum-

---

[1]Translated by C. M. BOWRA.

[2]Eisen und Blut.
[3]Die Politik ist die Lehre von Möglichen.

stances. No doctrine, involving more pernicious consequences, was ever invented by the wit of man than that any of its provisions can be suspended during any of the great exigencies of government.
Ex Parte Milligan, 4 Wallace 2, 120–121 [1866]

Daniel Decatur Emmett
1815–1904

1 I wish I was in de land ob cotton,
Old times dar am not forgotten.
  Look away, look away,
  Look away, Dixie[1] Land.
Dixie's Land [1859], st. 1

2 In Dixie's land, we'll took our stand,
To lib an' die in Dixie!   *Dixie's Land, chorus*

Johnson Jones Hooper
1815–1862

3 It is good to be shifty in a new country.
Some Adventures of Captain Simon Suggs [1845]

John Babsone Lane Soule
1815–1891

4 Go west, young man.[2]
Article in the Terre Haute (Indiana) Express [1851]

Elizabeth Cady Stanton
1815–1902

5 We hold these truths to be self-evident, that all men and women are created equal.
First Woman's Rights Convention, Seneca Falls, New York [July 19–20, 1848]. Declaration of Sentiments

6 Resolved, That it is the duty of the women of this country to secure to themselves their sacred right to the elective franchise.
First Woman's Rights Convention, Seneca Falls, New York. Resolution IX

7 The prejudice against color, of which we hear so much, is no stronger than that against sex. It is produced by the same cause, and manifested very much in the same way. The Negro's skin and the woman's sex are both prima facie evidence that they were intended to be in subjection to the white Saxon man.
Speech before the New York Legislature [February 18, 1860]

8 Woman's degradation is in man's idea of his sexual rights. Our religion, laws, customs, are all founded on the belief that woman was made for man. Come what will, my whole soul rejoices in the truth that I have uttered.[3]
Letter to Susan B. Anthony [June 14, 1860]

9 Our "pathway" is straight to the ballot box, with no variableness nor shadow of turning. . . . We demand in the Reconstruction suffrage for all the citizens of the Republic. I would not talk of Negroes or women, but of citizens.
Letter to Thomas Wentworth Higginson [January 13, 1868]

10 Women have crucified the Mary Wollstonecrafts, the Fanny Wrights, and the George Sands of all ages. Men mock us with the fact and say we are ever cruel to each other. . . . If this present woman [Victoria Woodhull] must be crucified, let men drive the spikes.   *Letter to Lucretia Mott [April 1, 1872]*

Anthony Trollope
1815–1882

11 The tenth Muse who now governs the periodical press.   *The Warden [1855], ch. 14*

12 One of her instructors in fashion had given her to understand that curls were not the thing. "They'll always pass muster," Miss Dunstable had replied, "when they are done up with bank notes."
Doctor Thorne [1858], ch. 16

13 There is no road to wealth so easy and respectable as that of matrimony.   *Doctor Thorne, 18*

14 I cannot hold with those who wish to put down the insignificant chatter of the world.
Framley Parsonage [1861]

---

[1]*Dixie* comes from the ten-dollar notes issued by the Citizens' Bank in bilingual Louisiana before the Civil War and bearing the French word *dix*, ten, on the reverse side. Soon New Orleans, then Louisiana and the entire South were called "The land of Dixie," and later *Dixieland* and *Dixie*. The word became immensely popular with the song "Dixie" (whose actual title is "Dixie's Land").—STUART BERG FLEXNER, *I Hear America Talking* [1976]

[2]Horace Greeley used the expression in an editorial in the *New York Tribune*. As the saying "Go west, young man, and grow up with the country" gained popularity, Greeley printed Soule's article, to show the source of his inspiration.
See Greeley, 489:9.

---

[3]Referring to resolutions she had introduced at the tenth National Woman's Rights Convention [May 10, 1860], declaring that under certain circumstances divorce was justifiable.

1   She understood how much louder a cock can crow in its own farmyard than elsewhere.
The Last Chronicle of Barset [1867], vol. I, ch. 17

2   Always remember . . . that when you go into an attorney's office door, you will have to pay for it, first or last.   *The Last Chronicle of Barset, I, 20*

3   It's dogged as does it. It ain't thinking about it.
The Last Chronicle of Barset, I, 61

4   It has been the great fault of our politicians that they have all wanted to do something.
Phineas Finn [1869], ch. 13

5   She knew how to allure by denying, and to make the gift rich by delaying it.   *Phineas Finn, 57*

6   There are worse things than a lie . . . I have found . . . that it may be well to choose one sin in order that another may be shunned.
Doctor Wortle's School [1879], ch. 6

7   He must have known me had he seen me as he was wont to see me, for he was in the habit of flogging me constantly. Perhaps he did not recognize me by my face.   *An Autobiography [1883], ch. 1*

8   Three hours a day will produce as much as a man ought to write.   *An Autobiography, 15*

9   It had at this time become my custom . . . to write with my watch before me, and to require from myself 250 words every quarter of an hour. I have found that the 250 words have been forthcoming as regularly as my watch went.
An Autobiography, 15

10   Of all the needs a book has, the chief need is that it be readable.   *An Autobiography, 19*

Philip James Bailey
1816–1902

11 Let each man think himself an act of God,
His mind a thought, his life a breath of God.
Festus [1839]. Proem

12 America, thou half-brother of the world;
With something good and bad of every land.
Festus. The Surface

Charlotte Brontë
1816–1855

13 We wove a web in childhood,
A web of sunny air.   *Retrospection [1846], st. 1*

14 The human heart has hidden treasures,
In secret kept, in silence sealed.
Evening Solace [1846], st. 1

15   Conventionality is not morality. Self-righteousness is not religion. To attack the first is not to assail the last.   *Jane Eyre [1847], preface*

16   Reader, I married him.   *Jane Eyre, ch. 38*

17   An abundant shower of curates has fallen upon the north of England.   *Shirley [1849], ch. 1*

18   Unromantic as Monday morning.
Shirley,

19   I am neither a man nor a woman but an author.
Letter to William Smith Williams [August 16, 1849]

Ellen Sturgis Hooper
1816–1848

20 I slept and dreamed that life was beauty.
I woke — and found that life was duty.
Beauty and Duty

Eugène Pottier
1816–1887

21 Arise, ye prisoners of starvation,
Arise, ye wretched of the earth,
For justice thunders condemnation —
A better world's in birth.
The Internationale [1871][1]

Henry David Thoreau
1817–1862

22 I am a parcel of vain strivings tied
By a chance bond together.
Sic Vita [1841], st. 1

23   We are as much as we see. Faith is sight and knowledge. The hands only serve the eyes.
Journal [1906]. April 10, 1841

24   The Indian . . . stands free and unconstrained in Nature, is her inhabitant and not her guest, and wears her easily and gracefully. But the civilized man has the habits of the house. His house is a prison.
Journal. April 26, 1841

25   It is a great art to saunter.[2]
Journal. April 26, 1841

---

[1] Music by PIERRE DEGEYTER [1848–1932].

[2] *Sauntering* . . . derived "from idle people who roved about the country, in the Middle Ages, and asked charity, under pretense of going *à la Sainte Terre,*" to the Holy Land, till the children exclaimed, "There goes a Sainte-Terrer." — THOREAU, *Walking* [1862]

1 A slight sound at evening lifts me up by the ears, and makes life seem inexpressibly serene and grand. It may be in Uranus, or it may be in the shutter.
Journal. July 10–12, 1841

2 For many years I was self-appointed inspector of snowstorms and rainstorms, and did my duty faithfully, though I never received one cent for it.
Journal. February 22 [1845–1847][1]

3 Some circumstantial evidence is very strong, as when you find a trout in the milk.
Journal. November 11, 1850

4 Nothing is so much to be feared as fear.
Journal. September 7, 1851

5 The bluebird carries the sky on his back.
Journal. April 3, 1852

6 The perception of beauty is a moral test.
Journal. June 21, 1852

7 The youth gets together his materials to build a bridge to the moon, or, perchance, a palace or temple on the earth, and, at length, the middle-aged man concludes to build a woodshed with them.
Journal. July 14, 1852

8 Fire is the most tolerable third party.
Journal. January 2, 1853

9 Nature is full of genius, full of the divinity; so that not a snowflake escapes its fashioning hand.
Journal. January 5, 1856

10 The same law that shapes the earth-star shapes the snow-star. As surely as the petals of a flower are fixed, each of these countless snow-stars comes whirling to earth.
Journal. January 5, 1856

11 That man is the richest whose pleasures are the cheapest.
Journal. March 11, 1856

12 The savage in man is never quite eradicated.
Journal. September 26, 1859

13 Talk of mysteries! Think of our life in nature— daily to be shown matter, to come in contact with it—rocks, trees, wind on our cheeks! the *solid* earth! the *actual* world! the *common sense! Contact! Contact! Who* are we? *where* are we?
The Maine Woods, Ktaadn [1848]

14 I think that we should be men first, and subjects afterward. It is not desirable to cultivate a respect for the law, so much as for the right.
Civil Disobedience [1849]

15 How does it become a man to behave toward this American government today? I answer that he cannot without disgrace be associated with it.
Civil Disobedience

16 A wise man will not leave the right to the mercy of chance, nor wish it to prevail through the power of the majority. There is but little virtue in the action of masses of men.
Civil Disobedience

17 I came into this world, not chiefly to make this a good place to live in, but to live in it, be it good or bad.
Civil Disobedience

18 Any man more right than his neighbors constitutes a majority of one.
Civil Disobedience

19 Under a government which imprisons any unjustly, the true place for a just man is also a prison . . . the only house in a slave State in which a free man can abide with honor.
Civil Disobedience

20 I saw that the State was half-witted, that it was timid as a lone woman with her silver spoons, and that it did not know its friends from its foes, and I lost all my remaining respect for it, and pitied it.
Civil Disobedience

21 The vessel, though her masts be firm,
Beneath her copper bears a worm.
A Week on the Concord and Merrimack Rivers [1849]. Monday [Though All the Fates Should Prove Unkind, st. 2]

22 Methinks my own soul must be a bright invisible green.
A Week on the Concord and Merrimack Rivers. Wednesday

23 It takes two to speak the truth—one to speak, and another to hear.
A Week on the Concord and Merrimack Rivers. Wednesday

24 Even the death of friends will inspire us as much as their lives. . . . Their memories will be encrusted over with sublime and pleasing thoughts, as monuments of other men are overgrown with moss; for our friends have no place in the graveyard.
A Week on the Concord and Merrimack Rivers. Wednesday

25 Go where we will on the *surface* of things, men have been there before us.
A Week on the Concord and Merrimack Rivers. Thursday

26 The frontiers are not east or west, north or south, but wherever a man *fronts* a fact.
A Week on the Concord and Merrimack Rivers. Thursday

27 A true account of the actual is the rarest poetry, for common sense always takes a hasty and superficial view.
A Week on the Concord and Merrimack Rivers. Thursday

---

[1]No year in Thoreau's dateline.

1 My life has been the poem I would have writ,
But I could not both live and utter it.
*A Week on the Concord and Merrimack
Rivers. My Life Has Been the Poem I Would
Have Writ*

2 As if our birth had at first sundered things, and
we had been thrust up through into nature like a
wedge, and not till the wound heals and the scar
disappears, do we begin to discover where we are,
and that nature is one and continuous everywhere.
*A Week on the Concord and Merrimack
Rivers. Friday*

3 What are the earth and all its interests beside the
deep surmise which pierces and scatters them?
*A Week on the Concord and Merrimack
Rivers. Friday*

4 It is so rare to meet with a man outdoors who
cherishes a worthy thought in his mind, which is independent of the labor of his hands.
*A Week on the Concord and Merrimack
Rivers. Friday*

5 The eye may see for the hand, but not for the
mind.
*A Week on the Concord and Merrimack
Rivers. Friday*

6 The fate of the country . . . does not depend on
what kind of paper you drop into the ballot box
once a year, but on what kind of man you drop
from your chamber into the street every morning.
Slavery in Massachusetts [1854]

7 I should not talk so much about myself if there
were anybody else whom I knew as well.
Walden [1854], ch. 1, Economy

8 I have traveled a good deal in Concord.
Walden, 1, Economy

9 Public opinion is a weak tyrant compared with
our own private opinion. What a man thinks of
himself, that it is which determines, or rather, indicates, his fate.   *Walden, 1, Economy*

10 As if you could kill time without injuring eternity.   *Walden, 1, Economy*

11 The mass of men lead lives of quiet desperation.
What is called resignation is confirmed desperation.
Walden, 1, Economy

12 It is a characteristic of wisdom not to do desperate things.   *Walden, 1, Economy*

13 It is never too late to give up our prejudices.
Walden, 1, Economy

14 Age is no better, hardly so well, qualified for an
instructor as youth, for it has not profited so much
as it has lost.   *Walden, 1, Economy*

15 Most of the luxuries, and many of the so-called
comforts, of life are not only not indispensable, but
positive hindrances to the elevation of mankind.
Walden, 1, Economy

16 To be a philosopher is not merely to have subtle
thoughts, nor even to found a school, but so to love
wisdom as to live accordingly to its dictates, a life of
simplicity, independence, magnanimity, and trust.
Walden, 1, Economy

17 Beware of all enterprises that require new clothes.
Walden, 1, Economy

18 In the long run men hit only what they aim at.
Walden, 1, Economy

19 The swiftest traveler is he that goes afoot.
Walden, 1, Economy

20 It is not necessary that a man should earn his living by the sweat of his brow unless he sweats easier
than I do.   *Walden, 1, Economy*

21 When a man dies he kicks the dust.
Walden, 1, Economy

22 As for doing good, that is one of the professions
which are full.   *Walden, 1, Economy*

23 There is no odor so bad as that which arises from
goodness tainted.   *Walden, 1, Economy*

24 There are a thousand hacking at the branches of
evil to one who is striking at the root.
Walden, 1, Economy

25 Philanthropy is almost the only virtue which is
sufficiently appreciated by mankind.
Walden, 1, Economy

26 A man is rich in proportion to the number of
things which he can afford to let alone.
*Walden, 2, Where I Lived, and What I
Lived For*

27 I know of no more encouraging fact than the
unquestionable ability of man to elevate his life by a
conscious endeavor.
*Walden, 2, Where I Lived, and What I
Lived For*

28 I went to the woods because I wished to live deliberately, to front only the essential facts of life, and
see if I could not learn what it had to teach, and not,
when I came to die, discover that I had not lived.
*Walden, 2, Where I Lived, and What I
Lived For*

29 Our life is frittered away by detail. . . . Simplify,
simplify.
*Walden, 2, Where I Lived, and What I
Lived For*

1 We do not ride on the railroad; it rides upon us.
Walden, 2, Where I Lived, and What I Lived For

2 Be it life or death, we crave only reality.
Walden, 2, Where I Lived, and What I Lived For

3 Time is but the stream I go a-fishing in.
Walden, 2, Where I Lived, and What I Lived For

4 Books must be read as deliberately and reservedly as they were written.
Walden, 3, Reading

5 How many a man has dated a new era in his life from the reading of a book.
Walden, 3, Reading

6 I love a broad margin to my life.
Walden, 4, Sounds

7 Our horizon is never quite at our elbows.
Walden, 5, Solitude

8 I never found the companion that was so companionable as solitude. We are for the most part more lonely when we go abroad among men than when we stay in our chambers. A man thinking or working is always alone, let him be where he will.
Walden, 5, Solitude

9 I had three chairs in my house: one for solitude, two for friendship, three for society.
Walden, 6, Visitors

10 I was determined to know beans.
Walden, 7, The Beanfield

11 Through want of enterprise and faith men are where they are, buying and selling, and spending their lives like serfs.   *Walden, 10, Baker Farm*

12 They [wood stumps] warmed me twice — once while I was splitting them, and again when they were on the fire.[1]   *Walden, 13, Housewarming*

13 Heaven is under our feet as well as over our heads.   *Walden, 16, The Pond in Winter*

14 While men believe in the infinite, some ponds will be thought to be bottomless.
Walden, 16, The Pond in Winter

15 Through our own recovered innocence we discern the innocence of our neighbors.
Walden, 17, Spring

16 It is not worth while to go round the world to count the cats in Zanzibar.
Walden, 18, Conclusion

17 As if there were safety in stupidity alone.
Walden, 18, Conclusion

18 If one advances confidently in the direction of his dreams, and endeavors to live the life which he has imagined, he will meet with a success unexpected in common hours.
Walden, 18, Conclusion

19 If a man does not keep pace with his companions, perhaps it is because he hears a different drummer. Let him step to the music which he hears, however measured or far away.
Walden, 18, Conclusion

20 It is life near the bone where it is sweetest.
Walden, 18, Conclusion

21 Rather than love, than money, than fame, give me truth.   *Walden, 18, Conclusion*

22 Only that day dawns to which we are awake. There is more day to dawn. The sun is but a morning star.   *Walden, 18, Conclusion*

23 I hear many condemn these men because they were so few. When were the good and the brave ever in a majority?
A Plea for Captain John Brown [1859]

24 I speak for the slave when I say that I prefer the philanthropy of Captain Brown to that philanthropy which neither shoots me nor liberates me.
A Plea for Captain John Brown

25 So we defend ourselves and our henroosts, and maintain slavery.
A Plea for Captain John Brown

26 He is not Old Brown any longer; he is an angel of light.   *A Plea for Captain John Brown*

27 Eastward I go only by force; but westward I go free.   *Walking [1862]*

28 In wildness is the preservation of the world.[2]
Walking

29 I believe in the forest, and in the meadow, and in the night in which the corn grows.   *Walking*

30 Life consists with wildness. The most alive is the wildest. Not yet subdued to man, its presence refreshes him.   *Walking*

31 Men will lie on their backs, talking about the fall of man, and never make an effort to get up.
Life Without Principle [1863]

32 A man may stand there [Cape Cod] and put all America behind him.   *Cape Cod [1865], ch. 10*

---

[1]Who splits his own wood warms himself twice. — *Saying*

[2]Motto of the Wilderness Society.
See John Muir, 572:13.

1   One world at a time.
Said a few days before his death

Alexei Konstantinovich Tolstoi
1817–1875

2   His pen is breathing revenge.
Vaska Shibanov [1855–1865]

3   No one can encompass the unencompassable.
Collected Works of Kosma Prutkov [1884][1]

4   If thou hast a fountain, shut it up: let even a fountain have a rest.
Collected Works of Kosma Prutkov

5   Many men are like unto sausages: whatever you stuff them with, that they will bear in them.
Collected Works of Kosma Prutkov

Alexander II
1818–1881

6   Better to abolish serfdom from above than to wait till it begins to abolish itself from below.
Speech in Moscow [March 30, 1856]

Cecil Frances Alexander
1818–1895

7   All things bright and beautiful,
All creatures great and small,
All things wise and wonderful,
The Lord God made them all.
All Things Bright and Beautiful [1848], st. 1

8   There is a green hill far away,
Without a city wall,
Where the dear Lord was crucified,
Who died to save us all.
There Is a Green Hill [1848], st. 1

9   Once in royal David's city
Stood a lowly cattle shed,
Where a mother laid her baby
In a manger for his bed:
Mary was that mother mild,
Jesus Christ her little child.
Once in Royal David's City [1848],[2] *st. 1*

Josh Billings
[Henry Wheeler Shaw]
1818–1885

10   A sekret ceases tew be a sekret if it iz once confided—it iz like a dollar bill, once broken, it iz never a dollar agin.
Josh Billings: His Sayings [1865]. Affurism

11   Love iz like the meazles; we kant have it bad but onst, and the later in life we have it the tuffer it goes with us.   *Josh Billings: His Sayings. Affurism*

12   Nature never makes any blunders; when she makes a fool she means it.
Josh Billings: His Sayings. Affurism

13   I don't care how much a man talks, if he only says it in a few words.
Josh Billings: His Sayings. Affurism

14   As scarce as truth is, the supply has always been in excess of the demand.
Josh Billings: His Sayings. Affurisms

15   Poverty iz the stepmother ov genius.
Josh Billings: His Sayings. Affurisms

16   The wheel that squeaks the loudest
Is the one that gets the grease.   *The Kicker*

17   It is better to know nothing than to know what ain't so.[3]   *Proverb [1874]*

18   If it want for faith, thare would be no living in this world. We couldn't even eat hash with enny safety, if it want for faith.
Essays [1876]. Faith

Emily Brontë
1818–1848

19   Sleep not, dream not; this bright day
Will not, cannot last for aye;
Bliss like thine is bought by years
Dark with torment and with tears.
Sleep Not [1846], st. 1

20   Cold in the earth—and fifteen wild Decembers
From those brown hills have melted into spring.
Remembrance [1846], st. 3

21   Once drinking deep of that divinest anguish,
How could I seek the empty world again?
Remembrance, st. 8

22   Yes, as my swift days near their goal,
'Tis all that I implore:

---

[1]Translated by B. G. GURNEY.
[2]Music by HENRY J. GAUNTLETT [1805–1876].

[3]Better know nothing than half-know many things—FRIEDRICH NIETZSCHE, *Thus Spake Zarathustra* [1883–1891], *pt. IV, 64*

In life and death a chainless soul,
With courage to endure.
The Old Stoic [1846], st. 3

1 No coward soul is mine,
No trembler in the world's storm-troubled sphere:
I see Heaven's glories shine,
And faith shines equal, arming me from fear.
Last Lines [1846], st. 1

2 There is not room for Death. *Last Lines, st. 7*

3 I *am* Heathcliff.
Wuthering Heights [1847], ch. 9

4 I lingered round them, under that benign sky:
watched the moths fluttering among the heath and
harebells; listened to the soft wind breathing through
the grass; and wondered how anyone could ever
imagine unquiet slumbers for the sleepers in that
quiet earth. *Wuthering Heights, last words*

Jacob Burckhardt
1818–1897

5 The picture I have formed of the *terribles simplificateurs* [terrible simplifiers] who are going to descend upon poor old Europe is not an agreeable one.
Letter to Friedrich von Preen [July 24, 1889][1]

Eliza Cook
1818–1889

6 I love it, I love it; and who shall dare
To chide me for loving that old armchair?
The Old Armchair

7 Better build schoolrooms for "the boy"
Than cells and gibbets for "the man."
A Song for the Ragged Schools, st. 12

Frederick Douglass
c. 1818–1895

8 Every tone [of the songs of the slaves] was a testimony against slavery, and a prayer to God for deliverance from chains.
*Narrative of the Life of Frederick Douglass
[1845], ch. 2*

9 You have seen how a man was made a slave; you
shall see how a slave was made a man.
Narrative of the Life of Frederick Douglass, 10

10 What, to the American slave, is your Fourth of
July? I answer: A day that reveals to him, more than

all other days in the year, the gross injustice and
cruelty to which he is the constant victim. To him
your celebration is a sham.
*Speech at Rochester, New York
[July 4, 1852]*

11 You profess to believe that "of one blood God
made all nations of men to dwell on the face of all
the earth" — and hath commanded all men, everywhere, to love one another — yet you notoriously
hate (and glory in your hatred!) all men whose skins
are not colored like your own!
Speech at Rochester, New York [July 4, 1852]

12 The ground which a colored man occupies in
this country is, every inch of it, sternly disputed.
*Speech at the American and Foreign Anti-
Slavery Society annual meeting, New York
City [May 1853]*

13 The whole history of the progress of human liberty shows that all concessions yet made to her august claims have been born of earnest struggle. . . .
If there is no struggle, there is no progress. Those
who profess to favor freedom, and yet deprecate agitation, are men who want crops without plowing
up the ground, they want rain without thunder and
lightning. They want the ocean without the awful
roar of its many waters.
*Speech at Canandaigua, New York [August 3,
1857]*

14 The destiny of the colored American . . . is the
destiny of America.
*Speech at the Emancipation League, Boston
[February 12, 1862]*

15 The relation subsisting between the white and
colored people of this country is the great, paramount, imperative, and all-commanding question
for this age and nation to solve.
*Speech at the Church of the Puritans, New
York City [May 1863]*

16 Despite of it all, the Negro remains . . . cool,
strong, imperturbable, and cheerful.
*Speech on the twenty-first anniversary of
Emancipation in the District of Columbia,
Washington, D.C. [April 1883]*

17 In all the relations of life and death, we are met
by the color line.
*Speech at the Convention of Colored Men,
Louisville, Kentucky [September 24, 1883]*

18 No man can put a chain about the ankle of his
fellow man without at last finding the other end fastened about his own neck.
*Speech at Civil Rights Mass Meeting,
Washington, D.C. [October 22, 1883]*

[1]Translated by ALEXANDER DRU.

1   The life of the nation is secure only while the nation is honest, truthful, and virtuous.

> *Speech on the twenty-third anniversary of Emancipation in the District of Columbia, Washington, D.C. [April 1885]*

2   Where justice is denied, where poverty is enforced, where ignorance prevails, and where any one class is made to feel that society is in an organized conspiracy to oppress, rob, and degrade them, neither persons nor property will be safe.

> *Speech on the twenty-fourth anniversary of Emancipation in the District of Columbia, Washington, D.C. [April 1886]*

George Duffield
1818–1888

3 Stand up!—stand up for Jesus!   *Hymn [1858]*

William Maxwell Evarts
1818–1901

4   The pious ones of Plymouth, who, reaching the Rock, first fell upon their own knees and then upon the aborigines.[1]

> *From HENRY WATTERSON in the Louisville Courier-Journal [July 4, 1913]*

Karl Marx
1818–1883

5   Religion . . . is the opium of the people.

> *Critique of the Hegelian Philosophy of Right [1844], introduction*

6   Hegel remarks somewhere[2] that all great world-historic facts and personages appear, so to speak, twice. He forgot to add: the first time as tragedy, the second time as farce.

> *The Eighteenth Brumaire of Louis Napoleon [1852],[3] pt. 1*

7   What was new in what I did was: (1) to demonstrate that the *existence of classes* is tied only to *defi-*

---

[1]This pun has also been attributed to Oliver Wendell Holmes, Bill Nye, and George Frisbie Hoar.
See William Bradford, 247:6.

[2]*Lectures on the Philosophy of History [1837], part III, sec. iii:* "Napoleon was twice defeated, and the Bourbons twice expelled. By repetition that which at first appeared merely a matter of chance and contingency, becomes a real and ratified existence."

[3]Translated by SAUL K. PADOVER.

---

nite historical phases of development of production; (2) that the class struggle necessarily leads to the *dictatorship of the proletariat;* (3) that this dictatorship is only a transition to the *dissolution of all classes* and leads to the formation of a *classless society.*

> *Letter to Joseph Weydemeyer [March 5, 1852]*

8   Nothing can have value without being an object of utility. If it be useless, the labor contained in it is useless, cannot be reckoned as labor, and cannot therefore create value.

> *Capital[4] [1867–1883], pt. II, ch. 2*

9   The intellectual desolation, artificially produced by converting immature human beings into mere machines.   *Capital, II, 10*

10   When commercial capital occupies a position of unquestioned ascendancy, it everywhere constitutes a system of plunder.   *Capital, II, 20*

11   From each according to his abilities, to each according to his needs.[5]

> *Critique of the Gotha Program [1875]*

12   The philosophers have only interpreted the world in various ways. The point, however, is to change it.

> *Theses on Feuerbach [1888], xi*

13   All I know is that I am not a Marxist.[7]

> *Quoted in FRIEDRICH ENGELS, Letter to Conrad Schmidt [August 3, 1890]*

Karl Marx
1818–1883
and
Friedrich Engels
1820–1895

14   A specter is haunting Europe—the specter of Communism. All the powers of old Europe have

---

[4]Abridged edition prepared by JULIAN BORCHARDT, translated by STEPHEN L. TRASK.

[5]This phrase is in quotation marks, and it is believed that Marx is quoting or paraphrasing either Louis Blanc [1811–1882] or Morelly [fl. 1773]:
Let each produce according to his aptitudes and his force; let each consume according to his need.—LOUIS BLANC, *Organisation du Travail* [1840]
Nothing in society will belong to anyone, either as a personal possession or as capital goods, except the things for which the person has immediate use, for either his needs, his pleasures, or his daily work. Every citizen will make his particular contribution to the activities of the community according to his capacity, his talent and his age; it is on this basis that his duties will be determined, in conformity with the distributive laws.—MORELLY, *Le Code de la Nature* [1755]

[6]Inscribed on his tomb at Highgate Cemetery, London.

[7]Translated by DONNA TORR.

entered into a holy alliance to exorcise this specter: Pope and Czar, Metternich and Guizot, French Radicals and German police spies.

The Communist Manifesto [1848],[1]
opening lines

1 The history of all hitherto existing society is the history of class struggles. Freeman and slave, patrician and plebeian, lord and serf, guild master and journeyman, in a word, oppressor and oppressed, stood in constant opposition to each other, carried on an uninterrupted, now hidden, now open fight, a fight that each time ended, either in a revolutionary reconstitution of society at large, or in the common ruin of the contending classes.

The Communist Manifesto, sec. 1

2 The executive of the modern state is but a committee for managing the common affairs of the whole bourgeoisie.[2] The bourgeoisie has, historically, played a most revolutionary role.

The Communist Manifesto, 1

3 The bourgeoisie, by the rapid improvement of all instruments of production, by the immensely facilitated means of communication, draws all, even the most barbarian, nations into civilization.

The Communist Manifesto, 1

4 Of all the classes that stand face to face with the bourgeoisie today, the proletariat alone is a really revolutionary class. The other classes decay and finally disappear in the race of modern industry; the proletariat is its special and essential product.[3]

The Communist Manifesto, 1

5 In this sense, the theory of the Communists may be summed up in the single sentence: Abolition of private property. *The Communist Manifesto, 2*

6 In proportion as the antagonism between classes within the nation vanishes, the hostility of one nation to another will come to an end.

The Communist Manifesto, 2

7 The ruling ideas of each age have ever been the ideas of its ruling class.

The Communist Manifesto, 2

8 The communists disdain to conceal their views and aims. They openly declare that their ends can

be obtained only by forcible overthrow of all existing social conditions. Let the ruling classes tremble at a communist revolution. The proletarians have nothing to lose but their chains. They have a world to win. Working men of all countries, unite![4]

The Communist Manifesto, 4

John Mason Neale
1818–1866

9 Good King Wenceslas looked out
On the feast of Stephen,
When the snow lay round about,
Deep and crisp and even.

Good King Wenceslas, st. 1

10 Brief life is here our portion.
Hymn from the Latin of SAINT BERNARD OF CLUNY *[c. 1145], pt. II, Hic Breve Vivitur [translated 1851], st. 1*

11 Jerusalem the golden, with milk and honey blest,
Beneath thy contemplation sink heart and voice oppressed.
Hymn from the Latin of SAINT BERNARD OF CLUNY, *III, Urbs Syon Aurea [translated 1858], st. 1*

12 O come, O come, Emmanuel,
And ransom captive Israel.
Hymn from the Latin, Veni, Veni, Emmanuel [twelfth century], st. 1 [translated 1861]

Francis Edward Smedley
1818–1864

13 You are looking as fresh as paint.
Frank Fairlegh [1850], ch. 41

14 All's fair in love and war.[5]
Frank Fairlegh, 50

Ivan Sergeyevich Turgenev
1818–1883

15 A nihilist is a man who does not bow to any authorities, who does not take any principle on trust, no matter with what respect that principle is surrounded. *Fathers and Sons [1862],*[6] *ch. 5*

---

[1] Translated by SAMUEL MOORE.

[2] By bourgeoisie is meant the class of modern capitalists, owners of the means of social production and employers of wage labor. — ENGELS, *notes to The Communist Manifesto* [1888 edition]

[3] By proletariat [is meant] the class of modern wage laborers who, having no means of production of their own, are reduced to selling their labor power in order to live. — ENGELS, *notes to The Communist Manifesto* [1888 edition]

[4] More familiar as: Workers of the world, unite!

[5] All policy's allowed in war and love. — SUSANNAH CENTLIVRE, *Love at a Venture* [1706], *act I*

[6] Translated by HARRY STEVENS.

1   That vague, crepuscular time, the time of regrets that resemble hopes, of hopes that resemble regrets, when youth has passed, but old age has not yet arrived. *Fathers and Sons, 7*

2   I share no man's opinions; I have my own. *Fathers and Sons, 13*

3   The courage not to believe in anything. *Fathers and Sons, 14*

4   A picture shows me at a glance what it takes dozens of pages of a book to expound. *Fathers and Sons, 16*

5   Whatever a man prays for, he prays for a miracle. Every prayer reduces itself to this: "Great God, grant that twice two be not four." *Prayer*

6   In days of doubt, in days of sad brooding on my country's fate, thou alone art my rod and my staff—mighty, true, free Russian speech! But for thee, how not to fall into despair, seeing all that happens at home? Yet who can think that such a tongue is not given to a great people? *Senilia [1882]*

Arthur Hugh Clough
1819–1861

7   Grace is given of God, but knowledge is bought in the market. *The Bothie of Tober-na-Vuolich [1848], pt. IV*

8   A world where nothing is had for nothing. *The Bothie of Tober-na-Vuolich, VIII*

9   And almost everyone when age,
Disease, or sorrows strike him,
Inclines to think there is a God,
Or something very like Him. *Dipsychus [1862], pt. I, sc. v*

10 Say not the struggle nought availeth,
The labour and the wounds are vain,
The enemy faints not, nor faileth,
And as things have been, things remain.

If hopes were dupes, fears may be liars;
It may be, in yon smoke concealed,
Your comrades chase e'en now the fliers,
And, but for you, possess the field.

For while the tired waves, vainly breaking,
Seem here no painful inch to gain,
Far back through creeks and inlets making
Came, silent, flooding in, the main,

And not by eastern windows only,
When daylight comes, comes in the light,

In front the sun climbs slow, how slowly,
But westward, look, the land is bright. *Say Not the Struggle Nought Availeth [1862]*

11 No graven images may be
Worshipped, except the currency. *The Latest Decalogue [1862], l. ?*

12 Thou shalt not covet, but tradition
Approves all forms of competition. *The Latest Decalogue, l. 19*

George Eliot [Marian Evans Cross]
1819–1880

13   'Tis God gives skill,
But not without men's hands: He could not make
Antonio Stradivari's violins
Without Antonio. *Stradivarius*

14 O may I join the choir invisible
Of those immortal dead who live again
In minds made better by their presence. *O May I Join the Choir Invisible*

15   These fellow mortals, every one, must be accepted as they are. *Adam Bede [1859], ch. 17*

16   There's no real making amends in this world, any more nor you can mend a wrong subtraction by doing your addition right. *Adam Bede, 18*

17   It's but little good you'll do a-watering the last year's crops. *Adam Bede, 18*

18   It was a pity he couldna be hatched o'er again, an' hatched different. *Adam Bede, 18*

19   A patronizing disposition always has its meaner side. *Adam Bede, 27*

20   It's them that take advantage that get advantage i' this world. *Adam Bede, 32*

21   He was like a cock who thought the sun had risen to hear him crow. *Adam Bede, 33*

22   Deep, unspeakable suffering may well be called a baptism, a regeneration, the initiation into a new state. *Adam Bede, 42*

23   We hand folks over to God's mercy, and show none ourselves. *Adam Bede, 42*

24   I'm not denyin' the women are foolish; God Almighty made 'em to match the men. *Adam Bede, 53*

25   The law's made to take care o' raskills. *The Mill on the Floss [1860], bk. III, ch. 4*

1 There is no hopelessness so sad as that of early youth, when the soul is made up of wants, and has no long memories, no superadded life in the life of others. *The Mill on the Floss, III, 5*

2 Not let them want bread, but only require them to eat it with bitter herbs. *The Mill on the Floss, IV, 1*

3 I've never any pity for conceited people, because I think they carry their comfort about with them.[1] *The Mill on the Floss, V, 4*

4 The happiest women, like the happiest nations, have no history. *The Mill on the Floss, VI, 3*

5 Nothing is so good as it seems beforehand. *Silas Marner [1861], ch. 18*

6 In our springtime every day has its hidden growths in the mind, as it has in the earth when the little folded blades are getting ready to pierce the ground. *Felix Holt, the Radical [1866], ch. 18*

7 One way of getting an idea of our fellow-countrymen's miseries is to go and look at their pleasures. *Felix Holt, the Radical, 28*

8 Prophecy is the most gratuitous form of error. *Middlemarch [1871–1872], ch. 10*

9 If we had a keen vision of all that is ordinary in human life, it would be like hearing the grass grow or the squirrel's heart beat, and we should die of that roar which is the other side of silence. *Middlemarch, 22*

10 If youth is the season of hope, it is often so only in the sense that our elders are hopeful about us. *Middlemarch, 55*

11 There is no creature whose inward being is so strong that it is not greatly determined by what lies outside it. *Middlemarch, Finale*

12 Hostesses who entertain much must make up their parties as ministers make up their cabinets, on grounds other than personal liking. *Daniel Deronda [1876], bk. I, ch. 5*

13 A difference of taste in jokes is a great strain on the affections. *Daniel Deronda, II, 15*

14 Men's men: gentle or simple, they're much of a muchness. *Daniel Deronda, IV, 31*

15 Blessed is the man who, having nothing to say, abstains from giving in words evidence of the fact. *Impressions of Theophrastus Such [1879]*

16 Biographies generally are a disease of English literature.
Letter to Mrs. Thomas Adolphus Trollope [December 19, 1879]

Thomas Dunn English
1819–1902

17 Oh! don't you remember sweet Alice, Ben Bolt?
Sweet Alice, whose hair was so brown.
Ben Bolt [1843]

Julia Ward Howe
1819–1910

18 Mine eyes have seen the glory of the coming of the Lord;
He is trampling out the vintage where the grapes of wrath are stored;
He hath loosed the fateful lightning of His terrible, swift sword;
His truth is marching on.
Battle Hymn of the Republic [1862], st. 1

19 In the beauty of the lilies Christ was born across the sea,
With a glory in His bosom that transfigures you and me;
As He died to make men holy, let us die to make men free.
Battle Hymn of the Republic, st. 5

Charles Kingsley
1819–1875

20 Give me the political economist, the sanitary reformer, the engineer; and take your saints and virgins, relics and miracles. The spinning-jenny and the railroad, Cunard's liners and the electric telegraph, are to me . . . signs that we are, on some points at least, in harmony with the universe.
Yeast [1848], ch. 5

21 Oh Mary, go and call the cattle home . . .
Across the sands of Dee.
The Sands of Dee [1849], st. 1

22 The cruel crawling foam.[2] *The Sands of Dee, st. 4*

23 For men must work, and women must weep,
And there's little to earn and many to keep,
Though the harbor bar be moaning.
The Three Fishers [1851], st. 1

---

[1] There is not enough of love and goodness in the world to throw any of it away on conceited people. —FRIEDRICH NIETZSCHE, *Human, All Too Human* [1878], *129*

[2] See Ruskin, 517:5.

1 And the sooner it's over, the sooner to sleep;
And good-bye to the bar and its moaning.
The Three Fishers, st. 3

2 Be good, sweet maid, and let who will be clever;
Do noble things, not dream them, all day long;
And so make Life, and Death, and that For Ever
One grand sweet song.
A Farewell [1856], st. 3

3 Clear and cool, clear and cool,
By laughing shallow, and dreaming pool.
Water Babies [1863]. Song I, st. 1

4 When all the world is young, lad,
And all the trees are green;
And every goose a swan, lad,
And every lass a queen;
Then hey for boot and horse, lad,
And round the world away:
Young blood must have its course, lad,
And every dog his day.
Water Babies. Song II, st. 1

5 God grant you find one face there
You loved when all was young!
Water Babies. Song II, st. 1

6   Science frees us in many ways . . . from the bodily
terror which the savage feels. But she replaces that,
in the minds of many, by a moral terror which is far
more overwhelming.
*Sermon, The Meteor Shower [November 26,
1866]*

7   Some say that the age of chivalry is past, that the
spirit of romance is dead. The age of chivalry is never
past, so long as there is a wrong left unredressed on
earth, or a man or woman left to say, I will redress
that wrong, or spend my life in the attempt.
*From Charles Kingsley: His Letters and
Memories of His Life [1879], vol. II, ch. 28*

James Russell Lowell
1819–1891

8 Blessed are the horny hands of toil!
A Glance Behind the Curtain [1843]

9 They are slaves who fear to speak
For the fallen and the weak.
Stanzas on Freedom [1843], st. 4

10 They are slaves who dare not be
In the right with two or three.
Stanzas on Freedom, st. 4

11 The nurse of full-grown souls is solitude.
Columbus [1844]

12 Once to every man and nation comes the moment
to decide,
In the strife of Truth with Falsehood, for the good
or evil side.   *The Present Crisis [1844], st. 5*

13 Truth forever on the scaffold, Wrong forever on
the throne—
Yet that scaffold sways the future, and, behind the
dim unknown,
Standeth God within the shadow, keeping watch
above his own.   *The Present Crisis, st. 8*

14 Not only around our infancy
Doth heaven with all its splendors lie;
Daily, with souls that cringe and plot,
We Sinais climb and know it not.
*The Vision of Sir Launfal [1848], prelude to
pt. I, st. 2*

15 For a cap and bells our lives we pay,
Bubbles we buy with a whole soul's tasking:
'Tis heaven alone that is given away,
'Tis only God may be had for the asking.
The Vision of Sir Launfal, st. 4

16 And what is so rare as a day in June?
Then, if ever, come perfect days.
The Vision of Sir Launfal, st. 5

17 In creating, the only hard thing's to begin;
A grass-blade's no easier to make than an oak.
A Fable for Critics [1848]

18 And I honor the man who is willing to sink
Half his present repute for the freedom to think,
And, when he has thought, be his cause strong or
weak,
Will risk t' other half for the freedom to speak.
A Fable for Critics

19 There comes Poe, with his raven, like Barnaby
Rudge,
Three fifths of him genius and two fifths sheer
fudge.   *A Fable for Critics*

20 Nature fits all her children with something to do,
He who would write and can't write, can surely review.   *A Fable for Critics*

21 Ez fer war, I call it murder—
There you hev it plain an' flat;
I don't want to go no furder
Than my Testament fer that.
The Biglow Papers. Series I [1848], no. 1, st. 5

22   You've gut to git up airly
Ef you want to take in God.
The Biglow Papers. I, 1, st. 6

23 A marciful Providence fashioned us holler
O' purpose thet we might our principles swaller.
The Biglow Papers. I, 4, st. 2

1 I du believe with all my soul
  In the gret Press's freedom,
  To pint the people to the goal
  An' in the traces lead 'em.
  The Biglow Papers. I, 6, st. 7

2 I *don't* believe in princerple,
  But oh I *du* in interest. *The Biglow Papers. I, 6, st. 9*

3 God makes sech nights, all white an' still,
  Fur'z you can look or listen,
  Moonshine an' snow on field an' hill,
  All silence an' all glisten.
  The Biglow Papers. Series II [1866]. The Courtin', st. 1

4 My gran'ther's rule was safer 'n 'tis to crow:
  Don't never prophesy—onless ye know.
  The Biglow Papers. II, 2

5 It's 'most enough to make a deacon swear.
  The Biglow Papers. II, 2

6 Ef you want peace, the thing you've gut tu du
  Is jes' to show you're up to fightin', tu.
  The Biglow Papers. II, 2

7 Bad work follers ye ez long's ye live.
  The Biglow Papers. II, 2

8 No, never say nothin' without you're compelled tu,
  An' then don't say nothin' thet you can be held tu.
  The Biglow Papers. II, 5

9 They came three thousand miles, and died,
  To keep the Past upon its throne;
  Unheard, beyond the ocean tide,
  Their English mother made her moan.
  Graves of Two English Soldiers on Concord Battleground [1849], st. 3

10 There is nothing so desperately monotonous as the sea, and I no longer wonder at the cruelty of pirates. *Fireside Travels [1864]. At Sea*

11 When I was a beggarly boy,
   And lived in a cellar damp,
   I had not a friend nor a toy,
   But I had Aladdin's lamp. *Aladdin [1868], st. 1*

12 Though old the thought and oft expressed,
   'Tis his at last who says it best.
   For an Autograph [1868]

13 For me Fate gave, whate'er she else denied,
   A nature sloping to the southern side.
   Epistle to George William Curtis [1874]. Postscript

14 The soil out of which such men as he are made is good to be born on, good to live on, good to die for and to be buried in.
   Garfield [September 24, 1881]

15 There is no good in arguing with the inevitable. The only argument available with an east wind is to put on your overcoat.
   Democracy [October 6, 1884]

16 These pearls of thought in Persian gulfs were bred,
   Each softly lucent as a rounded moon;
   The diver Omar plucked them from their bed,
   Fitzgerald strung them on an English thread.
   In a Copy of Omar Khayyám [1888], st. 1

17 Things always seem fairer when we look back at them, and it is out of that inaccessible tower of the past that Longing leans and beckons.
   Literary Essays, vol. I [1864–1890]. A Few Bits of Roman Mosaic

18 Mishaps are like knives, that either serve us or cut us, as we grasp them by the blade or the handle.
   Literary Essays, I. Cambridge Thirty Years Ago

19 What a sense of security in an old book which Time has criticized for us!
   Literary Essays, I. A Library of Old Authors

20 There is no better ballast for keeping the mind steady on its keel, and saving it from all risk of crankiness, than business.
   Literary Essays, II. New England Two Centuries Ago

21 Puritanism, believing itself quick with the seed of religious liberty, laid, without knowing it, the egg of democracy.
   Literary Essays, II. New England Two Centuries Ago

22 It was in making education not only common to all, but in some sense compulsory on all, that the destiny of the free republics of America was practically settled.
   Literary Essays, II. New England Two Centuries Ago

23 Every man feels instinctively that all the beautiful sentiments in the world weigh less than a single lovely action.
   Literary Essays, II. New England Two Centuries Ago

24 An umbrella is of no avail against a Scotch mist.
   Literary Essays, III [1870–1890]. On a Certain Condescension in Foreigners

25 A wise skepticism is the first attribute of a good critic.
   Literary Essays, III. Shakespeare Once More

Herman Melville
1819–1891

1   When the inhabitants of some sequestered island first descry the "big canoe" of the European rolling through the blue waters towards their shores, they rush down to the beach in crowds, and with open arms stand ready to embrace the strangers. Fatal embrace! They fold to their bosoms the viper whose sting is destined to poison all their joys.

                     Typee [1846], ch. 4

2   Genius all over the world stands hand in hand, and one shock of recognition runs the whole circle round.   *Hawthorne and His Mosses [1850]*

3   Are there no Moravians in the Moon, that not a missionary has yet visited this poor pagan planet of ours, to civilize civilization and christianize Christendom?   *White Jacket [1850], ch. 64*

4   The grand truth about Nathaniel Hawthorne. He says NO! in thunder; but the Devil himself cannot make him say *yes*.
    Letter to Nathaniel Hawthorne [April 16, 1851]

5   Call me Ishmael.   *Moby-Dick [1851], ch. 1*

6   Let the most absent-minded of men be plunged in his deepest reveries—stand that man upon his legs, set his feet a-going, and he will infallibly lead you to water, if water there be in all that region. . . . Meditation and water are wedded forever.
    Moby-Dick, 1

7   There floated into my inmost soul, endless processions of the whale, and, mid most of them all, one grand hooded phantom, like a snow hill in the air.   *Moby-Dick, 1*

8   Better sleep with a sober cannibal than a drunken Christian.   *Moby-Dick, 3*

9   Woe to him who seeks to pour oil upon the waters when God has brewed them into a gale! Woe to him who seeks to please rather than to appall!
    Moby-Dick, 9

10   A whale-ship was my Yale College and my Harvard.   *Moby-Dick, 24*

11   Thou great democratic God! . . . who didst pick up Andrew Jackson from the pebbles; who didst hurl him upon a war-horse; who didst thunder him higher than a throne!   *Moby-Dick, 26*

12   And this is what ye have shipped for, men! to chase that white whale on both sides of land, and over all sides of earth, till he spouts black blood and rolls fin out.   *Moby-Dick, 36*

13   All visible objects, man, are but as pasteboard masks . . . strike, strike through the mask!
    Moby-Dick, 3

14   All that most maddens and torments; all that stirs up the lees of things; all truth with malice in it; all that cracks the sinews and cakes the brain; all the subtle demonisms of life and thought; all evil, to crazy Ahab, were visibly personified, and made practically assailable in Moby Dick. He piled upon the whale's white hump the sum of all the general rage and hate felt by his whole race from Adam down; and then, as if his chest had been a mortar, he burst his hot heart's shell upon it.   *Moby-Dick, 41*

15   Though in many of its aspects this visible world seems formed in love, the invisible spheres were formed in fright.   *Moby-Dick, 42*

16   For as this appalling ocean surrounds the verdant land, so in the soul of man there lies one insular Tahiti, full of peace and joy, but encompassed by all the horrors of the half known life.
    Moby-Dick, 58

17   By heaven, man, we are turned round and round in this world, like yonder windlass, and Fate is the handspike.   *Moby-Dick, 132*

18   All collapsed, and the great shroud of the sea rolled on as it rolled five thousand years ago.
    Moby-Dick, 135

19   What we take to be our strongest tower of delight, only stands at the caprice of the minutest event—the falling of a leaf, the hearing of a voice, or the receipt of one little bit of paper scratched over with a few small characters by a sharpened feather.   *Pierre [1852], bk. IV*

20   One trembles to think of that mysterious thing in the soul, which seems to acknowledge no human jurisdiction, but in spite of the individual's own innocent self, will still dream horrid dreams, and mutter unmentionable thoughts.   *Pierre, IV*

21   A smile is the chosen vehicle for all ambiguities.
    Pierre, IV

22   I would prefer not to.
    Bartleby the Scrivener [1856]

23 The poor old Past,
The Future's slave.
    Battle-Pieces [1866]. The Conflict of Convictions, st. 6

24 All wars are boyish, and are fought by boys.
    Battle-Pieces. The March into Virginia

25   What troops
Of generous boys in happiness thus bred—

Saturnians through life's Tempe led,
Went from the North and came from the South,
With golden mottoes in the mouth,
To lie down midway on a bloody bed.
Battle-Pieces. On the Slain Collegians, st. 2

1 God bless Captain Vere!
Billy Budd, Sailor [1924], ch. 25

2 But me they'll lash in hammock, drop me deep.
Fathoms down, fathoms down, how I'll dream fast
  asleep.
I feel it stealing now. Sentry, are you there?
Just ease these darbies[1] at the wrist,
And roll me over fair!
I am sleepy, and the oozy weeds about me twist.
Billy Budd, Sailor, 25

John Ruskin
1819–1900

3 He is the greatest artist who has embodied, in
the sum of his works, the greatest number of the
greatest ideas.
Modern Painters, vol. I [1843], pt. I, ch. 2

4 To know anything well involves a profound sensation of ignorance.   *Modern Painters, I, I, 3*

5 The foam is not cruel.[2]...The state of mind
which attributes to it these characters of a living
creature is one in which the reason is unhinged by
grief. All violent feelings ... produce in us a false-
ness in all our impressions of external things, which
I would generally characterize as the "Pathetic
Fallacy."
Modern Painters, III [1856], IV, 12

6 The essence of lying is in deception, not in
words.   *Modern Painters, V, IX, 7*

7 Remember that the most beautiful things in the
world are the most useless; peacocks and lilies for
instance.
The Stones of Venice [1851–1853], vol. I, ch. 2

8 All great art is the work of the whole living creature, body and soul, and chiefly of the soul.
The Stones of Venice, I, 4

9 Blue color is everlastingly appointed by the Deity
to be a source of delight.
*Lectures on Architecture and Painting
[1853], I*

10 There is no wealth but life.
Unto This Last [1862], sec. 77

11 Let us reform our schools, and we shall find little
reform needed in our prisons.
Unto This Last, essay 2

12 Value is the life-giving power of anything; cost,
the quantity of labor required to produce it; price,
the quantity of labor which its possessor will take in
exchange for it.
Munera Pulveris [1862], ch. 1

13 There is no law of history any more than of a
kaleidoscope.
*Letter to James Anthony Froude [February
1864]*

14 Life being very short, and the quiet hours of it
few, we ought to waste none of them in reading valueless books.   *Sesame and Lilies [1865], preface*

15 All books are divisible into two classes: the books
of the hour, and the books of all time.
Sesame and Lilies. Of Kings' Treasuries, sec. 8

16 Borrowers are nearly always ill-spenders, and it is
with lent money that all evil is mainly done and all
unjust war protracted.
The Crown of Wild Olive [1866], lecture 1

17 Give a little love to a child, and you get a great
deal back.   *The Crown of Wild Olive, 1*

18 Taste ... is the *only* morality.... Tell me what
you like, and I'll tell you what you are.
The Crown of Wild Olive, 2

19 Life without industry is guilt, industry without
art is brutality.
*Lectures on Art [1870]. III, The Relation of
Art to Morals*

20 Every increased possession loads us with a new
weariness.   *The Eagle's Nest [1872], ch. 5*

21 Architecture ... the adaptation of form to resist
force.   *Val d'Arno [1874], ch. 6*

22 The first duty of government is to see that people have food, fuel, and clothes. The second, that
they have means of moral and intellectual education.   *Fors Clavigera [1876], letter 67*

23 Great nations write their autobiographies in three
manuscripts—the book of their deeds, the book of
their words, and the book of their art.
St. Mark's Rest [1877], preface

---

[1]Manacles.
[2]See Kingsley, 513:22.

Max Schneckenburger
1819–1849

1 Dear Fatherland, no danger thine:
Firm stands thy watch along the Rhine.[1]
> *The Watch on the Rhine (Die Wacht am Rhein) [1840], chorus*

Victoria
1819–1901

2　I will be good.
> *On first seeing a chart of the line of succession to the throne [March 11, 1830]*

3　*Great* events make me quiet and calm; it is only trifles that irritate my nerves.
> *Letter to King Leopold of Belgium [April 4, 1848]*

4　We are not interested in the possibilities of defeat.
> *To A. J. Balfour [December 1899]*

5　We are not amused.
> *Upon seeing an imitation of herself by the Honorable Alexander Grantham Yorke, groom-in-waiting to the Queen. From Notebooks of a Spinster Lady [January 2, 1900]*

6　He [William Gladstone] speaks to me as if I was a public meeting.
> *From GEORGE W. E. RUSSELL, Collections and Recollections [1898], ch. 14*

William Ross Wallace
1819–1881

7 The hand that rocks the cradle
Is the hand that rules the world.
> *The Hand That Rules the World, st. 1*

Walt Whitman
1819–1892

8　The United States themselves are essentially the greatest poem.
> *Preface to the first edition of Leaves of Grass [1855][2]*

---

[1]Lieb Vaterland, magst ruhig sein, / Fest steht und treu die Wacht am Rhein.

[2]The first edition of *Leaves of Grass*, published anonymously by its author in July 1855, contained a long preface and twelve untitled poems. Over the next four decades Whitman revised and enlarged his book. The texts and sequence of the verse quotations here are those of the so-called Deathbed Edition [Philadelphia, 1891–92].

9　All beauty comes from beautiful blood and beautiful brain.
> *Preface to the first edition of Leaves of Gra*

10　This is what you shall do: Love the earth and su and the animals, despise riches, give alms to ever one that asks, stand up for the stupid and crazy, de vote your income and labor to others, hate tyrants argue not concerning God.
> *Preface to the first edition of Leaves of Gras*

11　The proof of a poet is that his country absorb him as affectionately as he has absorbed it.
> *Preface to the first edition of Leaves of Gras*

12 One's-Self I sing, a simple separate person,
Yet utter the word Democratic, the word
　　En-Masse.
> *One's-Self I Sing*

13　O to be self-balanced for contingencies,
To confront night, storms, hunger, ridicule, accidents, rebuffs, as the trees and animals do.
> *Me Imperturb*

14 I hear America singing, the varied carols I hear.
> *I Hear America Singing*

15 I celebrate myself, and sing myself,
And what I assume you shall assume,
For every atom belonging to me as good belongs
　　to you.

I loafe and invite my soul,
I lean and loafe at my ease observing a spear of
　　summer grass.
> *Song of Myself, 1*

16 Stop this day and night with me and you shall possess the origin of all poems.
> *Song of Myself, 2*

17 Swiftly arose and spread around me the peace and
　　knowledge that pass all the argument of the
　　earth,
And I know that the hand of God is the promise of
　　my own,
And I know that the spirit of God is the brother of
　　my own,
And that all the men ever born are also my brothers, and the women my sisters and lovers,
And that a kelson of the creation is love.
> *Song of Myself, 5*

18 A child said *What is the grass?* fetching it to me
　　with full hands;
How could I answer the child? I do not know what
　　it is any more than he.

I guess it must be the flag of my disposition, out of
　　hopeful green stuff woven.
> *Song of Myself, 6*

19 And now it seems to me the beautiful uncut hair of
　　graves.
> *Song of Myself, 6*

1 Has any one supposed it lucky to be born?
  I hasten to inform him or her it is just as lucky to
    die, and I know it.

Song of Myself, 7

2 And the look of the bay mare shames silliness out
    of me.   *Song of Myself, 13*

3 This is the grass that grows wherever the land is
    and the water is,
  This is the common air that bathes the globe.

Song of Myself, 17

4 Have you heard that it was good to gain the day?
  I also say it is good to fall, battles are lost in the
    same spirit in which they are won.

Song of Myself, 18

5 I find no sweeter fat than sticks to my own bones.

Song of Myself, 20

6 My foothold is tenon'd and mortis'd in granite,
  I laugh at what you call dissolution,
  And I know the amplitude of time.

Song of Myself, 20

7 I am the poet of the Body and I am the poet of the
    Soul.   *Song of Myself, 21*

8 I am he that walks with the tender and growing
    night,
  I call to the earth and sea half-held by the night.

  Press close bare-bosom'd night—press close mag-
    netic nourishing night!
  Night of south winds—night of the large few stars!
  Still nodding night—mad naked summer night.

Song of Myself, 21

9 Walt Whitman, a kosmos, of Manhattan the son,
  Turbulent, fleshy, sensual, eating, drinking and
    breeding,
  No sentimentalist, no stander above men and
    women or apart from them,
  No more modest than immodest.

  Unscrew the locks from the doors!
  Unscrew the doors themselves from their jambs!

Song of Myself, 24

10 The scent of these arm-pits aroma finer than prayer,
  This head more than churches, bibles, and all the
    creeds.   *Song of Myself, 24*

11 I dote on myself, there is that lot of me and all so
    luscious.   *Song of Myself, 24*

12 Steep'd amid honey'd morphine, my windpipe
    throttled in fakes of death.

Song of Myself, 26

13 I merely stir, press, feel with my fingers, and am
    happy,

To touch my person to someone else's is about as
    much as I can stand.   *Song of Myself, 27*

14 Logic and sermons never convince,
  The damp of the night drives deeper into my soul.

Song of Myself, 30

15 I believe a leaf of grass is no less than the journey-
    work of the stars.   *Song of Myself, 31*

16 I think I could turn and live with animals, they are
    so placid and self-contain'd,
  I stand and look at them long and long.

  They do not sweat and whine about their
    condition,
  They do not lie awake in the dark and weep for
    their sins,
  They do not make me sick discussing their duty to
    God,
  Not one is dissatisfied, not one is demented with
    the mania of owning things,
  Not one kneels to another, nor to his kind that
    lived thousands of years ago,
  Not one is respectable or unhappy over the whole
    earth.   *Song of Myself, 32*

17 I am afoot with my vision.   *Song of Myself, 33*

18 I am the man, I suffer'd, I was there.

Song of Myself, 33

19 Agonies are one of my changes of garments.

Song of Myself, 33

20 I have said that the soul is not more than the body,
  And I have said that the body is not more than the
    soul,
  And nothing, not God, is greater to one than one's
    self is,
  And whoever walks a furlong without sympathy
    walks to his own funeral drest in his shroud.

Song of Myself, 48

21 Do I contradict myself?
  Very well then I contradict myself,
  (I am large, I contain multitudes.)

Song of Myself, 51

22 I sound my barbaric yawp over the roofs of the
    world.   *Song of Myself, 52*

23 I bequeath myself to the dirt to grow from the
    grass I love,
  If you want me again look for me under your
    boot-soles.   *Song of Myself, 52*

24 If anything is sacred the human body is sacred.

I Sing the Body Electric, 8

25 Through you I drain the pent-up rivers of myself,
  In you I wrap a thousand onward years.

A Woman Waits for Me

1 As Adam early in the morning,
  Walking forth from the bower refresh'd with sleep,
  Behold me where I pass, hear my voice, approach,
  Touch me, touch the palm of your hand to my
      body as I pass,
  Be not afraid of my body.
                          As Adam Early in the Morning

2 Afoot and light-hearted I take to the open road,
  Healthy, free, the world before me,
  The long brown path before me leading wherever I
      choose.

  Henceforth I ask not good-fortune, I myself am
      good-fortune.   *Song of the Open Road, 1*

3 The glories strung like beads on my smallest sights
      and hearings, on the walk in the street and the
      passage over the river.
                          Crossing Brooklyn Ferry, 2

4 A great city is that which has the greatest men and
      women,
  If it be a few ragged huts it is still the greatest city
      in the whole world.
                          Song of the Broad-Axe, 4

5 Come Muse migrate from Greece and Ionia,
  Cross out please those immensely overpaid
      accounts,
  That matter of Troy and Achilles' wrath, and
      Aeneas', Odysseus' wanderings,
  Placard "Removed" and "To Let" on the rocks of
      your snowy Parnassus.
                          Song of the Exposition, 2

6 We must march my darlings, we must bear the
      brunt of danger,
  We the youthful sinewy races, all the rest on us
      depend,
  Pioneers! O pioneers!   *Pioneers! O Pioneers!*

7 Out of the cradle endlessly rocking,
  Out of the mocking-bird's throat, the musical
      shuttle,
  Out of the Ninth-month midnight.
                          Out of the Cradle Endlessly Rocking

8 When I heard the learn'd astronomer,
  When the proofs, the figures, were ranged in
      columns before me,
  When I was shown the charts and diagrams, to add,
      divide, and measure them,
  When I sitting heard the astronomer where he lec-
      tured with much applause in the lecture-room,
  How soon unaccountable I became tired and sick,
  Till rising and gliding out I wander'd off by myself,
  In the mystical moist night-air, and from time to
      time,
  Look'd up in perfect silence at the stars.
                          When I Heard the Learn'd Astronomer

9 Words! book-words! what are you?
                          Song of the Banner at Daybrea

10 Young man I think I know you—I think this face
      is the face of the Christ himself,
  Dead and divine and brother of all, and here again
      he lies.
                          *A Sight in Camp in the Daybreak Gray
                          and Grim*

11 Many a soldier's loving arms about this neck have
      cross'd and rested,
  Many a soldier's kiss dwells on these bearded lips.
                          The Wound-Dresser

12 Give me the splendid silent sun with all his beams
      full-dazzling.
                          Give Me the Splendid Silent Sun, 1

13 Word over all, beautiful as the sky,
  Beautiful that war and all its deeds of carnage must
      in time be utterly lost,
  That the hands of the sisters Death and Night
      incessantly softly wash again, and ever again,
      this soil'd world;
  For my enemy is dead, a man divine as myself
      is dead.   *Reconciliation*

14 When lilacs last in the dooryard bloom'd,
  And the great star early droop'd in the western
      sky in the night,
  I mourn'd, and yet shall mourn with
      ever-returning spring.
                          When Lilacs Last in the Dooryard Bloom'd, 1

15 Nor for you, for one alone,
  Blossoms and branches green to coffins all I bring,
  For fresh as the morning, thus would I chant a
      song for you O sane and sacred death.
                          When Lilacs Last in the Dooryard Bloom'd, 7

16 Come lovely and soothing death,
  Undulate round the world, serenely arriving,
      arriving,
  In the day, in the night, to all, to each,
  Sooner or later delicate death.
                          When Lilacs Last in the Dooryard Bloom'd, 14

17 Dark mother always gliding near with soft feet,
  Have none chanted for thee a chant of fullest
      welcome?
                          When Lilacs Last in the Dooryard Bloom'd, 14

18 O Captain! my Captain! our fearful trip is done,
  The ship has weather'd every rack, the prize we
      sought is won,
  The port is near, the bells I hear, the people all
      exulting.   *O Captain! My Captain!, st. 1*

19 Exult O shores, and ring O bells!
  But I with mournful tread,

Walk the deck my Captain lies,
    Fallen cold and dead.
                    O Captain! My Captain!, st. 3

1 There was a child went forth every day,
    And the first object he look'd upon, that object he
        became.   *There Was a Child Went Forth*

2 The horizon's edge, the flying sea-crow, the
        fragrance of salt marsh and shore mud,
    These became part of that child who went forth
        every day, and who now goes, and will always
        go forth every day.
                    There Was a Child Went Forth

3 To me every hour of the light and dark is a miracle,
    Every cubic inch of space is a miracle.   *Miracles*

4 A batter'd, wreck'd old man,
    Thrown on this savage shore, far from home,
    Pent by the sea and dark rebellious brows, twelve
        dreary months,
    Sore, stiff with many toils, sicken'd and nigh to
        death,
    I take my way along the island's edge,
    Venting a heavy heart.   *Prayer of Columbus*

5 I dream in my dream all the dreams of the other
        dreamers,
    And I become the other dreamers.   *The Sleepers, 1*

6 I am she who adorn'd herself and folded her hair
        expectantly,
    My truant lover has come, and it is dark.
                            The Sleepers, 1

7 A noiseless patient spider,
    I mark'd where on a little promontory it stood
        isolated,
    Mark'd how to explore the vacant vast surrounding,
    It launch'd forth filament, filament, filament out of
        itself,
    Ever unreeling them, ever tirelessly speeding them.
                    A Noiseless Patient Spider

8 Camerado, this is no book,
    Who touches this touches a man.   *So Long!*

9   I depart from materials,
    I am as one disembodied, triumphant, dead.
                                So Long!

10   He [President Abraham Lincoln] has a face like a
    hoosier Michael Angelo, so awful ugly it becomes
    beautiful, with its strange mouth, its deep-cut, criss-
    cross lines, and its doughnut complexion.
                        Letter [March 19, 1863]

11   Never was there, perhaps, more hollowness of
    heart than at present, and here in the United States.
    Genuine belief seems to have left us.
                        Democratic Vistas [1871]

12   It [Democracy] is a great word, whose history, I
    suppose, remains unwritten, because that history
    has yet to be enacted.
                        Democratic Vistas

13   *The Real War Will Never Get in the Books.* And
    so good-bye to the war.
                *Specimen Days [1882]. The Real War Will
                Never Get in the Books*

14   Such was the war. It was not a quadrille in a ball-
    room. Its interior history will not only never be
    written — its practicality, minutiae of deeds and pas-
    sions, will never even be suggested.
                *Specimen Days. The Real War Will Never Get
                in the Books*

15   To have great poets, there must be great audi-
    ences, too.   *Collect [1882]. Notes Left Over*

16   So here I sit in the early candle-light of old
    age — I and my book — casting backward glances
    over our travel'd road.
                *November Boughs [1888]. A Backward
                Glance O'er Travel'd Roads*

17   The strongest and sweetest songs yet remain to
    be sung.
                *November Boughs. A Backward Glance O'er
                Travel'd Roads*

Susan B[rownell] Anthony
1820–1906

18   The men and women of the North are slave-
    holders, those of the South slaveowners. The guilt
    rests on the North equally with the South.
            Speech on No Union with Slaveholders [1857]

19   Cautious, careful people, always casting about to
    preserve their reputation and social standing, never
    can bring about a reform. Those who are really in
    earnest must be willing to be anything or nothing in
    the world's estimation.
            *On the campaign for divorce law reform
            [1860]*

20   Make [your employers] understand that you are
    in their service as workers, not as women.
            *The Revolution (woman suffrage newspaper),
            October 8, 1868*

21   Join the union, girls, and together say *Equal Pay
    for Equal Work.*
            *The Revolution (woman suffrage newspaper),
            March 18, 1869*

22   Woman must not depend upon the protection of
    man, but must be taught to protect herself.
            Speech in San Francisco [July 1871]

1   I shall work for the Republican party and call on all women to join me, precisely . . . for what that party has done and promises to do for women, nothing more, nothing less.
Letter to Elizabeth Cady Stanton [autumn 1872]

2   Here, in the first paragraph of the Declaration [of Independence], is the assertion of the natural right of all to the ballot; for how can "the consent of the governed" be given, if the right to vote be denied?
Is It a Crime for a Citizen of the United States to Vote? Speech [1873] before her trial for voting

3   Marriage, to women as to men, must be a luxury, not a necessity; an incident of life, not all of it. And the only possible way to accomplish this great change is to accord to women equal power in the making, shaping and controlling of the circumstances of life.
Speech on Social Purity [spring 1875]

Dion Boucicault
1820–1890

4   Yes, quit the house and never darken the threshold of its doors again.   *Flying Scud [1866], act I*

Florence Nightingale
1820–1910

5   It may seem a strange principle to enunciate as the very first requirement in a Hospital that it should do the sick no harm.[1]
Notes on Hospitals [1859], preface

Theodore O'Hara
1820–1867

6 On Fame's eternal camping ground
Their silent tents are spread,
And Glory guards, with solemn round,
The bivouac of the dead.
The Bivouac of the Dead[2] [1847], st. 1

7 Sons of the dark and bloody ground.[3]
The Bivouac of the Dead, st. 9

---

[1]See Hippocrates, 72:17.

[2]Written to commemorate Americans slain in the battle of Buena Vista [February 22–23, 1847].

[3]Kentucky, from its history as a hunting and burial territory for warring Indian tribes.

George Frederick Root
1820–1895

8 Tramp! Tramp! Tramp! the boys are marching,
Cheer up, comrades, they will come,
And beneath the starry flag
We shall breathe the air again
Of the free land in our own beloved home.
Tramp! Tramp! Tramp! [1862]

9 Yes, we'll rally round the flag, boys, we'll rally once again,
Shouting the battle cry of Freedom.
The Battle Cry of Freedom [1863]

Sir William Howard Russell
1820–1907

10   The Russians dashed on towards that thin red-line streak tipped with a line of steel.[4]
To The Times of London from the Crimea, describing the British infantry at Balaklava [October 25, 1854]

William Tecumseh Sherman
1820–1891

11   You cannot qualify war in harsher terms than I will. War is cruelty, and you cannot refine it.
Letter to James M. Calhoun, mayor of Atlanta, and others [September 12, 1864]

12   Hold the fort! I am coming![5]
Attributed signal from Kennesaw Mountain to General John Murray Corse at Allatoona Pass [October 5, 1864]

13   The legitimate object of war is a more perfect peace.   *Speech at St. Louis [July 20, 1865]*

14   War is at best barbarism. . . . Its glory is all moonshine. It is only those who have neither fired a shot nor heard the shrieks and groans of the wounded who cry aloud for blood, more vengeance, more desolation. War is hell.
Attributed to a graduation address at Michigan Military Academy [June 19, 1879]

---

[4]Soon the men of the column began to see that though the scarlet line was slender, it was very rigid and exact.—A. W. KINGLAKE [1809–1891], *Invasion of the Crimea, vol. III, p. 455*

It's "Thin red line of 'eroes" when the drums begin to roll.— RUDYARD KIPLING, *Tommy, st. 3*

[5]He actually said: "Hold out. Relief is coming." General Corse replied: "I am short a cheekbone and an ear, but am able to whip all hell yet."

Hold the fort, for I am coming!—PHILIP PAUL BLISS [1838–1876], *Hold the Fort, refrain*

1   I will not accept if nominated and will not serve if elected.[1]

> *Message to Republican National Convention [June 5, 1884]*

Herbert Spencer
1820–1903

2   Progress, therefore, is not an accident, but a necessity. . . . It is a part of nature.

> *Social Statics [1851], pt. I, ch. 2*

3   Education has for its object the formation of character.   *Social Statics, II, 17*

4   The poverty of the incapable, the distresses that come upon the imprudent, the starvation of the idle, and those shoulderings aside of the weak by the strong, which leave so many "in shallows and in miseries," are the decrees of a large, farseeing benevolence.   *Social Statics, III, 25*

5   Opinion is ultimately determined by the feelings, and not by the intellect.   *Social Statics, IV, 30*

6   No one can be perfectly free till all are free; no one can be perfectly moral till all are moral; no one can be perfectly happy till all are happy.

> *Social Statics, IV, 30*

7   Every cause produces more than one effect.

> *Essays on Education [1861]. On Progress: Its Law and Cause*

8   The tyranny of Mrs. Grundy is worse than any other tyranny we suffer under.

> *Essays on Education. On Manners and Fashion*

9   Old forms of government finally grow so oppressive that they must be thrown off even at the risk of reigns of terror.

> *Essays on Education. On Manners and Fashion*

10   The fact disclosed by a survey of the past that majorities have been wrong must not blind us to the complementary fact that majorities have usually not been entirely wrong.

> *First Principles [1861]*

11   Volumes might be written upon the impiety of the pious.   *First Principles*

12   We have unmistakable proof that throughout all past time, there has been a ceaseless devouring of the weak by the strong.

> *First Principles*

13   This survival of the fittest which I have here sought to express in mechanical terms, is that which Mr. Darwin has called "natural selection, or the preservation of favored races in the struggle for life."[2]

> *Principles of Biology [1864–1867], pt. III, ch. 12*

14   The Republican form of government is the highest form of government: but because of this it requires the highest type of human nature—a type nowhere at present existing.

> *Essays [1891]. The Americans*

15   The ultimate result of shielding men from the effects of folly is to fill the world with fools.

> *Essays. State Tamperings with Money Banks*

16   Time: That which man is always trying to kill, but which ends in killing him.   *Definitions*

Harriet Tubman
c. 1820–1913

17   When I found I had crossed that line,[3] I looked at my hands to see if I was the same person. There was such a glory over everything.

> *To her biographer Sarah H. Bradford [c. 1868]*

18   I started with this idea in my head, "There's two things I've got a right to . . . death or liberty."

> *To her biographer Sarah H. Bradford*

19   'Twant me, 'twas the Lord. I always told him, "I trust to you. I don't know where to go or what to do, but I expect you to lead me," and he always did.

> *To her biographer Sarah H. Bradford*

John Tyndall
1820–1893

20   Heat Considered as a Mode of Motion.

> *Title of treatise [1863]*

21   Life is a wave, which in no two consecutive moments of its existence is composed of the same particles.   *Fragments of Science, vol. II, Vitality*

22   The brightest flashes in the world of thought are incomplete until they have been proved to have their counterparts in the world of fact.

> *Fragments of Science. Scientific Materialism*

23   Charles Darwin, the Abraham of scientific men—a searcher as obedient to the command of truth as was the patriarch to the command of God.

> *Fragments of Science. Science and Man*

---

[1]The familiar version is: If nominated I will not run; if elected I will not serve.

[2]See Charles Darwin, 469:13.

[3]On her first escape from slavery [1845].

1   Superstition may be defined as constructive religion which has grown incongruous with intelligence.   *Fragments of Science. Science and Man*

2   Religious feeling is as much a verity as any other part of human consciousness; and against it, on the subjective side, the waves of science beat in vain.   *Fragments of Science. Professor Virchow and Evolution*

Henri-Frédéric Amiel
1821–1881

3   To know how to grow old is the masterwork of wisdom, and one of the most difficult chapters in the great art of living.   *Journal Intime [1883]*

4   An error is the more dangerous the more truth it contains.   *Journal Intime*

5   Charm: the quality in others that makes us more satisfied with ourselves.   *Journal Intime*

Sir Henry Williams Baker
1821–1877

6 The King of love my shepherd is,
Whose goodness faileth never;
I nothing lack if I am his,
And he is mine forever.   *Hymn [1868]*

Charles Baudelaire
1821–1867

7 Hypocrite lecteur—mon semblable—mon frère
[Hypocrite reader—my double—my brother]!   *Les Fleurs du Mal [1861]. Au Lecteur*

8 The poet is like the prince of the clouds
Who haunts the tempest and laughs at the archer;
Exiled on the ground in the midst of jeers,
His giant wings prevent him from walking.[1]   *Les Fleurs du Mal. L'Albatros, st. 4*

9 Perfumes, colors and sounds echo one another.[2]   *Les Fleurs du Mal. Correspondances*

10 Mother of memories, mistress of mistresses.[3]   *Les Fleurs du Mal. Le Balcon, st. 1*

11 There, there is nothing else but grace and measure,
Richness, quietness and pleasure.[4]   *Les Fleurs du Mal. L'Invitation au Voyage, refrain*

12 I have more memories than if I were a thousand years old.[5]   *Les Fleurs du Mal. Spleen, l. 1*

13 I am the wound and the knife!
I am the blow and the cheek!
I am the limbs and the wheel—
The victim and the executioner![6]   *Les Fleurs du Mal. L'Héautontimorouménos*

14 Here is the charming evening, the criminal's friend;
It comes like an accomplice, with stealthy tread.[7]   *Les Fleurs du Mal. Le Crépuscule du Soir*

15 What is that sad, dark island?—It is Cythera,
They tell us, a country famous in song,
Banal Eldorado of all the old bachelors.
Look! after all, it is a poor land![8]   *Les Fleurs du Mal. Un Voyage à Cythère*

16 O Death, old captain, it is time! raise the anchor![9]   *Les Fleurs du Mal. Le Voyage, VIII*

17 What do I care that you are good?
Be beautiful! and be sad![10]   *Nouvelles Fleurs du Mal [1866–1868]. Madrigal Triste, st. 1*

18   There can be no progress (real, that is, moral) except in the individual and by the individual himself.   *Mon Coeur Mis à Nu [1887], XV*

19   There are in every man, at every hour, two simultaneous postulations, one towards God, the other towards Satan.   *Mon Coeur Mis à Nu, XIX*

20   There exist only three beings worthy of respect: the priest, the soldier, the poet. To know, to kill, to create.[11]   *Mon Coeur Mis à Nu, XXII*

---

[1]Le Poète est semblable au prince des nuées / Qui hante la tempête et se rit de l'archer; / Exilé sur le sol au milieu des huées, / Ses ailes de géant l'empêchent de marcher.

[2]Les parfums, les couleurs, et les sons se répondent.

[3]Mère des souvenirs, maîtresse des maîtresses.

[4]Là, tout n'est qu'ordre et beauté, / Luxe, calme et volupté. Translated by Richard Wilbur.

[5]J'ai plus de souvenirs que si j'avais mille ans.

[6]Je suis la plaie et le couteau! / Je suis le soufflet et la joue! / Je suis les membres et la roue, / Et la victime et le bourreau!

[7]Voici le soir charmant, ami du criminel; / Il vient comme un complice, à pas de loup.

[8]Quelle est cette île triste et noire? —C'est Cythère, / Nous dit-on, un pays fameux dans les chansons, / Eldorado banal de tous les vieux garçons. / Regardez! après tout, c'est une pauvre terre.

[9]Ô Mort, vieux capitaine, il est temps! levons l'ancre!

[10]Que m'importe que tu sois sage? / Sois belle! et sois triste!

[11]Il n'existe que trois êtres respectables: le prêtre, le guerrier, le poète. Savoir, tuer, et créer.

1 To be a great man and a saint for oneself, that is the one important thing.
Mon Coeur Mis à Nu, LII

2 Theory of the true civilization. It is not to be found in gas or steam or table turning. It consists in the diminution of the traces of original sin.
Mon Coeur Mis à Nu, LIX

3 You must shock the bourgeois.[1]
Attributed

Sir Richard Francis Burton
1821–1890

4 Why meet we on the bridge of Time to 'change one greeting and to part?
The Kasîdah of Hájî Abdû El-Yezdí, pt. I, st. 11

5 Indeed he knows not how to know who knows not also how to un-know.
The Kasîdah of Hájî Abdû El-Yezdí, VI, st. 18

6 Do what thy manhood bids thee do, from none but self expect applause;
He noblest lives and noblest dies who makes and keeps his self-made laws.
The Kasîdah of Hájî Abdû El-Yezdí, VIII, st. 37

Crowfoot[2]
1821–1890

7 What is life? It is the flash of a firefly in the night. It is the breath of a buffalo in the wintertime. It is the little shadow which runs across the grass and loses itself in the sunset.
Last words [1890]

Fëdor Mikhailovich Dostoevski
1821–1881

8 Petersburg, the most theoretical and intentional town on the whole terrestrial globe.
Notes from the Underground [1864],[3] ch. 2

9 Man is sometimes extraordinarily, passionately, in love with suffering.
Notes from the Underground, 9

10 Man grows used to everything, the scoundrel!
Crime and Punishment [1866],[3] book I, ch. 2

11 If you were to destroy in mankind the belief in immortality, not only love but every living force maintaining the life of the world would at once be dried up.
The Brothers Karamazov [1879–1880],[3] bk. II, ch. 6

12 I want to tell you now about the insects to whom God gave "sensual lust." . . . I am that insect, brother, and it is said of me especially. All we Karamazovs are such insects, and, angel as you are, that insect lives in you too, and will stir a tempest in your blood. Tempests, because sensual lust is a tempest—worse than a tempest! Beauty is a terrible and awful thing! It is terrible because it has not been fathomed, for God sets us nothing but riddles. Here the boundaries meet and all contradictions exist side by side.
The Brothers Karamazov, III, 3

13 What to the mind is shameful is beauty and nothing else to the heart. Is there beauty in Sodom? Believe me, that for the immense mass of mankind beauty is found in Sodom. Did you know that secret? The awful thing is that beauty is mysterious as well as terrible. God and devil are fighting there, and the battlefield is the heart of man.
The Brothers Karamazov, III, 3

14 I want to travel in Europe . . . I know that I am only going to a graveyard, but it's a most precious graveyard.
The Brothers Karamazov, V, 3

15 If the devil doesn't exist, but man has created him, he has created him in his own image and likeness.
The Brothers Karamazov, V, 4

16 Is there in the whole world a being who would have the right to forgive and could forgive? I don't want harmony. From love of humanity I don't want it. . . . I would rather remain with my unavenged suffering and unsatisfied indignation, *even if I were wrong*. Besides, too high a price is asked for harmony; it's beyond our means to pay so much to enter on it. And so I hasten to give back my entrance ticket. . . . It's not God that I don't accept, Alyosha, only I most respectfully return Him the ticket.
The Brothers Karamazov, V, 4

17 Imagine that you are creating a fabric of human destiny with the object of making men happy in the end, giving them peace and rest at last, but that it was essential and inevitable to torture to death only one tiny creature . . . and to found that edifice on

---

[1] Il faut épater le bourgeois.
[2] Blackfoot warrior and orator.
[3] Translated by Constance Garnett.

its unavenged tears, would you consent to be the architect on those conditions? Tell me, and tell the truth.[1]   *The Brothers Karamazov, V, 4*

1   So long as man remains free he strives for nothing so incessantly and so painfully as to find someone to worship.   *The Brothers Karamazov, V, 5*

2   We have corrected Thy work and have founded it upon *miracle, mystery* and *authority*. And men rejoiced that they were again led like sheep, and that the terrible gift that brought them such suffering, was, at last, lifted from their hearts.
     The Brothers Karamazov, V, 5

3   Men reject their prophets and slay them, but they love their martyrs and honor those whom they have slain.   *The Brothers Karamazov, VI, 3*

4   The jealous are the readiest of all to forgive, and all women know it.
     The Brothers Karamazov, VIII, 3

5   Who doesn't desire his father's death?
     The Brothers Karamazov, XII, 5

6   They have their Hamlets, but we still have our Karamazovs!   *The Brothers Karamazov, XII, 9*

7   But profound as psychology is, it's a knife that cuts both ways.
     The Brothers Karamazov, XII, 10

8   For a moment the lie becomes truth.
     The Brothers Karamazov. Epilogue, ch. 2

9   We have all come out of Gogol's *Overcoat*.[2]
     Attributed

Mary Baker Eddy
1821–1910

10   Our Father-Mother God, all-harmonious.
     Science and Health with Key to the Scriptures [1875], p. 16

11   Jesus of Nazareth was the most scientific man that ever trod the globe. He plunged beneath the material surface of things, and found the spiritual cause.
     Science and Health with Key to the Scriptures, p. 313

12   Spirit is the real and eternal; matter is the unreal and temporal.
     Science and Health with Key to the Scriptures, p. 468

13   Disease is an experience of so-called mortal mind. It is fear made manifest on the body.
     Science and Health with Key to the Scriptures, p. 493

Gustave Flaubert
1821–1880

14   One must not always think that feeling is everything. Art is nothing without form.
     Letter to Madame Louise Colet [August 12, 1846]

15   What a horrible invention, the bourgeois, don't you think?[3]
     Letter to Madame Louise Colet [September 22, 1846]

16   One becomes a critic when one cannot be an artist, just as a man becomes a stool pigeon when he cannot be a soldier.
     Letter to Madame Louise Colet [October 22, 1846]

17   There was an air of indifference about them [the male guests], a calm produced by the gratification of every passion . . . that special brutality which comes from the habit of breaking down half-hearted resistances that keep one fit and tickle one's vanity — the handling of blooded horses, the pursuit of loose women.
     Madame Bovary [1857],[4] pt. I, ch. 8

18   It never occurred to her that if the drainpipes of a house are clogged, the rain may collect in pools on the roof; and she suspected no danger until suddenly she discovered a crack in the wall.
     Madame Bovary, II, 5

19   Human speech is like a cracked kettle on which we tap crude rhythms for bears to dance to, while we long to make music that will melt the stars.[5]
     Madame Bovary, II, 12

---

[1]"Do you remember the passage where he [Rousseau] asks the reader what he would do if he could make a fortune by killing an old mandarin in China by simply exerting his will, without stirring from Paris?" "Yes." "Well?" "Bah! I'm at my thirty-third mandarin." "Don't play the fool. Look here, if it were proved to you that the thing was possible and you only needed to nod your head, would you do it?" "Is your mandarin well stricken in years? But, bless you, young or old, paralytic or healthy, upon my word — The devil take it! Well, no." — HONORÉ DE BALZAC, *Le Père Goriot* [1835]

[2]This statement, traditionally attributed to Dostoevski and quoted by most writers on Dostoevski and on Russian realism, appears in Eugène Melchior, vicomte de Vogüé [1848–1910], *Le Roman Russe* [1886], ch. 3: "The more I read the Russians, the more I understand the observation one of them made to me: 'We have all come out of Gogol's *Overcoat*.'"

[3]Quelle atroce invention que celle du bourgeois, n'est-ce pas?

[4]Translated by FRANCIS STEEGMULLER.

[5]La parole humaine est comme un chaudron fêlé où nous battons des melodies à faire danser les ours, quand on voudrait attendrir les étoiles.

1   She [Madame Bovary] had that indefinable beauty that comes from happiness, enthusiasm, success—a beauty that is nothing more or less than a harmony of temperament and circumstances.
Madame Bovary, II, 12

2   We shouldn't maltreat our idols: the gilt comes off on our hands.[1]   *Madame Bovary, III, 6*

3   There isn't a bourgeois alive who in the ferment of his youth, if only for a day or for a minute, hasn't thought himself capable of boundless passions and noble exploits. The sorriest little woman-chaser has dreamed of Oriental queens; in a corner of every notary's heart lie the moldy remains of a poet.
Madame Bovary, III, 6

4   Of all the icy blasts that blow on love, a request for money is the most chilling and havoc-wreaking.
Madame Bovary, III, 8

5   Anyone's death always releases something like an aura of stupefaction, so difficult is it to grasp this irruption of nothingness and to believe that it has actually taken place.   *Madame Bovary, III, 9*

6   The writer in his work must be like God in his creation—invisible and all-powerful: he must be everywhere felt, but never seen.
Letter to Mademoiselle Leroyer de Chantepie [March 18, 1857]

7   The one way of tolerating existence is to lose oneself in literature as in a perpetual orgy.
Letter to Mademoiselle Leroyer de Chantepie [September 4, 1858]

8   Axiom: hatred of the bourgeois is the beginning of wisdom.
Letter to George Sand [May 10, 1867]

9   I call a bourgeois anyone whose thinking is vulgar.
Quoted by Maupassant

10   What is beautiful is moral, that is all there is to it.
Letter to Maupassant [October 26, 1880]

11   *I* am Madame Bovary.[2]
From RENÉ DESCHARNES, Flaubert [1909]

Nathan Bedford Forrest
1821–1877

12   Get there first with the most men.[3]
Reported by General Basil Duke and General Richard Taylor

Hermann Ludwig Ferdinand von Helmholtz
1821–1894

13   Nature as a whole possesses a store of force which cannot in any way be either increased or diminished . . . therefore, the quantity of force in Nature is just as eternal and unalterable as the quantity of matter. . . . I have named [this] general law "The Principle of the Conservation of Force."[4]
Über die Erhaltung der Kraft [1847]

14   Whoever, in the pursuit of science, seeks after immediate practical utility, may generally rest assured that he will seek in vain. All that science can achieve is a perfect knowledge and a perfect understanding of the action of natural and moral forces.
Academic discourse, Heidelberg [1862]

Nikolai Nekrasov
1821–1877

15   You do not have to be a poet, but you are obliged to be a citizen.
Poet and Citizen

16   Wretched and abundant,
Oppressed and powerful,
Weak and mighty,
Mother Russia!
Who Is Happy in Russia? [1873–1876]

William H[enry] Vanderbilt
1821–1885

17   The public be damned.
Reply to a newspaper reporter [October 2, 1882]

Rudolf Virchow
1821–1902

18   I formulate the doctrine of pathological generation . . . in simple terms: *omnis cellula e cellula.*[5]
Cellular Pathology [1858].[6] Disease, Life and Man

---

[1]Il ne faut pas toucher aux idoles: la dorure en reste aux mains.

[2]Madame Bovary, c'est moi!

[3]Erroneous version usually rendered: Git thar fustest with the mostest.

---

[4]Translated by E. ATKINSON.
Helmholtz's "force" is equivalent to the modern physicist's "energy."

[5]All cells come from [pre-existing] cells.

[6]Essays translated by LELLAND J. RATHER.

George John Whyte-Melville
1821–1878

1   In the choice of a horse and a wife, a man must please himself, ignoring the opinion and advice of friends.   *Riding Recollections [1878]*

Matthew Arnold
1822–1888

2   Be his[1]
My special thanks, whose even-balanced soul,
From first youth tested up to extreme old age,
Business could not make dull, nor passion wild:
Who saw life steadily and saw it whole.
    To a Friend [1849], l. 8

3   Others abide our question. Thou art free.
We ask and ask: Thou smilest and art still,
Out-topping knowledge.
    Shakespeare [1849], l. 1

4   Strong is the soul, and wise, and beautiful:
The seeds of godlike power are in us still:
Gods are we, bards, saints, heroes, if we will.
    Written in Emerson's Essays [1849], l. 11

5   Come, dear children, let us away;
Down and away below!
Now my brothers call from the bay,
Now the great winds shoreward blow,
Now the salt tides seaward flow;
Now the wild white horses play,
Champ and chafe and toss in the spray.
    The Forsaken Merman [1849], st. 1

6   Sand-strewn caverns, cool and deep,
Where the winds are all asleep.
    The Forsaken Merman, st. 4

7   Where great whales come sailing by,
Sail and sail, with unshut eye,
Round the world forever and aye.
    The Forsaken Merman, st. 4

8   Singing, "Here came a mortal,
But faithless was she.
And alone dwell forever
The kings of the sea."
    The Forsaken Merman, st. 8

9   Fate gave, what Chance shall not control,
His sad lucidity of soul.
    Resignation [1849], l. 197

10   The world in which we live and move
Outlasts aversion, outlasts love:
Outlasts each effort, interest, hope,
Remorse, grief, joy.   *Resignation, l. 215*

----

[1]Sophocles.

11   Yet they, believe me, who await
No gifts from Chance, have conquered Fate.
    Resignation, l. 247

12   We cannot kindle when we will
The fire that in the heart resides,
The spirit bloweth and is still,
In mystery our soul abides.
    Morality [1852], st. 1

13   Calm Soul of all things! make it mine
To feel, amid the city's jar,
That there abides a peace of thine,
Man did not make, and can not mar.
    Lines Written in Kensington Gardens [1852], st. 10

14   Goethe in Weimar sleeps, and Greece,
Long since, saw Byron's struggle cease.
    Memorial Verses, April 1850 [1852], st. 1

15   Physician of the Iron Age,
Goethe has done his pilgrimage.
He took the suffering human race,
He read each wound, each weakness clear;
And struck his finger on the place,
And said: Thou ailest here, and here!
    Memorial Verses, April 1850, st. 3

16   This iron time
Of doubt, disputes, distractions, fears.
    Memorial Verses, April 1850, st. 4

17   Hither and thither spins
The windborne, mirroring soul;
A thousand glimpses wins,
And never sees a whole.
    Empedocles on Etna [1852], act I, sc. ii, l. 82

18   Be neither saint- nor sophist-led, but be a man!
    Empedocles on Etna, I, ii, l. 136

19   Thou hast no *right* to bliss.
    Empedocles on Etna, I, ii, l. 160

20   We do not what we ought;
What we ought not, we do;
And lean upon the thought
That chance will bring us through.
    Empedocles on Etna, I, ii, l. 237

21   Nature, with equal mind,
Sees all her sons at play;
Sees man control the wind,
The wind sweep man away.
    Empedocles on Etna, I, ii, l. 257

22   So, loath to suffer mute,
We, peopling the void air,
Make Gods to whom to impute
The ills we ought to bear.
    Empedocles on Etna, I, ii, l. 277

1 Is it so small a thing
  To have enjoyed the sun,
  To have lived light in the spring,
  To have loved, to have thought, to have done;
  To have advanced true friends, and beat down
        baffling foes?   *Empedocles on Etna, II, l. 397*

2 The day in its hotness,
  The strife with the palm;
  The night in her silence,
  The stars in their calm.
                    Empedocles on Etna, II, l. 465

3 Yes, in the sea of life enisled,
  With echoing straits between us thrown,
  Dotting the shoreless watery wild,
  We mortal millions live *alone*.
            To Marguerite. Continued [1852], l. 1

4 But often in the world's most crowded streets,
  But often, in the din of strife,
  There rises an unspeakable desire
  After the knowledge of our buried life.
                    The Buried Life [1852], l. 45

5 And long we try in vain to speak and act
  Our hidden self, and what we say and do
  Is eloquent, is well — but 'tis not true!
                    The Buried Life, l. 64

6 What shelter to grow ripe is ours?
  What leisure to grow wise?
        Stanzas in Memory of the Author of
        "Obermann" [1852], st. 18

7 Ah! two desires toss about
  The poet's feverish blood;
  One drives him to the world without,
  And one to solitude.
        Stanzas in Memory of the Author of
        "Obermann," st. 24

8   What actions are the most excellent? Those, certainly, which most powerfully appeal to the great primary human affections: to those elementary feelings which subsist permanently in the race, and which are independent of time. These feelings are permanent and the same; that which interests them is permanent and the same also.
                    Preface to Poems [1853]

9 Go, for they call you, Shepherd, from the hill.
                    The Scholar Gypsy [1853], st. 1

10 Thou waitest for the spark from heaven: and we,
   Light half-believers of our casual creeds,
   Who never deeply felt, nor clearly willed . . .
   Who hesitate and falter life away,
   And lose tomorrow the ground won today —
   Ah! do not we, wanderer! await it too?
                    The Scholar Gypsy, st. 18

11   And amongst us one,
   Who most has suffered, takes dejectedly
   His seat upon the intellectual throne.
                    The Scholar Gypsy, st. 19

12 Oh, born in days when wits were fresh and clear,
   And life ran gaily as the sparkling Thames;
   Before this strange disease of modern life,
   With its sick hurry, its divided aims,
   Its heads o'ertaxed, its palsied hearts, was rife.
                    The Scholar Gypsy, st. 21

13 Still nursing the unconquerable hope,
   Still clutching the inviolable shade.
                    The Scholar Gypsy, st. 22

14 Strew on her roses, roses,
   And never a spray of yew!
   In quiet she reposes;
   Ah, would that I did too!
                    Requiescat [1853], st. 1

15 Her cabined, ample spirit
   It fluttered and failed for breath.
   Tonight it doth inherit
   The vasty hall of death.   *Requiescat, st. 4*

16 Truth sits upon the lips of dying men.
                    Sohrab and Rustum, l. 656

17   Sanity — that is the great virtue of the ancient literature; the want of that is the great defect of the modern, in spite of its variety and power.
                    Preface to Poems [1854]

18 For rigorous teachers seized my youth,
   And purged its faith, and trimmed its fire,
   Showed me the high, white star of Truth,
   There bade me gaze, and there aspire.
        Stanzas from the Grande Chartreuse [1855],
        st. 12

19 Wandering between two worlds, one dead,
   The other powerless to be born.
        Stanzas from the Grande Chartreuse, st. 15

20 And we forget because we must
   And not because we will.   *Absence [1857], st. 3*

21   The translator of Homer should above all be penetrated by a sense of four qualities of his author: that he is eminently rapid; that he is eminently plain and direct, both in the evolution of his thought and in the expression of it, that is, both in his syntax and in his words; that he is eminently plain and direct in the substance of his thought, that is, in his matter and ideas; and, finally, that he is eminently noble.
                    On Translating Homer [1861]

22   Of these two literatures [French and German], as of the intellect of Europe in general, the main effort, for now many years, has been a *critical* effort;

the endeavor, in all branches of knowledge — theology, philosophy, history, art, science — to see the object as in itself it really is.

On Translating Homer

1   The grand style arises in poetry, when a noble nature, poetically gifted, treats with simplicity or with severity a serious subject.

On Translating Homer

2   Nations are not truly great solely because the individuals composing them are numerous, free, and active; but they are great when these numbers, this freedom, and this activity are employed in the service of an ideal higher than that of an ordinary man, taken by himself.   *Democracy [1861]*

3   It is a very great thing to be able to think as you like; but, after all, an important question remains: *what* you think.   *Democracy*

4   For the creation of a masterwork of literature two powers must concur, the power of the man and the power of the moment, and the man is not enough without the moment.

The Function of Criticism at the Present Time [1864]

5   The critical power . . . tends, at last, to make an intellectual situation of which the creative power can profitably avail itself . . . to make the best ideas prevail.

The Function of Criticism at the Present Time

6   There is the world of ideas and there is the world of practice; the French are often for suppressing the one and the English the other; but neither is to be suppressed.

The Function of Criticism at the Present Time

7   Burke is so great because, almost alone in England, he brings thought to bear upon politics, he saturates politics with thought.

The Function of Criticism at the Present Time

8   The notion of the free play of the mind upon all subjects being a pleasure in itself, being an object of desire, being an essential provider of elements without which a nation's spirit, whatever compensations it may have for them, must, in the long run, die of inanition, hardly enters into an Englishman's thoughts.

The Function of Criticism at the Present Time

9   I am bound by my own definition of criticism: *a disinterested endeavor to learn and propagate the best that is known and thought in the world.*

The Function of Criticism at the Present Time

10   Whispering from her towers [Oxford] the last enchantments of the Middle Age. . . . Home of lost

causes, and forsaken beliefs, and unpopular names and impossible loyalties!

Essays in Criticism, first series [1865], preface

11   Poetry is simply the most beautiful, impressive and wisely effective mode of saying things, and hence its importance.

Essays in Criticism, first series. Heinrich Heine

12   *Philistine* must have originally meant, in the mind of those who invented the nickname, a strong, dogged, unenlightened opponent of the chosen people, of the children of the light.

Essays in Criticism, first series. Heinrich Heine

13   On the breast of that huge Mississippi of falsehood called *History*, a foam-bell more or less is no consequence.[1]

Essays in Criticism, first series. Literary Influence of Academies [1864]

14   The great apostle of the Philistines, Lord Macaulay.

Essays in Criticism, first series. Joubert

15   Are ye too changed, ye hills?
See, 'tis no foot of unfamiliar men
Tonight from Oxford up your pathway strays!
Here came I often, often, in old days —
Thyrsis[2] and I; we still had Thyrsis then.

Thyrsis [1866], st. 1

16   That sweet city[3] with her dreaming spires.

Thyrsis, st. 2

17   The bloom is gone, and with the bloom go I.

Thyrsis, st. 6

18   Yes, thou art gone! and round me too the night
In ever-nearing circle weaves her shade.

Thyrsis, st. 14

19   The sea is calm tonight.
The tide is full, the moon lies fair
Upon the straits; on the French coast, the light
Gleams, and is gone; the cliffs of England stand,
Glimmering and vast, out in the tranquil bay.

Dover Beach [1867], st. 1

20   Listen! you hear the grating roar
Of pebbles which the waves draw back, and fling,
At their return, up the high strand,
Begin, and cease, and then again begin,

---

[1]This passage appeared only in the first appearance of the essay in *Cornhill Magazine* [August 1864].

History is nothing more than the belief in the senses, the belief in falsehood. — FRIEDRICH NIETZSCHE, *The Twilight of the Idols* [1888], *"Reason" in Philosophy, I*

History is more or less bunk. — HENRY FORD [1863–1947], interview with Charles N. Wheeler, *Chicago Tribune* [May 25, 1916]

[2]Arthur Hugh Clough [1819–1861].

[3]Oxford.

With tremulous cadence slow, and bring
The eternal note of sadness in.   *Dover Beach, st. 1*

1 Sophocles long ago
Heard it on the Aegean.   *Dover Beach, st. 2*

2 The sea of faith
Was once, too, at the full, and round earth's shore
Lay like the folds of a bright girdle furled.
But now I only hear
Its melancholy, long, withdrawing roar,
Retreating, to the breath
Of the night-wind, down the vast edges drear
And naked shingles of the world.

Ah, love, let us be true
To one another! for the world, which seems
To lie before us like a land of dreams,
So various, so beautiful, so new,
Hath really neither joy, nor love, nor light,
Nor certitude, nor peace, nor help for pain;
And we are here as on a darkling plain
Swept with confused alarms of struggle and flight,
Where ignorant armies clash by night.
     Dover Beach, st. 3, 4

3 Creep into thy narrow bed,
Creep, and let no more be said!
     The Last Word [1867], st. 1

4 Let the long contention cease!
Geese are swans, and swans are geese.
     The Last Word, st. 2

5 Charge once more, then, and be dumb!
Let the victors, when they come,
When the forts of folly fall,
Find thy body by the wall.   *The Last Word, st. 4*

6 Cruel, but composed and bland,
Dumb, inscrutable and grand,
So Tiberius might have sat,
Had Tiberius been a cat.   *Poor Matthias [1867]*

7 Style . . . is a peculiar recasting and heightening,
under a certain condition of spiritual excitement, of
what a man has to say, in such a manner as to add
dignity and distinction to it.
     On the Study of Celtic Literature [1867], sec. 6

8 The Celts certainly have it [style] in a wonderful
measure.
     On the Study of Celtic Literature, sec. 6

9 The power of the Latin classic is in *character*,
that of the Greek is in *beauty*. Now character is capable of being taught, learnt, and assimilated: beauty
hardly.
     *Schools and Universities on the Continent
     [1868]*

10 The whole scope of the essay is to recommend
culture as the great help out of our present difficulties; culture being a pursuit of our total perfection
by means of getting to know, on all the matters
which most concern us, the best which has been
thought and said in the world.
     Culture and Anarchy [1869], preface

11 Our society distributes itself into Barbarians, Philistines, and Populace; and America is just ourselves,
with the Barbarians quite left out, and the Populace
nearly.   *Culture and Anarchy, preface*

12 I am a Liberal, yet I am a Liberal tempered by
experience, reflection, and renouncement, and I
am, above all, a believer in culture.
     Culture and Anarchy, introduction

13 Culture is then properly described not as having
its origin in curiosity, but as having its origin in the
love of perfection; it is *a study of perfection*.
     Culture and Anarchy. Sweetness and Light

14 Greatness is a spiritual condition worthy to excite love, interest, and admiration.
     Culture and Anarchy. Sweetness and Light

15 Not a having and a resting, but a growing and a
becoming is the character of perfection as culture
conceives it.
     Culture and Anarchy. Sweetness and Light

16 He who works for sweetness and light united,
works to make reason and the will of God prevail.
     Culture and Anarchy. Sweetness and Light

17 The men of culture are the true apostles of
equality.
     Culture and Anarchy. Sweetness and Light

18 Everything in our political life tends to hide from
us that there is anything wiser than our ordinary
selves.
     *Culture and Anarchy. Barbarians, Philistines,
     Populace*

19 The governing idea of Hellenism is spontaneity
of consciousness, that of Hebraism, strictness of
conscience.
     *Culture and Anarchy. Hebraism and
     Hellenism*

20 Below the surface stream, shallow and light,
Of what we say and feel—below the stream,
As light, of what we think we feel, there flows
With noiseless current, strong, obscure and deep,
The central stream of what we feel indeed.
     St. Paul and Protestantism [1870]

21 Conduct is three-fourths of our life and its largest concern.
     Literature and Dogma [1873], ch. 1

1   The freethinking of one age is the common sense of the next.   *God and the Bible [1875]*

2   Choose equality.
    Mixed Essays [1879]. Equality

3   Inequality . . . has the natural and necessary effect, under the present circumstances, of materializing our upper class, vulgarizing our middle class, and brutalizing our lower class.
    Mixed Essays. Equality

4   For poetry the idea is everything; the rest is a world of illusion, of divine illusion. Poetry attaches its emotion to the idea; the idea *is* the fact. The strongest part of our religion today is its unconscious poetry.
    Introduction to T. H. WARD, English Poets [1880]

5   *Eutrapelia.* "A happy and gracious flexibility," Pericles calls this quality of the Athenians . . . lucidity of thought, clearness and propriety of language, freedom from prejudice and freedom from stiffness, openness of mind, amiability of manners.
    Irish Essays [1882]. A Speech at Eton

6   English civilization—the humanizing, the bringing into one harmonious and truly humane life, of the whole body of English society—that is what interests me.
    Irish Essays. Ecce, Convertimur ad Gentes

7   That which in England we call the middle class is in America virtually the nation.
    A Word About America [1882]

8   The American Philistine was a livelier sort of Philistine than ours.
    A Word More About America [1885]

9   What really dissatisfies in American civilization is the want of the *interesting,* a want due chiefly to the want of those two great elements of the interesting, which are elevation and beauty.
    Civilization in the United States [1888]

10   The best poetry will be found to have a power of forming, sustaining, and delighting us, as nothing else can.
    Essays in Criticism, second series [1888]. The Study of Poetry

11   Coleridge, poet and philosopher wrecked in a mist of opium.
    Essays in Criticism, second series. Byron

12   [A] beautiful and ineffectual angel [Shelley], beating in the void his luminous wings in vain.
    Essays in Criticism, second series. Byron

Rudolf [Julius Emanuel] Clausius
1822–1888

13   Heat cannot of itself pass from a colder to a hotter body.
    The Second Law of Thermodynamics [1850][1]

Ulysses S[impson] Grant
1822–1885

14   No terms except an unconditional and immediate surrender can be accepted. I propose to move immediately upon your works.
    To General S. B. Buckner, Fort Donelson [February 16, 1862]

15   I propose to fight it out on this line, if it takes all summer.
    Dispatch to Washington, before Spottsylvania Court House [May 11, 1864]

16   Wherever the enemy goes let our troops go also.
    Dispatch to General Henry W. Halleck from City Point, Virginia [August 1, 1864]

17   The war is over—the rebels are our countrymen again.
    Upon stopping his men from cheering after Lee's surrender at Appomattox Court House [April 9, 1865]

18   Let us have peace.
    Accepting nomination for the presidency [May 29, 1868]

19   Let no guilty man escape, if it can be avoided. No personal considerations should stand in the way of performing a public duty.
    Indorsement of a letter relating to the Whiskey Ring [July 29, 1875]

20   Leave the matter of religion to the family altar, the church, and the private school, supported entirely by private contributions. Keep the church and the State forever separate.
    Speech at Des Moines, Iowa [1875]

Edward Everett Hale
1822–1909

21   Behind all these men you have to do with, behind officers, and government, and people even, there is the country herself, your country, and . . .

---

[1]Translated by WALTER D. BROWN.
    Heat will of its own accord flow only from a hot object to a cold object.—JOSIAH WILLARD GIBBS [1839–1903], *Scientific Papers* [1906], *The Second Law of Thermodynamics*

you belong to her as you belong to your own mother. Stand by her, boy, as you would stand by your mother.
The Man Without a Country [1863]

1   He loved his country as no other man has loved her, but no man deserved less at her hands.
The Man Without a Country. Epitaph of Philip Nolan

Thomas Hughes
1822–1896

2   Life isn't all beer and skittles; but beer and skittles, or something better of the same sort, must form a good part of every Englishman's education.
Tom Brown's Schooldays [1857], pt. I, ch. 2

3   He never wants anything but what's right and fair; only when you come to settle what's right and fair, it's everything that he wants and nothing that you want.   *Tom Brown's Schooldays, II, 2*

William Porcher Miles
1822–1899

4   "Vote early and vote often," the advice openly displayed on the election banners in one of our northern cities.
Speech in the House of Representatives [March 31, 1858]

Frederick Law Olmsted
1822–1903
and
Calvert Vaux
1824–1895

5   The Park [Central Park, New York City] throughout is a single work of art, and as such subject to the primary law of every work of art, namely, that it shall be framed upon a single, noble motive, to which the design of all its parts, in some more or less subtle way, shall be confluent and helpful.
Report submitted with "Greensward"[1] Plan, awarded first prize by the Board of Commissioners of the Central Park [April 28, 1858]

6   It is one great purpose of the Park to supply to the hundreds of thousands of tired workers, who have no opportunity to spend their summers in the country, a specimen of God's handiwork that shall be to them, inexpensively, what a month or two in the White Mountains or the Adirondacks is, at great cost, to those in easier circumstances.
Report submitted with "Greensward"[1] Plan, awarded first prize by the Board of Commissioners of the Central Park [April 28, 1858]

Louis Pasteur
1822–1895

7   No, a thousand times no; there does not exist a category of science to which one can give the name applied science. There are science and the applications of science, bound together as the fruit to the tree which bears it.[2]
Pourquoi la France n'a pas trouvé des hommes supérieurs au moment du péril. From Revue Scientifique [1871]

8   In the fields of observation chance favors only the prepared mind.[3]
Inaugural lecture, University of Lille [December 7, 1854]

Red Cloud[4]
1822–1909

9   We were told that they [federal troops] wished merely to pass through our country . . . to seek for gold in the Far West . . . Yet before the ashes of the council fire are cold, the Great Father is building his forts among us. You have heard the sound of the white soldier's axe upon the Little Piney. His presence here is . . . an insult to the spirits of our ancestors. Are we then to give up their sacred graves to be plowed for corn? Dakotas, I am for war.
Speech at council at Fort Laramie, Wyoming [1866]

Heinrich Schliemann
1822–1890

10   I have gazed on the face of Agamemnon.
Telegram to the king of Greece, upon excavating the fifth and last grave at Mycenae [August 1876]

---
[1]Pseudonym of Olmsted and Vaux in submitting their plan.

[2]Translated by I. BERNARD COHEN.
[3]Dans les champs de l'observation le hasard ne favorise que les esprits préparés.
[4]Mahpiua Luta, Oglala Sioux chief.

Théodore de Banville
1823–1891

1 We'll to the woods no more,
The laurels all are cut.[1]

Nous n'Irons Plus aux Bois

Julia A. Fletcher Carney
1823–1908

2 Little drops of water
Little grains of sand,
Make the mighty ocean
And the pleasant land.

Little Things [1845], st. 1

William Johnson Cory
1823–1892

3 They told me, Heraclitus, they told me you were
dead;
They brought me bitter news to hear and bitter
tears to shed.
I wept as I remembered how often you and I
Had tired the sun with talking and sent him down
the sky.
And now that thou art lying, my dear old Carian
guest,
A handful of gray ashes, long, long ago at rest,
Still are thy pleasant voices, thy *Nightingales,*
awake,
For Death, he taketh all away, but them he cannot
take.

Heraclitus. Translated from Callimachus[2]

Thomas Wentworth Higginson
1823–1911

4   When a thought takes one's breath away, a lesson on grammar seems an impertinence.

Preface to Emily Dickinson's *Poems, first
series [1890]*

William Walsham How
1823–1897

5 For all the saints, who from their labors rest.

Hymn [1864], st. 1

---

[1]Nous n'irons plus aux bois, / Les lauriers sont coupés.
Translated by A. E. Housman.
From an old nursery rhyme.
[2]See Callimachus, 85:14.

Leopold Kronecker
1823–1891

6   God made integers, all else is the work of man.

*Jahresberichte der Deutschen Mathematiker
Vereinigung, bk. 2*

George Martin Lane
1823–1897

7 The waiter roars it through the hall:
"We don't give bread with one fish ball!"

Lay of the Lone Fish Ball [1855], st. 10

Francis Parkman
1823–1893

8   The growth of New England was a result of the aggregate efforts of a busy multitude, each in his narrow circle toiling for himself, to gather competence or wealth. The expansion of New France was the achievement of a gigantic ambition striving to grasp a continent. It was a vain attempt.

*Pioneers of France in the New World [1865],
introduction*

9   A boundless vision grows upon us; an untamed continent; vast wastes of forest verdure; mountains silent in primeval sleep; river, lake, and glimmering pool; wilderness oceans mingling with the sky. Such was the domain which France conquered for civilization. Plumed helmets gleamed in the shade of its forests, priestly vestments in its dens and fastnesses of ancient barbarism. Men steeped in antique learning, pale with the close breath of the cloister, here spent the noon and evening of their lives, ruled savage hordes with a mild, parental sway, and stood serene before the direst shapes of death. Men of courtly nurture, heirs to the polish of a far-reaching ancestry, here, with their dauntless hardihood, put to shame the boldest sons of toil.

*Pioneers of France in the New World,
introduction*

10   Faithfulness to the truth of history involves far more than a research, however patient and scrupulous, into special facts. Such facts may be detailed with the most minute exactness, and yet the narrative, taken as a whole, may be unmeaning or untrue. The narrator must seek to imbue himself with the life and spirit of the time. He must study events in their bearings near and remote; in the character, habits, and manners of those who took part in them. He must himself be, as it were, a sharer or a spectator of the action he describes.

*Pioneers of France in the New World,
introduction*

1 For the student there is, in its season, no better place than the saddle, and no better companion than the rifle or the oar. *Autobiography [1868]*

2 The most momentous and far-reaching question ever brought to issue on this continent was: Shall France remain here or shall she not?
Montcalm and Wolfe [1884], introduction

3 The [French] Revolution began at the top—in the world of fashion, birth, and intellect—and propagated itself downwards.
Montcalm and Wolfe, introduction

Coventry Patmore
1823–1896

4 A Woman is a foreign land,
Of which, though there he settle young,
A man will ne'er quite understand
The customs, politics, and tongue.
The Angel in the House [1854–1856], bk. I, canto 9. Prelude 2, Woman

5 For want of me the world's course will not fail;
When all its work is done, the lie shall rot;
The truth is great, and shall prevail,
When none cares whether it prevail or not.
The Unknown Eros [1877]. Magna Est Veritas

William Brighty Rands [Matthew Browne]
1823–1882

6 Never do today what you can
Put off till tomorrow.[1] *Lilliput Levee*

7 Great wide, beautiful, wonderful world,
With the wonderful water round you curled,
And the wonderful grass upon your breast,
World, you are beautifully dressed.
The Child's World, st. 1

[Joseph] Ernest Renan
1823–1892

8 The whole of history is incomprehensible without him [Jesus].
La Vie de Jésus [1863], introduction

9 O Lord, if there is a Lord, save my soul, if I have a soul. *Prière d'un Sceptique*

10 Religion is not a popular error; it is a great instinctive truth, sensed by the people, expressed by the people. *Les Apôtres [1866]*

11 Immortality is to labor at an eternal task.
L'Avenir de la Science [1890], preface

12 Nothing great is achieved without chimeras.
L'Avenir de la Science, ch. 19

John Sherman
1823–1900

13 I have come home to look after my fences.
Speech to his neighbors, Mansfield, Ohio

William Marcy Tweed [Boss Tweed]
1823–1878

14 As long as I count the votes, what are you going to do about it?
Statement by the "Boss" of Tammany Hall on the ballot in New York City [November 1871]

William Allingham
1824–1889

15 Up the airy mountain,
Down the rushy glen,
We daren't go a-hunting
For fear of little men. *The Fairies, st. 1*

16 Four ducks on a pond,
A grass bank beyond,
A blue sky of spring,
White clouds on the wing;
What a little thing
To remember for years—
To remember with tears!

Four Ducks on a Pond

Barnard Elliott Bee
1824–1861

17 There is Jackson, standing like a stone wall!
Of General T. J. Jackson at the battle of Bull Run [July 21, 1861]

Phoebe Cary
1824–1871

18 And though hard be the task,
"Keep a stiff upper lip." *Keep a Stiff Upper Lip*

19 One sweetly solemn thought
Comes to me o'er and o'er;

---

[1] No idleness, no laziness, no procrastination; never put off till tomorrow what you can do today.—CHESTERFIELD, *Letters* [December 26, 1749]

I am nearer home today
Than I ever have been before.

Nearer Home, st. 1

[William] Wilkie Collins
1824–1889

1   "I haven't much time to be fond of anything," says Sergeant Cuff. "But when I *have* a moment's fondness to bestow, most times . . . the roses get it."
The Moonstone [1868]. First Period, ch. 12

Alexandre Dumas the Younger
1824–1895

2   Business? It's quite simple. It's other people's money.[1]
La Question d'Argent [1857], act II, sc. vii

Thomas Jonathan [Stonewall] Jackson
1824–1863

3   My duty is to obey orders.
A favorite aphorism

4   Let us cross over the river, and rest under the trees.
Last words [May 10, 1863]

William Thomson, Lord Kelvin
1824–1907

5   When you can measure what you are speaking about, and express it in numbers, you know something about it; but when you cannot measure it, when you cannot express it in numbers, your knowledge is of a meager and unsatisfactory kind: it may be the beginning of knowledge, but you have scarcely, in your thoughts, advanced to the stage of *science.*
Popular Lectures and Addresses [1891–1894]

Gustav Robert Kirchhoff
1824–1887

6   The highest object at which the natural sciences are constrained to aim, but which they will never reach, is the determination of the forces which are present in nature, and of the state of matter at any given moment—in one word, the reduction of all the phenomena of nature to mechanics.[2]
Über das Ziel der Naturwissenschaften [1865]

George Macdonald
1824–1905

7 Said the Wind to the Moon, "I will blow you out!"
The Wind and the Moon, st. 1

8 Here lie I, Martin Elginbrodde:
Hae mercy o' my soul, Lord God;
As I wad do, were I Lord God,
And ye were Martin Elginbrodde.
David Elginbrod [1863], bk. I, ch. 13

9   There is no feeling in a human heart which exists in that heart alone—which is not, in some form or degree, in every heart.
Unspoken Sermons, second series [1885]

10   You will be dead so long as you refuse to die.
What's Mine's Mine [1886], ch. 31

11   The world and my being, its life and mine, were one. The microcosm and macrocosm were at length atoned, at length in harmony. I lived in everything; everything entered and lived in me.
Lilith [1895], ch. 45

T[homas] H[enry] Huxley
1825–1895

12   I cannot but think that he who finds a certain proportion of pain and evil inseparably woven up in the life of the very worms, will bear his own share with more courage and submission.
On the Educational Value of the Natural History Sciences [1854]

13   To a person uninstructed in natural history, his country or seaside stroll is a walk through a gallery filled with wonderful works of art, nine-tenths of which have their faces turned to the wall.
On the Educational Value of the Natural History Sciences

14   Extinguished theologians lie about the cradle of every science as the strangled snakes beside that of Hercules.
Darwiniana. The Origin of Species [1860]

15   The method of scientific investigation is nothing but the expression of the necessary mode of working of the human mind.
Our Knowledge of the Causes of the Phenomena of Organic Nature [1863]

16   The improver of natural knowledge absolutely refuses to acknowledge authority, as such. For him, skepticism is the highest of duties, blind faith the one unpardonable sin.
On the Advisableness of Improving Natural Knowledge [1866]

---

[1]Les affaires, c'est bien simple, c'est l'argent des autres.
[2]Translated by J. B. STALLO.

1   The chess board is the world, the pieces are the phenomena of the universe, the rules of the game are what we call the laws of Nature. The player on the other side is hidden from us. We know that his play is always fair, just, and patient. But also we know, to our cost, that he never overlooks a mistake, or makes the smallest allowance for ignorance.
A Liberal Education [1868]

2   For every man the world is as fresh as it was at the first day, and as full of untold novelties for him who has the eyes to see them.
A Liberal Education

3   M. Comte's philosophy in practice might be compendiously described as Catholicism *minus* Christianity.   *On the Physical Basis of Life [1868]*

4   The great tragedy of Science—the slaying of a beautiful hypothesis by an ugly fact.
Biogenesis and Abiogenesis [1870]

5   If some great Power would agree to make me always think what is true and do what is right, on condition of being turned into a sort of clock and wound up every morning before I got out of bed, I should instantly close with the offer.
On Descartes' Discourse on Method [1870].
Method and Results

6   There is the greatest practical benefit in making a few failures early in life.
On Medical Education [1870]

7   That mysterious independent variable of political calculation, Public Opinion.
Universities, Actual and Ideal [1874]

8   Logical consequences are the scarecrows of fools and the beacons of wise men.
Animal Automatism [1874]

9   Size is not grandeur, and territory does not make a nation.   *On University Education [1876]*

10   If a little knowledge is dangerous, where is the man who has so much as to be out of danger?
On Elemental Instruction in Physiology [1877]

11   Irrationally held truths may be more harmful than reasoned errors.
The Coming of Age of The Origin of Species [1880]

12   It is the customary fate of new truths to begin as heresies and to end as superstitions.
The Coming of Age of The Origin of Species

13   I asserted—and I repeat—that a man has no reason to be ashamed of having an ape for his grandfather. If there were an ancestor whom I should feel shame in recalling it would rather be a man—a man of restless and versatile intellect—

who, not content with an equivocal success in his own sphere of activity, plunges into scientific questions with which he has no real acquaintance, only to obscure them by an aimless rhetoric, and distract the attention of his hearers from the real point at issue by eloquent digressions and skilled appeals to religious prejudice.
Reply to Wilberforce's question.[1] *From*
LEONARD HUXLEY, *Life and Letters of Thomas Henry Huxley [1900], vol. I*

George Edward Pickett
1825–1875

14   Up, men, and to your posts! Don't forget today that you are from Old Virginia.
Command at the beginning of his division's charge at Gettysburg [July 3, 1863]

Adelaide Anne Procter
1825–1864

15   Seated one day at the organ,
  I was weary and ill at ease,
  And my fingers wandered idly
  Over the noisy keys.   *A Lost Chord, st. 1*[2]

16   But I struck one chord of music
  Like the sound of a great Amen.
A Lost Chord, st. 2

Bayard Taylor
1825–1878

17   From the desert I come to thee
  On a stallion shod with fire,
  And the winds are left behind
  In the speed of my desire.   *Bedouin Song, st. 1*

18   Till the sun grows cold,
  And the stars are old,
  And the leaves of the Judgment Book unfold.
Bedouin Song, refrain

William Whiting
1825–1878

19   Eternal Father, strong to save,
  Whose arm doth bind the restless wave,

---

[1]If anyone were to be willing to trace his descent through an ape as his *grandfather,* would he be willing to trace his descent similarly on the side of his *grandmother?*—SAMUEL WILBERFORCE [1805–1873], *at the British Association for the Advancement of Science* [1860]
[2]Music by SIR ARTHUR SULLIVAN [1842–1900].

Who bidd'st the mighty ocean deep
Its own appointed limits keep,
O, hear us when we cry to Thee
For those in peril on the sea!
        The Hymn of the U.S. Navy [1860].[1] *Eternal*
        Father, Strong to Save, st. 1

Walter Bagehot
1826–1877

1   Writers, like teeth, are divided into incisors and
molars. Sydney Smith[2] was a "molar."
        Estimates of Some Englishmen and Scotchmen
        [1858]. The First Edinburgh Reviewers

2   The best reason why Monarchy is a strong
government is, that it is an intelligible government. The mass of mankind understand it, and
they hardly anywhere in the world understand any
other.
        The English Constitution [1867], ch. 3

3   [The British monarchy:]. Its mystery is its
life. We must not let in daylight upon magic. We
must not bring the Queen into the combat of politics, or she will cease to be reverenced by all combatants.
        The English Constitution, 4

4   One of the greatest pains to human nature is the
pain of a new idea.
        Physics and Politics [1869], ch. 5

5   The most melancholy of human reflections, perhaps, is that on the whole it is a question whether
the benevolence of mankind does most good or
harm.
        Physics and Politics, 5

6   A constitutional statesman is in general a man of
common opinions and uncommon abilities.
        Biographical Studies [1907]. Sir Robert Peel

7   You may talk of the tyranny of Nero and
Tiberius; but the real tyranny is the tyranny of your
next-door neighbor. . . . Public opinion is a perme-
ating influence, and it exacts obedience to itself;
it requires us to think other men's thoughts, to
speak other men's words, to follow other men's
habits.
        Biographical Studies. Sir Robert Peel

Dinah Maria Mulock Craik
1826–1887

8   Douglas, Douglas, tender and true!
        Douglas, Tender and True,[3] *refrain*

9   Oh, my son's my son till he gets him a wife,
But my daughter's my daughter all her life.
        Young and Old

John Ellerton
1826–1893

10 Now the laborer's task is o'er;
Now the battle day is past;
Now upon the farther shore
Lands the voyager at last.   *Hymn [1870],*[1] *st. 1*

11 Father, in thy gracious keeping
Leave we now thy servant sleeping.
        Hymn, refrain

12 The day thou gavest, Lord, is ended,
The darkness falls at thy behest;
To thee our morning hymns ascended,
Thy praise shall sanctify our rest.
        Hymn [1870], st. 1

Stephen Collins Foster
1826–1864

13 O, Susanna! O, don't you cry for me,
I've come from Alabama, with my banjo on my
        knee.   *O, Susanna*[4] *[1848], chorus*

14 Gwine to run all night!
Gwine to run all day!
I'll bet my money on de bobtail nag—
Somebody bet on de bay.
        Camptown Races [1850], chorus

15 Way down upon the Swanee River,
Far, far away,
There's where my heart is turning ever;
There's where the old folks stay.
        The Old Folks at Home [1851], st. 1

16 All the world is sad and dreary
Ev'rywhere I roam,
Oh! darkies, how my heart grows weary,
Far from the old folks at home.
        The Old Folks at Home, chorus

---

[3]O Douglas, O Douglas! / Tendir and trewe. —SIR RICHARD
HOLLAND [fl. 1450], *The Buke of the Howlat* [c. 1450], *st. 31*

[4]Sung for the first time by Nelson Kneass in Andrews' Eagle Ice
Cream Saloon, Pittsburgh, Pennsylvania [September 11, 1847]. It
quickly became a worldwide hit.

---

[1]Music by JOHN BACCHUS DYKES [1823–1876].
[2]See Sydney Smith, 398.

1 Weep no more, my lady,
  Oh! weep no more today!
We will sing one song for the old Kentucky home,
For the old Kentucky home far away.
           My Old Kentucky Home [1853], chorus

2 I dream of Jeanie with the light brown hair,
  Floating, like a vapor, on the soft summer air.
      Jeanie with the Light Brown Hair [1854], st. 1

3 I'm coming, I'm coming, for my head is bending
  low;
I hear those gentle voices calling, "Old Black Joe."
             Old Black Joe [1860], st. 3

4 Beautiful dreamer, wake unto me,
  Starlight and dewdrop are waiting for thee.
           Beautiful Dreamer [1864], st. 1

G[eorge] W[illiam] Hunt
c. 1829–1904

5 We don't want to fight, but, by jingo, if we do,
  We've got the ships, we've got the men, we've got
  the money, too.
                 Song [1878][1]

George B[rinton] McClellan
1826–1885

6 All quiet along the Potomac.
  Frequent report from his Union headquarters
  [1861]

Edward Stuyvesant Bragg
1827–1912

7 They love him most for the enemies he has made.
  Speech seconding the presidential nomination
  of Grover Cleveland [July 9, 1884]

[Samuel] Ward McAllister
1827–1895

8   There are only about 400 people in fashionable
New York Society. If you go outside that number

you strike people who are either not at ease in a
ballroom or else make other people not at ease.
      Quoted in New York Tribune [March 25, 1888]

Charles Eliot Norton
1827–1908

9   A knowledge of Greek thought and life, and of
the arts in which the Greeks expressed their thought
and sentiment, is essential to high culture. A man
may know everything else, but without this knowledge he remains ignorant of the best intellectual
and moral achievements of his own race.
           Letter to F. A. Tupper [1885]

10   The voice of protest, of warning, of appeal is
never more needed than when the clamor of fife
and drum, echoed by the press and too often by the
pulpit, is bidding all men fall in and keep step and
obey in silence the tyrannous word of command.
Then, more than ever, it is the duty of the good citizen not to be silent.
             True Patriotism [1898]

Lew[is] Wallace
1827–1905

11   A man is never so on trial as in the moment of
excessive good fortune.
     Ben Hur: A Tale of the Christ [1880], bk. V,
     ch. 7

12   Would you hurt a man keenest, strike at his self-
love.
       Ben Hur: A Tale of the Christ, VI, 2

Anna Bartlett Warner
1827–1915

13 Jesus loves me—this I know,
  For the Bible tells me so.
            The Love of Jesus [1858]

Septimus Winner
[Alice Hawthorne]
1827–1902

14 Listen to the mockingbird, listen to the
  mockingbird,
Still singing where the weeping willows wave.
        Listen to the Mockingbird [1855]

---

[1]Sung by Gilbert Hastings Macdermott (Farrell) [1845–1901], "the Great Macdermott." The song gave the terms "jingo" and "jingoism" to the political vocabulary, though the phrase "by jingo" had been used earlier by Goldsmith and Thomas Hood.

Henrik Ibsen
1828–1906

1   All or nothing.   *Brand [1866]*[1]

2   Look into any man's heart you please, and you will always find, in every one, at least one black spot which he has to keep concealed.
Pillars of Society [1877],[2] *act III*

3   The spirit of truth and the spirit of freedom— they are the pillars of society.
Pillars of Society, IV

4   There can be no freedom or beauty about a home life that depends on borrowing and debt.
A Doll's House [1879],[3] *act I*

5   Our house has never been anything but a play-room. I have been your doll wife, just as at home I was Daddy's doll child. And the children in turn have been my dolls. I thought it was fun when you came and played with me, just as they thought it was fun when I went and played with them. That's been our marriage, Torvald.
A Doll's House, III

6   If I'm ever to reach any understanding of myself and the things around me, I must learn to stand alone. That's why I can't stay here with you any longer.   *A Doll's House, III*

7   I have another duty equally sacred . . . My duty to myself.   *A Doll's House, III*

8   *Helmer:* First and foremost, you are a wife and mother.
Nora: That I don't believe any more. I believe that first and foremost I am an individual, just as much as you are.   *A Doll's House, III*

9   To crave for happiness in this world is simply to be possessed by a spirit of revolt. What right have we to happiness?   *Ghosts [1881]*,[2] *act I*

10   I am half inclined to think we are all ghosts, Mr. Manders. It is not only what we have inherited from our fathers that exists again in us, but all sorts of old dead ideas and all kinds of old dead beliefs and things of that kind. They are not actually alive in us; but there they are dormant, all the same, and we can never be rid of them. Whenever I take up a newspaper and read it, I fancy I see ghosts creeping between the lines. There must be ghosts all over the world. They must be as countless as grains of the sands, it seems to me. And we are so miserably afraid of the light, all of us.   *Ghosts, II*

11   Mother, give me the sun.   *Ghosts, III*

12   I hold that man is in the right who is most closely in league with the future.
Letter to Georg Brandes [January 3, 1882]

13   A community is like a ship; everyone ought to be prepared to take the helm.
An Enemy of the People [1882],[2] *act III*

14   The minority is always right.
An Enemy of the People, IV

15   You should never wear your best trousers when you go out to fight for freedom and truth.
An Enemy of the People, V

16   The strongest man in the world is he who stands most alone.   *An Enemy of the People, V*

17   Always do that, wild ducks do. Go plunging right to the bottom . . . as deep as they can get . . . hold on with their beaks to the weeds and stuff— and all the other mess you find down there. Then they never come up again.
The Wild Duck [1884],[4] *act II*

18   Take the life-lie away from the average man and straightaway you take away his happiness.
The Wild Duck, V

19   Our common lust for life.
Hedda Gabler [1890],[4] *act II*

20   Oh courage . . . oh yes! If only one had that . . . Then life might be livable, in spite of everything.
Hedda Gabler, II

21   Back he'll come . . . With vine leaves in his hair. Flushed and confident.   *Hedda Gabler, II*

22   Everything I touch seems destined to turn into something mean and farcical.   *Hedda Gabler, IV*

23   The younger generation will come knocking at my door.   *The Master Builder [1892]*,[5] *act I*

George Meredith
1828–1909

24   I expect that Woman will be the last thing civilized by Man.
The Ordeal of Richard Feverel [1859], ch. 1

---

[1]Translated by C. H. HERFORD.
[2]Translated by WILLIAM ARCHER.
[3]Translated by WILLIAM ARCHER.
See Dickens, 499:4.

[4]Translated by A. G. CHATER.
[5]Translated by EDMUND GOSSE and WILLIAM ARCHER.

1 Who rises from prayer a better man, his prayer is
answered.   *The Ordeal of Richard Feverel, 12*

2 The sun is coming down to earth, and the fields
and the waters shout to him golden shouts.
   The Ordeal of Richard Feverel, 19

3 Kissing don't last; cookery do!
   The Ordeal of Richard Feverel, 28

4 Speech is the small change of Silence.
   The Ordeal of Richard Feverel, 34

5 Not till the fire is dying in the grate,
Look we for any kinship with the stars.
Oh, wisdom never comes when it is gold,
And the great price we pay for it full worth;
We have it only when we are half earth.
   Modern Love [1862], st. 4

6 And if I drink oblivion of a day,
So shorten I the stature of my soul.
   Modern Love, st. 12

7 What are we first? First, animals; and next
Intelligences at a leap; on whom
Pale lies the distant shadow of the tomb.
   Modern Love, st. 30

8 In tragic life, God wot,
No villain need be! Passions spin the plot:
We are betrayed by what is false within.
   Modern Love, st. 43

9 Ah, what a dusty answer gets the soul
When hot for certainties in this our life!
   Modern Love, st. 50

10 Into the breast that gives the rose
Shall I with shuddering fall!
   The Spirit of Earth in Autumn [1862], st. 1

11 [Comedy] it is who proposes the correcting of
pretentiousness, of inflation, of dullness, and of the
vestiges of rawness and grossness yet to be found
among us. She is the ultimate civilizer, the polisher.
   The Egoist [1879]. Prelude

12 Cynicism is intellectual dandyism.
   The Egoist, ch. 7

13 In . . . the book of Egoism, it is written, possession without obligation to the object possessed approaches felicity.   *The Egoist, 14*

14 For singing till his heaven fills,
'Tis love of earth that he instills,
And ever winging up and up,
Our valley is his golden cup,
And he the wine which over flows
To lift us with him as he goes.
   The Lark Ascending [1881], l. 65

15 The song seraphically free
Of taint of personality.
   The Lark Ascending, l. 95

16 On a starred night Prince Lucifer uprose.
Tired of his dark dominion swung the fiend.
   Lucifer in Starlight [1883], l. 1

17 Around the ancient track marched, rank on rank,
The army of unalterable law.
   Lucifer in Starlight, l. 13

18 Enter these enchanted woods,
You who dare.
   The Woods of Westermain [1883], st. 1

19 She whom I love is hard to catch and conquer,
Hard, but O the glory of the winning were she
won!   *Love in the Valley [1883], st. 2*

20 A witty woman is a treasure; a witty beauty is a
power.   *Diana of the Crossways [1885], ch. 1*

21 What a woman thinks of women is the test of her
nature.   *Diana of the Crossways, 1*

22 Ireland gives England her soldiers, her generals
too.   *Diana of the Crossways, 2*

23 With patient inattention hear him prate.
   Bellerophon [1887], st. 4

24 Full lasting is the song, though he,
The singer, passes.
   The Thrush in February [1888], st. 17

25 Behold the life at ease; it drifts,
The sharpened life commands its course.
   Hard Weather [1888], l. 71

Dante Gabriel Rossetti
1828–1882

26 The blessed damozel leaned out
From the gold bar of Heaven;
Her eyes were deeper than the depth
Of waters stilled at even;
She had three lilies in her hand,
And the stars in her hair were seven.
   The Blessed Damozel [1850], st. 1

27 And the souls mounting up to God
Went by her like thin flames.
   The Blessed Damozel, st. 7

28 One thing then learned remains to me —
The woodspurge has a cup of three.
   The Woodspurge [1870], st. 4

29 Tell me now in what hidden way is
Lady Flora the lovely Roman?

Where's Hipparchia, and where is Thaïs,
Neither of them the fairer woman.
Where is Echo, beheld of no man
Only heard on river and mere—
She whose beauty was more than human? . . .
But where are the snows of yesteryear?
> *The Ballad of Dead Ladies (After François Villon) [1870], st. 1*

1 A sonnet is a moment's monument—
Memorial from the soul's eternity
To one dead deathless hour.
> *Sonnets from the House of Life [1870–1881]. Proem*

2 Beauty like hers is genius.
> *Sonnets from the House of Life, 18, Genius in Beauty*

3 And though thy soul sail leagues and leagues beyond—
Still, leagues beyond those leagues, there is more sea.
> *Sonnets from the House of Life, 73, The Choice—III*

4   My name is Might-have-been;
I am also called No-more, Too-late, Farewell.
> *Sonnets from the House of Life, 97, A Superscription*

5 When vain desire at last, and vain regret
Go hand in hand to death, and all is vain,
What shall assuage the unforgotten pain
And teach the unforgetful to forget?
> *Sonnets from the House of Life, 101, The One Hope*

6   The Stealthy School of Criticism.
> *Letter to the Athenaeum [1871]*

7 I have been here before,
But when or how I cannot tell;
I know the grass beyond the door,
The sweet keen smell,
The sighing sound, the lights around the shore.
> *Sudden Light [1881], st. 1*

Leo Nikolaevich Tolstoi
1828–1910

8   The hero of my tale, whom I love with all the power of my soul, whom I have tried to portray in all his beauty, who has been, is, and will be beautiful, is Truth.   *Sevastopol in May 1855 [1855]*

9   The old man . . . used to say that a nap "after dinner was silver—before dinner, golden."[1]
> *War and Peace [1865–1869], bk. I, ch. 15*

10   "What's this? am I falling? my legs are giving way under me," he thought, and fell on his back. He opened his eyes, hoping to see how the struggle of the French soldiers with the artilleryman was ending, and eager to know whether the red-haired artilleryman was killed or not, whether the cannons had been taken or saved. But he saw nothing of all that. Above him there was nothing but the sky— the lofty sky, not clear, but still immeasurably lofty, with gray clouds creeping quietly over it.
> *War and Peace,[2] III, 16*

11   Three days afterwards the little princess was buried, and Prince Andrey went to the steps of the tomb to take his last farewell of her. Even in the coffin the face was the same, though the eyes were closed. "Ah, what have you done to me?" it still seemed to say.   *War and Peace, IV, 9*

12   In historical events great men—so called—are but the labels that serve to give a name to an event, and like labels, they have the least possible connection with the event itself. Every action of theirs, that seems to them an act of their own free will, is in an historical sense not free at all, but in bondage to the whole course of previous history, and predestined from all eternity.   *War and Peace, IX, 1*

13   The strongest of all warriors are these two— Time and Patience.   *War and Peace, X, 16*

14   He [Platon Karataev] did not understand, and could not grasp the significance of words taken apart from the sentence. Every word and every action of his was the expression of a force uncomprehended by him, which was his life.
> *War and Peace, XII, 13*

15   For us, with the rule of right and wrong given us by Christ, there is nothing for which we have no standard. And there is no greatness where there is not simplicity, goodness, and truth.
> *War and Peace, XIV, 18*

16   Pure and complete sorrow is as impossible as pure and complete joy.
> *War and Peace, XV, 1*

17   The subject of history is the life of peoples and of humanity. To catch and pin down in words— that is, to describe directly the life, not only of humanity, but even of a single people, appears to be impossible.
> *War and Peace, epilogue, pt. II, ch. 1*

18   Happy families are all alike; every unhappy family is unhappy in its own way.
> *Anna Karenina [1875–1877], pt. I, ch. 1*

---

[1] Translated by LOUISE and AYLMER MAUDE.

[2] Translated by CONSTANCE GARNETT.

1 Ivan Ilych's life had been most simple and most ordinary and therefore most terrible.
The Death of Ivan Ilych [1886][1]

2 Ivan Ilych saw that he was dying, and he was in continuous despair.

In the depth of his heart he knew he was dying, but not only was he not accustomed to the thought, he simply did not and could not grasp it.

The syllogism he had learned from Kiezewetter's Logic: "Caius is a man, men are mortal, therefore Caius is mortal," had always seemed to him correct as applied to Caius, but certainly not as applied to himself. That Caius—man in the abstract—was mortal, was perfectly correct, but he was not Caius, not an abstract man, but a creature quite, quite separate from all others.
The Death of Ivan Ilych

3 Six feet of land was all that he needed.
How Much Land Does a Man Need? [1886]

4 The more is given the less the people will work for themselves, and the less they work the more their poverty will increase.[2]
Help for the Starving, pt. III [January 1892]

5 Art is a human activity having for its purpose the transmission to others of the highest and best feelings to which men have risen.
What Is Art? [1898], ch. 8

6 Man survives earthquakes, epidemics, the horrors of disease, and all the agonies of the soul, but for all time his most tormenting tragedy has been, is, and will be—the tragedy of the bedroom.
From Maksim Gorky. Reminiscences of Leo Nikolaevich Tolstoy [1920]

Geronimo
1829–1909

7 It [Arizona] is my land, my home, my father's land, to which I now ask to be allowed to return. I want to spend my last days there, and be buried among those mountains. If this could be I might die in peace, feeling that my people, placed in their native homes, would increase in numbers, rather than diminish as at present, and that our name would not become extinct.
To President Grant from the reservation at Fort Sill, Oklahoma, after surrender [1877]

Carl Schurz
1829–1906

8 Our country, right or wrong. When right, to be kept right; when wrong, to be put right.
Address, Anti-Imperialistic Conference, Chicago [October 17, 1899]

Ivan Mikhailovich Sechenov
1829–1905

9 All psychical acts without exception, if they are not complicated by elements of emotion . . . develop by way of reflex. Hence, all conscious movements resulting from these acts and usually described as voluntary, are reflex movements in the strict sense of the term.
Reflexes of the Brain [1863],[3] *ch. 2*

Charles Dudley Warner
1829–1900

10 To own a bit of ground, to scratch it with a hoe, to plant seeds, and watch the renewal of life—this is the commonest delight of the race, the most satisfactory thing a man can do.
My Summer in a Garden [1870]. Preliminary

11 No man but feels more of a man in the world if he have a bit of ground that he can call his own. However small it is on the surface, it is four thousand miles deep; and that is a very handsome property.
My Summer in a Garden. Preliminary

12 What a man needs in gardening is a cast-iron back, with a hinge in it.
My Summer in a Garden. Third Week

13 Politics makes strange bedfellows.
My Summer in a Garden. Fifteenth Week

14 What small potatoes we all are, compared with what we might be!
My Summer in a Garden. Fifteenth Week

15 The thing generally raised on city land is taxes.
My Summer in a Garden. Sixteenth Week

Thomas Edward Brown
1830–1897

16 A Garden is a lovesome thing, God wot!
My Garden

17 Not God! in Gardens! when the eve is cool?
Nay, but I have a sign:
'Tis very sure God walks in mine.　*My Garden*

---

[1]Translated by AYLMER MAUDE.

[2]If you stop supporting that crowd, it will support itself.—SENECA, *Epistles, 20, 7*

[3]Translated by S. BELSKY.

Initial of Creation, and
The Exponent of Earth.   *No. 917 [c. 1864]*

1 If I can stop one Heart from breaking
   I shall not live in vain
   If I can ease one Life the Aching
   Or cool one Pain
   Or help one fainting Robin
   Unto his Nest again
   I shall not live in Vain.   *No. 919 [c. 1864]*

2 A narrow Fellow in the Grass
   Occasionally rides—   *No. 986 [c. 1865], st. 1*

3 But never met this Fellow
   Attended or alone
   Without a tighter breathing
   And Zero at the Bone—   *No. 986, last stanza*

4 The Dying, is a trifle, past
   But living, this include
   The dying multifold—without
   The Respite to be dead.   *No. 1013 [c. 1865]*

5 'Twas my one Glory—
   Let it be
   Remembered
   I was owned of Thee—   *No. 1028 [c. 1865]*

6 I never saw a Moor—
   I never saw the Sea—
   Yet know I how the Heather looks
   And what a Billow be.

   I never spoke with God
   Nor visited in Heaven—
   Yet certain am I of the spot
   As if the Checks were given—
                              No. 1052 [c. 1865]

7 Experiment to me
   Is every one I meet
   If it contain a Kernel?
   The Figure of a Nut

   Presents upon a Tree
   Equally plausibly,
   But Meat within, is requisite
   To Squirrels, and to Me.   *No. 1073 [c. 1865]*

8 The Bustle in a House
   The Morning after Death
   Is solemnest of industries
   Enacted upon Earth—

   The Sweeping up the Heart,
   And putting Love away
   We shall not want to use again
   Until Eternity.   *No. 1078 [c. 1866]*

9 We never know how high we are
   Till we are called to rise

And then, if we are true to plan
Our statures touch the skies.
                              No. 1176 [c. 1870], st. 1

10 A word is dead
   When it is said,
   Some say.
   I say it just
   Begins to live
   That day.   *No. 1212 [c. 1872]*

11 There is no Frigate like a Book
   To take us Lands away
   Nor any Coursers like a Page
   Of prancing Poetry—
   This Traverse may the poorest take
   Without oppress of Toll—
   How frugal is the Chariot
   That bears the Human Soul!   *No. 1263 [c. 1873]*

12 I thought that nature was enough
   Till Human nature came
   But that the other did absorb
   As Parallax a Flame—   *No. 1286 [c. 1873], st. 1*

13 Until the Desert knows
   That Water grows
   His Sands suffice
   But let him once suspect
   That Caspian Fact
   Sahara dies.   *No. 1291 [c. 1873], st. 1*

14 Not with a Club, the Heart is broken
   Nor with a Stone—
   A Whip so small you could not see it
   I've known
   To lash the Magic Creature
   Till it fell.   *No. 1304 [c. 1874], st. 1*

15 A little Madness in the Spring
   Is wholesome even for the King.
                              No. 1333 [c. 1875]

16 Love's stricken "why"
   Is all that love can speak—
   Built of but just a syllable
   The hugest hearts that break.
                              No. 1368 [c. 1876]

17 Bees are Black, with Gilt Surcingles—
   Buccaneers of Buzz.   *No. 1405 [c. 1877], st. 1*

18 The Pedigree of Honey
   Does not concern the Bee—
   A Clover, any time, to him,
   Is Aristocracy.   *No. 1627 [c. 1884], version II*

19 A Drunkard cannot meet a Cork
   Without a Revery—
   And so encountering a Fly
   This January Day

Jamaicas of Remembrance stir
That send me reeling in.   *No. 1628 [c. 1884]*

1 Eden is that old-fashioned House
We dwell in every day
Without suspecting our abode
Until we drive away.   *No. 1657 [n.d.], st. 1*

2 I took one Draught of Life—
I'll tell you what I paid—
Precisely an existence—
The market price, they said.

They weighed me, Dust by Dust—
They balanced Film with Film,
Then handed me my Being's worth—
A single Dram of Heaven!   *No. 1725 [n.d.]*

3 My life closed twice before its close—
It yet remains to see
If Immortality unveil
A third event to me

So huge, so hopeless to conceive
As these that twice befell.
Parting is all we know of heaven,
And all we need of hell.   *No. 1732 [n.d.]*

4 That it will never come again
Is what makes life so sweet.   *No. 1741 [n.d.], st. 1*

5 The only secret people keep
Is Immortality.   *No. 1748 [n.d.]*

6 To make a prairie it takes a clover and one bee,
One clover, and a bee,
And revery.
The revery alone will do,
If bees are few.   *No. 1755 [n.d.]*

7 Elysium is as far as to
The very nearest Room
If in that Room a Friend await
Felicity or Doom—

What Fortitude the Soul contains,
That it can so endure
The accent of a coming Foot—
The opening of a Door—   *No. 1760 [n.d.]*

8 That Love is all there is,
Is all we know of Love;
It is enough, the freight should be
Proportioned to the groove.   *No. 1765 [n.d.]*

9 If I read a book and it makes my whole body so cold no fire can ever warm me, I know that is poetry. If I feel physically as if the top of my head were taken off, I know that is poetry. These are the only ways I know it. Is there any other way?
From MARTHA GILBERT DICKINSON BIANCHI, Life and Letters of Emily Dickinson [1924]

10   Little Cousins, Called back.
Last letter [May 1886]

Helen Hunt Jackson
1830–1885

11 O suns and skies and clouds of June,
And flowers of June together,
Ye cannot rival for one hour
October's bright blue weather.
October's Bright Blue Weather, st. 1

Mother Jones [Mary Harris Jones]
1830–1930

12   Pray for the dead and fight like hell for the living!
Autobiography [1925]

Alexander Muir
1830–1906

13   And joined in love together,
The Thistle, Shamrock, Rose entwine
The Maple Leaf forever!
The Maple Leaf Forever [1867]

Christina Georgina Rossetti
1830–1894

14 My heart is like a singing bird.
A Birthday [1861], st. 1

15   The birthday of my life
Is come, my love is come to me.
A Birthday, st. 2

16 When I am dead, my dearest,
Sing no sad songs for me;
Plant thou no roses at my head,
Nor shady cypress tree.
Be the green grass above me
With showers and dewdrops wet;
And if thou wilt, remember
And if thou wilt, forget.   *Song [1862], st. 1*

17 Remember me when I am gone away,
Gone far away into the silent land.
Remember [1862], l. 1

18 Better by far you should forget and smile
Than that you should remember and be sad.
Remember, l. 13

19 In the bleak midwinter
Frosty wind made moan,
Earth stood hard as iron,

Water like a stone;
Snow had fallen, snow on snow,
Snow on snow,
In the bleak midwinter,
Long ago.   *A Christmas Carol*

1 Oh roses for the flush of youth,
And laurel for the perfect prime;
But pluck an ivy branch for me
Grown old before my time.   *Song [1862]*

2 Who has seen the wind?
Neither you nor I:
But when the trees bow down their heads,
The wind is passing by.
                Who Has Seen the Wind? [1872], st. 2

3 Sleeping at last, the trouble and turmoil over,
Sleeping at last, the struggle and horror past,
Cold and white, out of sight of friend and of lover,
Sleeping at last.   *Sleeping at Last [1893], st. 1*

Robert Arthur Talbot Gascoyne-Cecil, Marquess of Salisbury
1830–1903

4   If you believe the doctors, nothing is wholesome; if you believe the theologians, nothing is innocent; if you believe the soldiers, nothing is safe.
Letter to Lord Lytton, Viceroy of India [June 15, 1877]

Alexander Smith
1830–1867

5   It is not of so much consequence what you say, as how you say it. Memorable sentences are memorable on account of some single irradiating word.
Dreamthorp [1863]. On the Writing of Essays

6   Death is the ugly fact which Nature has to hide, and she hides it well.
Dreamthorp. Of Death and the Fear of Dying

George Graham Vest
1830–1904

7   The one absolutely unselfish friend that man can have in this selfish world, the one that never deserts him, the one that never proves ungrateful or treacherous, is his dog. . . . When all other friends desert, he remains.[1]   *Speech in the Senate [1884]*

----

[1] If you want a friend in Washington, go buy a dog. — *Saying*

Ignatius Donnelly
1831–1901

8   The Democratic Party is like a mule — without pride of ancestry or hope of posterity.
Attribute

James A[bram] Garfield
1831–1881

9   Fellow citizens! God reigns, and the Government at Washington still lives!
Attributed speech on the assassination of Lincoln [April 15, 1865]

10   I am not willing that this discussion should close without mention of the value of a true teacher. Give me a log hut, with only a simple bench, Mark Hopkins[2] on one end and I on the other, and you may have all the buildings, apparatus and libraries without him.
Address to Williams College Alumni, New York [December 28, 1871]

Edward Robert Bulwer-Lytton, Earl of Lytton [Owen Meredith]
1831–1891

11 We may live without poetry, music and art;
We may live without conscience, and live without heart;
We may live without friends; we may live without books;
But civilized man cannot live without cooks.
                Lucile [1860], pt. I, canto 2, st. I

12 Genius does what it must, and talent does what it can.
                Last Words of a Sensitive Second-Rate Po

James Clerk Maxwell
1831–1879

13   All the mathematical sciences are founded on relations between physical laws and laws of number, so that the aim of exact science is to reduce the problems of nature to the determination of quantities by operations with numbers.
On Faraday's Lines of Force [1856

----

[2] Mark Hopkins [1802–1887], president of Williams College [1836–1872] and president of the American Board of Commissioners for Foreign Missions [1857–1881].

For Education is Making Men; / So is it now, so was it when / Mark Hopkins sat on one end of a log / And James Garfield sat on the other. — ARTHUR GUITERMAN, *Education*

1 When at last this little instrument appeared, consisting, as it does, of parts every one of which is familiar to us, and capable of being put together by an amateur, the disappointment arising from its humble appearance was only partially relieved on finding that it was really able to talk.

The Telephone [1878]

Philip Henry Sheridan
1831–1888

2 The only good Indians I ever saw were dead.[1]

Attributed remark at Fort Cobb, Indian Territory [January 1869]

Sitting Bull[2]
c. 1831–1890

3 What treaty that the white man ever made with us have they kept? Not one. When I was a boy the Sioux owned the world; the sun rose and set on their land; they sent ten thousand men to battle. Where are the warriors today? Who slew them? Where are our lands? Who owns them? . . . What law have I broken? Is it wrong for me to love my own? Is it wicked for me because my skin is red? Because I am a Sioux; because I was born where my father lived; because I would die for my people and my country? *Statement*

Louisa May Alcott
1832–1888

4 Christmas won't be Christmas without any presents. *Little Women [1868–1869], pt. I, ch. 1*

5 The spring sunshine streamed in like a benediction over the placid face upon the pillow—a face so full of painless peace, that those who loved it best smiled through their tears, and thanked God that Beth was well at last. *Little Women, II, 17*

6 If Mr. Clemens cannot think of something better to tell our pure-minded lads and lasses, he had best stop writing for them.

On Adventures of Huckleberry Finn [1885]

7 Resolved to take Fate by the throat and shake a living out of her.

From EDNAH D. CHENEY, Louisa May Alcott, Her Life, Letters, and Journals [1889], ch. 5

Elizabeth Akers Allen
1832–1911

8 Backward, turn backward, O Time, in your flight,
Make me a child again just for tonight!

Rock Me to Sleep [1860], st. 1

Lewis Carroll
[Charles Lutwidge Dodgson]
1832–1898

9 All in the golden afternoon
Full leisurely we glide,
For both our oars with little skill
By little arms are plied
While little hands make vain pretense
Our wanderings to guide.

Alice's Adventures in Wonderland [1865], introduction, st. 1

10 "What is the use of a book," thought Alice, "without pictures or conversations?"

Alice's Adventures in Wonderland, ch. 1

11 Do cats eat bats? . . . Do bats eat cats?

Alice's Adventures in Wonderland, 1

12 Curiouser and curiouser!

Alice's Adventures in Wonderland, 2

13 How doth the little crocodile
Improve his shining tail,
And pour the waters of the Nile
On every golden scale![3]

How cheerfully he seems to grin,
How neatly spreads his claws,
And welcomes little fishes in
With gently smiling jaws!

Alice's Adventures in Wonderland, 2

14 "I'll be judge, I'll be jury," said cunning old Fury;
"I'll try the whole cause, and condemn you to
death." *Alice's Adventures in Wonderland, 3*

15 Oh my fur and whiskers!

Alice's Adventures in Wonderland, 4

16 "I can't explain *myself*, I'm afraid, sir," said Alice, "because I'm not myself, you see."
"I don't see," said the Caterpillar.

Alice's Adventures in Wonderland, 5

---

[1]Edward Sylvester Ellis [1840–1916] reported that after Custer's fight with Black Kettle's band of Cheyenne Indians, the Comanche Chief Toch-a-way (Turtle Dove) was presented to General Sheridan. The Indian said: "Me Toch-a-way, me good Indian." The reply, as reported by Ellis but vehemently denied by Sheridan, is given in the text; the phrase is more often heard in the version: The only good Indian is a dead Indian.

[2]Tatanka Yotanka, Sioux warrior.

[3]See Watts, 304:1.

1 "You are old, Father William," the young man said,
   "And your hair has become very white;
   And yet you incessantly stand on your head—
   Do you think, at your age, it is right?"[1]
   Alice's Adventures in Wonderland
   [You Are Old, Father William, st. 1]

2 "In my youth," said his father, "I took to the law,
   And argued each case with my wife;
   And the muscular strength which it gave to my jaw,
   Has lasted the rest of my life."
   Alice's Adventures in Wonderland
   [You Are Old, Father William, st. 6]

3 "I have answered three questions, and that is
         enough,"
   Said his father. "Don't give yourself airs!
   Do you think I can listen all day to such stuff?
   Be off, or I'll kick you downstairs!"
   Alice's Adventures in Wonderland
   [You Are Old, Father William, st. 8]

4   Those serpents! There's no pleasing them!
   Alice's Adventures in Wonderland
   [You Are Old, Father William, st. 8]

5   "If everybody minded their own business," said
   the Duchess in a hoarse growl, "the world would
   go round a deal faster than it does."
   Alice's Adventures in Wonderland, 6

6   "Talking of axes," said the Duchess, "chop off
   her head!"
   Alice's Adventures in Wonderland, 6

7 Speak roughly to your little boy,
   And beat him when he sneezes:
   He only does it to annoy,
   Because he knows it teases.
   Alice's Adventures in Wonderland, 6

8   "If it had grown up," she said to herself, "it
   would have made a dreadfully ugly child; but it
   makes rather a handsome pig, I think."
   Alice's Adventures in Wonderland, 6

9   "All right," said the [Cheshire] Cat; and this
   time it vanished quite slowly, beginning with the
   end of the tail, and ending with the grin, which remained some time after the rest of it had gone.
   Alice's Adventures in Wonderland, 6

10   "Then you should say what you mean," the
   March Hare went on.
      "I do," Alice hastily replied; "at least—at least I
   mean what I say—that's the same thing, you know."
      "Not the same thing a bit!" said the Hatter.
   "Why, you might just as well say that 'I see what I
   eat' is the same thing as 'I eat what I see'!"
   Alice's Adventures in Wonderland, 7

11   "It was the *best* butter," the March Hare meekl
   replied.
   Alice's Adventures in Wonderland,

12 Twinkle, twinkle, little bat!
   How I wonder what you're at!
   Up above the world you fly,
   Like a teatray in the sky.[2]
   Alice's Adventures in Wonderland,

13   "Take some more tea," the March Hare said t(
   Alice, very earnestly.
      "I've had nothing yet," Alice replied in an of
   fended tone: "so I can't take more."
      "You mean you can't take *less*," said the Hatter
   "it's very easy to take *more* than nothing."
   Alice's Adventures in Wonderland, 7

14   They drew all manner of things—everything
   that begins with an M . . . such as mousetraps, anc
   the moon, and memory, and muchness—you know
   you say things are "much of a muchness."
   Alice's Adventures in Wonderland, 7

15   The Queen turned crimson with fury, and after
   glaring at her for a moment like a wild beast, began
   screaming, "Off with her head! Off with—"
   Alice's Adventures in Wonderland, 8

16   "Tut, tut, child," said the Duchess. "Everything's
   got a moral if only you can find it."
   Alice's Adventures in Wonderland, 9

17   Take care of the sense and the sounds will take
   care of themselves.[3]
   Alice's Adventures in Wonderland, 9

18   "We called him Tortoise because he taught us,"
   said the Mock Turtle angrily. "Really you are very
   dull!"
   Alice's Adventures in Wonderland, 9

19   "Reeling and Writhing, of course, to begin
   with," the Mock Turtle replied, "and the different
   branches of Arithmetic—Ambition, Distraction,
   Uglification, and Derision."
   Alice's Adventures in Wonderland, 9

20   Advance twice, set to partners . . . change lobsters, and retire in same order.
   Alice's Adventures in Wonderland, 10

21 "Will you walk a little faster?" said a whiting to a
         snail,
   "There's a porpoise close behind us, and he's
         treading on my tail."
   Alice's Adventures in Wonderland
   [The Lobster-Quadrille, st. 1]

---

[1] See Southey, 405:9.

[2] See Ann and Jane Taylor, 414:5.

[3] See Chesterfield, 314:21.

1 Will you, won't you, will you, won't you, will you
  join the dance?
  Alice's Adventures in Wonderland
  [The Lobster-Quadrille, st. 1]

2 The further off from England the nearer is to
  France —
  Then turn not pale, beloved snail, but come and
  join the dance.
  Alice's Adventures in Wonderland
  [The Lobster-Quadrille, st. 3]

3 'Tis the voice of the Lobster: I heard him declare
  "You have baked me too brown, I must sugar my
  hair."[1]
  Alice's Adventures in Wonderland
  ['Tis the Voice of the Lobster]

4 Soup of the evening, beautiful soup!
  Alice's Adventures in Wonderland
  [Turtle Soup]

5 Begin at the beginning . . . and go on till you
  come to the end: then stop.
  Alice's Adventures in Wonderland, 12

6 Sentence first — verdict afterwards.
  Alice's Adventures in Wonderland, 12

7 You're nothing but a pack of cards!
  Alice's Adventures in Wonderland, 12

8 Child of the pure, unclouded brow
  And dreaming eyes of wonder!
  Though time be fleet and I and thou
  Are half a life asunder,
  Thy loving smile will surely hail
  The love-gift of a fairy tale.
  Through the Looking-Glass [1872],
  introduction, st. 1

9 "The horror of that moment," the King went
  on, "I shall never, *never* forget!"
  "You will, though," the Queen said, "if you
  don't make a memorandum of it."
  Through the Looking-Glass, ch. 1

10 'Twas brillig, and the slithy toves
   Did gyre and gimble in the wabe;
   All mimsy were the borogoves,
   And the mome raths outgrabe.

   Beware the Jabberwock, my son!
   The jaws that bite, the claws that catch!
   Beware the Jubjub bird, and shun
   The frumious Bandersnatch!
   Through the Looking-Glass [Jabberwocky,
   st. 1, 2]

11 And, as in uffish thought he stood,
   The Jabberwock, with eyes of flame,

Came whiffling through the tulgey wood,
And burbled as it came!

One, two! One, two! And through and through
The vorpal blade went snicker-snack!
He left it dead, and with its head
He went galumphing back.

"And hast thou slain the Jabberwock?
Come to my arms, my beamish boy!
O frabjous day! Callooh! Callay!"
He chortled in his joy.
  Through the Looking-Glass [Jabberwocky,
  st. 4–6]

12 Curtsy while you're thinking what to say. It saves
time.   *Through the Looking-Glass, 2*

13 "Now! Now!" cried the Queen. "Faster! Faster!"
  Through the Looking-Glass, 2

14 "A slow sort of country!" said the Queen.
"Now, *here,* you see, it takes all the running you can
do, to keep in the same place. If you want to get
somewhere else, you must run at least twice as fast
as that!"   *Through the Looking-Glass, 2*

15 Speak in French when you can't think of the
English for a thing — turn out your toes when you
walk — and remember who you are!
  Through the Looking-Glass, 2

16 "If you think we're waxworks," he said, "you
ought to pay, you know. Waxworks weren't made to
be looked at for nothing. Nohow!"
  Through the Looking-Glass, 4

17 "Contrariwise," continued Tweedledee, "if it
was so, it might be; and if it were so, it would be;
but as it isn't, it ain't. That's logic."
  Through the Looking-Glass, 4

18 The sun was shining on the sea,
   Shining with all his might:
   He did his very best to make
   The billows smooth and bright —
   And this was odd, because it was
   The middle of the night.
   Through the Looking-Glass
   [The Walrus and the Carpenter, st. 1]

19 The Walrus and the Carpenter
   Were walking close at hand:
   They wept like anything to see
   Such quantities of sand:
   "If this were only cleared away,"
   They said, "it would be grand!"

   "If seven maids with seven mops
   Swept it for half a year,
   Do you suppose," the Walrus said,
   "That they could get it clear?"

---

[1]See Watts, 304:5.

"I doubt it," said the Carpenter,
And shed a bitter tear.
> *Through the Looking-Glass*
> *[The Walrus and the Carpenter, st. 4, 5]*

1 "O Oysters, come and walk with us!"
The Walrus did beseech.
"A pleasant walk, a pleasant talk,
Along the briny beach."
> *Through the Looking-Glass*
> *[The Walrus and the Carpenter, st. 6]*

2 And thick and fast they came at last,
And more, and more, and more—
All hopping through the frothy waves,
And scrambling to the shore.
> *Through the Looking-Glass*
> *[The Walrus and the Carpenter, st. 9]*

3 "The time has come," the Walrus said,
"To talk of many things:
Of shoes—and ships—and sealing wax—
Of cabbages—and kings—
And why the sea is boiling hot—
And whether pigs have wings."
> *Through the Looking-Glass*
> *[The Walrus and the Carpenter, st. 11]*

4 "But wait a bit," the Oysters cried,
"Before we have our chat;
For some of us are out of breath,
And all of us are fat!"
> *Through the Looking-Glass*
> *[The Walrus and the Carpenter, st. 12]*

5 The Carpenter said nothing but
"The butter's spread too thick!"
> *Through the Looking-Glass*
> *[The Walrus and the Carpenter, st. 16]*

6 "I weep for you," the Walrus said:
"I deeply sympathize."
With sobs and tears he sorted out
Those of the largest size,
Holding his pocket-handkerchief
Before his streaming eyes.
> *Through the Looking-Glass*
> *[The Walrus and the Carpenter, st. 17]*

7 But answer came there none[1]—
And this was scarcely odd, because
They'd eaten every one.
> *Through the Looking-Glass*
> *[The Walrus and the Carpenter, st. 18]*

8   Twopence a week, and jam every other day.
> *Through the Looking-Glass, 5*

---

[1]But answer came there none.—SIR WALTER SCOTT, *The Bridal of Triermain* [1813], *canto III, st. 10*

9   "The rule is, jam tomorrow, and jam yesterday—
but never jam today."
   "It must come sometimes to 'jam today,'" Alice
objected.
   "No, it can't," said the Queen. "It's jam every
other day: today isn't any other day, you know."
> *Through the Looking-Glass, 5*

10   "It's a poor sort of memory that only works
backwards," the Queen remarked.
> *Through the Looking-Glass, 5*

11   Consider anything, only don't cry!
> *Through the Looking-Glass, 5*

12   "There's no use trying," she said: "one *can't* believe impossible things."
   "I daresay you haven't had much practice," said
the Queen. "When I was your age, I always did it
for half-an-hour a day. Why, sometimes I've believed as many as six impossible things before breakfast."   *Through the Looking-Glass, 5*

13   They gave it me—for an unbirthday present.
> *Through the Looking-Glass, 6*

14   "But 'glory' doesn't mean 'a nice knockdown
argument,'" Alice objected.
   "When *I* use a word," Humpty Dumpty said, in
rather a scornful tone, "it means just what I choose
it to mean—neither more nor less."
   "The question is," said Alice, "whether you *can*
make words mean so many different things."
   "The question is," said Humpty Dumpty, "which
is to be master—that's all."
> *Through the Looking-Glass, 6*

15   It's as large as life and twice as natural.
> *Through the Looking-Glass, 7*

16 His answer trickled through my head,
Like water through a sieve.
> *Through the Looking-Glass, 8*

17   What's the French for fiddle-de-dee?
> *Through the Looking-Glass, 9*

18   It isn't etiquette to cut anyone you've been introduced to. Remove the joint!
> *Through the Looking-Glass, 9*

19 He would answer to "Hi!" or to any loud cry
Such as "Fry me!" or "Fritter my wig!"
To "What-you-may-call-um!" or
   "What-was-his-name!"
But especially "Thing-um-a-jig!"
> *The Hunting of the Snark [1876]. Fit I, st. 9*

20 "What's the good of Mercator's North Poles and
   Equators,
Tropics, Zones and Meridian Lines?"

So the Bellman would cry: and the crew would
    reply,
"They are merely conventional signs!"
> *The Hunting of the Snark, II, st. 3*

1 It frequently breakfasts at five-o'clock tea,
    And dines on the following day.
> *The Hunting of the Snark, II, st. 17*

2 There was silence supreme! Not a shriek, not a
    scream,
Scarcely even a howl or a groan,
As the man they called "Ho!" told his story of woe
In an antediluvian tone.
> *The Hunting of the Snark, III, st. 3*

3 It is this, it is this that oppresses my soul.
> *The Hunting of the Snark, III, st. 11*

4 They sought it with thimbles, they sought it with
    care;
They pursued it with forks and hope;
They threatened its life with a railway share;
They charmed it with smiles and soap.
> *The Hunting of the Snark, V, st. 1*

5 For the Snark *was* a Boojum, you see.
> *The Hunting of the Snark, VIII, st. 9*

6 He thought he saw an Elephant,
    That practiced on a fife:
He looked again, and found it was
A letter from his wife.
"At length I realize," he said,
"The bitterness of Life!"
> *Sylvie and Bruno [1889], ch. 5*

7 He thought he saw a Buffalo
Upon the chimneypiece:
He looked again, and found it was
His sister's husband's niece.
> *Sylvie and Bruno, 6*

8 He thought he saw an Albatross
That fluttered round the lamp:
He looked again, and found it was
A penny postage stamp.
"You'd best be getting home," he said,
"The nights are very damp."
> *Sylvie and Bruno, 12*

William Croswell Doane
1832–1913

9 Ancient of Days, who sittest throned in glory,
    To thee all knees are bent, all voices pray.
> *Hymn [1886], st. 1*

H[enry] C[lay] Work
1832–1884

10 Father, dear father, come home with me now,
    The clock in the belfry strikes one;
You said you were coming right home from the
    shop
As soon as your day's work was done.
> *Come Home, Father [1864], st. 1*

11 "Hurrah! hurrah! we bring the Jubilee!
Hurrah! Hurrah! the flag that makes you free!"
So we sang the chorus from Atlanta to the sea,
While we were marching through Georgia.
> *Marching Through Georgia [1865], chorus*

Wilhelm Max Wundt
1832–1920

12   We take issue . . . with every treatment of psychology that is based on simple self-observation or
on philosophical presuppositions.[1]
> *Grundzüge der Physiologischen Psychologie*
> *(Principles of Physiological Psychology) [1874]*

Isaac Hill Bromley
1833–1898

13 Conductor, when you receive a fare,
Punch in the presence of the passenjare! . . .
Punch, brothers! Punch with care!
Punch in the presence of the passenjare!
> *Punch, Brother, Punch [1875][2]*

Adam Lindsay Gordon
1833–1870

14 A little season of love and laughter,
    Of light and life, and pleasure and pain,
And a horror of outer darkness after,
And dust returneth to dust again.[3]
> *The Swimmer*

---

[1] Translated by EDWARD TITCHENER.

[2] Based on a New York streetcar sign. Erroneously attributed to Mark Twain, who wrote about the verse in *A Literary Nightmare* [1876].

[3] A little time for laughter, / A little time to sing, / A little time to kiss and cling, / And no more kissing after. —PHILIP BOURKE MARSTON [1850–1887], *After, st. 1*

John Marshall Harlan
1833–1911

1   Our Constitution is color-blind, and neither knows nor tolerates classes among citizens. In respect of civil rights, all citizens are equal before the law. The humblest is the peer of the most powerful.
Dissenting opinion, Plessy v. Ferguson 163 U.S. 537, 559 [1896]

Robert [Green] Ingersoll
1833–1899

2   Like an armed warrior, like a plumed knight, James G. Blaine marched down the halls of the American Congress and threw his shining lance full and fair against the brazen foreheads of the defamers of his country and the maligners of his honor.
Speech nominating Blaine for President, National Republican Convention [June 15, 1876]

3   I am the inferior of any man whose rights I trample under foot. Men are not superior by reason of the accidents of race or color. They are superior who have the best heart—the best brain.
Liberty

4   Every cradle asks us, "Whence?" and every coffin, "Whither?" The poor barbarian, weeping above his dead, can answer these questions as intelligently as the robed priest of the most authentic creed.
Address at a child's grave

5   We, too, have our religion, and it is this: Help for the living, hope for the dead.
Address at a child's grave

6   An honest God is the noblest work of man.
The Gods [1876]

7 Justice is the only worship.
Love is the only priest.
Ignorance is the only slavery.
Happiness is the only good.
The time to be happy is now,
The place to be happy is here,
The way to be happy is to make others so.
Creed

Petroleum V. Nasby [David Ross Locke]
1833–1888

8 The contract 'twixt Hannah, God and me,
Was not for one or twenty years, but for eternity.
Hannah Jane [1871], st. 29

Alfred Nobel
1833–1896

9   My factories may make an end of war sooner than your congresses. The day when two army corps can annihilate each other in one second, all civilized nations, it is to be hoped, will recoil from war and discharge their troops.
From Bertha von Suttner, Memoiren [Stuttgart, 1909]

Alfred von Schlieffen
1833–1913

10   When you march into France, let the last man on the right brush the channel with his sleeve.
Of his envelopment plan for the German invasion of France in World War I

John Emerich Edward Dalberg-Acton, Lord Acton
1834–1902

11   There is no error so monstrous that it fails to find defenders among the ablest men. Imagine a congress of eminent celebrities such as More, Bacon, Grotius, Pascal, Cromwell, Bossuet, Montesquieu, Jefferson, Napoleon, Pitt, etc. The result would be an Encyclopedia of Error.
Letter to Mary Gladstone [April 24, 1881]

12   Power tends to corrupt and absolute power corrupts absolutely.
Letter to Bishop Mandell Creighton [April 5, 1887]

13   Advice to Persons About to Write History—Don't.
Letter to Bishop Mandell Creighton, postscript

14   Liberty is not a means to a higher political end. It is itself the highest political end.
The History of Freedom and Other Essays [1907], ch. 1

15   Writers the most learned, the most accurate in details, and the soundest in tendency, frequently fall into a habit which can neither be cured nor pardoned—the habit of making history into the proof of their theories.
The History of Freedom and Other Essays, 8

George Arnold
1834–1865

1 Life for the living, and rest for the dead!
   The Jolly Old Pedagogue, st. 2

Sabine Baring-Gould
1834–1924

2 Onward, Christian soldiers,
Marching as to war,
With the Cross of Jesus
Going on before!
   Onward, Christian Soldiers [1864],[1] st. 1

3 Now the day is over,
Night is drawing nigh;
Shadows of the evening
Steal across the sky.
   Now the Day Is Over [1865], st. 1

4 Through the night of doubt and sorrow
Onward goes the pilgrim band,
Singing songs of expectation,
Marching to the promised land.
   Through the Night of Doubt and Sorrow [1867], st. 1[2]

Charles Farrar Browne [Artemus Ward]
1834–1867

5 I now bid you a welcome adoo.
   Artemus Ward: His Book [1862]. The Shakers

6 My pollertics, like my religion, bein of a exceedin accommodatin character.
   Artemus Ward: His Book. The Crisis

7 I girdid up my Lions & fled the Seen.
   Artemus Ward: His Book. A Visit to Brigham Young

8 Did you ever hav the measels, and if so how many?   *Artemus Ward: His Book. The Census*

9 The female woman is one of the greatest institooshuns of which this land can boste.
   Artemus Ward: His Book. Woman's Rights

10 I'm not a politician and my other habits air good.
   Artemus Ward: His Book. Fourth of July Oration

11 The prevailin weakness of most public men is to SLOP OVER! Washington never slopt over.
   Artemus Ward: His Book. Fourth of July Oration

12 The sun has a right to "set" where it wants to, and so, I may add, has a hen.
   Artemus Ward: His Travels [1865]. A Mormon Romance, ch. 4

13 I can't sing. As a singist I am not a success. I am saddest when I sing. So are those who hear me. They are sadder even than I am.
   Artemus Ward's Lecture [1866]

14 He [Brigham Young] is dreadfully married. He's the most married man I ever saw in my life.
   Artemus Ward's Lecture

15 Why is this thus? What is the reason of this thusness?   *Artemus Ward's Lecture*

16 The Puritans nobly fled from a land of despotism to a land of freedim, where they could not only enjoy their own religion, but could prevent everybody else from enjoyin his.[3]
   London Punch Letters, no. 5 [1866]

17 Let us all be happy and live within our means, even if we have to borrow the money to do it with.
   Natural History

Edgar Degas
1834–1917

18 A picture is something which requires as much knavery, trickery, and deceit as the perpetration of a crime. Paint falsely, and then add the accent of nature.   *Attributed*

George [Louis Palmella Busson] du Maurier
1834–1896

19 The wretcheder one is, the more one smokes; and the more one smokes, the wretcheder one gets—a vicious circle!
   Peter Ibbetson [1891]

20 Songs without words are best.   *Peter Ibbetson*

21 A little work, a little play,
To keep us going—and so, good day!

---

[1] Music by Sir Arthur Sullivan [1842–1900].
[2] Translated from the Danish of B. S. Ingemann [1825].

[3] The Puritan's idea of Hell is a place where everybody has to mind his own business. — *Attributed to* Wendell Phillips

A little warmth, a little light,
Of love's bestowing—and so, good night![1]

A little fun, to match the sorrow
Of each day's growing—and so, good morrow!

A little trust that when we die
We reap our sowing! and so—good-bye!
Trilby [1894], pt. VIII

Charles William Eliot
1834–1926

1   In the modern world the intelligence of public opinion is the one indispensable condition of social progress.
Inaugural address as president of Harvard [1869]

2   Enter to grow in wisdom.
Depart to serve better thy country and thy kind.
Inscriptions on the 1890 Gate to Harvard Yard

3   To the Fifty-fourth Regiment of Massachusetts Infantry:

The white officers, taking life and honor in their hands, cast in their lot with men of a despised race unproved in war, and risked death as inciters of servile insurrection if taken prisoners, besides encountering all the common perils of camp march and battle.

The black rank and file volunteered when disaster clouded the Union cause, served without pay for eighteen months till given that of white troops, faced threatened enslavement if captured, were brave in action, patient under heavy and dangerous labors, and cheerful amid hardships and privations.

Together they gave to the nation and the world undying proof that Americans of African descent possess the pride, courage, and devotion of the patriot soldier. One hundred and eighty thousand such Americans enlisted under the Union flag in 1863–1865.
Inscription on the Robert Gould Shaw Monument by Augustus Saint-Gaudens, Boston Common [1897][2]

Marshall Field
1834–1906

4   Give the lady what she wants!
Instruction to manager of his Chicago department store

Ernst Heinrich Haeckel
1834–1919

5   Ontogenesis, or the development of the individual, is a short and quick recapitulation of phylogenesis,[3] or the development of the tribe to which [ ] belongs, determined by the laws of inheritance and adaptation.   *The History of Creation [1868]*

6   The general theory of evolution . . . assume[s] that in nature there is a great, unital, continuou[s] and everlasting process of development, and that a[ll] natural phenomena without exception, from the mo[tion] of the celestial bodies and the fall of the rollin[g] stone up to the growth of the plant and the con[sciousness] of man, are subject to the same great law of causation—that they are ultimately to be re[duced] to atomic mechanics.
Freie Wissenschaft und Freie Lehre [1878]

Walter Kittredge
1834–1905

7 We're tenting tonight on the old campground,
Give us a song to cheer
Our weary hearts, a song of home
And friends we love so dear.
Tenting on the Old Campground [1864], st. [ ]

William Morris
1834–1896

8   Well, if this is poetry, it is very easy to write.
Remark [1854]. From J. W. MACKAIL, Life of William Morris [1899]

9 I was half mad with beauty on that day.
The Defense of Guenevere [1858], l. 109

10 Had she come all the way for this,
To part at last without a kiss?
Yea, had she borne the dirt and rain
That her own eyes might see him slain
Beside the haystack in the floods?
The Haystack in the Floods [1858], l. 1

11 I know a little garden close,
Set thick with lily and red rose,
Where I would wander if I might
From dewy morn to dewy night.
*The Life and Death of Jason [1867].
A Garden by the Sea, st. 1*

---

[1]La vie est vaine: / Un peu d'amour, / Un peu de haine . . . / Et puis—bonjour! / La vie est brève: / Un peu d'espoir, / Un peu de rêve / Et puis—bonsoir!—LEON MONTENAEKEN [b. 1859], *Peu de Chose*

[2]See Paul Laurence Dunbar, 660:3, and Robert Lowell, 801:11.

[3]Frequently quoted: Ontogeny recapitulates phylogeny. See Freud, 607:11.

[4]Translated by E. R. LANKESTER.

[5]Translated by J. B. STALLO.

1 The idle singer of an empty day.
The Earthly Paradise [1868–1870].
An Apology, st. 1

2 Dreamer of dreams, born out of my due time,
Why should I strive to set the crooked straight?
The Earthly Paradise. An Apology, st. 4

3 Love is enough, though the world be awaning.
Love Is Enough [1872]

4 If you want a golden rule that will fit everybody, this is it: Have nothing in your houses that you do not know to be useful, or believe to be beautiful.
The Beauty of Life [1880]

5 What I mean by Socialism is a condition of society in which there should be neither rich nor poor, neither master nor master's man, neither idle nor overworked, neither brain-sick brain workers nor heart-sick hand workers, in a word, in which all men would be living in equality of condition, and would manage their affairs unwastefully, and with the full consciousness that harm to one would mean harm to all—the realization at last of the meaning of the word *commonwealth.*
Written for "Justice" [1884]

6 The reward of labor is life.
News from Nowhere [1891], ch. 15

Frank [Richard] Stockton
1834–1902

7 Which came out of the opened door—the lady or the tiger?
The Lady or the Tiger? [1884]

8 The board money is in the ginger jar and our conscience is clear.
The Casting Away of Mrs. Lecks and Mrs. Aleshine [1886]

James Thomson
1834–1882

9 Statues and pictures and verse may be grand,
But they are not the Life for which they stand.
Art [1865], st. 3, l. 19

10 Give a man a horse he can ride,
Give a man a boat he can sail.
Sunday Up the River [1869], st. 15

11 The City is of Night; perchance of Death,
But certainly of Night.
The City of Dreadful Night [1874], st. 1

12 I find no hint throughout the Universe
Of good or ill, of blessing or of curse;
I find alone Necessity Supreme.
The City of Dreadful Night, st. 14

James McNeill Whistler
1834–1903

13 Two and two the mathematician continues to make four, in spite of the whine of the amateur for three, or the cry of the critic for five.
Whistler v. Ruskin [1878]

14 The rare few, who, early in life, have rid themselves of the friendship of the many.
The Gentle Art of Making Enemies [1890]

15 To say of a picture, as is often said in its praise, that it shows great and earnest labor, is to say that it is incomplete and unfit for view.
The Gentle Art of Making Enemies

16 The masterpiece should appear as the flower to the painter—perfect in its bud as in its bloom—with no reason to explain its presence—no mission to fulfill—a joy to the artist, a delusion to the philanthropist—a puzzle to the botanist—an accident of sentiment and alliteration to the literary man.
The Gentle Art of Making Enemies

17 Art should be independent of all claptrap—should stand alone, and appeal to the artistic sense of eye or ear, without confounding this with emotions entirely foreign to it, as devotion, pity, love, patriotism, and the like. All these have no kind of concern with it.
The Gentle Art of Making Enemies

18 One cannot continually disappoint a Continent.[1]
The Gentle Art of Making Enemies

19 I am not arguing with you—I am telling you.
The Gentle Art of Making Enemies

20 *Attorney-General Sir John Holker:* The labor of two days, then, is that for which you ask two hundred guineas?
Whistler: No;—I ask it for the knowledge of a lifetime.
The Gentle Art of Making Enemies. Messieurs Les Ennemis[2]

---

[1] Referring to a contemplated visit to the United States.

[2] Exchange in the 1878 trial of Whistler's libel suit against John Ruskin, who had written [*Fors Clavigera, Letter 79,* July 2, 1877] of the artist's *Nocturne in Black and Gold:* "I have seen, and heard, much of Cockney impudence before now; but never expected to hear a coxcomb ask two hundred guineas for flinging a pot of paint in the public's face."

1   *Wilde:* I wish I'd said that.
Whistler: You will, Oscar, you will.
From L. C. INGLEBY, *Oscar Wilde* [1907]

2   Had silicon been a gas I would have been a major general.
On failing chemistry at West Point. From
JOSEPH PENNELL, *The Life of James McNeill Whistler* [1908]

Thomas Brigham Bishop
1835–1905

3 John Brown's body lies a-moldering in the grave,
His soul is marching on.   *John Brown's Body, st. 1*

4 Shoo, fly! don't bodder me! I belong to Company G,
I feel like a morning star.   *Shoo, Fly. Refrain*

Phillips Brooks
1835–1893

5 O little town of Bethlehem!
How still we see thee lie;
Above thy deep and dreamless sleep
The silent stars go by;
Yet in thy dark streets shineth
The everlasting Light;
The hopes and fears of all the years
Are met in thee tonight.
O Little Town of Bethlehem [1867], *st. 1*

6   Life comes before literature, as the material always comes before the work. The hills are full of marble before the world blooms with statues.
Literature and Life

Samuel Butler
1835–1902

7   The man who lets himself be bored is even more contemptible than the bore.
The Fair Haven [1873]. *Memoir, ch. 3*

8   A hen is only an egg's way of making another egg.
Life and Habit [1877], *ch. 8*

9 Stowed away in a Montreal lumber room
The Discobolus standeth and turneth his face to
    the wall;
Dusty, cobweb-covered, maimed and set at naught,
Beauty crieth in an attic and no man regardeth.
O God! O Montreal!
A Psalm of Montreal [1884], *st. 1*

10 The Discobolus is put here because he is vulgar —
He has neither vest nor pants with which to cover
    his limbs.   *A Psalm of Montreal, st. 5*

11   It was very good of God to let Carlyle and Mrs
Carlyle marry one another and so make only two
people miserable instead of four.
*Letter to Miss E. M. A. Savage [November 21,
1884]*

12   It is far safer to know too little than too much.
People will condemn the one, though they will resent being called upon to exert themselves to follow
the other.   *The Way of All Flesh* [1903], *ch. 5*

13   Taking numbers into account, I should think
more mental suffering had been undergone in the
streets leading from St. George's, Hanover Square
than in the condemned cells of Newgate.
The Way of All Flesh, 13

14   Every man's work, whether it be literature or
music or pictures or architecture or anything else, is
always a portrait of himself.
The Way of All Flesh, 14

15   One great reason why clergymen's households
are generally unhappy is because the clergyman is so
much at home or close about the house.
The Way of All Flesh, 24

16   The advantage of doing one's praising for oneself is that one can lay it on so thick and exactly in
the right places.   *The Way of All Flesh, 34*

17   The best liar is he who makes the smallest
amount of lying go the longest way.
The Way of All Flesh, 39

18   A man's friendships are, like his will, invalidated
by marriage — but they are also no less invalidated
by the marriage of his friends.
The Way of All Flesh, 75

19   Life is the art of drawing sufficient conclusions
from insufficient premises.
Notebooks [1912]. *Life*

20   All progress is based upon a universal innate desire on the part of every organism to live beyond its
income.   *Notebooks. Life*

21   Though analogy is often misleading, it is the
least misleading thing we have.
Notebooks. Music, Pictures, and Books

22   The phrase "unconscious humor" is the one
contribution I have made to the current literature
of the day.   *Notebooks. Homo Unius Libri*

23   Genius . . . has been defined as a supreme capacity for taking trouble. . . . It might be more fitly
described as a supreme capacity for getting its possessors into pains of all kinds and keeping them
therein so long as the genius remains.
Notebooks. Genius

1 An apology for the Devil: It must be remembered that we have only heard one side of the case. God has written all the books.
Notebooks. Higgledy-Piggledy: An Apology for the Devil

2 God is Love—I dare say. But what a mischievous devil Love is!   *Notebooks. God Is Love*

3 [*The Ancient Mariner*] would not have taken so well if it had been called *The Old Sailor*.
Notebooks. Titles and Subjects

4 The public buys its opinions as it buys its meat, or takes in its milk, on the principle that it is cheaper to do this than to keep a cow. So it is, but the milk is more likely to be watered.
Notebooks. Sequel to "Alps and Sanctuaries"

5 I do not mind lying, but I hate inaccuracy.
Notebooks. Truth and Convenience: Falsehood

Andrew Carnegie
1835–1919

6 While the law [of competition] may be sometimes hard for the individual, it is best for the race, because it insures the survival of the fittest in every department. We accept and welcome, therefore, as conditions to which we must accommodate ourselves, great inequality of environment, the concentration of business, industrial and commercial, in the hands of a few, and the law of competition between these, as being not only beneficial, but essential for the future progress of the race.
Wealth. From the North American Review [June 1889]

7 Upon the sacredness of property civilization itself depends—the right of the laborer to his hundred dollars in the savings bank, and equally the legal right of the millionaire to his millions.
Wealth. From the North American Review

8 Surplus wealth is a sacred trust which its possessor is bound to administer in his lifetime for the good of the community.
Wealth. From the North American Review

9 Those who would administer wisely must, indeed, be wise, for one of the serious obstacles to the improvement of our race is indiscriminate charity.
Wealth. From the North American Review

.0 The man who dies . . . rich dies disgraced.
Wealth. From the North American Review

.1 Three generations from shirtsleeves to shirtsleeves.[1]   *Triumphant Democracy [1886]*

---

[1]There's nobbut three generations atween clog and clog.— *Lancashire proverb, which Carnegie liked to quote*

Mark Twain[2]
[Samuel Langhorne Clemens]
1835–1910

12 The serene confidence which a Christian feels in four aces.
Letter to The Golden Era (San Francisco) [May 22, 1864]

13 I *have* had a "call" to literature, of a low order— *i.e.* humorous. It is nothing to be proud of, but it is my strongest suit . . . seriously scribbling to excite the *laughter* of God's creatures.
Letter to Orion and Mary Clemens [October 19, 1865]

14 I don't see no p'ints about that frog that's any better'n any other frog.
The Notorious Jumping Frog of Calaveras County [1865][3]

15 I'll resk forty dollars that he can outjump any frog in Calaveras county.
The Notorious Jumping Frog of Calaveras County

16 They spell it Vinci and pronounce it Vinchy; foreigners always spell better than they pronounce.
The Innocents Abroad [1869], ch. 19

17 There's millions in it!
The Gilded Age (stage version) [1874]

18 Barring that natural expression of villainy which we all have, the man looked honest enough.
Sketches [1875]. A Mysterious Visit

19 Tom appeared on the sidewalk with a bucket of whitewash and a long-handled brush. He surveyed the fence, and all gladness left him and a deep melancholy settled down upon his spirit. Thirty yards of board fence nine feet high. Life to him seemed hollow, and existence but a burden.
The Adventures of Tom Sawyer [1876], ch. 2

20 Work consists of whatever a body is *obliged* to do. . . . Play consists of whatever a body is not obliged to do.   *The Adventures of Tom Sawyer, 2*

21 She makes me wash, they comb me all to thunder; she won't let me sleep in the woodshed. . . . The widder eats by a bell; she goes to bed by a bell; she gits up by a bell—everything's so awful reg'lar a body can't stand it.
The Adventures of Tom Sawyer, 35

22 There is a sumptuous variety about the New England weather that compels the stranger's admi-

---

[2]A pseudonym apparently derived from the Mississippi steamboating term signifying two fathoms (12 feet) of depth.

[3]Frequently cited as "The Celebrated Jumping Frog of Calaveras County."

ration — and regret. The weather is always doing something there; always attending strictly to business; always getting up new designs and trying them on the people to see how they will go. . . . Yes, one of the brightest gems in the New England weather is the dazzling uncertainty of it.

Speech. The Weather [1876]

1   I am a great & sublime fool. But then I am God's fool, & all His works must be contemplated with respect.

Letter to William Dean Howells [December 28(?), 1877]

2   I'm the man they call Sudden Death and General Desolation! Sired by a hurricane, dam'd by an earthquake. . . . When I'm playful I use the meridians of longitude and parallels of latitude for a seine, and drag the Atlantic Ocean for whales! I scratch my head with the lightning and purr myself to sleep with the thunder!

Life on the Mississippi [1883], ch. 3

3   The Child of Calamity.

Life on the Mississippi, 3

4   I can picture that old time to myself now, just as it was then: the white town drowsing in the sunshine of a summer's morning . . . the great Mississippi, the majestic, the magnificent Mississippi, rolling its mile-wide tide along, shining in the sun.

Life on the Mississippi, 4

5   I was gratified to be able to answer promptly, and I did. I said I didn't know.

Life on the Mississippi, 6

6   Your true pilot cares nothing about anything on earth but the river, and his pride in his occupation surpasses the pride of kings.

Life on the Mississippi, 7

7   By the Shadow of Death, but he's a lightning pilot!   *Life on the Mississippi, 7*

8   I'll learn him or kill him.

Life on the Mississippi, 8

9   When I find a well-drawn character in fiction or biography, I generally take a warm personal interest in him, for the reason that I have known him before — met him on the river.

Life on the Mississippi, 18

10   The first time I ever saw St. Louis, I could have bought it for six million dollars, and it was the mistake of my life that I did not do it.

Life on the Mississippi, 22

11   Give an Irishman lager for a month, and he's a dead man. An Irishman is lined with copper, and

the beer corrodes it. But whiskey polishes the copper and is the saving of him.

Life on the Mississippi, 2.

12   All the modern inconveniences.

Life on the Mississippi, 4.

13   Persons attempting to find a motive in this narrative will be prosecuted; persons attempting to find a moral in it will be banished; persons attempting to find a plot in it will be shot.

Adventures of Huckleberry Finn [1885]. Notice

14   You don't know about me, without you have read a book by the name of "The Adventures of Tom Sawyer," but that ain't no matter. That book was made by Mr. Mark Twain, and he told the truth, mainly. There was things which he stretched, but mainly he told the truth. That is nothing. never seen anybody but lied, one time or another.

Adventures of Huckleberry Finn, ch.

15   It was kind of solemn, drifting down the big still river, laying on our backs looking up at the stars, and we didn't ever feel like talking loud, and it warn't often that we laughed, only a little kind of low chuckle. We had mighty good weather, as general thing, and nothing ever happened to us at all, that night, nor the next, nor the next.

Adventures of Huckleberry Finn, 1.

16   "Pilgrim's Progress," about a man that left his family it didn't say why. I read considerable in it now and then. The statements was interesting, but tough.

Adventures of Huckleberry Finn, 1.

17   We said there warn't no home like a raft, after all. Other places do seem so cramped up and smothery, but a raft don't. You feel mighty free and easy and comfortable on a raft.

Adventures of Huckleberry Finn, 1.

18   It was a monstrous big river down there.

Adventures of Huckleberry Finn, 1.

19   All kings is mostly rapscallions.

Adventures of Huckleberry Finn, 2.

20   Hain't we got all the fools in town on our side? and ain't that a big enough majority in any town?

Adventures of Huckleberry Finn, 2.

21   You can't pray a lie.

Adventures of Huckleberry Finn, 3.

22   I studied a minute, sort of holding my breath, and then says to myself: "All right, then, I'll *go* to hell."

Adventures of Huckleberry Finn, 3.

1   He [George Washington Cable] has taught me to abhor and detest the Sabbath-day and hunt up new and troublesome ways to dishonor it.
     Letter to William Dean Howells [February 27, 1885]

2   The difference between the *almost*-right word & the *right* word is really a large matter—it's the difference between the lightning bug and the lightning.
     Letter to George Bainton [October 15, 1888]

3   We saw a faraway town sleeping in a valley by a winding river; and beyond it, on a hill, a vast gray fortress, with towers and turrets, the first I had ever seen, out of a picture.
     "Bridgeport?" said I, pointing.
     "Camelot," said he.
     A Connecticut Yankee in King Arthur's Court [1889]. A Word of Explanation

4   Whenever the literary German dives into a sentence, that is the last you are going to see of him till he emerges on the other side of his Atlantic with his verb in his mouth.
     A Connecticut Yankee in King Arthur's Court, ch. 22

5   There ain't no way to find out why a snorer can't hear himself snore.
     Tom Sawyer Abroad [1894], ch. 10

6   Tell the truth or trump—but get the trick.
     Pudd'nhead Wilson [1894]. Pudd'nhead Wilson's Calendar, ch. 1

7   Adam was but human—this explains it all. He did not want the apple for the apple's sake, he wanted it only because it was forbidden.
     Pudd'nhead Wilson. Pudd'nhead Wilson's Calendar, 2

8   Training is everything. The peach was once a bitter almond; cauliflower is nothing but cabbage with a college education.
     Pudd'nhead Wilson. Pudd'nhead Wilson's Calendar, 5

9   One of the most striking differences between a cat and a lie is that a cat has only nine lives.
     Pudd'nhead Wilson. Pudd'nhead Wilson's Calendar, 7

10   The holy passion of Friendship is of so sweet and steady and loyal and enduring a nature that it will last through a whole lifetime, if not asked to lend money.
     Pudd'nhead Wilson. Pudd'nhead Wilson's Calendar, 8

11   Why is it that we rejoice at a birth and grieve at a funeral? It is because we are not the person involved.
     Pudd'nhead Wilson. Pudd'nhead Wilson's Calendar, 9

12   When angry, count four; when very angry, swear.
     Pudd'nhead Wilson. Pudd'nhead Wilson's Calendar, 10

13   As to the Adjective: when in doubt, strike it out.
     Pudd'nhead Wilson. Pudd'nhead Wilson's Calendar, 11

14   Nothing so needs reforming as other people's habits.
     Pudd'nhead Wilson. Pudd'nhead Wilson's Calendar, 15

15   Put all your eggs in the one basket and—WATCH THAT BASKET.
     Pudd'nhead Wilson. Pudd'nhead Wilson's Calendar, 15

16   If you pick up a starving dog and make him prosperous, he will not bite you. This is the principal difference between a dog and a man.
     Pudd'nhead Wilson. Pudd'nhead Wilson's Calendar, 16

17   Few things are harder to put up with than the annoyance of a good example.
     Pudd'nhead Wilson. Pudd'nhead Wilson's Calendar, 19

18   It were not best that we should all think alike; it is difference of opinion that makes horse-races.
     Pudd'nhead Wilson. Pudd'nhead Wilson's Calendar, 19

19   [Citing a familiar "American joke":] In Boston they ask, How much does he know? in New York, How much is he worth? in Philadelphia, Who were his parents?
     What Paul Bourget Thinks of Us [1895]

20   He saw nearly all things as through a glass eye, darkly.
     Fenimore Cooper's Literary Offenses [1895]

21   Be good and you will be lonesome.
     Following the Equator [1897]. Pudd'nhead Wilson's New Calendar, frontispiece caption

22   When in doubt tell the truth.
     Following the Equator. Pudd'nhead Wilson's New Calendar, ch. 2

23   Noise proves nothing. Often a hen who has merely laid an egg cackles as if she had laid an asteroid.
     Following the Equator. Pudd'nhead Wilson's New Calendar, 5

1   Truth is the most valuable thing we have. Let us economize it.
      Following the Equator. Pudd'nhead Wilson's New Calendar, 7

2   It could probably be shown by facts and figures that there is no distinctly native American criminal class except Congress.
      Following the Equator. Pudd'nhead Wilson's New Calendar, 8

3   Everything human is pathetic. The secret source of Humor itself is not joy but sorrow. There is no humor in heaven.
      Following the Equator. Pudd'nhead Wilson's New Calendar, 10

4   We should be careful to get out of an experience only the wisdom that is in it—and stop there; lest we be like the cat that sits down on a hot stove-lid. She will never sit down on a hot stove-lid again—and that is well; but also she will never sit down on a cold one any more.
      Following the Equator. Pudd'nhead Wilson's New Calendar, 11

5   Pity is for the living, envy is for the dead.
      Following the Equator. Pudd'nhead Wilson's New Calendar, 19

6   It is by the goodness of God that in our country we have those three unspeakably precious things: freedom of speech, freedom of conscience, and the prudence never to practice either of them.
      Following the Equator. Pudd'nhead Wilson's New Calendar, 20

7   "Classic." A book which people praise and don't read.
      Following the Equator. Pudd'nhead Wilson's New Calendar, 25

8   Man is the only animal that blushes. Or needs to.
      Following the Equator. Pudd'nhead Wilson's New Calendar, 27

9   Each person is born to one possession which outvalues all his others—his last breath.
      Following the Equator. Pudd'nhead Wilson's New Calendar, 42

10   It takes your enemy and your friend, working together, to hurt you to the heart; the one to slander you and the other to get the news to you.
      Following the Equator. Pudd'nhead Wilson's New Calendar, 45

11   In statesmanship get the formalities right, never mind about the moralities.
      Following the Equator. Pudd'nhead Wilson's New Calendar, 65

12   Everyone is a moon, and has a dark side which he never shows to anybody.
      Following the Equator. Pudd'nhead Wilson's New Calendar, 66

13   The report of my death was an exaggeration.
      Note to London correspondent of the New York Journal [June 1, 1897]

14   Always do right. This will gratify some people and astonish the rest.
      Card sent to the Young People's Society, Greenpoint Presbyterian Church, Brooklyn [February 16, 1901]

15   I believe that our Heavenly Father invented man because he was disappointed in the monkey.
      Autobiographical Dictation [November 24, 1906]

16   Laws are sand, customs are rock. Laws can be evaded and punishment escaped, but an openly transgressed custom brings sure punishment.
      The Gorky Incident [1906]

17   Thunder is good, thunder is impressive; but it is the lightning that does the work.
      Letter to an Unidentified Person [August 28, 1908]

18   Power, money, persuasion, supplication, persecution—these can lift at a colossal humbug—push it a little—weaken it a little, century by century, but only laughter can blow it to rags and atoms at a blast. Against the assault of laughter nothing can stand.   *The Mysterious Stranger [1922], ch. 10*

19   O kind missionary, O compassionate missionary, leave China! come home and convert these Christians!
      Europe and Elsewhere [1923]. The United States of Lyncherdom

20   You tell me whar a man gits his corn pone, en I'll tell you what his 'pinions is.
      Europe and Elsewhere. Corn-Pone Opinions

21   Biographies are but the clothes and buttons of the man—the biography of the man himself cannot be written.   *Autobiography [1924], vol. I*

22   [Man] has imagined a heaven, and has left entirely out of it the supremest of all his delights . . . sexual intercourse! . . . His heaven is like himself: strange, interesting, astonishing, grotesque. I give you my word, it has not a single feature in it that he *actually values.*
      Letters from the Earth [1962], II

23   [The Bible] has noble poetry in it; and some clever fables; and some blood-drenched history;

and a wealth of obscenity; and upwards of a thousand lies.   *Letters from the Earth, III*

1   When I was younger I could remember anything, whether it happened or not; but I am getting old, and soon I shall remember only the latter.
  From ALBERT BIGELOW PAINE, Mark Twain, A Biography [1912]

2   Clothes make the man. Naked people have little or no influence in society.   *Attributed*

3   Everybody talks about the weather, but nobody does anything about it.[1]   *Attributed*

4   Golf is a good walk spoiled.   *Attributed*

Thomas Bailey Aldrich
1836–1907

5 In street and alley, what strange tongues are loud,
Accents of menace alien to our air,
Voices that once the Tower of Babel knew!
O Liberty, white Goddess! Is it well
To leave the gates unguarded?
                     The Unguarded Gates [1892]

6   Though I am not genuine Boston, I am Boston-plated.
  From FERRIS GREENSLET, The Life of Thomas Bailey Aldrich [1908]

Isabella Mary Beeton
1836–1865

7   A place for everything and everything in its place.[2]
                     The Book of Household Management [1861]

8   Clear as you go.
                     The Book of Household Management

Edward Ernest Bowen
1836–1901

9 Forty years on, when afar and asunder
Parted are those who are singing today.
                     Forty Years On [1872][3]

Joseph Chamberlain
1836–1914

10   The day of small nations has long passed away. The day of Empires has come.
                     Speech. Birmingham [May 12, 1904]

Sir W[illiam] S[chwenck] Gilbert
1836–1911

11 Oh, I am a cook and a captain bold
And the mate of the *Nancy* brig,
And a bo'sun tight, and a midshipmite,
And the crew of the captain's gig.
                     The "Bab" Ballads [1866–1871]. The Yarn of the "Nancy Bell," st. 3

12 As innocent as a new-laid egg.
                     Engaged [1877], act I

13 I'm called Little Buttercup — dear little Buttercup,
Though I could never tell why.
                     H.M.S. Pinafore [1878], act I

14 I am the Captain of the *Pinafore*;
And a right good captain too!
                     H.M.S. Pinafore, I

15 And I'm never, never sick at sea!
    What, never?
    No, never!
    What, *never*?
    Hardly ever!
He's hardly ever sick at sea!
Then give three cheers, and one cheer more
For the hardy Captain of the *Pinafore*!
                     H.M.S. Pinafore, I

16 And so do his sisters, and his cousins, and his aunts!
His sisters and his cousins,
Whom he reckons up by dozens,
And his aunts!   *H.M.S. Pinafore, I*

17 When I was a lad I served a term
    As office boy to an Attorney's firm.
    I cleaned the windows and I swept the floor
    And I polished up the handle of the big front door.
    I polished up that handle so carefullee
    That now I am the Ruler of the Queen's Navee!
                     H.M.S. Pinafore, I

18 Stick close to your desks and *never go to sea*,
And you all may be Rulers of the Queen's Navee!
                     H.M.S. Pinafore, I

19 Things are seldom what they seem,
Skim milk masquerades as cream.
                     H.M.S. Pinafore, II

20 He is an Englishman!
For he himself has said it,

---

[1]A famously moot quotation frequently attributed instead to Charles Dudley Warner (see 543). A variant version — "We all grumble about the weather but nothing is *done* about it" — appears in Robert Underwood Johnson's recollections of Mark Twain (*Remembered Yesterdays* [1923]).

[2]In a well-conducted man-of-war . . . everything is in its place, and there is a place for everything. — MARRYAT, *Masterman Ready* [1842]

[3]Harrow school song.

And it's greatly to his credit,
That he is an Englishman!   *H.M.S. Pinafore, II*

1 For he might have been a Roosian,
A French or Turk or Proosian,
Or perhaps Itali-an.
But in spite of all temptations
To belong to other nations,
He remains an Englishman.   *H.M.S. Pinafore, II*

2 It is, it is a glorious thing
To be a Pirate King.
    Pirates of Penzance [1879], act I

3 I am the very model of a modern Major-General.
I've information vegetable, animal, and mineral,
I know the Kings of England, and I quote the
    fights historical,
From Marathon to Waterloo, in order categorical.
    Pirates of Penzance, I

4 When the foeman bares his steel,
        Tarantara, tarantara!
We uncomfortable feel,
        Tarantara.   *Pirates of Penzance, II*

5 When constabulary duty's to be done,
The policeman's lot is not a happy one.
    Pirates of Penzance, II

6 Come, friends, who plow the sea,
        Truce to navigation,
        Take another station;
Let's vary piracee
With a little burglaree.[1]   *Pirates of Penzance, II*

7 Twenty love-sick maidens we,
Love-sick all against our will.
    Patience [1881], act I

8 You must lie upon the daisies and discourse in
        novel phrases of your complicated state of
        mind,
The meaning doesn't matter if it's only idle chatter
        of a transcendental kind.
And everyone will say,
As you walk your mystic way,
"If this young man expresses himself in terms too
        deep for *me*,
Why, what a very singularly deep young man this
        deep young man must be!"   *Patience, I*

9 Though the Philistines may jostle, you will rank as
        an apostle in the high aesthetic band,
If you walk down Piccadilly with a poppy or a lily
        in your medieval hand.
And everyone will say,
As you walk your flowery way,

"If he's content with a vegetable love, which would
        certainly not suit *me*,
Why, what a most particularly pure young man this
        pure young man must be!"   *Patience,*

10 Prithee, pretty maiden, will you marry me?
(Hey, but I'm hopeful, willow, willow, waly!)
    Patience,

11 While this magnetic,
Peripatetic
Lover he lived to learn,
By no endeavor,
Can magnet ever
Attract a silver churn!   *Patience, II*

12 Francesca da Rimini, miminy, piminy,
Je-ne-sais-quoi young man!   *Patience, II*

13 A greenery-yallery, Grosvenor Gallery,
Foot-in-the-grave young man!   *Patience, II*

14 I see no objection to stoutness, in moderation.
    Iolanthe [1882], act I

15 None shall part us from each other,
One in life and death are we:
All in all to one another—
I to thee and thou to me!
Thou the tree and I the flower—
Thou the idol; I the throng—
Thou the day and I the hour—
Thou the singer; I the song!   *Iolanthe, I*

16 Bow, bow, ye lower middle classes!
Bow, bow, ye tradesmen, bow, ye masses.
    Iolanthe, I

17 The Law is the true embodiment
Of everything that's excellent.
It has no kind of fault or flaw,
And I, my Lords, embody the Law.   *Iolanthe, I*

18 Pretty young wards in Chancery.   *Iolanthe, I*

19 For I'm not so old, and not so plain,
And I'm quite prepared to marry again.
    Iolanthe, I

20 Hearts just as pure and fair
May beat in Belgrave Square
As in the lowly air
        Of Seven Dials.   *Iolanthe, I*

21 When I went to the Bar as a very young man
(Said I to myself, said I).   *Iolanthe, I*

22 I often think it's comical
How nature always does contrive
That every boy and every gal,
That's born into the world alive,
Is either a little Liberal,
Or else a little Conservative!   *Iolanthe, II*

---

[1]The roistering chorus "Hail, hail, the gang's all here" is sung to
Sir Arthur Sullivan's music for these lines.

Here's a pretty kettle of fish!

Iolanthe, II

The House of Peers, throughout the war,
Did nothing in particular,
    And did it very well.   *Iolanthe, II*

When you're lying awake with a dismal headache,
    and repose is taboo'd by anxiety,
I conceive you may use any language you choose to
    indulge in, without impropriety.

Iolanthe, II

For you dream you are crossing the Channel, and
    tossing about in a steamer from Harwich—
Which is something between a large bathing ma-
    chine and a very small second-class carriage.

Iolanthe, II

Faint heart never won fair lady!
Nothing venture, nothing win—
Blood is thick, but water's thin—
In for a penny, in for a pound[1]—
It's Love that makes the world go round!

Iolanthe, II

I love my fellow creatures—I do all the good I
    can—
Yet everybody says I'm such a disagreeable man!
And I can't think why!

Princess Ida [1884], act I

A wandering minstrel I—
    A thing of shreds and patches,
    Of ballads, songs and snatches,
And dreamy lullaby!   *The Mikado [1885], act I*

I can't help it. I was born sneering.

The Mikado, I

As some day it may happen that a victim must be
    found,
I've got a little list—I've got a little list.
Of society offenders who might well be
    underground,
And who never would be missed—who never
    would be missed.   *The Mikado, I*

Then the idiot who praises, with enthusiastic tone,
All centuries but this, and every country but his
    own.   *The Mikado, I*

Three little maids from school are we,
Pert as a schoolgirl well can be,
Filled to the brim with girlish glee.

The Mikado, I

Ah, pray make no mistake,
We are not shy;

---

[1]Well, then o'er shoes, o'er boots. And in for a penny, in for a Pound.—EDWARD RAVENSCROFT [fl. 1671–1697], *The Canterbury Guests; Or, A Bargain Broken* [1695], act V, sc. i

We're very wide awake,
The moon and I!   *The Mikado, II*

13 Here's a pretty state of things!
Here's a pretty how-de-do!   *The Mikado, II*

14 My object all sublime
I shall achieve in time—
To let the punishment fit the crime.

The Mikado, II

15 A source of innocent merriment!   *The Mikado, II*

16   On a cloth untrue
      With a twisted cue
And elliptical billiard balls.   *The Mikado, II*

17 I seized him by his little pig-tail,
And on his knees fell he,
As he squirmed and struggled,
And gurgled and guggled,
I drew my snickersnee!   *The Mikado, II*

18   Merely corroborative detail, intended to give
artistic verisimilitude to an otherwise bald and unconvincing narrative.   *The Mikado, II*

19 The flowers that bloom in the spring, tra la,
Have nothing to do with the case.

The Mikado, II

20 On a tree by a river a little tomtit
Sang "Willow, titwillow, titwillow!"
And I said to him, "Dicky-bird, why do you sit
Singing 'Willow, titwillow, titwillow!'
"Is it weakness of intellect, birdie?" I cried,
"Or a rather tough worm in your little inside?"
With a shake of his poor little head he replied,
"Oh, willow, titwillow, titwillow!"

The Mikado, II

21   There's a fascination frantic
      In a ruin that's romantic;
Do you think you are sufficiently decayed?

The Mikado, II

22   He uses language that would make your hair
curl.   *Ruddigore [1887], act I*

23 When the footpads quail at the night-bird's wail,
    and black dogs bay at the moon,
Then is the specters' holiday—then is the ghosts'
    high noon!   *Ruddigore, II*

24 I have a song to sing, O!
Sing me your song, O!

The Yeomen of the Guard [1888], act I

25 It's a song of a merryman, moping mum,
Whose soul was sad, and whose glance was glum,
Who sipped no sup, and who craved no crumb,
As he sighed for the love of a lady.

The Yeomen of the Guard, I

1 He led his regiment from behind—
He found it less exciting.
The Gondoliers [1889], act I

2   That celebrated,
Cultivated,
Underrated
Nobleman,
The Duke of Plaza Toro!   *The Gondoliers, I*

3 No soldier in that gallant band
Hid half as well as he did.
He lay concealed throughout the war,
And so preserved his gore, O!   *The Gondoliers, I*

4 Of *that* there is no manner of doubt—
No probable, possible shadow of doubt—
No possible doubt whatever.   *The Gondoliers, I*

5 Life's a pudding full of plums;
Care's a canker that benumbs,
Wherefore waste our elocution
On impossible solution?
Life's a pleasant institution,
Let us take it as it comes!   *The Gondoliers, I*

6 The gratifying feeling that our duty has been done.
The Gondoliers, II

7 Take a pair of sparkling eyes.   *The Gondoliers, II*

8 When everyone is somebodee,
Then no one's anybody!   *The Gondoliers, II*

9 The world has joked incessantly for over fifty
centuries.
And every joke that's possible has long ago been
made.
His Excellency: The Played-Out Humorist
[1894]

Bret Harte
[Francis Brett Harte]
1836–1902

10   Tell the boys I've got the Luck with me now.
The Luck of Roaring Camp [1868]

11   Beneath this tree lies the body of JOHN
OAKHURST, who struck a streak of bad luck on the
23rd of November, 1850, and handed in his checks
on the 7th of December, 1850.
The Outcasts of Poker Flat [1869]

12 Which I wish to remark,
And my language is plain,
That for ways that are dark
And for tricks that are vain,
The heathen Chinee is peculiar,
Which the same I would rise to explain.
Plain Language from Truthful James [1870]

Jane Ellice Hopkins
1836–1904

13   Genius is an infinite capacity for taking pains.[1]
Work Amongst Working Men [187...

Cesare Lombroso
1836–1909

14   Klopstock was questioned regarding the mea...
ing of a passage in his poem. He replied, "God an...
I both knew what it meant once; now God alo...
knows."[2]   *The Man of Genius [1891], pt. I, ch.*

15   The appearance of a single great genius is mo...
than equivalent to the birth of a hundred medioc...
ties.   *The Man of Genius, II,*

16   "Lawsuit mania" . . . a continual craving to ...
to law against others, while considering themselv...
the injured party.   *The Man of Genius, III,*

John Burroughs
1837–1921

17 Serene, I fold my hands and wait,
Nor care for wind, nor tide, nor sea;
I rave no more 'gainst time or fate,
For lo! my own shall come to me.
Waiting [1876], st.

18   I was born with a chronic anxiety about t...
weather.   *Is It Going to Rain? [187...*

19   One goes to Nature only for hints and ha...
truths. Her facts are crude until you have absorb...
them or translated them. . . . It is not so much wh...
we see as what the thing seen suggests.
Signs and Seasons [1886]. A Sharp Looko...

20   It is always easier to believe than to deny. O...
minds are naturally affirmative.
The Light of Day [1900]. The Modern Skept...

21   Nature teaches more than she preaches. The...
are no sermons in stones. It is easier to get a spa...
out of a stone than a moral.
Time and Change [1912]. The Gospel of Natu...

22   I see on an immense scale, and as clearly as in...
demonstration in a laboratory, that good comes o...
of evil; that the impartiality of the Nature Pro...
dence is best; that we are made strong by what v...
overcome; that man is man because he is as free ...
do evil as to do good; that life is as free to devel...

---

[1]See Buffon, 321:11; Carlyle, 435:10; and Samuel But...
[1835–1902], 558:23.

[2]Also attributed to Robert Browning, apropos of his *Sordello.*

hostile forms as to develop friendly; that power waits upon him who earns it; that disease, wars, the unloosened, devastating elemental forces have each and all played their part in developing and hardening man and giving him the heroic fiber.

Accepting the Universe [1922]

Grover Cleveland
1837–1908

1   Your every voter, as surely as your chief magistrate, exercises a public trust.[1]

Inaugural Address [March 4, 1885]

George Dewey[2]
1837–1917

2   You may fire when you are ready, Gridley.

To the captain of Admiral Dewey's flagship at the battle of Manila Bay [May 1, 1898]

3   I am convinced that the office of the President is not such a difficult one to fill, his duties being mainly to execute the laws of Congress.

Interview in New York World [April 3, 1900]

William Dean Howells
1837–1920

4 Lord, for the erring thought
Not into evil wrought:
Lord, for the wicked will
Betrayed and baffled still:
For the heart from itself kept,
Our thanksgiving accept.   *A Thanksgiving*

5 He who sleeps in continual noise is wakened by
    silence.   *Pordenone, IV*

6   The wrecks of slavery are fast growing a fungus crop of sentiment.

Their Wedding Journey [1872]

7   We invite our novelists . . . to concern themselves with the more smiling aspects of life, which are the more American.

Editor's Study: Dostoievski's Latest Novel, in Harper's Monthly [September 1886]

8   The mortality of all inanimate things is terrible to me, but that of books most of all.

Letter to Charles Eliot Norton [April 6, 1903]

9   Clemens was sole, incomparable, the Lincoln of our literature.   *My Mark Twain [1910]*

10   Some people can stay longer in an hour than others can in a week.   *Attributed*

J[ohn] P[ierpont] Morgan
1837–1913

11   A man always has two reasons for what he does—a good one, and the real one.

From OWEN WISTER, Roosevelt: The Story of a Friendship [1930]

12   Any man who has to ask about the annual upkeep of a yacht can't afford one.   *Attributed*

13   Never be on the bear side but on the bull side when the United States is in question.[3]

Attributed

Horace Porter
1837–1921

14   A mugwump is a person educated beyond his intellect.

A slogan of the Cleveland-Blaine campaign [1884]

Innes Randolph
1837–1887

15 Oh, I'm a good old rebel, that's what I am.
A Good Old Rebel [c. 1870], st. 1

16 I won't be reconstructed, and I don't give a damn.
A Good Old Rebel, st. 4

Algernon Charles Swinburne
1837–1909

17 When the hounds of spring are on winter's traces,
    The mother of months in meadow or plain
Fills the shadows and windy places
With lisp of leaves and ripple of rain;
And the brown bright nightingale amorous
Is half assuaged for Itylus,
For the Thracian ships and the foreign faces,
The tongueless vigil, and all the pain.
Atalanta in Calydon [1865], chorus, st. 1

18 For winter's rains and ruins are over,
    And all the season of snows and sins;
The days dividing lover and lover,
The light that loses, the night that wins;
And time remembered is grief forgotten,

---

[1] "Public office is a public trust" was used by the Cleveland administration as its motto.

[2] See Ironquill, 580:2.

[3] Also attributed to Junius S. Morgan [1813–1890].

And frosts are slain and flowers begotten,
And in green underwood and cover
Blossom by blossom the spring begins.
Atalanta in Calydon, st. 4

1 Before the beginning of years
There came to the making of man
Time, with a gift of tears;
Grief, with a glass that ran;
Pleasure, with pain for leaven;
Summer, with flowers that fell;
Remembrance fallen from heaven,
And madness risen from hell;
Strength without hands to smite;
Love that endures for a breath;
Night, the shadow of light,
And life, the shadow of death.
Atalanta in Calydon, chorus, st. 1

2 For words divide and rend;
But silence is most noble till the end.
Atalanta in Calydon, chorus, st. 1

3 Change in a trice
The lilies and languors of virtue
For the raptures and roses of vice.
Dolores [1866], st. 9

4 O splendid and sterile Dolores,
Our Lady of Pain.
Dolores, st. 9

5 The delight that consumes the desire,
The desire that outruns the delight.
Dolores, st. 14

6 For the crown of our life as it closes
Is darkness, the fruit there of dust.
Dolores, st. 20

7 What ailed us, O gods, to desert you
For creeds that refuse and restrain?
Come down and redeem us from virtue,
Our Lady of Pain.
Dolores, st. 35

8 Lo, this is she that was the world's delight.
Laus Veneris [1866], st. 3

9 Ah, yet would God this flesh of mine might be
Where air might wash and long leaves cover me;
Where tides of grass break into foam of flowers,
Or where the wind's feet shine along the sea.
Laus Veneris, st. 14

10 O sad kissed mouth, how sorrowful it is!
Laus Veneris, st. 79

11 To have known love, how bitter a thing it is.
Laus Veneris, st. 103

12 There will no man do for your sake, I think,
What I would have done for the least word said.
I had wrung life dry for your lips to drink,
Broken it up for your daily bread.
The Triumph of Time [1866], st. 12

13 At the door of life, by the gate of breath,
There are worse things waiting for men than death.
The Triumph of Time, st. 2

14 I will go back to the great sweet mother,
Mother and lover of men, the sea.
The Triumph of Time, st. 3

15 I shall never be friends again with roses;
I shall loathe sweet tunes.
The Triumph of Time, st. 4

16 I have lived long enough, having seen one thing,
that love hath an end.
Hymn to Proserpine [1866], l.

17 Thou hast conquered, O pale Galilean;[1] the world
has grown gray from thy breath;
We have drunken of things Lethean, and fed on the
fullness of death.
Laurel is green for a season, and love is sweet for a
day;
But love grows bitter with treason, and laurel
outlives not May.
Sleep, shall we sleep after all? for the world is not
sweet in the end;
For the old faiths loosen and fall, the new years
ruin and rend. *Hymn to Proserpine, l. 35*

18 I shall die as my fathers died, and sleep as they
sleep; even so.
For the glass of the years is brittle wherein we gaze
for a span. *Hymn to Proserpine, l. 100*

19 For there is no God found stronger than death;
and death is a sleep. *Hymn to Proserpine, l. 110*

20 If love were what the rose is,
And I were like the leaf,
Our lives would grow together
In sad or singing weather. *A Match [1866], st. 1*

21 If you were April's lady,
And I were lord in May. *A Match, st. 5*

22 If you were queen of pleasure,
And I were king of pain,
We'd hunt down love together,
Pluck out his flying feather,
And teach his feet a measure,
And find his mouth a rein. *A Match, st. 6*

23 Forget that I remember,
And dream that I forget. *Rococo [1866], st. 2*

24 For life is sweet, but after life is death.
This is the end of every man's desire.
A Ballad of Burdens [1866]. L'Envoy

25 Here, where the world is quiet;
Here, where all trouble seems

---

[1]See Julian, 117:14.

Dead winds' and spent waves' riot
In doubtful dreams of dreams.
The Garden of Proserpine [1866], st. 1

1 I am tired of tears and laughter,
And men that laugh and weep;
Of what may come hereafter
For men that sow and reap:
I am weary of days and hours,
Blown buds of barren flowers,
Desires and dreams and powers
And everything but sleep.
The Garden of Proserpine, st. 2

2 We are not sure of sorrow,
And joy was never sure.
The Garden of Proserpine, st. 10

3 From too much love of living,
From hope and fear set free,
We thank with brief thanksgiving
Whatever gods may be
That no life lives forever;
That dead men rise up never;
That even the weariest river
Winds somewhere safe to sea.
The Garden of Proserpine, st. 11

4 Ah that such sweet things should be fleet,
Such fleet things sweet!   *Félise [1866], st. 22*

5 I remember the way we parted,
The day and the way we met;
You hoped we were both broken-hearted
And knew we should both forget.
An Interlude [1866], st. 11

6 And the best and the worst of this is
That neither is most to blame,
If you have forgotten my kisses
And I have forgotten your name.
An Interlude, st. 14

7 I am that which began;
Out of me the years roll;
Out of me God and man;
I am equal and whole;
God changes, and man, and the form of them
bodily; I am the soul.   *Hertha [1871], st. 1*

8 A creed is a rod,
And a crown is of night;
But this thing is God,
To be man with thy might,
To grow straight in the strength of thy spirit, and
to live out thy life as the light.
Hertha, st. 15

9 In the gray beginning of years, in the twilight of
things that began,
The word of the earth in the ears of the world, was
it God? was it man?   *Hymn of Man [1871]*

10 Glory to Man in the highest! for Man is the master
of things.   *Hymn of Man*

11   A blatant Bassarid of Boston, a rampant Maenad
of Massachusetts.[1]
Under the Microscope [1872]

12 Poor splendid wings so frayed and soiled and torn!
A Ballad of François Villon [1878], st. 3

13 Villon, our sad bad glad mad brother's name.
A Ballad of François Villon, refrain

14 In a coign of the cliff between lowland and
highland,
At the sea-down's edge between windward and lee,
Walled round with rocks as an inland island,
The ghost of a garden fronts the sea.
A Forsaken Garden [1878], st. 1

15 Sleep; and if life was bitter to thee, pardon,
If sweet, give thanks; thou hast no more to live;
And to give thanks is good, and to forgive.
*Ave Atque Vale: In Memory of Charles
Baudelaire [1878], st. 17*

16 Body and spirit are twins: God only knows which is
which.
*The Higher Pantheism in a Nutshell [1880],
st. 7*

17 God, whom we see not, is: and God, who is not,
we see:
Fiddle, we know, is diddle: and diddle, we take it, is
dee.
The Higher Pantheism in a Nutshell, st. 12

18   Mr. Whitman's Eve is a drunken apple-woman,
indecently sprawling in the slush and gutter amid
the rotten refuse of her overturned fruit-stall. . . .
Mr. Whitman's Venus is a Hottentot wench under
the influence of cantharides and adulterated rum.
Studies in Prose and Poetry [1894]. Whitmania

Henry [Brooks] Adams
1838–1918

19   Accident counts for much in companionship as
in marriage.
The Education of Henry Adams [1907], ch. 4

20   Women have, commonly, a very positive moral
sense; that which they will, is right; that which they
reject, is wrong; and their will, in most cases, ends
by settling the moral.
The Education of Henry Adams, 6

---

[1]Harriet Beecher Stowe, whose accusations against Byron in
"The True Story of Lady Byron's Life" [*Atlantic Monthly*, September 1869] and in *Lady Byron Vindicated* [1870] aroused
strong protests in England.

1 All experience is an arch, to build upon.
The Education of Henry Adams, 6

2 Only on the edge of the grave can man conclude anything.   *The Education of Henry Adams, 6*

3 Although the Senate is much given to admiring in its members a superiority less obvious or quite invisible to outsiders, one Senator seldom proclaims his own inferiority to another, and still more seldom likes to be told of it.
The Education of Henry Adams, 7

4 Friends are born, not made.
The Education of Henry Adams, 7

5 A friend in power is a friend lost.
The Education of Henry Adams, 7

6 The effect of power and publicity on all men is the aggravation of self, a sort of tumor that ends by killing the victim's sympathies.
The Education of Henry Adams, 10

7 Young men have a passion for regarding their elders as senile.
The Education of Henry Adams, 11

8 Knowledge of human nature is the beginning and end of political education.
The Education of Henry Adams, 12

9 Intimates are predestined.
The Education of Henry Adams, 13

10 Chaos often breeds life, when order breeds habit.   *The Education of Henry Adams, 13*

11 At best, the renewal of broken relations is a nervous matter.
The Education of Henry Adams, 16

12 Sumner's[1] mind had reached the calm of water which receives and reflects images without absorbing them; it contained nothing but itself.
The Education of Henry Adams, 16

13 The difference is slight, to the influence of an author, whether he is read by five hundred readers, or by five hundred thousand; if he can select the five hundred, he reaches the five hundred thousand.
The Education of Henry Adams, 17

14 The progress of Evolution from President Washington to President Grant was alone evidence enough to upset Darwin.
The Education of Henry Adams, 17

15 A teacher affects eternity; he can never tell where his influence stops.
The Education of Henry Adams, 20

16 One friend in a lifetime is much; two are many; three are hardly possible. Friendship needs a certain parallelism of life, a community of thought, a rivalry of aim.   *The Education of Henry Adams, 2●*

17 What one knows is, in youth, of little moment; they know enough who know how to learn.
The Education of Henry Adams, 2●

18 He had often noticed that six months' oblivion amounts to newspaper death, and that resurrection is rare. Nothing is easier, if a man wants it, than rest profound as the grave.
The Education of Henry Adams, 22

19 Morality is a private and costly luxury.
The Education of Henry Adams, 22

20 Practical politics consists in ignoring facts.
The Education of Henry Adams, 24

21 Nothing in education is so astonishing as the amount of ignorance it accumulates in the form of inert facts.   *The Education of Henry Adams, 25*

22 Power when wielded by abnormal energy is the most serious of facts.
The Education of Henry Adams, 28

23 Modern politics is, at bottom, a struggle not of men but of forces.
The Education of Henry Adams, 28

24 We combat obstacles in order to get repose, and, when got, the repose is insupportable.
The Education of Henry Adams, 29

25 No one means all he says, and yet very few say all they mean, for words are slippery and thought is viscous.   *The Education of Henry Adams, 31*

26 Even in America, the Indian summer of life should be a little sunny and a little sad, like the season, and infinite in wealth and depth of tone — but never hustled.
The Education of Henry Adams, 35

John Wilkes Booth
1838–1865

27 Sic semper tyrannis! The South is avenged!
After shooting President Lincoln
[April 14, 1865]

James Bryce
1838–1922

28 Europeans often ask, and Americans do not always explain, how it happens that this great office [the presidency], the greatest in the world, unless

---

[1]Charles Sumner [1811–1874].

we except the Papacy, to which any man can rise by his own merits, is not more frequently filled by great and striking men.
> *The American Commonwealth [1888], vol. I, ch. 8*

1   The government of cities is the one conspicuous failure of the United States.
> *The American Commonwealth, I, 51*

2   To most people nothing is more troublesome than the effort of thinking.
> *Studies in History and Jurisprudence [1901]. Obedience*

3   The greatest liberty that man has taken with Nature.[1]
> *South America [1912]*

George Cooper
1838–1927

4   Sweet Genevieve,
The days may come, the days may go,
But still the hands of memory weave
The blissful dreams of long ago.
> *Sweet Genevieve [c. 1877]*[2]

John Milton Hay
1838–1905

5   I'll hold her nozzle agin the bank
Till the last galoot's ashore.
> *Pike County Ballads [1871]. Jim Bludso, st. 5*

6   And Christ ain't a-going to be too hard
On a man that died for men.
> *Pike County Ballads. Jim Bludso, st. 7*

7   And I think that saving a little child,
And fotching him to his own,
Is a derned sight better business
Than loafing around The Throne.
> *Pike County Ballads. Little Breeches, last stanza*

8   True luck consists not in holding the best of the cards at the table:
Luckiest he who knows just when to rise and go home.
> *Distichs, no. 15*

9   It [the Spanish-American War] has been a splendid little war, begun with the highest motives, carried on with magnificent intelligence and spirit, favored by that fortune which loves the brave.
> *Letter to Theodore Roosevelt [July 27, 1898]*

10   The open door.
> *To the Cabinet regarding completion of the trade policy he had negotiated with China [January 2, 1900]*

George Washington Johnson
1838–1917

11   Let us sing of the days that are gone, Maggie,
When you and I were young.
> *When You and I Were Young, Maggie [1866],[3] refrain*

William Edward Hartpole Lecky
1838–1903

12   The Augustinian doctrine of the damnation of unbaptized infants and the Calvinistic doctrine of reprobation . . . surpass in atrocity any tenets that have ever been admitted into any pagan creed.
> *History of European Morals [1869], vol. I, ch. 1*

13   It had been boldly predicted by some of the early Christians that the conversion of the world would lead to the establishment of perpetual peace. In looking back, with our present experience, we are driven to the melancholy conclusion that, instead of diminishing the number of wars, ecclesiastical influence has actually and very seriously increased it.
> *History of European Morals, II, 4*

George Leybourne
d. 1884

14   He flies through the air with the greatest of ease,
This daring young man on the flying trapeze;
His figure is handsome, all girls he can please,
And my love he purloined her away!
> *The Man on the Flying Trapeze [1860]*[4]

Lydia Kamekeha Liliuokalani
1838–1917

15   Farewell to thee, farewell to thee . . .
Until we meet again.
> *Aloha Oe (Farewell to Thee) [1878]*

---

[1]The Panama Canal.
[2]Music by HENRY TUCKER.

[3]Music by JAMES AUSTIN BUTTERFIELD.
[4]Music by ALFRED LEE.

Ernst Mach
1838–1916

1   Physics is experience, arranged in economical order.
The Economical Nature of Physical Inquiry [1882]

2   Intelligible as it is . . . that the efforts of thinkers have always been bent upon the "reduction of all physical processes to the motions of atoms," it must yet be affirmed that this is a chimerical ideal. This ideal has often played an effective part in popular lectures, but in the workshop of the serious inquirer it has discharged scarcely the least function.
On the Principle of the Conservation of Energy [1894]

John, Viscount Morley of Blackburn
1838–1923

3   Where it is a duty to worship the sun it is pretty sure to be a crime to examine the laws of heat.
Voltaire [1872]

4   Evolution is not a force but a process; not a cause but a law.   *On Compromise [1874]*

5   It is not enough to do good; one must do it the right way.   *Rousseau [1876]*

6   You have not converted a man because you have silenced him.   *Rousseau*

7   The great business of life is to be, to do, to do without, and to depart.
Address on Aphorisms [1887]

8   Simplicity of character is no hindrance to subtlety of intellect.
Life of Gladstone [1903]

9   No man can climb out beyond the limitations of his own character.
Critical Miscellanies [1908]. Robespierre

10   There are some books which cannot be adequately reviewed for twenty or thirty years after they come out.
Recollections [1917], vol. I, bk. 2, ch. 8

11   In my creed, waste of public money is like the sin against the Holy Ghost.   *Recollections, II, 5, 3*

12   Success depends on three things: who says it, what he says, how he says it; and of these three things, what he says is the least important.
Recollections, II, 5, 4

John Muir
1838–1914

13   In God's wildness lies the hope of the world— the great fresh unblighted, unredeemed wilderness.
Alaska Fragment [1890]

14   The clearest way into the Universe is through a forest wilderness.   *John of the Mountains [1938]*

15   The mountains are fountains of men as well as of rivers, of glaciers, of fertile soil. The great poets, philosophers, prophets, able men whose thoughts and deeds have moved the world, have come down from the mountains—mountain-dwellers who have grown strong there with the forest trees in Nature's workshops.   *John of the Mountains*

16   Most people are *on* the world, not in it—have no conscious sympathy or relationship to anything about them—undiffused, separate, and rigidly alone like marbles of polished stone, touching but separate.   *John of the Mountains*

17   How hard to realize that every camp of men or beast has this glorious starry firmament for a roof! In such places standing alone on the mountaintop it is easy to realize that whatever special nests we make—leaves and moss like the marmots and birds, or tents or piled stone—we all dwell in a house of one room—the world with the firmament for its roof—and are sailing the celestial spaces without leaving any track.   *John of the Mountains*

Philippe Auguste Villiers de L'Isle-Adam
1838–1889

18   Living? We'll leave that to the servants.[1]
Axel [1890]

19   I have thought too much to stoop to action![2]
Axel

Paul Cézanne
1839–1906

20   Treat nature in terms of the cylinder, the sphere, the cone, all in perspective.
From Emile Bernard, *Paul Cézanne [1925]*

21   Right now a moment of time is fleeting by! Capture its reality in paint! To do that we must put

---

[1]Vivre? Les serviteurs feront cela pour nous.

[2]J'ai trop pensé pour daigner agir!

all else out of our minds. We must become that moment, make ourselves a sensitive recording plate . . . give the image of what we actually see, forgetting everything that has been seen before our time.
> *From* Joachim Gasquet, *Paul Cézanne [1926]*[1]

1 The day is coming when a single carrot, freshly observed [in a painting], will set off a revolution.
> *From* Joachim Gasquet, *Paul Cézanne*

Francis Pharcellus Church
1839–1906

2 Yes, Virginia, there is a Santa Claus. . . . Thank God! he lives, and he lives forever. A thousand years from now, Virginia, nay ten times ten thousand years from now, he will continue to make glad the heart of childhood.[2]
> *Editorial in the New York Sun [September 21, 1897]*

Henry George
1839–1897

3 So long as all the increased wealth which modern progress brings goes but to build up great fortunes, to increase luxury and make sharper the contrast between the House of Have and the House of Want, progress is not real and cannot be permanent.
> *Progress and Poverty [1879]. Introductory: The Problem*

Walter Pater
1839–1894

4 Every intellectual product must be judged from the point of view of the age and the people in which it was produced.
> *Studies in the History of the Renaissance [1873]. Mirandola*

5 Hers is the head upon which all "the ends of the world are come," and the eyelids are a little weary. It is a beauty wrought out from within upon the flesh, the deposit, little cell by cell, of strange thoughts and fantastic reveries and exquisite passions. Set it for a moment beside one of those white

Greek goddesses or beautiful women of antiquity, and how would they be troubled by this beauty, into which the soul with all its maladies has passed?
> *Studies in the History of the Renaissance. Leonardo da Vinci [Mona Lisa]*

6 She is older than the rocks among which she sits; like the vampire, she has been dead many times, and learned the secrets of the grave; and has been a diver in deep seas, and keeps their fallen day about her; and trafficked for strange webs with Eastern merchants: and as Leda, was the mother of Helen of Troy, and, as Saint Anne, the mother of Mary; and all this has been to her but as the sound of lyres and flutes, and lives only in the delicacy with which it has molded the changing lineaments, and tinged the eyelids and the hands.
> *Studies in the History of the Renaissance. Leonardo da Vinci [Mona Lisa]*

7 All art constantly aspires towards the condition of music.
> *Studies in the History of the Renaissance. The School of Giorgione*

8 Not the fruit of experience, but experience itself, is the end.
> *Studies in the History of the Renaissance. Conclusion*

9 To burn always with this hard, gemlike flame, to maintain this ecstasy, is success in life.
> *Studies in the History of the Renaissance. Conclusion*

10 Art comes to you proposing frankly to give nothing but the highest quality to your moments as they pass.
> *Studies in the History of the Renaissance. Conclusion*

11 To know when one's self is interested, is the first condition of interesting other people.
> *Marius the Epicurean [1885], ch. 6*

12 It is the addition of strangeness to beauty that constitutes the romantic character in art.
> *Appreciation [1889]. Postscript*

Charles Sanders Peirce
1839–1914

13 Do not block the way of inquiry.
> *Collected Papers [1931–1958], vol. I, par. 135*

14 The idea does not belong to the soul; it is the soul that belongs to the idea.
> *Collected Papers, I, 216*

---

[1] Translated by Norbert Guterman.

[2] Responding to a letter from eight-year-old Virginia O'Hanlon: "Please tell me the truth; is there a Santa Claus?"

1   Every man is fully satisfied that there is such a thing as truth, or he would not ask any question.
Collected Papers, V, 211

2   Let us not pretend to doubt in philosophy what we do not doubt in our hearts.
Collected Papers, V, 265

3   All the evolution we know of proceeds from the vague to the definite.   *Collected Papers, VI, 191*

4   Our whole past experience is continually in our consciousness, though most of it sunk to a great depth of dimness. I think of consciousness as a bottomless lake, whose waters seem transparent, yet into which we can clearly see but a little way.
Collected Papers, VII, 547

5   Unless man have a natural bent in accordance with nature's, he has no chance of understanding nature at all.
A Neglected Argument for the Reality of God [Hibbert Journal VII: 90]

James Ryder Randall
1839–1908

6 Avenge the patriotic gore
That flecked the streets of Baltimore,
And be the battle queen of yore,
Maryland! My Maryland!
Maryland! My Maryland! [1861], st. 1

Thomas Brackett Reed
1839–1902

7   They [two fellow congressmen] never open their mouths without subtracting from the sum of human knowledge.
From Samuel W. McCall, *The Life of Thomas Brackett Reed [1914], ch. 21*

John Davison Rockefeller
1839–1937

8   God gave me my money. I believe the power to make money is a gift from God. . . . I believe it is my duty to make money and still more money and to use the money I make for the good of my fellow man according to the dictates of my conscience.[1]
In an interview [1905]

---

[1]He's kind iv a society f'r the previntion of croolty to money. If he finds a man misusing his money he takes it away fr'm him an' adopts it. — Finley Peter Dunne, *Mr. Dooley Says* [1910]

Wilfrid Scawen Blunt
1840–1922

9 Ay, this is the famed rock, which Hercules
And Goth and Moor bequeathed us. At this door
England stands sentry.   *Gibralta*

Timothy J. Campbell
1840–1904

10   What's the Constitution between friends?[2]
Attributed [c. 1885

[Henry] Austin Dobson
1840–1921

11 Time goes, you say? Ah no!
Alas, Time stays, *we* go.
The Paradox of Time [1875], st. 1

12 The ladies of St. James's!
They're painted to the eyes;
Their white it stays forever,
Their red it never dies:
But Phyllida, my Phyllida!
Her color comes and goes;
It trembles to a lily —
It wavers to a rose.
The Ladies of St. James's [1883], st. 4

Thomas Hardy
1840–1928

13 These purblind Doomsters had as readily strown
Blisses about my pilgrimage as pain.
Hap [1866]

14 When I set out for Lyonnesse,
A hundred miles away,
The rime was on the spray,
And starlight lit my lonesomeness.
When I Set Out for Lyonnesse [1870], st. 1

15   Good, but not religious-good.
Under the Greenwood Tree [1872], ch. 2

16   Like the British Constitution, she owes her success in practice to her inconsistencies in principle.
The Hand of Ethelberta [1876]

17   A lover without indiscretion is no lover at all.
The Hand of Ethelberta

18   In fact, precisely at this transitional point of its nightly roll into darkness the great and particular

---

[2]Reported comment to President Cleveland, who refused to support a bill on the grounds that it was unconstitutional.

glory of the Egdon waste began, and nobody could be said to understand the heath who had not been there at such a time. It could best be felt when it could not clearly be seen.

The Return of the Native [1878], ch. 1

1   The place became full of a watchful intentness now; for when other things sank brooding to sleep the heath appeared slowly to awake and listen.

The Return of the Native, 1

2   The great inviolate place had an ancient permanence which the sea cannot claim. Who can say of a particular sea that it is old? Distilled by the sun, kneaded by the moon, it is renewed in a year, in a day, or in an hour. The sea changed, the fields changed, the rivers, the villages, and the people changed, yet Egdon remained.

The Return of the Native, 1

3   The hard, half-apathetic expression of one who deems anything possible at the hands of Time and Chance, except, perhaps, fair play.

The Mayor of Casterbridge [1886], ch. 1

4   And all her shining keys will be took from her, and her cupboards opened, and little things 'a didn't wish seen, anybody will see; and her wishes and ways will be as nothing!

The Mayor of Casterbridge, 18

5   Who is such a reprobate as I [Michael Henchard]! And yet it seems that even I be in Somebody's hand!   *The Mayor of Casterbridge, 41*

6   That Elizabeth-Jane Farfrae be not told of my death, or be made to grieve on account of me. And that I be not buried in consecrated ground. And that no sexton be asked to toll the bell. And that nobody is wished to see my dead body. And that no murners walk behind me at my funeral. And that no flours be planted on my grave. And that no man remember me.

The Mayor of Casterbridge, 45
[Henchard's will]

7   That cold accretion called the world, which, so terrible in the mass, is so unformidable, even pitiable, in its units.

Tess of the D'Urbervilles [1891], ch. 13

8   The chronic melancholy which is taking hold of the civilized races with the decline of belief in a beneficent power.   *Tess of the D'Urbervilles, 18*

9   "Justice" was done, and the President of the Immortals (in Aeschylean phrase) had ended his sport with Tess.   *Tess of the D'Urbervilles, 59*

10   But nobody did come, because nobody does.

Jude the Obscure [1895], pt. I, ch. 4

11   The fundamental error of their matrimonial union; that of having based a permanent contract on a temporary feeling.

Jude the Obscure, I, 11

12   But sometimes a woman's love of being loved gets the better of her conscience.

Jude the Obscure, IV, 5

13   Done because we are too menny.

Jude the Obscure, VI, 2

14   Do not do an immoral thing for moral reasons.

Jude the Obscure, VI, 3

15 I leant upon a coppice gate
When Frost was specter-gray,
And Winter's dregs made desolate
The weakening eye of day.

The Darkling Thrush [1900], st. 1

16 An aged thrush, frail, gaunt, and small,
In blast-beruffled plume.

The Darkling Thrush, st. 3

17 So little cause for carolings
Of such ecstatic sound
Was written on terrestrial things
Afar or nigh around,
That I could think there trembled through
His happy good-night air
Some blessed hope, whereof he knew
And I was unaware.

The Darkling Thrush, st. 4

18 Yes; quaint and curious war is!
You shoot a fellow down
You'd treat if met where any bar is,
Or help to half-a-crown.

The Man He Killed [1902], st. 5

19 What of the Immanent Will and its designs?
It works unconsciously as heretofore,
External artistries in circumstance.

The Dynasts [1904–1908], pt. I, forescene

20 A local cult called Christianity.

The Dynasts, I, Spirit of the Years, sc. vi

21 Ere systemed suns were globed and lit
The slaughters of the race were writ.

The Dynasts, II, v, semichorus

22   My argument is that War makes rattling good history; but Peace is poor reading.

The Dynasts, II, Spirit Sinister

23 We two kept house, the Past and I,
The Past and I;
Through all my tasks it hovered nigh,
Leaving me never alone.

The Ghost of the Past, st. 1

1 And as the smart ship grew
  In stature, grace, and hue,
  In shadowy silent distance grew the Iceberg too.
    *The Convergence of the Twain (Lines on the
    Loss of the Titanic) [1912], st. 8*

2 Woman much missed, how you call to me, call to me,
  Saying that now you are not as you were
  When you had changed from the one who was all
      to me,
  But as at first, when our day was fair.
    The Voice [1912], st. 1

3 What of the faith and fire within us
  Men who march away
  Ere the barn cocks say
  Night is growing gray,
  Leaving all that here can win us.
    Men Who March Away [1914], st. 1

4 That night your great guns, unawares,
  Shook all our coffins as we lay,
  And broke the chancel window-squares,
  We thought it was the Judgment Day.
    Channel Firing [1914], st. 1

5 Only a man harrowing clods
  In a slow silent walk
  With an old horse that stumbles and nods
  Half asleep as they stalk.

  Only thin smoke without flame
  From the heaps of couch grass:
  Yet this will go onward the same
  Though dynasties pass.

  Yonder a maid and her wight
  Come whispering by;
  War's annals will cloud into night
  Ere their story die.
    In Time of "The Breaking of Nations" [1915]

6 Ah, no; the years, the years;
  Down their chiseled names the raindrop plows.
    During Wind and Rain, st. 4

7 This is the weather the shepherd shuns,
  And so do I.   *Weathers [1922], st. 2*

8 And meadow rivulets overflow,
  And drops on gate bars hang in a row,
  And rooks in families homeward go,
  And so do I.   *Weathers, st. 2*

Fanny Dixwell Holmes
1840–1929

9   Washington is full of famous men and the women
they married when they were young.
    From CATHERINE DRINKER BOWEN, *Yankee
    from Olympus [1944]*

Chief Joseph[1]
c. 1840–1904

10   Our chiefs are killed. . . . The old men are all
dead. . . . The little children are freezing to death.
My people, some of them have run away to the hills
and have no blankets, no food. No one knows
where they are, perhaps freezing to death. I want to
have time to look for my children and see how
many of them I can find. Maybe I can find them
among the dead. Hear me, my chiefs. My heart is
sick and sad. From where the sun now stands I will
fight no more forever.
    *To the Nez Percé tribe after surrender to
    General Nelson A. Miles [battle of Bear Paw
    Mountains, Montana, September 30–October
    5, 1877]*

Alfred Thayer Mahan
1840–1914

11   The world has never seen a more impressive
demonstration of the influence of sea power upon
its history. Those far distant, storm-beaten ships,
upon which the Grand Army never looked, stood
between it and the dominion of the world.
    *The Influence of Sea Power upon the French
    Revolution and Empire, 1793–1812 [1892],
    vol. II, p. 118*

12   Whether they will or no, Americans must begin
to look outward.
    The Interest of America in Sea Power [1897]

William Graham Sumner
1840–1910

13   The Forgotten Man . . . delving away in patient
industry, supporting his family, paying his taxes,
casting his vote, supporting the church and the
school . . . but he is the only one for whom there is
no provision in the great scramble and the big divide. Such is the Forgotten Man. He works, he
votes, generally he prays — but his chief business in
life is to pay. . . . Who and where is the Forgotten
Man in this case, who will have to pay for it all?
    Speech. The Forgotten Man [1883]

John Addington Symonds
1840–1893

14 These things shall be — a loftier race
  Than e'er the world hath known shall rise

---

[1]Hinmaton-Yalaktit: Thunder Rolling in the Mountains.

With flame of freedom in their souls,
And light of knowledge in their eyes.
The Days That Are to Be, st. 1

1 They shall be gentle, brave and strong
To spill no drop of blood, but dare
All that may plant man's lordship firm
On earth and fire and sea and air.
The Days That Are to Be, st. 2

John Wilson
d. 1889

2 Oh for a book and a shady nook, either in door or
out.
Poem for a catalogue of secondhand books

Elizabeth Wordsworth
1840–1932

3 If all the good people were clever,
And all clever people were good,
The world would be nicer than ever
We thought that it possibly could.
Good and Clever [1890]

Émile Zola
1840–1902

4 I am little concerned with beauty or perfection. I
don't care for the great centuries. All I care about is
life, struggle, intensity. I am at ease in my generation. *My Hates [1866]*

5 A work of art is a corner of creation seen through
a temperament. *My Hates*

6 My own art is a negation of society, an affirmation of the individual, outside all rules and demands
of society. *My Hates*

7 Truth is on the march and nothing can stop it.
Article in Le Figaro [November 25, 1897]

8 J'accuse.
*Title of letter to the president of the French
Republic, L'Aurore [January 13, 1898]*

Robert Buchanan
1841–1901

9 The Fleshly School of Poetry.
Title of article [1871][1]

Georges Clemenceau
1841–1929

10 The good Lord had only ten.
*In reference to Woodrow Wilson's Fourteen
Points*

11 America is the only nation in history which
miraculously has gone directly from barbarism to
degeneration without the usual interval of civilization. *Attributed*

12 It is easier to make war than peace.[2]
Speech [1919]

Oliver Wendell Holmes, Jr.
1841–1935

13 The life of the law has not been logic: it has been
experience. *The Common Law [1881], Lecture I*

14 The law embodies the story of a nation's development through many centuries, and it cannot be
dealt with as if it contained only the axioms and
corollaries of a book of mathematics.
The Common Law, I

15 I think that, as life is action and passion, it is required of a man that he should share the passion
and action of his time at peril of being judged not
to have lived. *Memorial Day Address [1884]*

16 Through our great good fortune, in our youth
our hearts were touched with fire.
Memorial Day Address

17 I say to you in all sadness of conviction, that to
think great thoughts you must be heroes as well as
idealists. *The Profession of the Law [1886]*

18 Certainty generally is illusion, and repose is not
the destiny of man.
The Path of the Law [1897]

19 The remoter and more general aspects of the law
are those which give it universal interest. It is through
them that you not only become a great master in
your calling, but connect your subject with the universe and catch an echo of the infinite, a glimpse of
its unfathomable process, a hint of the universal law.
The Path of the Law

20 The rule of joy and the law of duty seem to me
all one.
*Speech at Bar Association Dinner, Boston
[1900]*

---

[1]Attack on the Pre-Raphaelites occasioned by some sonnets in
Dante Gabriel Rossetti's *The House of Life.*

[2]Il est plus facile de faire la guerre que la paix.

1   Life is an end in itself, and the only question as to whether it is worth living is whether you have enough of it.
Speech at Bar Association Dinner, Boston

2   A great man represents a great ganglion in the nerves of society, or, to vary the figure, a strategic point in the campaign of history, and part of his greatness consists in his being *there*.
John Marshall [1901]

3   Taxes are what we pay for civilized society.
Compañia de Tabacos v. Collector, 275 U.S. 87, 100 [1904]

4   Great cases like hard cases make bad law.
Northern Securities Co. v. United States, 193 U.S. 197, 400 [1904]

5   The Fourteenth Amendment does not enact Mr. Herbert Spencer's *Social Statics*.
Lochner v. New York, 198 U.S. 45, 75 [1905]

6   General propositions do not decide concrete cases. The decision will depend on a judgment or intuition more subtle than any articulate major premise.
Lochner v. New York, 198 U.S. 45, 78

7   Life is painting a picture, not doing a sum.
The Class of '61. From Speeches [1913]

8   The only prize much cared for by the powerful is power. The prize of the general is not a bigger tent, but command.
Law and the Court [1913]

9   The attacks upon the Court are merely an expression of the unrest that seems to wonder vaguely whether law and order pay. When the ignorant are taught to doubt, they do not know what they safely may believe.
Law and the Court

10   I recognize without hesitation that judges do and must legislate, but they can do so only interstitially; they are confined from molar to molecular motions.
Southern Pacific Co. v. Jensen, 244 U.S. 205, 221 [1917]

11   The common law is not a brooding omnipresence in the sky but the articulate voice of some sovereign or quasi sovereign that can be identified.
Southern Pacific Co. v. Jensen, 244 U.S. 205, 222 [1917]

12   Certitude is not the test of certainty.
Natural Law [1918]

13   The most stringent protection of free speech would not protect a man in falsely shouting fire in a theater and causing a panic.... The question in every case is whether the words used are used in such circumstances and are of such a nature as to create a clear and present danger that they will bring about the substantive evils that Congress has a right to prevent.
Schenck v. United States, 249 U.S. 47 [1919]

14   When men have realized that time has upset many fighting faiths, they may come to believe even more than they believe the very foundations of their own conduct that the ultimate good desired is better reached by free trade in ideas — that the best test of truth is the power of the thought to get itself accepted in the competition of the market, and that truth is the only ground upon which their wishes safely can be carried out. That at any rate is the theory of our Constitution. It is an experiment, as all life is an experiment.
Abrams v. United States, 250 U.S. 616, 630 [1919]

15   I dare say that I have worked off my fundamental formula on you that the chief end of man is to frame general propositions and that no general proposition is worth a damn.
Letter to Sir Frederick Pollock [1920]

16   If my fellow citizens want to go to Hell I will help them. It is my job.
Letter to Harold J. Laski [1920]

17   Have faith and pursue the unknown end.
Letter to John C. H. Wu [1924]

18   Upon this point a page of history is worth a volume of logic.
New York Trust Co. v. Eisner, 256 U.S. 345, 349 [1921]

19   It is said that this manifesto is more than a theory, that it was an incitement. Every idea is an incitement.
Gitlow v. New York, 268 U.S. 652, 673 [1925]

20   Three generations of imbeciles are enough.
Buck v. Bell, 274 U.S. 200, 207 [1927]

21   But if we are to yield to fashionable conventions, it seems to me that theaters are as much devoted to public use as anything well can be. We have not that respect for art that is one of the glories of France. But to many the superfluous is the necessary, and it seems to me that Government does not go beyond its sphere in attempting to make life livable for them.
Tyson & Bro. v. Banton, 273 U.S. 418, 447 [1927]

22   The power to tax is not the power to destroy while this Court sits.
Panhandle Oil Co. v. Knox, 277 U.S. 223 [1928]

23   For my part I think it a less evil that some criminals should escape than that the government should

play an ignoble part. . . . If the existing code does not permit district attorneys to have a hand in such dirty business [wiretapping], it does not permit the judge to allow such iniquities to succeed.

> *Olmstead v. United States, 277 U.S. 438, 470 [1928]*

1   If there is any principle of the Constitution that more imperatively calls for attachment than any other it is the principle of free thought—not free thought for those who agree with us but freedom for the thought that we hate.

> *United States v. Schwimmer, 279 U.S. 644, 653 [1928]*

2   The riders in a race do not stop short when they reach the goal. There is a little finishing canter before coming to a standstill. There is time to hear the kind voice of friends and to say to one's self: "The work is done." But just as one says that, the answer comes: "The race is over, but the work never is done while the power to work remains." The canter that brings you to a standstill need not be only coming to rest. It cannot be, while you still live. For to live is to function. That is all there is in living.

> *Radio address on his ninetieth birthday [March 8, 1931]*

3   Young man, the secret of my success is that at an early age I discovered I was not God.

> *Reply to a reporter's question on his ninetieth birthday [March 8, 1931]*

4   Oh, to be seventy again![1]

> *At ninety, upon seeing a beautiful young woman. Attributed*

5   A second-class intellect. But a first-class temperament!

> *On President Franklin Delano Roosevelt [March 8, 1933]*

W[illiam] H[enry] Hudson
1841–1922

6   I . . . thanked the Author of my being for the gift of that wild forest, those green mansions where I had found so great a happiness!

> *Green Mansions [1904], ch. 5*

7   In this wild solitary girl [Rima] I had at length discovered the mysterious warbler that so often followed me in the wood.

> *Green Mansions, 5*

Joaquin [Cincinnatus Hiner or Heine] Miller
c. 1841–1913

8 Behind him lay the gray Azores,
Behind the Gates of Hercules;
Before him not the ghost of shores,
Before him only shoreless seas.   *Columbus, st. 1*

9 He gained a world; he gave that world
Its grandest lesson: "On! sail on!"[2]

> *Columbus, st. 5*

Pierre Auguste Renoir
1841–1919

10   I have a predilection for painting that lends joyousness to a wall.

> *From AMBROISE VOLLARD, Renoir [1919]*

11   In a few generations you can breed a racehorse. The recipe for making a man like Delacroix is less well known.

> *From JEAN RENOIR, Renoir My Father [1958]*

Clement William Scott
1841–1904

12 Oh, promise me that some day you and I
Will take our love together to some sky
Where we can be alone and faith renew,
And find the hollows where those flowers grew.

> *Oh, Promise Me [1888][3]*

Edward Rowland Sill
1841–1887

13 At the punch bowl's brink
Let the thirsty think
What they say in Japan:
"First the man takes a drink,
Then the drink takes a drink,
Then the drink takes the man!"

> *An Adage from the Orient*

14   But Lord,
Be merciful to me, a fool!   *The Fool's Prayer*

---

[1]If only one were eighty! — COUNT FRIEDRICH VON WRANGEL [1784–1877]; *attributed*

[2]Actually, it was MARTÍN ALONSO PINZÓN [C. 1440–1493] who said, "Adelante, adelante, I can't hold with turning back without sighting land."

[3]Set to music by REGINALD DE KOVEN [1859–1920] and interpolated in his opera *Robin Hood* [1890].

Sir Henry Morton Stanley
1841–1904

1   Doctor Livingstone, I presume?
*On meeting David Livingstone in Ujiji,
Central Africa [November 10, 1871]*[1]

Ironquill [Eugene Fitch Ware]
1841–1911

2 O Dewey[2] was the morning
Upon the first of May,
And Dewey was the Admiral
Down in Manila Bay;
And Dewey were the Regent's eyes,
"Them" orbs of royal blue!
And Dewey feel discouraged?
I Dew not think we Dew.
*In the Topeka (Kansas) Daily Capital
[May 3, 1898]*

3 No evil deed live oN.   *The Palindrome*

George Frederick Baer
1842–1914

4   The rights and interests of the laboring man will
be protected and cared for—not by the labor agitators, but by the Christian men to whom God in His
infinite wisdom has given the control of the property interests of the country.
Letter [July 17, 1902]

Ambrose Bierce
1842–c. 1914

5 Mark how my fame rings out from zone to zone:
A thousand critics shouting: "He's unknown!"
Couplet

6   Peyton Farquhar was dead; his body, with a broken neck, swung gently from side to side beneath
the timbers of the Owl Creek bridge.
In the Midst of Life [1891].[3] *An Occurrence
at Owl Creek Bridge*

7 To men a man is but a mind. Who cares
What face he carries or what form he wears?
But woman's body is the woman. O
Stay thou, my sweetheart, and do never go.
The Devil's Dictionary [1906][4]

---

[1]"I couldn't think what else to say," Stanley admitted many
years later.

[2]See George Dewey, 567.

[3]First published as *Tales of Soldiers and Civilians*, retitled in
1892.

[4]First published as *The Cynic's Word Book*, retitled in 1911.

8   *Achievement, n.* the death of endeavor and the
birth of disgust.   *The Devil's Dictionary*

9   *Advice, n.* the smallest current coin.
The Devil's Dictionary

10   *Bore, n.* a person who talks when you wish him
to listen.   *The Devil's Dictionary*

11   *Cynic, n.* a blackguard whose faulty vision sees
things as they are, not as they ought to be.
The Devil's Dictionary

12   *Edible, adj.* good to eat, and wholesome to digest, as a worm to a toad, a toad to a snake, a snake
to a pig, a pig to a man, and a man to a worm.
The Devil's Dictionary

13   *Habit, n.* a shackle for the free.
The Devil's Dictionary

14   *Labor, n.* one of the processes by which A acquires property for B.
The Devil's Dictionary

15   *Lawsuit, n.* a machine which you go into as a pig
and come out as a sausage.
The Devil's Dictionary

16   *Marriage, n.* a community consisting of a master, a mistress, and two slaves, making in all, two.
The Devil's Dictionary

17   *Prejudice, n.* a vagrant opinion without visible
means of support.
The Devil's Dictionary

18   *Saint, n.* a dead sinner revised and edited.
The Devil's Dictionary

19   Woman would be more charming if one could
fall into her arms without falling into her hands.
Epigrams

20   You are not permitted to kill a woman who has
wronged you, but nothing forbids you to reflect
that she is growing older every minute. You are
avenged 1440 times a day.   *Epigrams*

21   Self-denial is indulgence of a propensity to forego.
Epigrams

22   The covers of this book are too far apart.
Capsule book review. Attributed

Charles Edward Carryl
1842–1920

23 A capital ship for an ocean trip
Was the *Walloping Window Blind*—
No gale that blew dismayed her crew
Or troubled the captain's mind.
The man at the wheel was taught to feel
Contempt for the wildest blow.

And it often appeared, when the weather had cleared,
That he'd been in his bunk below.
> *Davy and the Goblin: A Nautical Ballad*
> *[1886], st. 1*

Sir James Dewar
1842–1923

1   Minds are like parachutes. They only function when they are open.   *Attributed*

William James
1842–1910

2   I have often thought that the best way to define a man's character would be to seek out the particular mental or moral attitude in which, when it came upon him, he felt himself most deeply and intensely active and alive. At such moments there is a voice inside which speaks and says: "This is the real me!"
> *The Letters of William James [1920]. To his*
> *wife, Alice Gibbons James, 1878*

3   Most people live, whether physically, intellectually or morally, in a very restricted circle of their potential being. They *make use* of a very small portion of their possible consciousness, and of their soul's resources in general, much like a man who, out of his whole bodily organism, should get into a habit of using and moving only his little finger. Great emergencies and crises show us how much greater our vital resources are than we had supposed.
> *The Letters of William James. To*
> *W. Lutoslawski, May 6, 1906*

4   The moral flabbiness born of the exclusive worship of the bitch-goddess SUCCESS. That—with the squalid cash interpretation put on the word success—is our national disease.
> *The Letters of William James. To H. G. Wells,*
> *September 11, 1906*

5   The concrete man has but one interest—to be right. That to him is the art of all arts, and all means are fair which help him to it.
> *The Sentiment of Rationality [1882]*

6   All our scientific and philosophic ideals are altars to unknown gods.
> *The Dilemma of Determinism [1884]*

7   Habit is . . . the enormous flywheel of society, its most precious conservative agent. It alone is what keeps us all within the bounds of ordinance.
> *The Principles of Psychology [1890], ch. 4*

8   There is no more miserable human being than one in whom nothing is habitual but indecision.
> *The Principles of Psychology, 4*

9   Keep the faculty of effort alive in you by a little gratuitous exercise every day. That is, be systematically ascetic or heroic in little unnecessary points, do every day or two something for no other reason than that you would rather not do it, so that when the hour of dire need draws nigh, it may find you not unnerved and untrained to stand the test.
> *The Principles of Psychology, 4*

10   The hell to be endured hereafter, of which theology tells, is no worse than the hell we make for ourselves in this world by habitually fashioning our characters in the wrong way.
> *The Principles of Psychology, 4*

11   We are spinning our own fates, good or evil, and never to be undone. Every smallest stroke of virtue or of vice leaves its never so little scar . . . Nothing we ever do is, in strict scientific literalness, wiped out.
> *The Principles of Psychology, 4*

12   Consciousness . . . does not appear to itself chopped up in bits. . . . A "river" or a "stream" are the metaphors by which it is most naturally described. In talking of it hereafter, let us call it the stream of thought, of consciousness, or of subjective life.
> *The Principles of Psychology, 9*

13   As we take, in fact, a general view of the wonderful stream of our consciousness, what strikes us first is this different pace of its parts. Like a bird's life, it seems to be made of an alternation of flights and perchings.
> *The Principles of Psychology, 9*

14   As the brain changes are continuous, so do all these consciousnesses melt into each other like dissolving views. Properly they are but one protracted consciousness, one unbroken stream.
> *The Principles of Psychology, 9*

15   The last peculiarity of consciousness to which attention is to be drawn in this first rough description of its stream is that . . . it is always interested more in one part of its object [thought] than in another, and welcomes and rejects, or chooses, all the while it thinks.
> *The Principles of Psychology, 9*

16   An act has no ethical quality whatever unless it be chosen out of several all equally possible.
> *The Principles of Psychology, 9*

17   In its widest possible sense, however, a man's Self is the sum total of all that he *can* call his, not only his body and his psychic powers, but his clothes and his house, his wife and children, his ancestors and friends, his reputation and works, his lands and horses, and yacht and bank account. All these things give him the same emotions. If they wax and prosper, he feels triumphant; if they dwindle and die away, he feels cast down.
> *The Principles of Psychology, 10*

1   Let anyone try, I will not say to arrest, but to notice or attend to, the *present* moment of time. One of the most baffling experiences occurs. Where is it, this present? It has melted in our grasp, fled ere we could touch it, gone in the instant of becoming.
The Principles of Psychology, 15

2   Genius . . . means little more than the faculty of perceiving in an unhabitual way.
The Principles of Psychology, 19

3   The art of being wise is the art of knowing what to overlook.   *The Principles of Psychology, 22*

4   The more rational statement is that we feel sorry because we cry, angry because we strike, afraid because we tremble, and not that we cry, strike, or tremble because we are sorry, angry, or fearful, as the case may be. Without the bodily states following on the perception, the latter would be purely cognitive in form, pale, colorless, destitute of emotional warmth.   *The Principles of Psychology, 25*

5   A purely disembodied human emotion is a nonentity.   *The Principles of Psychology, 25*

6   In the deepest heart of all of us there is a corner in which the ultimate mystery of things works sadly.
The Will to Believe [1897]. Is Life Worth Living?

7   It is only by risking our persons from one hour to another that we live at all. And often enough our faith beforehand in an uncertified result is the only thing that makes the result come true.
The Will to Believe. Is Life Worth Living?

8   This life is worth living, we can say, since it is what we make it, from the moral point of view.
The Will to Believe. Is Life Worth Living?

9   Be not afraid of life. Believe that life *is* worth living, and your belief will help create the fact.
The Will to Believe. Is Life Worth Living?

10   All the higher, more penetrating ideals are revolutionary. They present themselves far less in the guise of effects of past experience than in that of probable causes of future experience.
The Will to Believe. The Moral Philosopher and the Moral Life

11   There is but one unconditional commandment, which is that we should seek incessantly, with fear and trembling, so to vote and to act as to bring about the very largest total universe of good which we can see.
The Will to Believe. The Moral Philosopher and the Moral Life

12   An unlearned carpenter of my acquaintance once said in my hearing: "There is very little difference between one man and another; but what little there is, is very important." This distinction seems to me to go to the root of the matter.
The Will to Believe. The Importance of Individuals

13   Religion . . . shall mean for us the feelings, acts, and experiences of individual men in their solitude.
The Varieties of Religious Experience [1902], lecture 2

14   Religion . . . is a man's total reaction upon life.
The Varieties of Religious Experience, 2

15   We can act *as if* there were a God; feel *as if* we were free; consider Nature *as if* she were full of special designs; lay plans *as if* we were to be immortal; and we find then that these words do make a genuine difference in our moral life.
The Varieties of Religious Experience, 3

16   The God whom science recognizes must be a God of universal laws exclusively, a God who does a wholesale, not a retail business. He cannot accommodate his processes to the convenience of individuals.
The Varieties of Religious Experience, 20

17   The philosophy which is so important in each of us is not a technical matter; it is our more or less dumb sense of what life honestly and deeply means. It is only partly got from books; it is our individual way of just seeing and feeling the total push and pressure of the cosmos.
Pragmatism [1907],[1] lecture 1

18   No particular results then, so far, but only an attitude of orientation, is what the pragmatic method means. The attitude of looking away from first things, principles, "categories," supposed necessities; and of looking toward last things, fruits, consequences, facts.   *Pragmatism, 2*

19   I myself believe that the evidence for God lies primarily in inner personal experiences.
Pragmatism, 3

20   Our minds thus grow in spots; and like grease spots, the spots spread. But we let them spread as little as possible: we keep unaltered as much of our old knowledge, as many of our old prejudices and beliefs, as we can. We patch and tinker more than we renew. The novelty soaks in; it stains the ancient mass; but it is also tinged by what absorbs it.
Pragmatism, 5

---

[1]The term [pragmatism] . . . was first introduced into philosophy by Mr. Charles Peirce in 1878 [in] an article entitled "How to Make Our Ideas Clear" in the *Popular Science Monthly* for January of that year. — *Pragmatism* [1907], *lecture 1*
See Charles Sanders Peirce, 573.

1 Truth *happens* to an idea. It *becomes* true, is *made* true by events. Its verity *is* in fact an event, a process: the process namely of its verifying itself, its veri-*fication*. Its validity is the process of its valid-*ation*.   *Pragmatism, 6*

2 Pluralism lets things really exist in the each-form or distributively. Monism thinks that the all-form or collective-unit form is the only form that is rational.   *A Pluralistic Universe [1909], lecture 8*

3 So long as antimilitarists propose no substitute for war's disciplinary function, no *moral equivalent* of war, analogous, as one might say, to the mechanical equivalent of heat, so long they fail to realize the full inwardness of the situation.   *Memories and Studies [1911]. The Moral Equivalent of War*

4 The "through-and-through" universe seems to suffocate me with its infallible impeccable all-pervasiveness. . . . It seems too buttoned-up and white-chokered and clean-shaven a thing to speak in the name of the vast slow-breathing unconscious Kosmos with its dread abysses and its unknown tides.   *Essays in Radical Empiricism [1912], ch. 12, Absolutism and Empiricism*

5 The union of the mathematician with the poet, fervor with measure, passion with correctness, this surely is the ideal.   *Collected Essays and Reviews [1920], ch. 11, Clifford's "Lectures and Essays" [1879]*

6 I wished, by treating Psychology *like* a natural science, to help her to become one.   *Collected Essays and Reviews. A Plea for Psychology as a Natural Science [1892]*

John Alexander Joyce
1842–1915

7 I shall love you in December
With the love I gave in May![1]
                           Question and Answer, st. 8

Prince Pëtr Alekseevich Kropotkin
1842–1921

8 Sociability is as much a law of nature as mutual struggle . . . mutual aid is as much a law of animal life as mutual struggle.   *Mutual Aid [1902]*

---

[1]Will you love me in December as you do in May? —JAMES J. WALKER [1881–1946]; *set to music by* ERNEST R. BALL [1905]

Sidney Lanier
1842–1881

9 Ye marshes, how candid and simple and nothing-withholding and free
Ye publish yourselves to the sky and offer yourselves to the sea!
                           The Marshes of Glynn [1877], l. 65

10 As the marsh hen secretly builds on the watery sod,
Behold I will build me a nest on the greatness of God:
I will fly in the greatness of God as the marsh hen flies
In the freedom that fills all the space 'twixt the marsh and the skies:
By so many roots as the marsh grass sends in the sod
I will heartily lay me a-hold on the greatness of God:
Oh, like to the greatness of God is the greatness within
The range of the marshes, the liberal marshes of Glynn.   *The Marshes of Glynn, l. 71*

11 Out of the hills of Habersham,
Down the valleys of Hall.
                           Song of the Chattahoochee [1877], st. 1

12 Into the woods my Master went,
Clean forspent, forspent.
Into the woods my Master came,
Forspent with love and shame.
                           A Ballad of Trees and the Master [1877], st. 1

Stéphane Mallarmé
1842–1898

13 The flesh is sad, alas, and I have read all the books.[2]   *Poésies. Brise Marine*

14 Such as into himself at last Eternity has changed him.[3]   *Poésies. Le Tombeau d'Edgar Poe*

15 A Throw of the Dice Will Never Abolish Chance.[4]
                           Poésies. Title of poem

16 To *name* an object is to take away three-fourths of the pleasure given by a poem. This pleasure consists in guessing little by little: to *suggest* it, that is the ideal.[5]
                           Réponse à une Enquête sur l'Évolution Littéraire [1891]

---

[2]La chair est triste, hélas! et j'ai lu tous les livres.

[3]Tel qu'en Lui-Même enfin l'éternité le change.

[4]Un coup de dés n'abolira jamais le hasard.

[5]*Nommer* un objet, c'est supprimer les trois-quarts de la jouissance du poème qui est fait peu à peu: le *suggérer*.

1   You don't make a poem with ideas, but with words.[1]

From PAUL VALÉRY, *Degas, Danse, Dessin*

Alfred Marshall
1842–1924

2   We might as reasonably dispute whether it is the upper or the under blade of a pair of scissors that cuts a piece of paper, as whether value is governed by utility or cost of production.

Principles of Economics [1890]

T. A. Palmer
fl. 1868–1882

3   Dead, dead, dead! and he never knew me, never called me mother!   *East Lynne [1874], act III*[2]

George Washington Plunkitt
1842–1924

4   I seen my opportunities and I took 'em.

Definition of "honest graft." From WILLIAM L. RIORDON, *Plunkitt of Tammany Hall [1905]*

5   The politician who steals is worse than a thief. He is a fool. With all the grand opportunities around for the man with a political pull, there's no excuse for stealin' a cent.

Definition of "honest graft." From WILLIAM L. RIORDON, *Plunkitt of Tammany Hall*

Hugh Antoine D'Arcy
1843–1925

6   "Say, boys! if you give me just another whiskey I'll be glad,
And I'll draw right here a picture of the face that drove me mad.
Give me that piece of chalk with which you mark the baseball score,
You shall see the lovely Madeleine upon the bar-room floor."

The Face upon the Floor [1887][3]

---

[1] Ce n'est point avec des idées que l'on fait des vers, c'est avec des mots.

[2] Adapted from the novel *East Lynne* [1861] by ELLEN (Mrs. Henry) WOOD.

[3] Often called "The Face on the Barroom Floor."

Henry James
1843–1916

7   The face of nature and civilization in this our country is to a certain point a very sufficient literary field. But it will yield its secrets only to a really *grasping* imagination. . . . To write well and worthily of American things one need even more than elsewhere to be a *master*.

Letter to Charles Eliot Norton [January 16, 1871]

8   It's a complex fate, being an American, and one of the responsibilities it entails is fighting against a superstitious valuation of Europe.

Letter [1872] quoted in PERCY LUBBOCK, *Letters of Henry James [1920], vol. I, biographical note*

9   It takes a great deal of history to produce a little literature.   *Hawthorne [1879], ch. 1*

10   Whatever question there may be of his [Thoreau's] talent, there can be none, I think, of his genius. It was a slim and crooked one, but it was eminently personal. He was unperfect, unfinished, inartistic; he was worse than provincial—he was parochial.   *Hawthorne, 4*

11   Cats and monkeys, monkeys and cats—all human life is there.

The Madonna of the Future [1879]

12   The real offense, as she ultimately perceived, was her having a mind of her own at all. Her mind was to be his—attached to his own like a small garden plot to a deer park.

The Portrait of a Lady [1881]

13   The only reason for the existence of a novel is that it does attempt to represent life.

The Art of Fiction [1888]

14   The only obligation to which in advance we may hold a novel, without incurring the accusation of being arbitrary, is that it be interesting.

The Art of Fiction

15   If I should certainly say to a novice, "Write from experience and experience only," I should feel that this was rather a tantalizing monition if I were not careful immediately to add, "Try to be one of the people on whom nothing is lost."

The Art of Fiction

16   We must grant the artist his subject, his idea, his *donnée:* our criticism is applied only to what he makes of it. . . . If we pretend to respect the artist at all, we must allow him his freedom of choice, in the face, in particular cases, of innumerable presump-

tions that the choice will not fructify. Art derives a considerable part of its beneficial exercise from flying in the face of presumptions.

The Art of Fiction

1   There are few things more exciting to me . . . than a psychological reason.   *The Art of Fiction*

2   The practice of "reviewing" . . . in general has nothing in common with the art of criticism.

Criticism [1893]

3   The critical sense is so far from frequent that it is absolutely rare, and the possession of the cluster of qualities that minister to it is one of the highest distinctions. . . . In this light one sees the critic as the real helper of the artist, a torchbearing outrider, the interpreter, the brother. . . . Just in proportion as he is sentient and restless, just in proportion as he reacts and reciprocates and penetrates, is the critic a valuable instrument.   *Criticism*

4   We work in the dark — we do what we can — we give what we have. Our doubt is our passion, and our passion is our task. The rest is the madness of art.   *The Middle Years [1893]*

5   The time-honored bread sauce of the happy ending.   *Theatricals: Second Series [1895]*

6   Vereker's secret . . . the general intention of his books: the string the pearls were strung on, the buried treasure, the figure in the carpet.

The Figure in the Carpet [1896]

7   I caught him, yes, I held him — it may be imagined with what passion; but at the end of a minute I began to feel what it truly was that I held. We were alone with the quiet day, and his little heart, dispossessed, had stopped.

The Turn of the Screw [1898], ending

8   Live all you can; it's a mistake not to. It doesn't so much matter what you do in particular, so long as you have your life. If you haven't had that what *have* you had? . . . What one loses one loses; make no mistake about that. . . . The right time is *any* time that one is still so lucky as to have. . . . Live!

The Ambassadors [1903], bk. V, ch. 2

9   There is, I think, no more nutritive or suggestive truth . . . than that of the perfect dependence of the "moral" sense of a work of art on the amount of felt life concerned in producing it. The question comes back thus, obviously, to the kind and the degree of the artist's prime sensibility, which is the soil out of which his subject springs.

Prefaces [1907–1909]. The Portrait of a Lady

10   Life being all inclusion and confusion, and art being all discrimination and selection, the latter, in search of the hard latent *value* with which it alone is concerned, sniffs round the mass as instinctively and unerringly as a dog suspicious of some buried bone.

Prefaces. The Spoils of Poynton

11   The fatal futility of Fact.

Prefaces. The Spoils of Poynton

12   The effort really to see and really to represent is no idle business in face of the *constant* force that makes for muddlement. The great thing is indeed that the muddled state too is one of the very sharpest of the realities, that it also has color and form and character, has often in fact a broad and rich comicality.   *Prefaces. What Maisie Knew*

13   To criticize is to appreciate, to appropriate, to take intellectual possession, to establish in fine a relation with the criticized thing and to make it one's own.   *Prefaces. What Maisie Knew*

14   The historian, essentially, wants more documents than he can really use; the dramatist only wants more liberties than he can really take.

Prefaces. The Aspern Papers

15   The ever importunate murmur, "Dramatize it, dramatize it!"   *Prefaces. The Altar of the Dead*

16   In art economy is always beauty.

Prefaces. The Altar of the Dead

17   The terrible *fluidity* of self-revelation.

Prefaces. The Ambassadors

18   I'm glad you like adverbs — I adore them; they are the only qualifications I really much respect.

Letter to Miss M. Betham Edwards [January 5, 1912]

19   We must know, as much as possible, in our beautiful art . . . what we are talking about — and the only way to know is to have lived and loved and cursed and floundered and enjoyed and suffered. I think I don't regret a single "excess" of my responsive youth — I only regret, in my chilled age, certain occasions and possibilities I didn't embrace.

Letter to Hugh Walpole [August 21, 1913]

20   I still, in presence of life . . . have reactions — as many as possible. . . . It's, I suppose, because I am that queer monster, the artist, an obstinate finality, an inexhaustible sensibility. Hence the reactions — appearances, memories, many things, go on playing upon it with consequences that I note and "enjoy" (grim word!) noting. It all takes doing — and I *do*. I believe I shall do yet again — it is still an act of life.

Letter to Henry Adams [March 21, 1914]

21   It is art that *makes* life, makes interest, makes importance, for our consideration and application of

these things, and I know of no substitute whatever for the force and beauty of its process.

Letter to H. G. Wells [July 10, 1915]

1   So it has come at last—the Distinguished Thing.   *Of his final illness [December 2, 1915]*

2   The full, the monstrous demonstration that Tennyson was not Tennysonian.

The Middle Years (autobiography) [1917], ch. 6

3   Summer afternoon—summer afternoon; to me those have always been the two most beautiful words in the English language.

Quoted by EDITH WHARTON, *A Backward Glance [1934], ch. 10*

William McKinley
1843–1901

4   There was nothing left for us to do but to take them all, and to educate the Filipinos, and uplift and civilize and Christianize them, and by God's grace do the very best we could for them, as our fellowmen for whom Christ also died.

On his decision to claim the Philippine Islands for the United States [1899]

Robert Bridges
1844–1930

5 Whither, O splendid ship, thy white sails crowding,
Leaning across the bosom of the urgent West,
That fearest nor sea rising, nor sky clouding,
Whither away, fair rover, and what thy quest?

Shorter Poems, bk. II [1879], no. 2 (A Passer-By), st. 1

6 When men were all asleep, the snow came flying,
In large white flakes falling on the city brown,
Stealthily and perpetually settling and loosely lying,
Hushing the latest traffic of the drowsy town.

Shorter Poems, III [1880], 2 (London Snow)

7 I love all beauteous things,
I seek and adore them;
God hath no better praise,
And man in his hasty days
Is honored for them.

Shorter Poems, IV [1890], 1, st. 1

Robert Jones Burdette
1844–1914

8   There are two days in the week about which and upon which I never worry. Two carefree days, kept

sacredly free from fear and apprehension. One o these days is Yesterday. . . . And the other day I de not worry about is Tomorrow.

The Golden Da

Anatole France [Jacques Anatole François Thibault]
1844–1924

9   I do not know any reading more easy, more fas cinating, more delightful than a catalogue.

*The Crime of Sylvestre Bonnard [1881].[1]
The Log, December 24, 1849*

10   To know is nothing at all; to imagine is every thing.

The Crime of Sylvestre Bonnard, pt. II, ch. 2

11   He flattered himself on being a man without any prejudices; and this pretension itself is a very grea prejudice.

The Crime of Sylvestre Bonnard, II,

12   Those who have given themselves the most con cern about the happiness of peoples have made thei neighbors very miserable.

The Crime of Sylvestre Bonnard, II, 4

13   Man is so made that he can only find relaxatior from one kind of labor by taking up another.

The Crime of Sylvestre Bonnard, II, 4

14   People who have no weaknesses are terrible there is no way of taking advantage of them.

The Crime of Sylvestre Bonnard, II, 4

15   The whole art of teaching is only the art o awakening the natural curiosity of young minds fo the purpose of satisfying it afterwards.

The Crime of Sylvestre Bonnard, II, 4

16   The good critic is one who tells of his mind's ad ventures among masterpieces.

La Vie Littéraire [1888], preface

17   We reproach people for talking about them selves; but it is the subject they treat best.

La Vie Littéraire. Journal des Goncourt

18   The law, in its majestic equality, forbids the rich as well as the poor to sleep under bridges, to beg ir the streets, and to steal bread.

The Red Lily [1894], ch. 7

19   A tale without love is like beef without mustard insipid.   *The Revolt of the Angels [1914], ch. 8*

---

[1]Translated by LAFCADIO HEARN.

Gerard Manley Hopkins
1844–1889

1 And I have asked to be
　　Where no storms come,
Where the green swell is in the havens dumb,
　　And out of the swing of the sea.
　　　Poems [1918].[1] *No. 20, Heaven-Haven, st. 2*

2 Elected Silence, sing to me
　And beat upon my whorlèd ear,
　Pipe me to pastures still and be
　The music that I care to hear.
　　　Poems. No. 24, The Habit of Perfection, st. 1

3　　　Thou mastering me
　　God! giver of breath and bread;
　　World's strand, sway of the sea;
　　　Lord of living and dead;
Thou hast bound bones and veins in me, fastened
　　me flesh,
And after it almost unmade, what with dread,
　　Thy doing: and dost thou touch me afresh?
Over again I feel thy finger and find thee.
　　　Poems. No. 28, The Wreck of the Deutschland,
　　　st. 1

4 The world is charged with the grandeur of God.
　　　Poems. No. 31, God's Grandeur, l. 1

5 Look at the stars! look, look up at the skies!
　O look at all the fire-folk sitting in the air!
　　　Poems. No. 32, The Starlight Night, l. 1

6 I caught this morning morning's minion, kingdom
　　of daylight's dauphin, dapple-dawn-drawn
　　　Falcon, in his riding
　　Of the rolling level underneath him steady air,
　　and striding
High there, how he rung upon the rein of a
　　wimpling wing
In his ecstasy!
　　　Poems. No. 36, The Windhover, l. 1

7 The achieve of, the mastery of the thing!
　　　Poems. No. 36, The Windhover, l. 8

8 Brute beauty and valor and act, oh, air, pride,
　　plume, here
Buckle!　　　*Poems. No. 36, The Windhover, l. 9*

9 Glory be to God for dappled things.
　　　Poems. No. 37, Pied Beauty, l. 1

10 All things counter, original, spare, strange;
　　Whatever is fickle, freckled (who knows how?)
　　With swift, slow; sweet, sour; adazzle, dim;

He fathers-forth whose beauty is past change:
　　Praise him.
　　　Poems. No. 37, Pied Beauty, l. 7

11 Summer ends now; now, barbarous in beauty, the
　　stooks arise
　　Around; up above, what wind-walks! what
　　lovely behavior
Of silk-sack clouds! Has wilder, willful-wavier
Meal-drift molded ever and melted across skies?
　　　Poems. No. 38, Hurrahing in Harvest, st. 1

12 Felix Randal the farrier, O he is dead then? My
　　duty all ended,
Who have watched his mold of man, big-boned
　　and hardy-handsome,
Pining, pining.
　　　Poems. No. 53, Felix Randal, st. 1

13 When thou at the random grim forge, powerful
　　amidst peers,
Didst fettle for the great gray drayhorse his bright
　　and battering sandal!
　　　Poems. No. 53, Felix Randal, st. 4

14 Margaret, are you grieving
　Over Goldengrove unleaving?
　　　Poems. No. 55, Spring and Fall: To A Young
　　　Child, l. 1

15 It is the blight man was born for,
　It is Margaret you mourn for.
　　　Poems. No. 55, Spring and Fall: To A Young
　　　Child, l. 12

16 As kingfishers catch fire, dragonflies draw flame.
　　　Poems. No. 57, l. 1

17 How to keep — is there any any, is there none such,
　　nowhere known some, bow or brooch or braid
　　or brace, lace, latch or catch or key to keep
Back beauty, keep it, beauty, beauty, beauty . . .
　　from vanishing away?
　　　Poems. No. 59, The Leaden Echo and the
　　　Golden Echo, l. 1

18 I say that we are wound
　With mercy round and round
　As if with air.
　　　Poems. No. 60, The Blessed Virgin Compared
　　　to the Air We Breathe, l. 34

19 World-mothering air, air wild,
　Wound with thee, in thee isled,
　Fold home, fast fold thy child.
　　　Poems. No. 60, The Blessed Virgin Compared
　　　to the Air We Breathe, l. 124

20 Not, I'll not, carrion comfort, Despair, not feast on
　　thee;
　Not untwist — slack they may be — these last
　　strands of man

---

[1]First published in 1918, edited by ROBERT BRIDGES. Poem numbers are from the third edition [1948], edited by W. H. GARDNER.

In me or, most weary, cry *I can no more*. I can;
Can something, hope, wish day come, not choose
not to be.
Poems. No. 64, Carrion Comfort, l. 1

1   That night, that year
Of now done darkness I wretch lay wrestling with
(my God!) my God.
Poems. No. 64, Carrion Comfort, l. 13

2 No worst, there is none. Pitched past pitch of grief,
More pangs will, schooled at forepangs, wilder
wring.   *Poems. No. 65, No Worst, l. 1*

3 O the mind, mind has mountains; cliffs of fall
Frightful, sheer, no-man-fathomed.
Poems. No. 65, No Worst, l. 9

4 I wake and feel the fell of dark, not day.
What hours, O what black hours we have spent
This night.
Poems. No. 69, I Wake and Feel, l. 1

5 I am gall, I am heartburn.
Poems. No. 69, I Wake and Feel, l. 9

6 I am all at once what Christ is, since he was what I
am, and
This Jack, joke, poor potsherd, patch, matchwood,
immortal diamond,
    Is immortal diamond.
*Poems. No. 72, That Nature Is a Heraclitean
Fire and of the Comfort of the Resurrection,
l. 22*

7   No doubt my poetry errs on the side of oddness.
I hope in time to have a more balanced and
Miltonic style. But as air, melody, is what strikes me
most of all in music, and design in painting, so design, pattern, or what I am in the habit of calling
inscape is what I above all aim at in poetry. Now it is
the virtue of design, pattern, or inscape to be distinctive, and it is the vice of distinctiveness to become queer. This vice I cannot have escaped.
Letter to Robert Bridges [February 15, 1879]

Andrew Lang
1844–1912

8 You can cover a great deal of country in books.
To the Gentle Reader, st. 5

9 The surge and thunder of the Odyssey.
Sonnet, The Odyssey

James Hilary Mulligan
1844–1916

10 The moonlight is the softest, in Kentucky,
Summer days come oftest, in Kentucky,

Friendship is the strongest,
Love's fires glow the longest,
Yet a wrong is always wrongest,
    In Kentucky.   *In Kentucky, st. 1*

Friedrich Wilhelm Nietzsche
1844–1900

11   Our destiny exercises its influence over us even
when, as yet, we have not learned its nature: it is
our future that lays down the law of our today.
Human, All Too Human [1878],[1] *sec. 7*

12   One must have a good memory to be able to
keep the promises one makes.
Human, All Too Human, 59

13   One will rarely err if extreme actions be ascribed
to vanity, ordinary actions to habit, and mean actions to fear.   *Human, All Too Human, 74*

14   Every tradition grows ever more venerable — the
more remote is its origin, the more confused that
origin is. The reverence due to it increases from
generation to generation. The tradition finally becomes holy and inspires awe.
Human, All Too Human, 96

15   When Zarathustra was alone . . . he said to his
heart: "Could it be possible! This old saint in the
forest hath not yet heard of it, that God *is dead!*"[2]
Thus Spake Zarathustra [1883–1891],[3]
prologue, ch. 2

16   Man is a rope stretched between the animal and
the Superman — a rope over an abyss.
Thus Spake Zarathustra, prologue, 3

17   I want to teach men the sense of their existence,
which is the Superman, the lightning out of the
dark cloud man.
Thus Spake Zarathustra, prologue, 7

18   This is the hardest of all: to close the open hand
out of love, and keep modest as a giver.
Thus Spake Zarathustra, pt. II, ch. 23

19   Distrust all in whom the impulse to punish is
powerful.   *Thus Spake Zarathustra, II, 29*

20   We ought to learn from the kine one thing: ruminating.   *Thus Spake Zarathustra, IV, 68*

21   If ye would go up high, then use your own legs!
Do not get yourselves *carried* aloft; do not seat
yourselves on other people's backs and heads!
Thus Spake Zarathustra, IV, 73

---

[1] Translated by ALEXANDER HARVEY.
[2] God is dead. God remains dead. And we have killed him. — NIETZ-
SCHE, *The Gay Science (Die Fröhliche Wissenschaft)* [1882], *ch. 125*
[3] Translated by THOMAS COMMON.

1 It is certainly not the least charm of a theory that it is refutable.
Beyond Good and Evil [1885–1886],[1] *pt. I, sec. 18*

2 No one is such a liar as the indignant man.
Beyond Good and Evil, II, 26

3 It is not the strength but the duration of great sentiments that makes great men.
Beyond Good and Evil, IV, 72

4 In revenge and in love woman is more barbarous than man. *Beyond Good and Evil, IV, 139*

5 Whoever fights monsters should see to it that in the process he does not become a monster. And when you look long into an abyss, the abyss also looks into you. *Beyond Good and Evil, IV, 146*

6 The thought of suicide is a great consolation: by means of it one gets successfully through many a bad night. *Beyond Good and Evil, IV, 157*

7 Blessed are the forgetful: for they get the better even of their blunders.
Beyond Good and Evil, IV, 217

8 Is not life a hundred times too short for us to bore ourselves? *Beyond Good and Evil, IV, 227*

9 One does not know—cannot know—the best that is in one. *Beyond Good and Evil, IV, 240*

10 Mozart, the last chord of a centuries-old great European taste. *Beyond Good and Evil, IV, 245*

11 The melancholia of everything completed!
Beyond Good and Evil, IX, 277

12 The masters have been done away with; the morality of the common man has triumphed.
Genealogy of Morals [1887], essay 1, aphorism 9

13 At the core of all these aristocratic races the beast of prey is not to be mistaken, the magnificent *blond beast,* avidly rampant for spoil and victory.
Genealogy of Morals, 1, 11

14 The broad effects which can be obtained by punishment in man and beast are the increase of fear, the sharpening of the sense of cunning, the mastery of the desires; so it is that punishment tames man, but does not make him "better."
Genealogy of Morals, 2, 15

15 The sick are the greatest danger for the healthy; it is not from the strongest that harm comes to the strong, but from the weakest.
Genealogy of Morals, 3, 14

16 A strong and well-constituted man digests his experiences (deeds and misdeeds all included) just as he digests his meats, even when he has some tough morsels to swallow.
Genealogy of Morals, 3, 16

17 Two great European narcotics, alcohol and Christianity.
The Twilight of the Idols [1888]. Things the Germans Lack, sec. 2

18 What is it: is man only a blunder of God, or God only a blunder of man?
The Twilight of the Idols. Things the Germans Lack, 2

19 If a man have a strong faith he can indulge in the luxury of skepticism.
The Twilight of the Idols. Things the Germans Lack, 12

20 Liberal institutions straightway cease from being liberal the moment they are soundly established: once this is attained no more grievous and more thorough enemies of freedom exist than liberal institutions.
The Twilight of the Idols. Things the Germans Lack, 38

21 It is my ambition to say in ten sentences what everyone else says in a whole book—what everyone else does *not* say in a whole book.
The Twilight of the Idols. Things the Germans Lack, 51

22 Love is the state in which man sees things most widely different from what they are. The force of illusion reaches its zenith here, as likewise the sweetening and transfiguring power. When a man is in love he endures more than at other times; he submits to everything.
The Antichrist [1888],[2] *aphorism 23*

23 God created woman. And boredom did indeed cease from that moment—but many other things ceased as well! Woman was God's *second* mistake.
The Antichrist, 48

24 Life always gets harder toward the summit—the cold increases, responsibility increases.
The Antichrist, 57

25 I call Christianity the one great curse, the one enormous and innermost perversion, the one great instinct of revenge, for which no means are too venomous, too underhand, too underground and too petty—I call it the one immortal blemish of mankind. *The Antichrist, 62*

26 My doctrine is: Live that thou mayest desire to live again—that is thy duty—for in any case thou wilt live again! *Eternal Recurrence,*[2] *sec. 27*

---

[1]Translated by HELEN ZIMMERN.

[2]Translated by ANTHONY M. LUDOVICI.

1   Even a thought, even a possibility, can shatter us and transform us.   *Eternal Recurrence, 30*

2   Nothing on earth consumes a man more quickly than the passion of resentment.   *Ecce Homo [1888]*[1]

3   I believe only in French culture, and regard everything else in Europe which calls itself "culture" as a misunderstanding. I do not even take the German kind into consideration.   *Ecce Homo*

4   Wherever Germany extends her sway, she ruins culture.   *Ecce Homo*

5   As an artist, a man has no home in Europe save in Paris.   *Ecce Homo*

6   Simply by being compelled to keep constantly on his guard, a man may grow so weak as to be unable any longer to defend himself.   *Ecce Homo*

7   My time has not yet come either; some are born posthumously.   *Ecce Homo*

8   No one can draw more out of things, books included, than he already knows. A man has no ears for that to which experience has given him no access.   *Ecce Homo*

9   The Germans are like women, you can scarcely ever fathom their depths — they haven't any.[2]   *Ecce Homo*

10   All prejudices may be traced back to the intestines. A sedentary life is the real sin against the Holy Ghost.[3]   *Ecce Homo*

11   One must separate from anything that forces one to repeat No again and again.   *Ecce Homo*

12   The Will to Power.[4]   *Title of book [1888]*

John Boyle O'Reilly
1844–1890

13   They who see the Flying Dutchman never, never reach the shore.   *The Flying Dutchman*

14   The red rose whispers of passion
And the white rose breathes of love;
O, the red rose is a falcon,
And the white rose is a dove.
    A White Rose, st. 1

---

15   The organized charity, scrimped and iced,
In the name of a cautious, statistical Christ.
    In Bohemia, st. 5

Arthur William Edgar O'Shaughnessy
1844–1881

16   We are the music-makers,
And we are the dreamers of dreams,
Wandering by lone sea breakers,
And sitting by desolate streams;
World-losers and world-forsakers,
On whom the pale moon gleams:
Yet we are the movers and shakers
Of the world forever, it seems.   *Ode, st. 1*

William Archibald Spooner[5]
1844–1930

17   Kinquering Congs their titles take.
    Announcing the hymn in college chapel

18   You have deliberately tasted two worms and you can leave Oxford by the next town drain.
    Dismissing a student. Attributed

19   I remember your name perfectly, but I just can't think of your face.   *Attributed*

Paul Verlaine
1844–1896

20   The long sobs
Of the violins
Of autumn
Pierce my heart
With monotonous languor.[6]
    Poèmes Saturniens [1866]. Chanson d'Automne

21   There is weeping in my heart
Like the rain falling on the city.[7]
    Romances sans Paroles [1874], III

22   Here are fruits, flowers, leaves and branches,
And here is my heart which beats only for you.[8]
    Romances sans Paroles. Green

---

[1]Translated by Anthony M. Ludovici.

[2]Man thinks woman profound — why? Because he can never fathom her depths. Woman is not even shallow. — Nietzsche, *The Twilight of the Idols, Maxims and Missiles, 27*

[3]Translated by Clifton P. Fadiman.

[4]Der Wille zur Macht.

[5]Canon Spooner, for many years warden of New College, Oxford, was famous for unintentional transposition of (usually initial) word sounds, giving rise to the term "spoonerism."

[6]Les sanglots longs / Des violons / De l'automne / Blessent mon coeur / D'une langueur / Monotone.

[7]Il pleure dans mon coeur / Comme il pleut sur la ville.

[8]Voici des fruits, des fleurs, des feuilles et des branches, / Et puis voici mon coeur qui ne bat que pour vous.

1 What have you done, you there
Weeping without cease,
Tell me, yes you, what have you done
With all your youth?[1]

Sagesse [1881], III, st. 6

2 Music above all, and for this
Choose the irregular.[2]

Jadis et Naguère [1884]. L'Art Poétique

3 Take eloquence and wring its neck![3]

Jadis et Naguère. L'Art Poétique

4 And all else is literature.[4]

Jadis et Naguère. L'Art Poétique

John B. Bogart[5]
1845–1921

5   When a dog bites a man, that is not news, because it happens so often. But if a man bites a dog, that is news.

From Frank M. O'Brien, *The Story of The (New York) Sun [1918]*

Will[iam McKendree] Carleton
1845–1912

6 Worm or beetle — drought or tempest — on a
    farmer's land may fall,
Each is loaded full o' ruin, but a mortgage beats
    'em all.   *The Tramp's Story*

7 Over the hill to the poorhouse I'm trudgin' my
    weary way.

Over the Hill to the Poorhouse, st. 1

William Kingdon Clifford
1845–1879

8   Remember, then, that it [science] is the guide of action; that the truth which it arrives at is not that which we can ideally contemplate without error, but that which we may act upon without fear; and you cannot fail to see that scientific thought is not an accompaniment or condition of human progress, but human progress itself.

Aims and Instruments of Scientific Thought [1872]

---

[1] Qu'as-tu fait, O toi que voilà / Pleurant sans cesse, / Dis, qu'as-tu fait, toi que voilà / De ta jeunesse?

[2] De la musique avant toute chose, / Et pour cela préfère l'Impair.

[3] Prends l'éloquence et tords-lui son cou!

[4] Et tout le reste est littérature.

[5] City editor [1873–1890] of *The Sun*, New York.

Daniel Webster Hoyt
1845–1936

9 Why should good words ne'er be said
Of a friend till he is dead?

A Sermon in Rhyme [1878], st. 1

George Kennan
1845–1924

10   Heroism, the Caucasian mountaineers say, is endurance for one moment more.

Letter to Henry Munroe Rogers [July 25, 1921]

John Banister Tabb
1845–1909

11 Out of the dusk a shadow,
    Then a spark;
Out of the clouds a silence,
    Then a lark;
Out of the heart a rapture,
    Then a pain;
Out of the dead, cold ashes,
    Life again.   *Evolution*

Punch

12   Advice to persons about to marry. — "Don't."

Vol. VIII, p. 1 [1845]

13   You pays your money and you takes your choice.

X, 16 [1846]

14   What is Matter? — Never mind.
What is Mind? — No matter.

XXIX, 19 [1855]

15   It ain't the 'unting as 'urts 'un, it's the 'ammer, 'ammer, 'ammer along the 'ard 'igh road.

XXX, 218 [1856]

16 There was an old owl lived in an oak,
The more he heard, the less he spoke;
The less he spoke, the more he heard,
O, if men were all like that wise bird!

LXVIII, 155 [1875]

17   It's worse than wicked, my dear, it's vulgar.

Almanac [1876]

18   Don't look at me, sir, with — ah — in that tone of voice.   *XCVII, 38 [1884]*

19   I'm afraid you've got a bad egg, Mr. Jones.
Oh no, my Lord, I assure you! Parts of it are excellent!   *CIX, 222 [1895]*

Charles Dupee Blake
1846–1903

1 Rock-a-bye-baby on the tree top,
When the wind blows the cradle will rock,
When the bough breaks the cradle will fall,
And down will come baby, cradle and all.
Attributed

Léon Bloy
1846–1917

2   Suffering is an auxiliary of creation.
Pages de Léon Bloy [1951]

3   When you ask God to send you trials, you may
be sure your prayer will be granted.
Pages de Léon Bloy. Pensées Détachées

Daniel Hudson Burnham
1846–1912

4   Make no little plans; they have no magic to stir
men's blood.   *Attributed*[1]

Charles Prestwich Scott
1846–1932

5   The primary office of a newspaper is the gathering of news . . . comment is free, but facts are sacred.
In the Manchester Guardian [May 6, 1926]

Edward Noyes Westcott
1846–1898

6   They say a reasonable amount o' fleas is good fer
a dog—keeps him from broodin' over *bein'* a dog.
David Harum [1898], ch. 32

7   The' ain't nothin' truer in the Bible 'n that
sayin' thet them that has gits.
David Harum, 35

Alexander Graham Bell
1847–1922

8   Mr. Watson, come here, I want you.[2]
To his assistant [March 10, 1876]

---

[1]This quotation is now doubted. See HENRY M. SAYLOR, "'Make
No Little Plans': Daniel Burnham Thought It but Did He Say
It?," *Journal of the American Institute of Architects, 27* [1957]: 3.

[2]The first intelligible words transmitted by telephone.

Thomas A[lva] Edison
1847–1931

9   There is no substitute for hard work.
Life [1932], ch. 2

10   Genius is one percent inspiration and ninet
nine percent perspiration.   *Life, 2*

Henry Demarest Lloyd
1847–1903

11   Monopoly is Business at the end of its journey.
Wealth Against Commonwealth [1894

12   Corporations have no souls, but they can lov
each other.   *Wealth Against Commonwealt*

John Locke
1847–1889

13 O Ireland, isn't it grand you look—
Like a bride in her rich adornin'?
And with all the pent-up love of my heart
I bid you the top o' the mornin'!
*The Exile's Return (Th' an'am an Dhia: My
Soul to God), st. 1*

Alice Meynell
1847–1922

14 She walks—the lady of my delight—
A shepherdess of sheep.   *The Shepherdess, st.*

15 I must not think of thee; and, tired yet strong,
I shun the thought that lurks in all delight—
The thought of thee—and in the blue Heaven's
height,
And in the sweetest passage of a song.
Renouncemen

Julia A. Moore
1847–1920

16 Leave off the agony, leave off style,
Unless you've got money by you all the while.
Leave Off the Agony in Sty

Milton Nobles
1847–1924

17 The villain still pursued her.
The Phoenix [1875], act I, sc. i

George Robert Sims
1847–1922

1 It was Christmas Day in the workhouse.
Christmas Day in the Workhouse, st. 1

Arthur James Balfour
1848–1930

2 His Majesty's Government view with favor the establishment in Palestine of a national home for the Jewish people, and will use their best endeavors to facilitate the achievement of this object, it being clearly understood that nothing shall be done which may prejudice the civil and religious rights of existing non-Jewish communities in Palestine, or the rights and political status enjoyed by Jews in any other country.
The Balfour Declaration. Letter to Lionel Walter, Lord Rothschild [November 2, 1917]

Sir Francis Darwin
1848–1925

3 But in science the credit goes to the man who convinces the world, not to the man to whom the idea first occurs.
First Galton Lecture before the Eugenics Society [1914]

Ludwig Max Goldberger
1848–1913

4 America, the land of unlimited possibilities.
Land of Unlimited Possibilities: Observations on Economic Life in the United States of America [1903]

Joel Chandler Harris
1848–1908

5 Hit look lak sparrer-grass, hit feel lak sparrer-grass, hit tas'e lak sparrer-grass, en I bless ef 'taint sparrer-grass.
Nights with Uncle Remus [1883], ch. 27

6 Tar-baby ain't sayin' nuthin', en Brer Fox, he lay low.   *Uncle Remus and His Friends [1892]*

7 Ez soshubble ez a baskit er kittens.
Uncle Remus and His Friends

8 Bred en bawn in a brier-patch, Brer Fox.
Uncle Remus and His Friends

9 You do de pullin', Sis Cow, en I'll do de gruntin'.
Uncle Remus and His Friends

10 W'en ole man Rabbit say "scoot," dey scooted, en w'en old Miss Rabbit say "scat," dey scatted.
Uncle Remus and His Friends

11 Lazy fokes' stummucks don't git tired.
Uncle Remus: Plantation Proverbs

12 Jaybird don't rob his own nes'.
Uncle Remus: Plantation Proverbs

13 Licker talks mighty loud w'en it gits loose fum de jug.   *Uncle Remus: Plantation Proverbs*

14 Hongry rooster don't cackle w'en he fine a wum.
Uncle Remus: Plantation Proverbs

15 Youk'n hide de fier, but w'at you gwine do wid de smoke?   *Uncle Remus: Plantation Proverbs*

16 Watch out w'en youer gittin' all you want. Fattenin' hogs ain't in luck.
Uncle Remus: Plantation Proverbs

17 Hop light, ladies,
Oh, Miss Loo!
Oh, swing dat yaller gal!
Do, boys, do!   *Plantation Play Song*

Joris Karl Huysmans
1848–1907

18 The loveliest tune imaginable becomes vulgar and insupportable as soon as the public begins to hum it and the hurdy-gurdies make it their own.
À Rebours (Against the Grain) [1884],[1] ch. 9

19 Art is the only clean thing on earth, except holiness.   *Crowds of Lourdes [1906]*

Alice James
1848–1892

20 When will women begin to have the first glimmer that above all other loyalties is the loyalty to Truth, *i.e.,* to yourself, that husband, children, friends and country are as nothing to that?
Diary [November 19, 1889]

Richard Jefferies
1848–1887

21 It is eternity now. I am in the midst of it. It is about me in the sunshine; I am in it, as the butterfly in the light-laden air. Nothing has to come; it is now. Now is eternity; now is the immortal life.
The Story of My Heart [1883]

---

[1]Translated by JOHN HOWARD.

Vilfredo Pareto
1848–1923

1   Give me a fruitful error any time, full of seeds, bursting with its own corrections. You can keep your sterile truth for yourself.
Comment on Kepler

Eben Eugene Rexford
1848–1916

2   Darling, I am growing old,
Silver threads among the gold
Shine upon my brow today;
Life is fading fast away.
Silver Threads Among the Gold [1873],[1] st. 1

Frederic Edward Weatherly
1848–1929

3   Always the same, Darby, my own,
Always the same to your old wife Joan.
Darby and Joan,[2] refrain

Bernhard von Bülow
1849–1929

4   A place in the sun.
A Promise for Germany. Speech before the Reichstag [December 6, 1897]

Lord Randolph Spencer Churchill
1849–1895

5   The old gang [members of the Conservative government].
Speech in the House of Commons [March 7, 1878]

Sir Edmund [William] Gosse
1849–1928

6   My father's theory[3] . . . was defined by a hasty press as being this—that God hid the fossils in the rocks in order to tempt geologists into infidelity.
Father and Son [1907], ch. 5

---

[1]Music by HART PEASE DANKS [1834–1903].

[2]Old Darby with Joan by his side, / You've often regarded with wonder; / He's dropsical, she is sore-eyed, / Yet they're ever uneasy asunder.— *Gentleman's Magazine* [March 1735]

[3]British naturalist Philip Henry Gosse [1810–1888], who opposed the uniformitarian geological theory of Charles Lyell [1797–1875].

William Ernest Henley
1849–1903

7   Bland as a Jesuit, sober as a hymn.
In Hospital [1888], no. 16, House Surgeon

8   Valiant in velvet, light in ragged luck,
Most vain, most generous, sternly critical,
Buffoon and poet, lover and sensualist:
A deal of Ariel, just a streak of Puck,
Much Antony, of Hamlet most of all,
And something of the Shorter-Catechist.
In Hospital, 25, Apparition (Robert Louis Stevenson)

9   As dust that drives, as straws that blow,
Into the night go one and all.
Ballade of Dead Actors [1888], l. 27

10   Out of the night that covers me,
Black as the Pit from pole to pole,
I thank whatever gods may be
For my unconquerable soul.

In the fell clutch of circumstance,
I have not winced nor cried aloud;
Under the bludgeonings of chance
My head is bloody, but unbowed.
Echoes [1888], no. 4, In Memoriam R. T. Hamilton Bruce ("Invictus"), st. 1, 2

11   I am the master of my fate;
I am the captain of my soul.
Echoes, 4, In Memoriam R. T. Hamilton Bruce ("Invictus"), st. 4

12   Night with her train of stars
And her great gift of sleep.
Echoes, 35, In Memoriam Margaritae Sororis, st. 2

13   Or ever the knightly years were gone
With the old world to the grave,
I was a King in Babylon
And you were a Christian Slave.
Echoes, 37, To W. A., st. 1

Sarah Orne Jewett
1849–1909

14   Captain Littlepage had overset his mind with too much reading.
The Country of the Pointed Firs [1896], ch. 5

15   Wrecked on the lee shore of age.
The Country of the Pointed Firs, 7

16   We were standing where there was a fine view of the harbor and its long stretches of shore all covered by the great army of the pointed firs, darkly

cloaked and standing as if they waited to embark. As we looked far seaward among the outer islands, the trees seemed to march seaward still, going steadily over the heights and down to the water's edge.   *The Country of the Pointed Firs, 7*

1   Tact is after all a kind of mind-reading.
                    The Country of the Pointed Firs, 10

2   In the life of each of us, I said to myself, there is a place remote and islanded, and given to endless regret or secret happiness.
                    The Country of the Pointed Firs, 15

3   'Tain't worthwhile to wear a day all out before it comes.   *The Country of the Pointed Firs, 16*

4   So we die before our own eyes; so we see some chapters of our lives come to their natural end.
                    The Country of the Pointed Firs, 21

5   The thing that teases the mind over and over for years, and at last gets itself put down rightly on paper — whether little or great, it belongs to Literature.
     Letter to Willa Cather. Quoted in preface to
     The Country of the Pointed Firs and Other
     Stories [1925]

Emma Lazarus
1849–1887

6   Give me your tired, your poor,
Your huddled masses yearning to breathe free,
The wretched refuse of your teeming shore,
Send these, the homeless, tempest-tost to me:
I lift my lamp beside the golden door.[1]
     The New Colossus: Inscription for the Statue of
     Liberty, New York Harbor [1883]

Sir William Osler
1849–1919

7   The greater the ignorance the greater the dogmatism.   *Montreal Medical Journal [1902]*

8   The natural man has only two primal passions, to get and to beget.
                    Science and Immortality [1904], ch. 2

9   The desire to take medicine is perhaps the greatest feature which distinguishes man from animals.
                    Science and Immortality, 14

10   Things cannot always go your way. Learn to accept in silence the minor aggravations, cultivate the

---
[1]Set to music by IRVING BERLIN for *Miss Liberty*.

gift of taciturnity and consume your own smoke with an extra draught of hard work, so that those about you may not be annoyed with the dust and soot of your complaints.
     From HARVEY CUSHING, The Life of Sir
     William Osler [1925], vol. I, ch. 22

11   Take the sum of human achievement in action, in science, in art, in literature — subtract the work of the men above forty, and while we should miss great treasures, even priceless treasures, we would practically be where we are today. . . . The effective, moving, vitalizing work of the world is done between the ages of twenty-five and forty.[2]
     From HARVEY CUSHING, The Life of Sir
     William Osler, I, 24 [The Fixed Period]

12   My second fixed idea is the uselessness of men above sixty years of age, and the incalculable benefit it would be in commercial, political, and in professional life, if as a matter of course, men stopped work at this age.[3]
     From HARVEY CUSHING, The Life of Sir
     William Osler, I, 24 [The Fixed Period]

13   Nothing in life is more wonderful than faith — the one great moving force which we can neither weigh in the balance nor test in the crucible.
     From HARVEY CUSHING, The Life of Sir
     William Osler, II, 30

Ivan Petrovich Pavlov
1849–1936

14   The naturalist must consider only one thing: what is the relation of this or that external reaction of the animal to the phenomena of the external world?
     Scientific Study of So-Called Psychical Processes
     in the Higher Animals [1906]

15   Mankind will possess incalculable advantages and extraordinary control over human behavior when the scientific investigator will be able to subject his fellow men to the same external analysis he would employ for any natural object, and when the human mind will contemplate itself not from within but from without.
     Scientific Study of So-Called Psychical Processes
     in the Higher Animals

---
[2]Address at Johns Hopkins University, Baltimore [February 22, 1905].

[3]This valedictory address caused much discussion and misquotation. It was headlined in the press: OSLER RECOMMENDS CHLOROFORM AT SIXTY, and occasioned many columns of letters, caustic cartoons, and the like, until to "Oslerize" became a byword.

James Whitcomb Riley
1849–1916

1 O'er folded blooms
On swirls of musk,
The beetle booms adown the glooms
And bumps along the dusk.   *The Beetle, st. 7*

2 The ripest peach is highest on the tree.
                    The Ripest Peach, st. 1

3 There! little girl; don't cry!   *A Life Lesson, st. 3*

4 That old sweetheart of mine.
                    An Old Sweetheart of Mine, st. 12

5 An' all us other children, when the supper things is
        done,
We set around the kitchen fire an' has the mostest
        fun
A-list'nin' to the witch-tales 'at Annie tells about,
An' the Gobble-uns 'at gits you
Ef you
    Don't
    Watch
        Out!   *Little Orphant Annie [1883], st. 1*

6 'Long about knee-deep in June,
'Bout the time strawberries melts
On the vine.   *Knee-Deep in June [1883], st. 1*

7 Oh! the old swimmin' hole! When I last saw the
        place,
The scenes was all changed, like the change in my
        face.   *The Old Swimmin' Hole [1883], st. 5*

8 O, it sets my heart a-clickin' like the tickin' of a
        clock,
When the frost is on the punkin and the fodder's in
        the shock.
                    When the Frost Is on the Punkin [1883], st. 3

August Strindberg
1849–1912

9 I loathe people who keep dogs. They are cowards
who haven't got the guts to bite people themselves.
                    A Madman's Diary [1895], pt. 3

Edward Bellamy
1850–1898

10 We hold the period of youth sacred to education, and the period of maturity, when the physical
forces begin to flag, equally sacred to ease and
agreeable relaxation.
                    Looking Backward, 2000–1887 [1888], ch. 6

11 The nation guarantees the nurture, education
and comfortable maintenance of every citizen from
the cradle to the grave.
                    Looking Backward, §

12 Love of money . . . was the general impulse to
effort in your day.   *Looking Backward, §*

13 Badly off as the men . . . were in your day, they
were more fortunate than their mothers and wives.
                    Looking Backward, 1.

14 An American credit card . . . is just as good in
Europe as American gold used to be.
                    Looking Backward, 1.

15 Equal wealth and equal opportunities of
culture . . . have simply made us all members of one
class.   *Looking Backward, 14*

16 Your system was liable to periodical convulsions . . . business crises at intervals of five to ten
years, which wrecked the industries of the nation.
                    Looking Backward, 22

17 On no other stage are the scenes shifted with
swiftness so like magic as on the great stage of history when once the hour strikes.
                    Looking Backward, author's postscrip

18 *Looking Backward* was written in the belief that
the Golden Age lies before us and not behind us.
                    Looking Backward, author's postscrip

Augustine Birrell
1850–1933

19 Libraries are not made; they grow.
                    Obiter Dicta. Book Buying

20 That great dust heap called "history."
                    Obiter Dicta. Carlyl

Hermann Ebbinghaus
1850–1909

21 From the most ancient subject we shall produce
the newest science.[1]
        *Inscription on the title page of Über das
        Gedachtnis (Memory) [1885]*

22 Psychology has a long past, but only a short history.
        *Abriss der Psychologie (Summary of
        Psychology) [1908], opening sentence*

---

[1] De subjecto vetustissimo novissimam promovemus scientiam.

Eugene Field
1850–1895

1 He could whip his weight in wildcats.
Modjesky as Cameel, st. 10

2 The best of all physicians
Is apple pie and cheese!
Apple Pie and Cheese, st. 5

3 It always was the biggest fish I caught that got away.
Our Biggest Fish, st. 2

4 When I demanded of my friend what viands he preferred,
He quoth: "A large cold bottle, and a small hot bird!"
The Bottle and the Bird, st. 1

5 Wynken, Blynken, and Nod one night
Sailed off in a wooden shoe—
Sailed on a river of crystal light
Into a sea of dew.
Wynken, Blynken, and Nod, st. 1

6 The little toy dog is covered with dust,
But sturdy and staunch he stands;
And the little toy soldier is red with rust,
And his musket molds in his hands;
Time was when the little toy dog was new,
And the soldier was passing fair;
And that was the time when our Little Boy Blue
Kissed them and put them there.
Little Boy Blue, st. 1

7 The gingham dog went "Bow-wow-wow!"
And the calico cat replied "Mee-ow!"
The air was littered, an hour or so,
With bits of gingham and calico.
The Duel, st. 2

8 'Most all the time, the whole year round, there ain't no flies on me,
But jest 'fore Christmas I'm as good as I kin be!
Jest 'Fore Christmas, st. 1

Fred Gilbert
1850–1903

9 The Man Who Broke the Bank at Monte Carlo.
Title of song [1892]

Samuel Gompers
1850–1924

10 To protect the workers in their inalienable rights to a higher and better life; to protect them, not only as equals before the law, but also in their health, their homes, their firesides, their liberties as men, as workers, and as citizens; to overcome and conquer prejudices and antagonism; to secure to them the right to life, and the opportunity to maintain that life; the right to be full sharers in the abundance which is the result of their brain and brawn, and the civilization of which they are the founders and the mainstay. . . . The attainment of these is the glorious mission of the trade unions.
Speech [1898]

Mary Ellen [Mary Elizabeth] Lease
1850–1933

11 Raise less corn and more hell!
Attributed. Advice to Kansas farmers [1890]

Henry Cabot Lodge
1850–1924

12 Let us have done with British-Americans and Irish-Americans and German-Americans, and so on, and all be Americans. . . . If a man is going to be an American at all let him be so without any qualifying adjectives; and if he is going to be something else, let him drop the word American from his personal description.
The Day We Celebrate (Forefathers' Day). Address, New England Society of Brooklyn [December 21, 1888]

13 It is the flag just as much of the man who was naturalized yesterday as of the man whose people have been here many generations.
Address [1915]

Guy de Maupassant
1850–1893

14 A man who looks a part has the soul of that part.[1]
Mont-Oriol [1887]

15 Conversation . . . is the art of never appearing a bore, of knowing how to say everything interestingly, to entertain with no matter what, to be charming with nothing at all.
Sur l'Eau (On the Water) [1888]

16 History, that excitable and lying old lady.[2]
Sur l'Eau (On the Water)

Bill [Edgar Wilson] Nye
1850–1896

17 Wagner's music is better than it sounds.
From Mark Twain's Autobiography [1924]

---

[1] Quand on a le physique d'un emploi, on en a l'âme.

[2] L'histoire, cette vieille dame exaltée et menteuse.

Laura E[lizabeth] Richards
1850–1943

1 Once there was an elephant
Who tried to use the telephant—
No! No! I mean an elephone
Who tried to use the telephone.
Eletelephony, l. 1

Robert Louis Stevenson
1850–1894

2   Mankind was never so happily inspired as when it made a cathedral.
An Inland Voyage [1878]. Noyon Cathedral

3   Every man is his own doctor of divinity, in the last resort.
An Inland Voyage. Noyon Cathedral

4   For my part, I travel not to go anywhere, but to go. I travel for travel's sake. The great affair is to move.   *Travels with a Donkey [1878]*

5   Marriage is like life in this—that it is a field of battle, and not a bed of roses.
Virginibus Puerisque [1881], pt. I, ch. 1

6   Man is a creature who lives not upon bread alone but principally by catchwords.
Virginibus Puerisque, I, 2

7   The cruelest lies are often told in silence.
Virginibus Puerisque, I, 4, Truth of Intercourse

8   Old and young, we are all on our last cruise.
Virginibus Puerisque, II, Crabbed Age and Youth

9   It is better to be a fool than to be dead.
Virginibus Puerisque, II, Crabbed Age and Youth

10   Books are good enough in their own way, but they are a mighty bloodless substitute for life.
Virginibus Puerisque, III, An Apology for Idlers

11   Perpetual devotion to what a man calls his business, is only to be sustained by perpetual neglect of many other things.
Virginibus Puerisque, III, An Apology for Idlers

12   There is no duty we so much underrate as the duty of being happy.
Virginibus Puerisque, III, An Apology for Idlers

13   To travel hopefully is a better thing than to arrive.
Virginibus Puerisque, VI, El Dorado

14 Fifteen men on the Dead Man's Chest—[1]
Yo-ho-ho, and a bottle of rum!
Drink and the devil had done for the rest—
Yo-ho-ho, and a bottle of rum!
Treasure Island [1883], ch. .

15   Doctors is all swabs.   *Treasure Island, .*

16   "What is the Black Spot, Captain?" . . . "That's summons, mate."   *Treasure Island, .*

17   Pieces of eight, pieces of eight, pieces of eight!
Treasure Island, 1.

18   Many's the long night I've dreamed of cheese—toasted, mostly.   *Treasure Island, 1.*

19   Them that die'll be the lucky ones.
Treasure Island, 2.

20 In winter I get up at night
And dress by yellow candlelight.
In summer, quite the other way,
I have to go to bed by day.
A Child's Garden of Verses [1885].
Bed in Summer, st. 1

21 A child should always say what's true
And speak when he is spoken to,
And behave mannerly at table;
At least as far as he is able.
A Child's Garden of Verses. Whole Duty
of Children

22 Whenever the moon and stars are set,
Whenever the wind is high,
All night long in the dark and wet,
A man goes riding by.
Late in the night when the fires are out,
Why does he gallop and gallop about?
A Child's Garden of Verses. Windy Nights,
st. 1

23 I have a little shadow that goes in and out with me
And what can be the use of him is more than I can
    see.
He is very, very like me from the heels up to the
    head;
And I see him jump before me, when I jump into
    my bed.
A Child's Garden of Verses. My Shadow, st. .

---

[1]Treasure Island came out of Kingsley's *At Last,* where I got th[e]
Dead Man's Chest—and that was the seed.—R. L. STEVENSON[,]
Letter to Sidney Colvin
    We were crawling slowly along, looking out for Virgin Gord[a,]
the first of those numberless isles which Columbus, so goes th[e]
tale, discovered on St. Ursula's day, and named them after the sai[nt]
and her eleven thousand mythical virgins. Unfortunately, Englis[h]
buccaneers have since given to most of them less poetic name[s.]
The Dutchman's Cap, Broken Jerusalem, The Dead Man's Ches[t,]
Rum Island, and so forth, mark a time and race more prosaic.—
CHARLES KINGSLEY, *At Last* [1870], *ch. 1*

1 The friendly cow all red and white,
  I love with all my heart:
  She gives me cream with all her might,
  To eat with apple tart.
  A Child's Garden of Verses. The Cow, st. 1

2 The world is so full of a number of things,
  I'm sure we should all be as happy as kings.
  A Child's Garden of Verses. Happy Thought

3   Dr. Jekyll and Mr. Hyde.
  Title of novel [1886]

4   Am I no a bonny fighter?
  Kidnapped [1886], ch. 10 (Alan Breck)

5 Let first the onion flourish there,
  Rose among roots, the maiden-fair,
  Wine-scented and poetic soul
  Of the capacious salad bowl.
  Underwoods [1887], bk. I, In English. To a Gardener

6 Under the wide and starry sky,
  Dig the grave and let me lie.
  Glad did I live and gladly die,
  And I laid me down with a will.

  This be the verse you grave for me:
  Here he lies where he longed to be;
  Home is the sailor, home from sea,
  And the hunter home from the hill.
  Underwoods, I, In English. Requiem

7 My body which my dungeon is,
  And yet my parks and palaces.
  Underwoods, I, In English. My Body Which My Dungeon Is

8 There's just ae thing I cannae bear,
  An' that's my conscience.
  Underwoods, II, In Scots. My Conscience

9   I have thus played the sedulous ape to Hazlitt, to Lamb, to Wordsworth, to Sir Thomas Browne, to Defoe, to Hawthorne, to Montaigne, to Baudelaire and to Obermann.
  Memories and Portraits [1887]. A College Magazine

10   A Penny Plain and Twopence Colored.
  Memories and Portraits. Essay About Skelt's Juvenile Drama

11 Wealth I ask not, hope nor love,
  Nor a friend to know me;
  All I ask, the heaven above
  And the road below me.
  Songs of Travel. The Vagabond, st. 4

12 The untented Kosmos my abode,
  I pass, a willful stranger;

My mistress still the open road
And the bright eyes of danger.
  Songs of Travel. Youth and Love, st. 3

13 I will make you brooches and toys for your delight
  Of birdsong at morning and starshine at night.
  Songs of Travel. Romance, st. 1

14 Bright is the ring of words
  When the right man rings them.
  Songs of Travel. No. 14, st. 1

15 Trusty, dusky, vivid, true,
  With eyes of gold and bramble dew,
  Steel-true and blade-straight
  The great artificer
  Made my mate.   *Songs of Travel. My Wife, st. 1*

16 Be it granted me to behold you again in dying,
  Hills of home!
  Songs of Travel. To S. R. Crockett, st. 3

17   Not every man is so great a coward as he thinks he is—nor yet so good a Christian.
  The Master of Ballantrae [1889]. Mr. Mackellar's Journey

18   Nothing like a little judicious levity.
  The Wrong Box [1889], ch. 7

19   Do you know what the Governor of South Carolina said to the Governor of North Carolina? It's a long time between drinks, observed that powerful thinker.[1]   *The Wrong Box, 8*

20   So long as we love we serve; so long as we are loved by others, I would almost say that we are indispensable; and no man is useless while he has a friend.   *Across the Plains [1892]. Lay Morals*

21   If your morals make you dreary, depend upon it, they are wrong. I do not say give them up, for they may be all you have, but conceal them like a vice lest they should spoil the lives of better and simpler people.   *Across the Plains. Lay Morals*

22   Here lies one who meant well, tried a little, failed much:—surely that may be his epitaph of which he need not be ashamed.
  Across the Plains. Lay Morals

23   Ice and iron cannot be welded.
  Weir of Hermiston [1896]

---

[1]Of the several traditions relating to the origin of this remark, the most reasonable one traces it to John Motley Morehead [1796–1866], who was Governor of North Carolina 1841–1845. He was visited by James H. Hammond [1807–1864], who was Governor of South Carolina 1842–1844. They engaged in discussion and argument, and when the latter waxed hot, Governor Morehead was reported by a servant to have exclaimed: "It's a long time between drinks."—JOHN MOTLEY MOREHEAD, *letter* [November 21, 1934]

1   Give us grace and strength to forbear and to persevere. . . . Give us courage and gaiety and the quiet mind, spare to us our friends, soften to us our enemies.
Prayer[1]

2   Youth is wholly experimental.
Letter to a Young Gentleman

Rose Hartwick Thorpe
1850–1939

3 She breathed the husky whisper—
"Curfew must not ring tonight."
Curfew Must Not Ring Tonight [1882], st. 2

4 Out she swung—far out; the city seemed a speck
of light below,
There 'twixt heaven and earth suspended as the
bell swung to and fro.
Curfew Must Not Ring Tonight, st. 7

Ella Wheeler Wilcox
1850–1919

5 One ship drives east and another drives west
With the selfsame winds that blow.
'Tis the set of sails and not the gales
Which tells us the way to go.   *Winds of Fate*

6 No! the two kinds of people on earth that I mean
Are the people who lift and the people who lean.
To Lift or to Lean

7 Laugh, and the world laughs with you;
Weep, and you weep alone.   *Solitude,*[2] *st. 1*

8 So many gods, so many creeds,
So many paths that wind and wind,
When just the art of being kind
Is all this sad world needs.   *The World's Need*

Kate Chopin [Katherine O'Flaherty]
1851–1904

9   Mrs. Pontellier was beginning to realize her position in the universe as a human being, and to recognize her relations as an individual to the world within and about her.
The Awakening [1899], pt. VI

10   For the first time in her life she stood naked in the open air, at the mercy of the sun, the breeze that beat upon her, and the waves that invited her.
The Awakening, XXXIX

Ferdinand Foch
1851–1929

11   My center is giving way, my right is pushed back, situation excellent, I am attacking.[3]
At the second battle of the Marne [1918].
From B. H. LIDDELL HART, Reputations Ten
Years After [1928]

Henry Arthur Jones
1851–1929
and
Henry Herman
1832–1894

12   Oh God! put back Thy universe and give me yesterday.
The Silver King [1882], act II, sc. 4

Edward Smith Ufford
1851–1929

13 Throw out the lifeline, throw out the lifeline,
Someone is sinking today.
Throw Out the Lifeline [1884], refrain

Francis William Bourdillon
1852–1921

14 The night has a thousand eyes,
And the day but one;
Yet the light of the bright world dies
With the dying sun.
The mind has a thousand eyes,
And the heart but one;
Yet the light of a whole life dies
When love is done.
Among the Flowers [1878]. The Night Has a
Thousand Eyes

[Charles Joseph] Paul Bourget
1852–1935

15   Ideas are to literature what light is to painting.[4]
La Physiologie de l'Amour Moderne [1890]

---

[1]On the bronze memorial to Stevenson in St. Giles Cathedral, Edinburgh, Scotland.

[2]Music by LOUIS MOREAU GOTTSCHALK [1829–1869].

[3]Mon centre cède, ma droite recule, situation excellente, j'attaque.

[4]La pensée est à la littérature ce que la lumière est à la peinture.

Robert Bontine Cunninghame-Graham
1852–1936

1   God forbid that I should go to any heaven in which there are no horses.
Letter to Theodore Roosevelt [1917]

Flying Hawk[1]
1852–1931

2   The tepee is much better to live in: always clean, warm in winter, cool in summer; easy to move . . . Indians and animals know better how to live than white man; nobody can be in good health if he does not have all the time fresh air, sunshine, and good water.
Statement in old age

Edwin Markham
1852–1940

3 Bowed by the weight of centuries he leans
Upon his hoe and gazes on the ground,
The emptiness of ages in his face,
And on his back the burden of the world.
The Man with the Hoe [1899],[2] st. 1

4 O masters, lords and rulers in all lands,
Is this the handiwork you give to God?
The Man with the Hoe, st. 3

5 A man to match the mountains[3] and the sea.
Lincoln, The Man of the People [1901], st. 1

6 The color of the ground was in him, the red earth,
The smack and tang of elemental things.
Lincoln, The Man of the People, st. 2

7   He went down
As when a lordly cedar, green with boughs,
Goes down with a great shout upon the hills,
And leaves a lonesome place against the sky.
Lincoln, The Man of the People, st. 4

George Moore
1852–1933

8   All reformers are bachelors — all extreme reformers have been bachelors.
The Bending of the Bough [1900], act I

---

[1]Oglala Sioux chief.

[2]Inspired by Jean-François Millet's painting.

[3]A man to match his mountains, not to creep / Dwarfed and abased below them. — JOHN GREENLEAF WHITTIER, *Among the Hills* [1869], *prelude*

Bring me men to match my mountains. — SAM WALTER FOSS, *The Coming American*

9 After all there is but one race — humanity.
The Bending of the Bough, III

10 A man travels the world over in search of what he needs and returns home to find it.
The Brook Kerith [1916], ch. 11

Henry Van Dyke
1852–1933

11 The lintel low enough to keep out pomp and pride:
The threshold high enough to turn deceit aside.
For the Friends at Hurstmont. The Door

12 Self is the only prison that can ever bind the soul.
The Prison and the Angel

13 The first day of spring is one thing, and the first spring day is another. The difference between them is sometimes as great as a month.
Fisherman's Luck [1899], ch. 5

James Davis [Owen Hall]
1853–1907

14 O tell me, pretty maiden, are there any more at home like you?
Florodora [1900], act II

Edgar Watson Howe
1853–1937

15 What people say behind your back is your standing in the community.
Country Town Sayings [1911]

16 There is nothing so well known as that we should not expect something for nothing — but we all do and call it Hope.
Country Town Sayings

José [Julian] Martí [y Perez]
1853–1895

17 Love is . . . born with the pleasure of looking at each other, it is fed with the necessity of seeing each other, it is concluded with the impossibility of separation!
Amor [1881]

18 A knowledge of different literatures is the best way to free one's self from the tyranny of any of them.
On Oscar Wilde [1882]

19 Man needs to suffer. When he does not have real griefs he creates them. Griefs purify and prepare him.
Adúltera (Adulterous Thoughts) [1883]

1   Terrible times in which priests no longer merit the praise of poets and in which poets have not yet begun to be priests.
On "El Poema de Niágara" of Pérez Bonalde [1883]

2   Men are products, expressions, reflections; they live to the extent that they coincide with their epoch, or to the extent that they differ markedly from it.   *Henry Ward Beecher [1887]*

3   A grain of poetry suffices to season a century.
Dedication of the Statue of Liberty [1887]

4   Others go to bed with their mistresses; I with my ideas.   *Letter [1890]*

5   Man needs to go outside himself in order to find repose and reveal himself.
Vivir en Sí (To Live in Oneself) [1891]

6   Mankind is composed of two sorts of men— those who love and create, and those who hate and destroy.   *Letter to a Cuban farmer [1893]*

7   Men have no special right because they belong to one race or another: the word man defines all rights.   *Mi Raza (My Race) [1893]*

8 I wish to leave the world
By its natural door;
In my tomb of green leaves
They are to carry me to die.
Do not put me in the dark
To die like a traitor;
I am good, and like a good thing
I will die with my face to the sun.
A Morir (To Die) [1894]

9   Only those who hate the Negro see hatred in the Negro.   *Manifesto of Montecristi [1895]*

10   The spirit of a government must be that of the country. The form of a government must come from the makeup of the country. Government is nothing but the balance of the natural elements of a country.   *Our America [1891]*

11   I have lived in the monster [the United States] and I know its insides; and my sling is the sling of David.   *Letter to Manuel Mercado [1895]*

Cecil [John] Rhodes
1853–1902

12   I desire to encourage and foster an appreciation of the advantages which will result from the union of the English-speaking peoples throughout the world, and to encourage in the students from the United States of America an attachment to the country from which they have sprung without I hope withdraw-

ing them or their sympathies from the land of their adoption or birth.
His will, establishing the Rhodes Scholarship

13   So little done—so much to do.   *Last word*

James A. Bland
1854–1911

14 Carry me back to old Virginny,
There's where the cotton and the corn and taters grow;
There's where the birds warble sweet in the springtime,
There's where this old darky's heart am longed to go.
Carry Me Back to Old Virginny [1875], st. 1

Sir James George Frazer
1854–1941

15   Dwellers by the sea cannot fail to be impressed by the sight of its ceaseless ebb and flow, and are apt, on the principles of that rude philosophy of sympathy and resemblance . . . to trace a subtle relation, a secret harmony, between its tides and the life of man. . . . The belief that most deaths happen at ebb tide is said to be held along the east coast of England from Northumberland to Kent.
The Golden Bough [1922],[1] ch. 3

16   The heaviest calamity in English history, the breach with America, might never have occurred if George the Third had not been an honest dullard.
The Golden Bough, 3

17   By religion, then, I understand a propitiation or conciliation of powers superior to man which are believed to direct and control the course of nature and of human life.   *The Golden Bough, 4*

18   It is a common rule with primitive people not to waken a sleeper, because his soul is away and might not have time to get back.
The Golden Bough, 18

19   The awe and dread with which the untutored savage contemplates his mother-in-law are amongst the most familiar facts of anthropology.
The Golden Bough, 18

20   When all is said and done our resemblances to the savage are still far more numerous than our differences from him.   *The Golden Bough, 23*

21   The world cannot live at the level of its great men.   *The Golden Bough, 37*

---

[1]Abridged one-volume edition. The original appeared in twelve volumes [1890–1915].

Thomas Riley Marshall
1854–1925

1 What this country needs is a really good five-cent cigar.[1]

Remark while presiding over the Senate

Jules Henri Poincaré
1854–1912

2 To doubt everything or to believe everything are two equally convenient solutions; both dispense with the necessity of reflection.

Quoted by BERTRAND RUSSELL *in preface to Science and Method [1913] (La Science et l'Hypothèse, 1903)*[2]

3 Science is built up with facts, as a house is with stones. But a collection of facts is no more a science than a heap of stones is a house.

Quoted by BERTRAND RUSSELL *in preface to Science and Method*

4 Sociology is the science with the greatest number of methods and the least results.

La Science et l'Hypothèse, ch. 1

Arthur Rimbaud
1854–1891

5 I went out under the sky, Muse! and I was your vassal.[3]

Ma Bohème. Fantaisie

6 My tavern was the Big Bear.
My stars in the sky rustled softly.[4]

Ma Bohème. Fantaisie

7 My sad heart foams at the stern.[5]

Le Coeur Volé

8 Lighter than a cork I danced on the waves.[6]

Le Bateau Ivre [1871]

9 Sweeter than apples to children
The green water spurted through my wooden hull.[7]

Le Bateau Ivre

10 I have bathed in the Poem
Of the Sea . . .
Devouring the green azures.[8]

Le Bateau Ivre

11 I have seen the sunset, stained with mystic horrors,
Illumine the rolling waves with long purple forms,
Like actors in ancient plays.[9]

Le Bateau Ivre

12 I long for Europe of the ancient parapets.[10]

Le Bateau Ivre

13 I have seen starry archipelagoes! and islands
Whose raving skies are opened to the voyager:
Is it in these bottomless nights that you sleep, in exile,
A million golden birds, O future Vigor?[11]

Le Bateau Ivre

14 Black A, white E, red I, green U, blue O: vowels,
Someday I shall recount your latent births.[12]

Voyelles [1871]

15 It is found again.
What? Eternity.
It is the sea
Gone with the sun.[13]

L'Éternité [1872]

16 O seasons, O châteaux,
What soul is without flaws?[14]

Bonheur, refrain

17 One evening, I sat Beauty in my lap.—And I found her bitter.—And I cursed her.

Une Saison en Enfer [1873]

18 I found I could extinguish all human hope from my soul.

Une Saison en Enfer

19 Baptism enslaved me.

Une Saison en Enfer. Nuit de l'Enfer

20 I am the master of fantasy.

Une Saison en Enfer. Nuit de l'Enfer

21 Old poetics played a large part in my alchemy of the word.

Une Saison en Enfer. Délires

22 I! I who fashioned myself a sorcerer or an angel, who dispensed with all morality, I have come back to the earth.

Une Saison en Enfer. Adieu

---

[1]What this country needs is a good five-cent nickel. — FRANKLIN P. ADAMS

[2]Translated by G. B. HALSTED.

[3]J'allais sous le ciel, Muse! et j'étais ton féal.

[4]Mon auberge était à la Grande Ourse. / Mes étoiles au ciel avaient un doux frou-frou.

[5]Mon triste coeur bave à la poupe.

[6]Plus léger qu'un bouchon j'ai dansé sur les flots.

[7]Plus douce qu'aux enfants la chair des pommes sures, / L'eau verte pénétra ma coque de sapin.

[8]Je me suis baigné dans le Poème / De la Mer . . . / Dévorant les azurs verts.

[9]J'ai vu le soleil bas, taché d'horreurs mystiques, / Illuminant de longs figements violets, / Pareils à des acteurs des drames très antiques.

[10]Je regrette l'Europe aux anciens parapets!

[11]J'ai vu des archipels sidéraux! et des îles / Dont les cieux délirants sont ouverts au voyageur: / Est-ce en ces nuits sans fonds que tu dors et t'exiles, / Million d'oiseaux d'or, ô future Vigueur?

[12]A noir, E blanc, I rouge, U vert, O bleu: voyelles, / Je dirai quelque jour vos naissances latentes!

[13]Elle est retrouvée, / Quoi? — L'Éternité. / C'est la mer allée / Avec le soleil.

[14]O saisons, O châteaux / Quelle âme est sans défauts?

1   One must be absolutely modern.
Une Saison en Enfer. Adieu

2   I have embraced the summer dawn.
Illuminations [1874]. Aube

3   It rains softly on the town.[1]   *From a lost poem*

4   I say one must be a *seer*, make oneself a *seer*. The poet makes himself a *seer* by an immense, long, deliberate *derangement* of all the senses.[2]
Letter to Paul Demeny [May 15, 1871]

Willard Duncan Vandiver
1854–1932

5   I come from a state that raises corn and cotton and cockleburs and Democrats, and frothy eloquence neither convinces nor satisfies me. I am from Missouri. You have got to show me.
Speech at a naval banquet in Philadelphia [1899]

Oscar [Fingal O'Flahertie Wills] Wilde
1854–1900

6 Tread lightly, she is near
Under the snow,
Speak gently, she can hear
The daisies grow.   *Requiescat, st. 1*

7 And down the long and silent street,
The dawn, with silver-sandaled feet,
Crept like a frightened girl.
The Harlot's House, st. 6

8   A poet can survive everything but a misprint.
The Children of the Poets

9   Meredith is a prose Browning, and so is Browning. He used poetry as a medium for writing in prose.
The Critic as Artist [1891], pt. I

10   As long as war is regarded as wicked, it will always have its fascination. When it is looked upon as vulgar, it will cease to be popular.
The Critic as Artist, II

11   There is no such thing as a moral or an immoral book. Books are well written, or badly written. That is all.
The Picture of Dorian Gray [1891], preface

12   All art is quite useless.
The Picture of Dorian Gray, preface

13   There is only one thing in the world worse tha[n] being talked about, and that is not being talke[d] about.   *The Picture of Dorian Gray, ch.*

14   A man cannot be too careful in the choice of h[is] enemies.   *The Picture of Dorian Gray,*

15   The only way to get rid of a temptation is t[o] yield to it.   *The Picture of Dorian Gray,*

16   He knew the precise psychological momen[t] when to say nothing.
The Picture of Dorian Gray,

17   The only difference between a caprice and a life-long passion is that the caprice lasts a little longer.
The Picture of Dorian Gray,

18   Children begin by loving their parents; as the[y] grow older they judge them; sometimes they fo[r]give them.   *The Picture of Dorian Gray,*

19   Over the piano was printed a notice: Please d[o] not shoot the pianist. He is doing his best.
Personal Impressions of America (Leadville) [1883]

20   Nowadays we are all of us so hard up that the on[ly] pleasant things to pay are compliments. They're th[e] only things we can pay.
Lady Windermere's Fan [1892], act

21   I can resist everything except temptation.
Lady Windermere's Fan,

22   We are all in the gutter, but some of us are look-ing at the stars.   *Lady Windermere's Fan, II*

23   In this world there are only two tragedies. On[e] is not getting what one wants, and the other is ge[t]ting it.   *Lady Windermere's Fan, II*

24   What is a cynic? A man who knows the price [of] everything, and the value of nothing.
Lady Windermere's Fan, II

25   Experience is the name everyone gives to the[ir] mistakes.   *Lady Windermere's Fan, II*

26   I have never admitted that I am more than twenty-nine, or thirty at the most. Twenty-nine when ther[e] are pink shades, thirty when there are not.[4]
Lady Windermere's Fan, I

---

[1]Il pleut doucement sur la ville.
Paul Verlaine used this as an epigraph for his *Ariettes Oubliées, III.*

[2]Je dis qu'il faut être *voyant*, se faire *voyant*. Le poète se fait *voyant* par un long, immense et raisonné *dérèglement* de tous les sens.

[3]In all considerations the psychological momentum or fact[or] must be allowed to play a prominent part, for without its cooper[a]tion there is little to be hoped from the work of the artillery.—
Neue Preussische Kreuzzeitung [December 16, 1870], *commentin[g] upon the siege of Paris*
An error in translation gave us "psychological moment" (i.[e.] the critical moment). The Parisians ridiculed the phrase as an e[x]ample of German pedantry, but it speedily became universal.

[4]When you come to write my epitaph, Charles, let it be in the[se] delicious words, "She had a long twenty-nine." —SIR JAMES BA[R]RIE, *Rosalind*

1 *Mrs. Allonby:* They say, Lady Hunstanton, that when good Americans die they go to Paris.[1]

Lady Hunstanton: Indeed? And when bad Americans die, where do they go to?

Lord Illingworth: Oh, they go to America.

  A Woman of No Importance [1893], act I

2 The youth of America is their oldest tradition. It has been going on now for three hundred years.

  A Woman of No Importance, I

3 *Lord Illingworth:* The Book of Life begins with a man and a woman in a garden.

Mrs. Allonby: It ends with Revelations.

  A Woman of No Importance, I

4 I suppose society is wonderfully delightful. To be in it is merely a bore. But to be out of it simply a tragedy. *A Woman of No Importance, III*

5 Really, if the lower orders don't set us a good example, what on earth is the use of them?

  The Importance of Being Earnest [1895], act I

6 Her hair has turned quite gold from grief.

  The Importance of Being Earnest, I

7 I have invented an invaluable permanent invalid called Bunbury, in order that I may be able to go down into the country whenever I choose.

  The Importance of Being Earnest, I

8 Of course the music is a great difficulty. You see, if one plays good music, people don't listen, and if one plays bad music people don't talk.

  The Importance of Being Earnest, I

9 To lose one parent, Mr. Worthing, may be regarded as a misfortune; to lose both looks like carelessness. *The Importance of Being Earnest, I*

10 Relations are simply a tedious pack of people, who haven't got the remotest knowledge of how to live, nor the smallest instinct about when to die.

  The Importance of Being Earnest, I

11 I never travel without my diary. One should always have something sensational to read in the train. *The Importance of Being Earnest, II*

12 Thirty-five is a very attractive age. London society is full of women of the very highest birth who have, of their own free choice, remained thirty-five for years. *The Importance of Being Earnest, III*

13 The fact is, that civilization requires slaves. The Greeks were quite right there. Unless there are slaves to do the ugly, horrible, uninteresting work, culture and contemplation become almost impossible. Human slavery is wrong, insecure, and demoralizing. On mechanical slavery, on the slavery of the machine, the future of the world depends.

  The Soul of Man Under Socialism [1895]

14 Charity creates a multitude of sins.

  The Soul of Man Under Socialism

15 Anybody can make history. Only a great man can write it. *Aphorisms*

16 I never saw a man who looked
With such a wistful eye
Upon that little tent of blue
Which prisoners call the sky.

  The Ballad of Reading Gaol [1898], pt. I, st. 3

17 When a voice behind me whispered low,
"That fellow's got to swing."

  The Ballad of Reading Gaol, I, st. 4

18 Yet each man kills the thing he loves,
By each let this be heard,
Some do it with a bitter look,
Some with a flattering word.
The coward does it with a kiss,
The brave man with a sword!

  The Ballad of Reading Gaol, I, st. 7

19 It is sweet to dance to violins
When Love and Life are fair:
To dance to flutes, to dance to lutes
Is delicate and rare:
But it is not sweet with nimble feet
To dance upon the air!

  The Ballad of Reading Gaol, II, st. 9

20 Something was dead in each of us,
And what was dead was Hope.

  The Ballad of Reading Gaol, III, st. 31

21 And the wild regrets, and the bloody sweats,
None knew so well as I:
For he who lives more lives than one
More deaths than one must die.

  The Ballad of Reading Gaol, III, st. 37

22 I know not whether laws be right,
Or whether laws be wrong;
All that we know who lie in gaol
Is that the wall is strong;
And that each day is like a year,
A year whose days are long.

  The Ballad of Reading Gaol, V, st. 1

23 The vilest deeds like poison weeds
Bloom well in prison air:
It is only what is good in man
That wastes and withers there:
Pale Anguish keeps the heavy gate
And the Warder is Despair.

  The Ballad of Reading Gaol, V, st. 5

---

[1]Good Americans, when they die, go to Paris. — THOMAS GOLD APPLETON [1812–1884]; *from* OLIVER WENDELL HOLMES, *The Autocrat of the Breakfast-Table* [1858]

1 How else but through a broken heart
May Lord Christ enter in?
The Ballad of Reading Gaol, V, st. 14

2   Where there is sorrow there is holy ground.
De Profundis [1905]

3   The English country gentleman galloping after a
fox—the unspeakable in full pursuit of the uneatable.   *De Profundis*

4   One must have a heart of stone to read the death
of Little Nell without laughing.
From RICHARD ELLMANN, Oscar Wilde [1988]

5   My wallpaper and I are fighting a duel to the
death. One or the other of us has to go.
From RICHARD ELLMANN, Oscar Wilde

William Cowper Brann[1]
1855–1898

6   Boston runs to brains as well as to beans and
brown bread. But she is cursed with an army of
cranks whom nothing short of a straitjacket or a
swamp elm club will ever control.
From The Iconoclast. Beans and Blood

Henry Cuyler Bunner
1855–1896

7 Off with your hat as the flag goes by!
Airs from Arcady [1888]. The Old Flag, st. 1

Eugene V[ictor] Debs
1855–1926

8   While there is a lower class I am in it, while there
is a criminal element I am of it; while there is a soul
in prison, I am not free.
Speech at trial for sedition [September 14, 1918]

Margaret Wolfe Hungerford
1855–1897

9   Beauty is in the eye of the beholder.
Molly Bawn [1878]

Sir Arthur Wing Pinero
1855–1934

10   From forty till fifty a man is at heart either a stoic
or a satyr.
The Second Mrs. Tanqueray [1893], act I

---

[1]Known as "The Iconoclast" from the name of his paper, first
published in Austin, Texas, and later in Waco.

Olive Schreiner [Ralph Iron]
1855–1920

11   The barb in the arrow of childhood suffering i
this: its intense loneliness, its intense ignorance.
The Story of an African Farm [1884], ch. I

12   There never was a man who said one word fo
woman but he said two for man and three for the
whole human race.
The Story of an African Farm, 4

William Sharp [Fiona Macleod]
1855–1905

13 My heart is a lonely hunter that hunts on a lonely
hill.   *The Lonely Hunter, st. 6*

L[yman] Frank Baum
1856–1919

14   The wicked Witch of the East.
The Wonderful Wizard of Oz[2] [1900], ch. 2

15   The road to the City of Emeralds is paved with
yellow brick.   *The Wonderful Wizard of Oz, 2*

16   I'm really a very good man; but I'm a very bad
Wizard.   *The Wonderful Wizard of Oz, 15*

Francis Bellamy
1856–1931

17   I pledge allegiance to the flag of the United
States of America and to the republic for which it
stands, one nation under God, indivisible, with liberty and justice for all.
The Pledge of Allegiance to the Flag [1892][3]

Theobald von Bethmann-Hollweg
1856–1921

18   Just for a word—"neutrality," a word which in
wartime has so often been disregarded, just for a
scrap of paper—Great Britain is going to make war.
To Sir Edward Goschen [August 4, 1914]

---

[2]See Harburg, 752:1, and Langley, 786.

[3]In 1888 JAMES B. UPHAM [1845–1905] wrote a draft that Bel-
lamy, chairman of a national celebration of the 400th anniversary
of America's discovery, helped put in final form:

I pledge allegiance to my flag and to the republic for which it
stands: one nation indivisible, with liberty and justice for all.

More than thirty years later, "my flag" was changed to "the flag
of the United States of America"; in 1954 an act of Congress
added "under God."

Louis D[embitz] Brandeis
1856–1941

1   Those who won our independence believed that the final end of the State was to make men free to develop their faculties; and that in its government the deliberative forces should prevail over the arbitrary. They valued liberty both as an end and as a means. They believed liberty to be the secret of happiness and courage to be the secret of liberty.
> *Whitney v. California, 274 U.S. 357, 375 [1927]*

2   Fear of serious injury cannot alone justify suppression of free speech and assembly. Men feared witches and burned women. It is the function of speech to free men from the bondage of irrational fears.   *Whitney v. California, 274 U.S. 357, 376*

3   They [the makers of the Constitution] conferred, as against the Government, the right to be let alone—the most comprehensive of rights and the right most valued by civilized men.
> *Olmstead v. United States, 277 U.S. 438, 478 [1928]*

4   If we would guide by the light of reason, we must let our minds be bold.
> *New State Ice Co. v. Liebmann, 285 U.S. 262, 311 [1932]*

5   The Court bows to the lessons of experience and the force of better reasoning, recognizing that the process of trial and error, so fruitful in the physical sciences, is appropriate also in the judicial function.
> *Burnet v. Coronado Oil and Gas Co., 285 U.S. 393, 406 [1932]*

6   There is in most Americans some spark of idealism, which can be fanned into a flame. It takes sometimes a divining rod to find what it is; but when found, and that means often, when disclosed to the owners, the results are often most extraordinary.   *The Words of Justice Brandeis [1953]*

Sigmund Freud[1]
1856–1939

7   The new psychoanalytic method [is] . . . somewhat subtle but irreplaceable, so fruitful has it proved to be in explaining obscure unconscious mental processes.[2]
> *Heredity and the Aetiology of the Neuroses [1896]*

8   The interpretation of dreams is the royal road to a knowledge of the unconscious activities of the mind.
> *The Interpretation of Dreams [1900], ch. 7*

9   When a member of my family complains to me of having bitten his tongue, pinched a finger, or the like, he does not get the sympathy he hopes for but instead the question: "Why did you do that?"
> *The Psychopathology of Everyday Life [1901], ch. 8*

10   Our hysterical patients suffer from reminiscences.
> *Five Lectures on Psychoanalysis [1910]. I*

11   The psychic development of the individual is a short repetition of the course of development of the race.[3]   *Leonardo da Vinci [1910]*

12   At bottom God is nothing other than an exalted father.   *Totem and Taboo [1913]. Pt. 4*

13   We believe that civilization has been created under the pressure of the exigencies of life at the cost of satisfaction of the instincts.
> *Introductory Lectures on Psychoanalysis [1916–1917]. Lecture I*

14   If a man has been his mother's undisputed darling he retains throughout life the triumphant feeling, the confidence in success, which not seldom brings actual success with it.
> *A Childhood Memory of Goethe's [1917]*

15   A culture which leaves unsatisfied and drives to rebelliousness so large a number of its members neither has a prospect of continued existence nor deserves it.
> *The Future of an Illusion [1927]*

16   Before the problem of the creative writer, analysis must lay down its arms.
> *Dostoevsky and Parricide [1928]*

17   Men have gained control over the forces of nature to such an extent that with their help they could have no difficulty in exterminating one another to the last man. They know this, and hence comes a large part of their current unrest, their unhappiness and their mood of anxiety.
> *Civilization and Its Discontents [1930], pt. VIII*

18   The ego's relation to the id might be compared with that of a rider to his horse. The horse supplies the locomotive energy, while the rider has the privilege of deciding on the goal and of guiding the powerful animal's movement. But only too often there arises between the ego and the id the not pre-

---

[1]Translated under the general editorship of JAMES STRACHEY, except for 607:7 and 608:4.

[2]Translated by M. MEYER.
   Apparently Freud's first published use of the root term "psychoanalytic."

[3]See Haeckel, 556:5.

cisely ideal situation of the rider being obliged to guide the horse along the path by which it itself wants to go.

New Introductory Lectures on Psycho-analysis [1933], lecture 31

1   The poor ego ... serves three severe masters and does what it can to bring their claims and demands into harmony with one another. No wonder that the ego so often fails in its task. Its three tyrannical masters are the external world, the super-ego and the id.

New Introductory Lectures on Psycho-analysis, 31

2   Where id was, there ego shall be.

New Introductory Lectures on Psycho-analysis, 31

3   Religion is an illusion and it derives its strength from its readiness to fit in with our instinctual wishful impulses.

New Introductory Lectures on Psycho-analysis, 35

4   It almost looks as if analysis were the third of those "impossible" professions in which one can be quite sure of unsatisfying results. The other two, much older-established, are the bringing-up of children and the government of nations.[1]

Analysis Terminable and Interminable [1937]

5   Judaism had been a religion of the father; Christianity became a religion of the son. The old God the Father fell back behind Christ; Christ, the Son, took his place, just as every son had hoped to do in primeval times.

Moses and Monotheism [1938], pt. III, sec. 1

6   The great question ... which I have not been able to answer, despite my thirty years of research into the feminine soul, is "What does a woman want?"[2]

From ERNEST JONES, Life and Work of Sigmund Freud, vol. II [1955], ch. 16

7   The poets and philosophers before me discovered the unconscious; what I discovered was the scientific method by which the unconscious can be studied.

On his seventieth birthday [1926]. From LIONEL TRILLING, The Liberal Imagination [1957]

8   Yes, America is gigantic, but a giant mistake.

From ERNEST JONES, Free Associations [1962]

9   To love and to work.[3]

From ERIK H. ERIKSON, Childhood and Society [1963]

10   Sometimes a cigar is just a cigar.   *Attributed*

Edmond Haraucourt
1856–1941

11 To leave is to die a little;
To die to what we love.
We leave behind a bit of ourselves
Wherever we have been.[4]

Choix de Poésies [1891]. Rondel de l'Adieu

Elbert Hubbard
1856–1915

12   It is not book learning young men need, nor instruction about this and that, but a stiffening of the vertebrae which will cause them to be loyal to a trust, to act promptly, concentrate their energies, do a thing — "carry a message to Garcia."[5]

A Message to Garcia [March 1899]

Robert E[dwin] Peary
1856–1920

13   The Eskimo, Ootah, had his own explanation. Said he: "The devil is asleep or having trouble with his wife, or we should never have come back so easily."

The North Pole [1910]

Henri Philippe Pétain
1856–1951

14   They shall not pass.[6]

Attributed. Verdun [February 26, 1916]

---

[3]Lieben und arbeiten.
Describing "what he thought a normal person should be able to do well" [Erikson].

[4]Partir, c'est mourir un peu; / C'est mourir à ce qu'on aime. / On laisse un peu de soi-même / En toute heure et dans tout lieu.
Translated by NORBERT GUTERMAN. The first line is a French proverb.

[5]After the declaration of the Spanish-American War, Andrew Summers Rowan, then lieutenant, United States Bureau of Military Intelligence, was sent to communicate with General Calixto Garcia. He landed in an open boat near Turquino Peak [April 24, 1898], executed the mission, and brought back information regarding the insurgent army.

[6]Ils ne passeront pas.
The first official record of the expression appears in General Nivelle's Order of the Day [June 23, 1916] to his troops at the height of battle: Vous ne les laisserez pas passer [You will not let them pass]! — ALAN HORNE, *New York Times Magazine* [February 20, 1966].
The inscription on the Verdun medal is: On ne passe pas.

---

[1]Translated by JOAN RIVIERE.
[2]Was will das Weib?

George Bernard Shaw
1856–1950

1   My method is to take the utmost trouble to find the right thing to say, and then to say it with the utmost levity.   *Answers to Nine Questions*

2   It's well to be off with the Old Woman before you're on with the New.
The Philanderer [1893], act II

3   The fickleness of the women I love is only equaled by the infernal constancy of the women who love me.   *The Philanderer, II*

4   The test of a man or woman's breeding is how they behave in a quarrel.   *The Philanderer, IV*

5   People are always blaming their circumstances for what they are. I don't believe in circumstances. The people who get on in this world are the people who get up and look for the circumstances they want, and, if they can't find them, make them.
Mrs. Warren's Profession [1893], act II

6   There are no secrets better kept than the secrets that everybody guesses.
Mrs. Warren's Profession, III

7   A great devotee of the Gospel of Getting On.
Mrs. Warren's Profession, IV

8   We have no more right to consume happiness without producing it than to consume wealth without producing it.   *Candida [1898], act I*

9   I'm only a beer teetotaler, not a champagne teetotaler. I don't like beer.   *Candida, III*

10   We don't bother much about dress and manners in England, because as a nation we don't dress well and we've no manners.
You Never Can Tell [1898], act I

11   The great advantage of a hotel is that it's a refuge from home life.   *You Never Can Tell, II*

12   There is only one religion, though there are a hundred versions of it.
*Plays Pleasant and Unpleasant [1898],
vol. II, preface*

13   You're not a man, you're a machine.
Arms and the Man [1898], act III

14   The worst sin towards our fellow creatures is not to hate them, but to be indifferent to them: that's the essence of inhumanity.
The Devil's Disciple [1901], act II

15   This is the true joy in life, the being used for a purpose recognized by yourself as a mighty one; the being thoroughly worn out before you are thrown on the scrap heap; the being a force of nature instead of a feverish selfish little clod of ailments and grievances complaining that the world will not devote itself to making you happy.
Man and Superman [1903], epistle dedicatory

16   A lifetime of happiness! No man alive could bear it: it would be hell on earth.
Man and Superman, act I

17   The more things a man is ashamed of, the more respectable he is.   *Man and Superman, I*

18   Marry Ann; and at the end of a week you'll find no more inspiration in her than in a plate of muffins.
Man and Superman, II

19   Hell is full of musical amateurs: music is the brandy of the damned.
Man and Superman, III

20   An Englishman thinks he is moral when he is only uncomfortable.   *Man and Superman, III*

21   There are two tragedies in life. One is to lose your heart's desire. The other is to gain it.[1]
Man and Superman, IV

22   The golden rule is that there are no golden rules.
Man and Superman. Maxims for Revolutionists

23   He who can, does. He who cannot, teaches.
Man and Superman. Maxims for Revolutionists

24   Marriage is popular because it combines the maximum of temptation with the maximum of opportunity.
Man and Superman. Maxims for Revolutionists

25   If you strike a child, take care that you strike it in anger, even at the risk of maiming it for life. A blow in cold blood neither can nor should be forgiven.
Man and Superman. Maxims for Revolutionists

26   Virtue consists, not in abstaining from vice, but in not desiring it.
Man and Superman. Maxims for Revolutionists

27   The greatest of our evils and the worst of our crimes is poverty.
Major Barbara [1905], preface

28   I am a Millionaire. That is my religion.
Major Barbara, act II

29   With the single exception of Homer, there is no eminent writer, not even Sir Walter Scott, whom I can despise so entirely as I despise Shakespeare when I measure my mind against his. . . . It would posi-

---

[1]See Wilde, 604:23.

tively be a relief to me to dig him up and throw stones at him.
> *Dramatic Opinions and Essays [1907].*
> *Blaming the Bard*

1   When two people are under the influence of the most violent, most insane, most delusive, and most transient of passions, they are required to swear that they will remain in that excited, abnormal, and exhausting condition continuously until death do them part.   *Getting Married [1908], preface*

2   I like a bit of a mongrel myself, whether it's a man or a dog; they're the best for every day.
> *Misalliance [1910], episode I*

3   If parents would only realize how they bore their children!   *Misalliance, I*

4   It is impossible for an Englishman to open his mouth, without making some other Englishman hate or despise him; English is not accessible even to Englishmen.   *Pygmalion [1913],*[1] *preface*

5   Women upset everything. When you let them into your life, you find that the woman is driving at one thing and you're driving at another.
> *Pygmalion, act II*

6   *Pickering:* Have you no morals, man?
> *Doolittle:* Can't afford them, Governor.
> *Pygmalion, II*

7   I'm one of the undeserving poor.   *Pygmalion, II*

8   Gin was mother's milk to her.   *Pygmalion, III*

9   All great truths begin as blasphemies.
> *Annajanska [1919]*

10   You see things; and you say, "Why?" But I dream things that never were; and I say, "Why not?"
> *Back to Methuselah [1921], pt. I, act I*

11   The nauseous sham goodfellowship our democratic public men get up for shop use.
> *Back to Methuselah, II*

12   Everything happens to everybody sooner or later if there is time enough.   *Back to Methuselah, V*

13   Assassination is the extreme form of censorship.
> *The Rejected Statement, pt. I*

14   One man that has a mind and knows it can always beat ten men who haven't and don't.
> *The Apple Cart [1929], act I*

15   An American has no sense of privacy. He does not know what it means. There is no such thing in the country.   *Speech at New York [April 11, 1933]*

---

[1]The play upon which the musical *My Fair Lady* is based. See Lerner, 803:6–803:13.

Louis Henri Sullivan
1856–1924

16   Form ever follows function.
> *The Tall Office Building Artistically*
> *Considered. From Lippincott's Magazine*
> *[March 1896]*

Frederick Winslow Taylor
1856–1915

17   In the past the man has been first. In the futur the System must be first.
> *The Principles of Scientific Management*
> *[1911], ch. 1*

Brandon Thomas
1856–1914

18   I am Charley's aunt from Brazil, where the nut come from.   *Charley's Aunt [1892], act*

Booker T[aliaferro] Washington
1856–1915

19   In all things that are purely social we [black an white] can be as separate as the fingers, yet one a the hand in all things essential to mutual progress.
> *Speech at the Cotton States and International*
> *Exposition, Atlanta [September 18, 1895]*

20   No race can prosper till it learns that there is a much dignity in tilling a field as in writing a poem.
> *Up from Slavery [1901*

21   You can't hold a man down without stayin down with him.   *Attribute*

Woodrow Wilson
1856–1924

22   The United States must be neutral in fact as we as in name. . . . We must be impartial in thought a well as in action.
> *Message to the Senate [August 19, 1914*

23   You deal in the raw material of opinion, and, my convictions have any validity, opinion ultimate governs the world.
> *Address to the Associated Press [April 20,*
> *1915]*

1 There is such a thing as a man being too proud to fight.
> *Address to Foreign-Born Citizens [May 10, 1915]*

2 [The Civil War] created in this country what had never existed before—a national consciousness. It was not the salvation of the Union; it was the re-birth of the Union.
> *Memorial Day Address [1915]*

3 We have stood apart, studiously neutral.
> *Message to Congress [December 7, 1915]*

4 America cannot be an ostrich with its head in the sand.
> *Speech at Des Moines [February 1, 1916]*

5 It must be a peace without victory. . . . Only a peace between equals can last.
> *Address to the Senate [January 22, 1917]*

6 A little group of willful men, representing no opinion but their own, have rendered the great Government of the United States helpless and con-temptible.
> *Statement made in reference to certain members of the Senate [March 4, 1917]*[1]

7 Armed neutrality is ineffectual enough at best.
> *Address to Congress, asking for a declaration of war [April 2, 1917]*

8 The world must be made safe for democracy.
> *Address to Congress, asking for a declaration of war [April 2, 1917]*

9 The day has come when America is privileged to spend her blood and her might for the principles that gave her birth and happiness and the peace which she has treasured.
> *Address to Congress, asking for a declaration of war [April 2, 1917]*

10 1. Open covenants of peace, openly arrived at.
2. Absolute freedom of navigation upon the seas. . . .
5. A free, open-minded, and absolutely impartial adjustment of all colonial claims.
> *Address to Congress (The Fourteen Points) [January 8, 1918]*[2]

11 14. A general association of nations must be formed . . . for the purpose of affording mutual guarantees of political independence and territorial integrity to great and small states alike.
> *Address to Congress (The Fourteen Points) [January 8, 1918]*

12 If I am to speak for ten minutes, I need a week for preparation; if fifteen minutes, three days; if half an hour, two days; if an hour, I am ready now.
> *From* JOSEPHUS DANIELS, *The Wilson Era: Years of War and After [1946]*

13 It is like writing history with lightning. And my only regret is that it is all so terribly true.
> *Attributed. On seeing D. W.* GRIFFITH's *movie The Birth of a Nation, at the White House [February 18, 1915]*

Edward F[rancis] Albee
1857–1930

14 Never give a sucker an even break.[3]   *Remark*

Joseph Conrad
1857–1924

15 A work that aspires, however humbly, to the condition of art should carry its justification in every line.
> *The Nigger of the Narcissus [1898], preface*

16 But the artist appeals to that part of our being which is not dependent on wisdom; to that in us which is a gift and not an acquisition—and, there-fore, more permanently enduring. He speaks to our capacity for delight and wonder, to the sense of mystery surrounding our lives: to our sense of pity, and beauty, and pain.
> *The Nigger of the Narcissus, preface*

17 The ship, a fragment detached from the earth, went on lonely and swift like a small planet.
> *The Nigger of the Narcissus, ch. 2*

18 Goodbye, brothers! You were a good crowd. As good a crowd as ever fisted with wild cries the beat-ing canvas of a heavy foresail; or tossing aloft, invis-ible in the night, gave back yell for yell to a westerly gale.   *The Nigger of the Narcissus, 5*

19 I am a great foe to favoritism in public life, in private life, and even in the delicate relationship of an author to his works.
> *Lord Jim [1900], author's note*

20 There is a weird power in a spoken word. . . . And a word carries far—very far—deals destruc-tion through time as the bullets go flying through space.   *Lord Jim, ch. 15*

---

[1]Eleven senators had conducted a filibuster against a bill author-izing the arming of American merchant vessels.

[2]See Clemenceau, 577:10.

[3]According to the *Morris Dictionary of Word and Phrase Origins* [1977], this is often attributed to W. C. Fields, who uttered it in *Poppy* [1923]. He made the quote famous.

1   That faculty of beholding at a hint the face of his desire and the shape of his dream, without which the earth would know no lover and no adventurer.
Lord Jim, 16

2   Only a moment; a moment of strength, of romance, of glamour—of youth! . . . A flick of sunshine upon a strange shore, the time to remember, the time for a sigh, and—goodbye!—Night—Goodbye . . . !
Youth [1902]

3   She strode like a grenadier, was strong and upright like an obelisk, had a beautiful face, a candid brow, pure eyes, and not a thought of her own in her head.
Tales of Unrest [1902]. The Return

4   Running . . . all over the sea trying to get behind the weather.
Typhoon [1902], ch. 2

5   We live, as we dream—alone.
Heart of Darkness [1902],[1] *I*

6   I don't like work—no man does—but I like what is in work—the chance to find yourself. Your own reality—for yourself, not for others—what no other man can ever know.
Heart of Darkness, I

7   No fear can stand up to hunger, no patience can wear it out, disgust simply does not exist where hunger is; and as to superstition, beliefs, and what you may call principles, they are less than chaff in a breeze.
Heart of Darkness, II

8   Exterminate all the brutes![2]
Heart of Darkness, II

9   The horror! The horror!
Heart of Darkness, III

10   Mistah Kurtz—he dead.
Heart of Darkness, III

11   The air of the New World seems favorable to the art of declamation.
Nostromo [1904], ch. 6

12   The terrorist and the policeman both come from the same basket. Revolution, legality—countermoves in the same game; forms of idleness at bottom identical.
The Secret Agent [1907], ch. 4

13   A man's real life is that accorded to him in the thoughts of other men by reason of respect or natural love.
Under Western Eyes [1911], pt. I, ch. I

14   Let a fool be made serviceable according to his folly.
Under Western Eyes, I, 3

15   The belief in a supernatural source of evil is not necessary; men alone are quite capable of every wickedness.
Under Western Eyes, II, 4

16   All ambitions are lawful except those which climb upward on the miseries or credulities of mankind.
A Personal Record [1912], preface

17   Only in men's imagination does every truth find an effective and undeniable existence. Imagination, not invention, is the supreme master of art as of life.
A Personal Record, ch. 1

18   Historian of fine consciences.
Notes on Life and Letters [1921]. Henry James, An Appreciation

Émile Coué
1857–1926

19   Every day, in every way, I'm getting better and better.[3]
Formula of his faith cures, inscribed in his sanitarium, Nancy, France

Clarence [Seward] Darrow
1857–1938

20   I do not consider it an insult, but rather a compliment to be called an agnostic. I do not pretend to know where many ignorant men are sure—that is all that agnosticism means.
Scopes trial, Dayton, Tennessee [July 13, 1925]

21   I don't believe in God because I don't believe in Mother Goose.
Speech at Toronto [1930]

22   There is no such thing as justice—in or out of court.
Interview at Chicago [April 1936]

John Davidson
1857–1909

23   In anguish we uplift
A new unhallowed song:
The race is to the swift;
The battle to the strong.
War Song, st. 1

---

[1]"Heart of Darkness" is experience . . . but it is experience pushed a little (and only very little) beyond the actual facts of the case for the perfectly legitimate, I believe, purpose of bringing it home to the minds and bosoms of the readers. . . . That somber theme had to be given a sinister resonance, a tonality of its own, a continued vibration that, I hoped, would hang in the air and dwell on the ear after the last note had been struck.—CONRAD, *Youth: A Narrative, and Two Other Stories, author's preface*

[2]For two hundred years, the Judges of England sat on the Bench, condemning to the penalty of death every man, woman, and child who stole property to the value of five shillings; and, during all that time, not one Judge ever remonstrated against the law. We English are a nation of brutes, and ought to be exterminated to the last man.—JOHN BRIGHT [1880]; in HENRY ADAMS, *The Education of Henry Adams* [1907], ch. 12

---

[3]Tous les jours, à tous les points de vue, je vais de mieux en mieux.

1 And blood in torrents pour
  In vain—always in vain,
  For war breeds war again.   *War Song, st. 7*

Benjamin Franklin King, Jr.
1857–1894

2 Nowhere to go but out,
  Nowhere to come but back.   *The Pessimist, st. 4*

Edgar Smith
1857–1938

3 You may tempt the upper classes
  With your villainous demitasses,
  But Heaven will protect the working girl.
                Heaven Will Protect the Working Girl

Frank Lebby Stanton
1857–1927

4 Jest a-wearyin' fer you—
  All the time a-feelin' blue.
                Wearyin' for You,[1] *st. 1*

5 Sweetes' li'l' feller—
  Everybody knows;
  Dunno what ter call 'im,
  But he's mighty lak' a rose!
                Mighty Lak' a Rose,[2] *st. 1*

Thorstein Veblen
1857–1929

6 Conspicuous consumption of valuable goods is a means of reputability to the gentleman of leisure.
                The Theory of the Leisure Class [1899], ch. 4

7 With the exception of the instinct of self-preservation, the propensity for emulation is probably the strongest and most alert and persistent of the economic motives proper.
                The Theory of the Leisure Class, 5

8 The dog . . . commends himself to our favor by affording play to our propensity for mastery, and as he is also an item of expense, and commonly serves no industrial purpose, he holds a well-assured place in men's regard as a thing of good repute.
                The Theory of the Leisure Class, 6

9 The office of the leisure class in social evolution is to retard the movement and to conserve what is obsolescent.   *The Theory of the Leisure Class, 7*

---

[1] Music by CARRIE JACOBS BOND.
[2] Music by ETHELBERT NEVIN [1862–1901].

10 Priestly vestments show, in accentuated form, all the features that have been shown to be evidence of a servile status and a vicarious life.
                The Theory of the Leisure Class, 7

11 The walking-stick serves the purpose of an advertisement that the bearer's hands are employed otherwise than in useful effort, and it therefore has utility as an evidence of leisure. But it is also a weapon and it meets a felt need of barbarian man on that ground.
                The Theory of the Leisure Class, 10

12 In point of substantial merit the law school belongs in the modern university no more than a school of fencing or dancing.
                The Higher Learning in America [1918]

Franz Boas
1858–1942

13 The behavior of an individual is therefore determined not by his racial affiliation, but by the character of his ancestry and his cultural environment.
                Race and Democratic Society [1945], ch. 4

14 No one has ever proved that a human being, through his descent from a certain group of people, must of necessity have certain mental characteristics.   *Race and Democratic Society, 7*

Sam Walter Foss
1858–1911

15 The woods were made for the hunters of dreams,
   The brooks for the fishers of song;
   To the hunters who hunt for the gunless game
   The streams and the woods belong.
                The Bloodless Sportsman, st. 3

16 Let me live in my house by the side of the road
   And be a friend to man.
                The House by the Side of the Road, st. 5

H[enry] W[atson] Fowler
1858–1933
and
F[rancis] G[eorge] Fowler
1870–1918

17 Prefer geniality to grammar.
                The King's English [1906], ch. 2

18 HACKNEYED PHRASES. . . . The purpose with which these phrases are introduced is for the most part that of giving a fillip to a passage that might be

humdrum without them . . . but their true use when they come into the writer's mind is as danger signals; he should take warning that when they suggest themselves it is because what he is writing is bad stuff, or it would not need such help; let him see to the substance of his cake instead of decorating with sugarplums.

A Dictionary of Modern English Usage [1926][1]

1   QUOTATION. . . . A writer expresses himself in words that have been used before because they give his meaning better than he can give it himself, or because they are beautiful or witty, or because he expects them to touch a chord of association in his reader, or because he wishes to show that he is learned and well read. Quotations due to the last motive are invariably ill-advised; the discerning reader detects it and is contemptuous; the undiscerning is perhaps impressed, but even then is at the same time repelled, pretentious quotations being the surest road to tedium.

A Dictionary of Modern English Usage

2   THAT, *relative pronoun* . . . The two kinds of relative clause, to one of which *that* and to the other of which *which* is appropriate, are the defining and the nondefining;[2] and if writers would agree to regard *that* as the defining relative pronoun, and *which* as the nondefining, there would be much gain both in lucidity and in ease. Some there are who follow this principle now, but it would be idle to pretend that it is the practice either of the most or of the best writers.

A Dictionary of Modern English Usage

Remy de Gourmont
1858–1915

3   Aesthetic emotion puts man in a state favorable to the reception of erotic emotion. Art is the accomplice of love. Take love away and there is no longer art.   *Décadence*[3]

4   Man is a successful animal, that's all.

Promenades Philosophiques

Ruggiero Leoncavallo
1858–1919

5   The comedy is finished.[4]

I Pagliacci (The Clowns) [1892], last words

John Trotwood Moore
1858–1929

6   Only the gamefish swims upstream.

The Unafrai

Adolph S[imon] Ochs
1858–1935

7   All the news that's fit to print.

Motto of the New York Time

Ohiyesa
[Charles Alexander Eastman][5]
1858–1939

8   [The Indian] sees no need for setting apart one day in seven as a holy day, since to him all days are God's.   *The Soul of the Indian [1911]*

Max Planck
1858–1947

9   We have no right to assume that any physical laws exist, or if they have existed up to now, that they will continue to exist in a similar manner in the future.

The Universe in the Light of Modern Physics [1931]

10   Anybody who has been seriously engaged in scientific work of any kind realizes that over the entrance to the gates of the temple of science are written the words: *Ye must have faith*. It is a quality which the scientist cannot dispense with.

Where Is Science Going? [1932]

11   An important scientific innovation rarely makes its way by gradually winning over and converting its opponents: it rarely happens that Saul becomes Paul. What does happen is that its opponents gradually die out and that the growing generation is familiarized with the idea from the beginning.

The Philosophy of Physics [1936]

Theodore Roosevelt
1858–1919

12   I wish to preach, not the doctrine of ignoble ease, but the doctrine of the strenuous life.

Speech before the Hamilton Club, Chicago [April 10, 1899]

13   Far better it is to dare mighty things, to win glorious triumphs, even though checkered by failure,

---

[1]To the memory of my brother Francis George Fowler . . . who shared with me the planning of this book, but did not live to share the writing. — H. W. FOWLER, *preface to the first edition*

[2]In American English, restrictive and nonrestrictive.

[3]Translated by W. A. BRADLEY.

[4]La commedia è finita.

[5]Santee Dakota.

than to take rank with those poor spirits who neither enjoy much nor suffer much, because they live in the gray twilight that knows not victory nor defeat.
Speech before the Hamilton Club, Chicago [April 10, 1899]

1   I am as strong as a bull moose and you can use me to the limit.
Letter to Marcus Alonzo Hanna [June 27, 1900][1]

2   No man is justified in doing evil on the ground of expediency.
The Strenuous Life: Essays and Addresses [1900]. The Strenuous Life

3   In life, as in a football game, the principle to follow is: Hit the line hard.
The Strenuous Life: Essays and Addresses. The American Boy

4   There is a homely adage which runs, "Speak softly and carry a big stick; you will go far." If the American nation will speak softly and yet build and keep at a pitch of the highest training a thoroughly efficient navy, the Monroe Doctrine will go far.
Speech at Minnesota State Fair [September 2, 1901]

5   The first requisite of a good citizen in this Republic of ours is that he shall be able and willing to pull his weight.
Speech at New York City [November 11, 1902]

6   A man who is good enough to shed his blood for his country is good enough to be given a square deal afterwards. More than that no man is entitled to, and less than that no man shall have.
Speech at Springfield, Illinois [July 4, 1903]

7   No man is above the law and no man is below it; nor do we ask any man's permission when we require him to obey it. Obedience to the law is demanded as a right; not asked as a favor.
Third Annual Message [December 7, 1903]

8   The men with the muckrakes are often indispensable to the well-being of society, but only if they know when to stop raking the muck, and to look upward to the celestial crown above them. . . . If they gradually grow to feel that the whole world is nothing but muck their power of usefulness is gone.[2]
Address on the laying of the cornerstone of the House Office Building, Washington, D.C. [April 14, 1906]

9   Malefactors of great wealth.
Speech at Provincetown, Massachusetts [August 20, 1907]

10   Nature-faker.
Everybody's Magazine [September 1907]

11   To waste, to destroy, our natural resources, to skin and exhaust the land instead of using it so as to increase its usefulness, will result in undermining in the days of our children the very prosperity which we ought by right to hand down to them amplified and developed.
Message to Congress [December 3, 1907]

12   Every man holds his property subject to the general right of the community to regulate its use to whatever degree the public welfare may require it.
Speech at Osawatomie, Kansas [August 31, 1910]

13   I took the Isthmus, started the Canal, and then left Congress—not to debate the Canal, but to debate me. . . . While the debate goes on the Canal does too.
Speech at University of California, Berkeley [March 23, 1911]

14   We stand at Armageddon and we battle for the Lord.
Speech at Progressive Party Convention, Chicago [June 17, 1912]

15   The lunatic fringe in all reform movements.
Autobiography [1913]

16   There is no room in this country for hyphenated Americanism. . . . The one absolutely certain way of bringing this nation to ruin, of preventing all possibility of its continuing to be a nation at all, would be to permit it to become a tangle of squabbling nationalities.
Speech before the Knights of Columbus, New York City [October 12, 1915]

17   One of our defects as a nation is a tendency to use what have been called "weasel words." When a weasel sucks eggs the meat is sucked out of the egg. If you use a "weasel word" after another there is nothing left of the other.
Speech at St. Louis [May 31, 1916]

18   Put out the light.
Last words [January 6, 1919]

Langdon Smith
1858–1908

19 When you were a tadpole and I was a fish,
In the Paleozoic time.
Evolution [1895], st. 1

---

[1]Now look, that damned cowboy is President of the United States.—MARCUS ALONZO HANNA [1837–1904], *on Theodore Roosevelt's accession [September 1901].*

[2]See Bunyan, 282:2.

Graham Wallas
1858–1932

1   The little girl had the making of a poet in her who, being told to be sure of her meaning before she spoke, said, "How can I know what I think till I see what I say?"

The Art of Thought [1926], ch. 4

Sir William Watson
1858–1935

2 April, April,
Laugh thy girlish laughter;
Then, the moment after,
Weep thy girlish tears.   *Song*

Katharine Lee Bates
1859–1929

3 O beautiful for spacious skies,
For amber waves of grain,
For purple mountain majesties
Above the fruited plain!
America! America!
God shed his grace on thee
And crown thy good with brotherhood
From sea to shining sea!

America the Beautiful [1893],[1] st. 1

Henri Bergson
1859–1941

4   Laughter has no greater foe than emotion. . . . To produce the whole of its effect, then, the comic demands something like a momentary anesthesia of the heart.[2]   *Laughter [1900], ch. 1, i*

5   The major task of the twentieth century will be to explore the unconscious, to investigate the sub-soil of the mind.   *Le Rêve (The Dream) [1901]*

6   The present contains nothing more than the past, and what is found in the effect was already in the cause.

L'Evolution Créatrice (Creative Evolution) [1907], ch. 1

7   Intelligence . . . is the faculty of making artificial objects, especially tools to make tools.

L'Evolution Créatrice, 2

8   L'élan vital [the vital spirit].

L'Evolution Créatrice,

Harold Edwin Boulton
1859–1935

9 Speed, bonnie boat, like a bird on the wing;
Onward, the sailors cry:
Carry the lad that's born to be king
Over the sea to Skye.   *Skye Boat Song, st.*

Carrie Chapman [Lane] Catt
1859–1947

10   No written law has ever been more binding tha[n] unwritten custom supported by popular opinion.

Speech, Why We Ask for the Submission of an Amendment, at Senate hearing on woman's suffrage [February 13, 1900]

11   When a just cause reaches its flood tide . . whatever stands in the way must fall before its over whelming power.

Speech at Stockholm, Is Woman Suffrage Progressing? [1911]

John Dewey
1859–1952

12   We naturally associate democracy . . . with free dom of action, but freedom of action without free capacity of thought behind it is only chaos.

Democracy in Education, in The Elementary School Teacher [December 1903]

13   Every great advance in science has issued from new audacity of imagination.

The Quest for Certainty [1929], ch. I

14   Education is not preparation for life; education life itself.   *Attribute*

Sir Arthur Conan Doyle
1859–1930

15   London, that great cesspool into which all th loungers of the Empire are irresistibly drained.

A Study in Scarlet [188?

16   When you have eliminated the impossible, wha ever remains, *however improbable*, must be th truth.   *The Sign of Four [1890], ch.*

17   The unofficial force—the Baker Street irregular

The Sign of Four,

---

[1]Music by SAMUEL A. WARD [1848–1903].
[2]Translated by CLOUDESLEY BRERETON and FRED ROTHWELL.

1   You see, but you do not observe. The distinction is clear.
> *The Adventures of Sherlock Holmes [1891].*
> *A Scandal in Bohemia*

2   To Sherlock Holmes she [Irene Adler] is always *the* woman.
> *The Adventures of Sherlock Holmes.*
> *A Scandal in Bohemia*

3   Singularity is almost invariably a clue. The more featureless and commonplace a crime is, the more difficult is it to bring it home.
> *The Adventures of Sherlock Holmes.*
> *The Boscombe Valley Mystery*

4   My name is Sherlock Holmes. It is my business to know what other people don't know.
> *The Adventures of Sherlock Holmes.*
> *The Adventure of the Blue Carbuncle*

5   The Speckled Band.
> *The Adventures of Sherlock Holmes.*
> *Title of story*

6   The lowest and vilest alleys of London do not present a more dreadful record of sin than does the smiling and beautiful countryside.
> *The Adventures of Sherlock Holmes.*
> *The Adventure of the Copper Beeches*

7   "... the curious incident of the dog in the nighttime."
  "The dog did nothing in the nighttime."
  "That was the curious incident," remarked Sherlock Holmes.
> *The Memoirs of Sherlock Holmes [1894].*
> *Silver Blaze*

8   Like all Holmes's reasoning the thing seemed simplicity itself when it was once explained.
> *The Memoirs of Sherlock Holmes.*
> *The Stock-Broker's Clerk*

9   You know my methods, Watson.
> *The Memoirs of Sherlock Holmes.*
> *The Crooked Man*

10   "Excellent!" I [Watson] cried.
  "Elementary," said he [Holmes].
> *The Memoirs of Sherlock Holmes.*
> *The Crooked Man*

11   [Professor Moriarty] is the Napoleon of crime, Watson. He is the organizer of half that is evil and of nearly all that is undetected in this great city.
> *The Memoirs of Sherlock Holmes.*
> *The Final Problem*

12   They were the footprints of a gigantic hound!
> *The Hound of the Baskervilles [1902], ch. 2*

13   Come, Watson, come! The game is afoot.
> *The Return of Sherlock Holmes [1904].*
> *The Adventure of the Abbey Grange*

14   The fair sex is your department.
> *The Return of Sherlock Holmes.*
> *The Second Stain*

15   We are dealing with an exceptionally astute and dangerous man . . . one of the most unscrupulous rascals that Australia has ever evolved—and for a young country it has turned out some very finished types.
> *His Last Bow [1917]. The Disappearance of*
> *Lady Frances Carfax*

16   The giant rat of Sumatra, a story for which the world is not yet prepared.
> *The Case Book of Sherlock Holmes [1927].*
> *The Adventure of the Sussex Vampire*

Havelock Ellis
1859–1939

17   To be a leader of men one must turn one's back on men.
> *Introduction to Joris Karl Huysmans,*
> *À Rebours (Against the Grain) [1884]*

18   The text of the Bible is but a feeble symbol of the Revelation held in the text of Men and Women.
> *Impressions and Comments*

19   The omnipresent process of sex, as it is woven into the whole texture of our man's or woman's body, is the pattern of all the process of our life.
> *The New Spirit*

20   Every artist writes his own autobiography.
> *The New Spirit*

21   All civilization has from time to time become a thin crust over a volcano of revolution.
> *Little Essays of Love and Virtue [1922], ch. 7*

22   The greatest task before civilization at present is to make machines what they ought to be, the slaves, instead of the masters of men.
> *Little Essays of Love and Virtue, 7*

23   Dancing is the loftiest, the most moving, the most beautiful of the arts, because it is no mere translation or abstraction from life; it is life itself.
> *The Dance of Life [1923], ch. 2*

24   The place where optimism most flourishes is the lunatic asylum.
> *The Dance of Life, 3*

25   A man must not swallow more beliefs than he can digest.
> *The Dance of Life, 5*

1   The Promised Land always lies on the other side of a wilderness.   *The Dance of Life, 5*

2   The sun and the moon and the stars would have disappeared long ago . . . had they happened to be within the reach of predatory human hands.   *The Dance of Life, 7*

3   Had there been a lunatic asylum in the suburbs of Jerusalem, Jesus Christ would infallibly have been shut up in it at the outset of his public career. That interview with Satan on a pinnacle of the Temple would alone have damned him, and everything that happened after could but have confirmed the diagnosis.   *Impressions and Comments, series 3*

Kenneth Grahame
1859–1932

4   There is *nothing*—absolutely nothing—half so much worth doing as simply messing about in boats . . . or with boats. . . . In or out of 'em, it doesn't matter.   *The Wind in the Willows [1908], ch. 1*

5   The clever men at Oxford
Know all that there is to be knowed.
But they none of them know one half as much
As intelligent Mr. Toad!
    The Wind in the Willows, 10

A[lfred] E[dward] Housman[1]
1859–1936

6   Loveliest of trees, the cherry now
Is hung with bloom along the bough.
    A Shropshire Lad [1896], no. 2, st. 1

7   Now, of my threescore years and ten,
Twenty will not come again,
And take from seventy springs a score,
It only leaves me fifty more.

And since to look at things in bloom
Fifty springs are little room,
About the woodlands I will go
To see the cherry hung with snow.
    A Shropshire Lad, 2, st. 2, 3

8   Clay lies still, but blood's a rover;
Breath's a ware that will not keep.
Up, lad: when the journey's over
There'll be time enough to sleep.
    A Shropshire Lad, 4 (Reveille), st. 6

9   Lovers lying two and two
Ask not whom they sleep beside,
And the bridegroom all night through
Never turns him to the bride.
    A Shropshire Lad, 12, st. 2

10   When I was one-and-twenty
I heard a wise man say,
"Give crowns and pounds and guineas
But not your heart away."
    A Shropshire Lad, 13, st. 1

11   When I was one-and-twenty
I heard him say again,
"The heart out of the bosom
Was never given in vain;
'Tis paid with sighs aplenty
And sold for endless rue."
And I am two-and-twenty,
And Oh, 'tis true, 'tis true.
    A Shropshire Lad, 13, st. 2

12   His folly has not fellow
Beneath the blue of day
That gives to man or woman
His heart and soul away.
    A Shropshire Lad, 14, st. 3

13   Oh, when I was in love with you,
Then I was clean and brave,
And miles around the wonder grew
How well I did behave.

And now the fancy passes by,
And nothing will remain,
And miles around they'll say that I
Am quite myself again.
    A Shropshire Lad, 18, st. 1, 2

14   And silence sounds no worse than cheers
After earth has stopped the ears.
    A Shropshire Lad, 19 (To an Athlete Dying Young), st. 4

15   The bells they sound on Bredon,
And still the steeples hum.
"Come all to church, good people"—
Oh, noisy bells, be dumb;
I hear you, I will come.
    A Shropshire Lad, 21, st. 7

16   The lads that will die in their glory and never be old.
    A Shropshire Lad, 23, st. 4

17   And fire and ice within me fight
Beneath the suffocating night.
    A Shropshire Lad, 30, st. 4

---

[1]I am not a pessimist but a pejorist (as George Eliot said she was not an optimist but a meliorist); and that philosophy is founded on my observation of the world, not on anything so trivial and irrelevant as personal history.—HOUSMAN, *autobiographical note written for a French translation of his poems*

1 There, like the wind through woods in riot,
  Through him the gale of life blew high;
  The tree of man was never quiet:
  Then 'twas the Roman, now 'tis I.
                    A Shropshire Lad, 31, st. 4

2 Oh tarnish late on Wenlock Edge,
  Gold that I never see.
                    A Shropshire Lad, 39, st. 3

3 Into my heart an air that kills
  From yon far country blows:
  What are those blue remembered hills,
  What spires, what farms are those?

  That is the land of lost content,
  I see it shining plain,
  The happy highways where I went
  And cannot come again.
                    A Shropshire Lad, 40, st. 1, 2

4 Earth and high heaven are fixed of old and founded
      strong.
                    A Shropshire Lad, 48, st. 1

5 Far in a western brookland
  That bred me long ago
  The poplars stand and tremble
  By pools I used to know.
                    A Shropshire Lad, 52, st. 1

6 With rue my heart is laden
  For golden friends I had,
  For many a rose-lipped maiden
  And many a lightfoot lad.
                    A Shropshire Lad, 54, st. 1

7 By brooks too broad for leaping
  The lightfoot boys are laid.
                    A Shropshire Lad, 54, st. 2

8 In all the endless road you tread
  There's nothing but the night.
                    A Shropshire Lad, 60, st. 2

9 Oh many a peer of England brews
  Livelier liquor than the Muse,
  And malt does more than Milton can
  To justify God's ways to man.[1]
  Ale, man, ale's the stuff to drink
  For fellows whom it hurts to think.
                    A Shropshire Lad, 62, st. 2

10 Mithridates, he died old.[2]
                    A Shropshire Lad, 62, st. 4

---

[1]See Milton, 263:21 and 269:3.

[2]Housman's passage is based on the belief of the ancients that Mithridates the Great [c. 135–63 B.C.] had so saturated his body with poisons that none could injure him. When captured by the Romans he tried in vain to poison himself, then ordered a Gallic mercenary to kill him.

11 Pass me the can, lad; there's an end of May.
                    Last Poems [1922], 9, st. 1

12 The troubles of our proud and angry dust
  Are from eternity, and shall not fail.
  Bear them we can, and if we can we must.
  Shoulder the sky, my lad, and drink your ale.
                    Last Poems, 9, st. 7

13 The laws of God, the laws of man,
  He may keep that will and can;
  Not I: let God and man decree
  Laws for themselves and not for me.
                    Last Poems, 12, l. 1

14 And how am I to face the odds
  Of man's bedevilment and God's?
  I, a stranger and afraid
  In a world I never made.   *Last Poems, 12, l. 15*

15 Strapped, noosed, nighing his hour,
  He stood and counted them and cursed his luck;
  And then the clock collected in the tower
  Its strength, and struck.
                    Last Poems, 15 (Eight O'Clock), st. 2

16 Happy bridegroom, Hesper brings
  All desired and timely things.
  All whom morning sends to roam,
  Hesper loves to lead them home.
  Home return who him behold,
  Child to mother, sheep to fold,
  Bird to nest from wandering wide:
  Happy bridegroom, seek your bride.
                    Last Poems, 24 (Epithalamium), st. 3

17 These, in the day when heaven was falling,
  The hour when earth's foundations fled,
  Followed their mercenary calling
  And took their wages and are dead.
            *Last Poems, 37 (Epitaph on an Army of
              Mercenaries),[3] st. 1*

18 What God abandoned, these defended.
                    Last Poems, 37, st. 2

19 They say my verse is sad: no wonder;
  Its narrow measure spans
  Tears of eternity, and sorrow,
  Not mine, but man's.
                    More Poems [1936], foreword

20 Hope lies to mortals
  And most believe her,
  But man's deceiver
  Was never mine.   *More Poems, 6, st. 1*

21 The rainy Pleiads wester,
  Orion plunges prone,

---

[3]The British regulars who made the retreat from Mons, beginning August 24, 1914.

And midnight strikes and hastens,
And I lie down alone.[1]   *More Poems, 11, st. 1*

1 Life, to be sure, is nothing much to lose,
  But young men think it is, and we were young.
                              More Poems, 36, l. 3

2 We now to peace and darkness
  And earth and thee restore
  Thy creature that thou madest
  And wilt cast forth no more.
              More Poems, 47 (For My Funeral), st. 3

3 Good night; ensured release,
  Imperishable peace,
  Have these for yours.[2]
  While sky and sea and land
  And earth's foundations stand
  And heaven endures.
              More Poems, 48 (Alta Quies), st. 1

4 Oh they're taking him to prison for the color of his
  hair.   *Additional Poems [1937], 18, st. 1*

5   Experience has taught me, when I am shaving of
  a morning, to keep watch over my thoughts, because, if a line of poetry strays into my memory, my
  skin bristles so that the razor ceases to act. . . . The
  seat of this sensation is the pit of the stomach.
              The Name and Nature of Poetry [1933]

Jerome K[lapka] Jerome
1859–1927

6   Let your boat of life be light, packed with only
  what you need—a homely home and simple pleasures, one or two friends, worth the name, someone
  to love and someone to love you, a cat, a dog, and a
  pipe or two, enough to eat and enough to wear, and
  a little more than enough to drink; for thirst is a
  dangerous thing.
              Three Men in a Boat [1889], ch. 3

7   I like work: it fascinates me. I can sit and look at
  it for hours. I love to keep it by me; the idea of getting rid of it nearly breaks my heart.
              Three Men in a Boat, 15

8   "Nothing, so it seems to me," said the stranger,
  "is more beautiful than the love that has weathered
  the storms of life. . . . The love of the young for the
  young, that is the beginning of life. But the love of
  the old for the old, that is the beginning of—of
  things longer."
              The Passing of the Third Floor Back [1908]

---

[1]See Sappho, 58:3.

[2]These three lines are on the tablet over Housman's grave in the
parish church at Ludlow, Shropshire, England.

William James Lampton
1859–1917

9 Same old slippers,
  Same old rice,
  Same old glimpse of
  Paradise.   *June Weddings, st. 1*

10 Where the corn is full of kernels
   And the colonels full of corn.   *Kentuck*

Charles E. Stanton
1859–1933

11 Lafayette, we are here.[3]
              *Address at the tomb of Lafayette, Picpus
              Cemetery, Paris [July 4, 1917]*

James Kenneth Stephen
1859–1892

12 When the Rudyards cease from Kipling
   And the Haggards ride no more.
              Lapsus Calami. To R. K

13 Of sentences that stir my bile,
   Of phrases I detest,
   There's one beyond all others vile:
   "He did it for the best."
              Lapsus Calami. The Malefactor's Plea, st.

Francis Thompson
1859–1907

14 The fairest things have fleetest end,
   Their scent survives their close:
   But the rose's scent is bitterness
   To him that loved the rose.
              Daisy [1893], st. 1

15 Nothing begins, and nothing ends,
   That is not paid with moan;
   For we are born in other's pain,
   And perish in our own.   *Daisy, st. 1*

16 Look for me in the nurseries of Heaven.[4]
              To My Godchil

17 I fled Him, down the nights and down the days;
   I fled Him, down the arches of the years;
   I fled Him, down the labyrinthine ways
   Of my own mind; and in the mist of tears
   I hid from Him, and under running laughter.
              The Hound of Heaven [1893], l.

---

[3]The remark has also been attributed to GENERAL JOHN JOSEP
PERSHING [1860–1948]; in *My Experiences in the World Wa*
[1931], Pershing denied having said "anything so splendid."

[4]Inscribed on Thompson's tombstone in Kensal Green Cemeter

1 But with unhurrying chase,
  And unperturbèd pace,
  Deliberate speed, majestic instancy,
  They beat — and a Voice beat
  More instant than the Feet —
  "All things betray thee, who betrayest Me."
  The Hound of Heaven, l. 10

2 Across the margent of the world I fled,
  And troubled the gold gateways of the stars.
  The Hound of Heaven, l. 25

3 I said to dawn, Be sudden; to eve, Be soon.
  The Hound of Heaven, l. 30

4 My days have crackled and gone up in smoke.
  The Hound of Heaven, l. 122

5 All which I took from thee I did but take,
  Not for thy harms,
  But just that thou might'st seek it in My arms.
  The Hound of Heaven, l. 171

6 O world invisible, we view thee,
  O world intangible, we touch thee,
  O world unknowable, we know thee.
  The Kingdom of God ("In No Strange Land")
  [1913], st. 1

7 The angels keep their ancient places;
  Turn but a stone, and start a wing!
  'Tis ye, 'tis your estrangèd faces,
  That miss the many-splendored thing.
  The Kingdom of God, st. 4

8 Upon thy so sore loss
  Shall shine the traffic of Jacob's ladder
  Pitched betwixt Heaven and Charing Cross.
  The Kingdom of God, st. 5

9 And lo, Christ walking on the water
  Not of Gennesareth, but Thames!
  The Kingdom of God, st. 6

10 Short arm needs man to reach to Heaven
  So ready is Heaven to stoop to him.
  Grace of the Way, st. 6

Sidney Webb, Lord Passfield
1859–1947

11 The inevitability of gradualness.
  Address to British Labor Party [1923]

Jane Addams
1860–1935

12 Private beneficence is totally inadequate to deal
  with the vast numbers of the city's disinherited.
  Twenty Years at Hull House [1910]

13 The common stock of intellectual enjoyment
  should not be difficult of access because of the economic position of him who would approach it.
  Twenty Years at Hull House

Sir James M[atthew] Barrie
1860–1937

14 Them that has china plates themsels is the maist
  careful no to break the china plates of others.
  The Little Minister [1891], ch. 26

15 We never understand how little we need in this
  world until we know the loss of it.
  Margaret Ogilvy [1896], ch. 8

16 Shall we make a new rule of life from tonight: always to try to be a little kinder than is necessary?
  The Little White Bird [1902], ch. 4

17 His lordship may compel us to be equal upstairs,
  but there will never be equality in the servants' hall.
  The Admirable Crichton [1903], act I

18 Do you believe in fairies? . . . If you believe, clap
  your hands!
  Peter Pan [1904], act IV

19 It's a sort of bloom on a woman. If you have it
  [charm], you don't need to have anything else, and
  if you don't have it, it doesn't much matter what
  else you have. Some women, the few, have charm
  for all; and most have charm for one. But some have
  charm for none.
  What Every Woman Knows [1908], act I

20 The tragedy of a man who has found himself out.
  What Every Woman Knows, IV

21 One's religion is whatever he is most interested
  in, and yours is Success.
  The Twelve-Pound Look [1910]

John Collins Bossidy
1860–1928

22 And this is good old Boston,
  The home of the bean and the cod,
  Where the Lowells talk to the Cabots
  And the Cabots talk only to God.[1]
  Toast, Holy Cross Alumni Dinner [1910]

---

[1]Patterned on the toast given at the twenty-fifth anniversary dinner of the Harvard Class of 1880, by a Westerner:

Here's to old Massachusetts, / The home of the sacred cod, /
Where the Adamses vote for Douglas, / And the Cabots walk with
God.

William Jennings Bryan
1860–1925

1   The humblest citizen of all the land, when clad in the armor of a righteous cause, is stronger than all the hosts of Error.
> *Speech at the National Democratic Convention, Chicago [1896]*

2   Destroy our farms and the grass will grow in the streets of every city in the country.
> *Speech at the National Democratic Convention, Chicago [1896]*

3   You shall not press down upon the brow of labor this crown of thorns. You shall not crucify mankind upon a cross of gold.[1]
> *Speech at the National Democratic Convention, Chicago [1896]*

Haddon Chambers
1860–1921

4   The long arm of coincidence.
> *Captain Swift [1888], act II*

Anton Pavlovich Chekhov
1860–1904

5   I feel more confident and more satisfied when I reflect that I have two professions and not one. Medicine is my lawful wife and literature is my mistress. When I get tired of one I spend the night with the other. Though it's disorderly it's not so dull, and besides, neither really loses anything through my infidelity.
> *Letter to A. S. Suvorin [September 11, 1888][2]*

6   I would like to be a free artist and nothing else, and I regret God has not given me the strength to be one.
> *Letter to Alexei Pleshcheev [October 4, 1888][2]*

7   My holy of holies is the human body, health, intelligence, talent, inspiration, love, and the most absolute freedom imaginable, freedom from violence and lies, no matter what form the latter two take. Such is the program I would adhere to if I were a major artist.
> *Letter to Alexei Pleshcheev [October 4, 1888]*

8   An artist must pass judgment only on what he understands; his range is limited as that of any other specialist — that's what I keep repeating and insisting upon. Anyone who says that the artist's field is all answers and no questions has never done any writing or had any dealings with imagery. An artist observes, selects, guesses and synthesizes.
> *Letter to A. S. Suvorin [October 27, 1888][2]*

9   One must not put a loaded rifle on the stage if no one is thinking of firing it.[3]
> *Letter to A. S. Lazarev-Gruzinsky [November 1, 1889]*

10   I am in mourning for my life. I am unhappy.
> *The Seagull [1896],[4] act I*

11   I try to catch every sentence, every word you and I say, and quickly lock all these sentences and words away in my literary storehouse because they might come in handy.
> *The Seagull, I*

12   People should be beautiful in every way — in their faces, in the way they dress, in their thoughts and in their innermost selves.
> *Uncle Vanya [1897],[4] act I*

13   We shall find peace. We shall hear the angels, we shall see the sky sparkling with diamonds.
> *Uncle Vanya, IV*

14   To Moscow, to Moscow, to Moscow!
> *Three Sisters [1901], act II*

15   All Russia is our orchard.
> *The Cherry Orchard [1904],[4] act II*

Baron Corvo
[Frederick William Rolfe]
1860–1913

16   He took one long slow breath: crossed right hand over left upon his breast: became like a piece of a pageant; and responded "I will."
> *Hadrian the Seventh [1904], ch. 3*

17   Pray for the repose of his soul. He was so tired.
> *Hadrian the Seventh, closing line*

---

[1] I shall not help crucify mankind upon a cross of gold. I shall not aid in pressing down upon the bleeding brow of labor this crown of thorns. — BRYAN, *speech in the House of Representatives* [December 22, 1894]

[2] Translated by SIMON KARLINSKY.

[3] A fuller version: If you say in the first chapter that there is a rifle hanging on a wall, in the second or third chapter it absolutely must go off. If it's not going to be fired, it shouldn't be hanging there. — S. SHCHUKIN, *Memoirs* [1911]

[4] Translated by RONALD HINGLY.

Harry M[icajah] Daugherty
1860–1941

1   In a smoke-filled room in some hotel.[1]
Attributed

Charlotte Perkins Gilman
1860–1935

2   There are things in that wallpaper that nobody knows about but me, or ever will.
Behind that outside pattern the dim shapes get clearer every day.
It is always the same shape, only very numerous.
And it is like a woman stooping down and creeping about behind that pattern.
The Yellow Wallpaper [1892]

3   The labor of women in the house, certainly, enables men to produce more wealth than they otherwise could; and in this way women are economic factors in society. But so are horses.
Women and Economics [1898], ch. 1

4   There is no female mind. The brain is not an organ of sex. As well speak of a female liver.
Women and Economics, 8

5   Cried all, "Before such things can come,
You idiotic child,
You must alter human nature!"
And they all sat back and smiled.
In This Our World [1893]. Similar Cases

6   "I do not want to be a fly!
I want to be a worm!"
In This Our World. A Conservative, st. 6

7   I ran against a Prejudice
That quite cut off the view.
In This Our World. An Obstacle, st. 1

8   There's a whining at the threshold—
There's a scratching at the floor—
To work! To work! In Heaven's name!
The wolf is at the door!
In This Our World. The Wolf at the Door, st. 6

9   The people people have for friends
Your common sense appall,

---

[1]According to the *New York Times* [February 21, 1920], Daugherty, presidential campaign manager for Senator Warren G. Harding, predicted that the convention would be deadlocked and would be decided by a group of men who "will sit down about two o'clock in the morning around a table in a smoke-filled room." Daugherty maintained that he had not said "smoke-filled." The room was in the suite occupied by George Harvey, rooms 804–805 in the Blackstone Hotel.

But the people people marry
Are the queerest folk of all.
Queer People

William Ralph Inge
1860–1954

10   A man may build himself a throne of bayonets, but he cannot sit on it.
From Wit and Wisdom of Dean Inge, edited by MARCHANT, *no. 108*

James Ball Naylor
1860–1945

11   King David and King Solomon
Led merry, merry lives,
With many, many lady friends
And many, many wives;
But when old age crept over them—
With many, many qualms,
King Solomon wrote the Proverbs
And King David wrote the Psalms.
Ancient Authors

Sir D'Arcy Wentworth Thompson
1860–1948

12   Numerical precision is the very soul of science.
On Growth and Form [1917], ch. 1

13   The harmony of the world is made manifest in Form and Number, and the heart and soul and all the poetry of Natural Philosophy are embodied in the concept of mathematical beauty.
On Growth and Form, epilogue

Owen Wister
1860–1938

14   When you call me that, *smile!*
The Virginian [1902], ch. 2

[William] Bliss Carman
1861–1929

15   No fidget and no reformer, just
A calm observer of ought and must.
The Joys of the Road, st. 22

16   The scarlet of the maples can shake me like a cry
Of bugles going by.   *A Vagabond Song, st. 2*

1 There is something in October sets the gypsy blood
astir.
A Vagabond Song, st. 3

Louise Imogen Guiney
1861–1920

2 He has done with roofs and men,
Open, Time, and let him pass.
Ballad of Kenelm

3 A short life in the saddle, Lord!
Not long life by the fire.
The Knight Errant, st. 2

John Luther Long
1861–1927

4   To die with honor when one can no longer live
with honor.[1]
Madame Butterfly [1897]

Sir Walter Raleigh
1861–1922

5 I wish I loved the human race;
I wish I loved its silly face;
I wish I liked the way it walks;
I wish I liked the way it talks;
And when I'm introduced to one
I wish I thought, *What jolly fun!*
*Wishes of an Elderly Man; wished at a garden
party [June 1914]*

Rabindranath Tagore
1861–1941

6   When one knows thee, then alien there is none,
then no door is shut. Oh, grant me my prayer that I
may never lose the touch of the one in the play of
the many.
Gitanjali [1913]

7 At my dying hour, and over my long life,
A clock strikes somewhere at the city's edge.
Poem [1941]

---

[1]Inscription on Samurai blade.
   One should die proudly when it is no longer possible to live
proudly. — FRIEDRICH NIETZSCHE, *The Twilight of the Idols* [1888],
Skirmishes in a War with the Age, 36

Frederick Jackson Turner
1861–1932

8   The frontier is the outer edge of the wave — the
meeting-point between savagery and civilization . .
the line of most rapid and effective Americaniza-
tion. The wilderness masters the colonist.
*The Significance of the Frontier in American
History [1894]*

Alfred North Whitehead
1861–1947

9   The study of mathematics is apt to commence in
disappointment. . . . We are told that by its aid the
stars are weighed and the billions of molecules in a
drop of water are counted. Yet, like the ghost of
Hamlet's father, this great science eludes the efforts
of our mental weapons to grasp it.
An Introduction to Mathematics [1911], ch. 1

10   Civilization advances by extending the number
of important operations which we can perform
without thinking about them.
An Introduction to Mathematics, 5

11   The science of pure mathematics, in its modern
developments, may claim to be the most original
creation of the human spirit.
Science and the Modern World [1925], ch. 2

12   The greatest invention of the nineteenth century
was the invention of the method of invention.
Science and the Modern World, 6

13   The religious vision, and its history of persistent
expansion, is our one ground for optimism. Apart
from it, human life is a flash of occasional enjoyments lighting up a mass of pain and misery, a
bagatelle of transient experience.
Science and the Modern World, 12

14   Rationalism is an adventure in the clarification of
thought.
Process and Reality [1929], pt. I, ch. 1, sec. 3

15   The safest general characterization of the
European philosophical tradition is that it consists
of a series of footnotes to Plato.
Process and Reality, II, 1, I

16   The human body is an instrument for the production of art in the life of the human soul.
Adventures of Ideas [1933], ch. 18

17   A general definition of civilization: a civilized society is exhibiting the five qualities of truth, beauty,
adventure, art, peace.   *Adventures of Ideas, 19*

1   The deliberate aim at Peace very easily passes into its bastard substitute, Anesthesia.
Adventures of Ideas, 20

2   There are no whole truths; all truths are half-truths. It is trying to treat them as whole truths that plays the devil.
Dialogues of Alfred North Whitehead [1953],[1] *prologue*

3   The vitality of thought is in adventure. *Ideas won't keep.* Something must be done about them. When the idea is new, its custodians have fervor, live for it, and, if need be, die for it.
Dialogues of Alfred North Whitehead, ch. 12, April 28, 1938

4   A culture is in its finest flower before it begins to analyze itself.
Dialogues of Alfred North Whitehead, 22, August 17, 1941

5   What is morality in any given time or place? It is what the majority then and there happen to like, and immorality is what they dislike.
Dialogues of Alfred North Whitehead, August 30, 1941

6   The ideas of Freud were popularized by people who only imperfectly understood them, who were incapable of the great effort required to grasp them in their relationship to larger truths, and who therefore assigned to them a prominence out of all proportion to their true importance.
Dialogues of Alfred North Whitehead, 28, June 3, 1943

7   A philosopher of imposing stature doesn't think in a vacuum. Even his most abstract ideas are, to some extent, conditioned by what is or is not known in the time when he lives.
Dialogues of Alfred North Whitehead, 29, June 10, 1943

8   Intellect is to emotion as our clothes are to our bodies; we could not very well have civilized life without clothes, but we would be in a poor way if we had only clothes without bodies.
Dialogues of Alfred North Whitehead, 29, June 10, 1943

9   No period of history has ever been great or ever can be that does not act on some sort of high, idealistic motives, and idealism in our time has been shoved aside, and we are paying the penalty for it.
Dialogues of Alfred North Whitehead, 32, January 13, 1944

10   The English never abolish anything. They put it in cold storage.
Dialogues of Alfred North Whitehead, 36, January 19, 1945

A[rthur] C[hristopher] Benson
1862–1925

11 Land of hope and glory, mother of the free,
How shall we extol thee, who are born of thee?
Wider still and wider shall thy bounds be set;
God, who made thee mighty, make thee
   mightier yet.
Land of Hope and Glory [1902],[2] *chorus*

Albert [Jeremiah] Beveridge
1862–1927

12   This party comes from the grass roots. It has grown from the soil of the people's hard necessities.
Address at the Bull Moose Convention, Chicago [August 5, 1912]

James W. Blake
1862–1935

13 East Side, West Side, all around the town,
The tots sang "Ring-a-rosie," "London Bridge is
   falling down";
Boys and girls together, me and Mamie O'Rorke,
Tripped the light fantastic on the sidewalks of New
   York.   *The Sidewalks of New York [1894]*[3]

Carrie Jacobs Bond
1862–1946

14 Well, this is the end of a perfect day,
Near the end of a journey, too.
A Perfect Day, st. 2

15 For memory has painted this perfect day
With colors that never fade,
And we find at the end of a perfect day
The soul of a friend we've made. *A Perfect Day, st. 2*

Nicholas Murray Butler
1862–1947

16   An expert is one who knows more and more about less and less.
Commencement address, Columbia University

---

[1]As recorded by Lucien Price.

[2]First *Pomp and Circumstance* march by Sir Edward Elgar.
[3]Music by Charles B. Lawlor.

John Jay Chapman
1862–1933

1   The New Testament, and to a very large extent the Old, *is* the soul of man. You cannot criticize it. It criticizes you.   *Letter [March 26, 1898]*

2   The present in New York is so powerful that the past is lost.   *Letter [1909]*

3   Everybody in America is soft, and hates conflict. The cure for this, both in politics and social life, is the same—hardihood. Give them raw truth.
Practical Agitation [1898]

4   You get the satisfaction of being heard, and that is the whole possible scope of human ambition.
Learning and Other Essays [1910]. The Unity of Human Nature

Edward, Viscount Grey of Fallodon
1862–1933

5   The lamps are going out all over Europe; we shall not see them lit again in our lifetime.
Comment [August 3, 1914], on the eve of World War I

O. Henry [William Sydney Porter]
1862–1910

6   Perhaps there is no happiness in life so perfect as the martyr's.
The Trimmed Lamp [1907]. The Country of Elusion

7   It was beautiful and simple as all truly great swindles are.
The Gentle Grafter [1908]. The Octopus Marooned

8   Life is made up of sobs, sniffles, and smiles, with sniffles predominating.
The Gentle Grafter. The Octopus Marooned

9   Busy as a one-armed man with the nettle-rash pasting on wallpaper.
The Gentle Grafter. The Ethics of Pig

10   Bagdad-on-the-Subway.[1]
Roads of Destiny [1909]. The Discounters of Money

11   History is bright and fiction dull with homely men who have charmed women.
Roads of Destiny. Next to Reading Matter

12   She plucked from my lapel the invisible strand of lint (the universal act of woman to proclaim ownership).
Strictly Business [1910]. A Ramble in Aphasia

13   East is East, and West is San Francisco, according to Californians. Californians are a race of people; they are not merely inhabitants of a State.
Strictly Business. A Municipal Report

14   It couldn't have happened anywhere but in little old New York.[2]
Whirligigs [1910]. A Little Local Color

15   A straw vote only shows which way the hot air blows.   *Rolling Stones [1913]. A Ruler of Men*

16   Take it from me—he's got the goods.
The Unprofitable Servant

17   Turn up the lights—I don't want to go home in the dark.[3]
Last words [June 5, 1910]

Charles Evans Hughes
1862–1948

18   We are under a Constitution, but the Constitution is what the judges say it is, and the judiciary is the safeguard of our liberty and of our property under the Constitution.
Speech at Elmira, New York [May 3, 1907]

19   How amazing it is that, in the midst of controversies on every conceivable subject, one should expect unanimity of opinion upon difficult legal questions! . . . The history of scholarship is a record of disagreements. And when we deal with questions relating to principles of law and their applications, we do not suddenly rise into a stratosphere of icy certainty.
Speech to the American Law Institute [May 7, 1936]

Auguste Lumière
1862–1954

20   It [film] can be exploited for a certain time as a scientific curiosity but, apart from that, it has no commercial future whatsoever.
On the invention of motion pictures [1895]

---

[1]Also in *A Madison Square Arabian Night, A Night in New Arabia,* and *What You Want.*

[2]Also in *A Midsummer Knight's Dream, Past One at Rooney's,* and *The Rubber Plant's Story.*

[3]I'm Afraid to Go Home in the Dark.—Harry H. Williams [1879–1922], *title of song* [1907]

Maurice Maeterlinck
1862–1949

1   It is always a mistake not to close one's eyes, whether to forgive or to look better into oneself.
Pelléas et Mélisande [1892]

2   There are no dead.
The Blue Bird [1909], act IV, sc. ii

Sir Henry Newbolt
1862–1938

3 To set the cause above renown,
To love the game beyond the prize,
To honor, while you strike him down,
The foe that comes with fearless eyes;
To count the life of battle good
And dear the land that gave you birth,
And dearer yet the brotherhood
That binds the brave of all the earth.
The Island Race. Clifton Chapel, st. 2

4 *Qui procul hinc,* the legend's writ,
The frontier grave is far away—
Qui ante diem periit:
Sed miles, sed pro patria.[1]
The Island Race. Clifton Chapel, st. 4

5 Now the sunset breezes shiver,
And she's fading down the river,
But in England's song forever
She's the Fighting Téméraire.
The Fighting Téméraire, st. 6

6 Play up! play up! and play the game!
Vitai Lampada

7 Keep the Nelson touch.   *Minora Sidera*

Robert Cameron Rogers
1862–1912

8 The hours I spent with thee, dear heart,
Are as a string of pearls to me;
I count them over, every one apart,
My rosary, my rosary.   *The Rosary [1894], st. 1*[2]

Edith [Newbold Jones] Wharton
1862–1937

9 There are two ways of spreading light: to be
The candle or the mirror that reflects it.
Vesalius in Zante

---

[1]Who died far away, before his time: but as a soldier, for his country.

[2]Music by ETHELBERT NEVIN [1862–1901].

10   Everything about her was at once vigorous and exquisite, at once strong and fine. He had a confused sense that she must have cost a great deal to make, that a great many dull and ugly people must, in some mysterious way, have been sacrificed to produce her.
The House of Mirth [1905], bk. I, ch. 1

11   He seemed a part of the mute melancholy landscape, an incarnation of its frozen woe, with all that was warm and sentient in him fast bound below the surface.   *Ethan Frome [1911]*

12   Almost everybody in the neighborhood had "troubles," frankly localized and specified; but only the chosen had "complications." To have them was in itself a distinction, though it was also, in most cases, a death warrant. People struggled on for years with "troubles," but they almost always succumbed to "complications."
Ethan Frome

13   Mrs. Ballinger is one of the ladies who pursue Culture in bands, as though it were dangerous to meet it alone.   *Xingu [1916]*

14   An unalterable and unquestioned law of the musical world required that the German text of French operas sung by Swedish artists should be translated into Italian for the clearer understanding of English-speaking audiences.
The Age of Innocence [1920], ch. 1

15   In the rotation of crops there was a recognized season for wild oats; but they were not sown more than once.   *The Age of Innocence, 31*

16   It was the old New York way of taking life "without effusion of blood": the way of people who dreaded scandal more than disease, who placed decency above courage, and who considered that nothing was more ill-bred than "scenes," except the behavior of those who gave rise to them.
The Age of Innocence, 33

17   The worst of doing one's duty was that it apparently unfitted one for doing anything else.
The Age of Innocence, 34

18   There's no such thing as old age; there is only sorrow.
A Backward Glance [1934]. A First Word

19   In spite of illness, in spite even of the archenemy sorrow, one *can* remain alive long past the usual date of disintegration if one is unafraid of change, insatiable in intellectual curiosity, interested in big things, and happy in small ways.
A Backward Glance. A First Word

20   I was never allowed to read the popular American children's books of my day because, as my

mother said, the children spoke bad English *without the author's knowing it.*
> *A Backward Glance, ch. 3*

Black Elk [Hehaka Sapa]
1863–1950

1   Everything an Indian does is in a circle, and that is because the power of the world always works in circles, and everything tries to be round. In the old days when we were a strong and happy people, all our power came to us from the sacred hoop of the nation, and so long as the hoop was unbroken the people flourished.
> *Black Elk Speaks, Being the Life Story of a Holy Man of the Oglala Sioux, as told through* JOHN G. NEIHARDT *[1961]*

C[onstantine] P[eter] Cavafy
1863–1933

2 But Argos can do without the sons of Atreus.
Ancient houses are not eternal.
> *When the Watchman Saw the Light*[1] *[1900]*

3   We won't be deceived
by titles such as Indispensable and Unique and
   Great.
Someone else indispensable and unique and great
can always be found at a moment's notice.
> *When the Watchman Saw the Light*

4 Pleasure will have much to teach him.
He will not be afraid of the destructive act;
one half of the house must be pulled down.
This way he will grow virtuously into knowledge.
> *Strengthening the Spirit [1903]*

5 What are we all waiting for
gathered together like this on the public square?
   The Barbarians are coming today.
> *Waiting for the Barbarians [1904]*,[2] *l. 1*

6 You'll not find another place, you'll not find another sea.
This city is going to follow you.
> *The City [1910]*,[3] *l. 9*

7 Setting out on the voyage to Ithaca
you must pray that the way be long,
full of adventures and experiences.
> *Ithaca [1911]*,[4] *l. 11*

8 Body, remember not only how much you were loved,
not only the beds you lay on,
but also those desires glowing openly
in eyes that looked at you,
trembling for you in voices.
> *Body, Remember [1918]*

9 I created you while I was happy, while I was sad,
with so many incidents, so many details.

And, for me, the whole of you has been transformed into feeling.
> *In the Same Space [1929]*

William Randolph Hearst
1863–1951

10   You furnish the pictures and I'll furnish the war.
> *Attributed instructions to artist* FREDERIC REMINGTON *in Havana, Cuba [March 1898]*[6]

Sir Arthur Thomas Quiller-Couch
1863–1944

11   Whenever you feel an impulse to perpetuate a piece of exceptionally fine writing, obey it — wholeheartedly — and delete it before sending your manuscript to press. Murder your darlings.
> *On the Art of Writing [1916]. On Style*

James Harvey Robinson
1863–1936

12   Political campaigns are designedly made into emotional orgies which endeavor to distract attention from the real issues involved, and they actually paralyze what slight powers of cerebration man can normally muster.
> *The Human Comedy [1937], ch. 9*

13   With supreme irony, the war to "make the world safe for democracy" ended by leaving democracy more unsafe in the world than at any time since the collapse of the revolutions of 1848.
> *The Human Comedy, 9*

---

[1]Translated by EDMUND KEELEY and GEORGE SAVIDIS.

[2]Translated by W. H. AUDEN and MARGUERITE YOURCENAR.

[3]Translated by ROBERT LIDDELL.

[4]Translated by JOHN MAVROGORDATO.

[5]Translated by EDMUND KEELEY and PHILLIP SHERRARD.

[6]Hearst always denied sending such a telegram, and there is no proof that he ever did, even though it accurately reflects his views at the time. — JOYCE MILTON, *The Yellow Kids: Foreign Correspondents in the Heyday of Yellow Journalism* [1989]

George Santayana
1863–1952

1 O World, thou choosest not the better part!
It is not wisdom to be only wise,
And on the inward vision close the eyes,
But it is wisdom to believe the heart.
O World, Thou Choosest Not [1894]

2 Beauty as we feel it is something indescribable: what it is or what it means can never be said.
The Sense of Beauty [1896], pt. IV, Expression

3 Even the most inspired verse, which boasts not without a relative justification to be immortal, becomes in the course of ages a scarcely legible hieroglyphic; the language it was written in dies, a learned education and an imaginative effort are requisite to catch even a vestige of its original force. Nothing is so irrevocable as mind.
The Life of Reason [1905–1906], vol. I, Reason in Common Sense

4 Happiness is the only sanction of life; where happiness fails, existence remains a mad and lamentable experiment.
The Life of Reason, I, Reason in Common Sense

5 That life is worth living is the most necessary of assumptions, and, were it not assumed, the most impossible of conclusions.
The Life of Reason, I, Reason in Common Sense

6 Fanaticism consists in redoubling your efforts when you have forgotten your aim.
The Life of Reason, I, Reason in Common Sense

7 Those who cannot remember the past are condemned to repeat it.
The Life of Reason, I, Reason in Common Sense

8 When Socrates and his two great disciples composed a system of rational ethics they were hardly proposing practical legislation for mankind . . . They were merely writing an eloquent epitaph for their country.
The Life of Reason, V, Reason in Science

9 Let a man once overcome his selfish terror at his own finitude, and his finitude is, in one sense, overcome.
The Ethics of Spinoza [1910], introduction

10 Perhaps the only true dignity of man is his capacity to despise himself.
The Ethics of Spinoza, introduction

11 Miracles are propitious accidents, the natural causes of which are too complicated to be readily understood.   *The Ethics of Spinoza, introduction*

12 The Bible is literature, not dogma.
The Ethics of Spinoza, introduction

13 American life is a powerful solvent. It seems to neutralize every intellectual element, however tough and alien it may be, and to fuse it in the native good will, complacency, thoughtlessness, and optimism.
Character and Opinion in the United States [1920]

14 All his life he [the American] jumps into the train after it has started and jumps out before it has stopped; and he never once gets left behind, or breaks a leg.
Character and Opinion in the United States

15 There is no cure for birth and death save to enjoy the interval.
Soliloquies in England and Later Soliloquies [1922]. War Shrines

16 I like to walk about amidst the beautiful things that adorn the world; but private wealth I should decline, or any sort of personal possessions, because they would take away my liberty.
Soliloquies in England and Later Soliloquies. The Irony of Liberalism

17 My atheism, like that of Spinoza, is true piety towards the universe and denies only gods fashioned by men in their own image, to be servants of their human interests.
Soliloquies in England and Later Soliloquies. On My Friendly Critics

18 Scepticism is the chastity of the intellect, and it is shameful to surrender it too soon or to the first comer.
Scepticism and Animal Faith [1923], ch. 9

19 The young man who has not wept is a savage, and the old man who will not laugh is a fool.
Dialogues in Limbo [1926], ch. 3

20 Religion in its humility restores man to his only dignity, the courage to live by grace.
Dialogues in Limbo, 4

21 There is nothing impossible in the existence of the supernatural: its existence seems to me decidedly probable.
The Genteel Tradition at Bay [1931]

22 There is no God and Mary is His Mother.
From ROBERT LOWELL, Life Studies. For George Santayana [1953]

Konstantin Sergeevich Alekseev Stanislavski
1863–1938

1   Our type of creativeness is the conception and birth of a new being—the person in the part. It is a natural act similar to the birth of a human being.
An Actor Prepares [1936],[1] *ch. 16*

2   In the creative process there is the father, the author of the play; the mother, the actor pregnant with the part; and the child, the role to be born.
An Actor Prepares, 16

Ernest L[awrence] Thayer
1863–1940

3 There was ease in Casey's manner as he stepped into his place,
There was pride in Casey's bearing, and a smile on Casey's face,
And when, responding to the cheers, he lightly doffed his hat,
No stranger in the crowd could doubt 'twas Casey at the bat.
Casey at the Bat [1888], st. 6

4 Oh! somewhere in this favored land the sun is shining bright;
The band is playing somewhere, and somewhere hearts are light;
And somewhere men are laughing and somewhere children shout,
But there is no joy in Mudville—mighty Casey has struck out.
Casey at the Bat, st. 13

Sir Roger Casement
1864–1916

5   Where all your rights become only an accumulated wrong; where men must beg with bated breath for leave to subsist in their own land, to think their own thoughts, to sing their own songs, to garner the fruits of their own labors . . . then surely it is braver, a saner and truer thing, to be a rebel in act and deed against such circumstances as these than tamely to accept it as the natural lot of men.
Statement from prison [June 29, 1916]

Joseph Hayden
fl. 1896

6 There'll be a hot time in the old town tonight.
A Hot Time in the Old Town [1896][2]

Richard Hovey
1864–1900

7 For it's always fair weather
When good fellows get together
With a stein on the table and a good song ringing clear.
A Stein Song [1898], st. 1

8 O, Eleazer Wheelock was a very pious man;
He went into the wilderness to teach the Indian. . . .
Eleazer was the faculty, and the whole curriculum
Was five hundred gallons of New England rum.
Eleazer Wheelock, st. 1

Andrew Barton [Banjo] Paterson
1864–1941

9 Once a jolly swagman camped by a billabong,
Under the shade of a coolibah tree,
And he sang as he sat and waited for his billy-boil,
"Who'll come a-waltzing Matilda with me?"[3]
Waltzing Matilda

Jules Renard
1864–1910

10   To succeed you must add water to your wine, until there is no more wine.   *Journal*

11   There are moments when everything goes well; don't be frightened, it won't last.   *Journal*

12   I am not sincere even when I am saying that I am not sincere.   *Journal*

13   We don't understand life any better at forty than at twenty, but we know it and admit it.   *Journal*

---

[2]Hayden's text for a march, *A Hot Time in the Old Town Tonight* [1886], by Theodore August Metz [1848–1936], later a favorite of Theodore Roosevelt's Rough Riders in Cuba, and still later Roosevelt's campaign song.

[3]Swagman: tramp. Billabong: waterhole. Coolibah: eucalyptus. Billy: container used for brewing tea. Matilda: a bundle containing personal belongings.
Music by Marie Cowan.

---

[1]Translated by Elizabeth Reynolds Hapgood.

Miguel de Unamuno
1864–1936

1 Consciousness is a disease.
The Tragic Sense of Life [1913], ch. 1

2 True science teaches, above all, to doubt and be ignorant.
The Tragic Sense of Life, 5

3 To believe in God is to yearn for His existence and, furthermore, it is to act as if He did exist.
The Tragic Sense of Life, 8

4 Martyrs create faith, faith does not create martyrs.
The Tragic Sense of Life, 9

5 My work . . . is to shatter the faith of men here, there, and everywhere, faith in affirmation, faith in negation, and faith in abstention from faith, and this for the sake of faith in faith itself.[1]
The Tragic Sense of Life, conclusion

6 Warmth, warmth, more warmth! for we are dying of cold and not of darkness. It is not the night that kills, but the frost.
The Tragic Sense of Life, conclusion

7 The devil is an angel too.
Two Mothers

8 And killing time is perhaps the essence of comedy, just as the essence of tragedy is killing eternity.
San Manuel Bueno, prologue

9 I would say that teleology is theology, and that God is not a "because," but rather an "in order to."
San Manuel Bueno, prologue

10 Let us go on committing suicide by working among our people, and let them dream life just as the lake dreams the sky.
San Manuel Bueno, prologue

11 Every peasant has a lawyer inside of him, just as every lawyer, no matter how urbane he may be, carries a peasant within himself.
Civilization Is Civilism

12 These terrible sociologists, who are the astrologers and alchemists of our twentieth century.
Fanatical Skepticism

13 Faith which does not doubt is dead faith.
The Agony of Christianity

Max Weber
1864–1920

14 Charisma knows only inner determination and inner restraint. . . . The charismatic leader gains and maintains authority solely by proving his strength in life.[2]
Wirtschaft und Gesellschaft (Economy and Society) [1922], pt. III, ch. 9

Israel Zangwill
1864–1926

15 Scratch the Christian and you find the pagan—spoiled.
Children of the Ghetto [1892]

16 America is God's crucible, the great melting pot where all the races of Europe are melting and re-forming![3]
The Melting Pot [1908], act I

Mrs. Patrick Campbell
[Beatrice Stella Tanner Campbell]
1865–1940

17 My dear, I don't care what they do, as long as they don't do it in the street and frighten the horses.
Attributed

Edith [Louisa] Cavell
1865–1915

18 I realize that patriotism is not enough. I must have no hatred or bitterness towards anyone.
Last words [October 12, 1915], before her execution by the Germans

H[erbert] A[lbert] L[aurens] Fisher
1865–1940

19 All political decisions are taken under great pressure, and if a treaty serves its turn for ten or twenty years, the wisdom of its framers is sufficiently confirmed.
Political Prophecies [1918]

20 It is easier for eight or nine elderly men to feel their way towards unanimity if they are not com-

---

[1] Translated by J. E. CRAWFORD FLITCH.

[2] Translated by H. H. GERTH and C. WRIGHT MILLS.

[3] The point about the melting pot . . . is that it did not happen. —NATHAN GLAZER [1925–] and DANIEL PATRICK MOYNIHAN [1927–], *Beyond the Melting Pot* [1963]
See Crèvecoeur, 352:7.

pelled to conduct their converging maneuvers under the microscopes and telescopes of the press, but are permitted to shuffle about a little in slippers.

An International Experiment [1] *[1921]*

1   Purity of race does not exist. Europe is a continent of energetic mongrels.

A History of Europe [1934], ch. 1

2   Politics is the art of human happiness.

A History of Europe, 31

George V
1865–1936

3   How is the Empire?

Attributed last words [January 21, 1936] [2]

Frederic William Goudy
1865–1947

4   I am the voice of today, the herald of tomorrow. . . . I am the leaden army that conquers the world—I am TYPE.

The Type Speaks [1938]

Laurence Hope
[Adela Florence Cory Nicolson]
1865–1904

5 To have—to hold—and—in time—let go!

India's Love Lyrics. The Teak Forest, st. 10

6 Pale hands I loved beside the Shalimar.

India's Love Lyrics. Kashmiri Song, st. 1

Rudyard Kipling
1865–1936

7 I have eaten your bread and salt.
I have drunk your water and wine.
The deaths ye died I have watched beside
And the lives ye led were mine.

Departmental Ditties [1886]. Prelude, st. 1

8 Little Tin Gods on Wheels.

Departmental Ditties. Public Waste, st. 4

9 The toad beneath the harrow knows
Exactly where each tooth point goes;
The butterfly upon the road
Preaches contentment to that toad.

Departmental Ditties. Pagett, M.P., prelude

10 And a woman is only a woman, but a good cigar is a smoke.

Departmental Ditties. The Betrothed, st. 25

11   It takes a great deal of Christianity to wipe out uncivilized Eastern instincts, such as falling in love at first sight.

Plain Tales from the Hills [1888]. Lispeth

12   Never praise a sister to a sister, in the hope of your compliments reaching the proper ears.

Plain Tales from the Hills. False Dawn

13   Many religious people are deeply suspicious. They seem—for purely religious purposes, of course—to know more about iniquity than the unregenerate.

Plain Tales from the Hills. Watches of the Night

14   The silliest woman can manage a clever man; but it needs a very clever woman to manage a fool!

Plain Tales from the Hills. Three and—an Extra

15   Lalun is a member of the most ancient profession in the world.

In Black and White [1888]. On the City Wall

16   Steady the Buffs.

Soldiers Three [1888]

17 Down to Gehenna or up to the Throne,
He travels the fastest who travels alone. [3]

Soldiers Three. The Winners (L' Envoi: What Is the Moral?), st. 1

18   More men are killed by overwork than the importance of the world justifies.

The Phantom 'Rickshaw [1888]

19 Oh, East is East, and West is West, and never the twain shall meet,
Till Earth and Sky stand presently at God's great Judgment Seat;
But there is neither East nor West, border, nor breed, nor birth,
When two strong men stand face to face, though they come from the ends of the earth!

The Ballad of East and West [1889]

20   Bite on the bullet, old man, and don't let them think you're afraid.

The Light That Failed [1890–1891]

---

[1] The League of Nations.

[2] As reported by Buckingham Palace. As reported in the diary of LORD DAWSON, the king's physician, however, George's last words were "God damn you."

---

[3] He may well win the race that runs by himself. — BENJAMIN FRANKLIN, *Poor Richard's Almanac* [1757]

1 If I were damned of body and soul,
　I know whose prayers would make me whole,
　Mother o' mine, O mother o' mine.
　　　　　　　　　Mother o' Mine [1891]

2 And the end of the fight is a tombstone white with
　　the name of the late deceased,
　And the epitaph drear: "A Fool lies here who tried
　　to hustle the East."
　　　　　　　　　The Naulahka [1892], ch. 5

3 When Earth's last picture is painted, and the tubes
　　are twisted and dried,
　When the oldest colors have faded, and the
　　youngest critic has died,
　We shall rest, and, faith, we shall need it — lie down
　　for an eon or two,
　Till the Master of All Good Workmen shall put us
　　to work anew.
　　　　　　When Earth's Last Picture Is Painted [1892]

4 They rise to their feet as He passes by, gentlemen
　　unafraid.
　　　　　　Ballads and Barrack Room Ballads [1892,
　　　　　　1893]. Dedication, st. 5

5 "What are the bugles blowin' for?" said Files-on-
　　Parade.
　"To turn you out, to turn you out," the Color-
　　Sergeant said.
　　　　　　Ballads and Barrack Room Ballads. Danny
　　　　　　Deever,[1] st. 1

6 They've taken of his buttons off an' cut his stripes
　　away,
　An' they're hangin' Danny Deever in the mornin'.
　　　　　　Ballads and Barrack Room Ballads. Danny
　　　　　　Deever, st. 1

7 We aren't no thin red 'eroes.
　　　　　　Ballads and Barrack Room Ballads. Tommy,
　　　　　　st. 4

8 For it's Tommy this, an' Tommy that, an' "Chuck
　　'im out, the brute!"
　But it's "Savior of 'is country" when the guns
　　begin to shoot.
　　　　　　Ballads and Barrack Room Ballads. Tommy,
　　　　　　st. 5

9 So 'ere's *to* you, Fuzzy-Wuzzy, at your 'ome in the
　　Soudan;
　You're a pore benighted 'eathen but a first-class
　　fightin' man.
　　　　　　Ballads and Barrack Room Ballads. Fuzzy-
　　　　　　Wuzzy, st. 1

10 Though I've belted you an' flayed you,
　By the livin' Gawd that made you,
　You're a better man than I am, Gunga Din!
　　　　　　Ballads and Barrack Room Ballads. Gunga
　　　　　　Din, st. 5

11 'Ave you 'eard o' the Widow at Windsor
　With a hairy gold crown on 'er 'ead?
　　　　　　Ballads and Barrack Room Ballads. The
　　　　　　Widow at Windsor, st. 1

12 By the old Moulmein Pagoda, lookin' eastward to
　　the sea,
　There's a Burma girl a-settin', and I know she
　　thinks o' me;
　For the wind is in the palm trees, and the temple
　　bells they say:
　"Come you back, you British soldier; come you
　　back to Mandalay!"
　　　　　　Ballads and Barrack Room Ballads.
　　　　　　Mandalay,[2] st. 1

13 On the road to Mandalay,
　Where the flyin' fishes play,
　An' the dawn comes up like thunder outer China
　　'crost the Bay!
　　　　　　Ballads and Barrack Room Ballads.
　　　　　　Mandalay, st. 1

14 Ship me somewheres east of Suez, where the best is
　　like the worst,
　Where there aren't no Ten Commandments, an' a
　　man can raise a thirst.
　　　　　　Ballads and Barrack Room Ballads.
　　　　　　Mandalay, st. 6

15 The Devil whispered behind the leaves, "It's pretty,
　　but is it Art?"
　　　　　　Ballads and Barrack Room Ballads. The
　　　　　　Conundrum of the Workshops, st. 1

16 To the legion of the lost ones, to the cohort of the
　　damned.
　　　　　　Ballads and Barrack Room Ballads.
　　　　　　Gentlemen Rankers, st. 1

17 We're poor little lambs who've lost our way,
　　Baa! Baa! Baa!
　We're little black sheep who've gone astray,
　　Baa — aa — aa!
　Gentlemen rankers out on the spree,
　Damned from here to Eternity,
　God ha' mercy on such as we,
　　Baa! Yah! Baa!
　　　　　　Ballads and Barrack Room Ballads.
　　　　　　Gentlemen Rankers, refrain

---

[1]Music by WALTER DAMROSCH [1862–1950].

[2]Music by OLEY SPEAKS [1874–1948].

1 We have done with Hope and Honor, we are lost
    to Love and Truth,
We are dropping down the ladder rung by rung;
And the measure of our torment is the measure of
    our youth.
God help us, for we knew the worst too young!
    Ballads and Barrack Room Ballads.
    Gentlemen Rankers, st. 4

2 And what should they know of England who only
    England know?
    Ballads and Barrack Room Ballads. The
    English Flag, st. 1

3 The sin ye do by two and two ye must pay for one
    by one.
    Ballads and Barrack Room Ballads.
    Tomlinson, l. 60

4 There's a legion that never was 'listed,
    That carries no colors or crest.
    Ballads and Barrack Room Ballads. The Lost
    Legion, st. 1

5 There are nine and sixty ways of constructing tribal
    lays,
    And every single one of them is right.
    Ballads and Barrack Room Ballads. In the
    Neolithic Age, st. 5

6 There be triple ways to take, of the eagle or the
    snake,
Or the way of a man with a maid;
But the sweetest way to me is a ship's upon the sea
In the heel of the Northeast Trade.
    Ballads and Barrack Room Ballads. The Long
    Trail, st. 5

7 When you're wounded and left on Afghanistan's
    plains,
And the women come out to cut up what remains,
Jest roll to your rifle and blow out your brains
An' go to your Gawd like a soldier.
    The Young British Soldier [1892]

8   He wrapped himself in quotations—as a beggar
would enfold himself in the purple of emperors.
    Many Inventions [1893]. The Finest Story in
    the World

9 When 'Omer smote 'is bloomin' lyre,
    He'd 'eard men sing by land an' sea;
An' what he thought 'e might require,
    'E went an' took—the same as me!
    When 'Omer Smote 'Is Bloomin' Lyre [1894],
    st. 1

10 Back to the Army again, sergeant,
    Back to the Army again.
Out o' the cold an' the rain.
    Back to the Army Again [1894], refrain

11   We be of one blood, ye and I.
    The Jungle Book [1894]. Kaa's Hunting

12 Brother, thy tail hangs down behind.
    The Jungle Book. Road Song of the
    Bandar-Log, refrain

13 Now this is the Law of the Jungle—as old and as
    true as the sky;
And the Wolf that shall keep it may prosper, but
    the Wolf that shall break it must die.
    The Second Jungle Book [1895]. The Law of
    the Jungle, st. 1

14 When Pack meets with Pack in the Jungle, and
    neither will go from the trail,
Lie down till the leaders have spoken—it may be
    fair words shall prevail.
    The Second Jungle Book. The Law of the
    Jungle, st. 6

15 Now these are the Laws of the Jungle, and many
    and mighty are they;
But the head and the hoof of the Law and the
    haunch and the hump is—Obey!
    The Second Jungle Book. The Law of the
    Jungle, st. 19

16 They change their skies above them,
    But not their hearts that roam.
    The Nativeborn [1895], st. 2

17 The Liner she's a lady, an' she never looks nor
    'eeds—
The Man-o'-War's 'er 'usband, an' 'e gives 'er all
    she needs,
But, oh, the little cargo boats that sail the wet seas
    roun',
They're just the same as you an' me a-plyin' up and
    down!
    The Liner She's a Lady [1895], st. 1

18 I've taken my fun where I've found it.
    The Ladies [1895], st. 1

19 For the Colonel's Lady an' Judy O'Grady
    Are sisters under their skins!   *The Ladies, st. 8*

20 'E's a sort of a bloomin' cosmopolouse—soldier
    an' sailor too.
    Soldier an' Sailor Too [1896], st. 2

21 A fool there was and he made his prayer
    (Even as you and I!)
To a rag and a bone and a hank of hair
    (We called her the woman who did not care)
But the fool he called her his lady fair—
    (Even as you and I!)   *The Vampire [1897], st. 1*

22 Daughter am I in my mother's house;
    But mistress in my own.
    Our Lady of the Snows [1898], st. 1

1 God of our fathers, known of old,
  Lord of our far-flung battle line,
  Beneath whose awful Hand we hold
  Dominion over palm and pine—
  Lord God of Hosts, be with us yet,
  Lest we forget—lest we forget!
                              Recessional [1899], st. 1

2 The tumult and the shouting dies;
  The captains and the kings depart.
                              Recessional, st. 2

3 Lo, all our pomp of yesterday
  Is one with Nineveh and Tyre!   *Recessional, st. 3*

4 Lesser breeds without the Law.   *Recessional, st. 4*

5 For frantic boast and foolish word—
  Thy mercy on Thy People, Lord!
                              Recessional, st. 5

6 Take up the White Man's burden,[1]
  Send forth the best ye breed—
  Go, bind your sons to exile
  To serve your captives' need.
                    The White Man's Burden [1899], st. 1

7   Little Friend of All the World.
                              Kim [1901], ch. 1

8 The flanneled fools at the wicket or the muddied
     oafs at the goals.   *The Islanders [1902], l. 31*

9 I keep six honest serving men
  (They taught me all I knew);
  Their names are What and Why and When
  And How and Where and Who.
                    *The Just-So Stories [1902]. The Elephant's
                    Child*

10   The great gray-green, greasy Limpopo River, all
      set about with fever-trees.
                    The Just-So Stories. The Elephant's Child

11 Rolling down to Rio.
                    *The Just-So Stories. The Beginning of the
                    Armadilloes, st. 2*

12   The Cat. He walked by himself, and all places
      were alike to him.
                    *The Just-So Stories. The Cat That Walked By
                    Himself*

13   He went back through the wet wild woods, wav-
      ing his wild tail, and walking by his wild lone. But
      he never told anybody.
                    *The Just-So Stories. The Cat That Walked By
                    Himself*

14 Who hath desired the sea?—the sight of salt water
     unbounded.
                    The Sea and the Hills [1903], st. 1

15 Something hidden. Go and find it. Go and look
     behind the Ranges—
   Something lost behind the Ranges. Lost and
     waiting for you. Go![2]
                    The Explorer [1903], st. 2

16 Boots—boots—boots—boots—movin' up and
     down again!
   There's no discharge in the war!
                    Boots [1903], st. 1

17   'Tisn't beauty, so to speak, nor good talk neces-
      sarily. It's just It. Some women'll stay in a man's
      memory if they once walked down a street.
                    Traffics and Discoveries [1904]. Mrs. Bathurst

18 Of all the trees that grow so fair,
   Old England to adorn,
   Greater are none beneath the Sun,
   Than oak, and ash, and thorn.
                    Puck of Pook's Hill [1906]. A Tree Song, st. 1

19 Brothers and Sisters, I bid you beware
   Of giving your heart to a dog to tear.
                    The Power of the Dog [1909]

20 If you can meet with Triumph and Disaster
   And treat those two impostors just the same.
                    Rewards and Fairies [1910]. If, st. 2

21 If you can talk with crowds and keep your virtue,
   Or walk with Kings—nor lose the common touch.
                    Rewards and Fairies. If, st. 4

22 Yours is the Earth and everything that's in it,
   And—which is more—you'll be a Man, my son!
                    Rewards and Fairies. If, st. 4

23 The female of the species is more deadly than the
     male.
                    The Female of the Species [1911], st. 1

24 Oh, Adam was a gardener, and God who made him
     sees
   That half a proper gardener's work is done upon
     his knees.   *The Glory of the Garden, st. 8*

25 For all we have and are,
   For all our children's fate,
   Stand up and take the war.
   The Hun is at the gate!
                    For All We Have and Are [1914], st. 1

26 What stands if Freedom fall?
   Who dies if England live?
                    For All We Have and Are, st. 4

---

[1]Pile on the brown man's burden / To gratify your greed.—JOHN
HOLLINGSHEAD, *published by* HENRY LABOUCHÈRE *in London Truth;
reprinted in Middlebury (Vermont) Register* [March 17, 1899]

---

[2]Because it is there.—GEORGE LEIGH MALLORY [1886–1924],
when asked why he wanted to climb Mount Everest

1 Hot and bothered.
> *Independence. Rectorial Address at St. Andrews [October 10, 1923]*

2 When your Daemon is in charge, do not try to think consciously. Drift, wait, and obey.
> *Something of Myself for My Friends Known and Unknown [1937], ch. 8*

Baroness Emmuska Orczy
1865–1947

3 We seek him here, we seek him there,
Those Frenchies seek him everywhere.
Is he in heaven?—Is he in hell?
That demmed, elusive Pimpernel?
> *The Scarlet Pimpernel [1905], ch. 12*

Logan Pearsall Smith
1865–1946

4 There are two things to aim at in life: first, to get what you want; and, after that, to enjoy it. Only the wisest of mankind achieve the second.
> *Afterthoughts [1931]*

5 How awful to reflect that what people say of us is true!   *Afterthoughts*

6 Solvency is entirely a matter of temperament and not of income.   *Afterthoughts*

7 There are few sorrows, however poignant, in which a good income is of no avail.
> *Afterthoughts*

8 The indefatigable pursuit of an unattainable perfection, even though it consist in nothing more than in the pounding of an old piano, is what alone gives a meaning to our life on this unavailing star.
> *Afterthoughts*

9 What I like in a good author is not what he says, but what he whispers.   *Afterthoughts*

10 People say that life is the thing, but I prefer reading.   *Afterthoughts*

11 There is more felicity on the far side of baldness than young men can possibly imagine.
> *Afterthoughts*

12 Thank heavens, the sun has gone in, and I don't have to go out and enjoy it.   *Afterthoughts*

Arthur Symons
1865–1945

13 And I would have, now love is over,
An end to all, an end:

I cannot, having been your lover,
Stoop to become your friend!
> *After Love [1892], st. 3*

14 My soul is like this cloudy, flaming opal ring.
> *Opals [1896]*

15 He knew that the whole mystery of beauty can never be comprehended by the crowd, and that while clearness is a virtue of style, perfect explicitness is not a necessary virtue.
> *The Symbolist Movement in Literature [1899]. Gérard de Nerval*

16 Without charm there can be no fine literature, as there can be no perfect flower without fragrance.
> *The Symbolist Movement in Literature. Stéphane Mallarmé*

17 The mystic too full of God to speak intelligibly to the world.
> *The Symbolist Movement in Literature. Arthur Rimbaud*

William Butler Yeats[1]
1865–1939

18 The woods of Arcady are dead,
And over is their antique joy;
Of old the world on dreaming fed;
Gray Truth is now her painted toy.
> *Crossways [1889]. The Song of the Happy Shepherd, st. 1*

19 Down by the salley gardens my love and I did meet;
She passed the salley gardens with little snow-white feet.
She bid me take love easy, as the leaves grow on the tree;
But I, being young and foolish, with her would not agree.
> *Crossways. Down by the Salley Gardens*

20 She bid me take life easy, as the grass grows on the weirs;
But I was young and foolish, and now am full of tears.   *Crossways. Down by the Salley Gardens*

21 The years like great black oxen tread the world,
And God the herdsman goads them on behind,
And I am broken by their passing feet.
> *The Countess Cathleen [1892], last lines*

22 Red Rose, proud Rose, sad Rose of all my days!
Come near me, while I sing the ancient ways.
> *The Rose [1893]. To the Rose Upon the Rood of Time, st. 1*

---

[1]See Auden, 775:14.

1 I will arise and go now, and go to Innisfree,
  And a small cabin build there, of clay and wattles
    made:
  Nine bean-rows will I have there, a hive for the
    honeybee,
  And live alone in the bee-loud glade.
          The Rose. The Lake Isle of Innisfree,[1] *st. 1*

2 A pity beyond all telling
  Is hid in the heart of love.
                    The Rose. The Pity of Love

3 The brawling of a sparrow in the eaves,
  The brilliant moon and all the milky sky,
  And all that famous harmony of leaves,
  Had blotted out man's image and his cry.
                The Rose. The Sorrow of Love, st. 1

4 When you are old and gray and full of sleep,
  And nodding by the fire, take down this book.[2]
                The Rose. When You Are Old, st. 1

5 How many loved your moments of glad grace,
  And loved your beauty with love false or true,
  But one man loved the pilgrim soul in you,
  And loved the sorrows of your changing face.
                The Rose. When You Are Old, st. 2

6   The Land of Faery,
  Where nobody gets old and godly and grave,
  Where nobody gets old and crafty and wise,
  Where nobody gets old and bitter of tongue.
              The Land of Heart's Desire [1894], l. 48

7   Land of Heart's Desire,
  Where beauty has no ebb, decay no flood,
  But joy is wisdom, time an endless song.
                The Land of Heart's Desire, l. 373

8 All things uncomely and broken, all things worn
    out and old,
  The cry of a child by the roadway, the creak of a
    lumbering cart,
  The heavy steps of the plowman, splashing the
    wintry mold,
  Are wronging your image that blossoms a rose in
    the deeps of my heart.
          *The Wind Among the Reeds [1899]. The
          Lover Tells of the Rose in His Heart, st. 1*

9 And God stands winding His lonely horn,
  And time and the world are ever in flight.
          The Wind Among the Reeds. Into the Twilight

---

[1]I had still the ambition, formed in Sligo in my teens, of living in imitation of Thoreau on Innisfree, a little island in Lough Gill, and when walking through Fleet Street very homesick I heard a little tinkle of water and saw a fountain in a shop window which balanced a little ball upon its jet, and began to remember lake water. From the sudden remembrance came my poem Innisfree. —YEATS, *The Trembling of the Veil* [1926]

[2]See Ronsard, 151:1.

10 And pluck till time and times are done
   The silver apples of the moon,
   The golden apples of the sun.
          *The Wind Among the Reeds. The Song of
          Wandering Aengus, st. 3*

11 Had I the heavens' embroidered cloths,
   Enwrought with gold and silver light.
          *The Wind Among the Reeds. He Wishes for the
          Cloths of Heaven*

12 But I, being poor, have only my dreams;
   I have spread my dreams under your feet;
   Tread softly because you tread on my dreams.
          *The Wind Among the Reeds. He Wishes for the
          Cloths of Heaven*

13 When I play on my fiddle in Dooney,
   Folk dance like a wave of the sea.
          *The Wind Among the Reeds. The Fiddler of
          Dooney, st. 1*

14 O heart! O heart! if she'd but turn her head,
   You'd know the folly of being comforted.
          *In the Seven Woods [1904]. The Folly of Being
          Comforted*

15 Never give all the heart, for love
   Will hardly seem worth thinking of
   To passionate women if it seem
   Certain, and they never dream
   That it fades out from kiss to kiss;
   For everything that's lovely is
   But a brief, dreamy kind delight.
          In the Seven Woods. Never Give All the Heart

16 I said, "A line will take us hours maybe;
   Yet if it does not seem a moment's thought,
   Our stitching and unstitching has been naught.
   Better go down upon your marrow-bones
   And scrub a kitchen pavement, or break stones."
                In the Seven Woods. Adam's Curse, st. 1

17 For to articulate sweet sounds together
   Is to work harder than all these, and yet
   Be thought an idler by the noisy set
   Of bankers, schoolmasters, and clergymen
   The martyrs call the world.
                In the Seven Woods. Adam's Curse, st. 1

18   It's certain there is no fine thing
   Since Adam's fall but needs much laboring.
                In the Seven Woods. Adam's Curse, st. 3

19 I heard the old, old men say,
   "All that's beautiful drifts away
   Like the waters."
          *In the Seven Woods. The Old Men Admiring
          Themselves in the Water*

20 The friends that have it I do wrong
   When ever I remake a song

Should know what issue is at stake,
It is myself that I remake.
> *The Collected Works in Verse and Prose of*
> *William Butler Yeats [1908], II, preliminary*
> *poem*

1 Why, what could she have done, being what
    she is?
Was there another Troy for her to burn?
> *The Green Helmet and Other Poems [1910].*
> *No Second Troy*

2 The fascination of what's difficult
Has dried the sap out of my veins, and rent
Spontaneous joy and natural content
Out of my heart.
> *The Green Helmet and Other Poems. The*
> *Fascination of What's Difficult*

3 Wine comes in at the mouth
And love comes in at the eye;
That's all we shall know for truth
Before we grow old and die.
> *The Green Helmet and Other Poems. A*
> *Drinking Song*

4 Though leaves are many, the root is one;
Through all the lying days of my youth
I swayed my leaves and flowers in the sun;
Now I may wither into the truth.
> *The Green Helmet and Other Poems. The*
> *Coming of Wisdom with Time*

5 In dreams begins responsibility.
> *Responsibilities [1914], epigraph (from an old*
> *play)*

6 Pardon, old fathers.
> *Responsibilities, preliminary poem*

7 Was it for this the wild geese spread
The gray wing upon every tide;
For this that all that blood was shed,
For this Edward Fitzgerald died,
And Robert Emmet and Wolfe Tone,
All that delirium of the brave?
Romantic Ireland's dead and gone,
It's with O'Leary in the grave.
> *Responsibilities. September 1913, st. 3*

8 Be secret and exult,
Because of all things known
That is most difficult.
> *Responsibilities. To a Friend Whose Work Has*
> *Come to Nothing*

9 The uncontrollable mystery on the bestial floor.
> *Responsibilities. The Magi, last line*

10 I made my song a coat
Covered with embroideries
Out of old mythologies

From heel to throat;
But the fools caught it,
Wore it in the world's eyes
As though they'd wrought it.
Song, let them take it,
For there's more enterprise
In walking naked.
> *Responsibilities. A Coa*

11 Upon the brimming water among the stones
Are nine-and-fifty swans.
> *The Wild Swans at Coole [1919]. The Wild*
> *Swans at Coole, st. 1*

12 Unwearied still, lover by lover,
They paddle in the cold
Companionable streams or climb the air;
Their hearts have not grown old.
> *The Wild Swans at Coole. The Wild Swans at*
> *Coole, st. 4*

13 Some burn damp faggots, others may consume
The entire combustible world in one small room.
> *The Wild Swans at Coole. In Memory of*
> *Major Robert Gregory, st. 11*

14 What made us dream that he could comb gray
    hair?
> *The Wild Swans at Coole. In Memory of*
> *Major Robert Gregory, st. 11*

15   A thought
Of that late death took all my heart for speech.
> *The Wild Swans at Coole. In Memory of*
> *Major Robert Gregory, st. 12*

16 I know that I shall meet my fate
Somewhere among the clouds above;
Those that I fight I do not hate,
Those that I guard I do not love;
My country is Kiltartan Cross,
My countrymen Kiltartan's poor.
> *The Wild Swans at Coole. An Irish Airman*
> *Foresees His Death, l. 1*

17 Nor law, nor duty bade me fight,
Nor public men, nor cheering crowds,
A lonely impulse of delight
Drove to this tumult in the clouds.
> *The Wild Swans at Coole. An Irish Airman*
> *Foresees His Death, l. 9*

18 And I may dine at journey's end
With Landor and with Donne.
> *The Wild Swans at Coole. To a Young Beauty,*
> *st. 3*

19 All the wild witches, those most noble ladies,
For all their broomsticks and their tears,
Their angry tears, are gone.
> *The Wild Swans at Coole. Lines Written in*
> *Dejection, l. 4*

1 I knew a phoenix in my youth, so let them have
  their day.
> *The Wild Swans at Coole. His Phoenix, refrain*

2 Hands, do what you're bid:
  Bring the balloon of the mind
  That bellies and drags in the wind
  Into its narrow shed.
> *The Wild Swans at Coole. The Balloon of the*
> *Mind*

3 We have lit upon the gentle, sensitive mind
  And lost the old nonchalance of the hand;
  Whether we have chosen chisel, pen or brush,
  We are but critics, or but half create.
> *The Wild Swans at Coole. Ego Dominus Tuus,*
> *l. 12*

4 All changed, changed utterly:
  A terrible beauty is born.
> *Michael Robartes and the Dancer [1921].*
> *Easter 1916, st. 1*

5 Too long a sacrifice
  Can make a stone of the heart.
  O when may it suffice?
> *Michael Robartes and the Dancer. Easter*
> *1916, st. 4*

6 Turning and turning in the widening gyre
  The falcon cannot hear the falconer;
  Things fall apart; the center cannot hold;
  Mere anarchy is loosed upon the world,
  The blood-dimmed tide is loosed, and
    everywhere
  The ceremony of innocence is drowned;
  The best lack all conviction, while the worst
  Are full of passionate intensity.
> *Michael Robartes and the Dancer. The Second*
> *Coming, st. 1*

7   Now I know
  That twenty centuries of stony sleep
  Were vexed to nightmare by a rocking cradle,
  And what rough beast, its hour come round
    at last,
  Slouches towards Bethlehem to be born?
> *Michael Robartes and the Dancer. The Second*
> *Coming, st. 2*

8 Imagining in excited reverie
  That the future years had come,
  Dancing to a frenzied drum,
  Out of the murderous innocence of the sea.
> *Michael Robartes and the Dancer. A Prayer*
> *for My Daughter, st. 2*

9   For such,
  Being made beautiful overmuch,
  Consider beauty a sufficient end,
  Lose natural kindness and maybe

The heart-revealing intimacy
That chooses right, and never find a friend.
> *Michael Robartes and the Dancer. A Prayer*
> *for My Daughter, st. 3*

10 It's certain that fine women eat
   A crazy salad with their meat.
> *Michael Robartes and the Dancer. A Prayer*
> *for My Daughter, st. 4*

11 In courtesy I'd have her chiefly learned;
   Hearts are not had as a gift but hearts are earned.
> *Michael Robartes and the Dancer. A Prayer*
> *for My Daughter, st. 5*

12 And many a poor man that has roved,
   Loved and thought himself beloved,
   From a glad kindness cannot take his eyes.
> *Michael Robartes and the Dancer. A Prayer*
> *for My Daughter, st. 5*

13 If there's no hatred in a mind
   Assault and battery of the wind
   Can never tear the linnet from the leaf.
> *Michael Robartes and the Dancer. A Prayer*
> *for My Daughter, st. 7*

14 An intellectual hatred is the worst,
   So let her think opinions are accursed.
   Have I not seen the loveliest woman born
   Out of the mouth of Plenty's horn,
   Because of her opinionated mind
   Barter that horn and every good
   By quiet natures understood
   For an old bellows full of angry wind?
> *Michael Robartes and the Dancer. A Prayer*
> *for My Daughter, st. 8*

15   All hatred driven hence,
   The soul recovers radical innocence
   And learns at last that it is self-delighting,
   Self-appeasing, self-affrighting,
   And that its own sweet will is Heaven's will.
> *Michael Robartes and the Dancer. A Prayer*
> *for My Daughter, st. 9*

16 That is no country for old men. The young
   In one another's arms, birds in the trees
   —Those dying generations—at their song,
   The salmon-falls, the mackerel-crowded seas,
   Fish, flesh, or fowl, commend all summer long
   Whatever is begotten, born, and dies.
   Caught in that sensual music all neglect
   Monuments of unaging intellect.
> *The Tower [1928]. Sailing to Byzantium, st. 1*

17 An aged man is but a paltry thing,
   A tattered coat upon a stick, unless
   Soul clap its hands and sing, and louder sing
   For every tatter in its mortal dress.
> *The Tower. Sailing to Byzantium, st. 2*

1 Consume my heart away; sick with desire
And fastened to a dying animal
It knows not what it is; and gather me
Into the artifice of eternity.
The Tower. Sailing to Byzantium, st. 3

2 Once out of nature I shall never take
My bodily form from any natural thing,
But such a form as Grecian goldsmiths make
Of hammered gold and gold enameling
To keep a drowsy Emperor awake;
Or set upon a golden bough to sing
To lords and ladies of Byzantium
Of what is past, or passing, or to come.[1]
The Tower. Sailing to Byzantium, st. 4

3 What shall I do with this absurdity—
O heart, O troubled heart—this caricature,
Decrepit age that has been tied to me
As to a dog's tail?
The Tower. The Tower, I

4 Does the imagination dwell the most
Upon a woman won or a woman lost?
The Tower. The Tower, II, st. 13

5 The night can sweat with terror as before
We pieced our thoughts into philosophy,
And planned to bring the world under a rule,
Who are but weasels fighting in a hole.
*The Tower. Nineteen Hundred and Nineteen,
I, st. 4*

6 But is there any comfort to be found?
Man is in love and loves what vanishes,
What more is there to say?
*The Tower. Nineteen Hundred and Nineteen,
I, st. 6*

7 O but we dreamed to mend
Whatever mischief seemed
To afflict mankind, but now
That winds of winter blow
Learn that we were crack-pated when we dreamed.
*The Tower. Nineteen Hundred and Nineteen,
III, st. 3*

8 Come let us mock at the great
That had such burdens on the mind
And toiled so hard and late
To leave some monument behind,
Nor thought of the leveling wind.
*The Tower. Nineteen Hundred and Nineteen,
V, st. 1*

9 Much did I rage when young,
Being by the world oppressed,

But now with flattering tongue
It speeds the parting guest.
The Tower. Youth and Age

10 Odor of blood when Christ was slain
Made all Platonic tolerance vain
And vain all Doric discipline.
The Tower. Two Songs from a Play, II, st. 1

11 Everything that man esteems
Endures a moment or a day.
Love's pleasure drives his love away,
The painter's brush consumes his dreams.
The Tower. Two Songs from a Play, II, st. 2

12 Whatever flames upon the night
Man's own resinous heart has fed.
The Tower. Two Songs from a Play, II, st. 2

13 Locke sank into a swoon;
The Garden died;
God took the spinning-jenny
Out of his side.
The Tower. Fragments, I

14 A shudder in the loins engenders there
The broken wall, the burning roof and tower
And Agamemnon dead.
The Tower. Leda and the Swan, st. 3

15 Labor is blossoming or dancing where
The body is not bruised to pleasure soul,
Nor beauty born out of its own despair,
Nor blear-eyed wisdom out of midnight oil.
O chestnut tree, great-rooted blossomer,
Are you the leaf, the blossom or the bole?
O body swayed to music, O brightening glance,
How can we know the dancer from the dance?
The Tower. Among School Children, st. 8

16 Never to have lived is best, ancient writers say;
Never to have drawn the breath of life, never to
     have looked into the eye of day;
The second best's a gay goodnight and quickly
     turn away.
From "Oedipus at Colonus," st. 3

17   That toil of growing up;
The ignominy of boyhood; the distress
Of boyhood changing into man;
The unfinished man and his pain.
*The Winding Stair and Other Poems [1933].
A Dialogue of Self and Soul, II, st. 1*

18 I am content to live it all again
And yet again, if it be life to pitch
Into the frog-spawn of a blind man's ditch.
*The Winding Stair and Other Poems. A
Dialogue of Self and Soul, II, st. 3*

19 When such as I cast out remorse
So great a sweetness flows into the breast

---

[1] I have read somewhere that in the Emperor's palace at Byzantium was a tree made of gold and silver, and artificial birds that sang. —YEATS's *note*

We must laugh and we must sing,
We are blest by everything,
Everything we look upon is blest.
> *The Winding Stair and Other Poems. A
> Dialogue of Self and Soul, II, st. 4*

1   But what is Whiggery?
A leveling, rancorous, rational sort of mind
That never looked out of the eye of a saint
Or out of drunkard's eye.
> *The Winding Stair and Other Poems. The
> Seven Sages*

2   Only God, my dear,
Could love you for yourself alone
And not your yellow hair.
> *The Winding Stair and Other Poems. For
> Anne Gregory, st. 3*

3 Swift has sailed into his rest;
Savage indignation there
Cannot lacerate his breast,
Imitate him if you dare,
World-besotted traveler; he
Served human liberty.
> *The Winding Stair and Other Poems. Swift's
> Epitaph*[1]

4 The intellect of man is forced to choose
Perfection of the life, or of the work,
And if it take the second must refuse
A heavenly mansion, raging in the dark.
> *The Winding Stair and Other Poems. The
> Choice, st. 1*

5 The unpurged images of day recede;
The Emperor's drunken soldiery are abed;
Night resonance recedes, night-walkers' song
After great cathedral gong.
> *The Winding Stair and Other Poems.
> Byzantium, st. 1*

6 At midnight on the Emperor's pavement flit
Flames that no faggot feeds, nor steel has lit.
> *The Winding Stair and Other Poems.
> Byzantium, st. 4*

7 An agony of flame that cannot singe a sleeve.
> *The Winding Stair and Other Poems.
> Byzantium, st. 4*

8 That dolphin-torn, that gong-tormented sea.
> *The Winding Stair and Other Poems.
> Byzantium, st. 5*

9 No man has ever lived that had enough
Of children's gratitude or woman's love.
> *The Winding Stair and Other Poems.
> Vacillation, III, st. 1*

10 Things said or done long years ago,
Or things I did not do or say
But thought that I might say or do,
Weigh me down, and not a day
But something is recalled,
My conscience or my vanity appalled.
> *The Winding Stair and Other Poems.
> Vacillation, V, st. 2*

11 Homer is my example and his unchristened
      heart.
> *The Winding Stair and Other Poems.
> Vacillation, VIII*

12 Somewhere beyond the curtain
Of distorting days
Lives that lonely thing
That shone before these eyes
Targeted, trod like Spring.
> *The Winding Stair and Other Poems. Quarrel
> in Old Age, st. 2*

13 I had wild Jack for a lover.
> *The Winding Stair and Other Poems.
> Words for Music Perhaps, V, Crazy Jane
> on God, st. 4*

14 "Fair and foul are near of kin,
And fair needs foul," I cried.
"My friends are gone, but that's a truth
Nor grave nor bed denied."
> *The Winding Stair and Other Poems. Words
> for Music Perhaps, VI, Crazy Jane Talks with
> the Bishop, st. 2*

15 But Love has pitched his mansion in
The place of excrement
For nothing can be sole or whole
That has not been rent.
> *The Winding Stair and Other Poems. Words
> for Music Perhaps, VI, Crazy Jane Talks with
> the Bishop, st. 3*

16 What were all the world's alarms
To mighty Paris when he found
Sleep upon a golden bed
That first dawn in Helen's arms?
> *The Winding Stair and Other Poems.
> Words for Music Perhaps, XVI, Lullaby,
> st. 1*

17 Speech after long silence; it is right,
All other lovers being estranged or dead . . .
That we descant and yet again descant
Upon the supreme theme of Art and Song:
Bodily decrepitude is wisdom; young
We loved each other and were ignorant.
> *The Winding Stair and Other Poems.
> Words for Music Perhaps, XVII, After Long
> Silence*

---

[1]See Swift, 299:29.

1 I carry the sun in a golden cup,
  The moon in a silver bag.[1]
      *The Winding Stair and Other Poems. Words
      for Music Perhaps, XIX, Those Dancing Days
      Are Gone*

2 I gave what other women gave
  That stepped out of their clothes,
  But when this soul, its body off,
  Naked to naked goes,
  He it has found shall find therein
  What none other knows.
      *The Winding Stair and Other Poems. A
      Woman Young and Old, IX, A Last
      Confession, st. 3*

3 He that sings a lasting song
  Thinks in a marrowbone.
      *A Full Moon in March [1935]. A Prayer for
      Old Age, st. 1*

4 I pray — for fashion's word is out
  And prayer comes round again —
  That I may seem, though I die old,
  A foolish, passionate man.
      *A Full Moon in March. A Prayer for Old Age,
      st. 3*

5   Whence had they come,
  The hand and lash that beat down frigid Rome?
  What sacred drama through her body heaved
  When world-transforming Charlemagne was
      conceived?
      *A Full Moon in March. Supernatural Songs,
      VIII, Whence Had They Come?*

6 All perform their tragic play,
  There struts Hamlet, there is Lear.
      Last Poems [1936–1939]. Lapis Lazuli, st. 2

7   Heaven blazing into the head:
  Tragedy wrought to its uttermost.
  Though Hamlet rambles and Lear rages,
  And all the drop-scenes drop at once
  Upon a hundred thousand stages,
  It cannot grow by an inch or an ounce.
      Last Poems. Lapis Lazuli, st. 2

8 Their eyes mid many wrinkles, their eyes,
  Their ancient, glittering eyes, are gay.
      Last Poems. Lapis Lazuli, st. 5

9 If soul may look and body touch,
  Which is the more blest?
      Last Poems. The Lady's Second Song, st. 3

10 My temptation is quiet.
  Here at life's end
  Neither loose imagination,

Nor the mill of the mind
  Consuming its rag and bone,
  Can make the truth known.
      Last Poems. An Acre of Grass, st. 2

11 Grant me an old man's frenzy,
  Myself must I remake
  Till I am Timon and Lear
  Or that William Blake
  Who beat upon the wall
  Till Truth obeyed his call.
      Last Poems. An Acre of Grass, st. 3

12 An old man's eagle mind.
      Last Poems. An Acre of Grass, st. 4

13 Hurrah for revolution and more cannon-shot!
  A beggar upon horseback lashes a beggar on foot.
  Hurrah for revolution and cannon come again!
  The beggars have changed places, but the lash
      goes on.
      Last Poems. The Great Day

14 You think it horrible that lust and rage
  Should dance attention upon my old age;
  They were not such a plague when I was young;
  What else have I to spur me into song?
      Last Poems. The Spur

15 John Synge, I and Augusta Gregory, thought
  All that we did, all that we said or sang
  Must come from contact with the soil, from that
  Contact everything Antaeus-like grew strong.
      *Last Poems. The Municipal Gallery Revisited,
      st. 6*

16 Think where man's glory most begins and ends,
  And say my glory was I had such friends.
      *Last Poems. The Municipal Gallery Revisited,
      st. 7*

17 Down the mountain walls
  From where Pan's cavern is
  Intolerable music falls.
  Foul goat-head, brutal arm appear,
  Belly, shoulder, bum,
  Flash fishlike; nymphs and satyrs
  Copulate in the foam.
      Last Poems. News for the Delphic Oracle, st. 3

18 Like a long-legged fly upon the stream
  His mind moves upon silence.
      Last Poems. Long-Legged Fly, refrain

19 What shall I do for pretty girls
  Now my old bawd is dead?
      *Last Poems. John Kinsella's Lament for Mrs.
      Mary Moore, refrain*

20 Fifteen apparitions have I seen;
  The worst a coat upon a coat-hanger.
      Last Poems. The Apparitions, refrain

---

[1] "The sun in a golden cup" . . . though not "the moon in a silver bag," is a quotation from the last of Mr. Ezra Pound's *Cantos.* — YEATS's note in *The Winding Stair and Other Poems*

1 Players and painted stage took all my love,
   And not those things that they were emblems of.
   Last Poems. The Circus Animals' Desertion,
   II, st. 3

2   Now that my ladder's gone,
   I must lie down where all the ladders start,
   In the foul rag-and-bone shop of the heart.
   Last Poems. The Circus Animals'
   Desertion, III

3 Irish poets, learn your trade,
   Sing whatever is well made.
   Last Poems. Under Ben Bulben, V

4 Under bare Ben Bulben's head
   In Drumcliff churchyard Yeats is laid.
   Last Poems. Under Ben Bulben, VI

5 On limestone quarried near the spot
   By his command these words are cut:
       Cast a cold eye
       On life, on death.
       Horseman, pass by![1]
   Last Poems. Under Ben Bulben, VI

6   I am still of opinion that only two topics can be
   of the least interest to a serious and studious
   mood—sex and the dead.
   The Letters of W. B. Yeats

7   If a poet interprets a poem of his own he limits
   its suggestibility. *The Letters of W. B. Yeats*

8   We poets would die of loneliness but for women,
   and we choose our men friends that we may have
   somebody to talk about women with.
   The Letters of W. B. Yeats. Letter to Olivia
   Shakespeare [1936]

9   In life courtesy and self-possession, and in the
   arts style, are the sensible impressions of the free
   mind, for both arise out of a deliberate shaping of
   all things and from never being swept away, whatever the emotion, into confusion or dullness.
   Essays and Introductions [1961]. Poetry and
   the Tradition

George W. Young
fl. 1900

10 The lips that touch liquor must never touch mine!
   The Lips That Touch Liquor, st. 5

George Ade
1866–1944

11   In uplifting, get underneath.
   Fables in Slang [1899]. The Good Fairy

12   Stay with the procession or you will never catch
   up.
   Forty Modern Fables [1901]. The Old-Time
   Pedagogue

13   Draw your salary before spending it.
   Forty Modern Fables. The People's Choice

14 Last night at twelve I felt immense,
   But now I feel like thirty cents.
   The Sultan of Sulu [1902]. Remorse

15 But, R - e - m - o - r - s - e!
   The water-wagon is the place for me; . . .
   It is no time for mirth and laughter,
   The cold, gray dawn of the morning after!
   The Sultan of Sulu. Remorse

Tristan Bernard
1866–1947

16   To live happily with other people one should ask
   of them only what they can give.
   L'Enfant Prodigue du Vesinet [1921]

17   Men are always sincere. They change sincerities,
   that's all.[2]
   Ce Que l'On Dit aux Femmes [1922], act III

Gelett Burgess
1866–1951

18 I never saw a purple cow,
   I never hope to see one;
   But I can tell you, anyhow,
   I'd rather see than be one.
   The Purple Cow [1895]

19 Ah, yes, I wrote the "Purple Cow"—
   I'm sorry, now, I wrote it!
   But I can tell you, anyhow,
   I'll kill you if you quote it.
   Cinq Ans Après [1914]

Harry Dacre
d. 1922

20 Daisy, Daisy, give me your answer, do!
   I'm half crazy, all for the love of you!
   It won't be a stylish marriage,
   I can't afford a carriage,
   But you'll look sweet upon the seat
   Of a bicycle built for two! *Daisy Bell [1892]*

---

[1]The last three lines are inscribed on Yeats's gravestone.

[2]Les hommes sont toujours sincères. Ils changent de sincérité,
voilà tout.

Thomas Lansing Masson
1866–1934

1   A Safe and Sane Fourth.   *Slogan*

Beatrix Potter
1866–1943

2   Once upon a time there were four little Rabbits, and their names were—Flopsy, Mopsy, Cottontail, and Peter.   *The Tale of Peter Rabbit [1902]*

3   But don't go into Mr. McGregor's garden.
    The Tale of Peter Rabbit

4   No more twist!
    The Tailor of Gloucester [1903]

5   The water was all slippy-sloppy in the larder and the back passage. But Mr. Jeremy liked getting his feet wet; nobody ever scolded him, and he never caught a cold.
    The Tale of Mr. Jeremy Fisher [1906]

Henry J. Sayers
d. 1932

6 Ta-ra-ra-boom-de-ay!
    Title of minstrel show number [1891], made famous by Lottie Collins [1892]

Lincoln Steffens
1866–1936

7   "So you've been over into Russia?" said Bernard Baruch, and I answered very literally, "I have been over into the future, and it works."[1]
    Autobiography [1931], ch. 18

Sun Yat-sen[2]
1866–1925

8   The Chinese people have only family and clan solidarity; they do not have national spirit . . . they are just a heap of loose sand. . . . Other men are the carving knife and serving dish; we are the fish and the meat.
    China as a Heap of Loose Sand [1924]

---

[1]On Steffens's return from revolutionary Russia in 1919. Its more familiar form is: I have seen the future, and it works.—Steffens, *letter to* Marie Howe [April 3, 1919].

[2]From *Sources of Chinese Tradition* [1960], edited by William Theodore de Bary.

Bert Leston Taylor
1866–1921

9   A bore is a man who, when you ask him how he is, tells you.
    The So-Called Human Race [1922]

H[erbert] G[eorge] Wells
1866–1946

10   The Social Contract is nothing more or less than a vast conspiracy of human beings to lie to and humbug themselves and one another for the general Good. Lies are the mortar that bind the savage individual man into the social masonry.
    Love and Mr. Lewisham [1899], ch. 23

11   The past is but the beginning of a beginning, and all that is and has been is but the twilight of the dawn.   *The Discovery of the Future [1901]*

12   Nothing could have been more obvious to the people of the early twentieth century than the rapidity with which war was becoming impossible. And as certainly they did not see it. They did not see it until the atomic bombs burst in their fumbling hands.   *The World Set Free [1914]*

13   The catastrophe of the atomic bombs which shook men out of cities and businesses and economic relations, shook them also out of their old established habits of thought, and out of the lightly held beliefs and prejudices that came down to them from the past.   *The World Set Free*

14   [A novel by Henry James] is like a church lit but without a congregation to distract you, with every light and line focused on the high altar. And on the altar, very reverently placed, intensely there, is a dead kitten, an egg-shell, a bit of string.
    Boon [1915], ch. 4, sec. 3

15   The professional military mind is by necessity an inferior and unimaginative mind; no man of high intellectual quality would willingly imprison his gifts in such a calling.
    The Outline of History [1920], ch. 40

16   Human history becomes more and more a race between education and catastrophe.
    The Outline of History, 41

17   Life begins perpetually. Gathered together at last under the leadership of man . . . unified, disciplined, armed with the secret powers of the atom and with knowledge as yet beyond dreaming, Life, forever dying to be born afresh, forever young and eager, will presently stand upon this earth as upon a footstool, and stretch out its realm amidst the stars.
    The Outline of History, 41

1   Queen Victoria was like a great paper-weight that for half a century sat upon men's minds, and when she was removed their ideas began to blow all over the place haphazardly.

> *From* NORMAN *and* JEAN MACKENZIE, H. G. Wells [1973]

Stanley Baldwin
1867–1947

2   When you think about the defense of England you no longer think of the chalk cliffs of Dover. You think of the Rhine. That is where our frontier lies today.

> *Speech in the House of Commons [July 30, 1934]*

[Enoch] Arnold Bennett
1867–1931

3   Being a husband is a whole-time job.

> *The Title [1918], act I*

4   Pessimism, when you get used to it, is just as agreeable as optimism.

> *Things That Have Interested Me [1918]*

5   The price of justice is eternal publicity.

> *Things That Have Interested Me, second series [1923]*

Vicente Blasco-Ibáñez
1867–1928

6   It was the roar of the real, the only beast [the crowd in the arena].

> *Sangre y Arena (Blood and Sand) [1908]*

7   Los Cuatro Jinetes del Apocalipsis [The Four Horsemen of the Apocalypse].[1]

> *Title of book [1916]*

Ernest Dowson
1867–1900

8 Last night, ah, yesternight, betwixt her lips and
   mine
There fell thy shadow, Cynara! thy breath was shed
Upon my soul between the kisses and the wine;
And I was desolate and sick of an old passion,
Yea, I was desolate and bowed my head:

I have been faithful to thee, Cynara! in my
   fashion.[2]

> *Non Sum Qualis Eram Bonae Sub Regno Cynarae [1896],[3] st. 1*

9 I have forgot much, Cynara! gone with the wind,
Flung roses, roses riotously with the throng.

> *Non Sum Qualis Eram Bonae Sub Regno Cynarae, st. 3*

10 I cried for madder music and for stronger wine,
But when the feast is finished and the lamps expire,
Then falls thy shadow, Cynara! the night is thine.

> *Non Sum Qualis Eram Bonae Sub Regno Cynarae, st. 4*

11 They are not long, the weeping and the laughter,
Love and desire and hate:
I think they have no portion in us after
We pass the gate.

They are not long, the days of wine and roses;
Out of a misty dream
Our path emerges for a while, then closes
Within a dream.

> *Vitae Summa Brevis Spem Nos Vetat Incohare Longam[4] [1896]*

Finley Peter Dunne [Mr. Dooley]
1867–1936

12   Life'd not be worth livin' if we didn't keep our inimies.

> *Mr. Dooley in Peace and in War [1898]. On New Year's Resolutions*

13   Th' dead ar-re always pop'lar. I knowed a society wanst to vote a monyment to a man an' refuse to help his fam'ly, all in wan night.

> *Mr. Dooley in Peace and in War. On Charity*

14   "I think," said Mr. Dooley, "that if th' Christyan Scientists had some science an' th' doctors more Christianity, it wudden't make anny diff'rence which ye called in — if ye had a good nurse."

> *Mr. Dooley's Opinions [1900]. Christian Science*

15   No matther whether th' constitution follows th' flag or not, th' supreme coort follows th' iliction returns.

> *Mr. Dooley's Opinions. The Supreme Court's Decisions*

16   I think a lie with a purpose is wan iv th' worst kind an' th' mos' profitable.

> *Mr. Dooley's Opinions. On Lying*

---

[1]Phrase derived from the four allegorical horses in the Bible (*Revelation 6:1–8*).
See Rice, 692:6.

[2]See Cole Porter, 732:15.
[3]See Horace, 100:12.
[4]See Horace, 99:6.

1   Th' dimmycratic party ain't on speakin' terms with itsilf.

Mr. Dooley's Opinions. Mr. Dooley Discusses Party Politics

2   Th' raypublican party broke ye, but now that ye're down we'll not turn a cold shoulder to ye. Come in an' we'll keep ye — broke.

Mr. Dooley's Opinions. Mr. Dooley Discusses Party Politics

3   Hogan's r-right whin he says: "Justice is blind." Blind she is, an' deef an' dumb an' has a wooden leg.

Mr. Dooley's Opinions. Cross-Examinations

4   No wan cares to hear what Hogan calls "Th' short an' simple scandals iv th' poor."

Mr. Dooley's Opinions. Cross-Examinations

5   'Twas founded be th' Puritans to give thanks f'r bein' presarved fr'm th' Indyans, an' . . . we keep it to give thanks we are presarved fr'm th' Puritans.

Mr. Dooley's Opinions. Thanksgiving

6   Vice . . . is a creature of such heejous mien . . . that th' more ye see it th' betther ye like it.

Mr. Dooley's Opinions. The Crusade Against Vice

7   "D' ye think th' colledges has much to do with th' progress iv th' wurruld?" asked Mr. Hennessy.
"D' ye think," said Mr. Dooley, "'tis th' mill that makes th' wather run?"

Mr. Dooley's Opinions. Colleges and Degrees

8   If ye live enough befure thirty ye won't care to live at all afther fifty.

Mr. Dooley's Opinions. Casual Observations

9   Among men, Hinnissy, wet eye manes dhry heart.

Mr. Dooley's Opinions. Casual Observations

10   A fanatic is a man that does what he thinks th' Lord wud do if He knew th' facts iv th' case.

Mr. Dooley's Opinions. Casual Observations

11   'Tis as hard f'r a rich man to enther th' kingdom iv Hiven as it is f'r a poor man to get out iv Purgatory.

Mr. Dooley's Opinions. Casual Observations

12   Thrust ivrybody, but cut th' ca-ards.

Mr. Dooley's Opinions. Casual Observations

13   A man that'd expict to thrain lobsters to fly in a year is called a loonytic; but a man that thinks men can be tu-rrned into angels be an iliction is called a rayformer an' remains at large.

Mr. Dooley's Opinions. Casual Observations

14   Miracles are laughed at be a nation that r-reads thirty millyon newspapers a day an' supports Wall sthreet.

Mr. Dooley's Opinions. Casual Observation

15   If a man is wise, he gets rich, an' if he gets rich he gets foolish, or his wife does. That's what keeps the money movin' around.

Observations by Mr. Dooley [1902]. Newport

16   But th' best thing about a little judicyous swearin' is that it keeps th' temper. 'Twas intinded as a compromise between runnin' away an' fightin'. Befure it was invinted they was on'y th' two ways out iv an argymint.   *Observations by Mr. Dooley. Swearing*

17   I don't think we injye other people's sufferin', Hinnissy. It isn't acshally injyement. But we feel betther f'r it.

Observations by Mr. Dooley. Enjoyment

18   Th' newspaper does ivrything f'r us. It runs th' polis foorce an' th' banks, commands th' milishy, conthrols th' ligislachure, baptizes th' young, marries th' foolish, comforts th' afflicted, afflicts th' comfortable, buries th' dead an' roasts thim afterward.

Observations by Mr. Dooley. Newspaper Publicity

19   "Ye know a lot about [raising children]," said Mr. Hennessy.
"I do," said Mr. Dooley. "Not bein' an author, I'm a gr-reat critic."

Dissertations by Mr. Dooley [1906]. The Bringing Up of Children

20   Th' prisidincy is th' highest office in th' gift iv th' people. Th' vice-prisidincy is th' next highest an' th' lowest. It isn't a crime exactly. Ye can't be sint to jail f'r it, but it's a kind iv a disgrace. It's like writin' anonymous letters.

Dissertations by Mr. Dooley. The Vice-President

21   This home iv opporchunity where ivry man is th' equal iv ivry other man befure th' law if he isn't careful.

Dissertations by Mr. Dooley. The Food We Eat

22   "Ye ra-ally do think dhrink is a nicissry evil?" said Mr. Hennessy.
"Well," said Mr. Dooley, "if it's an evil to a man, it's not nicissry, an' if it's nicissry it's an evil."

Dissertations by Mr. Dooley. The Bar

23   "He made [money]," said Mr. Dooley, "because he honestly loved it with an innocint affiction. He was thrue to it. Th' reason ye have no money is because ye don't love it f'r itsilf alone. Money won't iver surrender to such a flirt."

Mr. Dooley on Making a Will and Other Evil Necessities [1919]. On Making a Will

John Galsworthy
1867–1933

1   Nobody tells me anything.
Repeatedly spoken by James Forsyte in The Man of Property [1906] and In Chancery [1920]

2   Justice is a machine that, when someone has once given it the starting push, rolls on of itself.
Justice [1910], act II

3   Public opinion's always in advance of the law.
Windows [1922], act I

4   The value of a sentiment is the amount of sacrifice you are prepared to make for it.
Windows, II

5   A man of action forced into a state of thought is unhappy until he can get out of it.
Maid in Waiting [1931], ch. 3

6   The beginnings and endings of all human undertakings are untidy, the building of a house, the writing of a novel, the demolition of a bridge, and, eminently, the finish of a voyage.
Over the River [1933], ch. 1

7   How to save the old that's worth saving, whether in landscape, houses, manners, institutions, or human types, is one of our greatest problems, and the one that we bother least about.
Over the River, 39

Edith Hamilton
1867–1963

8   They [the Greeks] were the first Westerners; the spirit of the West, the modern spirit, is a Greek discovery and the place of the Greeks is in the modern world.
The Greek Way [1930], ch. 1

9   To rejoice in life, to find the world beautiful and delightful to live in, was a mark of the Greek spirit which distinguished it from all that had gone before. It is a vital distinction.
The Greek Way, 1

Kaethe [Schmidt] Kollwitz
1867–1945

10   I am gradually approaching the period in my life when work comes first. . . . No longer diverted by other emotions, I work the way a cow grazes.
Diary[1] [April 1910]

---

[1]Translated by RICHARD and CLARA WINSTON.

Charles Edward Montague
1867–1928

11   I was born below par to th' extent of two whiskies.
Fiery Particles [1923]

Luigi Pirandello
1867–1936

12   Life is a very sad piece of buffoonery, because we have . . . the need to fool ourselves continuously by the spontaneous creation of a reality (one for each and never the same for everyone) which, from time to time, reveals itself to be vain and illusory.
Autobiographical Sketch in Le Lettere, Rome [October 15, 1924][2]

Henry L[ewis] Stimson
1867–1950

13   Gentlemen do not read each other's mail.[3]
On Active Service in Peace and War [1948]

Joseph Weber
1867–1942
and
Lew Fields
1867–1941

14 Who was that lady I saw you with last night? She ain't no lady; she's my wife.
Vaudeville routine [1887]

Harry Leon Wilson
1867–1939

15   I can be pushed just so far.
Ruggles of Red Gap [1915]

Wilbur Wright
1867–1912
and
Orville Wright
1871–1948

16   Success. Four flights Thursday morning. All against twenty-one-mile wind. Started from level

---

[2]Translated by WILLIAM MURRAY.

[3]Explaining his 1929 decision, as Secretary of State, to close down the department's codebreaking agency (the American "black chamber").

with engine power alone. Average speed through air thirty-one miles. Longest fifty-nine seconds. Inform press. Home Christmas.

Telegram to the Reverend Milton Wright,
from Kitty Hawk, N.C. [December 17, 1903]

Émile Auguste Chartier [Alain]

1868–1951

1   To think is to say *no*.

Le Citoyen contre les Pouvoirs

2   We prove what we want to prove, and the real difficulty is to know what we want to prove.

Système des Beaux-Arts [1920]

3   Nothing is more dangerous than an idea, when it's the only one we have.   *Libres-propos*

Paul Claudel

1868–1955

4   You explain nothing, O poet, but thanks to you all things become explicable.

La Ville [1897], act I

5 The words I use
Are everyday words and yet are not the same!
You will find no rhymes in my verse, no magic.
There are your very own phrases.

La Muse Qui Est la Grace [1910]

6   When man tries to imagine Paradise on earth, the immediate result is a very respectable Hell.

Conversations dans le Loir-et-Cher [1929]

Norman Douglas

1868–1952

7   You can tell the ideals of a nation by its advertisements.   *South Wind [1917], ch. 7*

8   Many a man who thinks to found a home discovers that he has merely opened a tavern for his friends.   *South Wind, 24*

William Edward Burghardt Du Bois

1868–1963

9   The problem of the twentieth century is the problem of the color line.

To the Nations of the World; address to Pan-
African conference, London [1900]

10   Herein lies the tragedy of the age: not that men are poor — all men know something of poverty; not

that men are wicked — who is good? Not that men are ignorant — what is truth? Nay, but that men know so little of men.

The Souls of Black Folk [1903]

11   It is a peculiar sensation, this double-consciousness, this sense of always looking at one's self through the eyes of others. . . . One feels his twoness — an American, a Negro; two Souls, two thoughts, two unreconciled strivings; two warring ideals in one dark body, whose dogged strength alone keeps it from being torn asunder.

The Souls of Black Folk

12   The cost of liberty is less than the price of repression.

John Brown [1909]. The Legacy of John Brown

13   Liberty trains for liberty. Responsibility is the first step in responsibility.

John Brown. The Legacy of John Brown

14   The dark world is going to submit to its present treatment just as long as it must and not one moment longer.

Darkwater [1920]. The Souls of White Folk

15   The return from your work must be the satisfaction which that work brings you and the world's need of that work. With this, life is heaven, or as near heaven as you can get. Without this — with work which you despise, which bores you, and which the world does not need — this life is hell.

To His Newborn Great-Grandson; address on
his ninetieth birthday [1958]

16   Believe in life! Always human beings will live and progress to greater, broader, and fuller life.

Last message to the world [written 1957].
Read at his funeral [1963]

John Nance Garner

1868–1967

17   The vice-presidency isn't worth a pitcher of warm piss.   *Attributed*

Maxim Gorki[1]
[Aleksei Maksimovich Peshkov]

1868–1936

18   Let the storm rage ever stronger![2]

Song of a Stormy Petrel [1901]

---

[1]Gorki, "the bitter one," was the writer's pseudonym for his first sketch in a Tiflis newspaper [1892].

[2]This became a rallying cry of the revolutionaries.

1 Lies—there you have the religion of slaves and taskmasters.[1]   *The Lower Depths [1903]*

2 How marvelous is Man! How proud the word rings—Man!   *The Lower Depths*

3 In time I came to understand that out of the misery and murk of their lives the Russian people had learned to make sorrow a diversion, to play with it like a child's toy; seldom are they diffident about showing their happiness. And so, through their tedious weekdays, they made a carnival of grief; a fire is entertainment; and on a vacant face a bruise becomes an adornment.
Autobiography [1913]. Childhood

4 The proletarian state must bring up thousands of excellent "mechanics of culture," "engineers of the soul."[2]   *Speech at the Writers' Congress [1934]*

5 The basic hero of our books should be labor; that is, man organized by the processes of labor.
Speech at the Writers' Congress

Frank McKinney "Kin" Hubbard [Abe Martin]
1868–1930

6 It's no disgrace t' be poor, but it might as well be.
Abe Martin's Sayings and Sketches [1915]

7 When a fellow says it hain't the money but the principle o' the thing, it's th' money.
Hoss Sense and Nonsense [1926]

8 Nobuddy ever fergits where he buried a hatchet.
Abe Martin's Broadcast [1930]

9 If capital an' labor ever do git t'gether it's good night fer th' rest of us.   *Saying*

10 Now and then an innocent man is sent to the legislature.   *Saying*

E[dward] V[errall] Lucas
1868–1938

11 The French never allow a distinguished son of France to lack a statue.
Wanderings and Diversions [1926]. Zigzags in France

12 Americans are people who prefer the Continent to their own country, but refuse to learn its languages.
Wanderings and Diversions. The Continental Dictionary

13 People in hotels strike no roots. The French phrase for chronic hotel guests even says so: they are called dwellers *sur la branche*.
Wanderings and Diversions. To Be Let or Sold

Edmond Rostand
1868–1918

14 A great nose indicates a great man—
Genial, courteous, intellectual,
Virile, courageous.
Cyrano de Bergerac [1897],[3] act I

15 I fall back dazzled at beholding myself all rosy red,
At having, I myself, caused the sun to rise.
Chantecler [1910], act II, sc. iii

Robert Falcon Scott
1868–1912

16 Had we lived, I should have had a tale to tell of the hardihood, endurance, and courage of my companions which would have stirred the heart of every Englishman. These rough notes and our dead bodies must tell the tale.[4]
Diary of the Terra Nova Expedition to the Antarctic.[5] Message to the Public

17 It was blowing a blizzard. He [Capt. Lawrence E. G. Oates] said, "I am just going outside and may be some time." He went out into the blizzard and we have not seen him since.
Scott's Last Expedition: Journals [March 12, 1912]

18 Every day we have been ready to start for our depot *eleven miles* away, but outside the door of the tent it remains a scene of whirling drift. I do not think we can hope for any better things now. We shall stick it out to the end, but we are getting weaker, of course, and the end cannot be far.

It seems a pity, but I do not think I can write more.

R. Scott

For God's sake look after our people.
Diary of the Terra Nova Expedition to the Antarctic. Thursday, March 29, 1912 (last entry)

---

[1]The censor forbade this line to be spoken on the stage.

[2]Attributed to Joseph Stalin in conversation with Gorki [October 26, 1934].

[3]Translated by Brian Hooker.

[4]Inscribed on the memorial to Captain Scott and his companions, Waterloo Place, London.

[5]Found by searching party [November 1912]. First published [1913] as *Scott's Last Expedition: Journals*.

Luther Standing Bear[1]
1868–1939

1   Only to the white man was nature a "wilderness" and only to him was the land "infested" with "wild" animals and "savage" people. To us it was tame. Earth was bountiful and we were surrounded with the blessings of the Great Mystery. Not until the hairy man from the east came and with brutal frenzy heaped injustices upon us and the families that we loved was it "wild" for us. When the very animals of the forest began fleeing from his approach, then it was that for us the "Wild West" began.

Land of the Spotted Eagle [1933]

André Suarès
1868–1948

2   Heresy is the lifeblood of religions. It is faith that begets heretics. There are no heresies in a dead religion.   *Péguy*

William Allen White
1868–1944

3   Tinhorn politicians.

Emporia Gazette, Kansas [October 25, 1901]

4   All dressed up, with nowhere to go.

Of the Progressive party in 1916, after Theodore Roosevelt retired from presidential competition

5   The talent of a meat-packer, the morals of a moneychanger and the manners of an undertaker.

Obituary of Frank A. Munsey [December 23, 1925]

Laurence Binyon
1869–1943

6 They shall grow not old, as we that are left grow old:
Age shall not weary them, nor the years condemn.
At the going down of the sun and in the morning
We will remember them.

For the Fallen [1914], st. 4

Neville Chamberlain
1869–1940

7   For the second time in our history, a British Prime Minister has returned from Germany bringing peace with honor. I believe it is peace for our time. . . . Go home and get a nice quiet sleep.

Address from 10 Downing Street, London [September 30, 1938], after returning from the Munich Conference

8   Hitler has missed the bus.

Speech in the House of Commons [April 4, 1940]

Mohandas Karamchand [Mahatma] Gandhi[2]
1869–1948

9   Nonviolence is the first article of my faith. It is also the last article of my creed.

Defense against charge of sedition [March 23, 1922]

10   The term *Satyagraha* was coined by me . . . in order to distinguish it from the movement then going on . . . under the name of Passive Resistance.

    Its root meaning is "holding on to truth," hence "force of righteousness." I have also called it love force or soul force. In the application of *Satyagraha*, I discovered in the earliest stages that pursuit of truth did not permit violence being inflicted on one's opponent, but that he must be weaned from error by patience and sympathy. For what appears truth to the one may appear to be error to the other. And patience means self-suffering. So the doctrine came to mean vindication of truth, not by the infliction of suffering on the opponent, but on one's self.[3]

Defense against charge of sedition [March 23, 1922]

11   Nonviolence and truth *(Satya)* are inseparable and presuppose one another. There is no god higher than truth.

True Patriotism: Some Sayings of Mahatma Gandhi [1939][4]

---

[1]Chief of the Oglala Tribe of the Sioux Nation.

[2]Mahatma: Great Soul.
[3]See Martin Luther King, Jr., 823:5.
[4]Edited by S. Hobhouse.

André Gide
1869–1951

1 Families, I hate you! Shut-in homes, closed doors, jealous possessions of happiness.[1]
Les Nourritures Terrestres (Fruits of the Earth) [1897], bk. IV

2 What another would have done as well as you, do not do it. What another would have said as well as you, do not say it; written as well, do not write it. Be faithful to that which exists nowhere but in yourself—and thus make yourself indispensable.
Les Nourritures Terrestres. Envoi

3 The most decisive actions of our life . . . are most often unconsidered actions.
Les Faux Monnayeurs (The Counterfeiters) [1926]

4 It is with noble sentiments that bad literature gets written.[2] *Letter to François Mauriac [1928]*

Strickland Gillilan
1869–1954

5 Bilin' down 's repoort, wuz Finnigin!
An' he writed this here: "Musther Flannigan—
Off agin, on agin,
Gone agin.—FINNIGIN."
Finnigin to Flannigan, st. 6

6 Adam
Had 'em.   *Lines on the Antiquity of Microbes[3]*

Emma Goldman
1869–1940

7 Anarchism, then, really stands for the liberation of the human mind from the dominion of religion; the liberation of the human body from the shackles and restraints of government. Anarchism stands for a social order based on the free grouping of individuals for the purpose of producing real social wealth.
Anarchism: What It Really Stands For [1911]

8 If I can't dance I don't want to be in your revolution.   *Attributed[4]*

Stephen [Butler] Leacock
1869–1944

9 He flung himself from the room, flung himself upon his horse and rode madly off in all directions.
Nonsense Novels [1911]. Gertrude the Governess

10 The parent who could see his boy as he really is, would shake his head and say: "Willie is no good; I'll sell him."
Essays and Literary Studies [1916]. The Lot of the Schoolmaster

Edgar Lee Masters
1869–1950

11 All, all, are sleeping on the hill.
Spoon River Anthology [1915]. The Hill, refrain

12 Seeds in a dry pod, tick, tick, tick,
Tick, tick, tick, what little iambics,
While Homer and Whitman roared in the pines!
Spoon River Anthology. Petit, the Poet

13 Degenerate sons and daughters,
Life is too strong for you—
It takes life to love life.
Spoon River Anthology. Lucinda Matlock

14 Out of me unworthy and unknown
The vibrations of deathless music.
Spoon River Anthology. Anne Rutledge

15 I am Anne Rutledge who sleep beneath these weeds,
Beloved in life of Abraham Lincoln.
Spoon River Anthology. Anne Rutledge

Henri Matisse
1869–1954

16 I want to reach that state of condensation of sensations which constitutes a picture.
Notes d'un Peintre [1908]

17 What interests me most is neither still life nor landscape, but the human figure. It is through it that I best succeed in expressing the almost religious feeling I have towards life.
Notes d'un Peintre

---

[1]Familles, je vous hais! foyers clos; portes refermées; possessions jalouses du bonheur.

[2]C'est avec de beaux sentiments qu'on fait de la mauvaise littérature.

[3]Said to be the shortest poem in the language.

[4]A T-shirt slogan [1973] compatible with Goldman's ideas but with no supporting source in her speeches or writings. See ALIX KATES SHULMAN, "Dances with Feminists," *The Women's Review of Books* [December 1991].

William Vaughn Moody
1869–1910

1   Gigantic, willful, young,
Chicago sitteth at the northwest gates.
An Ode in Time of Hesitation [1901], st. 3

2   O ye who lead,
Take heed!
Blindness we may forgive, but baseness we will
smite.
An Ode in Time of Hesitation, st. 9

Edwin Arlington Robinson
1869–1935

3 I would have rid the earth of him
Once, in my pride.
I never knew the worth of him
Until he died.
An Old Story, st. 3

4 Life is the game that must be played.
Ballade by the Fire. Envoy

5 There is ruin and decay
In the House on the Hill:
They are all gone away,
There is nothing more to say.
The House on the Hill [1897], last stanza

6 Miniver Cheevy, child of scorn,
Grew lean while he assailed the seasons;
He wept that he was ever born,
And he had reasons.
Miniver Cheevy [1910], st. 1

7 Miniver Cheevy, born too late,
Scratched his head and kept on thinking;
Miniver coughed and called it fate,
And kept on drinking.
Miniver Cheevy, st. 8

8 I shall have more to say when I am dead.
John Brown, last line

9 Here where the wind is always north-northeast
And children learn to walk on frozen toes.
New England, st. 1

10 He glittered when he walked.
Richard Cory, st. 2

11 So on we worked, and waited for the light,
And went without the meat, and cursed the bread;
And Richard Cory, one calm summer night,
Went home and put a bullet through his head.
Richard Cory, st. 4

William Strunk, Jr.
1869–1946

12   Omit needless words.
Vigorous writing is concise. A sentence should
contain no unnecessary words, a paragraph no unnecessary sentences, for the same reason that a
drawing should have no unnecessary lines and a machine no unnecessary parts. This requires not that
the writer make all his sentences short, or that he
avoid all detail and treat his subjects only in outline,
but that every word tell.
The Elements of Style [1918], ch. 2, sec. 13

Booth Tarkington
1869–1946

13   There are two things that will be believed of any
man whatsoever, and one of them is that he has
taken to drink.   *Penrod [1914], ch. 10*

14   They were upon their great theme: "When I get
to be a man!" Being human, though boys, they
considered their present estate too commonplace to
be dwelt upon. So, when the old men gather, they
say: "When I was a boy!" It really is the land of
nowadays that we never discover.   *Penrod, 26*

Frank Lloyd Wright
1869–1959

15   No house should ever be *on* any hill or on anything. It should be *of* the hill, belonging to it, so
hill and house could live together each the happier
for the other.   *An Autobiography [1932]*

16   The physician can bury his mistakes, but the architect can only advise his client to plant vines.
New York Times Magazine [October 4, 1953]

Bernard M[annes] Baruch
1870–1965

17   Behind the black portent of the new atomic age
lies a hope which, seized upon with faith, can work
out salvation. . . . Let us not deceive ourselves: we
must elect world peace or world destruction.
*Address to the United Nations Atomic Energy
Commission [June 14, 1946]*

18   We are in the midst of a cold war[1] which is getting warmer.
Speech before the Senate Committee [1948]

---

[1]The phrase was first used by Baruch in 1947.

Hilaire Belloc
1870–1953

1 Child! do not throw this book about;
Refrain from the unholy pleasure
Of cutting all the pictures out!
Preserve it as your chiefest treasure.
*A Bad Child's Book of Beasts [1896],
dedication*

2 When people call this beast to mind,
They marvel more and more
At such a little tail behind,
So large a trunk before.
A Bad Child's Book of Beasts. The Elephant

3 Whatever happens we have got
The Maxim Gun, and they have not.
The Modern Traveller [1898], VI

4 A smell of burning fills the startled air —
The Electrician is no longer there!
Newdigate Poem

5 How slow the shadow creeps: but when 'tis past
How fast the shadows fall. How fast! How fast!
For a Sundial

6 Of courtesy, it is much less
Than courage of heart or holiness,
Yet in my walks it seems to me
That the Grace of God is in courtesy.
Courtesy

7 Do you remember an inn,
Miranda? *Tarantella*

8 The chief defect of Henry King
Was chewing little bits of string.
Cautionary Tales [1907]. Henry King

9 Matilda told such dreadful lies,
It made one gasp and stretch one's eyes;
Her aunt, who, from her earliest youth,
Had kept a strict regard for truth,
Attempted to believe Matilda:
The effort very nearly killed her.
Cautionary Tales. Matilda

10 For every time she shouted "Fire!"
They only answered "Little liar!"
And therefore when her aunt returned,
Matilda, and the house, were burned.
Cautionary Tales. Matilda

11 Here richly, with ridiculous display,
The Politician's corpse was laid away.
While all of his acquaintance sneered and slanged
I wept: for I had longed to see him hanged.
Epitaph on the Politician Himself

12 I'm tired of Love: I'm still more tired of Rhyme.
But Money gives me pleasure all the time.
Fatigue

13 The Devil, having nothing else to do,
Went off to tempt My Lady Poltagrue.
My Lady, tempted by a private whim,
To his extreme annoyance, tempted him.
On Lady Poltagrue, a Public Peril

14 Of this bad world the loveliest and the best
Has smiled and said "Good Night," and gone
    to rest. *On a Dead Hostess*

15 When I am dead, I hope it may be said:
"His sins were scarlet, but his books were read."
On His Books

Benjamin Nathan Cardozo
1870–1938

16 What has once been settled by a precedent will not be unsettled overnight, for certainty and uniformity are gains not lightly to be sacrificed.
The Paradoxes of Legal Science [1928]

17 As I search the archives of my memory, I seem to discern six types or methods [of judicial writing] which divide themselves from one another with measurable distinctness. There is the type magisterial or imperative; the type laconic or sententious; the type conversational or homely; the type refined or artificial, smelling of the lamp, verging at times upon preciosity or euphuism; the type demonstrative or persuasive; and finally the type tonsorial or agglutinative, so called from the shears and the pastepot which are its implements and emblem.
Law and Literature [1931]

18 [The Constitution] was framed upon the theory that the peoples of the several states must sink or swim together, and that in the long run prosperity and salvation are in union and not division.
Baldwin v. Seelig, 294 U.S. 511, 523 [1935]

19 Freedom of expression is the matrix, the indispensable condition, of nearly every other form of freedom.
Palko v. Connecticut, 302 U.S. 319, 327 [1937]

Lord Alfred Bruce Douglas
1870–1945

20 I am the Love that dare not speak its name.
Two Loves [1894]

Arthur J. Lamb
1870–1928

1 Her beauty was sold for an old man's gold,
She's a bird in a gilded cage.
A Bird in a Gilded Cage [1900]

Sir Harry Lauder
1870–1950

2 Oh, it's nice to get up in the mornin',
But it's nicer to lie in bed.   *Song*

3 Just a wee doch-an'-dorris
Before we gang awa' . . .
If y' can say
It's a braw brecht moonlecht necht,
Yer a' recht, that's a'.   *Song*

4 Roamin' in the gloamin'.   *Song*

5   I Love a Lassie.   *Title of song*

Vladimir Ilyich Lenin
[Vladimir Ilyich Ulyanov]
1870–1924

6 "The revolution's decisive victory over tsarism"
means the establishment of the *revolutionary-democratic dictatorship of the proletariat and the peasantry*.
Two Tactics of Social-Democracy [1905], ch. 6

7 We shall now proceed to construct the socialist
order.
Speech at the Congress of Soviets [October 26, 1917][1]

8 Every cook has to learn how to govern the state.
Will the Bolsheviks Retain Government Power? [1917]

9 The war is relentless: it puts the alternative in a
ruthless relief: either to perish, or to catch up with
the advanced countries and outdistance them, too,
in economic matters.
The Impending Catastrophe and How to Fight It [1917]

10 The suppression of the bourgeois state by the
proletarian state is impossible without a violent revolution.   *The State and Revolution [1918], ch. 1*

11 So long as the state exists there is no freedom.
When there is freedom, there will be no state.
The State and Revolution, 5

---

[1]Translated by MAX EASTMAN.

12 Communism is Soviet government plus the elec
trification of the whole country.
*New External and Internal Position and the
Problems of the Party [1920]*

13 It is true that liberty is precious—so preciou
that it must be rationed.
Attributed. Quoted by SIDNEY AND BEATRICE
WEBB, *Soviet Communism: A New
Civilization? [1936], p. 1036*

Rosa Luxemburg
1870–1919

14 I hope to die at my post: in the streets or in prison
Letter from prison [c. 1917

15 Freedom is always freedom for the one who
thinks differently.
The Russian Revolution [1922

Albert Jay Nock
1870–1945

16 As sheer casual reading matter, I still find th
English dictionary the most interesting book in ou
language.
*Memoirs of a Superfluous Man [1943], ch. 1,
pt. 4*

17 All Souls College, Oxford, planned better than i
knew when it limited the number of its undergradu
ates to four; four is exactly the right number for an
college which is really intent on getting results.
Memoirs of a Superfluous Man, 3, ...

18 Money does not pay for anything, never has
never will. It is an economic axiom as old as the hill
that goods and services can be paid for only wit
goods and services.
Memoirs of a Superfluous Man, 13, ...

Watty Piper
[Mabel Caroline Bragg]
1870–1945

19 I think I can. I think I can. I think I can.
The Little Engine That Could [1930

Roscoe Pound
1870–1964

20 The law must be stable, but it must not stan
still.
Introduction to the Philosophy of Law [1922

Saki [Hector Hugh Munro]
1870–1916

1 The cook was a good cook, as cooks go; and as cooks go she went.
Reginald [1904]. Reginald on Besetting Sins

2 Women and elephants never forget an injury.
Reginald. Reginald on Besetting Sins

3 I might have been a goldfish in a glass bowl for all the privacy I got.
Reginald. The Innocence of Reginald

4 The Western custom of one wife and hardly any mistresses.
Reginald in Russia [1910]. A Young Turkish Catastrophe

5 Poverty keeps together more homes than it breaks up.
The Chronicles of Clovis [1911]. Esmé

6 Sredni Vashtar went forth,
His thoughts were red thoughts and his teeth were white.
His enemies called for peace, but he brought them death.
Sredni Vashtar the Beautiful.
The Chronicles of Clovis. Sredni Vashtar

7 The sacrifices of friendship were beautiful in her eyes as long as she was not asked to make them.
Beasts and Super-Beasts [1914]. Fur

8 A little inaccuracy sometimes saves tons of explanation.
The Square Egg [1924]. Clovis on the Alleged Romance of Business

T. Laurence Seibert
fl. 1900

9 Casey Jones! Orders in his hand.
Casey Jones! Mounted to the cabin,
Took his farewell journey to that promised land.
Casey Jones [1909]. Adapted from verses by WALLACE SAUNDERS,[1] *set to music by* EDDIE NEWTON

---

[1]Of the many versions of this traditional ballad, the most familiar is printed in CARL SANDBURG, *The American Songbag* [1927]. It begins: Come all you rounders, for I want you to hear / The story of a brave engineer. / Casey Jones was the rounder's name, / On a big eight-wheeler of a mighty fame.

To the memory of the locomotive engineer whose name as "Casey Jones" became a part of folklore and the American language. "For I'm going to run till she leaves the rail — or make it on time with the southbound mail." — *Inscription on monument to* JOHN LUTHER JONES [1864–1900], *in Calvary Cemetery, Jackson, Tennessee*

Stephen Crane
1871–1900

10 The cold passed reluctantly from the earth, and the retiring fogs revealed an army stretched out on the hills, resting. As the landscape changed from brown to green, the army awakened, and began to tremble with eagerness at the noise of rumors.
The Red Badge of Courage [1895], opening sentences

11 They were going to look at war, the red animal — war, the blood-swollen god.
The Red Badge of Courage, 3

12 At times he regarded the wounded soldiers in an envious way. He conceived persons with torn bodies to be peculiarly happy. He wished that he, too, had a wound, a red badge of courage.
The Red Badge of Courage, 9

13 The red sun was pasted in the sky like a wafer.
The Red Badge of Courage, 9

14 He had fought like a pagan who defends his religion.
The Red Badge of Courage, 17

15 He had been to touch the great death, and found that, after all, it was but the great death. He was a man.
The Red Badge of Courage, 24

16 None of them knew the color of the sky.
The Open Boat [1897], first line

17 In the desert
I saw a creature, naked, bestial,
Who, squatting upon the ground,
Held his heart in his hands,
And ate of it.
I said, "Is it good, friend?"
"It is bitter — bitter," he answered;
"But I like it
"Because it is bitter,
"And because it is my heart."
The Black Riders [1895], III

18 Should the wide world roll away
Leaving black terror
Limitless night,
Nor God, nor man, nor place to stand
Would be to me essential
If thou and thy white arms were there
And the fall to doom a long way.
The Black Riders, X

19 Do not weep, maiden, for war is kind.
Because your lover threw wild hands toward the sky
And the affrighted steed ran on alone,
Do not weep.
War is kind.
War Is Kind [1899]. War Is Kind, st. 1

1 A man said to the universe:
   "Sir, I exist!"
   "However," replied the universe,
   "The fact has not created in me
   A sense of obligation."

> *War Is Kind. War Is Kind, fragment*

W[illiam] H[enry] Davies
1871–1940

2 What is this life if, full of care,
   We have no time to stand and stare?   *Leisure*

Theodore Dreiser
1871–1945

3   Our civilization is still in a middle stage, scarcely
beast, in that it is no longer wholly guided by instinct; scarcely human, in that it is not yet wholly
guided by reason.   *Sister Carrie [1900], ch. 8*

4   In your rocking chair by your window shall you
dream such happiness as you may never feel.

> *Sister Carrie, 50*

5   I acknowledge the Furies, I believe in them, I
have heard the disastrous beating of their wings.

> *To Grant Richards [1911]*

6   An American Tragedy.   *Title of novel [1925]*

7 Oh, the moonlight's fair tonight along the Wabash,
   From the fields there comes the breath of new-
      mown hay;
   Through the sycamores the candle lights are
      gleaming
   On the banks of the Wabash, far away.

> *On the Banks of the Wabash, chorus*[1]

Arthur Guiterman
1871–1943

8 Amoebas at the start
   Were not complex;
   They tore themselves apart
   And started Sex.   *Sex, st. 1*

9 Of all cold words of tongue or pen
   The worst are these: "I knew him when —"[2]

> *Prophets in Their Own Country*

---

[1]Written by Dreiser but credited to his songwriter brother, PAUL
DRESSER (1857–1906).

[2]See Whittier, 468:12.

Ralph Hodgson
1871–1962

10 'Twould ring the bells of Heaven
    The wildest peal for years,
    If Parson lost his senses
    And people came to theirs,
    And he and they together
    Knelt down with angry prayers
    For tamed and shabby tigers
    And dancing dogs and bears,
    And wretched, blind pit ponies,
    And little hunted hares.

> *The Bells of Heaven*

11 Time, you old gypsy man,
    Will you not stay,
    Put up your caravan
    Just for one day?

> *Time, You Old Gypsy Man, st. 1*

12 Oh, had our simple Eve
    Seen through the make-believe!
    Had she but known the
    Pretender he was!   *Eve, st. 5*

13 How they all pitied
    Poor motherless Eve!   *Eve, st. 7*

14 I saw in vision
    The worm in the wheat,
    And in the shops nothing
    For people to eat;
    Nothing for sale in
    Stupidity Street.   *Stupidity Street, st. 2*

James Weldon Johnson
1871–1938

15 We have come over a way that with tears has been
       watered,
    We have come, treading our path through the
       blood of the slaughtered.

> *Lift Every Voice and Sing [1900], st. 3*

16   The colored people of this country know and
understand the white people better than the white
people know and understand them.

> *The Autobiography of an Ex-Colored Man
> [1912], ch. 2*

17   Every race and every nation should be judged by
the best it has been able to produce, not by the
worst.

> *The Autobiography of an Ex-Colored Man, 10*

18 O black and unknown bards of long ago,
    How came your lips to touch the sacred fire?

How, in your darkness, did you come to know
The power and beauty of the minstrels' lyre?
O Black and Unknown Bards [1917], st. 1

1 And God stepped out on space,
And He looked around and said,
"I'm lonely—
I'll make me a world."
God's Trombones [1927]. The Creation, st. 1

2 With His head in His hands,
God thought and thought,
Till He thought: I'll make me a man!
God's Trombones. The Creation, st. 10

3   Find Sister Caroline . . .
And she's tired—
She's weary—
Go down, Death, and bring her to me.
God's Trombones. Go Down, Death, st. 5

4   It is from the blues that all that may be called
American music derives its most distinctive characteristic.   *Black Manhattan [1930], ch. 11*

Herbert George Ponting
1871–1935

5 On the outside grows the furside, on the inside
grows the skinside;
So the furside is the outside, and the skinside is the
inside.[1]   *The Sleeping Bag*[2]

Marcel Proust
1871–1922

6   For a long time I used to go to bed early.[3]
Remembrance of Things Past [1913–1927].[4]
Swann's Way, opening line

7   Once I had recognized the taste of the crumb of
madeleine soaked in her decoction of lime flowers
which my aunt used to give me . . . immediately the
old gray house upon the street, where her room
was, rose up like the scenery of a theater.
Remembrance of Things Past. Swann's Way

8   In his younger days a man dreams of possessing
the heart of the woman whom he loves; later, the
feeling that he possesses the heart of a woman may
be enough to make him fall in love with her.
Remembrance of Things Past. Swann's Way

9   What artists call posterity is the posterity of the
work of art.
*Remembrance of Things Past. Within a
Budding Grove, pt. I*

10   Not only does one not retain all at once the truly
rare works, but even within such works it is the least
precious parts that one perceives first. Less deceptive than life, these great masterpieces do not give
us their best at the beginning.
*Remembrance of Things Past. Within a
Budding Grove, I*

11   The time which we have at our disposal every
day is elastic; the passions that we feel expand it,
those that we inspire contract it; and habit fills up
what remains.
*Remembrance of Things Past. Within a
Budding Grove, I*

12   All the great things we know have come to us
from neurotics. It is they and only they who have
founded religions and created great works of art.
*Remembrance of Things Past. The
Guermantes Way. My Grandmother's
Illness*

13   Like everybody who is not in love, he imagined
that one chose the person whom one loved after
endless deliberations and on the strength of various
qualities and advantages.
*Remembrance of Things Past. Cities of the
Plain, pt. I*

14   They buried him, but all through the night of
mourning, in the lighted windows, his books
arranged three by three kept watch like angels with
outspread wings and seemed, for him who was no
more, the symbol of his resurrection.
*Remembrance of Things Past. The Captive,
pt. I*

15   The bonds that unite another person to ourself
exist only in our mind. Memory as it grows fainter
relaxes them, and notwithstanding the illusion by
which we would fain be cheated and with which,
out of love, friendship, politeness, deference, duty,
we cheat other people, we exist alone. Man is the
creature that cannot emerge from himself, that
knows his fellows only in himself; when he asserts
the contrary, he is lying.
*Remembrance of Things Past. The Sweet
Cheat Gone*

---

[1]He, to get the cold side outside, / Put the warm side fur side inside. / That's why he put the fur side inside, / Why he put the skin
side outside, / Why he turned them inside outside. —ANONYMOUS,
The Modern Hiawatha

[2]For the *South Polar Times,* Midwinter Day [June 22, 1911], prepared by the men of Captain Robert Falcon Scott's last Antarctic
expedition. Ponting was the photographer for the Scott expedition.

[3]*Longtemps je me suis couché de bonne heure.*

[4]*À la Recherche du Temps Perdu,* translated by C. K. SCOTT
MONTCRIEFF, except the last volume, *The Past Recaptured,* translated by FREDERICK A. BLOSSOM.

1   There is not a woman in the world the possession of whom is as precious as that of the truths which she reveals to us by causing us to suffer.
Remembrance of Things Past. The Sweet Cheat Gone

2   We are healed of a suffering only by experiencing it to the full.
Remembrance of Things Past. The Sweet Cheat Gone

3   Happiness is beneficial for the body but it is grief that develops the powers of the mind.
Remembrance of Things Past. The Past Recaptured

4   Only through art can we get outside of ourselves and know another's view of the universe which is not the same as ours and see landscapes which would otherwise have remained unknown to us like the landscapes of the moon. Thanks to art, instead of seeing a single world, our own, we see it multiply until we have before us as many worlds as there are original artists.
The Maxims of Marcel Proust [1948][1]

5   A book is the product of a different *self* from the self we manifest in our habits, in our social life, in our vices.
Contre Sainte-Beuve [1954]. The Method of Sainte-Beuve[2]

Ernest Rutherford
1871–1937

6   We cannot control atomic energy to an extent which would be of any value commercially, and I believe we are not likely ever to be able to do so.
Speech to the British Association for the Advancement of Science [1933]

John Millington Synge
1871–1909

7   What is the price of a thousand horses against a son where there is one son only?
Riders to the Sea [1904]

8   When I was writing *The Shadow of the Glen* . . . I got more aid than any learning could have given me from a chink in the floor of the old Wicklow house where I was staying, that let me hear what was being said by the servant girls in the kitchen.
The Playboy of the Western World [1907], preface

9   May I meet him with one tooth and it aching and one eye to be seeing seven and seventy divils in the twists of the road, and one old timber leg on him to limp into the scalding grave. There he is now crossing the strands, and that the Lord God would send a high wave to wash him from the world.[3]
The Playboy of the Western World, act I

10   Oh my grief, I've lost him surely. I've lost the only Playboy of the Western World.
The Playboy of the Western World, III, curtain line

11   A man who is not afraid of the sea will soon be drowned, he said, for he will be going out on a day he shouldn't. But we do be afraid of the sea, and we do only be drownded now and again.
The Aran Islands [1907]

12   There is no language like the Irish for soothing and quieting.   *The Aran Islands*

13   A translation is no translation, he said, unless it will give you the music of a poem along with the words of it.   *The Aran Islands*

Paul Valéry
1871–1945

14   The folly of mistaking a paradox for a discovery, a metaphor for a proof, a torrent of verbiage for a spring of capital truths, and oneself for an oracle, is inborn in us.
Introduction to the Method of Leonardo da Vinci [1895][4]

15   Collect all the facts that can be collected about the life of Racine and you will never learn from them the art of his verse. All criticism is dominated by the outworn theory that the man is the cause of the work as in the eyes of the law the criminal is the cause of the crime. Far rather are they both the effects.
Introduction to the Method of Leonardo da Vinci

16   The sea, the ever renewing sea![5]
Charmes [1922]. Le Cimetière Marin

---

[1]Edited and translated by JUSTIN O'BRIEN.
[2]Translated by SYLVIA TOWNSEND WARNER.

[3]May the grass grow at your door and the fox build his nest on your hearthstone. May the light fade from your eyes, so you never see what you love. May your own blood rise against you, and the sweetest drink you take be the bitterest cup of sorrow. May you die without benefit of clergy; may there be none to shed a tear at your grave, and may the hearthstone of hell be your best bed forever. — *Traditional Wexford curse*
[4]Translated by THOMAS MCGREEVY.
[5]La mer, la mer toujours recommencée!

1   The wind is rising . . . we must attempt to live.[1]
Charmes. Le Cimetière Marin

2   Poetry is simply literature reduced to the essence of its active principle. It is purged of idols of every kind, of realistic illusions, of any conceivable equivocation between the language of "truth" and the language of "creation."   *Littérature [1930]*

3   An intelligent woman is a woman with whom one can be as stupid as one wants.
Mauvaises Pensées et Autres [1941]

4   That which has always been accepted by everyone, everywhere, is almost certain to be false.
Tel Quel [1943]

5   God created man, and finding him not sufficiently alone, gave him a female companion so that he might feel his solitude more acutely.
Tel Quel

6   A poem is never finished, only abandoned.
From W. H. AUDEN, A Certain World [1970]

Sir Max Beerbohm
1872–1956

7   Most women are not so young as they are painted.   *A Defense of Cosmetics*

8   To give an accurate and exhaustive account of that period would need a far less brilliant pen than mine.   *Eighteen Eighty [1895]*

9   Zuleika, on a desert island, would have spent most of her time in looking for a man's footprint.
Zuleika Dobson [1911], ch. 2

10   She was one of the people who say: "I don't know anything about music really, but I know what I like."   *Zuleika Dobson, 9*

11   Of all the objects of hatred, a woman once loved is the most hateful.   *Zuleika Dobson, 13*

12   The Socratic manner is not a game at which two can play. Please answer my question, to the best of your ability.   *Zuleika Dobson, 15*

13   I have known no man of genius who had not to pay, in some affliction or defect either physical or spiritual, for what the gods had given him.
No. 2. The Pines

14   To say that a man is vain means merely that he is pleased with the effect he produces on other people. A conceited man is satisfied with the effect he produces on himself.   *Quia Imperfectum*

15   Strange, when you come to think of it, that of all the countless folk who have lived before our time on this planet not one is known in history or in legend as having died of laughter.   *Laughter*

Léon Blum
1872–1950

16   Life does not give itself to one who tries to keep all its advantages at once. I have often thought morality may perhaps consist solely in the courage of making a choice.   *On Marriage*

Patrick Reginald Chalmers
1872–1942

17   What's lost upon the roundabouts we pulls up on the swings!   *Roundabouts and Swings, st. 2*

Calvin Coolidge
1872–1933

18   There is no right to strike against the public safety by anybody, anywhere, any time.
Telegram to Samuel Gompers, president of the American Federation of Labor, on the Boston police strike [September 14, 1919]

19   The chief business of the American people is business.
Speech to the American Society of Newspaper Editors [January 17, 1925]

20   I do not choose to run for President in 1928.[2]
Statement to reporters [August 2, 1927]

21   He said he was against it.
On being asked what a clergyman preaching on sin had said

22   They hired the money, didn't they?
Attributed. Comment on European war debts [1925]

23   When a great many people are unable to find work, unemployment results.   *Attributed*

[Edward] Gordon Craig
1872–1966

24   That is what the title of artist means: one who perceives more than his fellows, and who records more than he has seen.
On the Art of the Theatre [1911]

---

[1]Le vent se lève . . . il faut tenter de vivre.

[2]See Will Rogers, 685:17.

Sergei Pavlovich Diaghilev

1872–1929

1   Astound me! I'll wait for you to astound me.
     To Jean Cocteau [1912]. From JEAN
     COCTEAU, *Journals, ed. Wallace Fowlie
     [1956], ch. 1*

Paul Laurence Dunbar

1872–1906

2 It is not a carol of joy or glee,
   But a prayer that he sends from his heart's deep
     core . . .
   I know why the caged bird sings!
                                     Sympathy [1899], st. 3

3 Since thou[1] and those who died with thee for right
   Have died, the Present teaches, but in vain!
                                     Robert Gould Shaw, st. 2

4 It's easy 'nough to titter w'en de stew is smokin'
     hot,
   But hit's mighty ha'd to giggle w'en dey's nuffin'
     in de pot.   *Philosophy*

Learned Hand

1872–1961

5   This much I think I do know — that a society so
riven that the spirit of moderation is gone, no court
can save; that a society where that spirit flourishes,
no court *need* save; that in a society which evades its
responsibility by thrusting upon the courts the nurture of that spirit, that spirit in the end will perish.
     *The Contribution of an Independent
     Judiciary to Civilization [1942]*

6   "I beseech ye in the bowels of Christ, think that
ye may be mistaken."[2] I should like to have that
written over the portals of every church, every
school, and every courthouse, and, may I say, of
every legislative body in the United States. I should
like to have every court begin, "I beseech ye in the
bowels of Christ, think that we may be mistaken."
     Morals in Public Life [1951]

7   I had rather take my chance that some traitors
will escape detection than spread abroad a spirit of
general suspicion and distrust, which accepts rumor

---

[1]Colonel Robert Gould Shaw, white commander of the 54th
Massachusetts regiment (first enlisted black regiment in the Civil
War), died with many others of the regiment at Fort Wagner [July
18, 1863].
     See Charles W. Eliot, 556:3, and Robert Lowell, 801:11.
[2]See Cromwell, 254:12.

and gossip in place of undismayed and unintimi-
dated inquiry.
     *Speech to the Board of Regents, University of
     the State of New York [October 24, 1952]*

8   That community is already in the process of dissolution where each man begins to eye his neighbor
as a possible enemy, where nonconformity with the
accepted creed, political as well as religious, is a
mark of disaffection; where denunciation, without
specification or backing, takes the place of evidence;
where orthodoxy chokes freedom of dissent; where
faith in the eventual supremacy of reason has become so timid that we dare not enter our convictions in the open lists, to win or lose.
     *Speech to the Board of Regents, University of
     the State of New York [October 24, 1952]*

John McCrae

1872–1918

9 In Flanders fields the poppies blow
   Between the crosses, row on row.
                                     In Flanders Fields [1915], st.

10 Take up our quarrel with the foe;
   To you from failing hands we throw
   The Torch: be yours to hold it high!
   If ye break faith with us who die
   We shall not sleep, though poppies grow
   In Flanders fields.   *In Flanders Fields, st.*

Bertrand Russell, Earl Russell

1872–1970

11   Mathematics may be defined as the subject in
which we never know what we are talking about,
nor whether what we are saying is true.
     *Recent Work on the Principles of Mathematics
     [1901]. In International Monthly, vol. 4,
     p. 84*

12   Mathematics, rightly viewed, possesses not only
truth, but supreme beauty — a beauty cold and austere, like that of sculpture, without appeal to any
part of our weaker nature, without the gorgeous
trappings of painting or music, yet sublimely pure
and capable of a stern perfection such as only the
greatest art can show.
     The Study of Mathematics [1902]

13   Mathematics takes us still further from what is
human, into the region of absolute necessity, to
which not only the actual world, but every possible
world, must conform.
     The Study of Mathematics

1 It is undesirable to believe a proposition when there is no ground whatever for supposing it to be true.   *Skeptical Essays [1928], ch. 1*

2 The psychology of adultery has been falsified by conventional morals, which assume, in monogamous countries, that attraction to one person cannot coexist with a serious affection for another. Everybody knows that this is untrue.
Marriage and Morals [1929], ch. 16

3 In 1744 he [David Hume] made an unsuccessful attempt to obtain a professorship at Edinburgh; having failed in this, he became first tutor to a lunatic and then secretary to a general. Fortified by these credentials he ventured again into philosophy.
A History of Western Philosophy [1945], ch. 17

4 Fear is the main source of superstition, and one of the main sources of cruelty. To conquer fear is the beginning of wisdom.
An Outline of Intellectual Rubbish [1950]

5 Three passions, simple but overwhelmingly strong, have governed my life: the longing for love, the search for knowledge, and unbearable pity for the suffering of mankind.
Autobiography [1967], prologue

Ellery Sedgwick
1872–1960

6 Autobiographies ought to begin with Chapter Two.
The Happy Profession [1946], ch. 1

7 In America, getting on in the world means getting out of the world we have known before.
The Happy Profession, 1

Carl [Lotus] Becker
1873–1945

8 Economic distress will teach men, if anything can, that realities are less dangerous than fancies, that fact-finding is more effective than fault-finding.
Progress and Power [1935]

9 The significance of man is that he is that part of the universe that asks the question, What is the significance of Man? He alone can stand apart imaginatively and, regarding himself and the universe in their eternal aspects, pronounce a judgment: The significance of man is that he is insignificant and is aware of it.
Progress and Power

George Bennard
1873–1958

10 I will cling to the old rugged cross,
And exchange it some day for a crown.
The Old Rugged Cross [1913], refrain

Willa [Sibert] Cather
1873–1947

11 No one can build his security upon the nobleness of another person.
Alexander's Bridge [1912], ch. 8

12 There are only two or three human stories, and they go on repeating themselves as fiercely as if they had never happened before.
O Pioneers! [1913], pt. II, ch. 4

13 The history of every country begins in the heart of a man or a woman.   *O Pioneers!, II, 4*

14 I like trees because they seem more resigned to the way they have to live than other things do.
O Pioneers!, II, 8

15 I tell you there is such a thing as creative hate!
The Song of the Lark [1915], pt. I

16 If there was a road I could not make it out in the faint starlight. There was nothing but land: not a country at all, but the material out of which countries are made.   *My Ántonia [1918], bk. I, ch. 1*

17 That is happiness; to be dissolved into something complete and great.[1]   *My Ántonia, I, 2*

18 Winter lies too long in country towns; hangs on until it is stale and shabby, old and sullen.
My Ántonia, II, 7

19 In New Mexico he always awoke a young man; not until he rose and began to shave did he realize that he was growing older. His first consciousness was a sense of the light dry wind blowing in through the windows, with the fragrance of hot sun and sagebrush and sweet clover; a wind that made one's body feel light and one's heart cry "To-day, to-day," like a child's.
Death Comes for the Archbishop [1927], bk. IX, ch. 3

20 Only solitary men know the full joys of friendship. Others have their family; but to a solitary and an exile his friends are everything.
Shadows on the Rock [1931], bk. III, ch. 5

---

[1]Inscribed on Willa Cather's gravestone in Jaffrey Center, New Hampshire.

Arthur Chapman
1873–1935

1 Out where the handclasp's a little stronger,
Out where the smile dwells a little longer,
That's where the West begins.
Out Where the West Begins, st. 1

Colette [Sidonie Gabrielle Colette]
1873–1954

2   Those pleasures so lightly called physical.
Mélanges

3   Whether you are dealing with an animal or a child, to convince is to weaken.
Le Pur et l'Impur [1932]

4   It was towards the end of June that incompatibility became established between them like a new season of the year.   *The Cat [1933], ch. 7*

5   One of the best things about love is just recognizing a man's step when he climbs the stairs.
Occupation [1941][1]

6   The three great stumbling blocks in a girl's education . . . *homard a l'Américaine,* a boiled egg, and asparagus.   *Gigi [1942]*

7   The day after that wedding night I found that a distance of a thousand miles, abyss and discovery and irremediable metamorphosis, separated me from the day before.   *Noces [1945]*

Walter de la Mare
1873–1956

8 Slowly, silently, now the moon
Walks the night in her silver shoon.   *Silver*

9 Here lies a most beautiful lady,
Light of step and heart was she;
I think she was the most beautiful lady
That ever was in the West Country.   *An Epitaph*

10 "Is there anybody there?" said the Traveler,
Knocking on the moonlit door;
And his horse in the silence champed the grasses
Of the forest's ferny floor.   *The Listeners*

11 "Tell them that I came, and no one answered,
That I kept my word," he said.   *The Listeners*

12 Look thy last on all things lovely,
Every hour—let no night
Seal thy sense in deathly slumber

Till to delight
Thou hast paid thy utmost blessing.
Fare Well [1918], st.

13 Nought but vast sorrow was there—
The sweet cheat gone.   *The Gho*

14 Who said "Peacock Pie"?
The old king to the sparrow:
Who said "Crops are ripe"?
Rust to the harrow.   *The Song of the Mad Prin*

15 Poor Jim Jay
Got stuck fast
In Yesterday.   *Jim Ja*

16 It's a very odd thing—
As odd as can be—
That whatever Miss T. eats
Turns into Miss T.   *Miss*

17 Bang! Now the animal
Is dead and dumb and done.
Nevermore to peep again, creep again, leap again,
Eat or sleep or drink again, oh, what fun!   *Hi*

Mark Fenderson
1873–1944

18   What's the use? Yesterday an egg, tomorrow feather duster.
Caption for cartoon: The Dejected Rooste

Ford Madox [Hueffer] Ford
1873–1939

19   A fervent young admirer exclaimed: "By Jove the Good Soldier is the finest novel in the Englis language!" whereupon my friend John Rodke who has always had a properly tempered admiratio for my work, remarked in his clear, slow drawl: "Ah yes. It is, but you have left out a word. It is th finest French novel in the English language!"
The Good Soldier [1915]. Dedicatory lette

20   This is the saddest story I have ever heard.
The Good Soldier, first lin

21   Only two classes of books are of universal appea the very best and the very worst.
Joseph Conrad [1924

22   No more Hope, no more Glory, no more pa rades for you and me. . . . Na poo, finny![2]
No More Parades [1925

---

[1]Translated by DAVID LE VAY.

[2]World War I slang version of Il n'y a plus, fini.

Lena Guilbert Ford
d. 1918

1 Keep the home fires burning,[1]
While your hearts are yearning;
Though your lads are far away
They dream of home.
There's a silver lining
Through the dark cloud shining;
Turn the dark cloud inside out,
Till the boys come home.
Keep the Home Fires Burning [1915]

Ellen Glasgow
1873–1945

2 No idea is so antiquated that it was not once modern. No idea is so modern that it will not some-day be antiquated.
Address to the Modern Language Association [1936]

3 Preserve, within a wild sanctuary, an inaccessible valley of reveries. *A Certain Measure [1943]*

W[illiam] C[hristopher] Handy
1873–1958

4 I hate to see the evenin' sun go down.
The St. Louis Blues [1914]

Otto Harbach
1873–1963

5 When a lovely flame dies,
Smoke gets in your eyes.
Roberta [1933].[2] Smoke Gets In Your Eyes

G[eorge] E[dward] Moore
1873–1958

6 It appears to me that in Ethics, as in all other philosophical studies, the difficulties and disagree-ments, of which history is full, are mainly due to a very simple cause: namely to the attempt to answer questions, without first discovering precisely *what* question it is which you desire to answer.
Principia Ethica [1903], preface

Charles Péguy
1873–1914

7 Surrender is essentially an operation by means of which we set about explaining instead of acting.
Les Cahiers de la Quinzaine [1905]

8 Homer is new and fresh this morning, and noth-ing, perhaps, is as old and tired as today's newspaper.[3]
Note sur M. Bergson et la Philosophie Bergsonienne [1914]

9 Freedom is a system based on courage.
From HALÉVY, *Life of Charles Péguy*

Sime Silverman
1873–1933

10 Wall St. Lays an Egg.
Headline announcing stock market crash, Variety [October 30, 1929]

Alfred [Emanuel] Smith[4]
1873–1944

11 The kiss of death.
Alluding to William Randolph Hearst's support of Ogden Mills, Smith's unsuccessful opponent for governor of New York State [1926]

12 Let's look at the record.
Campaign speeches [1928]

13 The Governor of New York State does not have to be an acrobat.
Speech in behalf of Franklin D. Roosevelt [1928]

14 Nobody shoots at Santa Claus.
Campaign speeches [1936]

15 No matter how thin you slice it, it's still baloney.
Campaign speeches [1936]

H[enry] M[ajor] Tomlinson
1873–1958

16 The sea is at its best at London, near midnight, when you are within the arms of a capacious chair, before a glowing fire, selecting phases of the voy-ages you will never make.
The Sea and the Jungle [1912]

---

[1]First line attributed to IVOR NOVELLO [1893–1951], who com-posed the music.

[2]Music by JEROME KERN.

[3]Homère est nouveau ce matin, et rien n'est peut-être aussi vieux que le journal d'aujourd'hui.

[4]He is the Happy Warrior of the political battlefield. —FRANKLIN D. ROOSEVELT, *nominating speech, Democratic National Conven-tion* [June 26, 1924]. See Wordsworth, 394:15.

1   As to the sea itself, love it you cannot. Why should you? I will never believe again the sea was ever loved by anyone whose life was married to it. It is the creation of Omnipotence, which is not of humankind and understandable, and so the springs of its behavior are hidden.   *The Sea and the Jungle*

Maurice Baring
1874–1945

2   All theories of what a good play is, or how a good play should be written, are futile. A good play is a play which when acted upon the boards makes an audience interested and pleased. A play that fails in this is a bad play.   *Have You Anything to Declare?*

Charles A[ustin] Beard
1874–1948
and
Mary R[itter] Beard
1876–1958

3   At no time, at no place, in solemn convention assembled, through no chosen agents, had the American people officially proclaimed the United States to be a democracy. The Constitution did not contain the word or any word lending countenance to it, except possibly the mention of "We, the people," in the preamble . . . When the Constitution was framed no respectable person called himself or herself a democrat.
    America in Midpassage [1939], ch. 17

Arthur Henry Reginald Buller
1874–1944

4 There was a young lady named Bright,
Whose speed was far faster than light;
    She set out one day
    In a relative way,
And returned home the previous night.
    Limerick. In Punch [December 19, 1923]

G[ilbert] K[eith] Chesterton
1874–1936

5   The Christian ideal has not been tried and found wanting. It has been found difficult; and left untried.
    What's Wrong with the World [1910], pt. I, ch. 5

6   Nothing sublimely artistic has ever arisen out of mere art, any more than anything essentially reasonable has ever arisen out of pure reason. There must

always be a rich moral soil for any great aesthetic growth.   *A Defense of Nonsense [1911]*

7 For the great Gaels of Ireland
Are the men that God made mad,
For all their wars are merry,
And all their songs are sad.
    The Ballad of the White Horse [1911], bk. II

8   The whole difference between construction and creation is exactly this: that a thing constructed can only be loved after it is constructed; but a thing created is loved before it exists.
    Preface to DICKENS, Pickwick Papers

9   A good joke is the one ultimate and sacred thing which cannot be criticized. Our relations with a good joke are direct and even divine relations.
    Preface to DICKENS, Pickwick Papers

10 Strong gongs groaning as the guns boom far
(Don John of Austria is going to the war);
Stiff flags straining in the night blasts cold
In the gloom black-purple, in the glint old gold;
Torchlight crimson on the copper kettledrums,
Then the tuckets, then the trumpets, then the cannon, and he comes.   *Lepanto [1915]*

11 Cervantes on his galley sets the sword back in the sheath
(Don John of Austria rides homeward with a wreath).
And he sees across a weary land a straggling road in Spain,
Up which a lean and foolish knight forever rides in vain.   *Lepanto*

12 To an open house in the evening
Home shall men come,
To an older place than Eden
And a taller town than Rome.
    The House of Christmas

13 Burn from my brain and from my breast
Sloth, and the cowardice that clings,
And stiffness and the soul's arrest:
And feed my brain with better things.
    A Ballade of a Book Reviewer

14 St. George he was for England,
And before he killed the dragon
He drank a pint of English ale
Out of an English flagon.   *The Englishman*

15 Step softly, under snow or rain,
To find the place where men can pray;
The way is all so very plain
That we may lose the way.   *The Wise Men*

16 And Noah he often said to his wife when he sat down to dine,
"I don't care where the water goes if it doesn't get into the wine."   *Wine and Water*

1 Fools! For I also had my hour;
One far fierce hour and sweet:
There was a shout about my ears,
And palms before my feet.   *The Donkey*

Sir Winston Spencer Churchill[1]
1874–1965

2   I pass with relief from the tossing sea of Cause and Theory to the firm ground of Result and Fact.
                    The Malakand Field Force [1898]

3   It is better to be making the news than taking it; to be an actor rather than a critic.
                    The Malakand Field Force

4   Nothing in life is so exhilarating as to be shot at without result.   *The Malakand Field Force*

5   There are men in the world who derive as stern an exaltation from the proximity of disaster and ruin, as others from success.
                    The Malakand Field Force

6   Terminological inexactitude.
     Speech in the House of Commons [February 22, 1906]

7   The maxim of the British people is "Business as usual."
     Speech at the Guildhall [November 9, 1914]

8   Politics are almost as exciting as war, and quite as dangerous. In war you can only be killed once, but in politics many times.   *Remark [1920]*

9   By being so long in the lowest form [at Harrow] I gained an immense advantage over the cleverer boys. . . . I got into my bones the essential structure of the ordinary British sentence — which is a noble thing. . . . Naturally I am biased in favor of boys learning English; I would make them all learn English: and then I would let the clever ones learn Latin as an honor, and Greek as a treat.
     Roving Commission: My Early Life [1930]

10   It is a good thing for an uneducated man to read books of quotations. Bartlett's *Familiar Quotations* is an admirable work, and I studied it intently. The quotations when engraved upon the memory give you good thoughts. They also make you anxious to read the authors and look for more.
     Roving Commission: My Early Life

11   You will make all kinds of mistakes; but as long as you are generous and true, and also fierce, you cannot hurt the world or even seriously distress her. She was made to be wooed and won by youth.
     Roving Commission: My Early Life

12   Decided only to be undecided, resolved to be irresolute, adamant for drift, solid for fluidity, all-powerful to be impotent.[2]
                    While England Slept [1936]

13   Dictators ride to and fro upon tigers which they dare not dismount. And the tigers are getting hungry.[3]   *While England Slept*

14   I have watched this famous island descending incontinently, fecklessly, the stairway which leads to a dark gulf.   *While England Slept*

15   The German dictator, instead of snatching the victuals from the table, has been content to have them served to him course by course.
     Speech on the Munich agreement, House of Commons [October 5, 1938]

16   That long [Canadian] frontier from the Atlantic to the Pacific Oceans, guarded only by neighborly respect and honorable obligations, is an example to every country and a pattern for the future of the world.
     Speech in honor of R. B. Bennett, Canada Club, London [April 20, 1939]

17   I cannot forecast to you the action of Russia. It is a riddle wrapped in a mystery inside an enigma.
                    Radio broadcast [October 1, 1939]

18   For each and for all, as for the Royal Navy, the watchword should be, "Carry on, and dread nought."
     Speech on traffic at sea, House of Commons [December 6, 1939]

19   I have nothing to offer but blood, toil, tears and sweat.[4]
     First Statement as Prime Minister, House of Commons [May 13, 1940]

20   Victory at all costs, victory in spite of all terror, victory however long and hard the road may be; for without victory there is no survival.
     First Statement as Prime Minister, House of Commons [May 13, 1940]

---

[2] Of Stanley Baldwin's policies.

[3] He who rides a tiger is afraid to dismount. — WILLIAM SCARBOROUGH [fl. c. 1875], *Chinese Proverbs* [1875], *no. 2082*

[4] Mollify it with thy tears, or sweat, or blood. — JOHN DONNE, *An Anatomy of the World* [1611], *I, 430–431*
Year after year they voted cent per cent, / Blood, sweat, and tear-wrung millions — why? for rent! — LORD BYRON, *The Age of Bronze* [1823], *XIV*
Their sweat, their tears, their blood bedewed the endless plain. — CHURCHILL, *The Unknown War* [1931], referring to the armies of the czar before the Russian Revolution.
Churchill alluded to his promise of blood, toil, tears, and sweat in subsequent speeches on October 8, 1940, May 7 and December 2, 1941, and January 27 and November 10, 1942.

---

[1] See Franklin D. Roosevelt and Sir Winston Churchill, 699.

1   We shall not flag or fail. We shall go on to the end. We shall fight in France, we shall fight on the seas and oceans, we shall fight with growing confidence and growing strength in the air, we shall defend our island, whatever the cost may be, we shall fight on the beaches, we shall fight on the landing grounds, we shall fight in the fields and in the streets, we shall fight in the hills; we shall never surrender.
Speech on Dunkirk, House of Commons [June 4, 1940]

2   Let us . . . brace ourselves to our duties, and so bear ourselves that if the British Empire and its Commonwealth last for a thousand years, men will still say: "This was their finest hour."
Speech in the House of Commons [June 18, 1940]

3   We shall defend every village, every town and every city. The vast mass of London itself, fought street by street, could easily devour an entire hostile army; and we would rather see London laid in ruins and ashes than that it should be tamely and abjectly enslaved.   *Radio broadcast [July 14, 1940]*

4   Never in the field of human conflict was so much owed by so many to so few.
Tribute to the Royal Air Force, House of Commons [August 20, 1940]

5   The British Empire and the United States will have to be somewhat mixed up together in some of their affairs for mutual and general advantage. For my own part, looking out upon the future, I do not view the process with any misgivings.
Tribute to the Royal Air Force, House of Commons [August 20, 1940]

6   Death and sorrow will be the companions of our journey; hardship our garment; constancy and valor our only shield. We must be united, we must be undaunted, we must be inflexible.
Report on the war, House of Commons [October 8, 1940]

7   We are waiting for the long-promised invasion. So are the fishes.
Radio broadcast to the French people [October 21, 1940]

8   Here is the answer which I will give to President Roosevelt. . . . Give us the tools, and we will finish the job.   *Radio broadcast [February 9, 1941]*

9   This is one of those cases in which the imagination is baffled by the facts.
Remark in the House of Commons following the parachute descent in Scotland of Rudolf Hess [May 13, 1941]

10   The British nation is unique in this respect. The are the only people who like to be told how ba things are, who like to be told the worst.
Report on the war, House of Commons [June 10, 1941]

11   A vile race of quislings[1] — to use the new wor which will carry the scorn of mankind down th centuries.
Speech at St. James's Palace, London [June 12 1941]

12   The destiny of mankind is not decided by mate rial computation. When great causes are on th move in the world . . . we learn that we are spirit not animals, and that something is going on i space and time, and beyond space and time, which whether we like it or not, spells duty.
Radio broadcast to America on receiving the honorary degree of Doctor of Laws from the University of Rochester, New York [June 16, 1941]

13   Hitler is a monster of wickedness, insatiable in hi lust for blood and plunder. Not content with havin all Europe under his heel, or else terrorized into vari ous forms of abject submission, he must now carry hi work of butchery and desolation among the vast multi tudes of Russia and of Asia. . . . So now this blood thirsty guttersnipe must launch his mechanized armie upon new fields of slaughter, pillage and devastation.
Radio broadcast on the German invasion of Russia [June 22, 1941]

14   We will have no truce or parley with you [Hitler] or the grisly gang who work your wicked will. You do your worst — and we will do our best.
Speech to the London County Council [July 14 1941]

15   The V sign is the symbol of the unconquerable will of the occupied territories, and a portent of th fate awaiting the Nazi tyranny.
Message to the people of Europe on launching the V for Victory propaganda campaign [July 20, 1941]

16   Nothing is more dangerous in wartime than to live in the temperamental atmosphere of a Gallu Poll,[2] always feeling one's pulse and taking one' temperature.
Report on the war, House of Commons [September 30, 1941]

[1]Vidkun Quisling, head of the Nasjonal Samling party in Nor way, who cooperated and collaborated with the Nazis when Ger many invaded Norway [April 9, 1940]. Quisling was execute [October 23, 1945].

[2]Dr. George H. Gallup [1901–1984] founded the American In stitute of Public Opinion in 1935.

1   Never give in, never give in, never, never, never, never—in nothing, great or small, large or petty—never give in except to convictions of honor and good sense.
Address at Harrow School [October 29, 1941]

2   Do not let us speak of darker days; let us speak rather of sterner days. These are not dark days: these are great days—the greatest days our country has ever lived; and we must all thank God that we have been allowed, each of us according to our stations, to play a part in making these days memorable in the history of our race.
Address at Harrow School [October 29, 1941]

3   In the past we have had a light which flickered, in the present we have a light which flames, and in the future there will be a light which shines over all the land and sea.
Speech on war with Japan, House of Commons [December 8, 1941]

4   What kind of people do they [the Japanese] think we are?
Speech to the U.S. Congress [December 26, 1941]

5   We have not journeyed all this way across the centuries, across the oceans, across the mountains, across the prairies, because we are made of sugar candy.
Speech to the Canadian Senate and House of Commons, Ottawa [December 30, 1941]

6   When I warned [the French] that Britain would fight on alone whatever they did, their generals told their prime minister and his divided cabinet, "In three weeks England will have her neck wrung like a chicken." Some chicken; some neck.
Speech to the Canadian Senate and House of Commons, Ottawa [December 30, 1941]

7   The late M. Venizelos[1] observed that in all her wars England—he should have said Britain, of course—always wins one battle—the last.
Speech at the Lord Mayor's Day Luncheon, London [November 10, 1942]

8   Now this is not the end. It is not even the beginning of the end. But it is, perhaps, the end of the beginning.
Speech at the Lord Mayor's Day Luncheon, London [November 10, 1942]

9   I have not become the King's First Minister in order to preside over the liquidation of the British Empire.
Speech at the Lord Mayor's Day Luncheon, London [November 10, 1942]

10   The soft underbelly of the Axis.
Report on the war, House of Commons [November 11, 1942]

11   In war-time, truth is so precious that she should always be attended by a bodyguard of lies.
Remark at Teheran Conference [December 1943]

12   "Not in vain" may be the pride of those who have survived and the epitaph of those who fell.[2]
Speech in the House of Commons [September 28, 1944]

13   The United States is a land of free speech. No where is speech freer—not even here where we sedulously cultivate it even in its most repulsive form.
Speech in the House of Commons [September 28, 1944]

14   He [President Franklin D. Roosevelt] died in harness, and we may well say in battle harness, like his soldiers, sailors, and airmen, who side by side with ours are carrying on their task to the end all over the world. What an enviable death was his.
Speech in the House of Commons [April 17, 1945]

15   I think "No comment" is a splendid expression. I am using it again and again. I got it from Sumner Welles.
To reporters at the Washington, D.C., airport, after conferring with President Truman at the White House [February 12, 1946]

16   From Stettin in the Baltic to Trieste in the Adriatic an iron curtain[3] has descended across the Continent.
Address at Westminster College, Fulton, Missouri [March 5, 1946]

---

[2]The eight thousand paratroopers of the First British Airborne Division who landed in Arnhem, Holland, behind the German lines and held the area for nine days and nights, with a loss of six thousand [September 1944]. MAJOR GENERAL R. E. URQUHART, the division commander, radioed to Field Marshal Bernard Montgomery: All will be ordered to break out rather than surrender.

[3]An iron curtain had dropped between him and the outer world—H. G. WELLS, *The Food of the Gods* [1904]

France . . . a nation of forty millions with a deep-rooted grievance and an iron curtain at its frontier.—GEORGE WASHINGTON CRILE [1864–1943], *A Mechanistic View of War and Peace* [1915]

With a rumble and a roar, an iron curtain is descending on Russian history.—VASILI ROZANOV [1856–1919], *Apocalypse of Our Time* [1918]

We were behind the "iron curtain" at last.—ETHEL ANNAKIN SNOWDEN [1881–1951], *Through Bolshevik Russia* [1920]

The Nazi minister of enlightenment and propaganda, PAUL JOSEPH GOEBBELS, used the phrase "iron curtain" in reference to the USSR in *Das Reich* [February 23, 1945].

CHURCHILL used it in a top-secret telegram to President Truman [May 12, 1945].

---

[1]Eleutherios Venizelos [1864–1936], Greek statesman.

1   In War: Resolution. In Defeat: Defiance. In Victory: Magnanimity. In Peace: Good Will.
The Second World War: Moral of the Work, vol. I, The Gathering Storm [1948]

2   No one can guarantee success in war, but only deserve it.
The Second World War: Moral of the Work, II, Their Finest Hour [1949]

3   When you have to kill a man it costs nothing to be polite.
The Second World War: Moral of the Work, III, The Grand Alliance [1950]

4   Everyone has his day and some days last longer than others.
Speech in the House of Commons [January 1952]

5   To jaw-jaw is always better than to war-war.
At a White House luncheon [June 26, 1954]

6   A fanatic is one who can't change his mind and won't change the subject.   *Saying*

7   The inherent vice of capitalism is the unequal sharing of blessings; the inherent virtue of socialism is the equal sharing of miseries.   *Saying*

8   Short words are best and the old words when short are best of all.   *Saying*

9   It is hard, if not impossible, to snub a beautiful woman—they remain beautiful and the rebuke recoils.   *Saying*

10   This is the sort of English up with which I will not put.   *Attributed*

Francis Macdonald Cornford
1874–1973

11   Every public action which is not customary, either is wrong, or, if it is right, is a dangerous precedent. It follows that nothing should ever be done for the first time.
Microcosmographia Academica: Being a Guide for the Young Academic Politician [1908], ch. 7

Clarence Day
1874–1935

12   What fairy story, what tale from the Arabian Nights of the jinns, is a hundredth part as wonderful as this true fairy story of simians! It is so much more heartening, too, than the tales we invent. A

universe capable of giving birth to many such accidents is—blind or not—a good world to live in, promising universe. . . . We once thought we lived on God's footstool; it may be a throne.
This Simian World [1920]. XIX

13   Aside from a few odd words in Hebrew, I took i completely for granted that God had never spoker anything but the most dignified English.
Life with Father [1935]. Father Interferes with the Twenty-third Psalm

14   "If you don't go to other men's funerals," h told Father stiffly, "they won't go to yours."
Life with Father. Father Plans to Get Ou

Robert Frost
1874–1963

15 They would not find me changed from him they knew—
Only more sure of all I thought was true.
Into My Own [1913], st. 4

16 Ah, when to the heart of man
Was it ever less than a treason
To go with the drift of things,
To yield with a grace to reason,
And bow and accept the end
Of a love or a season?
Reluctance [1913], st. 4

17 I'm going out to clean the pasture spring;
I'll only stop to rake the leaves away
(And wait to watch the water clear, I may):
I shan't be gone long.—You come too.
The Pasture [1914], st. 1

18 Something there is that doesn't love a wall.
Mending Wall [1914

19 My apple trees will never get across
And eat the cones under his pines, I tell him.
He only says, "Good fences make good neighbors."[1]   *Mending Wal*

20 Before I built a wall I'd ask to know
What I was walling in or walling out.
Mending Wal

21 And nothing to look backward to with pride,
And nothing to look forward to with hope.
The Death of the Hired Man [1914

22 Home is the place where, when you have to go there,
They have to take you in.
The Death of the Hired Man

[1]See George Herbert, 251:12.

1   The nearest friends can go
   With anyone to death, comes so far short
   They might as well not try to go at all.
                              Home Burial [1914]

2 Most of the change we think we see in life
   Is due to truths being in and out of favor.
                              The Black Cottage [1914]

3 Pressed into service means pressed out of shape.
                              The Self-Seeker [1914]

4 I shall be telling this with a sigh
   Somewhere ages and ages hence:
   Two roads diverged in a wood, and I—
   I took the one less traveled by,
   And that has made all the difference.
                              The Road Not Taken [1916], st. 4

5 I'd like to get away from earth awhile
   And then come back to it and begin over.
   May no fate willfully misunderstand me
   And half grant what I wish and snatch me away
   Not to return. Earth's the right place for love:
   I don't know where it's likely to go better.
                              Birches [1916]

6 One could do worse than be a swinger of birches.
                              Birches

7 I shall set forth for somewhere,
   I shall make the reckless choice
   Some say when they are in voice
   And tossing so as to scare
   The white clouds over them on,
   I shall have less to say,
   But I shall be gone.   *The Sound of the Trees [1916]*

8   Do you know,
   Considering the market, there are more
   Poems produced than any other thing?
   No wonder poets sometimes have to *seem*
   So much more businesslike than businessmen.
   Their wares are so much harder to get rid of.
                              New Hampshire [1923]

9 The snake stood up for evil in the Garden.
                              The Ax-Helve [1923]

10 Why make so much of fragmentary blue
   In here and there a bird, or butterfly,
   Or flower, or wearing-stone, or open eye,
   When heaven presents in sheets the solid hue?
                              Fragmentary Blue [1923], st. 1

11 Some say the world will end in fire,
   Some say in ice.
   From what I've tasted of desire
   I hold with those who favor fire.
   But if it had to perish twice,
   I think I know enough of hate
   To say that for destruction ice

Is also great
And would suffice.   *Fire and Ice [1923]*

12 The way a crow
   Shook down on me
   The dust of snow
   From a hemlock tree

   Has given my heart
   A change of mood
   And saved some part
   Of a day I had rued.   *Dust of Snow [1923]*

13 Whose woods these are I think I know.
   His house is in the village though;
   He will not see me stopping here
   To watch his woods fill up with snow.
                              *Stopping by Woods on a Snowy Evening
                              [1923], st. 1*

14 My little horse must think it queer
   To stop without a farmhouse near.
                              Stopping by Woods on a Snowy Evening, st. 2

15 The woods are lovely, dark and deep.
   But I have promises to keep,
   And miles to go before I sleep,
   And miles to go before I sleep.
                              Stopping by Woods on a Snowy Evening, st. 4

16 Love at the lips was touch
   As sweet as I could bear;
   And once that seemed too much;
   I lived on air.   *To Earthward [1923], st. 1*

17 Now no joy but lacks salt
   That is not dashed with pain
   And weariness and fault;
   I crave the stain

   Of tears, the aftermark
   Of almost too much love,
   The sweet of bitter bark
   And burning clove.   *To Earthward, st. 5, 6*

18 Keep cold, young orchard. Goodbye and keep
      cold.
   Dread fifty above more than fifty below.
                              Goodbye and Keep Cold [1923]

19 It looked as if a night of dark intent
   Was coming, and not only a night, an age.
   Someone had better be prepared for rage.
   There would be more than ocean-water broken
   Before God's last *Put out the Light* was spoken.
                              Once by the Pacific [1928]

20 Tree at my window, window tree,
   My sash is lowered when night comes on;
   But let there never be curtain drawn
   Between you and me.
                              Tree at My Window [1928], st. 1

1 That day she put our heads together,
 Fate had her imagination about her,
 Your head so much concerned with outer,
 Mine with inner, weather. *Tree at My Window, st. 4*

2 I have been one acquainted with the night.
   Acquainted with the Night [1928]

3 If, as they say, some dust thrown in my eyes
 Will keep my talk from getting overwise,
 I'm not the one for putting off the proof.
 Let it be overwhelming. *Dust in the Eyes [1928]*

4 Don't join too many gangs. Join few if any.
 Join the United States and join the family—
 But not much in between unless a college.
   Build Soil [1932]

5 The sun was warm but the wind was chill.
 You know how it is with an April day
 When the sun is out and the wind is still,
 You're one month on in the middle of May.
 But if you so much as dare to speak,
 A cloud comes over the sunlit arch,
 A wind comes off a frozen peak,
 And you're two months back in the middle of March.
   Two Tramps in Mud Time [1936], st. 3

6 But yield who will to their separation,
 My object in living is to unite
 My avocation and my vocation
 As my two eyes make one in sight.
 Only where love and need are one,
 And the work is play for mortal stakes,
 Is the deed ever really done
 For Heaven and the future's sakes.
   Two Tramps in Mud Time, st. 9

7 No memory of having starred
 Atones for later disregard,
 Or keeps the end from being hard.

 Better to go down dignified
 With boughten friendship by your side
 Than none at all. Provide, provide!
   Provide, Provide [1936], st. 6, 7

8 The old dog barks backward without getting up.
 I can remember when he was a pup.
   The Span of Life [1936]

9 I never dared to be radical when young
 For fear it would make me conservative when old.
   Precaution [1936]

10 The land was ours before we were the land's.
 She was our land more than a hundred years
 Before we were her people.
   The Gift Outright [1941][1]

---

[1]Read first before the Phi Beta Kappa Society at William and Mary College [December 5, 1941], later at the inauguration of President John F. Kennedy [January 20, 1961].

11 She is as in a field a silken tent
 At midday when a sunny summer breeze
 Has dried the dew and all its ropes relent,
 So that in guys it gently sways at ease.
   The Silken Tent [1942]

12 But strictly held by none, is loosely bound
 By countless silken ties of love and thought
 To everything on earth the compass round,
 And only by one's going slightly taut
 In the capriciousness of summer air
 Is of the slightest bondage made aware.
   The Silken Tent

13 Happiness Makes Up in Height for What It
 Lacks in Length. *Title of poem [1942]*

14 Far in the pillared dark
 Thrush music went—
 Almost like a call to come in
 To the dark and lament.

 But no, I was out for stars:
 I would not come in.
 I meant not even if asked,
 And I hadn't been.
   Come In [1942], st. 4, 5

15 And were an epitaph to be my story
 I'd have a short one ready for my own.
 I would have written of me on my stone:
 I had a lover's quarrel with the world.
   The Lesson for Today [1942]

16 We dance round in a ring and suppose,
 But the Secret sits in the middle and knows.
   The Secret Sits [1942]

17 Back out of all this now too much for us,
 Back in a time made simple by the loss
 Of detail, burned, dissolved, and broken off
 Like graveyard marble sculpture in the weather,
 There is a house that is no more a house
 Upon a farm that is no more a farm
 And in a town that is no more a town.
   Directive [1947]

18 First there's the children's house of make believe,
 Some shattered dishes underneath a pine,
 The playthings in the playhouse of the children.
 Weep for what little things could make them glad.
   Directive

19 Here are your waters and your watering place.
 Drink and be whole again beyond confusion.
   Directive

20 Have I not walked without an upward look
 Of caution under stars that very well
 Might not have missed me when they shot and fell?
 It was a risk I had to take—and took.
   Bravado [1947]

1   Any eye is an evil eye
That looks in on to a mood apart.
A Mood Apart [1947]

2   All those who try to go it sole alone,
Too proud to be beholden for relief,
Are absolutely sure to come to grief.
Haec Fabula Docet [1947]

3   It asks a little of us here.
It asks of us a certain height,
So when at times the mob is swayed
To carry praise or blame too far,
We may take something like a star
To stay our minds on and be staid.
Take Something Like a Star [1949]

4   Forgive, O Lord, my little jokes on Thee
And I'll forgive Thy great big one on me.
From In the Clearing [1962]

5   I am assured at any rate
Man's practically inexterminate.
Someday I must go into that.
There's always been an Ararat
Where someone someone else begat
To start the world all over at.
A-Wishing Well [1962]

6   It takes all sorts of in and outdoor schooling
To get adapted to my kind of fooling.
It Takes All Sorts [1962]

7   Unless I'm wrong
I but obey
The urge of a song:
I'm — bound — away!

And I may return
If dissatisfied
With what I learn
From having died.
Away! [1962], st. 5, 6

8   A poem . . . begins as a lump in the throat, a sense
of wrong, a homesickness, a lovesickness. . . . It
finds the thought and the thought finds the words.
Letter to Louis Untermeyer [January 1, 1916]

9   It is absurd to think that the only way to tell if a
poem is lasting is to wait and see if it lasts. The right
reader of a good poem can tell the moment it
strikes him that he has taken an immortal wound—
that he will never get over it.
*The Poetry of Amy Lowell. From the Christian
Science Monitor [May 16, 1925]*

10   The figure a poem makes. It begins in delight
and ends in wisdom . . . in a clarification of life—
not necessarily a great clarification, such as sects and
cults are founded on, but in a momentary stay
against confusion.
Collected Poems [1939]. Preface

11   No tears in the writer, no tears in the reader.
Collected Poems. Preface

12   Like a piece of ice on a hot stove the poem must
ride on its own melting. . . . Read it a hundred
times; it will forever keep its freshness as a metal
keeps its fragrance. It can never lose its sense of a
meaning that once unfolded by surprise as it went.
Collected Poems. Preface

13   How many times it thundered before Franklin
took the hint! How many apples fell on Newton's
head before he took the hint! Nature is always hint-
ing at us. It hints over and over again. And suddenly we take the hint.
Comment

14   It is only a moment here and a moment there
that the greatest writer has.
Comment

15   Poetry is a way of taking life by the throat.
Comment

16   Talking is a hydrant in the yard and writing is a
faucet upstairs in the house. Opening the first takes
all the pressure off the second.
Comment

17   The greatest thing in family life is to take a hint
when a hint is intended—and not to take a hint
when a hint isn't intended.
Comment

18   Always fall in with what you're asked to accept.
Take what is given, and make it over your way. My
aim in life has always been to hold my own with
whatever's going. Not against: with.
Comment

19   I've given offense by saying I'd as soon write
free verse as play tennis with the net down.
Interview [1959]

20   Education is . . . hanging around until you've
caught on.   *Comment [1963]*

Harry Graham
1874–1936

21   Billy, in one of his nice new sashes,
Fell in the fire and was burnt to ashes;
Now, although the room grows chilly,
I haven't the heart to poke poor Billy.
Ruthless Rhymes [1901]. Tender-Heartedness

Herbert [Clark] Hoover
1874–1964

1   The American system of rugged individualism.[1]
*Campaign speech, New York City
[October 22, 1928]*

2   The grass will grow in the streets of a hundred cities.   *Speech [October 31, 1932]*

3   A good many things go around in the dark besides Santa Claus.
Address to the John Marshall Republican Club, St. Louis, Missouri [December 16, 1935]

4   Older men declare war. But it is youth that must fight and die. And it is youth who must inherit the tribulation, the sorrow, and the triumphs that are the aftermath of war.
Speech at the Republican National Convention, Chicago [June 27, 1944]

Harold L[eClair] Ickes
1874–1952

5   I am against government by crony.
On resigning as secretary of the interior [February 1946]

Karl Kraus[2]
1874–1936

6   I and my public understand each other very well: it does not hear what I say, and I don't say what it wants to hear.   *Aphorism*

7   When the end of the world comes, I want to be living in retirement.   *Aphorism*

8   Heinrich Heine so loosened the corsets of the German language that today every little salesman can fondle her breasts.   *Aphorism*

9   An aphorism never coincides with the truth: it is either a half-truth or one-and-a-half truths.
Aphorism

10   Psychoanalysis is that mental illness for which it regards itself as therapy.   *Aphorism*

---

[1]While I can make no claim for having introduced the term "rugged individualism," I should be proud to have invented it. It has been used by American leaders for over a half-century in eulogy of those God-fearing men and women of honesty whose stamina and character and fearless assertion of rights led them to make their own way in life. —HERBERT HOOVER, *The Challenge to Liberty* [1934], *ch. 5*

[2]Translated by HARRY ZOHN.

11   A woman is, occasionally, quite a serviceable substitute for masturbation. It takes an abundance of imagination, to be sure.   *Aphorism*

Amy Lowell
1874–1925

12   A pattern called a war.
Christ! What are patterns for?   *Patterns*

13 Sappho would speak, I think, quite openly,
And Mrs. Browning guard a careful silence,
But Emily would set doors ajar and slam them
And love you for your speed of observation.
The Sisters

14 Heart-leaves of lilac all over New England,
Roots of lilac under all the soil of New England,
Lilac in me because I am New England.   *Lilacs*

W[illiam] Somerset Maugham
1874–1965

15   Like all weak men he laid an exaggerated stress on not changing one's mind.
Of Human Bondage [1915], ch. 39

16   People ask you for criticism, but they only want praise.   *Of Human Bondage, 50*

17   There is nothing so degrading as the constant anxiety about one's means of livelihood. . . . Money is like a sixth sense without which you cannot make a complete use of the other five.
Of Human Bondage, 51

18   I forget who it was that recommended men for their soul's good to do each day two things they disliked . . . it is a precept that I have followed scrupulously; for every day I have got up and I have gone to bed.
The Moon and Sixpence [1919], ch. 2

19   Conscience is the guardian in the individual of the rules which the community has evolved for its own preservation.   *The Moon and Sixpence, 14*

20   Do you know that conversation is one of the greatest pleasures in life? But it wants leisure.
The Trembling of a Leaf [1921], ch. 3

21   The tragedy of love is indifference.
The Trembling of a Leaf, 4

22   No one can be a humbug for five-and-twenty years. Hypocrisy is the most difficult and nerve-racking vice that any man can pursue; it needs an unceasing vigilance and a rare detachment of spirit.

It cannot, like adultery or gluttony, be practiced at spare moments; it is a whole-time job.
Cakes and Ale [1930], ch. 1

1   I [Death] was astonished to see him in Baghdad, for I had an appointment with him tonight in Samarra.   *Sheppy [1933], act III*

2   She [Sadie Thompson] gathered herself together. No one could describe the scorn of her expression or the contemptuous hatred she put into her answer. "You men! You filthy dirty pigs! You're all the same, all of you. Pigs! Pigs!"
Altogether [1934]. Rain

3   I would sooner read a timetable or a catalogue than nothing at all. They are much more entertaining than half the novels that are written.
The Summing Up [1938]

4   If a nation values anything more than freedom, it will lose its freedom; and the irony of it is that if it is comfort or money that it values more, it will lose that too.   *Strictly Personal [1941], ch. 31*

Alice Duer Miller
1874–1942

5 The white cliffs of Dover, I saw rising steeply
Out of the sea that once made her [England]
    secure.   *The White Cliffs [1940], I*

6 But in a world where England is finished and dead,
I do not wish to live.
The White Cliffs, LII

L[ucy] M[aud] Montgomery
1874–1908

7   A graveyard of buried hopes is about as romantic a thing as one can imagine.
Anne of Green Gables [1908], ch. 5

Robert William Service
1874–1958

8 This is the Law of the Yukon, that only the strong
    shall thrive;
That surely the weak shall perish, and only the fit
    survive.
Dissolute, damned and despairful, crippled and
    palsied and slain,
This is the Will of the Yukon — Lo, how she makes
    it plain!   *The Law of the Yukon*

9 Back of the bar, in a solo game, sat Dangerous Dan
    McGrew,
And watching his luck was his light-o'-love, the
    lady that's known as Lou.
The Shooting of Dan McGrew [1907], st. 1

10 The Northern Lights have seen queer sights,
But the queerest they ever did see
Was that night on the marge of Lake Lebarge
I cremated Sam McGee.
The Cremation of Sam McGee [1907], st. 1

Gertrude Stein
1874–1946

11   Rose is a rose is a rose is a rose.
Sacred Emily [written 1913]

12   You are all a lost generation.[1]
Used by ERNEST HEMINGWAY as an epigraph for The Sun Also Rises [1926]

13   Pigeons on the grass alas.
Four Saints in Three Acts [written 1927]

14   Before the Flowers of Friendship Faded Friendship Faded.   *Title [written 1930]*

15   I murmured to Picasso that I liked his portrait of Gertrude Stein. Yes, he said, everybody says that she does not look like it but that does not make any difference, she will.
The Autobiography of Alice B. Toklas [1933]

16   Remarks are not literature [said to Hemingway].
The Autobiography of Alice B. Toklas

17   [Ezra Pound] was a village explainer, excellent if you were a village, but if you were not, not.
The Autobiography of Alice B. Toklas

18   America is my country and Paris is my home town.   *An American and France [1936]*

19   In the United States there is more space where nobody is than where anybody is.
This is what makes America what it is.
The Geographical History of America [1936]

20   [Of Oakland, California:] There is no there there.
Everybody's Autobiography [1937], ch. 4

21 I am Rose my eyes are blue
I am Rose and who are you
I am Rose and when I sing
I am Rose like anything.
The World Is Round [1939]

---

[1]Ernest Hemingway stated that the remark was originally made by a garage owner in the Midi to Gertrude Stein in reference to his young mechanics, who were "une génération perdue."

1   What is the answer? [*I was silent.*] In that case, what is the question?
> *Last words. From* ALICE B. TOKLAS, *What Is Remembered [1963]*

Harry Williams
1874–1924

2 It's a long way to Tipperary, it's a long way to go;
It's a long way to Tipperary, to the sweetest girl I know!
Goodbye, Piccadilly, farewell, Leicester Square,
It's a long, long way to Tipperary, but my heart's right there!   *Tipperary [1908]*

E[dmund] C[lerihew][1] Bentley
1875–1956

3 The Art of Biography
Is different from Geography.
Geography is about Maps,
But Biography is about Chaps.
> *Biography for Beginners. Introduction*

4 Sir Christopher Wren
Said "I am going to dine with some men.
If anybody calls
Say I am designing St. Paul's."
> *Biography for Beginners. Sir Christopher Wren*[2]

5 John Stuart Mill
By a mighty effort of will
Overcame his natural bonhomie
And wrote *Principles of Political Economy.*
> *Biography for Beginners. John Stuart Mill*

6 George the Third
Ought never to have occurred.
One can only wonder
At so grotesque a blunder.[3]
> *Biography for Beginners. George III*

Mary McLeod Bethune
1875–1955

7   What does the Negro want? His answer is very simple. He wants only what all other Americans want. He wants opportunity to make real what the Declaration of Independence and the Constitution and the Bill of Rights say, what the Four Freedoms establish. While he knows these ideals are open to no man completely, he wants only his equal chance to obtain them.
> *"Certain Unalienable Rights." From What the Negro Wants [1944], edited by* RAYFORD W. LOGAN

8   If we accept and acquiesce in the face of discrimination, we accept the responsibility ourselves and allow those responsible to salve their conscience by believing that they have our acceptance and concurrence. We should, therefore, protest openly everything . . . that smacks of discrimination or slander.
> *"Certain Unalienable Rights." From What the Negro Wants, edited by* RAYFORD W. LOGAN

John Buchan, Lord Tweedsmuir
1875–1940

9   We can only pay our debt to the past by putting the future in debt to ourselves.
> *Address to the people of Canada, on the coronation of George VI [May 12, 1937]*

10   Public life is regarded as the crown of a career, and to young men it is the worthiest ambition. Politics is still the greatest and the most honorable adventure.   *Pilgrim's Way [1940]*

Edgar Rice Burroughs
1875–1950

11   As the body rolled to the ground Tarzan of the Apes placed his foot upon the neck of his lifelong enemy, and raising his eyes to the full moon threw back his fierce young head and voiced the wild and terrible cry of his people.
> *Tarzan of the Apes [1914], ch. 7*

12   I am Tarzan of the Apes. I want you. I am yours. You are mine.[4]   *Tarzan of the Apes, ch. 18*

Hasegawa Nyozekan[5]
1875–1969

13   The war was started as the result of a mistaken intuitive "calculation" which transcended mathe-

---

[1]A humorous quatrain in the form Bentley popularized is known as a clerihew.

[2]See Wren, 287.

[3]George the First was always reckoned / Vile, but viler George the Second; / And what mortal ever heard / Any good of George the Third? / When from earth the Fourth descended / God be praised, the Georges ended! —WALTER SAVAGE LANDOR, *epigram after hearing Thackeray's lectures, The Four Georges* [1855]

[4]Me Tarzan, you Jane. —Spoken by Johnny Weissmuller in the movie *Tarzan the Ape Man* [1932].

[5]From *Sources of Japanese Tradition* [1960], edited by WILLIAM THEODORE DE BARY.

matics. We believed with a blind fervor that we could triumph over scientific weapons and tactics by means of our mystic will. . . . The characteristic reliance on intuition by Japanese had blocked the objective cognition of the modern world.

The Lost Japan [1952]

Carl Gustav Jung
1875–1961

1 Without this playing with fantasy no creative work has ever yet come to birth. The debt we owe to the play of imagination is incalculable.

Psychological Types [1923], ch. 1, p. 82

2 The great problems of life — sexuality, of course, among others — are always related to the primordial images of the collective unconscious. These images are really balancing or compensating factors which correspond with the problems life presents in actuality. This is not to be marveled at, since these images are deposits representing the accumulated experience of thousands of years of struggle for adaptation and existence.

Psychological Types, 5, p. 271

3 The meeting of two personalities is like the contact of two chemical substances: if there is any reaction, both are transformed.

Modern Man in Search of a Soul [1933], p. 57

4 The great decisions of human life have as a rule far more to do with the instincts and other mysterious unconscious factors than with conscious will and well-meaning reasonableness. The shoe that fits one person pinches another; there is no recipe for living that suits all cases. Each of us carries his own life-form — an indeterminable form which cannot be superseded by any other.

Modern Man in Search of a Soul, p. 69

5 Aging people should know that their lives are not mounting and unfolding but that an inexorable inner process forces the contraction of life. For a young person it is almost a sin — and certainly a danger — to be too much occupied with himself; but for the aging person it is a duty and a necessity to give serious attention to himself.

Modern Man in Search of a Soul, p. 125

6 All ages before ours believed in gods in some form or other. Only an unparalleled impoverishment in symbolism could enable us to rediscover the gods as psychic factors, which is to say, as archetypes of the unconscious. No doubt this discovery is hardly credible as yet.

The Integration of the Personality [1939], p. 72

7 If there is anything that we wish to change in the child, we should first examine it and see whether it is not something that could better be changed in ourselves. *The Integration of the Personality, p. 285*

8 The conscious mind allows itself to be trained like a parrot, but the unconscious does not — which is why St. Augustine thanked God for not making him responsible for his dreams.

Psychology and Alchemy [1953], p. 51

9 The unconscious is not just evil by nature, it is also the source of the highest good: not only dark but also light, not only bestial, semihuman, and demonic but superhuman, spiritual, and, in the classical sense of the word, "divine."

The Practice of Psychotherapy [1953], p. 364

10 The little world of childhood with its familiar surroundings is a model of the greater world. The more intensively the family has stamped its character upon the child, the more it will tend to feel and see its earlier miniature world again in the bigger world of adult life.

From Psychological Reflections: A Jung Anthology [1953],[1] p. 83: Collected Works, vol. 4, The Theory of Psychoanalysis [1913]

11 This whole creation is essentially subjective, and the dream is the theater where the dreamer is at once scene, actor, prompter, stage manager, author, audience, and critic.

From Psychological Reflections: A Jung Anthology, p. 58: Collected Works, vol. 8, General Aspects of Dream Psychology [1916]

12 The dream is the small hidden door in the deepest and most intimate sanctum of the soul, which opens into that primeval cosmic night that was soul long before there was a conscious ego and will be soul far beyond what a conscious ego could ever reach.

From Psychological Reflections: A Jung Anthology, p. 46: Collected Works, vol. 10, The Meaning of Psychology for Modern Man [1934]

13 Emotion is the chief source of all becoming-conscious. There can be no transforming of darkness into light and of apathy into movement without emotion.

From Psychological Reflections: A Jung Anthology, p. 32: Collected Works, vol. 9, Psychological Aspects of the Mother Archetype [1938]

14 No one can flatter himself that he is immune to the spirit of his own epoch, or even that he pos-

---

[1] Edited by JOLANDE JACOBI.

sesses a full understanding of it. Irrespective of our conscious convictions, each one of us, without exception, being a particle of the general mass, is somewhere attached to, colored by, or even undermined by the spirit which goes through the mass. Freedom stretches only as far as the limits of our consciousness.

> *From Psychological Reflections: A Jung Anthology, p. 143: Collected Works, vol. 15, Paracelsus the Physician [1941]*

1   Where love rules, there is no will to power; and where power predominates, there love is lacking. The one is the shadow of the other.

> *From Psychological Reflections: A Jung Anthology, p. 87: Collected Works, vol. 7, On Psychology of the Unconscious [1943]*

Thomas Mann
1875–1955

2   We are most likely to get angry and excited in our opposition to some idea when we ourselves are not quite certain of our own position, and are inwardly tempted to take the other side.

> *Buddenbrooks [1903], pt. VIII, ch. 2*

3   Beauty can pierce one like a pain.

> *Buddenbrooks, XI, 2*

4   Space, like time, engenders forgetfulness; but it does so by setting us bodily free from our surroundings and giving us back our primitive, unattached state. . . . Time, we say, is Lethe; but change of air is a similar draught, and, if it works less thoroughly, does so more quickly.

> *The Magic Mountain [1924],[1] ch. 1*

5   A man lives not only his personal life, as an individual, but also, consciously or unconsciously, the life of his epoch and his contemporaries.

> *The Magic Mountain, 2*

6   The only religious way to think of death is as part and parcel of life; to regard it, with the understanding and the emotions, as the inviolable condition of life.

> *The Magic Mountain, 5*

7   Time has no divisions to mark its passage, there is never a thunderstorm or blare of trumpets to announce the beginning of a new month or year. Even when a new century begins it is only we mortals who ring bells and fire off pistols. *The Magic Mountain, 5*

8   Order and simplification are the first steps toward the mastery of a subject—the actual enemy is the unknown. *The Magic Mountain, 5*

9   Opinions cannot survive if one has no chance to fight for them. *The Magic Mountain, (*

10   All interest in disease and death is only another expression of interest in life. *The Magic Mountain, (*

11   The invention of printing and the Reformation are and remain the two outstanding services of central Europe to the cause of humanity.

> *The Magic Mountain, (*

12   Speech is civilization itself. The word, even the most contradictory word, preserves contact—it is silence which isolates. *The Magic Mountain, (*

13   A man's dying is more the survivors' affair than his own. *The Magic Mountain, (*

14   What we call mourning for our dead is perhaps not so much grief at not being able to call them back as it is grief at not being able to want to do so.

> *The Magic Mountain, 7*

15   Time cools, time clarifies; no mood can be maintained quite unaltered through the course of hours.

> *The Magic Mountain, 7*

16   In almost every artist nature is inborn a wanton and treacherous proneness to side with the beauty that breaks hearts, to single out aristocratic pretensions and pay them homage.

> *Stories of Three Decades [1936].*
> *Death in Venice*

17   In the Word is involved the unity of humanity, the wholeness of the human problem, which permits nobody to separate the intellectual and artistic from the political and social, and to isolate himself within the ivory tower of the "cultural" proper.

> *Letter to the dean of the Philosophical Faculty, Bonn University [January 1937][2]*

18   Hold fast the time! Guard it, watch over it, every hour, every minute! Unregarded it slips away, like a lizard, smooth, slippery, faithless, a pixy wife. Hold every moment sacred. Give each clarity and meaning, each the weight of thine awareness, each its true and due fulfillment. *The Beloved Returns [1939]*

Hughes Mearns
1875–1965

19 As I was going up the stair
I met a man who wasn't there.
He wasn't there again today.
I wish, I wish he'd stay away.   *The Psychoe*

---

[1]Translated by H. T. Lowe-Porter.

[2]Mann, who had left Germany [1933], wrote from Zurich after being informed that his name had been struck off the list of Honorary Doctors.

Rainer Maria Rilke
1875–1926

1   He was a poet and hated the approximate.
The Journal of My Other Self[1]

2   Love consists in this, that two solitudes protect and touch and greet each other.
Letters to a Young Poet[2]

3   The future enters into us, in order to transform itself in us, long before it happens.
Letters to a Young Poet

4   Beauty's nothing
but beginning of Terror we're still just able to bear,
and why we adore it so is because it serenely
disdains to destroy us. Each single angel is terrible.
Duino Elegies,[3] *1*

5   We're never single-minded, unperplexed, like migratory birds.   *Duino Elegies, 4*

6   The most visible joy can only reveal itself to us when we've transformed it, within.
Duino Elegies, 7

7   Death is the side of life which is turned away from us.   *Letter to W. von Hulewicz*

8   A good marriage is that in which each appoints the other guardian of his solitude.   *Letters*[4]

9   Once the realization is accepted that even between the *closest* human beings infinite distances continue to exist, a wonderful living side by side can grow up, if they succeed in loving the distance between them which makes it possible for each to see the other whole against the sky.   *Letters*

10   In the difficult are the friendly forces, the hands that work on us.   *Letters*

11   Works of art are indeed always products of having been in danger, of having gone to the very end in an experience, to where man can go no further.
Letters

Naomi Royde-Smith
c. 1875–1964

12 I know two things about the horse
And one of them is rather coarse.
The Horse [1928]

[1]Translated by JOHN LINTON.

[2]Translated by M. D. HERTER NORTON.

[3]Translated by J. B. LEISHMAN and STEPHEN SPENDER.

[4]Translated by JANE BARNARD GREENE and M. D. HERTER NORTON.

Rafael Sabatini
1875–1950

13   He was born with a gift of laughter and a sense that the world was mad. And that was all his patrimony.   *Scaramouche [1921], ch. 1*

Albert Schweitzer
1875–1965

14   Late on the third day, at the very moment when, at sunset, we were making our way through a herd of hippopotamuses, there flashed upon my mind, unforeseen and unsought, the phrase, "Reverence for Life."
Out of My Life and Thought [1949]

15   Affirmation of life is the spiritual act by which man ceases to live unreflectively and begins to devote himself to his life with reverence in order to raise it to its true value. To affirm life is to deepen, to make more inward, and to exalt the will to live.
Out of My Life and Thought

16   Truth has no special time of its own. Its hour is now — always.
Out of My Life and Thought

17   You don't live in a world all alone. Your brothers are here too.
On Receiving the Nobel Prize [1952]

Sherwood Anderson
1876–1941

18   All of the men and women the writer had ever known had become grotesques.
Winesburg, Ohio [1919]. The Book of the Grotesque

19   Everyone in the world is Christ and they are all crucified.   *Winesburg, Ohio. The Philosopher*

20   I am a lover and have not found my thing to love.   *Winesburg, Ohio. Tandy*

Sarah N[orcliffe] Cleghorn
1876–1959

21 The golf links lie so near the mill
That almost every day
The laboring children can look out
And watch the men at play.
The Golf Links Lie So Near the Mill [1915]

Irvin S[hrewsbury] Cobb
1876–1944

1   It smells like gangrene starting in a mildewed silo, it tastes like the wrath to come, and when you absorb a deep swig of it you have all the sensations of having swallowed a lighted kerosene lamp. A sudden, violent jolt of it has been known to stop the victim's watch, snap his suspenders and crack his glass eye right across.

Definition of "corn licker" given to the Distillers' Code Authority, NRA

Max Jacob
1876–1944

2   The poet's expression of joy conceals his despair at not having found the reality of joy.

La Défense de Tartufe [1919]

3   When you get to the point where you cheat for the sake of beauty, you're an artist.[1]

Art Poétique [1922]

4   What is called a sincere work is one that is endowed with enough strength to give reality to an illusion.   *Art Poétique*

Charles F[ranklin] Kettering
1876–1958

5   We should all be concerned about the future because we will have to spend the rest of our lives there.   *Seed for Thought [1949]*

Maxim Maximovich Litvinov
1876–1951

6   Peace is indivisible.[2]

Speech to the League of Nations, Geneva, condemning Italian aggression in Ethiopia [July 1, 1936]

Jack [John Griffith] London
1876–1916

7   A good idea, he thought, to sleep off to death. It was like taking an anaesthetic. Freezing was not so bad as people thought. There were lots worse ways

to die. . . . Then the man drowsed off into what seemed to him the most comfortable and satisfying sleep he had ever known.   *To Build a Fire [1908]*

Wilson Mizner
1876–1933

8   Life's a tough proposition, and the first hundred years are the hardest.   *Saying*

9   Be nice to people on your way up because you'll meet them on your way down.   *Saying*

10   When you steal from one author, it's plagiarism; if you steal from many, it's research.   *Saying*

11   You sparkle with larceny.   *Saying*

12   You're a mouse studying to be a rat.   *Saying*

13   To my embarrassment, I was born in bed with a lady.   *Saying*

Pope Pius XII [Eugenio Pacelli]
1876–1958

14   Private property is a natural fruit of labor, a product of intense activity of man, acquired through his energetic determination to ensure and develop with his own strength his own existence and that of his family, and to create for himself and his own an existence of just freedom, not only economic, but also political, cultural and religious.

Radio broadcast [September 1, 1944]

G[eorge] M[acaulay] Trevelyan
1876–1962

15   A man and what he loves and builds have but a day and then disappear; nature cares not—and renews the annual round untired. It is the old law, sad but not bitter. Only when man destroys the life and beauty of nature, there is the outrage.

Grey of Fallodon [1937], bk. I, ch. 3

16   Disinterested intellectual curiosity is the lifeblood of real civilization.

English Social History [1942], Introduction

17   Education . . . has produced a vast population able to read but unable to distinguish what is worth reading.   *English Social History, ch. 18*

Anthony [Henderson] Euwer
1877–1955

18 As a beauty I'm not a great star.
There are others more handsome, by far,

---

[1] C'est au moment où l'on triche pour le beau que l'on est artiste.

[2] In an earlier speech at the League [September 5, 1935] during the Italian preparations for the invasion, Litvinov used a similar phrase: "The thesis of the indivisibility of peace. . . . It has now become clear to the whole world that each war is the creation of a preceding war and the generator of new present or future wars."

But my face—I don't mind it
For I am behind it;
It's the people in front get the jar.
Limeratomy

Rose Fyleman
1877–1957

1 There are fairies at the bottom of our garden!
The Fairies, st. 1

Sir James Hopwood Jeans
1877–1946

2 Taking a very gloomy view of the future of the human race, let us suppose that it can only expect to survive for two thousand million years longer, a period about equal to the past age of the earth. Then, regarded as a being destined to live for three-score years and ten, humanity, although it has been born in a house seventy years old, is itself only three days old. *The Wilder Aspects of Cosmogony [1928]*

3 From the intrinsic evidence of his creation, the Great Architect of the Universe now begins to appear as a pure mathematician.
The Mysterious Universe [1930]

4 Physics tries to discover the pattern of events which controls the phenomena we observe. But we can never know what this pattern means or how it originates; and even if some superior intelligence were to tell us, we should find the explanation unintelligible.
Physics and Philosophy [1942]

McLandburgh Wilson
fl. 1915

5 'Twixt the optimist and pessimist
The difference is droll:
The optimist sees the doughnut
But the pessimist sees the hole.
Optimist and Pessimist

John M[unro] Woolsey
1877–1945

6 I am quite aware that owing to some of its scenes [James Joyce's] *Ulysses* is a rather strong draught to ask some sensitive, though normal, persons to take. But my considered opinion, after long reflection, is that whilst in many places the effect of *Ulysses* on the reader is somewhat emetic, nowhere does it tend to be an aphrodisiac.

Ulysses may, therefore, be admitted into the United States.
U.S. v. One Book Called "Ulysses," 5 Federal Supplement 182, 184 [1933], III

Emiliano Zapata
c. 1877–1919

7 Men of the South! It is better to die on your feet than to live on your knees![1] *Attributed*

Martin Buber
1878–1965

8 How would man exist if God did not need him, and how would you exist? You need God in order to be, and God needs you—for that is the meaning of your life. *I and Thou[2] [1923]*

George M[ichael] Cohan
1878–1942

9 Always Leave Them Laughing When You Say Goodbye. *Mother Goose [1903], title of song*

10 Give my regards to Broadway,
Remember me to Herald Square,
Tell all the gang at Forty-second Street
That I will soon be there.
Little Johnny Jones [1904]. Give My Regards to Broadway

11 I'm a Yankee Doodle dandy,
A Yankee Doodle do or die;
A real live nephew of my Uncle Sam's
Born on the Fourth of July.
Little Johnny Jones. Yankee Doodle Dandy

12 The Yanks are coming,
The drums rum-tumming everywhere.
Over There [1917]

13 And we won't come back till it's over over there.
Over There

14 What's all the shootin' for? *The Tavern [1920]*

Adelaide Crapsey
1878–1914

15 These be
Three silent things:

---

[1]Mejor morir a pie que vivir en rodillas.
Later a Republican watchword in the Spanish Civil War [1936–1939], especially identified with a speech at Madrid [July 18, 1936] by La Pasionaria [Dolores Ibarruri], 744.
See Franklin D. Roosevelt, 698:16.

[2]Translated by Walter Kauffmann.

The falling snow . . . the hour
Before the dawn . . . the mouth of one
Just dead.   *Cinquain: Triad*

Harry Emerson Fosdick
1878–1969

1   The Sea of Galilee and the Dead Sea are made of
the same water. It flows down, clear and cool, from
the heights of Hermon and the roots of the cedars
of Lebanon. The Sea of Galilee makes beauty of it,
for the Sea of Galilee has an outlet. It gets to give.
It gathers in its riches that it may pour them out
again to fertilize the Jordan plain. But the Dead Sea
with the same water makes horror. For the Dead
Sea has no outlet. It gets to keep.
                    The Meaning of Service [1920]

Don[ald Robert Perry] Marquis
1878–1937

2 I love you as New Englanders love pie!
            Sonnets to a Red-Haired Lady [1922], XII

3 dedicated to babs
     with babs knows what
     and babs knows why
                    archy[1] *and mehitabel [1927]*[2]

4 oh i should worry and fret
   death and i will coquette
   there s a dance in the old dame yet
   toujours gai toujours gai
            archy and mehitabel. the song of mehitabel

5 procrastination is the
   art of keeping
   up with yesterday
        archy and mehitabel. certain maxims of archy

6 an optimist is a guy
   that has never had
   much experience
        archy and mehitabel. certain maxims of archy

7   what in hell
   have i done to deserve
   all these kittens
        archy and mehitabel. mehitabel and her kittens

8 dance mehitabel dance
   caper and shake a leg

what little blood is left
will fizz like wine in a keg
        *archy and mehitabel. mehitabel dances with
        boreas*

9 i have noticed
   that when
   chickens quit
   quarrelling over their
   food they often
   find that there is
   enough for all of them
   i wonder if
   it might not
   be the same way
   with the
   human race
        *archy's life of mehitabel [1933]. random
        thoughts by archy*

10   it is a cheering thought to think
   that god is on the side of the best digestion[3]
            archy does his part [1935]. the big bad wolf

11   there is always
   a comforting thought
   in time of trouble when
   it is not our trouble
            archy does his part. comforting thought.

12 it wont be long now it wont be long
   man is making deserts of the earth
   it wont be long now
   before man will have it used up
   so that nothing but ants
   and centipedes and scorpions
   can find a living on it
            archy does his part. what the ants are saying

13 what man calls civilization
   always results in deserts
            archy does his part. what the ants are saying

14 it wont be long now it wont be long
   till earth is barren as the moon
   and sapless as a mumbled bone
            archy does his part. what the ants are saying

John Masefield
1878–1967

15 I must down to the seas again, to the lonely sea
          and the sky,
   And all I ask is a tall ship and a star to steer her by,
   And the wheel's kick and the wind's song and the
          white sail's shaking,

---

[1]Archy, a cockroach, is unable to use the shift key on the typewriter for capitals and punctuation.

[2]Published later with other works by archy as *the lives and times
of archy and mehitabel* [1943].

[3]Give me a good digestion, Lord, / And also something to digest. —ANONYMOUS, *A Pilgrim's Grace*, st. 1

And a gray mist on the sea's face and a gray dawn
    breaking.   *Sea Fever [1902], st. 1*

1 I must down to the seas again, for the call of the
    running tide
Is a wild call and a clear call that may not be
    denied.   *Sea Fever, st. 2*

2 I must down to the seas again, to the vagrant
    gypsy life,
To the gull's way and the whale's way where the
    wind's like a whetted knife;
And all I ask is a merry yarn from a laughing
    fellow rover,
And quiet sleep and a sweet dream when the long
    trick's over.   *Sea Fever, st. 3*

3 It's a warm wind, the west wind, full of birds' cries.
                        The West Wind [1902], st. 1

4 Quinquireme of Nineveh from distant Ophir,
Rowing home to haven in sunny Palestine,
With a cargo of ivory,
And apes and peacocks,
Sandalwood, cedarwood, and sweet white wine.
                                    Cargoes, st. 1

5 Dirty British coaster with a salt-caked smokestack,
Butting through the Channel in the mad March
    days,
With a cargo of Tyne coal,
Road rail, pig lead,
Firewood, ironware, and cheap tin trays.
                                    Cargoes, st. 3

Paul Reynaud
1878–1966

6   We shall win because we are the stronger.[1]
        Radio Speech [September 10, 1939]

Carl Sandburg
1878–1967

7 I am the people—the mob—the crowd—the mass.
Do you know that all the great work of the world is
    done through me?
        I Am the People, the Mob [1916]

8 Hog butcher for the world,
Tool maker, stacker of wheat,
Player with railroads and the nation's freight
    handler;
Stormy, husky, brawling,
City of the big shoulders.   *Chicago [1916]*

9 The fog comes
on little cat feet.
It sits looking
over harbor and city
on silent haunches
and then moves on.   *Fog [1916]*

10 Pile the bodies high at Austerlitz and Waterloo.
Shovel them under and let me work—
I am the grass; I cover all.   *Grass [1918]*

11 I tell you the past is a bucket of ashes.
                                Prairie [1918]

12 When Abraham Lincoln was shoveled into the
    tombs, he forgot the copperheads and the
    assassin . . . in the dust, in the cool tombs.
                            Cool Tombs [1918]

13 Lay me on an anvil, O God.
Beat me and hammer me into a crowbar.
Let me pry loose old walls.
Let me lift and loosen old foundations.
                        Prayers of Steel [1920]

14 Drum on your drums, batter on your banjos, sob
    on the long cool winding saxophones.
Go to it, O jazzmen.   *Jazz Fantasia [1920]*

15 The republic is a dream.
Nothing happens unless first a dream.
                Washington Monument by Night [1922]

16 Sometime they'll give a war and nobody will
    come.[2]   *The People, Yes [1936]*

17   The people will live on.
The learning and blundering people will live on.
They will be tricked and sold and again sold
And go back to the nourishing earth for rootholds.
                                The People, Yes

18 The people know the salt of the sea
and the strength of the winds
lashing the corners of the earth.
The people take the earth
as a tomb of rest and a cradle of hope.
Who else speaks for the Family of Man?
                                The People, Yes

19 This old anvil laughs at many broken hammers.
There are men who can't be bought.
                    The People Will Live On [1936]

---

[1]*Nous vaincrons parce que nous sommes les plus forts.*
The phrase became a war slogan.

[2]Suppose They Gave a War, and No One Came. —CHARLOTTE
KEYES [1914–], *article in McCall's* [October 1966]

Upton [Beall] Sinclair
1878–1968

1   Now and then a visitor wept, to be sure; but this slaughtering machine went on, visitors or no visitors. It was like some horrible crime committed in a dungeon, all unseen and unheeded, buried out of sight and of memory.   *The Jungle [1906], ch. 3*

2   I aimed at the public's heart, and by accident I hit it in the stomach.[1]
On The Jungle [in Cosmopolitan, October 1906]

Louis Edwin Thayer
1878–1956

3 I fancy when I go to rest someone will bring to light
Some kindly word or goodly act long buried out of sight;
But, if it's all the same to you, just give to me, instead,
The bouquets while I'm living and the knocking when I'm dead.
Of Post-Mortem Praises, st. 1

John Broadus Watson
1878–1958

4   Give me a dozen healthy infants, well-formed, and my own specified world to bring them up in and I'll guarantee to take any one at random and train him to become any type of specialist I might select — doctor, lawyer, artist, merchant chief and, yes, even beggarman and thief, regardless of his talents, penchants, tendencies, abilities, vocations, and race of his ancestors.   *Behaviorism [1925], ch. 5*

5   The universe will change if you bring up your children, not in the freedom of the libertine, but in behavioristic freedom.   *Behaviorism, 12*

Hans Zinsser
1878–1940

6   The scientist takes off from the manifold observations of predecessors, and shows his intelligence, if any, by his ability to discriminate between the important and the negligible, by selecting here and there the significant steppingstones that will lead across the difficulties to new understanding. The one who places the last stone and steps across to the terra firma of accomplished discovery gets all the credit.   *As I Remember Him [1940], ch. 20*

Nancy [Witcher Langhorne] Astor
1879–1964

7   I married beneath me. All women do.
Attributed

Ethel Barrymore
1879–1959

8   That's all there is, there isn't any more.
Signature curtain line added by her to the play Sunday [1904] by Thomas Raceward

Sir William Henry Beveridge
1879–1963

9   There is no inherent mechanism in our present system which can with certainty prevent competitive sectional bargaining for wages from setting up a vicious spiral of rising prices under full employment.
Full Employment in a Free Society [1945]

Louis Brownlow
1879–1963

10   They [the President's aides] should be possessed of high competence, great physical vigor, and a passion for anonymity.[2]
Administrative Management in the Government of the United States: Report of the President's Committee on Administrative Management [January 1937]

James Branch Cabell
1879–1958

11   I am willing to taste any drink once.
Jurgen [1919], ch. 16

---

[1]I haven't been able to ate anything more nourishin' thin a cucumber in a week. A little while ago no wan cud square away at a beefsteak with better grace thin mesilf. Today th' wurrud resthrant makes me green in the face. How did it all come about? A young fellow wrote a book. — Finley Peter Dunne *("Mr. Dooley") in Collier's* [1906]

[2]Tell the President that the way to solve his problem is to find that one man who would turn out to be . . . possessed of high competence, great physical vigor, and a passion for anonymity. — Tom Jones *(private secretary to Prime Minister Stanley Baldwin) to Brownlow* [1936]

1   The optimist proclaims that we live in the best of all possible worlds; and the pessimist fears this is true.   *The Silver Stallion [1926], ch. 26*

Ch'en Tu-hsiu[1]
1879–1942

2   The pulse of modern life is economic and the fundamental principle of economic production is individual independence.
          The New Youth [December 1916]

3   Man's happiness in life is the result of man's own effort and is neither the gift of God nor a spontaneous natural product.
          The New Youth [February 1918]

Albert Einstein
1879–1955

4   E = mc².
          Statement of the mass-energy equivalence relationship[2]

5   The most beautiful thing we can experience is the mysterious. It is the source of all true art and science.   *What I Believe [1930]*

6   Concern for man himself and his fate must always form the chief interest of all technical endeavors, concern for the great unsolved problems of the organization of labor and the distribution of goods— in order that the creations of our mind shall be a blessing and not a curse to mankind. Never forget this in the midst of your diagrams and equations.
          Address, California Institute of Technology [1931]

7   The whole of science is nothing more than a refinement of everyday thinking.
          Physics and Reality [1936]

8   Physical concepts are free creations of the human mind, and are not, however it may seem, uniquely determined by the external world.
          Evolution of Physics [1938]

9   Some recent work by E. Fermi and L. Szilard, which has been communicated to me in manuscript, leads me to expect that the element uranium may be turned into a new and important source of energy in the immediate future. Certain aspects of the situation which has arisen seem to call for watchfulness and, if necessary, quick action on the part of the Administration.
          Letter to President Franklin D. Roosevelt [August 2, 1939] (the letter that resulted in the assignment of government funds for developing the atom bomb)

10   This new phenomena [atomic energy] would also lead to the construction of bombs. . . . A single bomb of this type, carried by boat and exploded in a port, might very well destroy the whole port, together with some of the surrounding territory. However, such bombs might very well prove to be too heavy for transportation by air.
          Letter to President Franklin D. Roosevelt [August 2, 1939] (the letter that resulted in the assignment of government funds for developing the atom bomb)

11   As long as there are sovereign nations possessing great power, war is inevitable.
          Einstein on the atomic bomb. From the Atlantic Monthly [November 1945]

12   I do not believe that civilization will be wiped out in a war fought with the atomic bomb. Perhaps two thirds of the people of the earth might be killed, but enough men capable of thinking, and enough books, would be left to start again, and civilization could be restored.
          Einstein on the atomic bomb. From the Atlantic Monthly [November 1945]

13   Since I do not foresee that atomic energy is to be a great boon for a long time, I have to say that for the present it is a menace. Perhaps it is well that it should be. It may intimidate the human race into bringing order into its international affairs, which, without the pressure of fear, it would not do.
          Einstein on the atomic bomb. From the Atlantic Monthly [November 1945]

14   I shall never believe that God plays dice with the world.
          From PHILIPP FRANK, Einstein, His Life and Times [1947]

15   The Lord God is subtle, but malicious he is not.[3]
          Inscription in Jones Hall, Princeton University

16   Every intellectual who is called before one of the committees ought to refuse to testify, i.e., he must be prepared . . . for the sacrifice of his personal welfare in the interest of the cultural welfare of his country. . . . This kind of inquisition violates the spirit of the Constitution.
   If enough people are ready to take this grave step they will be successful. If not, then the intellec-

---

[1]From *Sources of Chinese Tradition* [1960], edited by WILLIAM THEODORE DE BARY. Ch'en was the founder [1921] of the Chinese Communist Party.

[2]Energy equals mass times the speed of light squared.
The original statement is: If a body gives off the energy L in the form of radiation, its mass diminishes by L / c². — EINSTEIN, *Ist die Tragheit eines Korpers von Seinem Energieghalt Abhangig?* [1905]

[3]Raffiniert ist der Herr Gott, aber Boshaft ist er nicht.

tuals of this country deserve nothing better than the slavery which is intended for them.
> *Letter to William Frauenglass [May 16, 1953]*[1]

1   The unleashed power of the atom has changed everything save our modes of thinking, and we thus drift toward unparalleled catastrophes.
> *From* RALPH E. LAPP, *The Einstein Letter That Started It All. In the New York Times Magazine [August 2, 1964]*

2   Something deeply hidden had to be behind things.
> *From* RALPH E. LAPP, *The Einstein Letter That Started It All. In the New York Times Magazine [August 2, 1964] [autobiographical handwritten note]*

E[dward] M[organ] Forster
1879–1970

3   Only connect! That was the whole of her sermon. Only connect the prose and the passion, and both will be exalted, and human love will be seen at its height. Live in fragments no longer. Only connect, and the beast and the monk, robbed of the isolation that is life to either, will die.
> *Howards End [1910], ch. 22*

4   The echo began in some indescribable way to undermine her hold on life. Coming at a moment when she chanced to be fatigued, it had managed to murmur, "Pathos, piety, courage—they exist, but are identical, and so is filth. Everything exists, nothing has value." If one had spoken vileness in that place, or quoted lofty poetry, the [echo's] comment would have been the same—"Ou-boum."
> *A Passage to India [1924]*

5   If I had to choose between betraying my country and betraying my friend, I hope I should have the guts to betray my country.
> *Two Cheers for Democracy [1951]. What I Believe*

6   Two cheers for Democracy: one because it admits variety and two because it permits criticism. Two cheers are quite enough: there is no occasion to give three.
> *Two Cheers for Democracy. What I Believe*

[Stella Maria] Miles Franklin
1879–1954

7   Weariness! Weariness! This was life—my life—my career, my brilliant career! I was fifteen—fifteen!

A few fleeting hours and I would be as old as those around me.
> *My Brilliant Career [1901], ch. 5*

Edmund L. Gruber
1879–1941

8   Over hill, over dale, we have hit the dusty trail
And those caissons go rolling along.
> *The Caisson Song*[2] *[1908]*

9   Oh, it's hi-hi-yee! for the field artilleree,
Shout out your numbers loud and strong,
And where'er we go, you will always know
That those caissons are rolling along.
> *The Caisson Song*

Joe Hill [Joseph Hillstrom]
1879–1915

10   Work and pray, live on hay,
You'll get pie in the sky when you die.
> *The Preacher and the Slave*

11   Don't waste any time mourning—organize!
> *Letter to William D. Haywood [November 18, 1915, the day before Hill's execution]*

John Haynes Holmes
1879–1964

12   If Christians were Christians, there would be no anti-Semitism. Jesus was a Jew. There is nothing that the ordinary Christian so dislikes to remember as this awkward historical fact.
> *The Sensible Man's View of Religion [1933]*

13   The universe is not hostile, nor yet is it friendly. It is simply indifferent.
> *The Sensible Man's View of Religion*

Vachel Lindsay
1879–1931

14   Booth died blind and still by faith he trod,
Eyes still dazzled by the ways of God.
> *General William Booth Enters into Heaven [1913], II*

---

[1]Einstein's letter was published in the *New York Times* [June 12, 1953]. Frauenglass had been subpoenaed to testify before the Senate Internal Security Subcommittee.

[2]The 1st Battalion of the 5th Field Artillery relieved the 2nd Battalion in the Philippines [April 1908]. Gruber, then a lieutenant in the 5th, was asked to write a song that would symbolize the spirit of the reunited regiment. There are many variant wordings.

1 Sleep softly . . . eagle forgotten . . . under the
stone.
The Eagle That Is Forgotten[1] *[1913], st. 5*

2 Factory windows are always broken.
Somebody's always throwing bricks,
Somebody's always heaving cinders,
Playing ugly Yahoo tricks. *Factory Windows, st. 1*

3 Fat black bucks in a wine-barrel room,
Barrel-house kings; with feet unstable,
Sagged and reeled and pounded on the table,
Pounded on the table,
Beat an empty barrel with the handle of a broom.
The Congo [1914], pt. I

4 Then I saw the Congo, creeping through the black,
Cutting through the forest with a golden track.
The Congo, I

5 Be careful what you do,
Or Mumbo-Jumbo, God of the Congo,
And all of the other
Gods of the Congo,
Mumbo-Jumbo will hoo-doo you. *The Congo, I*

6 A bronzed, lank man! His suit of ancient black,
A famous high top-hat and plain worn shawl
Make him the quaint great figure that men love,
The prairie-lawyer, master of us all.
*Abraham Lincoln Walks at Midnight [1914],
st. 3*

7 Spring came on forever,
Spring came on forever,
Said the Chinese nightingale.
The Chinese Nightingale [1917], end

8 Planting the trees that would march and train
On, in his name to the great Pacific,
Like Birnam Wood to Dunsinane,
Johnny Appleseed[2] swept on.
In Praise of Johnny Appleseed

Dixon Lanier Merritt
1879–1972

9 A wonderful bird is the pelican,
His bill will hold more than his belican.
He can take in his beak

Food enough for a week,
But I'm damned if I see how the helican.
The Pelican [1910]

Jack Norworth
1879–1959

10 Take me out to the ball game,
Take me out with the crowd.
Buy me some peanuts and cracker-jack—
I don't care if I never get back.
Take Me Out to the Ball Game [1908][3]

11 For it's one, two, three strikes you're out
At the old ball game.
Take Me Out to the Ball Game

Will[iam Penn Adair] Rogers
1879–1935

12 All I know is just what I read in the papers.
Prefatory remark

13 I tell you folks, all politics is applesauce.
The Illiterate Digest [1924], p. 30

14 Everything is funny as long as it is happening to
somebody else. *The Illiterate Digest, p. 131*

15 More men have been elected between sundown
and sunup than ever were elected between sunup
and sundown. *The Illiterate Digest, p. 152*

16 A comedian can only last till he either takes himself serious or his audience takes him serious.
Syndicated newspaper article

17 I not only "don't choose to run"[4] [for President]
but I don't even want to leave a loophole in case I
am drafted, so I won't "choose." I will say "won't
run" no matter how bad the country will need a comedian by that time.
Syndicated newspaper article

18 Politics has got so expensive that it takes lots of
money to even get beat with.
Syndicated newspaper article

19 My forefathers didn't come over on the *Mayflower,* but they met the boat.[5] *Remark*

20 I joked about every prominent man in my lifetime, but I never met one I didn't like. *Epitaph*

---

[1]John Peter Altgeld [1847–1902; governor of Illinois, 1893–
1897], widely criticized for pardoning, in June 1893, the anarchists who had been serving life terms since the Haymarket riot in
Chicago on May 4, 1886. In pardoning them, Altgeld declared
that "the judge conducted the trial with malicious ferocity."

[2]John Chapman [1774–1847].
Remember Johnny Appleseed, / All ye who love the apple; / He
served his kind by word and deed, / in God's grand greenwood
chapel. — WILLIAM HENRY VENABLE [1836–1920], *Johnny Appleseed, st. 25*

[3]Music by ALBERT VON TILZER [1878–1956].
[4]See Coolidge, 659:20.
[5]Rogers was part Cherokee.

Joseph Stalin
[Iosif Vissarionovich Dzhugashvili]
1879–1953

1   Print is the sharpest and the strongest weapon of our party.

Speech [April 19, 1923]

2   The most remarkable thing about socialist competition is that it creates a basic change in people's view of labor, since it changes the labor from a shameful and heavy burden into a matter of honor, matter of fame, matter of valor and heroism.

Speech [June 27, 1930]

3   The Hitlerite blackguards . . . have turned Europe into a prison of nations,[1] and this they call the new order in Europe.

Address to the Moscow Soviet [November 6, 1942]

4   The Pope! How many divisions has *he* got?

From WINSTON CHURCHILL, *The Gathering Storm [1948]*

5   You cannot make a revolution with silk gloves.

Attributed

6   A single death is a tragedy, a million deaths is a statistic.

Attributed

Bessie Anderson Stanley
1879–1952

7   He has achieved success who has lived well, laughed often and loved much; who has enjoyed the trust of pure women and the love of little children; who has filled his niche and accomplished his task; who has left the world better than he found it, whether by an improved poppy, a perfect poem, or a rescued soul; who has never lacked appreciation of earth's beauty or failed to express it; who has always looked for the best in others and given them the best he had; whose life was an inspiration; whose memory a benediction.

Success [1904]. Prize-winning definition in contest conducted by the Brown Book Magazine, Boston

Wallace Stevens
1879–1955

8   Twenty men crossing a bridge,
Into a village,

---
[1] . . . The saying that Russia is a prison of nations. —VLADIMIR ILYICH LENIN, *On the Question of National Policy* (and elsewhere)

Are twenty men crossing twenty bridges,
Into twenty villages,
Or one man
Crossing a single bridge into a village.

Metaphors of a Magnifico [1923]

9   The book of moonlight is not written yet.

The Comedian as the Letter C [1923], III, I

10   And as he came he saw that it was spring,
A time abhorrent to the nihilist
Or searcher for the fecund minimum.

The Comedian as the Letter C, III, 4

11   The natives of the rain are rainy men.

The Comedian as the Letter C, IV, I

12   The plum survives its poems.

The Comedian as the Letter C, V, I

13   Green crammers of the green fruits of the world.

The Comedian as the Letter C, VI, 2

14   Poetry is the supreme fiction, madame.

A High-Toned Old Christian Woman [1923]

15   Let be be finale of seem.
The only emperor is the emperor of ice-cream.

The Emperor of Ice-Cream [1923]

16   Only, here and there, an old sailor,
Drunk and asleep in his boots,
Catches tigers
In red weather.

Disillusionment of Ten O'Clock [1923]

17   Complacencies of the peignoir, and late
Coffee and oranges in a sunny chair.

Sunday Morning [1923], st. 1

18   She says, "But in contentment I still feel
The need of some imperishable bliss."
Death is the mother of beauty; hence from her,
Alone, shall come fulfillment to our dreams
And our desires.

Sunday Morning, st. 5

19   We live in an old chaos of the sun,
Or old dependency of day and night,
Or island solitude, unsponsored, free,
Of that wide water, inescapable.
Deer walk upon our mountains, and the quail
Whistle about us their spontaneous cries;
Sweet berries ripen in the wilderness;
And, in the isolation of the sky,
At evening, casual flocks of pigeons make
Ambiguous undulations as they sink,
Downward to darkness, on extended wings.

Sunday Morning, st. 8

20   Chieftain Iffucan of Azcan in caftan
Of tan with henna hackles, halt!

Bantams in Pine Woods [1923], st. 1

1 Damned universal cock, as if the sun
  Was blackamoor to bear your blazing tail.
  Bantams in Pine Woods, st. 2

2 I placed a jar in Tennessee,
  And round it was, upon a hill.
  It made the slovenly wilderness
  Surround that hill.
  Anecdote of the Jar [1923], st. 1

3   Frogs Eat Butterflies. Snakes Eat Frogs. Hogs
  Eat Snakes. Men Eat Hogs.
  Title of poem [1923]

4 Just as my fingers on these keys
  Make music, so the self-same sounds
  On my spirit make a music, too.
  Peter Quince at the Clavier [1923], I

5 Beauty is momentary in the mind —
  The fitful tracing of a portal;
  But in the flesh it is immortal.

  The body dies; the body's beauty lives.
  Peter Quince at the Clavier, IV

6 Susanna's music touched the bawdy strings
  Of those white elders; but, escaping,
  Left only Death's ironic scraping.
  Now, in its immortality, it plays
  On the clear viol of her memory,
  And makes a constant sacrament of praise.
  Peter Quince at the Clavier, IV

7 I do not know which to prefer,
  The beauty of inflections
  Or the beauty of innuendoes,
  The blackbird whistling
  Or just after.
  Thirteen Ways of Looking at a Blackbird
  [1923], st. 5

8 She sang beyond the genius of the sea.
  The water never formed to mind or voice,
  Like a body wholly body, fluttering
  Its empty sleeves; and yet its mimic motion
  Made constant cry, caused constantly a cry,
  That was not ours although we understood,
  Inhuman, of the veritable ocean.
  The Idea of Order at Key West [1936], st. 1

9 Poetry is the subject of the poem.
  The Man with the Blue Guitar [1937],
  XXII

10 I am a native in this world
  And think in it as a native thinks.
  The Man with the Blue Guitar, XXVIII

11   Light
  Is the lion that comes down to drink.
  The Glass of Water [1942], st. 2

12 A. A violent order is disorder; and
  B. A great disorder is an order. These
  Two things are one.
  Connoisseur of Chaos [1942], st. 1

13 One's grand flights, one's Sunday baths,
  One's tootings at the weddings of the soul
  Occur as they occur.
  The Sense of the Sleight-of-Hand Man [1942],
  st. 1

14 And, capable, created in his mind,
  Eventual victor, out of the martyrs' bones
  The ultimate elegance: the imagined land.
  Mrs. Alfred Uruguay [1942], st. 4

15 The prologues are over. It is a question, now,
  Of final belief. So, say that final belief
  Must be in a fiction. It is time to choose.
  Asides on the Oboe [1942], st. 1

16   To get at the thing
  Without gestures is to get at it as
  Idea.
  So-and-So Reclining on Her Couch [1947],
  st. 6

17 It was the last nostalgia: that he
  Should understand.
  Esthétique du Mal [1947], X

18 The greatest poverty is not to live
  In a physical world, to feel that one's desire
  Is too difficult to tell from despair.
  Esthétique du Mal, XV

19 Thus the theory of description matters most.
  It is the theory of the word for those

  For whom the word is the making of the world,
  The buzzing world and lisping firmament.

  It is a world of words to the end of it,
  In which nothing solid is its solid self.
  Description Without Place [1947], VII

20   Torn by dreams,

  By the terrible incantations of defeats
  And by the fear that defeats and dreams
    are one.

  The whole race is a poet that writes down
  The eccentric propositions of its fate.
  Men Made Out of Words [1947]

21 The inconceivable idea of the sun.

  You must become an ignorant man again
  And see the sun again with an ignorant eye
  And see it clearly in the idea of it.
  Notes Toward a Supreme Fiction [1947]. It
  Must Be Abstract, I

1 The death of one god is the death of all.
Notes Toward a Supreme Fiction. It Must Be Abstract, I

2 It is the celestial ennui of apartments
That sends us back to the first idea.
Notes Toward a Supreme Fiction. It Must Be Abstract, II

3 And still the grossest iridescence of ocean
Howls hoo and rises and howls hoo and falls.
Notes Toward a Supreme Fiction. It Must Be Abstract, III

4 We are the mimics. Clouds are pedagogues.
Notes Toward a Supreme Fiction. It Must Be Abstract, IV

5 The President ordains the bee to be
Immortal.
Notes Toward a Supreme Fiction. It Must Change, II

6 Booming and booming of the new-come bee.
Notes Toward a Supreme Fiction. It Must Change, II

7   He chose to include the things
That in each other are included, the whole,
The complicate, the amassing harmony.
Notes Toward a Supreme Fiction. It Must Give Pleasure, VI

8 These external regions, what do we fill them with
Except reflections, the escapades of death,
Cinderella fulfilling herself beneath the roof.
Notes Toward a Supreme Fiction. It Must Give Pleasure, VIII

9   Perhaps
The man-hero is not the exceptional monster,
But he that of repetition is most master.
Notes Toward a Supreme Fiction. It Must Give Pleasure, IX

10 They will get it straight one day at the Sorbonne.
Notes Toward a Supreme Fiction. It Must Give Pleasure, X

11 And one trembles to be so understood and, at last,
To understand, as if to know became
The fatality of seeing things too well.
The Novel [1950], st. 16

12 We keep coming back and coming back
To the real: to the hotel instead of the hymns
That fall upon it out of the wind.
An Ordinary Evening in New Haven [1950], IX

13 Total grandeur of a total edifice,
Chosen by an inquisitor of structures

For himself. He stops upon this threshold
As if the design of all his words takes form
And frame from thinking and is realized.
To an Old Philosopher in Rome [1950], st. 16

14 Light the first light of evening, as in a room
In which we rest and, for small reason, think
The world imagined is the ultimate good.
Final Soliloquy of the Interior Paramour [1950], st. 1

15 We say God and the imagination are one . . .
How high that highest candle lights the dark.
Final Soliloquy of the Interior Paramour, st. 5[1]

16 There it was, word for word,
The poem that took the place of a mountain.
The Poem That Took the Place of a Mountain [1952], st. 1

17 That scrawny cry—It was
A chorister whose *c* preceded the choir.
It was part of the colossal sun.
Not Ideas About the Thing but the Thing Itself [1954], st. 5

18 The palm at the end of the mind,
Beyond the last thought, rises . . .

A gold-feathered bird
Sings in the palm.   *Of Mere Being [1957], st. 1, 2*

19   The essential gaudiness of poetry.
Stevens's note to The Emperor of Ice-Cream

20   The essential thing in form is to be free in whatever form is used. A free form does not assure freedom. As a form, it is just one more form. So that it comes to this, I suppose, that I believe in freedom regardless of form.   *A Note on Poetry [1937]*

21   What makes the poet the potent figure that he is, or was, or ought to be, is that he creates the world to which we turn incessantly and without knowing it and that he gives to life the supreme fictions without which we are unable to conceive of it.
The Noble Rider and the Sound of Words [1942]

22   The subject matter of poetry is not that "collection of solid, static objects extended in space" but the life that is lived in the scene that it composes; and so reality is not that external scene but the life that is lived in it. Reality is things as they are.
The Necessary Angel [1951]

23   His [the poet's] function is to make his imagination theirs [the people's] and he fulfills himself only as he sees his imagination become the light in the minds of others. His role, in short, is to help people to live their lives.   *The Necessary Angel*

---
[1]Ellipses are in the original text.

1   The humble are they that move about the world with the lure of the real in their hearts.
> *The Necessary Angel. About One of Marianne Moore's Poems*

2   Poetry is poetry, and one's objective as a poet is to achieve poetry precisely as one's objective in music is to achieve music.
> *On selecting Domination of Black as his best poem*

3   A poem is a meteor.
> *Opus Posthumous [1957]. Adagia*

4   A poet looks at the world as a man looks at a woman.   *Opus Posthumous. Adagia*

5   All history is modern history.
> *Opus Posthumous. Adagia*

6   All poetry is experimental poetry.
> *Opus Posthumous. Adagia*

7   Poetry is a purging of the world's poverty and change and evil and death. It is a present perfecting, a satisfaction in the irremediable poverty of life.
> *Opus Posthumous. Adagia*

8   In the world of words, the imagination is one of the forces of nature.   *Opus Posthumous. Adagia*

9   God is in me or else is not at all (does not exist).
> *Opus Posthumous. Adagia*

10   The world is a force, not a presence.
> *Opus Posthumous. Adagia*

11   Poetry is a search for the inexplicable.
> *Opus Posthumous. Adagia*

Simeon Strunsky
1879–1948

12   Famous remarks are very seldom quoted correctly.   *No Mean City [1944], ch. 38*

Leon Trotsky
[Lev Davidovich Bronstein]
1879–1940

13   The literary "fellow travelers" of the Revolution.   *Literature and Revolution [1923], ch. 2*

14   The dictatorship of the Communist Party is maintained by recourse to every form of violence.
> *Terrorism and Communism [1924], p. 71*

15   It was the supreme expression of the mediocrity of the apparatus that Stalin himself rose to his position.   *My Life [1930], ch. 40*

16   The vengeance of history is more terrible than the vengeance of the most powerful General Secretary.
> *Stalin [1946], ch. 12*

Guillaume Apollinaire
[Wilhelm Apollinaris de Kostrowitsky]
1880–1918

17   Shepherdess, O Eiffel Tower, your flock of bridges is bleating this morning.[1]
> *Alcools [1913].[2] Zone*

18   Come night, strike hour.
Days go, I endure.[3]
> *Alcools. Le Pont Mirabeau (Mirabeau Bridge), refrain*

19   I hibernated in my past.[4]
> *Alcools. La Chanson du Mal-Aimé (Song of the Poorly Loved), st. 10*

20   O Milky Way, sister in whiteness
To Canaan's rivers and the bright
Bodies of lovers drowned,
Can we follow toilsomely
Your path to other nebulae?[5]
> *Alcools. La Chanson du Mal-Aimé (Song of the Poorly Loved), st. 13 (also st. 27)*

21   Pass on, let us pass, all is passing,
And I will look back many times:
The sound of hunting horns, when it dies
On the wind, is like our memories.[6]
> *Alcools. Cors de Chasse (Hunting Horns), st. 2, 3*

George Asaf [George H. Powell]
1880–1951

22   What's the use of worrying?
It never was worthwhile,
So, pack up your troubles in your old kit-bag,
And smile, smile, smile.
> *Pack Up Your Troubles in Your Old Kit-Bag [1915][7]*

---

[1] Bergère ô tour Eiffel le troupeau des ponts bêle ce matin.

[2] Translated by WILLIAM MEREDITH.

[3] Vienne la nuit sonne l'heure / Les jours s'en vont je demeure.

[4] J'ai hiverné dans mon passé.
Translated by ROGER SHATTUCK.

[5] Voie lactée ô soeur lumineuse / Des blancs ruisseaux de Chanaan / Et des corps blancs des amoureuses / Nageurs morts suivrons-nous d'ahan / Ton cours vers d'autres nébuleuses.

[6] Passons passons puisque tout passe / Je me retournerai souvent / Les souvenirs sont cors de chasse / Dont meurt le bruit parmi le vent.

[7] Music by FELIX POWELL.

Alexander Blok
1880–1921

1   With your whole body, with your whole heart, with your whole conscience, listen to the Revolution. . . . This is the music everyone who has ears should hear.
The Intelligentsia and the Revolution [1918]

W[illiam] C[laude] Fields
1880–1946

2   It ain't a fit night out for man or beast.
The Fatal Glass of Beer

3   Anyone who hates children and dogs can't be all bad.[1]   *Attributed*

4   On the whole, I'd rather be in Philadelphia.
Attributed epitaph

George [Joseph] Herriman
1880–1944

5   I ain't a Kat . . . and I ain't Krazy . . . it's what's behind me that I am . . . it's the idea behind me, Ignatz, and that's wot I am.
Krazy Kat (comic strip) [1913 and after]

6   In my Kosmis there will be no feeva of discord . . . all my immotions will function in hominy and kind feelings.   *Krazy Kat*

Helen Keller
1880–1968

7   The mystery of language was revealed to me. I knew then that "w-a-t-e-r" meant the wonderful cool something that was flowing over my hand. That living word awakened my soul, gave it light, joy, set it free!   *The Story of My Life [1902], ch. 4*

Douglas MacArthur
1880–1964

8   I shall return.
On arriving in Australia from the Philippines [March 30, 1942]

9   I have returned. By the grace of Almighty God, our forces stand again on Philippine soil.
On landing on Leyte [October 17, 1944]

10   I see that the old flagpole still stands. Have your troops hoist the colors to its peak, and let no enemy ever haul them down.
To Colonel George M. Jones and 503rd Regimental Combat Team, who recaptured Corregidor [March 2, 1945]

11   In war there is no substitute for victory.
Address to a Joint Meeting of Congress [April 19, 1951]

12   I still remember the refrain of one of the most popular barracks ballads of that day, which proclaimed most proudly that old soldiers never die; they just fade away. I now close my military career and just fade away.[2]
Address to a Joint Meeting of Congress [April 19, 1951]

George C[atlett] Marshall
1880–1959

13   If man does find the solution for world peace it will be the most revolutionary reversal of his record we have ever known.
Biennial Report of the Chief of Staff, United States Army [September 1, 1945]

14   Our policy is directed not against any country or doctrine but against hunger, poverty, desperation and chaos. Its purpose should be the revival of a working economy in the world so as to permit the emergence of political and social conditions in which free institutions can exist.
Address at Harvard University [June 5, 1947], announcing the European Recovery Plan (Marshall Plan)

15   It is not enough to fight. It is the spirit which we bring to the fight that decides the issue. It is morale that wins the victory.
Military Review [October 1948]

H[enry] L[ouis] Mencken
1880–1956

16   The virulence of the national appetite for bogus revelation.   *A Book of Prefaces [1917], ch. 1*

17   Time is a great legalizer, even in the field of morals.   *A Book of Prefaces, 4*

18   The public . . . demands certainties. . . . But there *are* no certainties.
Prejudices, First Series [1919], ch. 3

---

[1]Anyone who hates babies and dogs can't be all bad. —Leo C. Rosten [1908–1997], *in tribute to Fields at a banquet* [1939]
    The quip has become more familiar in the form attributed to Fields.

[2]See Anonymous, 850:20.

1 All successful newspapers are ceaselessly querulous and bellicose. They never defend anyone or anything if they can help it; if the job is forced upon them, they tackle it by denouncing someone or something else.

Prejudices, First Series, 13

2 The great artists of the world are never Puritans, and seldom even ordinarily respectable.

Prejudices, First Series, 16

3 Philadelphia is the most pecksniffian of American cities, and thus probably leads the world.

The American Language [1919]

4 If, after I depart this vale, you ever remember me and have thought to please my ghost, forgive some sinner and wink your eye at some homely girl.

Epitaph. From Smart Set [December 1921]

5 There are no mute, inglorious Miltons, save in the hallucinations of poets. The one sound test of a Milton is that he functions as a Milton.

Prejudices, Third Series [1922], ch. 3

6 Nine times out of ten, in the arts as in life, there is actually no truth to be discovered; there is only error to be exposed.

Prejudices, Third Series, 3

7 Injustice is relatively easy to bear; what stings is justice. *Prejudices, Third Series, 3*

8 The older I grow the more I distrust the familiar doctrine that age brings wisdom.

Prejudices, Third Series, 3

9 Faith may be defined briefly as an illogical belief in the occurrence of the improbable.

Prejudices, Third Series, 14

10 To be happy one must be (*a*) well fed, unhounded by sordid cares, at ease in Zion, (*b*) full of a comfortable feeling of superiority to the masses of one's fellow men, and (*c*) delicately and unceasingly amused according to one's taste. It is my contention that, if this definition be accepted, there is no country in the world wherein a man constituted as I am—a man of my peculiar weakness, vanities, appetites, and aversions—can be so happy as he can be in the United States.

On Being An American [1922]

11 The difference between a moral man and a man of honor is that the latter regrets a discreditable act, even when it has worked and he has not been caught.

Prejudices, Fourth Series [1924], ch. 11

12 Out where the grass grows high, and the horned cattle dream away the lazy afternoons, and men still fear the powers and principalities of the air—out there between the corn-rows he held his old puissance to the end.

In Memoriam: W[illiam] J[ennings] B[ryan] [1925]

13 No one in this world, so far as I know . . . has ever lost money by underestimating the intelligence of the great masses of the plain people.[1]

Notes on journalism, Chicago Tribune [September 19, 1926]

14 Of all escape mechanisms, death is the most efficient. *A Book of Burlesques [1928]*

15 When A annoys or injures B on the pretense of saving or improving X, A is a scoundrel.

Newspaper Days: 1899–1906 [1941]

16 Conscience is the inner voice which warns us somebody may be looking.

A Mencken Chrestomathy [1949]. Sententiae

17 Puritanism—The haunting fear that someone, somewhere, may be happy.

A Mencken Chrestomathy. Sententiae

18 There are some people who read too much: the bibliobibuli. I know some who are constantly drunk on books, as other men are drunk on whiskey or religion. They wander through this most diverting and stimulating of worlds in a haze, seeing nothing and hearing nothing.

Minority Report: H. L. Mencken's Notebooks [1956]

19 The booboisie. *Passim*

Robert [von Edler] Musil
1880–1942

20 One spent tremendous amounts on the army; but just enough to assure one of remaining the second weakest among the great powers.

The Man Without Qualities [1930],[2] bk. I, ch. 8

21 The number of portraits one saw of [Emperor Franz Joseph] was almost as great as the number of inhabitants of his realms. . . . Believing in his existence was rather like seeing certain stars although they ceased to exist thousands of years ago.

The Man Without Qualities, I, 20

---

[1]Often misquoted as "No one ever went broke underestimating the intelligence of the American people."

[2]Translated by EITHNE WILKINS and ERNST KAISER.

Alfred Noyes
1880–1958

1 Go down to Kew in lilac time (it isn't far from
London!)
And you shall wander hand in hand with love in
summer's wonderland.   *Barrel Organ, st. 5*

2 The wind was a torrent of darkness among the
gusty trees,
The moon was a ghostly galleon tossed upon
cloudy seas,
The road was a ribbon of moonlight over the
purple moor,
And the highwayman came riding—
Riding—riding—
The highwayman came riding, up to the old
inn-door.   *The Highwayman*

3 I'll come to thee by moonlight, though hell should
bar the way.   *The Highwayman*

Grantland Rice
1880–1954

4 When the One Great Scorer comes to write against
your name—
He marks—not that you won or lost—but how
you played the game.   *Alumnus Football*

5 All wars are planned by old men
In council rooms apart.   *Two Sides of War, st. 1*

6   Outlined against a blue-gray October sky, the
Four Horsemen[1] rode again. In dramatic lore they
were known as Famine, Pestilence, Destruction,
and Death. These are only aliases. Their real names
are Stuhldreher, Miller, Crowley, and Layden.
*Story on Notre Dame football victory over
Army, New York Tribune [October 19, 1924]*

Richard Rowland
1880–1947

7   The lunatics have taken charge of the asylum.
*Comment on the formation of United Artists
film corporation [1920]*

[Giles] Lytton Strachey
1880–1932

8   The art of biography seems to have fallen on evil
times in England. . . . With us, the most delicate
and humane of all the branches of the art of writing
has been relegated to the journeymen of letters; we

---

[1]Referring to the four allegorical horses in Revelation 6:1–8.

do not reflect that it is perhaps as difficult to write a
good life as to live one.
Eminent Victorians [1918]. Preface

9   If this is dying, then I don't think much of it.
*Last words. From MICHAEL HOLROYD, Lytton
Strachey [1968], vol. II*

Richard Henry Tawney
1880–1962

10   Industrialized communities neglect the very objects for which it is worth while to acquire riches in
their feverish preoccupation with the means by
which riches can be acquired.
The Acquisitive Society [1920]

T[homas] R[ussell] Ybarra
1880–1971

11 A Christian is a man who feels
Repentance on a Sunday
For what he did on Saturday
And is going to do on Monday.   *The Christian*

Franklin P[ierce] Adams [F.P.A.]
1881–1960

12   Christmas is over and Business is Business.
For the Other 364 Days

13 Up, to the office . . . and so to bed.
A Ballade of Mr. Samuel Pepys. Refrain

14 Ruthlessly pricking our gonfalon bubble,
Making a Giant hit into a double,
Words that are weighty with nothing but trouble:
"Tinker to Evers to Chance."
Baseball's Sad Lexicon

15 The best you get is an even break.
Ballade of Schopenhauer's Philosophy

16 Of making many books there is no end—
So Sancho Panza said, and so say I.
Thou wert my guide, philosopher and friend
When only one is shining in the sky.
*Lines on and from Bartlett's Familiar
Quotations*

17 Go, lovely Rose that lives its little hour!
Go, little booke! and let who will be clever!
Roll on! From yonder ivy-mantled tower
The moon and I could keep this up forever.
*Lines on and from Bartlett's Familiar
Quotations*

Daisy Ashford
[Margaret Mary Norman]
1881–1972

1   Bernard always had a few prayers in the hall and some whiskey afterwards as he was rarther pious.
The Young Visiters [1919], ch. 3

2   Here on a golden chair was seated the prince of Wales in a lovely ermine cloak and a small but costly crown.
The Young Visiters, 6

3   Taking the bull by both horns he kissed her violently on her dainty face. My bride to be he murmured several times.
The Young Visiters, 9

Joseph Campbell
1881–1944

4 As a white candle
In a holy place,
So is the beauty
Of an aged face.
The Old Woman, st. 1

Padraic Colum
1881–1972

5   A little house—a house of my own—
Out of the wind's and the rain's way.
An Old Woman of the Roads, st. 6

Sir Alexander Fleming
1881–1955

6   It is the lone worker who makes the first advance in a subject: the details may be worked out by a team, but the prime idea is due to the enterprise, thought and perception of an individual.
Address at Edinburgh University [1951]

Edgar A[lbert] Guest
1881–1959

7 Somebody said that it couldn't be done,
But he with a chuckle replied
That maybe it couldn't, but he would be one
Who wouldn't say so till he'd tried.
It Couldn't Be Done

8 It takes a heap o' livin' in a house t' make it home,
A heap o' sun an' shadder, an' ye sometimes have t' roam
Afore ye really 'preciate the things ye lef' behind,
An' hunger fer 'em somehow, with 'em allus on yer mind.
Home

Pope John XXIII
[Angelo Giuseppe Roncalli]
1881–1963

9   The social progress, order, security and peace of each country are necessarily connected with the social progress, order, security and peace of all other countries.
Pacem in Terris. Encyclical letter [April 11, 1963]

10   The representative of the highest spiritual authority of the earth is glad, indeed boasts, of being the son of a humble but robust and honest laborer.
Remark to the mayor of Fleury-sur-Loire. From Wit and Wisdom of Good Pope John, collected by Henri Fesquet *[1963]*[1]

11   Learn how to be a policeman, because that cannot be improvised. As regards being pope, you will see later. Anybody can be pope; the proof of this is that I have become one.
Letter to a young boy. From Wit and Wisdom of Good Pope John, collected by Henri Fesquet

Pablo Picasso
1881–1973

12   God is really only another artist. He invented the giraffe, the elephant, and the cat. He has no real style. He just keeps on trying other things.
From Françoise Gilot *and* Carlton Lake, *Life with Picasso [1964], ch. 1*

13   Painting isn't an aesthetic operation; it's a form of magic designed as a mediator between this strange hostile world and us, a way of seizing the power by giving form to our terrors as well as our desires.
From Françoise Gilot *and* Carlton Lake, *Life with Picasso, VI*

14   I am only a public entertainer who has understood his time.
Remark

Pierre Teilhard de Chardin[2]
1881–1955

15   We have only to believe. And the more threatening and irreducible reality appears, the more firmly and desperately must we believe. Then, little by little, we shall see the universal horror unbend, and then smile upon us, and then take us in its more than human arms.
The Divine Milieu [1957], pt. III, ch. 3, sec. B

---

[1]Translated by Salvator Attanasio.
[2]Translated by Bernard Wall.

1   If there were no internal propensity to unite, even at a prodigiously rudimentary level—indeed in the molecule itself—it would be physically impossible for love to appear higher up.

The Phenomenon of Man [1959], bk. IV, ch. 2, sec. 2

2   From an evolutionary point of view, man has stopped moving, if he ever did move.

The Phenomenon of Man, postscript

William Temple
1881–1944

3   There is no structural organization of society which can bring about the coming of the Kingdom of God on earth, since all systems can be perverted by the selfishness of man.

The Malvern Manifesto [1941]

Ludwig Edler von Mises
1881–1973

4   Unemployment as a mass phenomenon is the outcome of allegedly "pro-labor" policies of the governments and of labor union pressure and compulsion.   *Bureaucracy [1944]*

5   The market economy as such does not respect political frontiers. Its field is the world.

Human Action [1949]

6   Everybody thinks of economics whether he is aware of it or not. In joining a political party and in casting his ballot, the citizen implicitly takes a stand upon essential economic theories.   *Human Action*

7   Statistical figures referring to economic events are historical data. They tell us what happened in a nonrepeatable historical case.   *Human Action*

[Sir] P[elham] G[renville] Wodehouse
1881–1975

8 So always look for the silver lining
And try to find the sunny side of life.

Sally [1920].[1] Look for the Silver Lining

9   "Sir Jasper Finch-Farrowmere?" said Wilfred.
    "ffinch-ffarrowmere," corrected the visitor, his sensitive ear detecting the capital letters.

Meet Mr. Mulliner [1927]. A Slice of Life

---

[1]Music by JEROME KERN.
BUDDY DE SYLVA may have contributed lyrics.

10   No good can come of association with anything labelled Gwladys or Ysobel or Ethyl or Mabelle or Kathryn. But particularly Gwladys.

Very Good, Jeeves [1930]

11   Into the face of the young man who sat on the terrace of the Hotel Magnifique at Cannes there had crept a look of furtive shame, the shifty, hangdog look which announces that an Englishman is about to talk French.

The Luck of the Bodkins [1936]. The Luck of the Bodkins

12   I could see that if not actually disgruntled, he was far from being gruntled.

The Code of the Woosters [1938]. The Code of the Woosters

13   "I hate you, I hate you!" cried Madeline, a thing I didn't know anyone ever said except in the second act of a musical comedy.

Stiff Upper Lip, Jeeves [1963]

Max Born
1882–1970

14   The human race has today the means for annihilating itself—either in a fit of complete lunacy, i.e. in a big war, by a brief fit of destruction, or by careless handling of atomic technology, through a slow process of poisoning and of deterioration in its genetic structure.

Bulletin of the Atomic Scientists [June 1957]

Georges Braque
1882–1963

15   Art upsets, science reassures.   *Pensées sur l'Art*

16   Truth exists, only falsehood has to be invented.

Pensées sur l'Art

Percy Williams Bridgman
1882–1961

17   The concept of length is . . . fixed when the operations by which length is measured are fixed . . . The concept is synonymous with the corresponding set of operations.

The Logic of Modern Physics [1927]

Edward Arthur Burroughs, Bishop of Ripon
1882–1934

18   The sum of human happiness would not necessarily be reduced if for ten years every physical and

chemical laboratory were closed and the patient and resourceful energy displayed in them transferred to the lost art of getting on together and finding the formula for making both ends meet in the scale of human life.

Sermon to the British Association for the Advancement of Science, Leeds [September 4, 1927]

Father Divine [George Baker]

c. 1882–1965

1 Peace, it's wonderful.

Motto of the Peace Mission Movement

Sir Arthur Stanley Eddington

1882–1944

2 It is one thing for the human mind to extract from the phenomena of nature the laws which it has itself put into them; it may be a far harder thing to extract laws over which it has no control. It is even possible that laws which have not their origin in the mind may be irrational, and we can never succeed in formulating them.

Space, Time, and Gravitation [1920], ch. 12

3 If an army of monkeys were strumming on typewriters they *might* write all the books in the British Museum.

The Nature of the Physical World [1928], ch. 4

4 The road to a knowledge of the stars leads through the atom; and important knowledge of the atom has been reached through the stars.

Stars and Atoms [1928], lecture 1

Felix Frankfurter

1882–1965

5 The [Fifteenth] Amendment nullifies sophisticated as well as simple-minded modes of discrimination.

Lane v. Wilson, 307 U.S. 268, 275 [1939]

6 The history of liberty has largely been the history of the observance of procedural safeguards.

McNabb v. United States, 318 U.S. 332, 347 [1943]

7 One who belongs to the most vilified and persecuted minority in history is not likely to be insensible to the freedoms guaranteed by our Constitution. . . . But as judges we are neither Jew nor Gentile, neither Catholic nor agnostic.

Flag Salute Cases, 319 U.S. 624, 646 [1943]

8 After all, this is the Nation's ultimate judicial tribunal, not a super-legal-aid bureau.

Uveges v. Pennsylvania, 335 U.S. 437, 449 [1948]

9 In a democratic society like ours, relief must come through an aroused popular conscience that sears the conscience of the people's representatives.

Baker v. Carr, 369 U.S. 186, 270 [1962]

10 I know of no title that I deem more honorable than that of Professor of the Harvard Law School.

Of Law and Life and Other Things [1965]

Jean Giraudoux

1882–1944

11 There are truths which can kill a nation.

Electra

12 Faithful women are all alike, they think only of their fidelity, never of their husbands.

Amphitryon 38 [1929]

Samuel Goldwyn[1]

1882–1974

13 Include me out. *Attributed*

14 In two words: im-possible. *Attributed*

15 I read part of it all the way through.

Attributed

16 Anybody who goes to see a psychiatrist ought to have his head examined. *Attributed*

17 We've passed a lot of water since then.

Attributed

18 Anything that man says you've got to take with a dose of salts. *Attributed*

19 A verbal agreement isn't worth the paper it's written on. *Attributed*

William Frederick Halsey, Jr.

1882–1959

20 Attack — Repeat — Attack.

Dispatch to the South Pacific Force before the battle of Santa Cruz Islands [October 26, 1942]

---

[1]Goldwynisms — as his colorful misuses of English were popularly referred to — abounded. With so many gag writers working for him, hardly a lunch in Hollywood went by without somebody's concocting a malapropism and passing it off as something Sam Goldwyn had just said to him. — A. Scott Berg, *Goldwyn: A Biography* [1989], p. 396

1   Hit hard, hit fast, hit often.
Formula for waging war

2   Our ships have been salvaged and are retiring at high speed toward the Japanese fleet.
Radio message after Japanese claims that most of the U.S. Third Fleet had either been sunk or had retired [October 1944]

James Joyce
1882–1941

3   He was outcast from life's feast.
Dubliners [1916]. A Painful Case

4   Snow was general all over Ireland. It was falling on every part of the dark central plain, on the treeless hills, falling softly upon the Bog of Allen and, farther westward, softly falling into the dark mutinous Shannon waves. It was falling, too, upon every part of the lonely churchyard on the hill where Michael Furey lay buried. It lay thickly drifted on the crooked crosses and headstones, on the spears of the little gate, on the barren thorns. His soul swooned slowly as he heard the snow falling faintly through the universe and faintly falling, like the descent of their last end, upon all the living and the dead.
Dubliners. The Dead

5   Ireland is the old sow that eats her farrow.
A Portrait of the Artist as a Young Man [1916], ch. 5

6   The artist, like the God of the creation, remains within or behind or beyond or above his handiwork, invisible, refined out of existence, indifferent, paring his fingernails.
A Portrait of the Artist as a Young Man, 5

7   Welcome, O life! I go to encounter for the millionth time the reality of experience and to forge in the smithy of my soul the uncreated conscience of my race.
April 27. Old father, old artificer, stand me now and ever in good stead.
A Portrait of the Artist as a Young Man, concluding words of Stephen Dedalus

8   The snotgreen sea. The scrotumtightening sea.
Ulysses [1922]

9   Agenbite of inwit.[1] Conscience.   *Ulysses*

10   History, Stephen said, is a nightmare from which I am trying to awake.   *Ulysses*

11   My patience are exhausted [Martha Clifford].
Ulysses

12   A man of genius makes no mistakes. His errors are volitional and are the portals of discovery.
Ulysses

13   I thought well as well him as another and then I asked him with my eyes to ask again yes and then he asked me would I yes to say yes my mountain flower and first I put my arms around him yes and drew him down to me so he could feel my breasts all perfume yes and his heart was going like mad and yes I said yes I will Yes.   *Ulysses, last words*

14   riverrun, past Eve and Adam's, from swerve of shore to bend of bay, brings us by a commodius vicus of recirculation back to Howth Castle and Environs.
Finnegans Wake [1939], pt. I (opening)

15   O
        tell me all about
      Anna Livia! I want to hear all
about Anna Livia. Well, you know Anna Livia? Yes, of course, we all know Anna Livia. Tell me all. Tell me now.   *Finnegans Wake, I*

16   Can't hear with bawk of bats, all thim liffeying waters of. Ho, talk save us! My foos won't moos. I feel as old as yonder elm. A tale told of Shaun or Shem? All Livia's daughtersons. Dark hawks hear us. Night! Night! My ho head halls. I feel as heavy as yonder stone. Tell me of John or Shaun? Who were Shem and Shaun the living sons or daughters of? Night now! Tell me, tell me, tell me, elm! Night night! Telmetale of stem or stone. Beside the rivering waters of, hitherandthithering waters of. Night!
Finnegans Wake, I

17   Three quarks[2] for Muster Mark!
Finnegans Wake, II

18   I am passing out. O bitter ending! I'll slip away before they're up. They'll never see. Nor know. Nor miss me. And it's old and old it's sad and old it's sad and weary I go back to you, my cold father, my cold mad father, my cold mad feary father, till the near sight of the mere size of him, the moyles and moyles of it, moananoaning, makes me seasilt saltsick and I rush, my only, into your arms, I see them rising! Save me from those therrble prongs!
Finnegans Wake, IV

Fiorello H[enry] La Guardia
1882–1947

19   Ticker tape ain't spaghetti.
Speech to the United Nations Relief and Rehabilitation Administration [March 29, 1946]

---

[1] *Ayenbite of Inwyt* [remorse of conscience]. — Title of treatise on the seven deadly sins by DAN MICHEL OF NORTHGATE [fourteenth century]

[2] The origin of physicist Murray Gell-Mann's name [1964] for the basic building block of matter.

1   When I make a mistake it's a beaut!
On an indefensible appointment

Winifred M[ary] Letts
1882–c. 1936

2   I saw the spires of Oxford
As I was passing by,
The gray spires of Oxford
Against a pearl-gray sky.
My heart was with the Oxford men
Who went abroad to die.
The Spires of Oxford, st. 1

Jacques Maritain
1882–1973

3   In the modern social order, the *person* is sacrificed to the *individual.* The individual is given universal suffrage, equality of rights, freedom of opinion; while the person, isolated, naked, with no social armor to sustain and protect him, is left to the mercy of all the devouring forces which threaten the life of the soul, exposed to relentless actions and reactions of conflicting interests and appetites.... It is a homicidal civilization.
Three Reformers [1925]

A[lan] A[lexander] Milne[1]
1882–1956

4 James James
Morrison Morrison
Weatherby George Dupree
Took great care of his Mother
Though he was only three.
James James
Said to his Mother,
"Mother," he said, said he,
"You must never go down to the end of the town if
    you don't go down with me."
When We Were Very Young [1924].
Disobedience

5 I do like a little bit of butter to my bread!
When We Were Very Young. The King's
Breakfast

6   I am a Bear of Very Little Brain, and long words
Bother me.   *Winnie-the-Pooh [1926], ch. 4*

7   Time for a little something.
Winnie-the-Pooh, 6

---

[1]See Dorothy Parker, 738:16.

Sam [Taliaferro] Rayburn
1882–1961

8   A jackass can kick a barn down, but it takes a carpenter to build one.   *Remark [c. 1953]*

9   To get along, go along.
Attributed

Franklin Delano Roosevelt[2]
1882–1945

10   There is nothing I love as much as a good fight.
Interview in the New York Times [January 22, 1911]

11   These unhappy times call for the building of plans ... that build from the bottom up and not from the top down, that put their faith once more in the forgotten man[3] at the bottom of the economic pyramid.
Radio address [April 7, 1932]

12   The country needs and, unless I mistake its temper, the country demands bold, persistent experimentation. It is common sense to take a method and try it. If it fails, admit it frankly and try another. But above all, try something.
Address at Oglethorpe University, Atlanta, Georgia [May 22, 1932]

13   I pledge you, I pledge myself, to a new deal for the American people.[4]
Speech accepting the Democratic nomination for the presidency, Chicago [July 2, 1932]

14   There is no indispensable man.[5]
Campaign speech, New York City [November 3, 1932]

15   The only thing we have to fear is fear itself.
First Inaugural Address [March 4, 1933]

16   In the field of world policy I would dedicate this nation to the policy of the good neighbor.[6]
First Inaugural Address [March 4, 1933]

17   If I were asked to state the great objective which Church and State are both demanding for the sake of every man and woman and child in this country,

---

[2]See Oliver Wendell Holmes, Jr., 579:5, and Lippmann, 727:3.

[3]All honor to the one that in this hour / Cries to the world as from a lighted tower — / Cries for the Man Forgotten. — EDWIN MARKHAM, *The Forgotten Man*

[4]It seemed to me that what the nine hundred and ninety-four dupes needed was a new deal. — MARK TWAIN, *A Connecticut Yankee in King Arthur's Court* [1889], ch. 13

[5]Il n'y a point d'homme nécessaire. — *French proverb*

[6]I am as desirous of being a good neighbor as I am of being a bad subject. — HENRY DAVID THOREAU, *Civil Disobedience* [1849]

I would say that that great objective is "a more abundant life."

Address to the Federal Council of Churches of Christ [December 6, 1933]

1   We are moving forward to greater freedom, to greater security for the average man than he has ever known before in the history of America.

Fireside Chat [September 30, 1934]

2   Out of this modern civilization economic royalists carved new dynasties. . . . The royalists of the economic order have conceded that political freedom was the business of the Government, but they have maintained that economic slavery was nobody's business.

Speech accepting renomination [June 27, 1936]

3   This generation of Americans has a rendezvous with destiny.

Speech accepting renomination [June 27, 1936]

4   I have seen war. . . . I hate war.

Address at Chautauqua, New York [August 14, 1936]

5   I should like to have it said of my first Administration that in it the forces of selfishness and of lust for power met their match. I should like to have it said of my second Administration that in it these forces met their master.

Speech at Madison Square Garden [October 31, 1936]

6   I see one-third of a nation ill-housed, ill-clad, ill-nourished.

Second Inaugural Address [January 20, 1937]

7   The test of our progress is not whether we add more to the abundance of those who have much; it is whether we provide enough for those who have too little.

Second Inaugural Address [January 20, 1937]

8   The epidemic of world lawlessness is spreading. When an epidemic of physical disease starts to spread, the community approves and joins in a quarantine of the patients in order to protect the health of the community against the spread of the disease.

Speech at Chicago [October 5, 1937][1]

9   The only sure bulwark of continuing liberty is a government strong enough to protect the interests of the people, and a people strong enough and well enough informed to maintain its sovereign control over its government.

Fireside Chat [April 14, 1938]

10   A program whose basic thesis is not that the system of free private enterprise for profit has failed in this generation, but that it has not yet been tried.

Message on Concentration of Economic Power [April 29, 1938]

11   The Soviet Union, as everybody who has the courage to face the fact knows, is run by a dictatorship as absolute as any other dictatorship in the world.

Address to the American Youth Congress [February 10, 1940]

12   On this tenth day of June 1940 the hand that held the dagger has struck it into the back of its neighbor.[2]

Address at the University of Virginia, Charlottesville [June 10, 1940]

13   I have said this before, but I shall say it again and again and again: Your boys are not going to be sent into any foreign wars.

Campaign speech in Boston [October 30, 1940]

14   We must be the great arsenal of democracy.

Fireside Chat [December 29, 1940]

15   We look forward to a world founded upon four essential human freedoms. The first is freedom of speech and expression—everywhere in the world. The second is freedom of every person to worship God in his own way—everywhere in the world. The third is freedom from want . . . everywhere in the world. The fourth is freedom from fear . . . anywhere in the world.[3]

Message to Congress [January 6, 1941]

16   We, too, born to freedom, and believing in freedom, are willing to fight to maintain freedom. We and all others who believe as deeply as we do, would rather die on our feet than live on our knees.[4]

On receiving the degree of Doctor of Civil Law from Oxford University [June 19, 1941]

17   Yesterday, December 7, 1941—a date which will live in infamy—the United States of America was suddenly and deliberately attacked by naval and air forces of the Empire of Japan.

War Message to Congress [December 8, 1941]

18   Books cannot be killed by fire. People die, but books never die. No man and no force can abolish memory. . . . In this war, we know, books are weapons.

Message to the American Booksellers Association [April 23, 1942]

---

[1]The "Quarantine the Aggressors" speech.

[2]Italian Foreign Minister Count Galeazzo Ciano had just notified the French ambassador that Italy considered herself at war with France beginning June 11.

[3]See Franklin D. Roosevelt and Sir Winston Churchill, 699:8.

[4]See Zapata, 679:7.

1 It is not a tax bill but a tax relief bill providing relief not for the needy but for the greedy.
Tax bill veto message [February 22, 1944]

2 I think I have a right to resent, to object to libelous statements about my dog.[1]
Speech at the Teamsters' Dinner, Washington, D.C. [September 23, 1944]

3 All of our people all over the country—except the pure-blooded Indians—are immigrants or descendants of immigrants, including even those who came over here on the *Mayflower.*
Campaign speech in Boston [November 4, 1944]

4 The American people are quite competent to judge a political party that works both sides of a street.
Campaign speech in Boston [November 4, 1944]

5 We have learned that we cannot live alone, at peace; that our own well-being is dependent on the well-being of other nations, far away. We have learned that we must live as men, and not as ostriches, nor as dogs in the manger. We have learned to be citizens of the world, members of the human community.
Fourth Inaugural Address [January 20, 1945]

6 More than an end to war, we want an end to the beginnings of all wars.
Address written for Jefferson Day broadcast [April 13, 1945][2]

Franklin Delano Roosevelt and Winston Churchill

7 First, their countries seek no aggrandizement, territorial or other.
Second, they desire to see no territorial changes that do not accord with the freely expressed wishes of the peoples concerned.
Atlantic Charter, drawn up aboard the U.S.S. Augusta in Argentia Harbor, Newfoundland [issued August 14, 1941]

8 Sixth, after the final destruction of the Nazi tyranny, they hope to see established a peace which will afford to all nations the means of dwelling in safety within their own boundaries, and which will afford assurance that all the men in all the lands may live out their lives in freedom from fear and want.
Atlantic Charter, drawn up aboard the U.S.S. Augusta in Argentia Harbor, Newfoundland [issued August 14, 1941]

9 Eighth, they believe that all of the nations of the world, for realistic as well as spiritual reasons, must come to the abandonment of the use of force. Since no future peace can be maintained if land, sea or air armaments continue to be employed by nations which threaten, or may threaten, aggression outside of their frontiers, they believe, pending the establishment of a wider and permanent system of general security, that the disarmament of such nations is essential.
Atlantic Charter, drawn up aboard the U.S.S. Augusta in Argentia Harbor, Newfoundland [issued August 14, 1941]

James Stephens
1882–1950

10 I hear a sudden cry of pain!
There is a rabbit in a snare.   *The Snare*

11 Forgive us all our trespasses,
Little creatures, everywhere!   *Little Things, st. 5*

12 And, in cloud, and clod, to Sing
Of Everything and Anything!   *The Pit of Bliss*

13 Women are wiser than men because they know less and understand more.
The Crock of Gold [1912], ch. 2

14 They fell out over pigs, let them fall in over pigs.
In the Land of Youth [1924]

Virginia Woolf
1882–1941

15 On or about December, 1910, human character changed. I am not saying that one went out, as one might into a garden, and there saw that a rose had flowered, or that a hen had laid an egg. The change was not sudden and definite like that.
Mr. Bennett and Mrs. Brown [1924]

16 In people's eyes, in the swing, tramp, and trudge; in the bellow and uproar; the carriages, motor cars, omnibuses, vans, sandwich men shuffling and swinging; brass bands; barrel organs; in the triumph and the jingle and the strange high singing of some aeroplane overhead was what she loved; life; London; this moment in June.
Mrs. Dalloway [1925]

---

[1]It had been charged that the President's Scottie, Fala, allegedly stranded in the Aleutian Islands, had been brought home by a destroyer at a cost of millions.

[2]President Roosevelt died on April 12, at Warm Springs, Georgia.

1   Those comfortably padded lunatic asylums which are known, euphemistically, as the stately homes of England.[1]

The Common Reader [1925]. Lady Dorothy Nevill

2   Trivial personalities decomposing in the eternity of print.   *The Common Reader. The Modern Essay*

3   There is no room for the impurities of literature in an essay.   *The Common Reader. The Modern Essay*

4   That complete statement which is literature.

The Common Reader. How It Strikes a Contemporary

5   The word-coining genius, as if thought plunged into a sea of words and came up dripping.

The Common Reader. An Elizabethan Play

6   A biography is considered complete if it merely accounts for six or seven selves, whereas a person may well have as many thousand.

Orlando [1928], ch. 6

7   A woman must have money and a room of her own if she is to write fiction.

A Room of One's Own [1929], ch. 1

8   The beauty of the world which is so soon to perish, has two edges, one of laughter, one of anguish, cutting the heart asunder.   *A Room of One's Own, 2*

9   Women have served all these centuries as looking-glasses possessing the magic and delicious power of reflecting the figure of man at twice its natural size.

A Room of One's Own, 2

10   It is the masculine values that prevail . . . This is an important book, the critic assumes, because it deals with war. This is an insignificant book because it deals with the feelings of women in a drawing-room.   *A Room of One's Own, 4*

11   Death is the enemy. . . . Against you I will fling myself, unvanquished and unyielding, O Death.

The Waves [1931]

12   Surely it was time someone invented a new plot, or that the author came out from the bushes.

Between the Acts [1941]

Eubie [James Herbert] Blake
1883–1983

13   If I'd known I was going to live this long, I'd have taken better care of myself.

Attributed [1983]

---

[1]See Hemans, 431:19 and note.

Coco [Gabrielle] Chanel
1883–1971

14   How many cares one loses when one decides not to be something but to be someone.   *Remark*

15   There are people who have money and people who are rich.   *Remark*

16   As long as you know that most men are like children you know everything.   *Remark*

17   Fashion is architecture: it is a matter of proportions.   *Remark*

18   I wanted to give a woman comfortable clothes that would flow with her body. A woman is closest to being naked when she is well dressed.   *Remark*

Kahlil Gibran
1883–1931

19   Let there be spaces in your togetherness.

The Prophet [1923]. On Marriage

20   Work is love made visible. And if you cannot work with love but only with distaste, it is better that you should leave your work and sit at the gate of the temple and take alms of those who work with joy.

The Prophet. On Work

21   You pray in your distress and in your need; would that you might pray also in the fullness of your joy and in your days of abundance.

The Prophet. On Prayer

22   I have learned silence from the talkative, toleration from the intolerant, and kindness from the unkind; yet strange, I am ungrateful to those teachers.

Sand and Foam [1926]

Willie Howard
1883–1949

23   Comes de revolution, we'll eat strawberries and cream!   *Ballyhoo of 1932 (vaudeville) [1932]*

Franz Kafka
1883–1924

24   As Gregor Samsa awoke one morning from uneasy dreams he found himself transformed in his bed into a gigantic insect.[1]

The Metamorphosis [1915],[2] opening line

---

[1]When I read the line I thought to myself I didn't know anyone was allowed to write things like that. If I had known, I would have started writing a long time ago. So I immediately started writing short stories. — Gabriel García Márquez

[2]Translated by Willa and Edwin Muir.

1 No one else could ever be admitted here, since this gate was made only for you. I am now going to shut it. *Parables. Before the Law*[1]

2 The Messiah will come only when he is no longer necessary; he will come only on the day after his arrival; he will come, not on the last day, but on the very last. *Parables. The Coming of the Messiah*

3 This village belongs to the Castle, and whoever lives here or passes the night here does so in a manner of speaking in the Castle itself. Nobody may do that without the Count's permission. *The Castle [1926]*[1]

4 The true way goes over a rope which is not stretched at any great height but just above the ground. It seems more designed to make people stumble than to be walked upon. *The Great Wall of China. Reflections*

5 You do not need to leave your room. Remain sitting at your table and listen. Do not even listen, simply wait. Do not even wait, be quite still and solitary. The world will freely offer itself to you to be unmasked, it has no choice, it will roll in ecstasy at your feet. *The Great Wall of China. Reflections*

6 Only our concept of time makes it possible for us to speak of the Day of Judgment by that name; in reality it is a summary court in perpetual session. *The Great Wall of China. Reflections*

7 I think we ought to read only the kind of books that wound and stab us. . . . We need the books that affect us like a disaster, that grieve us deeply, like the death of someone we loved more than ourselves, like being banished into forests far from everyone, like a suicide. A book must be the axe for the frozen sea inside us. *Letter to Oskar Pollak [January 27, 1904]*

Nikos Kazantzakis
1883–1957

8 How simple and frugal a thing is happiness: a glass of wine, a roast chestnut, a wretched little brazier, the sound of the sea. . . . All that is required to feel that here and now is happiness is a simple, frugal heart. *Zorba the Greek [1946]*,[2] *ch. 7*

9 "Life is trouble," Zorba continued. "Death, no. To live — do you know what that means? To undo your belt and look for trouble!" *Zorba the Greek, 8*

10 The highest point a man can attain is not Knowledge, or Virtue, or Goodness, or Victory, but something even greater, more heroic and more despairing: Sacred Awe! *Zorba the Greek, 24*

11 The doors of heaven are adjacent and identical: both green, both beautiful. Take care, Adam! *The Last Temptation of Christ [1960]*,[3] *ch. 18*

John Maynard Keynes
1883–1946

12 He [Clemenceau] had one illusion — France; and one disillusion — mankind, including Frenchmen. *Economic Consequences of the Peace [1919], ch. 3*

13 He [Woodrow Wilson] could write Notes from Sinai or Olympus; he could remain unapproachable in the White House or even in the Council of Ten and be safe. But if he once stepped down to the intimate equality of the Four, the game was evidently up. *Economic Consequences of the Peace, 3*

14 *Long run* is a misleading guide to current affairs. *In the long run* we are all dead. *A Tract on Monetary Reform [1923], ch. 3*

15 Marxian Socialism must always remain a portent to the historians of opinion — how a doctrine so illogical and so dull can have exercised so powerful and enduring an influence over the minds of men, and, through them, the events of history. *The End of Laissez-Faire [1925], ch. 3*

16 The engine which drives Enterprise is not Thrift, but Profit. *A Treatise on Money [1930]*

17 Lenin is said to have declared that the best way to destroy the capitalist system was to debauch the currency. By a continuing process of inflation, governments can confiscate, secretly and unobserved, an important part of the wealth of their citizens. . . . Lenin was certainly right. *Essay in Persuasion [1931], pt. II*

18 The love of money as a possession — as distinguished from the love of money as a means to the enjoyments and realities of life — will be recognized for what it is, a somewhat disgusting morbidity, one of those semi-criminal, semi-pathological propensities which one hands over with a shudder to the specialists in mental disease. *Essay in Persuasion, V*

19 Words ought to be a little wild for they are the assault of thoughts on the unthinking. *In the New Statesman and Nation [July 15, 1933]*

---

[1]Translated by WILLA and EDWIN MUIR.
[2]Translated by CARL WILDMAN.

[3]Translated by P. A. BIEN.

1   His [Newton's] peculiar gift was the power of holding continuously in his mind a purely mental problem until he had seen through it.
Essays in Biography [1933]

2   Of the maxims of orthodox finance, none, surely, is more antisocial than the fetish of liquidity. . . . It forgets that there is no such thing as liquidity of investment for the community as a whole.
The General Theory of Employment, Interest and Money [1936], ch. 12

3   There are no intrinsic reasons for the scarcity of capital.
The General Theory of Employment, Interest and Money, 24

4   Practical men, who believe themselves to be quite exempt from any intellectual influences, are usually the slaves of some defunct economist. Madmen in authority, who hear voices in the air, are distilling their frenzy from some academic scribbler of a few years back.
The General Theory of Employment, Interest and Money, 24

Alfred Hart Miles
1883–1956

5 Anchors aweigh, my boys,
Anchors aweigh!
Farewell to college joys,
We sail at break of day.

Anchors Aweigh [1907][1]

Benito Mussolini
1883–1945

6   The Italian proletariat needs a blood bath for its force to be renewed.
Editorial, Popolo d'Italia [1920]

7   War alone brings up to its highest tension all human energy and puts the stamp of nobility upon the peoples who have the courage to face it.
Written for The Italian Encyclopedia. From GEORGE SELDES, *Sawdust Caesar [1935]*

8   We have buried the putrid corpse of liberty.
Speech. From MAURICE PARMELEE, *Bolshevism, Fascism and the Liberal-Democratic State [1934]*

---

[1]Music by CHARLES A. ZIMMERMAN.

José Ortega y Gasset
1883–1955

9   Rancor is an outpouring of a feeling of inferiority.
Meditations on Quixote [1911]

10   I am myself and what is around me, and if I do not save it, it shall not save me.
Meditations on Quixote

11   The Mediterraneans, who do not think clearly, do see clearly.
Meditations on Quixote

12   Culture is not life in its entirety, but just the moment of security, strength, and clarity.
Meditations on Quixote

13   Nations are formed and are kept alive by the fact that they have a program for tomorrow.
Invertebrate Spain [1922], ch. 2

14   A society without an aristocracy, without an elite minority, is not a society.   *Invertebrate Spain, 4*

15   Conversation is the socializing instrument par excellence, and in its style one can see reflected the capacities of a race.   *Invertebrate Spain, 7*

16   The choice of a point of view is the initial act of a culture.   *The Modern Theme [1923], ch. 7*

17   Order is not pressure which is imposed on society from without, but an equilibrium which is set up from within.   *Mirabeau and Politics [1927]*

18   Europe is really a swarm: many bees on a single course.   *The Revolt of the Masses [1930], prologue*

19   Minorities are individuals or groups of individuals especially qualified. The masses are the collection of people not specially qualified.
The Revolt of the Masses, ch. 1

20   A revolution only lasts fifteen years, a period which coincides with the effectiveness of a generation.   *The Revolt of the Masses, 10*

21   War is not an instinct but an invention.
The Revolt of the Masses, epilogue

22   The person portrayed and the portrait are two entirely different things.
The Dehumanization of Art [1948]

23   The masses feel that it is easy to flee from reality, when it is the most difficult thing in the world.
The Dehumanization of Art

24   The metaphor is probably the most fertile power possessed by man.   *The Dehumanization of Art*

25   I am a Spaniard, that is to say, a man without imagination.   *Esthetic Essays [1956]*

1   Primitive man is by definition tactile man.
Esthetic Essays

Joseph Alois Schumpeter
1883–1950

2   Entrepreneurial profit . . . is the expression of the value of what the entrepreneur contributes to production in exactly the same sense that wages are the value expression of what the worker "produces." It is not a profit of exploitation any more than are wages.
The Theory of Economic Development [1934], ch. 4

3   Marxism is essentially a product of the bourgeois mind.
Capitalism, Socialism and Democracy [1942], ch. 1

4   Capitalism inevitably and by virtue of the very logic of its civilization creates, educates and subsidizes a vested interest in social unrest.
Capitalism, Socialism and Democracy, 13

5   As a matter of practical necessity, socialist democracy may eventually turn out to be more of a sham than capitalist democracy ever was.
Capitalism, Socialism and Democracy, 23

Joseph Warren Stilwell
1883–1946

6   I claim we got a hell of a beating. We got run out of Burma and it is humiliating as all hell. I think we ought to find out what caused it, go back and retake it.
Statement [New Delhi, May 24, 1942] on the American retreat from Burma

William Carlos Williams
1883–1963

7   No wreaths please —
especially no hothouse flowers.
Some common memento is better,
something he prized and is known by:
his old clothes — a few books perhaps.
Tract [1917]

8   Hell take curtains! Go with some show
of inconvenience; sit openly —
to the weather as to grief.
Or do you think you can shut grief in?   *Tract*

9   Who shall say I am not
the happy genius of my household?
Danse Russe [1917]

10   so much depends
upon

a red wheel
barrow

glazed with rain
water

beside the white
chickens   *Spring and All [1923], no. XXI*

11   I have eaten
the plums
that were in
the icebox

and which
you were probably
saving
for breakfast

Forgive me
they were delicious
so sweet
and so cold   *This Is Just to Say [1934]*

12   Mothlike in mists, scintillant in the minute

brilliance of cloudless days, with broad bellying
sails
they glide to the wind tossing green water
from their sharp prows while over them the crew
crawls.   *The Yachts [1935], st. 2, 3*

13   It's the anarchy of poverty
delights me.   *The Poor [1938], st. 1*

14   THESE
are the desolate, dark weeks
when nature in its barrenness
equals the stupidity of man.

The year plunges into night
and the heart plunges
lower than night.   *These [1938], st. 1, 2*

15   It is difficult
to get the news from poems,
yet men die miserably every day
for lack
of what is found there.
Asphodel, That Greeny Flower [1955]

Will[iam Jacob] Cuppy
1884–1949

16   The Dodo never had a chance. He seems to have been invented for the sole purpose of becoming extinct and that was all he was good for.
How to Become Extinct [1941]. The Dodo

Texas [Mary Louise Cecilia] Guinan
1884–1933

1   Hello, sucker!

Greeting to nightclub patrons

Bert Kalmar
1884–1947
Harry Ruby
1895–1974
and
S[idney] J[oseph] Perelman
1904–1979

2   I'd horsewhip you if I had a horse.

Horse Feathers (screenplay) [1932], spoken by Groucho Marx

Alice [Lee] Roosevelt Longworth
1884–1980

3   Harding was not a bad man. He was just a slob.

Crowded Hours [1933]

4   I do wish [Calvin Coolidge] did not look as if he had been weaned on a pickle.

Crowded Hours. Attributing the remark to a fellow-patient of her doctor's

5   If you can't say anything good about someone, sit right here by me.

Embroidered on a pillow in her sitting room

Sean O'Casey
1884–1964

6   The whole worl's in a state o' chassis.

Juno and the Paycock [1924], act I and passim

7   One minute with him is all I ask; one minute alone with him, while you're runnin' for th' priest an' th' doctor.

The Plough and the Stars [1926], act II

8   A few hundhred scrawls o' chaps with a couple o' guns and Rosary beads, again' a hundhred thousand thrained men with horse, fut an' artillery . . . an' he wants us to fight fair!

The Plough and the Stars, IV

[Anna] Eleanor Roosevelt[1]
1884–1962

9   No one can make you feel inferior without your consent.   *This Is My Story [1937]*

10   You gain strength, courage and confidence by every experience in which you really stop to look fear in the face. You are able to say to yourself, "I lived through this horror. I can take the next thing that comes along." . . . You must do the thing you think you cannot do.   *You Learn by Living [1960]*

[Alfred] Damon Runyon
1884–1946

11   Always try to rub up against money, for if you rub up against money long enough, some of it may rub off on you.

Guys and Dolls [1931].[2] A Very Honorable Guy

12   I long ago come to the conclusion that all life is 6 to 5 against.

Money from Home [1935]. A Nice Price

13   A freeloader is a confirmed guest. He is the man who is always willing to come to dinner.

Short Takes [1946]. Freeloading Ethics

Sara Teasdale
1884–1933

14 When I am dead and over me bright April
Shakes out her rain-drenched hair,
Though you should lean above me broken-hearted,
I shall not care.   *I Shall Not Care, st. 1*

Norman [Mattoon] Thomas
1884–1968

15   I'd rather see America save her soul than her face.

Speech before antiwar protest, Washington, D.C. [November 27, 1965]

---

[1]She would rather light candles than curse the darkness and her glow has warmed the world. —ADLAI E. STEVENSON [November 7, 1962]

It is better to light one candle than curse the darkness. —Motto of the Christopher Society

[2]One of these days in your travels a guy is going to come to you and show you a nice brand-new deck of cards on which the seal is not yet broken, and that guy is going to offer to bet you that he can make the Jack of Spades jump out of the deck and squirt cider in your ear. But, son, do not bet that man, for as sure as you stand there you are going to wind up with an earful of cider. —FRANK LOESSER, JO SWERLING, and ABE BURROWS. *Guys and Dolls: A Musical Fable of Broadway* [1951], act I, sc. i

Harry S. Truman
1884–1972

1   When they told me yesterday what had happened, I felt like the moon, the stars and all the planets had fallen on me.
To reporters the day after his accession to the presidency [April 13, 1945]

2   When Kansas and Colorado have a quarrel over the water in the Arkansas River they don't call out the National Guard in each state and go to war over it. They bring a suit in the Supreme Court of the United States and abide by the decision. There isn't a reason in the world why we cannot do that internationally.   *Speech in Kansas City [April 1945]*

3   Sixteen hours ago an American airplane dropped one bomb on Hiroshima. . . . The force from which the sun draws its power has been loosed against those who brought war to the Far East.
First announcement of the atomic bomb [August 6, 1945]

4   The release of atomic energy constitutes a new force too revolutionary to consider in the framework of old ideas.
Message to Congress on atomic energy [October 3, 1945]

5   Means of destruction hitherto unknown, against which there can be no adequate military defense, and in the employment of which no single nation can in fact have a monopoly.
Declaration on Atomic Energy by President Truman and Prime Ministers Clement Attlee (Britain) and W. L. Mackenzie King (Canada) [November 15, 1945]

6   If you can't stand the heat, get out of the kitchen.
Saying

7   Once a decision was made, I did not worry about it afterward.
Memoirs [1955], vol. II, Years of Trial and Hope, ch. 1

8   The Marshall Plan will go down in history as one of America's greatest contributions to the peace of the world.   *Memoirs, II, Years of Trial and Hope, 8*

9   To me, party platforms are contracts with the people.   *Memoirs, II, Years of Trial and Hope, 13*

10   If there is one basic element in our Constitution, it is civilian control of the military.
Memoirs, II, Years of Trial and Hope, 19

11   There is a right kind and wrong kind of victory, just as there are wars for the right thing and wars that are wrong from every standpoint. . . . The kind of victory MacArthur had in mind — victory by the bombing of Chinese cities, victory by expanding the conflict to all of China — would have been the wrong kind of victory.
Memoirs, II, Years of Trial and Hope, 19

12   The buck stops here.
Sign on Truman's desk when President. From ALFRED STEINBERG, The Man from Missouri [1962]

13   The only thing new in the world is the history you don't know.
From MERLE MILLER, Plain Speaking: An Oral Biography of Harry S. Truman [1974], ch. 23

14   Secrecy and a free, democratic government don't mix.
From MERLE MILLER, Plain Speaking: An Oral Biography of Harry S. Truman, 35

Charter of the United Nations

15   We, the peoples of the United Nations
Determined to save succeeding generations from the scourge of war, which twice in our lifetime has brought untold sorrow to mankind, and
To reaffirm faith in fundamental human rights, in the dignity and worth of the human person, in the equal right of men and women and of nations large and small, and . . . for these ends
To practice tolerance and live together in peace with one another as good neighbors, and
To unite our strength to maintain international peace and security . . .
Have resolved to combine our efforts to accomplish these aims.
Charter of the United Nations [June 1945], preamble[1]

Sophie Tucker[2]
c. 1884–1966

16   From birth to age eighteen, a girl needs good parents. From eighteen to thirty-five, she needs good looks. From thirty-five to fifty-five, she needs a good personality. From fifty-five on, she needs good cash.
Said at sixty-nine

17   I have been poor and I have been rich. Rich is better.   *Attributed*

---

[1]The preamble is based on a draft by JAN CHRISTIAN SMUTS [1870–1950].

[2]Known as "The Last of the Red-Hot Mamas" from the title of a song by JACK YELLEN, which she introduced in 1928.

Niels Bohr
1885–1962

1   In our description of nature the purpose is not to disclose the real essence of the phenomena but only to track down, so far as it is possible, relations between the manifold aspects of our experience.
Atomic Theory and the Description of Nature [1934]

Arthur Wallace Calhoun
1885–1978

2   Gentlemen of the old régime in the South would say, "A woman's name should appear in print but twice—when she marries and when she dies."
Social History of the American Family [1918], citing MYRTA LOCKETT AVARY, *Dixie After the War [1906]*

Zechariah Chafee, Jr.
1885–1957

3   The press is a sort of wild animal in our midst—restless, gigantic, always seeking new ways to use its strength. . . . The sovereign press for the most part acknowledges accountability to no one except its owners and publishers.
The Press Under Pressure [Nieman Reports, April 1948]

Isak Dinesen [Karen Blixen]
1885–1962

4   What is man, when you come to think upon him, but a minutely set, ingenious machine for turning with infinite artfulness, the red wine of Shiraz into urine?   *Seven Gothic Tales [1934]. The Dreamers*

5   That old saying which the peasants call the bachelors' prayer: "I pray thee, good Lord, that I may not be married. But if I am to be married, that I may not be a cuckold. But if I am to be a cuckold, that I may not know. But if I am to know, that I may not mind."   *Seven Gothic Tales. The Poet*

6   I had seen a herd of elephant traveling through dense native forest . . . pacing along as if they had an appointment at the end of the world.
Out of Africa [1937], pt. I, ch. 1

7   If I know a song of Africa—I thought—of the giraffe, and the African new moon lying on her back, of the plows in the fields, and the sweaty faces of the coffee-pickers, does Africa know a song of me? Would the air over the plain quiver with a color that I had had on, or the children invent a game i which my name was, or the full moon throw shadow over the gravel of the drive that was lik me, or would the eagles of Ngong look out for me
Out of Africa, I,

8   I have before seen other countries, in the sam manner, give themselves to you when you are abou to leave them.   *Out of Africa, V,*

9   Man and woman are two locked caskets, c which each contains the key to the other.
Winter Tales [1942]. A Consolatory Ta

Will Durant
1885–1981

10   Once more, in the great systole and diastole c history, an age of freedom ended and an age of dis cipline began.   *Caesar and Christ [1944], ch. 1*

11   A great civilization is not conquered from with out until it has destroyed itself within. The essentia causes of Rome's decline lay in her people, he morals, her class struggle, her failing trade, her bu reaucratic despotism, her stifling taxes, her consum ing wars.   *Caesar and Christ, epilogu*

William Norman Ewer
1885–1976

12 How odd
Of God
To choose
The Jews.   *How Odd*[1]

Karen Horney
1885–1952

13   Fortunately [psycho]analysis is not the only wa to resolve inner conflicts. Life itself still remains very effective therapist.
Our Inner Conflicts [1945], conclusio

Frank Hyneman Knight
1885–1974

14   Market competition is the only form of organi zation which can afford a large measure of freedon to the individual.
Freedom and Reform [1947], ch. 1.

---

[1]But not so odd / As those who choose / A Jewish God, / Bu spurn the Jews. — CECIL BROWNE [1932–]

Not odd / Of God. / Goyim / Annoy 'im. — LEO C. ROSTE [1908–1997]

1 Large scale collective bargaining . . . is merely a seductive name for bilateral monopoly . . . and means either adjudication of conflicts in terms of power, or deadlock and stoppage, usually injuring outside people more than the immediate parties to the dispute.
Freedom and Reform, 13

Ring Lardner
1885–1933

2 "Are you lost, daddy?" I arsked tenderly. "Shut up," he explained.
The Young Immigrunts [1920]

3 A good many young writers make the mistake of enclosing a stamped, self-addressed envelope, big enough for the manuscript to come back in. This is too much of a temptation to the editor.
How to Write Short Stories [1924]

D[avid] H[erbert] Lawrence
1885–1930

4 You love me so much, you want to put me in your pocket. And I should die there smothered.
Sons and Lovers [1913], ch. 15

5 Not I, not I, but the wind that blows through me! A fine wind is blowing the new direction of Time.
Song of a Man Who Has Come Through [1920]

6 If only I am keen and hard like the sheer tip of a wedge
Driven by invisible blows,
The rock will split, we shall come at the wonder, we shall find the Hesperides.
Song of a Man Who Has Come Through

7   The glamor
Of childish days is upon me, my manhood is cast
Down in the flood of remembrance, I weep like a child for the past.   *Piano [1920]*

8 He was a little model, was Benjamin. Doctor Franklin. Snuff-colored little man! Immortal soul and all!
Studies in Classic American Literature [1922], ch. 2

9 I never saw a wild thing
Sorry for itself.   *Self-Pity [1923]*

10 A snake came to my water trough
On a hot, hot day, and I in pajamas for the heat,
To drink there.   *Snake [1923]*

11 For he seemed to me again like a king,
Like a king in exile, uncrowned in the underworld,
Now due to be crowned again.   *Snake*

12 Necessary, forever necessary, to burn out false shames and smelt the heaviest ore of the body into purity.
Lady Chatterley's Lover [1928]

13 This is John Thomas marryin' Lady Jane.
Lady Chatterley's Lover

14 How beastly the bourgeois is
especially the male of the species.
How Beastly the Bourgeois Is [1929]

15 Now in November nearer comes the sun
down the abandoned heaven.
November by the Sea [1929]

16 Beauty is a mystery. You can neither eat it nor make flannel out of it.
Sex Versus Loveliness [1930]

17 Sex and beauty are inseparable, like life and consciousness. And the intelligence which goes with sex and beauty, and arises out of sex and beauty, is intuition.   *Sex Versus Loveliness*

18 How the horse dominated the mind of the early races, especially of the Mediterranean! You were a lord if you had a horse. Far back, far back in our dark soul the horse prances. . . . The horse, the horse! The symbol of surging potency and power of movement, of action, in man.
Apocalypse [1931]

19 For man, as for flower and beast and bird, the supreme triumph is to be most vividly, most perfectly alive.   *Apocalypse*

20   Whales in mid-ocean, suspended in the waves of the sea
great heaven of whales in the waters, old hierarchies.
And enormous mother whales lie dreaming suckling their whale-tender young
and dreaming with strange whale eyes wide open in the waters of the beginning and the end.
Whales Weep Not! [1932]

21 Reach me a gentian, give me a torch!
Let me guide myself with the blue, forked torch of a flower
down the darker and darker stairs, where blue is darkened on blueness
even where Persephone goes, just now, from the frosted September
to the sightless realm where darkness is awake upon the dark.
Bavarian Gentians [1932]

22 Build then the ship of death, for you must take the longest journey, to oblivion.
The Ship of Death [1932], V

Sam M. Lewis
1885–1959
and
Joe Young
1889–1939

1   How You Gonna Keep 'Em Down on the Farm After They've Seen Paree?
Title and refrain of song [1919][1]

Sinclair Lewis
1885–1951

2   His name was George F. Babbitt [and] . . . he was nimble in the calling of selling houses for more than people could afford to pay.
Babbitt [1922], ch. 1

3   A sensational event was changing from the brown suit to the gray the contents of his pockets. He was earnest about these objects. They were of eternal importance, like baseball or the Republican Party.
Babbitt, 1

4   I've never done a single thing I've wanted to in my whole life! I don't know 's I've accomplished anything except just get along.   *Babbitt, 34*

5   Every compulsion is put upon writers to become safe, polite, obedient, and sterile. In protest, I declined election to the National Institute of Arts and Letters some years ago, and now I must decline the Pulitzer Prize.[2]
Letter declining the Pulitzer Prize for his novel Arrowsmith [1926]

6   What is love? . . . It is the morning and the evening star.   *Elmer Gantry [1927], ch. 20*

7   Our American professors like their literature clear and cold and pure and very dead.
The American Fear of Literature. Address in Stockholm on receiving the Nobel Prize for Literature [December 12, 1930]

8   It Can't Happen Here.   *Title of book [1935]*

André Maurois
1885–1967

9   The minds of different generations are as impenetrable one by the other as are the monads of Leibniz.   *Ariel [1924],[3] ch. 12*

10   Modesty and unselfishness—these are virtues which men praise—and pass by.   *Ariel, 24*

Chester William Nimitz
1885–1966

11   Uncommon valor was a common virtue.
Of the Marines at Iwo Jima [February–May 1945]

George S[mith] Patton
1885–1945

12   Wars may be fought with weapons, but they are won by men. It is the spirit of the men who follow and of the man who leads that gains the victory.
In the Cavalry Journal [September 1933]

13   Battle is the most magnificent competition in which a human being can indulge. It brings out all that is best; it removes all that is base.
Message to his troops [1943]

14   A pint of sweat will save a gallon of blood.[4]
War As I Knew It [1947], Appendix D, letter [April 3, 1944]

Ezra Pound
1885–1972

15   Your mind and you are our Sargasso Sea.
Portrait d'une Femme [1916]

16   The apparition of these faces in the crowd;
Petals on a wet, black bough.
In a Station of the Metro [1916]

17   Winter is icumen in,
Lhude sing Goddamm,
Raineth drop and staineth slop,
And how the wind doth ramm!
Sing: Goddamm.[5]   *Ancient Music*

18   The leaves fall early this autumn, in wind.
The paired butterflies are already yellow with
    August
Over the grass in the West garden;
They hurt me. I grow older.
The River Merchant's Wife: A Letter (After Rihaku)

19   For three years, out of key with his time,
He strove to resuscitate the dead art
Of poetry; to maintain "the sublime"
In the old sense. Wrong from the start—

---

[1]Music by WALTER DONALDSON [1893–1947].

[2]Lewis became a member of the Institute in 1935.

[3]Translated by ELLA D'ARCY.

[4]A drop of sweat on the drill ground will save many drops of blood on the battlefield.—AUGUST WILLICH [1810–1878], *The Army: Standing Army or National Army?* [1866]

[5]See Anonymous, 843:5.

No, hardly, but seeing he had been born
In a half savage country, out of date.
    Hugh Selwyn Mauberley. E.P. Ode pour
    l'élection de son sepulchre [1920], I

1 His true Penelope was Flaubert,
He fished by obstinate isles.
    Hugh Selwyn Mauberley. E.P. Ode pour
    l'élection de son sepulchre, I

2 The age demanded an image
Of its accelerated grimace,
Something for the modern stage,
Not, at any rate, an Attic grace.
    Hugh Selwyn Mauberley. E.P. Ode pour
    l'élection de son sepulchre, II

3 Better mendacities
Than the classics in paraphrase!
    Hugh Selwyn Mauberley. E.P. Ode pour
    l'élection de son sepulchre, II

4 Some quick to arm,
some for adventure,
some from fear of weakness,
some from fear of censure,
some for love of slaughter, in imagination,
learning later . . .
some in fear, learning love of slaughter;
Died some, pro patria,
    non "dulce" non "et decor" . . .
walked eye-deep in hell
believing in old men's lies, the unbelieving
came home, home to a lie.
    Hugh Selwyn Mauberley. E.P. Ode pour
    l'élection de son sepulchre, IV[1]

5 There died a myriad,
And of the best, among them,
For an old bitch gone in the teeth,
For a botched civilization.

Charm, smiling at the good mouth,
Quick eyes gone under earth's lid,

For two gross of broken statues,
For a few thousand battered books.
    Hugh Selwyn Mauberley. E.P. Ode pour
    l'élection de son sepulchre, V

6   As for literature
It gives no man a sinecure.
And no one knows, at sight, a masterpiece.
"And give up verse, my boy,
There's nothing in it."
    Hugh Selwyn Mauberley. E.P. Ode pour
    l'élection de son sepulchre, IX. Mr. Nixon

7 And the betrayers of language
    ......n and the press gang
And those who had lied for hire;

The perverts, the perverters of language, the
    perverts, who have set money-lust
Before the pleasures of the senses;
howling, as of a hen-yard in a printing-house,
    the clatter of presses,
the blowing of dry dust and stray paper,
foetor, sweat, the stench of stale oranges.
    Cantos [1925–1959], XIV

8 With *Usura*
With usura hath no man a house of good stone
each block cut smooth and well fitting.
    Cantos, XLV

9 No picture is made to endure nor to live with
but it is made to sell and sell quickly
with usura, sin against nature,
is thy bread ever more of stale rags
is thy bread dry as paper.
    Cantos, XLV

10 What thou lovest well remains, the rest is dross
What thou lov'st well shall not be reft from thee
What thou lov'st well is thy true heritage
Whose world, or mine or theirs or is it of none?
First came the seen, then thus the palpable
    Elysium, though it were in the halls of hell.
What thou lovest well is thy true heritage.
    Cantos, LXXXI

11 The ant's a centaur in his dragon world.
Pull down thy vanity, it is not man
Made courage, or made order, or made grace,
    Pull down thy vanity, I say pull down.
Learn of the green world what can be thy place
In scaled invention or true artistry,
Pull down thy vanity,
    Paquin pull down!
The green casque has outdone your elegance.
    Cantos, LXXXI

12   The history of an art is the history of masterwork, not of failures, or mediocrity.
    The Spirit of Romance [1910]

13   Poetry must be as well written as prose.
    Letter to Harriet Monroe [January 1915]

14   Objectivity and again objectivity, and expression:
no hindside-before-ness, no straddled adjectives (as
"addled mosses dank"), no Tennysonianness of
speech; nothing—nothing that you couldn't, in
some circumstance, in the stress of some emotion,
actually say.
    Letter to Harriet Monroe [January 1915]

15   Literature is language charged with meaning.
    ABC of Reading [1934], ch. 2

16   Literature is news that *stays* news.
    ABC of Reading, 2

---

[1]Ellipses are in the original text.

1   America, my country, is almost a continent and hardly yet a nation.   *Patria Mia*

Humbert Wolfe
1885–1940

2 Like a small gray
coffee pot
sits the squirrel.   *The Gray Squirrel [1924], st. 1*

3 Listen! the wind is rising,
and the air is wild with leaves,
We have had our summer evenings,
now for October eves!
                    Autumn (Resignation) [1926], st. 2

4 You cannot hope
to bribe or twist,
thank God! the
British journalist.

But, seeing what
the man will do
unbribed, there's
no occasion to.
                    The Uncelestial City [1930], bk. I, ii, 2.
                    Over the Fire

Elinor Hoyt Wylie
1885–1928

5 We shall walk in velvet shoes:
Wherever we go
Silence will fall like dews
On white silence below.   *Velvet Shoes [1921], st. 4*

6 Avoid the reeking herd,
Shun the polluted flock,
Live like that stoic bird
The eagle of the rock.
                    The Eagle and the Mole [1921], st. 1

7 If you would keep your soul
From spotted sight or sound,
Live like the velvet mole;
Go burrow underground.

And there hold intercourse
With roots of trees and stones,
With rivers at their source,
And disembodied bones.
                    The Eagle and the Mole, st. 5, 6

8 I was, being human, born alone;
I am, being woman, hard beset;
I live by squeezing from a stone
The little nourishment I get.
                    Let No Charitable Hope [1923], st. 2

9 If any have a stone to throw
It is not I, ever or now.   *The Pebble*

10 The worst and best are both inclined
To snap like vixens at the truth;
But, O, beware the middle mind
That purrs and never shows a tooth!
                    Nonsense Rhyme, st. 2

11   Honeyed words like bees,
Gilded and sticky, with a little sting.   *Pretty Words*

Karl Barth
1886–1968

12   Conscience is the perfect interpreter of life.
       The Word of God and the Word of Man [1957]

13   We have before us the fiendishness of business
competition and the world war, passion and wrongdoing, antagonism between classes and moral depravity within them, economic tyranny above and
the slave spirit below.
                    The Word of God and the Word of Man

William Rose Benét
1886–1950

14 And now there is merely silence, silence, silence,
       saying
All we did not know.   *Sagacity*

David Ben-Gurion
1886–1973

15   In Israel, in order to be a realist you must believe
in miracles.   *Interview [October 5, 1956]*

Hugo La Fayette Black
1886–1971

16   No higher duty, or more solemn responsibility,
rests upon this Court than that of translating into
living law and maintaining this constitutional shield
deliberately planned and inscribed for the benefit of
every human being subject to our Constitution —
of whatever race, creed or persuasion.
       Chambers v. Florida, 309 U.S. 227 [1938]

17   The First Amendment has erected a wall between church and state. That wall must be kept
high and impregnable. We could not approve the
slightest breach.
       Everson v. Board of Education, 330 U.S. 1
       [1947]

1 It is my belief that there *are* "absolutes" in our Bill of Rights, and that they were put there on purpose by men who knew what words meant and meant their prohibitions to be "absolutes."
Interview Before the American Jewish Congress [April 14, 1962]

2 An unconditional right to say what one pleases about public affairs is what I consider to be the minimum guarantee of the First Amendment.
New York Times Company v. Sullivan, 376 U.S. 254 [1964]

3 In revealing the workings of government that led to the Vietnam War, the newspapers nobly did precisely that which the Founders hoped and trusted they would do.
Concurring opinion on the publication of the Pentagon Papers [1971]

Randolph Silliman Bourne
1886–1918

4 War is the health of the state. It automatically sets in motion throughout society those irresistible forces for uniformity, for passionate cooperation with the Government in coercing into obedience the minority groups and individuals which lack the larger herd sense.   *The State [1918]*

Apsley [George Benet] Cherry-Garrard
1886–1959

5 Polar exploration is at once the cleanest and most isolated way of having a bad time which has been devised.
The Worst Journey in the World [1922]. Introduction

6 I now see very plainly that though we achieved a first-rate tragedy, which will never be forgotten because it was a tragedy, tragedy was not our business.
The Worst Journey in the World. Never Again

Frances Cornford
1886–1960

7 Magnificently unprepared
For the long littleness of life.
Rupert Brooke[1] [1915]

8 O why do you walk through the fields in gloves,
Missing so much and so much?

O fat white woman whom nobody loves,
Why do you walk through the fields in gloves
When the grass is as soft as the breast of doves
And shivering-sweet to the touch?
To a Fat Lady Seen from the Train [1915]

Al Jolson
1886–1950

9 You ain't heard nothin' yet, folks.
Ad lib remark in the first talking motion picture, The Jazz Singer [July 1927]

Gus Kahn
1886–1941
and
Raymond B. Egan
1890–1952

10 There's nothing surer,
The rich get rich and the poor get poorer,
In the meantime, in between time,
Ain't we got fun.

Ain't We Got Fun [1921]

Joyce Kilmer
1886–1918

11 I think that I shall never see
A poem lovely as a tree.
Trees[2] [1913], l. 1

12 Poems are made by fools like me,
But only God can make a tree.

Trees, l. 11

Aldo Leopold
1886–1948

13 We abuse land because we regard it as a commodity belonging to us. When we see land as a community to which we belong, we may begin to use it with love and respect.
A Sand County Almanac [1949], foreword

14 Conservation is a state of harmony between men and land.
A Sand County Almanac, part III, The Land Ethic

---

[1]See Rupert Brooke, 712.

[2]See Broun, 716:18, and Nash, 763:9.

Siegfried Sassoon
1886–1967

1 Soldiers are citizens of death's gray land.
> *Dreamers [1918]*

2 Soldiers are dreamers; when the guns begin
They think of firelit homes, clean beds, and wives.
> *Dreamers*

3 And when the war is done and youth stone dead
I'd toddle safely home and die — in bed.
> *Base Details [1918]*

4 Who will remember, passing through this gate,
The unheroic dead who fed the guns?
Who shall absolve the foulness of their fate —
Those doomed, conscripted, unvictorious ones?
> *On Passing the New Menin Gate [1918]*

5 I believe that the war, upon which I entered as a war of defense and liberation, has now become a war of aggression and conquest. . . . I have seen and endured the sufferings of the troops, and I can no longer be a party to prolong these sufferings for ends which I believe to be evil and unjust.
> *Finished with the War: A Soldier's Declaration [July 1917]*

Paul [Johannes] Tillich
1886–1965

6 The name of this infinite and inexhaustible depth and ground of all being is *God*.
> *The Shaking of the Foundations [1948], ch. 7*

7 Grace strikes us when we are in great pain and restlessness. . . . Sometimes at that moment a wave of light breaks into our darkness, and it is as though a voice were saying: "You are accepted."
> *The Shaking of the Foundations, 19*

8 The basic anxiety, the anxiety of a finite being about the threat of non-being, cannot be eliminated. It belongs to existence itself.
> *The Courage to Be [1952], ch. 2*

Ruth [Fulton] Benedict
1887–1948

9 From the moment of his birth the customs into which [an individual] is born shape his experience and behavior. By the time he can talk, he is the little creature of his culture.
> *Patterns of Culture [1934], ch. 1*

10 Our children are not individuals whose rights and tastes are casually respected from infancy, as they are in some primitive societies. . . . They are fundamentally extensions of our own egos and give a special opportunity for the display of authority.
> *Patterns of Culture, 7*

11 In world history, those who have helped to build the same culture are not necessarily of one race, and those of the same race have not all participated in one culture. In scientific language, culture is not a function of race.
> *Race: Science and Politics [1940], ch. 2*

12 Racism is the dogma that one ethnic group is condemned by nature to congenital inferiority and another group is destined to congenital superiority.
> *Race: Science and Politics, 7*

13 The tough-minded . . . respect difference. Their goal is a world made safe for differences, where the United States may be American to the hilt without threatening the peace of the world, and France may be France, and Japan may be Japan on the same conditions.
> *The Chrysanthemum and the Sword [1946], ch. 1*

Rupert Brooke[1]
1887–1915

14 Breathless, we flung us on the windy hill,
Laughed in the sun, and kissed the lovely grass.
> *The Hill [1910]*

15 And then you suddenly cried, and turned away.
> *The Hill*

16 Oh! yet
Stands the church clock at ten to three?
And is there honey still for tea?
> *The Old Vicarage, Grantchester [1912]*

17 Fish say, they have their stream and pond;
But is there anything beyond?
> *Heaven [1913]*

18 Then, the cool kindliness of sheets, that soon
Smooth away trouble; and the rough male kiss
Of blankets; grainy wood; live hair that is
Shining and free; blue-massing clouds; the keen
Unpassioned beauty of a great machine;
The benison of hot water; furs to touch;
The good smell of old clothes.
> *The Great Lover [1914]*

19 If I should die, think only this of me:
That there's some corner of a foreign field
That is forever England.
> *The Soldier [1914]*

---

[1]See Frances Cornford, 711:7.

1 Now, God be thanked, Who has matched us with
  His hour,
  And caught our youth, and wakened us from
  sleeping.   *Peace*

2 Blow out, you bugles, over the rich dead!
  There's none of these so lonely and poor of old,
  But, dying, has made us rarer gifts than gold.
                                    The Dead [1914], I

Marc Chagall
1887–1985

3   Do not leave my hand without light.
                                    Interview [1977]

Marcus Garvey
1887–1940

4   We are not engaged in domestic politics, in
church building or in social uplift work, but we are
engaged in nation building.
    Speech, The Principles of the Universal Negro
    Improvement Association, at New York City
    [November 25, 1922]

Isaac Goldberg
1887–1938

5 Diplomacy is to do and say
  The nastiest thing in the nicest way.   *The Reflex*

Martin Luis Guzmán
1887–1976

6   Here lay the dilemma: either Villa would submit
to the idea of the revolution without understanding
it, in which case he and the true revolution would
succeed; or Villa would follow his instincts blindly,
and the revolution and he would both fail.[1]
    El Aguila y la Serpiente (The Eagle and the
    Serpent) [1928], pt. II, bk. I, ch. 1

Robinson Jeffers
1887–1962

7 Lend me the stone strength of the past and I will
  lend you
  The wings of the future, for I have them.
    To the Rock That Will Be a Cornerstone
    [1924]

8   The deep dark-shining
  Pacific leans on the land,
  Feeling his cold strength
  To the outmost margins.   *Night [1925]*

9 The world's God is treacherous and full of
  unreason.   *Birth-Dues [1928]*

10 I'd sooner, except the penalties, kill a man than a
  hawk.   *Hurt Hawks [1928]*

11   I have grown to believe
  A stone is a better pillow than many visions.
                                Clouds of Evening [1930]

12 The strong lean upon death as on a rock.
                                Gale in April [1930]

13 Well: the day is a poem but too much
  Like one of Jeffers's, crusted with blood and
      barbaric omens,
  Painful to excess, inhuman as a hawk's cry.
    The Day Is a Poem (September 19, 1939)
    [1941]

14   As for me, I would rather
  Be a worm in a wild apple than a son of man.
                                Original Sin [1948]

Le Corbusier
[Charles Édouard Jeanneret]
1887–1965

15   A house is a machine for living in.[2]
                                Vers une Architecture [1923]

Emilio Mola
1887–1937

16   Fifth column.[3]
    Phrase, Spanish Civil War [1936–1939]

Sir Bernard Law Montgomery,
Viscount Montgomery of Alamein
1887–1976

17   To us is given the honor of striking a blow for
freedom which will live in history, and in the better
days that lie ahead men will speak with pride of our
doings.
    Message to his troops, on the eve of the Allied
    invasion of Europe [June 5, 1944]

---

[1]Translated by RACHEL PHILLIPS.

[2]Une maison est une machine-à-habiter.

[3]Mola, one of Franco's generals, boasted that he had four
columns of troops to lead against Madrid and a fifth column of
sympathizers inside Madrid.

Marianne Moore
1887–1972

1 Dürer would have seen a reason for living in a town
  like this.
                        The Steeple-Jack [1935], st. 1

2   The sweet air coming into your house on a
fine day, from water etched
    with waves as formal as the scales on a fish.
                        The Steeple-Jack, st. 1

3 Of the crow-blue mussel shells, one keeps
adjusting the ash heaps;
    opening and shutting itself like

an
injured fan.   *The Fish [1935], st. 1, 2*

4 I, too, dislike it.
    Reading it, however, with a perfect contempt
      for it, one discovers in
    it, after all, a place for the genuine.
                 Poetry [1935; revised 1967]

5 Nor till the poets among us can be
  "literalists of
the imagination"—above
    insolence and triviality and can present

for inspection, "imaginary gardens with real
      toads in them," shall we have
    it.   *Poetry, st. 4, 5 (excluded in 1967 revision)*[1]

6 I wonder what Adam and Eve
think of it by this time.
                   Marriage [1935]

7   Ecstasy affords
the occasion and expediency determines the form.
         The Past Is the Present [1935]

8 My father used to say,
  "Superior people never make long visits,
have to be shown Longfellow's grave
or the glass flowers at Harvard."   *Silence [1935]*

9 "The deepest feeling always shows itself in silence;
not in silence, but restraint."
Nor was he insincere in saying, "Make my house
    your inn."[2]
Inns are not residences.   *Silence*

10   There is a great amount of poetry in unconscious fastidiousness.
         Critics and Connoisseurs [1935]

---

[1] Omissions are not accidents.—MARIANNE MOORE, *Complete Poems* [1967], *author's note*

[2] Author's note: Edmund Burke, in *Burke's Life*, by James Prior: "Throw yourself into a coach," said he. "Come down and make my house your inn."

11   What is our innocence,
what is our guilt? All are
    naked, none is safe.   *What Are Years? [1941]*

12 The power of the visible
is the invisible.
         He "Digesteth Harde Yron" [1941], st.

13 I am troubled, I'm dissatisfied, I'm Irish.
        Spenser's Ireland [1941], last line

14 Another armored animal—scale
    lapping scale with spruce cone regularity until they
form the uninterrupted central
    tail row!   *The Pangolin [1941], st.*

15   Bedizened or stark
naked, man, the self, the being we call human,
    writing
master to this world.   *The Pangolin, st.*

16   Among animals, *one* has a sense of humor.
Humor saves a few steps, it saves years.
               The Pangolin, st.

17   The prey of fear, he, always
    curtailed, extinguished, thwarted by the dusk,
      work partly done,
says to the alternating blaze,
    "Again the sun!
anew each day; and new and new and new,
that comes into and steadies my soul."
               The Pangolin, st.

18   What sap
went through that little thread
to make the cherry red!
         Nevertheless [1944], st. 1

19 They say there is a sweeter air
    where it was made, than we have here.
        A Carriage from Sweden [1944]

20   THE MIND IS AN ENCHANTING THING
is an enchanted thing,
    like the glaze on a
katydid-wing
    subdivided by sun
    till the nettings are legion.
    The Mind Is an Enchanting Thing [1944], st.

21 I inwardly did nothing.
O Iscariot-like crime!
       In Distrust of Merits [1941], st.

22 We don't like flowers that do
    not wilt; they must die, and nine
    she-camel hairs aid memory.
        The Sycamore [1956], st.

23   O to be a dragon,
a symbol of the power of Heaven—of silkworm

size or immense; at times invisible.
  Felicitous phenomenon!
                              O To Be a Dragon [1959]

1 To wear the arctic fox
  you have to kill it.
                    The Arctic Ox (Or Goat) [1959], st. 1

2 Camels are snobbish
  and sheep, unintelligent;
      water buffaloes, neurasthenic—
  even murderous.
  Reindeer seem over-serious.
                    The Arctic Ox (Or Goat), st. 9

3   Why an inordinate interest in animals and athletes? They are subjects for art and exemplars of it,
are they not? minding their own business. Pangolins,
hornbills, pitchers, catchers, do not pry or prey—
or prolong the conversation; do not make us self-
conscious; look their best when caring least.
          A Marianne Moore Reader [1961], foreword

Samuel Eliot Morison
1887–1976

4   A tough but nervous, tenacious but restless race
[the Yankees]; materially ambitious, yet prone to introspection, and subject to waves of religious emotion. . . . A race whose typical member is eternally
torn between a passion for righteousness and a desire to get on in the world.
          Maritime History of Massachusetts [1921], ch. 2

5   A few hints as to literary craftsmanship may be
useful to budding historians. First and foremost, *get
writing!*
          *History as a Literary Art. Old South Leaflets,
          series II, no. 1 [1946]*

6   America was discovered accidentally by a great
seaman who was looking for something else; when
discovered it was not wanted; and most of the exploration for the next fifty years was done in the
hope of getting through or around it. America was
named after a man who discovered no part of the
New World. History is like that, very chancy.
          *The Oxford History of the American People
          [1965], ch. 2*

Edwin Muir
1887–1959

7 The killing beast that cannot kill
  Swells and swells in his fury till
  You'd almost think it was despair.
                    Collected Poems [1952]. The Combat

8 Since then they have pulled our ploughs and borne
      our loads,
  But that free servitude still can pierce our hearts.
  Our life is changed; their coming our beginning.
                    Collected Poems. The Horses.

Georgia O'Keeffe
1887–1986

9   Where I was born and where and how I have
lived is unimportant. It is what I have done with
where I have been that should be of interest.
                    Georgia O'Keeffe [1976]

10   I find that I have painted my life—things happening in my life—without knowing.
                    Georgia O'Keeffe [1976]

11   I had to create an equivalent for what I felt
about what I was looking at—not copy it.
                    Georgia O'Keeffe [1976]

Edith Sitwell
1887–1964

12 Lily O'Grady,
  Silly and shady,
  Longing to be
  A lazy lady.   *Facade [1923].[1] Popular Song*

13 Still falls the Rain—
  Dark as the world of man, black as our loss—
  Blind as the nineteen hundred and forty nails
  Upon the Cross.   *Still Falls the Rain [1940]*

14   Rhythm is one of the principal translators between dream and reality. Rhythm might be described as, to the world of sound, what light is to the
world of sight. It shapes and gives new meaning.
          *The Canticle of the Rose [1949]. Some Notes
          on My Own Poetry*

Alexander Woollcott
1887–1943

15   The two oldest professions in the world—
ruined by amateurs.
          *The Knock at the Stage Door. The Actor and
          the Streetwalker*

16   All the things I really like to do are either immoral, illegal, or fattening.   *Remark*

17   Germany was the cause of Hitler just as much as
Chicago is responsible for the Chicago *Tribune.*
          *Last words before the microphone [January 23,
          1943], on the People's Platform program*

---

[1]Music by WILLIAM WALTON.

Maxwell Anderson
1888–1959

1 Oh, it's a long, long while
From May to December,
But the days grow short,
When you reach September.
Knickerbocker Holiday [1938].[1]
September Song

2 Oh, the days dwindle down
To a precious few . . .
And these few precious days
I'll spend with you.
Knickerbocker Holiday. September Song

Bruce Bairnsfather
1888–1959

3   Well, if you knows of a better 'ole, go to it.
Fragments from France [1915]. Caption for cartoon

Irving Berlin
1888–1989

4 You've got to get up, you've got to get up,
You've got to get up this morning!
Oh! How I Hate to Get Up in the Morning [1918]

5   A Pretty Girl Is Like a Melody.
Ziegfeld Follies [1919], title of song

6 God bless America,
Land that I love.
God Bless America [1938]

7 From the mountains to the prairies,
To the oceans white with foam,
God bless America,
My home sweet home!
God Bless America

8 I'm dreaming of a white Christmas.
Holiday Inn [1942]. White Christmas

9 This is the army, Mr. Jones,
No private baths or telephones.
This Is the Army [1942], title song

10   There's No Business Like Show Business.
Annie Get Your Gun [1946], title of song

11   Anything You Can Do, I Can Do Better.
Annie Get Your Gun, title of song

Georges Bernanos
1888–1948

12   Hell, Madame, is to love no longer.
Le Journal d'un Curé de Campagne (The Diary of a Country Priest) [1936]

13   Democracies cannot dispense with hypocrisy any more than dictatorships can with cynicism.
Nous Autres Français (We French)

14   The most dangerous of our calculations are those we call illusions.
Dialogue des Carmélites [1949]

Henry Beston
1888–1968

15   The world today is sick to its thin blood for lack of elemental things, for fire before the hands, for water welling from the earth, for air, for the dear earth itself underfoot.
The Outermost House [1928], ch. 1

16   The three great elemental sounds in nature are the sound of rain, the sound of wind in a primeval wood, and the sound of outer ocean on a beach.
The Outermost House, 3

17   For a moment of night we have a glimpse of ourselves and of our world islanded in its stream of stars — pilgrims of mortality, voyaging between horizons across the eternal seas of space and time.
The Outermost House, 3

Heywood Broun
1888–1939

18   "Trees" maddens me, because it contains the most insincere line ever written by mortal man. Surely the Kilmer tongue must have been not far from the Kilmer cheek when he wrote, "Poems are made by fools like me."[2]
It Seems to Me [1935]. "Trees," "If," and "Invictus"

19   Life is a copycat and can be bullied into following the master artist who bids it come to heel.
It Seems to Me. Nature the Copycat

Dale Carnegie
1888–1955

20   How to Win Friends and Influence People.
Title of book [1938]

---

[1]Music by KURT WEILL.

[2]See Kilmer, 711:12.

Joyce Cary [Arthur Joyce Lunel]
1888–1957

1   She had a mannish manner of mind and face, able to feel hot and think cold.
Herself Surprised [1941], ch. 7

2   Sara could commit adultery at one end and weep for her sins at the other, and enjoy both operations at once.   *The Horse's Mouth [1944], ch. 8*

Raymond Chandler
1888–1959

3   A blonde to make a bishop kick a hole in a stained glass window.   *Farewell, My Lovely [1940], ch. 13*

4   Down these mean streets a man must go who is not himself mean.
The Simple Art of Murder [1950]

John Foster Dulles
1888–1959

5   You have to take chances for peace, just as you must take chances in war. . . . The ability to get to the verge without getting into the war is the necessary art. If you try to run away from it, if you are scared to go to the brink,[1] you are lost.
From JAMES SHEPLEY, *How Dulles Averted War, in* Life *[January 16, 1956]*

T[homas] S[tearns] Eliot
1888–1965

6 Let us go then, you and I,
When the evening is spread out against the sky
Like a patient etherized upon a table.
The Love Song of J. Alfred Prufrock [1917]

7 In the room the women come and go
Talking of Michelangelo.
The Love Song of J. Alfred Prufrock

8 There will be time to murder and create.
The Love Song of J. Alfred Prufrock

9 And indeed there will be time
To wonder, "Do I dare?" and, "Do I dare?"
The Love Song of J. Alfred Prufrock

10 I have measured out my life with coffee spoons.
The Love Song of J. Alfred Prufrock

11 I should have been a pair of ragged claws
Scuttling across the floors of silent seas.
The Love Song of J. Alfred Prufrock

12 Should I, after tea and cakes and ices,
Have the strength to force the moment to its crisis?
The Love Song of J. Alfred Prufrock

13 I have seen the moment of my greatness flicker,
And I have seen the eternal Footman hold my coat, and snicker,
And in short, I was afraid.
The Love Song of J. Alfred Prufrock

14 No! I am not Prince Hamlet, nor was meant to be;
Am an attendant lord, one that will do
To swell a progress, start a scene or two,
Advise the prince; no doubt, an easy tool,
Deferential, glad to be of use,
Politic, cautious, and meticulous;
Full of high sentence, but a bit obtuse;
At times, indeed, almost ridiculous—
Almost, at times, the Fool.
The Love Song of J. Alfred Prufrock

15 I grow old . . . I grow old. . . .
I shall wear the bottoms of my trousers rolled.
The Love Song of J. Alfred Prufrock

16 Shall I part my hair behind? Do I dare to eat a peach?
I shall wear white flannel trousers, and walk upon the beach.
I have heard the mermaids singing, each to each.

I do not think that they will sing to me.
The Love Song of J. Alfred Prufrock

17 Till human voices wake us, and we drown.
The Love Song of J. Alfred Prufrock

18 And I must borrow every changing shape
To find expression.   *Portrait of a Lady [1917], III*

19 I am aware of the damp souls of housemaids
Sprouting despondently at area gates.
Morning at the Window [1917]

20 The readers of the *Boston Evening Transcript*
Sway in the wind like a field of ripe corn.
The Boston Evening Transcript [1917]

21 Upon the glazen shelves kept watch
Matthew and Waldo, guardians of the faith,
The army of unalterable law.
Cousin Nancy [1917]

22 His laughter tinkled among the teacups.
Mr. Apollinax [1917]

23 Stand on the highest pavement of the stair—
Lean on a garden urn—
Weave, weave the sunlight in your hair.
La Figlia Che Piange [1917], st. 1

24 Simple and faithless as a smile and shake of the hand.   *La Figlia Che Piange, st. 2*

---

[1]From the phrase "to the brink" developed "brinkmanship."

1 Sometimes these cogitations still amaze
  The troubled midnight and the noon's repose.
                              La Figlia Che Piange, st. 3

2 Here I am, an old man in a dry month,
  Being read to by a boy, waiting for rain.
                              Gerontion [1920]

3 After such knowledge, what forgiveness? Think
      now
  History has many cunning passages, contrived
      corridors
  And issues, deceives with whispering ambitions,
  Guides us by vanities.   *Gerontion*

4 Neither fear nor courage saves us. Unnatural vices
  Are fathered by our heroism. Virtues
  Are forced upon us by our impudent crimes.
  These tears are shaken from the wrath-bearing tree.
                              Gerontion

5 The hippopotamus's day
  Is passed in sleep; at night he hunts;
  God works in a mysterious way—
  The Church can sleep and feed at once.
                              The Hippopotamus [1920], st. 6

6 Webster was much possessed by death
  And saw the skull beneath the skin.
                              Whispers of Immortality [1920], st. 1

7 He knew the anguish of the marrow
  The ague of the skeleton;
  No contact possible to flesh
  Allayed the fever of the bone.
                              Whispers of Immortality, st. 4 [of Donne]

8 Uncorseted, her friendly bust
  Gives promise of pneumatic bliss.
                              Whispers of Immortality, st. 5

9 Reorganized upon the floor
  She yawns and draws a stocking up.
                              Sweeney Among the Nightingales [1920], st. 4

10 The nightingales are singing near
  The Convent of the Sacred Heart,

  And sang within the bloody wood
  When Agamemnon cried aloud,
  And let their liquid siftings fall
  To stain the stiff dishonored shroud.
                              Sweeney Among the Nightingales, st. 9, 10

11 April is the cruellest month, breeding
  Lilacs out of the dead land, mixing
  Memory and desire, stirring
  Dull roots with spring rain.
                              *The Waste Land [1922]. I, The Burial of
                              the Dead*

12   You know only
  A heap of broken images, where the sun beats,

And the dead tree gives no shelter, the cricket no
    relief,
And the dry stone no sound of water. Only
There is shadow under this red rock,
(Come in under the shadow of this red rock),
And I will show you something different from
    either
Your shadow at morning striding behind you
Or your shadow at evening rising to meet you;
I will show you fear in a handful of dust.
                              The Waste Land. I, The Burial of the Dead

13 I had not thought death had undone so many.[1]
  Sighs, short and infrequent, were exhaled.[2]
                              The Waste Land. I, The Burial of the Dead

14 I think we are in rats' alley
  Where the dead men lost their bones.
                              The Waste Land. II, A Game of Chess

15 O O O O that Shakespeherian Rag—
  It's so elegant
  So intelligent.
                              The Waste Land. II, A Game of Chess

16 Hurry up please its time.
                              The Waste Land. II, A Game of Chess

17 But at my back from time to time I hear[3]
  The sound of horns and motors, which shall bring
  Sweeney to Mrs. Porter in the spring.
  O the moon shone bright on Mrs. Porter
  And on her daughter
  They wash their feet in soda water.
                              The Waste Land. III, The Fire Sermon

18   At the violet hour, when the eyes and back
  Turn upward from the desk, when the human
      engine waits
  Like a taxi throbbing waiting,
  I Tiresias, though blind, throbbing between two
      lives.   *The Waste Land. III, The Fire Sermon*

19 When lovely woman stoops to folly[4] and
  Paces about her room again, alone,
  She smooths her hair with automatic hand,
  And puts a record on the gramophone.
                              The Waste Land. III, The Fire Sermon

20 Phlebas the Phoenician, a fortnight dead,
  Forgot the cry of gulls, and the deep sea swell
  And the profit and loss.
                              The Waste Land. IV, Death by Water

21 Here is no water but only rock.
                              The Waste Land. V, What the Thunder Said

---

[1]Dante, *Inferno, canto III, ll. 55–57.*
[2]Dante, *Inferno, canto IV, ll. 25–27.*
[3]See Marvell, 277:1.
[4]See Goldsmith, 341:20.

1 Who is the third who walks always beside you?
The Waste Land. V, What the Thunder Said

2 *Dayadhvam:* I have heard the key
Turn in the door once and turn once only
We think of the key, each in his prison
Thinking of the key, each confirms a prison.
The Waste Land. V, What the Thunder Said

3 These fragments I have shored against my ruins.
The Waste Land. V, What the Thunder Said

4 We are the hollow men
We are the stuffed men
Leaning together
Headpiece filled with straw. Alas!
The Hollow Men [1925], I

5 Shape without form, shade without color,
Paralyzed force, gesture without motion;

Those who have crossed
With direct eyes, to death's other Kingdom
Remember us—if at all—not as lost
Violent souls, but only
As the hollow men
The stuffed men.   *The Hollow Men, I*

6 Between the idea
And the reality
Between the motion
And the act
Falls the Shadow.   *The Hollow Men, V*

7 This is the way the world ends
Not with a bang but a whimper.
The Hollow Men, V

8 A cold coming we had of it,
Just the worst time of the year.
Journey of the Magi [1927]

9 Because I do not hope to turn again[1]
Because I do not hope
Because I do not hope to turn.
Ash-Wednesday [1930], I

10 Because these wings are no longer wings to fly
But merely vans to beat the air
The air which is now thoroughly small and dry
Smaller and dryer than the will
Teach us to care and not to care
Teach us to sit still.   *Ash-Wednesday, I*

11 Terminate torment
Of love unsatisfied
The greater torment
Of love satisfied.   *Ash-Wednesday, II*

12 Blown hair is sweet, brown hair over the mouth
blown,

---

[1]Guido Cavalcanti [c. 1250–1300], *Perch' lo Non Spero.*

Lilac and brown hair;
Distraction, music of the flute, stops and steps of
the mind over the third stair,
Fading, fading; strength beyond hope and despair
Climbing the third stair.   *Ash-Wednesday, III*

13   Redeem
The time. Redeem
The unread vision in the higher dream
While jeweled unicorns draw by the gilded hearse.
Ash-Wednesday, IV

14 Against the Word the unstilled world still whirled
About the center of the silent Word.
Ash-Wednesday, V

15 Wavering between the profit and the loss
In this brief transit where the dreams cross
The dreamcrossed twilight between birth and
dying.   *Ash-Wednesday, VI*

16 The white sails still fly seaward, seaward flying
Unbroken wings.

And the lost heart stiffens and rejoices
In the lost lilac and the lost sea voices
And the weak spirit quickens to rebel
For the bent goldenrod and the lost sea smell.
Ash-Wednesday, VI

17 Even among these rocks,
Our peace in His will.   *Ash-Wednesday, VI*

18 What seas what shores what gray rocks and what
islands
What water lapping the bow
And scent of pine and the woodthrush singing
through the fog
What images return
O my daughter.   *Marina [1930]*

19   I'll convert *you!*
Into a stew.
A nice little, white little, missionary stew!
Sweeney Agonistes

20 Birth, and copulation, and death.
That's all the facts when you come to brass tacks.
Sweeney Agonistes

21 Two live as one
One live as two
Two live as three
Under the bam
Under the boo
Under the bamboo tree.   *Sweeney Agonistes*

22 Stone, bronze, stone, steel, stone, oakleaves,
horses' heels
Over the paving.   *Coriolan I. Triumphal March*

23 O hidden under the dove's wing, hidden in the
turtle's breast,

Under the palmtree at noon, under the running
    water
At the still point of the turning world. O hidden.
                Coriolan I. Triumphal March

1 How unpleasant to meet Mr. Eliot![1]
With his features of clerical cut,
And his brow so grim
And his mouth so prim.   *Five-Finger Exercises, V*

2 Yet we have gone on living,
Living and partly living.
                Murder in the Cathedral [1935], pt. I

3 They know and do not know, what it is to act or
    suffer.
They know and do not know, that acting is
    suffering.   *Murder in the Cathedral, I*

4 Saint and Martyr rule from the tomb.
                Murder in the Cathedral, I

5 The last temptation is the greatest treason:
To do the right deed for the wrong reason.
                Murder in the Cathedral, I

6 Human kind cannot bear very much reality.[2]
                Murder in the Cathedral, II

7 Time present and time past
Are both perhaps present in time future,
And time future contained in time past.
                Four Quartets. Burnt Norton [1935], pt. I

8 Footfalls echo in the memory
Down the passage which we did not take
Towards the door we never opened
Into the rose garden.
                Four Quartets. Burnt Norton, I

9 Garlic and sapphires in the mud
Clot the bedded axle-tree.
The trilling wire in the blood
Sings below inveterate scars
And reconciles forgotten wars.
                Four Quartets. Burnt Norton, II

10 At the still point of the turning world.
        Neither flesh nor fleshless.
                Four Quartets. Burnt Norton, II

11   Except for the point, the still point,
There would be no dance, and there is only the
    dance.   *Four Quartets. Burnt Norton, II*

12 Only through time time is conquered.
                Four Quartets. Burnt Norton, II

13 Sudden in a shaft of sunlight
Even while the dust moves

There rises the hidden laughter
Of children in the foliage
Quick now, here, now, always—
Ridiculous the waste sad time
Stretching before and after.
                Four Quartets. Burnt Norton, V

14 Macavity, Macavity, there's no one like Macavity,
He's broken every human law, he breaks the law of
    gravity.
His powers of levitation would make a fakir stare,
And when you reach the scene of the crime—
Macavity's not there!
                Old Possum's Book of Practical Cats [1939].
                Macavity: The Mystery Cat

15 In my beginning is my end.
                Four Quartets. East Coker [1940], pt. I

16   Keeping time,
Keeping the rhythm in their dancing
As in their living in the living seasons
The time of the seasons and the constellations
The time of milking and the time of harvest
The time of the coupling of man and woman
And that of beasts. Feet rising and falling.
Eating and drinking. Dung and death.
                Four Quartets. East Coker, I

17 What is the late November doing
With the disturbance of the spring.
                Four Quartets. East Coker, II

18 A periphrastic study in a worn-out poetical fashion,
Leaving one still with the intolerable wrestle
With words and meanings. The poetry does not
    matter.   *Four Quartets. East Coker, II*

19 The only wisdom we can hope to acquire
Is the wisdom of humility: humility is endless.
                Four Quartets. East Coker, II

20 The houses are all gone under the sea.
                Four Quartets. East Coker, II

21 The dancers are all gone under the hill.
                Four Quartets. East Coker, II

22 O dark dark dark.[3] They all go into the dark,
The vacant interstellar spaces, the vacant into the
    vacant.   *Four Quartets. East Coker, III*

23 And we all go with them, into the silent funeral,
Nobody's funeral, for there is no one to bury.
I said to my soul, be still,[4] and let the dark come
    upon you
Which shall be the darkness of God.
                Four Quartets. East Coker, III

---

[1]See Lear, 499:12.

[2]Also in ELIOT'S *Four Quartets. Burnt Norton, pt. I.*

[3]See Milton, 268:32.

[4]See *Psalms 46:10,* 17:23.

1 To arrive where you are, to get from where you are
    not,
  You must go by a way wherein there is no ecstasy.
  In order to arrive at what you do not know
  You must go by the way which is the way of
    ignorance.   *Four Quartets. East Coker, III*

2 The whole earth is our hospital
  Endowed by the ruined millionaire.
              Four Quartets. East Coker, IV

3 We call this Friday good.
              Four Quartets. East Coker, IV

4   And so each venture
  Is a new beginning, a raid on the inarticulate
  With shabby equipment always deteriorating
  In the general mess of imprecision of feeling,
  Undisciplined squads of emotion.
             Four Quartets. East Coker, V

5 Home is where one starts from. As we grow older
  The world becomes stranger, the pattern more
    complicated
  Of dead and living. Not the intense moment
  Isolated, with no before and after,
  But a lifetime burning in every moment
  And not the lifetime of one man only
  But of old stones that cannot be deciphered.
             Four Quartets. East Coker, V

6 Love is most nearly itself
  When here and now cease to matter.
  Old men ought to be explorers[1]
  Here and there does not matter
  We must be still and still moving
  Into another intensity
  For a further union, a deeper communion
  Through the dark cold and the empty desolation,
  The wave cry, the wind cry, the vast waters
  Of the petrel and the porpoise. In my end is my
    beginning.   *Four Quartets. East Coker, V*

7 I do not know much about gods; but I think that
    the river
  Is a strong brown god—sullen, untamed and
    intractable.
  Four Quartets. The Dry Salvages [1941], pt. I

8 The sea is the land's edge also, the granite
  Into which it reaches, the beaches where it tosses
  Its hints of earlier and other creation:
  The starfish, the hermit crab, the whale's
    backbone;
  The pools where it offers to our curiosity
  The more delicate algae and the sea anemone.
  It tosses up our losses, the torn seine,
  The shattered lobsterpot, the broken oar

And the gear of foreign dead men. The sea has
  many voices.
      Four Quartets. The Dry Salvages, I

9 There is no end of it, the voiceless wailing,
  No end to the withering of withered flowers.
      Four Quartets. The Dry Salvages, II

10 The backward look behind the assurance
  Of recorded history, the backward halflook
  Over the shoulder, towards the primitive terror.
      Four Quartets. The Dry Salvages, II

11 Time the destroyer is time the preserver.
      Four Quartets. The Dry Salvages, II

12   Not fare well,
  But fare forward, voyagers.
      Four Quartets. The Dry Salvages, III

13   Music heard so deeply
  That it is not heard at all, but you are the music
  While the music lasts.
      Four Quartets. The Dry Salvages, V

14   Only undefeated
  Because we have gone on trying;
  We, content at the last
  If our temporal reversion nourish
  (Not too far from the yew tree)
  The life of significant soil.
      Four Quartets. The Dry Salvages, V

15 What the dead had no speech for, when living,
  They can tell you, being dead: the communication
  Of the dead is tongued with fire beyond the
    language of the living.
    Four Quartets. Little Gidding [1942], pt. I

16 Ash on an old man's sleeve
  Is all the ash the burnt roses leave.
  Dust in the air suspended
  Marks the place where a story ended.
  Dust inbreathed was a house—
  The wall, the wainscot and the mouse
  The death of hope and despair,
    This is the death of air.
      Four Quartets. Little Gidding, II

17 Water and fire shall rot
  The marred foundations we forgot,
  Of sanctuary and choir.
    This is the death of water and fire.
      Four Quartets. Little Gidding, II

18 In the uncertain hour before the morning
  Near the ending of interminable night
  At the recurrent end of the unending
  After the dark dove with the flickering tongue
  Had passed below the horizon of his homing.
      Four Quartets. Little Gidding, II

---

[1]See Roethke, 781:2.

1 Since our concern was speech, and speech
impelled us
To purify the dialect of the tribe.[1]
Four Quartets. Little Gidding, II

2 Who then devised the torment? Love.
Love is the unfamiliar Name
Behind the hands that wove
The intolerable shirt of flame
Which human power cannot remove.
    We only live, only suspire
    Consumed by either fire or fire.
Four Quartets. Little Gidding, IV

3   A people without history
Is not redeemed from time, for history is a pattern
Of timeless moments. So, while the light fails
On a winter's afternoon, in a secluded chapel
History is now and England.
Four Quartets. Little Gidding, V

4 We shall not cease from exploration
And the end of all our exploring
Will be to arrive where we started
And know the place for the first time.
Four Quartets. Little Gidding, V

5 A condition of complete simplicity
(Costing not less than everything)
And all shall be well and
All manner of thing shall be well[2]
When the tongues of flame are infolded
Into the crowned knot of fire
And the fire and the rose are one.
Four Quartets. Little Gidding, V

6   It [tradition] cannot be inherited, and if you
want it you must obtain it by great labor.
Tradition and the Individual Talent [1919]

7   The progress of an artist is a continual self-sacrifice, a continual extinction of personality.
Tradition and the Individual Talent

8   Poetry is not a turning loose of emotion, but an
escape from emotion; it is not the expression of personality, but an escape from personality. But, of
course, only those who have personality and emotions
know what it means to want to escape from these
things.   *Tradition and the Individual Talent*

9   The only way of expressing emotion in the form
of art is by finding an "objective correlative"; in
other words, a set of objects, a situation, a chain of
events which shall be the formula of that *particular*
emotion.   *Hamlet and His Problems [1919]*

10   Immature poets imitate; mature poets steal.
Philip Massinger [1920]

11   Every vital development in language is a development of feeling as well.   *Philip Massinger*

12   In the seventeenth century a dissociation of sensibility set in, from which we have never recovered;
and this dissociation, as is natural, was aggravated
by the influence of the two most powerful poets of
the century, Milton and Dryden.
The Metaphysical Poets [1921]

13   Poets in our civilization, as it exists at present,
must be *difficult*. . . . The poet must become more
and more comprehensive, more allusive, more indirect, in order to force, to dislocate if necessary, language into its meaning.   *The Metaphysical Poets*

14   The great poet, in writing himself, writes his time.
Shakespeare and the Stoicism of Seneca [1927]

15   We know too much, and are convinced of too
little. Our literature is a substitute for religion, and
so is our religion.
A Dialogue on Dramatic Poetry [1928]

16   The general point of view may be described as
classicist in literature, royalist in politics, and Anglo-
Catholic in religion.
For Lancelot Andrewes [1928], preface

17   We fight for lost causes because we know that
our defeat and dismay may be the preface to our
successors' victory, though that victory itself will be
temporary; we fight rather to keep something alive
than in the expectation that anything will triumph.
*For Lancelot Andrewes. Francis Herbert
Bradley*

18   Genuine poetry can communicate before it is
understood.   *Dante [1929]*

19   More can be learned about how to write poetry
from Dante than from any English poet. . . . The
language of each great English poet is his own language; the language of Dante is the perfection of a
common language.   *Dante*

20   Sometimes, however, to be a "ruined man" is itself a vocation.
*The Use of Poetry and the Use of Criticism
[1933]. Wordsworth and Coleridge*

21   As things are, and as fundamentally they must always be, poetry is not a career, but a mug's game.
No honest poet can ever feel quite sure of the permanent value of what he has written: he may have
wasted his time and messed up his life for nothing.
*The Use of Poetry and the Use of Criticism,
conclusion*

---

[1]Donner un sens plus pur aux mots de la tribu. —STÉPHANE
MALLARMÉ, *Le Tombeau d'Edgar Poe*

[2]See Juliana of Norwich, 133:4.

1   Most editors are failed writers—but so are most writers.

From ROBERT GIROUX, *The Education of An Editor [1982]*

Jules Furthman
1888–1960
and
William Faulkner
1897–1962

2   Maybe just whistle. You know how to whistle, don't you, Steve? You just put your lips together and blow.

To Have and Have Not (screenplay) [1944], spoken by Lauren Bacall

Joseph [Patrick] Kennedy
1888–1969

3   Don't get mad, get even.   *Attributed*

Ronald Arbuthnott Knox
1888–1957

4 There once was a man who said, "God
Must think it exceedingly odd
If he finds that this tree
Continues to be
When there's no one about in the Quad."

Limerick on idealism[1]

William L[eonard] Laurence
1888–1977

5   A great ball of fire about a mile in diameter, changing colors as it kept shooting upward, from deep purple to orange, expanding, growing bigger, rising as it was expanding, an elemental force freed from its bonds after being chained for billions of years.

On the first atom bomb explosion.[2] *In the New York Times [September 26, 1945]*

6   At first it was a giant column that soon took the shape of a supramundane mushroom.

On the first atom bomb explosion. In the New York Times [September 26, 1945]

T[homas] E[dward] Lawrence[3]
1888–1935

7 I loved you, so I drew these tides of men into my
    hands and wrote my will across the sky in stars.
To earn you Freedom, the seven-pillared worthy
    house, that your eyes might be shining for me
When we came.

Seven Pillars of Wisdom[4] *[1926], dedication*

8   There could be no honor in a sure success, but much might be wrested from a sure defeat.

Revolt in the Desert [1927], ch. 19

Katherine Mansfield
1888–1923

9   If there was one thing that he hated more than another it was the way she had of waking him in the morning. She did it on purpose, of course. It was her way of establishing her grievance for the day.

Bliss [1920]. Mr. Reginald Peacock's Day

10   I want, by understanding myself, to understand others. I want to be all that I am capable of becoming. . . . This all sounds very strenuous and serious. But now that I have wrestled with it, it's no longer so. I feel happy—deep down. *All is well.*

Journal [1922], last entry

Eugene O'Neill
1888–1953

11   Dat ole davil, sea.

Anna Christie [1922], act I

12   Gimme a whiskey—ginger ale on the side. And don't be stingy, baby.[5]   *Anna Christie, I*

13   We's all poor nuts and things happen, and we yust get mixed in wrong, that's all.

Anna Christie, IV

14   For de little stealin' dey gits you in jail soon or late. For de big stealin' dey makes you emperor and puts you in de Hall o' Fame when you croaks. If dey's one thing I learns in ten years on de Pullman cars listenin' to de white quality talk, it's dat same fact.   *The Emperor Jones [1920], sc. i*

15   *Yank:* Sure! Lock me up! Put me in a cage! Dat's de on'y answer yuh know. G'wan, lock me up!
Policeman: What you been doin'?

---

[1] Dear Sir, Your astonishment's odd: / I am always about in the Quad; / And that's why the tree / Will continue to be, / Since observed by Yours Faithfully, God.— *Anonymous rejoinder*

[2] At Alamogordo, New Mexico [July 16, 1945]. See also Oppenheimer, 768:15.

[3] Lawrence changed his name to T. E. Shaw in 1927.

[4] See *Proverbs 9:1, 21:11.*

[5] Made famous in the movie version (1930) as silent film star Greta Garbo's first speech in a talkie.

Yank: Enough to gimme life for! I was born, see? Sure, dat's de charge. Write it in de blotter. I was born, get me!   *The Hairy Ape [1922], sc. vii*

1   Desire Under the Elms.   *Title of play [1924]*

2   God is a Mother.
         Strange Interlude [1928], pt. I, act V

3   Strange interlude! Yes, our lives are merely strange dark interludes in the electrical display of God the Father!   *Strange Interlude, II, IX*

4   Mourning Becomes Electra.
         Title of dramatic trilogy [1931]

5   The sea hates a coward.
         Mourning Becomes Electra [1931]. The Hunted, act IV

6   The damned don't cry.
         Mourning Becomes Electra. The Haunted, act III

7   The dead! Why can't the dead die!
         Mourning Becomes Electra. The Haunted, IV

8   A Long Day's Journey into Night.
         Title of play [1956]

9   Born in a goddam hotel room and dying in a hotel room!
         Last words. From Louis Shaeffer, *O'Neill: Son and Artist [1973]*

John Crowe Ransom
1888–1974

10 Two evils, monstrous either one apart,
      Possessed me, and were long and loath at going:
      A cry of Absence, Absence, in the heart,
      And in the wood the furious winter blowing.
         Winter Remembered

11 The lazy geese, like a snow cloud
      Dripping their snow on the green grass,
      Tricking and stopping, sleepy and proud,
      Who cried in goose, Alas.
         Bells for John Whiteside's Daughter

12 Here lies a lady of beauty and high degree.
      Of chills and fever she died, of fever and chills,
      The delight of her husband, her aunts, an infant of three,
      And of medicos marveling sweetly on her ills.
         Here Lies a Lady

13 God have mercy on the sinner
      Who must write with no dinner,
      No gravy and no grub,
      No pewter and no pub,

No belly and no bowels,
Only consonants and vowels.   *Survey of Literature*

14 Captain Carpenter rose up in his prime
Put on his pistols and went riding out.
         Captain Carpenter, st. 1

Knute [Kenneth] Rockne
1888–1931

15 Show me a good and gracious loser and I'll show you a failure.[1]
         Remark to Wisconsin basketball coach Walter Meanwell [1920s]

16 Win this one for the Gipper.   *Attributed[2]*

Alan Seeger
1888–1916

17 I have a rendezvous with Death
At some disputed barricade,
When spring comes back with rustling shade
And apple blossoms fill the air.
         I Have a Rendezvous with Death [1916]

18 And I to my pledged word am true,
I shall not fail that rendezvous.
         I Have a Rendezvous with Death

Bartolomeo Vanzetti
1888–1927

19 If it had not been for this thing, I might have lived out my life talking at street corners to scorning men. I might have died unmarked, unknown, a failure. Now we are not a failure. This is our career and our triumph. Never in our full life could we hope to do such work for tolerance, for justice, for man's understanding of man, as now we do by accident.
         Letter to his son [April 1927]

20 Our words—our lives—our pains: nothing! The taking of our lives—lives of a good shoemaker and a poor fish peddler—all! That last moment belongs to us—that agony is our triumph.
         Letter to his son [April 1927]

21 I found myself compelled to fight back from my eyes the tears, and quanch my heart trobling to my throat to not weep before him. But Sacco's name

---

[1]More familiar version: Show me a good loser and I'll show you a loser.

[2]See Buckner, 774:6.

will live in the hearts of the people when your name, your laws, institutions and your false god are but a dim rememoring of a cursed past in which man was wolf to the man.

Last speech to the court[1]

Henry A[gard] Wallace
1888–1965

1   The century on which we are entering can be and must be the century of the common man.

Address, The Price of Free World Victory [May 8, 1942]

Conrad Aiken
1889–1973

2 Music I heard with you was more than music,
And bread I broke with you was more than bread.
Now that I am without you, all is desolate;
All that was once so beautiful is dead.

Bread and Music [1914]

3 All lovely things will have an ending,
All lovely things will fade and die,
And youth, that's now so bravely spending,
Will beg a penny by and by.   *All Lovely Things*

4   The hiss was now becoming a roar—the whole world was a vast moving screen of snow—but even now it said peace, it said remoteness, it said cold, it said sleep.   *Silent Snow, Secret Snow [1932]*

5 Ice is the silent language of the peak;
and fire the silent language of the star.

And in the Human Heart. Sonnet 10

Anna Akhmatova[2]
1889–1966

6 If you can't give me love and peace,
Then give me bitter fame.

Rosary [composed 1913, published 1914]

7 Who will grieve for this woman? Does she not seem too insignificant for our concern?
Yet in my heart I never will deny her,
Who suffered death because she chose to turn.

Lot's Wife [composed 1922–1924]

8 No foreign sky protected me,
no stranger's wing shielded my face.
I stand as witness to the common lot,
survivor of that time, that place.

*Requiem [composed mainly 1935–1940].
Epigraph [composed 1961]*

9   In the terrible years of the Yezhov terror I spent seventeen months waiting in line outside the prison in Leningrad. One day somebody in the crowd identified me . . . and asked me in a whisper . . . "Can you describe this?" And I said: "I can."

*Requiem. Instead of a Preface
[composed 1957]*

10 That was a time when only the dead
could smile.

Requiem. Prologue [composed 1935–1940]

11 I should be proud to have my memory graced,
but only if the monument be placed . . .
here, where I endured three hundred hours
in line before the implacable iron bars.

Requiem. Epilogue [composed 1940], II

Robert [Charles] Benchley
1889–1945

12   Why don't you get out of that wet coat and into a dry martini?   *Attributed*[3]

13   Tell us your phobias and we will tell you what you are afraid of.   *Phobias*

14   In America there are two classes of travel—first-class, and with children.   *Kiddie-Kar Travel*

15   A great many people have come up to me and asked me how I manage to get so much work done and still keep looking so dissipated. My answer is "Don't you wish you knew?"

How to Get Things Done

16   Streets full of water. Please advise.

Telegram from Venice (attributed)

Charlie [Sir Charles Spencer] Chaplin
1889–1977

17   [The tramp character:] A tramp, a gentleman, a poet, a dreamer, a lonely fellow, always hopeful of romance and adventure.

My Autobiography [1964], ch. 10

---

[1]Vanzetti and Nicola Sacco, Italian anarchists, were executed August 23, 1927, by the Commonwealth of Massachusetts on charges, never conclusively proved, of murder and robbery.

[2]Translated by STANLEY KUNITZ with MAX HAYWARD.

[3]Spoken by him in the movie *The Major and the Minor* [1942] but, according to his account, borrowed from a similar line spoken by his friend Charles Butterworth in the Mae West movie *Every Day's a Holiday* [1937].

1   All I need to make a comedy is a park, a police-man, and a pretty girl.   *My Autobiography, 10*

2   I am known in parts of the world by people who have never heard of Jesus Christ.[1]
From LITA GREY CHAPLIN, My Life with Chaplin [1966]

Jean Cocteau
1889–1963

3   Mirrors should reflect a little before throwing back images.   *Des Beaux-Arts*

4   The worst tragedy for a poet is to be admired through being misunderstood.
Le Rappel à l'Ordre [1926]

5 The matters I relate
Are true lies.[2]
The Journals of Jean Cocteau [1956]. Quoted by WALLACE FOWLIE in the introduction

Christopher [Henry] Dawson
1889–1970

6   As soon as men decide that all means are permit-ted to fight an evil, then their good becomes indistin-guishable from the evil that they set out to destroy.
The Judgment of the Nations [1942]

Philip Guedalla
1889–1944

7   The work of Henry James has always seemed di-visible by a simple dynastic arrangement into three reigns: James I, James II, and the Old Pretender.
Supers and Supermen [1920]

Adolf Hitler
1889–1945

8   My adversaries . . . applied the one means that wins the easiest victory over reason: terror and force.
Mein Kampf (My Battle) [1933], vol. I, ch. 2

9   A majority can never replace the man. . . . Just as a hundred fools do not make one wise man, an heroic decision is not likely to come from a hundred cowards.   *Mein Kampf, I, 3*

10   Strength lies not in defense but in attack.
Mein Kampf, I, 3

11   All propaganda has to be popular and has to adapt its spiritual level to the perception of the least intelligent of those towards whom it intends to di-rect itself.   *Mein Kampf, I, 6*

12   The great masses of the people . . . will more easily fall victims to a big lie than to a small one.
Mein Kampf, I, 10

13   Never tolerate the establishment of two conti-nental powers in Europe.   *Mein Kampf, II, 14*

14   After all, who remembers the Armenians?
Attributed remark, prior to the invasion of Poland [1939]

15   After fifteen years of work I have achieved, as a common German soldier and merely with my fanat-ical will power, the unity of the German nation, and have freed it from the death sentence of Versailles.[3]
Proclamation to the troops on taking over the leadership of the German armed forces [December 21, 1941]

16   This war no longer bears the characteristics of former inter-European conflicts. It is one of those elemental conflicts which usher in a new millen-nium and which shake the world once in a thousand years.   *Speech to the Reichstag [April 26, 1942]*

17   Is Paris burning?[4]
Asked at the Oberkommando der Wehrmacht, Rastenburg, Germany [August 25, 1944]

George S. Kaufman
1889–1961

18   Satire is what closes Saturday night.   *Saying*

Stoddard King
1889–1933

19 There's a long, long trail a-winding
Into the land of my dreams,
Where the nightingales are singing
And a white moon beams.
The Long, Long Trail[5] [1913]

---

[1]See Lennon, 834:11.

[2]Les choses que je conte / Sont des mensonges vrais.

[3]The Allied and Associated Governments affirm and Germany accepts the responsibility of Germany and her Allies for causing all the loss and damage to which the Allied and Associated Govern-ments and their nationals have been subjected as a consequence of the war imposed upon them by the aggression of Germany and her Allies. — *Article 231 (the "war guilt clause"), Treaty of Versailles* [June 28, 1919]

[4]Brennt Paris?

[5]Music by ZO ELLIOTT.

Walter Lippmann
1889–1974

1   What each man does is based not on direct and certain knowledge, but on pictures made by himself or given to him. . . . The way in which the world is imagined determines at any particular moment what men will do.

Public Opinion [1922], ch. 1, The World Outside and the Pictures in Our Heads

2   In the great blooming, buzzing confusion of the outer world we pick out what our culture has already defined for us, and we tend to perceive that which we have picked out in the form stereotyped for us by our culture.

Public Opinion, 6, Stereotypes

3   Franklin D. Roosevelt is no crusader. He is no tribune of the people. He is no enemy of entrenched privilege. He is a pleasant man who, without any important qualifications for the office, would very much like to be President.

Today and Tomorrow [January 8, 1932]

4   In government offices which are sensitive to the vehemence and passion of mass sentiment public men have no sure tenure. They are in effect perpetual office seekers, always on trial for their political lives, always required to court their restless constituents.   *Essays in the Public Philosophy [1935]*

5   A free press is not a privilege but an organic necessity in a great society. . . . A great society is simply a big and complicated urban society.

Address at the International Press Institute Assembly, London [May 27, 1965]

6   Responsible journalism is journalism responsible in the last analysis to the editor's own conviction of what, whether interesting or only important, is in the public interest.

Address at the International Press Institute Assembly, London [May 27, 1965]

Jawaharlal Nehru
1889–1964

7   I want nothing to do with any religion concerned with keeping the masses satisfied to live in hunger, filth, and ignorance. I want nothing to do with any order, religious or otherwise, which does not teach people that they are capable of becoming happier and more civilized, on this earth, capable of becoming true *man*, master of his fate and captain of his soul.

From EDGAR SNOW, Journey to the Beginning [1958]

Arnold Joseph Toynbee
1889–1975

8   Civilizations, I believe, come to birth and proceed to grow by successfully responding to successive challenges. They break down and go to pieces if and when a challenge confronts them which they fail to meet.   *Civilization on Trial [1948], ch. 4*

9   America is a large, friendly dog in a very small room. Every time it wags its tail it knocks over a chair.   *Attributed*

Ludwig [Josef Johann] Wittgenstein
1889–1951

10   The world is all that is the case.[1]

Tractatus Logico-Philosophicus [1922]. 1

11   What we cannot speak about we must pass over in silence.[2]   *Tractatus Logico-Philosophicus, 7*

Vannevar Bush
1890–1974

12   It was through the Second World War that most of us suddenly appreciated for the first time the power of man's concentrated efforts to understand and control the forces of nature. We were appalled by what we saw.   *Science Is Not Enough [1967]*

Karel Čapek
1890–1938

13   Rossum's Universal Robots.[3]

R.U.R. [1920]

Agatha Christie
1890–1976

14   "This affair must all be unraveled from within." He [Hercule Poirot] tapped his forehead. "These little gray cells. It is 'up to them'—as you say over here."

The Mysterious Affair at Styles [1920], ch. 10

15   Every murderer is probably somebody's old friend.   *The Mysterious Affair at Styles, 11*

16   It is completely unimportant. That is why it is so interesting.   *The Murder of Roger Ackroyd [1926]*

---

[1] Die Welt ist alles, was der Fall ist.
Translated by D. F. PEARS and B. F. McGUINNESS.

[2] Wovon man nicht sprechen kann, darüber muss man schweigen.

[3] The term "robot" came into English through Čapek's play.

1   I don't think necessity is the mother of invention — invention, in my opinion, arises directly from idleness, possibly also from laziness. To save oneself trouble.
An Autobiography [1977], pt. III,
Growing Up

2   If you love, you will suffer, and if you do not love, you do not know the meaning of a Christian life.   *An Autobiography, III, Growing Up*

Marc[us Cook] Connelly
1890–1980

3   Gangway for de Lawd God Jehovah!
The Green Pastures[1] *[1930]*

4   *God:* I'll jest r'ar back an' pass a miracle.
The Green Pastures

5   *Gabriel:* How about cleanin' up de whole mess of 'em and sta'tin' all over ag'in wid some new kind of animal?
God: An' admit I'm licked?
The Green Pastures

6   Even bein' Gawd ain't a bed of roses.
The Green Pastures

Charles [André Joseph Marie] de Gaulle
1890–1970

7   France has lost a battle. But France has not lost the war.
Broadcast from London to the French people
after the fall of France [June 18, 1940]

8   Since those whose duty it was to hold the sword of France have let it fall, I have picked up its broken point.   *Radio address [July 13, 1940]*

9   If I live, I will fight, wherever I must, as long as I must, until the enemy is defeated and the national stain washed clean.
Les Mémoires de Guerre, vol. I [1954]

10   France cannot be France without greatness.
Les Mémoires de Guerre, I

11   I always thought I was Jeanne d'Arc and Bonaparte. How little one knows oneself.
Reply to speaker who compared him to
Robespierre. From Figaro Littéraire [1958]

12   When I want to know what France thinks, I question myself.
From JEAN-RAYMOND TOURNOUX, Sons of
France [1966]

13   Only peril can bring the French together. One can't impose unity out of the blue on a country that has 265 different kinds of cheese.   *Attributed*

Marjory Stoneman Douglas
1890–1998

14   There are no other Everglades in the world. . . . The miracle of the light pours over the green and brown expanse of saw grass and of water, shining and slow-moving below, the grass and water that is the meaning of the central fact of the Everglades of Florida. It is a river of grass.
The Everglades: River of Grass [1947], ch. 1

Dwight D[avid] Eisenhower
1890–1969

15   People of Western Europe: A landing was made this morning on the coast of France by troops of the Allied Expeditionary Force. This landing is part of the concerted United Nations plan for the liberation of Europe, made in conjunction with our great Russian allies. . . . I call upon all who love freedom to stand with us now. Together we shall achieve victory.   *Broadcast on D-Day [June 6, 1944]*

16   This conjunction of an immense military establishment and a large arms industry is new in the American experience. We must guard against the acquisition of unwarranted influence, whether sought or unsought, by the military-industrial complex. The potential for the disastrous rise of misplaced power exists and will persist.
Farewell Radio and Television Address to the
American People [January 17, 1961]

17   Biggest damfool mistake I ever made.
Recalling his appointment [1953] of Earl
Warren as Chief Justice of the United States

Gene Fowler
1890–1960

18   Writing is easy. All you do is stare at a blank sheet of paper until drops of blood form on your forehead.   *Attributed*[2]

---

[1]Suggested by Roark Bradford's stories, *Ol' Man Adam an' His Chillun* [1928].

[2]Also attributed (in a variant form) to sports columnist RED [WALTER WELLESLEY] SMITH [1905–1982].

Sir Alan Patrick Herbert
1890–1971

1   The Common Law of England has been laboriously built upon a mythical figure—the figure of "The Reasonable Man."
Uncommon Law [1935], p. 1

2   The critical period in matrimony is breakfast-time.
Uncommon Law, p. 98

3   An Act of God was defined as something which no reasonable man could have expected.
Uncommon Law, p. 316

Samuel Hoffenstein
1890–1947

4 Babies haven't any hair;
Old men's heads are just as bare;
Between the cradle and the grave
Lies a haircut and a shave.
Songs of Faith in the Year After Next, VIII

Gerald White Johnson
1890–1980

5   Heroes are created by popular demand, sometimes out of the scantiest materials, or none at all.
American Heroes and Hero-Worship [1943], ch. 1

6   In revolutionary times the rich are always the people who are most afraid.
American Freedom and the Press [1958]

Hanns Johst
1890–1978

7   When I hear the word "culture" . . . I reach for my pistol.[1]
Schlageter [1933]

Robert Ley
1890–1945

8   Strength through joy.[2]
Instruction for the German Labor Front [December 2, 1933]

H[oward] P[hillips] Lovecraft
1890–1937

9   The most merciful thing in the world, I think, is the inability of the human mind to correlate all its contents.
The Call of Cthulhu [1928], ch. 1

William A. Maguire
1890–1953

10   Praise the Lord and pass the ammunition.[3]
Attributed

Claude McKay
1890–1948

11 Upon the clothes behind the tenement,
That hang like ghosts suspended from the lines,
Linking each flat, but to each indifferent,
Incongruous and strange the moonlight shines.
A Song of the Moon

12 Although she feeds me bread of bitterness,
And sinks into my throat her tiger's tooth,
Stealing my breath of life, I must confess
I love this cultured hell that tests my youth!
Her vigor flows like tides into my blood,
Giving me strength erect against her hate.
Her bigness sweeps my being like a flood.
America

13 If we must die, let it not be like hogs
Hunted and penned in an inglorious spot.
If We Must Die

Christopher Morley
1890–1957

14   There is only one success—to be able to spend your life in your own way.
Where the Blue Begins [1922]

15   Life is a foreign language; all men mispronounce it.
Thunder on the Left [1925], ch. 14

16 There was so much handwriting on the wall
That even the wall fell down.
Around the Clock [1943]

17 Chattering voltage like a broken wire
The wild cicada cried, Six weeks to frost!
End of August

---

[1]Wenn ich Kultur höre . . . entsichere ich meinen Browning. Often attributed to HERMANN GOERING.

[2]Kraft durch Freude.

---

[3]Basis of the popular World War II song [1942] of that title by FRANK LOESSER [1910–1969].

1   Why do they put the Gideon Bibles only in the bedrooms, where it's usually too late, and not in the barroom downstairs?

Contribution to a Contribution

Boris Pasternak
1890–1960

2   Art is unthinkable without risk and spiritual self-sacrifice.

On Modesty and Bravery [1936]. Speech at Writers' Conference [1]

3   I am alone; all drowns in the Pharisees' hypocrisy.
To live your life is not as simple as to cross a field. [2]

Hamlet [1946] [3]

4   You are eternity's hostage
A captive of time.   *Night [1957]* [3]

5   But what are pity, conscience, or fear
To the brazen pair, compared
With the living sorcery
Of their hot embraces?

Bacchanalia [1957], [3] *st. 4*

6   During the last years of Mayakovski's life, [4] when all poetry had ceased to exist . . . literature had stopped.   *I Remember [1958]* [5]

7   It snowed and snowed, the whole world over,
Snow swept the world from end to end.
A candle burned on the table;
A candle burned.

Doctor Zhivago [1958]. [6] *The Poems of Yurii Zhivago (ch. 17),* [7] *Winter Night, st. 1*

8   A corner draft fluttered the flame
And the white fever of temptation
Upswept its angel wings that cast
A cruciform shadow.

Doctor Zhivago. The Poems of Yurii Zhivago (ch. 17) [7], *Winter Night, st. 7*

9   Man is born to live, not to prepare for life. Life itself, the phenomenon of life, the gift of life, is so breathtakingly serious!   *Doctor Zhivago, ch. 9*

10   And when the war broke out, its real horrors, its real dangers, its menace of real death were a bless-ing compared with the inhuman reign of the lie, and they brought relief because they broke the spell of the dead letter.   *Doctor Zhivago, epilogue*

11   Departure beyond the borders of my country is for me equivalent to death.

Letter to Nikita Khrushchev [1958] [1]

12 I am caught like a beast at bay.
Somewhere are people, freedom, light,
But all I hear is the baying of the pack,
There is no way out for me.

The Nobel Prize [1959] [3]

"Red" Rowley
fl. 1915

13 Mademoiselle from Armenteers,
Hasn't been kissed in forty years,
Hinky dinky, parley-voo.

Mademoiselle from Armentières [8]

14 Mademoiselle from St. Nazaire,
She never heard of underwear.

Mademoiselle from Armentières

Casey [Charles Dillon] Stengel
c. 1890–1975

15   I had many years that I was not so successful as a ballplayer, as it is a game of skill.

Testimony before U.S. Senate Subcommittee on Antitrust and Monopoly [July 9, 1958]

16   There comes a time in every man's life and I've had many of them.   *Remark*

17   Most people my age are dead.   *Remark*

Joseph N[ye] Welch
1890–1960

18   Until this moment, Senator, I think I never really gauged your cruelty or your recklessness. . . . Have you no sense of decency, sir, at long last? Have you left no sense of decency?

Response to Senator Joseph R. McCarthy during Senate hearings on alleged subversive activities in the U.S. Army [June 9, 1954]

---

[1] Translated by ELENA LEVIN.

[2] See Anonymous: Russian, 861:18.

[3] Translated by MAX HAYWARD.

[4] Vladimir Mayakovski [1893–1930].

[5] Translated by MANYA HARARI.

[6] Translated by MAX HAYWARD and MANYA HARARI.

[7] *The Poems of Yurii Zhivago* translated by BERNARD GUILBERT GUERNEY.

[8] Soldiers' song of World War I, with innumerable versions. The tune and verse structure were based on a British Army song composed by ALFRED JAMES WALDEN ["HARRY WINCOTT," 1867–1947].

Charles E[rwin] Wilson
1890–1961

1   For years I thought what was good for our country was good for General Motors, and vice versa. The difference did not exist.
To the Senate Committee on Armed Services [1953]

Waldemar Young
1890–1938

2   We have ways of making men talk.
Lives of a Bengal Lancer (screenplay) [1935]

Ely Culbertson
1891–1955

3   The bizarre world of cards . . . a world of pure power politics where rewards and punishments were meted out immediately. A deck of cards was built like the purest of hierarchies, with every card a master to those below it and a lackey to those above it. And there were "masses"—long suits—which always asserted themselves in the end, triumphing over the kings and aces.
Total Peace [1943], ch. 1

Karl Kelchner Darrow
1891–1982

4   One of the things which distinguishes ours from all earlier generations is this, that we have seen our atoms.   *The Renaissance of Physics [1936]*

Al Dubin
1891–1945

5   Tip-Toe Thru' the Tulips with Me.
Title of song [1939][1]

Antonio Gramsci
1891–1937

6   State = political society + civil society, in other words hegemony protected by the armor of coercion.   *Prison Notebooks [1933–1934]*

Jack McGowan
1891–1977

and

Kay Van Riper
d. 1948

7   Come on, kids, let's put on a show!
Babes in Arms (screenplay) [1939], spoken by Mickey Rooney

Haile Selassie
1891–1975

8   Outside the kingdom of the Lord there is no nation which is greater than any other. God and history will remember your judgment.
Speech, the League of Nations [1936][2]

Hu Shih[3]
1891–1962

9   Only when we realize that there is no eternal, unchanging truth or absolute truth can we arouse in ourselves a sense of intellectual responsibility.
La Jeunesse Nouvelle [April 1919]

Jomo Kenyatta [Kamau Wa Ngengi]
1891–1978

10   The African is conditioned, by the cultural and social institutions of centuries, to a freedom of which Europe has little conception, and it is not in his nature to accept serfdom forever. He realizes that he must fight unceasingly for his own complete emancipation; for without this he is doomed to remain the prey of rival imperialisms.
Facing Mount Kenya: The Tribal Life of the Gikuyu (Kikuyu) [1938], conclusion

11   We must try to trust one another. Stay and cooperate.[4]
Statement, as first president of the Republic of Kenya, to the white settlers [1964]

---

[2]He sought sanctions against Italy, which had invaded Ethiopia.
[3]From *Sources of Chinese Tradition* [1960], edited by WILLIAM THEODORE DE BARY.
[4]Harambee [Swahili for "Let's pull together"].—*National motto of Kenya*

---

[1]Music by JOE BURKE.

David Low
1891–1963

1   I have never met anybody who wasn't against war. Even Hitler and Mussolini were, according to themselves.
From the New York Times [February 10, 1946]

Osip Emilevich Mandelstam
1891–1938

2 We live, deaf to the land beneath us,
Ten steps away no one hears our speeches,

But where there's so much as half a conversation
The Kremlin's mountaineer will get his mention.
Stalin [1934], st. 1, 2

3 One by one forging his laws, to be flung
Like horseshoes at the head, the eye, or the groin.

And every killing is a treat
For the broad-chested Ossete.   *Stalin, st. 7, 8*

Irene Rutherford McLeod
1891–1964

4 I'm a lean dog, a keen dog, a wild dog, and lone.
Songs to Save a Soul [1919]. Lone Dog

Henry Miller
1891–1980

5   Every man with a bellyful of the classics is an enemy to the human race.   *Tropic of Cancer [1934]*

6   It's good to be just plain happy; it's a little better to know that you're happy; but to understand that you're happy and to know why and how . . . and still be happy, be happy in the being and the knowing, well that is beyond happiness, that is bliss.
The Colossus of Maroussi [1941], pt. I

Elliot Paul
1891–1958

7   The last time I see Paris will be on the day I die. The city was inexhaustible, and so is its memory.
The Last Time I Saw Paris [1942], pt. II, 23

Michael Polanyi
1891–1976

8   An art which has fallen into disuse for the period of a generation is altogether lost. . . . It is pathetic to watch the endless efforts—equipped with microscopy and chemistry, with mathematics and electronics—to reproduce a single violin of the kind the half-literate Stradivarius turned out as a matter of routine more than two hundred years ago.
Personal Knowledge [1958]

Cole [Albert] Porter
1891–1964

9 You do something to me,
Something that simply mystifies me.
Fifty Million Frenchmen [1929]. You Do Something to Me

10 Night and day you are the one,
Only you beneath the moon and under the sun.
Gay Divorce [1932]. Night and Day

11 I get no kick from champagne.
Mere alcohol doesn't thrill me at all,
So tell me why should it be true
That I get a kick out of you.
Anything Goes [1934]. I Get a Kick Out of You

12 You're the Nile,
You're the Tower of Pisa,
You're the smile
On the Mona Lisa. . . .
But if, Baby, I'm the bottom you're the top!
Anything Goes. You're the Top!

13 It was great fun,
But it was just one of those things.
Jubilee [1935]. Just One of Those Things

14 It's delightful, it's delicious, it's de-lovely.
Red, Hot and Blue [1936]. It's De-Lovely

15 But I'm always true to you, darlin', in my fashion,
Yes, I'm always true to you, darlin', in my way.
Kiss Me, Kate [1948]. Always True to You in My Fashion

Nicola Sacco[1]
1891–1927

16   Help the weak ones that cry for help, help the prosecuted and the victim . . . they are the comrades that fight and fall . . . for the conquest of the joy of freedom for all the poor workers. In this struggle for life you will find more love and you will be loved.   *Letter to his son Dante*

---

[1]See Vanzetti, 725:*n*1.

Earl Warren
1891–1974

1   To separate [black children] from others of similar age and qualifications solely because of their race generates a feeling of inferiority as to their status in the community that may affect their hearts and minds in a way unlikely ever to be undone. . . . We conclude that in the field of public education the doctrine of "separate but equal"[1] has no place. Separate educational facilities are inherently unequal.

Brown v. Board of Education of Topeka, 347 U.S. 483 [1954][2]

2   When an individual is taken into custody or otherwise deprived of his freedom by the authorities and is subjected to questioning . . . he must be warned prior to any questioning that he has the right to remain silent, that anything he says can be used against him in a court of law, that he has the right to the presence of an attorney, and that if he cannot afford an attorney one will be appointed for him prior to any questioning if he so desires.

Miranda v. Arizona, 384 U.S. 436 [1965]

George Aiken
1892–1984

3   The United States could well declare unilaterally that this stage of the Vietnam war is over — that we have "won" in the sense that our Armed Forces are in control of most of the field and no potential enemy is in a position to establish its authority over South Vietnam.

Speech in the U.S. Senate [October 19, 1966]

Walter Benjamin
1892–1940

4   Of all the ways of acquiring books, writing them oneself is regarded as the most praiseworthy method. . . . Writers are really people who write books not because they are poor, but because they are dissatisfied with the books which they could buy but do not like.   *Unpacking My Library [1931][3]*

---

[1]All railway companies carrying passengers in their coaches in the state shall provide equal but separate accommodations for the white and colored races. — *Louisiana Acts of 1890, no. III, p. 152;* quoted by Mr. Justice HENRY B. BROWN in *Plessy v. Ferguson, 163 U.S. 537* [1896]

[2]In a later implementation of the same case (*349 U.S. 294* [1955]), the Supreme Court asked that desegregation proceed "with all deliberate speed."

[3]Translated by HARRY ZOHN.

5   The products of art and science owe their existence not merely to the effort of the great geniuses that created them, but also to the unnamed drudgery of their contemporaries. There is no document of culture which is not at the same time a document of barbarism.

Edward Fuchs: Collector and Historian [1937]

Stella Benson
1892–1933

6 Call no man foe, but never love a stranger.

To the Unborn, st. 3

Charles Brackett
1892–1969

and

Billy [Samuel] Wilder
1906–2002

7   [Joe Gillis]: You used to be in silent pictures. You used to be big.

   [Norma Desmond]: I *am* big. It's the *pictures* that got small.

Sunset Boulevard (screenplay) [1950], spoken by William Holden and Gloria Swanson

Pearl S[ydenstricker] Buck
1892–1973

8   Our society must make it right and possible for old people not to fear the young or be deserted by them, for the test of a civilization is the way that it cares for its helpless members.

My Several Worlds [1954]

Walter C. Hagen
1892–1969

9   You're only here for a short visit. Don't hurry. Don't worry. And be sure to smell the flowers along the way.   *The Walter Hagen Story [1956]*

John Burdon Sanderson Haldane
1892–1964

10   Now, my suspicion is that the universe is not only queerer than we suppose, but queerer than we *can* suppose. . . . I suspect that there are more things in

heaven and earth than are dreamed of, in any philosophy. That is the reason why I have no philosophy myself, and must be my excuse for dreaming.
Possible Worlds [1927]

Robert H[oughwout] Jackson
1892–1954

1   If there is any fixed star in our constitutional constellation, it is that no official, high or petty, can prescribe what shall be orthodox in politics, nationalism, religion, or other matters of opinion or force citizens to confess by word or act their faith therein.
West Virginia State Board of Education v. Barnett, 319 U.S. 642 [1943]

2   The first trial in history for crimes against the peace of the world imposes a grave responsibility. The wrongs which we seek to condemn and punish have been so calculated, so malignant and so devastating that civilization cannot tolerate their being ignored because it cannot survive their being repeated.
Opening address before the International Military Tribunal, Nuremberg [1945]

3   There is danger that, if the Court does not temper its doctrinaire logic with a little practical wisdom, it will convert the constitutional Bill of Rights into a suicide pact.
Terminiello v. Chicago, 337 U.S. 1, 37 [1949]

4   The day that this country ceases to be free for irreligion, it will cease to be free for religion.
Dissenting opinion, Zorach v. Clausor, 343 U.S. 306, 325 [1952]

Robert S[taughton] Lynd
1892–1970

and

Helen Merrell Lynd
1896–1982

5   It is characteristic of mankind to make as little adjustment as possible in customary ways in the face of new conditions; the process of social change is epitomized in the fact that the first Packard car body delivered to the manufacturer had a whipstock on the dashboard.   *Middletown [1929], pt. VI, ch. 29*

Archibald MacLeish
1892–1982

6 There with vast wings across the canceled skies,
There in the sudden blackness the black pall
Of nothing, nothing, nothing—nothing at all.
The End of the World [1926]

7 A poem should not mean
But be.   *Ars Poetica [1926]*

8 And here face downward in the sun
To feel how swift how secretly
The shadow of the night comes on.
You, Andrew Marvell [1930]

9 We were the first that found that famous country:
We marched by a king's name: we crossed the
    sierras:
Unknown hardships we suffered: hunger.
Conquistador [1932]. Bernál Díaz' Preface

10 She lies on her left side her flank golden:
Her hair is burned black with the strong sun.
The scent of her hair is of rain in the dust on her
    shoulders:
She has brown breasts and the mouth of no other
    country.
Frescoes for Mr. Rockefeller's City [1933]. Landscape as a Nude, st. 1

11 America was promises . . .
It was Man who had been promised.
America Was Promises [1939]

12   Races didn't bother the Americans. They were something a lot better than any race. They were a People. They were the first self-constituted, self-created People in the history of the world.
The American Cause [1940]

13 old age
level light
evening in the afternoon
love without the bitterness and so
good-night   *Definitions of Old Age [1976]*

Edna St. Vincent Millay
1892–1950

14 All I could see from where I stood
Was three long mountains and a wood.
Renascence [1912], l. 1

15 The world stands out on either side
No wider than the heart is wide;
Above the world is stretched the sky,—
No higher than the soul is high.
The heart can push the sea and land
Farther away on either hand;
The soul can split the sky in two,
And let the face of God shine through.
But East and West will pinch the heart
That can not keep them pushed apart;
And he whose soul is flat—the sky
Will cave in on him by and by.

Renascence, last lines

1 O world, I cannot hold thee close enough!
>> *God's World [1917], st. 1*

2 My candle burns at both ends;
>> It will not last the night;
>> But, ah, my foes, and, oh, my friends—
>> It gives a lovely light.[1]
>> *A Few Figs from Thistles [1920]. First Fig*

3 We were very tired, we were very merry—
>> We had gone back and forth all night on the ferry.
>> *A Few Figs from Thistles. Recuerdo*

4 Whether or not we find what we are seeking
>> Is idle, biologically speaking.
>> *A Few Figs from Thistles. I Shall Forget You
>> Presently, l. 13*

5 Death devours all lovely things;
>> Lesbia with her sparrow
>> Shares the darkness—presently
>> Every bed is narrow.
>> *Passer Mortuus Est [1921], st. 1*

6 I know I am but summer to your heart,
>> And not the full four seasons of the year.
>> *I Know I Am But Summer [1923], l. 1*

7 I only know that summer sang in me
>> A little while, that in me sings no more.
>> *What Lips My Lips Have Kissed [1923], l. 13*

8 Euclid alone
>> Has looked on Beauty bare. Fortunate they
>> Who, though once only and then but far away,
>> Have heard her massive sandal set on stone.
>> *Euclid Alone Has Looked on Beauty Bare
>> [1923], l. 11*

9 If ever I said, in grief or pride,
>> I tired of honest things, I lied.
>> *The Goose Girl [1923], l. 5*

10 How strange a thing is death, bringing to his
>> knees, bringing to his antlers
>> The buck in the snow . . .
>> Life, looking out attentive from the eyes of
>> the doe.
>> *The Buck in the Snow [1928]*

11 I am not resigned to the shutting away of loving
>> hearts in the hard ground.
>> So it is, and so it will be, for so it has been, time
>> out of mind:
>> Into the darkness they go, the wise and the lovely.
>> Crowned
>> With lilies and with laurel they go; but I am not
>> resigned.
>> *Dirge Without Music [1928], st. 1*

12 Love is not all: it is not meat nor drink
>> Nor slumber nor a roof against the rain;
>> Nor yet a floating spar to men that sink.
>> *Love Is Not All [1931], l. 1*

Reinhold Niebuhr
1892–1971

13 God, give us grace to accept with serenity the things that cannot be changed, courage to change the things which should be changed, and the wisdom to distinguish the one from the other.
>> *The Serenity Prayer [1943]*

14 Goodness, armed with power, is corrupted; and pure love without power is destroyed.
>> *Beyond Tragedy [1938]*

15 The prophet himself stands under the judgment which he preaches. If he does not know that, he is a false prophet. *Beyond Tragedy*

16 Humor is a prelude to faith and
>> Laughter is the beginning of prayer.
>> *Discerning the Signs of the Times [1949]*

17 Nothing worth doing is completed in our lifetime; therefore, we must be saved by hope. Nothing true or beautiful or good makes complete sense in any immediate context of history; therefore, we must be saved by faith. Nothing we do, however virtuous, can be accomplished alone; therefore, we are saved by love.
>> *The Irony of American History [1952]*

Martin Niemoeller
1892–1984

18 In Germany they came first for the Communists, and I didn't speak up because I wasn't a Communist. Then they came for the Jews, and I didn't speak up because I wasn't a Jew. Then they came for the trade unionists, and I didn't speak up because I wasn't a trade unionist. Then they came for the Catholics, and I didn't speak up because I was a Protestant. Then they came for me, and by that time no one was left to speak up.

>> *Attributed*

Harold [Wallace] Ross
1892–1951

19 *The New Yorker* will not be edited for the old lady from Dubuque.[2]
>> *Upon founding The New Yorker [1925]*

---

[1]I burned my candle at both ends, / And now have neither foes nor friends.—SAMUEL HOFFENSTEIN, *Songs of Fairly Utter Despair, 8*

[2]Later this became "the little old lady from Dubuque."

1   Is Moby Dick the whale or the man?
    From JAMES THURBER, *The Years with Ross*
    [1958]

2   I understand the hero [of Ernest Hemingway's *A Farewell to Arms*] keeps getting in bed with women, and the war wasn't fought that way.
    From JAMES THURBER, *The Years with Ross*

J[ohn] R[onald] R[euel] Tolkien
1892–1973

3   In a hole in the ground there lived a hobbit. Not a nasty, dirty, wet hole, filled with the ends of worms and an oozy smell, nor yet a dry, bare, sandy hole with nothing in it to sit down on or to eat: it was a hobbit-hole, and that means comfort.
    The Hobbit; or There and Back Again [1937],
    ch. 1

4   One Ring to rule them all, One Ring to find them,
    One Ring to bring them all and in the darkness
        bind them.
    The Fellowship of the Ring [1965], bk. I, ch. 2

Mae West
1892–1980

5   Goodness had nothing to do with it.[1]
    Night After Night (screenplay) [1932]

6   Why don't you come up sometime and see me?[2] . . . Come on up, I'll tell your fortune.
    She Done Him Wrong (screenplay) [1933]

7   Beulah, peel me a grape.
    I'm No Angel (screenplay) [1933]

8   When I'm good, I'm very good, but when I'm bad I'm better.   *I'm No Angel*

9   When caught between two evils, I generally like to take the one I never tried.
    Klondike Annie (screenplay) [1936]

10   You're no oil painting, but you're a fascinating monster.   *Klondike Annie*

Wendell L[ewis] Willkie
1892–1944

11   Freedom is an indivisible word. If we want to enjoy it, and fight for it, we must be prepared to extend it to everyone, whether they are rich or poor, whether they agree with us or not, no matter what their race or the color of their skin.
    One World, ch. 13

12   The Constitution does not provide for first and second class citizens.
    An American Program [1944], ch. 2

Jack Yellen
1892–1991

13 Happy days are here again,
    The skies above are clear again:
    Let us sing a song of cheer again,
    Happy days are here again!
    Happy Days Are Here Again [1929][3]

Omar Bradley
1893–1981

14   The world has achieved brilliance without conscience. Ours is a world of nuclear giants and ethical infants.   *Address on Armistice Day [1948]*

15   In war there is no second prize for the runner-up.
    In the Military Review [February 1950]

16   Red China is not the powerful nation seeking to dominate the world. Frankly, in the opinion of the Joint Chiefs of Staff, this strategy would involve us in the wrong war, at the wrong place, at the wrong time, and with the wrong enemy.
    Testimony to the Committee on Armed Services and Committee on Foreign Affairs, U.S. Senate [May 15, 1951]

Lew Brown
1893–1958

and

Buddy [George Gard] De Sylva
1895–1950

17 And love can come to everyone,
    The best things in life are free.
    Good News [1927].[4] The Best Things in Life Are Free

18 Keep your sunny side up.
    Sunny Side Up [1929],[4] title song

---

[1]In reply to "Goodness, what beautiful diamonds!"
Also the title of her autobiography [1959].

[2]Frequently misquoted as "Come up and see me sometime."

---

[3]With music by MILTON AGER [1893–1979], this song was played at the 1932 Democratic presidential convention and became a campaign song for Franklin D. Roosevelt.

[4]Music by RAY HENDERSON.

James Bryant Conant
1893–1978

1   He who enters a university walks on hallowed ground.
Notes on the Harvard Tercentenary [1936]

2   There is only one proved method of assisting the advancement of pure science — that of picking men of genius, backing them heavily, and leaving them to direct themselves.
Letter to the New York Times [August 13, 1945]

Jimmy [James Francis] Durante
1893–1980

3   Goodnight, Mrs. Calabash, wherever you are.
Radio series sign-off [1942]

4   Dese are de conditions dat prevail.   *Saying*

5   Stop da music!   *Saying*

Hermann Goering
1893–1946

6   Shoot first and inquire afterwards, and if you make mistakes, I will protect you.
Instruction for the Prussian police [1933]

7   Submit to me as soon as possible a draft showing . . . measures already taken for the execution of the intended final solution of the Jewish question.
Directive (drafted by Adolf Eichmann)[1] to Reinhard Heydrich [July 31, 1941]

Harold [Joseph] Laski
1893–1950

8   We live under a system by which the many are exploited by the few, and war is the ultimate sanction of that exploitation.   *Plan or Perish [1945]*

9   It would be madness to let the purposes or the methods of private enterprise set the habits of the age of atomic energy.   *Plan or Perish*

Anita Loos
1893–1981

10   Gentlemen always seem to remember blondes.
Gentlemen Prefer Blondes [1925], ch. 1

11   She always believed in the old adage, "Leave them while you're looking good."
Gentlemen Prefer Blondes, 1

12   Kissing your hand may make you feel very, very good, but a diamond and sapphire bracelet lasts forever.
Gentlemen Prefer Blondes, 4

Mao Tse-tung
1893–1976

13   A revolution is not the same as inviting people to dinner, or writing an essay, or painting a picture . . . A revolution is an insurrection, an act of violence by which one class overthrows another.
Selected Works of Mao Tse-tung [1965], vol. I, p. 28

14   Every Communist must grasp the truth: "Political power grows out of the barrel of a gun."
Selected Works of Mao Tse-tung, II, 224

15   Weapons are an important factor in war, but not the decisive one; it is man and not materials that counts.
Lecture [1938]

16   War cannot for a single minute be separated from politics.
Lecture

17   The people are like water and the army is like fish.
Aspects of China's Anti-Japanese Struggle [1948]

18   The policy of letting a hundred flowers blossom and a hundred schools of thought contend is designed to promote the flourishing of the arts and the progress of science; it is designed to enable a socialist culture to thrive in our land.
Speech at Peking [February 27, 1957]

John P[hillips] Marquand
1893–1960

19   It is worthwhile for anyone to have behind him a few generations of honest, hard-working ancestry.
The Late George Apley [1937], ch. 3

20   Marriage . . . is a damnably serious business, particularly around Boston.
The Late George Apley, 11

---

[1]See Eichmann, 773:*n2.*

Vladimir Vladimirovich Mayakovski
1893–1930

1 If you wish,
  I shall grow irreproachably tender:
  Not a man, but a cloud in trousers!
  Cloud in Trousers [1915][1]

2 Citizen!
  Consider my traveling expenses:
  Poetry—
      all of it—
          is a journey to the unknown.
  *Conversation with a Tax Collector About
  Poetry [1926]*[2]

3 Then there's amortization,
          the deadliest of all,
  Amortization
          of the heart and soul.
  *Conversation with a Tax Collector About
  Poetry*

4 But I subdued myself,
          setting my heel
  On the throat
          of my own song.   *At the Top of My Voice*[1]

Wilfred Owen
1893–1918

5 Above all, this book is not concerned with Poetry,
  The subject of it is War, and the pity of War.
  The Poetry is in the pity.
  All a poet can do is warn.[3]   *Poems [1920], preface*

6 What passing bells for these who die as cattle?
  Only the monstrous anger of the guns.
  Only the stuttering rifles' rapid rattle
  Can patter out their hasty orisons.
  The Anthem for Doomed Youth, st. 1

7 And each slow dusk a drawing-down of blinds.
  The Anthem for Doomed Youth, st. 1

8 Red lips are not so red
  As the stained stones kissed by the English dead.
  Greater Love

9 Courage was mine, and I had mystery,
  Wisdom was mine, and I had mastery:
  To miss the march of this retreating world
  Into vain citadels that are not walled.
  Strange Meeting

---

³Translated by GEORGE REAVEY.

²Translated by MAX HAYWARD.

³The last three lines serve as the motto for Benjamin Britten's
War Requiem (Op. 66), which uses the Latin text of the Mass for
the Dead and some of the poems of Wilfred Owen.

Dorothy Parker
1893–1967

10 Four be the things I am wiser to know:
  Idleness, sorrow, a friend, and a foe.
  Enough Rope [1927]. Inventory, st. 1

11 Four be the things I'd been better without:
  Love, curiosity, freckles, and doubt.
  Enough Rope. Inventory, st. 2

12 Scratch a lover, and find a foe.
  *Enough Rope. Ballade of a Great Weariness,
  st. 1*

13 Men seldom make passes
  At girls who wear glasses.
  Enough Rope. News Item

14 Guns aren't lawful;
  Nooses give;
  Gas smells awful;
  You might as well live.   *Enough Rope. Résumé*

15 Why is it no one ever sent me yet
  One perfect limousine, do you suppose?
  Ah no, it's always just my luck to get
      One perfect rose.
  Enough Rope. One Perfect Rose, st. 3

16   Tonstant Weader Fwowed up.
     *Review of A. A. MILNE, The House at Pooh
     Corner [1928]*[4]

17   Runs the gamut of emotions from A to B.
     *Attributed theater review, comment on a
     player*

18   One more drink and I'll be under the host.
                                          Attributed

19   Excuse my dust.   *Epitaph, suggested by herself*

Frederick Salomon Perls
1893–1970

20 I do my thing, and you do your thing . . .
  You are you and I am I,
  And if by chance we find each other, it's beautiful;
  If not, it can't be helped.
  Gestalt Therapy Verbatim [1969]

Dorothy L[eigh] Sayers
1893–1957

21   The worst sin—perhaps the only sin—passion
can commit, is to be joyless.
  Gaudy Night [1936], ch. 23

---

⁴See Milne, 697.

Albert Szent-Györgyi von Nagyrapolt
1893–1986

1   The real scientist . . . is ready to bear privation and, if need be, starvation rather than let anyone dictate to him which direction his work must take.
Science Needs Freedom. From World Digest [1943]

2   Discovery consists of seeing what everybody has seen and thinking what nobody has thought.
From I. J. Good (ed.), The Scientist Speculates [1962]

Fred Allen [John Florence Sullivan]
1894–1956

3   I have just returned from Boston. It is the only sane thing to do if you find yourself up there.
Letter to Groucho Marx [June 12, 1953]

4   California's a wonderful place to live—if you happen to be an orange.
From Robert Taylor, Fred Allen [1989]

Isaac [Emmanuelovich] Babel
1894–1941

5   A phrase is born into the world both good and bad at the same time. The secret lies in a slight, an almost invisible twist. The lever should rest in your hand, getting warm, and you can only turn it once, not twice.   *Guy de Maupassant [1924]*[1]

6   No steel can pierce the human heart so chillingly as a period at the right moment.[2]
Guy de Maupassant

7   Speaking of silence, we can't help talking about me, the past master of this genre.
Speech at First Writers' Congress [1934]

8   The right to write badly was the privilege we widely used.   *Speech at First Writers' Congress*

Louis Ferdinand Céline [Louis Ferdinand Destouches]
1894–1961

9   Those who talk about the future are scoundrels. It is the present that matters. To evoke one's posterity is to make a speech to maggots.
Voyage au Bout de la Nuit (Journey to the End of the Night) [1932]

---

[1] Translated by Walter Morison.
[2] Translated by Max Hayward.

E[dward] E[stlin] Cummings
1894–1962

10   All in green went my love riding
on a great horse of gold
into the silver dawn.
       All in green went my love riding [1923]

11   in Just-
spring when the world is mud-
luscious the little
lame balloonman
whistles far and wee
       Chansons Innocentes [1923], 1

12   when the world is puddle-wonderful
       Chansons Innocentes, 1

13   Buffalo Bill's
defunct
    who used to
    ride a watersmooth-silver
         stallion
and break onetwothreefourfive pigeonsjustlikethat
      Jesus
he was a handsome man
    and what i want to know is
how do you like your blueeyed boy
Mister Death   *Portraits [1923], 8*

14   the Cambridge ladies who live in furnished souls
are unbeautiful and have comfortable minds.
       Sonnets—Realities [1923], I

15   take it from me kiddo
believe me
my country, 'tis of

you, land of the Cluett
Shirt Boston Garter and Spearmint
Girl With The Wrigley Eyes (of you
land of the Arrow Ide
and Earl &
Wilson
Collars) of you i
sing: land of Abraham Lincoln and Lydia
    E. Pinkham,
land above all of Just Add Hot Water And
    Serve—
from every B.V.D.

let freedom ring

amen.   *Poem, Or Beauty Hurts Mr. Vinal [1926]*

16   And there're a
hun-dred-mil-lion-oth-ers, like
all of you successfully if
delicately gelded (or spaded)
gentlemen (and ladies)
       Poem, Or Beauty Hurts Mr. Vinal

1 next to of course god america i
love you land of the pilgrims' and so forth
next to of course god america i [1926]

2 i sing of Olaf glad and big
whose warmest heart recoiled at war
i sing of Olaf glad and big [1931]

3 "I will not kiss your f.ing flag"
i sing of Olaf glad and big

4 "there is some s. I will not eat"
i sing of Olaf glad and big

5 unless statistics lie he was
more brave than me:more blond than you.
i sing of Olaf glad and big

6 somewhere i have never traveled, gladly beyond
any experience, your eyes have their silence.
somewhere I have never traveled [1931]

7 nobody, not even the rain, has such small hands
somewhere I have never traveled

8 anyone lived in a pretty how town
(with up so floating many bells down)
spring summer autumn winter
he sang his didn't he danced his did.
anyone lived in a pretty how town [1940]

9 my father moved through dooms of love
through sames of am through haves of give,
singing each morning out of each night
my father moved through depths of height
my father moved through dooms of love [1940]

10 and nothing quite so least as truth
—i say though hate were why men breathe—
because my father lived his soul
love is the whole and more than all
my father moved through dooms of love

11 a politician is an arse upon
which everyone has sat except a man
One Times One [1944], 10

12 mr u will not be missed
who as an anthologist
sold the many on the few
not excluding mr u   *One Times One, 11*

13 pity this busy monster, manunkind,
not. Progress is a comfortable disease.
One Times One, 14

14 A world of made
is not a world of born   *One Times One, 14*

15 We doctors know
a hopeless case if—listen: there's a hell
of a good universe next door; let's go
One Times One, 14

16 —when skies are hanged and oceans drowned,
the single secret will still be man
One Times One, 20

17 For he has the territory of harmonicas, the acres
of flutes, the meadows of clarinets, the domain of
violins. And God says: Why did they put you in
prison? What did you do to the people? "I made
them dance and they put me in prison."
The Enormous Room [1922]. Surplice

18 Take me up into your mind once or twice before
I die (you know why: just because the eyes of you
and me will be full of dirt some day). Quickly take
me up into the bright child of your mind.
The Enormous Room. Jean Le Nègre

Arthur Freed
1894–1973

19 Singin' in the rain, just singin' in the rain.
What a glorious feeling, I'm happy again.
Singin' in the Rain [1929][1]

Dashiell Hammett
1894–1961

20 That's the part of it I [Sam Spade] always liked.
He [Flitcraft] adjusted himself to beams falling, and
then no more of them fell, and he adjusted himself
to their not falling.
The Maltese Falcon [1930], ch. 7

21 The Thin Man.   *Title of novel [1934]*

Ben Hecht
1894–1964
and
Charles MacArthur
1895–1956

22 Go on, Heathcliff, run away. Bring me back the
world!
*Wuthering Heights (screenplay) [1939],
spoken by Merle Oberon*

Herman Hupfeld
1894–1951

23 You must remember this, a kiss is still a kiss,
A sigh is just a sigh;

---

[1]Music by NACIO HERB BROWN.

The fundamental things apply,
As time goes by.
> *Everybody's Welcome [1931]. As Time
> Goes By*[1]

[1] It's still the same old story,
A fight for love and glory,
A case of do or die!
The world will always welcome lovers,
As time goes by.
> *Everybody's Welcome. As Time Goes By*[1]

Aldous [Leonard] Huxley
1894–1963

[2] Christ-like in my behavior,
Like every good believer,
I imitate the Savior,
And cultivate a beaver.
> *Antic Hay [1923], ch. 4*

[3]   A bad book is as much of a labor to write as a good one; it comes as sincerely from the author's soul.   *Point Counter Point [1928], ch. 13*

[4]   Chastity—the most unnatural of all the sexual perversions.   *Eyeless in Gaza [1936], ch. 27*

[5] A poor degenerate from the ape,
Whose hands are four, whose tail's a limb,
I contemplate my flaccid shape
And know I may not rival him
Save with my mind.
> *First Philosopher's Song*

Nikita Sergeyevich Khrushchev
1894–1971

[6]   Cult of personality.
> *Special Report to Twentieth Party Congress
> [February 1956]*

[7]   About the capitalist states, it doesn't depend on you whether or not we exist. If you don't like us, don't accept our invitations, and don't invite us to come and see you. Whether you like it or not, history is on our side. We will bury you.[2]
> *Reported statement at reception for
> Wladyslaw Gomulka at the Polish Embassy,
> Moscow [November 18, 1956]*

---

[1]Also in the film *Casablanca* [1943].

[2]Neither the original nor the translation of the last two sentences appeared in either *Pravda* or the *New York Times,* which carried the rest of the text. Another possible translation of the last sentence is: We shall be present at your funeral; i.e., we shall outlive you; but the above is the familiar version.

Elzie Crisler Segar
1894–1938

[8]   I yam what I yam, an' that's all I yam!
> *Thimble Theatre (comic strip) [c. 1932],
> Popeye speaking*

[9]   I will gladly pay you Tuesday for a hamburger today.
> *Thimble Theatre (comic strip) [c. 1933],
> J. Wellington Wimpy speaking*

Genevieve Taggard
1894–1948

[10] Try tropic for your balm,
Try storm,
And after storm, calm.
Try snow of heaven, heavy, soft, and slow,
Brilliant and warm.
Nothing will help, and nothing do much harm.
> *Of the Properties of Nature for Healing an
> Illness, st. 1*

James Thurber
1894–1961

[11]   Well, if I called the wrong number, why did you answer the phone?
> *Caption for cartoon in The New Yorker*

[12]   I love the idea of there being two sexes, don't you?   *Caption for cartoon in The New Yorker*

[13]   He knows all about art, but he doesn't know what he likes.
> *Caption for cartoon in The New Yorker*

[14]   It's a naive domestic Burgundy without any breeding, but I think you'll be amused by its presumption.
> *Caption for cartoon in The New Yorker*

[15]   The War Between Men and Women.
> *Series of cartoons*

[16]   Early to rise and early to bed makes a male healthy and wealthy and dead.
> *Fables for Our Time [1940]. The Shrike and
> the Chipmunks*

[17]   You might as well fall flat on your face as lean over too far backward.
> *Fables for Our Time. The Bear Who Let It
> Alone*

[18]   Don't count your boobies until they are hatched.
> *Fables for Our Time. The Unicorn in the
> Garden*

1   You Could Look It Up.[1]   *Title of story [1941]*

2   Red Barber announces the Dodger games and he uses those expressions—picked them up down South. . . . "Tearing up the pea patch" means going on a rampage; "sitting in the catbird seat" means sitting pretty, like a batter with three balls and no strikes on him.
    The Thurber Carnival [1945]. The Catbird Seat

3   It is better to know some of the questions than all of the answers.   *Saying*

Jean Toomer
1894–1967

4 O can't you see it, O can't you see it,
    Her skin is like dusk on the eastern horizon
    . . . When the sun goes down.
        Cane [1923]. Karintha

5 Wind is in the cane. Come along.
    Cane leaves swaying, rusty with talk,
    Scratching choruses above the guinea's squawk,
    Wind is in the cane. Come along.
        Cane. Carma

6 A feast of moon and men and barking hounds,
    An orgy for some genius of the South
    With blood-hot eyes and cane-lipped scented
        mouth,
    Surprised in making folk songs from soul sounds.
        Cane. Georgia Dusk, st. 2

7 Beyond plants are animals,
    Beyond animals is man,
    Beyond man is the universe.

    The Big Light,
    Let the Big Light in!   *The Blue Meridian*

8 What use bombs and antibombs,
    Sovereign powers, brutal lives, ugly deaths?
    Are men born to go down like this?
        The Blue Meridian

9 Men,
    Men and women—
    Liberate!   *The Blue Meridian*

Mark Van Doren
1894–1972

10 Wit is the only wall
    Between us and the dark.   *Wit, st. 1*

Norbert Wiener
1894–1964

11   We have decided to call the entire field of control and communication theory, whether in the machine or in the animal, by the name of Cybernetics, which we form from the Greek [for] steersman.
        Cybernetics [1948]

12   The independent scientist who is worth the slightest consideration as a scientist has a consecration which comes entirely from within himself: a vocation which demands the possibility of supreme self-sacrifice.
        The Human Use of Human Beings [1950]

13   The future offers very little hope for those who expect that our new mechanical slaves will offer us a world in which we may rest from thinking. Help us they may, but at the cost of supreme demands upon our honesty and our intelligence. The world of the future will be an ever more demanding struggle against the limitations of our intelligence, not a comfortable hammock in which we can lie down to be waited upon by our robot slaves.
        God and Golem, Inc. [1964]

Edward, Duke of Windsor [Edward VIII]
1894–1972

14   I have found it impossible to carry the heavy burden of responsibility and to discharge my duties as King as I would wish to do without the help and support of the woman I love.[2]
    Farewell broadcast after abdication [December 11, 1936]

Bud [William] Abbott
1895–1974

and

Lou Costello [Louis Francis Cristillo]
1906–1959

15   Who's on first, What's on second, I Don't Know's on third—
        The Naughty Nineties [1945]

---

[1]Subsequently popularized by and associated with Casey Stengel, 730, who used it as a conversation clincher.

[2]Apparently written for Edward by Winston Churchill. See Sarah Bradford, *George VI* [1989], p. 202.

Jack [William Harrison] Dempsey
1895–1983

1   Honey, I just forgot to duck.
To his wife, after losing the heavyweight title to Gene Tunney [September 23, 1926]

Paul Éluard [Eugène Grindel]
1895–1952

2   I was born to know you
To give you your name
Freedom.[1]   *Poésie et Vérité [1942]. Liberté*

3   Farewell sadness
Good morning sadness.[2]
Poésie et Vérité. La Vie Immédiate

R[ichard] Buckminster Fuller
1895–1983

4   Don't fight forces; use them.   *Shelter [1932]*

5   God is a verb.
No More Secondhand God [1963]

6   For at least two million years men have been re-producing and multiplying on a little automated Spaceship Earth.   *Prospect for Humanity [1964]*

7   Synergy means behavior of whole systems unpre-dicted by the behavior of their parts.
What I Have Learned [1966]. How Little I Know

8   Thinking is a momentary dismissal of irrelevan-cies.   *Utopia or Oblivion [1969]*

9   Change the environment; do not try to change man.   *Design Science [1969]*

10   Either man is obsolete or war is.
I Seem to Be a Verb [1970]

11   I am the only guinea pig I have.
Address to Engineering Society at Tel Aviv [June 16, 1972]

12   Dare to be naive.
Synergetics [1975]. Moral of the Work

13   Unity is plural and, at minimum, is two.
Synergetics, sec. 224.12

14   Nature is trying very hard to make us succeed, but nature does not depend on us. We are not the only experiment.
Interview in the Minneapolis Tribune [April 30, 1978]

15   Universe to each must be
All that is, including me.
Environment in turn must be
All that is, excepting me.
Synergetics 2 [1979], sec. 100.12, Universal Requirements

Robert [Ranke] Graves
1895–1985

16   As you are woman, so be lovely:
As you are lovely, so be various,
Merciful as constant, constant as various,
So be mine, as I yours for ever.
Pygmalion to Galatea

17   Take your delight in momentariness,
Walk between dark and dark—a shining space
With the grave's narrowness, though not its peace.
Sick Love

18   Impossible men: idle, illiterate,
Self-pitying, dirty, sly,
For whose appearance even in City Parks
Excuses must be made to casual passers-by.

Has God's supply of tolerable husbands
Fallen, in fact, so low
Or do I always over-value woman
At the expense of man?
Do I?
It might be so.
A Slice of Wedding Cake

19   I suddenly realized with my first shudder of gen-tility that two sorts of Christians existed—our-selves, and the lower classes.
Good-bye to All That [1929], ch. 2

20   A well-chosen anthology is a complete dispen-sary of medicine for the more common mental dis-orders, and may be used as much for prevention as cure.   *On English Poetry, 29*

21   The reason why the hairs stand on end, the eyes water, the throat is constricted, the skin crawls and a shiver runs down the spine when one writes or reads a true poem is that a true poem is necessarily an invocation of the White Goddess, or Muse, the Mother of All Living, the ancient power of fright and lust—the female spider or the queen bee whose embrace is death.[3]
The White Goddess [1948], ch. 1

---

[1]Je suis né pour te connaître / Pour te nommer / Liberté.
[2]Adieu tristesse / Bonjour tristesse.

---

[3]See Emily Dickinson, 547:9, and Housman, 620:5.

Oscar Hammerstein II
1895–1960

1   Ol' Man River[1]
He just keeps rollin' along.
Show Boat [1927].[2] Ol' Man River

2 Can't help lovin' that man of mine.
Show Boat. Can't Help Lovin' That Man

3 The last time I saw Paris, her heart was warm and
gay.
I heard the laughter of her heart in every street
café.   *The Last Time I Saw Paris [1940][3]*

4 Oh, what a beautiful mornin'
Oh, what a beautiful day.
I got a beautiful feelin'
Everything's going my way.
*Oklahoma! [1943].[4] Oh, What a Beautiful
Mornin'*

5 The corn is as high as an elephant's eye,
An' it looks like it's climbin' clear up to the sky.
Oklahoma! Oh, What a Beautiful Mornin'

6 Ev'rythin's up to date in Kansas City.
They've gone about as fur as they c'n go!
Oklahoma! Kansas City

7 Some enchanted evening . . .
You may see a stranger
Across a crowded room.
*South Pacific [1949].[5] Some Enchanted
Evening*

8   I'm Gonna Wash That Man Right Outa My Hair.
South Pacific. Title of song

9   There Is Nothing Like a Dame.
South Pacific. Title of song

Lorenz [Milton] Hart
1895–1943

10 We'll have Manhattan,
The Bronx and Staten
Island too.   *Manhattan [1925][4]*

11   That's why the lady is a tramp.
Babes in Arms [1937].[4] The Lady Is a Tramp

12   Bewitched, Bothered and Bewildered.
Pal Joey [1940].[4] Bewitched

---

[1]The Mississippi.

[2]Based on the novel *Show Boat* [1926], by EDNA FERBER. Music by JEROME KERN.

[3]Music by JEROME KERN.
See Paul, 732:7.

[4]Music by RICHARD RODGERS.

[5]Based on *Tales of the South Pacific* [1947], by JAMES A. MICHENER. Music by RICHARD RODGERS.

L[esley] P[oles] Hartley
1895–1972

13   The past is a foreign country; they do things differently there.   *The Go-Between [1953], prologue*

Dolores Ibarruri [La Pasionaria][6]
1895–1989

14   No pasarán [They shall not pass]![7]
*Republican watchword in the Spanish Civil
War [1936–1939]*

Basil Henry Liddell Hart
1895–1970

15   Keep strong, if possible. In any case, keep cool. Have unlimited patience. Never corner an opponent, and always assist him to save his face. Put yourself in his shoes—so as to see things through his eyes. Avoid self-righteousness like the devil— nothing so self-blinding.
*Deterrent or Defense [1960]. Advice to
Statesmen*

Groucho [Julius Henry] Marx
1895–1977

16   I never forget a face, but in your case I'll make an exception.   *Saying*

17   Please accept my resignation. I don't care to belong to any club that will accept me as a member.
The Groucho Letters [1967]

John McNulty
1895–1956

18   They were talking about a certain hangout and Johnny said, "Nobody goes there anymore. It's too crowded."[8]
*Some Nights When Nothing Happens Are the
Best Nights in This Place [1943]*

Lewis Mumford
1895–1990

19   The clock, not the steam-engine, is the key-machine of the modern industrial age.
Technics and Civilization [1934]

---

[6]See Zapata, 679:7 and note.

[7]End of radio speech [July 18, 1936] calling on the women of Spain to help defend the Republic.

[8]Often attributed to YOGI BERRA, 814.

1   Layer upon layer, past times preserve themselves in the city until life itself is finally threatened with suffocation; then, in sheer defense, modern man invents the museum.   *The Culture of Cities [1938]*

Edward E. Paramore, Jr.
1895–1956

2 Oh, the North Countree is a hard countree
That mothers a bloody brood;
And its icy arms hold hidden charms
For the greedy, the sinful and lewd.
And strong men rust, from the gold and the lust
That sears the Northland soul.
    The Ballad of Yukon Jake [1921]

3 Oh, tough as a steak was Yukon Jake —
Hard-boiled as a picnic egg.
    The Ballad of Yukon Jake

Andy Razaf
1895–1973

4 Ain't misbehavin',
I'm savin' my love for you.
    Ain't Misbehavin' [1929][1]

5 Just 'cause you're black folks think you lack,
They laugh at you and scorn you too,
What did I do to be so black and blue?
    Black and Blue [1929][1]

Morrie Ryskind
1895–1985

6   One morning I shot an elephant in my pajamas. How he got into my pajamas I'll never know.
    Animal Crackers (screenplay) [1930], spoken by Groucho Marx

7   The calla lilies are in bloom again, mother. Such a strange flower, suitable for every occasion.
    Stage Door (screenplay) [1937],[2] *spoken by Katharine Hepburn*

Edmund Wilson
1895–1972

8   I have had a good many more uplifting thoughts, creative and expansive visions — while soaking in comfortable baths or drying myself after bracing showers — in well-equipped American bathrooms than I have ever had in any cathedral.
    A Piece of My Mind [1956], ch. 4

9   The cruellest thing that has happened to Lincoln since he was shot by Booth has been to fall into the hands of Carl Sandburg.[3]
    Patriotic Gore [1962], ch. 3

10   I attribute such success as I have had to the use of the periodic sentence.
    An Interview with Edmund Wilson [1962]

11   We tended to imagine Canada as a kind of vast hunting preserve convenient to the United States.
    O Canada [1965]

J[oseph] R[andolph] Ackerley
1896–1967

12   What strained and anxious lives dogs must lead, so emotionally involved in the world of men, whose affections they strive endlessly to secure, whose authority they are expected unquestioningly to obey, and whose minds they can never do more than imperfectly reach and comprehend.
    My Dog Tulip [1965]. Appendix

Edmund Blunden
1896–1974

13 I am for the woods against the world,
But are the woods for me?   *The Kiss*

14 Then is not Death at watch
Within those secret waters?
What wants he but to catch
Earth's heedless sons and daughters?
    The Midnight Skaters

André Breton
1896–1966

15   Subjectivity and objectivity commit a series of assaults on each other during a human life out of which the first one suffers the worse beating.[4]
    Nadja [1928], preface

16   It is at the movies that the only absolutely modern mystery is celebrated.
    From J. H. MATHEWS, Surrealism and Film

Everett McKinley Dirksen
1896–1969

17   A billion here, a billion there, and pretty soon you're talking about real money.   *Attributed*

---

[1]Music by THOMAS [FATS] WALLER and HARRY BROOKS.
[2]Written with ANTHONY VEILLER [1903–1965].

[3]Referring to Sandburg's six-volume biography, *Abraham Lincoln* [1926–1939].
[4]Translated by CESAR ALBINI.

John [Roderigo] Dos Passos
1896–1970

1   Make sure he ain't a dinge, boys.
Make sure he ain't a guinea or a kike,
how can you tell a guy's a hunredpercent when
all you've got's a gunnysack full of bones, bronze
buttons stamped with the screaming eagle and a
pair of roll puttees?
1919 [1932]. The Body of an American

2   America our nation has been beaten by strangers
who have bought the laws and fenced off the meadows and cut down the woods for pulp and turned
our pleasant cities into slums and sweated the wealth
out of our people and when they want to they hire
the executioner to throw the switch.
*The Big Money [1936]. They have clubbed us
off the streets*

F[rancis] Scott [Key] Fitzgerald
1896–1940

3   The victor belongs to the spoils.
The Beautiful and Damned [1922]

4   Everyone suspects himself of at least one of the
cardinal virtues, and this is mine: I am one of the
few honest people that I have ever known.
The Great Gatsby [1925], ch. 3

5   Jay Gatsby of West Egg, Long Island, sprang
from his Platonic conception of himself. He was a
son of God—a phrase which, if it means anything,
means just that—and he must be about His Father's
business, the service of a vast, vulgar, and meretricious beauty.
The Great Gatsby, 6

6   Her voice is full of money.
The Great Gatsby, 7

7   They were careless people, Tom and Daisy—
they smashed up things and creatures and then re-
treated back into their money or their vast carelessness, or whatever it was that kept them together,
and let other people clean up the mess they had
made.
The Great Gatsby, 9

8   Gatsby believed in the green light, the orgiastic
future that year by year recedes before us.
The Great Gatsby, 9

9   So we beat on, boats against the current, borne
back ceaselessly into the past.
The Great Gatsby, last line

10   Let me tell you about the very rich.[1] They are
different from you and me. They possess and enjoy

early, and it does something to them, makes them
soft where we are hard, and cynical where we are
trustful.
The Rich Boy [1926]

11   I remember riding in a taxi one afternoon between very tall buildings under a mauve and rosy
sky; I began to bawl because I had everything I
wanted and knew I would never be so happy again.
My Lost City [1932]

12   The hangover became a part of the day as well
allowed-for as the Spanish siesta.   *My Lost City*

13   The test of a first-rate intelligence is the ability to
hold two opposed ideas in the mind at the same
time, and still retain the ability to function.
The Crack-up [1936]

14   In a real dark night of the soul it is always three
o'clock in the morning.   *The Crack-up*

15   It was about then [1920] that I wrote a line
which certain people will not let me forget: "She
was a faded but still lovely woman of twenty-
seven."
Early Success [1937]

16 Egyptian Proverb: The worst things:
To be in bed and sleep not,
To want for one who comes not,
To try to please and please not.
Notebooks [1978]

17   Show me a hero and I will write you a tragedy.
Notebooks

18   There are no second acts in American lives.
Notebooks

19   Draw your chair up close to the edge of the
precipice and I'll tell you a story.   *Notebooks*

20   It is in the thirties that we want friends. In the
forties we know they won't save us any more than
love did.   *Notebooks*

21   All good writing is swimming under water and
holding your breath.   *Undated letter*

Ira Gershwin[2]
1896–1983

22 Oh, lady be good
To me.   *Lady Be Good [1924]. Oh, Lady Be Good*

23 'S wonderful! 'S marvelous—
You should care for me!
Funny Face [1927]. 'S Wonderful

24 I got rhythm,
I got music,

---

[1]See Hemingway, 754:14 and note 3.

[2]Music for all the lyrics is by GEORGE GERSHWIN.

I got my man—
Who could ask for anything more?
Girl Crazy [1930]. I Got Rhythm

1   Wintergreen for President.
Of Thee I Sing [1931], title of song

2   Love Is Sweeping the Country.
Of Thee I Sing, title of song

3 Of thee I sing, baby,
You have got that certain thing, baby,
Shining star and inspiration
Worthy of a mighty nation,
Of thee I sing!   *Of Thee I Sing, title song*

4 Summertime
And the livin' is easy.
Porgy and Bess [1935].[1] Summertime

5   A Woman Is a Sometime Thing.
Porgy and Bess, title of song

6 I got plenty of nothin',
And nothin's plenty for me.
Porgy and Bess, I Got Plenty of Nothin'

7 It ain't necessarily so—
The things that you're liable
To read in the Bible—
It ain't necessarily so.
Porgy and Bess, It Ain't Necessarily So

8   Let's Call the Whole Thing Off!
Shall We Dance [1937], title of song

9 The memory of all that—
No, no! They can't take that away from me.
Shall We Dance. They Can't Take That Away from Me

10 Nice work if you can get it,
And you can get it if you try.
A Damsel in Distress [1937]. Nice Work

Joe Jacobs
1896–1940

11   We wuz robbed!
After the heavyweight title fight between Max Schmeling and Jack Sharkey [June 21, 1932]

12   I should of stood in bed.
After leaving a sickbed to attend the World Series in Detroit [October 1935] and betting on the loser

---

[1]*Porgy and Bess.— Title of play* [1927] *by* DuBose Heyward [1885–1940] *and* Dorothy Heyward [1890–1961], *and of opera* [1935] *by* George Gershwin

Liam O'Flaherty
1896–1984

13   He [the informer] was a poor weak human being like themselves, a human soul, weak and helpless in suffering, shivering in the toils of the eternal struggle of the human soul with pain.
The Informer [1925]

Jean Piaget
1896–1980

14   If only we could know what was going on in a baby's mind while observing him in action we could certainly understand everything there is to psychology.   *La Première Année de l'Enfant [1927]*

Robert E[mmet] Sherwood
1896–1955

15   The trouble with me is, I belong to a vanishing race. I'm one of the intellectuals.
The Petrified Forest [1934]

16   Poor, dear God. Playing Idiot's Delight. The game that never means anything, and never ends.
Idiot's Delight [1936]

Lewis L[ichtenstein] Strauss
1896–1974

17   Our children will enjoy in their homes electrical energy too cheap to meter.
Speech on atomic energy [September 16, 1954]

Joseph Auslander
1897–1965

18 So there are no more words and all is ended;
The timbrel is stilled, the clarion laid away;
And Love with streaming hair goes unattended
Back to the loneliness of yesterday.
So There Are No More Words [1924]

Louise Bogan
1897–1970

19 I burned my life, that I might find
A passion wholly of the mind,
Thought divorced from eye and bone,
Ecstasy come to breath alone.
The Alchemist, st. 1

1 Women have no wilderness in them,
They are provident instead,
Content in the tight hot cell of their hearts
To eat dusty bread.   *Women, st. 1*

2 Up from the bronze, I saw
Water without a flaw
Rush to its rest in air,
Reach to its rest, and fall.   *Roman Fountain, st. 1*

3 —O remember
In your narrowing dark hours
That more things move
Than blood in the heart.   *Night, st. 4*

Bernard De Voto
1897–1955

4 The West begins where the average annual rainfall drops below twenty inches. When you reach the line which marks that drop—for convenience, the one hundredth meridian—you have reached the West.
The Plundered Province. In Harper's Magazine [August 1934]

5 Art is the terms of an armistice signed with fate.
Mark Twain at Work [1942]

6 The achieved West had given the United States something that no people had ever had before, an internal, domestic empire.
The Year of Decision [1943]

7 You can no more keep a martini in the refrigerator than you can keep a kiss there. The proper union of gin and vermouth is a great and sudden glory; it is one of the happiest marriages on earth and one of the shortest-lived.   *The Hour [1951]*

8 The dawn of knowledge is usually the false dawn.   *The Course of Empire [1952], ch. 2*

William Faulkner
1897–1962

9 Time is dead as long as it is being clicked off by little wheels; only when the clock stops does time come to life.
The Sound and the Fury [1929]. June Second 1910

10 I've seed de first en de last. . . . I seed de beginnin, en now I sees de endin.
The Sound and the Fury. April Eighth 1928

11 Because no battle is ever won he said. They are not even fought. The field only reveals to man his own folly and despair, and victory is an illusion of philosophers and fools.
The Sound and the Fury. April Eighth 1928

12 They [the Negroes] will endure. They are better than we are. Stronger than we are. Their vices are vices aped from white men or that white men and bondage have taught them: improvidence and intemperance and evasion—not laziness: evasion: of what white men had set them to, not for their aggrandizement or even comfort but his own.
The Bear [1932], pt. IV

13 Poor man. Poor mankind.
Light in August [1932], ch. 4

14 Too much happens. . . . Man performs, engenders, so much more than he can or should have to bear. That's how he finds that he can bear anything. . . . That's what's so terrible.
Light in August, 13

15 Tell about the South. What's it's like there. What do they do there. Why do they live there. Why do they live at all.
Absalom, Absalom! [1936], ch. 6

16 Gettysburg.[1] . . . You cant understand it. You would have to be born there.
Absalom, Absalom!, 9

17 Why do you hate the South?
I dont hate it. . . . I dont hate it. . . . *I dont hate it* he thought, panting in the cold air, the iron New England dark; *I dont. I dont! I dont hate it! I dont hate it!*   *Absalom, Absalom!, 9*

18 JEFFERSON, YOKNAPATAWPHA CO., Mississippi. Area, 2400 Square Miles. Population, Whites, 6298; Negroes, 9313. WILLIAM FAULKNER, Sole Owner & Proprietor.
Absalom, Absalom!, inscription on endpaper map drawn by author

19 He [the writer] must teach himself that the basest of all things is to be afraid; and, teaching himself that, forget it forever, leaving no room in his workshop for anything but the old verities and truths of the heart, the old universal truths lacking which any story is ephemeral and doomed—love and honor and pity and pride and compassion and sacrifice.
Speech upon receiving the Nobel Prize [December 10, 1950]

20 I decline to accept the end of man.
Speech upon receiving the Nobel Prize

21 I believe that man will not merely endure: he will prevail.   *Speech upon receiving the Nobel Prize*

---

[1]Representing, in context, the South.

1   He is immortal, not because he alone among creatures has an inexhaustible voice, but because he has a soul, a spirit capable of compassion and sacrifice and endurance.
Speech upon receiving the Nobel Prize

2   It is his [the poet's, the writer's] privilege to help man endure by lifting his heart, by reminding him of the courage and honor and hope and pride and compassion and pity and sacrifice which have been the glory of his past. The poet's voice need not merely be the record of man, it can be one of the props, the pillars to help him endure and prevail.
Speech upon receiving the Nobel Prize

3   The writer's only responsibility is to his art. He will be completely ruthless if he is a good one. . . . If a writer has to rob his mother, he will not hesitate; the "Ode on a Grecian Urn" is worth any number of old ladies.
From Writers at Work: The Paris Review Interviews [1959]

4   Really the writer doesn't want success. . . . He knows he has a short span of life, that the day will come when he must pass through the wall of oblivion, and he wants to leave a scratch on that wall — Kilroy was here — that somebody a hundred, or a thousand years later will see.
From Faulkner in the University [1959], Session 8

Paul Joseph Goebbels
1897–1945

5   We can do without butter, but, despite all our love of peace, not without arms. One cannot shoot with butter but with guns.[1]
Address in Berlin [January 17, 1936]

Herman J[acob] Mankiewicz
1897–1953

and

Orson Welles
1915–1985

6   Mr. Kane was a man who got everything he wanted, and then lost it. Maybe Rosebud was something he couldn't get or something he lost. Anyway, it wouldn't have explained anything. I don't think any word can explain a man's life. No, I guess Rosebud is just a piece in a jigsaw puzzle, a missing piece.
Citizen Kane (screenplay) [1941]

David McCord
1897–1997

7 By and by
God caught his eye.   *Epitaphs: The Waiter*

8 Still for us where Cottons mather
In the spring the Willas cather
    As of yore.
And What's More: On Stopping at a New Hampshire Inn [1941]

9 The decent docent doesn't doze;
He teaches standing on his toes.
His student dassn't doze and does,
And that's what teaching is and was.
What Cheer [1945]

10   Life is the garment we continually alter, but which never seems to fit.
Whereas to Mr. Franklin [1956]

Horace McCoy
1897–1955

11   "Why did you kill her?" the policeman in the rear seat asked. . . . "They shoot horses, don't they?" I said.   *They Shoot Horses, Don't They? [1935]*

Thornton [Niven] Wilder
1897–1975

12   Even memory is not necessary for love. There is a land of the living and a land of the dead and the bridge is love, the only survival, the only meaning.
The Bridge of San Luis Rey [1927], last lines

13 George Brush is my name
America's my nation
Luddington's my dwelling place
And Heaven's my destination.
Heaven's My Destination [1934], title page poem[2]

14   Most everybody in the world climbs into their graves married.   *Our Town [1938], act II*

15   The dead don't stay interested in us living people for very long. Gradually, gradually, they let go hold of the earth . . . and the ambitions they had . . . and the pleasures they had . . . and the things they suffered . . . and the people they loved. They get weaned away from earth — that's the way I put it — weaned away.[3]   *Our Town, III*

---

[1]Probably the origin of the slogan: Guns or butter.

[2]Labeled by Wilder: Doggerel verse which children of the Middle West were accustomed to write in their schoolbooks.

[3]Ellipses are in the original text.

1   Oh, earth, you're too wonderful for anybody to realize you. . . . Do any human beings ever realize life while they live it?—every, every minute?

Our Town, III

2   My advice to you is not to inquire why or whither, but just enjoy your ice cream while it's on your plate—that's my philosophy.

The Skin of Our Teeth [1942], act I

3   Ninety-nine percent of the people in the world are fools and the rest of us are in great danger of contagion.   *The Matchmaker [1954], act I*

4   The best part of married life is the fights. The rest is merely so-so.   *The Matchmaker, II*

Walter Winchell
1897–1972

5   Good evening, Mr. and Mrs. America and all the ships at sea! This is Walter Winchell in New York. Let's go to press.

Signature opening lines for his weekly radio broadcasts

Stephen Vincent Benét
1898–1943

6 And I died in my boots like a pioneer
With the whole wide sky above me.
A Ballad of William Sycamore, 1790–1880 [1923], st. 16

7 Go play with the towns you have built of blocks,
The towns where you would have bound me!
I sleep in my earth like a tired fox,
And my buffalo have found me.
The Ballad of William Sycamore, 1790–1880, st. 19

8 Oh, Georgia booze is mighty fine booze,
The best yuh ever poured yuh,
But it eats the soles right offen yore shoes,
For Hell's broke loose in Georgia.
The Mountain Whippoorwill [1923], st. 48

9 I have fallen in love with American names,
The sharp names that never get fat,
The snakeskin titles of mining claims,
The plumed war bonnet of Medicine Hat,
Tucson and Deadwood and Lost Mule Flat.
American Names [1927], st. 1

10 Bury my heart at Wounded Knee.
American Names, st. 7

11 American Muse, whose strong and diverse heart
So many men have tried to understand
But only made it smaller with their art,

Because you are as various as your land.
John Brown's Body [1928]. Invocation, st. 1

12 Stonewall Jackson, wrapped in his beard and his silence.   *John Brown's Body, bk. IV*

13   If two New Hampshiremen aren't a match for the devil, we might as well give the country back to the Indians.

The Devil and Daniel Webster [1936]

14   Even the damned may salute the eloquence of Mr. Webster.

The Devil and Daniel Webster

15 When Daniel Boone goes by at night
The phantom deer arise
And all lost, wild America
Is burning in their eyes.   *Daniel Boone [1942]*

Bertolt Brecht
1898–1956

16 Oh, the shark has pretty teeth, dear—
And he shows them pearly white—
Just a jackknife has Macheath, dear—
And he keeps it out of sight.
The Threepenny Opera (Die Dreigroschenoper) [1928].[1] The Ballad of Mack the Knife (Moritat)

17   Till you feed us, right and wrong can wait.
The Threepenny Opera, act II, sc. 3

18 Oh! Moon of Alabama
We now must say good-bye
We've lost our good old mama
And must have whiskey
Oh, you know why!
Rise and Fall of the City of Mahagonny (Aufstieg und Fall der Stadt Mahagonny) [1931].[2] Alabama Song

19   Alas, we
Who wished to lay the foundations of kindness,
Could not ourselves be kind.
But you, when at last it comes to pass
That man can help his fellow man,
Do not judge us
Too harshly.
To Those Born Later (An Die Nachgeborenen) [1938][3]

20   What they could do with round here is a good war. What else can you expect with peace running

---

[1]Music by KURT WEILL. Translated by MARC BLITZSTEIN. Based on the libretto of *The Beggar's Opera* by JOHN GAY.

[2]Music by KURT WEILL.

[3]Translated by H. R. HAYS.

wild all over the place? You know what the trouble with peace is? No organization.

> *Mother Courage and Her Children [1941], act I*

1 One can describe the world of today to the people of today only if one describes it as capable of alteration.

> *Can Today's World Become Restored Through Theater? [1955]*

William O[rville] Douglas
1898–1980

2 The Fifth Amendment is an old friend and a good friend. It is one of the great landmarks in man's struggle to be free of tyranny, to be decent and civilized.   *An Almanac of Liberty [1954]*

Federico García Lorca
1898–1936

3 In the parched path
I have seen the good lizard
(one drop of crocodile)
meditating.

> *The Old Lizard (El Lagarto Viejo) [1921]*[1]

4 Green, how much I want you green.
Green wind. Green branches.
The ship upon the sea
and the horse in the mountain.

> *Somnambule Ballad (Romance Sonámbulo) [1928]*[2]

5 But I am no more I,
nor is my house now my house.

> *Somnambule Ballad*

6 I touched her sleeping breasts,
and they opened to me suddenly
like spikes of hyacinth.

> *The Faithless Wife (La Casada Infiel) [1928]*[2]

7 Without silver light on their foliage
the trees had grown larger
and a horizon of dogs
barked very far from the river.   *The Faithless Wife*

8 Black are the horses.
The horseshoes are black.
On the dark capes glisten
stains of ink and of wax.
Their skulls are leaden,
which is why they don't weep.

With their patent leather souls
they come down the street.

> *Ballad of the Spanish Civil Guard (Romance de la Guardia Civil Española) [1928]*[3]

9 At five in the afternoon.
Ah, that fatal five in the afternoon!
It was five by all the clocks!
It was five in the shade of the afternoon!

> *Lament for Ignacio Sanchez Mejias (Llanto por Ignacio Sanchez Mejias) [1935]*,[2] *I*

10 I will not see it!

Tell the moon to come
for I do not want to see the blood
of Ignacio on the sand.

> *Lament for Ignacio Sanchez Mejias, II*

11 The New York dawn has
four columns of mud
and a hurricane of black doves
that paddle in putrescent waters.

> *The Poet in New York (Poeta en Nueva York) [1940]. The Dawn (La Aurora),*[2] *st. 1*

12 The light is buried under chains and noises
in impudent challenge of rootless science.
Through the suburbs sleepless people stagger,
as though just delivered from a shipwreck of blood.

> *The Poet in New York. The Dawn, st. 5*

George Gershwin
1898–1937

13 True music . . . must repeat the thought and inspirations of the people and the time. My people are Americans. My time is today.

> *From* Edward Jablonski *and* Lawrence D. Stewart, *The Gershwin Years [1926]*

Horace Gregory
1898–1982

14 My boyhood saw
Greek islands floating over Harvard Square.[4]

> *Chorus for Survival [1935], 12*

Edgar Y. Harburg
1898–1981

15 Once I built a railroad, now it's done.
Brother, can you spare a dime?

> *Americana [third edition, 1932].*[5] *Brother, Can You Spare a Dime?*

---

[1]Translated by Lysander Kemp.

[2]Translated by Stephen Spender and Joan Gili.

[3]Translated by A. L. Lloyd.

[4]The speaker in the poem is Ralph Waldo Emerson.

[5]Music by Jay Gorney.

1 Somewhere over the rainbow
Bluebirds fly.
Birds fly over the rainbow—
Why then, oh why can't I?
The Wizard of Oz [1939].[1] Over the Rainbow

2 We gotta be free—
The eagle and me.
Bloomer Girl [1944].[2] The Eagle and Me

3 How are things in Glocca Morra this fine day?
Finian's Rainbow [1947].[3] How Are Things in Glocca Morra?

C[live] S[taples] Lewis
1898–1963

4   The safest road to Hell is the gradual one—the gentle slope, soft underfoot, without sudden turnings, without milestones, without signposts.
The Screwtape Letters [1941], letter 12

5   The Future . . . something which everyone reaches at the rate of sixty minutes an hour, whatever he does, whoever he is.   *The Screwtape Letters, 25*

6   The long, dull, monotonous years of middle-aged prosperity or middle-aged adversity are excellent campaigning weather [for the Devil].
The Screwtape Letters, 28

Golda Meir
1898–1978

7   We only want that which is given naturally to all peoples of the world, to be masters of our own fate, only of our fate, not of others, and in cooperation and friendship with others.
Address to Anglo-American Committee of Inquiry [March 25, 1946]

Gunnar Myrdal
1898–1987

8   The American Negro problem is a problem in the heart of the American. It is there that the interracial tension has its focus. It is there that the decisive struggle goes on.
An American Dilemma [1944]

---

[1] Music by HAROLD ARLEN.
See Baum, 606:14.

[2] Music by HAROLD ARLEN.
The emancipation of woman from intemperance, injustice, prejudice, and bigotry.—AMELIA JENKS BLOOMER [1818–1894], *masthead of her paper The Lily*

[3] Music by BURTON LANE.

9   The treatment of the Negro is America's greatest and most conspicuous scandal.
An American Dilemma

Amelia Earhart [Putnam]
1898–1937

10 Courage is the price that life exacts for granting peace.
The soul that knows it not, knows no release
From little things;
Knows not the livid loneliness of fear,
Nor mountain heights where bitter joy can hear
The sound of wings.   *Courage*

Erich Maria Remarque
1898–1970

11   Monotonously the lorries sway, monotonously come the calls, monotonously falls the rain. It falls on our heads and on the heads of the dead up the line, on the body of the little recruit with the wound that is so much too big for his hip; it falls on Kemmerich's grave; it falls in our hearts.
All Quiet on the Western Front (Im Westen Nichts Neues) [1929]

Ben Shahn
1898–1969

12   Ever since I could remember I'd wished I'd been lucky enough to be alive at that great time—when something big was going on, like the Crucifixion. And suddenly I realized I was. Here I was living through another crucifixion. Here was something to paint!
On painting a gouache: Bartolomeo Vanzetti and Nicola Sacco [1932]

Jorge Luis Borges
1899–1986

13 Patio, heaven's watercourse.
The patio is the slope
down which the sky flows into the house.
Serenely
eternity waits at the crossway of the stars.
Fervor of Buenos Aires (Fervor de Buenos Aires) [1923]. Un Patio[4]

---

[4] Translated by ROBERT FITZGERALD.

1 A man gradually identifies himself with the form of his fate; a man is, in the long run, his own circumstances.

El Aleph [1949]. La Escritura de Dios

2 It would be exaggerating to say that our relationship is hostile; I live, I let myself live, so that Borges can weave his literature and that literature justifies me. . . . I don't know which of us is writing this page.[1]

Personal Anthology (Antologia Personal) [1961]. Borges and Myself (Borges y Yo)

3 I have known what the Greeks did not: uncertainty. *Ficciones [1962]. The Babylon Lottery*[2]

4 Writing is nothing more than a guided dream.

Doctor Brodie's Report [1972]. Preface[3]

5 The Falklands thing was a fight between two bald men over a comb.

On the 1982 Britain-Argentina conflict

Noël Coward
1899–1973

6 Mad dogs and Englishmen go out in the midday sun. *Mad Dogs and Englishmen*

7 I'll see you again,
Whenever spring breaks through again.

Bittersweet [1929], act I, sc. ii

8 Strange how potent cheap music is.

Private Lives [1930], act I

9 Don't Let's Be Beastly to the Germans.

Title of song

10 Learn the lines and don't bump into the furniture. *Attributed. Advice on acting*

Hart Crane
1899–1932

11 And yet this great wink of eternity,
Of rimless floods, unfettered leewardings.

Voyages [1926], II, st. 1

12 It was a kind and northern face
That mingled in such exile guise
The everlasting eyes of Pierrot
And, of Gargantua, the laughter.

Praise for an Urn: In Memoriam Ernest Nelson [1926]

13 Down Wall, from girder into street noon leaks,
A rip-tooth of the sky's acetylene.

The Bridge [1930]. To Brooklyn Bridge

14 And biased by full sails, meridians reel
Thy purpose—still one shore beyond desire!
The sea's green crying towers a-sway, Beyond.

The Bridge. Ave Maria

15 Damp tonnage and alluvial march of days . . .
Tortured with history, its one will—flow!

The Bridge. The River (Mississippi)

16 The swift red flesh, a winter king—
Who squired the glacier woman down the sky?
She ran the neighing canyons all the spring;
She spouted arms; she rose with maize—to die.

The Bridge. The Dance

17 The phonographs of hades in the brain
Are tunnels that re-wind themselves, and love
A burnt match skating in a urinal—

The Bridge. The Tunnel

18 And why do I often meet your visage here,
Your eyes like agate lanterns—on and on
Below the toothpaste and the dandruff ads?
And did their riding eyes right through your side,
And did their eyes like unwashed platters ride?
And Death, aloft—gigantically down[4]
Probing through you—toward me, O evermore!

The Bridge. The Tunnel

Duke [Edward Kennedy] Ellington
1899–1974

19 It Don't Mean a Thing If It Ain't Got That Swing.

Title of song [1932]

Friedrich August von Hayek
1899–1992

20 The system of private property is the most important guaranty of freedom, not only for those who own property, but scarcely less for those who do not. *The Road to Serfdom [1944], ch. 8*

21 I am certain that nothing has done so much to destroy the juridical safeguards of individual freedom as the striving after this mirage of social justice.

Economic Freedom and Representative Government [1973]

---

[1]Translated by RACHEL PHILLIPS.
[2]Translated by ANTHONY KERRIGAN.
[3]Translated by NORMAN THOMAS DI GIOVANNI.

[4]See Poe, 478:6.

Ernest Hemingway
1899–1961

1   You and me, we've made a separate peace.
In Our Time [1924], ch. 6

2   It makes one feel rather good deciding not to be a bitch. . . . It's sort of what we have instead of God.   *The Sun Also Rises [1926], ch. 19*

3   "Oh, Jake," Brett said, "we could have had such a damned good time together." . . .
"Yes," I said. "Isn't it pretty to think so?"
The Sun Also Rises, last lines

4   I had seen nothing sacred, and the things that were glorious had no glory and the sacrifices were like the stockyards at Chicago if nothing was done with the meat except to bury it . . . Abstract words such as glory, honor, courage, or hallow were obscene.   *A Farewell to Arms [1929], ch. 27*

5   The world breaks everyone and afterward many are strong at the broken places. But those that will not break it kills. It kills the very good and the very gentle and the very brave impartially. If you are none of these you can be sure that it will kill you too but there will be no special hurry.
A Farewell to Arms, 34

6   You never had time to learn. They threw you in and told you the rules and the first time they caught you off base they killed you.
A Farewell to Arms, 41

7   It was like saying good-bye to a statue. After a while I went out and left the hospital and walked back to the hotel in the rain.
A Farewell to Arms, 41

8   Grace under pressure.[1]
Definition of "guts." From DOROTHY PARKER, *The Artist's Reward, in The New Yorker [November 30, 1929]*

9   I know only that what is moral is what you feel good after and what is immoral is what you feel bad after.   *Death in the Afternoon [1932], ch. 1*

10   I was trying to write then and I found the greatest difficulty, aside from knowing truly what you really felt, rather than what you were supposed to feel, had been taught to feel, was to put down what really happened in action; what the actual things were which produced the emotion that you experienced . . . the real thing, the sequence of motion and fact which made the emotion and which would be as valid in a year or in ten years or, with luck and if you stated it purely enough, always.
Death in the Afternoon, 1

11   If he wrote it he could get rid of it. He had gotten rid of many things by writing them.
Winner Take Nothing [1933]. Fathers and Sons

12   All good books are alike in that they are truer than if they had really happened and after you are finished reading one you will feel that all that happened to you and afterwards it all belongs to you: the good and the bad, the ecstasy, the remorse and sorrow, the people and the places and how the weather was. If you can get so that you can give that to people, then you are a writer.
Old Newsman Writes. From Esquire [December 1934]

13   All modern American literature comes from one book by Mark Twain called *Huckleberry Finn.*
Green Hills of Africa [1935], ch. 1

14   The rich were dull and they drank too much. . . . He remembered poor Julian[2] and his romantic awe of them and how he had started a story once that began, "The very rich are different from you and me." And how someone had said to Julian, Yes, they have more money.[3]
The Fifth Column and The First Forty-Nine Stories [1938]. The Snows of Kilimanjaro

15   Kilimanjaro is a snow-covered mountain 19,710 feet high, and is said to be the highest mountain in Africa. Its western summit is called the Masai "Ngàje Ngài," the House of God. Close to the western summit there is the dried and frozen carcass of a leopard. No one has explained what the leopard was seeking at that altitude.
The Fifth Column and The First Forty-Nine Stories. The Snows of Kilimanjaro, epigraph

16   But did thee feel the earth move?
For Whom the Bell Tolls [1940], ch. 13

17   If we win here we will win everywhere. The world is a fine place and worth the fighting for and I hate very much to leave it.
For Whom the Bell Tolls, 43

---

[1]After skiing with the Hemingways in 1926, Gerald Murphy was "absolutely elated" when Hemingway praised his courage in venturing down the slopes for the first time as "grace under pressure." See HONORIA MURPHY DONNELLY with RICHARD N. BILLINGS, *Sara & Gerald* [1982].

[2]In original publication, "poor Scott Fitzgerald" [*Esquire*, August 1936].

[3]In 1936 Maxwell Perkins, the legendary editor of Fitzgerald and Hemingway at Charles Scribner's Sons, lunched with Hemingway and the critic Mary Colum. When Hemingway announced, "I am getting to know the rich," Mary Colum replied, "The only difference between the rich and other people is that the rich have more money." —MATTHEW J. BRUCCOLI [1931–], *Scott and Ernest* [1978]
See F. Scott Fitzgerald, 746:10.

1 Cowardice, as distinguished from panic, is almost always simply a lack of ability to suspend the functioning of the imagination.
Men at War [1942], introduction

2 Time is the least thing we have of.
From The New Yorker profile by LILLIAN ROSS *[May 13, 1950]*[1]

3 I must be worthy of the great DiMaggio who does all things perfectly even with the pain of the bone spur in his heel.
The Old Man and the Sea [1952]

4 A man can be destroyed but not defeated.
The Old Man and the Sea

5 The most essential gift for a good writer is a built-in, shock-proof, shit detector. This is the writer's radar and all great writers have had it.
Interview in Paris Review [Spring 1958]

6 You write until you come to a place where you still have your juice and know what will happen next and you stop and try to live through until the next day when you hit it again.
Interview in Paris Review

7 If you are lucky enough to have lived in Paris as a young man, then wherever you go for the rest of your life, it stays with you, for Paris is a moveable feast.
A Moveable Feast [1964], epigraph

Alfred Hitchcock
1899–1980

8 The "MacGuffin" is the term we use to cover all that sort of thing: to steal plans or documents, or discover a secret, it doesn't matter what it is. And the logicians are wrong in trying to figure out the truth of a MacGuffin, since it's beside the point. The only thing that really matters is that in the picture the plans, documents, or secrets must seem to be of vital importance to the characters.
In FRANÇOIS TRUFFAUT, *Hitchcock (1985)*

Robert Maynard Hutchins
1899–1977

9 The death of democracy is not likely to be an assassination from ambush. It will be a slow extinction from apathy, indifference, and undernourishment.
Great Books [1954]

Nadezhda Mandelstam
1899–1980

10 I decided it is better to scream. This pitiful sound, which sometimes, goodness knows how, reaches into the remotest prison cell, is a concentrated expression of the last vestige of human dignity. It is a man's way of leaving a trace, of telling people how he lived and died. By his screams he asserts his right to live, sends a message to the outside world demanding help and calling for resistance. If nothing else is left, one must scream. Silence is the real crime against humanity.
Hope Against Hope [1970],[2] *ch. 11*

Charles W. Morton
1899–1967

11 It was around two decades ago, in the city room of the Boston *Evening Transcript,* that I first became aware of the elongated-yellow-fruit school of writing. The phrase turned up in a story . . . about some fugitive monkeys and the efforts of police to recapture them by using bananas as bait.
The Elongated Yellow Fruit [1954]

Vladimir Nabokov
1899–1977

12 The cradle rocks above an abyss, and common sense tells us that our existence is but a brief crack of light between two eternities of darkness.
Speak, Memory [1947], ch. 1

13 I reject completely the vulgar, shabby, fundamentally medieval world of Freud, with its crankish quest for sexual symbols (something like searching for Baconian acrostics in Shakespeare's work) and its bitter little embryos spying, from their natural nooks, upon the love life of their parents.
Speak, Memory, 1

14 Lolita, light of my life, fire of my loins. My sin, my soul.
Lolita [1955], pt. I, ch. 1

15 You can always count on a murderer for a fancy prose style.
Lolita, I, 1

16 Between the age limits of nine and fourteen there occur maidens who, to certain bewitched travelers, twice or many times older than they, reveal their nature, which is not human, but nymphic (that is, demoniac); and these chosen creatures I propose to designate as "nymphets."
Lolita, I, 5

---

[1]Reprinted in book form: *Portrait of Hemingway* [1961].

[2]Translated by MAX HAYWARD.

1   I am thinking of aurochs and angels, the secret of durable pigments, prophetic sonnets, the refuge of art. And this is the only immortality you and I may share, my Lolita.   *Lolita, last paragraph*

2   In pornographic novels, action has to be limited to the copulation of clichés. Style, structure, imagery should never distract the reader from his tepid lust.   *On a Book Entitled Lolita [1956]*

3   For me a work of fiction exists only insofar as it affords me what I shall bluntly call aesthetic bliss.   *On a Book Entitled Lolita*

4   He never attempted to sleep on his left side, even in those dismal hours of the night when the insomniac longs for a third side after trying the two he has.   *Pnin [1957], ch. 1, sec. 2*

5   With the help of the janitor he screwed onto the side of the desk a pencil sharpener — that highly satisfying, highly philosophical implement that goes ticonderoga-ticonderoga, feeding on the yellow finish and sweet wood, and ends up in a kind of soundlessly spinning ethereal void as we all must.   *Pnin, 3, 4*

6   Like so many aging college people, Pnin had long since ceased to notice the existence of students on the campus.   *Pnin, 3, 6*

7   In high art and pure science detail is everything.   *Strong Opinions [1973]*

8   Literature was born not the day when a boy crying wolf, wolf came running out of the Neanderthal valley with a big gray wolf at his heels: literature was born on the day when a boy came crying wolf, wolf and there was no wolf behind him.   *Lectures on Literature [1980]*

E[lwyn] B[rooks] White
1899–1985

9   "It's broccoli, dear."
    "I say it's spinach, and I say the hell with it."
    Caption for cartoon by Carl Rose in The New Yorker [December 8, 1928]

10   I have occasionally had the exquisite thrill of putting my finger on a little capsule of truth, and heard it give the faint squeak of mortality under my pressure.   *Letter to Stanley Hart White [January 1929]*

11   I don't know which is more discouraging, literature or chickens.   *Letter to James Thurber [November 18, 1938]*

12   When Mrs. Frederick C. Little's second son was born, everybody noticed that he was not much bigger than a mouse. The truth of the matter was, the baby looked very much like a mouse in every way. He was only two inches high; and he had a mouse's sharp nose, a mouse's tail, a mouse's whiskers, and the pleasant, shy manner of a mouse. Before he was many days old he was not only looking like a mouse but acting like one, too — wearing a gray hat and carrying a small cane.   *Stuart Little [1945], ch. 1*

13   "My name is Margalo," said the bird, softly, in a musical voice. "I come from fields once tall with wheat, from pastures deep in fern and thistle; I come from vales of meadowsweet, and I love to whistle."   *Stuart Little, 8*

14   Democracy is the recurrent suspicion that more than half of the people are right more than half of the time.   *The Wild Flag [1946]*

15   I am a member of a party of one, and I live in an age of fear. Nothing lately has unsettled my party and raised my fears so much as your editorial, on Thanksgiving Day, suggesting that employees should be required to state their beliefs in order to hold their jobs. The idea is inconsistent with our constitutional theory and has been stubbornly opposed by watchful men since the early days of the Republic.   *Letter to the New York Herald Tribune [November 29, 1947]*

16   The city, for the first time in its long history, is destructible. A single flight of planes no bigger than a wedge of geese can quickly end this island fantasy, burn the towers, crumble the bridges, turn the underground passages into lethal chambers, cremate the millions. The intimation of mortality is part of New York now: in the sound of jets overhead, in the black headlines of the latest edition.   *Here Is New York [1949]*

17   It was the best place to be, thought Wilbur, this warm delicious cellar, with the garrulous geese, the changing seasons, the heat of the sun, the passage of swallows, the nearness of rats, the sameness of sheep, the love of spiders, the smell of manure, and the glory of everything.   *Charlotte's Web [1952], ch. 22*

18   None of the new spiders ever quite took her place in his heart. She was in a class by herself. It is not often that someone comes along who is a true friend and a good writer. Charlotte was both.   *Charlotte's Web, 22*

19   An unhatched egg is to me the greatest challenge in life.   *Letter to Reginald Allen [March 5, 1973]*

Louis [Satchmo] Armstrong
1900–1971

1   Man, if you gotta ask you'll never know.[1]
Reply when asked what jazz is

D[enis] W[illiam] Brogan
1900–1974

2   A people that has licked a more formidable enemy than Germany or Japan, primitive North America . . . a country whose national motto has been "root, hog, or die."
The American Character [1944]

3   Any well-established village in New England or the northern Middle West could afford a town drunkard, a town atheist, and a few Democrats.
The American Character

Herbert Butterfield
1900–1979

4   It [the scientific revolution] outshines everything since the rise of Christianity and reduces the Renaissance and Reformation to the rank of mere episodes, mere internal displacements, within the system of medieval Christendom. . . . It looms so large as the real origin of the modern world and of the modern mentality that our customary periodization of European history has become an anachronism and an encumbrance.
The Origins of Modern Science [1949]

Lenore Coffee
1900–1984

5   What a dump!
Beyond the Forest (screenplay) [1949], spoken by Bette Davis

Theodosius Dobzhansky
1900–1975

6   Nature's stern discipline enjoins mutual help at least as often as warfare. The fittest may also be the gentlest.   *Mankind Evolving [1962]*

Elizabeth, Queen Mother of England
1900–2002

7   The princesses would never leave without me, and I couldn't leave without the king, and the king will never leave.
Reported reply as to whether the princesses would leave England after the bombing of Buckingham Palace [1940]

8   I am almost glad we have been bombed. Now I feel I can look the East End in the face.
Comment on the German bombing of Buckingham Palace [September 1940]

Hans Frank
1900–1946

9   Our Constitution is the will of the Fuehrer.
In Volkischer Beobachter [May 20, 1936]

10   A thousand years will pass and the guilt of Germany will not be erased.
Before he was hanged at Nuremberg [October 16, 1946]

Erich Fromm
1900–1980

11   Freedom, although it has brought [modern man] independence and rationality, has made him isolated and, thereby, anxious and powerless.
Escape from Freedom [1941]. Foreword

12   Man's nature, his passions and anxieties, are a cultural product; as a matter of fact, man himself is the most important creation and achievement of the continuous human effort, the record of what we call history.   *Escape from Freedom, ch. 1*

James Edward Grant
1900–1966

13   "Republic" is one of those words that makes me tight in the throat. Same tightness a man gets when his baby makes his first step, or his boy first shaves, makes his first sound like a man. Some words can give you a feeling that makes your heart warm. "Republic" is one of those words.
The Alamo (screenplay) [1960], spoken by John Wayne

---

[1]Lady, if you got to ask you ain't got it. —THOMAS [FATS] WALLER [1904–1943], *when asked to explain rhythm*

Abel Green
1900–1973

1   Sticks Nix Hick Pix.
Headline about rural audiences' rejection of movies with rural themes, Variety [July 17, 1935]

James Hilton
1900–1954

2   The austere serenity of Shangri-La. Its forsaken courts and pale pavilions shimmered in repose from which all the fret of existence had ebbed away, leaving a hush as if moments hardly dared to pass.
Lost Horizon [1933], ch. 5

3   Anno domini — that's the most fatal complaint of all in the end.   *Goodbye, Mr. Chips [1934], ch. 1*

[Ayatolla] Ruholla Khomeini
1900–1989

4   The author of the Satanic Verses book [Salman Rushdie[1]], which is against Islam, the Prophet, and the Koran, and all those involved in its publication who were aware of its content, are sentenced to death. I ask all Moslems to execute them wherever they find them.   *Statement [February 14, 1989]*

Raphael Lemkin
1900–1959

5   By genocide[2] we mean the destruction of a nation or of an ethnic group.
Axis Rule in Occupied Europe [1944]

Margaret Mitchell
1900–1949

6   The usual masculine disillusionment in discovering that a woman has a brain.
Gone With the Wind [1936], pt. IV, ch. 36

7   Death and taxes and childbirth! There's never any convenient time for any of them.
Gone With the Wind, IV, 38

8   My dear, I don't give a damn [Rhett Butler to Scarlett O'Hara].[3]   *Gone With the Wind, V, 63*

9   I'll think of some way to get him back. After all, tomorrow is another day.
Gone With the Wind, last line

Wayne [Lyman] Morse
1900–1974

10   The liberal, emphasizing the civil and property rights of the individual, insists that the individual must remain so supreme as to make the state his servant.
Definition contributed to Nine Definitions of Liberalism. In the New Republic [July 22, 1946]

V[ictor] S[awdon] Pritchett
1900–1997

11   The detective novel is the art-for-art's sake of our yawning Philistinism, the classic example of a specialized form of art removed from contact with the life it pretends to build on.
Books in General [1953]. The Roots of Detection

12   I come from a set of storytellers and moralists. . . . The storytellers were forever changing the tale and the moralists tampering with it in order to put it in an edifying light.
A Cab at the Door [1967], ch. 1

Ernie Pyle
1900–1945

13   I write from the worm's-eye point of view.
Here Is Your War [1943]

Leo Robin
1900–1984

14   Diamonds Are a Girl's Best Friend.
Gentlemen Prefer Blondes [1949],[4] title of song

Antoine de Saint-Exupéry
1900–1944

15   Although human life is priceless, we always act as if something had an even greater price than life. . . . But what is that something?
Night Flight [1931], ch. 14

---

[1]See Rushdie, 841:1.

[2]Lemkin coined the word (by combining a Greek and a Latin root) and introduced it in this passage.

[3]Frankly, my dear, I don't give a damn. — SIDNEY HOWARD [1891–1939], *screenplay for Gone With the Wind* [1939].

[4]See Loos, 737:10.
Music by JULE STYNE.

1 Love does not consist in gazing at each other but in looking outward together in the same direction.   *Wind, Sand and Stars [1939]*

2 And it was at that moment that you pronounced your first intelligible sentence, a speech admirable in its human pride: "I swear that what I went through, no animal would have gone through."   *Wind, Sand and Stars*

3 Grown-ups never understand anything for themselves, and it is tiresome for children to be always and forever explaining things to them.   *The Little Prince [1943],[1] ch. 1*

4 It is only with the heart that one can see rightly; what is essential is invisible to the eye.   *The Little Prince, 21*

George Seferis [Giorgios Sefiriades]
1900–1971

5 Three years
we waited intently for the herald
closely watching
the pines the shore and the stars.   *Mythistorema [1935],[2] I*

6 We were searching to rediscover the first seed
so that the ancient drama could begin again.   *Mythistorema, I*

7 We have no rivers, we have no wells, we have no
   springs,
only a few cisterns—and these empty—that echo,
   and we worship them.
A stagnant hollow sound, the same as our
   loneliness
the same as our love, the same as our bodies.   *Mythistorema, X*

8 They were lovely, your eyes, but you didn't know
   where to look.   *Mythistorema, XVI*

9 They're a burden for us
the friends who no longer know how to die.   *Mythistorema, XIX*

10 Wherever I travel Greece wounds me.   *In the Manner of G.S. [1936]*

11 Each of us earns his death, his own death,
   which belongs to no one else
and this game is life.   *The Last Day [1939]*

12 Here where one meets the path of rain, wind, and
   ruin
does there exist the movement of the face, shape of
   the tenderness

of those who've shrunk so strangely in our lives,
those who remained the shadow of waves and
   thoughts with the sea's boundlessness
or perhaps no, nothing is left but the weight
the nostalgia for the weight of a living existence . . .
the poet a void.   *The King of Asine [1940]*

13 Sometimes it crosses my mind that the things I
   write here are nothing
other than images that prisoners or sailors tattoo
   on their skin.   *Logbook II [1944], epigraph*

14 Great suffering descended on Greece.
So many bodies thrown
into the jaws of the sea, the jaws of the earth . . .
all for a linen undulation, a bit of cloud,
a butterfly's flicker, a swan's down,
an empty tunic—all for a Helen.   *Helen [1953]*

15 He grew old between the fires of Troy
and the quarries of Sicily.   *Euripides the Athenian [1953]*

16 They are children of many men, our words.   *On Stage [1966],[3] 6*

17 As pines
   keep the shape of the wind
   even when the wind has fled and is no longer
     there,
   so words
guard the shape of man
even when man has fled and is no longer there.   *On Stage, 6*

18 When, on the road to Thebes, Oedipus met the Sphinx, who asked him her riddle, his answer was: *Man*. This simple word destroyed the monster. We have many monsters to destroy. Let us think of Oedipus' answer.   *Speech upon receiving the Nobel Prize [1963]*

Ignazio Silone [Secondo Tranquilli]
1900–1978

19 Liberty is the possibility of doubting, the possibility of making a mistake, the possibility of searching and experimenting, the possibility of saying "No" to any authority—literary, artistic, philosophic, religious, social, and even political.   *Essay in The God That Failed [1950][4]*

---

[1]Translated by Katherine Woods.
[2]Translated by Edmund Keeley and Philip Sherrard.

[3]Translated by Walter Kaiser.
[4]Edited by Richard Crossman.

Adlai E[wing] Stevenson
1900–1965

1   The problem of cat versus bird is as old as time. If we attempt to resolve it by legislation who knows but what we may be called upon to take sides as well in the age old problems of dog versus cat, bird versus bird, and even bird versus worm. . . . The State of Illinois and its local governing bodies already have enough to do without trying to control feline delinquency.

As governor of Illinois, vetoing a bird-protection bill [April 23, 1949]

2   Let's talk sense to the American people.
Speech accepting the Democratic presidential nomination [July 26, 1952]

Thomas Wolfe
1900–1938

3   A stone, a leaf, an unfound door.
Look Homeward, Angel [1929], foreword

4   Which of us has known his brother? Which of us has looked into his father's heart? Which of us has not remained forever prison-pent? Which of us is not forever a stranger and alone?
Look Homeward, Angel, foreword

5   O lost, and by the wind grieved, ghost, come back again.
Look Homeward, Angel, foreword

6   If a man has a talent and cannot use it, he has failed. If he has a talent and uses only half of it, he has partly failed. If he has a talent and learns somehow to use the whole of it, he has gloriously succeeded, and won a satisfaction and a triumph few men ever know.
The Web and the Rock [1939], ch. 30

7   I believe that we are lost here in America, but I believe we shall be found.
You Can't Go Home Again [1940], ch. 48

Roy Campbell
1901–1957

8 You praise the firm restraint with which they
     write —
I'm with you there, of course.
They use the snaffle and the curb all right;
But where's the bloody horse?
On Some South African Novelists

Margaret Craven
1901–1980

9   The Indian knows his village and feels for his village as no white man for his country, his town, or even for his own bit of land. His village is not the strip of land four miles long and three miles wide that is his as long as the sun rises and the moon sets. The myths are the village, and the winds and rains. The river is the village, and . . . the talking bird, the owl, who calls the name of the man who is going to die.
I Heard the Owl Call My Name [1973], pt. I

René Jules Dubos
1901–1982

10   The general formula of [ecological] management for the future might be, think globally and act locally.
The Wooing of Earth [1980]. Humankind and the Earth

Werner Karl Heisenberg
1901–1976

11   The more precisely we determine the position [of an electron], the more imprecise is the determination of velocity at this instant, and vice versa.[1]
On the Perceptual Content of Quantum Theoretical Kinematics and Mechanics [1927]

12   Every tool carries with it the spirit by which it has been created.   *Physics and Philosophy [1958]*

13   Since the measuring device has been constructed by the observer . . . we have to remember that what we observe is not nature in itself but nature exposed to our method of questioning.
Physics and Philosophy

Zora Neale Hurston
c. 1901–1960

14   I am not tragically colored. There is no great sorrow dammed up in my soul, nor lurking behind my eyes. . . . I do not weep at the world — I am too busy sharpening my oyster knife.
How It Feels to Be Colored Me [1928]

15   Women forget all those things they don't want to remember, and remember everything they don't want to forget. The dream is the truth. Then they act and do things accordingly.
Their Eyes Were Watching God [1937], ch. 1

---

[1]Heisenberg's "uncertainty principle."

1 De nigger woman is de mule uh de world so fur as Ah can see. Ah been prayin' fuh it tuh be different wid you. *Their Eyes Were Watching God, 2*

James Michael Kieran, Jr.
1901–1952

2 The brains trust.
In conversation with Franklin D. Roosevelt [August 1932], referring to the professors and other such advisers who served Roosevelt in his first campaign. The phrase later became "brain trust."

André Malraux
1901–1976

3 The great mystery is not that we should have been thrown down here at random between the profusion of matter and that of the stars; it is that from our very prison we should draw, from our own selves, images powerful enough to deny our nothingness.
Man's Fate (La Condition Humaine) [1933]

4 One cannot create an art that speaks to men when one has nothing to say.
Man's Hope (L'Espoir) [1938]

5 All art is a revolt against man's fate.
The Voices of Silence (Les Voix du Silence) [1951]

6 The human mind invents its Puss-in-Boots and its coaches that change into pumpkins at midnight because neither the believer nor the atheist is completely satisfied with appearances.
Anti-Memoirs [1967], preface

7 The genius of Christianity is to have proclaimed that the path to the deepest mystery is the path of love. *Anti-Memoirs. Anti-Memoirs, sec. 6*

8 The extermination camps, in endeavoring to turn man into a beast, intimated that it is not life alone which makes him man.
Anti-Memoirs. La Condition Humaine, sec. 2

9 The attempt to force human beings to despise themselves . . . is what I call hell.
Anti-Memoirs. La Condition Humaine, sec. 2

Margaret Mead
1901–1978

10 As the traveler who has once been from home is wiser than he who has never left his own doorstep, so a knowledge of one other culture should sharpen our ability to scrutinize more steadily, to appreciate more lovingly, our own.
Coming of Age in Samoa [1928], introduction

11 If we are to achieve a richer culture, rich in contrasting values, we must recognize the whole gamut of human potentialities, and so weave a less arbitrary social fabric, one in which each diverse human gift will find a fitting place.
Sex and Temperament in Three Primitive Societies [1935], conclusion

12 We know of no culture that has said, articulately, that there is no difference between men and women except in the way they contribute to the creation of the next generation.
Male and Female [1948]

13 The mind is not sex-typed.
Blackberry Winter [1972], ch. 5

14 Because of their age-long training in human relations — for that is what feminine intuition really is — women have a special contribution to make to any group enterprise, and I feel it is up to them to contribute the kinds of awareness that relatively few men . . . have incorporated through their education.
Blackberry Winter, 14

Linus [Carl] Pauling
1901–1994

15 Science is the search for truth — it is not a game in which one tries to beat his opponent, to do harm to others. We need to have the spirit of science in international affairs, to make the conduct of international affairs the effort to find the right solution, the just solution of international problems, not the effort by each nation to get the better of other nations, to do harm to them when it is possible.
No More War! [1958]

Arna Bontemps
1902–1973

16 Yet what I sowed and what the orchard yields
My brother's sons are gathering stalk and root,
Small wonder then my children glean in fields
They have not sown, and feed on bitter fruit.
A Black Man Talks of Reaping [1963], st. 3

17 Yet would we die as some have done:
Beating a way for the rising sun.
The Daybreakers [1963]

Thomas E[dmund] Dewey
1902–1971

1   That's why it's time for a change.[1]
*Campaign speech at San Francisco
[September 21, 1944]*

Erik [Homburger] Erikson
1902–1994

2   This sense of identity provides the ability to experience one's self as something that has continuity and sameness, and to act accordingly.
Childhood and Society [1950]

3   The identity crisis . . . occurs in that period of the life cycle when each youth must forge for himself some central perspective and direction, some working unity, out of the effective remnants of his childhood and the hopes of his anticipated adulthood.   *Young Man Luther [1958], ch. 1*

Stella Gibbons
1902–1989

4   The farm was crouched on a bleak hillside, whence its fields, fanged with flints, dropped steeply to the village of Howling a mile away.
Cold Comfort Farm [1932], ch. 3

5   Something nasty in the woodshed.
Cold Comfort Farm, 8

Wolcott Gibbs
1902–1958

6   Backward ran sentences until reeled the mind.
More in Sorrow [1958]. Time . . . Fortune . . . Life . . . Luce

7   Where it will all end, knows God!
More in Sorrow. Time . . . Fortune . . . Life . . . Luce

Langston Hughes
1902–1967

8   It is the duty of the younger Negro artist . . . to change through the force of his art that old whispering "I want to be white," hidden in the aspira-

tions of his people, to "Why should I want to be white? I am a Negro—and beautiful!"
*The Negro Artist and the Racial Mountain.
In The Nation [June 23, 1926]*

9   I've known rivers:
I've known rivers ancient as the world and older
      than the flow of human blood in human
      veins.
My soul has grown deep like the rivers.
The Negro Speaks of Rivers [1926]

10   I am a Negro:
      Black as the night is black,
      Black like the depths of my Africa.
Negro [1926]

11   Rest at pale evening . . .
A tall slim tree . . .
Night coming tenderly
Black like me.   *Dream Variations [1926]*

12   I got the Weary Blues
And I can't be satisfied.   *The Weary Blues [1926]*

13   Listen, Christ,
You did alright in your day, I reckon—
But that day's gone now.
They ghosted you up a swell story, too,
Called it Bible—
But it's dead now.   *Goodbye Christ [1932]*

14   Wear it
Like a banner
For the proud—
Not like a shroud.   *Color [1943]*

15   Good morning, daddy!
Ain't you heard
The boogie-woogie rumble
Of a dream deferred?
Dream Boogie [1951]

16   What happens to a dream deferred?
      Does it dry up
      like a raisin in the sun?
      Or fester like a sore—
      And then run?
      Does it stink like rotten meat?
      Or crust and sugar over—
      like a syrupy sweet?

      Maybe it just sags
      like a heavy load.

      Or does it explode?   *Harlem [1951]*

17   As I learn from you,
      I guess you learn from me—
      although you're older—and white—
      and somewhat more free.
Theme for English B [1951]

---

[1]The phrase was used extensively in the campaigns of 1944, 1948, and 1952.

1   Negro blood is sure powerful—because just *one* drop of black blood makes a colored man. *One* drop—you are a Negro! . . . Black is powerful.[1]

Simple Takes a Wife [1953]

Charles A[ugustus] Lindbergh[2]
1902–1974

2   We (that's my ship and I) took off rather suddenly. We had a report somewhere around 4 o'clock in the afternoon before that the weather would be fine, so we thought we would try it.

Lindbergh's Own Story. In the New York Times [May 23, 1927]

3   I saw a fleet of fishing boats. . . . I flew down almost touching the craft and yelled at them, asking if I was on the right road to Ireland.

They just stared. Maybe they didn't hear me. Maybe I didn't hear them. Or maybe they thought I was just a crazy fool. An hour later I saw land.

Lindbergh's Own Story. In the New York Times

Norman Maclean
1902–1990

4   In our family, there was no clear line between religion and fly fishing.

A River Runs Through It [1976]

Ogden Nash
1902–1971

5   Candy
Is dandy
But liquor
Is quicker.

Hard Lines [1931]. Reflections on Ice-Breaking

6   The turtle lives 'twixt plated decks
Which practically conceal its sex.
I think it clever of the turtle
In such a fix to be so fertile.

Hard Lines. The Turtle

7   The Bronx?
No, thonx!

Hard Lines. Geographical Reflection

8   A bit of talcum
Is always walcum.

Free Wheeling [1931]. The Baby

9   I think that I shall never see
A billboard lovely as a tree.
Indeed, unless the billboards fall
I'll never see a tree at all.[3]

Happy Days [1933]. Song of the Open Road

10   There is something about a Martini,
Ere the dining and dancing begin,
And to tell you the truth,
It is not the vermouth—
I think that perhaps it's the gin.

The Primrose Path [1935]. A Drink with Something in It

11   There was a young belle of old Natchez
Whose garments were always in patchez.
When comment arose
On the state of her clothes,
She drawled, When Ah itchez, Ah scratchez!

I'm a Stranger Here Myself [1938]. Requiem

12   The trouble with a kitten is
THAT
Eventually it becomes a
CAT.   *The Face Is Familiar [1941]. The Kitten*

13   I believe a little incompatibility is the spice of life, particularly if he has income and she is pattable.   *Versus [1949]. I Do, I Will, I Have*

14   He tells you when you've got on too much lipstick, And helps you with your girdle when your hips stick.   *Versus. The Perfect Husband*

15   A door is what a dog is perpetually on the wrong side of.

The Private Dining Room [1953]. A Dog's Best Friend Is His Illiteracy

16   How confusing the beams from memory's lamp are;
One day a bachelor, the next a grampa.
What is the secret of the trick?
How did I get so old so quick?

You Can't Get There from Here [1957]. Preface to the Past

17   Here lies my past. Good-bye I have kissed it;
Thank you, kids. I wouldn't have missed it.

You Can't Get There from Here. Preface to the Past

18   Maybe I couldn't be dafter,
But I keep wondering if this time we couldn't settle our differences before a war instead of after.

Everyone but Thee and Me [1962]. Is There an Oculist in the House?

---

[1]See Carmichael and Hamilton, 835:11.

[2]In the spring of '27, something bright and alien flashed across the sky. A young Minnesotan [Lindbergh] who seemed to have had nothing to do with his generation did a heroic thing, and for a moment people set down their glasses in country clubs and speakeasies and thought of their old best dreams.—F. SCOTT FITZGERALD

---

[3]See Kilmer, 711:11.

1 I myself am more and more inclined to agree with
Omar and Satchel Paige as I grow older:
Don't try to rewrite what the moving finger has
writ, and don't ever look over your shoulder.
There's Always Another Windmill [1968]. If a
Boder Meet a Boder, Need a Boder Cry? Yes

2 Linguistics becomes an ever eerier area, like I feel
like I'm in Oz,
Just trying to tell it like it was.[1]
The Old Dog Barks Backwards [1972]. What
Do You Want, A Meaningful Dialogue or a
Satisfactory Talk?

Curt Siodmak
1902–2000

3 Even a man who's pure in heart
And says his prayers at night
May become a wolf when the wolfbane blooms
And the autumn moon is bright.
The Wolf Man [1941], film script

Stevie [Margaret Florence] Smith
1902–1971

4 I was much too far out all my life
And not waving but drowning.
Not Waving but Drowning [1957]

5 Why does my Muse only speak when she is
unhappy?
She does not, I only listen when I am unhappy.
My Muse [1962]

6 Yet a time may come when a poet or any person
Having a long life behind him, pleasure and
sorrow . . .
May fancy life comes to him with love and says:
We are friends enough now for me to give you
death;
Then he may commit suicide, then
He may go.   *Exeat [1966]*

John [Ernst] Steinbeck
1902–1968

7   Man, unlike any other thing organic or inorganic
in the universe, grows beyond his work, walks up
the stairs of his concepts, emerges ahead of his accomplishments.
The Grapes of Wrath [1939], ch. 14

---

[1]Tell it like it is. — *Youth slogan* [1960s]

8   Okie use' ta mean you was from Oklahoma. Now
it means you're scum. Don't mean nothing itself, it's
the way they say it.
The Grapes of Wrath, 18

Meredith Willson
1902–1984

9 Ya got trouble, folks,
Right here in River City.
Trouble with a capital "T"
And that rhymes with "P"
And that stands for Pool!
The Music Man [1957]. Ya Got Trouble

10   River City's gonna have her Boys Band! As sure
as the Lord made little green apples, and that band's
gonna be in uniform!
The Music Man

Tallulah [Brockman] Bankhead
1903–1968

11   There is less in this than meets the eye.
Remark to Alexander Woollcott at Aglavaine
and Selysette by MAURICE MAETERLINCK
[January 3, 1922]

Count Galeazzo Ciano
1903–1944

12   As always, victory finds a hundred fathers but
defeat is an orphan.[2]
The Ciano Diaries, 1939–1943 [1946].
September 9, 1942

Cyril [Vernon] Connolly
1903–1974

13   Obesity is a mental state, a disease brought on
by boredom and disappointment.
The Unquiet Grave [1945], pt. I

14   Imprisoned in every fat man a thin one is wildly
signaling to be let out.[3]
The Unquiet Grave, II

---

[2]There's an old saying that victory has a hundred fathers and defeat is an orphan. — JOHN F. KENNEDY, *after the debacle at the Bay*
of Pigs, Cuba [April 21, 1961]

[3]Outside every fat man there was an even fatter man trying to
close in. — KINGSLEY AMIS [1922–1995], *One Fat Englishman*
[1963]

Countee Cullen
1903–1946

1 One three centuries removed
From the scenes his fathers loved,
Spicy grove, cinnamon tree,
What is Africa to me?
Heritage [1925]

2 Jesus of the twice-turned cheek,
Lamb of God, although I speak
With my mouth thus, in my heart
Do I play a double part.
Even at Thy glowing altar
Must my heart grow sick and falter
Wishing He I served were black. *Heritage*

3 Not yet has my heart or head
In the least way realized
They and I are civilized. *Heritage*

William Thomas Cummings
1903–1944

4 There are no atheists in the foxholes.
Field sermon, Bataan [1942]. From Carlos
P. Romulo, *I Saw the Fall of the Philippines*
[1942]

Malcolm Muggeridge
1903–1990

5 As Man alone, Jesus could not have saved us; as
God alone, he would not; Incarnate, he could and
did. *Jesus [1975], pt. I*

Anaïs Nin
1903–1977

6 It's all right for a woman to be, above all, human. I am a woman first of all.
The Diary of Anaïs Nin, vol. I [1966],
June 1933

7 Dreams are necessary to life.
The Diary of Anaïs Nin, II [1967], June
1936 (letter to her mother)

8 Each friend represents a world in us, a world
possibly not born until they arrive, and it is only by
this meeting that a new world is born.
The Diary of Anaïs Nin, II, March 1937

9 There are very few human beings who receive
the truth, complete and staggering, by instant illumination. Most of them acquire it fragment by fragment, on a small scale, by successive developments,
cellularly, like a laborious mosaic.
The Diary of Anaïs Nin, III [1969], Fall 1943

George Orwell [Eric Blair]
1903–1950

10 As for [Stanley] Baldwin, one could not even
dignify him with the name of stuffed shirt. He was
simply a hole in the air.
The Lion and The Unicorn [1940]

11 All animals are equal, but some animals are more
equal than others. *Animal Farm [1945], ch. 10*

12 The great enemy of clear language is insincerity.
Politics and the English Language [1946]

13 Political language . . . is designed to make lies
sound truthful and murder respectable, and to give
an appearance of solidity to pure wind.
Politics and the English Language

14 It was a bright cold day in April and the clocks
were striking thirteen. *1984 [1948], opening line*

15 Big Brother is watching you. *1984, pt. I, ch. 1*

16 War is peace. Freedom is slavery. Ignorance is
strength. *1984, I, 1*

17 Power is not a means; it is an end. One does not
establish a dictatorship in order to safeguard a revolution; one makes the revolution in order to establish the dictatorship. The object of persecution is
persecution. The object of torture is torture. The
object of power is power. *1984, III, 3*

18 If you want a picture of the future, imagine a
boot stamping on a human face—forever.
1984, III, 3

Casey [Kenneth C.] Robinson
1903–1979

19 Where's the rest of me?
Kings Row (screenplay) [1942], spoken by
Ronald Reagan[1]

20 Oh, Jerry, don't ask for the moon. We have the
stars.
Now Voyager (screenplay) [1942], spoken by
Bette Davis

Benjamin [McLane] Spock
1903–1998

21 Trust yourself. You know more than you think
you do.
The Common Sense Book of Baby and Child
Care [1946], ch. 1

---

[1]Also the title of Reagan's autobiography [1965].

1   The more people have studied different methods of bringing up children the more they have come to the conclusion that what good mothers and fathers instinctively feel like doing for their babies is the best after all.

The Common Sense Book of Baby and Child Care, 1

Evelyn Waugh
1903–1966

2   I expect you'll be becoming a schoolmaster, sir. That's what most of the gentlemen does, sir, that gets sent down for indecent behavior.

Decline and Fall [1928], Prelude

3   Anyone who has been to an English public school will always feel comparatively at home in prison. It is the people brought up in the gay intimacy of the slums . . . who find prison so soul destroying.   *Decline and Fall, pt. III, ch. 4*

4   *"What war?"* said the Prime Minister sharply. "No one has said anything to me about a war. I really think I should have been told. I'll be damned," he said defiantly, "if they shall have a war without consulting me. What's a cabinet for, if there's not more mutual confidence than that? What do they want a war for, anyway?"   *Vile Bodies [1930], ch. 8*

5   We will not have any Dickens today . . . but tomorrow, and the day after that, and the day after that. Let us read *Little Dorrit* again.

A Handful of Dust [1934], ch. 6

6   Feather-footed through the plashy fen passes the questing vole.   *Scoop [1938], bk. I, ch. 2, sec. 1*

7   He had aroused three irreconcilable feuds in Capri; he had practiced black art in Cefalu; he had been cured of drug taking in California and of an Oedipus complex in Vienna.

Brideshead Revisited [1945], bk. I, ch. 2

8   I caught a thin bat's squeak of sexuality, inaudible to any but me.

Brideshead Revisited, I, 3

9   Her eyes greenish and remote, with a rich glint of lunacy. . . . "What did your Loved One pass on from?" she asked.

The Loved One [1948], ch. 3

10   Randolph Churchill went into hospital . . . to have a lung removed. It was announced that the trouble was not "malignant." . . . It was a typical triumph of modern science to find the only part of Randolph that was not malignant and remove it.

Diaries [March 1964]

Nathanael West
1903–1940

11   Are you in trouble? — Do-you-need-advice? — Write-to-Miss-Lonelyhearts-and-she-will-help-you.

Miss Lonelyhearts [1933]

12   The Miss Lonelyhearts are the priests of twentieth-century America.   *Miss Lonelyhearts*

Peter Arno
1904–1968

13   I consider your conduct unethical and lousy.

Caption for cartoon

14   Well, back to the old drawing board.

Caption for cartoon showing designer walking away from crashed plane

Joseph Campbell
1904–1987

15   Myth is the secret opening through which the inexhaustible energies of the cosmos pour into human cultural manifestation. Religions, philosophies, arts, the social forms of primitive and historic man, prime discoveries in science and technology, the very dreams that blister sleep, boil up from the basic, magic ring of myth.

The Hero with a Thousand Faces [1949]. Prologue

16   Follow your bliss.   *The Power of Myth [1988]*

Deng Xiaoping
1904–1997

17   Yellow cat, black cat, as long as it catches mice, it is a good cat.[1]   *Speech [1962]*

Richard Eberhart
1904–

18   I stood there in the whirling summer,
My hand capped a withered heart,
And thought of China and of Greece,
Of Alexander in his tent;
Of Montaigne in his tower,
Of Saint Theresa in her wild lament.

Collected Poems, 1930–1960 [1960]. The Groundhog

---

[1]Translated by ROSS TERRILL.
Deng identified this as "a saying from Sichuan Province."

1　It is what man does not know of God
Composes the visible poem of the world.
　　Collected Poems, 1930–1960. On a Squirrel
　　Crossing the Road in Autumn in New
　　England

Bergen [Baldwin] Evans
1904–1978

2　Freedom of speech and freedom of action are meaningless without freedom to think. And there is no freedom of thought without doubt.
　　The Natural History of Nonsense [1946],
　　ch. 19

Clifton Fadiman
1904–1999

3　When you reread a classic you do not see more in the book than you did before; you see more in *you* than there was before.
　　Any Number Can Play [1957]

Cary Grant
[Archibald Alexander Leach]
1904–1986

4　Everybody wants to be Cary Grant. Even *I* want to be Cary Grant.　　*Attributed*

5　Old Cary Grant fine. How you?
　　Attributed answer to telegraphed query,
　　How old Cary Grant?

Graham Greene
1904–1991

6　There is always one moment in childhood when the door opens and lets the future in.
　　The Power and the Glory [1940], ch. 1

7　In human relations kindness and lies are worth a thousand truths.
　　The Heart of the Matter [1948], pt. I, ch. 2,
　　sec. iv

8　No human being can really understand another, and no one can arrange another's happiness.
　　The Heart of the Matter, III, 1, i

9　If we had not been taught how to interpret the story of the Passion, would we have been able to say from their actions alone whether it was the jealous Judas or the cowardly Peter who loved Christ?
　　The End of the Affair [1951], ch. 3

10　Have you seen a room from which faith has gone? . . . Like a marriage from which love has gone. . . . And patience, patience everywhere like a fog.　　*The Potting Shed [1957], act III*

11　Catholics and Communists have committed great crimes, but at least they have not stood aside, like an established society, and been indifferent. I would rather have blood on my hands than water like Pilate . . . if you have abandoned one faith, do not abandon all faith. There is always an alternative to the faith we lose. Or is it the same faith under another mask?
　　The Comedians [1966], pt. III, ch. 4, sec. 4

12　Our worst enemies here are not the ignorant and the simple, however cruel; our worst enemies are the intelligent and corrupt.
　　The Human Factor [1978], pt. III, ch. 3

Moss Hart
1904–1961

13　Boredom is the keynote of poverty . . . for where there is no money there is no change of any kind, not of scene or of routine.　　*Act One [1959], pt. I*

14　The only credential the city [New York] asked was the boldness to dream. For those who did, it unlocked its gates and its treasures, not caring who they were or where they came from.　　*Act One, II*

Roman Lee Hruska
1904–1999

15　Even if he is mediocre, there are a lot of mediocre judges and people and lawyers. They are entitled to a little representation, aren't they, and a little chance? We can't all have Brandeises, Cardozos and Frankfurters and stuff like that there.
　　Defending President Richard M. Nixon's
　　proposed appointment of G. Harrold Carswell
　　to the Supreme Court [1970]

Christopher [William
Bradshaw] Isherwood
1904–1986

16　I am a camera with its shutter open, quite passive, recording, not thinking. Recording the man shaving at the window opposite and the woman in the kimono washing her hair. Some day, all this will have to be developed, carefully printed, fixed.
　　Goodbye to Berlin [1939], A Berlin Diary

George F[rost] Kennan
1904–

1   The main element of any United States policy toward the Soviet Union must be that of a long-term, patient but firm and vigilant containment of Russian expansive tendencies.

The Sources of Soviet Conduct, in Foreign Affairs [July 1947]

2   If we are to regard ourselves as a grown-up nation—and anything else will henceforth be mortally dangerous—then we must, as the Biblical phrase goes, put away childish things; and among these childish things the first to go, in my opinion, should be self-idealization and the search for absolutes in world affairs: for absolute security, absolute amity, absolute harmony.

Russia and the West under Lenin and Stalin [1961], ch. 25

3   There is no political or ideological difference between the Soviet Union and the United States—nothing which either side would like, or would hope, to achieve at the expense of the other—that would be worth the risks and sacrifices of a military encounter.

The Cloud of Danger [1977], ch. 11

4   A war regarded as inevitable or even probable, and therefore much prepared for, has a very good chance of eventually being fought.

The Cloud of Danger, 13

A[bbott] J[oseph] Liebling
1904–1963

5   Freedom of the press is guaranteed only to those who own one.

Do You Belong in Journalism? in The New Yorker [May 14, 1960]

Pablo Neruda
[Neftalí Ricardo Reyes y Basualto]
1904–1973

6   Treacherous
generals:
look at my dead house,
look at broken Spain.

Residencia en la Tierra (Residence on Earth), series III [1947]. Explico Algunas Cosas (I Explain a Few Things)[1]

7   But from each hollow of Spain
Spain comes forth.

Residencia en la Tierra, III. Explico Algunas Cosas

8   But from each crime are born bullets
that will one day seek out in you
where the heart lies.

Residencia en la Tierra, III. Explico Algunas Cosas

9   What a great language I have, it's a fine language we inherited from the fierce Conquistadors . . . They carried everything off and left us everything . . . They left us the words.

Confieso Que He Vivido: Memorias (Memoirs) [1974],[2] *ch. 2*

10   Poetry is an act of peace. Peace goes into the making of a poet as flour goes into the making of bread.

Confieso Que He Vivido: Memorias, 6

11   I continue to work with the materials I have, the materials I am made of. With feelings, beings, books, events, and battles, I am omnivorous. I would like to swallow the whole earth. I would like to drink the whole sea.

Confieso Que He Vivido: Memorias, 11

12   Poetry is a deep inner calling in man; from it came liturgy, the psalms, and also the content of religions.

Confieso Que He Vivido: Memorias, 11

J[ulius] Robert Oppenheimer
1904–1967

13   It did not take atomic weapons to make man want peace, a peace that would last. But the atomic bomb was the turn of the screw. It has made the prospect of future war unendurable.

The Atomic Bomb and College Education [1946]

14   In some sort of crude sense which no vulgarity, no humor, no overstatement can quite extinguish, the physicists have known sin; and this is a knowledge which they cannot lose.

Physics in the Contemporary World, lecture at Massachusetts Institute of Technology [November 25, 1947]

15   We knew the world would not be the same. A few people laughed, a few people cried. Most people were silent. I remembered the line from the Hindu scripture, the *Bhagavad Gita*. . . . "I am be-

---

[1]Translated by Donald D. Walsh.

[2]Translated by Hardie St. Martin.

come Death, the destroyer of worlds." I suppose we all thought that, one way or another.

Recalling the explosion of the first atomic bomb near Alamogordo, New Mexico [July 16, 1945].[1] From Len Giovanitti *and* Fred Freed, The Decision to Drop the Bomb [1965]

S[idney] J[oseph] Perelman
1904–1979

1   I have Bright's Disease and he has mine.

Caption for cartoon, in Judge *[November 16, 1926]*

2   Philomène was a dainty thing, built somewhat on the order of Lois De Fee, the lady bouncer. She had the rippling muscles of a panther, the stolidity of a water buffalo, and the lazy insolence of a shoe salesman.   *Crazy Like a Fox [1944].* Kitchen Bouquet

3   Outside of a spring lamb trotting into a slaughterhouse, there is nothing in the animal kingdom as innocent and foredoomed as the new purchaser of a country place. The moment he scratches his signature on the deed, it is open season and no limit to the bag.   *Acres and Pains [1947], ch. 2*

4   The mere mention of Hollywood induces a condition in me like breakbone fever. It was a hideous and untenable place when I dwelt there, populated with few exceptions by Yahoos, and now that it has become the chief citadel of television, it's unspeakable.   *Interview in* Paris Review *[1964]*

5   There are nineteen words in Yiddish that convey gradations of disparagement from a mild, fluttery helplessness to a state of downright, irreconcilable brutishness. All of them can be usefully employed to pinpoint the kind of individuals I write about.

Interview in Paris Review

6   Button-cute, rapier-keen, wafer-thin and pauper-poor.   *Self-description*

Dr. Seuss [Theodor Seuss Geisel]
1904–1991

7 I meant what I said
And I said what I meant . . .[2]
An elephant's faithful
One hundred per cent!

Horton Hatches the Egg [1940]

8 You will see something new.
Two things. And I call them
Thing One and Thing Two.

The Cat in the Hat [1957]

Isaac Bashevis Singer
1904–1991

9   When literature becomes overly erudite, it means that interest in the art has gone and curiosity about the artist is what's most important. It becomes a kind of idolatry.

Isaac Bashevis Singer Talks . . . About Everything, interview with Richard Burgin in the New York Times Magazine *[November 26, 1978]*

10   It seems that the analysis of character is the highest human entertainment. And literature does it, unlike gossip, without mentioning real names.

Isaac Bashevis Singer Talks . . . About Everything, interview with Richard Burgin in the New York Times Magazine

11   There is a quiet humor in Yiddish and a gratitude for every day of life, every crumb of success, each encounter of love. . . . In a figurative way, Yiddish is the wise and humble language of us all, the idiom of a frightened and hopeful humanity.

Nobel lecture, Stockholm [December 8, 1978]

12   Children don't read to find their identity. They don't read to free themselves of guilt, to quench the thirst for rebellion, or to get rid of alienation. They have no use for psychology. They detest sociology. . . . They still believe in good, the family, angels, devils, witches, goblins, logic, clarity, punctuation and other such obsolete stuff.

Address at Nobel Prize banquet, Stockholm [December 10, 1978]

13   Buildings will collapse, power plants will stop generating electricity. Generals will drop atomic bombs on their own populations. Mad revolutionaries will run in the streets, crying fantastic slogans. I have often thought it would begin in New York. This metropolis has all the symptoms of a mind gone berserk.

Collected Stories [1986]. The Cafeteria[3]

B[urrhus] F[rederic] Skinner
1904–1990

14   The one fact that I would cry from every housetop is this: the Good Life is waiting for us—here and now! . . . At this very moment we have the nec-

---

[1]Oppenheimer also recalled another line from the *Bhagavad Gita*, "If the radiance of a thousand suns. . . ." See 87:8.

Now we are all sons of bitches. —Kenneth Tompkins Bainbridge [1904–1996]. Oppenheimer later remarked that this was "the best thing anyone said after the test."

[2]Ellipses are in the original text.

[3]Translated by Isaac Bashevis Singer and Dorothea Straus.

essary techniques, both material and psychological, to create a full and satisfying life for everyone.
Walden Two [1948], ch. 23

1   The real problem is not whether machines think but whether men do.
Contingencies of Reinforcement [1969], ch. 9

2   We are all controlled by the world in which we live, and part of that world has been and will be constructed by men. The question is this: are we to be controlled by accidents, by tyrants, or by ourselves in effective cultural design?
Cumulative Record [third edition, 1972], ch. 1

Betty [Wehner] Smith
1904–1972

3   There's a tree that grows in Brooklyn. Some people call it the Tree of Heaven. No matter where its seed falls, it makes a tree which struggles to reach the sky.   *A Tree Grows in Brooklyn [1943]*

Jane Ace
1905–1974

4   Time wounds all heels.[1]
From GOODMAN ACE, *The Fine Art of Hypochondria; or, How Are You? [1966]*

J[ames] William Fulbright
1905–1995

5   A policy that can be accurately, though perhaps not prudently, defined as one of "peaceful coexistence."   *Speech in the Senate [March 27, 1964]*

6   We must dare to think "unthinkable" thoughts. We must learn to explore all the options and possibilities that confront us in a complex and rapidly changing world. We must learn to welcome and not to fear the voices of dissent. We must dare to think about "unthinkable things" because when things become unthinkable, thinking stops and action becomes mindless.
Speech in the Senate [March 27, 1964]

Greta Garbo [Greta Gustafson]
1905–1990

7   I want to be alone.[2]   *Attributed*

---

[1]Also attributed to FRANK CASE, proprietor of the Algonquin Hotel.

[2]Garbo maintains that her most famous remark has always been misquoted. . . . "I only said, 'I want to be *let* alone!'" — JOHN BAINBRIDGE, *in Life* [January 24, 1955]

Dag Hammarskjöld
1905–1961

8   What gives life its value you can find — and lose. But never possess. This holds good above all for "the Truth about Life."   *Markings 1964*

9 The longest journey
Is the journey inwards
Of him who has chosen his destiny.
Markings 1964

Lillian Hellman
1905–1984

10   There are people who eat the earth and eat all the people on it like in the Bible with the locusts. And other people who stand around and watch them eat it.   *The Little Foxes [1939], act III*

11   For every man who lives without freedom, the rest of us must face the guilt.
Watch on the Rhine [1941], act II

12   Lonely people talking to each other can make each other lonelier.
The Autumn Garden [1951], act I

13   I am most willing to answer all questions about myself . . . But . . . I am not willing, now or in the future, to bring bad trouble to people who, in my past association with them, were completely innocent of any talk or any action that was disloyal or subversive.
Letter to the House Committee on Un-American Activities [May 19, 1952]

14   I cannot and will not cut my conscience to fit this year's fashions.
Letter to the House Committee on Un-American Activities

15   A man should be jailed for telling lies to the young.   *Candide [1956],[3] act II, sc. iii*

16   We will not think noble because we are not noble. We will not live in beautiful harmony because there is no such thing in this world, nor should there be. We promise only to do our best and live out our lives. Dear God, that's all we can promise in truth.   *Candide, II, iii*

Arthur Koestler
1905–1983

17   One may not regard the world as a sort of metaphysical brothel for emotions.
Darkness at Noon [1941].[4] The Second Hearing

---

[3]A comic operetta based upon Voltaire's satire. See Voltaire, 316:2–316:9, and Wilbur, 809:5.

[4]Translated by DAPHNE HARDY.

1   The definition of the individual was: a multitude of one million divided by one million.
> *Darkness at Noon. The Grammatical Fiction*

2   The Yogi and the Commissar.
> *Title of book [1945]*

Stanley Kunitz
1905–

3   On the royal road to Thebes
I had my luck, I met a lovely monster,
And the story's this: I made the monster me.
> *The Approach to Thebes [1958]*

4 I recognize the gods' capricious hand
And write this poem for money, rage, and love.
> *The Thief [1958]*

5 The thing that eats the heart is mostly heart.
> *The Thing That Eats the Heart [1958],*
> *last line*

6 Slime, in the grains of the State,
like smut in the corn,
from the top infected.
Hatred made law.
> *Around Pastor Bonhoeffer [1971]. Next to*
> *Last Things*

7 That pack of scoundrels
tumbling through the gate
emerges
as the Order of the State.   *The System [1971]*

8 *Liebchen,*
with whom should I quarrel
except in the hiss of love,
that harsh, irregular flame?   *The Quarrel [1979]*

9 In every house of marriage
there's room for an interpreter.
> *Route Six [1979]*

10 After all,
we are partners in this land,
co-signers of a covenant.
At my touch the wild
braid of creation
trembles.
> *Next-to-Last Things [1985]. The Snakes of*
> *September*

11 Our lives are spinning out
from world to world;
the shapes of things
are shifting in the wind.
What do we know
beyond the rapture and the dread?
> *Next-to-Last Things. The Abduction*

12   You have become like us,
disgraced and mortal.
> *Next-to-Last Things. The Wellfleet Whale*

Phyllis McGinley
1905–1977

13 Meek-eyed parents hasten down the ramps
To greet their offspring, terrible from camps.
> *Ode to the End of Summer*

14 Prince, I warn you, under the rose,
Time is the thief you cannot banish.
These are my daughters, I suppose.
But where in the world did the children vanish?
> *Ballade of Lost Objects [1954]*

15 Always on Monday morning the press reports
God as revealed to His vicars in various guises—
Benevolent, stormy, patient, or out of sorts.
God knows which God is the God God recognizes.
> *The Day After Sunday [1954]*

16 A mother's hardest to forgive.
Life is the fruit she longs to hand you,
Ripe on a plate. And while you live,
Relentlessly she understands you.   *The Adversary*

John O'Hara
1905–1970

17   Hot lead can be almost as effective coming from a linotype as from a firearm.
> *The Portable F. Scott Fitzgerald [1945],*
> *introduction*

18   An artist is his own fault.
> *The Portable F. Scott Fitzgerald, introduction*

Anthony Powell
1905–2000

19   All women are stimulated by the news that any wife has left any husband.
> *The Acceptance World [1955], ch. 4*

20   In the break-up of a marriage the world inclines to take the side of the partner with the most vitality, rather than the one apparently least to blame.
> *The Acceptance World, 5*

Ayn Rand
1905–1982

21   Civilization is the progress toward a society of privacy. The savage's whole existence is public,

ruled by the laws of his tribe. Civilization is the process of setting man free from men.
The Fountainhead [1943]

1   Great men can't be ruled.   *The Fountainhead*

2   Kill reverence and you've killed the hero in man.
The Fountainhead

3   If you ask me to name the proudest distinction of Americans—I would choose—because it contains all the others—the fact that they were the people who created the phrase "to *make* money." No other language or nation had ever used these words before. . . . Americans were the first to understand that wealth has to be created.
Atlas Shrugged [1957]

Jean Paul Sartre
1905–1980

4   Everything is gratuitous, this garden, this city and myself. When you suddenly realize it, it makes you feel sick and everything begins to drift . . . that's nausea.   *La Nausée (Nausea) [1938]*

5   Man is not the sum of what he has but the totality of what he does not yet have, of what he might have.   *Situations [1939], I*

6   We do not do what we want and yet we are responsible for what we are—that is the fact.
Situations, II

7   Man can will nothing unless he has first understood that he must count on no one but himself; that he is alone, abandoned on earth in the midst of his infinite responsibilities, without help, with no other aim than the one he sets himself, with no other destiny than the one he forges for himself on this earth.
L'Être et le Néant (Being and Nothingness) [1943]

8 Hell is—other people![1]
Huis-Clos (No Exit) [1944], sc. v

9   I was escaping from Nature and at last becoming myself, that Other whom I was aspiring to be in the eyes of others.   *Les Mots (The Words) [1964][2]*

10   All the same, they [books] do serve some purpose. Culture doesn't save anything or anyone, it doesn't justify. But it's a product of man: he projects himself into it, he recognizes himself in it; that critical mirror alone offers him his image.
Les Mots

11   Never have I thought that I was the happy possessor of a "talent"; my sole concern has been to save myself by work and faith.   *Les Mots*

12   If I relegate impossible Salvation to the prop-room, what remains? A whole man, composed of all men and as good as all of them and no better than any.   *Les Mots*

Wallace Stanley Sayre
1905–1972

13   In any dispute, the intensity of feeling is inversely proportional to the value of the stakes at issue. That is why academic politics are so bitter.   *Saying[3]*

Sir C[harles] P[ercy] Snow
1905–1980

14   Literary intellectuals at one pole—at the other scientists. . . . Between the two a gulf of mutual incomprehension.
The Two Cultures and the Scientific Revolution [1959]

15   No one is fit to be trusted with power. . . . No one. . . . Any man who has lived at all knows the follies and wickedness he's capable of. If he does not know it, he is not fit to govern others. And if he does know it, he knows also that neither he nor any man ought to be allowed to decide a single human fate.   *The Light and the Dark [1961]*

Lionel Trilling
1905–1976

16   The poet is in command of his fantasy, while it is exactly the mark of the neurotic that he is possessed by his fantasy.
The Liberal Imagination [1950]. Freud and Literature

17   There is no connection between the political ideas of our educated class and the deep places of the imagination.
The Liberal Imagination. The Function of the Little Magazine

18   Occasions are rare when the best literature becomes, as it were, the folk literature, and generally speaking literature has always been carried on within small limits and under great difficulties.
The Liberal Imagination. The Function of the Little Magazine

---

[1] L'enfer, c'est les Autres.
[2] Translated by BERNARD FRECHTMAN.

[3] "Sayre's Law" is sometimes cited as: "The politics of the university are so intense because the stakes are so low." Often but mistakenly attributed to HENRY A. KISSINGER.

1 We are all ill [i.e., neurotic]: but even a universal sickness implies an idea of health.

The Liberal Imagination. Art and Neurosis

2 The poet . . . may be used as the barometer, but let us not forget that he is also part of the weather.

The Liberal Imagination. The Sense of the Past

Harold Adamson
1906–1980

3 Comin' In on a Wing and a Prayer.

Title of song [1943][1]

Hannah Arendt
1906–1975

4 Aristotle explicitly assures us that man, insofar as he is a natural being and belongs to the species of mankind, possesses immortality; through the recurrent cycle of life, nature assures the same kind of being-forever to things that are born and die as to things that are and do not change.

Between Past and Future [1961], ch. 2

5 It was as though in those last minutes he [Eichmann][2] was summing up the lessons that this long course in human wickedness had taught us — the lesson of the fearsome, word-and-thought-defying *banality of evil.*

Eichmann in Jerusalem: A Report on the Banality of Evil [1963], ch. 15

6 No punishment has ever possessed enough power of deterrence to prevent the commission of crimes. On the contrary, whatever the punishment, once a specific crime has appeared for the first time, its reappearance is more likely than its initial emergence could have been.

Eichmann in Jerusalem: A Report on the Banality of Evil, epilogue

7 The hypocrite's crime is that he bears false witness against himself. What makes it so plausible to assume that hypocrisy is the vice of vices is that integrity can indeed exist under the cover of all other vices except this one. Only crime and the criminal, it is true, confront us with the perplexity of radical evil; but only the hypocrite is really rotten to the core.

On Revolution [1963], ch. 2

---

[1]Music by JIMMY McHUGH.

[2]To sum it all up, I must say I regret nothing. — [KARL] ADOLF EICHMANN [1906–1962], *while awaiting trial in Israel*

Richard Armour
1906–1989

8 Shake and shake
The catsup bottle.
None will come,
And then a lot'll.   *Going to Extremes [1949]*

Samuel Beckett
1906–1989

9 That's how it is on this bitch of an earth.

Waiting for Godot [1952], act I

10 Nothing happens, nobody comes, nobody goes, it's awful!   *Waiting for Godot, I*

11 He can't think without his hat.

Waiting for Godot, I

12 We are all born mad. Some remain so.

Waiting for Godot, II

13 *Estragon:* I can't go on like this.
Vladimir: That's what you think.

Waiting for Godot, II

14 *Clov:* Do you believe in the life to come?
Hamm: Mine was always like that.

Endgame [1957]

15 Nothing is funnier than unhappiness.

Endgame [1958]

16 Where I am, I don't know, I'll never know, in the silence you don't know, you must go on, I can't go on, I'll go on.

The Unnamable [1959], closing words

17 I could not have gone through the awful wretched mess of life without having left a stain upon the silence.

From DEIRDRE BAIR, *Samuel Beckett [1978]*

John Betjeman
1906–1984

18 He rose, and he put down The Yellow Book.
He staggered — and, terrible-eyed,
He brushed past the palms on the staircase
And was helped to a hansom outside.

The Arrest of Oscar Wilde at the Cadogan Hotel [1937], st. 9

19 Gracious Lord, oh bomb the Germans.
Spare their women for Thy Sake,
And if that is not too easy
We will pardon Thy Mistake.
But, gracious Lord, whate'er shall be,
Don't let anyone bomb me.

In Westminster Abbey [1940]

1 The sort of girl I like to see
Smiles down from her great height at me.
The Olympic Girl [1954]

2 Oh! would I were her racket pressed
With hard excitement to her breast.
The Olympic Girl

William J[oseph] Brennan, Jr.
1906–1997

3   Debate on public issues should be uninhibited, robust, and wide open, and that . . . may well include vehement, caustic, and sometimes unpleasantly sharp attacks on government and public officials.   *New York Times Co. v. Sullivan [1964]*

4   If the right of privacy means anything, it is the right of the individual, married or single, to be free from unwarranted governmental intrusion into matters so fundamentally affecting a person as the decision whether to bear or beget a child.
Eisenstadt v. Baird [1972]

5   Our nation has had a long and unfortunate history of sex discrimination . . . rationalized by an attitude of "romantic paternalism" which, in practical effect, put women not on a pedestal, but in a cage.
Frontiero v. Richardson [1973]

Robert Buckner
1906–

6   Some day, when things are tough, maybe you can ask the boys to go in there and win just one for the Gipper![1]
Knute Rockne — All-American (screenplay) [1940], spoken by Ronald Reagan as George Gipp

Curtis [Emerson] LeMay
1906–1990

7   My solution to the problem [of North Vietnam] would be to tell them frankly that they've got to draw in their horns and stop their aggression, or we're going to bomb them back into the Stone Age.   *Mission with LeMay [1965]*

Anne Morrow Lindbergh
1906–2001

8   The wave of the future is coming and there is no fighting it.   *The Wave of the Future [1940]*

---

[1]See Rockne, 724:16.

9   I . . . understand why the saints were rarely married women. I am convinced it has nothing inherently to do, as I once supposed, with chastity or children. It has to do primarily with distractions. . . . Woman's normal occupations in general run counter to creative life, or contemplative life or saintly life.
Gift from the Sea [1955], ch. 2

10   By and large, mothers and housewives are the only workers who do not have regular time off. They are the great vacationless class.
Gift from the Sea, 3

Satchel [Leroy] Paige
c. 1906–1982

11   Avoid fried meats which angry up the blood. If your stomach disputes you, lie down and pacify it with cool thoughts. Keep the juices flowing by jangling around gently as you move. Go very light on the vices, such as carrying on in society. The social ramble ain't restful. Avoid running at all times. Don't look back. Something might be gaining on you.   *How to Stay Young [1953]*

Roberto Rossellini
1906–1977

12   I am not a pessimist; to perceive evil where it exists is, in my opinion, a form of optimism.
Interview in Cahiers du Cinéma [1954]

Laurens Van der Post
1906–1996

13   Life is its own journey, presupposes its own change and movement, and one tries to arrest them at one's eternal peril.
Venture to the Interior [1951], pt. III, ch. 12

14   Africa has always walked in my mind proudly upright, an African giant among the other continents, toes well dug into the final ocean of one hemisphere, rising to its full height in the graying skies of the other; head and shoulders broad, square and enduring, making light of the bagful of blue Mediterranean slung over its back as it marches patiently through time.

Flamingo Feather [1955], ch. 3

15   Human beings are perhaps never more frightening than when they are convinced beyond doubt that they are right.
The Lost World of the Kalahari [1958], ch. 3

Elmer Wheeler
1906–1968

1   Don't sell the steak; sell the sizzle. It is the sizzle that sells the steak and not the cow, although the cow is, of course, mighty important.
Principle number 1 of salesmanship [c. 1936]

Henny Youngman
1906–1998

2   Take my wife . . . please!   *Comedy line*

W[ystan] H[ugh] Auden[1]
1907–1973

3 Let us honor if we can
The vertical man
Though we value none
But the horizontal one.
Epigraph for Poems [1930]

4 Sir, no man's enemy, forgiving all
But will his negative inversion, be prodigal.
Sir, No Man's Enemy [1930]

5 Harrow the house of the dead; look shining at
New styles of architecture, a change of heart.
Sir, No Man's Enemy

6 He was my North, my South, my East and West,
My working week and my Sunday rest,
My noon, my midnight, my talk, my song;
I thought that love would last forever: I was
    wrong.   *Twelve Songs. IX [1936]*

7 The greater the love, the more false to its object,
Not to be born is the best for man;
After the kiss comes the impulse to throttle,
Break the embraces, dance while you can.
O Who Can Ever Gaze His Fill [1936]

8 The stars are dead. The animals will not look.
We are left alone with our day, and the time is
    short, and History to the defeated
May say Alas but cannot help or pardon.
Spain [1937]

9 O plunge your hands in water,
Plunge them in up to the wrist;
Stare, stare in the basin
And wonder what you've missed.

The glacier knocks in the cupboard,
The desert sighs in the bed,

---
[1]Dates of composition follow *Collected Poems*, *ed.* EDWARD MENDELSOHN [London, 1991].

And the crack in the tea cup opens
A lane to the land of the dead.
As I Walked Out One Evening [1937],
st. 10, 11

10 Lay your sleeping head, my love,
Human on my faithless arm.
Lullaby [1937], st. 1

11 Every farthing of the cost,
All the dreaded cards foretell,
Shall be paid, but from this night
Not a whisper, not a thought,
Not a kiss nor look be lost.   *Lullaby, st. 3*

12 About suffering they were never wrong,
The Old Masters: how well they understood
Its human position; how it takes place
While someone else is eating or opening a window
    Or just walking dully along.
Musée des Beaux Arts [1938]

13 I sit in one of the dives
On Fifty-second Street
Uncertain and afraid
As the clever hopes expire
Of a low dishonest decade:
Waves of anger and fear
Circulate over the bright
And darkened lands of the earth,
Obsessing our private lives;
The unmentionable odor of death
Offends the September night.
September 1, 1939 [1939], st. 1

14 Earth, receive an honored guest;
William Yeats is laid to rest.
Let the Irish vessel lie
Emptied of its poetry.
In Memory of W. B. Yeats [1939], III, st. 1

15 In the nightmare of the dark
All the dogs of Europe bark.
In Memory of W. B. Yeats, III, st. 2

16 Intellectual disgrace
Stares from every human face,
And the seas of pity lie
Locked and frozen in each eye.
In Memory of W. B. Yeats, III, st. 3

17 To us he is no more a person
Now but a whole climate of opinion.
In Memory of Sigmund Freud [1939], st. 17

18 One rational voice is dumb: over a grave
The household of Impulse mourns one dearly
    loved.
Sad is Eros, builder of cities,
And weeping anarchic Aphrodite.
In Memory of Sigmund Freud, st. 28

1 Law, says the judge as he looks down his nose,
  Speaking clearly and most severely,
  Law is as I've told you before,
  Law is as you know I suppose,
  Law is but let me explain it once more,
  Law is The Law.   *Law Like Love [1939], st. 4*

2 Like love we don't know where or why
  Like love we can't compel or fly
  Like love we often weep
  Like love we seldom keep.
                    Law Like Love, last stanza

3 Our researchers into Public Opinion are content
  That he held the proper opinions for the time of
      year;
  When there was peace, he was for peace; when
      there was war, he went.
          *The Unknown Citizen (To JS/07/M/378
          This Marble Monument Is Erected by the
          State) [1939]*

4 Was he free? Was he happy? The question is absurd:
  Had anything been wrong, we should certainly
      have heard.
          *The Unknown Citizen (To JS/07/M/378
          This Marble Monument Is Erected by the
          State)*

5 At Dirty Dick's and Sloppy Joe's
  We drank our liquor straight,
  Some went upstairs with Margery,
  And some, alas, with Kate.
          *The Sea and the Mirror [1944]. Master and
          Boatswain*

6 And children swarmed to him like settlers. He
      became a land.   *Edward Lear [1945]*

7 Thou shalt not sit
  With statisticians nor commit
  A social science.
                    Under Which Lyre [1946], st. 27

8 If thou must choose
  Between the chances, choose the odd;
  Read the *New Yorker;* trust in God;
  And take short views.
                    Under Which Lyre, last stanza

9 Sob, heavy world,
  Sob as you spin,
  Mantled in mist, remote from the happy.
                    The Age of Anxiety [1946]

10 She looked over his shoulder
   For vines and olive trees,
   Marble well-governed cities
   And ships upon untamed seas,
   But there on the shining metal
   His hands had put instead

An artificial wilderness
And a sky like lead.
          The Shield of Achilles [1952], st. 1

11 The mass and majesty of this world, all
   That carries weight and always weighs the same,
   Lay in the hands of others; they were small
   And could not hope for help, and no help came;
   What their foes liked to do was done, their shame
   Was all the worst could wish: they lost their pride
   And died as men before their bodies died.
          The Shield of Achilles, st. 6

12   Some books are undeservedly forgotten; none
   are undeservedly remembered.
          The Dyer's Hand [1962]. Pt. I, Reading

13   It takes little talent to see clearly what lies under
   one's nose, a good deal of it to know in which direction to point that organ.
          The Dyer's Hand, I, Writing

14   Speaking for myself, the questions which interest
   me most when reading a poem are two. The first is
   technical: "Here is a verbal contraption. How does it
   work?" The second is, in the broadest sense, moral:
   "What kind of a guy inhabits this poem? What is his
   notion of the good life or the good place? His notion of the Evil One? What does he conceal from the
   reader? What does he conceal even from himself?"
          *The Dyer's Hand, II, Making, Knowing and
          Judging*

15   Whatever its actual content and overt interest,
   every poem is rooted in imaginative awe. Poetry can
   do a hundred and one things, delight, sadden, disturb, amuse, instruct—it may express every possible
   shade of emotion, and describe every conceivable
   kind of event, but there is only one thing that all
   poetry must do; it must praise all it can for being
   and for happening.
          *The Dyer's Hand, II, Making, Knowing and
          Judging*

Jacques Barzun
1907–

16   Whoever wants to know the heart and mind of
   America had better learn baseball, the rules and realities of the game—and do it by watching first
   some high school or small-town teams.
          God's Country and Mine [1954], ch. 8

Lesley Blanch
1907–

17   She was an Amazon. Her whole life was spent
   riding at breakneck speed along the wilder shores of

love. For her, each new affair was an encampment set up along the way; sometimes a palace, sometimes a tent, but always the supreme refuge.

The Wilder Shores of Love [1954]. The Honorable Jane Digby el Mezrah

Rachel [Louise] Carson
1907–1964

1   The sea lies all about us. The commerce of all lands must cross it. The very winds that move over the lands have been cradled on its broad expanse and seek ever to return to it. The continents themselves dissolve and pass to the sea, in grain after grain of eroded land. So the rains that rose from it return again in rivers. In its mysterious past it encompasses all the dim origins of life and receives in the end, after, it may be, many transmutations, the dead husks of that same life. For all at last returns to the sea—to Oceanus, the ocean river, like the ever-flowing stream of time, the beginning and the end.

The Sea Around Us [1951], ch. 14, ending

2   As crude a weapon as the cave man's club, the chemical barrage has been hurled against the fabric of life.   *Silent Spring [1962]*

Richard Crossman
1907–1974

3   Six intellectuals describe the journey into Communism and the return. They saw it first from a long way off . . . as a vision of the Kingdom of God on earth.

The God That Failed [1950]. Introduction

Daphne du Maurier
1907–1989

4   Last night I dreamt I went to Manderley again.

Rebecca [1938], first line

Christopher Fry
1907–

5 I travel light; as light,
That is, as a man can travel who will
Still carry his body around because
Of its sentimental value.

The Lady's Not for Burning [1950], act I

6 Religion
Has made an honest woman of the supernatural.

The Lady's Not for Burning, II

7 Try thinking of love or something.
Amor vincit insomnia.[1]

A Sleep of Prisoners [1951]

Louis MacNeice
1907–1963

8 It's no go my honey love, it's no go my poppet;
Work your hands from day to day, the winds will blow the profit.
The glass is falling hour by hour, the glass will fall forever,
But if you break the bloody glass you won't hold up the weather.   *Bagpipe Music, last stanza*

John Wayne
1907–1979

9   Talk low, talk slow, and don't say too much.

Advice on acting

Simone de Beauvoir
1908–1986

10   I wish that every human life might be pure transparent freedom.   *The Blood of Others [1946]*

11   This has always been a man's world, and none of the reasons hitherto brought forward in explanation of this fact has seemed adequate.

The Second Sex [1949–1950], pt. II, ch. 4

12   It is not in giving life but in risking life that man is raised above the animal; that is why superiority has been accorded in humanity not to the sex that brings forth but to that which kills.

The Second Sex, II, 4

13   One is not born a woman, one becomes one.[2]

The Second Sex, IV, 12

14   When we abolish the slavery of half of humanity, together with the whole system of hypocrisy that it implies, then the "division" of humanity will reveal its genuine significance and the human couple will find its true form.   *The Second Sex, VII, conclusion*

15   It is for man to establish the reign of liberty in the midst of the world of the given. To gain the supreme victory, it is necessary, for one thing, that by and through their natural differentiation men and women unequivocally affirm their brotherhood.

The Second Sex, VII, conclusion

---

[1]See Virgil, 96:*n*1.

[2]On ne naît pas femme, on le devient.

1   The moment a woman gets power, she loses the solidarity she had with other women. She will want to be equal in a man's world and will become ambitious for her own sake.   *Interview [1984]*

Harry A[ndrew] Blackmun
1908–1999

2   The right of privacy . . . is broad enough to encompass a woman's decision whether or not to terminate her pregnancy.
    Roe v. Wade, 410 U.S. 153 [1973]

Jacob Bronowski
1908–1974

3   Man is a singular creature. He has a set of gifts which make him unique among the animals: so that, unlike them, he is not a figure in the landscape — he is a shaper of the landscape. In body and in mind he is the explorer of nature, the ubiquitous animal, who did not find but has made his home in every continent.   *The Ascent of Man [1973], ch. 1*

4   Nature — that is, biological evolution — has not fitted man to any specific environment. . . . Among the multitude of animals which scamper, fly, burrow, and swim around us, man is the only one who is not locked into his environment. His imagination, his reason, his emotional subtlety and toughness, make it possible for him not to accept the environment but to change it. And that series of inventions by which man from age to age has remade his environment is a different kind of evolution — not biological, but cultural evolution. I call that brilliant sequence of cultural peaks *The Ascent of Man*.   *The Ascent of Man, 1*

Johnny Burke
1908–1964

5   Ev'ry time it rains it rains pennies from Heaven. Don't you know each cloud contains pennies from Heaven?   *Pennies from Heaven [1936][1]*

M[ary] F[rances] K[ennedy] Fisher
1908–1992

6   When I write of hunger, I am really writing about love and the hunger for it, and warmth and the love of it and the hunger for it . . . and then the warmth and richness and fine reality of hunger satisfied . . . and it is all one.[2]
    The Gastronomical Me [1943]. Foreword

Ian [Lancaster] Fleming
1908–1964

7   I would like a medium Vodka dry Martini — with a slice of lemon peel. Shaken and not stirred, please.   *Dr. No [1958], ch. 14*

John Kenneth Galbraith
1908–

8   One can relish the varied idiocy of human action during a panic to the full, for, while it is a time of great tragedy, nothing is being lost but money.
    The Great Crash, 1929 [1955], ch. 1

9   Wealth is not without its advantages and the case to the contrary, although it has often been made, has never proved widely persuasive.
    The Affluent Society [1958], ch. 1

10   Originality is something that is easily exaggerated, especially by authors contemplating their own work.   *The Affluent Society, 1*

11   The hallmark of the conventional wisdom is acceptability. It has the approval of those to whom it is addressed.   *The Affluent Society, 2*

12   The leisure class has been replaced by another and much larger class to which work has none of the older connotation of pain, fatigue, or other mental or physical discomfort. We have failed to observe the emergence of this New Class, as it may be simply called.

    The Affluent Society, 24

13   The superior confidence which people repose in the tall man is well merited. Being tall, he is more visible than other men and being more visible, he is much more closely watched. In consequence, his behavior is far better than that of smaller men.
    The Scotch [1964]

14   We are becoming the servants in thought, as in action, of the machine we have created to serve us.
    The New Industrial State [1967], ch. 1

15   The individual serves the industrial system not by supplying it with savings and the resulting capital; he serves it by consuming its products.
    The New Industrial State, 4

---

[1]Music by ARTHUR JOHNSTON.

[2]Ellipses are in the original text.

1   Much of the world's work, it has been said, is done by men who do not feel quite well. [Karl] Marx is a case in point.
The Age of Uncertainty [1977], ch. 3

Lyndon B[aines] Johnson
1908–1973

2   Come now, let us reason together.   *Saying*

3   All I have I would have given gladly not to be standing here today.
First address to Congress as President [November 27, 1963]

4   We have talked long enough in this country about equal rights. We have talked for a hundred years or more. It is time now to write the next chapter—and to write in the books of law.
First address to Congress as President

5   We still seek no wider war.
Radio/television speech [August 4, 1964] on the Gulf of Tonkin resolution

6   This nation, this generation, in this hour has man's first chance to build a Great Society, a place where the meaning of man's life matches the marvels of man's labor.
Address, accepting the presidential nomination [August 1964]

7   We are not about to send American boys nine or ten thousand miles away from home to do what Asian boys ought to be doing for themselves.
Remark at Akron University, Akron, Ohio [October 21, 1964]

Otto Kerner, Jr.
1908–1976

8   Our nation is moving toward two societies, one black, one white—separate and unequal.
Report of the National Advisory Commission on Civil Disorders [1968], p. 1

Claude Lévi-Strauss
1908–

9   The world began without the human race and it will end without it. . . . Man has never—save only when he reproduces himself—done other than cheerfully dismantle million upon million of structures and reduce their elements to a state in which they can no longer be reintegrated.
Tristes Tropiques [1955].[1] Conclusion

10   I therefore claim to show, not how men think in myths, but how myths operate in men's minds without their being aware of the fact.
The Raw and the Cooked [1964].[2] Overture

Abraham H[arold] Maslow
1908–1970

11   A musician must make music, an artist must paint, a poet must write, if he is to be ultimately at peace with himself. What a man can be, he must be.
Motivation and Personality [1954]

12   It is tempting, if the only tool you have is a hammer, to treat everything as if it were a nail.
The Psychology of Science [1966]

Joseph R[aymond] McCarthy
1908–1957

13   I have here in my hand a list of two hundred and five [people] that were known to the Secretary of State as being members of the Communist Party and who nevertheless are still working and shaping the policy of the State Department.
Speech, Wheeling, West Virginia [February 9, 1950]

Edward R[oscoe] Murrow
1908–1965

14   This—is London.
Opening phrase for broadcasts from London during World War II [1939–1945]

15   I pray you to believe what I have said about Buchenwald. I have reported what I saw and heard, but only part of it. For most of it I have no words.
Broadcast report from London on Buchenwald concentration camp [April 15, 1945]

16   We must not confuse dissent with disloyalty.
See It Now (broadcast). Report on Senator Joseph R. McCarthy [March 7, 1954]

17   We will not be driven by fear into an age of unreason if we . . . remember that we are not descended from fearful men, not from men who feared to write, to speak, to associate and to defend causes which were, for the moment unpopular.
See It Now (broadcast). Report on Senator Joseph R. McCarthy [March 7, 1954]

18   Unless we get off our fat surpluses and recognize that television in the main is being used to distract,

---

[1]Translated by JOHN RUSSELL.

[2]Translated by JOHN and DOREEN WEIGHTMAN.

delude, amuse and insulate us, then television and those who finance it, those who look at it and those who work at it, may see a totally different picture too late.

*Speech at the Radio and Television News
Directors Convention, Chicago
[October 15, 1958]*

Frank S. Nugent
1908–1965

and

Laurence Stallings
1894–1968

1   Never apologize and never explain—it's a sign of weakness.[1]

*She Wore a Yellow Ribbon (screenplay) [1949],
spoken by John Wayne*

Theodore Roethke
1908–1963

2 My secrets cry aloud.
  I have no need for tongue.
  My heart keeps open house,
  My doors are widely flung.
                          Open House [1941], st. 1

3 This urge, wrestle, resurrection of dry sticks,
  Cut stems struggling to put down feet,
  What saint strained so much,
  Rose on such lopped limbs to a new life?
                          Cuttings (later) [1948]

4 Nothing would sleep in that cellar.
                          Root Cellar [1948]

5 Nothing would give up life:
  Even the dirt kept breathing a small breath.
                          Root Cellar

6 Tugging all day at perverse life:
  The indignity of it!   *Weed Puller [1948]*

7 The whiskey on your breath
  Could make a small boy dizzy;
  But I hung on like death:
  Such waltzing was not easy.
                          My Papa's Waltz [1948], st. 1

8 I study the lives on a leaf: the little
  Sleepers, numb nudgers in cold dimensions,

---

[1]Never contradict. Never explain. Never apologize. (Those are the secrets of a happy life!)—JOHN ARBUTHNOT FISHER [1841–1920], *Letter to The Times of London* [September 5, 1919]

Beetles in caves, newts, stone-deaf fishes,
Lice tethered to long limp subterranean weeds,
Squirmers in bogs,
And bacterial creepers.   *The Minimal [1948]*

9 At Woodlawn I heard the dead cry;
  I was lulled by the slamming of iron,
  A slow drip over stones,
  Toads brooding in wells.
  All the leaves stuck out their tongues;
  I shook the softening chalk of my bones,
  Saying,
  Snail, snail, glister me forward,
  Bird, soft-sigh me home.
  Worm, be with me.
  This is my hard time.
                The Lost Son [1948], 1. The Flight

10 Fear was my father, Father Fear.
   His look drained the stones.
                The Lost Son, 3. The Gibber

11 A lively understandable spirit
   Once entertained you.
   It will come again.
   Be still.
   Wait.   *The Lost Son, 5. "It was beginning winter"*

12 And the new plants, still awkward in their soil,
   The lovely diminutives.
   I could watch! I could watch!
   I saw the separateness of all things!
                A Field of Light [1948], III

13 I remember the neckcurls, limp and damp as
       tendrils,
   And her quick look, a sidelong pickerel smile.
                Elegy for Jane [1953]

14 I take this cadence from a man named Yeats;
   I take it, and I give it back again.
       Four for Sir John Davies [1953], I. The Dance

15 I wake to sleep, and take my waking slow.
   I feel my fate in what I cannot fear.
   I learn by going where I have to go.
                The Waking [1953]

16 I knew a woman, lovely in her bones,
   When small birds sighed, she would sigh back at
       them;
   Ah, when she moved, she moved more ways than
       one:
   The shapes a bright container can contain!
                I Knew a Woman [1958]

17 Each one's himself yet each one's everyone.
                The Sententious Man [1958], st. 6

18 When I was a lark, I sang;
   When I was a worm, I devoured.
                What Can I Tell My Bones? [1958]

1 I long for the imperishable quiet at the heart of
     form.   *The Longing [1964]*

2 Old men should be explorers?[1]
  I'll be an Indian.
  Ogalala?
  Iroquois.   *The Longing*

3 What I love is near at hand,
  Always, in earth and air.
        The Far Field [1964], III

4 In a dark time, the eye begins to see.
        In a Dark Time [1964], st. 1

5 The soul has many motions, body one.
        The Motion [1964], I

6 Love begets love. This torment is my joy.
        The Motion, II

7 What's the worst portion in this mortal life?
  A pensive mistress, and a yelping wife.
        The Marrow [1964], I

8 Brooding on God, I may become a man.
  Pain wanders through my bones like a lost fire;
  What burns me now? Desire, desire, desire.
        The Marrow, II

9 Lord, hear me out, and hear me out this day:
  From me to Thee's a long and terrible way.
        The Marrow, III

10 Now I adore my life
  With the Bird, the abiding Leaf,
  With the Fish, the questing Snail,
  And the Eye altering all;
  And I dance with William Blake
  For love, for Love's sake.
        Once More, the Round [1964]

William Saroyan
1908–1981

11   If you give to a thief he cannot steal from you,
and he is then no longer a thief.
        The Human Comedy [1943], ch. 4

Victor [Frederick] Weisskopf
1908–

12   In man's brain the impressions from outside are
not merely registered; they produce concepts and
ideas. They are the imprint of the external world
upon the human brain. Therefore, it is not surpris-
ing that, after a long period of searching and erring,
some of the concepts and ideas in human thinking
should have come gradually closer to the fundamental laws of this world, that some of our thinking
should reveal the true structure of atoms and the
true movements of the stars. Nature, in the form of
man, begins to recognize itself.
        Knowledge and Wonder [1962]

Richard Wright
1908–1960

13   Goddammit, look! We live here and they live
there. We black and they white. They got things
and we ain't. They do things and we can't. It's just
like living in jail.   *Native Son [1940], bk. I*

14   Who knows when some slight shock, disturbing
the delicate balance between social order and thirsty
aspiration, shall send the skyscrapers in our cities
toppling?   *Native Son, I*

15   If we had been allowed to participate in the vital
processes of America's national growth, what would
have been the textures of our lives, the pattern of
our traditions, the routine of our customs, the state
of our arts, the code of our laws, the function of our
government! . . . We black folk say that America
would have been stronger and greater.
        12 Million Black Voices [1941]

James Agee
1909–1955

16   If I could do it, I'd do no writing at all here. It
would be photographs; the rest would be fragments
of cloth, bits of cotton, lumps of earth, records of
speech, pieces of wood and iron, phials of odors,
plates of food and of excrement. . . . A piece of the
body torn out by the root might be more to the
point.
        Let Us Now Praise Famous Men [1941].
        Preamble

17   All over Alabama the lamps are out. Every leaf
drenches the touch; the spider's net is heavy. The
roads lie there with nothing to use them. The fields
lie there, with nothing at work in them, neither
man nor beast.
        Let Us Now Praise Famous Men. On the
        Porch: 1

18   Nature, Mr. Allnut, is what we are put into this
world to rise above.
        The African Queen (screenplay) [1951],
        spoken by Katharine Hepburn

---

[1]See T. S. Eliot, 721:6.

Nelson Algren
1909–1981

1   [Algren] shunts aside all rules, regulations, and dicta, except for three laws that he says a nice little old Negro lady once taught him: Never play cards with any man named "Doc." Never eat at any place called "Mom's." And never, ever, no matter what else you do in your life, *never* sleep with anyone whose troubles are worse than your own.

> From H. E. F. DONOHUE, *Conversations with Nelson Algren [1964]*

Eric Ambler
1909–1998

2   The important thing to know about an assassination or an attempted assassination is not who fired the shot, but who paid for the bullet.

> *A Coffin for Demetrios [1939], ch. 2*

Sir Isaiah Berlin
1909–1997

3   There exists a great chasm between those, on one side, who relate everything to a single, central vision, one system more or less coherent or articulate, in terms of which they understand, think and feel . . . and, on the other side, those who pursue many ends, often unrelated and even contradictory. . . . The first kind of intellectual and artistic personality belongs to the hedgehogs, the second to the foxes. . . . Dante belongs to the first category, Shakespeare to the second.

> *The Hedgehog and the Fox [1953], pt. 1*[1]

4   One belief, more than any other, is responsible for the slaughter of individuals on the altars of the great historical ideals. . . . This is the belief that somewhere, in the past or in the future, in divine revelation or in the mind of an individual thinker, in the pronouncements of history or science, or in the simple heart of an uncorrupted good man, there is a final solution.   *Two Concepts of Liberty [1958]*

Paul Brooks
1909–

5   In America today you can murder land for private profit. You can leave the corpse for all to see, and nobody calls the cops.

> *The Pursuit of Wilderness [1971], ch. 1*

Dazai Osamu [Tsushima Shuji]
1909–1948

6   My unhappiness was the unhappiness of a person who could not say no.

> *No Longer Human*

Julius J. Epstein
1909–2000
and
Philip G. Epstein
1909–1952
and
Howard Koch
1916–1995

7   Of all the gin joints in all the towns in all the world, she walks into mine!

> *Casablanca (screenplay) [1943], spoken by Humphrey Bogart*

8   Play it, Sam.[2]

> *Casablanca (screenplay), spoken by Ingrid Bergman*

9   Here's looking at you, kid.

> *Casablanca (screenplay), spoken by Humphrey Bogart*

10   I'm *shocked, shocked* to discover that gambling is going on here!

> *Casablanca (screenplay), spoken by Claude Rains*

11   Round up the usual suspects.

> *Casablanca (screenplay), spoken by Claude Rains*

12   Louis, I think this is the beginning of a beautiful friendship.

> *Casablanca (screenplay), closing line, spoken by Humphrey Bogart*

Edwin [Herbert] Land
1909–1991

13   The bottom line is in heaven.

> *Reply [1977] rejecting view that only the bottom line of the balance sheet shows the worth of a product*

---

[1]See Archilochus, 56:22.

[2]Play it! — *Casablanca*, spoken by Humphrey Bogart.

Stanislaw J[erzy] Lec
1909–1966

1   One has to multiply thoughts to the point where there aren't enough policemen to control them.
Unkempt Thoughts [1962][1]

2   Proverbs contradict each other. That is the wisdom of a nation.   *Unkempt Thoughts*

3   No snowflake in an avalanche ever feels responsible.   *More Unkempt Thoughts [1968]*[1]

4   Get out of the way of justice. She is blind.
More Unkempt Thoughts

5   Prolong human life only when you can shorten its miseries.   *More Unkempt Thoughts*

6   Most of the sighs we hear have been edited.
More Unkempt Thoughts

Malcolm Lowry
1909–1957

7 Malcolm Lowry
Late of the Bowery
His prose was flowery
And often glowery
He lived, nightly, and drank, daily,
And died playing the ukelele.   *Epitaph*

8   How alike are the groans of love, to those of the dying.   *Under the Volcano [1947], ch. 12*

9   Somebody threw a dead dog after him down the ravine.   *Under the Volcano, last line*

10 Success is like some horrible disaster
Worse than your house burning.
After publication of Under the Volcano [1962]

Joseph Leo Mankiewicz
1909–1993

11   Fasten your seatbelts. It's going to be a bumpy night.
All About Eve (screenplay) [1950], spoken by Bette Davis

Elting E[lmore] Morison
1909–1995

12   The computer is no better than its program.
Men, Machines and Modern Times [1966]

C[yril] Northcote Parkinson
1909–1993

13   Work expands so as to fill the time available for its completion.   *Parkinson's Law [1957], ch. 1*

David Riesman
1909–

14   While all people want and need to be liked by some of the people some of the time, it is only the modern other-directed types who make this their chief source of direction and chief area of sensitivity.
The Lonely Crowd [1950], ch. 1

15   The idea that men are created free and equal is both true and misleading: men are created different; they lose their social freedom and their individual autonomy in seeking to become like each other.
The Lonely Crowd, 18

Stephen Spender
1909–1995

16 I think continually of those who were truly
great . . .
The names of those who in their lives fought for life,
Who wore at their hearts the fire's center.
Born of the sun they traveled a short while towards the sun,
And left the vivid air signed with their honor.
I Think Continually of Those

17   He's still half with us
Conniving slyly, yet he knows he's gone
Into that cellar where they'll never find him,
Happy to be alone, his last work done,
Word freed from world, into a different wood.
Collected Poems [1986]. Auden's Funeral, sec. 1

Simone Weil
1909–1943

18   Attachment is the great fabricator of illusions; reality can be attained only by someone who is detached.
Gravity and Grace (La Pesanteur et la Grâce) [1947]

19   Purity is the ability to contemplate defilement.
Gravity and Grace

20   Man alone can enslave man.
Oppression and Liberty [1958]. Reflections Concerning the Causes of Liberty and Social Oppression

1   What a country calls its vital economic interests are not the things which enable its citizens to live, but the things which enable it to make war. Gasoline is much more likely than wheat to be a cause of international conflict.

The Need for Roots (L'Enracinement) [1949]

Eudora Welty
1909–2001

2   I haven't a literary life at all, not much of a confession, maybe. But I do feel that the people and things I love are of a true and human world, and there is no clutter about them. . . . I would not understand a literary life.

Selected Stories of Eudora Welty [1943], introduction

3   The storm had rolled away to faintness like a wagon crossing a bridge.

A Curtain of Green [1941]. A Piece of News

4   The excursion is the same when you go looking for your sorrow as when you go looking for your joy.   *The Wide Net [1943]. The Wide Net*

5   All they could see was sky, water, birds, light, and confluence. It was the whole morning world.

The Optimist's Daughter [1978]

6   Writing fiction has developed in me an abiding respect for the unknown in a human lifetime and a sense of where to look for the threads, how to follow, how to connect, find in the thick of the tangle what clear line persists. The strands are all there: to the memory nothing is ever really lost.

One Writer's Beginnings [1984]. Finding a Voice

7   I am a writer who came of a sheltered life. A sheltered life can be a daring life as well. For all serious daring starts from within.

One Writer's Beginnings. Finding a Voice

Jean Anouilh
1910–1987

8   Orpheus—they've gone on now, the good as well as the bad. . . . They've done their little song and dance in your life. . . . They are that way in you now, forever.

Eurydice [1942]

9   This horror and all these useless gestures, this grotesque adventure is ours. We must live it. Death is absurd also.

Romeo and Jeannette [1946]

10   And under this carnival disguise the heart of an old youngster who is still waiting to give his all. But how to be recognized under this mask? This is what they call a fine career.

The Waltz of the Toreadors [1952]. English version

Jacques-Yves Cousteau
1910–1997

11   Sometimes we are lucky enough to know that our lives have been changed, to discard the old, embrace the new, and run headlong down an immutable course. It happened to me at Le Mourillon on that summer's day, when my eyes were opened to the sea.   *The Silent World [1953], ch. 1*

12   We must go and see for ourselves.[1]

Motto of his ship Calypso

Peter De Vries
1910–1993

13   We know the human brain is a device to keep the ears from grating on one another.

Comfort Me with Apples [1956], ch. 1

Tony [Two-Ton] Galento
1910–1979

14   I'll moider de bum.

Before his unsuccessful fight with Joe Louis for the heavyweight championship [June 28, 1939]

Jean Genet
1910–1986

15   To achieve harmony in bad taste is the height of elegance.

The Thief's Journal (Le Journal du Voleur) [1949]

16   I was already refusing to have taste. I forbade myself to have it. I knew that the cultivation of it would have not refined me but softened me.

The Thief's Journal

17   I call saintliness not a state but the moral procedure leading to it.

Quoted by Jean Paul Sartre in Saint Genet [1952]

---

[1] Il faut aller voir.

Frank Loesser
1910–1969

1 See what the boys in the back room will have
And tell them I'm having the same.
*Destry Rides Again [1939]. See What the Boys
in the Back Room Will Have*[1]

2 I'd love to get you
On a slow boat to China.
All to myself alone.
On a Slow Boat to China [1948]

Robert King Merton
1910–

3 The self-fulfilling prophecy is, in the beginning,
a *false* definition of the situation evoking a new behavior which makes the originally false conception
come *true*. The specious validity of the self-fulfilling
prophecy perpetuates a reign of error. For the prophet
will cite the actual course of events as proof that he
was right from the very beginning.
The Self-Fulfilling Prophecy [1948]

Wright Morris
1910–1998

4 In the dry places . . . towns, like weeds, spring
up when it rains, dry up when it stops. But in a dry
climate the husk of the plant remains. The stranger
might find, as if preserved in amber, something of
the green life that was once lived there, and the
ghosts of men who have gone on to a better place.
The withered towns are empty, but not uninhab-
ited. *The Works of Love [1952], ch. 1*

Mother Teresa
[Agnes Gonxha Bojaxhiu]
1910–1997

5 Let us do something beautiful for God. *Motto*

6 The greatest disease in the West today is not TB
or leprosy; it is being unwanted, unloved, and uncared for. We can cure physical diseases with medicine, but the only cure for loneliness, despair, and
hopelessness is love. *A Simple Path [1995]*

Elizabeth Bishop
1911–1979

7 This iceberg cuts its facets from within.
Like jewelry from a grave

---

[1]Music by FREDERICK HOLLANDER.

it saves itself perpetually and adorns
Only itself. *The Imaginary Iceberg [1946], st. 3*

8 Icebergs behoove the soul
(both being self-made from elements least visible)
to see them so: fleshed, fair, erected, indivisible.
The Imaginary Iceberg, st. 3

9 Until everything
was rainbow, rainbow, rainbow!
And I let the fish go. *The Fish [1946]*

10 Cold dark deep and absolutely clear,
element bearable to no mortal,
to fish and to seals . . . *At the Fishhouses [1955]*

11 It is like what we imagine knowledge to be:
dark, salt, clear, moving, utterly free,
drawn from the cold hard mouth
of the world, derived from the rocky breasts
forever, flowing and drawn, and since
our knowledge is historical, flowing, and flown.
At the Fishhouses

12 From Brooklyn, over the Brooklyn Bridge, on this
fine morning, please come flying.
*Invitation to Miss Marianne Moore [1955],
st. 1*

13 Should we have stayed at home,
wherever that may be?
Questions of Travel [1965]

14 *Time to plant tears,* says the almanac.
The grandmother sings to the marvelous stove
and the child draws another inscrutable house.
Sestina [1965]

15 The staring sailor
that shakes his watch
that tells the time
of the poet, the man
that lies in the house of Bedlam.
Visits to St. Elizabeths [1965], st. 11

16 I knew that nothing stranger
had ever happened.
In the Waiting Room [1976]

17 How had I come to be here
like them, and overhear
a cry of pain that could have
got loud and worse but hadn't?
In the Waiting Room

18 Home-made, home-made! But aren't we all?
Crusoe in England [1976]

19 I'd have
nightmares of other islands
stretching away from mine, infinities
of islands, islands spawning islands
like frogs' eggs turning into polliwogs

of islands, knowing that I had to live
on each and every one, eventually,
for ages, registering their flora,
their fauna, their geography.

Crusoe in England

1 —And Friday, my dear Friday, died of measles
seventeen years ago come March.

Crusoe in England

2 The art of losing isn't hard to master;
so many things seem filled with the intent
to be lost that their loss is no disaster.

Lose something every day. Accept the fluster
of lost door keys, the hour badly spent.
The art of losing isn't hard to master.

Geography III [1976]. One Art

3 Life and the memory of it cramped,
dim, on a piece of Bristol board.   *Poem [1976]*

Max Frisch
1911–1991

4   Technology . . . the knack of so arranging the
world that we don't have to experience it.

Homo Faber [1957]

William Golding
1911–1993

5   Ralph wept for the end of innocence, the darkness of man's heart, and the fall through the air of
the true, wise friend called Piggy.

The Lord of the Flies [1954], ch. 12

Hubert H[oratio] Humphrey
1911–1978

6   The politics of joy.

Presidential campaign slogan [1968]

Clark Kerr
1911–

7   The university has become the multiversity and the
nature of the presidency has followed this change. . . .
The president of the multiversity is leader, educator,
wielder of power, pump; he is also officeholder,
caretaker, inheritor, consensus seeker, persuader, bottleneck. But he is mostly a mediator.

*The Uses of the University. The Godkin
Lectures at Harvard University [1963]*

Noel Langley
1911–1981

8   Toto, I've a feeling we're not in Kansas anymore.
The Wizard of Oz (screenplay) [1939],[1] *spoken
by Judy Garland*

9   I'll get you, my pretty, and your little dog, too.
*The Wizard of Oz, spoken by Margaret
Hamilton*

Marshall [Herbert] McLuhan
1911–1980

10   The medium is the message.
*Understanding Media [1964], title of first
chapter*

11   There is a basic principle that distinguishes a hot
medium like radio from a cool one like the telephone, or a hot medium like the movie from a cool
one like TV. . . . Hot media are . . . low in participation, and cool media are high in participation or
completion by the audience.

Understanding Media, ch. 2

12   The new electronic interdependence recreates the
world in the image of a global village.

The Medium Is the Massage [1967]

Czeslaw Milosz
1911–

13 May the gentle mountains and the bells of the
   flocks
Remind us of everything we have lost,
For we have seen on our way and fallen in love
With the world that will pass in a twinkling.

Collected Poems 1931–1987[2]*. On Pilgrimage.*

14 Human reason is beautiful and invincible.
No bars, no barbed wire, no pulping of books,
No sentence of banishment can prevail against it.

Collected Poems 1931–1987[2]*. Incantation.*

David Ogilvy
1911–1999

15   The best headline I ever wrote contained *eighteen*
words: At Sixty Miles an Hour the Loudest Noise in
the New Rolls-Royce comes from the electric clock.

*Confessions of an Advertising Man [1963],
ch. 6*

---

[1]Written with Florence Ryerson and Edgar Allan Wolfe.
See Baum, 606.

[2]Translated from the Polish by Czeslaw Milosz and Robert
Hass.

Kenneth Patchen
1911–1972

1 Let us have madness openly, O men
Of my generation. Let us follow
The footsteps of this slaughtered age.
Let Us Have Madness Openly [1936]

2 I'd like to die like this . . .
with the dark fingers of the water
closing and unclosing over these sleepy lights
and a sad bell somewhere murmuring good night.
Crossing on Staten Island Ferry [1939]

3 Do I not deal with angels
When her lips I touch. *For Miriam [1942]*

4 Great mother of big apples it is a pretty
World! *I Feel Drunk All the Time [1945]*

5 I don't know how the rest of you feel,
But I feel drunk all the time.
I Feel Drunk All the Time

6 I am the magical mouse
I don't eat cheese
I eat sunsets
And the tops of trees.
The Magical Mouse [1952], st. 1

7 Oh lonesome's a bad place
To get crowded into.
Lonesome Boy Blues [1952]

Ronald [Wilson] Reagan
1911–

8 Government is like a big baby — an alimentary
canal with a big appetite at one end and no responsibility at the other.
*Remark while campaigning for governor of
California [1965]*

9 We're the party that wants to see an America in
which people can still get rich.
*Remark at Republican congressional dinner,
Washington, D.C. [May 4, 1982]*

10 [It is] the march of freedom and democracy
which will leave Marxism-Leninism on the ash heap
of history as it has left other tyrannies which stifle
the freedom and muzzle the self-expression of the
people.
Address to British Parliament [June 8, 1982]

11 Let us beware that while [Soviet rulers] preach
the supremacy of the state, declare its omnipotence
over individual man, and predict its eventual domination over all the peoples of the earth, they are the
focus of evil in the modern world. . . . I urge you to
beware the temptation . . . to ignore the facts of

history and the aggressive impulses of all evil empires, to simply call the arms race a giant misunderstanding and thereby remove yourself from the
struggle between right and wrong, good and evil.
*Speech to the National Association of
Evangelicals [March 8, 1983]*

12 It's difficult to believe that people are starving in
this country because food isn't available.
Press conference [June 11, 1986]

13 Come here to this gate! Mr. Gorbachev, open
this gate! Mr. Gorbachev, tear down this wall!
*Remarks at the Brandenburg Gate, West
Berlin [June 12, 1987]*

E[rnst] F[riedrich] Schumacher
1911–1977

14 Small Is Beautiful: Economics As If People
Mattered. *Title of book [1973]*

John Archibald Wheeler
1911–

15 There is nothing in the world except empty
curved space. Matter, charge, electromagnetism and
other fields are only manifestations of the curvature
of space.
Quoted in New Scientist [September 26, 1974]

Tennessee [Thomas Lanier] Williams
1911–1983

16 Knowledge — Zzzzzp! Money — Zzzzzp! —
Power! That's the cycle democracy is built on!
The Glass Menagerie [1945], sc. vii

17 Whoever you are — I have always depended on
the kindness of strangers.
A Streetcar Named Desire [1947], sc. xi

18 Time rushes toward us with its hospital tray of
infinitely varied narcotics, even while it is preparing
us for its inevitably fatal operation.
*The Rose Tattoo [1950]. Foreword, The
Timeless World of a Play*

19 It is a terrible thing for an old woman to outlive
her dogs. *Camino Real [1953]. Prologue*

20 *Make voyages! — Attempt them!* — there's nothing else . . . *Camino Real, block 8*

21 Nothing's more determined than a cat on a tin
roof — is there? Is there, baby?
Cat on a Hot Tin Roof [1955], act III, last line

Jorge Amado
1912–2001

1 Color of cinnamon
Clove's sweet smell,
I've come a long way
To see Gabrielle.
> *Gabriela, Clove and Cinnamon (Gabriela,*
> *Cravo e Canela) [1958], epigraph*

John Cheever
1912–1982

2   Fear tastes like a rusty knife and do not let her into your house. Courage tastes of blood. Stand up straight. Admire the world. Relish the love of a gentle woman. Trust in the Lord.
> *The Wapshot Chronicle [1957], ch. 36, end*

3   The sea that morning was iridescent and dark. My wife and my sister were swimming—Diana and Helen—and I saw their uncovered heads, black and gold in the dark water. I saw them come out and I saw that they were naked, unshy, beautiful, and full of grace, and I watched the naked women walk out of the sea.   *Stories [1978]. Goodbye, My Brother*

4   Then it is dark; it is a night where kings in golden suits ride elephants over the mountains.
> *Stories. The Country Husband*

5   It was at the highest point in the arc of a bridge that I became aware suddenly of the depth and bitterness of my feelings about modern life, and of the profoundness of my yearning for a more vivid, simple, and peaceable world.
> *Stories. The Angel of the Bridge*

Lawrence [George] Durrell
1912–1990

6 So the riders of the darkness pass
On their circuit: the luminous island
Of the self trembles and waits,
Waits for us all, my friends,
Where the sea's big brush recolors
The dying lives, and the unborn smiles.
> *Fangbrand [1946], last stanza*

7   I felt once more the strange equivocal power of the city—its flat alluvial landscape and exhausted airs . . . Alexandria; which is neither Greek, Syrian nor Egyptian, but a hybrid: a joint.
> *Justine [1957], pt. I*

8   We are the children of our landscape; it dictates behavior and even thought in the measure to which we are responsive to it.   *Justine, I*

Milton Friedman
1912–

9   Positive economics is in principle independent of any particular ethical position or normative judgments . . . In short, positive economics is or can be an "objective" science.
> *Essays in Positive Economics [1953], pt. I, 1*

10   Freedom in economic arrangements is itself a component of freedom broadly understood, so economic freedom is an end in itself. . . . Economic freedom is also an indispensable means toward the achievement of political freedom.
> *Capitalism and Freedom [1962], ch. 1*

11   There's no such thing as a free lunch.[1]
> *Attributed*

Woody [Woodrow Wilson] Guthrie
1912–1967

12 This land is your land, this land is my land,
From California to the New York island,
From the redwood forest to the Gulf Stream
    waters,
This land was made for you and me.
> *This Land Is Your Land [1956]*

Eugène Ionesco
1912–1994

13   Take a perfect circle, caress it and you'll have a vicious circle.
> *The Bald Soprano (La Cantatrice Chauve)*
> *[1950]*

14   There are more dead people than living. And their numbers are increasing. The living are getting rarer.   *Rhinoceros [1960],[2] act I*

15   We haven't the time to take our time.
> *Exit the King (Le Roi Se Meurt) [1963]*

Pope John Paul I [Albino Luciani]
1912–1978

16   He is Father. Even more, God is Mother, who does not want to harm us.
> *At Sunday Angelus blessing, St. Peter's Square*
> *[September 17, 1978]*

17   I am only a poor man, accustomed to small things and silence.   *Illustrissimi [1978], epilogue*

---

[1]Also attributed to economist Alvin H. Hansen [1887–1975].
[2]Translated by DEREK PROUSE.

Mary [Therese] McCarthy
1912–1989

1 Every word she [Lillian Hellman] writes is a lie, including "and" and "the."

Television interview [1980]

[Salvator] Aubrey [Clarence] Menen
1912–1989

2 There are three things which are real: God, human folly, and laughter. Since the first two pass our comprehension, we must do what we can with the third.

The Ramayana as Told by Aubrey Menen [1954]

Thomas P. [Tip] O'Neill, Jr.
1912–1994

3 All politics is local. *Saying*

Studs [Louis] Terkel
1912–

4 Perhaps it is this specter that most haunts working men and women: the planned obsolescence of people that is of a piece with the planned obsolescence of the things they make. Or sell.

Working [1972], introduction

Alan Mathison Turing
1912–1954

5 I propose to consider the question, "Can machines think?"

Computing Machinery and Intelligence [October 1950]

Patrick White
1912–1990

6 There's many benefits from a good read, just as some must sing a lungful of psalm, or take the bottle down from the shelf.

The Tree of Man [1955], ch. 1

7 Inspiration descends only in flashes, to clothe circumstances; it is not stored up in a barrel, like salt herrings, to be doled out. *Voss [1957], ch. 2*

George Barker
1913–1991

8 She will not glance up at the bomber or
     condescend
To drop her gin and scuttle to a cellar,
But lean on the mahogany table like a mountain
Whom only faith can move, and so I send
O all my faith and all my love to tell her
That she will move from mourning into morning.

Eros in Dogma [1944]. To My Mother

Menachem Begin
1913–1992

9 A great day in the annals of two ancient nations, Egypt and Israel, whose sons met in battle five times, fighting and falling. . . . It is thanks to our fallen heroes that we could have reached this day.

On signing the Egyptian-Israeli peace treaty, Washington, D.C. [March 26, 1979][1]

10 No more wars, no more bloodshed. Peace unto you. Shalom, salaam, forever.

On signing the Egyptian-Israeli peace treaty, Washington, D.C.

Sammy Cahn
1913–1993

11 Love and marriage, love and marriage,
Go together like a horse and carriage.

*Our Town (television musical) [1955].[2]
Love and Marriage*

Albert Camus
1913–1960

12 Mother died today, or maybe it was yesterday.

The Stranger (L'Étranger) [1942], I

13 For the first time, the first, I laid my heart open to the benign indifference of the universe. To feel it so like myself, indeed, so brotherly, made me realize that I'd been happy, and that I was happy still.

The Stranger, IV

14 There is but one truly serious philosophical problem, and that is suicide. Judging whether life is or is not worth living amounts to answering the fundamental question of philosophy.

The Myth of Sisyphus (Le Mythe de Sisyphe) [1942]

---

[1]See Sadat, 804:7.

[2]Music by Jimmy Van Heusen.

1 The absurd is the essential concept and the first truth. *The Myth of Sisyphus*

2 The struggle to reach the top is itself enough to fulfill the heart of man. One must believe that Sisyphus is happy. *The Myth of Sisyphus*

3 It is not rebellion itself which is noble but the demands it makes upon us. *The Plague (La Peste) [1947]*

4 Can one be a saint if God does not exist? That is the only concrete problem I know of today. *The Plague*

5 In the depth of winter, I finally learned that within me there lay an invincible summer. *Summer (L'Été) [1954]. Return to Tipasa*

6 I shall tell you a great secret, my friend. Do not wait for the last judgment. It takes place every day. *The Fall (La Chute) [1956]*

7 A single sentence will suffice for modern man: he fornicated and read the papers. *The Fall*

8 Freedom of the press is perhaps the freedom that has suffered the most from the gradual degradation of the idea of liberty. *Resistance, Rebellion, and Death [1960]*[1]

9 A free press can of course be good or bad, but, most certainly, without freedom it will never be anything but bad. . . . Freedom is nothing else but a chance to be better, whereas enslavement is a certainty of the worse. *Resistance, Rebellion, and Death*

Robertson Davies
1913–1995

10 Vaudeville audiences . . . could give the loudest sighs I have ever heard. Prisoners in the Bastille couldn't have touched them. *World of Wonders [1976]. A Bottle in the Smoke, pt. VIII*

11 The magician Merlin had a strange laugh, and it was heard when nobody else was laughing. . . . He laughed because he knew what was coming next. *World of Wonders. A Bottle in the Smoke, VIII*

12 She was worse than a blabber; she was a hinter. It gave her pleasure to rouse curiosity and speculation about dangerous things. *What's Bred in the Bone [1985]. What Would Not Out of the Flesh?*

13 About 60 years ago, I said to my father, "Old Mr. Senex is showing his age; he sometimes talks

---
[1]Translated by JUSTIN O'BRIEN.

quite stupidly." My father replied, "That isn't age. He's always been stupid. He is just losing his ability to conceal it." *You're Not Getting Older, You're Getting Nosier, in the New York Times Book Review [May 12, 1991]*

Gerald R[udolph] Ford
1913–

14 I'm a Ford, not a Lincoln. *Comment after his nomination for the vice-presidency [October 12, 1973]*

15 Our long national nightmare is over. *On being sworn in as President [August 9, 1974]*

16 There is no Soviet domination of Eastern Europe. *Television debate with Jimmy Carter [October 6, 1976]*

Donald Francis Mason
1913–

17 Sighted sub, sank same. *Radio message to U.S. Navy Base [January 28, 1942]*

Richard M[ilhous] Nixon
1913–1994

18 The kids, like all kids, loved the dog [Checkers], and I just want to say this, right now, that regardless of what they say about it, we are going to keep it. *Radio and TV speech responding to allegations of a political slush fund [September 23, 1952]*

19 You won't have Nixon to kick around anymore, because, gentlemen, this is my last press conference. *To the press [November 7, 1962]*

20 Bring us together again. *Speech in New York City [October 31, 1968]*

21 The great silent majority. *Speech [November 3, 1969]*

22 The Chinese are a great and vital people who should not remain isolated from the international community. . . . It is certainly in our interest, and in the interest of peace and stability in Asia and the world, that we take what steps we can toward improved practical relations with Peking. *First Foreign Policy Report to Congress [February 1970]*

23 If when the chips are down, the world's most powerful nation . . . acts like a pitiful, helpless giant,

the forces of totalitarianism and anarchy will threaten free nations and free institutions throughout the world.

Televised speech [April 30, 1970] announcing major United States offensive into Cambodia

1   I want you all to stonewall it.

Presidential transcript [March 22, 1973]

2   People have got to know whether or not their President is a crook. Well, I'm not a crook.

Press conference [November 11, 1973]

3   Always give your best, never get discouraged, never be petty; always remember, others may hate you. Those who hate you don't win unless you hate them. And then you destroy yourself.

Address to members of the administration on leaving office [August 9, 1974]

4   When the President does it, that means that it is not illegal.

Interview with David Frost [May 19, 1977]

Tillie Olsen
1913–

5   She would not exchange her solitude for anything. Never again to be forced to move to the rhythms of others.

Tell Me a Riddle [1961], title story, sec. 1

6   Only help her to know—help make it so there is cause for her to know—that she is more than this dress on the ironing board, helpless before the iron.

Tell Me a Riddle. I Stand Here Ironing

7   Women are traditionally trained to place others' needs first . . . their satisfaction to be in making it possible for others to use their abilities.

Silences [1978], pt. I

Rosa Parks
1913–

8   I had felt for a long time, that if I was ever told to get up so a white person could sit, that I would refuse to do so.

Recalling her refusal to give up her seat on a Montgomery, Alabama, bus [December 1, 1955]

Muriel Rukeyser
1913–1980

9 Fly down, Death: Call me:
I have become a lost name.

Madboy's Song, refrain

10 What would happen if one woman told the truth about her life?
The world would split open.

Käthe Kollwitz, sec. III

Delmore Schwartz
1913–1966

11 Time is the school in which we learn,
Time is the fire in which we burn.

For Rhoda [1938]

12 That inescapable animal walks with me.
Has followed me since the black womb held,
Moves where I move, distorting my gesture,
A caricature, a swollen shadow,
A stupid clown of the spirit's motive,
Perplexes and affronts with his own darkness,
The secret life of belly and bone.

The Heavy Bear Who Goes with Me, st. 3

Karl Shapiro
1913–2000

13 One day beside some flowers near his nose
He will be thinking, *When will I look at it?*
And pain, still in the middle distance, will reply
At what? and he will know it's gone,
O where! and begin to tremble and cry.
He will begin to cry as a child cries
Whose puppy is mangled under a screaming wheel.

V-Letter [1944]. The Leg

Lewis Thomas
1913–1993

14   What is [the earth] *most* like? . . . It is *most* like a single cell.

The Lives of a Cell [1974]. The Lives of a Cell

15   There is really no such creature as a single individual; he has no more life of his own than a cast-off cell marooned from the surface of your skin.

The Lives of a Cell. Antaeus in Manhattan

16   Viewed from the distance of the moon, the astonishing thing about the earth . . . is that it is alive. . . . Aloft, floating free beneath the moist, gleaming membrane of bright blue sky, is the rising earth, the only exuberant thing in this part of the cosmos. . . . It has the organized, self-contained look of a live creature, full of information, marvelously skilled in handling the sun.

The Lives of a Cell. The World's Biggest Membrane

1   We are a spectacular, splendid manifestation of life. We have language . . . We have affection. We have genes for usefulness, and usefulness is about as close to a "common goal" of nature as I can guess at. And finally, and perhaps best of all, we have music.
The Medusa and the Snail [1979]. The Youngest and Brightest Thing Around

2   We are, perhaps, uniquely among the earth's creatures, the worrying animal. We worry away our lives, fearing the future, discontent with the present, unable to take in the idea of dying, unable to sit still.
The Medusa and the Snail. The Youngest and Brightest Thing Around

Philip Yordan
1913–

3   Lie to me. Tell me all these years you've waited. Tell me.
Johnny Guitar (screenplay) [1954], spoken by Sterling Hayden

John Berryman
1914–1972

4   Mountainous, woman not breaks and will bend: sways God nearby: anguish comes to an end. Blossomed Sarah, and I blossom. Is that thing alive? I hear a famisht howl.
Homage to Mistress Bradstreet [1953], st. 21

5   Huffy Henry hid   the day, Unappeasable Henry sulked.
77 Dream Songs [1964], poem no. 1

6   I don't see how Henry, pried open for all the world to see, survived.
77 Dream Songs, 1

7   Life, friends, is boring. We must not say so.
77 Dream Songs, 14

8   Two daiquiris withdrew into a corner of the gorgeous room and one told the other a lie.   *77 Dream Songs, 16*

9   But never did Henry, as he thought he did, end anyone and hacks her body up and hide the pieces, where they may be found. He knows: he went over everyone, & nobody's missing. Often he reckons, in the dawn, them up. Nobody is ever missing.   *77 Dream Songs, 29*

10 He stared at ruin. Ruin stared straight back. He thought they were old friends.
77 Dream Songs, 45

11   Something can (has) been said for sobriety but very little.   *77 Dream Songs, 57*

12 But I do guess mos peoples gonna *lose*.
77 Dream Songs, 60

13 The world is gradually becoming a place where I do not care to be any more.
His Toy, His Dream, His Rest [1968], poem no. 149

14 It is a true error to marry with poets or to be by them.
His Toy, His Dream, His Rest, 187

15   Decent fall the cloths over a high income.
His Toy, His Dream, His Rest, 196

16 I saw in my dream the great lost cities, Machu Picchu, Cambridge Mass., Angkor.
His Toy, His Dream, His Rest, 197

17 What was it missing, then, at the man's heart so that he does not wound?
His Toy, His Dream, His Rest, 219 (So Long? Stevens)

18 Perhaps God resembles one of the last etchings of Goya & not Velasquez, never Rembrandt no.
His Toy, His Dream, His Rest, 238 (Henry's Programme for God)

19 I always wanted to be old, I wanted to say "O I haven't read that for fifteen years."
His Toy, His Dream, His Rest, 264

20 I haven't lost a battle yet but I am tense for the first losing.
His Toy, His Dream, His Rest, 315

21 Offering dragons quarter is no good, they regrow all their parts & come on again, they have to be killed.
His Toy, His Dream, His Rest, 316

22 When will indifference come.
His Toy, His Dream, His Rest, 384

Daniel [Joseph] Boorstin
1914–

23   A pseudo-event . . . comes about because someone has planned, planted, or incited it. Typically, it is not a train wreck or an earthquake, but an interview.   *The Image [1962], ch. 1*

24   The celebrity is a person who is known for his well-knownness.   *The Image, 1*

William Seward Burroughs
1914–1997

1 The title means exactly what the words say: NAKED Lunch—a frozen moment when everyone sees what is on the end of every fork.

Naked Lunch [1959]. Introduction

Ralph [Waldo] Ellison
1914–1994

2 I am an invisible man. . . . I am a man of substance, of flesh and bone, fiber and liquids—and I might even be said to possess a mind. I am invisible, understand, simply because people refuse to see me.

Invisible Man [1952], prologue

3 Live with your head in the lion's mouth. I want you to overcome 'em with yeses, undermine 'em with grins, agree 'em to death and destruction, let 'em swoller you till they vomit or bust wide open.

Invisible Man, ch. 1

John Hersey
1914–1993

4 There was no sound of planes. The morning was still; the place was cool and pleasant.

Then a tremendous flash of light cut across the sky. Mr. Tanimoto has a distinct recollection that it traveled from east to west, from the city toward the hills. It seemed a sheet of sun. Both he and Mr. Matsuo reacted in terror. . . . Under what seemed to be a local dust cloud, the day grew darker and darker. *Hiroshima [1946], ch. 1*

5 There, in the tin factory, in the first moment of the atomic age, a human being was crushed by books. *Hiroshima, 1*

Randall Jarrell
1914–1965

6 From my mother's sleep I fell into the State,
And I hunched in its belly till my wet fur froze.
Six miles from earth, loosed from its dream of life,
I woke to black flak and the nightmare fighters.
When I died they washed me out of the turret with
   a hose.

The Death of the Ball Turret Gunner [1944]

7 The saris go by me from the embassies.
Cloth from the moon. Cloth from another planet.
They look back at the leopard like a leopard.

The Woman at the Washington Zoo [1960]

8 You know what I was,
You see what I am: change me, change me!

The Woman at the Washington Zoo

9 But I identify myself, as always,
With something that there's something wrong
   with,
With something human.

The One Who Was Different [1965]

Joe Louis [Joseph Louis Borrow]
1914–1981

10 He can run, but he can't hide.

Remark before his heavyweight title fight with Billy Conn [June 19, 1946]

Bernard Malamud
1914–1986

11 Levin wanted friendship and got friendliness; he wanted steak and they offered spam.

A New Life [1961]

12 There comes a time in a man's life when to get where he has to go—if there are no doors or windows—he walks through a wall.

Rembrandt's Hat [1972]. Man in the Drawer

13 There is no life that can be recaptured wholly; as it was. Which is to say that all biography is ultimately fiction. What does that tell you about the nature of life, and does one really want to know?

Dubin's Lives [1979], ch. 1

14 One's fantasy goes for a walk and returns with a bride. *Long Work, Short Life [1985]*

Norman Panama
1914–
and
Melvin Frank
1913–1983

15 The pellet with the poison is in the vessel with the pestle, the chalice from the palace has the brew that is true.

The Court Jester (screenplay) [1956], spoken by Danny Kaye

Ross Parker
1914–1974

and

Hughie Charles
1907–

1 There'll always be an England
While there's a country lane,
Wherever there's a cottage small
Beside a field of grain.
There'll Always Be an England [1939]

Octavio Paz
1914–1998

2   Would it not be true to say that North Americans prefer to use reality rather than to know it?
The Labyrinth of Solitude (El Labrinto de la Soledad) [1950],[1] ch. 1

3   Solitude lies at the lowest depth of the human condition. Man is the only being who feels himself to be alone and the only one who is searching for the Other.   *The Labyrinth of Solitude, appendix*

4   Touched by poetry, language is more fully language and at the same time is no longer language: it is a poem.   *Claude Lévi-Strauss [1967],[1] ch. 3*

5 We are condemned
to kill time:
Thus we die
bit by bit   *Cuento de los Jardines [1968]*

6   The supreme value is not the future but the present. The future is a deceitful time that always says to us, "Not yet," and thus denies us. The future is not the time of love: what man truly wants he wants *now*. Whoever builds a house for future happiness builds a prison for the present.
Postscript (Posdata) [1970]

7   And the world is changed
if two people shaken by dizziness and enlaced
are fallen among the grass.
Configurations [1971]. Sun Stone (Piedra de Sol),[2] l. 432

8 My steps along this street
Resound
        in another street
In which
        I hear my steps
Passing along this street

In which
Only the mist is real.
Configurations. Here (Aqui)[3]

9 The absolutes the eternities
Their outlying districts
        Are not my theme
I am hungry for life and for death also
I know what I know and I write it.
Configurations. Vrindaban,[4] l. 152

10   Western civilization should be feminized.
Seven Voices [1972], interview

11   There can be a "boom" in petroleum or wheat, but there can't be a boom in the novel and less still in poetry.   *Seven Voices, interview*

Henry Reed
1914–1986

12 To-day we have naming of parts. Yesterday,
We had daily cleaning. And to-morrow morning,
We shall have what to do after firing. But to-day,
To-day we have naming of parts.
Lessons of the War [1946]. I, Naming of Parts

13 The early bees are assaulting and fumbling the
        flowers:
They call it easing the Spring.
Lessons of the War. I, Naming of Parts

14 And the various holds and rolls and throws and
        breakfalls
Somehow or other I always seemed to put
In the wrong place. And as for war, my wars
Were global from the start.
Lessons of the War. III, Unarmed Combat

Budd Schulberg
1914–

15   I could've been a contender. I could've had class and been somebody. Real class. Instead of a bum, let's face it, which is what I am.
On the Waterfront (screenplay) [1954], spoken by Marlon Brando

---

[1]Translated by RACHEL PHILLIPS.
[2]Translated by MURIEL RUKEYSER.

[3]Translated by CHARLES TOMLINSON.
[4]Translated by LYSANDER KEMP.

Jerry Siegel

1914–1996

and

Joe Shuster

1914–1992

1 Faster than a speeding bullet, more powerful than a locomotive, able to leap tall buildings at a single bound — look, up there in the sky, it's a bird, it's a plane, it's Superman!

Superman (comic strip) [June 1938]

Dylan Thomas

1914–1953

2 The force that through the green fuse drives the
  flower
Drives my green age; that blasts the roots of trees
Is my destroyer.
And I am dumb to tell the crooked rose
My youth is bent by the same wintry fever.

*The Force That Through the Green Fuse Drives
the Flower [1934]*

3 Light breaks where no sun shines;
Where no sea runs, the waters of the heart
Push in their tides.

Light Breaks Where No Sun Shines [1934]

4 The hand that signed the paper felled a city;
Five sovereign fingers taxed the breath,
Doubled the globe of dead and halved a country;
These five kings did a king to death.

The Hand That Signed the Paper [1936]

5 And death shall have no dominion.

Refrain and title of poem [1943]

6 After the first death there is no other.

*A Refusal to Mourn the Death, by Fire, of a
Child in London [1946]*

7 Forgotten mornings when he walked with his
  mother
  Through the parables
  Of sunlight
And the legend of the green chapels.

Poem in October [1946]

8 Now as I was young and easy under the apple
  boughs
About the lilting house and happy as the grass was
  green.

Fern Hill [1946], st. 1

9 And honored among wagons I was prince of the
  apple towns.

Fern Hill, st. 1

10 In the sun that is young once only,
  Time let me play and be
Golden in the mercy of his means.

Fern Hill, st. 1

11   And the sabbath rang slowly
In the pebbles of the holy streams.

Fern Hill, st. 2

12 And honored among foxes and pheasants by the
  gay house
Under the new-made clouds and happy as the heart
  was long,
  In the sun born over and over,
  I ran my heedless ways.   *Fern Hill, st. 5*

13   Time held me green and dying
Though I sang in my chains like the sea.

Fern Hill, st. 6

14 Do not go gentle into that good night,
Old age should burn and rave at close of day;
Rage, rage against the dying of the light.

*Do Not Go Gentle into That Good Night
[1952]*

15 One Christmas was so much like another, in those years around the seatown corner now and out of all sound except the distant speaking of the voices I sometimes hear a moment before sleep, that I can never remember whether it snowed for six days and six nights when I was twelve or whether it snowed for twelve days and twelve nights when I was six.

*Quite Early One Morning [1954]. A Child's
Christmas in Wales*

16 It is spring, moonless night in the small town, starless and bible-black.

Under Milk Wood [1954]

E[dward] Digby Baltzell

1915–1996

17 There is a crisis in American leadership in the middle of the twentieth century that is partly due, I think, to the declining authority of an establishment which is now based on an increasingly castelike White-Anglo Saxon-Protestant (WASP) upper class.

The Protestant Establishment [1964], ch. 1

Roland Barthes

1915–1980

18 I think that cars today are almost the exact equivalent of the great Gothic cathedrals: I mean the supreme creation of an era, conceived with passion by unknown artists, and consumed in image if not

in usage by a whole population which appropriates them as a purely magical object.

Mythologies [1972].[1] *The New Citroën*

Saul Bellow
1915–

1   There was a disturbance in my heart, a voice that spoke there and said, *I want, I want, I want!* It happened every afternoon, and when I tried to suppress it it got even stronger. . . . It never said a thing except *I want, I want, I want!*

Henderson the Rain King [1959]

2   I am simply a human being, more or less.

Herzog [1964]

3   As though to be Jewish weren't trouble enough, the poor woman was German, too.

Mr. Sammler's Planet [1970], pt. I

4   The idea of making the century's great crime look dull is not banal. Politically, psychologically, the Germans had an idea of genius. The banality was only camouflage. What better way to get the curse out of murder than to make it look ordinary, boring, or trite? . . . Banality is the adopted disguise of a very powerful will to abolish conscience.

Mr. Sammler's Planet, I

5   New York makes one think of the collapse of civilization, about Sodom and Gomorrah, the end of the world. The end wouldn't come as a surprise here. Many people already bank on it.

Mr. Sammler's Planet, VI

6   The body, she says, is subject to the forces of gravity. But the soul is ruled by levity, pure.

Him with His Foot in His Mouth [1984], title story

7   Who is the Tolstoy of the Zulus? The Proust of the Papuans? I'd be glad to read him.

Remark [1988], telephone interview

Jerome [Seymour] Bruner
1915–

8   The shrewd guess, the fertile hypothesis, the courageous leap to a tentative conclusion—these are the most valuable coin of the thinker at work.

The Process of Education [1960]

9   Any subject can be taught effectively in some intellectually honest form to any child at any stage of development.   *The Process of Education*

---

[1]Translated by ANNETTE LAVERS.

Alfred Kazin
1915–1998

10   A classic is a book that survives the circumstances that made it possible yet alone keeps those circumstances alive.

Review in The New Republic [August 29, 1988]

Sir Peter Brian Medawar
1915–1987

11   The scientist values research by the size of its contribution to that huge, logically articulated structure of ideas which is already, though not yet half built, the most glorious accomplishment of mankind.

The Art of the Soluble [1967]

12   Among scientists are collectors, classifiers, and compulsive tidiers-up; many are detectives by temperament and many are explorers; some are artists and others artisans. There are poet-scientists and philosopher-scientists and even a few mystics.

The Art of the Soluble

Arthur Miller
1915–

13   I don't say he's a great man. Willy Loman never made a lot of money. His name was never in the paper. He's not the finest character that ever lived. But he's a human being, and a terrible thing is happening to him. So attention must be paid. He's not to be allowed to fall into his grave like an old dog. Attention, attention must be finally paid to such a person.   *Death of a Salesman [1949], act I*

14   Never fight fair with a stranger, boy. You'll never get out of the jungle that way.

Death of a Salesman, I

15   I have not moved from there to here without I think to please you, and still an everlasting funeral marches round your heart.

The Crucible [1953], act II

16   I am inclined to notice the ruin in things, perhaps because I was born in Italy.

A View from the Bridge [1955], act I

Paul A. Samuelson
1915–

17   Wall Street indexes predicted nine out of the last five recessions.

Column in Newsweek [September 19, 1966]

1   Man does not live by GNP alone.

Economics [1973], ch. 40

Jean Stafford
1915–1979

2   To her own heart, which was shaped exactly like a valentine, there came a winglike palpitation, a delicate exigency, and all the fragrance of all the flowery springtime love affairs that ever were seemed waiting for them in the whiskey bottle.

*Children Are Bored on Sundays [1953],
title story*

Potter Stewart
1915–1985

3   I shall not today attempt further to define [pornography] . . . But I know it when I see it; and the motion picture involved in this case is not that.

*Concurring opinion in U.S. Supreme Court,
Jacobellis v. Ohio [1964]*

Orson Welles
1915–1985

4   In Italy for thirty years under the Borgias they had warfare, terror, murder, bloodshed, but they produced Michelangelo, Leonardo da Vinci, and the Renaissance. In Switzerland they had brotherly love, they had five hundred years of democracy and peace. And what did that produce? The cuckoo-clock.

*Speech written into The Third Man
(screenplay by Graham Greene and Carol
Reed) [1949]*

John Malcolm Brinnin
1916–1998

5 I seek a father who most need a son.

Oedipus: His Cradle Song [1963]

6 In their big peppermint hotels.

News from the Islands [1963]

7 Another hill town;
    another dry Cinzano in the sun.

Hotel Paradiso è Commerciale [1963]

8 We have all done this before; we're bored
    and terrified.   *Flight 539 [1963]*

9 All of a sudden came the pelicans:
    crazy old men in baseball caps, who flew
    like jackknives and collapsed like fans.

Skin Diving in the Virgins [1970]

Walter Cronkite
1916–

10   And that's the way it is.

Sign-off sentence, CBS Evening News

Gavin Ewart
1916–1996

11 Miss Twye was soaping her breasts in her bath
    When she heard behind her a meaning laugh
    And to her amazement she discovered
    A wicked man in the bathroom cupboard.

Miss Twye

Elizabeth Hardwick
1916–

12   Collaborating in the very private way of love or the highest kind of friendship . . . is the way for gifted, energetic wives of writers to a sort of composition of their own, this peculiar illusion of collaboration.

*Seduction and Betrayal: Women in Literature
[1974]. Amateurs*

13   This is the unspoken contract of a wife and her works. In the long run wives are to be paid in a peculiar coin — consideration for their feelings. And it usually turns out this is an enormous, unthinkable inflation few men will remit, or if they will, only with a sense of being overcharged.

*Seduction and Betrayal: Women in Literature.
Amateurs*

Shirley Jackson
1916–1965

14   "It isn't fair, it isn't right," Mrs. Hutchinson screamed, and then they were upon her.

The Lottery [1948], last line

Florynce Rae Kennedy
1916–2000

15   Niggerization is the result of oppression — and it doesn't just apply to black people. Old people, poor people, and students can also get niggerized.

*From GLORIA STEINEM, The Verbal Karate of
Florynce R. Kennedy, Esq. [1973]*

16   If men could get pregnant, abortion would be a sacrament.

*From GLORIA STEINEM, The Verbal Karate of
Florynce R. Kennedy, Esq.*

Robert S[trange] McNamara
1916–

1   We of the Kennedy and Johnson administrations who participated in the decisions on Vietnam acted according to what we thought were the principles and traditions of this nation. We made our decisions in the light of those values. Yet we were wrong, terribly wrong. We owe it to future generations to explain why.   *In Retrospect [1995], preface*

C[harles] Wright Mills
1916–1962

2   By the power elite, we refer to those political, economic, and military circles which as an intricate set of overlapping cliques share decisions having at least national consequences. In so far as national events are decided, the power elite are those who decide them.
The Power Elite [1956], ch. 1,
The Higher Circles

3   The sociological imagination enables us to grasp history and biography and the relations between the two within society.
The Sociological Imagination [1959], ch. 1

Walker Percy
1916–1990

4   The fact is I am quite happy in a movie, even a bad movie. Other people, so I have read, treasure memorable moments in their lives.   *The Moviegoer [1961]*

Gwendolyn Brooks
1917–2000

5   Maud went to college.
Sadie stayed at home.
Sadie scraped life
With a fine-tooth comb.
A Street in Bronzeville [1945]. Sadie and
Maud, st. 1

6   Abortions will not let you forget.
You remember the children you got that you did not
get.   *A Street in Bronzeville. The Mother, st. 1*

7   What shall I give my children? who are poor,
Who are adjudged the leastwise of the land.
Annie Allen [1949]. The Womanhood. The
Children of the Poor, sonnet 2

8   Exhaust the little moment. Soon it dies.
And be it gash or gold it will not come
Again in this identical disguise.
Annie Allen. Exhaust the Little Moment

9   And remembering . . .
Remembering, with twinklings and twinges,
As they lean over the beans in their rented back
room that is full of beads and receipts and
dolls and cloths, tobacco crumbs, vases and
fringes.
The Bean Eaters [1960]. The Bean Eaters,
st. 3

10   We real cool. We
Left school. We
Lurk late. We
Strike straight. We
Sing sin. We
Thin gin. We
Jazz June. We
Die soon.   *The Bean Eaters. We Real Cool*

11   What else is there to say but everything?
In the Mecca [1968], st. 16

12   He opened us—
who was a key,
who was a man.
In the Mecca. After Mecca. Malcolm X

13   The time
cracks into furious flower. Lifts its face
all unashamed. And sways in wicked grace.
In the Mecca. The Second Sermon on the
Warpland, st. 4

14   Big Bessie's feet hurt like nobody's business,
but she stands—bigly—under the unruly scrutiny,
stands in the wild weed.
In the wild weed
she is a citizen.
In the Mecca. The Second Sermon on the
Warpland, st. 4

15   Beware the easy griefs
that fool and fuel nothing.
Beckonings [1975]. Boys. Black, st. 7

Anthony Burgess
[John Anthony Burgess Wilson]
1917–1993

16   What's it going to be then, eh?
A Clockwork Orange [1962], passim

17   That shut her up real horrorshow and lovely.
A Clockwork Orange

18   You have no idea how pleasant it is not to have any future. It's like having a totally efficient contraceptive.
Honey for the Bears [1964], pt. II, ch. 6

Joe Darion
1917–2001

1 To dream the impossible dream,
To reach the unreachable star!
The Impossible Dream [1965][1]

Katharine [Meyer] Graham
1917–2001

2   What I essentially did was to put one foot in front of the other, shut my eyes, and step off the ledge. The surprise was that I landed on my feet.
Personal History [1997], ch. 18 (on becoming president of the Washington Post Co. in September 1963)

John Fitzgerald Kennedy
1917–1963

3   It was involuntary. They sank my boat.
Remark when asked how he became a hero. Quoted in ARTHUR M. SCHLESINGER, JR., A Thousand Days [1965], ch. 4

4   The New Frontier of which I speak is not a set of promises — it is a set of challenges. It sums up not what I intend to offer the American people, but what I intend to ask of them.
Speech accepting the Democratic presidential nomination [July 15, 1960]

5   I am not the Catholic candidate for President. I am the Democratic Party's candidate for President, who happens also to be a Catholic.
Speech to Greater Houston Ministerial Association [September 12, 1960]

6   For of those to whom much is given, much is required. And when at some future date the high court of history sits in judgment on each of us, recording whether in our brief span of service we fulfilled our responsibilities to the state, our success or failure, in whatever office we hold, will be measured by the answers to four questions: First, were we truly men of courage . . . Second, were we truly men of judgment . . . Third, were we truly men of integrity . . . Finally, were we truly men of dedication?
Speech to the Massachusetts State Legislature [January 9, 1961]

7   Let the word go forth from this time and place, to friend and foe alike, that the torch has been passed to a new generation of Americans, born in this century, tempered by war, disciplined by a hard

and bitter peace, proud of our ancient heritage, and unwilling to witness or permit the slow undoing of those human rights to which this nation has always been committed, and to which we are committed today at home and around the world.
    Let every nation know, whether it wishes us well or ill, that we shall pay any price, bear any burden, meet any hardship, support any friend, oppose any foe to assure the survival and the success of liberty.
Inaugural address [January 20, 1961]

8   Let us never negotiate out of fear, but let us never fear to negotiate.
Inaugural address [January 20, 1961]

9   All this will not be finished in the first one hundred days. Nor will it be finished in the first one thousand days, nor in the life of this Administration, nor even perhaps in our lifetime on this planet. But let us begin.   *Inaugural address [January 20, 1961]*

10   And so, my fellow Americans, ask not what your country can do for you; ask what you can do for your country.[2]
Inaugural address [January 20, 1961]

11   I believe this nation should commit itself to achieving the goal, before this decade is out, of landing a man on the moon and returning him safely to earth.
Address to joint session of Congress [May 25, 1961]

12   There is always inequity in life. Some men are killed in a war and some men are wounded, and some men never leave the country . . . Life is unfair.
Press conference [March 21, 1962]

13   I think this is the most extraordinary collection of talent, of human knowledge, that has ever been gathered together at the White House, with the

---

[2]For, stripped of the temporary associations which gave rise to it, it is now the moment when by common consent we pause to become conscious of our national life and to rejoice in it, to recall what our country has done for each of us, and to ask ourselves what we can do for our country in return.—OLIVER WENDELL HOLMES, JR., *Address Before John Sedgwick Post No. 4, Grand Army of the Republic* [May 30, 1884]
    As has often been said, the youth who loves his Alma Mater will always ask, not "What can she do for me?" but "What can I do for her?"—LE BARON RUSSELL BRIGGS [1855–1934], *Routine and Ideals* [1904], *College Life*
    In the great fulfillment we must have a citizenship less concerned about what the government can do for it and more anxious about what it can do for the nation.—WARREN G[AMALIEL] HARDING [1865–1923], *Republican National Convention, Chicago* [June 7, 1916]
    This thought had lain in Kennedy's mind for a long time. As far back as 1945 he had noted down in a looseleaf notebook a quotation from Rousseau: "As soon as any man says of the affairs of the state, What does it matter to me? the state may be given up as lost."—ARTHUR M. SCHLESINGER, JR., *A Thousand Days* [1965], *prologue, footnote*

---

[1]Music by MITCH LEIGH.

possible exception of when Thomas Jefferson dined alone.

> *Address at a White House dinner and*
> *reception honoring Nobel Prize winners*
> *[April 1962]*

1   My father always told me that all businessmen were sons of bitches, but I never believed it till now.

> *Comment on price increases proposed by U.S.*
> *Steel [April 1962]*

2   We don't see the end of the tunnel, but I must say I don't think it is darker than it was a year ago, and in some ways lighter.[1]

> *Press conference [December 12, 1962]*

3   If we cannot end now our differences, at least we can help make the world safe for diversity.

> *Address at American University, Washington,*
> *D.C. [June 10, 1963]*

4   No one has been barred on account of his race from fighting or dying for America — there are no "white" or "colored" signs on the foxholes or graveyards of battle.

> *Message to Congress on proposed civil rights*
> *bill [June 19, 1963]*

5   All free men, wherever they may live, are citizens of Berlin. And therefore, as a free man, I take pride in the words "Ich bin ein Berliner."

> *Address at City Hall, West Berlin*
> *[June 26, 1963]*

6   Yesterday, a shaft of light cut into the darkness. . . . For the first time, an agreement has been reached on bringing the forces of nuclear destruction under international control.

> *Television address in Washington*
> *[July 26, 1963][2]*

7   When power leads man toward arrogance, poetry reminds him of his limitations. When power narrows the areas of man's concern, poetry reminds him of the richness and diversity of his existence. When power corrupts, poetry cleanses, for art establishes the basic human truths which must serve as the touchstone of our judgment.

> *Address at Amherst College [October 26, 1963]*

8   Washington is a city of southern efficiency and northern charm.

> *Remark. Quoted in* ARTHUR M.
> SCHLESINGER, JR., *A Thousand Days [1965],*
> *ch. 25*

---

[1]If we see a light at the end of the tunnel, / It's the light of an oncoming train. — ROBERT LOWELL, *Since 1939* [1977]

[2]In Moscow on July 25, Averell Harriman, Lord Hailsham, and Andrei Gromyko initialed the nuclear test ban treaty.

Robert [Traill Spence] Lowell
1917–1977

9 Christ walks on the black water. In Black Mud
  Darts the kingfisher. On Corpus Christi, heart,
  Over the drum-beat of St. Stephen's choir
  I hear him, *Stupor Mundi*, and the mud
  Flies from his hunching wings and beak — my
    heart,
  The blue kingfisher dives on you in fire.

> *Colloquy in Black Rock [1946], st. 5*

10 I will catch Christ with a greased worm.

> *The Drunken Fisherman [1946], st. 5*

11 I saw the spiders marching through air,
   Swimming from tree to tree that mildewed day
     In latter August when the hay
     Came creaking to the barn.[3]

> *Mr. Edwards and the Spider [1946], st. 1*

12 This is the Black Widow, death.

> *Mr. Edwards and the Spider, st. 5*

13 I saw the sky descending, black and white,
   Not blue, on Boston.

> *Where the Rainbow Ends [1946], st. 1*

14 Now Paris, our black classic, breaking up
   like killer kings on an Etruscan cup.

> *Beyond the Alps [1959]*

15 You said:
   "We poets in our youth begin in sadness;
   thereof in the end come despondency and
     madness."

> *To Delmore Schwartz (Cambridge 1946)*
> *[1959]*

16 Who asks for me, the Shelley of my age,
   must lay his heart out for my bed and board.

> *Words for Hart Crane [1959]*

17 I doodle handlebar
   moustaches on the last Russian Czar.

> *Grandparents [1959]*

18 We are old-timers,
   each of us holds a locked razor.

> *Waking in the Blue [1959]*

19 I keep no rank nor station.
   Cured, I am frizzled, stale and small.

> *Home After Three Months Away [1959]*

20 Only teaching on Tuesdays, bookworming
   in pajamas fresh from the washer each morning,

---

[3]Jonathan Edwards [1703–1758], the Calvinist theologian, wrote at the age of twelve a series of scientific observations on the spider. See Edwards, 318:16.

I hog a whole house on Boston's
"hardly passionate Marlborough Street."[1]
　　　　Memories of West Street and Lepke [1959]

1 These are the tranquillized *Fifties,*
　and I am forty. Ought I to regret my seedtime?
　I was a fire-breathing Catholic C.O.,
　and made my manic statement,
　telling off the state and president, and then
　sat waiting sentence in the bull pen
　beside a Negro boy with curlicues
　of marijuana in his hair.
　　　　Memories of West Street and Lepke

2 Flabby, bald, lobotomized,
　he drifted in a sheepish calm,
　where no agonizing reappraisal
　jarred his concentration on the electric chair —
　hanging like an oasis in his air
　of lost connections.
　　　　Memories of West Street and Lepke

3 Tamed by *Miltown,* we lie on Mother's bed.
　　　　Man and Wife [1959]

4 　　Oh my *Petite,*
　clearest of all God's creatures, still all air and nerve.
　　　　Man and Wife

5 your old-fashioned tirade —
　loving, rapid, merciless —
　breaks like the Atlantic Ocean on my head.
　　　　Man and Wife

6 Gored by the climacteric of his want,
　he stalls above me like an elephant.
　　　　"To Speak of Woe That Is in Marriage" [1959]

7 My mind's not right.

　A car radio bleats,
　"Love, O careless Love. . . ." I hear
　my ill-spirit sob in each blood cell,
　as if my hand were at its throat. . . .
　I myself am hell;
　nobody's here.[2]　　　　*Skunk Hour [1959], st. 5, 6*

8 Father, forgive me
　my injuries,
　as I forgive
　those I
　have injured!

　You never climbed
　Mount Sion, yet left
　dinosaur

---

[1]The quotation is from Henry James.

[2]Ellipses are in the original text.

death-steps on the crust,
where I must walk.　　　*Middle Age [1964], st. 3, 4*

9 We are like a lot of wild
　spiders crying together,
　but without tears.　　　*Fall 1961 [1964], st. 4*

10 I am tired. Everyone's tired of my turmoil.
　　　　Eye and Tooth [1964], st. 9

11 Two months after marching through Boston,
　half the regiment was dead;
　at the dedication,
　William James could almost hear the bronze
　　　Negroes[3] breathe.

　Their monument sticks like a fishbone
　in the city's throat.
　Its Colonel is as lean
　as a compass-needle.

　He has an angry wrenlike vigilance,
　a greyhound's gentle tautness;
　he seems to wince at pleasure,
　and suffocate for privacy.
　　　　For the Union Dead [1964], st. 7–9

12 on Boylston Street, a commercial photograph
　shows Hiroshima boiling.
　　　　For the Union Dead, st. 14

13 When I crouch to my television set,
　the drained faces of Negro school-children rise like
　　balloons.　　　*For the Union Dead, st. 15*

14 The Aquarium is gone. Everywhere,
　giant finned cars nose forward like fish;
　a savage servility
　slides by on grease.　　　*For the Union Dead, st. 17*

15 We beg delinquents for our life.
　　　　Central Park. In the New York Review
　　　　[October 1965]

16 O to break loose, like the chinook
　salmon jumping and falling back,
　nosing up to the impossible
　stone and bone-crushing waterfall.
　　　　Waking Early Sunday Morning [1967], st. 1

17 Pity the planet, all joy gone
　from this sweet volcanic cone;
　peace to our children when they fall
　in small war on the heels of small
　war.　　　*Waking Early Sunday Morning, last stanza*

---

[3]On the Saint-Gaudens monument to Colonel Robert Gould
Shaw and the 54th Massachusetts Regiment.
　　There on foot go the dark outcasts, so true to nature that one
can almost hear them breathing as they march. —WILLIAM JAMES,
Oration at Dedication of the Monument [May 31, 1897]
　　See Charles W. Eliot, 556:3, and Paul L. Dunbar, 660:3.

1 Rome, if built at all, must be built in a day.
Marcus Cato 234–149 B.C. *[1973]*

2 No one like one's mother and father ever lived.
Returning [1973]

3 After loving you so much, can I forget
you for eternity, and have no other choice?
Obit [1973]

4 The line must terminate.
Yet my heart rises, I know I've gladdened a lifetime
knotting, undoing a fishnet of tarred rope;
the net will hang on the wall when the fish are
eaten,
nailed like illegible bronze on the futureless future.
Fishnet [1973]

5 If I could go through it all again,
the slender iron rungs of growing up,
I would be as young as any,
a child lost
in unreality and loud music.   *Realities [1977]*

6 It has taken me the time since you died
to discover you are as human as I am . . .
if I am.   *To Mother [1977]*

7 I—
really I can do little,
as little now as then,
about the infernal fires—
I cannot blow out a match.   *Grass Fires [1977]*

8 We are poor passing facts,
warned by that to give
each figure in the photograph
his living name.   *Epilogue [1977]*

Carson [Smith] McCullers
1917–1967

9   This was the summer when for a long time she
had not been a member. She belonged to no club
and was a member of nothing in the world. Frankie
had become an unjoined person who hung around
in the doorways, and she was afraid.
The Member of the Wedding [1946], ch. 1

10   If you walk along the main street on an August
afternoon there is nothing whatsoever to do.
The Ballad of the Sad Cafe [1951]

Jessica Mitford
1917–1996

11   O grave, where is thy victory? Where, indeed.
Many a badly stung survivor, faced with the aftermath of some relative's funeral, has ruefully concluded that the victory has been won hands down
by a funeral establishment.
The American Way of Death [1963], ch. 1

Arthur M[eier] Schlesinger, Jr.
1917–

12   Above all he [John F. Kennedy] gave the world
for an imperishable moment the vision of a leader
who greatly understood the terror and the hope,
the diversity and the possibility, of life on this planet
and who made people look beyond nation and race
to the future of humanity.
A Thousand Days [1965], ch. 37

13   The answer to the runaway Presidency is not the
messenger-boy Presidency. The American democracy must discover a middle ground between making the President a czar and making him a puppet.
The Imperial Presidency [1973], preface

14   Suppose . . . that Lenin had died of typhus in
Siberia in 1895 and Hitler had been killed on the
western front in 1916. What would the twentieth
century have looked like now?
The Cycles of American History [1986]

William H[ollingsworth] Whyte, Jr.
1917–1999

15   This book is about the organization man. If the
term is vague, it is because I can think of no other
way to describe the people I am talking about. . . .
They are the ones of our middle class who have left
home, spiritually as well as physically, to take the
vows of organization life, and it is they who are the
mind and soul of our great self-perpetuating institutions.   *The Organization Man [1956], pt. I, ch. 1*

Spiro T[heodore] Agnew
1918–1996

16   To some extent, if you've seen one city slum
you've seen them all.
*Election campaign speech at Detroit
[October 18, 1968]*

Leonard Bernstein
1918–1990

17   The key to the mystery of a great artist: that for
reasons unknown to him or to anyone else, he will
give away his energies and his life just to make sure

that one note follows another inevitably. . . . The composer, by doing this, leaves us at the finish with the feeling that something is right in the world, that something checks throughout, something that follows its own laws consistently, something we can trust, that will never let us down.

The Joy of Music [1959]. Beethoven's Fifth Symphony

[James] Harlan Cleveland
1918–

1   The Revolution of Rising Expectations.[1]
Title of speech at Colgate University [1949]

Richard P[hillips] Feynman
1918–1988

2   You know how it always is, every new idea, it takes a generation or two until it becomes obvious that there's no real problem. I cannot define the real problem, but I'm not sure there's no real problem. *Simulating Physics with Computers [1982]*

3   For a successful technology, reality must take precedence over public relations, for nature cannot be fooled.
Report on space shuttle Challenger disaster [1986]

Corita Kent
1918–1986

4   There are so many hungry people that God cannot appear to them except in the form of bread.
Enriched Bread (silkscreen) [1965]

Ann Landers [Esther P. Lederer]
1918–2002

5   Women complain about sex more often than men. Their gripes fall into two major categories: (1) Not enough. (2) Too much.
Truth Is Stranger . . . [1968], ch. 2

Alan Jay Lerner
1918–1986

6 Oh, wouldn't it be loverly?
My Fair Lady [1956],[2] act I, Wouldn't It Be Loverly?

7 They're always throwing goodness at you
But with a little bit of luck
A man can duck.
My Fair Lady, I, With a Little Bit of Luck

8   The rain in Spain stays mainly in the plain.
My Fair Lady, I, The Rain in Spain

9   In Hertford, Hereford and Hampshire, hurricanes hardly happen.
My Fair Lady, I, The Rain in Spain

10 I could have danced all night!
My Fair Lady, I, I Could Have Danced All Night!

11 Get me to the church on time!
My Fair Lady, II, Get Me to the Church on Time

12 Why can't a woman be more like a man?
My Fair Lady, II, A Hymn to Him

13 I've grown accustomed . . . to her face.[3]
My Fair Lady, II, I've Grown Accustomed to Her Face

14 Don't let it be forgot
That once there was a spot
For one brief shining moment that was known
As Camelot. *Camelot [1960],[2] end*

Nelson [Rolihlahla] Mandela
1918–

15   I have fought against white domination, and I have fought against black domination. I have cherished the ideal of a democratic and free society in which all persons will live together in harmony and with equal opportunities. It is an ideal which I hope to live for and achieve. But, if needs be, it is an ideal for which I am prepared to die.
Statement in the dock [April 20, 1964][4]

16   Only free men can negotiate; prisoners cannot enter into contracts.
Statement from prison [February 10, 1985]

---

[1]Remembering Edmund Burke's famous commentary on the turbulence of his time, I called [a speech at Colgate University] "Reflections on the Revolution of Rising Expectations." The phrase has since been attributed to nearly every literate American of our time, but I think this was the first time that phrase saw the light of day.—HARLAN CLEVELAND, *The Evolution of Rising Responsibility, address before the U.N.* [December 13, 1964]

[2]Music by FREDERICK LOEWE.
Musical based on GEORGE BERNARD SHAW's *Pygmalion*. See Shaw, 610:4–610:8.

[3]Ellipses are in the original text.

[4]Also quoted by him on his release from prison [February 11, 1990].

1   I am not truly free if I am taking away someone else's freedom, just as surely as I am not free when my freedom is taken away from me. The oppressed and the oppressor alike are robbed of their humanity.
Long Walk to Freedom [1994]

Edwin O'Connor
1918–1968

2   "God be good to the man," she said. "He was mean as a panther, but good luck to him."
The Last Hurrah [1956], ch. 8

3   I'm not just an elected official of the city; I'm a tribal chieftain as well.   *The Last Hurrah, 8*

Anwar al-Sadat
1918–1981

4   Land is immortal, for it harbors the mysteries of creation.   *In Search of Identity [1978], ch. 1*

5   A man's village is his peace of mind.
In Search of Identity, 2

6   Peace is much more precious than a piece of land.   *Speech in Cairo [March 8, 1978]*

7   Let there be no more war or bloodshed between Arabs and Israelis. Let there be no more suffering or denial of rights. Let there be no more despair or loss of faith.
On signing the Egyptian–Israeli peace treaty, Washington, D.C. [March 26, 1979][1]

Alexander Isayevich Solzhenitsyn
1918–

8   A great writer is, so to speak, a second government in his country. And for that reason no regime has ever loved great writers, only minor ones.
The First Circle [1964][2]

9   There was peace in their hearts. They were filled with the fearlessness of those who have lost *everything*, the fearlessness which is not easy to come by but which endures.   *The First Circle*

10   The sole substitute for an experience which we have not ourselves lived through is art and literature.   *Nobel Lecture [1972]*

---

[1]See Begin, 789:9.

[2]Translated by THOMAS P. WHITNEY.

11   Literature transmits incontrovertible condensed experience . . . from generation to generation. In this way literature becomes the living memory of a nation.
Nobel Lecture

12   Violence does not and cannot exist by itself; it is invariably intertwined with *the lie*.   *Nobel Lecture*

13   The Kolyma was the greatest and most famous island, the pole of ferocity of that amazing country of Gulag, which, though scattered in an archipelago geographically, was, in the psychological sense, fused into a continent—an almost invisible, almost imperceptible country inhabited by the Zek people.
The Gulag Archipelago 1918–1956 [1974, in translation],[2] I, preface

14   The Western world has lost its civil courage, both as a whole and separately, in each country, each government, each political party, and of course in the United Nations.
The Exhausted West. Commencement address at Harvard University [June 8, 1978]

15   I have spent all my life under a Communist regime, and I will tell you that a society without any objective legal scale is a terrible one indeed. But a society with no other scale but the legal one is not quite worthy of man either.
The Exhausted West. Commencement address at Harvard University

Muriel Spark
1918–

16   The one certain way for a woman to hold a man is to leave him for religion.
The Comforters [1957], ch. 1

17   I am putting old heads on your young shoulders . . . and all my pupils are the *crème de la crème*.
The Prime of Miss Jean Brodie [1962], ch. 1

18   Give me a girl at an impressionable age, and she is mine for life.   *The Prime of Miss Jean Brodie, 1*

19   One's prime is elusive. You little girls, when you grow up, must be on the alert to recognize your prime at whatever time of your life it may occur.
The Prime of Miss Jean Brodie, 1

20   It is one of the secrets of Nature in its mood of mockery that fine weather lays a heavier weight on the mind and hearts of the depressed and the inwardly tormented than does a really bad day with dark rain sniveling continuously and sympathetically from a dirty sky.
Territorial Rights [1979], ch. 3

Daniel Bell
1919–

1   Capitalism, it is said, is a system wherein man exploits man. And communism—is vice versa.
The End of Ideology [1960]

Robert L. Heilbroner
1919–

2   [The great economists] can be called the worldly philosophers, for they sought to embrace in a scheme of philosophy the most worldly of all of man's activities—his drive for wealth.
The Worldly Philosophers [1953]. Introduction

3   Less than seventy-five years after it officially began, the contest between capitalism and socialism is over: capitalism has won.
Reflections: The Triumph of Capitalism, in The New Yorker [January 23, 1989]

Pauline Kael
1919–2001

4   The words "Kiss Kiss Bang Bang," which I saw on an Italian movie poster, are perhaps the briefest statement imaginable of the basic appeal of movies.
Kiss Kiss Bang Bang [1968]. A Note on the Title

Doris Lessing
1919–

5   A woman without a man cannot meet a man, any man, of any age, without thinking, even if it's for a half-second, Perhaps this is *the* man.
The Golden Notebook [1962]. Free Women, 5

6   None of you [men] ask for anything—except everything, but just for so long as you need it.
The Golden Notebook. Free Women, 5

Primo Levi
1919–1987

7   The dark echoed with outlandish orders in that curt, barbaric barking of Germans in command which seems to give vent to a millennial anger.
Survival in Auschwitz [1960],[1] ch. 2

8   I am not even alive enough to know how to kill myself.   *Survival in Auschwitz, 15*

9   Today I think that if for no other reason than that an Auschwitz existed, no one in our age should speak of Providence.   *Survival in Auschwitz, 17*

[Wladziu Valentino; Lee] Liberace
1919–1987

10   I cried all the way to the bank.
Liberace: An Autobiography [1973], ch. 2

Laurence J[ohnston] Peter
1919–1990

11   In a hierarchy, every employee tends to rise to his level of incompetence.
The Peter Principle [1969]

12   If you don't know where you're going, you will probably end up somewhere else.
The Peter Principle

13   *Lateral Arabesque*—a pseudo-promotion consisting of a new title and a new work place.
The Peter Principle

J[erome] D[avid] Salinger
1919–

14   I keep picturing all these little kids playing some game in this big field of rye. . . . If they're running and they don't look where they're going I have to come out from somewhere and *catch* them. That's all I'd do all day. I'd just be the catcher in the rye and all. I know it's crazy.[2]
The Catcher in the Rye [1951], ch. 22

15   There isn't anyone *anywhere* that isn't Seymour's Fat Lady. Don't you know that? Don't you know that goddam secret yet? And don't you know—*listen* to me, now—*don't you know who that Fat Lady really is?* . . . Ah, buddy. Ah, buddy. It's Christ Himself. Christ Himself, buddy.[3]
Franny and Zooey [1961]

Pete [Peter] Seeger
1919–

16 Where have all the flowers gone?
The girls have picked them every one.
Oh, when will they ever learn?
Where Have All the Flowers Gone? [1961]

---

[1]Translated by STUART WOOLF.

[2]See Anonymous, 845:20.

[3]Ellipses are in the original text.

1 We're waist deep in the Big Muddy
And the big fool says to push on.
Waist Deep in the Big Muddy [1967]

May Swenson
1919–1989

2 Body my house
my horse my hound
what will I do
when you are fallen

Question [1954], st. 1

3 Where can I go
without my mount
all eager and quick
How will I know
in thicket ahead
is danger or treasure
when Body my good
bright dog is dead

Question, st. 3

4 The summer that I was ten—
Can it be there was only one
summer that I was ten?

The Centaur [1958]

5 Youth is given. One must put it away
like a doll in a closet,
take it out and play with it only
on holidays.   *How to Be Old [1963]*

6 It's done
on a diamond,
and for fun.
It's about
home, and it's
about run.   *Analysis of Baseball [1963]*

7 My face
a negative in the slate
window,
I sit
in a lit
corridor that races
through a dark
one.   *Riding the "A" [1963]*

George [Corley] Wallace
1919–1998

8   I draw the line in the dust and toss the gauntlet before the feet of tyranny. And I say, Segregation now! Segregation tomorrow! Segregation forever!
*Inaugural address as governor of Alabama
[January 14, 1963]*

Bella [Savitzky] Abzug
1920–1998

9   There are those who say I'm impatient, impetuous, uppity, rude, profane, brash and overbearing. . . . But whatever I am—and this ought to be made very clear at the outset—I am a very serious woman.
Bella! [1972]

Paul Celan [Antschel]
1920–1970

10 Black milk of daybreak we drink you at night
we drink you at noon death is a master from
Germany
we drink you at sundown and in the morning
we drink
and we drink you
death is a master from Germany his eyes are
blue . . .
he sets his pack on to us he grants us a grave in
the air
he plays with the serpents and daydreams death
is a master
from Germany   *Death Fugue [1952]*[1]

P[hyllis] D[orothy] [White] James
1920–

11   That's all one asks of a sermon. No possible relevance to anything but itself.
The Skull Beneath the Skin [1982], bk. V, ch. 1

Pope John Paul II [Karol Wojtyla]
1920–

12   The greatness of work is inside man.
*Easter Vigil and Other Poems [1979].
The Quarry, I, Material*

13   We must ask ourselves whether there will continue to accumulate over the heads of this new generation of children the threat of common extermination. . . . Are the children to receive the arms race from us as a necessary inheritance?
*Speech at the United Nations
[October 2, 1979]*

14   You are our dearly beloved brothers, and in a certain way, it could be said that you are our elder brothers.
*On visit to the Synagogue of Rome
[April 13, 1986]*

---

[1]Translated from the German, *Todesfuge*, by MICHAEL HAMBURGER.

Timothy Leary
1920–1996

1   Turn On, Tune In, Drop Out.
     Slogan (title of lecture) [1967]

Ernest Lehman
1920–

2   I allowed the soothing music and the muted sounds of the city and the rich, sweet smell of success that permeated the room to lull my senses.
     Tell Me about It Tomorrow (novella) [1950], retitled The Sweet Smell of Success [1957][1]

Howard Nemerov
1920–1991

3   Flaubert wanted to write a novel
     About nothing.   *Style [1967]*

4   His lordly darkness decked in filth
     Bearded with weed like a lady's favor,
     He is a black planet.
     The Blue Swallows [1967]. The Mud Turtle

5   There is in space a small black hole
     Through which, say our astronomers,
     The whole damn thing, the universe,
     Must one day fall. That will be all.
     Cosmic Comics [1975]

6   When Moses in Horeb struck the rock,
     And water came forth out of the rock,
     Some of the people were annoyed with Moses
     And said he should have used a fancier stick.
     On Certain Wits [1977]

7   The world is full of mostly invisible things,
     And there is no way but putting the mind's eye,
     Or its nose, in a book, to find them out,
     Things like the square root of Everest
     Or how many times Byron goes into Texas,
     Or whether the law of the excluded middle
     Applies west of the Rockies.
     To David, about His Education [1977]

Mario Puzo
1920–1999

8   I'll make him an offer he can't refuse.
     The Godfather [1969]

John Paul Stevens
1920–

9   Although we may never know with complete certainty the identity of the winner of this year's presidential election, the identity of the loser is perfectly clear. It is the nation's confidence in the judge as an impartial guardian of the rule of law.
     Dissenting opinion in U.S. Supreme Court, Bush v. Gore [December 12, 2000]

Stewart [Lee] Udall
1920–

10   The most common trait of all primitive peoples is a reverence for the lifegiving earth, and the native American shared this elemental ethic: the land was alive to his loving touch, and he, its son, was brother to all creatures.
     The Quiet Crisis [1963], ch. 1

11   A land ethic for tomorrow should be as honest as Thoreau's *Walden,* and as comprehensive as the sensitive science of ecology. It should stress the oneness of our resources and the live-and-help-live logic of the great chain of life. If, in our haste to "progress," the economics of ecology are disregarded by citizens and policy makers alike, the result will be an ugly America.   *The Quiet Crisis, 14*

Sloan Wilson
1920–

12   The Man in the Gray Flannel Suit.
     Title of novel [1955]

Rodney Dangerfield [Jacob Cohen]
1921–

13   I can't get no respect.   *Comedy signature line*

Alexander Dubček
1921–1992

14   Socialism with a human face.
     Slogan of the Prague Spring [1968]

Betty [Naomi] Friedan
1921–

15   The problem lay buried, unspoken, for many years in the minds of American women. It was a strange stirring, a sense of dissatisfaction, a yearning that

---

[1] *Sweet Smell of Success (screenplay) [1957], (musical) [2002]*

women suffered in the middle of the twentieth century in the United States. Each suburban wife struggled with it alone. As she made the beds, shopped for groceries, matched slipcover material, ate peanut butter sandwiches with her children, chauffeured Cub Scouts and Brownies, lay beside her husband at night—she was afraid to ask even of herself the silent question—"Is this all?"

The Feminine Mystique [1963], ch. 1

1   The problem that has no name—which is simply the fact that American women are kept from growing to their full human capacities—is taking a far greater toll on the physical and mental health of our country than any known disease.

The Feminine Mystique, 14

2   This uneasy sense of battles won, only to be fought over again, of battles that should have been won, according to all the rules, and yet are not, of battles that suddenly one does not really want to win, and the weariness of battle altogether—how many women feel it?   *The Second Stage [1981]*

Bill [William Henry] Mauldin
1921–

3   I feel like a fugitive from th' law of averages.

Up Front [1945]. Caption for cartoon

4   Look at an infantryman's eyes and you can tell how much war he has seen.

Up Front. Caption for cartoon

5   Beautiful view. Is there one for the enlisted men?

Up Front. Caption for cartoon

Julius K[ambarage] Nyerere
1921–1999

6   The survival of our wildlife is a matter of grave concern to all of us in Africa. These wild creatures amid the wild places they inhabit are not only important as a source of wonder and inspiration but are an integral part of our natural resources and of our future livelihood and well-being.

The Arusha Declaration, Tanganyika [September 1961]

Gene [Eugene Wesley] Roddenberry
1921–1991

7   Space—the final frontier . . . These are the voyages of the starship *Enterprise*. Its five-year mission: to explore strange new worlds, to seek out new life

and new civilizations, to boldly go where no man has gone before.

Star Trek (television series) [1966–1969]

Andrei Dmitrievich Sakharov
1921–1989

8   A thermonuclear war cannot be considered a continuation of politics by other means. It would be a means to universal suicide.

Progress, Coexistence, and Intellectual Freedom [1968]

9   Intellectual freedom is the only guarantee of a scientific-democratic approach to politics, economic development, and culture.

Progress, Coexistence, and Intellectual Freedom

10   Profound thoughts arise only in debate, with a possibility of counterargument, only when there is a possibility of expressing not only correct ideas but also dubious ideas.

Progress, Coexistence, and Intellectual Freedom

Peter Ustinov
1921–

11   The young need old men. They need men who are not ashamed of age, not pathetic imitations of themselves. . . . Parents are the bones on which children sharpen their teeth.   *Dear Me [1977], ch. 18*

Richard [Purdy] Wilbur
1921–

12 But up in his room by artificial light
My father paints the summer.

My Father Paints the Summer [1947]

13 The beautiful changes as a forest is changed
By a chameleon's tuning his skin to it.

The Beautiful Changes [1947], st. 2

14 I dreamt the past was never past redeeming:
But whether this was false or honest dreaming
I beg death's pardon now. And mourn the dead.

The Pardon [1950], last stanza

15   The eyes open to a cry of pulleys,
And spirited from sleep, the astounded soul
Hangs for a moment bodiless and simple
as false dawn.

Outside the open window
The morning air is all awash with angels.

Love Calls Us to the Things of This World [1956]

1   The soul shrinks

From all that it is about to remember,
From the punctual rape of every blessèd day,
And cries,
   "Oh, let there be nothing on earth but laundry,
Nothing but rosy hands in the rising steam
And clear dances done in the sight of heaven."
   Love Calls Us to the Things of This World

2 Mind in its purest play is like some bat
That beats about in caverns all alone,
Contriving by a kind of senseless wit
Not to conclude against a wall of stone.

It has no need to falter or explore;
Darkly it knows what obstacles are there,
And so may weave and flitter, dip and soar
In perfect courses through the blackest air.

And has this simile a like perfection?
The mind is like a bat. Precisely. Save
That in the very happiest intellection
A graceful error may correct the cave.
   Mind [1956]

3 The werewolf's painful change. Turning his head
   away
On the sweaty bolster, he tries to remember
The mood of manhood,

But lies at last, as always,
Letting it happen, the fierce fur soft to his face,
Hearing with sharper ears.   *Beasts [1956], st. 3, 4*

4 Ask us, prophet, how we shall call
Our natures forth when that live tongue is all
Dispelled, that glass obscured or broken

In which we have said the rose of our love and the
   clean
Horse of our courage, in which beheld
The singing locust of the soul unshelled,
And all we mean or wish to mean.
   Advice to a Prophet [1961], st. 7, 8

5 All bitter things conduce to sweet,
   As this example shows;
Without the little spirochete
We'd have no chocolate to eat,
Nor would tobacco's fragrance greet
   The European nose.
   Pangloss's Song: A Comic Opera Lyric [1961][1]

6 What can I do but move
From folly to defeat,
And call that sorrow sweet
That teaches us to see
The final face of love
In what we cannot be?
   Someone Talking to Himself [1961], last stanza

7 All that we do
Is touched with ocean, yet we remain
On the shore of what we know.
   For Dudley [1969]

8   What you hope for
Is that at some point of the pointless journey,
Indoors or out, and when you least expect it,
Right in the middle of your stride, like that,
So neatly that you never feel a thing,
The kind assassin Sleep will draw a bead
And blow your brains out.
   Walking to Sleep [1969]

9 In her room at the prow of the house
Where light breaks, and the windows are tossed
   with linden,
My daughter is writing a story.
   The Writer [1976]

Whitney M[oore] Young, Jr.
1921–1971

10   Black is beautiful when it is a slum kid studying to enter college, when it is a man learning new skills for a new job, or a slum mother battling to give her kids a chance for a better life. But white is beautiful, too, when it helps change society to make our system work for black people also. White is ugly when it oppresses blacks—and so is black ugly when black people exploit other blacks. No race has a monopoly on vice or virtue, and the worth of an individual is not related to the color of his skin.
   Beyond Racism: Building an Open Society [1969], ch. 4

Sir Kingsley Amis
1922–1995

11   A dusty thudding in his head made the scene before him beat like a pulse. His mouth had been used as a latrine by some small creature of the night, and then as its mausoleum. During the night, too, he'd somehow been on a cross-country run and then been expertly beaten up by secret police. He felt bad.   *Lucky Jim [1954], ch. 6*

12 Death has got something to be said for it:
There's no need to get out of bed for it;
Wherever you may be,
They bring it to you, free.
   Delivery Guaranteed [1979]

[1]See Hellman, 770:15.

Jack Kerouac
1922–1969

1   We're a *beat* generation.[1]
*Remark [November 1948]. From John
Clellon Holmes, Nothing More to Declare
[1967]*

2   But then they danced down the street like dingledodies, and I shambled after as I've been doing
all my life after people who interest me, because the
only people for me are the mad ones, the ones who
are mad to live, mad to talk, mad to be saved, desirous of everything at the same time, the ones who
never yawn or say a commonplace thing, but burn,
burn, burn like fabulous yellow roman candles exploding like spiders across the stars and in the middle you see the blue centerlight pop and everybody
goes "Awww!"   *On the Road [1957]*

Philip Larkin
1922–1985

3 Why should I let the toad *work*
Squat on my life?
Can't I use my wit as a pitchfork
And drive the brute off?   *Toads [1955]*

4 Marrying left your maiden name disused.
Maiden Name [1955]

5 Give me your arm, old toad;
Help me down Cemetery Road.
Toads Revisited [1964]

6 Sexual intercourse began
In nineteen sixty-three
(Which was rather late for me)—
Between the end of the *Chatterley* ban
And the Beatles' first LP.
Annus Mirabilis [1974]

7 One of those old-type *natural* fouled-up guys.
Posterity [1974]

8 They fuck you up, your mum and dad.
They may not mean to, but they do.
They fill you with the faults they had
And add some extra, just for you.
This Be The Verse [1974]

9 Perhaps being old is having lighted rooms
Inside your head, and people in them, acting.
People you know, yet can't quite name.
The Old Fools [1974]

10   Deprivation is for me what daffodils were for
Wordsworth.[2]   *Remark in interview [1979]*

John G[illespie] Magee, Jr.
1922–1941

11 Oh! I have slipped the surly bonds of Earth
And danced the skies on laughter-silvered wings;
Sunward I've climbed, and joined the tumbling
    mirth
Of sun-split clouds,—and done a hundred things
You have not dreamed of—wheeled and soared
    and swung
High in the sunlit silence. Hov'ring there,
I've chased the shouting wind along, and flung
My eager craft through footless halls of air . . .

Up, up the long, delirious, burning blue
I've topped the wind-swept heights with easy grace
Where never lark nor ever eagle flew—
And, while with silent lifting mind I've trod
The high untrespassed sanctity of space,
Put out my hand, and touched the face of God.
High Flight [1941][3]

Bob Merrill
1922–1998

12 People, people who need people
Are the luckiest people in the world.
People [1963][4]

John A. Powers
1922–1980

13   All systems go. Everything is A-OK.
*Statement as public information officer for
U.S. space program [1959–1964]*

Alain Robbe-Grillet
1922–

14   The true writer has nothing to say. What counts
is the way he says it.[5]
For a New Novel [1963]

---

[1]A man is beat whenever he goes for broke and wagers the sum
of his resources on a single number; and the young generation has
done that continually from early youth. — John Clellon Holmes
[1906–1988], *"This Is the Beat Generation," New York Times Magazine* [November 16, 1952].

[2]See Wordsworth, 394:4–394:8.

[3]Ellipses are in the original text.

[4]Music by Jule Styne.

[5]Le véritable écrivain n'a rien à dire, il a seulement une manière
de le dire.

Alice S[chaerr] Rossi
1922–

1   The single most impressive fact about the attempt by American women to obtain the right to vote is how long it took.
The Feminist Papers [1973]. Along the Suffrage Trail

Charles M[onroe] Schulz
1922–2000

2   *It was a dark and stormy night.*[1] *Suddenly a scream pierced the air. . . .* Good writing takes enormous concentration.   *Peanuts (comic strip)*

3   That's the only dog I know who can smell someone just *thinking* about food.
Peanuts (comic strip)

4   Big sisters are the crab grass in the lawn of life.
Peanuts (comic strip)

5   [*Linus*]: After you've died, do you get to come back?
[*Charlie Brown*]: If they stamp your hand.
Peanuts (comic strip)

Joseph Stefano
1922–

6   A boy's best friend is his mother.
Psycho (screenplay) [1960], spoken by Anthony Perkins

Jesse Marvin Unruh
1922–1987

7   Money is the mother's milk of politics.
Remark

Kurt Vonnegut, Jr.
1922–

8   So it goes.
Slaughterhouse-Five [1969], ch. 1 and passim

9   You know—we've had to imagine the war here, and we have imagined that it was being fought by aging men like ourselves. We had forgotten that wars were fought by babies. When I saw those freshly shaved faces, it was a shock. "My God, my God—" I said to myself, "it's the Children's Crusade."
Slaughterhouse-Five, 5

10   High school is closer to the core of the American experience than anything else I can think of.
From his introduction to Our Time Is Now: Notes from the High School Underground, edited by JOHN BIRMINGHAM [1970]

Italo Calvino
1923–1985

11   I have tried to remove weight, sometimes from people, sometimes from heavenly bodies, sometimes from cities; above all I have tried to remove weight from the structure of stories and from language.
Six Memos for the Next Millennium [1988]

Paddy Chayevsky
1923–1981

12   I'm mad as hell, and I'm not going to take it any more.   *Network, screenplay [1976]*

James Dickey
1923–1997

13 A shudder of joy runs up
The trunk: the needles tingle;
One bird uncontrollably cries.
The wind changes round, and I stir
Within another's life. Whose life?
In the Tree House at Night [1962]

14 And I to my motorcycle
Parked like the soul of the junkyard
Restored, a bicycle fleshed
With power, and tore off
Up Highway 106, continually
Drunk on the wind in my mouth,
Wringing the handlebar for speed,
Wild to be wreckage forever.
Cherrylog Road [1963]

15 All families lie together, though some are burned
alive.
The others try to feel
For them. Some can, it is often said.
The Firebombing [1965]

16   I saw for a blazing moment
The great grassy world from both sides,
Man and beast in the round of their need,
And the hill wind stirred in my wool.
The Sheep Child [1967]

17   All day I climb myself
Bowlegged up those damned poles   rooster-
heeled in all
Kinds of weather.   *Power and Light [1967]*

---

[1]See Bulwer-Lytton, 452:12.

1 And this is the house I pass through on my way
To power and light.   *Power and Light*

2 We have all been in rooms
We cannot die in.   *Adultery [1967]*

3   Nothing can come
of this   nothing can come

Of us: of me with my grim techniques
Or you who have sealed your womb
With a ring of convulsive rubber:

Although we come together,
Nothing will come of us.   *Adultery [1967]*

4   Your moves are exactly right
For a few things in this world.
                        Encounter in the Cage Country [1967]

Robert B. Elliott
1923–

and

Raymond H. Goulding
1922–1990

5   Hang by your thumbs, everybody! Write if you
get work!
          *Bob and Ray radio show [1946], signature
          closing lines*

Nadine Gordimer
1923–

6   That was one of the things she held against missionaries: how they stressed Christ's submission to
humiliation, and so had conditioned the people of
Africa to humiliation by the white man.
              Not for Publication [1965], title story

7   She filled her house with blacks, and white parsons who went around preaching Jesus was a revolutionary, and then when the police walked in she
was surprised.   *The Conservationist [1974]*

Joseph Heller
1923–1999

8   He had decided to live forever or die in the attempt, and his only mission each time he went up
was to come down alive.
                        Catch-22 [1961], ch. 3

9   There was only one catch and that was Catch-
22, which specified that a concern for one's own
safety in the face of dangers that were real and immediate was the process of a rational mind. Orr was

crazy and could be grounded. All he had to do was
ask; and as soon as he did, he would no longer be
crazy and would have to fly more missions. . . . If he
flew them he was crazy and didn't have to; but if he
didn't want to he was sane and had to. . . . "That's
some catch, that Catch-22," he [Yossarian] observed. "It's the best there is," Doc Daneeka
agreed.   *Catch-22, 5*

Henry [Alfred] Kissinger
1923–

10   Power is the great aphrodisiac.[1]
              In the New York Times [January 19, 1971]

11   History knows no resting places and no plateaus.
                        White House Years [1979], ch. 3

12   A conventional army loses if it does not win. The
guerrilla army wins if it does not lose.
              *The Vietnam Negotiation, in Foreign Affairs
              [January 1969]*

13   [Richard Nixon] would have been a great, great
man had somebody loved him.
              Quoted in STEPHEN AMBROSE, *Nixon: Ruin
              and Recovery 1973–1990 [1991]*

Denise Levertov
1923–1999

14 I like to find
what's not found
at once, but lies
within something of another nature
in repose, distinct.   *Pleasures [1959]*

15 Marvelous Truth, confront us
at every turn,
in every guise.   *Matins [1962], VII*

16 Two by two in the ark of
the ache of it.
                        The Ache of Marriage [1964]

Norman Mailer
1923–

17   In the air the Pentagon would then, went the
presumption, turn orange and vibrate until all evil
emissions had fled this levitation. At that point the
war in Vietnam would end.
              The Armies of the Night [1968], pt. III, ch. 5

18   A night journey on a bus was one of the few
times when everything ambitious, wild, overcon-

---

[1]Also quoted as: Power is the ultimate aphrodisiac.

ceived, hopeless, garish, and suffocatingly technical in American life nonetheless came together long enough to give the citizens a little peace, for it was only when they were on the move that Americans could feel anchored in their memories.

The Armies of the Night, IV, 5

1 So we think of Marilyn who was every man's love affair with America, Marilyn Monroe who was blonde and beautiful and had a sweet little rinky-dink of a voice and all the cleanliness of all the clean American backyards. She was our angel, the sweet angel of sex, and the sugar of sex came up from her like a resonance of sound in the clearest grain of a violin.   *Marilyn [1973], ch. 1*

2 Then the Warden said, "Do you have anything you'd like to say?" and Gary looked up at the ceiling and hesitated, then said, "Let's do it." That was it.

The Executioner's Song [1979], ch. 38

Hank Williams
1923–1953

3 Hear that lonesome whippoorwill?
He sounds too blue to fly.
The midnight train is whining low,
I'm so lonesome I could cry.

I'm So Lonesome I Could Cry [1942]

James Baldwin
1924–1987

4 My life, my *real* life, was in danger, and not from anything other people might do but from the hatred I carried in my own heart.

Notes of a Native Son [1955], title essay

5 Harlem had needed something to smash. To smash something is the ghetto's chronic need.

Notes of a Native Son, title essay

6 If we do not now dare everything, the fulfillment of that prophecy, re-created from the Bible in song by a slave, is upon us: *God gave Noah the rainbow sign, No more water, the fire next time!*

The Fire Next Time [1963], end

Robert Bolt
1924–1995

7 The law is not a "light" for you or any man to see by; the law is not an instrument of any kind. The law is a causeway upon which, so long as he keeps to it, a citizen may walk safely.

A Man for All Seasons [1960], act II

George [Herbert Walker] Bush
1924–

8 Voodoo economics.
Remark, presidential primary campaign [1980]

9 We are a nation of communities, of tens and tens of thousands of ethnic, religious, social, business, labor union, neighborhood, regional and other organizations, all of them varied, voluntary, and unique . . . a brilliant diversity spread like stars, like a thousand points of light in a broad and peaceful sky.[1]

Acceptance speech, Republican National Convention, New Orleans [August 18, 1988]

10 The Congress will push me to raise taxes, and I'll say no, and they'll push, and I'll say no, and they'll push again. And all I can say to them is read my lips: No New Taxes.

Acceptance speech, Republican National Convention, New Orleans [August 18, 1988]

11 I want a kinder, gentler nation.
Acceptance speech, Republican National Convention, New Orleans [August 18, 1988]

Truman Capote
1924–1984

12 It was a terrible, strange-looking hotel. But Little Sunshine stayed on: it was his rightful home, he said, for if he went away, as he had once upon a time, other voices, other rooms, voices lost and clouded, strummed his dreams.

Other Voices, Other Rooms [1948], ch. 5

13 [It] isn't writing at all—it's typing.
Comment [1959] on Beat Generation writers. From GERALD CLARKE, *Capote [1988]*

14 I didn't want to harm the man. I thought he was a very nice gentleman. Soft-spoken. I thought so right up to the moment I cut his throat.

In Cold Blood [1966]

Jimmy [James Earl, Jr.] Carter
1924–

15 We believe that the first time we're born, as children, it's human life given to us; and when we ac-

---

[1] Instantly he could see the town below now, coiling in a thousand fumes of homely smoke, now winking into a thousand points of friendly light its glorious small design, its aching passionate assurances of walls, warmth, comfort, food, and love. — THOMAS WOLFE, *The Web and the Rock* [1939]

cept Jesus as our Savior, it's a new life. That's what "born again" means.

In an interview with Robert L. Turner [March 16, 1976]

1   I've looked on a lot of women with lust. I've committed adultery in my heart many times. This is something that God recognizes I will do—and I have done it—and God forgives me for it.

Interview in Playboy magazine [October 1976]

2   Two problems of our country—energy and malaise.

Remark at town meeting, Bardstown, Kentucky [July 31, 1979]

Arthur Charles Erickson
1924–

3   North American civilization is one of the ugliest to have emerged in human history, and it has engulfed the world. Asphalt and exhaust fumes clog the villages. . . . This great, though disastrous, culture can only change as we begin to stand off and see . . . the inveterate materialism which has become the model for cultures around the globe.

Speech at Simon Fraser University [1973]

4   What the West has thrown on the waters of the world drifts back to us on a tide of cultural pollution appalling to behold.

Speech at International Congress of Architecture in Iran [1974]

Zbigniew Herbert
1924–1998

5 The pebble
is a perfect creature

equal to itself
mindful of its limits

filled exactly
with a pebbly meaning   *Pebble [1966]*[1]

Russell Baker
1925–

6   The only thing I was fit for was to be a writer, and this notion rested solely on my suspicion that I would never be fit for real work, and that writing didn't require any.

Growing Up [1982], ch. 9

---

[1]Translated from the Polish by CZESLAW MILOSZ and PETER DALE SCOTT.

Yogi [Lawrence Peter] Berra
1925–

7   It ain't over till it's over.

Comment on National League pennant race [1973]

8   How can you think and hit at the same time?

Remark

9   In baseball, you don't know nothing.   *Remark*

10   Slump? I ain't in no slump. I just ain't hitting.

Remark

11   You can observe a lot by watching.   *Remark*

12   If people don't want to come out to the ball park, nobody's going to stop them.   *Attributed*

13   It was déjà vu all over again.   *Attributed*

14   When you come to a fork in the road, take it.

Attributed

Lenny Bruce [Leonard Alfred Schneider]
1925–1966

15   People should be taught what is, not what should be. All my humor is based on destruction and despair. If the whole world were tranquil, without disease and violence, I'd be standing in the breadline.

The Essential Lenny Bruce [1967]. Epigraph

16   I'll die young, but it's like kissing God.

On his drug addiction

Barbara Pierce Bush
1925–

17   Somewhere out in this audience may even be someone who will one day follow in my footsteps, and preside over the White House as the President's spouse. I wish him well!

Remarks at Wellesley College Commencement [June 1, 1990]

John [Daniel] Ehrlichman
1925–1999

18   It'll play in Peoria.[2]   *Phrase [1970]*

19   I think we ought to let him [Patrick Gray] hang there. Let him twist slowly, slowly in the wind.

Telephone conversation with John Dean [March 7/8, 1973]

---

[2]Meaning politically acceptable to "Middle America."

Frantz Fanon
1925–1961

1   When I search for man in the technique and the style of Europe, I see only a succession of negations of man, and an avalanche of murders.
The Wretched of the Earth[1] *[1961].*
Conclusion

Maxine [Winokur] Kumin
1925–

2 I took the lake between my legs.
Morning Swim [1965]

3 Something went crabwise
across the snow this morning.
The Presence [1970]

4 Love, we are a small pond.   *We Are [1970]*

5 Meanwhile
let us cast one shadow
in air or water.   *Turning To [1972]*

6 Our daughters and sons have burst
from the marionette show
leaving a tangle of strings
and gone into the unlit audience.
The Absent Ones [1972]

7 Can it be
I am the only Jew residing in Danville, Kentucky,
looking for matzoh in the Safeway and the A & P?
Living Alone with Jesus [1972]

8 When Sleeping Beauty wakes up
she is almost fifty years old.
Time to start planning her retirement cottage.
The Archaeology of a Marriage [1978]

Malcolm X
[El-Hajj Malik El-Shabazz]
1925–1965

9   If you're born in America with a black skin, you're born in prison.
Interview [June 1963]

10   We are not fighting for integration, nor are we fighting for separation. We are fighting for recognition as human beings. We are fighting for . . . human rights.
Speech, Black Revolution, New York [1964]

---

[1]Translated by Constance Farrington.
See Pottier, 504:21.

11   The day that the black man takes an uncompromising step and realizes that he's within his rights, when his own freedom is being jeopardized, to use any means necessary to bring about his freedom or put a halt to that injustice, I don't think he'll be by himself.
Oxford Union Society debate
[December 3, 1964]

12   [On the assassination of President John F. Kennedy:] It was, as I saw it, a case of "the chickens coming home to roost." I said that the hate in white men had not stopped with the killing of defenseless black people, but that hate, allowed to spread unchecked, had finally struck down this country's Chief Magistrate.
Autobiography (as told to Alex Haley*)*
[1964], ch. 16

Zhores Aleksandrovich Medvedev
1925–

13   Science and technology, and the various forms of art, all unite humanity in a single and interconnected system. As science progresses, the worldwide cooperation of scientists and technologists becomes more and more of a special and distinct intellectual community of friendship, in which, in place of antagonism, there is growing up a mutually advantageous sharing of work, a coordination of efforts, a common language for the exchange of information, and a solidarity, which are in many cases independent of the social and political differences of individual states.
The Medvedev Papers [1970], preface

Flannery O'Connor
1925–1964

14   Does one's integrity ever lie in what he is not able to do? I think that usually it does, for free will does not mean one will, but many wills conflicting in one man. Freedom cannot be conceived simply.
Wise Blood [1952], foreword

15   "She would of been a good woman," The Misfit said, "if it had been somebody there to shoot her every minute of her life."
A Good Man Is Hard to Find [1953]

16   Besides the neutral expression she wore when she was alone, Mrs. Freeman had two others, forward and reverse, that she used for all her human dealings. Her forward expression was steady and driving like the advance of a heavy truck.
Good Country People [1955]

1   Mrs. Broadwater [Mary McCarthy] said when she was a child and received the Host, she thought of it as the Holy Ghost, He being the "most portable" person of the Trinity; now she thought of it as a symbol and implied it was a pretty good one. I then said, in a very shaky voice, "Well, if it's a symbol, to hell with it."

Letter to A. [December 10, 1955]

2   The novel is an art form and when you use it for anything other than art, you pervert it. . . . If you manage to use it successfully for social, religious, or other purposes, it is because you make it art first.

Letter to Father John McCown
[May 9, 1956]

3   I doubt if the texture of Southern life is any more grotesque than that of the rest of the nation, but it does seem evident that the Southern writer is particularly adept at recognizing the grotesque; and to recognize the grotesque, you have to have some notion of what is not grotesque and why.

Talk at Notre Dame University [spring 1957]

4   Knowing who you are is good for one generation only.

Everything That Rises Must Converge [1965],
title story

5   I have settled, in short, from reading my own writings, that my subject in fiction is the action of grace in territory held largely by the devil.

Mystery and Manners [1969]. On Her
Own Work

Frank R. Pierson
1925–

6   What we've got here is failure to communicate.

Cool Hand Luke (screenplay) [1967]

Margaret [Hilda Roberts] Thatcher
1925–

7   I like Mr. Gorbachev. We can do business together.

On their meeting [December 17, 1984]

8   If you lead a country like Britain . . . you have to have a touch of iron about you.

On her reputation as The Iron Lady
[March 21, 1986]

9   In politics, if you want anything said, ask a man. If you want anything done, ask a woman.

Saying

Gore Vidal
1925–

10   The theater needs continual reminders that there is nothing more debasing than the work of those who do well what is not worth doing at all.

Quoted in Newsweek [March 25, 1968]

11   Some writers take to drink, others take to audiences.

Interview in Paris Review [1981]

12   He turned being a Big Loser into a perfect triumph by managing to lose the presidency in a way bigger and more original than anyone else had ever lost it before.

Richard Nixon in Esquire [December 1983]

A[rchie] R[andolph] Ammons
1926–2001

13   Though I have looked everywhere
I can find nothing lowly
in the universe.

Still [1972]

14   In nature there are few sharp lines.

Corson's Inlet [1972], l. 31

15   No humbling of reality to precept.

Corson's Inlet, l. 116

16   Counting my numberless fingers.

Mountain Talk [1972]

17   Not so much looking for the shape
as being available
to any shape that may be
summoning itself
through me
from the self not mine but ours.

Poetics [1972]

18   I attended the burial of all my rosy feelings:
I performed the rites, simple and decisive.

Transaction [1972]

19   The stones are
prepared: they are round and ready.

Upland [1972]

20   I don't know about you,
but I'm sick of good poems, all those little rondures
splendidly brought off, painted gourds on a shelf.

Sphere [1974]

Chuck Berry
[Charles Edward Anderson]
1926–

1 Roll over Beethoven
And tell Tchaikovsky the news.
Roll Over Beethoven [1956]

2 He never learned to read or write so well
But he could play a guitar just like ringing a bell.
Johnny B. Goode [1958]

Robert Bly
1926–

3 I have wandered in a face, for hours,
Passing through dark fires.
I have risen to a body
Not yet born,
Existing like a light around the body,
Through which the body moves like a sliding
moon.
The Light Around the Body [1967].
Looking into a Face

4 The sound of the rampaging Missouri,
Bending the reeds again and again — something
inside us
Like a ghost train in the Rockies
About to be buried in snow!
Its long hoot
Making the owl in the Douglas fir turn his head.
The Light Around the Body. Asian Peace
Offers Rejected Without Publication

Mel Brooks [Melvin Kaminsky]
1926–

5 That's it, baby, if you've got it, flaunt it.
The Producers (screenplay) [1968]

6 Springtime for Hitler and Germany,
Deutschland is happy and gay.
We're moving to a faster pace,
Look out, here comes the Master Race!
The Producers (screenplay)

7 Where did we go right?
The Producers (screenplay)

Fidel Castro
1926–

8 History will absolve me.[1]
At his trial for raid on Moncada barracks
[October 16, 1953]

---
[1]La Historia me absolvera.

9 We are not only a Latin-American nation; we are
an Afro-American nation also.
Speech in Havana [1977]

Allen Ginsberg
1926–1997

10 I saw you, Walt Whitman, childless, lonely old
grubber, poking among the meats in the refrigerator and eyeing the grocery boys.
I heard you asking questions of each: Who killed
the pork chops? What price bananas? Are you my
Angel? *A Supermarket in California [1955]*

11 America I'm putting my queer shoulder to the
wheel. *America [1956]*

12 I saw the best minds of my generation destroyed by
madness, starving hysterical naked,
dragging themselves through the negro streets at
dawn looking for an angry fix
angelheaded hipsters burning for the ancient
heavenly connection to the starry dynamo in
the machinery of night. *Howl [1956]*

13 This is the end, the redemption from Wilderness,
way for the Wonderer, House sought for All, black
handkerchief washed clean by weeping.
Kaddish [1959], I

14 O mother
what have I left out
O mother
what have I forgotten *Kaddish, IV*

James [Ingram] Merrill
1926–1995

15 Always that same old story —
Father Time and Mother Earth,
A marriage on the rocks.
The Broken Home (1966)

16 Again last night I dreamed the dream called
Laundry. *The Mad Scene [1966]*

17 I knew
That life was fiction in disguise.
Days of 1935 (1969)

18 Proust's Law (are you listening?) is twofold:
(a) What least thing our self-love longs for most
Others instinctively withhold;

(b) Only when time has slain desire
Is his wish granted to a smiling ghost
Neither harmed nor warmed, now, by the fire.
Days of 1971 (1969)

19 I yearned for the kind of unseasoned telling found
In legends, fairy tales, a tone licked clean

Over the centuries by mild old tongues,
Grandam to cub, serene, anonymous.
The Book of Ephraim [1976], sec. A

1 What we dream up must be lived down, I think.
The Book of Ephraim, I

2   HE PREFERS
LIVE MUSIC TO A PATRON'S HUMDRUM SPHERES
Is this permitted? WHEN U ARE MOZART YES
He's living *now*? As what? A BLACK ROCK STAR
WHATEVER THAT IS.   *The Book of Ephraim, P*

Newton N[orman] Minow
1926–

3   When television is bad, nothing is worse. I invite
you to sit down in front of your television set when
your station goes on the air . . . and keep your eyes
glued to that set until the station signs off. I can assure you that you will observe a vast wasteland.
*Speech as chairman of the Federal
Communications Commission to National
Association of Broadcasters, Washington, D.C.
[May 9, 1961]*

Frank O'Hara
1926–1966

4 It is 12:20 in New York a Friday
three days after Bastille Day, yes
it is 1959 and I go get a shoeshine
because I will get off the 4:19 in Easthampton
at 7:15 and then go straight to dinner
and I don't know the people who will feed me
Lunch Poems [1964]. The Day Lady Died

5 If anyone was looking
for me I hid behind a
tree and cried out "I am
an orphan."

And here I am, the
center of all beauty!
writing these poems!
Imagine!
*Collected Poems [1967]. Autobiographia
Literaria*

6 "Sun, don't go!" I was awake
at last. "No, go I must, they're calling
me."
"Who are they?"
            Rising he said, "Some
day you'll know. They're calling to you
too." Darkly he rose, and then I slept.
*Collected Poems [1967]. A True Account of
Talking to the Sun at Fire Island*

Peter Shaffer
1926–

7   We keep saying old people are square. Then when
they suddenly aren't—we don't like it!
Equus [1973], act II, sc. 31

William D[eWitt] Snodgrass
1926–

8 It was the nature of the thing:
No moon outlives its leaving night,
No sun its day. And I went on
Rich in the loss of all I sing
To the threshold of waking light,
To larksong and the live, gray dawn.
So night by night, my life has gone.
Orpheus [1959]

9 The sleek, expensive girls I teach,
Younger and pinker every year,
Bloom gradually out of reach.
April Inventory [1959]

10 Though trees turn bare and girls turn wives,
We shall afford our costly seasons;
There is a gentleness survives
That will outspeak and has its reasons.
There is a loveliness exists,
Preserves us, not for specialists.
April Inventory

John Ashbery
1927–

11 As I sit looking out of a window of the building
I wish I did not have to write the instruction
        manual on the uses of a new metal.
The Instruction Manual [1956]

12   You and I
Are suddenly what the trees try
To tell us we are:
That their merely being there
Means something; that soon
We may touch, love, explain.
Some Trees [1956]

13 As Parmigianino did it, the right hand
Bigger than the head, thrust at the viewer
And swerving easily away, as though to protect
What it advertises.
Self-Portrait in a Convex Mirror [1975]

14 Something like living occurs, a movement
Out of the dream into its codification.
Self-Portrait in a Convex Mirror

Cesar [Estrada] Chavez
1927–1993

1   Viva la huelga [Long live the strike]!
Slogan of the United Farm Workers [the 1960s]

Günter [Wilhem] Grass
1927–

2   You can declare at the very start that it's impossible to write a novel nowadays, but then, behind your back, so to speak, give birth to a whopper, a novel to end all novels.
The Tin Drum [1959],[1] bk. I, The Wide Skirt

3   Even bad books are books and therefore sacred.
The Tin Drum. Rasputin and the Alphabet

Galway Kinnell
1927–

4   the rest of my days I spend
wandering, wondering
what, anyway,
was that sticky infusion, that rank flavor of blood,
   that poetry by which I lived?
Body Rags [1968]. The Bear

5   In the half darkness we look at each other
and smile
and touch arms across his little, startlingly muscled
   body—
this one whom habit of memory propels to the
   ground of his making,
sleeper only the mortal sounds can awake,
this blessing love gives again into our arms.
Mortal Acts, Mortal Words [1980]. After Making Love We Hear Footsteps

R[onald] D[avid] Laing
1927–1989

6   We are born into a world where alienation awaits us.   *The Politics of Experience [1967], introduction*

7   Madness need not be all breakdown. It may also be breakthrough. It is potentially liberation and renewal as well as enslavement and existential death.
The Politics of Experience, ch. 6

W[illiam] S[tanley] Merwin
1927–

8   You came back to us in a dream and we were not
   here.   *Come Back [1967]*

9   The dead will think the living are worth it we will
   know
Who we are
And we will all enlist again.
When the War Is Over [1967]

10   Every year without knowing it I have passed the
   day.   *For the Anniversary of My Death [1967]*

11   Of course there is nothing the matter with the stars
It is my emptiness among them
While they drift farther away in the invisible
   morning.
In the Winter of My Thirty-Eighth Year [1967]

12   I think I was cold in the womb.
The Forebears [1971]

13   I am the son of the first fish who climbed ashore
   but the news has not yet reached my bowels.
Psalm: Our Fathers [1971]

14   Like shadows
of the plumbing
that is all that is left
of the great city.   *The Plumbing [1971]*

15   Some alien blessing
is on its way to us.
Midnight in Early Spring [1971]

16   Oh pile of white shirts who is coming
to breathe in your shapes.
The Night of the Shirts [1971]

Andy Warhol
1927–1987

17   In the future everyone will be world-famous for fifteen minutes.
Catalogue of his photo exhibition in Stockholm [1968]

James Wright
1927–1980

18   Shake out the ruffle, turn and go,
Over the trellis blow the kiss.
Some of the guests will never know
Another night to shadow this.
Some of the birds awake in vines
Will never see another face

---

[1]Translated by RALPH MANHEIM.

So frail, so lovely anyplace
Between the birdbath and the bines.
                    To a Hostess Saying Good Night

1 I will putter as though I had not heard,
And lift him into my arms and sing
Whether he hears my song or not.
                    Mutterings over the Crib of a Deaf Child

2 I lean back, as the evening darkens and comes on.
A chicken hawk floats over, looking for home.
I have wasted my life.
                    *Lying in a Hammock at William Duffy's
                    Farm in Pine Island, Minnesota*

3 Suddenly I realize
That if I stepped out of my body I would break
Into blossom.
                    The Branch Will Not Break [1963]. A Blessing

Edward [Franklin] Albee
1928–

4   *George:* Who's afraid of Virginia Woolf . . .
    Martha: I . . . am . . . George . . . I am.
    Who's Afraid of Virginia Woolf?[1] *[1962].
    The Exorcism*

5   You gotta have a swine to show you where the
truffles are.
                    *Who's Afraid of Virginia Woolf?, act II,
                    Walpurgisnacht*

Maya Angelou
[Marguerite Johnson]
1928–

6 You may trod me in the very dirt
But still, like dust, I'll rise.
                    Still I Rise [1978]. And Still I Rise

7 History, despite its wrenching pain,
Cannot be unlived, but if faced
With courage, need not be lived again.
                    On the Pulse of Morning [1993][2]

[Avram] Noam Chomsky
1928–

8   Colorless green ideas sleep furiously.[3]
                    Syntactic Structures [1957], ch. 2

---

[1]*Who's Afraid of the Big Bad Wolf? — Title of song,* WALT DIS-
NEY *film cartoon Three Little Pigs* [1933]. Ellipses are in the original text.

[2]Read at the inauguration of PRESIDENT BILL CLINTON [January
20, 1993].

[3]Illustrating how meaning and syntax are independent of each
other.

Mary Daly
1928–

9   If God is male, then the male is God. The divine
patriarch castrates women as long as he is allowed
to live on in the human imagination.
                    Beyond God the Father [1973], ch. 1

Gabriel García Márquez
1928–

10   It was foreseen that the city of mirrors (or mirages) would be wiped out by the wind and exiled
from the memory of men at the precise moment
when Aureliano Babilonia would finish deciphering
the parchments, and that everything written on
them was unrepeatable since time immemorial and
forevermore, because races condemned to one hundred years of solitude did not have a second opportunity on earth.
                    *One Hundred Years of Solitude (Cien Años de
                    Soledad) [1967]*[4]

Michael Harrington
1928–1989

11   The other America, the America of poverty, is
hidden today in a way that it never was before. Its
millions are socially invisible to the rest of us. . . .
The very development of American society is creating a new kind of blindness about poverty. The
poor are increasingly slipping out of the very experience and consciousness of the nation.
                    *The Other America: Poverty in the United
                    States [1962], ch. 1*

12   For the urban poor the police are those who arrest you. In almost any slum there is a vast conspiracy against the forces of law and order.
                    *The Other America: Poverty in the United
                    States, 1*

Tom [Thomas Andrew] Lehrer
1928–

13 Remember the war against Franco?
That's the kind where each of us belongs.
Though he may have won all the battles,
We had all the good songs.
                    The Folk Song Army [1965]

14 "Once the rockets are up, who cares where they
      come down?
That's not my department," says Wernher von
Braun.   *Wernher von Braun [1965]*

---

[4]Translated by GREGORY RABASSA.

1   It is a sobering thought that when Mozart was my age, he had been dead for two years.
That Was the Year That Was [1965]

Philip Levine
1928–

2 Give me back my young brother, hard
and furious, with wide shoulders and a curse
for God and burning eyes that look upon
all creation and say, You can have it.
You Can Have It

Desmond Morris
1928–

3   There are one hundred and ninety-three living species of monkeys and apes. One hundred and ninety-two of them are covered with hair. The exception is a naked ape self-named *Homo sapiens.*
The Naked Ape [1967], introduction

Cynthia Ozick
1928–

4   The whole peninsula of Florida was weighted down with regret. Everyone had left behind a real life.
Rosa [1984]

5   I wanted to use what I was, to be what I was born to be—not to have a "career," but to be that straightforward obvious unmistakable animal, a writer.
Metaphor and Memory [1989]

Robert M[aynard] Pirsig
1928–

6   Other people can talk about how to expand the destiny of mankind. I just want to talk about how to fix a motorcycle. I think that what I have to say has more lasting value.
Zen and the Art of Motorcycle Maintenance [1974], pt. III, ch. 25

Anne Sexton
1928–1974

7   You, Doctor Martin, walk
from breakfast to madness. Late August,
I speed through the antiseptic tunnel where the
    moving dead still talk
of pushing their bones against the thrust
of cure. And I am queen of this summer hotel

or the laughing bee on a stalk
of death.
You, Doctor Martin [1960], st. 1

8 I have gone out, a possessed witch,
haunting the black air, braver at night.
Her Kind [1960]

9 A woman like that is not a woman, quite.
I have been her kind.   *Her Kind*

10 Leaving the page of the book carelessly open,
something unsaid, the phone off the hook
and the love, whatever it was, an infection.
Wanting to Die [1966], last stanza

11   Little Girl, My Stringbean, My Lovely Woman.
Title of poem [1966]

12 Beauty is a simple passion,
but, oh my friends, in the end
you will dance the fire dance in iron shoes.
Snow White and the Seven Dwarfs [1971]

13 Though they washed her with wine
and rubbed her with butter
it was to no avail.
She lay as still as a gold piece.
Snow White and the Seven Dwarfs

14 I would like a simple life
yet all night I am laying
poems away in a long box.
The Ambition Bird [1973], st. 4

L[ouis] E[dward] Sissman
1928–1976

15 Struck dumb by love among the walruses
And whales, the off-white polar bear with stuffing
Missing, the mastodons like muddy buses,
I sniff the mothproof air and lack for nothing.
Dying: An Introduction [1967]. The Museum of Comparative Zoology

16   Through my
Invisible new veil
Of finity, I see
November's world—
Low scud, slick street, three giggling girls—
As, oddly, not as sombre
As December,
But as green
As anything:
As spring.
Dying: An Introduction. Outbound

Alvin Toffler
1928–

1   Future shock . . . the shattering stress and disorientation that we induce in individuals by subjecting them to too much change in too short a time.
Future Shock [1970], Introduction

James Dewey Watson
1928–
and
Francis Harry Compton Crick
1916–

2   This [double helix] structure has novel features which are of considerable biological interest. . . . It has not escaped our notice that the specific pairing we have postulated immediately suggests a possible copying mechanism for the genetic material.
Molecular Structure of Nucleic Acids, in Nature [April 25, 1953][1]

Elie Wiesel
1928–

3   I was the accuser, God the accused. My eyes were open and I was alone — terribly alone in a world without God and without man.
Night [1958][2]

4   You'll try to reveal what should remain hidden, you'll try to incite people to learn from the past and rebel, but they will refuse to believe you. They will not listen to you. . . . You'll possess the truth, you already do; but it's the truth of a madman.
A Beggar in Jerusalem [1970], ch. 5[3]

5   Rejected by mankind, the condemned do not go so far as to reject it in turn. Their faith in history remains unshaken, and one may well wonder why. They do not despair. The proof: they persist in surviving not only to survive, but to testify.
The victims elect to become witnesses.
One Generation After [1970]. Readings[3]

Anne Frank
1929–1945

6   Whoever is happy will make others happy too. He who has courage and faith will never perish in misery!
Anne Frank: The Diary of a Young Girl [1952].[4] March 7, 1944

7   What *one* Christian does is his own responsibility, what *one* Jew does is thrown back at all Jews.
Anne Frank: The Diary of a Young Girl. May 22, 1944

8   [Daddy] said: "All children must look after their own upbringing." Parents can only give good advice or put them on the right paths, but the final forming of a person's character lies in their own hands.
Anne Frank: The Diary of a Young Girl. July 15, 1944

9   It's really a wonder that I haven't dropped all my ideals, because they seem so absurd and impossible to carry out. Yet I keep them, because in spite of everything I still believe that people are really good at heart. I simply can't build up my hopes on a foundation consisting of confusion, misery, and death. I see the world gradually being turned into a wilderness, I hear the ever approaching thunder, which will destroy us too, I can feel the sufferings of millions.
Anne Frank: The Diary of a Young Girl. July 15, 1944

X. J[oseph] Kennedy
1929–

10   One-woman waterfall, she wears
Her slow descent like a long cape
And pausing, on the final stair
Collects her motions into shape.
Nude Descending a Staircase, last stanza

11   I rang them up while touring Timbucktoo,
Those bosom chums to whom you're known as
"Who?"
To Someone Who Insisted I Look Up Someone

Martin Luther King, Jr.
1929–1968

12   The Negro's great stumblingblock is not the White Citizen's Counciler or the Ku Klux Klanner,

---

[1]We told her [the typist of their article] that she was participating in perhaps the most famous event in biology since Darwin's book. — WATSON, *The Double Helix* [1968].

[2]Translated by STELLA RODWAY.

[3]Translated by LILY EDELMAN and ELIE WIESEL.

---

[4]Translated by B. M. MOOYART.

but the white moderate who is more devoted to "order" than to justice, . . . who paternalistically believes he can set the timetable for another man's freedom.

Letter from Birmingham jail
[April 16, 1963]

1   If a man hasn't discovered something that he will die for, he isn't fit to live.

Speech in Detroit [June 23, 1963]

2   I have a dream that one day on the red hills of Georgia the sons of former slaves and the sons of former slaveowners will be able to sit down together at the table of brotherhood.

Speech at Civil Rights March on Washington
[August 28, 1963]

3   I have a dream that my four little children will one day live in a nation where they will not be judged by the color of their skin, but by the content of their character.

Speech at Civil Rights March on Washington
[August 28, 1963]

4   When we let freedom ring, when we let it ring from every village and every hamlet, from every state and every city, we will be able to speed up that day when all of God's children, black men and white men, Jews and Gentiles, Protestants and Catholics, will be able to join hands and sing in the words of the old Negro spiritual, "Free at last! Free at last! Thank God Almighty, we are free at last!"[1]

Speech at Civil Rights March on Washington
[August 28, 1963]

5   Nonviolence is the answer to the crucial political and moral questions of our time; the need for man to overcome oppression and violence without resorting to oppression and violence.

Man must evolve for all human conflict a method which rejects revenge, aggression and retaliation. The foundation of such a method is love.[2]

Speech accepting the Nobel Peace Prize
[December 11, 1964]

6   The tortuous road which has led from Montgomery to Oslo is a road over which millions of Negroes are traveling to find a new sense of dignity. It will, I am convinced, be widened into a superhighway of justice.

Speech accepting the Nobel Peace Prize
[December 11, 1964]

7   I refuse to accept the idea that the "isness" of man's present nature makes him morally incapable of reaching up for the "oughtness" that forever confronts him.

Speech accepting the Nobel Peace Prize
[December 11, 1964]

8   I refuse to accept the cynical notion that nation after nation must spiral down a militaristic stairway into the hell of nuclear destruction. I believe that unarmed truth and unconditional love will have the final word in reality.

Speech accepting the Nobel Peace Prize
[December 11, 1964]

9   The Negro was willing to risk martyrdom in order to move and stir the social conscience of his community and the nation . . . he would force his oppressor to commit his brutality openly, with the rest of the world looking on. . . . Nonviolent resistance paralyzed and confused the power structures against which it was directed.

Why We Can't Wait [1964]

10   Like anybody, I would like to live a long life. Longevity has its place. But I'm not concerned about that now. I just want to do God's will. And He's allowed me to go up to the mountain. And I've looked over, and I've seen the promised land. I may not get there with you, but I want you to know tonight that we as a people will get to the promised land. . . .

So I'm happy tonight. I'm not worried about anything. I'm not fearing any man.

Address to sanitation workers, Memphis, Tennessee [April 3, 1968], the night before his assassination

Milan Kundera

1929–

11   The struggle against power is the struggle of memory against forgetting.

The Book of Laughter and Forgetting [1980],[3]
pt. I, sec. ii

12   The only reason people want to be masters of the future is to change the past.

The Book of Laughter and Forgetting, I, xvii

13   Her drama was a drama not of heaviness but of lightness. What fell to her lot was not the burden but the unbearable lightness of being.

The Unbearable Lightness of Being [1984],[3]
pt. III

---

[1]King's epitaph, South View Cemetery, Atlanta, Georgia. See Anonymous: Spirituals, 863:2.

[2]See Gandhi, 650:10.

[3]Translated by MICHAEL HENRY HEIM.

1   Kitsch excludes everything from its purview which is essentially unacceptable in human existence.
The Unbearable Lightness of Being, VI

2   The wisdom of the novel comes from having a question for everything. When Don Quixote went out into the world, that world turned into a mystery before his eyes. That is the legacy of the first European novel.
A Talk with the Author by PHILIP ROTH *[1980]*[1]

Ursula K[roeber] Le Guin
1929–

3   The king was pregnant.
The Left Hand of Darkness [1969], ch. 8

4   He had grown up in a country run by politicians who sent the pilots to man the bombers to kill the babies to make the world safer for children to grow up in.   *The Lathe of Heaven [1971], ch. 6*

Claes Oldenburg
1929–

5   I am for an art that tells you the time of day, or where such and such a street is. I am for an art that helps old ladies across the street.
Statement for exhibition catalogue [1961]

John [James] Osborne
1929–1994

6   Oh heavens, how I long for a little ordinary human enthusiasm. Just enthusiasm—that's all. I want to hear a warm, thrilling voice cry out Hallelujah! Hallelujah! I'm alive.   *Look Back in Anger, act I*

7   It's no good trying to fool yourself about love. You can't fall into it like a soft job, without dirtying up your hands. It takes muscle and guts. And if you can't bear the thought of messing up your nice, clean soul, you'd better give up the whole idea of life and become a saint.   *Look Back in Anger, III, ii*

Adrienne Rich
1929–

8 Your mind now, moldering like wedding-cake, heavy with useless experience, rich

with suspicion, rumor, fantasy,
crumbling to pieces under the knife-edge
of mere fact.
Snapshots of a Daughter-in-Law [1963], st. 1

9 A thinking woman sleeps with monsters.
The beak that grips her, she becomes.
Snapshots of a Daughter-in-Law, st. 3

10 Piece by piece I seem
to re-enter the world.   *Necessities of Life [1966]*

11 My visionary anger cleansing my sight.
The Stranger [1973]

12 I am the androgyne.   *The Stranger*

13 There is a ladder.
The ladder is always there
hanging innocently
close to the side of the schooner.
Diving into the Wreck [1973]

14 I came to explore the wreck.
Diving into the Wreck

15 I came to see the damage that was done
and the treasures that prevail.
I stroke the beam of my lamp
slowly along the flank
of something more permanent
than fish or weed.   *Diving into the Wreck*

16   Re-vision—the act of looking back, of seeing with fresh eyes, of entering an old text from a new critical direction—is for women more than a chapter in cultural history: it is an act of survival.
On Lies, Secrets, and Silence [1979]. When We Dead Awaken

Chinua Achebe
1930–

17   In such a regime, I say, you died a good death if your life had inspired someone to come forward and shoot your murderer in the chest—without asking to be paid.
A Man of the People [1966], closing sentence

Neil [Alden] Armstrong
1930–

18   Houston, Tranquility Base here. The Eagle has landed.   *On reaching the moon [July 20, 1969]*

19   That's one small step for [a] man, one giant leap for mankind.
On first stepping on the moon [July 20, 1969]

---

[1]Translated by VERA KUNDERA and PETER KUSSI.

Buck Henry [Henry Zuckerman]
1930–
and
Calder Willingham
1922–

1   Ben—I want to say one word to you—just one word: plastics.
The Graduate (screenplay) [1967][1]

Ted [Edward J.] Hughes
1930–1998

2 Stare at the monster: remark
How difficult it is to define just what
Amounts to monstrosity in that
Very ordinary appearance.
Famous Poet [1957]

3 I imagine this midnight moment's forest:
Something else is alive
Beside the clock's loneliness
And this blank page where my fingers move.
The Hawk in the Rain [1957].
The Thought-Fox

4 . . . with a sudden sharp hot stink of fox,
It enters the dark hole of the head.
The window is starless still; the clock ticks,
The page is printed.
The Hawk in the Rain.
The Thought-Fox

5 My feet are locked upon the rough bark.
It took the whole of Creation
To produce my foot, my each feather:
Now I hold Creation in my foot
Or fly up, and revolve it all slowly—
I kill where I please because it is all mine.
Hawk Roosting [1960]

6 Daylong this tomcat lies stretched flat
As an old rough mat, no mouth and no eyes,
Continual wars and wives are what
Have tattered his ears and battered his head.
Esther's Tomcat [1960]

7 The rat is in the trap, it is in the trap,
And attacking heaven and earth with a mouthful
of screeches like torn tin.
The Rat's Dance [1967]

8 At twenty-five I was dumbfounded afresh
By my ignorance of the simplest things.
Birthday Letters [1998]. Fulbright Scholars

Frank [Francis] McCourt
1930–

9   Worse than the ordinary miserable childhood is the miserable Irish childhood, and worse yet is the miserable Irish Catholic childhood.
Angela's Ashes [1996], ch. 1

Harold Pinter
1930–

10   I said to this monk . . . I heard you got a stock of shoes here. Piss off, he said to me.
The Caretaker [1960], act I

11   If only I could get down to Sidcup! I've been waiting for the weather to break. He's got my papers, this man I left them with, it's got it all down there, I could prove everything.   *The Caretaker, I*

The earth's about five million years old, at least.
12 Who can afford to live in the past?
The Homecoming [1965], act III

13   I don't think we don't love each other.
Betrayal [1978], sc. 3

Wilfrid Sheed
1930–

14   If God had died in the blare of the twentieth century and in houses too new and cheap to be haunted, one must seek him in the old quiet places, where he might still live on in retirement.
The Good Word [1978], pt. I, ch. 12

15   Suicide . . . is about life, being in fact the sincerest form of criticism life gets.   *The Good Word, I, 15*

Stephen Sondheim
1930–

16 Tonight, tonight, won't be just any night.
Tonight there will be no morning star.
West Side Story [1957].[2] *Tonight*

17 I like to be in America!
O.K. by me in America!
Ev'rything free in America
For a small fee in America!
West Side Story. America

18   Everything's Coming Up Roses.
Gypsy [1959].[3] *Title of song*

19 Every day a little death,
In the parlor, in the bed,

---

[1]From the novel [1962] by CHARLES WEBB [1939–].

[2]Music by LEONARD BERNSTEIN.
[3]Music by JULE STYNE.

In the curtains, in the silver,
In the buttons, in the bread.
Every day a little sting,
In the heart and in the head.
    A Little Night Music [1973].[1] *Every Day*
    A Little Death

1 Isn't it rich?
Are we a pair?
Me here at last on the ground,
You in mid-air.
Send in the clowns.
    A Little Night Music. Send in the Clowns

Derek Walcott
1930–

2 I who am poisoned with the blood of both,
Where shall I turn, divided to the vein?
I who have cursed
The drunken officer of British rule, how choose
Between this Africa and the English tongue I love?
    A Far Cry from Africa [1962]

3 These palms are greater than Versailles,
for no man made them.
    Names [1976], II

4 Then after Eden,
was there no surprise?
O yes, the awe of Adam
at the first bead of sweat.
    Sea Grapes [1976]. The New World

5 The tourist archipelagoes of my South
are prisons too, corruptible, and though
there is no harder prison than writing verse,
what's poetry, if it is worth its salt,
but a phrase men can pass from hand to mouth?
    Forest of Europe [1979]

6 The Caribbean was borne like an elliptical basin
in the hands of acolytes, and a people were
    absolved
of a history which they did not commit.
    The Star-Apple Kingdom [1979]

7   I am tired of words,
and literature is an old couch stuffed with fleas.
    North and South [1981]

Mikhail Sergeyevich Gorbachev
1931–

8   The guilt of Stalin and his immediate entourage
before the Party and the people for the mass repres-

sions and lawlessness they committed is enormous
and unforgivable.
    Speech on the seventieth anniversary of the
    Russian Revolution [November 2, 1987]

9   The idea of restructuring [*perestroika*] . . . combines continuity and innovation, the historical experience of Bolshevism and the contemporaneity of
socialism.
    Speech on the seventieth anniversary of the
    Russian Revolution [November 2, 1987]

Toni Morrison
[Chloe Anthony Wofford]
1931–

10   I know what every colored woman in this country is doing. . . . Dying. Just like me. But the difference is they dying like a stump. Me, I'm going
down like one of those redwoods. I sure did live in
this world.   *Sula [1973], 1940*

11   When am I happy and when am I sad and what is
the difference? What do I need to know to stay
alive? What is true in the world? Her mind traveled
crooked streets and aimless goat paths, arriving
sometimes at profundity, other times at the revelations of a three-year-old.
    Song of Solomon [1977], ch. 5

12   When you know your name, you should hang on
to it, for unless it is noted down and remembered, it
will die when you do.   *Song of Solomon, 15*

13   At no point in my life have I ever felt as though I
were an American.
    In the New York Times [January 5, 1986]

Mordecai Richler
1931–2001

14   "I'm world-famous," Dr. Parks said, "all over
Canada."   *The Incomparable Atuk [1963], ch. 4*

Tom [Thomas Kennerly, Jr.] Wolfe
1931–

15   The Life—that *feeling*—The Life—the late
1940s early 1950s American Teenage Drive-In Life.
    The Electric Kool-Aid Acid Test[2] *[1968], ch. 4*

16   A glorious place, a glorious age, I tell you! A very
Neon Renaissance—And the myths that actually
touched you at that time—not Hercules, Orpheus,
Ulysses and Aeneas—but Superman, Captain Marvel,
Batman.   *The Electric Kool-Aid Acid Test, 4*

---

[1] Music by STEPHEN SONDHEIM.

[2] See Kesey, 831:12.

1 Radical Chic, after all, is only radical in style; in its heart it is part of Society and its traditions.
Radical Chic & Mau-Mauing the Flak Catchers [1970]

2 The Me Decade and the Third Great Awakening.
Title of essay [1976]

3 The idea was to prove at every foot of the way up that you were one of the elected and anointed ones who had *the right stuff* and could move higher and higher and even — ultimately, God willing, one day — that you might be able to join that special few at the very top, that elite who had the capacity to bring tears to men's eyes, the very Brotherhood of the Right Stuff itself.
The Right Stuff [1979], ch. 2

4 On Wall Street he and a few others — how many? — three hundred, four hundred, five hundred? — had become precisely that . . . Masters of the Universe.
The Bonfire of the Vanities [1987], ch. 1, The Master of the Universe

Aharon Appelfeld
1932–

5 The Holocaust is a central event in many people's lives, but it has also become a metaphor for our century. There cannot be an end to speaking and writing about it.
In the New York Times [November 15, 1986]

Carl Perkins
1932–1998

6 You can do anything,
But don't step on my blue suede shoes.
Blue Suede Shoes [1956]

Sylvia Plath
1932–1963

7 The silence drew off, baring the pebbles and shells and all the tatty wreckage of my life. Then, at the rim of vision, it gathered itself, and in one sweeping tide, rushed me to sleep.
The Bell Jar [1963]

8 A living doll, everywhere you look.
It can sew, it can cook,
It can talk, talk, talk. . . .
My boy, it's your last resort.
Will you marry it, marry it, marry it.
The Applicant [1963]

9 I have done it again.
Lady Lazarus [1963], st. 1

10 Dying
Is an art, like everything else.
I do it exceptionally well.

I do it so it feels like hell.
I do it so it feels real.
I guess you could say I've a call.
Lady Lazarus, st. 15, 16

11 Out of the ash
I rise with my red hair
And I eat men like air.
Lady Lazarus, last stanza

12 The woman is perfected.
Her dead

Body wears the smile of accomplishment,
The illusion of a Greek necessity

Flows in the scrolls of her toga,
Her bare

Feet seem to be saying:
We have come so far, it is over.   *Edge [1963]*

13 What a thrill —
My thumb instead of an onion.   *Cut [1963]*

14 You do not do, you do not do
Any more, black shoe
In which I have lived like a foot
For thirty years, poor and white,
Barely daring to breathe or Achoo.
Daddy [1963], st. 1

15 I have always been scared of *you*,
With your Luftwaffe, your gobbledygoo.
And your neat mustache
And your Aryan eye, bright blue.
Panzer-man, panzer-man, O You —
Daddy, st. 9

16 Every woman adores a Fascist,
The boot in the face, the brute
Brute heart of a brute like you.   *Daddy, st. 10*

17 White
Godiva, I unpeel —
Dead hands dead stringencies.   *Ariel [1965]*

18 And now I
Foam to wheat, a glitter of seas.   *Ariel*

Shel[by] Silverstein
1932–1999

19 Well, my daddy left home when I was three,
And didn't leave much to Ma and me,
Just this old guitar and an empty bottle of booze.

Now I don't blame him because he run and hid,
But the meanest thing he ever did was
Before he left, he went and named me Sue.
A Boy Named Sue [1969]

François Truffaut
1932–1984

1   Airing one's dirty linen never makes for a masterpiece.[1]   *Bed and Board [1972]*

John Updike
1932–

2   Our noise for some seconds passed beyond excitement into a kind of immense open anguish, a cry to be saved. But immortality is nontransferable. The papers said that the other players, and even the umpires on the field, begged him to come out and acknowledge us in some way, but he never had and did not now. Gods do not answer letters.
Hub Fans Bid Kid[2] Adieu, in The New Yorker [October 22, 1960]

3   A healthy male adult consumes each year one and a half times his own weight in other people's patience.
Assorted Prose [1965]. Confessions of a Wild Bore

4   That's one of my Goddam precious American rights, not to think about politics.
Rabbit Redux [1971]

5   We are cruel enough without meaning to be.
Rabbit Is Rich [1981]

Vine [Victor] Deloria, Jr.[3]
1933–

6   Tribalism is the strongest force at work in the world today.
Custer Died for Your Sins [1969], ch. 11

7   This country was a lot better off when the Indians were running it.
In the New York Times Magazine, March 3, 1970

---

[1]Les rendements de contes ne font jamais un chef d'oeuvre.

[2]Ted Williams of the Boston Red Sox, who played his last Fenway Park game on September 28, 1960.

[3]A Standing Rock Sioux.

Jerry Leiber
1933–

and

Mike Stoller
1933–

8   You ain't nothin' but a hound dog cryin' all the time.
Well, you ain't never caught a rabbit and you ain't no friend of mine.   *Hound Dog [1956]*

Joe Orton [John Kingsley]
1933–1967

9   I'd the upbringing a nun would envy and that's the truth. Until I was fifteen I was more familiar with Africa than my own body.
Entertaining Mr. Sloane [1964], act I

10   You were born with your legs apart. They'll send you to the grave in a Y-shaped coffin.
What the Butler Saw [1969], act I

Ann Willis Richards
1933–

11   Poor George, he can't help it—he was born with a silver foot in his mouth.
On Republican candidate George Bush [July 18, 1988]

Philip Roth
1933–

12   Doctor Spielvogel, this is my life, my only life, and I'm living it in the middle of a Jewish joke! I am the son in the Jewish joke—*only it ain't no joke!*
Portnoy's Complaint [1969]. Whacking Off

13   A Jewish man with parents alive is a fifteen-year-old boy, and will remain a fifteen-year-old boy *till they die!*   *Portnoy's Complaint. Cunt Crazy*

14   So [said the doctor]. Now vee may perhaps to begin Yes?   *Portnoy's Complaint. Punch Line*

Susan Sontag
1933–

15   Camp is a vision of the world in terms of style—but a particular kind of style. It is the love of the exaggerated, the "off," of things-being-what-they-are-

not. . . . The ultimate Camp statement: "it's good because it's awful."

Against Interpretation [1966]. Notes on Camp

1   Illness is the night-side of life, a more onerous citizenship. Everyone who is born holds dual citizenship, in the kingdom of the well and in the kingdom of the sick.   *Illness as Metaphor [1978]*

2   The AIDS crisis is evidence of a world in which nothing important is regional, local, limited; in which everything that can circulate does, and every problem is, or is destined to become, worldwide.

AIDS and Its Metaphors [1989]

Andrei Andreevich Voznesenski
1933–

3 I am Goya
of the bare field, by the enemy's beak gouged
till the craters of my eyes gape
I am grief

I am the tongue
of war, the embers of cities
on the snows of the year 1941
I am hunger   *I Am Goya [1960],[1] st. 1, 2*

4 They carried him[2] not to bury him:
They carried him down to crown him. . . .
The poet flourished here, disheveled,
Who would not bow before votive lamps
But to the common spade.

Leaves and Roots [1960][1]

5 The urge to kill, like the urge to beget,
Is blind and sinister. Its craving is set
Today on the flesh of a hare: tomorrow it can
Howl the same way for the flesh of a man.

Hunting a Hare [1964],[3] st. 5

6 Along a parabola life like a rocket flies,
Mainly in darkness, now and then on a rainbow.

Parabolic Ballad [1960][3]

Steven Weinberg
1933–

7   It is very hard to realize that this present universe has evolved from an unspeakably unfamiliar early condition, and faces a future extinction of endless cold or intolerable heat. The more the uni-

verse seems comprehensible, the more it also seems pointless.

The First Three Minutes [1977]. Epilogue

Yevgeny Alexandrovich Yevtushenko
1933–

8 There is no Jewish blood in my veins,
But I am hated with a scabby hatred
By all the anti-Semites,
        like a Jew.
And therefore
        I am a true Russian.   *Babi Yar [1961]*

Amiri Baraka [LeRoi Jones]
1934–

9 Lately, I've become accustomed to the way
The ground opens up and envelops me
Each time I go out to walk the dog.

Preface to a Twenty Volume Suicide Note [1961]

10 Saturday mornings we listened to *Red Lantern* &
        his undersea folk.
At 11, *Let's Pretend* / & we did / & I, the poet, still
        do, Thank God!   *In Memory of Radio [1961]*

11 Walk it slow
where you go
walk it slow . . .
We in the world
Poor as dirt
        Don't get some rhythm
    Somebody'll get hurt
    the world is black
    the world is green
    the world is red, yellow, brown
    the world is mean

3rd World Blues [1979]

James Brown
1934–

12 Say It Loud: "I'm Black and I'm Proud."
Some people say we've got a lot of malice,
Some say it's a lot of nerve.
But I say we won't quit moving
Until we get what we deserve.

Say It Loud: "I'm Black and I'm Proud" [1968] (song)

---

[1]Translated by STANLEY KUNITZ.
[2]Boris Pasternak.
[3]Translated by W. H. AUDEN.

Joan Didion
1934–

1   Writers are always selling somebody out.
Slouching Towards Bethlehem [1968], preface

2   We tell ourselves stories in order to live.
The White Album [1979]

Janet Malcolm
1934–

3   Every journalist who is not too stupid or too full of himself to notice what is going on knows that what he does is morally indefensible. He is a kind of confidence man, preying on people's vanity, ignorance, or loneliness, gaining their trust and betraying them without remorse.
The Journalist and the Murderer [1990], pt. I

Jonathan [Wolfe] Miller
1934–

4   I'm not a Jew. I'm Jew-*ish*. I don't go the whole hog.   *Beyond the Fringe [1960]*

N[avarre] Scott Momaday
1934–

5   Words were medicine; they were magic and invisible. They came from nothing into sound and meaning. They were beyond price; they could neither be bought nor sold.
House Made of Dawn [1968], January 26

Carl Sagan
1934–1996

6   We are an intelligent species and the use of our intelligence quite properly gives us pleasure. In this respect the brain is like a muscle. When it is in use we feel very good. Understanding is joyous.
Broca's Brain [1979], ch. 2

Gloria Steinem
1934–

7   Any woman who chooses to behave like a full human being should be warned that the armies of the status quo will treat her as something of a dirty joke; that's their natural and first weapon.
Sisterhood, in Ms. [spring 1972]

8   I can sometimes deal with men as equals and therefore can afford to like them.
Sisterhood, in Ms.

9   Some of us are becoming the men we wanted to marry.
Speech at Yale University [September 1981]

Mark Strand
1934–

10   Ink runs from the corners of my mouth.
There is no happiness like mine.
I have been eating poetry.
Eating Poetry [1968]

11   Wherever I am
I am what is missing.
Keeping Things Whole [1969]

12   Nothing could stop you.
Not the best day. Not the quiet. Not the ocean rocking.
You went on with your dying.
Elegy for My Father [1970]. 3. Your Dying

13   Nobody knows you. You are the neighbor of nothing.
Elegy for My Father. 6. The New Year

14   Now you invent the boat of your flesh and set it upon the waters
and drift in the gradual swell, in the laboring salt.
Now you look down. The waters of childhood are there.
Where Are the Waters of Childhood? [1978]

15   If a man publicly denounces poetry,
His shoes will fill with urine.
The New Poetry Handbook, st. 10

16   If a man finishes a poem,
he shall bathe in the blank wake of his passion
and be kissed by white paper.
The New Poetry Handbook, st. 21

17   I gaze upon the roast,
that is sliced and laid out
on my plate
and over it
I spoon the juices
of carrot and onion.
And for once I do not regret
the passage of time.
Selected Poems 1979. Pot Roast

Woody Allen [Allen Stuart Konigsberg]
1935–

1 Not only is there no God, but try getting a plumber on weekends.
    Getting Even [1972]. My Philosophy

2 How wrong Emily Dickinson was! Hope is not "the thing with feathers."[1] The thing with feathers has turned out to be my nephew. I must take him to a specialist in Zurich.
    Without Feathers [1975]. From the Allen Notebooks

3 It's not that I'm afraid to die. I just don't want to be there when it happens.
    Without Feathers. Death (A Play)

4 On the plus side, death is one of the few things that can be done as easily lying down.
    Without Feathers. The Early Essays

5 [Sex:] The most fun I've ever had without laughing.[2]   *Annie Hall (screenplay) [1977][3]*

6 More than any other time in history, mankind faces a crossroads. One path leads to despair and utter hopelessness. The other, to total extinction. Let us pray we have the wisdom to choose correctly.
    Side Effects [1980]. My Speech to the Graduates

7 Eighty percent of success is showing up.
    Interview

Susan Brownmiller
1935–

8 Man's discovery that his genitalia could serve as a weapon to generate fear must rank as one of the most important discoveries of prehistoric times, along with the use of fire and the first crude stone axe.
    Against Our Will: Men, Women, and Rape [1975], ch. 1

[Leroy] Eldridge Cleaver
1935–1998

9 Rape was an insurrectionary act. . . . I wanted to send waves of consternation throughout the white race.   *Soul on Ice [1968]. On Becoming*

10 You're either part of the solution or part of the problem.   *Speech, San Francisco [1968]*

Ken Kesey
1935–2001

11 A sound of cornered-animal fear and hate and surrender and defiance . . . like the last sound the treed and shot and falling animal makes as the dogs get him, when he finally doesn't care any more about anything but himself and his dying.
    One Flew over the Cuckoo's Nest [1962], pt. IV

12 There are going to be times when we can't wait for somebody. Now, you're either on the bus or off the bus. If you're on the bus, and you get left behind, then you'll find it again. If you're off the bus in the first place—then it won't make a damn.
    Quoted by Tom Wolfe *in The Electric Kool-Aid Acid Test [1968],[4] ch. 6*

W[illiam] P. Kinsella
1935–

13 If you build it, he will come.
    Shoeless Joe [1982][5]

Mary Oliver
1935–

14 When it's over, I want to say: all my life
I was a bride married to amazement.
I was the bridegroom taking the world into my
    arms.   *New and Selected Poems [1992]. When Death Comes*

15 The world where the owl is endlessly hungry and endlessly on the hunt is the world in which I live too.   *Blue Pastures [1995]. Owls*

Elvis Presley
1935–1977

16 Well since my baby left me
Well I found a new place to dwell
Well it's down at the end of lonely street
At Heartbreak Hotel.   *Heartbreak Hotel [1956][6]*

17 Love me tender, love me sweet,
Never let me go.   *Love Me Tender [1956][7]*

Simon Gray
1936–

18 *Stephen:* . . . What have you got against having children?

---

[1]See Emily Dickinson, 544:11.

[2]Giving canonical form to a quip already familiar on American college campuses for several decades.

[3]Written with Marshall Brickman [1941–].

[4]See Tom Wolfe, 826:15 and 826:16.

[5]Basis for the movie *Field of Dreams* [1989].

[6]Written with Mae Boren Axton [1907–1997] and Tommy Durden [1920–1999].

[7]Written with Vera Matson.

Simon: Well Steve, in the first place there isn't enough room. In the second place they seem to start by mucking up their parents' lives, and then go on in the third place to muck up their own. In the fourth place it doesn't seem right to bring them into a world like this in the fifth place and in the sixth place I don't like them very much in the first place. OK.   *Otherwise Engaged [1975], act II*

1   In my experience, the worst thing you can do to an important problem is discuss it. You know, I really do think this whole business of non-communication is one of the more poignant fallacies of our zestfully overexplanatory age.   *Otherwise Engaged, II*

Václav Havel
1936–

2   A specter is haunting eastern Europe:[1] the specter of what in the West is called "dissent."
    The Power of the Powerless [1978][2]

3   God—I don't know why—wanted me to be a Czech. It was not my choice. But I accept it, and I try to do something for my country because I live here.   *Interview [1988]*

Abbie [Abbott] Hoffman
1936–1989

4   Sacred cows make the tastiest hamburger.
    Remark. Recalled at his death

Barbara C. Jordan
1936–1996

5   "We, the people." It is a very eloquent beginning. But when that document[3] was completed on the seventeenth of September in 1787 I was not included in that "We, the people." I felt somehow for many years that George Washington and Alexander Hamilton, just left me out by mistake. But through the process of amendment, interpretation and court decision I have finally been included in "We, the people."
    Statement at Debate on Articles of Impeachment, Committee on the Judiciary, House of Representatives, Ninety-third Congress [July 25, 1974]

---

[1]See Marx and Engels, 510:14.

[2]Translated by P. WILSON.

[3]Preamble to the Constitution of the United States.

Kris Kristofferson
1936–

and

Fred Foster

6 Freedom's just another word for nothin' left to lose,
    And nothin' ain't worth nothin' but it's free.
    Me and Bobby McGee [1969]

Claude Brown
1937–

7   The children of these disillusioned colored pioneers inherited the total lot of their parents—the disappointments, the anger. To add to their misery, they had little hope of deliverance. For where does one run to when he's already in the promised land?
    Manchild in the Promised Land [1965]

Thomas Pynchon
1937–

8   Yet who can presume to say *what* the war wants, so vast and aloof it is . . . so *absentee*.
    Gravity's Rainbow [1973]

Erich Segal
1937–

9   Love means not ever having to say you're sorry.[4]
    Love Story [1970]

Tom Stoppard
1937–

10   You're familiar with the tragedies of antiquity, are you? The great homicidal classics?
    Rosencrantz and Guildenstern Are Dead [1967], act I

11   Though an arrow is always approaching its target, it never quite gets there, and Saint Sebastian died of fright.   *Jumpers [1972], act I*

12   If rationality were the criterion for things being allowed to exist, the world would be one gigantic field of soya beans!   *Jumpers, I*

---

[4]Love means never having to say you're sorry.—*Love Story (screenplay) [1970]*, spoken by Ali MacGraw.

1   An essentially private man [James Joyce] who wished his total indifference to public notice to be universally recognized.   *Travesties [1975], act I*

2   I learned three things in Zurich during the war. I wrote them down. Firstly, you're either a revolutionary or you're not, and if you're not you might as well be an artist as anything else. Secondly, if you can't be an artist, you might as well be a revolutionary . . . I forget the third thing.
   Travesties, last lines

John Dean
1938–

3   We have a cancer within, close to the Presidency, that is growing.
From The [Nixon] Presidential Transcripts [March 21, 1973]

A. Bartlett Giamatti
1938–1989

4   [Baseball] breaks your heart. It is designed to break your heart. The game begins in the spring, when everything else begins again, and it blossoms in the summer, filling the afternoons and evenings, and then as soon as the chill rains come, it stops, and leaves you to face the fall alone.
The Green Fields of the Mind [1977]

John Guare
1938–

5   Everybody on this planet is separated by only six other people. Six degrees of separation. Between us and everybody else on this planet.
Six Degrees of Separation [1990]

Joyce Carol Oates
1938–

6   This is a work of history in fictional form — that is, in personal perspective, which is the only kind of history that exists.   *Them [1969]. Author's Note*

Margaret Atwood
1939–

7 I would like to be the air
that inhabits you for a moment

only. I would like to be that unnoticed
& that necessary.   *Variation on the Word "Sleep"*

Raymond Carver
1939–1988

8   Maxine said it was another tragedy in a long line of low-rent tragedies.
What We Talk About When We Talk About Love [1981]. One More Thing

9   You have to eat and keep going. Eating is a small, good thing in a time like this.
Cathedral [1983]. A Small, Good Thing

10   Maybe I just don't understand poetry. I admit it's not the first thing I reach for when I pick up something to read.   *Cathedral. Title story*

Francis Ford Coppola
1939–

11   I love the smell of napalm in the morning. It smells like victory.
Apocalypse Now (screenplay) [1979], spoken by Robert Duvall

Germaine Greer
1939–

12   Is it too much to ask that women be spared the daily struggle for superhuman beauty in order to offer it to the caresses of a subhumanly ugly mate?
The Female Eunuch [1970]. Loathing and Disgust

Seamus [Justin] Heaney
1939–

13 Between my finger and my thumb
The squat pen rests.
I'll dig with it.   *Death of a Naturalist [1966]. Digging*

14 I shouldered a kind of manhood
stepping in to lift the coffins
of dead relations.   *North [1975]. Funeral Rites, I*

15 It all came back to me last night, stirred
By the sootfall of your things at bedtime,
Your head-down, tail-up hunt in a bottom drawer
For the black plunge-line nightdress.
   Field Work [1979]. The Skunk

1 And that moment when the bird sings very close
To the music of what happens.
Field Work [1979]. Song

2 You lose more of yourself than you redeem
Doing the decent thing.
Station Island [1984], XII

3 Two rafters and a cross-tie on the slate
Are the letters some call *ah,* some call *ay.*
There are charts, there are headlines, there is a
    right
Way to hold the pen and a wrong way.

First it is 'copying out,' and then 'English'
Marked correct with a little leaning hoe.
Smells of inkwells rise in the classroom hush.
A globe in the window tilts like a coloured O.
The Haw Lantern [1987]. Alphabets, I

William Least Heat-Moon [William Lewis Trogdon]
1939–

4   On the old highway maps of America, the main
routes were red and the back roads blue. Now even
the colors are changing. But in those brevities just
before dawn and a little after dark—times neither
day nor night—the old roads return to the sky
some of its color. Then, in truth, they cast a mysterious shadow of blue, and it's that time when the
pull of the blue highway is strongest, when the
open road is a beckoning, a strangeness, a place
where a man can lose himself.
Blue Highways [1982]. Preface

James Rado
1939–

and

Gerome Ragni
1942–1991

5 When the moon is in the seventh house
And Jupiter aligns with Mars,
Then peace will guide the planets,
And love will steer the stars;
This is the dawning of the age of Aquarius,
The age of Aquarius.
Hair [1966].[1] Aquarius

Grace Slick
1939–

6 One pill makes you larger
And one pill makes you small
And the ones that mother gives you
Don't do anything at all.
Go ask Alice
When she's ten feet tall.
White Rabbit [1967]

Thomas Harris
1940–

and

Ted [Theodore] Tally
1952–

7   I ate his liver with some fava beans and a nice
Chianti.
*The Silence of the Lambs (screenplay) [1991],
spoken by Anthony Hopkins*

Michael Herr
1940–

8   There was a famous story, some reporters asked
a door gunner, "How can you shoot women and
children?" and he'd answered, "It's easy, you just
don't lead 'em so much."
Dispatches [1977]. Breathing In

9   I think Vietnam was what we had instead of
happy childhoods.
Dispatches. Colleagues

10   Out on the street I couldn't tell the Vietnam
veterans from the rock and roll veterans. The sixties
had made so many casualties, its war and its music
had run power off the same circuit for so long they
didn't even have to fuse.
Dispatches. Breathing Out

John [Ono] Lennon
1940–1980

11   We're more popular than Jesus now.[2] I don't know
which will go first—rock 'n' roll or Christianity.
*Interview in London Evening Standard
[March 4, 1966]*

---

[1]Music by GALT MACDERMOT.

[2]See Chaplin, 726:2.

John Lennon
1940–1980

and

Sir Paul McCartney
1942–

1   I'll tell you something
I think you'll understand,
Then I'll say that something,
I want to hold your hand.
I Want to Hold Your Hand [1963]

2 There's a shadow hanging over me,
Oh yesterday came suddenly.
Yesterday [1965]

3 All the lonely people, where do they all belong?
Eleanor Rigby [1966]

4 Oh I get by with a little help from my friends
Mmm get high with a little help from my friends.
With a Little Help from My Friends [1967]

5 How does it feel to be one of the beautiful people?
Baby You're a Rich Man [1967]

6 You say you want a revolution
Well you know
we all want to change the world . . .
But when you talk about destruction
Don't you know that you can count me out
Don't you know it's gonna be alright.
Revolution [1968]

Phil Ochs
1940–1976

7 I'm sure it wouldn't interest anybody
Outside of a small circle of friends.
A Small Circle of Friends [1967]

Jack Weinberg
1940–

8   We have a saying in the movement that we don't trust anybody over thirty.
Interview on Free Speech movement at University of California, Berkeley [1964]

Paul Anka
1941–

9 I've lived a life that's full, I traveled each and ev'ry highway,
And more, much more than this, I did it my way.
My Way [1969][1]

Philip [Joseph] Caputo
1941–

10   You're going to learn that one of the most brutal things in the world is your average nineteen-year-old American boy.   *A Rumor of War [1977]*

Stokely Carmichael [Kwame Toure]
1941–1998

and

Charles [Vernon] Hamilton
1929–

11   Black power[2] . . . is a call for black people in this country to unite, to recognize their heritage, to build a sense of community. It is a call for black people to begin to define their own goals, to lead their own organizations and to support those organizations. It is a call to reject the racist institutions and values of this society.
Black Power! [1967], ch. 2

12   Before a group can enter the open society, it must first close ranks.   *Black Power!, 2*

Billy Collins
1941–

13 Of all the questions you might want to ask
about angels, the only one you ever hear
is how many can dance on the head of a pin.

---

[1]Music by CLAUDE FRANÇOIS, JACQUES REVAUX, and GILES THIBAUT.
    Signature song of FRANK SINATRA [1915–]. In November 1989 Soviet leader Mikhail Gorbachev announced (through a Foreign Ministry spokesman) that "the Sinatra Doctrine" had replaced the "Brezhnev Doctrine" for the east bloc nations: "Hungary and Poland are doing it their way."

[2]Carmichael had used the phrase "Black power" in a speech in Greenwood, Mississippi [June 17, 1966].
    To demand these God-given rights is to seek black power — what I call audacious power — the power to build black institutions of splendid achievement. — ADAM CLAYTON POWELL, JR. [1908–1972], *Baccalaureate address at Howard University* [May 29, 1966]
    See Langston Hughes, 763:1.

No curiosity about how they pass the eternal time
besides circling the Throne chanting in Latin
or delivering a crust of bread to a hermit on earth
or guiding a boy and a girl across a rickety wooden
    bridge.   *Questions about Angels [1991].*
                Questions about Angels

1 I love the sound of the bone against the plate
and the fortress-like look of it
lying before me in a moat of risotto,
the meat soft as the leg of an angel
who has lived a purely airborne existence.
        The Art of Drowning [1995]. Osso Buco

2 The one in the upper left-hand corner
is giving me a look
that says I know you are here
and I have nothing better to do
for the remainder of human time
than return your persistent but engaging stare.
      Picnic, Lightning [1998]. Victoria's Secret

Richard Dawkins
1941–

3   We are survival machines—robot vehicles blindly
programmed to preserve the selfish molecules known
as genes. This is a truth which still fills me with astonishment.   *The Selfish Gene [1976]. Preface*

Bob Dylan [Robert Zimmerman]
1941–

4 How many roads must a man walk down
Before you call him a man? . . .
The answer, my friend, is blowin' in the wind,
The answer is blowin' in the wind.
          Blowin' in the Wind [1962]

5 When your rooster crows at the break of dawn
Look out your window and I'll be gone
You're the reason I'm trav'lin' on
Don't think twice, it's all right
      Don't Think Twice, It's All Right [1963]

6 The order is
Rapidly fadin'.
And the first one now
Will later be last
For the times they are a-changin'.
      The Times They Are A-Changin' [1963]

7 Hey! Mr. Tambourine Man, play a song for me,
I'm not sleepy and there is no place I'm going to.
          Mr. Tambourine Man [1964]

8 How does it feel
To be on your own

With no direction home
Like a complete unknown
Like a rolling stone?   *Like a Rolling Stone [1965]*

9 You don't need a weather man
To know which way the wind blows
    Subterranean Homesick Blues [1965]

Nora Ephron
1941–

10   I'll have what she's having.
    When Harry Met Sally (screenplay) [1989],
    spoken by Estelle Reiner

Robert Hass
1941–

11 All the new thinking is about loss.
In this it resembles the old thinking.
The idea, for example, that each particular erases
the luminous clarity of a general idea.
      Praise [1979]. Meditation at Lagunitas

Jesse Jackson
1941–

12   My right and my privilege to stand here before
you has been won—won in my lifetime—by the
blood and the sweat of the innocent.
    Speech at Democratic National Convention,
    Atlanta [July 19, 1988]

13   When I look out at this convention, I see the face
of America, red, yellow, brown, black and white. We
are all precious in God's sight—the real rainbow
coalition.
    Speech at Democratic National Convention,
    Atlanta [July 19, 1988]

Helen Reddy
1941–

14 If I have to, I can do anything.
I am strong, I am invincible, I am woman.
           I Am Woman [1972]

Muhammad Ali[1]
1942–

15   I am the greatest.
    Slogan, inspired by wrestler Gorgeous George

16   Float like a butterfly, sting like a bee.
    Boxing credo, devised by aide Drew "Bundini"
    Brown

---

[1]Formerly Cassius Clay.

1 Not only do I knock 'em out, I pick the round.
Statement [December 1962]

2 I ain't got no quarrel with them Viet Cong.
On the draft [February 1966]

Stephen [William] Hawking
1942–

3 If we do discover a complete [unified] theory [of the universe], it should in time be understandable in broad principle by everyone, not just a few scientists. Then we shall all, philosophers, scientists, and just ordinary people, be able to take part in the discussion of the question of why it is that we and the universe exist. If we find the answer to that, it would be the ultimate triumph of human reason — for then we should know the mind of God.
A Brief History of Time [1988]. Conclusion

Erica Jong
1942–

4 The zipless fuck is absolutely pure. It is free of ulterior motives. There is no power game. The man is not "taking" and the woman is not "giving." No one is attempting to cuckold a husband or humiliate a wife. No one is trying to prove anything or get anything out of anyone. The zipless fuck is the purest thing there is. And it is rarer than the unicorn.
Fear of Flying [1973], ch. 1

Garrison Keillor
1942–

5 That's the news from Lake Wobegon, where all the women are strong, the men are good-looking, and all the children are above average.
A Prairie Home Companion [1974–1987], signature line

6 The little town that time forgot, that the decades cannot improve.
A Prairie Home Companion

Paul Simon
1942–

7 Hello darkness my old friend
I've come to talk with you again.
The Sounds of Silence [1964]

8 The words of the prophets
Are written on the subway walls
And tenement halls
And whispered in the sounds of silence.
The Sounds of Silence

9 Where have you gone, Joe DiMaggio?
A nation turns its lonely eyes to you.
Mrs. Robinson [1966]

10 I'm empty and aching and I don't know why.
Counting the cars on the New Jersey Turnpike.
They've all come to look for America.
America [1967]

11 Like a bridge over troubled water
I will lay me down.
Bridge over Troubled Water [1969]

12 If you'll be my bodyguard
I can be your long lost pal,
I can call you Betty
and, Betty, you can call me
You can call me Al.   *You Can Call Me Al [1985]*

13 The Mississippi Delta was shining
like a National guitar.   *Graceland [1986]*

Brendan V. Sullivan, Jr.
1942–

14 I'm not a potted plant. I'm here as the lawyer. That's my job.
Response to Senator Daniel Inouye during Senate hearings on Irangate [July 9, 1987]

Tammy Wynette
[Virginia Wynette Pugh]
1942–1998

15 But if you love him you'll forgive him
Even though he's hard to understand.
And if you love him, oh be proud of him
'Cause after all he's just a man.
Stand By Your Man [1968][1]

H. Rap [Hubert Gerold] Brown
1943–

16 Violence is as American as cherry pie.
Press conference [July 27, 1967]

---

[1]Written with her producer BILLY SHERRILL.
In 1992 her name and best-known song entered the presidential campaign when Hillary Rodham Clinton, stressing that her defense of her husband against charges of adultery was more than routine, said in a "60 Minutes" interview: "I'm not sitting here like some little woman standing by my man like Tammy Wynette." — *New York Times* [April 8, 1998]

R[obert] Crumb
1943–

1   Keep on truckin'.   *Slogan of cartoon character*

Nikki Giovanni
1943–

2 show me someone not full of herself and i'll show
    you a hungry person
        Poem for a Lady Whose Voice I Like [1970],
        last line

3   I really hope no white person ever has cause
to write about me
because they never understand
Black love is Black wealth and they'll
probably talk about my hard childhood
and never understand that
all the while I was quite happy.
        Nikki-Rosa [1970]

Mick [Michael Philip] Jagger
1943–

and

Keith Richards
1943–

4 I can't get no satisfaction . . .
I can't get no girl reaction.
        (I Can't Get No) Satisfaction [1965]

5 Please allow me to introduce myself,
I'm a man of wealth and taste.
I've been around for long, long years,
Stolen many a man's soul and faith.
        Sympathy for the Devil [1968]

6 Well, we all need someone we can lean on,
And if you want it, well, you can lean on me.
        Let It Bleed [1969]

7 You can't always get what you want
But if you try sometimes
You just might find
You get what you need.
        You Can't Always Get What You Want [1969]

Janis Joplin
1943–1970

8 Down on me, down on me,
Looks like everybody in this whole round world
Is down on me.
        Down on Me [1967]

9 Lord, won't you buy me a Mercedes-Benz,
My friends all drive Porsches,
I must make amends.   *Mercedes-Benz [1970]*

Joni Mitchell
1943–

10 They paved paradise
And put up a parking lot.   *Big Yellow Taxi [1969]*

11 We are stardust,
We are golden,
And we've got to get ourselves
Back to the garden.   *Woodstock [1969]*

James Carville
1944–

12   It's the economy, stupid.
        Political campaign motto [1992]

Rudolph W[illiam] Giuliani
1944–

13   Our hearts are broken, but they continue to beat,
and the spirit of our City has never been stronger.
        One Nation: America Remembers September
        11, 2001 [2001], introduction

14   Show your confidence. Show you're not afraid.
Go to restaurants. Go shopping.
        News conference [September 12, 2001]

Bill Griffith
1944–

15   Are we having fun yet?
        Zippy the Pinhead (comic strip) [1979]

George [W.] Lucas [Jr.]
1944–

16   Evil Empire.   *Star Wars (screenplay) [1977]*

17   May the Force be with you!
        Star Wars (screenplay), spoken by Alec Guinness

18   The Force will be with you . . . always!
        Star Wars (screenplay), spoken by Alec Guinness

19   Rebel spaceships, striking from a hidden base,
have won their first victory against the evil galactic
empire.   *Star Wars (title crawl)*

Alice Walker
1944–

1 Guided by my heritage of a love of beauty and a respect for strength—in search of my mother's garden, I found my own.
In Search of Our Mothers' Gardens [1974]

2 I think it pisses God off if you walk by the color purple in a field somewhere and don't notice it.
The Color Purple [1982]

3 I'm pore, I'm black, I may be ugly and can't cook, a voice say to everything listening. But I'm here.
The Color Purple

Annie Dillard
1945–

4 I had been my whole life a bell, and never knew it until at that moment I was lifted and struck.
Pilgrim at Tinker Creek [1974], ch. 2

5 The second before the sun went out we saw a wall of dark shadow come speeding at us. We no sooner saw it than it was upon us, like thunder. . . . It was as if an enormous, loping god in the sky had reached down and slapped the earth's face.
Teaching a Stone to Talk [1982]. Total Eclipse

Bob Marley
1945–1981

6 We're leaving Babylon
We're going to our Father's land.
Movement of Jah People [1977]

Don[ald] McLean
1945–

7 Bye, Bye, Miss American Pie
Drove my Chevy to the levee but the levee was dry
Them good old boys were drinkin'
Whiskey and Rye
Singin' this'll be the day that I die
This'll be the day that I die
American Pie [1971]

Peter Townshend
1945–

8 Hope I die before I get old.
This is my generation.
My Generation [1965]

August Wilson, Jr.
1945–

9 As long as the colored man look to white folks to put the crown on what he say . . . as long as he looks to white folks for approval . . . then he ain't never gonna find out who he is and what he's about.[1]
Ma Rainey's Black Bottom [1984], act 1

Julian Barnes
1946–

10 Why does the writing make us chase the writer? Why can't we leave well enough alone? Why aren't the books enough?
Flaubert's Parrot [1984], ch. 1

Steve [Stephen Bantu] Biko
1946–1977

11 The most potent weapon in the hands of the oppressor is the mind of the oppressed.
Statement as witness [May 3, 1976][2]

12 The basic tenet of black consciousness is that the black man must reject all value systems that seek to make him a foreigner in the country of his birth and reduce his basic human dignity.
Statement as witness [May 3, 1976][2]

George W[alker] Bush
1946–

13 Whether we bring our enemies to justice, or bring justice to our enemies, justice will be done.
Address to joint session of Congress [September 20, 2001]

Bill [William Jefferson] Clinton
1946–

14 I'll be with you until the last dog dies.
Primary campaign speech, Dover, New Hampshire [February 12, 1992]

15 I feel your pain.
Remark at a primary campaign rally [March 26, 1992]

16 I experimented with marijuana a time or two. And I didn't like it, and didn't inhale, and never tried it again.
Television interview [March 29, 1992]

---

[1] Ellipses are in the original text.
[2] From *Black Consciousness in South Africa* [1979], edited by MILLARD ARNOLD.

1   I do not believe that the politics of personal destruction is what the American people are interested in.   *News conference [March 8, 1994]*

2   I am going to say this again: I did not have sexual relations with that woman, Miss Lewinsky.   *News conference [January 26, 1998]*

3   It depends on what the meaning of the word "is" is. If the—if he—if "is" means is and never has been, that is not—that is one thing. If it means there is none, that was a completely true statement.   *Grand jury testimony [August 17, 1998]*

Paul Schrader
1946–

4   You talkin' to me?   *Taxi Driver (screenplay) [1976], spoken by Robert De Niro*

David Allen Stockman
1946–

5   None of us really understands what's going on with all these numbers.   *On the U.S. budget [1981]*

Oliver Stone
1946–

6   Greed is good! Greed is right! Greed works! Greed will save the U.S.A.![1]   *Wall Street (screenplay) [1987], spoken by Michael Douglas*

Hillary Rodham Clinton
1947–

7   I suppose I could have stayed home and baked cookies and had teas.   *Press interview on conflict of interest [March 17, 1992]*

8   We've been married for twenty-two years. And I have learned a long time ago that the only two people who count in any marriage are the two who are in it.   *The Today show (television interview) [January 27, 1998]*

---

[1]Greed is all right. . . . Greed is healthy. You can be greedy and still feel good about yourself.—IVAN FREDERICK BOESKY [1937–], *commencement address at University of California, Berkeley* [May 18, 1986]

9   The great story . . . is this vast right-wing conspiracy that has been conspiring against my husband since the day he announced for President.   *The Today show (television interview) [January 27, 1998]*

Larry David
1947–

10   It's about nothing, everything else is about something; this, it's about nothing.   *Seinfeld (television series). The Pitch [September 16, 1992]*

Arlo Guthrie
1947–

11 You can get anything you want at Alice's Restaurant.   *Alice's Restaurant [1966]*

Sir Elton John [Reginald Kenneth Dwight]
1947–

and

Bernie Taupin
1950–

12 They crawled out of the woodwork
And they whispered into your brain.
They set you on a treadmill
And they made you change your name.
And it seems to me you lived your life
Like a candle in the wind.
    Candle in the Wind (Goodbye Norma Jean) [1973]

Jane Kenyon
1947–1995

13 Let it come, as it will, and don't
be afraid. God does not leave us
comfortless, so let evening come.
    Let Evening Come [1990]

14 I slept in a bed
in a room with paintings
on the walls, and
planned another day
just like this day.
But one day, I know,
it will be otherwise.   *Otherwise [1993]*

[Ahmed] Salman Rushdie[1]
1947–

1   Literature is the one place in any society where, within the secrecy of our own heads, we can hear voices talking about everything in every possible way.   *Is Nothing Sacred? [1990]*

Joseph C. Stinson
1947–

2   Go ahead, make my day.[2]
Sudden Impact (screenplay) [1983], spoken by Clint Eastwood

Charles Philip Arthur George, Prince of Wales
1948–

3   Give this much to the Luftwaffe. When it knocked down our buildings, it didn't replace them with anything more offensive than rubble. *We* did that.
Speech in London [December 1987]

Jimmy Cliff
1948–

4 As sure as the sun will shine
I'm going to get it, what's mine
And then the harder they come
The harder they fall,
One and all.   *The Harder They Come [1972]*

Leslie Marmon Silko
1948–

5 It's only a matter of time, Indian
   you can't sleep with the river forever.
Storyteller [1981]. Indian Song: Survival

Martin Amis
1949–

6   My head is a city, and various pains have taken up residence in various parts of my face. A gum-and-bone ache has launched a cooperative on my upper west side. Across the park, neuralgia has rented a duplex in my fashionable east seventies. Downtown,

my chin throbs with lofts of jaw-loss. As for my brain, my hundreds, it's Harlem up there, expanding in the summer fires.   *Money [1985]*

Bruce Springsteen
1949–

7 We gotta get out while we're young
'Cause tramps like us, baby, we were born to run.
Born to Run [1975]

8 Down in the shadow of the penitentiary,
Out by the gas fires of the refinery;
I'm ten years burning down the road,
Nowhere to run, ain't nowhere to go.
Born in the U.S.A. [1984]

Melissa Mathison
1950–

9   E.T. phone home.
E.T.: The Extra Terrestrial (screenplay) [1982]

Rita Dove
1952–

10 You start out with one thing, end
up with another, and nothing's
like it used to be, not even the future.
The Yellow House on the Corner [1980]. O

11 Every day a wilderness—no
shade in sight. Beulah
patient among knickknacks,
the solarium a rage
of light, a grainstorm
as her gray cloth brings
dark wood to life.   *Museum [1983]. Dusting*

12   If you can't be free, be a mystery.
Grace Notes [1989]. Canary

Mary [Theresa] Schmich
1953–

13   Ladies and gentlemen of the class of 'ninety-seven: Wear sunscreen.
   If I could offer you only one tip for the future, sunscreen would be it. The long-term benefits of sunscreen have been proved by scientists, whereas the rest of my advice has no basis more reliable than my own meandering experience.
Mock commencement address.[3] Chicago Tribune [June 1, 1997]

---

[1]See Khomeini, 758:4.

[2]I have only one thing to say to the tax increasers: "Go ahead and make my day." — RONALD REAGAN [March 13, 1985]

---

[3]Erroneously attributed to KURT VONNEGUT, JR.

[Karen] Louise Erdrich
1954–

1   I was in love with the whole world and all that lived in its rainy arms.
Love Medicine [1984]. The Good Tears

James Gleick
1954–

2   Tiny differences in input could quickly become overwhelming differences in output. . . . In weather, for example, this translates into what is only half-jokingly known as the Butterfly Effect—the notion that a butterfly stirring the air today in Peking can transform storm systems next month in New York.
Chaos [1987], Prologue

Jerry [Jerome] Seinfeld
1954–

3   Everybody lies about sex. People lie during sex. If it weren't for lies, there'd be no sex.
New York Times [December 18, 1998]

Tony Kushner
1956–

4   People in a boat, waiting, terrified, while im-placable, unsmiling men, irresistibly strong, seize . . . maybe the person next to you, maybe you, and with no warning at all, with time only for a quick intake of air you are pitched into freezing, turbulent water and salt and darkness to drown.
Angels in America, pt. I: Millennium Approaches [1992], act I, sc. viii

Larry Charles
1957–

5   Not that there's anything wrong with that.
Seinfeld (television series). The Outing [February 11, 1993]

Cameron Crowe
1957–

6   Show me the money!
Jerry Maguire (screenplay) [1997], spoken by Cuba Gooding, Jr.

Michael Jackson
1958–

and

Lionel Richie
1950–

7   We are the world,
We are the children,
We are the ones
To make a better day.   *We Are the World [1985]*

Diana [Frances Spencer], Princess of Wales
1961–1997

8   There were three of us in this marriage, so it was a bit crowded.
BBC television interview [November 20, 1995]

9   I'd like to be a queen in people's hearts . . . someone's got to go out there and love people and show it.
BBC television interview [November 20, 1995]

J[oanne] K[athleen] Rowling
1965–

10   Before we begin our banquet, I would like to say a few words. And here they are: Nitwit! Oddment! Tweak!
Harry Potter and the Sorcerer's Stone [1998], ch. 7

11   I hope you're pleased with yourselves. We could all have been killed—or worse, expelled.
Harry Potter and the Sorcerer's Stone, 9

The Doors
1967

12   Come on, baby, light my fire
Try to set the night on fire.   *Light My Fire [1967]*

Monty Python's Flying Circus
1969–1974[1]

13   This parrot is no more. It has ceased to be. It's expired and gone to meet its maker. This is a late parrot. It's a stiff. Bereft of life, it rests in peace. If

---

[1]Series first shown on BBC television between 1969 and 1974. Written and conceived by Graham Chapman, John Cleese, Terry Gilliam, Eric Idle, Terry Jones, and Michael Palin.

you hadn't nailed it to the perch, it would be pushing up the daisies. It's rung down the curtain and
joined the choir invisible. This is an ex-parrot.

Episode 8 [1969]

1 I cut down trees, I skip and jump,
  I like to press wild flowers.
  I put on women's clothing
  And hang around in bars.   *Episode 9 [1969]*

2   I'd like to welcome the pommy bastard to God's
own earth and I'd like to remind him that we don't
like stuck-up sticky-beaks here.

Episode 22 [1970]

Sesame Street

1969–

3   Me want cookie!   *Spoken by Cookie Monster*[1]

4   It's not that easy bein' green.
               Bein' Green.[2] *Sung by Kermit the Frog*

Anonymous

5 Sumer is icumen in,
  Lhude sing cuccu!
  Groweth sed, and bloweth med,
  And springth the wude nu —
  Sing cuccu!³   *Cuckoo Song [c. 1250]*

6   A new broom sweeps clean.
                         Saying [13th century]

7 Ich am of Irlonde
  Ant of the holy lande
       Of Irlonde.
  Gode sire, pray ich the,
  For of saynte charite,
  Come ant dance wyth me
       In Irlonde.   *Ich Am of Irlonde [14th century]*[4]

8 When Adam delved and Eve span
  Who was then a gentleman?
     Text used by JOHN BALL *for his speech at
     Blackheath to the men in Wat Tyler's Rebellion
     [1381]*

9   Hew not too high lest the chips fall in thine eye.
                         Proverb [14th century]

10 I sing of a maiden
   That is makeles;
   King of all kings
   To her son she ches.
             Carol. I Sing of a Maiden [15th century]

11 For in my mind, of all mankind
   I love but you alone.
         The Nut-Brown Maid [15th century], refrain

12 For I must to the greenwood go,
   Alone, a banished man.
                 The Nut-Brown Maid, refrain

13 No burial this pretty pair
   Of any man receives,
   Till Robin Redbreast piously
   Did cover them with leaves.
                   The Children in the Wood, st. 16

14   Before you trust a man, eat a peck of salt with
him.   *Proverb*[5]

15   A fool's paradise.
                   Paston Letters [1462], no. 457

16   O Death, thou comest when I had thee least in
mind.   *Everyman [before 1500], l. 119*

17 Everyman, I will go with thee, and be thy guide,
   In thy most need to go by thy side.
                 Everyman [before 1500], l. 522

18 O Western wind, when wilt thou blow,
   That the small rain down can rain?
   Christ, that my love were in my arms
   And I in my bed again!
                     O Western Wind [c. 1530]

19 Crabbed age and youth cannot live together.
   Youth is full of pleasance, age is full of care.
               The Passionate Pilgrim [1599]

20 Love me little, love me long,
   Is the burden of my song.
               Love Me Little [1569–1570], refrain

21 Multiplication is vexation,
   Division is as bad;
   The rule of three doth puzzle me,
   And practice drives me mad.
                     Elizabethan MS [1570]

22 Alas, my Love! ye do me wrong
   To cast me off discourteously:
   And I have loved you so long,
   Delighting in your company.
         *From A Handful of Pleasant Delights [1584],
         st. 1*

---

[1]Character created by JEFFREY A. MOSS [1942–1998].

[2]Words and music by JOE RAPOSO [1937–1989].

[3]See Pound, 708:17.

[4]"I am of Ireland, / And the Holy Land of Ireland, / And time
runs on," cried she. / "Come out of charity, / Come dance with
me in Ireland." — YEATS, *The Winding Stair and Other Poems*
[1933], *Words for Music Perhaps, no. 20, "I Am of Ireland," refrain*

[5]An adage originating before Cicero, who quotes a version of it
in *De Amicitia 19, 67.*

1 Greensleeves was all my joy,
　Greensleeves was my delight;
　Greensleeves was my heart of gold,
　And who but Lady Greensleeves.
　　　　From A Handful of Pleasant Delights, refrain

2 Where griping griefs the heart would wound
　And doleful dumps the mind oppress,
　There music with her silver sound
　With speed is wont to send redress.[1]
　　　　A Song to the Lute in Musicke, st. 1

3 The blinded boy that shoots so trim,
　From heaven down did hie.
　　　　King Cophetua and the Beggar Maid, st. 2

4 It was a friar of orders gray
　Walked forth to tell his beads.
　　　　The Friar of Orders Gray,[2] *st. 1*

5 Our joys as winged dreams do fly;
　Why then should sorrow last?
　Since grief but aggravates thy loss,
　Grieve not for what is past.
　　　　The Friar of Orders Gray, st. 13

6 King Stephen was a worthy peer,
　His breeches cost him but a crown.
　　　　Take Thy Old Cloak About Thee,[3] *st. 7*

7 It's pride that puts this country down;
　Man, take thine old cloak about thee.
　　　　Take Thy Old Cloak About Thee, st. 7

8　　A fool and his money are soon parted.
　　　　English proverb

9 April is in my mistress' face,
　And July in her eyes hath place,
　Within her bosom is September,
　But in her heart a cold December.
　　　　*From Thomas Morley, Madrigals to Four
　　　　Voices [1594]*

10　　Hobson's choice.[4]　　*Phrase meaning no choice*

11 Lo here a new Aurora!
　　　　*From Thomas Morley, The First Book of
　　　　Canzonets to Two Voices [1595]*

12 Kill then, and bliss me,
　But first come kiss me.
　　　　*From Thomas Morley, The First Book of
　　　　Ballets to Five Voices [1595]*

13 Shoot, false Love, I care not.
　Spend thy shafts and spare not.
　　　　*From Thomas Morley, The First Book of
　　　　Ballets to Five Voices*

14 I was more true to Love than Love to me.
　　　　*From John Dowland, The First Book of Songs
　　　　or Airs [1597]*

15 Jerusalem, my happy home,
　When shall I come to thee?
　When shall my sorrows have an end?
　Thy joys when shall I see?
　　　　The Song of Mary [1601]

16 What poor astronomers are they
　Take women's eyes for stars!
　　　　*From John Dowland, The Third Book of
　　　　Songs or Airs [1603]*

17 And let all women strive to be
　As constant as Penelope.
　　　　Constant Penelope, st. 18

18 Turn again, Whittington,
　Lord Mayor of London.[5]
　　　　*Refrain of Bow Bells heard by Dick
　　　　Whittington [c. 1605]*

19 From the hag and hungry goblin
　That into rags would rend ye,
　And the spirit that stands by the naked man
　In the book of Moons defend ye!
　　　　Tom o' Bedlam [17th century], st. 1

20 The law locks up both man and woman
　Who steals the goose from off the common,
　But lets the greater felon loose
　Who steals the common from the goose.
　　　　*From Edward Potts Cheyney, Social and
　　　　Industrial History of England [1901],
　　　　introduction*

21 There is a lady sweet and kind,
　Was never face so pleased my mind;
　I did but see her passing by,
　And yet I love her till I die.
　　　　*From Thomas Ford, Music of Sundry Kinds
　　　　[1607], st. 1*

22 Love not me for comely grace,
　For my pleasing eye or face,
　Nor for any outward part,
　No, nor for a constant heart.
　　　　*From John Wilbye, Second Set of Madrigals
　　　　[1609]*

23 The silver swan, who living had no note,
　When death approached unlocked her silent throat;
　Leaning her breast against the reedy shore,

---

[1]Another version is used by Shakespeare in *Romeo and Juliet*, act IV, sc. v.

[2]Composed by Thomas Percy [1728–1811] from fragments of ancient ballads in Shakespeare; published in his *Reliques of Ancient English Poetry* [1765].

[3]Quoted in Shakespeare, *Othello*, act II, sc. iii, l. 93.

[4]Liveryman Thomas Hobson [1544–1631] obliged customers "to take the horse which stood near the stable door," according to Richard Steele, *The Spectator*, no. 509 [October 14, 1712].

[5]Richard Whittington, son of a London mercer, rose to be mayor of London three times before his death [1423].

Thus sung her first and last, and sung no more:
Farewell, all joys; O death, come close mine eyes;
More geese than swans now live, more fools than
    wise.
From ORLANDO GIBBONS, *The First Set of*
Madrigals and Motets of Five Parts [1612], I

1 Stay, O sweet, and do not rise!
The light that shines comes from thine eyes;
The day breaks not: it is my heart,
Because that you and I must part.
Stay, or else my joys will die,
And perish in their infancy.[1]
From JOHN DOWLAND, *A Pilgrim's Solace*
[1612]

2 We gather together to ask the Lord's blessing;
He chastens and hastens his will to make known;
The wicked oppressing now cease from distressing:
Sing praises to his Name; he forgets not his own.
Hymn [1625][2]

3 If there is a paradise on the face of the earth,
It is this, oh! it is this, oh! it is this.
Mogul Inscription in the Red Fort at Delhi
[1640]

4   Hear no evil, see no evil, speak no evil.
Legend related to the "Three Wise Monkeys"
carved over door of Sacred Stable, Nikko,
Japan [17th century]

5 Over the mountains and over the waves,
Under the fountains and under the graves;
Under floods that are deepest, which Neptune
    obey,
Over rocks that are steepest, Love will find out
    the way.   *Love Will Find Out the Way, st. 1*

6 Begone, dull Care! I prithee begone from me!
Begone, dull Care! Thou and I shall never agree.
From JOHN PLAYFORD, *Musical Companion*
[1687]

7 Though little, I'll work as hard as a Turk,
If you'll give me employ,
To plow and sow, and reap and mow,
And be a farmer's boy.
The Farmer's Boy [before 1689], st. 2

8 Carriages without horses shall go,
And accidents fill the world with woe.
Attributed to Mother Shipton[3]

9 Around the world thoughts shall fly
In the twinkling of an eye.
Attributed to Mother Shipton

10 Under water men shall walk,
Shall ride, shall sleep, and talk;
In the air men shall be seen
In white, in black, and in green.
Attributed to Mother Shipton

11 Iron in the water shall float
As easy as a wooden boat.
Attributed to Mother Shipton

12 A swarm of bees in May
Is worth a load of hay;
A swarm of bees in June
Is worth a silver spoon;
A swarm of bees in July
Is not worth a fly.   *Old English proverb*

13   When poverty comes in at the door, love flies
out the window.   *Saying [17th century]*

14 Please to remember the fifth of November,
Gunpowder treason and plot.
Guy Fawkes rhyme [17th century]

15 A zealous locksmith died of late,
And did arrive at heaven gate,
He stood without and would not knock,
Because he meant to pick the lock.
Epitaph upon a Puritanical Locksmith; from
WILLIAM CAMDEN, *Remains Concerning*
Britain [1637]

16   All the brothers were valiant, and all the sisters
virtuous.
From the inscription on the tomb of the Duchess
of Newcastle in Westminster Abbey [1673]

17 It is so soon that I am done for,
I wonder what I was begun for.
For a child aged three weeks, Cheltenham
Churchyard

18   Live and let live.   *Scottish proverb*

19   When I rest I rust [Rast ich, so rost ich].
German proverb

20   Coming through the rye.[4]
The Bob-tailed Lass, refrain

21 Sabina has a thousand charms
To captivate my heart;
Her lovely eyes are Cupid's arms,
And every look a dart:
But when the beauteous idiot speaks,

---

[1]Attributed also to JOHN DONNE, and included in a variant form in the seventh edition of his poems [1669].

[2]Translated by THEODORE BAKER.
  Written by an unknown author in celebration of Dutch freedom from Spanish sovereignty at the end of the sixteenth century. — *The Hymnal 1940 Companion*

[3]Prophecies ascribed to the fictitious Mother Shipton first appeared in 1641.

[4]Gin a body meet a body / Coming through the rye; / Gin a body kiss a body, / Need a body cry? — ROBERT BURNS, *Coming Through the Rye, st. 1*
  See Salinger, 805:14.

She cures me of my pain;
Her tongue the servile fetters breaks
And frees her slave again.
From Amphion Anglicus [1700]

1 God rest you merry, gentlemen,
Let nothing you dismay;
Remember Christ our Savior,
Was born on Christmas Day.   *Carol*

2 The holly and the ivy,
When they are both full grown,
Of all the trees that are in the wood,
The holly bears the crown:
The rising of the sun
And the running of the deer,
The playing of the merry organ,
Sweet singing in the choir.   *Carol*

3   Rain cats and dogs.   *Saying*

4   Sister Anne, do you see anyone coming?
Bluebeard; the cry of Fatima

5   Who will change old lamps for new?
The Arabian Nights (A Thousand and One Nights).[1] The History of Aladdin

6   Open sesame!
The Arabian Nights (A Thousand and One Nights). The History of Ali Baba

7   Drive a coach and six through an Act of Parliament.
Credited to Sir Stephen Rice [1637–1715], Chief Baron of the Exchequer, by MACAULAY *in History of England [1849–1861], ch. 12*

8 The Campbells are comin', oho, oho.
Song [c. 1715]

9 Fools' names, like fools' faces,
Are often seen in public places.[2]   *Saying*

10 And this is law, I will maintain,
Unto my dying day, sir,
That whatsoever king shall reign,
I'll still be the Vicar of Bray, sir!
The Vicar of Bray [1734], chorus

11 Some talk of Alexander, and some of Hercules;
Of Hector, and Lysander, and such great names as these;
But of all the world's brave heroes, there's none that can compare
With a tow, row, row, row, row, row for the British Grenadier.
The British Grenadiers [c. 1750]

12   The Girl I Left Behind Me.
Title of song [1759]

13   The united voice of all His Majesty's free and loyal subjects in America—liberty and property, and no stamps.
Motto of various American colonial newspapers [1765–1766]

14 Yankee Doodle came to town
Riding on a pony,
He stuck a feather in his hat
And called it macaroni.

Yankee Doodle, keep it up,
Yankee Doodle dandy,
Mind the music and the step,
And with the girls be handy.
Yankee Doodle,[3] st. 1 and chorus

15   It's all in the day's work.
Current since the 18th century

16 Man may work from sun to sun,
But woman's work is never done.   *Saying*

17 Count that day lost whose low descending sun
Views from thy hand no worthy action done.[4]
Saying

18   Don't tread on me.
Motto of the first official American flag; first raised by Lieutenant John Paul Jones in Commodore Esek Hopkins's flagship Alfred [December 3, 1775]

19   Rebellion to tyrants is obedience to God.[5]
Motto on Thomas Jefferson's seal [c. 1776]

20 Lost is our old simplicity of times,
The world abounds with laws, and teems with crimes.
On the Proceedings Against America,[6] st. 1

21 Our cargoes of meat, drink, and clothes beat the Dutch.   *Siege of Boston [1775]*

22 There were three gypsies a-come to my door,
And downstairs ran this lady, O!

---

[1]First European translation (ANTOINE GALLAND), 1704–1717.

[2]Collected by THOMAS FULLER [1654–1734], in *Gnomologia* [1732].

[3]This version was sufficiently popular in America in 1767 to be used in the ballad opera *The Disappointment; or, The Force of Credulity* by ANDREW BARTON.
Father and I went up to camp, / Along with Captain Goodwin, / And there we saw the men and boys, / As thick as hasty pudding. / Yankee doodle do.— *Version used by* ROYALL TYLER [1757–1826], *in The Contrast* [1790]

[4]An earlier version, signed by JAMES BOBART [December 8, 1697], begins "Think" rather than "Count."

[5]The motto of one, I believe, of the regicides of Charles I.— *Letter from Thomas Jefferson to Edward Everett* [February 24, 1823]
Jefferson's reference probably is to John Bradshaw [1602–1659].

[6]In the *Pennsylvania Gazette* [February 8, 1775], "from a late London Magazine."

One sang high and another sang low,
And the other sang bonny, bonny Biscay, O!
The Wraggle-Taggle Gypsies, O!, st. 1

1 She's gone with the wraggle-taggle gypsies, O!
The Wraggle-Taggle Gypsies, O!, st. 2

2 Down in the valley, the valley so low,
Hang your head over, hear the wind blow.
Down in the Valley

3 The goose hangs high.[1]   *Saying*

4 O Paddy dear, an' did ye hear the news that's goin'
   round?
The shamrock is by law forbid to grow on Irish
   ground!
No more St. Patrick's Day we'll keep, his color
   can't be seen,
For there's a cruel law agin the wearin' o' the
   Green!
The Wearing o' the Green [c. 1795]

5 For they're hangin' men an' women there for
   wearin' o' the Green.
The Wearing o' the Green

6 With drums and guns, and guns and drums
The enemy nearly slew ye.
My darling dear, you look so queer,
Oh, Johnny, I hardly knew ye.
Irish folk song, st. 1

7 Here we are on Tom Tiddler's ground
Picking up gold and silver.
Children's game

8 Christmas is coming, the geese are getting fat,
Please to put a penny in the old man's hat;
If you haven't got a penny, a ha'penny will do,
If you haven't got a ha'penny, God bless you!
Beggar's rhyme

9 From ghoulies and ghosties and long-leggety
   beasties
And things that go bump in the night, Good Lord,
   deliver us!
Cornish prayer

10 O God, thy sea is so great, and my boat is so
small.
Breton fishermen's prayer

11 Rest and be thankful.
*Inscription on stone seat in the Scottish
Highlands, and title of one of William
Wordsworth's poems*

12 The wisdom of many and the wit of one.
Definition of a proverb[2]

13 Don't cross the bridge until you come to it.
Proverb

14 It's gude to be merry and wise,
It's gude to be honest and true;
It's gude to be off with the old love,
Before you are on with the new.[3]
Rhyme

15 Oh, ye'll tak' the high road an' I'll tak' the low
   road,
An' I'll be in Scotland before ye;
But me and my true love will never meet again,
On the bonnie, bonnie banks o' Loch Lomond.
Loch Lomond, refrain

16 The woods are full of them.
*Quoted by ALEXANDER WILSON, American
Ornithology [1808], preface*

17 I wooed her in the wintertime
And in the summer too;
And the only, only thing I did that was wrong
Was to keep her from the foggy, foggy dew.
The Foggy, Foggy Dew, st. 1

18 Turkey in the straw, turkey in the hay,
Roll 'em up and twist 'em up a high tuckahaw,
And hit 'em up a tune called Turkey in the Straw.
Turkey in the Straw,[4] st. 1 and refrain

19 Sugar in the gourd and honey in the horn,
I never was so happy since the hour I was born.
Turkey in the Straw, st. 6

20 Jimmie crack corn and I don't care,
Old Massa's gone away.
The Blue-tail Fly, chorus

21 Give me that old-time religion,
It's good enough for me.
Hymn

22 It was good for Paul and Silas
And it's good enough for me.
Hymn

23 I expect to pass through this world but once;
any good thing therefore that I can do, or any kind-

---

[1][Meaning:] All is wonderful, 1866. Sometimes said to be from
"The goose honks high," referring to the fact that geese fly higher
in good weather, but there is no evidence this is the origin of the
term. —STUART BERG FLEXNER, *Listening to America* [1982]

[2]Probably based on the definition of a proverb which LORD
JOHN RUSSELL gave one morning at breakfast at Mardock's: "One
man's wit, and all men's wisdom." —*Memoirs of Sir James Mackin-
tosh, vol. 1, p. 473*

[3]Quoted as an old song by ANTHONY TROLLOPE in *Barchester
Towers* [1857], *ch. 46.*

[4]The classical American rural tune . . . steps around like an
apple-faced farmhand . . . as American as Andrew Jackson, Johnny
Appleseed, and Corn on the Cob. —CARL SANDBURG, *The American Songbag* [1927]

ness that I can show to any fellow creature, let me do it now; let me not defer or neglect it, for I shall not pass this way again.[1]   *Proverbial saying*

1 I've been working on the railroad
All the livelong day,
I've been working on the railroad
To pass the time away.
Don't you hear the whistle blowing?
Rise up so early in the morn.
Don't you hear the captain shouting,
"Dinah blow your horn."
    I've Been Working on the Railroad

2   When [or Since] Hector was a pup.
    American saying

3   OK.
    Abbreviation for humorous misspelling, "oll korrect" [1838][2]

4 'Tis the gift to be simple,
'Tis the gift to be free,
'Tis the gift to come down
Where we ought to be.
    Simple Gifts. Shaker song [c. 1848], st. 1

5 Buffalo gals, won't you come out tonight,
And dance by the light of the moon?
    Buffalo Gals

6   Women and children first.
    The Birkenhead Drill[3] [February 26, 1852]

7   You can't use tact with a Congressman! A Congressman is a hog! You must take a stick and hit him on the snout!   *Remark[4]*

8 Up and down the City Road,
In and out the Eagle,
That's the way the money goes—
Pop goes the weasel!
    Pop Goes the Weasel[5] [c. 1853]

9   Free soil, free men, free speech, Frémont.[6]
    Republican party rallying cry [1856]

---

[1]This saying has been attributed to many authors, most especially to STEPHEN GRELLET [Étienne de Grellet du Mabillier, 1773–1855], although it has not been found in any of Grellet's writings.

[2]For the history of this "most popular typical American expression," see STUART BERG FLEXNER, *I Hear America Talking* [1976], pp. 261–262.

[3]The women and children were the first to be removed from the sinking ship *Birkenhead*.

[4]Made by an unidentified cabinet member (possibly Secretary of the Interior JACOB DOLSON COX [1828–1900]), quoted by HENRY ADAMS, *The Education of Henry Adams*, ch. 17.

[5]The weasel was a hatter's tool, and "pop" was a term meaning to pawn or "hock." The Eagle was a music hall in the City Road. The song is attributed to W. R. MANDALE.

[6]John Charles Frémont [1813–1890] was the party's candidate for President.

10   Muscular Christianity.[7]
    Popular term in the 19th century for Christian social reform in England

11   It is a newspaper's duty to print the news and raise hell.   *The Chicago Times [1861]*

12   Dirty work at the crossroads.
    Attributed to WALTER MELVILLE's melodrama The Girl Who Took the Wrong Turning; or, No Wedding Bells for Him

13 The man on horseback.
    Popular term for General Georges Ernest Boulanger [1837–1891]

14   All I want of you is a little seevility, and that of the commonest goddamnedest kind.[8]
    The New Bedford Classic, as reported in ZEPHANIAH W. PEASE, The History of New Bedford [1918]. Supposed to be said by the mate of a whaler to his ill-humored captain

15 John Henry told his captain,
Says, "A man ain't nothin' but a man,
And before I'd let your steam drill beat me down, Lord,
I'd die with this hammer in my hand.
    John Henry [1873]

16 You-all means a race or section,
Family, party, tribe, or clan;
You-all means the whole connection
Of the individual man.
    You-All; from the Richmond Times-Dispatch

17 From the halls of Montezuma,
To the shores of Tripoli,
We fight our country's battles
On the land as on the sea.
    The Marines' Hymn [1847],[9] st. 1

18 There is a tavern in the town,
And there my true love sits him down,
And drinks his wine with laughter and with glee,
And never, never thinks of me.
    There Is a Tavern in the Town, st. 1

19 Adieu, adieu, kind friends, adieu, adieu, adieu,
I can no longer stay with you.
I'll hang my harp on a weeping willow-tree,
And may the world go well with thee.
    There Is a Tavern in the Town, refrain

---

[7]A term applied (from about 1857) to the ideal of religious character exhibited in the writings of Charles Kingsley. — *Oxford English Dictionary*

His Christianity was muscular. — BENJAMIN DISRAELI, *Endymion* [1880], ch. 14

[8]Another traditional version, repudiated by a New Bedford authority, is that the skipper said: "All I want out of you is silence, and damn little of that."

[9]See Anonymous, 851:20.

1 I belong to that highly respectable tribe
Which is known as the Shabby Genteel . . .
Too proud to beg, too honest to steal.
   The Shabby Genteel; sung by Sol Smith Russell
   [1848–1901] in A Poor Relation

2 The sons of the prophet are brave men and bold,
And quite unaccustomed to fear,
But the bravest by far in the ranks of the Shah
Was Abdullah Bulbul Amir.
   Abdullah Bulbul Amir [1877], st. 1

3 Now the heroes were plenty and well known to
      fame
In the troops that were led by the Czar,
And the bravest of these was a man by the name
Of Ivan Petrofski Skevar.
   Abdullah Bulbul Amir, st. 3

4 Is that Mr. Reilly, can anyone tell?
Is that Mr. Reilly that owns the hotel?
Well, if that's Mr. Reilly, they speak of so highly,
Upon me soul, Reilly, you're doin' quite well.
   Is That Mr. Reilly?[1] *[1882], chorus*

5 Sow a thought, and you reap an act;
Sow an act, and you reap a habit;
Sow a habit, and you reap a character;
Sow a character, and you reap a destiny.
   Quoted by SAMUEL SMILES *[1812–1904], in*
   Life and Labor *[1887]*

6   Now is the time for all good men to come to the
aid of the party.   *Practice sentence used in typing*[2]

7   The quick brown fox jumps over the lazy dog.
   Practice sentence used in typing (using whole
   alphabet)

8   As Maine goes, so goes the nation.[3]
   American political maxim [c. 1888]

9   Slide, Kelly, Slide.
   Title of song by J. W. KELLY *[1889]*

10 Lizzie Borden took an ax
And gave her mother forty whacks;
When she saw what she had done
She gave her father forty-one!
   Rhyme popular after the murder trial of
   Lizzie Borden, Fall River, Massachusetts
   [June 1893]

11 Out in the fields with God!
   Out in the Fields

12 Oh, why don't you work like other men do?
How the hell can I work when there's no work
      to do?   *Hallelujah, I'm a Bum [c. 1897]*[4]

13   Remember the Maine!*[5]
   Slogan in the Spanish-American War [1898]

14 Frankie and Johnny were lovers, my gawd, how
      they could love,
Swore to be true to each other, true as the stars
      above;
He was her man, but he done her wrong.
   Frankie and Johnny,[6] *st. 1*

15 The halls of fame are open wide
And they are always full;
Some go in by the door called "push,"
And some by the door called "pull."
   Quoted by STANLEY BALDWIN *[1867–1947] in*
   a speech in the House of Commons

16 The codfish lays ten thousand eggs,
The homely hen lays one.
The codfish never cackles
To tell you what she's done.
And so we scorn the codfish,
While the humble hen we prize,
Which only goes to show you
That it pays to advertise.
   It Pays to Advertise

17 One white foot — try him,
Two white feet — buy him,
Three white feet — look well about him;
Four white feet — go without him.[7]
   Rhyme for a horse-buyer

18   An apple a day keeps the doctor away.
   Current since the 19th century

19   Time is of the essence.   *Saying*

20   All the world is queer save me and thee; and
sometimes I think thee is a little queer.
   Attributed to a Quaker, speaking to his wife

21   Everyone has at least one sermon in him.
   Saying

---

[1]Assumed origin of "the life of Riley" (an easy life).

[2]Charles Weller, a court reporter, originated this expression
in . . . 1867 to test the efficiency of the first practical typewriter
which his friend Christopher Sholes had constructed. — *Life* [April
11, 1955]

[3]As Maine goes, so goes Vermont. — JAMES A. FARLEY [1888–
1976], *statement to press* [November 4, 1936], *after predicting cor-*
rectly that Franklin D. Roosevelt would carry all but two states in the
presidential election

[4]Also attributed to Harry McClintock.

[5]Derived from cartoon caption by CLIFFORD K. BERRYMAN
[1869–1949] in *The Washington Post* [April 3, 1898]: If the row
comes, REMEMBER THE MAINE, and show the world how American
sailors can fight.

[6]Traditional ballad; there are innumerable versions and verses.

[7]Three white feet and a white nose, / Rip off his skin and throw
him to the crows. — *New Hampshire version of last two lines*

1   You can always tell a Harvard man, but you can't tell him much.
        Attributed to JAMES BARNES *[1866–1936]*

2   I seen my duty and I done it.
        Current since the 19th century

3   There's a sucker born every minute.   *Saying*[1]

4   Keeping up with the Joneses.   *Popular saying*

5   Paying through the nose.
        Popular phrase for excessive payment

6   Doesn't amount to Hannah Cook.[2]
        Saying common in Maine and on Cape Cod

7   Hit's a lot worse to be soul-hungry than to be body-hungry.
        A Kentucky mountain woman asking for her granddaughter to be admitted to Berea College high school [c. 1900]. Quoted by CARL R. WOODWARD *in The Wonderful World of Books, edited by Alfred Stefferud [1953]*

8   There ain't no such animal.
        Caption for cartoon of a farmer at the circus looking at a dromedary. From Life [November 7, 1907], credited to Everybody's Magazine

9   How old is Ann?
        Popular phrase for "who knows?" [early 20th century][3]

10   The Pyramids first, which in Egypt were laid;
     Next Babylon's Gardens, for Amytis made;
     Then Mausolos' Tomb of affection and guilt;
     Fourth, the Temple of Dian in Ephesus built;
     The Colossus of Rhodes, cast in brass, to the Sun;
     Sixth, Jupiter's Statue, by Phidias done;
     The Pharos of Egypt comes last, we are told,
     Or the Palace of Cyrus, cemented with gold.
        Seven Wonders of the Ancient World

11   Use it up, wear it out;
     Make it do, or do without.
        New England maxim

12   Earned a precarious living by taking in one another's washing.   *Saying*

13   Something old, something new,
     Something borrowed, something blue,
     And a lucky sixpence in her shoe.[4]
        Wedding rhyme

14   God looks after fools, drunkards, and the United States.   *Epigram*

15   Church ain't out till the fat lady sings.[5]
        From FABIA RUE SMITH *and* CHARLES RAYFORD SMITH, *Southern Words and Sayings [1976]*

16   Would you like to sin
     With Elinor Glyn
     On a tiger skin?

     Or would you prefer
     To err with her
     On some other fur?
        On Elinor Glyn's romantic novel, Three Weeks (1907), and its episode of illicit sex on a tiger skin

17   We want bread and roses too.
        Slogan of women strikers, Lawrence, Massachusetts [1912]

18   "Shine, Shine, save poor me!
     I'll give you all the pussy a Shine can see."
     Shine says, "Now pussy's good, but pussy don't last—
     Shine's going to save his own black ass."
     And Shine swam on.   *Shine and the Titanic*[6]

19   Monkey in the tree,
     Lion on the ground.
     Monkey kept on signifying
     But he didn't come down.   *The Signifying Monkey*

20   Old soldiers never die;
     They only fade away![7]
        British Army song [c. 1915]

21   I didn't raise my boy to be a soldier.
        A Mother's Plea for Peace [1915]

22   She was poor but she was honest,
     And her parents was the same,
     Till she met a city feller,
     And she lost her honest name.   *Song [c. 1915]*

---

[1]Often attributed, but without substantiation, to P. T. Barnum [1810–1891]; possibly derived from the line in a popular nineteenth-century song, "There's a new jay [meaning, rube or mark] born every day." — RALPH KEYES, *Nice Guys Finish Seventh* [1992].

[2]Variously explained as a character who once lived on Campobello Island; a corruption of a phrase in Indian dialect; and a comparison with the worthlessness (for navigation) of a cook on board ship.

[3]"Mary is 24 years old. She is twice as old as Ann was when Mary was as old as Ann is now. How old is Ann?" — *Brainteaser in the New York Press* [October 16, 1903]
     Answer: Ann is 18.

[4]There are variants for the less familiar last line, such as: And a silver sixpence in each shoe.

---

[5]Proverbial lore current in several variant forms, the most familiar and recent of which is: The opera ain't over till the fat lady sings. — DANIEL JOHN COOK [1926–], *television newscast, San Antonio, Texas* [April 1978]

[6]"Undoubtedly the most popular poem in the black vernacular. In this version of events, the sole survivor of the *Titanic* is a black menial referred to as Shine, who turns out to be a champion swimmer." — HENRY LOUIS GATES, JR., "Sudden Def," *The New Yorker* [June 19, 1995]

[7]See Douglas MacArthur, 690:12.

1 It's the same the whole world over,
It's the poor wot gets the blame,
It's the rich wot gets the pleasure,
Ain't it all a bloomin' shame?

Song, chorus

2 Fifty million Frenchmen can't be wrong.[1]
Saying popular with American soldiers during World War I [1917–1918]

3 Say it ain't so, Joe.
Small boy to "Shoeless Joe" Jackson of the Chicago White Sox, as he emerged from a grand jury session [1920] on corruption in the 1919 World Series

4 One picture is worth a thousand words.
Misattributed "Chinese proverb"[2]

5 Don't sell America short.
Saying [c. 1925]

6 Don't lose
Your head
To gain a minute
You need your head
Your brains are in it.
Burma-Shave, roadside advertisement [1925–1963]

7 No woman can be too rich or too thin.
Saying[3]

8 No good deed goes unpunished.
Saying

9 God is in the details.
Saying[4]

10 Tennis, anyone?
Saying[5]

11 Lord, through this hour
Be Thou our Guide,
So by Thy power
No foot shall slide.
Westminster Chimes

12 Climb high
Climb far
Your goal the sky
Your aim the star.
Inscription on Hopkins Memorial Steps, Williams College, Williamstown, Massachusetts

13 Mother, may I go out to swim?
Yes, my darling daughter:
Hang your clothes on a hickory limb
And don't go near the water.
Rhyme

14 See the happy moron,
He doesn't give a damn.
I wish I were a moron—
My God, perhaps I am!
Rhyme

15 The difficult we do immediately. The impossible takes a little longer.
Slogan of United States Army Service Forces

16 Loose lips sink ships.
Government slogan, World War II

17 Kilroy was here.   *Army saying, World War II*

18 SNAFU (Situation Normal All Fucked Up).
Army saying, World War II

19 G.I. Joe.   *World War II term for infantryman[6]*

20 And when he goes to heaven
To Saint Peter he will tell:
Another Marine reporting, sir;
I've served my time in hell![7]
Epitaph on grave of Pfc. Cameron of the Marine Corps, Guadalcanal [1942]

21 Stay with me, God. The night is dark,
The night is cold: my little spark
Of courage dies. The night is long;
Be with me, God, and make me strong.
A Soldier—His Prayer,[8] st. 1

22 We sure liberated the hell out of this place.
American soldier in the ruins of a French village [1944]; quoted by MAX MILLER, The Far Shore [1945]

---

[1]Sometimes "forty" or "thirty" is heard instead of "fifty." When Texas Guinan and her troupe were refused entry into France [1931], she was quoted as saying: "It goes to show that fifty million Frenchmen *can* be wrong." She promptly renamed her show *Too Hot for Paris,* and toured the United States with it.

[2]"One look is worth a thousand words." Fred R. Barnard, in *Printers' Ink,* 8 Dec., 1921, p. 96. He changed it to "One picture is worth a thousand words" in *Printers' Ink,* 10 March, 1927, p. 114, and called it "a Chinese proverb, so that people would take it seriously." —BURTON STEVENSON, ed., *The Home Book of Proverbs, Maxims, and Familiar Phrases* [1948]

[3]Frequently attributed to the DUCHESS OF WINDSOR and others. Tell a female she's thin and she's yours for life. —ANNE BERNAYS [1930–], *Professor Romeo* [1989]

[4]A popular aphorism with the architect Ludwig Mies van der Rohe and the art historian Aby Warburg; attributed [*Le bon Dieu est dans le détail*] to GUSTAVE FLAUBERT but without verification; possibly derived from seventeenth-century humanist CASPAR BARLAEUS [1584–1648] [God hides in the smallest pieces].

[5]Frequently attributed to actor HUMPHREY BOGART, who resolutely denied saying it in any play or movie.

[6]This name, chosen for the soldier in LIEUTENANT DAVE BREGER'S comic strip for *Yank,* the Army weekly, first appeared in the issue of June 17, 1942. Writing in *Time* [February 26, 1945], Lieutenant Breger said: "I decided on 'G.I. Joe,' the 'G.I.' [Government Issue] because of its prevalence in Army talk, and the 'Joe' for the alliterative effect."

[7]From *The Marines' Hymn;* see Anonymous, 848:17.

[8]This poem, found on a scrap of paper in a slit trench in Tunisia during the battle of El Agheila, was printed in *Poems from the Desert,* by members of the British Eighth Army [1944].

1   Spartan simplicity must be observed. Nothing will be done merely because it contributes to beauty, convenience, comfort, or prestige.

From the Office of the Chief Signal Officer, U.S. Army [May 29, 1945]

2   Education is what you have left over after you have forgotten everything you have learned.

Saying

3   Time is a river without banks.   *Saying*

4   Till Hell freezes over.   *Saying*

5   One man, one vote.   *Civil rights slogan*

6   We shall overcome, we shall overcome,
We shall overcome some day
Oh, deep in my heart I do believe
We shall overcome some day.

Adapted [1960s] for the civil rights movement from an old religious song[1]

7   This is the grave of Mike O'Day
Who died maintaining his right of way.
His right was clear, his will was strong,[2]
But he's just as dead as if he'd been wrong.

Rhyme [20th century]

8   Do not fold, spindle, or mutilate.

Instructions on punch cards and computer cards [c. 1950s]

9   That's the way the cookie crumbles.

Saying [1950s]

10   "Murphy's Law": If something can go wrong, it will.   *Saying [1950s]*[3]

11   Winning isn't everything, it's the only thing.

Saying [1953], often attributed to U.C.L.A. football coach Henry ("Red") Sanders [1905–1958][4]

12   What, Me Worry?

Mad magazine ("Alfred E. Neuman") motto [1955], adapted from a turn-of-the-century advertising slogan

13   Black is beautiful.   *Slogan [1960s]*

14   We are the people of this generation, bred in at least modest comfort, housed now in universities, looking uncomfortably to the world we inherit.

Students for a Democratic Society, Port Huron Statement [1962], Preamble

15   Eyeball to eyeball.[5]   *Common expression*

16   Carnation Milk is the best in the land;
Here I sit with a can in my hand—
No tits to pull, no hay to pitch,
You just punch a hole in the son of a bitch.

The Virtues of Carnation Milk. From David Ogilvy, Confessions of an Advertising Man [1963]

17   America, love it or leave it.   *Slogan [1960s]*

18   It became necessary to destroy the town in order to save it.

Attributed to an American officer firing on Ben Tre, Vietnam [February 8, 1968]

19   Here men from the planet Earth first set foot on the moon, July 1969 A.D. We came in peace for all mankind.

Plaque on moon marking the U.S. landing there [July 1969]

20   Today is the first day of the rest of your life.

Wall slogan [1970s]

21   Beam me up, Scotty. There's no intelligent life down here.

Invented [early 1970s] by fans of Star Trek television series[6]

22   A mind is a terrible thing to waste.

United Negro College Fund advertising slogan [1972][7]

23   Expletive deleted.

White House transcripts [published 1974]

24   The most fundamental lesson of Three Mile Island, one that must be continually emphasized, is that accidents can happen.

Report of Congressional Subcommittee on Energy Research and Production [1980]

25   A woman without a man is like a fish without a bicycle.   *Feminist slogan [1980s]*

---

[1]Originating in pre–Civil War days, this song was adapted [c. 1900] by C. ALBERT TINDLEY as a Baptist hymn called "I'll Overcome Some Day." It became famous as a protest theme when sung by black workers on picket lines in Charleston, S.C. [1946].

[2]In some versions: He was right, dead right, as he sped along.

[3]Included in Arthur Bloch's collection of popular sayings, *Murphy's Law* [1977]. In its original form [1949] by EDWARD ALOYSIUS MURPHY, JR. [1917–]: "If there is more than one way to do a job, and one of those ways will end in disaster, then someone will do it that way."—BRIAN BURRELL, *The Words We Live By* [1997], pp. 146–149

[4]Compare: Winning isn't everything, but wanting to win is.— VINCE [VINCENT THOMAS] LOMBARDI [1913–1970], *interview* [1962]

[5]We're eyeball to eyeball, and I think the other fellow just blinked.—DEAN RUSK [1909–1994], *Conversation* [October 24, 1962] *during the Cuban missile crisis*

[6]Catchphrase based on a line from *Star Trek* scripts: Beam us up, Mr. Scott.

[7]What a waste it is to lose one's mind or not to have a mind is very wasteful.—DAN [J. DANFORTH] QUAYLE [1947–], *address to United Negro College Fund* [May 1989]

Anonymous: African

1 In the time when Dendid created all things,
  He created the sun,
  And the sun is born, and dies, and comes again.
  Old Song (Dinka)

2 He created man,
  And man is born, and dies, and does not come
      again.   *Old Song (Dinka)*

3 Somewhere the Sky touches the Earth, and the
  name of that place is the End.
  Saying (Wakamba)

4 All animals of the forest are alike, though we eat
  some and not others, because we the Dorobo and
  the animals all live side by side in the forest.
  From a Dorobo

5 Everything has an end.   *Saying (Masai)*

6 When elephants fight it is the grass that suffers.
  Proverb (Kikuyu)

7 Haste, haste, has no blessing.
  Proverb (Swahili)

8 To the person who seizes two things, one always
  slips from his grasp!   *Proverb (Swahili)*

9 The lie has seven endings.   *Proverb (Swahili)*

10 Goodness sold itself, badness flaunted itself about.
  Proverb (Swahili)

11 Speak silver, reply gold.   *Proverb (Swahili)*

12 The prayer of the chicken hawk does not get him
  the chicken.   *Proverb (Swahili)*

13 Wisdom is not bought.   *Proverb (Akan)*

14 Not even God is wise enough.
  Proverb (Yoruba)

15 Leave a log in the water as long as you like: it
  will never be a crocodile.
  Proverb (Guinea-Bissau)

Anonymous: Ballads

16 The king sits in Dunfermline town
  Drinking the blude-red wine.
  Sir Patrick Spens, st. 1

17 To Noroway, to Noroway,
  To Noroway o'er the faem;
  The king's daughter o' Noroway,
  'Tis thou must bring her hame.
  Sir Patrick Spens, st. 4

18 I saw the new moon late yestreen
  Wi' the auld moon in her arm;

And if we gang to sea, master,
  I fear we'll come to harm.
  Sir Patrick Spens, st. 10

19 O laith, laith were our gude Scots lords
  To wet their cork-heel'd shoon;
  But lang or a' the play was play'd
  They wat their hats aboon.
  Sir Patrick Spens, st. 15

20 Half owre, half owre to Aberdour,
  'Tis fifty fathoms deep;
  And there lies gude Sir Patrick Spens,
  Wi' the Scots lords at his feet!
  Sir Patrick Spens, st. 19

21 "And what will ye leave to your ain mither dear,
  Edward, Edward?"   *Edward, Edward, st. 7*

22 "The curse of hell frae me sall ye bear,
  Sic counsels ye give to me, O!"
  Edward, Edward, st. 7

23 Fight on, my merry men all;
  For why, my life is at an end.[1]   *Chevy Chase*

24 A fairer lady there never was seen
  Than the blind beggar's daughter of Bethnal
      Green.
  *The Beggar's Daughter of Bethnal Green,[2]
  st. 33*

25 When captains courageous, whom death could not
      daunt,
  Did march to the siege of the city of Gaunt,
  They mustered their soldiers by two and by three,
  And the foremost in battle was Mary Ambree.
  Mary Ambree,[3] st. 1

26 "I'll rest," said he, "but thou shalt walk";
  So doth this wandering Jew
  From place to place, but cannot rest
  For seeing countries new.
  The Wandering Jew, st. 9

27 Glasgerion swore a full great oath,
  By oak, and ash and thorn.   *Glasgerion, st. 19*

28 In Scarlet town, where I was born,
  There was a fair maid dwellin',
  Made every youth cry Well-a-day!
  Her name was Barbara Allen.

---

[1]Says Johnnie, "Fight on, my merry men all, / I'm a little
wounded, but I am not slain; / I will lay me down for to bleed a
while, / Then I'll rise and fight with you again." — *Johnnie Armstrong's Last Goodnight, st. 18; from* DRYDEN's *Miscellanies* [1702]

[2]This very house was built by the blind beggar of Bednall Green,
so much talked of and sung in ballads. — SAMUEL PEPYS, *Diary*
[June 26, 1663]

[3]BEN JONSON calls any virago Mary Ambree, and JOHN
FLETCHER alludes to Mary Ambree in *The Scornful Lady* [1616].

All in the merry month of May,
When green buds they were swellin',
Young Jemmy Grove on his deathbed lay,
For love of Barbara Allen.
Barbara Allen's Cruelty, st. 1, 2

1 So slowly, slowly rase she up,
And slowly she came nigh him,
And when she drew the curtain by—
"Young man, I think you're dyin'."
Barbara Allen's Cruelty, st. 4

2 True Thomas lay on Huntlie Bank;
A ferlie he spied wi' his e'e;
And there he saw a lady bright
Come riding down by the Eildon Tree.
Thomas the Rhymer, st. 1

3 "A bed, a bed," Clerk Saunders said,
"A bed for you and me!"
"Fye na, fye na," said may Margaret,
"Till anes we married be!"
Clerk Saunders, st. 2

4 There were twa sisters sat in a bour;
Binnorie, O Binnorie!
There came a knight to be their wooer,
By the bonnie milldams o' Binnorie.
Binnorie, st. 1

5 There were three ravens sat on a tree,
They were as black as they might be.

The one of them said to his mate,
"Where shall we our breakfast take?"
The Three Ravens, st. 1, 2

6 Down there came a fallow doe
As great with young as she might go.
The Three Ravens, st. 6

7 She buried him before the prime,
She was dead herself ere evensong time.

God send every gentleman
Such hounds, such hawks, and such leman.
The Three Ravens, st. 9, 10

8 Mony a one for him maks mane,
But nane sall ken where he is gane:
O'er his white banes, when they are bare,
The wind sall blaw for evermair.
The Twa Corbies, st. 5

9 Ye Highlands and ye Lawlands,
O where hae ye been?
They hae slain the Earl of Murray,
And laid him on the green.
The Bonny Earl of Murray, st. 1

10 O waly, waly, up the bank,
And waly, waly, doun the brae,

And waly, waly, yon burnside,
Where I and my Love wont to gae!
Waly, Waly, st. 1

11 "What gat ye to your dinner, Lord Randal, my son?
What gat ye to your dinner, my handsome young
    man?"
"I gat eels boil'd in broo'; mother, make my bed
    soon,
For I'm weary wi' hunting, and fain wald lie
    down."   *Lord Randal*

Anonymous: Cowboy Songs

12 As I was a-walking one morning for pleasure,
I spied a cowpuncher a-riding along.
Whoopee Ti Yi Yo, Git Along, Little Dogies

13 Whoopee ti yi yo, git along, little dogies,
It's your misfortune and none of my own,
Whoopee ti yi yo, git along, little dogies,
For you know Wyoming will be your new home.
Whoopee Ti Yi Yo, Git Along, Little Dogies

14 My foot in the stirrup, my pony won't stand,
Good-bye, Old Paint, I'm a-leavin' Cheyenne.
Good-bye, Old Paint

15 Foot in the stirrup and hand on the horn,
Best damned cowboy ever was born.
Come-a ti yi youpy, youpy yea, youpy yea,
Come-a ti yi youpy, youpy yea.
The Old Chisholm Trail

16 Last night as I lay on the prairie,
And looked at the stars in the sky,
I wondered if ever a cowboy
Would drift to that sweet bye-and-bye.
The Cowboy's Dream

17 As I walked out in the streets of Laredo,
As I walked out in Laredo one day,
I spied a poor cowboy wrapped up in white linen,
Wrapped up in white linen as cold as the clay.
The Cowboy's Lament, st. 1

18 Oh, beat the drum slowly[1] and play the fife lowly,
Play the Dead March as you carry me along;
Take me to the green valley, there lay the sod o'er
    me,
For I'm a young cowboy and I know I've done
    wrong.   *The Cowboy's Lament, refrain*

19 Oh bury me not on the lone prairie
Where the wild coyotes will howl o'er me.
The Dying Cowboy

---

[1]Also familiar as: Oh, bang the drum slowly.

1 Oh, bury me out on the prairie,
  Where the coyotes may howl o'er my grave.
  Bury Me out on the Prairie

2   Remember the Red River Valley
  And the cowboy that loves you so true.
  Red River Valley

3 Oh, give me a home where the buffalo roam,
  Where the deer and the antelope play,
  Where seldom is heard a discouraging word
  And the skies are not cloudy all day.
  Home on the Range [1873][1]

Anonymous: French

4   Revenons à nos moutons [Let us return to our
  sheep—i.e., subject].
  Maître Pathelin (15th-century farce)

5   Il ne faut pas être plus royaliste que le roi [One
  must not be more royalist than the king].
  Saying from the time of Louis XVI

6   Ça ira, ça tiendra [That will be, that will last].
  *Revolutionary song, based on a phrase of
  Benjamin Franklin's*

7   Liberté! Égalité! Fraternité! [Liberty! Equality!
  Fraternity!]
  *Phrase from before the French Revolution,
  officially adopted in 1793*

8   Tout passe, tout casse, tout lasse [Everything
  passes, everything perishes, everything palls].
  Proverb

9   Ah, les bons vieux temps où nous étions si malheureux [Oh, the good old times when we were so
  unhappy]!   *Saying*

10   L'amour, l'amour fait tourner le monde [It's
  love, it's love that makes the world go round].
  Song

11   On ne saurait faire une omelette sans casser des
  oeufs [You can't make an omelet without breaking
  eggs].   *Proverb*

12 Ami, entends-tu
  Le vol noir—des corbeaux—sur nos plaines . . .

  Ami, entends-tu
  Les cris sourds—du pays—qu'on enchaine.[2]
  Song of the Partisans [1940s]

13 Au clair de la lune,
  Mon ami Pierrot,

Prête-moi ta plume
Pour écrire un mot.   *Au Clair de la Lune*[3]

Anonymous: North American Indian

14 Screaming the night away
  With his great wing feathers
  Swooping the darkness up;
  I hear the Eagle bird
  Pulling the blanket back
  Off from the eastern sky.
  Invitation Song (Iroquois)

15   Holy Mother Earth, the trees and all nature are
  witnesses of your thoughts and deeds.
  Saying (Winnebago)

16   A people without history is like the wind on the
  buffalo grass.   *Saying (Sioux)*

17 Out of the earth
  I sing for them
  a Horse nation . . .
  I sing for them
  the animals.   *I Sing for the Animals (Teton Sioux)*

18 O our Mother the Earth, O our Father the Sky,
  Your children are we, and with tired backs
  We bring you gifts.   *Song of the Sky Loom (Tewa)*

19 May the warp be the white light of morning,
  May the weft be the red light of evening,
  May the fringes be the falling rain,
  May the border be the standing rainbow.
  Thus weave for us a garment of brightness.
  Song of the Sky Loom (Tewa)

20 Lovely! See the cloud, the cloud appear!
  Lovely! See the rain, the rain draw near!
  Who spoke?
  It was the little corn ear
  High on the tip of the stalk.
  Corn-grinding Song (Zuñi)

21 Big Blue Mountain Spirit,
  The home made of blue clouds . . .
  I am grateful for that mode of goodness there.
  Chant (Apache)[4]

22 The black turkey gobbler, the tips of his beautiful
      tail; above us the dawn becomes yellow.
  The sunbeams stream forward.
  Black Turkey Gobbler Chant (Apache)[5]

---

[1]Possibly written by BREWSTER HIGLEY.

[2]Friend, do you hear / The black flight—of our crows—on our
plains . . . / Friend, do you hear / The faint cries—of the country—
in chains.

[3]By the light of the moon, / My friend Pierrot, / Lend me your
pen / To write a word.

  This song, with music by JEAN-BAPTISTE LULLY [1632–1687],
has been popular since the time of Louis XIV [1638–1715].

[4]Translated by HARRY HOIJER.

[5]Translated by PLINY E. GODDARD.

1 House made of dawn,
House made of evening light,
House made of the dark cloud. . . .
Dark cloud is at the house's door,
The trail out of it is dark cloud,
The zigzag lightning stands high upon it.
Night Chant (Navaho)[1]

2 Happily may I walk.
May it be beautiful before me.
May it be beautiful behind me.
May it be beautiful below me.
May it be beautiful above me.
May it be beautiful all around me.
In beauty it is finished.   *Night Chant (Navaho)*

3 Lo, the Turquoise Horse of Johano-ai . . .
There he spurneth dust of glittering grains—
How joyous his neigh.
Song of the Horse (Navaho)

4 Hi! ni! ya! Behold the man of flint, that's me!
Four lightnings zigzag from me, strike and return.
War Chant (Navaho)

5 The ancient folk with evil spells, dashed to earth,
plowed under!   *War Chant (Navaho)*

6 Quarry mine, blessed am I
In the luck of the chase.
Comes the deer to my singing.
Hunting Song (Navaho)

7 Idlers and cowards are here at home now,
But the youth I love is gone to war, far hence.
Weary, lonely, for me he longs.
Wind Song (Kiowa)

8   In the beginning God gave to every people a cup
of clay, and from this cup they drank their life.
Proverb (Northern Paiute)

9 As long as the moon shall rise,
As long as the rivers shall flow,
As long as the sun shall shine,
As long as the grass shall grow.
Expression for term of a treaty

10 It ended . . .
With his body changed to light,
A star that burns forever in that sky.
The Flight of Quetzalcoatl (Aztec)[2]

11 I was out in my kayak . . .
and the seal came gently toward me.
Why didn't I harpoon him?
Was I sorry for him?

Was it the day, the spring day, the seal
playing in the sun
like me?   *Spring Fjord (Eskimo)*[3]

Anonymous: Nursery Rhymes

12 A man of words and not of deeds
Is like a garden full of weeds.
A Man of Words and Not of Deeds

13 It's like a lion at the door;
And when the door begins to crack,
It's like a stick across your back;
And when your back begins to smart,
It's like a penknife in your heart;
And when your heart begins to bleed,
You're dead, and dead, and dead, indeed.
A Man of Words and Not of Deeds

14 Cock a doodle doo!
My dame has lost her shoe;
My master's lost his fiddle stick,
And knows not what to do.   *Cock a Doodle Doo*

15 Three blind mice, see how they run!
They all ran after the farmer's wife,
She cut off their tails with a carving knife,
Did you ever see such a sight in your life,
As three blind mice?   *Three Blind Mice*

16 A frog he would a-wooing go.
Sing heigh-ho says Rowley.
A Frog He Would A-Wooing Go

17 With a rowley powley gammon and spinach,
Heigh-ho says Anthony Rowley.
A Frog He Would A-Wooing Go, chorus

18 Old King Cole
Was a merry old soul,
And a merry old soul was he,
He called for his pipe,
And he called for his bowl,
And he called for his fiddlers three.
Old King Cole

19 The King of France went up the hill
With forty thousand men;
The King of France came down the hill
And ne'er went up again.   *The King of France*

20 Jack Sprat could eat no fat,
His wife could eat no lean;
And so betwixt them both,
They licked the platter clean.   *Jack Sprat*

21 Rain, rain, go away,
Come again another day.   *Rain, Rain*

---

[1]Translated by WASHINGTON MATTHEWS.
[2]Translated by JEROME ROTHENBERG.

[3]Translated by ARMAND SCHWERNER.

1 Pat-a-cake, pat-a-cake, baker's man,
　Bake me a cake as fast as you can;
　Pat it and prick it, and mark it with B,
　Put it in the oven for baby and me.　　*Pat-a-Cake*

2 The lion and the unicorn
　Were fighting for the crown;
　The lion beat the unicorn
　All round about the town.
　Some gave them white bread,
　And some gave them brown;
　Some gave them plum cake,
　And sent them out of town.
　　　　　The Lion and the Unicorn

3 Little Jack Horner sat in the corner,
　Eating a Christmas pie.
　He put in his thumb, and pulled out a plum,
　And said, "What a good boy am I!"
　　　　　Little Jack Horner

4 London Bridge is falling down,
　My fair lady.　　*London Bridge*

5 Tell tale tit,
　Your tongue shall be slit,
　And all the dogs in our town
　Shall have a bit.　　*Tell Tale Tit*

6 As I was going to St. Ives,
　I met a man with seven wives,
　Each wife had seven sacks,
　Each sack had seven cats,
　Each cat had seven kits:
　Kits, cats, sacks, and wives,
　How many were there going to St. Ives?
　　　　　As I Was Going to St. Ives

7 The man in the wilderness asked of me
　How many strawberries grew in the sea.
　I answered him as I thought good,
　"As many as red herrings grow in the wood."
　　　　　The Man in the Wilderness

8 Ladybug, ladybug, fly away home,
　Your house is on fire, and your children will burn.
　　　　　Ladybug, Ladybug

9 Hickory dickory dock,
　The mouse ran up the clock,
　The clock struck one,
　The mouse ran down;
　Hickory dickory dock.　　*Hickory Dickory Dock*

10 Baa, baa, black sheep,
　Have you any wool?
　Yes, sir, yes, sir,
　Three bags full:
　One for my master,
　And one for my dame,

And one for the little boy
Who lives down the lane.　　*Baa, Baa, Black Sheep*

11 Mary, Mary, quite contrary,
　How does your garden grow?
　With silver bells, and cockleshells,
　And pretty maids all in a row.
　　　　　Mary, Mary, Quite Contrary

12 Oranges and lemons,
　Say the bells of St. Clement's.
　You owe me five farthings,
　Say the bells of St. Martin's.
　When will you pay me?
　Say the bells of Old Bailey.
　When I grow rich,
　Say the bells of Shoreditch.　　*Oranges and Lemons*

13 Here comes a candle to light you to bed,
　Here comes a chopper to chop off your head.
　　　　　Oranges and Lemons

14 "Who killed Cock Robin?"
　"I," said the sparrow,
　"With my bow and arrow,
　I killed Cock Robin."　　*Who Killed Cock Robin?*

15 "Who saw him die?"
　"I," said the fly,
　"With my little eye,
　I saw him die."　　*Who Killed Cock Robin?*

16 This little pig went to market;
　This little pig stayed home;
　This little pig had roast beef;
　This little pig had none;
　And this little pig cried, Wee, wee, wee!
　All the way home.　　*This Little Pig*

17 Little boy blue, come blow your horn,
　The sheep's in the meadow, the cow's in the corn;
　But where is the boy who looks after the sheep?
　He's under the haystack fast asleep.
　Will you wake him? No, not I,
　For if I do, he'll be sure to cry.　　*Little Boy Blue*

18 Simple Simon met a pieman
　Going to the fair:
　Says Simple Simon to the pieman,
　"Let me taste your ware."　　*Simple Simon*

19 Ding dong bell,
　Pussy's in the well.
　Who put her in?
　Little Johnny Green.　　*Ding Dong Bell*

20 Little Tom Tucker
　Sings for his supper;
　What shall he eat?
　White bread and butter.

How will he cut it
Without e'er a knife?
How will he be married
Without e'er a wife?   *Little Tom Tucker*

1 Crosspatch, draw the latch,
   Set by the fire and spin:
   Take a cup and drink it up,
   Then call your neighbors in.   *Crosspatch*

2 High diddle diddle
   The cat and the fiddle,
   The cow jumped over the moon;
   The little dog laughed
   To see such craft
   And the dish ran away with the spoon.
                           High Diddle Diddle

3 Three wise men of Gotham
   Went to sea in a bowl:
   And if the bowl had been stronger,
   My song had been longer.
                    Three Wise Men of Gotham

4 Jack and Jill went up the hill
   To fetch a pail of water;
   Jack fell down and broke his crown,
   And Jill came tumbling after.   *Jack and Jill*

5 Seesaw, Margery Daw,
   Jacky shall have a new master;
   Jacky must have but a penny a day,
   Because he can work no faster.
                        Seesaw, Margery Daw

6 Taffy was a Welshman, Taffy was a thief;
   Taffy came to my house and stole a piece of beef.
   I went to Taffy's house, Taffy wasn't in;
   Taffy came to my house and stole a silver pin.
   I went to Taffy's house; Taffy wasn't home.
   Taffy came to my house and stole a marrow bone.
   I went to Taffy's house and Taffy was in bed;
   So I picked up the poker and hit him in the head.
                        Taffy Was a Welshman

7 The Queen of Hearts
   She made some tarts,
   All on a summer's day;
   The Knave of Hearts
   He stole the tarts,
   And took them clean away.
                         The Queen of Hearts

8 Bye baby bunting,
   Daddy's gone a-hunting.
   Gone to get a rabbit skin
   To wrap the baby bunting in.
                            Bye Baby Bunting

9 Come, let's to bed,
   Says Sleepyhead;
   Tarry awhile, says Slow;

Put on the pot,
Says Greedy-gut,
We'll sup before we go.
                              Let's to Bed

10 Four and twenty tailors went to kill a snail,
    The best man among them durst not touch her tail.
    She put out her horns like a little Kyloe cow,
    Run, tailors, run, or she'll kill you all e'en now.
                       Four and Twenty Tailors

11 Goosey goosey gander,
    Whither shall I wander?
    Upstairs and downstairs,
    And in my lady's chamber;
    There I met an old man who wouldn't say his
       prayers;
    I took him by the left leg
    And threw him down the stairs.
                         Goosey Goosey Gander

12 Sing a song of sixpence,
    A pocket full of rye,
    Four and twenty blackbirds,
    Baked in a pie;
    When the pie was opened,
    The birds began to sing;
    Wasn't that a dainty dish
    To set before a king?

    The king was in his countinghouse
    Counting out his money;
    The queen was in the parlor
    Eating bread and honey;
    The maid was in the garden
    Hanging out the clothes,
    Along came a blackbird,
    And snipped off her nose.
                        Sing a Song of Sixpence

13 There was an old woman who lived in a shoe,
    She had so many children she didn't know what
       to do;
    She gave them some broth without any bread,
    She whipped them all soundly and put them to
       bed.   *There Was an Old Woman*

14 Ride a cockhorse to Banbury Cross,
    To see a fine lady upon a white horse;
    Rings on her fingers and bells on her toes,
    She shall have music wherever she goes.
                             Ride a Cockhorse

15 Tom, Tom, the piper's son,
    He learned to play when he was young.
    But all the tune that he could play
    Was "Over the hills and far away."
                      Tom, Tom, the Piper's Son

16 Tom, Tom, the piper's son,
    Stole a pig, and away he run;

The pig was eat, and Tom was beat,
And Tom went howling down the street.
Tom, Tom, the Piper's Son

1 "Where are you going to, my pretty maid?"
"I'm going a-milking, sir," she said.
Where Are You Going To, My Pretty Maid?

2 "My face is my fortune, sir," she said.
Where Are You Going To, My Pretty Maid?

3 "Nobody asked you, sir," she said.
Where Are You Going To, My Pretty Maid?

4 One a penny, two a penny, hot cross buns;
If you have no daughters, give them to your sons.
Hot Cross Buns

5 Pease-porridge hot, pease-porridge cold,
Pease-porridge in the pot, nine days old.
Pease-Porridge Hot

6 Curlylocks, Curlylocks,
Wilt thou be mine?
Thou shalt not wash dishes
Nor yet feed the swine,
But sit on a cushion
And sew a fine seam,
And feed upon strawberries,
Sugar and cream.
Curlylocks

7 I had a little nut tree, nothing would it bear
But a silver nutmeg and a golden pear;
The king of Spain's daughter came to visit me,
And all for the sake of my little nut tree.
I Had a Little Nut Tree

8 Humpty Dumpty sat on a wall,
Humpty Dumpty had a great fall;
All the king's horses
And all the king's men
Couldn't put Humpty Dumpty together again.
Humpty Dumpty

9 Little Bo-peep has lost her sheep,
And cannot tell where to find them;
Leave them alone, and they'll come home,
And bring their tails behind them.
Little Bo-peep

10 Little Polly Flinders
Sat among the cinders,
Warming her pretty little toes.
Her mother came and caught her,
And whipped her little daughter
For spoiling her nice new clothes.
Little Polly Flinders

11 There was an old woman tossed in a blanket,
Seventeen times as high as the moon;
But where she was going no mortal could tell,
For under her arm she carried a broom.

Old woman, old woman, old woman, said I,
Whither, ah whither, ah whither so high?
To sweep the cobwebs from the sky,
And I'll be with you by and by.
There Was an Old Woman

12 The north wind doth blow,
And we shall have snow,
And what will poor robin do then,
Poor thing? He'll sit in a barn,
To keep himself warm,
And hide his head under his wing,
Poor thing!
The North Wind Doth Blow

13 Old mother Hubbard
Went to the cupboard,
To fetch her poor dog a bone;
But when she came there
The cupboard was bare,
And so the poor dog had none.
Old Mother Hubbard

14 Pussy cat, pussy cat, where have you been?
I've been to London to look at the queen.
Pussy cat, pussy cat, what did you there?
I frightened a little mouse under the chair.
Pussy Cat

15 Peter Piper picked a peck of pickled peppers;
A peck of pickled peppers Peter Piper picked.
If Peter Piper picked a peck of pickled peppers,
Where's the peck of pickled peppers Peter Piper
   picked? *Peter Piper*

16 Monday's child is fair of face,
Tuesday's child is full of grace,
Wednesday's child is full of woe,
Thursday's child has far to go,
Friday's child is loving and giving,
Saturday's child has to work for its living,
But a child that's born on the Sabbath day
Is fair and wise and good and gay.
Monday's Child Is Fair of Face

17 Solomon Grundy,
Born on a Monday,
Christened on Tuesday,
Married on Wednesday,
Took ill on Thursday,
Worse on Friday,
Died on Saturday,
Buried on Sunday:
This is the end
Of Solomon Grundy.   *Solomon Grundy*

18 What are little boys made of?
Snips and snails, and puppy dogs' tails;
That's what little boys are made of.
What Are Little Boys Made Of?

1 What are little girls made of?
Sugar and spice, and everything nice;
That's what little girls are made of.

What Are Little Girls Made Of?

2 Hickety pickety, my black hen,
She lays eggs for gentlemen.
Gentlemen come every day
To see what my black hen doth lay.

Hickety Pickety[1]

3 Little Miss Muffet
Sat on a tuffet,
Eating some curds and whey.
Along came a spider,
And sat down beside her,
And frightened Miss Muffet away.

Little Miss Muffet

4 Peter, Peter Pumpkin-Eater,
Had a wife and couldn't keep her.
He put her in a pumpkin shell,
And there he kept her very well.

Peter, Peter Pumpkin-Eater

5 Jack, be nimble,
Jack, be quick,
Jack, jump over the candlestick.   *Jack Be Nimble*

6 There was a crooked man, and he went a crooked
       mile,
He found a crooked sixpence against a crooked
       stile;
He bought a crooked cat, which caught a crooked
       mouse,
And they all lived together in a little crooked
       house.   *There Was a Crooked Man*

7 Diddle diddle dumpling, my son John,
He went to bed with his stockings on;
One shoe off, one shoe on;
Diddle diddle dumpling, my son John.

Diddle Diddle Dumpling

8 Rub-a-dub-dub,
Three men in a tub,
And who do you think they be?
The butcher, the baker,
The candlestick-maker;
And all of them went to sea!   *Rub-a-Dub-Dub*

9 I saw three ships come sailing by,
Come sailing by, come sailing by,
I saw three ships come sailing by,
On New Year's Day in the morning.

I Saw Three Ships

10 In fir tar is,
In oak none is.

---

[1] Higgledy-piggledy my white hen, / She lays eggs for gentlemen; / She cannot be persuaded by gun or lariat / To come across
for the proletariat. — DOROTHY PARKER

In mud eel is,
In clay none is.
Goats eat ivy.
Mares eat oats.   *In Fir Tar Is*

11 Lucy Locket lost her pocket,
Kitty Fisher found it;
There was not a penny in it,
But a ribbon round it.   *Lucy Locket*

12 There were three jolly huntsmen,
As I have heard them say,
And they would go a-hunting
Upon St. David's Day.

There Were Three Jolly Huntsmen

13 All day they hunted,
And nothing did they find,
But a ship a-sailing,
A-sailing with the wind.

There Were Three Jolly Huntsmen

14 O do you know the muffin man,
The muffin man, the muffin man,
O do you know the muffin man,
That lives in Drury Lane?   *The Muffin Man*

15 To market, to market, to buy a fat pig,
Home again, home again, jiggety-jig.

To Market, To Market

16 Doctor Foster went to Gloucester
In a shower of rain;
He stepped in a puddle, up to his middle,
And never went there again.   *Doctor Foster*

17 There was an old woman
Lived under a hill;
And if she's not gone,
She lives there still.   *There Was an Old Woman*

18 There was a little man, and he had a little gun,
And his bullets were made of lead, lead, lead;
He went to the brook, and saw a little duck,
And shot it through the head, head, head.

There Was a Little Man

19 Lavender's blue, dilly dilly, lavender's green;
When I am king, dilly dilly, you shall be queen.

Lavender's Blue

20 A dillar, a dollar,
A ten o'clock scholar,
What makes you come so soon?
You used to come at ten o'clock,
And now you come at noon.   *A Dillar, a Dollar*

21 One flew east, one flew west,
One flew over the cuckoo's nest.   *One Flew East*

22 I had a little pony,
His name was Dapple Gray;
I lent him to a lady

To ride a mile away.
She whipped him, she slashed him,
She rode him through the mire;
I would not lend my pony now
For all the lady's hire.   *I Had a Little Pony*

1 Polly, put the kettle on,
We'll all have tea.   *Polly, Put the Kettle On, st. 1*

2 Sukey, take it off again,
They've all gone away.
                Polly, Put the Kettle On, st. 1

3 Little Tommy Tittlemouse
Lived in a little house;
He caught fishes
In other men's ditches.
                Little Tommy Tittlemouse

4 The farmer in the dell, the farmer in the dell,
Heigho! the derry oh, the farmer in the dell.
                The Farmer in the Dell

5 Hark! Hark! The dogs do bark,
The beggars are coming to town;
Some in rags, some in tags,
And some in velvet gowns.   *Hark! Hark!*

6 Ten little Indians standing in a line —
One went home, and then there were nine.
                Ten Little Indians

7 When good King Arthur ruled this land,
He was a goodly king,
He bought three pecks of barley meal,
To make a bag pudding.   *Good King Arthur*

8 One misty, moisty morning,
When cloudy was the weather,
I chanced to meet an old man
Clothed all in leather;
He began to compliment,
And I began to grin —
"How do you do?" and "How do you do?"
And "How do you do?" again!
                One Misty, Moisty Morning

9 Bobby Shaftoe's gone to sea,
Silver buckles on his knee;
He'll come back and marry me,
Pretty Bobby Shaftoe.   *Bobby Shaftoe*

10 Fe fi fo fum!
I smell the blood of an Englishman;
Be he alive or be he dead,
I'll grind his bones to make my bread.
                Fe Fi Fo Fum

11 Sing, sing! What shall I sing?
The cat's run away with the pudding-bag string.
                Sing, Sing! What Shall I Sing?

12 Shoe the horse, shoe the mare,
But let the little colt go bare.   *Shoe the Horse*

13 There was a man in our town,
And he was wondrous wise;
He jumped into a bramble bush
And scratched out both his eyes.
                There Was a Man in Our Town

14 There were two blackbirds,
Sitting on a hill,
The one named Jack,
The other named Jill;
Fly away, Jack! Fly away, Jill!
Come again, Jack! Come again, Jill!
                Two Blackbirds

15 This is the farmer sowing the corn,
That kept the cock that crowed in the morn,
That waked the priest all shaven and shorn,
That married the man all tattered and torn,
That kissed the maiden all forlorn,
That milked the cow with the crumpled horn,
That tossed the dog
That worried the cat
That killed the rat
That ate the malt
That lay in the house that Jack built.
                The House That Jack Built

Anonymous: Russian

16   Let the woman into Paradise, she'll bring her
cow along.   *Proverb*

17   An egg is dear on Easter Day.   *Proverb*

18   To live a life through is not like crossing a field.[1]
                Proverb

19   The eggs do not teach the hen.   *Proverb*

20   Without a shepherd sheep are not a flock.
                Proverb

21   Live with wolves, howl like a wolf.   *Proverb*

22   Don't hang noodles on my ears.   *Saying*

Anonymous: Shanties

23 Whiskey is the life of man,
Whiskey, Johnny!
Oh, I'll drink whiskey while I can,
Whiskey for my Johnny!   *Whiskey Johnny*

24 Oh, blow the man down, bullies, blow the man
down!
To me way-aye, blow the man down.
Oh, blow the man down, bullies, blow him right
down!

---

[1]See Boris Pasternak, 730:3.

Give me some time to blow the man down!
Blow the Man Down

1 What shall we do with the drunken sailor,
  Early in the morning?   *The Drunken Sailor*

2 Hooray and up she rises
  Early in the morning.   *The Drunken Sailor, chorus*

3 Oh, Shenandoah, I long to hear you,
  Way-hay, you rolling river!
  Oh, Shenandoah, I long to hear you,
  Ha-ha, we're bound away,
  'Cross the wide Missouri!   *Shenandoah*

4 A-roving, a-roving,
  Since roving's been my ru-i-in,
  I'll go no more a-roving
  With you, fair maid!   *A-Roving*

5 Glos'ter girls they have no combs,
  Heave away, heave away!
  They comb their hair with codfish bones.
  The Codfish Shanty

6 Oh, you New York girls, can't you dance the polka?
  Can't You Dance the Polka?

7   Good-bye, fare you well!
  We're homeward bound for New York town,
  Hurrah, my boys, we're homeward bound!
  Good-bye, Fare You Well

8 Oh, the times are hard and the wages low;
  Leave her, Johnny, leave her!
  I'll pack my bag and go below.
  It's time for us to leave her!   *Leave Her, Johnny*

9 There were two lofty ships, from old England they
      set sail,
  Blow high, blow low, and so sailed we! . . .
  Cruising down along the shores of High Barbaree!
  High Barbaree

10 There was a ship came from the north country,
  And the name of the ship was the Golden Vanity.
  And they feared she might be taken by the Turkish
      enemy,
  That sails upon the Lowland, Lowland, Lowland,
  That sails upon the Lowland sea.
  The Golden Vanity

11 Then blow ye winds, heigh-ho!
  A-roving I will go,
  I'll stay no more on England's shore,
  To hear the music play.
  I'm off on the morning train
  To cross the raging main,
  I'm taking a trip on a Government ship,
  Ten thousand miles away!
  Ten Thousand Miles Away

12 There is a flash packet, flash packet of fame,
  She hails from New York and the *Dreadnought*'s
      her name.   *The Dreadnought*

13 She's the Liverpool packet—O Lord, let her go!
  The Dreadnought

Anonymous: Spanish

14   A enemigo que huye puente de plata [If your enemy turns to flee, give him a silver bridge].
  Proverb

15   Al que madruga Dios le ayuda [God helps those
  who get up early].   *Proverb*

16   Con pan y vino se anda el camino [With bread
  and wine you can walk your road].   *Proverb*

17   El pez muere por la boca [The fish dies because
  he opens his mouth].   *Proverb*

18   El que se sienta en la puerta de su casa verá pasar
  el cadáver de su enemigo [He who sits at the door
  of his house will watch his enemy's corpse go by].
  Proverb

19   En boca cerrada no entran moscas [The closed
  mouth swallows no flies].   *Proverb*

20   En casa del leñero cuchillo de palo [In the woods-
  man's house the knives are of wood].
  Proverb

21   No por mucho madrugar amanece más temprano
  [Dawn comes no sooner for the early riser].
  Proverb

22   Quien bien te quiere te hará llorar [Whoever really loves you will make you cry].   *Proverb*

23   El oro y amores eran malos de encubrir [Gold
  and love affairs are difficult to hide].   *Proverb*

24   Dios te tenga en su santa mano [God keep you
  in his holy hand].   *A farewell*

Anonymous: Spirituals

25 Nobody knows the trouble I've seen,
  Nobody knows but Jesus.
  Nobody Knows the Trouble I've Seen

26 Joshua fit the battle of Jericho,
  And the walls come tumbling down.
  Joshua Fit the Battle of Jericho

27 Sometimes I feel like a motherless child,
  A long ways from home,
  A long ways from home.   *Motherless Child*

28 Go tell it on the mountain,
  Over the hills and everywhere;

Go tell it on the mountain,
That Jesus Christ is born.
Go Tell It on the Mountain

1 Go down, Moses,
  Way down in Egypt land,
  Tell old Pharaoh,
  Let my people go.   *Go Down, Moses*

2 Free at last, free at last,
  Thank God Almighty, we're free at last.[1]
Free at Last

3 I looked over Jordan, and what did I see? . . .
  A band of angels coming after me,
  Coming for to carry me home.
Swing Low, Sweet Chariot, st. 1

4 Swing low, sweet chariot,
  Coming for to carry me home.
Swing Low, Sweet Chariot, refrain

5 Michael row the boat ashore,
  Hallelujah!   *Michael Row the Boat Ashore*

6 Rise and shine and give God the glory
  For the year of Jubilee.   *Rise and Shine*

7 My Lord, what a morning,
  When the stars begin to fall.
My Lord, What a Morning

8 You'll hear the trumpet sound,
  To wake the nations underground,
  Look in my God's right hand,
  When the stars begin to fall.
My Lord, What a Morning

9 One more river,
  And that's the river of Jordan,
  One more river,
  There's one more river to cross.   *One More River*

10 Oh, freedom! Oh, freedom!
   Oh, freedom over me!
   And before I'd be a slave, I'll be buried in my
       grave,
   And go home to my Lord and be free.
Oh, Freedom!

11 Get on board, little children,
   There's room for many a more.
Get on Board, Little Children

12 The Gospel train's a-coming.
Get on Board, Little Children

13 Just like a tree that's standing by the water,
   We shall not be moved.
We Shall Not Be Moved

14 O Lord, I want to be in that number
   When the saints go marching in.
When the Saints Go Marching In

---

[1]See Martin Luther King, Jr., 823:4.

INDEX

INDEX

*Please see the Index section of the Guide to
the use of* Bartlett's Familiar Quotations,
page xi.

A

, black A white E, 603:14
emotions from A to B, 738:17
first write a crowned A, 134:23
injures B to improve X, 691:15
on gown letter A, 460:6
', for a. that and a. that, 380:14
-angling, be quiet and go a., 253:9
aron's rod, 8:12
b Iove principium, 95:*n*13
ovo, 101:*n*10
urbe condita, 123:4
bandon, all hope a. who enter here, 130:3
do not fear to a. faults, 62:13
government which kept us free, 358:10
learning and no sorrow, 58:18
to cries and lamentations, 108:4
bandoned, down the a. heaven, 707:15
God a. these defended, 619:18
man a. on earth, 772:7
poem never finished only a., 659:6
bandonment of force, 699:9
based, whoso exalt himself be a., 37:1
bashed the Devil stood, 266:25
batement and low price, 208:26
bbot of Aberbrothok, 405:11
bbots purple as their wines, 313:24
bdullah Bulbul Amir, 849:2
bednego, Shadrach Meshach and A., 30:3
-begging, truth goes a., 144:13
bel was keeper of sheep, 6:12
berbrothok, Abbot of A., 405:11
berdour, half owre to A., 853:20
bhor detest Sabbath-Day, 561:1
makers and laws approve, 284:25
bhorred in my imagination, 206:24
shears, 261:19
that senseless tribe, 299:2
bhors, God a. you, 318:16
nature a. a vacuum, 286:14
bide, fates impose that men a., 173:5
nowhere did a., 400:11
others a. our question, 528:3
tyme nyl no man a., 137:1
under the shadow of the Almighty, 18:25
who shall a. in thy tabernacle, 16:5
with me, 432:5
bides, in mystery soul a., 528:12
there a. peace of thine, 528:13
bideth, earth a. forever, 23:32
faith hope charity, 44:20
biding Leaf, 781:10
shepherds a. in field, 39:3
biezer, vintage of A., 10:37

Abiit ad plures, 109:*n*2
excessit evasit erupit, 90:*n*4
Abilities below mediocrity rewarded, 405:1
common opinions uncommon a., 538:6
from each according to a., 510:11
possible for others to use a., 791:7
splendid a. but utterly corrupt, 405:2
Ability, answer question to best of a., 659:12
charge not soul save to its a., 121:20
distressed by want of a., 63:18
laughter a. and Sighing, 545:18
lean and low a., 210:14
retain a. to function, 746:13
they never perform, 208:5
to get to verge, 717:5
Abject are usually ambitious, 287:8
submission, 349:14
Abjure my so much loved variety, 235:19
this rough magic I here a., 230:11
Able and willing to pull weight, 615:5
at least as far as a., 598:21
be a. for thine enemy, 210:20
rather a. than learned, 152:13
Ablest navigators, 353:11
Ablution round earth's shores, 439:11
Abner a prince and a great man, 11:40
smote him under the fifth rib, 11:39
Abode destined Hour, 471:7
dread a., 335:4
Last A. is Life, 122:3
Olympus a. of the gods, 54:21
untented Kosmos my a., 599:12
Abodes, peaceful a. of the gods, 54:*n*2
Abolish, English never a. anything, 625:10
right to alter or a. it, 357:2
serfdom from above, 508:6
slavery of half of humanity, 777:14
tyranny and vice, 350:14
Abolition of private property, 511:5
Abominable, newspapers the most a., 367:33
Abominably, imitated humanity so a., 204:14
Abomination, Mass an a., 144:15
of desolation, 37:7
Abora, singing of Mount A., 401:18
Aborigines, fell on knees then on a., 510:4
Abortion, men pregnant a. a sacrament,
797:16
will not give pessary to cause a., 72:16
Abortions will not let you forget, 798:6
Abou Ben Adhem, 417:12
Abound, grace a., 42:44
joys a. as seasons fleet, 172:9
Abounded, where sin a., 42:44
About about in reel and rout, 400:1
how did it all come a., 682:*n*l
it and about but evermore, 471:13

Above, at once a. beneath around, 337:16
economic tyranny a., 710:13
every good gift is from a., 47:11
insolence and triviality, 714:5
may it be beautiful a. me, 856:2
world stretched the sky, 734:15
Abraham, God of A. not of philosophers,
280:12
of scientific men, 523:23
that which has been sent down on A.,
120:13
thy name shall be A., 7:5
we are coming Father A., 488:6
Abraham's, beggar in A. bosom, 40:2
liest in A. bosom, 392:16
sleep in A. bosom, 174:11
Abram dwelled in Canaan, 7:2
O father A., 188:11
Abreast, one but goes a., 208:10
Abreuve nos sillons, 383:8
Abridging freedom of speech, 361:1
Abridgment of freedom, 367:2
Abroad for good of my country, 305:6
know own country before goes a., 332:29
lie a. for commonwealth, 232:19
obsequious a., 416:11
purchase great alliance, 173:2
schoolmaster is a., 409:18
what should not be published a., 72:16
when he next doth ride a., 347:24
Absalom my son my son, 12:7
Absence, conspicuous by a., 427:12
cry of A. A. in heart, 724:10
cure of love, 157:3
darkness death, 234:21
diminishes mediocre passions, 273:31
dote on his very a., 187:33
doth breed continual remembrance,
138:*n*5
like a winter my a., 227:7
love cannot admit a., 235:1
love rekindled by a., 324:22
makes heart fonder, 104:24
of mind we have borne, 407:28
of occupation not rest, 347:16
of romance in my history, 73:16
peace not a. of war, 286:13
seemed my flame to qualify, 227:13
Ulysses' a., 224:18
Absent, friends a. speak, 235:25
from Him I roam, 396:1
if to be a. were to be away, 276:5
in body present in spirit, 44:3
in the spring, 227:8
let no one speak ill of a., 104:22
one from another, 7:18

867

Absent *(continued)*
    room of a. child, 178:9
    thee from felicity, 207:13
Absentee, war vast aloof a., 832:8
Absentes, in a. felicior aestus amantes, 104:*n*5
Absenti nemo non nocuisse velit, 104:*n*4
Absentminded, most a. of men
    plunged in reveries, 516:6
Absents, les a. ont toujours tort, 305:*n*3
    presents endear a., 407:19
Absit omen, 123:5
Absolute and in herself complete, 267:22
    atoms preserved by a. solidity, 92:16
    be a. for death, 211:17
    built a. trust, 219:9
    dictatorship a. as any other, 698:11
    foreknowledge a., 265:13
    freedom of navigation, 611:10
    how a. the knave is, 206:22
    idea of knowledge, 78:5
    Johannes fac totum, 165:18
    mark you his a. shall, 224:26
    natures or kinds, 78:5
    notion of a. beauty, 76:8
    power corrupts absolutely, 554:12
    power in majority, 352:3
    power over wives, 361:12
    security, 768:2
    truth forever a., 489:17
Absolutely, corrupts a., 554:12
    nothing a. straight can be wrought, 339:3
Absolutes in Bill of Rights, 711:1
    in world affairs, 768:2
    meant prohibitions to be a., 711:1
    the a. the eternities, 794:9
Absolutism tempered by assassination, 385:5
Absolve, compensate bad in man a. him so,
    495:2
    foulness of their fate, 712:4
    history will a. me, 817:8
    pray God a. us all, 139:21
Absolved from allegiance, 349:11
    judge condemned when criminal a.,
    103:10
    people a. of history, 826:6
Absorb as Parallax a Flame, 546:12
Absorbing, reflects images without a., 570:12
Absorbs, country a. him affectionately,
    518:11
    tinged by what a. it, 582:20
Abstain from fleshly lusts, 47:27
    from intentional wrongdoing, 72:16
Abstains from words, 513:15
    Abstention, faith in a. from faith, 631:5
Abstinence easy to me, 326:4
    lean and sallow a., 261:7
    lend easiness to next a., 205:29
    sows sand all over, 373:11
Abstinete, a fabis a., 240:12
Abstract concepts, 359:15
    ideas conditioned by time, 625:7
    liberty not found, 344:9
    love of beauty in a., 440:10
    man in the a., 543:2
    words obscene, 754:4
Abstracts and brief chronicles, 203:25
Absurd, death a. also, 784:9
    is essential concept, 790:1
    lick a. pomp, 204:15

Absurd *(continued)*
    poets creatures most a., 313:5
    question is a., 776:4
    the a. not the improbable, 501:9
    to be believed because a., 116:19
Absurdity, dull without a single a., 341:9
    man only subject to a., 246:8
    privilege of a., 246:8
    what to do with this a., 640:3
Abundance, add more to a., 698:7
    full sharers in a., 597:10
    if thou hast a., 31:10
    out of a. mouth speaketh, 35:38
    possesses virtue in a., 59:8
    pray in days of a., 700:21
    will not suffer him to sleep, 24:13
Abundant, more a. life, 697:17
    shower of curates, 504:17
    wretched and a. Russia, 527:16
Abundantly, have life more a., 41:16
Abuse, how long Catiline a. our patience,
    90:7
    land as commodity, 711:13
    of greatness, 195:29
    wicked dreams a., 220:9
    you cause what you a., 293:12
Abused, by himself a. or disabused, 311:9
Abuses, evils exist only in a., 386:14
    excites hatred to conceal a., 409:10
Abusing, abstain from a. bodies, 72:16
    of God's patience, 190:20
    stop a. my verses or publish, 110:17
Abydos, Sestos and A. of her breasts, 235:21
Abysm of time, 229:10
Abysmal dark of center, 441:10
Abyss, cradle rocks above a., 755:12
    discovery metamorphosis, 662:7
    look long into a., 589:5
    looks into you, 589:5
    man is rope over a., 588:16
Abysses, dread a. unknown tides, 583:4
Abyssinia, Rasselas Prince of A., 324:24
Abyssinian maid, 401:18
Academe, groves of A., 101:12
    olive grove of A., 268:26
Academes, they are the books the a., 177:8
Academi, inter silvas A., 101:*n*4
Academic life, 239:6
    politics are so bitter, 772:13
Academy, Frenchman in A., 326:*n*6
Accelerated grimace, 709:2
Acceleration proportional to applied force,
    291:*n*2
Accents, aged a. untimely words, 169:4
    caught his clear a., 491:21
    yet unknown, 196:17
Accept, bow and a. end, 668:16
    decline to a. end of man, 748:20
    fall in with what asked to a., 671:18
    God a. him, 484:23
    I will not a. if nominated, 523:1
    learn to a. in silence, 595:10
    never a. thing as true, 254:2
    not God I don't a., 525:16
    our thanksgiving a., 567:4
    tamely a., 630:5
    things that cannot be changed, 735:13
    universe, 488:2
    will for deed a., 146:*n*5

Acceptability, hallmark of conventional
    wisdom a., 778:11
Acceptable, be a. in thy sight, 16:14
    offices a. here, 358:7
Acceptation, news worthy of a., 295:25
Accepted, fellow mortals a. as they are,
    512:15
    now is a. time, 45:7
    that which a. false, 659:4
    you are a., 712:7
Accepting, charms by a., 310:9
    not by a. favors, 74:3
Access and passage to remorse, 219:11
Accessible, English not a. to Englishmen,
    610:4
Accident, by a. got its liberty, 143:4
    counts for much, 569:19
    found out by a., 408:3
    happy a., 243:18
    of sentiment, 557:16
    progress not a. but necessity, 523:2
    shot of a., 214:23
    what seems a. springs from destiny,
    381:23
Accidentally, America discovered a., 715:6
    only a. am I French, 314:10
Accidents can happen, 852:24
    chapter of a. very long, 315:10
    confront ridicule a. rebuffs, 518:13
    controlled by a. or by ourselves, 770:2
    fill world, 845:8
    in best-regulated families, 498:7
    miracles propitious a., 629:11
    moving a. by flood, 212:29
    omissions are not a., 714:*n*1
    shackles a., 224:3
    universe capable of such a., 668:12
Accommodating vice, 278:12
Accommodations, equal but separate a.,
    733:*n*1
Accompany old age, 222:11
Accomplice, art a. of love, 614:3
    evening comes like a., 524:14
Accomplish little, 382:16
Accomplished anything except get along,
    708:4
    desire a. is sweet, 21:26
    her warfare is a., 27:38
    nothing a. alone, 735:17
    nothing great a. without passion, 390:8
    plan of Zeus was being a., 52:2
Accomplisher, Zeus a., 65:31
Accomplishes without any action, 59:7
Accomplishing, armorers a. the knights,
    193:11
    their appointed courses, 71:24
Accomplishment, smile of a., 827:12
Accomplishments, emerges ahead of a., 764:
    give luster, 315:7
Accord, someone whom we a. with, 364:3
Accordance, activity in a. with excellence,
    80:18
According, acted a. to what we thought,
    798:1
    to every man a. to his work, 18:2
    to the fixed law of gravity, 470:3
Account, closing your a. and mine, 471:18
    give accurate exhaustive a., 659:8
    of her life to clod, 194:15

Account *(continued)*
    sent to my a., 202:19
    whatever you lose no a., 102:22
Accountability to no one, 706:3
Accounting, death the final a., 124:7
    no a. for tastes, 123:18
Accounts, cross out overpaid a., 520:7
Accumulate, horrors a., 214:11
    sage does not a., 59:21
Accumulated experience, 675:2
    wrong, 630:5
Accumulates, where wealth a., 341:29
Accuracy tried by severe tests, 73:16
Accurate, give a. exhaustive account, 659:8
    in his judgment, 350:*n*1
Accursed craving for gold, 97:15
    fear most a. of base passions, 172:1
    he that first invented war, 170:2
    night she bore me, 69:19
    opinions are a., 639:14
Accuse, j'a., 577:8
    not a. me before the God, 3:12
    not Nature, 267:23
    not servant to his master, 23:23
Accused, I accuser God a., 822:3
Accuser, I a. God accused, 822:3
    no a. so terrible, 88:9
Accuses, excuses himself a. himself, 151:8
Accusing Spirit, 332:28
Accustomed to deliberate when drunk, 71:11
    to her face, 803:13
    to way ground opens up, 829:9
Aces, confidence in four a., 559:12
    triumphing over kings and a., 731:3
Acetylene, rip-tooth of sky's a., 753:13
Achaeans, brought upon the A. myriad woes, 52:1
    well-greaved A., 52:22
Achates, faithful A., 97:24
    fidus A., 97:*n*11
Ache, age a. penury, 211:24
    ark of the a. of it, 812:16
    charm a. with air, 195:6
    gum-and-bone a., 841:6
    my fingers a., 408:9
Acheron, fear of A. be sent packing, 93:7
Aches, my heart a., 437:5
    sense a. at thee, 214:28
    when the head a., 157:26
Achieve and cherish peace, 477:4
    some a. greatness, 209:30
    the a. of the thing, 587:7
Achieved a first-rate tragedy, 711:6
    by others' death, 178:17
    matchless deed's a., 338:2
    nothing a. without enthusiasm, 456:4
    the a. West, 748:6
Achievement, bring it to a., 69:28
    death of endeavor, 580:8
    of continuous human effort, 757:12
    quality form Man of A., 440:3
    sum of human a., 595:11
    talent in every branch of a., 74:1
    wealth opportunity for a., 74:1
Achievements of intellect everlasting, 95:10
Achieveth, naught n' assaieth naught n' a., 134:4
Achieving, still a. still pursuing, 466:3

Achilles exists only through Homer, 387:5
    not even A. will bring all to fulfillment, 53:30
    O fortunate youth A., 83:8
    see the great A., 481:14
    what name A. assumed, 256:17
    wrath of A., 52:1
Achilles', matter of Troy and A. wrath, 520:5
    stood upon A. tomb, 424:7
Aching, bring my a. heart to rest, 89:17
    ease one Life the A., 546:1
    empty and a. and I don't know why, 837:10
    one tooth and it a., 658:9
    spare my a. sight, 335:14
    they have left a. void, 347:2
Achitophel, false A. was first, 283:8
Achoo, barely daring to A., 827:14
Acknowledge and bewail our sins, 50:18
    and confess our sins, 49:18
    I a. the Furies, 656:5
    restraint of reverence, 73:18
    thing of darkness I a. mine, 230:16
    us in some way, 828:2
Acknowledged, governments whose independence a., 377:1
Acknowledgment, transcribed without a., 108:1
A-clickin' like tickin' of a clock, 596:8
A-cold, owl a., 436:20
    poor Tom's a., 217:2
Acolytes, basin in hands of a., 826:6
A-coming, Gospel train's a., 863:12
Acorns, hogs eat a., 270:*n*2
    oaks from little a., 124:12
Acquaintance, creditable a., 298:1
    in which no new a., 329:19
    should auld a., 379:8
    sneered and slanged, 653:11
    visiting a., 367:12
Acquaintances, make new a., 326:14
Acquainted with grief, 28:20
    with the night, 670:2
Acquaints, misery a. with strange bedfellows, 229:29
Acquent, when we were first a., 379:4
Acquiesce, if we a. in discrimination, 674:8
Acquire and beget a temperance, 204:11
Acquired, fortune has a. him, 85:3
    knowledge a. under compulsion, 77:18
Acquiring and possessing property, 339:9
    ways of a. books, 733:4
Acquisition, desire increases with a., 332:14
Acquisitions or losses by nature, 362:7
Acre in Middlesex, 448:5
    of barren ground, 229:8
Acres, a few paternal a. bound, 308:3
    happy man works ancestral a., 98:27
    has a. of flutes, 740:17
    over whose a. blessed feet, 184:22
Acrobat, Governor of New York not an a., 663:13
Acrostics, Baconian a., 755:13
Act against Constitution, 340:1
    against natural equity, 340:1
    an a. of survival, 824:16
    and do things accordingly, 760:15
    as if God did exist, 631:3
    as if there were God, 582:15

Act *(continued)*
    beauty and valor and a., 587:8
    between motion and a., 719:6
    both a. and know, 276:25
    bring to light goodly a., 682:3
    but not rely on own ability, 58:13
    has no ethical quality unless chosen, 581:16
    heaven helps not men who will not a., 61:*n*1
    in doubt to a. or rest, 311:9
    in the noon, 372:19
    initial a. of culture, 702:16
    last a. crowns play, 249:12
    locally, 760:10
    lover's or Roman's part, 309:28
    no a. of kindness ever wasted, 60:11
    not afraid of destructive a., 628:4
    not criminal unless intent criminal, 123:7
    of fear, 201:16
    of God defined, 729:3
    of life, 585:20
    old age play's last a., 91:18
    only on that maxim, 339:6
    our Antipodes, 256:25
    perform every a. as though your last, 115:2
    poem of a. of mind, 403:*n*2
    power to live and a., 395:12
    prologues to swelling a., 219:4
    promptly, 608:12
    reap an a., 849:5
    sins they love to a., 225:7
    sleep an a. or two, 231:18
    think himself a. of God, 504:11
    two witnesses to overt a., 360:15
    virtue and prudent a., 344:14
    vote and a. to bring good, 582:11
    Way of sage is to a., 59:21
    what it is to a. or suffer, 720:3
Acta est fabula, 123:6
Actaeon ego sum dominum cognoscite, 105:*n*11
    I am A., 105:15
Acted according to what we thought, 798:1
    lofty scene be a. o'er, 196:17
Acting is suffering, 720:3
    of dreadful thing, 196:1
    only when off stage he was a., 343:4
    people inside your head a., 810:9
    surrender explaining not a., 663:7
Action, accomplishes without any a., 59:7
    advantage of taking no a., 59:5
    brave in a. patient under labors, 556:3
    faithful honor clear, 310:15
    feeling for single good a., 364:22
    fruit of a. not be motive, 87:3
    give a. its character, 75:29
    horse symbol of a., 707:18
    imitate a. of the tiger, 192:30
    imitation of a. that is serious, 81:10
    impartial in thought and a., 610:22
    in a. how like an angel, 203:17
    in bondage to history, 542:12
    in thought as in a., 778:14
    knowledge must come through a., 68:13
    life a. and passion, 577:15
    lose the name of a., 203:33
    lust in a., 227:22

Action *(continued)*
  made to follow path of a., 63:4
  makes the a. fine, 251:1
  man is origin of his a., 80:14
  man of a. forced into thought, 647:5
  mindless a., 770:6
  moment not of a. or inaction, 87:*n*4
  no worthy a. done, 846:17
  nor utterance nor speech, 197:4
  nothing more terrible than ignorance in a., 366:7
  of masses of men, 505:16
  on a. alone be thy interest, 87:3
  pious a. sugar o'er, 203:32
  pious fraud as with bad a., 355:4
  predestined from eternity, 542:12
  proud men of a., 442:14
  science guide of a., 591:8
  sense of honor in a., 74:5
  sentiments weigh less than a., 515:23
  spectator of a. he describes, 534:10
  suit a. to the word, 204:12
  Tao takes no a., 59:3
  test lies in a., 65:29
  thought too much for a., 572:19
  to every a. equal reaction, 291:4
  vice by a. dignified, 183:17
Actions, decisive a. unconsidered, 651:3
  exceeds in his a., 63:14
  extreme a. ascribed to vanity, 588:13
  morality of his a., 331:14
  must be his spirit, 81:17
  mutual a. of two bodies, 291:4
  my a. are my ministers', 282:11
  not always a. show man, 310:2
  not always true sons, 271:8
  of the just, 254:7
  society exists for noble a., 80:29
  speaks according to his a., 62:15
  speech is image of a., 57:9
  think beforehand that a. be resolute, 82:7
  thousand a. once afoot, 192:22
  what a. most excellent, 529:8
  when our a. do not, 221:31
  work good of agent, 287:6
Active, deeply and intensely a., 581:2
  experimentation a. science, 500:16
  free a. individuals, 530:2
  through form and figure, 403:17
  to the vigilant a. brave, 353:2
Activest, his a. part, 272:13
Activities, knowledge of unconscious a. of mind, 607:8
Activity in accordance with excellence, 80:18
  property product of a., 678:14
Actor, better be a. than critic, 665:3
  condemn fault and not a., 211:9
  dreamer is a., 675:11
  pregnant with part, 630:2
  well-graced a. leaves, 180:13
Actors, like a. in ancient plays, 603:11
  these our a. were spirits, 230:9
Acts before he speaks, 62:15
  four a. already past, 306:19
  his a. being seven ages, 198:25
  let a play have five a., 101:27
  nameless unremembered a., 390:20
  no second a. in American lives, 746:18
  our lives in a. exemplary, 165:8

Acts *(continued)*
  psychical a. develop by reflex, 543:9
  to keep good a. refresh with new, 167:3
  with such a. fill a pen, 169:13
Actual, solid earth a. world, 505:13
  true account of a. is poetry, 505:27
Actuality of thought is life, 80:6
Actus non facit reum, 123:7
Acute inquisitive dexterous, 344:10
Acutely, companion so feel solitude a., 659:5
Ad astra per aspera, 123:8
  maiorem Dei gloriam, 149:*n*13
  unguem factus homo, 98:*n*10
Ad infinitum, so proceed a., 299:4
Adage, poor cat i' the a., 219:20
Adam, all that A. had, 454:19
  and his wife, 480:13
  as A. early in morning, 520:1
  awe of A., 826:4
  called his wife's name Eve, 6:10
  deep sleep upon A., 5:21
  had 'em, 651:6
  in A. all die, 44:24
  offending A., 192:17
  old A., 51:17
  son of A. and Eve, 297:7
  take care A., 701:11
  the goodliest man, 266:12
  was a gardener, 172:21, 635:24
  was but human, 561:7
  when A. delved, 843:8
  wonder what A. and Eve think, 714:6
  young A. Cupid, 182:27
Adamant for drift, 665:12
Adamantine chains, 263:23
Adam's dream, 439:14
  from Pyrrha's pebbles or A. seed, 436:15
  hold up A. profession, 206:15
  in A. ear left voice, 267:17
  in A. fall sinned, 296:7
  riverrun past Eve and A., 696:14
  since A. fall, 637:18
  sons conceived in sin, 241:8
Adamses vote for Douglas, 621:*n*1
Adaptation, struggle for a., 675:2
Adapted, means plainly a. to end, 371:4
  to my kind of fooling, 671:6
Adazzle dim, 587:10
Add hue to rainbow, 178:14
  more to abundance, 698:7
  one cubit to stature, 34:18
  power to a. or detract, 476:7
  some extra just for you, 810:8
  to these retired Leisure, 260:1
  to those with too much, 698:7
Added, all these things a. unto you, 34:21
Adder, like the deaf a., 17:34
  stingeth like an a., 22:38
  tread upon the lion and a., 18:26
Adding insult to injury, 330:15
Addison, volumes of A., 325:5
Addled mosses dank, 709:14
Address, prefer to a. myself to one man, 127:5
Addressed her winged words, 52:6
  is must a word to be a. to princes, 152:4
Addressing popular audiences, 81:9
Adds precious seeing to the eye, 177:6
Adelante adelante, 579:*n*2

Adequate, no a. military defense, 705:5
  strength not a. to resist, 81:21
Adeste fideles, 123:9
Adhere, time nor place did then a., 219:22
Adieu, bid you welcome a., 555:5
  chers tableaux, 255:*n*2
  fair day a., 178:5
  forevermore my dear, 379:3
  hand at lips bidding a., 438:16
  kind friends, 848:19
  she cries and waved, 307:1
  tristesse, 743:*n*2
Adjacent, doors of heaven a. identical, 701:1
Adjective when in doubt strike out, 561:13
Adjectives, American without qualifying a., 597:12
  no straddled a., 709:14
Adjoining, lain in a. Room, 545:4
Adjunct, learning an a. to ourself, 177:4
Adjusted in the Tomb, 545:4
Adjustment of colonial claims, 611:10
Adler, Irene A. always the woman, 617:2
Administer wealth for good, 559:8
Administration, conduct affairs of a., 477:1
  during my a. no blood shed, 359:4
  life of this A., 799:9
  said of first A., 698:5
  said of second A., 698:5
Administrations, Kennedy and Johnson a., 798:1
Admirable, express and a., 203:17
  something howsoever strange and a., 182:4
Admirably, those which most a. flourish, 227:*n*1
Admiral cheered them holding out hope, 140:3
  Dewey was the A., 580:2
  from time to time kill one a., 316:6
Admiration, as great in a. as herself, 231:16
  from critics, 447:20
  greatness worthy to excite a., 531:14
  jumps from a. to love, 406:5
  of the poet, 403:11
  only of weak minds, 268:20
  season your a., 201:13
Admire, many a. few know, 73:12
  most men a. virtue, 268:18
  that riches grow in hell, 264:23
  the world, 788:2
  to a. we should not understand, 300:19
  too simple to a. it, 447:20
  we like those who a. us, 273:32
  where none a., 329:25
Admired, celerity never more a., 223:23
  few a. by own households, 153:15
  that she might a. be, 176:12
  through being misunderstood, 726:4
Admires, coral lip a., 253:18
  meanly a. mean things, 490:9
Admiring Bog, 544:13
  in gloomy shade, 257:21
  Senate a. its members, 570:3
Admit I'm licked, 728:5
  impediments, 227:17
  never a. them in sight, 406:11
  no kind of traffic would I a., 229:25
Admitted, good pun may be a., 355:16
  no one else a. here, 701:1

Affection's, to me-wards your a. strong, 248:5
Affections dark as Erebus, 190:7
  great primary human a., 529:8
  great strain on a., 513:13
  hath not a Jew a., 188:30
  holiness of Heart's a., 439:13
  life history of a., 416:14
  old offenses of a. new, 227:15
  run to waste, 421:19
  t' a. and to faculties, 235:5
  they strive to secure, 745:12
  which attend human life, 303:8
Affects to nod, 285:8
  to renounce principles, 360:10
Affirm life, 677:15
  uprising unveiling a., 478:15
  what seems to be truth, 78:8
Affirmation, faith in a., 631:5
  of individual, 577:6
  of life, 677:15
Affirmative, minds naturally a., 566:20
  speak the a., 457:27
Affixed, thou deemest mountains a., 122:1
Afflict, coward conscience a. me, 174:20
  the best, 334:1
Afflicted, commend those who are a., 50:7
  neither oppress the a., 22:29
  newspaper comforts a., 646:18
Affliction alters, 229:3
  bread of a., 12:38
  consoling in depths of a., 474:16
  day of a., 32:22
  forgetfulness of a., 32:22
  furnace of a., 28:12
  have their A. by drops, 289:23
  one day smile again, 176:25
  pay in a. or defect, 659:13
  remembering mine a. and misery, 29:29
  saveth in time of a., 31:26
  water of a., 12:38, 27:26
Afflicts the comfortable, 646:18
Afford, ask upkeep of yacht can't a. one, 567:12
  can a. to like them, 830:8
  can't a. them Governor, 610:6
  our costly seasons, 818:10
  purest treasure mortal times a., 178:30
  selling houses for more than people could a., 708:2
Affords market for other products, 387:2
Affright air at Agincourt, 192:16
  the bad a., 334:1
Affrighted, rend the a. skies, 309:13
  steed ran on alone, 655:19
Affronts with his own darkness, 791:12
Afghanistan's, wounded and left on A. plains, 634:7
A-fishing, east wind never blow when he goes a., 252:23
  gone a., 252:20
  time is stream I go a. in, 507:3
Afloat, golden lilies a., 464:6
A-flowing, every sluice of knowledge set a., 350:18
A-flying, old Time is still a., 248:8
Afoot and light-hearted, 520:2
  game is a., 617:13
  game's a., 193:2

Afoot *(continued)*
  swiftest traveler goes a., 506:19
  thousand actions once a., 192:22
  with my vision, 519:17
Afraid, basest of things to be a., 748:19
  be not a. neither dismayed, 10:18
  be not a. of greatness, 209:30
  be not a. of life, 582:9
  be not a. of sudden fear, 20:27
  be not a. to give that little, 31:10
  because we tremble, 582:4
  contempt for governor who is a., 67:14
  death is a. of him, 122:28
  don't be a., 840:13
  don't let them think you're a., 632:20
  dying to be a. of thee, 545:20
  for the terror by night, 18:25
  Frankie was a., 802:9
  happiness makes heart a., 445:17
  in short I was a., 717:13
  it is I be not a., 36:16
  man not a. of sea, 658:11
  more a. than hurt, 147:17
  neither let it be a., 41:30
  not a. to die for friends, 100:16
  not a. to follow truth, 359:7
  not a. to go, 350:13
  not so much a. of death as ashamed, 255:20
  not that I'm a. to die, 831:3
  of fear, 388:23
  of the light, 540:10
  of whom shall I be a., 16:22
  Public a. of itself, 410:8
  rich people most a., 729:6
  she was a. to ask, 807:15
  show you're not a., 838:14
  small men a. of writings, 349:9
  so I was a., 491:14
  sore a., 39:3
  stranger and a., 619:14
  tell you what a. of, 725:13
  to do if last hour, 318:13
  to go home in dark, 626:*n3*
  to look upon God, 8:5
  to stand ridicule, 301:9
  to strike, 312:4
  uncertain and a., 775:13
  whistling to keep from being a., 285:2
  who's a. of Virginia Woolf, 820:4
  wife and children stand a., 255:20
Afresh, I was dumbfounded a., 825:8
  kiss a., 248:7
Africa, all A. and her prodigies, 255:13
  always something new out of A., 108:10
  Asia and A. expelled freedom, 354:9
  black like depths of my A., 762:10
  choose between A. and English tongue, 826:2
  conditioned people of A. to humiliation, 812:6
  does A. know song of me, 706:7
  ex A. semper aliquid novi, 108:*n5*
  Kilimanjaro highest in A., 754:15
  more familiar with A., 828:9
  song of A., 706:7
  survival of wildlife in A., 808:6
  walked proudly upright, 774:14
  what is A. to me, 765:1

African, Americans of A. descent, 556:3
  conditioned to freedom, 731:10
  giant among continents, 774:14
  new moon lying on back, 706:7
  where still A. complains, 368:12
Afric's burning shore, 404:7
  sunny fountains, 416:3
Afro-American, not only Latin-American nation but A., 817:9
After, before war instead of a., 763:18
  blackbird whistling or just a., 687:7
  man a. his own heart, 11:22
  old man looks before and a., 52:20
  that out of all whooping, 199:10
  this therefore because of this, 124:16
  us the deluge, 337:6
After-dinner talk, 480:10
After-dinner's sleep, 211:19
Aftermark of too much love, 669:17
Aftermath of war, 672:4
Afternoon, all in golden a., 549:9
  evening in a., 734:13
  fatal five in a., 751:9
  land in which always a., 480:16
  rude multitude call a., 177:11
  summer a. most beautiful words, 586:3
  winter's a. in chapel, 722:3
Afternoons, Winter A., 544:12
Afterthoughts, stronger than all a., 69:27
After-times, leave something to a., 262:11
Afton, flow gently sweet A., 379:10
Again, it was déjà vu all over a., 814:13
  off a. on a., 651:5
Against, all life 6 to 5 a., 704:12
  every sword a. his fellow, 11:23
  he not with me a. me, 35:36
  hope believed in hope, 42:43
  in confederacy a. him, 298:4
  kick a. the pricks, 65:12
  not a. with, 671:18
  who can be a. us, 43:9
Agamemnon, brave men before A., 100:15
  cried aloud, 718:10
  dead, 640:14
  gazed on face of A., 533:10
Agate, eyes like a. lanterns, 753:18
  no bigger than a.-stone, 182:22
Age, accompany old a., 222:11
  ache penury, 211:24
  and body of the time, 204:13
  at your a. heyday in blood, 205:22
  atomic a., 652:17, 793:5
  Augustan, 336:5
  beats off louring Old A., 142:7
  belongs only to own a., 433:4
  best in four things, 167:1
  cannot wither her, 223:15
  carefulness bringeth a., 32:43
  cast me not off in the time of old a., 18:8
  centuries roll back to a. of gold, 100:13
  childhood manhood and decrepit a., 249:13
  come to thy grave in full a., 13:40
  comfort to my a., 198:3
  contribution according to a., 510:*n5*
  crabbed a. and youth, 843:19
  dance attention on old a., 642:14
  decrepit a. tied to me, 640:3
  demanded an image, 709:2

Age *(continued)*

disease or sorrows strike, 512:9
distrust that a. brings wisdom, 691:8
does not make us childish, 365:2
drives my green a., 795:2
early candle-light of old a., 521:16
education best provision for old a., 79:17
employed in edging steel, 368:13
enchantments of the Middle A., 530:10
every a. has its pleasures, 289:8
father of all in every a., 313:7
first moment of atomic a., 793:5
folly in all of every a., 289:12
fool in every a., 312:18
forehead of the a. to come, 435:20
foreign nations and the next a., 168:19
fortify thy name against old a., 169:5
freethinking of one a. common sense of
   next, 532:1
full of care, 843:19
given to men of middle a., 228:26
gods have neither a. nor death, 68:19
Golden A., 95:22
golden a. in imagination, 448:17
good God what an a., 288:6
green old a., 283:4
habits of a. of atomic energy, 737:9
hardly feel pressure of a., 77:1
he hath not forgotten my a., 405:10
how tasteless and ill-bred, 94:12
if youth but knew if old a. but could,
   151:11
ill layer-up of beauty, 194:1
in a good old a., 7:3
in a. I bud again, 250:22
in the flower of their a., 11:15
in wintry a. no chill, 348:17
in year of his a., 123:10
infirmity of his a., 215:25
is grown so picked, 206:23
key-machine of modern industrial a.,
   744:19
labor of an a., 259:3
lady of certain a., 424:11
leaves friends and wine, 412:9
lee shore of a., 594:15
make a. to come my own, 275:2
master spirits of this a., 196:19
middle a. time of improving, 270:7
mind torpid in old a., 328:10
most people my a. are dead, 730:17
my a. lusty winter, 198:5
no falsehood lingers to old a., 69:4
no old a. only sorrow, 627:18
no other difference than a., 383:6
nor sword nor a. destroy, 105:21
not by a. is wisdom acquired, 86:6
not numbered by years, 155:7
not of an a. but for all time, 238:9
not one continued faithful until old a.,
   78:17
not only a night an a., 669:19
not profited so much as lost, 506:14
not so well qualified as youth, 506:14
not weary them, 650:6
of antiquity youth of world, 166:n2
of Aquarius, 834:5
of chivalry gone, 345:13
of chivalry past, 514:7

Age *(continued)*

of discord and strife, 172:3
of ease, 342:2
of fear, 756:15
of freedom ended discipline began,
   706:10
of gold, 100:13
of Gold, 258:19
of iron, 315:18
of Miracles, 434:19
of revolution and reformation, 358:13
of unreason, 779:17
Old A. and Experience, 293:5
Old A. coming bolt door, 123:3
old a. crown of life, 91:18
old a. in universal man, 166:n3
old a. is woman's hell, 276:6
old a. lacking neither honor nor lyre,
   99:16
old a. level light, 734:13
old a. only disease, 456:3
old a. play's last act, 91:18
old a. should burn, 795:14
old a. time of spending, 270:7
old Mr. Senex showing a., 790:13
olives of endless a., 227:12
or grief or sickness, 249:1
pays us with a. and dust, 160:14
peaceful as old a., 493:5
perform promises of youth, 324:24
physician of Iron A., 528:15
prayers which are a. his alms, 164:10
preferable to youth, 303:9
regret in chilled a., 585:19
restored of the Antonines, 353:n2
returns the Golden A., 95:22
shakes rooted folly of a., 289:16
shall be clearer than noonday, 14:8
Shelley of my a., 800:16
sign of old a., 399:7
smack of a. in you, 191:12
soon comes a., 161:5
soul of the a., 238:5
spirit of a., 316:26
tested to extreme old a., 528:2
the a. is dull and mean, 468:11
the harbor of all ills, 84:18
therefore summon a., 494:11
think at your a. it is right, 550:1
thinks better of gilded fool, 233:5
thirty-five attractive a., 605:12
this slaughtered a., 787:1
thou hast nor youth nor a., 211:19
'tis well an old a. is out, 285:22
to age succeeds, 480:7
too late or cold climate, 267:25
toys of a., 311:11
tragedy of the a., 648:10
veracity with old a., 274:10
very staff of my a., 188:16
view a. of poverty, 189:25
war dearth a. agues, 236:5
weak evils a. and hunger, 198:24
what was done in remote a., 455:4
when a. in wit out, 194:36
when Mozart was my a., 821:1
when old a. crept over, 623:11
when old a. shall generation waste, 438:5
when Thule no more ultimate, 107:11

Age *(continued)*

will fade beauty's flower, 151:3
with stealing steps, 150:7
without a name, 346:12
wives companions for middle a., 167:15
world's great a. begins, 429:22
worst of woes wait on a., 420:12
youth and a. equally a burden, 77:1
youth passed old a. not arrived, 512:1
Aged, beauty of a. face, 693:4
   certain age means a., 424:11
   man paltry thing, 639:17
   matched with a. wife, 481:7
   thrush frail gaunt, 575:16
   youth becomes as a., 211:19
Agenbite of inwit, 696:9
Agent, actions work good of a., 287:6
   free a. you were before, 115:29
   imagination a. of perception, 403:3
   Nature a. and patient at once, 79:18
   thus the poor a. despised, 208:24
   trust no a., 194:18
Agents of men of thought, 442:14
Age's, poison for a. tooth, 177:21
Ages, all a. believed in gods, 675:6
   and ages hence, 669:4
   before history, 348:24
   cycle of the a. renewed, 95:22
   emptiness of a. in face, 601:3
   famous to all a., 262:18
   God our help in a. past, 304:6
   gone a. long ago, 437:4
   heir of all a., 482:7
   how many a. hence, 196:17
   now he belongs to the a., 502:7
   Rock of A., 356:2
   seven a., 198:25
   thousand a. in Thy sight, 304:7
   three poets in three a., 284:27
   through a. one purpose, 482:3
   trace events of a., 443:5
   value from esteem of a., 282:8
   what thing not thought of a. long ago,
      365:16
   ye unborn a., 335:14
Agglomeration called Holy Roman Empire,
   316:1
Agglutinative, tonsorial or a. type, 653:17
Aggrandizement, no a. territorial or other,
   699:7
Aggravate, I will a. my voice, 181:1
Aggravation of self, 570:6
Aggravations, accept minor a., 595:10
Aggregate efforts of busy multitude, 534:8
   interests of community, 366:18
Aggression of Germany, 726:n3
   stop their a., 774:7
   threaten a., 699:9
   war of a. and conquest, 712:5
Aggressions, when a. require war, 358:14
Aggressors, quarantine the a., 698:n1
Agin, off a. on a., 651:5
Agincourt, affright air at A., 192:16
Aging people in contraction of life, 675:5
   person give attention to self, 675:5
Agir, j'ai trop pensé pour a., 572:n2
Agitation, peace at heart of endless a.,
   395:5
   those who deprecate a., 509:13

All *(continued)*

harm to one harm to a., 557:5
have not gift of martyrdom, 284:21
having nothing yet hath a., 232:15
hell broke loose, 266:26
his faults observed, 197:12
home-made but aren't we a., 785:18
honorable men, 196:28
hope abandon who enter here, 130:3
I and you and a. of us, 197:1
I could see from where I stood, 734:14
I dare do a., 219:21
I have is thine, 39:38
I know you a., 184:36
I want out of you, 848:n8
I write Poets A., 545:7
in all, 201:12, 486:21
in a. things charity, 274:22
in all to one another, 564:15
in confederacy against him, 298:4
in day's work, 846:15
in green went my love, 739:10
in the Downs, 306:22
in valley of death, 484:24
is best though we doubt, 269:16
is but toys, 220:25
is done that men can do, 379:2
is ephemeral, 115:15
is flux, 64:1
is mended, 182:15
is not lost, 264:3
is not well, 201:20
is passing, 689:21
is this a, 807:15
is vanity, 23:32
is well, 723:10
know a. except myself, 140:1
learned all drunk, 348:7
lord of a. yet prey to a., 311:9
lost save honor, 145:8
mankind love lover, 455:21
men created equal, 357:2, 476:7
men have need of gods, 54:15
men my compatriots, 153:21
moderation in a. things, 88:10
my days are trances, 478:10
my pretty ones, 222:1
news fit to print, 614:7
noblest Roman of them a., 197:21
not a. capable of everything, 95:24
ocean the source of a., 53:17
on our meat and on us a., 248:20
once so beautiful is dead, 725:2
one for a. a. for one, 175:4
one from a., 117:9
one law for a., 345:9
or nothing, 540:1
our yesterdays have lighted fools, 222:16
our youth our joys our a., 160:14
passion spent, 269:17
perform tragic play, 642:6
persons share in government, 80:30
quiet along Potomac, 539:6
quiet on western front, 752:11
readiness is a., 207:8
ripeness is a., 217:32
root and a., 486:21
round the town, 857:2
safely gathered in, 487:7

All *(continued)*

sees Me in a., 87:6
shall be well, 133:4, 722:5
shall die, 191:38
should cry Beware, 401:19
silence an' all glisten, 515:3
Souls College limited undergraduates, 654:17
take him for a. in a., 201:12
that is and shall be, 67:22
that live must die, 200:28
that makes a man, 486:8
that we see or seem, 477:11
that's beautiful drifts, 637:19
the brothers too, 209:27
the brothers valiant, 845:16
the lonely people, 835:3
the perfumes of Arabia, 222:7
the way home, 857:16
the winds of doctrine, 263:5
the world and his wife, 299:25
the world's a stage, 198:25
things are one, 64:3
things bright and beautiful, 508:7
things come of you Nature, 115:12
things come to who wait, 455:n1
things full of signs, 117:8
things how small soever, 286:2
things to all men, 44:9
things work together, 43:7
this above a., 201:27
this and heaven too, 295:26
this now too much for us, 670:17
this the world well knows, 227:22
time takes a. gives a., 159:8
unkindest cut of a., 196:34
waiting to give his a., 784:10
warts and a., 254:n1
was light, 313:10
was lost, 267:30
we are sinners a., 172:14
we can do, 469:15
we have and are, 635:25
we hope in Heaven, 477:10
we know for truth, 638:3
we know of Love, 547:8
we need of hell, 547:3
well that ends well, 148:4
which will not pass away, 420:19
who love freedom, 728:15
with one voice, 42:24
with thee all with thee, 466:20
work and no play, 253:11
world queer, 849:20
ye know on earth, 438:5
ye that pass by, 29:28
Allay, glowing axle doth a., 260:19
Allayed fever of bone, 718:7
no voice divine storm a., 348:22
Allaying fury and my passion, 229:19
no a. Thames, 276:3
not a drop of a. Tiber, 224:20
Allegiance, not bound to swear a., 100:18
to British, 349:11
to the South, 409:11
Allegory, life continual a., 440:15
on banks of Nile, 367:10
Allegra, laughing A., 467:12

Alleluia, Jesus Christ risen today A., 294:8
Allemand, je parle a. a mon cheval, 149:n12
Allen, name was Barbara A., 853:28
snow on Bog of A., 696:4
Alleviates, legacy a. sorrow, 159:4
Alley, in bowling a. bowled sun, 292:7
rats' a., 718:14
Sally in our a., 307:23
Titanic of cypress, 479:13
Alleys, lowest and vilest a. of London, 617:6
All-form only form rational, 583:2
All-good, must a. too follow, 424:30
All-harmonious, Father-Mother God a., 526:10
Alliance, holy a. to exorcise specter, 510:14
unless abroad purchase a., 173:2
Alliances, entangling a., 358:13
permanent a., 350:11
Allied Expeditionary Force, 728:15
great wits to madness a., 283:8
remembrance and reflection how a., 283:n2
Allies, great Russian a., 728:15
no eternal a., 417:20
thou hast great a., 393:2
All-in-all, intellectual A., 392:3
Alliteration, sentiment and a., 557:16
Alliteration's artful aid, 346:17
All-night vigil in soft face of girl, 68:1
Allnut, Nature Mr. A. we rise above, 781:18
Allons enfants de la patrie, 383:8
Allow not nature more than needs, 216:15
that you do not know it, 62:17
Allowance, no a. for ignorance, 537:1
Allowed, anyone a. to write like that, 700:n2
have merit handsomely a., 329:8
on every hand a. be, 378:1
the soothing music, 807:2
All-pervasiveness, infallible impeccable a., 583:4
All-powerful must all-good follow, 424:30
should fear everything, 257:8
to be impotent, 665:12
All's fair in love and war, 511:14
right with world, 491:2
well that ends well, 210:29
All-shaking, thou a. thunder, 216:18
Allure, to a. by denying, 504:5
Allure si vagabonde, 152:n14
Allured to brighter worlds, 342:6
Allures, war where wealth a., 284:22
Alluring, sea shows false a. smile, 93:5
Allusive, poet become more a., 722:13
Alluvial march of days, 753:15
Alma Mater, youth who loves A., 799:n2
Almanac, look in a. find out moonshine, 181:19
plant tears says a., 785:14
Almighty dollar, 416:18
gave dog, 398:8
gold, 238:1
shadow of the A., 18:25
thank God A. free at last, 823:4
that the A. would answer me, 14:41

Almighty's, arrow from A. bow, 375:4
  form glasses itself, 422:1
  God A. gentlemen, 283:17
  orders to perform, 301:12
Almond, peach once bitter a., 561:8
  tree shall flourish, 25:8
Almoner, best a. keeps nothing, 118:15
Almost glad we have been bombed,
  757:8
  everybody had troubles, 627:12
  right word and right word, 561:2
  thou persuadest me, 42:38
Alms, beg a. of palsied eld, 211:19
  for oblivion, 208:8
  give a. accordingly, 31:10
  give a. to every one that asks, 518:10
  of those who work with joy, 700:20
  when thou doest a., 34:10
Alms-basket of words, 177:10
Almsman's gown, 180:4
Aloft, Death a., 753:18
  invisible in night, 611:18
Aloha oe, 571:15
Alone a banished man, 843:12
  alone all all alone, 400:10
  and palely loitering, 439:3
  art should stand a., 557:17
  as sparrow a. upon house top, 19:5
  be a. on earth, 420:12
  being human born a., 710:8
  better to live a., 66:19
  beweep my outcast state, 226:5
  born unto himself a., 249:4
  Britain fight on a., 667:6
  cannot live a. at peace, 699:5
  clouded you will be a., 105:25
  don't live in world a., 677:17
  dwell kings of sea, 528:8
  go it sole a., 671:2
  grief mine a., 425:8
  heaven a. given away, 514:15
  here at gate a., 485:8
  how said I am a., 181:11
  I a. sit lingering here, 279:7
  I am a., 730:3
  I did it, 225:3
  I lie down a., 619:21
  I only am escaped a., 13:25
  I sleep a., 58:3
  I want to be a., 770:7
  in bee-loud glade, 637:1
  in the midst of the earth, 26:19
  in world without God, 822:3
  Jacob was left a., 7:19
  learn to stand a., 540:6
  leaving me never a., 575:23
  let her a. she will court you, 237:23
  let me a., 14:4
  let us a., 480:19
  long way I tread a., 432:11
  love but you a., 843:11
  love lives not a. in brain, 177:5
  loved him for himself a., 367:22
  man a. at moment of birth, 108:4
  man is a., 772:7
  man not sufficiently a., 659:5
  man only feels a., 794:3
  man thinking or working is a., 507:8
  man with God strive, 421:9

Alone *(continued)*
  never a. accompanied with noble
    thoughts, 163:20
  never a. with poet in pocket, 351:15
  never less a. than wholly a., 91:9
  never less a. than when a., 384:6
  nor for you for one a., 520:15
  not a. God is within, 112:6
  not good that man be a., 5:20
  not live by bread a., 10:*n*1
  nothing accomplished a., 735:17
  on wide wide sea, 400:10, 400:23
  one minute a. with him, 704:7
  paces about room a., 718:19
  right to be let a., 607:3
  sometimes be a., 249:19
  soon find himself a., 326:14
  strange city lying a., 478:4
  stranger and a., 760:4
  strongest stands a., 540:16
  though in wilderness never a., 112:*n*4
  through seas of thought a., 391:9
  travels fastest a., 632:17
  trodden the winepress a., 28:32
  virtue not left to stand a., 62:24
  we exist a., 657:15
  we live as we dream a., 612:5
  we millions live a., 529:3
  we perished each a., 348:22
  we shall die a., 279:22
  weep and you weep a., 600:7
  white man will never be a., 419:5
  withouten compaignye, 136:1
  you a. are you, 226:26
Along came a spider, 860:3
  to get a. go a., 697:9
Aloof in order to gain reputation, 78:10
Aloud, all a. wind doth blow, 177:18
  not winced nor cried a., 594:10
  secrets cry a., 780:2
  think a., 455:25
  to fight a. very brave, 544:4
Alpes, au-delà des A. l'Italie, 102:*n*8
  in conspectu A. alterum latus Italiae,
    102:*n*8
Alph the sacred river, 401:13
Alpha, I am A. and Omega, 49:4
Alphabet of flowers, 235:16
Alpine mountains cold, 263:15
Alps, beyond A. lies Italy, 102:12
Already with thee, 437:9
Alright, it's gonna be a., 835:6
  listen Christ you did a., 762:13
Altar, even at Thy glowing a., 765:2
  every light focused on high a.,
    644:14
  family a., 532:20
  great world's a. stairs, 484:5
  of freedom, 477:2
  what green a., 438:3
  with this inscription, 42:17
Altars of great historical ideals, 782:4
  their a. their hearths, 95:8
  to unknown gods, 581:6
Alter, circumstances a. cases, 442:3
  ego, 84:*n*5
  human nature, 623:5
  life garment we a., 749:10
  make and a. constitutions, 350:8

Alter *(continued)*
  right to a. or abolish it, 357:2
  when Hills do, 545:16
Alteration, alters when it a. finds, 227:17
  world capable of a., 751:1
Altereth, law of the Medes and Persians
  which a. not, 30:7
Alteri seculo, 88:*n*4
Altering, Eye a. all, 781:10
Alters, affliction a., 229:3
  love a. not, 227:17
  when it alteration finds, 227:17
Altitude, what leopard seeking at a., 754:15
Altitudo O a., 255:11
Alway, I would not live a., 14:4
  Lo I am with you a., 38:13
Always be an England, 794:1
  believed a. everywhere by all, 119:23
  count on a murderer, 755:15
  fair weather, 630:7
  Force will be with you a., 838:18
  I am with you a., 38:13
  in earth and air, 781:3
  poor a. with you, 37:21
  said my eyes were blue, 408:9
  suspect everybody, 496:33
  that same old story, 817:15
  they were a. making discoveries, 336:3
  three o'clock, 746:14
  you know how it is, 803:2
Am, I a. not what I was, 297:6
  I a. that I a., 8:7
  I a. what I a., 44:23
  I a. what I yam that's all I yam, 741:8
  my God perhaps I a., 851:14
  not I a fly, 374:4
  sames of a., 740:9
  tell them I A., 337:16
  what I a. so shall thou be, 125:4
Amanece no más temprano, 862:21
Amantium irae amoris integratio est, 88:*n*7
Amaryllis, anger of A. a sad thing, 95:19
  sport with A., 261:19
Amassing harmony, 688:7
Amateur, whine of a. for three, 557:13
Amateurs, hell full of musical a., 609:19
  ruined by a., 715:15
Amaze the unlearned, 308:14
Amazed and curious, 379:20
  gazing rustics, 342:9
  I am a. methinks, 178:22
  wise a. temperate furious, 220:26
Amazement, married to a., 831:14
Amazing grace how sweet the sound, 339:12
Amazon, she was an A., 776:17
Ambassador from Britain's crown, 487:10
  is an honest man, 232:19
Ambassadors in every quarter, 490:13
Amber, bee preserved in a., 110:20
  flies preserved in a., 110:*n*11
  scent of odorous perfume, 269:6
  waves of grain, 616:3
Amber-dropping hair, 261:10
Ambiguities, smile vehicle for a., 516:21
Ambiguous undulations, 686:19
Ambition a species of madness, 287:12
  all the pride cruelty and a., 160:13
  bookish a., 239:16

Apparition, lovely a. sent, 394:1
    of these faces, 708:16
    that a. sole of men he saw, 428:3
Apparitions, fifteen a. seen, 642:20
Appeal, basic a. of movies, 805:4
    books of universal a., 662:21
    I a. to any white man, 339:8
    I a. unto Caesar, 42:34
Appeals to religious prejudice, 537:13
Appear, fishermen a. like mice, 217:18
    small vices do a,, 217:24
    things not what a. to be, 112:11
    to be and appear not to be, 78:8
    while these visions did a., 182:15
Appearance, in a. at friendship, 288:26
    judge not according to a., 41:6
    looketh on the outward a., 11:25
    monstrosity in ordinary a., 825:2
    never attain reality, 382:8
    of new beings, 469:10
    takes on a. of nearby rock, 61:13
Appearances, judging people by a., 276:16
    keep up a., 496:40
    neither satisfied with a., 761:6
    often are deceiving, 60:8
    to mind are four kinds, 112:11
Appeared, there a. a chariot of fire, 12:39
Appears, God A. and God is Light, 375:16
    thine in mine a., 233:12
    when true Genius a., 298:4
Appeaseth strife, 21:37
Appendix, idleness an a. to nobility,
    240:15
Appetite a feeling and a love, 391:3
    a universal wolf, 207:27
    alimentary canal with big a., 787:8
    breakfast with a., 230:30
    cloy hungry edge of a., 179:6
    comes with eating, 146:1
    for bogus revelation, 690:16
    good digestion wait on a., 221:10
    increase of a., 201:4
    makes eating a delight, 270:3
    man given to a., 22:32
    may sicken, 208:25
    not meat but a., 270:3
    quench a. keep reason under control,
      116:4
    sharpen with cloyless sauce his a.,
      223:12
    umble pie with a., 498:11
    will into a., 207:27
    with keen a. he sits down, 188:19
Appetites, cloy a. they feed, 223:15
    conflicting interests and a., 697:3
    man of my a., 691:10
    not their a., 214:4
    subdue a. my dears, 496:16
Appius, that which A. says, 95:13
Applaud, old people a. it, 157:27
    thee to the very echo, 222:13
    world forever a., 476:3
Applause, deference and a. deserve, 355:8
    delight wonder of our stage, 238:5
    from none but self a., 525:6
    joy pleasance revel and a., 213:26
    lectured with much a., 520:8
    not least in honor or a., 162:*n*1
    sit attentive to own a., 312:4

Apple a day, 849:18
    as an a. reddens, 58:5
    blossoms fill air, 724:17
    candied a. quince plum gourd, 437:2
    cleft through core, 382:18
    did not want a. for a.'s sake, 561:7
    easy under the a. boughs, 795:8
    my a. trees never eat cones, 668:19
    of the eye, 16:8
    pickers passed it by, 58:5
    pie and cheese, 597:2
    prince of a. towns, 795:9
    rotten at the heart, 188:7
    round as a. was his face, 133:10
    to eat with a. tart, 599:1
    tree among the trees, 25:15
    worm in wild a., 713:14
    ye who love a., 685:*n*2
Apple-bearing Hesperian coast, 70:5
Apple-faced farmhand, 847:*n*4
Apple's cleft through core, 382:18
Apples, comfort me with a., 25:16
    golden a. of sun, 637:10
    great mother of big a., 787:4
    of gold in pictures of silver, 23:2
    on Dead Sea's shore, 420:18
    on Newton's head, 671:13
    silver a. of moon, 637:10
    since Eve ate a., 424:21
    small choice in rotten a., 175:22
    sure as Lord made little green a.,
      764:1
    sweeter than a., 603:9
Applesauce, politics is a., 685:13
Appleseed, Johnny A., 685:8
Apple-tree, bare branch of mossy a., 401:11
Apple-woman, Mr. Whitman's Eve drunken
    a., 569:18
Appliance, by desperate a. relieved, 205:32
Appliances, with all a. to boot, 191:34
Application, lays in a. on it, 497:27
Applied, acceleration proportional to a. force,
    291:*n*2
    science not exist, 533:7
Applies west of Rockies, 807:7
Apply our hearts unto wisdom, 18:23
    thine heart unto my knowledge, 22:27
Applying thought one finds, 457:*n*1
Appointed for my second race, 279:2
    house a. for all living, 14:39
    limits keep, 537:19
    their a. courses, 71:24
Appointeth the moon for seasons, 19:11
Appointment at end of world, 706:6
    in Samarra, 673:1
    never yields by a., 416:21
Appreciate things left behind, 693:8
    to criticize is to a., 585:13
Appreciates what others comprehend, 142:17
Appreciation of earth's beauty, 686:7
Apprehend some joy, 182:3
    we a. good clearly, 69:28
Apprehended, next world as closely a.,
    256:14
Apprehension, death most in a., 211:20
    in a. how like a god, 203:17
    of the good, 179:6
Apprenticehood, serve long a., 179:3
Appris, rien a. ni rien oublié, 369:*n*3

Approach, drum beats my a. tells thee I
    come, 249:2
    like rugged bear, 221:14
    see a. proud Edward's, 380:10
    snuff a. of tyranny, 344:10
    sweet a. of even or morn, 265:25
    touch me, 520:1
Approaching, arrow always a. target, 832:11
    ever a. thunder, 822:9
Approbation, cold a., 323:15
    from Sir Hubert Stanley, 384:13
Appropriate, all means which are a., 371:4
    to criticize is to a., 585:13
Approval, colored man looks to white folks
    for a., 839:9
Approve, abhor makers and laws a., 284:25
    by his loved mansionry, 219:15
    gods a. the depth, 395:10
    not a. slightest breach, 710:17
Approximate, hated the a., 677:1
Approximate, hated the a., 677:1
Après nous le déluge, 337:6
April, bright cold day in A., 765:14
    eighteenth of A., 467:14
    he smells A. and May, 190:28
    hoarfrost spread, 400:12
    how it is with A. day, 670:5
    in mistress' face, 844:9
    is the cruellest month, 718:11
    laugh thy girlish laughter, 616:2
    love resembleth A. day, 176:6
    lovely A. of her prime, 225:29
    men A. when they woo, 199:29
    of A. May of June, 247:14
    proud-pied A., 227:8
    shakes out her hair, 704:14
    showers May flowers, 151:6
    thirty days hath A., 150:8
    those that A. wears, 212:*n*1
    uncertain glory of A. day, 176:6
    with his shoures soote, 134:15
April's breeze unfurled, 453:11
    if you were A. lady, 568:21
    now that A. there, 492:4
Aprons, sewed fig leaves and made a., 6:5
Apt alliteration's aid, 346:17
    words have power, 269:2
Aptitude, genius a. for patience, 321:11
Aptitudes, produce according to a., 510:*n*5
Aquarium is gone, 801:14
Aquarius, age of A., 834:5
A-quarreling, set them a., 330:8
Aquitaine, Prince of A., 469:4
Arab in desert, 326:*n*6
Arabesque, Lateral A. a pseudo-promotion,
    805:13
Arabia, all the perfumes of A., 222:7
Arabian, as fast as A. trees, 215:13
Arabs, fold tents like A., 466:14
    no more war between A. Israelis, 804:7
    of the desert, 122:11
Arahat Buddhas who appear in world, 66:21
Ararat, always been an A., 671:5
Arbeiten, lieben und a., 608:*n*3
Arbiter is taste, 480:1
    of everyone's fortune, 95:*n*11
    of taste, 113:23
Arbitrary, deliberative forces over a., 607:1
Arbitrator, old common a. Time, 208:21
Arboreal, hairy quadruped probably a., 470:5

Arbores, serit a. quae alteri seculo, 88:*n*4

Arcadia, et in A. ego, 123:24
    I too am in A., 123:24

Arcady, woods of A. dead, 636:18

Arch, broken a. of London Bridge, 448:7
    experience a. to build upon, 570:1
    experience is an a., 481:9
    of ranged empire fall, 222:27
    sunlit a., 670:5

Archangel a little damaged, 407:9
    angel and a. join, 312:23
    ruined, 264:17

Archangels, with angels and a., 50:19

Arched flood, 453:11
    heaven-gates not so a., 244:8

Archer, feat of Tell the a., 382:18
    laughs at a., 524:8
    mark a. little meant, 397:17

Arches, fled Him down a. of years, 620:17

Archetypes of unconscious, 675:6

Archipelago, Gulag a., 804:13

Archipelagoes, starry a. and islands, 603:13
    tourist a. of South, 826:5

Archipels sidéraux et des îles, 603:*n*11

Architect advise to plant vines, 652:16
    every man a. of his fortune, 95:13
    fate of a., 364:19
    man his own a., 495:7
    of Universe a mathematician, 679:3
    venture to call himself a., 397:19

Architecture adaptation of form, 517:21
    fashion is a., 700:17
    frozen music, 364:28
    give children right to study a., 351:14
    love's a. is his own, 272:17
    man that has taste of a., 302:9
    music in space, 364:*n*1
    new styles of a., 775:5
    wondrous A. of world, 170:4

Archives, language the a. of history, 456:9
    of memory, 653:17

Arcs, on earth broken a., 494:4

Arctic, to wear a. fox, 715:1

Arcturus, guide A. with his sons, 15:11

Arden, now am I in A., 198:7

Ardent, love of glory most a., 303:8

Ardeur dans mes veines cachée, 290:*n*5

Ardor gives the charge, 205:23
    learning must be sought with a., 362:4

Are and are not, 78:8
    compared with might be, 543:14
    I shall tell you what you a., 370:4
    we a. the world, 842:7
    we know what we a., 206:6

Area, he who controls a. controls religion, 123:17

Arena, only beast in a. the crowd, 645:6

Aren't I a woman, 443:10

Arethusa grant me this labor, 96:1

Argent, les affaires l'a. des autres, 536:*n*1

Argos do without sons of Atreus, 628:2

Argosies of magic sails, 481:23

Argue, good man does not a., 59:21
    hard to a. with belly, 88:1
    liberty to a. freely, 263:4
    not against Heaven's hand, 263:16
    not concerning God, 518:10
    though vanquished a. still, 342:9

Argued each case with wife, 550:2

Argues, not to know me a. yourselves
        unknown, 266:24
    who a. is not a good man, 59:21

Arguing, in a. parson owned skill, 342:9
    much a. much writing, 263:1
    no a. with Johnson, 343:8
    not a. I am telling, 557:19
    with inevitable, 515:15

Arguit, stilus virum a., 240:5

Argument and intellects too, 341:12
    conduct right a. wrong, 343:3
    exact and priggish a., 461:14
    finer than staple of his a., 177:9
    for a week, 185:14
    heard great a., 471:13
    height of this great a., 263:21
    I have found a., 329:16
    in a. with men, 269:7
    knockdown, 285:1, 552:14
    knowest thou what a., 452:16
    maintain his a., 193:5
    makes thee beat wings, 92:*n*13
    metermaking a., 456:8
    necessity a. of tyrants, 381:4
    needs no reason, 60:6
    not stir without great a., 206:2
    of earth, 518:17
    overrefines a. brings self to grief, 132:12
    sheathed swords for lack of a., 193:1
    with east wind, 515:15

Arguments, no time for catch a., 476:2
    sure experiments and demonstrated a., 155:12

Argus, dark death seized A., 55:18

A-riding, cowpuncher a. along, 854:12

Ariel, deal of A., 594:8
    I A. will be correspondent, 229:16

Ariosto of North, 421:10

A-ripening, greatness is a., 231:2

Aris, pro a. atque focis, 95:*n*6

Arise, ah for man to a., 485:6
    arise from death, 236:4
    awake a., 264:11
    Barak and lead captivity captive, 10:30
    from dreams of thee, 429:8
    how shall the dead a., 256:1
    I will a. and go, 637:1
    my lady sweet a., 225:12
    Phoebus 'gins a., 225:12
    prisoners of starvation, 504:21
    shine for thy light is come, 28:29
    soldiers of Christ a., 322:26
    take up thy bed, 38:15
    thoughts that a. in me, 482:15
    wretched of earth, 504:21

Arises, democracy a. out of notion, 81:2

Ariseth a little cloud like a man's hand, 12:30
    sun also a., 23:32
    sun a. they gather themselves, 19:11

Aristocracy, Clover any time A., 546:18
    natural a. among men, 358:19
    not society without a., 702:14
    of Moneybag, 434:6
    untitled a., 473:17

Aristocratic, beast of prey in a. races, 589:13
    single out a. pretensions, 676:16

Aristotle and all you philosophers, 425:*n*2
    assures us man possesses immortality, 773:4
    bookes of A. and his philosophie, 134:36
    is it A. Pliny Buffon, 331:10

Aristotle's, live and die in A. works, 170:17

Arithmetic, branches of A., 550:19
    wealth a. cannot number, 245:1

Arithmetical, subsistence increases in a. ratio, 385:4

Arizona is my land, 543:7

Ark, into Noah's a., 347:18
    make thee an a., 6:26
    of bulrushes, 8:1
    of God is taken, 11:19
    of the ache of it, 812:16
    straight out of a., 398:18
    Uzzah put hand to a., 11:42

Arkansaw, rest anywhere it would be in A., 418:17

Arks, these are the a., 169:5

Arm and burgonet of men, 223:6
    brutal a. appear, 642:17
    can honor set to a., 186:35
    clothed in white samite, 139:3
    doth bind restless wave, 537:19
    faithless a., 775:10
    give me your a. old toad, 810:5
    I bit my a., 400:2
    is very long, 71:25
    it in rags, 217:24
    long a. of coincidence, 622:4
    maketh flesh his a., 29:17
    mortal a. and nerve feel, 397:22
    my bended a. for pillow, 62:27
    on bended a. doglike, 65:3
    reared a. crested world, 224:4
    seal upon thine a., 26:3
    short a. to reach to Heaven, 621:10
    slumbering on own right a., 436:4
    some quick to a., 709:4
    soon shall thy a., 348:23
    the obdured breast, 265:15
    under a. carried broom, 859:11
    wreath of hair which crowns my a., 235:9

Arma, cedant a. togae, 91:*n*3
    virumque cano, 96:*n*11

Armageddon, place called A., 48:34
    we stand at A., 615:14

Armchair, old a., 509:6

Armed at points exactly, 201:15
    Forces in control, 733:3
    goeth on to meet the a. men, 15:14
    goodness a. with power, 735:14
    neutrality, 611:7
    peace, 255:4
    rhinoceros, 221:14
    so strong in honesty, 197:10
    thrice a. that hath quarrel just, 172:12
    thy want as an a. man, 21:5

Armenians, who remembers A., 726:14

Armentières, mademoiselle from A., 730:13

Armes, aux a. citoyens, 383:8

Armies, anarchy scatters a., 67:24
    disbanding hired a., 433:9
    ignorant a. clash by night, 531:2
    mechanized a., 666:13
    of ransomed saints, 487:8
    resisted but not an idea, 451:4

Artists, as many worlds as a., 658:4
   great a. never Puritans, 691:2
   scientists a. and artisans, 796:12
   what a. call posterity, 657:9
Artless, full of a. jealousy, 206:3
Art's, art for a. sake, 427:4, 461:16
Arts, Athens mother of a. eloquence, 268:25
   babblative and scribblative, 405:20
   degrade first the a., 374:13
   flourishing of the a., 737:18
   Imagination with Reason mother of a.,
     362:*n*3
   in the a. style, 643:9
   in which wise excel, 293:7
   inglorious a. of peace, 276:22
   liberal a. study humanizes, 105:28
   medicine most distinguished of a., 73:5
   no a. no letters no society, 246:12
   no relish of those a., 302:9
   nurse of a. plenties, 193:25
   state of our a., 781:15
   stomach teacher of a., 108:16
   that caused to rise, 312:4
   they are the books the a., 177:8
   three a. with all things, 78:1
Aryan, neat mustache and A. eye, 827:15
As if, 582:15
A-sailing with the wind, 860:13
Ascend, base degrees by which a., 195:30
   if I a. up into heaven, 20:13
   into the hill of the Lord, 16:19
   Muse of fire a., 192:15
Ascendancy, capital in a. system of plunder,
   510:10
Ascended, bright pomp a. jubilant, 267:16
   into heaven, 50:3
   morning hymns a., 538:12
Ascending, angels a. and descending, 7:14,
   40:37
Ascendit, quanto plus a., 128:*n*5
Ascends to mountaintops, 420:20
Ascent, no a. too steep for mortals, 99:4
   of Man, 778:4
Ascetic in unnecessary points, 581:9
   systematically a., 581:9
Asclepius cured the body, 76:*n*3
   I swear by A., 72:16
   owe a cock to A., 72:11
Ash heap of history, 787:10
   oak a. and thorn, 635:18, 853:27
   on old man's sleeve, 721:16
   one adjusting a. heaps, 714:3
   out of a. I rise, 827:11
Ashamed, epitaph of which not a., 599:22
   more a. more respectable, 609:17
   naked and were not a., 6:2
   no reason to be a. of ape, 537:13
   not a. to defend a friend, 32:36
   not a. to fail, 324:4
   of death, 255:20
   of having been in love, 273:11
   shame is a. to sit, 184:1
   to be seen with him, 288:23
   to die, 441:13
   to look upon one another, 253:3
   white men ought to be a., 386:9
   workman that needeth not to be a.,
     46:31
Ashen, skies a. and sober, 479:11

Ashes, all a. to taste, 420:18
   am I and dust, 125:4
   beauty for a., 28:31
   cinders a. dust, 436:16
   earth will dissolve in a., 49:9
   e'en in our a. live, 334:25
   fell in fire and burnt to a., 671:21
   from his a. made, 483:16
   handful of gray a. at rest, 534:3
   in a. olde is fyr yreke, 136:6
   in a. rather than enslaved, 666:3
   into a. all my lust, 277:2
   new-create another heir, 231:16
   of his fathers, 448:14
   of Napoleon Bonaparte, 389:5
   out of a. life again, 591:11
   past a bucket of a., 681:11
   put on sackcloth with a., 13:18
   speak to your silent a., 94:28
   splendid in a., 256:22
   to ashes, 51:14
   turn to a. on lips, 412:14
   well-wrought urn becomes greatest a.,
     234:7
   yesterday embryo tomorrow a., 115:19
Ashore, till last galoot's a., 571:5
Asia and Africa expelled freedom, 354:9
   peace and stability in A., 790:22
   seven churches in A., 48:3
   vast multitudes of A., 666:13
Asian, do what A. boys ought to be doing,
   779:7
Aside, not idly stand a., 74:5
   to step a. is human, 378:18
Asinorum, pons a., 84:*n*6
Ask, all I a. is merry yarn, 681:2
   all I a. is tall ship, 680:15
   and it shall be given, 35:3
   and ye shall receive, 41:34
   cease to a. what morrow will bring, 99:11
   don't a. me to take none, 497:3
   drink divine, 238:2
   for anything except time, 387:13
   for me tomorrow, 183:28
   for the old paths, 29:6
   how he is he tells you, 644:9
   I do not a. you much, 178:27
   if you got to a. you ain't got it, 757:*n*1
   me blessing, 218:1
   me no more, 483:5
   me no more where Jove bestows, 253:13
   me no questions, 342:23
   never a. refuse resign office, 321:6
   not a dinner to a. a man to, 327:4
   not a. for what you wish you had not,
     106:27
   not offer people but a. of, 799:4
   not what country can do for you, 799:10
   not whom sleep beside, 618:9
   of him will they a. more, 39:31
   of thee forgiveness, 218:1
   only what they can give, 643:16
   she was afraid to a., 807:15
   the beasts, 14:11
   the Lord's blessing, 845:2
   us prophet, 809:4
   we a. not, 528:3
   wealth I a. not, 599:11
   what you can do for country, 799:10

Ask *(continued)*
   where a. is have, 338:1
   who could a. for more, 746:24
   why I have no statue, 88:3
   wilt thou go a. the Mole, 372:12
   you might want to a., 835:13
Asked a lithe lady, 373:9
   for it Georges Dandin, 278:16
   how pearls did grow, 248:2
   no other thing, 545:10
   not come even if a., 670:14
   Oliver a. for more, 496:7
   one another the reason, 200:3
   thief to steal me peach, 373:9
   to be where no storms, 587:1
Askelon, publish it not in the streets of A.,
   11:35
Asking, keep a. over and over, 442:19
   only God had for a., 514:15
   shoot murderer without a. to be paid,
     824:17
   too much, 389:18
Asks a little of us here, 671:3
   of us certain height, 671:3
Asleep, athwart noses as they lie a., 182:22
   awake and a. the same, 64:13
   birds are a. in trees, 365:25
   devil is a., 608:13
   drunk and a. in boots, 686:16
   half a. as they stalk, 576:5
   in lap of legends, 436:23
   is in world of his own, 111:17
   keep it quiet till it falls a., 282:9
   lips of those that are a. to speak, 26:1
   my Mary's a., 379:10
   on furrow sound a., 438:12
   sucks the nurse a., 224:12
   tide moving seems a., 487:2
   under haystack a., 857:17
   very houses seem a., 392:13
   when men were all a., 586:6
   where winds all a., 528:6
Asparagus stumbling block in girl's
   education, 662:6
Aspect, lend the eye terrible a., 192:30
   meet in her a. and eyes, 422:13
   sweet a. of princes, 231:2
Aspects, relations between a. of experience,
   706:1
   smiling a. of life, 567:7
Aspen, as a. leef gan to quake, 133:22
   light quivering a., 397:1
Asphalt and exhaust fumes, 814:3
Aspics' tongues, 214:14
Aspiration, social order and thirsty a.,
   781:14
Aspirations, right a., 66:24
Aspire, by due steps a., 260:13
   light and will a., 173:19
   mind a. to higher things, 163:24
   on what wings date he a., 374:5
   smile we would a. to, 231:2
   there bade me a., 529:18
   to what greater character can mortal a.,
     350:14
Aspired to be and was not, 494:10
Aspires, art a. towards condition of music,
   573:7
Aspiring, all to have a. minds, 170:4

woke and behold it was dream, 282:1
   and found it truth, 439:14
   and found myself famous, 422:5
   one night from dream, 417:12
-wooing, frog a. go, 856:16
wry, currents turn a., 203:33
   leaning all a., 472:1
www, everybody goes A., 810:2
x, Lizzie Borden took ax., 849:10
   to grind, 413:8
xe, book a. for frozen sea inside us, 701:7
   fitter to bruise, 270:8
   laid unto the root, 33:27
   neither hammer nor a., 12:16
xe's edge did try, 276:23
xes, talking of a., 550:6
xiom hatred of bourgeois, 527:8
   old as hills, 654:18
xioms, derives a. from particulars, 166:12
   flies from particulars to a., 166:12
   of mathematics, 577:14
   proved upon our pulses, 440:8
xis of earth sticks out, 473:14
   soft underbelly of A., 667:10
xle, glowing a. doth allay, 260:19
xletree, clot bedded a., 720:9
yenbite of inwyt, 696:*n*1
ylmer, Rose A. whom these eyes, 408:5
yuda, al que madruga Dios a., 862:15
zcan, Chieftain Iffucan of A., 686:20
zores, behind lay gray A., 579:8
   Fiores in the A., 486:22
ztecs by no means would give up, 145:1
zure, arose from out a. main, 318:8
   riding o'er a. realm, 335:13
   ringed with a. world, 484:19
   robe of night, 435:14
zure-lidded, slept an a. sleep, 437:2
zores, devouring green a., 603:10
zurs, dévorant les a. verts, 603:*n*8

B

, emotions from A to B, 738:17
   mark it with B, 857:1
ame, no use to b. looking-glass, 472:16
aa baa baa, 633:17
   baa black sheep, 857:10
aalim, Peor and B., 259:2
abbitt, his name was B., 708:2
abblative, arts b. and scribblative, 405:20
abbled of green fields, 192:27
abling drunkenness, 210:15
   gossip of the air, 209:10
abblings, profane and vain b., 46:29
abe, birth-strangled b., 221:22
   let mighty b. alone, 272:17
   love b. that milks me, 219:23
   pity like new-born b., 219:18
   pretty B. all burning bright, 168:26
   whose birth embraves morn, 272:17
abel, name of it called B., 6:36
   stir of the great B., 348:5
   voices once Tower of B. knew, 563:5
abes, out of the mouth of b., 15:32
abies, anyone who hates b., 690:*n*1
   bit b. in cradles, 491:16
   feel like doing for b., 766:1

Babies *(continued)*
   haven't hair, 729:4
   kill b. make world safer, 824:4
   wars fought by b., 811:9
Baboon who saved comrade, 470:6
Babs knows what and babs knows why, 680:3
Baby and me, 857:1
   bunting, 858:8
   down come b. and all, 592:1
   figure of giant mass, 207:29
   government like big b., 787:8
   looked like mouse, 756:12
   makes his first step, 757:13
   mother laid her b., 508:9
   my b. at my breast, 224:12
   of thee I sing b., 747:3
   rock-a-bye-b., 592:1
   since my b. left me, 831:16
   Tar-b. ain't sayin' nuthin', 593:6
Babylon, ere B. was dust, 428:3
   I was King in B., 594:13
   is fallen, 27:8, 48:32
   king of B. stood at the parting, 29:33
   we're leaving B., 839:6
Babylonish dialect, 270:20
Babylon's Gardens, 850:10
Baby's, know what going on in b. mind,
   747:14
Bacchus ever fair and ever young, 285:10
   that first, 260:16
   with pink eyne, 223:21
Bachelor, die a b., 194:28
   got acquainted with a b., 407:6
   one day b. next grampa, 763:16
   see b. of threescore, 194:10
Bachelors, reformers are b., 601:8
Bachelors' prayer, 706:5
Back, African moon lying on b., 706:7
   and side go bare, 151:10
   at b. from time to time hear, 718:17
   at my b. I always hear, 277:1
   begins to smart, 856:13
   borne me on his b., 206:24
   care not who sees your b., 185:23
   carries sky on b., 505:5
   cast-iron b. with hinge, 543:12
   dagger into b. of neighbor, 698:12
   die with harness on our b., 222:18
   eyes and b. turn upward, 718:18
   far b. in soul horse prances, 707:18
   follow and not see its b., 58:16
   got over Devil's b., 243:8
   I lean b., 820:2
   in a time made simple, 670:17
   mermaid on dolphin's b., 181:8
   never came b. to me, 499:20
   nowhere to come but b., 613:2
   on b. burden of world, 601:3
   on bat's b. I do fly, 230:13
   see what boys in b. room will have, 785:1
   shop entirely free, 152:17
   showed his b. above element, 224:4
   so much upon his b., 239:5
   speed today put b. tomorrow, 161:23
   think of some way to get him b., 758:9
   to Army again, 634:10
   to loneliness of yesterday, 747:18
   to the old drawing board, 766:14
   to you cold father, 696:18

Back *(continued)*
   unto ladder turns his b., 195:30
   wallet at his b., 208:8
Backbone, whale's b., 721:8
Backed like a weasel, 205:9
Back-friend a shoulder-clapper, 174:37
Background, if people keep me in b., 474:1
   slumbers in b. of the times, 381:12
Backing men of genius, 737:2
   plague upon such b., 185:23
Backs, birthrights proudly on b., 177:22
   making beast with two b., 212:21
   not seat on others' b., 588:21
Backslidings, our b. are many, 29:13
Backward, angel of b. look, 468:19
   casting b. glances, 521:16
   dark b. and abysm of time, 229:10
   goes who toils most, 131:15
   halflook over shoulder, 721:10
   I by b. steps move, 279:4
   lean over too far b., 741:17
   life must be understood b., 501:8
   look b. to ancestors, 345:11
   look b. to with pride, 668:21
   look behind assurance, 721:10
   old dog barks b., 670:8
   ran sentences, 762:6
   revolutions never go b., 450:7
   turn b. O Time, 549:8
Backwards, memory that only works b., 552:10
Backyards, cleanliness of clean American b.,
   813:1
Bacon, accept views Cicero Locke B. have
   given, 454:21
   celebrities such as B., 554:11
   not written Hamlet, 435:13
   secretary of Nature and learning, 253:10
Baconian acrostics, 755:13
Bacterial creepers, 780:8
Bad Americans die go to America, 605:1
   as for b. all theirs dies, 70:23
   beginning makes bad ending, 70:18
   better b. epitaph, 203:25
   better for being a little b., 212:10
   bold b. man, 160:18, 230:24
   book as much labor, 741:3
   breeding, 74:12
   can't be all b., 690:*n*1
   cause supported by bad means, 354:13
   charm to make b. good, 212:1
   circumstance makes action good or b.,
   75:29
   details whether good or b., 470:12
   even b. books are books, 819:3
   free press good or b., 790:9
   fustian's so sublimely b., 312:3
   good and b. angel, 240:11
   good and b. of every land, 504:12
   good b. indifferent, 287:9, 332:20
   good b. worst best, 478:4
   good die early b. late, 295:6
   great cases make b. law, 578:4
   grow into likeness of b. men, 78:13
   Harding not a b. man just a slob, 704:3
   hates children can't be all b., 690:3
   he felt b., 809:11
   he is writing b. stuff, 613:18
   herdsmen ruin flocks, 55:16
   I have b. dreams, 203:15

Bad *(continued)*
  immoral what you feel b. after, 754:9
  laws bring about worse, 331:4
  mad b. and dangerous, 418:7
  man who brings b. news, 67:15
  man's good knowing he is b., 494:24
  man's refuge, 59:11
  meaning good or b., 283:20
  means and bad men, 354:13
  men live that they may eat, 72:9
  moral character, 320:24
  neighbor is misfortune, 56:13
  never b. man good service, 345:6
  never good to bring b. news, 223:19
  never good war or b. peace, 320:33
  no benefit in gifts of b. man, 69:24
  no man who laughed b., 433:8
  nothing either good or b., 203:14
  obstinacy in b. cause, 255:15, 332:9
  of this b. world, 653:14
  persecution b. way to plant religion,
    255:16
  phrase good and b. at same time, 739:5
  pious fraud as with b. action, 355:4
  play not please audience, 664:2
  prosperity comes to a b. man, 61:12
  provide b. examples, 273:17
  sad and b. and mad, 494:17
  sad b. brother's name, 569:13
  start assuming that men are b., 143:3
  streak of b. luck, 566:11
  the b. affright, 334:1
  things ill got had b. success, 172:27
  truth told with b. intent, 375:9
  two nations good b., 277:6
  very b. Wizard, 606:16
  war never slays b. man, 68:16
  when b. men combine, 343:15
  when b. she was horrid, 468:4
  when good very good when b. better,
    736:8
  when television is bad, 818:3
  work follers ye, 515:7
  world is grown so b., 173:35
Badge, mercy nobility's true b., 175:13
  of all our tribe, 188:8
  red b. of courage, 655:12
Badine, on ne b. pas avec l'amour, 488:*n*4
Badness flaunted itself, 853:10
  you can get easily, 56:12
Baffled get up begin again, 492:16
  imagination b. by facts, 666:9
  to fight better, 495:15
Baffling, beat down b. foes, 529:1
Bag and baggage, 199:9
  empty b. cannot stand, 319:23
  moon in silver b., 642:1
  pack b. and go below, 862:8
  sealed b. of ducats, 188:24
  to make b. pudding, 861:7
  your old kit-b., 689:22
Bagatelle of transient experience, 624:13
Bagdad-on-the-Subway, 626:10
Bagful of blue Mediterranean, 774:14
Baggage, bag and b., 199:9
Bags, three b. full, 857:10
  two sealed b. of ducats, 188:24
Bah humbug, 497:13
Bahamas, arrived at island of B., 140:4

Bahram that great Hunter, 471:8
Bail, excessive b. nor excessive fines, 361:7
  no b. no demurrer, 367:20
Bailey, bells of Old B., 857:12
  unfortunate Miss B., 384:1
Bait, as a swallowed b., 227:22
  hook well, 194:27
  hook without b., 457:3
  melancholy b., 187:22
  your b. of falsehood, 202:30
Baited like eagles, 186:22
Baits, good news b., 269:13
Bake me a cake, 857:1
Baked, funeral b. meats, 201:10
  in a pie, 858:12
  me too brown, 551:3
  stayed home and b. cookies, 840:7
Baker, butcher b. candlestick-maker, 860:8
  not from benevolence of b., 338:13
  Street irregulars, 616:17
Baker's man, 857:1
Bakestone, cat upon hot b., 281:11
Balaam, ass said unto B., 9:22
Balance between order and aspiration, 781:14
  not weigh faith in b., 595:13
  of power, 304:16
  or reconciliation of opposite, 403:11
  redress b. of the Old, 390:1
  small dust of the b., 28:6
  uncertain b. of proud time, 165:19
Balanced and Miltonic style, 588:7
  Film with Film, 547:2
Balances, weighed in the b., 30:6
Balbec, editions of B. and Palmyra, 336:5
Bald, fight between two b. men, 753:5
  now your brow is b. John, 379:4
  old b. cheater Time, 237:11
  otherwise b. unconvincing narrative,
    565:18
  wish b. eagle not chosen, 320:24
Baldness, felicity on far side of b., 636:11
Baldwin simply hole in air, 765:10
Bales, down with costly b., 481:23
Balfour Declaration, 593:2
Ball, balm scepter and b., 193:16
  earthly b. a peopled garden, 364:3
  great b. of fire, 723:5
  one fish b., 534:7
  take me out to b. game, 685:10
Ballad, I love a b. in print, 228:31
  in the street, 454:27
  to mistress' eyebrow, 198:25
Ballad-mongers, meter b., 186:6
Ballads, permitted to make all b., 294:13
  songs and snatches, 565:7
  stuck about wall, 252:29
Ballast, more sail than b., 292:4
  no better b. than business, 515:20
Balloon of the mind, 639:2
Balloonman, little lame b., 739:11
Balloons, faces rise like b., 801:13
  have b. pass over to Europe, 413:7
Ballot, joining political party casting b.,
    694:6
  natural right to b., 522:2
  paper you drop in b. box, 506:6
  pathway to b. box, 503:9
  rap at b. box, 450:12
  stronger than bullet, 474:8

Ballplayer, many years not successful as b.,
    730:15
Ballroom, not at ease in a b., 539:8
  war not quadrille in b., 521:14
Balls, elliptical billiard b., 565:16
Balm in Gilead, 29:9
  not the b. the scepter, 193:16
  of hurt minds, 220:16
  the hydroptic earth hath drunk,
    234:20
  tropic for your b., 741:10
  wash b. from anointed king, 179:24
Balmy sleep, 305:23
  spring brings back b. warmth, 94:13
Baloney, it's still b., 663:15
Baltimore, gore that flecked streets of B.,
    574:6
Bam, under the b., 719:21
Bamboo, under the b. tree, 719:21
'Ban 'Ban Ca-Caliban, 229:32
Ban, in every voice every b., 374:7
  spreading ruin scattering b., 464:6
Banal Eldorado of old bachelors, 524:15
Banality of evil, 773:5
  was only camouflage, 796:4
Bananas as bait, 755:11
  what price b., 817:10
Banbury Cross, 858:14
Band, heaven-born b., 390:13
  no soldier in gallant b., 566:3
  of angels, 863:3
  of brothers, 193:20
  pilgrim b., 555:4
  playing somewhere, 630:4
  River City gonna have Boys B., 764:10
  speckled b., 617:5
Bandersnatch, frumious B., 551:10
Bands, brass b. barrel organs, 699:16
  dissolve political b., 357:2
  drew them with b. of love, 30:19
  end of life cancels b., 186:16
  her hands as b., 24:23
  iron b., 466:7
  loose the b. of Orion, 15:10
  pursue Culture in b., 627:13
Bandusian, O fount B., 100:6
Bane of all genius, 427:13
  precious b., 264:23
  suspicion b. of good society, 354:7
Baneful spirit of party, 350:9
Banes, o'er his white b., 854:8
Bang, Kiss Kiss B. B., 805:4
  not with b. but whimper, 719:7
  now animal is dead, 662:17
  the drum slowly, 854:*n*1
Banish all the world, 185:32
  pleasures b. pain, 304:11
  plump Jack, 185:32
  thief you cannot b., 771:14
  think not king did b. thee, 179:4
  understanding from his mind, 71:*n*3
  wisdom, 82:28
  with night we b. sorrow, 239:11
Banished, alone a b. man, 843:12
  find moral in narrative be b., 560:13
  yet true-born Englishman, 179:7
Banishment, bitter bread of b., 179:23
  no sentence of b., 786:14
Banjo on my knee, 538:13

Banjos, batter on your b., 681:14
Bank and shoal of time, 219:16
    breathes upon b. of violets, 208:25
    broke b. at Monte Carlo, 597:9
    contemplate entangled b., 470:2
    cried all the way to b., 805:10
    curls done up with b. notes, 503:12
    grass b. beyond, 535:16
    many people already b. on it, 796:5
    moonlight sleeps upon this b., 190:5
    waly up the b., 854:10
    whereon wild thyme blows, 181:12
Bankers schoolmasters clergymen, 637:17
Bankrupt of life, 283:9
Banks, allegory on b. of Nile, 367:10
    and braes o' bonny Doon, 378:21
    Brignal b., 397:16
    newspaper runs b., 646:18
    o' Loch Lomond, 847:15
    of Wabash far away, 656:7
    Tiber trembled underneath b., 195:15
    time river without b., 852:3
    vast surplus in b., 414:1
Banner, blood-red b. streams, 416:2
    over me was love, 25:16
    royal b. and all quality, 214:8
    that b. in sky, 473:3
    torn but flying, 421:18
    wear it like b. for proud, 762:14
    with strange device, 466:11
    yet Freedom yet thy b., 421:18
Banners, all thy b. wave, 408:20
    confusion on thy b. wait, 335:11
    flout the sky, 218:25
    hang b. on outward walls, 222:14
    terrible as an army with b., 25:27
Banquet, before we begin our b., 842:10
    behave in life as at b., 112:17
    hall deserted, 412:8
    partaken in anxiety, 60:15
    sated with b. of life, 93:13
Banqueting, speak of b. delights, 232:1
    upon borrowing, 32:31
Baptism enslaved me, 603:19
    suffering may be b., 512:22
Baptist's, John B. head in a charger,
    36:12
Baptizing in name of Father, 38:12
Bar, back of b. in solo game, 673:9
    crossed the b., 487:4
    gold b. of Heaven, 541:26
    harbor b. moaning, 513:23
    no moaning of b., 487:2
    to B. as very young man, 564:21
Barabbas a publisher, 425:10
    stock of B., 189:26
    was a robber, 41:37
Barak, arise B. and lead captivity captive,
    10:30
Barb in arrow of childhood, 606:11
Barbara, name was B. Allen, 853:28
Barbarian, meets need of b. man, 613:11
    Scythian bond nor free, 46:3
    weeping above dead, 554:4
Barbarians Philistines Populace, 531:11
    the B. are coming, 628:5
Barbaric omens, 713:13
    pearl and gold, 264:25
    sound my b. yawp, 519:22

Barbarism and despotism, 359:9
    document of b., 733:5
    fanaticism to b. one step, 331:27
    fastnesses of ancient b., 534:9
    from b. to degeneration, 577:11
    my native land prey to b., 118:4
    war is at best b., 522:14
Barbarous dissonance, 261:4
    in beauty stooks arise, 587:11
    multitude, 188:26
    triumph o'er her b. foes, 323:14
    woman more b. than man, 589:4
Barber, imprudently married b., 336:12
Bard, hear voice of the B., 373:16
    here dwelt, 318:10
    is envious of bard, 56:8
    music sent up by lover and b., 494:5
    old or modern b., 260:15
    whom none to praise, 392:*n*1
Bards, black and unknown b., 656:18
    gild lapses of time, 435:16
    have a share of honor, 55:1
    in fealty to Apollo, 435:19
    name me among lyric b., 99:2
    of Passion, 438:9
    saints heroes, 528:4
    sublime, 466:13
Bare, back and side go b., 151:10
    Ben Bulben's head, 643:4
    bodkin, 203:33
    cupboard was b., 859:13
    Goya of the b. field, 829:3
    imagination of feast, 179:6
    let little colt go b., 861:12
    looked on Beauty b., 735:8
    old men's heads b., 729:4
    on b. earth he lies, 285:12
    poor b. forked animal, 216:30
    ruined choirs, 226:24
    trees turn b., 818:10
Bare-bosomed, press close b. night, 519:8
Barefaced poverty drove me to verses, 101:13
Barefoot boy, 468:9
    dance b. on wedding day, 175:27
    dervishes, 453:18
    him that makes shoes go b., 148:*n*10
Barère's, not read B. Memoirs, 448:16
Bares, foeman b. steel tarantara, 564:4
Bargain catch cold and starve, 225:10
    in the way of b., 186:8
    necessity never good b., 319:11
    never better b. driven, 163:22
Bargaining, collective b. bilateral monopoly,
    707:1
    for wages, 682:9
Barge, Arthur from the b., 486:12
    drag the slow b., 348:23
    like burnished throne, 223:14
Bark, all dogs of Europe b., 775:15
    and bite, 303:17
    attendant sail, 311:16
    band of exiles moored b., 431:21
    bitter b. burning clove, 669:17
    fatal and perfidious b., 261:21
    feet locked upon rough b., 825:5
    hark dogs do b., 861:5
    is on the sea, 422:26
    let no dog b., 187:20
    moor b. with two anchors, 102:19

Bark *(continued)*
    off shot the specter b., 400:5
    seal on cold ice with piteous b., 436:19
    see they b. at me, 217:5
    star to every wandering b., 227:17
    watchdog's honest b., 423:11
    worse than bite, 252:16
    yond tall anchoring b., 217:18
Barked, dogs b. far from river, 751:7
Barking, crowing of cocks and b. of dogs,
    59:20
Barkis is willin', 497:30
Barks, Hylax b. in doorway, 95:26
    Nicean b. of yore, 478:2
    old dog b. backward, 670:8
Barley, land of wheat and b., 10:3
Barleycorn, inspiring bold John B., 379:19
    John B. got up again, 378:16
Barn, hay creaking to b., 800:11
    jackass can kick b. down, 697:8
    sit in a b., 859:12
    stack or the b. door, 259:13
Barnaby, like B. Rudge, 514:19
Barns, neither reap nor gather into b., 34:17
Barometer, poet b. but also weather, 773:2
Barrage, chemical b. against life, 777:2
Barred on account of race, 800:4
    recognize good but be b., 66:2
Barrel, beat an empty b., 685:3
    inspiration not stored up in b., 789:7
    of meal wasted not, 12:27
    organs, 699:16
Barrel-house kings, 685:3
Barren, acre of b. ground, 229:8
    after summer b. winter, 172:9
    among b. crags, 481:7
    bosom starves birth, 334:5
    bride, 310:5
    buds of b. flowers, 569:1
    earth b. as moon, 680:14
    imagination cold and b., 344:4
    leave this b. spot, 409:4
    live a b. sister all your life, 180:18
    small model of b. earth, 179:28
    superfluity of words, 295:10
    'tis all b., 333:4
    weep b. tears, 428:4
Barrenness, nature in its b., 703:14
Barricade, disputed b., 724:17
Barrier, escaped b. of your teeth, 52:25
Barriers against tyranny of political, 462:12
Barroom floor, 584:6
    Gideon Bibles not in b., 730:1
Bars, contentions are like b. of a castle, 22:11
    I hang around in b., 843:1
    implacable iron b., 725:11
    nor iron b. a cage, 276:4
Barter, government founded on b., 344:14
    that horn, 639:14
Bartlett's Familiar Quotations, 665:10
Base, army would be b. rabble, 344:17
    authority from others' books, 176:20
    battle removes all b., 708:13
    beetles o'er his b., 202:8
    contagious clouds, 184:36
    fall to the b. earth, 179:22
    first time caught off b., 754:6
    fly from firm b., 397:11
    keep down b. in man, 486:8

Base *(continued)*
    laws of servitude began, 282:19
    like the b. Indian, 215:13
    limps after in b. imitation, 179:10
    men being in love, 213:15
    of b. passions fear most accursed, 172:1
    sale of chapmen's tongues, 176:27
    scorning the b. degrees, 195:30
    small things make b. men proud,
      172:16
    to what b. uses return, 206:25
Baseball breaks your heart, 833:4
    chalk mark b. score, 584:6
    eternal importance like b., 708:3
    in b. don't know nothing, 814:9
    pelicans old men in b. caps, 797:9
    to know America learn b., 776:16
Baseless fabric of this vision, 230:9
Basely, spend that shortness b., 187:3
Baseness to write fair, 207:6
    we will smite, 652:2
Baser, fellows of b. sort, 42:16
Basest, our b. beggars, 216:15
Bashful, maiden of b. fifteen, 367:29
    stream hath seen God, 272:n2
Basic element in Constitution, 705:10
    hero of books labor, 649:5
Basilisk is sure to kill, 307:16
Basin, elliptical b. in hands of acolytes, 826:6
    stare in b., 775:9
Basis, no b. more reliable, 841:13
    of democratic state, 81:6
Basket, eggs in one b., 156:34, 561:15
    terrorist and policeman from same b.,
      612:12
    watch that b., 561:15
Bassarid, blatant B. of Boston, 569:11
Bassoon, flute violin b., 485:10
    heard the loud b., 399:15
Bastard, soft b. Latin, 423:4
    substitute Anesthesia, 625:1
    truth comes like b., 262:15
    welcome pommy b. to God's earth,
      843:2
Bastards, now gods stand up for b., 215:27
Bastille, prisoners in B. couldn't have touched
    them, 790:10
    three days after B. Day, 818:4
Bat beats about in caverns, 809:2
    black b. night, 485:8
    Casey at the b., 630:3
    ere b. hath flown, 221:6
    mind is like b., 809:2
    twinkle little b., 550:12
    weak-eyed b., 337:2
    wool of b. tongue of dog, 221:21
Bataillons, formez vos b., 383:8
Bate, nor b. one jot of heart, 263:16
Bated breath and whispering humbleness,
    188:9
Bath, blood b., 702:6
    sore labor's b., 220:16
Bathe in fiery floods, 211:23
    in the blank wake, 830:16
Bathed in Poem of Sea, 603:10
    like eagles lately b., 186:22
Bathes, common air b. globe, 519:3
Bathing, caught Whigs b., 459:8
    large b. machine, 565:4

Bathroom, wicked man in b. cupboard,
    797:11
Bathrooms, well-equipped American b.,
    745:8
Baths, army no private b., 716:9
    grand flights Sunday b., 687:13
    of all western stars, 481:14
    uplifting thoughts in b., 745:8
Batman, not Hercules but B., 826:16
Baton, French soldier carries marshal's b.,
    388:18
Bat's, on b. back I do fly, 230:13
    thin b. squeak of sexuality, 766:8
Bats, bawk of b., 696:16
    cast idols to moles and b., 26:12
    do b. eat cats, 549:11
Battalions, God for big b., 275:n1
    God with strongest b., 330:13
    sorrows come in b., 206:8
Battening our flocks, 261:16
Batter my heart, 236:11
    on your banjos, 681:14
Battered Caravanserai, 471:7
    cottage b. and decayed, 258:3
    few thousand b. books, 709:5
    tattered ears and b. head, 825:6
    wrecked old man, 521:4
Battering sandal, 587:13
Battery, assault and b. of wind, 639:13
Battiades, tomb of B., 85:13
Battle and the breeze, 408:16
    be the b. queen of yore, 574:6
    borne the b., 477:4
    Britain wins last b., 667:7
    common perils of b., 556:3
    cry of Freedom, 522:9
    day is past, 538:10
    drunk delight of b., 481:9
    each b. sees other's face, 193:11
    far-flung b. line, 535:1
    first blow half the b., 342:21
    flags were furled, 481:21
    foremost in b. Mary Ambree, 853:25
    France has lost b., 728:7
    from b. and murder, 50:13
    harness like soldiers, 667:14
    haven't lost b. yet, 792:20
    life a b. and sojourning, 115:6
    life of b. good, 627:3
    marriage field of b., 598:5
    most magnificent competition, 708:13
    no b. ever won, 748:11
    noise of b. rolled, 486:11
    not to the strong, 24:30, 353:2
    nothing except b. lost, 388:21
    of first rank, 451:10
    of Jericho, 862:26
    of Waterloo won on fields, 389:6
    one b. or by degrees, 354:15
    puts armor off b. done, 467:20
    see b. from castle, 92:n12
    see front o' b. lour, 380:10
    set Uriah in forefront of b., 12:2
    shout, 473:3
    sing tongue the glorious b., 129:n1
    smelleth the b. afar off, 15:15
    so melancholy as b. won, 388:21
    sons met in b. five times, 789:9
    Te Deum before b. begun, 449:14

Battle *(continued)*
    to the strong, 612:23
    Troy walls famed in b., 97:9
    we b. for the Lord, 615:14
    who prepare himself to b., 44:21
Battled, dream of b. fields, 397:7
Battlefield heart of man, 525:13
    is holy ground, 424:12
    met on great b., 476:7
Battlements, entrance under my b., 219:11
    fate sits on dark b., 384:15
    towers and b. it sees, 259:15
Battle's, no war or b. sound, 258:18
    when b. lost and won, 218:23
Battles, feelings beings books events b.,
    768:11
    fight our country's b., 848:17
    he lives not long who b. immortals,
      52:27
    lost in spirit in which won, 519:4
    O God of b., 193:17
    sieges fortunes, 212:28
    though he won all b., 820:13
    transacted by mechanism, 434:2
    uneasy sense of b. won, 808:2
    when someone b. hard, 53:5
    witness I have fought b., 282:5
Bauble, pleased with b. still, 311:11
    shallow b. boats, 207:23
Baudelaire, sedulous ape to B., 599:9
Baukunst eine erstarrte Musik nenne, 364:n1
Bawd, call b. a b., 84:n1
    now my old b. is dead, 642:19
    opportunity is great b., 319:13
Bawds, clocks the tongues of b., 184:23
Bawdy strings of elders, 687:6
Bawk of bats, 696:16
Bawl, I began to b., 746:11
Bawn, bred en b. in brier-patch, 593:8
Bay, brothers call from b., 528:5
    China 'crost the b., 633:13
    cliffs vast in tranquil b., 530:19
    deep-mouthed welcome, 423:11
    like b. of Portugal, 199:30
    look of b. mare shames silliness, 519:2
    no fetters in B. State, 468:5
    rather be dog and b. moon, 197:8
    reeking into Cadiz B., 492:6
    San Francisco b. center of prosperity,
      502:17
    sings in boat on b., 482:15
    somebody bet on b., 538:14
    spreading himself like a green b. tree,
      17:7
Bayed the whispering wind, 342:3
Baying, hear b. of pack, 730:12
Bayonets, by push of b., 330:10
    leave at point of b., 366:16
    throne of b., 623:10
Bays, lingering b., 323:15
    no b. to crown it, 250:15
Be, appear to b. and appear not to b., 78:8
    better not to b., 480:5
    bold, 161:11
    business of life is to b., 572:7
    cheerful while you are alive, 3:8
    first say what you would b., 112:16
    he is or was or has to b., 317:1
    let b. b. finale of seem, 686:15

Beast *(continued)*
   maw-crammed b., 494:8
   more subtile than any b., 6:3
   multitude b. of many heads, 100:*n*13
   no b. so fierce but knows pity, 173:32
   no more, 205:35
   of prey in aristocratic races, 589:13
   only b. in arena the crowd, 645:6
   only connect b. and monk, 684:3
   owest b. no hide, 216:30
   Pellinore followed questing b., 139:2
   people a many-headed b., 100:21
   people resemble wild b., 143:4
   righteous man regardeth the life of his b.,
     21:22
   second b. like a calf, 48:16
   serpent subtlest b., 267:26
   strangest b. ever he saw, 139:2
   that wants discourse of reason, 201:7
   third b. had a face as a man, 48:16
   what rough b., 639:7
   with many heads butts me, 224:29
   would act angel acts b., 280:5
Beastie, tim'rous b., 377:10
Beasties, long-leggety b., 847:9
Beastly, how b. bourgeois is, 707:14
   to the Germans, 753:9
Beast's, man's life cheap as b., 216:15
Beasts, ape vilest of b., 87:14
   ask the b., 14:11
   browse on their herbs, 4:10
   coupling of b., 720:16
   fly to wilderness, 82:1
   four b. had six wings, 48:16
   giant of b., 236:2
   invent new b. so terrible, 442:16
   judgment fled to b., 196:30
   man lived with birds and b., 82:27
   nature teaches b. to know friends, 224:19
   of all wild b. preserve me from tyrant,
     237:12
   of the forest creep forth, 19:11
   pair of very strange b., 200:6
   shall be at peace with thee, 13:39
   small and great b., 19:11
   transform ourselves into b., 213:26
   upon earth draw us to kingdom, 117:5
Beasts', not God's not b., 494:14
Beat an empty barrel, 685:3
   a path to your door, 454:*n*1
   Blake b. upon wall, 642:11
   down baffling foes, 529:1
   downward b. thy wings, 92:*n*13
   earth with unfettered foot, 99:18
   generation, 810:1
   gold to airy thinness b., 235:2
   heart hear her and b., 485:12
   him when he sneezes, 550:7
   his breast, 399:15
   man is b. when goes for broke, 810:*n*1
   me and hammer me, 681:13
   my people to pieces, 26:15
   our hearts continue to b., 838:13
   so we b. on, 746:9
   sound trumpet b. drums, 318:19
   sound trumpets b. drums, 285:9
   swords into plowshares, 26:11
   the bush, 147:11, 246:19
   the drum slowly, 854:18

Beat *(continued)*
   the Dutch, 846:21
   the ground, 260:23
   they b. and Voice b., 621:1
   Turk b. a Venetian, 215:14
   upon whorled ear, 587:2
   water they b., 223:14
   waves of science b. in vain, 524:2
   with fist instead of stick, 270:14
   you b. your pate, 310:17
Beaten at all points, 74:9
   poop was b. gold, 223:14
   till they know, 271:14
   up by secret police, 809:11
Beatific, enjoyed in vision b., 264:22
   vision, 129:*n*4
Beating, disastrous b. of wings, 656:5
   got a hell of a b., 703:6
   in void luminous wings, 532:12
   way for rising sun, 761:17
Beatitude, ninth b., 310:16
Beatles', between Chatterley ban and B. first
   LP, 810:6
Beatrice a light between truth and intellect,
   131:13
Beats about in caverns, 809:2
   all lies you can invent, 375:9
   back envious siege, 179:13
   drum b. my approach tells thee I come,
    249:2
   light b. on throne, 485:16
   upon high shore of world, 193:16
Beaumont, not bid B. lie, 238:5
   rare B., 247:11
Beaut, when I make mistake it's a b., 697:1
Beauteous, commands the b. files, 279:6
   dear b. death, 279:9
   evening calm and free, 392:15
   eye of heaven to garnish, 178:14
   idiot speaks, 845:21
   kindness not b. looks, 175:36
   love all b. things, 586:7
   pearls in b. ladies' eyes, 176:14
   prove a b. flower, 183:11
Beauties, glory of honors b. wits, 234:17
   in small proportions b. see, 238:14
   meaner b. of the night, 232:16
Beautifier, rank great b., 452:8
Beautiful a faery's child, 439:4
   all b. drifts away, 637:19
   all b. sentiments in world, 515:23
   all once so b. is dead, 725:2
   all things bright and b., 508:7
   and ineffectual angel, 532:12
   and therefore to be wooed, 172:2
   art for sake of b., 461:16
   as the sky, 520:13
   be b. and be sad, 524:17
   beauty comes from b. blood b. brain,
    518:9
   beauty making b. old rime, 227:11
   black is b., 852:13
   changes as forest, 808:13
   childish but divinely b., 381:13
   dancing most b. art, 617:23
   dreamer, 539:4
   face candid brow, 612:3
   find each other it's b., 738:20
   for spacious skies, 616:3

Beautiful *(continued)*
   friendship, 782:12
   from perceived harmony, 402:19
   how b. they are, 402:3
   how b. they stand, 431:19
   how b. they stood, 431:*n*1
   human reason is b., 786:14
   I am Negro and b., 762:8
   identification with b., 431:9
   in faces dress thoughts, 622:12
   may it be b. before me, 856:2
   mind more b. than earth, 391:13
   most b. among gods, 56:5
   most b. lady, 662:9
   most b. most useless, 517:7
   most b. mouth in world, 315:11
   most b. thing is mysterious, 683:5
   nothing b. makes complete sense, 735:17
   nothing in houses not b., 557:4
   oh what a b. mornin', 744:4
   overmuch, 639:9
   palace B., 281:19
   pea-green boat, 499:15
   people, 835:5
   poetry most b. mode, 530:11
   Pussy you are, 499:15
   quarto page, 367:27
   sacrifices of friendship b., 655:7
   scorn looks b., 210:5
   small is b., 787:14
   so awful ugly becomes b., 521:10
   so various so b. so new, 531:2
   something b. for God, 785:5
   sorrow more b., 438:18
   soup, 551:4
   Sredni Vashtar the B., 655:6
   swindles b. and simple, 626:7
   thing raises man, 143:10
   things adorn world, 629:16
   this is b. country, 447:5
   time of young love, 382:7
   too b. to live, 496:18
   true words are not b., 59:21
   uncut hair of graves, 518:19
   upon the mountains, 28:18
   what is b. is moral, 527:10
   when I was b., 150:13
   wise and b., 528:4
   women indisputably b. or ugly, 315:2
   wonderful world, 535:7
   words are not true, 59:21
Beauty, addition of strangeness to b., 573:12
   adventure art, 624:17
   all b. comes from blood and brain, 518:9
   all that b. all that wealth, 334:15
   and high degree, 724:12
   and majesty of ships, 467:8
   and virtue rarely together, 132:15
   and wisdom rarely conjoined, 109:10
   appreciation of earth's b., 686:7
   as b. not great star, 678:18
   as feel it indescribable, 629:2
   as much b. as could die, 237:22
   barbarous in b. stooks, 587:11
   beholding b. with eye of mind, 76:9
   bereft of b., 176:1
   body's b. lives, 687:5
   born of own despair, 640:15
   bought by judgment of eye, 176:27

Beauty *(continued)*

brute b. and valor, 587:8
by b. and by fear, 391:6
calls, 294:11
center of all b., 818:5
cheat for sake of b., 678:3
clad in b. of thousand stars, 171:1
come near your b. with nails, 172:5
concept of mathematical b., 623:13
convenience comfort, 852:1
creation of B., 480:1
crieth in attic, 558:9
daily b. in his life, 215:4
dead black chaos, 173:26
Death mother of b., 686:18
definition of b., 402:18
doth of itself persuade, 175:2
draws with single hair, 309:7
dreamed life b., 504:20
elevation and b., 532:9
ever ancient and ever new, 119:11
exists in mind, 330:5
extent of b. and power, 447:17
facts in naked simple b., 169:20
fatal gift of b., 421:11
flattered upon b., 315:2
for ashes, 28:31
fruits of life and b., 373:11
gift of God, 79:12
give b. in the inward soul, 76:6
good nature more amiable than b.,
    302:14
grows familiar to lover, 301:20
half mad with b., 556:9
half the b. you possess, 385:15
has not been fathomed, 525:12
Helen's b. in brow of Egypt, 182:3
her b. and her chivalry, 420:16
I died for B., 545:4
ill layer-up of b., 194:1
images of b., 76:9
in all things, 441:4
in art economy is b., 585:16
in b. it is finished, 856:2
in eye of beholder, 606:9
in naked b. more adorned, 266:20
is a mystery, 707:16
is a simple passion, 821:12
is there b. in Sodom, 525:13
is there in truth no b., 250:8
is truth, 438:5
is vain, 23:31
keep back b., 587:17
know b. as b., 58:8
left b. on shore, 452:17
light from her own b., 429:15
like hers is genius, 542:2
little concerned with b., 577:4
looked on B. bare, 735:8
love b. truth we seek, 428:17
love built on b., 235:14
loved your b., 637:5
lust not after her b., 21:6
makes b. because outlet, 680:1
making beautiful old rime, 227:11
mathematics supreme b., 660:12
momentary in mind, 687:5
must be truth, 439:13
mystery of b., 636:15

Beauty *(continued)*

Nature's brag, 261:9
Nature's coin, 261:8
ne'er enjoys, 312:8
neither heat limb nor b., 211:19
no excellent b., 168:12
no spring nor summer b., 235:18
notion of absolute b., 76:8
of aged face, 693:4
of good old cause, 392:14
of great machine, 712:18
of holiness, 16:25
of inflections, 687:7
of innuendoes, 687:7
of minstrels' lyre, 656:18
of own b. mind diseased, 421:20
of the lilies, 513:19
of world has edges, 700:8
one's b. another's ugliness, 456:2
orators dumb when b. pleadeth, 175:7
own excuse for being, 453:4
perception of b. moral test, 505:6
pierce like pain, 676:3
power of Greek in b., 531:9
principal b. in a building, 258:9
provoketh thieves, 197:34
renown which riches or b. confer, 95:2
sat B. in my lap, 603:17
sense of pity b. pain, 611:16
sex and b. inseparable, 707:17
she walks in b., 422:13
Sleeping B. wakes up, 815:8
smother up his b., 184:36
so long as b. shall be, 117:10
sold for old man's gold, 654:1
source of b. is in itself, 115:11
stands in admiration only, 268:20
stone to b. grew, 452:19
struggle for superhuman b., 833:12
sublimely pure, 660:12
such b. as you master, 227:11
such seems your b. still, 227:10
sufficient end, 639:9
take winds of March with b., 228:27
teaches such b. as woman's eye, 177:4
terrible and awful, 525:12
terrible b. is born, 639:4
that breaks hearts, 676:16
that comes from happiness, 527:1
that dost consecrate, 427:15
that must die, 438:16
their b. might declare, 400:13
thing of b. joy, 436:8
though injurious, 269:9
thy b. is to me, 478:2
'tisn't b. nor good talk, 635:17
to mind shameful to heart b., 525:13
too rich for use, 182:25
troubled by this b., 573:5
truly blent, 209:8
unadorned, 290:21
unmask her b. to moon, 201:22
vast vulgar meretricious b., 746:5
what b. is never be said, 629:2
where b. has no ebb, 637:7
where perhaps some b. lies, 259:15
whose b. past change, 587:10
wit high birth, 208:12
with him b. slain, 173:26

Beauty *(continued)*

withdraws mind from love of b., 62:10
without extravagance, 74:1
without grace, 457:3
without vanity, 419:10
witty b. a power, 541:20
worship in b. of holiness, 16:25
wrought out from within, 573:5
Beauty's, age will fade b. flower, 151:3
blazon of sweet b. best, 227:11
but skin deep, 231:20
ensign yet is crimson, 184:16
none of B. daughters, 422:23
nothing but beginning of Terror, 677:4
orient deep, 253:13
parallels in b. brow, 226:17
rose might never die, 225:27
sing smoothly with thy b. silent music,
    232:2
sorrow more beautiful than B. self,
    438:18
thy b. field, 225:28
Beaux, where none are b., 329:25
Beaver, cultivate a b., 741:2
on account of his B. Hat, 500:3
young Harry with b. on, 186:23
Became, first object looked upon b., 521:1
first tutor to a lunatic, 661:3
nothing b. him like leaving, 219:8
Because, God not a b., 631:9
I do not hope, 719:9
it is bitter because it is my heart, 655:17
it is there, 635:*n*2
Beckoning, open road is b., 834:4
shadows dire, 260:24
what b. ghost, 309:27
Beckons, Longing leans and b., 515:17
Becks, nods and b., 259:9
our minds to fellowship, 436:10
Become a kind of machine, 470:11
a saint, 824:7
all that may b. a man, 219:21
I have b. lost name, 791:9
ignorant man again, 687:21
let each b. all capable of, 434:9
man to behave toward government,
    505:15
not b. King's First Minister, 667:9
other dreamers, 521:5
them with half so good grace, 211:10
vilest things b. themselves, 223:15
you have b. like us, 771:12
Becomes, beak grips her she b., 824:9
blessed youth b. as aged, 211:19
that which is not b., 116:9
throned monarch better, 189:19
Becoming, growing and a b., 531:15
limit of b. mirth, 176:28
present gone instant of b., 582:1
some b. men we wanted to marry, 830:9
Becoming-conscious, emotion source of b.,
    675:13
Bed, a b. Clerk Saunders said, 854:3
and so to b., 288:2, 692:13
be blest that I lie on, 274:20
be in b. and sleep not, 746:16
born in b. with a lady, 678:13
brimstone b., 405:22
by night, 342:10

Behoved that there should be sin, 133:4
Behovely, sin is B., 133:*n*1
Being a little flesh a little breath, 115:1
   all things come from b., 59:3
   and happening, 776:15
   anxiety of finite b., 712:8
   art has reason for b., 457:9
   Beauty own excuse for b., 453:4
   broodin' over b. dog, 592:6
   chain of b., 457:10
   changes control our b., 481:5
   circle of potential b., 581:3
   currents of Universal B., 454:15
   depth ground of all b. God, 712:6
   each organic b. is striving, 469:15
   ends of B., 463:17
   ennobled by own exertions, 382:24
   human b. more or less, 796:2
   human b. through descent from group,
     613:14
   intellectual b., 265:4
   let there always be b., 58:7
   merely b. there means something, 818:12
   move and have our b., 42:19
   no creature whose inward b., 513:11
   offered B. for it, 545:10
   perfection in becoming intelligent b.,
     127:6
   place in chain of b., 457:10
   pleasing anxious b., 334:24
   receives reproach of b., 227:21
   things come into b., 300:7
   unbearable lightness of b., 823:13
   what she is, 638:1
   woman behave like full human b., 830:7
Being-forever, nature assures b., 773:4
Being's, my B. worth, 547:2
Beings, all b. thou shouldst not mourn, 87:2
   are honey of this Self, 51:21
   burn books burn human b., 442:10
   distances between human b., 677:9
   human b. ever realize life, 750:1
   human b. into machines, 510:9
   human b. living in den, 77:14
   new b. on this earth, 469:10
   of mind are not of clay, 421:8
   rights over human b., 364:18
   three b. worthy respect, 524:20
   which compose nature, 366:13
Beld, now your brow is b. John, 379:4
Belfry, clock in b. strikes one, 553:10
Belgium's capital gathered then, 420:16
Belgrave Square, hearts beat in B., 564:20
Belial, sons of B., 264:13
   thus B. counseled, 265:7
Belican, bill hold more than b., 685:9
Belie all corners of world, 225:17
   state one fact b. another, 455:6
Belief, final b. in fiction, 687:15
   genuine b. seems to have left us, 521:11
   help create fact, 582:9
   illogical b. in improbable, 691:9
   not within prospect of b., 218:32
   ripened into faith, 395:6
   that God created Universe, 127:8
Beliefs, bombs shook men out of b., 644:13
   dead ideas and b., 540:10
   employees required to state b., 756:15
   forsaken b., 530:10

Beliefs *(continued)*
   keep as many old b. as we can, 582:20
   less than chaff, 612:7
   more b. than can digest, 617:25
Believe a lie, 376:*n*1
   also in me, 41:26
   an expert, 98:11
   as it is convenient let us b., 105:7
   attempted to b. Matilda, 653:9
   because it is impossible, 116:*n*7
   children b. in good family angels,
     769:12
   courage not to b., 512:3
   deep in heart b., 852:6
   don't b. no sich person, 497:10
   easier to b. than deny, 566:20
   good tidings to people who b., 121:1
   her though I know she lies, 228:2
   I b. and take it, 152:3
   I b. in God the Father, 50:3
   if you b. clap hands, 621:18
   in freedom regardless of form, 688:20
   in God yearn for His existence, 631:3
   in incomprehensibility of God, 445:9
   in Israel you must b. in miracles, 710:15
   in life, 648:16
   in the life to come, 773:14
   in the forest and meadow and night,
     507:29
   know what he ought to b., 129:7
   leads you to b. a lie, 376:9
   Lord I b., 38:27
   man ready to b. what is told, 109:5
   me if all those endearing young charms,
     411:12
   me my country 'tis of you, 739:15
   men b. what they wish, 91:23
   more firmly desperately b., 693:15
   my own stories, 416:17
   ne'er b. do what you please, 375:14
   never b. God plays dice, 683:14
   no evil till evil's done, 276:7
   not know what safely b., 578:9
   oft repeating they b. 'em, 297:4
   only possibilities, 256:1
   own thought genius, 455:7
   people are good, 822:9
   rather b. fables in legends, 167:21
   rather b. God not exist, 461:17
   Robert who has tried it, 98:*n*4
   sailors won't b. it, 398:6
   Sisyphus happy, 790:2
   they half b. in it, 59:4
   to be evil and unjust, 712:5
   to doubt or b. everything, 603:2
   undesirable to b. proposition, 661:1
   we have only to b., 693:15
   what he can, 470:12
   what I said about Buchenwald, 779:15
   wisdom to b. heart, 629:1
   with all my soul, 515:1
   woman or epitaph, 419:16
   ye b. in God, 41:26
   ye do by no means b., 122:11
Believed, against hope b. in hope, 42:43
   always everywhere by all, 119:23
   because he b. in his God, 30:9
   I wept and I b., 387:3
   juggling fiends no more b., 222:22

Believed *(continued)*
   not seen yet b., 41:43
   to be b. because absurd, 116:19
   truth never understood and not b.,
     373:4
   what is least known, 152:15
Believer, above all a b. in culture, 531:12
   like every good b., 741:2
   not satisfied with appearances, 761:6
Believers, half b. of casual creeds,
    529:10
   O true b., 122:10
   true b. break eggs at convenient end,
    298:13
Believes, atheist half b. God, 306:9
   each b. his own, 308:7
   he who b. nothing, 357:5
   what each wishes he b., 81:16
Believeth, he that b. shall live, 41:19
   liveth and b., 41:19
   neither b. that it is sound of the trumpet,
    15:15
   whosoever b. in him, 40:46
Believing, be not faithless but b., 41:42
   in old men's lies, 709:4
   slave better than idolater, 120:14
   to b. souls gives light, 172:7
   where cannot prove, 483:10
Bell book and candle, 178:6
   book b. and candle, 139:11
   ding dong b., 857:19
   eats goes to bed by b., 559:21
   fancy from flower b., 493:8
   foam-b. no consequence, 530:13
   for whom the b. tolls, 236:19
   hear the surly sullen b., 226:23
   heart sound as b., 194:30
   I had been my whole life a b., 839:4
   in cowslip's b. I lie, 230:13
   invites me, 220:11
   just like ringing a b., 817:2
   merry as marriage b., 420:16
   middle b. trills out, 472:24
   sad b. murmuring good night, 787:2
   sexton tolled b., 445:14
   silence that dreadful b., 213:20
   some cost passing-b., 452:2
   strikes one, 306:2
   swung to and fro, 600:4
   the cat, 61:1, 133:2
   tongue sounds as sullen b., 191:8
   twilight and evening b., 487:3
   very word like b., 437:14
   who shall b. cat, 61:1
Belle Aurore, 495:4
   Dame sans Merci, 439:6
   of old Natchez, 763:11
   sois b. et sois triste, 524:*n*10
   vain to be a b., 329:25
Bellicose, newspapers querulous and b.,
    691:1
Bellies and drags in wind, 639:2
   fills their b., 58:9
Belligerent ants, 387:*n*5
Bellman, fatal b., 220:12
   would cry crew reply, 552:20
Bellow, in b. and uproar, 699:16
Bellows full of angry wind, 639:14
   like sea combated by winds, 130:11

ells bells bells bells, 479:21
  bonfires illuminations, 351:9
  floating many b. down, 740:8
  for cap and b. lives pay, 514:15
  for these who die, 738:6
  in your parlors, 213:8
  knolled to church, 198:22
  noisy b. be dumb, 618:15
  of Old Bailey, 857:12
  of Shoreditch, 857:12
  of St. Clement's, 857:12
  of St. Martin's, 857:12
  of the flocks, 786:13
  on her toes, 858:14
  port is near b. I hear, 520:18
  ring b. for new century, 676:7
  ring b. of Heaven, 656:10
  ring happy b., 484:14
  ring O b., 520:19
  ring out wild b., 484:13
  ring out your b., 163:23
  silver b. cockleshells, 857:11
  sound on Bredon, 618:15
  sweet b. jangled, 204:9
  temple b. they say, 633:12
Belly, eye bigger than b., 252:15
  fill his b. with east wind, 14:18
  God send thee good ale, 151:10
  hard to argue with b., 88:1
  has no ears, 88:1
  hunched in b. till wet fur froze, 793:6
  if it is well with your b., 101:4
  increasing b., 191:16
  injured by hunger, 82:19
  Jonah was in the b. of the fish, 30:27
  justice in fair round b., 198:25
  like a heap of wheat, 25:29
  men's only God their b., 118:4
  no b. no bowels, 724:13
  noise in the beast's b., 139:2
  secret life of b., 791:12
  shoulder bum, 642:17
  spent under b., 243:8
  upon thy b. shalt thou go, 6:7
  wears his wit in his b., 207:30
  whose God is their b., 45:36
Bellyful, man with b. of classics is enemy, 732:5
  of fighting, 225:11
Bellying, broad b. sails, 703:12
Belong, don't care to b., 744:17
  idea does not b. to soul, 573:14
  land to which we b., 711:13
  secret things b. unto the Lord, 10:11
  to Company G, 558:4
  to oneself, 152:18
  to vanishing race, 747:15
  where do they all b., 835:3
Belonging, atom b. to me belongs to you, 518:15
Belongs, death b. to no one else, 759:11
  kind where each of us b., 820:13
  now he b. to ages, 502:7
Beloved, ah my B. fill Cup, 471:10
  creature that is b., 209:21
  escape me never b., 492:15
  from pole to pole, 400:14
  he giveth his b. sleep, 20:5
  let my b. come into his garden, 25:24

Beloved (continued)
  never be b. by men, 375:8
  of Abraham Lincoln, 651:15
  our dearly b. brothers, 806:14
  our own b. home, 522:8
  Pan, 76:6
  perfection in b., 416:20
  physician, 46:6
  so is my b. among the sons, 25:15
  Son, 33:29
  this is my b., 25:26
  thought himself b., 639:12
Beloved's, heaped for b. bed, 430:19
  I am my b., 26:2
Below, down and away b., 528:5
  fast bound b. the surface, 627:11
  insure position by giving to those b., 5:1
  joy to pass to world b., 97:20
  may it be beautiful b. me, 856:2
  my thoughts remain b., 205:17
  no safety here b., 144:n3
  serfdom abolish itself from b., 508:6
  shining and slow-moving b., 728:14
  slave spirit b., 710:13
  thy element's b., 216:11
Belshazzar made a great feast, 30:5
Belt, undo b. look for trouble, 701:9
Belted, prince can mak b. knight, 380:13
  you an' flayed you, 633:10
Belua multorum es capitum, 100:n13
Bemocked, beams b. sultry main, 400:12
Ben Adhem's name led rest, 417:15
  Bolt, 513:17
  Bulben's head, 643:4
  Jonson his best poetry, 237:21
  O rare B. Jonson, 237:n2
Bench, log hut with simple b., 548:10
Bend, grass must b. when wind blows, 63:8
  I b. but do not break, 276:12
  if I cannot b. Heaven, 98:5
  shall I b. low, 188:9
  soften rocks or b. oak, 300:20
  woman not breaks will b., 792:4
Bended, on b. arm doglike, 65:3
Bendemeer's stream, 412:11
Bending sickle's compass, 227:17
  to your wool, 150:13
Bends, blue sky b. over all, 401:8
  gallant mast, 417:7
  though she b. him, 467:2
  with remover to remove, 227:17
Beneath a rougher sea, 348:22
  at once above b. around, 337:16
  married b. me all women do, 682:7
  rung battle shout, 473:3
Benedick the married man, 194:12
Benediction, face like a b., 156:9
  streamed like a b., 549:5
  whose memory a b., 686:7
Benefaction, calling to mind previous b., 73:2
Benefactor, less to blame than b., 273:18
Beneficence, private b. inadequate, 621:12
Beneficent, belief in b. power, 575:8
  mother of gods and men, 4:6
Beneficial, the opposite is b., 64:9
Benefit, find man to b. kingdom, 81:24
  from illnesses, 73:9
  from literary accomplishments in women, 361:14

Benefit (continued)
  government for common b., 339:10
  human b. and enjoyment, 344:14
  if men stop work at sixty, 595:12
  means of acquiring knowledge greatest b., 386:6
  no b. in gifts of bad man, 69:24
  of clergy, 658:n3
  of ill, 227:19
  poor b. of bewildering minute, 239:15
  practical b. in failures, 537:6
  trees to b. another generation, 88:7
  Way of Heaven to b. others, 59:21
Benefits, caution in refusing b., 287:14
  disable b. of your country, 199:25
  doubly b. who gives quickly, 102:14
  gratitude a desire for b., 273:33
  many b. from good read, 789:6
  memory of b. fades, 67:7
  of sunscreen, 841:13
  water b. all things, 58:12
Benevolence, beans and b., 458:12
  calls his trusting b., 341:23
  decrees of farseeing b., 523:4
  is man's mind, 82:13
  not from b. of butcher brewer baker, 338:13
  not infused from without, 82:12
  peace a disposition for b., 286:13
  tranquil habitation of man, 82:2
  whether b. does good, 538:5
Benevolent, heart b. and kind, 378:17
  people turn to b. rule, 82:1
  stormy patient, 771:15
Benighted, pore b. 'eathen, 633:9
Benign indifference of universe, 789:13
Benison of hot water, 712:18
  to fall, 248:20
Benjamin, little model was B., 707:8
Benjamin's, fell upon B. neck and wept, 7:32
  mess five times theirs, 7:28
Bennet called us Quakers, 280:15
  Mrs. B. stirring fire, 406:7
Bent, affection cannot hold b., 209:23
  as twig b. tree's inclined, 310:3
  bow cannot stand b., 157:24
  find out natural b., 77:19
  fool me to top of my b., 205:10
  goldenrod, 719:16
  idly b. on him that enters next, 180:13
  man who has b. himself, 81:25
  natural b. in accordance with nature's, 574:5
  thoughts downward b., 264:22
  to be b. is to become straight, 58:19
Benumbs, care's a canker that b., 566:5
Bequeath my soul to God, 168:19
  myself to dirt, 519:23
Bereaved, black as if b. of light, 372:1
Bereavement, anguish of b., 477:2
Bereft, muddy ill-seeming b. of beauty, 176:1
Bergère ô tour Eiffel, 689:n1
Berkeley, Bishop B. said no matter, 424:14
Berlin, citizens of B., 800:5
Berliner, ich bin ein B., 800:5
Bermudas, remote B. ride, 277:9
Bernard had prayers in hall whiskey afterwards, 693:1

Birth *(continued)*
    starves her generous b., 334:5
    sunshine a glorious b., 393:9
Birthday of my life, 547:15
Birthplace of valor, 379:5
Birthright, Esau sold his b., 7:11
Birthrights, bearing b. proudly, 177:22
Births, joyful b., 193:25
    vowels latent b., 603:14
Birth-strangled babe, 221:22
Bis dat qui cito dat, 123:11
Biscay, bonny bonny B. O, 846:22
Bishop, blonde to make b. kick hole in
    window, 717:3
    hypocrisy of b., 360:8
Bit, a b. crowded marriage, 842:8
    babies in cradles, 491:16
    by him that comes behind, 299:4
    dogs have a b., 857:5
    hair of dog that b. us, 148:23
    I b. my arm sucked blood, 400:2
    though he had b. me, 217:28
    went mad and b. the man, 341:18
Bitch, deciding not to be a b., 754:2
    gone in the teeth, 709:5
    how it is on b. of earth, 773:9
    punch hole in son of a b., 852:16
    son of mongrel b., 216:7
Bitches, businessmen sons of b., 800:1
    now we are all sons of b., 769:n1
    sons of b. want to live forever, 330:n2
Bitch-goddess Success, 581:4
Bite, bark and b., 303:17
    bark worse than b., 252:16
    bullet, 632:20
    dead man cannot b., 91:21
    dog prosperous will not b., 561:16
    hand that fed them, 346:1
    haven't guts to b. people themselves,
      596:9
    jaws that b., 551:10
    man recovered of the b., 341:19
    smaller still to b. 'em, 299:4
    sorrow hath less power to b., 179:5
    this fish will b., 194:27
Bites, air b. shrewdly, 202:2
Biteth like a serpent, 22:38
Biting, eager soul b. for anger, 258:6
Bitten, complains of having b. tongue, 607:9
Bitter, academic politics are so b., 772:13
    as coloquintida, 213:4
    as wormwood, 21:3
    bark and burning clove, 669:17
    because it is b. because is my heart,
      655:17
    bread of banishment, 179:23
    chill it was, 436:20
    do it with b. look, 605:18
    every b. thing is sweet, 23:12
    feed on b. fruit, 761:16
    feel by turns b. change, 265:17
    found Beauty b., 603:14
    from fountain wells up b. taste, 93:16
    give me b. fame, 725:6
    groan of martyr's woe, 375:4
    herbs, 8:17
    if life b. pardon, 569:15
    it is b. he answered, 655:17
    joy hear sound of wings, 752:10

Bitter *(continued)*
    known love how b., 568:11
    laugh my b. laugh, 473:2
    little embryos, 755:13
    love b. with treason, 568:17
    make oppression b., 203:30
    more b. than death, 24:23
    mortals make earth b., 434:1
    most b. is scornful jest, 323:12
    nailed on b. cross, 184:22
    news to hear, 534:3
    O b. ending, 696:18
    old and b. of tongue, 637:6
    old law sad not b., 678:15
    read in the b. letter, 212:24
    shed b. tear, 551:19
    sweet and b. fancy, 199:32
    things conduce to sweet, 809:5
    'tis b. cold, 200:12
    to look into happiness, 200:4
Bitterest, this lot is b., 66:2
Bitterness, by convention b., 72:14
    feeds me bread of b., 729:12
    gall of b., 42:5
    heart knoweth his own b., 21:29
    I must have no b., 631:18
    love without b., 734:13
    mingles sweet b. with her cares, 94:20
    of feelings about modern life, 788:5
    of Life, 553:6
    of my soul, 27:36
    of things, 395:17
    rose's scent b., 620:14
Bitters, mawkishness and b., 436:7
Bivouac of the dead, 522:6
Bizarre world of cards, 731:3
Blabber, she was worse than b., 790:12
Blabbing eastern scout, 260:22
    gaudy b. and remorseful day, 172:15
Blabs, when my tongue b., 208:27
Black A white E red I, 603:14
    and unknown bards, 656:18
    and white not blue, 800:13
    and white separate as fingers, 610:19
    as hell, 228:7
    as if bereaved of light, 372:1
    as night is black, 762:10
    as our loss, 715:13
    as Pit from pole to pole, 594:10
    as the devil, 369:9
    as they might be, 854:5
    bat night flown, 485:8
    beautiful when, 809:10
    black's not so b., 389:15
    born with b. skin, 815:9
    burned b. with sun, 734:10
    but comely, 25:12
    consciousness, 839:12
    creeping through the b., 685:4
    devil damn thee b., 222:9
    drop of b. blood, 763:1
    eyes and lemonade, 412:6
    fat b. bucks, 685:3
    folk say America been stronger, 781:15
    fought against b. domination, 803:15
    handkerchief washed clean, 817:13
    he is a b. planet, 807:4
    headlines of the latest edition, 756:16
    Hecate's summons, 221:6

Black *(continued)*
    horseshoes are b., 751:8
    hung be heavens with b., 171:11
    I am b. but O my soul is white, 372:1
    I'm B. and I'm Proud, 829:12
    I'm pore I'm b., 839:3
    in B. Mud kingfisher, 800:9
    in space small b. hole, 807:5
    institutions of splendid achievement,
      835:n2
    is beautiful, 852:13
    is powerful, 763:1
    just 'cause you're b., 745:5
    killing defenseless b. people, 815:12
    let b. flower blossom, 460:9
    let the devil wear b., 204:20
    like me, 762:11
    little b. sheep, 633:17
    love is Black wealth, 838:3
    man takes uncompromising step, 815:11
    men are pearls, 176:14
    men fought on Coromandel, 448:11
    milk of daybreak, 806:10
    my b. hen, 860:2
    niggerization not just to b. people, 797:15
    not so b. as painted, 164:16
    Old B. Joe, 539:3
    pall of nothing, 734:6
    people unite, 835:11
    plunge-line nightdress, 833:15
    portent of atomic age, 652:17
    pot calls kettle b., 158:28
    power, 835:11
    practiced b. art in Cefalu, 766:7
    ram tupping your ewe, 212:19
    rank and file, 556:3
    rock star, 818:2
    secret b. midnight hags, 221:24
    seek b. power, 835:n2
    since b. womb held, 791:12
    so b. and blue, 745:5
    spirits and white, 243:22
    spot to keep concealed, 540:2
    star-studded lute wears b. sun, 469:4
    suit of ancient b., 685:6
    suits of solemn b., 200:29
    swan rare bird, 113:9
    these b. bodies, 372:2
    thou readest b., 376:8
    till he spouts b. blood, 516:12
    turkey gobbler, 855:22
    two societies one b. one white, 779:8
    ugly when black exploit blacks, 809:10
    we b. and they white, 781:13
    wet b. bough, 708:16
    what is B. Spot, 598:16
    white not neutralize b., 495:2
    Widow death, 800:12
    wings one b. other white, 269:8
    wires grow on her head, 228:1
    wishing He I served were b., 765:2
    with Gilt Surcingles, 546:17
    world b. green red yellow, 829:11
    years like great b. oxen, 636:21
    yellow b. pale hectic red, 428:21
Black Hawk fought for countrymen, 386:9
    last sun shone on B., 386:8
Blackamoor, as if sun b., 687:1
Blackberries, reasons as plenty as b., 185:25

Blackbird snipped off nose, 858:12
   than b. 'tis to whistle, 270:15
   whistling or just after, 687:7
Blackbirds, four and twenty b., 858:12
   sitting on a hill, 861:14
Blackens every blot, 485:16
   skuttle fish b. water, 302:20
Blackest, Cerberus and b. Midnight, 259:7
   perfect through b. air, 809:2
Blackguard whose faulty vision, 580:11
Blackguards, Hitlerite b., 686:3
Blackness, faces all gather b., 30:29
   faces as b. of a kettle, 30:*n*2
   in sudden b. the pall, 734:6
   of darkness, 48:1
   of death, 93:7
Black-purple, in gloom b., 664:10
Black's not so black, 389:15
Blacks, enemies of persecuted b., 462:3
   filled her house with b., 812:7
Bladder, blows man up like a b., 185:28
Bladders, boys that swim on b., 231:2
   of philosophy, 293:4
Blade, first b. then ear, 38:18
   grasp by b. or handle, 515:18
   knife without a b., 356:12
   of grass always blade of grass, 241:*n*1
   trenchant b. Toledo trusty, 271:5
   upper or under b. of scissors, 584:2
   vorpal b., 551:11
Blades, two b. of grass grow, 298:15
   which b. bears better temper, 171:16
Blade-straight, steel-true and b., 599:15
Blaine marched down halls, 554:2
Blaize, lament for Madame B., 340:10
Blake, dance with William B., 781:10
   William B. beat upon wall, 642:11
Blame, alike reserved to b., 312:4
   bloody full of b., 227:22
   I don't b. him, 827:19
   needless to b. things past, 62:18
   neither is most to b., 569:6
   no dispraise or b., 269:15
   no reason to b. Trojans, 52:22
   or b. it too much, 343:2
   partner apparently least to b., 771:20
   poor wot gets b., 851:1
   praise at morning b. at night, 308:22
   praise nor b. writings, 308:20
   praise or b. momentary, 440:10
   praise or b. too far, 671:3
   secret thoughts without b., 246:10
   ungrateful man less to b., 273:18
Blame-all and Praise-all blockheads, 319:7
Blameless life, 485:16
   vestal's lot, 309:26
Blameworthy, the other strife is b., 56:7
Blaming, always b. circumstances, 609:5
   mortals are b. the gods, 54:9
Blanch, Tray B. and Sweetheart, 217:5
Bland as a Jesuit, 594:7
   cruel composed b., 531:6
Blandishing persuasion, 53:15
Blandishments not fascinate us, 362:9
Blank, a b. my lord, 209:26
   bumbast out b. verse, 165:18
   page, 825:3
   pain has Element of B., 545:14
   universal b., 265:25

Blanket of the dark, 219:12
   old woman tossed in b., 859:11
   pulling b. from eastern sky, 855:14
   sleeping is a wool b., 75:21
Blankets, people have no b., 576:10
   rough male kiss of b., 712:18
Blaspheme what they do not know, 280:10
Blasphemies, great truths begin as b., 610:9
Blasphemy, in soldier is flat b., 211:14
   Mass the greatest b., 144:15
Blast, contrary b. proclaims, 269:8
   drives wicked spirits, 130:12
   heard in the trances of b., 401:11
   midnight b., 424:22
   of no b. he died, 283:5
   of war blows in our ears, 192:30
   one b. upon bugle horn, 397:13
   stormy b., 304:6
   striding the b., 219:18
Blast-beruffled plume, 575:16
Blasted with antiquity, 191:17
   with excess of light, 335:9
   with the east wind, 7:26
Blastments, contagious b. imminent, 201:22
Blasts, hollow b. of wind, 306:21
   icy b. blow on love, 527:4
   newborn infant's tear, 374:8
   night b. cold, 664:10
   roots of trees, 795:2
Blatant Bassarid of Boston, 569:11
Blaw, up an' gie them a b., 385:8
Blaze, burst out into sudden b., 261:19
   dark amid b. of noon, 268:32
   heavens b. forth, 196:9
   the sapphire b., 335:9
Blazing evidence of immortality, 454:11
   heaven b. into head, 642:7
   in Gold quenching in Purple, 544:10
   moment, 811:16
   no more b. hearth, 334:13
   potentates b. in the heavens, 65:3
   tail, 687:1
Blazon of sweet beauty's best, 227:11
Blazoning, quirks of b. pens, 213:7
Bleak December, 479:1
   in b. midwinter frosty wind, 547:19
Bleakness, country of b., 472:23
Blear-eyed wisdom, 640:15
Bleat the one at the other, 228:10
Bleats articulate monotony, 394:*n*2
Bled, buried Caesar b., 471:9
   in Freedom's cause, 390:13
   Scots wha hae wi' Wallace b., 380:10
Bleed a while, 853:*n*1
   carcasses b. at sight of murderer, 137:*n*3
   heart begins to b., 856:13
   I fall upon thorns I b., 429:3
   if you prick us do we not b., 188:31
Bleeding brow of labor, 622:*n*1
   piece of earth, 196:21
   purple testament of b. war, 180:2
Blemish, Christianity immortal b., 589:25
   formed without b., 62:1
   lamb shall be without b., 8:16
Blent, beauty truly b., 209:8
Bless bed I lie on, 274:*n*3
   except thou b. me, 7:20
   God b. Captain Vere, 517:1
   God b. the Pretender, 314:12

Bless (continued)
   God b. us every one, 497:19
   God b. you, 847:8
   God b. you my dear, 329:20
   hand that gave blow, 283:23
   her when she is riggish, 223:15
   his name, 19:3
   hous from wikked wight, 136:3
   I b. God in libraries, 338:3
   Lord b. and keep thee, 9:17
   squire and relations, 497:23
   thee Bottom, 181:20
   them that curse you, 34:7
   turf that wraps clay, 336:16
   ye the Lord, 33:12
Blessed Abbot of Aberbrothok, 405:11
   all generations call me b., 38:38
   always to be b., 311:4
   are the dead, 48:33
   are the forgetful, 589:7
   are the meek, 33:33
   are the merciful, 33:33
   are the peacemakers, 33:33, 172:6
   are the poor in spirit, 33:33
   are the pure in heart, 33:33
   are they that mourn, 33:33
   are they that put their trust in him, 15:27
   are they which are persecuted, 33:33
   are they which hunger and thirst, 33:33
   are ye when men revile you, 33:33
   art thou among women, 38:34
   be he that cometh, 19:27
   be Lord God of Israel, 38:41
   be man that spares these stones, 231:19
   be the name of the Lord, 13:26
   bed be b. that I lie on, 274:20
   by country's wishes b., 336:15
   by everything, 640:19
   by yonder b. moon, 183:8
   candles of night, 190:12
   children call her b., 23:30
   come what may been b., 422:7
   damozel, 541:26
   endless sabbaths b. ones see, 126:5
   fell upon knees and b. God, 247:6
   green groves of the b., 97:28
   half part of b. man, 177:27
   hope whereof he knew, 575:17
   horny hands of toil, 514:8
   I had lived a b. time, 220:25
   is man who expects nothing, 310:16
   is the fruit of thy womb, 38:36
   is the man that trusteth, 29:17
   is the man that walketh not in counsel of
      ungodly, 15:27
   judge none b., 32:23
   kings may be b., 379:17
   little b. with soft phrase, 212:25
   Lord b. the latter end of Job, 15:26
   love of God had b., 417:15
   man who possesses keen mind, 75:22
   memory of the just is b., 21:15
   mood, 391:1
   more b. to give, 42:25
   mother of us all, 359:13
   mutter of Mass, 492:8
   over whose acres b. feet, 184:22
   part to heaven, 231:10
   plot this earth, 179:12

Blessed (*continued*)

quarry mine b. am I, 856:6
sanctified by reason b. by faith, 391:13
seeming b. they grow, 341:3
soul or body more b., 642:9
them unaware, 400:13
they that have not seen, 41:43
thou fallest a b. martyr, 231:7
thrice and four times b., 96:27
to put cares away, 94:9
twice b., 189:19
were but as b. as I, 305:9
who have no talent, 454:8
who having nothing to say, 513:15
whom thou blessest is b., 9:21
with milk and honey b., 511:11
youth becomes as aged, 211:19

Blessedness, perfect b. vision of God, 129:9
Blesses stars and thinks it luxury, 301:18
Blessest, whom thou b. is blessed, 9:21
Blesseth him that gives and him that takes, 189:19
Blessing, alien b. on its way, 819:15

and cursing, 10:12
ask me b., 218:1
brother hath taken away thy b., 7:13
creations of mind b. not curse, 683:6
good neighbor is great b., 56:13
haste haste has no b., 853:7
I had most need of b., 220:15
love gives, 819:5
makes a b. dear, 270:5
money cannot buy, 253:8
national debt b., 370:7, 414:15
no harm in b., 314:12
of Saint Peter's Master, 253:9
out of God's b. into sun, 149:3
paid thy utmost b., 662:12
public debt a public b., 370:n2
society is a b., 354:6
unqualified b., 386:14
war b. compared with reign of lie, 730:10

Blessings, free trade one of b., 447:9

God from whom all b. flow, 289:22
health and intellect the two b., 84:5
health greatest of b., 73:9
on him who invented sleep, 158:31
on thee little man, 468:9
on this house, 351:17
on your frosty pow, 379:4
one of evils and another of b., 54:6
reap b. of freedom, 354:14
secure b. of liberty, 360:13
two supreme b., 70:11
unequal sharing of b., 668:7
upon head of the just, 21:15
use b. of gods with wisdom, 100:16
without number, 304:4

Blew, fair breeze b., 399:20

great guns, 498:18
slug-horn to lips set and b., 217:n2

Blight man was born for, 587:15
Blighted, seared and b. heart, 477:12
Blights with plagues, 374:8
Blind and ignorant in all, 233:2

and naked Ignorance, 485:24
as nails upon Cross, 715:13
beggar's daughter, 853:24
Booth died b., 684:14

Blind (*continued*)

eyes of the b. shall be opened, 27:32
eyes to the b., 14:38
for being b. God prepare me, 288:28
Fortune painted b. with muffler, 168:n1
Fortune though b. not invisible, 168:10
Fury with abhorred shears, 261:19
guides, 37:3
halt and b., 39:32
he was as often seene, 135:24
hearts, 92:20
Homer sing to me, 170:22
I was b., 41:14
in country of b. one-eyed man king, 142:6
justice b. deef an' dumb, 646:3
justice is b., 783:4
leaders of the blind, 36:20
leading blind to pit, 118:5
love is b., 137:8, 188:20
love needs be b., 180:n1
love to faults always b., 373:10
man's ditch, 640:18
mouths, 262:1
none so b., 295:21
oblivion swallowed cities, 208:7
old mad b. despised king, 429:11
right to be b. sometimes, 377:3
three b. mice, 856:15
till some b. hand, 374:4
Tiresias though b., 718:18
to faults a little b., 296:19
urge to kill b., 829:5
was b. but now I see, 339:12
winged Cupid painted b., 180:21
wretched b. pit ponies, 656:10

Blinded boy, 844:3
Blindly, had we never loved sae b., 378:24
Blindness about poverty, 820:11

heathen in his b., 416:5
left to native b., 331:24
we may forgive, 652:2

Blinds, drawing-down of b., 738:7
Blindworms, newts and b. do no wrong, 181:15
Blinked, other fellow b., 852:n5
Bliss, beyond happiness is b., 732:6

bought by years, 508:19
contrary bringeth b., 172:3
cuckold lives in b., 213:34
deprived of everlasting b., 170:19
follow your b., 766:16
happy be and have immortal b., 161:8
he lives in b., 380:17
heart intoxicated with b., 382:7
in our brows bent, 223:1
in proof, 227:22
kill and b. me, 844:12
mutual and partaken b., 261:8
need of imperishable b., 686:18
never parted b. or woe, 268:4
no right to b., 528:19
not beds of down, 249:5
of dying, 309:3
of solitude, 394:8
perfect b. and sole felicity, 170:4
pneumatic b., 718:8
shadow's b., 188:28
soul in b., 217:29

Bliss (*continued*)

source of all my b., 342:13
sum of earthly b., 267:21
waking b., 260:28
was it in that dawn, 391:11
where ignorance is b., 333:22
work of fiction affords aesthetic b., 756:3

Blisses about my pilgrimage, 574:13
Blissful dreams of long ago, 571:4
Blister, never had b. in hand, 75:2

thirst b. easier, 544:14

Blithe, buxom b. and debonair, 259:8

Irish lad, 408:15
no lark more b. than he, 352:5
spirit, 429:16

Blizzard, it was blowing a b., 649:17
Block, chip of old b., 345:4

do not b. way of inquiry, 573:13
each b. cut smooth, 709:8
escaped the auction b., 501:6
mind a b. of wax, 78:11

Blockhead, no man but a b., 328:3
Blockheads, Blame-all Praise-all b., 319:7

read what blockheads wrote, 315:8

Blocks, stumbling b. in girl's education, 662:6

towns you built of b., 750:7

Blond beast, 589:13

more b. than you, 740:5

Blonde to make bishop kick hole in window, 717:3
Blondes, gentlemen prefer b., 737:10
Blood, after book of circulation of b., 280:20

all nations one b., 42:18
bath, 702:6
be on your own heads, 42:20
beauty comes from beautiful b., 518:9
bit arm sucked b., 400:2
blow in cold b., 609:25
by man shall his b. be shed, 6:33
chalice of My B., 49:14
Christ's b. streams, 171:4
courage tastes of b., 788:2
created Man of b. clot, 122:19
created you of b. clot, 121:19
crusted with b., 713:13
cry aloud for b., 522:14
delivered from shipwreck of b., 751:12
devise laws for b., 187:28
drenched in fraternal b., 415:2
drops of b. form on forehead, 728:18
ears gushed b., 436:19
earth one mighty b. spot, 460:3
effusion of b., 627:16
every drop of b. drawn, 477:4
fizz like wine, 680:8
flesh and b. so cheap, 446:6
for this all that b. shed, 638:7
freeze thy young b., 202:12
fried meats angry up b., 774:11
future smells of b., 442:17
glories of our b. and state, 254:9
good enough to shed b., 615:6
guiltless of country's b., 334:21
hand raised to shed b., 311:2
heart dry of b., 439:2
her young suck up b., 15:16
heyday in the b. is tame, 205:22
his b. be on us, 38:5

Blood *(continued)*

I that am of your b. taken from you, 243:13
impure b. drench field, 383:*n*1
in b. stepped in so far, 221:19
in torrents pour, 613:1
inhabits our frail b., 210:15
iron and b., 502:8
is nipped and ways be foul, 177:17
is their thinking, 69:8
it will have b. they say, 221:17
liquors in my b., 198:4
lust for b. and plunder, 666:13
magic to stir men's b., 592:4
make thick my b., 219:11
man whose b. is snow-broth, 211:1
man whose b. is warm, 187:18
meditate on b., 193:26
mingle b. with b. of children, 447:4
more stirs to rouse lion, 185:8
more things move than b. in heart, 748:3
Negro b. sure powerful, 763:1
new testament in my b., 44:16
no Jewish b. in my veins, 829:8
no sure foundation on b., 178:17
nor can b. be in sticks, 93:10
Norman b., 480:14
not a drop of b. shed, 359:4
not against flesh and b., 45:31
not see b. of Ignacio, 751:10
odor of b. when Christ slain, 640:10
of an Englishman, 861:10
of Christians is seed, 116:14
of martyrs seed of Church, 116:*n*3
of our heroes, 358:13
of patriots and tyrants, 357:15
of the lamb, 48:24
of the new testament, 37:27
of the slaughtered, 656:15
of this just person, 38:4
oh b. that freezes b. that burns, 492:11
old man had so much b., 222:5
on hands rather than water, 767:11
one b. ye and I, 634:11
own b. rise against you, 658:*n*3
pint of sweat save gallon of b., 708:14
poet's feverish b., 529:7
poisoned with b. of both, 826:2
present joys more to flesh and b., 284:24
pure and eloquent b., 236:1
rank flavor of b., 819:4
rivers older than flow of b., 762:9
sets gypsy b. astir, 624:1
shed by immortal King, 129:2
shed for you and for many, 49:14
sheds his b. with me, 193:20
sign to know gentle b., 162:6
smell b. of British man, 217:3
spend her b. and might, 611:9
spill no drop of b., 577:1
sprinkled upon garments, 28:32
still b. is strong, 444:10
stir men's b., 197:4
strong as flesh and b., 394:21
strong wyn reed as b., 135:14
summon up the b., 192:30
sun's o'ercast with b., 178:5
sweat and tear-wrung millions, 665:*n*4

Blood *(continued)*

sweat on drill ground save b. on battlefield, 708:*n*4
tears sweat or b., 665:*n*4
that strange mixture of b., 352:7
thick water's thin, 565:5
thicker than water, 281:9
thicks man's b. with cold, 400:3
this is my b., 37:27
till he spouts black b., 516:12
to drink, 460:16
toil tears sweat, 665:19
tree of liberty refreshed with b., 357:15
trilling wire in b., 720:9
up to eyes in b., 343:19
vigor flows into my b., 729:12
voice of thy brother's b., 6:14
wash this b. from hand, 220:19
watered by b. of tyrants, 370:1
weltering in his b., 285:12
what little b. is left, 680:8
when the b. burns, 201:31
whoso sheddeth man's b., 6:33
will have blood, 221:17
without shedding of b., 46:41
won by b. and sweat of innocent, 836:12
young b. have its course, 514:4
Blood-dimmed tide loosed, 639:6
Blood-hot eyes, 742:6
Bloodless substitute for life, 598:10
week of repose, 75:*n*3
Blood-red banner, 416:2
sunset glorious b., 492:6
wine, 853:16
Blood's a rover, 618:8
Bloodshed, fear and b., 394:16
no more wars no more b., 789:10
Blood-swollen, war b. god, 655:11
Bloodthirsty guttersnipe, 666:13
Bloody and invisible hand, 221:7
be b. bold and resolute, 221:26
book of law, 212:24
but unbowed, 594:10
dark and b. ground, 522:7
even so my b. thoughts, 214:15
full of blame, 227:22
mothers a b. brood, 745:2
often wipe b. nose, 307:7
sang within the b. wood, 718:10
sweats, 605:21
treason flourished, 197:1
where's the b. horse, 760:8
Bloom along the bough, 618:6
barred clouds b. soft-dying day, 438:13
flowers that b. in spring, 565:19
full on thy b., 378:8
gradually out of reach, 818:9
how can ye b., 378:21
is gone, 530:17
its b. is shed, 379:18
lemon trees b., 363:16
look at things in b., 618:7
now withering in my b., 309:25
of young Desire, 335:6
perfect in bud as in b., 557:16
sight of vernal b., 265:25
sort of b. on woman, 621:19
water lily b., 480:26

Bloom *(continued)*

well in prison air, 605:23
with the b. go I, 530:17
Bloomed, when lilacs in dooryard b., 520:14
Bloomin' cosmopolouse, 634:20
lyre, 634:9
shame, 851:1
Blooming, left b. alone, 411:15
Blooms each thing, 232:7
o'er folded b., 596:1
when the wolfbane b., 764:3
Bloomy, nightingale on b. spray, 262:7
Blossom, blossomed Sarah and I b., 792:4
by blossom spring begins, 567:18
desert b. as the rose, 27:31
in purple and red, 485:12
in their dust, 254:7
leaf b. or bole, 640:15
let black flower b., 460:10
letting hundred flowers b., 737:18
May when lusty heart b., 139:8
that hangs on bough, 230:13
Blossomed Sarah and I blossom, 792:4
Blossomer, great-rooted b., 640:15
Blossoming, labor b. or dancing, 640:15
Blossoms a rose in my heart, 637:8
and branches to coffins I bring, 520:15
apple b. fill air, 724:17
birds and bowers, 247:14
break into b., 820:3
of my sin, 202:19
tomorrow b., 231:2
Blot, art to b., 313:3
blackens every b., 485:16
discreetly b., 258:2
in thy scutcheon, 158:23
Lord b. out his name, 286:*n*4
out his name, 48:13
Blotted from life's page, 420:12
out man's image, 637:3
Shakespeare never b. line, 238:15
unpleasantest words that b. paper, 189:9
word out forever, 332:28
would he had b. a thousand, 238:15
Blotter, write in b. I was born, 723:15
Blow, all aloud wind doth b., 177:18
and swallow at same moment, 86:16
as straws that b., 594:9
bless hand that gave b., 283:23
breathe and b., 482:18
bugle blow, 482:19
but a word and a b., 285:1
come from moon and b., 482:18
death loves signal b., 306:11
east wind never b., 252:23
first b. half battle, 342:21
for freedom, 713:17
great winds shoreward b., 528:5
high blow low and so sailed we, 862:9
him again to me, 482:18
horrid deed in every eye, 219:18
hot and cold, 61:2
I the b. and cheek, 524:13
I will b. you out, 536:7
ideas began to b. all over, 645:1
in cold blood not forgiven, 609:25
know what wood by the b., 271:14
liberty's in every b., 380:11
might be the be-all, 219:16

ow *(continued)*
　north wind doth b., 859:12
　on whom I please, 198:20
　out you bugles, 713:2
　out your brains, 634:7
　pay with a deadly b., 65:16
　pealing organ b., 260:10
　perhaps may turn his b., 389:16
　put your lips together and b., 723:2
　selfsame winds that b., 600:5
　struck a deep mortal b., 65:9
　the kiss, 819:18
　the man down, 861:24
　thou winter wind, 199:1
　trumpet to arms, 354:5
　up an' gie them a b., 385:8
　upon my garden, 25:24
　when wilt thou b., 843:18
　who would be free strike b., 420:10
　wind come wrack, 222:18
　wind sail b., 854:8
　winds crack your cheeks, 216:18
　word and a b., 183:27
　wreathed horn, 394:19
　ye winds heigh-ho, 862:11
　your trumpets angels, 236:4
loweth, ill wind b. no man good, 149:14
　med, 843:5
　spirit b. and is still, 528:12
　wind b. where it listeth, 40:44
lowin' in the wind, 836:4
　what bugles b. for, 633:5
lowing, Elfland faintly b., 482:20
　furious winter b., 724:10
　it was b. a blizzard, 649:17
　new direction of Time, 707:5
　noise of tongues, 480:7
　of dry dust, 709:7
　what bugles b. for, 633:5
lown buds of barren flowers, 569:1
　by wind of criticism, 329:17
　crimes broad b., 205:16
　dust that is b. away, 31:19
　hair is sweet, 719:12
　pipe b. by surmises, 191:6
　what though mast b. overboard, 173:12
　with restless violence, 211:23
lows, apostolic b. and knocks, 271:3
　blast of war b. in ears, 192:30
　Dick the shepherd b. his nail, 177:17
　driven by invisible b., 707:6
　dust b. in your face, 217:12
　feather for each wind that b., 228:17
　from yon far country b., 619:3
　grass must bend when wind b., 63:8
　it in my face, 203:29
　man up like a bladder, 185:28
　meanest flower that b., 393:19
　never b. so red, 471:9
　soft zephyr b., 335:13
　taught by rod and b., 144:10
　vile b. and buffets, 221:1
　which way hot air b., 626:15
　which way the wind b., 836:9
　wild thyme b., 181:12
　wind b. cradle rock, 592:1
　wind b. it back again, 375:2
　wind from blue heaven b., 363:16
　wind that b. through me, 707:5

Blude-red wine, 853:16
Bludgeonings of chance, 594:10
Blue, all the time a-feelin' b., 613:4
　always said my eyes were b., 408:9
　and gold mistake, 544:5
　Aryan eye bright b., 827:15
　Beard's chaplain said, 495:25
　beneath b. of day, 618:12
　Big B. Mountain Spirit, 855:21
　breeches b., 405:23
　buff and the b., 380:19
　color source of delight, 517:9
　daisies pied and violets b., 177:16
　darkened on blueness, 707:21
　ethereal sky, 301:14
　forked torch of flower, 707:21
　fragmentary b., 669:10
　grappling in central b., 481:23
　hands b., 499:19
　Heaven's height, 592:15
　home made of b. clouds, 855:21
　I am Rose my eyes are b., 673:21
　inns of Molten B., 544:8
　kingfisher dives, 800:9
　lavender's b., 860:19
　little boy b. blow horn, 857:17
　Little Boy B. kissed them, 597:6
　little tent of b., 605:16
　living air and b. sky, 391:4
　not b. on Boston, 800:13
　O, 603:14
　October's bright b. weather, 547:11
　pine needles, 291:15
　Presbyterian true b., 271:1
　promontory with trees, 223:33
　pull of the b. highway, 834:4
　remembered hills, 619:3
　roses red violets b., 161:7
　rushing of arrowy Rhone, 420:25
　sky bends over all, 401:8
　sky of spring, 535:16
　so black and b., 745:5
　something b., 850:13
　suede shoes, 827:6
　true b., 271:1
　twitched his mantle b., 262:6
　unholy b., 411:14
　wave rolls nightly, 422:14
　wings were b., 499:20
Bluebird carries sky, 505:5
Bluebirds, over rainbow b. fly, 752:1
Blueeyed boy, 739:13
Blue-fringed lids, 401:12
Blue-massing clouds, 712:18
Blueness, blue darkened on b., 707:21
Blues, from b. American music, 657:4
　I got the Weary B., 762:12
Bluestocking, sagacious b., 448:12
Blume, du bist wie eine B., 442:*n*5
Blunder, frae monie a b. free us,
　378:6
　man b. of God or God of man,
　589:18
　so grotesque a b., 674:6
　worse than crime it is b., 383:9
Blunderbuss against religion, 326:12
Blundered, someone had b., 484:26
Blundering kind of melody, 283:20
　learning b. people live on, 681:17

Blunders, forgetful get better of b., 589:7
　like ropes, 451:12
　nature never makes b., 508:12
　round meaning, 312:3
Blunt monster with uncounted heads,
　191:6
　plain b. man, 197:3
Blush, born to b. unseen, 334:20
　fair regions raise our b., 368:12
　shame where is thy b., 205:23
　to give it in, 332:*n*2
　to make man b., 422:11
　truth does not b., 116:18
Blushed at herself, 212:27
　saw its God and b., 272:4
Blushes into wine, 272:*n*2
　man only animal that b., 562:8
Blushful Hippocrene, 437:7
Blushing, bears his b. honors, 231:2
　flowers shall rise, 308:5
　Religion b. veils fires, 313:25
Blustering, pity from b. wind, 276:5
Blut, Eisen und B., 502:*n*2
　O Haupt vol B. und Wunden, 258:*n*1
Blynken, Wynken B. and Nod, 597:5
Boanerges, neigh like B., 545:9
Board, back to the old drawing b., 766:14
　dim on Bristol b., 786:3
　get on b. little children, 863:11
　heart for bed and b., 800:16
　money in ginger jar, 557:8
　struck the b., 250:15
　well-benched ships, 57:12
Boards, ships are but b., 188:1
Boast, frantic b., 635:5
　having my freedom b. of nothing,
　179:3
　let not him that girdeth on his harness b.,
　12:33
　not b. who puts armor on, 467:20
　not of what thou wouldst have done,
　269:11
　not thyself of tomorrow, 23:9
　now b. thee death, 224:13
　of heraldry, 334:15
　of this I can, 179:7
　such is the patriot's b., 341:1
Boasters, great nations not b., 456:23
Boasteth, when he is gone his way then he b.,
　22:20
Boastful, high and b. neighs, 193:11
　in war daring b., 426:1
Boasting, strength without b., 358:5
Boasts, that which b. his birth, 425:5
Boat, carry Caesar in your b., 92:2
　forefathers met the b., 685:19
　give man b. he can sail, 557:10
　is on the shore, 422:26
　Michael row b. ashore, 863:5
　news of the b., 454:27
　of life be light, 620:6
　of your flesh, 830:14
　pea-green b., 499:15
　people in a b., 842:4
　sea so great b. so small, 847:10
　sings in b. on bay, 482:15
　slow b. to China, 785:2
　speed bonnie b., 616:9
　they sank my b., 799:3

Boats against the current, 746:9
   messing about in b., 618:4
   oh the little cargo b., 634:17
   shallow bauble b., 207:23
   that are not steered, 225:25
Boatswain, memory of B. a dog, 419:10
   tight and midshipmite, 563:11
Bobolink for Chorister, 544:17
Bobtail nag, 538:14
Boca, el pez muere por la b., 862:17
   en b. cerrada no entran moscas, 862:19
Bodes some strange eruption, 200:15
Bodice, loosens fragrant b., 437:1
Bodies a living sacrifice, 43:15
   abstain from abusing b., 72:16
   are buried in peace, 33:10
   as clothes to b., 625:8
   as imagination b. forth, 182:3
   clothes without b., 625:8
   died before b. died, 776:11
   elements or principles of b., 359:16
   freedom of living b., 501:1
   gave b. to commonwealth, 74:5
   ghosts of defunct b. fly, 270:23
   hollow sound same as our b., 759:7
   molecules that compose b., 359:16
   movements of largest b., 366:13
   mutual actions of two b., 291:4
   nature works by b. unseen, 92:15
   of unburied men, 244:3
   our b. are our gardens, 213:2
   our selves our souls and b., 51:1
   persons with torn b. happy, 655:12
   pile b. at Austerlitz, 681:10
   princes like to heavenly b., 167:24
   remove weight from heavenly b., 811:11
   rough notes and dead b., 649:16
   single soul in two b., 79:14
   soldiers bore dead b. by, 185:3
   these black b., 372:2
   thrown into sea, 759:14
   unclothed, 235:24
   we have seen dead b., 447:1
Bodiless and simple, 808:15
Bodily decrepitude wisdom, 641:17
   exercise when compulsory, 77:18
   form from natural thing, 640:2
   form of them b., 569:7
   states following perception, 582:4
Boding tremblers, 342:8
Bodkin, bare b., 203:33
Body, absent in b. present in spirit, 44:3
   age and b. of the time, 204:13
   and spirit twins, 569:16
   art work of b. and soul, 517:8
   Asclepius cured the b., 76:n3
   be not afraid of my b., 520:1
   book makes b. cold, 547:9
   carry b. for sentimental value, 777:5
   changed to light, 856:10
   clog of his b., 258:6
   continues in state of rest, 291:2
   damned of b. and soul, 633:1
   demd damp b., 496:23
   dies body's beauty lives, 687:5
   distressed in mind b. or estate, 50:7
   each petty artery in b., 202:9
   employ b. to serve, 95:1
   fear made manifest on b., 526:13

Body *(continued)*
   filled and vacant mind, 193:16
   find thy b. by wall, 531:5
   for this is My B., 49:13
   gave b. to country's earth, 180:6
   gin a b. meet a b., 845:n4
   give b. to be burned, 44:18
   happiness beneficial for b., 658:3
   having seen his b. borne before her,
     490:18
   health intelligence talent, 622:7
   her b. thought, 236:1
   her dead b. wears smile, 827:12
   here in the b. pent, 396:1
   human b. sacred, 519:24
   I have risen to a b., 817:3
   ideals in one dark b., 648:11
   infirm and exhausted, 140:10
   instrument for art, 624:16
   is his book, 235:6
   is Nature God is soul, 311:7
   is not b. more than raiment, 34:17
   its b. brevity, 402:2
   John Brown's b., 558:3
   joint and motive of b., 208:19
   lean b. and visage, 258:6
   liberation of the human b., 651:7
   light around the b., 817:3
   light of the b., 34:14
   like b. wholly b., 687:8
   little b. mighty heart, 192:25
   loves world as his b., 58:14
   man member of b., 465:3
   marry my b. to that dust, 249:1
   material fortune associated with b., 114:17
   mind or b. to prefer, 311:9
   more familiar with Africa than own b.,
     828:9
   my b. my dungeon is, 599:7
   my good bright dog, 806:3
   my house, 806:2
   no riches above sound b., 32:41
   not b. enough to cover mind, 398:19
   not bruised to pleasure soul, 640:15
   not more than soul, 519:20
   of Benjamin Franklin Printer, 319:2
   of each creature different, 73:13
   of little recruit, 752:11
   of this death, 43:4
   old in b. but never mind, 91:16
   one motion, 781:5
   oppressions of b. and mind, 359:3
   part of man's Self, 581:17
   pass from colder to hotter b., 532:13
   perfectly spherical, 499:14
   piece of b. torn out by root, 781:16
   Poet filling other B., 440:14
   poet of B. poet of Soul, 519:7
   politic like human body, 331:3
   power lies in mind and b., 95:1
   presence of b. in question, 407:28
   pygmy-b., 283:8
   reading to mind as exercise to b., 301:13
   remember, 628:8
   Resurrection of the b., 50:3
   ruler having human b. as subject, 77:2
   sex woven into whole b., 617:19
   sickness-broken b., 258:5
   so young b. with so old head, 189:18

Body *(continued)*
   soul gentle companion of b., 114:12
   soul is form and doth b. make, 162:5
   soul its b. off, 642:2
   soul look b. touch, 642:9
   sound mind in sound b., 113:17
   sound of b. and mind, 99:16
   startlingly muscled b., 819:5
   stepped out of my b., 820:3
   subject to forces of gravity, 796:6
   swayed to music, 640:15
   swung gently, 580:6
   this is my b., 37:27, 44:15
   'tis mind makes b. rich, 175:37
   to be buried obscurely, 168:19
   touch palm of hand to my b., 520:1
   whole b. not be cast into hell, 34:4
   wind made one's b. feel light, 661:19
   with whole b. listen, 690:1
   without spirit dead, 47:15
   woman's b. the woman, 580:7
   worms destroy this b., 14:25
Bodyguard, army is McClellan's b.,
     475:12
   if you'll be my b., 837:12
   of lies, 667:11
Body-hungry, soul-hungry worse than b.,
   850:7
Body's beauty lives, 687:5
   casting b. vest aside, 277:5
   go Soul the b. quest, 160:7
   hardly in a b. power, 378:2
Boffin the Golden Dustman, 499:3
Bog, snow falling on B. of Allen, 696:4
   to an admiring B., 544:13
Bogus revelation, 690:16
Boil, dreams b. up from ring of myth,
   766:15
   maketh the deep b. like a pot, 15:22
   we b. at different degrees, 457:11
Boilers, love so hot as nigh to burst my b.,
   418:16
Boiling, Hiroshima b., 801:12
   why sea b. hot, 552:3
Boils round naked isles, 318:5
Bois, cor au fond des b., 443:n2
   n'irons plus aux b., 534:n1
Boisterously, as b. maintained as gained,
   178:12
Bold, alive and so b. O earth, 429:24
   and turbulent of wit, 283:8
   bad man, 160:18, 230:24
   be bloody b. and resolute, 221:26
   be b., 161:11
   be not too b., 161:12
   brave men and b., 849:2
   cook and captain b., 563:11
   in conscious virtue b., 309:14
   inspiring b. John Barleycorn, 379:19
   jockey of Norfolk not too b., 161:n4
   let our minds be b., 607:4
   look with favor on b. beginning, 96:5
   maiden never b., 212:27
   man first eat oyster, 299:14
   peasantry, 341:29
   persistent experimentation, 697:12
   righteous are b. as a lion, 23:15
   story of Cambuscan b., 260:8
   too b. to imagine, 348:24

Book *(continued)*

little b. go without me, 134:*n*3
little b. I cast thee on waters, 134:*n*3
Macaulay a b. in breeches, 399:1
makes my body cold, 547:9
may be very amusing, 341:9
mine adversary had written a b., 14:41
nature's infinite b. of secrecy, 222:28
never read b. not year old, 457:4
new era in life from b., 507:5
no b. so bad but some good, 114:7
no Frigate like B., 546:11
no moral or immoral b., 604:11
not at his picture but his b., 238:4
not concerned with Poetry, 738:5
not more in b. than before, 767:3
note it in a b., 27:25
note you in b. of memory, 171:17
of a certain Cicero, 119:8
of deeds words and art, 517:23
of Egoism, 541:13
of female logic, 490:20
of knowledge fair, 265:25
of Life begins, 605:3
of life was opened, 48:37
of moonlight not written, 686:9
of Moons defend ye, 844:19
of Nature, 155:*n*5
of nature, 281:5
of Songs and Sonnets, 190:16
of Verses underneath Bough, 471:5
oh for b. and shady nook, 577:2
one b. furnishes treatise, 331:10
only one b. in them, 398:27
page of b. carelessly open, 821:10
present new b. to Cornelius, 93:22
product of a different self, 658:5
putting mind's eye in b., 807:7
read b. of fate, 191:36
reads but one b., 252:18
recognizes me in my b., 153:18
same today and forever, 489:2
say in sentences what others in b., 589:21
sealed with seven seals, 48:18
sour misfortune's b., 184:14
take down this b., 637:4
that they were printed in a b., 14:24
that wonderful b., 447:20
the world the b. of God, 232:11
this is an important b., 700:10
this grand b. the universe, 169:18
thou art the b., 248:21
throw whole b. in fire, 461:7
Time criticized for us, 515:19
to be read in twilight, 460:14
turn over library make b., 327:24
well-chosen b. or friend, 232:14
what is this marvelous b., 331:10
what is use of b., 549:10
what thou seest write in a b., 48:3
what you don't know make b., 399:4
when nobleman writes b., 329:*n*1
which does not sell, 408:1
who reads American b., 398:12
without pictures or conversations,
  549:10
works at body of b., 340:9
written in God's b., 121:5
young fellow wrote a b., 682:*n*1

Bookish ambition, 239:16
  theoric, 212:14
Bookmen, you two are b., 176:36
Book's a book although nothing in 't, 419:13
Books about books, 154:5
  all b. else so poor, 293:8
  all good b. alike, 754:12
  ambition to be stored with b., 239:16
  are weapons, 698:18
  as schoolboys from b., 183:12
  authority from others' b., 176:20
  bear him up, 293:4
  belong to eyes, 456:10
  best b. universal appeal, 662:21
  bloodless substitute, 598:10
  borrowers of b., 407:12
  burn b. burn human beings, 442:10
  by persons in America, 487:12
  by which printers have lost, 258:10
  children of brain, 297:16
  clad in blak or reed, 134:30
  consumed midnight oil, 307:3
  cover country in b., 588:8
  crushed by b., 793:5
  deep versed in b., 268:29
  do serve some purpose, 772:10
  do with friends as b., 455:29
  do you read b. through, 327:18
  dreams b. each a world, 394:21
  drunk on b., 691:18
  even bad b. are b., 819:3
  feelings beings b. events battles, 768:11
  few friends and many b., 275:5
  few thousand battered b., 709:5
  from b. of honor razed, 226:4
  gentleman not in your b., 194:8
  God written all the b., 559:1
  good b. truer than real, 754:12
  Homer all b. you need, 293:8
  I cannot live without b., 359:1
  I have read all the b., 583:13
  I'll burn my b., 171:6
  in lighted windows b. kept watch,
    657:14
  in running brooks, 197:37
  knowing I loved my b., 229:15
  lard their lean b., 240:2
  learn anatomy not from b., 242:11
  Learning wiser without b., 348:11
  legacies genius leaves, 302:13
  like men their authors, 297:15
  lineaments of Gospel b., 171:9
  live without b., 548:11
  magic preservation in b., 434:20
  many b. and never use them, 239:16
  men read as b. too much, 310:1
  monkeys write b. in British Museum,
    695:3
  more in woods than in b., 126:7
  never die, 698:18
  never read children's b., 627:20
  new French b., 493:9
  next o'er his b., 313:17
  no b. but score and tally, 172:22
  no pulping of b., 786:14
  not in your b., 194:8
  not killed by fire, 698:18
  of all time, 517:15
  of making many b., 25:10, 692:16

Books *(continued)*

of quotations, 665:10
of the hour, 517:15
old clothes a few b., 703:7
old manners b. wines, 342:15
only b. woman's looks, 412:5
out of olde b. newe science, 133:12
read deliberately as written, 507:4
read only b. that wound us, 701:7
readers like my b., 168:24
reading valueless b., 517:14
receive value from esteem, 282:8
rural quiet friendship b., 318:2
sins scarlet b. read, 653:15
some b. not adequately reviewed, 572:10
some b. to be tasted, 168:15
spectacles of b., 282:17
sweet serenity of b., 467:21
they are the b. the arts, 177:8
think for me, 407:26
trees shall be my b., 199:2
twenty b. at his beddes heed, 134:30
two classes of b., 517:15
undeservedly forgotten, 776:12
university a collection of b., 434:21
ways of acquiring b., 733:4
well or badly written, 604:11
why aren't the b. enough, 839:10
worst b. universal appeal, 662:21
you may carry to fire, 326:2
Booksellers, for all b. in world, 338:3
Bookstore, human nature weak in b.,
  500:13
Book-words what are you, 520:9
Bookworming in pajamas, 800:20
Boom, guns b. far, 664:10
  in petroleum but not in poetry, 794:11
Booming of new-come bee, 688:6
  surge of Aegean, 76:5
Booms, beetle b. adown glooms, 596:1
Boon, sordid b., 394:18
Boone, when Daniel B. goes by, 750:15
Boot, hey for b. and horse, 514:4
  saddle to horse, 491:13
  stamping on human face forever, 765:18
Booted, ready b. and spurred, 448:20
Booth died blind, 684:14
  since Lincoln shot by B., 745:9
Bootless cries, 226:5
Boots boots boots, 635:16
  died in b. like pioneer, 750:6
  drunk and asleep in b., 686:16
  gunpowder ran out heels of b., 336:12
  not to resist wind and tide, 173:5
  well then o'er shoes o'er b., 565:*n*1
  what b. it at one gate to make defense,
    269:4
  what b. with incessant care, 261:19
Boot-soles, look for me under b., 519:23
Booze, empty bottle of b., 827:19
  Georgia b., 750:8
Bo-peep, as if they played at b., 248:10
  little B., 859:9
Borden, Lizzie B. took ax, 849:10
Border nor breed nor birth, 632:19
  not move markers on b., 5:6
  through all wide B., 396:17
Borders, departure beyond b. death, 730:11
  invade b. of my realm, 151:13

Bosom *(continued)*
   I must not see, 277:22
   in ocean's b. unespied, 277:9
   in your fragrant b. dies, 253:15
   let me to Thy b. fly, 322:24
   liest in Abraham's b., 392:16
   loosened from her b. the girdle, 53:15
   of his Father and his God, 335:4
   of urgent West, 586:5
   sleep in Abraham's b., 174:11
   stuffed b. of perilous stuff, 222:12
   swell b. with thy fraught, 214:14
   third in your b., 183:20
   thorns that in b. lodge, 202:20
   warm cheek and rising b., 335:6
   which thy frozen b. bears, 212:n1
   wife of thy b., 10:5
   within b. is September, 844:9
   wring his b., 341:21
   write sorrow on b. of earth, 179:27
Bosomed deep in vines, 313:24
   high in tufted trees, 259:15
Bosoms, fold to their b. the viper, 516:1
   hair hang and brush b., 493:14
   men's business and b., 167:4
   waters lift their b., 207:26
   white b. of actresses, 326:7
Bossuet, celebrities such as B., 554:11
Boston, a Thucydides at B., 336:5
   blatant Bassarid of B., 569:11
   Cluett Shirt B. Garter, 739:15
   Concord Lexington, 414:16
   Evening Transcript, 717:20
   good old B., 621:22
   in B. ask how much does he know,
      561:19
   joined the church at B., 270:12
   just returned from B., 739:3
   marching through B., 801:11
   marriage serious around B., 737:20
   not blue on B., 800:13
   runs to brains, 606:6
   solid man of B., 467:13
   State-House hub, 473:13
   though I am not genuine B., 563:6
Boston-plated, I am B., 563:6
Boston's Marlborough Street, 800:20
Bo'sun tight and midshipmite, 563:11
Botanist, puzzle to b., 557:16
Botanize, peep and b., 392:2
Botany, all their b. Latin, 453:10
Botch of it trying to swap, 476:10
Botched civilization, 709:5
Boteler, Dr. B. said of strawberries, 253:5
Both, by adventuring b., 187:24
   I am with b., 178:5
   plague o' b. houses, 183:29
   wear b. for b. are thine, 173:33
Bother, long words B. me, 697:6
Bothered, bewitched b. bewildered,
      744:12
   hot and b., 636:1
Bottle, a little for the b., 362:10
   fragrance in whiskey b., 797:2
   friend in need nor b., 497:25
   large cold b., 597:4
   leave b. on chimleypiece, 497:3
   my b. of salvation, 160:8
   of hay, 181:25

Bottle *(continued)*
   shake and shake catsup b., 773:8
   take b. down from shelf, 789:6
Bottled lightning, 496:24
Bottleneck, president is b., 786:7
Bottles, narrow-necked b., 313:13
   new wine in old b., 35:21
   stay the b. of heaven, 15:12
Bottom, bless thee B., 181:20
   build from b. up, 697:11
   dive into b. of deep, 185:9
   every vat stand upon b., 281:17
   from shore sees sea b., 132:4
   I see not the b. of it, 208:14
   line is in heaven, 782:13
   not in one b. trusted, 187:14
   of the monstrous world, 262:3
   of the worst, 207:31
   sees into b. of my grief, 184:7
   sit on our own b., 154:7
   strike rock and go to b., 376:13
   unknown b. like bay of Portugal, 199:30
Bottomless, consciousness as b. lake, 574:4
   in b. nights you sleep, 603:13
   perdition, 263:23
   some ponds thought b., 507:14
Bouchon, plus léger qu'un b., 603:n6
Bough, apple reddens on high b., 58:5
   bloom along b., 618:6
   blossom that hangs on b., 230:13
   Book of Verses underneath B., 471:5
   breaks cradle fall, 592:1
   golden b., 640:2
   old forsaken b., 473:19
   sings on orchard b., 492:4
   touch not single b., 451:22
   wet black b., 708:16
Boughs, bird that lives in the b., 363:14
   cedar green with b., 601:7
   easy under the apple b., 795:8
   incense hangs upon b., 437:10
   lowest b. brushwood sheaf, 492:4
   off many a tree, 250:7
   shade of melancholy b., 198:22
   soul into b. does glide, 277:5
   which shake against cold, 226:24
Bought, beauty b. by judgment of eye,
      176:27
   bliss b. by years, 508:19
   crooked cat, 860:6
   Dickon thy master b., 161:n4
   golden opinions, 219:19
   good names to be b., 184:30
   honest politician stays b., 445:11
   knowledge b. in market, 512:7
   men who can't be b., 681:19
   neither b. nor sold, 830:5
   soul b. and paid for, 489:20
   strangers who b. laws, 746:2
   three pecks of meal, 861:7
   wisdom is not b., 853:13
Boughten friendship by side, 670:7
Bouillabaisse noble dish is, 490:17
Bouncer, Lois De Fee lady b., 769:2
Bound bones and veins in me, 587:3
   born under one law to another b., 162:16
   bourn b. of land, 229:25
   by countless ties, 670:12
   by own definition of criticism, 530:9

Bound *(continued)*
   each to each, 392:7
   I'm b. away, 671:7
   in icy chains by thee, 212:n1
   in shallows and miseries, 197:13
   in to saucy doubts, 221:9
   in with triumphant sea, 179:13
   leap tall buildings at single b., 795:1
   nothing but hath his b., 174:27
   of the everlasting hills, 7:38
   towns where you would have b. me,
      750:7
   upon wheel of fire, 217:29
   utmost b. of thought, 481:11
   we're b. away, 862:3
   with red tape, 498:13
Boundaries, Great Spirit knows no b., 387:6
   here b. meet, 525:12
   in safety within b., 699:8
   which divide Life, 478:17
   without war because no b., 387:n5
Bounded in a nutshell, 203:15
   our Country however b., 487:5
   waters lift bosoms, 207:26
Boundless as we wish our souls, 428:15
   contiguity of shade, 347:26
   drew from b. deep, 487:2
   endless sublime, 422:2
   his wealth, 396:11
   vision grows, 534:9
Bounds, living know no b., 254:5
   of place and time, 335:9
   wider b. be set, 625:11
Bountiful, Lady B., 305:4
Bounty, for his b. no winter, 224:4
   large was his b., 335:3
   lust of goat b. of God, 372:17
   those his former b. fed, 285:12
Bouquets while I'm living, 682:3
Bourbon or Nassau go higher, 297:7
Bourgeois anyone whose thinking vulgar,
      527:9
   épater le b., 525:n1
   hatred of b. beginning of wisdom, 527:8
   horrible invention the b., 526:15
   how beastly b. is, 707:14
   in ferment of youth, 527:3
   Marxism product of b. mind, 703:3
   quelle atroce invention b., 526:n3
   suppression of b. state, 654:10
   you must shock b., 525:3
Bourgeoisie class of modern capitalists,
      511:n2
   draws nations into civilization, 511:3
   face to face with b., 511:4
   played revolutionary role, 511:2
Bourn bound of land, 229:25
   country from whose b., 203:33
   lambs bleat from hilly b., 438:13
Bourreau, la victime et le b., 524:n6
Bout, notes with many a winding b., 259:20
   with love, 61:17
Bovary, I am Madame B., 527:11
   Madame B. had beauty, 527:1
Bow, always made awkward b., 441:6
   and accept end, 668:16
   arrow from Almighty's b., 375:4
   as unto b. cord is, 467:2
   better to b. than break, 147:24

Bow *(continued)*
bow lower middle classes, 564:16
cannot stand bent, 157:24
down thine ear, 22:27
draw b. ride and speak truth, 424:25
he bar and arwes brighte, 135:24
many strings to b., 148:14
nor does Apollo always stretch b., 99:25
of burning gold, 375:17
or brooch or braid, 587:17
set my b. in the cloud, 6:34
strong men shall b. themselves, 25:7
tensely strung easily broken, 103:7
themselves when he did sing, 230:27
to that whose course run, 335:21
what water lapping b., 719:18
when trees b. heads, 548:2
with my b. and arrow, 857:14
Bowed, at her feet he b., 10:33
by weight of centuries, 601:3
he fell where he b., 10:33
his comely head down, 276:24
to idolatries patient knee, 421:3
with grief and shame b. down, 258:4
Bowels, fatal b. of deep, 174:9
news not yet reached my b., 819:13
no belly no b., 724:13
of Christ, 254:12, 660:6
of compassion, 47:40
were moved for him, 25:25
Bower, as Adam walking from from b., 520:1
charmed alike tilt-yard and b., 417:11
in hall or b., 260:15
in heaven's high b., 372:8
keep b. quiet for us, 436:8
of roses by Bendemeer's, 412:11
Bowers, blossoms birds and b., 247:14
Bowery, Malcolm Lowry of B., 783:7
Bowl, called for his b., 856:18
capacious salad b., 599:5
golden b. be broken, 25:8
goldfish in glass b., 655:3
inverted B. we call Sky, 471:22
Love in a golden b., 372:12
lurk I in gossip's b., 181:5
of Night, 470:14
onion atoms lurk in b., 399:2
roasted crabs hiss in b., 177:18
went to sea in b., 858:3
Bowled, in bowling alley b. sun, 292:7
Bowlegged, climb myself b. up poles, 811:17
Bowling, poor Tom B., 362:11
Bows down to wood and stone, 416:5
Bowwow, big B. strain, 406:*n*1
Bowwows, demnition b., 496:27
Box, alabaster b. of ointment, 37:19
laying poems away in long b., 821:14
paper you drop in ballot b., 506:6
pathway to ballot b., 503:9
twelve good men into b., 409:19
where sweets compacted lie, 250:10
Boxin' Day, beadle on B., 495:29
Boy, barefoot b., 468:9
be a farmer's b., 845:7
beamish b., 551:11
beggarly b., 515:11
blueeyed b., 739:13
Chatterton marvelous b., 392:9
close upon the growing b., 393:11

Boy *(continued)*
crying wolf, 756:8
didn't raise b. to be soldier, 850:21
eternal, 228:9
every b. and every gal, 564:22
first shaves, 757:13
guiding a b. and a girl, 835:13
if b. have not woman's gift, 175:20
imagination of b. healthy, 436:7
is most powerful of Hellenes, 64:20
Jewish man remain fifteen-year-old b.,
   828:13
lad of mettle a good b., 185:19
let b. win his spurs, 132:17
like b. playing on seashore, 291:6
lily-livered b., 222:10
little b. blue, 857:11
Little B. Blue kissed them, 597:6
little tiny b., 210:19
love is a b., 271:17
make a small b. dizzy, 780:7
Minstrel B., 411:16
most unmanageable of all animals, 78:14
my greatness, 224:6
my lovely living b., 155:8
nineteen-year-old American b., 835:10
office b. to Attorney's firm, 563:17
only way to make b. sharp, 495:24
parent see b. as he really is, 651:10
parlous b., 174:6
purblind wayward b., 176:33
read to by a b., 718:2
schoolrooms for b., 509:7
smiling b. fell dead, 491:8
speak roughly to little b., 550:7
stood on burning deck, 432:1
that shoots so trim, 844:3
too much hope of thee loved b., 237:20
well for fisherman's b., 482:15
what a good b. am I, 857:3
when I was a b., 445:16, 652:14
who lives down lane, 857:10
who looks after sheep, 857:17
will you marry it, 827:8
wine dear b. and truth, 57:13
Boyhood changing into man, 640:17
ignominy of b., 640:17
saw Greek islands, 751:14
Boyhood's years, 412:7
Boyish, all wars b., 516:24
Boylston Street, on B. photograph, 801:12
Boy's best friend is mother, 811:6
love, 217:4
will wind's will, 467:7
Boys, all wars fought by b., 516:24
and girls level with men, 224:1
and girls together, 625:13
are marching, 522:8
as b. do sparrows, 297:17
as flies to wanton b., 217:11
ask b. to go win just one, 774:6
being human though b., 652:14
claret the liquor for b., 328:20
do what Asian b. ought to be doing,
   779:7
generous b. in happiness bred, 516:25
lightfoot b., 619:7
little b. made of, 859:18
mealy b. beef-faced b., 496:12

Boys *(continued)*
not about to send American b., 779:7
not sent into foreign wars, 698:13
rally round flag b., 522:9
River City's gonna have B. Band, 764:10
say b. another whiskey, 584:6
see what b. in back room will have, 785:1
steady b. steady, 335:22
that swim on bladders, 231:2
them good old b., 839:7
there we saw men and b., 846:*n*3
three merry b. are we, 242:15
throw stones at frogs, 85:4
till b. come home, 663:1
Bozzy, come to me my dear B., 329:5
Brace lace latch or catch, 587:17
ourselves to duties, 666:2
Bracelet of bright hair, 235:10
Brach, Lady the b., 216:1
rather hear Lady my b., 186:11
Bracing, drying after b. showers, 745:8
Bradford, there goes John B., 150:4
Brae, waly doun the b., 854:10
Braes, banks and b. o' bonny Doon, 378:21
green b., 379:10
Brag, beauty is Nature's b., 261:9
left this vault to b. of, 220:25
one went to b., 272:5
Bragg, more grape Captain B., 417:22
Bragging, bray of b. tongues, 67:12
Brahmin caste of New England, 473:17
hymn B. sings, 453:23
Braid, bow or brooch or b., 587:17
of creation trembles, 771:10
Braids, twisted b. of lilies, 261:10
Brain, abundance result of b., 597:10
all that cakes b., 516:14
as for my b., 841:6
Bear of Very Little B., 697:6
beauty comes from beautiful b., 518:9
book and volume of my b., 202:23
books children of b., 297:16
brain-sick b. workers, 557:5
burn from b. and breast, 664:13
changes continuous, 581:14
children of an idle b., 182:23
device to keep ears from grating, 784:13
disillusionment that woman has b., 758:6
feed b. with better things, 664:13
gladness thy b. know, 429:20
heat-oppressed b., 220:8
him with lady's fan, 185:17
imprint of external world on b., 781:12
in what furnace thy b., 374:6
intoxicate the b., 308:11
is like a muscle, 830:6
light broke upon b., 422:22
love not alone immured in b., 177:5
may devise laws, 187:28
memory warder of b., 220:2
not an organ of sex, 623:4
of feathers heart of lead, 313:18
paper bullets of the b., 194:28
pen gleaned teeming b., 439:8
Plato's b., 453:24
possess a poet's b., 169:17
schoolmasters puzzle b., 342:17
superior have best b., 554:3
unquiet heart and b., 483:15

Breathe *(continued)*
    hate were why men b., 740:10
    hear bronze Negroes b., 801:11
    heart pause to b., 423:1
    his native air, 308:3
    if such there b., 396:11
    not his name, 411:9
    slaves cannot b. in England, 347:27
    thou thereon didst only b., 238:3
    thoughts that b., 335:10
    yearning to b. free, 595:6
    you but knock b. shine, 236:11
Breathed, first true gentleman that b., 233:7
    still b. in sighs, 309:24
Breathes, hell itself b. out, 205:12
    of nations saved, 424:12
    there the man, 396:11
    upon bank of violets, 208:25
    with human breath, 480:9
Breathing, almost hear them b. as they
        march, 801:*n*3
    health and quiet b., 436:8
    household laws, 392:14
    music b. from her face, 275:*n*5
    revenge, 508:2
    talking coeval with b., 300:5
    whether b. is eating, 75:21
    without a tighter b., 546:3
Breathless, hanging b. on fate, 466:19
    we flung us on hill, 712:14
    with adoration, 392:15
Breath's a ware that will not keep, 618:8
Bred, dainties b. of a book, 176:34
    en bawn in brier-patch, 593:8
    me long ago, 619:5
    where is fancy b., 189:3
Bredon, bells sound on B., 618:15
Breeches, coat red b. blue, 405:23
    cost a crown, 844:6
    hand in b. pocket, 440:4
    Macaulay a book in b., 399:1
    women wear the b., 240:8
Breed and haunt, 219:15
    border nor b. nor birth, 632:19
    feared by their b., 179:12
    happy b. of men, 179:12
    if sun b. maggots, 203:6
    more careful of b. of horses, 292:2
    or England b. again, 169:13
    use doth b. habit, 176:15
Breeding, bad b. and vulgar manner, 74:12
    Burgundy without b., 741:14
    eating drinking and b., 519:9
    lilacs out of dead land, 718:11
    test of man or woman's b., 609:4
    write with ease to show b., 368:6
Breeds, familiarity b. contempt, 60:13
    lesser b. without Law, 635:4
Breeze, Athena sent favorable b., 54:13
    battle and the b., 408:16
    fair b. blew, 399:20
    flag to April's b., 453:11
    folds rippling in b., 490:2
    free as the b., 395:22
    ghost fled like fluttering b., 97:14
    midday summer b., 670:11
    of morning moves, 485:9
    plastic and vast one intellectual b.,
        399:10

Breeze *(continued)*
    that beat upon her, 600:10
    tyranny in tainted b., 344:10
Breezes, sunset b. shiver, 627:5
Breezy call of Morn, 334:12
Brekekekex, 75:18
Brennt Paris, 726:*n*4
Brent, bonie brow was b., 379:4
Brer Fox he lay low, 593:6
Brethren, firstborn among many b., 43:8
    for b. to dwell together, 20:10
    forget love to friends and b., 31:5
    least of these my b., 37:18
    our b. already in field, 353:3
    we be b., 7:1
Brève, la vie est b., 556:*n*1
Brevis, vita b. est, 73:*n*2
Brevity, its body b., 402:2
    soul of wit, 202:33
Brew, soup or broth or b., 490:17
    that is true, 793:16
Brewed, taste liquor never b., 544:7
Brewer, not from benevolence of b., 338:13
Brewer's, I am a b. horse, 186:17
Brews, as he b. so shall he drink, 237:5
    livelier liquor than Muse, 619:9
Bribe, cannot hope to b. or twist, 710:4
    too poor for b., 335:18
Bribery, treason b. or other high crimes,
        360:14
Bribes, tell everyone I take b., 472:19
Brick, no more straw to make b., 8:10
    road paved with yellow b., 606:15
Bricks, Rome a city of b., 102:7
    somebody's always throwing b., 685:2
Bridal, bridegrooms brides and b. cakes,
        247:14
    of earth and sky, 250:9
Bride, barren b., 310:5
    bridegroom seek your b., 619:16
    encounter darkness as a b., 211:21
    goes for walk returns with b., 793:14
    holy city as a b., 48:38
    I was a b., 831:14
    in her rich adornin', 592:13
    my b. to be he murmured, 693:3
    never turns to b., 618:9
    of quietness, 437:16
    paced into the hall, 399:16
Bride-bed, thought b. to have decked,
        206:30
Bridechamber, can children of b. mourn,
        35:20
Bridegroom all night through, 618:9
    coming out of his chamber, 16:11
    fresh as a b., 185:2
    happy b. Hesper brings, 619:16
    I was the b., 831:14
    in my death, 223:35
    mourn as b. with them, 35:20
    went forth to meet b., 37:12
Bridegrooms brides and bridal cakes, 247:14
Brides, as lion woos his b., 337:13
    bridegrooms b. and bridal cakes, 247:14
Bridge, and the b. is love, 749:12
    asses' b., 84:*n*6
    at highest point in arc of b., 788:5
    body swung beneath b., 580:6
    broken arch of London B., 448:7

Bridge *(continued)*
    don't cross b. until come to it, 847:13
    give him silver b., 862:14
    London B. falling down, 625:13, 857:4
    of Sighs, 421:5
    of Time, 525:4
    over troubled water, 837:11
    rickety wooden b., 835:13
    rude b. that arched the flood, 453:11
    twenty men crossing b., 686:8
    youth build b. to moon, 505:7
Bridgeport said I pointing, 561:3
Bridges, crossing twenty b., 686:8
    crumble the b., 756:16
    flock of b. bleating, 689:17
    forbids to sleep under b., 586:18
Bridle, between spur and b., 252:3
    gae his b. reins a shake, 379:3
Bridled, millions saddled and b., 448:20
Brief as lightning in collied night, 180:20
    as woman's love, 205:1
    chronicles of the time, 203:25
    December day, 468:17
    dreamy kind delight, 637:15
    hours and weeks, 227:17
    life here our portion, 511:10
    little b. authority, 211:13
    out out b. candle, 222:16
    thanksgiving, 569:3
    transit where dreams cross, 719:15
    when b. I become obscure, 101:18
    when our b. light has set, 94:4
Brier, bred en bawn in b.-patch, 593:8
    thorough bush thorough b., 181:3
Briers, full of b. is working-day world, 197:33
Brig, mate of Nancy b., 563:11
Brigade, Light B., 484:25
Bright, all calm all b., 427:10
    all calm as it was b., 279:5
    all things b. beautiful, 508:7
    and battering sandal, 587:13
    and violet-crowned, 66:10
    angels are b. still, 221:33
    Apollo's lute, 177:7
    April shakes out her hair, 704:14
    autumn moon is b., 764:3
    best of dark and b., 422:13
    billows smooth and b., 551:18
    bodies of lovers drowned, 689:20
    bracelet of b. hair, 235:10
    container can contain, 780:16
    countenance of truth, 262:12
    creature scorn not one, 395:20
    dark with excessive b., 265:27
    day is done, 224:5
    day so cool so calm so b., 250:9
    early b. transient chaste, 285:*n*4
    exhalation in the evening, 230:31
    eye of heaven shined b., 161:1
    eyes of danger, 599:12
    girdle furled, 531:2
    gleam of noble deeds, 66:8
    goddess excellently b., 237:10
    harmony in her b. eye, 275:21
    he saw lady b., 854:2
    honor b., 208:9
    is the ring of words, 599:14
    keep up your b. swords, 212:22
    ladies whose b. eyes, 259:19

Bull, a Cock and a B., 333:2
  be on b. side, 567:13
  cloud that looked like b., 74:14
  greatest of all is John B., 424:29
  handsome as b. that kidnapped Europa, 91:1
  John B. or Englishman's Fireside, 383:15
  moose, 615:1
  savage b. bear yoke, 194:11
  taking b. by both horns kissed her, 693:3
Bullen's, dawned from B. eyes, 334:7
Bullet, ballot stronger than b., 474:8
  bite b., 632:20
  faster than speeding b., 795:1
  has its billet, 293:11
  that will kill me not cast, 388:6
  through his head, 652:11
  who paid for the b., 782:2
Bullets made of lead, 860:18
  paper b. of the brain, 194:28
  seek out where heart lies, 768:8
  word as b. flying, 611:20
Bullied into following master artist, 716:19
  out of vice, 458:14
Bullocks, whose talk is of b., 33:7
Bullpen, waiting sentence in b., 801:1
Bulls, plowman's story of b., 104:19
Bulrush, seeking knot in a b., 86:7
Bulrushes, ark of b., 8:1
Bulwark, floating b. of our island, 338:9
  never failing, 144:9
  of continuing liberty, 698:9
  of Greece famous Athens, 66:10
Bulwarks, Britannia needs no b., 408:17
  greatest b. of liberty, 339:11
Bum, belly shoulder b., 642:17
  I'll moider de b., 784:14
  let's face it I am, 794:15
Bumbast out blank verse, 165:18
Bumble, the law is a ass said Mr. B., 496:14
Bump, don't b. into furniture, 753:10
  go b. in the night, 847:9
Bumper of good liquor, 367:24
Bumping, love b. against obstacles of civilization, 461:4
Bumps along the dusk, 596:1
Bumpy, fasten seatbelts b. night, 783:11
Bunbury, invaluable invalid B., 605:7
Bunch-backed, curse this pois'nous b. toad, 173:36
Buncombe and millions mostly fools, 435:8
Bunghole, stopping a b., 206:25
Bunk, been in his b. below, 580:23
  history more or less b., 530:n1
Bunker Hill, there is Boston and B., 414:16
Buns, hot cross b., 859:4
Bunting, baby b., 858:8
Buoy too small for sight, 217:18
Burbled as it came, 551:11
Burden, bear any b., 799:7
  bear his own b., 45:23
  borne the b., 36:36
  brown man's b., 635:n1
  changes labor from b. to honor, 686:2
  grasshopper shall be a b., 25:8
  great b. upon his back, 281:14
  grievous b. was thy birth, 174:12
  her lot not b., 823:13
  my b. is light, 35:35

Burden *(continued)*
  not b. our remembrances, 230:15
  of his song, 352:6
  of incommunicable, 418:1
  of my song, 843:20
  of nothing to do, 289:20
  of the desert of the sea, 27:7
  of the mystery, 391:1
  of them is intolerable, 50:18
  on back b. of world, 601:3
  they're a b. for us, 759:9
  vapors weep their b., 485:14
  weight of another's b., 252:9
  White Man's b., 635:6
  years are still a b., 69:14
  youth and age equally a b., 77:1
Burdens, had such b. on mind, 640:8
  they that bare b., 13:15
Burdensome, school in which nothing b., 120:1
  when life is b., 71:21
Bureau, super-legal-aid b., 695:8
Burgeoning wood brings forth, 52:31
Burglaree, with a little b., 564:6
Burglary, flat b. as ever committed, 195:2
  vary piracee with b., 564:6
Burgonet, arm and b. of men, 223:6
Burgundy, naive domestic B., 741:14
  treat wretch with B., 296:2
Burial, no b. this pretty pair, 843:13
  of my rosy feelings, 816:18
Buried, bodies are b. in peace, 33:10
  body to be b. obscurely, 168:19
  Caesar bled, 471:9
  dies and is b. with them, 70:23
  graveyard of b. hopes, 673:7
  hatchet, 649:8
  here children born one b., 475:2
  him before prime, 854:7
  lie deep b., 61:14
  life, 529:4
  not b. in consecrated ground, 575:6
  old Adam b., 51:17
  on Sunday, 859:17
  problem lay b., 807:15
  putrid corpse of liberty, 702:8
  soil good to be b. in, 515:14
  they b. him, 657:14
  want to be b. among mountains, 543:7
  was crucified dead and b., 50:3
  where Michael Furey b., 696:4
Buries empires in common grave, 353:12
  universal darkness b. all, 313:25
Burke great because brings thought, 530:7
  said Reporters' Gallery Fourth Estate, 433:n1
Burma girl a-settin', 633:12
  got run out of B., 703:6
Burn and rave, 795:14
  another Troy to b., 638:1
  better to marry than b., 44:6
  books burn human beings, 442:10
  children will b., 857:8
  everything or throw into water, 145:1
  fire b. cauldron bubble, 221:20
  flag yet terrific b., 408:18
  from brain and breast, 664:13
  frost itself doth b., 205:23
  great sphere thou movest in, 223:36

Burn *(continued)*
  heart b. within us, 40:27
  I'll b. my books, 171:6
  like fabulous roman candles, 810:2
  no blazing hearth b., 334:13
  old wood b. brightest, 244:1
  old wood to b., 167:1
  out false shames, 707:12
  some b. damp faggots, 638:13
  stars that round her b., 301:15
  the towers, 756:16
  time the fire in which we b., 791:11
  to the socket, 395:4
  violent fires soon b. out, 179:11
  we b. daylight, 182:21
  what thou hast worshipped, 119:25
  with hard gemlike flame, 573:9
  words that b., 335:10
  you bid me b. letters, 351:7
Burned, and his feet not be b., 21:7
  black with sun, 734:10
  bush b. with fire, 8:3
  candle b. on the table, 730:7
  feared witches and b. women, 607:2
  feet as if b. in a furnace, 48:5
  give my body to be b., 44:18
  half his Troy was b., 191:7
  heart ne'er within b., 396:11
  is Apollo's laurel bough, 171:7
  Matilda and house b., 653:10
  money b. out his purse, 143:16
  my life, 747:19
  on the water, 223:14
  some b. alive, 811:15
  take fire and his clothes not be b., 21:7
  topless towers of Ilium, 170:23
  while I was musing the fire b., 17:11
  word b. like a lamp, 33:11
  worship what thou hast b., 119:25
Burning and shining light, 40:49
  bow of b. gold, 375:17
  boy stood on b. deck, 432:1
  burns out another's b., 182:18
  candle b. while sleeping, 239:16
  clove, 669:17
  eyes, 821:2
  fire in mind ever b., 160:2
  for ancient connection, 817:12
  I'm ten years b. down the road, 841:8
  is Paris b., 726:17
  keep home fires b., 663:1
  lifetime in moment, 721:5
  marle, 264:9
  pretty Babe all b. bright, 168:26
  roof and tower, 640:14
  Sappho, 423:24
  seraphim in b. row, 262:9
  smell of b. fills air, 653:4
  success worse than house b., 783:10
  three words as with b. pen, 381:9
  Tyger Tyger b. bright, 374:5
  your lights b., 39:30
Burnished, barge like b. throne, 223:14
  livery of b. sun, 188:13
Burns, blood that freezes blood that b., 492:11
  candle b. at both ends, 735:2
  it b. your clothes, 369:16
  not she which b. in 't, 228:16

Buy (*continued*)

dispraise thing you desire to b., 208:15
full and fair ones come and b., 247:17
I will b. with you, 188:2
lose it that b. it with care, 187:16
never b. what you do not want, 359:11
no man might b. or sell, 48:30
nor can b. tomorrow, 233:9
two white feet b. him, 849:17
what would you b., 452:2
Buyer, city to perish if it finds b., 95:11
it is naught saith the b., 22:20
let b. beware, 123:14
needs a hundred eyes, 251:26
Buying and selling, 507:11
it's no fish ye're b., 397:20
Buys, who b. a minute's mirth, 175:5
Buzz, buccaneers of B., 546:17
crowd b. and murmurings, 275:4
the witty and fair annoys, 312:8
Buzzing world lisping firmament, 687:19
B.V.D., from every B., 739:15
By and by easily said, 205:11
and by God caught eye, 749:7
I get b. with a little help, 835:4
Bye baby bunting, 858:8
Bye-and-bye, sweet b., 854:16
Byron, close thy B., 433:19
cuts a figure, 440:15
from poetry of B. ethics, 447:22
mad bad dangerous to know, 418:7
times B. goes into Texas, 807:7
Byron's struggle cease, 528:14
Byway to heaven, 295:2
Byword, proverb and a b., 12:17
story and b. through world, 246:17
thou shalt become a b., 10:9
Byzantium, lords and ladies of B., 640:2

C

C Major of this life, 494:6
Caballero, el C. de la Triste Figura, 156:n5
Cabbage, cauliflower c. with college
education, 561:8
cut a c. leaf, 336:12
Cabbages and kings, 552:3
death find me planting c., 152:8
happy those who plant c., 146:10
no c. sprouting out, 474:10
Cabin, enter Logan's c. hungry, 339:8
mounted to the c., 655:9
small c. build there, 637:1
willow c. at gate, 209:9
Cabined ample spirit, 529:15
cribbed confined, 221:9
from her c. loophole peep, 260:22
Cabinet, post offices and c. appointments,
474:n1
Cabinets, make parties as ministers c., 513:12
Cable broke anchor lost, 173:12
no c. draw forcibly as love, 241:17
on seventh day scrape c., 502:16
taught me to abhor detest Sabbath, 561:1
Cabots talk only to God, 621:22
Cackle, don't c. w'en fine wum, 593:14
Cackles, codfish never c., 849:16
groans and dies, 431:17

Cadence from man named Yeats, 780:14
harsh c. of rugged line, 284:5
to his verse a smooth c., 289:6
tremulous c. slow, 530:20
Cadiz, reeking into C. Bay, 492:6
Cadmean victory, 71:12
Caecorum, in regione c. rex est luscus,
142:n4
Caelia has undone me, 333:16
Caelum, quid si nunc c. ruat, 88:n12
Caesar, all that C. could, 454:19
appeal unto C., 42:34
buried C. bled, 471:9
carry C. in your boat, 92:2
every wound of C., 197:5
great C. fell, 197:1
had his Brutus, 352:11
I come to bury C., 196:27
imperious C. dead, 206:26
not that I loved C. less, 196:24
O mighty C., 196:18
poor cried C. wept, 196:29
render unto C., 36:42
thou art mighty yet, 197:19
upon what meat C. feed, 195:21
word of C. stood, 196:31
Caesar's, all is C., 272:11
dead C. trencher, 223:27
hand Plato's brain, 453:24
I am, 150:3
poison from C. crown, 375:13
self is God's, 272:11
wife must be above suspicion, 91:n13
Caesars, how many C. and Pompeys,
332:10
Café, every street c., 744:3
Caftan of tan with henna, 686:20
Cage, gilded c., 654:1
nor iron bars a c., 276:4
put me in a c., 723:15
robin redbreast in c., 375:6
sing like birds i' the c., 218:1
women put not on pedestal but in c.,
774:5
Caged, know why c. bird sings, 660:2
Cages, marriage as with c., 153:17
Cain, land God gave to C., 145:4
set a mark upon C., 6:17
terre Dieu donna à C., 145:n2
was tiller of the ground, 6:12
went out from presence of the Lord,
6:18
Caissons go rolling along, 684:8
Caius is a man, 543:2
Cake, bake c. fast as can, 857:1
eat c. and have it, 149:16
Heaven's sugar c., 292:10
let them eat c., 331:19
see to substance of c., 613:18
some gave plum c., 857:2
Cakes and ale, 209:17
bridegrooms brides and bridal c., 247:14
Calabash, goodnight Mrs. C., 737:3
Calais, find C. lying in my heart, 150:11
Calamities of life, 295:7
of war, 324:21
Calamitous in drawn-out witticism, 408:6
necessity of going on, 355:4
to the conquered, 74:19

Calamity, Child of C., 560:3
fortune not satisfied with one c., 102:27
in English history, 602:16
makes c. of so long life, 203:33
man's true touchstone, 245:12
no c. greater than lavish desires, 59:6
Calamus, hinc quam sic c. saevior ense patet,
241:2
Calaveras, celebrated jumping frog of C.
county, 559:n3
outjump any frog in C. county, 559:15
Calcaria, de c. in carbonarium, 116:n8
Calculate, no wisdom can c. end, 354:18
Calculated, nicely c. less or more, 395:16
so c. so malignant, 734:2
Calculation shining out of other, 496:38
sum defies c., 364:16
Calculations, most dangerous c. we call
illusions, 716:14
Calculators, age of c., 345:13
Calculus, common sense reduced to c.,
366:14
Caldron of dissolute loves, 119:6
Caledonia stern and wild, 396:12
Caledonia's, support C. cause, 380:19
Calendar, a c. look in almanack, 181:19
striking from C., 471:20
year of Julian C. 710, 244:13
Calf and young lion together, 26:34
bring fatted c., 39:36
false as wolf to c., 208:7
killed c. in high style, 280:23
second beast like a c., 48:16
Calf's-skin on recreant limbs, 178:4
Caliban, 'Ban 'Ban Ca-C., 229:32
Calico cat replied Mee-ow, 597:7
Jam, 500:1
Pie, 499:20
tree, 499:20
California, cured of drug taking in C., 766:7
from C. to New York island, 788:12
if C. becomes prosperous country,
502:17
wonderful place to live if orange,
739:4
Californians race of people, 626:13
Caligula's horse made Consul, 405:1
Calix sanguinis mei, 49:14
Call, almost like c. to come, 670:14
back yesterday, 179:25, 239:10
bawd a bawd, 84:n1
brothers c. from bay, 528:5
cattle home, 513:21
delicate creatures ours, 214:4
don't c. out National Guard, 705:2
dunno what to c. 'im, 613:5
fig a fig, 84:1
for robin redbreast, 244:3
forth thundering Aeschylus, 238:8
gods to witness, 218:11
grief at not wanting to c. dead back,
676:14
had c. to literature, 559:13
heaven and earth to witness, 9:28
her blessed, 23:30
him a man, 836:4
how you c. to me c. to me, 576:2
in and invite God, 236:22
in thy death's head, 250:16

Candle (*continued*)
highest c. lights dark, 688:15
hold c. to my shames, 188:21
hold farthing c. to sun, 241:*n*4
how far c. throws beams, 190:8
light c. to the sun, 278:28
lights gleaming, 656:7
lived like c. in wind, 840:12
not care a farthing c., 407:22
of understanding, 31:9
one small c. light a thousand, 247:10
out out brief c., 222:16
put c. under a bushel, 34:2
scarcely fit to hold c., 314:13
set a c. in the sun, 241:18
this day light such a c., 145:2
to be c. or mirror, 627:9
to light you to bed, 857:13
two chairs half c., 500:4
white c. in holy place, 693:4
Candlelight, colors by c., 463:14
dress by yellow c., 598:20
sit in early c. of old age, 521:16
Candlelit, old at evening c., 150:13
Candles are all out, 220:5
blessed c. of night, 190:12
burn like fabulous roman c., 810:2
night's c. burnt out, 184:5
rather light c., 704:*n*1
when c. out all women fair, 111:20
Candlestick, jump over c., 860:5
put candle on a c., 34:2
Candlestick-maker, butcher baker c., 860:8
Candlesticks, seven golden c., 48:4
Candor and amicable relations, 377:1
Candy deal of courtesy, 185:10
is dandy, 763:5
not made of sugar c., 667:5
Cane, carrying a small c., 756:12
wind is in the c., 742:5
Canem, cave c., 123:13
Canker, as killing as c. to rose, 261:18
galls infants of spring, 201:22
loathesome c., 226:11
that benumbs, 566:5
this c. Bolingbroke, 185:6
worm c. and grief, 425:8
Cankers in musk-rose buds, 181:13
of calm world, 186:27
Cannes, Hotel Magnifique at C., 694:11
Cannibal, better sleep with sober c., 516:8
Cannibals that each other eat, 212:31
Cannikin, why clink c., 491:18
Cannon come again, 642:13
then c. and he comes, 664:10
to right of them, 485:1
Cannon's, burst c. roar, 473:3
mouth, 198:25
Cannons taken or saved, 542:10
Cannon-shot, revolution more c., 642:13
Cannot define the real problem, 803:2
he who c. teaches, 609:23
history c. be unlived, 820:7
it c. like adultery or gluttony, 672:22
killing beast that c. kill, 715:7
mind my wheel, 408:9
nature c. be fooled, 803:3
Canoe of the European, 516:1
paddle own c., 427:9

Canon 'gainst self-slaughter, 201:1
Canopy, most excellent c. the air, 203:17
who spread its c., 292:7
Canst, give all thou c., 395:16
Can't, I c. go on, 773:16
if you c. be free, 841:12
Cant, clear your mind of c., 329:14
nothing but c., 418:10
of criticism, 332:22
of hypocrites the worst, 332:22
of Not men but measures, 343:16
Cantankerous, small speech c., 82:21
Canted in this canting world, 332:22
Canter, little finishing c., 579:2
Canters, as they c. awaäy, 486:19
Cantharides, Hottentot wench under
influence of c., 569:18
Cantie wi' mair, 378:20
Canting, canted in this c. world, 332:22
Cants, clear myself of c., 433:22
which are canted, 332:22
Canvas of heavy foresail, 611:18
sail even with c. rent, 106:17
set your full c. flying, 85:16
Canyons, neighing c., 753:16
Cap, feather in his c., 332:25
for c. and bells lives pay, 514:15
riband in c. of youth, 206:13
Capability and godlike reason, 205:35
Negative C., 440:3
Capable, all I am c. of becoming, 723:10
and wide revenge, 214:15
become all c. of, 434:9
created in his mind, 687:14
hand now warm and c., 439:2
mathematician c. of reasoning, 77:16
not all c. of everything, 95:24
of being in uncertainties, 440:3
of every wickedness, 612:15
of greatest vices, 254:1
of nothing but dumbshows, 204:11
Capacious salad bowl, 599:5
Capacities, growing to full human c., 808:1
Capacity, by c. is wisdom acquired, 86:6
contribution according to c., 510:*n*5
for delight and wonder, 611:16
for taking pains, 566:13
for taking trouble, 321:*n*5, 558:23
freed c. of thought, 616:12
functional c., 362:7
of taking trouble, 435:10
receiveth as the sea, 208:26
to despise himself, 629:10
Cap-a-pe, 201:15
Caparisons, no c. if you please, 367:13
Cape, nobly C. Saint Vincent, 492:6
round c. of a sudden, 492:3
wears descent like long c., 822:10
Cape Cod, man may stand there [C.], 507:32
Caper and shake a leg, 680:8
Capers, he c. he dances, 190:28
nimbly in lady's chamber, 173:30
strange c., 198:9
Capes, on dark c. glisten ink wax, 751:8
Capitaine, Ô Mort vieux c., 524:*n*9
Capital an' labor git t'gether, 649:9
Belgium's c. gathered, 420:16
bring c. into competition, 339:2
fruit of labor, 475:11

Capital (*continued*)
has its rights, 475:11
in ascendancy system of plunder, 510:10
labor not ask patronage of c., 414:10
labor prior to c., 475:11
not by savings and c., 778:15
reasons for scarcity of c., 702:3
sensitive ear detecting c. letters, 694:9
ship for ocean trip, 580:23
where kingly Death, 430:3
Capitalism, contest between c. and socialism
over, 805:3
creates social unrest, 703:4
inherent vice of c., 668:7
system where man exploits man, 805:1
Capitalist, more sham than c. democracy,
703:5
way to destroy c. system, 701:17
Capitalists owners of means of production,
511:*n*2
Capitol, musing amidst ruins of C., 354:4
woman betrayed the C., 293:20
Capon, belly with good c. lined, 198:25
Capons, unless minutes c., 184:23
you cannot feed c. so, 204:19
Capri, three irreconcilable feuds in C.,
766:7
Caprice and lifelong passion, 604:17
lasts a little longer, 604:17
of minutest event, 516:19
Capricious, gods' c. hand, 771:4
Capriciousness of summer air, 670:12
Caps, threw their c., 224:17
Capsule, finger on c. of truth, 756:10
Captain, captive good attending c. ill,
226:22
Carpenter rose up, 724:14
chief c. answered, 42:28
cook and c. bold, 563:11
Death old c., 524:16
don't you hear c. shouting, 848:1
his c. Christ, 180:6
no c. do very wrong, 377:5
O C. my C., 520:18
of all these men of death, 282:7
of Hampshire grenadiers, 354:3
of his soul, 727:7
of my soul, 594:11
of second rank, 451:10
of the Pinafore, 563:14
right good c. too, 563:14
should be judged as a c., 140:9
soul of c. of life, 95:9
walk deck my C. lies, 520:19
Captain's choleric word, 211:14
crew of c. gig, 563:11
troubled c. mind, 580:23
Captains and kings depart, 635:2
courageous, 853:25
of industry, 435:4
thunder of the c., 15:15
Captive, carried us away c., 20:11
good attending captain ill, 226:22
Israel, 511:12
jailer another kind of c., 469:3
lead captivity c., 10:30
of time, 730:4
today unbind c., 453:14
weak minds led c., 268:20

Captivity is Consciousness, 544:22
    lead c. captive, 10:30
    power to cancel his c., 195:27
Capture of men by women, 490:*n*1
Captured, faced enslavement if c., 556:3
Capulet, I'll no longer be a C., 183:2
Car, drive the rapid c., 348:23
    gilded c. of day, 260:19
    radio bleats, 801:7
    rattling o'er stony street, 420:17
Caravan, innumerable c. which moves,
    432:10
    put up your c., 656:11
Caravanserai, battered C., 471:7
Carcass fit for hounds, 196:3
    honey in the c. of the lion, 10:39
    of leopard, 754:15
    where c. is eagles gather, 37:8
Carcasses bleed at sight of murderer, 137:*n*3
Card, clear conscience is sure c., 163:8
    he's a sure c., 283:24
    insipid as queen on c., 486:16
    master to those below, 731:3
    speak by the c., 206:22
Cardozos, can't all have Brandeises C.,
    767:15
Cards, cheat at c. genteelly, 327:23
    deck of c., 704:*n*2
    dreaded c. foretell, 775:11
    luck not holding best c., 571:8
    never play c. with man named Doc, 782:1
    nothing but pack of c., 551:7
    patience and shuffle c., 158:16
    played c. for kisses, 163:15
    thrust ivrybody but cut c., 646:12
    world of c., 731:3
Care a farthing candle, 407:22
    age full of c., 843:19
    and not to care, 719:10
    begone dull C., 845:6
    careless with artful c., 300:29
    cast away c., 156:29, 233:9
    deliberation and public c., 265:8
    driveth away sleep, 32:44
    feeling c. of law, 162:18
    fig for c. fig for woe, 147:3
    for who shall have borne battle, 477:4
    full of c. no time, 656:2
    golden c., 192:6
    happy whose wish and c., 308:3
    housewife ply evening c., 334:13
    I c. for nobody, 352:6
    I don't c. one straw, 89:6
    I don't c. what they do, 631:17
    I prayed and did God C., 544:20
    I sae weary fu' o' c., 378:21
    I shall not c., 704:14
    insensate c. of mortals, 92:*n*13
    irks c. the crop-full bird, 494:8
    Jimmie crack corn I don't c., 847:20
    keeps his watch, 183:18
    killed a cat, 195:9
    lose it that buy it with much c., 187:16
    nor c. beyond today, 333:20
    nor for itself hath c., 374:1
    not who sees your back, 185:23
    nought but c. on ev'ry han', 378:12
    of discipline is love, 31:20
    of life and happiness, 358:15

Care *(continued)*
    of the poor, 287:15
    of this world, 36:5
    punch with c., 553:13
    raveled sleave of c., 220:16
    Reason is past c., 228:6
    rest that knows no c., 93:13
    sat on his faded cheek, 264:19
    so wan with c., 184:21
    sought it with c., 553:4
    sounds take c. of themselves, 550:17
    taken better c. of myself, 700:13
    things past redress past c., 179:21
    tiresome verse-reciter C., 431:7
    weep away life of c., 428:2
    what boots it with incessant c., 261:19
    what c. I how fair she be, 246:18
    what is life if full of c., 656:2
    where c. lodges sleep never lie, 183:18
    windy side of c., 194:21
    woman who did not c., 634:21
    wrinkled C. derides, 259:10
    your sex's earliest latest c., 329:23
Care-charmer Sleep, 169:3
Cared as much as Bird, 544:20
    not to be at all, 264:27
Career, awe man from c. of his humor,
    194:28
    close military c. fade away, 690:12
    my c. my brilliant c., 684:7
    poetry not c., 722:21
    public life crown of c., 674:10
    this is our c., 724:19
    what they call fine c., 784:10
Careful, be c. what you do, 685:5
    ivry man equal if isn't c., 646:21
    not c. what they mean, 175:17
    o' widders, 495:23
    so c. of type, 484:4
    surgeons must be c., 544:2
Carefulness bringeth age, 32:43
Careless, be not c. in deeds, 116:1
    desolation, 199:17
    ease from tree to tree, 305:9
    first fine c. rapture, 492:5
    I tasted c. then, 544:14
    love, 801:7
    merits or faults to scan, 342:5
    of single life, 484:4
    on granary floor, 438:12
    people Tom and Daisy, 746:7
    shoestring, 248:4
    trifle, 219:8
    with artful care, 300:29
Carelessly, fleet the time c., 197:24
Carelessness, lose both parents c., 605:9
Care's an enemy to life, 209:1
    canker that benumbs, 566:5
    check and curb, 278:29
Cares and joys abound, 172:9
    blessed to put c. away, 94:9
    cast all c. on God, 486:15
    eating c., 259:20
    happy man void of c., 304:15
    heart depressed with c., 307:14
    kingdoms are but c., 139:16
    no one c. for me, 352:6
    now all ended, 192:11
    partisan c. nothing about rights, 76:18

Cares *(continued)*
    prime of youth a frost of c., 164:17
    soothe c. lift thoughts, 436:5
    that infest day, 466:14
    to fret thy soul with c., 161:24
    unbounded by sordid c., 691:10
    who c. or knows, 431:14
Caress, take perfect circle and c. it, 788:13
Caretaker, president is c., 786:7
Cargo, little c. boats, 634:17
    of ivory, 681:4
    of Tyne coal, 681:5
Cargoes of meat drink clothes, 846:21
Carian, dear old C. guest, 534:3
Caribbean borne like elliptical basin, 826:6
Caricature a swollen shadow, 791:12
    decrepit age, 640:3
Caritas, in omnibus c., 274:*n*4
Carlyle, God let C. and Mrs. C. marry,
    558:11
    loves silence platonically, 433:*n*2
Carnage and conquests cease, 422:8
    war and c. be lost, 520:13
Carnal, pearl for c. swine, 271:19
Carnation Milk best in land, 852:16
Carnival, make c. of grief, 649:3
Carol, it was c. of bird, 422:22
    not c. of joy or glee, 660:2
Caroline, find Sister C., 657:3
Carolings, so little cause for c., 575:17
Carols, varied c. I hear, 518:14
Carp at weakness of human mind, 286:19
    of truth, 202:30
Carpe diem, 99:*n*7
Carpent tua poma nepotes, 95:*n*18
Carpenter, Captain C. rose up, 724:14
    hewing wood for master c., 59:18
    said nothing but, 552:5
    takes c. to build barn, 697:8
    Walrus and the C., 551:19
Carpenter's, is not this the c. son, 36:9
Carpet, figure in the c., 585:6
Carriage, can't afford c., 643:20
    held just Ourselves, 545:15
    King in c. ride, 472:7
    love and marriage like horse and c.,
      789:11
    small second-class c., 565:4
Carriages motorcars omnibuses, 699:16
    without horses go, 845:8
    women helped into c., 443:10
Carried, beggar c. by angels, 40:2
    not get self c. aloft, 588:21
    pardon slowly c., 210:33
    though the mountains be c. into the sea,
      17:21
    us away captive, 20:11
    with every wind of doctrine, 45:27
Carrière ouverte aux talents, 388:12
Carries no colors or crest, 634:4
Carriest, thou c. them away as with a flood,
    18:20
Carrion comfort Despair, 587:20
    god kissing c., 203:6
Carrot, juices of c. and onion, 830:17
    single c. freshly observed, 573:1
Carry all he knew, 342:9
    big stick, 615:4
    Caesar in your boat, 92:2

Catch a falling star, 233:13
    another Antony, 224:15
    as catch can, 336:12
    bargain c. cold and starve, 225:10
    Christ with worm, 800:10
    claws that c., 551:10
    conscience of the king, 203:31
    earth's heedless sons, 745:14
    hard to c. and conquer, 541:19
    him once upon hip, 188:4
    I have to c. them, 805:14
    nets to c. the wind, 244:10
    only one c. Catch-22, 812:9
    perdition c. my soul, 213:30
    springes to c. woodcocks, 201:30
    the manners living, 310:21
    the nearest way, 219:10
    up with advanced countries, 654:9
    when pleasure can be had c. it, 328:7
    with his surcease success, 219:16
    you will never c. up, 643:12
Catch-22, some catch that C., 812:9
Catched, swallow gudgeons ere they're c., 60:n4
Catcher in the rye, 805:14
Catches, slow man c. up with swift, 54:27
Catching, poverty's c., 290:19
Catchwords, man lives by c., 598:6
Catechism, so ends my c., 186:35
Catechist, something of Shorter-C., 594:8
Categorical imperative, 339:6
    order c., 564:3
Categories, gripes fall into two c., 803:5
Category, Dante belongs to first c., 782:3
Caterpillar, I don't see said C., 549:16
Caterpillars of the commonwealth, 179:20
Caters for the sparrow, 198:3
Catharsis, tragedy a c., 81:10
Cathay, cycle of C., 482:9
Cathedral, after great c. gong, 641:5
    in vast c. leave him, 484:23
    mankind inspired made c., 598:2
    needs more than opinion to erect c., 442:15
    Tunes, 544:12
    uplifting thoughts in bathrooms than c., 745:8
Cathedrals, cars equivalent of Gothic c., 795:18
Cather, Willas c., 749:8
Catholic, candidate who happens also to be C., 799:5
    C.O., 801:1
    Church understands enthusiasts, 448:8
    holy C. Church, 50:3
    Irish C. childhood, 825:9
    judges neither C. nor agnostic, 695:7
    not C. candidate for President, 799:5
Catholicism minus Christianity, 537:3
Catholics and Communists, 767:11
    they came for C., 735:18
Catiline, how long C., 90:7
    prodigal of own possessions, 95:3
Cato, like C. give Senate laws, 312:4
    vanquished had C., 110:1
Cat's a cat and Rolet a knave, 289:10
    pull chestnuts with c. paw, 277:13
    run away with string, 861:11
    what c. averse to fish, 334:3

Cats, all c. gray when candles out, 111:n11
    and monkeys monkeys and cats, 584:11
    count c. in Zanzibar, 507:16
    do c. eat bats, 549:11
    each sack had seven c., 857:6
    fought dogs killed c., 491:16
    have two holes in coat, 356:19
    nation of c. wild and tame, 141:21
    rain c. and dogs, 846:3
    those who'll play with c., 156:32
Catsup, shake and shake c. bottle, 773:8
Cattle beneath shadow of oak, 345:16
    call c. home, 513:21
    cursed above all c., 6:7
    die as c., 738:6
    if c. and horses had hands, 61:21
    lowly c. shed, 508:9
    upon a thousand hills, 17:24
    would draw gods like cattle, 61:21
Catullus be resolved and firm, 94:6
    worst of all poets, 94:14
    you should cease folly, 94:5
Caucasus, thinking on frosty C., 179:6
Caught, ain't never c. a rabbit, 828:8
    at God's skirts, 491:14
    between two evils, 736:9
    God c. his eye, 749:7
    hanging around until you've c. on, 671:20
    him yes I held him, 585:7
    his clear accents, 491:21
    in that sensual music, 639:16
    like beast at bay, 730:12
    man of honor regrets even if not c., 691:11
    morning's minion, 587:6
    mother came and c. her, 859:10
    my heavenly jewel, 164:1
    our youth, 713:1
    she c. him by his garment, 7:25
    trout c. with tickling, 209:28
    with his sweet perfections c., 171:10
Cauldron, fire burn c. bubble, 221:20
Cauliflower cabbage with college education, 561:8
Causa latet vis notissima, 105:n12
Causation, law of c., 556:6
Cause, armor of righteous c., 622:1
    bad c. bad means, 354:13
    be c. strong or weak, 514:18
    beauty of good old c., 392:14
    calledst me dog before c., 189:10
    common c. decays, 73:17
    common c. to save Union, 475:3
    died in virtue's c., 175:15
    effect defective comes by c., 203:2
    effect whose c. is God, 348:13
    evolution not c. but law, 572:4
    final c. produces motion, 80:5
    full c. of weeping, 216:17
    Germany the c. of Hitler, 715:17
    good old c. is gone, 392:14
    Great First C., 348:24
    griefs we c. ourselves, 68:7
    hear me for my c., 196:23
    hidden but result well known, 105:16
    idea of oneself as c., 287:4
    if any man show just c., 51:8
    if world astray c. is in you, 131:18
    is there any c. in nature, 217:6

Cause *(continued)*
    it is just, 411:2
    Jesus found spiritual c., 526:11
    laws or kings c. or cure, 325:3
    little grace my c., 212:26
    no warrants but upon probable c., 361:3
    not a field but a c., 354:15
    not be judge in own c., 103:n7
    not jealous for the c., 214:17
    nothing comes without c., 318:17
    obstinacy in bad c., 255:15, 332:9
    of Freedom cause of God, 383:11
    of this effect, 203:2
    or men of Emerald Isle, 369:7
    perseverance in good c., 332:9
    produces more than one effect, 523:7
    report me and my c., 207:11
    sea of C. and Theory, 665:2
    set c. above renown, 627:3
    support Caledonia's c., 380:19
    tenacious of purpose in rightful c., 99:28
    try c. condemn to death, 549:14
    turn him to c. of policy, 192:19
    water-colors to impaint c., 186:33
    what in effect already in c., 616:6
    when just c. reaches flood tide, 616:11
    wherein tongue confuted, 258:8
    wit in other men, 191:9
    you c. what you abuse, 293:12
    Zeus first c., 65:11
Caused the widow's heart to sing, 14:37
Causes célèbres, 303:12
    defend c. which were unpopular, 779:17
    fight for lost c., 722:17
    flowers as in c. sleep, 253:13
    from amorous c. springs, 309:4
    great c. on move, 666:12
    happy man who could search out c., 96:13
    hidden c. of things, 233:4
    home of lost c., 530:10
    investigation of hidden c., 155:12
    of destruction, 331:3
    which impel separation, 357:2
    why and where fore, 193:22
Causeway, law is a c., 813:7
Caution in refusing benefits, 287:14
    scars of others teach c., 118:20
    upward look of c., 670:20
Cautious people never bring reform, 521:19
    politic c. and meticulous, 717:14
    seldom err, 62:23
    statistical Christ, 590:15
Cavalry of Woe, 544:4
Cave, courts thee in some pleasant c., 99:7
    error correct c., 809:2
    Idols of the C., 166:13
    shadows on opposite wall of C., 77:14
    sky will c. in on him, 734:15
    Stygian c. forlorn, 259:7
    vacant interlunar c., 268:33
Cave ab homine unius libri, 123:12
    canem, 123:13
Caveat emptor, 123:14
Cavern, mossy c., 438:10
    Pan's c., 642:17

Caverns, in c. all alone, 809:2
   measureless to man, 401:13
   sand-strewn c. cool and deep, 528:6
   twice ten thousand c., 439:7
Caves, beetles in c., 780:8
   dark unfathomed c., 334:20
   of ice, 401:17, 401:19
Caviar to the general, 203:24
Cavil on ninth part of hair, 186:8
Cawdor, Glamis thou art and C., 219:10
   I am Thane of C., 219:5
   shall sleep no more, 220:17
Cease and then again begin, 530:20
   ask whether happy c. to be, 465:8
   Byron's struggle c., 528:14
   Catullus you should c. folly, 94:5
   day and night shall not c., 6:32
   efforts to find where last rose lingers,
     99:20
   fears that I may c., 439:8
   from mental fight, 375:17
   from thine own wisdom, 22:33
   long contention c., 531:4
   man I am c. to be, 485:6
   not c. from exploration, 722:4
   poor shall never c., 10:6
   sing or c. to sing, 313:5
   the wicked c. from troubling, 13:31
   time c. and midnight never come,
     171:3
   to ask what morrow will bring, 99:11
   to be free for religion, 734:4
   upon the midnight, 437:12
   weeping without c., 591:1
   ye from man, 26:13
Ceased, God created woman boredom c.,
   589:23
   Pnin c. to notice students, 756:6
   this parrot has c. to be, 842:13
   when Lucy c. to be, 391:18
Ceaseless devouring of weak by strong,
   523:12
   thoughts of roaming, 291:12
   turns with c. pain, 340:15
Ceases, forbearance c. to be virtue, 343:13
   happiness c. like dream, 254:21
   to be free for irreligion, 734:4
Ceasing, O swiftness never c., 164:9
   pray without c., 46:12
Cedant arma togae, 91:n3
Cedar, as c. tall and slender, 363:4
   grow like a c. in Lebanon, 18:27
   lordly c. green with boughs, 601:7
Cedars of Lebanon, 19:10
   roots of c. of Lebanon, 680:1
Cedarwood, sandalwood c., 681:4
Cefalu, practiced black art in C., 766:7
Ceiling, Gary looked at c. hesitated, 813:2
Célébrait, Ronsard me c., 150:n7
Celebrate, I c. myself, 518:15
   not c. funeral with weeping, 87:13
Celebrated cultivated Duke of Plaza Toro,
   566:2
   Savior's birth c., 200:22
Celebrates pale Hecate's offerings, 220:9
Célèbres, causes c., 303:12
Celebrities, congress of c., 554:11
Celebrity person known for well-knownness,
   792:24

Celeriter, sat c. fieri satis bene, 102:n5
Celerity never more admired, 223:23
Celestial, apparreled in c. light, 393:7
   ennui of apartments, 688:2
   pattern of c. peace, 172:3
   sailing c. spaces, 572:17
   sate itself in c. bed, 202:17
   so c. article as Freedom, 354:10
   Wisdom calms the mind, 324:11
Celia, come my C., 237:14
   has undone me, 333:16
Celibacy has no pleasures, 324:27
Cell, deposit little c. by c., 573:5
   dwell on rock or in c., 160:10
   earth most like single c., 791:14
   ill-spirit sob in each blood c., 801:7
   in narrow c. forever laid, 334:11
   thine eternal c., 207:16
   tight hot c., 748:1
Cellar, born in a c., 336:9
   drop gin scuttle to c., 789:8
   gone into c. where never find him,
     783:17
   lived in c. damp, 515:11
   nothing sleep in that c., 780:4
   warm delicious c., 756:17
Cells, all c. from pre-existing c., 527:n5
   better schoolrooms than c., 509:7
   condemned c. of Newgate, 558:13
   little gray c., 727:14
Cellula, omnis c. e c., 527:18
Celts certainly have style, 531:8
Cement glue and lime of love, 247:15
Cemetery, help me down C. Road, 810:5
Censorship, assassination extreme c., 610:13
   if c. reigns, 349:9
Censure, durst not c., 323:15
   every trade save c., 419:14
   fear of c., 709:4
   freely who have written well, 308:8
   mankind c. injustice, 77:4
   pardons raven, 113:3
   take each man's c., 201:26
   tax for being eminent, 298:5
Census, test of civilization not c., 457:8
Cent, no excuse for stealin' a c., 584:5
   not one c. for tribute, 384:16
Centaur, cloud that looked like c., 74:14
   in dragon world, 709:11
Center cannot hold, 639:6
   in universe neither c. nor circumference,
     159:11
   intention stabs the c., 228:12
   many lines in dial's c., 192:22
   my c. giving way, 600:11
   of all beauty, 818:5
   of my sinful earth, 228:4
   of silent Word, 719:14
   unfathomed c., 441:10
   wore fire's c., 783:16
Centerlight, blue c. pop, 810:2
Centipedes, ants c. and scorpions, 680:12
Central stream of what we feel, 531:20
Central Park, one great purpose of C.,
   533:6
   single work of art, 533:5
Centre cède ma droite recule, 600:n3
Cents, feel like thirty c., 643:14
   hours and minutes dollars and c., 320:n1

Centuries, across c. across oceans, 667:5
   all c. but this, 565:10
   bowed by weight of c., 601:3
   don't care for great c., 577:4
   forty c. look down, 387:12
   joked over fifty c., 566:9
   lie through c., 492:8
   of folly noise sin, 492:11
   of stony sleep, 639:7
   roll back to age of gold, 100:13
   three c. removed, 765:1
   wish days to be as c., 456:31
   wit lasts two c., 417:4
   years roll into c., 486:9
Century, born in this c., 799:7
   fantastic c. move, 368:13
   grain of poetry season c., 602:3
   Holocaust metaphor for c., 827:5
   lain for c. dead, 485:12
   live for more than one c., 93:23
   of common man, 725:1
   of sonnets, 493:24
   problem of twentieth c. color line, 648:9
   ring bells for new c., 676:7
   seventeenth c. dissociation, 722:12
   what would twentieth c. look like, 802:14
Cerberus and blackest Midnight, 259:7
   give sop to C., 122:24
   like C. three gentlemen, 367:14
Cerebration, slight powers of c., 628:12
Ceremonies, hampering with c. and music,
   82:26
Ceremony, idol c., 193:15
   love useth enforced c., 197:6
   of innocence drowned, 639:6
   save c. save general c., 193:15
   that to great ones 'longs, 211:10
   thrice gorgeous c., 193:16
Ceres, which cost C. all that pain, 266:8
Certain am I of the spot, 546:6
   because impossible, 116:20
   fill c. portion of uncertain paper, 423:15
   is birth for the dead, 87:1
   is death for the born, 87:1
   no c. life achieved, 178:17
   nothing c. except death and taxes, 321:3
   of his fate, 213:34
   of nothing but affection, 439:13
   permanent and c. characteristics, 324:12
   signs should prefigure events, 91:2
   there is no fine thing, 637:18
   way for woman to hold a man, 804:16
Certainties, begin with c. end in doubts,
   166:4
   begin with doubts end in c., 166:4
   hot for c., 541:9
   public demands c., 690:18
   there are no c., 690:18
Certainty, certitude not rest of c., 578:12
   enslavement c. of worse, 790:9
   generally illusion, 577:18
   no such thing as absolute c., 464:11
   not lightly sacrificed, 653:16
   of the words of truth, 22:28
   pass from suspicion to c., 273:6
   principles of icy c., 626:19
   quit c. for uncertainty, 324:23
   sober c. of waking bliss, 260:28
   without doubt, 128:11

Change (*continued*)
speech small c. of Silence, 541:4
stamp of nature, 205:29
the many c. and pass, 430:17
the more things c., 468:23
them when we will, 483:9
things that are and do not c., 773:4
time for a c., 762:1
time will c. your opinions, 78:15
times c. and move continually, 161:21
times c. and we c. with them, 124:27
to virtue and worthiness, 195:28
too much c. too short time, 822:1
unafraid of c., 627:19
universe is c., 115:9
we all want to c. the world, 835:6
we think we see, 669:2
werewolf's painful c., 809:3
what should be changed, 735:13
when worse it must c., 144:8
Changé, nous avons c. tout cela, 278:*n1*
Changeable, young men's minds are c., 52:20
Changed, accept things that cannot be c., 735:13
changed utterly, 639:4
Eternity has c. him, 583:14
from the one all to me, 576:2
I c. my condition, 270:12
innocence for innocence, 228:10
like change in my face, 596:7
mind not to be c., 264:7
minds of gods not c. suddenly, 54:16
not c. from him they knew, 668:15
our life is c., 715:8
our lives have been c., 784:11
sea c. Egdon remained, 575:2
something better c. in ourselves, 675:7
we have c. all that, 278:2
we shall be c., 44:31
whole world have been c., 279:20
ye too c. ye hills, 530:15
Changeful mind of mortals, 66:14
presuming on c. potency, 208:17
Changes, agonies one of my c. of garments, 519:19
cause great c. in the world, 352:7
control our being, 481:5
follow c. of the moon, 213:36
God c. and man and form, 569:7
God c. not people until they change, 121:6
monthly c. in circled orb, 183:8
sky c. when wives, 199:29
woman often c., 97:*n8*
world's a scene of c., 275:7
Changeth, old order c., 486:12
sweareth to his own hurt and c. not, 16:6
Changing, borrow every c. shape, 717:18
scenes of life, 294:6
shallow c. woman, 174:15
stress on not c. mind, 672:15
Chankly Bore, 500:8
Channel, brush c. with sleeve, 554:10
butting through the C., 681:5
crossing C. and tossing, 565:4
man merely c. for food, 140:11
Chant, do use to c. it, 209:24
how can ye c., 378:21
none chanted c. of welcome, 520:17

Chanted, none c. chant of welcome, 520:17
Chanticleer, lungs crow like c., 198:17
Chanting, exaltation in c. of Muses, 69:21
faint hymns to moon, 180:18
in Latin, 835:13
Chants doleful hymn, 178:25
Chaos and old Night, 264:15
beauty dead black c., 173:26
bounded by primeval c., 487:*n1*
breeds life, 570:10
freedom of action without freed thought c., 616:12
infinite c. which separated us, 279:23
is come again, 213:30
of the sun, 686:19
of thought and passion, 311:9
our policy against c., 690:14
rough unordered mass, 105:12
this is why there is c., 82:29
thy dread empire C., 313:25
what a c. is man, 280:8
Chaos-like together crushed, 309:16
Chapel, afternoon in secluded c., 722:3
Devil builds c. there, 294:16
Devil would build c., 144:14
God's greenwood c., 685:*n2*
Chapels had been churches, 187:27
legend of green c., 795:7
Chapfallen, quite c., 206:24
Chaplain, Blue Beard's c., 495:25
Chapman, heard C. speak out loud and bold, 435:19
Chapmen, you do as c. do, 208:15
Chapmen's, not uttered by c. tongues, 176:27
Chaps, Biography is about C., 674:3
with couple o' guns, 704:8
Chapter, autobiographies begin C. Two, 661:6
of accidents very long, 315:10
of knowledge very short, 315:10
said he could repeat c., 328:11
say in first c. rifle hanging on wall, 622:*n3*
write the next c., 779:4
Chapters in art of living, 524:3
of lives to natural end, 595:4
Character, accommodation c., 555:6
adopt c. of octopus, 61:13
analysis of c. highest entertainment, 769:10
bearing on excellence of c., 80:17
best way to define c., 581:2
bird of bad moral c., 320:24
December 1910 human c. changed, 699:15
education for c., 523:3
energy of c., 383:3
family stamped c. on child, 675:10
find well-drawn c., 560:9
formed in world's torrent, 364:12
give action its c., 75:29
good c. remembered, 3:11
habits and manners, 534:10
higher than intellect, 454:23
his c. arbiter of everyone's fortune, 95:*n11*
liberal arts humanizes c., 105:28
lies in own hands, 822:8

Character (*continued*)
limitations of own c., 572:9
man that makes c., 305:21
man's c. is his fate, 64:16
men of contrary c., 62:22
never mind the c., 496:2
of mistress from dress of maids, 118:18
of perfection, 531:15
poetical c., 440:13
power of Latin in c., 531:9
reap a c., 849:5
simplicity of c., 572:8
Characteristics, have certain mental c., 613:14
of popular politician, 74:12
of vigorous mind, 324:12
Characterless, mighty states c., 208:7
Characters, attributes c. of living creature, 517:5
fashioning our c. wrong, 581:10
high c. cries one, 269:22
impressed on our c. and conduct, 332:10
knowledge of c. of rulers, 350:17
most women have no c., 310:4
not in calm that great c. are formed, 362:2
of hell to trace, 335:12
Charge Chester charge, 397:2
compulsive ardor gives c., 205:23
Cromwell I c. thee, 231:6
give his angels c. over thee, 18:26
give lie to slander c., 419:3
lunatics taken c. of asylum, 692:7
not soul save to its ability, 121:20
once more be dumb, 531:5
prepared lawyers met, 307:18
such is the c., 76:10
with all thy chivalry, 408:20
within the bosom, 544:4
Charged, language c. with meaning, 709:15
troops of error, 255:8
Charger, John Baptist's head in c., 36:12
Charges, die to save c., 240:20
Chariest maid prodigal enough, 201:22
Charing Cross, Heaven and C., 621:8
went out to C. to see Harrison hanged, 288:4
Chariot, appeared a c. of fire, 12:39
flying-c. through air, 348:23
maketh clouds his c., 19:8
of fire, 375:17
of Israel, 12:40
swing low sweet c., 863:4
that bears Human Soul, 546:11
Time's winged c., 277:1
why is his c. so long in coming, 10:34
Chariots, why tarry the wheels of his c., 10:34
Charisma inner determination inner restraint, 631:14
Charismatic leader gains authority, 631:14
Charitable, intents wicked or c., 202:5
men's c. speeches, 168:19
Charite, of saynte c., 843:7
Charities of kiss or smile, 404:3
Charity, affecting c. and devotion, 82:26
and have not c., 44:17
anticipate c. by preventing poverty, 127:3
beareth all things, 44:19

Charity *(continued)*
  begins at home, 88:13, 256:5
  believeth all things, 44:19
  come out of c., 843:*n*4
  crawling for c., 82:27
  creates multitude of sins, 605:14
  degrades, 461:8
  edifieth, 44:8
  endureth all things, 44:19
  envieth not, 44:18
  for all, 477:4
  greatest is c., 44:20
  hopeth all things, 44:19
  I am in c. with world, 299:9
  in all things c., 274:22
  in c. no excess, 167:17
  in c. to all mankind, 386:4
  in love and c. with neighbors, 50:17
  indiscriminate c., 559:9
  is kind, 44:18
  justice not c. wanting in world, 382:27
  little earth for c., 231:9
  love friendship c., 208:12
  never faileth, 44:19
  not puffed up, 44:18
  now abideth c., 44:20
  of saynte c., 843:7
  pity gave ere c. began, 342:5
  rarity of Christian c., 446:8
  scrimped and iced, 590:15
  shall cover multitude of sins, 47:31
  suffereth long, 44:18
  towards each other, 353:4
  towards others, 256:5
  vaunteth not, 44:18
  where c. neither fear nor ignorance,
    128:4
Charity's golden ladder, 127:3
Charlemagne, world-transforming C., 642:5
Charles, gentlehearted C., 407:*n*1
  immense empire of C. the Fifth, 381:*n*4
  navy of C. the Second, 448:19
  successors of C. the Fifth, 353:14
  the First his Cromwell, 352:11
Charles's, King C. head, 498:3
Charley's, I am C. aunt from Brazil, 610:18
Charlie is my darling, 385:7
  live and die wi' C., 390:12
  o'er the water to C., 390:12
Charlotte true friend good writer, 756:18
  went on cutting bread and butter, 490:18
Charm ache with air, 195:6
  by thought supplied, 391:3
  in melancholy, 384:8
  music oft hath such a c., 212:1
  northern c., 800:8
  object in possession seldom retains c.,
    114:6
  of all the Muses, 486:23
  of earliest birds, 266:17
  one native c., 342:11
  quality in others, 524:5
  simplicity and c., 98:23
  smiling at good mouth, 709:5
  some have c. for none, 621:19
  some women c. all, 621:19
  strengthen and teach, 466:22
  touching all the muses' c., 92:17
  wasted on sky, 453:4

Charm *(continued)*
  what c. soothe melancholy, 341:20
  witch hath power to c., 200:22
  without c. no literature, 636:16
Charmed alike tilt-yard and bower, 417:11
  bear a c. life, 222:20
  it with smiles and soap, 553:4
  magic casements, 437:13
  water burnt alway, 400:12
  with foolish whistlings, 275:17
Charmer, were t'other dear c. away, 307:17
Charmers, will not hearken to voice of c.,
    17:34
Charmian is this well done, 224:14
Charming, be c. with nothing, 597:15
  evening criminal's friend, 524:14
  form of government, 77:21
  friendly and c. relationship, 144:16
  how c. divine philosophy, 261:3
  left his voice, 267:17
  never so wisely, 17:34
  to totter into vogue, 336:4
Charm's, peace the c. wound up, 218:29
Charms, Aphrodite with intricate c., 57:*n*9
  by accepting, 310:9
  do not all c. fly, 436:17
  endearing young c., 411:12
  freedom has thousand c., 347:6
  icy arms hold c., 745:2
  music has c. to soothe, 300:20
  O Solitude where are c., 347:21
  or ear or sight, 402:7
  other maids' surpass, 368:15
  power obtained by c., 382:26
  Sabina has thousand c., 845:21
Charon could not prevent me, 69:12
Charter, large a c. as wind, 198:20
  this was c. of land, 318:8
Chartered libertine, 192:19
Charts, there are c., 834:3
Charybdis, I fall into C., 189:11
  implacable C. guards left, 189:*n*1
  on starboard beam C., 189:*n*1
Chase, blessed in luck of c., 856:6
  glowing hours, 420:17
  had a beast in view, 285:22
  lead a wild-goose c., 156:26
  my gloom away, 384:8
  panting syllable, 347:18
  piteous c., 198:1
  the sport of kings, 304:14
  to c. white whale, 516:12
  unhurrying c., 621:1
  when heated in the c., 294:7
  writing make us c. the writer, 839:10
Chased shouting wind along, 810:11
Chasm, there exists a great c., 782:3
Chassis, state o' c., 704:6
Chaste and fair, 237:10
  as ice, 204:5
  as the icicle, 224:31
  as unsunned snow, 225:13
  early bright transient c., 285:*n*4
  fair c. unexpressive she, 199:3
  modest and commonly c., 426:1
  nunnery of c. breast, 275:22
  to her husband, 310:5
  was she not c., 111:8
Chasten, power to c. and subdue, 391:4

Chasteneth, he that loveth c. him, 21:27
  whom the Lord loveth he c., 47:2
Chastening in hour of pride, 474:16
Chastise, I will c. with scorpions, 12:22
Chastised, father hath c. you, 12:22
  having been a little c., 31:16
Chastity, give me c. but not now, 119:9
  most unnatural sexual perversion, 741:4
  my brother Chastity, 261:2
  scepticism c. of intellect, 629:18
Chat, before we have our c., 552:4
Chat, la patte du c., 277:*n*2
Châteaux, O seasons O c., 603:16
Chatter against bird of Zeus, 65:28
  harebrained c., 459:24
  insignificant c. of world, 503:14
  of transcendental kind, 564:8
  those who have learned art c., 65:28
Chattering voltage, 729:17
Chatterley, between C. ban and Beatles' LP,
    810:6
Chatterton marvelous boy, 392:9
Chaucer, Dan C. first warbler, 480:22
  nigh to learned C., 247:11
  not lodge thee by C., 238:5
  well of English, 161:13
  whose sweet breath, 480:22
Chaucer's, corruption since C. days, 243:17
Chaud comme l'enfer, 369:*n*2
Chaudron, parole humaine comme un c. fêlé,
    526:*n*5
Chauffered Cub Scouts, 807:15
Cheap, electrical energy too c. to meter,
    747:17
  flesh and blood so c., 446:6
  good counsel c., 241:9
  greet c. holde at litel prys, 136:17
  hold c. the strain, 494:9
  how potent c. music is, 753:8
  ill ware is never c., 251:6
  life not c. but sacred, 456:31
  man's life c. as beast's, 216:15
  never buy because c., 359:11
  sitting as standing, 299:8
  sleep a c. pleasure, 158:31
  sold c. what is most dear, 227:15
  tin trays, 681:5
  what we obtain too c., 354:10
Cheaper than keep cow, 559:4
Cheapest, man richest whose pleasures c.,
    505:11
Cheat at cards genteelly, 327:23
  came to c. them, 386:9
  for sake of beauty, 678:3
  life 'tis all a c., 282:21
  out of love c. others, 657:15
  pleasure as great as to c., 271:22
  sweet c. gone, 662:13
  undertaken to c. me, 432:17
Cheated, illusion by which c., 657:15
  pleasure of being c., 271:22
Cheater, old bald c. Time, 237:11
Check, care's c. and curb, 278:29
  judicial power a c., 351:11
  rod to c. the erring, 394:10
Checked, be c. for silence, 210:20
Checkerboard of Nights and Days, 471:19
Checkered shade, 259:16
Checkers, kids loved the dog C., 790:18

Child *(continued)*

if you strike a c., 609:25
in simplicity a c., 310:19
in the name of this C., 51:5
is father of the man, 392:7
is known by his doings, 22:19
Jesus Christ her little c., 508:9
keeps secret well, 451:15
lie down like tired c., 428:2
life like froward c., 282:9
like three years' c., 399:13
little c. shall lead them, 26:34
look upon a little c., 322:25
lost in unreality, 802:5
Magus Zoroaster my dead c., 428:3
make c. able man, 152:13
meet nurse for poetic c., 396:12
Monday's c. fair of face, 859:16
more hideous in a c., 216:4
my c.-wife, 498:14
ne'er spend fury on c., 173:14
of Calamity, 560:3
of my right hand, 237:20
of our grandmother Eve, 176:24
of pure unclouded brow, 551:8
of scorn, 652:6
old man twice a. c., 203:21
on a cloud I saw a c., 371:13
painted c. of dirt, 312:8
role to be born, 630:2
room of absent c., 178:9
Rowland to dark tower, 217:3
said What is the grass, 518:18
saving little c., 571:7
seemed a small ungainly c., 58:2
seen a curious c., 395:5
Shakespeare Fancy's c., 259:20
shall play on hole of the asp, 26:34
spare rod and spoil c., 83:n7, 271:17
take me into bright c. of mind, 740:18
teach c. to doubt, 375:11
thankless c., 216:5
there is a man c. conceived, 13:29
there was a c. went forth, 521:1
thought as a c., 44:20
to mother sheep to fold, 619:16
train up a c. in the way, 22:25
tyrant is c. of Pride, 68:6
understood as a c., 44:20
unto us a c. is born, 26:31
virgin shall be with c., 33:17
warble c., 176:30
when I was a c., 44:20
when she was a c., 816:1
white as angel English c., 372:1
wise father knows own c., 188:17
would have made ugly c., 550:8
you are like a flower, 442:8
young c. with Mary, 33:19

Childbirth, death taxes c., 758:7

Childhood, barb in arrow of c., 606:11
eye of c. fears painted devil, 220:18
in my days of c., 407:1
little world of c., 675:10
make glad heart of c., 573:2
manhood and decrepit age, 249:13
model of greater world, 675:10
one moment in c., 767:6
ordinary miserable c., 825:9

Childhood *(continued)*

remnants of c. hopes of adulthood, 762:3
scenes of my c., 418:13
shows the man, 268:24
talk about my hard c., 838:3
waters of c. are there, 830:14
wove web in c., 504:13

Childhood's hour, 412:13, 477:13

Childhoods, had Vietnam instead of happy c., 834:9

Childish but divinely beautiful, 381:13
glamor of childish days, 707:7
practice c. ways, 54:11
put away c. things, 768:2
religion but a c. toy, 170:9
sweet c. days, 392:8
things, 44:20
treble, 198:25

Childishly, sucked on pleasures c., 233:10

Childishness, second c., 198:25

Childless and crownless, 421:17
saw Whitman c. lonely, 817:10

Children, age finds us true c. still, 365:2
all God's c. join hands, 823:4
an' all us other c., 596:5
and fools cannot lie, 148:18
and fools want everything, 288:29
as c. fear in darkness, 93:9
become as little c., 36:28
begin by loving parents, 604:18
believe in good family angels, 769:12
blood on us and on our c., 38:5
bones on which c. sharpen teeth, 808:11
books c. of brain, 297:16
breed of horses dogs c., 292:2
bring forth c. in sorrow, 6:9
bring up c. in behavioristic freedom, 682:5
bringing up c., 766:1
bringing-up of c., 608:4
can c. of bridechamber mourn, 35:20
can't form c. on own concepts, 364:13
come dear c. let us away, 528:5
don't read to find identity, 769:12
dream that my four c., 823:3
drinkest tears of c., 418:2
extensions of our egos, 712:10
familiarity breeds contempt and c., 60:n6
fear death as c. fear dark, 167:7
forever explaining to grown-ups, 759:3
freezing to death, 576:10
get on board little c., 863:11
give c. right to study painting, 351:14
Great Spirit make: them all for his c., 387:10
had so many c., 858:13
hates c. and dogs can't be all bad, 690:3
her c. arise, 23:30
herd c. home to mothers, 58:6
here my c. born, 475:2
how can you shoot women c., 834:8
husband c. friends nothing to that, 593:20
I and my c. are now free, 501:7
in days of our c., 615:11
in peace c. inter parents, 71:10
in the foliage, 720:13
in the wood, 843:13
indifferent c. of earth, 203:12

Children *(continued)*

iniquity of the fathers upon the c., 8:33
invent a game; 706:7
king over c. of pride, 15:24
laboring c. look out, 677:21
listen my c., 467:14
little c. cried in streets, 502:5
look after own upbringing, 822:8
love of little c., 686:7
most men are like c., 700:16
my c. glean, 761:16
nature fits c., 514:20
Nature's c. given into slavery, 141:12
Negro school-c., 801:13
no longer any c., 278:25
nor do c. prattle about his knees, 52:27
not one of her c. escaped, 501:6
of an idle brain, 182:23
of disillusioned colored pioneers, 832:7
of kingdom cast out, 35:13
of larger growth, 315:1
of light, 39:40, 530:12
of light and day, 46:10
of Men full of wiles, 75:8
of the day, 46:10
of this world wiser, 39:40
old men are c., 75:1
parents bore their c., 610:3
peace to our c. when they fall, 801:17
playthings in playhouse of c., 670:18
provoke not c. to anger, 46:4
Rachel weeping for her c., 33:21
receive arms race from us, 806:13
red c. acknowledge no boundaries, 387:6
remember c. you did not get, 798:6
return ye c. of men, 18:20
Revolution eats own c., 501:4
second wife hateful to c., 69:10
shall wander in the wilderness, 9:19
sins of fathers upon c., 71:5
so act toward c. so toward wife, 112:17
so are c. of the youth, 20:6
suffer little c., 38:28
swarmed like settlers, 776:6
sweeter than apples to c., 603:9
tale which holdeth c. from play, 163:26
teach them diligently unto thy c., 9:30
terrible c., 460:2
their country their c., 95:8
they shall be called c. of God, 33:33
travel first-class and with c., 725:14
walk on frozen toes, 652:9
we are c. of our landscape, 788:8
we are the c., 842:7
wealth and c. adornment of life, 121:16
weeping O brothers, 463:11
were all thy c. kind, 192:25
what give my c., 798:7
what have you got against c., 831:18
when voices of c., 372:10
where c. above average, 837:5
where did c. vanish, 771:14
wife and c. impediments, 167:14
wife and c. stand afraid, 255:20
will burn, 857:8
will enjoy electrical energy, 747:17
wisdom exalteth her c., 32:2
wisdom justified of c., 35:34
women and c. first, 848:6

Children *(continued)*
    words c. of many men, 759:16
    world safer for c. grow up in, 824:4
    your c. are we, 855:18
Children's, all our c. fate, 635:25
    books of my day, 627:20
    children think they are alone, 419:5
    gratitude woman's love, 641:9
    Hour, 467:10
    house of make believe, 670:18
    lips shall echo, 420:19
    my God the C. Crusade, 811:9
    teeth set on edge, 29:23
Child's amang you takin' notes, 380:6
    credulity c. strength, 407:16
    no c. pley to take wyf, 137:7
Child's-heart, not lose his c., 82:8
Chill and drear, 396:13
    bitter c. it was, 436:20
    in wintry age feel no c., 348:17
    mantle of wind and c. and rain, 138:15
    penury, 334:19
    sun was warm wind c., 670:5
    thy dreaming nights, 439:2
    wind is c., 396:21
Chilling, on love request for money c., 527:4
Chills, of c. and fever died, 724:12
Chilly, I feel c. and old, 493:14
    room grows c., 671:21
Chime, faintly as tolls evening c., 411:7
    higher than the sphery c., 261:12
    hours to which Heaven c., 278:29
    to guide their c., 277:11
Chimera, what a c. is man, 280:8
Chimeras, how many vain c. have you
        created, 141:11
    nothing achieved without c., 535:12
Chimerical, reduction to atoms c. ideal,
        572:2
Chimes at midnight, 192:1
    little jingle little c., 307:22
Chimleypiece, bottle on c., 497:3
Chimney, as c-sweepers come to dust, 225:23
    hung by c. with care, 411:5
    makes c. of your nose, 369:16
    old men from c. corner, 163:26
Chimneypiece, Buffalo upon c., 553:7
Chimneys, your c. I sweep, 372:4
Chin, close-buttoned to the c., 348:14
    dogs shame the gray c., 53:32
    my c. throbs, 841:6
    new-reaped, 185:2
China, break c. plates of others, 621:14
    'crost the Bay, 633:13
    leave C. convert Christians, 562:19
    mankind from C. to Peru, 324:5
    not seeking to dominate world, 736:16
    slow boat to C., 785:2
    though c. fall, 310:10
    thought of C. and Greece, 766:18
Chinee, heathen C. is peculiar, 566:12
Chinese, bombing of C. cities, 705:11
    great and vital people, 790:22
    nightingale, 685:7
    people have solidarity, 644:8
Chink, importunate c., 345:16
    in floor of Wicklow house, 658:8
Chinks of her sickness-broken body, 258:5
    that Time has made, 258:3

Chinook, break loose like c. salmon, 801:16
Chip of old block, 345:4
Chips down nation acts helpless, 790:23
    lest c. fall in eye, 843:9
Chirurgery, what c. relieve conscience, 242:7
Chisel, whether c. pen or brush, 639:3
Chiseled, down their c. names, 576:6
Chivalrous, proud and c. spirit, 81:17
Chivalry, age of c. gone, 345:13
    age of c. past, 514:7
    charge with all thy c., 408:20
    her beauty and her c., 420:16
    smiled c. away, 424:18
Chocolate, no c. to eat, 809:5
Choice and master spirits, 196:19
    brave man's c. is danger, 70:9
    can I have no other c., 802:3
    careful in c. of enemies, 604:14
    courage of making c., 659:16
    grain into this wilderness, 286:1
    Hobson's c., 844:10
    in the worth and c., 237:9
    it was not my c., 832:3
    life's business c., 495:2
    of horse and wife, 528:1
    of point of view, 702:16
    pays money takes c., 591:13
    reckless c., 669:7
    small c. in rotten apples, 175:22
    with freedom of c. and honor, 142:1
    word measured phrase, 392:10
Choir, chorister whose *c* preceded c., 688:17
    full-voiced c. below, 260:10
    invisible, 512:14
    of saints, 236:13
    sanctuary and c., 721:17
    singing in the c., 846:2
    St. Stephen's c., 800:9
    wailful c., 438:13
Choirs, bare ruined c., 226:24
Choix, le c. fait les amis, 355:n3
Choke them amid flowers, 93:16
Choked with ambition of meaner sort,
        171:19
Choleric, captain's c. word, 211:14
Chondria, Russia's c. for short, 446:15
Choose, any language you c., 565:3
    author as you c. friend, 287:20
    between Africa and English tongue,
        826:2
    between betraying country and friend,
        684:5
    do not c. to run, 659:20
    don't c. to run, 685:17
    equality, 532:2
    fool multitude c. by show, 188:25
    ground and take thy rest, 425:9
    if thou must c. the odd, 776:8
    if you dare, 257:13
    intellect forced to c., 641:4
    it is time to c., 687:15
    let's c. executors, 179:27
    likely man in preference to rich, 64:21
    not alone proper mate, 348:20
    not c. not to be, 587:20
    odd of God to c. Jews, 706:12
    path leading wherever I c., 520:2
    slavery or death, 301:21
    the irregular, 591:2

Choose *(continued)*
    therefore c. life, 10:12
    to live without friends, 80:15
    we c. our friends, 355:10
    what becomes Castilian, 442:1
Choosers, beggars should be no c., 148:9
Chooses, consciousness c. object, 581:15
    intimacy that c. right, 639:9
    no man c. evil, 382:20
Choosest not better part, 629:1
Chop off her head, 550:6
    off your head, 857:13
Chopper to chop off your head, 857:13
Chord in melancholy, 445:18
    in unison is touched, 348:10
    struck c. of music, 537:16
Chords that vibrate pleasure, 378:22
Chorister, bobolink for C., 544:17
    whose *c* preceded choir, 688:17
Chortled in his joy, 551:11
Chorus ending from Euripides, 493:8
    from Atlanta to sea, 553:11
    what a c., 408:8
Choruses above guinea's squawk, 742:5
Chose, David c. him five smooth stones,
        11:29
Chosen, few are c., 36:41
    I have c. you, 41:32
    Lord hath c. thee, 9:32
    only c. had complications, 627:12
    people children of light, 530:12
    people of God, 357:10
    vessel, 42:9
Choses que je conte, 726:n2
Choughs that wing air, 217:18
Choux, que la mort me trouve plantant mes
        c., 152:n7
Christ ain't a-going to be too hard, 571:6
    all at once what C. is, 588:6
    blood when C. slain, 640:10
    born across the sea, 513:19
    born in Bethlehem, 323:1
    bowels of C., 254:12, 660:6
    came from God and a woman, 443:11
    came to save sinners, 46:15
    catch C. with worm, 800:10
    cautious statistical C., 590:15
    deep did rot O C., 399:23
    Don Quixote and I, 415:21
    everyone in world is C., 677:19
    face is face of C. himself, 520:10
    half a drop ah my C., 171:4
    Himself buddy, 805:15
    his captain, 180:6
    I believe in Jesus C., 50:3
    in C. all made alive, 44:24
    is all and in all, 46:3
    is C. thy advocate, 292:12
    it is the Inchcape Rock, 405:12
    Jesus C. her little child, 508:9
    Jesus C. is born, 862:28
    Jesus C. the righteous, 47:38
    Jesus C. the same yesterday, 47:6
    joint heirs with C., 43:5
    Judas or Peter who loved C., 767:9
    keep your hearts through C. Jesus, 45:37
    kingdom and patience of Jesus C., 48:2
    kingdoms of his C., 48:27
    listen C. you did alright, 762:13

Christ *(continued)*
Lord C. enter in, 606:1
our Lord, 51:2
our Passover sacrificed, 44:5
our Savior, 846:1
people who never heard of Jesus C., 726:2
receive him, 484:23
redemption by Jesus C., 50:8
risen from dead, 44:24
rule given by C., 542:15
save us all, 466:6
Savior which is C., 39:3
see the C. stand, 493:21
show me dear C. Thy spouse, 236:12
shut up in asylum, 618:3
so Judas did to C., 180:8
soldiers of C. arise, 322:26
testimony of Jesus C., 48:2
that it were possible, 485:13
that my love in my arms, 843:18
the Lord risen today, 322:23
the Son took Father's place, 608:5
thief said last word to C., 494:25
thou art the C., 36:24
to live is C., 45:32
took the kindness, 494:25
vision of C. thou see, 376:7
walking on the water, 621:9
walks on black water, 800:9
what are patterns for, 672:12
Christendom, christianize C., 516:3
in C. where Christian, 455:16
live in any place in C., 151:14
wisest fool in C., 162:14
Christened on Tuesday, 859:17
Christian, any husband rather than C., 189:26
bear other's misfortunes like C., 313:12
charity, 446:8
confidence C. feels in four aces, 559:12
darkness fell upon C., 281:28
enterprise for glory of C. religion, 140:6
feels repentance on Sunday, 692:11
fled with a C., 188:24
forgive them as C., 406:11
hate him for a C., 188:3
honorable style of C., 255:6
I am a C. faithful man, 174:2
I mean the C. religion, 322:15
ideal found difficult, 664:5
if victory I shall become C., 119:26
in what peace a C. can die, 302:24
inconsistent with C. religion, 336:15
meaning of C. life, 728:2
men control property interests, 580:4
not so good a C. as thinks, 599:17
O my C. ducats, 188:24
only C. come to these parts, 140:6
pagan spoiled, 631:15
persuadest me to be C., 42:38
practice C. forbearance, 353:4
principle of suffering, 461:6
richest monarch in C. world, 381:15
Scientists some science, 645:14
scratch C. find pagan, 631:15
sleep with drunken C., 516:8
soldiers, 555:2
what one C. does, 822:7
where C. in Christendom, 455:16
witness of soul naturally C., 116:12

Christian *(continued)*
wonders of C. religion, 296:4
word of gentleman and C., 157:14
you are Ciceronian not C., 118:8
you were a C. Slave, 594:13
Christianity blemish of mankind, 589:25
Catholicism minus C., 537:3
cult called C., 575:20
doctors more C., 645:14
enormous perversion, 589:25
genius of C., 761:7
is an idea, 442:13
muscular C., 848:10
narcotics alcohol and C., 589:17
one great curse, 589:25
religion of the son, 608:5
since introduction of C., 357:8
takes great deal of C., 632:11
which go first rock and roll or C., 834:11
Christianize Christendom, 516:3
Filipinos, 586:4
Christians, all C. agree, 326:17
blood of C. is seed, 116:14
good C. good citizens, 414:9
have burnt each other, 423:9
have little difference, 327:10
missionary leave China convert C., 562:19
not born but made, 118:26
predicted conversion lead to peace,
571:13
see how C. love one another, 116:13
two sorts of C., 743:19
what these C. are, 188:11
Christ-like in my behavior, 741:2
Christmas, at C. no more desire rose, 176:21
at C. play, 151:4
born on C. Day, 846:1
comes but once a year, 151:4
Day in workhouse, 593:1
dreaming of white C., 716:8
Ghost of C. Past, 497:15
Ghost of C. Present, 497:17
Ghost of C. Yet to Come, 497:20
happy C. to all, 411:6
home, 647:16
is coming, 847:8
it was C. Day, 169:1
jest 'fore C., 597:8
keep C. all the year, 497:21
keep our C. merry still, 396:21
night before C., 411:5
one C. much like another, 795:15
over and Business is Business, 692:12
pie, 857:3
won't be Christmas, 549:4
Christom child, 192:27
Christ's blood streams, 171:4
in C. coach, 292:8
lady of C. College, 280:22
loore and his apostles twelve, 135:11
Lord C. heart, 453:24
progress and His prayer-time, 278:29
stamp, 250:3
submission to humiliation, 812:6
Chromis did not save himself, 52:18
Chronic anxiety about weather, 566:18
do not weep it's c., 496:39
hotel guests, 649:13
melancholy of civilized, 575:8

Chronicle of wasted time, 227:11
pride his own c., 208:1
small beer, 213:12
wars of kites, 269:18
Chronicles, brief c. of the time, 203:25
transcribe my c., 446:18
Chronology, according to our c., 244:13
Chrysanthemum, white c. immaculate,
291:14
Chuang-tzu, Begone cried C., 83:2
Chuck 'im out the brute, 633:8
Chuckle, he with c. replied, 693:7
little kind of low c., 560:15
Chuds, the C. Slavs and Krivchians, 125:12
Chums, bosom c., 822:11
Church ain't out till fat lady sings, 850:15
and State demand for country, 697:17
and State separate, 532:20
authority of C. moved me, 119:14
bells knolled to c., 198:22
blood of martyrs seed of C., 116:n3
built God a c., 347:17
come to c. good people, 618:15
get me to c. on time, 803:11
holy Catholic C., 50:3
I like a c., 452:18
I like silent c., 455:14
joined c. at Boston, 270:12
keep Sabbath going to C., 544:17
Mother C., 116:16
nearer to c. further from God, 147:22
new and great period in His C., 263:2
no other C. understood, 448:8
not forgotten inside of c., 186:17
not God for father if not C. for mother,
117:6
novel by Henry James like c., 644:14
of England, 322:15
persecuted c. of God, 44:23
plain as way to parish c., 198:21
prayers of c. to preserve travel, 299:21
saw a wedding in the c., 288:14
see a c. by daylight, 194:16
sleep and feed at once, 718:5
some to c. repair, 308:16
stands c. clock at ten to three, 712:16
take care of the c., 46:16
to be of no c. dangerous, 325:6
to c. and with my mourning very
handsome, 288:21
two lanterns in North C., 352:10
upon this rock build my c., 36:25
wall between c. and state, 710:17
where God built c., 144:14
wide as a c. door, 183:28
Churches, chapels had been c., 187:27
head more than c. bibles creeds, 519:10
in flat countries, 395:n1
scab of c., 233:1
seven c. in Asia, 48:3
Churchill, Randolph C. went into hospital,
766:10
Churchman, I that cowled c. be, 452:18
Churchyard abounds with images, 325:9
Drumcliff c., 643:4
where Michael Furey buried, 696:4
Churchyards yawn, 205:12
Churlish, reply c., 200:9
Churn, silver c., 564:11

Cibus, ali c. aliis venenum, 93:*n*5
Cicada, wild c. cried, 729:17
Cicadas, cries of c., 291:13
    like c. so leaders of Trojans, 52:21
    pour out their piping voices, 52:21
Cicala to cicala is dear, 85:9
Cicero, accept views C. Locke Bacon have
    given, 454:21
    book of a certain C., 119:8
Ciceronian, you are C. not Christian, 118:8
Cider, squirt c. in your ear, 704:*n*2
Ciel, j'allais sous le c. Muse, 603:*n*3
Cigar, good c. is a smoke, 632:10
    good five-cent c., 603:1
    sometimes c. just a c., 608:10
Cilicia, Tarsus in C., 42:26
Cinara, reign of the good C., 100:12
Cincinnatus of the West, 422:11
Cinderella fulfilling herself, 688:8
Cinders ashes dust, 436:16
    sat among the c., 859:10
    somebody's always heaving c., 685:2
Cinnamon, color of c., 788:1
    nutmegs ginger c. cloves, 249:15
    tinct with c., 437:2
    tree, 765:1
Cinzano, another dry C. in sun, 797:7
Cipher, write and c. too, 342:8
Circle, all within this c. move, 257:23
    close the c. of felicities, 358:12
    ever-nearing c. weaves shade, 530:18
    everything Indian does is in a c., 628:1
    glory like a c. in water, 171:14
    if you have formed a c., 376:1
    live in small c. as we will, 364:20
    of potential being, 581:3
    of the golden year, 481:6
    of wedding ring, 301:7
    outside a small c. of friends, 835:7
    perfect c. and vicious c., 788:13
    restricted c. of potential, 581:3
    shock of recognition whole c. round,
      516:2
    vicious c., 555:19
    weave c. round him, 401:19
    wheel is come full c., 218:4
Circled, monthly changes in c. orb, 183:8
Circles, power of world works in c., 628:1
    produce perfect c., 81:27
    share decisions of consequences, 798:2
    triangles c. and other geometrical figures,
      169:18
Circling, busy whisper c. round, 342:8
    morn waked by c. hours, 267:10
    the Throne, 835:13
Circuit, his c. unto the ends of it, 16:11
Circulate, everything that can c. does, 829:2
Circulation, after book of c. of blood, 280:20
Circumcised, took by throat the c. dog,
    215:14
Circumcision, neither c. nor uncircumcision,
    46:3
Circumference, in universe neither center nor
    c., 159:11
Circumlocution Office, 498:26
Circumscribed, not c. in one self place,
    170:20
Circumspection deliberation fortitude,
    337:10

Circumspections, truth has c. and limits,
    154:6
Circumstance and proper timing, 75:29
    artistries in c., 575:19
    envisage c. calm, 438:19
    fell clutch of c., 594:10
    of glorious war, 214:8
    some c. to please us, 274:*n*2
    unsifted in perilous c., 201:29
Circumstances, all classes times c., 502:18
    alter cases, 442:3
    classic survives c., 796:10
    fortuitous c., 398:1
    harmony of temperament and c., 527:1
    man is own c., 753:1
    people always blaming c., 609:5
    rule men, 71:22
    same c. same phenomena, 300:7
    war train of c., 354:18
Circumstantial, lie c., 200:9
    some c. evidence strong, 505:3
    things essential or things c., 281:22
Circumvent God, 206:19
Circuses, bread and c., 113:15
Cistern contains, 372:18
    wheel broken at the c., 25:8
Cisterns, we have c. and worship them, 759:7
Citadel, did not go to c. of Troy, 57:12
    sacked the holy c. of Troy, 54:7
    towered c. pendant rock, 223:33
Citadels, vain c. not walled, 738:9
Citations, avoid c. from poets, 73:3
Cite, devil can c. Scripture, 188:6
Cité, le buste survit à la c., 489:*n*1
Cities, anarchy why c. tumble, 67:24
    buries c. in common grave, 353:12
    embers of c., 829:3
    Eros builder of c., 775:18
    government of c. failure of United States,
      571:1
    grass in a hundred c., 672:2
    great lost c., 792:16
    hum of c. torture, 420:26
    London flower of C. all, 142:2
    man's skill built c., 90:4
    marble well-governed c., 776:10
    most pecksniffian of c., 691:3
    never have rest from evils, 77:12
    oblivion swallowed c. up, 208:7
    of men and manners, 481:9
    of the plain, 7:2
    place philosophy in c., 91:6
    remove weight from c., 811:11
    say unto the c. of Judah, 28:4
    towered c. please us then, 259:18
    turned pleasant c. into slums, 746:2
    two c. formed by two loves, 119:22
    warred for Homer dead, 239:13
Citizen consider traveling expenses, 738:2
    first requisite of good c., 615:5
    free nation great, 451:16
    good c. not silent, 539:10
    humblest c. of land, 622:1
    I am a Roman c., 90:10
    in wild weed she is c., 798:14
    may walk safely on law, 813:7
    nation guarantees maintenance of c.,
      596:11
    obliged to be c., 527:15

Citizen *(continued)*
    of no mean city, 42:26
    of the world, 72:10, 167:18
    takes stand upon economic theories,
      694:6
Citizen's, White C. Counciler, 822:12
Citizens clamoring for what is wrong, 99:28
    demean themselves as good c., 350:6
    equal before law, 554:1
    faction a number of c., 366:18
    fat and greasy c., 198:2
    force c. to confess, 734:1
    frenzy of his fellow c., 99:28
    good Christians good c., 414:9
    not women or Negroes but c., 503:9
    of Berlin, 800:5
    of death's land, 712:1
    of middle class, 81:1
    of the world, 699:5
    people born in U.S. are c., 361:8
    rights of other c., 366:18
    second class c., 736:12
    to arms c., 383:*n*1
    want to go to Hell I will help them,
      578:16
Citizenship anxious about what do for nation,
    799:*n*2
    illness onerous c., 829:1
Citoyens, aux armes c., 383:8
City, all that is left of c., 819:14
    and proud seat of Lucifer, 268:7
    appearance in C. Parks, 743:18
    Athens divine c., 66:10
    Babylon that great c., 48:32
    bust survives c., 489:8
    defend village town c., 666:3
    education to Greece, 74:4
    entire c. has suffered, 56:10
    except the Lord keep the c., 20:4
    failing that the rest of the c., 77:8
    famous Hanover c., 491:15
    flakes falling on c. brown, 586:6
    for sale, 95:11
    God made first c., 275:15
    grass will grow in streets of every c.,
      622:2
    great c. greatest men, 520:4
    happy c. which in peace thinks of war,
      241:12
    harder to be won than a strong c., 22:11
    he that taketh a c., 22:3
    hell c. like London, 429:9
    honor once at home in c., 246:2
    how doth the c. sit solitary, 29:26
    in country you praise c., 98:26
    in the c. of David, 39:3
    is destructible, 756:16
    is teacher of the man, 62:2
    like rain falling on c., 590:21
    long in populous c. pent, 267:28
    looking over harbor and c., 681:9
    make glad the c. of God, 17:22
    men make the c., 74:8
    most glorious c. of God, 119:21
    my head is a c., 841:6
    no continuing c., 47:7
    no mean c., 42:26
    obedient to his will, 77:13
    of big shoulders, 681:8

City *(continued)*

of mirrors, 820:10
of Night perchance Death, 557:11
of the soul, 421:16
one long in c. pent, 435:17
raised on c. land taxes, 543:15
road to the C. of Emeralds, 606:15
Rome a c. of bricks, 102:7
rose-red c., 501:5
royal David's c., 508:9
seen one c. slum seen all, 802:16
set on an hill, 34:2
since the founding of the c., 123:4
sounds of the c., 807:2
speck of light below, 600:4
spirit of our C. never stronger, 838:13
sweet c. dreaming spires, 530:16
taking in hand a c., 64:17
this c. going to follow you, 628:6
this great hive the c., 275:4
throne in a strange c., 478:4
to the c. and the world, 124:30
up and down C. Road, 848:8
upon a hill, 246:17
what is the c. but people, 224:27
without a c. wall, 508:8
Zion c. of our God, 339:13
City's disinherited, 621:12
feel amid c. jar, 528:13
Civet, give me an ounce of c., 217:22
in the room, 347:13
Civic, some c. manhood, 483:9
Civil, assent with c. leer, 312:4
discord, 302:2
engaged in great c. war, 476:7
founder of c. society, 330:17
fury first grew high, 270:13
in respect of c. rights, 554:1
over violent or over c., 283:16
rights of Englishman, 360:3
sea grew c. at her song, 181:8
state = political society + c. society, 731:6
text of c. instruction, 358:13
too c. by half, 367:11
Civil War rebirth of Union, 611:2
Civilian control of military, 705:10
Civility, a little c., 848:14
wild c., 248:4
Civilization advances by operations we
perform without thinking, 624:10
advances poetry declines, 447:12
botched c., 709:5
bourgeoisie draws nations into c., 511:3
cannot tolerate wrongs, 734:2
civilize c., 516:3
could be restored, 683:12
created under pressure of exigencies,
607:13
curiosity lifeblood of c., 678:16
definition of c., 624:17
elements of modern c., 434:10
English c. humanizing, 532:6
farmers founders of c., 415:9
France conquered for c., 534:9
homicidal c., 697:3
ignorant free in state of c., 359:2
in middle stage, 656:3
meeting-point between savagery and c.,
624:8

Civilization *(continued)*

nature and c. literary field, 584:7
New York the collapse of c., 796:5
not conquered from without, 706:11
not wiped out by atomic war, 683:12
obstacles of c., 461:4
poets in our c. difficult, 722:13
progress toward privacy, 771:21
provision for poor is test of c., 327:9
requires slaves, 605:13
resources of c. not exhausted, 472:12
results in deserts, 680:13
speech is c., 676:12
test of c. way cares for helpless, 733:8
theory of true c., 525:2
thin crust over revolution, 617:21
true test of c. is man, 457:8
usual interval of c., 577:11
western c. be feminized, 794:10
what dissatisfies in American c., 532:9
workers mainstay of c., 597:10
Civilizations break down fail to meet
challenge, 727:8
grow by responding to challenges, 727:8
Civilize civilization, 516:3
educate Filipinos uplift c. them, 586:4
Civilized man cannot live without cooks,
548:11
man has habits of house, 504:24
no c. life without clothes, 625:8
society five qualities, 624:17
they and I are c., 765:3
valued by c. men, 607:3
Woman last thing c., 540:24
Civilizer, comedy the ultimate c., 541:11
Civilizers, two c. of man, 459:18
Civis Romanus sum, 90:*n5*
Clad in beauty of thousand stars, 171:1
in complete steel, 261:2
in sober livery c., 266:15
morn in russet mantle c., 200:23
naked every day he c., 341:16
with native honor c., 266:9
Claim that our city is education, 74:4
woman takes off c. to respect, 71:9
Claims, adjustment of colonial c., 611:10
of long descent, 480:13
snakeskin titles of mining c., 750:9
Clamor, not in c. of crowded street, 467:22
Clamoring, citizens c. for what is wrong,
99:28
Clamorous owl that nightly hoots, 181:14
Clamors, immortal Jove's dread c., 214:8
venom c. of jealous woman, 174:38
Clan, family party tribe c., 848:16
leaf last of its c., 401:5
Clangor, trumpet's loud c., 284:15
Clap, if you believe c. hands, 621:18
padlock on her mind, 296:19
soul c. hands and sing, 639:17
Clapper, his tongue the c., 194:30
Claps, at heaven's gates c. wings, 163:16
Claptrap, art independent of c., 557:17
Claret liquor for boys, 328:20
Clarification, adventure in c. of thought,
624:14
poem ends in c. of life, 671:10
Clarifies, time cools time c., 676:15
Clarinets, has meadows of c., 740:17

Clarion laid away, 747:18
Clarity, culture moment of c., 702:12
give each moment c., 676:18
of a general idea, 836:11
Clarum et venerabile nomen, 110:*n6*
Clash, bring to our ears c. of arms, 353:3
ignorant armies c., 531:2
Clasp, dare deadly terrors c., 374:6
thrice tried to c. her image, 55:2
Clasps crag with crooked hands, 484:19
Class, brutalizing lower c., 532:3
could've had c. been somebody, 794:15
equal wealth made us one c., 596:15
ideas of ruling c., 511:7
leisure c. replaced by New C., 778:12
materializing upper c., 532:3
middle c. best political community, 81:1
middle c. in America the nation, 532:7
middle c. safety of England, 490:25
no criminal c. except Congress, 562:2
of 'ninety-seven, 841:13
office of leisure c., 613:9
one c. overthrows another, 737:13
ones of middle c. who left home, 802:15
proletariat revolutionary c., 511:4
Rome's decline lay in c. struggle, 706:11
second c. citizens, 736:12
she was in c. by herself, 756:18
struggle, 510:7
struggles, 511:1
taking from one c., 316:14
vulgarizing middle c., 532:3
while lower c. I am in it, 606:8
White-Anglo Saxon-Protestant upper c.,
795:17
Classes, all c. times circumstances, 502:18
antagonism between c., 511:6, 710:13
back masses against c., 472:13
bow lower middle c., 564:16
dissolution of all c., 510:7
draw powers into higher c., 359:10
four c. of Idols, 166:13
let ruling c. tremble, 511:8
no c. among citizens, 554:1
noblest work she o. O, 378:13
of travel first-class and with children,
725:14
other c. decay disappear, 511:4
ourselves and the lower c., 743:19
ruin of contending c., 511:1
tempt upper c., 613:3
tied to historical phases, 510:7
Classic book people praise don't read, 562:7
face, 478:2
Paris our black c., 800:14
reread c., 767:3
survives circumstances, 796:10
tread on c. ground, 301:11
Classical quotation, 329:7
Classicist in literature, 722:16
royalist Anglo-Catholic, 722:16
Classics, great homicidal c., 832:10
in paraphrase, 709:3
man with bellyful of c. enemy, 732:5
Classified, objects c., 364:22
Classless, formation of c. society, 510:7
Classroom hush, 834:3
Clatter of presses, 709:7
they make with his coach, 288:22

Clause, servant with this c., 251:1
two kinds of relative c., 614:2
Clavichord, stately at the c., 493:12
Claw, from c. can tell a lion, 123:25
red in tooth and c., 484:6
Clawed, age c. me in his clutch, 150:7
Claws, neatly spreads c., 549:13
pair of ragged c., 717:11
that catch, 551:10
Clay, beings of mind are not of c., 421:8
bless turf that wraps c., 336:16
dead and turned to c., 206:26
feet of c., 30:2
in c. none is, 860:10
kingdoms are c., 222:27
lies still, 618:8
of c. and wattles made, 637:1
porcelain c. of humankind, 284:28
Potter thumping his wet C., 471:17
power over the c., 43:13
say to him that fashioneth it, 28:11
tenement of c., 283:8
to every people cup of c., 856:8
weak creatures of c., 75:9
white linen cold as c., 854:17
Clean, art only c. thing, 593:19
bid them keep teeth c., 224:23
create in me a c. heart, 17:27
cry that it isn't c., 293:13
he that hath c. hands, 16:19
hearth, 407:13
horse of courage, 809:4
let other people c. up mess, 746:7
passed c. over Jordan, 10:19
pasture spring, 668:17
purge me and I shall be c., 17:26
starved for a look, 226:25
then c. and brave, 618:13
things holy profane c. obscene, 246:10
think of c. beds, 712:2
tumbler and corkscrew, 496:24
wash blood c. from hand, 220:19
Cleaned windows swept floor, 563:17
Cleanest and most isolated way, 711:5
Cleaning, yesterday had daily c., 794:12
Cleanliness next to godliness, 318:23
of all clean American backyards, 813:1
who of late for c., 244:15
Cleanly, leave sack and live c., 187:12
not too c. manger, 272:16
room lavender in windows, 252:29
thus so c. I myself can free, 169:14
Cleanse stuffed bosom of perilous stuff, 222:12
thou me from secret faults, 16:13
thoughts of our hearts, 50:16
Cleansed, what God hath c., 42:11
Cleanses, poetry c., 800:7
Clean-shaven, buttoned-up and c., 583:4
Clean-winged hearth, 468:18
Clear, action faithful honor c., 310:15
and cool clear and cool, 514:3
and present danger, 578:13
as a whistle, 314:14
as crystal, 499:8
as nose in face, 146:n7
as the sun, 25:27
as you go, 563:8
brown twilight atmosphere, 460:14

Clear *(continued)*
but one rule to be c., 417:3
coast was c., 169:15
conscience is sure card, 163:8
deep and absolutely c., 785:10
distinction is c., 617:1
doctrines plain and c., 271:25
enemy of c. language is insincerity, 765:12
fire clean hearth, 407:13
honor purchased by merit, 188:27
in cool September morn, 468:13
in his great office, 219:18
literature c. and cold, 708:7
loser is perfectly c., 807:9
my sad thoughts doth c., 279:7
no c. line, 763:4
one c. call for me, 487:2
read my title c., 304:10
religion of heaven, 436:10
spouse so bright and c., 236:12
summers wet and winters c., 96:6
they could get it c., 551:19
though deep yet c., 274:23
viol of her memory, 687:6
what is not c. is not French, 369:1
wild call and c. call, 681:1
your mind of cant, 329:14
Cleared, if this were only c., 551:19
ship cheered harbor c., 399:14
Clearer, age c. than noonday, 14:8
view ourselves with c. eyes, 248:22
Clearest of God's creatures, 801:4
way into Universe through forest, 572:14
who have c. vision, 74:2
Clearly, I see so c., 365:5
well conceived c. said, 289:7
Clearness, chief merit of language c., 116:6
virtue of style, 636:15
Clears today of past Regrets, 471:10
Cleave, man c. to his like, 32:27
thou canst not c. the earth, 121:12
to sunnier side of doubt, 486:24
tongue c. to the roof of my mouth, 20:11
unto his wife, 6:2
wood there am I, 117:4
Cleft, apple's c. through core, 382:18
Rock of Ages for me, 356:2
who c. Devil's foot, 233:13
Clemenceau had one illusion, 701:12
Clemency a species of nobility, 287:6
Clemens cannot think of something better, 549:6
Lincoln of literature, 567:9
Clement's, bells of St. C., 857:12
Cleopatra, every man's C., 283:2
squeaking C., 224:6
Cleopatra's nose, 279:20
Clergy, without benefit of c., 658:n3
Clergyman, avoid c. who is man of business, 118:12
proud c., 322:16
so much at home, 558:15
who never refuses dinner, 118:14
Clergymen, bankers schoolmasters c., 637:17
men women and c., 398:22
Clergymen's households unhappy, 558:15
Cleric before and Lay behind, 271:13
Clerical, features of c. cut, 720:1

Clerk, a bed C. Saunders said, 854:3
no difference 'twixt Priest and C., 248:6
ther was of Oxenford, 134:28
Clerks, gretteste c. noght wisest men, 136:7
Clever, encouraging c. pupil, 322:20
hopes expire, 775:13
if all c. people good, 577:3
let who will be c., 514:2, 692:17
men at Oxford, 618:5
of the turtle, 763:6
silliest woman manage c. man, 632:14
think oneself more c., 273:21
wet mind and say something c., 74:11
woman manage fool, 632:14
young poets, 403:20
Cleverer, advantage over c. boys, 665:9
Clichés, action limited to copulation of c., 756:2
Clicked behind the door, 342:10
off by little wheels, 748:9
Clickin' like tickin' of clock, 596:8
Client, art thou his c., 292:12
Clients, good counselors lack no c., 210:35
Cliff between lowland and highland, 569:11
dreadful summit of the c., 202:8
Cliffs of Dover, 645:2
of England stand, 530:19
of fall frightful sheer, 588:3
white c. of Dover, 673:5
would I were under the c., 70:4
Climacteric of his want, 801:6
Climate, age too late or cold c., 267:25
coal portable c., 456:25
difference of soil and c., 391:15
whole c. of opinion, 775:17
Climate's sultry, 423:8
Climates councils governments, 481:9
Climb, all day c. myself bowlegged, 811:17
back to upper air, 97:23
but I must c. the tree, 250:6
fain c. yet fear to fall, 160:4
high climb far, 851:12
if heart fails c. not, 160:n2
no man c. beyond limitations, 572:9
Sinais c. and know it not, 514:14
teach ye how to c., 261:12
Climbed, never c. Mount Sion, 801:8
to top of greasy pole, 459:13
Climber-upward turns face, 195:30
Climbest, moon c. skies, 163:29
Climbing, down thou c. sorrow, 216:11
liken fame to c. up a hill, 423:15
shakes his dewy wings, 257:16
still c. after knowledge infinite, 170:4
third stair, 719:12
Climbs, everybody c. into graves married, 749:14
higher monkey c. more see of behind, 128:10
in front sun c. slow, 512:10
Clime, change c. not disposition, 101:3
love no season knows nor c., 234:3
of unforgotten brave, 422:6
that lieth sublime, 478:18
Climes, cloudless c. starry skies, 422:13
Cling, bough where I c., 473:19
kiss and c., 553:n3
to old rugged cross, 661:10
together in one society, 391:7

Cold (*continued*)

bargain catch c. and starve, 225:10
blow hot and c., 61:2
blow in c. blood, 609:25
book makes my body c., 547:9
boughs which shake against c., 226:24
cast c. eye, 643:5
comfort, 178:27
comfort like c. porridge, 229:24
coming we had of it, 719:8
companionable streams, 638:12
dark deep clear, 785:10
dined upon c. meat, 288:16
doth not sting, 232:7
dull c. ear of death, 334:17
every drop of ink ran c., 336:2
fallen c. and dead, 520:19
feel hot and think c., 717:1
feeling his c. strength, 713:8
foot and hand go c., 151:10
friendship sounds too c., 412:10
fruitless moon, 180:18
goodbye and keep c., 669:18
gray dawn of morning after, 643:15
gray stones O Sea, 482:15
hand of death, 187:5
he makes c. as he wishes, 4:6
heart grown c. in vain, 430:13
heat flow from hot to c. object, 532:*n*1
her empty room is c., 89:17
his limbs c. in death, 98:12
hot c. moist and dry, 265:20
imagination c. and barren, 344:4
in the earth, 508:20
in the womb, 819:12
in thy c. bed, 249:1
iron, 419:3
it grew wondrous c., 399:17
keep c. young orchard, 669:18
large c. bottle, 597:4
lie in c. obstruction, 211:23
light and hot shade, 374:13
literature clear and c., 708:7
mad father, 696:18
meddles with c. iron, 161:*n*1
morn and c. indifference, 303:14
my lodging on c. ground, 307:2
neither c. nor hot, 48:14
neutrality, 345:20
never caught a c., 644:5
night blasts c., 664:10
night is c., 851:21
no such c. thing, 250:20
not more c. to you than I, 480:12
out o' c. an' rain, 634:10
out of dead c. ashes life, 591:11
owl a-c., 436:20
pain darkness and c., 494:19
passed reluctantly from earth, 655:10
pease-porridge c., 859:5
poor Tom's a-c., 217:2
principle, 252:*n*2
put it in c. storage, 625:10
side outside, 657:*n*1
sleep in dull c. marble, 231:5
sleep is heat for c., 158:31
snow said c. said sleep, 725:4
so c. no fire warm, 547:9
so sweet and so c., 703:11

Cold (*continued*)

sweat bathes me, 57:20
temper leaps over c. decree, 187:28
thicks man's blood with c., 400:3
through dark c. and desolation, 721:6
till sun grows c., 537:18
'tis bitter c., 200:12
to distant misery, 353:10
trembling c. in ghastly fears, 373:8
upon dead Caesar's trencher, 223:27
war getting warmer, 652:18
waters to a thirsty soul, 23:4
way long wind c., 396:3
we are dying of c., 631:6
winter with wrathful nipping c., 172:9
words of tongue or pen, 656:9
years grow c. to love, 96:17
Colder, heat cannot pass from c., 532:13
Coldly furnish forth marriage tables, 201:10
Coldness of my dear, 307:2
Cole, old King C., 856:18
Coleridge poet and philosopher, 532:11
Coliseum, while stands C. Rome stand, 421:23
Collaboration, peculiar illusion of c., 797:12
Collapse, New York the c. of civilization, 796:5
Collapsed, all c. and sea rolled on, 516:18
Collar, braw brass c., 378:4
Collars, Earl & Wilson C., 739:15
Collateral, with intellect only c. relations, 480:1
Collection of facts not science, 603:3
Collections, large c. of facts, 470:11
   mutilators of c., 407:12
   not c. of pictures but of fruit, 90:2
Collective bargaining is bilateral monopoly, 707:1
   unconscious, 675:2
Collective-unit only form, 583:2
Collectors, scientists c. classifiers, 796:12
Collects motions into shape, 822:10
College, aging c. people, 756:6
   cauliflower cabbage with c. education, 561:8
   endow c. or cat, 310:13
   farewell to c. joys, 702:5
   intent on getting results, 654:17
   it is a small c., 414:8
   lady of Christ's C., 280:22
   Maud went to c., 798:5
   not much between unless c., 670:4
Colleges to do with progress, 646:7
Collied night, 180:20
Collins, Mr. C. had only to change, 406:7
Collision, avoid foreign c., 409:8
Colonel lean as compass-needle, 801:11
Colonel's Lady an' Judy O'Grady, 634:19
Colonels full of corn, 620:10
Colonial, adjustment of c. claims, 611:10
Colonies are and ought to be free, 351:8
   commerce with our c., 344:4
   these united c., 349:11
Colonist, wilderness masters the c., 624:8
Colonization, American continents not for c., 376:16
Colony, dissenting c., 351:8
Coloquintida, bitter as c., 213:4

Color, air quiver with c., 706:7
blue c. delight, 517:9
by convention there is c., 72:14
her c. comes and goes, 574:12
his c. can't be seen, 847:4
horse of different c., 209:*n*1
horse of that c., 209:19
in the cup, 22:38
loves and skin, 233:17
met by c. line, 509:17
no matter c. of skin, 736:11
none knew c. of the sky, 655:16
not judged by c. of skin, 823:3
not superior by c., 554:3
of ground in him, 601:6
prejudice against c., 503:7
prison for c. of hair, 620:4
problem of c. line, 648:9
right to vote not denied on account of c., 361:9
Sergeant said, 633:5
shade without c., 719:5
that paints morning and evening clouds, 132:8
till heart tinged with c., 403:18
walk by c. purple in a field, 839:2
white is their c., 250:23
Colorado, Kansas and C. have quarrel, 705:2
Color-blind, Constitution is c., 554:1
Colored, as long as c. man look to white folks, 839:9
destiny of c. American, 509:14
disillusioned c. pioneers, 832:7
every c. woman is dying, 826:10
globe tilts like a c. O, 834:3
ground c. man occupies, 509:12
I am not tragically c., 760:14
no white or c. signs, 800:4
people understand white people, 656:16
relation between white and c. people, 509:15
skins not c. like your own, 509:11
twopence c., 599:10
Coloring, sober c. from eye, 393:19
Colorless green ideas sleep, 820:8
Colors, all c. suffusion from light, 402:7
changing c. shooting upward, 723:5
coat of many c., 7:23
embroidered girdle of many c., 53:15
hoist c. to peak, 690:10
nailed c. to the mast, 396:14
no c. or crest, 634:4
of imagination, 403:6
oldest c. have faded, 633:3
perfumes c. sounds echo, 524:9
seen by candlelight, 463:14
so like your own, 151:2
that never fade, 625:15
their c. and their forms, 391:3
under whose c. he fought so long, 180:6
Colossus, bestride world like C., 195:20
of Rhodes, 850:10
Colt, let little c. go bare, 861:12
Columbia, hail C., 390:13
Column, fifth c., 713:16
fountain's silvery c., 401:21
rising toward heaven, 414:11
throws up a steamy c., 348:4
took shape of mushroom, 723:6

Consul, Caligula's horse made C., 405:1
    my youth when Plancus was c., 100:7
Consule, fortunatam natam me c. Romam,
    91:*n*4
Consuls, each year new c., 114:14
Consulship, Rome natal neath my c., 91:10
Consult concerning great goddess, 389:9
    first c. our private ends, 274:*n*2
Consume according to need, 510:*n*5
    engines of despotism, 359:9
    entire combustible world, 638:13
    my heart away, 640:1
    own smoke, 434:22
    time c. strongest cord, 397:22
    without producing, 609:8
    your own smoke, 595:10
Consumed, bush was not c., 8:3
    by either fire or fire, 722:2
    days are c. like smoke, 19:4
    in image if not in usage, 795:18
    them as stubble, 8:28
Consumedly, they laughed c., 305:5
Consumer, promoting interest of c., 339:1
Consumes, delight that c. desire, 568:5
    male c. each year, 828:3
    painter's brush c. dreams, 640:11
Consumeth, watching for riches c. flesh,
    32:44
Consuming rag and bone, 642:10
    serves industrial system by c., 778:15
Consummated, marriages c. on earth, 163:18
Consummation devoutly to be wished,
    203:33
    quiet c. have, 225:24
Consumption, captain of men of death was
    C., 282:7
    conspicuous c., 613:6
    of the purse, 191:21
    purpose of all production, 339:1
Contact contact, 505:13
    possible to flesh, 718:7
    with the soil, 642:15
    word preserves c., 676:12
Contagion, foul c. spread, 262:2
    of world's slow stain, 430:13
    rest of us in danger of c., 750:3
    to this world, 205:12
Contagious, base c. clouds, 184:36
    blastments imminent, 201:22
Contain, I c. multitudes, 519:21
    margin too narrow to c., 255:1
    one the other will c., 545:11
    show c. and nourish all world, 177:8
Contained nothing but itself, 570:12
Container, bright c. can contain, 780:16
Containment of Russian expansive
    tendencies, 768:1
Contains, the cistern c., 372:18
    what Fortitude Soul c., 547:7
Contemneth small things, 32:32
Contemplate entangled bank, 470:2
    my flaccid shape, 741:5
    our forefathers, 337:10
Contemplation, beneath thy c., 511:11
    everything object of c., 403:16
    he for c. formed, 266:10
    her best nurse C., 260:29
    mind serene for c., 301:*n*1
    more than reading, 280:21

Contemplation *(continued)*
    right c., 66:24
    sundry c. of my travels, 199:23
Contemplative or saintly life, 774:9
Contemporaries, drudgery of their c., 733:5
    man lives life of c., 676:5
Contempt against majesty of Heaven, 318:15
    and anger of lip, 210:5
    comes from head, 425:13
    familiarity breeds c., 60:13
    for c. too high, 275:3
    for governor who is afraid, 67:14
    for wildest blow, 580:23
    no weakness no c., 269:15
    of God contempt of self, 119:22
    reading it with perfect c., 714:4
    silence is c., 461:3
    speak of moderns without c., 314:23
    treating with c. all from God, 144:18
Contemptible, bored more c. than bore,
    558:7
    rendered United States c., 611:6
    ridiculous c. animal, 322:16
    struggle, 343:15
Contemptuous, discerning reader c., 614:1
Contend, gods c. in vain, 382:12
    no more Love, 492:9
    seven towns c. for Homer, 239:*n*2
    ye powers of heaven, 272:16
Contender, could've been a c., 794:15
Contending, calm c. kings, 175:8
    fierce c. nations, 302:2
    for liberty, 349:13
    leaders ambitiously c., 366:19
    with adversity, 241:6
Content at the last, 721:14
    be c. with your lot, 60:21
    farewell c., 214:8
    humble livers in c., 230:25
    I am c., 386:7
    if reversion nourish, 721:14
    in health and mind's c., 288:19
    in tight hot cell, 748:1
    in whatsoever state to be c., 45:39
    land of lost c., 619:3
    majority of men c., 142:16
    make c. with fortunes fit, 216:25
    mind c. both crown and kingdom,
      165:17
    money means and c., 199:5
    my crown is called c., 172:30
    natural c., 638:2
    nothing less will c. me, 344:8
    poor and c. is rich, 213:35
    shut up in measureless c., 220:7
    that we might procreate like trees, 256:6
    thoughts that savor of c., 165:16
    to breathe his native air, 308:3
    to entertain lag-end of my life, 186:31
    to live it all again, 640:18
    travelers must be c., 198:7
    with life retire from world, 98:18
    with my harm, 199:9
    with vegetable love, 564:9
    with your lot, 60:21
Contented, always c. with his life, 446:13
    live on little with c. mind, 93:17
    men employed best c., 321:8
    most enjoy c. least, 226:6

Contented *(continued)*
    slaves howe'er c., 347:6
    white people never c., 387:9
    wi' little, 378:20
Contentedness, procurer of c., 252:25
Contention, let long c. cease, 531:4
    man of strife and c., 29:15
Contentions are like bars of a castle, 22:11
    fat c., 262:17
    of a wife, 22:15
Contentious, petty wisdom c., 82:21
Contentment fails, 341:2
    in c. still feel need, 686:18
    nor poorest receive c., 237:3
    preaches c. to toad, 632:9
    recover through c. with physician, 73:2
Contents, inability of mind to correlate all c.,
    729:9
    torn out and stripped, 319:2
Contest between capitalism and socialism
    over, 805:3
    end a c. quicker, 367:24
    this is a people's c., 475:10
Contests, what mighty c. rise, 309:4
Context, immediate c. of history, 735:17
Contiguity, boundless c. of shade, 347:26
Continence, give me c. but not now, 119:9
Continent allotted by Providence, 501:11
    almost a c. hardly a nation, 710:1
    Americans prefer C., 649:12
    brought forth on c., 476:7
    disappoint a C., 557:18
    heart no island but c., 167:18
    iron curtain across C., 667:16
    man home in every c., 778:3
    man is a piece of the c., 236:19
    most momentous question on c., 535:2
    our c. the old one, 366:10
    striving to grasp c., 534:8
    untamed c., 534:9
Continental, Jehovah and C. Congress, 355:9
    never tolerate two c. powers, 726:13
Continents, African giant among c., 774:14
    American c. not subjects for colonization,
      376:16
    dissolve into sea, 777:1
Contingencies, O to be self-balanced for c.,
    518:13
Continual comfort in a face, 171:9
    contentions of wife are c. dropping,
      22:15
    endeavor in c. motion, 192:20
    feast, 21:36
    live in c. mortification, 318:14
    small have c. plodders won, 176:20
Continually, think c. of truly great, 783:16
    times change and move c., 161:21
Continuation, thermonuclear war not c. of
    politics, 808:8
Continue, our hearts c. to beat, 838:13
Continued, not one c. faithful until old age,
    78:17
Continues, tree c. to be, 723:4
Continueth, he fleeth and c. not, 14:15
Continuing, faculty of c. to improve, 348:24
    no c. city, 47:7
Continuity, restructuring combines c.
    innovation, 826:9
    self has c. and sameness, 762:2

Continuous and seems always existing, 58:11
   as stars that shine, 394:5
   brain changes c., 581:14
   nature one and c., 506:2
   use of any organ, 362:7
Contraceptive, like having totally efficient c., 798:18
Contract, passions we inspire c. time, 657:11
   permanent c. on temporary feeling, 575:11
   Social C. vast conspiracy, 644:10
   succession bourn none, 229:25
   'twixt Hannah God and me, 554:8
   unspoken c. of wife and her works, 797:13
Contraction of life, 675:5
Contracts, prisoners cannot enter into c., 803:16
   with the people, 705:9
Contradict, do I c. myself, 519:21
   never c., 780:n1
   proverbs c. each other, 783:2
Contradiction, phrase long poem c., 479:22
   what a c. is man, 280:8
   when we risk no c., 307:5
   woman's a c. still, 310:11
Contradictions exist side by side, 525:12
Contraption, verbal c., 776:14
Contraries, by c. execute all things, 229:25
Contrariously, work c., 192:22
Contrariwise, 551:17
Contrary blast proclaims, 269:8
   bringeth bliss, 172:3
   everythink c. with me, 497:29
   Mary quite c., 857:11
   men of c. character, 62:22
   runneth not to the c., 338:10
   Spirit and flesh c., 45:21
   to the c. notwithstanding, 360:16
Contribute to diversion or improvement of country, 302:5
Contribution according to capacity, 510:n5
   to current literature, 558:22
Contributions to peace of world, 705:8
Contrite, broken and c. heart, 17:30
Contrivance of human wisdom, 345:12
   to raise prices, 338:15
Contrivances, wisdom of human c., 344:6
Contrive, head to c., 269:19
   our fees to pilfer, 75:2
Contrived corridors, 718:3
   double debt to pay, 342:10
Control and communication theory, 742:11
   cannot c. atomic energy, 658:6
   Chance shall not c., 528:9
   civilian c. of military, 705:10
   forces of nature, 727:12
   grammar c. even kings, 278:22
   lease of my true love c., 227:12
   man c. the wind, 528:21
   men gained c. over nature, 607:17
   nuclear c., 800:6
   over human behavior, 595:15
   stops at the shore, 421:26
   straitjacket or club c., 606:6
   without c. over ourselves, 366:9
Controlled by world constructed by men, 770:2
   events c. me, 476:9

Controlling intelligence understands, 115:24
Controls, love of other sights c., 233:11
Controversy, hearts of c., 195:19
Contumely, proud man's c., 203:33
Conturbat, Timor Mortis c. me, 142:4
Convenience comfort prestige, 852:1
   he that for c. takes oath, 271:20
Convenient, a c. season, 42:33
   break eggs at c. end, 298:13
   never c. time for any, 758:7
   that there be gods, 105:7
Convent of the Sacred Heart, 718:10
Convention, by c. there is color, 72:14
   is ruler of all, 66:13
   when I look out at c., 836:13
Conventional army, 812:12
   hallmark of c. wisdom acceptability, 778:11
   merely c. signs, 552:20
Conventionality not morality, 504:15
Convent's narrow room, 394:17
   solitary gloom, 309:25
Convents, happy c., 313:24
Conversation art of never appearing a bore, 597:15
   for c. well endued, 298:20
   good nature agreeable in c., 302:14
   hinges in French c., 333:5
   is but carving, 299:5
   Johnson's c. was mustard, 356:9
   of most searching sort, 455:27
   of select companions, 302:7
   one of greatest pleasures, 672:20
   preaching word for dull c., 398:15
   smaller excellencies of c., 355:16
   socializing instrument, 702:15
   three cannot take part in c., 455:27
   unforced as c. passed, 446:12
   wants leisure, 672:20
   when you fall into a man's c., 303:7
   where there's half a c., 732:2
   writing name for c., 332:15
Conversational or homely type, 653:17
Conversations, without pictures or c., 549:10
Converse and live with ease, 312:4
   formed by thy c., 311:15
   high c. with mighty dead, 317:16
Conversing I forget all time, 266:17
Conversion of world lead to perpetual peace, 571:13
   refuse till c. of Jews, 276:27
Convert Bill of Rights, 734:3
   you into stew, 719:19
Converted and become as children, 36:28
   love c. from thing it was, 226:14
   silenced man not c., 572:6
Converting human beings to machines, 510:9
Convey the wise it call, 190:17
Convicted, Daniel had c. them, 33:13
Conviction, do evil from religious c., 280:11
   editor's c., 727:6
   faithful to c. to old age, 78:17
   impeachment for and c. of high crimes, 360:14
   sadness of c., 577:17
   the best lack all c., 639:6
   we are loved, 451:7
Convictions, enter c. in open lists, 660:8
   people in old times had c., 442:15

Convince hearers of own assertions, 76:18
   logic and sermons never c., 519:14
   to c. is to weaken, 662:3
Convinced, frightening when c. they are right, 774:15
   it was the way of God, 270:12
   of too little, 722:15
Convinces, credit to man who c. world, 593:3
Convincing while they thought of dining, 343:2
Conviviality, taper of c., 496:28
Convolutions of smooth-lipped shell, 395:5
Convulsions, system liable to c., 596:16
Conwiviality, taper of c., 496:28
Cook, amount to Hannah C., 850:6
   and captain bold, 563:11
   every c. learn to govern, 654:8
   good c. as cooks go, 655:1
   ill c. that cannot lick fingers, 184:9
   makes his c. his merit, 278:5
Cookery is an art a noble science, 240:13
   kissing don't last c. do, 541:3
Cookie, me want c., 843:3
   the way c. crumbles, 852:9
Cookies, stayed home and baked c., 840:7
Cooks are gentlemen, 240:13
   as c. go she went, 655:1
   cannot live without c., 548:11
   Epicurean c., 223:12
   God sends meat Devil sends c., 147:n11
   guests praise it not c., 168:24
Cooks' own ladles, 491:16
Cool, caverns c. and deep, 528:6
   clear and c. clear and c., 514:3
   day so c. so calm, 250:9
   glassy c. translucent wave, 261:10
   in any case keep c., 744:15
   in dust in c. tombs, 681:12
   in Gardens when eve c., 543:17
   keep c. it will be all one, 456:20
   kept breath to c. pottage, 56:25
   kindliness of sheets, 712:18
   Negro c. strong imperturbable, 509:16
   of the day, 6:5
   one Pain, 546:1
   place was c. and pleasant, 793:4
   sequestered vale of life, 334:23
   we real c., 798:10
   winding saxophones, 681:14
Cooled a long age, 437:7
Coolibah tree, 630:9
Coolidge look as if weaned on pickle, 704:4
Cooling streams, 294:7
Coolness, wind to bring c. to men, 54:20
Cools, till husband c., 310:9
   time c. time clarifies, 676:15
Coon, gone c., 419:1
Cooped we live and die, 471:22
Cooperate, stay and c., 731:11
Cooperation with Government, 711:4
Cooperative on my upper west side, 841:6
Coort, supreme c. follows iliction, 645:15
Coot, haunts of c., 485:3
Cope, starry c. of heaven, 266:28
Cophetua loved the beggarmaid, 182:27
   sware oath, 482:13
Copious Dryden, 313:3

Copper, beneath her c. a worm, 505:21
    Irishman lined with c., 560:11
    kettledrums, 664:10
Copperheads, forgot c. and assassin, 681:12
Coppice, leant upon c. gate, 575:15
Copulate in the foam, 642:17
Copulation, action limited to c. of clichés,
    756:2
    birth c. and death, 719:20
    let c. thrive, 217:21
Copy, create equivalent not c., 715:11
    leave the world no c., 209:8
Copycat, life is a c., 716:19
Copying, mechanism for genetic material,
    822:2
Copyists, shortened labor of c., 433:9
Coquette, death and i c., 680:4
Cor, j'aime le son du c., 443:*n1*
    lacerare nequit, 299:29
Coral is far more red, 228:1
    lip admires, 253:18
    of his bones c. made, 229:20
Corbeaux, le vol noir des c., 855:12
Cord, as unto bow c. is, 467:2
    no c. draw forcibly as love, 241:17
    silver c. be loosed, 25:8
    stretch c. however fine, 432:18
    threefold c. not quickly broken, 24:9
    time consume strongest c., 397:22
Cordelia, such sacrifices my C., 218:2
Cordial, gold in phisik is a c., 135:7
    restore with c. fruit, 250:15
Cords, draw iniquity with c. of vanity, 26:21
    scourge of small c., 40:41
Core, apple's cleft through c., 382:18
    boredom at c. of life, 281:4
    hypocrite rotten to the c., 773:7
    red heart's c., 436:14
    wear him in heart's c., 204:17
Corinth, not everyone can get to C., 101:7
Corinthian a lad of mettle, 185:19
Corioli, Volscians in C., 225:3
Coriolanus, Volscians in C., 225:3
Cork, Drunkard cannot meet C., 546:19
    lighter than c. danced, 603:8
Cork-heeled shoon, 853:19
Corkscrew, clean rumbler and c., 496:24
Cormorant devouring Time, 176:16
    sat like a c., 266:5
Corn, alien c., 437:13
    before my tears did drown it, 250:15
    colonels full of c., 620:10
    cotton c. and taters, 602:14
    cow's in the c., 857:17
    crop of c. a field of tares, 164:17
    ear on tip of stalk, 855:20
    farmer sowing the c., 861:15
    field of ripe c., 717:20
    fields of c. where Troy was, 105:11
    full c. in the ear, 38:18
    full of kernels, 620:10
    high as elephant's eye, 744:5
    hope c. in chaff, 419:16
    Jimmie crack c., 847:20
    licker stop victim's watch, 678:1
    like smut in c., 771:6
    meadows rich with c., 468:13
    never thrust sickle in another's c., 103:27
    night in which c. grows, 507:29
    no use of metal c. or wine, 229:25

Corn *(continued)*
    not move sickle unto neighbor's c., 10:7
    not muzzle ox when treadeth c., 10:8
    out of olde feldes newe c., 133:12
    rain on c. a sad thing, 95:19
    raise less c. more hell, 597:11
    sent not c. for rich men only, 224:16
    shock of c. cometh in season, 13:40
    staff of life, 295:*n4*
    state that raises c., 604:5
    two ears of c. grow, 298:15
    was orient, 290:2
    whar man gits c. pone, 562:20
Cornelia said these are my jewels, 241:19
Cornelius, my new book to you C., 93:22
Corner, better to dwell in a c., 22:23
    draft fluttered flame, 730:8
    driven from every other c., 337:12
    head stone of the c., 19:25
    in deepest heart, 582:6
    in the thing I love, 214:4
    never c. opponent, 744:15
    of foreign field, 712:19
    of nonsense, 404:2
    old men from chimney c., 163:26
    sits wind in that c., 194:26
    thing not done in c., 42:37
    work of art c. of creation, 577:5
    years around seatown c., 795:15
Cornered-animal fear, 831:11
Corners, belie all c. of world, 225:17
    come three c. of world, 178:29
    four angels on c. of earth, 48:21
    four c. to my bed, 274:*n3*
    in his hand c. of earth, 49:24
    not wholly reap the c., 9:13
    old fantastical duke of dark c., 212:3
    round earth's imagined c., 236:4
Cornets, played before Lord on c., 11:41
Cornfield, o'er green c. did pass, 200:5
Cornish, twenty thousand C. men, 458:5
Corn-rows, between c. held old puissance,
    691:12
Corollaries, axioms and c., 577:14
Coromandel, black men fought on C.,
    448:11
    coast of C., 500:4
Coronation, kind as kings upon c. day,
    284:20
Coronets, kind hearts more than c., 480:14
Corporal, in c. sufferance, 211:20
Corporation of the Goosequill, 490:13
Corporations cannot commit treason,
    159:18
    have no souls, 159:18, 592:12
Corps, army c. annihilate each other,
    554:9
Corpse, frozen c. was he, 466:5
    make a lovely c., 497:6
    of Public Credit, 415:5
    Politician's c. laid away, 653:11
    putrid c. of liberty, 702:8
    slovenly unhandsome c., 185:3
    watch enemy's c. go by, 862:18
Corpses, behold they were dead c., 13:6
Corpulent man of fifty, 417:8
Corpus, habeas c., 124:1, 358:13
    hoc est c., 317:*n4*
    hoc est enim C. meum, 49:13

Corpus Christi, on C. heart, 800:9
Correct, easier to be critical than c., 459:11
    ideas also dubious ideas, 808:10
    what all mortals may c., 299:2
Corrected, revised and c. by Author, 319:2
Corrections, error bursting with c., 594:1
Correctness, passion with c., 583:5
Correggios and stuff, 343:6
Correlate, inability of mind to c. all contents,
    729:9
Correlative, objective c., 722:9
Correspondent to command, 229:16
Corridor, lit c. races through dark one, 806:7
Corridors, contrived c., 718:3
    of Time, 466:13
Corroborative, merely c. detail, 565:18
Corrupt a saint, 184:31
    abilities utterly c., 405:2
    enemies intelligent and c., 767:12
    evil communications c., 44:26
    influence, 345:3
    judge no king can c., 230:28
    moth and rust doth c., 34:12
    one good custom c. world, 486:12
    peace c., 268:15
    plea tainted and c., 189:4
    power tends to c., 554:12
    progeny yet more c., 100:2
    unlimited power apt to c., 323:6
    word like corrupt tree, 121:8
Corrupted, conscience with injustice c.,
    172:12
    goodness with power c., 735:14
    sun not c., 79:*n5*
    traitorously c. youth, 172:22
Corruptible put on incorruption, 44:31
Corruption, guilty of c. and renounce
    defense, 166:16
    honest words suffered c., 243:17
    I have said to c., 14:21
    man coffer full of c., 140:11
    sown in c., 44:29
    strong c. inhabits blood, 210:15
    symptom of liberty, 353:9
    wins not more than honesty, 231:7
Corruptly, offices not derived c., 188:27
Corrupts, absolute power c. absolutely,
    554:12
    power c. poetry cleanses, 800:7
    Socrates c. the youth, 76:10
Corse, dead c. in complete steel, 202:6
    to rampart we hurried, 427:1
Corsets, Heine loosened c. of German
    language, 672:8
Cortesía, la mesma, 158:*n2*
Cortez, stout C., 435:19
Cory, Richard C. one summer night,
    652:11
Corydon what madness has caught you,
    95:17
Co-signers of a covenant, 771:10
Cosmic night, 675:12
Cosmographers, physicians by their love
    grown c., 236:14
Cosmopolite, best C. loves country, 486:25
Cosmopolouse, bloomin' c., 634:20
Cosmos, energies of c. into cultural
    manifestation, 766:15
    push and pressure of c., 582:17

Cost, every farthing of c., 775:11
  give and not count c., 145:5
  good words c. little, 251:15
  is labor to produce anything, 517:12
  little less than new, 301:6
  loved and c. me so much, 255:2
  sitteth and counteth c., 39:33
  utility or c. of production, 584:2
Costing not less than everything, 722:5
Costly, attire comely not c., 163:1
  morality private c. luxury, 570:19
  seasons, 818:10
  so c. a sacrifice, 477:2
  thy habit, 201:26
Costs, good counsel c. nothing, 241:9
  nothing to be polite, 668:3
Cottage, hides not visage from our c., 229:1
  modest looks c. adorn, 342:12
  planning retirement c., 815:8
  poor man in mean c., 32:40
  poorest man in his c., 323:3
  soul's dark c., 258:3
  small, 794:1
Cottages, poor men's c. palaces, 187:27
Cotton, corn and c. and cockleburs, 604:5
  is king, 450:15
  land of c., 503:1
  spinning noble, 435:1
  where c. and taters grow, 602:14
Cottons mather, 749:8
Cottontail and Peter, 644:2
Couch, frowsy c. in sorrow steep, 380:18
  literature old c. stuffed with fleas, 826:7
  when owls do cry, 230:13
  wraps drapery of c., 432:10
Couché, longtemps je me suis c. de bonne
    heure, 657:n3
Cough, love and a c., 251:5
Coughed and called it fate, 652:7
Coughing drowns parson's saw, 177:18
Could all have been killed, 842:11
  if youth but knew if old age but c.,
    151:11
  nor even thing I c. be, 380:16
  have stayed home, 840:7
Couldn't, I c. think what else to say,
    580:n1
Couleurs, les parfums les c., 524:n2
Council, before ashes of c. fire cold, 533:9
  in c. rooms apart, 692:5
  outcome of words is in the c., 53:21
  power in aristocratical c., 352:3
  unapproachable in C. of Ten, 701:13
  Zeus god of c., 52:14
Counciler, White Citizen's C., 822:12
Councilor ought not to sleep, 52:13
Councils, takes wisdom from c., 345:3
Counsel, good c. cheap, 241:9
  how hard for women to keep c., 196:12
  if this c. be of men, 42:3
  love overwhelms wise c., 56:5
  man who c. can bestow, 309:2
  of thine own heart, 33:4
  princely c. in his face, 265:8
  sometimes c. take, 309:8
  spirit of c. and might, 26:33
  three keep c. if two away, 148:32
  took sweet c. together, 17:32
  two may keep c., 148:n15

Counsel *(continued)*
  walketh not in c. of ungodly, 15:27
  who darkeneth c. by words, 15:4
Counseled ignoble ease, 265:7
Counselor, name shall be called C., 26:31
Counselors, good c. lack no clients, 210:35
  kings and c. of the earth, 13:30
  multitude of c., 21:17
  wisest of c. Time, 67:2
Counsels, close designs crooked c., 283:8
  excellent things in c., 22:28
  hate c. not in such quality, 189:1
  how monie c. sweet, 379:15
  sic c. ye give, 853:22
Count, as long as I c. votes, 535:14
  cats in Zanzibar, 507:16
  chickens before hatched, 60:9
  don't c. your boobies, 741:18
  let me c. the ways, 463:17
  let us c. our spoons, 326:20
  milestones till haze dances, 472:24
  myself in nothing else so happy, 179:17
  myself king of space, 203:15
  on a murderer, 755:15
  only sunny hours, 410:n1
  that day lost, 846:21
  them over every one apart, 627:8
  until nothing else to c., 457:15
  when angry c. ten, 359:12
  you can c. me out, 835:6
Counted as the small dust, 28:6
  them and cursed luck, 619:15
  two and seventy stenches, 402:13
Countenance, bright c. of truth, 262:12
  cannot lie, 171:9
  chide God for c., 199:25
  damned disinheriting c., 367:30
  did the C. Divine, 375:17
  heart changeth his c., 32:29
  his c. like richest alchemy, 195:28
  human c. composed of ten parts, 108:9
  Knight of the Sorrowful C., 156:18
  lift up his c. upon thee, 9:17
  lift up the light of thy c., 15:30
  like lightning, 38:11
  merry heart maketh a cheerful c., 21:35
  more in sorrow than anger, 201:17
  of all Science, 391:14
  soon brightened, 395:5
  that in your c. would call master, 215:31
  tyrant's threatening c., 99:28
Counter original spare strange, 587:10
  stake c. boldly, 493:15
Counteracts Devil who is Death, 338:7
Counterargument, possibility of c., 808:10
Countercheck quarrelsome, 200:9
Counterfeit a gloom, 260:5
  Jove's dread clamors c., 214:8
  sleep death's c., 220:24
Counterfeited, laughed with c. glee, 342:8
Countermoves, revolution legality c. in same
    game, 612:12
Counterparts in world of fact, 523:22
Counters, wise men's c., 246:7
Countesses had no outlines, 496:22
Counteth, sitteth and c. cost, 39:33
Counting cars on New Jersey Turnpike,
    837:10
  my numberless fingers, 816:16

Countinghouse, king in c., 858:12
Countless infinitesimals of feeling, 404:3
  thousands mourn, 377:14
Countree, is this mine own c., 400:18
  North C. hard c., 745:2
Countries, churches in flat c., 395:n2
  give themselves to you, 706:8
  material out of which c. made, 661:16
  outdistance advanced c., 654:9
  peace of all c. connected, 693:9
  preferreth all c. before his own, 244:12
  seek no aggrandizement, 699:7
  wandering through many c., 94:28
Country, abroad for good of c., 305:6
  absorbs poet, 518:11
  all places all airs one c., 256:4
  America my c., 673:18, 710:1
  anything for good of c., 305:6
  as soldier for c., 627:n1
  ask not what c. do for you, 799:10
  behind people your c., 532:21
  belongs to people, 475:6
  best c. is at home, 341:1
  betraying c. betraying friend, 684:5
  better off when Indians running it, 828:7
  cannot ask success even for c., 385:16
  ceases to be free for irreligion, 734:4
  cherished in hearts, 487:5
  cover c. in books, 588:8
  cries of c. in chains, 855:n2
  defamers of his c., 554:2
  defended by our hands, 487:5
  departed into their own c., 33:19
  die but once to serve c., 301:24
  die in defense of his c., 53:19
  disable benefits of your c., 199:25
  diversion, 300:24
  divine nature gave us c., 90:4
  dreary tract of c., 478:11
  epitaph for their c., 629:8
  essential service to c., 298:15
  every c. but his own, 565:10
  every C. hath its Machiavel, 142:n5
  fame noised throughout c., 10:22
  fate of c. not in ballot, 506:6
  father of your c., 349:n7
  fight for one's c., 53:10
  fight to set c. free, 354:16
  find my c. in the right, 410:n2
  Flora and c. green, 437:7
  foreign troop in my c., 323:10
  fornication but in another c., 170:13
  fortunes of my c., 387:8
  found that famous c., 734:9
  friend of every c. but own, 389:14
  from yon far c. blows, 619:3
  genius is of no c., 346:14
  gentleman galloping, 606:3
  give c. back to Indians, 750:13
  God made the c., 347:25
  good for c. good for General Motors,
    731:1
  good news from a far c., 23:4
  good to be shifty in new c., 503:3
  governed by despot, 328:13
  grow up with c., 503:n2
  half savage c., 708:19
  has 265 different kinds of cheese, 728:13
  history of c. begins in heart, 661:13

Court *(continued)*
    hear rogues talk of c. news, 218:1
    in beauty and decay, 430:3
    keeps Death his c., 179:28
    let her alone she will c. you, 237:23
    moderation gone no c. can save, 660:5
    no justice in or out of c., 612:22
    starry threshold of Jove's C., 260:11
    summary c. in perpetual session, 701:6
    sun that shines upon his c., 229:1
    supreme c. follows iliction, 645:15
    temper doctrinaire logic, 734:3
    the camp the grove, 396:9
    though lewdness c. it, 202:17
    used against him in c., 733:2
    what's the new news at new c., 197:23
    world history is world's c., 381:10
Courte, n'ai pas loisir de la faire plus c.,
    279:*n*1
Courted by all the winds, 269:6
Courteous, gracious and c. to strangers,
    167:18
    intellectual virile, 649:14
    lowely and servysable, 134:20
    retort c., 200:9
Courtesan, word love in mouth of c., 454:9
Courtesies, sweet c. of life, 333:6
Courtesy, always time for c., 457:17
    and self-possession, 643:9
    candy deal of c., 185:10
    Grace of God in c., 653:6
    greater man greater c., 486:5
    high-erected thoughts in heart of c.,
    163:9
    in c. have her learned, 639:11
    mirour of alle c., 136:10
    mirror of all c., 230:22
    pink of c., 158:6, 183:22
Courthouse, portals of every c., 660:6
Courtier, heel of c., 206:23
Courtier's soldier's scholar's, 204:7
Courtliness and desire of fame, 486:8
Courtly nurture, 534:9
Courts, brawling c., 484:10
    case still before c., 101:19
    day in thy c., 18:17
    forsaken c. pale pavilions, 758:2
    hollow murmurs through c., 384:15
    into his c. with praise, 19:3
    laws conflict c. decide, 371:1
    shown in c. at feasts, 261:9
    thee on roses, 99:7
    thrusting on c. nurture of spirit, 660:5
    where Jamshyd gloried, 471:8
Cousins, Little C. Called back, 547:10
    sisters c. and aunts, 563:16
Coûte, il n'y a que le premier pas qui c.,
    317:*n*3
Couvrez ce sein que je ne saurais voir, 277:*n*4
Covenant, co-signers of a c., 771:10
    new and eternal c., 49:14
    token of a c., 6:34
    with death, 27:22, 462:6
    words of the c., 9:9
Covenanted with him for silver, 37:22
Covenants, open c. of peace, 611:10
Cover country in books, 588:8
    cunning sin c. itself, 194:38
    her face, 244:9

Cover *(continued)*
    I c. all, 681:10
    like c. of old book, 319:2
    only art guilt to c., 341:21
    paste and c. to our bones, 179:28
    that bosom I must not see, 277:22
    thee with his feathers, 18:25
    them with leaves, 843:13
Covered up our names, 545:5
Covers of book too far apart, 580:22
    out of night that c., 594:10
    who c. faults, 215:24
Covert from the tempest, 27:29
Covet, sin to c. honor, 193:18
    thou shalt not c., 9:1, 512:12
Coveted her and me, 479:18
Covetous desires of the world, 51:5
    man ever in want, 100:23
    of others' possessions, 95:3
    sordid fellow, 314:21
Covetousness, wealth cause of c., 170:11
    when old guard against c., 63:26
Cow and bear shall feed, 26:34
    cheaper than keep c., 559:4
    good animal in field, 327:15
    jumped over moon, 858:2
    little Kyloe c., 858:10
    purple c., 643:18
    red and white, 599:1
    she'll bring her c. along, 861:16
    sizzle sells steak not c., 775:1
    till the c. comes home, 245:7
    with crumpled horn, 861:15
    work way c. grazes, 647:10
    you do be pullin' Sis C., 593:9
Coward and brave held in same honor, 53:5
    conscience dost afflict, 174:20
    does it with kiss, 605:18
    had not resolution to fire it, 326:12
    never forgave, 332:1
    no c. soul mine, 509:1
    not so great a c. as thinks, 599:17
    sea hates c., 724:5
    turns away, 70:9
    worth little more than c., 386:11
Cowardice distinguished from panic, 755:1
    here all c. be ended, 130:4
    that clings, 664:13
Cowardly, war spares the c., 61:19
Cowards, conscience but word c. use, 174:22
    conscience does make c., 203:33
    die many times, 196:10
    hundred c., 726:9
    idlers and c. at home, 856:7
    in reasoning, 301:9
    mannish c., 197:35
    plague of all c., 185:21
    Public greatest of c., 410:8
Cowboy, best damned c., 854:15
    damned c. President of United States,
    615:*n*1
    I wondered if ever a c., 854:16
    I'm a young c., 854:18
    that loves you so true, 855:2
    wrapped in white linen, 854:17
Cowl does not make monk, 123:16
    I like a c., 452:18
    take wife or c., 156:*n*3
Cowled, I that c. churchman be, 452:18

Cowpuncher a-riding along, 854:12
Cow'rin', wee sleekit c., 377:10
Cow's in the corn, 857:17
Cows are my passion, 497:26
    sacred c. make tastiest hamburger, 832:4
    till the c. come home, 245:*n*4
Cowslip's, hang pearl in c. ear, 181:4
    in c. bell I lie, 230:13
    sweet c. grace, 363:4
Coxcomb ask two hundred guineas, 557:*n*2
Coxcombs, some made c. nature meant fools,
    308:9
Coy and hard to please, 397:1
    denial vain and c. excuse, 261:15
    sometimes coming sometimes c., 290:16
    yielded with c. submission, 266:11
Coyness, this c. were no crime, 276:26
Coyotes howl o'er grave, 855:1
    wild c. howl o'er me, 854:19
Crab, hermit c. whale's backbone, 721:8
    teach c. to walk straight, 75:4
    very likeness of roasted c., 181:5
Crabbed age and youth, 843:19
    philosophy not harsh and c., 261:3
    talk of c. old men, 94:4
Crab-grass, big sisters are c., 811:4
Crabs, roasted c. hiss in bowl, 177:18
Crabwise, something c. across snow, 815:3
Crack any of those old jokes, 75:17
    blow winds c. cheeks, 216:18
    door begins to c., 856:13
    glass eye across, 678:1
    hear the mighty c., 301:16
    heaven's vaults should c., 218:5
    in tea cup opens, 775:9
    nature's molds, 216:18
    sail-yards tremble masts c., 165:11
    she discovered c. in wall, 526:18
    stretch out to c. of doom, 221:30
Crack-brained, believed by vulgar that he was
    c., 280:20
Cracked growled roared howled, 399:18
    the mirror c., 480:26
Cracker-jack, buy peanuts and c., 685:10
Crackled and gone up in smoke, 621:4
Crackling of thorns under a pot, 24:18
Crack-pated when we dreamed, 640:7
Cracks, now c. a noble heart, 207:15
    sinews cakes brain, 516:14
Cradle asks whence, 554:4
    between c. and grave, 317:12, 729:4
    bough breaks c. fall, 592:1
    earth c. of hope, 681:18
    endlessly rocking, 520:7
    from c. to grave, 428:13, 596:11
    hand that rocks c., 518:7
    murder infant in c., 373:3
    of every science, 536:14
    of liberty, 415:16
    of the deep, 419:7
    procreant c., 219:15
    rocks above abyss, 755:12
    stands in the grave, 239:7
    vexed to nightmare by c., 639:7
    will rock, 592:1
Cradled into poetry by wrong, 428:19
Cradles, bit babies in c., 491:16
Craft, flung eager craft, 810:11
    lyf so short c. so long, 133:11

Creatures, all c. here below, 289:22
   brother to all c., 807:10
   by rule in nature teach, 192:20
   clearest of God's c., 801:4
   delicate c. ours, 214:4
   England breeds valiant c., 193:9
   essences of seasons became myriad c.,
     89:14
   from fairest c. desire increase, 225:27
   generations of living c. changed, 93:2
   God's c., 478:n1
   great and small, 508:7
   Leviathan hugest of c., 267:15
   little c. everywhere, 699:11
   love my fellow c., 565:6
   make fellow c. happy, 355:3
   makes meaner c. kings, 174:17
   of a day, 66:3
   poets c. most absurd, 313:5
   praise for all thy c., 128:2
   smashed up c., 746:7
   soul same in all c., 73:13
   spiritual c. walk unseen, 266:19
   that creep swim or fly, 289:15
   weak c. of clay, 75:9
   widows most perverse c., 302:17
   wild c. wild places natural resources,
     808:6
Creatures', human c. lives, 446:5
Credential, only c. New York asked, 767:14
Credentials, fortified by these c., 661:3
Credit, American c. card, 596:14
   an't much c. in that, 496:37
   dead corpse of Public C., 415:5
   done my c. much wrong, 472:3
   greatly to his c. that he is Englishman,
     563:20
   having more c. than money, 363:12
   his own lie, 229:11
   in science c. to man who convinces,
     593:3
   let the C. go, 471:6
   places last stone gets c., 682:6
   plans c. and Muse, 453:8
   shadow of authority and c., 345:3
   used my c., 184:27
Creditable acquaintance, 298:1
Creditors, we are debtors or c., 364:20
Credo quia impossibile, 116:n7
Credulities, ambitions climb on c., 612:16
Credulity, a little c. helps, 488:4
   falsehoods which c. encourages, 324:21
   listen with c. to fancy, 324:24
   man's weakness, 407:16
   youth the season of c., 323:5
Credulous, hatred renders votaries c.,
    331:18
Creed, Athanasian C. lyric, 459:25
   fundamental article of political c., 352:3
   is a rod, 569:8
   life to neighbor's c., 452:16
   most authentic c., 554:4
   necessity the c. of slaves, 381:4
   nonviolence article of c., 650:9
   of our political faith, 358:13
   sapping solemn c., 421:1
   suckled in c. outworn, 394:19
   tenets admitted into pagan c., 571:12
   whatever race c. or persuasion, 710:16

Creeds, casual c., 529:10
   dust of c. outworn, 428:6
   dust of systems and c., 480:7
   head more than churches bibles c.,
     519:10
   so many gods so many c., 600:8
   than in half the c., 484:11
   that refuse and restrain, 568:7
Creeks, back through c. and inlets, 512:10
Creep and let no more be said, 531:3
   beasts of the forest c. forth, 19:11
   dwarfed and abased, 601:n3
   feet like snails did c., 248:10
   flesh c., 495:21
   in one dull line, 308:16
   into narrow bed, 531:3
   learn to c. ere learn to go, 148:15
   let music c. in our ears, 190:5
   men c. not walk, 468:11
   nevermore to c. again, 662:17
   swim or fly, 289:15
   wit that can c., 312:10
Creepers, bacterial c., 780:8
Creeping, gray clouds c. quietly, 542:10
   hours of time, 198:22
   like snail to school, 198:25
   things c. innumerable, 19:11
   through the black, 685:4
   woman stooping down c. about, 623:2
Creeps, how slow shadow c., 653:5
   in this petty pace, 222:16
Creetur, lone lorn c., 497:29
Cremate the millions, 756:16
Cremated Sam McGee, 673:10
Crème, my pupils c. de la c., 804:17
Crepidam, ne supra c. sutor iudicaret, 83:n4
Crept into bosom of the sea, 172:15
   like frightened girl, 604:7
   music c. by upon waters, 229:19
   night c. upon our talk, 197:15
Crepuscular time, 512:1
Cressid, as false as C., 208:7
   where C. lay that night, 190:4
Crest, no colors or c., 634:4
Crested, reared arm c. the world, 224:4
Cretans, all C. are liars, 60:1
Crew, Bellman cry c. reply, 552:20
   crawls, 703:12
   darling of our c., 362:11
   dismayed her c., 580:23
   immediately the cock c., 37:35
   Mirth admit me of thy c., 259:12
   of captain's gig, 563:11
Crib, ass knoweth his master's c., 26:6
Cribbed, cabined c. confined, 221:9
Cricket, merry as c., 148:10
   no relief, 718:12
   on the hearth, 260:5
Cried A sail a sail, 400:2
   Agamemnon c. aloud, 718:10
   all the way to bank, 805:10
   for madder music, 645:10
   Give Me, 544:20
   in goose Alas, 724:11
   mercy to myself I c., 391:17
   No more, 250:15
   not winced nor c. aloud, 594:10
   out of the depths have I c., 20:7
   Peter denied Lord c., 296:10

Cried *(continued)*
   poor c. Caesar wept, 196:29
   you suddenly c., 712:15
Crier, good c. of green sauce, 146:8
   town-c. spoke my lines, 204:11
Cries, as a child c., 791:13
   bootless c., 226:5
   damned that c. Hold enough, 222:24
   fisted with wild c., 611:18
   man who turnips c., 325:21
   my fate c. out, 202:9
   of cicadas, 291:13
   of country in chains, 855:n2
   out Where is it, 401:12
   pitying the tender c., 372:9
   rump-fed ronyon c., 218:26
   to world from tower, 697:n3
   voice of Nature loudly c., 379:12
   whistle spontaneous c., 686:19
   wind full of birds' c., 681:3
Crieth, brother's blood c., 6:14
   in the wilderness, 27:38
   wisdom c. without, 20:24
Crillon, hang yourself brave C., 162:13
Crime appeared reappearance likely, 773:6
   committed in a dungeon, 682:1
   could not tell all forms of c., 97:27
   criminal cause of c., 658:15
   curious c. wickedness, 494:29
   fear of death never deterred c., 383:2
   from c. born bullets, 768:8
   from single c. know nation, 97:7
   hypocrite's c. bears false witness against
     self, 773:7
   Iscariot-like c., 714:21
   like virtue has degrees, 290:14
   more featureless commonplace a c.,
     617:3
   Moriarty the Napoleon of c., 617:11
   of being young man, 323:2
   places c. committed, 460:3
   popularity a c., 289:1
   poverty a c., 452:7
   prevention of mutual c., 80:29
   punishment fit c., 565:14
   scene of c. Macavity's not there, 720:14
   servitude consequence of c., 366:17
   silence real c. against humanity, 755:10
   successful c. called virtue, 107:10
   this coyness were no c., 276:26
   to be nobly born now c., 244:20
   to examine laws of heat, 572:3
   to love too well, 309:28
   vice-prisidincy isn't c. exactly, 646:20
Crimes against peace, 734:2
   and misfortunes, 316:20
   broad blown, 205:16
   committed c. but not stood aside, 767:11
   committed in thy name, 369:8
   high c. and misdemeanors, 360:14
   history register of c., 353:8
   no punishment prevent c., 773:6
   teems with c., 846:20
   virtues forced upon us by c., 718:4
   worst of our c. is poverty, 609:27
Criminal cause of crime, 658:15
   element I am of it, 606:8
   judge condemned when c. absolved,
     103:10

Crowley, Stuhldreher Miller C. Layden, 692:6
Crown, allegiance to c., 349:11
　　ambassador from Britain's c., 487:10
　　becomes monarch better than c., 189:19
　　breeches cost a c., 844:6
　　Caesar's laurel c., 375:13
　　carried him c. him, 829:4
　　chance may c. me, 219:6
　　contrary to c. built paper-mill, 172:22
　　cross for c., 661:10
　　defiance to forces of the C., 323:3
　　fell down broke c., 858:4
　　fighting for c., 857:2
　　fill me from c. to toe, 219:11
　　from c. of head to sole, 194:29
　　golden c. like a deep well, 180:9
　　good with brotherhood, 616:3
　　Greece with freedom, 62:5
　　hairy gold c. on 'ead, 633:11
　　hath worn the c., 32:21
　　have I no bays to c. it, 250:15
　　head that wears a c., 191:35
　　hoary head a c. of glory, 22:3
　　hollow c., 179:28
　　holly bears the c., 846:2
　　immortal c., 318:12
　　is called content, 172:30
　　is in my heart, 172:30
　　is love and friendship, 436:11
　　is of night, 569:8
　　kingly c. to gain, 416:2
　　laurel c. yield to praise, 91:8
　　many a c. spotless now, 381:22
　　mind content both c. and kingdom, 165:17
　　no cross no c., 249:5, 291:18
　　not the king's c. nor sword, 211:10
　　of glory, 47:32
　　of life, 47:10, 48:10
　　of life as it closes, 568:6
　　of thorns, 435:2
　　of thorns on brow of labor, 622:3
　　old age c. of life, 91:18
　　old Winter's head, 272:9
　　ourselves with rosebuds, 31:14
　　quiet mind richer than c., 165:16
　　small but costly c., 693:2
　　sorrow's c. of sorrow, 481:19
　　still the fine's the c., 210:29
　　sweet fruition of earthly c., 170:4
　　sword mace c. imperial, 193:16
　　that seldom kings enjoy, 172:30
　　the watery glade, 333:18
　　themselves assured, 227:12
　　thorns thy only c., 258:4
　　though they possess c., 295:4
　　virtuous woman is a c., 21:21
Crowned, due to be c. again, 707:11
　　Ghost sitting c. upon grave, 246:13
　　knot of fire, 722:5
　　Peace c. with smiles, 279:6
　　with lilies, 735:11
　　with stars, 290:1
　　with the sickle, 318:3
Crownest year with thy goodness, 18:4
Crownets, walked crowns and c., 224:4
Crowning, reason God's c. gift, 67:25
Crownless in voiceless woe, 421:17

Crowns and pounds and guineas, 618:10
　　are empty things, 295:4
　　end c. all, 208:21
　　end c. the work, 123:27
　　end c. us not fight, 248:1
　　if store of c. be scant, 239:3
　　in shades like these, 342:2
　　last act c. play, 249:12
　　not c. but men, 413:10
　　walked c. and crownets, 224:4
Crows and choughs that wing air, 217:18
　　at the break of dawn, 836:5
　　black flight of c., 855:*n2*
　　throw him to c., 849:*n7*
　　wars of kites or c., 269:18
Crow's-feet, til c. be growen, 133:19
Cru, j'ai pleuré et j'ai c., 387:*n2*
Crucible, God's c., 631:16
　　not test faith in c., 595:13
Crucified dead and buried, 50:3
　　everyone Christ and all c., 677:19
　　if this woman must be c., 503:10
　　let him be c., 38:3
　　where dear Lord c., 508:8
Crucifixion, living through another c., 752:12
Cruciform shadow, 730:8
Crucify mankind on cross of gold, 622:3
　　Son of God afresh, 46:40
Crude, berries harsh and c., 261:13
　　no c. surfeit reigns, 261:3
Cruel and unrelenting enemy, 349:14
　　and unusual punishment, 361:7
　　as death, 317:15
　　but composed and bland, 531:6
　　crawling foam, 513:22
　　death of Pyramus, 180:22
　　doubts more c. than truths, 278:8
　　enough without meaning to, 828:5
　　foam is not c., 517:5
　　I must be c. to be kind, 205:30
　　jealousy is c. as the grave, 26:3
　　mother of sweet loves, 100:12
　　never be c., 498:1
　　savage extreme rude c., 227:22
　　say we are c. to each other, 503:10
　　slain by fair c. maid, 209:25
　　tender mercies of the wicked are c., 21:22
Cruelest lies told in silence, 598:7
　　she alive, 209:8
Cruellest, April c. month, 718:11
　　thing happened to Lincoln, 745:9
Cruelly, Fortune c. scratched, 210:30
Cruelty, all the pride c. and ambition, 160:13
　　farewell fair c., 209:11
　　fear source of c., 661:4
　　full of direst c., 219:11
　　has human heart, 374:12
　　Mr. C., 281:24
　　never gauged your c., 730:18
　　of pirates, 515:10
　　to load falling man, 231:*n1*
　　war is c., 522:11
Cruise, all on our last c., 598:8
Cruising down shores of High Barbaree, 862:9
Crumb, craved no c., 565:25
　　just a C. to Me, 545:17
　　of madeleine, 657:7

Crumble the bridges, 756:16
Crumbled out again to his atomies, 235:26
Crumbles, the way cookie c., 852:9
　　Time c. things, 80:1
Crumbling, mind c. to pieces, 824:8
Crumbs, dogs eat of c., 36:21
Crumpetty Tree, 500:3
Crumpled, cow with c. horn, 861:15
Crusade, my God the Children's C., 811:9
Crusader, Franklin Roosevelt no c., 727:3
Cruse, little oil in a c., 12:26
Crush amang the stoure, 378:7
　　man shall man no longer c., 368:12
　　the infamous thing, 316:12
Crushed, human being c. by books, 793:5
　　most fragrant when c., 167:13
　　the sweet poison, 260:16
　　to ground diffuse sweets, 167:*n2*
　　together c. and bruised, 309:16
　　truth c. to earth, 432:16
Crushes, friend supports whom Fortune c., 110:6
Crusoe, Robinson C., 295:7, 331:10
Crust and sugar over, 762:16
　　dinosaur death-steps on c., 801:8
　　eaten in peace, 60:15
　　of bread and liberty, 312:17
　　over volcano of revolution, 617:21
　　upper c., 426:3, 442:2
　　water and c., 436:16
Crusted with blood, 713:13
Cry, all should c. Beware, 401:19
　　at a play to laugh or c., 298:19
　　battle c. of Freedom, 522:9
　　Bellman c. crew reply, 552:20
　　bubbling c. of swimmer, 423:17
　　but behold a c., 26:19
　　caused constantly a c., 687:8
　　cherry-ripe themselves do c., 232:5
　　consider anything don't c., 552:11
　　couch when owls do c., 230:13
　　damned don't c., 724:6
　　don't you c. for me, 538:13
　　every infant's c. of fear, 374:7
　　feel sorry because c., 582:4
　　for being born, 168:22
　　for restful death I c., 226:20
　　forgot c. of gulls, 718:20
　　God for Harry, 193:2
　　great c. in Egypt, 8:21
　　harlot's c. from street, 375:15
　　Havoc, 196:22
　　hear us when we c., 537:19
　　heard the dead c., 780:9
　　he'll be sure to c., 857:17
　　Hi or any loud c., 552:19
　　Hold hold, 219:12
　　hounds join in glorious c., 321:18
　　I can no more, 587:20
　　inhuman as hawk's c., 713:13
　　is still They come, 222:14
　　kitten and c. mew, 186:6
　　laugh for fear of having to c., 349:5
　　man's image and his c., 637:3
　　much c. no wool, 138:17
　　mum, 158:*n6*
　　my eyes out, 157:11
　　need a body c., 845:*n4*
　　nor swooned nor uttered c., 483:4

Cry *(continued)*
 not when father dies, 325:21
 of Absence Absence in heart, 724:10
 of bugles going by, 623:16
 of child by roadway, 637:8
 of pulleys, 808:15
 onward sailors c., 616:9
 out Hallelujah, 824:6
 out liberty freedom, 196:16
 out Olivia, 209:10
 raise a hue and c., 156:33
 scarcely c. 'weep, 372:4
 scrawny c. was a chorister, 688:17
 secrets c. aloud, 780:2
 shake me like a c., 623:16
 so lonesome I could c., 813:3
 stone shall c. out of wall, 30:31
 stones c. out, 40:11
 sudden c. of pain, 699:10
 that was not ours, 687:8
 the more it made them c., 342:22
 there little girl don't c., 596:3
 too big to c., 476:1
 voice c. Sleep no more, 220:16
 voiced c. of his people, 674:11
 war war still the c., 420:7
 wave c. wind c., 721:6
 we c. that we are come, 217:26
 we still should c., 168:22
 what shall I c., 28:2
 whoever loves you make you c., 862:22
Cryin' all the time, 828:8
 at the lock, 488:7
Crying, boy c. wolf, 756:8
 first voice was c., 31:21
 in the wilderness, 33:24
 infant c. in night, 484:3
 no more c., 49:1
 spiders c. together, 801:9
 watchmen on the heights are c., 164:6
 with sighing and c., 154:14
Crystal, golden sands c. brooks, 234:22
 river of c. light, 597:5
 soul pure as c., 499:8
Crystallization action of mind, 416:20
Cub, grandam to c., 817:19
Cubic inch of space a miracle, 521:3
Cubit, add one c. to stature, 34:18
Cuccu, lhude sing c., 843:5
Cuckold lives in bliss, 213:34
 not be c., 706:5
Cuckoo, as c. is in June, 186:14
 Cloud-C.-Land, 75:10
 jug-jug pu-we, 232:7
 lhude sing c., 843:5
 thus sings he C., 177:16
Cuckoo-buds of yellow hue, 177:16
Cuckoo-clock, Switzerland produced c., 797:4
Cuckoo's, one flew over c. nest, 860:21
Cucullus non facit monachum, 123:16
Cucumber, more nourishin' thin a c., 682:*n*1
Cucumbers, cold as c., 245:6
 lodge in garden of c., 26:8
 sunbeams out of c., 298:16
Cud, chew c. and are silent, 345:16
 whatsoever cheweth the c., 9:10
Cudgel thy brains no more, 206:16
Cudgel's, know what wood a c. of, 271:14

Cue is villainous melancholy, 215:30
 twisted c., 565:16
Cueillez les roses de la vie, 151:*n*1
 votre jeunesse, 151:*n*3
Cuff, the roses get it says Sergeant C., 536:1
Cui bono fuerit, 90:*n*7
Culled, nosegay of c. flowers, 154:4
Culpa, mea c. mea c., 49:6
 O felix c., 49:15
Culprit, stirs C. Life, 544:2
Cult called Christianity, 575:20
 of personality, 741:6
Cultivate a beaver, 741:2
 peace and harmony, 350:10
 sedulously c. free speech, 667:13
 we must c. our garden, 316:9
Cultivated, celebrated c. Duke, 566:2
Cultivates the golden mean, 99:23
Cultivation, equal in rights and in c., 465:7
Cultiver, il faut c. notre jardin, 316:*n*5
Cults, clarification c. founded on, 671:10
Cultural, character of c. environment, 613:13
 effective c. design, 770:2
 evolution, 778:4
 freedom, 678:14
 ivory tower of c., 676:17
 man's nature c. product, 757:12
 tide of c. pollution, 814:4
Culture, above all believer in c., 531:12
 believe only in French c., 590:3
 doesn't save anyone, 772:10
 equal opportunities of c., 596:15
 European c. a misunderstanding, 590:3
 Germany ruins c., 590:4
 great law of c., 434:9
 great though disastrous c., 814:3
 Greek essential to c., 539:9
 hear word c. reach for pistol, 729:7
 in finest flower, 625:4
 individual creature of his c., 712:9
 initial act of c., 702:16
 knowledge of other c., 761:10
 leaves unsatisfied drives to rebelliousness, 607:15
 mechanics of c., 649:4
 men of c. true apostles, 531:17
 moment of clarity, 702:12
 no prospect of continued existence, 607:15
 not function of race, 712:11
 pick out what c. has defined, 727:2
 politics economic development c., 808:9
 pursue C. in bands, 627:13
 pursuit of perfection, 531:10
 socialist c. thrive, 737:18
 soul takes nothing but education and c., 76:20
 study of perfection, 531:13
 to achieve richer c., 761:11
Cultures, materialism model for c., 814:3
Cum grano salis, 108:*n*8
Cumbered with much serving, 39:25
Cumin, tithe of anise and c., 37:2
Cunard's liners and telegraph, 513:20
Cunning, Esau was a c. hunter, 7:10
 history has c. passages, 718:3
 Hocus old c. attorney, 317:*n*4
 in war boastful c., 426:1
 livery of hell, 211:22

Cunning *(continued)*
 men pass for wise, 167:26
 more c. to be strange, 183:7
 nature's sweet c. hand, 209:8
 old Fury, 549:14
 punishment sharpens c., 589:14
 right hand forget her c., 20:11
 sin cover itself, 194:38
 truth which c. times put on, 189:6
 what plighted c. hides, 215:24
Cunningest pattern, 215:7
Cunningly, little world made c., 236:3
Cup, between c. and lip, 241:10
 come fill the C., 471:2
 come fill up my c., 398:11
 drained c. of Lethe, 99:1
 dregs of the C., 289:23
 drowned Glory in C., 472:3
 Etruscan c., 800:14
 fear at heart as at c., 400:6
 giveth his color in the c., 22:38
 he took the c., 37:27
 is new testament in my blood, 44:16
 leave a kiss but in the c., 238:2
 let this c. pass, 37:29
 life's enchanted c., 420:14
 man in whose hand the c. is found, 7:31
 my c. runneth over, 16:18
 o' kindness yet, 379:9
 of hot wine, 224:20
 of trembling, 28:16
 sun in golden c., 642:1
 take c. drink it up, 858:1
 that clears today, 471:10
 to every people c. of clay, 856:8
 valley his golden c., 541:14
 woodspurge has c. of three, 541:28
Cupboard, glacier knocks in c., 775:9
 was bare, 859:13
 wicked man in bathroom c., 797:11
Cupboards, keys took and c. opened, 575:4
Cupid and my Campaspe, 163:15
 bolt of C. fell, 181:9
 has his camps, 105:2
 it has long stood void, 249:8
 paid, 163:15
 senior-junior Dan C., 176:33
 silent note C. strikes, 256:7
 winged C. painted blind, 180:21
 young Adam C., 182:27
Cupiditas, radix malorum est c., 46:*n*1
Cupido upon his shuldres wynges, 135:24
Cupid's arms, 845:21
 concludes with C. curse, 164:8
Cups, flowing c. run swiftly, 276:3
 that cheer, 348:4
 when they are in their c., 31:5
Cur, ears of the old c., 271:9
Cur ergo haec ipse non facis, 118:*n*4
Curates, shower of c., 504:17
Curb, care's check and c., 278:29
 use snaffle c. all right, 760:8
 your magnanimity, 441:5
Curd, white c. of ass's milk, 312:7
Curdied by frost from snow, 224:31
Curds and whey, 860:3
Cure, absence c. of love, 157:3
 disease kill patient, 168:5
 for loneliness is love, 785:6

Cure *(continued)*
  laws or kings cause or c., 325:3
  no c. for birth and death, 629:15
  not worth the pain, 103:*n*1
  on exercise depend, 285:19
  past c. I am, 228:6
  past hope past c. past help, 184:8
  tale would c. deafness, 229:12
  the c. is freedom, 447:14
  thrust of c., 821:7
Cured, Asclepius c. the body, 76:*n*3
  I am frizzled stale, 800:19
  I treated him God c. him, 150:5
  more than Galen c., 251:19
  of every folly but vanity, 331:12
Cures, endure neither evils nor c., 102:10
  me of my pain, 845:21
  opposites c. for opposites, 73:4
  to fear worst c. worse, 208:4
Cureth, quiet mind c. all, 242:7
Curfew, far-off c. sound, 260:4
  must not ring tonight, 600:3
  tolls knell, 334:8
Curiosity, culture origin not in c., 531:13
  do well in closet by way of c., 314:25
  insatiable intellectual c., 627:19
  intellectual c., 678:16
  love c. freckles doubt, 738:11
  natural c. of young, 586:15
  offers to our c., 721:8
  order awakened c., 454:13
  permanent and certain, 324:12
  pleasure to rouse c., 790:12
Curious, amazed and c., 379:20
  busy c. thirsty fly, 317:7
  crime, 494:29
  in unnecessary matters, 31:30
  incident of dog, 617:7
  quaint and c. war is, 575:18
  seen a c. child, 395:5
  volume of forgotten lore, 478:20
Curiouser and curiouser, 549:12
Curl, had a little c., 468:4
  make your hair c., 565:22
Curled, wealthy c. darlings, 212:23
  wonderful water c., 535:7
Curlicues of marijuana, 801:1
Curls done up with bank notes, 503:12
  Frocks and C., 545:18
  Hyperion's c., 205:21
  natural c., 109:12
Curlylocks wilt be mine, 859:6
Currency, debauch c., 701:17
  no graven images except c., 512:11
Current, azure c. floweth, 502:3
  boats against the c., 746:9
  genial c. of soul, 334:19
  icy c. compulsive course, 214:15
  misleading guide to c. affairs, 701:14
  noiseless c. strong, 531:20
  swollen c. masses of ice, 489:18
  take c. when it serves, 197:14
  time a river of strong c., 115:17
Currents, fresh c. of life, 487:12
  turn awry, 203:33
Curriculum was rum, 630:8
Curried, short horse soon c., 147:27
Currite, lente c. noctis equi, 105:*n*3, 171:4

Curs of low degree, 341:17
Curse astonishment hissing and reproach, 29:22
  began to c., 37:35
  bless them that c. you, 34:7
  Christianity one great c., 589:25
  creations of mind blessing not c., 683:6
  for God, 821:2
  get the c. out of murder, 796:4
  God and die, 13:28
  has come upon me, 480:26
  his better angel, 215:10
  I know how to c., 229:17
  much knowledge a c., 83:1
  O c. of marriage, 214:4
  of hell frae me, 853:22
  on his virtues, 301:23
  primal eldest c., 205:14
  the darkness, 704:*n*1
  this pois'nous bunch-backed toad, 173:36
  with book bell and candle, 139:11
  youthful harlot's c., 374:8
Cursed above all cattle, 6:7
  be he that moves my bones, 231:19
  be man that trusteth in man, 29:17
  be my tribe, 188:5
  be the verse, 312:6
  Boston c. with cranks, 606:6
  counted and c. luck, 619:15
  drunken officer, 826:2
  Fate has c. you, 69:20
  floundered enjoyed, 585:19
  hard reading, 368:6
  me with his eye, 400:8
  name to all ages c., 283:8
  O c. spite, 202:29
  past, 724:21
  plagues with which mankind c., 295:3
  sat Beauty in lap c. her, 603:17
  the bread, 652:11
  thoughts, 220:6
Curses all Eve's daughters, 191:2
  like young chickens, 405:13
  not loud but deep, 222:11
  of the firmament, 286:*n*4
  rigged with c. dark, 261:21
Cursing, blessing and c., 10:12
Cursores vitae lampada tradunt, 93:*n*1
Curtailed, always c. thwarted, 714:17
Curtain, Anarch lets c. fall, 313:25
  close his eyes and draw c., 172:14
  iron c., 667:16
  never c. between you and me, 669:20
  Priam's c., 191:7
  purple c., 479:3
  somewhere beyond c., 641:12
  when she drew c. by, 854:1
Curtained, dreams abuse c. sleep, 220:9
Curtains, fringed c. of thine eye, 229:21
  hell take c., 703:8
  let fall the c., 348:4
  of Solomon, 25:12
  spread canopy or c. spun, 292:7
  through c. call on us, 234:2
Curtius Rufus seems descended from himself, 78:*n*1
Curtsied when you have, 229:18

Curtsy, nice customs c. to great kings, 194:2
  while you're thinking, 551:12
Curved, empty c. space, 787:15
Cushion, sit on a c., 859:6
Custodians of new ideas have fervor, 625:3
Custody, individual taken into c., 733:2
Custom, age cannot wither nor c. stale, 223:15
  conform to tyrant c., 155:6
  despot of mankind, 446:14
  follow c. of church where you are, 117:*n*8
  Fortune more kind than her c., 189:25
  gods' c. to bring low greatness, 71:19
  guide of human life, 330:6
  in all line of order, 207:24
  made property of easiness, 206:18
  make it their perch, 211:3
  more honored in breach, 202:3
  nature her c. holds, 206:14
  no law more binding than c., 616:10
  of Branksome Hall, 396:5
  old c. made life sweet, 197:36
  one good c. corrupt, 486:12
  reconciles to everything, 343:12
  sitting at receipt of c., 35:17
  stern C. spreads afar, 381:8
  to whom c. due, 43:24
  whereof memory of man, 338:*n*1
Customary fate of new truths, 537:12
  suits of solemn black, 200:29
Customer, tough c., 496:34
Customers, empire for raising c., 338:19
  sign brings c., 276:18
Customs, language manners laws c., 391:15
  laws are sand c. rock, 562:16
  nice c. curtsy to great kings, 194:2
  oh the times the c., 90:8
  politics and tongue, 553:4
  shape experience and behavior, 712:9
Cut and came again, 369:5
  anyone introduced to, 552:18
  diamond c. diamond, 246:3
  features of clerical c., 720:1
  him out in little stars, 183:32
  I c. down trees skip and jump, 843:1
  if thy hand offend thee c. it off, 34:4
  in the evening it is c. down, 18:20
  is branch that might have grown, 171:7
  it is soon c. off and we fly away, 18:22
  it without e'er knife, 857:20
  knives that serve or c., 515:18
  laurels all c., 534:1
  like a flower and is c. down, 14:15
  moment I c. his throat, 813:14
  my coat after my cloth, 147:21
  not c. conscience to fit fashions, 770:14
  off in blossoms of sin, 202:19
  off tails, 856:15
  stems struggling, 780:3
  strangers who c. down woods, 746:2
  stripes away, 633:6
  unkindest c. of all, 196:34
  up what remains, 634:7
  ways of men c. off, 265:25
  where were the righteous c. off, 13:32
  with beard of formal c., 198:25
Cuts, psychology c. both ways, 526:7

Dance *(continued)*
>   round in ring and suppose, 670:16
>   rouses him up to d., 55:12
>   sweet d. to violins, 605:19
>   the antic hay, 170:14
>   there is only the d., 720:11
>   time to d., 24:6
>   tipsy d. and jollity, 260:20
>   to flutes dance to lutes, 605:19
>   tossing heads in sprightly d., 394:6
>   upon the air, 605:19
>   walk before they d., 312:20
>   when you do d., 228:29
>   while you can, 775:7
>   with me in Ireland, 843:n4
>   with William Blake, 781:10
>   wyth me in Irlonde, 843:7

Danced by light of moon, 499:18
>   daughter of Herodias Salome d., 36:11
>   David d. before the Lord, 11:43
>   death fires d., 400:1
>   his did, 740:8
>   I could have d. all night, 803:10
>   like dingledodies, 810:2
>   moon on Monan's rill, 397:4
>   on waves, 603:8
>   Salome d., 36:11
>   star d., 194:22
>   till doomsday, 300:17
>   to see that banner, 473:3

Dancer from dance, 640:15

Dancers all gone under hill, 720:21
>   dancing in tune, 485:10

Dances as often as dance it can, 401:5
>   he capers he d., 190:28
>   in hamlets d. on green, 396:9
>   in sight of heaven, 809:1
>   in what ethereal d., 478:10
>   lulled with d. and delight, 181:12
>   oh she d. such a way, 269:23
>   when she d. in the wind, 284:8

Dancing dancers d. in tune, 485:10
>   days are done, 182:n2
>   dining and d. begin, 763:10
>   dogs and bears, 656:10
>   emptier ever d. in air, 180:9
>   in the checkered shade, 259:16
>   is life itself, 617:23
>   keeping rhythm in d., 720:16
>   labor blossoming or d., 640:15
>   loftiest of arts, 617:23
>   no more than school of d., 613:12
>   on volcano, 433:2
>   past our d. days, 182:24
>   to frenzied drum, 639:8
>   very merry d. drinking, 285:20

Dandin, asked for it Georges D., 278:16
Dandruff, toothpaste and d. ads, 753:18
Dandy, candy is d., 763:5
>   I'm a Yankee Doodle d., 679:11
>   Yankee Doodle d., 846:14

Dandyism, intellectual d., 541:12
Dane, more antique Roman than D., 207:12
Danger, above noise and d., 279:6
>   bear brunt of d., 520:6
>   brave man's choice is d., 70:9
>   bright eyes of d., 599:12
>   clear and present d., 578:13
>   days of d., 397:7

Danger *(continued)*
>   dear Fatherland no d. thine, 518:1
>   difficulty and d., 360:7
>   feared no d. knew no sin, 284:18
>   foretold that d. lurks within, 173:7
>   glory and d. alike, 74:2
>   hackneyed phrases d. signals, 613:18
>   in view of d. give up life, 63:12
>   is in discord, 466:23
>   my life was in d., 813:4
>   nettle d., 185:16
>   of faction, 367:1
>   of violent death, 246:12
>   or treasure, 806:3
>   pleased with d., 283:8
>   she suspected no d., 526:18
>   spur of all great minds, 165:12
>   there is d. from all men, 351:2
>   when fatherland in d., 380:20
>   where is man out of d., 537:10

Dangerous, astute and d. man, 617:15
>   delays d. in war, 163:n1
>   delays have d. ends, 171:20
>   demur you're d., 545:2
>   edge of things, 493:9
>   errors in religion d., 330:3
>   have in me something d., 207:1
>   idea d. when only one, 648:3
>   if a little knowledge d., 537:10
>   into d. world I leapt, 374:10
>   little learning d., 308:11
>   mad bad d. to know, 418:7
>   most d. calculations we call illusions, 716:14
>   politics as d. as war, 665:8
>   realities less d. than fancies, 661:8
>   rouse speculation about d. things, 790:12
>   say nothing in d. times, 245:27
>   show thy d. brow by night, 196:2
>   such men are d., 195:22
>   thirst d. thing, 620:6
>   to be of no church d., 325:6
>   to meet Culture alone, 627:13
>   to our peace and safety, 377:1
>   who make no noise are d., 276:19

Danger's troubled night, 408:18

Dangers, concern for safety in face of d., 812:9
>   defend us from d. of night, 50:10
>   delays breed d., 163:3
>   in what great d. ye spend little span, 92:20
>   of the seas, 254:22
>   she loved me for the d., 212:32
>   thorns and d. of world, 178:22
>   what d. thou make us scorn, 379:19
>   with d. compassed round, 267:13

Daniel, cast D. into the den of lions, 30:8
>   come to judgment, 189:21
>   had convicted them, 33:13
>   second D., 190:1

Dank, addled mosses d., 709:14
>   tarn of Auber, 479:12

Danny, hangin' D. Deever, 633:6
Dante belongs to the first category, 782:3
>   language of D. common language, 722:19
>   more learned from D., 722:19
>   of dread Inferno, 494:2

Daphnis, my songs draw D. home, 95:25
Dapple, name was D. Gray, 860:22
Dappled things, 587:9
Dapple-dawn-drawn Falcon, 587:6
Darbies, ease d. at wrist, 517:2
Darby, always same D. my own, 594:3
Dare all that may plant man's lordship, 577:1
>   ask just God's assistance, 477:3
>   call soul my own, 464:1
>   choose if you d., 257:13
>   deadly terrors clasp, 374:6
>   do duty as understand it, 475:1
>   endure greater than d., 490:23
>   enter you who d., 541:18
>   first ponder then d., 449:3
>   heart would deny and d. not, 222:11
>   I d. do all, 219:21
>   imitate him if you d., 641:3
>   is highest wisdom, 413:1
>   letting I d. not, 219:20
>   love that and say so too, 234:1
>   Love that d. not speak its name, 653:20
>   mighty things, 614:13
>   never d. utter untruth, 90:16
>   never grudge throe, 494:9
>   none d. call it treason, 168:23
>   O what men d. do, 194:37
>   slaves who d. not be, 514:10
>   soul to d., 397:6
>   speak truth as much as I d., 153:14
>   think unthinkable, 770:6
>   to be ahead of the world, 59:14
>   to be naive, 743:12
>   to be true, 249:18
>   to be wise, 100:22
>   to eat a peach, 717:16
>   what hand d. seize fire, 374:5
>   what man d. I d., 221:14
>   wonder Do I d., 717:9

Dared, determined d. and done, 338:2
>   never d. be radical when young, 670:9
>   none d. thou hast, 160:13

Daren't go a-hunting, 535:15
Dares, come before swallow d., 228:27
>   life d. send challenge, 272:8
>   who d. do more is none, 219:21

Darest thou then, 396:22
Darien, peak in D., 435:19
Daring, in war d. boastful, 426:1
>   pilot in extremity, 283:8
>   serious d. starts from within, 784:7
>   well-doing and d., 326:n6
>   young man on trapeze, 571:14

Dark, abysmal d. of center, 441:10
>   afraid to go home in d., 626:n3
>   after that the d., 487:3
>   all night in d. and wet, 598:22
>   and bloody ground, 522:7
>   and his d. secret love, 374:3
>   and lonely hiding place, 401:12
>   and stormy night, 452:12, 811:2
>   as Erebus, 190:7
>   as good in the d., 248:6
>   as world of man, 715:13
>   at one stride comes the d., 400:5
>   backward and abysm of time, 229:10
>   best of d. and bright, 422:13
>   between d. and daylight, 467:10
>   blanket of the d., 219:12

Dark *(continued)*

　blue ocean roll, 421:26
　Chromis did not save himself from d.
　　death, 52:18
　clear moving utterly free, 785:11
　cloud at house's door, 856:1
　cold and empty desolation, 721:6
　come to d. and lament, 670:14
　dark dark amid blaze, 268:32
　dark dark spaces, 720:22
　dove with flickering tongue, 721:18
　dull d. soundless day, 478:11
　echoed with outlandish orders, 805:7
　ever-during d., 265:25
　everyone is a moon has d. side, 562:12
　fate sits on d. battlements, 384:15
　fear death as children fear d., 167:7
　fell of d. not day, 588:4
　go home in d., 626:17
　great leap in the d., 246:16
　hawks hear us, 696:16
　highest candle lights d., 688:15
　hole of the head, 825:4
　horse, 458:23
　hour or twain, 220:29
　hunt it in the d., 347:18
　in d. time eye begins to see, 781:4
　in nightmare of the d., 775:15
　in the d. and silent grave, 160:14
　inscrutable workmanship, 391:7
　iron New England d., 748:17
　irrecoverably d., 268:32
　let d. come upon you, 720:23
　lie in d. weep for sins, 519:16
　life one long struggle in d., 93:1
　Maid and her Lord, 69:12
　mother always gliding near, 520:17
　mutinous Shannon waves, 696:4
　narrowing d. hours, 748:3
　night is d., 449:18, 851:21
　night of d. intent, 669:19
　night of the soul, 154:12, 746:14
　not d. days great days, 667:2
　not put me in d. to die, 602:8
　o'er d. silver mantle threw, 266:16
　old fantastical duke of d. corners, 212:3
　on d. theme trace verses of light, 92:17
　pillared d., 670:14
　raging in the d., 641:4
　rebellious brows, 521:4
　road whence no one returns, 94:2
　Satanic mills, 375:17
　sea iridescent and d., 788:3
　some days d. and dreary, 466:10
　soul's d. cottage, 258:3
　sun to me is d., 268:33
　then it is d., 788:4
　they all go into d., 720:22
　things in d. besides Santa Claus, 672:3
　to d. tower came, 217:3
　unconscious not only d. but light, 675:9
　unfathomed caves, 334:20
　violets are d. too, 96:2
　walk between d. and d., 743:17
　wall between us and d., 742:10
　wandering in d. labyrinth, 169:18
　ways that are d., 566:12
　we are for the d., 224:5
　we work in d., 585:4

Dark *(continued)*

　what if Amyntas is d., 96:2
　what in me is d. illumine, 263:21
　who art d. as night, 228:7
　with excessive bright, 265:27
　with torment and tears, 508:19
　wood where straight way lost, 129:17
　woods lovely d. deep, 669:15
　world and wide, 263:12
　world present treatment, 648:14
Darken, never d. threshold of doors, 522:4
Darkened, blue d. on blueness, 707:21
　hurtles in d. air, 335:17
　sun or light be not d., 25:7
　windows be d., 25:7
Darkeneth, who d. counsel by words, 15:4
Darkens, evening d., 820:2
Darker and darker stairs, 707:21
　as d. grows the night, 340:13
　the tinge that saddens, 460:8
Darkest before day dawneth, 258:15
　day will have passed, 348:18
　sun breaks through d. clouds, 175:37
Dark-heaving boundless, 422:2
Darkies how heart grows weary, 538:16
Darkling I listen, 437:12
　plain, 531:2
　roll d. down torrent, 324:9
　stand varying shore, 223:36
Darkly he rose, 818:6
　it knows obstacles, 809:2
　saw through glass eye d., 561:20
　see through glass d., 44:20
　wise and rudely great, 311:9
Darkness, absence d. death, 234:21
　affronts with his own d., 791:12
　again and silence, 467:18
　and light alike to thee, 20:14
　and shadow of death, 14:6, 19:13, 39:1
　as children fear in d., 93:9
　awake upon dark, 707:21
　awful d. silence reign, 500:7
　blackness of d., 48:1
　cast into outer d., 35:13
　comprehended it not, 40:30
　crown of our life is d., 568:6
　curse the d., 704:*n*1
　dawn on our d., 416:1
　deep but dazzling d., 279:1
　deep things out of d., 14:13
　deepens, 432:5
　distant voice in d., 467:18
　downward to d. on wings, 686:19
　dying of cold not d., 631:6
　embalmed d., 437:10
　encounter d. as a bride, 211:21
　falls at thy behest, 538:12
　falls from wings, 466:12
　fell upon Christian, 281:28
　gives light in d., 172:7
　hello d. my old friend, 837:7
　horror of outer d., 553:14
　hovers earth is silent, 4:9
　how great that d., 34:15
　how in your d. know, 656:18
　if light in thee be d., 34:15
　in d. and with dangers, 267:13
　in d. bind them, 736:4
　in him is no d., 47:36

Darkness *(continued)*

　in what d. of life spend little span, 92:20
　instruments of d., 219:3
　into d. peering, 479:4
　into d. they go, 735:11
　into eternal d. fire and ice, 130:9
　jaws of d. do devour it, 180:20
　land of d. and shadow, 14:6
　lead me from d. to light, 51:20
　leaves world to d. to me, 334:8
　lest d. come, 41:23
　light excelleth d., 24:3
　light shineth in d., 40:30
　lighten our d., 50:10
　lordly d. decked in filth, 807:4
　love in spite of d., 234:16
　mainly in d., 829:6
　man ever in d., 122:6
　no d. but ignorance, 210:17
　no d. into light without emotion, 675:13
　no light but d. visible, 264:1
　not walk in d., 41:10
　of God, 720:23
　of man's heart, 786:5
　outer d., 35:13, 37:15, 553:14
　over spirits of damned, 474:12
　pain d. and cold, 494:19
　peace and d., 620:2
　people that walked in d., 26:30
　people which sat in d., 33:31
　pestilence that walketh in d., 18:25
　prince of d. a gentleman, 217:1
　raven down of d., 260:27
　rulers of the d., 45:31
　scatters rear of d. thin, 259:13
　shaft of light in d., 800:6
　shares the d., 735:5
　sit in d. here, 265:9
　such as sit in d., 19:13
　swooping d. up, 855:14
　them that sit in d., 39:1
　this thing of d., 230:16
　thou makest d., 19:11
　through d. up to God, 484:5
　two eternities of d., 755:12
　universal d. buries all, 313:25
　upon face of the deep, 5:9
　wave of light breaks into d., 712:7
　we are not of d., 46:10
　where d. let me sow light, 128:5
　which may be felt, 8:14
　wind torrent of d., 692:2
　works of d., 43:26
　worms and shrouds, 436:5
　year of now done d., 588:1
Dark-shining Pacific, 713:8
Darky's heart longed to go, 602:14
Darling buds of May, 226:2
　Charlie is my d., 385:7
　daughter, 851:13
　I am growing old, 594:2
　man been mother's undisputed d.,
　　607:14
　my d. dear, 847:6
　my d. from the lions, 17:3
　Nature's D., 335:7
　of men and gods, 92:8
　of my heart, 307:23
　of our crew, 362:11

Day *(continued)*

every dog has his d., 452:5
every dog his d., 514:4
every year passed d., 819:10
everyone has his d., 668:4
exact d.-labor light denied, 263:13
faint in the d. of adversity, 23:1
fair d. adieu, 178:5
famous d. and year, 467:14
fate put heads together, 670:1
fell of dark not d., 588:4
first last everlasting d., 234:17
first spring d., 601:13
fogs prevail upon the d., 284:3
follow as night the d., 201:27
forever and a d., 199:28
frabjous d., 551:11
friends I have lost a d., 111:6
from our immortal d., 372:9
from this d. forward, 51:10
gaudy blabbing remorseful d., 172:15
gilded car of d., 260:19
given thee till break of d., 373:17
go ahead make my d., 841:2
go to bed by d., 598:20
God is d. night winter summer, 64:7
good to gain d., 519:4
got tired of Me, 545:1
great and dreadful d. of the Lord, 31:4
guest that tarrieth but a d., 31:19
gwine to run all d., 538:14
happiest d. happiest hour, 477:12
hath brightest d. a cloud, 172:9
he announced for President, 840:9
he that outlives this d., 193:19
health and a d., 454:16
hippopotamus's d., 718:5
home being washing-d., 288:16
how it is with April d., 670:5
I had rued, 669:12
I hate the d., 161:26
idle singer of empty d., 557:1
if she be a d., 299:12
in d. of adversity consider, 24:20
in d. of prosperity be joyful, 24:20
in its hotness, 529:2
in the d. of vengeance, 21:8
in the posteriors of this d., 177:11
in thy courts, 18:17
in which ye came out, 8:22
infinite d. excludes the night, 304:11
is a poem, 713:13
is at hand, 43:26
is done and darkness falls, 466:12
is for honest men, 70:10
is short labor long, 120:8
it is his d., 139:7
it was Christmas D., 169:1
jocund d. stands tiptoe, 184:5
joint-laborer with d., 200:17
July's d. short as December, 228:13
just for one d., 656:11
kings upon coronation d., 284:20
knell of parting d., 334:8
known a better d., 396:3
left alone with our d., 775:8
lengthens not a d., 233:9
let every man consider last d., 68:10
let the d. perish, 13:29

Day *(continued)*

let them have their d., 639:1
light of common d., 393:12
little systems have d., 483:11
long weary d. have end, 162:4
looked into eye of d., 640:16
love resembleth April d., 176:6
maddest merriest d., 480:15
makes d. seep into night, 122:7
meditate d. and night, 15:27
men die miserably every d., 703:15
merry as d. is long, 194:14
merry heart goes all d., 228:24
mildewed d. in August, 800:11
most wasted d. of all, 356:3
mounting at break of d., 394:20
night and d. you are the one, 732:10
Night mother of D., 468:6
night of time surpasseth d., 256:21
night thousand eyes d. one, 600:14
not a d. without a line, 83:10
not as dawning of d., 236:21
not look same by d., 463:14
not the best d., 830:12
not to me returns d., 265:25
not up soon as I, 178:24
now d. over, 555:3
now's the d., 380:10
of adversity, 24:20
of affliction, 32:22
of death better than birth, 24:15
of deliverance, 351:9
of Empires come, 563:10
of glory has come, 383:*n*1
of Judgment, 701:6
of my destiny's over, 422:25
of one's birth, 24:15
of prosperity, 32:22
of small things, 30:36
of spirits, 278:29
of the great reckoning, 3:12
of the Lord, 46:9
of vengeance, 21:8
of wrath, 49:9
on seventh d. God ended his work, 5:15
on that d. no soul wronged, 122:8
one d. beside some flowers, 791:13
pack clouds away and welcome d., 239:11
past and yet I saw no sun, 164:17
perfect d., 625:14
petty pace from d. to d., 222:16
planned another d., 840:14
precincts of cheerful d., 334:24
proper man as see in summer's d., 181:2
rain it raineth every d., 210:19, 216:25
rape of every blessed d., 809:1
rare as d. in June, 514:16
remember the sabbath d., 8:34
returns too soon, 423:1
Rome must be built in d., 802:1
Rome not built in one d., 148:13
rose with delight to us, 249:3
runs through roughest d., 219:7
saw my evil d., 386:8
seize the d., 99:12
set down as gain each d., 99:11
seventh d. thou shalt not work, 8:34
shall declare it, 43:36
shall stand at the latter d., 14:25

Day *(continued)*

she set out one d., 664:4
shineth unto perfect d., 21:1
sleep neither night nor d., 218:27
so cool so calm, 250:9
so foul and fair a d., 218:30
some d. you'll know, 818:6
soundless d. in autumn, 478:11
specter night and d., 374:15
spent but one d. thoroughly well, 138:11
St. Patrick's D., 847:4
sufficient unto d. is evil, 34:22
sun anew each d., 714:17
sun gone down while it was d., 29:14
sun shall not smite thee by d., 19:30
sunbeam in winter's d., 317:12
superfluous to demand time of d., 184:23
support us all d. long, 450:1
tender eye of pitiful d., 221:7
thanks to heroes reached this d., 789:9
that I die, 839:7
that is dead, 482:16
that shall burn as oven, 31:2
think every d. your last, 101:1
third d. comes a frost, 231:2
third d. he rose again, 50:3
third d. he will raise us up, 30:14
this d. for a memorial, 8:19
this d. we must part, 447:7
this January D., 546:19
those eyes the break of d., 211:31
those who dream by d., 478:13
thou d. I hour, 564:15
thou gavest Lord is ended, 538:12
thought it Judgment D., 576:4
three days after Bastille D., 818:4
tire the d. in toil, 249:6
'tis true 'tis d., 234:16
today first d. of rest of life, 852:20
today isn't any other d., 552:9
tomorrow a new d., 158:18
tomorrow as today, 228:9
tomorrow is another d., 758:9
trysting d., 448:13
turn by night or d., 393:7
two nights to every d., 250:12
unpurged images of d., 641:5
until the d. break, 25:19
unto day uttereth speech, 16:10
up by break of d., 250:7
vulgarize d. of judgment, 458:8
was it the spring d., 856:11
we the ones to make better d., 842:7
weakening eye of d., 575:15
wear d. out before comes, 595:3
wedding d. fixed, 322:15
well-spent d. happy sleep, 141:1
what a d. may bring, 23:9
when a boy came crying wolf, 756:8
when heaven was falling, 619:17
which the Lord hath made, 19:26
while it is d., 41:13
will come thou shalt wish for me,
  173:36
without all hope of d., 268:32
withstand in the evil d., 45:31
wrestled until breaking of d., 7:19
year and a d., 499:16
yield d. to night, 171:11

Dead *(continued)*

certain is birth for the d., 87:1
Christ risen from d., 44:24
close wall with English d., 192:30
communication of d., 721:15
corpse of Public Credit, 415:5
corse in complete steel, 202:6
crucified d. buried, 50:3
day that is d., 482:16
days among d. past, 405:16
dead dead indeed, 856:13
dead dead and never knew me, 584:3
dear d. women, 493:14
Death once d., 228:5
deathless hour, 542:1
descent of last end on d., 696:4
desire d. be near us, 483:23
dishonor not trouble once I am d., 69:16
divine brother of all, 520:10
dooms imagined for d., 436:9
doubled globe of d., 795:4
earth that bears thee d., 187:6
earth to living not d., 358:18
England finished and d., 673:6
envy for the d., 562:5
envy of the d., 69:19
faith d. which does not doubt, 631:13
faith without works is d., 47:15
fallen cold and d., 520:19
fame sun of d., 445:5
fell at his feet as d., 48:6
for a ducat dead, 205:18
for Love is d., 163:23
for Lycidas sorrow not d., 262:5
forgotten as a d. man out of mind, 16:27
full of d. men's bones, 37:4
gear of foreign d. men, 721:8
God is d., 588:15
govern living, 444:3
great god Pan is d., 112:2
greatest service or injury to d. man,
  76:20
half d. a living death, 269:1
half regiment d., 801:11
hands dead stringencies, 827:17
harrow house of d., 775:5
heads of d. up line, 752:11
healthy wealthy and d., 741:16
heard the d. cry, 780:9
Hector is d., 208:23
help for living hope for d., 554:5
her d. body wears smile, 827:12
her warrior d., 483:4
herself ere evensong, 854:7
high converse with mighty d., 317:16
himself must be d., 406:24
honor dies man d., 468:8
how fares it with happy d., 483:20
how possible that d. be brought alive,
  121:17
how shall the d. arise, 256:1
I am every d. thing, 234:21
ideas and dead beliefs, 540:10
if Lucy should be d., 391:17
immortal d. who live again, 512:14
in long run all d., 701:14
in praise of ladies d., 227:11
is at rest, 33:6
is God d., 443:9

Dead *(continued)*

is the king d., 174:16
just as d. as if wrong, 852:7
kissed by English d., 738:8
knocking when I'm d., 682:3
know not any thing, 24:28
lain for century d., 485:12
land of d., 749:12, 775:9
law hath not been d., 211:11
left it d. and with head, 551:11
let d. bury their d., 35:15
life is shrunk d. and interred, 234:20
lift coffins of d. relations, 833:14
light in dust lies d., 431:4
like vampire d. many times, 573:6
lilacs out of d. land, 718:11
living and d. are same, 64:13
living dog better than d. lion, 24:28
living scarce able to bury d., 247:8
look at my d. house, 768:6
Lord of living and d., 587:3
loses past and d. for future, 71:4
love never sick old d., 160:2
Magus Zoroaster my d. child, 428:3
maid not d. but sleepeth, 35:22
man cannot bite, 91:21
Man's Chest, 598:14
men rise up never, 569:3
men tell no tales, 283:26
mie love ys d., 368:10
mighty d., 317:16
mindful of unhonored d., 335:1
Mistah Kurtz he d., 612:10
more d. people than living, 788:14
more to say when d., 652:8
most lovely d., 478:8
most people my age are d., 730:17
mourn the d., 808:14
mouth of one just d., 679:15
moving d. still talk of pushing bones,
  821:7
Mozart had been d. two years, 821:1
my enemy is d. man divine d., 520:13
my lady's sparrow is d., 94:1
nature seems d., 220:9
ne'er said till friend d., 591:9
newspaper buries d., 646:18
no longer mourn when I am d., 226:23
noble Living and noble D., 391:12
not a house where not one d., 8:21
not d. but gone before, 106:*n*10
not God of d., 40:12
not interested in living, 749:15
not make war on d., 149:22
not reverence of d. but envy of living,
  246:14
now he is d. should I fast, 12:5
O he is d. then, 587:12
objects essentially d., 403:4
of d. nothing but good, 57:*n*1
old bawd is d., 642:19
old men are all d., 576:10
once d. never return, 471:16
one d. other powerless, 529:19
only d. who do not return, 370:2
only good Indians d., 549:2
out of d. cold ashes life, 591:11
outrage brave man d., 67:11
pattern of d. and living, 721:5

Dead *(continued)*

people so d. to liberty, 323:4
perfection, 485:5
Phlebas a fortnight d., 718:20
plucks d. lions by beard, 177:24
poetry of earth never d., 436:1
Poets d. and gone, 438:10
poets in misery d., 392:11
praised the d. already d., 24:7
pray for d. fight like hell for living,
  547:12
professors like literature d., 708:7
quick and the d., 50:3
renown and grace is d., 220:25
Respite to be d., 546:4
rest for the d., 555:1
rest her soul she's d., 206:21
resurrection of the d., 44:24
revisit in dreams the dear d., 69:11
right d. right as sped along, 852:*n*2
romantic Ireland's d., 638:7
rough notes and d. bodies, 649:16
rule over the departed d., 55:9
say I'm sick I'm d., 311:19
Sea and Sea of Galilee, 680:1
Sea fruits, 412:14
Sea's shore, 420:18
seek living among d., 40:25
shall be raised, 44:31
shall live living die, 284:17
sheeted d., 200:18
shores will swarm with invisible d., 419:5
smiling the boy fell d., 491:8
so dull so d. in look, 191:7
so long as refuse to die, 536:10
soldiers bore d. bodies by, 185:3
somebody threw d. dog down ravine,
  783:9
something d. in each of us, 605:20
soul so d., 396:11
Spartan d., 424:3
speak ill of the d., 57:2
stars are d., 775:8
stepping-stones of d. selves, 483:13
tell 'em Queen Anne's d., 383:12
there are no d., 627:2
there he fell down d., 10:33
these d. not died in vain, 476:7
these honored d., 476:7
think living worth it, 819:9
thirty is as good as d., 365:15
though d. shall he live, 41:19
three keep secret if two d., 319:12
thy greatest enemy d., 32:14
time is d., 748:9
time you have to spend d., 152:10
told me Heraclitus d., 534:3
took wages and are d., 619:17
topics of sex and the d., 643:6
travel to home among d., 429:25
tree gives no shelter, 718:12
trophies and d. things, 244:10
truth never fell d., 488:12
unhonored d., 335:1
until he is d. do not call man happy,
  57:11
vast and middle of night, 201:14
voices of d. like torrent's fall, 424:4
warred for Homer being d., 239:13

Death (*continued*)

Exodus of d., 467:6
faithful unto d., 48:10
Falstaff sweats to d., 185:15
Famine Pestilence Destruction D., 692:6
fear and danger of violent d., 246:12
fear d. as children fear dark, 167:7
fear d. feel fog, 494:18
fear of d. more dreaded than d., 103:16
fear of D. troubles me, 142:*n*2
fear of ignominious d., 383:2
fed on fullness of d., 568:17
feed on D., 228:5
fell sergeant d., 207:10
final accounting, 124:7
find me planting cabbages, 152:8
fly down D., 791:9
for restful d. I cry, 226:20
for thirty pence my d., 250:5
foretaste of d., 425:15
fortune favored him in moment of d., 114:3
found d. in life, 404:4
fraternity or d., 356:*n*3
friends enough now for d., 764:6
from d. to immortality, 51:20
from sudden d., 50:13
fruit threw d., 236:6
gallop Pegasus to d., 312:19
gates of dark D. stand wide, 97:23
give me liberty or d., 353:3
giving life by d. of others, 140:11
go down D. bring her, 657:3
go hand in hand to d., 542:5
go with anyone to d., 669:1
gods have neither age nor d., 68:19
gone to her d., 446:7
good d. does honor to whole life, 132:13
good thing to escape d., 67:19
great d., 655:15
grim d., 245:2
grim D. my son and foe, 265:19
had appointment in Samarra, 673:1
had undone so many, 718:13
half dead a living d., 269:1
halls of d., 432:10
has broached him to, 362:11
hath no more dominion, 42:45
hath ten thousand doors, 244:7
he brought them d., 655:6
he taketh all away, 534:3
heaven gives favorites early d., 83:*n*6
here find life in d., 404:4
how can you know about d., 63:5
how little room we take in d., 254:5
how strange a thing is d., 735:10
how they pray for d., 69:14
hungry for life and d., 794:9
I am near to d., 57:20
I here importune d., 223:37
I hung on like d., 780:7
idle and who has done much meet d. alike, 53:5
if D. knew how to forgive, 96:20
immortal D. has taken mortal life, 93:12
in d. daylight finish, 495:10
in d. they were not divided, 11:36
in his d. all things appear fair, 53:32
in itself is nothing, 282:20

in ranks of d. find him, 411:16
in sterres writen d. of every man, 136:11
in the midst of life d., 51:13
in the pot, 13:1
in the shadow of d., 19:13, 39:1
in vain to wish for d., 68:15
interest in d. interest in life, 676:10
intricate as d., 237:1
is a master from Germany, 806:10
is a sleep, 568:19
is afraid of him, 122:28
is as lover's pinch, 224:11
is dead not he, 430:14
is generally prompt, 469:15
is knowledge, 382:9
is most efficient, 691:14
is not D. at watch, 745:14
is nothing to us, 93:11
is slumber, 427:16
is swallowed up, 44:32
is the enemy, 700:11
jaws of d., 155:5, 485:2
judge none blessed before his d., 32:23
just d. kind umpire, 171:18
just that distance from d., 57:16
keeps D. his court, 179:28
keys of hell and d., 48:7
kingly D. keeps court, 430:3
kings did king to d., 795:4
kiss of d., 663:11
land of darkness and shadow of d., 14:6
land of the shadow of d., 26:30
last enemy is d., 44:25
last guerdon of d., 94:28
laugh myself to d., 229:31
lays icy hand on kings, 254:9
leaves body at d., 87:7
Life D. and that For Ever, 514:2
life or d. crave reality, 507:2
life perfected by d., 463:10
life shadow of d., 256:24, 568:1
life that which men call d., 71:3
life well used brings happy d., 141:1
like sleep steal on me, 428:2
like this, 466:6
limbs cold in d., 98:12
lively form of d., 164:12
looks gigantically, 478:6
love better after d., 463:18
love is strong as d., 26:3
Love posterior to D., 545:21
loves shining mark, 306:11
made d. his ladder, 161:27
makes equal high and low, 147:3
makes life live, 495:3
men at point of d., 184:15
men of d., 282:7
milder fate than tyranny, 65:10
Mister D., 739:13
more bitter than d., 24:23
mother of beauty, 686:18
mourned at birth not d., 314:6
naked in d. on unknown shore, 97:21
nativity chance or d., 191:4
neither fear nor long for d., 111:1
never taste of d. but once, 196:10
newspaper d., 570:18
no cure for d., 629:15

no God stronger than d., 568:19
no life by others' d., 178:17
no more d., 49:1
no trouble, 701:9
nor life nor angels, 43:12
not born for d., 437:13
not d. but dying is terrible, 322:14
not D. but Love, 463:15
not D. for I stood up, 545:6
not room for D., 509:2
not stop for D., 545:15
not the worst, 68:15
nothing call our own but d., 179:28
nothing to us, 84:8
now boast thee d., 224:13
now to D. devote, 268:3
O d. I will be thy plagues, 30:21
O D. in Life, 482:22
O D. thou comest, 843:16
O sane and sacred d., 520:15
odor of d., 775:13
of a dear friend, 182:11
of air, 721:16
of democracy, 755:9
of each day's life, 220:16
of endeavor birth of disgust, 580:8
of friends inspire us, 505:24
of hope and despair, 721:16
of one god death of all, 688:1
of the most noblest knights, 139:12
of water and fire, 721:17
old captain, 524:16
on else immortal us, 236:6
on his pale horse, 268:9
on life on d., 643:5
once dead, 228:5
one in life and d. are we, 564:15
one of few things done easily, 831:4
one of things Nature wills, 116:2
one studied in his d., 219:8
one talent d. to hide, 263:12
or dreamful ease, 480:20
our souls survive d., 104:*n*6
out of jaws of d., 155:*n*3
owe God a d., 192:2
pale horse and on him was D., 48:20
pang preceding d., 340:12
part and parcel of life, 676:6
parting foretaste of d., 425:15
past so he waited, 493:17
people given over to d., 93:21
play to you d. to us, 274:24
posterior to D., 545:21
precious is the d. of his saints, 19:24
preferred d. before slavery, 109:20
protracting life not deduct from d., 93:14
proud d., 207:16
proud to take us, 224:2
quick even in d., 159:9
quiet us in d. so noble, 269:15
read d. of Little Nell, 606:4
reared himself throne, 478:4
reasonable moderator D., 255:19
redeem them from d., 30:21
remain until d. do part, 610:1
remembered kisses after d., 482:22
rendezvous with D., 724:17
report of my d. an exaggeration, 562:13

Deceitful, damnable d. woman, 293:20
    favor is d., 23:31
    heart is d., 29:18
    kisses of enemy d., 23:11
Deceitfully, who hath not sworn d., 16:19
Deceitfulness of riches, 36:5
Deceits, from all d. of the world, 50:12
Deceive, dreams at length d. 'em, 297:4
    falsehood no longer d., 360:7
    not thy physician, 251:8
    pleasure to d. deceiver, 276:13
    practice to d., 396:23
    we d. ourselves, 47:37, 331:9
Deceived, be not d., 45:24
    good sense in country not d., 360:4
    more ignominious to mistrust than be d., 273:15
    the mother of mankind, 263:22
    true way to be d., 273:21
    world wants to be d., 141:15
Deceiver, gay d., 384:2
    man dupe d. decay, 428:13
    man's d. never mine, 619:20
    pleasure to deceive d., 276:13
Deceivers, men were d. ever, 194:25
Deceives, everything that d. enchants, 77:7
    nature never d. us, 331:9
    with whispering ambitions, 718:3
Deceiveth, serpent d. whole world, 48:29
Deceiving, appearances often are d., 60:8
December, brief D. day, 468:17
    from May to D., 716:1
    in heart cold D., 844:9
    in the bleak D., 479:1
    July's day short as D., 228:13
    love you in D., 583:7
    1910 human character changed, 699:15
    seek roses in D., 419:16
    wallow naked in D. snow, 179:6
    when they wed, 199:29
    yesterday D. 7, 1941, 698:17
Decembers, fifteen wild D., 508:20
Decency, no sense of d. sir, 730:18
    placed d. above courage, 627:16
    want of d. want of sense, 287:21
Decent and manly examination, 404:12
    docent doesn't doze, 749:9
    doing the d. thing, 834:2
    easy men, 353:15
    fall cloths over high income, 792:15
    provision for poor, 327:9
    respect to opinions, 357:2
Decently and in order, 44:22
Deception, lying is d. not words, 517:6
    military operation involves d., 83:3
Deceptive, masterpieces less d. than life, 657:10
Decide, comes moment to d., 514:12
    laws conflict courts d., 371:1
    reason can d. nothing here, 279:23
    wise men speak fools d., 57:18
Decided, matter d. considered true, 124:21
    on what they will not do, 82:6
    only to be undecided, 665:12
    to live forever, 812:8
Decides, doctors differ who d., 310:*n*1
Deciding not to be bitch, 754:2
Deciphered, stones that cannot be d., 721:5

Decision by majorities expedient, 472:9
    heroic d. not from cowards, 726:9
    once a d. made, 705:7
    valley of d., 30:23
    woman's d. to terminate pregnancy, 778:2
Decisions, careful resolutions unerring d., 112:13
    great d. of life, 675:4
    more of instincts than will, 675:4
    on Vietnam, 798:1
    political d. under pressure, 631:19
Decisive, performed rites simple and d., 816:18
    struggle goes on, 752:8
Deck, boy stood on burning d., 432:1
    of cards, 704:*n*2
    of cards hierarchies, 731:3
    walk d. my Captain lies, 520:19
Decked, bride-bed to have d., 206:30
    crown not d. with diamonds, 172:30
    lordly darkness d. in filth, 807:4
Decks, holystone d., 502:16
    turtle 'twixt plated d., 763:6
Declamation, New World favorable to d., 612:11
    roared Passion slept, 324:1
Declaration, for support of this d., 357:4
    make real D. of Independence, 674:7
Declare, day shall d. it, 43:36
    fishes shall d. unto thee, 14:11
    heavens d. glory of God, 16:10
    if thou hast understanding, 15:5
    older men d. war, 672:4
Decline and fall of Rome, 354:4
    of belief, 575:8
    to accept end of man, 748:20
    to buy repentance, 81:18
Declined election some years ago, 708:5
    into vale of years, 214:3
    star of fate d., 422:25
Declines, glow of early thought d., 422:16
Declineth, shadow when it d., 19:17
Declining, without d. West, 233:12
Déclose, la rose qui avoit d., 151:*n*2
Decompose, not yet been able to d., 359:16
Decomposing in eternity of print, 700:2
Decorum, dulce et d. est, 99:*n*18
Découvrir saint Pierre pour couvrir saint Paul, 148:*n*5
Decoyed into our condition, 288:14
Decreasing leg increasing belly, 191:16
Decree, God and man d., 619:13
    stately pleasure dome d., 401:13
    temper leaps over cold d., 187:28
Decreed, my own soul has d., 436:2
Decrees of farseeing benevolence, 523:4
Decrepit age tied to me, 640:3
    childhood manhood and d. age, 249:13
Decrepitude, bodily d. wisdom, 641:17
Dedde, mie love ys d., 368:10
Dedicate, we cannot d., 476:7
Dedicated here to unfinished work, 476:7
    nation so d., 476:7
    to babs, 680:3
    to great task remaining, 476:7
    to proposition men equal, 476:7
Dedication, were we men of d., 799:6
Deduced, not d. from phenomena, 290:26

Dee, diddle we take it is d., 569:17
    lived on River D., 352:5
    sands of D., 513:21
Deed, attempt and not the d., 220:13
    better day better d., 243:6
    by thought word and d., 50:18
    do a d. without God's knowledge, 65:26
    everything glory nothing, 365:18
    foul d. which she plotted, 55:5
    good d. in naughty world, 190:8
    him who has done d. to suffer, 65:16
    horrid d. in every eye, 219:18
    is d. really done for Heaven, 670:6
    look for d. soul performed, 122:16
    makes no noise over good d., 115:21
    nameless d., 384:15
    no evil d. live on, 580:3
    no good d. goes unpunished, 851:8
    of dreadful note, 221:6
    right d. wrong reason, 720:5
    so I may do d., 436:2
    unsung noblest d. will die, 66:11
    whereat valor will weep, 225:4
    without a name, 221:25
    word shadow of d., 72:15
Deed's, matchless d. achieved, 338:2
Deeds, a god has given d. of war, 53:13
    bright gleam of noble d., 66:8
    die however nobly done, 161:22
    evil d. do not prosper, 54:27
    foul d. will rise, 201:21
    fruitful of golden d., 265:26
    gentil that dooth gentil d., 136:23
    gentle mind by gentle d., 161:17
    great d. wrought at great risks, 71:23
    how many are your d., 4:11
    ill d. doubled with evil word, 174:36
    like poison weeds, 605:23
    looks quite through d. of men, 195:23
    man of words not d., 856:12
    man witness unto his d., 122:18
    matter for virtuous d., 165:8
    means to do ill d., 178:20
    minutiae of d. and passions, 521:14
    names d. legends events, 438:20
    noise of tongues and d., 480:7
    not let d. belie words, 118:11
    pinions of great d., 364:8
    pryvee to do gentil d., 136:22
    render the d. of mercy, 189:19
    sager sort our d. reprove, 231:21
    speaker of words and doer of d., 53:6
    thing that ends other d., 224:3
    unlucky d. relate, 215:13
    war and d. of carnage, 520:13
    who aim at great d. must suffer, 90:5
    whosoever performs good d., 122:4
    words are no d., 230:29
    words are women d. men, 252:7
    words have longer life than d., 66:5
Deef, justice blind d. an' dumb, 646:3
Deem himself god or beast, 311:9
    this which you d. of no moment, 78:16
Deep and crisp and even, 511:9
    and dark blue ocean, 421:26
    and dreamless sleep, 558:5
    and gloomy wood, 391:3
    as first love, 482:22
    attention like d. harmony, 179:8

Dell, farmer in the d., 861:4
De-lovely, delightful delicious d., 732:14
Delta, Mississippi D., 837:13
Delude, television used to distract d., 779:18
Deluding, vain d. Joys, 259:22
Deluge, after us the d., 337:6
   pedigree far back as D., 490:19
Déluge, après nous le d., 337:6
Delusion, Solon was under a d., 77:17
   to the philanthropist, 557:16
   trial by jury a d., 410:21
Delusive, most d. of passions, 610:1
Delved, Adam d., 843:8
Delves parallels in beauty's brow, 226:17
Delving in patient industry, 576:13
Demand for products, 387:2
   heroes created by popular d., 729:5
   superfluous to d. time of day, 184:23
   supply of truth in excess of d., 508:14
Demanded an image, 709:2
Demands, heavenly race d. zeal, 318:12
   rebellion makes upon us, 790:3
Demd damp moist unpleasant body, 496:23
   dowager's a d. outline, 496:22
   horrid grind, 496:26
Demean themselves as good citizens, 350:6
Demented, not one is d., 519:16
Demesne, deep-browed Homer ruled as d.,
   435:19
Demeter, goddess D. or Earth, 70:11
Demi-Atlas of this earth, 223:6
Demi-paradise, this other Eden d., 179:12
Demirep that loves, 493:9
Demitasses, villainous d., 613:3
Demmed elusive Pimpernel, 636:3
Demnition bowwows, 496:27
Democracies cannot dispense with hypocrisy,
   716:13
   security to d. against despots, 366:n6
Democracy, American d. discover middle
   ground, 802:13
   arises out of notion, 81:2
   arsenal of d., 698:14
   associate d. with freedom of action,
   616:12
   charming form of government, 77:21
   constitution named a d., 73:18
   cycle d. built on, 787:16
   death of d., 755:9
   direct self-government, 488:n5
   egg of d., 515:21
   freedom and d., 787:10
   government of people, 488:13
   if liberty and equality found in d., 80:30
   is a great word, 521:12
   more unsafe than ever, 628:13
   my idea of d., 474:11
   neither despotism nor d., 370:10
   passes into despotism, 77:22
   recurrent suspicion, 756:14
   self-canceling business, 434:7
   shuts past opens future, 463:3
   socialist d. may be sham, 703:5
   Switzerland years of d. and peace, 797:4
   true d. never existed, 331:2
   two cheers for D., 684:6
   United States not proclaimed d., 664:3
   whatever differs from this no d., 474:11
   world safe for d., 611:8

Democrat, no person called self d., 664:3
Democratic, basis of d. state, 81:6
   cherished ideal of d. society, 803:15
   created new d. world, 433:9
   establishes d. regime kill sons of Brutus,
   143:5
   nations not care for past, 463:3
   party ain't on speakin' terms, 646:1
   Party like mule, 548:8
   Party's candidate for President, 799:5
   public men, 610:11
   secrecy and d. government, 705:14
   society like ours, 695:9
   thou great d. God, 516:11
   utter word D., 518:12
Democrats, afford a few D., 757:3
   all saloon keepers D., 489:11
   raises corn and D., 604:5
Demon, when your D. in charge, 636:2
   you have roused, 474:12
Demoniac frenzy, 268:10
Demonic, semihuman and d., 675:9
Demonisms, subtle d. of life, 516:14
Demon-lover, wailing for her d., 401:14
Demons down under sea, 479:19
Demonstrandum, quod erat d., 84:16
Demonstrating careless desolation, 199:17
Demonstration, full monstrous d., 586:2
   truly marvellous d., 255:1
Demonstrative or persuasive type, 653:17
Demoralizing, human slavery d., 605:13
   nothing so d. as money, 67:16
Demur you're dangerous, 545:2
Demure, sober steadfast and d., 259:24
Demurrer, no bail no d., 367:20
Den, beard lion in his d., 396:22
   cast Daniel into the d. of lions, 30:8
   cockatrice' d., 26:34
   living in underground d., 77:14
   made it a d. of thieves, 36:39
   seven sleepers' d., 233:10
Dendid, when D. created all things, 853:1
Denial vain and coy excuse, 261:15
Denied, call may not be d., 681:1
   exact day-labor light d., 263:13
   justice delayed justice d., 472:15
   no other was d., 545:10
   Peter d. Lord, 296:10
   the faith, 46:22
   this only d. to God, 75:27
Denies, court a mistress she d. you, 237:23
   heaven to gaudy day d., 422:13
   Spirit that always d., 365:7
   voyager further sailing, 70:5
Denieth, antichrist d. the Father, 47:39
Denmark, ne'er villain in D., 202:25
   something rotten in D., 202:11
   sure it may be so in D., 202:24
Denoted foregone conclusion, 214:13
Denounces, if man publicly d. poetry, 830:15
Denouncing someone or something else,
   691:1
Dens and fastnesses of barbarism, 534:9
   lay them down in their d., 19:11
Denunciation in place of evidence, 660:8
Deny, easier to believe than d., 566:20
   me thrice, 37:35
   oh was no d., 373:8
   participation of freedom, 344:16

Deny (continued)
   poor heart would fain d., 222:11
   themselves nothing, 490:5
   thy father, 183:2
   us for our good, 223:11
Denying, to allure by d., 504:5
Deo erexit Voltaire, 347:n1
   gloria in excelsis D., 49:11
Deos fortioribus adesse, 113:n16
Depart, ah she doth d., 373:8
   be off, 90:n4
   captains and kings d., 635:2
   come like shadows so d., 221:29
   from evil, 17:2
   I d. from materials, 521:9
   I say let us have done, 254:13
   loth to d., 297:2
   ready to d., 408:11
   servant d. in peace, 39:5
   this vale, 691:4
   to be to do to d., 572:7
   to d. from evil is understanding, 14:36
   to serve better, 556:2
   when old he will not d. from it, 22:25
   when ye d. shake off dust, 35:26
Departed, all but he d., 412:8
   ghosts of d. quantities, 306:16
   glory is d. from Israel, 11:19
   he has d. withdrawn gone away, 90:9
   his spirit is d., 33:6
   into their own country, 33:19
   minds me o' d. joys, 378:21
   never to return, 378:21
   rule over the d. dead, 55:9
   sacred to d. spirit, 123:21
   souls d. shadows of living, 256:24
Departeth, heart d. from the Lord, 29:17
Departing, knolling d. friend, 191:8
   leave behind us, 466:2
Department, duty of judicial d., 371:1
   fair sex your d., 617:14
   that's not my d., 820:14
Departure beyond borders death, 730:11
   hour of d. has arrived, 76:14
   is taken for misery, 31:16
Depend, all rest on us d., 520:6
Depended, always d. on kindness of strangers,
   787:17
Dependence, in marriage d. mutual, 432:6
   of art on felt life, 585:9
   upon militia, 350:2
   women educated for d., 382:23
Dependency, old d. of day and night,
   686:19
Dependent, mortals live d. upon another,
   93:2
Depends, happiness d. as Nature shows,
   347:5
   on what the meaning is, 840:3
   so much d. upon, 703:10
Deplore, though still I do d., 236:15
Deploring, damsel lay d., 306:21
Deportment, model of D., 498:22
Depose my state but not my griefs, 180:10
Deposed, ghosts they have d., 179:28
   some have been d., 179:28
Deposit for substantial virtue, 357:10
   little cell by cell, 573:5
Deposited, near this spot d., 419:10

Devil (continued)
　　showed him kingdoms, 39:9
　　speak truth and shame D., 146:14
　　sugar o'er d. himself, 203:32
　　take her, 269:21
　　take the hindmost, 245:10
　　territory held by the d., 816:5
　　thou wast made d., 242:16
　　to pay, 157:19
　　walketh about as roaring lion, 47:33
　　what the d. was he doing in that galley, 278:21
　　whispered behind leaves, 633:15
　　why d. have all good tunes, 362:6
　　wi' usquebae face the d., 379:19
　　would build chapel, 144:14
　　your father the d., 41:12
Devil-and-all to pay, 157:19
Devilish and damned tobacco, 241:14
　　sly, 497:24
　　this wisdom is d., 47:18
Devil's, got over D. back, 243:8
　　true poet and of D. party, 372:13
　　who cleft the D. foot, 233:13
Devils, as many d. in Worms as tiles, 144:19
　　being offended, 213:8
　　fight like d., 193:10
　　in twists of road, 658:9
　　more d. than hell hold, 182:3
　　not so black as painted, 164:16
　　seven and seventy d., 658:9
　　to ourselves, 208:17
　　wrote at liberty when of D., 372:13
Devils', one more d.-triumph, 491:23
Devise, for thirty pence my death d., 250:5
　　laws for blood, 187:28
　　wit write pen, 176:26
Devised to keep strong in awe, 174:22
　　who d. torment, 722:2
Deviseth, man's heart d. his way, 22:1
Devoid of sense and motion, 265:4
Devote himself to life, 677:15
　　now to Death d., 268:3
Devotion, affecting charity and d., 82:26
　　farewel my bok and my d., 134:13
　　ignorance mother of d., 242:1
　　increased d. to cause, 476:7
　　last full measure of d., 476:7
　　no concern with art, 557:17
　　of patriot soldier, 556:3
　　to something afar, 430:21
Devotion's visage, 203:32
Devotions, I beheld your d., 42:17
Devour, crocodiles shed tears when would d., 168:3
　　entire hostile army, 666:3
　　jaws of darkness do d. it, 180:20
　　seeking whom he may d., 47:33
　　which d. widows' houses, 38:29
Devoured, great ones d. the small, 225:n1
　　when I was a worm I d., 780:18
Devourer, time d. of all things, 105:20
Devouring, cormorant d. Time, 176:16
　　green azures, 603:10
　　of weak by strong, 523:12
Devours, animal which d. own kind, 357:13
　　death d. lovely things, 735:5

Devoutly to be wished, 203:33
Dew, as sun the morning d., 285:27
　　begotten drops of d., 15:9
　　bespangling herb and tree, 248:16
　　breeze dried the d., 670:11
　　Daffodil doth of D., 545:16
　　Debauchee of D., 544:8
　　fearfully o'ertrip the d., 190:4
　　foggy foggy d., 847:17
　　ghastly d., 481:23
　　gold and bramble d., 599:15
　　honey-heavy d. of slumber, 196:5
　　I D. not think we D., 580:2
　　into a sea of d., 597:5
　　like d. on mountain, 397:9
　　liquid d. of youth, 201:22
　　of thy birth, 161:n3
　　of yon high eastern hill, 200:23
　　of youth, 19:18, 201:22
　　pour sweet d. on his tongue, 56:4
　　smell d. and rain, 250:22
　　thaw and resolve into a d., 201:1
　　which in sleep fallen on you, 429:14
　　will rust them, 212:22
　　womb of morning d., 161:6
Dewdrop, lingering d., 395:20
　　starlight and d., 539:4
Dewdrops, seek some d. here, 181:4
　　with showers and d. wet, 547:16
Dewey feel discouraged, 580:2
　　was the morning, 580:2
Dew-pearled, hillside's d., 491:2
Dews, fresh d. of night, 261:16
　　of evening shun, 315:13
　　silence fall like d., 710:5
Dewy, from noon to d. eve, 264:24
　　morn to dewy night, 556:11
　　shakes his d. wings, 257:16
Dexterous, acute inquisitive d., 344:10
Dhamma, hold fast to d. as a lamp, 66:20
Dhrink is nicissry evil, 646:22
Dhry, wet eye d. heart, 646:9
Diable, noir comme le d., 369:n2
　　que d. allait-il faire dans cette galère, 278:n5
　　s'est fait femme, 451:n1
Diadems and fagots, 453:18
Diagrams, charts d. to add divide measure, 520:8
　　in midst of d. and equations, 683:6
Dial, drew d. from his poke, 198:15
　　laugh an hour by his d., 198:17
　　true as d. to sun, 271:27
Dialect, Babylonish d., 270:20
　　purify d. of tribe, 722:1
Dialogue, wooden d. and sound, 207:28
Dial's, many lines in d. center, 192:22
Dials signs of leaping houses, 184:23
Diamond cut diamond, 246:3
　　done on a d., 806:6
　　immortal d. is immortal d., 588:6
　　in the sky, 414:5
　　lasts forever, 737:12
　　O D. thou little knowest the mischief done, 291:7
　　point of a d., 29:16
　　rough d., 314:25
　　sixty d. minutes, 441:12
　　spots of d. form, 348:6

Diamonds, crown not decked with d., 172:30
　　girl's best friend, 758:14
　　goodness what beautiful d., 736:n1
　　graven with d. in letters plain, 150:3
　　sky sparkling with d., 622:13
Dian, Temple of D., 850:10
Diana of the Ephesians, 42:24
Diana's foresters, 184:24
Dian's, hangs on D. temple, 224:31
Diapason closing full in Man, 284:13
Diary, never travel without d., 605:11
Diastole, great systole and d. of history, 706:10
Dice, God plays d. with world, 683:14
　　human bones, 425:4
　　never abolish chance, 583:15
Dicers', false as d. oaths, 205:19
Dick, evil assailable in Moby D., 516:14
　　the shepherd blows his nail, 177:17
Dickens, not have any D. today, 766:5
　　what the d. his name is, 190:27
Dickinson, how wrong Emily D. was, 831:2
Dickon thy master bought and sold, 161:n4
Dick's, Dirty D., 776:5
Dickybird why do you sit, 565:20
Dictate direction work must take, 739:1
　　of common sense, 318:18
　　terms between old and new world, 370:11
Dictates of conscience, 353:4
Dictation, I merely did His d., 489:21
Dictator, German d., 665:15
Dictators ride on tigers, 665:13
Dictatorship as absolute as any other, 698:11
　　of Communist Party, 689:14
　　of proletariat, 510:7
　　of the proletariat, 654:6
　　revolution to establish the d., 765:17
　　Soviet Union run by d., 698:11
Dictatorships cannot dispense with cynicism, 716:13
Dictatress, might become d. of world, 385:18
Dictionaries and temporary poems, 324:18
　　are like watches, 326:1
　　writer of d., 324:19
Dictionary, English d. best reading, 654:16
Did, danced his d., 740:8
　　it for the best, 620:13
　　Lucrece swears he d. her wrong, 175:12
　　till we loved, 233:10
Diddle diddle, 858:2
　　diddle dumpling, 860:7
　　we take it is dee, 569:17
Didn't, sang his d., 740:8
Dido with willow in her hand, 190:4
Die a bachelor, 194:28
　　adoring God loving friends, 317:3
　　all die merrily, 186:26
　　all shall d., 191:38
　　all that live must d., 200:28
　　Americans d. go to Paris, 605:1
　　and endow college, 310:13
　　and go we know not where, 211:23
　　and rise the same, 234:6
　　anything but d. for Tobacco, 407:23
　　appetite sicken and d., 208:25
　　as cattle, 738:6
　　as much beauty as could d., 237:22
　　as my fathers died, 568:18

Die *(continued)*

as some have done, 761:17
at the top, 299:27
be ashamed to d., 441:13
beast and monk d., 684:3
beauty that must d., 438:16
beauty's rose never d., 225:27
because a woman's fair, 246:18
been in rooms we cannot d. in, 812:2
before grow old and d., 638:3
before I wake, 296:15
before our own eyes, 595:4
before we laugh, 292:17
begins to d. from birth, 331:3
being born to d., 168:22
better to suffer than d., 276:10
bit by bit, 794:5
books never d., 698:18
born but to d., 311:9
break faith with us who d., 660:10
broke d. in molding Sheridan, 422:20
but once to d., 249:11
but once to serve country, 301:24
by famine die by inches, 295:16
by feigned deaths to d., 234:10
cooped we live and d., 471:22
cowards d. many times, 196:10
curse God and d., 13:28
dead live the living d., 284:17
dead so long as refuse to d., 536:10
dead which d. in the Lord, 48:33
dear I, 234:13
death thou shalt d., 236:9
deeds d. however nobly done, 161:22
do or d., 243:4, 380:11, 741:1
dry death, 229:9
easy live quiet d., 397:27
ere their story d., 576:5
fifteen-year-old till parents d., 828:13
fighting in defense of his country, 53:19
flowers must d., 714:22
for friends or fatherland, 100:16
for love, 210:22
for my people my country, 549:3
for such a long time, 277:14
for the people, 41:21
friends who no longer know how to d.,
    759:9
frogs do not d. in sport, 85:4
gladly d., 599:6
go since I needs must d., 160:7
good d. early bad late, 295:6
good d. first, 395:4
greatly think or bravely d., 309:28
gross flesh sinks here to d., 180:17
Guards d. but never surrender, 389:11
hang there till tree d., 225:26
haven't instinct about when to d.,
    605:10
hazard of the d., 174:24
here in rage, 299:1
honorable to d. for one's country, 99:27
hope I d. before I get old, 839:8
hope to d. at my post, 654:14
how can man d. better, 448:14
how to d. harder lesson, 152:n8
I am sick I must d., 232:9
I d. but have possessed, 422:7
I d. hard, 350:13

Die *(continued)*

I shall not wholly d., 100:11
I to d. and you to live, 76:14
I will show you how to d., 152:n8
I'd like to d. like this, 787:2
if be with that which seek, 430:17
if I must d., 211:21
if I should d., 712:19
if it were now to d., 213:14
if man d. shall he live, 14:17
if we must d., 729:13
if you poison us do we not d., 188:31
I'll d. young, 814:16
in Adam all d., 44:24
in bed, 712:3
in evening without regret, 62:20
in last dike, 345:8
in music, 76:n6
in the last ditch, 293:10
in this faith I will live and d., 139:19
in what peace a Christian can d., 302:24
is cast, 92:1
it will d. when you do, 826:12
jealousy not d. with love, 274:6
joys will d., 845:1
king tomorrow shall d., 32:18
lads that d. in glory, 618:16
lest we d., 9:2
let friendship d., 329:11
let us d. like men, 469:7
lib and d. in Dixie, 503:2
like Douglas d., 337:15
live and d. for idea, 625:3
live and d. in Aristotle's works, 170:17
live and d. r-r-rich, 499:6
live and d. wi' Charlie, 390:12
live forever or d. in attempt, 812:8
live like a wretch and d. rich, 240:21
live through time or d. by suicide, 474:3
lives on hope d. fasting, 320:8
living know they shall d., 24:28
look about us and to d., 310:20
love me sure to d., 412:13
lovely things fade and d., 725:3
lucky to d. and I know it, 519:1
man can d. but once, 192:2
men d. fast enough, 293:16
men d. miserably every day, 703:15
more deaths than one must d., 605:21
music when soft voices d., 430:19
must d. at last, 234:10
names not born to d., 426:7
never know life till d., 495:3
no young man ever thinks he shall d.,
    410:14
nobly to d., 67:5
not d. before we have explained
    ourselves, 352:2
not poor death, 236:7
not quickened except it d., 44:27
not that I'm afraid to d., 831:3
not willingly let it d., 262:11
of nothing but rage to live, 310:6
of remedies, 278:26
of rose in aromatic pain, 311:6
of that roar, 513:9
oh do not d., 234:14
old soldiers never d., 690:12, 850:20
on feet not live on knees, 698:16

Die *(continued)*

on feet than live on knees, 679:7
on gallows or of pox, 340:8
on mine own sword, 222:19
only art is to d., 341:21
or let me d., 392:7
or rest at last, 429:23
pattern to live and d., 491:21
perceives it d. away, 393:12
pie in sky when you d., 684:10
poets d. of loneliness, 643:8
praise that will never d., 74:5
pray as if to d. tomorrow, 320:6
proudly, 624:n1
remember that we d. all, 32:14
reptiles carried thither d., 124:34
resolve to conquer or d., 349:14
reverences age d. with it, 433:4
rich, 328:16
root hog or d., 757:2
rose with maize to d., 753:16
sail until I d., 481:14
seem though I d. old, 642:4
seems rich to d., 437:12
shall never d., 41:19
shall Trelawny d., 458:5
sink or swim live or d., 414:12
soil good to d. for, 515:14
something he will d. for, 823:1
spirit d. of inanition, 530:8
Tamburlaine must d., 170:5
teach men to d., 152:9
teach us how to d., 421:9
tells me I must d., 439:1
the death of the righteous, 9:23
theirs but to do and d., 484:27
there smothered, 707:4
they seemed to d., 31:16
things that are born and d., 773:4
this'll be day that I d., 839:7
thou shalt surely d., 5:19
time to d., 24:6
to d. a debt we must discharge, 249:n1
to d. honorably greatest virtue, 62:5
to d. is gain, 45:32, 76:12
to d. to sleep, 203:33
to itself it live and d., 227:4
to leave to d. a little, 608:11
to make men free, 513:19
to save charges, 240:20
toddle home d. in bed, 712:3
trust that when we d., 555:21
unlamented let me d., 308:4
unsung noblest deed will d., 66:11
unto the Lord, 43:29
we about to d. salute you, 114:11
we d. and we live, 122:9
we d. only once, 277:14
we d. soon, 798:10
we must, 173:10
we must be free or d., 393:5
we must needs d., 12:6
we shall d. alone, 279:22
we will d. free men, 362:9
weep or she will d., 483:4
went abroad to d., 697:2
when beggars d., 196:9
when good men d., 70:23
when he shall d. cut him in stars, 183:32

Difficult *(continued)*
  even those d. to please, 253:22
  excellent things d. as rare, 287:17
  fascination of what's d., 638:2
  found d. left untried, 664:5
  in d. are friendly forces, 677:10
  judgment d., 73:10, 364:4
  living up to it d., 490:14
  nothing so d. but may be found, 88:17
  of things known most d., 638:8
  Olympian is a d. foe, 52:11
  people d. to govern, 59:13
  poetry d. to read, 494:26
  poets must be d., 722:13
  remark how d. to define, 825:2
  to believe people starving, 787:12
  to get the news from poems, 703:15
  to flee from reality, 702:23
  to lay aside long-cherished love, 94:25
  to speak, 345:7
  to write good life as to live one, 692:8
  too d. to think nobly, 331:17
  when you do it reluctantly, 89:1
Difficulties of any individual, 406:18
Difficulty and danger, 360:7
  daunted by no d., 490:23
  govern tongues with d., 287:1
  makes d. his first business, 62:26
Diffused knowledge immortalizes, 384:17
Diffuses, dissolves d. dissipates, 403:4
  numbness d. my senses, 99:1
Diffusion, increase and d. of knowledge,
    385:2
Dig deep trenches in beauty's field, 225:28
  forbear to d. dust enclosed here, 231:19
  grave and let me lie, 599:6
  I cannot d., 39:39
  I'll d. with it, 833:13
  them up again, 244:4
Digest, edible wholesome to d., 580:12
  inwardly d. the Scriptures, 51:4
  more beliefs than can d., 617:25
  no more than able to d., 299:5
  of anarchy, 345:10
  some writers cannot them d., 168:24
  something to d., 680:*n*3
Digested, few books to be d., 168:15
Digestion, give me good d. Lord, 680:*n*3
  god on side of best d., 680:10
  good d. wait on appetite, 221:10
  prove in d. sour, 179:2
  sleep from pure d. bred, 266:29
  with sound d. man may front much,
    433:15
Digestions, unquiet meals make ill d., 174:39
Digests experiences as digests meats, 589:16
Diggeth a pit, 23:8
Dight, storied windows richly d., 260:10
Dignified, anything but d. English, 668:13
  better go down d., 670:7
  vice by action d., 183:17
Dignitate, cum d. otium, 90:*n*8
Dignities, earthly d., 231:3
Dignity and worth of person, 705:15
  contrary to d. built paper-mill, 172:22
  human d., 839:12
  in effort of patriots, 351:3
  in tilling field, 610:20
  last vestige of human d., 755:10

Dignity *(continued)*
  leisure with d., 90:14
  Negroes find new sense of d., 823:6
  of high calling, 345:2
  of history, 304:21
  of truth lost with protesting, 237:17
  restores man to d., 629:20
  true d. of man, 629:10
  wear undeserved d., 188:27
Digression, began a lang d., 378:5
Digressions, eloquent d., 537:13
  sunshine of reading, 332:12
Dike, last d. of prevarication, 345:8
Dilemma, here lay the d., 713:6
  horns of my d., 332:24
Diligence, best of me is d., 215:32
  keep thy heart with all d., 21:2
  learning must be attended to with d.,
    362:4
  mother of good fortune, 158:26
  observe physician with same d., 236:16
  work out salvation with d., 66:22
Diligent dispensation of pleasure, 416:15
  in his business, 22:31
Diligently, teach them d. unto thy children,
    9:30
  they d. practice it, 59:4
Dillar, a d. a dollar, 860:20
Dim and joyless if not shared, 412:15
  behind d. unknown, 514:13
  forsake their temples d., 259:2
  in intense inane, 428:11
  on Bristol board, 786:3
  religious light, 260:10
  spot which men call earth, 260:12
  sun in d. eclipse, 264:18
  windows of the soul, 376:9
DiMaggio, where have you gone Joe D.,
    837:9
  worthy of great D., 755:3
Dim-discovered, ships d., 317:17
Dime, brother can you spare d., 751:15
Dimension, sickness enlarges d. of self,
    407:27
Dimensions, hath not a Jew d., 188:30
Dim-glimmering, moon d. through window-
    pane, 402:14
Diminish, joys with age d., 495:10
  some nations increase others d., 93:2
Diminished, force in Nature not d., 527:13
  hide your d. rays, 266:*n*1
  stars hide their d. heads, 266:2
  to her cock, 217:18
Diminishes, any man's death d. me, 236:19
  functional capacity, 362:7
Diminution of original sin, 525:2
  without increase or d., 404:8
Diminutives, lovely d., 780:12
Dimitri, Long live D. Ivanovich, 447:1
Dimmycratic party ain't on speakin' terms,
    646:1
Dimness, most experience sunk to d., 574:4
Din, cock with lively d., 259:13
  hear the merry d., 399:12
  of strife, 529:4
Dinah blow your horn, 848:1
Dine at journey's end, 638:18
  at ten sup at six, 451:18
  going to d. with men, 674:4

Dine *(continued)*
  hang that jurymen d., 309:10
  when Noah sat down to d., 664:16
  with some men, 674:4
Dined, I have d. today, 399:3
  on mince, 499:18
  upon cold meat, 288:16
  when Jefferson d. alone, 799:13
Diners-out from whom we guard spoons,
    448:2
Dines on following day, 553:1
Ding dong bell, 857:19
  hey d. a d. d., 200:5
Dinge, make sure not a d. boys, 746:1
Dinginess, country of d., 472:23
Dingledodies, danced like d., 810:2
Dining and dancing begin, 763:10
  while they thought of d., 343:2
Dinner, after d. is after d., 298:2
  among old soakers, 288:11
  better is a d. of herbs, 21:36
  go straight to d., 818:4
  good d. and feasting, 288:13
  his life d. wife, 446:13
  lubricates business, 362:12
  man always willing to come to d., 704:13
  much depends on d., 424:21
  nap after d. silver before d. golden, 542:9
  not a d. to ask a man to, 327:4
  revolution not same as inviting to d.,
    737:13
  that we expect our d., 338:13
  three hours' march to d., 410:13
  what gat ye to d., 854:11
  write with no d., 724:13
Dinner's, glasses' edge when d. done,
    493:6
Dinners, true Amphitryon gives d., 278:14
  visits his d. not him, 278:5
Dinosaur death-steps, 801:8
Diogenes, if not Alexander would be D., 83:9
  plucked a cock, 79:4
  struck father when son swore, 241:20
Diomede, this sodeyn D., 134:7
Dios te tenga en su mano, 862:24
Diplomacy is to do and say, 713:5
Diplomats, pens of d. not ruin, 356:11
Dipped into the future, 481:23
  Jonathan d. rod in honeycomb, 11:24
Dirck galloped, 492:2
Dire, beckoning shadows d., 260:24
  effects from civil discord, 302:2
  gorge of salt sea tide, 189:*n*1
  offense from amorous causes, 309:4
Direct and honest not safe, 214:12
  eminently plain and d., 529:21
  him where to look for it, 235:26
  leaving to d. themselves, 737:2
  lie d., 200:9
  relations with good joke, 664:9
  understanding to d., 360:9
Direction, advances in d. of dreams, 507:18
  chief source of d., 783:14
  dictate d. work must take, 739:1
  great thing is what d., 473:10
  in which education starts, 77:10
  new critical d., 824:16
  new d. of Time, 707:5
  of right line, 291:3

Direction *(continued)*
   which thou canst not see, 311:8
   with no d. home, 836:8
Directions, by indirections find d., 202:30
   rode off in all d., 651:9
Director, can be d. of opponent's fate, 83:6
Directs the storm, 301:12, 313:20
Direful spring of Grecian woes, 309:18
Direst, full of d. cruelty, 219:11
   shapes of death, 534:9
Dirge, by forms unseen d. sung, 336:16
   for most lovely dead, 478:8
   in marriage, 200:25
   of dying year, 429:2
Dirt, bequeath myself to d., 519:23
   breathing a small breath, 780:5
   eyes of you and me full of d., 740:18
   instead of d. and poison, 297:19
   loss of wealth loss of d., 147:2
   painted child of d., 312:8
   trod me in the very d., 820:6
Dirty, airing d. linen never masterpiece,
      828:1
   all d. and wet, 299:26
   British coaster, 681:5
   business wiretapping, 578:23
   Dick's and Sloppy Joe's, 776:5
   self-pitying d. sly, 743:18
   treat woman as d. joke, 830:7
   wash d. linen at home, 388:4
   work at crossroads, 848:12
Dirtying up your hands, 824:7
Dis, by gloomy D. was gathered, 266:8
Dis aliter visum, 97:n4
   manibus sacrum, 123:21
Disable benefits of your country, 199:25
Disabused, by himself abused or d., 311:9
Disaffection, nonconformity mark of d.,
      660:8
Disagree, doctors d., 310:12
Disagreeable, such a d. man, 565:6
Disagreements, scholarship record of d.,
      626:19
Disagrees, what agrees d., 64:10
Disappearance, law master after my d., 66:23
Disappeared, sun would have d., 618:2
Disappoint a Continent, 557:18
Disappointed in monkey, 562:15
   unhouseled d. unaneled, 202:19
   who expects nothing never d., 310:16
Disappointment, boredom and d., 764:13
   mathematics commence in d., 624:9
Disappointments, too familiar with d.,
      474:1
Disappoints, man appoints God d., 138:n4
Disapprove of what you say, 317:2
Disarmament is essential, 699:9
Disaster clouded Union cause, 556:3
   evil gains equivalent of d., 56:14
   exaltation from d. and ruin, 665:5
   loss is no d., 786:2
   no greater d. than greed, 59:6
   one way will end in d., 852:n3
   success like d., 783:10
   Triumph and D., 635:20
Disasters, day's d. in morning face, 342:8
   make guilty of our d., 215:29
   middle station fewest d., 295:7
   weary with d., 221:2

Disastrous beating of wings, 656:5
   born to d. end, 161:24
   spake of d. chances, 212:29
   twilight sheds, 264:18
Disbelief in great men, 434:16
   suspension of d., 403:7
Disbranch, sliver and d., 217:13
Discard knowledge, 82:28
   the old, 784:11
Discarded, welcome home d. faith, 178:23
Discern infinite passion, 492:14
   innocence of neighbors, 507:15
Discerner of the thoughts, 46:38
Discerning, gives genius better d., 342:17
   to a d. Eye, 545:2
Discharge, no d. in war, 24:26, 635:16
   to die a debt we must d., 249:n1
Discharged, debt d. through eternity, 364:16
   with greater ease, 249:9
Discharging less than tenth, 208:5
Disciple not above master, 35:29
   true teacher has no d., 444:14
Disciples, gave bread to d., 37:27
   masters ashamed to become d., 232:10
   threatening against d., 42:6
Discipline, age of d. began, 706:10
   care of d. is love, 31:20
   desire of d., 31:20
   Doric d. vain, 640:10
   organization and d. of war, 142:12
   soul of army, 349:12
   that I have established, 66:23
Disciplined by peace, 799:7
   inaction, 385:1
Disciplines, I know d. of wars, 193:6
Disclose, merits to d., 335:4
   not d. essence of phenomena, 706:1
Disclosed, before buttons be d., 201:22
Discobolus standeth face to wall, 558:9
Discomforts accompany my being blind,
      288:28
Discontent, but only want and d., 272:1
   want of self-reliance, 455:15
   waste nights in d., 161:23
   wealth and poverty parents of d., 77:9
   winter of our d., 173:28
   yields nothing but d., 343:19
Discontented, stirs of d. strife, 239:6
Discontentment, no greater guilt than d.,
      59:6
Discord, age of d. and strife, 172:3
   civil d., 302:2
   danger in d., 466:23
   cke d. doth sow, 151:16
   harmony in d., 101:5
   harmony not understood, 311:8
   in my Kosmis no feeva of d., 690:6
   music must investigate d., 111:11
   so musical a d., 181:28
   what d. follows, 207:26
Discordant, concordant is d., 64:10
   reconciles d. elements, 391:7
   reconciliation of d. qualities, 403:11
   wavering multitude, 191:6
Discourage and abolish tyranny and vice,
      350:14
Discouraged, Dewey feel d., 580:2
   lest they be d., 46:4
   never get d., 791:3

Discouragement, there's no d., 282:4
Discouraging, which more d. literature or
      chickens, 756:11
Discourse, bid me d., 173:18
   everybody's d. of death, 288:12
   excellent dumb d., 230:7
   good company good d., 252:28
   in novel phrases, 564:8
   made us with large d., 205:35
   of fools is irksome, 32:38
   of reason, 201:7
   of the elders, 32:15
   rather thy d. than play, 241:15
   showers of sweet d., 272:9
Discourteously, cast me off d., 843:22
Discover everybody's face but own, 297:18
   I had not lived, 506:28
   never d. land of nowadays, 652:14
   shocked to d. gambling, 782:10
   who could d. God, 107:14
   you are human as I, 802:6
Discovered a truly marvellous demonstration,
      255:1
   America d. accidentally, 715:6
   I was not God, 579:3
   plant whose virtues not d., 457:25
   poets philosophers d. unconscious, 608:7
   when d. not wanted, 715:6
   wicked man in bathroom cupboard,
      797:11
Discoverers among them as comets,
      322:20
   ill d. think there is no land, 166:8
   sea-d. to new worlds, 233:11
Discovereth, he d. deep things, 14:13
Discoveries, they were always making d.,
      336:3
Discovering, only two ways of d. truth,
      166:12
Discovers, flute in dying notes d., 284:16
   fresh perfection, 416:20
Discovery, abyss d. metamorphosis, 662:7
   errors portals of d., 696:12
   man's d. genitalia a weapon, 831:8
   mistaking paradox for d., 658:14
   new dish does more than d. of star, 370:5
   seeing what everybody seen nobody
      thought, 739:2
   terra firma of accomplished d., 682:6
Discredit what they do not excel in, 82:29
Discreditable, regrets d. act, 691:11
Discreet, too d. to run amuck, 312:13
Discreetest, virtuousest d. best, 267:22
Discreetly blot, 258:2
   entered into reverently d. advisedly, 51:7
Discretion, better part of valor d., 187:9
   dronkenesse sepulture of his d., 137:18
   fair woman without d., 21:18
   inform their d., 359:6
   should be thrown aside, 83:15
   to the young man knowledge and d.,
      20:22
Discriminate between important and
      negligible, 682:6
Discriminating, keen d. sight, 389:15
Discrimination, art d. and selection, 585:10
   nation has history of sex d., 774:5
   protest d. and slander, 674:8
   sophisticated modes of d., 695:5

Diversion or improvement of country, 302:5
    present life a d., 122:3
    walking 'tis a country d., 300:24
Diversity, brilliant d. spread like stars, 813:9
    universal quality is d., 153:12
    world safe for d., 800:3
Diverter of sadness, 252:25
Dives, I sit in one of the d., 775:13
Divest, deprive or d. posterity, 339:9
Divide and rule, 123:22
    biped class, 79:*n*2
    distinguish and d., 270:16
    et impera, 123:22
    great scramble and big d., 576:13
    Life from Death, 478:17
    mountains d. us, 444:10
    never d. upon opinion, 255:7
    not d. Sunday from week, 200:16
    sense from thought d., 283:*n*2
    therefore doth heaven d., 192:20
    thin partitions their bounds d., 283:8
    to d. is not to take away, 429:25
    two almost d. the kind, 310:7
    words d. and rend, 568:2
Divided an inheritance with him, 356:6
    duty, 212:33
    fair d. excellence, 177:27
    Gaul d. into three parts, 91:22
    have they not d. the prey, 10:35
    house d. against itself, 38:17, 474:9
    in death they were not d., 11:36
    mankind into parties, 366:19
    thy kingdom is d., 30:6
    we fall, 349:*n*5
Dividends, comfortable man with d., 467:13
Dividing asunder of soul and spirit, 46:38
    by d. we fall, 349:10
    lover and lover, 567:18
    your sweet d. throat, 253:14
Divine, against thy D. Majesty, 50:18
    all things by law d., 429:7
    and terrible radiance, 451:8
    ask a drink d., 238:2
    Athens d. city, 66:10
    bird of Zeus, 65:28
    comfortable words, 485:18
    Countenance D. shine forth, 375:17
    dead d. brother of all, 520:10
    despair, 482:21
    discovery of d. truths, 305:1
    drink d., 238:2
    event, 484:18
    fear of some d. powers, 242:2
    fellowship d., 436:10
    God the Father a school-d., 312:23
    good amiable or sweet, 268:3
    human face d., 265:25
    I myself more d., 487:11
    illusion, 532:4
    Love the human form d., 372:6
    love which greybeards call d., 173:17
    Majority, 544:15
    makes drudgery d., 251:1
    man d. as myself is dead, 520:13
    nature gave us country, 90:4
    no government by d. right, 404:11
    no voice d. the storm allayed, 348:22
    nor glimpse d., 313:25
    one who shares in the d., 107:14

Divine *(continued)*
    philosophy, 261:3
    Philosophy, 484:1
    reborn into highest forms which are d.,
      142:1
    relations with good joke, 664:9
    reliance on d. providence, 357:4
    revelation, 782:4
    Right D. of Kings, 313:22
    right of kings, 474:13
    sign indicates future, 72:7
    superhuman spiritual and d., 675:9
    tale of Troy d., 260:6
    Terror the human form d., 374:12
    thought thinks of itself, 80:7
    to forgive d., 308:23
    tobacco d. rare, 241:14
    truth is precious and d., 271:19
    what the form d., 408:4
    whatever poet writes with d. inspiration,
      72:12
Divinely, childish but d. beautiful, 381:13
    in the wrong, 305:18
    tall, 480:23
Divineness, Poesy participation of d., 166:7
Diviner air, 395:11
Divinest anguish, 508:21
    Madness d. Sense, 545:2
    Melancholy, 259:23
Divining, takes d. rod to find, 607:6
Divinities, new d. of his own, 76:10
Divinity, all the d. I understand, 158:11
    doth hedge a king, 206:10
    dry volumes of d., 356:21
    gives wealth even to wicked man, 61:11
    gossip a kind of d., 56:19
    in odd numbers, 191:4
    man own doctor of d., 598:3
    nature full of d., 505:9
    piece of d. in us, 256:7
    that shapes our ends, 207:5
    wingy mysteries in d., 255:10
Divisa, Gallia est omnis d. in partes tres,
    91:*n*10
Division, equal d. of unequal earnings,
    413:12
    is as bad, 843:21
    salvation not in d., 653:18
    same as creation, 82:22
    saw d. grow together, 207:18
Divisions, how many d. has Pope got, 686:4
Divorce, long d. of steel, 230:23
Divorced from eye and bone, 747:19
Divulge, I will never d. such things, 72:16
Dix, French word d. on reverse, 503:*n*1
Dixie comes from ten-dollar notes, 503:*n*1
    Land, 503:1
    lib and die in D., 503:2
Dixit, ipse d., 124:4
Dizziness, two people shaken by d., 794:7
Dizzy, how fearful and d., 217:18
    make a small boy d., 780:7
Do, a' is done that men can d., 379:2
    all the good you can, 319:1
    all we can d., 469:15
    anything you can d. I can d., 716:11
    as chapmen do, 208:15
    as I say not as I do, 245:28

Do *(continued)*
    as you would be done by, 314:19
    boys do, 593:17
    damned if you d., 409:14
    decided on what they will not d., 82:6
    don't d. it in street, 631:17
    each day two things disliked, 672:18
    go and d. likewise, 39:24
    great right do little wrong, 189:20
    his arms might d. what this has done,
      257:22
    how not to d. it, 498:26
    I dare d. all, 219:21
    I d. it more natural, 209:15
    if to d. as easy as to know, 187:27
    it after high Roman fashion, 224:2
    it as for thee, 250:24
    it with thy might, 24:29
    just as one pleases, 410:12
    justice, 3:10
    justly and love mercy, 30:28
    know not what they d., 40:19
    know what he ought to d., 129:7
    let's d. it, 813:2
    make it d. or d. without, 850:11
    nastiest thing in nicest way, 713:5
    never d. today what can put off, 535:6
    no one knows what he can d., 104:5
    noble things not dream, 514:2
    not as some pastors, 201:23
    not choose to run, 659:20
    not do thing they most do show, 227:3
    not do to others, 63:20
    not do what we want, 772:6
    not go gentle, 795:14
    not kill, 3:10
    not we wanderer await, 529:10
    not what we ought, 528:20
    nothing we d. wiped out, 581:11
    now I'll d. 't, 205:15
    O what men dare d., 194:37
    one must be to d., 364:26
    or die, 243:4, 380:11, 741:1
    other men for they do you, 497:1
    reckless what I d., 221:1
    seeks little thing to d., 492:24
    so much to d., 484:8, 602:13
    strong d. what they can, 74:7
    that thou doest d. quickly, 41:24
    the evil I d., 43:3
    the very best I can, 477:8
    theirs but to d. and die, 484:27
    they d. things we can't, 781:13
    they know not what they d., 40:19
    thing I was born to d., 169:7
    thing that ends other deeds, 224:3
    thing think you cannot, 704:10
    things I did not d., 641:10
    things worth the writing, 319:20
    this in remembrance, 40:15
    this one thing I d., 45:35
    this will never d., 395:*n*1
    thou but thine, 267:23
    to be to d. to d. without, 572:7
    to will and to d. his pleasure, 45:34
    two things is to do neither, 102:15
    unto others as would have others do,
      35:*n*1
    we d. what we can, 585:4

Do *(continued)*

well what not worth doing, 816:10
what country d. for you, 799:10
what d. about it, 535:14
what have you or I to d. with it, 332:5
what he may, 207:4
what I will with mine, 36:37
what man would d. exalts, 493:20
what manhood bids, 525:6
what then thou would'st, 269:11
what d. they d. there, 748:15
what thou wilt, 146:4
what will I d. when you fallen, 806:2
what you can d. for country, 799:10
what you d. still betters what is done, 228:28
what you have to do, 112:16
whatsoever thy hand findeth to d., 24:29
will to d., 397:6
without being commanded, 79:15
write what men d., 166:10
ye even so unto them, 35:5
you d. not d., 827:14

Doc, never play cards with man named D., 782:1
Docent, decent d., 749:9
Doch-an'-dorris, wee d., 654:3
Docile and omnipotent, 545:9
Doctor and Saint, 471:13
apple keeps d. away, 849:18
Diet Quiet Merryman, 299:19
every man own d. of divinity, 598:3
fee d. for nauseous draught, 285:19
Foster went to Gloucester, 860:19
kills more than general, 292:22
Livingstone I presume, 580:1
while runnin' for d., 704:7
Doctor's, outlived the d. pill, 307:16
Doctors, believe d. nothing wholesome, 548:4
best d. in the world, 299:19
if d. had more Christianity, 645:14
is all swabs, 598:15
we d. know hopeless case, 740:15
when d. disagree, 310:12
Doctrinaire logic, 734:3
Doctrine, all the winds of d., 263:5
Augustinian d. Calvinistic d., 571:12
every wind of d., 45:27
from women's eyes this d., 177:8
go for refuge to D., 67:1
hidden under strange verses, 130:20
involving pernicious consequences, 502:18
little difference in d., 327:10
not for d. but music, 308:16
of pathological generation, 527:18
of separate but equal, 733:1
of strenuous life, 614:12
or practice or interpretation, 115:30
prove their d. orthodox, 271:3
so illogical and dull, 701:15
that each one select, 429:25
yesterday fact today d., 360:2
Doctrines, makes d. plain and clear, 271:25
Document of barbarism, 733:5
Documents, historian wants d., 585:14
Dodger, artful D., 496:8
Dodo never had a chance, 703:16

Doe, came a fallow d., 854:6
life looking out from eyes of d., 735:10
Doer, speaker of words and d. of deeds, 53:6
Doers of the word, 47:13
talkers no good d., 174:1
Does, dogged as d. it, 504:3
he who can d., 609:23
sees it and d. it, 492:24
two reasons for what man d., 567:11
what man d. based not on knowledge, 727:1
Doeth, what thy right hand d., 34:10
whatsoever he d. shall prosper, 15:27
with youre owene thyng, 137:2
Doff it for shame, 178:4
Doffed, lightly d. hat, 630:3
Dog, absolutely unselfish friend is d., 548:7
Almighty gave d., 398:8
America friendly d. in small room, 727:9
and your little d. too, 786:9
better than his d., 481:18
beware of d., 123:13
bites man not news, 591:5
Boatswain a d., 419:10
Body my good bright d., 806:3
breed maggots in dead d., 203:6
broodin' over bein' a d., 592:6
cat d. pipe or two, 620:6
circumcised d., 215:14
commends himself to our favor, 613:8
cut-throat d., 188:8
did nothing in nighttime, 617:7
dies like a d., 468:16
door what d. on wrong side of, 763:15
drunken d. ragged head, 407:2
each time I walk the d., 829:9
every d. his day, 514:4
fall in grave like old d., 796:13
fetch poor d. a bone, 859:13
gingham d. went Bow-wow, 597:7
go buy a d., 548:*n*1
grim king's d., 69:12
hair of d. that bit us, 148:23
has his day, 452:5
hath a day, 148:22
heart to d. to tear, 635:19
hold-fast the only d., 192:29
hound d. cryin' all the time, 828:8
I am his Highness' d., 313:9
I'm a lean d. keen d., 732:4
in life firmest friend, 419:11
in the manger, 60:19
is thy servant a d., 13:2
it was that died, 341:19
jumps over lazy d., 849:7
kids loved the d., 790:18
let no d. bark, 187:20
libelous statements about d., 699:2
like d. hunts in dreams, 481:20
little d. laughed, 858:2
living d. better than dead lion, 24:28
man bites d., 591:5
might as well speculate, 470:12
mine enemy's d., 217:28
more ridiculous than a d., 469:5
offers drowning d. drink, 251:7
old d. barks backward, 670:8
old d. Tray, 408:*n*2
old wife old d. ready money, 319:19

Dog *(continued)*

only d. I know, 811:3
pick up starving d., 561:16
poor d. Tray, 408:15
rather be d. and bay the moon, 197:8
returneth to his vomit, 23:7
since I am a d. beware, 189:10
so poor he could not keep a d., 117:11
somebody threw dead d. down ravine, 783:9
starved at master's gate, 375:7
suspicious of buried bone, 585:10
this d. my d., 182:9
thou calledst me d., 189:10
to gain private ends, 341:18
to this d. praise, 463:13
tossed d. that worried cat, 861:15
toy d. covered with dust, 597:6
truth's a d. must to kennel, 216:1
turned to his own vomit, 47:35
until the last d. dies, 839:14
whose d. are you, 313:9
why should a d. have life, 218:7
will have his day, 207:4
wool of bat tongue of d., 221:21
Dogged as does it, 504:3
strength, 648:11
strong d. unenlightened, 530:12
Doggedly, set himself d. to it, 326:8
Doggerel, rym d., 137:20
Dogies, git along little d., 854:13
Doglike, on bended arm d., 65:3
Dogma, Bible literature not d., 629:12
Dogmatism, greater ignorance greater d., 595:7
puppyism its full growth, 458:7
Dog's, more deadly than mad d. tooth, 174:38
walking on hinder legs, 327:3
Dogs, all d. of Europe bark, 775:15
all the d. in town, 857:5
as many d. there be, 341:17
black d. bay at moon, 565:23
crowing of cocks and barking of d., 59:20
dancing d. and bears, 656:10
delight to bark and bite, 303:17
drink running at the Nile, 106:7
eat of crumbs, 36:21
fought d. killed cats, 491:16
hark d. do bark, 861:5
hates babies and d., 690:*n*1
hates children and d., 690:3
horizon of d., 751:7
leave Now for d. and apes, 492:22
let slip d. of war, 196:22
lies with d. riseth with fleas, 251:24
little d. and all, 217:5
loathe people who keep d., 596:9
mad d. and Englishmen, 753:6
more careful of breed of d., 292:2
more I admire my d., 426:12
not live as d. in manger, 699:5
rain cats and d., 846:3
shall eat Jezebel, 12:35
shame the gray head, 53:32
sleeping d. lie, 498:12
strained anxious lives d. lead, 745:12
straw d., 58:10

Doom (*continued*)
  regardless of their d., 333:20
  stretch out to crack of d., 221:30
Doomed conscripted ones, 712:4
  story ephemeral and d., 748:19
  to company with pain, 394:16
Dooms imagined for mighty dead, 436:9
  of love, 740:9
Doomsday, danced till d., 300:17
  is near, 186:26
Doomsters, purblind D., 574:13
Doon, banks and braes o' bonny D., 378:21
Dooney, play on fiddle in D., 637:13
Door, at its own stable d., 545:9
  at the d. of life, 568:13
  at this d. England stands sentry, 574:9
  before his cottage d., 405:4
  begins to crack, 856:13
  called push, 849:15
  came out by same d., 471:13
  clicked behind d., 342:10
  dark cloud at house's d., 856:1
  dream hidden d. of soul, 675:12
  ever-open d., 52:*n*2
  foot wear steps of his d., 32:12
  form from off d., 479:7
  golden d., 595:6
  handle of big front d., 563:17
  he who sits at d. of house, 862:18
  hell of good universe next d., 740:15
  I am the d., 41:15
  know grass beyond d., 542:7
  leave world by natural d., 602:8
  lion at the d., 856:13
  moonlit d., 662:10
  no d. is shut, 624:6
  no right to open d., 76:15
  nor so wide as church d., 183:28
  of all subtleties, 58:7
  Old Age coming bolt d., 123:3
  open d., 571:10
  open to remedy, 156:12
  opening of a D., 547:7
  opens and lets future in, 767:6
  over that same d. was writ, 161:11
  put in his hand by the hole of the d., 25:25
  rapping at chamber d., 478:20
  shut shut the d., 311:19
  sits on horse at hostess' d., 177:26
  stack or the barn d., 259:13
  stand at the d. and knock, 48:15
  steed stolen shut stable d., 148:6
  stone leaf unfound d., 760:3
  then shuts the D., 544:15
  three gypsies a-come to d., 846:22
  to which no Key, 471:15
  turn in d. once only, 719:2
  up to old inn-d., 692:2
  we never opened, 720:8
  what dog on wrong side of, 763:15
  what is wind in that d., 139:5
  whining of a d., 236:22
  wide as a church d., 183:28
  wolf from d., 141:18
  wolf is at the d., 623:8
  world make path to d., 454:*n*1
  younger generation knocking at d., 540:23

Doorkeeper in the house of my God, 18:17
Doors are widely flung, 780:2
  as yet shut upon me, 440:9
  be ye lift up ye everlasting d., 16:20
  for men to take their exits, 244:7
  if no d. or windows, 793:12
  in to the upper d., 453:12
  never darken threshold of d., 522:4
  of heaven adjacent identical, 701:11
  open d. of his face, 15:20
  open your living d., 267:16
  pictures out of d., 213:8
  shut d. against setting sun, 218:15
  shut in the streets, 25:7
  shut-in homes closed d., 651:1
  ten thousand several d., 244:7
  to let out life, 244:*n*1
  unscrew d. themselves from jambs, 519:9
  unscrew locks from d., 519:9
Doorway, Hylax barks in d., 95:26
Doorways, unjoined person who hung in d., 802:9
Dooryard, lilacs last in d. bloomed, 520:14
Dorian mood of flutes, 264:16
Doric discipline, 640:10
Dorking, Hens of D., 500:5
Dormons, veillons dormants et veillants d., 153:*n*5
Dorobo and animals live side by side, 853:4
Dorure en reste aux mains, 527:*n*1
Dose, anything man says take with d. of salts, 695:18
Dotages, plagues and d. of human kind, 240:22
Dote, I d. on myself, 519:11
  on his very absence, 187:33
  on scraps of learning d., 305:16
Dotes yet doubts, 213:34
Double debt to pay, 342:10
  double toil and trouble, 221:20
  ducats stolen by daughter, 188:24
  eyes upon d. string, 235:4
  for all her sins, 27:38
  Giant hit into d., 692:14
  grew like a d. cherry, 181:22
  halve rights d. duties, 425:12
  health to thee, 422:26
  helix structure, 822:2
  hypocrite reader my d., 524:7
  make assurance d. sure, 221:27
  of orient pearl a d. row, 232:6
  palter with us in d. sense, 222:22
  pleasure to deceive deceiver, 276:13
  single nature's d. name, 207:17
  snakes with d. tongue, 181:15
Double-consciousness peculiar sensation, 648:11
Doubled globe of dead, 795:4
Double-faced, fame if not d., 269:8
Double-lived in regions new, 438:9
Double-mouthed, fame is d., 269:8
Doubly benefits who gives quickly, 102:14
  dying, 396:11
  seconded with will and power, 207:27
Doubt, all best though oft d., 269:16
  doubter and d., 453:23
  explain till all men d., 313:23
  faith dead which does not d., 631:13

Doubt (*continued*)
  faith in honest d., 484:11
  frets d. maw-crammed beast, 494:8
  grows with knowledge, 366:2
  hesitation and pain, 491:24
  I d. it said Carpenter, 551:19
  I d. some foul play, 201:20
  I show you d., 493:10
  ignorant taught to d., 578:9
  in d. to act or rest, 311:9
  iron time of d., 528:16
  let us not pretend to d., 574:2
  loop to hang d. on, 214:10
  love curiosity freckles d., 738:11
  modest d. called beacon, 207:31
  more d. stronger faith, 493:10
  my days of endless d., 159:21
  never. I love, 203:3
  never stand to d., 248:15
  new philosophy calls all in d., 235:26
  night of d. and sorrow, 555:4
  no freedom of thought without d., 767:2
  no longer could I d. him true, 408:9
  no manner of d., 566:4
  one may prove a fool, 460:20
  our d. is our passion, 585:4
  read to d., 398:3
  road to resolution lies by d., 249:10
  sun and moon should d., 375:14
  sunnier side of d., 486:24
  teach child to d., 375:11
  that sun doth move, 203:3
  thou stars are fire, 203:3
  time d. of Rome, 424:7
  to be once in d., 213:36
  to d. everything or believe, 603:2
  true science teaches d., 631:2
  truth to be liar, 203:3
  when in d. tell truth, 561:22
  when in d. win trick, 303:1
  where d. let me sow faith, 128:5
  wherefore didst thou d., 36:17
Doubted, never d. clouds break, 495:15
Doubter and the doubt, 453:23
Doubtful disputations, 43:27
  dreams of dreams, 568:25
  in d. things liberty, 274:22
  nice hazard of d. hour, 186:21
  thinking about thing no longer d., 464:13
  thoughts, 189:7
Doubting Castle, 281:26
  dreaming dreams, 479:4
  liberty is possibility of d., 759:19
Doubtless come again with rejoicing, 20:3
  God never did, 253:5
Doubts are traitors, 211:2
  begin with certainties end in d., 166:4
  begin with d. end in certainties, 166:4
  dotes yet d., 213:34
  from what he sees, 375:14
  littlest d. are fear, 205:2
  more cruel than truths, 278:8
  saucy d. and fears, 221:9
Doughnut, face with d. complexion, 521:10
  optimist sees d., 679:5
Douglas, Adamses vote for D., 621:*n*1
  in his hall, 396:22
  like D. conquer, 337:15

Dust *(continued)*

    earth and grave and d., 160:14
    equal but in d., 237:3
    even while d. moves, 720:13
    excuse my d., 738:19
    forbear to dig d. enclosed here, 231:19
    formed man of d. of the ground, 5:16
    guilty of d. and sin, 251:2
    handful of d., 718:12
    hath closed Helen's eye, 232:9
    heap called history, 596:20
    heap of d. alone remains, 309:29
    hear her and beat, 485:12
    hearts dry as summer d., 395:4
    I shall lie in the d., 53:27
    if as they say some d., 670:3
    in air suspended, 721:16
    in the d. the cool tombs, 681:12
    into D. and under D., 471:12
    kicks d., 506:21
    lay mightily in whirl of d., 53:22
    lick the d., 18:10
    light in d. lies, 431:4
    like d. I'll rise, 820:6
    limns on water writes in d., 168:21
    love reachest but to d., 163:24
    make d. of all things, 256:16
    make d. our paper, 179:27
    maniac scattering d., 483:22
    marry my body to that d., 249:1
    mouth filled with d., 237:3
    mysteries beyond thy d., 279:9
    name not perish in d., 405:17
    noble d. of Alexander, 206:25
    not without d. and heat, 262:23
    of creeds outworn, 428:6
    of glittering grains, 856:3
    of snow, 669:12
    of systems and creeds, 480:7
    on marble pavement d. grows, 89:17
    pays us with age and d., 160:14
    plummets to d. of hope, 68:6
    pride that licks the d., 312:10
    proud and angry d., 619:12
    quaint honor turn to d., 277:2
    quintessence of d., 203:18
    rain in d. on her shoulders, 734:10
    return to the earth, 25:8
    returneth to d. again, 553:14
    seemed to be local d. cloud, 793:4
    shake off d. of your feet, 35:26
    shalt thou eat, 6:7
    silent d., 334:17
    small d. of the balance, 28:6
    so nigh grandeur to d., 453:16
    that is a little gilt, 208:13
    that is blown away, 31:19
    this quiet D., 545:18
    thou art to dust returneth, 465:17
    thou art unto dust return, 6:10
    thrown in my eyes, 670:3
    to dust, 51:14
    toy dog covered with d., 597:6
    unto d. return, 6:10
    valiant d., 194:15
    vile d. whence he sprung, 396:11
    was Gentlemen and Ladies, 545:18
    we are but d. and shadow, 100:14
    we too into D. descend, 471:12

Dust *(continued)*

    weighed me D. by D., 547:2
    what a d. I raise, 433:3
    what is pomp but earth and d., 173:10
    with d. is dark and dim, 392:*n*2
    write good in d., 144:2
    you are not worth the d., 217:12
    you've long been d., 85:14
Duster, tomorrow feather d., 662:18
Dustman, Golden D., 499:3
Dusty answer, 541:9
    cobweb-covered maimed, 558:9
    eat d. bread, 748:1
    grated to d. nothing, 208:7
    hit the d. trail, 684:8
    purlieus of law, 484:10
    thudding in his head, 809:11
    way to d. death, 222:16
Dutch, beat the D., 846:21
    donkey like horse translated into D., 356:15
    fault of the D., 389:18
Dutchman, see Flying D., 590:13
Dutchman's, icicle on D. beard, 210:7
Duties, brace ourselves to d., 666:2
    halve rights double d., 425:12
    live without d. obscene, 457:26
    property has d., 459:6
    to execute the laws, 567:3
Duty, astray from d. and interest, 350:10
    better one's own d., 87:4
    brave man inattentive to d., 386:11
    daily stage of d. run, 289:21
    dare do d. as we understand it, 475:1
    dead then my d. ended, 587:12
    discussing d. to God, 519:16
    divided d., 212:33
    do your d., 257:5
    doing d. unfitted one for anything else, 627:17
    done my d. and no more, 321:14
    essence of judicial d., 371:1
    expects every man will do d., 377:6
    fight required of d., 87:2
    gratifying d. done, 566:6
    knowledge of their d., 74:5
    laid on me a sinner, 446:18
    lies in what is near, 82:3
    limping with d., 82:27
    lively sense of filial d., 356:21
    love is then our d., 307:15
    my d. to obey orders, 536:3
    neatness a d., 318:23
    no concern with d. or truth, 480:1
    nor law nor d. bade fight, 638:17
    not to be silent, 539:10
    of being happy, 598:12
    of judicial department, 371:1
    of younger Negro artist, 762:8
    out of d. cheat others, 657:15
    performing public d., 532:19
    rule of joy and d. one, 577:20
    sacred d. to myself, 540:7
    seen d. and done it, 850:2
    some sense of d., 483:9
    stern daughter of voice of God, 394:9
    subject's d. is king's, 193:14
    such d. as subject owes, 176:2
    thank God I have done d., 377:7

Duty *(continued)*

    to love those who wrong him, 115:27
    to worship sun, 572:3
    transforms obedience into d., 330:21
    trespasses against d., 343:18
    we owe Creator, 353:4
    whispers low, 453:16
    whole d. of man, 25:10
    woke found life d., 504:20
Duty's, constabulary d. to be done, 564:5
    faithful child, 445:2
Dux femina facti, 96:*n*14
    O vitae philosophia d., 91:*n*1
    vitae animus est, 95:*n*7
Dwarf on shoulders of giant, 240:4
Dwarfed and abased below, 601:*n*3
Dwarfish thief, 222:8
    whole, 402:2
Dwell a weeping hermit, 336:16
    awake and sing ye that d. in dust, 27:18
    better to d. in a corner, 22:23
    critic d. on excellencies, 302:16
    House we d. in every day, 547:1
    I but in suburbs of your pleasure, 196:6
    I found a new place to d., 831:16
    in house of the Lord, 16:18
    in midst of people of unclean lips, 26:25
    in the tents of wickedness, 18:17
    in the uttermost parts of the sea, 20:13
    not to d. in constantly, 290:24
    not d. in temples, 280:13
    nothing ill d. in such a temple, 229:23
    on heights of mankind, 382:11
    peace and rest never d., 264:2
    shall I like a hermit d., 160:10
    such as d. in tents, 6:19
    to perdition there to d., 263:23
    together in unity, 20:10
    two souls d. in my breast, 365:6
    where Israfel, 478:3
    who shall d. in thy holy hill, 16:5
    with vilest worms to d., 226:23
    world and they that d. therein, 16:19
Dwelled, Abram d. in Canaan, 7:2
    Lot d. in the cities, 7:2
Dwellers by the sea, 602:15
    sur la branche, 649:13
Dwelleth in the secret place, 18:25
    not in temples, 42:18
Dwellin', fair maid d., 853:28
Dwelling, desert my d. place, 421:24
    much on right, 289:18
    of the blest, 97:28
    single soul d. in two bodies, 79:14
    there God is d. too, 372:7
    thou hast been our d. place, 18:20
    whose d. is light of suns, 391:4
Dwells, heart place devil d. in, 256:2
    in me d. no greatness, 486:2
    water d. in lowly places, 58:12
    wherever Roman conquers he d., 107:7
    with gods above, 208:6
Dwelt among untrodden ways, 391:18
    by the brook Cherith, 12:24
    child who d. upon tract, 395:5
    in marble halls, 441:9
    Judah and Israel d. safely, 12:13
    like star and d. apart, 393:4
    too long have d. on thee, 234:18

E

Eases, time e. all things, 68:8
Easier go through eye of needle, 36:34
  grass-blade's no e. than oak, 514:17
  nothing e. than rest, 570:18
  nothing e. than self-deceit, 81:16
  played on than pipe, 205:8
  swallowed than flap-dragon, 177:10
  sweats e. than I, 506:20
  Thirst blister e., 544:14
  to be critical than correct, 459:11
  to believe than deny, 566:20
  to get favor from Fortune, 103:3
  to get into enemy's toils, 61:8
  to make war than peace, 577:12
  to resist at beginning, 141:7
Easiest, move e. who learned to dance,
  308:18
Easily, by and by e. said, 205:11
  never have come back so e., 608:13
Easiness, lend a kind of e., 205:29
  property of e., 206:18
Easing, they call it e. Spring, 794:13
East and West will pinch heart, 734:15
  argument with e. wind, 515:15
  blasted with the e. wind, 7:26
  cherubims e. of the garden, 6:11
  fashionable e. seventies, 841:6
  fill his belly with e. wind, 14:18
  from e. to western Ind, 199:7
  gorgeous e. in fee, 393:1
  gorgeous E. with richest hand, 264:25
  he was my E., 775:6
  I can look E. End in face, 757:8
  i' the E. my pleasure lies, 223:17
  is East and West is San Francisco, 626:13
  is East and West is West, 632:19
  it is the e. Juliet the sun, 182:28
  of Suez, 633:14
  one flew e., 860:21
  one ship e. another west, 600:5
  or west Phoenix builds, 253:15
  Side West Side, 625:13
  somewheres e. of Suez, 633:14
  star in the e., 33:18
  tried to hustle the E., 633:2
  west south north, 448:13
  wicked Witch of the E., 606:14
  wind never blow, 252:23
  youth who from e. travel, 393:12
Easter, egg dear on E. Day, 861:17
Easter-day, no sun upon an E., 269:23
Eastern, blabbing e. scout, 260:22
  dew of yon high e. hill, 200:23
  dusk on e. horizon, 742:4
  no Soviet domination of E. Europe,
  790:16
  not by e. windows only, 512:10
  pulling blanket off e. sky, 855:14
  specter haunting e. Europe, 832:2
  wipe out E. instincts, 632:11
Easthampton, the 4:19 in E., 818:4
Eastward, a garden e. in Eden, 5:17
  I go only by force, 507:27
  to the sea, 633:12
Easy, abstinence e. to me, 326:4
  all zeal Mr. E., 427:6
  as e. to marry rich woman, 490:12
  as grass grows on weirs, 636:20
  bid me take love e., 636:19

Easy *(continued)*
  criticism e. art difficult, 305:14
  decent e. men, 353:15
  evil is e., 280:6
  false man does e., 220:27
  give throne would be e., 81:24
  how e. bush supposed a bear, 182:3
  if to do as e. as to know, 187:27
  it's not e. bein' green, 843:4
  jolly and e. in minds, 490:5
  leap to pluck bright honor, 185:9
  live quiet die, 397:27
  my yoke is e., 35:35
  nothing so e. but becomes difficult, 89:1
  poetry e. to write, 556:8
  Rabelais' e. chair, 313:15
  road to Hades e. to travel, 85:2
  smooth e. inoffensive down to Hell,
  85:*n*1
  so e. and so plain a stop, 191:6
  summertime and livin' e., 747:4
  there life is supremely e., 54:20
  to blow and swallow not e., 86:16
  to go down into Hell, 97:23
  words are e. like the wind, 239:3
  writing's curst hard reading, 368:6
  young and e., 795:8
Eat and keep going, 833:9
  bread in sweat of thy face, 6:10
  bread without scarceness, 10:3
  cake and have it, 149:16
  Cannibals that each other e., 212:31
  cannot e. but little meat, 151:9
  cones under his pines, 668:19
  dare to e. a peach, 717:16
  did e. and were filled, 36:14
  dogs shall e. Jezebel, 12:35
  don't e. your heart, 60:3
  drink be merry, 24:27, 39:28
  drink for tomorrow we die, 27:10
  dust shalt thou e., 6:7
  dusty bread, 748:1
  eat me soul, 292:11
  enough to e. and wear, 620:6
  fine women e. crazy salad, 639:10
  frogs e. butterflies, 687:3
  great ones e. up little ones, 225:9
  he hath not e. paper, 176:34
  his pleasant fruits, 25:24
  I earn that I e., 199:6
  I e. and e. I swear, 193:23
  I e. the air, 204:19
  I e. what I see, 550:10
  I'll e. my head, 496:11
  in orchard enough to e., 307:21
  in the evening, 372:19
  it in haste, 8:18
  let them e. cake, 331:19
  like wolves fight like devils, 193:10
  men like air, 827:11
  Nebuchadnezzar did e. grass, 30:4
  neither e. it nor make flannel, 707:16
  never e. at place called Mom's, 782:1
  nevermore to e. again, 662:17
  no beans, 240:12
  no fat, 856:20
  no onions nor garlic, 182:2
  not to dullness, 321:5
  not to e. not for love, 454:2

Eat *(continued)*
  of fish that fed of worm, 205:33
  of the habitation, 188:2
  of the tree I did e., 6:6
  peck of salt with him, 843:14
  people who e. the earth, 770:10
  plant vineyards and e. the fruit, 28:37
  poor when anything to e., 79:*n*3
  so I did sit and e., 251:3
  some hae meat canna e., 380:7
  some s. I will not e., 740:4
  strive mightily e. as friends, 175:26
  take e. this is my body, 37:27, 44:15
  tell me what you e., 370:4
  that shall ye e., 9:10
  that they may live, 72:9
  the fat of the land, 7:33
  their flesh shall ye not e., 9:11
  they shall e. the flesh, 8:17
  thou shalt not e. of it, 5:19
  to e. thy heart, 161:24
  to e. with apple tart, 599:1
  to live and live to eat, 72:*n*3
  to live not live to eat, 278:13, 319:3
  up himself, 207:27
  wad e. that want it, 380:7
  we hae meat we can e., 380:7
  will not e. with you, 188:2
  worm that e. of a king, 205:33
Eaten a sour grape, 29:23
  crust e. in peace, 60:15
  God made and e., 492:8
  have we e. on insane root, 219:2
  I have e. the plums, 703:11
  me out of house and home, 191:27
  thee for a word, 177:10
  they'd e. every one, 552:7
  to death with rust, 191:20
  worms have e. them, 199:27
  your bread and salt, 632:7
Eater, great e. of beef, 209:3
  out of the e. came meat, 11:1
Eateth grass as an ox, 15:18
'Eathen, pore benighted 'e., 633:9
Eating air on promise of supply, 191:22
  appetite comes with e., 146:1
  appetite makes e. delight, 270:3
  bitter bread of banishment, 179:23
  bread and honey, 858:12
  cares, 259:20
  Christmas pie, 857:3
  curds and whey, 860:3
  drinking and breeding, 519:9
  drinking dung death, 720:16
  is a small good thing, 833:9
  poetry, 830:10
  produce of the land, 53:31
  proof of pudding in e., 157:21
  Son of man came e., 35:34
  whether breathing is e., 75:21
  while someone else is e., 775:12
  wise men know art of e., 370:3
  worn out with e. time, 283:5
Eats, believes he e. God, 333:12
  proud e. up himself, 208:1
  Revolution e. own children, 501:4
  seeking the food he e., 198:13
  she-wolf's young, 400:20
  soles offen shoes, 750:8

Elementary feelings permanently in race, 529:8
   said Holmes, 617:10
Elemented, things which e. it, 235:1
Element's, thy e. below, 216:11
Elements and angelic sprite, 236:3
   by term e. we mean, 359:16
   dismantle structures reduce e., 779:9
   essential provider of e., 530:8
   framed us of four e., 170:4
   government balance of natural e., 602:10
   heaven earth and all the e., 138:8
   I tax not you you e., 216:19
   least visible, 785:8
   reconciles discordant e., 391:7
   so mixed in him, 197:22
   something in us before e., 256:9
   weak and beggarly e., 45:18
Elephant, God invented giraffe e. cat, 693:12
   leans or stands, 250:14
   like e. roaming at will, 66:19
   Nature's great masterpiece an E., 236:2
   shot e. in my pajamas, 745:6
   stalls above like e., 801:6
   that practiced on fife, 553:6
   traveling through dense forest, 706:6
   tried to use telephant, 598:1
Elephant's, corn high as e. eye, 744:5
   faithful one hundred per cent, 769:7
Elephants endorsed with towers, 268:22
   kings ride e. over mountains, 788:4
   place e. for want of towns, 111:n5
   when e. fight grass suffers, 853:6
   women and e., 655:2
Elephone tried to use telephone, 598:1
Elevate condition of men, 475:10
   life by conscious endeavor, 506:27
Elevated, joy of e. thoughts, 391:4
Elevation and beauty, 532:9
   drink not to e., 321:5
   removal of hindrances to her e., 432:6
Eleven, possession e. points, 301:1
Elfin from green grass, 477:14
Elfland, horns of E., 482:20
Elginbrodde, here lie I Martin E., 536:8
Elgin's, stands in E. place, 487:10
Eli Eli lama sabachthani, 38:9
Elijah, mantle of E., 12:41
   the prophet, 31:4
   went up by a whirlwind, 12:39
Eliminated impossible, 616:16
Eliot, meet Mr. E., 720:1
Elisha took up mantle of Elijah, 12:41
Elite had capacity to bring tears, 827:3
   minority, 702:14
   power e. decide national events, 798:2
Elixir, bright e. peerless I had drunk, 438:20
Eliza made desperate retreat, 489:18
Elizabeth, from Jane to E., 406:7
   great E., 480:22
   Servant to Queen E., 162:17
Elizabeth-Jane Farfrae not told of my death, 575:6
Ell, give an inch take an e., 149:15
Ellen, wed fair E., 396:19
Elliptical billiard balls, 565:16
   Caribbean borne like e. basin, 826:6

Elm, expect pears from an e., 103:n12
   old as yonder e., 696:16
   round e. tree bole, 492:4
   tell me tell me e., 696:16
Elms, desire under the e., 724:1
   immemorial e., 483:8
Elocution, wherefore waste e., 566:5
Elongated-yellow-fruit school of writing, 755:11
Eloquence, army not halted by e., 502:12
   fill winepress of e., 118:28
   frothy e., 604:5
   gods do not give all men e., 54:26
   mother of arts and e., 268:25
   of Mr. Webster, 750:14
   silence more e., 489:1
   take e. wring neck, 591:3
   talking and e. not same, 238:19
   thou has inspired with, 126:4
   true e. takes no heed of, 279:13
Éloquence, prends l'é. tords-lui son cou, 591:n3
Eloquent but 'tis not true, 529:5
   digressions, 537:13
   epitaph for country, 629:8
   feeling and imagination make us e., 109:16
   just and mighty Death, 160:13
   pure and e. blood, 236:1
   what an e. manikin, 94:16
Else, leave all e. to the gods, 99:10
   think what e. to say, 580:n1
Elusive, The Vague and E., 58:16
Elves, make my small e. coats, 181:13
   whose little eyes glow, 248:11
Elysian, send you to E. plain, 54:20
Elysium as far as nearest Room, 547:7
   daughter of E., 381:8
   palpable E., 709:10
   what E. known, 438:10
Emanation, my e. far within, 374:15
Emancipates, everything that e. spirit, 366:9
Emancipating all nations, 361:12
Emancipation, African fight for e., 731:10
   of individual, 499:10
   of slavish part of mankind, 350:16
   of woman, 752:n2
Embalmed and treasured up to life, 262:22
   darkness, 437:10
Embalms, precedent e. principle, 459:10
Embark, firs cloaked as if to e., 594:16
Embarras des richesses, 316:n9
Embarrassment of riches, 316:25
   to my e. born in bed with lady, 678:13
Embassies, saris go by me from e., 793:7
Embattled farmers stood, 453:11
Embellish adventures, 355:8
Embellished, no part Nature has not e., 116:8
Ember, each separate dying e., 479:1
Embers, glowing e. through the room, 260:5
   O joy that in our e., 393:14
   of cities, 829:3
Emblem, shears and pastepot e., 653:17
Emblems of untimely graves, 348:6
   those things they were e. of, 643:1
Embodiment of everything excellent, 564:17
Embody the Law, 564:17
Emboldens, nothing e. sin as mercy, 218:17

Embosomed in the deep, 341:4
Embrace, arms take your last e., 184:17
   as to e. me she inclined, 263:18
   endure then pity then e., 311:10
   fatal e., 516:1
   is death, 743:21
   my dead mother's ghost, 55:2
   none do there e., 277:2
   Pole as Frenchman, 153:21
   possibilities I didn't e., 585:19
   principles or mistresses, 340:8
   ready to e. the strangers, 516:1
   rest that knows no care, 93:13
   simplicity, 58:17
   the new, 784:11
   time to e., 24:6
Embraced, ghost e. fled, 97:14
   summer dawn, 604:2
Embraces, break e., 775:7
   sorcery of hot e., 730:5
   your e. give life, 4:3
Embraves this morn, 272:17
Embroidered, heavens' e. cloths, 637:11
   loosened the e. girdle, 53:15
   speech like e. tapestries, 64:23
Embroideries, coat covered with e., 638:10
Embroil earth about fancied line, 289:18
Embryo, yesterday e. tomorrow ashes, 115:19
Embryos, bitter little e., 755:13
Emerald, cause or men of E. Isle, 369:7
   green as e., 399:17
Emeralds, road to the City of E., 606:15
Emergencies, government in e., 476:12
   great e. show resources, 581:3
Emerges ahead of accomplishments, 764:7
   path e. then closes, 645:11
   with verb in mouth, 561:4
Emetic, Ulysses somewhat e., 679:6
Emily set doors ajar and slam them, 672:13
Eminence, raised to that bad e., 264:25
Eminent, censure is tax for being e., 298:5
Eminently noble, 529:21
   plain and direct, 529:21
Emissions, until all evil e. had fled, 812:17
Emits a brighter ray, 340:13
Emmanuel, call his name E., 33:17
   O come O come E., 511:12
Emmet, Robert E. and Wolfe Tone, 638:7
Emotion, disembodied e. a nonentity, 582:5
   expressing e. in art, 722:9
   formula of that particular e., 722:9
   intellect is to e. as clothes, 625:8
   laughter has no greater foe than e., 616:4
   more than usual e., 403:11
   motion fact made e., 754:10
   no transforming without e., 675:13
   poetry escape from e., 722:8
   poetry express every e., 776:15
   recollected in tranquillity, 391:16
   source of becoming-conscious, 675:13
   undisciplined squads of e., 721:4
   weave e. thought sound, 446:12
Emotional, destitute of e. warmth, 582:4
   orgies, 628:12
   subtlety and toughness, 778:4
Emotions, foreign to art, 557:17
   from A to B, 738:17
   metaphysical brothel for e., 770:17

End *(continued)*

if e. brings me out, 477:8
in e. despondency and madness, 800:15
in my beginning is my e., 720:15
in my e. my beginning, 154:13, 721:6
in one purpose, 192:22
in the e. truth will conquer, 133:3
is bitter as wormwood, 21:3
is not yet, 37:6
is the renown, 210:29
journey's e., 215:11
journeys e. in lovers meeting, 209:13
justifying means by the e., 118:10
keep e. in view, 110:3
keeps e. from being hard, 670:7
knocks you with butt e., 343:8
last e. be like his, 9:23
latter e. of a fray, 186:29
laws e. tyranny begins, 323:6
let e. try the man, 191:28
let the e. be legitimate, 371:4
liberty as e. and means, 607:1
long weary day have e., 162:4
losses restored and sorrows e., 226:9
love hath an e., 568:16
made finer e. and went away, 192:27
make me to know mine e., 17:12
makes a swanlike e., 189:2
minutes hasten to their e., 226:16
must justify the means, 296:18
my wrath did e., 374:11
New York the e. of the world, 796:5
no e. in wandering mazes, 265:13
no e. of it the voiceless wailing, 721:9
no e. to withering, 721:9
no prospect of an e., 340:4
not e. to writing about Holocaust, 827:5
of every man's desire, 568:24
of exploring to arrive, 722:4
of fight tombstone white, 633:2
of journey too, 625:14
of life cancels bands, 186:16
of making many books there is no e., 25:10, 692:16
of perfect day, 625:14
of that man is peace, 17:8
of the beginning, 667:8
of the tunnel, 800:2
of the unending, 721:18
of the world, 38:13
of this day's business, 197:18
one must consider the e., 276:15
only when life comes to e., 65:8
pleasure the beginning and e., 84:9
pursue the unknown e., 578:17
quiet-colored e. of evening, 492:10
remember the e., 32:13
right true e. of love, 235:20
sans E., 471:12
served no private e., 310:15
sleep itself must e., 256:25
snow swept world e. to e., 730:7
some say world e. in fire, 669:11
something ere the e., 481:13
stay a while e. the sooner, 166:22
stick it out to e., 649:18
their words to the e. of the world, 16:11
there's an e. of May, 619:11
there's an e. on 't, 327:21

End *(continued)*

this is not the e., 667:8
this island fantasy, 756:16
till I e. my Song, 162:7
Time will one day e. it, 208:21
to all an e., 636:13
to beginnings of wars, 699:6
to make the e. most sweet, 178:33
to pause to make e., 481:10
to war, 699:6
true beginning of our e., 182:6
true lover therefore had good e., 139:9
truth to the e. of reckoning, 212:7
up somewhere else, 805:12
up with another, 841:10
we shall go on to e., 666:1
when e. of world comes, 672:7
where e. knows God, 762:7
where Sky touches Earth is E., 853:3
where you begun, 343:19
whole has beginning middle and e., 81:11
whose e. is destruction, 45:36
world without e., 49:25, 348:24
End-all, be-all and e., 219:16
Endanger, power to e. public liberty, 351:2
Endearing elegance of female friendship, 325:2
young charms, 411:12
Endearment, each fond e. tries, 342:6
Endeavor, achievement death of e., 580:8
by no e. can magnet, 564:11
disinterested e. to learn, 530:9
elevate life by conscious e., 506:27
in continual motion, 192:20
it were a vain e., 402:4
Endeavors to live life imagined, 507:18
Ended, God be praised Georges e., 674:*n*3
his cares now all e., 192:11
our revels now are e., 230:9
so e. Sicilian expedition, 74:9
with his body changed to light, 856:10
Endin, now sees de e., 748:10
Ending, all lovely things have e., 725:3
bad beginning makes bad e., 70:18
bread sauce of happy e., 585:5
hard beginning good e., 147:15
is despair, 230:17
O bitter e., 696:18
of interminable night, 721:18
Endings, beginnings and e. untidy, 647:6
lie has seven e., 853:9
Endless, humility is e., 720:19
in e. error hurled, 311:9
my days of e. doubt, 159:21
night, 248:18, 335:9
olives of e. age, 227:12
perpetual posterity, 409:12
pure and e. light, 279:5
regret or happiness, 595:2
road you tread, 619:8
summer days, 544:8
time an e. song, 637:7
whole vocation e. imitation, 393:13
Endlessly, cradle e. rocking, 520:7
owl is e. hungry, 831:15
Endorsed, elephants e. with towers, 268:22
Endow college or cat, 310:13
with all my goods I thee e., 51:19

Endowed by ruined millionaire, 721:2
by their creator, 357:2
Ends, all well that e. well, 148:4
all's well that e. well, 210:29
candle burns at both e., 735:2
come from e. of earth, 632:19
consult our private e., 274:*n*2
delays have dangerous e., 171:20
dog to gain private e., 341:18
filled with e. of worms, 736:3
formula for making e. meet, 694:18
game that never e., 747:16
his circuit unto the e. of it, 16:11
Law e. Tyranny begins, 286:7
man's glory most begins and e., 642:16
means requisite to e., 370:14
my story e. with freedom, 501:7
needless Alexandrine e. song, 308:17
of Being and ideal Grace, 463:17
of world come, 573:5
one e. other begins, 478:17
smile upon fingers' e., 192:27
strange eventful history, 198:25
thing that e. other deeds, 224:3
those who pursue many e., 782:3
thou aimest at, 231:7
violent delights have violent e., 183:24
watch that e. night, 304:7
way the world e., 719:7
which I believe to be evil, 712:5
with Revelations, 605:3
your family history e. with you, 78:18
Endurance and courage, 649:16
for one moment more, 591:10
Endure accent of coming Foot, 547:7
all deaths I could e., 268:1
all that human hearts e., 325:3
courage to e., 508:22
days go I e., 689:18
for ages to come, 371:3
greater than dare, 490:23
his name shall e. for ever, 18:11
if I e. you a little longer, 300:26
knows how to e. poverty, 100:16
man will not merely e., 748:21
men must e. their going, 217:32
misfortunes of others, 273:2
my heart, 55:23
my own despair, 296:6
Negroes will e., 748:12
neither evils nor cures, 102:10
no picture made to e., 709:9
not e. husband with beard, 194:13
not yet a breach, 235:2
nought e. but Mutability, 427:17
philosopher e. toothache, 195:7
privilege to help man e., 749:2
so long shall your honor e., 97:3
testing whether nation e., 476:7
then pity then embrace, 311:10
weeping may e. for a night, 16:26
what Malherbe writes will e., 164:5
youth's a stuff will not e., 209:14
Endured, moon hath her eclipse e., 227:12
much e. little enjoyed, 324:26
remembers all that he wrought and e., 55:14
something more dreadful, 55:23
sufferings of troops, 712:5

England *(continued)*
    knuckle-end of E., 398:14
    let not E. forget precedence, 262:16
    light candle in E., 145:2
    many a peer of E. brews, 619:9
    mariners of E., 408:16
    martial airs of E., 415:6
    men of E. wherefore plow, 429:6
    meteor flag of E., 408:18
    middle class in E., 532:7
    middle class safety of E., 490:25
    model to inward greatness, 192:25
    navy of E., 338:9
    neck wrung like chicken, 667:6
    never at foot of conqueror, 178:28
    nor E. did I know, 392:6
    of a king of E. too, 151:13
    oh to be in E., 492:4
    old E. to adorn, 635:18
    or E. breed again, 169:13
    paradise of women, 162:9
    poorest he in E., 246:6
    rightwise king of E., 139:1
    roast beef of E., 321:15
    roast beef of old E., 321:*n6*
    sea once made E. secure, 673:5
    shower of curates on E., 504:17
    slaves cannot breathe in E., 347:27
    St. George for E., 664:14
    stately homes of E., 431:19, 700:1
    such night in E., 448:4
    there I find flag of E., 388:9
    think about defense of E., 645:2
    this realm this E., 179:12
    what is left of E., 450:*n1*
    who dies if E. live, 635:26
    who only E. know, 634:2
    whoever wakes in E., 492:4
    wins last battle, 667:7
    with all thy faults, 346:*n5*
    wont to conquer others, 179:14
    world where E. dead, 673:6
    youth of E. are on fire, 192:24
England's green and pleasant land, 375:17
    mountains green, 375:17
    old E. winding sheet, 375:15
    pleasant pastures, 375:17
    song forever, 627:5
    stay no more on E. shore, 862:11
English, among E. Poets after death, 440:12
    anyone been to E. public school, 766:3
    attain E. style, 325:5
    biographies disease of E. literature,
      513:16
    can't think of E., 551:15
    Chaucer well of E., 161:13
    children spoke bad E., 627:20
    civilization humanizing, 532:6
    close wall with E. dead, 192:30
    dictionary best reading, 654:16
    father of E. criticism, 325:7
    for suppressing other, 530:6
    gentleman after a fox, 606:3
    God had never spoken anything but E.,
      668:13
    Good Soldier finest French novel in E.,
      662:19
    his E. sweete upon his tonge, 134:27
    in an E. lane, 492:12

English *(continued)*
    in favor of boys learning E., 665:9
    king's E., 190:20
    kissed by E. dead, 738:8
    language of E. poet, 722:19
    most beautiful words in E. language,
      586:3
    mother made moan, 515:9
    never abolish anything, 625:10
    not accessible even to Englishmen,
      610:4
    not Turkish court, 192:12
    one pair of E. legs, 193:7
    pint of E. ale, 664:14
    principle of E. constitution, 338:11
    strung on E. thread, 515:16
    take their pleasures sadly, 165:15
    tongue I love, 826:2
    trick of our E. nation, 191:19
    up with which not put, 668:10
    we E. nation of brutes, 612:*n2*
    white as angel E. child, 372:1
    winter ending in July, 424:19
Englishman beat three Frenchmen, 302:19
    blood of an E., 861:10
    content to say nothing, 329:2
    either for E. or Jew, 376:10
    every E. paid his way, 338:*n2*
    hangdog look of E. about to talk French,
      694:11
    he is an E., 563:20
    if I were American as I am E., 323:10
    impossible for E. to open mouth, 610:4
    last great E., 484:21
    prejudices of true E., 302:19
    rights of E., 360:3
    stirred heart of E., 649:16
    thinks moral when uncomfortable,
      609:20
    true-born E., 179:7
    vain ill-natured E., 294:17
Englishman's, part of every E. education,
    533:2
    thoughts, 530:8
Englishmen, mad dogs and E., 753:6
    O when shall E., 169:13
    reveal first to His E., 263:2
English-speaking, clearer understanding of E.
    audiences, 627:14
    union of E. peoples, 602:12
Engraven, deep on his front e., 265:8
Enigma, riddle in mystery inside e., 665:17
Enisled, in sea of life e., 529:3
Enjoy both operations at once, 717:2
    crown that seldom kings e., 172:30
    delight with liberty, 161:25
    don't have to go e. it, 636:12
    get what want and e. it, 636:4
    grudge what they cannot e., 60:19
    her while she's kind, 284:8
    honey-heavy dew of slumber, 196:5
    ice cream while it's on plate, 750:2
    indifferent and cannot e. it, 326:10
    interval, 629:15
    most e. contented least, 226:6
    neither e. nor suffer, 614:13
    other people's sufferin', 646:17
    private men e., 193:15
    prize not whiles we e. it, 194:39

Enjoy *(continued)*
    resources within thy reach, 66:1
    things we ought, 80:17
Enjoyed, hours I once e., 347:2
    in vision beatific, 264:22
    much endured little e., 324:26
    no sooner but despised, 227:22
    supinely e. gifts of founder, 353:15
    the lady, 373:9
    to have e. sun, 529:1
    trust of pure women, 686:7
Enjoyment, communal e. of fruits of earth,
    383:7
    human benefit and e., 344:14
    intellectual e., 621:13
    life not from e. to e., 328:4
    of life and liberty, 339:9
    of riches parade of riches, 338:16
    variety mother of E., 458:21
Enjoyments, occasional e. lighting pain,
    624:13
    seasoning of all e., 278:11
Enjoys, beauty ne'er e., 312:8
Enlaced are fallen among grass, 794:7
Enlarge, circle never ceaseth to e., 171:14
    my life, 324:8
Enlarges, develops and e. organ, 362:7
Enlighten people generally, 359:3
Enlightened enough to exercise control,
    359:6
    his eyes were e., 11:24
    who knows himself is e., 59:1
Enlist, we will all e. again, 819:9
Enlisted, is there view for e. men, 808:5
En-Masse, utter word E., 518:12
Enmity between thee and the woman, 6:8
    three classes of friendship and e., 114:18
Enna, not that fair field of E., 266:8
Ennoble, we must e. our works, 129:13
Ennobled by own exertions, 382:24
Ennui, celestial e. of apartments, 688:2
Enoch walked with God, 6:22
Enormous, guilt is e., 826:8
    knowledge e., 438:20
    writing takes e. concentration, 811:2
Enough as good as feast, 149:20
    damned that cries Hold e., 222:24
    for all, 680:9
    for my life, 32:5
    if something, 395:12
    know what is more than e., 373:1
    love is e., 557:3
    never know what is e., 373:1
    not e. to fight, 690:15
    not e. to help feeble up, 218:10
    of children's gratitude, 641:9
    or too much, 373:5
    time e. for that, 229:6
    'tis e. 'twill serve, 183:28
    to have died once e., 98:7
    why aren't the books e., 839:10
    word to wise e., 158:25
Enrage those paying your annuities, 316:27
Enrich yourselves, 419:6
Enriched, pension never e. young man,
    251:30
Enriches, that which not e. him, 213:33
Enrichissez-vous, 419:*n3*
Ensanguined hearts, 348:6

Ensign, beauty's e. yet is crimson, 184:16
　　full high advanced, 264:14
　　tear tattered e., 473:3
Enskyed, thing e. and sainted, 210:37
Enslave, man alone e. man, 783:20
　　people impossible to e., 410:2
　　we fight not to e., 354:16
Enslaved, baptism e. me, 603:19
　　destiny alike for free and e., 65:15
　　London in ruins rather than e., 666:3
　　tamely and abjectly e., 666:3
Enslavement and existential death, 819:7
　　certainty of worse, 790:9
　　faced e. if captured, 556:3
Ensnare, man's imperial race e., 309:7
Ensured release, 620:3
Entails, when truth e. ruin, 69:1
Entangling alliances, 358:13
　　what so e. as death, 237:1
Enter, all hope abandon who e. here, 130:3
　　enchanted woods, 541:18
　　into his gates with thanksgiving, 19:3
　　into joy, 37:13
　　into kingdom of heaven, 35:10
　　Lord Christ e. in, 606:1
　　nation which keepeth truth may e., 27:17
　　not into temptation, 37:30
　　storm rain may e., 323:3
　　they that e. must go on knees, 244:8
　　to grow in wisdom, 556:2
　　ye shall not e. into heaven, 36:28
Entered, I have e. on enterprise, 331:15
　　into springs of sea, 15:8
　　into unadvisedly, 51:7
Entergraft our hands, 235:4
Enterprise for glory of Christian, 140:6
　　is sick, 207:25
　　life-blood of our e., 186:20
　　more e. in walking naked, 638:10
　　private e. not yet tried, 698:10
　　Profit engine of E., 701:16
　　set habits of age, 737:9
　　voyages of starship E., 808:7
　　want of e. and faith, 507:11
　　without precedent, 331:15
Enterprises, in mighty e. determination
　　　enough, 104:21
　　of great pith, 203:33
　　that require new clothes, 506:17
Enters dark hole of the head, 825:4
　　idly bent on him that e. next, 180:13
　　nought e. there, 208:26
　　war seldom e. but where wealth allures,
　　　284:22
Entertain all comers, 52:30
　　lag-end of my life, 186:31
　　strangers, 47:4
　　this starry stranger, 272:16
Entertained angels unawares, 47:4
　　spirit once e. you, 780:11
Entertainer who understood his time,
　　693:14
Entertaining, more e. than half the novels,
　　673:3
Entertainment, analysis of character highest
　　e., 769:10
Entertains harmless day, 232:14
Enthroned, mercy e. in hearts of kings,
　　189:19

Enthusiasm, faith an excitement and e.,
　　461:14
　　human e., 824:6
　　nothing great without e., 456:4
　　whatever poet writes with e., 72:12
Enthusiasts, how to deal with e., 448:8
Entice, if sinners e. thee, 20:23
Entière, Vénus toute e., 290:n5
Entire, that ye may be perfect and e., 47:9
Entirely a free-labor nation, 450:6
Entities not multiplied unnecessarily, 132:10
Entitled, more no man e. to, 615:6
Entity and quiddity, 270:23
Entrails, in our own proper e., 197:19
　　webs from e. spin, 155:n2
Entrance, all men have one e. into life,
　　31:22
　　beware e. to quarrel, 201:26
　　fatal e. of Duncan, 219:11
　　give God back e. ticket, 525:16
Entrances, exits and their e., 198:25
Entrap, seeming truth to e. wisest, 189:6
Entrapped, love of you e. me, 4:2
Entreats, Hesperus e. thy light, 237:10
Entrepreneur, what e. contributes, 703:2
Entrepreneurial profit, 703:2
Entreprise, c'est une épineuse e., 152:n14
Entrusted, man to whom populace is e.,
　　52:13
　　with great concerns, 63:22
Entrusts life to one hole only, 86:11
Entwine itself verdantly, 411:12
Envelope, mistake of enclosing e., 707:3
Enveloping earth, 402:6
Envelops, ground opens and e. me, 829:9
Enviable death was his, 667:14
Envied, better e. than pitied, 71:15
Envieth, charity e. not, 44:18
Envious and calumniating time, 208:12
　　beggar is e. of beggar, 56:8
　　Casca, 196:33
　　humble are usually e., 287:8
　　more free than e. court, 197:36
　　regarded wounded soldiers in e. way,
　　　655:12
　　serpents e., 236:6
　　siege of watery Neptune, 179:13
　　silence e. tongues, 231:7
　　ungrateful Public, 410:8
Enviously, fate so e. debars, 277:8
Environ, what perils do e., 161:n1
Environment, ancestry and cultural e.,
　　613:13
　　change e. not man, 743:9
　　freedom in relation to e., 501:1
　　inequality of e., 559:6
　　internal e., 501:2
　　is all excepting me, 743:15
　　man not locked into e., 778:4
Environs, Howth Castle and E., 696:14
Envisage circumstance all calm, 438:19
Envoys, her e. ubiquitous, 490:13
　　two punctilious e. Thine and Mine,
　　　289:18
Envy and wrath shorten life, 32:43
　　attracts e. of world, 344:3
　　born from the start, 71:16
　　calumny hate pain, 430:13
　　dared not hate, 422:11

Envy *(continued)*
　　for the dead, 562:5
　　from e. hatred and malice, 50:11
　　golden mean avoids e. of palace, 99:23
　　honor without e. friend who prospered,
　　　65:7
　　no man's happiness, 199:6
　　not reverence of dead but e. of living,
　　　246:14
　　of less happier lands, 179:12
　　of the dead, 69:19
　　of the devil, 31:15
　　Pride E. Avarice three sparks, 130:18
　　slayeth the silly, 13:36
　　slays itself by own arrows, 122:23
　　stirred up with e., 263:22
　　strongly rooted as e., 367:32
　　toil e. want, 324:6
　　too low for e., 275:3
　　void of e. guile lust, 318:10
　　whim e. or resentment, 346:20
Envying, strife and e., 43:26
Enwrought with gold and silver, 637:11
Eon, lie down for e. or two, 633:3
Épater le bourgeois, 525:n1
Epecho [Επεχω], 153:3
Ephemeral, fame is e., 115:15
　　story e. and doomed, 748:19
Ephesus, Temple of Dian in E., 850:10
Ephraim, gleaning of grapes of E., 10:37
Epicure, serenely full e. say, 399:3
Epicurean cooks sharpen his appetite,
　　223:12
Epicurus, he was E. owene sone, 135:3
　　set forth highest good, 93:20
Epicurus', hog of E. herd, 101:1
Epidemic of world lawlessness, 698:8
Epidemical love of flattery, 303:10
Epidemics, man survives e., 543:6
Epigram, what is an e., 402:2
Epigrams, France despotism tempered by e.,
　　433:23
　　your e. are shorter, 110:18
Epigram-surprise, or with e., 446:12
Epilogue, no e. I pray you, 182:13
Episode, love an e. in man's life, 385:12
Episodes, Renaissance and Reformation e.,
　　757:4
Epitaph, believe woman or e., 419:16
　　better bad e., 203:25
　　drear, 633:2
　　for their country, 629:8
　　me who am their e., 234:20
　　not remembered in thy e., 187:7
　　of those who fell, 667:12
　　of which not ashamed, 599:22
　　to be my story, 670:15
Epitaphs, let's talk of e., 179:27
　　nice derangement of e., 367:9
Epithet belongs to gentleman, 407:2
　　his surname e. for knave, 142:n5
Epithets, stuffed with e. of war, 212:12
Epitome, all mankind's e., 283:15
Epoch, coincide with e. or differ, 602:2
　　man lives life of e., 676:5
　　no one immune to spirit of e.,
　　　675:14
　　spirit of e., 675:14
Epocha in history, 351:3

Eternity *(continued)*

    pleasing dreadful thought, 301:26

    predestined from all e., 542:12

    responsible through e., 476:2

    sells e. to get toy, 175:5

    shut in a span, 272:18

    silence deep as E., 433:*n*1

    sole one who traverses e., 4:5

    teacher affects e., 570:15

    tears of e., 619:19

    thoughts that wander through e., 265:4

    throughout all e., 375:1

    time the image of e., 116:10

    travelers of e., 291:12

    waits at crossway of stars, 752:13

    wants nothing but e., 225:1

    was in our lips and eyes, 223:1

    was in that moment, 300:10

    white radiance of e., 430:17

    wink of e., 753:11

Eternity's, lives in e. sunrise, 373:13

    you are e. hostage, 730:4

Ether, ampler e., 395:11

    falls through clear e. silently, 435:18

Ethereal, blue e. sky, 301:14

    flushed and like throbbing star, 437:3

    mildness come, 317:19

    sky, 263:23

    void, 756:5

    what e. dances, 478:10

Etherized upon a table, 717:6

Ethic, land e. for tomorrow, 807:11

Ethical, act has no e. quality unless chosen, 581:16

    nuclear giants e. infants, 736:14

Ethics, difficulties in E., 663:6

    dry volumes of e., 356:21

    of misanthropy and voluptuousness, 447:22

    system of rational e., 629:8

Ethiopian change his skin, 29:12

Ethiop's, rich jewel in E. ear, 182:25

Ethnic, dogma of e. superiority, 712:12

    genocide destruction of nation e. group, 758:5

Ethyl or Mabelle, 694:10

Etiam periere ruinae, 110:*n*7

Etiquette, isn't e. to cut anyone, 552:18

Étoiles, on voudrait attendrir les é., 526:*n*5

Eton, Waterloo won on fields of E., 389:6

Êtres, n'existe que trois ê. respectables, 524:*n*11

Etruscan cup, 800:14

Étude, la vraie é. de l'homme, 311:*n*1

Étudié, hé Dieu si j'eusse é., 139:*n*3

Euboea, Athens nigh to E., 76:5

Euclid looked on Beauty bare, 735:8

Euphemistically, asylums known e., 700:1

Euphuism, preciosity or e., 653:17

Eureka I have found it, 86:1

Euripides, all Greece the monument of E., 69:*n*1

    chorus ending from E., 493:8

    drew men as they were, 67:*n*2, 69:*n*1

Europa, bull that kidnapped E., 91:1

Europe a precious graveyard, 525:14

    all dogs of E. bark, 775:15

    artist no home in E. save Paris, 590:5

    continent of energetic mongrels, 632:1

Europe *(continued)*

    depravations of E., 296:4

    fifty years of E., 482:9

    glory of E. extinguished, 345:13

    governments of E., 357:13

    if clod washed away E. less, 236:19

    lamps going out over E., 626:5

    liberation of E., 728:15

    liberties of E., 359:9

    longest kingly line in E., 315:*n*3

    new order in E., 686:3

    no Soviet domination of Eastern E., 790:16

    noblest river in E., 302:19

    of ancient parapets, 603:12

    old tyrannical governments of E., 398:12

    pass over to E. between sun and sun, 413:7

    people of Western E., 728:15

    powers of old E., 510:14

    prison of nations, 686:3

    races of E. melting, 631:16

    really a swarm, 702:18

    regards her like stranger, 354:9

    Russia's future a danger for E., 499:10

    simplifiers going to descend upon E., 509:5

    specter haunting eastern E., 832:2

    specter haunting E., 510:14

    superstitious valuation of E., 584:8

    technique and style of E., 815:1

    thrilled with joy, 391:10

    two continental powers in E., 726:13

    under his heel, 666:13

    United States of E., 451:19

    window on E., 447:2

European, canoe of the E., 516:1

    colonization by E. powers, 376:16

    descendant of E., 352:7

    instruments of E. greatness, 370:11

    legacy of first E. novel, 824:2

    Mozart last of great E. taste, 589:10

    narcotics, 589:17

    nose, 809:5

    periodization of E. history, 757:4

    philosophical tradition footnotes to Plato, 624:15

    United States and E. power, 377:1

    wars of E. powers, 376:17

Europeans often ask, 570:28

Eurydice, half-regained E., 259:21

Eutrapelia happy flexibility, 532:5

Euxine, more dangerous breakers than E., 424:8

Evade erump, 90:*n*4

Evanescent, velocities of e. increments, 306:16

Evangelical, things moral or things e., 281:22

Evasion of what white men set them, 748:12

Evasit, abiit excessit e. erupit, 90:*n*4

Eve, called his wife's name E., 6:10

    child of our grandmother E., 176:24

    fairest of daughters E., 266:12

    from noon to dewy e., 264:24

    like toad at ear of E., 266:23

    motherless E., 656:13

    Mr. Whitman's E. drunken apple-woman, 569:18

    obey voice at e., 453:21

Eve *(continued)*

    oh had simple E., 656:12

    pensive E., 337:1

    riverrun past E. and Adam's, 696:14

    said to e. Be soon, 621:3

    since E. ate apples, 424:21

    son of Adam and E,, 297:7

    span, 843:8

    St. Agnes' E., 436:20

    stag at e., 397:4

    warblest at e., 262:7

    wonder what Adam and E. think, 714:6

Even, approach of e. or morn, 265:25

    as you and I, 634:21

    break, 611:14, 692:15

    deep and crisp and e., 511:9

    don't get mad get e., 723:3

    such is time, 160:14

    waters stilled at e., 541:26

    would God it were e., 10:10

Even-balanced soul, 528:2

Even-handed justice, 219:17

Evening and morning were first day, 5:10

    beauteous e. calm free, 392:15

    Boston E. Transcript, 717:20

    bright exhalation in the e., 230:31

    charming e. criminal's friend, 524:14

    come in the e., 501:15

    darkens, 820:2

    dews of e. carefully shun, 315:13

    die in e. without regret, 62:20

    eat in the e., 372:19

    expects his e. prey, 335:13

    fairer than e. air, 171:1

    gracious e. star, 501:12

    grateful e. mild, 266:18

    hate to see e. sun go down, 663:4

    house made of e. light, 856:1

    housewife ply e. care, 334:13

    in afternoon, 734:13

    in the e. it is cut down, 18:20

    is come rise up, 94:18

    isolation of sky at e., 686:19

    it was a summer e., 405:4

    light first light of e., 688:14

    like an e. gone, 304:7

    love morning and e. star, 708:6

    man that was in e. made, 257:21

    morning incense e. meal, 369:2

    must usher night, 430:8

    now came still e. on, 266:15

    of their lives, 534:9

    open house in e., 664:12

    quickly come as the E. Star, 90:6

    quiet-colored end of e., 492:10

    rainy e. to read this discourse, 252:23

    red light of e., 855:19

    rest at pale e., 762:11

    shades of e. drew on, 478:11

    shades prevail, 301:15

    shadow at e. rising, 718:12

    shadows of the e., 555:3

    slight sound at e., 505:1

    some enchanted e., 744:7

    soup of the e., 551:4

    spread out against sky, 717:6

    star love's harbinger, 268:13

    star you shine on dead, 430:*n*1

    sunset and e. star, 487:2

Evening *(continued)*
  to his labor until e., 19:11
  twilight and e. bell, 487:3
  until e. comes, 450:1
  walks at e. on three feet, 68:*n*3
  welcome peaceful e. in, 348:4
  when it is e. fair weather, 36:22
  withhold not thine hand in the e., 25:5
Evenings, we have had summer e., 710:3
Evensong, at last ring to e., 149:10
  at length ringeth to e., 149:*n*5
  dead ere e., 854:7
Event, caprice of minutest e., 516:19
  divine e., 484:18
  greatest e. in war, 74:9
  haunt spot of great e., 460:8
  Holocaust central e., 827:5
  how much the greatest e., 363:8
  men labels that name e., 542:12
  one e. happeneth to all, 24:4
  prophets make sure of e., 336:7
  thinking too precisely on e., 206:1
  unveil third e. to me, 547:3
  verity is an e., 583:1
Eventful, strange e. history, 198:25
Eventide, fast falls e., 432:5
Events cast shadows before, 408:19
  controlled me, 476:9
  course of human e., 357:2
  great e. make me calm, 518:3
  names deeds legends e., 438:20
  national e. decided by power elite, 798:2
  signs should prefigure e., 91:2
  some great e. some mean hypocrisies,
    351:13
  spirits of great e., 408:*n*3
  study e. in bearings, 534:10
  three e. in life, 292:19
Eventual domination over all, 787:11
Ever-during dark surrounds me, 265:25
  power, 395:5
  sleep one e. night, 231:21
Everest, square root of E., 807:7
Ever-fixed mark, 227:17
Everglades, no other E. in the world, 728:14
Ever-increasing wonder and awe, 339:4
Everlasting, achievements of intellect e.,
    95:10
  bonfire, 220:20
  composed to be e. possession, 73:16
  condemned into e. redemption, 195:3
  deprived of e. bliss, 170:19
  doors, 16:20
  eyes of Pierrot, 753:12
  farewells, 418:4
  Father, 26:31
  first last e. day, 234:17
  from e. to e. thou art God, 18:20
  funeral marches round your heart,
    796:15
  God the E. Refuge, 122:21
  had not fixed canon, 201:1
  here set up my e. rest, 184:17
  hills, 7:38
  his mercy is e., 19:3
  life, 40:46
  no, 433:14
  open ye e. gates, 267:16
  stood from e. to e., 290:2

Everlasting *(continued)*
  the e. arms, 10:16
  yea, 433:17
Everlastingness, bright shoots of e., 279:3
Ever-living, our e. poet, 225:*n*2
Evermore, probing through you O e., 753:18
Ever-nearing circle weaves shade, 530:18
Ever-returning spring, 520:14
Ever-rolling, time like e. stream, 304:8
Evers, Tinker to E. to Chance, 692:14
Ever-whirling wheel, 161:19
Every, assimilates e. thing to itself, 332:19
  day a little death, 825:19
  day a wilderness, 841:11
  day in every way, 612:19
  day's news, 211:28
  feature works, 406:17
  inch a king, 217:20
  man architect of his fortune, 95:13
  man for himself, 149:17
  new idea, 803:2
  over and over e. year, 406:1
  sooner e. party breaks up, 406:19
  war of e. man against e. man, 246:11
Everybody, almost e. had troubles, 627:12
  everything happens to e., 610:12
  goes Awww, 810:2
  hard to please e., 104:1
  he who praises e., 355:14
  if e. minded business, 550:5
  lies about sex, 842:3
  looks like e. is down on me, 838:8
  most e. climbs into graves married,
    749:14
  on this planet, 833:5
  suspect e., 496:33
  wants to be Cary Grant, 767:4
Everybody's business nobody's business,
    252:27
Everyday, refinement of e. thinking, 683:7
Everyman I will go with thee, 843:17
Everyone, each one's himself yet e.,
    780:1
  Future something e. reaches, 752:5
  has one sermon, 849:20
  in world is Christ, 677:19
  is a moon has dark side, 562:12
  love come to e., 736:17
  not e. can get to Corinth, 101:7
  satisfying life for e., 769:14
  understandable by e. not just scientists,
    837:3
  upon which e. has sat, 740:11
  went over e. nobody's missing, 792:9
  when e. is somebodee, 566:8
  will say, 564:9
  world breaks e., 754:5
Everyone's tired of turmoil, 801:10
  true worship, 76:1
Everything, a bore to tell e., 315:21
  about her was vigorous, 627:10
  and Anything, 699:12
  as resulting from laws, 470:12
  autumn in e., 493:2
  belongs to fatherland, 380:20
  conscience in e., 332:18
  costing not less than e., 722:5
  custom reconciles to e., 343:12
  deed e. glory nothing, 365:18

Everything *(continued)*
  detail is e., 756:7
  don't tell her e., 55:7
  else is about something, 840:10
  else is still, 372:10
  esteem e. esteem nothing, 278:3
  exists nothing has value, 684:4
  fearlessness of those who lost e., 804:9
  feeling not always e., 526:14
  for e. missed gained something, 455:19
  for poetry idea e., 532:4
  glory of e., 756:17
  God not willing to do e., 143:2
  good for something, 283:25
  good in e., 197:37
  grayness silvers e., 493:1
  grows old under power of Time, 80:1
  had e. I wanted, 746:11
  happens to everybody, 610:12
  hard to attain easily assailed, 114:15
  has an end, 853:7
  has two handles, 112:19
  he is superior to e. he possesses, 316:7
  he wants nothing you want, 533:3
  hear voices talking about e., 841:1
  I could prove e., 825:11
  I have e. yet nothing, 89:4
  I touch mean and farcical, 540:22
  if you win you win e., 279:23
  in its place, 563:7
  in relation to nothing, 279:16
  includes itself in power, 207:27
  is A-OK, 810:13
  is for the best, 316:2
  is gratuitous, 772:4
  is up to date in Kansas City, 744:6
  know e. forgive e., 385:*n*4
  lived in me, 536:11
  man esteems, 640:11
  man grows used to e., 525:10
  mean between nothing and e., 279:16
  men ask for e., 805:6
  moments when e. goes well, 630:11
  not all capable of e., 95:24
  now dare e., 813:6
  of one hidden stuff, 455:20
  passes, 855:8
  passes art alone eternal, 489:8
  practice is e., 103:*n*5
  public opinion e., 474:15
  sans e., 198:25
  smattering of e., 495:17
  spirit of youth in e., 227:8
  that can circulate does, 829:2
  that emancipates spirit, 366:9
  that pretty is, 225:12
  that's lovely is, 637:15
  treat e. as if a nail, 779:12
  tries e. before arms, 89:8
  understand e. makes tolerant, 385:14
  was rainbow, 785:9
  we have lost, 786:13
  we look upon blest, 640:19
  what else to say but e., 798:11
  what is God e., 66:12
  winning isn't e. it's only thing, 852:11
  worth what purchaser will pay, 104:7
Everything's coming up roses, 825:18
  got a moral, 550:16

Exactly, moves are e. right, 812:4

Exactness, facts detailed with e., 534:10

Exaggerated, love of the e., 828:15
  originality easily e., 778:10
  stress on not changing mind, 672:15

Exaggeration, chargeable with no e., 409:19
  report of my death an e., 562:13

Exalt him above all, 33:12
  himself shall be abased, 37:1
  will to live, 677:15

Exaltation from proximity of disaster, 665:5
  in chanting of Muses, 69:21

Exalted, both will be e., 684:3
  every valley shall be e., 28:1
  God an e. father, 607:12
  no very e. opinion, 344:2
  Satan e. sat, 264:25
  them of low degree, 38:39
  whoso humble himself be e., 37:1

Exalteth, righteousness e. a nation, 21:33
  wisdom e. her children, 32:2

Exalts, not what man does e., 493:20

Examination, decent and manly e., 404:12
  of acts of government, 404:12
  on minute e., 406:24

Examine, crime to e. laws of heat, 572:3
  turn inwards and e., 62:22

Examined, ought to have head e., 695:16

Example, annoyance of good e., 561:17
  from others take e., 89:13
  from the monkey, 128:10
  Homer is my e., 641:11
  if lower orders don't set good e., 605:5
  is school of mankind, 345:22
  more efficacious than precept, 325:1
  profit by their e., 352:11
  salutary influence of e., 325:6

Examples, no longer able to provide bad e.,
    273:17

Excalibur, so fell the brand E., 481:2

Exceed, flies worms e. me still, 304:3
  never e. your rights, 330:18
  reach e. grasp, 493:4

Exceedeth, thy wisdom and prosperity e. the
    fame, 12:19

Exceeding, grind e. small, 255:5
  honest e. poor man, 188:15
  wise fair-spoken, 231:14

Exceeds, far e. all earthly bliss, 155:*n*1
  man's might, 208:6

Excel, arts in which wise e., 293:7
  bees for government, 155:2
  discredit what they do not e. in, 82:29
  not e. because they labor, 410:18
  teach who themselves e., 308:8
  thou shalt not e., 7:36
  useless to e., 329:25

Excellence, activity in accordance with e.,
    80:18
  bearing on e. of character, 80:17
  fair divided e., 177:27
  fame of her e., 55:25
  in front of e. gods put sweat, 56:12
  long time to bring e. to maturity, 104:4
  mental e. a splendid possession, 95:2
  not exchange e. for riches, 57:6
  not only know e. but use it, 80:20
  stewards of their e., 227:4
  to few men comes e., 61:11

Excellencies, smaller e. of conversation,
    355:16
  true critic dwell on e., 302:16

Excellent angler now with God, 253:1
  dumb discourse, 230:7
  everything that's e., 564:17
  fancy, 206:24
  first e. second good, 142:17
  foppery of the world, 215:29
  hard to be truly e., 62:1
  how e. is thy name, 16:1
  how e. is thy lovingkindness, 17:4
  I cried, 617:10
  if you were a village, 673:17
  man of understanding is of e. spirit, 22:8
  most e. canopy the air, 203:17
  parts of it are e., 591:19
  situation e. I am attacking, 600:11
  so e. a king, 201:3
  so so is e. good, 200:1
  the e. lies before us, 385:3
  thing in woman, 218:6
  things difficult as rare, 287:17
  things in counsels, 22:28
  things that are more e., 42:41
  to have giant's strength, 211:12
  to make a poet e., 272:1
  well a fishmonger, 203:4
  what actions most e., 529:8
  wretch, 213:30

Excellently, goddess e. bright, 237:10

Excellest, thou e. them all, 23:31

Excelleth, light e. darkness, 24:3
  wisdom e. folly, 24:3

Excelling, cunningest pattern of e. nature,
    215:7

Excels dunce kept at home, 347:10
  quirks of blazoning pens, 213:7

Excelsior, 466:11

Excelsis, gloria in e. Deo, 49:11

Except a man be born again, 40:43
  it die, 44:27
  the Lord build the house, 20:4
  the Lord keep the city, 20:4
  the present company, 363:5
  thou bless me, 7:20

Exception, in your case make e., 744:16
  no rule admits not some e., 240:14
  proves rule, 240:*n*3

Exceptional, glorious to be e., 488:11

Exceptionally fine writing, 628:11

Excess, blasted with e. of light, 335:9
  desire of power in e., 167:19
  don't regret a single e., 585:19
  give me e. of it, 208:25
  in charity no e., 167:17
  not drinking but e., 245:17
  nothing in e., 124:9
  of glory obscured, 264:17
  of wealth cause of covetousness, 170:11
  reform carried to e. needs reforming,
    402:22
  reproach to religion, 291:21
  road of e. leads to palace of wisdom,
    372:14
  such e. of stupidity, 327:2
  surprise by fine e., 440:5
  wasteful and ridiculous e., 178:14
  when love is in e., 69:25

Excessit, abiit e. evasit erupit, 90:*n*4

Excessive, bail nor e. fines, 361:7
  dark with e. bright, 265:27
  good fortune, 539:11
  if national debt not e., 370:7
  laughter, 32:34

Exchange, atheist-laugh's a poor e., 378:11
  by just e. one for other, 163:22
  cross for crown, 661:10
  excellence for riches, 57:6

Exchequer of the poor, 179:18

Excise hateful tax, 324:17
  those to whom e. paid, 324:17

Excitabat enim fluctus in simpulo, 91:*n*6

Excite my amorous propensities, 326:7

Excited abnormal condition, 610:1
  passions not at will e., 478:19
  reverie, 639:8

Excitement, beyond e. into anguish, 828:2
  faith an e. and enthusiasm, 461:14
  spiritual e., 531:7

Excites us to arms, 284:15

Exciting, found it less e., 566:1
  politics almost e. as war, 665:8

Exclamation, by way of e., 141:21

Excluded, law of e. middle, 807:7

Excludes, kitsch e. everything, 824:1

Excommunicate, corporations cannot be e.,
    159:18

Excrement, place of e., 641:15

Excursion same for sorrow as joy, 784:4

Excuse, any e. will serve tyrant, 60:23
  came prologue, 268:2
  denial vain and coy e., 261:15
  fault worse by e., 178:15
  for the glass, 367:29
  I will not e., 462:5
  my dust, 738:19
  never e., 182:13
  play needs no e., 182:13

Excused from it as against my conscience,
    336:14

Excuses himself accuses himself, 151:8
  ignorance e. no man, 245:18
  must be made, 743:18

Excusing, love shows by e. nothing, 278:7
  make fault worse, 178:15

Execrable shape, 265:18
  sum of all villainies, 318:21

Execute, by contraries e., 229:25
  hand to e., 269:19, 360:9
  laws of Congress, 567:3
  villainy you teach me, 188:32

Executed, successfully e., 364:15

Execution of final solution of Jewish
    question, 737:7
  seeing evildoers taken to e., 150:4

Executioner, hire e. to throw switch, 746:2
  I victim and e., 524:13
  man his own e., 256:5
  mine own e., 236:17
  the master e., 59:18

Executioners would be most learned, 144:6

Executions far from useful examples, 383:2
  for the master executioner, 59:18

Executive, judicial distinct from e., 351:11
  legislative nominated by e., 353:6
  of modern state, 511:2

Executors, let's choose e., 179:27

Exegi monumentum aere perennius, 100:*n*8

Exemplary, our lives in acts e., 165:8

Exemplum de simia, 128:*n*5

Exempt from public haunt, 197:37
    true nobility e. from fear, 172:17

Exercise, bodily e. when compulsory, 77:18
    each e. art he knows, 75:3
    free e. of religion, 353:4
    gratuitous e. every day, 581:9
    prohibiting free e. thereof, 361:1
    reading to mind as e. to body, 301:13
    sad mechanic e., 483:15
    their constitutional right, 475:6
    wise for cure on e. depend, 285:19

Exercises his mind with suffering, 82:17

Exertions, ennobled by own e., 382:24
    what people attained with e., 356:11

Exhalation, bright e. in evening, 230:31

Exhaled, he was e., 285:27
    sighs infrequent e., 718:13

Exhaust the little moment, 798:8

Exhausted, my body infirm and e., 140:10
    my patience are e., 696:11
    resources of civilization not e., 472:12
    Time winds th' e. chain, 379:11
    worlds imagined new, 323:14

Exhaustive, give accurate e. account, 659:8

Exhibited, human relations perfectly e., 81:27

Exhilarating to be shot at without result, 665:4

Exhilaration, enjoyed perfect e., 454:14

Exigencies, great e. of government, 502:18
    pressure of e. of life, 607:13

Exile guise, 753:12
    king in e., 707:11
    kiss long as my e., 224:30
    men in e. feed on dreams, 65:13
    sleep in e., 603:13
    to e. friends everything, 661:20

Exiled on ground in jeers, 524:8

Exile's life is no life, 85:15

Exiles, band of e. moored bark, 431:21
    Paradise of e. Italy, 428:16

Exist, criterion for being allowed to e., 832:12
    God is in me or does not e., 689:9
    how would man e. if God did not need him, 679:8
    if God did not e., 316:22
    pathos piety courage e., 684:4
    rather believe God not e., 461:17
    saint if God does not e., 790:4
    seeing stars that ceased to e., 691:21
    since earth began to e., 348:24
    sir I e., 656:1
    time did not e. previously, 127:8
    true democracy never will e., 331:2
    we e. alone, 657:15
    why we and universe e., 837:3

Existed, true democracy never e., 331:2
    two sorts of Christians e., 743:19

Existence, anxiety belongs to e., 712:8
    believing in his e., 691:21
    brief crack of light, 755:12
    called New World into e., 390:1
    ceased to notice e. of students, 756:6
    closing your account, 471:18
    conscious of our own e., 80:16
    consecutive moments of e., 523:21

Existence *(continued)*
    culture no prospect of continued e., 607:15
    determination to develop own e., 678:14
    essential relationship to e., 501:10
    fret of e., 758:2
    knowledge enlarges sphere of e., 386:6
    life hollow e. burden, 559:19
    lived purely airborne e., 836:1
    more beloved e., 421:8
    nature owes me another e., 364:27
    of supernatural probable, 629:21
    one way of tolerating e., 527:7
    precisely an e., 547:2
    real and ratified e., 510:*n*2
    saw him spurn reign, 323:14
    spoke herself into e. as nation, 385:17
    Struggle for E., 469:14
    struggle for e., 675:2
    teach men sense of e., 588:17
    truth find e., 612:17
    unacceptable in human e., 824:1
    woman's whole e., 423:14

Existential, enslavement and e. death, 819:7

Existing like light around body, 817:3

Exists a great chasm, 782:3
    everything e. nothing has value, 684:4
    language for something that already e., 402:14
    nowhere but in yourself, 651:2

Exit pursued by a bear, 228:19
    wheresoever called to make e., 362:9

Exits and their entrances, 198:25
    doors for men to take their e., 244:7

Exodus, mysterious E. of death, 467:6

Expand, passions we feel e. time, 657:11

Expanding conflict to all China, 705:11
    in summer fires, 841:6

Expanse, green and brown e., 728:14
    oft of one wide e. had I been told, 435:19

Expansion, not a breach but an e., 235:2

Expansive, containment of Russian e. tendencies, 768:1

Ex-parrot, this is an e., 842:13

Expatiate free o'er scene of man, 310:20

Expect Saint Martin's summer, 171:13
    something for nothing, 601:16

Expectantly, folded her hair, 521:6

Expectation, better bettered e., 194:3
    makes a blessing dear, 270:5
    oft e. fails, 210:24
    rise, 340:12
    songs of e., 555:4
    whirls me round, 208:2

Expectations, revolution of rising e., 803:1

Expected, least e. happens, 459:1
    no reasonable man e., 729:3

Expects, blessed man who e. nothing, 310:16
    England e., 377:6

Expediency determines form, 714:7
    evil on ground of e., 615:2

Expedient, all things not e., 44:12
    as lighting by gas, 472:9
    that one die, 41:21

Expedition, so ended Sicilian e., 74:9

Expeditionary, Allied E. Force, 728:15

Expeditions, dyspepsy ruin of e., 418:5

Expelled, Asia and Africa e. freedom, 354:9
    Bourbons twice e., 510:*n*2
    or worse e., 842:11

Expend, silkworm e. her yellow labors, 239:15

Expende Hannibalem, 113:*n*11

Expense, at the e. of man, 743:18
    dog is item of e., 613:8
    great e. may be essential, 345:23
    of spirit in waste of shame, 227:22
    pretend to restrain e., 338:17

Expenses, consider my traveling e., 738:2
    work stops e. run on, 87:19

Expensive, nothing so e. as glory, 398:16
    politics e., 685:18
    sleek e. girls I teach, 818:9

Experience, accumulated e., 675:2
    an arch, 481:9
    arch to build upon, 570:1
    arranged in order, 572:1
    believe one who has e., 98:*n*4
    causes of future e., 582:10
    Court bows to e., 607:5
    customs shape e., 712:9
    effects of past e., 582:10
    encounter reality of e., 696:7
    get out of e. wisdom, 562:4
    gladly beyond any e., 740:6
    gone to end in e., 677:11
    has given no access, 590:8
    home where small e. grows, 175:23
    ignorant in spite of e., 323:2
    keeps dear school, 319:25
    knowledge not personal e., 77:6
    lamp of e., 353:1
    Liberal tempered by e., 531:12
    life of law, 577:13
    literature transmits e., 804:11
    make me sad, 199:24
    mind heavy with useless e., 824:8
    Mother of Sciences, 156:27
    my own meandering e., 841:13
    name for mistakes, 604:25
    no knowledge beyond e., 286:4
    not fruit of e. but e., 573:8
    of this sweet life, 132:5
    Old Age and E., 293:5
    optimist never had much e., 680:6
    pushed beyond facts, 612:*n*1
    relations between aspects of e., 706:1
    substitute for e. is art and literature, 804:10
    tells in every soil, 341:7
    travel part of e., 167:23
    triumph of hope over e., 327:8
    what e. and history teach, 390:4
    whole past e. in consciousness, 574:4
    wisdom acting upon e., 325:23
    write from e. only, 584:15

Experienced, nothing real till e., 440:18

Experiences, evidence for God in inner e., 582:19
    in solitude, 582:13
    shared e., 388:1
    strong man digests e., 589:16
    way full of adventures and e., 628:7

Experiencing suffering to full, 658:2

Experientia docet, 497:*n*1
    does it, 497:31

Eye *(continued)*

easier to go through e. of needle, 36:34
equal e. as God, 311:3
essential is invisible to e., 759:4
every old man's e., 183:18
evil e. that looks to mood apart, 671:1
far as human e. see, 481:23
fettered to her e., 276:2
for eye, 9:4
fringed curtains of thine e., 229:21
glad me with soft black e., 412:13
glittering e., 399:11
God caught e., 749:7
gray e. glances, 478:10
great e. of heaven, 161:1
had but one e., 496:15
half hidden from the e., 391:18
harmony in her bright e., 275:21
harvest of a quiet e., 392:4
hath not seen, 43:33
hearing ear seeing e., 22:19
heavenly rhetoric of thine e., 177:3
I have good e. uncle, 194:16
I have only one e., 377:3
if thy right e. offend, 34:4
ignorant e., 687:21
in my mind's e. Horatio, 201:11
intent on mazy plan, 379:13
interest unborrowed from e., 391:3
inward e., 394:8
is not satisfied with seeing, 23:34
jaundiced e., 308:24
lack-luster e., 198:15
language in her e., 208:19
lend e. terrible aspect, 192:30
less than meets e., 764:11
lifting up a fearful e., 168:26
light of the body is e., 34:14
like Mars, 205:21
locked and frozen in e., 775:16
locked up from mortal e., 272:7
looked into e. of day, 640:16
looks with threatening e., 178:11
love comes in at e., 638:3
made quiet by power, 391:2
many an e. danced, 473:3
mild and magnificent e., 491:21
moist e. dry hand, 191:16
mote in brother's e., 34:24
my face in thine e., 233:12
my great Taskmaster's e., 259:5
my striving e. dazzles, 279:10
Nature's walks, 310:21
negotiate for itself, 194:18
neighbor as possible enemy, 660:8
never e. did see that face, 171:10
no e. to watch, 412:3
nothing situate under heaven's e., 174:27
now mine e. seeth thee, 15:25
of childhood, 220:18
of heaven shined bright, 161:1
of heaven to garnish, 178:14
of lip of e. of brow, 227:11
of man hath not heard, 182:1
of newt toe of frog, 221:21
of saint, 641:1
of trilobite, 465:11
one auspicious e., 200:25
places e. of heaven visits, 179:4

Eye *(continued)*

poet's e. in fine frenzy, 182:3
putting mind's e. in book, 807:7
rude e. of rebellion, 178:23
sail with unshut e., 528:7
saw through glass e. darkly, 561:20
see e. to e., 28:19
see for hand not mind, 506:5
see out of needle's e., 497:4
see with e. serene, 394:2
see with half an e., 158:19
see with not through e., 376:9
seeing seven and seventy divils, 658:9
sees open heaven, 382:7
seller needs not one e., 251:26
set honor in one e., 195:17
smile in her e., 443:3
smile on lips tear in e., 396:20
sober coloring from e., 393:19
soul fix intellectual e., 443:7
still-soliciting e., 215:23
such a wistful e., 605:16
such beauty as woman's e., 177:4
tender e. of pitiful day, 221:7
that sun thine e., 226:14
thoughts legible in the e., 171:9
to a discerning E., 545:2
tongue sword, 204:7
twinkling of e., 44:31
vacant heart hand e., 397:27
vanquished by space, 159:10
view with hollow e., 189:25
wearing-stone or open e., 669:10
wet e. dhry heart, 646:9
what immortal hand or e., 374:5
when first your e. I eyed, 227:10
which girls hath merriest e., 171:16
wishing his foot equal with e., 172:32
with my little e., 857:15

Eyeball, I become transparent e., 454:15
to eyeball, 852:15
Eye-beams, our e. twisted, 235:4
Eyebrow, mistress' e., 198:25
Eyed, when first your eye I e., 227:10
Eye-deep in hell, 709:4
Eyeless in Gaza, 268:31
Eyelids a little weary, 573:5
from e. dripped love, 56:6
from e. wiped tear, 198:22
heavy and red, 446:2
of the morn, 261:16
slumber to mine e., 20:9
take thee with her e., 21:6
tinged e. and hands, 373:6
tired e. upon tired eyes, 480:17
weigh e. down, 191:33
Eyes, all things flourish where you turn e.,
308:5
ancient glittering e., 642:8
and back turn upward, 718:18
and see not, 29:3
as in a theater of men, 180:13
asked him with e. to ask again, 696:13
attentive e., 325:19
avenged for my two e., 11:7
before streaming e., 552:6
began to roll, 313:17
beheld God nature through their e.,
454:12

Eyes *(continued)*

black e. and lemonade, 412:6
blood-hot e., 742:6
bright e. of danger, 599:12
Bullen's e., 334:7
burning e., 821:2
burnt fire of thine e., 374:5
buyer needs a hundred e., 251:26
candid brow pure e., 612:3
cast mine e. and see, 248:19
cast one's e. so low, 217:18
close e. with holy dread, 401:19
close up his e. and draw curtain, 172:14
closed e. in endless night, 335:9
confess secrets of heart, 118:19
craters of my e. gape, 829:3
crossed with direct e., 719:5
cry my e. out, 157:11
cynosure of neighboring e., 259:15
death come close e., 844:23
deeper than depth, 541:26
desires in e. that looked at you, 628:8
die before our own e., 595:4
dreaming e. of wonder, 551:8
drink to me only with thine e., 238:2
dry e. laugh at fall, 492:16
dust thrown in my e., 670:3
eagle e., 435:19
elves whose little e. glow, 248:11
eternity was in our e., 223:1
everlasting e. of Pierrot, 753:12
eyelids upon tired e., 480:17
face facts with both e. open, 143:7
fields have e. woods have ears, 135:21
fix e. on greatness of Athens, 74:5
foe with fearless e., 627:3
fortune and men's e., 226:5
fountains fraught with tears, 164:12
from kindness cannot take e., 639:12
from starlike e. seek, 253:18
from those great e., 468:8
from women's e. this doctrine, 177:8
full of e. within, 48:16
gasp and stretch e., 653:9
gather to the e., 482:21
get thee glass e., 217:25
gone under earth's lid, 709:5
good for sore e., 299:7
greenish and remote, 766:9
had I your tongues and e., 218:5
hands and e. and heart, 421:21
hands only serve e., 504:23
hath not a Jew e., 188:30
have seen glory, 513:18
have their silence, 740:6
have they but see not, 19:22
having e. see not, 352:13
he always said my e. were blue, 408:9
he has ears and two e., 499:13
he turned up his e., 373:9
Heaven before mine e., 260:10
her aspect and her e., 422:13
her e. were wild, 439:4
him who has e. to see, 537:2
his e. are blue, 806:10
his e. are in his mind, 180:*n1*
his e. were enlightened, 11:24
his flashing e., 401:19
I will lift up mine e., 19:30

F

Face (*continued*)

look on her f., 309:6
look the East End in the f., 757:8
magic of a f., 253:21
make f. of heaven so fine, 183:32
mind's construction in f., 219:9
mirror of mind, 118:19
mist in my f., 494:18
moment that his f. I see, 400:22
morning f., 342:8
Moses hid his f., 8:5
music breathing from her f., 275:*n*5
my f. I don't mind it, 678:18
my f. in thine eye, 233:12
negative in slate window, 806:7
never eye did see that f., 171:10
night's starred f., 439:9
no more spoil upon my f., 194:1
no stranger's wing shielded my f., 725:8
nose on man's f., 176:7
of God shine through, 734:15
on barroom floor, 584:*n*3
open doors of his f., 15:20
open f. of heaven, 435:17
pardoned all except f., 424:10
Pity has a human f., 372:6
placid f. upon the pillow, 549:5
plain as nose in f., 146:15
poor lean lank f., 474:10
prism and silent f., 391:9
round jolly fruitful f., 474:*n*1
sages have seen in thy f., 347:21
saw manners in f., 325:19
sea's f. and gray dawn, 680:15
see another f. so frail, 819:18
sees other's umbered f., 193:11
set my ten commandments in your f., 172:5
she has a lovely f., 481:1
shining morning f., 198:25
smiling f. dream of Spring, 402:11
smiling in my f., 219:23
so pleased my mind, 844:21
socialism with human f., 807:14
soft f. of a girl, 68:1
something in a f., 304:13
sorrows of changing f., 637:5
strong men f. to f., 632:19
surrenders his f. to God, 122:4
that drove me mad, 584:6
that launched a thousand ships, 170:23
this fair f. the cause, 170:*n*5
this sunburnt f., 372:2
thou canst not see my f., 9:8
thy classic f., 478:2
touched f. of God, 810:11
truth showing its f. undisguised, 66:6
turned f. with ghastly pang, 400:8
visit her f. too roughly, 201:3
whole f. of world changed, 279:20
why bidest thou thy f. from me, 18:19
wish I loved silly f., 624:5
with twain he covered his f., 26:23
worst thing about him, 211:8
you could not see, 500:3
Faced, history f. with courage, 820:7
Face's, viewed in her fair f. field, 175:3

Faces all gather blackness, 30:29
bid them wash their f., 224:23
draw living f. from marble, 97:31
dusk f. with silken turbans, 268:23
estranged f., 621:7
fools' names like fools' f., 846:9
grind the f. of the poor, 26:15
hearts do in the f. rest, 233:12
in the crowd, 708:16
lords and owners of their f., 227:4
millions of f. none alike, 108:*n*4
of coffee-pickers, 706:7
of Negro school-children, 801:13
old familiar f., 407:1
put on two several f., 288:6
sea of upturned f., 397:23
sweat of other men's f., 477:3
Thracian ships foreign f., 567:17
Facets, iceberg cuts f. from within, 785:7
Facias ipse quod faciamus suades, 86:*n*9
Facile, plus f. de faire la guerre, 577:*n*2
Facilis descensus Averni, 97:*n*10
Facility of octosyllabic verse, 422:9
Facing fearful odds, 448:14
man who sits f. you, 57:20
Façon, je veux qu'on m'y voit en ma f., 152:*n*3
Fact, awkward historical f., 684:12
belief help create f., 582:9
Caspian F., 546:13
death ugly f. Nature hides, 548:6
falsehood more miraculous than f., 330:7
fatal futility of F., 585:11
firm ground of F., 665:2
frontiers wherever man fronts f., 505:26
idea is the f., 532:4
impressive f. about American women, 811:1
irritable reaching after f., 440:3
knife-edge of mere f., 824:8
natural f. spiritual, 454:17
of the Everglades, 728:14
slaying of hypothesis by ugly f., 537:4
state one f. belie another, 455:6
superiority in f. of conservatism, 456:7
that great f., 469:10
thought counterparts in f., 523:22
yesterday f. today doctrine, 360:2
Fact-finding more effective than fault-finding, 661:8
Faction a number of citizens, 366:18
danger of f., 367:1
Factions, old religious f., 345:19
Factor, timing is most important f., 56:18
Factories may make end of war, 554:9
Factors, gods as psychic f., 675:6
women economic f. in society, 623:3
Factory windows always broken, 685:2
Facts alarm more than principles, 360:11
all f. when come to brass tacks, 719:20
alone wanted in life, 498:23
are sacred, 592:5
are stubborn things, 300:6, 351:1
at first seem improbable, 169:20
collection of f. not science, 603:3
detailed with exactness, 534:10
drop cloak stand forth naked, 169:20
emphatic f. of history, 455:5
front essential f. of life, 506:28

Facts (*continued*)

if Lord knew f. iv case, 646:10
ignorance inert f., 570:21
ignore f. of history, 787:11
imagination baffled by f., 666:9
imagination for f., 368:8
inert f., 570:21
judges of f. not laws, 306:15
large collections of f., 470:11
looking toward f., 582:18
passions cannot alter f., 351:1
personages appear twice, 510:6
politics ignoring f., 570:20
power most serious of f., 570:22
science built with f., 603:3
we poor passing f., 802:8
what I want is F., 498:23
Faculties, borne his f. so meek, 219:18
men free to develop f., 607:1
t' affections and to f., 235:5
whose f. can comprehend, 170:4
Faculty, Eleazer was f., 630:8
infinite in f., 203:17
of continuing to improve, 348:24
unshackled exercise of every f., 450:14
Fade as a leaf, 28:33
colors that never f., 625:15
far away, 437:8
first to f. away, 412:13
into light of common day, 393:12
loveliness f., 411:12
lovely things f. and die, 725:3
may flourish or may f., 341:29
nothing of him that doth f., 229:20
old soldiers f. away, 690:12, 850:20
thy eternal summer not f., 226:3
Faded and gone, 411:15
but still lovely woman, 746:15
care sat on his f. cheek, 264:19
flowers of friendship f., 673:14
friendship f., 673:14
insubstantial pageant f., 230:9
oldest colors f., 633:3
on crowing of the cock, 200:22
Fades glimmering landscape, 334:9
out from kiss to kiss, 637:15
Fadeth, crown of glory that f. not, 47:32
flower f., 28:3
Fading, bestows the f. rose, 253:13
down the river, 627:5
fading, 719:12
in music, 189:2
life f. fast away, 594:2
order is rapidly f., 836:6
Faery, Land of F., 637:6
lands forlorn, 437:13
Faery's child, 439:4
Faggot, flames no f. feeds, 641:6
Faggots, some burn damp f., 638:13
Fagots, diadems and f., 453:18
Fail, audience never f. to laugh, 75:17
desire shall f., 25:8
from eternity shall not f., 619:12
if we should f., 220:1
let no man's heart f., 11:27
no such word as f., 452:11
not ashamed to f., 324:4
not f. that rendezvous, 724:18
not flag or f., 666:1

Fairy *(continued)*

fruits and flowers, 478:9
gifts fading away, 411:12
gold, 228:20
love-gift of f. tale, 551:8
no f. takes, 200:22
queen, 181:15
silly f. tale, 336:3
story of simians, 668:12
'tis almost f. time, 182:14
wide enough to wrap a f., 181:12
Fais ce que voudras, 146:*n*3
Faith, alternative to f. we lose, 767:11
an excitement and enthusiasm, 461:14
and fire within us, 576:3
and justice toward nations, 350:10
and morals hold, 393:5
animated by f. and hope, 325:6
be alone and f. renew, 579:12
become intuition, 395:6
begets heretics, 650:2
blind f. unpardonable sin, 536:16
break f. with us who die, 660:10
breastplate of f., 46:11
confess f. therein, 734:1
creed of our political f., 358:13
dead which does not doubt, 631:13
denied the f., 46:22
dying for f. not hard, 490:14
for all defects supplying, 129:3
for the sake of f. in f., 631:5
foundation of our f., 127:8
fresh and full of f., 459:9
fruit of Spirit is f., 45:22
good fight of f., 46:27
guardians of the f., 717:21
have f. and pursue end, 578:17
he mauna fa' that, 380:13
he who has courage and f., 822:6
holy f., 501:16
humor prelude to f., 735:16
if f. o'ercomes doubt, 493:10
if it want for f., 508:18
if scholar have not f., 82:16
if strong f. indulge in skepticism, 589:19
illogical belief in improbable, 691:9
in result makes result, 582:7
in some nice tenets, 275:20
in this f. I will live and die, 139:19
is sight and knowledge, 504:23
is the substance of things hoped for, 46:42
kept the f., 46:33
many a man's soul and f., 838:5
martyrs create f., 631:4
more f. in honest doubt, 484:11
mountain whom only f. can move, 789:8
mystery of f., 49:14
no f. in immortality, 469:2
no more despair or loss of f., 804:7
nonviolence article of f., 650:9
nor love nor law, 428:8
not create martyrs, 631:4
not f. but philosophy, 256:1
not for all his f. see, 452:18
not yet entered your hearts, 122:11
nothing more wonderful than f., 595:13
now abideth f., 44:20
O thou of little f., 36:17

Faith *(continued)*

O ye of little f., 35:16
of our fathers, 501:16
passive or hereditary f., 413:2
pin f. in things not seen, 116:7
pity their want of f., 355:7
plain and simple f., 197:6
Punic f., 95:12
quality cannot dispense with, 614:10
reaffirm f. in human rights, 705:15
reason greatest enemy f. has, 144:18
room from which f. gone, 767:10
sanctified by reason blest by f., 391:13
save myself by work and f., 772:11
saved by f., 735:17
sea of f., 531:2
shatter f. of men, 631:5
shell universe is to ear of F., 395:5
shines equal arming me, 509:1
show doubt prove f., 493:10
simple f. than Norman blood, 480:14
something of a f., 483:9
staff of f. to walk upon, 160:8
stand fast in f., 45:1
still by f. he trod, 684:14
that could remove mountains, 44:18
that yields to none, 104:28
thy f. hath saved thee, 39:14
triumphant o'er fears, 466:20
under another mask, 767:11
unfaithful, 486:3
walk by f. not sight, 45:6
want of enterprise and f., 507:11
wears f. as fashion of hat, 194:7
welcome home discarded f., 178:23
when f. lost honor dies, 468:8
where f. in reason timid, 660:8
without works, 47:15
ye must have f., 614:10
you call for f., 493:10
Faithful Achates, 97:24
action f. honor clear, 310:15
among the faithless f., 267:9
are the wounds of a friend, 23:11
at all times f. husband, 303:4
Christian f. man, 174:2
Duty's f. child, 445:2
elephant's f. one hundred per cent, 769:7
ever f., 124:23
falling out of f. friends, 88:*n*7
fierce wars and f. loves, 160:16
friend is medicine, 32:11
friend is strong defense, 32:10
friends hard to find, 239:3
good and f. servant, 37:13
in least faithful in much, 40:1
in love, 396:18
long and f. service, 501:6
love is f., 138:13
O come all ye f., 123:9
Penelope, 55:25
three f. friends, 319:19
to conviction to old age, 78:17
to thee Cynara, 645:8
to what exists in yourself, 651:2
unto death, 48:10
women all alike, 695:12
Faithfully to serve State, 254:11

Faithfulness, His infinite f., 296:4
hold f. and sincerity, 62:11
to truth of history, 534:10
Faithless, among the f. faithful, 267:9
arm, 775:10
as a smile, 717:24
as winds or seas, 290:16
be not f., 41:42
but f. was she, 528:8
in friendship but f. haven, 67:9
Faith's Defender, 314:12
Faiths, fighting f., 578:14
men's f. wafer-cakes, 192:29
old f. loosen and fall, 568:17
Fakes, windpipe throttled in f. of death, 519:12
Fakir, powers of levitation make f. stare, 720:14
Falcon, dapple-dawn-drawn F., 587:6
gentle as f., 141:22
like a f. swooping, 4:1
not hear falconer, 639:6
red rose a f., 590:14
towering in her pride, 220:28
Falconer, falcon not hear f., 639:6
Falconer's, O for a f. voice, 183:13
Falcons, hopes like towering f., 296:17
Falklands, the F. thing, 753:5
Fall, a thousand shall f. at thy side, 18:25
Anarch lets curtain f., 313:25
as wrong as to f. short, 63:6
baseball leaves you face f. alone, 833:4
benison to f., 248:20
bigger they come harder f., 71:*n*7
both f. into ditch, 36:20
by dividing we f., 349:10
can't f. into love, 824:7
cradle will f., 592:1
decline and f. of Rome, 354:4
desire of power caused angels to f., 167:19
divided we f., 349:*n*5
down can f. no lower, 271:11
dying f., 208:25
fain climb yet fear to f., 160:4
fear no f., 282:3
flat on your face, 741:17
flower displayed doth f., 209:23
forts of folly f., 531:5
fruit that can f. without shaking, 314:4
glass f. forever, 777:8
good to gain day good to f., 519:4
half to rise half to f., 311:9
harder they come harder they f., 841:4
haughty spirit before a f., 22:2
he that trusteth in riches shall f., 21:19
hero perish or sparrow f., 311:3
Humpty Dumpty had f., 859:8
I f. into Charybdis, 189:11
I with shuddering f., 541:10
if Freedom f., 635:26
if you stay price will f., 167:25
in love with Athens, 74:5
in with what asked to accept, 671:18
into arms not hands, 580:19
into hands of Carl Sandburg, 745:9
into Scylla to avoid Charybdis, 189:*n*1
leaves f. early, 708:18
let f. the curtains, 348:4

Far West, seek gold in F., 533:9
Farce, facts personages appear second as f., 510:6
   is played, 146:20
Farced title 'fore king, 193:16
Farcical, everything I touch f., 540:22
Fardels, who would f. bear, 203:33
Fare, bread and Gospel good f., 295:20
   delicate f. in another's house, 32:40
   forward, 87:*n4*
   forward voyagers, 721:12
   good-bye f. you well, 862:7
   hard very hard is my f., 307:2
   last of Romans f. thee well, 197:20
   like my peers, 494:19
   thee well if forever, 422:19
   when you receive f., 553:13
Fares, how it f. with happy dead, 483:20
   ill f. the land, 341:29
Farewell all joys, 844:23
   also called F., 542:4
   and then forever, 378:23
   bid f. to every fear, 304:10
   bid joys f., 436:3
   content, 214:8
   dear paintings, 255:2
   distracting town f., 309:22
   fair cruelty, 209:11
   fear farewell remorse, 266:4
   forever f. Cassius, 197:17
   goes out sighing, 208:11
   hail and f. my brother, 94:29
   hope, 266:4
   Horace whom I hated, 421:15
   king, 180:1
   Leicester Square, 674:2
   lobster-nights f., 309:23
   Monsieur Traveler, 199:25
   Morning Star, 90:6
   my bok and my devocioun, 134:13
   neighing steed, 214:8
   only feel f., 419:9
   Othello's occupation's gone, 214:8
   plumed troop, 214:8
   renowned Eretria, 76:5
   rewards and fairies, 244:14
   sadness, 743:3
   sweets to the sweet f., 206:29
   the tranquil mind, 214:8
   thou art too dear, 226:27
   thou child of my right hand, 237:20
   to all my greatness, 231:2
   to college joys, 702:5
   to the Highlands, 379:5
   to thee farewell, 571:15
Farewells, as many f. as stars, 208:16
   everlasting f., 418:4
   should be sudden, 424:27
Far-flung battle line, 635:1
Farfrae, Elizabeth-Jane F. not told of my death, 575:6
Farm, best business father's f., 489:9
   crouched on hillside, 762:4
   is like a man, 87:18
   keep 'em down on f., 708:1
   Middlesex village and f., 467:15
   snug little f. the world, 405:22
   that is no more a f., 670:17

Farmer in the dell, 861:4
   sowing the corn, 861:15
Farmer's boy, 845:7
   on f. land may fall, 591:6
   wife, 856:15
Farmers, ah too fortunate f., 96:11
   embattled f. stood, 453:11
   founders of civilization, 415:9
   gentlemen f., 424:13
   mechanics and laborers, 386:13
   pray that summers be wet, 96:6
Farmhand, apple-faced f., 847:*n4*
Farmhouse, stop without f. near, 669:14
Farms, destroy f. grass will grow in streets, 622:2
   houses and f. pillaged, 349:14
   what spires what f., 619:3
Farmsteads, when people inspect f., 90:2
Farmyard, cock louder in own f., 504:1
Far-off curfew sound, 260:4
   divine event, 484:18
   spies a f. shore, 172:32
   touch of greatness, 486:2
Farquhar, Peyton F. was dead, 580:6
Far-reaching ancestry, 534:9
Farrier, Felix Randal the f., 587:12
Farrow, Ireland old sow that eats f., 696:5
Far-stretched, all the f. greatness, 160:13
Farther away on either hand, 734:15
   off from heaven, 445:16
Farthest Thule, 96:4
   Thulè, 318:5
   way home's the f. way, 249:10
Farthing, do not care a f. candle, 407:22
   every f. of cost, 775:11
   hold f. candle to sun, 241:*n4*
   two sparrows sold for f., 35:30
Farthings, Latin word for three f., 176:31
   owe me five f., 857:12
Fas est et ab hoste doceri, 105:*n13*
Fascinate, blandishments not f. us, 362:9
Fascinates, work f. me, 620:7
Fascinating, you're a f. monster, 736:10
Fascination frantic, 565:21
   of what's difficult, 638:2
   war regarded wicked will have f., 604:10
Fascist, woman adores F., 827:16
Fashion birth intellect, 535:3
   bravery never out of f., 490:24
   faithful in my f., 645:8
   glass of f. mould of form, 204:8
   high Roman f., 224:2
   is architecture, 700:17
   like rusty mail, 208:9
   mayest f. thyself in whatever shape, 142:1
   of these times, 198:6
   of this world passeth, 44:7
   out of world out of f., 300:30
   seen in my natural f., 152:5
   take pleasures sadly after f. of country, 165:15
   true to you in my f., 732:15
   wears faith as f. of hat, 194:7
   wears out more apparel, 194:35
   worn-out poetical f., 720:18
Fashionable east seventies, 841:6
   New York Society, 539:8
   other f. topics, 341:15

Fashionable *(continued)*
   supersede f. novel, 448:10
   time like f. host, 208:11
Fashioned, gods f. by men, 629:17
   Providunce f. us holler, 514:23
   so slenderly, 446:7
Fashion's word is out, 642:4
Fashions in proud Italy, 179:10
   not cut conscience to fit f., 770:14
   old f. please best, 175:30
Fast and furious, 379:20
   bound below the surface, 627:11
   driveth onward f., 480:19
   hit f. hit often, 696:1
   how f. shadows fall, 653:5
   ill weed groweth f., 148:8
   men die f. enough, 293:16
   now he is dead should I f., 12:5
   or come he f., 396:16
   ship that does not sail f., 363:1
   stumble that run f., 183:19
   they follow, 206:*n2*
   thick and f. came at last, 552:2
   thine arrows stick f. in me, 17:9
   wit speeds too f., 176:29
Fasted forty days and nights, 33:30
Fasten him as a nail, 27:11
   your seatbelts bumpy night, 783:11
Fastened me flesh, 587:3
   to dying animal, 640:1
   Venus f. to prey, 290:12
Faster, beat to follow f., 223:14
   faster, 551:13
   speed far f. than light, 664:4
   than speeding bullet, 795:1
   travel f. than stagecoach, 342:14
   walk a little f., 550:21
   world would go round f., 550:5
Fastest, travels f. alone, 632:17
Fastidious, most f. critics, 447:20
Fastidiousness, unconscious f., 714:10
Fasting, lives on hope die f., 320:8
   thank heaven f., 199:20
   when full talk of f. easy, 118:22
Fat, all of us are f., 552:4
   and bean-fed horse, 181:5
   and greasy citizens, 198:2
   and sleek a true hog, 101:1
   black bucks, 685:3
   church ain't out till f. lady sings, 850:13
   contentions, 262:17
   duller than f. weed, 202:14
   eat the f. of the land, 7:33
   fair and forty, 363:6
   feast of f. things, 27:15
   feed f. the ancient grudge, 188:4
   geese are getting f., 847:8
   if to be f. be hated, 185:31
   in every f. man a thin one, 764:14
   is in the fire, 147:8
   Jack Sprat eat no f., 856:20
   Jeshurun waxed f., 10:14
   laugh and grow f., 195:*n1*
   men about me that are f., 195:22
   more f. than bard beseems, 318:10
   no sweeter f. than sticks to bones, 519:5
   of others' works, 240:2
   oily man of God, 318:11
   one is f. and grows old, 185:22

Fat *(continued)*

    outside every f. man an even fatter man, 764:*n*3

    resolved to grow f., 363:*n*1

    Seymour's F. Lady, 805:15

    sharp names never f., 750:9

    should himself be f., 329:15

    take f. with lean, 498:16

    Venus grown f., 417:17

    white woman, 711:8

    who drives f. oxen, 329:15

Fatal and perfidious bark, 261:21

    bellman, 220:12

    bowels of deep, 174:9

    complaint, 758:3

    embrace, 516:1

    entrance of Duncan, 219:11

    facility of octosyllabic, 422:9

    futility of Fact, 585:11

    gift of beauty, 421:11

    vision, 220:8

    Waterloo, 420:19

    yes I am f. man, 490:11

Fatality of seeing things too well, 688:11

Fate, all our children's f., 635:25

    can be director of opponent's f., 83:6

    cannot harm me, 399:3

    certain of his f., 213:34

    chooses our relatives, 355:10

    complex f. being American, 584:8

    coughed and called it f., 652:7

    death milder f. than tyranny, 65:10

    determines or indicates f., 506:9

    eagle's f. and mine are one, 61:*n*3

    eccentric propositions of its f., 687:20

    fears his f. too much, 272:2

    fixed f. free will, 265:13

    forced by f., 285:6

    foulness of their f., 712:4

    gave his sad lucidity, 528:9

    gave whate'er denied, 515:13

    had imagination about, 670:1

    hanging breathless on f., 466:19

    has cursed you, 69:20

    have conquered F., 528:11

    heart for any f., 466:3

    heart for every f., 422:26

    hung on razor's edge, 62:6

    I feel my f., 780:15

    I thy f. shall overtake, 249:1

    is handspike, 516:17

    lead me Zeus and F., 84:15

    man identifies with his f., 753:1

    man's character is his f., 64:16

    man's f., 761:5

    master of f., 485:22, 727:7

    master of my f., 594:11

    masters of our own f., 752:7

    meet f. among clouds, 638:16

    men cannot suspend f., 295:6

    my f. cries out, 202:9

    no armor against f., 254:9

    no f. misunderstand me, 669:5

    nobly born must nobly meet f., 70:21

    not decide single human f., 772:15

    of all extremes, 310:1

    of architect, 364:19

    of nation in own power, 449:4

    of nation riding, 467:16

Fate *(continued)*

    of new truths, 537:12

    of unborn millions, 349:14

    Providence will and f., 265:13

    rave no more 'gainst f., 566:17

    read book of f., 191:36

    seemed to wind him up, 283:5

    seize f. by the throat, 389:8

    sits on dark battlements, 384:15

    slave to f., 236:8

    so enviously debars, 277:8

    stars of thy f., 382:4

    stronger than anything, 69:21

    summons monarchs obey, 284:2

    take a bond of f., 221:27

    take F. by throat, 549:7

    thy f. and mine sealed, 483:5

    torrent of his f., 324:9

    what f. predestined, 388:13

    why know their f., 333:22

Fateful lightning, 513:18

Fates have given a patient soul, 54:5

    impose that men abide, 173:5

    masters of their f., 195:20

    of dread death, 54:1

    spinning our own f., 581:11

Father Abraham, 488:6

    alone is God, 412:17

    and I went to camp, 846:*n*3

    and mither gae mad, 379:7

    answered never word, 466:5

    antichrist denieth the F., 47:39

    author of play, 630:2

    baptizing in the name of F., 38:12

    bosom of his F., 335:4

    called brother's f. dad, 177:28

    child f. of man, 392:7

    cold mad f., 696:18

    dear f. come home, 553:10

    deny thy f., 183:2

    disappointed in monkey, 562:15

    eternal F. strong to save, 537:19

    far greater than his f., 52:34

    fear was my f., 780:10

    fell back behind Christ, 608:5

    foolish son calamity of f., 22:15

    forgive my injuries, 801:8

    full fathom five thy f. lies, 229:20

    gave f. forty-one, 849:10

    ghost of Hamlet's f., 624:9

    glorify your F. in heaven, 34:2

    glory be to the F., 49:25

    God an exalted f., 607:12

    God F. even more Mother, 788:16

    Great F. building forts among us, 533:9

    Great Spirit is my f., 387:7

    greatness in f. overwhelms son, 238:17

    happy to be f. unto many sons, 172:31

    hath chastised you, 12:22

    have we not all one f., 30:41

    heard my f. say, 352:1

    held out golden scales, 54:1

    honor thy f. and thy mother, 9:1

    in my youth said f., 550:2

    in thy gracious keeping, 538:11

    into thy hands, 40:22

    liar and f. of it, 41:12

    lived his soul, 740:10

    mad feary f., 696:18

Father *(continued)*

    man shall leave f. and mother, 6:2

    many talks from great f., 346:11

    more than hundred schoolmasters, 252:2

    moved through dooms, 740:9

    my f. feeds flocks, 337:14

    my f. paints summer, 808:12

    my f. sold me, 372:4

    my f. wept, 374:10

    name called everlasting F., 26:31

    no one like one's f. ever lived, 802:2

    not God for f. if not Church for mother, 117:6

    of a family, 114:8

    of all in every age, 313:7

    of English criticism, 325:7

    of lights, 47:11

    of mankind, 468:21

    of many nations, 7:5

    of such as dwell in tents, 6:19

    of such as handle harp, 6:20

    of Waters unvexed to sea, 476:5

    of your country, 349:*n*7

    old f. antick the law, 184:28

    old f. old artificer, 696:7

    old F. William, 405:9, 550:1

    omnipotent F. with his thunder, 55:*n*1

    our F. the Sky, 855:18

    please world and f., 276:14

    prince subject F. Son, 235:26

    rather have turnip than f., 325:21

    resembled my f. as he slept, 220:14

    ruffian, 185:30

    Scylla your f., 189:11

    seek f. who need son, 797:5

    smile at his f., 94:17

    Son and Holy Ghost, 38:12, 289:22

    struck f. when son swore, 241:20

    Time and Mother Earth, 817:15

    to corruption thou art my f., 14:21

    told me businessmen sons of bitches, 800:1

    true-begotten f., 188:14

    used to say, 714:8

    was a butcher, 280:23

    which art in heaven, 34:11

    will of my F., 35:10

    wise son maketh a glad f., 21:14

    wish f. to thought, 192:8

    withered when my f. died, 206:12

    without f. bred, 259:22

    would strangle f., 331:24

    you think your f. does not, 69:15

    your f. the devil, 41:12

Fathered, so f. and so husbanded, 196:8

Fatherland, die for friends or f., 100:16

    everything belongs to f., 380:20

    no danger thine, 518:1

    O f. O Ilium, 97:9

Fatherless, judge the f., 26:10

Father-Mother God, 526:10

Father's, about my F. business, 39:7

    daughters of my f. house, 209:27

    desire f. death, 526:5

    drink in my F. kingdom, 37:27

    grave, 102:3

    house not house of merchandise, 40:42

    in my f. house, 41:26

    joy mother's pride, 397:15

Fen, feather-footed through plashy f., 766:6
   of stagnant waters, 393:3
Fence, only f. against the world, 286:12
   Tom surveyed thirty yards of board f.,
    559:19
Fenced in piece of land, 330:17
   strangers who f. off meadows, 746:2
Fences, come to look after f., 535:13
   good f. good neighbors, 668:19
Fencing, no more than school of f., 613:12
Fere libenter homines, 91:*n*11
Fergits, nobuddy f. where buried hatchet,
   649:8
Feri ut se mori sentiat, 107:*n*9
Ferlie he spied wi' his e'e, 854:2
Ferment, bourgeois in f. of youth, 527:3
   space in which soul in f., 436:7
Fermi, work by F. and Szilard, 683:9
Fern, pastures deep in f., 756:13
   sparkle out among f., 485:3
Ferocity, courage without f., 419:10
   malicious f., 685:*n*1
Ferry, back and forth all night on f., 735:3
Fertile hypothesis, 796:8
   metaphor f. power, 702:24
   miles of f. ground, 401:13
   to be so f., 763:6
Fertilize Jordan plain, 680:1
Fervent, effectual f. prayer, 47:23
Fervet opus, 96:*n*8
Fervor, stranger moral f., 293:13
   with measure, 583:5
Fester like a sore, 762:16
   lilies that f., 227:5
Festina lente, 102:*n*4
Festively she puts forth, 394:20
Festivity, Two Lands are in f., 4:9
Fetch pail of water, 858:4
   poor dog a bone, 859:13
   the Age of Gold, 258:19
Fetter in shackles of historian, 257:18
Fettered, poetry f. fetters race, 376:4
   to her eye, 276:2
Fetters, no f. in Bay State, 468:5
   poetry fettered f. race, 376:4
   reason Milton wrote in f., 372:13
   servile f. breaks, 845:21
Fettle for great gray drayhorse, 587:13
Feuds, rent with civil f., 415:2
   three irreconcilable f. in Capri, 766:7
Fever called Living, 479:16
   induces condition like breakbone f.,
    769:4
   is Nature's instrument, 280:17
   life's fitful f., 221:5
   of chills and f. died, 724:12
   of life over, 450:1
   of temptation, 730:8
   of the bone, 718:7
   passion a f. in mind, 292:5
   weariness f. fret, 437:8
   youth bent by wintry f., 795:2
Feverish preoccupation with riches, 692:10
   selfish little clod, 609:15
Fever-trees, set about with f., 635:10
Few admired by own households, 153:15
   and far between are the Tathagatas,
    66:21
   are chosen, 36:41

Few (*continued*)
   business in hands of a f., 559:6
   companions f. in serious business,
    61:10
   condemn men because f., 507:23
   could know when Lucy ceased, 391:18
   days precious f., 716:2
   err grossly as the f., 283:18
   far and f., 499:19
   give but f. thy voice, 201:26
   happy f., 193:20
   if bees are f., 547:6
   immortal names, 426:7
   in hands not of f. but many, 73:18
   join f. if any, 670:4
   join special f. at top, 827:3
   know how to be old, 274:11
   laborers are f., 35:23
   let thy words be f., 24:11
   many admire f. know, 73:12
   many exploited by f., 737:8
   men of f. words best, 193:4
   much in f. words, 33:1
   philosophy is for the f., 155:11
   small country with f. people, 59:20
   so much owed to so f., 666:4
   sold the many on the f., 740:12
   some f. books to be chewed, 168:15
   that f. is all the world, 169:6
   the f. and the many, 370:9
   the notes are f., 371:12
   there be that find, 35:6
   things in this world, 812:4
   to f. men comes excellence, 61:11
   very f. to love, 391:18
   ye are many they are f., 429:14
   yellow leaves or none or f., 226:24
Fewest, having f. wants, 72:5
Fezziwig, Mrs. F. one vast Smile, 497:16
ffinch-ffarrowmere corrected the visitor,
   694:9
Fiamma, conosco i segni dell' antica f.,
   131:*n*4
Fiat justitia pereat coelum, 385:16
   justitia ruat coelum, 123:26
   lux, 5:*n*5
   ruat coelum f. voluntas tua, 124:22
Fiber, show food in minutest f., 403:18
Fibers, made of multitude of f., 451:12
Fibs, I'll tell you no f., 342:23
Fickle, whatever is f. freckled, 587:10
   woman always a f. thing, 97:19
Fickleness of women I love, 609:3
Fico, a f. for the phrase, 190:17
Fiction, biography is ultimately f., 793:13
   by fairy f. dressed, 335:15
   final belief in f., 687:15
   if woman is to write f., 700:7
   in disguise, 817:17
   lags after truth, 344:4
   poetry supreme f., 686:14
   tongue to deal in f., 307:5
   truth stranger than f., 424:23
   work of f. affords aesthetic bliss, 756:3
   writing f. developed respect for unknown,
    784:6
Fictional, work of history in f. form, 833:6
Fictions only and false hair, 250:8
   supreme f. of life, 688:21

Fiddle, cat and f., 858:2
   de-dee, 500:9
   master's lost f. stick, 856:14
   play on f. in Dooney, 637:13
   robes riche or f., 134:30
   we know is diddle, 569:17
Fiddle-dee-dee, French for f., 552:17
Fiddler, in came a f., 497:16
   statesman and buffoon, 283:15
Fiddlers three, 856:18
Fide, Punica f., 95:*n*9
Fidelity, gossamer f. of Man, 478:16
   think of f. not husbands, 695:12
Fidget, no f. and no reformer, 623:15
Fidus Achates, 97:*n*11
Fie fie upon her, 208:19
   foh and fum, 217:3
   my lord fie, 222:4
   upon this quiet life, 185:20
Field, accidents by flood and f., 212:29
   as a flower of the f., 19:7
   betokened tempest to f., 173:22
   consider lilies of f., 34:19
   cow a good animal in f., 327:15
   crop of corn a f. of tares, 164:17
   dedicate portion of f., 476:7
   dignity in tilling f., 610:20
   Esau was a man of the f., 7:10
   fair f. full of folk, 133:1
   gigantic f. of soya beans, 832:12
   goodliness as the flower of the f., 28:2
   Goya of the bare f., 829:3
   happy f. mossy cavern, 438:10
   has sight, 135:*n*2
   hath eyen wode eres, 135:21
   hi-hi-yee for f. artilleree, 684:9
   his arms, 164:19
   in league with stones of f., 13:39
   lay f. to f., 26:19
   life is not like crossing f., 861:18
   little f. well tilled, 319:10
   man for the f., 483:3
   man tills f. lies beneath, 485:14
   market economy's f. is world, 694:5
   not a f. but a cause, 354:15
   not that fair f. of Enna, 266:8
   not wholly reap corners of f., 9:13
   of grain, 794:1
   of human conflict, 666:4
   of ripe corn, 717:20
   potter's f., 38:1
   Prussia hurried to the f., 368:*n*5
   ring with importunate chink, 345:16
   roamed from f. to f., 371:9
   she is as in a f., 670:11
   shepherds abiding in f., 39:3
   six Richmonds in the f., 174:24
   so Truth be in the f., 263:5
   thy beauty's f., 225:28
   to live not as simple as cross f., 730:3
   viewed in her fair face's f., 175:3
   what though f. be lost, 264:3
Fields, as long as f. green, 430:8
   babbled of green f., 192:27
   battle won on playing f., 389:6
   carrying you into f. of light, 69:12
   dream of battled f., 397:7
   earth's green f., 501:17
   fanged with flints, 762:4

Figure a poem makes, 671:10
    baby f. of giant mass, 207:29
    but not figurative, 440:15
    human f. interests me most, 651:17
    in the carpet, 585:6
    in the landscape, 778:3
    is handsome, 571:14
    make me a fixed f., 214:26
    of a Nut, 546:7
    quaint great f., 685:6
Figures pedantical, 177:12
    universe in geometrical f., 169:18
Filament, launched forth f., 521:7
    one living f., 348:24
Filches my good name, 213:33
File, black rank and f., 556:3
    marching in endless f., 453:18
Files, beauteous f., 279:6
    foremost f. of time, 482:7
Files-on-Parade, 633:5
Filial, lively sense of f. duty, 356:21
    youth should be f., 62:9
Filipinos, educate F. uplift and civilize them,
    586:4
Fill all penuries, 236:21
    all the glasses there, 275:9
    at beginning of cask take your f.,
      56:16
    Cup that clears, 471:10
    his belly with east wind, 14:18
    Ithaca full of moths, 224:18
    me from crown to toe, 219:11
    mum dad f. you with faults, 810:8
    shoes f. with urine, 830:15
    stag drunk his f., 397:4
    void world never f., 347:2
    woods f. up with snow, 669:13
    world with fools, 523:15
Filled, body f. and vacant mind, 193:16
    did eat and were f., 36:14
    her house with blacks, 812:7
    little house well f., 319:10
    mouth f. with dust, 237:3
    rosebuds f. with snow, 232:6
    sails f. streamers waving, 269:6
    the hungry, 38:40
    they shall be f., 33:33
    thicket with honeyed song, 75:5
    with ends of worms, 736:3
    with Holy Ghost, 41:45
    with pebbly meaning, 814:5
Fillet, solemn f., 453:19
Filleth, bird that f. own nest, 141:19
Filling, two buckets f. one another,
    180:9
Fillip, giving f. to passage, 613:18
Fills, grief f. room of absent child,
    178:9
    me with astonishment, 836:3
    shadows and windy places, 567:17
    white rustling sail, 417:7
Filly, likeness of f. foal, 181:5
Film, balanced F. with F., 547:2
    thought beneath slight f., 544:6
Filtered, opinion truth f., 489:17
Filth, decked in f., 807:4
    hunger f. and ignorance, 727:7
    identical and so is f., 684:4
Filths savor but themselves, 217:14

Filthy, fog and f. air, 218:24
    let him be f. still, 49:3
    lucre, 46:17
    righteousnesses are as f. rags, 28:33
    so f. nobody touched, 449:1
    tobacco f. weed, 369:16
Fin, commencement de la f., 369:*n*4
    gold f. in porphyry, 483:6
Final belief in fiction, 687:15
    cause produces motion, 80:5
    face of love, 809:6
    judged in light of f. issue, 81:15
    resting place, 476:7
    Ruin fiercely drives, 306:13
    solution, 782:4
    solution of Jewish question, 737:7
    word in reality, 823:8
Finale of seem, 686:15
Finance, maxims of orthodox f., 702:2
Financial, stranger in f. straits, 73:2
Finch-Farrowmere, Sir Jasper F., 694:9
Find at end of perfect day, 625:15
    but seldom use them, 455:29
    by searching f. out God, 14:7
    chance to f. yourself, 612:6
    directions out, 202:30
    faithful friends hard to f., 239:3
    felicity we make or f., 325:3
    few there be that f., 35:6
    go and f. it, 635:15
    gone into cellar where never f. him,
      783:17
    happiness she does not f., 324:11
    happy could he f. it, 252:17
    hard to f. one just suited, 409:3
    he f. you sleeping, 38:31
    he it found shall f., 642:2
    he that loseth life shall f. it, 35:32
    his mouth a rein, 568:22
    if we f. each other, 738:20
    if you try you just might f., 838:7
    in His ways f. Him not, 486:10
    like again, 396:15
    look for truth not f. it, 331:25
    Love f. out way, 845:5
    man to benefit kingdom difficult, 81:24
    moral if you can f. it, 550:16
    next morning it was someone else, 384:9
    none but Love f. me out, 159:21
    one Ring to f. them, 736:4
    ourselves dishonorable graves, 195:20
    out cause of this effect, 203:2
    out moonshine, 181:19
    out of good f. evil, 224:5
    place where men pray, 664:15
    search will f. it out, 248:15
    seek all day ere you f. them, 187:23
    seek and ye shall f., 35:3
    seeking shall f. Him, 492:24
    sure to f. use for it, 398:10
    sure your sin will f. you out, 9:27
    talk and f. fault, 156:10
    thee sitting careless, 438:12
    there is enough, 680:9
    thy body by wall, 531:5
    to strive seek f., 481:15
    touch and do not f. it, 58:15
    trout in milk, 505:3

Find (*continued*)
    turn to pleasure all they f., 317:6
    two better hemispheres, 233:12
    virtue possession would not show, 194:39
    we profit by losing prayers, 223:11
    what gives life value, 770:8
    what we are seeking, 735:4
    what's not found at once, 812:14
    where last rose lingers, 99:20
    where seek is f., 338:1
    you shall f. me grave man, 183:28
Findeth, he that f. his life, 35:32
Finding smoother pebble, 291:6
    withhold f. or conjecture, 365:1
Finds, alters when it alteration f., 227:17
    he can bear anything, 748:14
    mark archer little meant, 397:17
    pang as great, 211:20
    sixpence in her shoe, 244:15
    tongues in trees, 197:37
    too late men betray, 341:20
Fine, at once strong and f., 627:10
    camlet cloak, 288:1
    exceptionally f. writing, 628:11
    eye in f. frenzy rolling, 182:3
    first f. careless rapture, 492:5
    grave's f. private place, 277:2
    lady upon white horse, 858:14
    make face of heaven so f., 183:32
    makes the action f., 251:1
    not only f. feathers make f. birds, 60:17
    passage particularly f., 327:19
    poetry less subtle and f., 262:19
    puss-gentleman, 347:13
    put too f. a point, 159:6
    that f. madness, 169:17
    thing needs laboring, 637:18
    too f. point on it, 498:21
    wind blowing new direction, 707:5
    women eat crazy salad, 639:10
    words butter no parsnips, 397:28
Finemque tenere, 110:*n*3
Finer than staple of his argument, 177:9
Finery, dressed out in all her f., 342:19
Fine's, still the f. the crown, 210:29
Fines, nor excessive f. imposed, 361:7
Finest hour, 666:2
    spectacles in nature, 320:15
    woman in nature, 303:5
Finger, ambitious f., 230:18
    between f. thumb squat pen, 833:13
    don't rewrite what moving f. writ, 764:1
    feel thy f. and find thee, 587:3
    God's f. touched him, 484:9
    goodness in little f., 299:17
    his slow and moving f., 214:26
    in every pie, 156:21
    let our f. ache, 157:*n*3
    Moving F. writes, 471:21
    moving only little f., 581:3
    my ring encompasseth thy f., 173:33
    of birth-strangled babe, 221:22
    of God, 8:13
    on capsule of truth, 756:10
    pipe for fortune's f., 204:17
    silent f. points to heaven, 395:7
    struck f. on the place, 528:15
Fingering slave, 392:2
Fingernails, artist indifferent paring f., 696:6

Fingers, counting my numberless f., 816:16
  dark f. of the water, 787:2
  five sovereign f., 795:4
  he has ears and eyes and ten f., 499:13
  heavens the work of thy f., 15:32
  ill cook cannot lick own f., 184:9
  just as my f. on keys, 687:4
  made before forks, 299:16
  my f. ache, 408:9
  my f. move, 825:3
  on keys make music, 687:4
  paddling palms and pinching f., 228:11
  separate as f. one as hand, 610:19
  twirled f. madly, 500:6
  wandered idly, 537:15
  weary and worn, 446:2
  with forced f. rude, 261:13
Fingers', smile upon f. ends, 192:27
  two f. breadth of damnation, 57:*n6*
Fini, il n'y a plus f., 662:*n2*
Finis bonus totum bonum, 148:*n1*
  coronat opus, 123:27
Finish, give tools f. job, 666:8
  strive on to f., 477:4
  whether sufficient to f., 39:33
Finished all is finished, 487:8
  by such a she, 177:27
  it is f., 41:40
  my course, 46:33
  our hand f. it, 106:6
  poem never f. only abandoned, 659:6
  the comedy is f., 614:5
  turned out some very f. types, 617:15
  when feast f., 645:10
Finisher, author and f. of our faith, 47:1
  ourselves author and f., 474:3
Finishes, if a man f. a poem, 830:16
Finite, anxiety of f. being, 712:8
  cannot bury infinite under F., 433:18
  hearts that yearn, 492:14
Finitude overcome, 629:9
Finity, veil of f., 821:16
Finned cars nose forward, 801:14
Finnigin, gone agin F., 651:5
Finny, na poo f., 662:22
Fir, in f. tar is, 860:10
Fire and ice within me fight, 618:17
  and rose are one, 722:5
  and water, 190:30
  answers fire, 193:11
  appeared a chariot of f., 12:39
  as kingfishers catch f., 587:16
  because 'tis filled with f., 373:14
  before ashes of council f. cold, 533:9
  beside the f. bending, 150:13
  best of servants, 434:25
  books not killed by f., 698:18
  books you may carry to f., 326:2
  bound upon wheel of f., 217:29
  burn cauldron bubble, 221:20
  burnt child f. dreadeth, 148:25
  burnt f. of thine eyes, 374:5
  bush burned with f., 8:3
  can a man take f. in his bosom, 21:7
  chains and penal f., 263:23
  chariot of f., 375:17
  clear f. clean hearth, 407:13
  come on baby light my f., 842:12
  consumed by either f. or f., 722:2

Fire *(continued)*
  dance f. dance in iron shoes, 821:12
  death of water and f., 721:17
  dives on you in f., 800:9
  don't f. unless fired upon, 346:9
  don't f. until you see whites of eyes, 340:5
  doubt thou stars are f., 203:3
  drunk with f., 381:8
  dying in the grate, 541:5
  earth f. sea air, 577:1
  element of f. put out, 235:26
  ever-living F. being kindled and going
    out, 64:6
  every time she shouted F., 653:10
  falsely shouting f. in theater, 578:13
  faster and not give up ship, 413:13
  fat is in the f., 147:8
  fell in f. and burnt to ashes, 671:21
  follow good side to f., 153:13
  fretted with golden f., 203:17
  gold shines like f., 65:24
  great ball of f., 723:5
  heap coals of f., 23:3
  hearts touched with f., 577:16
  heretic that makes the f., 228:16
  hide f. but w'at do wid smoke, 593:15
  hold f. in his hand, 179:6
  house on f. children burn, 857:8
  if his pistol misses f., 343:8
  in asshen olde is f. yreke, 136:6
  in mind ever burning, 160:2
  in the f. of Spring, 471:2
  in the lake, 5:2
  into eternal darkness f. and ice, 130:9
  is test of gold, 107:2
  knot of f., 722:5
  like sparks of f. befriend thee, 248:11
  lips touch sacred f., 656:18
  liquid f., 384:10
  little f. kindleth great matter, 47:16
  little f. quickly trodden out, 173:8
  Lolita f. of my loins, 755:14
  Lord was not in the f., 12:32
  made smoke into f., 434:22
  maketh ministers flame of f., 46:37
  melt in her own f., 205:23
  Milton Proteus of f., 403:13
  moral man shines like f., 66:25
  most tolerable third party, 505:8
  motion of hidden f., 396:2
  Mrs. Bennet stirring f., 406:7
  Muse of f., 192:15
  my heart consumed in f., 125:7
  neither wrath of love nor f., 105:21
  next time, 813:6
  no f. without smoke, 149:4
  not f. nor stars, 70:2
  not long life by f., 624:3
  not resolution to f. it, 326:12
  now stir the f., 348:4
  of life, 408:11
  of soul kindled, 496:28
  old and nodding by f., 637:4
  one f. burns out another's, 182:18
  out of frying pan into f., 116:21
  overcome heresy with f., 144:6
  pain wanders like lost f., 781:8
  pale his uneffectual f., 202:21
  pillar of f., 8:23

Fire *(continued)*
  pull chestnuts out of f., 277:13
  revealed by f., 43:36
  run through f. and water, 190:30
  sacred f. of liberty, 350:5
  sea or f., 200:21
  set around kitchen f., 596:5
  set by f. and spin, 858:1
  set f. to Thames, 336:10
  set house on f. to roast eggs, 168:2
  shadows which f. throws, 77:14
  shall try man's work, 43:36
  silent language of star, 725:5
  smell f. whose gown burns, 251:11
  some say world end in f., 669:11
  spark o' Nature's f., 377:17
  sparkle right Promethean f., 177:8
  spirit all compact of f., 173:19
  stallion shod with f., 537:17
  stand by the f. and stink, 216:1
  stood against my f., 217:28
  that in heart resides, 528:12
  thorough flood thorough f., 181:3
  those who favor f., 669:11
  three removes as bad as f., 320:9
  through f. and through water, 18:6
  throw whole book in f., 461:7
  time the f. in which we burn, 791:11
  tongued with f. beyond living, 721:15
  tongues of f., 41:45
  tree is cast into f., 33:27
  true love a durable f., 160:2
  two irons in the f., 245:5
  view what f. was near, 168:26
  virtue more than water or f., 63:23
  water and f. shall rot, 721:17
  what hand dare seize f., 374:5
  what of faith and f., 576:3
  when ready Gridley, 567:2
  whether in sea or f., 200:21
  which seems extinguished, 257:12
  while I was musing the f. burned, 17:11
  world is ever-living F., 64:6
  worthy of nothing but to be cast into f.,
    318:16
  years steal f. from mind, 420:14
  youth of England on f., 192:24
Firearm, lead from linotype as from f., 771:17
Firebell, like f. in the night, 359:5
Firebrand to smoke, 140:5
Fire-breathing Catholic C.O., 801:1
Fired another Troy, 285:14
  don't fire unless f. upon, 346:9
  if not f. shouldn't be hanging there,
    622:*n3*
  not who f. the shot, 782:2
  shot heard round world, 453:11
Firefly, life flash of f. in night, 525:7
  wakens, 483:6
Fire-folk sitting in the air, 587:5
Firelit, think of f. homes, 712:2
Fire-red cherubynnes face, 135:13
Fire's, wore f. center, 783:16
Fires, death f. danced, 400:1
  do little about infernal f., 802:7
  fuel to maintain his f., 253:18
  keep home f. burning, 663:1
  late when the f. out, 598:22
  live their wonted f., 334:25

Fires *(continued)*
 of Troy, 759:15
 out by gas f. of the refinery, 841:8
 passing through dark f., 817:3
 show remnant of their f., 289:14
 thought-executing f., 216:18
 true Genius kindles, 312:4
 veils her sacred f., 313:25
 violent f. soon burn out, 179:11
 wine inspires and f. us, 307:13
Fireside, Englishman's f., 383:15
 king by your own f., 155:13
 sit by f. with Sorrow, 431:7
Firesides, protect health homes f., 597:10
Firewood ironware and trays, 681:5
Firing, if no one thinking of f. it, 622:9
 no f. till you see whites of eyes, 330:10
 to-morrow have what to do after f., 794:12
Firkin, meal in the f., 454:27
Firm against the crowd, 483:9
 and stable earth, 247:6
 Catullus be resolved and f., 94:6
 fly from f. base, 397:11
 ground of Result, 665:2
 heart f. as stone, 15:21
 how take f. hold, 82:16
 my f. nerves never tremble, 221:14
 priests stood f. on dry ground, 10:19
 office boy to Attorney's f., 563:17
 praise f. restraint with which write, 760:8
 stands watch along Rhine, 518:1
 the f. are near to virtue, 63:10
 too f. a heart, 309:28
Firmament, brave o'erhanging f., 203:17
 buzzing world lisping f., 687:19
 Christ's blood streams in f., 171:4
 curses of the f., 285:n4
 fall to base earth from f., 179:22
 no fellow in f., 196:13
 now glowed the f., 266:16
 planets and the f., 235:26
 showeth his handiwork, 16:10
 spacious f. on high, 301:14
 starry f. for roof, 572:17
Firmer, tired ox treads with f. step, 118:27
Firm-footed by sea unchanging, 447:2
Firmness, in the right, 477:4
Firm-set earth, 220:10
Firs, pointed f. darkly cloaked, 594:16
First, absurd is the f. truth, 790:1
 after f. death no other, 795:6
 Amendment has erected wall, 710:17
 among equals, 124:17
 and foremost I am individual, 540:8
 and great commandment, 36:43
 and second class citizens, 736:12
 appearance of new beings, 469:10
 baby makes f. step, 757:13
 bead of sweat, 826:4
 became tutor to a lunatic, 661:3
 best country is at home, 341:1
 between acting and f. motion, 196:1
 blow half battle, 342:21
 born as children, 813:15
 came the seen, 709:10

First *(continued)*
 cannot be f. in everything, 60:21
 cast a stone, 41:8
 chance to build Great Society, 779:6
 come first served, 128:n2
 comes f. eats f., 128:1
 descry the big canoe, 516:1
 evening and morning were f. day, 5:10
 fine careless rapture, 492:5
 for which f. made, 494:7
 get there f., 527:12
 God f. planted garden, 168:13
 golden time of f. love, 382:7
 good die f., 395:4
 Great F. Cause, 348:24
 guarantee of F. Amendment, 711:2
 He is the f. and the last, 122:15
 him f. last midst, 267:3
 hundred days, 799:9
 in hearts of countrymen, 371:8
 in past man has been f., 610:17
 in the f. place, 831:18
 in war first in peace, 371:8
 is deep love, 59:14
 it is copying out, 834:3
 last everlasting day, 234:17
 last shall be f., 36:35
 light of evening, 688:14
 looking away from f. things, 582:18
 loved at f. sight, 170:15
 man among these than second in Rome, 91:26
 man who said This is mine, 330:17
 men f. subjects afterward, 505:14
 moment of atomic age, 793:5
 nothing be done for f. time, 668:11
 office of government splendid misery, 358:6
 one now will later be last, 836:6
 pay for it f. or last, 504:2
 poetry not f. thing I reach for, 833:10
 say what you would be, 112:16
 seed de f. en last, 748:10
 seems to Comprehend Whole, 545:7
 shall be last, 36:35
 shoot f. inquire afterwards, 737:6
 shudder of gentility, 743:19
 step is hardest, 317:9
 sweet sleep of night, 429:8
 that ever burst, 399:20
 that found famous country, 734:9
 the f. and the last, 49:4
 there is no last or f., 491:6
 thing let's kill lawyers, 172:19
 things the f. poets had, 169:16
 time in city's long history, 756:16
 thy f. love, 48:8
 true gentleman, 233:7
 two pass comprehension, 789:2
 we practice to deceive, 396:23
 what are we f., 541:7
 Who's on f., 742:15
 women and children f., 848:6
 youth tested to old age, 528:2
 Zeus f. cause, 65:11
Firstborn among many brethren, 43:8
 brought forth f. son, 39:2
 offspring of heaven f., 265:24
 smite all the f., 8:18

First-class fightin' man, 633:9
 second-class intellect f. temperament, 579:5
 travel f. and with children, 725:14
Firstfruits of them that slept, 44:24
Firstling of the infant year, 253:19
First-rate, test of f. intelligence, 746:13
 tragedy, 711:6
Fish, a poor f. peddler, 724:20
 all f. that cometh to net, 148:19
 and guests in three days, 86:n6
 army is like f., 737:13
 biggest f. got away, 597:3
 cannot live in fields, 93:10
 cars nose forward like f., 801:14
 dart before you, 4:10
 dies because he opens mouth, 862:17
 disputants put me in mind of skuttle f., 302:20
 dominion over f. of the sea, 5:14
 eat f. that fed of worm, 205:33
 fiddle de-dee, 500:9
 flesh or fowl, 639:16
 formal as scales on f., 714:2
 I let f. go, 785:9
 in troubled waters, 295:17
 it's no f. ye're buying, 397:20
 Jonah was in the belly of the f., 30:27
 kettle of f., 565:1
 little F. swam, 500:1
 nor flesh nor good red herring, 148:3
 not with melancholy bait, 187:22
 one f. ball, 534:7
 out of water, 291:10
 say they have stream, 712:17
 son of first f. ashore, 819:13
 teaching a f. to swim, 124:14
 this f. will bite, 194:27
 thou deboshed f. thou, 230:2
 to f. and to seals, 785:10
 we are f. and meat, 644:8
 what cat's averse to f., 334:3
 when you tadpole and I f., 615:19
 with F. questing Snail, 781:10
 with worm that eat king, 205:33
 without a bicycle, 852:25
Fishbone in city's throat, 801:11
Fished by obstinate isles, 709:1
Fisher, Kitty F. found it, 860:11
Fisherman's, well for f. boy, 482:15
Fishermen that walk upon the beach, 217:18
Fishers of men, 33:32
 of song, 613:15
Fishes, as f. taken in evil net, 24:30
 five loaves and two f., 36:13
 flyin' f. play, 633:13
 in other men's ditches, 861:3
 marvel how f. live in sea, 225:9
 men lived like f., 225:n1
 of sea draw us to kingdom, 117:5
 shall declare unto thee, 14:11
 stone-deaf f., 780:8
 talk like whales, 343:9
 thousand men that f. gnawed, 174:3
 waiting for invasion so are f., 666:7
 welcomes little f. in, 549:13
Fishified, flesh how art thou f., 183:21

Fishing, between religion and fly f., 763:4
 east wind never blow when he goes a-f., 252:23
 gone a-f., 252:20
 time is stream I go a-f. in, 507:3
Fishlike, ancient and f. smell, 229:28
 flash f., 642:17
Fishmonger, you are a f., 203:4
Fishnet, undoing f. of tarred rope, 802:4
Fist, feel army in my f., 381:5
 iron f., 389:3
 with f. instead of stick, 270:14
Fisted canvas, 611:18
Fit bed for this huge birth, 272:16
 content with fortunes f., 216:25
 dish f. for gods, 196:3
 for crooked counsels f., 283:8
 for public authority, 67:23
 for the kingdom of God, 39:16
 for treasons strategems, 190:7
 instruments of ill, 309:12
 life never seems to f., 749:10
 night for man or beast, 690:2
 not f. that men be compared with gods, 94:21
 only the f. survive, 673:8
 only to be writer, 814:6
 to one neutral thing both sexes f., 234:6
 which ordinary men f. for, 215:32
 why then I'll f. you, 164:14
Fitful, life's f. fever, 221:5
 tracing of portal, 687:5
Fitness, eternal f. of things, 322:7
Fits dull fighter, 186:29
 periodical f. of morality, 447:21
 shoe f. one pinches another, 675:4
 'twas sad by f., 337:3
 your thief, 212:2
Fitted him to a T, 146:*n*4
 in thy lips, 22:27
 nothing he not f. to bear, 115:22
Fitter love for me, 234:10
Fittest may also be gentlest, 757:6
 Survival of F., 469:13
 survival of f., 523:13, 559:6
Fitting and proper we do this, 476:7
 for princess descended of kings, 224:14
Fitzgerald, for this F. died, 638:7
 strung on English thread, 515:16
Fiunt non nascuntur Christiani, 118:*n*9
Five, Benjamin's mess was f. times as much, 7:28
 chose him f. smooth stones, 11:29
 cry of critic for f., 557:13
 fatal f. in the afternoon, 751:9
 full fathom f., 229:20
 kings did king to death, 795:4
 reasons we should drink, 292:23
 sons who died gloriously, 477:2
 sovereign fingers, 795:4
 were wise five foolish, 37:12
Five-cent, good f. cigar, 603:1
 good f. nickel, 603:*n*1
Five-pound note, 499:15
Fix eyes on greatness of Athens, 74:5
 in such f. be fertile, 763:6
 looking for angry f., 817:12

Fixed as an aim or butt, 192:20
 Everlasting had not f., 201:1
 fate free will, 265:13
 give name to every f. star, 176:20
 great gulf f., 40:3
 make me a f. figure, 214:26
 objects f. and dead, 403:4
 of old founded strong, 619:4
 sentinels almost receive, 193:11
 still stood f. to hear, 267:17
 thy soul the f. foot, 235:3
 wedding day f., 322:15
Fizz, blood f. like wine, 680:8
Flabbiness, moral f., 581:4
Flabby bald lobotomized, 801:2
Flaccid, contemplate my f. shape, 741:5
Flag, American f. floats, 343:11
 beneath starry f., 522:8
 braved a thousand years, 408:16
 companionship and country, 490:2
 death's pale f., 184:16
 goes by, 606:7
 in f. government and truths, 500:14
 meteor f. of England, 408:18
 not f. only but nation, 500:14
 not f. or fail, 666:1
 not kiss your f.ing f., 740:3
 of man naturalized yesterday, 597:13
 of my disposition, 518:18
 of our Union, 451:23
 party that does not carry f., 445:13
 pledge allegiance to f. of United States, 606:17
 rally round f. boys, 522:9
 spare country's f., 468:15
 that makes you free, 553:11
 there I find f. of England, 388:9
 there is National f., 490:2
 to April's breeze, 453:11
 was still there, 411:1
Flagon, out of English f., 664:14
Flagons, stay me with f., 25:16
Flagpole, old f. still stands, 690:10
Flagrant, fair and f. things, 272:12
Flagrante delicto, 123:28
Flags, battle f. furled, 482:1
 stiff f. straining, 664:10
Flak, woke to black f. nightmare fighters, 793:6
Flakes falling on city brown, 586:6
Flame, adding fuel to the f., 269:12
 as Parallax a F., 546:12
 courses beneath my skin, 57:20
 draft fluttered f., 730:8
 dragonflies draw f., 587:16
 feel spark of that ancient f., 97:17
 feel steady candle f., 492:8
 Fury slinging f., 483:22
 great f. follows little spark, 131:25
 hard gemlike f., 573:9
 idealism fanned into f., 607:6
 Jabberwock with eyes of f., 551:11
 love harsh irregular f., 771:8
 maketh ministers f. of fire, 46:37
 miserable mortals f. with life, 53:31
 my f. to qualify, 227:13
 nor public f. nor private, 313:25
 of freedom in souls, 576:14
 recognize signals of ancient f., 131:21

Flame (*continued*)
 sacred f., 401:22
 shirt of f., 722:2
 that cannot singe sleeve, 641:7
 thin smoke without f., 576:5
 tongues of f. infolded, 722:5
 vital spark of heavenly f., 309:3
 when lovely f. dies, 663:5
 words full of subtle f., 245:4
Flame-colored, hot wench in f. taffeta, 184:23
Flamens, here lies two f., 253:12
Flames have spread over globe, 359:9
 in forehead of sky, 262:5
 in present light f., 667:3
 must waste away, 253:18
 no faggot feeds, 641:6
 paly f., 193:11
 rich f. and hired tears, 256:13
 rolled on, 432:2
 went by her like thin f., 541:27
 whatever f. upon night, 640:12
Flaming bounds of place and time, 335:9
 hurled headlong f., 263:23
 ruddy limbs f. hair, 373:11
 sword which turned, 6:11
 thou f. minister, 215:7
 walls of heavens, 92:10
 youth, 205:23
Flammantia moenia mundi, 92:*n*6
Flanders, armies swore in F., 332:21
 in F. fields, 660:9
Flank golden, 734:10
 of something more permanent, 824:15
Flanks, silken f., 438:3
Flannel, neither eat it nor make f., 707:16
 wear white f. trousers, 717:16
Flanneled fools at wicket, 635:8
Flap bug with gilded wings, 312:8
Flap-dragon, easier swallowed than f., 177:10
Flare, quick to f. up, 54:25
Flash fishlike, 642:17
 mirth like f. of lightning, 302:18
 of light cut across sky, 793:4
 packet of fame, 862:12
Flashed and fell Excalibur, 481:2
 the living lightning, 309:13
Flashes, brightest f. of thought, 523:22
 inspiration descends only in f., 789:7
 occasional f. of silence, 399:1
 of merriment, 206:24
Flashing eyes, 401:19
Flat blasphemy, 211:14
 burglary as ever committed, 195:2
 churches in f. countries, 395:*n*2
 clothes lines linking each f., 729:11
 he whose soul is f., 734:15
 hev it plain an' f., 514:21
 how weary stale f., 201:1
 I their map lie f., 236:14
 in f. sea sunk, 260:29
 on your face, 741:17
 strike f. thick rotundity, 216:18
 the wall fell down f., 10:21
 with broad f. nails, 79:4
Flatter, more we love less we f., 278:7
 Neptune for his trident, 224:28
 not f. me at all, 254:16

Flies (*continued*)
see where it f., 170:23
shoot folly as it f., 310:21
through air with ease, 571:14
time's f., 218:18
unto you at last she f., 253:15
verse find who sermon f., 249:16
who f. can fight anew, 84:*n*3
wings of Time grief f., 276:17
worms and flowers, 304:3
Flieth, arrow that f. by day, 18:25
Flight, beetle wheels droning f., 334:9
black f. of crows, 855:*n*2
fellow of selfsame f., 187:24
flown his cloistered f., 221:6
from afar to view f., 296:17
his wild airy f., 269:8
life like f. of sparrow, 125:1
never-ending f. of days, 265:6
puts Stars to f., 470:14
single f. of planes, 756:16
struggle and f., 531:2
Sun scattered into f., 470:13
swift be thy f., 430:23
through sky thy certain f., 432:11
time and world in f., 637:9
time arrest f., 426:8
Time in your f., 549:8
Flights and perchings, 581:13
four f. Thursday, 647:16
grand f. Sunday baths, 687:13
of angels sing thee, 207:15
Flinch, we did not f., 62:6
Flinders, little Polly F., 859:10
Fling away ambition, 231:6
garment of Repentance f., 471:2
stone giant dies, 317:5
Flint, behold man of f., 856:4
firmest f. doth in continuance wear, 92:*n*9
weariness snore upon f., 225:19
Flints, fields fanged with f., 762:4
Flirt, money won't surrinder to f., 646:23
Flirtation, significant word f., 315:11
Flit on wings of borrowed wit, 247:1
Flits by on leathern wing, 337:2
Flitter dip and soar, 809:2
Flitting, Raven never f., 479:8
Float, how sweetly did they f., 260:27
iron in water f., 845:11
like a butterfly, 836:16
Floated into inmost soul, 516:7
web f. wide, 480:26
Floating bulwark of our island, 338:9
hair, 401:19
ice mast-high came f. by, 399:17
like vapor on air, 539:2
many bells down, 740:8
on the floor, 479:9
over Harvard Square, 751:14
spar to men that sink, 735:12
Floats, chicken hawk f. over, 820:2
on high o'er vales, 394:4
though unseen among us, 427:14
Flock, feed his f. like a shepherd, 28:5
keeping watch over their f., 39:3
of bridges bleating, 689:17
shun the polluted f., 710:6
silent f. in fold, 436:20
without shepherd sheep not f., 861:20

Flocks, bad herdsmen ruin their f., 55:16
battening our f., 261:16
bells of the f., 786:13
casual f. of pigeons, 686:19
my father feeds f., 337:14
or herds or human face, 265:25
while shepherds watched f., 294:4
Flogged, man never f. never taught, 83:16
she f. herself, 472:20
Flogging, habit of f. me constantly, 504:7
Flood, accidents by f. and field, 212:29
arched the f., 453:11
carriest them away as with a f., 18:20
decay no f., 637:7
enchafed f., 213:6
giant race before the f., 285:4
half our sailors swallowed in f., 173:12
land of mountain and f., 396:12
Milton Proteus of f., 403:13
of mortal ills, 144:9
of remembrance, 707:7
of words drop of reason, 319:15
taken at the f., 197:13
ten years before the F., 276:27
thorough f. thorough fire, 181:3
torn Naiad from f., 477:14
when just cause reaches f. tide, 616:11
Floods, bathe in fiery f., 211:23
haystack in f., 556:10
he hath established it upon the f., 16:19
neither can f. drown it, 26:4
passions like f. and streams, 160:5
rimless f., 753:11
stood upright as an heap, 8:28
that are deepest, 845:5
Floor, bar-room f., 584:6
careless on granary f., 438:12
cleaned windows swept f., 563:17
common sense on ground f., 473:18
forest's ferny f., 762:10
front of this small f., 272:19
mystery on bestial f., 638:9
nicely sanded f., 342:10
of heaven is inlaid, 190:5
reorganized upon f., 718:9
scratching at the f., 623:8
starry f., 373:17
sunk beneath watery f., 262:5
two jars on f. of Zeus, 54:6
wrought ghost upon f., 479:1
Floors of silent seas, 717:11
Flopsy Mopsy Cottontail Peter, 644:2
Flora and country green, 437:7
fauna geography, 785:19
Lady F. lovely Roman, 541:29
Flores in the Azores, 486:22
Florida, Everglades of F., 728:14
weighted with regret, 821:4
Flots, léger j'ai dansé sur les f., 603:*n*6
Floundered enjoyed suffered, 585:19
Flour, peace into poet as f. into bread, 768:10
Flourish, almond tree shall f., 25:8
first onion f. there, 599:5
may f. or may fade, 341:29
men f. only for a moment, 55:21
nations are destroyed or f., 376:4
poetry painting music f., 376:4
righteous shall f., 18:27

Flourish (*continued*)
set on youth, 226:17
those which most admirably f., 227:*n*1
where you turn eyes, 308:5
Flourished, bloody treason f., 197:1
hoop unbroken people f., 628:1
Flourishes, society where moderation f., 660:5
Flourisheth as flower of the field, 19:7
in the morning it f., 18:20
Flourishing like a green bay tree, 17:*n*1
of the arts, 737:18
Flours, no f. on grave, 575:6
Flout, banners f. the sky, 218:25
'em and scout 'em, 230:4
Flow, all pleasant fruits do f., 232:5
ceaseless ebb and f., 602:15
ebb and f. by the moon, 218:1
from discord f., 302:2
from my lips would f., 429:20
from whom all blessings f., 289:22
gently sweet Afton, 379:10
how well soe'er it f., 312:6
I within did f., 290:4
its one will f., 753:15
of soul, 312:14
oh could I f. like thee, 274:23
salt tides seaward f., 528:5
streams f. with ambrosia, 70:5
with tears of gold, 372:9
words to say it f., 289:7
Flower, age will fade beauty's f., 151:3
as a f. of the field, 19:7
bee does not hurt f., 66:25
blue forked torch of f., 707:21
crimson-tipped f., 378:7
culture in finest f., 625:4
displayed doth fall, 209:23
fadeth, 28:3
fancy from f. bell, 493:8
first f. of wilderness, 426:14
from every opening f., 304:1
full many a f., 334:20
glory in the f., 393:18
glory of man as f. of grass, 47:26
goodliness as the f. of the field, 28:2
he cometh forth like a f., 14:15
heaven in wild f., 375:5
herself a fairer f., 266:8
in crannied wall, 486:21
in the f. of their age, 11:15
let black f. blossom, 460:9
little f. if I understand, 486:21
little western f., 181:9
London f. of Cities all, 142:2
look like innocent f., 219:14
loved tree or f., 412:13
masterpiece appear as f., 557:16
meanest f. that blows, 393:19
merry Margaret as midsummer f., 141:22
moon like a f., 372:8
my love dropped like a f., 94:7
nipt my f. sae early, 380:5
of kings and knights destroyed, 139:13
of knyghthod and of fredom f., 137:22
of wickedness, 494:29
of wyfly pacience, 137:4
or wearing-stone, 669:10
prized beyond sculptured f., 432:13

Flying *(continued)*

    seaward f., 719:16
    snow came f., 586:6
    time f. never to return, 96:18
    trapeze, 571:14
    wild echoes f., 482:19
Foal, likeness of filly f., 181:5
Foam, born and die like f., 127:12
    copulate in f., 642:17
    cruel crawling f., 513:22
    is not cruel, 517:5
    like f. on river, 397:9
    now I f. to wheat, 827:18
    oceans white with f., 716:7
    of flowers, 568:9
    opening on the f., 437:13
    poetry new as f., 454:6
    sea folk turn into f., 461:21
    too full for sound and f., 487:2
    weeds and f., 452:17
    white f. flew, 399:20
Foam-bell no consequence, 530:13
Foaming out their own shame, 48:1
Foams, my sad heart f. at stern, 603:7
Focis, pro aris atque f., 95:*n6*
Focus of evil, 787:11
Focus of evil, 787:11
Fodder's in the shock, 596:8
Foe, angry with my f., 374:11
    at another gate let in the f., 269:4
    avowed erect manly f., 389:16
    call no man f., 733:6
    comes with fearless eyes, 627:3
    foils f. by effusion of ink, 338:4
    friend to her f., 386:10
    grim Death my son and f., 265:19
    heat not furnace for f., 230:20
    idleness sorrow friend f., 738:10
    laughter has no greater f. than emotion,
        616:4
    make one worthy man f., 312:6
    meet insulting f., 368:11
    met dearest f. in heaven, 201:10
    never made a f., 486:4
    Olympian a difficult f., 52:11
    overcome but half his f., 264:21
    perhaps a jealous f., 429:25
    scratch lover find f., 738:12
    someday to prove our f., 67:9
    sternest knight to f., 139:14
    support friend oppose f., 799:7
    take up quarrel with f., 660:10
    thou that seemest f., 144:*n3*
    timorous f., 312:4
    to favoritism, 611:19
    tyrants fall in every f., 380:11
    unrelenting f. to love, 318:7
    wolf that's f. to men, 244:4
Foeman bares steel tarantara, 564:4
Foeman's, beneath f. frown, 487:10
Foemen worthy of steel, 397:12
Foes, ah my f., 735:2
    beat down baffling f., 529:1
    learning's barbarous f., 323:14
    man that makes character makes f.,
        305:21
    not know friends from f., 505:20
    now have neither f. nor friends, 735:*n1*
    our f. press on, 129:5
    so far only hate our f., 67:9

Foes *(continued)*

    what their f. liked was done, 776:11
    will provide with arms, 97:12
Fog and filthy air, 218:24
    comes on cat feet, 681:9
    feel f. in throat, 494:18
    gleams through f., 333:10
    London particular a f., 498:20
    patience everywhere like f., 767:10
    woodthrush singing through f., 719:18
Foggy foggy dew, 847:17
Fogs, his rising f. prevail, 284:3
    retiring f. revealed an army, 655:10
Foh a fico for the phrase, 190:17
    Fie f. and fum, 217:3
Foiled, after thousand victories f., 226:4
Foils foe by effusion of ink, 338:4
Fold, all driven into same f., 99:22
    do not f. spindle or mutilate, 852:8
    flock in woolly f., 436:20
    hands and wait, 566:17
    home fast f. thy child, 587:19
    sheep not of this f., 41:18
    sheep to f., 619:16
    star that bids shepherd f., 260:18
    tents like Arabs, 466:14
    to their bosoms the viper, 516:1
    walking round the f., 372:9
    wolf in f. sad thing, 95:19
Folded her hair expectantly, 521:6
    lord of f. arms, 176:33
Folding of the hands to sleep, 21:5
Folds, lost f. of damasked gown, 151:2
    lull distant f., 334:9
    of bright girdle furled, 531:2
    rippling in breeze, 490:2
Foliage, children in f., 720:13
    silver light on f., 751:7
Folio, whole volumes in f., 176:26
Folk, ancient f. with evil spells, 856:5
    best literature becomes f. literature,
        772:18
    black f. say America been stronger,
        781:15
    dance like wave of sea, 637:13
    down there sea f. live, 461:20
    fair field full of f., 133:1
    messenger with language of his f., 121:7
    queerest f. of all, 623:9
    songs from soul sounds, 742:6
Folks, as long as colored man look to white f.,
        839:9
    O yonge fresshe f., 134:11
    rail against other folks, 322:2
    there's where old f. stay, 538:15
    think you lack, 745:5
Folks', lazy f. stummucks, 593:11
Follies and misfortunes of mankind, 353:8
    and wickedness, 772:15
    cease with youth, 323:2
    of town crept slowly, 342:14
    perished by their own f., 53:148
    that themselves commit, 188:20
    vices and f. of human kind, 300:12
    woes because of their own f., 54:9
Follow a shadow, 237:23
    admire virtue f. not her lore, 268:18
    after peace, 43:30
    and will not see its back, 58:16

Follow *(continued)*

    as night the day, 201:27
    beat to f. faster, 223:14
    even if disobedient I shall f., 84:15
    good to fire but not into it, 153:13
    goodness and mercy shall f. me, 16:18
    grasp subject words will f., 88:5
    him who sets you right, 115:29
    I f. but myself, 212:17
    if thou f. thy star, 130:23
    knowledge like star, 481:11
    lamb will never cease to f., 173:9
    let who loves country f., 465:13
    loves me let him f. me, 132:11
    me fishers of men, 33:32
    me let dead bury dead, 35:15
    nature, 110:3
    so fast they f., 206:*n2*
    spirit of men who f., 708:12
    still changes of the moon, 213:36
    the Gleam, 487:1
    the King, 485:20
    things which make for peace, 43:30
    this city going to f. you, 628:6
    thrift may f. fawning, 204:15
    truth wherever it may lead, 359:7
    us disquietly to graves, 215:28
    what is right he will f., 62:21
    your bliss, 766:16
    your desire, 3:6
    your spirit, 193:2
Followed, first f. it hymselve, 135:11
    him honored him, 491:21
    me since black womb held, 791:12
    mercenary calling, 619:17
    through all world she f. him, 482:10
Followeth, he that f. me, 41:10
    not after me, 35:32
Following, in f. him I follow myself, 212:17
    plow along mountainside, 392:9
    the master artist, 716:19
    the roc, 379:6
Follows but for form, 216:12
    God in his works, 305:1
    in His train, 416:2
Folly, according to his f., 612:14
    alone stays fugue of Youth, 142:7
    answer a fool according to his f., 23:6
    brood of F., 259:22
    call it madness f., 384:8
    cannot remedy f. of people, 143:15
    Catullus you should cease f., 94:5
    centuries of f. noise sin, 492:11
    every f. but vanity, 331:12
    fool returneth to his f., 23:7
    forts of f., 531:5
    from f. to defeat, 809:6
    has not fellow, 618:12
    Heaven itself we seek in our f., 99:4
    human f., 789:2
    in all of every age, 289:12
    joys to this are f., 239:17
    lovely woman stoops to f., 341:20,
        718:19
    nights wherein you spend f., 243:5
    noise of f., 260:2
    of being comforted, 637:14
    one's wisdom another's f., 456:2
    profit by f. of others, 108:13

Folly (*continued*)

remembered not slightest f., 198:8
reveals to man own f., 748:11
rid of f. beginning of wisdom, 100:19
shakes rooted f. of age, 289:16
shielding from effects of f., 523:15
shoot f. as it flies, 310:21
to be wise, 333:22
uses f. like stalking horse, 200:11
who lives without f., 273:25
wickedness or f., 475:8
wisdom excelleth f., 24:3
Folly's all they taught me, 412:5
at full length, 306:20
Fond, ae f. kiss, 378:23
and wayward thoughts, 391:17
foolish f. old man, 217:30
grow too f. of war, 465:14
I'm f. of lobsters, 469:5
lover, 269:20
prove so f., 218:14
too f. to rule alone, 312:4
trivial f. records, 202:22
Fonder, absence makes heart grow f., 104:24
Fondest hope decay, 412:13
Fondle, every salesman can f. her breasts, 672:8
Fondling she saith since I hemmed thee here, 173:20
Fondness, habitual hatred or f., 350:10
Fons Bandusiae splendidior vitro, 100:n4
Font, porphyry f., 483:6
Food as luscious as locusts, 213:4
chickens quit quarrelling over f., 680:9
crops the flowery f., 311:2
for worms, 319:2
gathereth her f. in the harvest, 21:4
government see that people have f., 517:22
homely was their f., 295:11
if music f. of love, 208:25
just thinking about f., 811:3
man merely a passage for f., 140:11
many companions for f. and drink, 61:10
moody f. of love, 223:18
music f. of love, 208:n1
my life my joy my f., 155:n4
of fancy, 199:32
of fools, 298:9
of love, 208:25
one f. for all, 383:6
people have no f., 576:10
poets' f. love and fame, 428:20
seeking the f. he eats, 198:13
starving because f. isn't available, 787:12
struggle for f., 469:n4
sweeping rain that leaveth no f., 289:23
sweet f. of knowledge, 163:25
thousand tables wanted f., 390:14
to one poison to others, 93:15
Tom's f. for seven year, 216:33
too fine for angels, 292:10
Fool all people all the time, 477:7
almost at times the F., 717:14
and his money, 844:8
answer a f. according to his folly, 23:6
at forty fool indeed, 305:17
at his end shall be a f., 29:19
better to be f. than dead, 598:9

Fool (*continued*)

big f. says push on, 806:1
busy old f. unruly Sun, 234:2
called her his lady fair, 634:21
clever woman manage f., 632:14
Don Quixote's a muddled f., 158:8
dullness of f. whetstone of wits, 197:25
enough to expunge, 328:19
every f. will be meddling, 22:18
every inch not f. is rogue, 283:21
gilded f., 233:5
great and sublime f., 560:1
greatest f. is man, 289:15
griefs that f. nothing, 798:15
has feathered his nest, 243:11
haste of f. slowest thing, 291:9
hath said in his heart, 16:4
he that trusteth in his own heart is a f., 23:17
hold tongue and pass for sage, 104:10
how ill white hairs become f., 192:13
I am Fortune's f., 183:30
I have played the f., 11:34
invented kissing, 299:18
laughter of the f., 24:18
learned f. more foolish, 278:24
lies here, 633:2
life time's f., 187:5
love's not Time's f., 227:17
made serviceable, 612:14
may prove self a f., 460:20
may talk wise man speaks, 238:19
me to top of my bent, 205:10
merciful to me a f., 579:14
met a f. i' the forest, 198:14
more hope of a f., 23:7
more knave than f., 157:18, 170:12
motley f., 198:14
multitude choose by show, 188:25
my poor f. is hanged, 218:7
nature makes f. she means it, 508:12
need to f. ourselves, 647:12
no f. like old f., 148:26
nor yet f. to fame, 312:1
now and then right, 347:11
O f. I shall go mad, 216:17
old doting f., 111:15
old man who will not laugh is f., 629:19
once harm done even f. understands, 53:23
one draught above heat makes him f., 209:7
patriot a f. in every age, 312:18
play the Roman f., 222:19
politician who steals is a f., 584:5
poor f. with all my lore, 365:4
rather have f. make me merry, 199:24
relenting f., 174:15
remains f. his life long, 368:9
resolved to live a f., 245:4
returneth to his folly, 23:7
said my muse to me, 163:28
satisfied, 465:2
some people all the time, 477:7
strumpet's f., 222:25
suspects himself a f., 306:5
talk sense to a f., 70:12
the more I, 198:7
there was made his prayer, 634:21

Fool (*continued*)

think he is wise, 200:2
this night thy soul, 39:29
though he be a f., 288:7
to fame, 312:1
uttereth all his mind, 23:19
way of a f., 21:23
when he holdeth his peace, 22:8
when we play the f., 408:8
wise enough to play f., 210:1
wise man dieth as the f., 24:5
wise man knows himself f., 200:2
wisest f. in Christendom, 162:14
with f. no companionship, 66:19
with foolish play the f., 83:15
with judges, 109:n8
yourself about love, 824:7
Fooled, nature cannot be f., 803:3
with hope, 282:21
Foolery governs whole world, 245:24
that wise men have, 197:26
walk about like sun, 209:32
Fool-gudgeon opinion, 187:22
Fooling, adapted to my f., 671:6
Foolish, an' f. notion, 378:6
and false as fame, 293:2
consistency, 455:11
fond old man, 217:30
fool calls you f., 70:12
forgive f. ways, 468:21
frantic boast f. word, 635:5
gets f. or wife does, 646:15
God hath chosen f. things, 43:32
hold that mortal f., 70:16
I being young and f., 636:19
lean and f. knight, 664:11
learned fool more f., 278:24
man built house on sand, 35:12
man who trusts woman, 97:n8
men who accuse a woman, 293:12
never said a f. thing, 292:24
newspaper marries f., 646:18
old and f. king, 24:10
passionate man, 642:4
penny wise pound f., 240:7
people without understanding, 29:3
seem f. among wise, 109:n8
son heaviness of his mother, 21:14
son is calamity of his father, 22:15
studied in my f. youth, 139:17
thing but a toy, 210:19
thing well done, 327:17
things to confound wise, 43:32
to make long prologue, 33:14
virgins, 37:12
when he had not pen, 329:4
whistlings of a name, 275:17
with f. play the fool, 83:15
women f. to match men, 512:24
wrath killeth the f., 13:36
young and f., 636:19
Foolishness, not fools but f., 244:17
Fool's errand, 332:8
mouth is his destruction, 22:9
paradise, 843:15
Fools, a little wise best f. be, 234:9
all f. on our side, 560:20
amongst f. a judge, 109:n8
are my theme, 419:12

Fools *(continued)*

but f. caught it, 638:10
by follies they perished the f., 54:8
by heavenly compulsion, 215:29
children and f. cannot lie, 148:18
children and f. want everything, 288:29
crabbed as dull f. suppose, 261:3
discourse of f. is irksome, 32:38
displeasing ten thousand f., 127:5
do not imitate successes, 88:2
do not know how much more is half than
    whole, 56:9
dreading e'en f., 312:4
effect of coercion to make f., 357:8
fill world with f., 523:15
flanneled f. at wicket, 635:8
food of f., 298:9
for I also had my hour, 665:1
God looks after f. and United States,
    850:14
great stage of f., 217:26
greatest f. most satisfied, 289:13
heart of f., 24:17
hundred f. not make wise man, 726:9
I am two f. I know, 234:8
illusion of f., 748:11
in all tongues called f., 200:6
in idle wishes f. stay, 369:4
laugh at men of sense, 292:18
learn in no other, 319:25
leaves 'em still two f., 300:14
let f. use talents, 209:6
lighted f. way to dusty death, 222:16
make a mock at sin, 21:28
millions mostly f., 435:8
more f. than wise, 844:23
ninety-nine percent of people f., 750:3
no more I'll tease, 309:22
not f. but foolishness, 244:17
of fortune, 218:18
of nature, 202:6
old men know young men f., 165:1
Paradise of F., 265:28
play the f. with time, 191:29
poems made by f. like me, 711:12
poor f. decoyed, 288:14
rush in, 309:1
say man has or has not principles, 445:7
scarecrows of f., 537:8
shoal of f. for tenders, 300:23
so deep-contemplative, 198:17
some made coxcombs nature meant f.,
    308:9
suckle f., 213:12
suffer f. gladly, 45:12
tedious old f., 203:11
the stop to busy f., 278:29
too green and only good for f., 60:*n*5
we f. of nature, 202:6
what f. call Nature, 494:30
what f. these mortals be, 106:12, 181:21
who came to scoff, 342:7
wise men profit more from f., 88:2
wise men speak f. decide, 57:18
wish to appear wise among f., 109:17
words are money of f., 246:7
young men think old men f., 165:1
Fools' experiments, 470:10
    names like f. faces, 846:9

Foos, my f. won't moos, 696:16
Foot, accent of coming F., 547:7
    and hand go cold, 151:10
    beat earth with unfettered f., 99:18
    beggar on f., 642:13
    better f. before, 178:18
    cannot put shoe on every f., 103:28
    crown to sole of f., 194:29
    dash f. against stone, 39:10
    dash thy f. against a stone, 18:26
    for foot, 9:4
    from the f. Hercules, 71:18
    her f. speaks, 208:19
    her f. was light, 439:4
    here men first set f. on moon, 852:19
    I hold Creation in my f., 825:5
    in front of the other, 799:2
    in the stirrup, 854:14, 854:15
    it featly, 229:18
    lived like f. for thirty years, 827:14
    my f. on my native heath, 397:25
    no f. of unfamiliar men, 530:15
    no f. slide, 851:11
    noiseless f. of time, 210:32
    of hand of f. of lip, 227:11
    one f. already in grave, 111:15
    one f. in sea one on shore, 194:25
    one white f. try him, 849:17
    print of naked f., 295:8
    proud f. of conqueror, 178:28
    rest for the sole of her f., 6:29
    silver f. in mouth, 828:11
    stamped f. and cried, 544:20
    suffer thy f. to be moved, 19:30
    thy soul the fixt f., 235:3
    wear steps of his door, 32:12
    who cleft Devil's f., 233:13
    wishing his f. equal with eye, 172:32
    with naked f. stalking my chamber, 150:2
Foot-and-a-half-long words, 101:20
Football, in life as in f., 615:3
Footfalls echo in memory, 720:8
Foothold tenoned and mortised in granite,
    519:6
Footing, 'twixt his stretched f., 207:28
Foot-in-the-grave young man, 564:13
Footless halls of air, 810:11
Footman, eternal F. snicker, 717:13
Footnotes to Plato, 624:15
Footpads, when f. quail, 565:23
Footpath, jog on the f. way, 228:24
Footprint, Zuleika looking for man's f.,
    659:9
Footprints of gigantic hound, 617:12
    on the sands of time, 466:2
Footstep, where thy f. gleams, 478:10
Footsteps, distant f. echo, 466:13
    home his f. turned, 396:11
    plants his f. in the sea, 347:3
    someone follow in my f., 814:17
Footstool, earth as f., 644:17
    earth is his f., 34:5
    God's f. may be throne, 668:12
Foppery, excellent f. of the world, 215:29
Fops, whole tribe of f., 215:26
Forbade me to put off my hat, 280:14
Forbear and persevere, 600:1
    be not too bold, 161:*n*4
    cruel mother, 100:12

Forbear *(continued)*

to dig dust enclosed here, 231:19
to judge, 172:14
Forbearance ceases to be virtue, 343:13
    practice Christian f., 353:4
Forbid, God f., 7:30
    it Almighty God, 353:3
    them not, 38:28
Forbidden by Constitution, 370:15
    tree whose mortal taste, 263:19
    wanted apple because was f., 561:7
    whatever not f. is permitted,
        381:20
Forbids, my mind f. to crave, 155:1
    rich as well as poor, 586:18
Force, abandonment of f., 699:9
    acceleration proportional to applied f.,
        291:*n*2
    adaptation of form to resist f., 517:21
    Allied Expeditionary F., 728:15
    and beauty of process, 585:21
    change from liberty to f., 385:18
    citizens to confess faith, 734:1
    Conservation of F., 527:13
    constant f. for muddlement, 585:12
    eastward I go only by f., 507:27
    elemental f. freed, 723:5
    evolution not a f., 572:4
    from which sun draws power, 705:3
    in Nature not increased, 527:13
    knowing f. of words, 63:29
    knowledge more than f., 166:*n*1
    language into meaning, 722:13
    love f., 650:10
    may the F. be with you, 838:17
    moment to its crisis, 717:12
    no f. however great, 432:18
    no motion has she no f., 392:1
    no place where need of skill, 71:17
    not by f. or violence, 353:4
    not remedy, 489:4
    of heaven-bred poesy, 176:11
    of his own merit, 230:19
    of righteousness, 650:10
    of temporal power, 189:19
    oppressor to commit brutality openly,
        823:9
    paralyzed f., 719:5
    passion spent novel f., 481:18
    produce according to f., 510:*n*5
    proportional to motive f., 291:3
    secret f. driving me, 472:23
    some patient f., 483:9
    soul f., 650:10
    spiritual f. stronger, 457:19
    terror and f., 726:8
    that through green fuse, 795:2
    them in spite of Nature, 271:7
    them to write, 271:7
    too revolutionary for old ideas, 705:4
    tribalism strongest f., 828:6
    uncomprehended which was his life,
        542:14
    use of f. but temporary, 344:7
    when one by f. subdues, 81:21
    who overcomes by f., 264:21
    will be with you, 838:18
    without wisdom falls of own weight,
        100:1

Foul *(continued)*
    rag-and-bone shop, 643:2
    shapes of f. disease, 484:15
    so f. and fair a day, 218:30
Fouled-up, old-type natural f. guys, 810:7
Foulness of their fate, 712:4
Found, came to ask what he had f., 405:5
    crooked sixpence, 860:6
    death in life, 404:4
    dove f. no rest, 6:29
    empire for raising customers, 338:19
    favor in thy sight, 7:6
    fresh Rhodora, 453:3
    fun where I f. it, 634:18
    has f. out thy bed, 374:3
    hast thou f. me O mine enemy, 12:34
    Him in shining of stars, 486:10
    I could extinguish hope, 603:18
    I f. a new world, 270:12
    I f. my wits you lost yours, 246:4
    I have f. it, 86:1
    I oft f. both, 187:24
    I once was lost now am f., 339:12
    in search of mother's garden f. my own,
        839:1
    in that town dog was f., 341:17
    in whose hand the cup is f., 7:31
    it is f. again, 603:15
    lack of what is f. there, 703:15
    looked inwards f. Nature, 282:17
    lost in America shall be f., 760:7
    lost time never f., 320:2
    man who has f. himself out, 621:20
    one man among a thousand, 24:24
    rebellion in way he f. it, 186:32
    Rome city of bricks, 102:7
    sense beneath rarely f., 308:13
    sheep which was lost, 39:34
    someone else can always be f., 628:3
    sought but f. him not, 25:20
    struggle to f. Roman state, 96:25
    that famous country, 734:9
    was lost and is f., 39:37
    weighed in the balances and f. wanting,
        30:6
    when f. make note, 497:25
    where shall wisdom be f., 14:33
    who loveliness within hath f., 233:17
    woman have I not f., 24:24
    you as a morsel, 223:27
Foundation consisting of confusion, 822:9
    is love, 823:5
    new government laying f., 357:2
    no sure f. on blood, 178:17
    of our faith, 127:8
    order our f., 444:1
Foundations, earth's f. fled, 619:17
    earth's f. stand, 620:3
    loosen old f., 681:13
    marred f. we forgot, 721:17
    of knowledge in mathematics, 128:11
    of states laws and arms, 142:11
    when I laid f. of earth, 15:5
    wished to lay f. of kindness, 750:19
Founded, earth and heaven f. strong, 619:4
    government f. on compromise, 344:14
    he hath f. it upon the seas, 16:19
    principle on which society not f.,
        333:11

Founded *(continued)*
    securely f., 364:15
    upon a rock, 35:11
Founder, supinely enjoyed gifts of f., 353:15
    true f. of civil society, 330:17
Founders, newspapers did that which F.
    hoped, 711:3
Foundest me poor, 342:13
Founding, since the f. of the city, 123:4
Fount Bandusian more sparkling than
    glass, 100:6
Fountain and a shrine, 478:9
    dying of thirst by the f., 138:14
    even f. have rest, 508:4
    from f. wells up bitter taste, 93:16
    like bubble on f., 397:9
    pitcher broken at the f., 25:8
    rise like f. for me, 486:13
    the f. overflows, 372:18
    troubled like f. stirred, 208:14
    woman moved like f. troubled, 176:1
Fountain's silvery column, 401:21
Fountains, Afric's sunny f., 416:3
    are within, 402:4
    fraught with tears, 164:12
    mountains are f. of men, 572:15
    silver f. have mud, 226:11
    under f. and graves, 845:5
    where the pleasant f. lie, 173:20
Four, age best in f. things, 167:1
    and twenty tailors, 858:10
    angels to my bed, 274:20
    ducks on a pond, 535:16
    freedoms, 698:15
    grant that twice two not f., 512:5
    hands are f., 741:5
    horsemen of Apocalypse, 645:7
    Horsemen rode again, 692:6
    intimate equality of the F., 701:13
    not f. friends in world, 279:17
    snakes gliding, 454:2
    spend in prayer, 159:20
    things better without, 738:11
    things wiser to know, 738:10
    two and two mathematician makes f.,
        557:13
    undergraduates right number, 654:17
    what F. Freedoms establish, 674:7
    winds of the heaven, 30:34
Fourfold, threefold f. tomb, 247:11
Four-in-hand, fiery f., 404:2
Fours, crawling on all f., 316:11
Fourscore and seven years ago, 476:7
    and upward, 217:30
    if by reason of strength they be f.,
        18:22
    wind him up for f. years, 283:5
Foursquare in hand and foot, 62:1
    to winds that blew, 484:22
Fourteen hundred years ago nailed, 184:22
Fourteenth Amendment not enact Spencer,
    578:5
Fourth, born on F. of July, 679:11
    Estate, 433:5
    estate, 447:16, 490:13
    estate in politics, 410:4
    Estate more important than all, 433:*n*1
    generation of them that hate me, 8:33
    safe and sane F., 644:1

Fourth *(continued)*
    this is the F., 359:14
    what to slave your F. of July, 509:10
Fowl, dominion over f. of the air, 5:14
    elegant f., 499:16
    fish flesh or f., 639:16
Fowler, snare of the f., 18:25
Fowls, May comen I here f. synge, 134:13
    of air draw us to kingdom, 117:5
    of the air shall tell, 14:11
    of the air sow not, 34:17
Fox, Aesop's f., 240:9
    be f. to recognize traps, 142:15
    Brer F. he lay low, 593:6
    build nest on hearthstone, 658:*n*3
    false as f. to lamb, 208:7
    from lair in morning, 435:15
    has many tricks, 56:*n*1
    knows many things, 56:22
    prince imitate f. and lion, 142:15
    prince must know how to play f.,
        111:*n*7
    quick brown f., 849:7
    says they are not ripe, 60:*n*5
    sleep in earth like tired f., 750:7
    stink of f., 825:4
    to wear arctic f., 715:1
    treason trusted like f., 187:1
Foxes, fellow f. cut off theirs, 240:9
    have holes, 35:14
    honored among f., 795:12
    little f. that spoil vines, 25:18
Foxey, maxim with F., 496:33
Foxholes, no atheists in f., 765:4
    no white or colored signs on f.,
        800:4
Fox's, patch lion's skin with f., 111:9
Frabjous day, 551:11
Fractions, happiness made of f., 404:3
Fragment, ship f. detached, 611:17
    truth f. by f., 765:9
Fragmentary blue, 669:10
Fragments, broken dishonored f., 415:2
    Death tramples it to f., 430:17
    gather up f., 41:3
    live in f. no longer, 684:3
    of the f. twelve baskets, 36:14
    shored against ruins, 719:3
Fragrance, as metal keeps f., 671:12
    jar will keep f., 412:*n*1
    no spicy f. while they grow, 167:*n*2
    of salt marsh shore mud, 521:2
    perfect flower without f., 636:16
    tobacco's f. greet, 809:5
    wind with f. of hot sun, 661:19
Fragrant bodice, 437:1
    centuries loaded f., 456:31
    in your f. bosom dies, 253:15
    most f. when crushed, 167:13
    thousand f. posies, 170:8
Frail, face so f., 819:18
    gaunt and small, 575:16
    inhabits our f. blood, 210:15
    may be f. its roof may shake, 323:3
    renown is fleeting and f., 95:2
    so f. a thing man, 296:14
    that I may know how f. I am, 17:12
    to f. mortality trust, 168:21
Frailties from dread abode, 335:4

Frailty, in f. consider last day, 68:10
  more flesh therefore more f., 186:19
  noblest f. of mind, 291:8
  tempt f. of our powers, 208:17
  thy name is woman, 201:5
Frame, heavens a shining f., 301:14
  I f. no hypotheses, 290:26
  mind mingles with whole f., 97:29
  of Nature break, 301:16
  out of three sounds f. star, 494:3
  quit this mortal f., 309:3
  stirs this mortal f., 401:22
  this goodly f. earth, 203:17
  this universal f. began, 284:13
  thy fearful symmetry, 374:5
  universal f. without mind, 167:21
Framed her last best work, 379:13
  Nature hath f. strange fellows, 187:15
  nature that f. us, 170:4
  speech finely f., 33:16
  to make women false, 213:5
Framers, wisdom of f. of treaty, 631:19
Français, je parle f. aux hommes, 149:*n*12
France a person, 444:8
  breasts that feed F., 165:14
  conquered for civilization, 534:9
  despotism tempered by epigrams, 433:23
  fair stood wind for F., 169:12
  fight in F. and on seas, 666:1
  forward sons of F., 383:*n*1
  get out of F. quickly, 333:*n*1
  glories of F., 578:21
  half of F. in mourning for other, 461:12
  has more need of me, 388:4
  has not lost the war, 728:7
  is invaded, 388:5
  King of F. went up hill, 856:19
  landing on coast of F., 728:15
  let sword of F. fall, 728:8
  nearer is to F., 551:2
  never go to F., 445:22
  not France without greatness, 728:10
  one illusion F., 701:12
  order matter better in F., 333:3
  save squadron honor F., 495:4
  shall F. remain here, 535:2
  son of F. never lack statue, 649:11
  standing on top of golden hours, 391:10
  want to know what F. thinks, 728:12
  when you march into F., 554:10
Francesca da Rimini miminy piminy, 564:12
Franchise, women to secure elective f., 503:6
Franco, remember war against F., 820:13
Frank, friendly and f., 489:3
  if heart just f. kindly, 278:10
  to all beside, 310:5
Frankfurters, can't all have Cardozos F., 767:15
Frankie and Johnny, 849:14
  had become unjoined person, 802:9
Frankincense, gold and f., 33:19
Franklin, before F. took hint, 671:13
  Benjamin F. Printer, 319:2
  Doctor F. snuff-colored little man, 707:8
  Roosevelt no crusader, 727:3
Franklin's quiet memory, 425:5

Frankly I don't give a damn, 758:*n*3
Frantic among thy servants, 32:4
  boast foolish word, 635:5
  fascination f., 565:21
  lover all as f., 182:3
Frantic-mad with evermore unrest, 228:6
Franz Joseph, portraits of F., 691:21
Fraternity, liberty equality f., 855:7
  of henpecked, 302:21
  or death, 356:*n*3
Fraud, pious f., 355:4
Fraught, swell bosom with thy f., 214:14
Fray, back from the dread f., 52:27
  latter end of f., 186:29
Frayed, poor wings so f., 569:12
Freckled, whatever is fickle f., 587:10
Freckles, love curiosity f. doubt, 738:11
Frederick, spires of F. stand, 468:14
Free active individuals, 530:2
  agent you were before, 115:29
  alchemized and f. of space, 436:10
  all men born f., 263:10
  all men should be f., 477:5
  and independent states, 349:11
  and independent States, 351:8
  and loyal subjects, 846:13
  as Nature first made man, 282:19
  as soon write f. verse, 671:19
  as the breeze, 395:22
  as the road, 250:15
  assure freedom to f., 476:3
  at last, 823:4, 863:2
  be f. all worthy spirits, 165:10
  be f. artist and nothing else, 622:6
  because equally f. absolutely equal, 81:2
  best things in life f., 736:17
  born f., 263:10
  born f. and equal, 357:*n*1
  but I was f. born, 42:28
  Colonies are and ought to be f., 351:8
  dark clear moving utterly f., 785:11
  days have been wondrous f., 305:9
  destiny alike for f. and enslaved, 65:15
  die to make men f., 513:19
  encounter, 263:5
  evening calm and f., 392:15
  everything f. in America, 825:17
  exercise of religion, 353:4, 361:1
  feel as if f., 582:15
  fight to set country f., 354:16
  fixed fate f. will, 265:13
  flag that makes you f., 553:11
  for irreligion, 734:4
  for religion, 734:4
  form not assure freedom, 688:20
  frae monie a blunder f. us, 378:6
  from all meaning, 283:20
  from hope and fear set f., 569:3
  furrow followed f., 399:20
  go home to my Lord and be f., 863:10
  God wills us f., 355:12
  government f. to people, 291:19
  government which kept us f., 358:10
  grouping of individuals, 651:7
  habit shackle for f., 580:13
  hair as f., 237:16
  half slave half f., 474:9
  healthy f. the world before me, 520:2
  her looks were f., 400:3

Free *(continued)*
  himself from God not f., 452:19
  his half-regained Eurydice, 259:21
  holiday-rejoicing spirit, 407:21
  I am not truly f., 804:1
  I and my children are now f., 501:7
  if you can't be f., 841:12
  in historical sense not f., 542:12
  in my soul am f., 276:4
  in whatever form used, 688:20
  Indian f. in Nature, 504:24
  Jesu set me f., 154:14
  land in beloved home, 522:8
  land of the f., 411:1
  let me gang f., 398:11
  like spirit animating universe, 443:5
  live hair shining and f., 712:18
  living word set soul f., 690:7
  love Virtue she alone is f., 261:12
  maids that weave thread, 209:24
  majestic f., 393:4
  man abide with honor, 505:19
  man f. to do evil as good, 566:22
  man is born f., 330:20
  me from this turbulent priest, 127:2
  men by nature equally f., 339:9
  men citizens of Berlin, 800:5
  mother of the f., 625:11
  my lines and life are f., 250:15
  nation ignorant and f., 359:2
  neither bond nor f., 46:3
  no one f. till all f., 523:6
  no such thing as f. lunch, 788:11
  not all f. who scorn chains, 346:7
  not happy unless f., 426:5
  nothin' ain't worth nothin' but it's f., 832:6
  nothing-withholding and f., 583:9
  now f. I once more weave, 446:17
  only educated are f., 112:12
  only f. men can negotiate, 803:16
  open-minded adjustment, 611:10
  ourselves subdue our masters, 361:12
  play of mind a pleasure, 530:8
  press good or bad, 790:9
  press necessity, 727:5
  principle of f. thought, 579:1
  principles of f. constitution lost, 353:6
  private enterprise, 698:10
  protection of f. speech, 578:13
  pure in life f. from sin, 99:15
  reason left f. to combat, 358:9
  Russian speech, 512:6
  servitude can pierce hearts, 715:8
  set bodily f. from surroundings, 676:4
  set my poor heart f., 212:*n*1
  should himself be f., 329:*n*2
  soil free men, 848:9
  solitude unsponsored f., 686:19
  soul in prison I am not f., 606:8
  speech in repulsive form, 667:13
  suppression of f. speech, 607:2
  take away our f. will and glory, 143:2
  that anchor and chain, 85:16
  that moment they are f., 347:27
  the human will, 313:8
  thenceforward and forever f., 475:15
  they bring it to you f., 809:12
  think they ought to be f., 343:19

Free (*continued*)

thou art f., 528:3
though thrall, 159:9
thought, 579:1
thought is f., 230:4
thus so cleanly I myself can f., 169:14
'tis the gift to be f., 848:4
to regulate industry, 358:12
to think speak write, 359:10
trade in ideas, 578:14
trade unpopular, 447:9
truth shall make you f., 41:11
unreproved pleasures f., 259:12
was he f. was he happy, 776:4
we gotta be f., 752:2
we must be f. or die, 393:5
we will die f. men, 362:9
westward I go f., 507:27
when evils most f., 196:2
white and somewhat more f., 762:17
who would be f. strike blow, 420:10
wish all men everywhere f., 475:14
woods more f. from peril, 197:36
yearning to breathe f., 595:6

Freed capacity of thought, 616:12

elemental force f., 723:5
no man's pie f. from his finger, 230:18

Freedom, abridging f. of speech, 361:1

abridgment of f., 367:2
African conditioned to f., 731:10
age of f. ended, 706:10
all solace to man gives, 132:18
all who love f., 728:15
altar of f., 477:2
and democracy, 787:10
another man's f., 822:12
associate democracy with f. of action, 616:12
assure f. to the free, 476:3
battle cry of F., 522:9
behavioristic f., 682:5
black f. jeopardized, 815:11
born to f., 698:16
born to give you your name F., 743:2
brought independence and rationality, 757:11
cause of F. cause of God, 383:11
chance to be better, 790:9
competition afford f. to individual, 706:14
crown Greece with f., 62:5
cultural f., 678:14
cure is f., 447:14
deny f. to others, 474:14
deny participation of f., 344:16
deprived of f. by authorities, 733:2
deserving of f. and life, 365:19
drawing f. and peace, 425:5
economic f., 678:14
every man who lives without f., 770:11
fight for f. and truth, 540:15
fight to maintain f., 698:16
fills space 'twixt marsh, 583:10
flame of f. in souls, 576:14
for all poor workers, 732:16
for one who thinks differently, 654:15
for thought we hate, 579:1
free form not assure f., 688:20
free press without f. bad, 790:9

Freedom (*continued*)

friends of f. doubt our sincerity, 474:7
from every B.V.D. f. ring, 739:15
from fear, 698:15, 699:8
from mountain height, 435:14
from prejudice, 532:5
from violence and lies, 622:7
from want, 698:15, 699:8
greater f. for average man, 698:1
greatest gift f. of will, 132:1
gret Press's f., 515:1
has a thousand charms, 347:6
having my f. boast of nothing, 179:3
history progress of f., 390:7
hunted round the globe, 354:9
idea of F., 488:13
if F. fall, 635:26
if I have f. in my love, 276:4
in economic arrangements, 788:10
in highest position least f., 95:7
indispensable condition of f., 653:19
indivisible word, 736:11
infringement of human f., 381:4
intellectual f. only guarantee, 808:9
is slavery, 765:16
is the prize, 386:2
law can only bring f., 365:23
let f. ring, 469:8, 823:4
liberal institutions enemies of f., 589:20
liberty f. enfranchisement, 196:16
life pure transparent f., 777:10
lose f. if value anything more, 673:4
lose social f. individual autonomy, 783:15
love not f. but license, 263:9
made man isolated anxious powerless, 757:11
my story ends with f., 501:7
nation which enjoys most f., 386:1
new birth of f., 476:7
no f. in borrowing, 540:4
no f. of thought without doubt, 767:2
none love f. but good men, 263:9
not conceived simply, 815:14
obedience bane of f., 427:13
of choice and with honor, 142:1
of expression matrix, 653:19
of f. he only is deserving, 365:19
of knyghthod and of f. flour, 137:22
of navigation, 611:10
of person, 358:13
of press, 358:13
of press bulwarks of liberty, 339:11
of press guaranteed those who own one, 768:5
of press has suffered most, 790:8
of religion, 358:13
of speech and expression, 698:15
of speech freedom of conscience, 562:6
of speech may be taken, 350:4
of thought, 337:12
of worship, 698:15
oh f. over me, 863:10
on mountains is f., 382:14
only to limits of consciousness, 675:14
people f. light, 730:12
political f., 678:14
political f. business of Government, 698:2
private property guaranty of f., 753:20
reap blessings of f., 354:14

Freedom (*continued*)

regardless of form, 688:20
religious f., 678:14
rhymes suggest wildest f., 454:3
safeguards of individual f., 753:21
secret of f. a brave heart, 74:5
secret of happiness, 74:5
seven-pillared house, 723:7
shall awhile repair, 336:16
shrieked as Kosciusko fell, 408:13
slaves fought for f., 450:10
so celestial article as F., 354:10
spirit of truth and f., 540:3
state exists is no f., 654:11
striking blow for f., 713:17
system based on courage, 663:9
taken away from me, 804:1
those who profess to favor f., 509:13
to speak, 514:18
to think, 514:18
tyrannies which stifle f., 787:10
unchartered f. tires, 394:11
values anything more than f., 673:4
wars which usurp standard of f., 385:18
wealth and f. reign, 341:2
what is F., 441:11
whose service is perfect f., 50:5
with great sum obtained f., 42:28
yet F. yet thy banner, 421:18

Freedom's, bled in F. cause, 390:13

holy light, 469:9
just another word, 832:6

Freedoms, four f., 698:15

insensible to f. of Constitution, 695:7
what Four F. establish, 674:7

Free-labor nation, 450:6
Freeloader confirmed guest, 704:13
Freely give, 35:25

lives at ease that f. lives, 132:18
offer itself to you, 701:5
serve because we freely love, 267:6
too dear for what's given f., 228:8
ye have received, 35:25

Freeman contending for liberty, 349:13

Mrs. F. had two others, 815:16
no f. taken except by legal judgment, 128:8
slave patrician plebeian, 511:1

Freemen, Americans f. or slaves, 349:14

nation of f., 474:3
who rules o'er f., 329:*n*2

Freer, nowhere is speech f., 667:13
Frees all faults, 230:17

her slave again, 845:21
one word f. us, 68:22

Freethinking of one age, 532:1
Freeze, mountain-tops that f., 230:27

thy young blood, 202:12

Freezes, till Hell f. over, 852:4
Freezing turbulent water, 842:4

was not so bad, 678:7

Freight, nation's f. handler, 681:8

proportioned to groove, 547:8

Freiheit, nur der verdient sich F., 365:*n*7
Frémont, free speech F., 848:9
French, believe only in F. culture, 590:3

Englishman about to talk F., 694:11
for fiddle-de-dee, 552:17
for suppressing one, 530:6

French *(continued)*
  German text of F. operas, 627:14
  gone to fight the F., 384:3
  Good Soldier finest F. novel, 662:19
  hinges in F. conversation, 333:5
  I speak F. to men, 149:23
  new F. books, 493:9
  of Parys to hir unknowe, 134:21
  on F. coast light gleams, 530:19
  only accidentally F., 314:10
  only peril can bring F. together, 728:13
  or Turk or Proosian, 564:1
  phrase for hotel guests, 649:13
  Radicals and German police spies,
    510:14
  Revolution began at top, 535:3
  Revolution inevitable yet completely
    unforeseen, 463:7
  soldier carries marshal's baton, 388:18
  spak ful faire and fetisly, 134:21
  speak F. when can't think of English,
    551:15
  stormed Ratisbon, 491:7
  struggle of F. soldiers, 542:10
  true German can't stand F., 365:10
  what is not clear is not F., 369:1
  word impossible not F., 388:3
Frenchies seek him everywhere, 636:3
Frenchman, embrace Pole as F., 153:21
  first man then a F., 314:10
  I praise the F., 347:19
  in Academy, 326:*n*6
  must be always talking, 329:2
Frenchmen, did march three F., 193:7
  Englishman beat three F., 302:19
  fifty million F., 851:2
  mankind including F., 701:12
Frenzied drum, 639:8
Frenzy, demoniac f., 268:10
  distilling f. from academic scribbler,
    702:4
  eye in fine f. rolling, 182:3
  not shaken from resolve by f., 99:28
  of his fellow citizens, 99:28
  old man's f., 642:11
Frequent, eagerly f. Doctor, 471:13
  more f. use of any organ, 362:7
  practicer of angling, 252:25
Frère, hypocrite lecteur mon f., 524:7
  sois mon f. ou je te tue, 356:*n*3
Fresh as a bridegroom, 185:2
  as a lark, 394:20
  as month of May, 134:18
  as paint, 511:13
  as the morning, 520:15
  complexion and heart together, 229:3
  dews of night, 261:16
  from brawling courts, 484:10
  heavens f. and strong, 394:12
  how quick and f. art thou, 208:26
  makes not f. again, 242:18
  perfection in beloved, 416:20
  sae f. and fair, 378:2
  streams meet in salt sea, 192:22
  suspicions, 213:36
  waste not f. tears, 70:20
  welcome faire f. May, 135:20
  woods and pastures new, 262:6
  world as f. as at first day, 537:2

Freshness, glory and f. of a dream, 393:7
  poem forever keep f., 671:12
Fret, i should worry and f., 680:4
  nuns f. not, 394:17
  of existence, 758:2
  passage through it, 258:6
  thy soul with crosses, 161:24
  weariness fever f., 437:8
Fretful, quills upon f. porpentine, 202:12
Frets doubt maw-crammed beast, 494:8
  struts and f. his hour, 222:16
Fretted the pygmy-body to decay, 283:8
  vault, 334:16
  with golden fire, 203:17
  your impatience so much f., 327:14
Freud, I reject world of F., 755:13
  ideas of F., 625:6
Freude, Kraft durch F., 729:*n*2
Friar of orders gray, 844:4
  ther was wantowne and merye,
    134:25
Friars, barefoot f. singing vespers, 354:4
Fribsbi, fatal man Madame F., 490:11
Friday, call this F. good, 721:3
  my dear Friday, 786:1
  my man F., 295:9
  three days after Bastille Day, 818:4
  worse on F., 859:17
Friday's child, 859:16
Friend, absolutely unselfish f. is dog, 548:7
  all he wished a f., 335:3
  angry with my f., 374:11
  answer my f. is blowin', 836:4
  at least one f. left, 477:1
  await Felicity or Doom, 547:7
  be a f. to man, 613:16
  best mirror an old f., 251:22
  betraying country betraying f., 684:5
  bosom-f. of sun, 438:11
  boy's best f. is mother, 811:6
  bring death to a f., 67:19
  cannot be known, 32:24
  choose author as choose f., 287:20
  death of f. make man look sad, 182:11
  diamonds girl's best f., 758:14
  do a f. service, 67:9
  do you hear, 855:*n*2
  dog the firmest f., 419:11
  down inside me, 477:1
  each f. a world, 765:8
  enemy and f. hurt you to heart, 562:10
  evening criminal's f., 524:14
  every man will be thy f., 239:3
  every murderer somebody's old f.,
    727:15
  faithful are wounds of f., 23:11
  fav'rite has no f., 334:4
  forsake not old f., 32:16
  good f. for Jesus' sake, 231:19
  good wine a f. or being dry, 292:23
  grant f. in my retreat, 347:19
  guide philosopher and f., 311:17, 692:16
  had not f. nor toy, 515:11
  happy house shelters f., 455:24
  hello darkness my old f., 837:7
  honor f. who prospered, 65:7
  house to lodge f., 312:16
  idleness sorrow f. foe, 738:10
  if I had a f. that loved her, 212:32

Friend *(continued)*
  if thou wouldest get a f., 32:9
  if you want f. in Washington, 548:*n*1
  in need, 86:14
  in need nor bottle, 497:25
  in power friend lost, 570:5
  is a second self, 91:15
  is medicine of life, 32:11
  is strong defense, 32:10
  keep thy f. under own key, 210:20
  keep tonge and keep f., 137:24
  knolling departing f., 191:8
  left exposed a F., 545:20
  little f. of all world, 635:7
  loan loses itself and f., 201:27
  lost every other f., 477:1
  lost no f., 310:15
  makes no f. never made foe, 486:4
  masterpiece of Nature, 455:26
  my f. judge not me, 159:13
  ne'er said till f. dead, 591:9
  never find a f., 639:9
  never known till need, 148:24
  never want f. in need, 497:25
  new f. is as new wine, 32:16
  no f. in misery, 239:3
  no man useless who has f., 599:20
  nor f. to know me, 599:11
  not a f. to close eyes, 285:12
  not ashamed to defend a f., 32:36
  of every country but own, 389:14
  of friendless name the f., 329:10
  of my better days, 426:6
  one chained f., 429:25
  one f. in lifetime much, 570:16
  person with whom sincere, 455:25
  poesy should be f., 436:5
  save me from Candid F., 389:16
  say Welcome f., 272:8
  sharpeneth countenance of his f., 23:14
  should bear friend's infirmities, 197:11
  single soul in two bodies, 79:14
  so great poet so good f., 285:17
  someone true f. good writer, 756:18
  soul of f. we've made, 625:15
  statesman yet f. to truth, 310:15
  stoop to become f., 636:13
  support f. oppose foe, 799:7
  supports whom Fortune crushes,
    110:6
  suspicious f., 312:4
  that sticketh closer than a brother,
    22:13
  think on thee dear f., 226:9
  this is my f., 25:26
  thou art not my f., 452:15
  to have f. be one, 455:28
  to her foe, 386:10
  to human race, 52:*n*2
  to man, 438:5
  to me fair f. never old, 227:10
  to public amusements, 327:12
  treat f. as if he might become enemy,
    103:8
  true wise f. called Piggy, 786:5
  well-chosen book or f., 232:14
  what is a f., 84:12
  wildly striking sometimes a f., 250:1
  you ain't no f. of mine, 828:8

Friendless, assist feeble and f., 350:14
    bodies of unburied men, 244:3
    of every f. name friend, 329:10
    omnipotent but f., 428:8
Friendliness, wanted friendship got f., 793:11
Friendly and charming relationship, 144:16
    and frank, 489:3
    bust, 718:8
    cow red and white, 599:1
    hath friends must show himself f., 22:13
    in difficult are f. forces, 677:10
    mingles with f. bowl, 312:14
    open and f. in private, 73:18
    social f. honest man, 377:18
    universe not hostile nor f., 684:13
Friend's, bear his f. infirmities, 197:11
    debauch f. wife genteelly, 327:23
Friends, a little help from my f., 835:4
    absent speak, 235:25
    adieu kind f., 848:19
    adversity tries f., 104:9
    age leaves f. and wine, 412:9
    are exultations, 393:2
    become bitter enemies, 240:6
    behave as we wish f. to behave, 79:16
    born not made, 570:4
    call that backing your f., 185:23
    choose men f., 643:8
    death of f. inspire us, 505:24
    defend me from my f., 389:*n*2
    die adoring God loving f., 317:3
    distresses of our f., 274:*n*2
    do with f. as books, 455:29
    enemies in war in peace f., 357:3
    enough now for death, 764:6
    ever been best of f., 498:33
    faithful f. hard to find, 239:3
    falling out of faithful f., 88:*n*7
    few f. and many books, 275:5
    forget love to f. and brethren, 31:5
    forsake me like memory, 431:14
    gain f. for when we awaken, 254:19
    golden f. I had, 619:6
    good book best of f., 489:2
    had been f. in youth, 401:9
    has thousand f. not friend to spare, 120:10
    have all in common, 76:7
    have no place in graveyard, 505:24
    he cast off his f., 343:5
    he that repeateth a matter separateth f., 22:5
    he thought they were old f., 792:10
    held up of his f., 32:28
    honor truth above f., 80:9
    humblest f., 395:20
    husband children f. nothing to that, 593:20
    in thirties want f., 746:20
    joy to their f., 54:22
    just f. and brave enemies, 358:14
    kindred days, 453:8
    lay down life for f., 41:31
    live without f., 548:11
    look with love as f., 288:6
    made fortune send for f., 75:23
    man that hath f., 22:13
    misfortune of our f., 274:15
    misfortune shows who not really f., 81:14

Friends *(continued)*
    multitude of f., 237:9
    my glory was I had such f., 642:16
    nature teaches beasts to know f., 224:19
    nearest f. can go, 669:1
    never f. with roses, 568:15
    no one would choose to live without f., 80:15
    not be four f. in world, 279:17
    not equal to yourself, 62:12
    of freedom doubt our sincerity, 474:7
    of my youth where are they, 123:1
    oh my f., 735:2
    old f. are best, 245:15
    old f. times manners, 342:15
    old f. to trust, 167:1
    ornament of house f., 457:12
    ought to forgive our f., 167:2
    outside a small circle of f., 835:7
    part of man's Self, 581:17
    people people have for f., 623:9
    preachers politicians f., 361:13
    precious all things from f., 85:11
    prosperity makes f., 104:9
    Romans countrymen, 196:27
    second glass for my f., 302:15
    secure f. by doing favors, 74:3
    secure you count many f., 105:25
    share all things, 60:2
    shifts of fortune test f., 91:14
    soul remembering my good f., 179:17
    spare to us our f., 600:1
    State not know f. from foes, 505:20
    strive mightily eat as f., 175:26
    that have it I do wrong, 637:20
    those f. thou hast, 201:25
    three faithful f., 319:19
    three f. hardly possible, 570:16
    thrust away by his f., 32:28
    to have advanced f., 529:1
    trencher-f., 218:18
    troops of f., 222:11
    two f. in lifetime many, 570:16
    tyranny's disease to trust no f., 65:19
    we choose our f., 355:10
    we love so dear, 556:7
    wealth maketh many f., 22:14
    were poor but honest, 210:23
    what became of f. I loved so, 128:13
    who go with the wind, 129:1
    who no longer know how to die, 759:9
    who plow sea, 564:6
    wife and children afraid, 255:20
    win f. and influence people, 716:20
    without three good f., 199:5
    women find few f., 329:22
    wounded in house of my f., 30:40
    wretched have no f., 283:1
    you and I long f., 320:17
Friendship, author demands your f., 408:1
    beautiful f., 782:12
    boughten f., 670:7
    commerce between equals, 341:25
    constant save in love, 194:18
    crown is love and f., 436:11
    elegance of female f., 325:2
    faded, 673:14
    from wine sudden f., 307:10
    hardly ever brings money, 406:20

Friendship *(continued)*
    highest kind of f., 797:12
    holy passion of F., 561:10
    in appearance at f. with me, 288:26
    in f. but faithless haven, 67:9
    in f. false, 283:11
    is the strongest, 588:10
    keep f. in repair, 326:14
    let f. die, 329:11
    Levin wanted f. got friendliness, 793:11
    like and dislike same things is f., 95:6
    love f. charity, 208:12
    Love without wings, 419:8
    moment when f. formed, 355:15
    needs no reason, 60:6
    needs parallelism of life, 570:16
    of the many, 557:14
    only solitary know joys of f., 661:20
    out of f. cheat others, 657:15
    paltry f. of Man, 478:16
    peace and honest f., 358:13
    rural quiet f. books, 318:2
    sacrifices of f., 655:7
    sets f. above public welfare, 67:14
    sheltering tree, 402:10
    sounds too cold, 412:10
    swear an eternal f., 278:19
    that can cease never real, 118:1
    three classes of f. and enmity, 114:18
    time strengthens f., 292:16
    true f. never serene, 281:1
    two chairs for f., 507:9
    wing of f. never moults, 496:28
    with a man, 82:9
Friendship's, true f. laws, 309:21
Friendships invalidated by marriage, 558:18
    keep f. in repair, 326:*n*5
Frieze, no jutty f. buttress, 219:15
Frigate, no F. like Book, 546:11
Fright, invisible spheres formed in f., 516:15
    power of f. and lust, 743:21
    Saint Sebastian died of f., 832:11
Frighted out of fear, 223:29
    sleep I have f. thee, 191:33
    the reign of Chaos, 264:15
Frighten, don't do it and f. horses, 631:17
    mountain cannot f. one born on it, 382:15
Frightened, crept like f. girl, 604:7
    don't be f. it won't last, 630:11
    little mouse under chair, 859:14
    Miss Muffet away, 860:3
    to death, 458:15
Frightening when convinced they are right, 774:15
Frightful fiend, 400:17
    vice a monster of f. mien, 311:10
Frights, it f. the isle, 213:20
Frigid, beat down f. Rome, 642:5
Fringe, lunatic f., 615:15
Fringed curtains of thine eye, 229:21
Fringes be falling rain, 855:19
Frippery, a little f. necessary, 362:3
Frisk i' the sun, 228:10
Frisson nouveau, 451:*n*4
Fritter my wig, 552:19
Frittered away by detail, 506:29
Frittering away his age, 398:20
Frivolity, irresponsible f., 459:24

Future *(continued)*
  shock, 822:1
  smells of Russian leather, 442:17
  something everyone reaches, 752:5
  spend rest of lives in f., 678:5
  those who talk about f., 739:9
  till F. dares forget Past, 430:2
  time f. in time past, 720:7
  transform itself in us, 677:3
  wave of f. is coming, 774:8
  wings of the f., 713:7
  world of f. a struggle, 742:13
Future's, Heaven and f. sakes, 670:6
  poor old Past the F. slave, 516:23
Futurity, shadows f. casts upon present,
  431:11
Fuzzy-Wuzzy, 'ere's to you F., 633:9
Fwowed, Tonstant Weader F. up, 738:16

G

G, belong to company G, 558:4
Gab, gift of g., 427:7
Gaberdine, Jewish g., 188:8
Gabrielle, long way to see G., 788:1
Gadarenes, country of the G., 38:20
Gadire, bound for Javan or G., 269:6
Gaels of Ireland, 664:7
Gage, one for all we g., 175:4
Gai, toujours g., 680:4
Gaiety, courage g. and quiet mind, 600:1
  eclipsed g. of nations, 325:10
Gain, better to incur loss than g., 86:9
  don't lose head to g. minute, 851:6
  every way makes my g., 215:3
  for everything g. lose something,
    455:19
  good to g. day, 519:4
  guile and lust of g., 318:10
  individual intends his own g., 338:18
  little patch of ground, 205:34
  madness of many for g. of few, 309:17,
    313:14
  man who in view of g., 63:12
  my good vain hope of g., 164:17
  necessity to glorious g., 394:16
  seen hungry ocean g. advantage, 226:18
  serves and seeks for g., 216:12
  set down as g. each day, 99:11
  strength by experience, 704:10
  the whole world, 36:27
  timely inn, 221:8
  to die is g., 45:32, 76:12
  tragedy to g. heart's desire, 609:21
Gained, boisterously maintained as g., 178:12
  for everything missed g. something,
    455:19
  from Heaven all he wished, 335:3
  no title lost no friend, 310:15
  this by philosophy, 79:15
  whatever he may have g., 63:21
Gaining, something might be g. on you,
  774:11
  trust and betraying, 830:3
Gains, do not seek evil g., 56:14
  evil g. equivalent of disaster, 56:14
  light g. make heavy purses, 165:2
  spirit that g. victory, 708:12

Gait, excessive laughter and g., 32:34
  forced g. of shuffling nag, 186:7
Gaiters, gas and g., 496:25
Gal, every g. born into world, 564:22
Galactic, evil g. empire, 838:19
Gale, no g. that blew, 580:23
  note that swells g., 335:5
  of life blew high, 619:1
  partake g., 311:16
  sun and summer g., 335:7
  that sweeps from north, 353:3
  waters God has brewed into g., 516:9
  yell for yell to g., 611:18
Galeed, name of it called G., 7:18
Galen, more than G. cured, 251:19
Galeotto was the book, 130:16
Galère, dans la g. d'un Turc, 278:*n5*
  que diable allait-il faire dans cette g.,
    278:*n5*
Gales, cool g. fan the glade, 308:5
  set of sails not g., 600:5
Galilean, O pale G., 568:17
  Pilot of the G. lake, 261:22
  you have conquered G., 117:14
Galilee, miracles in Cana of G., 40:40
  Sea of G. and Dead Sea, 680:1
  wave rolls nightly on deep G., 422:14
Galileo with his woes, 421:13
Gall, enough in thy ink, 210:8
  I am g. I am heartburn, 588:5
  lack g., 203:30
  of bitterness, 42:5
  take my milk for g., 219:11
  wormwood and the g., 29:29
Gallant, in g. trim vessel goes, 335:13
Gallanter I know, 544:4
Gallantly streaming, 411:1
Gallantry, conscience no more to do with g.,
  367:25
  what men call g., 423:8
Galled, let g. jade wince, 205:5
Galleon, moon ghostly g., 692:2
Gallery of works turned to wall, 536:13
Galley, Cervantes on g., 664:11
  on board a Turk's g., 278:*n5*
  slave to pen, 445:4
  what doing in that g., 278:21
Gallia est omnis divisa in partes tres, 91:*n10*
Gallio cared for none of those things, 42:21
Gallon, pint of sweat save g. of blood, 708:14
Gallop apace fiery-footed steeds, 183:31
  beggar will ride a g., 172:*n1*
  false g. of verses, 199:8
  go sit g., 387:13
  Pegasus to heath, 312:19
  why does he g. and g., 598:22
Galloped, I g. Dirck g., 492:2
Galloping after a fox, 606:3
Gallops, who Time g. withal, 199:15
Gallows, complexion is perfect g., 229:7
  die on g. or of pox, 340:8
  hanged Haman on the g., 13:20
  under the g. tree, 242:15
Galls, canker g. infants of spring, 201:22
  his kibe, 206:23
Gallup Poll feeling pulse, 666:16
Galoot's, till last g. ashore, 571:5
Gals, buffalo g. come out tonight, 848:5
Galumphing back, 551:11

Gamaliel, at feet of G., 42:27
Gambling is going on here, 782:10
Gambols, your g. your songs, 206:24
Game, back of bar in solo g., 673:9
  baseball is g. of skill, 730:15
  begins in the spring, 833:4
  gunless g., 613:15
  how you played g., 692:4
  in which my name was, 706:7
  is afoot, 617:13
  is being played, 279:23
  is done I've won I've won, 400:4
  is up, 225:16
  little pleasure of g., 296:17
  love g. beyond prize, 627:3
  play up and play g., 627:6
  poetry mug's g., 722:21
  rigor of the g., 407:13
  rules of g. laws of Nature, 537:1
  science not g., 761:15
  Socratic manner not a g., 659:12
  start g. on lone heaths, 410:13
  take me out to ball g., 685:10
  that must be played, 652:4
  that never means anything, 747:16
  this g. is life, 759:11
  war's a g., 348:9
  was empires, 425:4
  woman is his g., 483:2
Gamefish, only g. swims upstream, 614:6
Game's afoot, 193:2
Games, shows g. sports guns, 351:9
  victor in Olympic g. or announcer, 64:25
Gammon and spinach, 856:17
  and spinnage, 498:5
Gamp my name and Gamp my nater, 497:7
Gamut of emotions, 738:17
Gander, goosey g., 858:11
Gane, nane sall ken where he is g., 854:8
Gang aft a-gley, 377:12
  before we g. awa', 654:3
  grisly g., 666:14
  old g., 594:5
  tell g. at Forty-second Street, 679:10
Ganglion in nerves of society, 578:2
Gangrene in mildewed silo, 678:1
Gang's, hail hail g. all here, 564:*n1*
Gangs, don't join too many g., 670:4
Gangsters will stop, 82:28
Gangway for de Lawd, 728:3
Gaol, all we know who lie in g., 605:22
Gap appeared in the mountain, 60:22
  this great g. of time, 223:4
Gape, craters of my eyes g., 829:3
Gapes for drink again, 275:8
Gaping, love not a g. pig, 189:12
Garb, words in reason's g., 265:7
Garbage, prey on g., 202:17
Garcia, message to G., 608:12
Garde meurt mais ne se rend pas, 389:*n1*
Garden, blow upon my g., 25:24
  cherubims east of the g., 6:11
  come into g. Maud, 485:8
  cultivate our g., 316:9
  died, 640:13
  earthly ball a peopled g., 364:3
  fairies at bottom of g., 679:1
  flowers in g. meat in hall, 134:*n3*
  full of weeds, 856:12

Germany *(continued)*
    put G. in saddle, 502:10
    ruins culture, 590:4
    springtime for Hitler and G., 817:6
    the cause of Hitler, 715:17
Germens, all g. spill at once, 216:18
Gertrude, portrait of G. Stein, 673:15
Gesang, Wein Weib und G., 368:*n*2
Gesture, distorting my g., 791:12
    without motion, 719:5
Gestures, get at thing without g., 687:16
Get, accomplished anything except g. along,
    708:4
    and beget, 595:8
    at thing without gestures, 687:16
    can't always g. what you want, 838:7
    desire to g. on in world, 715:4
    from where you are not, 721:1
    gotta g. out while we're young, 841:7
    I can't g. no respect, 807:13
    I g. by with a little help, 835:4
    I'll g. you my pretty, 786:9
    men take best they can g., 328:12
    money still get money, 100:*n*12
    nice work if you can g. it, 747:10
    on board little children, 863:11
    out of kitchen, 705:6
    remember children you did not g.,
    798:6
    that I wear, 199:6
    thee behind me, 36:26
    thee glass eyes, 217:25
    thee to a nunnery, 204:3
    there first with most, 527:12
    time to g., 24:6
    to g. along go along, 697:9
    told to g. up so white person sit,
    791:8
    understanding, 20:28
    up begin again, 492:16
    up sweet Slug-a-bed, 248:16
    what we deserve, 829:12
    what you want, 636:4
    with child mandrake root, 233:13
    writing, 715:5
    you g. no more of me, 169:14
    you to my lady's chamber, 206:24
    you've got to g. up, 716:4
Gets, Dead Sea g. to keep, 680:1
    Galilee g. to give, 680:1
    him to rest, 193:16
    pleased with what he g., 198:13
    them that has g., 592:7
Getting along with women, 363:12
    and spending, 394:18
    better and better, 612:19
    Gospel of G. On, 609:7
    no g. rid of it, 406:1
    not g. what one wants, 604:23
    on in world, 661:7
    on together, 694:18
    out of world known before, 661:7
    prevent lower from g. more, 80:25
    to Heaven at last, 544:18
    what one wants, 604:23
    with all thy g. get understanding, 20:28
    youth is the time of g., 270:7
Gettysburg cant understand it, 748:16
Gewesen, wie es eigentlich g. ist, 441:*n*3

Ghastly dew, 481:23
    grim ancient Raven, 479:5
    long and g. kitchen, 500:17
    night full of g. dreams, 174:2
    trembling cold in g. fears, 373:8
    turned face with g. pang, 400:8
Ghetto's chronic need, 813:5
Ghost, before not g. of shores, 579:8
    embrace my mother's g., 55:2
    escapes from vanquished pyre, 104:25
    he gave up g., 40:23
    Holy G., 816:1
    lost and by wind grieved g., 760:5
    make g. of him that lets me, 202:10
    man giveth up the g., 14:16
    of Christmas Past, 497:15
    of Christmas Present, 497:17
    of Christmas Yet to Come, 497:20
    of deceased Roman Empire, 246:13
    of garden fronts sea, 569:14
    of Hamlet's father, 624:9
    please my g., 691:4
    some old lover's g., 235:7
    thrice the g. fled, 97:14
    vex not his g., 218:8
    what beckoning g., 309:27
    will not let me be, 442:7
    wish granted to smiling g., 817:18
    wrought g. upon floor, 479:1
    your g. will walk, 492:12
Ghosted you up a swell story, 762:13
Ghosties, ghoulies and g., 847:9
Ghostlike, haunt g. the spot, 460:8
Ghostly galleon, 692:2
Ghosts, clothes hang like g. from lines,
    729:11
    driven like g., 428:21
    from enchanter fleeing, 428:21
    haunted by g. deposed, 179:28
    of defunct bodies fly, 270:23
    of departed quantities, 306:16
    true love is like g., 273:12
    we are all g., 540:10
Ghosts' high noon, 565:23
Ghoul-haunted woodland of Weir, 479:12
Ghoulies and ghosties, 847:9
G.I. Joe, 851:19
Giant, America gigantic but g. mistake, 608:8
    as when a g. dies, 211:20
    Atlas upholds, 70:5
    baby figure of g. mass, 207:29
    branches tossed, 431:20
    Despair, 281:26
    dwarf on shoulders of g., 240:4
    fling stone g. dies, 317:5
    making G. hit into double, 692:14
    misunderstanding, 787:11
    nation like pitiful helpless g., 790:23
    of beasts, 236:2
    race before the flood, 285:4
    rat of Sumatra, 617:16
    tyrannous to use it like g., 211:12
    wings prevent walking, 524:8
Giant-dwarf, senior-junior g., 176:33
Giant's robe, 222:8
    strength, 211:12
Giants in the earth, 6:25
    standing on shoulders of G., 290:25
    strength of the ancient g., 55:*n*1

Gib, melancholy as g. cat, 184:29
Gibber, squeak and g., 200:18
Gibbets, better schoolrooms than g., 509:7
    keep lifted hand in awe, 305:20
Gibbon, eh Mr. G., 356:20
Gibe, call it humor when they g., 299:2
Gibeon, sun stand still upon G., 10:24
Gibes, where be your g. now, 206:24
Giddy, fancies are more g., 209:22
    habitation g. and unsure, 191:23
    I am g., 208:2
    thinks world turns round, 175:39
Giddy-paced, brisk and g. times, 209:20
Gideon Bibles only in bedrooms, 730:1
    sword of Lord and of G., 10:36
Gie me ae spark, 377:17
Gift, beauty the g. of God, 79:12
    born with g. of laughter, 677:13
    crave of thee g., 421:21
    every good g. and perfect g., 47:11
    every woman g. of world to me, 442:11
    fatal g. of beauty, 421:11
    gauntlet with g. in 't, 464:2
    great grace with little g., 85:11
    greatest g. freedom of will, 132:1
    have the g. to know it, 198:19
    hearts not had as g., 639:11
    heavenly g. of poesy, 284:11
    heaven's last best g., 267:1
    it is a god who gave you this g., 52:5
    love g. of fairy tale, 551:8
    love God's ultimate g., 493:19
    make g. rich by delaying, 504:5
    manner of giving worth more than g.,
    257:10
    most essential g. for good writer, 755:5
    Muses gave me honeyed g., 85:15
    never look g. horse in mouth, 119:1
    of excellence to few men, 61:11
    of God eternal life, 43:2
    of martyrdom, 284:21
    of sleep, 594:12
    of the gab, 427:7
    of tongues, 365:11
    reason God's crowning g., 67:25
    skilled poet through natural g., 65:28
    tablet a g. of Memory, 78:11
    terrible g. lifted from hearts, 526:2
    though small is precious, 54:23
    time with g. of tears, 568:1
    'tis the g. to be simple, 848:4
    to be well-favored g. of fortune, 194:33
    various g. to each, 466:22
    who know heaven save by heaven's g.,
    107:17
    woman's g. to rain shower, 175:20
    word better than g., 32:30
Gifted, poetically g., 530:1
Giftie, some power g. gie us, 378:6
Gifts, adore my g. instead of me, 250:18
    benefit in g. of bad man, 69:24
    enjoyed of founder, 353:15
    fairy g. fading away, 411:12
    fear Greeks even when they bring g., 97:6
    glorious g. of the gods, 52:19
    gods do not give all men g., 54:26
    liberality in g., 292:15
    more of his grace than g., 232:14
    my lady's admirable g., 129:16

Gifts *(continued)*

no g. from Chance, 528:11
people I cannot win with g., 280:16
presented unto him g., 33:19
rarer g. than gold, 713:2
rich g. wax poor, 204:2
riches to make g. to friends, 70:8
seven hundred pounds goot g., 190:15
spend not then his g. in vain, 237:14
thou only givest these g. to man, 418:3
two jars of the g. he gives, 54:6
with tired backs we bring g., 855:18
Gig, crew of captain's g., 563:11
Gigantic, America g. but giant mistake, 608:8
field of soya beans, 832:12
hound, 617:12
press restless g., 706:3
transformed into g. insect, 700:24
willful young, 652:1
Gigantically down, 478:6, 753:18
Giggle, ha'd to g. w'en nuffin' in pot, 660:4
Giggling, three g. girls, 821:16
Gild, bards g. lapses of time, 435:16
refined gold, 178:14
Gilded and sticky, 710:11
cage, 654:1
car of day, 260:19
eaves, 483:1
flap bug with g. wings, 312:8
fly does lecher, 217:21
fool, 233:5
gay g. scenes, 301:11
hearse, 719:13
laugh at g. butterflies, 218:1
not marble nor g. monuments, 226:15
throne is bit of wood g., 388:4
vessel goes, 335:13
Gilding, stripped of lettering and g., 319:2
Gilds, eternal summer g. them, 424:1
love g. the scene, 367:18
Gilead, no balm in G., 29:9
Gilpin long live he, 347:24
Gilt comes off on our hands, 527:2
dust that is a little g., 208:13
Surcingles, 546:17
Gimble, gyre and g., 551:10
Gimme a whiskey, 723:12
Gin, drop g. scuttle to cellar, 789:8
of all g. joints in all towns in world, 782:7
perhaps it's the g., 763:10
union of g. and vermouth, 748:7
was mother's milk to her, 610:8
Ginger ale on the side, 723:12
board money in g. jar, 557:8
hot i' the mouth, 209:17
nutmegs g. cinnamon cloves, 249:15
Gingham, bits of g. and calico, 597:7
dog went Bow-wow, 597:7
Gins, snares traps g. pitfalls, 490:*n*1
Gipper, win just one for the G., 774:6
win one for G., 724:16
Giraffe, God invented g. elephant cat, 693:12
Gird up thy loins like a man, 15:4
Girded, father's sword g. on, 411:16
he g. up his loins, 12:31
let loins be g., 39:30
with your loins g., 8:18
Girder, from g. into street noon leaks, 753:13
Girdeth, him that g. on his harness, 12:33

Girdid up my Lions & fled Seen, 555:7
Girdle, bright g. furled, 531:2
helps with g., 763:14
loosened the embroidered g., 53:15
round about earth, 181:10
round about world, 165:6
Girdled, walls and towers g. round, 401:13
Girl at impressionable age, 804:18
Burma g. a-settin', 633:12
crept like frightened g., 604:7
green g., 201:29
guiding a boy and a g., 835:13
Heaven protect working g., 613:3
I can't get no g. reaction, 838:4
I left behind me, 846:12
I like to see, 774:1
little g. had making of poet, 616:1
little g. my stringbean, 821:11
need park policeman pretty g., 726:1
needs good parents, 705:16
nice g. won't give an inch, 110:22
soft face of a g., 68:1
Spearmint G., 739:15
sweetest I know, 674:2
then spoke I to my g., 248:2
there little g. don't cry, 596:3
there was a little g., 468:4
unlessoned g. unschooled, 189:8
wild solitary g. Rima, 579:7
wink at homely g., 691:4
Girlish glee, 565:11
laughter, 616:2
Girl's, diamonds g. best friend, 758:14
stumbling blocks in g. education, 662:6
Girls, all g. he can please, 571:14
boys and g. level with men, 224:1
boys and g. together, 625:13
Dust was Lads and G., 545:18
Glos'ter g. they have no combs, 862:5
golden lads and g., 225:23
hear what servant g. said, 658:8
little g. made of, 860:1
little g. recognize your prime, 804:19
of all g. so smart, 307:23
oh you New York g., 862:6
sleek g. I teach, 818:9
three giggling g., 821:16
turn wives, 818:10
what shall I do for pretty g., 642:19
which g. hath merriest eye, 171:16
who wear glasses, 738:13
with g. be handy, 846:14
wretched un-ideaed g., 326:9
Git thar fustest with mostest, 527:*n*3
Gitche Gumee, shores of G., 466:24
Gits, them that has g., 592:7
Give a little love to child, 517:17
a man enough rope, 146:*n*8
a new commandment, 41:25
all that a man hath will he g., 13:27
all thou canst, 395:16
all to love, 453:8
an inch take an ell, 149:*n*8
and not count cost, 145:5
ask only what they can g., 643:16
Aztecs by no means would g. up, 145:1
bouquets while I'm living, 682:3
can't g. me love and peace, 725:6
countries g. themselves to you, 706:8

Give *(continued)*

country back to Indians, 750:13
cried G. Me, 544:20
crowns pounds guineas, 618:10
Dayrolles a chair, 315:14
delight and hurt not, 230:6
enemies means of our destruction, 61:9
eternal rest g. them, 49:8
every man thy ear, 201:26
fame for pot of ale, 193:3
freely received freely g., 35:25
Galilee gets to g., 680:1
great meals of beef, 193:10
hand and heart, 414:12
hautboys breath he comes, 285:9
haves of g., 740:9
him a little earth, 231:9
him death by inches, 225:2
his angels charge, 18:26
I generally had to g. in, 388:11
I will g. you rest, 35:35
I will not g. sleep to mine eyes, 20:9
if can g. that you are a writer, 754:12
in life did harbor g., 237:22
it an understanding, 201:19
kiss better than you g., 208:18
lady what she wants, 556:4
man horse can ride boat can sail, 557:10
me a kiss, 248:7
me a look, 237:16
me a thousand kisses, 94:4
me a torch, 707:21
me ae spark, 377:17
me again my hollow tree, 312:17
me an ounce of civet, 217:22
me another horse, 174:19
me back my heart, 420:2
me back my legions, 102:4
me back my young brother, 821:2
me bitter fame, 725:6
me but that, 156:28
me excess of it, 208:25
me good digestion Lord, 680:*n*3
me hand that is honest, 395:22
me handfuls of lilies, 98:1
me health and a day, 454:16
me John Baptist's head, 36:12
me liberty or give me death, 353:3
me liberty to know, 263:4
me more love or more disdain, 253:16
me my scallop shell, 160:8
me ocular proof, 214:9
me quoth I, 218:26
me that man, 204:17
me that old-time religion, 847:21
me the daggers, 220:18
me to drink mandragora, 223:4
me today take tomorrow, 122:25
me truth, 507:21
me where to stand, 86:2
me your answer do, 643:20
me your arm old toad, 810:5
me your tired your poor, 595:6
meanest flower can g., 393:19
more blessed to g., 42:25
mother g. me sun, 540:11
my regards to Broadway, 679:10
name to every fixed star, 176:20
Nature a chance, 154:8

Give *(continued)*

never g. all heart, 637:15
never g. in never, 667:1
no more g. the people straw, 8:10
no more to every guest, 299:5
not a windy night rainy morrow, 227:2
oh g. me a home, 855:3
peace I g. unto you, 41:30
peace in our time, 51:16
reason on compulsion, 185:25
some words g. you a feeling, 757:13
sop to Cerberus, 122:24
sorrow words, 221:35
thee peace, 9:17
them meat in due season, 19:11
these delights if thou canst g., 259:21
throne would be easy, 81:24
thy thoughts no tongue, 201:24
thy worst of thoughts, 213:32
to a thief, 781:11
to get esteem, 341:3
to spend to g. to want, 161:24
to the poor, 36:33
two daughters crying g. g., 23:24
up verse my boy, 709:6
up whole idea of life, 824:7
us a song to cheer, 556:7
us grace and strength, 600:1
us grace to accept, 735:13
us our daily bread, 34:11
us peace, 49:12
us rest or death, 480:20
us taste of your quality, 203:23
us the tools, 666:8
warning to world, 226:23
we g. what we have, 585:4
we receive but what we g., 402:5
what shall I g. my children, 798:7
what we g. and preserve, 476:3
what you command, 119:12
while we have praise to g., 238:5
world assurance of a man, 205:21
world the lie, 160:7
you all the pussy, 850:18
you some violets, 206:12

Given, as if Checks g., 546:6
ask and it shall be g., 35:3
gladly not to be standing here, 779:3
God has g. you one face, 204:6
hast thou g. the horse strength, 15:13
heart change of mood, 669:12
heaven alone g. away, 514:15
I have g. suck and know, 219:23
more g. less work, 543:4
much g. much required, 39:31
not have g. it for monkeys, 188:33
nothing g. nothing required, 321:19
of thine own have we g. thee, 13:12
our hearts away, 394:18
pay for what gods g., 659:13
take what is g., 671:18
thee till break of day, 373:17
them the slip, 295:22
thou hast g. him his heart's desire, 16:15
too dear for what's g. freely, 228:8

Given *(continued)*

unto every one that hath be g., 37:14
what scanted in hair g. in wit, 174:30

Giver, cheerful g., 45:10
keep modest as g., 588:18

Givers, when g. prove unkind, 204:2

Gives, blesseth him that g., 189:19
blessing love g., 819:5
but for another g. ease, 374:1
but greater feeling to worse, 179:6
doubly benefits who g. quickly, 102:14
'er all she needs, 634:17
he that lends g., 252:6
heart and soul away, 618:12
lovely light, 735:2
new meaning, 715:14
no man a sinecure, 709:6
secure whate'er he g., 324:10
sternest good-night, 220:12
the more he g. to others, 59:21
thoughts nature g. way to, 220:6
time takes all g. all, 159:8
to airy nothing, 182:3
twice who gives promptly, 123:11

Giveth his beloved sleep, 20:5
land the Lord g. thee, 9:1
life and breath, 42:18
man g. up the ghost, 14:16
not as world g., 41:30
unto the poor, 23:18

Giving enemies the slip, 332:7
heart to dog to tear, 635:19
in g. we receive, 128:5
insure position by g. generously, 5:1
manner of g. worth more, 257:10
not g. life but risking life, 777:12
not in g. vein today, 174:10
stealing and g. odor, 208:25

Gizzard, something in her g., 288:25

Glacier knocks in cupboard, 775:9
woman, 753:16

Glad, almost g. we have been bombed, 757:8
did I live gladly die, 599:6
heart too soon g., 491:10
kindness, 639:12
let us live and be g., 123:30
make g. the city of God, 17:22
me with soft black eye, 412:13
moments of g. grace, 637:5
never g. confident morning, 491:24
New Year, 480:15
not born before tea, 399:6
of other men's good, 199:6
Olaf g. and big, 740:2
sad g. brother's name, 569:13
show ourselves g., 49:23
some have what others would be g. of, 322:2
tidings of great joy, 294:5
to be of use, 717:14
to brink of fear, 454:14
to sleep with Aphrodite, 54:28
weep for what could make them g., 670:18
when they said unto me, 20:1
wine that maketh g. the heart, 19:9
wise son maketh a g. father, 21:14

Glad *(continued)*

with all my heart, 169:14
you like adverbs, 585:18

Glade, bee-loud g., 637:1
cool gales fan the g., 308:5
crown the watery g., 333:18
points to yonder g., 309:27

Gladly, be your wife g., 500:6
beyond any experience, 740:6
die, 599:6
lerne and gladly teche, 135:1
suffer fools g., 45:12

Gladness, begin in g., 392:9
garments of g., 31:11
I that in heill wes and g., 142:4
notes of g., 409:6
of the heart, 32:42
serve the Lord with g., 19:3
teach me half g., 429:20
wealth small aid for daily g., 70:8

Gladsome light of jurisprudence, 159:15

Glamis hath murdered sleep, 220:17
thou art and Cawdor, 219:10

Glamour, moment of romance of g., 612:2
of childish days, 707:7

Glance from heaven to earth, 182:3
glum, 565:25
O brightening g., 640:15
of the Lord, 422:15
she will not g. up at bomber, 789:8
ten thousand saw I at a g., 394:6
without a g. my way, 545:10

Glances, casting backward g., 521:16
gray eye g., 478:10

Glare, moths caught by g., 420:5
rockets' red g., 411:1
sunburnt by g. of life, 464:3
surrounds king hides him, 153:19

Glareth, not all gold that g., 127:n4

Glasgerion swore great oath, 853:27

Glass, bishop kick hole in stained g. window, 717:3
break bloody g., 777:8
dome of many-colored g., 430:17
drink not the third g., 249:17
excuse for the g., 367:29
failing hour by hour, 777:8
fill every g., 307:13
first g. for myself, 302:15
Fortune like g. easily broken, 103:2
fount more sparkling than g., 100:6
get thee g. eyes, 217:25
grief with g. that ran, 568:1
if your windows g., 319:18
made mouths in a g., 216:21
obscured or broken, 809:4
of brandy and water, 384:10
of fashion mould of form, 204:8
of years is brittle, 568:18
people in g. houses, 251:n2
pride is his own g., 208:1
satire a sort of g., 297:18
saw through g. eye darkly, 561:20
see through g. darkly, 44:20
shown g. flowers, 714:8
swift sandy g., 239:10
third g. thou canst not tame, 249:17
thou art thy mother's g., 225:29
Time turn up his g., 239:10

Glass (*continued*)

    turn down empty G., 472:6

    Venus take my votive g., 297:6

    wherein noble youth dress, 191:30

    whose house is g., 251:18

Glasses, fill all the g. there, 275:9

    girls who wear g., 738:13

    itself in tempests, 422:1

    Shakespeare and the musical g., 341:15

Glasses', peeps over g. edge, 493:6

Glassy cool translucent wave, 261:10

    his g. essence, 211:13

Glaze on katydid-wing, 714:20

Glazed with rain water, 703:10

Glazen, upon the g. shelves, 717:21

Gleam, bright g. of noble deeds, 66:8

    fled visionary g., 393:10

    follow the G., 487:1

Gleamed upon my sight, 394:1

Gleaming, like g. taper's light, 340:13

    twilight's last g., 411:1

Gleams, light g. and is gone, 530:19

    of remoter world, 427:16

    on whom pale moon g., 590:16

    through fog, 333:10

    thy footstep g., 478:10

    untraveled world, 481:9

Glean, let me g. after the reapers, 11:13

    shalt not g. thy vineyard, 9:13

Gleaned my teeming brain, 439:8

Gleaning of grapes of Ephraim, 10:37

Gleanings, shalt not gather the g., 9:13

Glee, counterfeited g., 342:8

    girlish g., 565:11

    piping songs of pleasant g., 371:13

Glen, down the rushy g., 535:15

Glenartney's, lone G. hazel shade, 397:4

Glib and oily art, 215:22

Glide, in sunny beams did g., 371:9

    leisurely we g., 549:9

    safe into haven g., 322:24

    soul into boughs does g., 277:5

    to wind tossing water, 703:12

Glided, mourns that day has g. by, 435:18

Glideth at own sweet will, 392:13

Gliding, dark mother always g. near, 520:17

    snakes g. up hollow, 454:2

Glimmer of twilight, 491:24

    women have g. of loyalty to Truth, 593:20

Glimmering, gone g., 420:8

    hold up tapers to sun, 241:*n*4

    mere g. and decays, 279:8

    now fades g. landscape, 334:9

    river lake g. pool, 534:9

Glimpse, nor g. divine, 313:25

    same old g. of Paradise, 620:9

Glimpses make me less forlorn, 394:19

    of forgotten dreams, 480:8

    revisitest g. of the moon, 202:6

    thousand g. wins, 528:17

Glint, in g. old gold, 664:10

Glisten, all silence an' g., 515:3

Glister me forward, 780:9

Glistering grief, 230:25

Glisters, all that g. not gold, 127:*n*4

Glitter of seas, 827:18

Glittered when he walked, 652:10

Glittering, ancient g. eyes, 642:8

    eye, 399:11

    how that g. taketh me, 248:19

Glitters, all that g. is not gold, 127:*n*4

Gloamin', roamin' in the g., 654:4

Global, my wars g. from the start, 794:14

    village, 786:12

Globally, think g., 760:10

Globe, common air bathes g., 519:3

    country spread over half g., 472:24

    distracted g., 202:22

    doubled g. of dead, 795:4

    flames have spread over g., 359:9

    freedom hunted round the g., 354:9

    great g. itself, 230:9

    in the window, 834:3

    interior of solid g., 443:5

    power dotted over g., 415:6

    sop of all this solid g., 207:26

    sway destinies of half the g., 463:2

Glocca Morra, how are things in G., 752:3

Gloire, le jour de g. est arrivé, 383:8

Gloom, chase my g. away, 384:8

    convent's solitary g., 309:25

    counterfeit a g., 260:5

    deep thicket's g., 363:16

    encircling g., 449:18

    in g. black-purple, 664:10

    moral g. of world, 460:4

    nor g. of night, 71:*n*8

    of earthquake and eclipse, 428:1

    tempted her out of g., 479:14

Glooms, beetle booms adown g., 596:1

    welcome kindred g., 317:14

Gloomy, deep and g. wood, 391:3

    view of future, 679:2

Gloria in excelsis Deo, 49:11

    mundi, 138:5

Gloriam, ad maiorem Dei g., 149:*n*13

Gloried and drank deep, 471:8

Glories, conquests g. triumphs spoils, 196:18

    Heaven's g. shine, 509:1

    my g. and state depose, 180:10

    of our blood and state, 254:9

    strung like beads, 520:3

    with their triumphs and their g., 492:11

Glorieth, let him that g. glory in me, 29:11

Glorified, whom he justified he g., 43:8

Glorify Father in heaven, 34:2

Glorious blood-red, 492:6

    by my sword, 272:*n*1

    circumstance of g. war, 214:8

    crowded hour of g. life, 346:12

    full many a g. morning, 226:10

    gifts of the gods, 52:19

    heaven's g. sun, 176:20

    honorable and g., 350:3

    how g. and painful, 488:11

    institution, 344:17

    king's daughter all g. within, 17:20

    made g. summer by sun of York, 173:28

    make thee g. by my pen, 272:3

    making city g. and great, 64:17

    mirror, 422:1

    mission of trade unions, 597:10

    morning for America, 337:11

    most g. city of God, 119:21

    most g. to victors, 74:9

    necessity to g. gain, 394:16

Glorious (*continued*)

    place glorious age, 826:16

    right hand is become g., 8:27

    shadow of g. name, 110:2

    song of old, 488:15

    sun in Heaven, 401:12

    sunshine a g. birth, 393:9

    Tam was g., 379:17

    the g. Ninety-two, 352:9

    the more g. the triumph, 354:10

    thing to be Pirate King, 564:2

    things g. had no glory, 754:4

    things of thee are spoken, 339:13

    war's g. art, 305:20

Gloriously drunk, 348:8

    he hath triumphed g., 8:25

    perjured, 100:5

    succeeded, 760:6

Glory, a light a g., 402:6

    and danger alike, 74:2

    and freshness of a dream, 393:7

    and nothing of a name, 422:17

    and shame of universe, 280:8

    and the dream, 393:10

    be the Perfect One, 545:16

    be to the Father, 49:25

    belongs to our ancestors, 111:13

    cataract leaps in g., 482:19

    crown of g., 47:32

    day of g. has come, 383:*n*1

    days of youth days of g., 424:26

    deed everything g. nothing, 365:18

    desire for g. clings, 113:26

    die in g. never old, 618:16

    doesn't mean argument, 552:14

    drowned G. in Cup, 472:3

    excess of g. obscured, 264:17

    fight for love and g., 741:1

    for country's g. fast, 396:14

    from gray hairs gone, 468:7

    from the earth, 393:9

    full meridian of my g., 230:31

    go where g. waits thee, 411:8

    guards bivouac of dead, 522:6

    heavens declare the g. of God, 16:10

    hoary head a crown of g., 22:3

    Homer herald of your g., 83:8

    hope of g., 50:8

    in His bosom, 513:19

    in one day fill stage, 249:13

    in the flower, 393:18

    is departed from Israel, 11:19

    is in their shame, 45:36

    jest and riddle of world, 311:9

    King of g. shall come in, 16:20

    land of hope and g., 625:11

    left him alone with g., 427:3

    let him that glorieth g. in me, 29:11

    like a circle in water, 171:14

    like a shooting star, 179:22

    long hair g. to woman, 44:14

    love of g. most ardent, 303:8

    my gown of g., 160:8

    myn the travaille thyn the g., 135:27

    no more Hope no more G., 662:22

    nothing so expensive as g., 398:16

    O what joy and g. must be, 126:5

    of Christian religion, 140:6

    of coming of Lord, 513:18

Go *(continued)*

sir gallop, 387:13
softly all my years, 27:36
Soul the body's quest, 160:7
Sun, don't g., 818:6
sweetest love I do not g., 234:10
tell the Spartans, 62:4
tell those who sent you, 366:16
then he may g., 764:6
they all g. into dark, 720:22
they'd immediately g. out, 375:14
through world safely g., 375:10
till the end, 551:5
Time stays we g., 574:11
to bed by day, 598:20
to boldly g. where no man gone before,
    808:7
to encounter reality, 696:7
to get along g. along, 697:9
to get where he has to g., 793:12
to g. beyond is wrong, 63:6
to grandfather's house we g., 450:11
to grass, 243:2
to it O jazzmen, 681:14
to it with delight, 223:30
to lost sheep of Israel, 35:24
to restaurants, 838:14
to pot, 343:10
to the ant, 21:4
travel to g., 598:4
try to g. it sole alone, 671:2
turn and g., 819:18
up and down as a talebearer, 9:14
waiting for you g., 635:15
walk it slow where you g., 829:11
we know not where, 211:23
we shall g. on to end, 666:1
we'll gather and g., 390:12
west young man, 503:4
when half-gods g., 453:9
where glory waits thee, 411:8
where money is, 486:20
where did we g. right, 817:7
where we will on surface, 505:25
who will g. for us, 26:26
will not let thee g., 7:20
with anyone to death, 669:1
with drift of things, 668:16
with me like good angels, 230:23
with night will g., 371:11
with show of inconvenience, 703:8
women come and g., 717:7
would not g. without father's word,
    432:2
write it before them, 27:25
ye and teach, 38:12
ye into all the world, 38:33
year going let him g., 484:14
you may call it madness, 384:8
Goä wheer munny is, 486:20
Goads them on behind, 636:21
    words of wise are as g., 25:9
Goal, do not turn back at g., 103:24
    good final g. of ill, 484:2
    grave not life's g., 465:17
    is living in agreement with nature, 84:13
    pint people to the g., 515:1
    progress our g., 444:1
    rider deciding on g., 607:18

Goal *(continued)*

riders not stop at g., 579:2
the sky, 851:12
Goals, black people define g., 835:11
    muddied oafs at g., 635:8
Goat, aimless g. paths, 826:11
    lust of g. bounty of God, 372:17
    splashing with hoofs of g., 464:6
    with g. feet dance antic hay, 170:14
Goat-head, foul g., 642:17
Goats, divideth sheep from g., 37:16
    eat ivy, 860:10
    lecherous g., 236:6
    you herd g., 58:6
Gobbledygoo, your Luftwaffe your g.,
    827:15
Gobbler, black turkey g., 855:22
Gobble-uns 'at gits you, 596:5
Goblet, upon first g., 451:13
Goblin, hag and hungry g., 844:19
Goblins 'at gits you, 596:5
    sprites and g., 228:14
God, a G. ready to pardon, 13:17
    a sea of infinite substance, 125:2
    abandoned these defended, 619:18
    abhors you, 318:16
    accept him, 484:23
    act as if G. exist, 631:3
    act as if there were G., 582:15
    act of G., 504:11
    Act of G. defined, 729:3
    afraid to look upon G., 8:5
    all mercy is God unjust, 306:8
    all service same with G., 491:6
    Almighty has hung sign, 415:17
    Almighty's gentlemen, 283:17
    alone knows, 566:14
    am I a g. I see so clearly, 365:5
    and angels as surety, 121:14
    and attributes eternal, 286:15
    and devil fighting, 525:13
    and history remember, 731:8
    and I knew once, 566:14
    and imagination one, 688:15
    and man decree, 619:13
    and nature do nothing uselessly, 80:n4
    and sinners reconciled, 323:1
    angler now with G., 253:1
    announced selves descended from a g.,
        416:7
    answers sharp, 464:2
    Appears and God is Light, 375:16
    argue not concerning G., 518:10
    as G. alone Jesus not saved us, 765:5
    as G. gives us to see right, 477:4
    as I wad do were I Lord G., 536:8
    as if G. wrote bill, 453:17
    as revealed to vicars, 771:15
    assumes the g., 285:8
    atheist half believes G., 306:9
    attribute to G. himself, 189:19
    be good to the man, 804:2
    be merciful, 40:9
    be praised Georges ended, 674:n3
    be still and know that I am G., 17:23
    be thanked, 713:1
    beauty the gift of G., 79:12
    became man devil woman, 451:2
    behold your G., 28:4

God *(continued)*

bein' G. ain't bed of roses, 728:6
being with thee, 392:16
believe in one G. and no more, 355:3
believes he eats G., 333:12
bequeath my soul to G., 168:19
bless America, 716:6, 716:7
bless Captain Vere, 517:1
bless the Pretender, 314:12
bless us every one, 497:19
bless you, 847:8
bless you my dear, 329:20
body Nature G. soul, 311:7
brewed waters into gale, 516:9
brooding on G., 781:8
built G. a church, 347:17
bush afire with G., 464:5
but for grace of G., 150:4
by G. Mr. Chairman, 339:7
by G. she'd better, 488:n1
by grace of G. forces on Philippine soil,
    690:9
Cabots talk only to G., 621:22
Cabots walk with G., 621:n1
cannot appear except in form of bread,
    803:4
cast all cares on G., 486:15
caught his eye, 749:7
cause of Freedom cause of G., 383:11
caused a deep sleep, 5:21
changes and man and form, 569:7
changes not people until they change,
    121:6
charged with grandeur of G., 587:4
chide G. for countenance, 199:25
chosen people of G., 357:10
Christ came from G. and a woman,
    443:11
circumvent G., 206:19
city of G., 119:21
closer walk with G., 347:1
comes as sun at noon, 236:21
comes G. behind them, 494:21
committed themselves to G., 247:5
Communism vision of Kingdom of G. on
    earth, 777:3
conscience a g. to all mortals, 84:7
contempt of G. love of G., 119:22
could have made a better berry, 253:5
course of Nature art of G., 255:n4
created heaven and earth, 5:9
created woman and boredom ceased,
    589:23
curse for G., 821:2
curse G. and die, 13:28
damn you, 632:n2
darkness of G., 720:23
dazzled by ways of G., 684:14
dear G. the very houses, 392:13
dear G. who loveth us, 401:2
dear to G. famous to all ages, 262:18
death of one g. death of all, 688:1
deem himself g. or beast, 311:9
defend the right, 172:8
depth of all being is G., 712:6
did G. Care, 544:20
die adoring G. loving friends, 317:3
die young like kissing G., 814:16
died before g. of love was born, 235:7

God *(continued)*

discovered I was not G., 579:3
discussing duty to G., 519:16
does not leave us, 840:13
don't believe in G. or Mother Goose, 612:21
doth G. exact day-labor, 263:13
dwells there among men, 126:1
ef you want to take in G., 514:22
effect whose cause is G., 348:13
either a beast or a g., 80:23
electrical display of G., 724:3
Enoch walked with G., 6:22
enormous loping g. in sky, 839:5
enter into kingdom of G., 36:34
equal to a g. sitting opposite you, 94:15
erects house of prayer, 294:16
eternal G. is thy refuge, 10:16
every g. set his seal, 205:21
every man G. or Devil, 283:16
evidence for G. in inner experiences, 582:19
except for G. our only lord, 169:11
face of G. shine through, 734:15
far be it from G., 15:1
Father-Mother G., 526:10
favor with G. and man, 39:8
fear G. and keep commandments, 25:10
fear G. and take own part, 452:4
fear G. honor the king, 47:28
fear G. nothing else, 502:15
fell upon knees and blessed G., 247:6
finding man not sufficiently alone, 659:5
finger of G., 8:13
first planted garden, 168:13
for G. sake hold your tongue, 234:5
for Harry, 193:2
for us all, 149:17
forbid it Almighty G., 353:3
foregoing generations beheld G., 454:12
forgive you but I never, 151:17
forgives me for it, 814:1
forgotten all I have done, 290:6
formed matter, 291:5
from the machine, 83:19
from whom blessings flow, 289:22
fulfills in many ways, 486:12
gave every people cup of clay, 856:8
gave Loaf to Bird, 545:17
gave me my money, 574:8
gave Noah rainbow sign, 813:6
gave the increase, 43:34
give him blood to drink, 460:16
give them wisdom, 209:6
give us grace to accept, 735:13
giver of breath and bread, 587:3
giveth both mouth and meat, 147:*n*11
glory to G., 39:4, 49:11
good fortune is g. among men, 65:14
good G. prepare me, 288:28
grace is given of G., 512:7
Grace of G. in courtesy, 653:6
grant you find one face, 514:5
granted it, 316:19
grants liberty, 415:7
great G. I'd rather be, 394:19
great G. our King, 469:9
great g. Pan, 112:2, 464:6
great G. to thee we tend, 120:5

God *(continued)*

greater than G. cannot be conceived, 126:3
greatness of G., 583:10
guideth whom He will, 122:2
ha' mercy on such as we, 633:17
had I but studied, 139:17
had never spoken anything but English, 668:13
hand of G. spirit of G., 518:17
handiwork you give G., 601:4
Hannah G. and me, 554:8
happiness not gift of G., 683:3
has brought us this peace, 95:14
has given you one face, 204:6
has G. sent a mortal as messenger, 121:14
has no real style, 693:12
has written all the books, 559:1
hates bray of bragging, 67:12
hath chosen foolish things, 43:32
hath given liberty, 366:17
hath made man upright, 24:25
hath made them so, 303:17
hath no better praise, 586:7
hath not given spirit of fear, 46:30
hath not one G. created us, 30:41
hath numbered thy kingdom, 30:6
hath said there is no G., 16:4
hath sifted a nation, 286:1
have mercy on sinner, 724:13
have mercy on such as we, 633:17
he for G. only, 266:10
he was a son of G., 746:5
heirs of G., 43:5
help us we knew worst too young, 634:1
helps them that help selves, 319:17
helps those who get up early, 862:15
herdsman goads, 636:21
here I stand G. help me, 144:7
hid fossils in rocks, 594:6
Himself can't kill words, 101:*n*3
himself from G. not free, 452:19
himself scarce seemed to be, 400:23
his Father and his G., 335:4
honest G. noblest work, 554:6
honest man noblest work of G., 311:13, 377:16
how odd of God, 706:12
how would man exist if G. did not need him, 679:8
I accuser G. accused, 822:3
I am a G., 428:5
I am a jealous G., 8:33
I am part or particle of G., 454:15
I am the Lord thy G., 8:31
I bless G. in libraries, 338:3
I think it pisses G. off, 839:2
I treated him G. cured him, 150:5
I who saw face of G., 170:19
I wretch wrestling with G., 588:1
if find answer mind of G., 837:3
if G. be for us, 43:9
if G. did not exist, 316:22
if G. died, 825:14
if G. is male, 820:9
if G. will, 121:15
if it be of G., 42:3
if triangles had g., 314:7
I'll leap up to my G., 171:4

God *(continued)*

in apprehension like a g., 203:17
in G. dazzling darkness, 279:1
in G. is our trust, 411:2
in mercy lend grace, 481:1
in name of most merciful G., 120:11
in the image of G., 6:33
in Three Persons, 416:6
in works and in word, 305:1
in youth remembered my G., 405:10
inclines to think there is G., 512:9
incomprehensibility of G., 445:9
insult to G., 491:23
invite G. and his angels, 236:22
is a Mother, 724:2
is a verb, 743:5
is an exalted father, 607:12
is an in order to, 631:9
is and all well, 468:20
is and is not voice of G., 312:22
is day night winter summer, 64:7
is dead, 588:15
is G. blunder of man, 589:18
is G. dead, 443:9
is in heaven, 24:11
is in me or does not exist, 689:9
is in the details, 851:9
is in the midst of her, 17:22
is light, 47:36
is love, 47:41
is Love I dare say, 559:2
is man blunder of G., 589:18
is no respecter of persons, 42:12
is not a because, 631:9
is not a man, 9:24
is not mocked, 45:24
is or He is not, 279:23
is our refuge and strength, 17:21
is seen God, 493:18
is swift at the reckoning, 121:22
is their belly, 45:36
is they are, 494:14
it is a g. who gave you this gift, 52:5
it's not G. I don't accept, 525:16
jealous G., 8:33
just are the ways of G., 269:3
justify ways of G. to men, 263:21
keep you in his holy hand, 862:24
keeps thee from G., 449:20
Kingdom of G. within you, 40:5
kissing carrion, 203:6
know what G. and man is, 486:21
know ye that the Lord he is G., 19:3
knowledge and love of G., 51:2
knowledge makes G. of me, 438:20
knows which God God recognizes, 771:15
lamb of G., 49:12
land G. gave to Cain, 145:4
laws of G. are forever, 67:20
laws of G. laws of man, 619:13
laws of nature and nature's G., 357:2
lay me on anvil O G., 681:13
let not G. speak with us, 9:2
let us worship G., 377:15
life of ease not for a g., 435:1
light is shadow of G., 256:24
light of heavens and earth, 121:21
light prime work of G., 265:*n*2

God (continued)

live innocently G. is here, 322:21
livin' G. that made you, 633:10
living G., 17:16
looks after fools, 850:12
looks up to Nature's G., 311:14
Lord G. Almighty, 416:6
Lord G. formed man, 5:16
Lord G. is subtle, 683:15
Lord G. made them all, 508:7
Lord G. of Hosts, 635:1
Lord G. planted a garden, 5:17
Lord G. send high wave, 658:9
Lord G. walking in garden, 6:5
Lord our G. is one Lord, 9:29
love not Pleasure love G., 433:20
love of G. had blessed, 417:15
loveth cheerful giver, 45:10
lust of goat bounty of G., 372:17
made him let him pass for man, 187:31
made integers, 534:6
made the country, 347:25
made the world, 42:18
make me strong, 851:21
make straight a highway for our G.,
     27:38
makes sech nights, 515:3
makes those who believe stand firm,
     121:8
man fallen g., 426:10
man g. in ruins, 454:18
man proposes G. disposes, 138:7
man sent from G., 40:31
man with G. always in majority, 150:10
man with G. strive, 421:9
man's word G. in man, 485:17
Masai House of G., 754:15
men G. made mad, 664:7
mighty fortress is our G., 144:9
mills of G. grind slowly, 255:5
most glorious city of G., 119:21
moved upon face of the waters, 5:9
moves in mysterious way, 347:3
music sent up to G., 494:5
must think it exceedingly odd, 723:4
my G. and King, 250:24
my G. have mercy, 154:9
my G. look not so fierce, 171:5
my G. why hast thou forsaken me, 16:16,
     38:9
my soul thirsteth for G., 17:16
nakedness of woman work of G., 372:17
name called the mighty G., 26:31
name of G. upon lips, 331:6
Nature and Nature's G., 305:1
nature is the art of G., 255:14
Nature's G., 311:14
nature's G. commands slave to rise, 386:2
nearer my G. to thee, 461:18
nearer to church further from G., 147:22
nest on greatness of G., 583:10
never made work for man to mend,
     285:19
never spoke with G., 546:6
next to of course g., 740:1
no G. and Mary His Mother, 629:22
no g. higher than truth, 650:11
no G. stronger than death, 568:19
no man hath seen G., 40:34

God (continued)

no more Aurora Leighs thank G., 472:8
no society bring Kingdom of G., 694:3
noblest work of G., 311:13
none other but the house of G., 7:16
nor G. nor man, 655:18
not alone G. is within, 112:6
not even G. is wise enough, 853:14
not G. for father if not Church for
     mother, 117:6
not G. in Gardens, 543:17
not G. of dead, 40:12
not only no G., 831:1
not serve G. if devil bid, 212:20
not willing to do everything, 143:2
O G. O Montreal, 558:9
O G. that bread so dear, 446:6
O G. that it were possible, 239:10
O Lamb of G., 49:12
of battles, 193:17
of Clotilda grant victory, 119:26
of fathers known of old, 635:1
of God, 50:4
of my idolatry, 183:9
of Nature, 250:18
of Nature placed in power, 353:2
of such is kingdom of G., 38:28
of the Congo, 685:5
of truth, 10:13
of universal laws, 582:16
Oh G. put back universe, 600:12
on right hand of G., 50:3
on seventh day G. ended his work, 5:15
on side of best digestion, 680:10
on side of big squadrons, 275:1
one G. even the Father, 412:17
one g. greatest among gods, 61:22
one G. law element, 484:18
one G. one principle of being, 115:26
One God the Everlasting Refuge, 122:21
one nation under G., 606:17
one that feared G., 13:21
only another artist, 693:12
only G. and angels lookers on, 166:9
only G. can make tree, 711:12
only G. had for asking, 514:15
only G. my dear, 641:2
only knows which is which, 569:16
our help in ages past, 304:6
out in fields with G., 849:11
out of me G. and man, 569:7
owe G. a death, 192:2
pairs off like with like, 55:15
patriarch obedient to G., 523:23
peace of G. passeth understanding, 45:37
Peace of G. which passeth all
     understanding, 51:2
perfect blessedness vision of G., 129:9
perhaps G. resembles etchings of Goya,
     792:18
plays dice with world, 683:14
pleased G. to visit us with death, 247:8
poor dear G., 747:16
poor Mexico so far from G., 544:1
praise be to G., 120:11
presume not G. to scan, 311:9
pride of peacock glory of G., 372:17
purlieu of g. of love, 235:8
put hand to ark of G., 11:42

God (continued)

rather believe G. not exist, 461:17
read New Yorker trust in G., 776:8
reason in man like G. in world, 129:10
rebellion obedience to G., 846:19
reflect that G. is just, 357:9
register of G., 256:20
reigns Government lives, 548:9
remains dead, 588:n2
render unto G., 36:42
rest you merry, 846:1
rib which Lord G. had taken, 5:21
rise and shine give G. glory, 863:6
round fat oily man of G., 318:11
said I am tired, 453:13
said Let Newton be, 313:10
said Let there be light, 5:9
said Let us make man, 5:12
saint if G. does not exist, 790:4
save the king, 11:21, 308:1
save the king say amen, 180:8
save the mark, 185:5
save the people, 413:11
save thee ancient Mariner, 399:19
saw that it was good, 5:11
say first of G. above, 311:1
says there is no G., 331:6
says why did they put you in prison,
     740:17
Scourge of G., 170:5
secluded from sight of G., 236:20
see G. made and eaten, 492:8
seek G. in old quiet places, 825:14
seen G. face to face, 7:21
sees G. in clouds, 311:5
self-reliance is reliance on G., 456:22
send every gentleman, 854:7
send them sorrow and shame, 141:21
sends meat Devil sends cooks, 147:n11
servant of G. well done, 267:11
servant of Living G., 338:6
served my G. with half the zeal, 231:8
service greater than the g., 207:32
sets nothing but riddles, 525:12
setteth the solitary in families, 18:7
shall any teach G., 14:29
shall smite thee, 42:29
shall wipe away tears, 49:1
she for G. in him, 266:10
shed grace on thee, 616:3
shield us, 181:18
shows sufficient light, 494:27
so commanded, 267:29
so loved the world, 40:46
so near is G. to man, 453:16
sole G. beside whom is none, 4:11
something beautiful for G., 785:5
Son of G. goes forth, 416:2
Son of the living G., 36:24
sons of G. shouted for joy, 15:6
sons of the living G., 30:12
Soul of each G. of all, 399:10
souls are in the hand of G., 31:16
souls mounting up to G., 541:27
Spirit of G. descending, 33:28
spirit shall return unto G., 25:8
standeth G. within shadow, 514:13
stands winding horn, 637:9
stay with me G., 851:21

Gold (*continued*)

cross of g., 622:3
eyes of g. and bramble dew, 599:15
fairy g., 228:20
fin in porphyry font, 483:6
fire is test of g., 107:2
flow with tears of g., 372:9
gateways of stars, 621:2
gild refined g., 178:14
gleaming in purple and g., 422:14
good as g., 497:18
great horse of g., 739:10
hair turned quite g. from grief, 605:6
hairy g. crown on 'ead, 633:11
hammered g., 640:2
harps of g., 488:15
if g. ruste what shal iren do, 135:10
in glint old g., 664:10
in itself useless, 143:13
in phisik is a cordial, 135:7
jewel of g. in swine's snout, 21:18
locks yellow as g., 400:3
lust of g., 484:15
man's the g. for all that, 380:12
more to be desired than g,, 16:12
names written in letters of g., 145:6
not all that shines as g., 127:11
old man's g., 654:1
orange glows, 363:16
path of g. for him, 492:3
patines of bright g., 190:5
picking up g. and silver, 847:7
plate sin with g., 217:24
poop was beaten g., 223:14
potable g., 241:14
purer than purest g., 237:18
purse of g. resolutely snatched, 184:25
quantity of g. temperate carry, 76:6
rarer gifts than g., 713:2
realms of g., 435:19
robe of g. and pearl, 193:16
roofs of g., 192:21
saint-seducing g., 182:17
scarfs garters g., 311:11
shines like fire, 65:24
shower of g., 433:25
silver and g. have I none, 42:1
silver threads among g., 594:2
so thin so pale yet g., 369:6
speak silver reply g., 853:11
still as a g. piece, 821:13
that I never see, 619:2
therefore lovede g. in special, 135:7
thombe of g., 135:12
to airy thinness beat, 235:2
trodden g., 264:22
troops pass through seek g., 533:9
truth with g. she weighs, 313:16
what female heart g. despise, 334:3
what is g. doing in holy place, 109:1
what's become of g., 493:14
wisdom never comes g., 541:5
wonder that g. esteemed, 143:13
Gold-bearing, crushed the g. Medes, 62:3
Golden Age before us not behind, 596:18
age exists in imagination, 448:17
all in g. afternoon, 549:9
Aphrodite, 54:28, 56:23
apples of sun, 637:10

Golden (*continued*)

as they did in g. world, 197:24
bindest in wreaths thy g. hair, 99:7
bough, 640:2
bought g. opinions, 219:19
bowl be broken, 25:8
care, 192:6
chain from heaven, 53:2
circle of g. year, 481:6
crown like a deep well, 180:9
days fruitful of golden deeds, 265:26
door, 595:6
Dustman, 499:3
every g. scale, 549:13
father held out g. scales, 54:1
fretted with g. fire, 203:17
friends I had, 619:6
goose with g. eggs, 61:3
hanging in a g. chain, 265:23
her flank g., 734:10
host of g. daffodils, 394:4
hours on angel wings, 380:4
in mercy of his means, 795:10
Jerusalem the g., 511:11
keep g. mean, 99:*n*16
key, 260:13
kings in g. suits ride elephants, 788:4
lads and girls, 225:23
lamps in a green night, 277:10
locks to silver turned, 164:9
Love in a g. bowl, 372:12
mean, 99:23
miller hath g. thumb, 135:*n*1
million b. birds, 603:13
mind stoops not, 188:22
mottoes in the mouth, 516:25
nap before dinner g., 542:9
on g. chair seated prince of Wales, 693:2
ope the g. eyes, 225:12
opes the iron shuts, 261:22
pear, 859:7
returns the G. Age, 95:22
Rule, 35:*n*1
rule is no golden rules, 609:22
rule will fit everybody, 557:4
sands and crystal brooks, 234:22
seven g. candlesticks, 48:4
Silence g., 433:21
sleep with g. Aphrodite, 54:28
stretches out my g. wing, 371:10
sun in g. cup, 642:1
time of first love, 382:7
track, 685:4
tree of life, 365:8
two g. hours, 441:12
Vanity, 862:10
we are g., 838:11
wear a g. sorrow, 230:25
what delight without g. Aphrodite, 56:23
years return, 429:22
Goldengrove unleaving, 587:14
Goldenrod, bent g., 719:16
Gold-feathered bird sings in palm, 688:18
Goldfish in glass bowl, 655:3
Goldsmith, here lies Nolly G., 335:23
Poet Naturalist Historian, 328:6
Goldsmiths, Grecian g. make, 640:2

Golf is a good walk spoiled, 563:4
links lie so near mill, 677:21
Golgotha, place called G., 38:6
Gondola, swam in a g., 199:25
Gone agin Finnigin, 651:5
all all are g., 407:1
and never must return, 261:17
and past help, 228:18
aye ages long ago, 437:4
before to unknown shore, 407:5
coon, 419:1
dead and g. lady, 206:5
down drain of eternity, 69:17
far away into silent land, 547:17
glimmering, 420:8
good old cause g., 392:14
goodness lives though they are g., 70:23
he has departed withdrawn g. away, 90:9
he will know it's g., 791:13
heaviness that's g., 230:15
heavy change now thou art g., 261:17
here and there, 227:15
here today g. tomorrow, 290:22
home art g., 225:23
I am g. like the shadow, 19:17
I shall be g., 669:7
I shan't be g. long, 668:17
I would have thee g., 183:15
if she's not g., 860:17
I'll be g., 836:5
into world of light, 279:7
line is g. out through all the earth, 16:11
mischief past and g., 212:34
my life has g., 818:8
not lost but g. before, 106:21
odds is g., 224:1
Othello's occupation's g., 214:8
Poets dead and g., 438:10
romantic Ireland's dead and g., 638:7
room from which faith g., 767:10
sea-discoverers to new worlds have g., 233:11
she's g. forever, 218:5
soon as she was g. from me, 373:8
sweet cheat g., 662:13
these things are past and g., 94:3
they are all g. away, 652:5
they've g. about as fur as c'n go, 744:6
thou art g. and forever, 397:9
Thursday come and week g., 251:33
to her death, 446:7
under earth's lid, 709:5
where have you g. Joe DiMaggio, 837:5
wind passeth over it and it is g., 19:7
with the wind, 645:9
yes thou art g., 530:18
Gonfalon bubble, 692:14
Gong, after great cathedral g., 641:5
Gongs, strong g. groaning, 664:10
Gong-tormented sea, 641:8
Good, a little fun and g. morrow, 555:21
a little work and g. day, 555:21
a thing moderately g., 355:2
abroad for g. of country, 305:6
all g. men, 849:6
all g. to me is lost, 266:4
Americans die go to Paris, 605:1
amiable or sweet, 268:3
and bad angel, 240:11

Good *(continued)*

and bad of every land, 504:12
and faithful servant, 37:13
any g. thing I can do, 847:23
any g. thing out of Nazareth, 40:36
apothecary, 217:22
apprehension of the g., 179:6
arrived in a g. harbor, 247:6
art for sake of g., 461:16
as all no better than any, 772:12
as gold, 497:18
as g. almost kill man as g. book, 262:21
as g. be out of world, 300:30
as g. in the dark, 248:6
as g. luck would have it, 190:32
as I can be, 597:8
as seems beforehand, 513:5
ask not g. fortune, 520:2
atom's weight of g., 122:20
bad book as much labor as g., 741:3
bad indifferent, 287:9, 332:20
bad worst best, 478:4
be g. and be lonesome, 561:21
be g. and happy today, 399:8
be g. sweet maid, 514:2
be of g. cheer, 36:16, 41:35
because it's awful, 828:15
becomes indistinguishable from evil,
  726:6
befriend themselves, 68:18
best is enemy of g., 316:16
best is g. enough, 364:10
book best of friends, 489:2
book lifeblood of spirit, 262:22
bringer of g. tidings, 121:1
bringeth thee into a g. land, 10:2
but not religious-good, 574:15
by evil and g. report, 45:8
by quiet natures understood, 639:14
call this Friday g., 721:3
cannot come to g., 201:8
can't say anything g., 704:5
captive g. attending captain ill, 226:22
catches mice g. cat, 766:17
character remembered, 3:11
charm to make bad g., 212:1
cheer is best physician, 66:4
chief g. and market, 205:35
cigar is a smoke, 632:10
circumstance makes action g. or bad,
  75:29
club assembly of g. fellows, 324:15
comes out of evil, 566:22
commodity of g. names, 184:30
company good discourse, 252:28
constituted for practice of g., 82:11
corn wood boards to sell, 454:10
counselors lack no clients, 210:35
crown g. with brotherhood, 616:3
day's work, 321:8
deed in naughty world, 190:8
deed to say well, 230:29
demean themselves as g. citizens, 350:6
deny us for our g., 223:11
depart from evil and do g., 17:2
desires be for what is g., 63:8
devil have all g. tunes, 362:6
die early bad late, 295:6
die first, 395:4

Good *(continued)*

digestion wait on appetite, 221:10
dinner and feasting, 288:13
do all the g. I can, 565:6
do all the g. you can, 319:1
do g. purify mind, 66:18
do g. the right way, 572:5
do g. to them that hate you, 34:7
doing g. one of professions full, 506:22
eating is a small g. thing, 833:9
enough for me, 847:21
enough to shed blood, 615:6
Epicurus set forth highest g., 93:20
evening Mr. Mrs. America, 750:5
every creature of God is g., 46:19
every evil hath g., 455:18
every g. gift, 47:11
everything in world g. for something,
  283:25
evil be thou my g., 266:4
evil reward punishment, 286:9
fair and learned and g. as she, 247:12
fair is by nature g., 162:6
faith toward nations, 350:10
familiar creature, 213:27
fell into g. ground, 36:4
fellows get together, 630:7
fences make good neighbors, 668:19
fight of faith, 46:27
five-cent cigar, 603:1
follow g. side to fire, 153:13
for a man that he bear the yoke, 29:30
for country good for General Motors,
  731:1
for sore eyes, 299:7
fortune is god among men, 65:14
Fortune may be short-lived, 247:3
fought a g. fight, 46:33
free press g. or bad, 790:9
friend for Jesus' sake, 231:19
general g. is plea of scoundrel, 376:5
gentle beast of a g. conscience, 182:8
glad of other men's g., 199:6
go gentle into that g. night, 795:14
go with me like g. angels, 230:23
God saw that it was g., 5:11
gods do not give all men g. looks, 54:26
gods how he will talk, 294:9
great poet so g. friend, 285:17
greed is g. greed is right, 840:6
half so g. a grace, 211:10
hand that made you g., 211:25
hanging too g. for him, 281:24
happiness the only g., 554:7
hard beginning g. ending, 147:15
have no need of advocate, 79:2
hay sweet hay, 181:25
he our g. will sever, 237:14
he who would do g., 376:5
hearkeners seldom hear g., 295:19
hell full of g. intentions, 126:9
hell full of g. meanings, 251:16
hell paved with g. intentions, 126:n4,
  251:n1
highest g., 91:7, 93:n7
him that bringeth g. tidings, 28:18
hold fast that which is g., 46:13
hold thou the g., 484:1
honest painful sermon, 288:5

Good *(continued)*

how g. and how pleasant, 20:10
how g. man's life, 493:16
I am the g. shepherd, 41:17
I have g. eye uncle, 194:16
I will be g., 518:2
if all g. people clever, 577:3
if g. why do I yield, 219:5
if he had not been born, 37:26
ill wind bloweth no man g., 149:14
in congruity of thing, 402:19
in everything, 197:37
in which mind at rest, 131:19
is it g. friend, 655:17
jest forever, 185:14
joke cannot be criticized, 664:9
judge men by g. fortune, 273:26
keep g. tongue in head, 230:3
King Arthur, 861:7
King Wenceslas, 511:9
kissing carrion, 203:n1
know g. as g., 58:8
know what were g. to do, 187:27
knowing g. and evil, 6:4
lad of mettle a g. boy, 185:19
lady be g. to me, 746:22
largest universe of g., 582:11
law is g., 46:14
law is good order, 81:7
laws lead to better, 331:4
laws where state armed, 142:11
leave while looking g., 737:11
left country for country's g., 305:n1
lie and humbug for general G., 644:10
life of battle g., 627:3
life or good place, 776:14
Life waiting for us, 769:14
like a g. thing die, 602:8
like every g. believer, 741:2
live in world g. or bad, 505:17
Lord deliver us, 50:11, 847:9
Lord is g., 19:3
lose g. we oft might win, 211:2
loser, 724:15
love as much as g. fight, 697:10
love g. pursue the worst, 105:n14
love sought is g., 210:6
loves what he is g. at, 291:11
luck in odd numbers, 191:4
luxury was doing g., 295:11
maintain g. government, 370:9
make g. thing too common, 191:19
maketh sun rise on evil and g., 34:8
man and a just, 40:24
man does not argue, 59:21
man's fortune, 216:9
man's g. knowing he is bad, 494:24
man's love, 199:20
man's sin, 332:n2
man's treasure, 59:11
many g. men are poor, 57:6
marriage, 677:8
Master of All G. Workmen, 633:3
meaning g. or bad, 283:20
men and true, 194:32
men desire the g., 80:27
men eat that they may live, 72:9
men of g. will, 49:11
men of ill judgment ignore g., 67:10

Good *(continued)*

men to do nothing, 346:2
mingled yarn g., and ill, 210:27
moral what you feel g. after, 754:9
Morning Midnight coming Home, 545:1
morning sadness, 743:3
morrow to our waking souls, 233:11
mothers and fathers, 766:1
mouth-filling oath, 186:12
music g. to melancholy, 287:9
must associate, 343:15
my g. vain hope of gain, 164:17
my religion is to do g., 355:1
name better than precious ointment,
    24:15
name in man and woman, 213:33
name is rather to be chosen, 22:24
name like precious ointment, 167:16
nature in conversation, 302:14
neighbor is great blessing, 56:13
neighbor policy, 697:16
neighbors, 705:15
neither honesty nor g. fellowship, 184:34
never bad man g. service, 345:6
never g. to bring bad news, 223:19
never g. war or bad peace, 320:23
news baits, 269:13
news worthy of acceptation, 295:25
no evil can happen to g. man, 76:13
no g. can come of association, 694:10
no physician considers own g., 77:2
noble be man helpful and g., 363:13
noble to be g., 480:14
noble type of g., 467:9
not enough to do g., 572:5
not enough to have g. mind, 253:23
not g. for swarm not g. for bee, 115:25
not g. that man should be alone, 5:20
not three g. men unhanged, 185:22
not to make g. place to live, 505:17
not too g. to be true, 295:25
nothing either g. or bad, 203:14
nothing g. alone, 452:16
nothing g. makes complete sense, 735:17
obstinacy in bad cause constancy in g.,
    255:15
of moral evil and of g., 390:19
of subjects end of kings, 295:4
oft interred with bones, 196:27
old age, 7:3
old Boston, 621:22
old paths where is the g. way, 29:6
old times are gone, 425:3
old times when unhappy, 855:9
one g. custom corrupt, 486:12
one g. knowledge, 72:6
one g. turn deserves another, 109:6
only what is g. in man, 605:23
or bad names, 332:10
or evil side, 514:12
orator a g. man skilled in speaking, 88:6
out of g. find evil, 264:5
overcome evil with g., 43:22
panics produce as much g., 354:11
Parent of g., 267:2
partial evil universal g., 311:8
people all with one accord, 340:10
people are g. at heart, 822:9
people's g. the highest law, 91:11

Good *(continued)*

perseverance in g. cause, 332:9
philosophy a g. horse, 341:22
phrase g. and bad at same time, 739:5
play audience pleased, 664:2
poet's made as well as born, 238:11
political g. carried to extreme, 383:1
portion of g. man's life, 390:20
poverty parts g. company, 398:5
prospect of distant g., 284:24
provoke to harm, 212:1
public g., 124:18
public g. and private rights, 367:1
pun may be admitted, 355:16
put on g. behavior, 424:9
quiet wise and g., 431:2
really a very g. man, 606:16
recognize g. but be barred, 66:2
relinquish life for g. of country, 388:7
reputation valuable, 102:18
return g. for evil, 297:10
rewarded evil for g., 7:29
rewardeth evil for g., 22:6
rich in g. works, 46:28
right reader of g. poem, 671:9
ripe and g. scholar, 231:14
sat at g. man's feast, 198:22
sat too long for any g., 254:13
Scots lords, 853:19
second class of intellect g., 142:17
see your g. works, 34:2
seize g. fortune, 365:22
sense equally distributed, 253:22
sense in country, 360:4
seven g. kine, 7:26
seven hundred pounds g. gifts, 190:15
shall not see when g. cometh, 29:17
shepherd, 41:17
smell of old clothes, 712:18
smiled and said G. Night, 653:14
so absolutely g. is truth, 495:6
Soldier finest French novel, 662:19
some g. some so-so, 110:15
some said It might do g., 281:12
so so is g., 200:1
soul remembering my g. friends, 179:17
speech more hidden than malachite, 3:4
speed to your youthful valor, 98:9
spinning fates g. or evil, 581:11
strong and of g. courage, 10:18
strong thick stupefying, 492:8
substantial world pure and g., 394:21
sum of g. government, 358:12
sustain g. fortune, 273:4
taste and see that the Lord is g., 17:1
tendency to g. like water, 82:10
the g. I do not, 43:3
the G. lies so near, 365:22
them g. old boys, 839:7
them that call evil g., 26:22
thing when an't woman's, 495:22
things fruits of originality, 464:16
things not had singly, 408:2
things strive to dwell, 229:23
things which belong to prosperity, 167:9
third glass for g. humor, 302:15
this time like all times g., 454:26
this world's g., 47:40
thought to aim at some g., 80:8

Good *(continued)*

time coming, 397:24, 502:4
to be born on, 515:14
to be merry and wise, 147:5, 380:19,
    847:14
to do g. and to communicate, 47:8
to gain day good to fall, 519:4
to love the unknown, 407:18
today better tomorrow, 462:15
too g. for any but anglers, 253:7
too much of g. thing, 156:4
traced lives of g. men, 395:14
tree of knowledge of g. and evil, 5:19
trust that somehow g., 484:2
two nations g. bad, 277:6
unconscious source of highest g., 675:9
undefined g. thirsted for, 413:1
universal license to be g., 441:11
value it next to g. conscience, 253:8
vote and act to bring g., 582:11
walk spoiled, 563:4
want power, 428:4
war slays g. man always, 68:16
wastes and withers there, 605:23
we had all g. songs, 820:13
we know the g., 69:28
week's labor, 243:20
what a g. boy am I, 857:3
what do I care you are g., 524:17
what g. came of it, 405:8
whatsoever things are of g. report, 45:38
when all men's g., 481:6
when Fortune means most g., 178:11
when g. men die, 70:23
when g. very g. when bad better, 736:8
when she was g., 468:4
when were g. in majority, 507:23
whether benevolence g., 538:5
whether it be g. or evil, 25:10
whosoever performs g. deeds, 122:4
why g. words ne'er said, 591:9
wine a good creature, 213:27
wine needs no bush, 104:*n*1
without three g. friends, 199:5
wits jump, 158:25
woman if five thousand a year, 490:7
word like good tree, 121:8
words worth much, 251:15
work together for g., 43:7
works better in sight of Lord, 121:16
world imagined ultimate g., 688:14
world kills the g., 754:5
write g. in dust, 144:2
Good-bye and keep cold, 669:18
brothers, 611:18
can scarcely bid g., 441:6
fare you well, 862:7
I have kissed it, 763:17
leave them laughing when say g., 679:9
like saying g. to statue, 754:7
Night Goodbye, 612:2
Old Paint, 854:14
Piccadilly, 674:2
proud world, 452:15
reap sowing and so g., 555:21
to bar and moaning, 514:1
to the war, 521:13
we now must say g., 750:18
Goodfellowship, nauseous sham g., 610:11

Good-humored stomach, 107:1
Goodliest, Adam the g. man, 266:12
Goodliness is as the flower of the field, 28:2
Good-looking, Lake Wobegon where men are g., 837:5
Goodly apple rotten at heart, 188:7
    how g. are thy tents, 9:26
    I have a g. heritage, 16:7
    outside falsehood hath, 188:7
    states and kingdoms, 435:19
    this g. frame earth, 203:17
Good-nature, full of g. as egg of meat, 183:n2
Good-natured woman, 407:6
Goodness and mercy shall follow me, 16:18
    armed with power, 735:14
    believe source of g. is sky, 140:7
    crownest the year with thy g., 18:4
    does not perish, 70:23
    felt how awful g. is, 266:25
    first acquired by child, 286:n3
    fruit of Spirit is g., 45:22
    grateful for mode of g., 855:21
    had nothing to do with it, 736:5
    her life filled with clouds of g., 361:n2
    highest point not G., 701:10
    how sad our Russia, 473:1
    if g. lead him not, 250:19
    in things evil, 193:13
    Infinite G. has wide arms, 131:9
    infinite power wisdom g., 296:4
    more g. in little finger, 299:17
    never fearful, 211:26
    no g. dies, 434:15
    no greatness where no g., 542:15
    powerful g. want, 428:4
    result of one's own merits, 126:10
    sold itself, 853:10
    tainted, 506:23
    thanks for all thy g., 50:8
    throw away g. on conceited, 513:n1
    throwing g. at you, 803:7
    thy fatherly g., 50:7
    what beautiful diamonds, 736:n1
    wisdom and g. to vile, 217:14
Good-night, a little warmth and g., 555:21
    and joy be wi' you, 385:9
    and so g., 734:13
    ensured release, 620:3
    fer th' rest of us, 649:9
    fortune g., 216:10
    gay g. and turn away, 640:16
    gives sternest g., 220:12
    Mrs. Calabash, 737:3
    my last g., 249:1
    sad bell murmuring g., 787:2
    sweet ladies, 206:7
    sweet prince, 207:15
    till it be morrow, 183:16
    to all a g., 411:6
    to each a fair g., 397:3
Goods, all his worldy g., 500:4
    and services paid with goods and services, 654:18
    compel philosophy to inquire about g., 91:6
    consumption of valuable g., 613:6
    distribution of g., 683:6
    got the g., 626:16

Goods (*continued*)
    not take g. with him, 3:2
    set not heart upon g., 32:5
    soul thou hast much g., 39:28
    with all my worldly g., 51:19
Goodwill complacency thoughtlessness, 629:13
    in peace g., 668:1
    men of g., 49:11
    to men, 488:15
    toward men, 39:4
Goodwin, along with Captain G., 846:n3
Goose, all gold the g. could give, 61:3
    cried in g. Alas, 724:11
    every g. a swan lad, 514:4
    hangs high, 847:3
    look, 222:9
    steals common from g., 844:20
    voice of wild g., 4:2
    wild-g. chase, 156:26
    with golden eggs, 61:3
Goosequill, Corporation of G., 490:13
Goosey goosey gander, 858:11
Goot, seven hundred pounds g. gifts, 190:15
Gopher, an ark of g. wood, 6:26
Gorbachev, I like Mr. G. we can do business, 816:7
    Mr. G. open this gate, 787:13
Gorboduc, niece of King G., 210:16
Gordian knot he will unloose, 192:19
Gore, avenge patriotic g., 574:6
    preserved his g. O, 566:3
Gored by climacteric of want, 801:6
    makes difference whose ox g., 144:20
    mine own thoughts, 227:15
Gorge, dire g. of salt sea tide, 189:n1
    my g. rises at it, 206:24
Gorgeous as sun at midsummer, 186:22
    east in fee, 393:1
    East with richest hand, 264:25
    palaces, 230:9
    so g. all London stared, 449:1
    thrice g. ceremony, 193:16
    Tragedy, 260:6
Gorgonized me, 485:7
Gorilla, distinguishable from g., 490:n1
Gory, shake thy g. locks at me, 221:11
    welcome to your g. bed, 380:10
Goshen, land of G., 7:34
Gospel, brown bread and the G., 295:20
    go and preach g., 38:33
    light first dawned, 334:7
    lineaments of G. books, 171:9
    of Getting On, 609:7
    train's a-coming, 863:12
Gossamer fidelity of Man, 478:16
Gossip, babbling g. of the air, 209:10
    in place of inquiry, 660:7
    is mischievous, 56:19
    no g. ever dies away, 56:19
Gossip's, lurk I in g. bowl, 181:5
Got it flaunt it, 817:5
    rhythm got music, 746:24
    the better of himself, 159:1
    they g. things we ain't, 781:13
    you've g. to get up, 716:4
Goth and Moor bequeathed us, 574:9
Gotham, wise men of G., 858:3

Gothic, cars equivalent of G. cathedrals, 795:18
    erect a G. cathedral, 442:15
    more than G. ignorance, 322:9
Gottbetrunkener, ein G. Mensch, 286:n4
Göttingen, University of G., 389:13
Gouged, by enemy's beak g., 829:3
Gourd, sugar in the g., 847:19
Gourds, painted g. on a shelf, 816:20
Gout kills more rich than poor, 280:18
Govern, angels to g., 358:11
    another without consent, 474:6
    dead g. living, 444:3
    easy to g. not to enslave, 410:2
    every cook learn to g., 654:8
    how can tyrants safely g., 173:2
    legitimate right to g., 404:11
    most make least noise, 245:25
    no man g. another, 474:6
    others first master himself, 244:19
    people difficult to g., 59:13
    reflect how you are to g., 343:19
    reigns but does not g., 154:15
    Right of Kings to g. wrong, 313:22
    stars g. our conditions, 217:16
    syllables g. the world, 245:26
    those that think must g., 341:7
    tongues with difficulty, 287:1
Governed, consent of g., 351:5
    consent of the g., 357:2, 522:2
    governments result of nature of g., 300:9
    grant of power from g., 404:11
    with how little wisdom world g., 245:n5
Governing governor, 416:8
Government, all persons share in g., 80:30
    at Washington lives, 548:9
    attachment to g., 344:17
    balance of natural elements, 602:10
    basis of g. opinion, 357:12
    behave toward g. today, 505:15
    behind g. and people, 532:21
    best g. make people happy, 447:8
    British g. best model, 370:8
    by crony, 672:5
    by means of his virtue, 62:14
    charming form of g., 77:21
    complain of injustice of g., 386:13
    consists in taking money, 316:14
    contrivance of wisdom, 345:12
    cooperation with G., 711:4
    excel the bees for g., 155:2
    excess a reproach to g., 291:21
    exigencies of g., 502:18
    first duty of g., 517:22
    first office of g. splendid misery, 358:6
    for common benefit, 339:10
    form of g. never take root, 388:1
    forming a republican g., 370:10
    founded on compromise, 344:14
    free to people, 291:19
    gives bigotry no sanction, 350:6
    good g. obtains, 63:9
    great writer second g., 804:8
    happiness end of g., 351:10
    happiness sole object of g., 353:7
    in carrying on your g., 63:8
    in flag g. and truths, 500:14
    in g. deliberative forces prevail, 607:1
    includes all the people, 462:9

Grain *(continued)*
  clearest g. of violin, 813:1
  Demeter gave nourishment of g., 70:11
  of mustard seed, 36:6
  of poetry season a century, 602:3
  say which g. will grow, 218:31
  see world in g. of sand, 375:5
  send g. into wilderness, 286:1
  spirits of land and g., 82:20
  with a g. of salt, 108:14
Grains, little g. of sand, 534:2
  two g. of wheat in chaff, 187:23
Grainy wood, 712:18
Grammar control even kings, 278:22
  corrupted youth in erecting g.-school, 172:22
  I am above g., 278:*n6*
  lesson on g. impertinence, 534:4
  nonsense and learning, 342:17
  prefer geniality to g., 613:17
Grammarian rhetorician geometrician, 113:5
Grammaticam, rex et supra g., 278:*n6*
Grammatici certant sub iudice lis est, 101:*n6*
Gramophone, puts record on g., 718:19
Grampa, one day bachelor next g., 763:16
Grampian, on the G. hills, 337:14
Granary, sitting on g. floor, 438:12
Grand, dumb inscrutable g., 531:6
  hooded phantom, 516:7
  O Ireland g. you look, 592:13
  Panjandrum, 336:12
  seek a g. perhaps, 146:20
  statues and pictures g., 557:9
  style, 530:1
  sweet song, 514:2
  they said it would be g., 551:19
  this g. book the universe, 169:18
  'tis g. 'tis solemn, 426:2
Grand Army, between G. and dominion, 576:11
Grandam, soul of g. inhabit a bird, 189:*n2*
  to cub, 817:19
Grandchild heir of the first, 238:17
Grandchildren come into world with thick skin, 442:17
Grande Ourse, mon auberge à la G., 603:*n4*
Grandest lesson On sail on, 579:9
  of all sepulchers, 74:5
Grandeur, feel every kind of g., 444:13
  hear with disdainful smile, 334:14
  in this view of life, 470:3
  of God, 587:4
  of the dooms, 436:9
  remains without intensity, 110:12
  Scotia's g. springs, 377:16
  size is not g., 537:9
  so nigh g. to dust, 453:16
  that was Rome, 478:2
Grandfather, ape for his g., 537:13
Grandfather's house, 450:11
  rule was safer, 515:4
Grandmother, ape as his g., 537:*n1*
  child of our g. Eve, 176:24
  sings to stove, 785:14
Grandmother's long and faithful service, 501:6
Grandsire cut in alabaster, 187:18
  proverbed with g. phrase, 182:20
Grandsires', sires' age worse than g., 100:2

Grange, moated g., 211:27, 480:3
Granite into which it reaches, 721:8
  tenoned and mortised in g., 519:6
Grant, everybody wants to be Cary G., 767:4
  Evolution from Washington to G., 570:14
  half g. what I wish, 669:5
  I may never prove so fond, 218:14
  may gods g. you all things, 54:22
  me old man's frenzy, 642:11
  me this last labor, 96:1
  O gods g. me this, 94:26
  of power from governed, 404:11
  old Cary G. fine, 767:5
  that twice two not four, 512:5
  us safe lodging, 450:1
  youth's heritage, 494:11
Granted, and God g. it, 316:19
  to behold you again, 599:16
Gran'ther's rule safer, 515:4
Granting our wish one of Fate's jokes, 61:*n2*
Grants, each day that Fortune g., 99:11
Grape, a little more g., 417:22
  burst Joy's g., 438:16
  eaten a sour g., 29:23
  first from out the purple g., 260:16
  for one g. the vine destroy, 175:5
  peel me a g., 736:7
  rich g. juice of good sense, 118:28
  shalt not gather every g., 9:13
Grapes are sour, 60:10
  gleaning of the g. of Ephraim, 10:37
  of thorns, 35:8
  our vines have tender g., 25:18
  where g. of wrath stored, 513:18
Grapeshot, whiff of g., 433:26
Grapple, let her and Falsehood g., 263:5
  them to thy soul, 201:25
Grappling in central blue, 481:23
Grasp it like a man of mettle, 307:20
  mathematics eludes our g., 624:9
  reach should exceed g., 493:4
  subject words will follow, 88:5
  this Sorry Scheme, 472:5
  what dread g., 374:6
  what they do not know, 82:29
Grasping, a really g. imagination, 584:7
  by g. at the shadow, 60:24
  capable of earnest g., 439:2
  Scrooge g. covetous, 497:12
Grasps in the comer, 208:11
Grass, all flesh is as g., 47:26
  all flesh is g., 28:2
  as long as g. grow, 856:9
  as soft as breast of doves, 711:8
  bank beyond, 535:16
  below above vaulted sky, 431:15
  between wind and g., 63:8
  blade of g. is blade of g., 241:*n1*
  child said What is the g., 518:18
  dripping snow on g., 724:11
  eateth g. as an ox, 15:18
  Elfin from green g., 477:14
  enlaced are fallen among g., 794:7
  from heaps of couch g., 576:5
  go to g., 243:2
  green g. above me, 547:16
  grow from g. I love, 519:23

Grass *(continued)*
  grow in streets, 672:2
  grows on weirs, 636:20
  grows wherever land water is, 519:3
  Guests Star-scattered on G., 472:6
  happy as g. was green, 795:8
  hearing g. grow, 513:9
  his days are as g., 19:7
  I am the g., 681:10
  kissed the lovely g., 712:14
  know g. beyond the door, 542:7
  like g. which groweth up, 18:20
  like rain upon mown g., 18:9
  may g. grow at door, 658:*n3*
  must bend when wind blows, 63:8
  narrow Fellow in the G., 546:2
  Nebuchadnezzar did eat g., 30:4
  no less than stars, 519:15
  observing spear of summer g., 518:15
  over g. in West garden, 708:18
  paler than g., 57:20
  pigeons on g. alas, 673:13
  river of g., 728:14
  roots, 625:12
  roots marsh g. sends, 583:10
  snake in the g., 95:20
  splendor in the g., 393:18
  stoops not, 173:27
  through frozen g., 436:20
  tides of g., 568:9
  two blades of g. grow, 298:15
  vaulter in sunny g., 417:10
  when elephants fight g. suffers, 853:6
  wind on buffalo g., 855:16
  withereth flower fadeth, 28:3
  withereth flower falleth, 47:26
  wonderful g. upon breast, 535:7
Grass-blade's no easier than oak, 514:17
Grasses of forest's floor, 662:10
  the spare few g., 444:12
Grass-green turf, 206:5
Grasshopper, ant and the g., 60:20
  shall be a burden, 25:8
Grasshoppers make field ring, 345:16
Grassy, great g. world, 811:16
Grate, fire dying in g., 541:5
Grated to dusty nothing, 208:7
Grateful, elderly mistress so g., 320:11
  evening mild, 266:18
Gratiano, but as the world G., 187:17
  speaks infinite deal of nothing, 187:23
Gratification from each component part, 403:8
  of every passion, 526:17
Gratified, Desire g. plants fruits, 373:11
  lineaments of G. Desire, 373:15
  sorry if wishes were g., 61:6
  to answer promptly, 560:5
  with mediocrity, 385:3
Gratify some astonish rest, 562:14
Gratifying feeling duty done, 566:6
Grating, brain device to keep ears from g., 784:13
  nor harsh nor g., 391:4
  roar of pebbles, 530:20
Gratitude, children's g. woman's love, 641:9
  desire for benefits, 273:33
  fruit of great cultivation, 325:18
  quiet humor in Yiddish and g., 769:11

Gratitude *(continued)*
    shall our g. sleep, 389:17
    soon grows old, 79:11
    still small voice of g., 335:20
Gratuities and privileges, 386:13
Gratuitous, everything is g., 772:4
    exercise every day, 581:9
Grave, airs martial brisk or g., 348:10
    Alcestis from the g., 263:17
    Alice, 467:12
    almost as go into g., 288:28
    a-moldering in the g., 558:3
    approach thy g., 432:10
    between cradle and g., 317:12, 729:4
    botanize upon mother's g., 392:2
    buries empires in common g., 353:12
    but she is in her g., 391:18
    come to thy g. in full age, 13:40
    conclude on edge of g., 570:2
    coyotes howl o'er my g., 855:1
    cradle stands in the g., 239:7
    cradle to g., 596:11
    defiled his father's g., 102:3
    dig g. and let me lie, 599:6
    Duncan is in his g., 221:5
    earth and g. and dust, 160:14
    expect of man this side g., 494:24
    fall in g. like old dog, 796:13
    from cradle to g., 428:13
    from g. to gay, 311:15
    from g. to light, 289:5
    frontier g. far, 627:4
    funeral marches to g., 466:1
    Ghost sitting crowned upon g., 246:13
    glory or g., 408:20
    gone with old world to g., 594:13
    hides things beautiful, 428:5
    hungry as the g., 317:15
    I will pay you in g., 431:7
    ignominy sleep with thee in g., 187:7
    I'll be buried in g., 863:10
    in law's g. study six, 159:20
    in the air, 806:10
    in the dark and silent g., 160:14
    is not life's goal, 465:17
    jealousy is cruel as the g., 26:3
    Kemmerich's g., 752:11
    lead but to g., 334:15
    lead these graces to g., 209:8
    learned secrets of g., 573:6
    little g. an obscure g., 180:5
    mummers, 313:19
    natural philosophy deep moral g., 168:17
    Nature a g., 443:15
    no flours on g., 575:6
    no wisdom in the g., 24:29
    none shed tear at g., 658:*n*3
    not g. nor bed denied, 641:14
    now with love now in colde g., 136:1
    O g. I will be thy destruction, 30:21
    of Mike O'Day, 852:7
    old and godly and g., 637:6
    one foot already in the g., 111:15
    peace is in g., 428:5
    pompous in the g., 256:22
    ransom them from the power of the g., 30:21
    renowned be thy g., 225:24

Grave *(continued)*
    rest profound as g., 570:18
    rotting g. ne'er get out, 375:11
    scalding g., 658:9
    secret as the g., 158:30
    secrets of the g., 573:6
    send to g. in Y-shaped coffin, 828:10
    shown Longfellow's g., 714:8
    soldier's g. for thee best, 425:9
    something beyond the g., 104:25
    strewed thy g., 206:30
    things holy profane g. and light, 246:10
    this verse g. for me, 599:6
    untimely g., 253:17
    unto a soul, 178:7
    where is thy victory, 44:32, 802:11
    where Laura lay, 160:9
    with O'Leary in g., 638:7
    with sorrow to the g., 7:27
    without a g., 421:27
    you shall find me g. man, 183:28
    Zeus grant g. restraint, 65:31
Graved inside of it Italy, 492:13
Gravel, mouth filled with g., 22:21
    pick about G., 440:2
    shadow over g. of drive, 706:7
Grave-makers, gardeners ditchers and g., 206:15
Grave-making, he sings at g., 206:17
Graven image, 8:32
    images of her gods, 27:8
Grave's a fine and private place, 277:2
Graves, beautiful uncut hair of g., 518:19
    climbs into g. married, 749:14
    dishonorable g., 195:20
    follow disquietly to g., 215:28
    from g. of our slain, 444:11
    let's talk of g., 179:27
    sacred g. plowed for corn, 533:9
    stood tenantless, 200:18
    under fountains and g., 845:5
    untimely g., 348:6
    watch from their g., 491:22
Graveyard, Europe a precious g., 525:14
    friends have no place in g., 505:24
    like g. marble sculpture, 670:17
    of buried hopes, 673:7
Graveyards, no white or colored signs on g., 800:4
Gravitation, Newtonian principle of g., 357:6
Gravity, body subject to forces of g., 796:6
    breaks law of g., 720:14
    fixed law of g., 470:3
    out of his bed, 185:27
    settled g., 226:14
    sometimes man of g., 144:5
    to practice g., 63:25
Gravy, no g. no grub, 724:13
    person who disliked g., 278:*n*4
Gray, all cats g. when candles out, 111:*n*11
    all theory is g., 365:8
    amice g., 268:30
    beginning of years, 569:9
    behind lay g. Azores, 579:8
    big g. wolf, 756:8
    bring down my g. hairs, 7:27
    changing from brown suit to g., 708:3
    cheerless over hills of g., 468:17
    cold g. stones O Sea, 482:15

Gray *(continued)*
    comb g. hair, 638:14
    dawn breaking, 447:6, 680:15
    dawn of morning after, 643:15
    death's g. land, 712:1
    dogs shame the g. head, 53:32
    flannel suit, 807:12
    friar of orders g., 844:4
    glory from g. hairs gone, 468:7
    great g. drayhorse, 587:13
    handful of g. ashes at rest, 534:3
    head grown g. in vain, 430:13
    iniquity, 185:30
    little g. cells, 727:14
    locks left are g., 405:9
    long g. beard, 399:11
    mist on sea's face, 680:15
    name was Dapple G., 860:22
    night is growing g., 576:3
    old and g. full of sleep, 637:4
    pilgrim g., 336:16
    red spirits and g., 243:22
    sad last g. hairs, 437:8
    set g. life, 481:4
    spires of Oxford, 697:2
    spirit yearning, 481:11
    still evening and twilight g., 266:15
    Truth her painted toy, 636:18
    where thy g. eye glances, 478:10
    wing upon every tide, 638:7
    withered cheek tresses g., 396:3
    world g. from thy breath, 568:17
Gray-eyed Athena, 54:13
Gray-fly winds her sultry horn, 261:16
Gray-green greasy Limpopo, 635:10
Gray-haired Saturn, 438:17
Gray-headed, old and g. error, 256:11
Grayness silvers everything, 493:1
Graze, as long as stars g., 97:3
    neither g. nor pierce, 214:23
    on my lips, 173:20
Grazes, work way cow g., 647:10
Grazing, men like satyrs g., 170:14
    tilling and g. feed France, 165:14
Grease, frye in owene g., 136:14
    lust melted him in own g., 136:*n*3
    servility slides by on g., 801:14
    wheel that squeaks gets g., 508:16
Greased worm, 800:10
Greasy, fat and g. citizens, 198:2
    gray-green g. Limpopo, 635:10
    Joan doth keel pot, 177:17
    top of g. pole, 459:13
Great, a g. g. man, 812:13
    age begins anew, 429:22
    Amen, 537:16
    and mighty resolutions, 271:8
    and original writer, 395:2
    and wide sea, 19:11
    apostle of Philistines, 530:14
    Architect of Universe mathematician, 679:3
    army of pointed firs, 594:16
    artificer made my mate, 599:15
    Babel, 348:5
    ball of fire, 723:5
    be g. be misunderstood, 455:12
    Beginning produced emptiness, 89:14
    Birnam wood, 221:28

Great *(continued)*

blew g. guns, 498:18
book that made g. war, 489:*n*4
Britain going to war, 606:18
build a G. Society, 779:6
burden upon his back, 281:14
Caesar fell, 197:1
ceremony that to g. ones 'longs, 211:10
chasm, 782:3
compare g. things with small, 95:15, 265:21
cost g. deal to make, 627:10
creatures g. and small, 508:7
crime look dull, 796:4
death, 655:15
deeds wrought at great risks, 71:23
deep to great deep, 486:14
desire to bottle of hay, 181:25
dissolved into something g., 661:17
do business in g. waters, 19:14
do g. right do little wrong, 189:20
duration of g. sentiments makes g. men, 589:3
Elizabeth, 480:22
empire and little minds, 345:1
Father building forts among us, 533:9
fault of our politicians, 504:4
feast of languages, 177:10
fell g. oaks, 320:4
finds pang as g., 211:20
First Cause, 348:24
fortune great slavery, 107:6
Gaels of Ireland, 664:7
geniuses, 733:5
globe itself, 230:9
God our King, 469:9
god Pan, 112:2, 464:6
grassy world, 811:16
gray-green greasy Limpopo, 635:10
Gromboolian plain, 500:7
gulf fixed, 40:3
have seen the wicked in g. power, 17:7
he is a g. observer, 195:23
hedgehog knows one g. thing, 56:22
heir of fame, 259:3
here thou g. Anna, 309:8
historical ideals, 782:4
horse of gold, 739:10
how g. that darkness, 34:15
ice also g. would suffice, 669:11
ill can he rule the g., 161:15
impotently g., 309:15
in admiration as herself, 231:16
indispensable unique g., 628:3
interests at stake, 81:4
is Diana, 42:24
is glory of the woman, 74:6
is truth, 31:6
know well I am not g., 486:2
leap in the dark, 246:16
let us mock at g., 640:8
live at level of g. men, 602:21
lives of g. men remind us, 466:2
making city glorious and g., 64:17
malefactors of g. wealth, 615:9
man does not lose child's-heart, 82:8
man does not think beforehand, 82:7
man's memory, 204:21
many dull ugly people, 627:10

Great *(continued)*

many talks from g. father, 346:11
manye smale maken a g., 138:1
mast of some g. ammiral, 264:9
matter or small, 32:8
meals of beef iron steel, 193:10
men are not always wise, 14:42
men can't be ruled, 772:1
men contending with adversity, 241:6
men great nations not boasters, 456:23
men texts of Revelation, 433:16
mother of big apples, 787:4
names as these, 846:11
nature's second course, 220:16
Neptune's ocean wash, 220:19
nice customs curtsy to g. kings, 194:2
none unhappy but g., 303:13
nose great man, 649:14
not g. pleasure to bring death, 67:19
nothing g. accomplished without passion, 390:8
nothing g. created suddenly, 112:7
O God thy sea is so g., 847:10
O that I were as g., 180:3
office not filled by great men, 570:28
ones eat up little ones, 225:9
only g. man write history, 605:15
Original proclaim, 301:14
our hearts are g., 485:21
packs and sets of g. ones, 218:1
pay g. deal too dear, 228:8
pearl of g. price, 36:7
persons great kindnesses, 158:20
pith and moment, 203:33
poet writes his time, 722:14
poets great audiences, 521:15
prince and a g. man fallen, 11:40
Prince in prison lies, 235:5
quaint g. figure, 685:6
rats small rats, 491:17
rightly to be g., 206:2
rough diamond, 314:25
rudely g., 311:9
seekest thou g. things, 29:25
silence alone g., 443:17
sleep out this g. gap, 223:4
small and g. beasts, 19:11
small thing analogy of g. things, 93:3
so clear in his g. office, 219:18
so g. a poet and friend, 285:17
so g. is his mercy, 19:6
society big complicated, 727:5
society on earth, 391:12
some are born g., 209:30
souls suffer in silence, 381:14
sphere thou movest in, 223:36
stage of fools, 217:26
suffer g. destruction, 469:15
sweet mother, 568:14
that g. fact, 469:10
that he is grown so g., 195:21
the g. story, 840:9
thereby the g. is achieved, 59:2
things are done, 375:18
things both g. and small, 401:2
things made of little, 494:21
those who were truly g., 783:16
thoughts come from heart, 333:13
to be a g. man, 525:1

Great *(continued)*

to do thing that ends all other, 224:3
truth g. and shall prevail, 535:5
truth is g. and endures, 3:5
whales sailing by, 528:7
whatever little seemed g., 448:3
when little fears grow g., 205:2
where love is g., 205:2
who is from Nature, 456:16
wide beautiful world, 535:7
winds shoreward blow, 528:5
wink of eternity, 753:11
with child and longing for prunes, 211:6
with young, 854:6
Great Spirit appointed place for us, 387:6
gave ancestors lands we possess, 387:11
is my father, 387:7
make them all for his children, 387:10
Greater, Brutus makes mine g., 197:11
far g. than his father, 52:34
ignorance greater dogmatism, 595:7
love false to object, 775:7
love hath no man, 41:31
man greater courtesy, 486:5
more strong far g., 227:20
none beneath Sun, 635:18
out of small beginnings g. things, 247:10
prey upon less, 317:4
punishment g. than I can bear, 6:16
service g. than the god, 207:32
than God cannot be conceived, 126:3
than Solomon, 36:1
than we know, 395:13
the g. the more humble, 31:27
thy necessity g. than mine, 164:2
to the g. glory of God, 149:24
Greatest, artist embodied g. ideas, 517:3
bears g. names, 269:8
disease in the West, 785:6
empty vessel g. sound, 193:21
event in war, 74:9
fool is man, 289:15
griefs those we cause, 68:7
happiness for greatest numbers, 315:15
how much the g. event, 363:8
I am the g., 836:15
man ever seen, 343:*n*3
men women greatest city, 520:4
minds capable of g. vices, 254:1
my vision's g. enemy, 376:7
of these is charity, 44:20
pass days in that skill g., 104:20
politics g. adventure, 674:10
question ever debated, 351:8
scandal waits on greatest state, 175:9
service or greatest injury, 76:20
sooner fail than not among g., 440:11
tell aloud g. failing, 298:20
vicissitude of things, 168:18
well-wrought urn becomes g. ashes, 234:7
Great-grandfather was but a waterman, 281:25
Greathearted gentlemen, 491:12
Great-hearted Stentor, 52:29
Greatly, they shall be g. rewarded, 31:16
think or bravely die, 309:28
to find quarrel in straw, 206:2

H

Habit *(continued)*
 of living, 256:18
 of making history proof, 554:15
 of memory, 819:5
 of moving little finger, 581:3
 order breeds h., 570:10
 ordinary actions ascribed to h., 588:13
 reap a h., 849:5
 second nature, 362:n2
 shackle for free, 580:13
 takes place of happiness, 446:16
 use doth breed a h., 176:15
 will encroach, 398:26
 with him test of truth, 369:3
Habitation, benevolence the tranquil h., 82:2
 eat of the h., 188:2
 giddy and unsure, 191:23
 heart h. large enough, 460:7
 local h. and name, 182:3
 of dragons, 27:30
Habits, character h. and manners, 534:10
 civilized man has h. of house, 504:24
 follow other men's h., 538:7
 form second nature, 362:8
 ill h. gather by degrees, 285:23
 manifest in our h., 658:5
 my other h. air good, 555:10
 of age of atomic energy, 737:9
 of peace and patience, 252:25
 reforming other people's h., 561:14
Habitual hatred or fondness, 350:10
 lie becomes h., 357:11
 nothing h. but indecision, 581:8
Hack, somebody to hew and h., 271:5
Hacking at branches of evil, 506:24
Hackles, henna h. halt, 686:20
Hackney, starved h. sonneteer, 308:21
Hackneyed phrases, 613:18
Had having and in quest to have, 227:22
Hades, descent to H. is same, 66:15
 hateful as gates of H., 53:4
 is relentless, 53:3
 no man takes wealth to H., 61:15
 pass gates of H., 61:14
 phonographs of h., 753:17
 road to H. easy to travel, 85:2
 sent to H. many valiant souls, 52:1
Hag and hungry goblin, 844:19
Haggard, if I do prove her h., 214:2
Haggards ride no more, 620:12
Hags, secret black midnight h., 221:24
Ha-ha we're bound away, 862:3
Hail and farewell my brother, 94:29
 Columbia, 390:13
 congenial horrors h., 317:14
 divinest Melancholy, 259:23
 Emperor we who are about to die, 114:11
 fellow well met, 299:26
 hail gang's all here, 564:n1
 holy light, 265:24
 let others h. rising sun, 335:21
 Liberty hail, 444:11
 love-gift of fairy tale, 551:8
 Master, 37:32
 thou highly favored, 38:34
 to the Chief, 397:8
 to thee blithe spirit, 429:16
 to you gods, 3:12

Hail *(continued)*
 wedded love, 266:22
 ye small sweet courtesies, 333:6
Hailed, so proudly we h., 411:1
Haine, un peu de h., 556:n1
Hair, amber-dropping h., 261:10
 as free, 237:16
 babies haven't h., 729:4
 beautiful uncut h. of graves, 518:19
 beauty draws with single h., 309:7
 bindest in wreaths thy golden h., 99:7
 blown h. is sweet, 719:12
 bracelet of bright h., 235:10
 brown h. and speaks small, 190:14
 burned black with sun, 734:10
 comb gray h., 638:14
 divide a h., 270:16
 draw you with single h., 241:n3
 Edith with golden h., 467:12
 fictions only and false h., 250:8
 folded her h. expectantly, 521:6
 hank of h., 634:21
 has become very white, 550:1
 his floating h., 401:19
 horrid image unfix h., 219:5
 hyacinth h., 478:2
 Jeanie with light brown h., 539:2
 lie tangled in her h., 276:2
 lilac and brown h., 719:12
 live h. shining and free, 712:18
 long h. glory, 44:14
 Love with streaming h., 747:18
 lute strung with his h., 177:7
 make your h. curl, 565:22
 my fell of h., 222:15
 ninth part of a h., 186:8
 not white h. that engenders wisdom, 84:3
 not your yellow h., 641:2
 of dog that bit us, 148:23
 of my flesh stood up, 13:34
 of yon gray head, 468:16
 part my h. behind, 717:16
 prison for color of h., 620:4
 rain-drenched h., 704:14
 recover h. that grows bald, 174:29
 rise with my red h., 827:11
 ruddy limbs flaming h., 373:11
 sacred h. dissever, 309:13
 scent of her h., 734:10
 smooths h. with automatic hand, 718:19
 soft-lifted, 438:12
 species covered with h., 821:3
 stand up, 68:23
 stars in h. seven, 541:26
 stroke his silver h., 372:3
 subtle wreath of h., 235:9
 sugar my h., 551:3
 swerve a h. from truth, 208:7
 tangles of Neaera's h., 261:19
 to stand an end, 202:12
 turned quite gold from grief, 605:6
 vine leaves in h., 540:21
 was long, 439:4
 wash that man outa my h., 744:8
 weave sunlight in h., 717:23
 what scanted in h. given in wit, 174:30
 with such h. too, 493:14
Hairbreadth missings of happiness, 322:12
 'scapes, 212:29

Haircut and a shave, 729:4
Hairs, bring down my gray h., 7:27
 glory from gray h. gone, 468:7
 how ill white h. become fool, 192:13
 if h. be wires, 228:1
 nine she-camel h. aid memory, 714:22
 of your head numbered, 35:30
 sad last gray h., 437:8
 stand on end, 743:21
 superfluity sooner by white h., 187:26
 those set our h. upright, 235:22
Hairy gold crown on 'ead, 633:11
 man from east, 650:1
Hal, 'tis my vocation H., 184:33
 would it were bed-time H., 186:34
Halcyon days, 75:11
 expect h. days, 171:13
Hale Father William, 405:9
Half a drop ah my Christ, 171:4
 a league, 484:24
 a life asunder, 551:8
 a loaf, 148:16
 angel half bird, 494:23
 as old as Time, 384:7
 as old as time, 501:5
 better be ignorant than h. know, 104:8
 better h., 163:21
 dead a living death, 269:1
 grant what I wish, 669:5
 he's still h. with us, 783:17
 his Troy was burned, 191:7
 how much more is h. than whole, 56:9
 how the other h. lives, 252:12
 in love with Death, 437:12
 light half shade, 481:3
 more than h. people right, 756:14
 of my own soul, 99:3
 of one order half another, 271:13
 one h. of the world, 406:15
 overcome but h. his foe, 264:21
 owre to Aberdour, 853:20
 part of blessed man, 177:27
 proper gardener's work, 635:24
 reveal half conceal, 483:14
 revolutions put h. of France in mourning, 461:12
 savage country, 708:19
 seas over, 299:10
 see with h. an eye, 158:19
 served God with h. the zeal, 231:8
 speak h. an hour need two days, 611:12
 the wit for half the beauty, 385:15
 they h. believe in it, 59:4
 to rise and half to fall, 311:9
 truth blackest lie, 486:18
 use h. talent, 760:6
 was not told me, 12:19
 well begun is h. done, 81:5
 who has begun has h. done, 100:22
Half-acre tombs, 234:7
Half-a-crown, help to h., 575:18
Half-alligator, half-horse h. breed, 418:17
Half-believers of casual creeds, 529:10
Half-brother of world, 504:12
Half-darkness, in the h., 819:5
Half-dozen, six of one h. of other, 427:8
Half-gods, when h. go, 453:9
Half-horse half-alligator breed, 418:17

Half-ignorant they turned an easy wheel, 436:19

Half-know, better know nothing than h., 508:*n3*

Half-look, backward h. over shoulder, 721:10

Half-reaped furrow, 438:12

Half-regained Eurydice, 259:21

Half-truth, aphorism a h., 672:9

Half-truths, all truths are h., 625:2
    Nature hints and h., 566:19

Half-witted, old h. sheep, 394:*n2*
    saw State was h., 505:20

Half-world, o'er one h. nature dead, 220:9

Halicarnassian, my H. friend, 85:14

Hall, bride paced into the h., 399:16
    dazzlingly lighted h., 500:17
    Douglas in his h., 396:22
    equality in servants' h., 621:17
    flowers in garden meat in h., 134:*n3*
    in h. or bower, 260:15
    Liberty H., 342:20
    o' Fame when you croaks, 723:14
    'tis merry in h., 151:7
    Tom bears logs into the h., 177:17
    vasty h. of death, 529:15
    waiter roars through h., 534:7

Hallelujah, cry out H. I'm alive, 824:6
    Michael row boat ashore H., 863:5

Halloo halloo loo loo, 216:28

Hallow the fiftieth year, 9:16
    we cannot h., 476:7
    words such as h. obscene, 754:4

Hallowed be thy name, 34:11
    ground, 737:1
    relics should be hid, 259:3
    so h. and so gracious, 200:22

Halls, footless h. of air, 810:11
    in h. in gay attire, 396:9
    marble h., 441:9
    my ho head h., 696:16
    of fame, 849:14
    of hell, 709:10
    of Montezuma, 848:17

Hallucinations of poets, 691:5

Halt and blind, 39:32
    henna hackles h., 686:20
    how long h. ye between opinions, 12:28
    I pray you make a little stay, 125:4
    no dishonor to h. at second place, 90:18
    put a h. to injustice, 815:11

Halted, army not h. by eloquence, 502:12

Halter, hope one will cut h., 258:12
    threats of h., 362:9

Halters, ill talking of h., 157:9

Halve rights double duties, 425:12

Halves, two h. of God, 451:1

Ham, Noah begat H., 6:24

Haman, they hanged H., 13:20

Hamburger, gladly pay you Tuesday for h. today, 741:9
    sacred cows make tastiest h., 832:4

Hamelin town's in Brunswick, 491:15

Hamlet, Bacon not written H., 435:13
    I am not Prince H., 717:14
    much Antony of H. most, 594:8
    O H. what a falling-off, 202:16
    rambles Lear rages, 642:7
    rude forefathers of h., 334:11
    there struts H., 642:6

Hamlet's, ghost of H. father, 624:9

Hamlets, in h. dances on green, 396:9
    they have H. we Karamazovs, 526:6

Hammer along 'ard 'igh road, 591:15
    die with h. in hand, 848:15
    iron when hot, 102:24
    me into crowbar, 681:13
    neither h. nor axe, 12:16
    only tool is a h., 779:12
    what the h., 374:6
    when you are a h. strike, 251:23

Hammered gold and gold enameling, 640:2

Hammers, busy h. closing rivets, 193:11
    laughs at broken h., 681:19

Hammock, future not a comfortable h., 742:13
    me they'll lash in h., 517:2

Hampden, some village H., 334:21

Hampering with ceremonies and music, 82:26

Hampshire, captain of H. grenadiers, 354:3

Hamstring, conceit lies in his h., 207:28

Han', prentice h. tried on man, 378:13

Hand against every man, 7:4
    against Heaven's h., 263:16
    and heart to this vote, 414:12
    and lash that beat Rome, 642:5
    as arrows in the h., 20:6
    automatic h., 718:19
    beneath awful H. we hold, 635:1
    bird in h. worth two in bush, 111:*n9*
    bite h. that fed, 346:1
    bless h. that gave blow, 283:23
    bloody and invisible h., 221:7
    bondman in h. bears power, 195:27
    book in his h., 281:14
    books you hold in h., 326:2
    Caesar's h., 453:24
    capped withered heart, 766:18
    child of my right h., 237:20
    close h. out of love, 588:18
    cloud like a man's h., 12:30
    cold h. of death, 187:5
    death lays icy h. on kings, 254:9
    died by the h. of the Lord, 8:29
    do not saw air with h., 204:11
    dry h. yellow cheek, 191:16
    dyer's h., 227:16
    each army hath a h., 178:5
    East with richest h., 264:25
    even I be in Somebody's h., 575:5
    every man's h. against him, 7:4
    eye see for h. not mind, 506:5
    farther away on either h., 734:15
    fear thy skinny h., 400:9
    findeth to do, 24:29
    foot and h. go cold, 151:10
    for hand, 9:4
    from h. no worthy action, 846:17
    God keep you in his h., 862:24
    gods' capricious h., 771:4
    handle toward my h., 220:8
    having put h. to plow, 39:16
    heart in h., 489:3
    heaving up my either h., 248:20
    her h. on her bosom, 215:1
    here's my h., 230:1
    his hat in his h., 326:3
    hold fire in his h., 179:6

Hand *(continued)*
    hold infinity in palm of h., 375:5
    hold your h. victorious, 70:14
    hop a little from her h., 183:15
    hour is at h., 37:31
    hurts my h., 214:20
    I want to hold your h., 835:1
    if they stamp your h., 811:5
    if thy right h. offend thee, 34:4
    in every honest h. a whip, 214:29
    in hand Americans all, 349:10
    in hand on edge of sand, 499:18
    in hand with wandering, 268:17
    in her left h. riches and honor, 20:25
    in his h. are the deep places, 18:29
    in one h. a stone, 86:8
    individual led by invisible h., 338:18
    infection and h. of war, 179:12
    iron h. in velvet glove, 149:21
    kingdom of heaven is at h., 33:23
    kissing h. may feel good, 737:12
    leans her cheek upon her h., 183:1
    left h. know what right h., doeth, 34:10
    left his garment in her h., 7:25
    lends h. to honest boldness, 84:2
    length of days in her right h., 20:25
    lifted h. in awe, 305:20
    like base Indian, 215:13
    like this hand, 493:21
    living from h. to mouth, 155:4
    made all to prosper in his h., 7:24
    man himself lend a h., 73:14
    man's h. not able to taste, 182:1
    medieval h., 564:9
    mortality's strong h., 178:16
    my thoughtless h., 374:4
    my times are in thy h., 16:28
    nature's sweet cunning h., 209:8
    never had blister in h., 75:2
    nonchalance of h., 639:3
    not h. but understanding, 157:25
    not leave my h. without light, 713:3
    of all that hate us, 38:42
    of God promise of my own, 518:17
    of h. of foot of lip, 227:11
    of Potter shake, 472:1
    Old Age and Experience h. in h., 293:5
    on the horn, 854:15
    orders in his h., 655:9
    our h. finished it, 106:6
    our times in his h., 494:7
    phrase men pass h. to mouth, 826:5
    prentice h. tried on man, 378:13
    put in his h. by the hole of the door, 25:25
    raised to shed blood, 311:2
    rash h. in evil hour, 267:30
    right h. bigger than head, 818:13
    right h. forget her cunning, 20:11
    right h. is become glorious, 8:27
    right h. of God, 50:3
    scepter snatched with unruly h., 178:12
    separate as fingers one as h., 610:19
    shake of the h., 717:24
    shakes parting guest by h., 208:11
    sheep of his h., 18:29
    shut when thou shouldest repay, 32:4
    souls of righteous in h. of God, 31:16
    stout of h., 396:6

Hand *(continued)*

stretched out to receive, 32:4
sweet Roman h., 210:10
sweeten this little h., 222:7
sword sleep in my h., 375:17
taking in h. a city, 64:17
ten thousand at thy right h., 18:25
that held dagger struck, 698:12
that I were glove upon that h., 183:1
that is honest and hearty, 395:22
that made you fair, 211:25
that mocked them, 427:18
that rocks cradle, 518:7
that rounded Peter's dome, 452:19
that signed the paper, 795:4
there shall thy h. lead me, 20:13
this living h., 439:2
thou openest thine h., 20:17
three lilies in her h., 541:26
thy h. great Anarch, 313:25
thy h. presseth me sore, 17:9
thy right h. shall hold me, 20:13
time hath taming h., 449:17
Time's fell h., 226:18
to execute, 269:19, 360:9
touch of vanished h., 482:15
tricks by sleight of h., 300:19
unfriendly to tyrants, 278:27
Uzzah put forth his h., 11:42
vacant heart h. eye, 397:27
wash blood from my h., 220:19
waved her lily h., 307:1
we are in God's h., 193:8
what immortal h. or eye, 374:5
what thy right h. doeth, 34:10
whatsoever thou takest in h., 32:13
with other h. held weapon, 13:15
with your staff in your h., 8:18
withhold not thine h. in the evening,
    25:5
work of thy h., 28:34
Hand-and-glove, 299:22
Handclasp's a little stronger, 662:1
Handed in his checks, 566:11
me my Being's worth, 547:2
Handel, not care candle for H., 407:22
scarcely fit to hold candle, 314:13
Handful of dust, 718:12
of gray ashes, 534:3
of meal in a barrel, 12:26
of silver, 491:20
until h. of earth stops mouths, 442:19
with quietness, 24:8
Handfuls, give me h. of lilies, 98:1
Handiwork, artist remains within behind h.,
    696:6
firmament showeth his h., 16:10
Park specimen of God's h., 533:6
you give to God, 601:4
Handkerchief, black h. washed clean, 817:13
holding pocket-h., 552:6
Handle, grasp by blade or h., 515:18
grasped the surest h., 122:4
jug without h., 500:4
knife for which h. missing, 356:12
lie a h. fits all tools, 473:12
of big front door, 563:17
right and wrong h. to everything, 112:*n*5
such as h. harp and organ, 6:20

Handle *(continued)*

touch not h. not, 46:1
toward my hand, 220:8
Handlebar moustaches on Czar, 800:17
wringing h. for speed, 811:14
Handled, vessels oft h. brightly shine, 170:16
with a Chain, 545:2
Handler, nation's freight h., 681:8
Handles, everything has two h., 112:19
Handling, tuning lyre and h. harp, 64:17
Handmaid, Nature's h. Art, 282:15
philosophy h. to religion, 166:11
riches good h. worst mistress, 166:19
Handmaiden, low estate of his h., 38:38
Hands and eyes and heart, 421:21
and hearts, 173:6
and then take h., 229:18
are four, 741:5
as bands, 24:23
bear thee up in their h., 18:26
believe in fairies clap h., 621:18
blue, 499:19
by fairy h. knell rung, 336:16
children join h. and sing, 823:4
clasps with crooked h., 484:19
clean h. and pure heart, 16:19
come knit h., 260:23
Country defended by h., 487:5
dead h. dead stringencies, 827:17
diadems and fagots in h., 453:18
do what you're bid, 639:2
entergraft our h., 235:4
establish the work of our h., 18:24
Father into thy h., 40:22
fold h. and wait, 566:17
folding of the h. to sleep, 21:5
from failing h. we throw, 660:10
fruit of her h., 23:31
gilt comes off on our h., 527:2
greedy h., 474:*n*1
had put instead, 776:10
hath not a Jew h., 188:30
held heart in h., 655:17
his h. formed the dry land, 18:29
horny h. of toil, 514:8
idle h., 304:2
in h. not of few but many, 73:18
into thy h. I commend my spirit, 40:22
issue is in God's h., 65:30
kills Scots washes his h., 185:20
large and sinewy h., 466:7
little h. make pretense, 549:9
little h. never made, 303:18
lives in h. of Great Spirit, 387:11
looked at h. see if I was same, 523:17
lover threw wild h. toward sky, 655:19
made before knives, 299:16
man's fortune in own h., 168:11
many h. make light work, 149:2
musket molds in his h., 597:6
my own fair h., 297:23
nobody has such small h., 740:7
not hearts, 214:16
not without men's h., 512:13
of Esau, 7:12
of memory weave, 571:4
of sisters Death and Night, 520:13
only serve eyes, 504:23
oozing out at palm of h., 367:16

Hands *(continued)*

pale h. I loved, 632:6
Pilate washed h., 38:4
plunge h. in water, 775:9
predatory human h., 618:2
pure of h., 3:12
rarely escapes injuring own h., 59:18
right h. of fellowship, 45:17
rosy h. in steam, 809:1
shake h. forever, 169:14
something from our h., 395:12
sore laborers have hard h., 270:10
soul clap h. and sing, 639:17
speak h. for me, 196:14
strength without h. to smite, 568:1
temples made with h., 42:18
that rod of empire, 334:18
that work on us, 677:10
that wove shirt of flame, 722:2
union of h., 451:23
union of h. and hearts, 274:18
with Pilate wash your h., 180:11
without dirtying your h., 824:7
work h. from day to day, 777:8
wounds in thine h., 30:40
Handsaw, know hawk from h., 203:20
Handsome as bull that kidnapped Europa,
    91:1
big-boned and hardy-h., 587:12
house to lodge friend, 312:16
in three hundred pounds, 190:29
is that handsome does, 341:11
Jesus he was a h. man, 739:13
man but gay deceiver, 384:2
not h. at twenty, 251:25
others more h. by far, 678:18
property, 543:11
rather a h. pig, 550:8
some women h. without adornment,
    90:19
strong rich or wise, 251:25
ugly thinks herself h., 315:2
wee thing, 380:3
with my mourning very h., 288:21
Handsomely, have merit h. allowed, 329:8
Handspike, Fate is h., 516:17
Handwriting on the wall, 729:16
Handy, with girls be h., 846:14
Handy-dandy which is the justice, 217:23
Hang by your thumbs, 812:5
calf's-skin on limbs, 178:4
caps on horns o' the moon, 224:17
clothes on hickory limb, 851:13
enough rope h. himself, 146:*n*8
feel his title h. loose, 222:8
go h. yourselves critics, 146:17
I h. around in bars, 843:1
in their own straps, 209:2
let him h. there, 814:19
like icicle on beard, 210:7
loop to h. doubt on, 214:10
my harp on willow-tree, 848:19
on to your name, 826:12
out our banners, 222:14
pearl in cowslip's ear, 181:4
she would h. on him, 201:4
so fretted you would h. yourself,
    327:14
sorrow, 195:*n*1

Hang *(continued)*
    that jurymen may dine, 309:10
    them up in silent icicles, 401:11
    themselves in hope one will cut halter, 258:12
    there like fruit my soul, 225:26
    together or hang separately, 320:18
    up philosophy, 184:3
    upon his pent-house lid, 218:27
    us every mother's son, 180:27
    when icicles h. by the wall, 177:17
    yellow leaves do h., 226:24
    your head over, 847:2
    yourself brave Crillon, 162:13
Hangdog, shifty h. look, 694:11
Hanged, house of a man h., 157:9
    I'll be h., 185:12
    knows he is to be h., 328:8
    longed to see him h., 653:11
    men h. that horses not be stolen, 289:3
    millstone h. about neck, 40:4
    my poor fool is h., 218:7
    our harps upon willows, 20:11
    they h. Haman, 13:20
    went out to see Harrison h., 288:4
    when skies are h., 740:16
Hangin' Danny Deever, 633:6
    men and women there, 847:5
Hanging and wiving by destiny, 147:*n9*
    around till you've caught on, 671:20
    breathless on thy fate, 466:19
    Danny Deever, 633:6
    in a golden chain, 265:23
    likewise destiny, 147:12
    men and women there, 847:5
    no man not deserve h., 154:1
    shadow h. over me, 835:2
    too good for him, 281:24
    worst use for man, 232:18
Hangman's, fear o' hell's a h. whip, 242:*n1*
Hangout, talking about certain h., 744:18
Hangover became part of day, 746:12
Hangs as mute on Tara's walls, 411:11
    blossom that h. on bough, 230:13
    bodiless as false dawn, 808:15
    goose h. high, 847:3
    he h. between in doubt, 311:9
    in shades the orange bright, 277:10
    in uncertain balance, 165:19
    on Dian's temple, 224:31
    on princes' favors, 231:2
    tail h. down behind, 634:12
    thereby h. a tale, 198:16
    upon cheek of night, 182:25
Hank of hair, 634:21
Hannah, amount to H. Cook, 850:6
    God and me, 554:8
Hannibal is at the gates, 124:2
    know how to win victory H., 86:18
    put H. in the scales, 113:16
Hanover, famous H. city, 491:15
    Saint George's H. Square, 558:13
Hansom, helped to h. outside, 773:18
Hap, from better h. to worse, 168:25
    my hope my h. my love, 155:8
Ha'penny will do, 847:8
Haphazardly, ideas blow h., 645:1
Haply I think on thee, 226:6

Happen, accidents can h., 852:24
    it can't h. here, 708:8
    know what will h. next, 755:6
    lies at last letting it h., 809:3
    melting pot did not h., 631:*n3*
    things you do not hope h., 86:15
    we's nuts and things h., 723:13
    what would h. if one woman told truth, 791:10
Happened, good books feel all h. to you, 754:12
    nothing ever h. at all, 560:15
    put down what really h., 754:10
    remember anything whether h. or not, 563:1
    show what actually h., 441:8
    this could have h. once, 494:20
Happening, being and h., 776:15
    funny if h. to somebody else, 685:14
Happens, don't want be there when h., 831:3
    future in us before it h., 677:3
    music of what h., 834:1
    nothing h. unless first a dream, 681:15
    too much h., 748:14
    truth h. to idea, 583:1
    unexpected always h., 86:*n8*
    whatever h. we have Maxim Gun, 653:3
Happier, envy of less h. lands, 179:12
    I am h. than I know, 267:19
    in passion we feel, 273:30
    people capable of becoming h., 727:7
    Pobbles h. without toes, 500:10
    remembering h. things, 481:19
    those who feel love most are h., 428:9
Happiest day happiest hour, 477:12
    intellection, 809:2
    martini one of h. marriages, 748:7
    of all men, 316:7
    time of New Year, 480:15
    treatise of natural education, 331:10
    women nations have no history, 513:4
Happily may I walk, 856:2
Happiness activity in accordance with excellence, 80:18
    avarice and h., 319:9
    beauty that comes from h., 527:1
    beneficial for body, 658:3
    best recipe for h., 406:14
    beyond h. is bliss, 732:6
    care of life and h., 358:15
    ceases like dream, 254:21
    consume h. without producing it, 609:8
    counting upon H., 440:2
    depends less on exterior things, 347:5
    dream h. you may never feel, 656:4
    enjoy h., 103:*n10*
    envy no man's h., 199:6
    freedom secret of h., 74:5
    great step towards h., 416:19
    greatest degree of h., 339:10
    greatest h. for greatest numbers, 315:15
    greatest h. for thinking man, 366:3
    Greatest H. Principle, 465:1
    habit takes place of h., 446:16
    hairbreadth missings of h., 322:12
    health foundation of h., 459:20
    hope for h. beyond life, 355:3
    how simple and frugal is h., 701:8
    ideal of h., 461:10

Happiness *(continued)*
    in hands of others, 410:7
    in married estate, 258:11
    is of retired nature, 302:7
    jealous possessions of h., 651:1
    liberty secret of h., 607:1
    lifetime of h. hell, 609:16
    look into h. through another's eyes, 200:4
    made of minute fractions, 404:3
    make ourselves worthy of h., 339:5
    makes up in height, 670:13
    man mistakes evil for h., 382:20
    mistaken path to h., 425:20
    new dish does more for human h., 370:5
    no h. like mine, 830:10
    no h. perfect as martyr's, 626:6
    no h. where no wisdom, 68:3
    no one can arrange another's h., 767:8
    not in multitude of friends, 237:9
    of human race, 345:2
    of peoples, 586:12
    of society end of government, 351:10
    on earth no sure h., 161:18
    on surer ground of mutual h., 460:13
    only one h. in life, 461:13
    pastime and our h., 394:21
    politics art of human h., 632:2
    principles to effect h., 357:2
    produced by good tavern, 328:2
    pursuing and obtaining h., 339:9
    pursuit of h., 357:2
    regret or secret h., 595:2
    result h., 497:34
    result of man's effort, 683:3
    secret of h. freedom, 74:5
    she does not find, 324:11
    sole object of government, 353:7
    sum of human h., 694:18
    supreme h. of life, 451:7
    take life-lie away take h., 540:18
    that makes heart afraid, 445:17
    the only good, 554:7
    the only sanction of life, 629:4
    thirst after h., 331:20
    to be dissolved into something great, 661:17
    to crave h. is revolt, 540:9
    too swiftly flies, 333:22
    two foes of human h., 425:17
    what right have we to h., 540:9
    wherein lies h., 436:10
Happy a man as any in world, 288:10
    accident, 243:18
    age when idle with impunity, 416:13
    alchemy of mind, 317:6
    all the while I was h., 838:3
    and I wrote my h. songs, 371:14
    as grass was green, 795:8
    as heart was long, 795:12
    as kings, 599:2
    as we imagine, 273:8
    ask yourself whether h., 465:8
    autumn fields, 482:21
    be and have immortal bliss, 161:8
    be good and h. today, 399:8
    best government make people h., 447:8
    bread sauce of h. ending, 585:5
    breed of men, 179:12

Happy *(continued)*

bridegroom Hesper brings, 619:16
call that man h., 65:8
Christmas to all, 411:6
combination of circumstances, 398:1
convents, 313:24
created you while h., 628:9
days here again, 736:13
deep down, 723:10
description of h. state, 286:8
duty of being h., 598:12
families alike, 542:18
fault, 49:12
few, 193:20
field mossy cavern, 438:10
genius of my household, 703:9
good government when those near made
    h., 63:9
good to be just plain h., 732:6
good-night air, 575:17
had Vietnam instead of h. childhoods,
    834:9
hail Columbia h. land, 390:13
he of calm and h. nature, 77:1
heart that sighed, 169:2
high majestical, 428:17
highways where I went, 619:3
horse to bear Antony, 223:5
hour wherein man might be h., 252:17
house shelters friend, 455:24
how h. he who crowns, 342:2
how h. vestal's lot, 309:26
how h. with either, 307:17
how we make ourselves h., 339:5
if all h. as we, 374:9
if ever wife h. in man, 270:11
I'm h. again, 740:19
I'm h. tonight, 823:10
in arms of chambermaid, 328:17
in being and knowing, 732:6
in even bad movie, 798:4
in nothing else so h., 179:17
in small ways, 627:19
in sorrow, 159:9
is he born and taught, 232:13
Isles, 481:14
Jerusalem h. home, 844:15
laugh before we are h., 292:17
let a lord once own the h. lines, 308:21
let us be h. as we can, 329:5
liking what they do, 333:11
little h. if say how much, 194:20
little needed to make h. life, 115:28
living things, 400:13
lucid intervals and h. pauses, 166:17
make fellow creatures h., 355:3
make two lovers h., 310:18
man be his dole, 147:*n*10
man happy dole, 147:13
man that hath his quiver full, 20:6
man who could search out causes, 96:13
man who works ancestral acres, 98:27
man's without a shirt, 147:2
master of himself a h. man, 100:9
mindful of h. time in misery, 130:15
moron, 851:14
never was so h., 847:19
no lad so h. as I, 408:15
no man h. who does not think so, 103:26

Happy *(continued)*

no one h. till all h., 523:6
not h. unless free, 426:5
not to seem too h., 494:16
O h. fault, 49:15
object of making men h., 525:17
old man, 95:16
pair, 266:14
people whose annals blank, 435:11
persons with torn bodies h., 655:12
place green groves of blest, 97:28
place to be h. here, 554:7
policeman's lot not h., 564:5
ports and h. havens, 179:4
possessor of talent, 772:11
prologues to swelling act, 219:4
prospects more pleasing than fruition,
    114:*n*3
Puritanism haunting fear someone h.,
    691:17
rarely find a h. life, 98:18
realize been h. was h. still, 789:13
remote from the h., 776:9
ring h. bells, 484:14
secrets of a h. life, 780:*n*1
so h. as America, 354:12
survive and multiply, 469:15
that we are not over happy, 203:13
the h. that have called thee so, 405:15
the man and happy he alone, 284:6
the man who void of cares, 304:15
the man whose wish, 308:3
they h. are and love, 257:2
thing to be father unto many sons,
    172:31
this h. country, 337:12
this the h. morn, 258:16
those early days when I, 279:2
those who plant cabbages, 146:10
those whose walls already rise, 96:33
time to be h. is now, 554:7
to be alone last work done, 783:17
to be h. be well fed, 691:10
to be h. make others so, 554:7
to have been h. most unhappy, 120:2
'twere now to be most h., 213:14
until dead not call man h., 57:11
Warrior, 394:15, 663:*n*4
was he free was he h., 776:4
when am I h., 826:11
where h. wing-beats are, 381:8
where one is h. there's homeland, 124:29
which of us h. in world, 490:8
who hath this only, 56:26
who in verse steer, 289:5
who knows rural gods, 96:14
who uses blessings with wisdom, 100:16
whoever h. make others h., 822:6
whom unbroken bond unites, 99:13
world not making you h., 609:15
world of h. days, 174:2
would never be so h. again, 746:11
Harangue, telling nothing in great h., 278:4
Harbinger, evening star love's h., 268:13
Harbingers are come, 250:23
    to heaven, 258:5
Harbor, age the h. of all ills, 84:18
    arrived in a good h., 247:6
    bar be moaning, 513:23

Harbor *(continued)*

cleared, 399:14
in life did h. give, 237:22
looking over h. and city, 681:9
run into a safe h., 57:15
ship comes into the h., 247:9
ship of state safely to h., 67:13
Hard as a piece of nether millstone, 15:21
    as nails, 496:9
    beginning good ending, 147:15
    brother h. and furious, 821:2
    cause that makes these h. hearts, 217:6
    Christ ain't a-going to be too h., 571:6
    curst h. reading, 368:6
    dealing teaches them suspect, 188:11
    for women to keep counsel, 196:12
    gemlike flame, 573:9
    heroic for earth too h., 494:5
    he's h. to understand, 837:15
    hit h. fast often, 696:1
    hit the line h., 615:3
    it is well I die h., 350:13
    it shall go h., 188:32
    keeps end from being h., 670:7
    latent value, 585:10
    like tip of wedge, 707:6
    makes them soft where we are h., 746:10
    not to write satire, 112:20
    nothing's so h. but search will find,
        248:15
    prove him with h. questions, 12:18
    sloth finds down pillow h., 225:19
    solid massy h. particles, 291:5
    stairs, 132:2
    things that are too h. for thee, 31:29
    this is my h. time, 780:9
    times h. and wages low, 862:8
    to argue with belly, 88:1
    to catch and conquer, 541:19
    to kick against pricks, 42:8
    to please everybody, 104:1
    very hard is my fare, 307:2
    was their lodging, 295:11
    way of transgressors is h., 21:25
Hard-boiled as picnic egg, 745:3
Hardened, he h. Pharaoh's heart, 8:12
Hardens, charity hardens, 461:8
    it h. a' within, 378:10
Harder, heart h. than stone, 55:24
    they come harder they fall, 841:4
Hardest, first hundred years h., 678:8
    first step is h., 317:9
    knife ill-used, 227:6
    of all to close hand, 588:18
    softest things overcome h., 59:5
Hard-favored rage, 192:30
Hardihood, cure for soft is h., 626:3
    dauntless h., 534:9
    endurance courage, 649:16
Harding not bad man just a slob, 704:3
Hardship, godlike h., 439:1
    meet any h., 799:7
    our garment, 666:6
Hardships, to stars through h., 123:8
    unknown h. we suffered, 734:9
Hard-working ancestry, 737:19
Hardy as Nemean lion's nerve, 202:9
    kiss me H., 377:8
Hardy-handsome, big-boned and h., 587:12

Hare and tortoise, 60:12
    hold with h. run with hound, 148:2
    limped trembling, 436:20
    mad March h., 141:16
    March H. went on, 550:10
    of whom proverb goes, 177:24
    rouse lion than start h., 185:8
    today on the flesh of a h., 829:5
Harebells, heath and h., 509:4
Harebrained chatter, 459:24
Hares, little hunted h., 656:10
    pull dead lions by beard, 177:*n*1
Hark deep sound strikes, 420:16
    do you hear sea, 439:*n*3
    hark dogs do bark, 861:5
    hark my soul, 501:17
    hark the lark, 225:12
    the herald angels sing, 323:1
Harlem, it's H. up there, 841:6
    needed something to smash, 813:5
Harlot's cry, 375:15
    youthful h. curse, 374:8
Harlots, ye h. sleep at ease, 309:22
Harm, content with my h., 199:6
    didn't want to h. the man, 813:14
    do h. to other nations, 761:15
    do me no h., 414:6
    do no h., 72:17
    do not h. subtle wreath of hair, 235:9
    do sick no h., 522:5
    does h. to another, 56:11
    does h. to my wit, 209:3
    fate cannot h. me, 399:3
    flea does all h. he can, 236:18
    good provoke to h., 212:1
    I abstain from intentional h., 72:16
    no one h. man who does self no wrong,
      119:3
    none shall h. Macbeth, 221:26
    nothing do much h., 741:10
    once h. has been done, 53:23
    to one harm to all, 557:5
    whether benevolence good or h., 538:5
    win us to our h., 219:3
Harmed, neither h. nor warmed, 817:18
Harmful, everything without control over
    selves h., 366:9
    more h. than reasoned errors, 537:11
Harmless as doves, 35:27
    drudge, 324:19
    entertains the h. day, 232:14
    inoffensive aristocracy, 473:17
    necessary cat, 189:13
    only h. great thing, 236:2
    pleasure, 325:10
Harmonicas, has territory of h., 740:17
Harmonies, tumult of mighty h., 429:4
Harmonious and humane life, 532:6
    dulcet and h. breath, 181:8
    Father-Mother God all-h., 526:10
    madness from my lips, 429:20
Harmoniously confused, 309:16
Harmonizes natural and artificial, 403:11
Harmony, absolute h., 768:2
    attention like deep h., 179:8
    between men and land, 711:14
    between tides and life, 602:15
    cultivate peace and h., 350:10
    disposed to h., 407:15

Harmony *(continued)*
    for you my Universe, 115:12
    from h. from heavenly h., 284:13
    I don't want h., 525:16
    in bad taste elegance, 784:15
    in discord, 101:5
    in h. with universe, 513:20
    is pure love, 169:10
    like h. in music, 391:7
    makes heaven drowsy with h., 177:7
    manifest in Form and Number, 623:13
    more h. in her bright eye, 275:21
    music wherever there is h., 256:7
    not live in h., 770:16
    not understood, 311:8
    of leaves, 637:3
    of temperament and circumstances, 527:1
    of the whole universe, 143:7
    perceived h. of object, 402:19
    power of h., 391:2
    such h. in immortal souls, 190:5
    too high price for h., 525:16
    touches of sweet h., 190:5
    whole complicate amassing h., 688:7
Harm's, in h. way, 363:1
Harms, beg often our own h., 223:11
    himself who does harm, 56:11
    lesse of two h., 53:*n*2
    took not for thy h., 621:5
Harness, die with h. on our back, 222:18
    died in h., 667:14
    him that girdeth on his h., 12:33
Harold stands on place of skulls, 420:15
Harp, as harper lays palm, 467:19
    hang h. on willow-tree, 848:19
    no h. like my own, 408:15
    not all who own h. are harpers, 90:3
    not on that string, 174:14
    once the h. of Innisfail, 409:6
    praise him with h., 20:21
    such as handle h., 6:20
    that once through Tara's halls, 411:11
    tuning lyre and handling h., 64:17
    wild h. slung behind him, 411:16
Harper, as h. lays palm on harp, 467:19
Harpers, not all who own harp are h., 90:3
Harping, still h. on my daughter, 203:7
Harpoon, why didn't I h. him, 856:11
Harps, hanged h. upon willows, 20:11
    of gold, 488:15
    organic h. diversely framed, 399:10
    played before the Lord on h., 11:41
Harris, words she spoke of Mrs. H., 497:11
Harrison, went out to see H. hanged, 288:4
Harrow house of dead, 775:5
    rust to the h., 662:14
    toad beneath h., 632:9
    up thy soul, 202:12
Harrowing clods, 576:5
Harry, cry God for H., 193:2
Harry succeeds, 192:12
    little touch of H., 193:12
    such a King H., 169:13
    young H. with beaver on, 186:23
Harsh as truth, 462:4
    berries h. and crude, 261:13
    cadence of a rugged line, 284:5
    in this h. world, 207:13
    life teaches us to be less h., 364:9

Harsh *(continued)*
    nor h. nor grating, 391:4
    out of tune and h., 204:9
    philosophy not h., 261:3
    school in which nothing h., 120:1
    words of Mercury are h., 177:19
Harsher, qualify war in h. terms, 522:11
Harshly, do not judge us too h., 750:19
    strings untouched will h. jar, 170:16
Harshness, no h. gives offense, 308:18
Hart, as h. panteth after water brooks,
    17:16
    as pants the h., 294:7
    be thou like to a young h., 26:5
    lame man leap as an h., 27:32
    ungalled play, 205:6
Harvard, always tell H. man, 850:1
    fair H., 426:13
    glass flowers at H., 714:8
    Law School, 695:10
    whale-ship was my Yale College and H.,
      516:10
Harvard Square, Greek islands over H.,
    751:14
Harvest, all the H. I reaped, 471:14
    gathereth her food in the h., 21:4
    God comes as sheaves in h., 236:21
    home, 185:2, 487:7
    is past, 29:8
    no h. but a thorn, 250:15
    of a quiet eye, 392:4
    reap the h. of your land, 9:13
    seedtime and h., 6:32
    shalt not gather the gleanings of h., 9:13
    time of h., 720:12
    truly is plenteous, 35:23
    your hour, 151:3
Harvests, wholesome h. reaps, 444:15
Harwich, steamer from H., 565:4
Has, what man h. he's sure of, 158:27
Hasard, coup de dés n'abolira le h., 583:*n*4
    l' h. ne favorise que les esprits préparés,
      533:*n*3
Hash, couldn't eat h. with enny safety,
    508:18
Haste, always in h., 318:22
    away so soon, 248:9
    brings failures, 71:20
    come time and h. day, 368:12
    eat it in h., 8:18
    haste has no blessing, 853:7
    I said in my h., 19:23
    in paying obligation, 273:28
    in wikked h. no profit, 147:*n*4
    make h. better foot before, 178:18
    make h. my beloved, 26:5
    maketh waste, 147:4
    married in h. repent at leisure, 300:11
    more h. less speed, 102:5
    now to my setting, 230:31
    of fool slowest thing, 291:9
    still pays haste, 212:9
    thee Nymph, 259:9
    this sweaty h., 200:17
    without h. but without rest, 366:11
    wooed in h. wed at leisure, 175:31
Hasten, minutes h. to their end, 226:16
Hastening, to h. ills a prey, 341:29
Hastens, midnight strikes and h., 619:21

Hastily, no werkman may werke wel and h., 137:10

nothing can be done h. and prudently, 103:21

Hasty, common sense takes h. view, 505:27

man in his h. days, 586:7

marriage seldom proveth well, 173:4

orisons, 738:6

Pudding, 369:2

pudding, 846:*n3*

start awa sae h., 377:10

Hat, cat in the h., 769:8

cockle h. and staff, 206:4

he can't think without h., 773:11

his h. in his hand, 326:3

lightly doffed h., 630:3

Lord forbade me to put off my h., 280:14

my h. upon my head, 326:3

not worse for wear, 347:23

off with your h., 606:7

on account of Beaver H., 500:3

penny in old man's h., 847:8

runcible h., 499:14

stuck feather in h., 846:14

wears faith as fashion of h., 194:7

Hatched, count chickens before h., 60:9

don't count boobies until h., 741:18

o'er an' hatched different, 512:18

silent when eggs h., 258:11

would grow mischievous, 195:31

Hatchet, buried h., 649:8

I did cut it with my h., 349:*n7*

Hatching vain empires, 265:9

Hate, cherish hearts that h. thee, 231:7

common herd, 99:26

counsels not in such quality, 189:1

creative h., 661:15

do good to them that h. you, 34:7

dumpy woman, 423:7

envy calumny h. pain, 430:13

envy dared not h., 422:11

families I h. you, 651:1

fear h. surrender defiance, 831:11

fly from not h. mankind, 420:24

for arts, 312:4

found only on stage, 424:6

freedom for thought we h., 579:1

gods h. the obvious, 51:22

hand of all that h. us, 38:42

him for a Christian, 188:3

I dont h. it, 748:17

I h. and I love, 94:27

I h. definitions, 458:20

I h. nobody, 299:9

I h. quotation, 454:7

I h. slavery, 474:7

I h. the day, 161:26

I h. war, 698:4

I h. ye all, 275:16

I h. you I h. you cried Madeline, 694:13

I know enough of h., 669:11

I shall h. all women, 234:14

immortal h., 264:3

implacable in h., 283:11

in white men, 815:12

inaccuracy, 559:5

ingratitude, 210:15

Hate *(continued)*

Juno's unrelenting h., 285:6

let them h. so long they fear, 89:16

love and desire and h., 645:11

love as though someday h., 67:*n3*

love treason but h. traitor, 91:24

loved him too much not to h., 290:8

making other Englishman h. him, 610:4

mankind, 218:21

no h. lost between us, 243:21

no sport in h., 431:3

nor love thy life nor h., 268:11

nought I did in h., 215:12

of those below, 420:20

one and love other, 34:16

one another and know it, 288:26

only love sprung from only h., 182:26

only those who h. Negro, 602:9

owe no man h., 199:6

Persian luxury I h., 99:19

rage and h. from Adam down, 516:14

religion enough to make us h., 298:3

scourge laid upon your h., 184:19

skins not like your own, 509:11

smile to those who h., 422:26

so far only should we h., 67:9

strength erect against her h., 729:12

the tree, 119:17

things we ought, 80:17

those I fight I do not h., 638:16

those who h. and destroy, 602:6

those who h. you don't win, 791:3

time to h., 24:6

to be unquiet at home, 288:27

to leave world, 754:17

to see evenin' sun go down, 663:4

traitors and treason love, 284:25

tyrants, 518:10

war, 698:4

were why men breathe, 740:10

whom they fear they h., 87:17

whom they have injured they h., 107:4

why do you h. the South, 748:17

Hated for my name's sake, 35:28

if to be fat be h., 185:31

past reason h., 227:22

quarrel in streets to be h., 440:17

the approximate, 677:1

to be h. needs but be seen, 311:10

way she had of waking him, 723:9

with hate found on stage, 424:6

with scabby hatred, 829:8

Hateful art how to forget, 249:3

as the gates of Hades, 53:4

pride is h. before God, 32:17

second wife h. to children, 69:10

self is h., 280:9

what h. to you do not to neighbor, 106:1

woman once loved h., 659:11

Hater, very good h., 325:22

Hates, anyone who h. babies, 690:*n1*

children can't be all bad, 690:3

God h. bray of bragging, 67:12

him that would stretch him, 218:8

tell him he h. flatterers, 196:4

thing he would not kill, 189:14

Hath, unto everyone that h., 37:14

Hating, die not h. enemies, 317:3

Hatred, all h. driven hence, 639:15

carried in my heart, 813:4

ceases by love, 66:17

comes from heart, 425:13

envy h. and malice, 50:11

excites h. to conceal abuses, 409:10

habitual h. or fondness, 350:10

hate Negro see h. in him, 602:9

hated with scabby h., 829:8

healthy h. of scoundrels, 435:9

I must have no h., 631:18

if no h. in mind, 639:13

intellectual h. worst, 639:14

love to h. turned, 300:22

made law, 771:6

not cease by hatred, 66:17

of bourgeois beginning of wisdom, 527:8

renders votaries credulous, 331:18

stalled ox and h. therewith, 21:36

stirreth up strifes, 21:16

through h. borne apart, 69:7

where h. let me sow love, 128:5

Hats off gentlemen a genius, 488:14

Seraphs swing snowy H., 544:9

war their h. aboon, 853:19

Hatter, can't take less said H., 550:13

Haughtiness of soul, 301:19

of the terrible, 27:2

Haughty, discountenance h. and lawless, 350:14

Juno's unrelenting hate, 285:6

nation proud in arms, 260:14

spirit before a fall, 22:2

vigilant resolute, 448:12

Hauling, crazy as h. timber into woods, 98:22

Haunch and hump is Obey, 634:15

Haunches, sits on silent h., 681:9

Haunt, breed and h., 219:15

exempt from public h., 197:37

ghostlike the spot, 460:8

murmurous h. of flies, 437:11

so h. thy days, 439:2

Haunted, beneath waning moon h., 401:14

by ghosts, 179:28

holy ground, 420:11

me like a passion, 391:3

passion in Lear me, 439:*n3*

summer eves by h. stream, 259:20

Haunters of cavern lake waterfall, 436:15

Haunting black air, 821:8

Puritanism h. fear someone may be happy, 691:17

Haunts about thy shape, 437:16

busy h. of men, 432:3

of coot and hem, 485:3

suspicion h. guilty mind, 173:16

tempest laughs at archer, 524:8

Haupt, O H. vol Blut und Wunden, 258:*n1*

Hautboys, give h. breath he comes, 285:9

Have, all I h. would h. given gladly, 779:3

all we h. and are, 635:25

curtsied when you h., 229:18

desire what we ought not to h., 103:22

everything yet nothing, 89:4

House of H., 573:3

in quest to h. extreme, 227:22

more than thou showest, 216:2

that which it fears to lose, 226:19

Have *(continued)*
  thee not yet see thee still, 220:8
  their Affliction by drops, 289:23
  these for yours, 620:3
  to h. and to hold, 51:10
  to h. to hold and let go, 632:5
  to h. what we would h., 211:15
  try to h. and use excellence, 80:20
  we h. Maxim Gun they h. not, 653:3
  what others would be glad of, 322:2
  what she's having, 836:10
  what we h. we prize not, 194:39
  where ask is h., 338:1
  you can h. it, 821:2
Haven, in friendship but faithless h., 67:9
  in sunny Palestine, 681:4
  safe into h. glide, 322:24
  under the hill, 482:15
Have-nots, Haves and H., 158:10
Havens, in h. dumb, 587:1
  ports and happy h., 179:4
Haves and Have-Nots, 158:10
  of give, 740:9
Having, are we h. fun yet, 838:15
  fewest wants, 72:5
  had h. and in quest to have, 227:22
  love not h. to say sorry, 832:9
  not a h. and resting, 531:15
  nothing possessing all, 45:9
Havoc, cry H., 196:22
Hawk, chicken h. floats over, 820:2
  gentle as falcon or h. of tower, 141:22
  know h. from handsaw, 203:20
  prayer of h. does not get chicken, 853:12
  sooner kill man than h., 713:10
Hawked, by mousing owl h. at, 220:28
Hawk's, inhuman as h. cry, 713:13
Hawks, dark h. hear us, 696:16
  such hounds such h., 854:7
  which h. flies higher pitch, 171:16
Hawthorn in the dale, 259:14
Hawthorne says NO in thunder, 516:4
  sedulous ape to H., 599:9
Hay, antic h., 170:14
  bottle of h., 181:25
  came creaking to barn, 800:11
  good h. sweet h., 181:25
  make h. when sun shineth, 147:9
  needle in bottle of h., 158:4
  new-mown h., 656:7
  no tits to pull no h. to pitch, 852:16
  work and pray live on h., 684:10
  world bundle of h., 424:29
Haydn, some cry up H., 407:22
Haystack in the floods, 556:10
  needle in h., 158:*n1*
  under h. asleep, 857:17
Hazard, men that h. all, 188:22
  nice h. of doubtful hour, 186:21
  of concealing, 378:10
  of new fortunes, 177:22
  of the die, 174:24
Hazel, lone Glenartney's h. shade, 397:4
Hazlitt, sedulous ape to H., 599:9
Hé Dieu si j'eusse étudié, 139:*n3*
He for God only, 266:10
  forget the H. and She, 234:1
  if you build it h. will come, 831:13
  is risen, 38:32, 49:17

He *(continued)*
  is the Rock, 10:13
  poorest h. in England, 246:6
  was he and I was I, 152:14
Head and hoof of Law, 634:15
  anointest my h. with oil, 16:18
  apples on Newton's h., 671:13
  at his h. a grass-green turf, 206:5
  bare Ben Bulben's h., 643:4
  behold my h., 250:23
  bending low, 539:3
  binds so dear a h., 430:1
  black wires grow on her h., 228:1
  blessings upon the h. of the just, 21:15
  bloody but unbowed, 594:10
  bowed comely h. down, 276:24
  bullet through his h., 652:11
  call in thy death's h., 250:16
  chop off her h., 550:6
  chop off your h., 857:13
  crotchets in thy h., 190:22
  crown in my heart not on h., 172:30
  crown of h. to sole, 194:29
  dark hole of the h., 825:4
  desolate and bowed h., 645:8
  dogs shame the gray h., 53:32
  don't lose your h., 851:6
  drunken dog ragged h., 407:2
  eat my h., 496:11
  feel as if top of h. off, 547:9
  four angels round my h., 274:20
  from heels up to h., 598:23
  from the fair h. forever, 309:13
  full of quarrels, 183:26
  gently falling on thy h., 304:4
  grown gray in vain, 430:13
  guts in his h., 207:30
  hairs of h. numbered, 35:30
  hang your h. over, 847:2
  heap coals of fire upon his h., 23:3
  heart runs away with h., 383:16
  heaven to weary h., 446:1
  her h. on her knee, 215:1
  here rests his h., 335:2
  hers is the h., 573:5
  hide h. under his wing, 859:12
  hitteth nail on h., 149:19
  hoary h. a crown of glory, 22:3
  if she'd but turn her h., 637:14
  imperfections on my h., 202:19
  in heart and h., 825:19
  in heart or in h., 189:3
  in lion's mouth, 793:3
  incessantly stand on h., 550:1
  it shall bruise thy h., 6:8
  Jezebel tired her h., 13:5
  John Baptist's h., 36:12
  keep good tongue in h., 230:3
  King Charles's h., 498:3
  lay sleeping h. my love, 775:10
  make you shorter by the h., 151:15
  man with the h., 483:3
  meet and not see its h., 58:16
  more than churches bibles creeds, 519:10
  my h. is a city, 841:6
  my hat upon my h., 326:3
  my ho h. halls, 696:16
  no bigger than his h., 217:18
  no roof to shroud his h., 239:13

Head *(continued)*
  not sound the rest not well, 157:*n3*
  not yet has heart or h., 765:3
  O sacred h. now wounded, 258:4
  of a pin, 835:13
  off with her h., 550:15
  off with his h., 174:8, 301:3
  on horror's h. horrors, 214:11
  one small h. could carry, 342:9
  ought to have h. examined, 695:16
  over h. and heels, 94:8
  picked up poker hit him in h., 858:6
  precious jewel in his h., 197:37
  right hand bigger than h., 818:13
  root of family is person of its h., 81:28
  sacred h. of thine, 261:21
  shake of his poor little h., 565:20
  shot it through the h., 860:18
  show my h. to the people, 381:2
  singe my white h., 216:18
  slide into lover's h., 391:17
  so young body with so old h., 189:18
  some once lovely H., 471:9
  Son of man nowhere to lay h., 35:14
  stone of the corner, 19:25
  strike stars with my exalted h., 99:2
  stuff the h. with reading, 313:23
  sudden if thing comes in his h., 173:15
  that wears crown, 191:35
  this old gray h., 468:15
  threw back fierce young h., 674:11
  thudding in his h., 809:11
  to contrive, 269:19
  trickled through h., 552:16
  turns no more his h., 400:17
  useful lesson to h., 348:11
  very staid h., 189:*n3*
  well-made rather than well-filled h.,
    152:13
  when the h. aches, 157:26
  whole h. is sick, 26:7
  wisdom of h. and heart, 498:24
  with its h. went galumphing, 551:11
  your h. concerned with outer weather,
    670:1
Headache, dismal h., 565:3
Head-down tail-up hunt, 833:15
Headings, good reduced to three h., 287:18
Headline, best h. ever wrote, 786:15
Headlines, black h. of the latest edition,
    756:16
  there are h., 834:3
Headlong down an immutable course,
    784:11
  hurled h. flaming, 263:23
Headpiece filled with straw, 719:4
Heads, beast of many h., 100:*n13*
  beast with many h., 224:29
  blood be on your h., 42:20
  brains of better h., 255:10
  day fate put h. together, 670:1
  diminished h., 266:2
  erect instead of bowing necks, 118:23
  green hands blue, 499:19
  grow beneath shoulders, 212:31
  heaven over our h., 507:13
  hills whose h. touch heaven, 212:30
  houseless h., 216:27
  lift up your h. O ye gates, 16:20

Heard (*continued*)

wise man say, 618:10
wished she had not h. it, 212:32

Hearers, convince h. of own assertions, 76:18
not h. only, 47:13
readers and h. like my books, 168:24
too deep for his h., 343:2

Hearest thou hardly a breadth, 365:25
why h. thou music sadly, 225:30

Heareth, thy servant h., 11:17

Hearing ear and the seeing eye, 22:19
grass grow, 513:9
heard of thee by h. of the ear, 15:25
make passionate my h., 176:30
mentioned in your h., 406:11
nor ear filled with h., 23:34
of a voice, 516:19

Hearings, smallest sights and h., 520:3

Hearken, will not h. to voice of charmers, 17:34

Hearkened, old men h. when he was young, 102:9
to my commandments, 28:13

Hearkeners seldom hear good, 295:19

Hears different drummer, 507:19
ear of him that h., 177:15
him in the wind, 311:5
monarch h., 285:8
neither h. nor sees, 392:1
other mainly h. the No, 364:7
step to music he h., 507:19
sun which h. all things, 52:24
you nearby sweetly speaking, 57:20

Hearse, gilded h., 719:13
marriage h., 374:8
underneath this sable h., 247:12

Heart, a man's h. deviseth his way, 22:1
absence makes h. grow fonder, 104:24
abundance of the h., 35:38
aimed at public's h. hit it in stomach, 682:2
all that mighty h., 392:13
all the h. soul senses, 493:16
all thy h. open, 483:7
although my h. is torn, 442:6
amortization of h. and soul, 738:3
and mind of America, 776:16
and voice oppressed, 511:11
apple rotten at the h., 188:7
apply h. unto my knowledge, 22:27
as he thinketh in his h., 22:35
baseball breaks your h., 833:4
batter my h., 236:11
battlefield h. of man, 525:13
because it is my h., 655:17
because my h. is pure, 482:11
begins to bleed, 856:13
benevolent and kind, 378:17
betray h. that loved her, 391:5
black spot in any h., 540:2
blessed are the pure in h., 33:33
blood around men's h., 69:8
book and h. never part, 296:8
break into flaws, 216:17
bring my aching h. to rest, 89:17
broken and contrite h., 17:30
brute h. of brute like you, 827:16
buildeth on vulgar h., 191:23

Heart (*continued*)

bullets seek out where h. lies, 768:8
burn within us, 40:27
bury my h. at Wounded Knee, 750:10
by sorrow of the h. the spirit is broken, 21:35
can push sea and land, 734:15
candle of understanding in thine h., 31:9
captivate my h., 845:21
caused the widow's h. to sing, 14:37
change of h., 775:5
clean hands and a pure h., 16:19
command my h. and me, 272:6
committed adultery in his h., 34:4
committed adultery in my h., 814:1
congenial to my h., 342:11
consume my h. away, 640:1
counsel of thine own h., 33:4
courage of h., 653:6
create in me a clean h., 17:27
Cruelty has human h., 374:12
cry of Absence in h., 724:10
cutting the h. asunder, 700:8
darkness of man's h., 786:5
darling of my h., 307:23
day breaks not it is my h., 845:1
deep in h. believe, 852:6
departeth from the Lord, 29:17
dispossessed had stopped, 585:7
do not submit in h., 81:21
don't eat your h., 60:3
East and West will pinch h., 734:15
eat thy h., 161:24
endure my h., 55:23
even in laughter the h. is sorrowful, 21:30
everlasting funeral marches round your h., 796:15
every h. prepare room, 304:9
executions hardening the h., 383:2
faint h. ne'er won fair lady, 158:2
faint h. never won fair lady, 565:5
falsehood of the h., 357:11
fear at my h. as at cup, 400:6
fed on truth, 403:18
find Calais lying in my h., 150:11
fire that in h. resides, 528:12
firm as stone, 15:21
followed delight with h. unsatisfied, 125:4
fool hath said in his h., 16:4
for any fate, 466:3
for every fate, 422:26
for h. from itself kept, 567:4
foul rag-and-bone shop of h., 643:2
fresh complexion and h., 229:3
getting rid of work breaks h., 620:7
give a loving h. to thee, 247:16
give lesson to head, 348:11
give me back my h., 420:2
give world another h., 435:20
given h. change of mood, 669:12
gives h. and soul away, 618:12
giving h. to dog to tear, 635:19
glad with all my h., 169:14
gladness of the h., 32:42
glows in every h., 305:15
grant all things your h. desires, 54:22
great thoughts come from h., 333:13

Heart (*continued*)

Greensleeves my h. of gold, 844:1
grieve his h., 221:29
grown cold in vain, 430:13
habitation large enough, 460:7
hands and eyes and h., 421:21
happiness makes h. afraid, 445:17
happy as h. was long, 795:12
happy the h. that sighed, 169:2
hardened Pharaoh's h., 8:12
has hidden treasures, 504:14
has its reasons, 280:1
hatred carried in my own h., 813:4
haven't h. to poke poor Billy, 671:21
he that is of a merry h., 21:36
hear her and beat, 485:12
held h. in hands, 655:17
help by lifting his h., 749:2
here is my h., 590:22
hid in h. of love, 637:2
hide what false h. know, 220:3
high as my h., 199:14
high-erected thoughts in h. of courtesy, 163:19
his h. was going like mad, 696:13
history begins in h. of man or woman, 661:13
hold me in thy h., 207:13
hope deferred maketh h. sick, 21:24
hot within me, 17:11
how but through broken h., 606:1
how dear to this h., 418:13
how h. grows weary, 538:16
human h. by which we live, 393:19
I am sick at h., 200:12
I have h. of a king, 151:13
I told her all my h., 373:8
if h. fails climb not, 160:n2
if h. just frank kindly, 278:10
imagination of man's h., 6:31
in h. and head, 825:19
in h. cold December, 844:9
in h. voice said I want, 796:1
in his pained h., 436:24
in my h. of h., 204:17
in my h. play double part, 765:2
in peril truth drawn from h., 93:8
in the h. or in the head, 189:3
into h. air that kills, 619:3
intoxicated with bliss, 382:7
is a lonely hunter, 606:13
is a treasury, 445:6
is deceitful, 29:18
is harder than stone, 55:24
is Highland, 444:10
is lying still, 392:13
is wounded within me, 19:17
keep green tree in h., 122:26
keep h. when all lost, 490:23
keep thy h. with all diligence, 21:2
keeps open house, 780:2
kindnesses makes h. run over, 355:15
knock at my ribs, 219:5
know truth by the h., 280:2
knoweth own bitterness, 21:29
laid h. open to indifference, 789:13
language of the h., 312:11
lay h. out for my board, 800:16
leaps up, 392:7

Heart *(continued)*

let no man's h. fail, 11:27
let not h. be troubled, 41:26, 41:30
level in her husband's h., 209:22
lies open unto me, 483:7
light of step and h., 662:9
like music on my h., 400:19
like singing bird, 547:14
little body mighty h., 192:25
live without h., 548:11
look in thy h. and write, 163:28
look into your h., 381:16
looked into father's h., 760:4
Lord Christ's h., 453:24
Lord looketh on the h., 11:25
lost h. stiffens, 719:16
love cow with all my h., 599:1
love Lord with h. soul and mind, 36:43
love the Lord with all thine h., 9:30
made h. cry To-day to-day, 661:19
make a stone of h., 639:5
make glad h. of childhood, 573:2
makes your h. warm, 757:13
man after his own h., 11:22
man who's pure in h., 764:3
man's own resinous h. fed, 640:12
May when lusty h. blossom, 139:8
meditation of my h., 16:14
meet mutual h., 318:7
mend the h., 309:14
Mercy has a human h., 372:6
merry h. doeth good, 22:7
merry h. goes all day, 228:24
merry h. maketh cheerful countenance, 21:35
mind is dupe of the h., 273:19
Mind lives on the H., 273:*n*1
mind thousand eyes h. one, 600:14
mine with my h. in it, 230:1
momentary anesthesia of h., 616:4
more knowledge of h. in Richardson's, 327:13
mortality touches the h., 96:34
moved more than with trumpet, 163:27
music in h. I bore, 393:6
must pause to breathe, 423:1
my crown is in my h., 172:30
my h. aches, 437:5
my h. consumed in fire, 125:7
my h. in my mouth, 109:9
my h. is at rest, 372:10
my h. is heavy, 365:12
my h. is not here, 379:6
my h. is pure, 482:11
my h. is sick and sad, 576:10
my h. is wax, 159:7
my h. leaps up, 392:7
my h. rose, 270:12
my h. shall not fear, 16:23
my h. with Oxford men, 697:2
my sad h. foams at stern, 603:7
my true-love hath my h., 163:22
naughtiness of thine h., 11:26
ne'er within him burned, 396:11
never give all h., 637:15
never given in vain, 618:11
never more hollowness of h., 521:11
never say I was false of h., 227:13
new opened, 231:2

no feeling in h. not in every h., 536:9
no island but continent, 167:18
no matter from the h., 208:22
no nor for constant h., 844:22
no wider than h. wide, 734:15
nor h. to report, 182:1
not with Club H. broken, 546:14
not yet has h. or head, 765:3
not your h. away, 618:10
now cracks a noble h., 207:15
O h. if she'd but turn, 637:14
O h. O troubled h., 640:3
obey thy h., 453:8
o'er-fraught h., 221:35
of a king, 151:13
of a lion, 122:28
of an old youngster, 784:10
of animals, 242:9
of bronze, 52:17
of fools, 24:17
of form, 781:1
of lead, 313:18
of man changeth countenance, 32:29
of man depressed, 307:14
of man place devil dwells, 256:2
of Muhammad, 122:13
of my mystery, 205:7
of oak our ships, 335:22
of Russia not forget, 458:17
of stone to read death of Little Nell, 606:4
of uncorrupted good man, 782:4
of wise, 24:17
oh h. oh blood that freezes, 492:11
old darky's h., 602:14
once woman has given h., 297:8
one jot of h. or hope, 263:16
only with h. one can see, 759:4
open my h. and see, 492:13
open unto me, 483:7
out of h. rapture, 591:11
peace at h. of endless agitation, 395:5
penknife in your h., 856:13
pent-up love of h., 592:13
people are good at h., 822:9
Pharaoh's h., 8:12
pierce h. with languor, 590:20
plunges lower than night, 703:14
poor h. would fain deny, 222:11
possessing h. of woman, 657:8
pourest thy full h., 429:16
preaching down daughter's h., 481:21
press thee to my h., 445:2
prithee send back my h., 270:2
quanch my h. trobling, 724:21
razors to my wounded h., 175:14
recoiled at war, 740:2
records of h. in pain, 446:11
recovered greenness, 250:21
red-leaved table of my h., 239:8
replies, 348:10
revolting and rebellious h., 29:4
rise in the h., 482:21
rises I've gladdened lifetime, 802:4
room my h. keeps empty, 249:1
rose in deeps of h., 637:8
rule my h., 449:21
runs away with head, 383:16

sad h. of Ruth, 437:13
savage indignation lacerate h., 299:29
seal upon thine h., 26:3
seared and blighted h., 477:12
secret anniversaries of h., 468:3
secret of freedom a brave h., 74:5
sesoun priketh every gentil h., 135:17
set my poor h. free, 212:*n*1
set not h. upon goods, 32:5
sets my h. a-clickin', 596:8
sets my h. to fluttering, 57:20
Shakespeare unlocked h., 395:19
shaped like valentine, 797:2
Shot straighter to H., 545:20
sick at h., 200:12
simple frugal h., 701:8
sound as bell, 194:30
soured kindness in my h., 219:*n*1
spring of love gushed from h., 400:13
squirrel's h. beat, 513:9
steady of h., 396:6
stick the h. of falsehood, 208:7
stirred h. of Englishman, 649:16
stop H. from breaking, 546:1
strike mine eyes but not my h., 237:16
strong and diverse h., 750:11
stubborn h. shall fare evil, 31:31
stuff which weighs upon h., 222:12
summer to your h., 735:6
superior have best h., 554:3
Sweeping up the H., 546:8
sweet to excess, 4:4
take beak from out my h., 479:7
that fed, 427:18
that loveth nought in May, 133:8
there will your h. be also, 34:13
there's where h. turning, 538:15
thing that eats h., 771:5
thinks tongue speaks, 194:30
though h. still as loving, 423:1
thou'll break my h., 378:21
through fire for kind h., 190:30
thy breast encloseth my h., 173:33
tickleth me aboute myn h. roote, 136:13
tiger's h. in player's hide, 165:18
tiger's h. in woman's hide, 172:24
Time laid hand on my h., 467:19
to conceive, 360:9
to mind shameful to h. beauty, 525:13
too soon made glad, 491:10
too tender or too firm h., 309:28
took all h. for speech, 638:15
trusteth in his own h., 23:17
turned to stone, 214:20
unchristened h., 641:11
unfortified, 200:31
unquiet h. and brain, 483:15
untraveled turns to thee, 340:15
vacant h. hand eye, 397:27
venting a heavy h., 521:4
verities and truths of h., 748:19
visit my sad h., 196:7
want of thought and h., 445:19
war in his h., 17:33
warm and gay, 744:3
warm h. within, 348:14
was one which most enamor, 423:3
waters of the h., 795:3

Heart *(continued)*

way to h. through stomach, 489:7
weaned h. from low desires, 143:11
wear h. upon my sleeve, 212:18
weeping in my h., 590:21
wet eye dhry h., 646:9
what dungeon dark as h., 460:18
what female h. gold despise, 334:3
what missing at the man's h., 792:17
what stronger breastplate than h., 172:12
when my h. hath 'scaped, 227:2
when to h. of man, 668:16
where h. lies brain lie, 494:1
which beats only for you, 590:22
whole h. is faint, 26:7
wine that maketh glad the h., 19:9
wisdom of head and h., 498:24
wisdom to believe h., 629:1
wise and understanding h., 12:11
with h. in hand, 489:3
with my whole h., 29:24
with rue h. laden, 619:6
with whole h. listen, 690:1
withered h., 766:18
woman whose h. is snares, 24:23
woman with the h., 483:3
words shall be in thine h., 9:30
wound h. that's broken, 397:17
wounded is wounding h., 272:13
Heartache, by sleep we end h., 203:33
Heartbreak, better chiding than h., 191:5
Hotel, 831:16
Heartburn, I am h., 588:5
Hearth, by this still h., 481:7
clean-winged h., 468:18
clear fire clean h., 407:13
cricket on the h., 260:5
no more blazing h., 334:13
woman for the h., 483:3
Hearths, their country their h., 95:8
Hearthstone, fox build nest on h., 658:*n*3
of hell best bed, 658:*n*3
Heartily know when half-gods go, 453:9
Heart-leaves of lilac all over New England,
672:14
Heart-revealing intimacy, 639:9
Heart's affections, 439:13
burst hot h. shell, 516:14
desire, 16:15
Desire, 472:5, 637:7
desires be with you, 197:28
his h. his mouth, 224:28
lose h. desire, 609:21
my h. in the Highlands, 379:6
my h. right there, 674:2
my h. undoing, 412:4
red h. core, 436:14
supreme ambition, 329:23
wear him in my h. core, 204:17
Hearts, affect h. and minds, 733:1
all that human h. endure, 325:3
and minds, 51:2
apply our h. unto wisdom, 18:23
as pure and fair, 564:20
beauty that breaks h., 676:16
blind h., 92:20
cash-boxes for h., 445:10
cause that makes hard h., 217:6
cheerful h. now broken, 412:7

Hearts *(continued)*

cherish h. that hate thee, 231:7
cleanse thoughts of our h., 50:16
come not to steal away h., 197:3
Country cherished in h., 487:5
day star arise in your h., 47:34
dry as summer dust, 395:4
ensanguined h., 348:6
find agonies strife of human h., 436:3
finite h. that yearn, 492:14
first in h. of countrymen, 371:8
given our h. away, 394:18
high in people's h., 195:28
hoard little h. great, 485:21
hugest h. that break, 546:16
human h. to chew, 429:13
in imagination of their h., 38:39
in love use own tongues, 194:18
in retiring draw h., 268:19
itch grows old in sick h., 113:13
keep your h. and minds, 45:37
keeps their h. vacuous, 58:9
kind h. more than coronets, 480:14
Knave of H., 858:7
Lord dwelt in people's h., 280:13
Lord searcheth all h., 13:10
mercy enthroned in h. of kings, 189:19
minds and h. of depressed, 804:20
neither have h. to stay, 271:29
new heraldry hands not h., 214:16
not had as gift are earned, 639:11
not their h. that roam, 634:16
of controversy, 195:19
of oak, 146:16
of the noble may be turned, 53:18
our h. all with thee, 466:20
our h. are broken, 838:13
palsied h., 529:12
pluck their h. from them, 193:17
queen in people's h., 842:9
Queen of H., 858:7
rain falls in h., 752:11
servitude can pierce our h., 715:8
shutting away of loving h., 735:11
somewhere h. are light, 630:4
steel my soldiers' h., 193:17
that beat as one, 464:7
that roam, 634:16
their bursting h. despond, 423:20
their h. not grown old, 638:12
though stout and brave, 466:1
thousand h. beat happily, 420:16
tight hot cell of h., 748:1
touched with heed, 577:16
true plain h., 233:12
union of hands and h., 274:18
union of h., 451:23
unto whom all h. are open, 50:16
what we do not doubt in h., 574:2
what your h. have amassed, 120:15
while your h. are yearning, 663:1
wine unto those of heavy h., 23:26
with your hands your h., 173:6
wore at h. the fire's center, 783:16
write upon h. of men, 381:9
Heartsease, infinite h., 193:15
Heart-sick hand workers, 557:5
Heartstrings are a lute, 478:*n*1
though jesses my dear h., 214:2

Heart-whole, warrant him h., 199:26
Hearty, hand that is honest and h., 395:22
humble and h. thanks, 50:8
old man, 405:9
Heat as mode of motion, 523:20
burden and h. of day, 36:36
cannot pass from colder, 532:13
cold and h., 6:32
crime to examine laws of h., 572:3
fantastic summer's h., 179:6
fear no more h. o' the sun, 225:23
flow from hot to cold object, 532:*n*1
he makes h. as he wishes, 4:6
if you can't stand h., 705:6
I'll shade him from h., 372:3
mechanical equivalent of h., 583:3
neither h. affection limb, 211:19
neither sun light on them nor h., 48:25
not furnace for foe, 230:20
not see when h. cometh, 29:17
not snow nor rain nor h., 71:24
one draught above h., 209:7
one h. drive out another, 165:5
Promethean h., 215:7
race not without h., 262:23
surprised was I with sudden h., 168:26
there is nothing hid from the h., 16:11
which made my heart to glow, 168:26
Heated in the chase, 294:7
Heath and harebells, 509:4
best felt not clearly seen, 574:18
brown h. and shaggy wood, 396:12
foot on my native h., 397:25
in the desert, 29:17
Heathcliff, go on H. run away, 740:22
I am H., 509:3
Heathen Chinee is peculiar, 566:12
human form in h. turk or jew, 372:7
in his blindness, 416:5
pore benighted h., 633:9
why do the h. rage, 15:28
Heather, know how H. looks, 546:6
Heaths, game on these lone h., 410:13
Heating, warm without h., 306:17
Heat-oppressed brain, 220:8
Heave away heave away, 862:5
Heaven about to confer great office, 82:17
above road below, 599:11
all h. around us, 412:3
all H. before mine eyes, 260:10
all hell that is not h., 170:21
all I ask h. above, 599:11
all places distant from h. alike, 241:11
all things in h., 45:40
all this and h. too, 295:26
all we hope in H., 477:10
alone given away, 514:15
and Charing Cross, 621:8
and earth pass away, 37:10
and earth to witness, 9:28
and future's sakes, 670:6
and home, 395:18
and nature sing, 304:9
angels in H. above, 479:19
as it is in h., 34:11
as the h. is high, 19:6
ascended into h., 50:3
attacking h. and earth, 825:7
blazing into head, 642:7

Heaven *(continued)*

bottom line is in h., 782:13
bread of h., 19:12
brightest h. of invention, 192:15
by h. I do love, 177:2
call h. and earth to witness, 9:28
clear religion of h., 436:10
combined essences of h. and earth, 89:14
confess yourself to h., 205:26
court it in shape of h., 202:17
crawling between h. and earth, 204:4
dances in sight of h., 809:1
did recompense send, 335:3
doors of h. adjacent identical, 701:11
down the abandoned h., 707:15
each goes own byway to h., 295:2
earth and high h., 619:4
earth nigher h. than now, 491:5
earth's crammed with h., 464:5
endures, 620:3
enter into kingdom of h., 35:10, 36:28
eye of h. to garnish, 178:14
eye sees open h., 382:7
farewells as stars in h., 208:16
farther off from h., 445:16
finds means to kill joys, 184:19
floor of h. is inlaid, 190:5
four winds of the h., 30:34
from h. did hie, 844:3
gained from H., 335:3
gate of h., 7:16
gems of h. starry train, 266:18
gentle rain from h., 189:19
getting to H. at last, 544:18
gives its favorites, 83:n6
glance from h. to earth, 182:3
God created h. and earth, 5:9
God is in h., 24:11
God's in his h., 491:2
going forth is from the end of the h., 16:11
gold bar of H., 541:26
great eye of h., 161:1
had made her such a man, 212:32
harbingers to h., 258:5
has no rage, 300:22
have ye souls in h., 438:9
hell I suffer seems a h., 266:3
helps not men who will not act, 61:n1
hills whose heads touch h., 212:30
his blessed part to h., 231:10
hours to which H. chime, 278:29
how long permit to H., 268:11
humbler h., 311:5
husbandry in h., 220:5
if earth be shadow of h., 267:7
if H. looked on riches, 298:11
if I ascend up into h., 20:13
if I cannot bend H., 98:5
in h. perfect round, 494:4
in Hell's despair, 374:1
in which no horses, 601:1
is above all yet, 230:28
is he in h., 636:3
is love, 396:9
it smells to h., 205:14
itself points out hereafter, 301:26
itself we seek in our folly, 99:4
itself would stoop to her, 261:12

Heaven *(continued)*

keys of kingdom of h., 36:25
kingdom of h. is at hand, 33:23
kingdom of h. like a net, 36:8
kingdom of h. like mustard seed, 36:6
kingdom of H. within you, 117:5
knows how to put price, 354:10
lay up treasures in h., 34:12
leave her to h., 202:20
leave the rest to h., 257:5
leaving mercy to h., 322:6
let justice be done though h. fall, 123:26
lies about us in infancy, 393:11
lift my soul to h., 230:23
light from h., 378:3
like egg earth like yolk, 114:13
Lord of h. and earth, 42:18
love is h., 396:9
made h. and earth,19:30
made thee neither of h. nor of earth, 142:1
majesty of H., 318:15
make a h. of hell, 264:7
make face of h. so fine, 183:32
Maker of h. and earth, 50:3
makes h. drowsy with harmony, 177:7
man is as H. made him, 157:29
marriages made in h., 163:18
matches made in h., 147:n9
measuring earth and h., 78:10
met my dearest foe in h., 201:10
more things in h. and earth, 202:26, 733:10
mount up to h., 19:15
near h. by sea as by land, 154:11
needs such men more than H. does, 356:16
new h. and new earth, 48:38
no humor in h., 562:3
not enter into kingdom of h., 36:28
not h. if we knew what it were, 270:5
not h. itself upon past has power, 284:7
nurseries of H., 620:16
of whales in waters, 707:20
offspring of h. firstborn, 265:24
on earth, 266:6
open face of h., 435:17
or near it, 429:16
ordinances of h., 63:27
our Father which art in h., 34:11
parting all we know of h., 547:3
peep through blanket, 219:12
Persian's h. easily made, 412:6
places eye of h. visits, 179:4
plays such tricks before h., 211:13
presents the solid hue, 669:10
prove that I and she ride together, 492:21
puts all H. in rage, 375:6
rains pennies from H., 778:5
reach port of h., 473:10
rejects the lore, 395:16
remembrance fallen from h., 568:1
rich man enther H., 646:11
ring bells of H., 656:10
same world hell h., 454:1
see h. in wildflower, 375:5
see h. open, 40:37
sends love of her, 4:1

Heaven *(continued)*

serve in h., 264:8
short arm to reach to H., 621:10
silent finger points to h., 395:7
sincerity the way of h., 82:4
single Dram of H., 547:2
smells to h., 205:14
so he goes to h., 205:15
some call it Tree of H., 770:3
spark from h., 529:10
spark from H. immortal, 381:8
spirit that fought in h., 264:26
star of unascended h., 428:11
starry cope of h., 266:28
stay the bottles of h., 15:12
steep and thorny way to h., 201:23
strange interesting astonishing grotesque, 562:22
such grace did lend her, 176:12
summons thee to h. or hell, 220:11
Sun drives Night from H., 470:13
swear neither by h. nor earth, 34:5
symbol of power of H., 714:23
take my soul, 178:21
tasted eternal joys of H., 170:19
tell little Greek to go to h., 113:5
thank h. fasting, 199:20
that leads men to hell, 227:22
theirs is the kingdom of h., 33:33
then Summer Then H. of God, 545:7
therefore doth h. divide, 192:20
things are sons of h., 324:14
though h. fall thy will be done, 124:22
though h. may perish, 385:n5
till h. and earth pass, 34:3
to be young was very h., 391:11
to gaudy day denies, 422:13
to h. being gone, 235:9
to throne in, 225:1
toward H. advancing, 381:8
treasure in h., 36:33
treasures in h., 34:12
trouble deaf h., 226:5
under feet as well as over heads, 507:13
unextinguishable laugh in h., 256:23
unfolds both h. and earth, 180:20
vain war with h., 264:25
visited in h., 546:6
war in h., 48:28
watered h. with tears, 374:6
way to h. of like length, 154:n4
what's a h. for, 493:4
when h. was falling, 619:17
wherever bright sun of h., 231:17
which giant Atlas upholds, 70:5
who know h. save by heaven's gift, 107:14
who sword of h. will bear, 211:29
will most incorrect to h., 200:31
will protect working girl, 613:3
wind from blue h. blows, 363:16
winds of h. visit face roughly, 201:3
winged seraphs of h., 479:18
wished Hell for ease from H., 376:3
with all splendors lie, 514:14
with the company of h., 50:19
words never to h. go, 205:17

Heaven-born band, 390:13
child, 258:17

Heaven-bred poesy, 176:11
Heaven-gates not so arched, 244:8
Heaven-kissing hill, 205:21
Heavenly blessings without number, 304:4
    can h. minds yield, 96:24
    caught my h. jewel, 164:1
    city formed by love of God, 119:22
    connection, 817:12
    Father disappointed in monkey, 562:15
    fools by h. compulsion, 215:29
    gift of poesy, 284:11
    harmony, 284:13
    paradise is that place, 232:5
    pen wherewith thou h. sing, 395:*n3*
    Powers, 363:15
    princes like to h. bodies, 167:24
    race demands zeal, 318:12
    refuse h. mansion, 641:4
    remove weight from h. bodies, 811:11
    rhetoric of thine eye, 177:3
    Rosalind, 197:32
    things h. or things earthly, 281:22
Heaven-rescued land, 411:2
Heaven's, against h. hand, 263:16
    all-gracious King, 488:15
    at h. gates claps wings, 163:16
    blue H. height, 592:15
    breath smells wooingly, 219:15
    cherubin horsed, 219:18
    command, 318:8
    despite, 374:2
    eternal King, 258:16
    eternal year is thine, 284:10
    glories shine, 509:1
    godfathers of h. lights, 176:20
    great lamps do dive, 231:21
    in h. high bower, 372:8
    lark at h. gate sings, 225:12
    last best gift, 267:1
    light forever shines, 430:17
    my destination, 749:13
    net is indeed vast, 59:17
    nothing situate under h. eye, 174:27
    own sweet will H. will, 639:15
    patio h. watercourse, 752:13
    riches of h. pavement, 264:22
    study like h. glorious sun, 176:20
    success found, 492:23
    sugar cake, 292:10
    vaults should crack, 218:5
    wide pathless way, 260:3
Heavens, ancient h., 394:12
    clothed with h., 290:1
    declare glory of God, 16:10
    distorts the h., 376:9
    fill with commerce, 481:23
    fill with shouting, 481:23
    flaming walls of h., 92:10
    God light of h. and earth, 121:21
    hung be h. with black, 171:11
    let justice be done though h. fall, 123:*n7*
    new h. and a new earth, 28:36
    oh h., 824:6
    offered this trust to h., 122:6
    potentates blazing in h., 65:3
    pure as naked h., 393:4
    rejoice in motion, 235:19
    show h. more just, 216:27
    sing ye h. earth reply, 322:23

Heavens *(continued)*
    spangled h., 301:14
    starry h. above me, 339:4
    thank h. sun gone in, 636:12
    themselves blaze forth, 196:9
    themselves the planets, 207:24
    when I consider thy h., 15:32
Heavens' embroidered cloths, 637:11
Heaviest ore of the body, 707:12
Heaviness, drama not of h. but of lightness,
    823:13
    foolish son the h. of his mother, 21:14
    garment of praise for spirit of h., 28:31
    that's gone, 230:15
Heaving up my either hand, 248:20
Heavy, advance of a h. truck, 815:16
    as yonder stone, 696:16
    change now thou art gone, 261:17
    eyelids h. and red, 446:2
    laden, 35:35
    light gains make h. purses, 165:2
    light wife h. husband, 190:11
    my heart is h., 365:12
    steps of plowman, 637:8
    toward school with h. looks, 183:12
    venting a h. heart, 521:4
    weight of world, 391:1
    wine unto those of h. hearts, 23:26
Hebraism strictness of conscience, 531:19
Hebrew, aside from few odd words in H.,
    668:13
    called in H. Armageddon, 48:34
Hebrides, in dreams behold H., 444:10
    stormy H., 262:3, 318:5
Hecate's, black H. summons, 221:6
    pale H. offerings, 220:9
Hector is dead, 208:23
    when H. was pup, 848:2
Hecuba, what's H. to him, 203:28
Hedge, divinity cloth h. a king, 206:10
    over h. before stile, 156:16
    pull not down your h., 251:12
Hedge-crickets sing, 438:13
Hedgehog knows one great thing, 56:22
Hedgehogs, belongs to the h., 782:3
    thorny h., 181:15
Heed, I will take h. to my ways, 17:10
    rumble of distant Drum, 471:6
    take h. lest he fall, 44:11
    take h. of loving me, 235:11
    ye who lead take h., 652:2
Heedless, earth's h. sons, 745:14
    ran my h. ways, 795:12
Heejous, creature of h. mien, 646:6
Heel, bids it come to h., 716:19
    coat from h. to throat, 638:10
    Europe under his h., 666:13
    of courtier, 206:23
    of Northeast Trade, 634:6
    on throat of my song, 738:4
    pain of bone spur in h., 755:3
    thou shalt bruise his h., 6:8
    tread upon another's h., 206:*n2*
Heels, at his h. a stone, 206:5
    follow truth too near h., 160:12
    fortune grow out at h., 216:9
    from h. up to head, 598:23
    gunpowder out at h., 336:12
    horses' h. over paving, 719:22

Heels *(continued)*
    out at h., 190:18
    over head and h., 94:8
    small war on h. of small war, 801:17
    time wounds all h., 770:4
    took to my h., 89:10
Heft of Cathedral Tunes, 544:15
Hegemony protected by armor of coercion,
    731:6
Heifer, if ye had not plowed with my h., 11:2
    lowing at skies, 438:3
Heifer's, false as wolf to h. calf, 208:7
Heigho the derry oh, 861:4
Height, asks of us certain h., 671:3
    depths of h., 740:9
    happiness makes up in h., 670:13
    my soul can reach, 463:17
    none can usurp h., 439:12
    nor depth, 43:12
    objects in an airy h., 296:17
    smiles from h. at me, 774:1
    stretch for greatness and h., 165:10
    worth's unknown although h. taken,
      227:17
Heights, dwell on h. of mankind, 382:11
    topped wind-swept h. with grace, 810:11
    towering h. of hills, 500:8
Heill, I that in h. wes and gladness, 142:4
Heine, Heinrich H. loosened corsets of
    German, 672:8
Heir as great in admiration as herself, 231:16
    grandchild h. of the first, 238:17
    great h. of fame, 259:3
    of all the ages, 482:7
    of mongrel bitch, 216:7
    that flesh is h. to, 203:33
    yourself sole h. of world, 290:1
Heirs, joint h. with Christ, 43:5
    of all eternity, 176:17
    of God, 43:5
Held, things she h. against missionaries,
    812:6
Helen brought her dowry destruction, 65:6
    did not board the ships, 57:12
    great suffering all for H., 759:14
    Leda mother of H., 573:6
    like another H., 285:14
    sweet H. make me immortal, 170:23
    threw into wine a drug, 54:19
    thy beauty is to me, 478:2
Helen's beauty in brow of Egypt, 182:3
    dawn in H. arms, 641:16
    dust hath closed H. eye, 232:9
Helican, damned if I see how h., 685:9
Helicon, muses of H., 56:1
    shepherding below holy H., 56:2
    watered our horses in H., 165:13
Helix, double h. structure, 822:2
Hell, agreement with h., 462:6
    all h. broke loose, 266:26
    all h. stir for this, 193:24
    all we need of h., 547:3
    better to reign in h., 264:8
    black as h., 228:7
    characters of h. to trace, 335:12
    citizens want to go to H. I will help,
      578:16
    city much like London, 429:9
    cunning livery of h., 211:22

Hell *(continued)*

curse of h. frae me, 853:22
do it so feels like h., 827:10
each bears his own H., 97:30
easy to go down into H., 97:23
England h. of horses, 162:9
entertained great scorn of H., 130:21
failure in great object, 436:6
fight like h. for living, 547:12
followed with him, 48:20
full of good intentions, 126:9
full of good meanings, 251:16
full of musical amateurs, 609:19
gates of h. not prevail, 36:25
give 'em h., 417:21
God holds you over pit of h., 318:16
got a h. of a beating, 703:6
halls of h., 709:10
hath no limits, 170:20
hearthstone of h. best bed, 658:*n*3
heaven that leads men to h., 227:22
hot as h., 369:9
I love this cultured h., 729:12
I myself am h., 801:7
I oft wished for H., 376:3
I shall move H., 98:5
I suffer seems a heaven, 266:3
I'm mad as h., 811:12
in Heaven's despite, 374:2
in h. roast like herrin, 380:2
into mouth of h., 485:2
is he in h., 636:3
is other people, 772:8
is to love no longer, 716:12
itself breathes out, 205:12
keys of h. and death, 48:7
lead apes in h., 175:27
liberated the h. out of place, 851:22
limbecks foul as h., 227:18
madness risen from h., 568:1
make a heaven of h., 264:7
make my bed in h., 20:13
more devils than h. hold, 182:3
myself am h., 266:3
never married that's his h., 241:4
no fury like woman scorned, 300:22
of a good universe, 740:15
of nuclear destruction, 823:8
old age is woman's h., 276:6
on earth, 609:16
out of h. leads to light, 265:11
passage broad to h., 85:*n*1
paved with good intentions, 126:*n*4,
251:*n*1
paved with priests' skulls, 119:2
pour milk of concord into h., 221:34
print news and raise h., 848:11
procuress to Lords of H., 484:1
Puritan's idea of H., 555:*n*3
raise less corn more h., 597:11
rebellious h., 205:23
reign in h., 264:8
riches grow in h., 264:23
rising from thousand thrones, 478:7
road to H. gradual, 752:4
same world h. heaven, 454:1
served my time in h., 851:20
spinach and the h. with it, 756:9
summons thee to heaven or h., 220:11

Hell *(continued)*

take curtains, 703:8
tell him to go to h., 417:23
this is h. nor am I out, 170:19
though h. bar way, 692:3
till H. freezes, 852:4
to h. with it, 816:1
tyranny like h., 354:10
very respectable H., 648:6
walked eye-deep in h., 709:4
war is h., 522:14
way I fly is h., 266:3
we make ourselves, 581:10
wedlock forced a h., 172:3
what h. in suing long, 161:23
what I call h., 761:9
what in h. have i done, 680:7
when one is in h., 316:4
where h. is there must we be, 170:20
where we are is h., 170:20
whip all h. yet, 522:*n*5
whole body not be cast into h., 34:4
with h. are we at agreement, 27:22
with work which bores you life is h.,
648:15
within him, 266:1
within myself, 256:2
wrote of Devils and H., 372:13
Hellas, confounded H., 74:10
of Hellas, 69:*n*1
Hellenes, boy is most powerful of H., 64:20
Hellenism spontaneity of consciousness,
531:19
Hellespont, Propontic and H., 214:15
Hell-kite, O h., 222:1
Hello darkness my old friend, 837:7
sucker, 704:1
Hell's broke loose in Georgia, 750:8
broken loose, 165:20
concave, 264:15
despair, 374:1
fear o' h. a hangman's whip, 242:*n*1
Hells, tormented with ten thousand h.,
170:19
Helm, everyone prepared to take h., 540:13
hold h. when sea calm, 103:6
Pleasure at the h., 335:13
Helmet and the plume, 480:26
for h. the hope of salvation, 46:11
now hive for bees, 164:10
Helmets gleamed in forests, 534:9
Help, a little h. from my friends, 835:4
a very present h. in trouble, 17:21
between hindrance and h., 392:5
cannot h. or pardon, 775:8
could not hope for h., 776:11
encumbers him with h., 326:10
feeble up, 218:10
for living hope for dead, 554:5
from whence cometh my h., 19:30
George can't h. it, 828:11
go love without the h., 376:2
God our h. in ages past, 304:6
God's h. and their valor, 388:5
her and that right early, 17:22
here I stand God h. me, 144:7
into Macedonia and h. us, 42:15
man endure, 749:2
man is without h., 772:7

Help *(continued)*

me down Cemetery Road, 810:5
mutual h. as often as warfare, 757:6
my h. cometh from the Lord, 19:30
no h. came, 776:11
nothing will h., 741:10
of the helpless, 432:5
one fainting Robin, 546:1
only h. her to know, 791:6
others out of fellow-feeling, 240:1
past hope past cure past h., 184:8
since there's no h., 169:14
them that help themselves, 61:5
thou mine unbelief, 38:27
thyself, 61:*n*1
to half-a-crown, 575:18
to h. or do no harm, 72:17
use treatment to h. sick, 72:16
what's gone past h., 228:18
when no h. in truth, 65:5
with h. of janitor, 756:5
with h. of surgeon recover, 182:12
Helped every one his neighbor, 28:9
to hansom outside, 773:18
Helper, Lord is my h., 47:5
Helpers fail and comforts flee, 432:5
Helpful, noble be man h. and good, 363:13
Helping, God h. me I can do no other,
144:*n*2
men to practice virtue, 81:22
so far from h. me, 16:16
Helpless before the iron, 791:6
justice without strength is h., 280:3
man in ignorance sedate, 324:9
naked piping loud, 374:10
rendered United States h., 611:6
test of civilization way cares for h., 733:8
Helpmeet, make him an h., 5:20
Helps, art h. old ladies across street, 824:5
fortune h. the brave, 89:11
God h. them that help selves, 319:17
God h. those who get up early, 862:15
Hemisphere, extend system to this h., 377:1
Hemispheres, where find two better h.,
233:12
Hemlock I had drunk, 437:5
snow from h. tree, 669:12
Hemlocks, murmuring pines and h., 466:16
Hemmed, since I have h. thee here, 173:20
Hemp, molders h. and steel, 397:22
Hempen, sing in a h. string, 242:15
Hen, as h. gathereth chickens, 37:5
cackles as if laid asteroid, 561:23
egg's way of making egg, 558:8
eggs do not teach h., 861:19
has right to set, 555:12
homely h. lays one, 849:16
laid an egg, 699:15
marsh h. secretly builds, 583:10
my black h., 860:2
my white h., 860:*n*1
two owls and h., 499:11
yard in printing house, 709:7
Hence all you vain delights, 243:5
endure their going h., 217:32
horrible shadow, 221:15
loathed Melancholy, 259:7
stay far h. you prudes, 105:4
these tears, 88:11

Hence *(continued)*
 vain deluding joys, 259:22
 with denial vain, 261:15
 ye profane, 275:16
Henna hackles halt, 686:20
Henpecked, fraternity of h., 302:21
 you all, 423:6
Henroosts, defend ourselves and h., 507:25
Henry, never did H. end anyone, 792:9
 pried open for all to see, 792:6
 unappeasable H. sulked, 792:5
Hens, milk-white H. of Dorking, 500:5
Hent, merrily h. the stile-a, 228:24
Heraclitus, told me H. dead, 534:3
 your death H., 85:14
Herald, hark the h. angels sing, 323:1
 Homer h. of your glory, 83:8
 lark h. of the morn, 184:4
 Morning Star h. of dawn, 90:6
 of tomorrow, 632:4
 owl night's h., 173:23
 silence perfectest h. of joy, 194:20
 station like h. Mercury, 205:21
 three years we waited for h., 759:5
Herald Square, remember me to H.,
 679:10
Heraldry, boast of h., 334:15
 new h. hands not hearts, 214:16
Herb, dew bespangling h. and tree, 248:16
Herba, latet anguis in h., 95:*n*14
Herbs and trees flourish in May, 139:8
 better is a dinner of h., 21:36
 bitter h., 8:17
 bread with bitter h., 513:2
 Medea gathered enchanted h., 190:4
 men with h. to smoke, 140:5
 of every joyous kind, 121:19
Hercules and Goth bequeathed us, 574:9
 behind Gates of H., 579:8
 from the foot H., 71:18
 let H. do what he may, 207:4
 not H. but Superman, 826:16
 snakes beside cradle of H., 536:14
Herd, avoid reeking h., 710:6
 groups individuals lack h. sense, 711:4
 hate the common h., 99:26
 Hesperus you h. homeward, 58:6
 imitators you slavish h., 101:11
 lowing h. wind slowly, 334:8
 of elephant traveling, 706:6
 ran into sea, 38:22
Herds, flocks or h. or human face, 265:25
Herdsman, God the h. goads, 636:21
Herdsmen, bad h. ruin flocks, 55:16
Here a little child I stand, 248:20
 a little there a little, 27:21
 a sheer hulk, 362:11
 am I, 11:16
 am I send me, 26:26
 and h. I am, 818:5
 and now cease to matter, 721:6
 and now is happiness, 701:8
 but I'm h., 839:3
 comes the trout, 209:28
 from h. to Eternity, 633:17
 gone h. and there, 227:15
 he lies where he longed, 599:6
 I am and here I stay, 469:1
 I have been h. before, 542:7

Here *(continued)*
 I know you are h., 836:2
 I stand, 144:7
 in the body pent, 396:1
 is God's plenty, 285:24
 is my space, 222:27
 is no water, 718:21
 it can't happen h., 708:8
 Kilroy was h., 749:4, 851:17
 Lafayette we are h., 620:11
 lies a King that ruled, 253:12
 lies a truly honest man, 272:19
 lies lady of beauty, 724:12
 lies Matthew Prior, 297:7
 lies my wife let her lie, 285:28
 no intelligent life down h., 852:21
 reason can decide nothing h., 279:23
 rests his head, 335:2
 thou ailest h. and h., 528:15
 today gone tomorrow, 290:22
 where wind north-northeast, 652:9
 where world is quiet, 568:25
Hereafter, heaven points out h., 301:26
 she should have died h., 222:16
 what is love 'tis not h., 209:14
 what may come h., 569:1
Hereditary, virtue is not h., 354:8
Here's looking at you kid, 782:9
Heresies, no h. in dead religion, 650:2
 truths begin as h., 537:12
Heresy lifeblood of religions, 650:2
 overcome h. with fire, 144:6
Heretic that makes the fire, 228:16
 they will proclaim me h., 142:8
Heretics, faith begets h., 650:2
Heritage, guided by my h., 839:1
 I have a goodly h., 16:7
 of woe, 422:12
 proud of ancient h., 799:7
 what thou lovest thy true h., 709:10
 youth's h., 494:11
Hermit crab whale's backbone, 721:8
 dwell a weeping h., 336:16
 old h. of Prague, 210:16
 poor in place obscure, 159:21
 shall I like a h. dwell, 160:10
Hermitage, give palace for h., 180:4
 take that for h., 276:4
Hermon, heights of H., 680:1
Hern, coot and h., 485:3
Hero, A H. of Our Time, 502:1
 basic h. of books labor, 649:5
 conquering h. comes, 318:19
 Conqueror Worm, 478:15
 every h. becomes bore, 456:17
 keeps getting in bed with women,
  736:2
 killed h. in man, 772:2
 millions a h., 349:2
 must drink brandy, 328:20
 of course Alexander h., 472:17
 perish or sparrow fall, 311:3
 show me a h., 746:17
 to his valet, 257:1
 Truth h. of my tale, 542:8
Herod, born in the days of H., 33:18
 out-herods H., 204:11
 Salome pleased H., 36:11
 should not return to H., 33:19

Herodias, daughter of H. danced, 36:11
Heroes as well as idealists, 577:17
 blood of our h., 358:13
 broods on her shining h., 444:12
 created by popular demand, 729:5
 hail ye h., 390:13
 hand in hand with my h., 472:22
 if we will, 528:4
 many valiant souls of h., 52:1
 peers h. of old, 494:19
 seeds of patriots and h., 340:*n*1
 statesmen philosophers, 361:14
 thanks to our fallen h., 789:9
 thin red h., 633:7
 thin red line of h., 522:*n*4
 were plenty, 849:3
 world's brave h., 846:11
Heroic decision not from cowards, 726:9
 for earth too hard, 494:5
 giving man h. fiber, 566:22
 little monkey, 470:6
 obstacle to being h., 460:20
 pleasures of h. poesy, 257:18
 poem a biography, 434:12
 sires, 289:14
 systematically h., 581:9
 womanhood, 467:9
Heroically mad, 283:20
Heroism endurance for moment more,
 591:10
 feels never reasons, 455:31
 labor matter of h., 686:2
 truest h. to resist doubt, 460:20
 vices fathered by h., 718:4
Héros pour les valets de chambre, 257:*n*1
Herring, fish nor flesh nor good red h.,
 148:3
 in hell roast like h., 380:2
Herrings, not stored in barrel like salt h.,
 789:7
 red h., 857:7
Herself, show me someone not full of h.,
 838:2
Hertford Hereford Hampshire, 803:9
Herz, mein H. ist schwer, 365:*n*5
 und wenn das H. auch bricht, 442:*n*3
Hesiod, Homer and H. attributed to gods,
 61:20
 might have kept his breath, 56:25
 taught H. beauteous song, 56:2
Hesitate and falter life away, 529:10
 dislike, 312:4
Hesitation, doubt h. pain, 491:24
 wager without h. that He is, 279:23
Hesper loves to lead home, 619:16
Hesperian, apple-bearing H. coast, 70:5
Hesperides, we shall find H., 707:6
Hesperus entreats thy light, 237:10
 it was schooner H., 466:4
 that led the starry host, 266:16
 you herd homeward, 58:6
Hessians, yonder are the H., 343:11
Heterodoxy another man's doxy, 317:11
 Thy-doxy, 434:4
Hew, not h. as carcass, 196:3
 somebody to h. and hack, 271:5
Hewers of wood, 10:23
Hewing wood for master carpenter,
 59:18

History *(continued)*
　has cunning passages, 718:3
　has yet to be enacted, 521:12
　hear by tale or h., 180:19
　immediate context of h., 735:17
　in all men's lives, 191:37
　incomprehensible without Jesus, 535:8
　influence of sea power on h., 576:11
　interior h. never be written, 521:14
　invented h., 317:8
　is more or less bunk, 530:*n*1
　is now and England, 722:3
　is on our side, 741:7
　is philosophy learned from examples,
　　104:17
　knows no plateaus, 812:11
　language the archives of h., 456:9
　lawyer without h. a mechanic, 397:19
　let h. answer question, 358:11
　life of peoples, 542:17
　like writing h. with lightning, 611:13
　love the h. of woman's life, 385:12
　Mississippi of falsehood H., 530:13
　must be false, 304:18
　no h. only biography, 455:5
　no law of h., 517:13
　of an art, 709:12
　of country begins in heart, 661:13
　of liberty history of safeguards, 695:6
　of masterwork not failures, 709:12
　of our race, 667:2
　of progress of human liberty, 509:13
　of society history of class struggles,
　　511:1
　of soldier's wound, 332:13
　ought to judge past, 441:8
　page of h. worth volume of logic,
　　578:18
　pattern of timeless moments, 722:3
　people never learned from h., 390:4
　people without h., 722:3, 855:16
　periodization of European h., 757:4
　Persons About to Write H., 554:13
　poetry more philosophic than h., 81:12
　portrayal of crimes and misfortunes,
　　316:20
　progress of freedom, 390:7
　proof of theories, 554:15
　psychology long past short h., 596:22
　read h. aright, 455:4
　read h. in nation's eyes, 334:22
　register of crimes, 353:8
　revolution in natural h., 470:1
　sacred thing, 157:28
　second time in our h., 650:7
　sons study natural h., 351:14
　stage of h., 596:17
　statements of h. are singulars, 81:12
　strange eventful h., 198:25
　systole and diastole of h., 706:10
　takes a great deal of h., 584:9
　Thucydides wrote h. of war, 73:15
　to the defeated, 775:8
　to ignore facts of h., 787:11
　tortured with h., 753:15
　triumphed over time, 160:11
　truth of h., 534:10
　uninstructed in natural h., 536:13
　vengeance of h. terrible, 689:16

History *(continued)*
　very chancy, 715:6
　War makes good h., 575:22
　what's her h., 209:26
　will absolve me, 817:8
　witness to passing time, 90:15
　work of h. in fictional form, 833:6
　world h. is world's court, 381:10
　you don't know, 705:13
History's purchased page, 420:22
Hit, a very palpable h., 207:9
　dusty trail, 684:8
　hard hit fast hit often, 696:1
　hard it rebounds, 327:22
　live until h. it again, 755:6
　nail on head, 149:19
　only what aim at, 506:18
　the line hard, 615:3
　think and h. same time, 814:8
Hitch wagon to star, 457:7
Hither and thither moves, 471:19
　and thither spins, 528:17
　come h., 198:11
　even as their coming h., 217:32
　let him come h., 282:4
　thither downward upward, 130:12
Hitherandthithering waters, 696:16
Hitherto shalt thou come but no further,
　15:7
Hitler, even H. against war, 732:1
　Germany the cause of H., 715:17
　missed bus, 650:8
　monster, 666:13
　springtime for H. and Germany,
　　817:6
　suppose H. killed in 1916, 802:14
Hitlerite blackguards, 686:3
Hitting, no slump just ain't h., 814:10
Hive for the honeybee, 637:1
　helmet now h. for bees, 164:10
　this great h. the city, 275:4
Hiven, rich man enther H., 646:11
Hiverné dans mon passé, 689:*n*4
Hives, fill h. with honey and wax, 297:19
Ho everyone that thirsteth, 28:24
　man they called H., 553:2
　my h. head halls, 696:16
　talk save us, 696:16
　with a hey and a h., 200:5
Hoard little hearts great, 485:21
　little h. of maxims, 481:21
Hoarded, beauty must not be h., 261:8
Hoarfrost, like April h. spread, 400:12
Hoarse, raven himself is h., 219:11
　unchanged to h. or mute, 267:13
Hoary, as I in h. winter night, 168:26
　head a crown of glory, 22:3
　my days dull and h., 279:8
　Sage replied, 325:20
Hobbes clearly proves, 299:3
Hobbit, in hole in ground lived h., 736:3
Hobbyhorse, rides h. peaceably, 332:5
Hobgoblin of little minds, 455:11
Hobson's choice, 844:10
Hoc erat in votis, 98:*n*12
　est enim Corpus meum, 49:13
　genus omne, 98:*n*8
　volo sic iubeo, 113:*n*6
Hock-carts, Maypoles H. wassails, 247:14

Hocus an old cunning attorney, 317:*n*4
Hocus-pocus, law a h. science, 317:10
Hoe, leans upon h. and gazes, 601:3
　scratch it with a h., 543:10
Hog butcher for world, 681:8
　Congressman is a h., 848:7
　I don't go whole h., 830:4
　of Epicurus' herd, 101:1
　root h. or die, 757:2
　whole house, 800:20
Hogan's r-right, 646:3
Hogs eat acorns, 270:*n*2
　eat snakes, 687:3
　fattenin' h. ain't in luck, 593:16
　let it not be like h., 729:13
　men eat h., 687:3
Hoist, troops h. colors to peak, 690:10
　with his own petar, 205:31
Hold, affection cannot h. bent, 209:23
　aloof to gain reputation, 78:10
　candle to my shames, 188:21
　cannot h. mortality's hand, 178:16
　cannot h. thee close enough, 735:1
　center cannot h., 639:6
　cry H. h., 219:12
　damned that cries H. enough, 222:24
　dominion over palm and pine, 635:1
　each thing his turn does h., 248:12
　eternal Footman h. my coat, 717:13
　faith h. which Milton held, 393:5
　farthing candle to sun, 241:*n*4
　fast that which is good, 46:13
　fast the time, 676:18
　fire in his hand, 179:6
　fort I am coming, 522:12
　glimmering tapers to sun, 241:*n*4
　gorgeous east in fee, 393:1
　how take firm h., 82:16
　I h. it towards you, 439:2
　I want to h. your hand, 835:1
　infinity in palm of hand, 375:5
　makes nice of no vile h., 178:12
　me in thy heart, 207:13
　mirror up to nature, 204:13
　more devils than hell can h., 182:3
　net to h. the wind, 244:*n*2
　nozzle agin the bank, 571:5
　opinion with Pythagoras, 189:17
　out relief is coming, 522:*n*5
　own with whatever's going, 671:18
　speak or forever h. his peace, 51:8
　that you know it, 62:17
　thou the good, 484:1
　thy right hand shall h. me, 20:13
　to have and to h., 51:10
　to have to h. and let go, 632:5
　to one despise other, 34:16
　torch high, 660:10
　up Adam's profession, 206:15
　water, 301:5
　with hare run with hound, 148:2
　world but as world, 187:17
　world wide enough to h. both, 332:16
　you as thing enskyed, 210:37
　you here root and all, 486:21
　your hand victorious, 70:14
　your tongue and let me love, 234:5
Hold, so h. und schön und rein, 442:*n*5
Hold-fast the only dog, 192:29

Home *(continued)*
> it was his rightful h., 813:12
> Jerusalem happy h., 844:15
> keep h. fires burning, 663:1
> keep only son at h., 337:14
> knock as you please nobody h., 310:17
> knows when to go h., 571:8
> life that depends on borrowing, 540:4
> longest way round shortest h., 249:*n*2
> love of h. love of country, 496:30
> made of blue clouds, 855:21
> make house h., 693:8
> man goeth to his long h., 25:8
> merriest when from h., 192:23
> my h. sweet h., 716:7
> my songs draw Daphnis h., 95:25
> Naiad airs brought h., 478:2
> nearer h. today, 535:19
> never change when love has found h., 104:18
> no h. like raft, 560:17
> no place like h., 426:15
> of bean and cod, 621:22
> of lost causes, 530:10
> of love, 227:14
> of the brave, 411:1
> of wild mirth, 460:4
> old Kentucky h., 539:1
> our eternal h., 304:6
> outlives day and comes safe h., 193:19
> Paris my h. town, 673:18
> place they have to take you in, 668:22
> pleasure never at h., 438:8
> returned h. previous night, 664:4
> returns h. to find needs, 601:10
> seek fortunes further than h., 175:23
> send h. my long strayed eyes, 234:18
> shall men come, 664:12
> show piety at h., 46:21
> sick for h., 437:13
> song of h. and friends, 556:7
> stayed h. and baked cookies, 840:7
> tavern for friends, 648:8
> they brought warrior, 483:4
> they'll come h., 859:9
> things foreign or things at h., 281:22
> this pig stayed h., 857:16
> till boys come h., 663:1
> till the cow comes h., 245:7
> to a lie, 709:4
> to my Lord and be free, 863:10
> toddle safely h., 712:3
> turns again h., 487:2
> welcome h. discarded faith, 178:23
> what does it leave at h., 502:2
> what is more agreeable than h., 90:25
> when you knock it never is h., 347:14
> where buffalo roam, 855:3
> wherever that may be, 785:13
> wish him safe at h., 384:3
> with no direction h., 836:8
> Wyoming will be your new h., 854:13

Home-keeping youth homely wits, 176:3
Homeland of patience, 458:18
> where happy there's h., 124:29
> wherever he prospers, 75:26

Homeless near thousand homes, 390:14
> tempest-tost, 595:6

Homely beauty of good old cause, 392:14
> conversational or h. type, 653:17
> definitions, 403:20
> features to keep home, 261:9
> hen lays one, 849:16
> home be it never so h., 426:*n*5
> home simple pleasures, 620:6
> home-keeping youth h. wits, 176:3
> joys, 334:14
> men who charmed women, 626:11
> slighted shepherd's trade, 261:19
> was their food, 295:11
> wink at h. girl, 691:4

Homemade but aren't we all, 785:18
Homer, Achilles exists only through H., 387:5
> all the books you need, 293:8
> and Hesiod attributed to the gods, 61:20
> and Whitman roared in pines, 651:12
> deep-browed H. ruled as demesne, 435:19
> even good old H. nods, 102:1
> found H. herald of your glory, 83:8
> is my example, 641:11
> learned root of H., 239:*n*2
> liken H. to setting sun, 110:12
> living H. begged bread, 239:*n*2
> made blind H. sing to me, 170:22
> new and fresh, 663:8
> nods, 102:1, 308:10
> our poets steal from H., 240:3
> read H. once, 293:8
> smote bloomin' lyre, 634:9
> there were poets before H., 90:21
> translator of H., 529:21
> warred for H. being dead, 239:13
> with single exception of H., 609:29
> you must not call it H., 295:13

Homère nouveau ce matin, 663:*n*3
Homer's rule best, 312:15
Homerus, quandoque dormitat H., 102:*n*1
Home's, way h. the farthest way, 249:10
Homes, homeless near thousand h., 390:14
> introduce philosophy into h., 91:6
> poverty keeps h. together, 655:5
> protect health h. firesides, 597:10
> shut-in h. closed doors, 651:1
> stately h. of England, 431:19, 700:1
> think of firelit h., 712:2

Homesickness, poem begins as h., 671:8
Homeward bound for New York town, 862:7
> Hesperus you herd h., 58:6
> look h. Angel, 262:4
> plowman h. plods, 334:8
> rooks in families h. go, 576:8

Homicidal civilization, 697:3
> great h. classics, 832:10

Homines, quot h. tot sententiae, 89:*n*4
Homing, horizon of his h., 721:18
Hominy, immotions function in h. kind feelings, 690:6
> white man filled with Indians' h., 346:10

Homme avec Dieu dans la majorité, 150:*n*5
> chaque h. porte la forme de l'humaine condition, 153:*n*6
> condition de l'h., 279:*n*3
> d'entendement n'a rien perdu, 152:*n*11
> la vraie étude de l'h., 311:*n*1
> le style c'est l'h. même, 321:*n*2

Homme *(continued)*
> l'h. c'est un roseau pensant, 280:*n*2
> l'h. est né libre, 330:*n*3
> l'h. ni ange ni bête, 280:*n*3
> ne saurait forger un ciron, 153:*n*3
> n'y a point h. nécessaire, 697:*n*5
> qu'est-ce que l'h. dans la nature, 279:*n*2
> vain divers et ondoyant, 152:*n*5

Hommes sont toujours sincères, 643:*n*2
Homo, ad unguem factus h., 98:*n*10
> ecce h., 41:*n*2
> naked ape H. sapiens, 821:3
> proponet Deus disponit, 138:*n*4
> sum humani nil a me alienum puto, 88:*n*9

Homos, became one of stately h. of England, 431:*n*1
Honest, a few h. men, 254:10
> ale-house, 252:29
> and wise men rule, 351:17
> angler, 252:23
> anglers or very h. men, 253:7
> armor is his h. thought, 232:13
> as world goes, 203:5
> day is for h. men, 70:10
> depository of public interests, 359:10
> dies an h. fellow, 242:*n*4
> direct and h. not safe, 214:12
> doubt, 484:11
> exceeding poor man, 188:15
> George Third h. dullard, 602:16
> God noblest work of man, 554:6
> good h. painful sermon, 288:5
> good to be h. and true, 380:19
> gude to be h. and true, 847:14
> hand that is h. and hearty, 395:22
> hard-working ancestry, 737:19
> here lies a truly h. man, 272:19
> I one of few h. people, 746:4
> in every h. hand a whip, 214:29
> labor bears lovely face, 233:6
> looking for h. man, 79:6
> man close-buttoned, 348:14
> man looked h. enough, 559:18
> man sent to lie abroad, 232:19
> man's aboon his might, 380:13
> man's the noblest work of God, 311:13, 377:16
> merry and yet h. too, 191:3
> nation secure only while h., 510:1
> no such thing as h. man, 306:18
> not h. that filleth own nest, 141:19
> peace and h. friendship, 358:13
> politician stays bought, 445:11
> politicians long step from h. men, 474:2
> poor but h., 210:23, 850:22
> prejudices of Englishman, 302:19
> religion made h. woman of supernatural, 777:6
> room for h. men, 354:16
> six h. serving men, 635:9
> social friendly h. man, 377:18
> soul that can be h., 242:17
> tale speeds plainly told, 174:13
> taught in intellectually h. form, 796:9
> thief tender murderer, 493:9
> tired of h. things, 735:9
> to no purpose, 105:27
> too h. to steal, 849:1

Honest *(continued)*
    twelve h. men, 306:15
    water, 218:13
    whatsoever things are h., 45:38
    win us with h. trifles, 219:3
    words suffered corruption, 243:17
Honesta turpitudo est pro causa bona, 102:*n*11
Honestly, let us walk h., 43:26
Honesty, armed so strong in h., 197:10
    corruption wins not more than h., 231:7
    is his fault, 218:16
    is praised and starves, 112:21
    love paradox without losing h., 456:6
    manhood nor fellowship, 184:34
    rich h. dwells like miser, 200:8
    root of h. in good education, 111:12
    thy h. and love, 213:22
Honesty's best policy, 158:21
Honey and plenty of money, 499:15
    eating bread and h., 858:12
    fill hives with h. and wax, 297:19
    gather h. all the day, 304:1
    I just forgot to duck, 743:1
    in the carcass of the lion, 10:39
    in the horn, 847:19
    land flowing with milk and h., 8:6
    land of h., 10:3
    locusts and wild h., 33:25
    milk and h., 8:6, 511:11
    no go my h. love, 777:8
    nor h. make nor pair, 402:11
    Pedigree of H., 546:18
    speech sweeter than h., 52:8
    still for tea, 712:16
    surfeited with h., 186:13
    sweeter than h. and honeycomb, 16:12
    this Self is h. of all beings, 51:21
    very h. of earthly joy, 275:4
    with milk and h. blessed, 511:11
Honeybee, hive for the h., 637:1
Honeybees, so work the h., 192:20
Honeycomb, dipped rod in h., 11:24
    lips of a strange woman drop as h., 21:3
    sweeter than honey and the h., 16:12
    Will H. calls ladies, 303:11
    wrath sweeter than h., 53:26
Honeydew, on h. hath fed, 401:19
Honeyed, filled thicket with h. song, 75:5
    Muses gave me h. gift, 85:15
    steeped amid h. morphine, 519:12
    words like bees, 710:11
Honey-heavy dew of slumber, 196:5
Honeyless, leave them h., 197:16
Honi soit qui mal y pense, 132:16
Honks, goose h. high, 847:*n*1
Honor, accompany old age as h., 222:11
    action faithful h. clear, 310:15
    all lost save h., 145:8
    all men, 47:28
    and greatness of his name, 231:17
    as valiant I h. him, 196:25
    bards have a share of h., 55:1
    before h. is humility, 21:39
    belongs to soul, 114:17
    bright, 208:9
    by h. and dishonor, 45:8
    can h. set a leg, 186:35
    changes labor from burden to h., 686:2

Honor *(continued)*
    Christmas in heart, 497:21
    comes a pilgrim gray, 336:16
    comes from Zeus, 52:14
    dearer than life, 157:13
    depends on opinion of mob, 287:13
    die with h., 624:4
    done with Hope and H., 634:1
    foe while you strike, 627:3
    free man abide with h., 505:19
    friend who prospered, 65:7
    from books of h. razed, 226:4
    full of days riches and h., 13:14
    giving h. unto the wife, 47:30
    good death does h. to whole life, 132:13
    his memory, 238:16
    hurt that H. feels, 481:22
    if we can vertical man, 775:3
    in her left hand riches and h., 20:25
    is a mere scutcheon, 186:35
    jealous in h., 198:25
    lacking neither h. nor lyre, 99:16
    let it look like perfect h., 223:2
    life and h. in hands, 556:3
    like an island, 289:17
    louder talked of h., 448:*n*1
    love in excess brings nor h., 69:25
    loved I not h. more, 276:1
    make one vessel unto h., 43:13
    maligners of his h., 554:2
    man of h. regrets discreditable act, 691:11
    man willing to sink, 514:18
    map of h. in thy face, 172:11
    may we h. law, 415:14
    men who have a sense of h., 53:20
    mine h. is my life, 178:31
    national h. national property, 376:15
    neither property nor h. touched, 142:16
    new-made h. doth forget, 177:20
    no h. in sure success, 723:8
    no longer live with h., 624:4
    not least in h. or applause, 162:*n*1
    not pay h. with tears, 87:13
    nought in hate all in h., 215:12
    of striking blow for freedom, 713:17
    or dishonor to last generation, 476:3
    our sacred h., 357:4
    peace with h., 459:21, 650:7
    peace without h. not peace, 427:11
    peasants carry h. in their hands, 246:2
    peereth in meanest habit, 175:37
    perseverance keeps h. bright, 208:9
    physician, 33:5
    pluck bright h. from moon, 185:9
    pluck up drowned h., 185:9
    post of h. is private station, 301:25
    pricks me on, 186:35
    prophet not without h., 36:10
    purchased by merit, 188:27
    quaint h. turn to dust, 277:2
    rooted in dishonor, 486:3
    sense of h. in action, 74:5
    set h. in one eye, 195:17
    shall uphold the humble, 23:21
    signed with their h., 783:16
    sin to covet h., 193:18
    sin to prefer life to h., 113:14
    sinks, 341:2

Honor *(continued)*
    so long shall your h. endure, 97:3
    stain in thine h., 33:3
    strength and h. are her clothing, 23:29
    subject of my story, 195:18
    take h. from me and life done, 178:31
    that h. would thee do, 192:25
    the king, 47:28
    those they have slain, 526:3
    through his h. I conquered him, 246:2
    thy father and mother, 9:1
    to whom honor due, 43:24
    travels in strait so narrow, 208:10
    truth above friends, 80:9
    what is h. a word, 186:35
    what is left when h. lost, 102:25
    when faith lost h. dies, 468:8
    whom king delighteth to h., 13:19
    with native h. clad, 266:9
    words such as h. obscene, 754:4
Honorable, all h. men, 196:28
    ancient and h., 26:32
    and glorious, 350:3
    Brutus is an h. man, 196:28
    conquests, 345:2
    designs were strictly h., 322:11
    get loose from h. engagement, 343:16
    have that which is truly h., 82:15
    intentions h., 349:6
    murderer, 215:12
    no title more h., 695:10
    not h. to tell lies, 69:1
    object only of war h., 354:17
    obstinate truthful man, 498:19
    only h. provision, 406:9
    politics most h. adventure, 674:10
    retreat, 199:9
    style of Christian, 255:6
    to die for one's country, 99:27
    true and h. wife, 196:7
    yet write verse badly, 278:9
Honorably, to die h. greatest virtue, 62:5
Honored among foxes, 795:12
    among wagons, 795:9
    bones, 259:3
    custom more h. in breach, 202:3
    followed him h. him, 491:21
    how loved how h. once, 309:29
    in their generations, 33:9
    man in hasty days h. for them, 586:7
    of them all, 481:9
    these h. dead, 476:7
Honorificabilitudinitatibus, 177:10
Honoring, not so much h. thee, 238:3
Honor's, can h. voice provoke, 334:17
    listen for dear h. sake, 261:10
    when h. at the stake, 206:2
Honors acquired by unrighteousness, 62:27
    bears his blushing h., 231:2
    beauties wits, 234:17
    female sex excluded from h. and offices, 362:5
    gave his h. to the world, 231:10
    mindless of its just h., 395:19
    people I cannot win with h., 280:16
Hood, him that wears a h., 151:9
    more than a h. to make monk, 123:*n*3
Hooded, one grand h. phantom, 516:7
Hoodoo, Mumbo-Jumbo will h. you, 685:5

Hoof, head and h. of Law, 634:15
  whatsoever parteth the h., 9:10
Hoofs of swinish multitude, 345:15
Hook, bait the h. well, 194:27
  draw out leviathan with a h., 15:19
  spares next swath, 438:12
  without bait, 457:3
Hook-nosed fellow of Rome, 192:5
Hooks, silver h., 234:22
Hoop of the nation, 628:1
Hoops, grapple with h. of steel, 201:25
Hooray and up she rises, 862:2
Hoosier, face like h. Michael Angelo,
  521:10
Hooting and shrieking, 195:26
  at glorious sun, 401:12
Hoots, owl that nightly h., 181:14
Hop, lets it h. a little, 183:15
  light ladies, 593:17
Hope, Admiral cheered them holding out h.,
  140:3
  against h. believed in h., 42:43
  all h. abandon who enter here, 130:3
  all we h. in Heaven, 477:10
  all will yet be well, 475:2
  Americans h. of world, 340:7
  and believe what he can, 470:12
  animated by faith and h., 325:6
  because I do not h., 719:9
  beyond h. and despair, 719:12
  beyond shadow of dream, 436:12
  blessed h. whereof he knew, 575:17
  break it to our h., 222:22
  certain h. of Resurrection, 51:14
  cradle of h., 681:18
  days are spent without h., 14:2
  death of h. and despair, 721:16
  deferred maketh the heart sick, 21:24
  Democratic Party without h. of posterity,
    548:8
  done with H. and Honor, 634:1
  extinguish h. from soul, 603:18
  farewell h., 266:4
  fear cannot be without h., 287:7
  feed on h., 161:23
  fondest h. decay, 412:13
  fooled with h., 282:21
  for a season, 408:13
  for helmet the h. of salvation, 46:11
  for the best, 398:17
  for years to come, 304:6
  forks and h., 553:4
  from h. and fear set free, 569:3
  frustrate of his h., 262:13
  full of immortality, 31:16
  good breakfast bad supper, 166:20
  help for living h. for dead, 554:5
  I die before I get old, 839:8
  if youth season of h., 513:10
  illusions of h., 352:13
  in the day of evil, 29:20
  in trembling h. repose, 335:4
  is there any better h., 475:7
  is to expect something for nothing,
    601:16
  is waking dream, 79:10
  land of h. and glory, 625:11
  last best h. of earth, 476:3
  lies to mortals, 619:20

Hope *(continued)*
  like taper's light, 340:13
  lined himself with h., 191:22
  little h. of deliverance, 832:7
  lives on h. die fasting, 320:8
  look forward with h., 668:21
  memory outlive his life, 204:21
  men in exile feed on h., 65:13
  my good vain h. of gain, 164:17
  my h. my hap my love, 155:8
  my h. my love, 257:23
  never comes, 264:2
  never to h. again, 231:2
  no more H. no more Glory, 662:22
  no other medicine but h., 211:16
  nor love nor friend, 599:11
  not endure another's h., 296:6
  not h. and no help came, 776:11
  not thing with feathers, 831:2
  now abideth h., 44:20
  nursing unconquerable h., 529:13
  of fair advantages, 188:22
  of glory, 50:8
  of pride and power, 477:12
  of the ungodly, 31:19
  on h. wretch relies, 340:12
  one jot of heart or h., 263:16
  one will cut halter, 258:12
  only h. lies in despair, 290:10
  past h. past cure past help, 184:8
  phantoms of h., 324:24
  plummets to dust of h., 68:6
  prisoners of h., 30:38
  ray of h. blown out, 474:12
  safety to h. not safety, 97:11
  saved by h., 735:17
  sin was too much h., 237:20
  springs eternal, 311:4
  that there it not withered be, 238:3
  the thing with feathers, 544:11
  things you do not h. happen, 86:15
  this government best h., 358:10
  to h. till H. creates, 428:14
  to see Pilot, 487:4
  to the end, 47:24
  to turn again, 719:9
  triumph of h. over experience, 327:8
  true h. is swift, 174:17
  understood terror and h., 802:12
  virtue flock to their aid, 455:3
  what was dead was H., 605:20
  whence this pleasing h., 301:26
  which guides changeful mind, 66:14
  while life there's h., 89:2, 90:24
  whose h. the Lord is, 29:17
  without all h. of day, 268:32
  without h. we live in desire, 130:10
  without object cannot live, 402:12
  work without H., 402:12
  you're pleased with yourselves, 842:11
Hoped, substance of things h. for, 46:42
  we were broken-hearted, 569:5
Hopeful, elders h. about us, 513:10
  green stuff woven, 518:18
  hey but I'm h., 564:10
Hopeless fancy feigned, 482:22
  grief passionless, 463:12
  passion, 490:11
  so huge so h., 547:3

Hopeless *(continued)*
  we doctors know h. case, 740:15
  woes of h. lovers, 284:16
Hopelessness of early youth, 513:1
  path leads to despair utter h., 831:6
Hope's true gage, 160:8
Hopes, adversity not without h., 167:11
  and fears of all years, 558:5
  clever h. expire, 775:13
  graveyard of buried h., 673:7
  hearts h. prayers tears, 466:20
  if h. were dupes fears may be liars, 512:10
  life's span forbids us enter on h., 99:6
  like towering falcons, 296:17
  no more change name, 394:11
  of future years, 466:19
  remnants of childhood h. of adulthood,
    762:3
  stirred up with high h., 262:18
  tender leaves of h., 231:2
  that resemble regrets, 512:1
  that St. Nicholas, 411:5
  vain h. like dreams of those who wake,
    109:15
  vanity of human h., 324:13
  wholly h. to be, 494:14
Hoping, tender yearning sweet h., 382:7
  trembling h. lingering, 309:3
Hopkins, Mark H. on one end, 548:10
Hopping, meager shriveled h., 345:16
  through frothy waves, 552:2
Horace, studied spontaneity of H., 109:11
  whom I hated so, 421:15
Horatii curiosa felicitas, 109:*n*3
Horatio, I knew him H., 206:24
  in my mind's eye H., 201:11
  more things in heaven H., 202:26
  speak to it H., 200:14
  thrift thrift H., 201:10
  to what base uses we may return H.,
    206:25
Horde, society one polished h., 424:20
Horeb, Moses in H. struck rock, 807:6
Horizon, dusk on eastern h., 742:4
  of dogs, 751:7
  of his homing, 721:18
  our h. never at our elbows, 507:7
Horizon's edge, 521:2
Horizontal, cord into h. line, 432:18
  one, 775:3
Horn, barter that h., 639:14
  beetle winds sullen h., 337:2
  blow wreathed h., 394:19
  come blow h., 857:17
  cow with crumpled h., 861:15
  Dinah blow your h., 848:1
  gate of h., 55:22, 98:2
  God winding lonely h., 637:9
  gray-fly winds sultry h., 261:16
  hand on h., 854:15
  honey in the h., 847:19
  hounds and h., 259:13
  huntsman winds his h., 321:18
  lusty h., 199:31
  mouth of Plenty's h., 639:14
  of hunter on hill, 447:6
  one blast upon bugle h., 397:13
  poured through mellow h., 337:4
  Roland sound your h., 126:11

Horn (*continued*)

 sound of h. at night, 443:13
 sound upon bugle h., 481:16
 tunes frozen up in h., 355:6
 with his hounds and h., 435:15
Horned Moon with one bright star, 400:7
Horner, little Jack H., 857:3
Hornets, bees for flies and h. for bees,
  144:8
 cobwebs let h. through, 297:20
Horns, hang caps on h. o' the moon,
  224:17
 like Kyloe cow, 858:10
 of Elfland, 482:20
 of my dilemma, 332:24
 sound of h. and motors, 718:17
 sound of hunting h., 689:21
 taking bull by both h. kissed her, 693:3
Horny hands of toil, 514:8
Horresco referens, 97:n3
Horrible, hence h. shadow, 221:15
 imaginings, 219:5
 invention the bourgeois, 526:15
 that lust and rage, 642:14
 voice, 74:12
Horribly, I will h. revenge, 193:23
 live by medicine live h., 322:18
 stuffed with epithets of war, 212:12
Horrid, blow h. deed in every eye, 219:18
 dream h. dreams, 516:20
 hideous notes of woe, 424:22
 image doth unfix hair, 219:5
 life demd h. grind, 496:26
 shapes and shrieks, 259:7
 when bad she was h., 468:4
Horridly to shake our disposition, 202:6
Horror, Dead Sea makes h., 680:1
 fell upon Christian, 281:28
 lived through this h., 704:10
 of falling into naught, 301:26
 of outer darkness, 553:14
 of that moment, 551:9
 screams of h. rend, 309:13
 soul of plot, 478:14
 the h. the h., 612:9
 this h. is ours, 784:9
 universal h. unbend, 693:15
Horror's, on h. head horrors, 214:11
Horrors accumulate, 214:11
 congenial h. hail, 317:14
 of half known life, 516:16
 sunset stained with mystic h., 603:11
 supped full with h., 222:15
Horrorshow, shut her up h. and lovely,
  798:17
Horse stood near stable door, 844n4
 a dog a h. a rat, 218:7
 and his rider hath he thrown, 8:25
 bean-fed h. beguile, 181:5
 beggars mounted run h. to death, 172:23
 body my h. my hound, 806:2
 boot saddle to h. and away, 491:13
 brewer's h., 186:17
 bring h. to water, 148:12
 Caligula's h. made Consul, 405:1
 call me h., 185:24
 cart before h., 149:8
 choice of h. and wife, 528:1
 dark h., 458:23

Horse (*continued*)

 dearer than his h., 481:18
 death on his pale h., 268:9
 difference of opinion makes h.-races,
  561:18
 dominated mind of early races, 707:18
 donkey like h. translated into Dutch,
  356:15
 ego's relation to id as rider to h., 607:18
 far back in soul h. prances, 707:18
 fine lady upon white h., 858:14
 flung himself on h., 651:9
 foot an' artillery, 704:8
 for want of h. rider lost, 251:29, 320:10
 for want of shoe h. lost, 251:29, 320:10
 give man h. he can ride, 557:10
 give me another h., 174:19
 great h. of gold, 739:10
 guide h. along path it wants to go,
  607:18
 happy h. to bear Antony, 223:5
 hast thou given the h. strength, 15:13
 hey for boot and h., 514:4
 horsewhip you if had a h., 704:2
 I am not so poor a h., 476:10
 in silence champed, 662:10
 in the mountain, 751:4
 know two things about the h., 677:12
 knows the way, 450:11
 leene as is a rake, 134:29
 lord if you had h., 707:18
 love and marriage like h. and carriage,
  789:11
 must think it queer, 669:14
 my h. my wife my name, 458:13
 my kingdom for a h., 174:23
 nation, 855:17
 never look gift h. in mouth, 119:1
 noblest conquest of man, 321:9
 nothing but talk of his h., 187:29
 O for a h. with wings, 225:15
 of different color, 209:n1
 of our courage, 809:4
 of that color, 209:19
 old h. stumbles and nods, 576:5
 pale h., 48:20, 268:9
 philosophy a good h., 341:22
 shoe the h., 861:12
 short h. soon curried, 147:27
 sits on h. at hostess' door, 177:26
 spur not unbroken h., 398:4
 Turquoise H. of Johano-ai, 856:3
 uses folly like stalking h., 200:11
 when h. stolen fool shuts stable, 148:n3
 where's the bloody h., 760:8
Horseback, beggar on h., 172:n1
 beggar upon h., 642:13
 man on h., 848:13
 on h. through dreary tract, 478:11
Horsed upon sightless couriers, 219:18
Horseleach hath two daughters, 23:24
Horseman pass by, 643:5
Horsemanship, forgetful of his h., 53:22
 witch world with noble h., 186:24
Horsemen, chariot and h. of Israel, 12:40
 four h. of Apocalypse, 645:7
Horsemill, desire a h., 240:18
Horse's, 'ear h. legs, 486:19
 trusts in h. health, 217:4

Horses, all the king's h., 859:8
 and poets not overfed, 159:12
 as fed h. in the morning, 29:2
 black are the h., 751:8
 carriages without h. go, 845:8
 chariot and h. of fire, 12:39
 come saddle your h., 398:11
 don't do it and frighten h., 631:17
 England hell of h., 162:9
 handling of blooded h., 526:17
 heaven in which no h., 601:1
 if cattle and h. had hands, 61:21
 if wishes were h., 281:7
 men hanged that h. not be stolen, 289:3
 more careful of breed of h. than children,
  292:2
 not swap h., 476:10
 oats in England given to h., 324:20
 of instruction, 372:20
 price of thousand h., 658:7
 run slowly h. of night, 105:3
 slowly run O h. of night, 171:n2
 they shoot h. don't they, 749:11
 they tend, 501:6
 watered our h. in Helicon, 165:13
 which h. bear him best, 171:16
 wild white h. play, 528:5
 women h. economic factors in society,
  623:3
 would draw gods like horses, 61:21
Horses' heels over paying, 719:22
Horseshoes, laws flung like h., 732:3
Horsewhip, I'd h. you if had a horse,
  704:2
Horus non numero nisi serenas, 410:15
Hose, washed me out of turret with h.,
  793:6
 youthful h. well saved, 198:25
Hospitable, in peace generous h., 426:1
 on h. thoughts intent, 267:5
Hospital, first requirement in H., 522:5
 tray of narcotics, 787:18
 whole earth our h., 721:2
 world not inn but h., 256:8
Hospitality, given to h., 43:18
Host, Hesperus led starry h., 266:16
 many an old h. damned, 185:31
 of golden daffodils, 394:4
 one more drink be under h., 738:18
 praise Him heavenly h., 289:22
 though an h. should encamp, 16:23
 tie of h. and guest, 65:17
 time like fashionable h., 208:11
 with angelic h. proclaim, 323:1
Hostage, you are eternity's h., 730:4
Hostages to fortune, 167:14
Hostess', sits on horse at h. door, 177:26
Hostesses make parties as ministers cabinets,
  513:12
Hostile, universe not h. nor friendly, 684:13
Hostilities, victory when opponent surrenders
  before h., 83:5
Hostility, eternal h. against tyranny, 358:8
 sorrow to disarm h., 467:3
Host's Canary wine, 438:10
Hosts, holy is the Lord of h., 26:24
 Lord God of H., 635:1
 Lord of h. King of glory, 16:21
 of Error, 622:1

Hot and bothered, 636:1
  and cold and moist and dry, 265:*n*1
  and rebellious liquors, 198:4
  as hell, 369:9
  blow h. and cold, 61:2
  can one go upon h. coals, 21:7
  cat on h. tin roof, 281:*n*1
  cold and h. moist and dry, 284:13
  cold light and h. shade, 374:13
  cold moist and dry, 265:20
  conscience seared with h. iron, 46:18
  cross buns, 859:4
  fair h. wench in taffeta, 184:23
  feel h. and think cold, 717:1
  for certainties, 541:9
  ginger h. i' the mouth, 209:17
  hammer iron when h., 102:24
  heat flow from h. to cold object,
    532:*n*1
  I would thou wert cold or h., 48:14
  in my h. youth, 100:7
  Just Add H. Water, 739:15
  lead effective from linotype, 771:17
  little pot and soon h., 175:33
  my heart was h. within me, 17:11
  my love was so h., 418:16
  neither cold nor h., 48:14
  pease-porridge h., 859:5
  sleep is cold for the h., 158:31
  small h. bird, 597:4
  snake came on h. h. day, 707:10
  so h. that it singe yourself, 230:20
  stink of fox, 825:4
  temper leaps over, 187:28
  time in old town tonight, 630:6
  w'en stew smokin' h., 660:4
  when iron is h. strike, 102:*n*12
  which way h. air blows, 626:15
  why sea boiling h., 552:3
  your wit's too h., 176:29
Hotel, back to h. in rain, 754:7
  born in goddam h. room dying in h.
    room, 724:9
  Heartbreak H., 831:16
  instead of hymns, 688:12
  queen of this summer h., 821:7
  refuge from home life, 609:11
  smoke-filled room in h., 623:1
  terrible strange-looking h., 813:12
Hotels, big peppermint h., 797:6
  people in h., 649:13
Hothouse, no h. flowers, 703:7
Hotness, day in its h., 529:2
Hotspur of the North, 185:20
Hottentot, Mr. Whitman's Venus H. wench,
    569:18
Hotter, pass from colder to h., 532:13
Hound dog cryin' all the time, 828:8
  footprints of gigantic h., 617:12
  hold with hare run with h., 148:2
  mongrel puppy whelp h., 341:17
  my horse my h., 806:2
  single H., 545:19
Hounds and horn, 259:13
  carcass fit for h., 196:3
  join in glorious cry, 321:18
  moon men and barking h., 742:6
  noise like questing of thirty h., 139:2
  of spring, 567:17

Hounds *(continued)*
  such h. such hawks, 854:7
  with his h. and horn, 435:15
Hour before dawn silent, 679:15
  books of the h., 517:15
  childhood's h., 412:13, 477:13
  Children's H., 467:10
  cometh and now is, 40:48
  crowded h. of glorious life, 346:12
  dark h. or twain, 220:29
  destined H., 471:7
  eternity in an h., 375:5
  every h. a miracle, 521:3
  every h. that passes O, 378:12
  fall that very h., 209:23
  far fierce h. and sweet, 665:1
  fluster of h. badly spent, 786:2
  fools for I also had my h., 665:1
  for one short h. see, 485:13
  from h. to h. we ripe, 198:16
  had I died h. before, 220:25
  happiest day happiest h., 477:12
  hazard of doubtful h., 186:21
  I have had my h., 284:7
  I was born, 847:19
  improve each shining h., 304:1
  inevitable h., 334:15
  is at hand, 37:31
  is not yet come, 40:38
  its h. come round at last, 639:7
  last h. of my life, 318:13
  laugh an h. by his dial, 198:17
  lives its little h., 432:13, 692:17
  living at this h., 393:3
  look on you when last h. comes, 104:26
  look thy last every h., 662:12
  Lord through this h., 851:11
  matched us with His h., 713:1
  met me in evil h., 378:7
  more desirable than fortunate h., 94:19
  nighing his h., 619:15
  not an h. more or less, 217:30
  not showpiece of an h., 73:16
  nothing can bring back h., 393:18
  now's the h., 380:10
  of adversity, 416:10
  of departure has arrived, 76:14
  of thoughtless youth, 391:4
  of truth now always, 677:16
  one bare h. to live, 171:3
  one dead deathless h., 542:1
  our h. is marked, 388:13
  rash hand in evil h., 267:30
  ripe, 192:9
  serve the future h., 395:12
  speak an h. ready now, 611:12
  stay longer in h., 567:10
  struts and frets his h., 222:16
  takes away things, 328:7
  that turns back longing of seafarers,
    131:14
  the wished the trysted h., 380:8
  this was their finest h., 666:2
  thou the day I the h., 564:15
  time and the h., 219:7
  torturing h., 334:1
  two hundred fifty words every quarter h.,
    504:9
  uncertain h. before morning, 721:18

Hour *(continued)*
  violet h., 718:18
  watch with me one h., 37:30
  what sweet h. yields, 431:7
  wherein man might be happy, 252:17
  who drowsy at that h., 256:25
  wonder of an h., 420:9
Hour's, never spent h. talk withal, 176:28
  sleep before midnight, 252:10
Hours, age not numbered by h., 155:7
  and minutes dollars and cents, 320:*n*1
  arrest your course, 426:8
  better three h. too soon, 190:26
  count only sunny h., 410:*n*1
  creeping h. of time, 198:22
  dismal h. of the night, 756:4
  entertain lag-end with quiet h., 186:31
  golden h. on angel wings, 380:4
  his brief h. and weeks, 227:17
  I once enjoyed, 347:2
  I spent with thee, 627:8
  life short quiet h. few, 517:14
  mournful midnight h., 363:15
  narrowing dark h., 748:3
  nor h. days months, 234:3
  redeem these h., 239:10
  seven h. to law, 159:*n*5
  six h. in sleep, 159:20
  sixteen h. ago Hiroshima, 705:3
  sorrow breaks reposing h., 174:5
  steal h. from night, 412:1
  success unexpected in common h.,
    507:18
  sweetest h. e'er I spend, 378:14
  three h. a day what man ought to write,
    504:8
  Time in h. days years, 279:5
  to which Heaven doth chime, 278:29
  two golden h., 441:12
  unless h. cups of sack, 184:23
  waked by circling h., 267:10
  weary of days and h., 569:1
  what h. O what black h., 588:4
  Woman in our h. of ease, 397:1
House, a h. no more a h., 670:17
  all the h. of Israel played, 11:41
  all through the h., 411:5
  appointed for all living, 14:39
  bear witness to his piety, 386:3
  blessings on this h., 351:17
  body my h. my horse my hound, 806:2
  built on sand, 35:12
  Bustle in a H. Morning after Death,
    546:8
  by the side of the road, 52:30, 613:16
  call upon my soul within the h., 209:9
  child draws inscrutable h., 785:14
  children's h. of make believe, 670:18
  civilized man's h. prison, 504:24
  clergyman so much about h., 558:15
  covet thy neighbor's h., 9:1
  crooked h., 860:6
  daughter in mother's h., 634:22
  daughters of my father's h., 209:27
  divided against itself, 38:17, 474:9
  doll in the doll's h., 499:4
  doorkeeper in h. of my God, 18:17
  dust inbreathed was h., 721:16
  dwell in h. of the Lord, 16:18

Humankind, lords of h. pass by, 341:5
  not bear much reality, 720:6
  of all tyrannies on h., 284:19
  porcelain clay of h., 284:28
  vices and follies of h., 300:12
Humble and hearty thanks, 50:8
  appearance of telephone, 549:1
  are usually envious, 287:8
  be it ever so h., 426:15
  frowned not on h. birth, 335:2
  heyday in blood is h., 205:22
  himself shall be exalted, 37:1
  honor shall uphold the h., 23:21
  livers in content, 230:25
  members of society, 386:13
  ne'er ebb to h. love, 214:15
  not only h. but umble, 498:*n*1
  pie, 498:11
  soft meek patient h., 233:7
  son of h. laborer, 693:10
  the greater the more h., 31:27
  through vainglory, 153:9
  very h. person, 498:2
  wisdom is h., 348:12
  with lure of the real, 689:1
Humbleness, whispering h., 188:9
Humbler heaven, 311:5
Humblest citizen of land, 622:1
  friends, 395:20
  peer of powerful, 554:1
Humbling, no h. of reality to precept,
  816:15
Humbly beseech you of pardon, 214:1
  walk h. with thy God, 30:28
Humbug, bah h., 497:13
  conspiracy to lie and h., 644:10
  government of H. or Humdrum, 459:3
  lift at colossal h., 562:18
  no one can be a h., 672:22
Humdrum, government of Humbug or H.,
  459:3
  passage might be h., 613:18
Humiliating, run out of Burma h. as hell,
  703:6
Humiliation, Christ's submission to h., 812:6
  valley of H., 281:20
Humility a thing commendable, 147:*n*13
  a virtue all preach, 245:16
  angling like virtue of h., 252:26
  before honor is h., 21:39
  is endless, 720:19
  modest stillness and h., 192:30
  proud in h., 240:24
  sense of reverence, 70:15
  where there is h., 128:4
Humor, awe man from career of his h.,
  194:28
  call it h. when they gibe, 299:3
  liveliest effusions of h., 406:21
  most when she obeys, 310:9
  my h. based on despair, 814:15
  one has sense of h., 714:16
  prelude to faith, 735:16
  quiet h. in Yiddish, 769:11
  saves a few steps, 714:16
  source of H. not joy but sorrow, 562:3
  that's the h. of it, 192:26
  third glass for good h., 302:15
  unconscious h., 558:22

Humor *(continued)*
  unyoked h. of idleness, 184:36
  woman in this h. wooed, 173:34
Humored, played with and h., 282:9
Humorous, call to h. literature, 559:13
  sadness, 199:23
  very beadle to h. sigh, 176:32
Hump, haunch and h. is Obey, 634:15
  whale's white h., 516:14
  without a positive h., 490:3
Humpty Dumpty, 859:8
  when I use word said H., 552:14
Hums, beetle with drowsy h., 221:6
Hun is at the gate, 635:25
Hunched in belly till wet fur froze, 793:6
Hunching wings and beak, 800:9
Hundred, a few h. scrawls, 704:8
  at three h. pence ointment prize, 250:5
  buyer needs a h. eyes, 251:26
  done h. things you not dreamed of,
    810:11
  father more than h. schoolmasters, 252:2
  first h. days, 799:9
  first h. years hardest, 678:8
  fourteen h. years ago nailed, 184:22
  had I a h. tongues, 97:27
  how tell guy's a h. percent, 746:1
  if very angry count h., 359:12
  of three h. grant three, 424:3
  one a h. years hence, 456:20
  one h. ninety-three species, 821:3
  ran a h. years to a day, 473:15
  rode the six h., 484:24
  ten jokes an h. enemies, 332:6
  thousand thrained men, 704:8
  thousand to that h., 248:7
  to that twenty add h. more, 248:7
  victory finds a h. fathers, 764:12
  wi' a h. pipers an' a', 385:8
Hundredfold, brought forth fruit h., 36:4
Hun-dred-mil-lion-oth-ers, 739:16
Hundred's soon hit, 492:24
Hung aloft the night, 439:11
  be heavens with black, 171:11
  here h. those lips, 206:24
  unjoined person who h. in doorways,
    802:9
  with bloom along bough, 618:6
Hungary and Poland doing it their way,
  835:*n*1
Hunger and thirst after righteousness, 33:33
  confront night storms h., 518:13
  fer 'em somehow, 693:8
  filth and ignorance, 727:7
  God is war peace surfeit h., 64:7
  he that cometh to me shall never h., 41:4
  I am h., 829:3
  I offer h. thirst battles, 465:13
  mouth and belly injured by h., 82:19
  no fear stand up to h., 612:7
  no sauce like h., 157:30
  once done with h. rich and poor as one,
    70:8
  they shall h. no more, 48:25
  toil h. nakedness, 442:1
  warmth richness reality of h. satisfied,
    778:6
  weak evils age and h., 198:24
  write of h. writing about love, 778:6

Hungered and ye gave meat, 37:17
Hungry and he gave him meat, 339:8
  as grave, 317:15
  ate when we were not h., 298:18
  cloy h. edge of appetite, 179:6
  for life and death, 794:9
  generations, 437:13
  hag and h. goblin, 844:19
  he hath filled h., 38:40
  if thine enemy be h., 23:3
  judges the sentence sign, 309:10
  lean and h. look, 195:22
  makes h. where most satisfies, 223:15
  owl is endlessly h., 831:15
  Pinch a h. lean-faced villain, 175:1
  rich when he is h., 79:*n*3
  sheep look up, 262:2
  show you h. person, 838:2
  sleep is meat for the h., 158:31
  so many h. people, 803:4
  soul, 23:12
  stomach cannot hear, 276:21
  tigers getting h., 665:13
Hungry-looking, fear pale and h. men,
  92:7
Hunredpercent, how tell guy's a h., 746:1
Hunt down love together, 568:22
  gunless game, 613:15
  head-down tail-up h., 833:15
  in fields for health, 285:19
  it in the dark, 347:18
Hunted and penned in inglorious spot,
  729:13
  freedom h. round globe, 354:9
  little h. hares, 656:10
  past reason h., 227:22
Hunter, Bahram that great H., 471:8
  Esau was a cunning h., 7:10
  home from hill, 599:6
  Lo H. of East caught, 470:14
  man is the h., 483:2
  Nimrod the mighty h., 6:35
Hunters who hunt gunless game, 613:15
  woods for h. of dreams, 613:15
Hunting, ain't h. as 'urts 'un, 591:15
  Canada a vast h. preserve, 745:11
  daddy's gone a-h., 858:8
  daren't go a-h., 535:15
  passion for h. something, 496:10
  upon St. David's Day, 860:12
  we will go, 321:18
  weary wi' h., 854:11
Huntlie, true Thomas on H. Bank, 854:2
Huntress, queen and h., 237:10
Hunts, at night hippopotamus h., 718:5
  in dreams, 481:20
  on a lonely hill, 606:13
Huntsman, as h. his pack, 343:5
  winds his horn, 321:18
Huntsmen are up in America, 256:25
  three jolly h., 860:12
  three jovial h., 321:*n*7
Hurdy-gurdies make tune their own, 593:18
Hurl, didst h. him upon a war-horse, 516:11
Hurled headlong flaming, 263:23
  in ruin and confusion h., 301:16
  into ruin h., 311:3
  world and her train h., 279:5
Hurlyburly's, when the h. done, 218:23

Hurrah for old Kentuck, 417:21
    for revolution, 642:13
    my boys we're homeward bound, 862:7
    we bring the Jubilee, 553:11
Hurricane of black doves, 751:11
    sired by h., 560:2
Hurricanes hardly happen, 803:9
Hurricanoes, cataracts and h., 216:18
Hurry, always in haste never in h., 318:22
    don't h. don't worry, 733:9
    Nature will h. back, 101:2
    sick h. divided aims, 529:12
    to see your lady, 4:1
    up please its time, 718:16
Hurt, balm of h. minds, 220:16
    enemy and friend h. you to heart, 562:10
    give delight and h. not, 230:6
    he who shall h. wren, 375:8
    if I don't h. her, 414:6
    man keenest in self-love, 539:12
    more afraid than h., 147:17
    no h. found upon Daniel, 30:9
    not the earth, 48:22
    panics produce as much good as h.,
      354:11
    power to h., 227:3
    somebody'll get h., 829:11
    sweareth to his own h., 16:6
    that Honor feels, 481:22
    their health it might h., 343:7
    they h. me I grow older, 708:18
    they shall not h. nor destroy, 26:34
    too badly h. to laugh, 476:1
    why should I h. thee, 332:16
Hurtles in darkened air, 335:17
Hurtless breaks, 217:24
Hurts, fellows it h. to think, 619:9
    it h. my hand, 214:20
    pinch which h. and is desired, 224:11
    truth never h. teller, 495:6
Husband and wife keep a household, 54:22
    any her h. rather than Christian, 189:26
    at all times faithful h., 303:4
    being h. whole-time job, 645:3
    chaste to her h., 310:5
    children friends nothing to that, 593:20
    conspiring against my h., 840:9
    delight of h. aunts infant, 724:12
    doth safely trust in her, 23:27
    easier to be lover than h., 445:3
    frae wife despises, 379:15
    give you h. and home, 54:22
    holy city adorned for h., 48:38
    I come, 224:10
    is known in the gates, 23:28
    lay beside her h., 807:15
    light wife heavy h., 190:11
    lover in h. lost, 329:24
    Man-o'-War's 'er h., 634:17
    no worse a h. than best of men, 223:13
    shape a h. out of, 490:*n*1
    sovereynetee over h., 136:21
    thankless h., 423:20
    till h. cools, 310:9
    virtuous woman a crown to her h., 21:21
    with beard, 194:13
    woman oweth duty to h., 176:2
    women stimulated by news wife left h.,
      771:19

Husbanded, so fathered and so h., 196:8
Husbandman waiteth for precious fruit,
    47:21
Husbandry, edge of h., 201:27
    in heaven, 220:5
    ye are God's h., 43:35
Husband's, level in her h. heart, 209:22
Husbands at chirche dore hadde fyve, 135:8
    friends lovers h., 361:13
    God's supply of tolerable h., 743:18
    think of fidelity not h., 695:12
    unlimited power into hands of h., 361:11
Hush, classroom h., 834:3
    hark deep sound strikes, 420:16
    my dear, 304:4
    with setting moon, 485:10
Hushed be every thought, 395:17
    in grim repose, 335:13
    in silence h. his soul, 395:5
    now air is h., 337:2
Hushing traffic of drowsy town, 586:6
Husks, dead h. of life, 777:1
    strewed with h., 208:20
Husky, stormy h. brawling, 681:8
Hustle, tried to h. the East, 633:2
Hustled, Indian summer never h., 570:26
Huswife's, tease the h. wool, 261:9
Hut, love in h. 436:16
Hutchinson, isn't fair Mrs. H. screamed,
    797:14
Huts, ragged h. greatest city, 520:4
Hyacinth, breasts like spikes of h., 751:6
    hair, 478:2
    sell bread and buy h., 123:2
    the Garden wears, 471:9
Hyacinths are dark too, 96:2
Hybla, words rob H. bees, 197:16
Hybrid, Alexandria a h., 788:7
Hyde, Dr. Jekyll and Mr. H., 599:3
Hydra, monstrosity more prodigious than H.,
    100:*n*13
Hydrant, talking is a h. in the yard, 671:16
Hydroptic earth hath drunk, 234:20
Hyena, song of siren nor voice of h., 165:4
Hylas, je ne vous aime pas H., 296:*n*1
Hylax barks in doorway, 95:26
Hymn Brahmin sings, 453:23
    chants doleful h., 178:25
    sober as a h., 594:7
Hymns, chanting faint h. to moon, 180:18
    hotel instead of h., 688:12
    psalms h. and spiritual songs, 45:29
    that fall out of wind, 688:12
    to thee morning h. ascended, 538:12
Hyperboles, three-piled h., 177:12
Hyperion to a satyr, 201:3
Hyperion's curls, 205:21
Hyphenated Americanism, 615:16
Hypocrisies, some great events some mean h.,
    351:13
Hypocrisy, democracies cannot dispense with
    h., 716:13
    drowns in Pharisees' h., 730:3
    from pride vainglory and h., 50:11
    has ample wages, 144:13
    homage vice pays to virtue, 273:27
    is most difficult vice, 672:22
    of bishop, 360:8
    panics touchstones of h., 354:11

Hypocrisy *(continued)*
    speaking lies in h., 46:18
    vice of vices, 773:7
Hypocrite lecteur, 524:7
    reader, 524:7
    rotten to the core, 773:7
    scoundrel h. flatterer, 376:5
    sometimes more sometimes less, 445:7
    thou h., 35:1
Hypocrites, cant of h. the worst, 332:22
    effect of coercion to make h., 357:8
    enemies taunt us as h., 474:7
    not h. in sleep, 410:19
    scribes and Pharisees h., 37:2
Hypocritic Days, 453:18
Hypotheses, I frame no h., 290:26
Hypothesis, fertile h., 796:8
    nature of an h., 332:19
    no need of that h., 866:15
    slaying of h. by ugly fact, 537:4
    whatever not deduced is h., 290:26
Hyrcan tiger, 221:14
Hyssop, purge me with h., 17:26
Hysterica passio, 216:11
Hysterical patients suffer from reminiscences,
    607:10
    starving h. naked, 817:12

I

I accept the universe, 488:2
    am, 8:7
    am a Jew, 188:30
    am a Liberal, 531:12
    am a Roman citizen, 90:10
    am Actaeon, 105:15
    am Alpha and Omega, 49:4
    am always about in the Quad, 723:*n*1
    am Duchess of Malfi still, 244:6
    am dying Egypt dying, 223:37
    am Fortune's fool, 183:30
    am from Missouri, 604:5
    am guilty of corruption, 166:16
    am he that liveth, 48:7
    am Heathcliff, 509:3
    am I you are you, 492:15
    am innocent of the blood, 38:4
    Am Jehovah said, 337:16
    am Madame Bovary, 527:11
    am master of my fate, 594:11
    am no more I, 751:5
    am not as other men, 40:8
    am not what I was, 100:12
    am only guinea pig I have, 743:11
    am quite myself again, 618:13
    am rising to a man's work, 115:20
    am Sir Oracle, 187:20
    am that I am, 8:7
    am that which began, 569:7
    am the androgyne, 824:12
    am the bread of life, 41:4
    am the door, 41:15
    am the good shepherd, 41:17
    am the grass, 681:10
    am the greatest, 836:15
    am the light of the world, 41:10
    am the Lord thy God, 8:31
    am the people, 681:7

I (continued)

am the resurrection, 41:19
am the state, 290:5, 388:4
am the way, 41:28
am what I am, 44:23
am what is missing, 830:11
am whatever was or is, 112:3
am with both, 178:5
am with you always, 38:13
am woman, 836:14
am yet what who cares, 431:14
and my Annabel Lee, 479:18
and public understand each other, 672:6
and so do I, 576:8
and you and all of us, 197:1
another I, 84:12
become transparent eyeball, 454:15
believe and take it, 152:3
bring you good tidings, 39:3
bucket full of tears am I, 180:9
but what am I, 484:3
came I saw I conquered, 92:5
came saw and overcame, 192:5
can do better, 716:11
can no more, 587:20
can't get no respect, 807:13
cleave wood there am I, 117:4
did cut it with hatchet, 349:n7
do it exceptionally well, 827:10
do my thing, 738:20
Don't Know's on third, 742:15
even as you and I, 634:21
fashioned myself sorcerer, 603:22
feel it and am in torment, 94:27
get a kick out of you, 732:11
have a dream, 823:2, 823:3
have found it, 86:1
have liberated my soul, 126:8
have not begun to fight, 363:2
have somewhat against thee, 48:8
he was he and I was I, 152:14
hear America singing, 518:14
heir of all ages, 482:7
here am I, 11:16
hid from Him, 620:17
in twelve thousand none, 180:8
infinite I Am, 403:3
it is I, 36:16
John, 48:2
knew him when, 656:9
know not the man, 37:35
know thee not old man, 192:13
letting I dare not, 219:20
longed to see him hanged, 653:11
Lord is it I, 37:25
man in the moon, 182:9
Muses' priest sing, 99:26
myself am hell, 801:7
one alone I am with him, 117:4
reader I married him, 504:16
red I green U, 603:14
rock fly as soon as I, 397:11
said the sparrow, 857:14
say it's spinach, 756:9
says the Quarterly, 425:1
shall return, 690:8
sing of brooks, 247:14
sleep alone, 58:3
stand at the door and knock, 48:15

I (continued)

stranger and afraid, 619:14
struck the board, 250:15
survived, 363:7
the more fool I, 198:7
the sole unbusy thing, 402:11
then Roman now I, 619:1
think therefore I am, 254:4
Tiresias, 718:18
to die and you to live, 76:14
told you so, 424:22
treated him God cured him, 150:5
want to be alone, 770:7
wasted time now doth time waste me,
     180:15
went to Taffy's house, 858:6
went to the woods, 506:28
when I am for myself what am I, 106:3
who saw face of God, 170:19
will be good, 518:2
will be heard, 462:5
will move the earth, 86:2
would prefer not to, 516:22
yam what I yam that's all I yam, 741:8
you and I are suddenly, 818:12
Iacta alea est, 92:n1
Iago, delight in conceiving I., 440:13
     pity of it I., 214:22
Iam ver egelidos refert tepores, 94:n5
Iambics, not escape my i., 94:30
     what little i., 651:12
Ibycus, cranes of I., 60:n2
Ice and iron not be welded, 599:23
     between Eliza and pursuer, 489:18
     caves of i., 401:17, 401:19
     chaste as i., 204:5
     fire and i. within fight, 618:17
     for destruction would suffice, 669:11
     into eternal darkness fire and i., 130:9
     mast-high, 399:12
     on hot stove, 671:12
     seek i. in June, 419:16
     silent language of peak, 725:5
     skating over thin i., 455:30
     smooth the i., 178:14
     thick-ribbed i., 211:23
     trust not one night's i., 251:28
     was here ice was there, 399:18
     will burn, 452:20
Ice cream, emperor of i., 686:15
     enjoy i. while it's on plate, 750:2
Iceberg cuts facets from within, 785:7
     in shadowy silent distance grew I., 576:1
Icebergs behoove the soul, 785:8
Icebox, plums that were in the i., 703:11
Iced, charity scrimped and i., 590:15
Iceland, from Rome to I., 289:15
Ich am of Irlonde, 843:7
     bin ein Berliner, 800:5
     grolle nicht, 442:n3
     weiss nicht was soll es bedeuten, 442:n4
Ichabod, named the child I., 11:19
Icicle, chaste as the i., 224:31
     on Dutchman's beard, 210:7
Icicles, silent i., 401:11
     when i. hang by the wall, 177:17
Icily regular, 485:5
Icumen, sumer is i. in, 843:5
     winter is i. in, 708:17

Icy arms hold hidden charms, 745:2
     bound in i. chains, 212:n1
     current compulsive course, 214:15
     death lays i. hand on kings, 254:9
     principles of i. certainty, 626:19
     reason's i. intimations, 446:11
     silence of tomb, 439:2
Id, ego's relation to i. as rider to horse,
     607:18
     external world super-ego and i., 608:1
     where i. was ego shall be, 608:2
Idea, a good i., 678:7
     absolute i. of knowledge, 78:5
     angry opposition to i., 676:2
     antiquated was once modern, 663:2
     between i. and reality, 719:6
     Christianity is an i., 442:13
     clarity of a general i., 836:11
     dangerous when only one, 648:3
     does not belong to soul, 573:14
     due to individual, 693:6
     every i. an incitement, 578:19
     every new i., 803:2
     every thing has determinate i., 78:6
     for poetry i. everything, 532:4
     get at it as i., 687:16
     give up whole i. of life, 824:7
     governing i. of Hellenism, 531:19
     grant artist his i., 584:16
     is the fact, 532:4
     is not banal, 796:4
     it's the i. behind me Ignatz, 690:5
     made true by events, 583:1
     nothing more dangerous than i.,
          648:3
     O the i. was childish, 381:13
     of Freedom, 488:13
     of genius, 796:4
     of sun, 687:21
     of what true and false, 286:17
     one i. and that wrong, 327:7
     original i. animate nation, 487:12
     pain of a new i., 538:4
     right i. of the gods, 78:16
     see clearly in i. of it, 687:21
     sends us back to first i., 688:2
     teach young i. to shoot, 318:1
     truth happens to i., 583:1
     when i. new custodians have fervor,
          625:3
     whose time come, 451:4
     with image, 403:11
Ideal, cherished i. for which prepared to die,
     803:15
     Christian i. found difficult, 664:5
     higher than ordinary man, 530:2
     Milton attracts into his i., 403:13
     of happiness, 461:10
     polity, 77:13
     reduction to atoms chimerical i.,
          572:2
     to be right by instinct, 67:26
     union fervor with measure, 583:5
Idealism shoved aside, 625:9
     spark of i. fanned, 607:6
Idealistic motives, 625:9
Idealists, heroes as well as i., 577:17
Idealize, secondary imagination struggles to
     i., 403:4

Inches, death by i., 225:2
   die by famine die by i., 295:16
Incident, curious i. of dog in nighttime, 617:7
Incidents, so many i. so many details, 628:9
Incidis in Scyllam cupiens, 189:*n*1
Incipit Vita Nova, 129:14
Incisions, underneath fine i., 544:2
Incisors, writers divided into i. and molars, 538:1
Incite people to learn from past, 822:4
Incited, pseudo-event someone i., 792:23
Incitement, every idea an i., 578:19
Inciters of servile insurrection, 556:3
Incivility and procrastination, 418:6
Inclement, raw i. summers, 298:16
Inclination, read as i. leads, 326:19
   to hear you, 303:7
Inclinations cannot alter evidence, 351:1
   worship God according to own i., 109:18
Incline thine ear O Lord, 27:35
   to which side shall we i., 279:23
Inclined, as to embrace me she i., 263:18
   as twig bent tree's i., 310:3
   sins they are i. to, 271:4
   to notice ruin in things, 796:16
   to snap like vixens, 710:10
Inclines to think there is God, 512:9
Include me out, 695:13
   things that included whole, 688:7
Included in We the people, 832:5
Includes itself in power, 207:27
Inclusion, life i. and confusion, 585:10
Income, annual i. twenty pounds, 497:34
   business with i. at heels, 347:15
   decent fall cloths over high i., 792:15
   devote i. labor to others, 518:10
   good i. of no avail, 636:7
   he has i. she pattable, 763:13
   however great i., 87:18
   just man will pay more i. tax, 77:3
   large i. is the best recipe, 406:14
   live beyond i., 558:20
   rent is sorrow i. tears, 249:8
   solvency not matter of i., 636:6
   twenty expenditure nineteen, 497:34
Incommunicable, burden of i., 418:1
Incomparable, Clemens sole i., 567:9
Incompatibility established between them, 662:4
   spice of life, 763:13
Incompetence, rise to level of i., 805:11
Incompetent, though competent appear i., 83:3
Incomplete and unfit for view, 557:15
Incomprehensibility of God, 445:9
Incomprehensible, history i. without Jesus, 535:8
Incomprehension, mutual i., 772:14
Inconceivable idea of sun, 687:21
Incongruous moonlight shines, 729:11
   with intelligence, 524:1
Inconsistencies in principle, 574:16
   of opinion justifiable, 415:12
Inconsolé, je suis le veuf l'i., 469:*n*2
Inconstancy, constant in Nature i., 275:7
   nothing constant but i., 297:21
   state of man i., 279:18

Inconstant, mob is varied and i., 287:13
   moon, 183:8
Inconvenience, go with show of i., 703:8
Inconveniences, modern i., 560:12
Incorrect, will most i. to heaven, 200:31
Incorruptible, dead raised i., 44:31
   sea-green I., 434:5
Incorruption, corruptible put on i., 44:31
   raised in i., 44:29
Increase and diffusion of knowledge, 385:2
   as if i. of appetite, 201:4
   from fairest creatures desire i., 225:27
   God gave i., 43:34
   his tribe i., 417:12
   in a geometrical ratio, 469:15
   of his government, 26:31
   some nations i. others diminish, 93:2
   without i. or diminution, 404:8
Increased devotion to cause, 476:7
   force in Nature not i., 527:13
   Jesus i. in wisdom, 39:8
   knowledge shall be i., 30:11
   means and leisure, 459:18
Increasers, one thing to say to tax i., 841:*n*2
Increases, absence i. great passions, 273:31
   in geometrical ratio, 385:4
   necessity of being ready i., 475:9
Increaseth, he that i. knowledge i. sorrow, 24:2
Increasing belly, 191:16
   purpose runs, 482:3
   store with loss, 226:18
   youth waneth by i., 164:9
Increment, unearned i., 464:22
Increments, velocities of evanescent i., 306:16
Incumbent, care of poor i. on society, 287:15
Incurable, disease is i., 191:21
   life is an i. disease, 275:13
   old age is an i. disease, 456:*n*1
Ind, from east to western I., 199:7
   wealth of Ormus and I., 264:25
Indebted to memory for his jests, 368:8
Indecency, prejudicial as public i., 158:13
Indecent, sent down for i. behavior, 766:2
Indecision, nothing habitual but i., 581:8
Indeed, friend in need friend i., 86:*n*7
Indefatigable pursuit of unattainable, 636:8
Indefensible, journalist morally i., 830:3
Indemnity for the past, 323:*n*3
Indenture, this oath and this i., 72:16
Independence, banners of foreign i., 385:18
   forever, 414:*n*5
   freedom brought i. rationality, 757:11
   governments whose i. acknowledged, 377:1
   in marriage i. will be equal, 432:6
   individual i. economic principle, 683:2
   magnanimity trust, 506:16
   make real Declaration of I., 674:7
   mutual guarantees of i., 611:11
   now Independence forever, 414:13
   of solitude, 455:10
Independent and have inherent rights, 339:9
   free and i. states, 349:11
   free and i. States, 351:8
   scientist, 742:12
   support renders i., 350:1
Indescribable, beauty i., 629:2

Indestructible, Christianity i. and immortal, 442:13
   Union indestructible States, 468:22
Indeterminable, life-form i., 675:4
Index, a dab at an i., 340:9
   marble i. of a mind, 391:9
Indexes baby figure of giant mass, 207:29
Indian, I'll be an I., 781:2
   knows his village, 760:9
   like the base I., 215:13
   lo the poor I., 311:5
   morn on the I. steep, 260:22
   not decked with I. stones, 172:30
   only a matter of time I., 841:9
   stands free in Nature, 504:24
   summer of life, 570:26
   to I. all days are God's, 614:8
   to wilderness to teach I., 630:8
   wilderness, 296:4
Indians, all immigrants except I., 699:3
   country better when I. running it, 828:7
   give country back to I., 750:13
   know better how to live, 601:2
   only good I. dead, 549:2
   ten little I., 861:6
   thanks f'r bein' presarved fr'm I., 646:5
Indians', called Guanahaní in I. tongue, 140:4
   white man warmed before I. fire, 346:10
India's coral strand, 416:3
Indicates, determines or i. man's fate, 506:9
Indictment against whole people, 344:11
Indies, had come to the I., 140:3
   wealth of I., 328:15
   went to I. to conquer a people, 140:9
Indifference, benign i. of universe, 789:13
   extinction from i., 755:9
   morn and cold i., 303:14
   total i. to public notice, 833:1
   tragedy of love i., 672:21
   when will i. come, 792:22
Indifferent, artist i. paring fingernails, 696:6
   children of earth, 203:12
   delayed till I am i., 326:10
   good bad i., 287:9, 332:20
   rather than believe God i., 461:17
   stood aside been i., 767:11
   to be i. essence of inhumanity, 609:14
   to each i., 729:11
   universe is i., 684:13
Indifferently, look on both i., 195:17
Indigested, irregular i. piece, 324:16
Indignant, no one such liar as i. man, 589:7
   spirit fled i. to shades, 98:12
Indignatio, ubi saeva i., 299:29
Indignation, provoking thy wrath and i., 50:18
   savage i., 299:29, 641:3
   unsatisfied i., 525:16
   until the i. be overpast, 27:19
   will produce verses, 113:1
Indignity, the i. of it, 780:6
Indirect, persecution i. way to plant religion, 255:16
   poet become more i., 722:13
Indirections, by i. find directions, 202:30
Indiscretion, lover without i., 574:17
Indiscriminate charity, 559:9

Infirm, Minstrel i. and old, 396:3
    my body i. and exhausted, 140:10
    of purpose, 220:18
    poor i. weak old man, 216:20
Infirmities, bear his friend's i., 197:11
    bear i. of weak, 43:31
Infirmity, feblit with i., 142:4
    first i. of weak minds, 261:*n*1
    last i. of noble mind, 261:19
    of his age, 215:25
    of will, 455:15
Inflamed with mutual animosity, 366:19
    with study of learning, 262:18
Inflation, continuing process of i., 701:17
Inflections, beauty of i., 687:7
Inflexible, important principles i., 477:6
    we must be i., 666:6
Inflicts, gentleman never i. pain, 450:3
Influence, cock has great i. on own dunghill, 103:5
    corrupt i., 345:3
    deprives republican example of just i., 474:7
    naked people have little i., 563:2
    planetary i., 215:29
    rain i. and judge prize, 259:19
    salutary i. of example, 325:6
    teacher's i. never stops, 570:15
    unwarranted i., 728:16
    win friends i. people, 716:20
Influences, servile to all skyey i., 211:18
    sweet i. of Pleiades, 15:10
    wide world-embracing i., 433:5
Infolded, tongues of flame i., 722:5
Inform, occasions i. against me, 205:35
    press home Christmas, 647:16
    their discretion, 359:6
Information, can find i., 327:26
    vegetable animal mineral, 564:3
    woman of little i., 406:4
Informed, correctly i. as to past, 448:17
    people well enough i., 698:9
Informer poor weak human being, 747:13
Infrequent, sighs short and i., 718:13
    worshipper of gods, 99:17
Infringement of human freedom, 381:4
Infuse, illustrious acts high raptures i., 257:19
    souls of animals i. into men, 189:17
Infuses that liberal obedience, 344:17
Infusing thoughts and passions, 403:16
Infusion, sticky i., 819:4
Ingiuria, chi fa i. non perdona, 107:*n*2
Inglorious arts of peace, 276:22
    mute i. Milton, 334:21
Ingrateful man, 216:18
Ingratitude, haste in paying is i., 273:28
    hate i. more than lying, 210:15
    man's i., 199:1
    thou marble-hearted fiend, 216:4
Inhabit, build houses and i. them, 28:37
    country belongs to people who i. it, 475:6
    house and all that i. it, 351:17
    parched places, 29:17
    soul of grandam i. bird, 189:*n*2
Inhabitant, Indian is Nature's i., 504:24
Inhabitants, Californians a race not i., 626:13
    not only i. of field, 345:16
    number of portraits as great as i., 691:21

Inhabitants *(continued)*
    of some sequestered island, 516:1
    proclaim liberty to all i., 9:16
Inhabits our frail blood, 210:15
    poem, 776:14
Inhale, I didn't i., 839:16
Inherent, decay i. in all component things, 66:22
    purpose i. in art so in nature, 79:18
    rights, 339:9
Inherit, all which it i. dissolve, 230:9
    flow'rets of Eden i., 412:12
    looking uncomfortably to world we i., 852:14
    meek shall i. the earth, 17:5, 33:33
    the wind, 21:20
    tonight doth i., 529:15
    with pain purchased i. pain, 176:18
Inheritance, divided an i. with him, 356:6
    not be destroyed, 360:5
Inherited total lot of parents, 832:7
    tradition cannot be i., 722:6
Inheritor, president is i., 786:7
Inhuman as hawk's cry, 713:13
    of the veritable ocean, 687:8
    reign of lie, 730:10
Inhumanity, indifferent is essence of i., 609:14
    man's i. to man, 377:14
Inimies, keep our i., 645:12
Iniquities, judge allow i., 578:23
Iniquity, bond of i., 42:5
    draw i. with cords of vanity, 26:21
    gray i., 185:30
    I was shapen in i., 17:25
    is pardoned, 27:38
    of oblivion, 256:19
    of the fathers, 8:33
    punish wicked for their i., 27:2
    reaped i., 30:18
    religious know more about i., 632:13
Initial of Creation, 545:21
Iniuria, volenti non fit i., 124:33
Injure, to benefit and not i., 59:21
Injured, forgiveness to i. does belong, 107:*n*2
    like i. fan, 714:3
    minds i. by hunger and thirst, 82:19
    no one i. save by himself, 119:*n*2
    party, 566:16
    those I have i., 801:8
    whom they have i. they hate, 107:4
Injures, never pardons those he i., 107:*n*2
Injuries, forgive me my i., 801:8
    saints in your i., 213:8
Injuring, at expense of i. their virtue, 63:16
    kill time without i. eternity, 506:10
    rarely escapes i. own hands, 59:18
    restrain men from i., 358:12
Injurious, beauty though i., 269:9
Injury, add insult to i., 106:10
    adding insult to i., 330:15
    fear of serious i., 607:2
    greatest service or greatest i., 76:20
    never forget i., 655:2
    never use treatment with view to i., 72:16
    recompense i. with justice, 63:15
    returns on him who began, 93:19

Injury *(continued)*
    sooner forgotten than insult, 314:18
    such i. vex a saint, 175:32
    where i. let me sow pardon, 128:5
Injustice, bear with patience i., 278:10
    complain of i. of government, 386:13
    conscience with i. corrupted, 172:12
    easy to bear, 691:7
    extreme justice extreme i., 124:26
    extreme justice often i., 88:*n*13
    extreme law often extreme i., 88:19
    fear of suffering i., 273:13
    man ever in darkness of i., 122:6
    mankind censure i., 77:4
    no i. to person who consents, 124:33
    nothing so felt as i., 498:32
    one man's justice another's i., 456:2
    put a halt to i., 815:11
    sometimes service to public, 360:11
Injustices, heaped i. upon us, 650:1
Injye other people's sufferin', 646:17
Ink, effusion of i., 338:4
    essential in painting, 125:8
    every drop of i. ran cold, 336:2
    gall enough in thy i., 210:8
    galley slave to i., 445:4
    hath not drunk i., 176:34
    never saw pen and i., 210:16
    runs from mouth, 830:10
    seven seas of i., 122:5
Inkwells, smells of i., 834:3
Inky, not alone my i. cloak, 200:29
Inlaid with patines of bright gold, 190:5
Inland island, 569:14
    though i. far we be, 393:17
Inn, gain timely i., 221:8
    happiness produced by i., 328:2
    make my house your i., 714:9
    no room in the i., 39:2
    remember i. Miranda, 653:7
    take mine ease in mine i., 147:19
    up to old i.-door, 692:2
    warmest welcome at an i., 328:*n*1
    world not i. but hospital, 256:8
Inner light will shine forth, 366:*n*4
    man, 45:26
    mine with i. weather, 670:1
    Temple's i. shrine, 392:16
    weather, 670:1
Innisfail, harp of I., 409:6
Innisfree, go to I., 637:1
Innocence and health, 342:1
    ceremony of i., 639:6
    changed i. for i., 228:10
    confession next thing to i., 104:14
    fearful i., 392:14
    has nothing to dread, 290:13
    her i. a child, 284:12
    ignorance not i., 495:9
    murderous i. of sea, 639:8
    never blossom into license, 290:14
    of love, 209:24
    of our neighbors, 507:15
    our peace our i., 392:14
    Ralph wept for end of i., 786:5
    recovered i., 507:15
    silence often of pure i., 228:15
    soul recovers i., 639:15
    what is our i., 714:11

Insurrection, never did i. want such water-
colors, 186:33
revolution is i., 737:13
servile i., 556:3
suffers nature of an i., 196:1
Intangible, world i. we touch, 621:6
Integer vitae scelerisque purus, 99:*n*9
Integers, God made i., 534:6
Integration, not fighting for i., 815:10
Integrity, clothed with i., 278:10
does one's i. lie, 815:14
in silence preserve i., 129:11
state of natural i., 82:27
territorial i., 611:11
were we men of i., 799:6
Intellect, achievements of i. everlasting, 95:10
adduces authority uses not i., 141:4
character higher than i., 454:23
conformity of object and i., 127:1
fashion birth i., 535:3
feather to tickle i., 407:29
find no i. comparable to my own, 487:13
forced to choose, 641:4
health i. the two blessings, 84:5
improperly exposed, 398:19
invisible to man who has none, 425:19
is to emotion as clothes, 625:8
light between truth and i., 131:13
man with godlike i., 470:7
march of i., 405:21
marks of God in liberal i., 412:18
mugwump educated beyond i., 567:14
of narrow normal amount, 425:18
opinion from feelings not i., 523:5
restless versatile i., 537:13
scepticism chastity of i., 629:18
scholar is delegated i., 454:20
second-class i. first-class temperament,
579:5
subtlety of i., 572:8
too profound for human i., 470:12
unaging i., 639:16
weakness of i., 565:20
Will and I. the same, 286:18
with i. or with conscience, 480:1
Intellection, happiest i., 809:2
Intellects, argument and i. too, 341:12
three classes of i., 142:17
Intellectual, a tear an i. thing, 375:4
All-in-all, 392:3
before committees, 683:16
being, 265:4
curiosity, 678:16
dandyism, 541:12
desolation, 510:9
disgrace, 775:16
enjoyment, 621:13
freedom only guarantee, 808:9
hatred worst, 639:14
lords of ladies i., 423:6
neutralize i. element, 629:13
Northwest Passage to i. world, 332:27
not separate i. from social, 676:17
ought to refuse to testify, 683:16
passion drives out sensuality, 140:12
product judged from age produced,
573:4
responsibility, 731:9
rights and powers, 413:2

Intellectual *(continued)*
take i. possession, 585:13
throne, 529:11
virile courageous, 649:14
Intellectuals at one pole, 772:14
deserve intended slavery, 683:16
I'm one of the i., 747:15
Intelligence, controlling i. understands,
115:24
even if superior i. tell us, 679:4
gods do not give all men i., 54:26
incongruous with i., 524:1
lost money underestimating i. of people,
691:13
making artificial objects, 616:7
overwhelms i. of all gods, 56:5
School I. make it a soul, 441:2
sensation instinct i., 443:6
struggle against limitations of i., 742:13
talent inspiration, 622:7
test of first-rate i., 746:13
use of i. pleasure, 830:6
vast enough to comprehend all forces,
366:13
which goes with sex, 707:17
Intelligences, first animals then i., 541:7
Intelligent, all i. thoughts already thought,
366:6
beam me up no i. life down here, 852:21
enemies i. and corrupt, 767:12
may be called i. indeed, 63:7
Mr. Toad, 618:5
perception of least i., 726:11
perfection in becoming i. being, 127:6
pleasing one i. man displeasing fools,
127:5
possesses keen i. mind, 75:22
so elegant so i., 718:15
woman, 659:3
Intelligible, monarchy an i. government,
538:2
your first i. sentence, 759:2
Intelligibly, speak i. to world, 636:17
Intend, what evil I i. to do, 69:27
Intended, take hint when i., 671:17
years damp my i. wing, 267:25
Intending to build tower, 39:33
Intense loneliness intense ignorance, 606:11
moment isolated, 721:5
Intensely, soul listened i., 395:5
Intensity, all I care about is i., 577:4
full of passionate i., 639:6
grandeur remains without i., 110:12
moving into another i., 721:6
of feeling, 772:13
Intent, eye i. on mazy plan, 379:13
forget not yet tried i., 149:25
his first avowed i., 282:4
is al, 134:9
love come with murderous i., 70:2
night of dark i., 669:19
not criminal unless i. criminal, 123:7
on hospitable thoughts i., 267:5
prick sides of my i., 219:18
truth told with bad i., 375:9
Intention stabs the center, 228:12
Intentional, abstain from i. wrongdoing,
72:16
Petersburg most i. town, 525:8

Intentions, hell full of good i., 126:9
hell paved with good i., 126:*n*4,
251:*n*1
honorable, 349:6
Intents are savage-wild, 184:12
discerner of thoughts and i., 46:38
wicked or charitable, 202:5
Inter, in hugger-mugger i. him, 206:9
in peace children i. parents, 71:10
Intercourse between tyrants and slaves,
341:25
hold i. with roots of trees, 710:7
in her i. with foreign nations, 410:*n*3
lived in social i., 327:11
open and friendly in private i., 73:18
sexual i. began, 810:6
supremest of delights sexual i.,
562:22
with foreign nations, 410:20
Interest, art makes life makes i., 585:21
duty and i., 350:10
exceed in i. knock at door, 407:17
features of biological i., 822:2
I du believe in i., 515:2
impulse of passion or i., 366:18
it wouldn't i. anybody, 835:7
of the producer, 339:1
promote public i., 338:18
public i., 727:6
pursue his own i. his own way, 339:2
regard to their own i., 338:13
take personal i. in well-drawn character,
560:9
unborrowed from the eye, 391:3
Interested in big things, 627:19
know one's self is i., 573:11
not i. in defeat, 518:4
what American people are i. in, 840:1
Interesting, American want of the i., 532:9
because unimportant, 727:16
obligation of novel be i., 584:14
other people, 573:11
statements i. but tough, 560:16
Interest's on dangerous edge, 493:9
Interests, Christian men control property i.,
580:4
eternal and perpetual i., 417:20
exposed to conflicting i., 697:3
great i. at stake, 81:4
human figure i. me most, 651:17
of community, 366:18
politicians have i. aside from people's,
474:2
various powerful i., 414:1
Interfered in behalf of rich, 447:3
Interfused, something far more i., 391:4
Intergraft our hands, 235:4
Interim like a phantasma, 196:1
Interlude, strange i., 724:3
Interludes, strange dark i., 724:3
Interlunar, vacant i. cave, 268:33
Intermeddle, stranger doth not i., 21:29
Interminable night, 721:18
Intermingle jest with earnest, 168:8
Intermission, laugh sans i., 198:17
pleasure is i. of pain, 245:23
Internal domestic empire, 748:6
environment, 501:2
medium, 501:1

Italy, beyond Alps lies I., 102:12
    far from I. I lie, 85:15
    fashions in proud I., 179:10
    graved inside of it I., 492:13
    Greece I. and England did adorn, 284:27
    had warfare terror murder, 797:4
    notice ruin because born in I., 796:16
    Paradise of exiles, 428:16
Itch, incurable i. for writing, 113:13
    of disputing, 233:1
Itchez, Ah i. Ah scratchez, 763:11
Itching palm, 197:7
Iteration, damnable i., 184:31
Ithaca, fill I. full of moths, 224:18
    setting out on voyage to I., 628:7
Ithers, see ourselves as i. see us, 378:6
Itself, illness which regards i. as therapy,
        672:10
    is it true in and for i., 390:11
    love is most nearly i., 721:6
    no relevance to anything but i., 806:11
    thou art the thing i., 216:30
Itylus, half assuaged for I., 567:17
Iucundior, quae est domestica sede i.,
        90:n12
Iudex damnatur ubi nocens absolvitur,
        103:n4
Iudicaret, ne supra crepidam sutor i., 83:n4
Iura, sunt superis sua i., 105:n15
Ius est ars boni et aequi, 124:5
    summum saepe summa est malitia,
        88:n13
Ivan Ilych dying, 543:2
    Ilych's life most simple, 543:1
    Petrofski Skevar, 849:3
Ives, going to St. I., 857:6
Ivory apes and peacocks, 12:20, 681:4
    bit of i. on which I work, 406:25
    gate of i., 55:22, 98:2
    neck is as a tower of i., 25:30
    tower, 676:17
    tower of i., 461:2
Ivy, goats eat i., 860:10
    holly and the i., 846:2
    myrtle and i., 424:26
    not hang i. over wine, 104:11
    pluck i. branch for me, 548:1
    with i. never sere, 261:13
Ivy-mantled tower, 334:10, 692:17

J

Jabal father of such as dwell in tents, 6:19
Jabberwock, beware J., 551:10
J'accuse, 577:8
Jack and Jill, 858:4
    banish plump J., 185:32
    be nimble, 860:5
    house that J. built, 861:15
    joke poor potsherd, 588:6
    little J. Horner, 857:3
    makes J. a dull boy, 253:11
    of Spades, 704:n2
    one named J. fly away J., 861:14
    Sprat eat no fat, 856:20
Jackass can kick barn down, 697:8
Jackknife, just a j. has Macheath, 750:16
Jackknives, pelicans flew like j., 797:9

Jackson standing like stone wall, 535:17
    Stonewall J. wrapped in beard, 750:12
    who didst pick up Andrew J. from
        pebbles, 516:11
Jacky have new master, 858:5
Jacob called the place Peniel, 7:21
    gave Esau bread and pottage, 7:11
    God of J. not philosophers, 280:12
    served seven years, 7:17
    sold his birthright unto J., 7:11
    that which has been sent down on J.,
        120:13
    thy tents O J., 9:26
    was a plain man, 7:10
    was left alone, 7:19
    wrestled as Angel with J., 252:19
Jacob's ladder, 621:8
    talk of J. ladder, 458:10
    voice is J. voice, 7:12
Jade, arrant j. on a journey, 341:22
    let galled j. wince, 205:5
Jael brought forth butter, 10:32
    took a nail, 10:28
J'ai vécu, 363:7
Jail, all we know who lie in j., 605:22
    can't be sint to j. for it, 646:20
    like living in j., 781:13
    little stealin' gits you in j., 723:14
    patron and the j., 324:6
    with chance of being drowned, 326:16
Jailed for telling lies to young, 770:15
Jailer another kind of captive, 469:3
    inexorable as self, 460:18
Jake, Yukon J., 745:3
Jam, Calico J., 500:1
    every other day, 552:8
    tomorrow jam yesterday, 552:9
Jamaicas of Remembrance, 546:19
Jambs, unscrew doors from j., 519:9
James could almost hear the bronze Negroes,
        801:11
    Councillor to King J., 162:17
    I James II Old Pretender, 726:7
    James Morrison Morrison, 697:4
    King J. used to call for old shoes, 245:15
    let J. rejoice, 338:4
    novel by Henry J. like church, 644:14
    work of Henry J., 726:7
James's, ladies of St. J., 574:12
Jamshyd gloried drank deep, 471:8
Jane, from J. to Elizabeth, 406:7
    John Thomas marryin' Lady J., 707:13
    me Tarzan you J., 674:n4
Jangled, sweet bells j., 204:9
Jangling, keep juices flowing by j. around,
        774:11
Janitor, with the help of the j., 756:5
January, a Fly this J. Day, 546:19
Japan, forces of Empire of J., 698:17
    from Paris to J., 289:15
    what they say in J., 579:13
Japanese reliance on intuition, 674:13
Japheth, Noah begat J., 6:24
Jar, feel amid city's j., 528:13
    in Tennessee, 687:2
    people in front get j., 678:18
    retains odor, 412:n1
    strings untouched will harshly j., 170:16
    wine j. when molding began, 101:17

Jardin, il faut cultiver notre j., 316:n5
Jargon of the schools, 296:16
Jars, two j. on floor of Zeus, 54:6
Jasper of jocundity, 142:3
Jaundiced eye, 308:24
Jaunts, Jorrocks' j. and jollities, 458:11
Javan, bound for J. or Gadire, 269:6
Jaw, muscular strength to j., 550:2
Jawbone of an ass, 11:4
Jaw-jaw better than to war-war, 668:5
Jaws, gently smiling j., 549:13
    of darkness do devour it, 180:20
    of death, 155:5, 485:2
    of sea and earth, 759:14
    that bite, 551:10
Jay, new j. born every day, 850:n1
Jay Gatsby of West Egg Long Island, 746:5
    poor Jim J., 662:15
Jaybird don't rob own nes', 593:12
Jazz, ask what j. is, 757:1
    we j. June, 798:10
Jazzmen, go to it O j., 681:14
Je connais tout fors moi-même, 140:n1
Jealous, art j. mistress, 456:27
    confirmations, 214:5
    for they are jealous, 214:17
    I am a j. God, 8:33
    in honor, 198:25
    law a j. mistress, 412:16
    not j. for the cause, 214:17
    one not easily j., 215:13
    possessions of happiness, 651:1
    readiest to forgive, 526:4
    scornful yet j. eyes, 312:4
    souls not answered, 214:17
    venom clamors of j. woman, 174:38
Jealousies, surmises j. conjectures, 191:6
Jealousy, beware my lord of j., 213:34
    born with love, 274:6
    ear of j. heareth all, 31:12
    feeds upon suspicion, 273:6
    full of artless j., 206:3
    green-eyed j., 189:7
    has a human face, 374:12
    in j. more self-love, 274:2
    is cruel as the grave, 26:3
    is the rage of a man, 21:8
    life of j., 213:36
    of rivals near throne, 361:15
    these are the forgeries of j., 181:7
Jeanie with light brown hair, 539:2
Jeanne d'Arc and Bonaparte, 728:11
Jeers, exiled on ground in j., 524:8
Jefferson, celebrities such as J., 554:11
    Thomas J. still surv—, 352:4
    when J. dined alone, 799:13
    Yoknapatawpha County, 748:18
Jeffers's, too much like one of J., 713:13
Jehovah, in name of great J., 355:9
    is my strength, 27:1
    Jove or Lord, 313:7
    Lawd God J., 728:3
    tell them I Am J. said, 337:16
Jehu, the driving of J., 13:4
Jekyll, Dr. J. and Mr. Hyde, 599:3
Jellies soother than creamy curd, 437:2
Jelly, distilled almost to j., 201:16
    out vile j., 217:8
Je-ne-sais-quoi young man, 564:12

Jenny kissed me, 417:16

Jeoffrey, consider my Cat J., 338:6

Jeopardized, black freedom j., 815:11

Jeopardy, nor be twice put in j., 361:4
    went in j. of their lives, 12:10

Jeremy, Mr. J. liked feet wet, 644:5

Jericho, from Jerusalem to J., 39:22
    Joshua fit battle of J., 862:26
    tarry at J. until beards be grown, 12:1

Jerusalem, daughters of J., 25:12
    from J. to Jericho, 39:22
    I saw the new J., 48:38
    I will wipe J., 13:8
    if I forget thee O J., 20:11
    meet in sweet J., 173:13
    my happy home, 844:15
    speak comfortably to J., 27:38
    temple of J., 121:10
    that killest prophets, 37:5
    the golden, 511:11
    thy sister calls, 376:6
    was J. builded here, 375:17
    wise men came to J., 33:18

Jeshurun waxed fat, 10:14

Jessamine, casement j. stirred, 485:10

Jesse, David the son of J., 12:9
    rod out of the stem of J., 26:33

Jesses my dear heart-strings, 214:2

Jessica, sit J. look, 190:5

Jest and youthful jollity, 259:9
    best to use myself in j., 234:10
    between j. and earnest, 157:7
    breaks no bones, 329:9
    fellow of infinite j., 206:24
    glory j. and riddle, 311:9
    good j. forever, 185:14
    I j. to Oberon, 181:5
    intermingle j. with earnest, 168:8
    life is a j., 307:19
    most bitter is scornful j., 323:12
    put his whole wit in a j., 245:4
    unseen inscrutable, 176:7

Jested quaffed and swore, 487:10

Jester, fool and j., 192:13

Jesting, no j. with edge tools, 243:3
    what is truth said j. Pilate, 167:5

Jest's prosperity lies in ear, 177:15

Jests, he j. at scars, 182:28
    indebted to memory for j., 368:8

Jesu, by will of J. into another place, 139:15
    Christ and seiynte Benedight, 136:3
    Lord J. blessed Pelican, 129:6
    my dearest one, 154:14

Jesuit, bland as a J., 594:7

Jesus, accept J. as Savior, 813:15
    as J. sat at meat, 37:19
    author and finisher, 47:1
    came to save sinners, 46:15
    Cross of J., 555:2
    gentle J. meek and mild, 322:25
    history incomprehensible without J., 535:8
    Incarnate saved us, 765:5
    increased in wisdom, 39:8
    keep your hearts through Christ J., 45:37
    king of Jews, 38:7
    lover of my soul, 322:24
    loves me this I know, 539:13
    man who says he is J., 333:12

Jesus *(continued)*
    miracles did J. in Cana, 40:40
    most scientific man, 526:11
    nobody knows but J., 862:25
    none but J. heard, 443:10
    of twice-turned cheek, 765:2
    parsons preaching J. a revolutionary, 812:7
    saith give me to drink, 40:47
    shut up in asylum, 618:3
    stand up stand up for J., 510:3
    sure this J. will not do, 376:10
    that which was given to J., 120:13
    took bread, 37:27
    was a Jew, 684:12
    was born in Bethlehem, 33:18
    went to them walking on the sea, 36:15
    wept, 41:20
    we're more popular than J. now, 834:11
    with J. we worship Father, 412:17

Jesus Christ, advocate with the Father J., 47:38
    Don Quixote and I, 415:21
    her little child, 508:9
    I believe in J., 50:3
    kingdom and patience of J., 48:2
    our Lord, 51:2
    people who never heard of J., 726:2
    redemption by our Lord J., 50:8
    risen today, 294:8
    testimony of J., 48:2
    that J. is born, 862:28
    the same yesterday today and for ever, 47:6

Jesus', good friend for J. sake, 231:19

Jets, sound of j. overhead, 756:16

Jeunesse, au temps de ma j. folle, 139:*n3*
    cueillez cueillez votre j., 151:*n3*
    qu'as-tu fait de ta j., 591:*n1*
    si j. savait, 151:11

Jew, because I wasn't J., 735:18
    either for Englishman or J., 376:10
    hated like a J., 829:8
    hath not a J. eyes, 188:30
    human form in heathen turk or j., 372:7
    I'm not a J. I'm Jew-ish, 830:4
    Jesus was a J., 684:12
    judges neither J. nor Gentile, 695:7
    much kindness in the J., 188:10
    neither Greek nor J., 46:3
    of Tarsus, 42:26
    only J. in Danville looking for matzoh, 815:7
    that Shakespeare drew, 313:11
    wandering J., 853:26
    what one J. does, 822:7
    yes I am a J., 458:24

Jewel, caught my heavenly j., 164:1
    immediate j. of souls, 213:33
    no j. like Rosalind, 199:7
    of gold in swine's snout, 21:18
    of the just, 279:9
    precious j. in his head, 197:37
    rich j. in Ethiop's ear, 182:25

Jeweled unicorns, 719:13

Jewelry, like j. from a grave, 785:7

Jewels five-words-long, 482:17
    give j. for set of beads, 180:4
    these are my j., 241:19
    unclasps warmed j., 437:1

Jewish, being J. trouble enough, 796:3
    choose a J. God, 706:*n1*
    establishment of home for J. people, 593:2
    final solution of J. question, 737:7
    gaberdine, 188:8
    living in middle of J. joke, 828:12
    man with parents alive, 828:13
    no J. blood in my veins, 829:8

Jew-ish, I'm not a Jew I'm J., 830:4

Jews, Jesus king of J., 38:7
    King of the J., 33:18
    kiss and infidels adore, 309:5
    odd of God to choose the J., 706:12
    Papists Protestants J. Turks in one ship, 255:3
    refuse till conversion of J., 276:27
    right and status of J. in any country, 593:2
    spurn the J., 706:*n1*
    thrown back at all J., 822:7

Jezebel, dogs shall eat J., 12:35
    painted her face, 13:5

Jiggety-jig, home again j., 860:15

Jigsaw, Rosebud missing piece in j. puzzle, 749:6

Jill, Jack and J., 858:4
    other named J. fly away J., 861:14

Jim, poor J. Jay, 662:15
    simple child dear brother J., 390:*n5*

Jimmie crack corn, 847:20

Jinetes, los cuatro j. del Apocalipsis, 645:7

Jingle, little j. little chimes, 307:22
    triumph and the j., 699:16

Jingling of guinea, 481:22

Jingly, Lady J. Jones, 500:5

Jingo, by j. if we do, 539:5
    repent by j., 445:22

Joan as my Lady, 248:6
    Darby same to old wife J., 594:3
    greasy J. keel pot, 177:17

Job, blessed the latter end of J., 15:26
    doth J. fear God for nought, 13:24
    fall into it like a soft j., 824:7
    give tools finish j., 666:8
    go to Hell will help them is my j., 578:16
    hypocrisy is whole-time j., 672:22
    more than one way to do j., 852:*n3*
    patience of J., 47:22
    poor as J., 191:14
    that's my j., 837:14

Joblillies, Picninnies and the J., 336:12

Jobs, right people in right j., 502:14

Jockey of Norfolk not too bold, 161:*n4*

Jocund, cocks and lions j. be, 235:13
    day stands tiptoe, 184:5
    rebecks sound, 259:16
    such a j. company, 394:7
    then be thou j., 221:6

Jocundity, jasper of j., 142:3

Joe, G.I. J., 851:19
    Old Black J., 539:3
    say it ain't so J., 851:3
    where have you gone J. DiMaggio, 837:9

Joe's, Sloppy J., 776:5

Jog on the footpath way, 228:24

Johannes, absolute J. fac totum, 165:18

Johano-ai, Turquoise Horse of J., 856:3

John and I are quit, 297:5
  Anderson my jo, 379:4
  awake my St. J., 310:20
  Baptist's head, 36:12
  Barleycorn got up again, 378:16
  Brown's body, 558:3
  Bull or Englishman's fireside, 383:15
  Don J. of Austria, 664:10
  Donne Anne Donne Un-done, 233:*n3*
  greatest of all is J. Bull, 424:29
  I J., 48:2
  I J. saw the holy city, 48:38
  inspiring bold J. Barleycorn, 379:19
  Matthew Mark Luke and J., 274:20
  my son J., 860:7
  or Shaun, 696:16
  Peel with coat so gay, 435:15
  shut the door good J., 311:19
  some said J. print it, 281:12
  speak for yourself J., 467:5
  Stuart Mill, 674:5
  there St. J. mingles, 312:14
  Thomas marryin' Lady Jane, 707:13
  who killed J. Keats, 425:1
  whose name was J., 40:31
John Henry told his captain, 848:15
Johnny, Frankie and J., 849:14
  I hardly knew ye, 847:6
  leave her J. leave her, 862:8
  little J. Green, 857:19
  whiskey J., 861:23
John's, bounded by St. J., 487:5
Johnson, great Chain of literature Samuel J.,
  337:8
  Kennedy and J. administrations, 798:1
  no arguing with J., 343:8
Join, children j. hands and sing, 823:4
  choir invisible, 512:14
  don't j. too many gangs, 670:4
  few gangs if any, 670:4
  hand in hand Americans, 349:10
  now j. your hands and hearts, 173:6
  the family, 670:4
  them that j. house to house, 26:19
  triumph of skies, 323:1
  union and say Equal Pay, 521:21
  United States, 670:4
  will you j. dance, 551:1
Joined, he has j. great majority, 109:4
  lawfully j. together, 51:8
  make third j. former two, 284:27
  my name j. to theirs, 105:10
  rogue and whore together, 299:6
  what God hath j., 36:32
  when issues are j., 59:15
  whom God hath j., 51:12
Joint, every j. and motive, 208:19
  heirs with Christ, 43:5
  remove the j., 552:18
  time is out of j., 202:29
Joint-laborer, night j. with day, 200:17
Joints, dividing j. and marrow, 46:38
  of all gin j. in all towns in world, 782:7
Joke, ain't no j., 828:12
  every j. long ago made, 566:9
  forgive Thy j. on me, 671:4
  good j. not criticized, 664:9
  Jack j. poor potsherd, 588:6
  living in middle of Jewish j., 828:12

Joke *(continued)*
  loses everything when joker laughs, 381:6
  many a j. had he, 342:8
  treat woman as dirty j., 830:7
Joked about every prominent man, 685:20
  world j. incessantly, 566:9
Joker, joke loses everything when j.
  laughs, 381:6
Jokes, crack any of these old j., 75:17
  difference of taste in j., 513:13
  Fate's saddest j., 61:*n2*
  little j. on Thee, 671:4
  standing j., 302:3
  ten j. an hundred enemies, 332:6
Jollities, Jorrocks' jaunts and j., 458:11
Jollity, jest and youthful j., 259:9
  tipsy dance and j., 260:20
  upon my yowthe and my j., 136:13
Jolly and easy in minds, 490:5
  miller, 352:5
  red nose, 249:15
  swagman, 630:9
  three j. huntsmen, 860:12
  What j. fun, 624:9
Jonah was in the belly of the fish, 30:27
Jonathan heard not his father's oath, 11:24
  loved him as his own soul, 11:32
Jones, Casey J., 655:9
  Lady Jingly J., 500:5
  this is the army Mr. J., 716:9
Joneses, keeping up with J., 850:4
Jonson, Ben J. his best poetry, 237:21
  O rare Ben J., 237:*n2*
Jonson's learned sock, 259:20
Jordan, fertilize J. plain, 680:1
  I looked over J., 863:3
  stood in midst of J., 10:19
  that's the river of J., 863:9
Joris and he, 492:3
Jorrocks' jaunts and jollities, 458:11
Joseph, king which knew not J., 7:39
  stript J. of his coat, 7:23
Joshua fit battle of Jericho, 862:26
  like J. commanded sun, 320:21
Jostle, though Philistines may j., 564:9
Jostling, no man lives without j., 434:13
  not done by j. in street, 375:18
Jot, one j. of former love retain, 169:14
  one j. of heart or hope, 263:16
  or tittle, 34:3
Jour, le j. de gloire est arrivé, 383:8
Journal, aussi vieux que le j. d'aujourd'hui,
  663:*n3*
Journalism, responsible j., 727:6
Journalist, bribe or twist British j., 710:4
  knows is morally indefensible, 830:3
Journey, arrant jade on a j., 341:22
  begin j. on Sundays, 299:21
  dawn speeds a man on j., 56:17
  death and sorrow on our j., 666:6
  end of j. too, 625:14
  going a j., 410:10
  he is in a j. or sleepeth, 12:29
  in middle of j. of life, 129:17
  intellectuals describe j. into Communism,
  777:3
  life is its own j., 774:13
  long day's j. into night, 724:8
  longest j. go, 429:25

Journey *(continued)*
  longest j. inwards, 770:9
  longest part of j., 90:1
  Monopoly Business at end of j., 592:11
  night j. on a bus, 812:18
  of a thousand miles, 59:12
  some point of pointless j., 809:8
  soul of j. liberty, 410:12
  to oblivion, 707:22
  to promised land, 655:9
  to unknown, 738:2
  universe in map, 157:34
  with my strange heroes, 472:22
Journeyed across centuries, 667:5
Journeyman to grief, 179:3
Journeymen, delicate art relegated to j.,
  692:8
  nature's j., 204:14
Journey's, dine at j. end, 638:18
  here is my j. end, 215:11
  when j. over, 618:8
Journeys end in lovers meeting, 209:13
Journeywork of stars, 519:15
Jours s'en vont je demeure, 689:*n3*
Jove, daughter of J., 334:1
  for his power to thunder, 224:28
  front of J. himself, 205:21
  in ancestral J. Troy's sons rejoice, 98:4
  Jehovah J. or Lord, 313:7
  laughs at lovers' perjuries, 183:5
  we descend from J., 98:4
  where J. bestows, 253:13
  with J. I begin, 95:18
Jove's, immortal J. dread clamors, 214:8
  of J. nectar sup, 238:2
  starry threshold of J. Court, 260:11
Jovi, eripuitque J. fulmen, 107:*n7*
Jovial, Autumn comes j. on, 318:3
  three j. huntsmen, 321:*n7*
Joy, all that j. can give, 310:6
  although our last, 215:16
  always to j. inclined, 373:10
  and Love triumphing, 265:26
  antique j., 636:18
  apprehend some j., 182:3
  at weeping, 194:4
  be unconfined, 420:17
  be wi' you a', 385:9
  bed of crimson j., 374:3
  before a j. proposed, 227:22
  bitter j., 752:10
  brightened with j., 395:5
  bringer of that j., 182:3
  chortled in his j., 551:11
  cometh in the morning, 16:26
  courage love j., 307:13
  deep power of j., 391:2
  delights in joy, 225:30
  dreme of j. all but in vayne, 138:*n8*
  enter into j., 37:13
  Europe thrilled with j., 391:10
  even his griefs are a j., 55:14
  every child may j. to hear, 371:14
  excursion same for sorrow as j., 784:4
  father's j. mother's pride, 397:15
  feast of j. a dish of pain, 164:17
  formed of j. and mirth, 376:2
  fruit of Spirit is j., 45:22
  gem of all j., 142:3

Joy *(continued)*

general j. of whole table, 221:13
glad tidings of great j., 294:5
good tidings of great j., 39:3
Greensleeves all my j., 844:1
have j. or power, 454:4
he who binds to himself a j., 373:13
honey of all earthly j., 275:4
I wish you j. of the worm, 224:8
in trouble and in j., 294:6
is the sweet voice, 402:7
is wisdom, 637:7
kisses j. as it flies, 373:13
lean in j. upon Father's knee, 372:3
man made for j. and woe, 375:10
marriage has more j. than pain, 69:9
masterpiece j. to artist, 557:16
meet with j. in sweet Jerusalem, 173:13
my j. my grief, 257:23
my life my j., 155:8
no j. but lacks salt, 669:17
no j. in Mudville, 630:4
nor love nor light, 531:2
not because troubles are delectable j.,
    92:19
not carol of j. or glee, 660:2
not intermeddle with his j., 21:29
now 'tis little j., 445:16
O j. that in our embers, 393:14
O what j. and glory must be, 126:5
Ocean and my j., 422:3
of elevated thoughts, 391:4
of life is variety, 324:22
of love too short, 139:6
oil of j. for mourning, 28:31
pain short j. eternal, 382:13
perfect j. therein I find, 155:*n*1
Phyllis is my only j., 290:16
pity planet all j. gone, 801:17
pleasance revel, 213:26
poet's j. conceals despair, 678:2
politics of j., 786:6
pray in j. and abundance, 700:21
pure and complete j. impossible, 542:16
reveal itself when transformed in us,
    677:6
rule of j. and duty one, 577:20
scrip of j. immortal diet, 160:8
senses forever in j., 493:16
shall reap in j., 20:3
shudder of j. runs up, 811:13
silence perfectest herald of j., 194:20
silly j. at silly things, 342:*n*1
snatch a fearful j., 333:19
sons of God shouted for j., 15:6
source of Humor not j. but sorrow, 562:3
spontaneous j., 638:2
stern j. warriors feel, 397:12
strength through j., 729:8
surprised by j., 395:9
Tahiti full of peace and j., 516:16
that your j. be full, 41:34
the luminous cloud, 402:7
thing of beauty j. forever, 436:8
this is alone Life J. Empire Victory,
    428:14
this torment my j., 781:6
thou spark from Heaven, 381:8
to pass to world below, 97:20

Joy *(continued)*

to the world, 304:9
to their friends, 54:22
true j. in life, 609:15
walked in glory and j., 392:9
was never sure, 569:2
weep at j., 194:4
where poverty and j., 128:4
whose hand is ever at lips, 438:16
work with j., 700:20
world can give, 422:16
Joyance everywhere, 399:9
Joyce, private man James J., 833:1
Joyful all ye nations rise, 323:1
    births, 193:25
    in day of prosperity be j., 24:20
    make a j. noise, 18:5, 18:29, 19:3
    shall my j. temples bind, 257:22
Joyfulness prolongeth his days, 32:42
Joyless, sin to be j., 738:21
Joyous, how j. his neigh, 856:3
    understanding is j., 830:6
Joyously, flowers through grass j. sprang,
    127:13
Joyousness, lends j. to a wall, 579:10
Joy's, burst J. grape, 438:16
    soul lies in doing, 207:21
Joys abound as seasons fleet, 172:9
    as winged dreams, 844:5
    be j. three parts pain, 494:9
    bid j. farewell, 436:3
    fairest j. give unrest, 436:13
    fall not to rich alone, 101:6
    homely j., 334:14
    in another's loss of ease, 374:2
    kill your j. with love, 184:19
    let j. be as May, 249:14
    minds me o' departed j., 378:21
    nakedness all j. are due to thee,
        235:24
    only solitary know j. of friendship,
        661:20
    our youth our j. our all, 160:14
    perish in infancy, 845:1
    present j. more to flesh and blood,
        284:24
    raise j. and triumphs high, 322:23
    sting destined to poison j., 516:1
    summer hath his j., 232:3
    taste whole j., 235:24
    tasted eternal j. of Heaven, 170:19
    tenderness its j. and fears, 393:19
    thy j. when shall I see, 844:15
    to this are folly, 239:17
    vain deluding j., 259:22
    with age diminish, 495:10
    youth's season for j., 307:15
Jubal father of such as handle harp, 6:20
Jubilant, bright pomp ascended j.,
    267:16
Jubilee, bring the J., 553:11
    fiftieth year j., 9:16
    sons to thy J. throng, 426:13
    year of J., 863:6
Jubjub bird, 551:10
Judah and Israel dwelt safely, 12:13
    say unto the cities of J., 28:4
    sin of J., 29:16
Judaism religion of the father, 608:5

Judas had given them the slip, 295:22
    if J. had not been born, 37:26
    jealous J. cowardly Peter, 767:9
    saith Why is ointment not sold,
        41:22
    so J. did to Christ, 180:8
Judea, Bethlehem of J., 33:18
Judge above his last, 83:11
    allow iniquities, 578:23
    amongst fools a j., 109:*n*8
    by sample we j. whole, 156:2
    children j. parents, 604:18
    condemned when criminal absolved,
        103:10
    do not j. us too harshly, 750:19
    forbear to j., 172:14
    I j. not thee, 159:13
    I'll be j. I'll be jury, 549:14
    impartial guardian of rule of law, 807:9
    impartial j., 345:20
    justice j. or vicar, 367:24
    law says j. as looks down nose,
        776:1
    listening like j. supreme, 446:12
    my friend j. not me, 159:13
    my witness and my j., 242:12
    never j. until other side heard, 70:6
    no king can corrupt, 230:28
    no one should j. own case, 103:19
    none blessed, 32:23
    not according to appearance, 41:6
    not play before done, 249:12
    not that we be not judged, 477:3
    not that ye be not judged, 34:23
    of all things, 280:8
    of authors' names, 308:20
    out of thy mouth will I j., 40:10
    people j. men by success, 273:26
    people seldom j. right, 370:9
    quick and the dead, 50:3
    rain influence j. prize, 259:19
    right j. judges wrong, 67:17
    setting yourself up as j., 78:15
    should not be young, 77:6
    sober as j., 321:16
    sole j. of truth, 311:9
    the fatherless, 26:10
    to j. events sanely, 416:19
    upright j. learned j., 189:27
Judged in light of final issue, 81:15
    intellectual product j. from age produced,
        573:4
    judge not that we be not j., 477:3
    judge not that ye be not j., 34:23
    not to have lived, 577:15
    should be j. as a captain, 140:9
Judge's robe, 211:10
Judges, a fool with j., 109:*n*8
    all ranged, 307:18
    as j. neither Jew nor Gentile, 695:7
    common j. of property, 324:17
    Constitution what j. say, 626:18
    do and must legislate, 578:10
    hungry j. sentence sign, 309:10
    in every state bound thereby, 360:16
    lots of mediocre j., 767:15
    of facts not laws, 306:15
    right judge j. wrong, 67:17
Judgest, thou j. another, 42:39

Justice *(continued)*

lance of j. hurtless breaks, 217:24
law of humanity j. equity, 345:9
let j. be done though heaven fall, 123:26
let j. be done though heaven perish, 385:*n*5
liberty plucks j., 210:36
love of j. simply fear, 273:13
machine rolls of itself, 647:2
made for sake of peace, 144:11
marriage placed under rule of equal j., 465:7
mercy seasons j., 189:19
mirage of social j., 753:21
moderation in j., 355:*n*1
no such thing as j., 612:22
not charity wanting in world, 382:27
not violate laws of j., 339:2
one man's j. another's injustice, 456:2
peace a disposition for j., 286:13
peace more important than j., 144:11
penetrates Eternal J. as eye into sea, 132:4
Poetic J., 313:16
price of j. publicity, 645:5
rails upon thief, 217:23
reason and j., 370:13
recompense injury with j., 63:15
returns, 95:22
revenge a wild j., 167:8
strength without j., 280:3
strong lance of j., 217:24
subject to God and J., 126:17
superhighway of j., 823:6
sword of j. has no scabbard, 368:17
sword of j. lay down, 295:4
temper j. with mercy, 268:6
temporary but conscience eternal, 144:12
the law my ducats, 188:24
there is none, 127:14
though j. be thy plea, 189:19
thunders condemnation, 504:21
Thwackum was for doing j., 322:6
to none sell j., 128:9
toward all nations, 350:10
uncompromising as j., 462:4
was done, 575:9
what stings is j., 691:7
where j. denied, 510:2
which is the j., 217:23
white moderate less devoted to j., 822:12
with liberty and j. for all, 606:17
without j. courage weak, 319:6
without strength, 280:3
work for tolerance for j., 724:19

Justifiable, inconsistencies often j., 415:12
ways of God j. to men, 269:3

Justification, work of art carry j., 611:15

Justified, not j. doing evil for expediency, 615:2
whom he called he j., 43:8
wisdom j. of her children, 35:34

Justifieth, it is God that j., 43:10

Justify, culture doesn't j., 772:10
end must j. the means, 296:18
God's ways to man, 619:9
he will not j. you without you, 119:20
thought to j. wrongdoings, 316:18
ways of God to men, 263:21

Justifying means by the end, 118:10
virtue debases in j., 315:17
Justitia, fiat j. ruat coelum, 123:26
Justly, do j. and love mercy, 30:28
Just-spring, in J., 739:11
Jutty, no j. frieze buttress, 219:15
J'y suis j'y reste, 469:*n*1

K

Kaleidoscope, no law of history than of k., 517:13
Kane man who got everything wanted, 749:6
Kansas and Colorado have quarrel, 705:2
I've feeling not in K. anymore, 786:8
Kansas City, ev'rythin's up to date in K., 744:6
Karamazovs, all we K. such insects, 525:12
they have Hamlets we K., 526:6
Kaspar's, old K. work was done, 405:4
Kat, I ain't a K., 690:5
Kate, kiss me K., 175:29
O K. nice customs curtsy to great kings, 194:2
some alas with K., 776:5
trust thee gentle K., 185:18
Kathleen Mavourneen, 447:6
Kathryn, or Mabelle or K., 694:10
Katydid, glaze on k.-wing, 714:20
Kayak, I was out in my k., 856:11
Keats, Tennyson outglittering K., 452:13
who killed John K., 425:1
Kedar, tents of K., 25:12
Keel, drinks water her k. plows air, 165:11
greasy Joan doth k. pot, 177:17
keep mind steady on k., 515:20
ship sink on even k., 106:24
thrill of life along k., 466:18
Keen and hard like wedge, 707:6
and quivering ratio, 544:3
blessed man who possesses k. mind, 75:22
discriminating sight, 389:15
dull fighter and k. guest, 186:29
love's k. arrows, 199:19
polished razor k., 314:3
with k. appetite he sits down, 188:19
Keener with constant use, 416:12
with his k. eye, 276:23
Keep and pass and turn again, 453:22
another thing hidden, 55:7
at times frae being sour, 378:2
bid them k. teeth clean, 224:23
breath's a ware will not k., 618:8
cold young orchard, 669:18
coming back and coming back, 688:12
company he is wont to k., 71:2
cool, 456:20
corner in thing I love, 214:4
Dead Sea gets to k., 680:1
down base in man, 486:8
easier to get than k. Fortune, 103:3
'em down on the farm, 708:1
England k. my bones, 178:21
except the Lord k. the city, 20:4
eyes open before marriage, 319:21
fear God and k. his commandments, 25:10

Keep *(continued)*

golden mean, 99:*n*16
good tongue in head, 230:3
goodbye and k. cold, 669:18
green tree in heart, 122:26
guard and k. them, 59:14
he may k. that will and can, 619:13
home fires burning, 663:1
how to k. is there any, 587:17
ideas won't k., 625:3
in adversity k. an even mind, 99:21
in despite of light k. us together, 234:16
keeping men off k. them on, 307:11
let it k. one shape, 211:3
like love seldom k., 776:2
Lord bless thee and k. thee, 9:17
many to k., 513:23
me as the apple of the eye, 16:8
Nelson touch, 627:7
on truckin', 838:1
our Christmas merry still, 396:21
own appointed limits k., 537:19
Past upon throne, 515:9
promises to k., 669:15
push on k. moving, 384:12
republic if you can k. it, 321:2
right to k. and bear arms, 361:2
Sabbath going to Church, 544:17
shop and shop keep thee, 165:2
six honest servingmen, 635:9
soul bought by one able to k. it, 489:20
state in wonted manner k., 237:10
stiff upper lip, 535:18
stop hole to k. wind away, 206:26
strong in any case keep cool, 744:15
sunny side up, 736:18
sword within scabbard k., 285:21
talk from getting overwise, 670:3
thee in all thy ways, 18:26
thee in the way, 9:5
thee only unto her, 51:9
them within thee, 22:27
thing seven years, 398:10
this up forever, 692:17
thou my feet, 449:18
thy friend under own key, 210:20
thy heart with all diligence, 21:2
thy tongue from evil, 17:2
time to k., 24:6
to moderation, 110:3
up appearances, 496:40
up your bright swords, 212:22
we are going to k. dog, 790:18
wolf from door, 141:*n*4
word of promise to our ear, 222:22
wrong to k. guest back, 55:13
yet I k. them, 822:9
you shall k. the key, 201:28
your hearts and minds, 45:37
your powder dry, 409:16
yourself to yourself, 495:28

Keeper, Abel was k. of sheep, 6:12
brother's k., 6:13
of warm lights, 68:1
the Lord is thy k., 19:30
Keepers of the house shall tremble, 25:7
Keepest ports of slumber open, 192:6

Kind *(continued)*

could not ourselves be k., 750:19
cruel only to be k., 205:30
enjoy her while she's k., 284:8
Fortune more k. than her custom, 189:25
had it been early had been k., 326:10
heart benevolent and k., 378:17
hearts more than coronets, 480:14
human k. not bear much reality, 720:6
I am a k. of burr, 212:4
I have been her k., 821:9
kindness not therefore k., 310:2
lady sweet and k., 844:21
less than k., 200:27
love is k., 44:18
no best in k. but degree, 466:22
not seek for k. relief, 372:11
plenty of the k., 480:6
serve country and thy k., 556:2
thief said last k. word, 494:25
through fire for k. heart, 190:30
two almost divide the k., 310:7
war is k., 655:19
were all thy children k., 192:25
where each of us belongs, 820:13
yet he was k., 342:8
Kinder, a little k. than necessary, 621:16
gentler nation, 813:11
Kindle, cannot k. when will, 528:12
soft desire, 285:15
truths k. light for t., 92:18
Kindled, anger of Lord k., 11:42
at taper of conwiviality, 496:28
earth, 425:5
light here k., 247:10
man like light k. and put out, 64:12
world Fire k., 64:6
Kindles, fires true Genius k., 312:4
in clothes a wantonness, 248:3
love kindled by virtue k. another, 131:20
Kindleth, how great a little fire k., 47:16
Kindliness of sheets, 712:18
Kindling her undazzled eyes, 263:3
Kindly, be k. affectioned, 43:17
earth slumber, 482:2
frosty but k., 198:5
fruits of the earth, 50:15
had we never loved sae k., 378:24
if heart just frank k., 278:10
Light, 449:18
Nature's k. law, 311:11
stopped for me, 545:15
to his fellow men, 52:30
word goodly act, 682:3
words do not enter so deeply, 82:18
Kindness, a God of great k., 13:17
acts of k. and of love, 390:20
always depended on k. of strangers,
787:17
and lies, 767:7
begets kindness, 67:7
Christ took k., 494:25
cup o' k. yet, 379:9
glad k., 639:12
in women not looks, 175:36
kill wife with k., 175:35
learned k. from unkind, 700:22
lose natural k., 639:9
milk of human k., 219:10

Kindness *(continued)*

much k. in the Jew, 188:10
no act of k. ever wasted, 60:11
not free from ridicule, 476:6
not therefore kind, 310:2
recompense k. with k., 63:15
reputation for k. enters deeply, 82:18
show k. to parents, 121:11
sincerity earnestness and k., 63:25
to fellow creature, 847:23
tongue is the law of k., 23:30
what wisdom greater than k., 331:8
wished to lay foundations of k., 750:19
Kindnesses, great persons great k., 158:20
of k. one makes heart run over, 355:15
thought of k. done, 94:24
Kindred, friends k. days, 453:8
never in such slavery as to forgo k.,
109:19
true to k. points, 395:18
welcome k. glooms, 317:14
Kindreds, all nations and k., 48:23
Kinds, absolute natures or k., 78:5
birds are k. of knowledge, 78:12
material objects of two k., 92:16
Kine, learn from k. ruminating, 588:20
Pharaoh's lean k. loved, 185:31
seven good k., 7:26
seven thin k., 7:26
King, a' for our rightfu' K., 379:1
a new k. over Egypt, 7:39
Arthur is not dead, 139:15
balm from an anointed k., 179:24
born to be k., 616:9
but thou the k. did banish, 179:4
by your own fireside, 155:13
Cambyses' vein, 185:29
can do no wrong, 338:11
cat may look on k., 149:5
catch conscience of k., 203:31
Charles' head, 498:3
chief defect of Henry K., 653:8
cometh unto thee lowly, 30:37
contrary to k. built paper-mill, 172:22
Cophetua loved beggarmaid, 182:27
cotton is k., 450:15
David and King Solomon, 623:11
divinity doth hedge a k., 206:10
earth receive her K., 304:9
every inch a k., 217:20
exists only as such, 153:19
farced title 'fore k., 193:16
farewell k., 180:1
first k. fortunate soldier, 315:24
follow the K., 485:20
George be a k., 491:1
glare surrounds k. hides him, 153:19
glorious to be Pirate K., 564:2
glory to newborn K., 323:1
God bless the K., 314:12
God save the K., 11:21, 308:1
God save the k. say amen, 180:8
good K. Wenceslas, 511:9
governs like a k., 331:21
great God our K., 469:9
great K. above all gods, 18:29
greater than K. himself, 323:7
half the zeal I served my k., 231:8
heart and stomach of a k., 151:13

King *(continued)*

heaven's all-gracious k., 488:15
here lies a K. that ruled, 253:12
here lies the k., 292:24
honor the k., 47:28
I am the Roman k., 278:*n6*
I couldn't leave without the k., 757:7
I was a K. in Babylon, 594:13
if chance will have me k., 219:6
impossible to discharge duties as K.,
742:14
in carriage may ride, 472:7
in country of blind one-eyed man is k.,
142:6
in exile, 707:11
in sleep a k., 227:1
is the k. dead, 174:16
Jesus K. of Jews, 38:7
kings did k. to death, 795:4
let there be one k., 52:15
little profits idle k., 481:7
Long live the k., 347:24
love is my lord and k., 484:16
made for quietness' sake, 246:1
Madness wholesome even for K., 546:15
mine eyes have seen the K., 26:25
mockery k. of snow, 180:12
Moloch sceptered k., 264:26
more royalist than k., 855:5
mortal temples of k., 179:28
my God and K., 250:24
niece of K. Gorboduc, 210:16
no k. in Israel, 11:11
not every year a k. born, 114:14
of a k. of England too, 151:13
of all kings, 843:10
of Babylon stood at the parting, 29:33
of France went up hill, 856:19
of glory shall come in, 16:20
of infinite space, 203:15
of kings, 48:35, 323:*n1*
of love my shepherd is, 524:6
of pain, 568:22
of shreds and patches, 205:24
of Spain's daughter, 859:7
of terrors, 14:22
of the Jews, 33:18
offends no law is k. indeed, 165:9
old and foolish k., 24:10
old k. to sparrow, 662:14
old mad blind despised k., 429:11
once and future k., 139:*n2*
over children of pride, 15:24
Ozymandias k. of kings, 427:18
pageantry of k., 360:8
passing brave to be a k., 170:3
Pirate K., 564:2
reigns but not govern, 154:15
rightwise k. of England, 139:1
ruthless K., 335:11
seemed to me like k., 707:11
shall reign in righteousness, 27:28
sigh sword of Angel K., 375:4
singer accompany the k., 382:11
sits in Dunfermline, 853:16
so excellent a k., 201:3
Son of Heaven's eternal K., 258:16
still I am k. of those, 180:10
stomach of a k., 151:13

Knotted and combined locks part, 202:12
Know a subject ourselves, 327:26
    all I k. is I am not Marxist, 510:13
    all there is to be knowed, 618:5
    all ye k. on earth, 438:5
    allow you do not k., 62:17
    arrive at what not k., 721:1
    as I am known, 44:20
    as if to k. became fatality, 688:11
    as much as possible, 585:19
    be still and k. that I am God, 17:23
    best that is in one, 589:9
    best things not learned, 333:15
    better be ignorant than half k., 104:8
    better k. nothing than what ain't so, 508:17
    better k. nothing than half-k., 508:*n*3
    blaspheme what they do not k., 280:10
    both act and k., 276:25
    by their fruits k. them, 35:9
    charms slaves never k., 347:6
    dancer from dance, 640:15
    determined to k. beans, 507:10
    disciplines of wars, 193:6
    disposition of women, 89:9
    do not k. much about gods, 721:7
    do you k. me my lord, 203:4
    does one really want to k., 793:13
    doesn't k. what he likes, 741:13
    don't k. where go better, 669:5
    dost k. who made thee, 371:15
    dost thou k. me fellow, 215:31
    enough who k. how to learn, 570:17
    every wise man's son, 209:13
    everything forgive everything, 385:*n*4
    for whom bell tolls, 236:19
    four things wiser to k., 738:10
    gallanter I k., 544:4
    go we k. not where, 211:23
    God with thee k. it not, 392:16
    greater than we k., 395:13
    have the gift to k. it, 198:19
    hawk from handsaw, 203:20
    he will k. it's gone, 791:13
    heartily k., 453:9
    how in your darkness k., 656:18
    how should I true love k., 206:4
    how tender 'tis to love babe, 219:23
    how to grow old, 524:3
    how to speak falsehoods, 56:3
    I am but summer, 735:6
    I am happier than I k., 267:19
    I k. a bank, 181:12
    I k. all worth knowing in America, 487:13
    I k. and world knows, 450:7
    I k. it when I see it, 797:3
    I k. myself a man, 233:3
    I k. not seems, 200:29
    I k. not the man, 37:35
    I k. that is poetry, 547:9
    I k. thy pride, 11:26
    I k. what I like, 659:10
    I k. you all, 184:36
    I k. you are here, 836:2
    I said I didn't k., 560:5
    I shall meet fate, 638:16
    if cuckold may not k., 706:5
    if don't k. where going, 805:12

Know *(continued)*
    if find answer k. mind of God, 837:3
    if to do as easy as to k., 187:27
    if you gotta ask you'll never k., 757:1
    if you want to k. yourself, 381:16
    I'm farther from heaven, 445:16
    in baseball don't k. nothing, 814:9
    in Boston ask how much does he k., 561:19
    in mathematics never k. what about, 660:11
    in part prophesy in part, 44:20
    in truth we k. nothing, 72:13
    it no more, 19:7
    Jesus loves me this I k., 539:13
    knows not how to k., 525:5
    less than all unknown, 242:10
    less understand more, 699:13
    let him not k. 't, 214:7
    let not left hand k., 34:10
    liberty to k., 263:4
    like love don't k. where or why, 776:2
    living k. no bounds, 254:5
    lucky to die and I k. it, 519:1
    make me to k. mine end, 17:12
    man not k. of God, 767:1
    many admire few k., 73:12
    men k. so little of men, 648:10
    much say little, 331:7
    my methods Watson, 617:9
    my soul hath power to k., 233:2
    neither shall his place k. him, 14:3
    never k. how high we are, 546:9
    never k. what is enough, 373:1
    never prophesy onless k., 515:4
    never see nor k. nor miss me, 696:18
    no such liberty, 276:2
    none of them k. one half as much, 618:5
    not enough to k., 80:20
    not k. I am a woman, 199:12
    not subtle ways, 453:22
    not utter what dost not k., 185:18
    not what they do, 40:19
    not what they mean, 482:21
    not what we may be, 206:6
    not whether laws be right, 605:22
    nothing except my ignorance, 72:8
    only broken images, 718:12
    only dog I k., 811:3
    only k. we loved in vain, 419:9
    only that he nothing knew, 268:28
    others that we k. not of, 203:33
    parting all we k. of heaven, 547:3
    people you k. yet can't name, 810:9
    place for first time, 722:4
    pleasure none but madmen k., 283:22
    pools I used to k., 619:5
    power to k. all things, 233:2
    reason from what we k., 311:1
    rest who does not k., 105:1
    safer to k. too little, 558:12
    say not you k. another, 356:6
    saying all we did not k., 710:14
    shall never k. how to Reply, 375:12
    she thinks o' me, 633:12
    shore of what we k., 809:7
    something of own country, 332:29
    strive to grasp what they do not k., 82:29

Know *(continued)*
    study great deal to k. little, 314:11
    subject of knowledge is to k., 78:12
    tell me what you k., 454:7
    that age to age succeeds, 480:7
    that I may k. how frail I am, 17:12
    that man might k. end, 197:18
    that men are like children, 700:16
    that my redeemer liveth, 14:25
    that the Lord is God, 19:3
    that you do not know, 59:16
    the best thought and said, 531:10
    the like no more, 471:18
    the right moment, 57:4
    them by their fruits, 35:8
    there is cause for her to k., 791:6
    they k. and do not k., 720:3
    this I k. full well, 296:1
    thought so now I k. it, 307:19
    thyself, 56:24, 311:9
    till then what love I bore thee, 392:6
    to k. is nothing, 586:10
    to k. men thoroughly, 416:19
    to k. to kill to create, 524:20
    to k. well involves ignorance, 517:4
    too much convinced of too little, 722:15
    trick worth two of that, 185:11
    we all k. Anna Livia, 696:15
    we are eternal, 287:16
    we k. the good, 69:28
    we k. what we are, 206:6
    well I am not great, 486:2
    what do I k., 153:4
    what do we k., 771:11
    what false heart doth k., 220:3
    what God and man is, 486:21
    what I know and write it, 794:9
    what I like, 659:10
    what I read in papers, 685:12
    what is past I k., 31:7
    what is to come I k. not, 31:7
    what no other man can k., 612:6
    what other people don't know, 617:4
    what should it k. of death, 390:15
    what should they k. of England, 634:2
    what 'tis to pity, 198:22
    what to do with this time, 454:26
    what want to prove, 648:2
    what wood a cudgel's of, 271:14
    what you don't k. make book, 399:4
    when one doesn't k. where going, 364:23
    when you k. your name, 826:12
    where'er I go, 393:9
    where I am I don't k., 773:16
    which way wind blows, 836:9
    who only England k., 634:2
    who speaks does not k., 59:9
    who we are enlist again, 819:9
    whose prayers make whole, 633:1
    whose woods I think I k., 669:13
    with complete certainty, 807:9
    world unknowable we k., 621:6
    world without going outdoors, 59:7
    worst and provide for it, 352:13
    wot lays afore us, 497:9
    ye not there is a prince fallen, 11:40
    you k. as well as we, 74:7
    you k. how it always is, 803:2
    you know more than you think, 765:21

Know *(continued)*
  you k. we French, 491:7
  you k. what I was, 793:8
Knowed, know all there is to be k., 618:5
Knowest, speak less than thou k., 216:2
  thou k. my downsitting, 20:12
  thou k. thy estimate, 226:27
  thou k. 'tis common, 200:28
  thou the land, 363:16
Knoweth, He k. all things, 122:15
  he k. not who shall gather them, 17:14
  no man k. of his sepulcher, 10:17
  sun k. his going down, 19:11
Knowing I loved my books, 229:15
  not k. what they do, 194:37
  of Devil's party without k. it, 372:13
  secret of happiness freedom, 74:5
  when to have done, 435:5
  who you are, 816:4
  without author's k. it, 627:20
Knowledge, absolute idea of k., 78:5
  acquired under compulsion, 77:18
  after such k., 718:3
  all k. and wonder is pleasure, 166:2
  all k. my province, 165:21
  and love of God, 51:2
  apply thine heart unto my k., 22:27
  ask it for k. of lifetime, 557:20
  birds are kinds of k., 78:12
  book of k. fair, 265:25
  born in possession of k., 63:1
  born to follow k., 131:2
  but no power, 71:26
  by suffering, 463:10
  causes to be without k., 58:9
  chapter of k. very short, 315:10
  climbing after k. infinite, 170:4
  comes wisdom lingers, 482:4
  conformity of object and intellect, 127:1
  dawn of k. false dawn, 748:8
  death is k., 382:9
  desirable of itself, 450:2
  desire more love and k., 197:31
  desire of k. caused man to fall, 167:19
  desire of k. increases, 332:14
  diffused k. immortalizes, 384:17
  diffusion of k. advantageous, 462:15
  discard k., 82:28
  do deed without God's k., 65:26
  doubt grows with k., 366:2
  dreadful k. of truth, 68:5
  earth full of k. of Lord, 26:34
  enormous makes God of me, 438:20
  essential k., 501:10
  every sluice of k. opened, 350:18
  exact k. of the past, 73:16
  excellent things in counsels and k., 22:28
  extraordinary collection of k., 799:13
  faith sight and k., 504:23
  fence against world is k., 286:12
  follow k. like star, 481:11
  foundations of k. in mathematics, 128:11
  furnish means of acquiring k., 386:6
  grow from more to more, 483:12
  grow virtuously into k., 628:4
  he that hath k. spareth his words, 22:8
  he that increaseth k., 24:2
  her ample page, 334:19
  highest point not K., 701:10

Knowledge *(continued)*
  if a little k. dangerous, 537:10
  improver of natural k., 536:16
  in traveling carry k., 328:15
  increase and diffusion of k., 385:2
  increaseth strength, 22:39
  is bought in market, 512:7
  is of two kinds, 327:26
  is power, 166:1
  is proud, 348:12
  is sufficient to attain, 63:21
  is the one only good, 72:6
  liberty not preserved without k., 350:17
  light of k. in eyes, 576:14
  like what we imagine k. to be, 785:11
  manners must adorn k., 314:25
  may give weight, 315:7
  meager and unsatisfactory, 536:5
  men by nature desire k., 80:4
  money power, 787:16
  more than force, 166:n1
  much k. a curse, 83:1
  multiplieth words without k., 15:2
  must come through action, 68:13
  never learned of schools, 468:10
  night unto night showeth k., 16:10
  no k. beyond experience, 286:4
  no work nor device nor k., 24:29
  not arrogant because of k., 3:4
  not infused from without, 82:12
  not true k. but only belief, 122:9
  of atom through stars, 695:4
  of God more than burnt offerings, 30:16
  of Greek thought, 539:9
  of human nature, 406:21, 570:8
  of itself a treasure, 450:2
  of nothing, 495:17
  of other culture appreciate our own,
    761:10
  of our buried life, 529:4
  of their duty, 74:5
  of unconscious activities of mind, 607:8
  of women of his own family, 465:4
  of world not in closet, 314:17
  opinion is k. in making, 263:1
  out-topping k., 528:3
  peace and k. pass argument, 518:17
  poetry finer spirit of k., 391:14
  profess not the k., 31:31
  puffeth up, 44:8
  rich storehouse, 166:6
  science achieve perfect k., 527:14
  science begets k., 73:6
  search for k. a passion, 661:5
  shall any teach God k., 14:29
  shall be increased, 30:11
  should be his guide, 77:6
  show tracks of k., 93:3
  sorrow is k., 423:2
  spirit of k. and fear of the Lord, 26:33
  subject of k. is to know, 78:12
  subjective and objective in k., 403:2
  subtracting from human k., 574:7
  sweetly uttered k., 163:25
  they have too much k., 59:13
  this is k., 62:17
  to be possessed of all this k., 350:14
  to the young man k. and discretion,
    20:22

Knowledge *(continued)*
  too much k. for skeptic, 311:9
  tree of k. of good and evil, 5:19
  under difficulties, 410:1
  virtue harder than k., 286:11
  what man does not based on k., 727:1
  wise man has no extensive k., 59:21
  wise man utter vain k., 14:18
  you have been given little k., 121:13
Knowledgeable of evils, 64:26
Knowledges, general k. idiots possess, 374:14
Known a better day, 396:3
  all writer had k. become grotesques,
    677:18
  among leaves never k., 437:8
  and do not want it, 326:10
  because of all things k., 638:8
  believed what is least k., 152:15
  best k. and thought, 530:9
  by company he keeps, 71:n1
  by people never heard of Jesus Christ,
    726:2
  cause hidden result well k., 105:16
  God of fathers k. of old, 635:1
  have ye not k., 28:7
  if k. going to live this long, 700:13
  know as I am k., 44:20
  lady k. as Lou, 673:9
  letters should not be k., 229:25
  much to be done little k., 325:15
  must have k. me had he seen me, 504:7
  no more than other men, 280:21
  searched me and k. me, 20:12
  too late, 182:26
  unto whom all desires k., 50:16
  what do to be forever k., 275:2
  what Greeks did not uncertainty, 753:3
  you're k. as who, 822:11
Knows, all this the world well k., 227:22
  babs k. what and babs k. why, 680:3
  but world end tonight, 492:20
  each exercise art he k., 75:3
  expert k. more about less, 625:16
  God's mouth k. not falsehood, 65:22
  greatness k. itself, 186:30
  happy who k. rural gods, 96:14
  how to confess, 319:22
  if you k. of a better 'ole, 716:3
  it k. not what it is, 640:1
  man says what he k., 331:13
  no beast but k. some pity, 173:32
  no one k. masterpiece, 709:6
  no one k. till he tries, 104:5
  not also to un-know, 525:5
  not draw out more than already k., 590:8
  not how other half lives, 252:12
  not what to do, 856:14
  now God alone k., 566:14
  reason k. nothing of, 280:1
  sage k. without going about, 59:7
  Secret sits in middle and k., 670:16
  sleep that k. not breaking, 397:7
  tale every schoolboy k., 333:17
  tell wife all he k., 258:7
  the less one k., 59:7
  the universe not himself, 276:20
  toad beneath harrow k., 632:9
  what none other k., 642:2
  what one k. of little moment, 570:17

Knows *(continued)*
  what's what, 496:3
  who k. does not speak, 59:9
  who k. himself is enlightened, 59:1
  who k. only his side k. little, 464:12
  who k. others is wise, 59:1
  wise father that k. child, 188:17
  wot's wot, 496:3
  you not Heavenly Powers, 363:15
Knuckle-end of England, 398:14
Ko-ax, brekekekex k. k., 75:18
Kolyma island of Gulag, 804:13
Kontinent, als unser K. das alte, 366:*n*3
Kosciusko, Freedom shrieked as K. fell,
    408:13
Kosmis, in my K. no feeva of discord, 690:6
    Walt Whitman a k., 519:9
    with dread abysses, 583:4
Kraft durch Freude, 729:*n*2
Krazy, ain't a Kat ain't K., 690:5
Kremlin's mountaineer, 732:2
Krieg, der K. ist nichts anderes, 413:*n*1
    ernährt den Krieg, 382:*n*1
Krishna, splendor of Mighty One K., 87:8
Krivchians, the Chuds Slavs and K., 125:12
Kronos, son of K., 52:10
Ku Klux Klanner, Negro's stumbling-block
    not K., 822:12
Kubla Khan, in Xanadu did K., 401:13
Kultur, wenn K. höre, 729:*n*1
Kunst, in der K. ist das Beste gut genug,
    364:*n*1
Kunti, son of K. goes, 87:7
Kurtz, Mistah K. he dead, 612:10
Kyloe, little K. cow, 858:10
Kyrie eleison, 49:10

L

Laban said heap of stones a witness, 7:18
Labeled Gwladys or Ysobel, 694:10
Labels, men are l. that give name to event,
    542:12
Labor, a youth of l., 342:2
  all ye that l., 35:35
  and intent study, 262:11
  and to wait, 466:3
  and wounds are vain, 512:10
  as another's serf, 55:9
  at eternal task, 535:11
  aversion to l., 293:18
  bad book as much l., 741:3
  basic hero l., 649:5
  because they excel, 410:18
  blossoming or dancing, 640:15
  bread from mouth of l., 358:12
  brow of l., 622:3
  capital an' l. git t'gether, 649:9
  capital fruit of l., 475:11
  capital solicits aid of l., 414:10
  capitalists employers of l., 511:*n*2
  changes l. from burden to honor, 686:2
  cost is l. to produce anything, 517:12
  devote income l. to others, 518:10
  exact day-l. light denied, 263:13
  genius intuitive talent for l., 321:*n*5
  good week's l., 243:20

Labor *(continued)*
  grant me this l., 96:1
  has natural and market price, 404:8
  honest l. bears a lovely face, 233:6
  in all l. there is profit, 21:32
  in the deep mid-ocean, 480:21
  in vain, 20:4
  independent and proud, 414:10
  independent of l. of hands, 506:4
  knowledge remuneration for l., 450:2
  learning without thought is l. lost,
    62:16
  little effect much l., 406:25
  long workers idle, 120:8
  look after souls in l., 78:9
  man organized by l., 649:5
  many must l. for one, 422:10
  marvels of man's l., 779:6
  mountain was in l., 60:*n*7
  mountains will be in l., 101:23
  my l. for my travail, 207:20
  no sin to l. in vocation, 184:33
  not ask for reward, 145:5
  not to be rich, 22:33
  nothing but l. for pains, 155:15
  obtain tradition by l., 722:6
  of an age, 259:3
  of love, 46:7
  of two days, 557:20
  of women in house, 623:3
  only relaxation another kind of l.,
    586:13
  organization of l., 683:6
  prior to capital, 475:11
  private property fruit of l., 678:14
  process which A acquires for B, 580:14
  pro-l. policies, 694:4
  reward of l. is life, 557:6
  rights protected not by l. agitators,
    580:4
  say picture shows l., 557:15
  selling l. power, 511:*n*3
  six days shalt thou l., 8:34, 502:16
  superior to capital, 475:11
  take nothing of his l., 24:14
  that has reference to want, 390:10
  those who l. in earth, 357:10
  thou and I waste, 150:1
  to his l. until evening, 19:11
  union pressure, 694:4
  useless if object useless, 510:8
  visible and invisible l., 451:14
  we delight in physics pain, 220:22
  what profit of all his l., 23:32
  why life all l. be, 480:18
  yet is their strength l. and sorrow, 18:22
Laborare, orare est l., 124:11
Laboratory, every l. closed ten years, 694:18
Labored not for myself only, 33:2
  nothings, 308:14
Laborer, I am a true l., 199:6
  right of l. to savings, 559:7
  son of robust l., 693:10
  worthy of hire, 39:19
Laborer's task o'er, 538:10
Laborers, enable l. to subsist, 404:8
  farmers mechanics and l., 386:13
  harvest plenteous but l. few, 35:23
  selling labor power to live, 511:*n*3

Laborers *(continued)*
  sore l. have hard hands, 270:10
  together with God, 43:35
Laboring children can look out, 677:21
  drift in l. salt, 830:14
  fine thing needs much l., 637:18
  rights and interests of l. man, 580:4
  sleep of a l. man, 24:13
  to produce bons mots, 278:6
Laborious, live l. days, 261:19
Labor's, sore l. bath, 220:16
Labors, garner fruits of l., 630:5
  notice you take of my l., 326:10
  patient under dangerous l., 556:3
  rest from their l., 48:33
  saints who from l. rest, 534:5
Labourage et pâturage deux mamelles,
    165:*n*5
Labyrinth, wandering in dark l., 169:18
Labyrinthical, perplexed l. soul, 237:2
Labyrinthine ways, 620:17
Lace, brace l. latch catch, 587:17
  Greek is like l., 329:3
Lacedemonians not wont to ask how many,
    72:3
Lacerare, cor l. nequit, 299:29
Lacerate, cannot l. his breast, 641:3
  savage indignation l. heart, 299:29
Laces just reveal surge, 544:6
Lacessit, nemo me impune l., 124:8
Lack, eternal l. of pence, 482:12
  gall, 203:30
  good counselors l. no clients, 210:35
  he that giveth unto the poor shall not l.,
    23:18
  if any l. wisdom, 47:9
  of many a thing sought, 226:8
  plentiful l. of wit, 203:9
  shalt not l. any thing, 10:3
  they l. a sacred poet, 100:15
Lacked, being l. and lost, 194:39
  if I l. anything, 251:2
Lackey, card l. to those above, 731:3
Lacking, in nature's inventions nothing l.,
    141:9
  little is never l., 93:17
  neither honor nor lyre, 99:16
Lackluster eye, 198:15
Lacks, what it l. in length, 670:13
Laconic or sententious type, 653:17
Lacrimae, hinc illae l., 88:*n*6
  rerum, 96:*n*15
Lad, blithe Irish l., 408:16
  born to be king, 616:9
  come to you my l., 379:7
  lightfoot l., 619:6
  of mettle a good boy, 185:19
  pass me the can l., 619:11
  up l. when journey's over, 618:8
  well for sailor l., 482:15
  when all world young l., 514:4
  when I was a l., 563:17
Ladder always close to schooner, 824:13
  behold a l., 7:14
  charity's golden l., 127:3
  down l. rung by rung, 634:1
  Jacob's l., 458:10, 621:8
  made death his l., 161:27
  make a l. of our vices, 119:16

Ladder (*continued*)
   talk of Jacob's l., 458:10
   to all high designs, 207:25
   unto l. turns his back, 195:30
   young ambition's l., 195:30
Ladders, lie down where l. start, 643:2
Laddie, your Highland l. gone, 384:3
Laden, with rue heart l., 619:6
Ladies and gentlemen of the class, 841:13
   art helps old l. across street, 824:5
   Cambridge l., 739:14
   Dust was Gentlemen and L., 545:18
   good night sweet l., 206:7
   Grecian Urn worth old l., 749:3
   if l. be but young and fair, 198:19
   in praise of l. dead, 227:11
   intellectual, 423:6
   lion among l., 181:18
   lords and l. of Byzantium, 640:2
   novel on tables of l., 448:10
   of St. James's, 574:1
   over-offended l., 303:11
   remember the l., 361:11
   when he has l. to please, 406:17
   whose bright eyes, 259:19
   wild witches noble l., 638:19
Ladies', kindling smiles in l. eyes, 446:12
   pearls in beauteous l. eyes, 176:14
   rime into l. favors, 193:27
Ladles, cooks' own l., 491:16
Lads, Dust was L. and Girls, 545:18
   golden l. and girls, 225:23
   pure-minded l. and lasses, 549:6
   that die in glory, 618:16
   though l. far away, 663:1
   thought no more behind, 228:9
Lady be good to me, 746:22
   born in bed with a l., 678:13
   Bountiful, 305:4
   by yonder blessed moon I swear, 183:8
   church ain't out till fat l. sings, 850:15
   Colonel's L. an' Judy O'Grady, 634:19
   Disdain, 194:9
   doth protest too much, 205:4
   downstairs ran l. 0, 846:22
   enjoyed the l., 373:9
   faint heart ne'er won fair l., 158:2
   faint heart never won fair l., 565:5
   fairer l. never seen, 853:24
   fine l. upon white horse, 858:14
   fool called her l. fair, 634:21
   for secrecy no l. closer, 185:18
   garmented in light, 429:15
   give l. what she wants, 556:4
   he saw a l. bright, 854:2
   hear l. sing in Welsh, 186:11
   here lies l. of beauty, 724:12
   here lies most beautiful l., 662:9
   history excitable old l., 597:16
   I asked a lithe l., 373:9
   if you got to ask, 757:*n*1
   if you were April's l., 568:21
   Jingly Jones, 500:5
   Joan as my L., 248:6
   John Thomas marryin' L. Jane, 707:13
   lent him to a l., 860:22
   Liner she's a l., 634:17
   longing for that lovely l., 89:17

Lady (*continued*)
   longing to be a lazy l., 715:12
   many many l. friends, 623:11
   met l. in meads, 439:4
   my fair l., 857:4
   my l. sweet arise, 225:12
   O l. we receive what we give, 402:5
   of certain age, 424:11
   of Christ's College, 280:22
   of my delight, 592:14
   of Shalott, 480:26, 481:1
   old l. from Dubuque, 735:19
   Old L. of Threadneedle Street, 376:11
   or the tiger, 557:7
   Our L. of Pain, 568:4
   rather hear L. howl in Irish, 186:11
   rob l. by marriage, 322:11
   Seymour's Fat L., 805:15
   sighed for love of l., 565:25
   sweet and kind, 844:21
   talking to Hens of Dorking, 500:5
   that's known as Lou, 673:9
   that's why l. is tramp, 744:11
   the brach may stand, 216:1
   weep no more my l., 539:1
   who was that l., 647:14
   with Lamp, 467:9
   you are the cruelest she, 209:8
   young l. named Bright, 664:4
Ladybug fly away home, 857:8
Lady's, brain him with l. fan, 185:17
   for all l. hire, 860:22
   get you to l. chamber, 206:24
   he capers nimbly in l. chamber, 173:30
   imagination rapid, 406:5
   in my l. chamber, 858:11
   in the case, 307:9
   love learned in l. eyes, 177:5
Ladyships, lordships sold to maintain l., 239:15
Lady-smocks all silver-white, 177:16
Lafayette we are here, 620:11
Lag-end of my life, 186:31
Lager, give Irishman l. for month, 560:11
Laggard in love, 396:19
Lags, fiction l. after truth, 344:4
Laid aside business, 252:20
   bait l. to make taker mad, 227:22
   him on the green, 854:9
   in a manger, 39:2
   in sad cypress l., 209:25
   me down with a will, 599:6
   my heart open to indifference, 789:13
   on with a trowel, 197:27
   sun is l. to sleep, 237:10
   when I am l. in earth, 294:3
   where wast thou when I l. foundations, 15:5
Lain for a century dead, 485:12
   should I have l. still, 13:30
Lair, deep his midnight l. made, 397:4
   rouse lion from his l., 398:7
   slugs leave their l., 402:11
Laisse un peu de soi-même, 608:*n*4
Laissez faire laissez passer, 315:16
Laith were gude Scots lords, 853:19
Lake, consciousness as bottomless l., 574:4
   dream life as l. dreams sky, 631:10
   fire in the l., 5:2

Lake (*continued*)
   goddess of the silver l., 261:10
   in l. an arm, 139:3
   Lebarge, 673:10
   Pilot of Galilean l., 261:22
   river l. glimmering pool, 534:9
   sedge withered from l., 439:3
   to Rydal L. that lead, 392:*n*1
   took l. between my legs, 815:2
   wind over l. image, 5:3
Lake Wobegon, that's the news from L., 837:5
Lakes, great l. of North America, 448:11
   light shakes across l., 482:19
Lalun member of ancient profession, 632:15
Lama, Eli Eli l. sabachthani, 38:9
Lamb, blood of the l., 48:24
   false as fox to l., 208:7
   go to bed with l., 163:9
   God will provide himself a l., 7:8
   he who made L. make thee, 374:6
   little L. I'll tell thee, 371:16
   little L. who made thee, 371:15
   Mary had a little l., 425:11
   of God, 40:35, 49:12
   of God although I speak, 765:2
   pipe song about a L., 371:13
   quiet as a l., 178:13
   save one little ewe l., 12:3
   sedulous ape to L., 599:9
   shall be without blemish, 8:16
   skin of innocent l. parchment, 172:20
   tempers wind to shorn l., 151:12, 333:7
   to the slaughter, 28:23
   was the holy L. of God, 375:17
   when lion fawns upon l., 173:9
   will never cease to follow, 173:9
   wolf shall dwell with the l., 26:34
Lambs could not forgive, 497:11
   gather the l. with his arm, 28:5
   little hills like l., 19:21
   loud bleat from hilly bourn, 438:13
   poor little l. lost way, 633:17
   we were as twinned l., 228:10
   wolves and l. have no concord, 54:2
Lame and impotent conclusion, 213:12
   feet to the l., 14:38
   little l. balloonman, 739:11
   man leap as an hart, 27:32
   wrinkled and slanting-eyed, 53:7
Lament, come to dark and l., 670:14
   for Madame Blaize, 340:10
   frogs drone their l., 96:9
   have I not reason to l., 390:16
   mistakes of good man, 360:10
   wild l., 766:18
Lamentable, most l. comedy, 180:22
   that skin of lamb parchment, 172:20
Lamentation, empire's l., 484:20
Lamentations, sighs l. and wailings, 130:5
Lamenting, last l. kiss, 235:12
Lamp, Aladdin's l., 424:17, 515:11
   beside the golden door, 595:6
   confusing beams from memory's l., 763:16
   fluttered round l., 553:8
   God's light like a l., 121:21
   I have but one l., 353:1
   Lady with L., 467:9

Laughter (*continued*)

laugh thy girlish l., 616:2
love and l., 553:14
myriad l. of ocean waves, 65:18
no one died of l., 659:15
no time for mirth and l., 643:15
of Gargantua the l., 753:12
of her heart, 744:3
of the fool, 24:18
present l., 209:14
seriously scribbling to excite l., 559:13
sudden glory maketh l., 246:9
that all can see, 472:22
tinkled among teacups, 717:22
tired of tears and l., 569:1
under running l., 620:17
weeping and the l., 645:11
when her lovely l. shows, 232:6
wine women mirth l., 423:18
with pain fraught, 429:19

Laughter-silvered wings, 810:11

Launched, face that l. a thousand ships, 170:23

forth filament, 521:7

Laundry, dreamed dream called L., 817:16

nothing but l., 809:1

Laura, grave where L. lay, 160:9

if L. Petrarch's wife, 423:22
rose-cheeked L. come, 232:2

Laurea, concedat l. laudi, 91:*n*3

Laurel and myrtle and rose, 363:16

burned is Apollo's l. bough, 171:7
crown yield to praise, 91:8
crowned with l., 735:11
for perfect prime, 548:1
green for a season, 568:17
no l. crown for outrunning burro, 111:2
outlives not May, 568:17
poison from Caesar's l. crown, 375:13

Laurels are cut, 534:1

in chains or in l., 489:16
Northern l. not change, 349:1
worth all your l., 424:26
yet once more O ye l., 261:13

Lavender in the windows, 252:29

mints savory marjoram, 228:26

Lavender's blue dilly dilly lavender's green, 860:19

Laver son linge sale, 388:*n*2

Lavish, liar always l. of oaths, 257:11

no calamity greater than l. desires, 59:6

Lavvy Minx or Sphinx, 499:5

Law agin wearin' o' Green, 847:4

all things by l. divine, 429:7
and order pay, 578:9
and the prophets, 35:5, 36:43
army of unalterable l., 541:17, 717:21
bloody book of l., 212:24
book of the l., 13:16
born under one l. to another bound, 162:16
broken every human l., 720:14
by transgressing kept l., 263:6
can only bring freedom, 365:23
common l. not omnipresence, 578:11
common l. nothing but reason, 159:14
Common L. of England, 729:1
Congress shall make no l., 361:1
conspiracy against l. and order, 820:12

Law (*continued*)

craving to go to l., 566:16
curses in Book of L., 286:*n*4
delight is in l. of the Lord, 15:27
despair l. chance hath slain, 236:5
do as adversaries in l., 175:26
due process of l., 361:4, 361:8
dusty purlieus of l., 484:10
embodies nation's development, 577:14
embody the L., 564:17
ends Tyranny begins, 286:7
equal before l., 554:1
eternal l., 66:17
evolution not cause but l., 572:4
extreme l. often extreme injustice, 88:19
faith nor love nor l., 428:8
first l. for historian, 90:16
for man law for thing, 453:7
for rulers and people, 502:18
fugitive from l. of averages, 808:3
future lays l. of today, 588:11
good l. is good order, 81:7
great cases make bad l., 578:4
great l. of culture, 434:9
has honored us, 415:14
hath not been dead, 211:11
hatred made l., 771:6
having not the l., 42:40
head and hoof of L., 634:15
hint of universal l., 577:19
hocus-pocus science, 317:10
I my Lords embody L., 564:17
ignorance of the l., 245:18
in his l. doth he meditate, 15:27
in l. what plea so tainted, 189:4
in majestic equality, 586:18
is a ass a idiot, 496:14
is a jealous mistress, 412:16
is good, 46:14
is order, 81:7
is The Law, 776:1
justice the l. my ducats, 188:24
lapped in universal l., 482:2
last result of wisdom, 325:23
lesser breeds without L., 635:4
life of l. is experience, 577:13
locks up man and woman, 844:20
love is fulfilling of l., 43:25
love l. to itself, 120:6
master after my disappearance, 66:23
mighty mightier necessity, 365:14
mob l., 474:4
moral l. within me, 339:4
murder by the l., 305:20
Murphy's L., 852:10
mysterious l. true source, 266:22
natural l. old nonsense, 417:2
Nature's kindly l., 311:11
nature's l. man made to mourn, 377:13
necessity has no l., 119:15
necessity hath no l., 254:14
necessity knows no l. except prevail, 103:20
nice sharp quillets of l., 171:16
no l. more binding than custom, 616:10
no l. of history, 517:13
no man above or below l., 615:7
nor l. bade me fight, 638:17

Law (*continued*)

not a light to see by, 813:7
not come to destroy l., 34:2
not concerned with trifles, 123:19
not exempted from power of l., 162:18
not l. so much as right, 505:14
not make scarecrow of l., 211:3
not one jot pass from l., 34:3
obedience to l. demanded, 615:7
of competition, 559:6
of excluded middle, 807:7
of gravity, 470:3
of humanity, 345:9
of musical world, 627:14
of nature and nations, 345:9
of our Creator, 345:9
of the Jungle, 634:13
of the land, 128:8
of the Medes and Persians, 30:7
of the Yukon, 673:8
old father antick the l., 184:28
old l. sad but not bitter, 678:15
one God l. element, 484:18
one l. and one truth, 115:26
one l. for all, 345:9
one L. for Lion and Ox, 373:6
ordinance of reason for common good, 129:8
others will plead at l., 97:31
ought to weed it out, 167:8
our reason is our l., 267:29
people fight for their l., 64:14
people's good the highest l., 91:11
perfection of reason, 159:14
Poetry not matured by l., 440:11
possession eleven points in l., 301:1
precedents constitute l., 360:2
primary l. of every work of art, 533:5
principles of l. and applications, 626:19
Professor of Harvard L. School, 695:10
protection by l., 386:13
Proust's L., 817:18
public opinion in advance of l., 647:3
reason the life of the l., 159:14
remoter aspects of l., 577:19
rich men rule the l., 341:8
rule nations under l., 97:31
rule of l., 807:9
same l. shapes earth-star and snow-star, 505:10
say what l. is, 371:1
says judge as looks down nose, 776:1
school no more than school of fencing, 613:12
seat of l. bosom of God, 162:18
seven hours to l., 159:*n*5
so general a study, 344:10
sociability l. of nature, 583:8
stable but not stand still, 654:20
stands mute in midst of arms, 90:11
Supreme L. of the land, 360:16
sword of war or l., 359:4
this is l. I maintain, 846:10
to windward of l., 346:19
tongue is the l. of kindness, 23:30
took to the l., 550:2
translating into living l., 710:16
true embodiment, 564:17
universal l., 339:6

Law *(continued)*
    unto themselves, 42:40
    voice of l. harmony of world, 162:18
    what others do from fear of l., 79:15
    where no l. no transgression, 42:42
    which governs all law, 345:9
    who to himself is l., 165:9
    windy side of the l., 194:*n*1
    write in books of l., 779:4
Lawd, gangway for de L., 728:3
Lawful, all ambitions l., 612:16
    all things l. for me, 44:12
    guns aren't l., 738:14
    is it not l., 36:37
    without some l. recreation, 157:24
Lawfully, if a man use it l., 46:14
Lawlands, ye Highlands and L., 854:9
Lawless attack upon liberty, 337:10
    discountenance haughty and l., 350:14
    linsey-woolsey brother, 271:13
    winged unconfined, 373:10
Lawlessness, world l., 698:8
Lawn, rivulets through l., 483:8
    sisters crab grass in l. of life, 811:4
    white as driven snow, 228:30
Lawns, like satyrs grazing on the l., 170:14
Law's delay, 203:33
    in l. grave study six, 159:20
    to take care o' raskills, 512:25
Laws, abhor makers and their l. approve, 284:25
    abounds with l. teems with crimes, 846:20
    acting around us, 470:2
    and arms foundations of states, 142:11
    and constitution of country, 360:9
    are like cobwebs, 297:20
    are sand customs rock, 562:16
    bad l. bring about worse, 331:4
    base l. of servitude, 282:19
    best l. teach to trample bad l., 489:13
    breathing household l., 392:14
    conflict courts decide, 371:1
    Constitution and l. of U.S., 360:16
    crime to examine l. of heat, 572:3
    devise l. for blood, 187:28
    doing what l. permit, 314:8
    end tyranny begins, 323:6
    equal protection of the l., 361:8
    execute the l. of Congress, 567:3
    fewer l. less power, 456:11
    flung at head, 732:3
    for themselves not me, 619:13
    forms all produced by l., 470:2
    found state and give it l., 143:3
    give little Senate l., 312:4
    God of universal l., 582:16
    good l. lead to better, 331:4
    government free where l. rule, 291:19
    government of l. not men, 351:4
    grind the poor, 341:8
    grinding general l. out, 470:11
    human mind put in nature, 695:2
    in which we have no voice, 361:11
    judges of facts not l., 306:15
    know not whether l. right, 605:22
    language manners l. customs, 391:15
    like spiders' webs, 57:17
    Nature and Nature's l. hid, 313:10

Laws *(continued)*
    never forget l. of forefathers, 109:19
    not assume physical l. exist, 614:9
    not care who make l., 294:13
    not good l. where not armed, 142:11
    not violate l. of justice, 339:2
    obedient to their l. we lie, 62:4
    of God are forever, 67:20
    of God laws of man, 619:13
    of nature and nature's God, 357:2
    of the Jungle, 634:15
    one by one forging l., 732:3
    or kings cause or cure, 325:3
    ought not to remain unaltered, 80:26
    physical l. and l. of numbers, 548:13
    power of making l., 370:12
    resulting from designed l., 470:12
    right from which l. derive authority, 360:6
    rules of game l. of Nature, 537:1
    secure equal justice, 73:18
    self-made l., 525:6
    sweeps a room as for thy l., 251:1
    the more l. are made prominent, 59:10
    three l. of righteousness, 65:1
    true friendship's l., 309:21
    two l. discrete, 453:7
    unequal l. to savage race, 481:7
    useless l. weaken necessary l., 314:9
    which ran like drinking songs, 74:10
Lawsuit machine you go into, 580:15
    mania, 566:16
Lawsuits, win l. and are happy, 74:11
Lawyer, deceive not thy l., 251:8
    has peasant inside, 631:11
    I'm here as the l., 837:14
    nor for every quarrel to l., 251:21
    not what l. tells me, 344:12
    peasant has l. inside, 631:11
    prairie-l. master of all, 685:6
    skull of a l., 206:20
    without history a mechanic, 397:19
Lawyers, charge prepared l. met, 307:18
    let's kill all the l., 172:19
    no l. among them, 143:14
    one hundred and fifty l. do business, 359:8
Lay aside long-cherished love, 94:25
    Cleric before and L. behind, 271:13
    down in her loveliness, 401:6
    down life for friends, 41:31
    down reins of power, 477:1
    dying in Algiers, 469:6
    earthly fancies down, 484:23
    enough to l. up, 307:21
    field to field, 26:19
    heart out for my board, 800:16
    her in the earth, 206:27
    his weary bones among ye, 231:9
    hold on eternal life, 46:27
    it on thick, 558:16
    like folds of bright girdle, 531:2
    like warrior taking rest, 427:2
    me down, 837:11
    me down in peace, 15:31
    me down to bleed, 853:*n*1
    me down to sleep, 296:15
    me on anvil O God, 681:13
    nature's l. idiot, 235:15

Lay *(continued)*
    not flattering unction, 205:25
    not up treasures, 34:12
    on Macduff, 222:24
    Pelion on Ossa, 55:*n*1
    proud usurpers low, 380:11
    sleeping head my love, 775:10
    them down in their dens, 19:11
    unpremeditated l., 396:4
    up treasures in heaven, 34:12
    upon thy lips, 223:37
    waste our powers, 394:18
Layden, Stuhldreher Miller Crowley L., 692:6
Layer upon layer in city, 745:1
Layer-up, ill l. of beauty, 194:1
Layeth beams of his chambers, 19:8
Lays, constructing tribal l., 634:5
    eggs for gentlemen, 860:2
Laziness, evasion not l., 748:12
    no l. no procrastination, 535:*n*1
Lazy dog, 849:7
    fokes' stummucks, 593:11
    geese like snow cloud, 724:11
    longing to be a l. lady, 715:12
    looking for something to do, 333:14
    Scheldt or wandering Po, 340:14
Lea, slowly o'er the l., 334:8
    standing on pleasant l., 394:19
Lead apes in hell, 175:27
    bullets made of l., 860:18
    but not master them, 58:13
    but to grave, 334:15
    country like Britain, 816:8
    easy to l., 410:2
    from death to immortality, 51:20
    from linotype as from firearm, 771:17
    he will infallibly l. you to water, 516:6
    heart of l., 313:18
    I expect you to l. me, 523:19
    in traces l. 'em, 515:1
    just don't l. 'em so much, 834:8
    kindly Light, 449:18
    little child shall l. them, 26:34
    me from darkness to light, 51:20
    me from unreal to real, 51:20
    me to rock higher than I, 17:37
    me Zeus and Fate, 84:15
    my steps aright, 432:11
    not take l. in all things, 53:13
    road rail pig l., 681:5
    sky like l., 776:10
    tears scald like molten l., 217:29
    there shall thy hand l. me, 20:13
    these graces to grave, 209:8
    those that are with young, 28:5
    us not into temptation, 34:11
    wild-goose chase, 156:26
    ye who l. take heed, 652:2
Leaden army conquers world, 632:4
    scepter, 305:24
Leaden-eyed despairs, 437:8
Leader and commander to people, 28:25
    because of not daring to be ahead, 59:14
    charismatic l. gains authority, 631:14
    educator wielder of power, 786:7
    philosophy you l. of life, 91:5
    that people may require l., 77:25

Leader *(continued)*
to be l. turn one's back, 617:17
who understood terror, 802:12
Leaders ambitiously contending, 366:19
blind l. of the blind, 36:20
lie down till l. have spoken, 634:14
Leadership, crisis in American l., 795:17
Leadest thou that heifer, 438:3
Leadeth me beside still waters, 16:18
me in paths of righteousness, 16:18
Leads, astronomy l. from this world, 77:15
heaven that l. men to hell, 227:22
on to fortune, 197:13
spirit of man who l., 708:12
you to believe a lie, 376:9
Leaf, abiding L., 781:10
blossom or bole, 640:15
cut a cabbage l., 336:12
every l. drenches touch, 781:17
fade as a l., 28:33
falling of a l., 516:19
falls with l. in October, 242:14
his l. shall not wither, 15:27
I were like the l., 568:20
in her mouth was an olive l., 6:30
last l. upon tree, 473:19
lift me as wave l. cloud, 429:3
lives on a l., 780:8
my days in yellow l., 425:8
never tear linnet from l., 639:13
November's l., 396:13
of grass no less than stars, 519:15
olive l. pacific sign, 268:16
one red l., 401:5
round elm tree bole in tiny l., 492:4
sere yellow l., 222:11
shall be green, 29:17
stone l. unfound door, 760:3
turn over a new l., 158:7
Leaf-fringed legend, 437:16
Leafy month of June, 400:15
roll up l. Olympus, 96:8
League, half a l. onward, 484:24
in l. with future, 540:12
in l. with the stones, 13:39
Leagues beyond those leagues, 542:3
land appeared at two l., 140:4
thousand l. a thousand years, 320:20
Leaks, from girder noon l., 753:13
Leal, land o' the l., 385:11
Lean above me broken-hearted, 704:14
and foolish knight, 664:11
and hungry look, 195:22
and loafe at my ease, 518:15
and low ability, 210:14
and sallow abstinence, 261:7
and slippered pantaloon, 198:25
as compass-needle, 801:11
body and visage, 258:6
dull privations and l. emptiness, 234:21
grew l. assailed seasons, 652:6
hors l. as is a rake, 134:29
I l. back, 820:2
I'm l. dog keen dog, 732:4
in joy upon Father's knee, 372:3
lard their l. books, 240:2
lards the l. earth, 185:15
on garden urn, 717:23
on mahogany table like mountain, 789:8

Lean *(continued)*
on me, 838:6
over too far backward, 741:17
people who l., 600:6
Pharaoh's l. kine loved, 185:31
poor l. lank face, 474:10
strong l. upon death, 713:12
take fat with l., 498:16
unwashed artificer, 178:19
we all need someone we can l. on, 838:6
wife eat no l., 856:20
Lean-faced, Pinch a hungry l. villain, 175:1
Leaning across bosom of West, 586:5
against the Sun, 544:9
on reedy shore, 844:23
stuffed men l. together, 719:4
Leans against the land, 341:4
elephant l. or stands, 250:14
her cheek upon her hand, 183:1
Longing l. and beckons, 515:17
Pacific l. on the land, 713:8
upon his hoe and gazes, 601:3
Leap, able to l. tall buildings, 795:1
giant l. for mankind, 824:19
I'll l. up to my God, 171:4
in order to stations l., 284:13
in the dark, 246:16
lame man l. as an hart, 27:32
look before you l., 271:21
look ere ye l., 147:6
nevermore to l. again, 662:17
of whale up Niagara, 320:15
to pluck bright honor, 185:9
to tentative conclusion, 796:8
Leaped, in Endymion I l., 440:11
into dangerous world I l., 374:10
out to wed with Thought, 483:18
Leaping, brooks too broad for l., 619:7
frog l. in, 291:16
signs of l. houses, 184:23
Leaps, cataract l. in glory, 482:19
my heart l. up, 392:7
nature not proceed by l., 322:19
Lear, Hamlet rambles L. rages, 642:7
passage in L. haunted me, 439:*n3*
pleasant to know Mr. L., 499:12
reading King L., 356:21
there struts Hamlet there L., 642:6
till I am Timon and L., 642:1
Learn about one thing from another, 117:8
and propagate best, 530:9
at no other, 345:22
by doing, 80:11
by going, 780:15
craft so long to l., 133:11
fools l. in no other, 319:25
from having died, 671:7
from our enemies, 105:17
from those who teach, 67:26
gladly he l. and gladly teche, 135:1
him or kill him, 560:8
how to forget, 249:3
I l. from you guess you l. from me,
762:17
in suffering teach in song, 428:19
Irish poets l. trade, 643:3
know how to l., 570:17
lines don't bump into furniture, 753:10
live and l., 297:14

Learn *(continued)*
man l. nothing without being taught,
108:6
neither shall they l. war, 26:11
never had time to l., 754:6
nor account pang, 494:9
not yet so old but she may l., 189:8
of the green world, 709:11
read mark l., 51:4
they l. to be idle, 46:23
to be policeman, 693:11
to bear beams of love, 372:2
to do well, 26:10
to labor and wait, 466:3
we were crack-pated, 640:7
what life had to teach, 506:28
when will they ever l., 805:16
wise l. from enemies, 75:7
Learned, all l. all drunk, 348:7
although men say he has not l., 62:10
and conned by rote, 197:12
angling never fully l., 252:21
fair and l. and good as she, 247:12
fool more foolish, 278:24
forgotten everything l., 852:2
grew within this l. man, 171:7
his great language, 491:21
I l. a long time ago, 840:8
in courtesy have her l., 639:11
Jonson's l. sock, 259:20
judge should have l. to know evil, 77:6
know best things not l., 333:15
libraries of the l., 338:3
love first l. in lady's eyes, 177:5
love trade you have l., 115:14
make the l. smile, 308:14
more l. from Dante, 722:19
never l. to read, 817:2
nothing forgotten nothing, 369:10
rather able than l., 152:13
root of Homer, 239:*n2*
thoughts of many men, 54:7
to look on nature, 391:4
to melt at others' woe, 334:2
upright judge l. judge, 189:27
we should have l. women, 361:14
when I heard l. astronomer, 520:8
without sense, 346:15
writer wishes to show he is l., 614:1
Learning, a' the l. I desire, 377:17
abandon l. and no sorrow, 58:18
Alcuin my name l. I loved, 125:5
angel's wit and singular l., 144:5
blundering people live on, 681:17
but an adjunct to ourself, 177:4
cast into mire, 345:15
enough l. to misquote, 419:15
grammar nonsense and l., 342:17
great end of l., 82:14
grow old l. many things, 57:8
hath gained most, 258:10
how to use eyes, 461:15
if I should not be l. now, 86:4
inclination towards l. strong, 293:15
inflamed with study of l., 262:18
knows all he is capable of l., 127:6
labored for them that seek l., 33:2
little l. dangerous, 308:11
love he bore to l., 342:8

Learning *(continued)*
   love of l., 467:21
   love of slaughter, 709:4
   much l. make mad, 42:35
   much l. not teach understanding, 64:5
   not attained by chance, 362:4
   on scraps of l. dote, 305:16
   pause from l. to be wise, 324:6
   polite l., 295:24
   red plague rid you for l. me your
      language, 229:17
   royal road to l., 84:*n7*
   secretary of Nature and all l., 253:10
   steeped in antique l., 534:9
   thought without l., 62:16
   wear l. like watch, 314:24
   weight of l., 484:17
   whence is thy l., 307:3
   who so neglects l. in youth, 71:4
   wiser without books, 348:11
   without thought, 62:16
Learning's triumph o'er her foes, 323:14
Learns, who l. must suffer, 65:5
Lease of my true love, 227:12
   summer's l. too short, 226:2
Least, faithful in l., 40:1
   I am l. of apostles, 44:23
   joy last not l., 215:16
   last not l. in love, 196:20
   love l. that let men know, 176:5
   most enjoy contented l., 226:6
   myself not l. but honored, 481:9
   not l. in honor or applause, 162:*n1*
   nothing so l. as truth, 740:10
   of the evils, 80:13
   of these my brethren, 37:18
   of two evils, 53:*n2*
   promise most given when l. said, 164:18
   said soonest mended, 157:*n1*
   though last not l., 162:1
   unjust in l., 40:1
   woman who occasions l. talk, 74:6
Leather, clothed all in l., 861:8
   future smells of Russian l., 442:17
   rest all l. or prunella, 311:12
   Spanish or neat's l., 271:14
   trod upon neat's l., 195:14
Leathern, flits by on l. wing, 337:2
   silken or l. purse, 304:15
   war with rere-mice for l. wings, 181:13
Leave all else to the gods, 99:10
   all meaner things, 310:20
   America love or l. it, 852:17
   at point of bayonets, 366:16
   behind bit of ourselves, 608:11
   bottle on chimleypiece, 497:3
   by next town drain, 590:18
   do not need l. your room, 701:5
   give themselves when you l., 706:8
   God does not l. us, 840:13
   her Johnny leave her, 862:8
   her to heaven, 202:20
   him for religion, 804:16
   I couldn't l. without the king, 757:7
   I must l. all that, 255:2
   king will never l., 757:7
   kiss but in the cup, 238:2
   living name behind, 244:10
   man shall l. father and mother, 6:2

Leave *(continued)*
   me a little, 481:16
   me O Love, 163:24
   me to repose, 335:16
   monument behind, 640:8
   no stone unturned, 70:7
   not a rack behind, 230:9
   not a stain, 33:3
   not l. you comfortless, 41:29
   off agony leave off style, 592:16
   off wishing to deserve thanks, 94:23
   peace I l. with you, 41:30
   princesses would never l. without me,
      757:7
   religion to family, 532:20
   sack and live cleanly, 187:12
   something to after-times, 262:11
   the rest to heaven, 257:5
   thee in the storm, 216:12
   them alone they'll come home, 859:9
   them for the poor and stranger, 9:13
   them honeyless, 197:16
   them in midst of his days, 29:19
   them laughing, 679:9
   them while looking good, 737:11
   to l. to die a little, 608:11
   took l. but was loth to depart, 297:2
   we thy servant sleeping, 538:11
   world no copy, 209:8
Leaven, a little l., 44:4
   pain for l., 568:1
Leaveneth the whole lump, 44:4
Leaves, air wash l. cover me, 568:9
   air wild with l., 710:3
   among l. never known, 437:8
   cane l. swaying, 742:5
   cover them with l., 843:13
   cover with l. and flowers, 244:3
   crisped and sere, 479:11
   dead driven like ghosts, 428:21
   easy as l. grow on tree, 636:19
   fall early, 708:18
   generation of men like l., 52:31
   harmony of l., 637:3
   lisp of l., 567:17
   mankind fleet of life like l., 75:9
   me fifty more, 618:7
   must walk over the l., 155:*n5*
   naturally as L. to tree, 440:6
   no l. no birds, 445:23
   oak l. horses' heels, 719:22
   of any author, 255:18
   of judgment Book unfold, 537:18
   of Life keep falling, 471:3
   piled against doors, 89:17
   sewed fig l. together, 6:5
   shady l. of destiny, 272:7
   shatter your l., 261:13
   stop to rake l. away, 668:17
   stuck out tongues, 780:9
   swayed my l. and flowers, 638:4
   tender l. of hopes, 231:2
   thick as autumnal l., 264:10
   though l. many the root is one, 638:4
   tomb of green l., 602:8
   vine l. in hair, 540:21
   what if my l. falling, 429:4
   where l. the rose, 471:4
   words are like l., 308:13

Leaves *(continued)*
   world to darkness, 334:8
   yellow l. or none or few, 226:24
Leaving all that here win us, 576:3
   country for country's sake, 305:*n1*
   Love behind, 545:20
   me never alone, 575:23
   nothing became him like l., 219:8
   to direct themselves, 737:2
   to take command of troops, 388:5
   we're l. Babylon, 839:6
Lebanon, cedars of L., 19:10, 680:1
   grow like a cedar in L., 18:27
   silken Samarcand to cedared L., 437:2
Lebarge, Lake L., 673:10
Lecher, gilded fly does l., 217:21
Lecherous goats, 236:6
Lecteur, hypocrite l., 524:7
Lecture, if you wish to hold a l., 73:3
Lectured, astronomer l. with applause, 520:8
Led, Bruce has aften l., 380:10
   dumb and silent be l., 350:4
   neither saint- nor sophist-l., 528:18
   regiment from behind, 566:1
   to believe a lie, 376:*n1*
Leda mother of Helen, 573:6
Ledge, step off the l., 799:2
Lee, between windward and l., 569:14
   I and my Annabel L., 479:18
   shore of age, 594:15
   the beautiful Annabel L., 479:19
Leek, by this l., 193:23
Leeks, wel loved he garleek oynons l.,
   135:14
Leer, assent with civil l., 312:4
Lees, drink life to l., 481:8
   mere l. is left, 220:25
   stirs up l. of things, 516:14
   wines on the l., 27:15
Leewardings, unfettered l., 753:11
Left behind a real life, 821:4
   better to be l., 483:*n3*
   booming surge of Aegean, 76:5
   cannon to l. of them, 485:1
   country for country's good, 305:*n1*
   fair Scotland's strand, 379:1
   for handful of silver l. us, 491:20
   his garment in her hand, 7:25
   implacable Charybdis guards l., 189:*n1*
   in her l. hand riches and honor, 20:25
   let not l. hand know, 34:10
   lies on her l. side, 734:10
   ne'er l. man i' mire, 218:13
   O mother what have I l. out, 817:14
   one taken the other l., 37:11
   sleep on his l. side, 756:4
   the warm precincts, 334:24
   the web left the loom, 480:26
   thou hast l. thy first love, 48:8
   vivid air signed with honor, 783:16
Leg, can honor set to l., 186:35
   caper and shake l., 680:8
   decreasing l. increasing belly, 191:16
   justice has wooden l., 646:3
   meat soft as l. of an angel, 836:1
   never breaks l., 629:14
   one old timber l., 658:9
   took him by left l., 858:11
Legacies, books l. genius leaves, 302:13

Legacy alleviates sorrow, 159:4
  charm in a good l., 159:4
  of first European novel, 824:2
Legal justice art of good and fair, 124:5
  no l. slaves except mistress of house, 465:6
  society without objective l. scale, 804:15
  super-l.-aid bureau, 695:8
  unanimity on l. questions, 626:19
Legality, revolution l. counter-moves in same game, 612:12
Legalizer, time great l., 690:17
Legend, ghost of ancient l., 442:7
  leaf-fringed l., 437:16
  of green chapels, 795:7
Legend's, qui procul hinc l. writ, 627:4
Legends, asleep in lap of l., 436:23
  fairy tales tone licked clean, 817:19
  names deeds gray l. events, 438:20
  rather believe fables in l., 167:21
Leges, silent enim l. inter arma, 90:n6
Leggemmo, quel giorno più non vi l. avante, 130:n5
Legible, thoughts l. in eye, 171:9
Legion, my name is L., 38:21
  of lost ones, 633:16
  soldier of the L., 469:6
  that never was 'listed, 634:4
Legiones redde, 102:n3
Legions, give me back my l., 102:4
Legislate, judges do and must l., 578:10
Legislation, female deprived of voice in l., 362:5
  great problem of l., 386:5
  solve problem of cat versus bird by l., 760:1
Legislative, every l. body in U.S., 660:6
  judicial distinct from l., 351:11
  nominated by executive, 353:6
Legislators, poets l. of world, 431:12
Legislature, innocent man sent to l., 649:10
  newspaper conthrols l., 646:18
Legitimate, let the end be l., 371:4
  object of government, 358:15
Legs, born with l. apart, 828:10
  'ear 'erse's l., 486:19
  giving way under me, 542:10
  his l. bestrid the ocean, 224:4
  if go high use own l., 588:21
  not natural to walk on two l., 356:18
  of iron, 30:2
  on his last l., 243:15
  on stilts we walk on our own l., 154:7
  one pair of English l., 193:7
  slimy things crawl with l., 399:23
  that bird never on l., 497:22
  took lake between my l., 815:2
  vast trunkless l., 427:18
  walk under his huge l., 195:20
Leibniz, monads of L., 708:9
Leicester, farewell L. Square, 674:2
Leisure answers leisure, 212:9
  be doon at l. parfitly, 137:10
  class replaced by New Class, 778:12
  conversation wants l., 672:20
  gentleman of l., 613:6
  has utility as evidence of l., 613:11

Leisure *(continued)*
  means and l. civilizers, 459:18
  no l. who useth it not, 252:11
  office of l. class, 613:9
  repent at l., 300:11
  retired L., 260:1
  to grow wise, 529:6
  with dignity, 90:14
  wooed in haste wed at l., 175:31
Leisurely, full l. we glide, 549:9
Leman, such l., 854:7
Lemon, be with you in squeezing of l., 342:18
  Martini with slice of l. peel, 778:7
  trees bloom, 363:16
  twelve miles from a l., 398:23
Lemonade, black eyes and l., 412:6
Lemons, oranges and l., 857:12
Lend a kind of easiness, 205:29
  eye a terrible aspect, 192:30
  eyes the glowworm l. thee, 248:11
  Friendship last if not asked to l. money, 561:10
  heaven such grace did l. her, 176:12
  less than thou owest, 216:2
  man himself l. a hand, 73:14
  me leave to come, 162:4
  me stone strength of past, 713:7
  me your ears, 196:27
  men who borrow men who l., 407:11
  us thine aid, 416:1
  you wings of future, 713:7
Lender, borrower is servant to the l., 22:26
  neither borrower nor l., 201:27
Lendeth, because it l. light, 161:26
  unto the Lord, 22:16
Lendings, off you l., 216:30
Lends hand to honest boldness, 84:2
  he that l. gives, 252:6
  soul l. tongue vows, 201:31
  three things I never l., 458:13
Leñero, en casa del l., 862:20
Length, concept of l., 694:17
  drags its slow l. along, 308:17
  Folly's at full l., 306:20
  in l. of days understanding, 14:12
  of days in her right hand, 20:25
  operations by which l. determined, 694:17
  what it lacks in l., 670:13
  words of learned l., 342:9
Lengthened sage advices, 379:15
  shadow of man, 455:13
Lengthening, drags l. chain, 340:15
Lengthens not a day, 233:9
Lenin, suppose L. died of typhus, 802:14
Lenity, what makes robbers bold but l., 172:29
Lenore, lost L., 479:2
Lent him to a lady, 860:22
  with l. money evil done, 517:16
Lente currite noctis equi, 105:n3, 171:4
  sois plus l., 426:n3
Lentils, gave Esau pottage of l., 7:11
Leonardo, Italy produced Michelangelo L., 797:4
Leonidas and Washington, 424:12
  my name L. will echo throughout time, 85:15

Leopard change his spots, 29:12
  cloud that looked like l., 74:14
  frozen carcass of l., 754:15
  look back at l. like a l., 793:7
  shall lie down with the kid, 26:34
Leopards, leaping like L. to Sky, 544:10
Leprosy, greatest disease not TB or l., 785:6
  skin white as l., 400:3
Lesbia, let us live and love my L., 94:4
  my sweetest L., 231:21
  with her sparrow, 735:5
Lesbos, Sappho of L. tenth muse, 57:n8
Less, can't take l. said Hatter, 550:13
  fears l. than imaginings, 219:5
  greater prey upon l., 317:4
  he spoke more he heard, 591:16
  how much l. man, 14:32
  if clod washed away Europe l., 236:19
  is more, 493:3
  more and more about l., 625:16
  more matter with l. art, 202:34
  nicely calculated l. or more, 395:16
  no man shall have, 615:6
  not that I loved Caesar l., 196:24
  of two evils, 53:n2
  rather than be l. cared not to be, 264:27
  small Latin and l. Greek, 238:7
  than kind, 200:27
  than meets the eye, 764:11
  the l. one knows, 59:7
  they have the more noise, 313:13
  weep to make l. depth of grief, 172:25
Lessened, one pain l. by another's, 182:18
Lessening, little things go l., 494:21
Lesser breeds without Law, 635:4
  than my name, 180:3
  woman l. man, 482:5
Lesson, draw from others the l., 88:15
  grandest l. On sail on, 579:9
  harder l. how to die, 152:n8
  heart give l. to head, 348:11
  of Three Mile Island, 852:24
  on grammar impertinence, 534:4
  seems to carry, 348:20
  you should heed, 414:3
Lessons, three l. I would write, 381:9
Let all her ways be unconfined, 296:19
  another man praise thee, 23:10
  at another l. in the foe, 269:4
  dead bury dead, 35:15
  dearly l. or l. alone, 249:8
  each man exercise art he knows, 75:3
  evening come, 840:13
  every thing that hath breath praise, 20:21
  face of God shine through, 734:15
  freedom ring, 469:8
  Greeks be Greeks, 270:6
  her not walk in the sun, 203:6
  him be just and deal kindly, 419:5
  him look to his bond, 188:29
  him never come back, 491:24
  him now speak, 51:8
  him pass for a man, 187:31
  it be let it pass, 315:n2
  it begin here, 346:9
  joys be as May, 249:14
  justice be done though heaven fall, 123:26
  me die death of righteous, 9:23

Let *(continued)*
  me have no lying, 229:4
  me love, 234:5
  me not to marriage of true minds, 227:17
  me tell the world, 187:2
  my people go, 8:9, 863:1
  never curtain drawn, 669:20
  never l. me go, 831:17
  no dog bark, 187:20
  no man's heart fail, 11:27
  no such man be trusted, 190:7
  not heart be troubled, 41:26, 41:30
  not poor Nelly starve, 282:12
  not the sun go down, 45:28
  sleeping dogs lie, 498:12
  slip dogs of war, 196:22
  thame say, 162:7
  the toast pass, 367:29
  the words of my mouth, 16:14
  them eat cake, 331:19
  them have their day, 639:1
  them say, 162:*n7*
  this cup pass, 37:29
  thy words be few, 24:11
  us all to meditation, 172:14
  us alone, 480:19
  us be happy as we can, 329:5
  us begin, 799:9
  us do something beautiful, 785:5
  us go into the house of the Lord, 20:1
  us go singing as far as we go, 95:29
  us go then, 717:6
  us have peace, 532:18
  us have tongs and bones, 181:24
  us live and love, 94:4, 231:21
  us now praise famous men, 33:8
  us reason together, 26:10
  us take it as it comes, 566:5
  us then be up, 466:3
  what will be said or done, 358:3
  who will be clever, 514:2, 692:17
  will not l. thee go, 7:20
  your light shine, 34:2
Lethal, turn underground passages into l.
    chambers, 756:16
Lethe, cup that brings sleep of L., 99:1
  go not to L., 438:14
  river of oblivion, 265:16
  rots in ease on L. wharf, 202:14
  time is L., 676:4
Lethean, drunken of things L., 568:17
Lethe-wards had sunk, 437:5
Let's call whole thing off, 747:8
  carve him as a dish, 196:3
  choose executors, 179:27
  contend no more Love, 492:9
  do it, 813:2
  kill all the lawyers, 172:19
  look at the record, 663:12
  Pretend and we did, 829:10
  talk of graves, 179:27
Lets, make ghost of him that l. me, 202:10
Letter and spirit of constitution, 371:4
  broke spell of dead l., 730:10
  killeth, 45:3
  last till you write your l., 233:15
  longer than usual, 279:12
  not l. but spirit, 45:3
  on gown appeared l. A, 460:6

Letter *(continued)*
  one l. of Richardson's, 327:13
  read in the bitter l., 212:24
  scarlet l. passport, 460:12
  to the World, 545:3
Lettered, locked l. collar, 378:4
Lettering, stripped of l. and gilding, 319:2
Letters, ass in three l., 277:19
  Gods do not answer l., 828:2
  graven with diamonds in l. plain, 150:3
  in your l. speak of me, 215:13
  like writin' anonymous l., 646:20
  man of l., 281:5
  mingle souls, 235:25
  no arts no l. no society, 246:12
  republic of l., 322:13
  sensitive ear detecting capital l., 694:9
  should not be known, 229:25
  some call ah, 834:3
  you bid me burn l., 351:7
Letter-writing, the great art o' l., 496:1
Letting hundred flowers blossom, 737:18
  I dare not, 219:20
Lettres, un sot en trois l., 277:*n3*
Levee, drove my Chevy to the l., 839:7
Level, boys and girls l. with men, 224:1
  in her husband's heart, 209:22
  levelers wish to l. down, 327:1
Leveled together by Tao, 82:22
Levelers wish to level down, 327:1
Leveling, cannot bear l. up, 327:1
  rancorous mind, 641:1
  wind, 640:8
Levels all ranks, 452:9
Lever you can only turn once, 739:5
Leviathan, draw out l. with a hook, 15:19
  hugest of creatures, 267:15
  that crooked serpent, 27:20
  whom thou hast made to play, 19:11
Levin wanted friendship got friendliness,
    793:11
Levitation, evil emissions fled l., 812:17
  powers of l. would make fakir stare,
    720:14
Levity, a little judicious l., 599:18
  say it with utmost l., 609:1
  soul ruled by l. pure, 796:6
  there should be no l., 325:16
Levy, foreign l., 221:5
Levying war, 360:15
Lewd fellows, 42:16
  the sinful and l., 745:2
Lewdness, though l. court it, 202:17
Lewinsky, that woman Miss L., 840:2
Lex, de minimis non curat l., 123:19
  salus populi suprema l., 91:*n5*
Lexicographer writer of dictionaries, 324:19
Lexicography, not yet so lost in l., 324:14
Lexicon of youth, 452:11
Lexington and Bunker Hill, 414:16
Lhude sing cuccu, 843:5
  sing Goddamm, 708:17
Liable, all men are l. to error, 286:6
Liar always lavish of oaths, 257:11
  and the father of it, 41:12
  best l., 558:17
  doubt truth to be l., 203:3
  either l. or madman, 331:6
  no one such l. as indignant man, 589:2

Liar *(continued)*
  of first magnitude, 300:16
  should have good memory, 109:14
  show me a l., 252:1
  they answered Little l., 653:10
Liars, all Cretans are l., 60:1
  all men are l., 19:23
  drunkards l. adulterers, 215:29
  fears may be l., 512:10
  when they speak truth, 79:9
Libelous statements about dog, 699:2
Liber, vade salutatum pro me l., 134:*n3*
Liberal arts study humanizes, 105:28
  education, 295:24
  emphasizing rights of individual, 758:10
  I am a L., 531:12
  infuses that l. obedience, 344:17
  institutions cease being liberal, 589:20
  little L., 564:22
  luxury of l. government, 502:9
  tempered by experience, 531:12
  to love her is l. education, 303:6
Liberality in gifts well timed, 292:15
Liberate, men and women l., 742:9
Liberated, I have l. my soul, 126:8
  the hell out of place, 851:22
Liberates, neither shoots nor l. me, 507:24
Liberation, madness potentially l., 819:7
  of Europe, 728:15
  of human mind, 651:7
Liberavi animam meam, 126:*n3*
Liberis, pro patria pro l., 95:*n6*
Libertas, in dubiis l., 274:*n4*
  ubi l. ibi patria, 340:3
Libertate, sub l. quietem, 278:*n7*
Liberté, je suis né pour te nommer L.,
    743:*n1*
Liberties, dramatist wants l., 585:14
  liberty above all l., 263:4
  not too strong for l., 476:12
  science and l. of Europe, 359:9
Libertine, chartered l., 192:19
  freedom of the l., 682:5
  puffed and reckless l., 201:23
Libertines, self-love makes more l., 331:11
Liberty, abstract l. not found, 344:9
  Americans love l., 323:8
  and glory of his country, 414:11
  and Union, 415:3
  arduous struggle for l., 352:13
  as end and means, 607:1
  assert and maintain l. and virtue, 350:14
  basis of democratic state is l., 81:6
  brightest in dungeons L., 422:21
  bulwark of continuing l., 698:9
  bulwarks of l., 339:11
  by accident got its l., 143:4
  cannot be preserved without knowledge,
    350:17
  Captivity is Consciousness so's L., 544:22
  change from l. to force, 385:18
  condition upon which given l., 366:17
  contending for l., 349:13
  corruption symptom of l., 353:9
  cost of l., 648:12
  courage secret of l., 607:1
  cradle of l., 415:16
  crust of bread and l., 312:17
  degradation of idea of l., 790:8

Liberty *(continued)*

deprive of life l. or property, 361:8
deprived of life l. or property, 361:4
doing what laws permit, 314:8
doing what one desires, 464:21
enjoy delight with l., 161:25
enjoy such l., 276:4
enjoyment of life and l., 339:9
equality fraternity, 855:7
establish our real l., 152:17
extremism in defense of l., 355:*n*1
freedom enfranchisement, 196:16
from despotism to l. in featherbed, 358:2
give me l. or death, 353:3
God who gave life gave l., 357:1
hail L. hail, 444:11
he served human l., 641:3
he that commands sea is at l., 168:14
headstrong l., 174:27
highest political end, 554:14
history of l. history of safeguards, 695:6
history of progress of human l., 509:13
I must have l. withal, 198:20
if l. found in democracy, 80:30
in doubtful things l., 274:22
in moderate governments, 370:10
in mouth of Webster, 454:9
in proportion to restraint, 415:13
individual l. individual power, 386:1
interfering with l., 464:9
is possibility of doubting, 759:19
judiciary safeguard of l., 626:18
know no such l., 276:2
knows nothing but victories, 489:16
lawless attack upon l., 337:10
life l. pursuit of happiness, 357:2
little is achieved through L., 495:13
love of l. love of others, 410:16
man establish reign of l., 777:15
mocks my loss of l., 371:10
mountain nymph sweet l., 259:11
my Soul at L., 544:21
nation conceived in L., 476:7
natural l. establishes itself, 339:2
neither in despotism or democracy, 370:10
neither l. nor safety, 320:13
of a poet, 257:18
of conscience, 255:3
of individual, 464:15
of press, 360:3, 462:14
of thought life of soul, 316:28
only to those who love it, 415:7
peace l. and safety, 358:13
people so dead to l., 323:4
placid repose under l., 278:27
plucks justice by nose, 210:36
possessions take away l., 629:16
power to endanger public l., 351:2
precious must be rationed, 654:13
price of l., 366:*n*6
proclaim l. throughout land, 9:16
property no stamps, 846:13
putrid corpse of l., 702:8
quick with seed of l., 515:21
right to death or l., 523:18
sacred fire of l., 350:5
secret of happiness, 607:1
secure blessings of l., 360:13

Liberty *(continued)*

seeking l. which is so dear, 131:6
so loving-jealous of his l., 183:15
soul of journey is l., 410:12
spirit of l., 344:6
survival of l., 799:7
sweet land of l., 469:8
taken with Nature, 571:3
this country to preserve l., 359:9
this is L. Hall, 342:20
to know, 263:4
to think feel do, 410:12
trains for liberty, 648:13
Tree, 354:5
tree of l. refreshed, 357:15
tree of l. watered by blood, 370:1
what crimes in thy name, 369:8
where l. there is my country, 340:3
where Slavery is L. cannot be, 490:1
white Goddess, 563:5
with l. and justice for all, 606:17
wrote at l. when of Devils, 372:13
Liberty's in every blow, 380:11
Libraries, have well-furnished l., 239:16
I bless God in l., 338:3
meek young men grow up in l., 454:21
not made they grow, 596:19
Library, furnished me from mine own l., 229:15
public l. affords conviction, 324:13
turn over half a l., 327:24
was dukedom large enough, 229:13
whereon I look, 248:21
Libre, l'homme est né l., 330:*n*3
Libri, cave ab homine unius l., 123:12
Lice tethered, 780:8
License, equal l. in bold invention, 101:16
innocence never blossom into l., 290:14
love not freedom but l., 263:9
poetic l., 90:17
universal l. to be good, 441:11
Licensing and prohibiting, 263:5
Licentiae, poetarum l. liberiora, 90:*n*9
Licentious, newspapers the most l., 367:33
soldiery, 345:5
Lick absurd pomp, 204:15
ill cook that cannot l. fingers, 184:9
it into form, 108:*n*7
the dust, 18:10
Valleys up, 545:8
Licked, admit I'm l., 728:5
platter clean, 856:20
soup from ladies, 491:16
Licker, corn l. stop victim's watch, 678:1
talks mighty loud, 593:13
Licks, bear l. them into proper shape, 108:12
hand raised to shed blood, 311:2
pride that l. the dust, 312:10
Lid, earth's l., 709:5
pent-house l., 218:27
Lids, drops blue-fringed l., 401:12
eternal l. apart, 439:11
Lie a thought more nigh, 247:11
abroad for commonwealth, 232:19
all the Dead l. down, 545:6
asked lady to l. her down, 373:9
asks no questions isn't told l., 342:*n*2
at proud foot of conqueror, 178:28
athwart noses as they l. asleep, 182:22

Lie *(continued)*

becomes habitual, 357:11
before us like land of dreams, 531:2
big l., 726:12
by emperor's side, 214:20
can't pray a l., 560:21
children and fools cannot l., 148:18
circumstantial, 200:9
contrive one noble l., 77:8
countenance cannot l., 171:9
credit his own l., 229:11
deep buried, 61:14
differences between cat and l., 561:9
dig grave let me l., 599:6
direct, 200:9
dost thou l. so low, 196:18
down because 'twas night, 234:16
down for eon or two, 633:3
down in green pastures, 16:18
down like tired child, 428:2
down till leaders spoken, 634:14
down where ladders start, 643:2
every word she writes is l., 789:1
fain wald l. down, 854:11
families l. together, 811:15
faults l. gently on him, 231:11
for a moment l. becomes truth, 526:8
give the world the l., 160:7
half a truth blackest, 486:18
handle which fits all, 473:12
has seven endings, 853:9
heaven with splendors l., 514:14
here let her l., 285:28
here obedient to their laws we l., 62:4
home to a l., 709:4
how l. through centuries, 492:8
how still we see thee l., 558:5
I can't tell a l., 349:*n*7
I l. down alone, 619:21
I shall l. in the dust, 53:27
I their map l. flat, 236:14
if I l. spit in my face, 185:24
in cold obstruction, 211:23
in cowslip's bell I l., 230:13
in dark weep for sins, 519:16
in your throat, 191:11
inhuman reign of l., 730:10
leads you to believe a l., 376:9
lightly gentle earth, 245:9
like bill on Nature's Reality, 433:24
nicer to l. in bed, 654:2
not a man that he should l., 9:24
not know what it is to l., 448:16
nothing can need a l., 249:18
on knees of the gods, 54:10
on Mother's bed, 801:3
one daiquiri told the other a l., 792:8
permits himself to tell l., 357:11
rather l. in woollen, 194:13
sergeant's widow told l., 472:20
shall rot, 535:5
sleep will never l., 183:18
sleeping dogs l., 498:12
still and slumber, 304:4
still ye thief, 186:11
stone tell where I l., 308:4
sweet compulsion in music l., 259:6
sweets compacted l., 250:10
talking of fall of man, 507:31

Lie *(continued)*

tangled in her hair, 276:2
thought uttered is l., 458:16
to me tell me you've waited, 792:3
truth in masquerade, 424:15
underneath this stone doth l., 237:22
unless statistics l., 740:5
upon the daisies, 564:8
violence intertwined with l., 804:12
what is a l., 424:15
where'er she l., 272:7
which is all a lie, 486:18
who loves to l. with me, 198:11
with a purpose worst, 645:16
with my fathers, 7:35
worse things than l., 504:6
yonder all before us l., 277:1
young shall l. down together, 26:34
Liebchen with whom should I quarrel, 771:8
Lieben und arbeiten, 608:n3
Lied, never seen anybody but l., 560:14
those who l. for hire, 709:7
Lief not be as be in awe, 195:18
Liege of loiterers, 176:33
we are men my l., 220:31
Lies are mortar, 644:10
at last as always, 809:3
believe her though she l., 228:2
Bible has thousand l., 562:23
bodyguard of l., 667:11
cruelest l. told in silence, 598:7
dalliance in wardrobe l., 192:24
death l. on my tongue, 187:5
everybody l. about sex, 842:3
exposed he l., 285:12
Fool l. here, 633:2
freedom from l., 622:7
full fathom five thy father l., 229:20
great Prince in prison l., 235:5
half truth blackest of l., 486:18
heaven l. about us, 393:11
here again he l., 520:10
here food for worms, 319:2
here l. a King that ruled, 253:12
here l. beautiful lady, 662:9
here l. Matthew Prior, 297:7
here l. my wife, 285:28
here l. one who meant well, 599:22
here l. one whose name, 441:7
here l. our good Edmund, 343:2
here l. truly honest man, 272:19
Hope l. to mortals, 619:20
in his bed walks with me, 178:9
in the rude manger l., 258:17
jailed for telling l. to young, 770:15
kindness and l., 767:7
long time l. in one word, 179:1
make l. sound truthful, 765:13
Matilda told dreadful l., 653:9
matters I relate are true l., 726:5
music on spirit l., 480:17
now l. he there, 196:31
old men's l., 709:4
on chaliced flowers that l., 225:12
on her left side, 734:10
poets tell many l., 57:7
religion of slaves, 649:1
speaking l. in hypocrisy, 46:18
steep my speech in l., 65:29

Lies *(continued)*

tells l. without attending, 357:11
that way madness l., 216:26
to hide it, 249:n5
to tell l. not honorable, 69:1
truth to cover l., 300:15
uneasy l. head that wears crown, 191:35
where he longed to be, 599:6
with dogs riseth with fleas, 251:24
you can invent, 375:9
Life a battle and sojourning, 115:6
a Fury slinging flame, 483:22
a man's real l., 612:13
academic l., 239:6
accept Jesus new l., 813:15
account of her l. to clod, 194:15
actuality of thought is l., 80:6
admits not of delays, 328:7
adore my l. with Bird, 781:10
affirmation of l., 677:15
after l. is death, 568:24
ain't all beer and skittles, 496:n1
all a man hath will he give for l., 13:27
all his l. in the wrong, 293:5
all human l. in monkeys and cats, 584:11
all I care about is l., 577:4
all inclusion and confusion, 585:10
all l. an experiment, 578:14
all l. is a dream, 254:18
all l. 6 to 5 against, 704:12
all my l. I was a bride, 831:14
along parabola l. flies, 829:6
American l. solvent, 629:13
among people who love each other, 461:10
and Death and For Ever, 514:2
and memory of it, 786:3
and power of increase, 286:2
and what's a l., 249:13
anyone whose l. married to sea, 664:1
anything for a quiet l., 243:19
anythin' for a quiet l., 496:5
art long l. short, 364:4
art makes l., 585:21
art of drawing conclusions, 558:19
as for future l. man judge, 470:9
as much as my l. was worth, 332:23
as to bed's-feet l. shrunk, 234:20
as to breathe were l., 481:10
at ease drifts, 541:25
at no point in l. felt American, 826:13
at the door of l., 568:13
awful wretched mess of l., 773:17
bagatelle of transient experience, 624:13
bankrupt of l., 283:9
be it l. or death crave reality, 507:2
be not afraid of l., 582:9
bear a charmed l., 222:20
beg delinquents for l., 801:15
begins perpetually, 644:17
believe in l., 648:16
believe in l. to come, 773:14
best of l. intoxication, 423:19
best part of married l. fights, 750:4
best portion of man's l., 390:20
best things in l. free, 736:17
birth l. and death, 292:19
birthday of my l., 547:15

Life *(continued)*

bitterness of feelings about modern l., 788:5
bitterness of L., 553:6
blameless l., 485:16
blot out of book of l., 48:13
boat of l. be light, 620:6
Book of L. begins, 605:3
book of l. opened, 48:37
books substitute for l., 598:10
boredom at core of l., 281:4
bread called staff of l., 295:18
bread of l., 41:4
bread of l. in mouth, 292:11
breath of l., 5:16
breathed by Creator, 470:3
breathtakingly serious, 730:9
brief l. our portion, 511:10
brisking about the l., 338:7
broad margin to my l., 507:6
broken l. up for bread, 568:12
buried l., 529:4
burrs and thorns of l., 436:5
but a span, 296:14
C Major of this l., 494:6
calamity of so long l., 203:33
cannot tear out page of l., 461:7
care of l. and happiness, 358:15
careless of single l., 484:4
care's an enemy to l., 209:1
cast cold eye on l. on death, 643:5
chain of l., 807:11
change we think we see in l., 669:2
changing scenes of l., 294:6
chaos breeds l., 570:10
charmed l., 222:20
clock stops time come to l., 748:9
closed twice before close, 547:3
comes a time in every man's l., 730:16
comes before literature, 558:6
comes to end in prosperity, 65:8
comes to him with love, 764:6
compared l. to a dream, 153:7
compel philosophy to inquire about l., 91:6
conduct three-fourths of l., 531:21
consists with wildness, 507:30
contraction of l., 675:5
control nature and human l., 602:17
controlling circumstances of l., 522:3
cool sequestered vale of l., 334:23
count l. of battle good, 627:3
crowded hour of l., 346:12
crown of l., 47:10, 48:10
crown of L. as it closes, 568:6
Culprit L., 544:2
custom guide of human l., 330:6
daily beauty in his l., 215:4
dancing is l. itself, 617:23
dead husks of l., 777:1
dear as light and l., 380:4
death after l. does please, 161:3
death makes l. live, 495:3
death nor l. nor angels, 43:12
death of each day's l., 220:16
death part of l., 676:6
death side of l. away from us, 677:7
defeat my l., 214:30
demd horrid grind, 496:26

Life *(continued)*

deprive of l. liberty or property, 361:8
deprived of l. liberty or property, 361:4
destroys single l. rescues single l., 120:9
devote his l. in serving his prince, 62:10
difficult to write good l. as live one, 692:8
digressions l. of reading, 332:12
dim origins of l., 777:1
disease of modern l., 529:12
does thy l. destroy, 374:3
done their song and dance in your l., 784:8
dost thou love l., 320:1
doth l. in tendance spend, 161:24
dream l. as lake dreams sky, 631:10
dream of l., 430:12
dreamed l. was beauty, 504:20
dreams necessary to l., 765:7
drink l. to lees, 481:8
earnest art gay, 381:19
ease one L. the Aching, 546:1
echo undermine hold on l., 684:4
education not preparation for l. is l., 616:14
education will determine future l., 77:10
effective therapist, 706:13
elevate l. by conscious endeavor, 506:27
empty dream, 465:17
end in itself, 578:1
end of l. cancels bands, 186:16
enjoyment of l. and liberty, 339:9
enlarge my l., 324:8
enough for my l., 32:5
entrusts l. to one hole, 86:11
envy and wrath shorten l., 32:43
eternal l. gift of God, 43:2
eternal l. in knowledge of God, 50:5
everlasting l., 40:46
everything in political l., 531:18
evidence of vicarious l., 613:10
exempt from public haunt, 197:37
exile's l. no l., 85:15
experience of this sweet l., 132:5
fabric of l., 777:2
fall upon thorns of l., 429:3
falter l. away, 529:10
fear of Acheron which troubles l., 93:7
feels l. in every limb, 390:15
felt l. in producing art, 585:9
fever of l. over, 450:1
fie upon this quiet l., 185:20
for l. six hundred pounds, 312:16
for l. to come, 228:23
for the living, 555:1
for why my l. at end, 853:23
force uncomprehended was his l., 542:14
fought for l., 783:16
free to develop hostile forms as friendly, 566:22
friend is medicine of l., 32:11
frittered away by detail, 506:29
from this cup they drank their l., 856:8
front essential facts of l., 506:28
fruit she longs to hand you, 771:16
fruits of l. and beauty, 373:11
gale of l. high, 619:1
game is l., 759:11
game that must be played, 652:4

Life *(continued)*

garment we alter, 749:10
gates of new l. to thee, 493:21
gave thee l. bid thee feed, 371:15
give to eat of the tree of l., 48:9
give up whole idea of l., 824:7
give us luxuries of l., 502:6
giveth his l. for sheep, 41:17
giving l. by death of others, 140:11
God gave l. gave liberty, 357:1
golden tree of l., 365:8
good death does honor to whole l., 132:13
Good L. waiting for us, 769:14
great business of l., 572:7
greater price than l., 758:15
greatest thing in family l., 671:17
Greek thought and l., 539:9
Greeks have dreamt dream of l. best, 366:8
green l. once lived there, 785:4
growth only evidence of l., 449:19
grunt and sweat under weary l., 203:33
half a l. asunder, 551:8
half spent before we know, 252:13
happy all his l., 252:17
harder toward summit, 589:24
harmonious and humane l., 532:6
have the light of l., 41:10
have you found l. distasteful, 495:10
he giveth l., 42:18
he that findeth l., 35:32
he that loveth her loveth l., 32:2
he who knows l., 293:16
here find l. in death, 404:4
high l., 341:15
high l. mistaken path, 425:20
his l. a breath of God, 504:11
his l. dinner wife, 446:13
his l. was gentle, 197:22
his l. was in the right, 275:20
honor dearer than l., 157:13
hope for happiness beyond l., 355:3
horrors of half known l., 516:16
hot for certainties in l., 541:9
house to be let for l. , 249:8
how good man's l., 493:16
human l. a large Mansion, 440:9
human l. a state in which much endured, 324:26
human l. priceless, 758:15
hungry for l. and death, 794:9
I am in mourning for my l., 622:10
I am the bread of l., 41:4
I believe in l. everlasting, 50:3
I burned my l., 747:19
I have painted my l., 715:10
I have wasted my l., 820:2
I haven't a literary l., 784:2
I would like simple l., 821:14
if it be l. to pitch, 640:18
if l. bitter pardon, 569:15
if one had courage l. livable, 540:20
if woman told truth about her l., 791:10
if you haven't had l., 585:8
ills scholar's l. assail, 324:6
imagination master of l., 612:17
immortal Death has taken mortal l., 93:12

Life *(continued)*

in internal environment, 501:2
in l. as in football, 615:3
in l. courtesy, 643:9
in l. did harbor give, 237:22
in London all l. can afford, 328:9
in middle of journey of l., 129:17
in our l. Nature live, 402:5
in sea of l. enisled, 529:3
in struggle for l. find love, 732:16
in the midst of l. death, 51:13
in whom standeth eternal l., 50:5
Indian summer of l., 570:26
inseparable like l. and consciousness, 707:17
intend to lead new l., 50:17
interest in death interest in l., 676:10
into each l. rain fall, 466:10
irremediable poverty of l., 689:7
is a copycat, 716:19
is a foreign language, 729:15
is a jest, 307:19
is a wave, 523:21
is action and passion, 577:15
is all beer and skittles, 496:n1
is an incurable disease, 275:13
is boring, 792:7
is but a span, 296:14
is fading fast away, 594:2
is made of sobs sniffles and smiles, 626:8
is or is not worth living, 789:14
is its own journey, 774:13
is l. so dear, 353:3
is not l. more than meat, 34:17
is only error, 382:9
is painting picture, 578:7
is real life is earnest, 465:17
is short art long, 73:10
is supremely easy for men, 54:20
is the thing, 636:10
is thorny, 401:9
is trouble Zorba continued, 701:9
is unfair, 799:12
is what we make it, 582:8
isn't all beer and skittles, 533:2
it pretends to build on, 758:11
it takes l. to love l., 651:13
it would be L., 545:12
joy of l. is variety, 324:22
jump the l. to come, 219:16
jury passing on l., 211:4
keep pure both l. and art, 72:16
keep way of the tree of l., 6:11
lag-end of my l., 186:31
large as l. twice as natural, 552:15
Last Abode is L., 122:3
last hour of my l., 318:13
last of l. best, 494:7
lasted the rest of my l., 550:2
lay down l. for friends, 41:31
lay hold on eternal l., 46:27
Leaves of L. falling, 471:3
left behind a real l., 821:4
length of l. leading among inquiries, 114:16
let thy l. be sincere, 32:7
liberty pursuit of happiness, 357:2
light l. pleasure pain, 553:14
light of l., 41:10

Life *(continued)*

light of whole l. dies, 600:14
like a dome of many-colored glass, 430:17
like a froward child, 282:9
like living l. over, 321:4
like runners pass on torch of l., 93:2
little l. rounded with sleep, 230:9
little needed to make happy l., 115:28
live all days of your l., 299:20
live l. he has imagined, 507:18
live l. not simple, 730:3
live l. through not like crossing field, 861:18
live out thy l. as light, 569:8
lived in scene it composes, 688:22
lived l. talking at street corners, 724:19
lively form of death, 164:12
Lolita light of my l., 755:14
London this moment, 699:16
long disease my l., 312:2
long littleness of l., 711:7
looking out from eyes of doe, 735:10
lose l. shall find it, 36:27
love an episode in man's l., 385:12
Love anterior to L., 545:21
love l. of their parents, 755:13
love long l. better than figs, 222:29
love of wisdom guide of l., 376:14
love only business in l., 417:6
love the history of woman's l., 385:12
loveth her loveth l., 32:2
lust for l., 540:19
made of marble and mud, 460:17
making ends meet in l., 694:18
man lives l. of epoch, 676:5
mankind fleet of l. like leaves, 75:9
man's l. cheap as beast's, 216:15
many-colored l. he drew, 323:14
married to sea, 664:1
married to single l., 272:10
may perfect be, 238:14
measured l. with coffee spoons, 717:10
medicine for l. which has fled, 60:5
memory without pain, 68:10
messed up l. for nothing, 722:21
mine honor is my l., 178:31
miserable mortals flame with l., 53:31
money as means to l., 701:18
more abundant l., 697:17
more lost than l., 110:5
more sweet than painted pomp, 197:36
most loathed worldly l., 211:24
much too far out all my l., 764:4
my l. has gone, 818:8
my l. is preserved, 7:21
my l. my joy, 155:8
my l. my real l. in danger, 813:4
my l. poem I would have writ, 506:1
my lines and l. are free, 250:15
my poems naughty my l. pure, 110:13
my way of l. is fallen, 222:11
near bone sweetest, 507:20
never know what l. means till you die, 495:3
never to have drawn breath of l., 640:16
new era in l. from book, 507:5
new l. begins, 129:14

Life *(continued)*

new l. when sin no more, 501:17
nightmare L.-in-Death was she, 400:3
no life but death, 164:12
no l. by others' death, 178:17
no l. can be recaptured wholly, 793:13
no l. lives forever, 569:3
no l. moves in empty passageways, 68:4
no man loses other l. than that he lives, 115:3
no man loves l. like old, 69:5
no no no l., 218:7
no wealth but l., 517:10
nobody write l. of man, 327:11
nor love thy l. nor hate, 268:11
not cheap but sacred, 456:31
not doing a sum, 578:7
not giving l. but risking l., 777:12
not keep advantages of l., 659:16
not l. alone makes man, 761:8
not L. for which they stand, 557:9
not long l. by fire, 624:3
not take his own l., 76:15
not to fancy what fair in l., 493:7
nothing give up l., 780:5
nothing in his l., 219:8
nothing much to lose, 620:1
novel attempt to represent l., 584:13
now I live now l. is done, 164:17
now is immortal l., 593:21
O Death in L., 482:22
O for L. of Sensations, 440:1
o' the building, 220:23
occupations few tranquil l., 115:13
ocean of l., 467:18
o'er ills o' l. victorious, 379:17
of jealousy, 213:36
of law not logic, 577:13
of l. he only is deserving, 365:19
of man heroic poem, 434:12
of man solitary, 246:12
of peoples and humanity, 542:17
of poor man in mean cottage, 32:40
of Riley, 849:*n*1
of significant soil, 721:14
of simplicity independence magnanimity, 506:16
of soul, 316:28
of this world, 122:9
old age crown of l., 91:18
on this unavailing star, 636:8
one Draught of L., 547:2
one entrance into l., 31:22
one in l. and death are we, 564:15
one l. to lose for country, 370:6
one long struggle in dark, 93:1
only one happiness in l., 461:13
our l. is changed, 715:8
out of ashes l. again, 591:11
out of it are the issues of l., 21:2
outlive his l. half a year, 204:21
over my long l., 624:7
over there behind Shelf, 545:12
part with l. cheerfully, 115:19
pass them for nobler l., 436:3
perceivers of terror of l., 456:23
perfect interpreter of l., 710:12
perfected by death, 463:10
perfection of l. or work, 641:4

Life *(continued)*

period in l. when work comes first, 647:10
philosophy you leader of l., 91:5
piece of buffoonery, 647:12
poem ends in clarification of l., 671:10
poet gives l. to fictions, 688:21
present l. a diversion and sport, 122:3
present l. like flight of sparrow, 125:1
pressure of exigencies of l., 607:13
price l. exacts for peace, 752:10
progress from want to want, 328:4
progress to fuller l., 648:16
prolong l. only when shorten miseries, 783:5
protracted is protracted woe, 324:8
protracting l. not deduct from death, 93:14
public l. crown of career, 674:10
public l. situation of power, 343:18
pulse of l. stood still, 306:1
pulse of modern l. economic, 683:2
pure in l. free from sin, 99:15
ran gaily as Thames, 529:12
rarely find a happy l., 98:18
realize l. while live it, 750:1
reason the l. of the law, 159:14
rejoice in l. mark of Greek spirit, 647:9
religion reaction upon l., 582:14
religious feeling toward l., 651:17
relinquish l. for good of country, 388:7
rest of his dull l., 245:4
resurrection and the l., 41:19
resurrection unto eternal l., 51:14
Reverence for L., 677:14
reward of labor is l., 557:6
rights to a better l., 597:10
rounded with a sleep, 230:9
rule of l. from tonight, 621:16
sated with banquet of l., 93:13
save l. shall lose it, 36:27
saw l. steadily saw it whole, 528:2
science of l. superb hall, 500:17
scraped l. with fine-tooth comb, 798:5
seas of l. like wine, 290:4
secret l. of belly and bone, 791:12
secrets of a happy l., 780:*n*1
sedentary l. sin, 590:10
see into l. of things, 391:2
seek not l. of immortals, 66:1
sense of what l. means, 582:17
set before you l. and death, 10:12
set gray l., 481:4
set l. at pin's fee, 202:7
set my l. on any chance, 221:2
set my l. upon cast, 174:24
sex pattern of process of l., 617:19
shadow of death, 256:24, 568:1
sharpened l. commands course, 541:25
she is mine for l., 804:18
sheltered l. can be daring l., 784:7
short l. in saddle, 624:3
short quiet hours few, 517:14
sin to prefer l. to honor, 113:14
slits the thin-spun l., 261:19
smooth road of l., 333:6
so short craft so long, 133:11
so was it when l. began, 392:7
soul the captain of l., 95:9
sound which tells of l., 407:*n*1

Light *(continued)*

apparreled in celestial l., 393:7
armor of l., 43:26
around the body, 817:3
a-roving by l. of moon, 423:1
at end of tunnel, 800:*n*1
be not darkened, 25:7
be the earth, 69:13
because it lendeth l., 161:26
better to l. one candle, 704:*n*1
black as if bereaved of l., 372:1
body changed to l., 856:10
breaks where no sun shines, 795:3
bringeth to l. the shadow of death, 14:13
broke upon brain, 422:22
buried under chains, 751:12
burning and shining l., 40:49
by her own radiant l., 260:29
by l. of moon, 855:*n*3
candle and put it under bushel, 34:2
candle of understanding, 31:9
candle to the sun, 278:28
carrying you into fields of l., 69:12
certain Slant of l., 544:12
children of l., 39:40, 530:12
children of l. and day, 46:10
cold l. and hot shade, 374:13
come on baby l. my fire, 842:12
comes from thine eyes, 845:1
common as l. is love, 428:9
consider how l. is spent, 263:12
danced by l. of moon, 499:18
darkness and l. alike to thee, 20:14
dawn's early l., 411:1
dear as l. and life, 380:4
dies before thy word, 313:25
dim religious l., 260:10
doth trample on my days, 279:8
echo and l. unto eternity, 430:2
enough for wot I've to do, 496:13
everlasting L., 558:5
exact day-labor l. denied, 263:13
excelleth darkness, 24:3
excess of l., 335:9
existence brief crack of l., 755:12
fade from eyes, 658:*n*3
fade into l. of common day, 393:12
fails on winter's afternoon, 722:3
fantastic round, 260:23
fantastic toe, 259:10
fierce l. beats on throne, 485:16
flash of l. cut across sky, 793:4
former l. restore, 215:7
forward the L. Brigade, 484:25
freedom's holy l., 469:9
from grave to l., 289:5
gains make heavy purses, 165:2
garmented in l., 429:15
gates of l., 267:10
Gatsby believed in the green l., 746:8
gives a lovely l., 735:2
gives l. in darkness, 172:7
gladsome l. of jurisprudence, 159:15
gleams and is gone, 530:19
God Appears and God is L., 375:16
God guideth to His l., 121:21
God is l., 47:36
God l. of heavens and earth, 121:21
God shows sufficient l., 494:27

Light *(continued)*

God's eldest daughter, 258:9
God's first creature l., 265:*n*2
gold and silver l., 637:11
gone into world of l., 279:7
gospel l. first dawned, 334:7
guide by l. of reason, 607:4
hail holy l., 265:24
half l. half shade, 481:3
half-believers, 529:10
have l. of life, 41:10
he is angel l., 507:26
heaven to day denies, 422:13
heaven's l. forever shines, 430:17
here kindled, 247:10
Hesperus entreats thy l., 237:10
hop l. ladies, 593:17
I am l. of the world, 41:10
if l. in thee be darkness, 34:15
if once we lose this l., 237:14
in despite of l. keep us together, 234:16
in minds of others, 688:23
in present l. flames, 667:3
in ragged luck, 594:8
in room by artificial l., 808:12
in sound sound-like power in light,
    399:9
in the dust lies dead, 431:4
infant crying for l., 484:3
inner l. will shine forth, 366:*n*4
is lion comes to drink, 687:11
is shadow of God, 256:24
it giveth l. unto all, 34:2
judged in l. of final issue, 81:15
law not a l. to see by, 813:7
lead kindly L., 449:18
lead me from darkness to l., 51:20
let perpetual l. shine, 49:8
let the Big L. in, 742:7
let there be l., 5:9
let your l. shine, 34:2
lift up the l. of thy countenance, 15:30
like gleaming taper's l., 340:13
little drops of l., 257:21
live and love in God's l., 143:12
live out thy life as l., 569:8
lived l. in spring, 529:1
Lolita l. of my life, 755:14
long l. shakes, 482:19
made l. of it, 36:40
man like l. kindled and put out, 64:12
many hands make l. work, 149:2
mass times speed of l. squared, 683:*n*2
men of inward l., 271:24
mocks at it and sets it l., 179:5
moralists put tale in edifying l., 758:12
more by number than your l., 232:16
more l., 366:12
my burden is l., 35:35
neither joy nor love nor l., 531:2
night shadow of l., 568:1
no darkness into l. without emotion,
    675:13
no l. but darkness visible, 264:1
no l. propitious shone, 348:22
Noose of L., 470:14
not leave my hand without l., 713:3
of bright world dies, 600:14
of Light, 50:4

Light *(continued)*

of light beguile, 176:19
of my understanding, 293:15
of oncoming train, 800:*n*1
of setting suns, 391:4
of step and heart, 662:9
of the body, 34:14
of the world, 34:2, 41:10
of things, 390:18
of thy sword, 444:11
of whole life dies, 600:14
old age level l., 734:13
on dark theme trace verses of l., 92:17
once set is our little l., 231:21
one small candle l. a thousand, 247:10
out of hell leads to l., 265:11
people have seen a great l., 26:30
people in darkness saw great l., 33:31
place void of all l., 130:11
pleasing dreams slumbers l., 397:3
power and l., 812:1
prime work of God, 265:*n*2
progeny of l., 267:8
pure and endless l., 279:5
purple l. of Love, 335:6
put out the l., 215:7, 615:18
Put out the L., 669:19
radiant l. rests on men, 66:3
rage against dying of l., 795:14
rather l. candles than curse darkness,
    704:*n*1
river of crystal l., 597:5
roving by l. of moon, 423:1
sadder l. than moon, 468:17
seeking light, 176:19
shaft of l. in darkness, 800:6
she loves, 485:9
she treads on it so l., 173:27
shines over land and sea, 667:3
shineth in darkness, 40:30
shower of l. is poesy, 436:4
solarium a rage of l., 841:11
something of angelic l., 394:3
speed far faster than l., 664:4
stand in your own l., 148:30
steeps of l., 487:8
strikes Sultan's Turret with L., 470:13
strong shadow where much l., 363:9
suffusion from that l., 402:7
sun gives l. soon as he rises, 321:1
sweetness and l., 297:19, 531:16
teach l. to counterfeit a gloom, 260:5
that cometh from her wisdom, 31:23
that green l. that lingers, 402:4
that led astray, 378:3
that lies in woman's eyes, 412:4
that loses night that wins, 567:18
that never was, 394:13
that shineth more and more, 21:1
the first light of evening, 688:14
the Lord is my l., 16:22
thickens and crow makes wing, 221:7
things holy profane grave and l., 246:10
those that rebel against the l., 14:30
thousand points of l., 813:9
threshold of waking l., 818:8
thy l. is come, 28:29
thy l. relume, 215:7

Light *(continued)*
>time's glory bring truth to l., 175:8
>to guide, 394:10
>to lighten Gentiles, 39:6
>to them in darkness, 39:1
>to those in darkness, 145:6
>to whom God assigns no l., 121:22
>tracings of eternal l., 381:9
>travel l., 777:5
>trifles l. as air, 214:5
>tripped l. fantastic, 625:13
>truth not sought for comes to l., 83:17
>truth will come to l., 137:n3
>truths kindle l. for truths, 92:18
>two ways of spreading l., 627:9
>unconscious not only dark but l., 675:9
>unto my path, 19:28
>unveiled her peerless l., 266:16
>upon them hath the l. shined, 26:30
>us down in honor or dishonor, 476:3
>Vesper now raising his l., 94:18
>void of l., 264:6
>waited for the l., 652:11
>walk while ye have l., 41:23
>wave of l. breaks into darkness, 712:7
>we fear in the l., 93:9
>we shall need no other l., 366:n4
>what l. is to painting, 600:15
>what l. through yonder window, 182:28
>when daylight comes comes in l., 512:10
>when my l. low, 483:21
>when our brief l. has set, 94:4
>which lighteth every man, 40:32
>white l. of morning, 855:19
>why rise because 'tis l., 234:16
>wife make heavy husband, 190:11
>winning make prize light, 229:22
>withdrawn which once he wore, 468:7
>world but thickened l., 458:2

Lighted fools way to dusty death, 222:16
>old is having l. rooms in head, 810:9

Lighten our darkness, 50:10

Lightened, thundered and l., 74:10
>weight of world l., 391:1

Lightens, cease to be ere it l., 183:10

Lighter than cork danced on waves, 603:8
>town is l. than vanity, 281:23

Lightest, movements of l. atom, 366:13
>sovereign is the l., 82:20
>word harrow soul, 202:12

Lightfoot, many a l. lad, 619:6

Light-hearted, afoot and l., 520:2

Lighthouse, below the l. top, 399:14
>took sitivation at l., 496:5

Lightland, rise in heaven's l., 4:7
>set in western l., 4:8

Lightly draws its breath, 390:15
>earth rest l. on you, 124:25
>entered into unadvisedly or l., 51:7
>lie l. gentle earth, 245:9
>rest, 69:13
>tread l. she is near, 604:6
>we esteem too l., 354:10

Lightness, drama not of heaviness but of l., 823:13

Lightning, bottled l., 496:24
>countenance like l., 38:11
>does the work, 562:17
>done like l., 237:6

Lightning *(continued)*
>fateful l., 513:18
>flashed the living l., 309:13
>he thence had riven, 425:5
>he's a l. pilot, 560:7
>in collied night, 180:20
>in thunder l. or in rain, 218:23
>like writing history with l., 611:13
>makes awful l., 463:19
>mirth like flash of l., 302:18
>outstare the l., 223:29
>Satan as l. fall, 39:20
>scratch head with l., 560:2
>strikes mountaintop, 99:24
>Superman the l., 588:17
>too like the l., 183:10
>vain to look for defense against l., 104:6
>zigzag l. stands high, 856:1

Lightnings, four l. zigzag from me, 856:4
>in the splendor of the moon, 481:2
>veiling l. of song, 430:9

Light-o'-love lady known as Lou, 673:9

Lights around the shore, 542:7
>Father of l., 47:11
>fled garlands dead, 412:8
>godfathers of heaven's l., 176:20
>highest candle l. dark, 688:15
>love is keeper of warm l., 68:1
>moon l. up the earth, 58:1
>Northern L. seen sights, 673:10
>of the world, 347:9
>ridicule one of principal l., 301:10
>that do mislead the morn, 211:31
>turn up l., 626:17
>water closing over sleepy l., 787:2
>your l. burning, 39:30

Light-winged Dryad, 437:6

Ligislachure, newspaper conthrols l., 646:18

Like a winter my absence, 227:7
>ape how l. to us, 87:14
>can afford to l. them, 830:8
>doth quit like, 212:9
>every good believer, 741:2
>find their l. again, 396:15
>God pairs l. with l., 55:15
>how do you l. your blueeyed boy, 739:13
>I didn't l. it, 839:16
>I don't l. them much, 831:18
>I don't l. you Sabidius, 110:16
>I know what I l., 659:10
>I l. to be in America, 825:17
>I would l. to be the air, 833:7
>look upon his l. again, 201:12
>lose freedom autonomy seeking to become l., 783:15
>me from heels to head, 598:23
>more ye see better l. it, 646:6
>never met one I didn't l., 685:20
>not fair terms, 188:12
>of each thing, 176:21
>one that stands on promontory, 172:32
>people like priest, 30:13
>poor cat i' the adage, 219:20
>same things is friendship, 95:6
>tell me what you l., 517:18
>those who admire us, 273:32
>to an hermit poor, 159:21
>to see it lap Miles, 545:8
>upon earth there is not his l., 15:23

Like *(continued)*
>very l. a whale, 205:9
>very very l. me, 598:23
>want it most l. it least, 314:22
>we don't l. it, 818:7
>what he loves never l. too much, 237:21
>will to like, 147:16

Liked, all people need be l. by some people, 783:14
>book the better, 342:22
>it not and died, 232:17
>several women, 229:33
>way it walks, 624:5

Likely impossibility preferable, 81:13
>man in preference to rich, 64:21
>we are all l. to go astray, 67:26

Likeness, devil created in man's l., 525:15
>gods in l. of men, 42:13
>grow into l. of bad men, 78:13
>let us make man after our l., 5:12
>of filly foal, 181:5
>very l. of roasted crab, 181:5

Likes, doesn't know what he l., 741:13
>nobody l. man who brings bad news, 67:15

Likewise, go and do l., 39:24

Liking, all love all l. all delight, 248:18
>grounds other than l., 513:12
>happy l. what they do, 333:11
>saves me trouble of l., 406:23

Lilac all over New England, 672:14
>and brown hair, 719:12
>lost l., 719:16
>time, 692:1

Lilacs last in dooryard bloomed, 520:14
>out of dead land, 718:11

Lilies and languors of virtue, 568:3
>beauty of the l., 513:19
>breaking golden l., 464:6
>calla l. in bloom again mother, 745:7
>crowned with l., 735:11
>feed among the l., 25:21
>handfuls of l. to scatter, 98:1
>of the field, 34:19
>peacocks and l., 517:7
>roses and white l. grow, 232:5
>silent war of l., 175:3
>that fester, 227:5
>three l. in her hand, 541:26
>twisted braids of l., 261:10
>wheat set about with l., 25:29

Lilting house, 795:8
>I've heard them l., 340:6

Lily maid of Astolat, 485:25
>of the valleys, 25:14
>paint the l., 178:14
>poppy or a l., 564:9
>take silver and buy l., 123:n1
>thick with l. and rose, 556:11
>trembles to a l., 574:12
>water l. bloom, 480:26

Lily-livered boy, 222:10

Lima, curious traveler from L., 336:5

Limb, feels life in every l., 390:15
>neither heat affection l., 211:19
>sound wind and l., 158:15
>tail's a l., 741:5

Limbecks foul as hell, 227:18

Limbo large and broad, 265:28

Live *(continued)*

in him we l., 42:19
in house by side of road, 613:16
in human imagination, 820:9
in old chaos of sun, 686:19
in our life Nature l., 402:5
in restricted circle, 581:3
in small circle as we will, 364:20
in this faith I will l. and die, 139:19
in world as spectator, 302:4
in world good or bad, 505:17
Indians know better how to l., 601:2
innocently God is here, 322:21
isn't fit to l., 823:1
it all again, 640:18
known going to l. this long, 700:13
leave sack l. cleanly, 187:12
let me l. unseen unknown, 308:4
let us l. and love, 94:4, 231:21
life he has imagined, 507:18
life through not like crossing field,
    861:18
like stoic bird, 710:6
like to l. a long life, 823:10
like velvet mole, 710:7
like wretch and die rich, 240:21
long l. our noble king, 308:1
long l. the strike, 819:1
love wisdom l. accordingly, 506:16
loves to l. i' the sun, 198:13
mad to l. mad to be saved, 810:2
make war to l. in peace, 80:19
man born to l., 730:9
man desires to l. long, 298:6
man does not l. by GNP alone, 797:1
man forgets to l., 292:19
martyrdom to l., 256:14
marvel how fishes l. in sea, 225:9
merrily shall I l. now, 230:13
mirth with thee I mean to l., 259:21
more virtue than doth l., 237:22
name shall l. behind me, 207:13
no evil deed l. on, 580:3
no longer l. with honor, 624:4
no man shall see me and l., 9:8
no picture made to l. with, 709:9
nobly to l., 67:5
not both l. and utter it, 506:1
not in myself, 420:26
not l. by bread only, 10:1
not l. if England finished, 673:6
not l. unto oneself, 83:18
not l. with living, 186:35
not three good men unhanged, 185:22
not to l. but to make war, 784:1
now I l. now life is done, 164:17
on knees, 679:7, 698:16
one bare hour to l., 171:3
only by risking we l., 582:7
or die, 414:12
out thy life as light, 569:8
peaceably, 43:20
pleasurably without living wisely, 84:10
power to l. and act, 395:12
prophets do they l. forever, 30:33
proudly, 624:n1
pure speak true, 485:20
rage to l., 310:6
rationally for time assigned, 115:19

Live *(continued)*

realize life while l. it, 750:1
says Death, 98:14
sea folk l. three hundred years, 461:21
see so much nor l. so long, 218:9
shall not l. in Vain, 546:1
she tried to l. without him, 232:17
so l. that when summons comes, 432:10
so long as ye both shall l., 51:9
so we'll l. pray sing, 218:1
so wise young never l. long, 174:7
soil good to l. on, 515:14
something that doth l., 393:14
take means whereby I l., 190:2
teach men to l., 152:9
teaching nations how to l., 262:16
ten times ten, 451:18
that nation might l., 476:7
that they may eat, 72:9
that thou desire to live again, 589:26
their wonted fires, 334:25
thou hast no more to l., 569:15
though dead shall he l., 41:19
through time or die by suicide, 474:3
till tomorrow, 348:18
to be in awe, 195:18
to be show and gaze, 222:23
to extent they coincide with epoch, 602:2
to fight another day, 84:n3
to itself it l. and die, 227:4
to l. is Christ, 45:32
to l. is to function, 579:2
to l. not as simple as cross field, 730:3
to please must please to live, 324:3
today, 110:14
together in peace, 705:15
too beautiful to l., 496:18
true as I l., 243:9
unable to l. in society, 80:23
undo belt look for trouble, 701:9
until next day when hit it again, 755:6
unto the Lord, 43:29
upon daily rations, 497:23
upon vapor of dungeon, 214:4
we die and we l., 122:9
we how we can, 173:10
we l. as we dream alone, 612:5
we l. here they l. there, 781:13
we must attempt to l., 659:1
we only l. only suspire, 722:2
we shall l. in his sight, 30:14
what thou livest l. well, 268:11
while ye may, 266:14
who dies if England l., 635:26
why do they l. there, 748:15
with ease, 312:4
with her and live with thee, 259:12
with me and be my love, 170:6, 234:22
with the gods, 115:23
with thee and be thy love, 160:3
with wolves howl like wolf, 861:21
with you love to l., 100:4
within no power to l. long, 106:16
within reach to l. nobly, 106:16
within sense they quicken, 430:19
without conscience, 548:11
without duties obscene, 457:26
without playing knave, 288:6
without poetry music art, 548:11

Live *(continued)*

world in which I l., 831:15
world not to l. but to die in, 256:8
would you l. forever, 330:11
you might as well l., 738:14
you will know how to l., 365:9
Live-and-help-live logic, 807:11
Lived, back above element they l. in, 224:4
discover I had not l., 506:28
everything l. in me, 536:11
for all times, 381:18
had we l. tale to tell, 649:16
history need not be l. again, 820:7
how I have l. unimportant, 715:9
I had l. a blessed time, 220:25
I have l. long enough, 222:11, 568:16
I have l. today, 284:6
I have not l. in vain, 302:5
I l. on air, 669:16
in cellar damp, 515:11
in his mild magnificent eye, 491:21
in little house, 861:3
in Paris as young man, 755:7
in pretty how town, 740:8
in tide of times, 196:21
I've l. a life that's full, 835:9
judged not to have l., 577:15
life l. in scene it composes, 688:22
light in spring, 529:1
like foot for thirty years, 827:14
long on alms-basket of words, 177:10
loved cursed floundered, 585:19
men l. like fishes, 225:n1
must be l. down, 818:1
my father l. his soul, 740:10
never to have l. is best, 640:16
nightly drank daily, 783:7
on River Dee, 352:5
poetry by which I l., 819:4
she l. unknown, 391:18
some l. long and l. little, 152:11
through this horror, 704:10
together in crooked house, 860:6
under a hill, 860:17
under my woodside, 254:15
who has l. well, 686:7
without disgrace without praise, 130:6
Livelier liquor than Muse, 619:9
plaything gives youth delight, 311:11
Livelihood, anxiety about l., 672:17
right l., 66:24
Lively, cock with l. din, 259:13
from l. to severe, 311:15
life l. form of death, 164:12
sense of filial duty, 356:21
understandable spirit, 780:11
Liver, as well speak of female l., 623:4
I ate his l., 834:7
Liverpool, she's the L. packet, 862:13
Livers, humble l. in content, 230:25
Livery, cunning l. of hell, 211:22
in his l. walked crowns, 224:4
in sober l. clad, 266:15
of burnished sun, 188:13
Lives at ease that freely lives, 132:18
body's beauty l., 687:5
brutal l. ugly deaths, 742:8
cat has only nine l., 561:9
competency l. longer, 187:26

Lizard, Lion and L. keep, 471:8
  seen the good l., 751:3
  time slips away like l., 676:18
Lizzie Borden took ax, 849:10
Llorar, quien te quiere te hará l., 862:22
Lo Christ walking on the water, 621:9
  I am with you always, 38:13
  the poor Indian, 311:5
  virtue is at hand, 63:2
Load, ass will carry l., 158:32
  cruelty to l. falling man, 231:n1
  every rift of subject, 441:5
  would sink a navy, 231:4
Loaded, centuries l. fragrant, 456:31
  not put l. rifle on stage, 622:9
Loads, laid many heavy l. on thee, 297:n1
Loaf, better half a l., 148:16
  of Bread and Thou, 471:5
  to every Bird, 545:17
Loafe, I l. and invite my soul, 518:15
Loafing around The Throne, 571:7
Loan oft loses friend, 201:27
Loaning, on ilka green l., 340:6
Loath, long and l. at going, 724:10
  to lay out money on rope, 240:20
  what maidens l., 437:17
Loathe, I l. the country, 300:24
  people who keep dogs, 596:9
  sweet tunes, 568:15
  taste of sweetness, 186:13
Loathed Melancholy, 259:7
  most l. worldly life, 211:24
Loathes, all outward l., 233:17
Loathing, deepest l. brings, 181:17
Loathsome canker in sweetest bud, 226:11
Loaves, five l. and two fishes, 36:13
Lobotomized, flabby bald l., 801:2
Lobster, voice of the L., 551:3
Lobster-nights, luxurious l., 309:23
Lobsterpot, shattered l., 721:8
Lobsters, change l. and retire, 550:20
  thrain l. to fly, 646:13
  I'm fond of l., 469:5
Local, all politics is l., 789:3
  cult Christianity, 575:20
  habitation and name, 182:3
  seemed to be l. dust cloud, 793:4
Locally, act l., 760:10
Loch, banks o' L. Lomond, 847:15
Lochinvar, young L., 396:17
Lock, cryin' at l., 488:7
  meant to pick l., 845:15
  sure l. me up, 723:15
Locke, accept views Cicero L. Bacon have
    given, 454:21
  sank into swoon, 640:13
Locked and frozen in eye, 775:16
  feet l. upon rough bark, 825:5
  lettered collar, 378:4
  man and woman two l. caskets, 706:9
  naked though l. up in steel, 172:12
  razor, 800:18
  'tis in my memory l., 201:28
  up from mortal eye, 272:7
Locket, Lucy L. lost pocket, 860:11
Locks are like the snaw, 379:4
  immortal l. fell forward, 52:10
  knotted and combined l., 202:12
  open l. whoever knocks, 221:23

Locks *(continued)*
  pluck drowned honor by l., 185:9
  shake thy gory l. at me, 221:11
  shaking her invincible l., 263:3
  time to silver turned, 164:9
  unscrew l. from doors, 519:9
  were like the raven, 379:4
  which are left are gray, 405:9
  yellow as gold, 400:3
Locksmith, zealous l. died, 845:15
Locomotive, more powerful than l., 795:1
Locust of soul unshelled, 809:4
  tossed up and down as the l., 19:17
Locusts and wild honey, 33:25
  food as luscious as l., 213:4
  like in Bible with l., 770:10
Lodge, house to l. friend, 312:16
  in garden of cucumbers, 26:8
  in some vast wilderness, 347:26
  not l. thee by Chaucer, 238:5
  thorns that in bosom l., 202:20
  where thou lodgest I will l., 11:12
Lodged, love l. in woman's breast, 232:12
  with me useless, 263:12
Lodges, where care l. sleep never lie, 183:18
Lodgest, where thou l. I will lodge, 11:12
Lodging, grant us safe l., 450:1
  hard was their l., 295:11
  my l. is on cold ground, 307:2
  Phoebus' l., 183:31
  place of wayfaring men, 29:10
Lo'ed, better l. ye canna be, 385:6
Loftier race than known, 576:14
  raise somewhat l. strain, 95:21
Loftiest peaks most wrapt, 420:20
Loftiness of thought surpassed, 284:27
Lofts of jaw-loss, 841:6
Lofty and sour, 231:14
  build the l. rhyme, 261:14
  scene be acted o'er, 196:17
  sky immeasurably l., 542:10
  towers I see down-rased, 226:18
Log hut with simple bench, 548:10
  Mark Hopkins at end of l., 548:n2
  roll my l. I roll yours, 107:8
  tough wedge for tough l., 104:2
  will never be crocodile, 853:15
Logan's, enter L. cabin hungry, 339:8
Logic and rhetoric able to contend, 168:17
  and sermons never convince, 519:14
  book of female l., 490:20
  doctrinaire l., 734:3
  is logic, 473:16
  of mind overtasked, 473:7
  page of history worth volume of l.,
    578:18
  that's l., 551:17
Logical, built in such l. way, 473:15
  consequences scarecrows of fools, 537:8
Logicians are wrong, 755:8
Logs, Tom bears l. into the hall, 177:17
Loins, gird up thy l. like a man, 15:4
  he girded up his l., 12:31
  let your l. be girded, 39:30
  Lolita fire of my l., 755:14
  shudder in l., 640:14
  with your l. girded, 8:18
Lois, built on order of L. De Fee, 769:2
Loiterers, liege of all l., 176:33

Loitering, alone and palely l., 439:3
Lolita, immortality you and I share L., 756:1
  light of my life, 755:14
Loman never made money, 796:13
Lomond, bonnie banks of Loch L., 847:15
London Bridge falling down, 625:13, 857:4
  broken arch of L. Bridge, 448:7
  don't send poet to L., 442:12
  flower of Cities all, 142:2
  great cesspool, 616:15
  hell city much like L., 429:9
  in ruins rather than enslaved, 666:3
  isn't far from L., 692:1
  Lord Mayor of L., 844:18
  loved life L., 699:16
  particular a fog, 498:20
  sea at best at L., 663:16
  this is L., 779:14
  tired of L. tired of life, 328:9
  to L. to look at queen, 859:14
  vilest alleys of L., 617:6
Lone Glenartney's hazel shade, 397:4
  lorn creetur, 497:29
  not in l. splendor, 439:11
  poor l. woman, 191:25
  sheiling, 444:10
  walking by wild l., 635:13
  worker makes first advance, 693:6
Lonelier, make each other l., 770:12
Loneliness, beside the clock's l., 825:3
  die of l., 643:8
  intense l. ignorance, 606:11
  of yesterday, 747:18
  only cure for l., 785:6
  our l. our love our bodies, 759:7
  people's ignorance or l., 830:3
Lonely, all the l. people, 835:3
  and poor of old, 713:2
  and swift like planet, 611:17
  dark and l. hiding place, 401:12
  down at end of l. street, 831:16
  flowering in l. word, 486:23
  God winding l. horn, 637:9
  hunts on l. hill, 606:13
  I'm l. I'll make world, 657:1
  impulse of delight, 638:17
  more l. among men, 507:8
  nation turns its l. eyes to you, 837:9
  people talking to each other, 770:12
  rapture on l. shore, 421:25
  sea and sky, 680:15
  sleep among l. hills, 395:1
  so l. 'twas that God, 400:23
  sun in l. lands, 484:19
  thing that shone, 641:12
  tramp l. fellow, 725:17
  wandered l. as a cloud, 394:4
Lonelyhearts, Miss L., 766:11
Lonesome, be good and be l., 561:21
  like one that on l. road, 400:17
  October, 479:11
  place against sky, 601:7
  road, 400:17
  whippoorwill, 813:3
Lonesomeness, starlight lit l., 574:14
Lonesome's a bad place, 787:7
Long and faithful service, 501:6
  and ghastly kitchen, 500:17
  and lank and brown, 400:9

Long *(continued)*

and loath at going, 724:10
and steep is the way, 56:12
and terrible way, 781:9
apprenticehood, 179:3
arm of coincidence, 622:4
art l. life short, 364:4
as l. as ever you can, 319:1
as l. as moon rise, 856:9
be day never so l., 149:10
calamity of so l. life, 203:33
cool winding saxophones, 681:14
day's journey into night, 724:8
day's task is done, 223:34
deliberate derangement, 604:4
divorce of steel, 230:23
for imperishable quiet, 781:1
for l. time used to go to bed early, 657:6
from l. to l. in solemn sort, 402:8
Gilpin l. live he, 347:24
gray beard glittering eye, 399:11
hair glory to woman, 44:14
happy as heart was l., 795:12
his arm is very l., 71:25
how l. a time in one word, 179:1
how l. to obtain vote, 811:1
how l. wilt thou forget me, 16:3
I have lived l. enough, 222:11
I learned l. time ago, 840:8
I loved you once l. ago, 58:2
I speak not loud or l., 162:*n*3
in l. run all dead, 701:14
it shan't be l., 315:12
it wont be l. now, 680:12, 680:14
kiss l. as my exile, 224:30
labor l. workers idle, 120:8
lane knows no turnings, 491:19
life how l. or short, 268:11
life is short art l., 73:10
life well spent is l., 141:2
light shakes, 482:19
littleness of life, 711:7
live our noble king, 308:1
live the strike, 819:1
long ago, 442:4
long thoughts, 467:7
long trail a-winding, 726:19
long wintry nights, 500:7
Lord how l., 26:27
love me little love me l., 248:5, 843:20
may land be bright, 469:9
mechanic pacings, 481:4
melancholy l. withdrawing roar, 531:2
merry as day is l., 194:14
never make l. visits, 714:8
nor that little l., 306:7
nor wants that little l., 341:13
not l. life by fire, 624:3
not l. the weeping and the laughter,
    645:11
poem does not exist, 479:22
pray that way be l., 628:7
pull strong pull, 498:9
run misleading guide to affairs, 701:14
see so much nor live so l., 218:9
seven l. year, 216:33
short and l. of it, 190:24
short meaning of l. speech, 382:2
small showers last l., 179:11

Long *(continued)*

suits, 731:3
that thy days may be l., 9:1
think life too l., 293:16
thought the travel l., 171:10
three l. mountains, 734:14
time between drinks, 599:19
to talk with lover's ghost, 235:7
trick's over, 681:2
Trochee trips from l. to short, 402:8
way l. wind cold, 396:3
way to Tipperary, 674:2
ways from home, 862:27
within no power to live l., 106:16
words Bother me, 697:6
Long Island, Jay Gatsby of West Egg L.,
    746:5
Long-drawn aisle, 334:16
Longed, lies where l. to be, 599:6
    to embrace mother's ghost, 55:2
    truly l. for death, 480:9
Longer, impossible takes l., 851:15
    letter l. than usual, 279:12
    no l. stay with you, 848:19
    smile dwells l., 662:1
    some days l., 668:4
    song had been l., 858:3
    stretch him out l., 218:8
    words have l. life than deeds, 66:5
Longest fifty-nine minutes, 647:16
    journey go, 429:25
    journey inwards, 770:9
    journey to oblivion, 707:22
    nights are l. there, 211:7
    part of the journey, 90:1
    way round shortest home, 249:*n*2
Longest-lived and shortest-lived die same,
    115:5
Longeth, my flesh l. for thee, 18:3
Longevity has its place, 823:10
Longfellow's, shown L. grave, 714:8
Long-haired, not these l. men I fear, 92:7
Longing after immortality, 301:26
    cast l. eye on offices, 358:7
    for stewed prunes, 211:6
    for that lovely lady, 89:17
    leans and beckons, 515:17
    lingering look behind, 334:24
    more l. wavering, 209:22
    what sweet thoughts what l., 130:14
Longings, I have immortal l. in me, 224:9
Longitude, in l. tho' scanty, 379:21
    use l. and latitude for seine, 560:2
Long-legged fly upon stream, 642:18
Long-leggety beasties, 847:9
Long-lost, I can be your l. pal, 837:12
Longmans', it's still in L. shop, 392:*n*1
Longs for a third side, 756:4
Long-strayed eyes, 234:18
Long-suffering and very pitiful, 31:26
    fruit of Spirit is l., 45:22
    love is l., 138:13
Longtemps je me suis couché de bonne
    heure, 657:*n*3
Longue, je n'ai fait celle-ci plus l., 279:*n*1
Loo, oh Miss L., 593:17
Look about us and die, 310:20
    afraid to l. upon God, 8:5
    after all it is a poor land, 524:15

Look *(continued)*

after our people, 649:18
after souls in labor, 78:9
all world here to l. on me, 181:11
and pass on, 130:7
angel of backward l., 468:19
around choose ground, 425:9
as they run l. behind, 333:19
ashamed to l. next morning, 253:3
astronomy compels soul to l. upwards,
    77:15
at all the fire-folk, 587:5
at the stars, 587:5
at things in bloom, 618:7
away Dixie Land, 503:1
back many times, 689:21
backward l. behind assurance, 721:10
before time to l. round, 364:20
before you leap, 271:21
behind the Ranges, 635:15
clean starved for a l., 226:25
come to l. for America, 837:10
direct him where to l. for it, 235:26
do it with bitter l., 605:18
don't l. back, 774:11
don't l. over your shoulder, 764:1
down on hate, 420:20
ere ye leap, 147:6
every l. a dart, 845:21
eyes l. your last, 184:17
eyes that would not l. on me, 367:21
fear in the face, 704:10
for circumstances, 609:5
for me in nurseries, 620:16
for me under boot-soles, 519:23
for truth but not find it, 331:25
fortress-like l. of it, 836:1
forty centuries l. down, 387:12
forward to posterity, 345:11
forward to with hope, 668:21
give me a l., 237:16
goose l., 222:9
her quick l., 780:13
her wanton spirits l. out, 208:19
homeward Angel, 262:4
how floor of heaven, 190:5
how others do it, 381:16
how ring encompasseth thy finger, 173:33
I had fixed my l. on his, 130:21
I'll not l. for wine, 238:2
in almanack find out moonshine, 181:19
in my God's right hand, 863:8
in that tone of voice, 591:18
in thy heart and write, 163:28
into happiness through another's eyes,
    200:4
into lives as into mirror, 89:13
into oneself, 627:1
into seeds of time, 218:31
into your heart, 381:16
lean and hungry l., 195:22
learned to l. on nature, 391:4
let him l. to his bond, 188:29
let it l. like perfect honor, 223:2
library whereon I l., 248:21
like innocent flower, 219:14
lingering l. behind, 334:24
look up at skies, 587:5
make man l. sad, 182:11

Look *(continued)*
  making crime l. dull, 796:4
  morn in russet mantle clad, 200:23
  my God l. not so fierce, 171:5
  ne'er l. back, 214:15
  no more upon't, 243:13
  not down but up, 494:12
  not thou upon the wine, 22:38
  of bay mare shames silliness out of me,
    519:2
  of love alarms, 373:14
  of soft deceit, 373:14
  on both indifferently, 195:17
  on my works ye Mighty, 427:18
  on you when last hour comes, 104:26
  only a l. and voice, 467:18
  or listen, 515:3
  out here comes Master Race, 817:6
  out your window, 836:5
  reader l., 238:4
  see monument l. around, 287:19
  shifty hangdog l., 694:11
  soul l. body touch, 642:9
  Stein does not l. like portrait, 673:15
  take a backward l., 544:5
  things fairer when we l. back, 515:17
  through a millstone, 163:12
  thy last on things lovely, 662:12
  to essence of a thing, 115:30
  to it, 475:9
  upon a little child, 322:25
  upon his like again, 201:12
  upon world as parish, 318:20
  upward l. of caution, 670:20
  we l. at each other, 819:5
  we l. before and after, 429:19
  westward l. land is bright, 512:10
  when will I l. at it, 791:13
  who comes here, 178:7
  with favor on bold beginning, 96:5
  with thine ears, 217:23
  ye there, 321:n7
  you could l. it up, 742:1
  you didn't know where to l., 759:8
Looked again found it was, 553:6
  and sighed again, 285:13
  as she did love, 439:5
  before thou leapt, 147:n5
  come when l. for, 501:15
  down to Camelot, 480:26
  God l. around and said, 657:1
  into eye of day, 640:16
  Lot's wife l. back, 7:7
  love to eyes which spake, 420:16
  no sooner l. but loved, 200:3
  on Beauty bare, 735:8
  on better days, 198:22
  on women with lust, 814:1
  out of eye of saint, 641:1
  over his shoulder, 776:10
  sideways up, 400:6
  to Government for bread, 346:1
  unutterable things, 317:18
  up in perfect silence, 520:8
  with such a wistful eye, 605:16
  with wild surmise, 435:19
Looker-on, patient l., 249:12
Lookers-on, only God and angels l.,
    166:9

Looketh, Lord l. on the heart, 11:25
  on the outward appearance, 11:25
  well to ways of her household, 23:30
Lookin' eastward to sea, 633:12
Looking, act of l. back, 824:16
  as if alive, 491:9
  as like one pea does another, 146:18
  at self through others, 648:11
  conscience warns somebody l., 691:16
  eastward to sea, 633:12
  even if gods should be l., 54:28
  for honest man, 79:6
  for something to do, 333:14
  fresh as paint, 511:13
  hand to plow and l. back, 39:16
  here's l. at you kid, 782:9
  leave them while l. good, 737:11
  one way rowing another, 281:25
  outward together, 759:1
  over harbor and city, 681:9
  pleasure of l. at each other, 601:17
  seaman l. for something else, 715:6
  see without l. through windows, 59:7
  well can't move her, 269:20
Looking Backward was written, 596:18
Looking-glass, no use to blame l., 472:16
Looking-glasses, women l. reflecting man,
    700:9
Looks, assurance given by l., 171:9
  commercing with the skies, 259:25
  dispatchful l., 267:5
  everybody's l. of death, 288:12
  gigantically down, 478:6
  gods do not give all men good l., 54:26
  in the clouds, 195:30
  kindness not beauteous l., 175:36
  love l. not with eyes, 180:21
  modest l. cottage adorn, 342:12
  more elder than thy l., 189:22
  never l. nor 'eeds, 634:17
  not deep-searched with saucy l., 176:20
  old man l. before and after, 52:20
  on alike, 229:1
  on tempests, 227:17
  patron l. with unconcern, 326:10
  poet l. at world as man at woman, 689:4
  puts on his pretty l., 178:9
  quite through deeds of men, 195:23
  she l. with threatening eye, 178:11
  she needs good l., 705:16
  through Nature up, 311:14
  toward school with heavy l., 183:12
  war of l. between them, 173:21
  were free, 400:3
  whole world in face, 466:8
Loom, I cannot ply the l., 58:4
  left the web left the l., 480:26
Loon, thou cream-faced l., 222:9
Loop to hang doubt on, 214:10
Looped and windowed raggedness, 216:27
Loophole, from her cabined l. peep, 260:22
  no l. in case drafted, 685:17
Loopholes of retreat, 348:5
Loose, all hell broke l., 266:26
  as the wind, 250:15
  feel his title hang l., 222:8
  hell's broken l., 165:20
  imagination, 642:10
  lips sink ships, 851:16

Loose *(continued)*
  the bands of Orion, 15:10
  w'en it gits l. fum jug, 593:13
Loosed, arrows l. several ways, 192:22
  blood-dimmed tide l., 639:6
  fateful lightning, 513:18
  silver cord be l., 25:8
Loosen, old faiths l. and fall, 568:17
  old foundations, 681:13
Loosened, Heine l. corsets of German
    language, 672:8
Loosens fragrant bodice, 437:1
Lopped limbs, 780:3
Lord, all ye works of the L., 33:12
  am an attendant l., 717:14
  among wits, 326:11
  and Father of mankind, 468:21
  angel of L. came down, 294:4
  angel of L. came upon them, 39:3
  anger of L. kindled, 11:42
  answered Job out of the whirlwind, 15:4
  be thankit, 380:7
  be with you, 49:7
  better is little with the fear of the L.,
    21:36
  bless thee and keep thee, 9:17
  bless ye the L., 33:12
  blessed be L. God, 38:41
  blessed the latter end of Job, 15:26
  blot out his name, 285:n4
  bringeth thee into good land, 10:2
  Cain went out from presence of the L.,
    6:18
  Christ the L. risen today, 322:23
  Christ's heart, 453:24
  climb tree L. to see, 296:13
  coming of the L., 513:18
  Dark Maid and her L., 69:12
  day of the L., 46:9
  day thou gavest L. is ended, 538:12
  day which the L. hath made, 19:26
  dead which die in the L., 48:33
  died by the hand of the L., 8:29
  directeth his steps, 22:1
  disciples of the L., 42:6
  do if He knew facts, 646:10
  eternal rest give them O L., 49:8
  fear of the L. is beginning of wisdom,
    19:19
  fear of the L. is wisdom, 14:36
  feast to the L., 8:19
  for the erring thought, 567:4
  forbade me to put off my hat, 280:14
  forgive O L. my jokes, 671:4
  from winter plague L. deliver us, 232:8
  gangway for L., 728:3
  gave and hath taken away, 13:26
  glory of the L. is risen, 28:29
  go and the L. be with thee, 11:28
  go home to my L. and be free, 863:10
  God Almighty, 48:16
  God caused a deep sleep, 5:21
  God formed man, 5:16
  God is subtle, 683:15
  God made them all, 508:7
  God of Hosts, 635:1
  God planted a garden, 5:17
  God send high wave, 658:9
  God walking in garden, 6:5

Lord *(continued)*

good L. deliver us, 50:11, 847:9
good L. had only ten, 577:10
good works better in sight of L.,
  121:16
Gracious L. bomb Germans, 773:19
great and dreadful day of the L., 31:4
hath chosen thee, 9:32
have mercy on us, 49:10, 232:9
hear me out, 781:9
hear word of the L., 29:21
holy is the L. of hosts, 26:24
how discourse is of death, 288:12
how long, 26:27
how world given to lying, 187:11
I am the L. thy God, 8:31
I believe, 38:27
I heard the voice of the L., 26:26
I replied My L., 250:17
I want to be in that number, 863:14
I were l. in May, 568:21
I will sing unto the L., 8:25
if you had horse, 707:18
in glance of the L., 422:15
is a man of war, 8:26
is come, 304:9
is good, 19:3
is in his holy temple, 30:32
is in this place, 7:15
is it I, 37:25
is my helper, 47:5
is my light, 16:22
is my rock, 12:8
is my shepherd, 16:18
is my strength and shield, 16:24
is my strength and song, 8:25
is nigh unto them that call, 20:18
is risen, 49:17
is risen indeed, 40:28
is the strength of my life, 16:22
is thy keeper, 19:30
is thy shade, 19:30
is with thee, 38:34
Jehovah Jove or L., 313:7
kingdoms of our L., 48:27
King's our only l., 169:11
know ye that the L. he is God, 19:3
land which the L. giveth thee, 9:1
lendeth unto the L., 22:16
lift up his countenance, 9:17
looketh on the heart, 11:25
love is my l. and king, 484:16
love the L. with all thine heart, 9:30
made all to prosper, 7:24
make a joyful noise unto the L., 19:3
make his face shine upon thee, 9:17
make me an instrument, 128:5
make my enemies ridiculous, 316:19
Mayor of London, 844:18
mercy on Thy People L., 635:5
methought what pain to drown, 174:3
my help cometh from the L., 19:30
my L. what a morning, 863:7
my soul doth magnify L., 38:37
name of the L. in vain, 8:33
neat and trimly dressed, 185:2
not everyone that saith L., 35:10
not in wind earthquake fire, 12:32
not tempt the L. your God, 9:31

Lord *(continued)*

not the weight of an ant escapes the L.,
  121:5
O L. if there is a L., 535:9
O L. let her go, 862:13
O L. my God I have trusted, 154:14
of all Being, 120:11
of all yet prey to all, 311:9
of far-flung battle line, 635:1
of folded arms, 176:33
of heaven and earth, 42:18
of himself, 232:15, 422:12
of hosts he is the King of glory, 16:21
of living and dead, 587:3
of lords, 48:35
of the Ocean, 70:5
of yourself, 285:18
once own happy lines, 308:21
our God is one L., 9:29
our maker, 18:29
oure l. dooth with youre owene thing,
  137:2
patient unto coming of L., 47:21
peace in our time O L., 51:16
praise L. pass ammunition, 729:10
pray L. soul to keep, 296:15
precious in the sight of the L., 19:24
prepare way of L., 27:38, 33:24
preserve thee, 19:30
raise me up I trust, 160:14
reason L. makes so many, 476:8
reigneth, 19:2
replied O L. Thou art, 337:16
rib which L. God had taken, 5:21
Savior which is Christ the L., 39:3
searcheth all hearts, 13:10
secret things belong unto the L., 10:11
seeth not as man, 11:25
servant in love l. in marriage, 137:15
servant not above l., 35:29
serve the L. with gladness, 19:3
serves good l. lives in luxury, 126:15
set a mark upon Cain, 6:17
shall preserve thy going and coming,
  19:30
short life in saddle L., 624:3
showed me so I did see, 280:13
sitting upon a throne, 26:23
soul is the concern of my L., 121:13
Spirit of the L. shall rest upon him, 26:33
support us all day long, 450:1
sword of the L. and of Gideon, 10:36
taste and see that the L. is good, 17:1
taught Man that he knew not, 122:19
through this hour, 851:11
thy God is with thee, 10:18
thy L. the most generous, 122:19
'twant me 'twas the L., 523:19
wait upon the L., 28:8
watch between me and thee, 7:18
we battle for the L., 615:14
went before them, 8:23
what fools these mortals be, 181:21
where dear L. crucified, 508:8
who created Man, 122:19
whom the L. loveth he chasteneth, 47:2
whose hope the L. is, 29:17
will wipe away tears, 27:16
with me abide, 432:5

Lord *(continued)*

woman that feareth the L., 23:31
won't you buy me a Mercedes-Benz,
  838:9
word of the L. endureth, 47:26
worship the L. in beauty of holiness,
  16:25
Lordly, butter in a l. dish, 10:32
cedar green with boughs, 601:7
darkness, 807:4
name is, 479:5
Lord's anointed temple, 220:23
ask the L. blessing, 845:2
earth is the L., 16:19, 44:13
it is the L. passover, 8:18
name is to be praised, 19:20
sing the L. song, 20:11
who is on the L. side, 9:7
Lords and ladies of Byzantium, 640:2
and owners of their faces, 227:4
but breath of kings, 377:16
gude Scots l., 853:19
Lord of l., 48:35
masters l. and rulers, 601:4
not kings and l., 413:10
o' the creation, 378:5
of Hell, 484:1
of humankind pass by, 341:5
of ladies intellectual, 423:6
princes and l., 341:29
Scots l. at his feet, 853:20
seemed l. of all, 266:9
who lay ye low, 429:6
wit among L., 326:11
Lordship, plant man's l., 577:1
Lordships sold to maintain ladyships, 239:15
Lordships', dance attendance on l. pleasures,
  231:15
Lore, admire virtue follow not her l., 268:18
Cristes l. and his apostles twelve, 135:11
gives me mystical l., 408:19
Heaven rejects the l., 395:16
poor fool with all my l., 365:4
volume of forgotten l., 478:20
Lorn, lone l. creetur, 497:29
Lorries, monotonously l. sway, 752:11
Lose and neglect creeping hours, 198:22
comfort or money too, 673:4
convictions to win or l., 660:8
don't l. your head, 851:6
for everything gain l. something, 455:19
freedom if value anything more, 673:4
gain world l. soul, 36:27
good we oft might win, 211:2
has no wits to l., 346:3
have what it fears to l., 226:19
having nothing nothing l., 173:3
he that findeth life shall l. it, 35:32
he who doesn't l. wits, 346:3
his child's-heart, 82:8
I would not l. you, 189:1
if once we l. this light, 237:14
if you l. you l. nothing, 279:23
it that buy it with care, 187:16
itself in sky, 494:5
knife ill-used l. edge, 227:6
life nothing much to l., 620:1
managing to l. presidency, 816:12
more of yourself than redeem, 834:2

Love *(continued)*

acts of kindness and of l., 390:20
alas how l. can trifle, 176:13
all beauteous things, 586:7
all for l. a little for bottle, 362:10
all for l. nothing for reward, 161:4
all in green went my l. riding, 739:10
all l. all liking all delight, 248:18
all love of other sights controls, 233:11
all l. sweet, 428:9
all must l. human form, 372:7
all policy's allowed in l., 511:*n5*
all she loves is l., 423:21
all trust a few, 210:20
all we know of L., 547:8
all's fair in l. and war, 511:14
almost too much l., 669:17
alters not, 227:17
am like to l. three more, 270:4
America l. or leave it, 852:17
Americans because they love liberty, 323:8
and a cough, 251:5
and all his pleasures toys, 232:3
and be loved by forever, 493:21
and be loved by me, 479:17
and be wise, 102:16
and desire and hate, 645:11
and fame to nothingness, 439:10
and fear hardly together, 142:10
and glory, 741:1
and good company, 305:7
and have not l., 44:*n1*
and laughter, 553:14
and man's unconquerable mind, 393:2
and marriage go together, 789:11
and scandal, 322:3
and still to l., 348:17
and thanks, 354:10
and War same thing, 158:12
and we will teach them how, 391:13
anger of lovers renews l., 88:*n7*
anterior to Life, 545:21
art accomplice of l., 614:3
ashamed of having been in l., 273:11
at first sight, 632:11
at the lips, 669:16
babe that milks me, 219:23
bade me welcome, 251:2
base men being in l., 213:15
beareth all things, 44:19
beautiful time of young l., 382:7
begets love, 781:6
believeth all things, 44:19
better is thy l. than wine, 25:23
beyond the world, 292:1
bid me take l. easy, 636:19
Black l. is Black wealth, 838:3
blessing l. gives, 819:5
born with pleasure of looking, 601:17
bout with l., 61:17
boy's l., 217:4
breastplate of faith and l., 46:11
bridge is l., 749:12
brief as woman's l., 205:1
bright particular star, 210:21
brings bewitching grace, 70:2
brook weather that l. not wind, 176:35

Love *(continued)*

brotherly l., 43:17, 47:4
built on beauty, 235:14
bumping against obstacles of civilization, 461:4
business that we l., 223:30
but her love forever, 378:24
but I do l. thee, 213:30
but you alone, 843:11
by heaven I do l., 177:2
calls to war, 164:19
can come to everyone, 736:17
care of discipline is l., 31:20
careless l., 801:7
cement glue and lime of l., 247:15
change old l. for new, 164:8
cherish and obey, 51:18
children's gratitude woman's l., 641:9
close hand out of l., 588:18
clouds of goodness and l., 361:*n2*
collaborating in private way of l., 797:12
come and take my l. away, 226:19
come unto my l., 162:4
comes in at eye, 638:3
comforteth like sunshine, 173:24
common as light is l., 428:9
concluded with impossibility of separation, 601:17
conquer L. that run away, 253:20
conquers all things, 96:3
contend no more l., 492:9
converted from thing it was, 226:14
corporations can l. each other, 592:12
could you and I conspire, 472:5
countless ties of l., 670:12
courage l. joy, 307:13
course of true l., 180:19
covereth all sins, 21:16
crime to l. too well, 309:28
crown is l. and friendship, 436:11
curiosity freckles doubt, 738:11
dare l. that and say so too, 234:1
dark secret l., 374:3
deep as first l., 482:22
demanded of genius l. of truth, 366:4
desire more l. and knowledge, 197:31
die for l., 210:22
die to what we l., 608:11
died before god of l. was born, 235:7
diminution of l. of truth, 324:21
dinner of herbs where l. is, 21:36
distills desire, 70:2
do justly and l. mercy, 30:28
do not trifle with l., 488:9
does not consist in gazing, 759:1
doesn't l. a wall, 668:18
dooms of l., 740:9
draw as l. with thread, 241:17
drew them with bands of l., 30:19
dropped like a flower, 94:7
dull sublunary lovers' l., 235:1
earth sun animals, 518:10
earth's place for l., 669:5
end of l. or season, 668:16
endureth all things, 44:19
envieth not, 44:18
episode in man's life, 385:12
eternity in l. with production of time, 372:15

Love *(continued)*

eyes silent tongues of L., 156:8
faith nor l. nor law, 428:8
faithful in l., 396:18
fall in l. with Athens, 74:5
falling out renewing is of l., 88:*n7*
false maids in l., 208:7
false or true, 637:5
fed with necessity of seeing, 601:17
few l. to hear sins they act, 225:7
fickleness of women I l., 609:3
final face of l., 809:6
first is deep l., 59:14
first learned in lady's eyes, 177:5
fitter l. for me, 234:10
flies out window, 845:13
food of l., 208:25
fool yourself about l., 824:7
for l. lead apes in hell, 175:27
for l. of Barbara Allen, 853:28
for Love's sake, 781:10
forbearance l. charity, 353:4
force, 650:10
forever lost, 442:6
forever wilt thou l., 438:1
forget l. to friends and brethren, 31:5
forgive us, 436:16
forspent with l. and shame, 583:12
foundation is l., 823:5
freedom in my l., 276:4
freely serve because we freely l., 267:6
friendship charity, 208:12
from eyelids dripped l., 56:6
fruit of Spirit is l., 45:22
fruits of l. gone, 425:8
fullness even of l., 53:12
game beyond prize, 627:3
gather Rose of l., 161:5
gilds the scene, 367:18
give a little l. to child, 517:17
give all to l., 453:8
give me more l. or more disdain, 253:16
go l. without the help, 376:2
go out and l. people, 842:9
God is, 47:41
God is L. I dare say, 559:2
gods l. the obscure, 51:22
goes toward love, 183:12
gold and l. affairs difficult to hide, 862:23
golden time of first l., 382:7
good man's l., 199:20
good to l. the unknown, 407:18
great l. grows there, 205:2
great secret of morals is l., 431:9
greater l. hath no man, 41:31
greater l. the more false, 775:7
greatest is l., 44:20
greatness worthy to excite l., 531:14
groans of l. like those of dying, 783:8
grown old in l., 376:3
grows bitter with treason, 568:17
gude to be off with old l., 847:14
hail wedded l., 266:22
half in l. with Death, 437:12
happiness to l. and be loved, 461:13
hardly worth thinking of, 637:15
harmony is pure l., 169:10
hate as though someday l., 67:*n3*

Love *(continued)*

hate foes as far as we soon might l. them, 67:9
hate one and l. other, 34:16
hate traitors treason l., 284:25
hath an end, 568:16
hath so long possessed me, 129:15
hatred as well as l., 331:18
hatred ceases by l., 66:17
he bore to learning, 342:8
he will then l. me, 372:3
hearts in l. use own tongues, 194:18
heaven is l., 396:9
heaven sends l. of her, 4:1
hell is to l. no longer, 716:12
her till I die, 844:21
hid in heart of l., 637:2
Highlands for ever I l., 379:5
him most for enemies, 539:7
him who in l. of Nature, 432:7
his banner over me was l., 25:16
hiss of l., 771:8
history of woman's life, 385:12
hold your tongue and let me l., 234:5
hollow sound same as our l., 759:7
hope nor l. nor friend, 599:11
hopeth all things, 44:19
how do I l. thee, 463:17
how should I true l. know, 206:4
how they could l., 849:14
human l. seen at its height, 684:3
hunt down l. together, 568:22
I am sick of l., 25:16
I both l. and do not l., 61:18
I do not l. thee Doctor Fell, 296:1
I don't think we don't l. each other, 825:13
I hate and I l., 94:27
I l. a lass, 363:4
I l. a lassie, 654:5
I l. broad margin to life, 507:6
I l. everything old, 342:15
I l. sound of bone, 836:1
I taught thee to l., 235:15
I was in l. with the whole world, 842:1
I'd l. to get you on slow boat, 785:2
idea of two sexes, 741:12
if ever thou shalt l., 209:21
if I l. you what business of yours, 364:1
if l. were what rose is, 568:20
if music food of l., 208:25
if no l. is what feel I so, 133:16
if she will not l., 269:21
if world and l. were young, 160:3
if you can't give me l., 725:6
if you l. him, 837:15
if you l. you suffer, 728:2
I'm savin' my l. for you, 745:4
impossible not to l. all things, 399:9
in a golden bowl, 372:12
in a hut, 436:16
in it was l. and desire, 53:15
in l. and charity with neighbors, 50:17
in l. illusion reaches zenith, 589:22
in l. two solitudes touch, 677:2
in l. with American names, 750:9
in l. with loving, 119:7
in l. with the world, 786:13

Love *(continued)*

in l. woman more barbarous, 589:4
in my bosom like a bee, 164:15
in others they l. l., 274:13
in our will to l. or not, 267:6
in spite of darkness, 234:16
in struggle for life find l., 732:16
in summer's wonderland, 692:1
inestimable l., 50:8
innocence of l., 209:24
inspiration l. and freedom, 622:7
instill l. of you into world, 3:11
is a boy, 271:17
is a sickness full of woes, 169:9
is agreement, 169:10
is all there is, 547:8
is best, 492:11
is blind, 188:20
is blynd, 137:8
is dead, 163:23
is enough, 557:3
is flower-like, 402:10
is fulfilling of law, 43:25
is heaven, 396:9
is intercourse between tyrants and slaves, 341:25
is kind, 44:18
is most beautiful among gods, 56:5
is most nearly itself, 721:6
is not all, 735:12
is not love which alters, 227:17
is strong as death, 26:3
is sweeping the country, 747:2
is the whole, 740:10
is then our duty, 307:15
it and who shall dare, 509:6
itself have rest, 423:1
itself slumber on, 430:19
iz like meazles, 508:11
jealousy born with l., 274:6
Joy and L. triumphing, 265:26
joy nor l. nor light, 531:2
joy of l. too short, 139:6
jumps from admiration to l., 406:5
keep corner in thing I l., 214:4
kelson of creation is l., 518:17
kill things they do not l., 189:14
kill your joys with l., 184:19
kindled by virtue, 131:20
kindness shall win my l., 175:36
King of l. my shepherd is, 524:6
King without the woman I l., 742:14
know the l. betwixt us, 275:14
knowledge and l. of God, 51:2
known l. how bitter, 568:11
labor of l., 46:7
laggard in l., 396:19
land that I l., 716:6
last not least in l., 196:20
law to itself, 120:6
lay aside long-cherished l., 94:25
learn to bear beams of l., 372:2
lease of my true l., 227:12
least that let men know, 176:5
leave me O L., 163:24
leaving L. behind, 545:20
lest thy l. prove variable, 183:8
let l. who never loved, 123:15

Love *(continued)*

let me l. river and woodland, 96:12
let thy l. be younger, 209:23
let us be true, 531:2
let us live and l., 94:4, 231:21
let us surrender to l., 96:3
let warm L. in, 438:7
life among people who l. each other, 461:10
life of their parents, 755:13
light dies when l. done, 600:14
like Death levels, 452:9
like everybody not in l., 657:13
like l. don't know where or why, 776:2
live and l. in God's light, 143:12
live with me and be my l., 170:6, 234:22
live with thee and be thy l., 160:3
lodged in woman's breast, 232:12
long life better than figs, 222:29
long l. doth so, 183:25
longing for l. a passion, 661:5
look at enemies with l., 288:6
look of l. alarms, 373:14
looked as she did l., 439:5
looks not with eyes, 180:21
Lord with all thy heart, 36:43
lore of l. deep learned, 436:14
lost to L. and Truth, 634:1
lovers' quarrels renewal of l., 88:12
Lyric L. half angel, 494:23
makes world go round, 565:5, 855:10
man in l. endures more, 589:22
man in l. with suffering, 525:9
man is in l., 640:6
mankind except American, 328:14
man's l. apart from life, 423:14
many waters cannot quench l., 26:4
Marilyn man's l. affair with America, 813:1
marriage from which l. gone, 767:10
marriage without l., 319:8
martyrs honor slain, 526:3
may perfectly l. thee, 50:16
me and keep my commandments, 8:33
me and my true l., 847:15
me in December, 583:*n*1
me little love me long, 248:5, 843:20
me not for grace, 844:22
me sure to die, 412:13
me tender, 831:17
means not having to say sorry, 832:9
medicines to make me l. him, 185:12
men died but not for l., 199:27
Mercy Pity Peace and L., 372:5
mercy unto them that l. me, 8:33
met you not with my true L., 160:1
mie l. ys dedde, 368:10
mighty pain to l., 275:10
ministers of L., 401:22
mischievous devil, 559:2
moderately, 183:25
money rage and l., 771:4
money the sinew of l., 91:*n*8
moody food of l., 223:18
more libertines than l., 331:11
more l. less we flatter, 278:7
more than love, 479:18
more true than L. to me, 844:14
morning and evening star, 708:6

Love (*continued*)

most important business, 417:6
music food of l., 223:18
musick thing I l. most, 288:17
my home of l., 227:14
my hope my hap my l., 155:8
my hope my l., 257:23
my lord and king, 484:16
my l. and I did meet, 636:19
my l. he purloined away, 571:14
my l. is come to me, 547:15
my L. like red red rose, 378:19
my L. like the melodie, 378:19
my l. of birth as rare, 277:7
my whole course of l., 212:26
mysterious by this l., 234:6
ne'er ebb to humble l., 214:15
neighbor as thyself, 9:15
neighbor yet pull not down hedge,
     251:12
never any that could escape l., 117:10
never change when l. has found home,
     104:18
never doubt I l., 203:3
never faileth, 44:19
never l. stranger, 733:6
never l. unless you can, 232:4
never see what you l., 658:*n*3
never seek to tell thy l., 373:8
never seeketh own, 138:13
never sick old dead, 160:2
never taint my l., 214:30
never told her l., 209:26
no concern with art, 557:17
no creature give orders to l., 461:5
no disguise conceal l., 273:10
no go my honey l., 777:8
no l. but vanity, 417:18
no l. lost, 158:14, 237:8
no more dear l., 483:5
no season knows, 234:3
noght oold as whan newe, 137:3
none but L. find me out, 159:21
none knew thee but to l., 426:6
nor l. thy life nor hate, 268:11
not a gaping pig, 189:12
not Death but L., 463:15
not enough religion to make us l., 298:3
not found thing to l., 677:20
not freedom but license, 263:9
not l. thee dear so much, 276:1
not man the less, 421:25
not my l. to see, 161:26
not Pleasure love God, 433:20
not puffed up, 44:18
not to be loved but to l., 128:5
not to eat not for l., 454:2
not to l. when we l., 156:23
not wise who buffet against l., 68:12
nothing I l. as much as fight, 697:10
nothing in l., 222:8
now abideth l., 44:20
now l. is over, 636:13
now warm in l., 309:25
now who never loved before, 305:12
now with l. now in colde grave, 136:1
O human l., 477:10
O ye that l. mankind, 354:9
obedience troops of friends, 222:11

Love (*continued*)

of a brute, 478:16
of beauty, 62:10
of British people, 344:17
of flattery, 303:10
of gentle woman, 788:2
of glory the most ardent, 303:8
of God, 45:16
of God in Christ, 43:12
of home love of country, 496:30
of justice simply fear, 273:13
of learning, 467:21
of little children, 686:7
of money as possession, 701:18
of money impulse to effort, 596:12
of money the root of evil, 46:26
of old for old, 620:8
of pleasure, 310:7
of praise, 305:15
of self love of God, 119:22
of slaughter, 709:4
of spiders, 756:17
of sway, 310:7
of the exaggerated, 828:15
of the virtuous, 62:10
of virtue, 331:14
of wisdom guide of life, 376:14
of you has entrapped me, 4:2
of young for young, 620:8
offender detest offense, 285:*n*3
on l. request for money chilling, 527:4
one another, 41:25, 43:24
one jot of former l. retain, 169:14
one of best things about l., 662:5
only l. sprung from only hate, 182:26
open rebuke better than secret l., 23:11
our l. hath no decay, 234:17
our occupations, 497:23
our principle, 444:1
out of l. cheat others, 657:15
out of l. with your nativity, 199:25
oyster may be crossed in l., 368:7
pain to l. in vain, 275:10
pains of l. sweeter far, 282:18
pangs of disprized l., 203:33
pardon to extent we l., 274:4
passed muse appeared, 446:17
passing the l. of women, 11:38
path to deepest mystery path of l., 761:7
paths to woman's l., 243:1
people and things I l., 784:2
perfect l. casteth out fear, 47:42
perhaps right to dissemble l., 376:12
pest of l., 436:13
physicians by their l. grown
     cosmographers, 236:14
pitched his mansion, 641:15
planet of L. on high, 485:9
Platonic l., 157:8
pleasure and l. are pinions, 364:8
pleasure drives l. away, 640:11
pleasure of l. in loving, 273:30
poets' food l. and fame, 428:20
possesses heart fall in l., 657:8
pray that l. may never come, 70:2
prophet of soul, 452:18
prosperity's very bond of l., 229:3
purlieu of god of l., 235:8
purple light of L., 335:6

Love (*continued*)

Pussy my l., 499:15
putting L., away, 546:8
quaint figure men l., 685:6
quantity of l., 207:2
quarrels in concord end, 269:10
quick-eyed L., 251:2
radiant with splendor, 128:3
rather than l. than money than fame,
     507:21
regain l. once possessed, 269:9
regent of l.-rimes, 176:33
rekindled by absence, 324:22
resembleth April day, 176:6
respect or natural l., 612:13
right true end of l., 235:20
rose of our l., 809:4
ruined l. when built anew, 227:20
rules the court, 396:9
rules the gods, 68:12
satisfied, 719:11
saved by l., 735:17
seals of l., 211:31
see how Christians l. one another, 116:13
seeketh not itself to please, 374:1
seeketh self to please, 374:2
seized this man for fair form, 130:13
separate us from l. of Christ, 43:11
servant in l. lord in marriage, 137:15
sets l. task like that, 417:18
shackles of old l., 486:3
shadow of power, 676:1
shall know no quarrels, 99:13
she whom I l. hard to catch, 541:19
shoot false L., 844:13
sigh to those who l. me, 422:26
sighed for l. of lady, 565:25
silence in l. bewrays woe, 160:6
sin who tell us l. die, 405:14
sit down says L., 251:3
sleep on my L., 249:1
smile of l., 375:3
so dear I l. him, 268:1
so full in my nature, 493:19
so hot as nigh to burst my boilers, 418:16
so long as we l. we serve, 599:20
someone to l. and l. you, 620:6
something tells me but not l., 189:1
sorrow of l. dureth overlong, 139:6
sought is good, 210:6
speak low if you speak l., 194:17
spirit all compact of fire, 173:19
spirit of l., 46:30
spirit of l. how quick and fresh, 208:26
sports of l., 237:14
spring of l. gushed from heart, 400:13
steer stars, 834:5
stony limits cannot hold l., 183:4
struck dumb by l., 821:15
study way to l. each other, 249:3
such I believe my l., 143:10
suffereth long, 44:18
swears she is made of truth, 228:2
sweet as l., 369:9
sweet for a day, 568:17
sweet lovers l. spring, 200:5
sweetest l. I do not go, 234:10
take l. away no art, 614:3
take l. together to sky, 579:12

Love *(continued)*

takes life to l. life, 651:13
tale without l., 586:19
teach monarch to be wise, 334:7
that can be reckoned, 222:26
that comes too late, 210:33
that dare not speak its name, 653:20
that endures for breath, 568:1
that L. is all is all we know of L., 547:8
that moves sun and other stars, 132:9
that my l. were in my arms, 843:18
that never seen twice, 443:16
that never told can be, 373:8
that winged seraphs coveted, 479:18
that word is l., 68:22
the brotherhood, 47:28
the good pursue the worst, 105:*n*14
the human form divine, 372:6
the Lord with all thine heart, 9:30
the only meaning, 749:12
the only priest, 554:7
thee better after death, 463:18
thee to the depth, 463:17
them as God gives them, 364:13
them that love me, 21:10
there are those who l. it, 414:8
they do not l. that do not show, 176:5
they happy are and l., 257:25
they l. a train, 206:*n*2
this bud of l., 183:11
this cultured hell, 729:12
those I guard I do not l., 638:16
those who always loved l. more, 305:12
those who l. and create, 602:6
those who l. want wisdom, 428:4
those who love you, 316:12
those who wrong him, 115:27
those who yearn for impossible, 365:17
thou wast all to me l., 478:9
though presst with ill, 348:17
through l. come together into one, 69:7
through our l. is my lord slain, 139:12
throw away l. on conceited, 513:*n*1
thy first l., 48:8
thy honesty and l., 213:22
thy l. to me was wonderful, 11:38
thy neighbor, 9:15
thy neighbor as thyself, 36:43
thy sweet l. remembered, 226:7
thyself last, 231:7
till I prince of l. beheld, 371:9
time to l., 24:6
time weakens l., 292:16
tired of L., 653:12
to be wise and l., 208:6
to be worst of company, 298:1
to begin journey on Sundays, 299:21
to faults always blind, 373:10
to hatred turned, 300:22
to lose myself, 407:25
to lose myself in a mystery, 255:11
to l. and to cherish, 51:10
to l. and to work, 608:9
to l. her a liberal education, 303:6
to matrimony in a moment, 406:6
to say how much l. is little l., 132:14
to see her was to l. her, 378:24
too much l. of living, 569:3

Love *(continued)*

took all my l., 643:1
trade you have learned, 115:14
tragedy of l. indifference, 672:21
treason but hate traitor, 91:24
true l. a durable fire, 160:2
true l. differs from gold and clay, 429:25
true l. is like ghosts, 273:12
true l. sits him down, 848:18
truth pardon error, 315:22
try thinking of l., 777:7
tunes shepherd's reed, 396:9
turns to thoughts of l., 481:17
unconditional l., 823:8
unconquerable waster, 68:1
unfamiliar Name, 722:2
unrelenting foe to l., 318:7
unsatisfied, 719:11
unsought is better, 210:6
up groweth with youre age, 134:11
vaunteth not, 44:18
vegetable l. grow, 276:27
vegetable l. not suit me, 564:9
very ecstasy of l., 202:32
very few to l., 391:18
Virtue she alone is free, 261:12
visible world formed in l., 516:15
waft her l. to Carthage, 190:4
we are a small pond, 815:4
we may touch l. explain, 818:12
weathered storms of life, 620:8
what I l. near at hand, 781:3
what is l., 708:6
what is l. 'tis not hereafter, 209:14
what l. I bore to thee, 392:6
whatever it was an infection, 821:10
when I l. thee not, 213:30
when I was in l. with you, 618:13
when L. and Life fair, 605:19
when l. begins to sicken, 197:6
when l. is in excess, 69:25
when L. speaks, 177:7
when my l. swears, 228:2
when we love not, 156:23
where I and my L. wont to gae, 854:10
where is l. beauty truth, 428:17
where l. and need one, 670:6
where l. is great, 205:2
where l. of man l. of art, 73:2
where l. rules no will to power, 676:1
where Mercy L. and Pity dwell, 372:7
where power predominates l. lacking, 676:1
which greybeards call divine, 173:17
which us doth bind, 277:8
white rose breathes of l., 590:14
whom the gods l., 83:14
why is all l. speak, 546:16
why L. needs be blind, 180:*n*1
wife Belle Aurore, 495:4
wilder shores of l., 776:17
will find out way, 845:5
wisdom live accordingly, 506:16
with all thy faults I l. thee, 346:*n*5
with delight discourses, 129:16
with streaming hair, 747:18
with you l. to live, 100:4
without bitterness, 734:13
without dissimulation, 43:16

Love *(continued)*

without his wings, 419:8
without marriage, 319:8
without power destroyed, 735:14
women l. lovers, 274:13
word l. in mouth of courtesan, 454:9
words of l. then spoken, 412:7
work is l. made visible, 700:20
world in l. with night, 183:32
world outlasts l., 528:10
worms eaten but not for l., 199:27
would be dried up, 525:11
write of hunger writing about l., 778:6
wroth with one we l., 401:9
wrought new alchemy, 234:21
ye do me wrong, 843:22
years grow cold to l., 96:17
yes I'm in l., 333:16
yields to business, 105:23
you as New Englanders love pie, 680:2
you for yourself alone, 641:2
you in December, 583:7
you l. me so much, 707:4
you l. the daylight, 69:15
you ten years before the Flood, 276:27
your enemies, 34:7
youth gave l. and roses, 412:9
Zeus's bed of l., 70:5

Loved, alas I l. you best, 293:9

alas that all we l. of him, 430:7
Alcuin my name learning I l., 125:5
and lost, 477:2, 483:19
and thought himself beloved, 639:12
as l. we are indispensable, 599:20
at first sight, 170:15
at home revered abroad, 377:16
betray heart that l. her, 391:5
better l. ye canna be, 385:6
better to have l. and lost, 483:19
burning Sappho l., 423:24
conviction we are l., 451:7
country as no other man, 533:1
cursed floundered, 585:19
did till we l., 233:10
each other and were ignorant, 641:17
God so l. world, 40:46
had somebody l. him, 812:13
happiness to love and be l., 461:13
him because he was he, 152:14
him for himself alone, 367:22
him like a brither, 379:16
him so followed him, 491:21
him that l. rose, 620:14
him too much not to hate him, 290:8
how l. how honored once, 309:29
I have l. beauty, 441:4
I have l. thee Ocean, 422:3
I l. her that she did pity, 212:32
I l. Ophelia, 207:2
I not honor more, 276:1
I saw and l., 353:17
if ever man l. by wife, 270:11
if I had a friend that l. her, 212:32
Jonathan l. him as his own soul, 11:32
King Cophetua l. beggarmaid, 182:27
know we l. in vain, 419:9
knowing I l. my books, 229:15
laughed often l. much, 686:7

Loved *(continued)*

life London this moment, 699:16
love and be l. by me, 479:17
love now who never l., 305:12
love of being l., 575:12
mansionry, 219:15
memory of l. and lost, 477:2
moments of glad grace, 637:5
money with affliction, 646:23
Muses l. me, 85:15
never l. tree or flower, 412:13
never time place l. one, 495:12
never to have l., 483:19
no man ever l., 227:17
no sooner looked but l., 200:3
not l. world nor world me, 421:3
not that I l. Caesar less, 196:24
not wisely but too well, 215:13
one blotted from page, 420:12
out upon it I have l., 270:4
pale hands I l., 632:6
passing well, 203:22
Pharaoh's lean kine l., 185:31
pilgrim soul in you, 637:5
produces motion through being l., 80:5
remember not only how l., 628:8
Rome more, 196:24
safer to be feared than l., 142:10
scenes his fathers l., 765:1
see souls we l., 485:13
she l. me for dangers, 212:32
she l. much, 39:13
sighed to many l. one, 420:4
so much cost me so much, 255:2
Solomon l. many strange women, 12:21
some we l. loveliest, 471:11
the man and honor memory, 238:16
those who always l. love more, 305:12
thou hast not l., 198:8
to be l. be lovable, 105:8
to have l. to have thought, 529:1
too late I l. you, 119:11
too much hope of thee l. boy, 237:20
twice or thrice had I l. thee, 234:15
use him as though you l. him, 253:6
we never l. sae kindly, 378:24
what did L. One pass on from, 766:9
when all was young, 514:5
wish I l. human race, 624:5
with more than love, 479:18
woman once l. hateful, 659:11
you once long ago, 58:2
you so I drew tides of men, 723:7
Love-darting eyes, 261:9
Love-gift of fairy tale, 551:8
Love-in-idleness, 181:9
Loveliest and best, 471:11
and best said Good Night, 653:14
despairing songs l., 488:10
of lovely things, 432:13
of trees, 618:6
village of the plain, 341:28
woman born, 639:14
Loveliness exists, 818:10
its l. increases, 436:8
lay down in her l., 401:6
let thy l. fade, 411:12
needs not ornament, 318:4
portion of the l., 430:16

Loveliness *(continued)*

this Adonis in l., 417:8
within, 233:17
your L. and my death, 441:3
Lovely, a single l. action, 515:23
all l. things have ending, 725:3
amiable l. death, 178:8
and pleasant in their lives, 11:36
apparition sent, 394:1
April of her prime, 225:29
as l. so be various, 743:16
as woman so be l., 743:16
billboard l. as a tree, 763:9
come l. soothing death, 520:16
corpse, 497:6
devours all l. things, 735:5
diminutives, 780:12
everything that's l. is, 637:15
faded but still l. woman, 746:15
flowers are l., 402:10
gentleman-like man, 181:2
gives a l. light, 735:2
go l. rose, 257:24
go l. Rose, 692:17
he is altogether l., 25:26
honest labor bears a l. face, 233:6
in her bones, 780:16
is the Rose, 393:8
ladies dead and l. knights, 227:11
look last on things l., 662:12
loveliness he made more l., 430:16
Mary Morison, 380:9
monster, 771:3
more l. and more temperate, 226:2
more l. than Pandora, 266:20
most l. dead, 478:8
Nature swears l. dears, 378:13
nothing but truth is l., 289:19
poem l. as a tree, 711:11
Richard sweet l. rose, 185:6
see cloud appear, 855:20
shut her up horrorshow and l., 798:17
so l. fair, 214:28
some once l. Head, 471:9
two l. berries on one stem, 181:22
virtue how l., 266:25
whatsoever things are l., 45:38
when her l. laughter shows, 232:6
wise and the l., 735:11
with me is to be l. still, 348:17
woman stoops to folly, 341:20, 718:19
woods l. dark and deep, 669:15
your eyes, 759:8
Lover all as frantic, 182:3
and sensualist, 594:8
angel appear to l., 305:10
beauty familiar to l., 301:20
cannot having been l., 636:13
dividing l. and l., 567:18
easier to be l. than husband, 445:3
every l. a warrior, 105:2
faithless l., 423:20
fond l., 269:20
found my l. on his bed, 4:4
give repentance to her l., 341:21
I am l., 677:20
in husband lost, 329:24
it was a l. and his lass, 200:5
Jesus l. of my soul, 322:24

Lover *(continued)*

love a l., 455:21
lunatic the l. the poet, 182:3
magnetic peripatetic l., 564:11
music sent up by l. and bard, 494:5
my truant l. has come, 521:6
no l. and no adventurer, 612:1
of all plagues l. bears, 296:5
of concord, 50:5
of men the sea, 568:14
scratch l. find foe, 738:12
sighed as l. obeyed as son, 354:1
sighing like furnace, 198:25
threw wild hands toward sky, 655:19
true l. therefore had good end, 139:9
wild Jack for a l., 641:13
without indiscretion no lover, 574:17
woman loves her l., 423:21
woman wailing for demon-l., 401:14
Wotton a most dear l., 252:25
you l. of trees, 492:12
Loverly, wouldn't it be l., 803:6
Lover's, act l. or Roman's part, 309:28
death as l. pinch, 224:11
quarrel with world, 670:15
run into it as to l. bed, 223:35
shall win l. hire, 373:14
slide into l. head, 391:17
some old l. ghost, 235:7
Lovers always talking about themselves,
274:1
among all her l. none to comfort,
29:27
bodies of l. drowned, 689:20
cannot see follies, 188:20
falling out of l. renewing of love, 88:n7
fled away into storm, 437:4
Frankie and Johnny l., 849:13
friends l. husbands, 361:13
journeys end in l. meeting, 209:13
lying two and two, 618:9
make two l. happy, 310:18
never tired of each other, 274:1
not of two l. but two loves, 235:21
of beauty without extravagance, 74:1
of virtue, 253:9
of wisdom without unmanliness, 74:1
old l. soundest, 244:1
other l. estranged or dead, 641:17
perjuries of l., 104:27
Romans countrymen and l., 196:23
star-crossed l., 182:16
such as I all true l., 209:21
swear more performance, 208:5
sweet l. love the spring, 200:5
thy l. were all untrue, 285:22
to bed, 182:14
true l. run into strange capers, 198:9
woes of hopeless l., 284:16
women born my sisters and l., 518:17
women love l., 274:13
world will welcome l., 741:1
Lovers', at l. perjuries Jove laughs, 183:5
dull sublunary l. love, 235:1
pure l. souls descend, 235:5
quarrels renewal of love, 88:12
seasons run, 234:2
silver-sweet sound l. tongues, 183:14
sonnets turned psalms, 164:10

Love's architecture is his own, 272:17
  evening star l. harbinger, 268:13
  fires glow longest, 588:10
  keen arrows, 199:19
  my l. richer than tongue, 215:15
  mysteries in souls grow, 235:6
  not Time's fool, 227:17
  passives, 272:13
  pleasure drives love, 640:11
  purple with l. wound, 181:9
  stricken why, 546:16
  such ever l. way, 494:13
  young dream, 411:13
Loves, all she l. is love, 423:21
  as lines so l. oblique, 277:8
  but their oldest clothes, 233:17
  caldron of dissolute l., 119:6
  change everything except l., 316:23
  color l. and skin, 233:17
  cowboy that l. you so true, 855:2
  cruel mother of sweet l., 100:12
  demirep that l., 493:9
  faint in light she l., 485:9
  fat woman nobody l., 711:8
  fierce wars and faithful l., 160:16
  he that l. a rosy cheek, 253:18
  he that l. sorrow, 233:9
  heart of woman he l., 657:8
  him better for faults, 341:24
  his fellow men, 417:14
  I have reigned with your l., 152:1
  if our l. remain, 492:12
  kills thing he l., 605:18
  man l. what he is good at, 291:11
  me best that calls me Tom, 239:12
  me let him follow me, 132:11
  mourn ye Graces and L., 94:1
  muse l. the race of bards, 55:1
  no man l. life like old, 69:5
  not his wronger, 213:34
  of two l. the nests, 235:21
  silence somewhat platonically, 433:*n2*
  suspects yet soundly l., 213:34
  to hear himself talk, 183:23
  to live i' the sun, 198:13
  to sit and hear me sing, 371:10
  two cities formed by two l., 119:22
  two l. I have, 228:3
  what he l. never like too much, 237:21
  who l. a garden, 348:3, 444:15
  who l. to lie with me, 198:11
  whoever really l. you, 862:22
  world as his body, 58:14
Lovesick, twenty l. maidens, 564:7
  winds were l., 223:14
Lovesickness, poem begins as l., 671:8
Lovesome, Garden l. thing, 543:16
  wee thing, 380:3
Lovest, canst not guide whom thou l.,
  122:2
  what thou l. well, 709:10
Loveth cheerful giver, 45:10
  dear God who l. us, 401:2
  he that l. her l. life, 32:2
  he that l. not knoweth not God, 47:41
  him whom my soul l., 25:20
  prayeth best who l. best, 401:2
  well both man bird beast, 401:1
  whom the Lord l. he chasteneth, 47:2

Loving, after l. you so much, 802:3
  can't help l. that man of mine, 744:2
  children begin l. parents, 604:18
  die adoring God l. friends, 317:3
  distance between human beings, 677:9
  for l. and for saying so, 234:8
  give a l. heart to thee, 247:16
  in love with l., 119:7
  mercy, 355:3
  night made for l., 423:1
  pardon for too much l. you, 214:1
  pleasure of love is in l., 273:30
  rapid merciless, 801:5
  shutting away of l. hearts, 735:11
  so l. to my mother, 201:3
  take heed of l. me, 235:11
  that old armchair, 509:6
Loving-jealous of his liberty, 183:15
Loving-kindness, goodness and l., 50:8
Lovingkindness, how excellent is thy l., 17:4
Low, abatement and l. price, 208:26
  ambition and pride of kings, 310:20
  Brer Fox he lay l., 593:6
  cast one's eyes so l., 217:18
  death makes equal high and l., 147:3
  descending sun, 846:17
  dost thou lie so l., 196:18
  exalted them of l. degree, 38:39
  foreheads villainous l., 230:10
  gods' custom to bring l. greatness, 71:19
  high and l. rich and poor, 386:14
  I'll tak' the l. road, 847:15
  last great Englishman l., 484:21
  lean and l. ability, 210:14
  low breathe and blow, 482:18
  man adding one to one, 492:24
  one sang high another l., 846:22
  scud, 821:16
  speak l., 194:17
  sweet and l., 482:18
  swing l. sweet chariot, 863:4
  swinging l. with sullen roar, 260:4
  talk l. talk slow, 777:9
  ten l. words, 308:16
  too l. for envy, 275:3
  too l. they build, 306:12
  valley so l., 847:2
  voice was gentle and l., 218:6
  what is l. raise and support, 263:21
  when my light l., 483:21
Lowells talk to Cabots, 621:22
Lower, a little l. than angels, 15:32
  brutalizing l. class, 532:3
  down can fall no l., 271:11
  middle classes, 564:16
  night beginning to l., 467:10
  orders don't set good example, 605:5
  part of mankind, 295:7
  prevent l. from getting more, 80:25
  see front o' battle l., 380:10
  take you a button-hole l., 177:13
  while there is a l. class, 606:8
Lowered, sash l. when night, 669:20
Lowest and most dejected thing, 217:9
  type hear Tao, 59:4
Lowing herd wind slowly, 334:8
Lowland, between l. and highland, 569:14
  sails upon L. sea, 862:10
Lowlands, ye Highlands and L., 854:9

Lowliness, man of l. and affability, 144:5
  young ambition's ladder, 195:30
Lowly air of Seven Dials, 564:20
  and riding upon an ass, 30:37
  better to be l. born, 230:25
  man bears stamp of l. origin, 470:7
  meek and l. in heart, 35:35
  nothing l. in universe, 816:13
  organized creatures, 470:8
Lowry, Malcolm L. of Bowery, 783:7
Low-vaulted past, 473:11
Loyal and neutral in a moment, 220:26
  nature noble mind, 486:7
  to a trust, 608:12
Loyalties, impossible l., 530:10
Loyalty, map of l. in thy face, 172:11
  women have l. to Truth to yourself,
  593:20
Lubricates, dinner l. business, 362:12
Lucan, line in which L. meant to rise, 110:10
Lucasta, then my L. might I crave, 276:5
Lucent, softly l. as moon, 515:16
Lucid, full of l. intervals, 158:8
  interval, 284:3
  intervals and happy pauses, 166:17
  moments, 442:18
Lucidity of thought, 532:5
  sad l. of soul, 528:9
Lucifer, he falls like L., 231:2
  Prince L. uprose, 541:16
  proud seat of L., 268:7
  son of the morning, 27:3
  spirits that fell with L., 170:18
Luck, as good l. would have it, 190:32
  blessed in l. of chase, 856:6
  counted and cursed his l., 619:15
  fattenin' hogs ain't in l., 593:16
  for good l. cast old shoe, 147:23
  good l. in odd numbers, 191:4
  had l. met monster, 771:3
  ill l. seldom alone, 156:25
  in odd numbers, 191:4, 443:4
  I've got the L. with me, 566:10
  light in ragged l., 594:8
  little bit of l., 803:7
  not holding best cards, 571:8
  run to meet ill l., 458:9
  spit on us for l., 85:8
  struck streak of bad l., 566:11
  watching l. his light-o'-love, 673:9
Luckiest knows when to go home, 571:8
  people in the world, 810:12
Lucky enough to know, 784:11
  not call man happy but l., 57:11
  sixpence in shoe, 850:13
  them that die'll be l. ones, 598:19
  to be alive at great time, 752:12
  to be born, 519:1
  to die and I know it, 519:1
  to have lived in Paris, 755:7
Lucre, filthy l., 46:17
Lucrece swears he did her wrong, 175:12
Lucy, if L. should be dead, 391:17
  Locket lost her pocket, 860:11
  when L. ceased to be, 391:18
Luddington's my dwelling place, 749:13
Luftwaffe, give this much to the L., 841:3
  your L. your gobbledygoo, 827:15
Lugged, melancholy as l. bear, 184:29

M

Macht, der Wille zur M., 590:*n*3
Mächte, ihr himmlischen M., 363:*n*4
Machu Picchu Cambridge Mass. Angkor,
    792:16
Mackerel, stinks like rotten m., 405:2
Mackerel-crowded seas, 639:16
Macrocosm, microcosm and m. atoned,
    536:11
Macte nova virtute puer, 98:*n*2
Mad, all poets are m., 240:10
    am m. and am not m., 61:18
    and lamentable experiment, 629:4
    as Bedlam, 497:35
    as March hare, 141:*n*2
    bad and dangerous, 418:7
    cold m. father, 696:18
    dogs and Englishmen, 753:6
    don't call a man m., 333:12
    don't get m. get even, 723:3
    face that drove me m., 584:6
    father and mither gae m., 379:7
    go m. or unstable, 71:14
    half m. with beauty, 556:9
    he first makes m., 71:6
    heroically m., 283:20
    I am not m., 42:36
    idolatry, 207:32
    if they behold a cat, 189:12
    I'm m. as hell, 811:12
    in pursuit, 227:22
    laid to make taker m., 227:22
    makes men m., 215:8
    man must be a little m., 154:2
    March days, 681:5
    March hare, 141:16
    men God made m., 664:7
    more deadly than m. dog's tooth,
        174:38
    much learning make m., 42:35
    naked summer night, 519:8
    nobly wild not m., 248:13
    north-northwest, 203:20
    O fool I shall go m., 216:17
    old m. blind despised king, 429:11
    pleasure in being m., 283:22
    practice drives m., 843:21
    prose run m., 312:3
    provided man not m., 331:12
    pursuit, 437:17
    sad and bad and m., 494:17
    sad m. brother's name, 569:13
    sense that world was m., 677:13
    some born m. some remain so, 773:12
    that he is m. 'tis true, 203:1
    that trusts in wolf, 217:4
    to live mad to be saved, 810:2
    undevout astronomer is m., 306:14
    we are m. nationally, 106:28
    went m. and bit the man, 341:18
    whom God wishes to destroy he makes
        m., 71:6, 124:19
    world, 497:35
    world mad kings, 178:1
Madam is there nothing else, 545:10
    says the earl immediately, 277:12
Madame Bovary had beauty, 527:1
    hell M. is to love no longer, 716:12
    I am M. Bovary, 527:11
    poetry the supreme fiction m., 686:14

Madcap, once in my days be a m., 184:35
Maddens, all that m. torments, 516:14
    Trees m. me, 716:18
Madder music stronger wine, 645:10
Maddest merriest day, 480:15
Madding, far from m. crowd's strife,
    334:23
Made a rural pen, 371:14
    and loveth all, 401:2
    annihilating all that's m., 277:4
    begotten not m., 50:4
    by whom all things m., 50:4
    Christians not born but m., 118:26
    confusion m. masterpiece, 220:23
    day which the Lord hath m., 19:26
    did he who m. Lamb, 374:6
    fearfully and wonderfully m., 20:15
    friends born not m., 570:4
    God m. and eaten, 492:8
    God m. him let him pass for man,
        187:31
    him a little lower than angels, 15:32
    his pendent bed, 219:15
    in wisdom hast thou m. all, 19:11
    incarnate and was m. man, 50:4
    it is he that hath m. us, 19:3
    little Lamb who m. thee, 371:15
    Lord God m. them all, 508:7
    marriages m. in heaven, 163:18
    men and not made them well, 204:14
    mouths in a glass, 216:21
    my song a coat, 638:10
    myself a motley, 227:15
    of sterner stuff, 196:29
    poet's m. as well as born, 238:11
    sea is his and he m. it, 18:29
    stuff as dreams are m. on, 230:9
    swears she is m. of truth, 228:2
    the best of this, 380:17
    this parting well m., 197:17
    us with large discourse, 205:35
    what man has m. of man, 390:16
    when or you or I are m., 248:18
    without fear, 15:23
    world I never m., 619:14
    world m. safe for democracy, 611:8
    world of m. not world of born, 740:14
Madeleine soaked in lime flowers, 657:7
    upon bar-room floor, 584:6
Madeline, I hate you I hate you cried M.,
    694:13
Madeline's fair breast, 436:25
Mademoiselle from Armenteers, 730:13
    from St. Nazaire, 730:14
Madest, creature that thou m., 620:2
Madly, stars shot m. from spheres, 181:8
    twirled fingers m., 500:6
Madman, either liar or m., 331:6
    if he like m. lived, 159:5
    that is the m., 182:3
    truth of a m., 822:4
Madmen in authority distilling frenzy,
    702:4
    which none but m. know, 283:22
Madness, a little M. in Spring, 546:15
    anger a short m., 100:24
    avarice a piece of m., 287:*n*1
    despondency and m., 392:9, 800:15
    destroyed by m., 817:12

Madness *(continued)*
    from breakfast to m., 821:7
    go you may call it m., 384:8
    great wits to m. allied, 283:8
    harmonious m. flow, 429:20
    in brain, 401:9
    let us have m. openly, 787:1
    life is a m., 254:18
    midsummer m., 210:11
    moon-struck m., 268:10
    much M. divinest Sense, 545:2
    much of M., 478:18
    need not be all breakdown, 819:7
    no genius without touch of m., 107:5
    of many for gain of few, 313:14
    risen from hell, 568:1
    Sense starkest M., 545:2
    species of m., 287:12
    sudden m. came upon Orpheus, 96:20
    that fine m., 169:17
    that way m. lies, 216:26
    the rest is m. of art, 585:4
    though this be m., 203:10
    'tis m. to defer, 306:3
    to let private enterprise set habits, 737:9
    to live like wretch, 240:21
    what m. has caught you, 95:17
Madonnas, Rafael of dear M., 494:2
Madrigal, woeful stuff this m., 308:21
Madrigals, melodious birds sing m., 170:7
Madruga, al que m. Dios ayuda, 862:15
Madrugar, no por mucho m., 862:21
Mads, music m. me, 180:16
    second m. him, 209:7
Maecenas, how comes it M., 98:15
Maenad of Massachusetts, 569:11
Maggots, breed m. in dead dog, 203:6
    make speech to m., 739:9
Magic, argosies of m. sails, 481:23
    casements, 437:13
    lash M. Creature, 546:14
    little plans no m., 592:4
    must not let daylight in upon m., 538:3
    no rhymes no m., 648:5
    numbers, 300:21
    of a face, 253:21
    of the sea, 467:8
    painting form of m., 693:13
    preservation in books, 434:20
    scenes shifted like m., 596:17
    sweet m. brings together, 381:8
    this rough m., 230:11
    thought and m. sound, 446:17
    to stir men's blood, 592:4
    with a m. like thee, 422:23
Magical, I am m. mouse, 787:6
    power imagination, 403:10
    purely m. object, 795:18
Magician Merlin had strange laugh, 790:11
    rope-dancer physician m., 113:5
Magick, strange kind of m. bias, 332:10
Magister artis ingenique largitor venter,
    108:*n*10
Magisterial or imperative type, 653:17
Magistrate, by m. equally useful, 353:5
    grown gray in office, 446:19
    no name of m., 229:25
Magna Carta will have no sovereign, 159:19
Magna est veritas et praevalet, 31:*n*2

Make *(continued)*

so much of fragmentary blue, 669:10
soul is form and doth body m., 162:5
straight a highway for our God, 27:38
sudden sally, 485:3
the Lord m. his face shine upon thee, 9:17
the most of it, 352:11
the phrase to m. money, 772:3
thee an ark, 6:26
thee mightier yet, 625:11
thick my blood, 219:11
unless philosophy m. a Juliet, 184:3
up my sum, 207:2
us do what we can, 457:1
us heirs of all eternity, 176:17
war to live in peace, 80:19
waves m. towards pebbled shore, 226:16
world safe for diversity, 800:3
worse appear the better, 74:13
yourselves another face, 204:6
Make-believe, children's house of m., 670:18
Eve seen through m., 656:12
Makeless, maiden that is m., 843:10
Maker, as though m. and molder of thyself, 142:1
Lord our m., 18:29
more pure than his m., 13:35
of Heaven and earth, 50:3
reproacheth his M., 22:4
rests in lightland, 4:9
tool m., 681:8
Makers, abhor m. and their laws approve, 284:25
Makes, another which m., 78:1
heaven drowsy with harmony, 177:7
heretic that m. the fire, 228:16
me or fordoes me quite, 215:5
me poor indeed, 213:33
men mad, 215:8
night hideous, 202:*n*1
one little room an everywhere, 233:11
or mars us, 215:2
swanlike end, 189:2
sweet music with stones, 176:8
thinking m. it so, 203:14
tongue of him that m. it, 177:15
whole world kin, 208:12
Makest, thou m. darkness, 19:11
what m. thou, 28:11
Maketh clouds his chariot, 19:8
he m. me to lie down, 16:18
the deep to boil, 15:22
Making green one red, 220:19
many books, 25:10, 692:16
news better than taking it, 665:3
night hideous, 202:6
shaping and controlling life, 522:3
Mal, honi soit qui m. y pense, 132:16
Malachite, good speech more hidden than m., 3:4
Maladies, soul with all its m., 573:5
Maladministration, secured against m., 339:10
Malady, he smiles it is a m., 94:10
medicine worse than m., 103:*n*1
of not marking, 191:13
Malaise, two problems energy and m., 814:2

Malcontents, liege of m., 176:33
Mars of m., 190:19
Male adult, 828:3
and female created he, 5:13
and female fuse into one solid, 73:13
cannot tolerate living with equal, 465:5
difference of education between m. and female, 361:15
especially m. of species, 707:14
healthy wealthy and dead, 741:16
if God is m., 820:9
kiss of blankets, 712:18
more deadly than m., 635:23
Malefactors of great wealth, 615:9
Malfi, I am Duchess of M. still, 244:6
Malherbe, at last comes M., 289:6
what M. writes will endure, 164:5
Malheur, de son âge tout le m., 316:*n*10
Malheureux, où nous étions si m., 855:9
Malice domestic, 221:5
from envy hatred and m., 50:11
much m. little wit, 284:23
never was his aim, 299:2
no m. or ill will, 386:4
no rampart against m., 277:17
no suspicion of m. in his writing, 90:16
nor set down aught in m., 215:13
ridicule without m., 476:6
toward none, 477:4
truth with m. in it, 516:14
we've got a lot of m., 829:12
Malicious ferocity, 685:*n*1
he is not, 683:15
wisdom entereth not in m. mind, 146:5
Malignant and turbaned Turk, 215:14
so m. so devastating, 734:2
trouble was not m., 766:10
Maligners of his honor, 554:2
Malignity, motiveless m., 402:17
Malitia, ius summum saepe summa est m., 88:*n*13
Mallecho, miching m., 204:22
Malorum, radix m. est cupiditas, 46:*n*1
Malt, ate the m., 861:15
does more than Milton can, 619:9
Maltreat, shouldn't m. our idols, 527:2
Mama, we've lost good old m., 750:18
Mamas, last of red-hot m., 705:*n*2
Mammon, cannot serve God and m., 34:16
is like fire, 434:*n*3
the least erected spirit, 264:22
wins his way, 420:5
Man, a certain m. went down, 39:22
a great great m., 812:13
a little mad if not stupid, 154:2
a little worse than a m., 187:32
a m. like me, 374:4
a m. zealous for nothing, 328:19
a social animal, 287:10
actions show m. we find, 310:2
Adam the goodliest m., 266:12
after all he's just a m., 837:15
after his own heart, 11:22
aged m. paltry thing, 639:17
ah for m. to arise, 485:6
ah when to heart of m., 668:16
ain't nothin' but a man, 848:15
all that a m. hath will he give, 13:27
all that makes m., 486:8

Man *(continued)*

all that may become a m., 219:21
alone abandoned on earth, 772:7
alone can enslave man, 783:20
always tell Harvard m., 850:1
am I not a m. and brother, 346:13
ambitious m. have no satisfaction, 237:3
an ape or angel, 459:12
and beast, 811:16
and bird and beast, 401:1
and brother, 346:13
and his fate, 683:6
and what he loves have but day, 678:15
and woman in garden, 605:3
and woman two locked caskets, 706:9
animal which devours own, 357:13
apparel oft proclaims m., 201:26
arms and the m. I sing, 96:23, 285:6
Art mediatress between nature and m., 403:16
as a m. wipeth a dish, 13:8
as happy a m. as any, 288:10
as M. alone Jesus not saved us, 765:5
as m. looks at woman, 689:4
as nature made him, 331:15
as old as his arteries, 280:19
Ascent of M., 778:4
assurance of a m., 205:21
at expense of m., 743:18
at thirty m. suspects himself fool, 306:5
at wheel taught to feel, 580:23
average m., 698:1
baker's m., 857:1
battered wrecked old m., 521:4
battlefield heart of m., 525:13
be a friend to m., 613:16
be m. be nonconformist, 455:9
bear with all the faults of m., 232:4
bears stamp of lowly origin, 470:7
beautiful thing raises m., 143:10
became a living soul, 5:16
become ignorant m. again, 687:21
been mother's undisputed darling, 607:14
before you trust a m., 843:14
behold m. of flint, 856:4
behold the m., 41:38
being his own physician, 79:18
being reasonable must get drunk, 423:19
belief woman made for m., 503:8
believe in equality of m., 355:3
Benedick the married m., 194:12
best m. like water, 58:12
best m. worst-natured muse, 292:25
better m. than I Gunga Din, 633:10
better spared better m., 187:8
beware m. of one book, 123:12
beyond m. is universe, 742:7
bites dog, 591:5
blessings on thee little m., 468:9
blest m. that spares these stones, 231:19
blood of a British m., 217:3
blow the m. down, 861:24
bold bad m., 160:18, 230:24
bold m. first eat oyster, 299:14
born dies and does not come again, 853:2
born to live not prepare for life, 730:9
boyhood changing into m., 640:17

Man (*continued*)

brave m. inattentive to duty, 386:11
brave m. with a sword, 605:18
breathes there the m., 396:11
bronzed lank m., 685:6
Brutus is an honorable m., 196:28
but be a m., 528:18
butterfly dreaming I am a m., 82:23
by m. came death, 44:24
by m. came resurrection, 44:24
by m. shall his blood be shed, 6:33
by nature political animal, 80:21
Caius is a m., 543:2
call no m. foe, 733:6
came to making of m., 568:1
can a m. take fire in his bosom, 21:7
can die but once, 192:2
can raise thirst, 633:14
cannot emerge from himself, 657:15
can't hold m. down without staying,
    610:21
capable of becoming true m., 727:7
cause of work, 658:15
caverns measureless to m., 401:13
cease ye from m., 26:13
cells and gibbets for m., 509:7
century of common m., 725:1
certain way to hold a m., 804:16
certainly crazy, 153:5
change environment not m., 743:9
child conceived, 13:29
child father of m., 392:7
childhood shows the m., 268:24
Christian faithful m., 174:2
city is teacher of the m., 62:2
civilized m. cannot live without cooks,
    548:11
civilized m. has habits of house, 504:24
clothed with rags, 281:14
comes with his torment, 382:14
common m. has triumphed, 589:12
commonest M. shows grace in quarrel,
    440:17
composed of all men, 772:12
concern for m. himself, 683:6
concrete m. has one interest, 581:5
conference maketh a ready m., 168:16
confidence in tall m. merited, 778:13
connection of individual m., 848:16
control the wind, 528:21
count on no one but himself, 772:7
country turns out, 457:8
coupling of m. and woman, 720:16
created M. of blood clot, 122:19
crime of being young m., 323:2
crooked m., 860:6
cruelty to load falling m., 231:*n*1
daring young m. on trapeze, 571:14
dark as world of m., 715:13
dark cloud m., 588:17
delights not me, 203:18
desire for desire of m., 404:1
desire of knowledge caused m. to fall,
    167:19
diapason closing in M., 284:13
did not make can not mar, 528:13
dieth and wasteth away, 14:16
dignity of m. capacity to despise self,
    629:10

Man (*continued*)

dispute it like a m., 222:2
do not bet that m., 704:*n*2
does not live by GNP alone, 797:1
doth not live by bread only, 10:1
dream past wit of m., 181:29
drest in brief authority, 211:13
drink takes m., 579:13
drove out the m., 6:11
drowsed off, 678:7
dull ear of drowsy m., 178:10
each m. act of God, 504:11
ear of m. hath not seen, 182:1
either m. obsolete or war is, 743:10
end of that m. is peace, 17:8
endeavoring to turn m. into beast, 761:8
errs as long as he strives, 365:3
Esau was a m. of the field, 7:10
escape from rope and gun, 307:16
establish reign of liberty, 777:15
even such a m. so faint, 191:7
every cry of every m., 374:7
every m. a piece of the continent, 236:19
every m. architect of his fortune, 95:13
every m. at his best state, 17:13
every m. for himself, 149:17
every m. has his fault, 218:16
every m. hath a good and bad angel,
    240:11
every m. his greatest enemy, 256:5
every m. is wanted, 456:13
every m. own architect, 495:7
every m. satisfied there is truth, 574:1
every m. under his vine, 12:13
every m. was God or Devil, 283:16
every m. will do duty, 377:6
expatiate o'er scene of m., 310:20
eye of m. hath not heard, 182:1
fallen god, 426:10
false m., 294:12
false m. does easy, 220:27
false to any m., 201:27
Family of M., 681:18
fashion wears out more than m., 194:36
favor with God and m., 39:8
first m. among these than second in
    Rome, 91:26
first-class fightin' m., 633:9
fit night for m. or beast, 690:2
foolish fond old m., 217:30
foolish passionate m., 642:4
foot-in-the-grave young m., 564:13
for all seasons, 144:5
for m. as for flower beast bird, 707:19
for the field, 483:3
for the sword, 483:3
forgotten as a dead m. out of mind,
    16:27
Forgotten M., 576:13
forgotten m., 697:11
formed for society, 338:8
formed m. of dust, 5:16
free as Nature made m., 282:19
free to do evil as good, 566:22
frees himself from bonds, 461:6
fresh from Natur's mold, 497:8
Friday, 295:9
frontiers wherever m. fronts fact, 505:26
gently scan brother m., 378:18

Man (*continued*)

get a new m., 229:32
gird up thy loins like a m., 15:4
give every m. thy ear, 201:26
giveth up the ghost, 14:16
glory to M. in highest, 569:10
go west young m., 503:4
goal of landing m. on moon, 799:11
God above or m. below, 311:1
God and m. decree, 619:13
God became m. devil woman, 451:2
god in ruins, 454:18
God is not a m., 9:24
God's ways to m., 619:9
goes riding by, 598:22
goeth forth unto his work, 19:11
goeth to his long home, 25:8
good for a m. that he bear the yoke,
    29:30
good m. and just, 40:24
good m. does not argue, 59:21
good name in m. and woman, 213:33
great m. great ganglion, 578:2
great nose great m., 649:14
greater m. greater courtesy, 486:5
greatest fool is m., 289:15
greatest m. ever seen, 343:*n*3
greatness of work inside m., 806:12
grew within this learned m., 171:7
ground colored m. occupies, 509:12
grows beyond his work, 764:7
grows used to everything, 525:10
half part of blessed m., 177:27
hand of a mighty m., 20:6
hand will be against every m., 7:4
happy citizen free, 451:16
happy m. be his dole, 147:*n*10
happy m. happy dole, 147:13
happy m. works ancestral acres, 98:27
happy old m., 95:16
happy the m. and he alone, 284:6
hardly a m. now alive, 467:14
harrowing clods, 576:5
has Forever, 492:22
has two primal passions, 595:8
has will woman way, 473:8
hath penance done, 400:16
having put hand to plow, 39:16
he created m., 853:2
he was a m., 655:15
he was a m. take him for all in all, 201:12
he was her m., 849:14
heard wise m. say, 618:10
heart of m. place devil dwells in, 256:2
hearty old m., 405:9
her wit was more than m., 284:12
himself important creation, 757:12
himself lend a hand, 73:14
his answer was M., 759:18
his own executioner, 256:5
honest exceeding poor m., 188:15
honest m. close-buttoned, 348:14
honest m. noblest work of God, 311:13,
    377:16
honest m. sent to lie abroad, 232:19
horse noblest conquest of m., 321:9
how dieth the wise m., 24:5
how many roads m. walk down, 836:4
how marvelous is M., 649:2

Man (*continued*)

how poor a thing is m., 169:8
how proud word M. rings, 649:2
how would m. exist if God did not need
   him, 679:8
howl for flesh of m., 829:5
humiliation by white m., 812:6
hungry sinner, 424:21
I am cease to be, 485:6
I am first a m., 314:10
I am the m., 519:18
I appeal to any white m., 339:8
I got my m., 746:24
I have been a m., 364:25
I know thee not old m., 192:13
I loved the m. and honor memory,
   238:16
I must feel it as a m., 222:2
I never writ nor no m. loved, 227:17
I the m. in the moon, 182:9
identifies with his fate, 753:1
if a m. die shall he live, 14:17
if a m. finishes a poem, 830:16
if a m. has talent, 760:6
if a m. publicly denounces poetry, 830:15
if not wedding day absolutely fixed on,
   322:15
if such a m. there be, 312:5
I'll make me a m., 657:2
I'm m. of wealth and taste, 838:5
improvable reason of M., 443:6
in armor slave, 495:5
in arms wish to be, 394:15
in every fat m. a thin one, 764:14
in every m. two postulations, 524:19
in gray flannel suit, 807:12
in his hasty days, 586:7
in love endures more, 589:22
in love with suffering, 525:9
in mind of m. a motion, 391:4
in our town, 861:13
in past m. has been first, 610:17
in subjection to white Saxon m., 503:7
in whose hand cup is found, 7:31
in wilderness, 857:7
in wit a m., 310:19
incarnate and was made m., 50:4
ingrateful m., 216:18
inner m., 45:26
insignificant and aware of it, 661:9
intellect of m. choose, 641:4
interpreter of nature, 432:19
intimates eternity to m., 301:26
invented m. because disappointed in
   monkey, 562:15
invisible m., 793:2
is a machine, 329:21
is a prisoner, 76:15
is a reasoning animal, 106:18
is a thinking reed, 280:4
is as Heaven made him, 157:29
is born for uprightness, 62:25
is born free, 330:20
is born unto trouble, 13:37
is God blunder of m., 589:18
is man and master, 485:22
is m. blunder of God, 589:18
is m. no more than this, 216:30
is not so good a Christian, 599:17

Man (*continued*)

is not so great a coward, 599:17
is one soul many tongues, 116:15
is origin of his action, 80:14
is raised above animal, 777:12
is singular creature, 778:3
is the hunter, 483:2
je-ne-sais-quoi young m., 564:12
Jewish m. with parents alive, 828:13
joked about every prominent m., 685:20
killed hero in m., 772:2
kills thing he loves, 605:18
know how to defy opinion, 385:13
know myself a m., 233:3
know the m. that must hear me, 400:22
know what God and m. is, 486:21
knoweth not his time, 24:30
known by company he keeps, 71:n1
lame m. leap as an hart, 27:32
large-hearted m., 463:9
last m. on right brush channel, 554:10
last strands of m., 587:20
laugh to scorn power of m., 221:26
law for m., 453:7
laws of God beyond m., 67:20
laws of God laws of m., 619:13
least considerable m., 360:9
leave his father and mother, 6:2
lengthened shadow of one m., 455:13
less no m. have, 615:6
let each m. hope and believe, 470:12
let end try the m., 191:28
let him pass for a m., 187:31
let m. outlive his wealth, 189:25
let no such m. be trusted, 190:7
let us make m. in our image, 5:12
life of m. solitary, 246:12
lightning out of cloud m., 588:17
like light kindled and put out, 64:12
little difference between m. and m.,
   582:12
little m. had little gun, 860:18
lived with birds and beasts, 82:27
lives by catchwords, 598:6
lives life of epoch, 676:5
living-dead m., 175:1
long as colored m. look to white folks,
   839:9
look no way but downwards, 282:2
looketh on the outward appearance,
   11:25
looking for honest m., 79:6
Lord is a m. of war, 8:26
Lord seeth not as m. seeth, 11:25
lose what he never had, 253:4
lot of m. but once to die, 249:11
love not m. the less, 421:25
lovely gentleman-like m., 181:2
loves what vanishes, 640:6
lovin' that m. of mine, 744:2
low m. seeks little thing, 492:24
made for joy and woe, 375:10
made her such a m., 212:32
made of ordinary things, 381:21
made the town, 347:25
made to mourn, 377:13
majority never replace m., 726:9
makes gods by the dozen, 153:5
making deserts of earth, 680:12

Man (*continued*)

manners maketh m., 132:19
man's inhumanity to m., 377:14
man's word God in m., 485:17
marks earth with ruin, 421:26
master of fate, 485:22, 727:7
master of himself a happy m., 100:9
may fish with worm, 205:33
measure of all things, 72:1
mere M., 478:16
merely a passage for food, 140:11
middle-aged m. build woodshed, 505:7
military m., 193:5
mind's the standard of m., 303:16
misfortunes of m. occasioned by m.,
   108:7
mistakes evil for happiness, 382:20
Mr. Tambourine M., 836:7
Moby Dick whale or m., 736:1
mollusk cheap edition of m., 457:16
more no m. entitled to, 615:6
more right than neighbors, 505:18
more sinned against, 216:23
muffin m., 860:14
must have faults, 109:7
my m. of men, 223:9
Nature formed one such m., 422:20
nature in form of m., 781:12
necessarily a m., 314:10
needs go outside himself, 602:5
needs to suffer, 601:19
ne'er left m. i' mire, 218:13
negations of m., 815:1
neither angel nor beast, 280:5
neither m. nor woman but author,
   504:19
never bad m. good service, 345:6
never is blest, 311:4
never met m. I didn't like, 685:20
never saw m. who looked, 605:16
new m. raised up in him, 51:17
nice m., 298:7
no angel, 445:7
no benefit in gifts of bad m., 69:24
no indispensable m., 697:14
no m. above or below law, 615:7
no m. born an angler, 252:22
no m. born unto himself, 249:4
no m. content with lot, 98:15
no m. deserved less at country's hands,
   533:1
no m. do for your sake, 568:12
no m. hero to his valet, 257:1
no m. is an island, 236:19
no m. not deserve hanging, 154:1
no m. remember me, 575:6
no m. see me more, 230:31
no m. should marry, 459:15
no m. takes with him wealth, 61:15
no m. useless who has friend, 599:20
no m. worth having true, 297:9
no reasonable m. expected, 729:3
no sin for m. to labor in vocation, 184:33
no such thing as honest m., 306:18
noble animal, 256:22
noble be m. helpful and good, 363:13
noblest work of m., 554:6
none more wonderful than m., 67:18
not a just m. upon earth, 24:22

Man *(continued)*

not a m. but cloud, 738:1
not good that m. be alone, 5:20
not happy unless free, 426:5
not lifetime of one m. only, 721:5
not locked into environment, 778:4
not materials that counts, 737:15
not passion's slave, 204:17
not sum of what he has, 772:5
not take goods with him, 3:2
not what kind of paper but m., 506:6
nothing feebler than a m., 55:20
nothing more wretched than a m., 53:25
nothing to do with just m., 38:2
nothing wears clothes but M., 250:13
O that m. might know end, 197:18
of action forced into thought, 647:5
of an unbounded stomach, 231:12
of cheerful yesterdays, 395:8
of comfort no m. speak, 179:27
of dust, 5:16
of genius had to pay, 659:13
of honor regrets discreditable act, 691:11
of letters, 281:5
of many resources, 54:7
of many wiles, 309:20
of morals tell me why, 275:9
of my kidney, 191:1
of my peculiar weakness, 691:10
of nasty ideas, 298:7
of sorrows, 28:20
of strife and contention, 29:15
of unclean lips, 26:25
of understanding, 32:12
of understanding is of excellent spirit,
    22:8
of understanding lost nothing, 152:16
of virtue, 62:26
of words not deeds, 856:12
Ol' M. River, 744:1
old age in universal m., 166:*n*3
old m. broken, 231:9
old m. had so much blood, 222:5
old m. in dry month, 718:2
old m. to whom old men hearkened,
    102:9
old m. twice a child, 203:21
old m. who will not laugh, 629:19
Old M. with beard, 499:11
old m. with something of young, 91:16
old m. wouldn't say prayers, 858:11
on horseback, 848:13
once a man who said God, 723:4
once to every m. and nation, 514:12
one m. among a thousand, 24:24
one m. crossing bridge, 686:8
one m. one vote, 852:5
one m. plays many parts, 198:25
one m. with courage a majority, 387:1
one more wrong to m., 491:23
one small step for m., 824:19
one-book m., 398:27
only animal that blushes, 562:8
only feels alone, 794:3
only great m. write history, 605:15
only m. harrowing clods, 576:5
only m. is vile, 416:4
only one that knows nothing, 108:6
organization m., 802:15

Man *(continued)*

organized by labor, 649:5
out of me God and m., 569:7
out of one m. a race, 267:14
outrage a brave m. dead, 67:11
outrage when m. destroys nature, 678:15
outside every fat m., 764:*n*3
owes not any m., 466:8
palms greater no m. made them, 826:3
Parliament of m., 482:1
particularly pure young m., 564:9
partly is, 494:14
people arose as one m., 11:10
perceives it die away, 393:12
perhaps this is the m., 805:5
picked out of ten thousand, 203:5
pig edible to m., 580:12
pious m. not less a m., 277:23
place and means for every m., 210:28
plain blunt m., 197:3
Plato's m., 79:4
play is tragedy M., 478:15
play the m. Master Ridley, 145:2
poetry inner calling in m., 768:12
poor despised old m., 216:20
poor m. accustomed to small things,
    788:17
poor m. being down, 32:28
poor m. get out iv Purgatory, 646:11
poor m. had nothing, 12:3
poor m. is Christ's stamp, 250:3
poor m. poor mankind, 748:13
poor m. that has loved, 639:12
poorest m. in his cottage, 323:3
possesses immortality, 773:4
power of m. and moment, 530:4
powers superior to m., 602:17
prayer of righteous m., 47:23
preached as dying m., 274:21
prejudiced unreasonable m., 498:19
prentice han' tried on m., 378:13
press not falling m., 231:1
primitive m. tactile m., 703:1
private m. James Joyce, 833:1
privilege to help m. endure, 749:2
projects himself into culture, 772:10
proper m. as see in summer's day, 181:2
proper study of mankind is m., 311:9
proposes God disposes, 138:7
prosperity comes to bad m., 61:12
proud yet wretched thing, 233:3
prudent m. looketh well to his going,
    21:31
rather be worm than son of m., 713:14
reading maketh a full m., 168:16
ready money makes the m., 304:12
ready to believe what is told, 109:5
really a very good m., 606:16
Reasonable M. mythical figure, 729:1
rebuke a wise m., 21:12
recovered of the bite, 341:19
register of God not record of m., 256:20
rejoice O young m. in youth, 25:6
rejoiceth as a strong m., 16:11
rich in things he can let alone, 506:26
rich m. beginning to fall, 32:28
rich m. enter into kingdom, 36:34
rich m. enther Hiven, 646:11
richest pleasures cheapest, 505:11

Man *(continued)*

righteous m. regardeth the life of his
    beast, 21:22
righteous m. to make fall, 161:2
Rights of M., 345:10
rope between animal and Superman,
    588:16
round fat oily m. of God, 318:11
rousing like strong m., 263:3
ruined m., 722:20
ruins of the noblest m., 196:21
rule will show the m., 57:5
sabbath made for m., 38:16
said to universe, 656:1
savage in m. never eradicated, 505:12
savage individual m., 644:10
says what he knows, 331:13
scholar is M. Thinking, 454:20
seeks for what is remote, 82:3
seen how m. made slave slave made m.,
    509:9
self-made m. and worships creator, 489:6
sent from God, 40:31
serve time to every trade, 419:14
setting m. free from men, 771:21
seven women shall take hold of one m.,
    26:17
severe he was, 342:8
shall m. be more pure than maker, 13:35
shall man no longer crush, 368:12
shall mortal m. be more just, 13:35
she knows her m., 241:*n*3
sight make old m. young, 481:3
significance of m., 661:9
silliest woman manage m., 632:14
single sentence for modern m., 790:7
singularly deep young m., 564:8
slothful m. saith, 23:7
small m. may not be entrusted, 63:22
smiling destructive m., 294:12
smiteth a m. so that he die, 9:3
so can any m., 186:5
so frail a thing m., 296:14
so in way in house, 488:3
so is it now I am a m., 392:7
so much one m. can do, 276:25
so near is God to m., 453:16
so unto m. woman, 467:2
so various, 283:15
social friendly honest m., 377:18
social world work of m., 300:8
solid m. of Boston, 467:13
something m. will die for, 823:1
son of m. that thou visitest him, 15:32
sooner kill m. than hawk, 713:10
soul of m. imperishable, 78:3
soul of m. larger, 441:10
spares neither m. nor his works, 353:12
spirit stands by naked m., 844:19
sprang to his feet, 491:14
stage where every m. play part, 187:17
stagger like a drunken m., 19:16
standing by my m., 837:*n*1
state of m. like kingdom, 196:1
stole the fruit, 250:6
stopped moving if ever did move, 694:2
strives for someone to worship, 526:1
strong m. digests experiences, 589:16
strongest m. stands alone, 540:16

Man (*continued*)

style is the m., 321:10
subtle knot which makes us m., 235:5
successful animal, 614:4
such a disagreeable m., 565:6
such master such m., 151:5
sum of all he has acquired, 333:9
superior m. acts before he speaks, 62:15
superior m. is modest, 63:14
survives earthquakes, 543:6
sweet slumbers of virtuous m., 302:1
system where m. exploits m., 805:1
takes drink drink takes man, 579:13
teach you more of m., 390:19
tempt not desperate m., 184:13
temptation but for m. to master, 495:1
that died for men, 571:6
that great and true Amphibium, 255:17
that hangs on favors, 231:2
that has mind and knows it, 610:14
that hath his quiver full, 20:6
that hath no music, 190:7
that hath tongue no man, 176:9
that is a worm, 14:32
that is born of a woman, 14:15
that makes character, 305:21
that m. to man the world o'er, 380:14
that mocks and sets it light, 179:5
that trusteth in man, 29:17
that trusteth in the Lord, 29:17
that was in evening made, 257:21
that which m. is made of, 339:3
that's married, 210:26
there did meet another m., 326:3
there is a m. child conceived, 13:29
thin m., 740:21
think mortal thoughts, 69:18
thinking or working is alone, 507:8
third beast had a face as a m., 48:16
this is Plato's m., 79:4
this is the state of m., 231:2
this m. shall be myself, 331:15
this was a m., 197:22
thou art the m., 12:4
though old m. young gardener, 358:17
thought young m. brings forth, 78:9
tills field lies beneath, 485:14
time ends in killing m., 523:16
time whereof memory of m., 338:10
Time you old gypsy m., 656:11
to a wise m. ports, 179:4
to all country dear, 342:4
to be a great m., 525:1
to be m. with thy might, 569:8
to command, 483:3
to every m. a damsel or two, 10:35
to every m. according to his work, 18:2
to every m. upon earth, 448:14
to laugh proper to m., 145:10
to man so oft unjust always to women, 423:20
to match mountains, 601:5
to men m. is mind, 580:7
to the young m. knowledge and discretion, 20:22
tool-using animal, 433:10
totality of what he might have, 772:5
tree of m. never quiet, 619:1
truly honest m., 272:19

Man (*continued*)

trust m. on his oath or bond, 218:14
try fortunes to last m., 192:4
two words for m., 606:12
tyranny over mind of m., 358:8
unaccommodated m., 216:30
uncorrupted good m., 782:4
unfinished m. and his pain, 640:17
use every m. after desert, 203:26
use money for good of fellow m., 574:8
vain diverse undulating, 152:6
various M., 379:13
vertical m., 775:3
very unclubable m., 327:5
victory shifts from m. to m., 52:33
vindicate ways of God to m., 310:21
want anything said ask m., 816:9
wants but little, 306:7, 341:13
war as is of every m. against every m., 246:11
was it God was it m., 569:9
was there m. dismayed, 484:25
wash that m. outa my hair, 744:8
way of m. with maid, 23:25, 634:6
We created M., 122:12
wealth even to a wicked m., 61:11
well-bred m. knows how to confess, 319:22
well-favored m., 194:33
went mad and bit the m., 341:18
went to Bar as very young m., 564:21
what a chimera is m., 280:8
what a piece of work is m., 203:17
what is American this new m., 352:7
what is m. in nature, 279:16
what is m. that thou art mindful, 15:32
what is m. what is he not, 66:3
what is significance of M., 661:9
what m. can be he must be, 779:11
what m. dare I dare, 221:14
what m. has made of m., 390:16
what m. not know of God, 767:1
what manner of m., 38:19
what may m. within hide, 211:30
what mean m. seeks, 63:19
what signifies life o' m., 378:12
what treaty white m. kept, 549:3
when honor dies m. dead, 468:8
when I get to be m., 652:14
when I search for m., 815:1
when m. can help fellow m., 750:19
when m. of rank an author, 329:8
when m. of real talent dies, 356:16
when right m. rings them, 599:14
where love of m. love of art, 73:2
whiskey life of m., 861:23
white m. warmed before Indians' fire, 346:10
who brings bad news, 67:15
who Broke Bank, 597:9
who craves more is poor, 106:13
who expects nothing, 310:16
who had been promised, 734:11
who has city obedient, 77:13
who has found himself out, 621:20
who is not himself mean, 717:4
who looks part has soul of part, 597:14
who never fought pilfers, 75:2
who owes nothing to land, 331:14

Man (*continued*)

who runs may fight again, 84:6
who said This is mine, 330:17
who sits facing you, 57:20
who touches this touches a m., 521:8
who turnips cries, 325:21
who was a key a m., 798:12
who wasn't there, 676:19
who wert once despot, 428:13
whole duty of m., 25:10
whole relation between m. and woman, 460:13
whom Fortune scratched, 210:30
whom king delighteth to honor, 13:19
who's master who's m., 299:26
who's pure in heart, 764:3
whose blood is snow-broth, 211:1
whose blood warm within, 187:18
why can't woman be more like m., 803:12
wicked m. in bathroom cupboard, 797:11
will cleave to like, 32:27
will no m. say amen, 180:8
will not merely endure, 748:21
wills us slaves, 355:12
wind sweep m. away, 528:21
wine a peep-hole on a m., 57:14
wise and moral m., 66:25
wise in his own conceit, 23:7
wise m. has no extensive knowledge, 59:21
wise m. is strong, 22:39
wise m. knows himself fool, 200:2
wise m. not leave right to chance, 505:16
wise m. speaks, 238:19
wisest m. does not fancy he is, 289:9
with God always in majority, 150:10
with God strive, 421:9
with great things to pursue, 492:24
with seven wives, 857:6
with the head, 483:3
without a flaw, 98:21
without a tear, 409:5
without imagination, 702:25
without money rather than money without man, 64:21
witness unto his deeds, 122:18
wolf to man, 724:21
woman lesser m., 482:5
woman more barbarous than m., 589:4
woman not depend on protection of m., 521:22
woman without m. cannot meet m., 805:5
woman without m. like fish without bicycle, 852:25
women looking-glasses reflecting m., 700:9
wonder and glory of universe, 470:4
word m. defines all rights, 602:7
words guard shape of m., 759:17
work for m. to mend, 285:19
work from sun to sun, 846:16
world without God and m., 822:3
worst use a m. could be put to, 232:18
worth makes the m., 311:12
wrathful m. stirreth up strife, 21:37
writing maketh exact m., 168:16
writing master to world, 714:15

Marrowbone, thinks in a m., 642:3
Marrowbones, better down on m., 637:16
Marry, advice to persons about to m., 591:12
  ancient people, 258:12
  Ann, 609:18
  as easy to m. rich woman, 490:12
  becoming men we wanted to m., 830:9
  better to m. than burn, 44:6
  boy will you m. it, 827:8
  certain person at certain time, 449:7
  error to m. with poets, 792:14
  every woman should m., 459:15
  God let Carlyle and Mrs. Carlyle m.,
    558:11
  he'll come back and m. me, 861:9
  is to halve rights double duties, 425:12
  maiden will you m. me, 564:10
  may m. whom she likes, 490:3
  my body to that dust, 249:1
  people people m., 623:9
  prepared to m. again, 564:19
  proper time to m., 348:20
  this is miching mallecho, 204:22
  your son when you will, 251:13
Marryin', John Thomas m. Lady Jane,
    707:13
Marrying left maiden name disused, 810:4
Mars, an eye like M., 205:21
  Jupiter aligns with M., 834:5
  makes us or m. us, 215:2
  of malcontents, 190:19
  this seat of M., 179:12
Marsh, fragrance of salt m., 521:2
  frogs in the m. mud, 96:9
  hen secretly builds, 583:10
  space 'twixt m. and skies, 583:10
Marshall Plan one of greatest contributions,
    705:8
Marshal's, French soldier carries m. baton,
    388:18
  truncheon, 211:10
Marshes how candid and simple, 583:9
  of Glynn, 583:10
Martha was cumbered with serving, 39:25
Martial, airs m. brisk or grave, 348:10
  airs of England, 415:6
  cloak around him, 427:2
  sounds, 264:15
  swashing and m. outside, 190:5
Martin Elginbrodde, 536:8
  you Doctor M., 821:7
Martini, get into a dry m., 725:12
  medium Vodka dry M., 778:7
  one of happiest marriages on earth, 748:7
  something about M., 763:10
Martin's, bells of St. M., 857:12
  expect Saint M. summer, 171:13
Martlet, temple-haunting m., 219:15
Martyr, deye a m. go to heaven, 134:1
  saint and M. rule from tomb, 720:4
  thou fallest a blessed m., 231:7
Martyrdom, all have not gift of m., 284:21
  Negro willing to risk m., 823:9
  not at all fond of m., 316:24
  to live, 256:14
  torches of m., 358:16
Martyrdoms have crowned church, 116:n3
Martyr's, groan of m. woe, 375:4
  no happiness perfect as m., 626:6

Martyrs, blood of m. seed of Church, 116:n3
  create faith, 631:4
  faith not create m., 631:4
  love m. honor slain, 526:3
  noble army of m., 50:2
  noisy set m. call world, 637:17
Martyrs', out of m. bones elegance, 687:14
Marvel how fishes live in sea, 225:9
  more and more, 653:2
  not Ulysses but Captain M., 826:16
Marveling sweetly on her ills, 724:12
Marvelous, Chatterton m. boy, 392:9
  how m. is Man, 649:2
  in all nature something m., 80:3
  's wonderful 's m., 746:23
  truly m. demonstration, 255:1
  Truth confront us, 812:15
  unknown taken for m., 113:28
  what does not first appear m., 108:8
  what is this m. book, 331:10
Marvels of man's labor, 779:6
Marx case in point, 779:1
Marxian Socialism portent to historians,
    701:15
Marxism, product of bourgeois mind, 703:3
Marxism-Leninism, 787:10
Marxist, all I know is I am not M., 510:13
Mary at thy window be, 380:8
  born of the Virgin M., 50:3
  call cattle home, 513:21
  had a little lamb, 425:11
  hath chosen good part, 39:26
  incarnate of the Virgin M., 50:4
  my M., 348:17
  my sweet Highland M., 380:4
  no God and M. His Mother, 629:22
  quite contrary, 857:11
  Saint Anne mother of M., 573:6
  was that mother mild, 508:9
  young child with M., 33:19
Mary-buds, winking M. begin, 225:12
Maryland, hills of M., 468:14
  my Maryland, 574:6
Mary's, my M. asleep, 379:10
Masai House of God, 754:15
Masculine, the usual m. disillusionment,
    758:6
  values that prevail, 700:10
Mask and antique pageantry, 259:20
  faith under another m., 767:11
  how recognized under m., 784:10
  like Castlereagh, 429:12
  no m. like truth, 300:15
  off reality remains, 93:8
  strike strike through m., 516:13
Masks and revels sweet youth make, 232:1
Mason, mere working m., 397:19
Masonry, lies mortar that bind man into
    social m., 644:10
Masons building roofs of gold, 192:21
Masquerade, truth in m., 424:15
Masquerades as cream, 563:19
Mass and majesty of world, 776:11
  baby figure of giant m., 207:29
  blessed mutter of M., 492:8
  chaos a rough unordered m., 105:12
  I am the m., 681:7
  lead lives of quiet desperation, 506:11
  novelty stains ancient m., 582:20

Mass *(continued)*
  of London itself, 666:3
  of the people, 370:9
  Paris well worth a M., 162:12
  particle of general m., 675:14
  rough unordered m., 105:12
  skies and earth a solid m., 121:18
  spirit which goes through m., 675:14
  the greatest blasphemy, 144:15
  times speed of light squared, 683:n2
  world terrible in m., 575:7
Massachusetts, here's to M., 621:n1
  House of Representatives of M. Bay,
    352:9
  rampant Maenad of M., 569:11
  there she is, 414:16
Massage, medium is m., 786:12
Massa's, old M. gone away, 847:20
Masses, as to what are called the m., 456:15
  back m. against classes, 472:13
  bow ye m., 564:16
  easily fall victims to lie, 726:12
  huddled m., 595:6
  little virtue in action of m., 505:16
  long suits, 731:3
Massive, heard her m. sandal, 735:8
Massy, solid m. hard particles, 291:5
  two m. keys he bore, 261:22
Mast, bends gallant m., 417:7
  like drunken sailor on m., 174:9
  nailed colors to the m., 396:14
  of some great ammiral, 264:9
  what though m. blown overboard,
    173:12
Master, accuse not a servant unto his m.,
    23:23
  artist who bids come to heel, 716:19
  behold m., 317:1
  blessing of Saint Peter's M., 253:9
  calls no man m., 413:2
  card m. to those below, 731:3
  death is m. from Germany, 806:10
  disciple not above m., 35:29
  everyone can m. grief, 194:31
  executioner, 59:18
  fire what a m., 434:25
  great M. said I see, 466:22
  has a new m., 229:32
  hewing wood for m. carpenter, 59:18
  I am m. of fantasy, 603:20
  in limitations the m., 365:23
  into the woods my M. went, 583:12
  Jacky have new m., 858:5
  law m. after my disappearance, 66:23
  lifeblood of m. spirit, 262:22
  look out here comes M. Race, 817:6
  Man is m. of things, 569:10
  man writing m. to world, 714:15
  mistress two slaves, 580:16
  need more to be m., 584:7
  no more subtle m., 486:8
  nor master's man, 557:5
  not be slave not be m., 474:11
  O worthy M., 466:17
  of All Good Workmen, 633:3
  of himself, 244:19
  of himself a happy man, 100:9
  of his fate, 485:22, 727:7
  of my fate, 594:11

Means (*continued*)
give enemies m. of our destruction, 61:9
God placed in our power, 353:2
heaven finds m. to kill joys, 184:19
it m. mischief, 204:22
justifying m. by the end, 118:10
liberty as end and m., 607:1
live within m., 555:17
love of money as m., 701:18
make money by any m., 100:20
mercy of his m., 795:10
not but blunders round meaning, 312:3
of destruction hitherto unknown, 705:5
requisite to ends, 370:14
take m. whereby I live, 190:2
thanks for m. of grace, 50:8
that wins easiest victory, 726:8
thermonuclear war m. to universal
    suicide, 808:8
to do ill deeds, 178:20
to make us one, 235:4
use any m. necessary, 815:11
war political relations by other m., 413:3
what beauty m., 629:2
what I choose it to mean, 552:14
Meant, I m. what I said said what I m., 769:7
more m. than meets ear, 260:9
well tried a little, 599:22
Measles and if so how many, 555:8
Friday died of m., 786:1
love iz like m., 508:11
Measure every wandering planet's course,
    170:4
fervor with m., 583:5
for Measure, 212:9
last full m. of devotion, 476:7
man is m. of all things, 72:1
narrow m. spans, 619:19
observe due m., 56:18
of my days, 17:12
of torment measure of youth, 634:1
shrunk to this little m., 196:18
teach his feet a m., 568:22
there is m. in all things, 98:17
to a merry m., 431:1
what you are speaking about, 536:5
with what m. ye mete, 34:24
Measured by my soul, 303:16
choice word m. phrase, 392:10
it shall be m. to you, 34:24
language, 483:15
motion, 391:8
out my life with coffee spoons, 717:10
Measureless, caverns m. to man, 401:13
rhythms m. and wild, 70:2
shut up in m. content, 220:7
Measures, in short m. life perfect be, 238:14
not men, 314:15, 341:27
Not men but m., 343:16
taken for execution of final solution,
    737:7
Measuring device constructed by observer,
    760:13
earth and heaven, 78:10
Meat, as egg is full of m., 183:26
buys opinions like m., 559:4
cannot eat but little m., 151:9
crazy salad with m., 639:10
dined upon cold m., 288:16

Meat (*continued*)
drink and cloth to us, 146:19
flowers in garden m. in hall, 134:*n*3
God sends m. Devil sends cooks,
    147:*n*11
hungered and ye gave m., 37:17
hungry and he gave him m., 339:8
in due season, 19:11
is not life more than m., 34:17
love not m. nor drink, 735:12
made worms' m. of me, 183:29
mock m. it feeds on, 213:34
not m. but appetite, 270:3
on our m. and on us all, 248:20
one appointed to buy m., 246:1
one man's poison another's m., 93:*n*5
out of the eater came m., 11:1
outdid the m., 248:14
provideth her m. in the summer, 21:4
seek their m. from God, 19:11
sendeth mouth sendeth m., 147:14
sit down and taste my m., 251:3
sleep is m. for the hungry, 158:31
snewed of m. and drynke, 135:4
soft as the leg of an angel, 836:1
some hae m. canna eat, 380:7
stink like rotten m., 762:16
strong m. to them of full age, 46:39
this dish of m. too good, 253:7
upon what m. Caesar feed, 195:21
was locusts and wild honey, 33:25
we are fish and m., 644:8
we hae m. we can eat, 380:7
went without the m., 652:11
within requisite, 546:7
Meat-packer, talent of m., 650:5
Meats, avoid fried m., 774:11
funeral baked m., 201:10
of all m. soonest cloy, 275:4
poking among the m., 817:10
Mecca, sacred temple of M., 121:10
Mechanic, lawyer without history a m.,
    397:19
long m. pacings, 481:4
made poetry m. art, 347:8
sad m. exercise, 483:15
Mechanical equivalent of heat, 583:3
slavery future of world, 605:13
Mechanics, farmers m. and laborers, 386:13
of culture, 649:4
paradise of mathematical sciences, 141:10
reduced to atomic m., 556:6
reduction of nature to m., 536:6
Mechanism, battles by m., 434:2
copying m. for genetic material, 822:2
Mechanisms, of all escape m., 691:14
vital m. have object, 501:2
Mechanized armies, 666:13
automaton, 427:13
Med, bloweth m., 843:5
Med'cinable gum, 215:13
Meddle, inclination to m., 410:6
not with him that flattereth, 22:22
wise men refrain to m., 143:15
Meddles with cold iron, 161:*n*1
Meddling, every fool will be m., 22:18
Medea gathered enchanted herbs, 190:4
Medes, crushed the gold-bearing M., 62:3
law of the M. and Persians, 30:7

Media, hot m. low in participation, 786:11
Medias, in m. res, 101:*n*11
Mediator, painting m. between world and us,
    693:13
president mostly a m., 786:7
Mediatory, reconciling m. power, 402:20
Mediatress, Art m. between nature and man,
    403:16
Medici created and destroyed me, 141:13
Medicinable gum, 215:13
some griefs are m., 225:14
Medicine, cure diseases with m., 785:6
distinguishes man from animals, 595:9
doeth good like m., 22:7
for life which has fled, 60:5
for mental disorders, 743:20
for misery, 70:11
has to examine disease, 111:11
in m. sins of commission mortal, 330:1
live by m. live horribly, 322:18
most distinguished of arts, 73:5
my lawful wife, 622:5
no m. but hope, 211:16
of life, 32:11
thee to sweet sleep, 214:6
words were m., 830:5
worse than malady, 103:*n*1
Medicine Hat, war bonnet of M., 750:9
Medicines to make me love him, 185:12
Medicos marveling sweetly, 724:12
Medieval hand, 564:9
world of Freud, 755:13
Medio tutissimus ibis, 105:*n*10
Mediocre, if you are m. and grovel, 349:7
lots of m. judges people lawyers, 767:15
minds, 274:7
passions, 273:31
Mediocrities, single genius hundred m.,
    566:15
Mediocrity, abilities below m. rewarded,
    405:1
gratified with m., 385:3
history of masterwork not m., 709:12
of apparatus, 689:15
solitude safeguard of m., 456:28
Meditate, in his law doth he m., 15:27
on blood, 193:26
thankless Muse, 261:19
Meditating, in path good lizard m., 751:3
upon whatsoever state, 87:7
Meditation and water wedded forever, 516:6
let us all to m., 172:14
maiden m. fancy-free, 181:9
of my heart, 16:14
where m. neither anxiety nor doubt,
    128:4
Mediterranean, bagful of blue M., 774:14
Mediterraneans see clearly, 702:11
Medium, hot m. like radio cool like
    telephone, 786:11
internal m., 501:1
is massage, 786:12
is message, 786:10
Meek and gentle with these butchers, 196:21
blessed are the m., 33:32
borne his faculties so m., 219:18
gentle Jesus m. and mild, 322:25
he is m. he is mild, 371:16
holy and m. she cries, 373:9

Men *(continued)*

heaven that leads m. to hell, 227:22
His ways with m., 486:10
history biography of great m., 434:17
hit only what they aim at, 506:18
hollow m., 719:4, 719:5
homely m. charmed women, 626:11
honor all m., 47:28
if all m. were just, 75:28
if m. are destroyed, 67:3
if m. could get pregnant, 797:16
if m. like that wise bird, 591:16
impossible m., 743:18
in catalogue ye go for m., 220:31
in m. we various passions find, 310:7
inflation few m. remit, 797:13
is there view for enlisted m., 808:5
keeping m. off keep them on, 307:11
knocking around with m., 363:12
know so little of men, 648:10
labels that give name to event, 542:12
Lake Wobegon where m. are good-
    looking, 837:5
lead lives of quiet desperation, 506:11
let us die like m., 469:7
let us praise famous m., 33:8
let your light shine before m., 34:2
like m. undergo fatigue, 354:14
like satyrs grazing, 170:14
little group of willful m., 611:6
live as m. not ostriches, 699:5
live at level of great m., 602:21
lived like fishes, 225:n1
lives of great m. remind us, 466:2
lodging place of wayfaring m., 29:10
looks quite through deeds of m., 195:23
love is waster of rich m., 68:1
made m. and not made them well,
    204:14
made spectacle to m., 44:2
man that died for m., 571:6
masters of their fates, 195:20
may come men may go, 485:4
may read strange matters, 219:13
measures not m., 314:15, 341:27
melancholy m. eat no beans, 240:12
melancholy m. most witty, 241:5
men's m., 513:14
merriest when from home, 192:23
merry m. all, 853:23
mice and m., 377:12
mighty m. of valor, 10:20
mighty m. which were of old, 6:25
mocks married m., 177:16
moon m. and barking hounds, 742:6
more fortunate than mothers, 596:13
more lonely among m., 507:8
more m. killed by overwork, 632:18
most m. are like children, 700:16
mountains are fountains of m., 572:15
must be decided, 82:6
must endure their going, 217:32
must work women weep, 513:23
my man of m., 223:9
natives of rain rainy m., 686:11
naturally in two parties, 359:10
need of world of m., 492:3
never be beloved by m., 375:8

Men *(continued)*

no common m., 456:15
no compacts between lions and m., 54:2
no country for old m., 639:16
no two m. cannot be distinguished, 108:9
no worse husband than best of m.,
    223:13
nor blame the writings but the m.,
    308:20
not ashamed of age, 808:11
not descended from fearful m., 779:17
not fit that m. be compared with gods,
    94:21
not laugh other men to scorn, 122:10
not m. but manners, 321:20
Not m. but measures, 343:16
not m. you took them for, 194:34
not similar are gods and m., 52:28
not three good m. unhanged, 185:22
O m. in the harbor lane, 85:16
O miserable minds of m., 92:20
O what m. dare do, 194:37
object of making m. happy, 525:17
of Athens, 42:17
of courtly nurture, 534:9
of culture true apostles, 531:17
of despised race, 556:3
of England wherefore plow, 429:6
of few words best, 193:4
of good will, 49:11
of ill judgment ignore good, 67:10
of less value than gold, 143:13
of like passions, 42:14
of my generation, 787:1
of other minds, 341:4
of polite learning, 295:24
of renown, 6:25
of sense are one religion, 277:12
of the South, 679:7
of understanding, 24:30
old m. are all dead, 576:10
old m. are children, 75:1
old m. from chimney corner, 163:26
old m. garrulous by nature, 91:17
old m. know young m. fools, 165:1
old m. ought to be explorers, 721:6
old m. shall dream dreams, 30:22
old m. should be explorers, 781:2
older m. declare war, 672:4
our democratic public m., 610:11
Oxford m. who went abroad to die,
    697:2
parole of literary m., 329:7
peace to m. of good will, 49:11
persuade eyes of m. without orator, 175:2
phrase m. pass hand to mouth, 826:5
place where m. can pray, 664:15
port liquor for m., 328:20
practical m. slaves of defunct economist,
    702:4
praise famous m., 33:8
preached as to dying m., 274:21
private m. enjoy, 193:15
prize the thing ungained, 207:22
proper m. as ever trod, 195:14
proud m. in old age, 68:3
proud m. of action, 442:14
public m. no sure tenure, 727:4
put enemy in their mouths, 213:26

Men *(continued)*

quit you like m., 45:1
quit yourselves like m., 11:18
ready booted and spurred, 448:20
real half-horse half-alligator breed,
    418:17
reject prophets, 526:3
rich m. rule the law, 341:8
rise on stepping-stones, 483:13
rivalship of wisest m., 303:5
roll of common m., 186:4
room for honest m., 354:16
sailors but m., 188:1
saints aid if m. call, 401:8
sandwich m. shuffling, 699:16
savage m. uncouth manners, 344:3
search land of living m., 396:15
see m. as trees walking, 38:26
seldom make passes, 738:13
sensible conscientious m., 326:n6
sensible m. never tell, 459:26
sent not corn for rich m. only, 224:16
setting man free from m., 771:21
should be what they seem, 213:31
shut doors against setting sun, 218:15
sing by land an' sea, 634:9
sit and hear each other groan, 437:8
slain a thousand m. with jawbone, 11:4
slave to fate chance desperate m., 236:8
sleek-headed m., 195:22
small m. afraid of writings, 349:9
small things make base m. proud, 172:16
so many m. so many opinions, 89:12
some m. killed wounded never leave,
    799:12
some m. love not a pig, 189:12
some to pleasure take, 310:8
sons of m. and angels say, 322:23
sons of m. snared in evil time, 24:30
speak with tongues of m., 44:17
spirit of m. who follow, 708:12
spirits of just m., 47:3
strange that m. fear, 196:10
strength of twenty m., 184:11
strong m. shall bow themselves, 25:7
subject m. to external analysis, 595:15
such as sleep o' nights, 195:22
such m. are dangerous, 195:22
take best they can get, 328:12
talk of crabbed old m., 94:4
talking of fall of man, 507:31
text of M. and Women, 617:18
that are ruined, 345:21
that hazard all, 188:22
that laugh and weep, 569:1
that sow and reap, 569:1
that strove with gods, 481:13
themselves m. wrong, 121:4
there before us, 505:25
there He makes m., 415:17
there is danger from all m., 351:2
think all men mortal but themselves,
    306:6
thoughts of m. decay, 161:22
thoughts of m. widened, 482:3
thousand m. that fishes gnawed, 174:3
three merry m. be we, 242:n5
tide in affairs of m., 197:13
tides of m., 723:7

Mighty *(continued)*
    so m. a Redeemer, 49:15
    some have called thee m., 236:7
    sound of m. wind, 41:44
    states characterless, 208:7
    things from small beginnings grow,
       282:15
    true free Russian speech, 512:6
    weak and m. Russia, 527:16
    weak things to confound m., 43:32
Mighty One, splendor of M. Krishna, 87:8
Mignonne allons voir si la rose, 151:*n*2
Migrate, come Muse m. from Greece, 520:5
Migration of the soul, 76:12
Migratory, unperplexed like m. birds, 677:5
Mild and magnificent eye, 491:21
    gentle Jesus meek and m., 322:25
    grateful evening m., 266:18
    he is meek he is m., 371:16
    Mary was mother m., 508:9
    peace on earth mercy m., 323:1
Milder fate than tyranny is death, 65:10
    term to governments, 357:13
Mildewed day in August, 800:11
    silo, 678:1
Mildness, ethereal m. come, 317:19
Mile, crooked m., 860:6
    every m. two in winter, 252:14
    lesson of Three M. Island, 852:24
    miss as good as m., 398:9
Mile-a, your sad tires in a m., 228:24
Miles around wonder grew, 618:13
    of fertile ground, 401:13
    sed m. sed pro patria, 627:4
    see it lap the M., 545:8
    six m. from earth, 793:6
    three thousand m. and died, 515:9
    to go before I sleep, 669:15
    twelve m. from a lemon, 398:23
Milestones, counting m. count on, 472:24
    road to Hell without m., 752:4
Milieu, un m. entre rien et tout, 279:*n*2
Milishy, newspaper commands m., 646:18
Militaristic stairway, 823:8
Military, civilian control of m., 705:10
    establishment, 728:16
    man, 193:5
    mind, 644:15
    no adequate m. defense, 705:5
    now close m. career fade away, 690:12
    operation involves deception, 83:3
    risks sacrifices of m. encounter, 768:3
    war too serious for m., 369:15
Military-industrial complex, 728:16
Militia, newspaper commands m., 646:18
    place dependence upon m., 350:2
    well-regulated m. necessary, 361:2
Milk, adversity's sweet m. philosophy, 184:2
    and honey blest, 511:11
    black m. of daybreak, 806:10
    Carnation M. best in land, 852:16
    comes frozen home in pail, 177:17
    find trout in m., 505:3
    gin was mother's m. to her, 610:8
    in the pan, 454:27
    land flowing with m. and honey, 8:6
    likely to be watered, 559:4
    money is mother's m., 811:7
    my ewes and weep, 229:2

Milk *(continued)*
    of human kindness, 219:10
    of Paradise, 401:19
    skim m. masquerades as cream, 563:19
    sweet m. of concord, 221:34
    take my m. for gall, 219:11
    takes m. cheaper than keep cow, 559:4
    white curd of ass's m., 312:7
Milked cow with crumpled horn, 861:15
Milking, going a-m. sir she said, 859:1
    lilting at ewe m., 340:6
    time of m., 720:16
Milks, love babe that m. me, 219:23
Milk-white, before m. now purple, 181:9
    Hens of Dorking, 500:5
Milky, all the m. sky, 637:3
    over Sado the M. Way, 291:17
    solar walk or m. way, 311:5
    twinkle on m. way, 394:5
    Way sister in whiteness, 689:20
Mill, at the m. with slaves, 268:31
    cannot grind with water that's past,
      251:14
    does m. make water run, 646:7
    God's m. grinds slow, 252:5
    golf links so near m., 677:21
    John Stuart M., 674:5
    much water goeth by m., 149:6
    of the mind, 642:10
    of truism, 455:3
Milldams o' Binnorie, 854:4
Mille, plus de souvenirs que si m. ans, 524:*n*5
Millennial, give vent to m. anger, 805:2
Millennium, war usher in new m., 726:16
Miller, honest m. hath golden thumb, 135:*n*1
    knoweth not of water, 149:6
    sees not all the water, 149:*n*4
    Stuhldreher M. Crowley Layden, 692:6
    there was a jolly m., 352:5
Milliard-headed throng, 310:*n*1
Milliner, perfumed like a m., 185:2
Million, bought St. Louis for six m. dollars,
    560:10
    earth's five m. years old, 825:12
    golden birds, 603:13
    high man aiming at m., 492:24
    make that thousand up a m., 248:7
    multitude of m. divided by m., 771:1
    play pleased not the m., 203:24
    second m., 330:19
Millionaire, I am a M. that is my religion,
    609:28
    right of m. to millions, 559:7
    ruined m., 721:2
Millions, cremate the m., 756:16
    fate of unborn m., 349:14
    for defense, 384:16
    of Bubbles like us, 471:18
    of debt, 345:3
    of spiritual creatures, 266:19
    of tongues record, 420:19
    one murder made villain m. a hero, 349:2
    ready saddled and bridled, 448:20
    right of millionaire to m., 559:7
    sufferings of m., 822:9
    tear-wrung m., 665:*n*4
    there's m. in it, 559:17
    we mortal m. live alone, 529:3
    with m. under his care, 4:5

Millions *(continued)*
    yearly multiplying m., 501:11
    yet unborn, 337:10
Millionth, encounter for m. time, 696:7
Mills, dark Satanic m., 375:17
    of God grind slowly, 255:5
Millstone hanged about neck, 40:4
    hard as a piece of nether m., 15:21
    look through a m., 163:12
Milton aggravated dissociation, 722:12
    attracts into unity of ideal, 403:13
    faith hold which M. held, 393:5
    function as M., 691:5
    malt does more than M., 619:9
    mute inglorious M., 334:21
    reason M. wrote in fetters, 372:13
    test of M. to function as M., 691:5
    thou shouldst be living, 393:3
    was for us, 491:22
Miltonic, balanced and M. style, 588:7
Milton's wormwood words, 262:*n*1
Miltons, no mute inglorious M., 691:5
Miltown, tamed by M., 801:3
Mimic motion made cry, 687:8
Mimics, we are the m., 688:4
Mimsy were borogoves, 551:10
Mince, not to m. the matter, 155:14
    this matter, 213:22
Mincing poetry, 186:7
    walking and m. as they go, 26:16
Mind, a certain unsoundness of m., 447:13
    absence of m. we have borne, 407:28
    accurate m. overtasked, 473:7
    acts of m. itself, 403:15
    all comes from the m., 66:16
    allus on yer m., 693:8
    and soul according, 483:12
    as a dead man out of m., 16:27
    as m. pitched ear pleased, 348:10
    aspire to higher things, 163:24
    aware of own rectitude, 97:2
    balloon of the m., 639:2
    beauty exists in m., 330:5
    beauty momentary in m., 687:5
    become aware of itself, 457:6
    beholding beauty with eye of m., 76:9
    beings of m. are not of clay, 421:8
    benevolence is man's m., 82:13
    best work the human m., 379:13
    beware the middle m., 710:10
    blessed man who possesses keen m.,
      75:22
    block of wax, 78:11
    body filled and vacant m., 193:16
    bonds only in m., 657:15
    breaks chains from every m., 373:10
    bright child of m., 740:18
    celestial Wisdom calms m., 324:11
    chance favors prepared m., 533:8
    changeful m. of mortals, 66:14
    characteristics of vigorous m., 324:12
    chaste breast quiet m., 275:22
    clap padlock on her m., 296:19
    clear your m. of cant, 329:14
    clothed and in right m., 38:23
    companion none like unto m., 150:6
    complicated state of m., 564:8
    concentrates his m. wonderfully, 328:8
    conjunction of the m., 277:8

Mind *(continued)*

conscious m. trained like parrot, 675:8
contemplate itself from without, 595:15
content, 165:17
courage gaiety quiet m., 600:1
creations of m. be blessing, 683:6
dagger of the m., 220:8
daylight in the m., 302:18
disdaining littlenesses, 78:10
disease experience of mortal m., 526:13
diseased always illusion, 501:3
distressed in m. body or estate, 50:7
dupe of the heart, 273:19
education forms common m., 310:3
employ m. to rule, 95:1
enabled to number worlds, 443:5
essay a loose sally of m., 324:16
exercises his m. with suffering, 82:17
extract laws from nature, 695:2
eye see for hand not m., 506:5
face so pleased my m., 844:21
face the mirror of the m., 118:19
fanatic can't change m., 668:6
farewell the tranquil m., 214:8
feed this m. of ours, 390:17
fiery particle, 424:16
first destroys their m., 71:*n*4
first from m. banish understanding,
    71:*n*4
fool uttereth all his m., 23:19
free m. guards rights, 413:2
free play of m., 530:8
frugal m., 347:22
gentle m. by gentle deeds, 161:17
gentle sensitive m., 639:3
gentleness of spirit serenity of m., 252:*n*3
golden m. stoops not, 188:22
good in which m. at rest, 131:19
good m. possesses kingdom, 107:12
great fortitude of m., 326:5
greatest powers of m., 406:21
grief develops m., 658:3
had such burdens on m., 640:8
happy alchemy of m., 317:6
has mountains cliffs, 588:3
has thousand eyes, 600:14
he that wants anger hath maimed m.,
    258:14
heart and m. of America, 776:16
heavy with useless experience, 824:8
her m. to be attached like garden, 584:12
his eyes are in his m., 180:*n*1
his own business, 156:31
household in oneness of m., 54:22
human m. invents Puss-in-Boots, 761:6
I am not in perfect m., 217:30
I had thee least in m., 843:16
idle m. knows not what it wants, 87:16
if find answer know m. of God, 837:3
if I am to know may not m., 706:5
if no hatred in m., 639:13
impatient, 200:31
impressions of free m., 643:9
in adversity keep an even m., 99:21
in another Zeus puts a good m., 53:13
in m. of man a motion, 391:4
in my m. of mankind, 843:11
in purest play like bat, 809:2
in the m. ever burning, 160:2

Mind *(continued)*

inability of m. to correlate, 729:9
inaction saps vigor of m., 141:5
Indian whose untutored m., 311:5
is an aviary, 78:12
is an enchanting thing, 714:20
is its own place, 264:7
is stayed on thee, 27:17
keep m. steady on keel, 515:20
know what going on in baby's m.,
    747:14
knowledge of unconscious activities of
    m., 607:8
known m. of the Lord, 43:14
labyrinthine ways of m., 620:17
last infirmity of noble m., 261:19
laugh that spoke vacant m., 342:3
let dauntless m. still ride, 173:1
leveling rancorous m., 641:1
liberation of the human m., 651:7
live on little with contented m., 93:17
lives on the Heart, 273:*n*1
look clean through the m., 163:12
love looks with the m., 180:21
love Lord with all thy m., 36:43
loyal nature noble m., 486:7
makes body rich, 175:37
man that has m. and knows it, 610:14
man's unconquerable m., 393:2
man's village is his peace of m., 804:5
marble index of a m., 391:9
march of human m. slow, 344:13
Marxism product of bourgeois m., 703:3
measure my mind against Shakespeare's,
    609:29
military m., 644:15
mill of the m., 642:10
mingles with whole frame, 97:29
minister to m. diseased, 222:12
mirror in every m., 325:9
mode of working of human m., 536:15
moldering like wedding-cake, 824:8
movement so wandering as that of m.,
    152:19
moves upon silence, 642:18
my m. forbids to crave, 155:1
my m. is troubled, 208:14
narrowed his m., 343:2
nature of m. mortal, 93:11
nature with equal m., 528:21
never brought to m., 379:8
never m. did m. his grace, 171:10
noble m. here o'erthrown, 204:7
nobler in m. to suffer, 203:33
noblest frailty of m., 291:8
not body enough to cover m., 398:19
not enough to have good m., 253:23
not rival save with m., 741:5
not set m. for or against, 62:21
not sex-typed, 761:13
not to be changed, 264:7
not yet of Percy's m., 185:20
nothing so irrevocable as m., 629:3
of individual thinker, 782:4
of man becomes more beautiful, 391:13
of own beauty m. diseased, 421:20
old in body but never m., 91:16
old man's eagle m., 642:12
one just suited to our m., 409:3

Mind *(continued)*

openness of m., 532:5
opinionated m., 639:14
oppressions of body and m., 359:3
or body to prefer, 311:9
our concern be peace of m., 85:8
out of sight out of m., 138:10
over matter, 443:6
overset m. with reading, 594:14
painter's m. with viewer, 444:6
palm at end of m., 688:18
passion a fever in m., 292:5
passion wholly of m., 747:19
peace is a state of m., 286:13
persecutes the m., 284:19
persuaded in his m., 43:28
poem of act of m., 403:*n*2
poetry fine-spun from m. at peace,
    105:24
power lies in m. and body, 95:1
presence of m. in danger, 287:6
prudent m. can see room, 68:11
purify the m., 66:18
quiet m. cureth all, 242:7
quiet m. richer than crown, 165:16
raise and erect the m., 166:7
reading to m. as exercise to body, 301:13
reason ignis fatuus of m., 293:3
reclothe us in our rightful m., 468:21
reeled the m., 762:6
rest to m. cheerer of spirits, 252:25
seek for the lost m., 82:14
seems to have become a machine, 470:11
serene for contemplation, 301:*n*1
sound m. in sound body, 113:17, 286:8
sound of body and m., 99:16
spirit of a sound m., 46:30
speculate on the m. of Newton, 470:12
Spirit of chainless M., 422:21
steal fire from m., 420:14
stops and steps of m., 719:12
stress on not changing m., 672:15
sublimity the echo of a noble m., 110:11
submitting things to desires of m., 166:7
subsoil of the m., 616:5
Sumner's m. contained itself, 570:12
suspicion haunts guilty m., 173:16
sweet to let m. unbend, 100:17
tact a kind of m.-reading, 595:1
terrible thing to waste, 852:22
the music and the step, 846:14
the music breathing, 275:*n*5
time out of m., 155:16
to me a kingdom is, 155:1
to men man is m., 580:7
to m. shameful to heart beauty, 525:13
torpid in old age, 328:10
tranquil m. a m. well ordered, 115:8
traveled crooked streets, 826:11
troubled captain's m., 580:23
troubled m. be stranger, 249:14
tumors of a troubled m., 269:2
tyranny over m. of man, 358:8
universal frame without m., 167:21
unsuitability of m. and purpose, 498:15
untutored m., 311:5
vacant is mind distressed, 347:16
villain's m., 188:12
was still unpledged, 70:3

Mind *(continued)*
water never formed to m., 687:8
weakness of human m., 286:19
weapon of oppressor m. of oppressed, 839:11
wet m. and say something clever, 74:11
what I am taught, 414:7
what is M. No matter, 591:14
what pleased to call m., 449:6
where is love but in m., 428:17
wisdom entereth not in malicious m., 146:5
words are physicians of m. diseased, 65:20
your m. and you, 708:15
your m. tossing on ocean, 187:13
Minded what they were about, 332:3
Mind-forged manacles I hear, 374:7
Mindful of unhonored dead, 335:1
what is man that thou art m., 15:32
Mindfulness, right m., 66:24
Mindless action, 770:6
of its just honors, 395:19
Mind-reading, tact a kind of m., 595:1
Mind's adventures among masterpieces, 586:16
find the m. construction, 219:9
in my m. eye Horatio, 201:11
my m. not right, 801:7
opaque depths of m. folds, 152:19
putting m. eye in book, 807:7
the standard of man, 303:16
Minds, admiration only of weak m., 268:20
affect hearts and m., 733:1
all their m. transfigured, 182:4
all to have aspiring m., 170:4
balm of hurt m., 220:16
becks m. to fellowship, 436:10
best m. of my generation, 817:12
can heavenly m. yield, 96:24
comfortable m., 739:14
danger spur of great m., 165:12
great empire and little m., 345:1
greatest m. capable of greatest vices, 254:1
grow in spots, 582:20
hearts and m., 51:2
hobgoblin of little m., 455:11
home in m. of men, 74:5
injured by hunger and thirst, 82:19
innocent and quiet, 276:4
keep your hearts and m., 45:37
let our m. be bold, 607:4
little things affect little m., 459:7
lose self in other m., 407:25
made better by presence, 512:14
marriage of true m., 227:17
me o' departed joys, 378:21
mediocre m., 274:7
men of other m., 341:4
mighty m. of old, 405:16
naturally affirmative, 566:20
never do more than imperfectly reach, 745:12
O miserable m. of men, 92:20
of American women, 807:15
of different generations, 708:9
of gods not changed, 54:16

Minds *(continued)*
only function when open, 581:1
paper-weight sat upon men's m., 645:1
reason freed men's m., 107:13
record of best m., 431:10
refuge of weak m., 315:4
religion of feeble m., 345:17
show how myths operate in m., 779:10
so many men so many m., 89:n4
speak m. of others to speak my own better, 152:12
stay our m. be staid, 671:3
steadiest m. to waver, 67:21
strongest m. world hears least, 395:3
themselves our m. impress, 390:17
to different m., 454:1
young men's m. are changeable, 52:20
Mine, because it is all mine, 825:5
every beast of the forest is m., 17:24
eyes have seen glory, 513:18
fatal words M. and Thine, 156:7
I am Tarzan I am yours you are m., 674:12
I'm going to get what's m., 841:4
lives ye led were m., 632:7
lovin' that man of m., 744:2
mother o' m., 633:1
she is m. for life, 804:18
was always like that, 773:14
was ever grief like m., 250:4
what is yours is m., 86:5
what's m. is yours, 212:11
why shouldst thou have m., 270:2
will defend what's m., 159:n4
with my heart in it, 230:1
Mineral, information vegetable animal m., 564:3
Minerals, poisonous m. and that tree, 236:6
Minerva, owl of M. spreads wings, 390:3
Mingle blood with blood of children, 447:4
in one spirit meet m., 429:7
letters m. souls, 235:25
you that m. may, 243:22
Mingled, respect m. with surprise, 397:12
yarn good and ill, 210:27
Mingles, mind m. with whole frame, 97:29
with friendly bowl, 312:14
with her cares sweet bitterness, 94:20
Mingling, understanding distorts by m., 166:14
Minikin won't set fire to Thames, 336:10
Minimum guarantee of First Amendment, 711:2
searcher for fecund m., 686:10
Mining, titles of m. claims, 750:9
Minion, morning's m., 587:6
Minions of the moon, 184:24
Minister, King's First M., 667:9
patient must m. to himself, 222:12
thou flaming m., 215:7
to mind diseased, 222:12
Ministering angel shall my sister be, 206:28
angel thou, 397:1
Ministers, maketh m. flame of fire, 46:37
of grace defend us, 202:4
of Love, 401:22
you murdering m., 219:11
Ministers', my actions are my m., 282:11

Ministry, by the m. of the prophets, 30:20
frost performs secret m., 401:10
secret m. of frost, 401:11
Miniver Cheevy, 652:6
Minnehaha Laughing Water, 467:1
Minnesotan, young M. did heroic thing, 763:n2
Minnows, Triton of the m., 224:26
Minorities are qualified individuals, 702:19
Minority always right, 540:14
coercing into obedience m. groups, 711:4
elite m., 702:14
majority deprive m., 475:5
most vilified m. in history, 695:7
Minstrel Boy to war has gone, 411:16
infirm and old, 396:3
no M. raptures swell, 396:11
wandering m. I, 565:7
Minstrel's, power of m. lyre, 656:18
Mint, tithe of m., 37:2
Mints, lavender m. savory marjoram, 228:26
Minute, do good in m. particulars, 376:5
don't lose head to gain m., 851:6
one m. with him, 704:7
poor benefit of bewildering m., 239:15
speak more in m., 183:23
too late, 190:26
Minutely organized particulars, 376:5
Minute's success pays failure, 495:14
who buys a m. mirth, 175:5
Minutes, five m. with that man, 343:n3
hasten to their end, 226:16
hours and m. dollars and cents, 320:n1
my thoughts are m., 180:15
round earth in forty m., 181:10
sixty diamond m., 441:12
speak for ten m. need week, 611:12
unless m. capons, 184:23
what damned m. tells he, 213:34
world-famous for fifteen m., 819:17
Minutiae of deeds never suggested, 521:14
Minx, don't care whether a M. or Sphinx, 499:5
Miracle, cubic inch of space a m., 521:3
every hour a m., 521:3
man always prays for m., 512:5
monstrosity and m. myself, 154:3
mystery and authority, 526:2
no testimony establish m., 330:7
of rare device, 401:17
of the light, 728:14
r'ar back pass m., 728:4
Miracles, Age of M., 434:19
are past, 210:25
did Jesus in Cana, 40:40
in Israel you must believe in m., 710:15
laughed at, 646:14
propitious accidents, 629:11
Miraculous, falsehood more m. than fact, 330:7
Mirage of social justice, 753:21
works of unbelievers a m., 121:22
Mirages, city of m., 820:10
Miranda, remember inn M., 653:7
Mire, learning cast into m., 345:15
ne'er left man i' m., 218:13
rode him through m., 860:22

Mirror, best m. an old friend, 251:22
cracked from side to side, 480:26
critical m. of culture, 772:10
face the m. of the mind, 118:19
hold m. up to nature, 204:13
in every mind, 325:9
look into lives as into m., 89:13
man's manners a m., 366:5
novel a m. that strolls along highway,
    417:1
of all courtesy, 230:22
of alle curteisye, 136:10
speech a m. of soul, 104:16
that reflects candle, 627:9
thou glorious m., 422:1
understanding is false m., 166:14
you who dirty the m., 293:13
Mirroring, windborne m. soul, 528:17
Mirrors, city of m., 820:10
of shadows futurity casts, 431:11
should reflect, 726:3
Mirth admit me of thy crew, 259:12
and fun fast furious, 379:20
as does not make ashamed, 253:3
bards of Passion and M., 438:9
formed of joy and m., 376:2
he is all m., 194:29
home of m. made desolate, 460:4
I'll use you for my m., 197:9
in funeral, 200:25
in the house of m., 24:17
like flash of lightning, 302:18
limit of becoming m., 176:28
man of marvelous m. and pastimes,
    144:5
May's newfangled m., 176:21
no time for m. and laughter, 643:15
present m., 209:14
required of us m., 20:11
resort of m., 260:5
songs of sadness and m., 466:21
string attuned to m., 445:18
sunburnt m., 437:7
tragical m., 182:5
tumbling m. of sun-split clouds, 810:11
vexed with m. ear of night, 420:3
who buys a minute's m., 175:5
wine women m. laughter, 423:18
with thee I mean to live, 259:21
Misanthropos, I am M., 218:21
Misanthropy and voluptuousness, 447:22
Misapplied, virtue turns vice being m.,
    183:17
Misbehaved once at funeral, 407:8
Misbehavin', ain't m. savin' love, 745:4
Misbeliever, you call me m., 188:8
Miscalled, simple truth m. simplicity,
    226:22
Mischance, ride in triumph over m., 173:1
Mischief, it means m., 204:22
little neglect great m., 320:10
mend whatever m., 640:7
O Diamond thou little knowest m.,
    291:7
Satan finds m., 304:2
that is past and gone, 212:34
virtuous do, 490:16
when to m. mortals bend, 309:12
Mischiefs, dreadful m. from wine, 293:18

Mischievous, gossip is m , 56:19
hatched would grow m., 195:31
Love a m. devil, 559:2
Misdeeds, murder and m., 164:12
Misdemeanors, high crimes and m., 360:14
Misdoings, heartily sorry for m., 50:18
Miser, rich honesty like m., 200:8
Miserable comforters are ye all, 14:19
have no other medicine, 211:16
I have passed m. night, 174:2
Irish childhood, 825:9
made neighbors m., 586:12
me m., 266:3
mercy on us m. offenders, 49:21
minds of men, 92:20
mortals like leaves, 53:31
nothing m. but what is thought so, 120:4
now made m. by white people, 387:9
render last part m., 292:20
sharers of the event, 337:10
sinners, 51:3
to be weak is m., 264:4
train, 394:16
Miserably, men die m. every day, 703:15
Miserere, 17:*n2*
nobis, 49:12
Miseries, ambitions which climb on m.,
    612:16
bound in shallows and m., 197:13
death umpire of men's m., 171:18
delivered from perils and m., 247:6
equal sharing of m., 668:7
getting idea of m., 513:7
of world are misery, 439:12
prolong life only when shorten m., 783:5
Miser's, heaps of m. treasure, 261:1
Misery acquaints with strange bedfellows,
    229:29
companions in m., 104:12
departure is taken for m., 31:16
distant m., 353:10
drink and remember m. no more, 23:26
gave to m. all he had, 335:3
in m. mindful of happy time, 130:15
loves company, 281:10
medicine for m., 70:11
mighty poets in m. dead, 392:11
miseries of world are m., 439:12
no friend in m., 239:3
one man's will all men's m., 162:19
result m., 497:34
so full of m., 480:5
splendid m., 358:6
still delights to trace, 348:21
vow eternal m. together, 294:1
Misfit, good woman The M. said, 815:15
Misfortune, bad neighbor is m., 56:13
in other countries poverty m., 452:7
it's your m. none of my own, 854:13
lose one parent m., 605:9
made throne her seat, 303:13
never delight in another's m., 103:13
of our best friends, 274:15
remembrance of former m., 157:2
shows who not really friends, 81:14
to have been happy is most unhappy m.,
    120:2
war national m., 449:5
Misfortune's, sour m. book, 184:14

Misfortunes, bear another's m. perfectly,
    313:12
by speaking relieve m., 257:9
come from wrong notions, 416:19
crimes and m., 316:20
endure m. of others, 273:2
follies and m. of mankind, 353:8
not unacquainted with m., 55:10
of man occasioned by man, 108:7
Misgiving, room for m., 68:11
Misgivings, not view process with m.,
    666:5
Misgovernment, augur m., 344:10
Mishaps like knives, 515:18
Mislead, lights that m. morn, 211:31
Misleading, analogy least m. thing, 558:21
long run m. guide, 701:14
Misled by fancy's meteor ray, 378:3
simplicity no longer m., 360:7
Mislike me not for complexion, 188:13
not my speeches you m., 172:4
Misprint, poet not survive m., 604:8
Mispronounce, all men m. it, 729:15
Misquote, enough learning to m., 419:15
Miss as good as mile, 398:9
many-splendored thing, 621:7
march of retreating world, 738:9
mine he cannot m., 163:22
Nature cannot m., 285:25
pain that pain to m., 275:10
see nor know nor m. me, 696:18
Miss Lonelyhearts priests of twentieth-
    century, 766:12
Miss T., whatever M. eats, 662:16
Missed, for everything m. gained something,
    455:19
I wouldn't have m. it, 763:17
it lost it forever, 494:20
mr u will not be m., 740:12
never would be m., 565:9
stars might not have m., 670:20
woman much m., 576:2
wonder what you've m., 775:9
Misses an unit, 492:24
Heaven's net m. nothing, 59:17
man who m. opportunity, 369:13
Missing, I am what is m., 830:11
nobody is ever m., 792:9
Rosebud m. piece in jigsaw puzzle,
    749:6
so much and so much, 711:8
what m. at the man's heart, 792:17
Mission, glorious m. of unions, 597:10
to come down alive, 812:8
Missionaries, things she held against m.,
    812:6
Missionary leave China convert Christians,
    562:19
not visited our planet, 516:3
stew, 719:19
Mississippi, commence travels in M.
    steamboat, 413:9
Delta, 837:13
of falsehood called History, 530:13
rolling mile-wide tide along, 560:4
Missouri, 'cross the wide M., 862:3
I am from M., 604:5
sound of rampaging M., 817:4
Misspending time a self-homicide, 289:2

Mist, came both m. and snow, 399:17
    dispelled when woman appears, 307:14
    gray m. on sea's face, 680:15
    in my face, 494:18
    mantled in m., 776:9
    of tears, 620:17
    only m. is real, 794:8
    Scotch m., 515:24
    swoln with rank m., 262:2
    white in blue m. on foam, 502:2
    wrecked in m. of opium, 532:11
Mistake, America giant m., 608:8
    biggest damfool m., 728:17
    blue and gold m., 544:5
    in translation, 297:10
    is has been shall be no m., 389:4
    never overlooks m., 537:1
    not to close eyes, 627:1
    of enclosing envelope, 707:3
    of my life, 560:10
    pardon Thy M., 773:19
    pray make no m., 565:12
    when I make m. it's a beaut, 697:1
    woman God's second m., 589:23
Mistaken, I pronounce m., 274:*n*1
    intuitive calculation, 674:13
    think that we may be m., 660:6
    think that you may be m., 254:12
Mistakes, experience name for m., 604:25
    if you make m. I will protect, 737:6
    man of genius no m., 696:12
    of good man, 360:10
    physician can bury m., 652:16
Mistaking paradox for discovery, 658:14
Mister Death, 739:13
Mistress, art a jealous m., 456:27
    as with maid so with her m., 27:13
    character of m. from dress of maids,
      118:18
    court a m. she denies you, 237:23
    in my own, 634:22
    law a jealous m., 412:16
    literature my m., 622:5
    moderately fair, 275:6
    my m. the open road, 599:12
    necessity m. of nature, 141:8
    no casual m. but wife, 484:7
    no legal slaves except m. of house,
      465:6
    O m. mine, 209:12
    of herself, 310:10
    of mistresses, 524:10
    or a friend, 429:25
    pensive m., 781:7
    riches good handmaid worst m.,
      166:19
    should be like a country retreat,
      290:24
    such m. such Nan, 151:5
    teeming m. barren bride, 310:5
Mistress' eyebrow, 198:25
    my m. eyes nothing like the sun, 228:1
    orders to perform, 313:20
Mistresses, embrace principles or m., 340:8
    hardly any m., 655:4
    mistress of m., 524:10
    others go to bed with m., 602:4
    wives young men's m., 167:15
Mistrust, more ignominious to m., 273:15

Mists, errors wanderings m. and tempests,
    92:*n*12
    foul and ugly m., 184:36
    mothlike in m., 703:12
    season of m., 438:11
    the Apennine, 544:6
Misty moisty morning, 861:8
    mountaintops, 184:5
    out of m. dream, 645:11
    sheiling of m. island, 444:10
Misunderstand, no fate willfully m., 669:5
Misunderstanding, culture a m. if not French,
    590:3
Misunderstands, how often he m. others,
    364:21
Misunderstood, admired through being m.,
    726:4
    to be great to be m., 455:12
Misuse, oft happeth to m. wit, 137:23
Misused, sweet poison of m. wine, 260:16
Mite, can't make m. makes gods, 153:5
Mites, widow threw in two m., 38:30
Mither, father and m. gae mad, 379:7
    leave to m. dear, 853:21
Mithridates, half M., 448:12
    he died old, 619:10
Mitte sectari rosa, 99:*n*13
Mixed, elements so m. in him, 197:22
    in wrong that's all, 723:13
Mixing memory and desire, 718:11
Mixture, good things come in m., 408:2
    that strange m. of blood, 352:7
Mizpah, name of it called M., 7:18
Moab is my washpot, 17:36
Moan, delicious m., 438:6
    English mother made m., 515:9
    frosty wind made m., 547:19
    made sweet m., 439:5
    of doves in elms, 483:8
    paid with m., 620:15
Moananoaning, moyles of it m., 696:18
Moaning, harbor bar m., 513:23
    no m. of the bar, 487:2
    now they are m., 340:6
Moans, amid no earthly m., 478:7
    round with many voices, 481:14
Moat defensive to a house, 179:12
    of risotto, 836:1
Moated grange, 211:27, 480:3
Mob, amphibious ill-born m., 294:17
    at times m. swayed, 671:3
    honor depends on opinion of m., 287:13
    I am the m., 681:7
    is varied and inconstant, 287:13
    not ask better only different, 144:8
    of gentlemen, 313:1
    redress of m. law, 474:4
    supreme governors the m., 336:1
Mobile, donna è m., 97:*n*8
Mobilized, when armies are m., 59:15
Moby Dick whale or man, 736:1
    evil assailable in M., 516:14
Mock, after I have spoken m. on, 14:28
    air with idle state, 335:11
    at the great, 640:8
    fools make a m. at sin, 21:28
    meat it feeds on, 213:34
    on Voltaire Rousseau, 375:2
    spirits of wise m. us, 191:29

Mock *(continued)*
    their own presage, 227:12
    their useful toil, 334:14
    time with fairest show, 220:3
    Turtle, 550:18, 550:19
    your own grinning, 206:24
Mocked, God is not m., 45:24
    my sense is m., 233:3
    smiles as if he m. himself, 195:24
Mocker, wine is a m., 22:17
Mockery king of snow, 180:12
    monumental m., 208:9
    of monumental stone, 430:11
    unreal m. hence, 221:15
Mocketh, whoso m. the poor, 22:4
Mockingbird, listen to the m., 539:14
Mockingbird's, out of m. throat, 520:7
Mocks, man that m. and sets it light, 179:5
    married men, 177:16
    my loss of liberty, 371:10
Model, Americans may become m., 340:7
    British government best m., 370:8
    little m. was Benjamin, 707:8
    of Deportment, 498:22
    of man from Natur's mold, 497:8
    of modern Major-General, 564:3
    republican m. of government, 350:5
    small m. of barren earth, 179:28
    to thy inward greatness, 192:25
Models, turn pages of Greek m., 101:28
Moderate, give m. alarm, 462:4
    liberty is in m. governments, 370:10
    white m. devoted to order, 822:12
Moderately, love m., 183:25
    love m., 183:25
    mistress m. fair, 275:6
    rescue wife, 462:4
Moderation, astonished at my own m., 339:7
    gone no court can save, 660:5
    in all things, 88:10
    in justice no virtue, 355:*n*1
    in principle a vice, 355:2
    in temper a virtue, 355:2
    keep to m., 110:3
    spirit of m. flourishes, 660:5
    stoutness in m., 564:14
    urge me not to m., 462:4
Moderator of passions, 252:25
    reasonable m. Death, 255:19
Modern, all history m., 689:5
    American literature from one book,
      754:13
    disease of m. life, 529:12
    evil in the m. world, 787:11
    feelings of m. life, 788:5
    idea antiquated once m., 663:2
    inconveniences, 560:12
    key-machine of m. industrial age, 744:19
    life economic, 683:2
    man invents museum, 745:1
    old or m. bard, 260:15
    one must be absolutely m., 604:1
    origin of m. world, 757:4
    single sentence for m. man, 790:7
    something for m. stage, 709:2
    spirit Greek discovery, 647:8
    wise saws and m. instances, 198:25
Moderns only have opinions, 442:15
    speak of m. without contempt, 314:23

Morals, code of modern m., 429:25
    conventional m., 661:2
    faith and m. hold, 393:5
    great secret of m. is love, 431:9
    have you no m. man, 610:6
    if your m. make you dreary, 599:21
    man of m. tell me why, 275:9
    of moneychanger, 650:5
    Rome's decline lay in m., 706:11
    time legalizer of m., 690:17
Moravians, no M. in Moon, 516:3
Morbidity, somewhat disgusting m., 701:18
Morbus, senectus insanabilis m. est, 456:*n1*
Mordecai rent his clothes, 13:18
More and more about less and less, 625:16
    and more and more, 552:2
    cantie wi' m., 378:20
    Cawdor shall sleep no m., 220:17
    celebrities such as M., 554:11
    come through alive, 53:20
    easy to take m. than nothing, 550:13
    for I have m., 236:15
    grow from m. to m., 483:12
    how much m. is half than whole, 56:9
    is man of angel's wit, 144:5
    know what is m. than enough, 373:1
    less he spoke m. he heard, 591:16
    little m. than kin, 200:27
    loved Rome m., 196:24
    Macbeth shall sleep no m., 220:17
    matter with less art, 202:34
    meant than meets ear, 260:9
    nicely calculated less or m., 395:16
    no man entitled to, 615:6
    no m. dear love, 483:5
    no m. of that, 215:13
    Oliver asked for m., 496:7
    say m. than this rich praise, 226:26
    sleep no m., 220:16
    the m. he uses for others, 59:21
    the m. the merrier, 149:9
    there isn't any m., 682:8
    to be desired than gold, 16:12
    to say when I am dead, 652:8
    you see m. in you, 767:3
Mores, O tempora O m., 90:8
Mori, pro patria m., 99:*n18*
    ut se m. sentiat, 107:*n9*
Moriarty Napoleon of crime, 617:11
Morir, mejor m. a pie, 679:*n1*
Morison, lovely Mary M., 380:9
Morituri, ave Caesar m. te salutamus, 114:*n8*
Morn and cold indifference, 303:14
    and liquid dew of youth, 201:22
    approach of even or m., 265:25
    as yet 'tis early m., 481:16
    cock trumpet to m., 200:20
    day's at m., 491:2
    dewy m. to dewy night, 556:11
    each M. a thousand Roses, 471:4
    fair laughs the m., 335:13
    from m. to noon he fell, 264:24
    healthy breath of m., 438:17
    in russet mantle clad, 200:23
    incense-breathing M., 334:12
    lark herald of the m., 184:4
    lights that mislead m., 211:31
    lived the space of a m., 164:3
    more bright than Mayday m., 368:15

Morn *(continued)*
    not waking till she sings, 163:16
    on the Indian steep, 260:22
    opening eyelids of the m., 261:16
    peeping in at m., 445:15
    red m. betokened wrack, 173:22
    rose the morrow m., 401:3
    rouse the slumbering m., 259:13
    September m., 468:13
    sweet is breath of m., 266:17
    this the happy m., 258:16
    tresses like the m., 261:9
    ushers in the m., 321:18
    waked by circling hours, 267:10
Morne plaine, 451:*n3*
Mornin', hangin' Danny Deever in m., 633:6
    nice to get up in m., 654:2
    top o' the m., 592:13
Morning after, 643:15
    after Death, 546:8
    air awash with angels, 808:15
    all whom m. sends to roam, 619:16
    almost at odds with m., 221:18
    always m. somewhere, 458:6
    as Adam early in the m., 520:1
    as fed horses in the m., 29:2
    as m. shows the day, 268:24
    as the sun the m. dew, 285:27
    a-walking one m. for pleasure, 854:12
    birdsong at m., 599:13
    breeze of m. moves, 485:9
    come in the m., 501:15
    day's disasters in m. face, 342:8
    Dewey was the m., 580:2
    dissolutely spent Tuesday m., 184:25
    early in m., 862:1
    early in the m. our song, 416:6
    evening and m. were first day, 5:10
    fair came forth, 268:30
    farewell M. Star, 90:6
    feel like m. star, 558:4
    forehead of the m. sky, 262:5
    fresh as the m., 520:15
    full many a glorious m., 226:10
    give him the m. star, 48:12
    glorious m. for America, 337:11
    glut sorrow on m. rose, 438:15
    Good M. Midnight coming Home, 545:1
    good m. sadness, 743:3
    hangin' Danny Deever in m., 633:6
    hear right way in the m., 62:20
    in Bowl of Night, 470:14
    in m. we remember them, 650:6
    in the m. it flourisheth, 18:20
    in the m. like grass, 18:20
    in the m. of the times, 166:*n3*
    in the m. we drink, 806:10
    it was whole m. world, 784:5
    joy cometh in the m., 16:26
    looketh forth as the m., 25:27
    love m. and evening star, 708:6
    matter for May m., 210:12
    misty moisty m., 861:8
    my Lord what a m., 863:7
    my m. incense, 369:2
    never glad confident m., 491:24
    nice to get up in m., 654:2
    of the world, 491:5
    oh what a beautiful m., 744:4

Morning *(continued)*
    penitence next m., 496:31
    praise at m. blame at night, 308:22
    quintessence of life, 425:21
    shadow at m. striding, 718:12
    she will move from mourning into m.,
      789:8
    shining m. face, 198:25
    singing each m., 740:9
    some m. unaware, 492:4
    son of the m., 27:3
    sons of the m., 416:1
    sorrow makes night m., 174:5
    sow thy seed in the m., 25:5
    star you shone among living, 430:*n1*
    stars drift away in invisible m., 819:11
    stars sang together, 15:6
    they that watch for m., 20:8
    think in the m., 372:19
    this m. came home cloak, 288:1
    tonight no m. star, 825:16
    two o'clock in m. courage, 388:14
    uncertain hour before m., 721:18
    white light of m., 855:19
    wings of the m., 20:13
    woe to them that rise early in m., 26:20
    womb of m. dew, 161:6
    would God it were m., 10:10
Morning's at seven, 491:2
    minion, 587:6
Mornings, forgotten m., 795:7
Moron, happy m., 851:14
Morose, obstinate pliant merry m., 111:3
    view of present, 448:17
Morphine, steeped amid honeyed m., 519:12
Morrison, James James M. M., 697:4
Morrow, a little fun and good m., 555:21
    cease to ask what m. will bring, 99:11
    desire of night for the m., 430:21
    every soul look upon m., 122:16
    good m. to our waking souls, 233:11
    good night till it be m., 183:16
    man's yesterday ne'er like m., 427:17
    misty m. a myrie someris day, 133:21
    night urge the m., 430:8
    put no trust in the m., 99:12
    rainy m., 227:2
    rash who reckons on m., 68:14
    rose the m. morn, 401:3
    take no thought for m., 34:22
Mors, nil igitur m. est ad nos, 93:*n3*
    ultima ratio, 124:7
Morsel for a monarch, 223:8
    I found you as a m., 223:27
    under tongue sweet m., 295:14
Morsels, tough m. to swallow, 589:16
Mort, Ô m. vieux capitaine, 524:*n9*
    que la m. me trouve plantant mes choux,
      152:*n7*
Mortal and may err, 254:6
    arm and nerve feel, 397:22
    behind m. Bone, 544:21
    coil, 203:33
    disease experience of m. mind, 526:13
    disgraced and m., 771:12
    dreams no m. dared, 479:4
    element bearable to no m., 785:10
    every tatter in m. dress, 639:17
    frame, 401:22

Mother-in-law, go not empty unto thy m., 11:14
  savage contemplates m., 602:19
Motherless, like a m. child, 862:27
  poor m. Eve, 656:13
Mother's, botanize upon m. grave, 392:2
  cannot bear a m. tears, 98:8
  daughter in m. house, 634:22
  embrace my dead m. ghost, 55:2
  from m. sleep fell into State, 793:6
  from m. womb untimely ripped, 222:21
  gin was m. milk to her, 610:8
  hang us every m. son, 180:27
  hardest to forgive, 771:16
  in search of my m. garden, 839:1
  lie on M. bed, 801:3
  man been m. undisputed darling, 607:14
  money is m. milk, 811:7
  naked out of my m. womb, 13:26
  pride father's joy, 397:15
  sons anchors of m. life, 69:2
  thou art thy m. glass, 225:29
Mothers a bloody brood, 745:2
  and housewives vacationless, 774:10
  good m. and fathers, 766:1
  herd children home to m., 58:6
  men more fortunate than m., 596:13
  men what m. made, 456:24
  men with m. and wives, 446:5
Mothlike in mists, 703:12
Mothproof air, 821:15
Moths among heath and harebells, 509:4
  fill Ithaca full of m., 224:18
  like m. caught by glare, 420:5
Motion and a spirit, 391:4
  between acting and first m., 196:1
  between m. and act, 719:6
  change of m. proportional, 291:3
  devoid of sense and m., 265:4
  endeavor in continual m., 192:20
  final cause produces m., 80:5
  gesture without m., 719:5
  heat as mode of m., 523:20
  heavens rejoice in m., 235:19
  her m. blushed at herself, 212:27
  in one sphere, 187:4
  life meets all m. becomes its soul, 399:9
  meandering with mazy m., 401:15
  measured m., 391:8
  mimic m. made cry, 687:8
  money sets world in m., 103:30
  no m. has she now, 392:1
  of hidden fire, 396:2
  picture involved, 797:3
  scoured with perpetual m., 191:20
  some men forward m. love, 279:4
  speculators about perpetual m., 141:11
  this sensible warm m., 211:23
  uniform m. in right line, 291:2
  what does awesome m. mean, 472:24
  with majestic m., 421:7
Motions, collects m. into shape, 822:10
  molar to molecular m., 578:10
  skittish in all m., 209:21
  soul has many m., 781:5
  stings and m. of sense, 211:1
  to thy m. lovers' seasons run, 234:2

Motive, art framed on single noble m., 533:5
  every joint and m., 208:19
  find m. in this narrative, 560:13
  fruit of action not be m., 87:3
  hunting, 402:17
  let not fruits of action be m., 87:3
  path m. guide, 120:5
  proportional to m. force, 291:3
Motiveless malignity, 402:17
Motives, act on high m., 625:9
  anatomizing of m., 457:6
  idealistic m., 625:9
  of more fancy, 210:34
  strongest of economic m., 613:7
  war begun with highest m., 571:9
  whereby men work, 286:9
Motley fool, 198:14
  made myself m. to the view, 227:15
Motley's the only wear, 198:18
Motor cars and omnibuses, 699:16
Motorcycle parked like soul of junkyard, 811:14
  talk about how to fix a m., 821:6
Motors, sound of horns and m., 718:17
Mots de la tribu, 722:*n*1
  fait des vers avec des m., 584:*n*1
Motto, national m. root hog, 757:2
  of sundial near Venice, 410:15
  that is mankind's m., 276:10
  that is our m., 450:16
  this be our m., 411:2
Mottoes, golden m. in the mouth, 516:25
Moulmein, by old M. Pagoda, 633:12
Moults, wing of friendship never m., 496:28
Mount all eager and quick, 806:3
  mount my soul, 180:17
  pure and disposed to m. to stars, 131:23
  singing of M. Abora, 401:18
  to paradise, 453:12
  up to the heaven, 19:15
  up with wings as eagles, 28:8
  whilst you m. up on high, 180:9
Mountain and deep gloomy wood, 391:3
  as long as shadows touch m. slopes, 97:3
  Big Blue M. Spirit, 855:21
  cannot frighten one born on it, 382:15
  don't care if I see m., 407:3
  down the m. walls, 642:17
  flee as a bird to your m., 16:2
  forked m. or blue promontory, 223:33
  Freedom from m. height, 435:14
  get thee up into the high m., 28:4
  go tell it on the m., 862:28
  God allowed me up the m., 823:10
  heights where bitter joy, 752:10
  huge gap appeared in m., 60:22
  Kilimanjaro highest m., 754:15
  land of m. and flood, 396:12
  lean on mahogany table like m., 789:8
  like dew on m., 397:9
  my holy m., 26:34
  nymph sweet liberty, 259:11
  poem that took place of m., 688:16
  purple m. majesties, 616:3
  rests on earth, 5:1
  robes m. in azure hue, 408:12
  say yes my m. flower, 696:13
  see one m. and see all, 241:3
  shall be made low, 28:1

Mountain *(continued)*
  sheep are sweeter, 418:9
  up the airy m., 535:15
  woods or steepy m. yields, 170:6
Mountaineer, Kremlin's m., 732:2
Mountainous woman not breaks will bend, 792:4
Mountain's, sun over m. rim, 492:3
Mountains, across m. across prairies, 667:5
  Alpine m. cold, 263:15
  at distance airy, 408:*n*1
  beautiful upon the m., 28:18
  before the m. were brought forth, 18:20
  by the winter sea, 486:11
  deer walk upon m., 686:19
  Delectable M., 281:27
  divide us, 444:10
  earth's monuments, 461:1
  England's m. green, 375:17
  faith that could remove m., 44:18
  fountains of men, 572:15
  from m. to prairies, 716:7
  gentle m. remind us, 786:13
  Greenland's icy m., 416:3
  high m. a feeling, 420:26
  in primeval sleep, 534:9
  kings ride elephants over m., 788:4
  labor mouse brought forth, 101:23
  look on Marathon, 424:2
  man to match m., 601:5
  match m. not creep below, 601:*n*3
  mind has m., 588:3
  not reach m. in height, 121:12
  of the Moon, 479:15
  offered this trust to m., 122:6
  on m. is freedom, 382:14
  one is of the sea one of m., 394:23
  over m. over waves, 845:5
  people live in sierras and m., 140:9
  skipped like rams, 19:21
  split m. with thunderbolt, 96:8
  thou deemest m. affixed, 122:1
  though the m. be carried into the sea, 17:21
  three long m., 734:14
  truth bounded by m., 153:6
  want to be buried among m., 543:7
  when men and m. meet, 375:18
  white man bestrode m., 346:10
  yonder m. stand upon base, 382:18
  young hart upon m. of spices, 26:5
Mountainside, following plow along m., 392:9
  from every m., 469:8
Mountaintop, lightning strikes m., 99:24
  standing alone on m., 572:17
Mountaintops, stands tiptoe on misty m., 184:5
  that freeze, 230:27
  who ascends to m., 420:20
Mountebank, mere anatomy a m., 175:1
Mounted, beggars m. run horse to death, 172:23
  to his cabin, 655:9
  Troilus m. Troyan walls, 190:4
Mounteth, courage m. with occasion, 177:23
Mounting at break of day, 394:20
  lives not m. and unfolding, 675:5
  souls m. to God, 541:27
Mounts, in war m. warrior's steed, 396:9

Moves *(continued)*

no life m. in empty passageways, 68:4
she stirs she starts she m., 466:18
sits looking then m. on, 681:9
to see sad sights m. more, 175:10
where I move, 791:12
whole creation m., 484:18
your m. are exactly right, 812:4

Movest, great sphere thou m. in, 223:36

Movie, happy in even bad m., 798:4
hot medium like m., 786:11

Movies, at m. the only modern mystery, 745:16
basic appeal of m., 805:4

Movin' up and down again, 635:16

Moving accidents by flood and field, 212:29
always m. as restless Spheres, 170:4
finger writes, 471:21
forward to greater freedom, 698:1
his slow and m. finger, 214:26
in m. how express, 203:17
into another intensity, 721:6
man has stopped m. if ever did move, 694:2
nightly pitch m. tent, 396:1
others themselves as stone, 227:3
push on keep m., 384:12
tide as m. seems asleep, 487:2
up and down again, 635:16
waters at priestlike task, 439:11
we won't quit m., 829:12

Mown, like rain upon m. grass, 18:9
we multiply whenever m. down, 116:14

Moyles and moyles of it, 696:18

Mozart last chord of European taste, 589:10
some cry up M., 407:22
when M. was my age, 821:1
when u are M., 818:2

Much, and this is m., 420:19
by m. too m., 186:13
don't say too m., 777:9
drinking little thinking, 298:2
enough or too m., 373:5
faithful in m., 40:1
given much required, 39:31, 799:6
have I seen and known, 481:9
have I traveled, 435:19
I do not ask you m., 178:27
in few words, 33:1
is force of heaven-bred poesy, 176:11
know too m. convinced of too little, 722:15
lady doth protest too m., 205:4
learning doth make thee mad, 42:35
learning not teach understanding, 64:5
little happy if I could say how m., 194:20
missing so m. and so m., 711:8
no man wanted m., 456:13
not many but m., 124:10
nothing too m., 57:1
of a muchness, 297:12, 513:14, 550:14
of Madness, 478:14
once that seemed too m., 669:16
safer too little than too m., 558:12
see so m. nor live so long, 218:9
so m. depends upon, 703:10
so m. for him, 200:26
so m. owed by so many, 666:4
so m. to do, 484:8, 602:13

Much *(continued)*

talk too m., 283:14
those who have too m., 698:7
too m. of good thing, 156:4
unjust in m., 40:1
what he loves never like too m., 237:21
wrested from sure defeat, 723:8

Muchness, much of a m., 297:12, 513:14, 550:14

Muck, all of a m. of sweat, 341:14
know when to stop raking m., 615:8
money is like m., 167:20
whole world is m., 615:8

Mucking up parents' lives, 831:18

Muckle, twice as m. 's a' that, 380:15

Muckrake in his hand, 282:2

Muckrakes, men with m. indispensable, 615:8

Mud, alive and wagging tail in m., 83:2
flies from wings, 800:9
fragrance of salt marsh shore m., 521:2
frogs in the marsh m., 96:9
garlic and sapphires in m., 720:9
in Black M. kingfisher, 800:9
in m. eel is, 860:10
life made of marble and m., 460:17
silk stocking filled with m., 388:16
silver fountains have m., 226:11

Muddied oafs at goals, 635:8

Muddle through, 489:5

Muddled, Don Quixote's a m. fool, 158:8
state sharpest of realities, 585:12

Muddlement, constant force for m., 585:12

Muddy ill-seeming thick, 176:1
mastodons like m. buses, 821:15
vesture of decay, 190:5
waist deep in Big M., 806:1

Mud-luscious, world is m., 739:11

Mudville, no joy in M., 630:4

Muffet, little Miss M., 860:3

Muffin man, 860:14

Muffins, no more inspiration than plate of m., 609:18

Muffled and dumb, 453:18
oars, 405:3

Muffler, Fortune painted blind with m., 168:n1

Mug's, poetry m. game, 722:21

Mugwump educated beyond intellect, 567:14

Muhammad, heart of M., 122:13
I M. am only a warner, 121:1

Mule, Democratic Party like m., 548:8
nigger woman m. uh de world, 761:1

Multa, non m. sed multum, 124:10

Multeity in Unity, 402:18

Multifold, dying m., 546:4

Multiplication is vexation, 843:21

Multiplied, deviation from truth is m., 80:2
entities not m. unnecessarily, 132:10
visions, 30:20

Multiplieth words without knowledge, 15:2

Multiply, be fruitful and m., 5:14
in us a brighter ray, 421:8
survive and m., 469:15
thanks to art see world m., 658:4
thoughts, 783:1
we m. whenever mown down, 116:14

Multitude a Hydra, 100:n13
always in the wrong, 287:22
as the sand by the sea in m., 12:12

Multitude *(continued)*

barbarous m., 188:26
beast of many heads, 100:n13
charity creates m. of sins, 605:14
charity shall cover m. of sins, 47:31
could not name the m., 52:17
discordant wavering m., 191:6
efforts of busy m., 534:8
many-headed m., 100:n13, 224:22
of counsellors, 21:17
of days, 324:8
of friends, 237:9
of million divided by million, 771:1
of rulers, 52:15
of sins, 47:31
rude m. call afternoon, 177:11
swinish m., 345:15
that choose by show, 188:25

Multitudes, against revolted m., 267:11
I am large contain m., 519:21
in the valley of decision, 30:23
pestilence-stricken m., 428:21
vast m. of Russia, 666:13

Multitudinous seas incarnadine, 220:19

Multiversity, university become m., 786:7

Mum, cry m., 158:n6
merryman moping on, 565:25
they fuck you up your m. and dad, 810:8

Mumbo-Jumbo God of the Congo, 685:5

Mumbo jumbos, soot-smeared M., 433:4

Mummers, grave m., 313:19

Mummy, yesterday embryo tomorrow a m., 115:19

Mum's the word, 158:29

Munch your good dry oats, 181:25

Munched and munched and munched, 218:26

Mundi, flammantia moenia m., 92:n6
Stupor M., 800:9

Mundus, fiat justitia et pereat m., 123:n7
quantilla prudentia m. regatur, 145:n1

Munich, wave M. all thy banners, 408:20

Munny, doänt marry for m., 486:20
goä wheer m. is, 486:20

Muove, e pur si m., 169:n3

Murder and misdeeds, 164:12
brother's m., 205:14
cannot be hid, 137:n3
contrived husband's m., 55:5
from battle and m., 50:13
get the curse out of m., 796:4
how easily m. discovered, 137:n3
I'll m. de bum, 784:14
indulges himself in m., 418:6
infant in cradle, 373:3
land for private profit, 782:5
Macbeth does m. sleep, 220:16
make m. respectable, 765:13
met M. on the way, 429:12
most foul, 202:13
one m. made a villain, 349:2
one to destroy is m., 305:20
sacrilegious m., 220:23
shrieks out, 137:n3
speak with miraculous organ, 137:n3
thousands, 305:20
time to m. and create, 717:8
war I call it m., 514:21

N

Names *(continued)*

  great n. as these, 846:11
  judge of authors' n., 308:20
  Moss covered up our n., 545:5
  never allow n. mentioned, 406:11
  new-made honor forget men's n., 177:20
  not born to die, 426:7
  of those who fought for life, 783:16
  sharp n. never get fat, 750:9
  their botany Latin n., 453:10
  tongues that syllable men's n., 260:24
  two most sacred n., 275:19
  unpopular n. impossible loyalties, 530:10
  What and Why and When, 635:9
  whom love of God blessed, 417:15
  written in letters of gold, 145:6
Naming, to-day we have n. of parts, 794:12
Nan, such mistress such N., 151:5
Nancy, mate of N. brig, 563:11
Nane sall ken where he is gane, 854:8
Nap after dinner silver before dinner golden,
    542:9
Napalm, smell of n. in morning, 833:11
Napoleon, ashes of N. Bonaparte, 389:5
  celebrities such as N., 554:11
  mighty somnambulist, 451:9
  Moriarty the N. of crime, 617:11
  sole obstacle to peace, 388:7
  was twice defeated, 510:*n*2
Napping, nodded nearly n., 478:20
Narcotics alcohol and Christianity, 589:17
  hospital tray of n., 787:18
  numbing pain, 483:15
  two great European n., 589:17
Narrative as whole untrue, 534:10
  bald and unconvincing n., 565:18
  motive in this n., 560:13
Narrator imbue self with the time, 534:10
Narrow, bestride the n. world, 195:20
  convent's n. room, 394:17
  creep into n. bed, 531:3
  every bed is n., 735:5
  Fellow in the Grass, 546:2
  honor in strait so n., 208:10
  in n. cell forever laid, 334:11
  into its n. shed, 639:2
  is the way, 35:6
  margin too n. to contain demonstration,
    255:1
  measure spans, 619:19
  track to highest good, 93:20
  two n. words Hic jacet, 160:13
  when find road n., 127:5
Narrowed his mind, 343:2
Narrowing lust of gold, 484:15
Narrow-mindedness, superior man will not
    manifest n., 81:23
Narrow-necked bottles, 313:13
Narrowness, grave's n., 743:17
Narrow-souled people, 313:13
Narvus, I have been rather n., 439:*n*3
Nascitur, poeta n. non fit, 114:*n*11
Nassau, can Bourbon or N. go higher, 297:7
Nastiest thing in nicest way, 713:5
Nastily, live meanly and n., 288:22
Nasty brutish and short, 246:12
  man of n. ideas, 298:7
  not n. dirty hole, 736:3
  something n. in woodshed, 762:5

Natal, Rome n. neath my consulship, 91:10
Natchez, belle of old N., 763:11
Nation, America's my n., 749:13
  as Maine so goes n., 849:8
  better one suffer than n. grieve, 283:13
  commit to landing man on moon, 799:11
  conceived in Liberty, 476:7
  darlings of our n., 212:23
  defects as n. to use weasel words, 615:17
  fate of n. in own power, 449:4
  fate of n. riding, 467:16
  favors from n. to n., 350:12
  from single crime know n., 97:7
  genocide destruction of n. ethnic group,
    758:5
  Germany a n. a race, 444:8
  God hath sifted a n., 286:1
  greatness of British N., 302:19
  grown-up n., 768:2
  guarantees maintenance of citizen,
    596:11
  guiding-star of whole brave n., 502:5
  hardly yet a n., 710:1
  has government it deserves, 368:16
  has history of sex discrimination, 774:5
  haughty n. proud in arms, 260:14
  hoop of n., 628:1
  Horse n., 855:17
  ignorant and free, 359:2
  judged by best not worst, 656:17
  kinder gentler n., 813:11
  light shone to whole n., 247:10
  like pitiful helpless giant, 790:23
  literature memory of n., 804:11
  look beyond n. and race, 802:12
  make all ballads of n., 294:13
  middle class in America the n., 532:7
  most important element in n., 82:20
  moving toward two societies, 779:8
  ne'er would thrive, 296:20
  no n. greater than any other, 731:8
  no n. ruined by trade, 320:22
  no single n. have monopoly, 705:5
  not flag only but n., 500:14
  not only Latin-American n., 817:9
  of brutes, 612:*n*2
  of communities, 813:9
  of freemen, 474:3
  of shopkeepers, 338:19
  once to every man and n., 514:12
  one n. under God, 606:17
  one-third of a n., 698:6
  paramount question for n., 509:15
  perpetually to be conquered, 344:7
  plant a n., 243:23
  preserved us a n., 411:2
  principles and traditions of this n., 798:1
  publish it to all the n., 297:5
  puissant n., 263:3
  righteousness exalteth a n., 21:33
  rise against nation, 37:6
  secure only while honest, 510:1
  serve my n. ruin another, 314:10
  shall not lift up sword, 26:11
  shopkeeping n., 331:22
  slave-holding n., 450:6
  small one become a strong n., 28:30
  so conceived so dedicated, 476:7
  social prosperity means n. great, 451:16

Nation *(continued)*

  supports Wall Street, 646:14
  tardy apish n., 179:10
  territory not make n., 537:9
  that that n. might live, 476:7
  this n. under God, 476:7
  trick of our English n., 191:19
  truths which can kill n., 695:11
  turns its lonely eyes to you, 837:9
  values anything more than freedom,
    673:4
  vengeance ask and cry on whole n.,
    141:21
  we are here by will of n., 366:16
  we are n. building, 713:4
  what it can do for n., 799:*n*2
  which enjoys most freedom most
    powerful, 386:1
  which keepeth the truth, 27:17
  worthy of mighty n., 747:3
National, Chinese not have n. spirit, 644:8
  compass of n. authority, 370:15
  consciousness, 611:2
  debt national blessing, 370:7, 414:15
  don't call out N. Guard, 705:2
  events decided by power elite, 798:2
  guitar, 837:13
  honor is national property, 376:15
  motto root hog, 757:2
  nightmare over, 790:15
  rock of n. resources, 415:5
  stain washed clean, 728:9
  there is N. flag, 490:7
Nationalism, orthodox in n., 734:1
Nationalities, squabbling n., 615:16
Nation's, bind up n. wounds, 477:4
  confidence, 807:9
  freight handler, 681:8
  law embodies n. development, 577:14
  read history in n. eyes, 334:22
  spirit die of inanition, 530:8
  ultimate judicial tribunal, 695:8
Nations abandon use of force, 699:9
  all n. and kindreds, 48:23
  all n. gathered, 37:16
  all n. one blood, 42:18
  are as a drop of a bucket, 28:6
  are destroyed or flourish, 376:4
  astonishment among all n., 10:9
  be and make new n., 231:17
  belong to other n., 564:1
  breathes of n. saved, 424:12
  civilized n. will recoil from war, 554:9
  day of small n. past, 563:10
  dwelling in safety, 699:8
  eclipsed gaiety of n., 325:10
  equal right of n., 705:15
  Europe prison of n., 686:3
  father of many n., 7:5
  fierce contending n., 302:2
  foreign n. and the next age, 168:19
  general association of n., 611:11
  get better of other n., 761:15
  go and teach all n., 38:12
  government of n., 608:4
  great n. not boasters, 456:23
  great when ideal higher, 530:2
  happiest n. have no history, 513:4
  individuals of all n., 352:7

Nature *(continued)*

habits form second n., 362:8
happiness depends as N. shows, 347:5
happiness of retired n., 302:7
hath framed strange fellows, 187:15
he is great who is from N., 456:16
he of calm and happy n., 77:1
heav'n and n. sing, 304:9
her custom holds, 206:14
her masterpiece designed, 379:13
highest type of human n., 523:14
hints and half-truths, 566:19
hold mirror up to n., 204:13
human n. finer, 440:7
human n. seeming born again, 391:10
I fear thy n., 219:10
I feel the link of n., 268:4
I loved, 408:11
I was escaping from N., 772:9
if n. conquers, 382:8
imagination one of forces of n., 689:8
impartiality of N. best, 566:22
in almost every artist n., 676:16
in her inventions, 141:9
in love of N. holds, 432:7
in n. few sharp lines, 816:14
in our life N. live, 402:5
in perfect n. no distinction of kind, 82:27
in state of war by n., 299:3
in terms of cylinder sphere cone, 572:20
in you stands on verge, 216:13
Indian unconstrained in N., 504:24
is but art unknown, 311:8
is the art of God, 255:14
is there any cause in n., 217:6
is wont to hide herself, 64:4
kindly bent to ease us, 274:*n*2
knowledge of human n., 406:21, 570:3
knows her business better than we do, 154:8
law of n. and nations, 345:9
laws of n. and nature's God, 357:2
laws which mind put into n., 695:2
learned to look on n., 391:4
liberty taken with N., 571:3
lies within something of another n., 812:14
limited n. infinite desires, 426:10
line in n. is not found, 452:20
link of n., 268:4
little we see in N., 394:18
living in agreement with n., 84:13
living N. not Art, 449:21
looking at objects of N., 402:14
looks through N. up, 311:14
losses wrought by n., 362:7
lost their original n., 82:26
loyal n. noble mind, 486:7
lusty stealth of n., 215:26
made a pause, 306:1
made him then broke mold, 143:8
made one with N., 430:15
made thee to temper man, 294:2
man as n. made him, 331:15
man by n. political animal, 80:21
man explorer of n., 778:3
man's efforts to control n., 727:12
man's n. cultural product, 757:12

Nature *(continued)*

means God of N. placed in our power, 353:2
men by n. desire knowledge, 80:4
men by n. equally free, 339:9
men gained control over n., 607:17
might stand up and say, 197:22
mingling its n. with n. of things, 166:14
mistress and guardian of n., 141:8
modesty of n., 204:12
more than n. needs, 216:15
mortal n. did tremble, 393:15
muse on N. with poet's eye, 408:14
must obey necessity, 197:15
my n. is subdued, 227:16
my Treatise of Human N., 330:9
needed not books to read N., 282:17
never deceives us, 331:9
never did betray, 391:5
never makes blunders, 508:12
no arrogant wonders of n., 472:23
no chance of understanding n., 574:5
no part N. has not touched, 116:8
no such thing in N., 269:*n*1
noble and incapable of deceit, 398:8
noble n. poetically gifted, 530:1
not from philosophers but n., 242:11
not man less but N. more, 421:25
not proceed by leaps, 322:19
nothing at prompting of n. but weep, 108:6
nothing in n. without purpose, 465:11
nothing purposeless trivial unnecessary, 127:7
observer of human n., 495:19
of an hypothesis, 332:19
of desire not to be satisfied, 80:25
of mind mortal, 93:11
of the thing, 818:8
often hidden, 168:9
once out of n., 640:2
one and continuous, 506:2
one touch of n., 208:12
outrage when man destroys n., 678:15
owes me another existence, 364:27
paint falsely add accent of n., 555:18
passing through n. to eternity, 200:28
passion could not shake, 214:23
pattern of excelling n., 215:7
progress part of n., 523:2
prophets of N., 391:13
qu'est-ce que l'homme dans la n., 279:*n*2
recover hair bald by n., 174:29
red in tooth and claw, 484:6
reduce problems of n. to numbers, 548:13
reduction of n. to mechanics, 536:6
renews annual round untired, 678:15
rest in N. not God, 250:18
reverence human n., 412:18
rich with spoils of N., 255:12
rules of game laws of N., 537:1
science of N., 289:4
science right interpretation of n., 432:19
secret of study of n., 461:15
secretary of N., 253:10
seems dead, 220:9
sighing through her works, 267:30
silent energy of n., 449:15

Nature *(continued)*

simple n. to his hope given, 311:5
simple News N. told, 545:3
sloping to southern side, 515:13
so priketh n. in hir corages, 134:16
sociability law of n., 583:8
some made coxcombs n. meant fools, 308:9
something marvelous in all n., 80:3
such stupidity not in N., 327:2
suffers n. of insurrection, 196:1
sullenness against N., 262:20
swears lovely dears, 378:13
teaches beasts to know friends, 224:19
teaches more than preaches, 566:21
tendency of man's n. to good, 82:10
that framed us, 170:4
things rank and gross in n., 201:2
think of our life in n., 505:13
thou and n. so gently part, 224:11
thoughts n. gives way to, 220:6
thrust into n. like wedge, 506:2
to advantage dressed, 308:12
to be commanded must be obeyed, 166:15
to him who in love of N., 432:7
to read N. he looked inwards, 282:17
to white man n. wilderness, 650:1
to write and read comes by n., 194:33
too noble for world, 224:28
trees and all n., 855:15
trying to make us succeed, 743:14
understanding distorts n. of things, 166:14
universal n. say, 323:*n*1
usura sin against n., 709:9
vicaire of almyghty lorde, 133:13
voice of n. cries, 334:25
voice of N. cries, 379:12
war of n., 470:3
war of n. is not incessant, 469:15
we fools of n., 202:6
what fools call N., 494:30
what is man in n., 279:16
what put into world to rise above, 781:18
what tell you about n. of life, 793:13
when n. makes fool she means it, 508:12
wherefore thus partial, 141:12
with equal mind, 528:21
without voice or sound, 337:16
words like N. half reveal, 483:14
works by means of bodies unseen, 92:15
write in spite of N., 271:7
yet do I fear thy n., 219:10
yet remembers, 393:14
you've conquered human n., 496:16
Nature-faker, 615:10
Nature's above art, 217:19
beauty is N. brag, 261:9
beauty is N. coin, 261:8
chief masterpiece, 293:7
crack n. molds, 216:18
Darling, 335:7
debt to N. quickly paid, 249:9
discipline enjoins mutual help, 757:6
eye N. walks, 310:21
fever is N. instrument, 280:17

Necks, heads erect instead of bowing n., 118:23
　walk with stretched forth n., 26:16
Nectar in a sieve, 402:12
　of Jove's n. sup, 238:2
Nectared, feast of n. sweets, 261:3
Need, all men have n. of gods, 54:15
　all we n. of hell, 547:3
　all ye n. to know, 438:5
　consume according to n., 510:n5
　deserted at utmost n., 285:12
　disposed to one another by n., 114:18
　distribution according to n., 42:2
　England hath n. of thee, 393:3
　everywhere we have n. of Zeus, 85:6
　France has more n. of me, 388:4
　friend in n., 86:14
　how little we n., 621:15
　how many things no n. of, 72:4
　I had most n. of blessing, 220:15
　in thy n. go by thy side, 843:17
　na start awa sae hasty, 377:10
　no n. for tongue, 780:2
　no n. of valor, 75:28
　no n. to get out of bed, 809:12
　nothing can n. a lie, 249:18
　of world of men, 492:3
　people who n. people, 810:12
　pray in distress and n., 700:21
　someone we can lean on, 838:6
　thy n. greater than mine, 164:n2
　to know to stay alive, 826:11
　we shall n. no other light, 366:n4
　what is natural is n., 417:2
　where love and n. one, 670:6
　you don't n. weather man, 836:9
　you get what you n., 838:7
　you n. God God needs you, 679:8
Needed, all n. by each, 452:16
　Harlem n. something to smash, 813:5
　six feet all he n., 543:3
　traitor no longer n., 254:20
Needful, one thing is n., 39:26
Needle, for the n. she, 483:3
　go through eye of n., 36:34
　in bottle of hay, 158:4
　in haystack, 158:n1
　lean as compass-n., 801:11
　plying n. and thread, 446:2
　true as n. to pole, 271:n1
Needle's, see out of n. eye, 497:4
Needles, into waves pine n., 291:15
Needless Alexandrine ends song, 308:17
　omit n. words, 652:12
　Show, 545:7
　to blame things past, 62:18
　to speak about things done, 62:18
Needs, country n. and demands, 697:12
　fair n. foul I cried, 641:14
　gives 'er all she n., 634:17
　go whom devil drive, 149:7
　man in search of what n., 601:10
　more than nature n., 216:15
　to each according to n., 510:11
　we must n. die, 12:6
Needy hollow-eyed sharp-looking wretch, 175:1
　I am poor and n., 19:17
　make not n. eyes to wait, 32:1

Needy *(continued)*
　not for n. but for greedy, 699:1
　store money in stomachs of n., 118:29
　strength to the n., 27:14
Negation, faith in n., 631:5
　my art n. of society, 577:6
Negations of man, 815:1
Negative Capability, 440:3
　feelings about marriage, 293:14
　inversion, 775:4
Neglect creeping hours, 198:22
　easier to mend n. than quicken love, 118:2
　God and his angels, 236:22
　heart's case must kings n., 193:15
　little n. great mischief, 320:10
　monuments of unaging intellect, 639:16
　perpetual n. of things, 598:11
　sweet n. more taketh me, 237:16
　wise and salutary n., 344:6
Neglectful Nature wherefore thus partial, 141:12
Neglects, whoso n. learning in youth, 71:4
Negligence, let friendship die by n., 329:11
Negligences, noble n., 297:3
Negligent, celerity admired by n., 223:23
Negligible, discriminate between important and n., 682:6
Negotiate, every eye n. for itself, 194:18
　never fear to n., 799:8
　never n. out of fear, 799:8
　only free men can n., 803:16
Negro, American N. problem in heart of American, 752:8
　blood sure powerful, 763:1
　boy with curlicues, 801:1
　cool strong imperturbable, 509:16
　dehumanizing the N., 474:12
　duty of younger N. artist, 762:8
　I am a N., 762:10
　I am N. and beautiful, 762:8
　school-children, 801:13
　those who hate N. see hatred in N., 602:9
　through n. streets, 817:12
　treatment of N. greatest scandal, 752:9
　two-ness an American a N., 648:11
　what does N. want, 674:7
　willing to risk martyrdom, 823:9
Negroes, hear bronze N. breathe, 801:11
　not women or N. but citizens, 503:9
Negro's great stumblingblock, 822:12
　skin prima facie evidence, 503:7
Neiges, où sont les n. d'antan, 139:n4
Neigh, how joyous his n., 856:3
　like Boanerges, 545:9
Neighbor, bad n. is misfortune, 56:13
　better a n. that is near, 23:13
　dagger into back of n., 698:12
　eye n. as enemy, 660:8
　false witness against thy n., 9:1
　good n. policy, 697:16
　hate your n., 447:22
　he promised to defend, 448:11
　helped every one his n., 28:9
　let n. carve for you, 299:5
　love n. yet pull not down hedge, 251:12
　love thy n., 36:43
　love thy n. as thyself, 9:15

Neighbor *(continued)*
　not look to see what n. does, 115:10
　of nothing, 830:13
　tyranny of next-door n., 538:7
　what hateful to you do not to n., 106:1
Neighboring communities overlook one another, 59:20
　cynosure of n. eyes, 259:15
Neighbor's, life to n. creed lent, 452:16
　neighed after his n. wife, 29:2
　not covet thy n. wife, 9:1
　not covet thy n. house, 9:1
　not move sickle unto n. corn, 10:7
　your concern when n. wall on fire, 101:9
Neighbors, borrowing everything of n., 288:22
　call n. in, 858:1
　first to attack their n., 277:18
　good fences good n., 668:19
　innocence of our n., 507:15
　live as good n., 705:15
　made n. miserable, 586:12
　make sport for n., 406:12
　more right than n., 505:18
　who practices virtue will have n., 62:24
Neighed after his neighbor's wife, 29:2
Neighing canyons, 753:16
　farewell the n. steed, 214:8
　in likeness of filly foal, 181:5
Neighs, high and boastful n., 193:11
Neither, do two things at once do n., 102:15
Nell, death of Little N. without laughing, 606:4
Nelly, let not poor N. starve, 282:12
Nelson touch, 627:7
Nemean, hardy as N. lion's nerve, 202:9
Nemo me impune lacessit, 124:8
　repente fuit turpissimus, 113:n3
Neon Renaissance, 826:16
Nephew of my Uncle Sam's, 679:11
　turned out to be my n., 831:2
Neptune, envious siege of watery N., 179:13
　flatter N. for trident, 224:28
　floods which N. obey, 845:5
　sink ship on even keel, 106:24
Neptune's ocean wash this blood, 220:19
Neque semper arcum, 99:n17
Nero, tyranny of N., 538:7
Nerve, a lot of n., 829:12
　all air and n., 801:4
　hardy as Nemean lion's n., 202:9
　iron n., 484:22
　mortal arm and n. feel, 397:22
　o'er which do creep, 428:18
　stretch every n., 318:12
Nerve-racking, hypocrisy is a n. vice, 672:22
Nerves, ganglion in n. of society, 578:2
　my firm n. never tremble, 221:14
　trifles irritate my n., 518:3
Nervous, I have been rather n., 439:n3
　renewal of relations n. matter, 570:11
　tough but n., 715:4
Nessus, shirt of N. upon me, 223:32
　shirts, 433:22
Nest, bird that filleth own n., 141:19
　builds phoenix' n., 272:17
　eagle make n. on high, 15:16
　feathered his n. well, 243:11
　good to keep n. egg, 158:1

Nightingale *(continued)*
    sings round it, 412:11
    that on yon bloomy spray, 262:7
    wakeful n., 266:16
    when May is past, 253:14
Nightingales are singing near Convent, 718:10
    silent when eggs hatched, 258:11
    thy N. awake, 534:3
    where n. singing, 726:19
Nightly on deep Galilee, 422:14
    owl that n. hoots, 181:14
    pitch moving tent, 396:1
    shore, 479:5
    sings the staring owl, 177:17
    to listening earth, 301:15
Nightmare from which trying to awake, 696:10
    in n. of the dark, 775:15
    Life-in-Death, 400:3
    national n. over, 790:15
    vexed to n., 639:7
    woke to flak n. fighters, 793:6
Nightmares of other islands, 785:19
Night's candles are burnt out, 184:5
    owl n. herald, 173:23
    piercing n. dull ear, 193:11
    Plutonian shore, 479:5
    rung n. yawning peal, 221:6
    starred face, 439:9
    sweet bird, 430:15
    trust not one n. ice, 251:28
Nights all white an' still, 515:3
    and feasts of gods, 98:25
    are longest there, 211:7
    are very damp, 553:8
    are wholesome, 200:22
    Checkerboard of N. and Days, 471:19
    chill thy dreaming n., 439:2
    days and n. to Addison, 325:5
    delights as short as n., 243:5
    fasted forty days and n., 33:30
    fled Him down the n., 620:17
    forty days and forty n., 6:28
    in bottomless n. you sleep, 603:13
    long wintry n., 500:7
    luxurious lobster-n., 309:23
    men such as sleep o' n., 195:22
    Moses was there forty days and forty n., 9:9
    no more profit of shining n., 176:20
    of waking, 397:7
    revels long o' n., 196:11
    shorten tedious n., 232:3
    two n. to every day, 250:12
    waste n. in discontent, 161:23
Night-side, illness is n. of life, 829:1
Nighttime, dog did nothing in n., 617:7
Night-walkers' song, 641:5
Nihil nimis, 124:9
    nos haec novimus esse n., 111:*n3*
Nihilist man who does not bow, 511:15
    spring abhorrent to n., 686:10
Nil desperandum, 99:*n4*
    habet infelix paupertas, 113:*n4*
    humani n. a me alienum puto, 88:*n9*
    igitur mors est ad nos, 93:*n3*
    posse creari de nilo, 92:*n8*
    tam difficile est, 88:*n11*
    terribile nisi ipse timor, 166:*n4*

Nile, allegory on banks of N., 367:10
    dogs drink running at the N., 106:7
    outvenoms worms of N., 225:17
    serpent of old N., 223:7
    waters of the N., 549:13
    you're the N., 732:12
Nimble airy servitors, 262:14
    in calling of selling, 708:2
    Jack be n., 860:5
    thought can jump, 226:13
    with n. feet dance on air, 605:19
    words so n., 245:4
Nimbly and sweetly, 219:15
    he capers n. in lady's chamber, 173:30
Nimis, ne quid n., 124:*n2*
Nimrod the mighty hunter, 6:35
Nine and fifty swans, 638:11
    and sixty ways, 634:5
    bean-rows have there, 637:1
    by N. Gods he swore, 448:13
    days old, 859:5
    lives like a cat, 148:27
    she-camel hairs aid memory, 714:22
    some say there are n. muses, 57:*n8*
    stitch in time saves n., 109:*n1*
    then there were n., 861:6
    thrice again to make up n., 218:29
Nineteen, average n.-year-old American boy, 835:10
    intercourse began in n. sixty-three, 810:6
Ninety and nine went not astray, 36:29
Ninety-nine percent of people fools, 750:3
Ninety-three, one hundred n. species, 821:3
Ninety-two, one hundred n. covered with hair, 821:3
    the glorious N., 352:9
Nineveh, one with N. and Tyre, 635:3
    quinquireme of N., 681:4
Ninny, compared to Handel's a n., 314:13
Ninth beatitude, 310:16
    part of a hair, 186:8
Ninth-month midnight, 520:7
Niobe, like N. all tears, 201:6
    of nations, 421:17
Nipped, blood is n. and ways foul, 177:17
    my flower sae early, 380:5
Nipping, winter with wrathful n. cold, 172:9
Nipple, plucked n. from his gums, 219:23
Nips his root then he falls, 231:2
Nix, sticks n. hick pix, 758:1
Nixon, won't have N. to kick, 790:19
No comment is splendid expression, 667:15
    continuing city, 47:7
    cross no crown, 249:5
    discharge in that war, 24:26
    effects, 433:24
    everlasting n., 433:14
    evil deed live on, 580:3
    forces one to repeat N., 590:11
    go not to Lethe, 438:14
    Hawthorne says N. in thunder, 516:4
    I was out for stars, 670:14
    in him is n. darkness, 47:36
    let me taste the whole, 494:19
    love lost, 158:14
    mainly hears the N., 364:7
    man content with lot, 98:15
    man is an island, 236:19
    man see me more, 230:31

No *(continued)*
    more trusting in women, 55:8
    New Taxes, 813:10
    new thing under the sun, 23:35
    nice girl won't say n., 110:22
    no no life, 218:7
    one about in the Quad, 723:4
    one can return from there, 3:1
    one cares for me, 352:6
    one goes and comes back, 3:2
    one means all he says, 570:25
    one should judge own case, 103:19
    others said N., 281:12
    person who could not say n., 782:6
    remembrance of former things, 23:36
    saying N. to authority, 759:19
    this morning sir I say, 463:14
    time like present, 296:3
    to think is say n., 648:1
No pasarán, 744:14
Noah begat Shem Ham Japheth, 6:24
    God gave N. rainbow sign, 813:6
    often said to wife, 664:16
Noah's, into N. ark, 347:18
Nobility, betwixt wind and n., 185:3
    idleness an appendix to n., 240:15
    in their natures, 213:15
    of style, 417:5
    species of n., 287:6
    true n. exempt from fear, 172:17
    war alone brings n., 702:7
Nobility's, mercy is n. true badge, 175:13
Nobis pereunt et imputantur, 110:*n12*
Noble and incapable of deceit, 398:8
    and most sovereign reason, 204:9
    and puissant nation, 263:3
    army of Martyrs, 50:2
    be man helpful and good, 363:13
    bright gleam of n. deeds, 66:8
    British sentence n. thing, 665:9
    contrive one n. lie, 77:8
    cookery a n. science, 240:13
    do n. things, 514:2
    dust of Alexander, 206:25
    efforts in last war, 323:8
    eightfold path, 66:24
    eminently n., 529:21
    false idol or n. true birth, 78:9
    he shall have a n. memory, 225:5
    hearts of the n. may be turned, 53:18
    horsemanship, 186:24
    in reason, 203:17
    invention, 356:18
    is he no more, 67:7
    last infirmity of n. mind, 261:19
    Living and noble Dead, 391:12
    long live our n. king, 308:1
    man a n. animal, 256:22
    mind here o'ethrown, 204:7
    nature passion not shake, 214:23
    nature poetically gifted, 530:1
    nature too n. for world, 224:28
    negligences teach, 297:3
    never alone accompanied with n. thoughts, 163:20
    not rebellion which is n., 790:3
    not think n., 770:16
    now cracks a n. heart, 207:15
    person attracts noble people, 364:11

Nonviolence and truth inseparable, 650:11
   first article of faith, 650:9
   is the answer, 823:5
Nonviolent resistance paralyzed, 823:9
Noodles, don't hang n. on my ears, 861:22
Nook, book and shady n., 577:2
Nooks, sequestered n., 467:21
Noon, act in the n., 372:19
   and evening of lives, 534:9
   athwart the n., 401:12
   dark amid blaze of n., 268:32
   far from fiery n., 438:17
   from girder n. leaks, 753:13
   from morn to n. he fell, 264:24
   from n. to dewy eve, 264:24
   ghosts' high n., 565:23
   he was my n., 775:6
   lying till n., 325:17
   now you come at n., 860:20
   riding near her highest n., 260:3
   sun at n., 236:21
   under the palmtree at n., 719:23
   we drink you at n., 806:10
Noonday, age clearer than n., 14:8
   bird of night at n., 195:26
   destruction that wasteth at n., 18:25
Noon's, troubled midnight and n. repose,
   718:1
Noontide, night morning and n. night, 174:5
Noose, marriage a n., 158:9
   of Light, 470:14
Noosed, strapped n. nighing hour, 619:15
Nooses give, 738:14
Normal, situation n. fucked up, 851:18
Norman blood, 480:14
Norman's, reef of N. Woe, 466:6
Noroway o'er the faem, 853:17
North, Ariosto of the N., 421:10
   awake O n. wind, 25:24
   Countree hard countree, 745:2
   elevation of the N. Star, 140:8
   fair weather cometh out of the n., 15:3
   farewell to the N., 379:5
   guilt on N. equally with South, 521:18
   he was my N., 775:6
   Hotspur of the N., 185:20
   infect to n. star, 194:19
   lanterns in N. Church, 352:10
   next gale from n., 353:3
   no N. no East no West, 409:11
   Poles and Equators, 552:20
   ship came from n. country, 862:10
   wind doth blow, 859:12
   without sharp N., 233:12
North America, native warrior of N., 426:1
North American civilization engulfed world,
   814:3
North Americans use reality, 794:2
North Carolina, said to Governor of N.,
   599:19
Northeast, heel of N. Trade, 634:6
Northern charm southern efficiency, 800:8
   constant as n. star, 196:13
   kind and n. face, 753:12
   laurels not change, 349:1
   Lights seen queer sights, 673:10
   ocean in vast whirls, 318:5
   States muddle through, 489:5
Northland soul, 745:2

North-northeast, wind always n., 652:9
North-northwest, but mad n., 203:20
Northwest, Chicago at n. gates, 652:1
   Passage to intellectual world, 332:27
   to n. died away, 492:6
Norval, my name is N., 337:14
Norway o'er the faem, 853:17
Norwegian, pine hewn on N. hills, 264:9
Nose, as n. on man's face, 176:7
   as sharp as pen, 192:27
   assert n. on face his own, 347:12
   blackbird snipped off n., 858:12
   Cleopatra's n., 279:20
   entuned in hir n. ful semely, 134:21
   European n., 809:5
   gave pouncet-box his n., 185:2
   great n. great man, 649:14
   innocent n., 198:1
   jolly red n., 249:15
   law says judge as looks down n., 776:1
   liberty plucks justice by n., 210:36
   makes chimney of your n., 369:16
   Marian's n. looks red, 177:18
   nose nose nose, 249:15
   often wipe bloody n., 307:7
   paying through n., 850:5
   plain as n. in face, 146:15
   putting mind's eye or n. in book, 807:7
   red n. makes me ashamed, 288:23
   ring at end of n., 499:16
   which direction to point n., 776:13
   with spectacles on n., 198:25
Nosegay of culled flowers, 154:4
Noses, athwart n. as asleep, 182:22
   hold n. to grindstone, 147:20
Nosing up to impossible stone, 801:16
Nostalgia for living existence, 759:12
   last n., 687:17
Nostrils, blast of thy n., 8:28
   breathed into his n., 5:16
   whose breath is in his n., 26:13
Not an Attic grace, 709:2
   as I will but thou, 37:29
   as the world giveth, 41:30
   for love, 199:27
   I not I, 707:5
   in vain, 667:12
   lost but gone before, 106:21
   my will but thine, 40:16
   so wild a dream, 460:7
   that I loved Caesar less, 196:24
   to eat not for love, 454:2
Notary's, in n. heart remains of poet, 527:3
Note and enjoy noting, 585:20
   bolder n. than this, 478:3
   deed of dreadful n., 221:6
   dreadful n. of preparation, 193:11
   eternal n. of sadness, 530:20
   it in a book, 27:25
   living had no n., 844:23
   make sure one n. follows another, 802:17
   silent n. Cupid strikes, 256:7
   take a n. of that, 449:6
   take n. O world, 214:12
   that swells gale, 335:5
   tu-who a merry n., 177:17
   when found make n., 497:25
   work of noble n., 481:13
   world little n., 476:7

Note *(continued)*
   wrapped in five-pound n., 499:15
   you in book of memory, 171:17
Notebook, set in a n., 197:12
Noted down and remembered, 826:12
Notes are few, 371:12
   as warbled to the string, 260:7
   by distance made sweet, 337:4
   child's amang you takin' n., 380:6
   curls done up with bank n., 503:12
   flute in dying n., 284:16
   he listens well who takes n., 130:25
   liquid n. close day, 262:8
   of gladness, 409:6
   rough n. and dead bodies, 649:16
   thrill deepest n. of woe, 378:22
   through all compass of n., 284:13
   trills thick-warbled n., 268:26
   with many a winding bout, 259:20
   write N. from Olympus, 701:13
Nothing, a man zealous for n., 328:19
   a worm a mere n., 318:15
   a year, 490:6
   achieved without chimeras, 535:12
   ain't heard n. yet, 711:9
   ain't worth nothin' but it's free, 832:6
   airy n., 182:3
   all for love n. for reward, 161:4
   all or n., 540:1
   before and nothing behind, 401:20
   begins and nothing ends, 620:15
   begot of n. but vain fantasy, 182:23
   beside remains, 427:18
   better know useless things than n.,
     106:26
   blessed man who expects n., 310:16
   book's a book though n. in 't, 419:13
   bring peace but yourself, 455:17
   brought n. into world, 46:25
   burden of n. to do, 289:20
   but hath been said, 240:3
   but pack of cards, 551:7
   but talk of his horse, 187:29
   but the night, 619:8
   but the truth, 157:17
   call our own but death, 179:28
   can be accomplished alone, 735:17
   can be created from nothing, 92:12
   can be done hastily and prudently,
     103:21
   can bring back hour, 393:18
   can come of this, 812:3
   can need a lie, 249:18
   can rescue me, 171:2
   can touch him further, 221:5
   cannot create when n. to say, 761:4
   certain except death and taxes, 321:3
   comes amiss so money comes, 175:25
   comes out, 455:3
   comes without cause, 318:17
   common law n. but reason, 159:14
   constant but inconstancy, 297:21
   could stop you, 830:12
   death in itself is n., 282:20
   death is n. to us, 84:8, 93:11
   deed everything glory n., 365:18
   did n. in particular, 565:2
   do much harm, 741:10
   do n. be a gentleman, 165:3

O (continued)
quanta qualia sunt illa sabbata, 126:n2
tell me all about Anna Livia, 696:15
tempora O mores, 90:8
terque quaterque beati, 96:n12
wooden O, 192:16
Oafs, muddied o. at goals, 635:8
Oak and ash and thorn, 635:18, 853:27
bend knotted o., 300:20
grass-blade's no easier than o., 514:17
heart of o. our ships, 335:22
hearts of o., 146:16
in o. none is, 860:10
many strokes fell the o., 163:n2
owl lived in o., 591:16
revolution growth natural as o., 489:12
shadow of British o., 345:16
under o. in stormy weather, 299:6
Oak-cleaving thunderbolts, 216:18
Oaken, old o. bucket, 418:14
Oakhurst, body of John O., 566:11
Oakland California no there there, 673:20
Oakleaves, stone steel stone o., 719:22
Oaks, fell great o., 320:4
from little acorns, 124:12
many strokes overthrow o., 163:5
Oar, broken o. and gear of dead, 721:8
never had o. or lance, 75:2
no better companion than o., 535:1
put in her o., 157:35
wind and wave and o., 480:21
Oars, both o. with little skill, 549:9
falling o. kept time, 277:11
keep time, 411:7
muffled o., 405:3
were silver, 223:14
Oasis in air of lost connections, 801:2
Oatcakes, Calvin o. and sulphur, 398:14
Oaten, if aught of o. stop, 337:1
Oath, blushed as he gave o., 332:28
break o. he never made, 271:20
Cophetua sware o., 482:13
good mouth-filling o., 186:12
he that imposes o., 271:20
in lapidary inscriptions not upon o.,
328:1
punishment if one swears false o., 53:29
swore full great o., 853:27
this o. and this indenture, 72:16
trust man on o. or bond, 218:14
whore's o., 217:4
Oaths are but words, 271:18
are straws, 192:29
false as dicers' o., 205:19
God not take you to task for O., 120:15
liar always lavish of o., 257:11
strange o., 198:25
Oats, definition of o. meant to vex, 324:n3
grain given to horses, 324:20
mares eat o., 860:10
munch your good dry o., 181:25
Obadias, young O., 296:9
Obdured, arm the o. breast, 265:15
Obedience bane of genius, 427:13
coercing into o., 711:4
enforced o., 215:29
fear keeps men in o., 242:2
infuses that liberal o., 344:17
love o. troops of friends, 222:11

Obedience (continued)
makes slaves of men, 427:13
principle of rule or o., 351:5
rebellion o. to God, 846:19
to law demanded, 615:7
to which is fixed o., 192:20
transforms o. into duty, 330:21
Obedient, city to his will, 77:13
compulsion to become o., 708:5
to their laws we lie, 62:4
to truth, 523:23
to whomsoever in authority, 73:18
Obelisk, strong upright like o., 612:3
Obermann, sedulous ape to O., 599:9
Oberon, I jest to O., 181:5
my O. what visions, 181:27
Obesity mental state, 764:13
Obey, Anna whom three realms o., 309:8
drift wait and o., 636:2
fate summons monarchs o., 284:2
haunch and hump is O., 634:15
I but o. urge of song, 671:7
in silence tyrannous word, 539:10
it wholeheartedly, 628:11
Music's power o., 284:13
my duty to o. orders, 536:3
nature must o. necessity, 197:15
thy heart, 453:8
to love cherish and o., 51:18
voice at eve, 453:21
weight of time o., 218:9
woman to o., 483:3
Obeyed at prime, 453:21
nature to be commanded must be o.,
166:15
parents insist on being o., 382:29
sighed as lover o. as son, 354:1
sun and moon o. him, 320:21
Truth o. his call, 642:11
Obeys, bends him but o. him, 467:2
has humor when she o., 310:9
whoever o. the gods, 52:7
Object all sublime, 565:14
conformity of o. and intellect, 127:1
consideration of public o., 73:17
first o. looked upon that o. became,
521:1
Hope without o., 402:12
in living to unite, 670:6
in possession seldom retains charm, 114:6
legitimate o. of government, 358:15
marriage had always been her o., 406:9
obligation to o. possessed, 541:13
of British government, 370:8
of war is peace, 522:13
only of war honorable, 354:17
paramount o. save Union, 475:13
perceived harmony of o., 402:19
purely magical o., 795:18
see o. as it is, 529:22
strange and high, 277:7
when gold becomes her o., 192:7
Objective and subjective united, 403:2
Church and State demand, 697:17
correlative, 722:9
economics can be o. science, 788:9
of poet to achieve poetry, 689:2
Objectivity and again objectivity, 709:14
subjectivity and o., 745:15

Objects, all o. of all thought, 391:4
all visible o. are pasteboard masks, 516:13
classified, 364:22
earnest about these o., 708:3
extended in space, 688:22
extracted from many o., 199:23
in an airy height, 296:17
industrialized communities neglect o.,
692:10
material o. are of two kinds, 92:16
Oblations, bring no more vain o., 26:9
Obligation, haste in paying o., 273:28
not created sense of o., 656:1
of novel be interesting, 584:14
to John owed, 297:5
to object possessed, 541:13
Obligations, in marriage o. reciprocal, 432:6
rank has its o., 384:11
Oblige, noblesse o., 384:11
Obliged, so obliging he ne'er o., 312:4
to be a citizen, 527:15
to struggle with world, 382:19
wealthy and relieved poor, 52:n2
whatever o. to do whatever not o. to do,
559:20
Obliging, so o. he ne'er obliged, 312:4
Oblique, as lines so loves o., 277:8
Oblivion, alms for o., 208:8
blind o. swallowed cities, 208:7
blindly scattereth poppy, 256:19
commend to cold o., 429:25
diffuses senses with o., 99:1
formless ruin of o., 208:20
Lethe the river of o., 265:16
longest journey to o., 707:22
my o. is a very Antony, 223:3
not to be hired, 256:20
of a day, 541:6
razure of o., 212:6
sacred to o., 239:14
second childishness and o., 198:25
six months' o., 570:18
wall of o., 749:4
Oblivioni sacrum, 239:14
Oblivious, sweet o. antidote, 222:12
Oblomovism, 499:8
Obscene, abstract words o., 754:4
live without duties o., 457:26
sailing on o. wings, 401:12
things holy profane clean o., 246:10
Obscenity, Bible has wealth of o., 562:23
Obscure, cloud o. science, 359:9
destiny o., 334:14
gods love the o., 51:22
hermit poor in place o., 159:21
little grave an o. grave, 180:5
regions of philosophy, 330:8
the palpable o., 265:10
unconscious mental processes, 607:7
when brief I become o., 101:18
Obscured, excess of glory o., 264:17
Obscurely, body to be buried o., 168:19
Obscures show of evil, 189:4
Obscurity, no defense but o., 302:10
origin involved in o., 416:7
Obsequies, come to these sorrowful O.,
94:28
solemnized their o., 256:13
Obsequious and conciliating abroad, 416:11

Old *(continued)*

beats off louring O. Age, 142:7
beauty making beautiful o. rime, 227:11
before we grow o. and die, 638:3
being o. having lighted rooms, 810:9
bellows full of angry wind, 639:14
bells of O. Bailey, 857:12
bitch gone in teeth, 709:5
Black Joe, 539:3
black ram tupping ewe, 212:19
books wines, 342:15
born o. and ugly, 496:36
busy o. fool unruly Sun, 234:2
Cary Grant fine, 767:5
cast me not off in the time of o. age, 18:8
change o. love for new, 164:8
chaos of sun, 686:19
chilly and grown o., 493:14
chip of o. block, 345:4
custom made life sweet, 197:36
dance attention on o. age, 642:14
dance in o. dame yet, 680:4
darling I am growing o., 594:2
despise not thy mother when she is o.,
    22:37
discard the o., 784:11
disease of o. men avarice, 243:12
dog barks backward, 670:8
dog Tray, 408:n2
dogs shame nakedness of o. man, 53:32
early candle-light of o. age, 521:16
education best provision for o. age, 79:17
ends stolen of holy writ, 173:37
England to adorn, 635:18
England's winding sheet, 375:15
every o. man's eye, 183:18
faiths loosen and fall, 568:17
familiar faces, 407:1
fashions please best, 175:30
father antick the law, 184:28
father old artificer, 696:7
Father William, 405:9, 550:1
few know how to be o., 274:11
foolish fond o. man, 217:30
former things grow o., 248:12
forsake not o. friend, 32:16
forsaken bough, 473:19
fortify thy name against o. age, 169:5
friends are best, 245:15
friends times manners, 342:15
friends to trust, 167:1
gang, 594:5
glorious song of o., 488:15
Glory, 452:14
glory of o. story is forever, 98:6
God of our fathers known of o., 635:1
God these o. men, 69:14
gratitude soon grows o., 79:11
green o. age, 283:4
grew o. between fires of Troy, 759:15
grow o. along with me, 494:7
grow o. in body but never mind, 91:16
grow o. learning many things, 57:8
grow o. without visiting, 59:20
growing o. in drawing nothing, 348:2
grown o. before my time, 548:1
grown o. in love, 376:3
half as o. as Time, 384:7
half as o. as time, 501:5

Old *(continued)*

half-witted sheep, 394:n2
happy o. man, 95:16
heads on young shoulders, 804:17
heard o. o. men say, 637:19
hearts not grown o., 638:12
hermit of Prague, 210:16
hope I die before I get o., 839:8
hot time in o. town, 630:6
houses mended, 301:6
how did I get o. so quick, 763:16
how o. is Ann, 850:9
I grow o. I grow o., 717:15
I have been young and now am o., 17:6
I know thee not o. man, 192:13
I love everything o., 342:15
if Ancient Mariner called O. Sailor, 559:3
if to be o. and merry be sin, 185:31
if youth but knew if o. age but could,
    151:11
in o. age learn to be wise, 68:3
in story, 482:19
Kentucky home, 539:1
kept thy truth so pure of o., 263:15
King Cole, 856:18
kit-bag, 689:22
know how to grow o., 524:3
lads that will never be o., 618:16
lady from Dubuque, 735:19
Lady of Threadneedle Street, 376:11
lamps for new, 846:5
last to lay o. aside, 308:15
like him that's growing o., 69:5
like to give good advice, 273:17
linen wash whitest, 244:1
little o. New York, 626:14
loosen o. foundations, 681:13
love never sick o. dead, 160:2
love noght o. as whan newe, 137:3
love of o. for o., 620:8
lovers soundest, 244:1
mad blind despised king, 429:11
make me conservative when o., 670:9
man as o. as his arteries, 280:19
man broken, 231:9
man had so much blood, 222:5
man in dry month, 718:2
man looks before and after, 52:20
man to whom old men hearkened, 102:9
man twice a child, 203:21
man weds tyrant, 71:1
man who will not laugh, 629:19
man who wouldn't say prayers, 858:11
Man with beard, 499:11
man with something of young, 91:16
man young gardener, 358:17
manners books wines, 342:15
man's eagle mind, 642:12
man's frenzy, 642:11
man's gold, 654:1
men are children, 75:1
men from chimney corner, 163:26
men garrulous by nature, 91:17
men know young men fools, 165:1
men ought to be explorers, 721:6
men shall dream dreams, 30:22
men should be explorers, 781:2
men's heads bare, 729:4
men's lies, 709:4

Old *(continued)*

mighty men of o., 6:25
Minstrel infirm and o., 396:3
Mithridates he died o., , 619:10
moon in her arm, 853:18
mother Hubbard, 859:13
nature abhors the o., 456:3
new way to pay o. debts, 245:3
new wine in o. bottles, 35:21
New World redress balance of O., 390:1
no country for o. men, 639:16
no falsehood lingers to o. age, 69:4
no fool like o. fool, 148:26
no man would be o., 298:6
no o. age only sorrow, 627:18
no time like o. time, 473:5
not criticize O. Testament, 626:1
not O. Brown any longer, 507:26
not one continued faithful until o. age,
    78:17
not so o. not so plain, 564:19
not yet so o. but she may learn, 189:8
now my o. bawd dead, 642:19
oaken bucket, 418:14
off with O. Woman, 609:2
offenses of affections new, 227:15
one is fat and grows o., 185:22
or modern bard, 260:15
order changeth, 486:12
pardon o. fathers, 638:6
peaceful as o. age, 493:5
penny in o. man's hat, 847:8
people are square, 818:7
people in o. times had convictions,
    442:15
people not to fear young or be deserted,
    733:8
pippins toothsomest, 244:1
poetics in my alchemy, 603:21
poor despised o. man, 216:20
Pretender, 726:7
prosperity blessing of O. Testament,
    167:10
pry loose o. walls, 681:13
religious factions, 345:19
resembles the o. thinking, 836:11
ring out the o., 484:14
roast beef of O. England, 321:n6
rugged cross, 661:10
same o. story, 817:15
save o. worth saving, 647:7
say I'm growing o., 417:16
saying wise and o., 161:n4
seem though I die o., 642:4
sight make o. man young, 481:3
sign of o. age, 399:7
so be it when I grow o., 392:7
so young body with so o. head, 189:18
soakers, 288:11
soldiers never die, 690:12, 850:20
soldiers surest, 244:1
some o. lover's ghost, 235:7
something o. something new, 850:13
speak truth more as I grow o., 153:14
stones that cannot be deciphered, 721:5
studies a delight to the o., 90:13
sublime in o. sense, 708:19
surgeon to o. shoes, 195:13
sweetheart of mine, 596:4

Particulars, do good in minute p., 376:5
   flies from p. to axioms, 166:12
   minutely organized p., 376:5
Parties, always two p., 457:5
   divided mankind into p., 366:19
   men naturally in two p., 359:10
Parting all we know of heaven, 547:3
   foretaste of death, 425:15
   if not this p. well made, 197:17
   is such sweet sorrow, 183:16
   king stood at p. of way, 29:33
   shakes p. guest by hand, 208:11
   speed the p. guest, 309:21
   speeds the p. guest, 640:9
Partir c'est mourir un peu, 608:n4
Partisan cares nothing about rights, 76:18
Partition, union in p., 181:22
Partitions, thin p., 283:8
Partner, take side of p. with most vitality, 771:20
Partners, our property subject to control of p., 362:5
   set to p. change lobsters, 550:20
   we are p. in this land, 771:10
Partridge sitteth on eggs, 29:19
Parts, Gaul divided into three p., 91:22
   here the p. shift, 493:19
   of good natural p., 156:30
   of it are excellent, 591:19
   one man plays many p., 198:25
   only Christian come to these p., 140:6
   remembers me his gracious p., 178:9
   to-day we have naming of p., 794:12
   uttermost p. of the sea, 20:13
   virtue on outward p., 189:5
Parturient montes nascetur mus, 101:n9
Party, come to aid of p., 849:6
   comes from grass roots, 625:12
   fire tolerable third p., 505:8
   guilt of Stalin before P., 826:8
   I am p. of one, 756:15
   injured p., 566:16
   is madness of many, 313:14
   joining political p. casting ballot, 694:6
   of Past party of Future, 457:5
   of revolution civilization, 451:19
   offices not for p., 413:14
   platforms are contracts, 705:9
   print strongest weapon of p., 686:1
   sooner every p. breaks up, 406:19
   spirit of p., 350:9
   that does not carry flag, 445:13
   that works both sides of street, 699:4
   to p. gave up, 343:2
   to prolong these sufferings, 712:5
   tribe or clan, 848:16
   true poet and of Devil's p., 372:13
   unshackled by p., 395:22
   wants to see people still get rich, 787:9
   what that p. has done for women, 522:1
Party-spirit at best madness, 309:17
Parvis e glandibus quercus, 124:12
Pas, du sublime au ridicule il n'y a qu'un p., 388:n1
   premier p. qui coûte, 317:n3
Pasarán, no p., 744:14
Pascal, celebrities such as P., 554:11

Pass, all which will not p. away, 420:19
   all ye that p. by, 29:28
   and turn again, 453:22
   by me as idle wind, 197:10
   by sight so touching, 392:12
   gates of Hades, 61:14
   he brings to p. every word, 65:22
   heaven and earth p., 34:3
   horseman p. by, 643:5
   how they p. eternal time, 835:13
   I p. a willful stranger, 599:12
   in angels say, 453:12
   in naked breadths of ocean, 467:n3
   into nothingness, 436:8
   joy to p. to world below, 97:20
   let him p. for a man, 187:31
   let it be let it p., 315:n2
   let the toast p., 367:29
   like night from land to land, 400:22
   loveliest soonest p. away, 432:13
   me the can lad, 619:11
   my words not p. away, 37:10
   not away, 7:6
   not p. save with My authority, 122:14
   not p. this way again, 847:23
   O let him p., 218:8
   o'er green corn-field did p., 200:5
   on let us pass, 689:21
   onward though dynasties p., 576:5
   open Time let him p., 624:2
   our comprehension, 789:2
   praise Lord p. ammunition, 729:10
   ships that p. in night, 467:18
   strangely p., 226:14
   these things come to p., 37:6
   they shall not p., 608:14, 744:14
   this too shall p. away, 474:16
   through land of Egypt, 8:18
   virtues men praise and p. by, 708:10
   we p. the gate, 645:11
   what cannot speak about p. over, 727:11
   world will p. in a twinkling, 786:13
Passage broad to Hell, 85:n1
   fret p. through it, 258:6
   man merely p. for food, 140:11
   Northwest P. to intellectual world, 332:27
   not regret p. of time, 830:17
   of angel's tear, 435:18
   over the river, 520:3
   sweetest p. of a song, 592:15
   to remorse, 219:11
   we did not take, 720:8
   you think particularly fine, 327:19
Passages, apprenticehood to foreign p., 179:3
   history has cunning p., 718:3
   turn underground p. into lethal chambers, 756:16
   which seem confidences, 457:14
Passageways, no life moves in empty p., 68:4
Passe, on ne p. pas, 608:n6
   tout p., 855:8
Passé, hiverné dans mon p., 689:n4
Passed away glory from earth, 393:9
   below horizon of homing, 721:18
   clean over Jordan, 10:19
   for dangers I had p., 212:32
   fortunes that I have p., 212:28
   over on dry ground, 10:19

Passed *(continued)*
   so he p. over, 282:6
   we've p. a lot of water since then, 695:17
Passenger e'er pukes in, 424:8
Passengers are just that distance from death, 57:16
Passenjare, punch in presence of p., 553:13
Passer deliciae meae puellae, 94:n1
Passer, laissez faire laissez p., 315:16
   ne les laisserez pas p., 608:n6
Passeront, ils ne p. pas, 608:n6
Passers-by, excuses made to casual p., 743:18
Passes among the impure, 79:n5
   bright youth p. swiftly, 61:16
   every hour that p. O, 378:12
   everything p. art eternal, 489:8
   everything p. perishes palls, 855:8
   men seldom make p., 738:13
   now fancy p. by, 618:13
   rise to feet as He p., 633:4
Passest, tell Spartans thou who p. by, 62:4
Passeth, fashion of world p., 44:7
   one generation p. away, 23:32
   peace which p. understanding, 45:37
   that within which p. show, 200:30
   wind p. over it, 19:7
Passing, all is p., 689:21
   bells for these who die, 738:6
   longest part of journey p. of gate, 90:1
   out O bitter ending, 696:18
   past or p. or to come, 640:2
   power p. from the earth, 394:22
   see her p. by, 844:21
   speak each other in p., 467:18
   the love of women, 11:38
   through nature to eternity, 200:28
   wind is p. by, 548:2
Passio, hysterica p., 216:11
Passion, all p. spent, 269:17
   and death of a friend, 182:11
   bards of P., 438:9
   beauty is a simple p., 821:12
   blank wake of his p., 830:16
   by p. driven, 378:3
   caprice and lifelong p., 604:17
   chaos of thought and p., 311:9
   connect prose and p., 684:3
   cows my p., 497:26
   drug which takes away p., 54:19
   fever in mind, 292:5
   for a scarlet coat, 298:19
   for anonymity, 682:10
   for hunting something, 496:10
   for righteousness, 715:4
   gratification of every p., 526:17
   grown man's p., 331:24
   happier in p. we feel, 273:30
   haunted me like a p., 391:3
   holy p. of Friendship, 561:10
   hopeless p., 490:11
   I must speak in p., 185:29
   impulse of p. or interest, 366:18
   in first p. woman loves lover, 423:21
   in first p. women love lovers, 274:13
   infinite p. and pain, 492:14
   intellectual p. drives out sensuality, 140:12
   interpret story of P., 767:9

Pay *(continued)*

just man will p. more tax, 77:3
law and order p., 578:9
make me able to p. for it, 288:1
man of genius had to p., 659:13
money not p. for anything, 654:18
new way to p. old debts, 245:3
no worship to garish sun, 183:32
not p. honor with tears, 87:13
only things we can p., 604:20
our lives we p., 514:15
piper, 300:17
remember to p. the debt, 72:11
rob Peter p. Paul, 148:11
served without p., 556:3
taxes p. for civilized society, 578:3
vow and not p., 24:12
we must anguish p., 544:3
we shall p. any price, 799:7
when will you p. me, 857:12
with a deadly blow, 65:16
with ratiocination, 270:17
words p. no debts, 208:3
you ought to p. you know, 551:16

Paying, enrage those p. your annuities, 316:27
through nose, 850:3

Pays, he that dies p. all debts, 230:5
he who p. piper, 300:*n*2
him in own coin, 299:24
money takes choice, 591:13
to advertise, 849:15
us with age and dust, 160:14

Pays, du p. qu'on enchaine, 855:12
fameux dans les chansons, 524:*n*8

Pea, looking as one p. does another, 146:18
princess felt p. through mattresses, 461:19
tearing up p. patch, 742:2

Peace, abides a p. of thine, 528:13
above all earthly dignities, 231:3
adventure art p., 624:17
all her paths are p., 20:26
and knowledge pass argument, 518:17
and rest can never dwell, 264:2
armed p., 255:4
as a river, 28:13
at p. with himself, 779:11
at the last, 450:1
author of p., 50:5
be American without threatening p., 712:13
be at p. henceforward, 466:23
be within thy walls, 20:2
beasts shall be at p. with thee, 13:39
between effect and it, 219:11
between equals, 611:5
bodies are buried in p., 33:10
bring p. to others, 138:12
calm world and long p., 186:27
cannot live alone at p., 699:5
carry gentle p., 231:7
cease not to advocate p., 320:*n*3
central p. at heart, 395:5
commerce honest friendship, 358:13
Constitution law in war and p., 502:18
contributions to p. of world, 705:8
conversion of world perpetual p., 571:13
corrupt, 268:15

Peace *(continued)*

crimes against p., 734:2
crowned with smiles, 279:6
crust eaten in p., 60:15
cultivate p. and harmony, 350:10
dangerous to p. and safety, 377:1
deep dream of p., 417:12
depart in p., 419:4
easier to make war than p., 577:12
end of that man is p., 17:8
enemies called for p., 655:6
enemies in war in p. friends, 357:3
face full of painless p., 549:5
first in war first in p., 371:8
follow after p., 43:30
fool when he holdeth p., 22:8
for our time, 650:7
fruit of Spirit is p., 45:22
gentlemen may cry P., 353:3
give citizens little p., 812:18
give to all nations p., 50:14
give us p., 49:12
go in p., 39:14, 124:31
go sleep with Turks, 180:7
god has brought this p., 95:14
God is war p. surfeit hunger, 64:7
guide planets, 834:5
habits of p. and patience, 252:25
hard and bitter p., 799:7
hath her victories, 263:11
hope to see p. established, 699:8
I am for p., 19:29
I give unto you, 41:30
I leave with you, 41:30
if you can't give me love and p., 725:6
if you want p., 515:6
imperishable p., 620:3
in His will is our p., 131:26
in our time, 51:16
in p. children inter parents, 71:10
in p. goodwill, 668:1
in p. just generous, 426:1
in p. Love tunes, 396:9
in p. nothing so becomes man, 192:30
in p. thinks of war, 241:12
in p. ye critics dwell, 309:22
in their hearts, 804:9
in what p. a Christian can die, 302:24
indivisibility of p., 678:*n*2
indivisible, 678:6
inglorious arts of p., 276:22
into poet as flour into bread, 768:10
is in grave, 428:5
is not absence of war, 286:13
is p. so sweet, 353:3
is poor reading, 575:22
its ten thousands, 349:3
it's wonderful, 695:1
just and lasting p., 477:4
justice made for sake of p., 144:11
keep him in perfect p., 27:17
keep p. within yourself, 138:12
lay me down in p., 15:31
let us have p., 532:18
liberty and safety, 358:13
live together in p., 705:15
make a desert call it p., 114:1
make war to live in p., 80:19
makes solitude calls it p., 422:8

Peace *(continued)*

man's village is his p. of mind, 804:5
may he rest in p., 124:20
means of preserving p., 350:7
Mercy Pity P. and Love, 372:5
more important than justice, 144:11
more precious than piece of land, 804:6
my p. is gone, 365:12
naked poor mangled P., 193:25
Napoleon sole obstacle to p., 388:7
never good war or bad p., 320:23
no p. unto the wicked, 28:14
nor help for pain, 531:2
nor shall this p. sleep with her, 231:16
not made for justice, 144:11
not p. but a sword, 35:31
not take atomic weapons to want p., 768:13
nothing bring p. but self, 455:17
nothing contributes more to p. of soul, 356:13
object of war p., 522:13
of all countries connected, 693:9
of God which passeth all understanding, 51:2
of p. there shall be no end, 26:31
on earth mercy mild, 323:1
on earth p. and good will, 39:4
on the earth, 488:15
order security and p., 693:9
our concern be p. of mind, 85:8
our p. in His will, 719:17
our p. our innocence, 392:14
passes into Anesthesia, 625:1
pattern of celestial p., 172:3
perpetual p., 258:16
poetry act of p., 768:10
poetry fine-spun from mind at p., 105:24
price life exacts for p., 752:10
Prince of P., 26:31
proclaims olives of age, 227:12
publisheth p., 28:18
rest in soft p., 237:21
righteousness and p. have kissed each other, 18:18
running wild all over, 750:20
seek p. and pursue it, 17:2
separate p., 754:1
servant depart in p., 39:5
slept in p., 231:10
snow said p., 725:4
soft phrase of p., 212:25
speak or forever hold his p., 51:8
star of p. return, 408:18
suffering evils of long p., 113:11
Tahiti full of p. and joy, 516:16
take chances for p., 717:5
the charm's wound up, 218:29
the human dress, 372:6
there is no p., 353:3
they are in p., 31:16
though make this marriage for my p., 223:17
thousand years of p., 484:15
time of p., 24:6
to him that is far off, 28:28
to men of good will, 49:11
to our children when they fall, 801:17
to this house, 39:18

Pen *(continued)*
 words as with burning p., 381:9
 worse than the sword, 241:2
 write p. for I am volumes, 176:26
 written with a p. of iron, 29:16
Penal, chains and p. fire, 263:23
Penalty, greatest p. of evildoing, 78:13
 paying p. for no idealism, 625:9
Penance, hath p. done, 400:16
 more will do, 400:16
Pence, eternal lack of p., 482:12
 for thirty p. my death, 250:5
 take care of p., 314:21
 three hundred p., 41:22
Pencil, he screwed on p. sharpener, 756:5
Pendent, blown about p. world, 211:23
 made his p. bed, 219:15
 towered citadel p. rock, 223:33
 world as a star, 265:23
Pends-toi brave Crillon, 162:*n*6
Penelope, constant as P., 844:17
 faithful P., 55:25
 true P. was Flaubert, 709:1
Penetrable to shower of gold, 433:25
Penetrates Eternal Justice as eye into sea,
 132:4
 non-being p. no space, 59:5
 sun p. privies, 79:7
Penetrating, fault of p. wit, 274:8
Peniel, called the place P., 7:21
Peninsula, whole p. of Florida, 821:4
Penitence, vague kind of p., 496:31
Penitentiary, down in shadow of the p.,
 841:8
Penknife in your heart, 856:13
Pennies, rains p. from Heaven, 778:5
Penniless, forgive man for being p., 445:6
 lass wi' lang pedigree, 385:10
Penny, beg p. by and by, 725:3
 for your thought, 148:28
 in for p. in for pound, 565:5
 in old man's hat, 847:8
 Jacky have p. a day, 858:5
 not a p. in it, 860:11
 one a p. two a p., 859:4
 Plain and Twopence Colored, 599:10
 postage stamp, 553:8
 wise pound foolish, 240:7
Pens, if trees in earth were p., 122:5
 natural right to use p., 316:15
 of diplomats not ruin, 356:11
 quirks of blazoning p., 213:7
 skewered with office p., 498:13
Pensant, un roseau p., 280:*n*2
Pense, honi soit qui mal y p., 132:16
 je p. donc je suis, 254:4
Pensée à littérature que lumière à peinture,
 600:*n*4
Pension never enriched young man,
 251:30
Pensive Eve, 337:1
 mistress, 781:7
 soul, 337:4
Pent by sea and dark brows, 521:4
 here in the body p., 396:1
 long in city p., 435:17
 long in populous city p., 267:28
Pentagon turn orange and vibrate, 812:17
Pentameter, in p. aye falling, 401:21

Penthouse, hang upon his p. lid, 218:27
Pent-up, drain p. rivers of myself, 519:25
 love of my heart, 592:13
Penuries, to fill all p., 236:21
Penury, age ache p., 211:24
 chill p., 334:19
 talk tendeth only to p., 21:32
People, a stiffnecked p., 9:6
 absolved of history, 826:6
 aging college p., 756:6
 all exulting, 520:18
 all p. and tongues, 48:23
 all p. need be liked by some p., 783:14
 all sorts of p., 219:19
 all the lonely p., 835:3
 all with one accord, 340:10
 Americans a P., 734:12
 annoyed with Moses, 807:6
 are like water, 737:17
 arose as one man, 11:10
 attentive unto book of law, 13:16
 be nice to p. on way up, 678:9
 beat my p. to pieces, 26:15
 behind p. the country, 532:21
 believe p. are really good, 822:9
 believe these p. from sky, 140:7
 black p. unite, 835:11
 brave new world that has such p., 230:14
 British p. like to be told worst, 666:10
 came to their senses, 656:10
 capable of becoming happier, 727:7
 cautious p. never bring reform, 521:19
 change what is in themselves, 121:6
 chief business of American p., 659:19
 chosen p. children of light, 530:12
 chosen p. of God, 357:10
 colored p. understand white p., 656:16
 come to church good p., 618:15
 come ye thankful p., 487:7
 comfort ye my p., 27:37
 common p. of the skies, 232:16
 common-looking p. best, 476:8
 complained of long voyage, 140:3
 conceited p. carry comfort, 513:3
 conditioned p. of Africa to humiliation,
 812:6
 confidence in justice of p., 475:7
 considered by p. equally true, 353:5
 contracts with the p., 705:9
 country belongs to p., 475:6
 dangerous who make no noise, 276:19
 descend to meet, 455:23
 differ in their discourse, 277:12
 difference between rich and other p.,
 754:*n*3
 difficult to believe p. starving, 787:12
 difficult to govern, 59:13
 dull and ugly p., 627:10
 easily becomes prey, 143:4
 economics as if p. mattered, 787:14
 experiment of American p., 350:5
 eyes of all p. upon us, 246:17
 fear and distrust the p., 359:10
 find p. have good sense, 274:5
 fool some p., 477:7
 freedom light, 730:12
 gift iv the p., 646:20
 given over in troops to disease and death,
 93:21

People *(continued)*
 glory of thy p. Israel, 39:6
 God save the p., 413:11
 good tidings to all p., 39:3
 government for benefit of p., 409:9
 government for the p., 415:1
 government includes all the p., 462:9
 government of by for p., 476:7, 488:13
 Government of p. Congress is p., 431:13
 greater part of rich p., 338:16
 grudge what they cannot enjoy, 60:19
 have always some champion, 77:23
 have right to knowledge, 350:17
 have right to rise up, 474:5
 hell is other p., 772:8
 his p. were his temple, 280:13
 hoop unbroken p. flourished, 628:1
 how you are to govern p., 343:19
 I am the p., 681:7
 I know all p. worth knowing in America,
 487:13
 I loathe p. who keep dogs, 596:9
 if p. don't want to come, 814:12
 imagine a vain thing, 15:28
 in a boat, 842:4
 in fashionable New York Society, 539:8
 in front get the jar, 678:18
 in glass houses, 251:*n*2
 in hotels strike no roots, 649:13
 in old times had convictions, 442:15
 included in We the p., 832:5
 indictment against whole p., 344:11
 is a great beast, 100:*n*13
 judging p. by appearances, 276:16
 known by p. never heard of Jesus Christ,
 726:2
 land of Russian p., 458:18
 laughed cried most silent, 768:15
 law for rulers and p., 502:18
 lazy p. looking for something to do,
 333:14
 leader and commander to the p., 28:25
 let go hold of p., 749:15
 let my p. go, 8:9, 863:1
 lie during sex, 842:3
 lift p. from dust, 453:14
 like p. like priest, 30:13
 lonely p. talking to each other, 770:12
 look after our p., 649:18
 love of British p., 344:17
 made the Constitution, 371:6
 maintain control of government, 698:9
 many p. unable to find work, 659:23
 many-headed beast, 100:21
 marry ancient p., 258:12
 masses of p. not qualified, 702:19
 may be made to follow path, 63:4
 may grow old without visiting, 59:20
 may walk but not throw stones at birds,
 325:16
 mercy on my poor p., 154:9
 mercy on Thy P. Lord, 635:5
 more dead p. than living, 788:14
 more than half p. right, 756:14
 most important element, 82:20
 most p. my age are dead, 730:17
 multitude of the gross p., 100:*n*13
 muzzle self-expression of p., 787:10
 my p. are Americans, 751:13

People *(continued)*

my p. would increase, 543:7
naked p. have little influence, 563:2
narrow-souled p., 313:13
never learned from history, 390:4
new deal for American p., 697:13
ninety-nine percent of p. fools, 750:3
no doubt but ye are the p., 14:9
no more give the p. straw, 8:10
not always what seem, 346:5
numerous and warlike, 140:9
O stormy p., 137:5
oats supports p., 324:20
of his pasture, 18:29
of p. by p. for p., 476:7, 488:13
of unclean lips, 26:25
of Western Europe, 728:15
old p. are square, 818:7
old p. not to fear young or be deserted,
    733:8
old p. poor p. also get niggerized, 797:15
on whom nothing lost, 584:15
on world not in it, 572:16
one man die for p., 41:21
one of beautiful p., 835:5
one should like to drop, 329:6
only p. for me mad, 810:2
only two p. who count, 840:8
our land before we her p., 670:10
our sovereign the p., 415:n1
people have for friends, 623:9
people marry, 623:9
planned obsolescence of p., 789:4
poet help p. live their lives, 688:23
power from the p., 458:22
protection of p., 339:10
put up with oppressive rule, 463:8
relation between white and colored p.,
    509:15
religion opium of p., 510:5
remove weight from p., 811:11
representatives of p., 426:12
resemble wild beast, 143:4
retain virtue and vigilance, 475:8
right of p. to make alter constitutions,
    350:8
right of trampling on p., 450:9
right p. in right jobs, 502:14
Rome's decline lay in p., 706:11
Sacco's name in hearts of p., 724:21
safe depository of powers, 359:6
say life is the thing, 636:10
seldom judge right, 370:9
sensed by p. expressed by p., 535:10
separated by six other p., 833:5
should be beautiful, 622:12
should be taught what is, 814:15
should fight for their law, 64:14
shouted with a great shout, 10:21
show my head to the p., 381:2
showed thy p. hard things, 17:35
signs for a god-fearing p., 121:3
small country with few p., 59:20
so dead to liberty, 323:4
so many hungry p., 803:4
special p. unto himself, 9:32
spoil lives of better p., 599:21
still in the gristle, 344:5
struggled on with troubles, 627:12

People *(continued)*

such tongue to great p., 512:6
sum married p. owe, 364:16
talebearer among thy p., 9:14
talk sense to American p., 760:2
that once bestowed commands, 113:15
that p. may require leader, 77:25
the p. will live on, 681:17
there is a p. risen, 280:16
thy p. shall be my p., 11:12
to all the p. you can, 319:1
to these p. I owe everything, 475:2
tricked and sold, 681:17
turn to benevolent rule, 82:1
two kinds of p., 600:6
two p. miserable instead of four, 558:11
two p. shaken by dizziness, 794:7
two thirds of p. killed, 683:12
under violent passions, 610:1
underestimating intelligence of p.,
    691:13
visited and redeemed his p., 38:41
voice of p. is voice of God, 125:3
want to be masters of future, 823:12
watch over economy of private p.,
    338:17
we are his p., 19:3
we p. will get to promised land, 823:10
we the p., 360:13
were passed clean over Jordan, 10:19
what did you do to the p., 740:17
what is the city but p., 224:27
what kind of p. do they think we are,
    667:4
what p. are like here, 363:11
what p. say behind back, 601:15
what p. say of us true, 636:5
where no vision the p. perish, 23:20
which sat in darkness, 33:31
who eat the earth, 770:10
who have money, 700:15
who know little, 331:7
who lift people who lean, 600:6
who love each other, 461:10
who need people, 810:12
who will feed me, 818:4
win friends influence p., 716:20
wish p. to think well of you, 279:14
with no weaknesses, 586:14
with rights in hands, 462:9
without history, 722:3, 855:16
witness to the p., 28:25
would die for my p., 549:3
would that Roman p. had single neck,
    107:16
you know yet can't name, 810:9
Peopled, earthly ball a p. garden, 364:3
    teach order to p. kingdom, 192:20
    world must be p., 194:28
People's good is highest law, 91:11
    in p. eyes life, 699:16
    nor p. judgment always true, 283:18
    not seat self on other p. backs, 588:21
    other p. money, 536:2
    queen in p. hearts, 842:9
    reforming other p. habits, 561:14
    sits high in p. hearts, 195:28
    soil of p. necessities, 625:12
    state worst of all states, 257:7

People's *(continued)*

this is a p. contest, 475:10
    voice odd, 312:22
Peoples, domination over all p., 787:11
    English-speaking p., 602:12
    happiness of p., 586:12
    history life of p., 542:17
    mos p. gonna lose, 792:12
    of United Nations, 705:15
    sink or swim together, 653:18
    who have courage to face war, 702:7
    wishes of p. concerned, 699:7
Peopling the void air, 528:22
Peor and Baalim, 259:2
Peoria, it'll play in P., 814:18
Peppercorn, I am a p., 186:17
Peppered two of them, 185:24
Peppermint, big p. hotels, 797:6
Peppers, peck of pickled p., 859:15
Per caputque pedesque, 94:n4
Perceive here a divided duty, 212:33
    in form stereotyped by culture, 727:2
    ye are too superstitious, 42:17
    yourself sole heir of world, 290:1
Perceived harmony of object, 402:19
Perceivers of terror of life, 456:23
Perceives, artist p. more than fellows, 659:24
    it die away, 393:12
Perceiving, conscious that we are p., 80:16
    genius p. in unhabitual way, 582:2
Percent, eighty p. of success, 831:7
Percents, elegant simplicity of three p., 362:13
Perception, imagination agent of p., 403:3
    of beauty moral test, 505:6
    pale colorless, 582:4
Perch, custom make it their p., 211:3
    if you hadn't nailed parrot to p., 842:13
    where eagles dare not p., 173:35
Perches in the soul, 544:11
Perchings, flights and p., 581:13
Percy, old song of P. and Douglas, 163:27
Percy's, not yet of P. mind, 185:20
Perdition, bottomless p., 263:23
    catch my soul, 213:30
Perdu, tout p. fors l'honneur, 145:n6
Perdue, une génération p., 673:n1
Pereant qui nostra ante nos dixerunt, 124:13
Pereat, fiat justitia et p. mundus, 123:n7
Peremptory, would not with p. tone, 347:12
Perennial pleasures plants, 444:15
    spring of prodigality, 345:3
Perestroika combines continuity innovation,
    826:9
Perfect and entire, 47:9
    be ye therefore p., 34:9
    circle and vicious circle, 788:13
    end of p. day, 625:14
    every p. gift, 47:11
    form a more p. Union, 360:13
    Glory be the P. One, 545:16
    happiness p. as martyr's, 626:6
    his work is p., 10:13
    I am not in p. mind, 217:30
    in bud as in bloom, 557:16
    in heaven p. round, 494:4
    in p. nature no distinction of kind, 82:27
    interpreter of life, 710:12
    keep him in p. peace, 27:17
    let patience have her p. work, 47:9

Perfect *(continued)*
life may p. be, 238:14
love casteth out fear, 47:42
made p. in weakness, 45:15
mark the p. man, 17:8
move in p. phalanx, 264:16
nothing quite new is p., 90:20
one p. limousine, 738:15
only p. man, 242:17
pebble is a p. creature, 814:5
practice makes p., 103:*n*5
produce p. circles, 81:27
shineth unto the p. day, 21:1
spirits of just men made p., 47:3
then if ever p. days, 514:16
visit p. in being too short, 406:16
when that which is p., 44:20
whether by a p. poem, 686:7
woman nobly planned, 394:3
world p. everywhere, 382:14
Perfected, woman is p., 827:12
Perfectest, silence p. herald of joy, 194:20
Perfectibility of man, 462:15
Perfection as culture conceives it, 531:15
culture study of p., 531:13
dead p., 485:5
fullness of p. in him, 177:27
holds in p. but moment, 226:1
law is p. of reason, 159:14
little concerned with p., 577:4
of life or of work, 641:4
of mathematics, 660:12
pink of p., 342:16
rides upon p. of his officials, 89:15
right praise true p., 190:9
spiritual p. of man, 127:6
stern p. as greatest art, 660:12
unattainable p., 636:8
vowing p. of ten, 208:5
Perfections, discovers p. in beloved, 416:20
sweet p. caught, 171:10
Perfectly, I remember your name p., 590:19
loser is p. clear, 807:9
Perfidious Albion, 388:19
fatal and p. bark, 261:21
Perform, ability they never p., 208:5
Almighty's orders to p., 301:12
every act as though it were your last,
115:2
his wonders to p., 347:3
never promise more than p., 103:18
Performance, desire outlive p., 191:32
lovers swear more p., 208:5
takes away the p., 220:21
Performed, look for deed soul p., 122:16
rites simple decisive, 816:18
to a T, 146:11
Performs, man p. engenders, 748:14
Perfume, amber scent of odorous p., 269:6
feel my breasts all p., 696:13
owest cat no p., 216:30
puss-gentleman all p., 347:13
throw p. on violet, 178:14
Perfumed like milliner, 185:2
old women should not be p., 56:21
sea, 478:2
so p. that winds love-sick, 223:14
Perfumes, all the p. of Arabia, 222:7
colors sounds echo, 524:9

Perhaps, seek a grand p., 146:20
Pericles calls quality lucidity, 532:5
in wrath the Olympian P., 74:10
Periclum ex aliis facito, 88:*n*10
Periculum in mora, 163:*n*1
Periit, qui ante diem p., 627:4
Peril, in p. mask is off, 93:8
those in p. on sea, 537:19
use our pens at our p., 316:15
woods more free from p., 197:36
Perilous, cleanse bosom of p. stuff, 222:12
fight, 411:1
nothing more p. than new order, 142:9
seas in faery lands forlorn, 437:13
thought without learning is p., 62:16
turns to p. waters, 130:1
unsifted in p. circumstance, 201:29
Perils, avoid p. by united forces, 287:11
defend us from all p., 50:10
how many p. do enfold, 161:2
of camp march and battle, 556:3
when our p. are past, 389:17
Period at the right moment, 739:6
new and great p. in His Church, 263:2
of effectiveness of generation, 702:20
Periodic, success to p. sentence, 745:10
Periodization of European history, 757:4
Peripatetic lover, 564:11
Periphrastic study, 720:18
Peris, sweets of Fairies P. Goddesses, 436:15
Perish, beauty so soon to p., 700:8
city to p. if it finds buyer, 95:11
drink unto him that is ready to p., 23:26
fame of her excellence will never p.,
55:25
hero p. or sparrow fall, 311:3
if it had to p. twice, 669:11
if we must p. in fight, 469:7
in our own, 620:15
in their infancy, 845:1
let justice be done though world p.,
123:*n*7
let the day p., 13:29
may they p. who used our words, 124:13
name not p. in dust, 405:17
or catch up, 654:9
shall not p. from earth, 476:7
should not p., 40:46
spirit of moderation will p., 660:5
surely weak p., 673:8
survive or p., 414:12
that one of thy members should p., 34:4
the thought, 301:4
their goodness does not p., 70:23
though heaven may p., 385:*n*5
thy money p., 42:4
truths wake to p. never, 393:16
twice, 669:11
weakly p. at another moment, 53:31
where no vision the people p., 23:20
with the sword, 37:33
Perished as they had never been, 33:9
by own follies they p., 53:148
in his pride, 392:9
the weapons of war p., 11:38
we p. each alone, 348:22
who p. being innocent, 13:32
Perishes, everything p., 855:8
Periuria ridet amantum Iupiter, 104:*n*8

Periwig, new p. make a great show, 288:21
Periwig-pated, robustious p. fellow, 204:11
Perjured, gloriously p., 100:5
murderous bloody, 227:22
Perjuries, at lovers' p. Jove laughs, 183:5
of lovers, 104:27
Perked up in glistering grief, 230:25
Permanence sea cannot claim, 575:2
Permanent alliances, 350:11
and certain characteristics, 324:12
and the same, 529:8
contract on temporary feeling, 575:11
disuse of any organ, 362:7
feelings p. and the same, 529:8
interests of community, 366:18
more p. than fish or weed, 824:15
nothing ought to be p., 462:15
share in government, 370:9
system of security, 699:9
Permission, nobody without Count's p.,
701:3
Permit base contagious clouds, 184:36
doing what laws p., 314:8
how long p. to Heaven, 268:11
Permitte divis cetera, 99:*n*6
Permitted to shuffle in slippers, 631:20
whatever not forbidden is p., 381:20
Pernicious consequences, 502:18
love of flattery, 303:10
race of odious vermin, 298:14
Perpetual, desire a p. rack, 240:18
devotion to business, 598:11
feast of nectared sweets, 261:3
kingdom of p. night, 174:4
let p. light shine, 49:8
neglect of other things, 598:11
night, 94:4, 237:14
office seekers, 727:4
orgy, 527:7
our interests eternal and p., 417:20
scoured with p. motion, 191:20
sleep of p. night, 94:4
speculators about p. motion, 141:11
summary court in p. session, 701:6
work us a p. peace, 258:16
Perpetually, life begins p., 644:17
nation p. to be conquered, 344:7
one hour then damned p., 171:3
saves itself p., 785:7
Perpetuate, any way to p. the World, 256:6
piece of fine writing, 628:11
Perpetuity, merit of p., 256:19
Perplexed in the extreme, 215:13
labyrinthical soul, 237:2
to have plenty is to be p., 58:19
Perplexes and affronts, 791:12
monarchs, 264:18
Perplexity of radical evil, 773:7
Persecute, despitefully use and p. you,
34:7
you for my sake, 33:33
Persecuted church of God, 44:23
for righteousness' sake, 33:33
most p. minority, 695:7
Persecutes the mind, 284:19
Persecutest, why p. thou me, 42:7
Persecution bad way to plant religion, 255:16
gives p. no assistance, 350:6
object of p. is p., 765:17

Physician *(continued)*
　　read book of Nature, 155:*n*5
　　recover through contentment with p., 73:2
　　rope-dancer p. magician, 113:5
　　whole need not p., 35:18
Physicians, all p. against his opinion, 280:20
　　best of all p., 597:2
　　by their love grown cosmographers 236:14
　　words are p. of mind diseased, 65:20
Physicists have known sin, 768:14
Physics experience arranged, 572:1
　　labor we delight in p. pain, 220:22
　　tries to discover pattern, 679:4
Pia mater of mine, 255:10
　　womb of p., 177:1
Pianist, do not shoot p., 604:19
Piano, pounding of old p., 636:8
Picasso, murmured to P. I liked portrait, 673:15
Piccadilly, goodbye P., 674:2
　　walk down P., 564:9
Pick about the Gravel, 440:2
　　knock out p. round, 837:1
　　not scruple to p. pocket, 294:14
　　out what culture has defined, 727:2
　　up starving dog, 561:16
Picked, age grown so p., 206:23
　　from leaves of any author, 255:18
　　man p. out of ten thousand, 203:5
　　peck of pickled peppers, 859:15
　　up broken point, 728:8
Pickerel, sidelong p. smile, 780:13
Pickety, hickety p., 860:2
Picking men of genius, 737:2
Pickle, Coolidge look as if weaned on p., 704:4
　　put you in this p., 156:3
Pickwickian sense, 495:18
Picnic, hard-boiled as p. egg, 745:3
Picninnies and the Joblillies, 336:12
Pictura, ut p. poesis, 102:*n*2
Picture condensation of sensations, 651:16
　　Earth's last p. painted, 633:3
　　fain paint p., 493:25
　　is not pornography, 797:3
　　life is painting p., 578:7
　　no p. made to endure, 709:9
　　not at his p. but his book, 238:4
　　of future, 765:18
　　of terribles simplificateurs, 509:5
　　one p. worth thousand words, 851:4
　　placed the busts between, 306:20
　　requires knavery trickery deceit, 555:18
　　say p. shows labor, 557:15
　　see a fine p., 364:2
　　see totally different p. too late, 779:18
　　shows what pages expound, 512:4
　　truly like me, 254:16
Pictures, apples of gold in p. of silver, 23:2
　　cutting all p. out, 653:1
　　in our eyes to get, 235:4
　　it's the p. that got small, 733:7
　　out of doors, 213:8
　　sleeping are but as p., 220:18
　　statues p. verse grand, 557:9
　　what man does based on p., 727:1

Pictures *(continued)*
　　without p. or conversations, 549:10
　　you furnish p. I furnish war, 628:10
Picturesque and gloomy wrong, 460:22
Pie, as New Englanders love p., 680:2
　　ate umble p., 498:11
　　baked in a p., 858:12
　　best physicians apple p. and cheese, 597:2
　　Calico P., 499:20
　　Christmas p., 857:3
　　finger in every p., 156:21
　　humble p., 498:11
　　in the sky, 684:10
　　Miss American P., 839:7
　　no man's p. is freed, 230:18
　　Peacock P., 662:14
　　violence as American as cherry p., 837:16
　　when p. opened, 858:12
Piebald linsey-woolsey brothers, 313:19
Piece, all of a p. throughout, 285:22
　　bleeding p. of earth, 196:21
　　by piece I re-enter world, 824:10
　　equal p. of justice Death, 255:19
　　fenced in p. of land, 330:17
　　irregular indigested p., 324:16
　　of exceptionally fine writing, 628:11
　　of the continent, 236:19
　　peace more precious than p. of land, 804:6
　　still as a gold p., 821:13
　　what a p. of work is man, 203:17
Pieces, all in p. all coherence gone, 235:26
　　beat my people to p., 26:15
　　chess p. phenomena of universe, 537:1
　　dashed in p. the enemy, 8:27
　　God hides in smallest p., 851:*n*4
　　of eight, 598:17
　　tear to p. that great bond, 221:7
　　thirty p. of silver, 30:39, 37:22
Pied, daisies p. shallow brooks, 259:15
　　daisies p. violets blue, 177:16
Pieman, met a p., 857:18
Pierce, beauty p. like pain, 676:3
　　free servitude can p. our hearts, 715:8
　　meeting soul may p., 259:20
　　neither graze nor p., 214:23
　　pigmy's straw does p. it, 217:24
Pierces, deep surmise p., 506:3
　　so that it assaults, 230:17
Piercing night's dull ear, 193:11
Pierian spring, 308:11
Pierre, découvrir saint P. pour couvrir saint Paul, 148:*n*5
Pierrot, eyes of P., 753:12
　　mon ami P., 855:13
　　my friend P., 855:*n*3
Piety, all your P. nor Wit, 471:21
　　bound by natural p., 392:7
　　first show p. at home, 46:21
　　grant this in return for p., 94:26
　　grow warmer in Iona, 325:4
　　pathos p. courage, 684:4
　　requires to honor truth, 80:9
　　towards universe, 629:17
Pig, buy a fat p., 860:15
　　dear P. are you willing, 499:17
　　eat Tom beat, 858:16
　　I am only guinea p. I have, 743:11
　　in a poke, 149:18

Pig *(continued)*
　　in as p. out as sausage, 580:15
　　little p. to market, 857:16
　　love not a gaping p., 189:12
　　rather a handsome p., 550:8
　　road rail p. lead, 681:5
　　satisfied, 465:2
　　snake edible to p., 580:12
Pigeon-livered, I am p., 203:30
Pigeons, casual flocks of p., 686:19
　　on grass alas, 673:13
　　onetwothreefourfive p., 739:13
　　tame p. peas, 270:*n*2
Piggy, said P. I will, 499:17
　　true wise friend called P., 786:5
Piggy-wig stood, 499:16
Pigments, secret of durable p., 756:1
Pigmy's straw does pierce it, 217:24
Pigs, fell out over p. fall in over p., 699:14
　　men filthy as p., 673:2
　　speak Greek naturally as p. squeak, 270:15
　　whether p. have wings, 552:3
Pigtail, seized him by little p., 565:17
Pike, holy text of p. and gun, 271:2
Pilate saith what is truth, 41:36
　　suffered under Pontius P., 50:3
　　washed his hands, 38:4
　　what is truth said jesting P., 167:5
　　with P. wash your hands, 180:11
Pile bodies at Austerlitz, 681:10
　　on brown man's burden, 635:*n*1
　　Ossa on Olympus, 55:3
　　Ossa on Pelion, 96:8
Piled, labor of an age in p. stones, 259:3
Pilfer, contrive our fees to p., 75:2
Pilgrim band, 555:4
　　came forth with p. steps, 268:30
　　gray, 336:16
　　intent to be a p., 282:4
　　my first p. has shown his face, 134:*n*3
　　of Eternity, 430:9
　　soul in you, 637:5
Pilgrimage, blisses about my p., 574:13
　　comforts of weary p., 329:11
　　Goethe done p., 528:15
　　life a weary p., 249:13
　　succeed me in my p., 282:5
　　thus I'll take my p., 160:8
Pilgrimages, longen folk to goon on p., 134:16
Pilgrim's Progress about man left family, 560:16
Pilgrims of mortality, 716:17
　　they knew they were p., 247:4
　　we p. passing to and fro, 136:2
Pilgrims', land of p. and so forth, 740:1
　　land of p. pride, 469:8
Pill, one p. makes you larger, 834:6
　　outlived doctor's p., 307:16
　　sugarcoat the p., 278:15
Pillage, slaughter p. devastation, 666:13
Pillaged, houses and farms p., 349:14
Pillar of cloud by day, 8:23
　　of fire by night, 8:23
　　of salt, 7:7
　　of state, 265:8
　　triple p. of the world, 222:25
　　twig and a p., 82:22

Pillared dark, 670:14

Pillars of society, 540:3
   wisdom hath hewn out her seven p.,
     21:11

Pillicock sat on Pillicock-hill, 216:28

Pillow, my bended arm for p., 62:27
   placid face upon the p., 549:5
   sloth finds down p. hard, 225:19
   stone better p. than visions, 713:11

Pilot cares about nothing but river, 560:6
   daring p. in extremity, 283:8
   great p. sail with canvas rent, 106:17
   he's a lightning p., 560:7
   in calm sea every man p., 281:6
   lives our p. still, 173:12
   no chance to p. Union, 475:3
   of the Galilean lake, 261:22
   see P. face to face, 487:4
   that weathered storm, 389:17
   unstable p. steers leaking ship, 118:5

Pilots man bombers to kill babies, 824:4
   of purple twilight, 481:23

Pimpernel, demmed elusive P., 636:3

Pimples warts and everything, 254:16

Pin, angels on head of a p., 835:13
   Taffy stole silver p., 858:6
   with a little p., 180:1

Pinafore, Captain of the P., 563:14

Pinch, death as lover's p., 224:11
   East and West will p. heart, 734:15
   hungry lean-faced villain, 175:1
   necessity's sharp p., 216:14
   set sharp racks to p., 436:19

Pinched, complains of having p. finger, 607:9

Pinches, none tell where shoe p. me, 111:8
   shoe fits one p. another, 675:4

Pinching, paddling palms and p. fingers,
   228:11

Pindar, flying abroad as P. says, 78:10

Pine because they lost virtue, 109:2
   dwindle peak and p., 218:28
   for what is not, 429:19
   for which soul did p., 478:9
   into waves p. needles, 291:15
   palm and p., 635:1
   scent of p., 719:18
   shall I ever sigh and p., 250:15
   shattered dishes underneath p., 670:18
   tall p. of the forest, 377:9
   tallest p., 264:9
   with fear and sorrow, 161:23
   yonder p. that sings, 85:7

Pineapple of politeness, 367:8

Pined and wanted food, 390:14
   she p. in thought, 209:26

Pines, cones under his p., 668:19
   keep shape of wind, 759:17
   murmuring p. hemlocks, 466:16
   roared in the p., 651:12
   watching p. shore and stars, 759:5

Pining pining, 587:12

Pinions of great deeds, 364:8

'Pinions, tell you what his 'p. is, 562:20

Pink, Bacchus with p. eyne, 223:21
   of courtesy, 158:6, 183:22
   of perfection, 342:16
   twenty-nine when p. shades, 604:26

Pinker, girls I teach younger p. every year,
   818:9

Pinkham, land of Lydia E. P., 739:15

Pinks that grow, 212:*n*1

Pinnace like fluttered bird, 486:22

Pinnacle, imagined p. and steep, 439:1

Pinnacled dim in inane, 428:11

Pinpoint, Yiddish words p. individuals, 769:5

Pin's, set life at p. fee, 202:7

Pint, come within p. of wine, 303:3
   of sweat save blood, 708:14
   people to goal, 515:1

Pioneer, died in boots like p., 750:6

Pioneers, disillusioned colored p., 832:7
   O pioneers, 520:6

Pious action sugar o'er, 203:32
   all were p., 296:9
   Bernard rarther p., 693:1
   Eleazer Wheelock p., 630:8
   feeling of gratitude, 414:11
   fraud as with bad action, 355:4
   impiety of p., 523:11
   love is p., 138:13
   man not less a man, 277:23
   not p. longer than rod behind, 144:10
   ones of Plymouth, 510:4
   thoughts as harbingers, 258:5
   times ere priestcraft, 283:6

Pipe but as linnets, 483:17
   called for p., 856:18
   cat dog p. or two, 620:6
   easier played on than p., 205:8
   for fortune's finger, 204:17
   me to pastures still, 587:2
   piped silly p., 440:11
   rumor is a p., 191:6
   song about a Lamb, 371:13

Piped silly pipe, 440:11
   with merry cheer, 371:13

Piper, followed the P., 491:17
   he who pays p., 300:*n*2
   pay the p., 300:17
   Peter P. picked peck, 859:15
   pipe song again, 371:13

Piper's son, 858:15

Pipers, wi' a hundred p. an' a', 385:8

Pipes and timbrels, 437:17
   and whistles in his sound, 198:25

Piping, cicadas pour out their p. voices, 52:21
   down valleys wild, 371:13
   helpless naked p. loud, 374:10
   songs forever new, 438:2
   songs of pleasant glee, 371:13
   weak p. time of peace, 173:31

Pippins, old p. toothsomest, 244:1

Piracee, vary p., 564:6

Piracy, let's vary p., 564:6

Pirate King, 564:2

Pirates, wonder at cruelty of p., 515:10

Pis, tant p. and tant mieux, 333:5

Pisa, you're the Tower of P., 732:12

Piscem natare doces, 124:14

Pisgah, greeted Moses from P., 441:15

Piss off he said to me, 825:10
   vice-presidency not worth pitcher of
     warm p., 648:17

Pisses, I think it p. God off, 839:2

Pistol, hear word culture reach for my p.,
   729:7
   if his p. misses fire, 343:8
   pun a p. not feather, 407:29

Pistols, fire p. for new century, 676:7
   put on p. went riding, 724:14

Pit, black as the P., 594:10
   Eagle know what is in p., 372:12
   many-headed monster of p., 313:4
   ponies, 656:10
   they'll fill a p., 186:28
   whoso diggeth a p., 23:8

Pitch, daubed with slime and p., 8:1
   he that toucheth p., 32:25
   into frog-spawn, 640:18
   nightly p. moving tent, 396:1
   pitched past p. of grief, 588:2
   they that touch p. defiled, 194:35
   what validity and p., 208:26
   which hawks flies higher p., 171:16

Pitch-black, night p. upon the deep, 96:26

Pitched, as mind p. ear pleased, 348:10
   betwixt Heaven and Charing Cross,
     621:8
   his tent toward Sodom, 7:2
   into freezing water, 842:4
   Love p. mansion, 641:15
   past pitch of grief, 588:2

Pitcher, as wheel runs why water p., 101:17
   broken at the fountain, 25:8
   vice-presidency not worth p. of warm
     piss, 648:17

Pitchers, small p. have wide ears, 149:1

Pitchfork, clothes thrown on with p., 299:13
   drive out Nature with p., 101:2
   use wit as p., 810:3

Piteous, coursed down in p. chase, 198:1
   thing among wretched mortals, 53:32

Pitfalls, snares traps gins p., 490:*n*1

Pith, enterprises of great p., 203:33

Pitiable, world p. in units, 575:7

Pitied, better envied than p., 71:15
   how they p. Eve, 656:13
   lost respect and p. it, 505:20
   pity and be p., 198:22

Pities plumage, 354:19

Pitiful helpless giant, 790:23
   long-suffering and very p., 31:26
   selfish Public, 410:8
   tender eye of p. day, 221:7
   'twas wondrous p., 212:32

Pitiless, pelting of p. storm, 216:27

Pitt, celebrities such as P., 554:11

Pity a human face, 372:6
   beyond all telling, 637:2
   deserveth double p., 160:6
   for suffering mankind, 661:5
   for the living, 562:5
   from blustering wind, 276:5
   gave ere charity began, 342:5
   hid in heart of love, 637:2
   his ignorance, 496:19
   know what 'tis to p., 198:22
   knows not wrath nor p., 446:19
   like naked new-born babe, 219:18
   loved her that she did p., 212:32
   Mercy P. Peace and Love, 372:5
   my simplicity, 322:25
   no beast but knows touch of p., 173:32
   no concern with art, 557:17
   no p. sitting in clouds, 184:7
   of it Iago, 214:22
   of War, 738:5

Plane, it's a bird p. Superman, 795:1
Planes, no sound of p., 793:4
　　single flight of p., 756:16
Planet, cloth from moon from another p.,
　　793:7
　　everybody on this p. is separated, 833:5
　　has gone cycling on, 470:3
　　he is a black p., 807:4
　　lifetime on this p., 799:9
　　of Love on high, 485:9
　　pity the p. all joy gone, 801:17
　　poor pagan p. of ours, 516:3
　　riming p., 195:10
　　ship like small p., 611:17
　　sojourners on p., 443:5
　　when new p. swims, 435:19
Planetary influence, 215:29
Planet's, wandering p. course, 170:4
Planets and the firmament, 235:26
　　had fallen on me, 705:1
　　in stations listening, 267:16
　　in their turn, 301:15
　　observe degree, 207:24
　　peace guide p., 834:5
　　then no p. strike, 200:22
Planned another day like this one, 840:14
　　obsolescence of people, 789:4
　　perfect woman nobly p., 394:3
　　pseudo-event someone p., 792:23
　　shield deliberately p., 710:16
Planner, evil plan most harmful to p., 56:11
Plans, all men's p. to fulfillment, 53:28
　　credit and Muse, 453:8
　　lay p. as if immortal, 582:15
　　make no little p., 592:4
　　that build from bottom up, 697:11
Plant a nation, 243:23
　　architect advise to p. vines, 652:16
　　error hardy p., 488:16
　　if tree dies p. another, 322:22
　　I'm not a potted p., 837:14
　　land set out to p. wood, 312:16
　　no more than cotton they p., 501:6
　　no roses at my head, 547:16
　　persecution bad way to p. religion,
　　　255:16
　　this thorn this canker, 185:6
　　time to p., 24:6
　　vineyards and eat the fruit, 28:37
　　we have become feeble p., 377:9
　　whose virtues not discovered, 457:25
Planted, God first p. a garden, 168:13
　　I have p., 43:34
　　pseudo-event someone p., 792:23
　　tree p. by rivers of water, 15:27
　　tree p. by the waters, 29:17
Planting trees that would march, 685:8
　　wheat for this p., 286:n1
Plants, as aromatic p. bestow, 167:n2
　　beyond p. are animals, 742:7
　　fruits of life and beauty, 373:11
　　he that p. trees loves others, 88:n4
　　his footsteps in the sea, 347:3
　　perennial pleasures p., 444:15
　　sickly p. niggard earth, 334:5
　　still awkward in soil, 780:12
　　suck in the earth, 275:8
　　trees to benefit another generation, 88:7
Plashy, feather-footed through p. fen, 766:6

Plastic and vast one intellectual breeze,
　　399:10
Plastics, one word p., 825:1
Plat of rising ground, 260:4
Plata, puente de p., 862:14
Plate, enjoy ice cream while it's on p., 750:2
　　life fruit ripe on p., 771:16
　　make ourselves recording p., 572:21
　　sin with gold, 217:24
　　sound of bone against p., 836:1
Plateaus, history knows no p., 812:11
Plates, break china of others, 621:14
　　dropped from his pocket, 224:4
Platforms contracts with the people, 705:9
Plato and truth are dear, 80:9
　　dear to me truth dearer, 80:n2
　　European philosophical tradition
　　　footnotes to P., 624:15
　　having defined man, 79:4
　　healer of the soul, 76:n3
　　rather be wrong with P., 91:4
　　rhetoric of rule of P., 262:19
　　thou reasonest well, 301:26
Platonic love, 157:8
　　sprang from P. conception of self, 746:5
　　tolerance vain, 640:10
Platonically, loves silence p., 433:n2
Plato's brain, 453:24
　　retirement, 268:26
　　this is P. man, 79:4
Platter, licked p. clean, 856:20
Platters, unwashed p. ride, 753:18
Plaudits, shouts and p., 467:22
Plausibly, Nut upon Tree equally p., 546:7
Play, a little work a little p., 555:21
　　a song for me, 836:7
　　affording p. to propensity for mastery,
　　　613:8
　　all her sons at p., 528:21
　　all work and no p., 253:11
　　anything possible except fair p., 575:3
　　at a p. to laugh or cry, 298:19
　　at Christmas p., 151:4
　　fair just and patient, 537:1
　　father author of p., 630:2
　　fool with the foolish, 83:15
　　fools with the time, 191:29
　　for mortal stakes, 670:6
　　foul p., 201:20
　　free p. of mind, 530:8
　　good p. audience pleased, 664:2
　　guitar like ringing a bell, 817:2
　　hart ungalled p., 205:6
　　I doubt some foul p., 201:20
　　if music food of love p. on, 208:25
　　in my heart p. double part, 765:2
　　is over, 123:6
　　is tragedy Man, 478:15
　　it Sam, 782:8
　　it'll p. in Peoria, 814:18
　　judge not p. before i.e. done, 249:12
　　kings would not p. at, 348:9
　　last act crowns p., 249:12
　　leviathan whom thou hast made to p.,
　　　19:11
　　life's poor p., 311:11
　　little victims p., 333:20
　　mind in its purest p., 809:2
　　needs no excuse, 182:13

Play *(continued)*
　　never p. cards with man named Doc,
　　　782:1
　　no harp so cheerily p., 408:15
　　not let my p. run, 294:15
　　of the many, 624:6
　　on fiddle in Dooney, 637:13
　　out the play, 186:1
　　perform tragic p., 642:6
　　played out, 490:8
　　pleased not the million, 203:24
　　rather thy discourse than p., 241:15
　　seem saint when most p. devil, 173:37
　　shouts with sister at play, 482:15
　　skillfully with a loud noise, 16:30
　　stage where every man p. part, 187:17
　　stake counter boldly if you p., 493:15
　　tale which holdeth children from p.,
　　　163:26
　　that fails a bad play, 664:2
　　the fool, 408:8
　　the man Master Ridley, 145:2
　　the Roman fool, 222:19
　　the swan and die in music, 76:n6
　　the villain, 213:28
　　theories of a good p., 664:2
　　thy summer's p., 374:4
　　time let me p., 795:10
　　to you death to us, 274:24
　　tune he could p., 858:15
　　up and play the game, 627:6
　　watch men at p., 677:21
　　whatever body not obliged to do, 559:20
　　when I p. with cat, 153:1
　　who goes to American p., 398:12
　　wise enough to p. fool, 210:1
　　with flowers and smile, 192:27
　　with towns you built of blocks, 750:7
　　young and old come forth to p., 259:16
Playboy of the Western World, 658:10
Played, as if they p. at bo-peep, 248:10
　　before the Lord on instruments, 11:41
　　easier p. on than pipe, 205:8
　　farce is p., 146:20
　　game is being p., 279:23
　　game that must be p., 652:4
　　how you p. game, 692:4
　　I have p. the fool, 11:34
　　on dulcimer p., 401:18
　　play p. out, 490:8
　　sedulous ape, 599:9
　　sweetly p. in tune, 378:19
　　with and humored, 282:9
Player on other side hidden, 537:1
　　strutting p., 207:28
　　that struts and frets, 222:16
　　with railroads, 681:8
Player's, tiger's heart in p. hide, 165:18
Players and painted stage, 643:1
　　and umpires begged, 828:2
　　in your housewifery, 213:8
　　men and women merely p., 198:25
　　mouth it as many p. do, 204:11
　　though the most be p., 238:18
Playhouse, playthings in p. of children,
　　670:18
Playing fields of Eton, 389:6
　　Idiot's Delight, 747:16
　　if year p. holidays, 184:36

Pleasure *(continued)*
  when p. can be had, 328:7
  wince at p., 801:11
  with pain for leaven, 568:1
  worldly ease or p., 318:14
  Youth and P. meet, 420:17
  youth of p. wasteful, 495:10
Pleasure's a sin, 423:13
Pleasures, after such p., 235:13
  and toils, 398:8
  banish pain, 304:11
  cannot understand p. of other, 406:15
  celibacy has no p., 324:27
  conversation one of greatest p., 672:20
  dance attendance on lordships' p., 231:15
  disciplined state of p. and pains, 286:*n3*
  English take their p. sadly, 165:15
  every age has its p., 289:8
  go look at their p., 513:7
  homely home simple p., 620:6
  let go hold of p., 749:15
  lightly called physical, 662:2
  like poppies spread, 379:18
  love and all his p. toys, 232:3
  man richest p. cheapest, 505:11
  'mid p. and palaces, 426:15
  money-lust before p., 709:7
  of heroic poesy, 257:18
  of youth, 303:9
  perennial p. plants, 444:15
  pretty p. might me move, 160:3
  some new p. prove, 234:22
  sucked on country p., 233:10
  than all other p. are, 282:18
  too refined to please, 310:6
  unreproved p. free, 259:12
  we will all the p. prove, 170:6
Pledge, I p. allegiance to flag, 606:17
  lives fortunes sacred honor, 357:4
  with mine, 238:2
  you I pledge myself, 697:13
Pleiades, moon has set and the P., 58:3
  sweet influences of P., 15:10
Pleiads, rainy P. wester, 619:21
Plenteous, harvest is p., 35:23
Plenties, nurse of arts p., 193:25
Plentiful lack of wit, 203:9
Plenty, here is God's p., 285:24
  heroes were p., 849:3
  in delay no p., 209:14
  just had p., 378:15
  laurels though ever so p., 424:26
  of nothin', 747:6
  of the kind, 480:6
  reasons as p. as blackberries, 185:25
  scatter p. o'er smiling land, 334:22
  to have p. is to be perplexed, 58:19
Plenty's, mouth of P. horn, 639:14
Pleure dans mon coeur, 590:*n6*
Pleuré, j'ai p. et j'ai cru, 387:*n2*
Pleurer, de peur d'en p., 349:*n3*
Pleut, comme il p. sur la ville, 590:*n6*
  doucement sur la ville, 604:*n1*
Pliable, name of other P., 281:15
Pliant, obstinate p. merry morose, 111:3
Plied, by little arms p., 549:9
  myself to fruitless poetry, 164:14
Plighted, what p. cunning hides, 215:24
Pliny, is it Aristotle P. Buffon, 331:10

Plis, les p. de sa robe pourprée, 151:*n2*
Plodders, small have p. won, 176:20
Plods, plowman homeward p., 334:8
Ploffskin Pluffskin Pelican jee, 500:11
Plot, blessed p. this earth, 179:12
  find p. in narrative be shot, 560:13
  gunpowder treason and p., 845:14
  Horror soul of p., 478:14
  melodious p., 437:6
  passions spin p., 541:8
  souls that cringe and p., 514:14
  thickens, 282:10
  time someone invented p., 700:12
  women guide the p., 367:18
Plotted, foul deed which she p., 55:5
Ploughs, they have pulled our p., 715:8
Plow ancient and valuable, 470:8
  following p. along mountainside, 392:9
  for lords who lay ye low, 429:6
  friends who p. sea, 564:6
  having put hand to p., 39:16
  sow reap mow, 845:7
  speed his p., 165:7
Plowed, dashed to earth p. under, 856:5
  I have p. and planted, 443:10
  if ye had not p. with my heifer, 11:2
  land p. before man, 470:8
  sea, 415:20
  wickedness, 30:18
Plowing, men want crops without p., 509:13
Plowman, heavy steps of p., 637:8
  homeward plods, 334:8
Plowman's story is of bulls, 104:19
Plows, drinks water her keel p. air, 165:11
  in the fields, 706:7
Plowshare, drives p. o'er creation, 306:13
  put not p. too deep, 398:4
  stern Ruin's p., 378:8
Plowshares, beat swords into p., 26:11
Pluck a crow together, 174:33
  bright honor from moon, 185:9
  from memory rooted sorrow, 222:12
  I come to p. your berries, 261:13
  it out and cast it from thee, 34:4
  love not flower they p., 453:10
  out heart of my mystery, 205:7
  out his flying feather, 568:22
  sworn to weed and p. away, 179:20
  their hearts from them, 193:17
  this flower safety, 185:16
  till time and times done, 637:10
  time to p. up, 24:6
  up drowned honor, 185:9
  you out of crannies, 486:21
Plucked, an olive leaf p. off, 6:30
  Diogenes p. a cock, 79:4
  fruit she p. she eat, 267:30
  lint from lapel, 626:12
  my nipple from his gums, 219:23
  violets p., 242:18
Plucker down of kings, 172:28
Plucks dead lions by beard, 177:24
  liberty p. justice, 210:36
  off my beard, 203:29
  with a thread p. it back, 183:15
Plum, pulled out p., 857:3
  some gave p. cake, 857:2
  survives its poems, 686:12
Plumage, pities p., 354:19

Plumber, try getting p. on weekends, 831:1
Plumbing, shadows of p. left of city, 819:14
Plume, blast-beruffled p., 575:16
  helmet and the p., 480:26
Plume, prête-moi ta p., 855:13
Plumed, farewell p. troop, 214:8
  helmets gleamed in forests, 534:9
  knight, 554:2
  war bonnet, 750:9
Plumes, borrowed p., 60:16
  feathered with eagle's p., 61:9
  her feathers, 260:29
Plummet, deeper than p. sound, 230:12
Plummets to dust of hope, 68:6
Plump, banish p. Jack, 185:32
Plumpskin Ploshkin Pelican jill, 500:11
Plumpy Bacchus with pink eyne, 223:21
Plums, I have eaten the p., 703:11
  life's a pudding full of p., 566:5
Plunder, capital in ascendancy system of p.,
    510:10
  lust for blood and p., 666:13
  public p., 414:*n1*
  years p. one thing after another, 101:14
Plunge hands in water, 775:9
Plunged, be p. in deepest reveries, 516:6
Plunge-line, black p. nightdress, 833:15
Plunges, heart p. lower than night, 703:14
  into scientific questions, 537:13
  Orion p. prone, 619:21
  year p. into night, 703:14
Plural, unity is p., 743:13
Pluralism lets exist in each-form, 583:2
Plus ça change, 468:*n3*
  est quam vita salusque, 110:*n5*
Pluto, won the ear of P., 259:21
Plutonian shore, 479:5
Pluto's, iron tears down P. cheek, 260:7
Ply, I cannot p. the loom, 58:4
  the sampler, 261:9
Plyin', boats a-p. up and down, 634:17
Plying needle and thread, 446:2
Plymouth, pious ones of P., 510:4
Pneumatic bliss, 718:8
Pnin ceased to notice students, 756:6
Po, wandering P., 340:14
Pobble who has no toes, 500:9
Pobbles happier without toes, 500:10
Pocket full of rye, 858:12
  learning in private p., 314:24
  Lucy Locket lost p., 860:11
  never alone with poet in p., 351:15
  not scruple to pick p., 294:14
  plates dropped from his p., 224:4
  put me in your p., 707:4
  save their own p., 73:17
Pocket-handkerchief, holding p., 552:6
Pockets, contents of his p., 708:3
Pod, seeds in dry p. tick, 651:12
Poe with his raven, 514:19
Poem a poem and nothing more, 479:23
  bathed in P. of Sea, 603:10
  begins as lump in throat, 671:8
  day is a p., 713:13
  dignity in writing p., 610:20
  does P. not merely says P., 435:6
  don't make p. with ideas, 584:1
  fain write p., 493:25
  feeling for single good p., 364:22

Poem *(continued)*

> figure a p. makes, 671:10
> finds the thought, 671:8
> for poem's sake, 479:23
> heroic p. a biography, 434:12
> if a man finishes a p., 830:16
> immediate object pleasure not truth, 403:8
> is a meteor, 689:3
> language touched by poetry is p., 794:4
> lovely as a tree, 711:11
> metermaking argument makes p., 456:8
> music of p. in translation, 658:13
> my life p. I would have writ, 506:1
> never finished only abandoned, 659:6
> of any length not all poetry, 403:9
> of the act of the mind, 403:n2
> of world, 767:1
> ought himself to be true p., 262:13
> phrase long p. contradiction, 479:22
> pleasure of p. guessing, 583:16
> poetry subject of p., 687:9
> pretty p. Mr. Pope, 295:13
> questions when reading p., 776:14
> read a good p., 364:2
> ride on own melting, 671:12
> right reader of good p., 671:9
> rooted in awe, 776:15
> should not mean, 734:7
> suggestibility of p., 643:7
> that took place of mountain, 688:16
> to which we return, 402:21
> true p. an invocation, 743:21
> United States greatest p., 518:8
> way to tell if p. lasting, 671:9
> what guy inhabits p., 776:14
> whether by a perfect p., 686:7
> who wants to understand p., 364:24
> write p. for money, 771:4

Poème, baigné dans le P., 603:n8

> supprimer la jouissance du p., 583:n5

Poem's, poem for p. sake, 479:23

Poems by water-drinkers, 101:10

> dictionaries and temporary p., 324:18
> get the news from p., 703:15
> here I am writing these p., 818:5
> I'm sick of good p., 816:20
> laying p. away in long box, 821:14
> made by fools like me, 711:12
> more p. produced, 669:8
> my p. naughty but life pure, 110:13
> plum survives its p., 686:12
> possess origin of all p., 518:16
> that's how book of p. made, 110:15

Poena, noxiae p., 91:n7

Poesis, ut pictura p., 102:n2

Poesy, force of heaven-bred p., 176:11

> heavenly gift of p., 284:11
> overwhelm myself in p., 436:2
> participation of divineness, 166:7
> pleasures of heroic p., 257:18
> should be friend, 436:5
> shower of light is p., 436:4

Poet a void, 759:12

> all p. can do is warn, 738:5
> and saint to thee alone, 275:19
> barometer but also part of weather, 773:2
> beneath this sod p. lies, 404:4

Poet *(continued)*

> binds together by passion, 391:15
> born not made, 114:n11
> brings soul into activity, 403:10
> buffoon and p., 594:8
> Coleridge p. and philosopher, 532:11
> comic p. paint follies, 300:12
> could not but be gay, 394:7
> creates world, 688:21
> don't send p. to London, 442:12
> every p. in his kind, 299:4
> flourished here disheveled, 829:4
> force language into meaning, 722:13
> gives life to fictions, 688:21
> Goldsmith P. Naturalist, 328:6
> great p. writes his time, 722:14
> had no p. and died, 313:6
> he was a true p., 372:13
> he was p. and hated approximate, 677:1
> I the p. still do Thank God, 829:10
> if p. interprets poem, 643:7
> in command of fantasy, 772:16
> in notary's heart remains of p., 527:3
> language of English p., 722:19
> like prince of clouds, 524:8
> limbs of a dismembered p., 98:20
> looks at world, 689:4
> lunatic the lover the p., 182:3
> make his imagination the people's, 688:23
> makes himself seer, 604:4
> man that lies in Bedlam, 785:15
> most unpoetical, 440:14
> must write, 779:11
> never alone with p. in pocket, 351:15
> never sure of value, 722:21
> no p. without unsoundness, 447:13
> not every year a p. born, 114:14
> not have to be p., 527:15
> not survive misprint, 604:8
> objective of p. achieve poetry, 689:2
> of Body poet of Soul, 519:7
> our ever-living p., 225:n2
> peace into p. as flour into bread, 768:10
> potent figure, 688:21
> priest soldier p., 524:20
> profound philosopher, 403:12
> proof of a p., 518:11
> retired in Tower of Ivory, 461:n1
> skilled p. through natural gift, 65:28
> so great a p. and friend, 285:17
> soaring in high region, 262:10
> take away liberty of p., 257:18
> they lack a sacred p., 100:15
> this truth p. sings, 481:19
> to make a p. excellent, 272:1
> to p. nothing useless, 324:25
> tragedy for p. be admired, 726:4
> union of mathematician with p., 583:5
> wasted time for nothing, 722:21
> whatever p. writes with enthusiasm, 72:12
> who wishes to understand p., 364:24
> whole race is a p., 687:20
> worthy name of P., 435:6
> you explain nothing p., 648:4

Poeta nascitur non fit, 114:n11

Poetarum licentiae liberiora, 90:n9

Poète semblable au prince, 524:n1

Poetic faith, 403:7

> fields encompass me, 301:11
> Justice, 313:16
> license, 90:17
> meet nurse for p. child, 396:12
> no p. raptures feel, 368:13
> pleasure in p. pains, 283:n4
> wine-scented and p. soul, 599:5

Poetical character, 440:13

> worn-out p. fashion, 720:18
> would gods made thee p., 199:18

Poetically, noble nature p. gifted, 530:1

Poetics, never indulge in, 87:11

> old p. in my alchemy, 603:21

Poetry act of peace, 768:10

> actual is rarest p., 505:27
> administers to effect, 431:9
> aim at inscape in p., 588:7
> all p. difficult, 494:26
> all p. experimental, 689:6
> antithesis to science, 402:15
> as in painting so in p., 102:2
> Ben Jonson his best p., 237:21
> best p. a power, 532:10
> best words in best order, 403:20
> Bible has noble p., 562:23
> book not concerned with P., 738:5
> boom in petroleum but not in p., 794:11
> breath of knowledge, 391:14
> by which I lived, 819:4
> civilization advances p. declines, 447:12
> cleanses, 800:7
> comes naturally as Leaves to tree, 440:6
> communicate before understood, 722:18
> communication of pleasure, 402:15
> dead art of p., 708:19
> do a hundred things, 776:15
> does not matter, 720:18
> emptied of its p., 775:14
> escape from emotion, 722:8
> essential p., 402:21
> fettered fetters race, 376:4
> fine-spun from mind at peace, 105:24
> fleshly school of p., 577:9
> for p. idea everything, 532:4
> from p. liturgy psalms religions, 768:12
> gaudiness of p., 688:19
> Genius of P., 440:11
> give children right to study p., 351:14
> grain of p. season a century, 602:3
> grand style in p., 530:1
> great and unobtrusive, 440:4
> hate p. with design on us, 440:4
> homely definitions of p., 403:20
> I have been eating p., 830:10
> I know that is p., 547:9
> I too dislike p., 714:4
> if a man publicly denounces p., 830:15
> if this is p. very easy, 556:8
> in unconscious fastidiousness, 714:10
> inner calling in man, 768:12
> is in the pity, 738:5
> is painting that speaks, 62:7
> is poetry, 689:2
> journey to unknown, 738:2
> knew well how to write p., 85:13
> language is fossil p., 456:9
> language touched by p., 794:4

Praising, advantage of p. oneself, 558:16
    lean and sallow abstinence, 261:7
    what is lost, 210:31
Prances, far back in soul horse p., 707:18
Prancing Poetry, 546:11
Prate, hear him p., 541:23
    stones p. of whereabout, 220:10
Prates, all she p. has nothing in it, 298:19
Prattle, nor do children p. about his knees,
    52:27
    thinking his p. tedious, 180:13
Praxed, Saint P. in a glory, 492:7
Praxiteles unable to reach all the material,
    116:8
Pray, after this manner p. ye, 34:11
    all p. in their distress, 372:5
    as if to die tomorrow, 320:6
    can't p. a lie, 560:21
    farmers p. that summers be wet, 96:6
    for dead fight like hell for living, 547:12
    for me and come not, 171:2
    for no man but myself, 218:14
    for repose of his soul, 622:17
    for them which despitefully use you, 34:7
    God absolve us all, 139:21
    God to keep me from being proud,
      287:23
    goes to bed and does not p., 250:12
    how they p. for death, 69:14
    I p. you in your letters, 215:13
    in distress and need, 700:21
    in fullness of joy, 700:21
    late and early p., 232:14
    Lord soul to keep, 296:15
    make me able to pay for it, 288:1
    make no mistake, 565:12
    one to watch one to p., 274:20
    place men can p., 664:15
    remained to p., 342:7
    so we'll live p. sing, 218:1
    that love may never come, 70:2
    that the way be long, 628:7
    to p. is to work, 124:11
    two went to p., 272:5
    watch and p., 37:30
    we do p. for mercy, 189:19
    will not p. with you, 188:2
    without ceasing, 46:12
    work and p. live on hay, 684:10
    you now forget, 217:31
    you undo this button, 218:7
Prayed, caught God's skirts p., 491:14
    of Course I p., 544:20
    to genius of the place, 98:3
Prayer, be relieved by p., 230:17
    be sure p. will be granted, 592:3
    Christ's progress and His p.-time, 278:29
    comes round again, 642:4
    effectual fervent p., 47:23
    every p. reduces to this, 512:5
    fool there was made p., 634:21
    for S.T.C., 404:4
    four spend in p., 159:20
    from heart's deep core, 660:2
    God erects house of p., 294:16
    indeed good, 73:14
    laughter beginning of p., 735:16
    more wrought by p., 486:13
    my house a house of p., 36:39

Prayer *(continued)*
    never made but one p., 316:19
    of hawk not get chicken, 853:12
    rises better man p. answered, 541:1
    sadness touches me with a p., 442:8
    same p. doth teach us all, 189:19
    scent of arm-pits finer than p., 519:10
    soul's sincere desire, 396:2
    which rises from heart in grace, 131:10
    wing and p., 773:3
Prayerbooks, beads and p., 311:11
Prayers, among p. a piece of land, 98:24
    angry p., 656:10
    are daughters of Zeus, 53:7
    Bernard had p. in hall whiskey afterwards,
      693:1
    fall to thy p., 192:13
    for a pretense make p., 38:29
    God answers sharp some p., 464:2
    hate enough to hear your p., 61:*n*2
    make of your p. one sacrifice, 230:23
    man who says his p. at night, 764:3
    mention of thee in my p., 46:36
    profit by losing our p., 223:11
    to preserve travel, 299:21
    to punish they answer p., 61:*n*2
    which are age his alms, 164:10
    whose p. make me whole, 633:1
    wouldn't say p., 858:11
Prayeth best who loveth best, 401:2
    well who loveth well, 401:1
Prayin' it tuh be different wid you, 761:1
Praying, dressing nursing p. and all's over,
    423:20
    now he is p., 205:15
Prays, thus the suppliant p., 324:8
Preach gospel to every creature, 38:33
    humility a virtue all p., 245:16
    practice what you p., 86:17, 118:11
    preached as never p. again, 274:21
    supremacy of the state, 787:11
Preached as never to preach again, 274:21
    law that I have p., 66:23
    up patience, 296:21
Preacher, vanity of vanities saith the P., 23:32
Preachers, deliver me from phlegmatic p.,
    361:13
    say Do as I say, 245:28
Preaches contentment to toad, 632:9
    nature teaches more than p., 566:21
    well that lives well, 158:11
Preaching down daughter's heart, 481:21
    silent church better than p., 455:14
    woman p., 327:3
    word for dull conversation, 398:15
Precarious living, 850:12
Precautions against disease of writing, 126:6
Precedence, England not forget p., 262:16
Precedent, dangerous p., 668:11
    embalms principle, 459:10
    not unsettled overnight, 653:16
    one p. creates another, 360:2
    supported by precedents will become p.,
      113:22
    without p. and imitator, 331:15
Precedents accumulate constitute law,
    360:2
    supported by p. will become precedent,
      113:22

Preceding, pang p. death, 340:12
Precept, example more efficacious than p.,
    325:1
    first p. never to accept thing as true,
      254:2
    must be upon precept, 27:21
    no humbling of reality to p., 816:15
    Poetry not by p., 440:11
    true business p., 497:1
'Preciate things left behind, 693:8
Precincts, warm p. of cheerful day, 334:24
Preciosity or euphuism, 653:17
Precious, adds p. seeing to the eye, 177:6
    all things from friends, 85:11
    as p. as truths she reveals, 658:1
    bane, 264:23
    bearing p. seed, 20:3
    better than p. ointment, 24:15
    box of p. ointment, 37:19
    days spend with you, 716:2
    Europe a p. graveyard, 525:14
    gift though small p., 54:23
    glory p. forever, 70:14
    good name like p. ointment, 167:16
    half so p. as they sell, 472:4
    husbandman waiteth for p. fruit, 47:21
    in the sight of the Lord, 19:24
    in war-time truth is so p., 667:11
    jewel in his head, 197:37
    liberty p., 654:13
    make vile things p., 216:24
    most p. thing, 331:14
    nothing so p. as time, 84:*n*4
    ointment, 37:19
    stone set in silver sea, 179:12
    things most p. to me, 222:2
    three unspeakably p. things, 562:6
    truth is p. and divine, 271:19
    virtue like p. odors, 167:13
Precipice, close to edge of p., 746:19
Precise, art too p. in every part, 248:4
    silken terms p., 177:12
Precisely, thinking too p. on event, 206:1
Precision, numerical p. soul of science,
    623:12
Precocity, for p. price demanded, 487:14
    to laugh a miracle of p., 108:5
Predatory human hands, 618:2
Predecessor, illustrious p., 322:*n*2
Predecessors, illustrious p., 322:17
    scientist takes off from p., 682:6
Predestinate, he also did p., 43:8
Predestined from all eternity, 542:12
    intimates p., 570:9
    what fate p., 388:13
Predict phenomena, 433:1
Predicted nine of last five recessions,
    796:17
Predicts ruin of the state, 375:7
Predilection, I have p. for painting, 579:10
Predominance, treachers by spherical p.,
    215:29
Predominating, with sniffles p., 626:8
Preeminence, contending for p., 366:19
Preeminent, to be bravest and p., 52:32
Pre-existing, cells from p. cells, 527:*n*5
Prefer geniality to grammar, 613:17
    gentlemen p. blondes, 737:10
    I would p. not to, 516:22

Press *(continued)*
  freedom of p. has suffered most, 790:8
  freedom of speech or of p., 361:1
  I like to p. wild flowers, 843:1
  inform p. home Christmas, 647:16
  let's go to p., 750:5
  liberty of p., 360:3, 462:14
  microscopes and telescopes of p., 631:20
  Monday p. reports, 771:15
  my last p. conference, 790:19
  not falling man, 231:1
  not p. upon brow of labor, 622:3
  sort of wild animal, 706:3
  stir p. feel with fingers, 519:13
  tenth Muse governs p., 503:11
  toward the mark, 45:35
  with vigor on, 318:12
Pressed into service out of shape, 669:3
  love though p. with ill, 348:17
Presses, clatter of p., 709:7
Presseth, thy hand p. me sore, 17:9
Press's, gret P. freedom, 515:1
Pressure, form and p., 204:13
  government relaxing p., 463:8
  grace under p., 754:8
  hardly feel p. of age, 77:1
  of cosmos, 582:17
  of exigencies of life, 607:13
  opening first p. off second, 671:16
Prestige, convenience comfort p., 852:1
Presume, Dr. Livingstone I p., 580:1
  not God to scan, 311:9
  yourself ignorant, 403:1
Presuming on changeful potency, 208:17
Presumption, amused by its p., 741:14
  in kings and ministers, 338:17
  in wisdom, 344:6
Presumptions, art flying in face of p., 584:16
Pretend, let us not p. to doubt, 574:2
  Let's P. and we did, 829:10
  to know when you do not, 59:16
Pretender, God bless the P., 314:12
  had she known p. he was, 656:12
  James I James II and Old P., 726:7
  who P. or who King, 314:12
Pretends, life it p. to build on, 758:11
Pretense, for a p. make prayers, 38:29
  to faint meaning make p., 284:3
Pretenses to break known rules by, 254:14
Pretension, this p. a prejudice, 586:11
Pretensions, aristocratic p., 676:16
Pretentiousness, correcting of p., 541:11
Prêtre guerrier poète, 524:*n*11
Prettier, pebble or p. shell, 291:6
Prettiest little parlor, 446:9
Pretty, all my p. ones, 222:1
  Babe all burning bright, 168:26
  birds do sing, 232:7
  Bobby Shaftoe, 861:9
  but is it Art, 633:15
  everything that p. is, 225:12
  Fanny's way, 305:11
  feet like snails, 248:10
  follies themselves commit, 188:20
  how town, 740:8
  how-de-do, 565:13
  I'll get you my p., 786:9
  it is a p. world, 787:4
  kettle of fish, 565:1

Pretty *(continued)*
  little toes, 859:10
  maids all in row, 857:11
  my p. maid, 859:1
  need park policeman p. girl, 726:1
  no burial this p. pair, 843:13
  only p. ring time, 200:5
  pleasures might me move, 160:3
  poem Mr. Pope, 295:13
  puts on his p. looks, 178:9
  state of things, 565:13
  tell me p. maiden, 601:14
  to see what money will do, 288:20
  to think so, 754:3
  what do for p. girls, 642:19
  young wards, 564:18
Prevail against human reason, 786:14
  conditions dat p., 737:4
  evening shades p., 301:15
  fair words p., 634:14
  gates of hell not p., 36:25
  God who is able to p., 252:19
  his rising fogs p., 284:3
  make best ideas p., 530:5
  man will p., 748:21
  masculine values that p., 700:10
  necessity knows no law except p., 103:20
  'tis the Majority p., 545:2
  truth shall p. when none cares, 535:5
  will looking ill p., 269:20
Prevailed, David p. over the Philistine, 11:30
  the dragon p. not, 48:28
  with double sway, 342:7
Prevails, when vice p., 301:25
  where commerce long p., 341:2
Prevarication, last dike of p., 345:8
Prevent, enjoy religion p. others, 555:16
  lower from getting more, 80:25
  me from carrying you up, 69:12
  surest way to p. war, 404:13
Prevention, anthology used for p., 743:20
  of mutual crime, 80:29
  society for p. of croolty to money, 574:*n*1
Prevents our being natural, 274:12
Previous, calling to mind p. benefaction, 73:2
  result of p. study, 406:6
  returned home p. night, 664:4
Prey, animals and athletes not p., 715:3
  at fortune, 214:2
  beast of p. in aristocratic races, 589:13
  eagle seeketh p., 15:16
  expects his evening p., 335:13
  fear birds of p., 211:3
  great lord yet p. to all, 311:9
  greater p. upon less, 317:4
  have they not divided the p., 10:35
  of fear, 714:17
  of rich on poor, 357:13
  of rival imperialisms, 731:10
  on garbage, 202:17
  people easily becomes p., 143:4
  smaller fleas on him p., 299:4
  to dumb forgetfulness a p., 334:24
  to hastening ills a p., 341:29
  universal p., 207:27
  Venus fastened to p., 290:12
  where eagles dare not perch, 173:35
  young lions roar after p., 19:11

Preying on people's vanity ignorance, 830:3
Priam's curtain, 191:7
Priapus, it is I P. crying, 85:16
  made of marble, 95:23
Price, abatement and low p., 208:26
  for precocity p. demanded, 487:14
  great p. for wisdom, 541:5
  greater p. than life, 758:15
  greet cheep holde at litel p., 136:17
  heaven put p. upon goods, 354:10
  is far above rubies, 23:27
  is labor in exchange for anything, 517:12
  life exacts for peace, 752:10
  market p. they said, 547:2
  men have their p., 304:17
  natural and market p., 404:8
  of everything, 604:24
  of justice eternal publicity, 645:5
  of liberty, 366:*n*6
  of thousand horses, 658:7
  of wisdom is above rubies, 14:35
  pay any p., 799:7
  pearl of great p., 36:7
  too high p. for harmony, 525:16
  weighed for my p., 30:39
  what p. bananas, 817:10
  will fall, 167:25
  words beyond p., 830:5
Priced, weighed measured p. everything, 498:25
Priceless, human life p., 758:15
Prices, contrivance to raise p., 338:15
  spiral of rising p., 682:9
Prick and sting her, 202:20
  if you p. us do we not bleed, 188:31
  it mark it with B, 857:1
  sides of my intent, 219:18
Pricking, gentle knight p. on plain, 160:17
  gonfalon bubble, 692:14
  of my thumbs, 221:23
Pricks, honor p. me on, 186:35
  kick against the p., 42:8, 65:12
  to subsequent volumes, 207:29
Pride, age that will p. deflower, 161:5
  aiming at blest abodes, 167:*n*3
  all the p. cruelty and ambition, 160:13
  and conceit original sin, 300:3
  and courage of patriot, 556:3
  bold peasantry country's p., 341:29
  chastening in hour of p., 474:16
  coy submission modest p., 266:11
  Democratic Party without p. of ancestry, 548:8
  Envy Avarice three sparks, 130:18
  fell with my fortunes, 197:30
  from p. vainglory and hypocrisy, 50:11
  goeth before destruction, 22:2
  he that is low no p., 282:3
  I know thy p., 11:26
  idleness and p., 320:14
  in Casey's bearing, 630:3
  in occupation, 560:6
  in their port, 341:5
  is hateful before God, 32:17
  is his own glass, 208:1
  is therefore pleasure, 287:2
  king over children of p., 15:24
  land of pilgrims' p., 469:8
  lintel low to keep out p., 601:11

Pride *(continued)*
 look backward with p., 668:21
 mother's p. father's joy, 397:15
 my high-blown p. broke under me, 231:2
 of country, 490:2
 of kings, 310:20
 of peacock glory of God, 372:17
 of power sink, 344:6
 of those who have survived, 667:12
 perished in his p., 392:9
 plume here buckle, 587:8
 pomp and circumstance, 214:8
 pomp and p., 601:11
 rank p., 301:19
 rid earth of him in my p., 652:3
 shall bring him low, 23:21
 soldier's p., 491:8
 solemn p. yours, 477:2
 speak with p. of our doings, 713:17
 speech admirable in human p., 759:2
 stoic's p., 311:9
 tasted all the summer's p., 371:9
 that licks the dust, 312:10
 that puts country down, 844:7
 they lost their p., 776:11
 to relieve wretched his p., 342:5
 touched to quick, 491:8
 towering in p. of place, 220:28
 tyrant is child of P., 68:6
 vain the sage's p., 313:6
 was not made for men, 32:19
 will have a fall, 68:n2
Priest all shaven and shorn, 861:15
 free me from turbulent p., 127:2
 God's high p., 42:30
 I the Muses' p. sing, 99:26
 like people like p., 30:13
 love the only p., 554:7
 no difference 'twixt P. and Clerk, 248:6
 O mysterious p., 438:3
 of most authentic creed, 554:4
 soldier poet, 524:20
 still is Nature's p., 393:12
 the true God's p., 253:12
 well ought p. example give, 201:n2
 while runnin' for p., 704:7
Priestcraft, pious times ere p., 283:6
Priestlike, waters at p. task, 439:11
Priestly vestments evidence of servile status,
   613:10
 vestments in dens, 534:9
Priests, ancestors p. in temple, 458:24
 bless her when she is riggish, 223:15
 by mightier hand, 447:10
 Miss Lonelyhearts p., 766:12
 not merit praise of poets, 602:1
 poets not yet p., 602:1
 stood firm on dry ground, 10:19
Priests', hell paved with p. skulls, 119:2
Priez Dieu que tous nous veuille absoudre,
   139:n6
Prim, mouth so p., 720:1
Primal eldest curse, 205:14
Primary, great p. human affections, 529:8
 imagination, 403:3
Prime, buried him before p., 854:7
 gather Rose whilst p., 161:5
 give him always of p., 299:5
 laurel for perfect p., 548:1

Prime *(continued)*
 light the p. work of God, 265:n2
 lovely April of her p., 225:29
 obeyed at p., 453:21
 of youth a frost of cares, 164:17
 one's p. elusive, 804:19
 rose up in his p., 724:14
 what is the p. of life, 77:11
 Zeus p. mover, 65:11
Prime Minister returned, 650:7
 what war said P., 766:4
Primer, armed with his p., 409:18
Primeval cosmic night, 675:12
 forest p., 466:16
 mountains in p. sleep, 534:9
Primitive impulses of heart, 479:n1
 man tactile man, 703:1
 North America, 757:2
 people not waken sleeper, 602:18
 terror, 721:10
 unattached state, 676:4
Primordial images of collective unconscious,
   675:2
Primrose path of dalliance treads, 201:23
 sweet as the p., 342:12
 way, 220:20
Primum non nocere, 72:n5
Primus inter pares, 124:17
Prince, advise the p., 717:14
 can mak belted knight, 380:13
 duty subject owes p., 176:2
 first servant of state, 330:12
 good night sweet p., 207:15
 great P. in prison lies, 235:5
 have no study but war, 142:12
 I am not P. Hamlet, 717:14
 I warn you, 771:14
 imitate fox and lion, 142:15
 in serving his p., 62:10
 keeps tortoise enclosed, 83:2
 Lucifer uprose, 541:16
 must be lion, 111:n7
 not propose it to my p., 314:10
 of apple towns, 795:9
 of Aquitaine, 469:4
 of clouds haunts tempest, 524:8
 of darkness a gentleman, 217:1
 of Peace, 26:31
 of Wales in small but costly crown, 693:2
 Rasselas P. of Abyssinia, 324:24
 semblable au p. des nuées, 524:n1
 subject Father Son, 235:26
 there is a p. fallen, 11:40
 till I p. of love beheld, 371:9
Princedoms Virtues Powers, 267:8
Princely counsel in his face, 265:8
Princerple, don't believe in p., 515:2
Princes, all p. I, 234:4
 ancestors p. of earth, 459:n1
 and lords may flourish, 341:29
 blaze forth death of p., 196:9
 but breath of kings, 377:16
 contentment in being equal to p., 237:3
 fall like one of the p., 18:14
 find few real friends, 329:22
 gilded monuments of p., 226:15
 hate traitor but love treason, 91:n12
 kings and p. have philosophy, 77:12
 like to heavenly bodies, 167:24

Princes *(continued)*
 must a word to be addressed to p., 152:4
 orgulous, 423:n2
 pale kings and p., 439:6
 put not your trust in p., 20:19
 sweet aspect of p., 231:2
 Three P. of Serendip, 336:3
 whose merchants are p., 27:12
Princes', cottages p. palaces, 187:27
 hangs on p. favors, 231:2
 not so arched as p. palaces, 244:8
Princess descended of kings, 224:14
 felt pea through mattresses, 461:19
 thoughtless saying of p., 331:19
 three days afterwards p. buried, 542:11
Princesses would never leave without me,
   757:7
Principal translators between dream and
   reality, 715:14
 wisdom is the p. thing, 20:28
Principalities, against p. and powers, 45:31
 men fear power p. of air, 691:12
 never known to exist, 142:14
 nor powers, 43:12
Principality in Utopia, 448:5
Principle, active p. of literature, 659:2
 but a cold p., 252:n2
 don't believe in p., 515:2
 general p. gives no help, 390:5
 Greatest Happiness P., 465:1
 hain't money but p., 649:7
 inconsistencies in p., 574:16
 love our p., 444:1
 moderation in p. a vice, 355:2
 necessary and fundamental p., 338:11
 nihilist takes no p. on trust, 511:15
 o' the thing, 649:7
 of Conservation of Force, 527:13
 old but true as fate, 91:n12
 on which society not founded, 333:11
 one God one p. of being, 115:26
 one p. make universe single creature,
   117:9
 precedent embalms p., 459:10
 rebels from p., 345:14
 same p. in whatever shape, 474:13
 strange p. as first requirement, 522:5
Principles and traditions of nation, 798:1
 elements or p. of bodies, 359:16
 embrace p. or mistresses, 340:8
 facts alarm more than p., 360:11
 faithfulness and sincerity as first p., 62:11
 first p. take deepest root, 361:14
 fools say man has or has not p., 445:7
 guide his life by true p., 93:17
 important p. inflexible, 477:6
 less than chaff, 612:7
 looking away from p., 582:18
 might p. swaller, 514:23
 of Political Economy, 674:5
 renounce his p., 360:10
 restless unfixed in p., 283:8
 that gave America birth, 611:9
 to effect safety, 357:2
Print, all news fit to p., 614:7
 eternity of p., 700:2
 faith he'll p. it, 380:6
 gentlehearted in p., 407:2
 I love a ballad in p., 228:31

Proclaims, apparel oft p. the man, 201:26
   peace p. olives of age, 227:12
Proconsuls, each year new p., 114:14
Procrastination, incivility and p., 418:6
   is thief of time, 306:4
   keeping up with yesterday, 680:5
   no idleness no p., 535:*n1*
Procreant cradle, 219:15
Procreate, that we might p. like trees, 256:6
Procul hinc procul este severi, 105:*n4*
Procurer of contentedness, 252:25
Procuress to Lords of Hell, 484:1
Prodigal, Catiline p. of own possessions, 95:3
   chariest maid p. enough, 201:22
   enemy be p., 775:4
   how p. the soul, 201:31
   of ease, 283:9
   son, 39:35
Prodigality, spring of p., 345:3
Prodigies, all Africa and her p., 255:13
Prodigy, what a p. is man, 280:8
Produce according to aptitudes, 510:*n5*
   but not take possession, 58:13
   eating p. of the land, 53:31
   laboring to p. bons mots, 278:6
   my foot my feather, 825:5
   perfect circles and squares, 81:27
   sacrificed to p. her, 627:10
   the person, 124:1
   things and to rear them, 58:13
Produced, after they are p., 58:7
   intellectual product judged from age p.,
    573:4
Producer, promoting interest of p., 339:1
Produces, final cause p. motion, 80:5
Producing, consume without p., 609:8
Product, book is p. of different self, 658:5
   happiness not spontaneous p., 683:3
   man's nature cultural p., 757:12
Production, consumption sole end of all p.,
   339:1
   entrepreneur contributes to p., 703:2
   eternity in love with p. of time, 372:15
   improvement of instruments of p., 511:3
   means of social p., 511:*n2*
   opens demand for products, 387:2
   principle of economic p., 683:2
   utility or cost of p., 584:2
Products, demand for p., 387:2
   of art and science, 733:5
Profanation to keep in, 248:17
Profane and old wives' fables, 46:20
   and vain babblings, 46:29
   for me to p. it, 430:20
   hence ye p., 275:16
   things holy p. clean obscene, 246:10
   things sacred or things p., 281:22
Profaned heavenly gift of poesy, 284:11
   one word too often p., 430:20
Profess not the knowledge, 31:31
   politics like ours p., 317:4
Profession, hold up Adam's p., 206:15
   is to disguise, 143:14
   most ancient p., 632:15
   people differ in discourse and p., 277:12
Professions, analysis third of impossible p.,
   608:4
   one of p. which are full, 506:22
   satisfied to have two p., 622:5

Professor encouraging clever pupil, 322:20
   of art of puffing, 368:2
   of Harvard Law School, 695:10
   profit p. naught, 164:14
Professors like literature dead, 708:7
   of Dismal Science, 435:7
Professorship, unsuccessful attempt to obtain
   p., 661:3
Proffer, fawning greyhound did p., 185:10
Profit, and the p. and loss, 718:20
   between p. and the loss, 719:15
   by folly of others, 108:13
   by losing our prayers, 223:11
   by their example, 352:11
   engine of Enterprise, 701:16
   entrepreneurial p., 703:2
   few p. by advice, 102:20
   in all labor there is p., 21:32
   murder land for private p., 782:5
   no more p. of shining nights, 176:20
   no p. but the name, 205:34
   no p. where no pleasure, 175:21
   private enterprise for p., 698:10
   professor naught, 164:14
   title and p. I resign, 301:*n1*
   truth as opposeth no p., 246:15
   what p. of all his labor, 23:32
   winds blow p., 777:8
   wise men p. more from fools, 88:2
Profitable, lie with purpose most p., 645:16
Profited, age not p. so much as lost, 506:14
   what is a man p., 36:27
Profits, keeping p. up by keeping wages
   down, 404:9
   little p. that idle king, 481:7
Profound, both may be called p., 58:7
   in his view, 350:*n1*
   man thinks woman p., 590:*n1*
   subtle and p. female, 58:11
   thoughts arise in debate, 808:10
   whole subject is too p., 470:12
Profoundness of yearning for more vivid
   world, 788:5
Profundity, arriving sometimes at p., 826:11
Profuse strains of unpremeditated art, 429:16
Progeny, Angels p. of light, 267:8
   give world corrupt p., 100:2
   of learning, 367:5
Prognostics not always prophecies, 336:7
Program, computer no better than its p.,
   783:12
   for tomorrow, 702:13
Programmed to preserve genes, 836:3
Progress based on universal desire, 558:20
   call P. Tomorrow, 451:11
   Christ's p. and His prayer-time, 278:29
   comfortable disease, 740:13
   competition essential for p., 559:6
   condition of social p., 556:1
   from want to want, 328:4
   history p. of freedom, 390:7
   in human virtue, 382:22
   man's mark, 494:14
   no p. except individual, 524:18
   no struggle no p., 509:13
   not accident but necessity, 523:2
   not real cannot be permanent, 573:3
   of all countries connected, 693:9
   of artist self-sacrifice, 722:7

Progress *(continued)*
   our goal, 444:1
   part of nature, 523:2
   Pilgrim's P. about man left family, 560:16
   promote p. of science, 737:18
   rake's p., 490:10
   scientific thought human p., 591:8
   separate yet one in mutual p., 610:19
   social p. of each country, 693:9
   swell a p., 717:14
   test of our p., 698:7
   to fuller life, 648:16
Prohibited, means which are not p., 371:4
Prohibiting free exercise thereof, 361:1
   licensing and p., 263:5
Prohibitions, meant p. to be absolutes, 711:1
Proie, à sa p. attachée, 290:*n5*
Project for extracting sunbeams, 298:16
Pro-labor policies of governments, 694:4
Proletarian state, 649:4
   suppression of bourgeois state by p.,
    654:10
Proletarians have nothing to lose, 511:8
Proletariat class of wage laborers, 511:*n3*
   come across for p., 860:*n1*
   dictatorship of the p., 510:7, 654:6
   Italian p., 702:6
   product of industry, 511:4
   revolutionary class, 511:4
Prologue, excuse came p., 268:2
   make a long p., 33:14
   what's past is p., 229:26
Prologues, happy p. to swelling act, 219:4
   over, 687:15
Prolongeth, joyfulness p. his days, 32:42
Promethean heat, 215:7
   sparkle right P. fire, 177:8
Prominent, the more laws are made p., 59:10
Promise, broke no p., 310:15
   eating air on p. of supply, 191:22
   keep word of p. to our ear, 222:22
   most given when least said, 164:18
   never p. more than perform, 103:18
   none relies on, 292:24
   of pneumatic bliss, 718:8
   oh p. me, 579:12
   only to do our best, 770:16
   years of p. rapidly roll round, 386:2
Promise-crammed, I eat the air p., 204:19
Promised, already in p. land, 832:7
   fruits outdo what flowers p., 164:4
   land, 441:15, 555:4
   Land beyond wilderness, 618:1
   Man who had been p., 734:11
   seen p. land, 823:10
   shalt be what thou art p., 219:10
Promises, age perform p. of youth, 324:24
   America was p., 734:11
   fails where most it p., 210:24
   good memory to keep p., 588:12
   to keep, 669:15
Promontory, as if a p. washed away, 236:19
   blue p. with trees, 223:33
   like one that stands on p., 172:32
   on little p. stood, 521:7
   once I sat upon p., 181:8
   see one p. and see all, 241:3
   seems to me sterile p., 203:17
   stretched like a p., 267:15

Promote flourishing of arts, 737:18
    general welfare, 360:13
    public interest, 338:18
Promoting, not by destroying but p., 345:2
Promotion, none sweat but for p., 198:6
Prompt, apology too p., 268:2
    death is generally p., 469:15
    in attack, 344:10
Prompter, dreamer is p., 675:11
Prompters, how many p., 408:8
Promptly, gives twice who gives p., 123:11
Prompts tongue to deal in fiction, 307:5
Prone to introspection, 715:4
Proneness to side with beauty, 676:16
Prongs, therrble p., 696:18
Pronoun, that relative p., 614:2
Pronounce, foreigners spell better than p.,
    559:16
Pronounced first intelligible sentence, 759:2
    speak as I p. it to you, 204:11
Pronouncements of history or science, 782:4
Proof, bliss in p., 227:22
    cite as p. he was right, 785:3
    give me ocular p., 214:9
    history p. of theories, 554:15
    mistaking metaphor for p., 658:14
    not one for putting off p., 670:3
    of a poet, 518:11
    of pudding in eating, 157:21
    that I have become pope, 693:11
    through the night, 411:1
    undying p., 556:3
Proofs, how I would correct p., 431:18
    of holy writ, 214:5
Proosian, French or Turk or P., 564:1
Prop, my very p., 188:16
    that doth sustain house, 190:2
Propaganda has to be popular, 726:11
Propagate, learn and p. best, 530:9
Propagated, Revolution p. downwards, 535:3
Propagation, all our p., 235:4
Propensities, excite my amorous p., 326:7
    natural p., 345:21
    semi-criminal p., 701:18
Propensity for emulation, 613:7
    for mastery, 613:8
    internal p. to unite, 694:1
    to forego, 580:21
Proper, circumstance and p. timing, 75:29
    fitting and p., 476:7
    gardener's work, 635:24
    in our own p. entrails, 197:19
    man as see in summer's day, 181:2
    mate, 348:20
    men as ever trod, 195:14
    opinions for time of year, 776:3
    price upon goods, 354:10
    silence gives p. grace to women, 67:4
    stations, 497:23
    study of mankind is man, 311:9
    time to marry, 348:20
    union of gin and vermouth, 748:7
    words in proper places, 298:10
Propertied as all tuned spheres, 224:4
Property, a very handsome p., 543:11
    abolition of private p., 511:5
    acquiring and possessing p., 339:9
    best ideas common p., 106:15
    Christian men control p. interests, 580:4

Property *(continued)*
    common judges of p., 324:17
    contempt for equality of p., 462:11
    deprive of life liberty p., 361:8
    deprived of life liberty or p., 361:4
    get hold of portable p., 498:34
    government resting on p., 77:20
    has duties, 459:6
    is theft, 480:2
    judiciary safeguard of p., 626:18
    liberty p. no stamps, 846:13
    national honor national p., 376:15
    neither persons nor p. safe, 510:2
    neither p. nor honor touched, 142:16
    of easiness, 206:18
    our p. subject to control and disposal,
      362:5
    private p. fruit of labor, 678:14
    proputty proputty, 486:19
    sacredness of p., 559:7
    subject to community, 615:12
    system of private p., 753:20
    they can call their own, 349:14
    unequal distribution of p., 366:19
    was thus appalled, 207:17
Prophecies, prognostics not always p., 336:7
Prophecy gratuitous error, 513:8
    re-created from Bible, 813:6
    self-fulfilling p. false definition, 785:3
    spirit of p. in me, 76:17
    trumpet of p. O Wind, 429:5
Prophesy, don't never p., 515:4
    in part, 44:20
    O I could p., 187:5
Prophesying war, 401:16
Prophet, ask us p., 809:4
    cite as proof he was right, 785:3
    Elijah the p., 31:4
    historian p. in reverse, 404:10
    not without honor, 36:10
    of the soul, 452:18
    said I, 479:6
    sons of the p., 849:2
    under judgment he preaches, 735:15
    your p. the Nazarite, 188:2
Prophetic, awful pause p. of end, 306:1
    O my p. soul, 202:15
    soul of the wide world, 227:12
Prophets and kings, 39:21
    best of p. is the past, 424:28
    beware false p., 35:7
    come down from mountains, 572:15
    do they live forever, 30:33
    is Saul among the p., 11:20
    Jerusalem that killest p., 37:5
    law and the p., 35:5, 36:43
    men reject p., 526:3
    ministry of the p., 30:20
    mouth of holy p., 38:42
    not destroy law or p., 34:2
    of Nature, 391:13
    that which was given to the P., 120:13
    wisest p. make sure, 336:7
    words of p. on subway walls, 837:8
Propitiation, he is p. for our sins, 47:38
    religion of powers, 602:17
Propitious hours, 426:8
    miracles p. accidents, 629:11
    no light p. shone, 348:22

Propontic and Hellespont, 214:15
Proportion, genius consummate sense of p.,
    321:*n*5
    insisture course p., 207:24
    music wherever there is p., 256:7
    preserving sweetness of p., 237:19
    some strangeness in p., 168:12
    when no p. kept, 180:14
Proportional, acceleration p. to applied force,
    291:*n*2
    to motive force, 291:3
Proportioned, freight p. to groove, 547:8
    to human constitution, 306:17
Proportions, fashion matter of p., 700:17
    in small p. beauties see, 238:14
Propose to fight it out, 532:15
Proposed, before a joy p., 227:22
Proposes, man p. God disposes, 138:7
Proposition, life's a tough p., 678:8
    no general p. worth damn, 578:15
    that all men equal, 476:7
    undesirable to believe p., 661:1
Propositions, general p. concrete cases, 578:6
    man to frame general p., 578:15
Propriété c'est le vol, 480:2
Propriety, frights isle from her p., 213:20
    not infused from without, 82:12
    rules of p., 63:28
Propter vitam vivendi perdere causas, 113:*n*9
Proputty proputty proputty, 486:19
Prorsus credibile est quia ineptum est,
    116:*n*6
Pro's, from p. and con's they fell, 157:4
Prose, all not p. is verse, 278:18
    Browning used poetry for writing p.,
      604:9
    connect p. and passion, 684:3
    fancy p. style, 755:15
    his p. was flowery, 783:7
    homely definitions of p., 403:20
    Meredith p. Browning, 604:9
    money p. of life, 456:12
    opposed to metre, 402:15
    poetry must be as well written as p.,
      709:13
    run mad, 312:3
    speaking p. without knowing it, 278:17
    unattempted yet in p. or rhyme, 263:20
    verse will seem p., 293:8
    words in best order, 403:20
Prosecuted, find motive in narrative be p.,
    560:13
    help p. and victim, 732:16
Proserpin, where P. gathering flowers,
    266:8
Prospect, dull p. of distant good, 284:24
    every p. pleases, 416:4
    no p. of an end, 340:4
    noblest p. Scotchman sees, 326:18
    not within p. of belief, 218:32
Prospects more pleasing than fruition,
    114:*n*3
    shining p. rise, 301:11
Prosper, evil deeds do not p., 54:27
    made all to p. in his hand, 7:24
    treason doth never p., 168:23
    whatsoever he doeth shall p., 15:27
    Wolf that keep it p., 634:13
Prospered, honor friend who p., 65:7

Prosperity and salvation in union, 653:18
    ben in p. and it remembren, 133:23
    best discover vice, 167:12
    blessing of Old Testament, 167:10
    comes to bad man, 61:12
    dormant in p., 416:10
    doth bewitch men, 244:5
    friend not known in p., 32:24
    good things which belong to p., 167:9
    in day of p. be joyful, 24:20
    in p. easy to find friend, 81:*n*2
    in the day of p., 32:22
    jest's p. lies in ear, 177:15
    life comes to end in p., 65:8
    makes friends, 104:9
    middle-aged p., 752:6
    not without fears, 167:11
    one man who can stand p., 434:23
    remembrance of p., 32:22
    social p. means man happy, 451:16
    studies are an ornament in p., 90:13
    thy p. exceedeth the fame, 12:19
    tries souls even of wise, 95:5
    undermining the very p., 615:11
    with more taste, 300:4
    within thy palaces, 20:2
    would not be so welcome, 270:9
Prosperity's very bond of love, 229:3
Prosperous, if California becomes p.
    country, 502:17
    make starving dog p., 561:16
    remorse sleeps in p. period, 331:16
Prospers, homeland is wherever he p.,
    75:26
    who p. one day suffer reverse, 68:11
Prostitute, I puff the p. away, 284:8
Protect, Heaven p. working girl, 613:3
    I will p. you, 737:6
    I'll p. it now, 451:22
    two solitudes p. each other, 677:2
    us by thy might, 469:9
    what it advertises, 818:13
    woman taught to p. herself, 521:22
Protected, hegemony p. by armor of
    coercion, 731:6
    rights of laboring man p., 580:4
Protection and security of people, 339:10
    equal p. of the laws, 361:8
    equally entitled to p., 386:13
    return for p. of society, 464:18
    to the oppressed, 73:18
Protector when he first appears, 77:23
Protects lingering dewdrop, 395:20
Protest, lady doth p. too much, 205:4
    openly discrimination slander, 674:8
    voice of p. needed, 539:10
Protestant, because I was P., 735:18
    gunpowder and P. religion, 434:10
    I mean the P. religion, 322:5
    thy P. to be, 247:16
Protestants Jews Turks in one ship, 255:3
Papists or P., 326:17
Protesting, dignity of truth lost with p.,
    237:17
Proteus of fire and flood, 403:13
    rising from sea, 394:19
Protracted, life p. is p. woe, 324:8
Protracting life not deduct from death,
    93:14

Proud, all p. and mighty have, 317:12
    and angry dust, 619:12
    and chivalrous spirit, 81:17
    apt the poor to be p., 210:3
    arrogancy of the p., 27:2
    befits p. birth, 67:5
    clergyman, 322:16
    death be not p., 236:7
    eats up himself, 208:1
    Edward's power, 380:10
    ever fair and never p., 213:11
    every cock p. on own dunghill, 103:*n*2
    fashions in p. Italy, 179:10
    foot of conqueror, 178:28
    grief is p., 178:3
    here shall thy p. waves be stayed, 15:7
    his name, 396:11
    how p. word Man rings, 649:2
    I'm Black and I'm P., 829:12
    in arms, 260:14
    in humility, 240:24
    instruct sorrows to be p., 178:3
    is spirit of Zeus-fostered kings, 52:14
    knowledge is p., 348:12
    lay p. usurpers low, 380:11
    make death p. to take us, 224:2
    man drest in authority, 211:13
    man's contumely, 203:33
    me no prouds, 184:6
    men in old age, 68:3
    men of action, 442:14
    mistress' orders to perform, 313:20
    O p. death, 207:16
    oh be p. of him, 837:15
    of ancient heritage, 799:7
    our purses shall be p., 175:37
    pray God to keep me from being p.,
        287:23
    Rose sad Rose, 636:22
    scattered the p., 38:39
    Science, 311:5
    seat of Lucifer, 268:7
    setter up and puller down of kings,
        172:*n*2
    sleepy and p., 724:11
    small things make base men p., 172:16
    that he learned so much, 348:12
    that they are not proud, 240:24
    'tis all the p. shall be, 309:29
    too p. for a wit, 343:2
    too p. for relief, 671:2
    too p. to beg, 849:1
    too p. to fight, 611:1
    too p. to importune, 335:18
    tower in the town, 478:6
    towers, 421:7
    uncertain balance of p. time, 165:19
    vain man may become p., 287:3
    wear it like banner for p., 762:14
    world said I, 272:17
    yet not p. to know, 309:2
    yet wretched thing, 233:3
Proudest distinction of Americans, 772:3
    of his works, 353:12
Proudly, bearing birthrights p., 177:22
    die p. if not live p., 624:*n*1
    what so p. we hailed, 411:1
Proud-pied April, 227:8
Prouds, proud me no p., 184:6

Proust of the Papuans, 796:7
Proust's Law, 817:18
Prove a beauteous flower, 183:11
    all things, 46:13
    believing where cannot p., 483:10
    came to p. him with hard questions,
        12:18
    fairy gold and 'twill p., 228:20
    him first, 32:9
    I could p. everything, 825:11
    if I do p. her haggard, 214:2
    I'll p. more true, 183:7
    mysterious by this love, 234:6
    one of the elected, 827:3
    show doubt p. faith, 493:10
    so fond, 218:14
    some new pleasures p., 234:22
    warrant she'll p. an excuse, 367:29
    we p. what we want to p., 648:2
    we will all the pleasures p., 170:6
    when givers p. unkind, 204:2
Proved a very woe, 227:22
    believe one who has p. it, 98:11
    benefits p. by scientists, 841:13
    error and upon me p., 227:17
    them and found them worthy, 31:16
    which was to be p., 84:16
Provençal song, 437:7
Provender, truly a peck of p., 181:25
Proverb, a p. and a byword, 12:17
    hare of whom p. goes, 177:24
    thou shalt become a p., 10:9
    till Life illustrated P., 440:18
Proverbed with grandsire phrase, 182:20
Proverbs, books like p., 282:8
    contradict each other, 783:2
    King Solomon wrote P., 623:11
    of Solomon, 497:25
    patch griefs with p., 195:5
    Solomon spake three thousand p., 12:14
Proveth, hasty marriage seldom p. well, 173:4
Provide, foes will p. with arms, 97:12
    for common defense, 360:13
    for human wants, 345:12
    for those with too little, 698:7
    God will p. himself a lamb, 7:8
    if any p. not for his own, 46:22
    know worst and p. for it, 352:13
    provide, 670:7
Provided, right that wants be p., 345:12
Providence, Auschwitz existed not speak of
    P., 805:9
    behind frowning p., 347:4
    behold now another p., 247:9
    Chance nickname for P., 356:4
    fashioned us holler, 514:23
    grand scene and design in p., 350:16
    may assert eternal P., 263:21
    on side of last reserve, 275:*n*1
    one thing in creation to demonstrate P.,
        112:8
    parsimony requires no p., 345:24
    reasoned high of P., 265:13
    reliance on divine p., 357:4
    special p., 207:8
    their guide, 268:17
    trust in P., 253:9
Provident, women p. instead, 748:1
Providently caters for sparrow, 198:3

Provider, essential p. of elements, 530:8

Provides, fury p. arms, 96:28

Provideth her meat in the summer, 21:4

Province, all knowledge my p., 165:21

Provinces, kissed away kingdoms and p., 223:24

    these limbs her p., 235:9

Provincial, worse than p. parochial, 584:10

Provision, decent p. for poor, 327:9

    education best p. for old age, 79:17

    for well-educated young women, 406:9

    make not p. for flesh, 43:26

Provisions not suspended in exigencies, 502:18

    spare nothing but p., 109:20

Provoke, good p. to harm, 212:1

    not children to anger, 46:4

    silent dust, 334:17

Provokes desire, 220:21

    no one p. me with impunity, 124:8

Provoketh, beauty p. thieves, 197:34

Provoking most justly thy wrath, 50:18

Prow of the house, 809:9

    youth on the p., 335:13

Prows, water from sharp p., 703:12

Proximity, exaltation from p. of disaster, 665:5

Proximus sum egomet mihi, 88:n8

Prudence, forced into p. in youth, 406:22

    never to practice either, 562:6

Prudent, love is p., 138:13

    man looketh well to his going, 21:31

    mind can see room, 68:11

    pushes his p. purpose, 306:5

    virtue and p. act, 344:14

Prudery a kind of avarice, 416:22

Prudes, stay far hence you p., 105:4

Prunella, rest all leather or p., 311:12

Prunes and prism, 498:27

    longing for stewed p., 211:6

Pruninghooks, spears into p., 26:11

Pruritus, disputandi p. ecclesiarum scabies, 233:n1

Prussia hurried to the field, 368:n5

Prussian, French or Turk or P., 564:1

Pry, animals and athletes not p., 715:3

    loose old walls, 681:13

Psalm, some must sing lungful of p., 789:6

Psalmist, sweet p. of Israel, 12:9

Psalms, from poetry p., 768:12

    King David wrote P., 623:11

    lovers' sonnets turned p., 164:10

    make joyful noise with p., 18:29

    show ourselves glad with p., 49:23

    speaking to yourselves in p., 45:29

Psalteries, played before the Lord on p., 11:41

Psaltery, praise him with p., 20:21

Psara, blackened spine of P., 444:12

Pseudo-event comes about because planned, 792:23

Pseudo-promotion, Lateral Arabesque a p., 805:13

Psyche my Soul, 479:13

Psychiatrist, anybody who goes to a p., 695:16

Psychic development of individual, 607:11

    gods as p. factors, 675:6

    powers part of man's Self, 581:17

Psychical acts develop by reflex, 543:9

Psychoanalysis is mental illness, 672:10

    not the only way, 706:13

Psychoanalytic, new p. method irreplaceable, 607:7

Psychological moment, 604:16

    momentum or factor, 604:n3

    reason, 585:1

Psychology based on self-observation, 553:12

    children no use for p., 769:12

    knife cuts both ways, 526:7

    know baby's mind understand p., 747:14

    long past short history, 596:22

    of adultery, 661:2

    treating P. like natural science, 583:6

Ptolemy, authority and researches of P., 140:8

Pub, no pewter no p., 724:13

Public action which is not customary, 668:11

    anyone been to English p. school, 766:3

    be damned, 527:17

    British p. in fits of morality, 447:21

    buys opinions like meat, 559:4

    care, 265:8

    consideration of p. object, 73:17

    conspiracy against the p., 338:15

    debate on p. issues uninhibited, 774:3

    debt public blessing, 370:n2

    demands certainties, 690:18

    entertainer who understood his time, 693:14

    exempt from p. haunt, 197:37

    fit for p. authority, 67:23

    for the p. good, 124:18

    friend to p. amusements, 327:12

    good and private rights, 367:1

    has crude ideas, 416:23

    I and p. understand each other, 672:6

    in field of p. education, 733:1

    indifferent to p. welfare, 362:5

    intelligence of p. opinion, 556:1

    interest, 727:6

    life crown of career, 674:10

    life situation of power, 343:18

    like a Frog, 544:13

    make the p. stare, 423:23

    mean animal, 410:8

    men governed by p. reasons, 357:7

    men no sure tenure, 727:4

    men nor cheering crowds, 638:17

    men Slop Over, 555:11

    microcosm of p. school, 458:19

    must and will be served, 292:6

    no personal considerations in p. duty, 532:19

    no strike against p. safety, 659:18

    nor p. flame nor private, 313:25

    odium and public hatred, 409:10

    office public trust, 567:n1

    offices p. trusts, 413:14

    opinion everything, 474:15

    opinion exacts obedience, 538:7

    opinion in advance of law, 647:3

    Opinion variable, 537:7

    opinion weak tyrant, 506:9

    opinion welcomes talent, 73:18

    power to endanger p. liberty, 351:2

    prejudicial as p. indecency, 158:13

Public *(continued)*

    promote p. interest, 338:18

    reproached me in p., 388:4

    researchers into P. Opinion, 776:3

    say what one pleases about p. affairs, 711:2

    scandal is wicked, 277:24

    schools nurseries of vice, 322:1

    seldom forgive twice, 356:8

    sets friendship above p. welfare, 67:14

    sharp attacks on p. officials, 774:3

    sound of p. scorn, 268:8

    speaks to me as if I were p. meeting, 518:6

    speedy and p. trial, 361:5

    strength individual security, 370:8

    tune vulgar if p. hums it, 593:18

    unite for p. safety, 388:8

    vexes p. men, 482:12

    waste of p. money, 572:11

    welfare, 615:12

Publican, fawning p., 188:3

    the other a p., 40:7

Publicans and sinners, 35:34

Publication, all involved in p. of Satanic Verses, 758:4

Publicity, effect of p. on men, 570:6

    price of justice p., 645:5

    withhold finding from p., 365:1

Publicly, if a man p. denounces poetry, 830:15

Public's, aimed at p. heart hit it in stomach, 682:2

Publish and be damned, 389:7

    it not in the streets, 11:35

    it to all the nation, 297:5

    right or wrong, 419:12

    yourselves to sky, 583:9

Published, what should not be p. abroad, 72:16

Publisher, Barabbas a p., 425:10

    no author genius to p., 443:2

Publisheth peace, 28:18

Puck, streak of P., 594:8

Pudding, hasty p., 846:n3

    life's a p., 566:5

    proof of p. in eating, 157:21

    solid p. empty praise, 313:16

    sweets of Hasty P., 369:2

    to make bag p., 861:7

Pudding-bag string, 861:11

Puddle, stepped in a p., 860:16

    world is p.-wonderful, 739:12

Puddles, novel reflects mud p. underfoot, 417:1

Puddle-wonderful, world is p., 739:12

Puff the prostitute away, 284:8

Puffed and reckless libertine, 201:23

    charity not p. up, 44:18

    love not p. up, 44:18

Puffeth, knowledge p. up, 44:8

Puffing, professor of art of p., 368:2

Puffins razorbills guillemots and kittiwakes, 387:n5

Puissance, between corn-rows held old p., 691:12

Puissant nation rousing herself, 263:3

Pukes, sea passenger p. in, 424:8

Puking, mewling and p., 198:25

Pulitzer, decline the P. Prize, 708:5

Pull all together, 498:9
  chestnuts out of fire, 277:13
  door called p., 849:14
  down thy vanity, 709:11
  long p. strong p., 498:9
  not down your hedge, 251:12
  opportunities around for political p.,
    584:5
  Paquin p. down, 709:11
  weight, 615:5
Pulled our ploughs and borne our loads,
  715:8
Puller down of kings, 172:n2
Pulleth sword out of stone, 139:1
Pulleys, cry of p., 808:15
Pullin', you do de p. Sis Cow, 593:9
Pullman, ten years on P. cars, 723:14
Pulls, who p. me down, 171:4
Pulping, no p. of books, 786:14
Pulpit drum ecclesiastic, 270:14
Pulpits, some to common p., 196:16
Pulse, my p. like soft drum, 249:2
  of life stood still, 306:1
  of modern life economic, 683:2
  of the machine, 394:2
  poll feeling p., 666:16
  scene beat like a p., 809:11
Pulses, axioms proved upon p., 440:8
  give world other p., 435:20
Pumice, smoothed with dry p. stone, 93:22
Pump, president is p., 786:7
Pumpkin, frost is on p., 596:8
  put her in p. shell, 860:4
Pumpkins, coaches that change into p.,
  761:6
  where early p. blow, 500:4
Pun, good p. may be admitted, 355:16
  make so vile a p., 294:14
  pistol not feather, 407:29
Punch bowl's brink, 579:13
  brothers, 553:13
  hole in son of a bitch, 852:16
  in presence of passenjare, 553:13
Punctilious envoys Thine and Mine, 289:18
Punctual as a Star, 545:9
  rape of every day, 809:1
Punctuality politeness of kings, 370:16
Punic faith, 95:12
Punica fide, 95:n9
Punish, distrust impulse to p., 588:19
  the world for evil, 27:2
  to p. they answer prayers, 61:n2
Punished as enemy of country, 386:10
  big words always p., 68:3
  in the sight of men, 31:16
Punishing anyone between them, 398:28
  beware of p. wrongfully, 3:10
Punishment, broad effects of p., 589:14
  could not name all types of p., 97:27
  cruel and unusual p., 361:7
  Erinyes exact p. underground, 53:29
  fit the crime, 565:14
  good evil reward p., 286:9
  is greater than I can bear, 6:16
  let p. match offense, 91:13
  no p. prevent crimes, 773:6
  pleasing p. women bear, 174:25
  reward rather than p., 447:3
  servitude p. of guilt, 366:17

Punishment *(continued)*
  tames man, 589:14
  transgressed custom brings p., 562:16
Punishments, for great wrongdoing great p.,
  71:13
  rewards and p. in cards, 731:3
Punkin, frost is on p., 596:8
Pup, remember when he was p., 670:8
  since Hector was p., 848:2
Pupil, encouraging clever p., 322:20
Pupils, my p. crème de la crème, 804:17
  true teacher defends p., 444:14
Puppet, making President czar making him
  p., 802:13
Puppets best and worst are we, 491:6
  shut up box and p., 490:8
Puppies, greyhound p., 472:19
Puppy dogs' tails, 859:18
  mangled under a screaming wheel,
    791:13
  mongrel p. whelp hound, 341:17
Puppyism, dogmatism p. its full growth,
  458:7
Pur comme un ange, 369:n2
Purblind Doomsters, 574:13
  wimpled whining p., 176:33
Purchase, unless abroad p. alliance, 173:2
  you p. pain, 310:6
Purchased at price of chains, 353:3
  by merit of the wearer, 188:27
  history's p. page, 420:22
  with pain p. inherit pain, 176:18
Purchaser, new p. of country place, 769:3
  worth what p. will pay, 104:7
Pure and complete sorrow impossible, 542:16
  and disposed to mount to stars, 131:23
  and eloquent blood, 236:1
  and endless light, 279:5
  as an angel, 369:9
  as naked heavens, 393:4
  as snow, 204:5
  beauty of mathematics, 660:12
  blessed are the p. in heart, 33:33
  clean hands and a p. heart, 16:19
  clear as crystal, 499:8
  enjoyed trust of p. women, 686:7
  harmony is p. love, 169:10
  hearts as p. and fair, 564:20
  I will keep p. and holy, 72:16
  immortals cannot escape, 68:1
  in high art and p. science, 756:7
  in life free from sin, 99:15
  land of p. delight, 304:11
  literature p. and dead, 708:7
  live p. speak true, 485:20
  love without power, 735:14
  lovers' souls descend, 235:5
  man who's p. in heart, 764:3
  mathematics original, 624:11
  my heart is p., 482:11
  my poems naughty my life p., 110:13
  of mouth pure of hands, 3:12
  particularly p. young man, 564:9
  religion breathing laws, 392:14
  shall man be more p. than maker, 13:35
  silence of p. innocence, 228:15
  Simon P., 297:13
  sleep from p. digestion bred, 266:29
  so sweet and p. and fair, 442:8

Pure *(continued)*
  soul unto captain Christ, 180:6
  stars are not p. in his sight, 14:32
  substantial world p. and good, 394:21
  thy truth so p. of old, 263:15
  unclouded brow, 551:8
  unto p. all things p., 46:35
  whatsoever things are p., 45:38
  whether his work be p., 22:19
  women innocent and p., 229:25
  young man, 564:9
Pure-minded, something better to tell p.,
  549:6
Purer than purest gold, 237:18
Purest, frost from p. snow, 224:31
  purer than p. gold, 237:18
  ray serene, 334:20
  treasure mortal times afford, 178:30
  virgin p. lipped, 436:14
Purgatory, England is p. of men, 162:9
  in erthe I was his p., 136:15
  poor man get out iv P., 646:11
Purge and leave sack, 187:12
  me with hyssop, 17:26
  melancholy, 229:5
Purging, poetry p. of world's poverty, 689:7
Purified, every creature p., 170:21
Purify dialect of tribe, 722:1
  the mind, 66:18
Puritan, devil a p. that he is, 209:18
  hated bear-baiting, 448:18
Puritanism haunting fear someone may be
  happy, 691:17
  laid egg of democracy, 515:21
Puritans founded to give thanks, 646:5
  great artists never P., 691:2
  nobly fled, 555:16
  thanks we are presarved fr'm P., 646:5
Purity ability to contemplate difilement,
  783:19
  of race does not exist, 632:1
  ore of body into p., 707:12
Purlieu of god of love, 235:8
Purlieus, dusty p. of law, 484:10
Purloined, love he p. her away, 571:14
Purple, abbots p. as their wines, 313:24
  beggar in p., 634:8
  beyond utmost p. rim, 482:10
  blossom in p. and red, 485:12
  cow, 643:18
  first from out the p. grape, 260:16
  gleaming in p. and gold, 422:14
  light of Love, 335:6
  mountain majesties, 616:3
  pilots of p. twilight, 481:23
  quenching in P., 544:10
  restore to whiteness wool dyed p.,
    118:25
  riot, 436:24
  rustling of p. curtain, 479:3
  testament of bleeding war, 180:2
  the sails, 223:14
  walk by color p. in a field, 839:2
  waves with long p. forms, 603:11
  with love's wound, 181:9
Purple-stained mouth, 437:7
Purpose a horse of that color, 209:19
  bait on p. laid, 227:22
  change ideas when served p., 500:18

Purpose *(continued)*
cite Scripture for his p., 188:6
dog serves no industrial p., 613:8
end in one p., 192:22
infirm of p., 220:18
inherent in art so in nature, 79:18
invented for sole p. of becoming extinct, 703:16
lie with p. worst, 645:16
my p. holds, 481:14
nothing in nature without p., 465:11
of producing social wealth, 651:7
one increasing p. runs, 482:3
poetry not p. but passion, 478:19
pushes his prudent p., 306:5
shake my fell p., 219:11
she did it on p., 723:9
speak plain and to p., 194:24
steady p. tranquilize mind, 443:7
tenacious of p. in rightful cause, 99:28
time to every p., 24:6
to speak and p. not, 215:22
to what p. this waste, 37:20
true joy being used for p., 609:15
unconquerable p. realized, 407:7
with p. of its own, 391:8
Purposed, linger out a p. overthrow, 227:2
Purposeless, in Nature nothing p., 127:7
Purposes, search out p. of gods, 66:9
use novel for other p., 816:2
Purrs and never shows tooth, 710:10
Purse, consumption of the p., 191:21
costly as p. can buy, 201:26
it drains your p., 369:16
money burned out his p., 143:16
of gold resolutely snatched, 184:25
put money in thy p., 213:3
silken or leathern p., 304:15
so little in his p., 239:5
who steals my p. steals trash, 213:33
Purses, light gains make heavy p., 165:2
our p. shall be proud, 175:37
Pursue Culture in bands, 627:13
love good p. the worst, 105:*n*14
man with great thing to p., 492:24
my Reason to O altitudo, 255:11
phantoms of hope, 324:24
seek peace and p. it, 17:2
seem to fly it it will p., 237:23
those who p. many ends, 782:3
triumph partake gale, 311:16
vain war with heaven, 264:25
Pursued, exit p. by a bear, 228:19
it with forks and hope, 553:4
villain still p. her, 592:17
Pursues fame at risk of losing self, 82:25
Pursueth, wicked flee when no man p., 23:15
Pursuing and obtaining happiness, 339:9
he is talking or he is p., 12:29
still achieving still p., 466:3
Pursuit, clear paths of laudable p., 475:10
culture a p. of perfection, 531:10
indefatigable p., 636:8
mad in p., 227:22
of happiness, 357:2
of knowledge, 410:1
of science, 527:14
of uneatable, 606:3

Pursuit *(continued)*
vain p. of human glory, 253:17
what mad p., 437:17
Pursy, fatness of these p. times, 205:27
Purview, kitsch excludes everything from p., 824:1
Push and pressure of cosmos, 582:17
big fool says p. on, 806:1
door called p., 849:14
heart can p. sea and land, 734:15
in their tides, 795:3
off, 481:14
on keep moving, 384:12
Pushed, I can be p. so far, 647:15
Pushes prudent purpose to resolve, 306:5
Pushing their bones, 821:7
Puss-gentleman all perfume, 347:13
Puss-in-Boots, human mind invents P., 761:6
Pussy, I like little p., 414:6
I'll give you all the p., 850:17
O lovely P., 499:15
Pussycat, Owl and P., 499:15
where have you been, 859:14
Pussy's in well, 857:19
Put a tongue in every wound, 197:5
antic disposition on, 202:27
away childish things, 768:2
blessed to p. cares away, 94:9
bullet through his head, 652:11
candle shall never be p. out, 145:2
candle which shall not be p. out, 31:9
down Richard, 185:6
down what really happened, 754:10
enemy in their mouths, 213:26
Germany in saddle, 502:10
her in pumpkin shell, 860:4
I p. away childish things, 44:20
in her oar, 157:35
me in a cage, 723:15
me in your pocket, 707:4
money in thy purse, 213:3
never do what can p. off, 535:6
not your trust in princes, 20:19
off thy shoes, 8:4
on armor of light, 43:26
on good behavior, 424:9
on Lord Jesus Christ, 43:26
on pistols went riding, 724:14
on whole armor of God, 45:30
one foot in front of the other, 799:2
out hand touched face of God, 810:11
out the light, 215:7, 615:18
out the Light, 669:19
plain tale p. you down, 185:26
shall be surely p. to death, 9:3
shoulder to the wheel, 61:4
too fine a point, 159:6, 498:21
up your caravan, 656:11
when I p. out to sea, 487:2
worst use a man could be p. to, 232:18
yourself in his shoes, 744:15
Putrefy, most swiftly p., 227:*n*1
Putrescent, paddle in p. waters, 751:11
Putrid corpse of liberty, 702:8
Puts all Heaven in a rage, 375:6
forth tender leaves of hopes, 231:2
he who p. armor off, 467:20
record on gramophone, 718:19
Puttees, pair of roll p., 746:1

Putter, I will p., 820:1
Putting, dispatch in p. end to it, 81:26
Love away, 546:8
mind's eye in book, 807:7
off the proof, 670:3
on breastplate of faith, 46:11
queer shoulder to wheel, 817:11
Puzzle, Rosebud missing piece in jigsaw p., 749:6
rule of three p., 843:21
schoolmasters p. brain, 342:17
to botanist, 557:16
Puzzled, thou art more p. than Egyptians, 210:17
Puzzles the will, 203:33
Puzzling, though p. not beyond conjecture, 256:17
Pye, shine with P., 420:1
Pygmy body, 283:8
Pyramid, bottom of economic p., 697:11
star-y-pointing p., 259:3
Pyramids first, 850:10
from summit of p., 387:12
Pyramus and Thisby, 180:22
cruel death of P., 180:22
Pyre, ghost escapes from vanquished p., 104:25
Pyrrha for whom bindest thou thy hair, 99:7
Pyrrha's, from P. pebbles, 436:15
Pyrrhic victory, 85:*n*2
Pythagoras, hold opinion with P., 189:17
opinion of P. concerning wildfowl, 189:*n*2
said to his scholars, 240:12
Pythagoreans, rather wrong with Plato than right with P., 91:4

Q.E.D., 84:16
Quad, I am always about in Q., 723:*n*1
when no one about in the Q., 723:4
Quadrangular, spots q. of diamond, 348:6
Quadrille, war not q. in ball-room, 521:14
Quadruped, hairy q. with tail, 470:5
Quae est domestica sede iucundior, 90:*n*12
Quaffed, jested q. and swore, 487:10
Quaffing, laughing q. unthinking time, 285:20
Quail and shake the orb, 224:4
when footpads q., 565:23
whistle about us, 686:19
Quails, he brought q., 19:12
Quaint and curious volume, 478:20
and curious war is, 575:18
great figure, 685:6
honor turn to dust, 277:2
wonders at q. spirits, 181:14
Quake, earth did q., 38:10
Quakers, first called us Q., 280:15
Qualifications, adverbs only q. I respect, 585:18
without any important q. for office, 727:3
Qualified, I am q., 215:32
masses are not q., 702:19
Qualify, my flame to q., 227:13
Qualis artifex pereo, 109:*n*10

Quick (*continued*)
true apothecary thy drugs q., 184:18
word of God is q., 46:38
Quicken, live within sense they q., 430:19
Quickened, not q. except it die, 44:27
Quickeneth, spirit that q., 41:5
Quickens to rebel, 719:16
Quicker, end a contest q., 367:24
liquor is q., 763:5
Quick-eyed Love observing me, 251:2
Quickly, behold I come q., 49:3
bring me beaker of wine, 74:11
do q. that thou doest, 41:24
doubly benefits who gives q., 102:14
little fire q. trodden, 173:8
nature falls into revolt, 192:7
to pass gates of Hades, 61:14
turn away, 640:16
'twere well it were done q., 219:16
well done is q. done, 102:6
Quickness, too much q. to be taught, 310:6
Quicksands, Soundings q. rocks, 440:11
Quid datur a divis felici optatius hora,
94:*n7*
si nunc caelum ruat, 88:*n12*
Quiddities, quips and q., 184:26
where be his q. now, 206:20
Quiddity, entity and q., 270:23
Quien bien te quiere, 862:22
Quiet, all q. along Potomac, 539:6
all q. on western front, 752:11
anything for a q. life, 243:19
as a lamb, 178:13
as a stone, 438:17
be q. and go a-angling, 253:9
bower q. for us, 436:8
breath, 437:12
by q. natures understood, 639:14
calm q. innocent recreation, 253:5
chaste breast and q. mind, 275:22
conscience stands brunt of life, 69:29
consummation have, 225:24
courage gaiety q. mind, 600:1
desperation, 506:11
Doctor Q., 299:19
easy live q. die, 397:27
enforced from q. sphere, 192:3
entertain lag-end with q. hours, 186:31
eye made q. by power, 391:2
fie upon this q. life, 185:20
harvest of a q. eye, 392:4
here where world q., 568:25
holy time q. as nun, 392:15
hours few, 517:14
I get very q. and rarely speak, 128:7
imperishable q., 781:1
in q. she reposes, 529:14
kiss me and be q., 314:2
lain still and been q., 13:30
limit of world, 485:15
mind cureth all, 242:7
mind richer than crown, 165:16
minds innocent and q., 276:4
my temptation q., 642:10
not the q., 830:12
o'er hilltops is q. now, 365:25
ornament of q. spirit, 47:29
retirement rural q. friendship, 318:2
rich q. and infamous, 448:9

Quiet (*continued*)
scallop shell of q., 160:8
shining to the q. moon, 401:11
singeth a q. tune, 400:15
sleep when the long trick's over, 681:2
sleepers in q. earth, 509:4
spirit so still and q., 212:27
still and q. conscience, 231:3
study to be q., 46:8
tree of man never q., 619:1
truth hath a q. breast, 178:34
wise and good, 431:2
Quiet-colored end of evening, 492:10
Quieting, soothing and q., 658:12
Quietly shining to quiet moon, 401:11
Quietness, bride of q., 437:16
handful with q., 24:8
richness q. and pleasure, 524:11
Quietness', king made for q. sake, 246:1
Quietus, he himself his q. make, 203:33
Quill from angel's wing, 395:*n3*
Quillets, his q. his cases, 206:20
nice sharp q. of law, 171:16
Quills, upon fretful porpentine, 202:12
Quince, slices of q., 499:18
Quinquireme of Nineveh, 681:4
Quintessence even from nothingness, 234:21
morning q. of life, 425:21
of dust, 203:18
Quintilian, made Q. stare and gasp, 263:7
Quintilius give me back my legions, 102:4
Quip modest, 200:9
Quippe secundae res sapientium animos
fatigant, 95:*n3*
Quips and cranks, 259:9
and quiddities, 184:26
shall q. and sentences awe, 194:28
Quire of bad verses, 448:12
Quiring to young-eyed cherubins, 190:5
Quirks of blazoning pens, 213:7
Quis custodiet ipsos custodes, 113:*n8*
Quislings, vile race of q., 666:11
Quit certainty for uncertainty, 324:23
house never darken threshold, 522:4
John and I are q., 297:5
oh quit this mortal frame, 309:3
quit for shame, 269:21
rats have q. it, 229:14
we won't q. moving, 829:12
you like men, 45:1
yourselves like men, 11:18
Quitter, il faut q. tout cela, 255:*n2*
Quiver, air q. with a color, 706:7
happy is the man that hath his q. full,
20:6
Quivering, light q. aspen, 397:1
ratio, 544:3
Quiver's choice, 424:24
Quixote, Don Q. a muddled fool, 158:8
when Don Q. went out into world, 824:2
Quixote's, youngsters read Don Q. story,
157:27
Quo usque Catilina abutere patientia, 90:*n3*
vadis, 41:*n1*
Quod erat demonstrandum, 84:16
semper quod ubique quod ab omnibus,
119:*n7*
Quos deus vult perdere, 124:19
Quot homines tot sententiae, 89:*n4*

Quotation, classical q., 329:7
I hate q., 454:7
Quotations, backed opinion with q., 296:21
Bartlett's Familiar Q., 665:10
book furnishes no q., 418:11
good to read books of q., 665:10
ill-advised, 614:1
pretentious q. tedium, 614:1
wrapped himself in q., 634:8
Quote fights historical, 564:3
grow immortal as they q., 305:16
kill you if you q. it, 643:19
we all q., 457:22
wise reader q. wisely, 444:16
Quoted, famous remarks seldom q. correctly,
689:12
odes and jewels, 482:17
Quoter, next to originator first q., 457:20
Quoth, give me q. I, 218:26
Raven Nevermore, 479:5, 479:7

R

R, months that have no r, 154:10
Rabbit, ain't never caught a r., 828:8
in a snare, 699:10
ole man R. say scoot, 593:10
skin to wrap baby, 858:8
thoughts of r. are rabbits, 458:3
Rabbits, four little r., 644:2
thoughts of rabbit are r., 458:3
Rabble, army would be base r., 344:17
Rabelais' easy chair, 313:15
Race, a simple r., 396:10
all run in r., 44:10
another r. hath been, 393:19
appointed for my second r., 279:2
arms r., 806:13
barred on account of r., 800:4
bellyful of classics enemy to human r.,
732:5
between education and catastrophe,
644:16
Californians a r., 626:13
call arms r. a misunderstanding, 787:11
competition essential for r., 559:6
conscience of my r., 696:7
consternation throughout white r.,
831:9
culture not function of r., 712:11
despised r., 556:3
development of individual repetition of r.,
607:11
dusky r., 482:6
fair chance in r. of life, 475:10
feelings permanently in r., 529:8
friend to human r., 52:*n2*
future of human r., 679:2
Germany a r., 444:8
giant r. before the flood, 285:4
happiness of human r., 345:2
heavenly r. demands zeal, 318:12
history of our r., 667:2
human r. born to fly upward, 131:17
human r. has means for annihilating itself,
694:14
human r. never have rest from evils,
77:12

Rain *(continued)*
   nobody not even the r., 740:7
   nor ever wet with r., 54:21
   nor winter storm nor r., 54:20
   number the drops of r., 31:24
   on corn a sad thing, 95:19
   out o' cold an' r., 634:10
   pack when it begins to r., 216:12
   people daily wet with r., 143:15
   rain go away, 856:21
   ripple of r., 567:17
   roof against the r., 735:12
   sendeth r. on just and unjust, 34:8
   shower of commanded tears, 175:20
   singin' in the r., 740:19
   small r. down can r., 843:18
   smell dew and r., 250:22
   snow nor r. nor heat, 71:24
   softly under snow or r., 664:15
   some r. must fall, 466:10
   still falls the R., 715:13
   sunshine after r., 173:24
   sweeping r. that leaveth no food, 289:23
   thirsty earth soaks up r., 275:8
   waiting for r., 718:2
   walked to hotel in r., 754:7
   was upon the earth, 6:28
   weeping like r. on city, 590:21
Rainbow, add hue to r., 178:14
   border be standing r., 855:19
   coalition, 836:13
   comes and goes, 393:8
   God gave Noah r. sign, 813:6
   in the sky, 392:7
   now and then on r., 829:6
   rainbow rainbow, 785:9
   somewhere over r., 752:1
Rainbow's glory shed, 431:4
Rain-drenched hair, 704:14
Raindrop, down names r. plows, 576:6
Rained ghastly dew, 481:23
Raineth drop staineth slop, 708:17
   rain it r. every day, 210:19, 216:25
Rainfall, West begins where r. drops, 748:4
Rain's, out of wind's and r. way, 693:5
Rains, ev'ry time r. r. pennies from Heaven,
   778:5
   long r. were falling, 125:6
   return in rivers, 777:1
   softly on the town, 604:3
   winter's r. and ruins, 567:18
Rainstorms, inspector of r., 505:2
Rainwater, glazed with r., 703:10
Rainy evening to read this discourse, 252:23
   eyes, 179:27
   love world and all in its r. arms, 842:1
   morrow, 227:2
   natives of rain r. men, 686:11
   Pleiads wester, 619:21
   weary of wench guest weather r., 319:4
Raise, Death old captain r. anchor, 524:16
   didn't r. boy to be soldier, 850:21
   hue and cry, 156:33
   joys and triumphs high, 322:23
   less corn more hell, 597:11
   Lord shall r. me up I trust, 160:14
   man can r. a thirst, 633:14
   Music r. and quell, 284:14
   print news and r. hell, 848:11

Raise *(continued)*
   somewhat loftier strain, 95:21
   song of harvest-home, 487:7
   stone cleave wood, 117:4
   the genius, 309:14
   what is low r. and support, 263:21
Raised a mortal to the skies, 285:16
   dead shall be r., 44:31
   in incorruption, 44:29
   new man r. up in him, 51:17
   not a stone, 427:3
Raiseth, cross that r. me, 461:18
Raisin in the sun, 762:16
Raising, empire for r. customers, 338:19
Raisons, le coeur a ses r., 280:n1
Rake among scholars, 448:15
   every woman at heart r., 310:8
   hors leene as is a r., 134:29
   stop to r. leaves away, 668:17
Rake's progress, 490:10
Rakes, scholar among r., 448:15
Raking, know when to stop r. muck, 615:8
Rally round the flag boys, 522:9
Ralph wept for end of innocence, 786:5
Ram, black r. tupping your ewe, 212:19
   caught in a thicket, 7:9
   how wind doth r., 708:17
Rambles, Hamlet r., 642:7
Rambling, be not r. in thought, 116:1
Ramm, how wind doth r., 708:17
Rampallian, away you r., 191:26
Rampant for spoil and victory, 589:13
   Maenad of Massachusetts, 569:11
Rampart, corse to r. we hurried, 427:1
   no r. against malice, 277:17
Ramparts we watched, 411:1
Ramps, hasten down r., 771:13
Rams, mountains skipped like r., 19:21
Ran a hundred years to a day, 473:15
   before Ahab, 12:31
   dismayed away, 190:4
   grief with glass that r., 568:1
   my heedless ways, 795:12
   neighing canyons, 753:16
   on ten winters more, 283:5
   sunset r. one glorious blood-red, 492:6
Rancor outpouring of inferiority, 702:9
   will out, 172:4
Rancorous rational mind, 641:1
Randal, Felix R. the farrier, 587:12
   Lord R. my son, 854:11
Randolph Churchill went into hospital,
   766:10
   thy wreath has lost rose, 397:18
Random grim forge, 587:13
   I am writing at r., 440:16
   shaft at r. sent, 397:17
   we thrown down here at r., 761:3
Rang, sabbath r. slowly, 795:11
   them while touring Timbucktoo,
   822:11
Range with humble livers, 230:25
Ranged his tropes, 296:21
   if I have r., 227:14
   wide arch of r. empire fall, 222:27
Ranges, something lost behind the r., 635:15
Rank, battle of the first r., 451:10
   black r. and file, 556:3
   but guinea's stamp, 380:12

Rank *(continued)*
   flavor of blood, 819:4
   great beautifier, 452:8
   has its obligations, 384:11
   keep no r. nor station, 800:19
   marched r. on r., 541:17
   me with barbarous multitude, 188:26
   my offense is r., 205:14
   swoln with r. mist, 262:2
   things r. and gross, 201:2
   when man of r. an author, 329:8
Rankers, gentlemen r., 633:17
Ranks, close r., 835:12
   for adoration all the r., 337:17
   of death, 411:16
   the same with God, 491:6
Rank-scented many, 224:25
Ransom captive Israel, 511:12
   them from the power of the grave,
   30:21
Rant, I'll r. as well as thou, 207:3
   when you r. and swear, 241:n3
Rapacious and licentious soldiery, 345:5
Rape an insurrectionary act, 831:9
   of every day, 809:1
Raphael made a century of sonnets,
   493:24
Raphaels, talked of their R., 343:6
Rapid, drive the r. car, 348:23
   Homer eminently r., 529:21
   lady's imagination r., 406:5
Rapidly, order is r. fadin', 836:6
Rapier-keen, button-cute r., 769:6
Rapping at chamber door, 478:20
Rapscallions, all kings mostly r., 560:19
Rapt ship run on side so low, 165:11
   soul sitting in thine eyes, 259:25
Rapture, beyond r. and dread, 771:11
   first fine careless r., 492:5
   on lonely shore, 421:25
   then a pain, 591:11
Raptures and roses of vice, 568:3
   illustrious acts high r. infuse, 257:19
   no Minstrel r. swell, 396:11
   no poetic r. feel, 368:13
R'ar back an' pass a miracle, 728:4
Rara avis in terris, 113:n5
Rare and bloodless week of repose, 75:n3
   and radiant maiden, 479:2
   are solitary woes, 206:n2
   as day in June, 514:16
   Beaumont, 247:11
   Ben Jonson, 237:n2
   bird on earth, 113:9
   delicate and r., 605:19
   detachment of spirit, 672:22
   excellent things r., 287:17
   few rid selves of friendship, 557:14
   my love of birth as r., 277:7
   somewhere a r. name, 75:10
   to meet man outdoors, 506:4
   tobacco divine r., 241:14
Rarely rarely comest thou, 430:24
Rarer gifts than gold, 713:2
   the living are getting r., 788:14
Rarity of Christian charity, 446:8
Rascal, biggest r. that walks, 114:4
   if r. have not given medicines, 185:12
Rascally yea-forsooth knave, 191:10

Rascals, lash the r. naked, 214:29
    law's to take care o' r., 512:25
    one of most unscrupulous r., 617:15
    would you live forever, 330:11
Rase, slowly r. she up, 854:1
Rash hand in evil hour, 267:30
    not splenetive and r., 207:1
    too r. too unadvised, 183:10
    who reckons on morrow, 68:14
Rash-embraced despair, 189:7
Rashes, green grow the r. O, 378:14
Rashly charged troops of error, 255:8
    importunate, 446:7
Rashness, beware of r., 476:4
Raskills, law's to take care o' r., 512:25
Rasselas Prince of Abyssinia, 324:24
Rast ich so rost ich, 845:19
Rat, a dog a horse a r., 218:7
    begin to smell a r., 157:20
    giant r. of Sumatra, 617:16
    how now a r., 205:18
    is in the trap, 825:7
    killed the r., 861:15
    mouse studying to be r., 678:12
    poisoned r. in hole, 299:1
Raths, mome r. outgrabe, 551:10
Ratified, real and r. existence, 510:*n*2
Ratio, increase in geometrical r., 469:15
    keen and quivering r., 544:3
    population increases in geometrical r., 385:4
    subsistence in arithmetical r., 385:4
Ratiocination, pay with r., 270:17
Rational ethics, 629:8
    I am r. therefore sing hymns, 112:9
    one r. voice dumb, 775:18
    rancorous r. mind, 641:1
    with men he can be r., 406:17
    world presents r. aspect, 390:6
Rationalism adventure in clarification of thought, 624:14
Rationality, freedom brought independence r., 757:11
    if r. were criterion, 832:12
Rationally, him who looks on world r., 390:6
    live r. for time assigned, 115:19
    till women more r. educated, 382:22
Rationed, so precious must be r., 654:13
Rations, live upon daily r., 497:23
Ratisbon, stormed R., 491:7
Rats came tumbling, 491:17
    desert sinking ship, 108:*n*6
    have quit it, 229:14
    land-r. and water-r., 188:1
    mice r. and such small deer, 216:33
    nearness of r., 756:17
    they fought dogs, 491:16
Rats' alley, 718:14
Rattle his bones over stones, 446:10
    pleased with a r., 311:11
    rifles' rapid r., 738:6
Rattling good history, 575:22
    he was as r. thunder, 224:4
    o'er stony street, 420:17
    of a coach, 236:22
Ravages, irreparable r. of time, 290:15
Rave at close of day, 795:14
    no more 'gainst time, 566:17
Raved, but as I r., 250:17

Raveled sleave of care, 220:16
Raven, censure pardons r., 113:3
    grim and ancient R., 479:5
    himself is hoarse, 219:11
    locks were like the r., 379:4
    never flitting, 479:8
    Poe with his r., 514:19
    smoothing the r. down, 260:27
Ravening, inwardly are r. wolves, 35:7
Ravens brought him bread, 12:25
    He that doth r. feed, 198:3
    three r. on a tree, 854:5
Ravine, threw dead dog down the r., 783:9
Raving skies opened to voyager, 603:13
Ravished ears, 285:8
    eyes, 301:11
Ravishing, what dear r. thing, 290:23
Raw, give them r. truth, 626:3
    inclement summers, 298:16
    Marian's nose red and r., 177:18
    material of opinion, 610:23
Ray, emits a brighter r., 340:13
    misled by fancy's meteor r., 378:3
    multiply a brighter r., 421:8
    purest r. serene, 334:20
    Shadwell's night admits no r., 284:3
Rayformer, called r. remains at large, 646:13
Rayless majesty, 305:24
Raypublican party broke ye, 646:2
Rays, hide your diminished r., 266:*n*1
    in vain produced all r. return, 452:20
    your r. in midst of sea, 4:10
Raze out troubles of brain, 222:12
Razed, from books of honor r., 226:4
    Nature's works to me r., 265:25
Razón, sueño de la r. monstruos, 362:14
Razor, each holds locked r., 800:18
    Occam's R., 132:*n*3
    satire like polished r., 314:3
Razor's, fate hung on r. edge, 62:6
Razors to my wounded heart, 175:14
Razure of oblivion, 212:6
Reach, above r. of ordinary men, 392:10
    apple pickers not r. it, 58:5
    bloom gradually out of r., 818:9
    enjoy resources within thy r., 66:1
    fool to follow what is out of r., 111:16
    I cannot r. it, 279:10
    man's r. exceed grasp, 493:4
    me a gentian, 707:21
    never more than imperfectly r., 745:12
    not condescending to anything within r., 78:10
    of wisdom and of r., 202:30
    unreachable star, 799:1
    until we r. ripest fruit, 170:4
    wishes for that beyond r., 293:19
Reached, god in sky r. down, 839:5
Reaches five hundred thousand readers, 570:13
    thoughts beyond r. of souls, 202:6
Reaching forth unto things before, 45:35
    irritable r. after fact, 440:3
Reaction, attack is the r., 327:22
    external r. to world, 595:14
    I can't get no girl r., 838:4
    if any r. both transformed, 675:3
    religion r. upon life, 582:14
    to every action equal r., 291:4

Reacts, critic r. reciprocates, 585:3
Read a good poem, 364:2
    a little I can r., 222:28
    a silly fairy tale, 336:3
    as deliberately as written, 507:4
    as inclination leads, 326:19
    aught I could ever r., 180:19
    best company when you r., 398:25
    better neither r. nor write, 410:5
    blockheads r. what blockheads wrote, 315:8
    book of fate, 191:36
    book people praise don't r., 562:7
    both r. the Bible, 376:8
    but not distinguish what worth it, 678:17
    children don't r. to find identity, 769:12
    damn authors they never r., 346:20
    each wound each weakness, 528:15
    gentlemen do not r. other's mail, 647:13
    haven't r. that for years, 792:19
    he that runs may r., 348:15
    history in nation's eyes, 334:22
    Homer once, 293:8
    I have r. all the books, 583:13
    in the bitter letter, 212:24
    know what I r. in papers, 685:12
    many benefits from good r., 789:6
    mark learn, 51:4
    my lips No New Taxes, 813:10
    my title clear, 304:10
    never learned to r., 817:2
    never r. book not year old, 457:4
    not poem we have r., 402:21
    not that I ever r. them, 367:33
    old authors to r., 167:1
    only books that wound us, 701:7
    part all through, 695:15
    poetry difficult to r., 494:26
    sins scarlet books r., 653:15
    strange matters, 219:13
    take up r., 119:10
    that day we r. no farther, 130:16
    timetable than nothing, 673:3
    to by a boy, 718:2
    to doubt or read to scorn, 398:3
    to r. comes by nature, 194:33
    very few to r., 392:*n*1
    what do you r. my lord, 203:8
    whoso that kan r. hem as they write, 133:15
    wits to r., 238:5
    youngsters r. men understand, 157:27
Readable, book chief need is be r., 504:10
Reader, delighting and instructing r., 101:29
    delights r. instructs too, 289:16
    exciting sympathy of r., 403:6
    good r. makes good book, 457:14
    hypocrite r., 524:7
    I married him, 504:16
    look, 238:4
    my story ends with freedom, 501:7
    no tears in r., 671:11
    poetry strike R. as own thoughts, 440:5
    right r. of good poem, 671:9
    take them not for mine, 134:*n*3
    what conceal from r., 776:14
    wise r. quote wisely, 444:16

Readers and hearers like my books, 168:24
become more indolent, 340:11
five hundred thousand r., 570:13
of Boston Evening Transcript, 717:20
Readest, thou r. black, 376:8
Readeth, he may run that I. it, 30:30
Readiness is all, 207:8
Reading, after r. your work, 316:11
contemplation more than r., 280:21
creative r. creative writing, 454:22
curst hard r., 368:6
digressions sunshine of r., 332:12
English dictionary best r., 654:16
it with perfect contempt, 714:4
life the thing but I prefer r., 636:10
maketh a full man, 168:16
my own writings, 816:5
new era in life from r., 507:5
no r. more fascinating than catalogue, 586:9
overset mind with r., 594:14
Peace makes poor r., 575:22
sheer casual r. matter, 654:16
such r. as never read, 313:23
tact a kind of mind-r., 595:1
theologian not born by r., 144:17
to mind as exercise to body, 301:13
valueless books, 517:14
write things worthy r., 319:20
Reads as task, 326:19
but one book, 252:18
he r. much great observer, 195:23
Ready, a God r. to pardon, 13:17
completely r. state, 502:9
conference maketh a r. man, 168:16
fire when r. Gridley, 567:2
for war way to avoid it, 293:17
in defense, 344:10
minds to fellowship, 436:10
money Aladdin's lamp, 424:17
money makes the man, 304:12
my tongue is the pen of a r. writer, 17:19
necessity of being r., 475:9
no r. way to virtue, 256:3
old wife old dog r. money, 319:19
rough sir but r., 497:28
to embrace the strangers, 516:1
to ride spread alarm, 467:15
to try our fortunes, 192:4
we always are r., 335:22
with every nod to tumble, 174:9
with you be r. to die, 100:4
Ready-made, critics all r., 419:14
Real, a man's r. life, 612:13
coming back to r., 688:12
dark night of soul, 746:14
do it so feels r., 827:10
lead me from unreal to r., 51:20
life r. life earnest, 465:17
lure of the r., 689:1
never fit for r. work, 814:6
no r. problem, 803:2
nothing r. except humanity, 444:2
nothing r. till experienced, 440:18
only mist is r., 794:8
producing r. social wealth, 651:7
Simon Pure, 297:13
spirit r. and eternal, 526:12
that is moral, 524:18

Real *(continued)*
thing which made the emotion, 754:10
this is the r. me, 581:2
three things which are r., 789:2
War Will Never Get in Books, 521:13
what is r. is reasonable, 390:2
Realist, in Israel to be r., 710:15
Realities and creators, 455:8
less dangerous than fancies, 661:8
muddled state sharpest of r., 585:12
not images of beauty but r., 76:9
Reality, appearance never attain r., 382:8
attained only by detached, 783:18
between idea and r., 719:6
capture its r. in paint, 572:21
final word in r., 823:8
fine r. of hunger satisfied, 778:6
flee from r., 702:23
give r. to illusion, 678:4
history illumines r., 90:15
human kind not bear much r., 720:6
in r. atoms and space, 72:14
is things as they are, 688:22
mask off r. remains, 93:8
must take precedence, 803:3
no humbling of r. to precept, 816:15
of distress, 354:19
of experience, 696:7
regulate imagination by r., 325:24
the more threatening r. appears, 693:15
three mirror same r., 359:15
translators between dream and r., 715:14
use r. rather than know it, 794:2
we crave only r., 507:2
your own r. for yourself, 612:6
Realize bitterness of Life, 553:6
earth too wonderful to r. you, 750:1
I'd been happy, 789:13
Mrs. Pontellier to r. position, 600:9
suddenly I r., 820:3
Realized, design of all his words r., 688:13
they and I civilized, 765:3
Realm, invade borders of my r., 151:13
mysterious r., 432:10
riding o'er azure r., 335:13
this r. this England, 179:12
turned out of R. in my petticoat, 151:14
Realms above, 401:9
and islands as plates, 224:4
Anna whom three r. obey, 309:8
of gold, 435:19
those who Dwell in R. of day, 375:16
whatever r. to see, 340:15
Reap an act, 849:5
as you sow ye r., 271:21
blessings of freedom, 354:14
harvest of your land, 9:13
he that regardeth the clouds not r., 25:4
in joy, 20:3
men that sow and r., 569:1
not wholly r. the corners, 9:13
sow not neither r., 34:17
that shall he also r., 45:24
the whirlwind, 30:17
we r. our sowing, 555:21
Reaped, all the harvest I r., 471:14
iniquity, 30:18
wheat never r. nor sown, 290:2
Reaping, autumn that grew by r., 224:4

Reappraisal, agonizing r., 801:2
Reaps, wholesome harvests r., 444:15
Rear my dusky race, 482:6
tender thought, 318:1
to produce and to r. them, 58:13
Reared arm crested the world, 224:4
himself a throne, 478:4
Rearward of a conquered woe, 227:2
Reason and experiment have been indulged, 357:6
and will of God prevail, 531:16
argument needs no r., 60:6
art has r. for being, 457:9
asked one another the r., 200:3
beast that wants discourse of r., 201:7
but from what we know, 311:1
by r. of strength, 18:22
can decide nothing here, 279:23
capability and godlike r., 205:35
common law nothing but r., 159:14
deeply when forcibly feel, 383:4
destroys book kills r., 262:21
discourse of r., 201:7
feast of r. flow of soul, 312:14
flood of words drop of r., 319:15
freed men's minds, 107:13
give r. on compulsion, 185:25
God's crowning gift, 67:25
greatest enemy faith has, 144:18
guide by light of r., 607:4
have I not r. to lament, 390:16
human r. is beautiful, 786:14
humanity r. and justice, 344:12
ignis fatuus of mind, 293:3
I'm trav'lin' on, 836:5
Imagination abandoned by R., 362:*n*3
immortal all else mortal, 60:4
improvable r. of Man, 443:6
in images of sense, 402:20
in itself confounded, 207:18
in man like God in world, 129:10
is of no use to us, 350:4
is past care, 228:6
keep r. under control, 116:4
know truth not only by r., 280:2
knows nothing of, 280:1
law is perfection of r., 159:14
law ordinance of r. for common good, 129:8
left free to combat error, 358:9
left free to combat it, 359:7
let my will take place of r., 113:10
let us r. together, 26:10, 779:2
lies between spur and bridle, 252:3
life of the law, 159:14
make worse appear better r., 74:13
men have lost their r., 196:30
Milton wrote in fetters, 372:13
most sovereign r., 204:9
no other but woman's r., 176:4
noble in r., 203:17
not listen to r., 488:5
not yet guided by r., 656:3
of this thusness, 555:15
or any other r. why, 292:23
our r. is our law, 267:29
panders will, 205:23
passions not conform to r., 370:13
past r. hunted, 227:22

Reason *(continued)*
  psychological r., 585:1
  pursue my R. to O altitudo, 255:11
  rather to feel than r., 382:26
  reaching after fact and r., 440:3
  rhyme nor r., 162:8
  right deed for wrong r., 720:5
  ruling passion conquers r., 310:14
  sanctified by r. blest by faith, 391:13
  shall enforce her sway, 368:12
  sleep of r. produces monsters,
      362:14
  still keeps its throne, 305:2
  takes the r. prisoner, 219:2
  teach thy necessity to r., 179:4
  tell me the r. I pray, 405:9
  theirs not to r. why, 484:27
  themselves out again, 193:27
  two worlds to r., 255:17
  victory over r., 726:8
  we bicker creates war, 153:2
  what someone else has to say, 488:5
  where faith in r. timid, 660:8
  why I cannot tell, 296:1
  with reasonable men, 462:7
  worse appear better r., 265:3
  yield with grace to r., 668:16
Reasonable amount o' fleas good for dog,
    592:6
  good ear in music, 181:24
  holy and living sacrifice, 51:1
  man being r. must get drunk, 423:19
  Man mythical, 729:1
  moderator Death, 255:19
  no r. man expected, 729:3
  nothing r. from pure reason, 664:6
  speak a few r. words, 364:2
  what is real is r., 390:2
Reasonableness, will and well-meaning r.,
    675:4
Reasoned errors, 537:11
Reasonest, Plato thou r. well, 301:26
Reasoning but to err, 311:9
  cowards in r., 301:9
  destroy power of r., 78:6
  infant's r., 331:24
  like all Holmes's r., 617:8
  man is a r. animal, 106:18
  mathematician capable of r., 77:16
  self-sufficing thing, 392:3
Reasonings, versed in r. of men, 69:21
Reason's icy intimations, 446:11
  in erring r. spite, 311:8
  words clothed in r. garb, 265:7
Reasons, and he had r., 652:6
  as two grains of wheat, 187:23
  find of settled gravity, 226:14
  for scarcity of capital, 702:3
  heart has its r., 280:1
  heroism never r., 455:31
  immoral thing for moral r., 575:14
  made his mouth water, 271:10
  man always has two r., 567:11
  plenty as blackberries, 185:25
  private as well as public r., 357:7
Reassures, science r., 694:15
Rebecks, jocund r. sound, 259:16
Re-begot, ruined me and I am r.,
    234:21

Rebel, aspiring to angels men r., 167:*n*3
  I'm a good old r., 567:15
  in act and deed, 630:5
  learn from past and r., 822:4
  quickens to r., 719:16
  spaceships, 838:19
  those that r. against the light, 14:30
Rebellion, a little r. a good thing, 357:14
  against United States, 475:15
  century and half without r., 357:15
  determined to foment r., 361:11
  lay in his way, 186:32
  not r. which is noble, 790:3
  now and then good, 357:14
  rude eye of r., 178:23
Rum Romanism R., 495:16
  to tyrants, 846:19
Rebellions, legends events r. majesties,
    438:20
Rebellious, dark r. brows, 521:4
  hell, 205:23
  hot and r. liquors, 198:4
  revolting and r. heart, 29:4
  storms it wooeth, 502:3
  stubborn and r. generation, 18:12
Rebelliousness, culture drives to r., 607:15
Rebels from principle, 345:14
  our countrymen again, 532:17
Rebirth, of Union, 611:2
Reborn, power to be r. into highest forms,
    142:1
Rebounds, hit hard it r., 327:22
Rebuff, welcome each r., 494:9
Rebuffs, confront accidents r., 518:13
Rebuke a wise man, 21:12
  is better than secret love, 23:11
  recoils, 668:9
Rebus, cedit amor r., 105:*n*17
  est modus in r., 98:*n*7
Recall a stone thrown, 101:*n*3
Recalled, word cannot be r., 101:8
Recant, if I do not r., 142:8
Recapitulation, ontogenesis r. of
    phylogenesis, 556:5
Recapture, never could r., 492:5
Recede, unpurged images r., 641:5
Recedes, orgiastic future that r. before us,
    746:8
Receipt of little bit of paper, 516:19
  sitting at r. of custom, 35:17
Receive, ask and ye shall r., 41:34
  Christ r. him, 484:23
  hand stretched out to r., 32:4
  if lungs r. our air, 347:27
  more blessed to give than r., 42:25
  my soul at last, 322:24
  the fugitive, 354:9
  wax to r., 423:3
  we r. but what we give, 402:5
Received, freely ye have r., 35:25
  the Host, 816:1
Receives comfort like cold porridge, 229:24
  reproach of being, 227:21
Receiveth, one r. prize, 44:10
Recessions, predicted nine of last five r.,
    796:17
Recht, yet a' r. that's a', 654:3
Recipe for making Delacroix, 579:11
  rare r. for melancholy, 407:4

Reciprocal in marriage obligations r., 432:6
Recirculation, commodius vicus of r., 696:14
Recite In the name of thy Lord, 122:19
Reck the rede, 201:*n*2
Reckless, make r. choice, 669:7
  puffed and r. libertine, 201:23
  what I do to spite world, 221:1
Recklessness, never gauged your cruelty r.,
    730:18
Reckon ill who leave me out, 453:23
  when I count at all, 545:7
Reckoned, love that can be r., 222:26
Reckoning, day of great r., 3:12
  God swift at the r., 121:22
  honor a trim r., 186:35
  no r. made, 202:19
  sense of r., 193:17
  truth to the end of r., 212:7
Reckons, rash who r. on morrow, 68:14
  up by dozens, 563:16
Recks not his own rede, 201:23
Reclined, all on a rock r., 306:21
Reclothe us in rightful mind, 468:21
Recognition of evil, 58:8
  of ugliness, 58:8
  shock of r., 516:2
Recognize a wise man, 61:23
  did not r. me by my face, 504:7
  gods' hand, 771:4
  good but be barred, 66:2
  relations to world, 600:9
Recognized, wished indifference universally
    r., 833:1
Recognizes, man r. himself in culture, 772:10
  my book in me, 153:18
  which God God r., 771:15
Recognizing man's step, 662:5
Recoiled, warmest heart r. at war, 740:2
Recoils, rebuke r., 668:9
Recollect, cannot r. ignorance in which born,
    333:8
  cannot r. when it begun, 545:14
  that Almighty gave dog, 398:8
Recollected, emotion r. in tranquillity, 391:16
Recollection, fond r. presents them, 418:13
  like living life over, 321:4
Recommencée, la mer toujours r., 658:*n*5
Recommendation, fair exterior a silent r.,
    102:26
Recommends, nimbly and sweetly r. itself,
    219:15
Recompense as largely send, 335:3
  injury with justice, 63:15
  no evil for evil, 43:19
  service beyond all r., 257:14
Reconciled, God and sinners r., 323:1
Reconciles, custom r. to everything, 343:12
  discordant elements, 391:7
  forgotten wars, 720:9
  good dinner r., 288:13
  world easily r. to death, 460:19
Reconciliation of opposite qualities, 403:11
Reconciling mediatory power, 402:20
Reconstructed, won't be r., 567:16
Reconstruction, demand in R. suffrage,
    503:9
Record, dreadful r. of sin, 617:6
  let's look at the r., 663:12
  one more the final r., 446:18

Record *(continued)*
   poetry r. of best happiest moments,
     431:10
   puts r. on gramophone, 718:19
   register of God not r. of man, 256:20
   weep to r., 332:*n*2
Recorded, assurance of r. history, 721:10
   by Muses live for ay, 161:22
   last syllable of r. time, 222:16
Recorders, flutes and soft r., 264:16
Recording Angel dropped a tear, 332:28
   make ourselves r. plate, 572:21
   man shaving, 767:16
Records that defy tooth of time, 305:22
   trivial fond r., 202:22
Recount, such bickerings to r., 269:18
Recover and prove an ass, 182:12
   hair that grows bald, 174:29
   health through contentment, 73:2
   that I may r. strength, 17:15
Recovered innocence, 507:15
   man r. of the bite, 341:19
   virtue if lost seldom r., 286:11
Recreant limbs, 178:4
Recreation, calm quiet innocent r., 253:5
   without some lawful r., 157:24
Recruit, body of little r., 752:11
Recruits in worldly warfare, 270:*n*1
Rectitude, marks of God in r., 412:18
   mind aware of own r., 97:2
Recure, woes time cannot r., 159:21
Recurrent end of unending, 721:18
Red animal war, 655:11
   as a rose is she, 399:16
   as stones kissed by dead, 738:8
   badge of courage, 655:12
   beauty whose r. and white, 209:8
   beholding myself rosy r., 649:15
   blossom in purple and r., 485:12
   China not seeking to dominate world,
     736:16
   coat r. breeches blue, 405:23
   coral is far more r., 228:1
   cow all r. and white, 599:1
   fair weather for sky is r., 36:22
   fortunes of my r. people, 387:8
   heart's core, 436:14
   her lips were r., 400:3
   herrings, 857:7
   I green U blue O, 603:14
   in him the r. earth, 601:6
   in r. cloth appeared letter A, 460:6
   in tooth and claw, 484:6
   jolly r. nose, 249:15
   Lantern and his undersea folk, 829:10
   leaf r. and sear, 396:13
   life stream again, 439:2
   lips not so red, 738:8
   lips r. and one was thin, 270:1
   making the green one r., 220:19
   Marian's nose looks r., 177:18
   men scalped each other, 448:11
   morn that betokened, 173:22
   my Luve like a r. r. rose, 378:19
   my sin is r., 292:13
   my skin is r., 549:3
   nose makes me ashamed, 288:23
   pale and hectic r., 428:21
   plague rid you, 229:17

Red *(continued)*
   remember R. River Valley, 855:2
   rise with my r. hair, 827:11
   rose is a falcon, 590:14
   Rose proud Rose, 636:22
   rose whispers of passion, 590:14
   roses r. and violets blue, 161:7
   sap make cherry r., 714:18
   shadow under r. rock, 718:12
   slayer, 453:22
   so r. the Rose, 471:9
   soldier r. with rust, 597:6
   spirits and gray, 243:22
   still and awful r., 400:12
   sun pasted in sky, 655:13
   swift r. flesh, 753:16
   tape, 498:13
   thin r. 'eroes, 633:7
   thin r.-line streak, 522:10
   thoughts were r. thoughts, 655:6
   tigers in r. weather, 686:16
   wheel barrow, 703:10
   when last r. man has vanished, 419:5
   wine when it is r., 22:38
Redbreast, call for robin r., 244:3
   robin r. in cage, 375:6
   Robin R. piously, 843:13
   sit and sing, 401:11
   whistles from garden-croft, 438:13
Reddens, as an apple r., 58:5
Rede, reck the r., 201:*n*2
   recks not his own r., 201:23
Redeem, lose more of yourself than r., 834:2
   the time, 719:13
   them from death, 30:21
   these hours, 239:10
   unread vision, 719:13
   us from virtue, 568:7
Redeemed of the Lord shall return, 28:15
   visited and r., 38:41
Redeemer, know that my r. liveth, 14:25
   my strength and my r., 16:14
   such and so mighty a R., 49:15
Redeeming, past never past r., 808:14
Redemption, condemned into everlasting r.,
     195:3
   from above did bring, 258:16
   from Wilderness, 817:13
   inestimable love in r., 50:8
Redemptorem, tantum meruit habere R.,
     49:15
Red-handed, 123:28
Red-hot, last of r. mamas, 705:*n*2
Rediscover gods as psychic factors, 675:6
Red-leaved table of my heart, 239:8
Red-letter days, 407:10
Red-line streak, 522:10
Redoubling efforts, 629:6
Redress balance of the Old, 390:1
   I will r. that wrong, 514:7
   music send r., 844:2
   no r. by mob law, 474:4
   of grievances, 361:1
   procure r. of wrongs, 350:14
   things past r. now past care, 179:21
Reduce selfishness, 58:17
Reduction of physical processes, 572:2
Redwood, from r. forest to Gulf Stream
    waters, 788:12

Redwoods, I'm going down like r., 826:10
Reed, be merciful to broken r., 166:16
   bruised r. shall he not break, 28:10
   Love tunes shepherd's r., 396:9
   man is a thinking r., 280:4
   staff of this broken r., 27:34
Reeds, bending r. again and again, 817:4
   down in r. by river, 464:6
Reedy shore, 844:23
Reef of Norman's Woe, 466:6
Reeking herd, 710:6
   into Cadiz Bay, 492:6
Reel, about in r. and rout, 400:1
   to and fro, 19:16
Réel, il n'y a de r. que l'humanité, 444:*n*1
Reeled mind, 762:6
   sagged and r., 685:3
Reeling, send me r. in, 546:19
   through summer days, 544:8
Re-enter, I r. world, 824:10
Reference to one consent, 192:22
References, money and goods best r., 499:2
   verify your r., 371:7
Refine, cannot r. war, 522:11
   if good sense r. her page, 289:16
   it ne'er so much, 237:18
Refined, artist r. out of existence, 696:6
   gild r. gold, 178:14
   or artificial type, 653:17
   pleasures too r., 310:6
   thee but not with silver, 28:12
Refinement of everyday thinking, 683:7
Refinery, out by gas fires of the r., 841:8
Refines, how the style r., 308:21
Refining, still went on r., 343:2
Reflect before throwing images, 726:3
   how awful to r., 636:5
   how you are to govern, 343:19
   on struggle for life, 469:15
Reflecting man twice natural size, 700:9
Reflection, dispense with necessity of r.,
     603:2
   Liberal tempered by r., 531:12
   on acts of mind, 403:15
   remembrance and r. allied, 283:*n*2
   you may come tomorrow, 431:7
Reflections, except r. escapades of death,
     688:8
   mortifying r., 470:*n*1
Reflects, novel r. blue of skies, 417:1
   who r. too much, 382:16
Reflex, conscious movements r., 543:9
Reform carried to excess needs reforming,
     402:22
   cautious people never bring r., 521:19
   is not to equalize property, 80:25
   let us r. schools, 517:11
   that you may preserve, 448:1
Reformation mere episode, 757:4
   printing and the R., 676:11
   reforming of R. itself, 263:2
   revolution and r., 358:13
Reformer, no fidget no r., 623:15
   remains at large, 646:13
Reformers, all r. are bachelors, 601:8
   of error, 358:16
Reforming of Reformation itself, 263:2
   other people's habits, 561:14
   reform carried to excess needs r., 402:22

Reforms, at forty r. plan, 306:5
Refrain from setting yourself judge, 78:15
  from unholy pleasure, 653:1
  time to r. from embracing, 24:6
  tonight, 205:29
Refresh, to keep good acts r. with new, 167:3
Refreshed, as Adam r. with sleep, 520:1
  tree of liberty r., 357:15
Refreshes, presence of wildness r., 507:30
Refrigerator, keep martini in r., 748:7
Refuge, bad man's r., 59:11
  be r. unto yourselves, 66:20
  death become sought-after r., 71:21
  each affair always supreme r., 776:17
  eternal God is thy r., 10:16
  go for r. to Buddha, 67:1
  God is our r. and strength, 17:21
  God the Everlasting R., 122:21
  he is my r. and fortress, 18:25
  home is safest r., 159:n4
  hotel r. from home life, 609:11
  idleness r. of weak minds, 315:4
  patriotism last r. of scoundrel, 327:25
  studies a r. in adversity, 90:13
Refugium, domus rutissimum r., 159:16
Refuse, amid rotten r. of overturned fruit-stall, 569:18
  creeds that r., 568:7
  heavenly mansion, 641:4
  I would r. to get up, 791:8
  make offer he can't r., 807:8
  never ask r. resign office, 321:6
  nothing r., 453:8
  profane fables, 46:20
  thy name, 183:2
  till conversion of Jews, 276:27
  wretched r. of shore, 595:6
Refused, stone which the builders r., 19:25
Refuses, what one r. in a minute, 381:11
Refusing, all remedies r., 169:9
  caution in r. benefits, 287:14
  says a lot in vain r., 364:7
Refutable, charm of theory r., 589:1
Refute, who can r. a sneer, 360:1
Regain love once possessed, 269:9
Regard, strict r. to conscience, 352:9
  two qualities inspire r., 80:24
  well-assured place in men's r., 613:8
  without remedy without r., 221:3
Regarded, heard not r., 186:14
Regardeth, he that r. the clouds, 25:4
Regardez c'est une pauvre terre, 524:n8
Regardless, alas r. of their doom, 333:20
Regards to Broadway, 679:10
  what is before his feet, 87:15
Regeneration, moral r. of mankind, 465:7
  suffering may be r., 512:22
Regent, of love-rimes, 176:33
Regent's, Dewey were R. eyes, 580:2
Regime, establishes democratic r. kill sons of Brutus, 143:5
  gentlemen of old r., 706:2
  no r. ever loved great writers, 804:8
Regiment, half the r. dead, 801:11
  led r. from behind, 566:1
  monstrous r. of women, 150:9
  warring within for r., 170:4
Regio, cuius r. eius religio, 123:17

Region, calm r. where no night, 248:22
  poet soaring in high r., 262:10
  thrilling r. of ice, 211:23
Regional, nothing important is r., 829:2
Regions, double-lived in r. new, 438:9
  in soft r. born soft men, 71:27
  obscure r. of philosophy, 330:8
  of sorrow doleful shades, 264:2
  these external r., 688:8
Register, history r. of crimes, 353:8
  of God, 256:20
Regret, die in evening without r., 62:20
  Florida weighted with r., 821:4
  I have but one life, 370:6
  I must say I r. nothing, 773:n2
  my seedtime, 801:1
  not r. passage of time, 830:17
  only r. is all so terribly true, 611:13
  or secret happiness, 595:2
  possibilities I didn't embrace, 585:19
  remember and r., 451:21
  trifling education of females, 361:16
  vain desire vain r., 542:5
  wild with all r., 482:22
Regrets, congratulatory r., 459:22
  past R. future Fears, 471:10
  that resemble hopes, 512:1
  wild r. bloody sweats, 605:21
Regrette l'Europe aux anciens parapets, 603:n10
Regretted speech never silence, 104:15
Regrow, dragons r. their parts, 792:21
Regular, everything's so awful r., 559:21
  icily r., 485:5
Regulate, free to r. industry, 358:12
  imagination by reality, 325:24
  my room, 325:12
  use of property, 615:12
Rehearse as ny as evere he kan, 135:16
Reign, awful darkness r., 500:7
  come to r. over us, 125:12
  existence saw him spurn r., 323:14
  in hell, 264:8
  king shall r. in righteousness, 27:28
  of error, 785:3
  of the good Cinara, 100:12
  to r. is worth ambition, 264:8
  to r. to be omnipotent but friendless, 428:8
  wealth and freedom r., 341:2
  what is pomp rule r., 173:10
  where saints immortal r., 304:11
Reigned, I have r. with your loves, 152:1
Reigneth, the Lord r., 19:2
Reigns but does not govern, 154:15
  God r. Government lives, 548:9
  if censorship r., 349:9
  no crude surfeit r., 261:3
  of terror, 523:9
Reilly, is that Mr. R., 849:4
Reimpressed by external ordinances, 325:6
Rein, find his mouth a r., 568:22
  not give dalliance r., 230:8
  rung upon r., 587:6
Rein, so hold und schön und r., 442:n5
Reindeer seem over-serious, 715:9
Reins, gae his bridle r. a shake, 379:3
  of power, 477:1

Reintegrated, reduce elements can no longer be r., 779:9
Reject, ignoring all you r., 457:27
  men r. prophets, 526:3
  that they r. is wrong, 569:20
  world of Freud, 755:13
Rejected, despised and r. of men, 28:20
Rejects, consciousness r. object, 581:15
  Heaven r. the lore, 395:16
Rejoice at birth grieve at funeral, 561:11
  desert shall r., 27:31
  for I have found sheep, 39:34
  heavens r. in motion, 235:19
  in ancestral Jove Troy's sons r., 98:4
  in life mark of Greek spirit, 647:9
  in thy youth, 25:6
  let James r., 338:4
  let the earth r., 19:2
  not over thy enemy, 32:14
  we in ourselves r., 402:7
Rejoices in the lost lilac, 719:16
Rejoiceth as a strong man, 16:11
  in his strength, 15:14
  more of that sheep, 36:29
Rejoicing, come again with r., 20:3
  see riches partake in r., 262:20
Relate and embellish adventures, 355:8
  these unlucky deeds r., 215:13
Related, to whom r. by whom begot, 309:29
Relation, all just supply and all r., 235:26
  enjoy original r. to universe, 454:12
  poor r. irrelevant, 407:24
  whole r. between man and woman, 460:13
Relations between aspects of experience, 706:1
  candor and amicable r., 377:1
  fundamental of social r., 465:7
  human r. perfectly exhibited, 81:27
  lift coffins of dead r., 833:14
  public r., 803:3
  renewal of r. nervous, 570:11
  sexual r. with that woman, 840:2
  squire and his r., 497:23
  tedious pack of people, 605:10
  with intellect only collateral r., 480:1
  women's training in human r., 761:14
Relationship, essential r. to existence, 501:10
  friendly and charming r., 144:16
  of author to works, 611:19
Relative, set out in r. way, 664:4
  that r. pronoun, 614:2
Relatives, fate chooses our r., 355:10
Relaxation, allowed himself fun and r., 71:14
  maturity sacred to r., 596:10
  only r. from labor, 586:13
  there may be r., 325:16
Release, deadly forfeit should r., 258:16
  ensured r., 620:3
  from little things, 752:10
  of atomic energy, 705:4
Relent, shall make him once r., 282:4
Relenting fool, 174:15
Relentless, Hades is r., 53:3
  power, 334:1
  war r., 654:9
Relents, my rigor r., 344:6
Relevance, sermon no r. to anything, 806:11

Reliability, shifts of Fortune test r. of friends, 91:14

Reliance on divine providence, 357:4
  self-reliance r. on God, 456:22

Relics, hallowed r. should be hid, 259:3
  unhonored his r. laid, 411:9

Relief, cricket no r., 718:12
  for greedy, 699:1
  for this r. much thanks, 200:12
  hold out r. coming, 522:*n5*
  not seek for kind r., 372:11
  to dig him up throw stones at him, 609:29
  too proud for r., 671:2

Relies, on hope wretch r., 340:12

Relieve misfortunes by speaking, 257:9
  the oppressed, 26:10
  to r. wretched his pride, 342:5
  what wealth r. conscience, 242:7

Relieved, by desperate appliance r., 205:32
  obliged wealthy and r. poor, 52:*n2*
  unless I be r. by prayer, 230:17

Religio, tantum r. potuit suadere malorum, 92:*n7*

Religion, airy subtleties in r., 255:10
  allowed to invade private life, 411:4
  Anglo-Catholic in r., 722:16
  any r. keeping masses satisfied, 727:7
  behold clear r., 436:10
  blunderbuss against r., 326:12
  blushing veils fires, 313:25
  breathing household laws, 392:14
  but a childish toy, 170:9
  Christianity r. of the son, 608:5
  depth in philosophy bringeth to r., 167:22
  different opinions concerning r., 366:19
  duty we owe Creator, 353:4
  enjoy r. prevent others, 555:16
  enough to make us hate, 298:3
  enterprise for glory of Christian r., 140:6
  errors in r. dangerous, 330:3
  establishment of r., 361:1
  evil deeds r. prompt, 92:11
  excess a reproach to r., 291:21
  feelings in solitude, 582:13
  for religion's sake, 427:4
  free exercise of r., 353:4
  free for r., 734:4
  freedom of r., 358:13
  he who controls area controls r., 123:17
  I am a Millionaire that is my r., 609:28
  I mean the Christian r., 322:5
  in r. so uneven, 295:2
  inconsistent with Christian r., 336:14
  is an illusion, 608:3
  Judaism r. of the father, 608:5
  knavery and change, 290:17
  leave him for r., 804:16
  leave r. to family, 532:20
  liberation from dominion of r., 651:7
  lies r. of slaves, 649:1
  line between r. and fly fishing, 763:4
  literature substitute for r., 722:15
  made honest woman, 777:6
  my r. is to do good, 355:1
  no heresies in dead r., 650:2
  no part of r. to compel r., 117:2
  not popular error, 535:10

Religion *(continued)*
  of feeble minds, 345:17
  of well-doing and daring, 326:*n6*
  of which rewards distant, 325:6
  one r. hundred versions, 609:12
  one r. true as another, 242:3
  one's r. neither harms nor helps another, 117:1
  opium of people, 510:5
  orthodox in r., 734:1
  pagan who defends r., 655:14
  persecution bad way to plant r., 255:16
  philosophy handmaid to r., 166:11
  politics like r., 358:16
  poverty a reproach to r., 291:21
  powerless to bestow, 457:18
  printing and Protestant r., 434:10
  propitiation of powers, 602:17
  restores man to dignity, 629:20
  rum and true r., 423:16
  self-righteousness not r., 504:15
  sensible men of same r., 459:26
  slovenliness no part of r., 318:23
  stands on tiptoe, 251:4
  superstition incongruous r., 524:1
  that old-time r., 847:21
  total reaction upon life, 582:14
  we too have our r., 554:5
  what r. is that, 277:12
  wonders of Christian r., 296:4
  your r. is Success, 621:21

Religions, from poetry r., 768:12
  heresy lifeblood of r., 650:2
  neurotics founded r., 657:12
  thirty-two r. one dish, 369:12
  vicissitude of sects and r., 168:18

Religious, appeals to r. prejudice, 537:13
  dim r. light, 260:10
  do evil from r. conviction, 280:11
  duties consist in justice, 355:3
  feeling a verity, 524:2
  feeling toward life, 651:17
  freedom, 678:14
  old r. factions, 345:19
  people suspicious, 632:13
  rather political than r., 326:17
  seed of r. liberty, 515:21
  suspended r. inquiries, 353:16
  vision our ground for optimism, 624:13
  waves of r. emotion, 715:4
  way to think of death, 676:6

Religious-good, good but not r., 574:15

Relinquish, time does not r. rights, 364:18

Relish him more in soldier, 213:13
  imaginary r. is so sweet, 208:2
  love of gentle woman, 788:2
  no r. of those arts, 302:9
  of saltness of time, 191:12
  versing, 250:22

Relished, taste by which r., 395:2

Reluctant sweet r. amorous delay, 266:11

Reluctantly, difficult when you do it r., 89:1

Relume, Promethean heat thy light r., 215:7

Rem tene verba sequentur, 88:*n3*

Remain, if our loves r., 492:12
  laws ought not to r. unaltered, 80:26
  my thoughts r. below, 205:17
  nothing will r., 618:13
  shall France r. here, 535:2

Remain *(continued)*
  sitting at your table, 701:5
  some born mad some r. so, 773:12
  thou shalt r., 438:5
  until death do part, 610:1
  with unavenged suffering, 525:16

Remainder of human time, 836:2

Remained to pray, 342:7

Remaineth, while the earth r., 6:32

Remaining second weakest among great powers, 691:20

Remains, heap of dust alone r., 309:29
  nothing done while aught r., 384:5
  the One r., 430:17
  what r. is bestial, 213:23
  what thou lovest well r., 709:10
  women cut up what r., 634:7

Remake, it is myself I r., 637:20
  myself must I r., 642:11

Remark, Frenchman r. shrewd, 347:19
  which I wish to r., 566:12

Remarkable, nothing r. beneath moon, 224:1

Remarks are not literature, 673:16
  Hegel r. somewhere, 510:6
  seldom quoted correctly, 689:12

Rembrandt, not Velasquez never R., 792:18

Remedies, all r. refusing, 169:9
  die of r. not illnesses, 278:26
  he that will not apply new r., 168:4
  worse than disease, 103:4

Remedy against consumption of purse, 191:21
  cannot r. folly of people, 143:15
  force not r., 489:4
  Fortune leaves door to r., 156:12
  is to inform discretion, 359:6
  patience best r. for trouble, 86:10
  sought the r., 200:3
  things without all r., 221:3
  tobacco sovereign r., 241:14
  too strong for disease, 68:24
  worse than disease, 103:*n1*

Remember, all it is about to r., 809:1
  and be sad, 547:18
  and regret, 451:21
  cannot r. past, 629:7
  children you did not get, 798:6
  Christ our Savior, 846:1
  distinctly I r., 479:1
  fifth of November, 845:14
  for years r. with tears, 535:16
  forget that I r., 568:23
  gentlemen r. blondes, 737:10
  God and history r., 731:8
  house where I was born, 445:15
  if I do not r. thee, 20:11
  if row comes R. the Maine, 849:*n5*
  if thou wilt r., 547:16
  in sweet pangs r. me, 209:21
  in your narrowing hours, 748:3
  inn Miranda, 653:7
  little note nor r., 476:7
  Lot's wife, 40:6
  me to Herald Square, 679:10
  me when I am gone, 547:17
  me when in thy kingdom, 40:20
  no man r. me, 575:6
  not only how much loved, 628:8
  not r. what I must be, 180:3

Repay, I will r., 43:21
    shut when thou shouldest r., 32:4
    tomorrow will r., 282:21
Repeat, condemned to r. past, 629:7
    No again and again, 590:11
Repeateth, he that r. a matter, 22:5
Repeating, human stories r., 661:12
    oft r. they believe 'em, 297:4
Repeats his words, 178:9
Repent at leisure, 300:11
    neither to change nor falter nor r.,
        428:14
    restore should I r. me, 215:7
    we do earnestly r., 50:18
    what's past, 205:26
    ye kingdom is at hand, 33:23
    ye who do truly and earnestly r., 50:17
    you will r. by jingo, 445:22
Repentance, call sinners to r., 35:19
    decline to buy r., 81:18
    fear of consequence, 273:24
    garment of R., 471:2
    give r. to her lover, 341:21
    on a Sunday, 692:11
    tears of r. you'll wipe, 373:12
Repented, strove and much r., 423:10
Repetition, of r. most master, 688:9
Repine, do not r. my friends, 496:39
Replace, no one could r. Franklin, 319:*n*1
Replenish the earth, 5:14
Replication of your sounds, 195:15
Replied Fish fiddle de-dee, 500:9
    O Lord Thou art, 337:16
    shade r., 479:15
    with chuckle r., 693:7
Replies, heart r., 348:10
Reply churlish, 200:9
    pause for a r., 196:26
    pain will r. at what, 791:13
    reply, 189:3
    shall never know how to R., 375:12
    sing ye heavens earth r., 322:23
    theirs not to r., 484:27
Report, by evil r. and good r., 45:8
    ill r. while you live, 203:25
    me and cause aright, 207:11
    nor heart to r., 182:1
    of fashions in proud Italy, 179:10
    of my death an exaggeration, 562:13
    vexation only to understand the r., 27:23
    whatsoever things are of good r., 45:38
    who knows how he may r., 269:12
Reported, their praises might be r., 33:9
Reporters sit in fourth estate, 447:16
Reporters' Gallery Fourth Estate, 433:*n*1
Repose, as well for defense as r., 159:17
    earned night's r., 466:9
    find r. reveal self, 602:5
    foster-nurse of nature is r., 217:17
    hushed in grim r., 335:13
    in r. distinct, 812:14
    in trembling hope r., 335:4
    leave me to r., 335:16
    long for a r., 394:11
    not destiny of man, 577:18
    placid r. under liberty, 278:27
    pray for r. of his soul, 622:17
    quenched in cold r., 430:6
    rare and bloodless week of r., 75:*n*3

Repose (*continued*)
    spirit of r., 449:15
    tabooed by anxiety, 565:3
    that ever is the same, 394:11
    thoughts nature gives way to in r., 220:6
    when got r. insupportable, 570:24
    worship but no r., 429:21
Reposes, in quiet she r., 529:14
Reposing, sorrow breaks r. hours, 174:5
Reprehend, if I r. anything in world, 367:9
Represent, effort to see and r., 585:12
    Muhammad did not falsely r., 122:13
Representation, laws in which we have no r.,
    361:11
    mediocre people entitled to r., 767:15
    taxation without r., 340:2
Representative, individual with r., 403:11
    of highest spiritual authority, 693:10
    owes you, 344:1
    proper office of r. assembly, 464:23
Representatives, conscience of r., 695:9
    House of R., 352:9
    more I see r. of people, 426:12
    women ought to have r., 382:28
Repressed their noble rage, 334:19
Repression, price of r., 648:12
Repressions, mass r. and lawlessness, 826:8
Reproach, curse astonishment hissing and r.,
    29:22
    everything that is a r. among men, 61:20
    mine ways without r., 104:28
    no defense against r., 302:10
    people talking about themselves, 586:17
    receives r. of being, 227:21
Reproached me in public, 388:4
Reproacheth his Maker, 22:4
Reproaching, without r. brethren, 412:17
Reprobate, who such r. as I, 575:5
Reprobation, doctrine of r., 571:12
    fall to r., 215:10
Reproduction, preserved by r., 362:7
Reproof on her lip, 443:3
    valiant, 200:9
Reprove, check erring and r., 394:10
    not a scorner, 21:12
    sager sort our deeds r., 231:21
Reproved each dull delay, 342:6
Reptiles, no r. found there, 124:34
Republic a raft, 376:13
    for which it stands, 606:17
    if you can keep it, 321:2
    is a dream, 681:15
    is one of those words, 757:13
    of letters, 322:13
    they died to save, 477:2
Republican, deprives r. example of just
    influence, 474:7
    eternal importance like R. Party, 708:3
    forming a r. government, 370:10
    highest government 523:14
    model of government, 350:5
    only form of government, 358:1
    party broke ye, 646:2
    work for R. party, 522:1
Republicans, we are all R., 358:9
    we are R., 495:15
Republics, destiny of r. settled, 515:22
    in small r. is stability, 415:19
    never known to exist, 142:14

Repulsive, free speech in r. form, 667:13
Reputation an idle imposition, 213:24
    at every word r. dies, 309:9
    better than my r., 382:10
    bubble r., 198:25
    for kindness enters deeply, 82:18
    gain forever r. among men, 72:16
    I have lost my r., 213:23
    men who survive their r., 153:8
    more valuable than money, 102:18
    not aloof in order to gain r., 78:10
    not carefully preserved, 287:13
    part of man's Self, 581:17
    reputation reputation, 213:23
    sold R. for Song, 472:3
    spotless r., 178:30
    written out of r., 295:12
Repute, sink present r. for freedom, 514:18
    thing of good r., 613:8
Reputed wise for saying nothing, 187:21
Request deed in silence, 131:1
Requiem aeternam dona eis, 49:8
    to thy high r., 437:12
Requiescat in pace, 124:20
Require, that people may r. leader, 77:25
    thought 'e might r., 634:9
    what is it men in women r., 373:15
Required, much given much r., 39:31, 799:6
    nothing given nothing r., 321:19
    of us a song, 20:11
    of us mirth, 20:11
    this night soul shall be r., 39:29
Requirement, first r. in Hospital, 522:5
Requisite, first r. of good citizen, 615:5
    Meat r. to Squirrels, 546:7
    right to means r., 370:14
Reread classic, 767:3
Rere-mice, some war with r., 181:13
Re-resolves then dies, 306:5
Rerum, sunt lacrimae r., 96:*n*15
Res iudicata pro veritate habetur, 124:21
Rescind, voted not to r., 352:9
Rescue me protect me, 3:12
    my soul from their destructions, 17:3
    nothing can r. me, 171:2
    trump of r. sound, 453:14
Rescues, whoever r. single life earns merit,
    120:9
Research contribution to ideas, 796:11
    steal from many authors is r., 678:10
Researchers into Public Opinion, 776:3
Resemblance neglects spirit of objects, 125:9
    showy r. of distress, 354:19
Resemblances, our r. to the savage, 602:20
Resembled my father as he slept, 220:14
Resembles, the most r. God, 378:17
Resembleth, love r. April day, 176:6
Resentment consumes a man, 590:2
    whim envy or r., 346:20
Reserve back shop all our own, 152:17
    side of last r., 275:*n*1
    thy judgment, 201:26
Reservedly, read books as r. as written, 507:4
Réserver une arrière boutique toute notre,
    152:*n*12
Reside in thrilling region, 211:23
Residence, forted r., 212:6
    pains have taken up r., 841:6
Residences, inns not r., 714:9

Reverence *(continued)*
　Hell do it r., 478:7
　human nature, 412:18
　humility sense of r., 70:15
　in deeper r. praise, 468:21
　kill r. you've killed hero, 772:2
　more of r. in us, 483:12
　none so poor to do him r., 196:31
　not r. of dead but envy of living, 246:14
　passions held in r., 478:19
　some r. for laws, 483:9
Reverenced, Queen in politics cease to be r.,
　538:3
Reverences gilt Popinjays, 433:4
Reverend vice, 185:30
Reverently, entered into r., 51:7
Reverie, excited r., 639:8
Reveries, be plunged into deepest r., 516:6
　fantastic r., 573:5
　so airy, 348:2
　valley of r., 663:3
Reverse, forward and r., 815:16
　time will r. your opinions, 78:15
　who prospers one day suffer r., 68:11
Reversion is the action of Tao, 59:3
　no bright r. in sky, 309:28
　temporal r., 721:14
Revery alone will do, 547:6
　cannot meet Cork without R., 546:19
　clover bee and r., 547:6
Review, can't write can r., 514:20
Reviewed, book r. after thirty years, 572:10
Reviewers would have been poets, 402:16
Reviewing not criticism, 585:2
Revile and persecute you, 33:33
Revilest God's high priest, 42:30
Revised and corrected by Author, 319:2
Re-vision act of looking back, 824:16
Revisit in dreams the dear dead, 69:11
Revisitest thus glimpses of moon, 202:6
Revisits, gladden him who r. it, 414:11
Revive, after two days will he r. us, 30:14
　could I r. within me, 401:19
　lamps straight again r., 231:21
Reviving old Desires, 471:1
Revolt, art r. against fate, 761:5
　inferiors r. to be equal, 81:3
　is it a r., 363:3
　nature falls into r., 192:7
Revolted, against r. multitudes, 267:11
Revolting and rebellious heart, 29:4
Revolution and reformation, 358:13
　call R. Progress, 451:11
　carrot in painting set off r., 573:1
　civilization crust over r., 617:21
　comes de r. eat strawberries and cream,
　700:23
　deprive minority justify r., 475:5
　eats own children, 501:4
　fellow travelers of R., 689:13
　French R. began at top, 535:3
　hurrah for r., 642:13
　I don't want to be in your r., 651:8
　image of r., 5:2
　in natural history, 470:1
　inward and outward r., 413:1
　is insurrection, 737:13
　is natural, 489:12
　lasts fifteen years, 702:20

Revolution *(continued)*
　legality counter-moves in same game,
　612:12
　like Saturn, 501:4
　listen to the R., 690:1
　not make r. with silk gloves, 686:5
　not same as inviting to dinner, 737:13
　of rising expectations, 803:1
　party of r. civilization, 451:19
　scientific r., 757:4
　served r. plowed sea, 415:20
　Sire it is a r., 363:3
　suppression impossible without r., 654:10
　to establish dictatorship, 765:17
　tremble at communist r., 511:8
　true r. would succeed, 713:6
　you say you want a r., 835:6
Revolutionaries, mad r. will run in streets,
　769:13
Revolutionary, atomic energy r. force, 705:4
　bourgeoisie historically r., 511:2
　either r. or not, 833:2
　higher ideals r., 582:10
　if not r. be artist, 833:2
　in r. times, 729:6
　parsons preaching Jesus a r., 812:7
　proletariat alone r., 511:4
　reconstitution of society, 511:1
　right to overthrow, 475:6
Revolutionary-democratic, establishment of r.
　dictatorship, 654:6
Revolution's victory over tsarism, 654:6
Revolutions, collapse of r. of 1848, 628:13
　in r. great interests at stake, 81:4
　never go backward, 450:7
　not made they come, 489:12
　put half of France in mourning, 461:12
　state which creates r., 81:3
Revolve it all slowly, 825:5
Revolving, grief with r. year, 430:5
　in course of one r. moon, 283:15
Reward according to his works, 46:34
　all for love nothing for r., 161:4
　angling r. to itself, 252:25
　good evil r. punishment, 286:9
　great Master urgent, 120:8
　if thou not thine own r., 252:*n2*
　labor not ask for r., 145:5
　neither have they any more a r., 24:28
　no r. offered, 441:12
　of knowing we do Thy will, 145:5
　of labor is life, 557:6
　of thing to have done it, 456:14
　of virtue is virtue, 455:28
　rather than punishment, 447:3
　virtue is her own r., 252:*n2*
Rewarded, abilities below mediocrity r.,
　405:1
　evil for good, 7:29
　for that which ye have done, 122:8
　they shall be greatly r., 31:16
Rewarder, who now will be my r., 282:5
Rewardeth evil for good, 22:6
Rewards and fairies, 244:14
　and punishments in cards, 731:3
　fortune's buffets and r., 204:16
　religion of which r. distant, 325:6
Rewrite, don't r. what moving finger writ,
　764:1

Rex, ego sum r., 278:*n6*
　quondam rexque futurus, 139:15
Rhadamanthys, fair-haired R., 54:20
Rhapsody of words, 205:20
Rhein, die Wacht am R., 518:*n1*
Rhetoric able to contend, 168:17
　for r. he could not ope, 270:18
　heavenly r. of thine eye, 177:3
　obscure by aimless r., 537:13
　of rule of Plato, 262:19
Rhetorician, grammarian r. geometrician,
　113:5
　sophisticated r., 459:23
Rhetorician's rules, 270:19
Rheumatics, unless down with r., 87:11
Rhine frontier of England, 645:2
　watch along the R., 518:1
　wide and winding R., 420:23
Rhinoceros, armed r., 221:14
Rhodes, Colossus of R., 850:10
Rhodora, fresh R. in woods, 453:3
Rhone, arrowy R., 420:25
Rhyme, beauty making beautiful old r.,
　227:11
　into ladies' favors, 193:27
　it hath taught me to r., 177:2
　lofty r., 261:14
　many a mused r., 437:12
　more sweetly than r., 437:16
　nor reason, 162:8
　outlive this powerful r., 226:15
　rudder of verses, 271:6
　Runic r., 479:21
　tired of Love more tired of R., 653:12
　unattempted yet in prose or r., 263:20
Rhymed dogerel, 137:20
Rhymes, Namby Pamby's little r.,
　307:22
　no r. in my verse, 648:5
　regent of love-r., 176:33
　suggest freedom, 454:3
　that r. with P, 764:9
Rhyming, planet, 195:10
Rhythm essential in painting, 125:8
　I got r., 746:24
　in all thought, 399:9
　keeping r. in dancing, 720:16
　one of principal translators, 715:14
　poor as dirt don't get r., 829:11
　to world of sound what light is, 715:14
Rhythmical creation of Beauty, 480:1
Rhythms measureless and wild, 70:2
　we tap crude r. for bears, 526:19
Rialto, what news on R., 188:2
Rib, smote him under the fifth r., 11:39
　which Lord God had taken, 5:21
Riband in cap of youth, 206:13
　to stick in coat, 491:20
Ribbed sea sand, 400:9
Ribbon, a R. at a time, 544:16
　in cap of youth, 206:13
　road r. of moonlight, 692:2
　round it, 860:11
Ribs, he took one of his r., 5:21
　heart knock at my r., 219:5
　of Death, 261:5
Rice, not stir r. though it sticks, 158:24
　same old r., 620:9
　with coarse r. to eat, 62:27

Rich, abundance of the r., 24:13
  America in which people still get r., 787:9
  and poor all as one, 70:8
  are different from you and me, 746:10
  as easy to marry r. woman, 490:12
  attire creeps rustling, 437:1
  beauty too r. for use, 182:25
  better live r. than die r., 328:16
  beyond dreams of avarice, 330:16
  blow bugles over r. dead, 713:2
  choose likely man in preference to r.,
    64:21
  company of just men better than r. estate,
    70:17
  dies r. dies disgraced, 559:10
  difference between r. and other people,
    754:n3
  different from you and me, 754:14
  dull and drank, 754:14
  few are r. and wellborn, 370:9
  flames and hired tears, 256:13
  folk ride on camels, 497:4
  freedom to r. or poor, 736:11
  get rich, 711:10
  gifts wax poor, 204:2
  gout kills more r. than poor, 280:18
  greater part of r. people, 338:16
  had I interfered for r., 447:3
  have more money, 754:n3
  have power and poor deprived, 77:20
  high and low r. and poor, 386:14
  honesty dwells like miser, 200:8
  if r. gets foolish, 646:15
  if r. whenever you please, 79:5
  in good works, 46:28
  in loss of all I sing, 818:8
  in poverty, 159:9
  in things he can let alone, 506:26
  is better, 705:17
  isn't it r., 826:1
  jewel in Ethiop's ear, 182:25
  joys fall not to r. alone, 101:6
  knowledge a r. storehouse, 166:6
  labor not to be r., 22:33
  law forbids r. as well as poor, 586:18
  laws broken by mighty and r., 57:17
  let him be r. and weary, 250:19
  live and die r-r-r., 499:6
  live like a wretch and die r., 240:21
  make r. richer, 386:13
  maketh haste to be r., 23:16
  man beginning to fall, 32:28
  man enther Hiven, 646:11
  man not glory in riches, 29:11
  man to enter into kingdom, 36:34
  many evil men are r., 57:6
  men rule the law, 341:8
  mind r. with suspicion, 824:8
  moral soil for aesthetic growth, 664:6
  neither r. nor poor, 557:5
  no woman can be too r. too thin, 851:7
  nor r. at forty, 251:25
  not gaudy, 201:26
  people most afraid, 729:6
  people who are r., 700:15
  poor and content is r., 213:35
  possessed by money, 240:19
  quiet and infamous, 448:9
  rob poor, 443:12

Rich *(continued)*
  say more than this r. praise, 226:26
  seems it r. to die, 437:12
  sent empty away, 38:40
  sent not corn for r. men only, 224:16
  snow year a r. year, 251:10
  something r. and strange, 229:20
  the treasure, 285:11
  'tis mind makes body r., 175:37
  to hear wooden dialogue, 207:28
  too r. a pearl for swine, 271:19
  two nations the r. and poor, 459:5
  waster of r. men, 68:1
  when he is hungry, 79:n3
  when men drink they are r., 74:12
  when thou art old and r., 211:19
  with corn, 468:13
  with forty pounds a year, 342:4
  with spoils of Nature, 255:12
  with spoils of time, 334:19
  wot gets pleasure, 851:1
Richard Cory one summer night, 652:11
  Sir R. Grenville lay, 486:22
  sweet lovely rose, 185:6
Richardson, if you read R. for story, 327:14
Richardson's, one letter of R., 327:13
Richer, for r. for poorer, 51:10
  love's r. than my tongue, 215:15
  make rich r., 386:13
  man held to be holier, 118:4
  quiet mind r. than crown, 165:16
  than all his tribe, 215:13
Riches and honors by unrighteousness, 62:27
  and power gifts of fate, 126:10
  are for spending, 168:6
  are ready snares, 139:15
  best r. ignorance of wealth, 342:1
  by theft will not stay, 5:8
  cover multitude of woes, 83:13
  deceitfulness of r., 36:5
  despise r., 518:10
  earth is full of thy r., 19:11
  embarrassment of r., 316:25
  enjoyment of r. parade of r., 338:16
  Fame and Pleasure, 287:18
  feverish preoccupation with r., 692:10
  full of days r. and honor, 13:14
  good handmaid worst mistress, 166:19
  good name rather than r., 22:24
  grow in hell, 264:23
  he heapeth up r., 17:14
  he that getteth r. not by right, 29:19
  he that trusteth in his r., 21:19
  house field and wife great r., 319:10
  if r. valuable to Heaven, 298:11
  in her left hand r. and honor, 20:25
  infinite r. in little room, 170:10
  make themselves wings, 22:34
  means by which r. acquired, 692:10
  neither poverty nor r., 23:22
  no r. above a sound body, 32:41
  nor r. to men of understanding, 24:30
  not exchange our excellence for r., 57:6
  not profit the sluggish, 3:6
  of heaven's pavement, 264:22
  Peru with its r., 442:1
  poverty and use of service, 229:25
  renown which r. or beauty confer, 95:2
  rich man not glory in r., 29:11

Riches *(continued)*
  see her r. partake in rejoicing, 262:20
  to live on little with contented mind,
    93:17
  to make gifts to friends, 70:8
  to make thy r. pleasant, 211:19
  to such a scoundrel, 298:11
  virtue and r. seldom on one man, 241:7
  watching for r., 32:44
Richesses, l'embarras des r., 316:n9
Richest alchemy, 195:28
  East with r. hand, 264:25
  man r. pleasures cheapest, 505:11
  monarch in Christian world, 381:15
  Spain is become r. of countries, 140:9
Richly, storied windows r. dight, 260:10
Richmond, on R. Hill a lass, 368:15
Richmonds, six R. in the field, 174:24
Richness, much r. in lytell space, 170:n3
  of soul, 79:8
  quietness and pleasure, 524:11
  warmth r. reality of hunger satisfied,
    778:6
Rich-wrought, Aphrodite on your r. throne,
    57:19
Rickety wooden bridge, 835:13
Rid, can't r. myself of spirits I summoned,
    364:14
  earth of him in my pride, 652:3
  getting r. of work breaks heart, 620:7
  mend it or be r. on 't, 221:2
  never r. of rest of her, 297:8
  no getting r. of annuity, 406:1
  of friendship of the many, 557:14
  of temptations by yielding, 445:8
  of things by writing them, 754:11
  poets' wares harder to get r., 669:8
  red plague r. you, 229:17
  to have got r. of folly, 100:19
Ridden, millions ready to be r., 448:20
  should nonetheless have r., 144:19
Riddle, glory jest and r., 311:9
  had not found out my r., 11:2
  of the Sphinx, 68:9
  Phoenix r. hath more wit, 234:6
  Sphinx asked Oedipus r., 759:18
  wrapped in mystery, 665:17
Riddles, God sets nothing but r., 525:12
Riddling perplexed soul, 237:2
Ride, a few to r. millions, 448:20
  and spread alarm, 467:15
  beggar will r. a gallop, 172:n1
  beggars might r., 281:7
  boldly ride, 479:15
  cockhorse, 858:14
  draw bow r. and speak truth, 424:25
  Germany knows how to r., 502:10
  Haggards r. no more, 620:12
  in triumph over mischance, 173:1
  in triumph through Persepolis, 170:3
  like unwashed platters r., 753:18
  mankind, 453:6
  midnight r. of Paul Revere, 467:14
  next doth r. abroad, 347:24
  not free horse to death, 158:32
  of the Valkyries, 501:14
  poem r. on own melting, 671:12
  remote Bermudas r., 277:9
  rough-shod, 498:8

Rise *(continued)*

my Shakespeare r., 238:5
not r. early never do good, 325:17
out of ash I r., 827:11
out of wreck r., 495:11
people have right to r. up, 474:5
stoop to r., 244:18
sun sets to r. again, 495:10
suns that set may r. again, 237:14
then we shall r., 248:22
though war should r. against me, 16:23
till we are called to r., 546:9
to feet as He passes by, 633:4
to r. love stoops, 494:13
truth crushed will r. again, 432:16
up at the voice of the bird, 25:7
up my love, 25:17
up so early in morn, 848:1
we die and r. the same, 234:6
we fall to r., 495:15
what are you when sun shall r., 232:16
why r. because 'tis light, 234:16
wilt thou therefore r. from me, 234:16
woe unto them that r. up early, 26:20

Risen, Christ r. from dead, 44:24
Christ the Lord r. today, 322:23
He is r., 38:32, 49:17
Jesus Christ r. today, 294:8
Lord is r. indeed, 40:28
the Lord is r., 49:17
there is a people r., 280:16

Riser, dawn comes no sooner for early r., 862:21

Rises from prayer better man, 541:1
hidden laughter, 720:13
hooray up she r., 862:2
howls hoo and r., 688:3
my gorge r. at it, 206:24
soul that r. with us, 393:11
sun gives light soon as he r., 321:1
unspeakable desire, 529:4

Riseth from feast with keen appetite, 188:19
late trot all day, 319:24
with fleas, 251:24

Rising, beating way for r. sun, 761:17
before the r. sun, 304:7
every land rejoices at his r., 4:6
fogs prevail upon day, 284:3
from r. of the sun unto going down, 19:20
I see them r., 696:18
let others hail r. sun, 335:21
listen the wind is r., 710:3
more worship r. than setting sun, 91:20
of the sun, 846:2
plat of r. ground, 260:4
Proteus r. from sea, 394:19
revolution of r. expectations, 803:1
shadow r. to meet you, 718:12
through change and storm, 426:14
warm cheek and r. bosom, 335:6
wind is r., 659:1

Risk, art unthinkable without r., 730:2
conquer without r., 257:2
flatterer r. everything, 300:2
I had to take and took, 670:20

Risk *(continued)*

of reigns of terror, 523:9
t'other half for freedom, 514:18

Risking, not giving life but r. life, 777:12
only by r. we live, 582:7

Risks, great deeds wrought at great r., 71:23

Risotto, moat of r., 836:1

Rites, performed r. simple decisive, 816:18

Rival, cannot r. for one hour, 547:11
know I may not r. him, 741:5
remains to r. what they have done, 74:5

Rivalry of aim, 570:16

Rivals are the worst, 296:5
jealousy of r. near throne, 361:15

Rivalship of wisest men, 303:5

River, Alph the sacred r., 401:13
among r. sallows, 438:13
at my garden's end, 312:16
can't sleep with the r. forever, 841:5
cross r. rest under trees, 536:4
down in reeds by r., 464:6
drifting down r., 560:15
Eliza across r., 489:18
glideth at own sweet will, 392:13
great r. take me to main, 483:5
in the ocean, 464:8
lake glimmering pool, 534:9
let me love r. and woodland, 96:12
Lethe the r. of oblivion, 265:16
like foam on r., 397:9
like snow falls in r., 379:18
lived on R. Dee, 352:5
met character on r., 560:9
monstrous big r. down there, 560:18
not step twice into same r., 64:*n2*
Oceanus the ocean r., 777:1
of grass, 728:14
of crystal light, 597:5
of oblivion, 265:16
Ol' Man R., 744:1
on a tree by a r., 565:20
one more r. to cross, 863:9
over r. through wood, 450:11
passage over the r., 520:3
peace as a r., 28:13
pilot cares about nothing but r., 560:6
see one r. and see all, 241:3
she's fading down r., 627:5
spreadeth out her roots by the r., 29:17
strong brown god, 721:7
swap horses crossing r., 476:10
Thames noblest r., 302:19
there is a r., 17:22
time a r. of strong current, 115:17
time r. without banks, 852:3
tirra lirra by r., 480:25
water of r. never the same, 127:12
way-hay you rolling r., 862:3
weariest r., 569:3

River City gonna have Boys Band, 764:10
trouble here in R., 764:9

Rivering, beside r. waters of, 696:16

Riverrun past Eve and Adam's, 696:14

Rivers, as brooks make r., 285:23
as long as r. flow, 856:9
as long as r. shall run, 97:3
at their source, 710:7

Rivers *(continued)*

by shallow r. birds sing, 170:7
by the r. of Babylon, 20:11
deepest r. least sound, 160:*n3*
drain pent-up r. of myself, 519:25
fire r. cannot quench, 173:8
I've known r., 762:9
my soul deep like r., 762:9
no r. no wells no springs, 759:7
not step twice into same r., 64:8
of water in a dry place, 27:29
rains return in r., 777:1
run into the sea, 23:33
run to seas, 285:23
shallow brooks and r. wide, 259:15
tree planted by r., 15:27

Rivets, busy hammers closing r., 193:11

Rivulet, neat r. of text, 367:27

Rivulets hurrying through lawn, 483:8
meadow r. overflow, 576:8

Road, 'ammer along 'ard 'igh r., 591:15
backward glances over traveled r., 521:16
broad hard-beaten r., 454:10
but one r. leads to Corinth, 101:*n2*
butterfly upon r., 632:9
by r. his ever-open door, 52:*n2*
come to fork in r. take it, 814:14
dark r. whence no one returns, 94:2
divils in twists of r., 658:9
free as the r., 250:15
from Montgomery, 823:6
heaven above r. below, 599:11
help me down Cemetery R., 810:5
high r. to England, 326:18
house by side of r., 52:30, 613:16
if r. could not make it out, 661:16
I'm ten years burning down the r., 841:8
is smooth, 56:12
lonesome r., 400:17
matrimony r. to wealth, 503:13
no r. or ready way to virtue, 256:3
no royal r. to geometry, 84:17
of excess leads to palace of wisdom, 372:14
open r., 599:12
poor slaves tread, 429:25
rail pig lead, 681:5
ribbon of moonlight, 692:2
right r. to Ireland, 763:3
rough r. leads to greatness, 106:23
royal r. to Thebes, 771:3
smooth r. of life, 333:6
straggling r. in Spain, 664:11
take to open r., 520:2
takes no private r., 311:14
to City of Emeralds, 606:15
to Hades easy to travel, 85:2
to Hell gradual, 752:4
to resolution, 249:10
to stars through atom, 695:4
up and down City R., 848:8
up and road down one and same, 64:11
virtue demands thorny r., 152:21
when find r. narrow, 127:5
which leads to peace, 358:13
will be less tedious, 95:29
winding r. before me, 410:13
with bread and wine walk r., 862:16
ye'll take the high r., 847:15

Roads, crooked r. are r. of genius, 373:2
    how many r., 836:4
    improvement makes straight r., 373:2
    lie with nothing to use them, 781:17
    old r. return to sky some color, 834:4
    open when you rise, 4:10
    two r. diverged, 669:4
Roadway, cry of child by r., 637:8
Roam, absent from Him I r. 396:1
    all morning sends to r., 619:16
    dunce sent to r., 347:10
    ever let fancy r., 438:8
    ev'rywhere I r., 538:16
    home where buffalo r., 855:3
    long wont to r., 478:2
    not their hearts that r., 634:16
    soar but never r., 395:18
    though we may r., 426:15
    where'er I r., 340:15
    wish to r. farther, 365:22
Roamed, how sweet I r., 371:9
    with my Soul, 479:13
Roamin' in the gloamin', 654:4
Roaming, ceaseless thoughts of r., 291:12
    mistress mine where r., 209:12
Roar, grating r. of pebbles, 530:20
    grievous r., 404:7
    hiss now becoming r., 725:4
    melancholy long withdrawing r., 531:2
    men want ocean without r., 509:13
    music in its r., 421:25
    of only beast in arena, 645:6
    other side of silence, 513:9
    set table on a r., 206:24
    swinging low with sullen r., 260:4
    think lion sleeping because he didn't r., 381:7
    welkin r., 191:31
    you as any nightingale, 181:1
    you gently as sucking dove, 181:1
    young lions r. after prey, 19:11
Roared, cracked growled r. howled, 399:18
    Declamation r., 324:1
    Homer and Whitman r., 651:12
    well r. Lion, 182:10
Roaring, devil as r. lion, 47:33
    empty tigers or r. sea, 184:12
    with hollow blasts, 306:21
    words of my r., 16:16
Roars it through the hall, 534:7
Roast beef of England, 321:15
    I gaze upon the r., 830:17
    in hell r. you like herrin, 380:2
    rules the r., 141:n3
    set house on fire to r. eggs, 168:2
    with fire, 8:17
Roasted crabs hiss in bowl, 177:18
    very likeness of r. crab, 181:5
Roasts, newspaper buries dead r. thim afterward, 646:18
Rob, if writer r. mother, 749:3
    jaybird don't r. own nes', 593:12
    lady by marriage, 322:11
    neighbor he promised to defend, 448:11
    not the poor, 22:29
    Peter pay Paul, 148:11
    rich r. poor, 443:12
    starve ere I'll r. further, 185:13
    words r. Hybla bees, 197:16

Robbed, he's not r. at all, 214:7
    not wanting what stolen, 214:7
    of their humanity, 804:1
    that smiles, 213:1
    we wuz r., 747:11
Robber, Barabbas a r., 41:37
Robbers, the more r. there will be, 59:10
    what makes r. bold but lenity, 172:29
Robbing, live by sharping and r., 320:24
    think little of r., 418:6
Robe, giant's r., 222:8
    intertissued r. of gold, 193:16
    judge's r., 211:10
    sa r. de pourpre au soleil, 151:n2
Robert, believe R. who has tried it, 98:n4
Robes and furred gowns, 217:24
    garland and singing r., 262:10
    loosely flowing, 237:16
    mountain in azure hue, 408:12
    riche or fithele, 134:30
    sky-r. spun of Iris' woof, 260:17
    washed r. in blood, 48:24
Robespierre sea-green Incorruptible, 434:5
Robin, call for r. redbreast, 244:3
    fainting R., 546:1
    redbreast in a cage, 375:6
    redbreast piously, 843:13
    what will poor r. do., 859:12
    who killed Cock R., 857:14
Robinson Crusoe, 295:7, 331:10
Robot vehicles blindly programmed, 836:3
    waited upon by r. slaves, 742:13
Robots, Rossum's Universal R., 727:13
Robs me of that which not enriches him, 213:33
Robust, debate on public issues r., 774:3
Robustious periwig-pated fellow, 204:11
Rock, all on a r. reclined, 306:21
    cradle will r., 592:1
    crag of the r., 15:16
    dwell on r. or in cell, 160:10
    eagle dwelleth on r., 15:16
    eagle of the r., 710:6
    founded upon r., 35:11
    he is the R., 36:25
    he only is my r., 18:1
    it is the Inchcape R., 405:12
    knew the perilous r., 405:11
    laws are sand customs r., 562:16
    lean upon death as on r., 713:12
    living as black r. star, 818:2
    Lord is my r., 12:8
    Moses in Horeb struck r., 807:6
    Moses smote r. twice, 9:20
    no water only r., 718:21
    of Ages, 356:2
    of offense, 26:29
    of our salvation, 18:29
    poetry old as r., 454:6
    sails well but strike r., 376:13
    shadow under red r., 718:12
    shadows of a great r. in a weary land, 27:29
    small r. holds back great wave, 54:17
    takes on appearance of nearby r., 61:13
    that is higher than I, 17:37
    the tall r. the mountain, 391:3
    this r. shall fly, 397:11
    towered citadel pendant r., 223:33

Rock *(continued)*
    upon this r. I will build, 36:25
    way of a serpent upon a r., 23:25
    which Hercules bequeathed, 574:9
    will split, 707:6
Rock-a-bye-baby, 592:1
Rock and roll, not tell Vietnam from r. veterans, 834:10
    which go first r. or Christianity, 834:11
Rockbound, stern and r. coast, 431:20
Rocked in cradle of deep, 419:7
Rocket, life like r. flies, 829:6
Rockets, once r. are up, 820:14
Rockets' red glare, 411:1
Rockies, applies west of R., 807:7
    ghost train in R. buried in snow, 817:4
Rocking, cradle endlessly r., 520:7
    in your r. chair by window, 656:4
Rock-ribbed, hills r., 432:9
Rocks and stones and trees, 392:1
    cries of cicadas sink into r., 291:13
    even among these r., 719:17
    hand that r. cradle, 518:7
    marriage on the r., 817:15
    nor can sap be in r., 93:10
    older than r., 573:6
    over r. wood and water, 449:15
    seas laugh when r. near, 244:5
    soften r. or bend oak, 300:20
    Soundings quicksands r., 440:11
    that are steepest, 845:5
    the r. rent, 38:10
    trees wind, 505:13
    walled round with r., 569:14
    what gray r., 719:18
Rocky shore beats back siege, 179:13
Rod, a chief a r., 311:13
    Aaron's r., 8:12
    and blows not much good, 144:10
    cast thy r. before Pharaoh, 8:11
    creed is a r., 569:8
    he that spareth his r., 21:27
    Jonathan put forth the r., 11:24
    not pious longer than r., 144:10
    of empire, 334:18
    of iron, 48:11
    out of the stem of Jesse, 26:33
    spare r. and spoil child, 83:n7, 271:17
    thy r. and thy staff, 16:18
    to check the erring, 394:10
    Wisdom be put in silver r., 372:12
Rode him through mire, 860:22
    off in all directions, 651:9
    the six hundred, 484:24
    upon a cherub, 16:9
Roderick, Saxon I am R. Dhu, 397:10
    where was R. then, 397:13
Rodillas, mejor morir que vivir en r., 679:n1
Roe, be thou like to a r., 26:5
    following the r., 379:6
Roes, breasts like two young r., 25:21
Roger, Sir R. made reflections, 302:19
Rogue and peasant slave, 203:27
    every inch not fool is r., 283:21
    joined this r. and whore, 299:6
Rogues, hear r. talk of court news, 218:1
Roi, plus royaliste que le r., 855:5
Rois, l'exactitude la politesse des r., 370:n4

Root and all in hand, 486:21
    axe laid unto the r., 33:27
    from which tyrant springs, 77:23
    get with child a mandrake r., 233:13
    government never take r., 388:1
    hog or die, 757:2
    insane r., 219:2
    learned r. of Homer, 239:n2
    leaves many r. one, 638:4
    love of money r. of evil, 46:26
    nips his r. then he falls, 231:2
    of heaven and earth, 58:11
    of honesty in good education, 111:12
    of the kingdom, 81:28
    of the matter, 14:26, 582:12
    of wisdom, 31:25
    one striking at r. of evil, 506:24
    piece of body torn out by r., 781:16
    square r. of Everest, 807:7
    tickleth me aboute myn herte r., 136:13
    tree whose r. is firmly fixed, 121:8
    what you are r. and all, 486:21
    withered because no r., 36:3
Rooted, great-r. blossomer, 640:15
    honor r. in dishonor, 486:3
    shakes r. folly of age, 289:16
    sorrow, 222:12
    strongly r. as envy, 367:32
    weeds are shallow-r., 172:10
Rootholds, go back to earth for r., 681:17
Roots, branch shall grow out of his r., 26:33
    grass r., 625:12
    marsh grass sends in sod, 583:10
    no r. in hotels, 649:13
    of lilac under soil, 672:14
    rose among r., 599:5
    spreadeth out her r. by the river, 29:17
    stirring dull r., 718:11
Rope between animal and Superman, 588:16
    draw sin with a cart r., 26:21
    enough till haltered themselves, 146:n8
    escape from r. and gun, 307:16
    just above ground, 701:4
    lay out money on a r., 240:20
    never want r. enough, 146:17
Rope-dancer physician magician, 113:5
Ropes, all its r. relent, 670:11
    blunders like r., 451:12
Rory O'More, says R., 443:4
Rosa, sub r., 256:n1
Rosalind, heavenly R., 197:32
    no jewel like R., 199:7
Rosary, couple o' guns and R. beads, 704:8
    my r. my r., 627:8
Rose again the third day, 50:3
    among thorns, 117:13
    and put down Yellow Book, 773:18
    at which my heart r., 270:12
    Aylmer whom these wakeful eyes, 408:5
    beauty's r. might never die, 225:27
    bestows the fading r., 253:13
    breast that gives r., 541:10
    cankers in musk-r. buds, 181:13
    cheerless over hills, 468:17
    come see if the r., 151:2
    darkly he r., 818:6
    desert shall blossom as the r., 27:31
    die of a r., 311:6

Rose *(continued)*
    fairest when budding, 163:n4
    familiar as r. in spring, 115:18
    find where last r. lingers, 99:20
    fire and r. are one, 722:5
    gather R. whilst prime, 161:5
    glut sorrow on r., 438:15
    go lovely r., 257:24
    go lovely R., 692:17
    him that loved r., 620:14
    I am R. my eyes are blue, 673:21
    if love were what r. is, 568:20
    immortal Shakespeare r., 323:14
    in deeps of my heart, 637:8
    into the r. garden, 720:8
    is a rose is a rose, 673:11
    killing as canker to r., 261:18
    last r. of summer, 411:15
    laurel and myrtle and r., 363:16
    leaves when r. dead, 430:19
    lovely is the R., 393:8
    mighty lak' a r., 613:5
    my Luve like a red red r., 378:19
    no more desire r., 176:21
    O R. thou art sick, 374:3
    of our love, 809:4
    of Sharon, 25:14
    of Yesterday, 471:4
    of youth, 223:25
    on such lopped limbs, 780:3
    one perfect r., 738:15
    onion r. among roots, 599:5
    red as a r. is she, 399:16
    red R. a falcon, 590:14
    red R. proud R. sad R., 636:22
    red r. whispers of passion, 590:14
    Richard sweet lovely r., 185:6
    saw r. had flowered, 699:15
    she lived as roses do, 164:3
    slowly r. she up, 854:1
    so red the R., 471:9
    sweeter in bud, 163:14
    tell the crooked r., 795:2
    tell you how Sun r., 544:16
    that lives little hour, 432:13, 692:17
    the morrow morn, 401:3
    thick with lily and red r., 556:11
    Thistle Shamrock R. entwine, 547:13
    thought like full-blown r., 436:24
    under the r., 256:10
    up in his prime, 724:14
    vernal bloom or summer's r., 265:25
    wavers to a r., 574:12
    white r. a dove, 590:14
    white r. breathes of love, 590:14
    without a thorn, 368:15
    without thorn the r., 266:7
    wreath has lost r., 397:18
Roseau, un r. pensant, 280:n2
Rosebud something he couldn't get, 749:6
Rosebuds, crown ourselves with r., 31:14
    filled with snow, 232:6
    gather ye r., 248:8
Rose-cheeked Laura come, 232:2
Rose-lipped maiden, 619:6
    young and r. cherubin, 214:27
Rosemary and rue, 228:25
    for remembrance, 206:11
Rose-red city half old as time, 501:5

Rose's scent bitterness, 620:14
Roses, all night r. heard, 485:10
    all the way, 492:1
    and white lilies grow, 232:5
    ash burnt r. leave, 721:16
    bein' Gawd ain't bed of r., 728:6
    by Bendemeer's stream, 412:11
    courts thee on r., 99:7
    days of wine and r., 645:11
    each Morn thousand R., 471:4
    everything's coming up r., 825:18
    flung r. riotously, 645:9
    for flush of youth, 548:1
    gather r. of life today, 151:1
    get it says Sergeant Cuff, 536:1
    have thorns fountains mud, 226:11
    love and r., 412:9
    make thee beds of r., 170:8
    marriage not bed of r., 598:5
    money beautiful as r., 456:12
    never friends with r., 568:15
    no r. at my head, 547:16
    raptures and r. of vice, 568:3
    red and violets blue, 161:7
    rose she lived as r. do, 164:3
    scent of r. hang still, 412:2
    seek r. in December, 419:16
    silent war of lilies and r., 175:3
    strew on her r., 529:14
    sweet days and r., 250:10
    sweet musk-r. and eglantine, 181:12
    we want bread and r. too, 850:17
    when we last gathered r., 246:4
    women are as r., 209:23
Rossum's Universal Robots, 727:13
Rost, rast ich so r. ich, 845:19
Rosy, 'cause another's r. are, 246:18
    hands in steam, 809:1
    he that loves a r. cheek, 253:18
    lips and cheeks, 227:17
    mauve and r. sky, 746:11
    wreath, 238:3
Rosy-fingered dawn, 52:9
Rot, deep did r., 399:23
    enough to r. upon ground, 307:21
    from hour to hour we r., 198:16
    inwardly, 262:2
    lie in cold obstruction and r., 211:23
    lie shall r., 535:5
    name of the wicked shall r., 21:15
    water and fire shall r., 721:17
Rote, learned and conned by r., 197:12
    phrases learned by r., 298:19
Rots in ease on Lethe wharf, 202:14
Rotten, apple r. at the heart, 188:7
    dead and r., 319:20
    mackerel by moonlight, 405:2
    navy would be r. timber, 344:17
    small choice in r. apples, 175:22
    something r. in state of Denmark, 202:11
Rottenness begins in conduct, 358:7
Rotting grave ne'er get out, 375:11
Rotundity, thick r. o' the world, 216:18
Rough but ready, 497:28
    diamond knowledge, 314:25
    male kiss of blankets, 712:18
    notes and our dead bodies, 649:16
    oil smooths what is r., 108:2
    places made plain, 28:1

Rough (*continued*)
rude sea, 179:24
spirit that on life's r. sea, 165:11
steep the way and r. at first, 56:12
this r. magic, 230:11
torrent of occasion, 192:3
turns smoothness r., 494:9
unordered mass, 105:12
what r. beast, 639:7
winds do shake, 226:2
winter and r. weather, 198:11
Rougher, I beneath a r. sea, 348:22
Roughest, runs through r. day, 219:7
Rough-hew them how we will, 207:5
Roughly, speak r. to little boy, 550:7
visit her face too r., 201:3
Roughnesses pimples and everything, 254:16
Roughs, among his fellow r., 487:10
Roughshod, ride r., 498:8
Round, attains upmost r., 195:30
earth's imagined corners, 236:4
everything tries to be r., 628:1
fat oily man of God, 318:11
giddy thinks world turns r., 175:39
I pick r., 837:1
in heaven perfect r., 494:4
in r. of their need, 811:16
justice in fair r. belly, 198:25
large and smooth and r., 405:5
life's dull r., 328:n1
light fantastic r., 260:23
longest way r. shortest home, 249:n2
nature renews r. untired, 678:15
ocean and living air, 391:4
square person in r. hole, 398:13
stones prepared r. ready, 816:19
the world away, 514:4
turned r. and r. in world, 516:17
unvarnished tale deliver, 212:26
up the usual suspects, 782:11
Roundabouts, lost on r., 659:17
Rounded Peter's dome, 452:19
with a sleep, 230:9
Roundelay, merry merry merry r., 164:8
Rounders, come all you r., 655:n1
Round-heads and Wooden-shoes, 302:3
Rounds, completion of their appointed r., 71:n8
Rouse, at dismal treatise r., 222:15
at name of Crispian, 193:19
lion from his lair, 398:7
lion than start hare, 185:8
the slumbering morn, 259:13
Roused, demon r. will rend you, 474:12
Rousing like a strong man, 263:3
Rousseau asks the reader, 526:n1
mock on R., 375:2
not ask Jean Jacques R., 348:19
Rout, about in reel and r., 400:1
ruin upon ruin r. on r., 265:22
Rove, wherever I r., 379:5
Rover, blood's a r., 618:8
laughing fellow r., 681:2
whither away fair r., 586:5
Roving, go no more a-r., 423:1
I'll go no more a-r., 862:4
Roving's been my ru-i-in, 862:4

Row, crosses r. on r., 660:9
Devil knows how to r., 400:21
if r. comes Remember the Maine, 849:n4
of orient pearl a double r., 232:6
one way look another, 112:n1
seraphim in burning r., 262:9
uninterrupted central tail r., 714:14
Rowed with muffled oars, 405:3
Rowers who advance backward, 112:n1
Rowing home to haven, 681:4
looking one way r. another, 281:25
Rowland, Child R. to dark tower, 217:3
Rowley, heigh-ho says Anthony R., 856:17
Rows, nine bean-r. have, 637:1
Royal banner and all quality, 214:8
David's city, 508:9
descended of so many r. kings, 224:14
Navy watchword, 665:18
road to geometry, 84:17
road to Thebes, 771:3
sware a r. oath, 482:13
teeming womb of r. kings, 179:12
throne of kings, 179:12
throne of r. state, 264:25
Royalist in politics, 722:16
more r. than king, 855:5
Royaliste, plus r. que le roi, 855:5
Royalists of economic order, 698:2
Ruant, fiat justitia r. coeli, 123:n7
Ruat coelum fiat voluntas tua, 124:22
fiat justitia r. coelum, 123:26
Rub, always r. against money, 704:11
let the world r., 156:28
there's the r., 203:33
Rub-a-dub-dub, 860:8
Rubbed her with butter, 821:13
Rubber, ring of convulsive r., 812:3
Rubble, anything more offensive than r., 841:3
Rubies, her price is above r., 23:27
price of wisdom is above r., 14:35
Rubric in book of my memory, 129:14
Rudder, rhyme r. of verses, 271:6
steer my r. true, 106:n11
Rudders, pain and pleasure r., 286:n3
Ruddy drops that visit heart, 196:7
limbs flaming hair, 373:11
there the lion's r. eyes, 372:9
Rude am I in my speech, 212:25
by r. bridge, 453:11
dust the r. wind blows, 217:12
engines whose r. throats, 214:8
eye of rebellion, 178:23
forefathers of the hamlet, 334:11
I'm uppity r. profane, 806:9
in speech, 45:11
in the r. manger lies, 258:17
mercy of a r. stream, 231:2
multitude call afternoon, 177:11
rough r. sea, 179:24
savage extreme r. cruel, 227:22
sea grew civil at her song, 181:8
with forced fingers r., 261:13
witty to be r., 298:20
Rudely great, 311:9
speke he never so r., 135:16
Rudge, like Barnaby R., 514:19
Rudis indigestaque moles, 105:n9
Rudyards cease from Kipling, 620:12

Rue, nought shall make us r., 178:29
rosemary and r., 228:25
sold for endless r., 618:11
wear r. with a difference, 206:12
with r. heart laden, 619:6
Rued, day I had r., 669:12
Ruerent, cur imbres r., 107:n7
Ruffian, father r., 185:30
Ruffle, shake out the r., 819:18
Ruffles, giving pair of laced r., 296:2
like sending them r., 343:7
Rufus, Curtius R. descended from himself, 78:n1
Rug, snug as bug in r., 320:16
Rugged and without a beach, 289:17
cadence of a r. line, 284:5
individualism, 672:1
old r. cross, 661:10
Russian bear, 221:14
Ruh', meine R. ist hin, 365:n5
Ruin and combustion, 263:23
around the dear r., 411:12
bad herdsmen r. flocks, 55:16
decay in House on Hill, 652:5
dyspepsy r. of most things, 418:5
exaltation from disaster and r., 665:5
final R. fiercely drives, 306:13
formless r. of oblivion, 208:20
hath taught me thus to ruminate, 226:19
he stared at r. r. stared back, 792:10
he that tastes woman r. meets, 307:16
here meets rain wind r., 759:12
I'll r. you, 432:17
in r. and confusion hurled, 301:16
into r. hurled, 311:3
majestic though in r., 265:8
man marks earth with r., 421:26
my country's r., 293:10
new years r. and rend, 568:17
notice r. in things, 796:16
of our sex, 337:7
pens of diplomats not r., 356:11
predicts r. of the state, 375:7
princes and their r., 231:2
rather than preservation, 142:14
science without conscience r. of soul, 146:5
seize thee ruthless King, 335:11
serve my nation r. another, 314:10
since roving's been my r., 862:4
spreading r. scattering ban, 464:6
that was my r., 365:13
that's romantic, 565:21
upon ruin rout on rout, 265:22
when truth entails r., 69:1
whom God to r. has designed, 71:n4
Ruined, archangel r., 264:17
bare r. choirs, 226:24
by amateurs, 715:15
love when built anew, 227:20
me and I am re-begot, 234:21
men that are r., 345:21
millionaire, 721:2
no nation r. by trade, 320:22
spend wealth at once you are r., 445:6
threshold of r. tenement, 323:3
to be r. man a vocation, 722:20
Ruinous, all r. disorders, 215:28
Ruin's, stern R. plowshare, 378:8

Rus I see you, 472:23
   said to people of R., 125:12
   similar to troika, 472:24
Rus in urbe, 111:*n2*
Rush down to the beach, 516:1
   fools r. in, 309:1
   my only into your arms, 696:18
   nations shall r. like many waters, 27:5
   to glory or grave, 408:20
Rush-candle, please to call it r., 175:38
Rushed to meet insulting foe, 368:11
Rushing of many waters, 27:5
   sound of r. wind, 41:44
Russet, morn in r. mantle clad, 200:23
Russia, all R. our orchard, 622:15
   been over into R., 644:7
   heart of R. not forget, 458:17
   homeland of patience, 458:18
   how sad our R., 473:1
   is a prison, 426:4
   last out night in R., 211:7
   Mother R., 527:16
   not forecast action of R., 665:17
   prison of nations, 686:*n1*
   seen R. content anywhere else, 426:5
   vast multitudes of R., 666:13
Russian, communism R. autocracy upside
    down, 499:9
   future smells of R. leather, 442:17
   great R. allies, 728:15
   I am true R., 829:8
   might have been R., 564:1
   mighty true free R. speech, 512:6
   people make sorrow diversion, 649:3
   rugged R. bear, 221:14
Russians and Americans, 463:2
   dashed towards line, 522:10
Russians' joy to drink, 126:2
Russia's chondria for short, 446:15
   future a danger, 499:10
Rust, better to wear out than r. out, 282:14
   dew will r. them, 212:22
   eaten to death with r., 191:20
   if gold r. what shal iren do, 135:10
   moth and r. doth corrupt, 34:12
   strong men r., 745:2
   that which never taketh r., 163:24
   time r. sharpest sword, 397:22
   to the harrow, 662:14
   toy soldier red with r., 597:6
   unburnished, 481:10
   when I rest I r., 845:19
Rustics, amazed gazing r., 342:9
Rustled, stars in sky r. softly, 603:6
Rustles, to him in fear everything r., 69:3
Rustling of purple curtain, 479:3
   spring with r. shade, 724:17
   to her knees, 437:1
Rusts, iron r. from disuse, 141:5
Rusty, cane leaves r. with talk, 742:5
   for want of fighting r., 271:5
   mail, 208:9
Ruth, melt with r., 262:4
   sad heart of R., 437:13
Ruthless, good writer r., 749:3
   in war cunning r., 426:1
   nor any wildcat so r., 75:13
   ruin seize thee r. King, 335:11
Ruthlessly pricking bubble, 692:14

Rutledge, I am Anne R., 651:15
Rydal, to R. Lake that lead, 392:*n1*
Rye, catcher in the r., 805:14
   coming through the r., 845:20
   pocket full of r., 858:12

S

Sabachthani, Eli Eli lama s., 38:9
Sabbath, child born on S., 859:16
   eternal S. of his rest, 284:1
   keep S. going to Church, 544:17
   made for man, 38:16
   rang slowly, 795:11
   remember the s. day, 8:34
Sabbath-breaking, drinking and S., 418:6
Sabbath-day, abhor detest S., 561:1
Sabbaths, endless s. blessed ones see, 126:5
Sabidius, I don't like you S., 110:16
Sabina has thousand charms, 845:21
Sabine, bounded by S., 487:5
Sabines, life the old S. knew, 96:15
Sable cloud, 260:25
   it was a s. silvered, 201:18
   night s. goddess, 305:24
   Sleep son of s. Night, 169:3
   underneath this s. hearse, 247:12
Sables, suit of s., 204:20
Sabrina fair, 261:10
Sacco's name will live, 724:21
Sack, each S. had seven cats, 857:6
   if s. and sugar be fault, 185:31
   intolerable deal of s., 186:2
   leave s. live cleanly, 187:12
   unless hours cups of s., 184:23
Sackcloth, put on s. with ashes, 13:18
Sacked the holy citadel of Troy, 54:7
Sacks, seven s., 857:6
Sacrament, men pregnant abortion a s.,
    797:16
   of praise, 687:6
   virtue of s. like light, 79:*n5*
Sacred, Alph the s. river, 401:13
   Awe, 701:10
   cod, 621:*n1*
   cows make tastiest hamburger, 832:4
   drama heaved, 642:5
   duty to myself, 540:7
   even bad books are s., 819:3
   facts are s., 592:5
   feed his s. flame, 401:22
   fire of liberty, 350:5
   hair dissever, 309:13
   head now wounded, 258:4
   head of thine, 261:21
   history a s. thing, 157:28
   hold every moment s., 676:18
   hoop of the nation, 628:1
   human body s., 519:24
   let there be s. silence, 99:26
   life not cheap but s., 456:31
   lips touch s. fire, 656:18
   nothing s., 754:4
   our s. honor, 357:4
   sane and s. death, 520:15
   source of sympathetic tears, 335:8
   they lack a s. poet, 100:15
   things s. or things profane, 281:22

Sacred *(continued)*
   to departed spirit, 123:21
   to oblivion, 239:14
   two most s. names, 275:19
   veils her s. fires, 313:25
Sacredness of property, 559:7
Sacrifice acceptable to God, 43:15
   coming to s., 438:3
   living s., 43:15, 51:1
   make one sweet s., 230:23
   mercy and not s., 30:16
   too long a s., 639:5
   you make for sentiment, 647:4
Sacrificed, certainty precedent not lightly s.,
    653:16
   Christ our Passover s., 44:5
   person s. to individual, 697:3
   to produce her, 627:10
Sacrifices it to your opinion, 344:1
   like stockyards, 754:4
   of friendship, 655:7
   such s. my Cordelia, 218:2
   with such s. God is pleased, 47:8
Sacrilegious murder hath broke ope, 220:23
Sacrum, oblivioni s., 239:14
Sad, a little sunny a little s., 570:26
   all their songs s., 664:7
   all world s. dreary, 538:16
   and bad and mad, 494:17
   and weary I go back, 696:18
   as angels, 332:*n2*
   augurs mock own presage, 227:12
   bad brother's name, 569:13
   be beautiful and be s., 524:17
   companion dull-eyed melancholy, 225:8
   created you while s., 628:9
   cypress, 209:25
   experience make me s., 199:24
   flesh is s. alas, 583:13
   heart foams at stern, 603:7
   heart of Ruth, 437:13
   how s. our Russia, 473:1
   is Eros builder of cities, 775:18
   kissed mouth, 568:10
   last gray hairs, 437:8
   lucidity of soul, 528:9
   make man look s., 182:11
   mechanic exercise, 483:15
   mine a s. one, 187:17
   my verse s. no wonder, 619:19
   name forever s., 309:24
   no s. songs for me, 547:16
   old law s. not bitter, 678:15
   or singing weather, 568:20
   remember and be s., 547:18
   Rose of all my days, 636:22
   say I'm s., 417:16
   soul s. glance glum, 565:25
   sound of horn, 443:14
   still s. music of humanity, 391:4
   stories of death of kings, 179:28
   sullen and s., 317:13
   tale's best for winter, 228:14
   tires in a mile-a, 228:24
   to see s. sights moves, 175:10
   'twas s. by fits, 337:3
   uncertain rustling, 479:3
   vicissitude of things, 332:2
   visit my s. heart, 196:7

Sad *(continued)*
    weight of this s. time, 218:9
    when am I s., 826:11
    words of tongue or pen, 468:12
Sadder and wiser man, 401:3
    light than waning moon, 468:17
    than owl songs, 424:22
    those who hear s. than I, 555:13
Saddest are these, 468:12
    of the year, 432:14
    story ever heard, 662:20
    sweetest songs s. thought, 429:19
    when I sing, 555:13
Saddle, boot s. to horse, 491:13
    come s. your horses, 398:11
    no better place than s., 535:1
    put Germany in s., 502:10
    short life in s., 624:3
    things are in s., 453:6
Saddled, millions s. and bridled, 448:20
Sadie stayed home, 798:5
    Thompson answer, 673:2
Sadly, part we s. in troublous world, 173:13
    why hearest thou music s., 225:30
Sadness, begin in s., 800:15
    diverter of s., 252:25
    eternal note of s., 530:20
    farewell s., 743:3
    humorous s., 199:23
    more prevailing s., 409:6
    of a vale, 438:17
    of conviction, 577:17
    songs of s. and mirth, 466:21
    soul taste s. of might, 438:16
    sweet though in s., 429:4
    touches me with a prayer, 442:8
    unmannerly s. in youth, 187:30
    where s. let me sow joy, 128:5
    wraps me in humorous s., 199:23
Sado, over S. the Milky Way, 291:17
Safe and sane Fourth, 644:1
    believe soldiers nothing s., 548:4
    compulsion to become s., 708:5
    depository of public interests, 359:10
    direct and honest not s., 214:12
    for democracy, 628:13
    he that's secure is not s., 320:3
    none is s., 714:11
    run into a s. harbor, 57:15
    see me s. up, 144:3
    shall wooden wall continue, 64:n3
    weariest river s. to sea, 569:3
    wish him s. at home, 384:3
    world s. for democracy, 611:8
    world s. for diversity, 800:3
Safeguard, judiciary s. of liberty, 626:18
    of the west, 393:1
Safeguards, history of procedural s., 695:6
Safely, but to be s. thus, 220:30
    citizen may walk s. on law, 813:7
    Judah and Israel dwelt s., 12:13
    ship of state s. to harbor, 67:13
    toddle s. home, 712:3
Safer to be feared than loved, 142:10
    world s. for children, 824:4
Safest, home is s. refuge, 159:n4
    in the middle, 105:14
    just when s. sunset touch, 493:8
    road to Hell, 752:4

Safety, as if s. in stupidity, 507:17
    concern for s. in face of dangers, 812:9
    dangerous to peace and s., 377:1
    fame for ale and s., 193:3
    greatest degree of s., 339:10
    in multitude of counsellors, 21:17
    in s. within boundaries, 699:8
    in skating s. is speed, 455:30
    neither liberty nor s., 320:13
    no s. here below, 144:n3
    no strike against public s., 659:18
    obtaining happiness and s., 339:9
    peace liberty and s., 358:13
    pluck this flower s., 185:16
    principles to effect s., 357:2
    to hope not safety, 97:11
    unite for public s., 388:8
    with which error tolerated, 358:9
Sagacious blue-stocking, 448:12
    bold and turbulent of wit, 283:8
    how s. the mouse, 86:11
Sagacity, by accidents and s., 336:3
    no s. no powers, 345:24
Sage, by saint by savage by s., 313:7
    daughters of Muses, 66:4
    does not accumulate, 59:21
    government of the s., 58:9
    hoary S. replied, 325:20
    hold tongue pass for s., 104:10
    Homer's rule best, 312:15
    knows without going about, 59:7
    lengthened s. advices, 379:15
    Milton's wormwood words, 262:n1
    never strives for the great, 59:2
    Way of s. is to act, 59:21
Sage, que m'importe que tu sois s., 524:n10
Sagebrush, wind with fragrance of s., 661:19
Sager sort our deeds reprove, 231:21
Sage's, vain the s. pride, 313:6
Sages appeared crawling for charity, 82:27
    by s. perfectly exhibited, 81:27
    error of the S., 82:27
    have seen in thy face, 347:21
    holy s. once did sing, 258:16
    than all the s. can, 390:19
    wisdom of our s., 358:13
Sagged and reeled, 685:3
Sags like heavy load, 762:16
Sahara dies, 546:13
Said, by and by easily s., 205:11
    death has something to be s. for it,
        809:12
    fool hath s. in his heart, 16:4
    he always s. my eyes were blue, 408:9
    he himself has s. it, 563:20
    he was against sin, 659:21
    I kept my word he s., 662:11
    I meant what I s. s. what I meant, 769:7
    I s. in my haste, 19:23
    I to myself said I, 564:21
    in grief or pride, 735:9
    inadvertently s. some evil thing, 79:1
    least s. soonest mended, 157:n1
    let no more be s., 531:3
    let what will be s., 358:3
    little s. soon amended, 157:5
    much s. on both sides, 302:11
    never to himself hath s., 396:11
    no sooner s. than done, 87:10

Said *(continued)*
    nothing s. that has not been s., 89:3
    so Sancho Panza s., 692:16
    the best thought and s., 531:10
    thing that is s. is s., 137:25
    thing which was not, 298:17
    'tis well s. again, 230:29
    to my soul be still, 720:23
    too late to say anything not s., 292:14
    want anything s. ask man, 816:9
    well as if I had s. it, 299:15
    when all is s. and done, 602:20
    who s. Peacock Pie, 662:14
    word dead when s., 546:10
Sail, all s. no anchor, 449:2
    at break of day, 702:5
    bark attendant s., 311:16
    beyond sunset and stars, 481:14
    cried A s. a s., 400:2
    even with canvas rent, 106:17
    give man boat he can s., 557:10
    here she comes full s., 300:23
    hoist s. while gale, 147:n7
    more s. than ballast, 292:4
    on, 579:9
    on O Ship of State, 466:19
    out on your trades again, 85:16
    sea-mark of my utmost s., 215:11
    shallow bauble boats dare s., 207:23
    solitary s. that rises, 502:2
    soul s. leagues beyond, 542:3
    time to take in s., 453:20
    tomorrow s. the Ocean Sea, 99:9
    two lofty ships set s., 862:9
    we must s. not drift, 473:10
    wet seas roun', 634:17
    white and rustling s., 417:7
    with unshut eye, 528:7
Sailed away year and day, 499:16
    off in wooden shoe, 597:5
    Swift s. into rest, 641:3
Sailing celestial spaces, 572:17
    denies voyager further s., 70:5
    great whales s. by, 528:7
    like a stately ship, 269:6
    on obscene wings, 401:12
    ship a-s. with the wind, 860:13
Sailor, drunken s. on mast, 174:9
    here and there old s., 686:16
    home is the s., 599:6
    if Ancient Mariner called Old S., 559:3
    soldier an' s. too, 634:20
    staring s. that shakes watch, 785:15
    well for s. lad, 482:15
    what shall we do with drunken s., 862:1
Sailor's wife had chestnuts, 218:26
Sailors but men, 188:1
    half our s. swallowed, 173:12
    images s. tattoo, 759:13
    onward s. cry, 616:9
    show world how American s. fight,
        849:n5
    soldiers s. airmen, 667:14
    Spanish s. with bearded lips, 467:8
    won't believe it, 398:6
Sail's shaking, 680:15
Sails, argosies of magic s., 481:23
    biased by full s., 753:14
    broad bellying s., 703:12

Sails *(continued)*
 filled streamers waving, 269:6
 filled with lusty wind, 165:11
 handed all s. and set treo, 140:4
 purple the s., 223:14
 set of s. not gales, 600:5
 swell full, 452:1
 thy white s. crowding, 586:5
 vessel of my genius now hoists s., 131:5
 well but strike rock, 376:13
 white s. fly seaward, 719:16
Sail-yards tremble masts crack, 165:11
Saint and Martyr rule from tomb, 720:4
 become a s., 824:7
 by s. by savage by sage, 313:7
 corrupt a s., 184:31
 dead sinner revised, 580:18
 Doctor and S., 471:13
 if God does not exist, 790:4
 lips would temp a s., 420:*n*1
 looked out of eye of s., 641:1
 neither s.- nor sophist-led, 528:18
 old s. in forest, 588:15
 poet and s. to thee alone, 275:19
 saw my late espoused s., 263:17
 Sebastian died of fright, 832:11
 seem s. when most play devil, 173:37
 strained so much, 780:3
 such injury vex a s., 175:32
 threadbare s., 233:5
 to be a s. for oneself, 525:1
Saint Agnes' Eve, 436:20
 moon hath set, 437:3
Saint Anne mother of Mary, 573:6
 yes by S., 209:17
Saint Augustine thanked God, 675:8
Saint Clement's, bells of S., 857:12
Saint George, England and S., 193:2
 for England, 664:14
 that swinged dragon, 177:26
Saint George's Hanover Square, 558:13
Saint Ives, going to S., 857:6
Saint James's, ladies of S., 574:12
Saint John, awake my S., 310:20
 ancient animal symbols of S., 442:16
 there S. mingles, 312:14
Saint John's, whether bounded by the S., 487:5
Saint Louis bought it for six million dollars, 560:10
Saint Martin's, expect S. summer, 171:13
Saint Nazaire, mademoiselle from S., 730:14
Saint Nicholas soon would be there, 411:5
Saint Paul's, designing S., 674:4
 ruins of S., 336:5, 448:7
Saint Peter's, blessing of S. Master, 253:9
Saint Stephen's choir, 800:9
Saint Theresa in wild lament, 766:18
Saint Vincent, nobly Cape S., 492:6
Sainted, thing enskyed and s., 210:37
Sainte-Terrer, there goes a S., 504:*n*2
Saintliness not a state, 784:17
Saintly, woman's normal occupations counter s. life, 774:9
Saints aid if men call, 401:8
 choir of s., 236:13
 Communion of S., 50:3
 for all the s., 534:5
 heroes if we will, 528:4

Saints *(continued)*
 in your injuries, 213:8
 men below and s. above, 396:9
 precious is the death of his s., 19:24
 rarely married women, 774:9
 slaughtered s., 263:15
 sweetly sing, 292:8
 take your s. and virgins, 513:20
 to windows run, 544:9
 when s. go marching in, 863:14
 where s. immortal reign, 304:11
Saint-seducing gold, 182:17
Saintship of an anchorite, 420:6
Sairey, oh S. S. little do we know, 497:9
Sais, que s.-je, 153:*n*2
Saisons, O s. O châteaux, 603:*n*14
Saith, he s. among the trumpets, 15:15
Sake, for God's s. sit upon ground, 179:28
 for his name's s., 16:18
 good friend for Jesus' sake, 231:19
 hated for my name's s., 35:28
 love for Love's s., 781:10
 persecute you for my s., 33:33
 poem for poem's s., 479:23
 wine for thy stomach's s., 46:24
Sakes, Heaven and future's s., 670:6
Saki, eternal S. from Bowl poured, 471:18
 O S. you pass, 472:6
Salaam, peace unto you shalom s. forever, 789:10
Salad, capacious s. bowl, 599:5
 crazy s. with meat, 639:10
 days, 223:10
 Garrick's a s., 343:1
Salads, ho 'tis time of s., 333:1
Salaputium disertum, 94:*n*6
Salary, draw s. before spending, 643:13
Sale, base s. of chapmen's tongues, 176:27
 city for s., 95:11
Salesman, every s. can fondle her breasts, 672:8
 lazy insolence of shoe s., 769:2
Salley, down by s. gardens, 636:19
Sallied flesh, 201:*n*1
Sallow, lean and s. abstinence, 261:7
Sallows, among river s., 438:13
Sally in our alley, 307:23
 loose s. of mind, 324:16
 make a sudden s., 485:3
 none like pretty S., 307:23
Salmon, like chinook s. jumping, 801:16
 wasn't wine was s., 495:20
 with first s. and first green peas, 467:13
Salmon-falls, 639:16
Salome danced, 36:11
Saloon, all s. keepers Democrats, 489:11
Salt, became a pillar of s., 7:7
 drift in laboring s., 830:14
 eat peck of s. with him, 843:14
 eaten your bread and s., 632:7
 fragrance of s. marsh, 521:2
 how s. is another's bread, 132:2
 if s. have lost savor, 34:1
 land and not inhabited, 29:17
 no joy but lacks s., 669:17
 not worth his s., 109:8
 of the earth, 34:1
 one s. sea, 192:22
 seasoned with Attic s., 278:23

Salt *(continued)*
 speech seasoned with s., 46:5
 tides seaward flow, 528:5
 upon their tails, 297:17
 water and s. and darkness, 842:4
 water unbounded, 635:14
 with a grain of s., 108:14
Salt-caked smokestack, 681:5
Salted, wherewith shall it be s., 34:1
Saltness of time, 191:12
 sugar and s. agree, 343:1
Salts, anything man says take with dose of s., 695:18
Saltsick, seasilt s., 696:18
Saltus, natura non facit s., 322:*n*3
Salus extra ecclesiam non est, 117:*n*3
 populi suprema lex, 91:*n*5
Salutary influence of example, 325:6
 wise and s. neglect, 344:6
Salute, we about to die s. you, 114:11
Salutes everyone in early days, 77:24
Salvaged, ships s. and retiring, 696:2
Salvation, concern temporal s., 352:13
 for helmet the hope of s., 46:11
 for him there is s., 365:20
 for our s. came down, 50:4
 Genius work out s., 440:11
 he is become my s., 8:25, 27:1
 he only is my rock and s., 18:1
 in union, 653:18
 my bottle of s., 160:8
 my light and my s., 16:22
 no s. outside Church, 117:7
 none should see s., 189:19
 rock of our s., 18:29
 three things necessary for s., 129:7
 waited for thy s., 7:37
 work out own s., 45:33
 work out s. with diligence, 66:22
Sam, play it S., 782:8
Samarcand, silken S. to cedared Lebanon, 437:2
Samaria, woman of S., 40:47
Samaritan had compassion, 39:23
Samarra, appointment in S., 673:1
Same, always s. old story, 817:15
 Darby always s. to Joan, 594:3
 descent to Hades is s., 66:15
 ever the s., 152:2
 looking outward in s. direction, 759:1
 men all the s., 673:2
 permanent and the s., 529:8
 precisely s. rocks, 469:11
 repose that ever is the s., 394:11
 self was not the s., 207:17
 the more they remain s., 468:23
 the s. as everywhere, 363:11
 think and hit s. time, 814:8
 whole world over, 851:1
 yesterday today and for ever, 47:6
Sameness of sheep, 756:17
 self has continuity and s., 762:2
 with difference, 403:11
Sames of am, 740:9
Samite, arm clothed in white s., 139:3
 clothed in white s. mystic, 485:19
Samphire, one that gathers s., 217:18
Sample, by s. we judge whole, 156:2
Sampler, serve to ply the s., 261:9

Sauce, bread s. of happy ending, 585:5
    cloyless s., 223:12
    good crier of green s., 146:8
    no s. like hunger, 157:30
Saucy doubts and fears, 221:9
    not deep-searched with s. looks, 176:20
Saul and Jonathan were lovely and pleasant,
        11:36
    becomes Paul, 614:11
    hath slain his thousands, 11:31
    is S. among the prophets, 11:20
    why persecutest thou me, 42:7
    yet breathing slaughter, 42:6
Saunders, a bed Clerk S. said, 854:3
Saunter, great art to s., 504:25
Sauntering from à la Sainte Terre, 504:n2
Sausage, in as pig out as s., 580:15
Sausages, men are like s., 508:5
Savage and Tartarly, 425:1
    breast, 300:20
    bull bear the yoke, 194:11
    by saint s. by sage, 313:7
    contemplates mother-in-law, 602:19
    delights to torture, 470:6
    dole laws unto s. race, 481:7
    extreme rude cruel, 227:22
    half s. country, 708:19
    if little s. left to himself, 331:24
    in man never eradicated, 505:12
    indignation, 299:29, 641:3
    individual man, 644:10
    is he who saves himself, 141:6
    men and uncouth manners, 344:3
    noble s., 282:19
    our resemblances to the s., 602:20
    place as holy and enchanted, 401:14
    ruled s. hordes, 534:9
    servility slides by, 801:14
    soothe a s. breast, 300:20
    take some s. woman, 482:6
    thrown on s. shore, 521:4
    wilderness into empire, 345:2
    young man who not wept s., 629:19
Savage-creating fellow, 75:19
Savageness, sing s. out of a bear, 214:21
Savagery, meeting-point between s. and
        civilization, 624:8
Savages, grow like s., 193:26
    in unknown island, 458:24
Savage-wild, time and intents are s., 184:12
Save, assist him to s. face, 744:15
    came to s. sinners, 46:15
    conquer but to s., 409:2
    destroy town to s. it, 852:18
    died to s. us all, 508:8
    eternal Father strong to s., 537:19
    God s. the king, 11:21, 180:8, 308:1
    God s. the mark, 185:5
    greed will s. the U.S.A., 840:6
    himself he cannot s., 38:8
    listen and s., 261:10
    me from Candid Friend, 389:16
    me from therrble prongs, 696:18
    my soul if I have soul, 535:9
    myself by work and faith, 772:11
    nobly s. or meanly lose, 476:3
    not s. it it not s. me, 702:10
    old worth saving, 647:7
    one drop would s. my soul, 171:4

Save *(continued)*
    Shine Shine s. poor me, 850:17
    squadron honor France, 495:4
    thee ancient Mariner, 399:19
    what is around me, 702:10
    whosoever s. life shall lose it, 36:27
    wish to s. their own pocket, 73:17
Saved by hope faith love, 735:17
    harvest is past and we are not s., 29:8
    he s. others, 38:8
    I have s. myself, 56:20
    part of day rued, 669:12
    there be souls must be s., 213:19
    youthful hose well s., 198:25
Saves, humor s. a few steps, 714:16
    itself perpetually, 785:7
    savage he who s. himself, 141:6
    soul in new French books, 493:9
Savin', I'm s. love for you, 745:4
Saving, not s. but selection, 345:24
    save old worth s., 647:7
Savings, not by s. and capital, 778:15
Savior at his sermon on mount, 492:7
    Christ our S., 846:1
    I imitate the S., 741:2
    of 'is country, 633:8
    which is Christ, 39:3
Savior's birth celebrated, 200:22
    sing tongue the S. glory, 129:2
Savoir être à soi, 152:n13
    tuer et créer, 524:n11
Savor, filths s. but themselves, 217:14
    fleeting delights, 426:8
    if salt have lost s., 34:1
    seeming and s. all winter, 228:25
    thoughts that s. of content, 165:16
Savory, lavender mints s. marjoram, 228:26
Saw, all at once I s. a crowd, 394:4
    coughing drowns parson's s., 177:18
    do not s. the air, 204:11
    expanse of s. grass and water, 728:14
    first one another s., 234:17
    heavens fill, 481:23
    him with my own eyes, 278:1
    I at a glance, 394:6
    I came I s. I conquered, 92:5
    I came s. and overcame, 192:5
    I s. and loved, 353:17
    last time I s. Paris, 744:3
    life steadily saw it whole, 528:2
    man clothed with rags, 281:14
    manners in face, 325:19
    ne'er s. I never felt, 392:13
    never s. a man who looked, 605:16
    never s. a Moor, 546:6
    never s. purple cow, 643:18
    not seen as others s., 477:13
    on a cloud I s. a child, 371:13
    skull beneath skin, 718:6
    spiders marching, 800:11
    spires of Oxford, 697:2
    then I s. the Congo, 685:4
    three ships, 860:9
    through glass eye darkly, 561:20
    water lily bloom, 480:26
    who was that lady I s., 647:14
    young Harry with beaver on, 186:23
Saws, full of wise s., 198:25
Sawyer, Adventures of Tom S., 560:14

Saxa, in spatio pertundere s., 92:n9
Saxon I am Roderick Dhu, 397:10
    in subjection to white S. man, 503:7
Saxophones, long cool winding s., 681:14
Say, cannot create when nothing to s., 761:4
    canst not s. I did it, 221:11
    can't s. anything good, 704:5
    defend right to s. it, 317:2
    disapprove of what you s., 317:2
    Do as I s. not as I do, 245:28
    don't s. too much, 777:9
    everything interestingly, 597:15
    find right thing to s., 609:1
    first of God above, 311:1
    good deed to s. well, 230:29
    good night till it be morrow, 183:16
    I don't s. what public wants, 672:6
    I shall have less to s., 669:7
    I want to s., 831:14
    I'd like to s. a few words, 842:10
    it ain't so Joe, 851:3
    it as you understand it, 382:5
    It Loud, 829:12
    it with utmost levity, 609:1
    know much s. little, 331:7
    light stream of what we s., 531:20
    love not having to s. sorry, 832:9
    more to s. when dead, 652:8
    nastiest thing in nicest way, 713:5
    never know what I'm going to s., 128:7
    never s. I was false of heart, 227:13
    never s. more than necessary, 367:6
    not struggle nought availeth, 512:10
    not what we ought to s., 218:9
    not what you s. but how, 548:5
    nothin' without compelled, 515:8
    nothin' you can be held to, 515:8
    nothing but what said, 240:3
    nothing to s., 513:15
    nothing to s. s. nothing, 413:4
    nothing you couldn't actually s., 709:14
    one may s. what one thinks, 113:24
    person who could not s. no, 782:6
    remember what we s. here, 476:7
    right to s. what one pleases, 711:2
    secure within can s., 284:6
    see what I s., 616:1
    shall my little bark, 311:16
    shame s. what it will, 206:14
    shudder to s. it, 97:8
    so long as we can s., 217:10
    some s. I'm impatient impetuous uppity,
        806:9
    some s. world end in fire, 669:11
    style of what man has to s., 531:7
    tale as said to me, 396:8
    temple bells they s., 633:12
    that's all I s., 473:16
    there is no more to s., 208:23
    there is nothing more to s., 652:5
    they s. my verse sad, 619:19
    things I did not do or s., 641:10
    this again, 840:2
    this with presence of mind, 89:7
    though I s. it that should not, 245:13
    to all the world, 197:22
    to the fleet, 377:n1
    too late to s. anything not said, 292:14
    way they s. it, 764:8

Say (*continued*)

wet mind and s. something clever, 74:11
what else to s. but everything, 798:11
what everyone else does not s., 589:21
what law is, 371:1
what more is there to s., 640:6
what others s. of them, 279:17
what people s. behind back, 601:15
what s. they let them s., 162:*n*7
what will Mrs. Grundy s., 384:14
what you mean, 550:10
what you would be, 112:16
which can s. more, 226:26
which grain will grow, 218:31
wouldn't s. so till tried, 693:7
you can have it, 821:2

Sayer, always seer is a s., 455:2

Saying all we did not know, 710:14
for loving and for s. so, 234:8
good-bye to statue, 754:7
is one thing, 153:11
mode of s. things, 530:11
reputed wise for s. nothing, 187:21
thoughtless s. of princess, 331:19
wise and old, 161:*n*4
Wrath by his meekness, 372:9

Says a lot in vain refusing, 364:7
no one means all he s., 570:25
she speaks yet s. nothing, 182:29
what he s. least important, 572:12
who is it that s. most, 226:26
who s. it what he s., 572:12

Scab of churches, 233:1

Scabbard, sword of justice has no s., 368:17
sword within the s. keep, 285:21

Scabby, hated with s. hatred, 829:8

Scabies, disputandi pruritus ecclesiarum s., 233:*n*1

Scaffold sways the future, 514:13
Truth forever on s., 514:13

Scaffoldage, 'twixt footing and s., 207:28

Scald, tears s. like molten lead, 217:29

Scalding grave, 658:9

Scale, every golden s., 549:13
he by geometric s., 270:21
in equal s. weighing, 200:25
lapping scale with regularity, 714:14
Poetic Justice with lifted s., 313:16
so shall you s. the stars, 98:9
society without objective legal s., 804:15

Scaled invention or artistry, 709:11

Scales are his pride, 15:20
father held out golden s., 54:1
fell from his eyes, 42:10
put Hannibal in the s., 113:16
waves as formal as s. on fish, 714:2

Scallop shell of quiet, 160:8

Scalped each other, 448:11

Scan, gently s. brother man, 378:18
merits or faults to s., 342:5
presume not God to s., 311:9

Scandal, dreaded s. more than disease, 627:16
greatest s. waits on greatest state, 175:9
love and s., 322:3
public s. is wicked, 277:24
tea and s., 300:13
treatment of Negro greatest s., 752:9

Scandalous and poor, 293:1

Scandals of th' poor, 646:4
short an' simple s., 646:4

Scant, if store of crowns be s., 239:3

Scanted, what s. in hair given in wit, 174:30

Scanter of your maiden presence, 202:1

Scanty, in longitude tho' s., 379:21

'Scape, who should 's. whipping, 203:26

'Scaped, heart 's. this sorrow, 227:2

Scapegoat, let him go for a s., 9:12

'Scapes, hair-breadth 's., 212:29

Scar, virtue or vice leaves s., 581:11
wound heals s. disappears, 506:2

Scarcely greet me with that sun, 226:14

Scarceness, eat bread without s., 10:3

Scarcity, on first s. will turn, 346:1
reasons for s. of capital, 702:3

Scare, white clouds on, 669:7

Scarecrow, not make s. of law, 211:3

Scarecrows of fools, 537:8

Scared, always been s. of you, 827:15
to go to brink, 717:5

Scarf up tender eye of day, 221:7

Scarfs garters gold, 311:11

Scarlet, in S. town, 853:28
letter her passport, 460:12
line slender rigid exact, 522:*n*4
of maples shake me, 623:16
passion for a s. coat, 298:19
sins s. books read, 653:15
though your sins be as s., 26:10

Scars, he jests at s., 182:28
I carry with me, 282:5
inveterate s., 720:9
of others teach caution, 118:20

Scat, w'en Miss Rabbit say s., 593:10

Scatted, Miss Rabbit say scat they s., 593:10

Scatter plenty o'er smiling land, 334:22

Scattered, he hath s. the proud, 38:39
Israel s. upon the hills, 12:37
to the wind, 480:6
when cloud s., 431:4

Scattering, maniac s. dust, 483:22

Scatters, anarchy s. armies, 67:24
deep surmise s., 506:3
rear of darkness thin, 259:13

Scene before him beat like pulse, 809:11
dreamer is dream s., 675:11
last s. of all, 198:25
live o'er each s., 309:14
lofty s. be acted o'er, 196:17
love gilds the s., 367:18
not ask to see distant s., 449:18
play one s. of excellent dissembling, 223:2
speaks a new s., 249:12
start a s. or two, 717:14

Scenery essential in painting, 125:8
fine human nature finer, 440:7

Scenes, changing s. of life, 294:6
from s. like these, 377:16
gay gilded s., 301:11
his fathers loved, 765:1
ill-bred s., 627:16
no more behind your s. David, 326:7
of my childhood, 418:13
shifted on stage of history, 596:17

Scent, amber s. of perfume, 269:6
of arm-pits aroma finer than prayer, 519:10
of her hair, 734:10

Scent (*continued*)
of pine, 719:18
of roses hang round it, 412:2
rose's s. bitterness, 620:14
survives their close, 620:14

Scepter, balm s. and ball, 193:16
leaden s., 305:24
shepherd's crook beside s., 452:9
shows force of power, 189:19
snatched with unruly hand, 178:12

Sceptered, in s. pall sweeping by, 260:6
isle, 179:12
mercy above s. sway, 189:19
Moloch s. king, 264:26
what avails the s. race, 408:4

Scheldt, lazy S. or wandering Po, 340:14

Scheme, for breakfast a s., 305:19
Sorry S. of Things, 472:5
yields no revenue, 343:19

Schemes, best laid s., 377:12

Schiller has material sublime, 403:19

Scholar among rakes, 448:15
determined s. and man of virtue, 63:16
he was a s., 231:14
if s. have not faith, 82:16
is delegated intellect Man Thinking, 454:20
more in soldier than s., 213:13
showed him gentleman an' s., 378:4
ten o'clock s., 860:20
thou art a s., 200:14
who cherishes love of comfort, 63:11
who pursues fame not s., 82:25

Scholar's, courtier's soldier's s., 204:7
ills s. life assail, 324:6

Scholars dispute and case still before courts, 101:19
God of Abraham not s., 280:12
land of s., 341:6
make mayors but not s., 241:1
Pythagoras said to his s., 240:12

Scholarship record of disagreements, 626:19

Schön, so hold und s. und rein, 442:*n*5
war ich auch, 365:*n*6

School, anyone been to English public s., 766:3
corrupted youth in erecting s., 172:22
creeping like snail to s., 198:25
elongated-yellow-fruit s. of writing, 755:11
experience keeps dear s., 319:25
fleshly s. of poetry, 577:9
high s. closer to core of experience, 811:10
in joyful s. days, 407:1
in my s.-days, 187:24
in which nothing harsh, 120:1
Intelligence make it a soul, 441:2
law s. no more than s. of fencing, 613:12
leave religion to private s., 532:20
microcosm of public s., 458:19
of mankind, 345:22
of Stratford atte Bowe, 134:21
Satanic s., 405:19
stealthy s. of criticism, 542:6
tales out of s., 148:1
threadbare saint in wisdom's s., 233:5
three little maids from s., 565:11
time the s. in which we learn, 791:11

School *(continued)*
  to s. not to travel, 167:23
  toward s. with heavy looks, 183:12
  we left s., 798:10
Schoolboy, every s. knows it, 274:17
  every s. knows, 448:6
  tale every s. knows, 333:17
  whining s. with satchel, 198:25
Schoolboy's tale, 420:9
Schoolboys, as s. from books, 183:12
School-children, Negro s., 801:13
School-divine, God the Father a s., 312:23
Schoolgirl, pert as s. can be, 565:11
Schooling, in and outdoor s., 671:6
Schoolman's subtle art, 312:11
Schoolmaster, becoming a s. sir, 766:2
  is abroad, 409:18
Schoolmasters, bankers s. clergymen, 637:17
  father more than hundred s., 252:2
  let s. puzzle brain, 342:17
Schoolrooms, better s. than cells, 509:7
Schools, hundred s. of thought contend,
    737:18
  jargon of the s., 296:16
  knowledge never learned of s., 468:10
  let us reform s., 517:11
  maze of s., 308:9
  nurseries of vice, 322:1
  old maxim in the s., 298:9
Schooner Hesperus, 466:4
  ladder close to s., 824:13
Schweigen ist golden, 433:21
Science achieve perfect knowledge, 527:14
  advance in s. audacity of imagination,
    616:13
  advancement of pure s., 737:2
  aim of exact s., 548:13
  and applications together, 533:7
  and opinion, 73:6
  and technology unite humanity, 815:13
  applied s. not exist, 533:7
  art and s. in particulars, 376:5
  astrology disease not s., 127:4
  built with facts, 603:3
  challenge of rootless s., 751:12
  Christyan Scientists some s., 645:14
  cloud obscures., 359:9
  communication of truth, 402:15
  cookery a noble s., 240:13
  countenance of all S., 391:14
  cradle of every s., 536:14
  Dismal S., 435:7
  dissociate language from s., 359:15
  experimentation active s., 500:16
  fair S. frowned not, 335:2
  falsely so called, 46:29
  first-rate furniture, 473:18
  frees us, 514:6
  from ancient subject newest s., 596:21
  God whom s. recognizes, 582:16
  great s. eludes our grasp, 624:9
  great tragedy of S., 537:4
  guide of action, 591:8
  impersonality of s., 500:19
  in high art and pure s., 756:7
  in s. credit to man who convinces, 593:3
  in s. experts differ, 626:19
  is ourselves, 500:19
  law a hocus-pocus s., 317:10

Science *(continued)*
  mysterious is source of art and s., 683:5
  natural s. involves three things, 359:15
  not safe for S. to divulge causes, 233:4
  numerical precision soul of s., 623:12
  object of s. truth, 402:15
  observation passive s., 500:16
  of life superb hall, 500:17
  of Nature, 289:4
  out of olde bokes newe s., 133:12
  physical s. not console me, 279:15
  poem opposed to works of s., 403:8
  poetry antithesis to s., 402:15
  products of art and s., 733:5
  promote progress of s., 737:18
  pronouncements of history or s., 782:4
  proud S., 311:5
  reassures, 694:15
  refinement of everyday thinking, 683:7
  right interpretation of nature, 432:19
  scarcely advanced to s., 536:5
  search for truth, 761:15
  shalt not commit a social s., 776:7
  spirit of s. in international affairs, 761:15
  temple of s., 614:10
  thought to aim at some good, 80:8
  treating Psychology like natural s., 583:6
  true s. teaches doubt, 631:2
  typical triumph of modern s., 766:10
  waves of s. beat in vain, 524:2
  which draws conclusions, 477:9
  with least results, 603:4
  without conscience ruin, 146:5
Sciences, experience Mother of S., 156:27
  mathematical s. founded, 548:13
  mathematics queen of s., 409:15
  mechanics paradise of mathematical s.,
    141:10
  natural s. aim never reach, 536:6
Scientia potestas est, 166:1
Scientiam, de subjecto vetustissimo
    novissimam s., 596:n1
Scientific, Abraham of s. men, 523:23
  exploited as a s. curiosity, 626:20
  ideals altars to unknown gods, 581:6
  innovation rarely converts opponents,
    614:11
  Jesus most s. man, 526:11
  method by which unconscious studied,
    608:7
  method of s. investigation, 536:15
  plunges into s. questions, 537:13
  revolution, 757:4
  thought is human progress, 591:8
Scientific-democratic, intellectual freedom s.
    approach, 808:9
Scientist cannot dispense with faith, 614:10
  independent s., 742:12
  ready to bear privation, 739:1
  takes off from predecessors, 682:6
  values research, 796:11
  wiser not to withhold, 365:1
Scientists at other pole, 772:14
  collectors classifiers tidiers-up, 796:12
  understandable by everyone not just s.,
    837:3
Scintillant in cloudless days, 703:12
Scissors, two halves of pair of s., 399:n1
  upper or under blade of s., 584:2

Scoff, fools who came to s., 342:7
Scolded, nobody ever s. him, 644:5
Scooped, Tankards s. in Pearl, 544:7
Scoot, old man Rabbit say s., 593:10
Scooted, Rabbit say scoot they s., 593:10
Scope had not been so short, 231:n2
  of my opinion, 200:15
  this man's art that man's s., 226:6
  whole possible s. of human ambition,
    626:4
  within s. of constitution, 371:4
Score, from seventy springs a s., 618:7
  give me a kiss and to that a s., 248:7
  no books but s. and tally, 172:22
Scored, our days are s. against us, 110:23
Scorer, One Great S., 692:4
Scorn, bright creatures. not one, 395:20
  child of s., 652:6
  dangers make us s., 379:19
  delights, 261:19
  figure for time of s., 214:26
  folks s. you too, 745:5
  foul s. that prince invade, 151:13
  her own image, 204:13
  laugh a siege to s., 222:14
  laugh to s. power of man, 221:26
  laughed His word to s., 347:17
  looks beautiful, 210:5
  mine ever name of s., 486:9
  not all free who s. chains, 346:7
  not laugh other men to s., 122:10
  not the sonnet, 395:19
  not thing to laugh to s., 199:31
  of mankind down centuries, 666:11
  read to s., 398:3
  sound of public s., 268:8
  the codfish, 849:15
  to change state with kings, 226:7
  to take offense, 308:19
  under solemn fillet saw s., 453:19
  upright man laughed to s., 14:10
Scorned his spirit, 195:24
  woman s., 300:22
Scorner, reprove not a s., 21:12
Scornful, most bitter is s. jest, 323:12
  sitteth in the seat of the s., 15:27
  yet jealous eyes, 312:4
Scorning base degrees, 195:30
Scorns, whips and s. of time, 203:33
Scorpion, under every stone a s., 75:n4
Scorpions, ants centipedes and s., 680:12
  I will chastise with s., 12:22
Scotch mist, 515:24
Scotched, we have s. the snake, 221:4
Scotchman, beggarly S., 326:12
  if caught young, 327:16
  noblest prospect S. sees, 326:18
Scotia's grandeur springs, 377:16
Scotland, be in S. before ye, 847:15
  in S. oats supports people, 324:20
Scotland's, left fair S. strand, 379:1
Scots, gude S. lords, 853:19
  kills six or seven dozen S., 185:20
  lords at his feet, 853:20
  wha hae wi' Wallace bled, 380:10
Scott, beam us up Mr. S., 852:n6
  no eminent writer not even S.,
    609:29
Scotty, beam me up S., 852:21

Sea (*continued*)

never loved by anyone married to it, 664:1
never never sick at s., 563:15
never saw the S., 546:6
never trust s. when calm, 93:5
never was on s. or land, 394:13
no land when see but s., 166:8
not all water in rough rude s., 179:24
nothing but hath bound in s., 174:27
nothing sure in s. fight, 377:4
number the sand of the s., 31:24
O God thy s. is so great, 847:10
ocean s. not sufficient room, 239:1
of Cause and Theory, 665:2
of dew, 597:5
of faith, 531:2
of Galilee and Dead Sea, 680:1
of troubles, 203:33
of upturned faces, 397:23
of words, 700:5
offer yourselves to s., 583:9
ole davil s., 723:11
on land as on the s., 848:17
once made England secure, 673:5
one foot in s. one on shore, 194:25
one is of the s., 394:23
one salt s., 192:22
or fire, 200:21
over great s. winds trouble waters, 92:19
over s. to Skye, 616:9
passenger e'er pukes in, 424:8
pent by s. and dark brows, 521:4
people know salt of s., 681:18
perfumed s., 478:2
plants footsteps in s., 347:3
plow the s., 564:6
Pontick s., 214:15
pouring oil on the s., 108:*n*1
praise s. on shore remain, 162:10
precious stone set in silver s., 179:12
Proteus rising from s., 394:19
raging waves of the s., 48:1
righteousness as waves of s., 28:13
rising nor sky clouding, 586:5
round cape sudden came s., 492:3
running all over s., 612:4
sailed wintry s., 466:4
sailor home from s., 599:6
sails upon Lowland s., 862:10
sang in my chains like s., 795:13
see one s. and see all, 241:3
sepulcher there by s., 479:20
served revolution plowed s., 415:20
shadows upon a s. obscure, 121:22
ship's way upon s., 634:6
ships of war at s., 486:22
shows false alluring smile, 93:5
sight of immortal s., 393:17
silent s., 399:20
sing by land and s., 634:9
singing over the wine-dark s., 54:13
sky and s. and land, 620:3
slimy s., 399:23
snotgreen scrotumtightening s., 696:8
spirit that on life's rough s., 165:11
summers in a s. of glory, 231:2
sun was shining on s., 551:18

Sea (*continued*)

sunless s., 401:13
swing of the s., 587:1
syllabub s., 500:1
the s. is his, 49:24
the s. the s., 76:2
there was no more s., 48:38
though the mountains be carried into the s., 17:21
thought jump s. and land, 226:13
thousand furlongs of s., 229:8
to sea through your expanse, 472:23
to s. to s., 452:1
tomb by sounding s., 479:20
tomorrow we sail the Ocean S., 99:9
trunk spouts out a s., 267:15
two if by s., 467:15
union with native s., 395:5
uttermost parts of the s., 20:13
voice whose sound like s., 393:4
walking on the s., 36:15
waters cover the s., 26:34
way of a ship in the s., 23:25
weariest river winds to s., 569:3
we'll o'er the s., 390:12
went to s. in sieve, 499:19
wet sheet flowing s., 417:7
whales in waves of s., 707:20
when I put out to s., 487:2
whether in s. or fire, 200:21
who can say s. is old, 575:2
who commands the s. has command, 64:24
who hath desired s., 635:14
who run across s. do not change disposition, 101:3
why s. boiling hot, 552:3
wind nor tide nor s., 566:17
wind of western s., 482:18
winds pierced solitudes, 453:3
wish you a wave o' the s., 228:29
wrinkled s. beneath, 484:19
you'll not find another s., 628:6
your mind and you Sargasso S., 708:15
Sea-banks, upon the wild s., 190:4
Sea-born treasures, 452:17
Sea-change, suffer a s., 229:20
Sea-crow, flying s., 521:2
Sea-discoverers, 233:11
Sea-down's edge, 569:14
Seafarers, hour that turns back longing of s., 131:14
Sea-green Incorruptible, 434:5
Seal, god seem to set his s., 205:21
impression as from s. of ring, 78:11
on cold ice full of darts, 436:19
playing in sun like me, 856:11
scales shut together as with close s., 15:20
sense in deathly slumber, 662:12
set me as a s., 26:3
slumber did my spirit s., 392:1
to such a bond, 188:10
up avenues of ill, 453:17
upon thine arm, 26:3
Sealed bag of ducats, 188:24
in vain, 211:31
thy fate and mine s., 483:5

Sealed (*continued*)

with seven seals, 48:18
your womb, 812:3
Sealing, come s. night, 221:7
shoes ships s. wax, 552:3
snapped off like s. wax, 497:22
Seals of love sealed in vain, 211:31
sealed with seven s., 48:18
to fish and to s., 785:10
Seam, sew a fine s., 859:6
Sea-maid's music, 181:8
Seaman, betokened wrack to s., 173:22
looking for something else, 715:6
Seaman's story is of tempest, 104:19
Sea-mark of my utmost sail, 215:11
Seamen were not gentlemen, 448:19
Sear, leaf red a s., 396:13
Search for inexplicable, 689:11
happy man who could s. out causes, 96:13
in s. of my mother's garden, 839:1
land of living men, 396:15
not worth the s., 187:23
out purposes of gods, 66:9
so painful and so long, 293:5
the scriptures, 41:1
their own glory, 23:5
things above thy strength, 31:29
walked in the s. of the depth, 15:8
will find it out, 248:15
Searched me and known me, 20:12
Searcher for fecund minimum, 686:10
obedient to truth, 523:23
Searches, tent that s., 207:31
unreasonable s. and seizures, 361:3
Searcheth, Lord s. all hearts, 13:10
Searching, by s. find out God, 14:7
to rediscover first seed, 759:6
Seared and blighted heart, 477:12
conscience s. with hot iron, 46:18
Sears Northland soul, 745:2
Sea's big brush recolors, 788:6
face and gray dawn, 680:15
green crying towers a-sway, 753:14
thoughts with s. boundlessness, 759:12
Seas, dangers of the s., 254:22
desperate s. long wont, 478:2
diver in deep s., 573:6
faithless as winds or s., 290:16
fight on s. and oceans, 666:1
floors of silent s., 717:11
freedom of s., 611:10
glitter of s., 827:18
guard our native s., 408:16
half s. over, 299:10
he hath founded it upon the s., 16:19
I must down to s., 680:15, 681:1, 681:2
incarnadine, 220:19
laugh when rocks near, 244:5
mackerel-crowded s., 639:16
of life like wine, 290:4
of pity lie, 775:16
of space and time, 716:17
perilous s., 437:13
port after stormy s., 161:3
rivers run to s., 285:23
roaring with blasts, 306:21
sail wet s. roun', 634:17
seven s. of ink, 122:5
shoreless s., 579:8

Security *(continued)*
    system of general s., 699:9
    to democracies against despots, 366:*n*6
Sed haec prius fuere, 94:*n*2
Sedate, ignorance s., 324:9
Sedentary life sin, 590:10
Sedge withered from lake, 439:3
Sedition, wine cause of s., 293:18
Sedulous ape, 599:9
Sedulously cultivate free speech, 667:13
See a fine picture, 364:2
    all could s. was sky water birds, 784:5
    all we s. or seem, 477:11
    and be seen, 105:6
    bachelor of threescore again, 194:10
    best not to s. beams of sun, 61:14
    blind now I s., 41:14
    bosom I must not s., 277:22
    but not observe, 617:1
    can I s. another's woe, 372:11
    change we think we s., 669:2
    cherry hung with snow, 618:7
    Christ stand, 493:21
    church by daylight, 194:16
    dagger I s. before me, 220:8
    direction which thou canst not s., 311:8
    dwarf on giant s. farther, 240:4
    eye begins to s., 781:4
    eye to eye, 28:19
    eyes and s. not, 29:3
    eyes have they but s. not, 19:22
    eyes weep but never s., 408:5
    from where I stood, 734:14
    full plain I s., 400:21
    girl I like to s., 774:1
    go and s. for ourselves, 784:12
    God made and eaten, 492:8
    God whom we s. not is, 569:17
    gold that I never s., 619:2
    happy moron, 851:14
    have thee not yet s. thee still, 220:8
    hear read or understand, 332:19
    Heaven's glories shine, 509:1
    here it is, 439:2
    here shall he s. no enemy, 198:11
    how she leans her cheek, 183:1
    how they run, 856:15
    how world goes, 217:23
    how world wags, 198:15
    how yond justice rails, 217:23
    how you would do, 376:1
    I don't s. said Caterpillar, 549:16
    I know pornography when I s. it, 797:3
    I now s. very plainly, 711:6
    I s. not feel how beautiful, 402:3
    I s. what I eat, 550:10
    I'll s. you again, 753:7
    image of what we actually s., 572:21
    in all things thee to s., 250:24
    in my flesh shall I s. God, 14:25
    in small proportions beauties s., 238:14
    into life of things, 391:2
    it clearly in the idea, 687:21
    it lap the Miles, 545:8
    it shining plain, 619:3
    it yet remains to s., 547:3
    kings have desired to s., 39:21
    let mine eyes not s., 208:27
    lofty towers I s. down-rased, 226:18

See *(continued)*
    little Tippler, 544:9
    lovers cannot s. follies, 188:20
    may I be there to s., 347:24
    me safe up, 144:3
    Mediterraneans s. clearly, 702:11
    meet and not s. its head, 58:16
    more people s. than weigh, 315:7
    more ye s. better like it, 646:6
    never s. nor know nor miss me, 696:18
    never s. tree at all, 763:9
    no evil, 845:4
    no man s. me more, 230:31
    none should s. salvation, 189:19
    none so blind as not s., 295:21
    not my love to s., 161:26
    not s. me stopping here, 669:13
    not the bottom of it, 208:14
    not worth going to s., 328:21
    O can't you s. it, 742:4
    object as it really is, 529:22
    oh say can you s., 411:1
    one mountain and see all, 241:3
    one-third of nation ill-housed, 698:6
    only their own shadows, 77:14
    only with heart one can s., 759:4
    other whole against sky, 677:9
    oursels as ithers see us, 378:6
    people refuse to s. me, 793:2
    really do not s. signal, 377:3
    sad sights moves, 175:10
    see their mark, 250:23
    seem to s. things thou dost not, 217:25
    she stirs, 466:18
    Shelley plain, 492:17
    smile his work to s., 374:6
    so much nor live so long, 218:9
    sons what things you are, 192:7
    sun with ignorant eye, 687:21
    taste and s. that the Lord is good, 17:1
    the conquering hero, 318:19
    the Way of Heaven, 59:7
    there shall no man s. me, 9:8
    they bark at me, 217:5
    they shall s. God, 33:33
    things as they are, 325:24
    things seen I s. no more, 393:7
    things through his eyes, 744:15
    think I shall never s., 711:11, 763:9
    those things ye see, 39:21
    thou canst not s. my face, 9:8
    through glass darkly, 44:20
    to s. her was to love her, 378:24
    Veil through which not s., 471:15
    Venus let me never s., 297:6
    was blind but now I s., 339:12
    we are as much as we s., 504:23
    what a rent, 196:33
    what can not s. over is infinite, 433:12
    what I say, 616:1
    what I see, 204:10
    what s. elsewhere not here, 138:8
    whatever you s. is Jupiter, 110:8
    whatsoever I shall s. or hear, 72:16
    where Christ's blood streams, 171:4
    where it flies, 170:23
    where she comes apparelled like spring, 225:6
    Winter comes, 317:13

See *(continued)*
    with half an eye, 158:19
    with not through the eye, 376:9
    world in grain of sand, 375:5
    you s. more in you, 767:3
    you s. things, and say Why, 610:10
    you s. what I am, 793:8
    young men shall s. visions, 30:22
    your good works, 34:2
Seed, bearing precious s., 20:3
    blood of Christians is s., 116:14
    blood of martyrs s. of Church, 116:*n*3
    broadcast catch somewhere, 488:12
    de first en last s. de beginnin, 748:10
    enmity between thy s. and her s., 6:8
    ground more malign with bad s., 131:22
    groweth s., 843:5
    heaven like to mustard s., 36:6
    money the s. of money, 330:19
    nor his s. begging bread, 17:6
    of religious liberty, 515:21
    searching to rediscover first s., 759:6
    sow thy s. in the morning, 25:5
    wonder the s. of knowledge, 166:2
    work is s. sown, 433:6
Seeds, fruitful error full of s., 594:1
    in dry pod tick, 651:12
    of godlike power, 528:4
    of patriots and heroes, 340:*n*1
    of time, 218:31
    plant s. watch renewal, 543:10
    some s. fell by way side, 36:2
    treason sows secret s., 127:14
Seedtime and harvest, 6:32
    fair s. had my soul, 391:6
    regret my s., 801:1
Seeing, adds precious s. to the eye, 177:6
    eye is not satisfied with s., 23:34
    eyes made for s., 453:4
    fatality of s. too well, 688:11
    hearing ear s. eye, 22:19
    individual way of s., 582:17
    my head is worth s., 381:2
    necessity of s. each other, 601:17
    the root of the matter, 14:26
    understands without s., 59:7
    what everybody seen nobody thought, 739:2
    with fresh eyes, 824:16
    worth s. not going to see, 328:21
Seek all day ere you find them, 187:23
    and adore them, 586:7
    and ye shall find, 35:3
    beauteous eye of heaven to garnish, 178:14
    by trophies and dead things, 244:10
    carry with us wonders we s., 255:13
    empty world again, 508:21
    flee from me that did me s., 150:2
    for Eldorado, 479:15
    for the lost mind, 82:14
    for truth in groves of Academe, 101:12
    fortunes further than home, 175:23
    going to s. grand perhaps, 146:20
    Heaven itself in our folly, 99:4
    it in My arms, 621:5
    judgment, 26:10
    knock breathe and s. to mend, 236:11

Seek (*continued*)

labored for them that s. learning, 33:2
never s. to tell thy love, 373:8
newer world, 481:14
no farther s. his merits, 335:4
not life of immortals, 66:1
not out things that are too hard, 31:29
not s. for kind relief, 372:11
out soldier's grave, 425:9
peace and pursue it, 17:2
poets that lasting marble s., 257:26
some dew drops here, 181:4
that which thou dost s., 430:17
their meat from God, 19:11
they s. a sign, 39:27
those that s. me early, 21:10
to bring largest good, 582:11
to s. her through the world, 266:8
to strive s. find, 481:15
we s. him here we s. him there, 636:3
we s. no wider war, 779:5
where s. is find, 338:1
why s. living among dead, 40:25
with fear and trembling, 582:11
world was not to s. me, 329:13
ye first the kingdom of God, 34:21
Seekest thou great things, 29:25
Seeketh, love never s. own, 138:13
love s. not itself to please, 374:1
love s. self to please, 374:2
Seeking bubble reputation, 198:25
find what we are s., 735:4
knot in a bulrush, 86:7
light s. light, 176:19
may be found by s., 88:17
new ways to use strength, 706:3
symbolical language, 402:14
the food he eats, 198:13
unperplexed s. find Him, 492:24
what leopard was s., 754:15
whom he may devour, 47:33
with the soul, 364:5
Seeks abroad may find, 438:12
man s. for what is remote, 82:3
serves and s. for gain, 216:12
Wisdom's self oft s., 260:29
with the sword repose, 278:27
Seeling, come s. night, 221:7
Seem a saint when most play devil, 173:37
all uses of this world, 201:1
all we see or s., 477:11
earth to me did s., 393:7
finale of s., 686:15
grow to what they s., 341:3
men should be what they s., 213:31
not always what they s., 346:5
not to s. but be best, 65:2
things not always what they s., 106:9
things not what they s., 465:17
things seldom what s., 563:19
though I die old, 642:4
to fly it, 237:23
to see things thou dost not, 217:25
Seemed, absence s. my flame to qualify, 227:13
but a few days, 7:17
part of the landscape, 627:11
scarce s. there to be, 400:23
that which once s. he, 404:4

Seemed (*continued*)

they s. to die, 31:16
to me like king, 707:11
Seeming and savor all winter, 228:25
beguile by s. otherwise, 213:10
Seemly for young man to lie mangled, 53:32
Seems, I know not s., 200:29
madam Nay it is, 200:29
no bigger than his head, 217:18
she hangs on cheek of night, 182:25
such s. your beauty still, 227:10
to shake the spheres, 285:8
Seen, after they've s. Paree, 708:1
artist records more than s., 659:24
atoms, 731:4
best of our time, 215:28
better days, 198:23, 218:19
better days who has not, 425:2
duty and done it, 850:2
ear of man hath not s., 182:1
ere I had s. that day, 201:10
everywhere felt but never s., 527:6
evidence of things not s., 46:42
eye hath not s., 43:33
first came the s., 709:10
future and it works, 644:*n1*
girdid up Lions and fled S., 555:7
hungry ocean gain advantage, 226:18
I have s. better faces, 216:8
I have s. further, 290:25
I have s. God face to face, 7:21
I have s. the sunset, 603:11
I have s. the wicked in great power, 17:7
known me had he s. me, 504:7
moment of greatness flicker, 717:13
no man hath s. God, 40:34
not s. as others saw, 477:13
not s. the righteous forsaken, 17:6
not s. yet believed, 41:43
nothing yet, 157:6
on our way, 786:13
one city slum seen all, 802:16
pin faith in things not s., 116:7
promised land, 823:10
starry archipelagoes, 603:13
thee oft amid store, 438:12
things not s. eternal, 45:5
things s. are temporal, 45:5
through make-believe, 656:12
to be hated needs but be s., 311:10
too early s. unknown, 182:26
touch scarcely felt or s., 314:3
war hate war, 698:4
we have not s. him since, 649:17
what I have seen, 204:10
Seer is a sayer, 455:2
must make oneself a s., 604:4
poet makes himself a s., 604:4
Sees, care not who s. your back, 185:23
doubts from what he s., 375:14
God who made him s., 635:24
into bottom of my grief, 184:7
it and does it, 492:24
man control wind, 528:21
Me in all, 87:6
nature s. all her sons at play, 528:21
neither hears nor s., 392:1
never s. a whole, 528:17
Present Past Future s., 373:16

Sees (*continued*)

some morning unaware, 492:4
sun which s. all things, 52:24
things as they are, 580:11
Seesaw Margery Daw, 858:5
Seest, what thou s. write, 48:3
Seeth, Lord s. not as man s., 11:25
now mine eye s. thee, 15:25
Seethe a thousand men in troubles, 436:19
Seevility, a little s., 848:14
Segregation now segregation tomorrow, 806:8
Seine, torn s. shattered lobsterpot, 721:8
Seize fate by the throat, 389:8
good fortune, 365:22
maybe person next to you, 842:4
ruin s. thee, 335:11
the day, 99:12
the flower, 379:18
what hand dare s. fire, 374:5
Seized, love s. me so strongly, 130:13
Seizures, unreasonable searches and s., 361:3
Seldom he smiles, 195:24
Seld-shaven odd-eyed, 407:2
Selection, art discrimination and s., 585:10
Natural S., 469:12
natural s., 523:13
not saving but s., 345:24
Selects, artist observes s. guesses, 622:8
Soul s. her own Society, 544:15
Self, applause from none but s., 525:6
concentered all in s., 396:11
earthly city formed by love of s., 119:22
experience one's s., 762:2
for my single s., 195:18
friend is a second s., 91:15
is hateful, 280:9
is honey of all beings, 51:21
love seeketh s. to please, 374:2
luminous island of s., 788:6
not mine but ours, 816:17
nothing greater than one's s., 519:20
One's-S. I sing, 518:12
only prison, 601:12
product of a different s., 658:5
swear by thy gracious s., 183:9
through eyes of others, 648:11
to thine own s. be true, 201:27
toll me back from thee to my sole s., 437:14
total of all he can call his, 581:17
try to speak hidden s., 529:5
was not the same, 207:17
what jailer inexorable as s., 460:18
Self-affrighting, learns it is s., 639:15
Self-appeasing, learns it is s., 639:15
Self-appointed inspector of snowstorms, 505:2
Self-balanced, O to be s. for contingencies, 518:13
Self-blinding, nothing so s., 744:15
Self-canceling, democracy s., 434:7
Self-circling energies, 402:20
Self-complacency is pleasure, 287:4
Self-conceit may lead to self-destruction, 60:18
philosophy to get rid of s., 112:14
Self-conscious, not make us s., 715:3

Self-constituted, Americans first s. People, 734:12

Self-contained, placid and s., 519:16

Self-control, self-knowledge s., 480:11

Self-deceit, nothing easier than s., 81:16

Self-delighting, learns it is s., 639:15

Self-denial indulgence, 580:21

Self-denying, in war ruthless s., 426:1

Self-destruction, self-conceit may lead to s., 60:18

Self-devoted, in war s., 426:1

Self-dissection introversion, 457:6

Self-evident, hold these truths s., 503:5
    hold truths to be s., 357:2

Self-expression, muzzle the s., 787:10

Self-fulfilling prophecy false definition, 785:3

Self-government, democracy direct s., 488:n5

Self-help root of growth, 500:12

Self-homicide, misspending time a s., 289:2

Self-idealization childish, 768:2

Self-interest speaks all tongues, 273:7

Selfish, art s. and perverse, 389:10
    being all my life, 406:13
    feverish s. little clod, 609:15
    molecules known as genes, 836:3
    spiteful Public, 410:8
    very old most s., 490:22

Selfishness, forces of s. met match, 698:5
    reduce s., 58:17
    systems perverted by s., 694:3

Self-knowledge self-control, 480:11

Self-love, address ourselves to their s., 338:13
    and social be made the same, 386:5
    and social the same, 311:18
    greatest of flatterers, 273:1
    in jealousy more s., 274:2
    makes more libertines, 331:11
    strike at s., 539:12
    thing our s. longs for, 817:18

Self-made from elements, 785:8
    laws, 525:6
    man and worships creator, 489:6

Self-observation, psychology based on s., 553:12

Self-perpetuating, mind soul of s. institutions, 802:15

Self-pitying dirty sly, 743:18

Self-possession, courtesy and s., 643:9

Self-preservation, instinct of s., 613:7

Self-protection sole end for interfering, 464:9

Self-reliance aversion to society, 455:8
    discontent want of s., 455:15
    reliance on God, 456:22

Self-respect, never break word or lose s., 115:7
    not manifest want of s., 81:23

Self-revelation, terrible fluidity of s., 585:17

Self-reverence self-knowledge, 480:11

Self-righteousness, avoid s., 744:15
    not religion, 504:15

Self-sacrifice, progress of artist s., 722:7
    risk and spiritual s., 730:2
    vocation demands s., 742:12

Self-sacrificing love of brute, 478:16

Selfsame, shot fellow s. way, 187:24
    song that found path, 437:13
    sun that shines upon court, 229:1
    winds that blow, 600:5

Self-slaughter, his canon 'gainst s., 201:1

Self-subsisting self-seeking me, 449:8

Self-suffering, patience means s., 650:10

Self-sufficing, reasoning s. thing, 392:3

Self-trust, in s. all virtues comprehended, 454:24
    teacher inspires s., 444:14

Sell a country, 387:10
    buy with you s. with you, 188:2
    did s. himself to work wickedness, 12:36
    don't s. America short, 851:5
    don't s. steak s. sizzle, 775:1
    for a shilling, 499:17
    go and s. that thou hast, 36:33
    made to s. and s. quickly, 709:9
    no branch over wine that will s., 104:11
    no man might buy or s., 48:30
    precious as stuff they s., 472:4
    to none s. right or justice, 128:9
    when you can, 199:21
    Willie is no good I'll s. him, 651:10

Seller needs not one eye, 251:26

Selling, buying and s. spending lives, 507:11
    nimble in s. houses, 708:2
    writers are always s. somebody out, 830:1

Sells eternity to get toy, 175:5

Selva, mi ritrovai per una s. oscura, 129:n7

Selves, beautiful in thoughts in s., 622:12
    biography accounts for six or seven s., 700:6
    our s. our souls and bodies, 51:1

Semblable au prince des nuées, 524:n1
    hypocrite lecteur mon s. mon frère, 524:7

Semblance in another's case, 348:21

Semel emissum volat irrevocabile verbum, 101:n3

Semen est sanguis christianorum, 116:n3

Semi-criminal semi-pathological, 701:18

Semihuman and demonic, 675:9

Semi-pathological propensities, 701:18

Semper eadem, 152:2
    fidelis, 124:23

Sempronius, we'll do more S., 301:17

Senate admiring its members, 570:3
    like Cato give S. laws, 312:4
    Roman s. long debate, 301:21

Senator seldom proclaims inferiority, 570:3

Send an Angel before thee, 9:5
    choice grain into this wilderness, 286:1
    fortune will s. it, 233:9
    here am I s. me, 26:26
    home my long strayed eyes, 234:18
    homeless tempest-tost, 595:6
    in the clowns, 826:1
    me reeling in, 546:19
    more grace than gifts to s., 232:14
    never s. to know for whom bell tolls, 236:19
    recompense as largely s., 335:3
    them that s. unto thee, 22:28
    whom shall I s., 26:26

Sending, before s. manuscript to press, 628:11

Senectus insanabilis morbus est, 456:n1

Senex, old Mr. S. showing age, 790:13

Senex, fortunate s., 95:n12

Senile, regarding elders as s., 570:7

Senior-junior giant-dwarf, 176:33

Sennacherib king of Assyria departed, 13:6

Sens, dormer un s. plus pur, 722:n1

Sensation instinct intelligence, 443:6

Sensational event changing from brown suit, 708:3
    something s. to read, 605:11

Sensations, condensation of s., 651:16
    rather than Thoughts, 440:1

Sense aches at thee, 214:28
    common s. appall, 623:9
    common s. hasty superficial, 505:27
    common s. not so common, 316:13
    common s. on ground floor, 473:18
    common s. plain dealing, 456:5
    common s. reduced to calculus, 366:14
    devoid of s. and motion, 265:4
    dictate of common s., 318:18
    divinest S., 545:2
    enchants my s., 208:2
    find people have good s., 274:5
    fools laugh at men of s., 292:18
    from thought divide, 283:n2
    fruit of s. beneath, 308:13
    genius s. and wit, 347:7
    good s. equally distributed, 253:22
    good s. in country, 360:4
    good s. of Americans, 462:13
    good s. refine her page, 289:16
    humility s. of reverence, 70:15
    in larger s. cannot dedicate, 476:7
    learned without s., 346:15
    lively s. of filial duty, 356:21
    money like sixth s., 672:17
    money speaks s., 290:20
    moral s. of work of art, 585:9
    much S. starkest Madness, 545:2
    my s. is mocked, 233:3
    no s. of decency sir, 730:18
    no s. of ills to come, 333:20
    not s. enough to come in, 143:n6
    nothing good makes complete s., 735:17
    of dissatisfaction, 807:15
    of death in apprehension, 211:20
    of future favors, 273:n2
    of honor in action, 74:5
    of it is anyhow, 494:26
    of obligation, 656:1
    of reckoning, 193:17
    of what life means, 582:17
    one has s. of humor, 714:16
    one that has another s., 302:9
    one world to s., 255:17
    palls upon the s., 301:20
    palter with us in double s., 222:22
    Pickwickian, 495:18
    rich grape juice of good s., 118:28
    satire or s., 312:7
    seal s. in slumber, 662:12
    Shadwell never deviates into s., 284:3
    sound an echo to s., 308:18
    stings and motions of s., 211:1
    sublime, 391:4
    sublime in old s., 708:19
    take care of s., 550:17
    talk s. to a fool, 70:12
    talk s. to American people, 760:2
    through s. and nonsense, 283:20
    want of decency want of s., 287:21
    whose soul is s., 235:1

Senseless, abhorred that s. tribe, 299:2
    kind of s. wit, 809:2

Senses, as long as I keep my s., 449:13
  derangement of all s., 604:4
  diffuses s. with oblivion, 99:1
  flies from s. and particulars to axioms, 166:12
  forever in joy, 493:16
  hath not a Jew s., 188:30
  if Parson lost s., 656:10
  lull my s., 807:2
  money-lust before s., 709:7
  our gentle s., 219:15
  steep s. in forgetfulness, 191:33
Sensibility, dissociation of s., 722:12
  inexhaustible s., 585:20
  soil of subject, 585:9
Sensible and conscientious men, 326:*n*6
  impressions of free mind, 643:9
  men never tell, 459:26
  this s. warm motion, 211:23
  to feeling as to sight, 220:8
Sensitive, gentle s. mind, 639:3
Sensitivity, chief area of s., 783:14
Sensual, caught in s. music, 639:16
  lust a tempest, 525:12
  this wisdom is s., 47:18
  turbulent fleshy s. eating drinking, 519:9
Sensualist, lover and s., 594:8
Sensuality, intellectual passion drives out s., 140:12
Sensuous, simple s. and passionate, 262:19
Sent, him that s. me, 41:13
  thee late a rosy wreath, 238:3
  to my account, 202:19
  to spy out the land, 9:18
Sentence, death s. of Versailles, 726:15
  every s. victory, 119:24
  first verdict afterwards, 551:6
  full of high s., 717:14
  German dives into s., 561:4
  hungry judges s. sign, 309:10
  I catch every s., 622:11
  my s. is for open war, 265:1
  no s. of banishment, 786:14
  no unnecessary words, 652:12
  not understand words apart from s., 542:14
  originator of good s., 457:20
  single s. for modern man, 790:7
  structure of British s., 665:9
  success to periodic s., 745:10
  true in all times, 474:16
  waiting s. in bull pen, 801:1
  your first intelligible s., 759:2
Sentenced, author sentenced to death, 758:4
Sentences, backward ran s., 762:6
  memorable s., 548:5
  paragraph no unnecessary s., 652:12
  say in ten s. what others in book, 589:21
  shall quips and s. awe, 194:28
  that stir bile, 620:13
Sententiae, quot homines tot s., 89:*n*4
Sententious, laconic or s. type, 653:17
Sentest, thou s. forth thy wrath, 8:28
Sentient, critic s. and restless, 585:3
Sentiment and alliteration, 557:16
  fungus crop of s., 567:6
  in s. public crude, 416:23

Sentiment (*continued*)
  living s. and dying s., 414:13
  offices sensitive to mass s., 727:4
  read Richardson for s., 327:14
  sacrifice you make for s., 647:4
Sentimental, carry body for s. value, 777:5
Sentimentalist, no s. no stander above, 519:9
Sentimentally disposed to harmony, 407:15
Sentiments, duration of great s., 589:3
  precluded from offering s., 350:4
  them's my s., 490:4
  to which bosom echo, 325:9
  weigh less than action, 515:23
  with noble s. bad literature, 651:4
Sentinels almost receive, 193:11
Sentry are you there, 517:2
  at this door England stands s., 574:9
  stands a winged s., 279:6
Separate and equal station, 357:2
  and unequal, 779:8
  but equal, 733:1
  church and State s., 532:20
  dying ember, 479:1
  educational facilities unequal, 733:1
  from forces to repeat No, 590:11
  he shall s. them, 37:16
  like marbles touching but s., 572:16
  peace, 754:1
  people s. rigidly alone, 572:16
  quite quite s., 543:2
  simple s. person, 518:12
  to s. because of race, 733:1
  us from love of Christ, 43:11
Separated by only six people, 833:5
  infinite chaos which s. us, 279:23
  war not s. from politics, 737:16
Separately, hang together or hang s., 320:18
Separateness of all things, 780:12
Separateth, he that repeateth a matter s. friends, 22:5
Separation, causes which impel s., 357:2
  not fighting for s., 815:10
  prepare definitely for s., 404:6
  six degrees of s., 833:5
  yield who will to s., 670:6
September, from frosted S. to sightless realm, 707:21
  morn, 468:13
  offends the S. night, 775:13
  thirty days hath S., 150:8
  when you reach S., 716:1
  within bosom S., 844:9
Sepulcher, night dome of vast s., 429:2
  no man knoweth of his s., 10:17
  there by the sea, 479:20
  whole earth s. of famous men, 74:5
Sepulchers, grandest of all s., 74:5
  shrouds and s. delight, 436:5
  whited s., 37:4
Sequel, unto God is the s., 122:4
Sequence, natural s. of unnatural beginning, 406:22
  of phenomena, 359:15
Sequestered, her wild s. seat, 337:4
  nooks, 467:21
  vale of life, 334:23
Seraphically, song s. free, 541:15
Seraphim, bright s. in burning row, 262:9

Seraphims, above it stood the s., 26:23
Seraphs swing snowy Hats, 544:9
  where s. might despair, 420:5
  winged s. of Heaven, 479:18
Sere, fallen into the s., 222:11
  leaf red and s., 396:13
  leaves crisped and s., 479:11
  meadows brown and s., 432:14
  with ivy never s., 261:13
Serendipity, now do you understand s., 336:3
Serene before direst death, 534:9
  count only hours s., 410:*n*1
  I fold my hands, 566:17
  mind s. for contemplation, 301:*n*1
  pure s., 435:19
  purest ray s., 334:20
  see with eye s., 394:2
  true friendship never s., 281:1
Serenely eternity waits at crossway of stars, 752:13
  full epicure would say, 399:3
Serenity, gentleness of spirit s. of mind, 252:*n*3
  grace to accept with s., 735:13
  steady and perpetual s., 302:18
  sweet s. of books, 467:21
  usual querulous s., 406:10
Serf, labor as another's s., 55:9
  patrician plebeian lord and s., 511:1
Serfdom, abolish s. from above, 508:6
  African not accept s. forever, 731:10
Serfs, spending lives like s., 507:11
  vassals and s., 441:9
Sergeant, back to Army again s., 634:10
  Color-S. said, 633:5
  this fell s. death, 207:10
Sergeant Cuff, the roses get it says S., 536:1
Sergeant's widow told lie, 472:20
Serious and alarming consequences, 350:4
  and the smirk, 496:17
  annuity is a s. business, 406:1
  audience takes him s., 685:16
  Cervantes' s. air, 313:15
  comedian takes himself s., 685:16
  companions few in s. business, 61:10
  I am a very s. woman, 806:9
  I never was more s., 407:2
  imitation of action that is s., 81:10
  insisted always on being s., 71:14
  life breathtakingly s., 730:9
  marriage damnably s. business, 737:20
  no human thing of s. importance, 78:2
  nothing s. in mortality, 220:25
  one who is s. all day, 3:7
  philosophical problem, 789:14
  strenuous and s., 723:10
  war too s. for military, 369:15
Sermon, all one asks of s., 806:11
  calls it a s., 398:15
  everyone has one s., 849:21
  good honest painful s., 288:5
  perhaps turn out a s., 378:9
  verse find who s. flies, 249:16
  whole of her s., 684:3
Sermons and soda water, 423:18
  in stones, 197:37
  logic and s. never convince, 519:14
  no s. in stones, 566:21

Seven ages, 198:25
 churches in Asia, 48:3
 cities warred, 239:13
 days shall ye eat unleavened bread, 8:20
 Dials, 564:20
 empty ears, 7:26
 everything left at six and s., 134:*n*1
 fourscore and s. years, 476:7
 from s. till s. times s., 376:3
 golden candlesticks, 48:4
 good kine, 7:26
 hours to law, 159:*n*5
 hundred pounds and possibilities, 190:15
 Jacob served s. years, 7:17
 keep thing s. years, 398:10
 lie has s. endings, 853:9
 long year, 216:33
 maids with seven mops, 551:19
 morning's at s., 491:2
 pounds tenpence a man, 343:11
 sealed with s. seals, 48:18
 sette world on six and s., 134:1
 seventy times s., 36:31
 sleepers' den, 233:10
 stars in hair s., 541:26
 thin kine, 7:26
 wisdom hath hewn out her s. pillars, 21:11
 years of famine, 7:26
 years would be insufficient, 406:2
Seven-pillared, Freedom s. house, 723:7
Seventeen times high as moon, 859:11
Seventeenth century dissociation, 722:12
Seventh day thou shalt not work, 8:34
 on s. holystone decks, 502:16
Seventy, oh to be s. again, 579:4
 times seven, 36:31
Sever, and then we s., 378:23
 he our good will s., 237:14
Several, for s. virtues s. women, 229:33
Severe, as holy as s., 211:29
 critic on own Works, 440:10
 ego serves three s. masters, 608:1
 eyes s. and beard, 198:25
 from lively to s., 311:15
 from pleasant to s., 289:5
 man s. he was, 342:8
 merely just is s., 315:23
 or if s. in aught, 342:8
 truth s., 335:15
Severed, our state cannot be s., 268:5
Severity, treats subject with s., 530:1
Sew a fine seam, 859:6
 time to s., 24:6
Sewer, common s. take it from distinction, 243:13
Sex, amoebas started S., 656:8
 and beauty inseparable, 707:17
 and the dead, 643:6
 brain not organ of s., 623:4
 conceal its s., 763:6
 everybody lies about s., 842:3
 fair s., 157:36
 fair s. your department, 617:14
 Marilyn sweet angel of s., 813:1

Sex (*continued*)
 most fun without laughing, 831:5
 nation has history of s. discrimination, 774:5
 no other difference than s., 383:6
 no stronger than my s., 196:8
 omnipresent process of s., 617:19
 ornament of her s., 496:29
 prejudice against color against s., 503:7
 right to vote not denied on account of s., 361:10
 ruin of our s., 337:7
 spirits either s. assume, 264:12
 superiority to s. that kills, 777:12
 to the last, 285:26
 woman's s. prima facie evidence, 503:7
 women complain about s. more than men, 803:5
Sexes, love idea of two s., 741:12
 there are three s., 398:22
 to one neutral thing both s. fit, 234:6
Sex's, your s. earliest care, 329:23
Sexton, no s. to toll bell, 575:6
 tolled the bell, 445:14
 went and told s., 445:14
Sex-typed, mind not s., 761:13
Sexual intercourse began, 810:6
 man's idea of s. rights, 503:8
 most unnatural of s. perversions, 741:4
 quest for s. symbols, 755:13
 relations with that woman, 840:2
 supremest of delights s. intercourse, 562:22
Sexuality, thin bat's squeak of s., 766:8
Seymour's Fat Lady, 805:15
Shabby equipment deteriorating, 721:4
 Genteel, 849:1
 tamed and s. tigers, 656:10
 winter hangs on till s., 661:18
Shackles accidents, 224:3
 and restraints of government, 651:7
 of a historian, 257:18
 of an old love, 486:3
 touch our country's. fall, 347:27
Shade, admiring in gloomy s., 257:21
 boundless contiguity of s., 347:26
 checkered s., 259:16
 cold light and hot s., 374:13
 fable song or fleeting s., 248:18
 gentlemen of the s., 184:24
 ghost along moonlight s., 309:27
 green thought in green s., 277:4
 I'll s. him from heat, 372:3
 inviolable s., 529:13
 let it sleep in the s., 411:9
 lone Glenartney's hazel s., 397:4
 no s. in sight, 841:11
 no s. no shine, 445:23
 of melancholy boughs, 198:22
 replied, 479:15
 round me night weaves s., 530:18
 sitting in a pleasant s., 239:2
 sport with Amaryllis in the s., 261:19
 spring with rustling s., 724:17
 the Lord is thy s., 19:30
 trees crowd into a s., 308:5
 variable as the s., 397:1
 without color, 719:5

Shaded, no s. stream, 368:13
Shades, crowns in s. like these, 342:2
 doleful s., 264:2
 evening s. prevail, 301:15
 of the prison-house, 393:11
 spirit fled indignant to s., 98:12
 twenty-nine when pink s., 604:26
Shadow, abide under the s. of the Almighty, 18:25
 another night to s. this, 819:18
 at evening rising, 718:12
 at morning striding, 718:12
 bringeth to light the s. of death, 14:13
 by grasping at the s., 60:24
 cruciform s., 730:8
 daisy by s. it casts, 395:20
 darkness and s. of death, 14:6, 19:13, 39:1
 days are as a s., 13:13
 down in s. of the penitentiary, 841:8
 every s. of authority, 345:3
 falls the S., 719:6
 falls thy s. Cynara, 645:10
 fell thy s. Cynara, 645:8
 fleeth as a s., 14:15
 follow a s., 237:23
 God within s., 514:13
 hanging over me, 835:2
 hence horrible s., 221:15
 hope beyond s. of dream, 436:12
 how slow s. creeps, 653:5
 I am gone like the s., 19:17
 I have a little s., 598:23
 if earth be s. of heaven, 267:7
 kills the growth, 238:17
 land of darkness and s. of death, 14:6
 land of the s. of death, 26:30
 lengthened s. of man, 455:13
 life is a s., 254:18
 life is little s., 525:7
 life s. of death, 256:24, 568:1
 life's but a walking s., 222:16
 light s. of God, 256:24
 like a s. like a dream, 55:2
 like a vast s. moved, 279:5
 mankind is dream of a s., 66:3
 meanwhile cast one s., 815:5
 night s. of light, 568:1
 no s. no antiquity, 460:22
 no s. of doubt, 566:4
 of British oak, 345:16
 of glorious name, 110:2
 of night comes on, 734:8
 of the Glen, 658:8
 of the tomb, 541:7
 of turning, 47:11
 of unseen Power, 427:14
 over gravel of drive, 706:7
 saw lion's s. ere himself, 190:4
 ship's huge s., 400:12
 sit in s. of death, 19:13, 39:1
 soul from out s., 479:9
 strong s. where much light, 363:9
 swift as a s., 180:20
 swollen s., 791:12
 then a spark, 591:11
 time is a very s., 31:13
 under red rock, 718:12
 under s. of thy wings, 16:8

Shape *(continued)*
  two of far nobler s., 266:9
  without form, 719:5
  words guard s. of man, 759:17
Shaped, feather whence pen was s., 395:14
Shapen, I was s. in iniquity, 17:25
Shapes and gives new meaning, 715:14
  behind outside pattern dim s., 623:2
  bright container can contain, 780:16
  calling s. and beckoning shadows, 260:24
  divinity that s. our ends, 207:5
  full of s. is fancy, 208:26
  horrid s. and shrieks, 259:7
  of foul disease, 484:15
  of things are shifting, 771:11
  poet's pen turns to s., 182:3
  ring out old s., 484:15
  shirts who coming to breathe s., 819:16
Shaping, deliberate s. of things, 643:9
Shard-borne beetle, 221:6
Share, all persons s. in government, 80:30
  bear own s. with courage, 536:12
  friends s. all things, 60:2
  no man's opinions, 512:2
  passion and action of time, 577:15
  threatened with railway s., 553:4
Shared experiences, 388:1
  joyless if not s. with him, 412:15
Sharer of action he describes, 534:10
Sharers, full s. in abundance, 597:10
  miserable s. of the event, 337:10
Shares the darkness, 735:5
Sharing, equal s. of miseries, 668:7
  unequal s. of blessings, 668:7
Shark has pretty teeth, 750:16
  went all naked to hungry s., 436:19
Sharon, rose of S., 25:14
Sharp as a two-edged sword, 21:3
  hot stink of fox, 825:4
  in nature few s. lines, 816:14
  names never get fat, 750:9
  necessity's s. pinch, 216:14
  nice s. quillets of law, 171:16
  nose as s. as pen, 192:27
  without s. North, 233:12
  wood has a s. ear, 135:*n*2
Sharpen with cloyless sauce his appetite,
    223:12
Sharpened life commands course, 541:25
  their tongues like a serpent, 20:16
Sharpeneth, iron s. iron, 23:14
Sharpening, busy s. my oyster knife, 760:14
Sharper, slander whose edge s. than sword,
    225:17
  than a serpent's tooth, 216:5
  than two-edged sword, 46:38
Sharpest, time rust s. sword, 397:22
Sharping, live by s. and robbing, 320:24
Sharp-looking, hollow-eyed s. wretch, 175:1
Sharp-sighted, fear is s., 156:20
Shatter faith of men, 631:5
  it to bits and then, 472:5
  possibility can s. us, 590:1
  vase if you will, 412:2
  your leaves, 261:13
Shattered lobsterpot, 721:8
  visage lies, 427:18
  when lamp is s., 431:4
Shaun, tale of S. or Shem, 696:16

Shave, began to s. realize growing older,
    661:19
  haircut and a s., 729:4
Shaven, all s. and shorn, 861:15
Shavers, two of a thousand s., 108:*n*4
Shaves, his boy first s., 757:13
Shaving, man s. at window, 767:16
Shawl, famous top-hat plain s., 685:6
Shawnee, I am a S., 387:8
Shay, one-hoss s., 473:15
She and comparisons are odious, 235:17
  cruelest s. alive, 209:8
  fair chaste unexpressive s., 199:3
  finished by such a s., 177:27
  for God in him, 266:10
  forget the He and S., 234:1
  that not impossible s., 272:6
Sheaf, brushwood s., 492:4
  sickle and wheaten s., 318:3
Shears, abhorred s., 261:19
  and pastepot, 653:17
  marriage resembles s., 398:28
Sheath, one sword keeps another in s., 252:4
  sets sword back in s., 664:11
  sword outwears s., 423:1
Sheathed swords for lack of argument, 193:1
Sheaves, after the reapers among the s., 11:13
  bringing his s. with him, 20:3
  God comes as s. in harvest, 236:21
Sheba, queen of S. heard of Solomon, 12:18
She-bear pops head into shop, 336:12
Shed, balloon of mind in s., 639:2
  bitter tear, 551:19
  bitter tears to s., 534:3
  by man shall his blood be s., 6:33
  for many for remission, 37:27
  for this all blood s., 638:7
  hand raised to s. blood, 311:2
  its bloom is s., 379:18
  lowly cattle s., 508:9
  prepare to s. them now, 196:32
Sheddeth, whoso s. man's blood, 6:33
Shedding, without s. of blood, 46:41
Sheds, disastrous twilight s., 264:18
  he that s. blood with me, 193:20
Sheelah, when S. was nigh, 408:15
Sheen of their spears, 422:14
Sheep, Abel was keeper of s., 6:12
  as s. that have not a shepherd, 12:37
  baa baa black s., 857:10
  Bo-peep has lost s., 859:9
  boy looks after s., 857:17
  divideth s. from goats, 37:16
  found s. which was lost, 39:34
  giveth life for s., 41:17
  glad to have kept s., 254:15
  hungry s. look up, 262:2
  like s. to slaughter, 350:4
  little black s., 633:17
  lost s. of house of Israel, 35:24
  men again led like s., 526:2
  mountain s. sweeter, 418:9
  noble ensample to his s., 135:9
  of his hand, 18:29
  of his pasture, 19:3
  old half-witted s., 394:*n*2
  other s. I have, 41:18
  owest s. no wool, 216:30
  rejoiceth more of that s., 36:29

Sheep *(continued)*
  return to our s., 855:4
  sameness of s., 756:17
  shepherd tells tale of s., 104:19
  shepherdess of s., 592:14
  shepherding s. below holy Helicon, 56:2
  strayed like lost s., 49:19
  to fold, 619:16
  unintelligent, 715:2
  valley s. fatter, 418:9
  we like s. have gone astray, 28:22
  which went not astray, 36:29
  wine, 451:13
  without shepherd s. not flock, 861:20
  you herd s., 58:6
Sheep-hook, know how to hold a s., 262:1
Sheepish calm, 801:2
Sheep's, casts a s. eye, 157:31
  come in s. clothing, 35:7
  in the meadow, 857:17
  wolf in s. clothing, 60:7
Sheer, frightful s. no-man-fathomed, 588:3
  here a s. hulk, 362:11
Sheet, old England's winding s., 375:15
  seemed a s. of sun, 793:4
  waters his winding s., 239:1
  wet s. flowing sea, 417:7
  who ever got out of winding s., 237:1
Sheeted dead, 200:18
Sheets, cool kindliness of s., 712:18
  fumble with the s., 192:27
Sheiling, lone s., 444:10
Shelf, dust of upper s., 447:11
  Life over there behind S., 545:12
  painted gourds on a s., 816:20
  take bottle down from s., 789:6
Shell, burst hot heart's s., 516:14
  kill him in the s., 195:31
  pebble or prettier s., 291:6
  scallop s. of quiet, 160:8
  smooth-lipped s., 395:5
  universe itself is, 395:5
  unseen within thy airy s., 260:26
Shelley beautiful ineffectual angel, 532:12
  Burns S. were with us, 491:22
  of my age, 800:16
  see S. plain, 492:17
Shells, crow-blue mussel s., 714:3
Shelter, dead tree no s., 718:12
  from the stormy blast, 304:6
  what s. to grow ripe, 529:6
  where storm drives I s., 100:18
Sheltered, in youth it s., 451:22
  life can be daring life, 784:7
Shelters, happy house s. friend, 455:24
Shelves, symmetry of s., 407:12
  upon the glazen s., 717:21
Shem, Noah begat S., 6:24
  tale of Shaun or S., 696:16
Shenandoah I long to hear you, 862:3
Shepherd, any philosophy in thee s., 199:4
  as sheep that have not a s., 12:37
  as s. divideth sheep, 37:16
  call you S. from hill, 529:9
  Dick the s. blows his nail, 177:17
  every s. tells his tale, 259:14
  feed his flock like a s., 28:5
  giveth his life, 41:17
  hears their thundering, 52:26

Shepherd *(continued)*
I am the good s., 41:17
King of love my s. is, 524:6
Lord is my s., 16:18
star that bids s. fold, 260:18
tells his tale of sheep, 104:19
valiant s. who drives flock, 4:6
weather s. shuns, 576:7
without s. sheep not flock, 861:20
Shepherdess O Eiffel Tower, 689:17
of sheep, 592:14
Shepherding below holy Helicon, 56:2
Shepherd's, homely slighted s. trade, 261:19
lays s. crook, 452:9
Love tunes s. reed, 396:9
truth in s. tongue, 160:3
Shepherds abiding in field, 39:3
watched flocks by night, 294:4
Shepherds', I who once played s. songs, 96:22
Sheridan, broke die molding S., 422:20
Sherlock, my name is S. Holmes, 617:4
to S. Holmes always the woman, 617:2
Sherry, cocktail and s. cobbler, 416:9
is dull, 327:2
She-wolf's, eats s. young, 400:20
Shibboleth, say now S., 10:38
Shield, constancy and valor s., 666:6
Constitution the s., 502:18
constitutional s., 710:16
God s. us, 181:18
his truth shall be thy s., 18:25
idle spear and s., 258:18
Lord is my strength and my s., 16:24
of its protection, 502:18
took spear but left s., 368:11
what care I for that s., 56:20
Shielding men from effects of folly, 523:15
Shift, here the parts s., 493:19
let me s. for myself, 144:3
onion will do well for such s., 175:20
thus times do s., 248:12
Shifted his trumpet, 343:6
Shifting, shapes s. in the wind, 771:11
Shifts of Fortune test friends, 91:14
victory s. from man to man, 52:33
Shifty, good to be s. in new country, 503:3
Shilling, sell for s. ring, 499:17
Splendid S., 304:15
Shillings, ducks and drakes with s., 165:3
rather than forty s., 190:16
Shine, all thou dost s. upon, 427:15
as sure as sun will s., 841:4
by side of path we tread, 348:15
continuous as stars that s., 394:5
face of God s. through, 734:15
for thy light is come, 28:29
forth upon clouded hills, 375:17
full alchemized and free, 436:10
Heaven's glories s., 509:1
if moon s. at full or no, 271:23
inner light will s. forth, 366:n4
let your light s., 34:2
make his face s. upon thee, 9:17
nor public flame dares s., 313:25
not to s. in use, 481:10
perpetual light s. upon them, 49:8
rise and s. give God glory, 863:6
S. S. save poor me, 850:17

Shine *(continued)*
traffic of Jacob's ladder, 621:8
upon my brow today, 594:2
vessels oft handled brightly s., 170:16
wherever bright sun shall s., 231:17
wind's feet s. along sea, 568:9
wit will s., 284:5
with Pye, 420:1
you but knock breathe s., 236:11
Shined, although not s. upon, 271:27
eye of heaven s. bright, 161:1
in my angel-infancy, 279:2
upon them hath the light s., 26:30
Shines and stinks, 405:2
faith s. equal arming me, 509:1
foolery s. everywhere, 209:32
gold s. like fire, 65:24
good deed, 190:8
incongruous moonlight s., 729:11
light where no sun s., 795:3
moon s. bright, 190:4
simile that solitary s., 313:2
upon court and cottage, 229:1
wise moral man s. like fire, 66:25
wit s. at expense of memory, 300:1
Shineth everlasting Light, 558:5
light s. in darkness, 40:30
light that s. unto perfect day, 21:1
when sun s. make hay, 147:9
Shingles, naked s. of world, 531:2
Shining Big-Sea-Water, 466:24
burning and s. light, 40:49
death loves s. mark, 306:11
eyes s. for me, 723:7
improve each s. hour, 304:1
improve s. tail, 549:13
like a National guitar, 837:13
live hair s. and free, 712:18
look s. at architecture, 775:5
morning face, 198:25
no more profit of s. nights, 176:20
nowhere but in the dark, 279:9
of the stars, 486:10
on broken fragments, 415:2
on the sea, 551:18
only one s. in sky, 391:18, 692:16
path of the just is as s. light, 21:1
prospects rise, 301:11
sea to s. sea, 616:3
see it s. plain, 619:3
spangled heavens s. frame, 301:14
through dark cloud s., 663:1
to the quiet moon, 401:11
with all his might, 551:18
Shins, break s. against wit, 198:10
Ship, anchor heaves s. swings free, 452:1
and I took off suddenly, 763:2
as the smart s. grew, 576:1
being in s. is being in jail, 326:16
build s. of death, 707:22
came from north country, 862:10
capital s. for ocean trip, 580:23
comes into the harbor, 247:9
community like s., 540:13
don't give up the s., 413:n3
fragment from earth, 611:17
idle as painted s., 399:21
land to which s. must go, 394:20
me east of Suez, 633:14

Ship *(continued)*
name of s. Golden Vanity, 862:10
never sink except on even keel, 106:24
not to give up s., 413:13
of state, 67:13
of State, 466:19
of Union, 475:3
one s. drives east, 600:5
Papists Protestants Jews Turks in one s., 255:3
places s. alongside enemy, 377:5
rapt s. run on side so low, 165:11
rats desert sinking s., 108:n6
sailing like a stately s., 269:6
tall s. and star to steer, 680:15
trip on Government s., 862:11
unstable pilot steers leaking s., 118:5
upon the sea, 751:4
was cheered, 399:14
way of a s. in the sea, 23:25
weathered every rack, 520:18
whither O splendid s., 586:5
whose weal and woe is common, 255:3
wish to have no connection with any s., 363:1
Shipped, and this is what ye have s. for, 516:12
Ship's huge shadow, 400:12
way upon the sea, 634:6
Ships are but boards, 188:1
are only hulls, 68:4
are swift as a bird, 54:24
beauty and majesty of s., 467:8
believe these s. from sky, 140:7
board the well-benched s., 57:12
by s. lies a dead man, 54:3
dim-discovered, 317:17
distant storm-beaten s., 576:11
face that launched a thousand s., 170:23
fare north, fare south, 4:10
go down to the sea in s., 19:14
guarded with s., 257:20
heart of oak our s., 335:22
how many s. my presence worth, 81:19
like s. steer courses, 271:6
loose lips sink s., 851:16
Mr. Mrs. America all s. at sea, 750:5
of war at sea, 486:22
salvaged and retiring, 696:2
saw three s. come sailing, 860:9
season of s. is here, 85:16
shoes s. sealing wax, 552:3
stately s. go on, 482:15
that pass in night, 467:18
there go the s., 19:11
there were two lofty s., 862:9
Thracian s. foreign faces, 567:17
upon untamed seas, 776:10
we've got the s., 539:5
wooden wall is your s., 64:18
Shipwreck, delivered from s. of blood, 751:12
Shipwrecked before I got aboard, 106:25
Shiraz, wine of S. into urine, 706:4
Shirt, happy man's without s., 147:2
land of the Cluett S., 739:15
naked truth is I have no s., 177:14
never s. on back, 296:2
not dignify with name of stuffed s., 765:10

Shirt *(continued)*
    of flame, 722:2
    of Nessus upon me, 223:32
    Song of the S., 446:3
    when wanting a s., 343:7
Shirtless, sleeveless some s. others, 313:19
Shirts, Nessus s., 433:22
    who is coming to breathe shapes, 819:16
Shirtsleeves, three generations s. to s., 559:11
Shit, built-in shock-proof s. detector, 755:5
Shiver runs down spine, 743:21
    sunset breezes s., 627:5
Shivering, stood s. in snow, 168:26
Shivering-sweet to touch, 711:8
Shoal, bank and s. of time, 219:16
    of fools for tenders, 300:23
Shock disturbing delicate balance, 781:14
    fodder's in the s., 596:8
    future s., 822:1
    like s. of corn cometh, 13:40
    of recognition, 516:2
    strikes with shivering s., 405:12
    we shall s. them, 178:29
    you must s. bourgeois, 525:3
Shocked to discover gambling, 782:10
Shocks, thousand natural s., 203:33
Shod, worse s. than shoemaker's wife, 148:20
Shoe, cannot put s. on every foot, 103:28
    dame has lost s., 856:14
    fits one pinches another, 675:4
    for want of nail s. lost, 251:29, 320:10
    none tell where s. pinches me, 111:8
    not do any more black s., 827:14
    old s. for good luck, 147:23
    old woman lived in s., 858:13
    one s. off one s. on, 860:7
    over Edom will I cast out my s., 17:36
    sailed in wooden s., 597:5
    sixpence in her s., 244:15, 850:13
    the horse, 861:12
    whether s. be Spanish, 271:14
Shoemaker, lives of s. and fish peddler,
    724:20
Shoemaker's, worse shod than s. wife, 148:20
Shoes and ships and sealing wax, 552:3
    blue suede s., 827:6
    dance fire dance in iron s., 821:12
    eats soles offen s., 750:8
    heard you got stock of s., 825:10
    him that makes s. go barefoot, 148:*n*10
    King James used to call for old s., 245:15
    latchet of whose s., 38:14
    nor scrip nor s., 39:17
    put off thy s., 8:4
    put yourself in his s., 744:15
    sold the poor for a pair of s., 30:24
    surgeon to old s., 195:13
    walk in velvet s., 710:5
    well then o'er s. o'er boots, 565:*n*1
    will fill with urine, 830:15
    with your s. on your feet, 8:18
Shoeshine, I go get a s., 818:4
Shoestring, careless s. in whose tie, 248:4
Shone, eyes that s. now dimmed, 412:7
    far off his coming s., 267:12
    glory s. around, 294:4
    glory s. round about them, 39:3
    light here kindled s. unto many, 247:10
    like meteor streaming, 264:14

Shone *(continued)*
    moon s. on Mrs. Porter, 718:17
    no light propitious s., 348:22
    princely counsel s., 265:8
    they s. not on poet's page, 100:*n*11
    with preeminent luster, 113:20
Shoo fly, 558:4
Shook all our coffins, 576:4
    softening chalk of bones, 780:9
Shoon, cork-heeled s., 853:19
    sandal s., 206:4
    silver s., 662:8
Shoot, cannot s. with butter, 749:5
    do not s. pianist, 604:19
    don't s. Colonel, 419:1
    don't s. the messenger, 67:*n*5
    false Love, 844:13
    fellow down, 575:18
    first inquire afterwards, 737:6
    folly as it flies, 310:21
    guns begin to s., 633:8
    her every minute, 815:15
    how can you s. women children, 834:8
    if you must, 468:15
    inspired someone to s. your murderer,
      824:17
    teach young idea to s., 318:1
    they s. horses don't they, 749:11
Shootin', what's all s. for, 679:14
Shooting, glory like a s. star, 179:22
    stars attend thee, 248:11
Shoots, boy that s. so trim, 844:3
    his wit, 200:11
    neither s. nor liberates, 507:24
    nobody s. at Santa Claus, 663:14
    of everlastingness, 279:3
Shop, back s. our own free, 152:17
    closed for other business, 477:8
    keep s. and s. keep thee, 165:2
    said you were coming from s., 553:10
    she-bear pops head into s., 336:12
Shopkeeper, what is true of s., 331:22
Shopkeepers, government influenced by s.,
    338:19
    nation of s., 338:19
Shopkeeping nation, 331:22
Shopped for groceries, 807:15
Shopping, go s., 838:14
Shops, in s. nothing to eat, 656:14
Shore, Afric's burning s., 404:7
    beats back envious siege, 179:13
    boat is on s., 422:26
    breast against reedy s., 844:23
    fast by their native s., 348:16
    fragrance of salt marsh s. mud, 521:2
    from s. sees sea bottom, 132:4
    gaze from s. on another's tribulation,
      92:19
    high s. of world, 193:16
    his own native s., 478:2
    I on opposite s., 467:15
    lee s. of age, 594:15
    left beauty on s., 452:17
    lights around s., 542:7
    man's control stops at s., 421:26
    naked in death on unknown s., 97:21
    never reach the s., 590:13
    Nightly s., 479:5
    ocean's wave-beat s., 501:17

Shore *(continued)*
    of what we know, 809:7
    one foot in sea one on s., 194:25
    one s. beyond desire, 753:14
    Plutonian s., 479:5
    praise sea on s. remain, 162:10
    rapture on lonely s., 421:25
    refuse of teeming s., 595:6
    roar echoed along s., 404:7
    round earth's s., 531:2
    scrambling to the s., 552:2
    spies a far-off s., 172:32
    stayed upon green s., 440:11
    sunshine on strange s., 612:2
    then on s. of world, 439:10
    thrown on savage s., 521:4
    unknown and silent s., 407:5
    upon farther s., 538:10
    upon the Irish s., 379:3
    varying s. o' the world, 223:36
    watery s., 373:17
    waves make towards pebbled s., 226:16
    wide-watered s., 260:4
    wild New England s., 431:21
Shoreditch, bells of S., 857:12
Shoreless seas, 579:8
    watery wild, 529:3
Shores and desert wildernesses, 260:24
    concave s., 195:15
    exult O s., 520:19
    not ghost of s., 579:8
    of Gitche Gumee, 466:24
    of Tripoli, 848:17
    pure ablution round s., 439:11
    rolling towards their s., 516:1
    what seas what s., 719:18
    whisperings around desolate s., 439:7
    wilder s. of love, 776:17
    will swarm with invisible dead, 419:5
Shoreward, great winds s. blow, 528:5
Shorn, tempers wind to s. lamb, 151:12
Short an' simple scandals, 646:4
    and long of it, 190:24
    and simple annals, 334:14
    arm to reach to Heaven, 621:10
    art long life s., 364:4
    as any dream, 180:20
    as watch that ends night, 304:7
    as wrong as to fall s., 63:6
    day s. labor long, 120:8
    full description of happy state, 286:8
    in s. I was afraid, 717:13
    in s. measures life perfect be, 238:14
    in the story itself, 33:14
    joy of love too s., 139:6
    July's day s. as December, 228:13
    lack time to make it s., 279:12
    let thy speech be s., 33:1
    life how long or s., 268:11
    life in saddle Lord, 624:3
    life is s. art long, 73:10
    life s. quiet hours few, 517:14
    life too s. to bore ourselves, 589:8
    meaning of long speech, 382:2
    my scope had not been so s., 231:*n*2
    nasty brutish and s., 246:12
    nearest comes so far s., 669:1
    not make sentences s., 652:12
    one ready for my own, 670:15

Shrouds, darkness worms and s., 436:5
Shrunk, as to bed's-feet life s., 234:20
    shank, 198:25
      those s. strangely in our lives, 759:12
      to this little measure, 196:18
      vanished and s. away, 169:1
Shudder, hands over with s., 701:18
    in loins, 640:14
    my first s. of gentility, 743:19
    to say it, 97:8
Shuddering fear green-eyed jealousy, 189:7
    I with s. fall, 541:10
Shuffle, patience and s. cards, 158:16
    permitted to s. in slippers, 631:20
Shuffled off this mortal coil, 203:33
Shuffling, forced gait of s. nag, 186:7
    sandwich men s., 699:16
Shulamite, return O S., 25:28
Shun, dews of evening s., 315:13
    frumious Bandersnatch, 551:10
    heaven that leads men to hell, 227:22
    let me s. that, 216:26
    polluted flock, 710:6
    studies in which work dies with worker,
      141:3
    thought that lurks, 592:15
    when I s. Scylla, 189:11
    who doth ambition s., 198:13
    wise men s. mistakes of fools, 88:2
Shuns, weather shepherd s., 576:7
Shut, am now going to s. gate, 701:1
    doors against setting sun, 218:15
    doors s. in the streets, 25:7
    eyes against painful truth, 352:13
    fountain up, 508:4
    her up horrorshow and lovely, 798:17
    in from world without, 468:18
    no door is s., 624:6
    shut the door, 311:19
    them in with their triumphs, 492:11
    up box and puppets, 490:8
    up he explained, 707:2
    up in measureless content, 220:7
    when thou shouldest repay, 32:4
Shut-in homes closed doors, 651:1
Shuts up story of our days, 160:14
Shutter, body borne before her on s.,
    490:18
    camera with s. open, 767:16
    it may be in the s., 505:1
Shutters, close s. fast, 348:4
Shutteth up bowels of compassion, 47:40
Shutting away of loving hearts, 735:11
Shuttle, musical s., 520:7
    swifter than weaver's s., 14:2
Shy, we are not s., 565:12
Sibboleth, he said S., 10:38
Sibyl, as David and the S. say, 49:9
Sic semper tyrannis, 124:24, 570:27
    sic iuvat ire sub umbras, 97:*n9*
    transit gloria mundi, 138:5
Sicilian, so ended S. expedition, 74:9
Sicily, quarries of S., 759:15
Sick and ye visited me, 37:17
    at heart, 200:12
    became tired and s., 520:8
    danger for the healthy, 589:15
    do s. no harm, 522:5
    enterprise is s., 207:25

Sick *(continued)*
    for home, 437:13
    hope deferred maketh heart s., 21:24
    I am s. at heart, 200:12
    I am s. I must die, 232:9
    I am s. of both, 328:5
    I'm s. of good poems, 816:20
    in fortune, 215:29
    kingdom of s., 829:1
    love never s. old dead, 160:2
    make me s. discussing duty, 519:16
    need physician, 35:18
    never never s. at sea, 563:15
    night but daylight s., 190:10
    nothing but to make him s., 235:20
    O Rose thou art s., 374:3
    of an old passion, 645:8
    of love, 25:16
    say I'm s. I'm dead, 311:19
    superintend s., 73:2
    that surfeit with too much, 187:25
    use treatment to help s., 72:16
    whole head is s., 26:7
    with desire, 640:1
Sicken, appetite may s. and die, 208:25
    when love begins to s., 197:6
Sickened and nigh to death, 521:4
Sickle, crowned with the s., 318:3
    never thrust s. in another's corn, 103:27
    not move s. unto neighbor's corn, 10:7
Sickle's, bending s. compass, 227:17
Sicklied o'er with thought, 203:33
Sickly plants niggard earth, 334:5
Sickness, age or grief or s., 249:1
    and troubled mind, 249:14
    by his health s., 372:9
    enlarges dimension of self, 407:27
    in s. and in health, 51:10
    love a s. full of woes, 169:9
    trublit now with gret s., 142:4
    universal s. implies idea of health, 773:1
Sickness-broken body, 258:5
Sidcup, if only I could get to S., 825:11
Side, a thousand shall fall at thy s., 18:25
    angel on outward s., 211:30
    back and s. go bare, 151:10
    cooperative on my upper west s., 841:6
    cracked from s. to s., 480:26
    curse angel from his s., 215:10
    East S. West S., 625:13
    far s. of baldness, 636:11
    God on s. of big squadrons, 275:1
    good or evil s., 514:12
    hear other s., 119:13
    heard other s., 70:6
    history is on our s., 741:7
    house by s. of road, 52:30, 613:16
    lies on her left s., 734:10
    on that s. toil hunger, 442:1
    proneness to s. with beauty, 676:16
    sleep on his left s., 756:4
    spinning-jenny out of s., 640:13
    stands out on either s., 734:15
    to which s. shall we incline, 279:23
    trumpets on other s., 282:6
    which s. that I must go, 178:5
    who is on the Lord's s., 9:7
    windy s. of care, 194:21
    windy s. of law, 194:*n1*

Side *(continued)*
    with pouch on s., 198:25
    wrong s. of thirty, 299:12
Sidelong pickerel smile, 780:13
Sides, god would have three s., 314:7
    Laughter holding both his s., 259:10
    much said on both s., 302:11
    prick s. of my intent, 219:18
    split s. with laughing, 157:12
    thorns in your s., 10:27
    two s. to every question, 72:2
    unfed s., 216:27
Sidewalk, Tom appeared on s., 559:19
Sidewalks of New York, 625:13
Sideways, listened and looked s. up, 400:6
Sidnaeian showers, 272:9
Sidney, Friend to Sir Philip S., 162:17
Sidney's sister Pembroke's mother, 247:12
Siege, envious s. of watery Neptune, 179:13
    how cam'st to be s. of this moon calf,
      229:30
    laugh a s. to scorn, 222:14
    of city of Gaunt, 853:25
Sieges, battles s. fortunes, 212:28
Sienta, el que s. en la puerta, 862:18
Sierras, crossed the s., 734:9
    people who live in s., 140:9
Siesta, hangover allowed-for as Spanish s.,
    746:12
Sieve, nectar in a s., 402:12
    to sea in s., 499:19
    water through a s., 552:16
Sifted, God hath s. a nation, 285:*n2*
Siftings, liquid s. fall, 718:10
Sigh back at them, 780:16
    is just a sigh, 740:23
    lack of many a thing, 226:8
    like Tom o' Bedlam, 215:30
    no more ladies, 194:25
    shall I ever s. and pine, 250:15
    some a light s., 452:2
    sword of Angel King, 375:4
    telling this with s., 669:4
    time for a s., 612:2
    to those who love me, 422:26
    very beadle to humorous s., 176:32
    weep no more nor s., 242:18
Sighed and looked and sighed again, 285:13
    and looked unutterable things, 317:18
    as lover obeyed as son, 354:1
    for love of lady, 565:25
    for such a one, 169:2
    no sooner loved but s., 200:3
    soul toward Grecian tents, 190:4
    to many though he loved one, 420:4
    when small birds s., 780:16
Sighing by a sycamore tree, 215:1
    farewell goes out s., 208:11
    laughter ability S., 545:18
    lover s. like furnace, 198:25
    plague of s. and grief, 185:28
    shall flee away, 27:33
    sound lights around shore, 542:7
    that Nature formed but one, 422:20
    through all her works, 267:30
    with s. and crying, 154:14
Sighs, before my s. did dry it, 250:15
    Bridge of S., 421:5
    his alarms, 164:19

Silent (*continued*)

halls of death, 432:10

haunches, 681:9

icicles, 401:11

impossible to be s., 345:7

in shadowy s. distance grew Iceberg, 576:1

in the dark and s. grave, 160:14

into the s. funeral, 720:23

language of peak, 725:5

lark that soars singing then s., 132:6

long and s. street, 604:7

majority, 790:21

my tongue falls s., 57:20

night holy night, 427:10

note Cupid strikes, 256:7

painting is s. poetry, 62:7

power in men to be s., 287:1

prism and s. face, 391:9

question is this all, 807:15

right to remain s., 733:2

sea, 399:20

slow and s. stream Lethe, 265:16

spectator of scene, 410:6

spring, 777:2

stars go by, 558:5

sweet s. thought, 226:8

tents are spread, 522:6

the truly s. who keep apart 5:5

these three s. things, 679:15

till you see whites of eyes, 340:*n3*

to be s. better than to speak, 111:14

unknown and s. shore, 407:5

upon peak in Darien, 435:19

used to be in s. pictures, 733:7

war of lilies, 175:3

what is still and s. all, 424:4

when eggs hatched, 258:11

why art thou s., 447:7

with s. delight, 372:8

wound deep in her breast, 97:18

Silently, falls through clear ether s., 435:18

how s. with how wan face, 163:29

invisibly, 373:8

now the moon, 662:8

steal away, 466:14

Silicon, had s. been gas, 558:2

Silk, not make revolution with s. gloves, 686:5

owest worm no s., 216:30

soft as s. remains, 307:20

sound of her s. skirt, 89:17

stocking filled with mud, 388:16

stockings and white bosoms, 326:7

suit which cost me much, 288:1

that thing of s., 312:7

Silken dalliance, 192:24

flanks, 438:3

in field s. tent, 670:11

lines silver hooks, 234:22

or in leathern purse, 304:15

sad uncertain, 479:3

terms precise, 177:12

ties of love, 670:12

white s. turbans wreathed, 268:23

Silks, in s. my Julia goes, 248:19

Silk-sack clouds, 587:11

Silkworm expend her yellow labors, 239:15

size or immense, 714:23

Silliest woman manage clever man, 632:14

Silliness, look of bay mare shames s. out of me, 519:2

Sillons, abreuve nos s., 383:8

Silly, envy slayeth the s., 13:36

fairy tale, 336:3

joy at silly things, 342:*n1*

Lily O'Grady s. and shady, 715:12

loved its s. face, 624:5

nothing more s. than s. laugh, 94:11

question, 332:4

sooth, 209:24

Silo, mildewed s., 678:1

Silver and gold have I none, 42:1

answer rang, 463:15

apples of gold in pictures of s., 23:2

apples of moon, 637:10

bells cockleshells, 857:11

buckles on knee, 861:9

churn, 564:11

cord be loosed, 25:8

foot in his mouth, 828:11

for handful of s. he left, 491:20

fountains have mud, 226:11

give him s. bridge, 862:14

goddess of the s. lake, 261:10

gold and s. ivory and apes, 12:20

gold and s. light, 637:11

hooks, 234:22

if you have two pieces of s., 123:*n1*

into s. dawn, 739:10

light on foliage, 751:7

lining on the night, 260:25

lining through cloud, 663:1

look for s. lining, 694:8

mantle threw, 266:16

moon in s. bag, 642:1

nap after dinner s., 542:9

nutmeg, 859:7

oars were s., 223:14

picking up gold and s., 847:7

precious stone set in s. sea, 179:12

refined thee but not with s., 28:12

seated in thy s. chair, 237:10

shoon, 662:8

sixpence in shoe, 850:*n4*

snarling trumpets, 436:21

sold the righteous for s., 30:24

speak s. reply gold, 853:11

spoon in mouth, 159:2

stroke his s. hair, 372:3

swan who living, 844:23

Taffy stole s. pin, 858:6

thirty pieces of s., 30:39, 37:22

threads among gold, 594:2

tips with s. fruit-tree tops, 183:8

Wisdom be put in s. rod, 372:12

Silvered, it was a sable s., 201:18

Silvern, Speech is s., 433:21

Silver-sandaled, dawn with s. feet, 604:7

Silver-sweet sound lovers' tongues, 183:14

Silver-white, lady-smocks all s., 177:16

Silvia, be by S. in the night, 176:10

who is S. what is she, 176:12

Simia, exemplum de s., 128:*n5*

quam similis nobis, 87:*n8*

Simiadae branched off, 470:4

Simians, true fairy story of s., 668:12

Similar, not s. are race of gods, 52:28

sons s. to their fathers, 54:12

to mortals neither in shape nor thought, 61:22

Simile a like perfection, 809:2

that solitary shines, 313:2

Similitudes, I have used s., 30:20

Simon Pure, 297:13

Simple S., 857:18

Simple, a s. child, 390:15

and faithless as smile, 717:24

as false dawn, 808:15

back in a time made s., 670:17

facts in naked s. beauty, 169:20

faith than Norman blood, 480:14

gout kills more wise than s., 280:18

great swindles s., 626:7

how s. and frugal is happiness, 701:8

I would like s. life, 821:14

Ivan Ilych's life most s., 543:1

justice rails upon yon s. thief, 217:23

my s. natural fashion, 152:5

natural s. affecting, 343:4

no vice so s., 189:5

ordinary therefore terrible, 543:1

performed rites s. and decisive, 816:18

plain and s. faith, 197:6

race, 396:10

sensuous and passionate, 262:19

separate person, 518:12

short and s. annals, 334:14

Simon, 857:18

the s. are near to virtue, 63:10

'tis the gift to be s., 848:4

to give subtilty to the s., 20:22

too s. to admire it, 447:20

truth his utmost skill, 232:13

truth miscalled simplicity, 226:22

Simple-minded modes of discrimination, 695:5

Simpler, better and s. people, 599:21

Simples, compounded of many s., 199:23

Simplest, ignorance of s. things, 825:8

note that swells gale, 335:5

Simplex munditiis, 99:*n3*

Simplicitas, O sancta s., 138:*n2*

venerationi sancta s., 118:*n7*

Simplicity and charm, 98:23

complete s., 722:5

embrace s., 58:17

in wit man s. child, 310:19

independence magnanimity, 506:16

makes s. a grace, 237:16

makes uneducated effective, 81:9

mine is unadorned s., 104:28

no greatness where no s., 542:15

no hindrance to subtlety, 572:8

no longer misled, 360:7

O holy s., 138:4

of three per cents, 362:13

old s. of times, 846:20

pity my s., 322:25

revered holy s., 118:21

seemed s. itself once explained, 617:8

simple truth miscalled s., 226:22

Spartan s., 852:1

treats with s. or severity, 530:1

Simplificateurs, terribles s., 509:5

Simplification first step to mastery of subject, 676:8

Simplify simplify, 506:29

Simulacrum, sun the dark s. of God, 256:24

Simulate, no disguise can s. love, 273:10

Sin, Adam's sons conceived in s., 241:8
against Holy Ghost, 572:11, 590:10
against s., 659:21
be ye angry and s. not, 45:28
before polygamy made a s., 283:6
behoved that there should be s., 133:4
blossoms of my s., 202:19
by that s. fell the angels, 231:6
choose one s., 504:6
cunning s. cover itself, 194:38
draw s. with cart rope, 26:21
dreadful record of s., 617:6
feared no danger knew no s., 284:18
fight with death and s., 487:8
folly noise and s., 492:11
fools make a mock at s., 21:28
go and s. no more, 41:9
good man's s., 332:n2
guilty of dust and s., 251:2
has many tools, 473:12
he that is without s., 41:8
hold it half a s., 483:14
human sympathy for s., 460:3
if old and merry be s., 185:31
ignorance not innocence but s., 495:9
in private not sin, 277:24
in s. did my mother conceive me, 17:25
in this be free from s., 440:16
is Behovely, 133:n1
learnt s. to fly, 296:11
much of Madness more of S., 478:14
my s. is red, 292:13
my s. my soul, 755:14
neatness a duty not s., 318:23
no s. but ignorance, 170:9
no s. to labor in vocation, 184:33
nothing emboldens s. as mercy, 218:17
of Judah, 29:16
original s., 525:2
original s. of man, 300:3
physicists have known s., 768:14
plate s. with gold, 217:24
pleasure's a s., 423:13
poverty is no s., 252:8
private s. not so prejudicial, 158:13
pure in life free from s., 99:15
sedentary life s., 590:10
shall be no more, 501:17
some rise by s., 211:5
sure your s. will find you out, 9:27
taketh away s. of world, 40:35
that I s. not with my tongue, 17:10
'tis s. nay profanation, 248:17
to covet honor, 193:18
to prefer life to honor, 113:14
usura s. against nature, 709:9
wages of s. is death, 43:2
waive quantum o' the s., 378:10
was too much hope, 237:20
we sing s., 798:10
weeps incessantly for my s., 374:15
where s. abounded, 42:44
who tell us love can die, 405:14
wilt thou forgive that s., 236:15

Sin *(continued)*
without s., without guilt, 3:12
worst s. passion can commit, 738:21
worst s. towards fellow creatures, 609:14
would you like to s., 850:14
ye do by two and two, 634:3

Sinai, Wilson write Notes from S., 701:13

Sinais, we S. climb, 514:14

Sincere flattery, 349:9
friend person with whom s., 455:25
his soul s., 335:3
if his words are s., 62:10
let thy life be s., 32:7
love is s., 138:13
men always s., 643:17
not s. even when saying not s., 630:12
of soul s., 310:15
officious innocent s., 329:10
prayer soul's s. desire, 396:2
think beforehand that words be s., 82:7
work give reality to illusion, 678:4

Sincerely from author's soul, 741:3

Sincerest, our s. laughter, 429:19

Sincérité, changent de s., 643:n2

Sincerities, men change s., 643:17

Sincerity, friends of freedom doubt our s., 474:7
hold faithfulness and s., 62:11
panics touchstones of s., 354:11
tell young men with great s., 325:17
to practice s., 63:25
way of heaven, 82:4
wrought in sad s., 452:19

Sinecure, gives no man a s., 709:6

Sinew, money the s. of love, 91:n8

Sinews, coin is s. of war, 146:2
cracks s. cakes brain, 516:14
exercises s. with toil, 82:17
money s. of war, 91:19
of soul, 258:14
of virtue, 252:28
stiffen s. summon blood, 192:30
wealth the s. of affairs, 85:1
what are s. of philosopher, 112:13

Sinewy, youthful s. races, 520:6

Sinful, center of my s. earth, 228:4
desires of the flesh, 51:5
greedy the s. and lewd, 745:2

Sing, a little time to s., 553:n3
all a green willow, 215:1
ancient ways, 636:22
and build the lofty rhyme, 261:14
and louder sing, 639:17
arms and the man I s., 96:23, 285:6
awake and s., 27:18
because I must, 483:17
bid soul of Orpheus s., 260:7
bow themselves when he did s., 230:27
by land and sea, 634:9
caused the widow's heart to s., 14:37
charmingly sweet you s., 499:16
dance and drink and s., 374:4
do not think they s. to me, 717:16
eagle suffers little birds to s., 175:17
elected Silence s. to me, 587:2
for Horse nation, 855:17
Grecian woes goddess s., 309:18
hark the herald angels s., 323:1

Sing *(continued)*
hear angels s., 488:15
hear lady s. in Welsh, 186:11
heaven and nature s., 304:9
heavenly s., 395:n3
heigh-ho says Rowley, 856:16
holy sages once did s., 258:16
I am Rose and when I s., 673:21
I can't s., 555:13
I s. as bird sings, 363:14
I s. myself, 518:15
I s. of brooks, 247:14
I s. with mortal voice, 267:13
I will s. unto the Lord, 8:25
in a hempen string, 242:15
in my brain I s. it, 494:2
let others s. of knights, 169:4
lhude s. cuccu, 843:5
Lhude s. Goddamm, 708:17
like birds i' the cage, 218:1
lift into my arms and s., 820:1
Long live king, 347:24
loss of all I s., 818:8
me your song O, 565:24
nightingale came to s., 461:23
no birds s., 439:3
no sad songs for me, 547:16
nor pair nor build nor s., 402:11
of a maiden, 843:10
of days that are gone, 571:11
of Everything and Anything, 699:12
of Olaf glad and big, 740:2
of thee I s., 469:8
of thee I s. baby, 747:3
of you i s., 739:15
one of the songs of Zion, 20:11
One's-Self I s., 518:12
or cease to sing, 313:5
pipe as linnets s., 483:17
praises to his Name, 845:2
pretty birds do s., 232:7
saddest when I s., 555:13
saints sweetly s., 292:8
savageness out of a bear, 214:21
set upon bough to s., 640:2
sit and hear me s., 371:10
so we'll live pray s., 218:1
so wildly well, 478:3
song of cheer again, 736:13
song of sixpence, 858:12
songs not heard before, 99:26
still wouldst thou s., 437:12
strange that death should s., 178:25
the Lord's song, 20:11
thee a song in thy praise, 379:10
thee to thy rest, 207:15
thou smoothly, 232:2
tongue of the dumb shall s., 27:32
tongue the Savior's glory, 129:2
unto him a new song, 16:30
unto the Lord a new song, 19:1
we must laugh and s., 640:19
we s. sin, 798:10
what shall I s., 861:11
whatever well made, 643:3
when birds do s., 200:5
willow willow willow, 215:1
wrath of Achilles, 52:1
ye heavens earth reply, 322:23

Singe, flame that cannot s. sleeve, 641:7
  my white head, 216:18
  so hot that it s. yourself, 230:20
Singe, ich s. wie der Vogel singt, 363:*n*3
Singer accompany the king, 382:11
  he the s. passes, 541:24
  idle s. of empty day, 557:1
  none bear beside the s., 408:10
  sans Wine Song S., 471:12
  thou s. I song, 564:15
Singers, God sent S. on earth, 466:21
  long ago was one of the s., 499:13
Singest of summer, 437:6
  soaring ever s., 429:17
Singeth all night long, 200:22
  quiet tune, 400:15
Singin' in the rain, 740:19
  this'll be day I die, 839:7
Singing and making melody, 45:29
  come before his presence with s., 19:3
  come with s. unto Zion, 28:15
  comes deer to my s., 856:6
  delight in s., 408:10
  each morning, 740:9
  garland and s. robes, 262:10
  go s. as far as we go, 95:29
  hear mermaids s., 233:13
  heard the mermaids s., 717:16
  heart like s. bird, 547:14
  hollaing and s. of anthems, 191:18
  I hear America s., 518:14
  in the choir, 846:2
  in the Wilderness, 471:5
  locust of soul, 809:4
  masons building roofs, 192:21
  of Mount Abora, 401:18
  perhaps s. bird come, 122:26
  sad or s. weather, 568:20
  sets even a wise man s., 55:12
  songs of expectation, 555:4
  still dost soar, 429:17
  those who are s. today, 563:9
  till his heaven fills, 541:14
  time of the s. of birds, 25:17
  we are nest of s. birds, 326:6
  where nightingales s., 726:19
  where weeping willows, 539:14
  with muses of Helicon begin s., 56:1
  woodthrush s. through fog, 719:18
Singist, as s. not success, 555:13
Single, beauty draws with s. hair, 309:7
  best augury is to fight, 53:10
  Dram of Heaven, 547:2
  draw you with s. hair, 241:*n*3
  eternity only a s. night, 76:12
  every s. one is right, 634:5
  flight of planes, 756:16
  for my s. self, 195:18
  from s. crime know nation, 97:7
  Hound, 545:19
  man in possession of fortune, 406:3
  married to s. life, 272:10
  must begin with a s. step, 59:12
  nature's double name, 207:17
  no s. nation have monopoly, 705:5
  no such creature as s. individual, 791:15
  not a s. kind of strife, 56:7
  nothing in world s., 429:7
  out aristocratic pretensions, 676:16

Single *(continued)*
  secret will be man, 740:16
  soul in two bodies, 79:14
  spies, 206:8
Single-minded like migratory birds, 677:5
Sings at grave-making, 206:17
  below inveterate scars, 720:9
  church ain't out till fat lady s., 850:15
  each song twice, 492:5
  for his supper, 857:20
  he that s. lasting song, 642:3
  in boat on bay, 482:15
  know why caged bird s., 660:2
  lark at heaven's gate s., 225:12
  like an angel s., 190:5
  moment when the bird s., 834:1
  morn not waking till she s., 163:16
  nightingale s. all day, 412:11
  nightly s. the staring owl, 177:17
  on orchard bough, 492:4
  this truth poet s., 481:19
  thus s. he Cuckoo, 177:16
  tune without the words, 544:11
  yonder pine that s., 85:7
Singularity almost invariably a clue, 617:3
  poetry surprise not by S., 440:5
Singulars, statements of history are s.,
    81:12
Sinister resonance, 612:*n*1
  urge to kill s., 829:5
Sink downward to darkness, 686:19
  heart and voice oppressed, 511:11
  hold you as I s., 104:26
  load would s. a navy, 231:4
  loose lips s. ships, 851:16
  Neptune s. ship on even keel, 106:24
  not gross to s. but light, 173:19
  of uncertainty and error, 280:8
  or swim, 185:7
  or swim live or die, 414:12
  or swim together, 653:18
  present repute for freedom, 514:18
  pride of power s., 344:6
  raft which will never s., 376:13
  to nothingness do s., 439:10
  tosses but doesn't s., 123:29
  who s. to rest, 336:15
Sinking into inferiority, 414:2
  kind of alacrity in s., 190:31
  knowledge like s. star, 481:11
  rats desert s. ship, 108:*n*6
  someone s. today, 600:13
Sinks and I am ready to depart, 408:11
  day-star in ocean bed, 262:5
  gross flesh s. downward, 180:17
  honor s., 341:2
  with bubbling groan, 421:27
Sinn, das kommt mir nicht aus dem S.,
    442:*n*4
Sinned against my brother the ass, 128:6
  in Adam's fall s., 296:7
  more s. against than sinning, 216:23
  we have s. against thee, 29:13
Sinner, dead s. revised and edited, 580:18
  desireth not death of s., 49:22
  forgive some s., 691:4
  merciful to me a s., 40:9
  of his memory, 229:11
  too weak to be a s., 218:13

Sinner *(continued)*
  whether he be s., 41:14
  who write with no dinner, 724:13
Sinners, call s. to repentance, 35:19
  came to save s., 46:15
  God and s. reconciled, 323:1
  if s. entice thee, 20:23
  miserable s., 51:3
  old s. have brawny consciences, 270:10
  publicans and s., 35:34
  Son of man betrayed to s., 37:31
  standeth in the way of s., 15:27
  we are s. all, 172:14
Sinning, more sinned against than s., 216:23
Sin's, sometimes s. a pleasure, 423:13
Sins, acknowledge our manifold s., 50:18
  be all my s. remembered, 204:1
  charity creates multitute of s., 605:14
  double for all her s., 27:38
  few love to hear s. they act, 225:7
  forgiveness of s., 49:14
  Forgiveness of s., 50:3
  forgiveth s. and saveth, 31:26
  her s. which are many, 39:13
  lie in dark weep for s., 519:16
  love covereth all s., 21:16
  manifold s. and wickedness, 49:18
  multitude of s., 47:31
  of commission mortal, 330:1
  of fathers upon children, 71:5
  of omission venial, 330:1
  of the world, 49:12
  oldest s. newest ways, 192:10
  other s. only speak, 137:*n*3
  remembrance of precedent s., 242:6
  scarlet books read, 653:15
  shed for remission of s., 37:27
  snows and s., 567:18
  takes away s. of the world, 49:12
  they are inclined to, 271:4
  though your s. be as scarlet, 26:10
  weep for her s. at other, 717:2
Sion, never climbed Mount S., 801:8
Sioux owned the world, 549:3
Sip, can't be tasted in s., 496:32
  lifeblood seemed to s., 400:6
Sipped no sup, 565:25
Sir Oracle, 187:20
Siren, listen to song of s., 352:13
  song of s. nor voice of hyena, 165:4
  tears, 227:18
Sirens, what song the S. sang, 256:17
Sires, heroic s., 289:14
Sires' age worse than grandsires', 100:2
Sisera, mother of S. looked out window,
    10:34
  stars fought against S., 10:31
Sister Anne do you see, 846:4
  art my mother and my s., 14:21
  Caroline, 657:3
  Jerusalem thy s. calls, 376:6
  live a barren s. all your life, 180:18
  Milky Way s. in whiteness, 689:20
  ministering angel my s., 206:28
  never praise s. to s., 632:12
  poverty is s. of beggary, 75:24
  shouts with s., 482:15
  Sidney's s. Pembroke's mother, 247:12
  still gentler s. woman, 378:18

Skinside is inside, 657:5
Skip, I cut down trees s. and jump, 843:1
Skipped, mountains s. like rams, 19:21
Skipper had taken daughter, 466:4
Skirmish of wit, 194:6
Skirt, sound of her silk s., 89:17
Skirts, God's s., 491:14
Skittish, unstaid and s. in motions, 209:21
Skittles, beer and s., 496:n1, 533:2
    porter and s., 496:4
Skugg, here S. lies, 320:16
Skull beneath the skin, 718:6
    of a lawyer, 206:20
    place of s., 38:6
    some poor fellow's s., 405:6
Skulls, hell paved with priests' s., 119:2
    leaden they don't weep, 751:8
    place of s., 420:15
Skuttle-Fish, rejoice with S., 338:4
Sky, above the vaulted s., 431:15
    above world stretched the s., 734:15
    against pearl-gray s., 697:2
    all could see was s. water birds, 784:5
    all the milky s., 637:3
    and sea and land, 620:3
    banners flout the s., 218:25
    beautiful as the s., 520:13
    believe power and goodness in s., 140:7
    believe these ships from s., 140:7
    blue ethereal s., 301:14
    blue s. bends over all, 401:8
    blue s. of spring, 535:16
    blue s. over my head, 410:13
    bluebird carries s., 505:5
    Brain wider than S., 545:11
    bridal of earth and s., 250:9
    broad and peaceful s., 813:9
    changes when wives, 199:29
    daffodil s., 485:9
    daily bread of eyes, 454:5
    descending black and white, 800:13
    diamond in the s., 414:5
    dusky night rides down s., 321:18
    Eagle looking at s., 439:1
    ethereal s., 263:23
    fair weather for s. is red, 36:22
    forehead of morning s., 262:5
    go forth under open s., 432:8
    goal the s., 851:12
    guides through s. thy flight, 432:11
    immeasurably lofty, 542:10
    inverted Bowl we call S., 471:22
    isolation of s., 686:19
    like lead, 776:10
    lingered under benign s., 509:4
    living air and blue s., 391:4
    lonely sea and s., 680:15
    lonesome place against s., 601:7
    lose itself in s., 494:5
    lyre within s., 478:3
    mauve and rosy s., 746:11
    measure pathways of s., 97:31
    membrane of bright blue s., 791:16
    moving moon went up s., 400:11
    Music shall untune s., 284:17
    no bright reversion in s., 309:28
    no foreign s. protected me, 725:8
    no limits but s., 156:14
    none knew color of the s., 655:16

Sky (*continued*)
    nothing but hath bound in s., 174:27
    nothing but s. and the ocean, 401:20
    November's s., 396:13
    old and true as s., 634:13
    only one shining in s., 391:18, 692:16
    our Father the S., 855:18
    peopling earth waters s., 289:15
    pie in s., 684:10
    prisoners call the s., 605:16
    publish yourselves to s., 583:9
    pulling blanket off eastern s., 855:14
    rain from dirty s., 804:20
    rainbow in the s., 392:7
    ring out to wild s., 484:13
    robes spun of Iris' woof, 260:17
    sea rising nor s. clouding, 586:5
    sent him down the s., 534:3
    shoulder s. drink ale, 619:12
    silence in starry s., 395:1
    slope down which s. flows, 752:13
    somewhere S. touches Earth, 853:3
    soul larger than s., 441:10
    sparkling with diamonds, 622:13
    split the s. in two, 734:15
    spread out against s., 717:6
    squired glacier woman down s., 753:16
    stand at Judgment Seat, 632:19
    star drooped in western s., 520:14
    star that burns forever in s., 856:10
    steal across the s., 555:3
    sweep cobwebs from s., 859:11
    take love together to s., 579:12
    tears of s., 315:13
    teatray in the s., 550:12
    threw wild hands toward s., 655:19
    tree cannot grow in s., 93:10
    tree struggles to reach s., 770:3
    under wide and starry s., 599:6
    went out under s. Muse, 603:5
    what if s. were to fall, 88:18
    wide s. above me, 750:6
    will cave in on him, 734:15
    wrote across s. in stars, 723:7
Skye, over sea to S., 616:9
Skyey, servile to s. influences, 211:18
Sky's, rip-tooth of s. acetylene, 753:13
    the limit, 156:n4
    whatever s. above me, 422:26
Skyscrapers, send s. toppling, 781:14
Slack, observing me grow s., 251:2
Slain a thousand men with jawbone, 11:4
    all whom war hath s., 236:5
    by fair cruel maid, 209:25
    crippled palsied s., 673:8
    death ere thou s. another, 247:12
    Earl of Murray, 854:9
    from graves of our s., 444:11
    frosts are s., 567:18
    her own eyes see him s., 556:10
    honor those they have s., 526:3
    if s. thinks he is s., 51:24
    Jabberwock, 551:11
    more come through alive than are s., 53:20
    time has s. desire, 817:18
    Saul hath s. his thousands, 11:31
    some s. in war, 179:28
    think he is slain, 453:22

Slain (*continued*)
    through our love is my lord s., 139:12
    where s. are there is she, 15:16
    with him beauty s., 173:26
    wounded but not s., 853:n1
Slam, Emily set doors ajar and s. them, 672:13
Slamming, lulled by s. of iron, 780:9
Slander, give lie to s., 419:3
    lives upon succession, 174:34
    one to s. other to get news to you, 562:10
    protest discrimination and s., 674:8
    that gradually soaks into mind, 63:7
    vindication against s., 476:11
    whose edge sharper than sword, 225:17
Slanderous, death by s. tongues, 195:12
Slanged, acquaintance sneered and s., 653:11
Slant, certain S. of light, 544:12
Slanting-eyed, lame wrinkled and s., 53:7
Slapped, god reached down s. earth's face, 839:5
Slashed, she s. him, 860:22
Slaughter, as an ox goeth to the s., 21:9
    as lamb to the s., 28:23
    like sheep to s., 350:4
    love of s., 709:4
    of individuals, 782:4
    pillage devastation, 666:13
    threatenings and s., 42:6
Slaughtered, blood of s., 656:15
    saints, 263:15
    this s. age, 787:1
Slaughtering machine went on, 682:1
Slaughters of race writ, 575:21
Slave, be no s. have no s., 474:14
    before I'd be a s., 863:10
    believing s. better than idolater, 120:14
    commonly called S. Trade, 318:21
    deserves to be a s., 386:10
    eternal s. to mortal rage, 226:18
    every sixth man a s., 398:12
    fingering s., 392:2
    freeman s. patrician plebeian, 511:1
    frees her s. again, 845:21
    galley s. to pen, 445:4
    God commands s. to rise, 386:2
    half s. half free, 474:9
    I speak for the s., 507:24
    in some degree a s., 350:10
    man in armor s., 495:5
    man once despot and s., 428:13
    no s. on our land, 468:5
    not be s. not be master, 474:11
    not like quarry-s., 432:10
    of Words, 433:11
    passion's s., 204:17
    prison only house in s. State, 505:19
    prisoner but not s., 276:n1
    rogue and peasant s., 203:27
    save Union without freeing s., 475:13
    seen how man made s. s. made a man, 509:9
    sleep soundly as wretched s., 193:16
    spirit below, 710:13
    this s. country, 447:4
    thought's s. of life, 187:5
    to animosity or affection, 350:10
    to fate chance kings, 236:8

Slave (*continued*)
to no sect, 311:14
to thousands, 213:33
Trade, 318:21
what to s. your Fourth of July, 509:10
you were a Christian S., 594:13
Slaveholders, men and women of North s., 521:18
Slaveholding nation, 450:6
Slavekeeping inconsistent, 336:14
Slaveowners, men and women of South s., 521:18
sons of former s., 823:2
Slavery, chains and s., 353:3, 380:10
children given into s., 141:12
children sold into s., 443:10
economic s. nobody's business, 698:2
economical relations of s., 450:15
every tone testimony against s., 509:8
freedom is s., 765:16
great fortune great s., 107:6
hear anyone arguing for s., 477:5
I hate s., 474:7
ignorance only s., 554:7
intellectuals deserve s., 683:16
mechanical s., 605:13
never in such s. as to forgo kindred, 109:19
of half of humanity, 777:14
of the machine, 605:13
or death, 301:21
preferred death before s., 109:20
price of chains and s., 353:3
they can have anywhere, 344:15
we maintain s., 507:25
when s. comes upon him, 55:17
where S. is Liberty cannot be, 490:1
wrecks of s., 567:6
writing instrument of s., 336:14
wrong and demoralizing, 605:13
Slaves, all persons held as s., 475:15
Americans freemen or s., 349:14
at the mill with s., 268:31
Britons never will be s., 318:8
cannot breathe in England, 347:27
civilization requires s., 605:13
fit instruments to make s., 323:4
fought for freedom, 450:10
howe'er contented, 347:6
if any should be s., 477:5
lies religion of s., 649:1
machines s. not masters, 617:22
man wills us s., 355:12
necessity the creed of s., 381:4
no legal s. except mistress of house, 465:6
our new mechanical s., 742:13
practical men s. of defunct economist, 702:4
save Union by freeing s., 475:13
songs of s. testimony, 509:8
sons of former s., 823:2
tired of ruling over s., 330:14
to do ugly horrible work, 605:13
tyrants and s., 341:25
who fear to speak, 514:9
Slavish, emancipation of s. part of mankind, 350:16
imitators you s. herd, 101:11
mercenary, 349:13

Slavs, Chuds S. and Krivchians, 125:12
Slay, reject prophets s. them, 526:3
though he s. me yet will I trust, 14:14
Slayer, if s. thinks he slays, 51:24
red s., 453:22
envy s. the silly, 13:36
Slaying of hypothesis by ugly fact, 537:4
Slays envy s. itself by own arrows, 122:23
if slayer thinks he s., 51:24
moves mates s., 471:19
slayer think he s., 453:22
war its thousands s., 349:3
war never s. bad man, 68:16
Sleave, ravelled s. of care, 220:16
Sleek expensive girls I teach, 818:9
fat and s. a true hog, 101:1
Sleek-headed men, 195:22
Sleekit, wee s. cow'rin', 377:10
Sleep a wink, 312:12
abundance will not suffer him to s., 24:13
after toil, 161:3
among lonely hills, 395:1
an act or two, 231:18
an after-dinner's s., 211:19
and a forgetting, 393:11
and feed, 205:35
and if life was bitter, 569:15
as they sleep even so, 568:18
ask not whom s. beside, 618:9
at ten, 451:18
azure-lidded s., 437:2
balmy s., 305:23
be in bed and s. not, 746:16
beneath these weeds, 651:15
better s. with sober cannibal, 516:8
blessings on him who invented s., 158:31
brother of death, 53:16
Brother to Death, 169:3
by a s. to say we end, 203:33
cannot break his s., 471:8
can't s. with the river forever, 841:5
care driveth away s., 32:44
care-charmer S., 169:3
centuries of stony s., 639:7
cheap pleasure, 158:31
Church s. and feed at once, 718:5
councilor ought not s. whole night, 52:13
covers man like cloak, 158:31
curtained s., 220:9
death an eternal s., 381:3
death is a s., 568:19
death like s. steal, 428:2
Death's brother S., 97:25
death's counterfeit, 220:24
Death's twin brother, 53:n1
deep and dreamless s., 558:5
Do I wake or s., 437:15
even in our s. pain, 65:5
exposition of s. upon me, 181:26
first sweet s. of night, 429:8
flowers as in causes s., 253:13
folding of the hands to s., 21:5
freed from everlasting s., 256:25
friend of woe, 405:15
from mother's s. fell into State, 793:6
full of sweet dreams, 436:8
fullness even of s., 53:12
gates of S., 98:2

Sleep (*continued*)
gentle s., 191:33
Glamis hath murdered s., 220:17
go home and get s., 650:7
God bless man who invented s., 158:n7
great gift of s., 594:12
green ideas s. furiously, 820:8
he giveth his beloved s., 20:5
Homer may s., 102:n1
hour's s. before midnight, 252:10
how s. the brave, 336:15
I always s. upon ale, 305:3
I s. alone, 58:3
I will not give s. to mine eyes, 20:9
ignominy s. with thee, 187:7
in Abraham's bosom, 174:11
in dull cold marble, 231:5
in exile, 603:13
in s. a king, 227:1
in soot I s., 372:4
in the night, 372:19
in the shade, 411:9
innocent s., 220:16
is drink for the thirsty, 158:31
is meat for the hungry, 158:31
it is a gentle thing, 400:14
itself must end, 256:25
kind assassin S., 809:8
lay me down in peace and s., 15:31
lay me down to s., 296:15
Lord God caused a deep s., 5:21
Macbeth does murder s., 220:16
Macbeth shall s. no more, 220:17
medicine thee to sweet s., 214:6
men such as s. o' nights, 195:22
miles to go before s., 669:15
most gentle s., 191:n1
most things s. lying, 250:14
mountains in primeval s., 534:9
nature's soft nurse, 191:33
neither night nor day, 218:27
neither slumber nor s., 19:30
never s. with anyone with worse troubles, 782:1
nevermore to s. again, 662:17
nice quiet s., 650:7
no more, 220:16
no s. till morn, 420:17
nor shall this peace s. with her, 231:16
not dream not, 508:19
not hypocrites in s., 410:19
not my design to s., 254:17
nothing s. in that cellar, 780:4
of a laboring man, 24:13
of death, 203:33
of Lethe, 99:1
of perpetual night, 94:4
of reason produces monsters, 362:14
off to death, 678:7
old and gray full of s., 637:4
on his left side, 756:4
on my Love in thy cold bed, 249:1
one ever-during night, 231:21
one short s. past, 236:9
only s., 492:9
out the thought of it, 228:23
out this great gap, 223:4
past first s. in Persia, 256:25
perchance to dream, 203:33

Slow *(continued)*
confidence plant of s. growth, 323:5
drag of days, 69:14
drag the s. barge, 348:23
drags its s. length along, 308:17
drip over stones, 780:9
he that is s. to anger, 21:37
how s. shadow creeps, 653:5
I am s. of speech, 8:8
I am s. of study, 180:26
in assembling, 73:17
man catches up with swift, 54:27
march of human mind s., 344:13
Meander's margent green, 260:26
melancholy s., 340:14
of a s. tongue, 8:8
rises worth, 323:13
silent walk, 576:5
sort of country, 551:14
Spondee stalks, 402:8
swift s. sweet sour, 587:10
talk low talk s., 777:9
tarry awhile says S., 858:9
tremulous cadence s., 530:20
vaster than empires and more s., 276:27
walk it s. where you go, 829:11
wisely and s., 183:19
Slow-breathing unconscious Kosmos, 583:4
Slowest, haste of fool s. thing, 291:9
Slowly, ever forward but s., 356:10
follies of town crept s., 342:14
let him twist s. s. in wind, 814:19
lowing herd wind s., 334:8
mills of God grind s., 255:5
night Pass more s., 426:9
rase she up, 854:1
run O horses of night, 171:*n*2
run s. horses of night, 105:3
silently now moon, 662:8
Slug-a-bed, sweet S., 248:16
Sluggard, go to the ant thou s., 21:4
voice of the s., 304:5
Sluggardy, May wol have no s. anyght, 135:17
Slughorn to my lips I set, 217:*n*2
Slugs leave their lair, 402:11
Sluice, every s. of knowledge opened, 350:18
Slum, see one city s. seen all, 802:16
Slumber, death is s., 427:16
did my spirit seal, 392:1
he that keepeth thee will not s., 19:30
honey-heavy dew of s., 196:5
I must s. again, 304:5
kindly earth s., 482:2
lie still and s., 304:4
love itself s. on, 430:19
more sweet than toil, 480:21
neither s. nor sleep, 19:30
nor s. nor a roof, 735:12
ports of s. open, 192:6
seal sense in s., 662:12
to mine eyelids, 20:9
to soothing s. seven, 159:*n*5
where s. abbots, 313:24
yet a little s., 21:5
Slumbered, you have but s. here, 182:15
Slumbering in open air, 402:11
might half s., 436:4
rouse the s. morn, 259:13

Slumbering *(continued)*
scepter o'er s. world, 305:24
thoughts, 256:25
Slumber's chain bound me, 412:7
Slumbers, fire extinguished often s., 257:12
how imagine unquiet s., 509:4
pleasing dreams s. light, 397:3
soul dead that s., 465:17
sweet s. of virtuous, 302:1
what s. in background, 381:12
Slump, ain't in no s., 814:10
Slums, gay intimacy of s., 766:3
turned cities into s., 746:2
Sly, Questioner who sits so s., 375:12
self-pitying dirty s., 743:18
tough and devilish s., 497:24
Smack and tang of elemental things, 601:6
my life s. sweet, 495:10
of age in you, 191:12
Small, air thoroughly s. and dry, 719:10
all things how s. soever, 286:2
and could not hope, 776:11
and great beasts, 19:11
buoy too s. for sight, 217:18
but sullen horn, 337:2
cabin build there, 637:1
candle light a thousand, 247:10
cannot reach the s., 161:15
choice in rotten apples, 175:22
chronicle s. beer, 213:12
compare great things with s., 95:15, 265:21
cottage s., 794:1
country with few people, 59:20
creatures great and s., 508:7
day of s. nations past, 563:10
day of s. things, 30:36
eating is s. good thing, 833:9
felony to drink s. beer, 172:18
frizzled stale and s., 800:19
gray coffee pot, 710:2
great matter or s., 32:8
grind exceeding s., 255:5
have plodders won, 176:20
home where s. experience grows, 175:23
hot bird, 597:4
house and large garden, 275:5
how s. of all hearts endure, 325:3
in s. proportions beauties see, 238:14
is beautiful, 787:14
is it so s. a thing, 529:1
Latin and less Greek, 238:7
make my s. elves coats, 181:13
man may not be entrusted, 63:22
manye s. maken a greet, 138:1
men afraid of writings, 349:9
mice and such s. deer, 216:33
mighty things from s. beginnings grow, 282:15
model of barren earth, 179:28
my house though s., 251:27
nobody has such s. hands, 740:7
one a strong nation, 28:30
one pill makes you s., 834:6
out of s. beginnings, 247:10
potatoes, 543:14
rain down can rain, 843:18
rock holds back great wave, 54:17
sea so great boat so s., 847:10

Small *(continued)*
service is true service, 395:20
showers last long, 179:11
speaks s. like a woman, 190:14
still s. voice, 12:32
still s. voice of gratitude, 335:20
sweet courtesies of life, 333:6
thing analogy of great things, 93:3
things and silence, 788:17
things both great and s., 401:2
things make base men proud, 172:16
vices do appear, 217:24
young women of s. fortune, 406:9
Smaller and dryer than will, 719:10
behavior better than that of s. man, 778:13
fleas that on him prey, 299:4
made s. with art, 750:11
Smallest, God hides in the s. pieces, 851:*n*4
orb like angel sings, 190:5
star of s. magnitude, 265:23
Small-knowing, unlettered s. soul, 176:23
Smart, as the s. ship grew, 576:1
girls that are so s., 307:23
shall s. for it, 21:17
some will s. for it, 195:8
Smash, Harlem needed something to s., 813:5
why s. the chairs, 472:17
Smashed up things, 746:7
Smattering of everything, 495:17
Smell, ancient and fish-like s., 229:28
begin to s. a rat, 157:20
blood of British man, 217:3
blood of Englishman, 861:10
dew and rain, 250:22
dog who can s. someone, 811:3
far worse than weeds, 227:5
fire whose gown burns, 251:11
flowers along the way, 733:9
good s. of old clothes, 712:18
I love the s. of napalm, 833:11
lilies that fester s. worse, 227:5
lost sea s., 719:16
of burning fills air, 653:4
of the lamp, 83:7
rose by any name s. as sweet, 183:3
sweet and blossom in dust, 254:7
sweet keen s., 542:7
yes to s. pork, 188:2
Smellest so sweet, 214:28
Smelleth the battle afar off, 15:15
Smelling of the lamp, 653:17
Smells, gas s. awful, 738:14
he s. April and May, 190:28
heaven's breath s. wooingly, 219:15
like gangrene, 678:1
not of itself but thee, 238:3
of inkwells rise, 834:3
to heaven, 205:14
Smelt heaviest ore of body, 707:12
Smile, affliction s. again, 176:25
and be a villain, 202:24
as I do now, 473:19
at claims of descent, 480:13
better last s., 297:*n*2
did he s. work to see, 374:6
disdainful s., 334:14
dwells longer, 662:1

Soldier's *(continued)*
pride touched to quick, 491:8
sound of white s. axe, 533:9
Soldiers are dreamers, 712:2
believe s. nothing safe, 548:4
bore dead bodies by, 185:3
by two and by three, 853:25
Christian s., 555:2
citizens of death's land, 712:1
French s. with artilleryman, 542:10
grow like savages as s. will, 193:26
Ireland gives England s., 541:22
of Christ arise, 322:26
old s. never die, 690:12, 850:20
old s. surest, 244:1
regarded wounded s. in envious way,
655:12
sailors and airmen, 667:14
Soldiers', steel my s. hearts, 193:17
Soldiery, Emperor's drunken s., 641:5
licentious s., 345:5
Sole arbiter is taste, 480:1
crown of head to s., 194:29
go it s. alone, 671:2
God beside whom is none, 4:11
rest for the s. of her foot, 6:29
unbusy thing, 402:11
Soleil bas taché d'horreurs mystiques, 603:n9
Solemn drifting down river, 560:15
fillet, 453:19
gorgeous palaces s. temples, 230:9
he says with s. air, 377:15
one sweetly s. thought, 535:19
pride yours, 477:2
sapping s. creed, 421:1
stillness lay, 488:15
suits of s. black, 200:29
this her s. bird, 266:18
Solemnest of industries, 546:8
Solemnities, feasts and high s., 261:9
Solemnized their obsequies, 256:13
with pomp and parade, 351:9
Soles, eats s. offen shoes, 750:8
Soliciting, still s. eye, 215:23
Solid earth actual world, 505:13
for fluidity, 665:12
heaven presents s. hue, 669:10
man of Boston, 467:13
massy hard particles, 291:5
nothing s. is its s. self, 687:19
pudding empty praise, 313:16
sop of all this s. globe, 207:26
this too too s. flesh, 201:1
virtue, 214:23
Solidarity, family and clan s., 644:8
independent of differences, 815:13
loses s. with other women, 778:1
Solidity, atoms preserved by absolute s.,
92:16
give appearance of s. to pure wind,
765:13
Solitary and cannot impart it, 326:10
as oyster, 497:12
be not s. be not idle, 242:8
convent's s. gloom, 309:25
God setteth the s. in families, 18:7
how doth the city sit s., 29:26
if idle be not s. if s. be not idle, 329:1
love all s. places, 428:15

Solitary *(continued)*
men know friendship, 661:20
poor nasty brutish, 246:12
quite still and s., 701:5
rare are s. woes, 206:n2
sail that rises, 502:2
shriek, 423:17
simile that s. shines, 313:2
stirred by s. cloud, 291:12
took their s. way, 268:17
Solitude at depth of human condition, 794:3
bliss of s., 394:8
companion so feel s. more, 659:5
companionable as s., 507:8
drives poet to s., 529:7
each guardian of other's s., 677:8
friend to genius, 456:28
how sweet is s., 347:19
I love tranquil s., 431:2
independence of s., 455:10
is sweet, 347:19
island s. unsponsored free, 686:19
makes s. calls it peace, 422:8
not exchange s. for anything, 791:5
nurse of souls s., 514:11
O S. where are charms, 347:21
of his own heart, 463:4
one chair for s., 507:9
one hundred years of s., 820:10
religion experiences in s., 582:13
safeguard to mediocrity, 456:28
sometimes best society, 267:27
Soul to S. retires, 471:1
sweet retired s., 260:29
teach us to die, 421:9
Solitudes, in love two s. touch, 677:2
pierced our s., 453:3
Solo game, 673:9
Solomon, behold a greater than S., 36:1
curtains of S., 25:12
Grundy, 859:17
in all his glory, 34:20
King David and King S., 623:11
loved many strange women, 12:21
priests in temple of S., 458:24
Proverbs of S., 497:25
wisdom of S., 12:15
Solomon's, song of songs which is S., 25:11
Solon was under a delusion, 77:17
Solution, dissatisfaction with other s., 454:11
final s., 782:4
final s. of Jewish question, 737:7
for world peace, 690:13
of international problems, 761:15
part of s. or of problem, 831:10
waste elocution on s., 566:5
Solutions, two equally convenient s., 603:2
Solvency a matter of temperament, 636:6
Solvent, American life powerful s., 629:13
Somber, I am the s. one, 469:4
not as s. as December, 821:16
Some are born great, 209:30
born mad some remain so, 773:12
born posthumously, 590:7
come to take their ease, 231:18
day you'll know, 818:6
for adventure, 709:4
gave white bread, 857:2
must watch some sleep, 205:6

Some *(continued)*
of you with Pilate, 180:11
quick to arm, 709:4
said John print it, 281:12
say world will end in fire, 669:11
talk of Alexander, 846:11
that shadows kiss, 188:28
the portion of s., 289:23
to kill cankers, 181:13
war with rere-mice, 181:13
will smart for it, 195:8
Somebody, could've had class been s., 794:15
had s. loved him, 812:13
how dreary to be S., 544:13
may be looking, 691:16
necessary to s., 457:2
said it couldn't be done, 693:7
to hew and hack, 271:12
when everyone is s., 566:8
Somebody's always throwing bricks, 685:2
even I be in S. hand, 575:5
Someday I must go into that, 671:5
inner light shine forth, 366:n4
love as though s. hate hate as though s.
love, 67:n3
to prove our foe, 67:9
Someone better be prepared, 669:19
dog who can smell s., 811:3
else's freedom, 804:1
find next morning it was s. else, 384:9
gently rapping, 478:20
had blundered, 484:26
is sinking today, 600:13
not be something but s., 700:14
someone else begat, 671:5
to love and someone to love you, 620:6
touch my person to s. else's, 519:13
we can lean on, 838:6
while s. else is eating, 775:12
Something about a martini, 763:10
attempted something done, 466:9
beautiful for God, 785:5
bright and alien, 763:n2
cool s. flowing over hand, 690:7
crabwise across snow, 815:3
dead in each of us, 605:20
death has s. to be said for it, 809:12
else is alive, 825:3
ere the end, 481:13
everything else is about s., 840:10
everything good for s., 283:25
expect s. for nothing, 601:16
fame created s. of nothing, 258:13
far more interfused, 391:4
for modern stage, 709:2
good and bad of every land, 504:12
had greater price than life, 758:15
have all wanted to do s., 504:4
have in me s. dangerous, 207:1
he prized and is known by, 703:7
hidden behind things, 684:2
hidden go and find it, 635:15
if s. can go wrong it will, 852:10
in her gizzard, 288:25
in the wind, 174:32
in this more than natural, 203:19
in us never dies, 379:12
like a star, 671:3
lost behind Ranges, 635:15

Something *(continued)*

might be gaining on you, 774:11
must be left to chance, 377:4
nasty in woodshed, 762:5
no reasonable man expected, 729:3
not be s. but someone, 700:14
of Shorter-Catechist, 594:8
old something new, 850:13
one must be s. to do s., 364:26
rich and strange, 229:20
right in world something we trust,
    802:17
rotten in state of Denmark, 202:11
tells me but not love, 189:1
that doesn't love a wall, 668:18
that doth live, 393:14
there is s. in a face, 304:13
time for a little s., 697:7
'tis s. nothing, 213:33
to do, 514:20
too much of this, 204:17
try do s. for my country, 832:3
very like Him, 512:9
what is that s., 758:15
would turn up, 459:9
wrong with something human, 793:9
you do s. to me, 732:9
you will see s. new, 769:8
Sometime, come up and see me s., 736:n2
come up s. and see me, 736:6
did me seek, 150:2
lofty towers down-rased, 226:18
woman a s. thing, 747:5
Sometimes, arriving s. at profundity, 826:11
I feel like a motherless child, 862:27
Somewhat, I have s. against thee, 48:8
Somewhere ages hence, 669:4
beyond the curtain, 641:12
end up s. else, 805:12
Hegel remarks s., 510:6
in favored land, 630:4
over the rainbow, 752:1
people freedom light, 730:12
set forth for s., 669:7
what with all these clouds, 75:10
Somewheres east of Suez, 633:14
Somnambulist of vanished dream, 451:9
Son, Absalom my s. my s., 12:7
and heir of mongrel bitch, 216:7
antichrist denieth Father and S., 47:39
be a Man my s., 635:22
bring forth a s., 33:17
brought forth firstborn s., 39:2
Christ the S. took Father's place, 608:5
crucify S. of God afresh, 46:40
David the s. of Jesse, 12:9
dear s. of memory, 259:3
do not bet that man, 704:n2
every s. hoped to do, 608:5
every wise man's s. doth know, 209:13
false as stepdame to s., 208:7
Father S. and Holy Ghost, 38:12, 289:22
foolish s. calamity of father, 22:15
foolish s. the heaviness of his mother,
    21:14
glory be to the S., 49:25
greatness in father overwhelms s., 238:17
grim Death my s. and foe, 265:19
hang us every mother's s., 180:27

Son *(continued)*

have his s. respect him, 286:10
he was a s. of God, 746:5
his only s. myself, 337:14
if s. ask bread, 35:4
in the Jewish joke, 828:12
knew my s. was mortal, 76:3
Lord Randal my s., 854:11
man is s. of own works, 95:n11
marry s. when you will, 251:13
my beloved S., 33:29
of a Pharisee, 42:31
of Atreus, 52:25
of Bharata, 87:2
of first fish ashore, 819:13
of God goes forth to war, 416:2
of Heaven's eternal king, 258:16
of humble laborer, 693:10
of Kronos, 52:10
of man came eating and drinking, 35:34
of man coming in cloud, 40:14
of man is betrayed, 37:31
of man nowhere to lay head, 35:14
of man that thou visitest him, 15:32
of man which is a worm, 14:32
of the living God, 36:24
of the morning, 27:3
of the Sun, 81:20
only begotten S., 40:46
out of Egypt called my s., 33:20
prince subject Father S., 235:26
prodigal s., 39:35
punch hole in s. of a bitch, 852:16
rather be worm than s. of man, 713:14
reverence for his s., 286:10
seek father who need s., 797:5
sighed as lover obeyed as s., 354:1
struck father when s. swore, 241:20
the carpenter's s., 36:9
this is my s. Telemachus, 481:12
this my s. was dead, 39:37
thou art ever with me, 39:38
thou art the S. of God, 36:18
till he gets wife, 538:9
to her s. she ches, 843:10
Tom the piper's s., 858:16
unfeathered thing a s., 283:10
unto us a s. is given, 26:31
virgin shall bear a s., 26:28
where one s. only, 658:7
wise s. maketh a glad father, 21:14
woman behold thy s., 41:39
wrath of Peleus' s., 309:18
you are young my s., 78:15
Son, j'aime le s. du cor, 443:n1
Song, a god has given the lyre and s., 53:13
all my s. would be, 461:18
burden of my s., 843:20
burthen of his s., 352:6
dance and Provençal s., 437:7
does Africa know s. of me, 706:7
echo of mournful s., 472:23
fable s. or fleeting shade, 248:18
famed in s. famous Athens, 66:10
filled thicket with honeyed s., 75:5
fishers of, 613:15
full lasting is s., 541:24
gentlemen singing this s., 491:12
give us s. to cheer, 556:7

Song *(continued)*

glorious s. of old, 488:15
good s. ringing clear, 630:7
had been longer, 858:3
hear a little s., 364:2
heel on throat of my s., 738:4
in England's s. forever, 627:5
in thy praise, 379:10
Jehovah is my s., 27:1
learn suffering teach in s., 428:19
let satire be my s., 419:12
let them take it, 638:10
listen to s. of siren, 352:13
Lord is my strength and s., 8:25
made s. a coat, 638:10
moralize my s., 160:16
needless Alexandrine ends s., 308:17
never heard in tale or s., 260:15
new unhallowed s., 612:23
night-walkers' s., 641:5
oaten stop or pastoral s., 337:1
of a merryman, 565:25
of Africa, 706:7
of faithful Penelope, 55:25
of Harvest-home, 487:7
of night's sweet bird, 430:15
of siren nor voice of hyena, 165:4
of sixpence, 858:12
of songs, 25:11
of the Shirt, 446:3
on wings of s., 442:5
one grand sweet s., 514:2
perhaps it may turn out s., 378:9
perhaps self-same s., 437:13
pipe s. about a Lamb, 371:13
play a s. for me, 836:7
read s. not sermon, 249:n4
remake a s., 637:20
required of us a s., 20:11
revive her symphony and s., 401:19
sans Wine S., 471:12
sea grew civil at her s., 181:8
seraphically free, 541:15
shall rise to Thee, 416:6
sing one s. for old Kentucky home, 539:1
sing the Lord's s., 20:11
sing unto him a new s., 16:30
sing unto the Lord a new s., 19:1
sings lasting s., 642:3
sings s. twice over, 492:5
sold Reputation for a s., 472:3
sounded by death, 426:11
spur me into s., 642:14
suck melancholy out of s., 198:12
sweetest passage of a s., 592:15
sweetest s. ever heard, 422:22
taught Hesiod beauteous s., 56:2
theme of Art and S., 641:17
thou singer I s., 564:15
till I end my S., 162:7
time an endless s., 637:7
to sing O, 565:24
unlike subject frame s., 315:12
urge of a s., 671:7
what is s. the Sirens sang, 256:17
when this s. sung and past, 150:1
whether he hears my s., 820:1
whose note sounded by death, 426:11
wind's s. sail's shaking, 680:15

Song *(continued)*
  wine women and s., 368:9
  wrote one s., 494:2
Songe, la vie apparié a un s., 153:*n*5
Songs, all their s. sad, 664:7
  and I wrote my happy s., 371:14
  angelic s. swelling, 501:17
  ballads s. snatches, 565:7
  Book of S. and Sonnets, 190:16
  composed of tears, 488:10
  despairing s. loveliest, 488:10
  folk s. from soul sounds, 742:6
  forever new, 438:2
  harsh after s. of Apollo, 177:19
  his s. were a thousand and five, 12:14
  I who once played shepherds' s., 96:22
  laws which ran like drinking s., 74:10
  leave to sing own s., 630:5
  make and well endyte, 134:19
  muse has taught them s., 55:1
  my s. draw Daphnis home, 95:25
  no sad s. for me, 547:16
  of expectation, 555:4
  of pleasant glee, 371:13
  of sadness and mirth, 466:21
  of slaves testimony, 509:8
  of Zion, 20:11
  psalms hymns and spiritual s., 45:29
  sage daughters of Muses, 66:4
  sing s. not heard before, 99:26
  song of s., 25:11
  strongest and sweetest s. remain, 521:17
  sweetest s. saddest thought, 429:19
  we had all good s., 820:13
  where are s. of Spring, 438:13
  without words best, 555:20
  your gambols your s., 206:24
Sonitum ventis concessit, 107:*n*7
Sonnet a moment's monument, 542:1
  scorn not the s., 395:19
Sonneteer, starved hackney s., 308:21
Sonnets, Book of Songs and S., 190:16
  century of s., 493:24
  lovers' s. turned psalms, 164:10
  onlie begetter of insuing s., 225:*n*2
  prophetic s., 756:1
  written s. all his life, 423:22
Sonorous metal blowing, 264:15
Son's son till he gets wife, 538:9
Sons, Adam's s. conceived in sin, 241:8
  all her s. at play, 528:21
  anchors of mother's life, 69:2
  bears all its s. away, 304:8
  brother's s. gathering stalk and root,
    761:16
  businessmen s. of bitches, 800:1
  degenerate s. and daughters, 651:13
  earth's heedless s., 745:14
  five s. died gloriously, 477:2
  forward s. of France, 383:*n*1
  give them to your s., 859:4
  guide Arcturus with his s., 15:11
  happy to be father unto many s., 172:31
  her patient s., 341:4
  kill s. of Brutus, 143:5
  more worthless than sires, 100:2
  now we are all s. of bitches, 769:*n*1
  of Atreus, 628:2
  of Belial, 264:13

Sons *(continued)*
  of bitches do you want to live forever,
    330:*n*2
  of dark and bloody ground, 522:7
  of Edward sleep, 174:11
  of former slaves, 823:2
  of God shouted for joy, 15:6
  of men and angels say, 322:23
  of the living God, 30:12
  of the morning, 416:1
  of the prophet, 849:2
  of toil, 534:9
  see s. what things you are, 192:7
  similar to their fathers, 54:12
  that my s. may have liberty to study,
    351:14
  things as s. of heaven, 324:14
  to thy Jubilee throng, 426:13
  who Shem and Shaun s. of, 696:16
Soon as once set is our little light, 231:21
  better three hours too s., 190:26
  late and s., 394:18
  little pot and s. hot, 175:33
  said to eve Be s., 621:3
  shall thy arm, 348:23
Sooner every party breaks up, 406:19
  it's over sooner to sleep, 514:1
  kill man than hawk, 713:10
  product is no s. created, 387:2
  stay a while end the s., 166:22
Soonest, least said s. mended, 157:*n*1
Soot, dust and s. of complaints, 595:10
  in s. I sleep, 372:4
Sootfall, stirred by s. of your things, 833:15
Sooth, silly s., 209:24
Soothe a savage breast, 300:20
  cares lift thoughts, 436:5
  flattery s. ear of death, 334:17
  or wound heart, 397:17
  songs s. with their touch, 66:4
  thine ear, 337:1
  what charm s. melancholy, 341:20
Soothed by unfaltering trust, 432:10
Soothing, come lovely s. death, 520:16
  Irish language for s., 658:12
  language, 358:3
  music, 807:2
Soothsayer, painter trainer s., 113:5
Soothsayers make better living than
    truthsayers, 356:17
Sop, give s. to Cerberus, 122:24
  of all this solid globe, 207:26
Sophist, saint- nor s.-led, 528:18
Sophisters, age of s., 345:13
Sophisticated modes of discrimination, 695:5
  three on 's are s., 216:30
Sophistries, old old s. of June, 544:5
Sophocles drew men as they ought to be,
    67:*n*2, 69:*n*1
  long said, 531:1
Sorbonne, straight one day at S., 688:10
Sorcerer, I who fashioned myself s., 603:22
Sorcery of hot embraces, 730:5
Sordid boon, 394:18
  covetous s. fellow, 314:21
Sore, good for s. eyes, 299:7
  laborers have hard hands, 270:10
  labor's bath, 220:16
  stiff with toils, 521:4

Sore *(continued)*
  task, 200:16
  thy hand presseth me s., 17:9
  thy so s. loss, 621:8
Sore-eyed, he's dropsical she s., 594:*n*2
Sorrow, a little fun to match s., 555:21
  abandon learning and no s., 58:18
  and sighing shall flee away, 27:33
  bitterest cup of s., 658:*n*3
  bread in s. ate, 363:15
  breaks seasons, 174:5
  bring forth children in s., 6:9
  by s. of the heart the spirit is broken,
    21:35
  calls no time that's gone, 242:18
  death and s. our companions, 666:6
  down thou climbing s., 216:11
  drink today and drown s., 242:13
  enough to disarm, 467:3
  ere s. comes with years, 463:11
  excursion same for s. as joy, 784:4
  find s. near at hand, 63:17
  for angels, 491:23
  for lost Lenore, 479:2
  for Lycidas s. not dead, 262:5
  frowsy couch in s. steep, 380:18
  give s. words, 221:35
  glut s. on rose, 438:15
  God send them s. and shame, 141:21
  hang s. care'll kill cat, 195:*n*1
  happy in s., 159:9
  hath less power to bite, 179:5
  he that increaseth knowledge increaseth
    s., 24:2
  he that loves s., 233:9
  I have known s., 97:4
  idleness s. friend foe, 738:10
  is knowledge, 423:2
  keep thy s. to thyself, 31:8
  legacy alleviates s., 159:4
  more beautiful, 438:18
  more in s. than anger, 201:17
  naught but vast s. there, 662:13
  never comes too late, 333:22
  night of doubt and s., 555:4
  no great s. dammed up in soul, 760:14
  no more s., 49:1
  no old age only s., 627:18
  not be in s. too, 372:11
  not mine but man's, 619:19
  of love dureth overlong, 139:6
  parting is such sweet s., 183:16
  pine with fear and s., 161:23
  pure and complete s. impossible, 542:16
  regions of s., 264:2
  rent is s. income tears, 249:8
  rooted s., 222:12
  Russian people make s. a diversion, 649:3
  see if there be s. like unto my s., 29:28
  sickness and troubled mind, 249:14
  sing away s., 156:29
  sit by fireside with S., 431:7
  sit thee down s., 176:25
  sorrow's crown of s., 481:19
  source of Humor not joy but s., 562:3
  sphere of our s., 430:21
  stranger to s., 69:20
  sweet that teaches, 809:6
  to think full of s., 437:8

Sorrow *(continued)*

    unfelt s., 220:27

    unspeakable s. you bid me renew, 97:5

    veiling song in s., 430:9

    we are not sure of s., 569:2

    wear a golden s., 230:25

    what s. was bad'st her know, 334:2

    when my heart 'scaped this s., 227:2

    where s. is holy ground, 606:2

    why should s. last, 844:5

    wilt Thou live with me, 484:7

    with night we banish s., 239:11

    with s. to the grave, 7:27

    write s. on bosom of earth, 179:27

    year wake year to s., 430:8

    yet is their strength labor and s., 18:22

Sorrowful, even in laughter the heart is s., 21:30

    O sad kissed mouth how s., 568:10

    soul s. unto death, 37:28

    they were exceeding s., 37:25

Sorrow's crown of sorrow, 481:19

Sorrows, carried our s., 28:21

    come not single spies, 206:8

    disease or s. strike him, 512:9

    few s. in which income no avail, 636:7

    instruct s. to be proud, 178:3

    losses restored and s. end, 226:9

    man of s., 28:20

    of your changing face, 637:5

    when gods bring s., 55:20

    when s. have end, 844:15

    women plunged into s., 382:26

Sorry, cheeks of s. grain, 261:9

    feel s. because we cry, 582:4

    heartily s. for misdoings, 50:18

    if our wishes were gratified, 61:6

    love not having to say s., 832:9

    man who is s. will win, 59:15

    now I wrote it, 643:19

    Scheme of Things, 472:5

    truly s. man's dominion, 377:11

    union of very s. men, 53:11

    wild thing s. for itself, 707:9

Sort, ambition of meaner s., 171:19

    sager s. our deeds reprove, 231:21

    two of every s., 6:27

Sort, le s. fait les parents, 355:*n*3

Sorted out largest size, 552:6

Sorts, all s. and conditions of men, 50:6

    all s. of people, 219:19

    two s. of Christians, 743:19

Soshubble ez baskit er kittens, 593:7

So-so is good, 200:1

    rest of married life s., 750:4

    some good some s., 110:15

Sot, vous êtes un s., 277:*n*3

Soudan, home in the S., 633:9

Sought, by night on my bed I s. him, 25:20

    he s. the storms, 283:8

    I never s. world, 329:13

    it with thimbles, 553:4

    less often s. than found, 425:9

    love s. is good, 210:6

    many a thing I s., 226:8

    out many inventions, 24:25

    popularity crime when s., 289:1

    the remedy, 200:3

Sought *(continued)*

    to men that s. him sweet, 231:14

    truth not s. for, 83:17

Soul, adventure most unto itself S., 545:19

    all the agonies of the s., 543:6

    America save s. rather than face, 704:15

    amortization of heart and s., 738:3

    and in my s. am free, 276:4

    architect expends s., 364:19

    art in life of s., 624:16

    art work of body and s., 517:8

    astounded s., 808:15

    astronomy compels s. to look upwards, 77:15

    awake my s., 289:21, 318:12

    beauty in inward s., 76:6

    belongs to the idea, 573:14

    bequeath my s. to God, 168:19

    beyond ego reach, 675:12

    bitterness of my s., 27:36

    body brevity wit s., 402:2

    body Nature is and God the s., 311:7

    brevity the s. of wit, 202:33

    call upon my s., 209:9

    calm S. of all things, 528:13

    can split sky in two, 734:15

    captain of his s., 727:7

    captain of life, 95:9

    captain of my s., 594:11

    chainless s., 508:22

    charge not s. save to its ability, 121:20

    Chariot that bears Human S., 546:11

    clap hands and sing, 639:17

    cold waters to a thirsty s., 23:4

    condemned to be, 545:19

    crowd not on my s., 335:14

    damned of body and s., 633:1

    damp of night drives deeper into s. 519:14

    dare call s. my own, 464:1

    dark night of the s., 154:12

    dead that slumbers, 465:17

    deep distress humanized my S., 394:14

    digressions s. of reading, 332:12

    discipline of army, 349:12

    dissever my s. from s. of Annabel Lee, 479:19

    dividing s. and spirit, 46:38

    dream is hidden door of s., 675:12

    dull would he be of s., 392:12

    dusty answer gets s., 541:9

    eager s. biting for anger, 258:6

    eat eat me s., 292:11

    engineers of s., 649:4

    eternally unslayable, 87:2

    even-balanced s., 528:2

    extinguish hope from s., 603:18

    extinguished his s., 474:12

    fair seedtime had my s., 391:6

    false words infect the s., 76:19

    far back in s. horse prances, 707:18

    fates have given a patient s., 54:5

    fiery s., 283:8

    find prison s. destroying, 766:3

    floated into my inmost s., 516:7

    flow of s., 312:14

    folk songs from s. sounds, 742:6

    for which s. did pine, 478:9

    force, 650:10

Soul *(continued)*

    forces which threaten s., 697:3

    from out that shadow, 479:9

    gain world lose s., 36:27

    genial current of s., 334:19

    gives heart and s. away, 618:12

    go S. the body's quest, 160:7

    God changes I am the s., 569:7

    grapple them to thy s., 201:25

    grave unto a s., 178:7

    half conceal S. within, 483:14

    half of my own s., 99:3

    hang like fruit my s., 225:26

    hark hark my s., 501:17

    harrow up thy s., 202:12

    has fled, 468:8

    has many motions, 781:5

    has to itself decreed, 436:2

    hath been alone, 400:23

    hath elbow-room, 178:26

    hath not lifted his s. unto vanity, 16:19

    hath power to know all things, 233:2

    haughtiness of s., 301:19

    he restoreth my s., 16:18

    he shall preserve thy s., 19:30

    he whose s. is flat, 734:15

    heart and s. and senses forever, 493:16

    heaven take my s., 178:21

    height my s. can reach, 463:17

    her lips suck forth my s., 170:23

    him whom my s. loveth, 25:20

    his s. sincere, 335:3

    honor belongs to s., 114:17

    Horror s. of plot, 478:14

    I have liberated my s., 126:8

    I hope his s. be in glorie, 136:15

    icebergs behoove the s., 785:8

    idea does not belong to s., 573:14

    if you would keep s., 710:7

    immortal because has s., 749:1

    immortal s. and all, 707:8

    in bliss, 217:29

    in mystery s. abides, 528:12

    in prison I am not free, 606:8

    in s. of man one insular Tahiti, 516:16

    in the s. and the clod, 493:18

    into boughs does glide, 277:5

    iron entered into his s., 51:15

    is form and doth body make, 162:5

    is his own, 193:14

    is in a ferment, 436:7

    is marching on, 558:3

    is the concern of my Lord, 121:13

    its body off, 642:2

    Jesus lover of my s., 322:24

    Jonathan loved him as his own s., 11:32

    joy's s. lies in doing, 207:21

    kindled at conwiviality, 496:28

    kiss my whole s., 171:*n*1

    knows no release, 752:10

    larger than sky, 441:10

    largest and most comprehensive s., 282:16

    lay not unction to s., 205:25

    lends tongue vows, 201:31

    life meets all motion becomes its s., 399:9

    life of s., 316:28

    lift my s. to heaven, 230:23

    like cloudy opal ring, 636:14

Soul *(continued)*

listened intensely, 395:5
little s. wandering guest, 114:12
loafe and invite my s., 518:15
locust of s. unshelled, 809:4
look and body touch, 642:9
look for deed s. performed, 122:16
looks part has s. of part, 597:14
love the Lord with all thy s., 9:30
made up of wants, 513:1
man became a living s., 5:16
many a man's s. and faith, 838:5
measured by my s., 303:16
meeting s. may pierce, 259:20
merry old s., 856:18
migration of the s., 76:12
mind and s. according, 483:12
mirroring s., 528:17
more stately mansions O s., 473:11
most offending s. alive, 193:18
motorcycle parked like s. of junkyard,
    811:14
mount mount my s., 180:17
my father lived his s., 740:10
my sin my s., 755:14
my s. an't yours Mas'r, 489:20
my S. at Liberty, 544:21
my s. bright invisible green, 505:22
my s. deep like rivers, 762:9
my s. doth magnify the Lord, 38:37
my s. there is a country, 279:6
my s. thirsteth for thee, 18:3
my s. waiteth for the Lord, 20:8
my unconquerable s., 594:10
mysterious thing in s., 516:20
never taught to stray, 311:5
new depths broken in s., 413:1
nice clean s., 824:7
no coward s. mine, 509:1
no higher than s. high, 734:15
Northland s., 745:2
not bruised to pleasure s., 640:15
not more than body, 519:20
not spoken of the s., 465:17
nothing contributes more to peace of s.,
    356:13
numerical precision s. of science, 623:12
O my prophetic s., 202:15
O my s. is white, 372:1
O s. be changed to waterdrops, 171:5
of Adonais like star, 430:18
of business, 315:6
of each God of all, 399:10
of friend we've made, 625:15
of goodness in things evil, 193:13
of grandam inhabit a bird, 189:n2
of man immortal, 78:3
of music shed, 411:11
of sleeper away, 602:18
of s. sincere, 310:15
of the age, 238:5
of the plot, 478:14
of wit, 202:33
offends me to the s., 204:11
on that day no s. wronged, 122:8
one s. though many tongues, 116:15
palace of the s., 258:1
pensive s., 337:4
perches in the s., 544:11

Soul *(continued)*

perdition catch my s., 213:30
pilgrim s. in you, 637:5
Plato healer of s., 76:n3
poet brings s. into activity, 403:10
poet of Body poet of S., 519:7
poetry should enter one's s., 440:4
poor intricated s., 237:2
poor s. sat sighing, 215:1
poor s. the center, 228:4
possess s. with patience, 284:26
pouring forth s., 437:12
pray for repose of his s., 622:17
pray Lord my s. keep, 296:15
prison that can bind s., 601:12
prophet of the s., 452:18
prophetic s. of world, 227:12
Psyche my S., 479:13
pure and clear as crystal, 499:8
rapt s. in thine eyes, 259:25
receive my s. at last, 322:24
recovers radical innocence, 639:15
rejoices in truth uttered, 503:8
remembering my good friends, 179:17
rescue my s. from their destructions, 17:3
rescued s., 686:7
research into feminine s., 608:6
rest her s. she's dead, 206:21
richness of s., 79:8
riddling perplexed s., 237:2
roamed with my S., 479:13
ruled by levity pure, 796:6
sad glance glum, 565:25
sad lucidity of s., 528:9
said to s. be still, 720:23
sail leagues and leagues, 542:3
same in all creatures, 73:13
sanctum of the s., 675:12
save my s. if I have s., 535:9
saves s. in new French books, 493:9
School Intelligence make it a s., 441:2
science without conscience ruin of s.,
    146:5
seeking with s. land of Greeks, 364:5
selects her Society, 544:15
shall be required of thee, 39:29
shorten stature of s., 541:6
shrinks from all to remember, 809:1
sighed s. toward Grecian tents, 190:4
sincerely from author's s., 741:3
sinews of s., 258:14
single s. in two bodies, 79:14
sleepless s. that perished, 392:9
smithy of s., 696:7
so dead, 396:11
so panteth my s. after thee, 17:16
sorrowful unto death, 37:28
speech a mirror of s., 104:16
stirred s. to inmost depths, 449:15
strains that might create a s., 261:5
strong is the s., 528:4
sun steadies my s., 714:17
sweet and virtuous s., 250:11
swell the s. to rage, 285:15
swooned slowly, 696:4
takes nothing with her, 76:20
taste sadness of might, 438:16
that can be honest, 242:17
that rises with us, 393:11

Soul *(continued)*

the hungry s., 23:12
thirst that from s. doth rise, 238:2
thirsteth for God, 17:16
this that oppresses s., 553:3
thou hast much goods, 39:28
thoughtful S. to Solitude, 471:1
thy s. the fixt foot, 235:3
time the s. of this world, 112:5
'tis my outward s., 235:9
to dare, 397:6
tumult of the s., 395:10
two to bear my s. away, 274:20
unlettered small-knowing s., 176:23
unto captain Christ, 180:6
upon my s. between kisses, 645:8
variety s. of pleasure, 290:18
wake s. by tender strokes, 309:14
was like a star, 393:4
wears out breast, 423:1
weddings of the s., 687:13
what Fortitude S. contains, 547:7
what of s. left I wonder, 493:13
what s. without flaws, 603:16
whispereth within him, 122:12
whose s. is sense, 235:1
why art thou cast down O my s., 17:17
why castest thou off my s., 18:19
why shrinks the s., 301:26
windows of the s., 376:9
wine-scented poetic s., 599:5
with all its maladies, 573:5
with all thy heart and s., 36:43
with my whole s., 29:24
witness of s. naturally Christian, 116:12
yet my s. drew back, 251:2
Soul-hungry, worse to be s., 850:7
Soul-making, vale of S., 441:1
Soul's arrest, 664:13
dark cottage, 258:3
for s. good do things disliked, 672:18
my s. calm retreat, 278:29
prayer s. sincere desire, 396:2
whole s. tasking, 514:15
Souls are in the hand of God, 31:16
beams of wit on other s., 284:3
beyond reaches of our s., 202:6
boundless as we wish our s., 428:15
conscience grinds our s., 242:6
corporations have no s., 159:18, 592:12
damp s. of housemaids, 717:19
departed shadows of living, 256:24
flame of freedom in s., 576:14
great s. suffer in silence, 381:14
have sight of sea, 393:17
immediate jewel of their s., 213:33
in s. sympathy with sounds, 348:10
jealous s. not answered, 214:17
left your s. on earth, 438:9
letters mingle s., 235:25
live in furnished s., 739:14
look after s. in labor, 78:9
love's mysteries in s. grow, 235:6
many valiant s. of heroes, 52:1
memory green in our s., 411:10
miserable state wretched s., 130:6
mounting up to God, 541:27
must not be saved, 213:19
numberless infinities of s., 236:4

Souls (*continued*)

nurse of full-grown s., 514:11
of animals infuse themselves, 189:17
of emperors and cobblers, 153:2
of Poets dead, 438:10
our selves our s. and bodies, 51:1
our s. survive death, 104:*n*6
our two s. which are one, 235:2
patent leather s., 751:8
possess s. in patience, 40:13
prosperity tries s. even of wise, 95:5
pure lovers' s. descend, 235:5
see s. we loved, 485:13
sit close and silently, 155:*n*2
such harmony in immortal s., 190:5
sucks two s., 235:12
suspicion companion of mean s., 354:7
that cringe and plot, 514:14
there be s. must be saved, 213:19
those poor S. who dwell in Night, 375:16
through such s. God shows light, 494:27
times that try men's s., 354:10
to believing s. gives light, 172:7
two s. alas dwell in my breast, 365:6
two s. with single thought, 464:7
unbodied, 235:24
violent s., 719:5
waking s., 233:11
wounded by such things, 277:22

Sound as of rushing wind, 41:44

believeth it is s. of trumpet, 15:15
bells s. on Bredon, 618:15
bitter joy hear s. of wings, 752:10
boy makes first s. like a man, 757:13
came o'er my ear like sweet s., 208:25
come back s., 158:15
deeper than plummet s., 230:12
empty vessel greatest s., 193:21
far-off curfew s., 260:4
full of s. and fury, 222:16
heal blows of s., 473:4
hearest the s. thereof, 40:44
heart s. as bell, 194:30
is forced, 371:12
let it s. no more, 180:16
let s. of it flee, 354:5
light in s. s.-like power in light, 399:9
mind in sound body, 113:17, 286:8
music with silver s., 844:2
must seem echo to sense, 308:18
my barbaric yawp, 519:22
nature without voice or s., 337:16
no riches above s. body, 32:41
no s. dissonant, 407:*n*1
no s. of planes, 793:4
no s. of water, 718:12
no war or battle's s., 258:18
noght but eyr ybroken, 133:6
not fourth s. but star, 494:3
of body and mind, 99:16
of bone against plate, 836:1
of great Amen, 537:16
of her silk skirt, 89:17
of horn at night, 443:13
of horns and motors, 718:17
of jets overhead, 756:16
of public scorn, 268:8
of revelry by night, 420:16
of the grinding is low, 25:7

Sound (*continued*)

of thunder heard remote, 265:12
of voice that is still, 482:15
persuasive s., 300:21
resonance of s. in violin, 813:1
rhythm to world of s., 715:14
silver-sweet s. lovers' tongues, 183:14
slight s. at evening, 505:1
stagnant hollow s., 759:7
sweet is every s., 483:8
thought and magic s., 446:17
thundering s., 342:9
too full for s., 487:2
trump of rescue s., 453:14
trumpet beat drums, 318:19
trumpet give uncertain s., 44:21
trumpet shall s., 44:31
trumpets beat drums, 285:9
upon bugle horn, 481:16
voice as s. of many waters, 48:5
voice whose s. like sea, 393:4
what stop she please, 204:17
wooden dialogue and s., 207:28

Sounded, trumpets s. for him, 282:6
Soundest, old lovers s., 244:1
Sounding brass or tinkling cymbal, 44:17
cataract haunted me, 391:3
Soundings, acquainted with S., 440:11
Soundless day in autumn, 478:11
Soundlessness, be mysterious to point of s., 83:6
Soundly, sleep s. as wretched slave, 193:16
suspects yet s. loves, 213:34
Soundness of observation, 289:4
Sounds and sweet airs, 230:6
army stilly s., 193:16
articulate sweet s., 637:17
concord of sweet s., 190:7
exceed knock at door, 407:17
let s. of music creep, 190:5
martial s., 264:15
muted s., 807:2
of silence, 837:8
only mortal s. can awake, 819:5
out of three s. frame, 494:3
perfumes colors s. echo, 524:9
replication of your s., 195:15
self-same s. on spirit, 687:4
sympathy with s., 348:10
take care of themselves, 550:17
that echo still, 480:22
three great elemental s., 716:16
Wagner's music better than it s., 597:17
Soup, beautiful s., 551:4
Bouillabaisse sort of s., 490:17
licked s. from ladles, 491:16
of the evening, 551:4
Sour, conscience made him s., 482:14
eaten a s. grape, 29:23
every sweet hath s., 455:18
grapes are s., 60:10
how s. sweet music is, 180:14
keep at times frae being s., 378:2
lofty and s., 231:14
misfortune's book, 184:14
prove in digestion s., 179:2
Source, little water in stream fault of s., 118:7
mysterious law true s., 266:22
mysterious s. of art and science, 683:5

Source (*continued*)

ocean the s. of all, 53:17
of all my bliss, 342:13
of innocent merriment, 565:15
of sympathetic tears, 335:8
Soured milk of human kindness, 219:*n*1
South, archipelagoes of my S., 826:5
called land of Dixie, 503:*n*1
come thou s. wind, 25:24
full of the warm S., 437:7
guilt on North equally with S., 521:18
he was my S., 775:6
is avenged, 570:27
know no S. no North, 409:11
men of the S., 679:7
night of s. winds, 519:8
some genius of S., 742:6
Swallow flying S., 483:1
tell about the S., 748:15
'twixt s. and southwest, 270:16
why do you hate the S., 748:17
South Carolina, Governor of S. said, 599:19
South Vietnam, no enemy to establish authority over S., 733:3
Southbound mail, 655:*n*1
Southerly, when wind s. know hawk, 203:20
Southern, bore me in s. wild, 372:1
change to S. willows, 349:1
efficiency, 800:8
nature to s. side, 515:13
writer adept at recognizing grotesque, 816:3
Southey's, four first rhymes are S., 134:*n*3
Southwest, 'twixt south and s. side, 270:16
Souvenirs, j'ai plus de s., 524:*n*5
Sovereign, common law voice of s., 578:11
five s. fingers, 795:4
life to s. power, 480:11
lightest element in nation, 82:20
lord the king, 292:24
Magna Carta will have no s., 159:19
nations possessing great power, 683:11
noble and most s. reason, 204:9
of sighs and groans, 176:33
our s. the people, 415:*n*1
power in government s., 370:14
powers brutal lives ugly deaths, 742:8
press, 706:3
Sovereignty, top of s., 438:19
unlimited s. in majority, 352:3
wommen desire s., 136:21
Soviet, no S. domination of Eastern Europe, 790:16
Soviet Union, no difference between S. and U.S. worth risks, 768:3
run by dictatorship, 698:11
United States policy toward S., 768:1
Sow a thought, 849:5
as you s. ye reap, 271:21
he that observeth wind not s., 25:4
Ireland old s. that eats farrow, 696:5
men that s. and reap, 569:1
they s. not, 34:17
they that s. in tears, 20:3
thy seed in the morning, 25:5
wrong s. by ear, 149:13
Sowed, what I s. what orchard yields, 761:16
Sowest, that which thou s., 44:27
Soweth, whatsoever a man s., 45:24

Spirit *(continued)*

lifeblood of master s., 262:22
lively understandable s., 780:11
Mammon least erected s., 264:22
man of understanding is of excellent s., 22:8
mark of Greek s., 647:9
meek and quiet s., 47:29
modern s. Greek discovery, 647:8
motion and a s., 391:4
motions of his s. dull, 190:7
my s. too weak, 439:1
nation's s. die of inanition, 530:8
naught so much s. calms, 423:16
no longer ruler of own s., 385:18
no s. can walk abroad, 200:22
not letter but s., 45:3
of age, 316:26
of Beauty that dost consecrate, 427:15
of counsel and might, 26:33
of Delight, 430:24
of fear, 46:30
of God brother of my own, 518:17
of God moved upon face of the waters, 5:9
of government must be of country, 602:10
of his own epoch, 675:14
of knowledge and fear of the Lord, 26:33
of liberty, 344:6
of love how quick and fresh, 208:26
of men who follow, 708:12
of moderation, 660:5
of Night, 430:22
of our City never stronger, 838:13
of party, 350:9
of popular government, 367:1
of prophecy in me, 76:17
of repose, 449:15
of science, 761:15
of suspicion and distrust, 660:7
of the time, 534:10
of the valley never dies, 58:11
of wisdom and understanding, 26:33
of youth in everything, 227:8
of Zeus-fostered kings, 52:14
original creation of s., 624:11
pardlike s. beautiful swift, 430:10
passed before my face, 13:34
perturbed s., 202:28
poetry finer s. of knowlege, 391:14
proud and chivalrous s., 81:17
rare detachment of s., 672:22
real and eternal, 526:12
renew a right s. within me, 17:27
resemblance neglects s. of objects, 125:9
revenge delight of mean s., 113:18
sacred to departed s., 123:21
scorned his s., 195:24
self-same sounds on s., 687:4
shall rest upon him, 26:33
shall return unto God, 25:8
shallow s. of judgment, 171:16
slave s. below, 710:13
slumber did my s. seal, 392:1
so still and quiet, 212:27
spur the clear s. cloth raise, 261:19
straight in strength of s., 569:8
strongest and fiercest, 264:26

Spirit *(continued)*

that always denies, 365:7
that on life's rough sea, 165:11
that quickeneth, 41:5
that stands by naked man, 844:19
thy s. walks abroad, 197:19
too much s. to be at ease, 310:6
tool carries s. by which created, 760:12
travail and vexation of s., 24:8
truth shows s. and substance, 125:9
vanity and vexation of s., 24:1
vital s., 616:8
weak s. quickens, 719:16
whatever anguish of s., 352:13
which goes through mass, 675:14
whither shall I go from thy s., 20:13
wild S. moving everywhere, 429:1
within me constraineth me, 14:43
within nourishes, 97:29
wounded s. who can bear, 22:10
yearning in desire, 481:11
yet a S. still and bright, 394:3
Spiriting, do my s. gently, 229:16
Spiritless, man so faint so s., 191:7
Spirit's, clown of s. motive, 791:12
Spirits, all s. and melted into air, 230:9
apothecary never out of s., 367:19
be free all worthy s., 165:10
black s. and white, 243:22
blast drives wicked s., 130:12
by our own s. defied, 392:9
call s. from vasty deep, 186:5
can either sex assume, 264:12
cheerer of s., 252:25
day of s., 278:29
good s. when well dressed, 496:37
her wanton s. look out, 208:19
how can you serve s., 63:5
I summoned up, 364:14
insult to s. of ancestors, 533:9
like two s. suggest me, 228:3
maketh his angels s., 46:37
master s. of this age, 196:19
not jump with common s., 188:26
of great events, 408:*n*3
of just men, 47:3
of land and grain, 82:20
of the damned, 474:12
of wise mock us, 191:29
other s. standing apart, 435:20
red s. and gray, 243:22
that fell with Lucifer, 170:18
that tend thoughts, 219:11
throng with returning s., 419:5
tribe of s. and of men, 122:14
unclean s. entered swine, 38:22
unhappy s. fell with Lucifer, 170:18
vanish like evil s., 359:3
we are s. not animals, 666:12
who live in twilight, 614:13
wonders at quaint s., 181:14
Spirit-stirring drum, 214:8
Spiritu, et cum s. tuo, 49:7
Spiritual excitement, 531:7
found s. cause, 526:11
highest s. authority, 693:10
inward and s. grace, 51:6
millions of s. creatures, 266:19
natural fact symbol of s., 454:17

Spiritual *(continued)*

Negro s. free at last, 823:4
perfection of man, 127:6
psalms hymns and s. songs, 45:29
risk and s. self-sacrifice, 730:2
stronger than material, 457:19
superhuman s. and divine, 675:9
wickedness in high places, 45:31
Spirochete, without little s., 809:5
Spit, if I lie s. in my face, 185:24
on us for luck, 85:8
upon my Jewish gaberdine, 188:8
Spite, force in s. of Nature, 271:7
in erring reason's s., 311:8
O cursed s., 202:29
of cormorant devouring Time, 176:16
the world, 221:1
Spiteful envious animal the Public, 410:8
Splashing wintry mold, 637:8
Spleen, in a s. unfolds heaven and earth, 180:20
that scourge of Britain, 446:15
Splendid abilities utterly corrupt, 405:2
and sterile Dolores, 568:4
by the vision s., 393:12
give me s. silent sun, 520:12
in ashes, 256:22
little war, 571:9
misery, 358:6
poor s. wings, 569:12
Shilling, 304:15
tear, 485:11
you rise, 4:7
Splendide mendax, 100:*n*2
Splendidly null, 485:5
Splendor falls on castle walls, 482:19
in the grass, 393:18
not in lone s., 439:11
of the Mighty One Krishna, 87:8
on earth no such s., 126:1
your s. like heaven's s., 4:5
Splendors, heaven with s. lie, 514:14
Splenetive and rash, 207:1
Split ears of groundlings, 204:11
mountains with thunderbolt, 96:8
sides with laughing, 157:12
the sky in two, 734:15
world would s. open, 791:10
Splits, who s. wood warms twice, 507:*n*1
Splitting, image of s. apart, 5:1
warmed while s. stumps, 507:12
Spoil it by trying to explain, 367:15
little foxes that s. the vines, 25:18
lives of better people, 599:21
no more s. upon my face, 194:1
rampant for s. and victory, 589:13
spare rod and s. child, 83:*n*7, 271:17
villanous company s. of me, 186:18
Spoiled, Christian a pagan s., 631:15
good walk s., 563:4
Spoiling nice new clothes, 859:10
Spoils, conquests glories triumphs s., 196:18
of time, 334:19
rich with s. of Nature, 255:12
to victor belong s., 419:2
treasons stratagems and s., 190:7
victor belongs to s., 746:3

Spoke, man who knew more s. less, 111:18
    more he heard less he s., 591:16
    never s. with God, 546:6
    of disastrous chances, 212:29
    town-crier s. my lines, 204:11
Spoken, glorious things of thee s., 339:13
    God had never s. anything but English, 668:13
    God's last Put out Light s., 669:19
    lie down till leaders s., 634:14
    not s. of soul, 465:17
    Rome has s. case closed, 119:19
    speak when s. to, 598:21
    weird power in s. word, 611:20
    word at random s., 397:17
    word comes not back, 101:*n3*
Spondee, slow S. stalks, 402:8
Spontaneity, Hellenism s. of consciousness, 531:19
    studied s. of Horace, 109:11
Spontaneous, happiness not s. product, 683:3
    joy and natural content, 638:2
    overflow of feelings, 391:16
Spoon, dish ran away with s., 858:2
    hire long s. eat with feend, 137:11
    juices of carrot and onion, 830:17
    runcible s., 499:18
    silver s. in mouth, 159:2
Spoons, faster counted s., 448:*n1*
    guard our s., 448:2
    let us count our s., 326:20
    measured life with coffee s., 717:10
    woman with silver s., 505:20
Sport, boys throw stones in s., 85:4
    ended his s. with Tess, 575:9
    make s. for neighbors, 406:12
    no s. in hate, 431:3
    of kings, 304:14
    present life a diversion and s., 122:3
    that wrinkled Care derides, 259:10
    they kill us for their s., 217:11
    to have enginer hoist, 205:31
    with Amaryllis, 261:19
    would be tedious, 184:36
Sported on the green, 405:4
Sports and plays with me, 371:10
    joy of youthful s., 422:3
    of love, 237:14
    shows games s. guns, 351:9
Sporus, let S. tremble, 312:7
Spot, black s. to keep concealed, 540:2
    certain am I of s., 546:6
    dim s. men call earth, 260:12
    do in that remote s., 388:10
    earth one mighty blood s., 460:3
    out damned s., 222:3
    stand on right s., 364:15
    there is no s. in thee, 25:22
    what is Black S., 598:16
Spotless reputation, 178:30
Spots, leopard change his s., 29:12
    minds grow in s., 582:20
    quadrangular of diamond, 348:6
Spotted sight or sound, 710:7
    snakes with double tongue, 181:15
Spouse, President's s. I wish him well, 814:17
    so bright and clear, 236:12
Spout till you have drenched, 216:18
Spouted arms, 753:16

Spouts black blood and rolls fin out, 516:12
    trunk s. out a sea, 267:15
Sprang to the stirrup, 492:2
Sprat, Jack S. eat no fat, 856:20
Sprawling in slush and gutter, 569:18
Spray, never a s. of yew, 529:14
    nightingale on bloomy s., 262:7
    rime was on the s., 574:14
    toss in the s., 528:5
Spread alarm, 467:15
    dreams under your feet, 637:12
    masters s. yourselves, 180:23
    money not good unless s., 167:20
    out against sky, 717:6
    silent tents s., 522:6
    truth from pole to pole, 301:15
    with her fan s., 300:23
Spreading, by broad s. disperse, 171:14
    chestnut tree, 466:7
    himself like a green bay tree, 17:7
Spreads, wrath s. through hearts of men, 53:26
Sprechen ist silbern, 433:21
    wovon man nicht s. kann, 727:*n2*
Spree, gentlemen rankers on s., 633:17
Sprightly, tossing heads in s. dance, 394:6
Spring, a little Madness in S., 546:15
    absent in the s., 227:8
    apparelled like the s., 225:6
    blossom by blossom s. begins, 567:18
    blue sky of s., 535:16
    breaks through again, 753:7
    brings back balmy warmth, 94:13
    brown hills melted into s., 508:20
    call it easing the S., 794:13
    came on forever, 685:7
    can s. be far behind, 429:5
    clean pasture s., 668:17
    come gentle s., 317:19
    comes slowly up this way, 401:4
    comes with rustling shade, 724:17
    direful s., 309:18
    disturbance of the s., 720:17
    ever-returning s., 520:14
    first day of s. one thing first s. day another, 601:13
    flowers that bloom in s., 565:19
    from her may violets s., 206:27
    full of sweet days, 250:10
    game begins in the s., 833:4
    hounds of s., 567:17
    in Just-s., 739:11
    in s. young man's fancy, 481:17
    in the fire of S., 471:2
    infants of s., 201:22
    last leaf in s., 473:19
    lived light in s., 529:1
    makest a s. to gush forth, 121:14
    Mrs. Porter in s., 718:17
    no season such delight as s., 247:13
    no s. nor summer beauty, 235:18
    not as in bud of s., 236:21
    of ever-flowing water, 98:24
    of love gushed from heart, 400:13
    of love resembleth April day, 176:6
    of prodigality, 345:3
    Pierian s., 308:11
    ran canyons all s., 753:16
    season of s. comes on, 52:31

Spring *(continued)*
    silent s., 777:2
    starless and bible-black, 795:16
    stirring roots with s. rain, 718:11
    summer autumn winter, 740:8
    sunshine streamed in, 549:5
    sweet lovers love the s., 200:5
    targeted trod like S., 641:12
    time abhorrent to nihilist, 686:10
    'tis s. and weeds shallow-rooted, 172:10
    where are songs of S., 438:13
    Winter mother of S., 468:6
    would not be so pleasant, 270:9
    year's at s., 491:2
    year's pleasant king, 232:7
Springes to catch woodcocks, 201:30
Springs, beside the s. of Dove, 391:18
    entered into s. of sea, 15:8
    every thought that s., 395:17
    fifty s. little room, 618:7
    from seventy s. a score, 618:7
    hope s. eternal, 311:4
    of behavior hidden, 664:1
    root from which tyrant s., 77:23
    Scotia's grandeur s., 377:16
    steeds to water at those s., 225:12
    we have no s., 759:7
Springth the wude nu, 843:5
Springtime, birds warble sweet in s., 602:14
    for Hitler and Germany, 817:6
    fragrance of all s., 797:2
    in s. every day growths, 513:6
    only pretty ring time, 200:5
Sprinkled, blood s. upon my garments, 28:32
Sprite, angelic s., 236:3
Sprites and goblins, 228:14
Sprouting despondently at gates, 717:19
    no cabbages s. out, 474:10
Spruce affectation, 177:12
    cone regularity, 714:14
Sprung, vile dust whence he s., 396:11
Spun, gods have s. the thread, 54:6
    of Iris' woof, 260:17
    yarn s. in Ulysses' absence, 224:18
Spur, avarice s. of industry, 330:4
    between s. and bridle, 252:3
    fame is the s., 261:19
    me into song, 642:14
    my dull revenge, 205:35
    no s. to my intent, 219:18
    not unbroken horse, 398:4
    pain of bone s. in heel, 755:3
    reward and punishment s., 286:9
    studies a s. to young, 90:13
Spurn, choose Jewish God s. Jews, 706:*n1*
    existence saw him s. reign, 323:14
Spurned, youth s. in vain, 164:9
Spurns that patient merit takes, 203:33
Spurred boldly on and dashed, 283:20
    ready booted and s., 448:20
Spurs, let boy win his s., 132:17
    now s. lated traveler, 221:8
Spy, prettiest little parlor you did s., 446:9
    sent to s. out the land, 9:18
Spying, bitter little embryos s., 755:13
Squabbling nationalities, 615:16
Squadron, save s. honor France, 495:4
Squadrons, God on side of big s., 275:1
Squads, undisciplined s. of emotion, 721:4

Steer (*continued*)
   star to s. her by, 680:15
   too nigh sands, 283:8
Steered, boats that are not s., 225:25
Steersman, Cybernetics from Greek s.,
   742:11
Stein on table, 630:7
   portrait of Gertrude S., 673:15
Stelle, a riveder le s., 131:*n*1
   l'amor che muove il sole e l'altre s.,
     132:*n*2
   puro e disposto a salire alle s., 131:*n*5
Stem or stone, 696:16
   rod out of the s. of Jesse, 26:33
   thy slender s., 378:7
   two berries on one s., 181:22
Stemming with hearts of controversy, 195:19
Stems, cut s. struggling, 780:3
Stench of stale oranges, 709:7
Stenches, two and seventy s., 402:13
Stentor, great-hearted S., 52:29
Step, don't s. on my blue suede shoes, 827:6
   fanaticism to barbarism one s., 331:27
   first s. is hardest, 317:9
   from sublime to ridiculous, 388:2
   highest s. of charity's golden ladder,
     127:3
   keep s. obey in silence, 539:10
   light of s. and heart, 662:9
   mind music and s., 846:14
   must begin with single s., 59:12
   not s. twice into same rivers, 64:8
   off the ledge, 799:2
   one small s. for man, 824:19
   one s. enough for me, 449:18
   recognizing man's s., 662:5
   softly under snow, 664:15
   to music he hears, 507:19
   to s. aside is human, 378:18
Stepdame, false as s. to son, 208:7
Stephen, feast of S., 511:9
   King S. worthy peer, 844:6
Stephen's, St. S. choir, 800:9
Stepmother, Nature a merciless s., 108:3
   Nature cruel and ruthless s., 141:12
   poverty s. ov genius, 508:15
   stony-hearted s., 418:2
Stepped down to the Four, 701:13
   if I s. out of my body, 820:3
   in a puddle, 860:16
   in blood s. in so far, 221:19
   out of their clothes, 642:2
Stepping-stones of dead selves, 483:13
Steppingstones to understanding, 682:6
Steps, age with stealing s., 150:7
   beware of desperate s., 348:18
   by due s. aspire, 260:13
   came forth with pilgrim s., 268:30
   foot wear s. of his door, 32:12
   hear not my s., 220:10
   heavy s. of plowman, 637:8
   humor saves a few s., 714:16
   I by backward s. move, 279:4
   invites my s. and points, 309:27
   lead my s. aright, 432:11
   Lord directeth his s., 22:1
   my s. along this street, 794:8
   same s. as Author, 440:8
   stops and s. of mind, 719:12

Steps (*continued*)
   wandering s. and slow, 268:17
   with how sad s. O Moon, 163:29
Stereotyped, perceive in form s. by culture,
   727:2
Sterile, compulsion to become s., 708:5
   earth seems a s. promontory, 203:17
   splendid and s. Dolores, 568:4
   truth for yourself, 594:1
Sterling, refine her s. page, 289:16
Stern, and rock-bound coast, 431:20
   Caledonia s. and wild, 396:12
   custom spreads afar, 381:8
   daughter of voice of God, 394:9
   joy warriors feel, 397:12
   man s. to view, 342:8
   my sad heart foams at s., 603:7
   Ruin's plowshare, 378:8
Sterner, ambition of s. stuff, 196:29
   days not darker days, 667:2
Sternest, gives s. good-night, 220:12
   knight to foe, 139:14
Stew, convert you into missionary s., 719:19
   w'en s. smokin' hot, 660:4
Stewards of their excellence, 227:4
Stewed, longing for s. prunes, 211:6
Stick across your back, 856:13
   carry a big s., 615:4
   coat upon a s., 639:17
   hips s., 763:14
   I am a burr I shall s., 212:4
   Moses should have fancier s., 807:6
   take s. hit him on snout, 848:7
   there I'll s., 156:28
   thine arrows s. fast in me, 17:9
   to s. the heart of falsehood, 208:7
   to your last, 83:*n*4
   with fist instead of s., 270:14
Sticketh closer than a brother, 22:13
Sticking, ay s. in a tree, 397:26
Sticking-place, screw your courage to s.,
   220:1
Sticks nix hick pix, 758:1
   no sweeter fat than s. to bones, 519:5
   resurrection of dry s., 780:3
Sticky, gilded and s., 710:11
   infusion, 819:4
Sticky-beaks, we don't like stuck-up s., 843:2
Stiff dishonored shroud, 718:10
   flags straining, 664:10
   in opinions, 283:15
   sore s. with toils, 521:4
   twin compasses, 235:3
   upper lip, 535:18
Stiffen sinews summon blood, 192:30
Stiffening of vertebrae, 608:12
Stiffens, heart s. and rejoices, 719:16
Stiffish cock-tail, 494:22
Stiffnecked, a s. people, 9:6
Stiffness and soul's arrest, 664:13
   freedom from s., 532:5
Stifle freedom of people, 787:10
   opinion endeavoring to s., 464:14
Stile, over hedge before s., 156:16
Stile-a, merrily hent the s., 228:24
Still and awful red, 400:12
   and quiet conscience, 231:3
   as a gold piece, 821:13
   as a maid, 373:9

Still (*continued*)
   be s. and know that I am God, 17:23
   be s. wait, 780:11
   beside the s. waters, 16:18
   everything else is s., 372:10
   falls the Rain, 715:13
   how s. we see thee lie, 558:5
   lute be s. I have done, 150:1
   mightest s. the enemy, 15:32
   mighty heart lying s., 392:13
   point of turning world, 719:23, 720:10
   quite s. and solitary, 701:5
   sad music of humanity, 391:4
   should I have lain s., 13:30
   small voice, 12:32
   small voice of gratitude, 335:20
   sound of voice that is s., 482:15
   spirit bloweth and is s., 528:12
   spirit so s. and quiet, 212:27
   take heed of s. waters, 160:*n*3
   to be neat, 237:15
   we must be s. and s. moving, 721:6
   when all woods are s., 262:7
   when sun out wind s., 670:5
Stille Nacht Heilige Nacht, 427:*n*1
Stillness, air solemn s. holds, 334:9
   modest s. and humility, 192:30
   soft s. and the night, 190:5
   solemn s. lay, 488:15
   such s., 291:13
   talent formed in s., 364:12
Stilly, army s. sounds, 193:11
Stilts, no matter mount on s., 154:7
Stimulated by news wife left husband, 771:19
Stilus virum arguit, 240:5
Sting, cold doth not s., 232:7
   death where is thy s., 44:32
   destined to poison joys, 516:1
   each s. that bids, 494:9
   every day a little s., 825:19
   how bitter a s. a little fault, 131:7
   like a bee, 836:16
   prick and s. her, 202:20
   serpent s. thee twice, 189:15
   with a little s., 710:11
Stinger, 'tis a s., 243:16
Stingeth like an adder, 22:38
Stings, stinks and s., 312:8
   wanton s. of sense, 211:1
   what s. is justice, 691:7
   you for your pains, 307:20
Stingy, don't be s. baby, 723:12
Stink, fish and visitors s., 86:*n*6
   like rotten meat, 762:16
   stand by the fire and s., 216:1
Stinks and stings, 312:8
   like rotten mackerel, 405:2
   several s., 402:13
Stir, all hell s. for this, 193:24
   at dismal treatise rouse and s., 222:15
   crown me without my s., 219:6
   Jamaicas of Remembrance s., 546:19
   men's blood, 197:4
   not s. rice though it sticks, 158:24
   now s. the fire, 348:4
   of the great Babel, 348:5
   press feel with fingers, 519:13
   smoke and s. of this dim spot, 260:12
   without great argument, 206:2

Streets *(continued)*

gibber in Roman s., 200:18
grass will grow in s., 622:2, 672:2
her mind traveled crooked s., 826:11
in thy dark s. shineth, 558:5
lion is in the s., 23:7
mourners go about the s., 25:8
of Laredo, 854:17
publish it not in the s. of Askelon, 11:35
through midnight s., 374:8
through negro s., 817:12
truth never fell dead in s., 488:12
world's most crowded s., 529:4
Strength, all your s. in union, 466:23
all your s. is weakness, 67:20
alone of Muses born, 436:5
ancient and natural s., 338:9
as thy days so thy s., 10:15
beyond hope and despair, 719:12
by experience with fear, 704:10
castle's s. will laugh, 222:14
collected s. and struck, 619:15
credulity child's s., 407:16
culture moment of s., 702:12
disease gained s. by delays, 105:22
dogged s., 648:11
erect against her hate, 729:12
exert his utmost s., 62:10
feeling his cold s., 713:8
fight beyond your s., 53:14
forsake me not when my s. faileth, 18:8
giant's s., 211:12
God is our refuge and s., 17:21
growing s. in air, 666:1
hast thou given the horse s., 15:13
hast thou ordained s., 15:32
he flourishes in his s., 55:20
he rejoiceth in his s., 15:14
if by reason of s. they be fourscore, 18:22
ignorance is s., 765:16
in life, 631:14
in union even of sorry men, 53:11
is as strength of ten, 482:11
is to sit still, 27:25
Jehovah is my s., 27:1
justice without s., 280:3
king's name a tower of s., 174:18
knowledge increaseth s., 22:39
lies in attack, 726:10
Lord is my s. and song, 8:25
Lord is my s. and my shield, 16:24
Lord is the s. of my life, 16:22
moment of s. of romance, 612:2
muscular s. to jaw, 550:2
my s. and my redeemer, 16:14
new ways to use s., 706:3
not given s. to be artist, 622:6
not s. of sentiment but duration, 589:3
of the ancient giants, 55:*n*1
of the hills is his, 18:29, 49:24
of twenty men, 184:11
perfect in weakness, 45:15
public s. individual security, 370:8
renew their s., 28:8
respect s. without fearing, 358:5
search things above thy s., 31:29
stone s. of past, 713:7
submit because s. not adequate, 81:21

Strength *(continued)*

that I may recover s., 17:15
they go from s. to s., 18:16
through joy, 729:8
to forbear and persevere, 600:1
to force the moment, 717:12
to the needy, 27:14
to the poor, 27:14
tower of s., 484:22
transforms s. into right, 330:21
union gives s., 61:7
unite s. to maintain peace, 705:15
what though s. fails, 104:21
without boasting, 358:5
without hands to smite, 568:1
without insolence, 419:10
without justice, 280:3
Strengthen, charm s. and teach, 466:22
me only this once, 11:7
Strengthens, bread s. man's heart, 295:18
time s. friendship, 292:16
Strenuous life, 614:12
sounds s. and serious, 723:10
tongue, 438:16
Stress and disorientation, 822:1
on not changing mind, 672:15
storm and s., 368:14
strives against s. of necessity, 70:16
Stretch every nerve, 318:12
far as coin would s., 184:27
him out longer, 218:8
nor does Apollo always s. bow, 99:25
will line s. out, 221:30
yourselves for greatness, 165:10
Stretched, above world s. the sky, 734:15
army s. out on the hills, 655:10
forefinger of Time, 482:17
pia mater of mine, 255:10
tomcat lies s. flat, 825:6
'twixt his s. footing, 207:28
walk with s. forth necks, 26:16
Stretches out my golden wing, 371:10
Stretching before and after, 720:13
Strew, flowers to s. Thy way, 250:7
on her roses, 529:14
Strewed thy grave, 206:30
with husks, 208:20
Stricken deer go weep, 205:6
love's s. why, 546:16
old and s. in years, 10:25
Strict, death s. in his arrest, 207:10
regard to conscience, 352:9
Strictly held by none, 670:12
meditate thankless Muse, 261:19
vow binds too s., 486:6
Strictness, for extreme diseases extreme s., 73:11
Hebraism s. of conscience, 531:19
Stride, at one s. comes dark, 400:5
right in middle of s., 809:8
Striding high there how he rung, 587:6
shadow s. behind you, 718:12
the blast, 219:18
Strife, age of discord and continual s., 172:3
all things born through s., 64:9
and envying, 43:26
appeaseth s., 21:37
clubs typical of s., 348:6
din of s., 529:4

Strife *(continued)*

find agonies s. of human hearts, 436:3
from the s. of tongues, 16:29
honor for a man to cease from s., 22:18
ignoble s., 334:23
man of s. and contention, 29:15
no s. between me and thee, 7:1
none worth my s., 408:11
not a single kind of s., 56:7
of love, 105:*n*2
of Truth with Falsehood, 514:12
stirs of discontented s., 239:6
with the palm, 529:2
wrathful man stirreth up s., 21:37
Strifes, hatred stirreth up s., 21:16
Strike, adjective when in doubt s. out, 561:13
afraid to s., 312:4
at self-love, 539:12
awe into beholders, 298:12
but hear me, 64:19
clock doth s. by algebra, 270:22
clock will s. Devil will come, 171:4
disease or sorrows s. him, 512:9
feel angry because we s., 582:4
flat thick rotundity, 216:18
honor foe while you s., 627:3
it and it hurts my hand, 214:20
long live the s., 819:1
mine eyes but not my heart, 237:16
out fine passage, 327:19
right to s. against public safety, 659:18
sails well but s. rock, 376:13
so he may feel he is dying, 107:15
spear to thrust club to s., 145:7
stars with my exalted head, 99:2
take care you s. in anger, 609:25
the tent, 465:15
then no planets s., 200:22
through the mask, 516:13
truth may s. out his teeth, 160:12
we s. straight, 798:10
when a hammer s., 251:23
when iron is hot, 102:*n*12
when s. at king must kill him, 458:4
Strikes, lightning s. mountaintop, 99:24
like rising knell, 420:16
midnight s. and hastens, 619:21
one two three s. you're out, 685:11
silent note Cupid s., 256:7
Striking blow for freedom, 713:17
great office not filled by great s. men, 570:28
so s. and grotesque, 448:12
sometimes a friend, 250:1
spaceships s. from hidden base, 838:19
String attuned to mirth, 445:18
chewing bits of s., 653:8
dead kitten egg-shell bit of s., 644:14
eyes upon double s., 235:4
harp not on that s., 174:14
notes as warbled to the s., 260:7
of pearls to me, 627:8
pearls strung on, 585:6
pudding-bag s., 861:11
sing in a hempen s., 242:15
untune that s., 207:26
Stringbean, Little Girl My S., 821:11
Stringencies, dead hands dead s., 827:17
Stringent protection of free speech, 578:13

Sudden *(continued)*
    from wine s. friendship, 307:10
    glory maketh laughter, 246:9
    if thing comes in his head, 173:15
    in shaft of sunlight, 720:13
    in s. blackness the pall, 734:6
    make s. sally, 485:3
    said to dawn Be s., 621:3
    sharp hot stink of fox, 825:4
    storms are short, 179:11
    this s. Diomede, 134:7
    too unadvised too s., 183:10
    violent and s. usurpations, 367:2
Suddenly I realize, 820:3
    lest coming s., 38:31
Sue, we were not born to s., 178:32
    went and named me S., 827:19
    won't s. you, 432:17
Suede, blue s. shoes, 827:6
Sueño de la razón monstruos, 362:14
    toda la vida es s., 254:*n*2
Sueños sueños son, 254:*n*2
Suez, east of S., 633:14
Suffer, act or s., 720:3
    all alike, 223:26
    better to s. than die, 276:10
    detraction will not s. it, 186:35
    fools gladly, 45:12
    for such a woman they s., 52:22
    great destruction, 469:15
    great souls s. in silence, 381:14
    hell I s. seems a heaven, 266:3
    him who has done deed to s., 65:16
    hysterical patients s. from reminiscences,
        607:10
    if you love you s., 728:2
    little children, 38:28
    man needs to s., 601:19
    me that I may speak, 14:28
    me to come, 322:25
    neither enjoy nor s., 614:13
    never s. evil in future, 55:20
    nobler in mind to s., 203:33
    one s. than nation grieve, 283:13
    rivalship of wisest men, 303:5
    sea-change, 229:20
    tamely lawless attack, 337:10
    than one innocent s., 338:12
    them and they'll o'ergrow garden,
        172:10
    though guiltless must s., 71:*n*2
    thy foot to be moved, 19:30
    truths woman reveals by causing to s.,
        658:1
    weak s. what they must, 74:7
    who aim at great deeds must s., 90:5
    who learns must s., 65:5
    woes Hope thinks infinite, 428:14
Sufferance badge of all our tribe, 188:8
    in corporal s., 211:20
Suffered, enjoyed and s., 585:19
    entire city has s., 56:10
    fire s. rivers cannot quench, 173:8
    I s. I was there, 519:18
    in his heart many woes, 54:7
    one who has most s., 529:11
    under Pontius Pilate, 50:3
    yearning that women s., 807:15
    you have s. worse things, 96:29

Sufferer, best of men was a s., 233:7
Sufferest more of mortal griefs, 193:15
Suffereth, charity s. long, 44:18
    love s. long, 44:18
Sufferin', injye other people's s., 646:17
Suffering, about s. they were never wrong,
        775:12
    acting is s., 720:3
    auxiliary of creation, 592:2
    Christian principle of s., 461:6
    exercises his mind with s., 82:17
    great s. on Greece, 759:14
    healed of s. by experiencing it, 658:2
    human race, 528:15
    injye other people's s., 646:17
    knowledge by s., 463:10
    learn s. teach song, 428:19
    man consume own smoke, 434:22
    man in love with s., 525:9
    may be called baptism, 512:22
    miserable doing or s., 264:4
    more mental s. in St. George's, 558:13
    no more s. or denial of rights, 804:7
    pity for s. a passion, 661:5
    relieve s. of brother, 127:9
    truth by s., 650:10
    unavenged s., 525:16
    weak helpless in s., 747:13
Sufferings, I can feel s. of millions, 822:9
    of the troops, 712:5
    poets by their s. grow, 272:1
    to each his s., 333:22
Suffers, eagle s. little birds to sing, 175:17
    then nature of insurrection, 196:1
Suffice, ice also would s., 669:11
    O when may it s., 639:5
    Sands s., 546:13
Sufficeth, God s. me, 121:2
Sufficiency, elegant s., 318:2
Sufficient, beauty s. end, 639:9
    ocean sea not s. room, 239:1
    unto the day is evil thereof, 34:22
    virtue s. of herself, 252:*n*2
    whether s. to finish, 39:33
Sufficiently decayed, 565:21
Suffocate for privacy, 801:11
Suffocating night, 618:17
Suffocation, life threatened with s., 745:1
Suffrage for all citizens, 503:9
    individual given universal s., 697:3
Suffuses all with blackness of death, 93:7
Suffusion from that light, 402:7
Sugar and spice, 860:1
    Heaven's s. cake, 292:10
    if sack and s. be fault, 185:31
    in the gourd, 847:19
    my hair, 551:3
    not made of s. candy, 667:5
    of sex, 813:1
    oil vinegar s., 343:1
    pious action s. o'er, 203:32
Sugarcoat the pill, 278:15
Sugarplums, decorating with s., 613:18
Suggest, like two spirits s. me, 228:3
    to s. is ideal of poem, 583:16
Suggested, minutiae of deeds never s.,
        521:14
Suggestibility, limits poem's s., 643:7
Suggestion, yield to that s., 219:5

Suicide, Bill of Rights into s. pact, 734:3
    committing s. by working, 631:10
    despair and s., 469:2
    is about life, 825:15
    is confession, 415:4
    live through time or die by s., 474:3
    philosophical problem is s., 789:14
    then he may commit s., 764:6
    thermonuclear war means to universal s.,
        808:8
    thought of s. consolation, 589:6
Suis, j'y s. j'y reste, 469:*n*1
Suit action to the word, 204:12
    bring s. in Supreme Court, 705:2
    certainly not s. me, 564:9
    changing from brown s. to gray, 708:3
    Man in Gray Flannel S., 807:12
    of ancient black, 685:6
    of sables, 204:20
    shall I be still in s., 250:15
    silk s. which cost much, 288:1
Suitable, flower s. for every occasion,
        745:7
Suits, kings in golden s. ride elephants,
        788:4
    long s., 731:3
    of solemn black, 200:29
    out of s. with fortune, 197:29
    these but s. of woe, 200:30
    wear strange s., 199:25
Sukey take it off again, 861:2
Sulky, our s. sullen dame, 379:14
Sullen and sad, 317:13
    beetle winds s. horn, 337:2
    hear the surly s. bell, 226:23
    our sulky s. dame, 379:14
    swinging low with s. roar, 260:4
    tongue sounds as s. bell, 191:8
    untamed intractable, 721:7
    winter hangs on till s., 661:18
Sullenness against Nature, 262:20
Sullied, crown s. in the winning, 381:22
    flesh, 201:*n*1
Sulphur, Calvin oatcakes and s., 398:14
Sulphurous and thought-executing, 216:18
Sultan after Sultan with his Pomp, 471:7
Sultan's Turret, 470:13, 470:14
Sultry, common where climate's s., 423:8
    gray-fly winds her s. horn, 261:16
    main, 400:12
Sum, life not doing s., 578:7
    make up my s., 207:2
    man not s. of what he has, 772:5
    married people owe, 364:16
    of all villainies, 318:2
    of earthly bliss, 267:21
    of good government, 358:12
    of human achievement, 595:11
    of human happiness, 694:18
    of things ever being renewed, 93:2
    statue s. of all it acquired, 333:9
    subtracting from s. of human knowledge,
        574:7
    with a great s. obtained freedom, 42:28
Sumatra, giant rat of S., 617:16
Sumer, dô der s. komen was, 127:*n*6
    is icumen in, 843:5
Summary court in perpetual session,
        701:6

Summer, after many a s. dies the swan, 485:14
after s. barren winter, 172:9
afternoon most beautiful words, 586:3
and winter shall not cease, 6:32
baseball blossoms in s., 833:4
being done, 247:7
capriciousness of s. air, 670:12
clothe general earth, 401:11
commend all s. long, 639:16
days oftest in Kentucky, 588:10
dream beneath tamarind, 477:14
embraced s. dawn, 604:2
ends now, 587:11
eternal s. gilds them, 424:1
eves by haunted stream, 259:20
expanding in s. fires, 841:6
expect Saint Martin's s., 171:13
fight if it takes all s., 532:15
flies on s. eves, 437:11
flowers of middle s., 228:26
fly after s. merrily, 230:13
God is day night winter s., 64:7
grace a s. queen, 397:16
hath his joys, 232:3
hearts dry as s. dust, 395:4
in s. the other way, 598:20
Indian s. of life, 570:26
is ended, 29:8
is icumen in, 843:5
it was a s. evening, 405:4
last rose of s., 411:15
mad naked s. night, 519:8
made s. by sun of York, 173:28
my father paints s., 808:12
no season such delight as s., 247:13
no spring nor s. beauty, 235:18
now s. came to pass, 127:13
observing spear of s. grass, 518:15
one swallow makes a s., 80:n3
one swallow not a s., 80:10
provideth her meat in the s., 21:4
reeling through s. days, 544:8
sang in me, 735:7
season when soft was the sun, 132:20
singest of s., 437:6
soldier sunshine patriot, 354:10
summer's flower to s. sweet, 227:4
sun and s. gale, 335:7
sweet as s., 231:14
that I was ten, 806:4
then S. Then Heaven of God, 545:7
this guest of s., 219:15
thy eternal s. not fade, 226:3
to your heart, 735:6
we have had s. evenings, 710:3
welcome s. with sonne softe, 133:14
when had not been a member, 802:9
whirling s., 766:18
with flowers that fell, 568:1
within me invincible s., 790:5
words in winter articulated next s., 111:19
Summer's, all on s. day, 858:7
compare thee to s. day, 226:2
day and with setting sun, 264:24
fantastic s. heat, 179:6
flower to summer sweet, 227:4
lease too short, 226:2

Summer's *(continued)*
proper man as see in s. day, 181:2
ripening breath, 183:11
tasted all the s. pride, 371:9
thy s. play, 374:4
vernal bloom or s. rose, 265:25
wonderland, 692:1
Summers, farmers pray that s. be wet, 96:6
in a sea of glory, 231:2
raw inclement s., 298:16
Summertime and livin' easy, 747:4
Summit, dreadful s. of the cliff, 202:8
from s. of pyramids, 387:12
life harder toward s., 589:24
lost in vapor, 423:15
Summits, snowy s. old in story, 482:19
Summon his array, 448:13
up remembrance of things past, 226:8
up the blood, 192:30
Summoned, spirits I s. up, 364:14
Summons, black Hecate's s., 221:6
Black Spot a s., 598:16
fate s. monarchs obey, 284:2
fearful s., 200:19
thee to heaven or hell, 220:11
when s. comes to join, 432:10
Summum bonum, 91:n2, 93:n6
ius summa iniuria, 124:26
Sumner's mind contained itself, 570:12
Sumptuous variety about New England weather, 559:22
Sun, again the s., 714:17
all except s. is set, 424:1
also ariseth, 23:32
and moon in flat sea sunk, 260:29
and moon should doubt, 375:14
and with the setting s., 264:24
ariseth they gather themselves, 19:11
as if s. blackamoor, 687:1
as long as s. shine, 856:9
as s. the morning dew, 285:27
as sure as s. will shine, 841:4
at going down of s., 650:6
at mercy of s., 600:10
at noon, 236:21
awake my soul and with s., 289:21
aweary of the s., 222:17
be not darkened, 25:7
beating way for rising s., 761:17
before the rising s., 304:7
best not to see beams of s., 61:14
black with strong s., 734:10
born dies comes again, 853:1
born of the s., 783:16
born over and over, 795:12
breaks through darkest clouds, 175:37
Brother S. who brings us day, 128:2
burn the great sphere, 223:36
cast in brass to S., 850:8
chaos of the s., 686:19
clear as the s., 25:27
common s. air skies, 335:5
dark simulacrum of God, 256:24
day past and yet I saw no s., 164:17
die with face to s, 602:8
distilled by the s., 575:2
don't go, 818:6
doubt that s. doth move, 203:3
duty to worship s., 572:3

Sun *(continued)*
evenin' s. go down, 663:4
eyes behold s. last time, 415:2
face downward in s., 734:8
fame s. of dead, 445:5
far from the s., 335:7
fear no more heat o' the s., 225:23
first Poets Then S., 545:7
foolery about orb like s., 209:32
force from which s. draws power, 705:3
frisk i' the s., 228:10
from rising of the s. unto going down, 19:20
fruit I bore was the s., 112:n2
gather round setting s., 393:19
give me splendid silent s., 520:12
gives light soon as he rises, 321:1
glorious s. in Heaven, 401:12
go out in midday, 753:6
golden apples of s., 637:10
gorgeous as s. at midsummer, 186:22
greater none beneath S., 635:18
he set a tabernacle for the s., 16:11
heap o' s. and shadder, 693:8
heart s. of their microcosm, 242:9
himself at center of universe, 143:7
himself fair hot wench, 184:23
hold farthing candle to s., 241:n4
hold glimmering tapers to s., 241:n4
I myself caused s. to rise, 649:15
I saw under the s., 24:30
if s. breed maggots, 203:6
images where s. beats, 718:12
imitate the s., 184:36
in bowling alley bowled s., 292:7
in dim eclipse, 264:18
in dominions never sets, 381:15
in front s. climbs slow, 512:10
in golden cup, 642:1
in lonely lands, 484:19
inconceivable idea of s., 687:21
is but a morning star, 507:22
is gone down while it was day, 29:14
is laid to sleep, 237:10
is lost and the earth, 235:26
itself which makes times, 234:17
Juliet is the s., 182:28
knitters in s., 209:24
knoweth his going down, 19:11
laughed in the s., 712:14
leaning against S., 544:9
leaves and flowers in s., 638:4
let not the s. go down, 45:28
let others hail rising s., 335:21
light candle to the s., 278:28
light dies with dying s., 600:14
light where no s. shines, 795:3
like ball of fire, 386:8
like Joshua commanded s., 320:21
liken Homer to setting s., 110:12
little window where s., 445:15
livery of burnished s., 188:13
looked over mountain's rim, 492:3
loss of s., 315:13
love earth s. animals, 518:10
Love that moves s. and other stars, 132:9
loves to live i' the s., 198:13
low descending s., 846:17
made summer by s. of York, 173:28

Sun (*continued*)

make guilty the s., 215:29
make our s. stand still, 277:3
maketh s. rise on evil and good, 34:8
man work s. to s., 846:16
marigold goes to bed wi' the sun, 228:26
maturing s., 438:11
moon or s. or what you please, 175:38
moon stars sweet, 452:3
more worship rising than setting s., 91:20
mother give me s., 540:11
my mistress' eyes nothing like the s., 228:1
nearer comes the s., 707:15
neither shall s. light on them, 48:25
never sets on empire, 381:*n*4
no better thing under the s., 24:27
no new thing under the s., 23:35
no s. its day, 818:8
no s. upon an Easter-day, 269:23
of righteousness arise, 31:3
only you under s., 732:10
out of God's blessing into s., 149:3
owes no homage unto s., 256:9
part of the colossal s., 688:17
pasted in sky, 655:13
pay no worship to garish s., 183:32
penetrates privies, 79:7
place in the s., 594:4
protects dewdrop from s., 395:20
question if His Glory, 545:16
raisin in the s., 762:16
ran s. down with talk, 85:14
remains pure through pollutions, 79:*n*5
risen to hear him crow, 512:21
rising of the s., 846:2
rose and set on Sioux land, 549:3
sand and wild uproar, 452:17
sea gone with s., 603:15
second before s. went out, 839:5
see s. with ignorant eye, 687:21
seemed a sheet of s., 793:4
self-same s. on court and cottage, 229:1
set a candle in the s., 241:18
sets to rise again, 495:10
setting s. and music at close, 179:9
setting s. set to rights, 440:2
shall not smite thee, 19:30
shineth upon dunghill, 79:*n*5
shut doors against setting s., 218:15
sitting in the s., 405:4
somewhere s. is shining, 630:4
Son of the S., 81:20
stain both moon and s., 226:11
stand a little out of my s., 79:3
stand still upon Gibeon, 10:24
steadies my soul, 714:17
study like heaven's glorious s., 176:20
subordinated s. and moon, 122:7
summer season when soft was s., 132:20
tell you how S. rose, 544:16
thank heavens s. gone in, 636:12
that brief December day, 468:17
that is young once only, 795:10
that s. thine eye, 226:14
till s. grows cold, 537:18
tired s. with talking, 534:3
to have enjoyed s., 529:1
to me is dark, 268:33

Sun (*continued*)

traveled short while towards s., 783:16
true as dial to s., 271:27
unruly S., 234:2
walk in the s., 203:6
was shining on the sea, 551:18
was warm wind chill, 670:5
what are you when s. shall rise, 232:16
when s. goes down, 742:4
when s. out wind still, 670:5
when s. shineth make hay, 147:9
wherever bright s. of heaven, 231:17
which sees all things, 52:24
who scattered into flight, 470:13
wind with fragrance of hot s., 661:19
wing subdivided by s., 714:20
wishes lengthen as our s. declines, 306:10
works done under the s., 24:1
worse than s. in March, 186:25
would have disappeared, 618:2
yesternight s. went hence, 234:11
Sunbeam impossible to be soiled, 79:*n*5
in winter's day, 317:12
thikke as motes in s., 136:20
Sunbeams, chances like s. pass, 319:*n*2
out of cucumbers, 298:16
stream forward, 855:22
Sunburnt by glare of life, 464:3
mirth, 437:7
this s. face, 372:2
Sunday, buried on S., 859:17
chicken in pot every S., 162:11
different from another day, 325:16
grand flights S. baths, 687:13
he was my S. rest, 775:6
not divide S. from week, 200:16
repentance on a S., 692:11
we will be married o' S., 175:29
Sundays, begin journey on S., 299:21
Sundered, as if birth s., 506:2
Sundering, love know no s. quarrels, 99:13
Sundial, motto of s., 410:15
Sundown, elected between s. and sunup, 685:15
we drink you at s., 806:10
Sundry contemplation of my travels, 199:23
moveth us in s. places, 49:18
Sung, by forms unseen dirge s., 336:16
first and last sung no more, 844:23
guardian angels s. this strain, 318:8
her amorous descant s., 266:16
Sappho loved and s., 423:24
strongest sweetest songs to be s., 521:17
Sunk, all s. beneath waves, 348:16
beneath watery floor, 262:5
in flat sea s., 260:29
Lethe-wards had s., 437:5
so low that sacred head, 261:21
world's whole sap is s., 234:20
Sunless sea, 401:13
Sunlight, golden s. glows, 502:3
moonlight unto s., 482:5
parables of s., 795:7
sudden in shaft of s., 720:13
weave s. in hair, 717:23
Sunlit arch, 670:5
Sunnier side of doubt, 486:24

Sunny, a little s. a little sad, 570:26
count only s. hours, 410:*n*1
dome, 401:19
in s. beams did glide, 371:9
Palestine, 681:4
pleasure dome, 401:17
side of life, 694:8
side up, 736:18
web of s. air, 504:13
Sunrise, lives in eternity's s., 373:13
lost between s. and sunset, 441:12
Sun's o'ercast with blood, 178:5
rim dips, 400:5
Suns, light of setting s., 391:4
process of the s., 482:3
radiance of a thousand s., 87:8
skies clouds of June, 547:11
systemed s. globed and lit, 575:21
that set may rise again, 237:14
Sunscreen, wear s., 841:13
Sunset and evening star, 487:2
between sunrise and s., 441:12
breezes shiver, 627:5
I have seen s., 603:11
life little shadow in s., 525:7
of life gives me lore, 408:19
ran one glorious blood-red, 492:6
sail beyond the s., 481:14
stained with horrors, 603:11
touch, 493:8
Sunsets, I eat s. and trees, 787:6
Sunshine and good water, 601:2
comforteth like s. after rain, 173:24
digressions s. of reading, 332:12
eternity about me in s., 593:21
fill sky with cloudless s., 100:9
glorious birth, 393:9
holiday, 259:16
if opened in s., 460:14
in the shady place, 161:1
Little S. stayed on, 813:12
on strange shore, 612:2
patriot, 354:10
spring s. streamed in, 549:5
white town drowsing in s., 560:4
Sun-split, tumbling mirth of s. clouds, 810:11
Sunt lacrimae rerum, 96:*n*15
Sun-thaw, thatch smokes in s., 401:11
Sunup, elected between sundown and s., 685:15
Sunward I've climbed, 810:11
Sup at six sleep at ten, 451:18
before we go, 858:9
of Jove's nectar s., 238:2
sipped no s., 565:25
Superannuated idol, 302:8
Supercilious hypocrisy of bishop, 360:8
Superego, external world s. and id, 608:1
Superexcellent, tobacco divine rare s., 241:14
Superficial, common sense hasty s., 505:27
Superfluity, barren s. of words, 295:10
sooner white hairs, 187:26
Superfluous, in nature's inventions nothing s., 141:9
in poorest thing s., 216:15
to demand time of day, 184:23
to many the s. is necessary, 578:21

Surrender *(continued)*
    to Him we s., 120:13
    unconditional s., 532:14
    we shall never s., 666:1
Surrenders, victory when opponent s. before
    hostilities, 83:5
    whosoever s. his face to God, 122:4
Surrounding, how to explore vacant vast s.,
    521:7
Surrounds, ever-during dark s. me, 265:25
Survey mankind, 324:5
    monarch of all I s., 347:20
    time takes s. of world, 187:5
Survival, assure s. of liberty, 799:7
    love the only s., 749:12
    of Fittest, 469:13
    of fittest, 523:13, 559:6
    of wildlife in Africa, 808:6
    re-vision an act of s., 824:16
    we are s. machines, 836:3
    without victory no s., 665:20
Survive and multiply, 469:15
    cannot s. wrongs repeated, 734:2
    monuments of wit s. monuments of
      power, 165:22
    only the fit s., 673:8
    opinions not s. without fight, 676:9
    or perish, 414:12
    our souls s. death, 104:*n6*
    passions which yet s., 427:18
Survived, don't see how Henry s., 792:6
    I s., 363:7
    pride of those who have s., 667:12
Survives, classic s. circumstances, 796:10
    plum s. its poems, 686:12
    Thomas Jefferson still s., 352:4
Survivor, many a stung s., 802:11
    of that time that place, 725:8
Survivors', dying more s. affair, 676:13
Susanna, O S., 538:13
Susanna's music, 687:6
Suspect everybody, 496:33
    once s. Caspian Fact, 546:13
    thoughts of others, 188:11
Suspected, new opinions always s., 286:3
    wished wife not so much as s., 91:25
Suspecting, without s. our abode, 547:1
Suspects himself of virtues, 746:4
    round up the usual s., 782:11
    yet soundly loves, 213:34
Suspend functioning of imagination, 755:1
    I s. my judgment, 153:3
    men cannot s. fate, 295:6
Suspended, I s. religious inquiries, 353:16
    'twixt heaven and earth s., 600:4
Suspense in news is torture, 269:14
Suspension of disbelief, 403:7
Suspicion always haunts guilty mind, 173:16
    Caesar's wife must be above s., 91:*n13*
    companion of mean souls, 354:7
    general s. and distrust, 660:7
    jealousy feeds upon s., 273:6
    more than half right, 756:14
    no s. of partiality in his writing, 90:16
    rumor fantasy, 824:8
    stuck full of eyes, 187:1
Suspicions, fresh s., 213:36
Suspicious friend, 312:4
    religious people s., 632:13

Suspire, we only live only s., 722:2
Sustain, prop that doth s. house, 190:2
Sustenance, White S. Despair, 545:13
Swabs, doctors is all s., 598:15
Swagman, jolly s., 630:9
Swain, frugal s., 337:14
Swains, that all our s. commend her, 176:12
Swaller, principles s., 514:23
Swallow a camel, 37:3
    blow and s. at same moment, 86:16
    come before s. dares, 228:27
    flying South, 483:1
    gudgeons ere they're catch'd, 60:*n4*
    more beliefs than digest, 617:25
    one s. makes a summer, 80:*n3*
    one s. not a summer, 80:10
    principles s., 514:23
    revenge s. them up, 214:15
    Swallow flying, 483:1
    up death in victory, 27:16
Swallowed, Aaron's rod s. their rods, 8:12
    as a s. bait, 227:22
    death s. up, 44:32
    easier s. than flap-dragon, 177:10
    half our sailors s., 173:12
    lighted kerosene lamp, 678:1
    oblivion s. cities up, 208:7
    other books to be s., 168:15
    up and lost, 265:4
    up in death, 76:16
Swalloweth the ground with fierceness,
    15:15
Swallowing, pity from s. wave, 276:5
Swallow's, hope flies with s. wings, 174:17
Swallows twitter in the skies, 438:13
    west wind and the s., 85:16
Swam in a gondola, 199:25
    little Fish s., 500:1
Swamped, atoms cannot be s. by force, 92:16
Swan, black s. rare bird, 113:9
    cygnet to pale faint s., 178:25
    dies the s., 485:14
    every goose s. lad, 514:4
    he himself was s., 462:1
    of Avon, 238:12
    play the s. and die in music, 76:*n6*
    silver s. living had no note, 844:23
    think thy s. a crow, 182:19
    were I s. sing like s., 112:9
Swanee, way down upon S. River, 538:15
Swanlike, makes a s. end, 189:2
Swans, all his geese are s., 336:8
    all our geese are s., 240:23
    as much spirit of prophecy as s., 76:17
    geese s. s. geese, 531:4
    more geese than s., 844:23
    nine-and-fifty s., 638:11
    of others are geese, 336:8
    sing more lustily, 76:17
Swap, botch trying to s., 476:10
    horses crossing river, 476:10
Swarm, Europe really a s., 702:18
    not good for s. not good for bee,
      115:25
    of bees and honey in the carcass, 10:39
    of bees in May, 845:12
Swashing and martial outside, 197:35
Swat, Akond of S., 500:2
Swath, spares next s., 438:12

Sway, a little rule a little s., 317:12
    in wind like corn, 717:20
    love of s., 310:7
    mercy above sceptered s., 189:19
    mild parental s., 534:9
    mortal things doth s., 161:19
    of the sea, 587:3
    prevailed with double s., 342:7
    sweeping whirlwind's s., 335:13
Swayed, at times mob s., 671:3
    body s. to music, 640:15
    leaves and flowers in sun, 638:4
    rod of empire might have s., 334:18
Sways, by submitting s., 310:9
    gently s. at ease, 670:11
    God nearby, 792:4
    so s. she level, 209:22
Swear an eternal friendship, 278:19
    began to curse and s., 37:35
    by Apollo Physician, 72:16
    by thy gracious self, 183:9
    by yonder blessed moon I s., 183:8
    do not s. at all, 183:9
    lovers s. more performance, 208:5
    make deacon s., 515:5
    no where woman true and fair, 233:14
    not at all, 34:5
    not bound to s. allegiance, 100:18
    not by the moon, 183:8
    that what I went through, 759:2
    when very angry s., 561:12
    when you rant and s., 241:*n3*
Sweareth to his own hurt, 16:6
Swearin', judicious s. keeps temper, 646:16
Swears, Lucrece s. he did her wrong, 175:12
    Nature s. lovely dears, 378:13
    punishment if one s. false oath, 53:29
    she is made of truth, 228:2
Sweat, all of a muck of s., 341:14
    and whine about condition, 519:16
    athlete crowned in s. of brow, 118:6
    awe at first bead of s., 826:4
    blood toil tears s., 665:19
    cold s. bathes me, 57:20
    drop of s. on drill ground, 708:*n4*
    earned with s. of brows, 156:1
    gods put s. in front of excellence, 56:12
    grunt and s., 203:33
    midday s., 249:6
    night s. with terror, 640:5
    none s. but for promotion, 198:6
    of his brow, 506:20
    of other men's faces, 477:3
    of thy face, 6:10
    save gallon of blood, 708:14
    tears s. or blood, 665:*n4*
    wet with honest s., 466:8
    who casts to write must s., 238:10
    won by blood and s. of innocent, 836:12
Sweated wealth out of our people, 746:2
Sweats, bloody s., 605:21
    easier than I do, 506:20
    Falstaff s. to death, 185:15
Sweaty faces of coffee-pickers, 706:7
    head on s. bolster, 809:3
    this s. haste, 200:17
Swede, strike terror in S., 447:2
Swedish, French operas sung by S. artists,
    627:14

Sweeney to Mrs. Porter, 718:17
Sweep clouds no more, 473:3
  cobwebs from sky, 859:11
  on you citizens, 198:2
  over thee in vain, 421:26
  wind s. man away, 528:21
  your chimneys I s., 372:4
Sweepers, as chimney-s. come to dust, 225:23
Sweeping, in sceptered pall s. by, 260:6
  love s. the country, 747:2
  rain that leaveth no food, 289:23
  up the Heart, 546:8
  whirlwind's sway, 335:13
Sweeps a room as for thy laws, 251:1
  next gale that s. from north, 353:3
Sweet, adversity's s. milk philosophy, 184:2
  air coming into house, 714:2
  Alice Ben Bolt, 513:17
  all love is s., 428:9
  all season shall be s., 401:11
  allaying both with its s. air, 229:19
  amazing grace how s. the sound, 339:12
  and bitter fancy, 199:32
  and honorable to die for country, 99:27
  and low, 482:18
  and musical as Apollo's lute, 177:7
  and pure and fair, 442:8
  and twenty, 209:14
  and virtuous soul, 250:11
  approach of even or morn, 265:25
  are uses of adversity, 197:37
  as by fancy feigned, 482:22
  as I could bear, 669:16
  as love, 369:9
  as my revenge, 224:30
  as summer, 231:14
  as the primrose, 342:12
  aspect of princes, 231:2
  attractive grace, 266:10
  attractive kind of grace, 171:9
  Auburn, 341:28
  be good s. maid, 514:2
  bells jangled, 204:9
  bird that shunnest noise, 260:2
  bird's throat, 198:11
  bitter conduce to s., 809:5
  blazon of s. beauty's best, 227:11
  blown hair is s., 719:12
  bread of deceit is s., 22:21
  bye-and-bye, 854:16
  came o'er my ear like s. sound, 208:25
  cement of love, 247:15
  chariot, 863:4
  cheat gone, 662:13
  childish days, 392:8
  city dreaming spires, 530:16
  coming my own my s., 485:12
  compulsion in music lie, 259:6
  concord of s. sounds, 190:7
  courtesies of life, 333:6
  cowslip's grace, 363:4
  day so cool so calm, 250:9
  disorder in the dress, 248:3
  dividing throat, 253:14
  doth suck his s., 164:15
  dream when trick's over, 681:2
  Echo sweetest nymph, 260:26
  every bitter thing is s., 23:12

Sweet *(continued)*
  every s. hath sour, 455:18
  experience of this s. life, 132:5
  fierce hour and s., 665:1
  flow gently s. Afton, 379:10
  food of knowledge, 163:25
  for s. grape vine destroy, 175:5
  for thy more s. understanding, 176:24
  Genevieve, 571:4
  glideth at own s. will, 392:13
  good amiable or s., 268:3
  good night s. prince, 207:15
  great s. mother, 568:14
  guess each s., 437:10
  he makes s. music with stones, 176:8
  heard melodies s., 437:18
  Helen make me immortal, 170:23
  his mouth is most s., 25:26
  how monie counsels s., 379:15
  how sour s. music is, 180:14
  how s. and fair she seems, 257:24
  how s. I roamed, 371:9
  how s. is solitude, 347:19
  how s. their memory still, 347:2
  if life s. give thanks, 569:15
  imaginary relish is so s., 208:2
  in s. pangs remember me, 209:21
  influences of Pleiades, 15:10
  is breath of vernal shower, 335:20
  is every sound, 483:8
  is peace so s., 353:3
  is pleasure after pain, 285:11
  is revenge, 423:12
  is the breath of morn, 266:17
  is the whispering music, 85:7
  keen smell, 542:7
  lady s. and kind, 844:21
  land of liberty, 469:8
  life s. brother, 452:3
  loathe s. tunes, 568:15
  look s. upon seat, 643:20
  love me s., 831:17
  love s. for a day, 568:17
  lovers love the spring, 200:5
  made s. moan, 439:5
  magic brings together, 381:8
  medicine thee to s. sleep, 214:6
  meet in s. Jerusalem, 173:13
  mercy nobility's badge, 175:13
  milk of concord, 221:34
  mingles s. bitterness with her cares, 94:20
  more s. than painted pomp, 197:36
  mountain nymph s. liberty, 259:11
  music's melting fall, 335:20
  musk-roses and eglantine, 181:12
  my Adonis hath a s. tooth, 163:13
  my home s. home, 716:7
  my lady s. arise, 225:12
  my life smack s., 495:10
  my s. Highland Mary, 380:4
  nature's s. cunning hand, 209:8
  naught so s. as melancholy, 239:17
  neglect more taketh me, 237:16
  never merry when hear s. music, 190:6
  not s. to dance on air, 605:19
  notes by distance made s., 337:4
  o' the year, 228:21
  oblivious antidote, 222:12
  of bitter bark, 669:17

Sweet *(continued)*
  one s. sacrifice, 230:23
  Parthenope nourished me, 96:21
  parting is such s. sorrow, 183:16
  Peace is crowned, 279:6
  perfections caught, 171:10
  plums so s. and so cold, 703:11
  poison for age's tooth, 177:21
  poison of misused wine, 260:16
  pour s. dew on his tongue, 56:4
  psalmist of Israel, 12:9
  reluctant amorous delay, 266:11
  retired solitude, 260:29
  retirement urges s. return, 267:27
  Richard s. lovely rose, 185:6
  Roman hand, 210:10
  rose by any name as s., 183:3
  serenity of books, 467:21
  showers of s. discourse, 272:9
  silent thought, 226:8
  singing in the choir, 846:2
  sleep of laboring man s., 24:13
  Slug-a-bed, 248:16
  slumbers of virtuous, 302:1
  smell of success, 807:2
  smell s. and blossom in dust, 254:7
  smellest so s., 214:28
  solitude is s., 347:19
  sounds and s. airs, 230:6
  sounds together, 637:17
  spring full of s. days, 250:10
  spring year's pleasant king, 232:7
  stay O s., 845:1
  stolen waters are s., 21:13
  such fleet things s., 569:4
  such s. thunder, 181:28
  summer's flower to summer s., 227:4
  swan of Avon, 238:12
  sweets to the s., 206:29
  sweets with s. war not, 225:30
  swore my lips were s., 408:9
  tell not s. I am unkind, 275:22
  Thames run softly, 162:7
  the coming on of evening, 266:18
  the moonlight sleeps, 190:5
  then how it was s., 494:17
  thing to revisit in dreams, 69:11
  things s. to taste prove sour, 179:2
  though in sadness, 429:4
  though wickedness be s., 14:27
  thoughts that savor of content, 165:16
  thy s. love remembered, 226:7
  to dance to violins, 605:19
  to know eye will mark, 423:11
  to let mind unbend, 100:17
  to look into fair, 435:17
  to make the end most s., 178:33
  took s. counsel together, 17:77
  touches of s. harmony, 190:5
  two-and-twenty, 424:26
  utter s. breath, 182:2
  wee wife o' mine, 380:3
  what makes life so s., 547:4
  where late s. birds sang, 226:24
  white wine, 681:4
  world not s. in end, 568:17
  yellow finish and s. wood, 756:5
  your most s. voices, 224:24
  Zeus grant s. delight, 65:31

Sweeten my imagination, 217:22
   this little hand, 222:7
Sweeteners of tea, 322:3
Sweeter air where it was made, 714:19
   mountain sheep s., 418:9
   no s. fat than sticks to bones, 519:5
   pains of love be s. far, 282:18
   rose is s. in bud, 163:14
   speech s. than honey, 52:8
   than apples to children, 603:9
   than honey and the honeycomb, 16:12
   than sound of instrument, 256:7
   world hath not a s. creature, 214:20
   wrath s. than honeycomb, 53:26
   yet is gratitude, 335:20
Sweetes' li'l' feller, 613:5
Sweetest, canker lives in s. bud, 226:11
   girl I know, 674:2
   hours e'er I spend, 378:14
   last taste s. last, 179:9
   Lesbia, 231:21
   life near bone s., 507:20
   li'l' feller, 613:5
   love I do not go, 234:10
   melancholy, 243:5
   passage of a song, 592:15
   rain makes not fresh, 242:18
   Shakespeare Fancy's child, 259:20
   song ear ever heard, 422:22
   songs saddest thought, 429:19
   strongest and s. songs remain, 521:17
   surfeit of the s. things, 181:17
   sweet Echo s. nymph, 260:26
   vibrate s. pleasure, 378:22
   voice of God's creatures, 478:n1
   way to me, 634:6
Sweetheart come see if the rose, 151:2
   stay my s. never go, 580:7
   that old s. of mine, 596:4
   Tray Blanch and S., 217:5
Sweetly, hears you nearby speaking, 57:20
   how s. did they float, 260:27
   marveling s. on ills, 724:12
   methinks how s. flows, 248:19
   more s. than rhyme, 437:16
   nimbly and s. recommends, 219:15
   one s. solemn thought, 535:19
   played in tune, 378:19
   so s. were forsworn, 211:31
   worm feed s. upon me, 237:3
   worm shall feed s. on him, 14:31
Sweetness and light, 297:19, 531:16
   by convention s., 72:14
   flows into breast, 640:19
   keeps with perfect s., 455:10
   linked s. long drawn out, 259:20
   loathe taste of s., 186:13
   of proportion, 237:19
   out of the strong came s., 11:1
   through mine ear, 260:10
   waste s. on desert air, 334:20
Sweets, brought'st Thy s. along, 250:7
   compacted lie, 250:10
   diffuse balmy s. around, 167:n2
   feast of nectared s., 261:3
   grown common lose delight, 227:9
   into your list, 417:16
   last taste of s., 179:9
   lost in the s., 307:16

Sweets *(continued)*
   of Hasty Pudding, 369:2
   stolen s. are best, 301:8
   to the sweet, 206:29
   wilderness of s., 267:4
   with sweet war not, 225:30
Swell a progress, 717:14
   bosom with thy fraught, 214:14
   deep sea s., 718:20
   drift in gradual s., 830:14
   from lyre within sky, 478:3
   ghosted you up a s. story, 762:13
   green s. in havens dumb, 587:1
   music with voluptuous s., 420:16
   no Minstrel raptures s., 396:11
   soul to rage, 285:15
Swelling and limitless billows, 401:20
   angelic songs s., 501:17
   prologues to the s. act, 219:4
Swells and s. in his fury, 715:7
   note that s. gale, 335:5
   pealing anthem s., 334:16
Swept, be not s. off feet by impression,
   112:15
   cleaned windows s. floor, 563:17
   it for half a year, 551:19
   with confused alarms, 531:2
Swerve a hair from truth, 208:7
   from s. of shore to bend of bay, 696:14
Swift as a bird or thought, 54:24
   as a shadow, 180:20
   be approaching flight, 430:23
   has sailed into rest, 641:3
   how s. how secretly, 734:8
   lonely and s. like planet, 611:17
   love is s., 138:13
   O time too s., 164:9
   race is not to the s., 24:30
   race is to the s., 612:23
   red flesh, 753:16
   sandy glass, 239:10
   slow man catches up with s., 54:27
   slow sweet sour, 587:10
   spirit beautiful and s., 430:10
   terrible s. sword, 513:18
   to hear, 47:12
   too s. arrives as tardy, 183:25
   true hope is s., 174:17
Swifter than eagles, 11:36
   than weaver's shuttle, 14:2
Swiftest traveler goes afoot, 506:19
Swiftly, bright youth passes s., 61:16
   flowing cups run s. round, 276:3
   happiness too s. flies, 333:22
   most s. fester or putrefy, 227:n1
   walk o'er wave, 430:22
Swiftness, O s. never ceasing, 164:9
Swig, absorb deep s. of it, 678:1
Swim, creep s. or fly, 289:15
   mother may I s., 851:13
   naughty night to s. in, 216:31
   sink or s., 185:7
   sink or s. live or die, 414:12
   sink or s. together, 653:18
   teaching a fish to s., 124:14
   wanton boys that s. on bladders, 231:2
   wherever wood can s., 388:9
   with bladders of philosophy, 293:4
Swimmer, strong s. in agony, 423:17

Swimmin', old s. hole, 596:7
Swimming from tree to tree, 800:11
   my wife and sister were s., 788:3
   under water, 746:21
Swims, into his ken, 435:19
   only gamefish s. upstream, 614:6
Swindles, great s. simple, 626:7
Swine, cast pearls before s., 35:2
   gotta have a s., 820:5
   is unclean, 9:11
   nor feed the s., 859:6
   pearl for carnal s., 271:19
   unclean spirits entered s., 38:22
   wine, 451:13
Swine's, jewel of gold in a s. snout, 21:18
Swing dat yaller gal, 593:17
   don't mean thing if ain't got s., 753:19
   low sweet chariot, 863:4
   of the sea, 587:1
   Seraphs s. snowy Hats, 544:9
   that fellow's got to s., 605:17
   tramp and trudge, 699:16
Swinged, Saint George that s. dragon, 177:26
Swinger of birches, 669:6
Swinging low with sullen roar, 260:4
Swings, lost on roundabouts pulls up on s.,
   659:17
Swinish, hoofs of s. multitude, 345:15
Swirls of musk, 596:1
Switch, hire executioner to throw s., 746:2
Switzerland had love democracy, 797:4
Swiveller, here's a state cried Mr. S., 496:32
Swollen shadow, 791:12
Swoller, let 'em s. you, 793:3
Swoon, Locke sank into s., 640:13
Swooned nor uttered cry, 483:4
   soul s. slowly, 696:4
Swoop, at one fell s., 222:1
Sword, another drawn with s., 477:4
   arm held fair s., 139:3
   brave man with s., 605:18
   deputed s., 211:10
   die on mine own s., 222:19
   every man's s. was against his fellow,
   11:23
   eye tongue, 204:7
   fallen by edge of the s., 32:39
   famous by my s., 272:3
   father's s. girded on, 411:16
   flaming s. which turned, 6:11
   fleshed thy maiden s., 187:10
   glorious by my s., 272:n1
   I with s. will open, 190:23
   is the s. unswayed, 174:16
   let s. of France fall, 728:8
   light of thy s., 444:11
   man for the s., 483:3
   nation shall not lift s., 26:11
   nor s. nor age destroy, 105:21
   not peace but a s., 35:31
   of heaven will bear, 211:29
   of justice has no scabbard, 368:17
   of justice lay down, 295:4
   of the Lord and of Gideon, 10:36
   of war or of law, 359:4
   one s. keeps another in sheath, 252:4
   outwears its sheath, 423:1
   pen mightier than s., 452:10
   pen preferable to s., 157:22

T

Take (continued)

any shape but that, 221:14
arms against sea of troubles, 203:33
arms t. your last embrace, 184:17
away art of writing, 387:5
beak from out heart, 479:7
bread from mouth of labor, 358:12
but degree away, 207:26
can't t. that away from me, 747:9
care of the sense, 550:17
chances for peace, 717:5
come to fork in road t. it, 814:14
each man's censure, 201:26
eat this is my body, 37:27
form from off my door, 479:7
from seventy springs score, 618:7
from them sense of reckoning, 193:17
give an inch t. an ell, 149:*n8*
give me today t. tomorrow, 122:25
heaven t. my soul, 178:21
heed of loving me, 235:11
her up tenderly, 446:7
him and cut him in stars, 183:32
him for all in all, 201:12
honor from me and life done, 178:31
I believe and t. it, 152:3
into air my breath, 437:12
it as it comes, 566:5
it from me, 626:16
it from me kiddo, 739:15
kiss you t. is better, 208:18
life easy, 636:20
love easy, 636:19
love together to sky, 579:12
me into bright child of mind, 740:18
my milk for gall, 219:11
my waking slow, 780:15
my wife please, 775:2
my yoke, 35:35
no thought for morrow, 34:22
not able to t. the lead, 53:13
not t. his own life, 76:15
not t. it any more, 811:12
not thy holy spirit from me, 17:28
note O world, 214:12
nothing of his labor, 24:14
nothing on looks, 499:1
O take those lips away, 211:31
one I never tried, 736:9
pair of sparkling eyes, 566:7
passage we did not t., 720:8
physic pomp, 216:27
pray Lord soul t., 296:15
risk I had to t. and took, 670:20
some come to t. their ease, 231:18
the wings of the morning, 20:13
thee with her eyelids, 21:6
them he cannot t., 534:3
they have to t. you in, 668:22
thine ease, 39:28
thine old cloak about thee, 844:7
this cadence from Yeats, 780:14
this cannot t. her, 269:21
thy rod, 8:11
Time will t. my love away, 226:19
to open road, 520:2
triple ways to t., 634:6
up our quarrel with the foe, 660:10
up read, 119:10

Take (continued)

up thy bed, 38:15
upon's mystery of things, 218:1
we must t. the current, 197:14
what course others may t., 353:3
what is given, 671:18
what sweet hour yields, 431:7
will for the deed, 146:13
winds of March, 228:27
you a button-hole lower, 177:13
you t. my house, 190:2
your delight in momentariness, 743:17
Taken, ark of God is t., 11:19
at the flood, 197:13
away that which he hath, 37:14
better care of myself, 700:13
from you for your better health, 243:13
fun where found it, 634:18
hath t. away thy blessing, 7:13
home gone and t. thy wages, 225:23
no profit where no pleasure t., 175:21
one t. the other left, 37:11
the Lord hath t. away, 13:26
to drink, 652:13
when t. to be shaken, 383:14
worth's unknown although height t., 227:17
Taker, laid to make t. mad, 227:22
Takes away the performance, 220:21
blesseth him that t., 189:19
no fairy t., 200:22
no man t. wealth with him, 61:15
no private road, 311:14
soul t. nothing with her, 76:20
the reason prisoner, 219:2
time t. all gives all, 159:8
Takest, bringing in secret whom thou t. away, 90:6
whatsoever thou t. in hand, 32:13
Taketh away sin of world, 40:35
he t. wise in craftiness, 13:38
sweet neglect more t. me, 237:16
Taking away someone else's freedom, 804:1
from one class to give to other, 316:14
in hand a city, 64:17
in one another's washing, 850:12
Talcum always walcum, 763:8
Tale, as a t. that is told, 18:21
every schoolboy knows, 333:17
every t. condemns me, 174:21
every tongue brings in t., 174:21
fair t. of a tub, 144:1
flowery t. more sweetly, 437:16
hear by t. or history, 180:19
I could a t. unfold, 202:12
love-gift of fairy t., 551:8
moon takes up wondrous t., 301:15
never heard in t. or song, 260:15
of hardihood endurance, 649:16
of Shaun or Shem, 696:16
of Troy divine, 260:6
out of season, 32:35
plain t. put you down, 185:26
point moral or adorn t., 324:7
round unvarnished t., 212:26
say t. as said to me, 396:8
schoolboy's t., 420:9
shepherd tells his t., 259:14
silly fairy t., 336:3

Tale (continued)

speeds best plainly told, 174:13
tell t. tit, 857:5
telle a t. after a man, 135:16
that I relate, 348:20
thereby hangs a t., 198:16
to him my t. I teach, 400:22
told by an idiot, 222:16
Truth hero of my t., 542:8
twice-told t., 178:10
which holdeth children from play, 163:26
without love, 586:19
would cure deafness, 229:12
yet often told a t., 409:6
Talebearer, go up and down as a t., 9:14
Talebearers as bad as tale-makers, 367:26
Tale-makers, tale-bearers as bad as t., 367:26
Talent, blessed who have no t., 454:8
blessed with each t., 312:4
contribution according to t., 510:*n5*
does what it can, 548:12
extraordinary collection of t., 799:13
formed in stillness, 364:12
grieved when man of t. dies, 356:16
happy possessor of t., 772:11
has t. cannot use it, 760:6
honors t. in every branch, 73:18
inspiration love, 622:7
of meat-packer, 650:5
succeeded using whole t., 760:6
to see what under nose, 776:13
which is death to hide, 263:12
Talents equal to business, 113:21
grounds are virtue and t., 358:19
la carrière ouverte aux t., 388:12
let fools use t., 209:6
reviewers tried t. failed, 402:16
Tale's, sad t. best for winter, 228:14
Tales already plainly told, 55:11
dead men tell no t., 283:26
natural fear increased with t., 167:7
out of school, 148:1
tell old t. and laugh, 218:1
to me so dear, 442:4
witch-t. Annie tells, 596:5
words as idle t., 40:26
Talk a little wild, 230:21
after-dinner t., 480:10
always t. who never think, 238:*n2*
and never think, 238:13
bad music people don't t., 605:8
Cabots t. only to God, 621:22
cane leaves rusty with t., 742:5
cannot t. with civet in room, 347:13
come after me let people t., 131:11
create do not t., 365:24
fishes t. like whales, 343:9
fool may t. wise man speaks, 238:19
from getting overwise, 670:3
good gods how he will t., 294:9
hear t. of court news, 218:1
innocent of t. or action, 770:13
I've come to t. with you again, 837:7
let's t. of graves, 179:27
let's t. of wills, 179:27
living doll can t. t. t., 827:8
loves to hear himself t., 183:23
low talk slow, 777:9

Talk (*continued*)

never spent hour's t. withal, 176:28
night crept upon our t., 197:15
no one would t. much in society, 364:21
not of other men's lives, 32:33
not to me of name, 424:26
nothing but t. of his horse, 187:29
of crabbed old men, 94:4
of degeneracy and decay, 448:17
of many things, 552:3
of mysteries, 505:13
of nothing but business, 140:2
of pushing their bones, 821:7
of things heavenly, 281:22
pleasant walk pleasant t., 552:1
ran sun down with t., 85:14
save us, 696:16
sense to a fool, 70:12
sense to American people, 760:2
small t. dies in agonies, 429:10
so much about myself, 506:7
some little t. awhile, 471:15
some t. of Alexander, 846:11
telephone really able to t., 549:1
tendeth only to penury, 21:32
'tisn't beauty nor good t., 635:17
to him of Jacob's ladder, 458:10
tongues have their t., 156:*n*3
too much, 283:14
true I t. of dreams, 182:23
two t. one hear, 455:27
ways of making men t., 731:2
what common t. of town is, 288:7
with crowds keep virtue, 635:21
with lover's ghost, 235:7
with you walk with you, 188:2
woman who occasions least t., 74:6
Talkative, learned silence from t., 700:22
Talked between the Rooms, 545:5
I believe they t. of me, 305:5
like poor Poll, 335:23
long enough about rights, 779:4
of their Raphaels, 343:6
worse than being t. about, 604:13
Talker, time is a t., 70:19
Talkers, know little great t., 331:7
no good doers, 174:1
Talkin', you t. to me, 840:4
Talking and eloquence not same, 238:19
Frenchman always t., 329:2
he is t. or is pursuing, 12:29
he will be t., 194:36
bear voices t. about everything, 841:1
hydrant in yard, 671:16
in mathematics never know what t.,
     660:11
is passion of woman, 300:5
keep people from t., 156:*n*3
know what we are t. about, 585:19
lived life t. at street corners, 724:19
lonely people t. to each other, 770:12
of axes, 550:6
of fall of man, 507:31
of Michelangelo, 717:7
people t. about themselves, 586:17
tired sun with t., 534:3
to Hens of Dorking, 500:5
Talks, don't care how much man t., 508:13
wish I liked way it t., 624:5

Tall, as cedar t. and slender, 363:4
ask Alice when ten feet t., 834:6
confidence in t. man merited, 778:13
divinely t., 480:23
ship and star to steer, 680:15
to reach the pole, 303:16
yond t. anchoring bark, 217:18
Taller by breadth of nail, 298:12
town than Rome, 664:12
Tallest pine, 264:9
Tally, no books but score and t., 172:22
Talmud, rather believe fables in T., 167:21
Tam, ah T. thou'll get thy fairin, 380:2
lo'ed him like brither, 379:16
was glorious, 379:17
Tamarind, dream beneath t. tree, 477:14
Tambourine, Mr. T. Man, 836:7
Tamburlaine must die, 170:5
the Scourge of God, 170:5
Tame a shrew, 241:13
glass thou canst not t., 249:17
heyday in the blood is t., 205:22
of all t. a flatterer, 237:12
though I seem t., 150:3
tongue can no man t., 47:17
Tamed and shabby tigers, 656:10
by Miltown, 801:3
Tamely, suffer t. lawless attack, 337:10
Tameness, trusts in t. of a wolf, 217:4
Tamer of human breast, 334:1
Tames, punishment t. man, 589:14
Tammie, as T. glowered, 379:20
Tammy, like T. Wynette, 837:*n*1
Tan, caftan of t., 686:20
cheek of t., 468:9
Tangere, noli me t., 41:*n*3
noli me t. for Caesar's I am, 150:3
Tangle of squabbling nationalities, 615:16
Tangled in amorous nets, 268:19
lie t. in her hair, 276:2
web we weave, 396:23
Tangles of Neaera's hair, 261:19
Tankards scooped in Pearl, 544:7
Tant pis and tant mieux, 333:5
pour tant, 148:*n*14
Tantum religio potuit suadere malorum,
     92:*n*7
Tao, action of T., 59:3
destruction of T. and virtue, 82:27
function of T., 59:3
is storehouse of all things, 59:11
leveled together by T., 82:22
look at T. and do not see it, 58:15
takes no action, 59:3
that can be told of, 58:7
when average hear T., 59:4
when highest hear T., 59:4
when lowest hear T., 59:4
why it is so near to T., 58:12
Tape, red t., 498:13
ticker t. ain't spaghetti, 696:19
Taper of conviviality, 496:28
Taper-light, with t. garnish heaven, 178:14
Taper's, like gleaming t. light, 340:13
Tapers, hold glimmering t. to sun, 241:*n*4
Tapestries, speech like embroidered t., 64:23
Tapestry, give children right to study t.,
     351:14
Tappertit, strings said Mr. T., 496:35

Tapping, suddenly there came t., 478:20
Tar, in fir t. is, 860:10
water proportioned, 306:17
Tarantara tarantara, 564:4
Ta-ra-ra-boom-de-ay, 644:6
Tara's halls, 411:11
Tar-baby ain't sayin' nuthin', 593:6
Tard dans un monde trop vieux, 488:*n*3
Tardy apish nation, 179:10
as t. as too slow, 183:25
Tarentum, far from my native T., 85:15
Tares, crop of corn a field of t., 164:17
of mine own brain, 255:18
Targeted trod like Spring, 641:12
Tarn, dank t. of Auber, 479:12
Tarnish late on Wenlock Edge, 619:2
Tarquin, great house of T., 448:13
viewed in her face's field, 175:3
Tarried, too long we t., 499:16
Tarrieth, guest that t. but a day, 31:19
tide t. no man, 147:10
time nor tide t., 147:*n*7
Tarry at Jericho until beards be grown, 12:1
awhile says Slow, 858:9
why t. the wheels of his chariots, 10:34
Tar's labor or Turkman's rest, 425:6
Tarsus, a Jew of T., 42:26
stately ship of T., 269:6
Tart, to eat with apple t., 599:1
Tartarly, savage and T., 425:1
Tarts, made some t., 858:7
Tarzan, I am T. of the Apes, 674:12
me T. you Jane, 674:*n*4
of the Apes, 674:11
Task, accomplished his t., 686:7
delightful t., 318:1
labor at eternal t., 535:11
laborer's t. o'er, 538:10
long day's t. is done, 223:34
my t. is smoothly done, 261:11
of pure ablution, 439:11
of twentieth century to explore
     unconscious, 616:5
remaining before us, 476:7
sore t., 200:16
there's the rub the t., 97:23
though hard be t., 535:18
what he reads as t., 326:19
worldly t. hast done, 225:23
Tasking, whole soul's t., 514:15
Taskmaster's, my great T. eye, 259:5
Taskmasters, lies religion of t., 649:1
Tassel-gentle, lure this t. back, 183:13
Taste, all ashes to the t., 420:18
and see that the Lord is good, 17:1
arbiter of t., 113:23
by which relished, 395:2
from fountain wells up bitter t., 93:16
good strong thick smoke, 492:8
is the only morality, 517:18
last t. of sweets, 179:9
liquor never brewed, 544:7
loathe t. of sweetness, 186:13
man of wealth and t., 838:5
man's hand not able to t., 182:1
never t. who always drink, 238:*n*2
no t. when you married me, 367:28
not Pierian spring, 308:11
of death but once, 196:10

Tear *(continued)*
    heart to dog to t., 635:19
    intellectual thing, 375:4
    man without a t., 409:5
    never t. linnet from leaf, 639:13
    newborn infant's t., 374:8
    passage of angel's t., 435:18
    Recording Angel dropped a t., 332:28
    shed bitter t., 551:19
    smile on lips t. in eye, 396:20
    splendid t., 485:11
    still ushered with t., 309:24
    sympathetic t., 334:6
    tattered ensign, 473:3
    to pieces that great bond, 221:7
    we shed though secret, 411:10
Tearing up pea patch, 742:2
Tears, angry t. gone, 638:19
    are on her cheeks, 29:27
    before my t. did drown it, 250:15
    big round t. coursed down, 198:1
    bitter t. to shed, 534:3
    blood toil t. sweat, 665:19
    blotted all over with t., 490:20
    broomsticks and t., 638:19
    bucket full of t. am I., 180:9
    cannot bear a mother's t., 98:8
    crave stain of t., 669:17
    crocodile t., 165:*n*3
    crocodiles shed t. when would devour,
        168:3
    crying but without t., 801:9
    dark with torment and t., 508:19
    drop t. as fast, 215:13
    fight from eyes t., 724:21
    flow with t. of gold, 372:9
    fountains fraught with t., 164:12
    from wrath-bearing tree, 718:4
    girlish t., 616:2
    hence these t., 88:11
    here are the t. of things, 96:34
    hired t., 256:13
    idle tears, 482:21
    if you have t., 196:32
    in t. amid alien corn, 437:13
    iron t. down Pluto's cheek, 260:7
    like Niobe all t., 201:6
    Lord God will wipe away t., 27:16
    mine own t. do scald, 217:29
    mist of t., 620:17
    no t. in writer no t. in reader, 671:11
    nor all your T. wash out, 471:21
    not pay honor with t., 87:13
    nothing is here for t., 269:15
    now am full of t., 636:20
    of eternity, 619:19
    of one tiny creature, 525:17
    of repentance you'll wipe, 373:12
    of sky for loss of sun, 315:13
    of things, 96:34
    rain shower of commanded t., 175:20
    remember with t., 535:16
    rent is sorrow income t., 249:8
    shall drown the wind, 219:18
    Siren t., 227:18
    smiled through their t., 549:5
    smiles t. of boyhood's years, 412:7
    smiling through t., 53:1
    songs composed of t., 488:10

Tears *(continued)*
    such as angels weep, 264:20
    sweat or blood, 665:*n*4
    sympathetic t., 335:8
    that speak, 275:18
    thaw not frost, 430:1
    they that sow in t., 20:3
    thoughts too deep for t., 393:19
    time to plant t., 785:14
    time with gift of t., 568:1
    tired of t. and laughter, 569:1
    unseen and unknown, 472:22
    waste not fresh t., 70:20
    watered heaven with t., 374:6
    way with t. watered, 656:15
    weep barren t., 428:4
    wipe away all t., 49:1
    with sobs and t. sorted, 552:6
    your death brought me t., 85:14
Tear-wrung millions, 665:*n*4
Teas, baked cookies and had t., 840:7
    where small talk dies, 429:10
Tease, fools no more I'll t., 309:22
    the huswife's wool, 261:9
Teases, he knows it t., 550:7
    mind over for years, 595:5
Teatray, like t. in sky, 550:12
Technique and style of Europe, 815:1
Techniques, me with my grim t., 812:3
    to create full life, 769:14
Technology, for a successful t., 803:3
    knack of arranging world, 786:4
Tecum vivere amem tecum obeam libens,
    100:*n*1
Tedious as twice-told tale, 178:10
    old fools, 203:11
    relations t. pack, 605:10
    returning as t. as go o'er, 221:19
    road will be less t., 95:29
    shorten t. nights, 232:3
    sport would be t., 184:36
    thinking his prattle t., 180:13
    to tell tales already told, 55:11
Tedium, pretentious quotations t., 614:1
Teeming brain, 439:8
    mistress barren bride, 310:5
    refuse of t. shore, 595:6
    womb of kings, 179:12
Teenage, American T. Drive-In Life, 826:15
Teeth, bid them keep t. clean, 224:23
    bitch gone in the t., 709:5
    children's t. set on edge, 29:23
    red thoughts t. white, 655:6
    sans t. sans eyes, 198:25
    shark has pretty t., 750:16
    terrible round about, 15:20
    truth may strike out his t., 160:12
    weeping and gnashing of t., 35:13
    what speech escaped your t., 52:25
    who made t. shall give bread, 147:*n*11
    with the skin of my t., 14:23
    writers like t. incisors molars, 538:1
Teetotaler, beer t. not champagne t., 609:9
Tehee quod she, 136:5
Tekel, Mene Mene T. Upharsin, 30:6
Telegraph, Cunard's liners and t., 513:20
Telemachus, mine own T., 481:12
Teleology is theology, 631:9
Telephant, elephant tried to use t., 598:1

Telephone, cool medium like t., 786:11
    elephone tried to use t., 598:1
    really able to talk, 549:1
Telephones, army no private baths or t.,
    716:9
Telescope ends microscope begins, 451:17
Telescopes of the press, 631:20
Television, chief citadel of t., 769:4
    crouch to t. set, 801:13
    used to distract delude amuse insulate,
        779:18
    vast wasteland, 818:3
Tell, a bore to t. everything, 315:21
    aloud greatest failing, 298:20
    can't t. him much, 850:1
    dead can t. you being dead, 721:15
    dead men t. no tales, 283:26
    don't t. they'd advertise, 544:13
    dream of not t., 401:7
    'em Queen Anne's dead, 383:12
    every word t., 652:12
    feat of T. the archer, 382:18
    fowls shall t. thee, 14:11
    her one thing and keep another, 55:7
    her that wastes her time, 257:24
    her what I tell to thee, 483:1
    him he hates flatterers, 196:4
    him to go to hell, 417:23
    if one but t. a thing well, 66:8
    I'll t. you no fibs, 342:23
    it like it is, 764:*n*1
    it like it was, 764:2
    it not in Gath, 11:35
    it on the mountain, 862:28
    kiss and t., 300:18
    little Lamb I'll t. thee, 371:16
    me all these years you've waited, 792:3
    me I ought to do, 344:12
    me muse, 54:7
    me Muse, 309:20
    me not in mournful numbers, 465:17
    me not sweet I am unkind, 275:22
    me of John or Shaun, 696:16
    me tales to me dear, 442:4
    me tell me elm, 696:16
    me thy company, 158:17
    me what thy name is, 479:5
    me what you eat, 370:4
    me what you know, 454:7
    me what you like, 517:18
    me where all past years are, 233:13
    me where fancy bred, 189:3
    my story, 207:13
    never seek to t. thy love, 373:8
    O t. me all about Anna Livia, 696:15
    old tales and laugh, 218:1
    sad stories of death of kings, 179:28
    tale tit, 857:5
    tales already told, 55:11
    Tchaikovsky the news, 817:1
    teach him to t. my story, 212:32
    that I cannot t. said he, 405:8
    that to the marines, 398:6
    the crooked rose, 795:2
    the world, 187:2
    them I Am, 337:16
    them I came, 662:11
    those who sent you, 366:16
    truth and shame devil, 146:*n*6

Tell (*continued*)
  us your phobias, 725:13
  we t. ourselves stories, 830:2
  what and where they be, 485:13
  what thou art, 158:17
  wife all he knows, 258:7
  you a great secret, 790:6
  you my drift, 194:23
  you what you are, 370:4, 517:18
  young men, 325:17
Teller, truth never hurts t., 495:6
Telleth number of the stars, 20:20
Telling, blessed strains t., 501:17
  I am not arguing I am t., 557:19
  nothing in great harangue, 278:4
  off state and president, 801:1
  pity beyond all t., 637:2
  this with sigh, 669:4
Tells lies without attending, 357:11
  nobody t. me anything, 647:1
  of a nameless deed, 384:15
  when too much lipstick, 763:14
Telmetale of stem or stone, 696:16
Téméraire, Fighting T., 627:5
Tempe, through life's T. led, 516:25
Temper doctrinaire logic, 734:3
  hot t. leaps over, 187:28
  judicious swearin' keeps t., 646:16
  justice with mercy, 268:6
  made thee to t. man, 294:2
  moderation in t. a virtue, 355:2
  unless I mistake its t., 697:12
  which blades bears better t., 171:16
  wit with morality, 302:6
  woman of uncertain t., 406:4
Temperament, creation seen through t., 577:5
  harmony of t. and circumstances, 527:1
  second-class intellect first-class t., 579:5
  solvency matter of t., 636:6
Temperamental atmosphere of Gallup Poll, 666:16
Temperance a species of courage, 287:6
  acquire and beget a t., 204:11
  as easy as t. difficult, 326:4
  fruit of Spirit is t., 45:22
Temperate affords me none, 253:16
  more lovely and more t., 226:2
  wise amazed t. furious, 220:26
Temperature, poll taking t., 666:16
Tempered, absolutism t. by assassination, 385:5
  by war, 799:7
Tempers wind to shorn lamb, 151:12, 333:7
Tempest, betokened t. to field, 173:22
  covert from the t., 27:29
  haunts t., 524:8
  in a teapot, 91:*n*6
  in the very torrent t., 204:11
  no more hear t. howling, 362:11
  on me t. falls, 65:23
  seaman's story is of t., 104:19
  sensual lust t., 525:12
  still is high, 322:24
Tempested, thou shalt not be t., 133:5
Tempests, errors wanderings mists and t., 92:*n*12
  fell all night, 250:22
  glasses itself in t., 422:1
  looks on t., 227:17

Tempest-tost, send t. to me, 595:6
Tempestuous petticoat, 248:4
Temple bells they say, 633:12
  drove out of t., 40:41
  hangs on Dian's t., 224:31
  his people were his t., 280:13
  his train filled the t., 26:23
  Lord is in his holy t., 30:32
  Lord's anointed t., 220:23
  many a t. half as old, 384:7
  no sooner t. built to God, 144:*n*4
  nothing ill in such t., 229:23
  of Delight, 438:16
  of Dian, 850:10
  of God is holy, 44:1
  of Jerusalem, 121:10
  of science, 614:10
  sacred t. of Mecca, 121:10
  singing vespers in T. of Jupiter, 354:4
  two went into t. to pray, 40:7
  veil of t. rent, 38:10
Temple-haunting martlet, 219:15
Temple's inner shrine, 392:16
Temples, forsake their t. dim, 259:2
  God's first t., 432:12
  gorgeous palaces solemn t., 230:9
  made with hands, 42:18
  mortal t. of king, 179:28
  of his gods, 448:14
  shall my joyful t. bind, 257:22
  smote the nail into his t., 10:28
  which men had commanded, 280:13
Tempora mutantur nos et mutamur, 124:27
  O t. O mores, 90:8
Temporal, concern t. salvation, 352:13
  force of t. power, 189:19
  matter unreal and t., 526:12
  reversion, 721:14
  things seen are t., 45:5
Temporary, dictionaries and t. poems, 324:18
  obtain a little t. safety, 320:13
  permanent contract on t. feeling, 575:11
  use of force but t., 344:7
Temps, ah les bons vieux t., 855:9
  au t. de ma jeunesse folle, 139:*n*3
  le t. a laissé son manteau, 138:*n*7
  O t. suspends vol, 426:*n*2
Tempt, Devil went off to t. Lady Poltagrue, 653:13
  frailty of our powers, 208:17
  its new-fledged offspring, 342:6
  not desperate man, 184:13
  shall not t. the Lord, 9:31
  upper classes, 613:3
Temptation, beware t. to ignore facts, 787:11
  blessed the man that endureth t., 47:10
  cold and to t. slow, 227:3
  enter not into t., 37:30
  last t. greatest treason, 720:5
  lead us not into t., 34:11
  maximum of t., 609:24
  my t. is quiet, 642:10
  resist everything except t., 604:21
  to get rid of t. yield, 604:15
  to the editor, 707:3
  white fever of t., 730:8
  why t. but for man to meet, 495:1
Temptations, rid of t. by yielding, 445:8
  to belong to other nations, 564:1

Tempted her out of gloom, 479:14
  My Lady t. by a private whim, 653:13
Tempus edax rerum, 105:*n*16
  omnia t. revelat, 107:*n*1
Ten, and David his t. thousands, 11:31
  aren't no T. Commandments, 633:14
  ask Alice when t. feet tall, 834:6
  better t. guilty escape, 338:12
  Council of T., 701:13
  death hath t. thousand doors, 244:7
  good Lord had only t., 577:10
  I'm t. years burning down the road, 841:8
  it's now t. o'clock, 488:7
  jokes an hundred enemies, 332:6
  little Indians, 861:6
  live t. times t., 451:18
  low words, 308:16
  men who haven't and don't, 610:14
  not if I had t. tongues, 52:17
  o'clock scholar, 860:20
  only one summer that I was t., 806:4
  set my t. commandments in your face, 172:5
  speak for t. minutes need week, 611:12
  strength as strength of t., 482:11
  thousand miles away, 862:11
  thousand saw I at a glance, 394:6
  thousand times ten thousand, 487:8
  thousand to go out of it, 297:15
  to the world allot, 159:*n*5
  vowing perfection of t., 208:5
  when angry count t., 359:12
  wrote words of t. commandments, 9:9
Tenacious but restless, 715:4
  of purpose in rightful cause, 99:28
Tenanted, by good angels t., 478:12
  differently t. islands, 469:11
Tenantless, graves stood t., 200:18
  save to wind, 420:21
Tend, great God to thee we t., 120:5
  no more than horses they t., 501:6
  on mortal thoughts, 219:11
Tendance, doth life in t. spend, 161:24
Tendencies, containment of Russian expansive t., 768:1
Tendency to good like water, 82:10
Tender and true, 538:8
  eye of pitiful day, 221:7
  for another's pain, 333:22
  grace of day dead, 482:16
  irreproachably t., 738:1
  is the night, 437:9
  know how t. 'tis, 219:23
  leaves of hopes, 231:2
  love me t., 831:17
  Majesty, 545:3
  mercies of the wicked are cruel, 21:22
  murderer, 493:9
  our vines have t. grapes, 25:18
  pitying the t. cries, 372:9
  rear t. thought, 318:1
  strokes of art, 309:14
  the t. mercy of God, 39:1
  too t. or too firm heart, 309:28
  walks with t. growing night, 519:8
  yearning sweet hoping, 382:7
Tender-handed stroke a nettle, 307:20
Tenderly, night coming t., 762:11

Tenderness its joys and fears, 393:19
    shape of t., 759:12
    thanks to its t., 393:19
Tenders, shoal of fools for t., 300:23
Tendrils, limp and damp as t., 780:13
    strong, 394:21
Ténébreux, je suis le t., 469:*n*2
Tenement of clay, 283:8
    threshold of ruined t., 323:3
    upon clothes behind t., 729:11
    words written on t. halls, 837:8
Teneriff or Atlas unremoved, 266:27
Tenets admitted into pagan creed, 571:12
    faith in some nice t., 275:20
    surpass in atrocity any t., 571:12
Tennessee, placed jar in T., 687:2
Tennis anyone, 851:10
    play t. with the net down, 671:19
Tennyson not Tennysonian, 586:2
    out-babying Keats, 452:13
Tennysonianness of speech, 709:14
Tenoned, foothold t. and mortised in granite, 519:6
Tenor, noiseless t. of their way, 334:23
Tenpence, seven pounds t. a man, 343:11
Tense for first losing, 792:20
Tension, interracial t. has focus, 752:8
Tent, Alexander in his t., 766:18
    I rede you t. it, 380:6
    in field silken t., 670:11
    little t. of blue, 605:16
    nightly pitch moving t., 396:1
    outside t. whirling drift, 649:18
    pitched his t. toward Sodom, 7:2
    prize of general not t., 578:8
    strike the t., 465:15
    that searches bottom of worst, 207:31
Tenth, be thou the t. Muse, 226:12
    less than t. part of one, 208:5
    Muse governs press, 503:11
Tenting tonight, 556:7
Tents, dwell in the t. of wickedness, 18:17
    dwelling in t., 7:10
    fold t. like Arabs, 466:14
    how goodly are thy t., 9:26
    of Kedar, 25:12
    sighed soul toward Grecian t., 190:4
    silent t. spread, 522:6
    such as dwell in t., 6:19
    to your t. O Israel, 12:23
Tenure, public men no sure t., 727:4
Tenures, his t. and his tricks, 206:20
Tepee warm in winter cool in summer, 601:2
Tepid, never distract reader from t. lust, 756:2
Term, MacGuffin is the t., 755:8
    served a t., 563:17
Termagant, whipped for o'erdoing T., 204:11
Terminate torment, 719:11
    woman's decision to t. pregnancy, 778:2
Termination, no government provides for its own t., 475:4
Terminations, terrible as her t., 194:19
Terminological inexactitude, 665:6
Terms between old and new world, 370:11
    fair t. and villain's mind, 188:12
    litigious t., 262:17

Terms *(continued)*
    of armistice with fate, 748:5
    silken t. precise, 177:12
    too deep for me, 564:8
    unconditional surrender, 532:14
    unfamiliar t., 116:6
Terra firma of accomplished discovery, 682:6
    in t. pax, 49:11
Terrace walk and half rood, 312:16
Terre, c'est une pauvre t., 524:*n*8
    Dieu donna à Caïn, 145:*n*2
Terrestrial, written on t. things, 575:17
Terrible as an army with banners, 25:27
    as her terminations, 194:19
    beauty born, 639:4
    beauty mysterious t., 525:13
    beauty t. and awful, 525:12
    burden of nothing to do, 289:20
    children, 460:2
    each angel is t., 677:4
    fluidity of self-revelation, 585:17
    for old woman to outlive her dogs, 787:19
    from a t. land, 27:7
    from camps, 771:13
    gift lifted from hearts, 526:2
    haughtiness of the t., 27:2
    invent new beasts so t., 442:16
    judges all ranged a t. show, 307:18
    lend the eye t. aspect, 192:30
    life ordinary most t., 543:1
    long and t. way, 781:9
    mind t. thing to waste, 852:22
    no accuser so t., 88:9
    not death but dying is t., 322:14
    nothing more t. than ignorance, 366:7
    nothing t. except fear itself, 166:18
    sociologists, 631:12
    swift sword, 513:18
    thing happening to him, 796:13
    times, 602:1
    years of Yezhov terror, 725:9
Terrible-eyed, staggered and t., 773:18
Terribles, enfants t., 460:2
    simplificateurs, 509:5
Terribly, armies swore t., 332:21
    we were wrong t. wrong., 798:1
Terrified, bored and t., 797:8
Terrifies, silence of spaces t. me, 279:21
Terrify, heart they ought to t., 383:2
Territorial aggrandizement, 699:7
    integrity, 611:11
    no t. changes, 699:7
Territories, occupied t., 666:15
Territory, grace in t. held by devil, 816:5
    has t. of harmonicas, 740:17
    not make nation, 537:9
Terror, afraid for the t. by night, 18:25
    and force, 726:8
    at own finitude, 629:9
    Beauty's beginning of T., 677:4
    human form divine, 374:12
    leaving black t., 655:18
    night sweat with t., 640:5
    no t. Cassius, 197:10
    perceivers of t. of life, 456:23
    perch and not t., 211:3

Terror *(continued)*
    primitive t., 721:10
    reigns of t., 523:9
    science frees from bodily t., 514:6
    strike t. in Swede, 447:2
    understood t. and hope, 802:12
    victory in spite of t., 665:20
Terrorist and policeman from same basket, 612:12
Terrors, dare deadly t. clasp, 374:6
    king of t., 14:22
    painting gives form to t., 693:13
Tertullian, every word of T. a sentence, 119:24
Tess, ended his sport with T., 575:9
Test, habit with him t. of truth, 369:3
    lies in action, 65:29
    no t. which is not fanciful, 68:13
    not t. faith in crucible, 595:13
    of civilization, 733:8
    of first-rate intelligence, 746:13
    of man or woman's breeding, 609:4
    of ridicule, 301:9
    of true theories to predict, 433:1
    perception of beauty moral t., 505:6
    true t. of civilization, 327:9, 457:8
    untrained to stand t., 581:9
Testament, blood of the new t., 37:27
    new t. in my blood, 44:16
    prosperity blessing of Old T., 167:10
    purple t. of bleeding war, 180:2
    than my T. fer that, 514:21
Testamenti, novi et aeterni t., 49:14
Tested, to extreme old age, 528:2
Testify, condemned survive to t., 822:5
    intellectual refuse to t., 683:16
Testimonial, provisions t. when we are dead, 109:20
Testimony, every tone t. against slavery, 509:8
    no t. establish miracle, 330:7
    of Jesus Christ, 48:2
Testing whether nation endure, 476:7
Testis unus testis nullus, 124:28
Tests, accuracy tried by severe t., 73:16
Testyment, than my T. fer that, 514:21
Tetchy and wayward thy infancy, 174:12
Tête d'armée, 388:*n*8
    plutôt la t. bien faite que bien pleine, 152:*n*9
Tether time or tide, 147:*n*7
Tethered, lice t., 780:8
Texas, times Byron goes into T., 807:7
Text, entering old t. from new direction, 824:16
    holy t. of pike and gun, 271:2
    is old orator green, 173:25
    neat rivulet of t., 367:27
    of civil instruction, 358:13
    of Men and Women, 617:18
Thai half said, 162:15
Thaïs, where is T., 541:29
Thalatta, 76:*n*1
Thames, life ran gaily as T., 529:12
    no allaying T., 276:3
    noblest river, 302:19
    not of Gennesareth but T., 621:9
    set fire to T., 336:10
    sweet T. run softly, 162:7

Thin *(continued)*

one wildly signaling, 764:14
partitions, 283:8
red 'eroes, 633:7
red-line streak, 522:10
ring becomes t. by wearing, 92:14
seven t. kine, 7:26
smoke without flame, 576:5
so t. so pale yet gold, 369:6
tell female she's t. she's yours, 851:n3
through thick and t., 136:n1, 283:20
thurgh thikke and t., 136:8
water's t., 565:5
we t. gin, 798:10

Thine, fatal words Mine and T., 156:7
is the kingdom, 13:11
not my will but t., 40:16
wear both for both are t., 173:33

Thing, a little learning is a dangerous t.,
    308:11
a tear an intellectual t., 375:4
acting of dreadful t., 196:1
aged man paltry t., 639:17
asked no other t., 545:10
awe of such t. as myself, 195:18
come at last the Distinguished T., 586:1
crush the infamous t., 316:12
dejected t. of fortune, 217:9
do not do t. they most do show, 227:3
doing is another t., 153:11
don't mean t. if ain't got swing, 753:19
dooth with your owene t., 137:2
each t. his turn does hold, 248:12
eating is a small good t., 833:9
enskyed and sainted, 210:37
every bitter t. is sweet, 23:12
every t. that lives is Holy, 373:7
excellent t. in woman, 218:6
far far better t., 498:31
fine t. needs laboring, 637:18
foolish t. but a toy, 210:19
good t. out of Nazareth, 40:36
guilty t. surprised, 393:15
hates t. he would not kill, 189:14
having seen one t., 568:16
hedgehog knows one great t., 56:22
hope not t. with feathers, 831:2
how poor a t. is man, 169:8
I am every dead t., 234:21
I do my t. you your t., 738:20
I have done one braver t., 233:16
I was born to do, 169:7
ill-favored t. but mine own, 200:7
is it so small a t., 529:1
keep corner in t. I love, 214:4
kills t. he loves, 605:18
law for t., 453:7
learn about one t. from another, 117:8
life is the t., 636:10
little learning dangerous t., 308:11
make good t. too common, 191:19
many a t. sought, 226:8
many-splendored t., 621:7
mastery of the t., 587:7
meanest t. he ever did, 827:19
men prize the t. ungained, 207:22
mind terrible t. to waste, 852:22
moderately good, 355:2
motion like living t., 391:8

Thing *(continued)*

necessary for triumph of evil, 346:2
never done single t. I wanted to, 708:4
never said a foolish t., 292:24
no new t. under the sun, 23:35
no such cold t., 250:20
no the t. I should be, 380:16
not done in a corner, 42:37
not t. to laugh to scorn, 199:31
of beauty joy forever, 436:8
of darkness, 230:16
of evil, 479:6
of shreds and patches, 565:7
One and Thing Two, 769:8
only t. to fear is fear, 697:15
pleasant t. if thou keep them within thee,
    22:27
poor t. but mine own, 200:n1
quite another t., 314:12
reasoning self-sufficing t., 392:3
reward of t. to have done it, 456:14
romantic a t. as one can imagine, 673:7
said t. which was not, 298:17
same t. good bad indifferent, 287:9
saying is one t., 153:11
sleep it is a gentle t., 400:14
small t. analogy of great things, 93:3
so neatly you never feel t., 809:8
started like a guilty t., 200:19
sudden if t. comes in his head, 173:15
surest way to get a t., 449:12
that eats the heart, 771:5
that ends all other deeds, 224:3
that hath been is that which shall be,
    23:35
that is one t., 840:3
that is your own, 80:24
the Falklands t., 753:5
the play's the t., 203:31
thou art the t. itself, 216:30
throw away dearest t. owed, 219:8
time least t. we have of, 755:2
to every t. there is a season, 24:6
to love, 677:20
too much of good t., 156:4
unfeathered two-legged t., 283:10
very odd t., 662:16
we may nat lightly have, 136:16
what t. of sea or land, 269:6
winning isn't everything only t., 852:11
winsome wee t., 380:3
with feathers, 544:11
you start out with one t., 841:10

Things, admires mean t. is Snob, 490:9

age best in four t., 167:1
all these t. added unto you, 34:21
all t. all day long, 485:24
all t. are artificial, 255:14
all t. are one, 64:3
all t. born through strife, 64:9
all t. bright beautiful, 508:7
all t. by law divine, 429:7
all t. come of thee, 13:12
all t. great and small, 401:2
all t. how small soever, 286:2
all t. taken from us, 480:19
all t. to all men, 44:9
all thinking t., 391:4
always best in beginning, 279:11

Things *(continued)*

are in saddle, 453:6
are not what they seem, 465:17
are of the snake, 453:5
are sons of heaven, 324:14
as language are attractive, 456:19
as they are, 688:22
as t. have been t. remain, 512:10
authentic tidings of invisible t., 395:5
beautiful and good, 428:5
beginnings of t. not distinguished by eye,
    92:13
best t. confused with ill, 428:4
best t. in life free, 736:17
bitterness of t., 395:17
both great and small, 401:2
by season seasoned, 190:9
by whom all t. were made, 50:4
calm Soul of all t., 528:13
cannot always go your way, 595:10
compare great t. with small, 95:15,
    265:21
counter original spare, 587:10
dappled t., 587:9
day of small t., 30:36
desired and timely t., 619:16
DiMaggio, does t. perfectly, 755:3
do noble t., 514:2
does away with ideas of t., 78:6
done a thousand dreadful t., 175:18
dream strange t., 460:5
dreaming on t. to come, 227:12
drift of t., 668:16
elemental t., 601:6
equal to all t., 343:2
eternal fitness of t., 322:7
evidence of t. not seen, 46:42
excellent t. in counsels, 22:28
facts are stubborn t., 300:6, 351:1
fair and flagrant t., 272:12
fairer when we look back, 515:17
fall apart, 639:6
feed brain with better t., 664:13
filled with intent to be lost, 786:2
for all t. unfit, 343:2
forms of t. unknown, 182:3
four t. come not back, 101:n3
friends share all t., 60:2
from all t. one and from one all t., 64:10
fundamental t. apply, 740:23
glorious t. of thee spoken, 339:13
good t. strive to dwell, 229:23
good t. which belong to prosperity, 167:9
great t. are done, 375:18
great t. from neurotics, 657:12
great t. made of little, 494:21
greatest vicissitude of t., 168:18
he can afford to let alone, 506:26
he is before all t., 45:40
here are the tears of t., 96:34
holy profane clean obscene, 246:10
holy revealed only to men holy, 73:7
how can these t. be, 40:45
how many t. I have no need of, 72:4
human t. subject to decay, 284:2
I did not do or say, 641:10
impossible t., 552:12
in all t. thee to see, 250:24
in the midst of t., 101:25

Thinking *(continued)*
  form and frame from t., 688:13
  greatest happiness for t. man, 366:3
  high t., 392:14
  highly of men or matrimony, 406:9
  human t. closer to laws of world, 781:12
  is dismissal of irrelevancies, 743:8
  it ain't t. about it, 504:3
  love hardly seem worth t., 637:15
  makes it so, 203:14
  man t. or working is alone, 507:8
  much drinking little t., 298:2
  new t. is about loss, 836:11
  of the key, 719:2
  on fantastic summer's heat, 179:6
  on frosty Caucasus, 179:6
  on thinking, 80:7
  operations we perform without t., 624:10
  reed, 280:4
  refinement of everyday t., 683:7
  scholar is Man T., 454:20
  scratched head kept t., 652:7
  stops action mindless, 770:6
  theologian not born by t., 144:17
  through t. few or none harmed, 150:6
  too highly of himself, 287:2
  too much t. to have common thought,
    310:6
  too precisely on event, 206:1
  what nobody has thought, 739:2
  woman sleeps with monsters, 824:9
Thinkings, speak as to thy t., 213:32
Thinks better of gilded fool, 233:5
  divine thought t. of itself, 80:7
  evil to him who evil t., 132:16
  freedom for one who t. differently,
    654:15
  he t. too much, 195:22
  heart t. tongue speaks, 194:30
  in a marrowbone, 642:3
  know she t. o' me, 633:12
  like a philosopher, 331:21
  never t. of me, 848:18
  not look to see what neighbor t., 115:10
  think as native t., 687:10
  to get a living, 331:17
  too little or too much, 311:9
  want to know what France t., 728:12
  what a man t. of himself, 506:9
Thinness, gold to airy t. beat, 235:2
Thin-spun, slits the t. life, 261:19
Third and fourth generation of them that
    hate me, 8:33
  day comes a frost, 231:2
  day he will raise us up, 30:14
  drink not the t. glass, 249:17
  drowns him, 209:7
  fire tolerable t. party, 505:8
  I Don't Know's on t., 742:15
  in your bosom, 183:20
  insomniac longs for t. side, 756:4
  is not to dare to be ahead, 59:14
  to make t. she joined former two, 284:27
  who walks beside you, 719:1
Thirst after happiness, 331:20
  dangerous thing, 620:6
  drank without t., 298:18
  dying of t. by the fountain, 138:14
  fame t. of youth, 421:2

Thirst *(continued)*
  goes away with drinking, 146:1
  he that believeth on me shall never t.,
    41:4
  hunger and t. after righteousness, 33:33
  man can raise t., 633:14
  mouth and belly injured by t., 82:19
  neither t. any more, 48:25
  nor for every t. to pot, 251:21
  that from soul doth rise, 238:2
  this T. blister easier, 544:14
Thirsteth, everyone that t., 28:24
  my soul t. for God, 17:16
  my soul t. for thee, 18:3
Thirsty and ye gave drink, 37:17
  busy curious t. fly, 317:7
  cold waters to a t. soul, 23:4
  earth soaks up the rain, 275:8
  if thine enemy be t., 23:3
  in a dry and t. land, 18:3
  let the t. think, 579:13
  sleep is drink for the t., 158:31
Thirteen, clocks striking t., 765:14
Thirties, in t. want friends, 746:20
Thirty, at t. man suspects himself fool, 306:5
  days hath November, 150:8
  don't trust anybody over t., 835:8
  feel like t. cents, 643:14
  for t. pence my death, 250:5
  live enough before t., 646:8
  never admitted I am more than t., 604:26
  nor strong at t., 251:25
  on the wrong side of t., 299:12
  once t. already old, 365:15
  pieces of silver, 30:39, 37:22
  years in man's life, 77:11
Thirty-five, from t. to fifty-five, 705:16
  very attractive age, 605:12
Thirtyfold, brought forth fruit t., 36:4
Thirty-four, this day t. years old, 288:19
Thirty-one, all the rest have t., 150:8
This above all, 201:27
  after t. therefore because of t., 124:16
  do in remembrance of me, 40:15
  hath not offended king, 144:4
  is London, 779:14
  is my beloved, 25:26
  is my beloved Son, 33:29
  is my body, 37:27
  is my friend, 25:26
  is my own my native land, 396:11
  is our gracious will, 143:6
  is the place, 450:8
  is the real me, 581:2
  is the way, 27:27
  is the worst, 217:10
  it is t. oh it is t., 845:3
  that it should come to t., 201:2
  too shall pass away, 474:16
  was a man, 197:22
Thisbe fearfully o'ertrip dew, 190:4
Thisby, Pyramus and T., 180:22
Thistle Shamrock Rose entwine, 547:13
Thistles, figs of t., 35:8
Thither, hither and t. spins, 528:17
Thomas, John T. marryin' Lady Jane, 707:13
  saith he to T., 41:42
  true T., 854:2
Thompson, Sadie T. answer, 673:2

Thonx, Bronx no t., 763:7
Thor, da stehe ich nun ich armer T., 365:*n*2
Thoreau, living like T., 637:*n*1
  unperfect unfinished, 584:10
Thoreau's, no question of T. genius, 584:10
Thorn in the flesh, 45:14
  no harvest but a t., 250:15
  oak and ash and t., 635:18, 853:27
  plant this t. this canker, 185:6
  primrose peeps beneath t., 342:12
  rose without a t., 368:15
  snail's on t., 491:2
  wantons thro' flowering t., 378:21
  without t. the rose, 266:7
Thornbush, this t. my t., 182:9
Thorns and dangers of this world, 178:22
  burrs and t. of life, 436:5
  crown of t. on labor, 622:3
  fall upon t. of life, 429:3
  grapes of t., 35:8
  in your sides, 10:27
  noble crown is of t., 435:2
  rose among t., 117:13
  roses have t., 226:11
  snow on barren t., 696:4
  that in bosom lodge, 202:20
  thy only crown, 258:4
  under a pot, 24:18
Thorny hedge-hogs, 181:15
  life is, 401:9
  undertaking to follow mind, 152:19
  virtue demands t. road, 152:21
  way to heaven, 201:23
Thou art the man, 12:4
  beside me singing, 471:5
  Duty whispers T. must, 453:16
  holier than t., 28:35
  shalt not sit with statisticians, 776:7
Though an host should encamp, 16:23
Thought, actuality of t. is life, 80:6
  adorns nature with new thing, 456:8
  adventure in clarification of t., 624:14
  agents of men of t., 442:14
  all I t. was true, 668:15
  all objects of all t., 391:4
  armor is his honest t., 232:13
  as a child, 44:20
  believe own t. genius, 455:7
  beneath slight film, 544:6
  best known and t., 530:9
  beyond utmost bound of t., 481:11
  brightest t. incomplete, 523:22
  by t. word and deed, 50:18
  can't bear the t., 824:7
  chaos of t. and passion, 311:9
  charm by t. supplied, 391:3
  community of t., 570:16
  depends on stomach, 316:21
  divine t. thinks of itself, 80:7
  divorced from eye, 747:19
  energy of t., 449:20
  erring t., 567:4
  essential in painting, 125:8
  even t. can shatter us, 590:1
  every t. that springs, 395:17
  evolution of t., 529:21
  finds the words, 671:8
  flashes in world of t., 523:22
  free t., 579:1

Thought *(continued)*

    freed capacity of t., 616:12
    freedom of t., 337:12
    glow of early t. declines, 422:16
    God t. and t., 657:2
    gods t. otherwise, 97:13
    Greek t. and life, 539:9
    green t. in green shade, 277:4
    he t. they were old friends, 792:10
    her body t., 236:1
    high t. amiable words, 486:8
    his mind a t. of God, 504:11
    his who says it best, 515:12
    human t. or form, 427:15
    I t. that love would last, 775:6
    in you boundless t. born, 472:23
    independent of labor, 506:4
    is as a death, 226:19
    is free, 230:4
    lean upon the t., 528:20
    leaped to wed with Thought, 483:18
    learning without t., 62:16
    liberty of t. life of soul, 316:28
    lies like burden, 455:2
    like full-blown rose, 436:24
    lived with no other t., 479:17
    loftiness of t. surpassed, 284:27
    lucidity of t., 532:5
    man of action forced into t., 647:5
    near to be t. so shortly, 195:1
    nimble t. can jump, 226:13
    no freedom of t. without doubt, 767:2
    nor t. of leveling wind, 640:8
    not a t. be lost, 775:11
    not t. death undone so many, 718:13
    not t. of own in head, 612:3
    of China and Greece, 766:18
    of kindnesses done, 94:24
    often original, 473:6
    old man had so much blood, 222:5
    one t. in breast another on tongue, 95:4
    pale cast of t., 203:33
    passes swiftly as a t., 61:16
    pearls of t., 515:16
    penny for your t., 148:28
    perish the t., 301:4
    pleasing dreadful t., 301:26
    plunged into sea of words, 700:5
    power in mysteries of t., 69:21
    practice and t. forge art, 96:7
    principle of free t., 579:1
    rear tender t., 318:1
    rhythm in all thought, 399:9
    Roman t. hath struck him, 222:30
    saturates politics with t., 530:7
    scientific t. human progress, 591:8
    seem a moment's t., 637:16
    sense from t. divide, 283:*n*2
    servants in t. as in action, 778:14
    she pined in t., 209:26
    sleep out the t. of it, 228:23
    sow a t., 849:5
    strange seas of t., 391:9
    stream of t., 581:12
    style dress of t., 295:27
    sweet silent t., 226:8
    sweetest songs saddest t., 429:19
    sweetly solemn t., 535:19
    swift as a bird or t., 54:24

Thought *(continued)*

    take no t. about what is distant, 63:17
    take no t. for morrow, 34:22
    taking t. add one cubit, 34:18
    that lurks in all delight, 592:15
    the best t. and said, 531:10
    thee bright, 228:7
    think so then t. so still, 500:11
    thinking what nobody t., 739:2
    third silence of t., 468:1
    tire the night in t., 249:6
    to have loved t. done, 529:1
    to justify wrongdoings, 316:18
    too much thinking to have common t.,
      310:6
    too much to stoop to action, 572:19
    traversed universe in t., 92:10
    tremble into t., 399:10
    two souls with single t., 464:7
    uffish t., 551:11
    understandest my t. afar off, 20:12
    unmeaning thing they call a t., 308:17
    uttered a lie, 458:16
    vitality of t., 625:3
    want of t. and heart, 445:19
    weave emotion t. sound, 446:17
    wed with Thought, 483:18
    What jolly fun, 624:5
    what oft was t., 308:12
    what thing not t. of ages long ago,
      365:16
    when t. takes breath away, 534:4
    wish father to t., 192:8
    without learning, 62:16
    words slippery t. viscous, 570:25
    would destroy paradise, 333:22
    young man brings forth, 78:9
Thought-executing fires, 216:18
Thoughtless, hour of t. youth, 391:4
    my t. hand, 374:4
    saying of great princess, 331:19
Thoughtlessness and optimism, 629:13
Thought's slave of life, 187:5
Thoughts, all intelligent t. already thought,
    366:6
    all t. all passions, 401:22
    and intents of heart, 46:38
    assault of t. on unthinking, 701:19
    beautiful in t., 622:12
    beyond reaches of souls, 202:6
    calmer of t., 252:25
    ceaseless t. of roaming, 291:12
    discerner of the t., 46:38
    doubtful t., 189:7
    fat paunch never breeds fine t., 118:13
    fly in twinkling of eye, 845:9
    fond and wayward t., 391:17
    fresh t. along shores, 487:12
    give thy t. no tongue, 201:24
    give thy worst of t., 213:32
    gored mine own t., 227:15
    great t. come from heart, 333:13
    high t. must have high language, 75:20
    high-erected t. in heart of courtesy,
      163:19
    holy profane clean obscene, 246:10
    in these t. myself despising, 226:6
    joy of elevated t., 391:4
    leave to think own t., 630:5

Thoughts *(continued)*

    legible in the eye, 171:9
    long long t., 467:7
    multiply t., 783:1
    my bloody t., 214:15
    my sad t. doth clear, 279:7
    my t. are minutes, 180:15
    my t. my trollops, 331:23
    my t. not your t., 28:27
    never alone accompanied with noble t.,
      163:20
    never spoken or written, 449:13
    of a turtle turtles, 458:3
    of earthly men, 55:20
    of men decay, 161:22
    of men widened, 482:3
    of other men, 612:13
    of youth long, 467:7
    on hospitable t. intent, 267:5
    pansies for t., 206:11
    pieced t. into philosophy, 640:5
    pious t. as harbingers, 258:5
    profound t. arise in debate, 808:10
    quotations give good t., 665:10
    remain below, 205:17
    rule the world, 457:19
    second t. are best, 70:1
    secret t. run over all things, 246:10
    Sensations rather than T., 440:1
    shroud of t., 421:4
    slumbering t., 256:25
    so thy t. when thou gone, 430:19
    soothe cares lift t., 436:5
    speech to conceal t., 316:18
    style the dress of t., 315:5
    suspect the t. of others, 188:11
    tend on mortal t., 219:11
    that arise in me, 482:15
    that breathe, 335:10
    that nature gives way to, 220:6
    that savor of content, 165:16
    think mortal t., 69:18
    think other men's t., 538:7
    to memory dear, 397:14
    to think great t. be heroes, 577:17
    too deep for tears, 393:19
    turns to t. of love, 481:17
    understandeth all imaginations of the t.,
      13:10
    unexpressed fall dead, 101:*n*3
    unmentionable t., 516:20
    unrighteous man forsake his t., 28:26
    unthinkable t., 770:6
    uplifting t. in baths, 745:8
    wander through eternity, 265:4
    were always downward bent, 264:22
    were red thoughts, 655:6
    what sweet t. what longing, 130:14
    which were not their thoughts, 421:4
    with sea's boundlessness, 759:12
    words without t., 205:17
    wrapped in my t., 138:16
Thousand, a t. shall fall at thy side, 18:25
    actions once afoot, 192:22
    after t. victories foiled, 226:4
    ages in Thy sight, 304:7
    cattle upon t. hills, 17:24
    conscience hath t. tongues, 174:21
    day in thy courts better than a t., 18:17

Ticks, the clock t., 825:4
Ticonderoga, implement that goes t.-t., 756:5
Tiddler's, Tom T. ground, 847:7
Tide, a-going out with t., 498:10
　blood-dimmed t. loosed, 639:6
　boots not to resist wind and t., 173:5
　call of running t., 681:1
　deaths at ebb t., 602:15
　dire gorge of salt sea t., 189:*n*1
　full moon lies fair, 530:19
　in affairs of men, 197:13
　of pomp that beats, 193:16
　of times, 196:21
　such t. as seems asleep, 487:2
　tarrieth no man, 147:10
　time nor t. tarrieth, 147:*n*7
　turning o' the t., 192:27
　under the whelming t., 262:3
　unheard beyond ocean t., 515:9
　when just cause reaches flood t., 616:11
　wind nor t. nor sea, 566:17
Tides and life of man, 602:15
　dread abysses unknown t., 583:4
　of grass foam of flowers, 568:9
　of men into my hands, 723:7
　push in their t., 795:3
　salt t. seaward flow, 528:5
Tidiers-up, scientists t., 796:12
Tidings, bringer of good t., 121:1
　confirm t. as they roll, 301:15
　dismal t. when he frowned, 342:8
　glad t. of great joy, 294:5
　good t. of great joy, 39:3
　him that bringeth good t., 28:18
　of invisible things, 395:5
Tie, careless shoestring in whose t., 248:4
　of host and guest, 65:17
　up the knocker, 311:19
　up thy fears, 250:16
Tied by chance bond together, 504:22
　I am t. to the stake, 217:7
　to me as to dog's tail, 640:3
Tiger, Hyrcan t., 221:14
　imitate action of the t., 192:30
　lady or t., 557:7
　rides t. afraid to dismount, 665:*n*3
　sin on a t. skin, 850:16
　Tiger burning bright, 374:5
Tiger's heart in player's hide, 165:18
　heart in woman's hide, 172:24
　sinks into my throat t. tooth, 729:12
Tigers, catches t. in red weather, 686:16
　empty t. or roaring sea, 184:12
　getting hungry, 665:13
　not daughters, 217:15
　of wrath, 372:20
　tamed and shabby t., 656:10
　they dare not dismount, 665:13
Tight hot cell, 748:1
　in the throat, 757:13
　little island, 395:21
Tighter, without t. breathing, 546:3
Tightfisted hand at the grindstone, 497:12
Tight-rooted, wolf's-bane t., 438:14
Tiles, as many devils in Worms as t., 144:19
Tillage begins other arts follow, 415:9
Tilled, little field well t., 319:10
Tiller, Cain was t. of ground, 6:12

Tilling and grazing feed France, 165:14
　dignity in t. field, 610:20
Tills, man t. field lies beneath, 485:14
Tilly-loo, sang T., 499:20
Tilt at all I meet, 312:13
Tilth vineyard none, 229:25
Tilting at windmills, 156:*n*2
Tilts, globe t. like a coloured O, 834:3
Tilt-yard, charmed alike t. and bower, 417:11
Tim, Tiny T. last of all, 497:19
Timber, crazy as hauling t. into woods, 98:22
　navy would be rotten t., 344:17
　one old t. leg, 658:9
　seasoned t. never gives, 250:11
Timbrel is stilled, 747:18
　praise him with t., 20:21
Timbrels, pipes and t., 437:17
　played before the Lord on t., 11:41
Timbucktoo, rang them while touring T., 822:11
Time, a little t. for laughter, 553:*n*3
　a t. when it was not, 545:14
　abysm of t., 229:10
　Africa marches patiently through t., 774:14
　age and body of the t., 204:13
　almighty t. disquiets, 68:19
　always t. for courtesy, 457:17
　an endless song, 637:7
　and chance happeneth to all, 24:30
　and intents are savage-wild, 184:12
　and Patience strongest of warriors, 542:13
　and the hour, 219:7
　and world ever in flight, 637:9
　annihilate space and t., 310:18
　arrest your flight, 426:8
　Art long T. fleeting, 466:1
　art that tells t. of day, 824:5
　as one born out of t., 44:23
　as t. goes by, 740:23, 741:1
　ask for anything except t., 387:13
　at hands of T. and Chance, 575:3
　at same t. good bad indifferent, 287:9
　author of authors, 166:3
　ay fleeth t., 137:1
　bank and shoal of t., 219:16
　bears away all things, 95:28
　beautiful t. of young love, 382:7
　bid t. return, 179:25
　Bird of T. has little way, 471:2
　book T. criticized for us, 515:19
　books of all t., 517:15
　born out of my due t., 557:2
　bounds of place and t., 335:9
　bridge of T., 525:4
　brief chronicles of the t., 203:25
　but little at a t., 299:5
　cancels young pain, 69:22
　captive of t., 730:4
　cease and midnight never come, 171:3
　chinks that T. has made, 258:3
　chronicle of wasted t., 227:11
　come t. and haste day, 368:12
　comes a t. in every man's life, 730:16
　condemned to kill t., 794:5
　consume strongest cord, 397:22
　convinced of imbecility by t., 325:14
　cools time clarifies, 676:15

Time *(continued)*
　cormorant devouring T., 176:16
　corridors of T., 466:13
　could have had damned good t., 754:3
　cracks in furious flower, 798:13
　creeping hours of t., 198:22
　crumbles things, 80:1
　daughters of T., 453:18
　Death old captain it is t., 524:16
　defy tooth of t., 305:22
　destroyer time preserver, 721:11
　devourer of all things, 105:20
　did not exist previously, 127:8
　die for such a long t., 277:14
　died far away before his t., 627:*n*1
　discovers truth, 107:3
　do not squander t., 320:1
　does not relinquish its rights, 364:18
　done his best for his t., 381:18
　don't waste t. mourning, 684:11
　doth transfix flourish, 226:17
　driveth onward fast, 480:19
　duty beyond space and t., 666:12
　eases all things, 68:8
　engenders forgetfulness, 676:4
　enough for sleep, 618:8
　enough for that, 229:6
　entertainer who understood his t., 693:14
　envious and calumniating t., 208:12
　eternity in love with production of t., 372:15
　ever-flowing stream of t., 777:1
　falling oars kept t., 277:11
　Father T. and Mother Earth, 817:15
　feet in ancient t., 375:17
　fire in which we burn, 791:11
　fleet the t. carelessly, 197:24
　flying never to return, 96:18
　fool some people all the t., 477:7
　footprints on sands of t., 466:2
　for a change, 762:1
　for a little something, 697:7
　for all good men, 849:6
　for long t. used to go to bed early, 657:6
　for many words, 55:4
　for quick intake of air, 842:4
　for remainder of human t., 836:2
　for sleep, 55:4
　for such a word, 222:16
　for us to leave her, 862:8
　foremost files of t., 482:7
　future in time past, 720:7
　get me to church on t., 803:11
　goes you say, 574:11
　good t. coming, 502:4
　great legalizer, 690:17
　great poet writes his t., 722:14
　grown old before my t., 548:1
　gude t. coming, 397:24
　half as old as T., 384:7
　half as old as t., 501:5
　happiest t. of New Year, 480:15
　has come Walrus said, 552:3
　has no divisions, 676:7
　has slain desire, 817:18
　hath taming hand, 449:17
　hath to silver turned, 164:9
　hath wallet at his back, 208:8

Tolerated, error of opinion t., 358:9
    not only t. but encouraged, 404:12
Tolerating, one way of t. existence, 527:7
Toleration, learned t. from intolerant, 700:22
Toll for the brave, 348:16
    greater t. on health of country, 808:1
    me back from thee, 437:14
    oppress of T., 546:11
Tolle lege tolle lege, 119:*n*4
Toiled, sexton t. bell, 445:14
Tolls, curfew t. knell, 334:8
    faintly t. evening chime, 411:7
    for whom the bell t., 236:19
    it t. for thee, 236:19
Tom appeared on sidewalk, 559:19
    bears logs into the hall, 177:17
    before I go T. Moore, 422:26
    Fool's errand, 332:8
    little T. Tucker, 857:20
    loves me best that calls me T., 239:12
    o' Bedlam, 215:30
    O T. Thumb, 183:*n*1
    poor T. Bowling, 362:11
Tom piper's son, 858:15
Tom Jones, more knowledge of heart than in
    all T., 327:13
    will outlive Escurial, 353:14
Tomb, Achilles' t., 424:7
    adjusted in the T., 545:4
    by sounding sea, 479:20
    distant shadow of t., 541:7
    earth t. of rest, 681:18
    e'en from t. nature cries, 334:25
    icy silence of t., 439:2
    man t. for other animals, 140:11
    Mausolos' T., 850:10
    monument without a t., 238:5
    of Battiades, 85:13
    of Callimachus, 85:13
    of green leaves, 602:8
    Prince Andrey went to t., 542:11
    room for Shakespeare in your t., 247:11
    room my heart keeps in thy t., 249:1
    saint and Martyr rule from t., 720:4
    sea was made for his t., 239:1
    threefold fourfold t., 247:11
Tombs, half-acre t., 234:7
    in dust in cool t., 681:12
    shoveled into the t., 681:12
Tombstone, end of fight t. white, 633:2
Tomcat lies stretched flat, 825:6
Tommy this and Tommy that, 633:8
    Tittlemouse, 861:3
Tomorrow and day after and day after, 766:5
    and t. and t., 222:16
    ask for me t., 183:28
    blossoms, 231:2
    boast not thyself of t., 23:9
    call Progress T., 451:11
    do thy worst, 284:6
    eat drink t. we die, 27:10
    fair adventure of t., 178:24
    feather duster, 662:18
    fill sky with clouds, 100:9
    give me today take t., 122:25
    gone down drain of eternity, 69:17
    happiest time, 480:15
    have what to do after firing, 794:12

Tomorrow *(continued)*
    herald of t., 632:4
    here today gone t., 290:22
    I am going to do that t., 121:15
    I purpose to regulate room, 325:12
    in today walks t., 408:*n*3
    is another day, 758:9
    is not, 68:14
    jam t. jam yesterday, 552:9
    king t. shall die, 32:18
    know nothing of t., 399:8
    land ethic for t., 807:11
    let him love, 123:15
    let us do or die, 243:*n*1
    live till t., 348:18
    lose t. ground won today, 529:10
    never put off till t., 535:*n*1
    new day, 158:18
    no t. nor yesterday, 234:17
    nor can buy t., 233:9
    not worry about T., 586:8
    once again sail Ocean Sea, 99:9
    perhaps not do 't t., 242:13
    prepare for wants of t., 60:20
    program for t., 702:13
    put off till t., 535:6
    segregation now segregation t., 806:8
    speed today be put back t., 161:23
    such day t. as today, 228:9
    to fresh woods, 262:6
    unborn T. dead Yesterday, 471:20
    wait not till t., 151:1
    why T. I may be, 471:10
    will be dying, 248:8
    will repay, 282:21
Tomorrow's falser than former day, 282:21
    life is too late, 110:14
Tomorrows, confident t., 395:8
Tom's food for seven long year, 216:33
    poor T. a-cold, 217:2
Tomtit, little t., 565:20
Tone, antediluvian t., 553:2
    deep autumnal t., 429:4
    licked clean over centuries, 817:19
    of some world far from ours, 431:8
    peremptory t., 347:12
    Robert Emmet and Wolfe T., 638:7
    take t. of company, 314:20
    testimony against slavery, 509:8
Tongs, let us have t. and bones, 181:24
Tongue, all-obliterated T., 471:17
    at will yet never loud, 213:11
    can no man tame, 47:17
    candied t. lick pomp, 204:15
    cleave to the roof of my mouth, 20:11
    cold words of t. or pen, 656:9
    confuted by conscience, 258:8
    could scarcely cry, 372:4
    customs politics and t., 535:4
    death lies on my t., 187:5
    dove with flickering t., 721:18
    every t. brings in tale, 174:21
    eye t. sword, 204:7
    fair words never hurt t., 147:*n*14
    fallen by the t., 32:39
    falls silent, 57:20
    falsehood of the t., 357:11
    fellows of infinite t., 193:27
    flattering t. speeds guest, 640:9

Tongue *(continued)*
    fool hold t. and pass for sage, 104:10
    from his t. flowed speech, 52:8
    give thy thoughts no t., 201:24
    great ox stands on my t., 65:4
    heart thinks t. speaks, 194:30
    her t. fetters breaks, 845:21
    his t. dropped manna, 265:3
    his t. must vent, 224:28
    hold your t. and let me love, 234:5
    hurteth not t. to give fair words, 147:25
    I am t. of war, 829:3
    iron t. of midnight, 182:14
    is the clapper, 194:30
    is the law of kindness, 23:30
    keep good t. in head, 230:3
    keep thy t. from evil, 17:2
    keep t. and keep freend, 137:24
    live t. all dispelled, 809:4
    love's richer than my t., 215:15
    man that hath t. no man, 176:9
    murder though no t. speak, 137:*n*3
    my t. is the pen of a ready writer, 17:19
    my t. swore, 70:3
    never ear did hear that t., 171:10
    never hold t. a minute, 298:19
    never in t. that makes it, 177:15
    never repented held t., 104:*n*2
    no need for t., 780:2
    no t. their beauty declare, 400:13
    no t. to wound us, 412:3
    not able to conceive, 182:1
    not far from Kilmer cheek, 716:18
    of a slow t., 8:8
    of the dumb shall sing, 27:32
    old and bitter of t., 637:6
    on his t. they pour sweet dew, 56:4
    one thought in breast another on t.,
      95:4
    outvenoms all worms of Nile, 225:17
    put a t. in every wound, 197:5
    rolls it under his t., 295:14
    sad words of t., 468:12
    Shakespeare spake, 393:5
    shall be slit, 857:5
    sharp t. grows keener, 416:12
    sing t. the Savior's glory, 129:2
    snakes with double t., 181:15
    soul lends t. vows, 201:31
    sounds as sullen bell, 191:8
    strenuous t., 438:16
    such t. to great people, 512:6
    that I sin not with my t., 17:10
    though he hide it under his t., 14:27
    thy own shame's orator, 174:35
    to deal in fiction, 307:5
    to persuade, 269:19
    trippingly on the t., 204:11
    truth in shepherd's t., 160:3
    understanding but no t., 201:19
    use of my oracular t., 367:9
    use our t. at our peril, 316:15
    wery good thing, 495:22
    when my t. blabs, 208:27
    with his t. win a woman, 176:9
    wool of bat t. of dog, 221:21
    would t. utter, 482:15
Tongued with fire beyond living, 721:15
Tongueless vigil, 567:17

Tongues, all people and t., 48:23
    and deeds, 480:7
    aspics' t., 214:14
    bray of bragging t., 67:12
    clocks the t. of bawds, 184:23
    conscience hath thousand t., 174:21
    evil days and evil t., 267:13
    eyes silent t. of Love, 156:8
    from the strife of t., 16:29
    gift of t., 365:11
    govern t. with difficulty, 287:1
    had I a hundred t., 97:27
    had I your t. and eyes, 218:5
    have their talk, 156:*n*3
    hearts in love use own t., 194:18
    in all t. called fools, 200:6
    in trees, 197:37
    leaves stuck out t., 780:9
    mild old t., 817:19
    millions of t. record, 420:19
    not if I had ten t., 52:17
    not uttered by chapmen's t., 176:27
    of Douglas and myself, 474:13
    of dying men, 179:8
    of fire, 41:45
    of flame infolded, 722:5
    of men and angels, 44:17
    one soul though many t., 116:15
    self-interest speaks all t., 273:7
    sharpened their t. like a serpent, 20:16
    silence envious t., 231:7
    silver-sweet sound lovers' t., 183:14
    slanderous t., 195:12
    speak with other t., 41:45
    strange t. are loud, 563:5
    that syllable men's names, 260:24
    whispering t. can poison truth, 401:9
    woods have t., 135:*n*2
Tongue-tied by authority, 226:21
Tonight, child again just for t., 549:8
    curfew not ring t., 600:3
    from Oxford strays, 530:15
    hot time in old town t., 630:6
    met in thee t., 558:5
    refrain t., 205:29
    tenting t. on campground, 556:7
    tonight won't be just any night, 825:16
    world may end t., 492:20
Tonnage, damp t., 753:15
Tonsorial or agglutinative type, 653:17
Tonstant Weader Fwowed up, 738:16
Took all heart for speech, 638:15
    all which I t. from thee, 621:5
    by throat circumcised dog, 215:14
    great care of his Mother, 697:4
    not men you t. them for, 194:34
    one Draught of Life, 547:2
    one less traveled by, 669:4
    seen my opportunities and t. 'em, 584:4
    suffering human race, 528:15
    to my heels, 89:10
    to the law, 550:2
    wages and are dead, 619:17
    went and t. same as me, 634:9
Tool carries spirit, 760:12
    grows keener with use, 416:12
    maker, 681:8
    nor any t. of iron, 12:16
    only t. is a hammer, 779:12

Too-late, also called T., 542:4
Tools, give us the t., 666:8
    no jesting with edge t., 243:3
    sin has many t., 473:12
    teach but to name t., 270:19
    to make tools, 616:7
    with t. he is all, 433:10
Tool-using animal, 433:10
Tooth, defy t. of time, 305:22
    for tooth, 9:4
    hadde alwey coltes t., 136:18
    more deadly than mad dog's t., 174:38
    my Adonis hath a sweet t., 163:13
    of time, 212:6
    one t. and it aching, 658:9
    poison for age's t., 177:21
    purrs and never shows t., 710:10
    red in t. and claw, 484:6
    sharper than serpent's t., 216:5
    sinks into throat tiger's t., 729:12
    where each t. point goes, 632:9
Toothache, philosopher endure t., 195:7
Toothpaste and dandruff ads, 753:18
Toothsomest, old pippins t., 244:1
Tootings at weddings of soul, 687:13
Top, die at the t., 299:27
    fool me to t. of my bent, 205:10
    o' the mornin', 592:13
    of head taken off, 547:9
    of sovereignty, 438:19
    Revolution began at t., 535:3
    special few at very t., 827:3
    struggle to reach t., 790:2
    you're the t., 732:12
Top-hat, famous high t., 685:6
Topics, only two serious t., 643:6
    other fashionable t., 341:15
    two t. yourself and me, 328:5
    while serious t. disputing, 446:12
Topless towers of Ilium, 170:23
Toppling, send skyscrapers t., 781:14
Tops, tips with silver fruit-tree t., 183:8
[Topsy] 'spect growed, 489:19
Torah, whole T. rest is commentary, 106:1
Torch be yours to hold it high, 660:10
    bright t. and casement, 438:7
    give me a t., 707:21
    like runners pass on t. of life, 93:2
    of a flower, 707:21
    passed to new generation, 799:7
    truth is t., 333:10
Torchbearing outrider, 585:3
Torches of martyrdom, 358:16
Torchlight crimson on kettledrums, 664:10
Tore, shout t. hell's concave, 264:15
Torment, dark with t. and tears, 508:19
    delicious t., 455:22
    I feel it and am in t., 94:27
    is my joy, 781:6
    man comes with his t., 382:14
    measure of our t., 634:1
    of love unsatisfied, 719:11
    there shall no t. touch them, 31:16
    what t. not a marriage bed, 236:20
    who devised the t., 722:2
Tormented with ten thousand hells, 170:19
Tormenting, cant of criticism most t., 332:22
Torments in wedding ring, 301:7
    most maddens and t., 516:14

Torn and beaten out he lies, 431:17
    between passion for righteousness, 715:4
    by dreams, 687:20
    Naiad from flood, 477:14
    persons with t. bodies happy, 655:12
    screeches like t. tin, 825:7
    seine shattered lobsterpot, 721:8
    wings frayed soiled and t., 569:12
Torpedoes, damn the t., 449:16
Torpid, mind t. in old age, 328:10
Torquatus stretching his baby hands, 94:17
Torrent, character formed in world's t.,
    364:12
    in the very t. tempest, 204:11
    of his fate, 324:9
    rough t. of occasion, 192:3
    wind t. of darkness, 692:2
Torrent's, voices of dead like t. fall, 424:4
Torrents, blood in t. pour, 613:1
Torrid or frozen zone, 253:16
Tortoise because he taught us, 550:18
    hare and t., 60:12
    prince keeps t. enclosed, 83:2
Tortuous road from Montgomery, 823:6
Torture, hum of cities t., 420:26
    no rack T. me, 544:21
    object of t. is t., 765:17
    one poor word, 284:4
    one tiny creature, 525:17
    suspense in news is t., 269:14
    touch him not t. not again, 430:13
Tortured, millions of innocent t., 357:8
    with history, 753:15
Torturing hour, 334:1
Toss in the spray, 528:5
    tut tut good enough to t., 186:28
    weariness t. him to my breast, 250:19
Tossed, I am t. up and down, 19:17
    old woman t. in blanket, 859:11
    the dog, 861:15
    them human hearts, 429:13
    windows t. with linden, 809:9
Tosses but doesn't sink, 123:29
    up our losses, 721:8
Tossing aloft invisible, 611:18
    crossing Channel t., 565:4
    green water, 703:12
    heads in sprightly dance, 394:6
    mind is t. on the ocean, 187:13
    sea of Cause and Theory, 665:2
    so as to scare clouds, 669:7
Total grandeur of total edifice, 688:13
    irrecoverably dark t. eclipse, 268:32
Totalitarianism threaten free nations, 790:23
Totality of what he might have, 772:5
Toto I've feeling not in Kansas anymore,
    786:8
Tots sang Ring-a-rosie, 625:13
Totter into vogue, 336:4
Touch, approach t. me t. palm of hand, 520:1
    at t. I yield, 483:5
    common t., 635:21
    fear not to t. the best, 160:7
    furs to t., 712:18
    great death, 655:15
    Happy Isles, 481:14
    harps of gold, 488:15
    have to have t. of iron, 816:8
    he wants the natural t., 221:32

Trouble *(continued)*
    with a capital T, 764:9
    with kitten, 763:12
    with peace is no organization, 750:20
    words weighty with t., 692:14
    ya got t. folks, 764:9
Troubled air, 264:*n*1
    be not t., 37:6
    bridge over t. water, 837:11
    by this beauty, 573:5
    captain's mind, 580:23
    fish in t. waters, 295:17
    gold gateways of stars, 621:2
    I am t., 714:13
    let not heart be t., 41:26, 41:30
    mind, 249:14
    my mind is t., 208:14
    see that ye be not t., 37:6
    tumors of a t. mind, 269:2
    woman moved like fountain t., 176:1
Troubles, almost everybody had t., 627:12
    fear of Acheron which t. life, 93:7
    never sleep with anyone with worse t.,
      782:1
    of proud and angry dust, 619:12
    pack up your t., 689:22
    sea of t., 203:33
    wide and dark, 436:19
    written t. of the brain, 222:12
Troublesome disguises which we wear,
    266:21
    effort of thinking t., 571:2
    loud and t. insects, 345:16
Troubling, the wicked cease from t., 13:31
Troublous, part we sadly in t. world, 173:13
Trough, snake came to water t., 707:10
Trousers, cloud in t., 738:1
    never wear best t. to fight, 540:15
    steam engine in t., 398:24
    wear bottoms of t. rolled, 717:15
    wear white flannel t., 717:16
Trout, find t. in milk, 505:3
    here comes the t., 209:28
Trowel, laid on with a t., 197:27
Troy, did not go to citadel of T., 57:12
    fields of corn where T. was, 105:11
    fired another T., 285:14
    fires of T., 759:15
    half his T. was burned, 191:7
    has been, 97:10
    heard T. doubted, 424:7
    sacked the holy citadel of T., 54:7
    tale of T. divine, 260:6
    that matter of T., 520:5
    walls famed in battle, 97:9
    was there another T., 638:1
    why Grecians sacked T., 170:*n*5
    windy T., 481:9
    woman laid T. in ashes, 293:20
    worn the stones of T., 208:7
Troyan, Troilus mounted T. walls, 190:4
Truant disposition, 201:9
    every t. knew, 342:8
    my t. lover has come, 521:6
Truce, no t. or parley with Hitler, 666:14
    to navigation, 564:6
Truck, like advance of a heavy t., 815:16
Truckin', keep on t., 838:1
Trudge, swing tramp and t., 699:16

Trudgin' my weary way, 591:7
True, advanced t. friends, 529:1
    all I thought was t., 668:15
    and honorable wife, 196:7
    and righteous altogether, 477:4
    apothecary thy drugs quick, 184:18
    art for sake of t., 461:16
    as dial to sun, 271:27
    as I live, 243:9
    as needle to pole, 271:*n*1
    as stars above, 849:14
    as stiel, 134:6
    as taxes, 498:4
    as turnips, 498:4
    beautiful words are not t., 59:21
    beggar t. king, 346:6
    beginning of our end, 182:6
    best not expected to go t., 326:1
    blue, 271:1
    both t. both wise, 275:5
    brew that is t., 793:15
    child always say what's t., 598:21
    children and fools speak t., 148:*n*8
    completely t. statement, 840:3
    considered by people equally t., 353:5
    course of t. love, 180:19
    dare to be t., 249:18
    definition of style, 298:10
    democracy never existed, 331:2
    distinguish t. from false, 286:17
    ease in writing, 308:18
    eloquent but 'tis not t., 529:5
    every t. man's apparel, 212:2
    everyone's t. worship, 76:1
    false idol or noble t. birth, 78:9
    falsely t., 486:3
    first t. gentleman, 233:7
    for you true for all, 455:7
    founder of civil society, 330:17
    free Russian speech, 512:6
    generous t. and fierce, 665:11
    Genius appears in World, 298:4
    good men and t., 194:32
    great Power make me think t., 537:5
    gude to be honest and t., 847:14
    guid to be honest and t., 380:19
    happiness not in multitude of friends,
      237:9
    how should I t. love know, 206:4
    how to speak t. things, 56:3
    I am a t. laborer, 199:6
    I am t. Russian, 829:8
    I have gone here and there, 227:15
    I talk of dreams, 182:23
    I to my pledged word t., 724:18
    idea of what t. and false, 286:17
    if England rest but t., 178:29
    if we are t. to plan, 546:9
    I'll prove more t., 183:7
    in mathematics never know what t.,
      660:11
    in print sure they are t., 228:31
    is it t. in and for itself, 390:11
    judgments of Lord t., 16:12, 477:4
    lease of my t. love, 227:12
    live pure speak t., 485:20
    love a durable fire, 160:2
    love is like ghosts, 273:12
    love sits him down, 848:18

True *(continued)*
    lovers run into strange capers, 198:9
    makes false conception come t., 785:3
    marriage of t. minds, 227:17
    matter decided considered t., 124:21
    matters I relate are t. lies, 726:5
    me and my t. love, 847:15
    Milton was a t. poet, 372:13
    more t. than Love to me, 844:14
    music repeat thought of people, 751:13
    mysterious law t. source, 266:22
    never accept thing as t., 254:2
    no ground for supposing it t., 661:1
    no longer could I doubt him t., 408:9
    no man worth having t., 297:9
    nobility exempt from fear, 172:17
    not too good to be t., 295:25
    nothing t. makes complete sense, 735:17
    nothing t. that may not seem false, 153:3
    Oh 'tis t. 'tis t., 618:11
    one religion t. as another, 242:3
    only regret is that all so terribly t., 611:13
    order of going, 76:8
    Penelope was Flaubert, 709:1
    people's judgment t., 283:18
    pessimist fears this is t., 683:1
    pity 'tis 'tis t., 203:1
    plain hearts, 233:12
    poem an invocation, 743:21
    proved t. before prove false, 271:25
    right praise t. perfection, 190:9
    right t. end of love, 235:20
    ring in the t., 484:14
    small service is t. service, 395:20
    so t. to thyself, 168:1
    so young my lord and t., 215:19
    strange but t., 424:23
    such as I all t. lovers, 209:21
    tender and t., 538:8
    that he is mad 'tis t., 203:1
    the blushful Hippocrene, 437:7
    the t. Light, 40:32
    theory of t. civilization, 525:2
    think of companions t., 389:13
    Thomas, 854:2
    'tis t. 'tis day, 234:16
    'tis t. 'tis pity, 203:1
    to kindred points, 395:18
    to thee till death, 501:16
    to thine own self be t., 201:27
    to t. occasion t., 484:22
    to you in my fashion, 732:15
    trusty dusky vivid t., 599:15
    way but yet untried, 166:12
    way goes over rope, 701:4
    what each wishes he believes t., 81:16
    what is t. in the world, 826:11
    what is t. of shopkeeper, 331:22
    what people say of us t., 636:5
    whatsoever things are t., 45:38
    when you met her, 233:15
    wit nature to advantage, 308:12
    woman t. and fair, 233:14
    words are not beautiful, 59:21
    worshippers shall worship, 40:48
    writ your annals t., 225:3
    writer has nothing to say, 810:14
True-begotten father, 188:14
True-born Englishman, 179:7

Try *(continued)*
  if you t. sometimes you just might, 838:7
  let end t. the man, 191:28
  might as well not t., 669:1
  one white foot t. him, 849:17
  then worms shall t., 277:2
  times that t. men's souls, 354:10
  to be one on whom nothing lost, 584:15
  tropic for your balm, 741:10
  try again, 414:3
  whole cause condemn you, 549:14
  with all my might to mind, 414:7
Trying, because we have gone on t., 721:14
  God keeps on t. other things, 693:12
  the two sides he has, 756:4
  to fool yourself about love, 824:7
Trysted, the wished the t. hour, 380:8
Trysting, named a t. day, 448:13
Tsarism, revolution's victory over t., 654:6
Tu, et t. Brute, 92:n3, 196:15
Tub, every t. stand upon bottom, 281:n2
  fair tale of a t., 144:1
  three men in a t., 860:8
Tubal-cain artificer in brass and iron, 6:21
Tubes twisted and dried, 633:3
Tuckahaw, high t., 847:18
Tucker, little Tom T., 857:20
Tuckets, then t. then trumpets, 664:10
Tucson and Deadwood, 750:9
Tuesday, christened on T., 859:17
  dissolutely spent T. morning, 184:25
  gladly pay you T. for hamburger today,
    741:9
Tuesday's child full of grace, 859:16
Tuesdays, only teaching on T., 800:20
Tuffet, sat on a t., 860:3
Tufted, bosomed high in t. trees, 259:15
Tug, then was the t. of war, 294:10
Tugged with fortune, 221:2
Tugging all day at perverse life, 780:6
Tugs, each t. in different way, 424:29
Tulgey wood, 551:11
Tulips, tip-toe thru' the t. with me, 731:5
Tumble, anarchy why cities t., 67:24
  ready with every nod to t., 174:9
Tumbler, clean t. corkscrew, 496:24
Tumbling, Jill t. after, 858:4
  joined t. mirth, 810:11
Tumor ends by killing sympathies, 570:6
Tumors of a troubled mind, 269:2
Tumult and shouting dies, 635:2
  in the clouds, 638:17
  of mighty harmonies, 429:4
  of the soul, 395:10
  whirling through air forever dark,
    130:5
Tumultuous privacy of storm, 453:2
Tune, all t. he could play, 858:15
  he who pays piper calls t., 300:n2
  incapable of t., 407:15
  instrument here at the door, 236:13
  loveliest t. becomes vulgar, 593:18
  of flutes kept stroke, 223:14
  out of t. and harsh, 204:9
  singeth a quiet t., 400:15
  sings t. without words, 544:11
  sweetly played in t., 378:19
  turn on t. in drop out, 807:1
  voices keep t. oars time, 411:7

Tuned like fifty stomachaches, 497:16
  spheres, 224:4
Tunes, Cathedral T., 544:12
  devil have all good t., 362:6
  frozen up in horn, 355:6
  loathe sweet t., 568:15
  Love t. shepherd's reed, 396:9
Tuning lyre and handling harp, 64:17
Tunnel, antiseptic t., 821:7
  end of t., 800:2
  light at end of t., 800:n1
Tunnels that re-wind themselves, 753:17
Tupping your white ewe, 212:19
Turbaned, malignant and t. Turk, 215:14
Turbans, white silken t. wreathed, 268:23
Turbulent fleshy sensual eating drinking,
    519:9
  free me from t. priest, 127:2
  freezing t. water, 842:4
  people t. and changing, 370:9
  sagacious and t. of wit, 283:8
Turc, la galère d'un T., 278:n5
Turf, bless t. that wraps clay, 336:16
  grass-green t., 206:5
  green be t. above thee, 426:6
  green t. beneath feet, 410:13
Turk, bear like the T., 312:4
  human form in heathen t. or jew, 372:7
  malignant and turbaned T., 215:14
  or Proosian, 564:1
  out-paramoured the T., 216:29
  work hard as T., 845:7
Turkey a more respectable bird, 320:24
  black t. gobbler, 855:22
  in the straw, 847:18
  it was a t., 497:22
  myrtle and t. part, 406:14
Turkish, be taken by T. enemy, 862:10
  English not T. court, 192:12
Turkman's rest, 425:6
Turk's, on board a T. galley, 278:n5
Turks, Papists Protestants Jews T. in one ship,
    255:3
  sleep with T. and infidels, 180:7
Turmoil, tired of my t., 801:10
Turn again Whittington, 844:18
  away no more, 373:17
  backward O Time, 549:8
  currents t. awry, 203:33
  dark cloud inside out, 663:1
  death because chose to t., 725:7
  do not hope to t. again, 719:9
  do not t. back at goal, 103:24
  down empty Glass, 472:6
  each thing his t. does hold, 248:12
  good t. asketh another, 148:21
  him to cause of policy, 192:19
  his merry note, 198:11
  in door once turn once only, 719:2
  Lordship t. it over, 449:6
  now t. different hue, 61:13
  on tune in drop out, 807:1
  one good t. deserves another, 109:6
  out your toes, 551:15
  over a new leaf, 158:7
  over half a library, 327:24
  pass and t. again, 453:22
  quickly t. away, 640:16
  smile once more t. thy wheel, 216:10

Turn *(continued)*
  something t. up, 459:9
  stone start a wing, 621:7
  the other cheek, 34:6
  thee behind me, 13:3
  to t. you out t. you out, 633:5
  up the lights, 626:17
  where shall I t., 826:2
  wheresoe'er I may, 393:7
  why wilt thou t. away, 373:17
  worm will t., 172:26
Turned aside to sleep, 234:12
  dead and t. to clay, 206:26
  face with ghastly pang, 400:8
  from one's course by opinions, 86:3
  having once t. walks on, 400:17
  he t. up his eyes, 373:9
  heart is t. to stone, 214:20
  him right and round about, 379:3
  home his footsteps t., 396:11
  in case anything t. up, 497:32
  one who never t. back, 495:15
  round and round in world, 516:17
  suddenly cried and t. away, 712:15
  sword which t. every way, 6:11
  them inside outside, 657:n1
  world t. upside downward, 240:8
Turnest, thou t. man to destruction, 18:20
Turning, from itself never t., 160:2
  gas steam or table t., 525:2
  in widening gyre, 639:6
  neither shadow of t., 47:11
  o' the tide, 192:27
  still point of t. world, 719:23
  wine into urine, 706:4
Turnings, long lane knows no t., 491:19
Turnip, rather have t. than father, 325:21
Turnips, man who t. cries, 325:21
  true as t., 498:4
Turnpike, counting cars on New Jersey T.,
    837:10
Turns again home, 487:2
  climber-upward t. face, 195:30
  earth's smoothness rough, 494:9
  giddy thinks world t. round, 175:39
  his necessity to gain, 394:16
  into Miss T., 662:16
  lightly to love, 481:17
  no more his head, 400:17
  over your papers, 356:7
  poet's pen t. to shapes, 182:3
  times go by t., 168:25
  to thoughts of love, 481:17
  unto ladder t. his back, 195:30
  with ceaseless pain, 340:15
Turpissima bestia, 87:n8
Turquoise Horse of Johano-ai, 856:3
Turret, Sultan's T. with Light, 470:13
  washed me out of t. with hose, 793:6
Turtle, clever of t., 763:6
  lives 'twixt decks, 763:6
  Mock T., 550:18, 550:19
  thoughts of t. turtles, 458:3
  voice of the t. is heard, 25:17
Turtledove, voice of the t., 4:4
Turtle's breast, 719:23
Tut done thousand dreadful things, 175:18
Tutor to a lunatic, 661:3
Tut-tut child said Duchess, 550:16

Tu-whit tu-who, 177:17
TV, cool medium like T., 786:11
Twa, lost but ane t. behin', 380:15
    sisters sat in bour, 854:4
Twain, book made by Mr. Mark T., 560:14
    from one book by Mark T., 754:13
    never t. meet, 632:19
Twangling, thousand t. instruments, 230:6
Tweedledee, contrariwise continued T.,
    551:17
Tweedledum and Tweedledee, 314:13
Twelve good men, 409:19
    honest men, 306:15
    I in t. thousand none, 180:8
    in sworn t. have thief, 211:4
    in t. found truth in all but one, 180:8
    iron tongue hath told t., 182:14
    parted between t. and one, 192:27
    snowed t. days and t. nights, 795:15
Twelvemonth's, run t. length again, 379:11
Twentieth, party make t. century, 451:19
    what would t. century look like, 802:14
Twenty ballads stuck about wall, 252:29
    cannot live on t. pound, 249:20
    love-sick maidens, 564:7
    men crossing bridge, 686:8
    not handsome at t., 251:25
    strength of t. men, 184:11
    substance of grief hath t. shadows,
      179:16
    sweet and t., 209:14
    to that t. add hundred more, 248:7
    understand life at t., 630:13
    will not come again, 618:7
    years in woman's life, 77:11
Twenty-eight, came to serve at t., 140:10
Twenty-five, at t. dumbfounded afresh, 825:8
    between t. and forty, 595:11
    first t. years worth all, 452:6
Twenty-nine, she had a long t., 604:*n4*
    when there are pink shades, 604:26
Twenty-one, confidence of t., 326:15
Twenty-seven, woman of t., 746:15
Twenty-third day of October in Julian
    Calendar, 244:13
Twice as muckle 's a' that, 380:15
    blessed, 189:19
    life closed t. before close, 547:3
    love that never seen t., 443:16
    Napoleon was t. defeated, 510:*n2*
    not step t. into same rivers, 64:8
    old man t. a child, 203:21
    or thrice had I loved thee, 234:15
    serpent sting thee t., 189:15
    who splits wood warms t., 507:*n1*
    woman's name in print t., 706:2
    wood stumps warmed me t., 507:12
Twice-told tale, 178:10
Twice-turned, Jesus of t. cheek, 765:2
Twig and a pillar, 82:22
    as t. bent tree's inclined, 310:3
Twilight and evening bell, 487:3
    between birth and dying, 719:15
    brown t. atmosphere, 460:14
    disastrous t. sheds, 264:18
    glimmer of t., 491:24
    live in gray t., 614:13
    of things that began, 569:9
    past is t. of dawn, 644:11

Twilight (*continued*)
    pilots of purple t., 481:23
    still evening and t. gray, 266:15
Twilight's last gleaming, 411:1
Twin, stiff t. compasses, 235:3
Twined flowers, 438:12
Twinkle little bat, 550:12
    little star, 414:5
    on milky way, 394:5
Twinkling of an eye, 44:31
    world will pass in a t., 786:13
Twinklings, remembering with t. and
    twinges, 798:9
Twinned, we were as t. lambs, 228:10
Twins, body and spirit t., 569:16
    two young roes that are t., 25:21
Twirled, Brazil he t. Button, 545:10
    fingers madly, 500:6
Twist, cannot hope to bribe or t., 710:4
    'em up, 847:18
    let him t. slowly in wind, 814:19
    no more t., 644:4
    Oliver T. asked for more, 496:7
    oozy weeds about me t., 517:2
    secret lies in invisible t., 739:5
    wolf's-bane, 438:14
Twisted braids of lilies, 261:10
    cue, 565:16
    our eye-beams t., 235:4
    prisoner in his t. gyves, 183:15
    tubes t. and dried, 633:3
Twisting, character of t. octopus, 61:13
Twitched his mantle blue, 262:6
Twitches, Death t. my ear, 98:14
Two and one are three, 394:*n2*
    and two mathematician makes four,
      557:13
    as stiff twin compasses, 235:3
    bicycle built for t., 643:20
    blackbirds, 861:14
    by two in ark of ache, 812:16
    can t. walk together, 30:25
    cheers for Democracy, 684:6
    do t. things do neither, 102:15
    fifths sheer fudge, 514:19
    gods Persuasion and Compulsion, 64:22
    grains of wheat in chaff, 187:23
    grant that twice t. not four, 512:5
    gross of broken statues, 709:5
    I am t. fools I know, 234:8
    if by sea, 467:15
    if ever t. were one, 270:11
    in right with t. or three, 514:10
    irons in the fire, 245:5
    kinds of people, 600:6
    lads that thought no more behind, 228:9
    lanterns in North Church, 352:10
    live as one, 719:21
    lost but ane t. behin', 380:15
    love idea of t. sexes, 741:12
    lovely berries on one stem, 181:22
    loves I have, 228:3
    may keep counsel, 148:*n15*
    may talk one hear, 455:27
    not without God, 117:4
    o'clock in morning courage, 388:14
    of every sort, 6:27
    of far nobler shape, 266:9
    of trade never agree, 307:6

Two (*continued*)
    oldest professions, 715:15
    one t. and third in your bosom, 183:20
    or three gathered together, 36:30
    our t. souls which are one, 235:2
    reasons good one real one, 567:11
    roads diverged in wood, 669:4
    seizes t. things one slips, 853:8
    sides to every question, 72:2
    sin ye do by t. and t., 634:3
    single soul in t. bodies, 79:14
    sisters sat in a bour, 854:4
    sleep an act or t., 231:18
    souls dwell in my breast, 365:6
    stars keep not motion, 187:4
    strings to bow, 148:*n7*
    supreme blessings, 70:11
    takes t. to speak truth, 505:23
    Thing One and Thing T., 769:8
    things believed of any man, 652:13
    unity at minimum is t., 743:13
    voices are there, 394:23
    we t. alone will sing, 218:1
    went to pray, 272:5
Two Lands are in festivity, 4:9
Two-and-twenty, I am t., 618:11
    sweet t., 424:26
Two-edged, sharp as a t. sword, 21:3
    sharper than t. sword, 46:38
Two-handed engine, 262:2
Two-legged, unfeathered t. thing, 283:10
Two-ness an American a Negro, 648:11
Twopence a week and jam, 552:8
    colored, 599:10
Twopenny, don't care t. damn, 389:5
    wi' t. fear nae evil, 379:19
Twye, Miss T. soaping breasts in bath, 797:11
Tyger Tyger burning bright, 374:5
Tygers of wrath, 372:20
Tyler, Tippecanoe and T., 404:*n2*
Tyne, cargo of T. coal, 681:5
Type, highest t. of human nature, 523:14
    I am T., 632:4
    of all her race, 487:10
    of the wise, 395:18
    so careful of t., 484:4
Types, movable t., 433:9
    of judicial writing, 653:17
Typewriters, monkeys strumming on t.,
    695:3
Typical, clubs t. of strife, 348:6
Typing, it isn't writing it's t., 813:13
Tyrannical, strength without justice is t.,
    280:3
    three t. masters, 608:1
Tyrannies, of all t. on human kind, 284:19
    war dearth age agues t., 236:5
    which stifle the freedom, 787:10
Tyrannis, sic semper t., 570:27
Tyrannous to use strength like giant, 211:12
    word of command, 539:10
Tyranny and oppressions vanish, 359:3
    death a milder fate than t., 65:10
    destruction of Nazi t., 699:8
    discourage and abolish t. and vice,
      350:14
    economic t. above, 710:13
    establishes t. kill Brutus, 143:5
    fate awaiting Nazi t., 666:15

Tyranny *(continued)*
  fortune's wayward t., 67:6
  government transformed to t., 415:19
  Law ends T. begins, 286:7
  laws end t. begins, 323:6
  like hell not easily conquered, 354:10
  not only t. but tyrant, 354:9
  of Mrs. Grundy, 523:8
  of next-door neighbor, 538:7
  of one literature, 601:18
  over mind of man, 358:8
  snuff approach of t., 344:10
  struggle to be free of t., 751:2
  taxation without representation t., 340:2
  toss gauntlet before feet of t., 806:8
Tyranny's disease, 65:19
  ecclesiastic t. worst, 295:3
Tyrant, any excuse will serve t., 60:23
  conform to t. custom, 155:6
  is child of Pride, 68:6
  little t. of fields, 334:21
  not only tyranny but t., 354:9
  old man weds t., 71:1
  preserve me from a t., 237:12
  public opinion weak t., 506:9
  root from which t. springs, 77:23
  when t. has disposed of enemies, 77:25
Tyrant's, Ercles' vein a t. vein, 180:24
  threatening countenance, 99:28
Tyrants, all men would be t., 295:5, 361:11
  and slaves, 341:25
  argument of t., 381:4
  blood of patriots and t., 357:15
  controlled by t. or by ourselves, 770:2
  fall in every foe, 380:11
  hand unfriendly to t., 278:27
  hate t., 518:10
  how can t. govern home, 173:2
  kings t. from policy, 345:14
  rebellion to t., 846:19
  their t. their historians, 450:10
  thunderbolts and t., 319:*n*1
  thus always to t., 124:24
  to t. no quarter, 462:7
  watered by blood of t., 370:1
Tyre, one with Nineveh and T., 635:3
Tyrian, no distinction between Trojan and T., 97:1

U

U, green U blue O, 603:14
  will not be missed, 740:12
Ubi bene ibi patria, 124:29
  libertas ibi patria, 340:3
  saeva indignatio, 299:29
Ubiquitous, her envoys u., 490:13
  man u. animal, 778:3
Uffish thought, 551:11
Ugliest man who came to Ilium, 52:16
  North American civilization one of u., 814:3
Uglification and Derision, 550:19
Ugliness, one's beauty another's u., 456:2
  recognition of u., 58:8
Ugly America, 807:11
  born old and u., 496:36
  caresses of subhumanly u. mate, 833:12

Ugly *(continued)*
  dirty bird u. and offensive, 462:1
  dull and u. people, 627:10
  fact Nature hides, 548:6
  foul and u. mists, 184:36
  I may be u. and can't cook, 839:3
  like toad u. and venomous, 197:37
  night full of u. sights, 174:2
  so awful u. becomes beautiful, 521:10
  what sights of u. death in eyes, 174:3
  woman not u., 315:2
  women indisputably u., 315:2
  Yahoo tricks, 685:2
Ukelele, died playing u., 783:7
Ultima Thule, 96:*n*2, 107:*n*6
Ultimate, depository of u. powers, 359:6
  mystery works sadly, 582:6
  power u. aphrodisiac, 812:*n*1
  sanction of exploitation, 737:8
Ulysses admitted into U.S., 679:6
  like U. made glorious voyage, 150:12
Ulysses' absence, 224:18
Umbered, sees other's u. face, 193:11
Umble, very u. person, 498:2
Umbrella against Scotch mist, 515:24
Umbris, ex u. in veritatem, 450:5
Umpire, death u. of men's miseries, 171:18
Umpires, players and u. begged, 828:2
Unable, people u. to find work, 659:23
  to live in society, 80:23
  to sit still in a room, 279:19
Unacceptable in human existence, 824:1
Unaccommodated man, 216:30
Unaccountable, how soon u., 520:8
Unaccustomed to fear, 849:2
Unacquainted, not u. with misfortunes, 55:10
Unacted, nurse u. desires, 373:3
Unadorned, beauty u., 290:21
  when u. adorned most, 318:4
Unadvised, too rash too u., 183:10
Unadvisedly, entered into u., 51:7
Unaffected, affecting to seem u., 300:29
  with men be rational and u., 406:17
Unafraid, gentlemen u., 633:4
  of change, 627:19
Unaging intellect, 639:16
Unalienable, certain u. rights, 357:2
  essential and u. rights, 357:*n*1
Unalterable, army of u. law, 541:17, 717:21
  quantity of force u., 527:13
Unaltered, laws ought not to remain u., 80:26
Unaneled, unhouseled disappointed u., 202:19
Unanimity, feel way toward u., 631:20
  on legal questions, 626:19
Unapproachable in White House, 701:13
Unarm Eros, 223:34
Unarmed, being u. be despised, 142:13
  truth, 823:8
Unashamed, brawling judgments u., 485:24
Unassisted merit advances slowly, 323:*n*4
Unattainable perfection, 636:8
Unattempted yet in prose or rhyme, 263:20
Unavailing star, 636:8
Unavenged suffering, 525:16
Unaware, hope he knew and I u., 575:17
  some morning u., 492:4

Unawares, entertained angels u., 47:4
Unbarred gates of light, 267:10
Unbearable lightness of being, 823:13
Unbeautiful and have comfortable minds, 739:14
Unbecoming, not u. men that strove, 481:13
Unbelief, help thou mine u., 38:27
Unbelievers, do not the u. see, 121:18
  works of u. a mirage, 121:22
Unbelieving came home, 709:4
Unbend, sweet to let mind u., 100:17
  universal horror u., 693:15
Unbidden guests welcomest when gone, 171:15
Unbirthday present, 552:13
Unblighted unredeemed wilderness, 572:13
Unbodied, souls u., 235:24
Unborn, fate of u. millions, 349:14
  millions yet u., 337:10
  posterity of those u., 302:13
  states u., 196:17
  ye u. ages, 335:14
Unborrowed, interest u. from the eye, 391:3
Unbought, health u., 285:19
Unbound, so are ye u., 453:14
Unbounded, man of an u. stomach, 231:12
  salt water u., 635:14
Unbowed, head bloody but u., 594:10
Unbreathed, virtue unexercised and u., 262:23
Unbribed, what man will do u., 710:4
Unbroken, seaward flying u. wings, 719:16
  spur not u. horse, 398:4
Unburied, bodies of u. men, 244:3
  unwept u. Patroclus, 54:3
Unburnished, rust u., 481:10
Unbusy, sole u. thing, 402:11
Unbutton, come u. here, 216:30
Uncared, unloved and u. for, 785:6
Uncaught, from world's snare u., 223:31
Uncertain and afraid, 775:13
  balance of proud time, 165:19
  coy hard to please, 397:1
  fill certain portion of u. paper, 423:15
  glory of April day, 176:6
  hour before morning, 721:18
  however u. of giving happiness, 406:9
  life's u. voyage, 218:22
  rustling of curtain, 479:3
  to it nothing u., 366:13
  trumpet give u. sound, 44:21
Uncertainties, capable of u., 440:3
Uncertainty, dazzling u. of New England weather, 559:22
  known what Greeks did not u., 753:3
  quit certainty for u., 324:23
  sink of u. and error, 280:8
Unchanging, no u. truth, 731:9
  Olympus ever u., 54:21
Uncharitable to ourselves, 256:5
Uncharitableness, from all u. deliver, 50:11
Unchartered freedom tires, 394:11
Unchecked, population u. increases, 385:4
Unchristened, Homer and his u. heart, 641:11
Uncircumcision, neither circumcision nor u., 46:3
Uncivilized Eastern instincts, 632:11
Unclasps her warmed jewels, 437:1

Uncle, I have good eye u., 194:16
    me no uncle, 179:19
    my prophetic soul my u., 202:15
    nephew of my U. Sam's, 679:11
Unclean, man of u. lips, 26:25
    people of u. lips, 26:25
    spirits entered swine, 38:22
    swine is u., 9:11
Unclose, began to u. damask gown, 151:2
Unclothed, bodies u. must be, 235:24
Unclouded, pure u. brow, 551:8
Unclubable, very u. man, 327:5
Uncoffined and unknown, 421:27
Uncomely, things u. and broken, 637:8
Uncomfortable feel tarantara, 564:4
    moral when only u., 609:20
Uncommon, common opinions u. abilities,
        538:6
    valor common virtue, 708:11
Uncompromising as justice, 462:4
Unconcern, patron looks with u., 326:10
Unconcerned hear mighty crack, 301:16
Unconditional and immediate surrender,
        532:14
    love, 823:8
    right to say what one pleases, 711:2
Unconfined, lawless winged u., 373:10
    let all her ways be u., 296:19
    let joy be u., 420:17
Unconquerable, love u. waster, 68:1
    man's u. mind, 393:2
    nursing u. hope, 529:13
    soul, 594:10
    will, 264:3, 666:15
Unconquered, thy arm u. steam, 348:23
Unconscionable time dying, 282:13
Unconscious, archetypes of u., 675:6
    collective u., 675:2
    explore u., 616:5
    fastidiousness, 714:10
    humor, 558:22
    knowledge of u. activities of mind, 607:8
    Kosmos, 583:4
    not only evil by nature, 675:9
    obscure u. mental processes, 607:7
    part of man's life, 434:14
    poetry, 532:4
    poets philosophers discovered u., 608:7
    source of highest good, 675:9
    studied, 608:7
Unconsidered, decisive actions often u.,
        651:3
    snapper-up of u. trifles, 228:22
Unconsoled widower, 469:4
Unconstitutional, power to pronounce u.,
        462:12
Uncontrollable laughter, 52:12
    mystery, 638:9
Unconvincing, preferable to u. possibility,
        81:13
Uncorrupted, heart of an u. good man, 782:4
Uncorseted her friendly bust, 718:8
Uncounted, monster with u. heads, 191:6
Uncouth, savage men u. manners, 344:3
Uncreated conscience of race, 696:7
    wide womb of u. night, 265:4
Uncreating word, 313:25
Uncrowned in the underworld, 707:11
Unction, flattering u., 205:25

Uncumbered with a wife, 285:18
Uncut, beautiful u. hair of graves, 518:19
Undaunted by villains in power, 352:9
    daughter of desires, 272:14
    we must be u., 666:6
Undazzled, kindling her u. eyes, 263:3
Undecided, decided only to be u., 665:12
Undefeated because we have gone on trying,
        721:14
Undefiled, well of English u., 161:13
Under blossom that hangs on bough,
        230:13
    every stone a politician, 75:15
    one more drink be u. host, 738:18
    the greenwood tree, 198:11
Underbelly, soft u. of Axis, 667:10
Underestimating, lost money by u.
        intelligence of people, 691:13
Underfoot, men tread u. what feared, 93:18
Undergraduates limited to four, 654:17
Underground, go burrow u., 710:7
    living in u. den, 77:14
    might well be u., 565:9
    turn u. passages into lethal chambers,
        756:16
    wake nations u., 863:8
Underjaw, most things move u., 250:14
Underlings, that we are u., 195:20
Undermine, echo u. her hold on life, 684:4
    'em with grins, 793:3
Undermining prosperity, 615:11
Underneath are the everlasting arms, 10:16
    in uplifting get u., 643:11
    this sable hearse, 247:12
    this stone doth lie, 237:22
Undernourishment, extinction from u., 755:9
Underrated nobleman, 566:2
Understand, Americans were first to u., 772:3
    and control nature, 727:12
    at last to u., 688:11
    Black love is Black wealth, 838:3
    both these do not u., 51:24
    everything makes tolerant, 385:14
    fury in your words, 214:24
    Gettysburg you cant u., 748:16
    grown-ups never u., 759:3
    how little we need, 621:15
    I and public u. each other, 672:6
    I u. thy kisses, 186:10
    if I could u., 486:21
    know less u. more, 699:13
    life at forty, 630:13
    mankind u. Monarchy, 538:2
    may not be made to u. it, 63:4
    maybe I just don't u. poetry, 833:10
    ne'er quite u. customs, 535:4
    no human being u. another, 767:8
    not to be understood but to u., 128:5
    now do you u. serendipity, 336:3
    say it as you u. it, 382:5
    so many tried to u., 750:11
    that he should u., 687:17
    they that trust in him shall u., 31:17
    though he's hard to u., 837:15
    to admire we should not u., 300:19
    vexation only to u. the report, 27:23
    want to u. others, 381:16, 723:10
    writer's ignorance, 403:1
    youngsters read men u., 157:27

Understandable by everyone not just
        scientists, 837:3
    spirit, 780:11
Understandest my thought afar off, 20:12
Understandeth, Lord u. all the imaginations,
        13:10
Understanding action of forces, 527:14
    begged Him to take away my u., 293:15
    candle of u., 31:9
    declare if thou hast u., 15:5
    first from mind banish u., 71:n4
    foolish people without u., 29:3
    for thy more sweet u., 176:24
    give it an u., 201:19
    gone a-woolgathering, 243:n6
    ignorant of his u., 403:1
    in length of days u., 14:12
    is false mirror, 166:14
    is joyous, 830:6
    man of u., 32:12
    man of u. is of excellent spirit, 22:8
    man of u. lost nothing, 152:16
    men of u., 24:30
    much learning not teach u., 64:5
    myself, 723:10
    no full u. of own epoch, 675:14
    not hand but u., 157:25
    not obliged to find u., 329:16
    of myself and things around me, 540:6
    Peace of God passeth all u., 51:2
    peace which passeth u., 45:37
    spirit of wisdom and u., 26:33
    steppingstones to u., 682:6
    to depart from evil is u., 14:36
    to direct, 360:9
    where is the place of u., 14:33
    wife, 244:11
    wise and u. heart, 12:11
    with all thy getting get u., 20:28
    with little u. world ruled, 145:3
    woman of mean u., 406:4
Understandings, best flattered upon u., 315:2
Understands, none of us really u., 840:5
    relentlessly she u. you, 771:16
    without seeing, 59:7
Understood as a child, 44:20
    by quiet natures u, , 639:14
    harmony not u., 311:8
    his time, 693:14
    interpreter hardest to be u., 368:1
    poetry communicate before u., 722:18
    trembles to be so u., 688:11
    truth never u. and not believed, 373:4
Undertake executions for master executioner,
        59:18
Undertaken, work we have u., 246:17
Undertaker, manners of u., 650:5
Undertaking, thorny u. to follow movement
        of mind, 152:19
Underwear, never heard of u., 730:14
Underwood, green u. and cover, 567:18
Underworld, uncrowned in the u., 707:11
Undescribable, describe u., 421:12
Undeserved, wear u. dignity, 188:27
Undeservedly forgotten, 776:12
Undeserving, one of the u. poor, 610:7
Undesirable to believe proposition, 661:1
Undetected, organizer of nearly all u., 617:11
Undevout astronomer is mad, 306:14

Unkindness, I tax not you with u., 216:19
  may defeat my life, 214:30
  may do much, 214:30
Unkissed, unknowe u. and lost, 133:17
Unknelled uncoffined, 421:27
Unknow, knows not also to u. , 525:5
Unknowable, world u. we know, 621:6
Unknown, accents yet u., 196:17
  affection hath u. bottom, 199:30
  altars to u. gods, 581:6
  and silent shore, 407:5
  behind dim u., 514:13
  black and u. bards, 656:18
  critics shouting He's u., 580:5
  developed respect for u. in lifetime, 784:6
  enemy is the u., 676:8
  forms of things u., 182:3
  good to love the u., 407:18
  hardships we suffered, 734:9
  know less than all u., 242:10
  let me live unseen u., 308:4
  like a complete u., 836:8
  loss no loss, 102:17
  means of destruction hitherto u., 705:5
  naked in death on u. shore, 97:21
  nature is but art u., 311:8
  not lived ill who passed u., 101:6
  not to know me argues yourselves u., 266:24
  out of me unworthy u., 651:14
  poetry journey to u., 738:2
  she lived u., 391:18
  taken for marvelous, 113:28
  things standing thus u., 207:13
  to fortune and fame u., 335:2
  to the u. god, 42:17
  too early seen u., 182:26
  traveled among u. men, 392:6
  unkist and lost, 133:17
  unknelled uncoffined u., 421:27
  worth's u. although height taken, 227:17
Unlamented let me die, 308:4
Unlearned, amaze th' u., 308:14
Unleashed power of the atom, 684:1
Unleavened bread and bitter herbs, 8:17
  seven days shall ye eat u. bread, 8:20
Unleaving, Goldengrove u., 587:14
Unless name is noted down, 826:12
  statistics lie, 740:5
Unlessoned girl unschooled, 189:8
Unlettered small-knowing soul, 176:23
Unlimited, land of u. possibilities, 593:4
  power apt to corrupt, 323:6
  rights will become u., 330:18
Unlived, history cannot be u., 820:7
Unlocked, Shakespeare u. heart, 395:19
  silent throat, 844:23
Unloose, Gordian knot u., 192:19
  not worthy to u., 38:14
Unloved and uncared for, 785:6
Unlovely, keep u. things afar, 85:8
Unlucky, these u. deeds relate, 215:13
Unmake, people can u. Constitution, 371:6
Unmanageable, most u. of all animals, 78:14
Unmanliness, wisdom without u., 74:1
Unmanly, 'tis u. grief, 200:31
Unmannerly, called them untaught u., 185:3
  sadness in youth, 187:30

Unmask her beauty to moon, 201:22
  time's glory to u. falsehood, 175:8
Unmasked, offer itself to be u., 701:5
Unmatchable, mastiffs of u. courage, 193:9
Unmeaning thing they call a thought, 308:17
Unmentionable odor of death, 775:13
  thoughts, 516:20
Unmoved cold and to temptation slow, 227:3
Unnat'ral, poetry's u., 495:29
Unnatural, most u. of sexual perversions, 741:4
  nothing u. that is not impossible, 368:4
  vices fathered by heroism, 718:4
Unnecessarily, entities not multiplied u., 132:10
Unnecessary, curious in u. matters, 31:30
  heroic in u. points, 581:9
  in Nature nothing u., 127:7
  sentence no u. words, 652:12
Unnerved and untrained, 581:9
Unnoticed, rather attacked than u., 328:18
  that u. & that necessary, 833:7
Unnumbered idle pebbles, 217:18
Unobtrusive, poetry should be u., 440:4
Unofficial force Baker Street irregulars, 616:17
Unordered, Chaos a rough u. mass, 105:12
Unpaid, you with u. bill, 431:7
Unparalleled catastrophes, 684:1
  in thought u., 410:15
  lass u., 224:13
Unpassioned beauty of great machine, 712:18
Unpeel, white Godiva I u., 827:17
Unperiphrastic, 75:19
Unperplexed like migratory birds, 677:5
  seeking find Him, 492:24
Unperturbed pace, 621:1
Unpitied sacrifice, 343:15
  unrespited u. unreprieved, 265:5
Unpleasant, demd u. body, 496:23
  to meet Mr. Eliot, 720:1
Unpleasantest words that blotted paper, 189:9
Unpleased, in power u., 283:8
Unpleasing to a married ear, 177:16
Unpledged, mind was still u., 70:3
Unpoetical, poet u., 440:14
Unpolluted, fair and u. flesh, 206:27
Unpopular, free trade u., 447:9
  names impossible loyalties, 530:10
Unpossessed, is empire u., 174:16
Unpracticed, unlessoned girl u., 189:8
Unpremeditated art, 429:16
  lay, 396:4
  strain, 318:10
  verse, 267:24
Unprepared courage, 388:14
  magnificently u., 711:7
Unprincipled for good of unprincipled, 63:8
Unprofitable, how weary stale flat u., 201:1
  servant, 37:15
Unpunished, no good deed goes u., 851:8
Unpurged images of day, 641:5
Unqualified blessing, 386:14
Unquenchable, gleam of noble deeds ever u., 66:8

Unquiet, hate to be u. at home, 288:27
  heart and brain, 483:15
  how imagine u. slumbers, 509:4
  meals make ill digestions, 174:39
Unravished bride of quietness, 437:16
Unread his works, 392:n1
  vision, 719:13
Unreadable forty years from now, 417:5
Unreal, lead me from u. to real, 51:20
  matter u. and temporal, 526:12
  mockery hence, 221:15
Unreality and loud music, 802:5
Unreason, age of u., 779:17
  world's God full of u., 713:9
Unreasonable, perfectly u. man, 498:19
Unredeemed, unblighted u. wilderness, 572:13
Unredressed, so long as wrong u. on earth, 514:7
Unreeling tirelessly speeding them, 521:7
Unreflectively, ceases to live u., 677:15
Unregarded time slips away, 676:18
Unregenerate, more about iniquity than u., 632:13
Unrelated and contradictory ends, 782:3
Unrelenting foe to love, 318:7
  haughty Juno's u. hate, 285:6
  our cruel and u. enemy, 349:14
Unremembered, nameless u. acts, 390:20
Unreprieved, unrespited unpitied u., 265:5
Unreproved pleasures free, 259:12
Unrequited toil, 477:4
Unrespited unpitied unreprieved, 265:5
Unrest, attacks on Court expression of u., 578:9
  capitalism creates social u., 703:4
  fairest joys give u., 436:13
  frantic-mad with evermore u., 228:6
  large part of current u., 607:17
  men miscall delight, 430:13
Unrighteous, if you know a thing is u., 81:26
  man forsake his thoughts, 28:26
Unrighteousness, riches and honors by u., 62:27
Unroll, page did ne'er u., 334:19
Unromantic as Monday morning, 504:18
Unruly, scepter snatched with u. hand, 178:12
  Sun, 234:2
  tongue an u. evil, 47:17
  wit's an u. engine, 250:1
Unsafe, democracy u., 628:13
Unsaid, something u., 821:10
Unsatisfied, culture leaves u. drives to rebelliousness, 607:15
  indignation, 525:16
  love u., 719:11
Unschooled, unlessoned girl u., 189:8
Unscottified, most u. of your countrymen, 327:20
Unscrew locks from doors, 519:9
Unscrupulous, one of most u. rascals, 617:15
Unsearchable dispose, 269:16
Unseasonable and immoderate sleep, 325:13
  to eat an oyster, 154:10
Unseasoned telling found in legends, 817:19
Unseemly, not u. to die in defense, 53:19

Unseen, all u. and unheeded, 682:1
 born to blush u., 334:20
 by forms u. dirge sung, 336:16
 counsel of the U. and Silent, 435:3
 down u. full of water, 180:9
 I walk u., 260:3
 ill habits by u. degrees, 285:23
 jest u. inscrutable, 176:7
 let me live u. unknown, 308:4
 nature works by bodies u., 92:15
 thou art u. yet I hear, 429:18
 walk the earth u., 266:19
 within thy airy shell, 260:26
Unselfish, absolutely u. friend is dog, 548:7
 love of brute, 478:16
Unselfishness, modesty and u., 708:10
Unsettled, precedent not u. overnight,
 653:16
Unsex me here, 219:11
Unshackled by party, 395:22
 exercise of every faculty, 450:14
Unshorn fields boundless beautiful, 432:15
Unshut eye, 528:7
Unsifted in perilous circumstance, 201:29
Unsightly noisome things, 452:17
Unslayable, soul eternally u., 87:2
Unsmiling, implacable u. men, 842:4
Unsmote by the sword, 422:15
Unsought, love u. is better, 210:6
Unsoundness of mind, 447:13
Unspeakable, citadel of television u., 769:4
 desire, 529:4
 in pursuit of the uneatable, 606:3
 is sorrow you bid me renew, 97:5
Unspoken problem for many years, 807:15
 words which were better u., 55:12
Unsponsored, solitude u. free, 686:19
Unspotted from the world, 47:14
Unstable as water, 7:36
 become u. without knowing it, 71:14
 feet u., 685:3
 woman always fickle u. thing, 97:19
Unstaid and skittish in motions, 209:21
Unsteadiness of second class, 370:9
Unstilled world whirled, 719:14
Unsubstantial as shadows, 75:9
Unsuccessful or successful war, 347:26
Unsung noblest deed will die, 66:11
 unwept unhonored u., 396:11
Unsunned, chaste as u. snow, 225:13
 heaps of miser's treasure, 261:1
Unsure, habitation giddy and u., 191:23
 what's to come still u., 209:14
Unsuspected isle in far-off seas, 491:4
Unswayed, is the sword u., 174:16
Untainted, what stronger breastplate than
 heart u., 172:12
Untamed continent, 534:9
 seas, 776:10
 sullen u. intractable, 721:7
Untaught, called them u. knaves, 185:3
Untell the days, 239:10
Untender, so young and so u., 215:19
Untented Kosmos my abode, 599:12
Unthinkable, dare to think u. thoughts,
 770:6
Unthinking, assault of thoughts on u.,
 701:19
 time, 285:20

Unthread rude eye of rebellion, 178:23
Untidy, beginnings and endings u., 647:6
Until the day break, 25:19
Untimely, from mother's womb u. ripped,
 222:21
 grave, 253:17
 graves, 348:6
'Unting, ain't 'u. as 'urts 'un, 591:15
Untitled aristocracy, 473:17
Untouched, strings u. will harshly jar,
 170:16
Untrained to stand test, 581:9
Untraveled, gleams u. world, 481:9
 heart u. turns to thee, 340:15
Untrespassed sanctity of space, 810:11
Untried found difficult left u., 664:5
Untrodden, dwelt among u. ways, 391:18
Untroubling and untroubled where I lie,
 431:15
Untrue, cloth u. twisted cue, 565:16
 might telle his tale u., 135:16
 narrative as a whole u., 534:10
 thy lovers were all u., 285:22
 unsad and evere u., 137:5
Untruth, never dare utter u., 90:16
Untune, Music shall u. the sky, 284:17
 that string, 207:26
Untuned, like u. strings women are, 170:16
Untutored, Indian whose u. mind, 311:5
Untwist last strands of man, 587:20
Unum, E pluribus u., 98:n5
Unus, E pluribus u., 98:n5
Unused, fust in us u., 205:35
 to the melting mood, 215:13
Unusual, cruel and u. punishment, 361:7
Unutterable, looked u. things, 317:18
Unuttered part of man's life, 434:14
Unvanquishable, in u. number, 429:14
Unvanquished, I u. and unyielding, 700:11
Unvarnished, round u. tale deliver, 212:26
Unveil, Immortality u. third event, 547:3
Unveiled her peerless light, 266:16
Unveiling, uprising u. affirm, 478:15
Unvexed to the sea, 476:5
Unvictorious, conscripted u. ones, 712:4
Unwanted, greatest disease is being u.,
 785:6
Unwashed, great u., 410:3
 lean u. artificer, 178:19
 platters ride, 753:18
Unwastefully, manage affairs u., 557:5
Unwearied still lover by lover, 638:12
Unwelcome, bringer of u. news, 191:8
Unwept in eternal night, 100:15
 unburied Patroclus, 54:3
 unhonored unsung, 396:11
Unwillingly I left your land, 97:26
 to school, 198:25
Unwomanly rags, 446:2
Unworthy, merit of the u. takes, 203:33
 out of me u. unknown, 651:14
Unwritten, history u. because yet to be
 enacted, 521:12
 ordinances, 73:18
 written and u. law, 116:11
Unwrung, our withers are u., 205:5
Unyielding, Hades is u., 53:3
 I unvanquished and u., 700:11
Unyoked humor of idleness, 184:36

Up and down City Road, 848:8
 cannot bear leveling u., 327:1
 game is u., 225:16
 go u. and down as a talebearer, 9:14
 lad when journey's over, 618:8
 look not down but u., 494:12
 men to your posts, 537:14
 nice to people on way u., 678:9
 road u. and road down one and same,
  64:11
 roos sonne and up roose Emelye, 135:26
 Satan walking u. and down, 13:23
 so floating many bells, 740:8
 success is showing u., 831:7
 sunny side u., 736:18
 you've got to get u., 716:4
Upbraid my falsehood, 208:7
Upbringing, children look after own u.,
 822:8
 nun would envy, 828:9
Upharsin, Mene Mene Tekel U., 30:6
Upholds, giant Atlas u., 70:5
Upkeep, annual u. of yacht, 567:12
Uplift, educate Filipinos u. civilize them,
 586:4
Uplifted, from despair thus high u., 264:25
 loud u. angel trumpets, 262:9
Uplifting, in u. get underneath, 643:11
 thoughts in baths, 745:8
Upmost, attains u. round, 195:30
Upon, and then they were u. her, 797:14
 me soul Reilly, 849:4
Upper crust, 426:3, 442:2
 materializing u. class, 532:3
 part of mankind, 295:7
 stiff u. lip, 535:18
Uppity, I'm u. rude profane brash, 806:9
Upraised, eyes u. as inspired, 337:4
Upright, behold the u., 17:8
 God hath made man u., 24:25
 judge learned judge, 189:27
 man is laughed to scorn, 14:10
 these set our flesh u., 235:22
 walketh u. in a straight way, 122:17
Uprightness, man is born for u., 62:25
Uprising, my downsitting and mine u., 20:12
 unveiling affirm, 478:15
Uproar, in bellow and u., 699:16
 sand and wild u., 452:17
 universal peace, 221:34
Uprose, Prince Lucifer u., 541:16
Upset, progress of Evolution u. Darwin,
 570:14
Upsets, art u., 694:15
Upside, world turned u. downward, 240:8
Upstairs and downstairs, 488:7
 downstairs in lady's chamber, 858:11
 equal u., 621:17
Upstart crow beautified with our feathers,
 165:18
Upstream, only gamefish swims u., 614:6
Upswept angel wings, 730:8
Upturned, sea of u. faces, 397:23
Upward, as the sparks fly u., 13:37
 human race born to fly u., 131:17
 look of caution, 670:20
Upwards, astronomy compels soul to look u.,
 77:15
Uranium new source of energy, 683:9

Uranus, it may be in U., 505:1
Urban, complicated u. society, 727:5
    for u. poor police arrest, 820:12
Urbi et orbi, 124:30
Urge of a song, 671:7
    to beware the temptation, 787:11
    to kill, 829:5
    wrestle resurrection, 780:3
Urgent, Master is u., 120:8
Uriah, set ye U. in forefront of battle, 12:2
Urinal, burnt match skating in u., 753:17
Urine, shoes will fill with u., 830:15
    turning wine into u., 706:4
Urn, bubbling loud-hissing u., 348:4
    Grecian U. worth old ladies, 749:3
    lean on garden u., 717:23
    storied u., 334:17
    well-wrought u. becomes greatest ashes, 234:7
U.S.A., greed will save the U., 840:6
Usage, consumed in image if not in u., 795:18
    tristement selon l'u. de leur pays, 165:*n6*
'Usband, Man-o'-War's 'er 'u., 634:17
Use a little wine for stomach's sake, 46:24
    again until Eternity, 546:8
    against the u. of nature, 219:5
    all gently, 204:11
    almost change nature, 205:29
    any language you choose, 565:3
    beauty too rich for u., 182:25
    cannot u. talent, 760:6
    come to deadly u., 217:13
    doth breed habit, 176:15
    every man after desert, 203:26
    find but seldom u. them, 455:29
    frequent u. of any organ, 362:7
    glad to be of u., 717:14
    him as though loved him, 253:6
    I'll u. you for my mirth, 197:9
    in measured language, 483:15
    it and never wear it out, 58:11
    it up wear it out, 850:11
    know not how to u. victory, 86:18
    living measured by u., 152:11
    main thing is u. it well, 253:23
    make proper u. of victories, 88:8
    many books and never u. them, 239:16
    me to the limit, 615:1
    no u. of metal, 229:25
    not poor who has enough to u., 101:4
    not to shine in u., 481:10
    of force but temporary, 344:7
    of him more than I see, 598:23
    rather in power than u., 210:20
    ring worn thin by u., 92:*n9*
    speak daggers but u. none, 205:13
    sure to find u. for it, 398:10
    treatment to help sick, 72:16
    try to have and u. excellence, 80:20
    tyrannous to u. strength like giant, 211:12
    want of u. mind torpid, 328:10
    what's the u., 662:18
    worship he found in u., 76:1
    worst u. a man could be put to, 232:18
Used, I am u. to it, 476:6
    I have u. similitudes, 30:20
    key always bright, 319:26

Used *(continued)*
    man grows u. to everything, 525:10
    mouth u. as a latrine, 809:11
    my credit, 184:27
    only witchcraft I have u., 212:32
    wine good if well u., 213:27
Useful, be u. where thou livest, 250:2
    books you may carry most u., 326:2
    by magistrate equally u., 353:5
    lesson to head, 348:11
    mock their u. toil, 334:14
    nothing in houses not u., 557:4
    villain would have been u., 383:3
Usefulness common goal of nature, 792:1
    power of u. gone, 615:8
Useless, art quite u., 604:12
    better know u. things than nothing, 106:26
    each without other, 467:2
    general maxim u., 447:15
    gold in itself u., 143:13
    if object u. labor u., 510:8
    laws weaken necessary laws, 314:9
    life is early death, 364:6
    lodged with me u., 263:12
    most beautiful most u., 517:7
    no man u. who has friend, 599:20
    other virtues would be u., 278:10
    second good third u., 142:17
    slip u. away, 435:12
    to excel, 329:25
    to poet nothing u., 324:25
Uselessly, nature does nothing u., 80:22
Uselessness of men above sixty, 595:12
Uses, corner for others' u., 214:4
    one art which u. things, 78:1
    panics have u., 354:11
    seem all u. of this world, 201:1
    sweet are u. of adversity, 197:37
    the more he u. for others, 59:21
    to what base u. return, 206:25
Usher, House of U., 478:11
Ushered, still u. with tear, 309:24
Ushers in the morn, 321:18
Usquebae, wi' u. face the devil, 379:19
Usual, not in the u. way, 501:7
Usura sin against nature, 709:9
    with U., 709:8
Usurpations, violent and sudden u., 367:2
Usurpers, lay proud u. low, 380:11
Usury, from all u. free, 98:27
Utility, as foundation of morals U., 465:1
    has u. as evidence of leisure, 613:11
    in science seek immediate u. in vain, 527:14
    nothing value but object of u., 510:8
    of futility, 82:24
    of useful things, 82:24
    or cost of production, 584:2
Utinam populus Romanus unam cervicem, 107:*n10*
Utmost bound of human thought, 481:11
    bound of the everlasting hills, 7:38
    Thule, 96:4
Utopia, principality in U., 448:5
Utter, liberty to u., 263:4
    not both live and u. it, 506:1
    not in u. nakedness, 393:11
    not u. what dost not know, 185:18

Utter *(continued)*
    nothing for which not responsible, 476:2
    sweet breath, 182:2
    wise man u. vain knowledge, 14:18
    would tongue u., 482:15
Utterance, action nor u., 197:4
    if u. denied thought a burden, 455:2
Uttered, not u. by chapmen's tongues, 176:27
    or unexpressed, 396:2
    part of man's life, 434:14
Uttereth, day unto day u. speech, 16:10
    fool u. all his mind, 23:19
    wisdom u. her voice, 20:24
Uttering such dulcet breath, 181:8
Utterly destroy power of reasoning, 78:6
Uttermost parts of the sea, 20:13
Uzzah put forth his hand, 11:42

V

V sign is symbol and portent, 666:15
Vacant, body filled and v. mind, 193:16
    heart hand eye, 397:27
    interlunar cave, 268:33
    interstellar spaces, 720:22
    into the vacant, 720:22
    laugh that spoke v. mind, 342:3
    mind distressed, 347:16
    stuffs out v. garments, 178:9
Vacationless, mothers and housewives v., 774:10
Vacuous, keeps their hearts v., 58:9
Vacuum, nature abhors a v., 286:14
    think in v., 625:7
Vade in pace, 124:31
    salutatum pro me liber, 134:*n3*
Vae victis, 124:32
Vagabond shalt thou be, 6:15
Vague, boundaries shadowy and v., 478:17
    crepuscular time, 512:1
    evolution from v. to definite, 574:3
    The V. and Elusive, 58:16
Vain, a' is done in v., 379:2
    all delights are v., 176:18
    all Doric discipline, 640:10
    ambition of kings, 244:10
    beauty is v., 23:31
    begot of v. fantasy, 182:23
    blood pour in v., 613:1
    bring no more v. oblations, 26:9
    citadels not walled, 738:9
    deluding Joys, 259:22
    denial v. and coy excuse, 261:15
    desire vain regret, 542:5
    dreme of joye all but in v., 138:*n8*
    every man walketh in a v. show, 17:14
    hatching v. empires, 265:9
    hence all you v. delights, 243:5
    I have not lived in v., 302:5
    I shall not live in V., 546:1
    ignobly v., 309:15
    ill-natured Englishman, 294:17
    in v. always in v., 613:1
    in v. to wish for death, 68:15
    know we loved in v., 419:9
    labour and wounds are v., 512:10
    man may become proud, 287:3

Vain *(continued)*
  man pleased with effect on people, 659:14
  man v. diverse undulating, 152:6
  mock on 'tis all in v., 375:2
  most v. most generous, 594:8
  name of the Lord in v., 8:33
  not in v., 667:12
  oblations, 26:9
  pain to love in v., 275:10
  people imagine a v. thing, 15:28
  pomp and glory, 51:5, 231:2
  profane and v. babblings, 46:29
  pursuit of human glory, 253:17
  says a lot in v. refusing, 364:7
  sealed in v., 211:31
  spend not then his gifts in v., 237:14
  the Present teaches in v., 660:3
  they are disquieted in v., 17:14
  they labor in v., 20:4
  to look for defense against lightning, 104:6
  tribute of a smile, 396:10
  tricks that are v., 566:12
  war with heaven, 264:25
  was the chief's pride, 313:6
  watchman waketh but in v., 20:4
  wisdom all, 265:14
  wise man utter v. knowledge, 14:18
  words in your oaths, 120:15
  youth is v., 401:9
Vaincrons parce que plus forts, 681:*n*1
Vaine, la vie est v., 556:*n*1
Vainglory, from pride v. and hypocrisy, 50:11
  humble through v., 153:9
  pleasance here all v., 142:5
Vainness, lying v. drunkenness, 210:15
Vale, depart this v., 691:4
  far sunken, 438:17
  meanest floweret of v., 335:5
  meet thee in hollow v., 249:1
  of Soul-making, 441:1
  of years, 214:3
  sequestered v. of life, 334:23
  violet-embroidered v., 260:26
Vale, ave atque v., 94:*n*9
Valentine, heart shaped like v., 797:2
Vales, hills v. woodland plain, 309:16
  o'er v. and hills, 394:4
  of meadowsweet, 756:13
Valet, hero to his v., 257:1
  not aware of this, 81:20
Valets, masters worthy v., 349:4
Valets de chambre, héros pour les v., 257:*n*1
Valiant, as v. I honor him, 196:25
  be v. not too venturous, 163:1
  brothers v., 845:16
  dust, 194:15
  England breeds v. creatures, 193:9
  if you are very v., 52:5
  in velvet, 594:8
  never taste of death but once, 196:10
  reproof v., 200:9
  souls of heroes, 52:1
  trencher-man, 194:5
Validation, validity process of v., 583:1
Validity process of validation, 583:1
  what v. and pitch, 208:26
Valkyries, ride of the V., 501:14

Valley, all in the v. of death, 484:24
  bicker down v., 485:3
  down in the v., 847:2
  every v. shall be exalted, 28:1
  faraway town sleeping in v., 561:3
  he paweth in the v., 15:14
  his golden cup, 541:14
  may v. streams content me, 96:12
  Neanderthal v., 756:8
  of Ajalon, 10:24
  of decision, 30:23
  of dry bones, 29:34
  of Humiliation, 281:20
  of reveries, 663:3
  of Shadow, 479:15
  of shadow of death, 16:18
  sheep fatter, 418:9
  spirit of the v. never dies, 58:11
  take me to green v., 854:18
Valleys, greenest of our v., 478:12
  groves hills fields, 170:6
  hills and v. dales and fields, 170:*n*1
  lick V. up, 545:8
  lily of the v., 25:14
  of Hall, 583:11
  piping down v. wild, 371:13
Vallombrosa, strow the brooks in V., 264:10
Valor, better part of v. discretion, 187:9
  birthplace of v., 379:5
  brute beauty and v., 587:8
  constancy and v. our shield, 666:6
  deed whereat v. will weep, 225:4
  God's help and their v., 388:5
  good speed to your youthful v., 98:9
  he for v. formed, 266:10
  mighty men of v., 10:20
  my v. is certainly going, 367:16
  no need of v., 75:28
  plucks dead lions, 177:24
  thy v. prevail, 444:11
  uncommon v. common virtue, 708:11
  who would true v. see, 282:4
Valorous, Roland v. Oliver wise, 126:12
Valuable coin of thinker, 796:8
  if riches v. to Heaven, 298:11
  reputation more v. than money, 102:18
  time most v. thing, 84:11
  what v. not new, 409:17
Valuation, government resting on v. of property, 77:20
  superstitious v. of Europe, 584:8
Value at a penny talk of old men, 94:4
  carry body for its sentimental v., 777:5
  cynic knows v. of nothing, 604:24
  dearness only gives v., 354:10
  easier discover deficiency than see v., 390:9
  from stamp of ages, 282:8
  full extent of its own v., 387:2
  governed by utility or cost, 584:2
  hard latent v., 585:10
  is life-giving power of anything, 517:12
  it next to good conscience, 253:8
  men of less v. than gold, 143:13
  no v. when possessed, 293:19
  none but horizontal, 775:3
  nothing has v., 684:4
  nothing v. but object of utility, 510:8
  of sentiment is sacrifice, 647:4

Value *(continued)*
  of stakes at issue, 772:13
  of what entrepreneur contributes, 703:2
  of what poet has written, 722:21
  supreme v. not future but present, 794:6
  then we rack the v., 194:39
  what gives life v., 770:8
  what I say more lasting v., 821:6
Valueless, reading v. books, 517:14
Values anything more than freedom, 673:4
  masculine v., 700:10
  not single feature in heaven he v., 562:22
Vampire, like v. dead many times, 573:6
Vanbrugh's, dead Sir John V. house of clay, 297:*n*1
Vanessa extraordinary woman, 298:*n*2
Vanilla of society, 398:21
Vanish like evil spirits, 359:3
  where did children v., 771:14
Vanished and shrunk away, 169:1
  Cheshire Cat v. slowly, 550:9
  touch of v. hand, 482:15
Vanishes, man loves what v., 640:6
Vanisheth, life a vapor that v., 47:20
Vanishing, keep beauty from v., 587:17
  race, 747:15
Vanitas vanitatum, 490:8
Vanities, guides us by v., 718:3
  man of my v., 691:10
Vanity, all is v., 23:32
  all others but v., 405:14
  and vexation of spirit, 24:1
  beauty without v., 419:10
  conscience or v. appalled, 641:10
  cords of v., 26:21
  cured of every folly but v., 331:12
  dispel v. with v., 117:3
  every man at his best state is v., 17:13
  extreme actions ascribed to v., 588:13
  Fair, 281:23, 490:5
  give no hollow aid, 421:9
  Golden V., 862:10
  hath not lifted his soul unto v., 16:19
  in years, 185:30
  my days are v., 14:4
  no love but v., 417:18
  of human hopes, 324:13
  of vanities, 23:32
  preying on people's v. ignorance, 830:3
  pull down thy v., 709:11
  repeyreth hom fro worldly v., 134:11
  tickle one's v., 526:12
  town is lighter than v., 281:23
Vanquished by desire, 58:4
  had Cato, 110:1
  Macbeth never v. be, 221:28
  one safety to v., 97:11
  though v. argue still, 342:9
Vans, omnibuses and v., 699:16
  to beat the air, 719:10
Vantage, coign of v., 219:15
  ground of truth, 92:*n*12
Vapor, floating like v. on air, 539:2
  life a v. that vanisheth, 47:20
  like bear or lion, 223:33
  live upon v. of dungeon, 214:4
  summit lost in v., 423:15

Vapors both away, 235:12
    congregation of v., 203:17
    strangle him, 184:36
    weep their burthen, 485:14
Variable as the shade, 397:1
    lest thy love prove v., 183:8
    mysterious independent v., 537:7
Variableness, with whom is no v., 47:11
Variation if useful preserved, 469:12
Varied, mob is v. and inconstant, 287:13
    rule the v. year, 317:13
Variety, abjure my so much loved v., 235:19
    about New England weather, 559:22
    Democracy admits v., 684:6
    democracy full of v., 77:21
    in spite of v. and power, 529:17
    infinite v., 223:15
    joy of life is v., 324:22
    mother of Enjoyment, 458:21
    no pleasure unseasoned by v., 103:9
    order in v. we see, 309:16
    soul of pleasure, 290:18
Variety's spice of life, 348:1
Various, a man so v., 283:15
    as lovely so be v., 743:16
    as your land, 750:11
    constant as v., 743:16
    distribution of property, 366:19
    gift to each, 466:22
    of v. stuff the v. Man, 379:13
    so v. so beautiful so new, 531:2
    speaks a v. language, 432:7
Varium et mutabile femina, 97:*n8*
Varnished clock, 342:10
Varying shore o' the world, 223:36
Vase, shatter v. if you will, 412:2
Vases, beads dolls cloths v., 798:9
Vassal, God how fine a v., 126:13
    Muse I was your v., 603:5
Vassals and serfs at side, 441:9
Vast and furious ocean, 247:6
    dead v. and middle of night, 201:14
    deserts of v. eternity, 277:1
    edges drear, 531:2
    heaven's net is v., 59:17
    intelligence were v. enough, 366:13
    like a v. shadow moved, 279:5
    lodge in v. wilderness, 347:26
    mass of London itself, 666:3
    more devils than v. hell, 182:3
    plastic and v. one intellectual breeze, 399:10
    right-wing conspiracy, 840:9
    slow-breathing unconscious, 583:4
    struggle to found Roman state, 96:25
    wings across skies, 734:6
Vaster, grow v. than empires, 276:27
Vasty, call spirits from v. deep, 186:5
    hall of death, 529:15
Vat, every v. stand upon bottom, 281:17
Vaterland, lieb V. magst ruhig sein, 518:*n1*
Vats, cheeses out of v., 491:16
Vaudeville audiences give loudest sighs, 790:10
Vault, fretted v., 334:16
    left this v. to brag of, 220:25
Vaulter in sunny grass, 417:10
Vaulting ambition, 219:18
Vaults, heaven's v. should crack, 218:5

Vaunt-couriers to thunderbolts, 216:18
Vaunteth, charity v. not, 44:18
Vauntie, her best and she was v., 379:21
Vaward of our youth, 191:15
Vécu, j'ai v., 363:7
    rose a v. ce que vivent les roses, 164:*n4*
Vegetable, information v. animal mineral, 564:3
    love not suit me, 564:9
    my v. love should grow, 276:27
Vegetate like the country, 410:11
Vehicles, robot v., 836:3
Veil, invisible new v. of finity, 821:16
    my v. no mortal ever took up, 112:3
    of temple rent, 38:10
    painted v. call Life, 428:*n1*
    through which not see, 471:15
Veiled Melancholy, 438:16
Veiling lightnings of song, 430:9
Veillons dormants et veillants dormons, 153:*n5*
Veils, Religion v. her fires, 313:25
Vein, divided to the v., 826:2
    Ercles' v. a tyrant's v., 180:24
    King Cambyses' v., 185:29
    not in giving v. today, 174:10
    of poetry in all men, 434:18
Veins, bound bones and v. in me, 587:3
    dried sap out of v., 638:2
    in my v. red life, 439:2
    sea itself floweth in v., 290:1
Velasquez, not V. never Rembrandt, 792:18
Velocities of evanescent increments, 306:16
Velocity, determination of v., 760:11
Velvet, gilded and covered with v., 388:4
    iron hand in v. glove, 149:21
    live like v. mole, 710:7
    some in v. gowns, 861:5
    valiant in v., 594:8
    walk in v. shoes, 710:5
Venenum, ali cibus aliis v., 93:*n5*
Venerable, every tradition grows v., 588:14
    parts of constitution, 345:3
Venerably dull, 346:15
Veneration, much v. but no rest, 167:24
Venerationi sancta simplicitas, 118:*n7*
Venetian, Turk beat a V., 215:14
Vengeance, blood v. desolation, 522:14
    I ask and cry, 141:21
    in the day of v., 21:8
    is mine, 43:21
    just my v. complete, 491:14
    nor one feeling of v., 369:7
    of history terrible, 689:16
Venial, sins of omission v., 330:1
Venice, at V. gave his body, 180:6
    commonwealth of V. this inscription, 241:12
    more than any man in V., 187:23
    on Bridge of Sighs, 421:5
    sate in state, 421:6
Venienti occurrite morbo, 109:*n1*
Venizelos observed, 667:7
Venom clamors of jealous woman, 174:38
Venomous, like toad ugly and v., 197:37
    no means too v., 589:25
Vent, his tongue must v., 224:28
Vent, le v. se lève, 659:*n1*

Venting heavy heart, 521:4
Ventre affamé, 276:*n3*
Ventricle of memory, 177:1
Venture, each v. new beginning, 721:4
    nothing v. nothing win, 565:5
    nought v. nought have, 148:17
    to call himself architect, 397:19
Ventured again into philosophy, 661:3
    like wanton boys, 231:2
    neck or nothing, 492:23
Ventures, lose our v., 197:14
    not in one bottom trusted, 187:14
Venturous, be valiant not too v., 163:1
Venus grown fat, 417:17
    herself fastened to prey, 290:12
    mingles sweet bitterness with cares, 94:20
    Mr. Whitman's V. Hottentot wench, 569:18
    nurturing V., 92:8
    take my votive glass, 297:6
Vénus toute entière, 281:*n5*
Veracity, entertain doubt of my v., 355:7
    which increases with age, 274:10
Verb, emerges with v. in mouth, 561:4
    God is a v., 743:5
Verba, rem tene v. sequentur, 88:*n3*
Verbal agreement isn't worth paper written on, 695:19
    poem a v. contraption, 776:14
Verbiage, mistaking v. for truths, 658:14
Verbosity, not crude v. but holy simplicity, 118:21
    thread of his v., 177:9
Verdant, ocean surrounds v. land, 516:16
Verdantly, entwine itself v., 411:12
Verderben, und das war mein V., 365:*n6*
Verdict afterwards, 551:6
Verdure, vast forest v., 534:9
Vere, God bless Captain V., 517:1
Vereker's secret, 585:6
Verge, ability to get to v., 717:5
    ample room and v. enough, 335:12
    on very v. of her confine, 216:13
Verification, verity process of v., 583:1
Verify your references, 371:7
Verisimilitude, artistic v., 565:18
Veritable ocean, 687:8
Véritable Amphitryon, 278:*n2*
Veritas, amicus Plato sed magis amica v., 80:*n2*
    in vino v., 57:*n5*, 124:3
    magna est v., 31:*n2*
    non erubescit, 116:*n5*
Veritatem dies aperit, 107:*n1*
Vérité que ces montagnes, 153:*n4*
Verities and truths of heart, 748:19
Verity is an event, 583:1
    religious feeling a v., 524:2
    verifying itself, 583:1
Vermeil-tinctured lip, 261:9
Vermin, pearls and v., 449:1
    race of odious v., 298:14
Vermont, as Maine so goes V., 849:*n3*
Vermouth, not the v., 763:10
    union of gin and v., 748:7
Vernal, breath of v. shower, 335:20
    one impulse from v. wood, 390:19
    seasons of the year, 262:20
    sight of v. bloom, 265:25

W

Wade, should I w. no more, 221:19
Wading up to eyes in blood, 343:19
Wafer, sun pasted like w., 655:13
Wafer-cakes, men's faiths w., 192:29
Wafer-thin, rapier-keen w., 769:6
Waft her love to Carthage, 190:4
Wag, let world w., 147:19
    where beards w. all, 151:7
Wage laborers having no means of
    production, 511:n3
Wägen, erst w. dann wagen, 449:n1
Wager, what will you w., 279:23
Wagers sum of resources, 810:n1
Wages are value expression, 703:2
    bargaining for w., 682:9
    home gone and ta'en thy w., 225:23
    keeping profits up by keeping w. down,
        404:9
    of sin is death, 43:2
    times hard and w. low, 862:8
    took w. and are dead, 619:17
Wagging, alive and w. tail in mud, 83:2
Wagner's music better than it sounds,
    597:17
Wagon, hitch your w. to star, 457:7
    storm like w. crossing bridge, 784:3
    water-w. place for me, 643:15
Wagons, honored among w., 795:9
Wags, see how world w., 198:15
    so w. the world, 198:n1
    tail knocks over chair, 727:9
Wail, new w. times' waste, 226:8
    night bird's w., 565:23
    or knock the breast, 269:15
    to w. such woes, 159:21
    who buys mirth to w. a week, 175:5
Wailful choir, 438:13
Wailing, voiceless w., 721:9
    winds naked woods, 432:14
    woman w. for demon-lover, 401:14
Wailings, sighs lamentations and w., 130:5
Waist deep in Big Muddy, 806:1
    slender w. confined, 257:22
Wait a bit Oysters cried, 552:4
    a man should w., 76:15
    all things come to who w., 455:n1
    be still w., 780:11
    digestion w. on appetite, 221:10
    do not listen simply w., 701:5
    do not w. be still, 701:5
    do not w. for last judgment, 790:6
    drift w. and obey, 636:2
    fold hands and w., 566:17
    for wisest of counselors, 67:2
    I almost had to w., 290:7
    labor and to w., 466:3
    right and wrong can w., 750:17
    stand and w., 263:14
    these w. all upon thee, 19:11
    times we can't w. for somebody, 831:12
    to fawn to crouch to w., 161:24
    to watch water clear, 668:17
    upon I would, 219:20
    upon the Lord, 28:8
    who only stand and w., 263:14
    why w. until next year, 81:26
Waited, death past so he w., 493:17
    for billy-boil, 630:9
    for the light, 652:11

Waited *(continued)*
    for thy salvation, 7:37
    three years w. for herald, 759:5
Waiter roars it through hall, 534:7
Waitest for spark from heaven, 529:10
Waiteth, my soul w. for the Lord, 20:8
Waiting for invasion so are fishes, 666:7
    for rain, 718:2
    taxi throbbing w., 718:18
    what are we all w. for, 628:5
    worse things w. than death, 568:13
Waits, destiny w. alike, 65:15
    human engine w., 718:18
Waive quantum o' the sin, 378:10
Wake and call me early, 480:15
    and feel fell of dark, 588:4
    awake for night is flying, 164:6
    blank w. of passion, 830:16
    die before I w., 296:15
    Do I w. or sleep, 437:15
    eternally, 236:9
    for the Sun, 470:13
    him no not I, 857:17
    human voices w. us, 717:17
    in durance vile I w., 380:18
    nations underground, 863:8
    sleep to w., 495:15
    sleeping w. and waking sleep, 153:7
    thou wilt not w., 249:1
    to sleep, 780:15
    truths w. to perish never, 393:16
    unto me, 539:4
Waked after long sleep, 230:6
    by the circling hours, 267:10
    I w. she fled, 263:18
    priest all shaven, 861:15
    to ecstasy living lyre, 334:18
    you have w. me too soon, 304:5
Wakeful nightingale, 266:16
Waken, not w. sleeper soul is away, 602:18
    thou with me, 483:6
Wakened by silence, 567:5
    us from sleeping, 713:1
Wakens, firefly w., 483:6
Wakes, Maypoles Hock-carts wassails w.,
    247:14
    Sleeping Beauty w. up, 815:8
    whoever w. in England, 492:4
Waketh, watchman w. but in vain, 20:4
Waking bliss, 260:28
    hope is w. dream, 79:10
    morn not w. till she sings, 163:16
    nights of w., 397:7
    no such matter, 227:1
    silence with w. bird, 485:10
    sleeping wake and w. sleep, 153:7
    souls, 233:11
    take my w. slow, 780:15
    threshold of w. light, 818:8
    vision or w. dream, 437:15
    way she had of w. him, 723:9
Walcum, talcum always w., 763:8
Waldo, Matthew and W. guardians, 717:21
Wales, prince of W. in small but costly crown,
    693:2
Walk a little faster, 550:21
    amidst beautiful things, 629:16
    and not faint, 28:8
    and wot not what they are, 176:20

Walk *(continued)*
    ask for old paths and w. therein, 29:6
    before they dance, 312:20
    between dark and dark, 743:17
    by faith, 45:6
    can two w. together, 30:25
    citizen may w. safely on law, 813:7
    closer w. with God, 347:1
    crust where I must w., 801:8
    cypress in palace w., 483:6
    deck my Captain lies, 520:19
    down Piccadilly, 564:9
    fantasy goes for w. returns with bride,
        793:14
    fishermen that w. beach, 217:18
    foolery does w. about, 209:32
    from breakfast to madness, 821:7
    good w. spoiled, 563:4
    happily may I w., 856:2
    humbly with thy God, 30:28
    I w. unseen, 260:3
    I'll rest but thou w., 853:26
    in fear and dread, 400:17
    in the street, 520:3
    in velvet shoes, 710:5
    into my parlor, 446:9
    it slow where you go, 829:11
    let her not w. in the sun, 203:6
    let us w. honestly, 43:26
    no spirit can w. abroad, 200:22
    not natural to w. on two legs, 356:18
    not on earth exultantly, 121:12
    on eggs, 239:9
    Oysters come w. with us, 552:1
    people may w. but not throw stones,
        325:16
    pleasant w. pleasant talk, 552:1
    race of men who w. upon earth, 52:28
    revealed her as true goddess, 96:32
    rise and w. with him, 69:14
    roads must man w. down, 836:4
    shall not w. in darkness, 41:10
    slow silent w., 576:5
    solar w. or milky way, 311:5
    take up bed and w., 38:15
    talk with you w. with you, 188:2
    teach crab to w. straight, 75:4
    the earth unseen, 266:19
    through fields in gloves, 711:8
    through valley of shadow, 16:18
    under water men w., 845:10
    upon England's mountains, 375:17
    upon the beach, 717:16
    where'er you w., 308:5
    which way they w., 220:10
    while ye have light, 41:23
    with Kings, 635:21
    with stretched forth necks, 26:16
    ye in it, 27:27
    your ghost will w., 492:12
    your mystic way, 564:8
Walked along the Strand, 326:3
    among ancient trees, 373:16
    Cat w. by himself, 635:12
    crowns and crownets, 224:4
    Enoch w. with God, 6:22
    eye-deep in hell, 709:4
    glittered when he w., 652:10
    him that w. the waves, 262:5

Water *(continued)*

flows clear from Lebanon, 680:1
give thine enemy w., 23:3
glory like circle in w., 171:14
grass grows wherever land w. is, 519:3
green w. spurted through hull, 603:9
grind with w. that's past, 251:14
he will infallibly lead you to w., 516:6
hears thy faintest word, 272:*n*2
heaven as near by w., 154:*n*4
honest w., 218:13
I came like W., 471:14
if British went by w., 352:10
imperceptible w., 445:24
into freezing turbulent w., 842:4
is best, 65:24
is good, 58:12
Just Add Hot W., 739:15
know worth of w., 319:27
land-rats and w.-rats, 188:1
land-thieves and w.-thieves, 188:1
Laughing W., 467:1
leave log in w., 853:15
like a stone, 547:19
lily bloom, 480:26
limns on w. writes in dust, 168:21
little drops of w., 534:2
little w. in stream fault of source, 118:7
more than ocean w. broken, 669:19
more w. glideth by mill, 149:*n*4
Moses struck rock w. came forth, 807:6
much w. goeth by mill, 149:6
name writ in w., 441:7
never formed to mind, 687:8
never hold w., 301:5
never miss w. till well dry, 319:*n*2
no more w., 813:6
no sound of w., 718:12
no w. only rock, 718:21
not all w. in rough rude sea, 179:24
not of Gennesareth but Thames, 621:9
o'er the w. to Charlie, 390:12
of affliction, 12:38, 27:26
of river never the same, 127:12
on hands like Pilate, 767:11
over rocks wood and w., 449:15
passed a lot of w. since then, 695:17
people are like w., 737:17
plunge hands in w., 775:9
quarrel over w. in Arkansas River, 705:2
reasons made mouth w., 271:10
reflects images, 570:12
rivers of w. in a dry place, 27:29
run through fire and w., 190:30
rush to rest in air, 748:2
salt w. unbounded, 635:14
saw grass and of w., 728:14
send down w. on earth, 121:19
skuttle fish blackens w., 302:20
slippy-sloppy in larder, 644:5
snake came to w. trough, 707:10
sound of w., 291:16
spring of ever-flowing w., 98:24
stagnant w. loses purity, 141:5
stained the w. clear, 371:14
steeds to w. at those springs, 225:12
stream smoothest w. deepest, 160:*n*3
street before the w. gate, 13:16
streets full of w., 725:16

Water *(continued)*

struggling for life in the w., 326:10
sunshine and good w., 601:2
supposes mirage to be w., 121:22
tar w. so mild and benign, 306:17
through a sieve, 552:16
through fire and through w., 18:6
to succeed add w. to wine, 630:10
tossing green w., 703:12
tree planted by rivers of w., 15:27
under running w., 719:23
under w. men walk, 845:10
unstable as w., 7:36
until Desert knows W., 546:13
virtue more than w. or fire, 63:23
virtues we write in w., 231:13
wait to watch w. clear, 668:17
was made wine, 40:39
wash feet in soda w., 718:17
water everywhere, 399:22
welling from earth, 716:15
what w. lapping bow, 719:18
which they beat, 223:14
whole stay of w., 26:14
wide w. inescapable, 686:19
with w. to drink, 62:27
without a flaw, 748:2
wonderful w. round you, 535:7
written in running w., 94:22
Watercolors to impaint his cause, 186:33
Watercourse, patio heaven's w., 752:13
Water-drinkers, no poems by w. please for
   long, 101:10
Waterdrops, soul be changed to w., 171:5
   women's weapons w., 216:16
   worn stones of Troy, 208:7
Watered, Apollos w., 43:34
   by blood of tyrants, 370:1
   heaven with tears, 374:6
   our horses in Helicon, 165:13
   with tears w., 36:15
Waterfall, from w. named her, 467:1
   nosing up to bone-crushing w., 801:16
   one-woman w., 822:10
Watering, a-w. last year's crops, 512:17
   pot and pruning knife, 488:1
   your waters and w. place, 670:19
Waterloo, Austerlitz and W., 681:10
   battle of first rank, 451:10
   dismal plain, 451:5
   every man meets W., 489:15
   from Marathon to W., 564:3
   thou fatal W., 420:19
   won on playing fields, 389:6
Waterman, great-grandfather was but a w.,
   281:25
Watermen look astern row ahead, 112:1
Water's thin, 565:5
Waters and their powers, 421:7
   at their priestlike task, 439:11
   beams of his chambers in w., 19:8
   beautiful drifts like w., 637:19
   beside the still w., 16:18
   cannot quench love, 26:4
   cast thy bread upon the w., 25:3
   cold w. to a thirsty soul, 23:4
   come ye to the w., 28:24
   cover the sea, 26:34
   do business in great w., 19:14

Waters *(continued)*

Father of W. unvexed to sea, 476:5
fen of stagnant w., 393:3
fish in troubled w., 295:17
here are your w., 670:19
hitherandthithering w., 696:16
liffeying w., 696:16
like music on w., 422:23
music crept by upon w., 229:19
nearer roll, 322:24
no other such majestic flow of w., 464:8
noise of many w., 18:28
of beginning and end, 707:20
of petrel and porpoise, 721:6
of the heart, 795:3
once more upon w., 420:13
over great sea winds trouble w., 92:19
over rolling w. go, 482:18
peopling earth w. and sky, 289:15
pour w. of Nile, 549:13
rivering w., 696:16
rushing of many w., 27:5
secret w., 745:14
set it upon w., 830:14
should lift their bosoms, 207:26
shout golden shouts, 541:2
Spirit of God moved upon w., 5:9
stilled at even, 541:26
stolen w. are sweet, 21:13
take heed of still w., 160:*n*3
tree planted by the w., 29:17
turns to perilous w., 130:1
voice as sound of many w., 48:5
voice of many w., 48:31
were a wall, 8:24
were gathered together, 8:28
were his winding sheet, 239:1
what West has thrown on w., 814:4
woe to him who seeks to pour oil upon
   w., 516:9
Watersmooth-silver stallion, 739:13
Water-wagon place for me, 643:15
Watery, crown the w. glade, 333:18
   envious siege of w. Neptune, 179:13
   nest, 257:16
   shore, 373:17
   sunk beneath w. floor, 262:5
Watson, know my methods W., 617:9
   Mr. W. come here, 592:8
Wattle, ever hear of Captain W., 362:10
Wattles, of clay and w. made, 637:1
Wave, all sunk beneath the w., 348:16
   as w. succeeds w., 206:*n*2
   blue w. rolls nightly, 422:14
   cry wind cry vast waters, 721:6
   dance like w. of sea, 637:13
   frontier outer edge of w., 624:8
   glassy cool translucent w., 261:10
   life is a w., 523:21
   lift me as w. leaf cloud, 429:3
   small rock holds back great w., 54:17
   star-spangled banner w., 411:1
   swiftly walk o'er w., 430:22
   to wash him from world, 658:9
   whose arm bind restless w., 537:19
   wind or swallowing w., 276:5
   winning w. deserving note, 248:4
   wish you a w. o' the sea, 228:29
   write woman's vows upon w., 69:6

Wave-beat shore, 501:17
Waved her lily hand, 307:1
 long has it w. on high, 473:3
Waver, steadiest minds to w., 67:21
Wavering between profit and loss, 719:15
 discordant w. multitude, 191:6
 more longing w., 209:22
Waves, amber w. of grain, 616:3
 bound as steed, 420:13
 breaking w. dashed, 431:20
 Britannia rule the w., 318:8
 come as the w. come, 397:21
 cypress in palace walk, 483:6
 formal as scales on fish, 714:2
 here shall thy proud w. be stayed, 15:7
 him that walked the w., 262:5
 hopping through frothy w., 552:2
 I danced on the w., 603:8
 into w. pine needles, 291:15
 laughter of ocean w., 65:18
 make towards pebbled shore, 226:16
 march o'er mountain w., 408:17
 mutinous Shannon w., 696:4
 of anger and fear, 775:13
 of religious emotion, 715:4
 of science beat in vain, 524:2
 on side of ablest navigators, 353:11
 over mountains over w., 845:5
 pebbles which w. fling, 530:20
 raging w. of the sea, 48:1
 remained shadow of w., 759:12
 righteousness as w. of sea, 28:13
 sunset illumine w., 603:11
 that invited her, 600:10
 tired w. vainly breaking, 512:10
 whales in w. of sea, 707:20
 when w. went high, 283:8
 wild w. whist, 229:18
Waves', spent w. riot, 568:25
Waving, not w. but drowning, 764:4
 sails filled streamers w., 269:6
 wild tail, 635:13
Wax, fill hives with honey and w., 297:19
 mind a block of w., 78:11
 my heart is w., 159:7
 rich gifts w. poor, 204:2
 shoes ships sealing w., 552:3
 snapped like sealing w., 497:22
 to flaming youth virtue w., 205:23
 to receive, 423:3
Waxed, Jeshurun w. fat, 10:14
Waxworks, if we're w. you pay, 551:16
Way, abode Hour and went his w., 471:7
 all the w. home, 857:16
 broad is the w., 35:6
 catch the nearest w., 219:10
 come all the w. for this, 556:10
 crow shook snow, 669:12
 died maintaining right of w., 852:7
 down upon Swanee River, 538:15
 every day in every w., 612:19
 every one his own w., 89:12
 every w. makes my gain, 215:3
 everything's going my w., 744:4
 for woman to hold a man, 804:16
 go not into every w., 32:6
 God moves in mysterious w., 347:3
 going the w. of all the earth, 10:26
 he should go, 22:25

Way *(continued)*
 hear right w. in the morning, 62:20
 heaven's wide pathless w., 260:3
 home's the farthest way, 249:10
 Hungary Poland doing it their w., 835:*n*1
 I did it my w., 835:9
 in dark wood where straight w. lost, 129:17
 in whatsoever w. any come to Me, 87:5
 is plain peaceful just, 476:3
 jog on the footpath w., 228:24
 king stood at parting of w., 29:33
 lambs who lost w., 633:17
 let each go his own w., 104:23
 let the wicked forsake his w., 28:26
 life's common w., 393:4
 like wild beast guards w., 374:15
 long and steep is the w., 56:12
 long is the w. and hard, 265:11
 long w. to Tipperary, 674:2
 long wind cold, 396:3
 longest w. round shortest home, 249:*n*2
 love find w., 845:5
 make it over your w., 671:18
 merit makes his w., 230:19
 met you not my Love by the w., 160:1
 my w. of life is fallen, 222:11
 narrow w., 35:6
 new w. to pay old debts, 245:3
 no ready w. to virtue, 256:3
 no w. out for me, 730:12
 noiseless tenor of their w., 334:23
 not pass this w. again, 847:23
 of a fool, 21:23
 of a man with a maid, 23:25, 634:6
 of a serpent upon a rock, 23:25
 of a ship in the sea, 23:25
 of all flesh, 244:2
 of an eagle in the air, 23:25
 of coming into world, 297:15
 of God, 270:12
 of Heaven has no favorites, 59:19
 of Heaven to benefit others, 59:21
 of ignorance, 721:1
 of sage is to act, 59:21
 of the tree of life, 6:11
 of transgressors is hard, 21:25
 old paths where is the good w., 29:6
 out of hell leads up, 265:11
 out of wind's and rain's w., 693:5
 plods his weary w., 334:8
 prepare the w. before me, 31:1
 prepare the w. of the Lord, 27:38, 33:24
 pretty Fanny's w., 305:11
 primrose w., 220:20
 rebellion lay in his w., 186:32
 roses all the w., 492:1
 see the W. of Heaven, 59:7
 set out in relative w., 664:4
 ship's w. upon sea, 634:6
 so plain we may lose way, 664:15
 solar walk or milky w., 311:5
 Spring comes slowly up this w., 401:4
 such ever love's w., 494:13
 sweetest w. to me, 634:6
 tells us the w. to go, 600:5
 that can be told of, 58:7
 that w. madness lies, 216:26

Way *(continued)*
 that's the w. it is, 797:10
 that's the w. to do it, 417:21
 the money goes, 848:8
 the truth and the life, 41:28
 there is a lion in the w., 23:7
 they say it, 764:8
 this is w. world ends, 719:7
 this the w. walk ye in it, 27:27
 thorny w. to heaven, 201:23
 though hell bar w., 692:3
 thoughts nature gives w. to, 220:6
 to bliss, 249:5
 to draw new mischief, 212:34
 to dusty death, 222:16
 to keep thee in the w., 9:5
 to man's heart, 489:7
 to tell if poem lasting, 671:9
 took their solitary w., 268:17
 trudgin' weary w., 591:7
 true w. but yet untried, 166:12
 true w. goes over rope, 701:4
 twinkle on milky w., 394:5
 unlikely to be undone, 733:1
 what counts is w. writer says it, 810:14
 win my w. to the coast, 70:5
 wisdom finds a w., 369:4
 with tears watered, 656:15
 world ends, 719:7
Wayfarer world renowned, 125:4
Wayfaring, lodging place of w. men, 29:10
Way-hay you rolling river, 862:3
Ways, amend your w., 29:7
 blood nipped and w. be foul, 177:17
 consider her w. and be wise, 21:4
 dazzled by w. of God, 684:14
 dwelt among untrodden w., 391:18
 from cheerful w. of men, 265:25
 God's w. to man, 619:9
 her w. are w. of pleasantness, 20:26
 his w. are judgment, 10:13
 I will take heed to my w., 17:10
 in all the w. you can, 319:1
 in His w. found Him not, 486:10
 just are the w. of God, 269:3
 keep thee in all thy w., 18:26
 labyrinthine w., 620:17
 lots worse w. to die, 678:7
 many w. meet in one town, 192:22
 nine and sixty w., 634:5
 of God justifiable, 269:3
 of God to man, 310:21
 of God to men, 263:21
 of making men talk, 731:2
 oldest sins newest w., 192:10
 possible to fail in many w., 80:12
 practice childish w., 54:11
 sing ancient w., 636:22
 stand ye in the w., 29:6
 that are dark, 566:12
 to lengthen our days, 412:1
 to make thy w. known, 50:6
 triple w. to take, 634:6
 your w. are not my w., 28:27
Wayside, seeds fell by w., 36:2
Wayward, clod of w. marl, 194:15
 fond and w. thoughts, 391:17
 fortune's w. tyranny, 67:6
 purblind w. boy, 176:33

Wayward *(continued)*
    sisters depart, 419:4
    terchy and w. thy infancy, 174:12
Wayworn, weary w. wanderer, 478:2
We about to die salute you, 114:11
    are Ancients of the earth, 166:*n*3
    are as much as we see, 504:23
    are his offspring, 42:19, 85:6
    are his people, 19:3
    are many, 38:21
    are not amused, 518:5
    are the hollow men, 719:4
    are the world, 842:7
    be brethren, 7:1
    content at the last, 721:14
    gather together, 845:2
    happy few, 193:20
    have ways of making men talk, 731:2
    must needs die, 12:6
    my ship and I., 763:2
    real cool, 798:10
    shall not be moved, 863:13
    shall overcome, 852:6
    that had loved him so, 491:21
    the peoples of United Nations, 705:15
    thought we would try, 763:2
    were very tired, 735:3
    would and would not, 212:5
Weader, Tonstant Weader Fwowed up,
    738:16
Weak and beggarly elements, 45:18
    and fruitless words, 477:2
    and mighty Russia, 527:16
    creatures of clay, 75:9
    devouring of w. by strong, 523:12
    evils age and hunger, 198:24
    fear to appear w., 281:3
    flesh is w., 37:30
    God hath chosen w., 43:32
    grow w. keeping on guard, 590:6
    infirmities of w., 43:31
    men not changing mind, 672:15
    my spirit too w., 439:1
    not w. if we use means, 353:2
    ones that cry for help, 732:16
    piping time of peace, 173:31
    pondered w. and weary, 478:20
    poor infirm w. old man, 216:20
    refuge of w. minds, 315:4
    shoulderings aside of w., 523:4
    speak for fallen and w., 514:9
    spirit quickens to rebel, 719:16
    success to the w., 349:12
    suffer what they must, 74:7
    surely w. perish, 673:8
    to be w. is miserable, 264:4
    too w. to be a sinner, 218:13
    without justice courage w., 319:6
    witness of thy name, 259:3
Weaken, to convince is to w., 662:3
Weakening eye of day, 575:15
Weakens, time w. love, 292:16
Weaker, we are getting w. of course, 649:18
    wife the w. vessel, 47:30
Weakest fruit drops earliest, 189:16
    goes to wall, 157:23
    harm to strong from w., 589:15
    spent enough to assure remaining second
        w., 691:20

Weak-eyed bat, 337:2
Weakly perish at another moment, 53:31
Weakness, all else is w., 443:17
    all your strength is w., 67:20
    amiable w., 322:10
    carp at w. of human mind, 286:19
    credulity man's w., 407:16
    fear of w., 709:4
    is function of Tao, 59:3
    is it w. of intellect, 565:20
    it's a sign of w., 780:1
    made perfect in w., 45:15
    man of my w., 691:10
    no w. no contempt, 269:15
    of children's limbs innocent, 119:5
    of most public men, 555:11
    power obtained by w., 382:26
    read each wound each w., 528:15
    stronger by w., 258:3
    too much w. for stoic's pride, 311:9
    you saw his w., 382:17
Weaknesses, people with no w. terrible,
    586:14
Weal and woe is common, 255:3
    come w. come woe, 390:12
Wealth, all that w. e'er gave, 334:15
    and children adornment of life, 121:16
    arithmetic cannot number, 245:1
    best riches ignorance of w., 342:1
    Black love is Black w., 838:3
    boundless his w., 396:11
    build up great fortunes, 573:3
    by any means get w., 312:21
    cause of covetousness, 170:11
    company of just men better than w.,
        70:17
    consume w. without producing it, 609:8
    drive for w., 805:2
    equal w. and opportunities, 596:15
    even to wicked man, 61:11
    governments confiscate w., 701:17
    has to be created, 772:3
    health and w. missed me, 417:16
    I ask not, 599:11
    if you spend w. at once, 445:6
    let man outlive his w., 189:25
    loss of w. loss of dirt, 147:2
    love of w. in all that Americans do, 463:6
    love remembered such w. brings, 226:7
    maketh many friends, 22:14
    malefactors of great w., 615:9
    man of w. and taste, 838:5
    matrimony road to w., 503:13
    men produce more w., 623:3
    no man takes w. to Hades, 61:15
    no w. but life, 517:10
    nor too much w. nor wit, 244:16
    not set heart on w., 5:8
    not without advantages, 778:9
    number and happiness, 345:2
    of Indies, 328:15
    of kings can give nothing more, 101:4
    of Ormus and of Ind, 264:25
    opportunity for achievement, 74:1
    parent of luxury, 77:9
    pauper in midst of w., 100:8
    piled by unrequited toil, 477:4
    private w. I decline, 629:16

Wealth *(continued)*
    real social w., 651:7
    set exact w. of states, 186:21
    sinews of affairs, 85:1
    small aid is w., 70:8
    so act toward office so toward w., 112:17
    surplus w. sacred trust, 559:8
    than w. in storehouse, 5:7
    war where w. allures, 284:22
    where w. accumulates, 341:29
    which all men desire, 145:6
    wisdom outweighs w., 68:2
Wealthily, come to wive it in Padua,
    175:24
Wealthy curled darlings, 212:23
    healthy w. and dead, 741:16
    healthy w. and wise, 319:14
    man and kindly, 52:30
    obliged w. and relieved poor, 52:*n*2
    reckon wise w., 76:6
Weaned away from earth, 749:15
    child shall put hand on cockatrice' den,
        26:34
    Coolidge look as if w. on pickle, 704:4
    from error, 650:10
    heart from low desires, 143:11
    were we not w. till then, 233:10
Weans, are w. in bed, 488:7
Weapon, every experiment like w., 145:7
    genitalia could serve as w., 831:8
    most potent w. in hands of oppressor,
        839:11
    natural and first w., 830:7
    print is strongest w., 686:1
    satire's my w., 312:13
    walking-stick also a w., 613:11
    with other hand held w., 13:15
Weapons, books are w., 698:18
    important in war, 737:15
    not take atomic w. to want peace,
        768:13
    of war perished, 11:38
    triumph over w. and tactics, 674:13
    women's w. waterdrops, 216:16
Wear an undeserved dignity, 188:27
    both for both are thine, 173:33
    bottoms of trousers rolled, 717:15
    day out before it comes, 595:3
    disguises which we w., 266:21
    golden sorrow, 230:25
    hat not worse for w., 347:23
    heart upon my sleeve, 212:18
    him in my heart's core, 204:17
    I get that I w., 199:6
    let the devil w. black, 204:20
    motley's the only w., 198:18
    not my dagger in my mouth, 225:22
    ourselves and never rest, 170:4
    out better than rust, 282:14
    out in a walled prison, 218:1
    such qualities as would w., 341:10
    sunscreen, 841:13
    thou w. lion's hide, 178:4
    use and never w. it out, 58:11
    use it up w. it out, 850:11
    weeds of Athens he doth w., 181:16
    white flannel trousers, 717:16
    women w. the breeches, 240:8
    your rue with a difference, 206:12

Well (*continued*)

servant of God w. done, 267:11
sing so wildly w., 478:3
spent but one day thoroughly w., 138:11
till the w. runs dry, 319:n2
to do w. is what matters, 254:19
work done by men who not feel w.,
    779:1
worth doing is worth doing w., 314:16
Well-a-day, youth cry W., 853:28
Well-being dependent on well-being of
    others, 699:5
instructions for, 5:4
Well-beloved, my w. hath a vineyard, 26:18
Well-benched, board the w. ships, 57:12
Wellborn, few are rich and w., 370:9
Well-bred man knows how to confess, 319:22
very strange and w., 300:25
Well-chosen anthology, 743:20
book or friend, 232:14
Well-conducted, like a w. person, 490:18
Well-doing, be not weary in w., 45:25
religion of w. and daring, 326:n6
Well-drawn, find w. character, 560:9
Well-dressed, sense of being perfectly w.,
    457:18
Well-educated young women, 406:9
Well-favored man, 194:33
Well-fed, not these w. men I fear, 92:7
Well-filled, well-made rather than w. head,
    152:13
Well-furnished libraries, 239:16
Well-governed, marble w. cities, 776:10
Well-graced actor leaves, 180:13
Well-greaved Achaeans, 52:22
Wellington's army, 338:n2
Well-knownness, celebrity person known for
    w., 792:24
Well-made rather than well-filled head,
    152:13
Well-read, writer to show he is w., 614:1
Well's, when the w. dry, 319:27
Wells, buckets into empty w., 348:2,
    398:20
toads brooding in w., 780:9
we have no w., 759:7
Well-spent, rare as w. Life, 434:8
Well-trod stage, 259:20
Well-wishing adventurer, 225:n2
Well-written Life rare, 434:8
Well-wrought urn becomes greatest ashes,
    234:7
Welsh, hear lady sing in W., 186:11
Welshman, Taffy was a W., 858:6
Welt, die W. ist alles was der Fall ist, 727:n1
Weltering in his blood, 285:12
Weltgeschichte ist das Weltgericht, 381:n3
Weltschmerz, 384:4
Wenceslas, good King W., 511:9
Wench, besides the w. is dead, 170:13
fair hot w. in taffeta, 184:23
one w. in the house, 245:n1
weary of w. guest weather, 319:4
Wenlock, tarnish late on W. Edge, 619:2
Went, as cooks go she w., 655:1
in jeopardy of their lives, 12:10
Lord w. before them, 8:23
ne'er w. up again, 856:19
same door wherein I w., 471:13

Went (*continued*)

to bed with stockings on, 860:7
to woods to live deliberately, 506:28
Wept as I remembered, 534:3
he w. to hear, 371:13
I w. and I believed, 387:3
I w. for I longed to see him hanged,
    653:11
Jesus w., 41:20
like anything to see, 551:19
my father w., 374:10
Peter w. bitterly, 37:35
remembering he w. bitterly, 54:4
that he was born, 652:6
when the poor cried Caesar w., 196:29
when we remembered Zion, 20:11
young man who has not w., 629:19
Were, Euripides drew men as they w., 67:n2
now you are not as you w., 576:2
Werewolf's painful change, 809:3
Wernher, not my department says W. von
    Braun, 820:14
West begins where rainfall drops, 748:4
bosom of urgent W., 586:5
Cincinnatus of W., 422:11
East and W. will pinch heart, 734:15
East is East W. W., 632:19
east or w. Phoenix builds, 253:15
East Side W. Side, 625:13
far down within dim W., 478:4
go w. young man, 503:4
greatest disease in the W., 785:6
he was my W., 775:6
is San Francisco, 626:13
Lochinvar out of the W., 396:17
most beautiful lady in W. Country, 662:9
one flew w., 860:21
one ship east another w., 600:5
open the W. Port, 398:11
safeguard of w., 393:1
specter in W. called dissent, 832:2
spirit of w. Greek discovery, 647:8
that's where W. begins, 662:1
the achieved W., 748:6
turn to great W., 489:9
what W. has thrown on waters, 814:4
Wild W. began, 650:1
wild W. Wind, 428:21
wind and the swallows, 85:16
wind full of cries, 681:3
without declining W., 233:12
West Egg, Jay Gatsby of W. Long Island,
    746:5
Westen, im w. nichts neues, 752:11
Wester, rainy Pleiads w., 619:21
Western, all quiet on w. front, 752:11
brookland, 619:5
civilization be feminized, 794:10
custom of one wife, 655:4
from east to w. Ind, 199:7
little w. flower, 181:9
many w. islands, 435:19
Playboy of the W. World, 658:10
walk o'er w. wave, 430:22
wind of w. sea, 482:18
wind when wilt thou blow, 843:18
world lost civil courage, 804:14
Westerners, Greeks first w., 647:8
Westminster Abbey or victory, 377:2

Westward I go free, 507:27
look the land is bright, 512:10
the course of empire, 306:19
Westward-ho, 210:4
Wet, all dirty and w., 299:26
all night in dark and w., 598:22
black bough, 708:16
eye manes dhry heart, 646:9
farmers pray that summers be w., 96:6
get out of that w. coat, 725:12
liked getting feet w., 644:5
my mind and say something clever, 74:11
nor ever w. with rain, 54:21
not nasty dirty w. hole, 736:3
sail w. seas roun', 634:17
sheet and flowing sea, 417:7
wild woods, 635:13
Whacks, forty w., 849:10
Whale, endless processions of the w., 516:7
eyes wide open in waters, 707:20
leap of w. up Niagara, 320:15
Moby Dick w. or man, 736:1
to chase that white w., 516:12
very like a w., 205:9
Whale's backbone, 721:8
white hump, 516:14
Whales, drag Atlantic Ocean for w., 560:2
great w. sailing by, 528:7
in mid-ocean, 707:20
talk like w., 343:9
Whale-ship was my Yale College and
    Harvard, 516:10
Wharf, rots in ease on Lethe w., 202:14
Wharves, remember black w. and slips, 467:8
What a dump, 757:5
ain't so, 508:17
and Why and When, 635:9
are they among many, 41:2
are you when sun shall rise, 232:16
art thou idol ceremony, 193:15
can I do for her, 799:n2
could she have done, 638:1
did Hand of Potter shake, 472:1
do I know, 153:4
does a woman want, 608:6
find out who he is w. he's about, 839:9
God hath joined, 36:32
hath God wrought, 9:25
have I done unto thee, 9:22
have I to do with thee, 40:38
I am so shall thou be, 125:4
I have done with where I have been,
    715:9
I'll have w. she's having, 836:10
is a man profited, 36:27
is Africa to me, 765:1
is city but people, 224:27
is left when honor lost, 102:25
is love 'tis not hereafter, 209:14
is man, 706:4
is so rare as day in June, 514:16
is that something, 758:15
is the night, 221:18
is this quintessence of dust, 203:18
is truth, 41:36
is truth said jesting Pilate, 167:5
is your life, 47:20
is yours is mine, 86:5
know wot's w., 496:3

What *(continued)*
    makest thou, 28:11
    me worry, 852:12
    needs my Shakespeare, 259:3
    news on the Rialto, 188:2
    no soap, 336:12
    of the night, 27:9
    say they let them say, 162:n7
    shall I cry, 28:2
    the anvil, 374:6
    the devil was he doing in that galley,
        278:21
    the hammer, 374:6
    thou seest write, 48:3
    who why which w., 500:2
    you have let it suffice, 5:8
Whatever begotten born and dies,
    639:16
    gods may be, 569:3
    I tried to write was verse, 105:26
    is fickle freckled, 587:10
    is in its causes just, 283:3
    is is right, 311:8
    Miss T. eats, 662:16
    stirs this mortal frame, 401:22
    you have spend less, 329:12
    you lose reckon no account, 102:22
Whatever's, hold own with w. going,
    671:18
What's done is done, 221:3
    gone and what's past help, 228:18
    Hecuba to him, 203:28
    her history, 209:26
    in a name, 183:3
    it going to be then eh, 798:16
    past and what's to come, 208:20
    past is prologue, 229:26
    the shootin' for, 679:14
    use of worrying, 689:22
Whatsoever, in w. way any come to Me,
    87:5
    ye would men do, 35:5
What-was-his-name, 552:19
What-you-may-call-um, 552:19
Wheat, belly is like a heap of w., 25:29
    fields tall with w., 756:13
    foam to w. glitter of seas, 827:18
    for this planting, 286:n1
    gasoline more than w. cause of conflict,
        784:1
    hid in two bushels of chaff, 187:23
    immortal w., 290:2
    land of w. and barley, 10:3
    stacker of w., 681:8
    worm in the w., 656:14
Wheaten, sickle and w. sheaf, 318:3
Wheel, as w. runs why water pitcher,
    101:17
    bound upon w. of fire, 217:29
    breaks butterfly upon w., 312:7
    broken at the cistern, 25:8
    cannot mind my w., 408:9
    ever-whirling w., 161:19
    I the limbs and w., 524:13
    in the middle of a wheel, 29:31
    is come full circle, 218:4
    man at w. taught to feel, 580:23
    queer shoulder to the w., 817:11
    shoulder to the w., 61:4

Wheel *(continued)*
    smile once more turn thy w., 216:10
    sofa round, 348:4
    that squeaks gets grease, 508:16
    turned an easy w., 436:19
Wheelbarrow, red w. glazed with rain, 703:10
Wheelock, Eleazer W. pious man, 630:8
Wheel's kick and winds' song, 680:15
Wheels, beetle w. droning flight, 334:9
    clicked off by little w., 748:9
    Little Tin Gods on W., 632:8
    of weary life, 283:5
    oil for its own w., 347:15
    why tarry the w. of his chariots, 10:34
Whelmed in deeper gulfs than he, 348:22
Whelming, under the w. tide, 262:3
Whelp, mongrel puppy w. hound, 341:17
When I heard learned astronomer, 520:8
    I knew him w., 656:9
    men drink they are rich, 74:11
    or how I cannot tell, 542:7
    shall we three meet again, 218:23
    that I was little tiny boy, 210:19
    What and Why and W., 635:9
    will I look at it, 791:13
    will they ever learn, 805:16
Whence and what art thou, 265:18
    comest thou, 13:23
    cradle asks w., 554:4
    had they come, 642:5
Whenever, if poor w. you can if rich w. you
        please, 79:5
    you feel an impulse, 628:11
Whensoever called to make exit, 362:9
Where and Oh where, 384:3
    are snows of yesteryear, 139:18
    are you going to, 859:1
    cries out W. is it, 401:12
    did we go right, 817:7
    fear to be we know not w., 282:20
    go without my mount, 806:3
    have all the flowers gone, 805:16
    hell is there must we be, 170:20
    How and W. and Who, 635:9
    I am I don't know, 773:16
    I am there ye may be, 41:27
    is fancy bred, 189:3
    is it now the glory, 393:10
    is she now, 222:6
    not how many but w. they are, 72:3
    was Roderick then, 397:13
    wast thou when I laid the foundations,
        15:5
    we are is hell, 170:20
    who are we w. are we, 505:13
    your treasure is, 34:13
Whereabout, stones prate of my w., 220:10
Whereas I was blind, 41:14
Where'er she lie, 272:7
    you walk, 308:5
Wherefore are these things hid, 209:4
    art thou Romeo, 183:2
    causes why and w., 193:22
    every why hath a w., 174:28
    stopp'st thou me, 399:11
Wherein lies happiness, 436:10
Where's my serpent of old Nile, 223:7
    rest of me, 765:19
Wheresoever called to make exit, 362:9

Wherever, home w. that may be, 785:13
    I am, 830:11
    there's a cottage small, 794:1
    they burn books, 442:10
    you may be, 809:12
Whether he hears my song or not, 820:1
Whetstone, finest edge with blunt w., 163:2
    of wits, 197:25
Whetted, wind's like w. knife, 681:2
Whey, curds and w., 860:3
Which, at odds with morning w. is w.,
    221:18
    God only knows w. is w., 569:16
    is the justice, 217:23
    of us has known brother, 760:4
    that and w., 614:2
    who why w. what, 500:2
Whiff of grapeshot, 433:26
Whiffling through tulgey wood, 551:11
Whiggery, what is W., 641:1
Whigs, caught the W. bathing, 459:8
While there's life there's hope, 89:2, 90:24
Whilst planet has gone cycling on, 470:3
Whim envy or resentment, 346:20
    just as the w. bites, 407:22
    tempted by a private w., 653:13
Whimper, not bang but w., 719:7
Whine, sweat and w. about condition, 519:16
Whining at threshold, 623:8
    born naked and falls a-w., 108:n3
    of a door, 236:22
    poetry, 234:8
    school-boy with satchel, 198:25
    wimpled w. purblind, 176:33
Whip all hell yet, 522:n5
    fear o' hell's a hangman's w., 242:n1
    in every honest hand a w., 214:29
    so small you could not see, 546:14
    weight in wildcats, 597:1
Whipped for overdoing Termagant, 204:11
    he must be w. out, 216:1
    her little daughter, 859:10
    offending Adam, 192:17
    she w. him, 860:22
    them all soundly, 858:13
Whipping, future smells of w., 442:17
    who should 'scape w., 203:26
Whippoorwill, hear that lonesome w., 813:3
Whips and scorns of time, 203:33
    my father chastised you with w., 12:22
Whipstock, first Packard had w. on
        dashboard, 734:5
Whirl asunder and dismember me, 178:5
    lay mightily in w. of dust, 53:22
Whirled in an arch, 481:2
    unstilled world w., 719:14
Whirligig of time, 210:18
Whirling summer, 766:18
Whirls, expectation w. me round, 208:2
    Northern ocean in vast w., 318:5
Whirlwind, Elijah went up by a w., 12:39
    home in your manes, 472:24
    Lord answered Job out of the w., 15:4
    of passion, 204:11
    reap the w., 30:17
    rides in the w., 301:12, 313:20
Whirlwind's, sweeping w. sway, 335:13
Whirlwinds in the south, 27:7
Whiskers, oh my fur and w., 549:15

Whiskey and Rye, 839:7
    for my Johnny, 861:23
    gimme a w. ginger ale on side, 723:12
    must have w. you know why, 750:18
    on your breath, 780:7
    polishes copper, 560:11
    prayers in hall w. afterwards, 693:1
    say boys another w., 584:6
Whiskies, born two w. below par, 647:11
Whisper, breathed the husky w., 600:3
    busy w. circling round, 342:8
    far-heard w. o'er the sea, 400:5
    not a w. be lost, 775:11
Whispered, Devil w. behind leaves, 633:15
    in sounds of silence, 837:8
    into your brain, 840:12
    voice behind me w. low, 605:17
Whispereth, soul w. within him, 122:12
Whispering ambitions, 718:3
    bayed the w. wind, 342:3
    from Oxford towers, 530:10
    humbleness, 188:9
    I will ne'er consent, 423:10
    maid and wight w. by, 576:5
    music of yonder pine, 85:7
    tongues can poison truth, 401:9
Whisperings, keeps eternal w., 439:7
Whispers, Duty w. low, 453:16
    listen to w. of fancy, 324:24
    o'er-fraught heart, 221:35
    of each other's watch, 193:11
    what good author w., 636:9
Whist, wild waves w., 229:18
Whistle and I'll come to you, 379:7
    and she'll come to you, 245:11
    blackbird 'tis to w., 270:15
    clear as a w., 314:14
    don't you hear w. blowing, 848:1
    go w. for the rest, 156:24
    hir joly w. wel ywet, 136:9
    I love to w., 756:13
    I'd w. her off, 214:2
    let it w. as it will, 396:21
    maybe just w., 723:2
    pay too much for w., 320:19
    quail w. about us, 686:19
    them back, 343:5
Whistles far and wee, 739:11
    pipes and w. in his sound, 198:25
    thrice, 400:4
Whistling, blackbird w. or just after, 687:7
    to bear courage up, 285:n1
    to keep from being afraid, 285:2
Whistlings, foolish w. of a name, 275:17
White, a moment w., 379:18
    and drifted snow, 450:11
    as angel English child, 372:1
    as driven snow, 228:30
    as leprosy, 400:3
    as long as colored man look to w. folks, 839:9
    beard decreasing leg, 191:16
    beautiful when it helps, 809:10
    beauty whose red and w., 209:8
    black and w. separate as fingers, 610:19
    Black Hawk fought against w. men, 386:9
    black spirits and w., 243:22
    black where I read w., 376:8
    bosoms of actresses, 326:7

White *(continued)*
    bread and butter, 857:20
    candle in holy place, 693:4
    chickens, 703:10
    chrysanthemum immaculate, 291:14
    Citizen's Counciler, 822:12
    cliffs of Dover, 673:5
    clothed in w. samite, 139:3, 485:19
    clouds on wing, 535:16
    colored people understand w. people, 656:16
    consternation throughout w. race, 831:9
    cow all red and w., 599:1
    crimson petal now w., 483:6
    dreaming of w. Christmas, 716:8
    end of fight tombstone w., 633:2
    fat w. woman, 711:8
    fever of temptation, 730:8
    fleece w. but 'tis too cold, 161:n4
    flower of blameless life, 485:16
    foam flew, 399:20
    fought against w. domination, 803:15
    get up so w. person could sit, 791:8
    Goddess, 743:21
    Godiva I unpeel, 827:17
    hair become very w., 550:1
    hate in w. men, 815:12
    how ill w. hairs become fool, 192:13
    humiliation by w. man, 812:6
    I appeal to any w. man, 339:8
    if snow be w., 228:1
    in subjection to w. Saxon man, 503:7
    in w. black and green, 845:10
    is their color, 250:23
    little missionary stew, 719:19
    made w. in blood, 48:24
    man warmed before Indians' fire, 346:10
    man will never be alone, 419:5
    Man's burden, 635:6
    moderate devoted to order, 822:12
    moon beams, 726:19
    nights all w. an' still, 515:3
    nor w. so very w., 389:15
    not neutralize black, 495:2
    O my soul is w., 372:1
    o'er his w. banes, 854:8
    officers cast lot, 556:3
    one w. foot try him, 849:17
    or colored signs, 800:4
    parsons preaching Jesus, 812:7
    prisoner to w. man, 386:8
    radiance of eternity, 430:17
    radiance stretches above it, 54:21
    raiment w. as snow, 38:11
    really hope no w. person, 838:3
    red thoughts teeth w., 655:6
    relation between w. and colored people, 509:15
    rose breathes of love, 590:14
    rose is a dove, 590:14
    roses and w. lilies grow, 232:5
    sails still fly seaward, 719:16
    samite, 139:3, 485:19
    scare w. clouds on, 669:7
    seas show w. when rocks near, 244:5
    silence below, 710:5
    singe my w. head, 216:18
    sins shall be w. as snow, 26:10
    sound of w. soldier's axe, 533:9

White *(continued)*
    superfluity comes by w. hairs, 187:26
    Sustenance despair, 545:13
    sweet w. wine, 681:4
    to chase that w. whale, 516:12
    to w. man nature wilderness, 650:1
    tupping; your w. ewe, 212:19
    two societies one black one w., 779:8
    ugly when oppresses blacks, 809:10
    we black and they w., 781:13
    wear w. flannel trousers, 717:16
    what treaty w. man kept, 549:3
    why should I want to be w., 762:8
    wild w. horses play, 528:5
    wings one black other W., 269:8
    you're older and w. and free, 762:17
White House, preside over W., 814:17
    unapproachable in w., 701:13
White-Anglo Saxon-Protestant upper class, 795:17
White-chokered and clean-shaven, 583:4
Whited sepulchers, 37:4
    thou w. wall, 42:29
Whiteness, Milky Way sister in w., 689:20
    restore to w. wool dyed purple, 118:25
Whiter, I shall be w. than snow, 17:26
Whites of their eyes, 330:10, 340:5
Whitest, old linen wash w., 244:1
Whitewash, bucket of w. and longhandled brush, 559:19
Whitewashed wall, 342:10
Whither, advice not to inquire why or w., 750:2
    away fair rover, 586:5
    coffin asks w., 554:4
    fled visionary gleam, 393:10
    goest thou, 41:33
    shall I go from thy spirit, 20:13
    so high, 859:11
    thou goest I will go, 11:12
Whithersoever, with thee w. thou goest, 10:18
Whiting, as w. said with tail in mouth, 356:n1
    to a snail, 550:21
Whitman, Homer and W. roared in pines, 651:12
    I saw you Walt W., 817:10
Walt W. a kosmos, 519:9
Whitman's, Mr. W. Eve Mr. W. Venus, 569:18
Whittington, turn again W., 844:18
Who are these coming, 438:3
    are they, 818:6
    are we where are we, 505:13
    can hold fire in his hand, 179:6
    doesn't desire father's death, 526:5
    doth ambition shun, 198:13
    ever got out of winding sheet, 237:1
    ever loved not at first sight, 170:15
    find out w. he is what he's about, 839:9
    follows in His train, 416:2
    has seen the wind, 548:2
    hath desired sea, 635:14
    hath known mind of Lord, 43:14
    How and Where and W., 635:9
    I'm Nobody w. are you, 544:13
    is in who's out, 218:1
    is Silvia what is she, 176:12

Who *(continued)*
    is the happy Warrior, 394:15
    is the third, 719:1
    is this King of glory, 16:21
    killed Cock Robin, 857:14
    killed John Keats, 425:1
    knows but world may end, 492:20
    loses and who wins, 218:1
    night and silence w. is here, 181:16
    ran to help me, 414:4
    said Peacock Pie, 662:14
    shall ascend into the hill of the Lord,
      16:19
    shall bell cat, 61:1
    shall deliver me, 43:4
    shall stand in his holy place, 16:19
    should 'scape whipping, 203:26
    then devised torment, 722:2
    to himself law no law doth need,
      165:9
    touches a hair, 468:16
    why which what, 500:2
    will bell cat, 133:2
    would have thought so much blood,
      222:5
    you're known as w., 822:11
Whoe'er has traveled, 328:*n*1
    she be, 272:6
Whoever really loves you, 862:22
    wishes to attain English style, 325:5
    you are behold your master, 317:1
Whole America nothing less, 344:8
    armor of God, 45:30
    by sample we judge w., 156:2
    climate of opinion, 775:17
    complicate amassing harmony, 688:7
    drink and be w. again, 670:19
    duty of man, 25:10
    earth is sepulcher of famous men,
      74:5
    earth our hospital, 721:2
    First Comprehend W., 545:7
    general joy of w. table, 221:13
    has beginning middle and end, 81:11
    how much more is half than w., 56:9
    I am equal and w., 569:7
    idea of life, 824:7
    indictment against w. people, 344:11
    love is the w., 740:10
    makes w. world kin, 208:12
    man composed of all men, 772:12
    my w. course of love, 212:26
    need not physician, 35:18
    never sees a w., 528:17
    nothing sole or w., 641:15
    one stupendous w., 311:7
    prayers make me w., 633:1
    saw life w., 528:2
    soul's tasking, 514:15
    subject is too profound, 470:12
    taste w. of it, 494:19
    tribe of fops, 215:26
    volumes in folio, 176:26
    wide sky above me, 750:6
    willing to know w. truth, 352:13
Wholeness of human problem, 676:17
Wholes, couples are w. and not w., 64:10
Wholesale, God who does w. business,
    582:16

Wholesome, believe doctors nothing w.,
    548:4
    even for King, 546:15
    harvests reaps, 444:15
    nights are w., 200:22
Wholesomest, old wine w., 244:1
Whole-time, husband a w. job, 645:3
Wholly, I shall not w. die, 100:11
Whom shall I fear, 16:22
    they fear they hate, 87:17
Whoopee ti yi yo git along little dogies,
    854:13
Whooping, out of all w., 199:10
Whoops, owlet w. to wolf below, 400:20
Whopper, give birth to w., 819:2
Whore, joined this rogue and w., 299:6
    pity she's a w., 246:5
    posture of a w., 224:6
    the woman's a w., 327:21
Whore's oath, 217:4
Whores, till all w. burnt alive, 296:20
Whorled ear, 587:2
Who's afraid of Virginia Woolf, 820:4
    in who's out, 218:1
    master who's man, 299:26
    on first, 742:15
Whose, to w. advantage, 90:12
    world or mine or theirs, 709:10
Why, causes w. and wherefore, 193:22
    did you do that, 607:9
    don't you speak for yourself, 467:5
    every w. hath a wherefore, 174:28
    I can't say w. I don't like you, 110:16
    I can't think w., 565:6
    I dream and say W. not, 610:10
    is plain as way to church, 198:21
    is this thus, 555:15
    love's stricken w., 546:16
    man of morals tell me w., 275:9
    men fell out knew not w., 270:13
    not inquire w. or whither, 750:2
    persecutest thou me, 42:7
    then oh why can't I, 752:1
    though I could never tell w., 563:13
    we and universe exist, 837:3
    What and W. and When, 635:9
    who w. which what, 500:2
    you see things and say W., 610:10
Wibrated, strings better not w., 496:35
Wicked are wicked no doubt, 490:16
    blast drives w. spirits, 130:12
    deceitful and desperately w., 29:18
    dreams abuse sleep, 220:9
    flee when no man pursueth, 23:15
    forsake his way, 28:26
    God help the w., 185:31
    I have seen the w. in great power, 17:7
    intents w. or charitable, 202:5
    little better than one of w., 184:32
    man in bathroom cupboard, 797:11
    men are w. who is good, 648:10
    name of the w. shall rot, 21:15
    no peace unto the w., 28:14
    public scandal is w., 277:24
    punish w. for their iniquity, 27:2
    something w. this way comes, 221:23
    sways in w. grace, 798:13
    tender mercies of the w. are cruel, 21:22
    the w. cease from troubling, 13:31

Wicked *(continued)*
    the w. oppressing, 845:2
    violence covereth the mouth of the w.,
      21:15
    war regarded as w., 604:10
    wealth even to a w. man, 61:11
    wickedness proceedeth from the w.,
      11:33
    will betrayed still, 567:4
    Witch of the East, 606:14
    work your w. will, 666:14
    worse than w. it's vulgar, 591:17
Wickedness, did sell himself to work w.,
    12:36
    dwell in the tents of w., 18:17
    far be it from God that he should do w.,
      15:1
    flower of w., 494:29
    follies and w., 772:15
    Hitler monster of w., 666:13
    manifold sins and w., 49:18, 50:18
    men capable of every w., 612:15
    method in man's w., 245:8
    of a woman, 32:37
    or folly, 475:8
    plowed w. reaped iniquity, 30:18
    proceedeth from the wicked, 11:33
    spiritual w. in high places, 45:31
    though w. be sweet, 14:27
    turn from w. and live, 49:22
Wicket, flanneled fools at w., 635:8
Wicklow, chink in floor of W. house,
    658:8
Wictim o' connubiality, 495:25
Widder eats by bell, 559:21
Widders, be wery careful o' w., 495:23
Wide and starry sky, 599:6
    and winding Rhine, 420:23
    arch of ranged empire fall, 222:27
    capable and w. revenge, 214:15
    dark world and w., 263:12
    enough to wrap a fairy, 181:12
    gates of dark Death stand w., 97:23
    great and w. sea, 19:11
    great w. beautiful world, 535:7
    is the gate, 35:6
    no wider than heart w., 734:15
    nor so w. as church door, 183:28
    shallow brooks and rivers w., 259:15
    sky above me, 750:6
    though its meshes are w., 59:17
    too w. for shrunk shank, 198:25
    water inescapable, 686:19
    wide sea, 400:10
    womb of uncreated night, 265:4
    world dreaming on things to come,
      227:12
    world w. enough to hold both, 332:16
Widely, doors are w. flung, 780:2
Widened, thoughts of men w., 482:3
Widening, ever w. slowly silence, 485:23
    turning in w. gyre, 639:6
Wider and permanent system, 699:9
    no w. than heart wide, 734:15
    seek no w. war, 779:5
    still and wider, 625:11
Wide-sounding Zeus, 53:13, 55:17
Wide-watered shore, 260:4
Wide-waving wings, 348:23

Wilderness *(continued)*
  oceans mingling with sky, 534:9
  of monkeys, 188:33
  of sweets, 267:4
  of this world, 281:13
  Promised Land beyond w., 618:1
  redemption from W., 817:13
  slovenly w., 687:2
  sweet berries in w., 686:19
  though in w. never alone, 112:*n*4
  to white man nature w., 650:1
  voice crying in the w., 33:24
  voice that crieth in the w., 27:38
  wander in the w. forty years, 9:19
  way into Universe through w., 572:14
  were Paradise enow, 471:5
  women have no w., 748:1
Wildernesses, desert w., 260:24
Wildest peal for years, 656:10
  rhymes suggest w. freedom, 454:3
Wildfowl, not a more fearful w., 181:18
  opinion of Pythagoras concerning w.,
    189:*n*2
Wild-goose chase, 156:26
Wildlife, survival of our w. in Africa, 808:6
Wildly, sing so w. well, 478:3
  striking sometimes a friend, 250:1
Wildness, in God's w. hope of world, 572:13
  in w. is preservation of world, 507:28
  life consists with w., 507:30
Wiles, full of w. full of guile, 75:8
  man of many w., 309:20
  wanton w., 259:9
Wilhelmine, little grandchild W., 405:4
Will, act according to w. of another, 382:23
  and Intellect the same, 286:18
  be there a w., 369:4
  boy's w. wind's w., 467:7
  built against w. of gods, 53:9
  city obedient to his w., 77:13
  committed to w. of God, 247:5
  complies against his w., 271:28
  conscious w. and reasonableness, 675:4
  Constitution w. of Fuehrer, 757:9
  creature of people's w., 371:6
  decisions more of instincts than w.,
    675:4
  does not make difference she w.,
    673:15
  doeth w. of my Father, 35:10
  dread puzzles the w., 203:33
  enchains us to ill, 428:17
  fixed fate free w., 265:13
  forget not because we w., 529:20
  free the human w., 313:8
  free w. not free at all, 542:12
  free w. not one but many wills, 815:14
  God's w. be done, 355:12
  good w. to men, 488:15
  good w. toward men, 39:4
  greatest gift freedom of w., 132:1
  here by w. of nation, 366:16
  his w. to make known, 845:2
  I pay thy poverty not thy w., 184:10
  I w. as God wills, 355:12
  if God w., 121:15
  Immanent W. and its designs, 575:19
  in His w. is our peace, 131:26
  infirmity of w., 455:15

Will *(continued)*
  into appetite, 207:27
  its one w. flow, 753:15
  killing by simply exerting w., 526:*n*1
  laid me down with a w., 599:6
  let my w. take place of reason, 113:10
  living lies in your w., 152:11
  love-sick against w., 564:7
  man has w. woman way, 473:8
  Mariner hath his w., 399:13
  men of good w., 49:11
  mighty effort of w., 674:5
  most incorrect to heaven, 200:31
  my fanatical w. power, 726:15
  my poverty but not my w. consents,
    184:10
  no malice or ill w., 386:4
  not as I w. but thou, 37:29
  not my w. but thine, 40:16
  of God prevail, 531:16
  of the Yukon, 673:8
  one man's w. all men's misery, 162:19
  our peace in His w., 719:17
  own sweet w., 392:13
  own sweet w. Heaven's w., 639:15
  power into w., 207:27
  Providence w. and fate, 265:13
  reason panders w., 205:23
  responded I w., 622:16
  serveth not another's w., 232:13
  smaller and dryer than w., 719:10
  take away our free w. and glory, 143:2
  that it become universal law, 339:6
  that which they w. is right, 569:20
  this is our gracious w., 143:6
  though heaven fall thy w. be done,
    124:22
  Thy w. be done, 34:11
  to abolish conscience, 796:4
  to do, 397:6
  to live, 677:15
  to power, 590:12
  to w. and to do his pleasure, 45:34
  triumph by mystic w., 674:13
  unconquerable w., 264:3, 666:15
  undisappointed, 112:13
  want to do God's w., 823:10
  was w. das Weib, 608:*n*2
  when you w. they won't, 89:9
  wicked w. baffled still, 567:4
  woman's cold perverted w., 431:16
  woman's w., 177:25
  word to thing when We w. it, 121:9
  work your wicked w., 666:14
  wrote w. across sky, 723:7
  you w. Oscar you w., 558:1
  you won't you, 551:1
Willas cather, 749:8
Wille zur Macht, 590:*n*3
Willed, little wife well w., 319:10
  never felt nor cried clearly w., 529:10
Willful, gigantic w. young, 652:1
  group of w. men, 611:6
  stranger, 599:12
Willful-wavier meal-drift, 587:11
William, old Father W., 405:9, 550:1
Willie is no good I'll sell him, 651:10
  wee W. Winkie, 488:7
Willin', Barkis is w., 497:30

Willing, able and w. to pull weight, 615:5
  faithfully to serve State, 254:11
  spirit is w., 37:30
  suspension of disbelief, 403:7
  to taste any drink once, 682:11
  to wound, 312:4
Willingly as one would kill fly, 175:18
Willow, all a green w., 147:1, 215:1
  all under the w. tree, 368:10
  cabin at gate, 209:9
  Dido with w. in her hand, 190:4
  hang harp on w.-tree, 848:19
  sing all a green w., 215:1
  titwillow, 565:20
  willow waly, 564:10
  willow willow, 215:1
Willows, change to Southern w., 349:1
  hanged harps upon w., 20:11
  weeping w. wave, 539:14
Wills, God w. it, 123:20
  God w. us free, 355:12
  let's talk of w., 179:27
  many w. in one man, 815:14
  our w. are gardeners, 213:2
Wilson could write from Sinai, 701:13
Wilt, do what thou w., 146:4
  flowers that do not w., 714:22
Wimpled whining purblind, 176:33
Wimpling wing, 587:6
Win, army loses if it does not w., 812:12
  because we are stronger, 681:6
  best to w. without fighting, 83:5
  convictions to w. or lose, 660:8
  defeated warriors then seek to w., 83:4
  friends and influence people, 716:20
  here win everywhere, 754:17
  if you w. you w. everything, 279:23
  just one for the Gipper, 774:6
  kindness shall w. my love, 175:36
  know how to w. victory Hannibal, 86:18
  lawsuits and are happy, 74:11
  lose good we oft might w., 211:2
  man who is sorry will w., 59:15
  my way to the coast, 70:5
  noble renown, 53:27
  nothing venture nothing w., 565:5
  one for Gipper, 724:16
  or lose it all, 272:2
  race runs by himself, 591:*n*1
  shall w. lover's hire, 373:14
  they laugh that w., 214:19
  those who hate you don't w., 791:3
  those who know how to w., 88:8
  us to our harm, 219:3
  us with honest trifles, 219:3
  victorious warriors w. first, 83:4
  wanting to w. is everything, 852:*n*4
  when in doubt w. trick, 303:1
  with his tongue w. a woman, 176:9
Wince, let galled jade w., 205:5
Winced, not w. nor cried aloud, 594:10
Winchell, this is Walter W. in New York,
    750:5
Wind a fiery Pegasus, 186:24
  all aloud w. cloth blow, 177:18
  always north-northeast, 652:9
  and clouds now here, 431:16
  and wave and oar, 480:21
  argument with cast w., 515:15

Wind *(continued)*

as large a charter as w., 198:20
a-sailing with the w., 860:13
assault and battery of w., 639:13
at a little w. dost thou fall, 131:17
awake O north w., 25:24
bayed the whispering w., 342:3
bellies and drags in w., 639:2
bellows full of angry w., 639:14
between w. and the grass, 63:8
betwixt w. and his nobility, 185:3
blasted with the east w., 7:26
blow thou winter w., 199:1
blow w. come wrack, 222:18
bloweth where it listeth, 40:44
blowin' in the w., 836:4
blowing at my door, 129:1
blowing new direction, 707:5
blows cradle rock, 592:1
blustering w. or swallowing wave, 276:5
breath of night-w., 531:2
brook weather that love not w., 176:35
chaff which w. driveth away, 15:27
changes and I stir, 811:13
chased shouting w. along, 810:11
come w. come weather, 282:4
comes off frozen peak, 670:5
crannying w., 420:21
doth ramm, 708:17
drunk on w. in my mouth, 811:14
dust blown away with the w., 31:19
dust the rude w. blows, 217:12
east w. never blow, 252:23
every w. of doctrine, 45:27
fair stood w. for France, 169:12
false as w., 208:7
fate seemed to w. him up, 283:5
feather for each w., 228:17
fill belly with east w., 14:18
flights against w., 647:16
fly upon wings of the w., 16:9
forgot to w. clock, 332:4
fresh west w., 54:13
friends who go with the w., 129:1
frosty w. made moan, 547:19
full of birds' cries, 681:3
gentle w, does move, 373:8
give appearance of solidity to pure w.,
    765:13
going down the w., 288:3
gone with the w., 645:9
green w. green branches, 751:4
gusts of clear-blowing west w., 54:20
he that observerh the w., 25:4
hear voice in every w., 333:19
hear w. blow, 847:2
hears him in the w., 311:5
hey ho w. and rain, 210:19, 216:25
hiding place from the w., 27:29
hollow blasts of w., 306:21
hymns that fall out of w., 688:12
ill w. bloweth no man good, 149:14
impatient as the w., 395:9
in trees a sad thing, 95:19
inherit w., 21:20
is chill, 396:21
is in palm trees, 633:12
is in the cane, 742:5
is passing by, 548:2

Wind *(continued)*

let her down the w., 214:2
leveling w., 640:8
light dry w. blowing in windows, 661:19
like W. I go, 471:14
listen the w. is rising, 710:3
lived like candle in w., 840:12
loose as the w., 250:15
Lord was not in the w., 12:32
lost and by w. grieved, 760:5
made heart cry To-day to-day, 661:19
man control w., 528:21
mantle of w. and chill and rain, 138:15
meteor streaming to w., 264:14
net to hold the w., 244:*n*2
nets to catch the w., 244:10
no 'twas but the w., 420:17
nor tide nor sea, 566:17
north w. doth blow, 859:12
O w. weder gynneth clere, 133:18
of criticism, 329:17
of doctrine, 45:27
of western sea, 482:18
on buffalo grass, 855:16
over lake inner truth, 5:3
pass by me as idle w., 197:10
passeth over it, 19:7
paths that w. and w., 600:8
pines keep shape of w., 759:17
renown but breath of w., 131:16
rising attempt to live, 659:1
said W. to Moon, 536:7
sails filled with lusty w., 165:11
sall blaw for evermair, 854:8
scattered to w., 480:6
scatters some leaves, 52:31
sits w. in that corner, 194:26
something in the w., 174:32
sound of rushing w., 41:44
sound w. and limb, 158:15
sown the w., 30:17
stop hole to keep w. away, 206:26
straw see which way w. is, 245:21
sun was warm w. chill, 670:5
sway in w. like corn, 717:20
sweep man away, 528:21
swoln with w. and mist, 262:2
tears shall drown the w., 219:18
tempers w. to shorn lamb, 151:12,
    333:7
that blows through me, 707:5
that follows fast, 417:7
through woods in riot, 619:1
throw sand against w., 375:2
thunderstorm against w., 421:18
torrent of darkness, 692:2
unhelped by any w., 401:10
up with earful of cider, 704:*n*2
warm w. the west w., 681:3
wave cry w. cry, 721:6
way long w. cold, 396:3
west w. and the swallows, 85:16
Western w. when wilt thou blow, 843:18
what is w. in that door, 139:5
what woman says written in w., 94:22
when she dances in the w., 284:8
when sun out w. still, 670:5
when w. southerly know hawk, 203:20
whenever w. is high, 598:22

Wind *(continued)*

where a w. ever soft, 363:16
which way the w. blows, 836:9
who has seen w., 548:2
wild West W., 428:21
wings of the w., 16:9, 19:8
winnow not with every w., 32:6
winnowing w., 438:12
wiped out by w., 820:10
words are but w., 271:18
words are easy like the w., 239:3
Windborne mirroring soul, 528:17
Winding, God w. lonely horn, 637:9
long cool w. saxophones, 681:14
long trail a-w., 726:19
notes with many a w. bout, 259:20
Winding-sheet of Edward's race, 335:12
old England's w., 375:15
waters were his w., 239:1
who ever got out of w., 237:1
Windlass, turned round like w., 516:17
Windlasses and assays of bias, 202:30
Windmills, tilting at w., 156:*n*2
Window, bishop kick hole in stained glass w.,
    717:3
clapte the w. to, 136:5
face negative in slate w., 806:7
in your rocking chair by w., 656:4
is starless still, 825:4
Jezebel looked out at a w., 13:5
light through yonder w., 182:28
little w. where sun, 445:15
look out your w., 836:5
love flies out in w., 845:13
Mary at thy w. be, 380:8
on Europe, 447:2
sit looking out of w., 818:11
tirlin' at w., 488:7
tree, 669:20
Walloping W. Blind, 580:23
Windowed, looped and w. raggedness,
    216:27
Windows be darkened, 25:7
cleaned w. swept floor, 563:17
dim w. of the soul, 376:9
factory w. always broken, 685:2
if no doors or w., 793:12
if your w. are glass, 319:18
in lighted w. books kept watch, 657:14
lavender in the w., 252:29
not by eastern w. only, 512:10
Saints to w. run, 544:9
see without looking through w., 59:7
storied w. richly dight, 260:10
through w. call on us, 234:2
Windows tossed with linden, 809:9
Windpipe throttled in fakes of death,
    519:12
Wind's feet shine along sea, 568:9
like whetted knife, 681:2
out of w. and rain's way, 693:5
will, 467:7
Winds are left behind, 537:17
ascribing to w. the noise, 107:13
beetle w. sullen horn, 337:2
beteem w. of heaven, 201:3
blow profit, 777:8
blow w. crack your cheeks, 216:18
blow ye w. heigh-ho, 862:11

Winds *(continued)*

breath rides on posting w., 225:17
come as the w. come, 397:21
courted by all the w., 269:6
cradled on sea, 777:1
faithless as w. or seas, 290:16
four w. of the heaven, 30:34
four-square to w., 484:22
gray-fly w. sultry horn, 261:16
great w. shoreward blow, 528:5
huntsman w. his horn, 321:18
imprisoned in viewless w., 211:23
lashing corners of earth, 681:18
neither shaken by w. nor wet, 54:21
of doctrine, 263:5
on side of ablest navigators, 353:11
over great sea w. trouble waters, 92:19
rough w. do shake, 226:2
sea w. pierced solitudes, 453:3
selfsame w. that blow, 600:5
somewhere safe to sea, 569:3
take w. of March with beauty, 228:27
time w. th' exhausted chain, 379:11
wailing w. naked woods, 432:14
were love-sick, 223:14
when w. breathing low, 429:8
where w. are all asleep, 528:6
Winds' and spent waves' riot, 568:25
Windsor, Widow at W., 633:11
Windswept, topped w. heights with grace, 810:11
Wind-walks, what w., 587:11
Windward, between w. and lee, 569:14
to w. of law, 346:19
Windy, flung us on w. hill, 712:14
night rainy morrow, 227:2
shadows and w. places, 567:17
side of care, 194:21
side of law, 194:n1
Troy, 481:9
Wine, age leaves friends and w., 412:9
and women go together, 240:22
and women mirth laughter, 423:18
as water unto w., 482:5
best w. that goeth down sweetly, 26:1
better is thy love than w., 25:23
between kisses and w., 645:8
blood fizz like w., 680:8
blushes into w., 272:n2
bored with good w., 459:4
bring me beaker of w., 74:11
bring water bring w., 61:17
Canary w., 438:10
come within pint of w., 303:3
comes in at mouth, 638:3
days of w. and roses, 645:11
dear boy and truth, 57:13
did not know the W., 544:14
drinking blude-red w., 853:16
drinks w. with laughter, 848:18
drunk your water and w., 632:7
drunken but not with w., 27:24
enjoy laughter over the w., 85:13
for thy stomach's sake, 46:24
frolic w., 248:14
from w. sudden friendship, 307:10
glass of w. happiness, 701:8
good w. a friend or being dry, 292:23
good w. a good creature, 213:27

Wine *(continued)*

good w. needs no bush, 104:n1
hard to hide ignorance over w., 64:15
Helen threw into w. a drug, 54:19
if it doesn't get into w., 664:16
I'll not look for w., 238:2
in w. is truth, 57:n5, 124:3
insolence and w., 264:13
inspires us and fires us, 307:13
inventing liquid w., 70:11
invisible spirit of w., 213:25
is a mocker, 22:17
is a peep-hole, 57:14
jar when molding began, 101:17
jug of W. Loaf of Bread, 471:5
leaving drinking of w., 288:9
lion w., 451:13
madder music stronger w., 645:10
maketh merry, 25:1
mischiefs from w., 293:18
monkey w., 451:13
murmured Snodgrass, 495:20
new friend as new w., 32:16
new w. in old bottles, 35:21
no use of metal corn or w., 229:25
not hang branch over w., 104:11
of astonishment, 17:35, 807:9
of life is drawn, 220:25
old w. to drink, 167:1
old w. wholesomest, 244:1
placed near my dying mouth, 127:10
poisonous w., 438:14
sans W. Song Singer, 471:12
seas of life like w., 290:4
sheep w., 451:13
some blithe w. I had drunk, 438:20
strong w. reed as blood, 135:14
sure there was w., 250:15
sweet poison of misused w., 260:16
sweet pomegranate w., 4:3
sweet white w., 681:4
swine w., 451:13
that maketh glad the heart, 19:9
to succeed add water to w., 630:10
turning w. into urine, 706:4
unto those of heavy hearts, 23:26
urges me on, 55:12
vows made in w., 199:22
walnuts and w., 480:10
washed her with w., 821:13
water made w., 40:39
when it is red, 22:38
when the w. goes in, 382:6
which over flows, 541:14
with bread and w. walk road, 862:16
with not a drop of Tiber, 224:20
women and song, 368:9
women and w., 307:13
Wine-barrel room, 685:3
Winebibber, gluttonous and a w., 35:34
Wine-dark, singing over the w. sea, 54:13
Winepress, fill w. of eloquence, 118:28
of fierceness and wrath, 48:36
trodden the w. alone, 28:32
Wines, abbots purple as their w., 313:24
feast of w. on the lees, 27:15
old times manners w., 342:15
willingly drinks their w., 365:10
Wine-scented poetic soul, 599:5

Wing and a prayer, 773:3
Bird is on the W., 471:2
Conquest's crimson w., 335:11
crow makes w. to rooky wood, 221:7
crows that w. midway air, 217:18
damp my intended w., 267:25
dropped from angel's w., 395:14
flits by on leathern w., 337:2
gray w. upon tide, 638:7
hidden under dove's w., 719:23
hide head under his w., 859:12
inconstant w. as winds, 427:14
lark's on w., 491:2
of friendship never moults, 496:28
of submission, 121:11
quill from angel's w., 395:n3
shall brush my w., 374:4
speed like bird on w., 616:9
stretches out my golden w., 371:10
turn stone start w., 621:7
wimpling w., 587:6
Wing-beats, where happy w. are, 381:8
Winged, change me to w. bird, 70:4
Cupid painted blind, 180:21
does w. life destroy, 373:13
he addressed her w. words, 52:6
lawless w. unconfined, 373:10
seraphs of Heaven, 479:18
stands a w. sentry, 279:6
Time's w. chariot, 277:1
Winging, ever w. up and up, 541:14
Wings across canceled skies, 734:6
angel w. cast shadow, 730:8
at heaven's gates claps w., 163:16
beating luminous w. in vain, 532:12
books like angels with outspread w., 657:14
bug with gilded w., 312:8
disastrous beating of w., 656:5
downward beat thy w., 92:n13
downward on extended w., 686:19
each had six w., 26:23
fly upon w. of the wind, 16:9
four beasts had each six w., 48:16
giant w. prevent walking, 524:8
golden hours on angel w., 380:4
healing in his w., 31:3
hear sound of w., 752:10
hope flies with swallow's w., 174:17
I am the w., 453:23
if he soars with own w., 372:16
laughter-silvered w., 810:11
lets grow her w., 260:29
Love without his w., 419:8
mount up with w. as eagles, 28:8
no longer wings to fly, 719:10
O for a horse with w., 225:15
obscene w., 401:12
of borrowed wit, 247:1
of Night, 466:12
of silence, 260:27
of the dove, 422:18
of the future, 713:7
of the morning, 20:13
of the wind, 16:9, 19:8
on what w. dare he aspire, 374:5
on w. of song, 442:5
on w. of Time grief flies, 276:17
one black other white, 269:8

Woman *(continued)*

hate a dumpy w., 423:7
have I not found, 24:24
he that tastes w. ruin meets, 307:16
heart of w. he loves, 657:8
I am a very serious w., 806:9
I am a w. first, 765:6
I am w., 836:14
in argument with men a w. worse, 269:7
in hours of ease, 397:1
in kimono, 767:16
in this humor wooed, 173:34
is a dish for gods, 224:7
is at heart a rake, 310:8
is his game, 483:2
is one of greatest instituooshuns, 555:9
is only a woman, 632:10
is perfected, 827:12
know how to submit, 385:13
large-brained w., 463:9
last thing civilized, 540:24
lesser man, 482:5
let w. into Paradise, 861:16
let w. then go on, 432:6
like some little w., 837:*n*1
like that not woman quite, 821:9
like w. stooping down creeping about, 623:2
lips of a strange w. drop as honeycomb, 21:3
Little Girl My Stringbean My Lovely W., 821:11
little w. who wrote the book, 489:*n*4
lived in shoe, 858:13
lone w. with silver spoons, 505:20
long hair glory to w., 44:14
look for the w., 450:18
love improves a w., 305:7
loveliest w. born, 639:14
lovely in her bones, 780:16
lovely w. stoops to folly, 341:20, 718:19
made he a w., 5:21
made mouths in a glass, 216:21
man and w. in garden, 605:3
man and w. two locked caskets, 706:9
man that is born of a w., 14:15
man's desire for w., 404:1
mighty ills done by w., 293:20
mist dispelled when w. appears, 307:14
modest w. in finery, 342:19
more barbarous than man, 589:4
more charming if not fall into hands, 580:19
mortifying when w. considers difference of education, 361:15
mountainous w. not breaks will bend, 792:4
moved like fountain troubled, 176:1
much missed, 576:2
must have money and a room, 700:7
nakedness of w. work of God, 372:17
neither man nor w. but author, 504:19
nigger w. mule uh de world, 761:1
no animal more invincible than w., 75:13
no w. as precious as truths, 658:1
no w. can be too rich too thin, 851:7
none of w. born, 221:26
not born w. becomes one, 777:13
not even shallow, 590:*n*1

Woman *(continued)*

not kill w. who wronged you, 580:20
not know I am a w., 199:12
not ugly thinks herself handsome, 315:2
nothing worse than shameless w., 75:16
O w. lovely w., 294:2
O w. perfect w., 242:16
of mean understanding, 406:4
of Samaria, 40:47
off with Old W. before New, 609:2
often changes, 97:*n*8
old w. lived under hill, 860:17
old w. tossed in blanket, 859:11
once loved hateful, 659:11
once w. has given heart, 297:8
one that was a w. sir, 206:21
one word for w., 606:12
one would bury for nothing, 497:5
organizer a w., 96:31
over-mastered with dust, 194:15
over-value w., 743:18
oweth duty to husband, 176:2
perfect w. nobly planned, 394:3
poor lone w., 191:25
poor w. was German too, 796:3
preaching, 327:3
proclaim ownership, 626:12
real w. lineal indeed, 436:15
rejoices in revenge, 113:18
sat in unwomanly rags, 446:2
says what will please, 331:13
scorned, 300:22
sexual relations with that w., 840:2
shallow changing w., 174:15
silliest w. manage man, 632:14
so unto man is w., 467:2
sort of bloom on w., 621:19
speaks small like a w., 190:14
still be a w. to you, 305:10
still gentler sister w., 378:18
stock rising in market, 450:12
stoops to folly, 341:20, 718:19
substitute for masturbation, 672:12
take elder than herself, 209:22
take some savage w., 482:6
takes off claim to respect, 71:9
talking passion of w., 300:5
taught to protect herself, 521:22
terrible for old w. to outlive her dogs, 787:19
that deliberates is lost, 301:22
that feareth the Lord, 23:31
the w. is a whore, 327:21
therefore to be won, 172:2
think man an angel, 490:15
thinking w. sleeps with monsters, 824:9
to obey, 483:3
to Sherlock Holmes always the w., 617:2
tremble to win w., 460:10
true and fair, 233:14
understanding harmful in w., 293:15
Vanessa extraordinary w., 298:*n*2
venom clamors of jealous w., 174:38
virtuous w. is a crown, 21:21
wailing for demon-lover, 401:14
want anything done ask w., 816:9
what a w. thinks of women, 541:21

Woman *(continued)*

what does a w. want, 608:6
what happen if one w. told truth, 791:10
what have I to do, 40:38
what w. says written in wind, 94:22
who can find a virtuous w., 23:27
who did not care, 634:21
who grieve for this w., 725:7
who has wronged you, 580:20
who occasions least talk, 74:6
who plans such deeds, 55:5
whole relation between man and w., 460:13
whom thou gavest, 6:6
whose heart is snares, 24:23
whosoever looketh on a w., 34:4
why can't w. be more like man, 803:12
wickedness of a w., 32:37
will not give w. pessary, 72:16
with fair opportunities, 490:3
with his tongue win a w., 176:9
with the heart, 483:3
with whom be stupid, 659:3
without man cannot meet man, 805:5
without man like fish without bicycle, 852:25
without w. I love, 742:14
witty w. a treasure, 541:20
woman's body is the w., 580:7
won or woman lost, 640:4
worthy w. al hir lyve, 135:8
would run through fire, 190:30
Woman-chaser, sorriest little w., 527:3
Womanhood, heroic w., 467:9
Womanly, manly deeds like words, 252:*n*1
Woman's a contradiction, 310:11
body is the woman, 580:7
brief as w. love, 205:1
children's gratitude w. love, 641:9
cold perverted will, 431:16
come to my w. breasts, 219:11
desire for desire of man, 404:1
die because a w. fair, 246:18
gift to rain tears, 175:20
life history of affections, 416:14
light lies in w. eyes, 412:4
love lodged in w. breast, 232:12
love of being loved, 575:12
love the history of w. life, 385:12
love w. whole existence, 423:14
name in print twice, 706:2
no other but w. reason, 176:4
normal occupations, 774:9
old age is w. hell, 276:6
only books w. looks, 412:5
paths to love, 243:1
right of privacy encompass w. decision, 778:2
sex prima facie evidence, 503:7
spark in w. heart, 416:10
such beauty as w. eye, 177:4
the w. a whore, 327:21
tiger's heart in w. hide, 172:24
time of opportunity short, 75:12
tongue good when an't w., 495:22
twenty years in w. life, 77:11
vows write upon wave, 69:6
will, 177:25
work never done, 846:16

Womb, came forth of mother's w., 24:14
  cold in the w., 819:12
  from mother's w. untimely ripped,
    222:21
  fruit of thy w., 38:36
  naked out of my mother's w., 13:26
  of morning dew, 161:6
  of pia mater, 177:1
  of uncreated night, 265:4
  sealed your w., 812:3
  shall forget him, 14:31
  since black w. held, 791:12
  teeming w. of royal kings, 179:12
Women, accord w. equal power, 522:3
  all men and w. had become grotesques,
    677:18
  American w. kept from growing, 808:1
  American w. to obtain right to vote,
    811:1
  and children first, 848:6
  and elephants, 655:2
  and wine, 307:13
  are angels wooing, 207:21
  are as roses, 209:23
  are like tricks, 300:19
  are seldom inventors, 316:17
  as workers not as w., 521:20
  attend men and not w., 78:9
  be spared struggle for beauty, 833:12
  better or worse than men, 292:21
  bevy of fair w., 268:12
  blessed among w., 38:34
  brought shame on all w., 55:6
  capture of men by w., 490:*n*1
  children of larger growth, 315:1
  come and go, 717:7
  come out to cut up what remains, 634:7
  compare with me ye w., 270:11
  complain about sex more than men,
    803:5
  dear dead w., 493:14
  degraded by trivial attentions, 382:25
  desiren sovereynetee, 136:21
  die of loneliness but for w., 643:8
  difference between men and w., 761:12
  divine patriarch castrates w., 820:9
  duty of w. to secure francise, 503:6
  economic factors in society, 623:3
  educated for dependence, 382:23
  England is paradise of w., 162:9
  equal right of men and w., 705:15
  especially to w., 423:12
  fair w. and brave men, 420:16
  fairest among w., 25:13
  faithful w. alike, 695:12
  feared witches burned w., 607:2
  feel weariness of battle, 808:2
  feelings of w., 700:10
  fickleness of w. I love, 609:3
  find few real friends, 329:22
  fine w. eat crazy salad, 639:10
  foolish to match men, 512:24
  for w. act of survival, 824:16
  forget what don't want to remember,
    760:15
  framed to make w. false, 213:5
  gave what other w. gave, 642:2
  Germans are like w., 590:9
  getting along with w., 363:12

Women *(continued)*
  given deplorable education, 461:6
  great city greatest men w., 520:4
  Greeks be Greeks and W. what they are,
    270:6
  guide the plot, 367:18
  hangin' men and w., 847:5
  happiest w. no history, 513:4
  hate all w. when thou art gone, 234:14
  have as much rights as man, 443:11
  have glimmer of loyalty to Truth, 593:20
  have no characters, 310:4
  have no wilderness, 748:1
  have positive moral sense, 569:20
  haven't any depths, 590:9
  hero keeps getting in bed with w., 736:2
  hid himself among w., 256:17
  homely men charmed w., 626:11
  how can you shoot w. children, 834:8
  how hard for w. to keep counsel, 196:12
  I know disposition of w., 89:9
  impressive fact about American w., 811:1
  in w. two divide, 310:7
  indisputably beautiful, 315:2
  innocent and pure, 229:25
  kindness in w. not looks, 175:36
  know jealous readiest to forgive, 526:4
  know less understand more, 699:13
  knowledge of w. of his own family, 465:4
  labor of w. in house, 623:3
  Lake Wobegon where w. are strong,
    837:5
  let w. into your life, 610:5
  like to be conquered, 490:21
  like untuned golden strings, 170:16
  liked several w., 229:33
  literary accomplishments in w., 361:14
  looking-glasses reflecting man, 700:9
  loses solidarity with other w., 778:1
  love lovers, 274:13
  make public judge, 416:23
  man always unjust to w., 423:20
  married beneath me all w. do, 682:7
  men and w. affirm brotherhood, 777:15
  men and w. created equal, 503:5
  men and w. liberate, 742:9
  men and w. merely players, 198:25
  men w. and clergymen, 398:22
  men work w. weep, 513:23
  minds of American w., 807:15
  monstrous regiment of w., 150:9
  more pangs than wars or w., 231:2
  musick and w. give way to, 288:15
  my sisters and lovers, 518:17
  no more trusting in w., 55:8
  not so young as painted, 659:7
  not w. or Negroes but citizens, 503:9
  old w. should not be perfumed, 56:21
  other w. cloy appetites, 223:15
  ought to have representatives, 382:28
  passing the love of w., 11:38
  passionate w., 637:15
  pleasing punishment w. bear, 174:25
  plunged into cares and sorrows, 382:26
  pursuit of loose w., 526:17
  put not on pedestal but in cage, 774:5
  remember what don't want to forget,
    760:15
  run to extremes, 292:21

Women *(continued)*
  saints were rarely married w., 774:9
  seven w. take hold of one man, 26:17
  silence gives grace to w., 67:4
  Solomon loved many strange w., 12:21
  some w. charm all, 621:19
  some w. handsome without adornment,
    90:19
  some w. stay in memory, 635:17
  spare w. for Thy Sake, 773:19
  special contribution awareness, 761:14
  stimulated by news wife left husband,
    771:19
  superiority of their w., 463:5
  text of Men and W., 617:18
  that's the nature of w., 156:23
  these impossible w., 75:14
  they married when young, 576:9
  thou fairest among w., 25:13
  till w. more rationally educated, 382:22
  trained to place others' needs first, 791:7
  upset everything, 610:5
  war between men and w., 741:15
  watched naked w. walk out of sea, 788:3
  we should have learned w., 361:14
  wear the breeches, 240:8
  what a woman thinks of w., 541:21
  what is it men in w. require, 373:15
  what that party promises w., 522:1
  when candles out all w. fair, 111:20
  who remained thirty-five, 605:12
  wine and w. go together, 240:22
  wine w. and song, 368:9
  wine w. mirth laughter, 423:18
  words are w. deeds men, 252:7
  young w. of small fortune, 406:9
Women's eyes for stars, 844:16
  from w. eyes this doctrine, 177:8
  I put on w. clothing, 843:1
  sooner lost than w. are, 209:22
  weapons waterdrops, 216:16
Won, battles lost in spirit in which w., 519:4
  battles that should been w., 808:2
  by captain of second rank, 451:10
  by men with courage, 74:5
  capitalism has w., 805:3
  game is done I've w., 400:4
  glory of winning were she w., 541:19
  lose ground w. today, 529:10
  not that you w. or lost, 692:4
  on playing fields of Eton, 389:6
  other palms are w., 393:19
  prize we sought is w., 520:18
  she that with poetry w., 271:16
  small have plodders w., 176:20
  so melancholy as battle w., 388:21
  the ear of Pluto, 259:21
  things w. are done, 207:21
  though he w. all battles, 820:13
  wars w. by men, 708:12
  was woman in this humor w., 173:34
  when battle's lost and w., 218:23
  woman therefore to be w., 172:2
  woman w. or woman lost, 640:4
  wooed and not unsought be w., 267:20
  world made to be w. by youth, 665:11
Wonder, a w. I haven't dropped ideals, 822:9
  all knowledge and w. is pleasure, 166:2
  all w. that would be, 481:23

Worse *(continued)*
  lots w. ways to die, 678:7
  make w. appear the better, 74:13
  medicine w. than malady, 103:*n1*
  most are w. than their fathers, 54:12
  no w. a husband than best, 223:13
  nothing w. than shameless woman, 75:16
  on Friday, 859:17
  or w. expelled, 842:11
  pen w. than the sword, 241:2
  pray gods they change for w., 164:8
  remedies w. than disease, 103:4
  than an infidel, 46:22
  than be swinger of birches, 669:6
  than being talked about, 604:13
  than crime it is blunder, 383:9
  than sun in March, 186:25
  than wicked it's vulgar, 591:17
  things than lie, 504:6
  things waiting than death, 568:13
  to fear worst cures w., 208:4
  you have suffered w. things, 96:29
Worship bitch-goddess Success, 581:4
  come to w. him, 33:18
  compelled from their w., 255:3
  duty to w. sun, 572:3
  everyone's true w., 76:1
  Father in spirit, 40:48
  freedom of w., 698:15
  God according to own inclinations,
    109:18
  in Roman world, 353:5
  justice the only w., 554:7
  let us w. and bow down, 18:29
  let us w. God, 377:15
  man strives for someone to w., 526:1
  more w. rising than setting sun, 91:20
  none save Him, 121:11
  of world but no repose, 429:21
  pay no w. to garish sun, 183:32
  stated calls to w., 325:6
  the Lord in beauty of holiness, 16:25
  Thee do we w., 120:11
  true worshippers shall w., 40:48
  what thou hast burned, 119:25
Worshipped, burn what thou hast w., 119:25
  fell down and w. him, 33:19
  neither w. with hands, 42:18
  no graven images w., 512:11
  stocks and stones, 263:15
Worshipper, grudging w. of the gods, 99:17
Worshippers, sufferest more than thy w.,
  193:15
  true w. shall worship, 40:48
Worst and best inclined to snap, 710:10
  are full of passionate intensity, 639:6
  best and w. of this is, 569:6
  bottom of the w., 207:31
  British like to be told w., 666:10
  Catullus w. of all poets, 94:14
  comes to the worst, 243:7
  death not the w., 68:15
  do your w. we our best, 666:14
  ecclesiastic tyranny's w., 295:3
  give thy w. of thoughts, 213:32
  good bad w. best, 478:4
  his face the w. thing, 211:8
  intellectual hatred w., 639:14
  is better than none, 326:1

Worst *(continued)*
  is death, 179:26
  is not, 217:10
  is yet to come, 486:17
  knew w. too young, 634:1
  know w. and provide for it, 352:13
  love good pursue the w., 105:*n14*
  no w. there is none, 588:2
  of all states, 257:7
  of the company, 298:1
  of words, 213:32
  persecutes the mind, 284:19
  portion in this life, 781:7
  race and nation judged by best not w.,
    656:17
  rivals are the w., 296:5
  thing is discuss problem, 832:1
  things present w., 191:24
  this is the w., 217:10
  to fear w. cures worse, 208:4
  tomorrow do thy w., 284:6
  treason has done his w., 221:5
  use a man could be put to, 232:18
  when w. little better than beast, 187:32
  where best like w., 633:14
Worsted, though right w., 495:15
Worst-natured muse, 292:25
Worth a thousand men, 397:13
  an age without a name, 346:12
  as much as my life was w., 332:23
  conscience of her w., 267:20
  country of w., 379:5
  dignity and w. of person, 705:15
  doing is worth doing well, 314:16
  good words w. much, 251:15
  how many ships my presence w., 81:19
  in New York ask how much w., 561:19
  in the w. and choice, 237:9
  little more than coward, 386:11
  makes the man, 311:12
  man w. as he esteems himself, 146:7
  my Being's w., 547:2
  never knew w. of him, 652:3
  nobler yet in his own w., 283:19
  not w. going to see, 328:21
  not w. his salt, 109:8
  not w. paper written on, 465:9
  not w. the search, 187:23
  not w. wooing not w. winning, 467:4
  nothing w. doing completed, 735:17
  of state worth of individuals, 464:20
  Paris well w. a Mass, 162:12
  show me but thy w., 193:15
  slow rises by w., 323:13
  spending more than Canada is w., 316:5
  trick w. two of that, 185:11
  what is w. in anything, 271:15
  what purchaser will pay, 104:7
  when we see men of w., 62:22
  wit nor words nor w., 197:4
  you are not w. the dust, 217:12
  Zeus takes away half a man's w., 55:17
Worthies, than all the W. did, 233:16
Worthily, write w. of American things, 584:7
Worthiness, change to virtue and w., 195:28
  love in excess brings nor w., 69:25
Worthless, sons more w. than sires, 100:2
Worth's unknown although height taken,
  227:17

Worthwhile, worrying never w., 689:22
Worthy, brave men and w. patriots, 262:18
  foemen w. of steel, 397:12
  I am not w. to unloose, 38:14
  laborer w. of hire, 39:19
  no w. action done, 846:17
  nothing w. departs, 434:15
  of great DiMaggio, 755:3
  of nothing but to be cast into fire, 318:16
  proved them and found them w., 31:16
  taketh not cross is not w., 35:32
  valets, 349:4
Wot, knows wot's w., 496:3
  walk and w. not what they are, 176:20
Wotton a most dear lover, 252:25
Would God I had died for thee, 12:7
  God it were even, 10:10
  God it were morning, 10:10
  he had blotted a thousand, 238:15
  that I did too, 529:14
  thou hadst ne'er been born, 214:28
  wait upon I w., 219:20
  we w. and we w. not, 212:5
Wound, earth felt the w., 267:30
  he will never get over, 671:9
  heal by degrees, 213:29
  heals scar disappears, 506:2
  history of soldier's w., 332:13
  honor take away grief of w., 186:35
  I the w. and knife, 524:13
  immortal w., 671:9
  jests that never felt w., 182:28
  much too big for hip, 752:11
  purple with love's w., 181:9
  put a tongue in every w., 197:5
  read each w. each weakness, 528:15
  read only books that w. us, 701:7
  red badge of courage, 655:12
  silent w. deep in her breast, 97:18
  soothe or w. heart, 397:17
  startle like a w., 63:7
  up every morning, 537:5
  what missing so he does not w., 792:17
  willing to w., 312:4
  with mercy round, 587:18
  with thee in thee isled, 587:19
  with touch scarcely felt, 314:3
Wounded and left on Afghanistan's plains,
  634:7
  but not slain, 853:*n1*
  in house of my friends, 30:40
  is the wounding heart, 272:13
  like a w. snake, 308:17
  my heart is w. within me, 19:17
  O sacred head now w., 258:4
  razors to my w. heart, 175:14
  regarded w. soldiers in envious way,
    655:12
  shrieks and groans of w., 522:14
  souls w. by such things, 277:22
  spirit who can bear, 22:10
  what a w. name, 207:13
  you're w., 491:8
Wounded Knee, bury my heart at W., 750:10
Wounding, wounded is the w. heart, 272:13
Wounds, bind up w. of friend, 174:19
  bind up nation's w., 477:4
  faithful are w. of friend, 23:11
  fight and not heed w., 145:5

X

Y

Years *(continued)*

knightly y. were gone, 594:13
like great black oxen, 636:21
may be for y., 447:7
months add themselves make y., 486:9
more memories than if thousand y. old, 524:12
new y. ruin and rend, 568:17
nor the y. draw nigh, 25:7
nor y. condemn, 650:6
not count man's y., 457:15
O for ten y., 436:2
old and stricken in y., 10:25
our hope for y. to come, 304:6
out of me y. roll, 569:7
plunder one thing after another, 101:14
ran a hundred y. to a day, 473:15
roll into centuries, 486:9
sea folk live three hundred y., 461:21
seven y. of famine, 7:26
seven y. would be insufficient, 406:2
short space of four y., 475:8
Sleeping Beauty fifty y. old, 815:8
sorrow comes with y., 463:11
spend our y. as a tale that is told, 18:21
spend this little span of y., 92:20
steal fire from mind, 420:14
survive two thousand million y., 679:2
ten y. on Pullman cars, 723:14
thousand leagues a thousand y., 320:20
thousand y. are as yesterday, 18:20
thousand y. of peace, 484:15
threescore y. and ten, 18:22, 618:7
Time in hours days y., 279:5
touch of earthly y., 392:1
twenty y. in woman's life, 77:11
vale of y., 214:3
vanity in y., 185:30
wander in the wilderness forty y., 9:19
where all past y. are, 233:13
wind him for fourscore y., 283:5
work as if to live hundred y., 320:6
wrap thousand onward y., 519:25
Yesterday's Seven thousand Y., 471:10
Yeats, cadence from man named Y., 780:14
in churchyard Y. laid, 643:4
William Y. laid to rest, 775:14
Yell, gave y. for y. to gale, 611:18
Yelled, flew down y. at craft, 763:3
Yellow, all looks y., 308:24
black pale hectic red, 428:21
cheek white beard, 191:16
come unto these y. sands, 229:18
commended y. stockings, 209:31
cuckoo-buds of y. hue, 177:16
dawn becomes y., 855:22
finish and sweet wood, 756:5
green and y. melancholy, 209:26
leaves or none or few, 226:24
locks y. as gold, 400:3
my days in y. leaf, 425:8
nodding o'er y. plain, 318:3
not your y. hair, 641:2
put down The Y. Book, 773:18
road paved with y. brick, 606:15
roman candles exploding, 810:2
silkworm expend her y. labors, 239:15
the sere the y. leaf, 222:11
with August, 708:18

Yelping wife, 781:7
Yeoman's service, 207:7
Yes by Saint Anne, 209:17
Devil cannot make Hawthorne say y., 516:4
I answered last night, 463:14
I said yes I will Yes, 696:13
my darling daughter, 851:13
vee may perhaps to begin y., 828:14
Virginia there is a Santa Claus, 573:2
Yeses, overcome 'em with y., 793:3
Yesterday bird of night did sit, 195:26
call back y., 179:25, 239:10
came suddenly, 835:2
egg tomorrow duster, 662:18
fact today doctrine, 360:2
great families of y., 295:1
had daily cleaning, 794:12
jam tomorrow jam y., 552:9
keeping up with y., 680:5
loneliness of y., 747:18
man's y. ne'er like morrow, 427:17
maybe it was y., 789:12
no tomorrow nor y., 234:17
not worry about Y., 586:8
pomp of y., 635:3
put back universe give me y., 600:12
Rose of Y., 471:4
same y. today and for ever, 47:6
sleep which thou owedst y., 214:6
stuck fast in Y., 662:15
thousand years are as y., 18:20
unborn Tomorrow dead Y., 471:20
who has seen y., 425:2
word of Caesar stood, 196:31
Yesterday's Seven thousand Years, 471:10
Yesterdays have lighted fools, 222:16
man of cheerful y., 395:8
Yesternight, last night ah y., 645:8
the sun went hence, 234:11
Yesteryear, where are snows of y., 139:18
where snows of y., 541:29
Yet a little while, 41:23
forget not y., 149:25
the end is not y., 37:6
Yew, never spray of y., 529:14
not too far from y., 721:14
Yezhov, terrible years of Y., 725:9
Yiddish, quiet humor in Y., 769:11
words in Y. gradations of disparagement, 769:5
Yield, and not to y., 481:15
at touch I y., 483:5
courage never to y., 264:3
neither y. to song of siren, 165:4
not neck to fortune's yoke, 173:1
not to evils, 97:22
to get rid of temptation y., 604:15
to that suggestion, 219:5
to y. is to be preserved, 58:19
who will to separation, 670:6
with grace to reason, 668:16
Yielded with coy submission, 266:11
Yielding place to new, 486:12
to temptations, 445:8
Yields nothing but discontent, 343:19
what sweet hour y., 431:7
woods or steepy mountain y., 170:6
Yin and Yang, 89:14

Yogi and the commissar, 771:2
Yo-ho-ho and bottle of rum, 598:14
Yoke, bear his mild y., 263:14
bear the y. in his youth, 29:30
my y. is easy, 35:35
savage bull bear y., 194:11
shake y. of inauspicious stars, 184:17
take my y., 35:35
yield not neck to fortune's y., 173:1
Yoknapatawpha County, 748:18
Yolk, heaven like egg earth like y., 114:13
Yonder all before us lie, 277:1
Yonghy-Bonghy-Bò, lived Y., 500:4
Yore, not now as of y., 393:7
Yorick, alas poor Y., 206:24
York, made summer by sun of Y., 173:28
Yorkshire, living in Y., 398:23
You ain't heard nothing yet, 711:9
alone are you, 226:26
also Brutus, 92:6
and I are suddenly, 818:12
and I past dancing days, 182:24
anything y. can do, 716:11
are neighbor of nothing, 830:13
are not for all markets, 199:21
are you and I am I, 738:20
are young my son, 78:15
as y. are woman, 743:16
asses made to bear so are y., 175:28
could look it up, 742:1
do as would have others do unto y., 35:*n*1
do not judge us too harshly, 750:19
do something to me, 732:9
do your thing, 738:20
Doctor Martin, 821:7
gate made only for y., 701:1
have conquered Galilean, 117:14
have named him, 290:11
I and y. and all of us, 197:1
I get a kick out of y., 732:11
I to die and y. to live, 76:14
knowing who y. are, 816:4
land made for y. and me, 788:12
money may rub off on y., 704:11
need God God needs you, 679:8
nothing could stop y., 830:12
story's about y., 98:16
two are book-men, 176:36
while I am I y. are y., 492:15
your mind and y., 708:15
You-all means race or section, 848:16
Young Adam Cupid, 182:27
affections run to waste, 421:19
ambition's ladder, 195:30
and easy, 795:8
and foolish, 636:19
and old come forth to play, 259:16
and old the same, 64:13
and rose-lipped cherubin, 214:27
and so fair, 446:7
Bacchus ever fair and y., 285:10
beautiful time of y. love, 382:7
blood have course, 514:4
bloom of y. Desire, 335:6
boys and girls level, 224:1
Brigham Y. dreadfully married, 555:14
caparisons don't become y. woman, 367:13

Z